SOCIAL SECURITY LEGISLATION 2016/17

VOLUME II: INCOME SUPPORT, JOBSEEKER'S ALLOWANCE, STATE PENSION CREDIT AND THE SOCIAL FUND

SOCIAL SECURITY LEGISLATION 2016/17

General Editor
Nick Wikeley, M.A. (Cantab)

VOLUME II: INCOME SUPPORT, JOBSEEKER'S ALLOWANCE, STATE PENSION CREDIT AND THE SOCIAL FUND

Commentary By

Penny Wood, LL.B., M.Sc.
District Tribunal Judge

Richard Poynter, B.C.L., M.A. (Oxon.)
District Tribunal Judge,
Judge of the Upper Tribunal

Nick Wikeley, M.A. (Cantab)
Judge of the Upper Tribunal,
Emeritus Professor of Law,
University of Southampton

John Mesher, B.A., B.C.L. (Oxon), LL.M. (Yale)

Consultant Editor
Child Poverty Action Group

SWEET & MAXWELL

THOMSON REUTERS

Published in 2016 by Thomson Reuters (Professional) UK Limited
trading as Sweet & Maxwell, Friars House,
160 Blackfriars Road, London, SE1 8EZ.
(Registered in England and Wales. Company No 1679046.
Registered office: 2nd Floor, 1 Mark Square, Leonard Street,
London EC2A 4EG)

For further information on our products and services, visit
http://www.sweetandmaxwell.co.uk

Typeset by Servis Filmsetting Ltd, Stockport, Cheshire
Printed and bound by CPI Group (UK) Ltd, Croydon, CR0 4YY

ISBN 978-0-414-05601-5

No natural forests were destroyed to make this product;
only farmed timber was used and replanted.

A CIP catalogue record for this book is available
from the British Library

CHILD POVERTY ACTION GROUP

The Child Poverty Action Group (CPAG) is a charity, founded in 1965, which campaigns for the relief of poverty in the United Kingdom. It has a particular reputation in the field of welfare benefits law derived from its legal work, publications, training and parliamentary and policy work, and is widely recognised as the leading organisation for taking test cases on social security law.

CPAG is therefore ideally placed to act as Consultant Editor to this 5-volume work—**Social Security Legislation 2016/17**. CPAG is not responsible for the detail of what is contained in each volume, and the authors' views are not necessarily those of CPAG. The Consultant Editor's role is to act in an advisory capacity on the overall structure, focus and direction of the work.

For more information about CPAG, its rights and policy publications or training courses, its address is 30 Micawber Street, London, N1 7TB (telephone: 020 7837 7979—website: *http://www.cpag.org.uk*).

CHILD POVERTY ACTION GROUP

FOREWORD

I am proud that in recent times our Tribunals have been exceedingly effective at adapting to change, embracing new technology and responding positively to the latest transformational innovations, often at the behest of external stakeholders. Yet at the same time it is comforting to be able to hold fast to that which is good in more traditional forms of communication. I am therefore more than happy to welcome these latest volumes of legislation with the accompanying commentary and recommend them to all those involved in the work of our Tribunals as we seek to deliver access to justice.

Judge John Aitken
President
Social Entitlement Chamber
First-tier Tribunal

PREFACE

Income Support, Jobseeker's Allowance, State Pension Credit and the Social Fund is Volume II of what is now a five-volume series: *Social Security Legislation 2016/17*. The companion volumes are: Hooker, Poynter, White, Wikeley, Williams and Wood, *Volume I: Non-Means Tested Benefits and Employment and Support Allowance*; Rowland and White, *Volume III: Administration, Adjudication and the European Dimension*; Wikeley, Williams and Hooker, *Volume IV: Tax Credits and HMRC-administered Social Security Benefits*; and Mesher, Poynter, Wikeley and Wood, *Volume V: Universal Credit*.

Each of the first four volumes in the series provides a legislative text, clearly showing the form and date of amendments, and commentary up to date to April 11, 2016 (Volume V is being published later and will be up to date to August). The commentary in this volume includes case law developments up to late July 2016.

April 2016/17 is the first year in which there has been only very limited up-rating of the benefits covered by this volume. This is due to two factors. Firstly, the Welfare Reform and Work Act 2016 received the Royal Assent on March 16, 2016. Many of the cuts made by this Act were previewed in last year's preface and are not yet in force. Sections 11 and 12 of, and Sch.1 to, the Act, however, which impose a four-year freeze on the rates of "the relevant sums" of certain social security benefits and "the relevant amounts" of tax credits, came into force on commencement. As far as the benefits covered by this volume are concerned, the relevant sums are the personal allowances for income support and income-based JSA and the age-related amounts for contribution-based JSA. The consequence is that these sums will remain at their 2015/16 rate until at least April 6, 2020.

Secondly, the freezing of these personal allowances and age-related amounts is compounded by the fact that, although not subject to the freeze, the income support and income-based JSA premiums remain at their 2015/16 rate, with the exception of the pensioner premiums and the higher pensioner premium. This is because when conducting the annual review of social security benefit rates required by s.150 of the Social Security Administration Act 1992 the Secretary of State decided that the benefits specified in s.150 of the Social Security Administration Act 1992 had maintained their value in relation to prices as measured by the Consumer Prices Index over the 12-month period ending September 2015 (which showed a negative growth rate of −0.1 per cent: see para.4.2 of the Explanatory Memorandum to the Social Security Benefits Up-rating Order 2016 (SI 2016/230)). No increase was therefore required. The benefits specified in s.150 include income support (see subs.(1)(h)) and JSA (see subs.(1)(k)).

However, the amounts for the pensioner and higher pensioner premiums in income support and income-based JSA and for the standard minimum guarantee and savings credit thresholds in state pension credit have been increased as a consequence of the "triple lock" commitment, whereby the basic state pension is up-rated each year by the higher of inflation, the increase in average earnings or 2.5 per cent. The rise in earnings was 2.9 per cent for the quarter ending July 2015 (as measured by the Average Weekly Earnings statistic) and was the highest of the three and so the standard minimum guarantee element was increased by that percentage. The premiums for pensioners have been increased by the cash increase for the standard minimum guarantee element of state pension credit (see paras 7.3 and 7.4 of the Explanatory Memorandum to the Social Security Benefits (Adjustment of Amounts and Thresholds) Regulations 2016 (SI 2016/242)).

In addition, the income bands which determine the level of non-dependant deductions from housing costs in income support, income-based JSA and state pension credit were up-rated in line with the rise in earnings and the amount of the deduction by the forecast growth (0.75 per cent) in rents for those eligible for housing benefit (see paras 7.13 and 7.14 of the Explanatory Memorandum to SI 2016/242). Otherwise all the rates for the benefits covered by this volume have stood still.

The main legislative developments during the last year, as far as the benefits covered by this volume are concerned, have been, firstly, the changes to state pension credit made by the Pensions Act 2014 with effect from April 6, 2016, in particular the abolition of the savings credit element and the assessed income period. The other significant change is the introduction of a single waiting period of 39 weeks for housing costs for new claims for income support and income-based JSA made on or after April 1, 2016.

In terms of case law, the Court of Appeal's judgment in *Secretary of State for Work and Pensions v Reilly and Hewstone* and *Secretary of State for Work and Pensions v Jeffrey and Bevan* [2016] EWCA Civ 413 is the latest development in relation to sanctions, in particular those imposed in connection with a "failure" under a scheme under s.17A of the Jobseekers Act 1995 ("Work for your benefit" schemes). The Court of Appeal allowed the Secretary of State's appeal against the decision of the majority of the Upper Tribunal Three-Judge panel (*SSWP v TJ (JSA)* [2015] UKUT 56 (AAC)) in relation to the effect of the Jobseekers (Back to Work Schemes) Act 2013. The Court agreed with the decision of the minority that the provision in s.1(1) of the Act that the JSA (Employment, Skills and Enterprise Scheme) Regulations 2011 (SI 2011/917) was to be treated "for all purposes" as made under s.17A of the Jobseekers Act 1995 was too clear and unequivocal to admit of the construction that had been favoured by the majority. The central issue therefore became whether Lang J's decision in *R. (on the application of Reilly (No. 2) and Hewstone) v Secretary of State for Work and Pensions* [2014] EWHC 2182 (Admin) to grant a declaration of incompatibility with the claimants' rights under art.6 of the ECHR in relation to the retrospective effect of the Jobseekers (Back to Work) Schemes Act 2013 had been correct. The Court upheld her decision. The Court of Appeal's judgment and the previous litigation are discussed in detail in the General Note at the beginning of the Jobseekers (Back to Work Schemes) Act 2013.

The right to reside test, as usual, continues to be a fertile source of court and Upper Tribunal decisions. This year has seen yet more important decisions, which include the CJEU decisions in *Jobcenter Berlin Neukölln v Alimanovic* (Case C–67/14), *Vestiche Arbeit Jobcenter Kreis Recklinghausen v Garcia-Nieto* (Case C–299/14), *Secretary of State for the Home Department v NA* (Case C–115/15) and *Commission v United Kingdom* (Case C–308/14), the Supreme Court's decision in *Mirga v Secretary of State for Work and Pensions* [2016] UKSC 1 and the Upper Tribunal's decision in *SSWP v SFF, ADR v SSWP, CS v London Borough of Barnet and SSWP* [2015] UKUT 502. The decision in *SFF* considers a number of legal and practical issues arising from the decision of the CJEU in *Saint Prix v Secretary of State for Work and Pensions* (Case C–507/12) [2014] AACR 18. These decisions and their implications are analysed in detail, as are all aspects of this complex test.

Besides these highlighted developments, there has also been the usual crop of more minor legislative changes and the continuing flow of Upper Tribunal decisions on various aspects of the means-tested benefits covered by this volume. This includes, for instance, a number of decisions on a range of issues concerning the treatment of capital, and on housing costs.

As always, revising and updating the legislative text and commentary has required considerable flexibility on the part of the publisher and a great deal of help from a number of sources, including CPAG as advisory editor to the series, for which we express our sincere appreciation. Thanks are also due to Peter Banks, Maggie Phelps, John Bourne and Martin Williams.

To maximise space for explanatory commentary we have provided lists of definitions only where the commentary to the provision is substantial, or where reference to definitions is essential for its proper understanding. Users of this book should always check whether particular words or phrases they are called on to apply have a particular meaning ascribed to them in the legislation. Generally, the first or second regulation in each set of regulations contains definitions of key terms (check the "Arrangement of Regulations" at the beginning of each major set of regulations for an indication of the subject matter covered by each regulation). There are also "definition" or "interpretation" sections in each of the Acts (check "Sections Reproduced" at the beginning of each Act for an indication of the subject matter covered by each section or Schedule).

Users of this series, and its predecessors, have over the years provided valuable comments which have invariably been helpful to us in ensuring that the selection of legislative material for inclusion and the commentary upon it reflect the sort of difficulties encountered in practice. In so doing, readers have thus helped shape the content of each of the volumes in this series and assisted in ensuring the accuracy of the material. We hope that readers will continue that tradition. Please write to the General Editor of this series, Nick Wikeley, c/o School of Law, University of Southampton, Highfield, Southampton S017 1BJ, email: njw@soton.ac.uk, who will pass on any comments received to the appropriate commentator.

Our gratitude also goes to the President of the First-tier Tribunal (Social Entitlement Chamber) and his staff for continuing the tradition of help and encouragement.

August 2016

Penny Wood
Richard Poynter
Nick Wikeley
John Mesher

CONTENTS

PART III
OLD STYLE JOBSEEKER'S ALLOWANCE

USING THIS BOOK: AN INTRODUCTION TO LEGISLATION AND CASE LAW

Introduction

This book is not a general introduction to, or general textbook on, the law relating to social security but it is nonetheless concerned with both of the principal sources of social security law—*legislation* (both primary and secondary) and *case law*. It sets out the text of the most important legislation, as currently in force, and then there is added commentary that refers to the relevant case law. Lawyers will be familiar with this style of publication, which inevitably follows the structure of the legislation.

This note is designed primarily to assist readers who are not lawyers to find their way around the legislation and to understand the references to case law, but information it contains about how to find social security case law is intended to be of assistance to lawyers too.

Primary legislation

Primary legislation of the United Kingdom Parliament consists of *Acts of Parliament* (also known as *statutes*). They will have been introduced to Parliament as *Bills*. There are opportunities for Members of Parliament and peers to debate individual clauses and to vote on amendments before a Bill is passed and becomes an Act (at which point the clauses become sections). No tribunal or court has the power to disapply, or hold to be invalid, an Act of Parliament unless it is inconsistent with European Union law.

An Act is known by its "short title", which incorporates the year in which it was passed (e.g. the Social Security Contributions and Benefits Act 1992), and is given a chapter number (abbreviated as, for instance, "c.4" indicating that the Act was the fourth passed in that year). It is seldom necessary to refer to the chapter number but it appears in the running heads in this book.

Each *section* (abbreviated as "s." or, in the plural, "ss.") of an Act is numbered and may be divided into *subsections* (abbreviated as "subs." and represented by a number in brackets), which in turn may be divided into *paragraphs* (abbreviated as "para." and represented by a lower case letter in brackets) and *subparagraphs* (abbreviated as "subpara." and represented by a small roman numeral in brackets). Subparagraph (ii) of para.(a) of subs.(1) of s.72 will usually be referred to simply as "s.72(1)(a)(ii)". Upper case letters may be used where additional sections or subsections are inserted by amendment and additional lower case letters may be used where new paragraphs and subparagraphs are inserted. This accounts for the rather ungainly s.171ZS of the Social Security Contributions and Benefits Act 1992 (in Vol.IV).

Sections of a large Act may be grouped into a numbered *Part*, which may even be divided into *Chapters*. It is not usual to refer to a Part or a Chapter unless referring to the whole Part or Chapter.

Where a section would otherwise become unwieldy because it is necessary to include a list or complicated technical provisions, the section may simply refer to a *Schedule* at the end of the Act. A Schedule (abbreviated as "Sch.") may be divided into paragraphs and subparagraphs and further divided into heads and subheads. Again, it is usual to refer simply to, say, "para.23(3)(b)(ii) of Schedule 3". Whereas it is conventional to speak of a section *of* an Act, it is usual to speak of a Schedule *to* an Act.

When Parliament wishes to change the law, it may do so by passing a new Act that amends a previous Act or it may do so by passing a freestanding Act, although even then consequential amendments to other legislation are usually required. Thus, for instance, when incapacity benefit was introduced by the Social Security (Incapacity for Work) Act 1994, the changes were largely made by inserting ss.30A to 30E and Pt XIIA into the Social Security Contributions and Benefits Act 1992 and repealing the provisions in that Act dealing with sickness and invalidity benefit. In contrast, when jobseeker's allowance was introduced by the Jobseekers Act 1995, it was decided that the main provisions relating to the new benefit would be found in the 1995 Act itself and the 1992 Act was amended only so as to repeal, or amend, the provisions dealing with, or referring to, unemployment benefit.

When there has been a proliferation of Acts or Acts have been very substantially amended, the legislation may be consolidated in a new Act, for which there is a fast track procedure in Parliament. Only limited amendments may be made by a consolidation Act but such an Act reorganises and tidies up the legislation. Because social security law is so frequently amended, it tends to be consolidated every decade or two. The last consolidation Acts relevant to this book were the Social Security Contributions and Benefits Act 1992 (in Vols I, II and IV) and the Social Security Administration Act 1992 (in Vol.III).

Secondary legislation

Secondary legislation (also known as *subordinate legislation* or *delegated legislation*) is made by *statutory instrument* in the form of a set of *Regulations* or a set of *Rules* or an *Order*. The power to make such legislation is conferred on ministers and other persons or bodies by Acts of Parliament. To the extent that a statutory instrument is made beyond the powers (in Latin, *ultra vires*) conferred by primary legislation, it may be held by a tribunal or court to be invalid and ineffective. Secondary legislation must be laid before Parliament. However, most secondary legislation is not debated in Parliament and, even when it is, it cannot be amended although an entire statutory instrument may be rejected.

A set of Regulations or Rules or an Order has a name indicating its scope and the year it was made and also a number, as in the Social Security (Disability Living Allowance) Regulations 1991 (SI 1991/2890) (the 2890th statutory instrument issued in 1991). Because there are over 3,000 statutory instruments each year, the number of a particular statutory instrument is important as a means of identification and it should usually be cited the first time reference is made to that statutory instrument.

Sets of Regulations or Rules are made up of individual *regulations* (abbreviated as "reg.") or *rules* (abbreviated as "r." or, in the plural, "rr."). An Order is made up of *articles* (abbreviated as "art."). Regulations, rules and articles may be divided into paragraphs, subparagraphs and heads. As in Acts, a set of Regulations or Rules or an Order may have one or more

Schedules attached to it. The style of numbering used in statutory instruments is the same as in sections of, and Schedules to, Acts of Parliament. As in Acts, a large statutory instrument may have regulations or rules grouped into Parts and, occasionally, Chapters. Statutory instruments may be amended in the same sort of way as Acts.

Northern Ireland legislation

Most of the legislation set out in this series applies only in Great Britain, social security not generally being an excepted or reserved matter in relation to Northern Ireland. However, Northern Irish legislation—both primary legislation, most relevantly in the form of *Orders in Council* (which, although statutory instruments, had the effect of primary legislation in Northern Ireland while there was direct rule from Westminster) and *Acts of the Northern Ireland Assembly*, and subordinate legislation, in the form of *statutory rules*—has, until recently, largely replicated legislation in Great Britain so that much of the commentary in this book will be applicable to equivalent provisions in Northern Ireland legislation. Latterly, there has been a greater reluctance to maintain parity with Great Britain and initially at least the provisions in the Welfare Reform Act 2012 were not replicated in Northern Ireland.

However, following a lengthy impasse, on November 18, 2015, the Northern Ireland Assembly consented to the stalled Northern Ireland (Welfare Reform) Bill 2015 being taken forward by the Westminster Parliament and approved the welfare clauses of the Welfare Reform and Work Bill as initially introduced at Westminster and the draft Welfare Reform (Northern Ireland) Order 2015. Subsequently, the Northern Ireland (Welfare Reform) Act 2015 received the Royal Assent on November 25, 2015. The purpose of the Act is to provide a power by Order in Council to legislate for welfare reform in Northern Ireland and confer power on the Secretary of State or on a Northern Ireland department to make further provision by regulations or order.

The Welfare Reform (Northern Ireland) Order 2015 (NISI 2015/2006) was duly made and came into force on December 10, 2015. The Order makes provision equivalent to the Welfare Reform Act 2012 and will implement the reforms contained in that Act in Northern Ireland with some limited specific changes. The Order confers powers on the Northern Ireland Department for Social Development (to be renamed the Department for Communities) to make regulations with respect to the reforms in Northern Ireland. The reforms are gradually being rolled out across the jurisdiction in 2016 and 2017 (see e.g. the Welfare Reform (Northern Ireland) Order 2015 (Commencement No. 1) Order 2016 (SR 2016/46)).

In addition, the Northern Ireland Act 1998 (Modification) Order 2016 (SI 2016/160) adds the Welfare Reform Act 2012 and the Welfare Reform (Northern Ireland) Order 2015, together with certain pensions legislation to the legislation listed in s.87(6) of the Northern Ireland Act 1998 (which requires the Secretary of State for Work and Pensions and the Minister with responsibility for social security in Northern Ireland to consult each other to ensure, to the extent they agree, that the relevant legislation achieves single systems of social security, child support and pensions for the UK). To that extent parity in welfare provision is maintained. Alongside these statutory changes, the Northern Ireland Executive has announced allocations from Executive funds to "top-up" the UK welfare arrangements in

Northern Ireland, so as to mitigate the effects of these changes, with a review planned for 2018/2019.

European Union legislation

The United Kingdom is a Member State of the European Union, and European Union legislation has effect within the United Kingdom. The primary legislation is in the form of the *Treaties* agreed by the Member States. Relevant subordinate legislation is in the form of *Regulations*, adopted to give effect to provisions of the Treaties, and *Directives*, addressed to Member States and requiring them to incorporate certain provisions into their domestic laws. Directives are relevant because, where a person brings proceedings against an organ of the State, as is invariably the case where social security is concerned, that person may rely on the Directive as having direct effect if the Member State has failed to comply with it. European Union Treaties, Regulations and Directives are divided into *Articles* (abbreviated as "art."). United Kingdom legislation that is inconsistent with European Union legislation may be disapplied. The most relevant provisions of European Union legislation are set out in Part III of *Vol.III: Administration, Appeals and the European Dimension*.

The outcome of the EU referendum of June 23, 2016 does not immediately alter the United Kingdom's membership of the Union; the United Kingdom will remain a Member State and European Union law will continue to apply until such time as the exit arrangements provided for in art.50 of the Treaty on European Union are completed.

Finding legislation in this book

If you know the name of the piece of legislation for which you are looking, use the list of contents at the beginning of each volume of this series which lists the pieces of legislation contained in the volume. That will give you the paragraph reference to enable you to find the beginning of the piece of legislation. Then, it is easy to find the relevant section, regulation, rule, article or Schedule by using the running heads on the right-hand pages. If you do not know the name of the piece of legislation, you will probably need to use the index at the end of the volume in order to find the relevant paragraph number but will then be taken straight to a particular provision.

The legislation is set out as amended, the amendments being indicated by numbered sets of square brackets. The numbers refer to the numbered entries under the heading "AMENDMENTS" at the end of the relevant section, regulation, rule, article or Schedule, which identify the amending statute or statutory instrument. Where an Act has been consolidated, there is a list of "DERIVATIONS" identifying the provisions of earlier legislation from which the section or Schedule has been derived.

Finding other legislation

Legislation in both its amended and its unamended form may now be found on *http://www.legislation.gov.uk* and so the "Blue Volumes" at *http://lawvolumes.dwp.gov.uk/the-law-relating-to-social-security/* are no longer being updated (as from October 2015). Northern Ireland social security legislation may be found at *http://www.communities-ni.gov/law_relating_to_social_security*. European Union legislation may be found at *http://eur-lex.europa.eu/collection/eu-law.html*

Interpreting legislation

Legislation is written in English and generally means what it says. However, more than one interpretation is often possible. Most legislation itself contains definitions. Sometimes these are in the particular provision in which a word occurs but, where a word is used in more than one place, any definition will appear with others. In an Act, an interpretation section is usually to be found towards the end of the Act or of the relevant Part of the Act. In a statutory instrument, an interpretation provision usually appears near the beginning of the statutory instrument or the relevant Part of it. In the more important pieces of legislation in this series, there is included after every section, regulation, rule, article or Schedule a list of "DEFINITIONS", showing where definitions of words used in the provision are to be found.

However, not all words are statutorily defined and there is in any event more to interpreting legislation than merely defining its terms. Decision-makers and tribunals need to know how to apply the law in different types of situations. That is where case law comes in.

Case law and the commentary in this book

In deciding individual cases, courts and tribunals interpret the relevant law and incidentally establish legal principles. Decisions on questions of legal principle of the superior courts and appellate tribunals are said to be binding on decision-makers and the First-tier Tribunal, which means that decision-makers and the First-tier Tribunal must apply those principles. Thus the judicial decisions of the superior courts and appellate tribunals form part of the law. The commentary to the legislation in this series, under the heading "GENERAL NOTE" after a section, regulation, rule, article or Schedule, refers to this *case law*.

The largest part of the case law regarding social security benefits is still in the form of decisions of Social Security Commissioners and Child Support Commissioners. However, while there are still Commissioners in Northern Ireland, which has a largely separate judiciary and tribunal system, the functions of Commissioners in Great Britain were transferred to the Upper Tribunal and allocated to the Administrative Appeals Chamber of that tribunal on November 3, 2008. Consequently, social security case law is increasingly to be found in decisions of the Upper Tribunal.

The commentary in this series is not itself binding on any decision-maker or tribunal because it is merely the opinion of the author. It is what is actually said in the legislation or in the judicial decision that is important. The legislation is set out in this series, but it will generally be necessary to look elsewhere for the precise words used in judicial decisions. The way that decisions are cited in the commentary enables that to be done.

The reporting of decisions of the Upper Tribunal and Commissioners

About 50 of the most important decisions of the Administrative Appeals Chamber of the Upper Tribunal are selected to be "reported" each year in the Administrative Appeals Chamber Reports (AACR), using the same criteria as were formerly used for reporting Commissioners' decisions in Great Britain. The selection is made by an editorial board of judges and decisions are selected for reporting only if they are of general importance and command the assent of at least a majority of the relevant judges. The term "reported" simply means that they are published in printed form as well as on the Internet (see *Finding case law*, below) with headnotes (i.e. summaries) and indexes, but there are two other important consequences of a decision being reported. Reported decisions are available in some tribunal venues and can be consulted in local social security offices and some main libraries. They also have a greater precedential status than ordinary decisions (see *Judicial precedent* below).

A handful of Northern Ireland Commissioners' decisions are also selected for reporting in the Administrative Appeals Chamber Reports each year, the selection being made by the Chief Social Security Commissioner in Northern Ireland.

Citing case law

As has been mentioned, the largest part of social security case law is still to be found in decisions of Social Security Commissioners and Child Support Commissioners, even though the Commissioners have now effectively been abolished in Great Britain.

Reported decisions of Commissioners were known merely by a number or, more accurately, a series of letters and numbers beginning with an "R". The type of benefit in issue was indicated by letters in brackets (e.g. "IS" was income support, "P" was retirement pension, and so on) and the year in which the decision was selected for reporting or, from 2000, the year in which it was published as a reported decision, was indicated by the last two digits, as in *R(IS) 2/08*. In Northern Ireland there was a similar system until 2009, save that the type of benefit was identified by letters in brackets after the number, as in *R 1/07 (DLA)*.

Unreported decisions of the Commissioners in Great Britain were known simply by their file numbers, which began with a "C", as in *CIS/2287/2008*. The letters following the "C" indicated the type of benefit in issue in the case. Scottish and, at one time, Welsh cases were indicated by a "S" or "W" immediately after the "C", as in *CSIS/467/2007*. The last four digits indicated the calendar year in which the case was registered, rather than the year it was decided. A similar system operated in Northern Ireland until 2009, save that the letters indicating the type of benefit appeared in brackets after the numbers and, from April 1999, the financial year rather than the calendar year was identified, as in *C 10/06-07 (IS)*.

Decisions of the Upper Tribunal, of courts and, since 2010, of the Northern Ireland Commissioners are generally known by the names of the parties (or just two of them in multi-party cases). Individuals are anonymised through the use of initials in the names of decisions of the Upper Tribunal and the Northern Ireland Commissioners and occasionally in the names of decisions of courts. In this series, the names of official bodies may also be abbreviated (e.g. "SSWP" for the Secretary of State for Work and Pensions, "HMRC" for Her Majesty's Revenue and Customs, "CMEC" for the Child Maintenance and Enforcement Commission and "DSD" for the Department for Social Development in Northern Ireland). Since 2010, decisions of the Upper Tribunal and of Northern Ireland Commissioners have also been given a "flag" in brackets to indicate the subject matter of the decision, which in social security cases indicates the principal benefit in issue in the case. Thus, the name of one jobseeker's allowance case is *SSWP v JB (JSA)*.

Any decision of the Upper Tribunal, of a court since 2001 or of a Northern Ireland Commissioner since 2010 that has been intended for publication has also given a *neutral citation number* which enables the decision to be more precisely identified. This indicates, in square brackets, the year the decision was made (although in relation to decisions of the courts it sometimes merely indicates the year the number was issued) and also indicates the court or tribunal that made the decision (e.g. "UKUT" for the Upper Tribunal, "NICom" for a Northern Ireland Commissioner, "EWCA Civ" for the Civil Division of the Court of Appeal in England and Wales, "NICA" for the Court of Appeal in Northern Ireland, "CSIH" for the Inner House of the Court of Session (in Scotland), "UKSC" for the Supreme Court and so on). A number is added so that the reference is unique and finally, in the case of the Upper Tribunal or the High Court in England and Wales, the relevant chamber of the Upper Tribunal or the relevant division or other part of the High Court is identified (e.g. "(AAC)" for the Administrative Appeals Chamber, "(Admin)" for the Administrative Court and so on). Examples of decisions of the Upper Tribunal and a Northern Ireland Commissioner with their neutral citation numbers are *SSWP v JB (JSA)* [2010] UKUT 4 (AAC) and *AR v DSD (IB)* [2010] NICom 6.

If the case is reported in the Administrative Appeals Chamber Reports or another series of law reports, a reference to the report usually follows the neutral citation number. Conventionally, this includes either the year the case was decided (in round brackets) or the year in which it was reported (in square brackets), followed by the volume number (if any), the name of the series of reports (in abbreviated form—see the Table of Abbreviations at the beginning of each volume of this series) and either the page number or the case number. However, before 2010, cases reported in the Administrative Appeals Chamber Reports or with Commissioners' decisions were numbered in the same way as reported Commissioners' decisions. *Abdirahman v Secretary of State for Work and Pensions* [2007] EWCA Civ 657; [2008] 1 W.L.R. 254 (also reported as *R(IS) 8/07*) is a Court of Appeal decision, decided in 2007 but reported in 2008 in volume 1 of the Weekly Law Reports at p.254 and also in the 2007 volume of reported Commissioners' decisions. *NT v SSWP* [2009] UKUT 37 (AAC), *R(DLA) 1/09* is an Upper Tribunal case decided in 2009 and reported in the Administrative Appeals Chamber Reports in the same year. *Martin v SSWP* [2009] EWCA Civ 1289; [2010] AACR 9 is a decision of the Court of Appeal that was decided in 2009 and was the ninth decision reported in the Administrative Appeals Chamber Reports in 2010.

It is usually necessary to include the neutral citation number or a reference to a series of reports only the first time a decision is cited in any document. After that, the name of the case is usually sufficient.

All decisions of the Upper Tribunal that are on their website have neutral citation numbers. If you wish to refer a tribunal or decision-maker to a decision of the Upper Tribunal that does not have a neutral citation number, contact the office of the Administrative Appeals Chamber (adminappeals@hmcts.gsi.gov.uk) who will provide a number and add the decision to the website.

Decision-makers and claimants are entitled to assume that judges of both the First-tier Tribunal and the Upper Tribunal have immediate access to reported decisions of Commissioners or the Upper Tribunal and they need not provide copies, although it may sometimes be helpful to do so.

However, where either a decision-maker or a claimant intends to rely on an unreported decision, it will be necessary to provide a copy of the decision to the judge and other members of the tribunal. A copy of the decision should also be provided to the other party before the hearing because otherwise it may be necessary for there to be an adjournment to enable that party to take advice on the significance of the decision.

Finding case law

The extensive references described above are used so as to enable people easily to find the full text of a decision. Most decisions of any significance since the late 1990s can be found on the Internet.

Decisions of the Upper Tribunal and of the Commissioners in Great Britain may be found on the HMCTS website at *http://www.osscsc.gov.uk/Decisions/decisions.htm*. This includes reported decisions since 1991 and other decisions considered likely to be of interest to tribunals and tribunal users since about 2000, together with a few older decisions. Decisions of Commissioners in Northern Ireland may be found on *http://www.dsdni.gov.uk/index/law_and_legislation.htm*.

The Administrative Appeals Chamber Reports, which include not only reported decisions of the Administrative Appeals Chamber of the Upper Tribunal but also reported decisions of the Northern Ireland Commissioners and decisions of the courts in related areas of law, are available on the HMCTS website at *http://www.osscsc.gov.uk/Decisions/adminAppealsChamberReports.htm*. They are also published by the Stationery Office in bound volumes which follow on from the bound volumes of Commissioners' decisions published from 1948.

Copies of decisions of the Administrative Appeals Chamber of the Upper Tribunal or of Commissioners that are otherwise unavailable may be obtained from the offices of the Upper Tribunal (Administrative Appeals Chamber) or, in Northern Ireland, from the Office of the Social Security and Child Support Commissioners.

Decisions of a wide variety of courts and tribunals in the United Kingdom may be found on the free website of the British and Irish Legal Information Institute, *http://www.bailii.org*. It includes all decisions of the Supreme Court and provides fairly comprehensive coverage of decisions given since about 1996 by the House of Lords and Privy Council and most of the higher courts in England and Wales, decisions given since 1998 by the Court of Session and decisions given since 2000 by the Court of Appeal and High Court in Northern Ireland. Some earlier decisions have been included, so it is always worth looking and, indeed, those decisions dating from 1873 or earlier and reported in the English Reports may be found through a link to *http://www.commonlii.org/uk/cases/EngR/*.

Decisions of the European Court of Justice (concerned with the law of the European Union) are all to be found on *http://www.curia.europa.eu*.

Decisions of the European Court of Human Rights are available at *http://www.echr.coe.int*.

Most decisions of the courts in social security cases, including decisions of the European Court of Justice on cases referred by United Kingdom courts and tribunals, are reported in the Administrative Appeals Chamber Reports or with the reported decisions of Commissioners and may therefore be found on the same websites and in the same printed series of reported decisions.

So, for example, *R(I)1/00* contains Commissioner's decision *CSI/12/1998*, the decision of the Court of Session upholding the Commissioner's decision and the decision of the House of Lords in *Chief Adjudication Officer v Faulds*, reversing the decision of the Court of Session. The most important decisions of the courts can also be found in the various series of law reports familiar to lawyers (in particular, in the *Law Reports*, the *Weekly Law Reports*, the *All England Law Reports*, the *Public and Third Sector Law Reports*, the *Industrial Cases Reports* and the *Family Law Reports*) but these are not widely available outside academic or other law libraries, although the *All England Law Reports* are occasionally to be found in the larger public libraries. See the Table of Cases at the beginning of each volume of this series for all the places where a decision mentioned in that volume is reported.

If you know the name or number of a decision and wish to know where in a volume of this series there is a reference to it, use the Table of Cases or the Table of Commissioners' Decisions in the relevant volume to find the paragraph(s) where the decision is mentioned.

Judicial precedent

As already mentioned, decisions of the Upper Tribunal, the Commissioners and the higher courts in Great Britain become *case law* because they set binding precedents which must be followed by decision-makers and the First-tier Tribunal in Great Britain. This means that, where the Upper Tribunal, Commissioner or court has decided a point of legal principle, decision-makers and appeal tribunals must make their decisions in conformity with the decision of the Upper Tribunal, Commissioner or court, applying the same principle and accepting the interpretation of the law contained in the decision. So a decision of the Upper Tribunal, a Commissioner or a superior court explaining what a term in a particular regulation means, lays down the definition of that term in much the same way as if the term had been defined in the regulations themselves. The decision may also help in deciding what the same term means when it is used in a different set of regulations, provided that the term appears to have been used in a similar context.

Only decisions on points of law set precedents that are binding and, strictly speaking, only decisions on points of law that were necessary to the overall conclusion reached by the Upper Tribunal, Commissioner or court are binding. Other parts of a decision (which used to be known as obiter dicta) may be regarded as helpful guidance but need not be followed if a decision-maker or the First-tier Tribunal is persuaded that there is a better approach. It is particularly important to bear this in mind in relation to older decisions of Social Security Commissioners because, until 1987, the right of appeal to a Commissioner was not confined to points of law.

Where there is a conflict between precedents, a decision-maker or the First-tier Tribunal is generally free to choose between decisions of equal status. For these purposes, most decisions of the Upper Tribunal and decisions of Commissioners are of equal status. However, a decision-maker or First-tier Tribunal should generally prefer a reported decision to an unreported one unless the unreported decision was the later decision and the Commissioner or Upper Tribunal expressly decided not to follow the earlier reported decision. This is simply because the fact that a decision has been reported shows that at least half of the relevant judges of the Upper

Tribunal or the Commissioners agreed with it at the time. A decision of a Tribunal of Commissioners (i.e. three Commissioners sitting together) or a decision of a three-judge panel of the Upper Tribunal must be preferred to a decision of a single Commissioner or a single judge of the Upper Tribunal.

A single judge of the Upper Tribunal will normally follow a decision of a single Commissioner or another judge of the Upper Tribunal, but is not bound to do so. A three-judge panel of the Upper Tribunal will generally follow a decision of another such panel or of a Tribunal of Commissioners, but similarly is not bound to do so, whereas a single judge of the Upper Tribunal will always follow such a decision.

Strictly speaking, the Northern Ireland Commissioners do not set binding precedent that must be followed in Great Britain but their decisions are relevant, due to the similarity of the legislation in Northern Ireland, and are usually regarded as highly persuasive with the result that, in practice, they are generally given as much weight as decisions of the Great Britain Commissioners. The same approach is taken in Northern Ireland to decisions of the Upper Tribunal on social security matters and to decisions of the Great Britain Commissioners.

Decisions of the superior courts in Great Britain and Northern Ireland on questions of legal principle are almost invariably followed by decision-makers, tribunals and the Upper Tribunal, even when they are not strictly binding because the relevant court was in a different part of the United Kingdom or exercised a parallel—but not superior—jurisdiction.

Decisions of the European Court of Justice come in two parts: the Opinion of the Advocate General and the decision of the Court. It is the decision of the Court which is binding. The Court is assisted by hearing the Opinion of the Advocate General before itself coming to a conclusion on the issue before it. The Court does not always follow its Advocate General. Where it does, the Opinion of the Advocate General often elaborates the arguments in greater detail than the single collegiate judgment of the Court. Decision-makers, tribunals and Commissioners must apply decisions of the European Court of Justice, where relevant to cases before them, in preference to other authorities binding on them.

The European Court of Human Rights in Strasbourg is quite separate from the European Court of Justice in Luxembourg and serves a different purpose: interpreting and applying the European Convention on Human Rights, which is incorporated into United Kingdom law by the Human Rights Act 1998. Since October 2, 2000, public authorities in the United Kingdom, including courts, Commissioners, tribunals and decision-makers, have been required to act in accordance with the incorporated provisions of the Convention, unless statute prevents this. They must take into account the Strasbourg case law and are required to interpret domestic legislation, so far as it is possible to do so, to give effect to the incorporated Convention rights. Any court or tribunal may declare secondary legislation incompatible with those rights and, in certain circumstances, invalidate it. Only the higher courts can declare a provision of primary legislation to be incompatible with those rights, but no court, tribunal or Upper Tribunal can invalidate primary legislation. The work of the Strasbourg Court and the impact of the Human Rights Act 1998 on social security are discussed in the commentary in Part IV of *Vol III: Administration, Appeals and the European Dimension*.

See the note to s.3(2) of the Tribunals, Courts and Enforcement Act 2007 in Part V of *Vol III: Administration, Appeals and the European Dimension* for a more detailed and technical consideration of the rules of precedent.

Other sources of information and commentary on social security law

For a comprehensive overview of the social security system in Great Britain, CPAG's *Welfare Benefits and Tax Credits Handbook*, published annually each spring, is unrivalled as a practical introduction from the claimant's viewpoint.

From a different perspective, the Department for Work and Pensions publishes the 14-volume *Decision Makers' Guide* at *https://www.gov.uk/government/collections/decision-makers-guide-staff-guide* and the new *Advice for Decision Making*, which covers personal independence payment, universal credit and the "new" versions of Jobseeker's Allowance and Employment and Support Allowance, at *https://www.gov.uk/government/publications/advice-for-decision-making-staff-guide*. Similarly, Her Majesty's Revenue and Customs publish manuals relating to tax credits, child benefit and guardian's allowance, which they administer, see *http://www.hmrc.gov.uk/thelibrary/manuals-a-z.htm*. (Note that the *Child Benefit Technical Manual* also covers guardian's allowance). These guides and manuals are extremely useful but their interpretation of the law is not binding on tribunals and the courts, being merely internal guidance for the use of decision-makers.

There are a number of other sources of valuable information or commentary on social security case law: see in particular publications such as the *Journal of Social Security Law*, CPAG's *Welfare Rights Bulletin*, *Legal Action* and the *Adviser*. As far as online resources go there is little to beat *Rightsnet* (*http://www.rightsnet.org.uk*). This site contains a wealth of resources for people working in the welfare benefits field but of special relevance in this context are the Commissioners/Upper Tribunal Decisions section of the "Toolkit" area and also the "Briefcase" area which contains summaries of the decisions (with links to the full decisions). Sweet and Maxwell's online subscription service *Westlaw* is another valuable source (*http://www.westlaw.co.uk*), as is the Merrill Corporation's *Casetrack* (*http://www.casetrack.com/ct/casetrack.nsf/index?openframeset*) and LexisNexis *Lexis* (*http://www.lexis.com*).

Conclusion

The Internet provides a vast resource but a search needs to be focused. Social security schemes are essentially statutory and so in Great Britain the legislation which is set out in this series forms the basic structure of social security law. However, the case law shows how the legislation should be interpreted and applied. The commentary in this series should point the way to the case law relevant to each provision and the Internet can then be used to find it where that is necessary.

CHANGE OF NAME FROM DEPARTMENT OF SOCIAL SECURITY TO DEPARTMENT FOR WORK AND PENSIONS

The Secretaries of State for Education and Skills and for Work and Pensions Order 2002 (SI 2002/1397) makes provision for the change of name from the Department of Social Security to Department for Work and Pensions. Article 9(5) provides:

"(5) Subject to article 12 [which makes specific amendments], any enactment or instrument passed or made before the coming into force of this Order shall have effect, so far as may be necessary for the purposes of or in consequence of the entrusting to the Secretary of State for Work and Pensions of the social security functions, as if any reference to the Secretary of State for Social Security, to the Department of Social Security or to an officer of the Secretary of State for Social Security (including any reference which is to be construed as such as reference) were a reference to the Secretary of State for Work and Pensions, to the Department for Work and Pensions or, as the case may be, to an officer of the Secretary of State for Work and Pensions."

CHANGES IN TERMINOLOGY CONSEQUENT UPON THE ENTRY INTO FORCE OF THE TREATY OF LISBON

The Treaty of Lisbon (Changes in Terminology) Order 2011 (SI 2011/1043) (which came into force on April 22, 2011) makes a number of changes to terminology used in primary and secondary legislation as a consequence of the entry into force of the Treaty of Lisbon on December 1, 2009. The Order accomplishes this by requiring certain terms in primary and secondary legislation to be read in accordance with the requirements of the Order. No substantive changes to the law are involved.

The changes are somewhat complex because of the different ways in which the term "Community" is used, and the abbreviations "EC" or "EEC" are used. References to the "European Community", "European Communities", "European Coal and Steel Communities", "the Community", "the EC" and "the EEC" are generally to be read as references to the "European Union".

The following table shows the more common usages involving the word "Community" in the first column which are now to be read in the form set out in the second column:

Original term	**To be read as**
Community treaties	EU treaties
Community institution	EU institution
Community instrument	EU instrument
Community obligation	EU obligation
Enforceable Community right	Enforceable EU right
Community law, or European Community law	EU law
Community legislation, or European Community legislation	EU legislation
Community provision, or European Community provision	EU provision

Provision is also made for changes to certain legislation relating to Wales in the Welsh language.

Relevant extracts from the Order can be found in Volume III, *Administration, Adjudication and the European Dimension*.

THE MARRIAGE (SAME SEX COUPLES) ACT 2013

The Marriage (Same Sex Couples) Act 2013 (c.30) provides in s.3 and Schs 3 and 4 that the terms "marriage", "married couple" and being "married" in existing and future legislation in England and Wales are to be read as references to a marriage between persons of the same sex. The same approach is taken to any legislation about couples living together as if married. This is subject to certain specified exclusions contained in Sch.4, and in any Order providing for a contrary approach to be taken.

Schedule 2 to The Marriage (Same Sex Couples) Act 2013 (Consequential and Contrary Provisions and Scotland) Order 2014 (SI 2014/560) contains a substantial list of contrary provisions to s.11(1) and (2) and paras 1 to 3 of Sch.3 to the 2013 Act. Most of these relate to specific enactments, but note that Pt 2 of the Schedule provides that s.11(1) and (2) do not apply to "EU instruments". This term is defined in Sch.1 to the European Communities Act 1972 (as amended) as "any instrument issued by an EU institution". It refers mainly to regulations, directives, decisions, recommendations and opinions issued by the institutions.

TABLE OF CASES

TABLE OF COMMISSIONERS' DECISIONS 1948–2009

TABLE OF ABBREVIATIONS USED IN THIS SERIES

1975 Act	Social Security Act 1975
1977 Act	Marriage (Scotland) Act 1977
1979 Act	Pneumoconiosis (Workers' Compensation) Act 1979
1986 Act	Social Security Act 1986
1996 Act	Employment Rights Act 1996
1998 Act	Social Security Act 1998
2002 Act	Tax Credits Act 2002
2004 Act	Gender Recognition Act 2004
2006 Act	Armed Forces Act 2006
2008 Act	Child Maintenance and Other Payments Act 2008
2013 Act	Marriage (Same Sex Couples) Act 2013
2014 Act	Marriage and Civil Partnership (Scotland) Act 2014
A1P1	Art.1 of Protocol 1 to the European Convention on Human Rights
AA	Attendance Allowance
AA 1992	Attendance Allowance Act 1992
AAC	Administrative Appeals Chamber
AACR	Administrative Appeals Chamber Reports
A.C.	Law Reports, Appeal Cases
A.C.D.	Administrative Court Digest
Admin	Administrative Court
Admin L.R.	Administrative Law Reports
Administration Act	Social Security Administration Act 1992
Administration Regulations	Statutory Paternity Pay and Statutory Adoption Pay (Administration) Regulations 2002
AIP	assessed income period
All E.R.	All England Reports
All E.R. (E.C.)	All England Reports (European Cases)
AMA	Adjudicating Medical Authorities
AO	Adjudication Officer
AOG	*Adjudication Officers Guide*
art.	article
Art.	Article
ASD	Autistic Spectrum Disorder
ASPP	Additional Statutory Paternity Pay

A.T.C.	Annotated Tax Cases
Attendance Allowance Regulations	Social Security (Attendance Allowance) Regulations 1991
AWT	All Work Test
BA	Benefits Agency
Benefits Act	Social Security Contributions and Benefits Act 1992
B.H.R.C.	Butterworths Human Rights Cases
B.L.G.R.	Butterworths Local Government Reports
Blue Books	*The Law Relating to Social Security*, Vols 1–11
B.P.I.R.	Bankruptcy and Personal Insolvency Reports
B.T.C.	British Tax Cases
BTEC	Business and Technology Education Council
B.V.C.	British Value Added Tax Reporter
B.W.C.C.	Butterworths Workmen's Compensation Cases
c.	chapter
C	Commissioner's decision
C&BA 1992	Social Security Contributions and Benefits Act 1992
CAA 2001	Capital Allowances Act 2001
CAB	Citizens Advice Bureau
CAO	Chief Adjudication Officer
CB	Child Benefit
CBA 1975	Child Benefit Act 1975
CBJSA	Contribution-Based Jobseeker's Allowance
C.C.L. Rep.	Community Care Law Reports
CCM	HMRC *New Tax Credits Claimant Compliance Manual*
C.E.C.	European Community Cases
CERA	cortical evoked response audiogram
CESA	Contribution-based Employment and Support Allowance
CFS	chronic fatigue syndrome
Ch.	Chancery Division Law Reports; Chapter
Citizenship Directive	Directive 2004/38/EC of the European Parliament and of the Council of April 29, 2004
CJEC	Court of Justice of the European Communities
CJEU	Court of Justice of the European Union
Claims and Payments Regulations	Social Security (Claims and Payments) Regulations 1987
Claims and Payments Regulations 1979	Social Security (Claims and Payments) Regulations 1979
Claims and Payments Regulations 2013	Universal Credit, Personal Independence Payment, Jobseeker's Allowance and Employment and Support Allowance (Claims and Payments) Regulations 2013

CM	Case Manager
CMA	Chief Medical Adviser
CMEC	Child Maintenance and Enforcement Commission
C.M.L.R.	Common Market Law Reports
C.O.D.	Crown Office Digest
COLL	*Collective Investment Schemes Sourcebook*
Community, The	European Community
Computation of Earnings Regulations	Social Security Benefit (Computation of Earnings) Regulations 1978
Computation of Earnings Regulations 1996	Social Security Benefit (Computation of Earnings) Regulations 1996
Consequential Provisions Act	Social Security (Consequential Provisions) Act 1992
Contributions and Benefits Act	Social Security Contributions and Benefits Act 1992
Contributions Regulations	Social Security (Contributions) Regulations 2001
COPD	chronic obstructive pulmonary disease
CP	Carer Premium; Chamber President
CPAG	Child Poverty Action Group
CPR	Civil Procedure Rules
Cr. App. R.	Criminal Appeal Reports
CRCA 2005	Commissioners for Revenue and Customs Act 2005
Credits Regulations 1974	Social Security (Credits) Regulations 1974
Credits Regulations 1975	Social Security (Credits) Regulations 1975
Crim. L.R.	Criminal Law Review
CRU	Compensation Recovery Unit
CSA 1995	Children (Scotland) Act 1995
CSIH	Inner House of the Court of Session (Scotland)
CSM	Child Support Maintenance
CS(NI)O 1995	Child Support (Northern Ireland) Order 1995
CSOH	Outer House of the Court of Session (Scotland)
CSPSSA 2000	Child Support, Pensions and Social Security Act 2000
CTA	Common Travel Area
CTA 2009	Corporation Tax Act 2009
CTA 2010	Corporation Tax Act 2010
CTB	Council Tax Benefit
CTC	Child Tax Credit
CTC Regulations	Child Tax Credit Regulations 2002
CTF	child trust fund
CTS	Carpal Tunnel Syndrome
DAC	Directive 2011/16/ EU (Directive on administrative co-operation in the field of taxation)

DAT	Disability Appeal Tribunal
dB	decibels
DCA	Department for Constitutional Affairs
DCP	Disabled Child Premium
Decisions and Appeals Regulations 1999	Social Security Contributions (Decisions and Appeals) Regulations 1999
Dependency Regulations	Social Security Benefit (Dependency) Regulations 1977
DfEE	Department for Education and Employment
DHSS	Department of Health and Social Security
Disability Living Allowance Regulations	Social Security (Disability Living Allowance) Regulations
DIY	do it yourself
DLA	Disability Living Allowance
DLA Regs 1991	Social Security (Disability Living Allowance) Regulations 1991
DLAAB	Disability Living Allowance Advisory Board
DLADWAA 1991	Disability Living Allowance and Disability Working Allowance Act 1991
DM	Decision Maker
DMA	Decision-making and Appeals
DMG	*Decision Makers' Guide*
DMP	Delegated Medical Practitioner
DP	Disability Premium
DPT	diffuse pleural thickening
DPTC	Disabled Person's Tax Credit
DRO	Debt Relief Order
DSD	Department for Social Development (Northern Ireland)
DSM IV; DSM-5	Diagnostic and Statistical Manual of Mental Disorders of the American Psychiatric Association
DSS	Department of Social Security
DTI	Department of Trade and Industry
DWA	Disability Working Allowance
DWP	Department for Work and Pensions
DWPMS	Department for Work and Pensions Medical Service
EAA	Extrinsic Allergic Alveolitis
EAT	Employment Appeal Tribunal
EC	European Community
ECHR	European Convention on Human Rights
ECJ	European Court of Justice
E.C.R.	European Court Reports
ECSC	European Coal and Steel Community
ECSMA	European Convention on Social and Medical Assistance

EEA	European Economic Area
EEC	European Economic Community
EESSI	Electronic Exchange of Social Security Information
E.G.	Estates Gazette
E.G.L.R.	Estates Gazette Law Reports
EHC plan	education, health and care plan
EHIC	European Health Insurance Card
EHRC	European Human Rights Commission
E.H.R.R.	European Human Rights Reports
EL	employers' liability
E.L.R	Education Law Reports
EMA	Education Maintenance Allowance
EMP	Examining Medical Practitioner
Employment and Support Allowance Regulations	Employment and Support Allowance Regulations 2008
EPS	extended period of sickness
Eq. L.R.	Equality Law Reports
ERA	evoked response audiometry
ERA scheme	Employment, Retention and Advancement scheme
ES	Employment Service
ESA	Employment and Support Allowance
ESA Regs 2013	Employment and Support Allowance Regulations 2013
ESA Regulations	Employment and Support Allowance Regulations 2008
ESA WCAt	Employment and Support Allowance Work Capability Assessment
ESE Scheme	Employment, Skills and Enterprise Scheme
ESE Regulations	Jobseeker's Allowance (Employment, Skills and Enterprise Scheme) Regulations 2011
ESES Regulations	Jobseeker's Allowance (Employment, Skills and Enterprise Scheme) Regulations 2011
ETA 1973	Employment and Training Act 1973
ETA(NI) 1950	Employment and Training Act (Northern Ireland) 1950
ETS	European Treaty Series
EU	European Union
Eu.L.R.	European Law Reports
EWCA Civ	Civil Division of the Court of Appeal (England and Wales)
EWHC Admin	Administrative Court Division of the High Court (England and Wales)
FA 1993	Finance Act 1993
FA 1996	Finance Act 1996

FA 2004	Finance Act 2004
Fam. Law	Family Law
FAS	Financial Assistance Scheme
F.C.R.	Family Court Reporter
FEV	forced expiratory volume
FIS	Family Income Supplement
FISMA 2000	Financial Services and Markets Act 2000
F.L.R.	Family Law Reports
FME	further medical evidence
F(No.2)A 2005	Finance (No.2) Act 2005
FOTRA	Free of Tax to Residents Abroad
FRAA	flat rate accrual amount
FSCS	Financial Services Compensation Scheme
FTT	First-tier Tribunal
General Benefit Regulations 1982	Social Security (General Benefit) Regulations 1982
General Regulations	Statutory Shared Parental Pay (General) Regulations 2014
GMP	Guaranteed Minimum Pension
GNVQ	General National Vocational Qualification
GP	General Practitioner
GRA	Gender Recognition Act 2004
GRB	Graduated Retirement Benefit
GRP	Graduated Retirement Pension
HB	Housing Benefit
HBRB	Housing Benefit Review Board
HCD	House of Commons Debates
HCP	healthcare professional
HCV	Hepatitis C virus
Health Service Act	National Health Service Act 2006
Health Service (Wales) Act	National Health Service (Wales) Act 2006
HIV	Human Immunodeficiency Virus
HL	House of Lords
H.L.R.	Housing Law Reports
HMIT	Her Majesty's Inspector of Taxes
HMRC	Her Majesty's Revenue and Customs
HMSO	Her Majesty's Stationery Office
Hospital In-Patients Regulations 1975	Social Security (Hospital In-Patients) Regulations 1975
HP	Health Professional
HPP	Higher Pensioner Premium
HRA 1998	Human Rights Act 1998
H.R.L.R.	Human Rights Law Reports
HRP	Home Responsibilities Protection

HSE	Health and Safety Executive
IAC	Immigration and Asylum Chamber
IAP	Intensive Activity Period
IB	Incapacity Benefit
IB PCA	Incapacity Benefit Personal Capability Assessment
IB Regs	Social Security (Incapacity Benefit) Regulations 1994
IB Regulations	Social Security (Incapacity Benefit) Regulations 1994
IB/IS/SDA	Incapacity Benefits Regime
IBJSA	Income-Based Jobseeker's Allowance
IBS	Irritable Bowel Syndrome
ICA	Invalid Care Allowance
I.C.R.	Industrial Cases Reports
ICTA 1988	Income and Corporation Taxes Act 1988
IFW Regulations	Incapacity for Work (General) Regulations 1995
IH	Inner House of the Court of Session
I.I.	Industrial Injuries
IIAC	Industrial Injuries Advisory Council
IIDB	Industrial Injuries Disablement Benefit
ILO	International Labour Organization
Imm. A.R.	Immigration Appeal Reports
Incapacity for Work Regulations	Social Security (Incapacity for Work) (General) Regulations 1995
Income Support General Regulations	Income Support (General) Regulations 1987
IND	Immigration and Nationality Directorate of the Home Office
I.N.L.R.	Immigration and Nationality Law Reports
I.O.	Insurance Officer
IPPR	Institute of Public Policy Research
IRESA	Income-Related Employment and Support Allowance
I.R.L.R.	Industrial Relations Law Reports
IS	Income Support
IS Regs	Income Support Regulations
IS Regulations	Income Support (General) Regulations 1987
ISA	Individual Savings Account
ISBN	International Standard Book Number
ITA 2007	Income Tax Act 2007
ITEPA 2003	Income Tax, Earnings and Pensions Act 2003
I.T.L. Rep.	International Tax Law Reports
I.T.R.	Industrial Tribunals Reports
ITS	Independent Tribunal Service

ITTOIA 2005	Income Tax (Trading and Other Income) Act 2005
IVB	Invalidity Benefit
IW (General) Regs	Social Security (Incapacity for Work) (General) Regulations 1995
IW (Transitional) Regs	Incapacity for Work (Transitional) Regulations
Jobseeker's Allowance Regulations	Jobseeker's Allowance Regulations 1996
Jobseeker's Regulations 1996	Jobseeker's Allowance Regulations 1996
JSA	Jobseeker's Allowance
JSA 1995	Jobseekers Act 1995
JSA (NI) Regulations	Jobseeker's Allowance (Northern Ireland) Regulations 1996
JSA (Transitional) Regulations	Jobseeker's Allowance (Transitional) Regulations 1996
JSA Regs 1996	Jobseeker's Allowance Regulations 1996
JSA Regs 2013	Jobseeker's Allowance Regulations 2013
JS(NI)O 1995	Jobseekers (Northern Ireland) Order 1995
J.S.S.L.	Journal of Social Security Law
J.S.W.L.	Journal of Social Welfare Law
K.B.	Law Reports, King's Bench
L.& T.R.	Landlord and Tenant Reports
LCW	limited capability for work
LCWA	Limited Capability for Work Assessment
LCWRA	limited capability for work-related activity
LEA	local education authority
LEL	Lower Earnings Limit
LET	low earnings threshold
L.G. Rev.	Local Government Review
L.G.L.R.	Local Government Reports
L.J.R.	Law Journal Reports
LRP	liable relative payment
L.S.G.	Law Society Gazette
Luxembourg Court	Court of Justice of the European Union (also referred to as CJEC and ECJ)
MA	Maternity Allowance
MAF	Medical Assessment Framework
Maternity Allowance Regulations	Social Security (Maternity Allowance) Regulations 1987
ME	myalgic encephalomyelitis
Medical Evidence Regulations	Social Security (Medical Evidence) Regulations 1976
MEN	Mandatory Employment Notification
Mesher and Wood	*Income Support, the Social Fund and Family Credit: the Legislation* (1996)
M.H.L.R.	Mental Health Law Reports

MHP	mental health problems
MIF	minimum income floor
MIG	minimum income guarantee
Migration Regulations	Employment and Support Allowance (Transitional Provisions, Housing Benefit and Council Tax Benefit (Existing Awards) (No.2) Regulations 2010
MP	Member of Parliament
MRSA	methicillin-resistant Staphylococcus aureus
MS	Medical Services
MWA Regulations	Jobseeker's Allowance (Mandatory Work Activity Scheme) Regulations 2011
MWAS Regulations	Jobseeker's Allowance (Mandatory Work Activity Scheme) Regulations 2011
NCB	National Coal Board
NDPD	Notes on the Diagnosis of Prescribed Diseases
NHS	National Health Service
NI	National Insurance
N.I..	Northern Ireland Law Reports
NICA	Northern Ireland Court of Appeal
NICom	Northern Ireland Commissioner
NICs	National Insurance Contributions
NINO	National Insurance Number
NIRS 2	National Insurance Recording System
N.L.J.	New Law Journal
NMC	Nursing and Midwifery Council
Northern Ireland Contributions and Benefits Act	Social Security Contributions and Benefits (Northern Ireland) Act 1992
N.P.C.	New Property Cases
NTC Manual	Clerical procedures manual on tax credits
NUM	National Union of Mineworkers
NUS	National Union of Students
OCD	obsessive compulsive disorder
Ogus, Barendt and Wikeley	A. Ogus, E. Barendt and N. Wikeley, *The Law of Social Security* (1995)
Old Cases Act	Industrial Injuries and Diseases (Old Cases) Act 1975
OPB	One Parent Benefit
O.P.L.R.	Occupational Pensions Law Reports
OPSSAT	Office of the President of Social Security Appeal Tribunals
Overlapping Benefits Regulations	Social Security (Overlapping Benefits) Regulations 1975
P	retirement pension case
P. & C.R.	Property and Compensation Reports
para.	paragraph

Pay Regulations	Statutory Paternity Pay and Statutory Adoption Pay (General) Regulations 2002; Statutory Shared Parental Pay (General) Regulations 2014
PAYE	Pay As You Earn
PC	Privy Council
PCA	Personal Capability Assessment
PD	Practice Direction; prescribed disease
Pens. L.R.	Pensions Law Reports
Pensions Act	Pension Schemes Act 1993
PEP	Personal Equity Plan
Persons Abroad Regulations	Social Security Benefit (Persons Abroad) Regulations 1975
Persons Residing Together Regulations	Social Security Benefit (Persons Residing Together) Regulations 1977
PIE	Period of Interruption of Employment
PILON	pay in lieu of notice
Pilot Scheme Regulations	Universal Credit (Work-Related Requirements) In Work Pilot Scheme and Amendment Regulations 2015
PIP	Personal Independence Payment
P.I.Q.R.	Personal Injuries and Quantum Reports
Polygamous Marriages Regulations	Social Security and Family Allowances (Polygamous Marriages) Regulations 1975
PPF	Pension Protection Fund
Prescribed Diseases Regulations	Social Security (Industrial Injuries) (Prescribed Diseases) Regulations 1985
PSCS	Pension Service Computer System
Pt	Part
PTA	pure tone audiometry
P.T.S.R.	Public and Third Sector Law Reports
PTWR 2000	Part-time Workers (Prevention of Less Favourable Treatment) Regulations 2000
PVS	private and voluntary sectors
Q.B.	Queen's Bench Law Reports
QBD	Queen's Bench Division
QCS Board	Quality Contract Scheme Board
QEF	qualifying earnings factor
QYP	qualifying young person
r.	rule
R	Reported Decision
R.C.	Rules of the Court of Session
REA	Reduced Earnings Allowance
reg.	regulation
RIPA	Regulation of Investigatory Powers Act 2000
RMO	Responsible Medical Officer

rr.	rules
RR	reference rate
RSI	repetitive strain injury
RTI	Real Time Information
R.V.R.	Rating & Valuation Reporter
s.	section
S	Scottish Decision
SAP	Statutory Adoption Pay
SAPOE Regulations	Jobseeker's Allowance (Schemes for Assisting Persons to Obtain Employment) Regulations 2013
SAWS	Seasonal Agricultural Work Scheme
SAYE	Save As You Earn
SB	Supplementary Benefit
SBAT	Supplementary Benefit Appeal Tribunal
SBC	Supplementary Benefits Commission
S.C.	Session Cases
S.C. (H.L.)	Session Cases (House of Lords)
S.C. (P.C.)	Session Cases (Privy Council)
S.C.C.R.	Scottish Criminal Case Reports
S.C.L.R.	Scottish Civil Law Reports
Sch.	Schedule
SDA	Severe Disablement Allowance
SDP	Severe Disability Premium
SEC	Social Entitlement Chamber
SEN	special educational needs
SERPS	State Earnings Related Pension Scheme
ShPP	statutory shared parental pay
ShPP Regulations	Statutory Shared Parental Pay (General) Regulations 2014
SI	Statutory Instrument
SIP	Share Incentive Plan
S.J.	Solicitors Journal
S.J.L.B.	Solicitors Journal Law Brief
S.L.T.	Scots Law Times
SMP	Statutory Maternity Pay
SMP (General) Regulations 1986	Statutory Maternity Pay (General) Regulations 1986
SPC	State Pension Credit
SPC Regulations	State Pension Credit Regulations 2002
SPCA 2002	State Pension Credit Act 2002
SPL Regulations	Shared Parental Leave Regulations 2014
SPP	Statutory Paternity Pay
ss.	sections

SS (No.2) A 1980	Social Security (No.2) Act 1980
SSA 1975	Social Security Act 1975
SSA 1977	Social Security Act 1977
SSA 1978	Social Security Act 1978
SSA 1979	Social Security Act 1979
SSA 1981	Social Security Act 1981
SSA 1986	Social Security Act 1986
SSA 1988	Social Security Act 1988
SSA 1989	Social Security Act 1989
SSA 1990	Social Security Act 1990
SSA 1998	Social Security Act 1998
SSAA 1992	Social Security Administration Act 1992
SSAC	Social Security Advisory Committee
SSAT	Social Security Appeal Tribunal
SSCBA 1992	Social Security Contributions and Benefits Act 1992
SSCB(NI)A 1992	Social Security Contributions and Benefits (Northern Ireland) Act 1992
SSCPA 1992	Social Security (Consequential Provisions) Act 1992
SSD	Secretary of State for Defence
SSHBA 1982	Social Security and Housing Benefits Act 1982
SSHD	Secretary of State for the Home Department
SSI	Scottish Statutory Instrument
SS(MP)A 1977	Social Security (Miscellaneous Provisions) Act 1977
SSP	Statutory Sick Pay
SSP (General) Regulations	Statutory Sick Pay (General) Regulations 1982
SSPA 1975	Social Security Pensions Act 1975
SSPP	statutory shared parental pay
SSWP	Secretary of State for Work and Pensions
State Pension Credit Regulations	State Pension Credit Regulations 2002
S.T.C.	Simon's Tax Cases
S.T.C. (S.C.D.)	Simon's Tax Cases: Special Commissioners' Decisions
S.T.I.	Simon's Tax Intelligence
STIB	Short-Term Incapacity Benefit
subpara.	subparagraph
subs.	subsection
T	Tribunal of Commissioners' Decision
T.C.	Tax Cases
TCA 1999	Tax Credits Act 1999
TCA 2002	Tax Credits Act 2002
TCC	Technology and Construction Court
TCEA 2007	Tribunals, Courts and Enforcement Act 2007

TCGA 1992	Taxation of Chargeable Gains Act 2002
TCTM	*Tax Credits Technical Manual*
TEC	Treaty Establishing the European Community
TENS	transcutaneous electrical nerve stimulation
TEU	Treaty on European Union
TFEU	Treaty on the Functioning of the European Union
TIOPA 2010	Taxation (International and Other Provisions) Act 2010
TMA 1970	Taxes Management Act 1970
T.R.	Taxation Reports
Transfer of Functions Act	Social Security Contributions (Transfer of Functions etc.) Act 1999
Tribunal Procedure Rules	Tribunal Procedure (First-tier Tribunal)(Social Entitlement Chamber) Rules 2008
UB	Unemployment Benefit
UC	Universal Credit
UC Regs 2013	Universal Credit Regulations 2013
UCITS	Undertakings for Collective Investments in Transferable Securities
UKAIT	UK Asylum and Immigration Tribunal
UKBA	UK Border Agency of the Home Office
UKCC	United Kingdom Central Council for Nursing, Midwifery and Health Visiting
UKFTT	United Kingdom First-tier Tribunal Tax Chamber
UKHL	United Kingdom House of Lords
U.K.H.R.R.	United Kingdom Human Rights Reports
UKSC	United Kingdom Supreme Court
UKUT	United Kingdom Upper Tribunal
UN	United Nations
Universal Credit Regulations	Universal Credit Regulations 2013
URL	uniform resource locator
USI Regs	Social Security (Unemployment, Sickness and Invalidity Benefit) Regulations 1983
USI Regulations	Social Security (Unemployment, Sickness and Invalidity Benefit) Regulations 1983
UT	Upper Tribunal
VAT	Value Added Tax
VCM	vinyl chloride monomer
Vol.	Volume
VWF	Vibration White Finger
W	Welsh Decision
WCA	Work Capability Assessment
WCAt	limited capability for work assessment
WFHRAt	Work-Focused Health-Related Assessment

WFI	work-focused interview
WFTC	Working Families Tax Credit
Wikeley, Annotations	N. Wikeley, "Annotations to Jobseekers Act 1995 (c.18)" in *Current Law Statutes Annotated* (1995)
Wikeley, Ogus and Barendt	Wikeley, Ogus and Barendt, *The Law of Social Security* (2002)
W.L.R.	Weekly Law Reports
Workmen's Compensation Acts	Workmen's Compensation Acts 1925 to 1945
WP	Widow's Pension
WPS	War Pensions Scheme
WRA 2007	Welfare Reform Act 2007
WRA 2009	Welfare Reform Act 2009
WRA 2012	Welfare Reform Act 2012
W-RA Regulations	Employment and Support Allowance (Work-Related Activity) Regulations 2011
WRAAt	Work-Related Activity Assessment
WRPA 1999	Welfare Reform and Pensions Act 1999
WRP(NI)O 1999	Welfare Reform and Pensions (Northern Ireland) Order 1999
WTC	Working Tax Credit
WTC Regulations	Working Tax Credit (Entitlement and Maximum Rate) Regulations 2002

PART I

BENEFITS ACTS

Social Security Contributions and Benefits Act 1992

(1992 c.4)

SECTIONS REPRODUCED

PART VII

INCOME-RELATED BENEFITS

General

Income support

Family credit

Disability working allowance

General

PART VIII

THE SOCIAL FUND

PART VII

INCOME-RELATED BENEFITS

General

Income-related benefits

1.2 **123.**—(1) Prescribed schemes shall provide for the following benefits (in this Act referred to as "income-related benefits")—

(a) income support;
(b) [4. . .];
(c) [4. . .];
(d) housing benefit; and
[1(e) council tax benefit.]

(2) The Secretary of State shall make copies of schemes prescribed under subsection (1)(a), (b) or (c) above available for public inspection at local offices of [3 the Department of Work and Pensions] at all reasonable hours without payment.

[Subss.(3)–(4) omitted as applying only to housing benefit and council tax benefit.]

AMENDMENTS

1. Local Government Finance Act 1992 Sch.9 para.1(1) (April 1, 1993).
2. Tax Credits Act 1999 Sch.1 paras 1 and 2(f) (October 5, 1999).
3. Secretaries of State for Education and Skills and for Work and Pensions Order 2002 (SI 2002/1397) art.12 and Sch. para.9 (June 27, 2002).
4. Tax Credits Act 2002 s.60 and Sch.6 (April 8, 2003).

Income support

124.—(1) A person in Great Britain is entitled to income support if— 1.3

[1(a) he is of or over the age of 16;]

[4(aa) he has not attained the qualifying age for state pension credit;]

(b) he has no income or his income does not exceed the applicable amount;

(c) he is not engaged in remunerative work and, if he is a member of a [6 couple], the other member is not so engaged; [1. . .]

[1(d) except in such circumstances as may be prescribed, he is not receiving relevant education;

(e) he falls within a prescribed category of person; [5 . . .]

(f) he is not entitled to a jobseeker's allowance and, if he is a member of a [6 couple], the other member of the couple is not [3, and the couple are not,] entitled to an income-based jobseeker's allowance.] [4 [9. . .]

(g) if he is a member of a [6 couple], the other member of the couple is not entitled to state pension credit.] [8 ; and

(h) he is not entitled to an employment and support allowance and, if he is a member of a couple, the other member of the couple is not entitled to an income-related employment and support allowance.]

[10(1A) Regulations under paragraph (e) of subsection (1) must secure that a person who-

(a) is not a member of a couple, and

(b) is responsible for, and a member of the same household as, a child under the age of 5,

falls within a category of person prescribed under that paragraph.]

(2) [2. . .].

(3) [2. . .].

(4) Subject to subsection (5) below, where a person is entitled to income support, then—

(a) if he has no income, the amount shall be the applicable amount; and

(b) if he has income, the amount shall be the difference between his income and the applicable amount.

(5) Where a person is entitled to income support for a period to which this subsection applies, the amount payable for that period shall be calculated in such manner as may be prescribed.

(6) Subsection (5) above applies—

(a) to a period of less than a week which is the whole period for which income support is payable; and

(b) to any other period of less than a week for which it is payable.

[8 (7) In this section, "income-related employment and support allowance" means an income-related allowance under Part 1 of the Welfare Reform Act 2007 (employment and support allowance).]

AMENDMENTS

1. Jobseekers Act 1995 Sch.2 para.30 (October 7, 1996).
2. Jobseekers Act 1995 Sch.3 (October 7, 1996).
3. Welfare Reform and Pensions Act 1999 Sch.8 para.28 (March 19, 2001).

4. State Pension Credit Act 2002 s.14 and Sch.2 paras 1 and 2 (October 6, 2003).
5. State Pension Credit Act 2002 s.21 and Sch.3 (October 6, 2003).
6. Civil Partnership Act 2004 s.254(1) Sch.24 para.42 (December 5, 2005).
7. Welfare Reform Act 2007 s.28 and Sch.3 para.9 (October 27, 2008).
8. Welfare Reform Act 2007 s.28 and Sch.3 para.10 (October 27, 2008).
9. Welfare Reform Act 2007 s.67 and Sch.8 (October 27, 2008).
10. Welfare Reform Act 2009 s.3(1) (May 21, 2012). (Note that s.3(1) had been amended before it came into force. Section 58(1) and (2) of the Welfare Reform Act 2012, brought into force on March 20, 2012 by art.2(1)(c) of the Welfare Reform Act 2012 (Commencement No. 1) Order 2012 (SI 2012/863) replaced "7" with "5" in the new subs.(1A)(b)).

DEFINITIONS

"Great Britain"—see s.172(a).
"income-based jobseeker's allowance"—see s.137(1) and Jobseekers Act s.35(1).
"couple"—see s.137(1).
"prescribed"—*ibid.*
"qualifying age for state pension credit"—*ibid.*

GENERAL NOTE

Subsection (1)

1.4 Here the general conditions of entitlement to income support are set out. Note the amendments made on October 7, 1996, on October 6, 2003, and on October 27, 2009 as a consequence of the introduction of, respectively, jobseeker's allowance ("JSA"), state pension credit ("SPC") and employment and support allowance ("ESA") (see below). All of the conditions must be satisfied for there to be entitlement to income support (*CIS 166/1994*). There is also a capital test under s.134(1).

If there is entitlement under this subsection, the amount of income support is laid down in subss.(4)–(6).

There is no contributions test or requirement of citizenship (but see s.115 of the Immigration and Asylum Act 1999 on "persons subject to immigration control"). However, although a person qualifies if he is in Great Britain, an habitual residence condition was introduced on August 1, 1994 and a right to reside condition on May 1, 2004. See the definition of "person from abroad" in reg.21AA of the Income Support (General) Regulations and the notes to that definition. Regulation 4 of the Income Support Regulations allows an award to continue for a short period of temporary absence from Great Britain, but otherwise income support cannot be paid to a person outside Great Britain. See *R(IS) 4/99* and *R(IS) 9/98*, which hold that income support is not a social security benefit within art.4(1) of EC reg.1408/71. Although income support has been listed by the UK Government as included in the new category of "special non-contributory benefits" to which reg.1408/71 applies from June 1, 1992 (see art.4(2a) and Annex IIa), such benefits cannot be "exported" (i.e. paid where the claimant is in another Member State) (art.10a). Article 10a provides for the granting of such benefits "exclusively in the territory of the Member State in which [the person] reside[s], in accordance with the legislation of that State". ("Resides" means "habitually resides": art.1(h).) It was argued in *Perry v Chief Adjudication Officer, The Times*, October 20, 1998, also reported as part of *R(IS) 4/99*, that art.10a conferred a positive right to income support on the claimant because of his habitual residence in the UK, and that he remained entitled to income support by virtue of that right, even during periods of temporary absence. However, the Court of Appeal rejected this argument. The language of art.10a made it clear that special non-contributory benefits were to be granted in accordance with the domestic law of the Member State. Presence in Great Britain was a requirement of the UK's legislation (subject to the exceptions in reg.4 of the Income Support Regulations) and this was not incompatible with art.10a. The Court of Appeal also agreed with the Commissioner that the claimant could not rely on art.2(4) of EC Regulation 1247/92 (the Regulation which introduced the June 1992 amendment) to export an entitlement to income support in respect of periods before June 1, 1992.

Paragraph (a)

From October 7, 1996 the minimum age for income support is again 16 (as it was until September 1988 before most 16- and 17-year-olds were excluded). But to be entitled a person must fall within a prescribed category (para.(e)). See reg.4ZA of and Sch.1B to the Income Support Regulations for these categories. Note that a person aged 16 to 18 in relevant education is still only entitled to income support in certain circumstances (para.(d) and reg.13 of the Income Support Regulations). 1.5

The reduction in the lower age limit is a consequence of the replacement from October 7, 1996 of income support by income-based JSA for people who are required to be available for work as a condition of receiving benefit. To be entitled to income-based JSA a person must in general be at least 18 (Jobseekers Act s.3(1)(f)(i)), although there are exceptions, which are similar, but not identical, to those that used to operate for income support (see the 1996 edition of J. Mesher and P. Wood, *Income Support, the Social Fund and Family Credit: the Legislation* for reg.13A of and Sch.1A to the Income Support Regulations and the further escape under s.25; these provisions were revoked on October 7, 1996). Entitlement to JSA, SPC or ESA excludes entitlement to income support (paras (f)–(h)).

Paragraph (aa)

State Pension Credit was introduced on October 6, 2003. Paragraph (aa) rules out any possibility that a claimant could be entitled to both state pension credit and income support by providing that no person who has reached "the qualifying age for state pension credit" can be entitled to income support. "The qualifying age for state pension credit" is defined by s.137(1) below. The effect of that definition is that the qualifying age was 60 for both men and women until April 2010 and will now increase by stages to 65 in line with the increase in pensionable age for a woman. It remains possible for the partner of a person over 60 to claim income support in some circumstances—see para.(g) below. 1.6

Paragraph (b)

The person's income (which includes the income of the claimant's family) must be less than the applicable amount (effectively the figure set for the family's requirements under s.135). However, note that as a consequence of the removal of amounts for children from income support (with effect from April 6, 2004, except in "transitional cases"—see the note to reg.17 of the Income Support Regulations), only a partner's income will count as that of the claimant and the applicable amount will no longer include any personal allowances for children, the family premium, the disabled child premium or an enhanced disability premium for a child. 1.7

CIS 166/1994 confirms that the conditions in subs.(1) are cumulative. The fact that the claimant was not working in his business and so para.(c) did not apply, did not mean that income from that business could not potentially disentitle him under para.(b). See the notes to reg.30 of the Income Support Regulations.

Paragraph (c)

The introduction of the condition in para.(c) marked an important change from the supplementary benefit rules. If either the claimant or his partner is in remunerative work (defined in regs 5 and 6 of the Income Support Regulations) there is no entitlement to income support. For supplementary benefit, this condition was only applied to the claimant. The transitional protection announced on April 28, 1988 (see p.198 of the 1998 edition of *Mesher and Wood*) has remained on an extra-statutory basis. 1.8

Note that from October 7, 1996 the limit for remunerative work in the case of a partner is 24 hours or more a week (Income Support Regulations reg.5(1A)). It remains 16 or more for the claimant.

Paragraph (d)

1.9 See regs 12 and 13 of the Income Support Regulations.

Paragraph (e)

1.10 From October 7, 1996 only certain categories of people are entitled to income support. See reg.4ZA of and Sch.1B to the Income Support Regulations for these categories. They are similar to those groups who formerly were exempt from the requirement to be available for work for the purposes of income support (see Sch.1 to the Income Support Regulations which was revoked on October 7, 1996), but there are some differences.

Paragraph (f)

1.11 Entitlement to JSA excludes entitlement to income support (any "top-up" to a person's contribution-based JSA will be by way of income-based JSA, not income support); if the claimant is a member of a couple, he will also not qualify for income support if his partner is entitled to income-based JSA or if he and his partner are entitled together to "joint-claim" JSA. But although entitlement to income support and JSA is mutually exclusive, some people may be eligible for either, i.e. those who fall into a prescribed category for income support but who also satisfy the labour market conditions for JSA. See the notes to reg.4ZA of the Income Support Regulations for discussion of the position of such claimants and of the fact that the raising of the limit for remunerative work for partners to 24 hours a week from October 7, 1996 may create a "better-off" problem for some claimants.

Paragraph (g)

1.12 By virtue of para.(aa) above, a claimant who has reached the qualifying age for state pension credit cannot be entitled to income support. Claimants who have not themselves reached the qualifying age for state pension credit, but who have partners above that age, may claim income support as long as their partners are not actually entitled to state pension credit. Since, under s.1 SSAA 1992, there can be no entitlement to state pension credit without making a claim, the effect is that couples with one member who has reached the qualifying age for state pension credit and one member who has not (and who are not already in receipt of state pension credit) can choose to claim either income support, JSA, or ESA (according to the circumstances of the member who has not reached pensionable age), or state pension credit. It will normally be advantageous to claim state pension credit.

Paragraph (h)

1.13 Entitlement to ESA excludes entitlement to IS (as does a partner's entitlement to income-related (but not contribution-related) ESA). See the note on the Introduction of ESA in the commentary to para.7 of Sch.1B (below).

Subsection (1A)

1.14 See para.1 of Sch.IB to the Income Support Regulations and the notes to that paragraph.

Subsection (4)

1.15 This provision sets out the basic means test calculation for income support. Providing that the conditions of entitlement imposed by subs.(1) and the capital test under s.134(1) are satisfied, the claimant's income is set against his applicable amount, calculated according to regs 17–22 of the Income Support (General) Regulations. The difference is the amount of benefit. The claimant's income includes that of the other members of his family, except in prescribed cases (s.136(1)). Note that as a consequence of the removal of amounts for children from income support (with effect from April 6, 2004, except in "transitional cases"—see further the note to reg.17 of the Income Support Regulations), only a partner's income will count as that of the claimant.

Subsections (5) and (6)

These provisions allow regulations to deal with entitlement for part-weeks. See regs 73–77 of the Income Support (General) Regulations. 1.16

Severe hardship cases

125.—[1. . .] 1.17

AMENDMENT

1. Jobseekers Act 1995 Sch.3 (October 7, 1996).

Trade disputes

126.—(1) This section applies to a person, other than a child or a person of a prescribed description— 1.18

(a) who [2 is prevented from being entitled to a jobseeker's allowance by section 14 of the Jobseekers Act 1995 (trade disputes)]; or

(b) who would be so [2 prevented] if otherwise entitled to that benefit, except during any period shown by the person to be a period of incapacity for work [1 . . .] or to be within the maternity period.

(2) In subsection (1) above "the maternity period" means the period commencing at the beginning of the 6th week before the expected week of confinement and ending at the end of the 7th week after the week in which confinement takes place.

(3) For the purposes of calculating income support—

(a) so long as this section applies to a person who is not a member of a family, the applicable amount shall be disregarded;

(b) so long as it applies to a person who is a member of a family but is not a member of a [4 couple], the portion of the applicable amount which is included in respect of him shall be disregarded;

(c) so long as it applies to one of the members of a [4 couple]—

(i) if the applicable amount consists only of an amount in respect of them, it shall be reduced to one half; and

(ii) if it includes other amounts, the portion of it which is included in respect of them shall be reduced to one-half and any further portion of it which is included in respect of the member of the couple to whom this section applies shall be disregarded;

(d) so long as it applies to both members of a [4 couple]—

(i) if neither of them is responsible for a child or person of a prescribed description who is a member of the same household, the applicable amount shall be disregarded; and

(ii) in any other case, the portion of the applicable amount which is included in respect of them and any further portion of it which is included in respect of either of them shall be disregarded.

(4) Where a reduction under subsection (3)(c) above would not produce a sum which is a multiple of 5p, the reduction shall be to the nearest lower sum which is such a multiple.

(5) Where this section applies to a person for any period, then, except so far as regulations provide otherwise—

(a) in calculating the entitlement to income support of that person or a member of his family the following shall be treated as his income and shall not be disregarded—
   (i) any payment which he or a member of his family receives or is entitled to obtain by reason of the person to whom this section applies being without employment for that period; and
   (ii) without prejudice to the generality of sub-paragraph (i) above, any amount which becomes or would on an application duly made, become available to him in that period by way of repayment of income tax deducted from his [3 taxable earnings (as defined by section 10 of the Income Tax (Earnings and Pensions) Act 2003 under PAYE regulations]; and
(b) any payment by way of income support for that period or any part of it which apart from this paragraph would be made to him, or to a person whose applicable amount is aggregated with his—
   (i) shall not be made if the weekly rate of payment is equal to or less than the relevant sum; or
   (ii) if it is more than the relevant sum, shall be at a weekly rate equal to the difference.

(6) In respect of any period less than a week, subsection (5) above shall have effect subject to such modifications as may be prescribed.

(7) Subject to subsection (8) below, the "relevant sum" for the purposes of subsection (5) above shall be [5£40.50].

(8) If an order under section 150 of the Administration Act (annual up-rating) has the effect of increasing payments of income support, from the time when the order comes into force there shall be substituted, in subsection (5)(b) above, for the references to the sum for the time being mentioned in it references to a sum arrived at by—
(a) increasing that sum by the percentage by which the personal allowance under paragraph 1(1) of Part I of Schedule 2 to the Income Support (General) Regulations 1987 for a single person aged not less than 25 has been increased by the order; and
(b) if the sum so increased is not a multiple of 50p, disregarding the remainder if it is 25p and, if it is not, rounding it up or down to the nearest 50p,

and the order shall state the substituted sum.

Amendments

1. Social Security (Incapacity for Work) Act 1994 Sch.1 para.31 (April 13, 1995).
2. Jobseekers Act 1995 Sch.2 para.31 (October 7, 1996).
3. Income Tax (Earnings and Pensions) Act 2003 Sch.6 Pt 2 para.179 (April 6, 2003).
4. Civil Partnership Act 2004 s.254 and Sch.24 para.43 (December 5, 2005).
5. Social Security Benefits Up-rating Order 2015 (SI 2015/457) art.16 (April 6, 2015).

Derivation

Social Security Act 1986 s.23.

Definitions

"child"—see s.137(1).
"couple"—*ibid.*

"family"—*ibid.*
"prescribed"—*ibid.*
"the Administration Act"—see s.174.

GENERAL NOTE

The trade dispute rule, long an important part of the supplementary benefit scheme, was considerably simplified in the income support rules, although most of the stringency remains. **1.19**

Subsection (1)

The rule applies to anyone other than a child or qualifying young person (Income Support Regulations reg.14) who is disentitled to JSA, or would be disentitled, under s.14 of the Jobseekers Act. Thus the income support rule depends directly on the JSA rule. Note that if the decision-maker considers that he does not have enough information to decide this question, it will be assumed that the person is involved in the trade dispute (Decisions and Appeals Regulations 1999 reg.13(2)). **1.20**

The rule does not apply when the person involved is incapable of work. The rule also does not apply in the maternity period, defined in subs.(2).

If the rule applies there are consequences for the way in which applicable amounts are calculated. This is dealt with in subs.(3). There are also consequences for the way in which income is calculated. This is dealt with in subs.(5) and in a number of regulations. The most immediate effect is that the person is treated as in remunerative work for the seven days following the first day of the stoppage of work or the day on which the claimant withdrew his labour (Income Support Regulations reg.5(4)). The result is that neither the person nor his partner can be entitled to income support at all for those days (s.124(1)(c)).

Subsection (3)

This provision sets out the effect on the applicable amount if the claimant is not excluded by the conditions of entitlement. **1.21**

(a) A single claimant with no child or qualifying young person in the household is to have no applicable amount, and so cannot be entitled to any benefit.

(b) For a single claimant with a child or qualifying young person in the household, the "portion of the applicable amount included in respect of" the claimant is disregarded. It is clear that the personal allowance for the claimant is taken out, and so is any premium payable on account of the claimant's disability or age or because she is a carer. Arguably the family premium and the lone parent element of the family premium (if payable) are not included "in respect of" the claimant and so remain, but the *Decision Makers Guide* only accepts this in the case of the basic family premium (see para.32639). But this point ceased to be relevant when the basic family premium and the family premium for lone parents became payable at the same rate.

(c) For a couple where the trade dispute rule applies to only one of them, if they have no premiums on top of their personal allowance, that allowance is reduced by a half. This is a different rule from supplementary benefit, which would have left the other partner with the appropriate personal allowance for a single claimant. If there are any premiums, then the rule in para. (b) applies. Thus any premium payable solely for the person involved in the dispute (e.g. a carer premium) is taken out, but according to para.32642 of the *Decision Makers Guide* such a premium will be included in full if it is for the person not involved in the dispute. Any premium paid for the couple (e.g. a pensioner premium) is reduced by half. But para.32642 accepts that the family premium is payable in full. It is easier to argue for the retention of the family premium here, since that would be paid to the remaining partner if the partner involved in the trade dispute disappeared.

(d) For a couple where the trade dispute rule applies to both of them, the applicable amount is nil if there is no child or qualifying young person in the house-hold. If there is a child or qualifying young person, then the family premium and any premium paid for that person's disability is allowed on top of the personal allowance for that person.

Note that housing costs are payable, provided that at least one member of the family (e.g. a child or qualifying young person) is not involved in the dispute. The housing costs are treated as the responsibility of the member or members not involved in the dispute (Income Support Regulations Sch.3 para.2(2)).

Further, note that the above explanation of the provisions in subs.(3) needs to be modified to take into account the removal of amounts for children and qualifying young persons from income support with effect from April 6, 2004, except for "transitional cases". Transitional cases in this context are income support claimants (i) who were in receipt of the child elements (see below) on April 6, 2004 and who have not subsequently been awarded child tax credit, or (ii) whose families included a child or young person on April 6, 2004, who have not been awarded child tax credit and who made a new claim for income support after that date but before September 8, 2005. Such claimants will continue to receive the child elements, that is, personal allowances, the family premium and premiums for their children as part of their income support until they apply for or are transferred onto child tax credit. This transfer was intended to start in October 2004 but was repeatedly delayed and it now seems the the transfer process will not take place at all and the situation will eventually be resolved by the abolition of income support and child tax credit and their replacement by universal credit. See further the note to reg.17 of the Income Support Regulations.

Subsection (5)

1.22 If the trade dispute rule applies, the normal rules about income are modified. Under para.(a) any payment that a member of the family receives, or is entitled to obtain by reason of the person involved in the trade dispute being without employment, must be taken into account. In *R(SB) 29/85* a loan from a local authority Social Work Department (the Scottish equivalent of a Social Services Department) to meet arrears of hire purchase repayments was held to be capable of being such a payment. The claimant had not been in arrears before the dispute and the loan was to be repaid on his return to work. However, on the facts it was a payment of capital, not income. Although reg.41(3) of the Income Support Regulations (now only still in force in "transitional cases"—see further the note to reg.41(3)) secures that, in trade dispute cases, payments under ss.17, 23B, 23C or 24A of the Children Act 1989 or s.12 of the Social Work (Scotland) Act 1968 or s.29 or s.30 of the Children (Scotland) Act 1995 (payments to families to prevent children being taken into care, etc.) are to be treated as income, not capital. Nor does the disregard of such income in para.28 of Sch.9 to the Income Support Regulations apply in trade dispute cases. Other categories of income normally disregarded but counted here are income in kind (para.21) and charitable, voluntary or personal injury payments (para.15). Holiday pay paid more than four weeks after the termination of employment (normally capital) is earnings (reg.35(1)(d)).

The other main category under para.(a) is income tax refunds paid or due. The effect of reg.48(2) is that in trade dispute cases refunds do not count as capital. The assumption is then that they count as income, but this does not seem to be provided for expressly.

Under para.(b) there is the final automatic deduction of the "relevant sum." This is the sum specified in subs.(6), as increased in future years under subs.(7). The sum was increased to £40.50 in April 2015 (not increased in April 2016). The relevant sum is often called "assumed strike pay," but is deducted regardless of whether the person involved is entitled to strike pay, a member of a union, or even on strike.

The "compensation" for this rule is that any payment from a trade union up to the amount of £40.50 is disregarded (Sch.9 para.34).

The cumulative result of these income rules, plus the reductions in applicable amounts, is that even married strikers will often receive very little benefit indeed (if any).

Effect of return to work

127.—If a person returns to work with the same employer after a period during which section 126 above applies to him, and whether or not his return is before the end of any stoppage of work in relation to which he is or would be [1 prevented from being entitled to a jobseeker's allowance]— 1.23

(a) that section shall cease to apply to him at the commencement of the day on which he returns to work; and

(b) until the end of the period of 15 days beginning with that day section 124(1) above shall have effect in relation to him as if the following paragraph were substituted for paragraph (c)—"(c) in the case of a member of a [2 couple], the other member is not engaged in remunerative work; and"; and

(c) any sum paid by way of income support for that period of 15 days to him or, where he is a member of a [2 couple], to the other member of that couple, shall be recoverable in the prescribed manner from the person to whom it was paid or from any prescribed person or, where the person to whom it was paid is a member of a [2 couple], from the other member of the couple.

AMENDMENTS

1. Jobseekers Act 1995 Sch.2 para.32 (October 7, 1996).
2. Civil Partnership Act 2004 s.254 and Sch.24 para.44 (December 5, 2005).

DERIVATION

Social Security Act 1986 s.23A.

DEFINITIONS

"couple"—see s.137(1).
"prescribed"—*ibid.*

GENERAL NOTE

This section allows income support to be paid for the first 15 days following a return to work from a trade dispute. Normally the work would exclude entitlement to benefit under s.124(1)(c) regardless of whether any wages were payable or not. The rules about the relevant sum and income tax refunds under s.126 do not apply, but the other adjustments to the income rules do apply. Applicable amounts are calculated in the ordinary way. Note that any advance of earnings or loan made by the employer counts as earnings (Income Support Regulations, reg.48(5) and (6)). In addition, any payment of benefit under this section is recoverable under subs.(c) and Pt VIII of the Payments Regulations. 1.24

Family credit

Family credit

1.25 **128.**—[1 . . .]

AMENDMENT

1. Tax Credits Act 2002 s.60 and Sch.6 (April 8, 2003).

Disability working allowance

Disability working allowance

1.26 **129.**—[1 . . .]

AMENDMENT

1. Tax Credits Act 2002 s.60 and Sch.6 (April 8, 2003).

GENERAL NOTE

1.27 Sections 128 and 129 originally dealt with family credit and disability working allowance respectively. As a result of amendments made by the Tax Credits Act 1999, these sections then provided the legislative basis for working families' tax credit (WFTC) and disabled person's tax credit (DPTC) with effect from October 5, 1999. However, the Tax Credits Act 2002 replaced WFTC and DPTC with a new tax credits regime comprising working tax credit (WTC) and child tax credit (CTC). Consequently, ss.128 and 129 were repealed with effect from April 8, 2003 by s.60 of and Sch.6 to the Tax Credits Act 2002 (see further Tax Credits Act 2002 (Commencement No.4, Transitional Provisions and Savings) Order 2003, art.2(4)(e) and Sch.2).

The text of and commentary on ss.128 and 129 have accordingly been omitted from this volume for 2003 and subsequent years. For the full annotated text of these provisions, see paras 1.34–1.62 of the 2002 edition of this volume; see also Pt IV of that volume for the Family Credit (General) Regulations 1987 (SI 1987/1973) and the Disability Working Allowance (General) Regulations 1991 (SI 1991/2887). The 2002 commentary on ss.128 and 129 and on those (and other relevant) regulations should be read together with the Updating Material at paras 6.1–6.35 in the 2003 edition. That section included the updating material on WFTC and DPTC in the 2002/2003 Supplement as well as subsequent developments.

For detailed commentary on WTC and CTC, see Vol.IV in this series, *Tax Credits and HMRC-administered Social Security Benefits.*

General

Exclusions from benefit

1.28 **134.**—(1) No person shall be entitled to an income-related benefit if his capital or a prescribed part of it exceeds the prescribed amount.

(2) Except in prescribed circumstances the entitlement of one member of a family to any one income-related benefit excludes entitlement to that benefit for any other member for the same period.

(3) [1 . . .]

(4) Where the amount of any income-related benefit would be less than

a prescribed amount, it shall not be payable except in prescribed circumstances.

AMENDMENT

1. Local Government Finance Act 1992 Sch.9 para.7 (April 1, 1993).

DERIVATION

Subs.(1): Social Security Act 1986 s.22(6).
Subs.(2): 1986 Act s.20(9).
Subs.(4): 1986 Act s.21(7).

DEFINITIONS

"family"—see s.137(1).
"prescribed"—*ibid.*

GENERAL NOTE

Subsection (1)

The capital limit for income support was raised to £16,000 for all claimants on April 10, 2006 (Income Support Regulations, reg.45). See the 2005 edition of this volume for the different capital limits that applied for most claimants before that date. This brings the capital limit for income support (and income-based JSA, which has also been increased to £16,000 from April 10, 2006—see reg.107 of the JSA Regulations) into line with that which applies for housing benefit and until the abolition of council tax benefit on April 1, 2103 applied for that benefit. The same capital limit applies for income-related ESA (see reg.110 of the ESA Regulations in Vol.I of this series) and for universal credit (see reg.18 of the Universal Credit Regulations in Vol.V of this series). There is no capital limit for working tax credit and child tax credit, nor for state pension credit. 1.29

Since the capital rule operates as an exclusion to benefit it is arguable that the burden of proof that a claimant's capital exceeds the limit is on the Secretary of State. The Tribunal of Commissioners in *CIS 417/1992*, reported as part of *R(IS) 26/95*, treat satisfaction of the capital rule as part of what the claimant has to prove in showing entitlement to income support. However, the contrary argument was not put to the Tribunal. But once it has been shown that the claimant possesses an item of capital, it is for him to prove that one of the disregards in Sch.10 applies (*CIS 240/1992*). Similarly, if it has been established that the claimant is the legal owner of a property, the burden is on him to show that the beneficial ownership does not follow the legal ownership (*CIS 30/1993*).

These decisions, however, need to be read in the light of the House of Lords' judgment in *Kerr v Department of Social Development for Northern Ireland* [2004] UKHL 23; [2004] 4 All E.R. 385, also reported as *R 1/04 (SF)*, in which Baroness Hale emphasised that the process of adjudication for social security benefits is a co-operative one in which both the Department and the claimant should play their part and that normally it ought not to be necessary to resort to more formal concepts such as the burden of proof.

In *MB v Royal Borough of Kensington & Chelsea (HB)* [2011] UKUT 321 (AAC) the claimant relied on *Chichester DC v B and SSWP* [2009] UKUT 34 (AAC) in which it was stated that it was for the Council to show that the claimant had a beneficial interest in the capital at issue (see para.28). Judge Wikeley, however, considered that the answer to this lay in the point made by Baroness Hale in *Kerr* that it was for each party (claimant or department) to provide such information as they reasonably can. The claimant in *MB v RB Kensington & Chelsea* was the one who had exclusive knowledge about the purchase of the property in issue and the mortgage payments and thus it was her responsibility to marshal what evidence she could to show that, although she was the legal owner, she was not the sole beneficial owner of the property.

Subsection (4)

See reg.26(4) of the Claims and Payments Regulations in Vol.III of this series. 1.30

The applicable amount

1.31 **135.**—(1) The applicable amount, in relation to any income-related benefit, shall be such amount or the aggregate of such amounts as may be prescribed in relation to that benefit.

(2) The power to prescribe applicable amounts conferred by subsection (1) above includes power to prescribe nil as an applicable amount.

(3) [[1][[3]. . .

(4) . . .]

(5) [[4] . . .] The applicable amount for a severely disabled person shall include an amount in respect of his being a severely disabled person.

(6) Regulations may specify circumstances in which persons are to be treated as being or as not being severely disabled.

AMENDMENTS

1. To be omitted until s.9 of the Social Security Act 1990 is brought into force: Social Security (Consequential Provisions) Act 1992 s.6 and Sch.4 Pt I.
2. Local Government Finance Act 1992 Sch.9 para.8 (April 1, 1993).
3. Health and Social Care Act 2001 s.67(2) and Sch.6 Pt 3 (April 15, 2002).
4. Tax Credits Act 2002 s.60 and Sch.6 (April 8, 2003).

DERIVATION

Social Security Act 1986 s.22(1)–(4).

DEFINITION

"prescribed"—see s.137(1).

GENERAL NOTE

Subsection (1)

1.32 See regs 17–22A of, and Sch.2 and Sch.7 to, the Income Support (General) Regulations.

CIS 683/1993 confirms that a claimant's applicable amount can only consist of elements specified in the relevant regulations. It cannot be increased by the amount of maintenance (or insurance premiums) the claimant is required to pay.

Subsection (2)

1.33 See reg.21 of and Sch.7 to the Income Support Regulations.

Subsections (5) and (6)

1.34 See para.13 of Sch.2 to the Income Support (General) Regulations. A provision requiring the payment of a community care addition to income support to very severely disabled people was put into the 1986 Act when it was going through the House of Lords. Although the Government did not wish to have this requirement in the legislation it did not seek to remove its spirit when the Bill returned to the House of Commons. However, it put in its own amendments, which have now become subss.(5) and (6).

In *R(IS) 22/93* the Commissioner held that s.22(4) of the 1986 Act (the predecessor of subs.(6)) did not authorise the making of regulations prescribing conditions to be satisfied before a person counts as severely disabled other than conditions relating to the extent of that person's disablement. Otherwise, the mandatory provision of s.22(3) (the predecessor of subs.(5)) would be undermined. He therefore went on to hold that heads (ii) and (iii) of para.13(2)(a) of Sch.2, on the severe disability premium, were not validly part of the General Regulations. This was because they referred to the presence of a non-dependant in the claimant's household and to the receipt of invalid care allowance by another person, and not to the claimant's disability.

On appeal, the majority of the Court of Appeal took the opposite view, that s.22(4) gave the Secretary of State power to specify financial and domestic conditions as part of the circumstances in which a person was or was not to be treated as severely disabled (*Chief Adjudication Officer v Foster* [1992] Q.B. 31; [1991] 3 All E.R. 846). Therefore the provisions were valid. Lord Donaldson MR dissented trenchantly, saying that if s.22(4) allowed regulations to specify conditions not relating to the severity of disability this would "emasculate the imperative contained in subs.(3) and indeed . . . render it otiose."

The House of Lords ([1993] A.C. 754; [1993] 1 All E.R. 705) also held the **1.35** provisions to be valid. Lord Bridge agreed that subs.(3) (now subs.(5)) required the applicable amount for a severely disabled person to include some amount in respect of being such a person. But subs.(4) (now subs.(6)) was a deeming provision that allowed the Secretary of State to define who was to be treated as severely disabled. He could do this by reference to circumstances that either related to the degree of disability or affected the extent of need for income support arising from the disability. If the only power intended to be given by subs.(4) was a power to define the degree of disability that qualified as severe, the language used was totally inappropriate for that purpose (especially compared with the precise code for determining the degree of disability which qualified someone for severe disablement allowance).

Lord Bridge would have reached this conclusion without looking at the Parliamentary history of the subsections in Hansard, but following *Pepper v Hart* [1993] A.C. 593; [1992] 3 W.L.R. 1032 this could be consulted. The statements of Ministers in both Houses of Parliament on the government amendments made clear that it was intended to use the regulation-making power to prescribe that the severe disability premium should only be applicable where the person was receiving the higher rate of attendance allowance, was living in a household with no other adult able to care for him and had no-one eligible for invalid care allowance in respect of him. Therefore, the ambiguity in the regulation-making power was to be resolved so as to authorise that use of the power.

The House of Lords' decision settled the scope of subss.(5) and (6). See the notes to para.13 of Sch.2 to the Income Support (General) Regulations for the conditions for the severe disability premium. On the powers of the Social Security Commissioners, tribunals and decision-makers to determine the validity or otherwise of regulations, see Vol.III of this series.

Income and capital

136.—(1) Where a person claiming an income-related benefit is a **1.36** member of a family, the income and capital of any member of that family shall, except in prescribed circumstances, be treated as the income and capital of that person.

(2) Regulations may provide that capital not exceeding the amount prescribed under section 134(1) above but exceeding a prescribed lower amount shall be treated, to a prescribed extent, as if it were income of a prescribed amount.

(3) Income and capital shall be calculated or estimated in such manner as may be prescribed.

(4) A person's income in respect of a week shall be calculated in accordance with prescribed rules; and the rules may provide for the calculation to be made by reference to an average over a period (which need not include the week concerned).

(5) Circumstances may be prescribed in which—

(a) a person is treated as possessing capital or income which he does not possess;
(b) capital or income which a person does possess is to be disregarded;
(c) income is to be treated as capital;
(d) capital is to be treated as income.

DEFINITIONS

"family"—see s.137(1).
"prescribed"—*ibid.*

GENERAL NOTE

Subsection (1)

1.37 This provides that the general rule for income support is that all of the family's (as defined in s.137(1)) income and capital should be aggregated together and treated as the claimant's. The modifications to this rule for children and young persons were in regs 44 and 47 of the Income Support Regulations (see the 2003 edition of this volume for those regulations and the notes to those regulations). However, as a consequence of the removal of amounts for children and young persons from income support (with effect from April 6, 2004, except in "transitional cases"—see the note to reg.17 of the Income Support Regulations), a child's income and capital will be totally ignored and only a partner's income and capital will count as that of the claimant (see the amended form of reg.23(1) of the Income Support Regulations).

Subsection (2)

1.38 See reg.53 of the Income Support Regulations. From April 10, 2006 this provides for an income to be assumed to be produced from capital between £6,000 and £16,000 (see the 2005 edition of this volume for the different lower and upper capital limits that applied for most claimants before that date). However, for claimants who live permanently in a care home, Abbeyfield Home or independent hospital (for the definitions of these terms see reg.2(1) of the Income Support Regulations) the tariff income rule only applies to capital over £10,000 (see reg.53(1A)).

Subsections (3)–(5)

1.39 Large parts of the regulations deal with the matters covered by these subsections.

Interpretation of Part VII and supplementary provisions

1.40 **137.**—(1) In this Part of this Act, unless the context otherwise requires —

[1"billing authority" has the same meaning as in Part I of the Local Government Finance Act 1992;]

"child" means a person under the age of 16;

[1. . .]

[4 [7 8 "couple" means—

(a) two people who are married to, or civil partners of, each other and are members of the same household; or
(b) two people who are not married to, or civil partners of, each other but are living together as a married couple otherwise than in prescribed circumstances;]]

"dwelling" means any residential accommodation, whether or not consisting of the whole or part of a building and whether or not comprising separate and self-contained premises;

"family" means—

(a) a [4 couple];

(b) a [4 couple] and a member of the same household for whom one of them is or both are responsible and who is a child or a person of a prescribed description;

(c) except in prescribed circumstances, a person who is not a member of a [4 couple] and a member of the same household for whom that person is responsible and who is a child or a person of a prescribed description;

[2"income-based jobseeker's allowance" has the same meaning as in the Jobseekers Act 1995;]

"industrial injuries scheme" means a scheme made under Schedule 8 to this Act or section 159 of the 1975 Act or under the Old Cases Act;

[1 5 . . .]

[6 "local authority" in relation to Scotland means a council constituted under section 2 of the Local Government etc. (Scotland) Act 1994;]

[4 . . .]

[3"pensionable age" has the meaning given by the rules in paragraph 1 of Schedule 4 to the Pensions Act 1995 (c.26);]

"prescribed" means specified in or determined in accordance with regulations;

[3"state pension credit" means state pension credit under the State Pension Credit Act 2002;

[4 . . .]

"the qualifying age for state pension credit" is (in accordance with section 1(2)(b) and (6) of the State Pension Credit Act 2002)—

(a) in the case of a woman, pensionable age; or

(b) in the case of a man, the age which is pensionable age in the case of a woman born on the same day as the man;]

[4 . . .]

"war pension scheme" means a scheme under which war pensions (as defined in section 25 of the Social Security Act 1989) are provided;

"week", in relation to [1council tax benefit], means a period of seven days beginning with a Monday.

[4 (1A) [7 . . .]]

(2) Regulations may make provision for the purposes of this Part of this Act—

(a) as to circumstances in which a person is to be treated as being or not being in Great Britain;

(b) continuing a person's entitlement to benefit during periods of temporary absence from Great Britain;

(c) as to what is or is not to be treated as remunerative work or as employment;

[2(d) as to circumstances in which a person is or is not to be treated as engaged or normally engaged in remunerative work;]

(e) as to what is or is not to be treated as relevant education;

(f) as to circumstances in which a person is or is not to be treated as receiving relevant education;

(g) specifying the descriptions of pension increases under war pension schemes or industrial injuries schemes that are analogous to the benefits mentioned in section 129(2)(b)(i) to (iii) above;

(h) as to circumstances in which a person is or is not to be treated as occupying a dwelling as his home;

(i) for treating any person who is liable to make payments in respect of a dwelling as if he were not so liable;
(j) for treating any person who is not liable to make payments in respect of a dwelling as if he were so liable;
(k) for treating as included in a dwelling any land used for the purposes of the dwelling;
(l) as to circumstances in which persons are to be treated as being or not being members of the same household;
(m) as to circumstances in which one person is to be treated as responsible or not responsible for another.

AMENDMENTS

1. Local Government Finance Act 1992 Sch.9 para.9 (April 1, 1993).
2. Jobseekers Act 1995 Sch.2 para.35 (October 7, 1996).
3. State Pension Credit Act 2002 s.14 and Sch.2 paras 1 and 4 (October 6, 2003).
4. Civil Partnership Act 2004 s.254(1) and Sch.24 para.46 (December 5, 2005).
5. Local Government etc. (Scotland) Act 1994 s.180 and Sch.13, para.174(5) and Sch.14 (April 1, 1996).
6. Welfare Reform Act 2007 Sch.5 para.1(4) (July 3, 2007).
7. Marriage (Same Sex Couples) Act 2013 (Consequential and Contrary Provisions and Scotland) Order 2014 (SI 560/2014) art.2 and Sch.1 para.22(8) (March 13, 2014).The amendment extends to England and Wales only (see SI 2014/107 art.1(4)).
8. Marriage and Civil Partnership (Scotland) Act 2014 and Civil Partnership Act 2004 (Consequential Provisions and Modifications) Order 2014 (SI 2014/3229) art.5(3) and Sch.4 para.2(13) (December 16, 2014). The amendment relates only to Scotland (see (SI 2014/3229) art.3(4)) but is in the same terms as the amendment made in relation to England and Wales by SI 2014/107 (see point 7 above).

DEFINITIONS

"the 1975 Act"—see s.174.
"the Old Cases Act"—*ibid.*

GENERAL NOTE

Subsection (1)

1.41 These definitions are important throughout the income support scheme:

"*Child*". Note the restricted definition that gives rise to the need to define "young persons" in regulations, to describe those aged 16 and over.

"*Couple*". See the notes to the definition in reg.2(1) of the Income Support Regulations.

"*Dwelling*". See the notes to the definition of "dwelling occupied as the home" in reg.2(1) of the Income Support Regulations.

"*Family*". The definition effectively covers couples with or without children and single claimants with children. It may be that some contexts in the regulations require that single claimants without children are also included where a "family" is referred to.

Paragraph (b) covers couples and any child or young person (see reg.14 of the Income Support Regulations) in the household for whom one of the couple is responsible. On the general test of membership of the household and children, see *England v Secretary of State for Social Services* [1982] 3 F.L.R. 222; *R(FIS) 4/83* and *R(SB) 14/87*. There are deeming rules in reg.16 of the Income Support Regulations.

Paragraph (c) covers a single claimant who is responsible for a child in the same household.

"*Income-based jobseeker's allowance*". See ss.35(1) and 1(4) of the Jobseekers Act. 1.42
"*The qualifying age for state pension credit*". See note to s.124(1)(aa) above.

PART VIII

THE SOCIAL FUND

Payments out of the social fund

[1 **138.**—(1) There may be made out of the social fund, in accordance with this Part of this Act— 1.43

(a) Payments of prescribed amounts, whether in respect of prescribed items or otherwise, to meet, in prescribed circumstances, maternity expenses and funeral expenses; and

(b) . . . *[Omitted as relating solely to the discretionary social fund.]*]

(2) Payments may also be made out of that fund, in accordance with this Part of this Act, of a prescribed amount or a number of prescribed amounts to prescribed descriptions of persons, in prescribed circumstances, to meet expenses for heating, which appear to the Secretary of State to have been or to be likely to be incurred in cold weather.

(3) . . . *[Omitted as relating solely to the discretionary social fund.]*

(4) In this section "prescribed" means specified in or determined in accordance with regulations.

(5) . . . *[Omitted as relating solely to the discretionary social fund.]*

AMENDMENT

1. Social Security Act 1998 s.70 (April 5, 1999).

GENERAL NOTE

This book cannot contain any real discussion of the general social fund scheme. It is concerned with claims that can lead to an appeal to a tribunal. Only the payments for maternity and funeral expenses under subs.(1)(a) and for cold weather and winter fuel under subs.(2) are dealt with by decision-makers and tribunals. 1.44

Subsection (1)(a)

Subsection (1)(a) is re-enacted by s.70(1)(a) of the 1998 Act with effect from April 5, 1999. This part of the social fund scheme was originally brought into operation in April 1987 to enable payments to be made for maternity and funeral expenses. These are made under the ordinary system of adjudication and under regulations required to be made by subs.(1)(a). They are not subject to any budget. See the Social Fund Maternity and Funeral Expenses (General) Regulations 2005. The death grant and the maternity grant, formerly payable under the Social Security Act 1975, were abolished (1986 Act ss.38 and 41) and the provisions for maternity and funeral expenses under the supplementary benefit regulations were removed in April 1987 (General Regulations regs 13–15). 1.45

Subsection (1)(a) does little more than provide the framework for the detailed entitlement set out in the General Regulations. See s.78(4) of the Administration Act on the recovery of funeral payments from the estate of the deceased.

New restrictions on payments for funeral expenses were introduced on June 5, 1995 and there was further clarification and tightening-up of the rules on April 7,

1997 (see regs 7 and 7A of the General Regulations and the notes to those regulations). Note also the changes introduced on November 17, 1997.

The argument that maternity (or funeral) expenses that do not qualify under subs. (1)(a) can be met from the discretionary social fund under subs.(1)(b) was rejected in *R. v Social Fund Inspector Ex p. Harper*, High Court, February 7, 1997. Harrison J held that subss.(1)(a) and (b) provided mutually exclusive methods of meeting particular needs and that maternity and funeral expenses were only intended to be met to the extent laid down in the General Regulations.

Subsection (2)

1.46 Although the predecessor of this subsection was in force from April 1988, the regulations it required were not in place until November 7, 1988 (Social Fund Cold Weather Payments (General) Regulations 1988). The form of the scheme, as embodied in the 1988 Regulations, has been amended several times. The current form does not require a separate claim to be made for a severe weather payment. As for maternity and funeral expenses, the decisions are made by decision-makers, with appeals to a tribunal, and are not subject to any budget.

See also the notes to the Social Fund Winter Fuel Payment Regulations 2000.

PART XIII

GENERAL

Interpretation

Application of Act in relation to territorial waters

1.47 **172.**—In this Act—

(a) any reference to Great Britain includes a reference to the territorial waters of the United Kingdom adjacent to Great Britain;

(b) any reference to the United Kingdom includes a reference to the territorial waters of the United Kingdom.

Age

1.48 **173.**—For the purposes of this Act a person—

(a) is over or under a particular age if he has or, as the case may be, has not attained that age; and

(b) is between two particular ages if he has attained the first but not the second;

and in Scotland (as in England and Wales) the time at which a person attains a particular age expressed in years is the commencement of the relevant anniversary of the date of his birth.

References to Acts

1.49 **174.**—In this Act—

"the 1975 Act" means the Social Security Act 1975;

"the 1986 Act" means the Social Security Act 1986;

"the Administration Act" means the Social Security Administration Act 1992;

"the Consequential Provisions Act" means the Social Security (Consequential Provisions) Act 1992;

"the Northern Ireland Contributions and Benefits Act" means the Social Security Contributions and Benefits (Northern Ireland) Act 1992;

"the Old Cases Act" means the Industrial Injuries and Diseases (Old Cases) Act 1975; and

"the Pensions Act" means the [1 Pension Schemes Act 1993].

AMENDMENT

1. Pension Schemes Act 1993 s.190 Sch.8 para.41.

Subordinate legislation

Regulations, orders and schemes

175.—(1) Subject to [2subsection (1A) below], regulations and orders under this Act shall be made by the Secretary of State. **1.50**

[2(1A) Subsection (1) above has effect subject to—

(a) any provision [3 . . .] providing for regulations or an order to be made by the Treasury or by the Commissioners of Inland Revenue, [3 . . .]

[3 . . .]

(2) Powers under this Act to make regulations, orders or schemes shall be exercisable by statutory instrument.

(3) Except in the case of an order under section 145(3) above and in so far as this Act otherwise provides, any power under this Act to make regulations or an order may be exercised—

(a) either in relation to all cases to which the power extends, or in relation to those cases subject to specified exceptions, or in relation to any specified cases or classes of case;

(b) so as to make, as respects the cases in relation to which it is exercised—

(i) the full provision to which the power extends or any less provision (whether by way of exception or otherwise),

(ii) the same provision for all cases in relation to which the power is exercised, or different provision for different cases or different classes of case or different provision as respects the same case or class of case for different purposes of this Act;

(iii) any such provision either unconditionally or subject to any specified condition;

and where such a power is expressed to be exercisable for alternative purposes it may be exercised in relation to the same case for any or all of those purposes; and powers to make regulations or an order for the purposes of any one provision of this Act are without prejudice to powers to make regulations or an order for the purposes of any other provision.

(4) Without prejudice to any specific provision in this Act, any power conferred by this Act to make regulations or an order (other than the power conferred in section 145(3) above) includes power to make thereby such incidental, supplementary, consequential or transitional provision as appears to the [2 person making the regulations or order] to be expedient for the purposes of the regulations or order.

(5) Without prejudice to any specific provisions in this Act, a power conferred by any provision of this Act except—

(a) sections 30, 47(6), [1 25B(2)(a)] and 145(3) above and paragraph 3(9) of Schedule 7 to this Act;

(b) section 122(1) above in relation to the definition of "payments by way of occupational or personal pension"; and

(c) Part XI,

to make regulations or an order includes power to provide for a person to exercise a discretion in dealing with any matter.

(6) *[Omitted as relating only to housing benefit and community charge benefit.]*

(7) Any power of the Secretary of State under any provision of this Act, except the provisions mentioned in subsection (5)(a) and (b) above and Part IX, to make any regulations or order, where the power is not expressed to be exercisable with the consent of the Treasury, shall if the Treasury so direct be exercisable only in conjunction with them.

(8) and (9) *[Omitted as relating only to ss.116 to 120.]*

(10) Any reference in this section or section 176 below to an order or regulations under this Act includes a reference to an order or regulations made under any provision of an enactment passed after this Act and directed to be construed as one with this Act; but this subsection applies only so far as a contrary intention is not expressed in the enactment so passed, and without prejudice to the generality of any such direction.

AMENDMENTS

1. Social Security (Incapacity for Work) Act 1994 Sch.1 para.36 (April 13, 1995).

2. Social Security Contributions (Transfer of Functions, etc.) Act 1999 s.2 and Sch.3 para.29 (April 1, 1999).

3. Tax Credits Act 2002 s.60 Sch.6 (April 1, 2003).

DERIVATION

Social Security Act 1986 ss.83(1) and 84(1).

Parliamentary control

1.51 **176.**—(1)–(2c) *[Omitted as not applying to income-related benefits.]*

(3) A statutory instrument—

(a) which contains (whether alone or with other provisions) any order, regulations or scheme made under this Act by the Secretary of State, [1 the Treasury or the Commissioners of Inland Revenue,] other than an order under section 145(3) above; and

(b) which is not subject to any requirement that a draft of the instrument shall be laid before and approved by a resolution of each House of Parliament,

[2 (bb) regulations prescribing a percentage rate for the purposes of—

(i) paragraph 3B(3) or 7B(3) of Schedule 5, or

(ii) paragraph 5(3) of Schedule 5A;]

shall be subject to annulment in pursuance of a resolution of either House of Parliament.

AMENDMENTS

1. Social Security Contributions (Transfer of Functions, etc.) Act 1999 s.2 and Sch.3 para.30 (April, 1999).
2. Pensions Act 2004 ss.297(4) and 322(3) and Sch.3 para.11 (April 6, 2005).

DERIVATION

Social Security Act 1986 s.83(4).

[Short title, commencement and extent]

Short title, commencement and extent

177.—(1) This Act may be cited as the as the Social Security Contributions and Benefits Act 1992. 1.52

(2) This Act is to be read, where appropriate, with the Administration Act and the Consequential Provisions Act.

(3) The enactments consolidated by this Act are repealed, in consequence of the consolidation, by the Consequential Provisions Act.

(4) Except as provided in Schedule 4 to the Consequential Provisions Act, this Act shall come into force on 1st July 1992.

(5) The following provisions extend to Northern Ireland—

section 16 and Schedule 2;
section 116(2); and
this section.

(6) Except as provided by this section, this Act does not extend to Northern Ireland.

DEFINITIONS

"the Administration Act"—see s.174.
"the Consequential Provisions Act"—*ibid.*

Jobseekers Act 1995

(1995 C.18)

SECTIONS REPRODUCED

PART I

THE JOBSEEKER'S ALLOWANCE

Entitlement

1. The jobseeker's allowance. 1.53
2. The contribution-based conditions.

An Act to provide for a jobseeker's allowance and to make other provision to promote the employment of the unemployed and the assistance of persons without a settled way of life. [June 28, 1995]

GENERAL NOTE

Old Style Jobseeker's Allowance: A Brief Overview

On October 7, 1996 ("commencement"), jobseeker's allowance ("JSA") replaced two separate benefits, unemployment benefit ("UB") and income support ("IS"), as the benefit for those unemployed persons whom the state requires to remain in the labour market as a condition of receiving state support. UB disappeared entirely. IS remained as means-tested assistance for those whose personal circumstances were such that they were not required to seek work as a condition of receiving state support: principally pensioners (but now see state pension credit), the sick and disabled, single parents. (For a full list see Income Support (General) Regulations 1987 reg.4ZA and Sch.1B.) 1.54

That remains the position in relation to cases in which universal credit under the Welfare Reform Act 2012 has not come into operation. In cases where that benefit has come into operation, the Act as consequently amended (called in this volume the new style Jobseekers Act 1995) is set out in Pt VI together with the Jobseeker's

Allowance Regulations 2013. What is set out in this Part is the Act (called in this volume the old style Jobseekers Act 1995) as it continues to apply in cases in which universal credit has not come into operation and to which the Jobseeker's Allowance Regulations 1996 (Pt III) remain relevant. The two forms of JSA are called in the legislation, and in this volume, new style JSA and old style JSA. See the introductory annotation to the JSA Regulations 2013 for the cases in which universal credit has come into operation. There are exceptionally complex transitional provisions on the transition from old style JSA to new style JSA and vice versa contained in WRA 2012 Commencement Orders (see the No.9 Order (SI 2013/983), as amended in particular by the No.11 Order (SI 2013/1511)). These Orders as amended down to December 31, 2014 are set out and briefly annotated in the Supplement to the 2014/15 edition of this series and subsequent Orders will be dealt with in the 2016/17 edition of Vol.V. The effect of those provisions on the JSA Regulations 1996 and on the JSA Regulations 2013 is noted in the appropriate places.

JSA was introduced by the Jobseekers Act 1995 ("the Act"), which remains a free-standing source rather than (on the model of incapacity benefit) effecting its ends by inserting new sections in the SSCBA 1992. The Act, however, is very much a skeleton, with the bulk of the key detail found in two sets of regulations: in the voluminous JSA Regulations 1996 (SI 1996/207) (originally 172 regulations and eight Schedules) and in the fortunately less extensive but somewhat complex Jobseeker's Allowance (Transitional Provisions) Regulations 1995 ("the JSA (Transitional) Regulations"). Both sets have been quite heavily amended.

1.55 The Government's aim in introducing JSA was to depart from the previous confusing regime under which the unemployed could be eligible for either or both of two different benefits (UB and IS), based on different principles (one a contributory benefit as of right, the other based on test of means), each with its own set of rules (albeit that there was a degree of commonality), one administered by the Employment Service ("ES"), the other by the Benefits Agency ("BA"). JSA as initially introduced and now as old style JSA is a single benefit, embodying both a contributory and a means-tested component, with unified rules on such key aspects as labour market tests, the treatment of earnings and days of benefit payment, and claimants dealing (so far as possible) with a single office. On the implications of JSA as a single benefit see further *Hockenjos v Secretary of State for Social Security*, Court of Appeal, May 2, 2001, approving *CJSA 1920/1999*. It was designed also to emphasise the responsibilities of the unemployed to take every advantage of the opportunities open to them to return to the world of work (*Jobseeker's Allowance*, Cmnd. 2687 (October 1994), Foreword by Peter Lilley and Michael Portillo, at p.2 ("White Paper")). The new benefit structure and administration were supposed to be simpler and clearer, affording better value for the taxpayer, and a better service to claimants. JSA was to help people return to work by strengthening incentives to work; by creating a framework of support within which the ES could give more effective advice and help; by increasing understanding among the unemployed about their obligations and encouraging effective action to meet them, in part by providing effective and timely sanctions for those who did not take the required steps; and by supporting the effectiveness for the unemployed of active labour market policies (White Paper para.2.9). Old style JSA, like incapacity benefit, was expected to help target available money on those who needed it most and effect significant financial savings (White Paper para.3.3).

This introductory overview examines the main elements of the conditions of entitlement to old style JSA, concentrating on conditions common to both components of JSA, and highlighting major areas of difference between JSA and the UB and/or IS regime of benefits for unemployed people.

JSA is a weekly benefit, payable on a weekly basis, with only limited provision for part-weeks. It thus emulates IS rather than UB, a daily benefit. But, following the UB pattern, claimants generally had to serve three (now seven) waiting days in any jobseeking period before entitlement begins (those intermittently unemployed being aided here by a 12-week "linking" rule and the provision for "linked periods" such as ones of incapacity or entitlement to maternity allowance or periods of training that do not "break" a jobseeking period) (s.21 Sch.1 para.4; JSA Regulations 1996 regs 46–49).

1.56 There are two types of old style JSA: contribution-based JSA (CBJSA) and income-based JSA (IBJSA). Both have common "core" conditions of entitlement, but also some peculiar to each type. The former focus only on the claimant, as do the conditions specific to CBJSA. IBJSA has a wider focus; it deploys the IS concept of aggregation of resources (those of members of his family being, generally, treated as those of the claimant) and applies some of its specific conditions of entitlement to members of the claimant's family.

To deal first with *the common "core" conditions*: a person in Great Britain, and under pensionable age, who is out of work (not working 16 or more hours per week) but capable of it, is not receiving relevant education, and satisfying the labour market conditions (available for employment; actively seeking employment; entry into a jobseeker's agreement), will be eligible for old style JSA. *Such a person will be entitled to CBJSA*, for a maximum of six months in an unbroken period of unemployment (longer in calendar terms with intermittent but "linked" unemployment)—a marked and controversial reduction from the one-year entitlement to UB—provided that the contribution conditions are satisfied (the insurance-based element, which will—save in unusual circumstances—exclude those under 18), that the person does not earn more than the prescribed amount each week and that he is not entitled to income support (ss.1, 2).

The rules on determining the amount of CBJSA payable were markedly different from UB. CBJSA is a basic benefit with no increases for dependants. More surprisingly for an insurance-based benefit, nominally paid as of right and commonly seen (albeit mistakenly) as "earned" by the payment of contributions into the insurance scheme, the amount will vary as between claimants who have satisfied the same contribution conditions to be eligible for it. The amount is determined by first ascertaining the age-related amount applicable to the claimant (a lower rate for those aged up to 24, and a higher rate for those aged 25 or over), and then making prescribed deductions in respect of the claimant's earnings and pension payments (no concept of aggregation of family resources is here applicable) (s.4(1)and (2); JSA Regulations 1996 regs 79–81). The concept of abatement of benefit (even to nil) in respect of pension payments is familiar to students of UB, but with CBJSA applies regardless of age, unlike UB where it affected only those aged 55 or over (SSCBA 1992 s.30 (now repealed)). Taken with s.2(1)(c) (earnings in excess of the prescribed amount precluding entitlement), these elements of age-relation and abatement on account of earnings as well as pension payments confirm the awkward hybrid nature of CBJSA: neither a fully-fledged contributory benefit receivable as of right and regardless of means, nor a fully-fledged income-related benefit. Although abatement of CBJSA because of earnings represents a further extension of means-testing into the contributory sphere, CBJSA cannot properly be described as an income-related benefit in the same sense as IS or IBJSA. These rules on CBJSA look to a much narrower range of "means": capital is totally ignored while, with respect to income only earnings are regarded for s.2(1)(c) purposes, although pension payments are in addition taken into account in terms of abatement or reduction of CBJSA.

1.57 *A claimant satisfying the common "core" conditions will be eligible for IBJSA* if neither he nor any member of his family is entitled to income support and no one else in his family is entitled to IBJSA (ss.1 3(1)(b)–(d)). Generally speaking, the claimant must be 18 or over, but certain 16 and 17-year-olds can be entitled in cases of hardship, if the Secretary of State so directs, or in a variety of prescribed circumstances (e.g. as a couple with a child, or as someone laid off from, or kept on short time in his employment, or as a person leaving care) (ss.3(1)(f) and 16; JSA Regulations 1996 Pt IV (Young Persons)). The claimant's partner, if any, must not be engaged in remunerative work (s.3(1)(e)). Capital over a prescribed limit precludes entitlement to IBJSA altogether (s.13; JSA Regulations 1996 reg.107 (£16,000) (see further reg.116(1ZA) and (1B)). But, as with other income-related benefits, the claimant's income (including tariff income from capital) must not exceed the applicable amount (here made up, on the IS model and following rules borrowed from that benefit, of appropriate personal allowances, premiums and eligible housing costs, with modifications in respect of persons in residential care and nursing homes and of special cases (e.g. persons from abroad)) (s.3(1)(a)).

In relation to IBJSA, the means test is broadly the same as that for income support and many of the other rules mirror those that apply to income support. Where there are differences, these are noted at the appropriate places in the commentary. One important change that was made to the income support rules alongside the introduction of JSA was that from October 7, 1996, in the case of a claimant's partner, remunerative work is defined as 24 (not 16) hours a week. This also applies to IBJSA.

An unemployed claimant may thus merely get CBJSA, having, for example, capital resources that preclude entitlement to IBJSA (although he may later move on to IBJSA when those resources fall below the capital limit), or having an income exceeding his IBJSA applicable amount. Or, because of an inadequate contribution record denying access to CBJSA, there may simply be entitlement to IBJSA. Alternatively, a claimant may be entitled to both components at the same time. In that situation, the amount of old style JSA payable is the income-based element unless that is lower than the contribution-based element, in which case the latter is the amount payable. Whatever the amount payable, however, the entitlement to CBJSA erodes the claimant's maximum six months' entitlement to that component of JSA (ss.4(6)–(11) and 5(1)).

1.58 An otherwise existing entitlement to old style JSA will be defeated where the claimant's unemployment is due to a stoppage of work due to a trade dispute, in which he has a direct interest, at his place of work, or because he has withdrawn his labour in furtherance of any trade dispute (s.14). The period affected, not being one of entitlement, will not count towards his six months' entitlement to CBJSA, thus reaffirming the benefit system's supposed neutrality in trade disputes.

Even where entitlement to old style JSA exists, the allowance is not payable for varying periods in a number of situations in which the person's unemployment might be said to be voluntary both in terms of how it came about and his behaviour whilst unemployed (ss.19–19B; JSA Regulations 1996 regs 69–75). Where in such situations there is an underlying entitlement to CBJSA, however, such periods of preclusion from payment eat into the maximum period of entitlement to CBJSA (s.5(1); JSA Regulations 1996 reg.47(4))—a position in marked contrast to UB where periods of disqualification for voluntary unemployment merely delayed the start of, or interrupted, the one year's maximum entitlement.

Unsurprisingly, non-entitlement to old style JSA generally means no allowance can be paid. In a number of situations there is no entitlement to JSA because of failure to meet one or more of the labour market conditions (availability; actively seeking employment; entry into a jobseeker's agreement). Nonetheless, a reduced rate of IBJSA is payable in cases of hardship (s.21 and Sch.1 para.8; JSA Regulations 1996 regs 140–146). JSA also remains payable pending determination of whether a sanction should be imposed but, once imposed, there is no automatic entitlement to a reduced rate of benefit; a reduced rate of IBJSA is only payable in cases of hardship (ss.19 and 20(4)–(6); JSA Regulations 1996 regs 140–146).

1.59 The basic rules are modified significantly in their application to share fishermen and members of the forces (s.21 and Sch.1 para.17; JSA Regulations 1996 Pt XII).

The standard JSA picture was as above for several years. From March 19, 2001, a new dimension was added: the requirement that a "joint-claim couple" make a joint claim for JSA (what by definition is a joint-claim IBJSA (s.1(4)). This aspect of the scheme goes beyond the familiar notion of aggregation of needs and resources (although "joint-claim JSA" embodies that too (see ss.3A and 4)) since that traditional model embodies the notion of one partner in a couple being dependent on the other, the latter being the claimant and having to fulfil the conditions of entitlement. The "joint-claim couple" aspect goes further than this in that each partner is party to the claim and each must satisfy the conditions of entitlement in s.1(2)(a)–(c) and (e)–(i). In other words, each partner of a joint-claim couple must: (i) be available for employment; (ii) have entered into a jobseeker's agreement; (iii) be actively seeking employment; (iv) not be engaged in remunerative work; (v) be capable of work; (vi) not be receiving relevant education; (vii) be under pensionable age; and (viii) be in Great Britain.

The "joint-claim" scheme has, legislatively speaking, required the adaptation of rules designed for a single claimant to deal instead with two people. Of particular note are the provisions for entitlement notwithstanding that one member of the couple does not meet the "labour market conditions" (see JSA Regulations 1996 reg.3D) and the provision enabling one member of the couple to receive a reduced rate of benefit where the other is caught by a sanction unders ss.19, 19A or 19B.

A "joint-claim couple" is defined in s.1(4) as a couple, of a prescribed descrip- **1.60** tion, who are not members of any family that includes someone for whom one of the members of the couple is entitled to child benefit. JSA Regulations 1996 reg.3A gives the prescribed description: initially where one of the members of the couple was born after March 19, 1976, but being 18 or over (reg.3A(1)). From October 28, 2002, subject to reg.3E(2)(l), it covers such a person born after October 28, 1957. Such a couple, however, will not be of a prescribed description if there is a child but no one is as yet entitled to child benefit, because there has been no claim or one has only just been made; if the couple has care of a child or young person as fosterers or with a view to adoption; or if a child or young person is living with the couple when he is away from home while at school (reg.3A(1)).

In short, the central idea of the "joint-claim scheme" is that certain childless couples—young childless couples at least one of whom is (in the initial scheme under 25, later extended to under 45)—will have to make joint claims for income-based jobseeker's allowance. The change is aimed at preventing benefits dependency at a young age by ensuring that both partners are directly involved in the labour market, so that, for example, each will have to be available for and actively seeking work. Rather than one being the dependant of the other, both members of the couple will be claimants having equal rights and responsibilities.

Note also the power in s.29 to pilot new regulations and the back to work bonus scheme introduced by s.26. See the notes to those sections.

PART I

THE JOBSEEKER'S ALLOWANCE

Entitlement

The jobseeker's allowance

1.—(1) An allowance, to be known as a jobseeker's allowance, shall be **1.61** payable in accordance with the provisions of this Act.

(2) Subject to the provisions of this Act, a claimant is entitled to a jobseeker's allowance if he—

(a) is available for employment;
(b) has entered into a jobseeker's agreement, which remains in force;
(c) is actively seeking employment;
[[1](d) satisfies the conditions set out in section 2;]
(e) is not engaged in remunerative work;
[[4](f) does not have limited capability for work;]
(g) is not receiving relevant education;

(h) is under pensionable age; and
(i) is in Great Britain.

[1(2A) Subject to the provisions of this Act, a claimant who is not a member of a joint-claim couple is entitled to a jobseeker's allowance if he satisfies—

(a) the conditions set out in paragraphs (a) to (c) and (e) to (i) of subsection (2); and
(b) the conditions set out in section 3.

(2B) Subject to the provisions of this Act, a joint-claim couple are entitled to a jobseeker's allowance if—

(a) a claim for the allowance is made jointly by the couple;
(b) each member of the couple satisfies the conditions set out in paragraphs (a) to (c) and (e) to (i) of subsection (2); and
(c) the conditions set out in section 3A are satisfied in relation to the couple.

(2C) Regulations may prescribe circumstances in which subsection (2A) is to apply to a claimant who is a member of a joint-claim couple.

(2D) Regulations may, in respect of cases where a person would (but for the regulations) be a member of two or more joint-claim couples, make provision for only one of those couples to be a joint-claim couple; and the provision which may be so made includes provision for the couple which is to be the joint-claim couple to be nominated—

(a) by the persons who are the members of the couples, or
(b) in default of one of the couples being so nominated, by the Secretary of State.]

(3) A jobseeker's allowance is payable in respect of a week.

(4) In this Act—

"a contribution-based jobseeker's allowance" means a jobseeker's allowance entitlement to which is based on the claimant's satisfying conditions, which include those set out in section 2; [2. . .]

"an income-based jobseeker's allowance" means a jobseeker's allowance entitlement to which is based on the claimant's satisfying conditions, which include those set out in section 3 [1 or a joint-claim jobseeker's allowance;

"a joint-claim couple" means a [3 couple] who—

(a) are not members of any family whose members include a person in respect of whom a member of the couple is entitled to child benefit, and
(b) are of a prescribed description;

"a joint-claim jobseeker's allowance" means a jobseeker's allowance entitlement to which arises by virtue of subsection (2B).]

AMENDMENTS

1. Welfare Reform and Pensions Act 1999 Sch.7 para.2 (March 19, 2001).
2. Welfare Reform and Pensions Act 1999 Sch.13 Pt V (April 2, 2000).
3. Civil Partnership Act 2004 s.254 and Sch.24 Pt 7 para.118 (December 5, 2005).
4. Welfare Reform Act 2007 Sch.3 para.12 (October, 27, 2008).

DEFINITIONS

"actively seeking employment"—see s.7(1).
"available for employment"—see s.6(1).
"claimant"—see s.35(1).
"couple"—see s.35(1).
"employment"—see s.35(1) and JSA Regulations 1996 reg.3.

"employment" (in section 7)—see s.7(8).
"entitled"—see s.35(1) and SSAA 1992 ss.1 and 68.
"Great Britain"—see s.35(1).
"jobseeker's agreement"—see ss.9(1) and 35(1).
"limited capability for work"—see s.35(2) and Sch.1 para.2 and SSCBA 1992 Pt XIIA.
"pensionable age"—see s.35(1) and JSA Regulations 1996 reg.3 and SSCBA 1992 s.122(1).
"relevant education"—see s.35(2) and Sch.1 para.14 and JSA Regulations 1996 reg.54.
"remunerative work"—see s.35(2) and Sch.1 para.1 and JSA Regulations 1996 reg.51.
"week"—see s.35(1).
"work"—*ibid.*

General Note

This section provides the legislative basis for payment of old style JSA, a weekly benefit (subs.(3)) and a single benefit (see *Hockenjos v Secretary of State for Social Security*, Court of Appeal, May 2, 2001, approving *CJSA 1920/1999*) taking two forms (subs.(4)): (1) a "contribution-based jobseeker's allowance" (in essence the replacement for the insurance based unemployment benefit); and (2) an "income-based jobseeker's allowance" (in essence the income-related benefit that took over the role that income support previously played for unemployed people of insufficient means). Subsection (2) sets out the conditions of entitlement to CBJSA and subss.(2A) and (2B) set out the conditions for IBJSA. Note that there are several common conditions (paras (a)–(c) and (e)–(i) of subs.(2)), that must be fulfilled, as well as a separate condition referring on to s.2 for CBJSA (subs.(2)(d)), to s.3 for IBJSA apart from members of a joint-claim couple (subs.(2A)(b)) and to s.3A for joint-claim couples (subs.(2B)(c)). On joint-claim couples see s.1(4) and "Overview of JSA" above. 1.62

Subsection (2)

This sets out the basic conditions of entitlement to old style JSA, in either of its forms, either directly or by reference. It is merely a "framework", amplified by other sections of and Schedules to the Act (subs.(2) begins, "Subject to the provisions of this Act") and in the detail of the Jobseeker's Allowance Regulations 1996 (the JSA Regulations 1996). Many of the central conditions will be familiar to those who previously dealt with UB and/or income support for the unemployed. But conditions previously only applicable to the income support aspect of benefits for the unemployed and not to UB are now applied also to the replacement for UB: CBJSA. In addition, and reflecting the ethos of a benefit for "jobseekers" rather than the "unemployed", a central condition for all types of old style JSA is that the claimant has entered into a jobseeker's agreement which remains in force (para.(b)). 1.63

The conditions of entitlement, the sources in which they are "fleshed out", and some of the principles they reflect and the problem areas they deal with are considered in the remainder of this annotation (unless stated otherwise, each condition must be satisfied by *both* members of a "joint-claim couple", on which see further "Overview of JSA", above, and the notes to subs.(4), below):

(1) "*Is available for employment*" (para.(a)): see further s.6 and the JSA Regulations 1996 Pt II, Chs I and II (regs 4–17). This "labour market" condition is one aspect of the central underlying principle, common to regimes of benefit for unemployed people, that the claimant's unemployment must be involuntary.

(2) "*Has entered into a jobseeker's agreement which remains in force*" (para.(b)): see further ss.9–10 and the JSA Regulations 1996 (regs 31–40). Note, in particular, that a claimant is to be treated as having satisfied this condition in any of the circumstances set out in JSA Regulations 1996 reg.34. This is a further aspect of the underlying principle, common in regimes of benefit for the unemployed, that 1.64

the claimant's unemployment must be involuntary: being a jobseeker, looking to return to work, and agreeing a programme of activity, the better to enable him to do so. The jobseeker's agreement is an integral part of identifying what steps back to work are appropriate for claimants and to enable regular and effective monitoring of their activities to that end, reviewing and altering the terms of the agreement as necessary over a period (see White Paper para.4.16 and ss.10 and 11). Note, in particular, that "employment officers" (usually Jobcentre Plus personnel: see the notes to the s.35(1) definition and s.9(13)) cannot enter into an agreement the terms of which are such that the claimant acting in accordance with them would fail to satisfy either of the key requirements to be available for and actively seeking work, thus placing such officers at the heart of policing these central requirements of the system (s.9(5)). See the notes to s.9 below for when an agreement has validly been entered into and the notes to s.10 for when it remains in force.

(3) "*Is actively seeking employment*" (para.(b)): see further s.7 and the JSA Regulations 1996 regs 18–22. This second "labour market" condition is a further aspect of the central underlying principle, common to regimes of benefit for unemployed people, that the claimant's unemployment must be involuntary. In any week a person is actively seeking employment if during that week they take such steps as they can reasonably be expected to take in order to have *the best prospects of securing employment*, thereby stressing the requirements of taking positive action to secure work.

(4) *Satisfies either: (a) the conditions set out in s.2; or (b)(i) (as a non-joint-claim claimant) those in s.3; or (ii) (as joint-claim couple) those in s.3A.*

1.65 *The conditions set out in s.2 (CBJSA) (para.(1)(d))*: The concept of "joint-claim couple" is not of relevance here. Each claimant is treated as a separate individual. The conditions enumerated in s.2 deal with the further particular conditions of entitlement, and JSA Regulations 1996 reg.56 provides some amplification. Regulations 47 and 48 are also relevant, and it is necessary to cross-refer to some of the provisions of the SSCBA 1992 dealing with contribution conditions. In essence the contribution conditions (the claimant's insurance record) are much the same as those under UB from 1988 onwards, but there is greater protection of the position of carers who left the labour market to care for an invalid and now wish to return to the world of employment. However, s.2 also establishes the mutual exclusivity of income support and CBJSA and in addition embodies a preclusive earnings rule.

1.66 *The conditions set out in s.3 (IBJSA for a claimant who is not a member of a joint-claim couple) (subs.(2A))*: those set out in s.3 are particular to IBJSA for a claimant who is not a member of a joint-claim couple. On "joint-claim couple" see "Overview of JSA", above, and notes to subs.(4), below. Amplification is found in the JSA Regulations 1996 regs 76–155. The rules on means test are essentially the same as for income support.

1.67 *The conditions set out in s.3A ((IBJSA for a joint-claim couple)(subss.(2B)–(2D))*: Broadly speaking, these adapt the means-test and other provisions in s.3 to become conditions to be met by both members of the joint-claim couple. On "joint-claim couple", see "Overview of JSA", above, and the notes to subs.(4), below.

(5) "*Is not engaged in remunerative work*", (para.(e)): see further s.21 and Sch.1 para.1, which together enabled the making of the amplificatory regulations, the JSA Regulations 1996 regs 51–53. It may seem obvious that those who have a job cannot be said to be unemployed. But previous regimes have always catered for partial unemployment, and it is inevitably a matter of controversy at what point a line is to be drawn saying claimants are working to such an extent that they cannot properly be said to be unemployed and need state support. The remunerative work rules draw that line; once the threshold is reached the old style JSA system will no longer regard a working claimant as "unemployed". The remunerative work rules as applicable to CBJSA set the threshold at 16 hours per week: "remunerative work" means in

the case of the claimant (the only person relevant for CBJSA), work in which he is engaged or, where hours of work fluctuate, is engaged on average, for not less than 16 hours per week; and work here means work for which payment is made or which is done in expectation of payment (JSA Regulations 1996 reg.51(1)(a)). Provision is made in JSA Regulations 1996 reg.51(2) and (3) for determining the number of hours for which a person is engaged in work, essentially along the same line as provisions applicable to the issue in income support prior to its replacement as a benefit for unemployed people (Income Support (General) Regulations 1987 reg.5).

JSA Regulations 1996 reg.52 deals with those who are to be treated as engaged in remunerative work, notwithstanding that they may not at the time at issue be doing any work at all and, indeed, may be wholly without employment. In this way, the remunerative work condition becomes a vehicle for excluding the following claimants from both types of old style JSA:

(a) those who are without good cause absent from what constitutes remunerative work under reg.51 (those on maternity leave or absent from work through illness are protected);
(b) those absent from what constitutes remunerative work under reg.51 by reason of a recognised, customary or other holiday (those on maternity leave or absent from work through illness are protected); and
(c) for the period in which the payment is taken into account, those who were, or were treated as being, in remunerative work whose employment has been suspended and who have been paid holiday pay in respect of it.

Regulation 53 protects a range of claimants who *are* working by treating them as **1.68**
not engaged in remunerative work: charity or voluntary workers paid only expenses; those engaged on a scheme for which a training allowance is paid; certain persons living in or temporarily absent from residential accommodation, a nursing home or a residential care home; (as regards the performance of their duties) part-time firemen, auxiliary coastguards, lifeboatmen, members of a fire brigade, members of a prescribed territorial or reserve force; councillors as regards the performance of their duties; those engaged in boarding and fostering children; those mentally or physically disabled whose earning capacity or hours of work are in consequence reduced below 75 per cent of the normal threshold.

As noted above, for CBJSA, only the claimant is relevant. Note in contrast that a claimant who is a member of a married or unmarried couple (but not a joint-claim couple) will be excluded from IBJSA, despite not being engaged (or treated as engaged) in remunerative work, if the partner is so engaged (or treated as so engaged), but the hours' threshold in respect of the partner is 24 rather than 16 (s.3(1)(e) and JSA Regulations 1996 reg.51(1)(b)). As regards a joint-claim couple, both must satisfy the remunerative work condition. Failure of one to do so would, in principle, be expected to result in disentitlement of both. But see JSA Regulations 1996 reg.3E, enabling the other member of a joint-claim couple to claim as a "standard" ss.1(2A) and 3 claimant in certain circumstances where the other member fails to meet one or more of the conditions of entitlement in s.1(2)(a)–(c) and (e)–(i). One such circumstance is where the "failing" member is engaged, or has agreed to be engaged, in remunerative work for more than 16 but less than 24 hours per week (JSA Regulations 1996 reg.3E(2)(g)).

(6) *"Does not have limited capability for work"* (para.(f)): this represents, as in the past, a demarcation line between benefits for those able to work but unable to find employment and benefits for those incapable of work (incapacity benefit and ESA). However, complications inevitably did occur when claimants had to transfer from one type of benefit to the other, particularly in respect of periods of short-term incapacity. Hence the demarcation is no longer as strict as in the past; s.21 and Sch.1 para.2 enabled the making of JSA Regulations 1996 reg.55, which allows someone to remain in receipt of old style JSA whilst incapable of work for up to two weeks. No more than two such periods are permitted in any jobseeking period of less than 12 months. Where a jobseeking period lasts longer than 12 months, in effect one is entitled to no more than two such "short-term incapacity periods" in any

12 months. Regulaation 55A now allows receipt to continue for a more extended period of up to 13 weeks in total, but only once in any 12 months.

1.69 (7) *"Is not receiving relevant education"* (para.(g)): see further s.21 and Sch.1 para.14 and the regulation they enabled, JSA Regulations 1996 reg.54, which defines it to cover only full-time education, not being a course of advanced education, which is undertaken by a child or young person. Someone treated as a child for child benefit purposes or who is receiving full-time education as far as the child benefit system is concerned (see SSCBA 1992 s.142) is treated as receiving full-time education for the purposes of jobseeker's allowance (JSA Regulations 1996 reg.54(2)). As this exclusion covers persons under 19, the effect of the contribution conditions (the claimant's insurance record) is to make this in practice a hurdle much more relevant to income-based than contribution-based JSA. Those on a full-time course of advanced education, it should be noted, will be excluded from old style JSA because they are treated as not available for employment (see s.6 and JSA Regulations 1996 regs 1(3) and 15(a)).

(8) *"Is under pensionable age"* (para.(h)): "pensionable age" is defined as in the SSCBA 1992 s.122(1) (see s.35(1) and JSA Regulations 1996 reg.3). This inability of those over pensionable age to obtain old style JSA represented a significant change from the UB regime, where those who had deferred retirement or had elected to "de-retire" in order to enhance their eventual retirement pension could receive UB while seeking work. The change, however, is thought to have affected a very small number of people each year (per Mr R. Evans, Parliamentary Under Secretary of State, *House of Commons Standing Committee Debates on the Jobseeker's Bill*, col.133).

(9) *"Is in Great Britain"* (para.(i)): see further s.21 and Sch.1 para.11, which enabled JSA Regulations 1996 reg.50 to treat temporary absence for certain specified purposes (e.g. to attend an employment interview) as presence in Great Britain and the amendment effected by JSA Regulations 1996 reg.165 to reg.11 of the Persons Abroad Regulations 1975 to enable entitlement notwithstanding absence in the circumstances covered by reg.11. Note that for CBJSA there is no requirement of "residence", whether ordinary or habitual; the condition is one of presence. However, rules on habitual residence apply to restrict or deny the access of some people to IBJSA. Note further that this condition of presence in Great Britain cannot prevail against the entitlements afforded under EC law: see, e.g. EC Regulation 883/2004 (Vol.III).

Subsection (2A)

1.70 This deals with what is termed in this commentary the "standard" claimant for IBJSA: that is, the claimant who is not a member of a joint-claim couple (on "joint-claim couple" see "Overview of JSA", above, and notes to subs.(4), below). In other words, broadly speaking, being a single person, a member of a couple with children, or a member of a childless couple neither of whom was born after March 19, 1976 (i.e. neither is under 25) or, since October 2002, neither of whom was born after October 28, 1957 (i.e. neither is under 45). This claimant must meet the common conditions of entitlement in s.1(2)(a)–(c) and (e)–(i), plus those in s.3.

Subsection (2B)

1.71 This deals with the entitlement of a joint-claim couple (see notes to subs.(4)) to IBJSA. The couple must make a claim for the allowance jointly. Each member of the couple must meet the common conditions of entitlement in s.1(2)(a)–(c) and (e)–(i), plus those in s.3A. An allowance, entitlement to which is obtained pursuant to this subsection, is called a "joint-claim jobseeker's allowance" (subs.(4)).

Subsection (2C)

1.72 This rule-making power enables regulations to stipulate circumstances in which a member of a joint-claim couple (see further notes to subs.(4)) is instead to be treated as a "standard" claimant under subs.(2A). JSA Regulations 1996 reg.3E is the product of the exercise of this power. It enables one member of a joint-claim couple to claim as a "standard" ss.1(2A) and 3 claimant in certain circumstances where the other member (described here as the "failing" member) does not satisfy one or more of the conditions of entitlement in s.1(2)(a)–(c) and (e)–(i). One such circumstance is where the "failing" member is engaged, or has agreed to be engaged, in remunerative work for more than 16 but less than 24 hours per week (JSA Regulations 1996 reg.3E(2)(g)). Others include where the "failing" member is pregnant and claiming maternity allowance or statutory maternity pay (reg.3E(2)(h)); or in receipt of statutory sick pay (reg.3E(2)(k)); or who is over pensionable age (reg.3E(2)(f)). See further the notes to that regulation.

Subsection (2D)

This power enables regulations to be made where someone would otherwise be a member of two joint-claim couples. JSA Regulations 1996 reg.3(2) is the product of the exercise of this power. Where someone would otherwise be a member of more than one joint-claim couple, he will be regarded as a member of the couple he nominates or (in default) that the Secretary of State nominates. That nominated couple operates to the exclusion of any other couple of which he may be a member. **1.73**

Subsection (3)

This stipulates that old style JSA is paid in respect of a week, whereas UB was, of course, a daily benefit. Note, however, that s.21 and Sch.1 para.5 enable the making of regulations to permit payment of JSA for a period of less than a week. The circumstances in which this may be done are contained in JSA Regulations 1996 regs 150–155. **1.74**

Subsection (4)

This specifies that there are two types of jobseeker's allowance: (1) a "contribution-based jobseeker's allowance", entitlement to which depends on fulfilling the common conditions in subs.(2) plus the specific ones in s.2; and (2) an "income-based jobseeker's allowance", entitlement to which is dependent on meeting the particular conditions set out in s.3 (standard claimant) or s.3A (joint-claim couple) as well as the common conditions in subs.(2). **1.75**

Just as with the old regime of benefits for unemployed people, where a person might, depending on the circumstances, be entitled to only one or to both of UB and income support, so with the old style JSA: s.4 contains complicated provisions on amounts of each type of allowance and the situation, common in practice, where the allowance received by an unemployed person looking for work is an amalgam of both types.

The subsection also defines "joint-claim couple" as a couple, *of a prescribed description*, who are not members of any family that includes someone for whom one of the members of the couple is entitled to child benefit. JSA Regulations 1996 reg.3A, as amended from October 28, 2002, gives the prescribed description: where one of the members of the couple was born after October 28, 1957, but being 18 or over. Subject to reg.3E(l), below, it thus now covers a member aged between 18 and 45. Initially coverage was for those aged between 18 and 25. Such a couple, however, will not be of a prescribed description if:

(a) under JSA Regulations 1996 reg.77(3), one of its members is treated as responsible for a child or young person (where no one is as yet entitled to child benefit, for example, because a claim has only just been made);
(b) the couple has care of a child or young person in one or more of the circumstances mentioned in JSA Regulations 1996 reg.78(4) (where they are fosterers or the child has been placed with them for adoption); and
(c) a child or young person is living with the couple in the circumstances mentioned in JSA Regulations 1996 reg.78(8) (a child living with the couple when he is away from home while at school).

"Joint-claim jobseeker's allowance" is also defined in this subsection. It means an allowance entitlement to which arises through subs.(2B), above. It then falls within the definition of IBJSA.

New style JSA

1.76 Note that in those cases and areas where universal credit has come into force, income-based JSA is abolished and replaced by new style JSA (which is contribution-based only). See Pt VI of this book for the legislation relating to new style JSA and for the cases and areas to which it applies.

The contribution-based conditions

1.77 **2.**—(1) The conditions referred to in [2 section 1(2)(d)] are that the claimant—

(a) has actually paid Class 1 contributions in respect of one ("the base year") of the last two complete years before the beginning of the relevant benefit year and satisfies the additional conditions set out in subsection (2);

(b) has, in respect of the last two complete years before the beginning of the relevant benefit year, either paid Class 1 contributions or been credited with earnings and satisfies the additional condition set out in subsection (3);

(c) does not have earnings in excess of the prescribed amount; and

(d) is not entitled to income support.

(2) The additional conditions mentioned in subsection (1)(a) are that—

(a) the contributions have been paid before the week for which the jobseeker's allowance is claimed;

[4 (b) the claimant's relevant earnings for the base year upon which primary Class 1 contributions have been paid or treated as paid are not less than the base year's lower earnings limit multiplied by 26.

(2A) Regulations may make provision for the purposes of subsection (2)(b) for determining the claimant's relevant earnings for the base year.

(2B)Regulations under subsection (2A) may, in particular, make provision—

(a) for making that determination by reference to the amount of a person's earnings for periods comprised in the base year;

(b) for determining the amount of a person's earnings for any such period by—

(i) first determining the amount of the earnings for the period in accordance with regulations made for the purposes of section 3(2) of the Benefits Act, and

(ii) then disregarding so much of the amount found in accordance with sub-paragraph (i) as exceeded the base year's lower earnings limit (or the prescribed equivalent).]

(3) The additional condition mentioned in subsection (1)(b) is that the earnings factor derived [3from so much of the claimant's earnings as did not exceed the upper earnings limit and] upon which primary Class 1 contributions have been paid or treated as paid or from earnings credited is not less, in each of the two complete years, than the lower earnings limit for the year multiplied by 50.

[1(3A) Where primary Class 1 contributions have been paid or treated as paid on any part of a person's earnings, [3subsection (3)] above shall have effect as if such contributions had been paid or treated as paid on so much of the earnings as did not exceed the upper earnings limit.]

[5(3B) Regulations may—

(a) provide for the first set of conditions to be taken to be satisfied in the case of persons—
   (i) who have been entitled to any prescribed description of benefit during any prescribed period or at any prescribed time, or
   (ii) who satisfy other prescribed conditions;

(b) with a view to securing any relaxation of the requirements of the first set of conditions in relation to persons who have been entitled as mentioned in paragraph (a)(i), provide for that set of conditions to apply in relation to them subject to prescribed modifications.

(3C) In subsection (3B)—

"the first set of conditions" means the condition set out in subsection (1) (a) and the additional conditions set out in subsection (2);

"benefit" means—

[6(za) universal credit,]

(a) any benefit within the meaning of section 122(1) of the Benefits Act,

(b) any benefit under Parts 7 to 12 of the Benefits Act,

(c) credits under regulations under section 22(5) of the Benefits Act,

(d) a contribution-based jobseeker's allowance, and

(e) working tax credit.]

(4) For the purposes of this section—

(a) "benefit year" means a period which is a benefit year for the purposes of Part II of the Benefits Act or such other period as may be prescribed for the purposes of this section;

(b) "the relevant benefit year" is the benefit year which includes—
   (i) the beginning of the jobseeking period, which includes the week for which a jobseeker's allowance is claimed, or
   (ii) (if earlier) the beginning of any linked period; and

(c) other expressions which are used in this section and the Benefits Act have the same meaning in this section as they have in that Act.

AMENDMENTS

1. Social Security Act 1998 Sch.7 para.133 (April 6, 1999).
2. Welfare Reform and Pensions Act 1999 Sch.7 para.3 (March 19, 2001).
3. National Insurance Contributions Act 2002 Sch.1 para.45 (April 6, 2003).
4. Welfare Reform Act 2009 s.12 (November 1, 2010).
5. Welfare Reform Act 2009 s.12(5) (November 29, 2011).
6. Welfare Reform Act 2012 Sch.2 para.35 (April 29, 2013).

DEFINITIONS

"the Benefits Act"—see s.35(1).
"benefit year"—see SSCBA 1992 s.21(6).
"claimant"—see s.35(1).
"earnings"—see s.35(3) and Sch.1 para.6; SSCBA 1992 s.3.
"earnings factor"—see SSCBA 1992 ss.22 and 23.
"jobseeking period"—see s.35(1) and JSA Regulations 1996 reg.47.
"linked period"—see s.35(2) and Sch.1 para.3; JSA Regulations 1996 reg.48(2).
"lower earnings limit"—see SSCBA 1992 s.5(1)(a).
"prescribed"—see s.35(1).
"primary Class 1 contributions"—see SSCBA 1992 ss.6, 8.
"upper earnings limit"—see SSCBA 1992 ss.122(1) and 5(1).

"week"—see s.35(1).
"year"—see subs.(4)(c) and s.35(1) and SSCBA 1992 s.122(1).

GENERAL NOTE

1.78 Section 1 stipulates that to be entitled to CBJSA, a person must fulfil not only the common conditions set out in s.1(2)(a)–(c) and (e)–(i), but also those particular to that contribution-based type of old style JSA set out in this section (see s.1(2)(d)).

The particular conditions are threefold. First, and unsurprisingly in an insurance or contribution-based benefit, the claimant must satisfy conditions as to past contributions in terms of a specified mixture of paid and credited Class 1 social security contributions (those paid by employed earners) in specified recent years (subs.(1)(a) and (b)). Secondly, any earnings with respect to the week of claim must not exceed a prescribed amount (subs.(1)(c)). Thirdly, the claimant must not be entitled to income support (subs.(1)(d)).

Each of these conditions will be examined in turn.

Subsections (1)(a) and (b), (2)–(4); particular condition one: the contribution conditions

1.79 These set out, or provide the necessary interpretative arrangements for, the insurance or contribution-based conditions of entitlement particular to CBJSA. In structure, they reproduce those that had been applicable to UB since 1988, when those contribution conditions were tightened (with at least one unintended effect, now remedied in the JSA system) to require a more recent and extensive contact with the world of employment (see SSCBA 1992 s.25(1) and (2)(a) and Sch.3 Pt I para.1 as in force immediately prior to commencement). The changes effected by s.12 of the Welfare Reform Act 2009 and regulations made in consequence significantly further tightened the contribution conditions for CBJSA from November 1, 2010. They mean that the requisite level of earnings in the tax year relied on for the first contribution condition is now 26 times that year's lower earnings limit (LEL), rather than 25, and the conditions now (by virtue of reg.45A of the JSA Regulations 1996) only count earnings as at that LEL so that new claimants will have to have worked for at least 26 weeks in one of the last two tax years. Prior to these amendments, when the level was 25 times the LEL and the scheme looked also to earnings between the lower and upper earnings limits, a high earner could qualify on less than four weeks' work in the tax year and someone at the national minimum wage could qualify in about 12 weeks.

As with all contributory benefits, whether someone satisfies the contribution conditions for the benefit is a decision for the Secretary of State and now appealable to a tribunal as a decision on a claim for or award of benefit not otherwise rendered non-appealable (SSA 1998, s.12 and Sch.2; Decisions and Appeals Regulations 1999 reg.27 and Sch.2). From April 1, 1999, this has to some extent been affected by the entry into force of the Social Security (Transfer of Functions, etc.) Act 1999 (Vol.III) which transfers certain functions from the Secretary of State to the Board of Inland Revenue, whose functions have now been transferred to Her Majesty's Revenue and Customs (HMRC) by s.5(2) of the Commissioners for Revenue and Customs Act 2005. Certain matters as to categorisation of earners, which class of contributions a person is liable or entitled to pay, and whether they have been paid in respect of any period become decisions for HMRC, thus impacting to some degree on the Secretary of State's decision as to whether the conditions specific to benefit entitlement are met. It would seem that for now such decisions on contribution conditions for benefit purposes remain ones for the Secretary of State. See the notes to s.8 of the Transfer of Functions Act in Vol.III. It would be inappropriate to go into much detail here, but a brief outline may be of assistance in understanding the nature of CBJSA and in considering the matter of when someone, having exhausted his title to such an allowance in accordance with the provisions of s.5(1) (after 26 weeks in a case of continuous unemployment), can become entitled to a further CBJSA in accordance with the provisions of s.5(2). Some knowledge is also useful to identify the groups excluded by these contribution conditions from access to CBJSA.

Applying the contribution conditions: the first step in applying the contribution conditions is to identify the relevant benefit year: by virtue of subs.(4)(b), the one including the beginning of the jobseeking period or any linked period (as will be seen below, the concept of linked period is crucial in helping qualify for CBJSA those persons who left the labour market in order to care for an invalid, many of whom who had inadvertently been ruled out of UB by the tightening of the contribution conditions in 1988). A benefit year runs generally from the first Sunday in January in one calendar year until the first Saturday in January in the next calendar year. So, if someone's first ever claim for any benefit was for JSA in October 2014, the relevant benefit year is 2014–2015. The second step in applying the conditions is to ascertain the two contribution/tax years (April 6 in one calendar year to April 5 in the next) in which the requisite level of contributions must be met: the last two *complete* tax/contribution years *before the start of the relevant benefit year*. So if the benefit year is 2014–2015 (Jan.–Jan.), the tax/contribution years are 2012–2013 and 2011–2012 (April–April), since tax/contribution year 2013–2014 was not complete at the start of the relevant benefit year. The final steps are to determine whether in one of those tax/contribution years (the "base year") the requisite level of *paid* contributions has been met (the first contribution condition) (subss.(1)(a) and (2)(b)) and, if so, whether the requisite level of paid and/or credited contributions has also been met in respect of each of the two tax years (the second contribution condition) (subss.(1)(b) and (3)). Paid (or treated as paid) means paid (or treated as paid) on so much of the earnings in the relevant years as did not exceed the upper earnings limit for contributions payment purposes (subs.(3A)). See further commentary to SSCBA 1992 Sch.3 in Vol. I. **1.80**

The effect of the contribution conditions (potentially problematic groups): although one must always be careful to avoid an over-simplistic approach in such a complex area, one can readily identify a number of groups either denied entitlement by the contribution conditions or who will have significant difficulties satisfying them: **1.81**

(a) *The self-employed*—it is too simplistic to say that no self-employed person can have title to a CBJSA; it depends on just when the person was in self-employment. Since the contribution conditions can only be satisfied by Class 1 contributions (those paid by employed earners or credited during periods of unemployment or incapacity), the effect is to exclude from CBJSA those who were self-employed throughout either of the relevant tax/contribution years.

(b) *Those who have never been employed*—the requirement in the first contribution condition for payment of contributions effectively excludes those who, whether through unemployment, incapacity or disability, have been unable to build a contribution record in terms of paid contributions.

(c) *Those unemployed or incapable of work during the relevant tax/contribution years but in work before the first year or since the end of the second year*—if insufficient contributions have been paid in either of the years to satisfy condition one, these groups will be excluded, despite a prior or subsequent full record in terms of paid contributions, unless the period of unemployment or incapacity forms a linked period with the current jobseeking period (see JSA Regulations 1996 reg.48): a gap of more than 12 weeks precludes linking.

(d) *Persons under 18*—the conditions of entitlement to CBJSA contain no explicit lower age limit, unlike IBJSA, which specifically excludes most persons under 18 (see s.3(1)(f)). The contribution conditions do, however, tend to preclude entitlement to CBJSA for those under 18 save in highly unusual circumstances; even a claim at the very beginning of a benefit year requires looking back to a tax year beginning almost three years earlier, so that for the bulk of the period focused on, the person will have been under 16, generating neither paid nor credited Class 1 contributions.

(e) *The low-paid*—those whose earnings fall below the lower earnings limit for the whole or the main part of a tax year will not satisfy the contribution conditions since there is no liability or ability to pay Class 1 contributions where earnings fall below that limit, and, because the person is in work, no Class 1 credits are generated.

(f) *Those married women or widows paying reduced rate contributions*—these do not generate any earnings factor (and so do not count) for UB/JSA purposes (SSCBA 1992 s.22(4)).

1.82 *Contribution-based JSA: an improved position for carers*: From 1988, the first contribution condition for UB required looking back to one of two recent tax years, rather than, as was the case prior to 1988, to any tax/contribution year. This impacted adversely on those (usually women) who, possibly with a full contribution record, left the secure world of employment to care for an invalid. Whilst receipt of invalid care allowance (now carer's allowance) produced credited Class 1 contributions to help fulfil the second contribution condition, a person who sought to return to the job market and claimed UB pending finding work, say, some five years later, would be precluded from entitlement since in neither of the relevant tax/contribution years would any actual contributions have been paid; from 1988 a complete record of paid contributions in earlier tax years did not count. This was an unintended effect of the 1988 changes (see Mr R. Evans, Parliamentary Under Secretary of State, *House of Commons Standing Committee B Debates on the Jobseeker's Bill*, cols 161–162 (1994–95)), and was not carried over into CBJSA because the concept of "linked period" (see subs.(4)(b)(ii), s.21 and Sch.1 para.3, and JSA Regulations 1996 reg.48) includes, for purposes of helping someone to satisfy the contribution conditions, periods of receipt of carer's allowance (see JSA Regulations 1996 reg.48(2) and (3)), so that in our example, provided the jobseeking period in respect of which the JSA claim is made falls within 12 weeks of the period of receipt of carer's allowance ending (see JSA Regulations 1996 reg.48(2A); *SSWP v Baker – CJSA/2168/2010*), the "relevant benefit year" becomes that in which the period of entitlement to carer's allowance began (see subs.(4)(b)), and the relevant tax/contribution years, being determined by reference to that benefit year, are years in which the person had a full contribution record of paid contributions. Accordingly, where a claimant had worked part time for a year after the ending of ICA before making his CBJSA claim, the "linked period" could not, because of the 12-week limit, enable him to rely on a period of pre-ICA paid contributions (*SSWP v Baker – CJSA/2168/2010*).

Subsection (1)(c): particular condition two: the earnings condition

1.83 In the 1994 White Paper, the Government presented CBJSA as a benefit receivable for a period, irrespective of means, by those unemployed people who had paid contributions whilst in employment (para.4.21). Despite that, but in line with other statements in the White Paper (*ibid.*), this second particular condition specifies that a claimant for CBJSA "must not have earnings in excess of the prescribed amount".

The idea is to preclude from entitlement to CBJSA those whose earnings, after taking account of any earnings disregards under the old style JSA scheme, would exceed their contributory entitlement. It is important to note that the earnings condition precludes entitlement, rather than allowing underlying entitlement but precluding payment. This preclusion of entitlement means that weeks covered by it do not eat into a claimant's maximum 182 days of entitlement to CBJSA (see s.5).

The prescribed amount is not the same for everyone, but is determined for a particular claimant in accordance with the formula set out in JSA Regulations 1996 reg.56: a level equal to the claimant's personal age-related rate of CBJSA (determined in accordance with s.4(1)(a) and JSA Regulations 1996 reg.79) plus the appropriate disregards from his earnings, minus one penny. Only the claimant's earnings are taken into account. On what constitutes "earnings" and their calculation, see s.35(3), which requires the term to be construed in accordance with SSCBA 1992 s.3 (earnings includes any remuneration or profit derived from an employment) and in accordance with Sch.1 para.6, which enables the making of regulations to treat as earnings limited categories of employment protection payments.

The definition in s.35(3) is subject to regulations made for the purposes of that provision. It is most likely that regs 98 (employed earners) and 100 (self-employed) of the JSA Regulations 1996 were not made under the powers in s.35(3), as had been submitted in previous editions, rather than under s.12 alone. Instead, the reference to "in accordance with" s.3 of the SSCBA 1992 appears to incorporate the provisions of the Computation of Earnings Regulations (Vol.I), as decided by Commissioner Howell in *CJSA/3928* and *3931/2003*. Regulations 9 (employed earners) and 12 (self-employment) of those Regulations define what does and does not count as earnings in generally similar, but by no means identical, terms to those of regs 98 and 100 (or of regs 35 and 38 of the Income Support Regulations). In particular, some of the specific employment-related rules in reg.98 are not replicated. Regulation 3(2) of the Computation of Earnings Regulations provides that earnings are to be the whole of a claimant's earnings, except to the extent that regs 10 (employed earners: deduction of disregards specified in Sch.1, child care charges and amounts for income tax, national insurance contributions and pension contributions) and 13 (self-employed: similar deductions) provide otherwise. It therefore seems clear enough that net, rather than gross, earnings are to be taken into account under s.2(1)(c), but the treatment of disregards raises a difficulty in relation to reg.56 of the JSA Regulations 1996. In fixing the prescribed limit which must not be exceeded for s.2(1)(c) to be satisfied reg.56 requires any amount disregarded from the claimant's earnings under reg.99(2) (employed earners) or 101(2) (self-employed) to be added back to the personal age-related rate of CBJSA. If disregards have already been taken into account in calculating the amount of earnings to be used for the purpose of s.2(1)(c), that appears to allow a double counting. Perhaps the answer then (if the references in reg.56 to regs 99(2) and 101(2) cannot be taken to influence the plain meaning of ss.2(1)(c) and 35(3)) is that for the purposes of CBJSA no amounts have or would be disregarded from the claimant's earnings under regs 99(2) or 101(2), so that only the Computation of Earnings Regulations disregards can be considered.

In *CJSA/3928 & 3931/2003*, Commissioner Howell applied this earnings condi- **1.84**
tion, using the Computation of Earnings Regulations so as to spread forward the payment received at the end of a month in respect of a range of past work (the claimant's hours were irregular), thus ruling out the particular weeks of claim because the earnings thus assessed were in each week above the prescribed amount.

One way of looking at this earnings condition (and to some extent reconciling the rule with conceptions of this as a benefit paid irrespective of means) might be to regard it as a statement that those earning in excess of the prescribed amount cannot in reality be said to be unemployed but are, in effect, deemed to be "employed". Thus the earnings rule plays a parallel role to that of the "remunerative work" condition in s.1(2)(e) which, as regards CBJSA, rules out claimants working 16 or more hours per week (see reg.5 of the JSA Regulations 1996). Both rules deal with the area of partial unemployment (the claimant actually works for some of the week). The remunerative work rule denies title to those working more than the specified hours, whilst the earnings rule denies entitlement to those whose part-week employment, albeit falling within the 15 hours permitted, is quite well-paid. Both rules thus deal with an area of difficulty once covered by the complexities and uncertainties of the "full extent normal rule" (see USI Regulations 1996 regs 7(1)(e) and (2), pp.719, 722 and 730–35 of the 1996 edition of *Non Means Tested Benefits: The Legislation*).

The remunerative work rule also contains some deeming of claimants to be in remunerative work for periods to which payments are attributed under reg.94 of the JSA Regulations 1996, but the only remaining provision in reg.52(3) is limited to holiday pay that is caught by reg.98(1)(c) in the case of a claimant whose employment meeting the 16-hour condition has been suspended rather than terminated (see reg.52(3A) and Sch.6 para.1). Otherwise, the amount of income from earnings may affect eligibility for CBJSA under s.4(1)(b) and for IBJSA through its means test, but these rules precluding entitlement will not be triggered.

Another way of looking at this earnings condition, however, especially when one reads it alongside the rules contained in s.4(1) on reduction or abatement of CBJSA because of earnings and pension payments, is to see it as a further intrusion of elements of "means-testing" into contributory benefits, something increasing stealthily since 1980 (see Vol.I, annotation to s.2 of the SSCBA 1992). That said, however, it is equally clear that, despite such elements of "means-testing", CBJSA cannot properly be regarded as an "income-related" or fully-fledged "means-tested benefit" in the same way as income support, working tax credit or IBJSA. These rules on CBJSA look to a much narrower range of "means": capital is totally ignored, while, with respect to income, only earnings are regarded for subs.(1)(c) purposes, although pension payments are in addition taken account of under s.4(1) (abatement or reduction of CBJSA). Furthermore, the rules look only to the claimant's resources and not, like income-related benefits, to those of a partner or dependants. In short, CBJSA is an uneasy hybrid benefit.

Subsection (1)(d): particular condition three: the claimant must not be entitled to income support

1.85 Read with s.3(1)(b) and SSCBA 1992 s.124(1)(f) (inserted by Sch.2 para.30 of this Act), this establishes that old style JSA and income support are mutually exclusive benefits: one cannot have both at the same time. JSA is the benefit for those who are expected to seek work as a condition of receiving state benefit; income support or State Pension Credit (universal credit by definition not being operative for the claimant in question) is the residual income-related benefit for those who are not: (for a full list see the Income Support (General) Regulations 1987 reg.4ZA and Sch.1B [prescribed categories of person] inserted by the Income Support (General) (Jobseeker's Allowance Consequential Amendments) Regulations 1996). So, under the income support scheme as amended by this Act and by regulations, requirements that (save in prescribed cases) claimants be available for and actively seeking work have gone, the minimum age of entitlement drops to 16, and persons able to claim entitlement (those in a prescribed category of person (see SSCBA 1992 s.124(1)(e)) are listed exhaustively in reg.4ZA of and Sch.1B to the Income Support (General) Regulations 1987. See the notes to reg.4ZA for discussion of the position of claimants who may be able to claim either old style JSA or income support and of the fact that the 24-hour limit for remunerative work for partners under JSA (the same limit applies to income support from October 7, 1996) may lead to a "better-off" problem for some claimants.

New style JSA

1.86 Note that in those cases and areas where universal credit has come into force, income-based JSA is abolished and replaced by new style JSA (which is contribution-based only). See Pt VI of this book for the legislation relating to new style JSA and for the cases and areas to which it applies.

The income-based conditions

1.87 **3.**—(1) The conditions referred to in [1 section 1(2A)(b)] are that the claimant—

(a) has an income which does not exceed the applicable amount (determined in accordance with regulations under section 4) or has no income;

(b) is not entitled to income support [2[4, state pension credit or an income-related employment and support allowance]];

(c) is not a member of a family one of whose members is entitled to income support;

(d) is not a member of a family one of whose members is entitled to an income-based jobseeker's allowance;

[2 (dd) is not a member of a [3 couple] the other member of which is entitled to state pension credit;]

[4 (de) is not a member of a couple the other member of which is entitled to an income-related employment and support allowance;]

(e) is not a member of a [3 couple] the other member of which is engaged in remunerative work; and

(f) is a person—

(i) who has reached the age of 18; or

(ii) in respect of whom a direction under section 16 is in force; or

(iii) who has, in prescribed circumstances to be taken into account for a prescribed period, reached the age of 16 but not the age of 18.

(2) Regulations may provide for one or both of the following conditions to be included in the income-based conditions, in the case of a person to whom subsection (1)(f)(ii) or (iii) applies—

(a) a condition that the claimant must register for employment;

(b) a condition that the claimant must register for training.

(3) In subsection (1)(f)(iii) "period" includes—

(a) a period of a determinate length;

(b) a period defined by reference to the happening of a future event; and

(c) a period of a determinate length but subject to earlier determination upon the happening of a future event.

(4) Regulations under subsection (2) may, in particular, make provision by reference to persons designated by the Secretary of State for the purpose of the regulations.

AMENDMENTS

1. Welfare Reform and Pensions Act 1999 s.59 and Sch.7 para.4(1) (March 19, 2001).
2. State Pension Credit Act 2002 s.14 and Sch.2 para.37 (October 6, 2003).
3. Civil Partnership Act 2004 s.254 and Sch.24 para.119 (December 5, 2005).
4. Welfare Reform Act 2007 s.28(1) and Sch.3 para.12(3) (October 27, 2008).

DEFINITIONS

"claimant"—see s.35(1).
"couple"—*ibid.*
"employment"—*ibid.* and JSA Regulations 1996 reg.4.
"family"—see s.35(1).
"income-based conditions"—*ibid.*
"income-based jobseeker's allowance"—see s.1(4).
"prescribed"—see s.35(1).
"training"—*ibid.*

GENERAL NOTE

Subsection (1)

This contains the further conditions for entitlement to income-based JSA for a claimant who is not a member of a "joint-claim couple" in addition to those in s.1 and the capital rule under s.13(1). See s.3A for the further conditions of entitlement for a joint-claim couple. For who constitutes a "joint-claim couple", see s.1(4) and reg.3A(1) of the JSA Regulations 1996. **1.88**

Under para.(a), the person's income (which includes the income of his family, except as prescribed: s.13(2) and reg.88(1) of the JSA Regulations 1996) must be less than the applicable amount (effectively the figure set for the family's requirements under s.4(5)). Note that as a consequence of the removal of amounts for children from income-based JSA (with effect from April 6, 2004, except in "transitional cases"—see the note to reg.17 of the Income Support Regulations and the note to reg.83 of the JSA Regulations 1996), only a partner's income will count as that of the claimant and the applicable amount will no longer include any personal allowances for children, the family premium, the disabled child premium or the enhanced disability premium for a child. The person must in general be at least 18 (para.(f)(i)), except if he comes within certain categories (para.(f)(iii)), or the Secretary of State has directed that he will otherwise suffer severe hardship (para.(f)(ii) and s.16). (See regs 57–68 of the JSA Regulations 1996 for those 16- and 17-year-olds who are entitled to income-based JSA and the conditions of their eligibility.) If the person is a member of a couple, his partner must not be engaged in remunerative work (in the case of a partner remunerative work is work of 24 hours or more a week: reg.51(1)(b) of the JSA Regulations 1996) (para. (e)). Paragraphs (b) and (c) confirm that income-based JSA is not payable if the claimant, or any member of his family, is entitled to income support. See the corresponding amendment to s.124(1) of the Contributions and Benefits Act as regards the conditions of entitlement to income support. In addition, para.(d) excludes entitlement if another member of the family is entitled to income-based JSA. Following the introduction of state pension credit on October 6, 2003, entitlement to income-based JSA is also excluded if the claimant is entitled to state pension credit (para.(b)) or if he is a member of a couple and his partner is entitled to state pension credit (para.(dd)). Similarly, from October 27, 2008, as a consequence of the start of the ESA scheme, entitlement is excluded if the claimant is entitled to income-related ESA (para.(b)) or if he is a member of a couple and his partner is entitled to income-related ESA (para.(de)).

Subsection (2)

1.89 See reg.62 of the JSA Regulations.

New style JSA

1.90 Note that in those cases and areas where universal credit has come into force, income-based JSA is abolished and replaced by new style JSA (which is contribution-based only). See Pt VI of this book for the legislation relating to new style JSA and for the cases and areas to which it applies.

[1 The conditions for claims by joint-claim couples

1.91 **3A.**—(1) The conditions referred to in section 1(2B)(c) are—

(a) that the income of the joint-claim couple does not exceed the applicable amount (determined in accordance with regulations under section 4) or the couple have no income;

(b) that no member of a family of which the couple are members is entitled to income support;

(c) that no member of any such family (other than the couple) is entitled to an income-based jobseeker's allowance;

[2 (cc) that neither member of the couple is entitled to state pension credit;]

[3 (cd) that neither member of the couple is entitled to an income-related employment and support allowance;]

(d) that at least one member of the couple has reached the age of 18; and

(e) that if only one member of the couple has reached the age of 18, the other member of the couple is a person—

(i) in respect of whom a direction under section 16 is in force; or

(ii) who has, in prescribed circumstances to be taken into account for a prescribed period, reached the age of 16.

(2) Subsections (2) and (4) of section 3 shall apply in relation to a member of the couple to whom subsection (1)(e)(i) or (ii) above applies as they apply in relation to a claimant to whom subsection (1)(f)(ii) or (iii) of that section applies.

(3) In subsection (1)(e)(ii) above "period" shall be construed in accordance with section 3(3).]

AMENDMENTS

1. Welfare Reform and Pensions Act 1999 s.59 and Sch.7 para.4(2) (March 19, 2001).
2. State Pension Credit Act 2002 s.14 and Sch.2 para.38 (October 6, 2003).
3. Welfare Reform Act 2007 s.28(1) and Sch.3 para.12(4) (October 27, 2008).

DEFINITIONS

"claimant"—see s.35(1).
"family"—*ibid.*
"income-based jobseeker's allowance"—see s.1(4).
"joint-claim couple"—*ibid.*
"prescribed"—see s.35(1).

GENERAL NOTE

Subsection (1)

In addition to the requirements in s.1 and the capital rule under s.13(1), this sets out the further conditions for entitlement to income-based JSA in the case of a joint-claim couple (defined in s.1(4) and see reg.3A(1) of the JSA Regulations 1996). For a claimant for income-based JSA who is not a member of a joint-claim couple, see. s.3. 1.92

The conditions in subs.(1) more or less mirror those in s.3(1), with the necessary adjustments in the wording due to the fact that this section is only concerned with claims by a couple who both have to meet the conditions (except in certain circumstances—see reg.3E of the JSA Regulations 1996). The amendment made on October 6, 2003 as a consequence of the introduction of state pension credit excludes entitlement to income-based JSA in the case of a joint-claim couple if either member of the couple is entitled to state pension credit (para.(cc)). A similar amendment was made on October 27, 2008 following the start of the ESA scheme excluding entitlement if either member of the couple is entitled to income-related ESA (para.(cd)).

New style JSA

Note that in those cases and areas where universal credit has come into force, income-based JSA is abolished and replaced by new style JSA (which is contribution-based only). See Pt VI of this book for the legislation relating to new style JSA and for the cases and areas to which it applies. 1.93

[1 Joint-claim couples: the nominated member

3B.—(1) Where a joint-claim couple make a claim for a joint-claim jobseeker's allowance, they may nominate one of them as the member of the couple to whom the allowance is to be payable. 1.94

(2) In default of one of them being so nominated, the allowance shall be payable to whichever of them is nominated by the Secretary of State.

(3) Subsections (1) and (2) have effect subject to section 4A(4) and (7).

(4) In this Act references to the nominated member of a joint-claim couple are, except where section 20A(7) applies, to the member of the couple nominated under subsection (1) or (2) above; and where section 20A(7) applies, references to the nominated member of such a couple are to the member of the couple to whom section 20A(7) provides for the allowance to be payable.

(5) Nothing in this section or section 20A(7) affects the operation of any statutory provision by virtue of which any amount of the allowance is required or authorised to be paid to someone other than the nominated member of the couple.]

AMENDMENT

1. Welfare Reform and Pensions Act 1999 s.59 and Sch.7 para.4(2) (March 19, 2001).

DEFINITIONS

"joint-claim couple"—see s.1(4).
"joint-claim jobseeker's allowance"—*ibid.*

GENERAL NOTE

New style JSA

1.95 Note that in those cases and areas where universal credit has come into force, income-based JSA is abolished and replaced by new-style JSA (which is contribution-based only). See Pt VI of this book for the legislation relating to new-style JSA and for the cases and areas to which it applies.

Amount payable by way of jobseeker's allowance

1.96 **4.**—(1) In the case of a contribution-based jobseeker's allowance, the amount payable in respect of a claimant ("his personal rate") shall be calculated by—
(a) determining the age-related amount applicable to him; and
(b) making prescribed deductions in respect of earnings [3, pension payments, PPF payments and FAS payments].

(2) The age-related amount applicable to a claimant, for the purposes of subsection (1)(a), shall be determined in accordance with regulations.

(3) In the case of an income-based jobseeker's allowance [2 (other than a joint-claim jobseeker's allowance)], the amount payable shall be—
(a) if a claimant has no income, the applicable amount;
(b) if a claimant has an income, the amount by which the applicable amount exceeds his income.

[2 (3A) In the case of a joint-claim jobseeker's allowance, the amount payable in respect of a joint-claim couple shall be—
(a) if the couple have no income, the applicable amount;
(b) if the couple have an income, the amount by which the applicable amount exceeds the couple's income.]

(4) Except in prescribed circumstances, a jobseeker's allowance shall not be payable where the amount otherwise payable would be less than a prescribed minimum.

(5) The applicable amount shall be such amount or the aggregate of such amounts as may be determined in accordance with regulations.

(6) Where a claimant [1is entitled to both a contribution-based jobseeker's allowance and an income-based jobseeker's allowance] but has no income, the amount payable [1 by way of a jobseeker's allowance] shall be—
(a) the applicable amount, if that is greater than his personal rate; and
(b) his personal rate, if it is not.

(7) Where the amount payable to a claimant to whom subsection (6) applies is the applicable amount, the amount payable to him by way of a jobseeker's allowance shall be taken to consist of two elements—
(a) one being an amount equal to his personal rate; and
(b) the other being an amount equal to the excess of the applicable amount over his personal rate.

(8) Where a claimant [1 is entitled to both a contribution-based jobseeker's allowance and an income-based jobseeker's allowance] and has an income, the amount payable [1 by way of a jobseeker's allowance] shall be—

(a) the amount by which the applicable amount exceeds his income, if the amount of that excess is greater than his personal rate; and

(b) his personal rate, if it is not.

(9) Where the amount payable to a claimant to whom subsection (8) applies is the amount by which the applicable amount exceeds his income, the amount payable to him by way of a jobseeker's allowance shall be taken to consist of two elements—

(a) one being an amount equal to his personal rate; and

(b) the other being an amount equal to the amount by which the difference between the applicable amount and his income exceeds his personal rate.

(10) The element of a jobseeker's allowance mentioned in subsection (7)(a) and that mentioned in subsection (9)(a) shall be treated, for the purpose of identifying the source of the allowance, as attributable to the claimant's entitlement to a contribution-based jobseeker's allowance.

(11) The element of a jobseeker's allowance mentioned in subsection (7)(b) and that mentioned in subsection (9)(b) shall be treated, for the purpose of identifying the source of the allowance, as attributable to the claimant's entitlement to an income-based jobseeker's allowance.

[2 (11A) In subsections (6) to (11) "claimant" does not include—

(a) a joint-claim couple, or

(b) a member of such a couple (other than a person to whom regulations under section 1(2C) apply);

but section 4A, which contains corresponding provisions relating to joint-claim couples, applies instead.]

(12) Regulations under subsection (5) may provide that, in prescribed cases, an applicable amount is to be nil.

AMENDMENTS

1. Welfare Reform and Pensions Act 1999 s.70 and Sch.8 para.29 (November 11, 1999).

2. Welfare Reform and Pensions Act 1999 Sch.7 para.5 (March 19, 2001).

3. Pensions Act 2004 (PPF Payments and FAS Payments) (Consequential Provisions) Order 2006 (SI 2006/343) art.2 and Sch. Pt 2 para.2(1) (February 14, 2006).

DEFINITIONS

"claimant"—see s.35(1).
"contribution-based conditions"—*ibid.*
"contribution-based jobseeker's allowance"—see s.1(4).
"earnings"—see s.35(3).
"FAS payments"—see s.35(1).
"income-based conditions"—*ibid.*
"income-based jobseeker's allowance"—see s.1(4).
"joint-claim couple"—see s.1(4).
"pension payments"—see s.35(1).
"PPF payments"—*ibid.*
"prescribed"—*ibid.*

General Note

1.97 This section is concerned with the amount of a jobseeker's allowance. The various rules it contains arise out of the fact that JSA is a single benefit with two different elements: contribution-based JSA and income-based JSA. Thus, for example, when both components are payable it is necessary to identify each element for accounting purposes, contribution-based JSA being payable out of the National Insurance Fund and income-based JSA out of general taxation (see subss.(7), (9), (10) and (11)), and because of the 182-day limit on entitlement for contribution-based JSA (see s.5(1)). Sub-section (1) provides the basic framework for the calculation of the amount payable by way of contribution-based JSA (the "personal rate") and subs. (3) does the same for income-based JSA (by setting the person's income, if any, against his applicable amount). If the claimant satisfies the conditions of entitlement for both contribution-based and income-based JSA and his personal rate is either greater than his applicable amount if he has no income, or is greater than his applicable amount minus his income, the amount of JSA payable will be the personal rate (subss.(6)(b) and (8)(b)). This reflects the fact that contribution-based JSA, although subject to increased (when compared with unemployment benefit) reduction in respect of the *claimant's* own earnings and pension payments, still falls considerably short of being a totally means-tested benefit.

Subsections (1) and (2)

1.98 If the claimant is entitled to contribution-based JSA, the amount payable ("his personal rate") is calculated by deducting from the age-related amount appropriate to him (see reg.79 of the JSA Regulations 1996) any earnings that he has (see reg.80) and pension, PPF and FAS payments under reg.81.

The end result may be that such deductions result in no amount being payable, despite an underlying entitlement. In other words, the concept of abatement of benefit, confined in unemployment benefit cases to pension payments in respect of claimants aged 55 or over, has been carried over into JSA, irrespective of the age of the claimant, and extended to also cover earnings. Further, it would appear that even where the personal rate is nil because of such abatement, nevertheless, because there remains an underlying entitlement, that period still counts towards the maximum period of entitlement to contribution-based JSA (182 days in any period for which the person's entitlement is established by reference (under s.2(1)(b)) to the same two years—see s.5(1)). This contrasts with the position under s.2(1)(c) where the weekly earnings (on their own) exceed the prescribed amount; in that situation there is no entitlement (the person in effect is treated as if employed) and the periods covered do not eat into the 182 days' maximum entitlement (26 weeks, assuming continuous unemployment).

Subsection (3)

1.99 This provision sets out the basic means test calculation for income-based JSA (other than a joint-claim jobseeker's allowance). Provided that the conditions of entitlement imposed by ss.1 and 3 and the capital test under s.13(1) are satisfied, the claimant's income is set against his applicable amount, calculated according to regs 82–87 of the JSA Regulations 1996. The difference is the amount of benefit. The claimant's income includes that of the other members of his family (s.13(2)), although note the modifications to this rule for children and young persons which were in regs 106 and 109 of the JSA Regulations 1996 (see the 2003 edition of this volume for those regulations and the notes to those regulations). However, as a consequence of the removal of amounts for children and young persons from income-based JSA (with effect from April 6, 2004, except in "transitional cases"—see further the note to reg.17 of the Income Support Regulations and the note to reg.83 of the JSA Regulations 1996), a child's income and capital will be totally ignored and only a partner's income and capital will count as that of the claimant (see the amended form of reg.88(1) of the JSA Regulations 1996).

Subsection (3A)

This sets out the basic means test calculation for a joint-claim jobseeker's allowance. Provided that the conditions of entitlement imposed by ss.1 and 3A–B and the capital test under s.13(1) are satisfied, the joint-claim couple's income is set against its applicable amount, calculated according to regs 86A–C of the JSA Regulations 1996. The difference is the amount of benefit, so that, if the couple has no income the amount payable is its applicable amount. **1.100**

Subsection (4)

See reg.87A of the JSA Regulations 1996. **1.101**

Subsection (5)

See regs 82 to 87 of, and Schs 1, 2, 5 and 5A to, the JSA Regulations 1996. These adopt the income support model, although there are some changes to the premiums to reflect the fact that people over pensionable age have never been entitled to JSA. **1.102**

Subsection (11A)

This provides that subss.(6)–(11) do not apply to a joint-claim couple. Instead, similar provision is made for such a couple in s.4A, below. **1.103**

Subsection (12)

See regs 85 and 85A of, and Schs 5 and 5A to, the JSA Regulations 1996. **1.104**

New style JSA

Note that in those cases and areas where universal credit has come into force, income-based JSA is abolished and replaced by new style JSA (which is contribution-based only). See Pt VI of this book for the legislation relating to new style JSA and for the cases and areas to which it applies. **1.105**

[1 Amount payable in respect of joint-claim couple

4A.—(1) This section applies where— **1.106**

(a) a joint-claim couple are entitled to a joint-claim jobseeker's allowance; and

(b) one or each of the members of the couple is in addition entitled to a contribution-based jobseeker's allowance;

and in such a case the provisions of this section have effect in relation to the couple in place of section 4(3A).

(2) If a joint-claim couple falling within subsection (1) have no income, the amount payable in respect of the couple by way of a jobseeker's allowance shall be—

(a) the applicable amount, if that is greater than the couple's personal rate; and

(b) the couple's personal rate, if it is not.

(3) Where the amount payable in accordance with subsection (2) is the applicable amount, the amount payable in respect of the couple by way of a jobseeker's allowance shall be taken to consist of two elements—

(a) one being an amount equal to the couple's personal rate; and

(b) the other being an amount equal to the excess of the applicable amount over the couple's personal rate.

(4) Where the amount payable in accordance with subsection (2) is the couple's personal rate, then—

(a) if each member of the couple is entitled to a contribution-based jobseeker's allowance, an amount equal to the member's own personal rate shall be payable in respect of the member by way of such an allowance;

(b) if only one of them is so entitled, an amount equal to that member's personal rate shall be payable in respect of the member by way of such an allowance;

and in either case nothing shall be payable in respect of the couple by way of a joint claim jobseeker's allowance.

(5) If a joint-claim couple falling within subsection (1) have an income, the amount payable in respect of the couple by way of a jobseeker's allowance shall be—

(a) the amount by which the applicable amount exceeds the couple's income, if the amount of that excess is greater than the couple's personal rate; and

(b) the couple's personal rate, if it is not.

(6) Where the amount payable in accordance with subsection (5) is the amount by which the applicable amount exceeds the couple's income, the amount payable in respect of the couple by way of a jobseeker's allowance shall be taken to consist of two elements—

(a) one being an amount equal to the couple's personal rate; and

(b) the other being an amount equal to the amount by which the difference between the applicable amount and the couple's income exceeds the couple's personal rate.

(7) Where the amount payable in accordance with subsection (5) is the couple's personal rate, subsection (4) shall apply as it applies in a case where the amount payable in accordance with subsection (2) is that rate.

(8) The element of a jobseeker's allowance mentioned in subsection (3)(a) and that mentioned in subsection (6)(a) shall be treated, for the purpose of identifying the source of the allowance, as attributable—

(a) in a case where only one member of the joint-claim couple is entitled to a contribution-based jobseeker's allowance, to that member's entitlement to such an allowance; and

(b) in a case where each member of the couple is entitled to a contribution-based jobseeker's allowance, rateably according to their individual entitlements to such an allowance.

(9) The element of a jobseeker's allowance mentioned in subsection (3)(b) and that mentioned in subsection (6)(b) shall be treated, for the purpose of identifying the source of the allowance, as attributable to the couple's entitlement to a joint-claim jobseeker's allowance.

(10) In this section, "the couple's personal rate", in relation to a joint-claim couple, means—

(a) where only one member of the couple is entitled to a contribution-based jobseeker's allowance, that member's personal rate;

(b) where each member of the couple is entitled to such an allowance, the aggregate of their personal rates.]

AMENDMENT

1. Welfare Reform and Pensions Act 1999 s.59 and Sch.7 para.6 (March 19, 2001).

DEFINITIONS

"contribution-based jobseeker's allowance"—see s.1(4).
"joint-claim couple"—*ibid.*
"joint-claim jobseeker's allowance"—*ibid.*

General Note

This section is concerned with the amount of JSA in the case of a joint-claim couple where either or both members of the couple are entitled to contribution-based JSA. If there is no entitlement to contribution-based JSA, see s.4(3A). Its provisions have a similar effect to those in s.4(6)–(11). See the notes to s.4 as to why there is a need for these rules. Note the definition of "the couple's personal rate" in subs.(10). The "personal rate" is the amount payable by way of contribution-based JSA (see s.4(1)). **1.107**

New style JSA

Note that in those cases and areas where universal credit has come into force, income-based JSA is abolished and replaced by new style JSA (which is contribution-based only). See Pt VI of this book for the legislation relating to new style JSA and for the cases and areas to which it applies. **1.108**

Duration of a contribution-based jobseeker's allowance

5.—(1) The period for which a person is entitled to a contribution-based jobseeker's allowance shall not exceed, in aggregate, 182 days in any period for which his entitlement is established by reference (under section 2(1)(b)) to the same two years. **1.109**

(2) The fact that a person's entitlement to a contribution-based jobseeker's allowance ("his previous entitlement") has ceased as a result of subsection (1), does not prevent his being entitled to a further contribution-based jobseeker's allowance if—

(a) he satisfies the contribution-based conditions; and
(b) the two years by reference to which he satisfies those conditions includes at least one year which is later than the second of the two years by reference to which his previous entitlement was established.

(3) Regulations may provide that a person who would be entitled to a contribution-based jobseeker's allowance but for the operation of prescribed provisions of, or made under, this Act shall be treated as if entitled to the allowance for the purposes of this section.

Definitions

"contribution-based conditions"—see ss.2 and 35(1).
"contribution-based jobseeker's allowance"—see ss.1(4) and 35(1).
"prescribed"—see s.35(1).
"regulations"—*ibid.*
"year"—*ibid.*

General Note

This section deals only with entitlement to CBJSA. It has no direct relevance to IBJSA, but will have consequences where there was entitlement to both types of old style JSA and the amount payable was, in effect, that from IBJSA (see further annotations to s.4(6)–(11)). See also the final part of this note about new style JSA. **1.110**

Entitlement to CBJSA (a benefit obtainable as of right rather than income-related) is time-limited, as was its predecessor, unemployment benefit. Title to the latter expired when someone had been entitled to it for 312 days in a single period of interruption of employment (after 12 months in a case of continuous unemployment, although the calendar period would be longer where the single period of unemployment was composed of several spells, separated in time, but "linked" for benefit purposes). However, that person could requalify for consideration for another "year" of entitlement (actual entitlement depending on satisfaction of the standard conditions of entitlement) by working for a specified number of hours per week for a specified number of weeks in a specified time period.

This section similarly provides for a time-based expiry of entitlement to CBJSA and for an ability to qualify for further, in turn time-limited, spells of entitlement to it. The rules in their specifics, however, afford a marked contrast with the UB regime. The time limit on entitlement is in effect halved to 26 weeks in a case of continuous unemployment (longer in calendar terms in cases of intermittent unemployment—see annotation to subs.(1)), and the rules on requalification for a further spell of entitlement are linked, not to hours of work done, but in essence to less readily understandable matters of the claimant's contribution record in particular years, albeit in a manner that in effect will tend to require a return to employment in order to requalify (see annotation to subs.(2)).

Tribunals will need more knowledge of contributions than before (if only to understand the Secretary of State's decision communicated to them), since both the "exhaustion rule" (subs.(1)) and the "requalification rule" (subs.(2)) refer to the contribution-based conditions in s.2, the central ones for requalification purposes being those dealing with the claimant's contribution record. See further the annotations to that section.

In *PL v SSWP (JSA)* [2016] UKUT 177 (AAC), Judge Markus gave the opinion that, in the light of the assistance that the claimant had received from her specialist disability employment adviser and specialist Work Choice provider, she had not been discriminated against under art.14 of the ECHR by the limit on the duration of CBJSA and the accepted evidence that those with disabilities take longer to find work than those without. Even if there had been discrimination, the judge had no doubt that it was justified, both in the initial introduction of the rule in 1996 and in its continuing application. The opinion was not a necessary part of the decision because, as the Upper Tribunal has no power to give a declaration of incompatibility of primary legislation under s.4 of the Human Rights Act 1998, the judge had no alternative to dismissing the claimant's appeal against the disallowance of benefit on the expiry of the 182-day limit.

Subsection (1): the exhaustion rule

1.111 This stipulates that the period for which a person can be entitled to CBJSA cannot exceed in total 182 days *in any period for which his entitlement is established by reference (under s.2(1)(b): the second contribution condition) to the same two tax/contribution years.*

In the simplest case of continuous unemployment, this effectively means that after serving the seven "waiting days" (s.21 and Sch.1 para.4; JSA Regulations 1996 reg.46) the exhaustion point is reached after 26 weeks, since old style JSA generally operates on a full week basis. This was, perhaps, the most striking change from the UB regime.

However, more complicated cases can arise. Some people suffer intermittent unemployment, with spells of unemployment being interspersed with a variety of other spells: periods of incapacity for work, spells of employment, periods of training, periods caring for an invalid, periods of pregnancy. How is one to ascertain whether the days in an initial spell of unemployment are to be aggregated with ones in a later spell for purposes of this exhaustion rule? The answer lies in the rubric: *182 days in any period for which his entitlement is established by reference (under s.2(1)(b): the second contribution condition) to the same two tax/contribution years.* Translating and applying this requires some understanding of the concepts, "jobseeking period" (see further, JSA Regulations 1996 reg.47) "linking" (see further JSA Regulations 1996 reg.48(1)) and "linked period" (see further, JSA Regulations 1996 reg.48(2) and (3)). It also requires some understanding of the contribution-record conditions in s.2 ("his entitlement is established by reference . . . to the same two years").

1.112 Basically a "jobseeking period" is one in which the claimant satisfies or is treated as satisfying the conditions of entitlement common to both types of old style JSA, set out in s.1(2)(a)–(c) and (e)–(i) (see JSA Regulations 1996 reg.47). Notions of "linking" may be familiar from the UB regime and from incapacity benefit. But the "linking rule" for JSA is somewhat different as to specifics. It requires two or more ostensibly distinct jobseeking periods to be treated as one period where they are separated by a period comprising only: (a) any period of not more than 12 weeks; (b) a linked period; (c) any period of not more than 12 weeks falling between any two linked periods or between a jobseeking period and a linked period; or (d) a period of summons for jury service requiring attendance at court (see JSA Regulations 1996 reg.48(1)). A "linked period" embraces periods of incapacity for work, of entitlement to a maternity allowance, of engagement in training for which a training allowance is payable and (for more limited purposes) of entitlement to carer's allowance (see JSA Regulations 1996 reg.48(2)). Note, however, that the rubric does not refer to "jobseeking period" or to "linked period" but deliberately to "*any period* for which his entitlement is established by reference (under s.2(1)(b)) to the same two [tax/contribution] years" (emphasis supplied by annotator). So days of entitlement to CBJSA in wholly separate jobseeking periods can still be aggregated for purposes of the exhaustion rule provided that entitlement to CBJSA in each is determined by reference to the same two tax/contribution years. Which brings us to the essentials of the contribution-record conditions (see further the annotations to s.2).

Under s.2, the two tax/contribution years (April–April) relevant for a claim are the last two *complete* tax/contribution years before the *start* of the benefit year (generally first Sunday in January in one calendar year to the first Saturday in January in the next), which includes the beginning of the *jobseeking period* in respect of which old style JSA is being claimed or, if earlier, the beginning of any *linked period* (see s.2(1) and (4)).

All this is much less readily understandable in terms of application to real life than the UB regime. For some illustrative examples see the notes in previous editions of this volume.

Interpreting and applying the rubric "any period for which a person is entitled to a contribution-based jobseeker's allowance" requires making and maintaining the important distinction between "entitled" and "payable". While an allowance cannot be payable without entitlement, a person can be entitled to an allowance but, nevertheless, it may not be payable to him. So, if weekly earnings exceed the prescribed amount, there is no entitlement (s.2(1)(c)). If, in contrast, a combination of earnings and pension payments merely reduce the amount otherwise payable to nil under the abatement provisions of s.4, there is entitlement, but no payable amount. Similarly, a claimant caught by the trade dispute provision is not entitled to an allowance, whereas in contrast the approach is that no allowance is payable to a person who loses his job through misconduct, despite his satisfying the conditions of entitlement to old style JSA. How does this relate to the exhaustion rule under subs.(1)? Obviously, days of entitlement to JSA count towards the period, days of non-entitlement cannot. So a period in which a person's earnings exceed the prescribed amount does not erode the maximum period of entitlement, although a period in which an amount otherwise payable to an entitled claimant is reduced to nil does count towards and eat into that 182-day maximum. The period in which the claimant is caught by the trade dispute provision does not affect the 182-day maximum, but one in which, despite entitlement to contribution-based JSA, an allowance is not payable because he is caught by s.19 (e.g. for leaving a job through misconduct) or s.19A, does erode the 182-day period (something confirmed, unnecessarily, by JSA Regulations 1996 reg.47(4)).

Note finally that regulations under subs.(3) can treat someone, for the purposes of the exhaustion and requalification rules, as entitled to CBJSA where specified provisions of the Act (that is, specified in regulations—"prescribed") or under the Act (i.e. contained in Regulations) have removed what would otherwise have been an actual underlying entitlement. See further the annotation to subs.(3), below.

Subsection (2): the requalification rule

1.113 Requalification here does not mean that the person will be entitled to benefit or that it will in fact be payable even if there is an entitlement. Actual entitlement will depend on fulfilling the conditions of entitlement, common to both types of old style JSA, which are set out in s.1, while the amount payable depends as normal on the principles in s.4. Requalification essentially means getting back on track for reconsideration of possible entitlement to CBJSA.

In order to requalify for consideration, the claimant must satisfy the conditions specific to CBJSA that are set out in s.2: not being entitled to income support (one cannot have IS and old style JSA at the same time); weekly earnings not exceeding a prescribed amount; and satisfying the contribution-record conditions (subs.(2)(a)). Further, however, the two tax/ contribution years by reference to which the contribution-record conditions are satisfied must include at least one tax/contribution year which is later than the second tax/contribution year by reference to which "his previous entitlement" to CBJSA (now exhausted applying subs.(1)) was established. So someone who remains continuously unemployed after exhausting his title, or whose spells of intermittent unemployment are not separated by periods that break the link, cannot requalify. Yet, in contrast, a claimant who breaks the link back to the previous period (for example by working for 16 or more hours per week for a continuous period of at least 13 weeks) in a way that moves the new claim into benefit year 2015/2016, if thereafter without work, or working less than 16 hours per week, can requalify, provided that: (i) the contribution record in tax/contribution years 2012/2013 and 2013/2014 reaches the requisite level; (ii) his weekly earnings do not exceed the prescribed amount; and (iii) he is not entitled to income support (one cannot have IS and old style JSA at the same time). The link would also be broken by not claiming JSA for a continuous 13-week period, since a period of no claim cannot be a jobseeking period (JSA Regulations 1996 reg.47(3)(a)), but that apparent ability to move a new claim into a benefit year more favourable for requalification purposes is not one open to those without work who need an income from the state in terms of IBJSA. Periods in excess of 12 weeks of non-entitlement because of being caught by the trade dispute provision (s.14 and JSA Regulations 1996 reg.47(3)(d)) or where entitlement ceased because of a failure to comply with, for example, attendance conditions (see JSA Regulations 1996 regs 25 and 47(3)(c)) also have the effect of breaking the link, but, given their effect on income replacement, will tend to do fortuitously rather than as a matter of deliberate choice to assist requalification.

Subsection (3)

1.114 The old style JSA regime draws a crucial distinction between entitlement to an allowance, on the one hand, and an allowance being payable on the other (see further the annotations to subs.(1), above). While an allowance cannot be payable without entitlement, a person can be entitled to an allowance but nevertheless it may not be payable to him. So, if weekly earnings exceed the prescribed amount, there is no entitlement (s.2(1)(c)). If in contrast, a combination of earnings and pension payments merely reduce the amount otherwise payable to nil under the abatement provisions of s.4, there is entitlement, but no payable amount. Similarly, a claimant caught by the trade dispute provision is not entitled to an allowance, whereas in contrast the approach is that no allowance is payable to a person who loses his job through misconduct, despite his satisfying the conditions of entitlement to JSA. Under subs.(1), obviously, days of entitlement to JSA count towards the period; days of non-entitlement cannot. So a period in which a person's earnings exceed the prescribed amount does not erode the maximum period of entitlement, although a period in which an amount otherwise payable to an entitled claimant is reduced to nil does count towards and eat into that 182-day maximum. The period in which the claimant is caught by the trade dispute provision does not affect the 182-day maximum but one in which, despite entitlement, an allowance is not payable because he is caught by s.19 (e.g. for leaving a job through misconduct) or s.19A does erode the 182-day period.

All this seems obvious but is a necessary precursor to understanding the role of this subsection and of the regulation made under it.

This subsection enables the making of regulations to treat someone, for the purposes of the exhaustion and requalification rules, as entitled to a CBJSA, where specified provisions of the Act (that is, specified in regulations—"prescribed") or under the Act (i.e. contained in regulations) have removed what would otherwise have been an actual underlying entitlement. In other words, although in the situation covered there may be no entitlement such as to enable the award of any or the full amount of benefit, nevertheless the period covered in the regulations will eat into the maximum 182 days' entitlement.

The regulation made under subs.(3) is JSA Regulations 1996 reg.47(4). Sub-paras (a) and (b) of reg.47(4) provide that a day in a jobseeking period (see reg.47(1)–(3)) in respect of which the person satisfies the contribution-record conditions (in s.2(1)(a) and (b)) counts for the purposes of the exhaustion rule in this section as a day of entitlement to CBJSA even though no benefit is payable by virtue of s.19 or s.19A. However, a day of entitlement in respect of which payment is precluded under s.19 or s.19A already ranks for the purposes of the exhaustion rule in subs.(1) by virtue of the "entitlement/payability" distinction discussed in the annotations to that subsection. Thus reg.47(4) was unnecessary to secure that aim. But whether this is taken from this subsection and reg.47(4)(a) and (b) or simply from the consequences of the distinction ss.19 and 19A draw between entitlement, on the one hand, and the allowance not being payable on the other (examined above), one thing is abundantly clear: the days for which someone is ruled out of receiving benefit under s.19 (e.g. because of losing employment through misconduct) or s.19A now count in determining when title to CBJSA is exhausted. So if someone with an underlying entitlement to CBJSA is denied payment for what is not now necessarily the maximum period of preclusion (26 weeks), that preclusion not only prevents payment, but extinguishes entitlement to such an allowance based on the tax/contribution years relevant to that claim and, to gain another period of entitlement, the claimant will have to satisfy the requalification rule (subs.(2)). So reaching the right and proper decision on what under the UB regime would have been called "disqualification" and determining the appropriate period of preclusion is even more important than before (see further the annotations to s.19).

Regulation 47(4)(a) and (c) read with para.(2) of that regulation achieves another purpose: that stated in the joint Employment Department/Department of Social Security memorandum to the House of Lords Select Committee on the Scrutiny of Delegated Powers (HL 50, 1994–1995, Annex I). That memorandum suggested that the subsection:

> "enables regulations to provide for certain classes of person to be treated as entitled to a contribution-based jobseeker's allowance. *It will be used to ensure that claimants who are receiving payments of an income-based jobseeker's allowance under the provisions of paragraphs 8 and 9 of Schedule 1 have their contributory entitlement of 182 days eroded, in cases where a contributory entitlement would have existed.*" (para.31, emphasis added by annotator.)

JSA Regulations 1996 reg.47(4)(a) and (c), read together, mean that any period in which someone who satisfies the contribution-record conditions (see s.2(1)(a) and (b)) is denied benefit because they are not available for or actively seeking work or because no jobseeker's agreement is in force, but nonetheless is awarded a reduced payment because of severe hardship (see JSA Regulations 1996 Pt IX), counts towards the 182-day maximum entitlement period to contribution-based jobseeker's allowance.

New style JSA

1.115 Note that in those cases and areas where universal credit has come into force, income-based JSA is abolished and replaced by new style JSA (which is contribution-based only). See Pt VI of this book for the legislation relating to new style JSA and for the cases and areas to which it applies.

The transition from new style JSA

1.116 In subss.(1) and (2) (the first reference), the references to contribution-based jobseeker's allowance are, where art.13(1) and (2) of the Welfare Reform Act 2012 (Commencement No.9 and Transitional and Transitory Provisions and Commencement No.8 and Savings and Transitional Provisions (Amendment)) Order 2013 (as amended and set out in the 2014/15 Supplement) applies, to be read as if they included a reference to a new style JSA award (art.13(4) of that Order).

Jobseeking

Availability for employment

1.117 **6.**—(1) For the purposes of this Act, a person is available for employment if he is willing and able to take up immediately any employed earner's employment.

(2) Subsection (1) is subject to such provisions as may be made by regulations; and those regulations may, in particular, provide that a person—

(a) may restrict his availability for employment in any week in such ways as may be prescribed; or

(b) may restrict his availability for employment in any week in such circumstances as may be prescribed (for example, on grounds of conscience, religious conviction or physical or mental condition or because he is caring for another person) and in such ways as may be prescribed.

(3) The following are examples of restrictions for which provision may be made by the regulations—

(a) restrictions on the nature of the employment for which a person is available;

(b) restrictions on the periods for which he is available;

(c) restrictions on the terms or conditions of employment for which he is available;

(d) restrictions on the locality or localities within which he is available.

(4) Regulations may prescribe circumstances in which, for the purposes of this Act, a person is or is not to be treated as available for employment.

(5) Regulations under subsection (4) may, in particular, provide for a person who is available for employment—

(a) only in his usual occupation,

(b) only at a level of remuneration not lower than that which he is accustomed to receive, or

(c) only in his usual occupation and at a level of remuneration not lower than that which he is accustomed to receive,

to be treated, for a permitted period, as available for employment.

(6) Where it has been determined [[1] . . .] that a person is to be treated, for the purposes of this Act, as available for employment in any week,

the question whether he is available for employment in that week may be subsequently determined [[1]under section 9 or 10 of the Social Security Act 1998].

(7) In this section "permitted period", in relation to any person, means such period as may be determined in accordance with the regulations made under subsection (4).

(8) Regulations under subsection (4) may prescribe, in relation to permitted periods—

(a) the day on which any such period is to be regarded as having begun in any case;

(b) the shortest and longest periods which may be determined in any case;

(c) factors which [[2]the Secretary of State] may take into account in determining the period in any case.

(9) For the purposes of this section "employed earner's employment" has the same meaning as in the Benefits Act.

AMENDMENTS

1. Social Security Act 1998 Sch.7 para.134(1) (October 18, 1999).
2. Social Security Act 1998 Sch.7 para.134(2) (October 18, 1999).

DEFINITIONS

"Benefits Act"—see s.35(1).
"claimant"—*ibid.*
"employed earner's employment"—see subs.(9) and SSCBA 1992 s.2(1)(a).
"employment"—see s.35(1) and JSA Regulations 1996 reg.4.
"prescribed"—see s.35(1).
"regulations"—*ibid.*
"week"—*ibid.*

GENERAL NOTE

This section and ss.7-10 expand on the "labour market conditions" for entitlement to old style JSA in s.1(2)(a)–(c). However, much of the key detail remains in the regulations made under these sections (see Pt II of the JSA Regulations 1996). Note that regulations made under ss.6 and 7 are subject to the affirmative procedure (s.37(1)(c)). See also s.19B for the possibility of a reduction in benefit on a new claim after the termination of entitlement because of ceasing to be available for employment. **1.118**

Note that there can be no entitlement to CBJSA or regular IBJSA at the beginning of a claim until the decision-maker is satisfied that the claimant meets the availability condition in s.1(2)(a). However, there may be eligibility for payments under the hardship provisions in regs 140–146H of the JSA Regulations 1996. In addition, if the issue is ultimately resolved in favour of the claimant, full benefit is to be paid from the date of claim.

The interaction of the hardship provisions and the rules on suspension of payment of benefit is complex. There appear to be two stages at the beginning of a claim. First, the decision-maker may defer the making of any decision until satisfied that there is sufficient evidence to do so, within the limits of reasonableness under s.8(1) of the SSA 1998 (see the annotation in Vol. I). In those circumstances, if the sole reason for the delay is that an issue arises as to satisfaction of one of the "labour market" conditions in s.1(2)(a)–(c) (reg.141(2) of the JSA Regulations 1996 and the equivalent provision for joint-claim couples in regs 146A–146H, not separately noted below) and the claimant falls into one of the vulnerable groups specified in reg.140(1), the claimant is to be treated as entitled to IBJSA at the hardship rate after the expiry of the seven waiting days. A person outside the vulnerable groups, if in hardship (reg.140(2)), can be so treated from the 15th day after the claim (reg.142). However, there seems a limited need for any delay in making a decision in such circumstances because reg.141(4), made under para.8 of Sch.1 to the old style Jobseekers Act 1995, allows a person within s.140(1), except where there is deemed non-availability under reg.15 of the JSA Regs 1996, to be entitled to IBJSA at the hardship rate without satisfying the conditions in s.1(2)(a)–(c), provided that the other conditions in s.1(2) are satisfied. There is no similar provision in reg.142. If a decision on entitlement can then be made under reg.141(4), the second stage comes into play. On the face of it, reg.16(2) of the Decisions and Appeals Regulations 1999 requires the Secretary of State to suspend payment of any benefit whenever an issue arises as to whether a JSA claimant is or was available for employment or is or was actively seeking employment. However, reg.141(5) specifically excludes the effect of that provision in the circumstances where reg.141(4) applies. These second-stage rules also apply where an issue as to availability arises during the course of an award of JSA. There in no equivalent to reg.12A of the USI Regulations, where full UB was payable pending resolution of an outstanding issue over availability during an award.

The benefits regimes for unemployed people have always embodied an underlying principle that the unemployment must be involuntary, one aspect of which is that a claimant without work must want to and seek to return to the world of employment. One element giving effect to that principle has been the requirement that the claimant, as a condition of receiving benefit, must be "available for employment" (examined here). The other is that the claimant must actively be seeking employment (examined in the annotations to s.7). The availability requirement formed an integral part both of UB and of income support. However, while the central concept of availability was the same for each benefit, the detailed rules and approaches were not.

This section, amplifying the basic statement of availability as a condition of entitlement to old style JSA (whether contribution or income-based) set out in s.1(2)(a), gives a basic definition of the "available for employment" requirement (subs.(1) and (9)). But that relatively straightforward approach, encapsulating the essence of case law (decisions of courts and Commissioners on the availability concept in its manifestations in earlier regimes of benefits for the unemployed) is itself made "subject to such provisions as may be made by regulations" made under the other provisions of this section, which consist of rule-making powers (subs.(2)–(5)), definitions (subs.(7) and (9)), and one dealing with the scope of revision or supersession of a decision that a person is to be treated as available (subs.(6)). The regulations made under this section are the JSA Regulations 1996 regs 4 and 5–17, which are detailed and rendered complex by "legislation by reference" and the manner in which they often qualify each other.

Subsection (1)

1.119 This sets out what might be called the general principle of availability; in effect a statutory endorsement of the basic case law propositions that to be available a claimant must be prepared to accept at once any offer of suitable employment brought to his notice (*R(U)1/53*) and must be able to accept such an offer (*Shaukat Ali v CAO, App. to R(U)1/85*). The general principle stated in the subsection requires a claimant:

(i) to be *willing* to take up *any employed earner's employment*;

(ii) to be *able* to take it up; and

(iii) to be willing and able to do so *immediately*.

Each of these elements requires some further comment, undertaken below. It must be recalled, however, that this general statement, important as it is in emphasising requirements to be flexible to meet the needs of the labour market, is qualified by regulations. The essence of those qualifications is set out in the annotation to this section, with the detail being reserved for the annotations to the particular regulations.

Non-availability precludes entitlement to old style JSA (see s.1(2)(a)). However it is not crystal clear from that provision or from subs.(1) whether the matter is to be looked at on a weekly or, like unemployment benefit, a daily basis. Granted s.1(3) further stipulates that JSA "is payable in respect of a week", but the scheme also provides for part-week entitlement (s.21 and Sch.1 para.5, JSA Regulations 1996 regs 150–155). The question arises whether a claimant unavailable on one or two days in a particular week loses entitlement for that whole week or just for the days of non-availability, retaining title to a proportionately reduced rate of benefit for the remaining days of the week on which he is available. The Departmental view is apparently that one must read this subsection with s.1. Taking the absolute availability rule ("a person is available for employment if he is willing and able to take up immediately any employed earner's employment") in this subsection with the weekly basis of JSA ("a jobseeker's allowance is payable in respect of a week": s.1(3)), the requirement is to be available throughout the week in the absolute terms set by this subsection, unless specifically relieved from that requirement by means of the concessions set out in the JSA Regulations 1996 dealing with availability: so that a single unprotected day of non-availability precludes entitlement for that benefit week. The matter is further explored in the annotations to JSA Regulations 1996 reg.7(3).

"Any employed earner's employment": As was the case with the previous regime of benefits for unemployed people (*R(U) 14/51*), availability for self-employment does not suffice; the section requires availability for employed earner's employment, on the definition of which see subs.(9) and SSCBA 1992 ss.2(1)(a) and 122(1). Note in contrast that in some circumstances a claimant can confine his jobsearch to self-employment and still be actively seeking employment under s.7 and JSA Regulations 1996 reg.20. But the claimant must always still be available for *employment* as opposed to *self-employment.* 1.120

The rubric refers to *"any"* employed earner's employment. The apparent width of this indicates graphically the need for claimants to be flexible in a changing labour market. Yet, subs.(2) and resultant regulations enable the imposition of a range of restrictions on availability, for the generality of claimants throughout their claim (JSA Regulations 1996 regs 7 and 8), for the generality of claimants during a "permitted period" of up to 13 weeks (JSA Regulations 1996 reg.16), for those laid off or kept on short-time (JSA Regulations 1996 reg.17) and for particular groups of claimants (JSA Regulations 1996 regs 13 and 13A), examined in more depth in the annotations to the particular regulations themselves.

The reasoning in *GP v SSWP (JSA)* [2015] UKUT 476 (AAC); [2016] AACR 14 discussed in the notes to s.7(1) below, would indicate that only availability for employed earner's employment in Great Britain can be required.

Under the previous regime of benefits for the unemployed, being available for part-time work only did not of itself necessarily preclude availability (*CU109/48(KL); CU22/91,* paras 9 and 10). That is *not* the position under old style JSA. Subject to regulations enabling restriction of hours to less, in order to be regarded as available for employment, a person must be willing and able (see below) to take up employment for a minimum of 40 hours per week (JSA Regulations 1996 reg.6(1)) but also be willing and able to take up employment of less than 40 hours per week (JSA Regulations 1996 reg.6(2)). In other words, being available merely for part-time employment (less than 40 hours per week) does not suffice but to be available one must not only be available for full-time employment (40 hours or more per week) but be willing and able to accept part-time employment (less than 40 hours per week), if offered. Generally, no claimant is able to restrict his availability to less than the 40 hours minimum (JSA Regulations 1996 reg.7(1)), although there are exceptions for those with caring responsibilities (reg.13(4) and (5)), for certain lone parents (reg.13A), for those on short-time (reg.17(2)) and for anyone whose physical or mental condition makes reasonable such a restriction (reg.13(3)). Furthermore, JSA Regulations 1996 reg.7 allows a claimant to agree a pattern of availability ("the times at which he is available to take up employment") for 40 hours or more across a week, even though this may effect some reduction in his prospects of securing employment, provided that the pattern of availability is such as to afford him reasonable prospects of securing employment and that those prospects are not reduced considerably by the restriction embodied in the pattern of availability.

1.121 *"Willing . . . to take up"*: What a claimant is willing and not willing to do can, of course, most obviously be judged from his professions of willingness on claim forms, in interviews with Jobcentre Plus, and in his jobseeker's agreement. But it can also be inferred from his conduct (see *R(U)4/53*).

1.122 *"Able to take up"*: Problem areas under previous regimes of benefits for unemployed people afford likely instances where this requirement will prove problematic. Because of the different wording of the primary legislation, and the detail of new specific regulations, however, it cannot readily be assumed that the case law solutions propounded under the old regime will necessarily carry over into the new. But, bearing that very much in mind, obvious instances of inability to take up employment are where immigration law precludes the claimant working (*Shaukat Ali v CAO,* Appendix to *R(U)1/85*), or the claimant is about to go abroad (*R(U)2/90(T)*—dealing with the position of wives of servicemen about to join their husbands for a posting abroad), or is contractually bound to another employer (*R(U)11/51*), for example, to be on call each working day. As regards this last category, note, however, the specific rules treating "a person who is laid-off " and "a person who is kept on short time" (both terms specifically defined in JSA Regulations 1996 reg.4) as available in certain circumstances (reg.17). Thus, it is arguable that a person subject to a zero hours contract who is given no hours of work could be available for employment but probably not if the contract contains an exclusivity clause (not outlawed until the coming into force of s.153 of the Small Business, Enterprise and Employment Act 2015 on May 26, 2015).

Another instance of possible inability would be going away on holiday. The position as respects UB, of course, was that a claimant could still be regarded as available if, having made prior arrangements with the Employment Service, he could be readily contacted, would be willing and able to cut short the holiday to accept employment and could show that there was nothing to prevent him accepting such suitable employment as might be notified (*R(U)1/55*). But there is now in the legislation itself an explicit statutory requirement of being able to take up *immediately* any employment, with only a few exceptions enshrined in legislation (JSA Regulations 1996 regs 5, 11 and 12). So it would appear that a harsher approach may have to be taken than under the UB regime (see *CJSA/1279/1998*). However, the existence of other provisions deeming claimants to be available for employment and to be actively seeking employment in certain circumstances may also be relevant to potential entitlement (regs 14 and 19).

On the general approach, there is helpful guidance on the relationship between the condition of availability and the contents of the jobseeker's agreement in *R(JSA) 2/07* and *AT v SSWP (JSA)* [2013] UKUT 73 (AAC). The critical provisions are regs 5(4) and 7(2) of the JSA Regulations 1996. Regulation 5(4) provides that a claimant who in accordance with reg.7 or some other provisions is only available for employment at certain times is not required to be able to take up employment at a time at which he is not available, provided that he is willing and able to take up employment immediately he is available. Regulation 7(2) allows a claimant to restrict the number of hours per week for which he is available, subject to a minimum of 40 hours except where use can be made of the exceptions in reg.7(1), if that pattern of availability leaves reasonable prospects of securing employment and (sub-para.(b)) the pattern of availability is recorded in the jobseeker's agreement, as originally signed or as varied. The great majority of claimants will have imposed such a restriction, by stating that they are not available every day of the week or for some hours out of the 24 or for some maximum weekly hours no less than 40. It was decided in *R(JSA) 2/07* that, for reg.7(2)(b) to have any practical application, it has to entail that a claimant whose actual pattern of availability is more restricted than recorded in the jobseeker's agreement (e.g. by going away on holiday and becoming unable to take up employment immediately) ceases to satisfy the conditions of entitlement in s.1(2)(a). And ceasing to satisfy that condition on one day in the benefit week eliminates entitlement for the whole week.

The application of those principles is well illustrated in *AT*, along with a very limited way out through the possibility of a retrospective amendment of the jobseeker's agreement. The Secretary of State decided that the claimant there had not been available for employment and therefore not entitled to JSA for the two benefit weeks ending on December 31, 2009 and January 7, 2010. After the Jobcentre had closed on December 31, 2009, the claimant decided to go away to Yorkshire, intending to return on January 3, 2010. Bad weather stopped him returning until January 8, 2010, so that he missed signing on on January 7, although he had informed the Jobcentre of the position on January 5. Judge Rowland agreed that the claimant had not been available for employment in the benefit week ending on January 7, 2010, but accepted the Secretary of State's submission that, since the claimant had been available for all of the week ending January 31, 2009 until the evening of that day, his travelling to Yorkshire did not significantly reduce his prospects of securing employment, so that there should be a retrospective variation of his jobseeker's agreement (which had originally contained no restriction on days or times of availability, only a maximum of 40 hours per week) to accord with the actual pattern of availability in that week. The claimant had also no doubt done enough in the week ending January 31, 2009 to satisfy the condition of actively seeking employment.

The circumstances of *AT* were unusual so that, while the decision shows a way out in a limited number of hard cases, it does not provide any great inroad into the basic holiday rule. It is possible that some exceptions and deemings might assist a wider range of claimants, in which case reg.7(2) of the JSA Regulations 1996 will not be a problem. Under reg.5(1), a person who has caring responsibilities for anyone needing care who is in the same household or a close relative need only be willing and able to take up employment on being given one week's notice and to attend an interview on 48 hours' notice. Under reg.5(1A), where the caring responsibilities are for a child and they would make it unreasonable for the claimant to keep to the para.(1) limits, the notice periods are extended to 28 and 7 days respectively. The definition of "caring responsibilities" in reg.4 does not require a person to have sole or main or even any particular degree of responsibility for caring for the child or other person. So could a claimant with a child or a relative etc who needs care, even if they have a partner, argue that while away on holiday they are to be regarded as available for employment if they can be called back for an interview or employment within the relevant limits? In addition, reg.14(1)(t) deems claimants to be available for employment while looking after a child for whom they have caring responsibilities during a school holiday or similar vacation period, if it is unreasonable to make other arrangements for care. Claimants who can take the benefit of any of those provisions might still have a problem with the condition of actively seeking employment, but reg.19(1)(p) deems claimants to be actively seeking employment in any week in respect of which they have given notice to an employment officer that they do not intend to be actively seeking employment and intend to be residing away from home (subject to a limit of two weeks in any 12 months in an ordinary holiday case). Regulation 19(1)(p) appears to require advance notice, as would obviously be sensible for anyone who wanted to take advantage of any of the provisions on availability.

"Immediately": Just as case law on UB generally required a claimant to be able to accept *at once* a suitable position, so the old style JSA statutory formulation of availability generally requires willingness and ability to take up *immediately* any employed earner's employment. A person is able to take up employment immediately even if 1.123

he first has to obtain clearance in respect of any job, where that clearance is more or less a formality and normally a telephone call would suffice (*CSU 182/1997*, which concerned a former Inland Revenue employee who had taken early retirement and so was subject to the "Rules on the acceptance of outside appointments by Crown Servants").

However, exceptions are provided in JSA Regulations 1996 reg.5, made under the width of the enabling power in subs.(2), below. The exceptions give the claimant varying periods of grace within which one must be willing and able to take up employment, for a range of groups: (a) for persons with caring responsibilities; (b) for those engaged in voluntary work; (c) for others providing a service with or without remuneration; and (d) for certain persons employed for less than 16 hours per week and under a specific statutory obligation to provide notice. It also prevents the "immediately" requirement being used to negate the protective effect of regs 7, 13 or 17, allowing certain claimants periods of non-availability (in effect agreeing a "pattern of availability") by providing that the "immediately" condition cannot be used to require a claimant to be available at a time of permitted non-availability pursuant to his pattern of availability, so long as he is willing and able to take up employment immediately that permitted spell ends. See further the annotations to JSA Regulations 1996 reg.5.

Subsections(2) and (3)

1.124 Subsection (2) enables the basic availability rule in subs.(1) to be modified by regulations, particularly (but not exclusively) by enabling a person to restrict his availability in prescribed ways and by enabling someone to restrict his availability both in prescribed circumstances (e.g. on grounds of his physical or mental condition) and in prescribed ways. Subsection (3) sets out examples of restrictions which can be provided for in regulations: on the nature of employment; on periods of availability; on terms and conditions of employment; and on the locality or localities of availability. But clearly neither subsection so limits the modifications that can be made in regulations.

Leaving aside the "deemed available" and "deemed not available" regulations examined under subs.(4), the regulations made: (a) provide for exceptions to the "immediately" available requirements (JSA Regulations 1996 reg.5), and (b) set out permitted restrictions (JSA Regulations 1996 regs 6–13A and 17). The former have been noted in the annotation to subs.(1). The latter set a standard minimum hours (40) per week requirement and enable a claimant to place a range of restrictions on his availability in a week without endangering his entitlement through failure to surmount the availability hurdle (see in particular regs 7, 8, 13 and 17). Some groups of claimants are allowed more restrictions than others. See further the annotations to the specific regulations, but note here a central requirement (not applicable to those who impose only restrictions reasonable in light of physical or mental condition) that the claimant establish that he has reasonable prospects of securing employment despite (generally all) the restrictions he has imposed.

Subsections(4), (5), (7) and (8)

1.125 Subsection (4) enables the making of regulations treating someone either as available or, as the case may be, not available for old style JSA purposes, whatever might be the result of applying the standard test of actual availability. See further JSA Regulations 1996 regs 14 and 14A (treated as available) and 15 (treated as not available, i.e. excluded from JSA). Subsection (5) provides that regulations under subs.(4) can in particular enable a claimant to restrict availability to his usual occupation for a "permitted period", defined in subs.(7) as "in relation to any person, such period as may be determined in accordance with regulations", which regulations, pursuant to subs.(8), can prescribe the day on which the period begins, its minimum and maximum lengths and the factors that a decision-maker may take into account in determining the period in any particular case. JSA Regulations 1996 reg.16 is the product. There is a specific "deeming" regulation dealing with those laid-off or kept on short time (reg.17). Other "deeming" regulations deal with full-time students following a "qualifying course" (an employment related course of further or higher education, or a standard above that, lasting no more than 12 months) (reg.17A) and lone parents with care of children aged 5 (reg.17B).

Subsection (6)

This provides that where it had been decided that a person is to be treated as available for employment in any benefit week, a subsequent revision or supersession of that decision can embrace also the question whether, in that week, the person was actually available for employment. **1.126**

Subsection (9)

This stipulates that "employed earner's employment" has the same meaning for purposes of this section as it does in SSCBA 1992, s.2. See Vol. I: *Non Means Tested Benefits*. **1.127**

See *GP v SSWP (JSA)* [2015] UKUT 476 (AAC); [2016] AACR 14, discussed in para.1.120 above and in detail in the notes to s.7(1) below.

New style JSA

Note that in those cases and areas where universal credit has come into force, income-based JSA is abolished and replaced by new style JSA (which is contribution-based only). See Pt VI of this book for the legislation relating to new style JSA and for the cases and areas to which it applies. **1.128**

Actively seeking employment

7.—(1) For the purposes of this Act, a person is actively seeking employment in any week if he takes in that week such steps as he can reasonably be expected to have to take in order to have the best prospects of securing employment, **1.129**

(2) Regulations may make provision—

(a) with respect to steps which it is reasonable, for the purposes of subsection (1), for a person to be expected to have to take in any week;

(b) as to circumstances (for example, his skills, qualifications, abilities and physical or mental limitations) which, in particular, are to be taken into account in determining whether, in relation to any steps taken by a person, the requirements of subsection (1) are satisfied in any week.

(3) Regulations may make provision for acts of a person which would otherwise be relevant for purposes of this section to be disregarded in such circumstances (including circumstances constituted by, or connected with, his behaviour or appearance) as may be prescribed.

(4) Regulations may prescribe circumstances in which, for the purposes of this Act, a person is to be treated as actively seeking employment.

(5) Regulations under subsection (4) may, in particular, provide for a person who is actively seeking employment—

(a) only in his usual occupation,

(b) only at a level of remuneration not lower than that which he is accustomed to receive, or

(c) only in his usual occupation and at a level of remuneration not lower than that which he is accustomed to receive,

to be treated, for the permitted period determined in his case for the purposes of section 6(5), as actively seeking employment during that period.

(6) Regulations may provide for this section, and any regulations made

under it, to have effect in relation to a person who has reached the age of 16 but not the age of 18 as if "employment" included "training".

(7) Where it has been determined [1. . .] that a person is to be treated, for the purposes of this Act, as actively seeking employment in any week, the question whether he is actively seeking employment in that week may subsequently be determined [1under section 9 or 10 of the Social Security Act 1998].

(8) For the purposes of this section—

"employment" means employed earner's employment or, in prescribed circumstances—

(a) self-employed earner's employment; or

(b) employed earner's employment and self-employed earner's employment;

and "employed earners employment" and "self-employed earner's employment" have the same meaning as in the Benefits Act.

AMENDMENT

1. Social Security Act 1998 Sch.7 para.135 (October 18, 1999).

DEFINITIONS

"the Benefits Act"—see s.35(1).
"employed earner's employment"—see subs.(8) and SSCBA 1992 ss.2(1)(a) and 122(1).
"prescribed"—see s.35(1).
"regulations"—*ibid.*
"self-employed earner's employment"—see subs.(8) and SSCBA 1992 ss.2(1)(b) and 122(1).
"training"—see s.35(1); JSA Regulations 1996 reg.65(6).
"week"—see s.35(1); JSA Regulations 1996 reg.4.

GENERAL NOTE

1.130 The actively seeking employment test as a "labour market" condition of entitlement to old style JSA, like availability for employment (the other "labour market" condition) set out in s.6, is a concrete manifestation of the underlying principle governing benefit regimes for unemployed people that the unemployment must be involuntary. Dropped from the regime in the 1930s, it was reintroduced amidst considerable controversy in 1989. Contrary to expectations, it did not generate a flood of appeals to tribunals. Note the possibility under s.19B of a reduction in benefit on a new claim after the termination of entitlement because of ceasing to be actively seeking employment.

Note that there can be no entitlement to CBJSA or regular IBJSA at the beginning of a claim until the decision-maker is satisfied that the claimant meets the condition in s.1(2)(c). However, there may be eligibility for payments under the hardship provisions in regs 140–146H of the JSA Regulations 1996. In addition, if the issue is ultimately resolved in favour of the claimant, full benefit is to be paid from the date of claim.

The interaction of the hardship provisions and the rules on suspension of payment of benefit is complex. There appear to be two stages at the beginning of a claim. First, the decision-maker may defer the making of any decision until satisfied that there is sufficient evidence to do so, within the limits of reasonableness under s.8(1) of the SSA 1998 (see the annotation in Vol. I). In those circumstances, if the sole reason for the delay is that an issue arises as to satisfaction of one of the "labour market" conditions in s.1(2)(a)–(c) (reg.141(2) of the JSA Regulations 1996 and the equivalent provision for joint claim couples in regs 146A–146H, not separately noted below) and the claimant falls into one of the vulnerable groups specified in reg.140(1), the claimant is to be treated as entitled to IBJSA at the hardship rate after the expiry of the seven waiting days. A person outside the vulnerable groups, if in hardship (reg.140(2)), can be so treated from the 15th day after the claim (reg.142). However, there seems a limited need for any delay in making a decision in such circumstances because reg.141(4), made under para.8 of Sch.1 to the old style Jobseekers Act 1995, allows a person within s.140(1), except where there is deemed non-availability under reg.15 of the JSA Regulations 1996, to be entitled to IBJSA at the hardship rate without satisfying the conditions in s.1(2)(a)–(c), provided that the other conditions in s.1(2) are satisfied. There is no similar provision in reg.142. If a decision on entitlement can then be made under reg.141(4), the second stage comes into play. On the face of it, reg.16(2) of the Decisions and Appeals Regulations 1999 requires the Secretary of State to suspend payment of any benefit whenever an issue arises as to whether a JSA claimant is or was available for employment or is or was actively seeking employment. However, reg.141(5) specifically excludes the effect of that provision in the circumstances where reg.141(4) applies. These second stage rules also apply where an issue as to actively seeking employment arises during the course of an award of JSA.

Note that regs 19–21B of the JSA Regulations 1996, made under subs.(4), prescribe circumstances in which a claimant is deemed to satisfy the actively seeking employment test and that reg.18, made under subs.(2), amplifies the test in subs.(1).

Subsection (1)

As regards UB, the test for actively seeking work was contained in subordinate legislation: to be actively seeking work in any week, persons had to take such steps, reasonable in their case, as to offer them *the best prospects of receiving offers of employment* (USI Regulations reg.12B(1)). For old style JSA, this subsection contains a similarly formulated test: in any week persons are actively seeking employment if during that week they takes such steps as they can reasonably be expected to take in order to have *the best prospects of securing employment,* perhaps thereby stressing more strongly the requirement of taking positive action to secure work. **1.131**

Note that here "employment" is not confined to "employed earner's employment" but can in some circumstances embrace self-employment (subs.(8)): see further JSA Regulations 1996 regs 18(3)(i), 19(1)(r) and 20(2) and (3)). However, it is significant that the definition of "employed earner's employment" in s.2(1)(a) of the SSCBA 1992, specifically imported into s.7 (and therefore the regulations made under it) by subs.(8) as part of the definition of "employment", is restricted to such employment in Great Britain. In *GP v SSWP (JSA)* [2015] UKUT 476 (AAC); [2016] AACR 14, Judge Gray held that that means that steps directed to securing employment that is not in Great Britain cannot count for the purpose of satisfying the test in s.7(1). In the particular case, the claimant was a highly qualified research scientist who, having been unsuccessful in seeking work in the UK in her field or in more menial jobs, was looking only for jobs in China and had in the period in question arranged two interviews there. The judge decided that the claimant's entitlement to JSA was rightly terminated. She mentioned the oddity that the s.2(1) definition is restricted to Great Britain, rather than the UK. That would on its face exclude from entitlement claimants taking steps only to secure employment in Northern Ireland. If that conclusion cannot be right, could it be argued that, despite the specific terms of s.7(8), the restriction to employment in Great Britain should be ignored? There is the further oddity that under reg.19(2)(m) of the JSA Regulations 1996 a person who is temporarily absent from Great Britain for at least three days in any week to attend an interview for employment, having notified an employment officer in writing, is deemed to be actively seeking employment for that week (and see regs 14(1)(a) and 50(6)). In that context, "employment" cannot sensibly be restricted to employment in Great Britain. It would be ludicrous if reg.19(2)(m) were restricted to interviews abroad for jobs in Great Britain. Is this a case where the context requires a different meaning to that specified in s.7(8) or does it indicate that that definition properly extends to something that would be employed earner's employment if carried on in Great Britain? There is no similar restriction in relation to the work search requirement in new style JSA.

It is for claimants to establish that they are actively seeking employment. As Northern Ireland Commissioner Brown stated in *C1/00–01(JSA)* and *C2/00–01 (JSA)*, "it is . . . in the claimant's interest to keep a record and to have as far as possible further corroborative proof of the steps he has taken to seek employment" (see para.29). Note, however, that the claimant's oral or written statement that he did this or that constitutes "evidence", so that in that case the tribunal erred insofar as it appeared to have rejected the claimant's statement merely because it was uncorroborated: "a claimant does not have to produce corroborative evidence though obviously his case will be strengthened if he can do so" (see para.30). These principles were followed and applied in *PC v SSWP (JSA)* [2016] UKUT 277 (AAC). Commissioner Brown continued:

> "the tribunal was of course entitled to reject any evidence if it did not find it reliable. What it was not entitled to do however was to conclude that the claimant's evidence was not evidence. The claimant's evidence could have been accepted by the Tribunal and could, at its height, have, if accepted, established that he was actively seeking work. Instead, however, the Tribunal appeared to ignore this evidence and appeared to have the view that corroborative evidence must always be produced" (see para.34).

As Commissioner Williams rightly points out in *CJSA/1814/2007* (at paras 9–15), this subsection requires the application of a positive rather than a negative test. It asks what the claimant did in the week in question, rather than what he did not do. It is not a matter of whether each of the steps in the claimant's jobseeker's agreement were met, but rather whether the tests in s.7(1) and JSA Regulations 1996 reg.18(1) are met by what the claimant actually did in the week at issue. The questions to be answered were thus:

> "(a) Should the claimant be expected to take at least three jobsearch steps that week, or is it reasonable that only one or two be taken?
> (b) What steps were taken?
> (c) In the light of that reasonable expectation and those findings, were the steps taken by the claimant "such steps as he can reasonably be expected to have to take in order to have the best prospects of securing employment" (s.7(1))?
> If the steps by the claimant taken meet that test, it is irrelevant that the claimant did not also take some other step, whether or not it is in the jobseeker's agreement". (at para.15)

That approach and the terms of reg.18 in general indicate that the stress should be more on reasonableness than on a view that there will always be something more that could be done to have the best prospects of securing employment. *CJSA/1814/2007* was followed and applied in *CJSA/3146/2009* in finding that a tribunal had gone wrong in law in focusing on whether the claimant had met the requirements of his jobseeker's agreement rather than on whether the steps that he had taken were such as he could reasonably have been expected to take to have the best prospects of securing employment.

Further, despite the general obligation on the claimant to show the positive steps taken in a week, if the Secretary of State asserts to a tribunal that the claimant has failed to take particular steps that were open, supporting evidence may be necessary, particularly where the relevant information is within the DWP's control. So, where it was asserted that there were suitable roles on the Universal Jobmatch website that the claimant could have applied for, but did not, the Secretary of State needed to produce evidence of such availability to validate that assertion (para.11 of *RD v SSWP (JSA)* [2015] UKUT 702 (AAC)).

In Commissioner's decision *CJSA/2162/2001* (see the notes to s.9 below), it was suggested that there might be circumstances in which the application of the s.7(1) test would result in a conclusion that there were no steps that it was reasonable for the claimant to take in a particular week, so that the test could be satisfied by taking no steps. It is now submitted that the endorsement of that view in past editions was wrong. Despite the view expressed there by Commissioner Williams that reg.18 read as a whole did not preclude such a conclusion, it is hard to read reg.18(1) as requiring anything less than an absolute minimum of one step in any week to satisfy s.7(1). See further the notes to reg.18 and note the deeming in reg.19.

Subsection (2)

This enabling power authorises regulations to be made with respect to the steps it is reasonable for someone to be expected to have to take in order to be regarded as actively seeking employment and as to the circumstances that in particular are to be taken into account in determining whether the steps actually taken by a person are such as to satisfy the actively seeking employment test. **1.132**

See the detailed provision in reg.18 and the notes to that provision. The non-exhaustive list in reg.18(2) of things that might count as reasonable steps is probably less significant than the non-exhaustive list in reg.18(3) of circumstances of the particular case to which regard is to be had in deciding whether the claimant has taken all reasonable steps in a week. As well as the claimant's skills, qualifications and abilities and physical or mental limitations, as specifically mentioned in subs. (2), account must be taken of the claimant's past work experience and the lapse of time since last working, steps taken in previous weeks and their effectiveness, the availability and location of employment vacancies and the special circumstances of homeless claimants. Taking part in various worthy activities and being deemed available for employment under reg.14 are relevant. More generally, time engaged in voluntary work (see reg.4) and the extent to which it may have improved prospects of employment is to be taken into account (reg.18(3)(g)).

Subsection (3)

This remarkable and controversial provision has no direct parallel in the predecessor provisions on actively seeking work that governed UB and income support for unemployed people. It enables regulations to be made prescribing circumstances in which acts of a person that would otherwise be relevant in applying the actively seeking employment test are to be disregarded. Those circumstances include ones constituted by, or connected with, the person's behaviour or appearance, but the range of circumstances is not restricted to those categories. The aim was to "enable a person's jobseeking activity to be disregarded if he behaves or presents himself in such a way as deliberately to reduce or extinguish his chance of receiving offers of employment" (DSS, *Notes on Clauses* [with respect to the Jobseeker's Bill]). JSA Regulations 1996 reg.18(4) is the material provision. It provides that an otherwise relevant act of a person is to be disregarded in a number of circumstances unless the circumstances were due to reasons beyond his control: (i) where in taking the act he acted in a violent or abusive manner; (ii) where the act comprised the completion of an application for employment and he spoiled the application; and (iii) where, by his behaviour or appearance he otherwise undermined his prospects of securing the employment in question. **1.133**

The regulation, particularly in head (iii), thus involves a more explicit "policing" of behaviour, appearance and, possibly, form-filling competence by Jobcentre Plus personnel, decision-makers and tribunals. The concept of "spoiled the application" in head (ii) is by no means crystal clear. The saving for reasons beyond one's control will presumably protect the dyslexic and the illiterate, but what about the semi-literate? Electoral law, of course, has the concept of the "spoilt ballot paper", which covers the situation in which the voter has inadvertently dealt with his ballot paper in such a manner that it cannot conveniently be used as a ballot paper, but whether that in any way provides a valid analogy for "spoiled" in this regulation remains to be seen. See also the decisions in *CJSA/4665/2001* and in *CJSA/2082/2002* and *CJSA/5415/2002*, discussed in the notes to s.19(2)(c) below. Given the aim of the provision, it might have been better to have worded it "deliberately spoiled". A further sanction for some such behaviour lies in the preclusion of payment of benefit under s.19(2)(d) in respect of the person having, without a good reason, neglected to avail himself of a reasonable opportunity of employment; the equivalent provision in the UB regime enabled disqualification of a claimant who had attended an interview for a job as a parcel porter in a "dirty and unshaven state" (*R(U)28/55*). Care will have to be taken to avoid applying the provision in a manner discriminatory on grounds of sex or race (e.g. to penalise men with long hair or Rastafarians with dreadlocks).

Subsections (4) and (5)

1.134 Subsection (4) enables the making of regulations treating a person as actively seeking employment. Subsection (5) amplifies this by providing that such regulations can, for the "permitted period" for availability purposes (see s.6(5) and JSA Regulations 1996 reg.16), enable a person to be treated as actively seeking employment where he is actually doing so only in his usual occupation, or only at a level of remuneration not lower than that which he is accustomed to receive, or only in that occupation and at such a level of remuneration. See JSA Regulations 1996 regs 19–21B.

There is a wide range of cases of deemed actively seeking employment specified in reg.19(1) (possibly subject to conditions in reg.19(2) or (2A)), which need to be looked at carefully. Some mirror cases of deemed availability for employment under regs 14 or 14A. Of particular interest is reg.19(1)(p), covering any week in respect of which the claimant has given (advance) notice to an employment officer of not intending to be actively seeking employment and intending to reside away from home (subject to varying limits within any 12 months: reg.19(2)).

Subsection (6)

1.135 This enables regulations to be made so that in respect of payment of IBJSA to 16 and 17-year-olds "employment" for actively seeking work purposes extends to training. See further JSA Regulations 1996 reg.65.

Subsection (7)

1.136 This deals with the situation where in accordance with the Act it has been decided that a person is to be treated as actively seeking employment in any week. It enables a subsequent revision or supersession of that decision to embrace also the question whether in that week the person was actually actively seeking employment.

Subsection (8)

1.137 This makes clear that employment, for actively seeking work purposes, covers both employed earner's and self-employed earner's employment. For definitions of these terms, see SSCBA 1992 ss.2(1) and 122(1).

See the discussion of *GP v SSWP (JSA)* [2015] UKUT 476 (AAC); [2016] AACR 14 in the notes to s.7(1) above, in relation to employment outside Great Britain.

See the somewhat unconvincing decision of the Court of Appeal in *Hakki v Secretary of State for Work and Pensions and Blair* [2014] EWCA Civ 530 on the application of the SSCBA 1992 definition of self-employed earner's employment in the child support context. The Court accepted the agreement on behalf of the mother with the Secretary of State's view that, despite the terms of s.2(1) of the SSCBA 1992 and the approach of the Upper Tribunal in *HH v CMEC (CSM)* [2011] UKUT 60 (AAC), the definition for child support and social security purposes should be the same as for income tax purposes, meaning that a person had to be engaged in a trade, profession, employment or vocation. In the case of a "professional" poker player it held, on the particular facts found by the First-tier Tribunal, that he did not have a sufficient degree of organisation in relation to his poker playing to constitute a trade. However, it was accepted that it was possible to conceive of cases in which there was sufficient organisation for a gambler's winnings to be taxable and for the person therefore to be a self-employed earner.

New style JSA

Note that in those cases and areas where universal credit has come into force, income-based JSA is abolished and replaced by new style JSA (which is contribution-based only). See Pt VI of this book for the legislation relating to new style JSA and for the cases and areas to which it applies. 1.138

Attendance, information and evidence

8.—(1) Regulations may make provision for requiring a claimant [2(other than a joint-claim couple claiming a joint-claim jobseeker's allowance)]— 1.139

(a) to [4participate in an interview in such manner, time and place] as [1an employment officer] may specify; and

(b) to provide information and such evidence as may be prescribed as to his circumstances, his availability for employment and the extent to which he is actively seeking employment.

[2(1A) Regulations may make provision—

(a) for requiring each member of a joint-claim couple claiming a joint-claim jobseeker's allowance to attend at such place and such time as [5an employment officer] may specify;

(b) for requiring a member of such a couple to provide information and such evidence as may be prescribed as to his circumstances, his availability for employment and the extent to which he is actively seeking employment;

(c) for requiring such a couple to jointly provide information and such evidence as may be prescribed as to the circumstances of each or either member of the couple, the availability for employment of each or either member of the couple and the extent to which each or either member of the couple is actively seeking employment;

(d) where any requirement to provide information or evidence is imposed on such a couple by virtue of paragraph (c), for the joint obligation of the couple to be capable of being discharged by the provision of the information or evidence by one member of the couple.]

(2) Regulations under subsection (1) or [2(1A)] may, in particular, [5provide for entitlement to a jobseeker's allowance to cease at such time as may be determined in accordance with any such regulations if, when a person fails to comply with such regulations, that person (or, if that person is a member of a joint-claim couple, either member of the couple) does not make prescribed contact with an employment officer within a prescribed period of the failure]

[3(ca)] [6 *Repealed.*]

[3(d)] [6 *Repealed.*]

[3(2A)] [6 *Repealed.*]

[1(3)] [6 *Repealed.*]

AMENDMENTS

1. Welfare Reform and Pensions Act 1999 s.70 and Sch.8 para.29 (November 11, 1999).
2. Welfare Reform and Pensions Act 1999 Sch.7 para.7 (March 19, 2001).
3. Welfare Reform Act 2009 s.33 (February 10, 2010).
4. Welfare Reform Act 2012 s.45 (October 8, 2012).
5. Welfare Reform Act 2012 s.48 and Sch.7 para.2 (October 22, 2012), replacing paras (a)–(c).
6. Welfare Reform Act 2012 s.147 and Sch.14 Pt 3 (October 22, 2012).

DEFINITIONS

"a joint-claim couple"—see s.1(4).
"a joint-claim jobseeker's allowance"—see s.1(4).
"claimant"—see s.35(1).
"employment"—see s.35(1) and JSA Regulations 1996 reg.4.
"employment officer"—see s.35(1).
"prescribed"—*ibid*
"regulations"—*ibid.*

GENERAL NOTE

1.140 This section provides a range of rule-making powers with respect to requiring a claimant (and each member of a joint-claim couple) to participate in an interview in such manner, time and place as an employment officer may specify and to provide information and evidence on the person's circumstances, availability for employment and the extent to which he is actively seeking employment (subs.(1)). In short, to provide through participation, etc. the wherewithal whereby the claim can continue to be monitored and assessed. The change from "attend" to "participate in", effected from October 8, 2012, as well as reflecting enhanced conditionality, also enables interviews to be conducted remotely.

The provision made under subs.(1)(a) is reg.23 of the JSA Regulations 1996 (subs.(1A)(a) and reg.23A for joint-claim couples). The provision made under subss.(1)(b) and (1A)(b)–(d) is reg.24, augmented by regs 24A and 24B. The immediate consequences of failing to comply with a requirement under s.8 are set out in regs 25–27. Subject to conditions, failures to participate in a properly notified interview or to provide a signed declaration under reg.24(6) and (10) (but not failures to comply with any other part of reg.24) lead to the ceasing of entitlement to old style JSA. A failure without a good reason to comply with regulations made under s.8(1) or (1A) is also a sanctionable failure under s.19A(2)(a), potentially leading to reduction of benefit for fixed periods under reg.69A of the JSA Regulations 1996. However, reg.70A(2) prevents there being a reduction in benefit for any failure to comply with any part of reg.24 and for many failures to comply with reg.23 or 23A. See the notes to regs 25 and 70A for the interaction between the sanction and the ceasing of entitlement under regs 25–27.

In *CS v SSWP (JSA)* [2015] UKUT 61 (AAC) Judge Wikeley drew an analogy in cases under regs 25–27 with the sanctions regime, so that the same principle as he had suggested in *DL v SSWP (JSA)* [2013] UKUT 295 (AAC) should apply, that the legislation should be construed strictly, giving the claimant the benefit of any doubt that might reasonably apply before imposing a penalty.

New style JSA

1.141 Note that in those cases and areas where universal credit has come into force, income-based JSA is abolished and replaced by new style JSA (which is contribution-based only). See Pt VI of this book for the legislation relating to new style JSA and for the cases and areas to which it applies.

The jobseeker's agreement

1.142 **9.**—(1) An agreement which is entered into by a claimant and an employment officer and which complies with the prescribed requirements in force at the time when the agreement is made is referred to in this Act as "a jobseeker's agreement".

(2) A jobseeker's agreement shall have effect only for the purposes of section 1.

(3) A jobseeker's agreement shall be in writing and be signed by both parties.

[[3](3A) The agreement may be in electronic form and signed by means of an electronic signature (within the meaning given in section 7(2) of the Electronic Communications Act 2000).]

(4) A copy of the agreement shall be given to the claimant.

(5) An employment officer shall not enter into a jobseeker's agreement with a claimant unless, in the officer's opinion, the conditions mentioned in section 1(2)(a) and (c) would be satisfied with respect to the claimant if he were to comply with, or be treated as complying with, the proposed agreement.

(6) The employment officer may, and if asked to do so by the claimant shall forthwith, refer a proposed jobseeker's agreement to [[1]the Secretary of State] for him to determine—

(a) whether, if the claimant concerned were to comply with the proposed agreement, he would satisfy—

(i) the condition mentioned in section 1(2)(a); or

(ii) the condition mentioned in section 1(2)(c); and

(b) whether it is reasonable to expect the claimant to have to comply with the proposed agreement.

(7) [[1]On a reference under subsection (6) the Secretary of State]—

(a) shall, so far as practicable, dispose of it in accordance with this section before the end of the period of 14 days from the date of the reference;

(b) may give such directions, with respect to the terms on which the employment officer is to enter into a jobseeker's agreement with the claimant, as [[1]the Secretary of State] considers appropriate;

(c) may direct that, if conditions as he considers appropriate are satisfied, the proposed jobseeker's agreement is to be treated (if entered into) as having effect on such date, before it would otherwise have effect, as may be specified in the direction.

(8) Regulations may provide—

(a) for such matters as may be prescribed to be taken into account by [[1]the Secretary of State] in giving a direction under subsection (7)(c); and

(b) for such persons as may be prescribed to be notified of—

(i) any determination of [[1] the Secretary of State] under this section;

(ii) any direction given by [[1] the Secretary of State] under this section.

(9) [[1] . . .].

(10) Regulations may provide that, in prescribed circumstances, a claimant is to be treated as having satisfied the condition mentioned in section 1(2)(b).

(11) Regulations may provide that, in prescribed circumstances, a jobseeker's agreement is to be treated as having effect on a date, to be determined in accordance with the regulations, before it would otherwise have effect.

(12) Except in such circumstances as may be prescribed, a jobseeker's agreement entered into by a claimant shall cease to have effect on the coming to an end of an award of a jobseeker's allowance made to him [[2]or to a joint-claim couple of which he is a member.].

(13) In this section and section 10 "employment officer" means an officer of the Secretary of State or such other person as may be designated for the purposes of this section by an order made by the Secretary of State.

AMENDMENTS

1. Social Security Act 1998 Sch.7 para.136 (October 18, 1999).

2. Welfare Reform and Pensions Act 1999 Sch.7 para.8 (March 19, 2001).

3. Social Security (Electronic Communications) Order 2011 (SI 2011/1498) art.2(2) (February 1, 2012).

DEFINITIONS

"a joint-claim couple"—see s.1(4).
"a joint-claim jobseeker's allowance"—see s.1(4).
"claimant"—see s.35(1).
"employment officer"—*ibid.*
"prescribed"—*ibid.*
"regulations"—*ibid.*

GENERAL NOTE

1.143 This section, containing and enabling the making of further important provisions on the jobseeker's agreement, needs to be read in the light of the amplification and clarification provided by JSA Regulations 1996 regs 31–36, made under it; and of s.10 supplemented by regs 37–40, which provide for the variation of a jobseeker's agreement. This note attempts to blend the provisions of this section and the JSA Regulations 1996 with statements in the White Paper and/or in Parliament on the administrative process, to give a coherent account of how the arrangements with respect to jobseeker's agreements operate. On some points of finer detail, however, readers will have to scrutinise closely the exact terms of the regulations referred to.

Perhaps the most obvious and striking difference between UB and old style JSA is the central requirement that, in order to be entitled to JSA, the claimant must have entered into a jobseeker's agreement that remains in force (s.1(2)(b)). Note, however, that a person may be treated as having done so in any of the circumstances set out in JSA Regulations 1996 reg.34. This provision covers various cases in which the claimant has not yet had an interview with an employment officer, for instance at the beginning of a claim that was allowed to be made without attending a Jobcentre Plus office (reg.34(a)), as well as some cases in which the claimant is deemed to be available for employment (reg.34(c) and (g)). Could an example of the application of reg.34(d) (normal operation of provisions or practice as to claiming impracticable or unduly difficult because of circumstances not peculiar to the claimant) be circumstances where the office is overwhelmed by claims on the closure of a town's major employer?

If reg.34 applies, s.1(2)(b) is satisfied and the actual absence of a signed agreement is not an obstacle to an award of old style JSA. If reg.34 does not apply, there cannot be any award of regular benefit until a jobseeker's agreement is signed (although, as seen below, the agreement may then operate from the date of claim and benefit will be payable after the waiting days if the other conditions of entitlement are satisfied). However, there may be eligibility for payments under the hardship provisions in regs 140–146H of the JSA Regulations 1996.

The interaction of the hardship provisions and the rules on suspension of payment of benefit is complex. There appear to be two stages at the beginning of a claim. First, the decision-maker may defer the making of any decision until satisfied that there is sufficient evidence to do so, within the limits of reasonableness under s.8(1) of the SSA 1998 (see the annotation in Vol. I). In those circumstances, if the sole reason for the delay is that an issue arises as to satisfaction of one of the "labour market" conditions in s.1(2)(a)–(c) (reg.141(2) of the JSA Regulations 1996 and the equivalent provision for joint claim couples in regs 146A–146H, not separately noted below) and the claimant falls into one of the vulnerable groups specified in reg.140(1), the claimant is to be treated as entitled to IBJSA at the hardship rate after the expiry of the seven waiting days. A person outside the vulnerable groups, if in hardship (reg.140(2)), can be so treated from the 15th day after the claim (reg.142). However, there seems a limited need for any delay in making a decision in such circumstances because reg.141(4), made under para.8 of Sch.1 to the old style Jobseekers Act 1995, allows a person within s.140(1), except where there is deemed non-availability under reg.15 of the JSA Regulations 1996, to be entitled to IBJSA at the hardship rate without satisfying the conditions in s.1(2)(a)–(c), provided that the other conditions in s.1(2) are satisfied. There is no similar provision in reg.142. If a decision on entitlement can then be made under reg.141(4), the second stage of possible suspension of payment could come into play. However, it appears that reg.16(1) and (3) of the Decisions and Appeals Regulations 1999 allowing the Secretary of State to suspend payment of any benefit whenever an issue arises as to whether a condition of entitlement is satisfied cannot bite in these circumstances. Unless and until a jobseeker's agreement is signed, there is no doubt that the condition of entitlement in s.1(2)(b) is not met, so that no "issue" arises. Thus the specific effect of reg.141(5) of the JSA Regulations 1996 in excluding the operation of reg.16 where reg.141(4) applies appears not to be necessary in the present context.

That a person must enter (or be treated as having entered) into such an agreement is the way in which previously voluntary arrangements (the Back to Work plan) were translated into legal requirements for the purposes of old style JSA. A jobseeker's agreement has effect only for the purposes of entitlement to JSA ("the purposes of section 1") (subs.(2)) and hence does not give rise to any contractual or other private law obligations or relationship.

Note that there is no direct sanction for a claimant's failure to comply with the commitments recorded in the jobseeker's agreement. The condition of entitlement in s.1(2)(b) is met by the mere existence of the agreement and there is nothing in ss.19–19B that specifically refers to the jobseeker's agreement. There is a link to the condition of entitlement in s.1(2)(a) (availability) through the requirement in reg.7(2)(b) of the JSA Regulations 1996 that the claimant at least keeps to the pattern of availability recorded in the agreement, discussed in para.1.146 below. There is also a link to the condition of entitlement in s.1(2)(c) (actively seeking employment) in that a failure to carry out the work-search steps recorded in the agreement *might* lead to a conclusion that that condition is not satisfied, but the test is that set out in s.7(1) above and reg.18 of the JSA Regulations 1996 (basically whether the claimant has taken such steps as can reasonably be expected to have the best prospects of employment), not merely falling below the level specified in the agreement (see the notes to s.7(1)).

Subsection (1) defines "a jobseeker's agreement" as one entered into by a claimant 1.144
and an "employment officer", complying with the "prescribed requirements" as in force at the time it is made. "Employment officer" is defined in subs.(13) in the same terms as in s.35(1) (see the notes on the definition there). The jobseeker's agreement must be in writing and signed by both parties to it (the claimant and the employment officer) (subs.(3)) or in electronic form with electronic signatures (subs.(3A)). The claimant signs a declaration that he understands and agrees to the conditions set out in the agreement (White Paper para.4.19), but the declaration is not specified in regulations as one of the "prescribed requirements".

The "prescribed requirements" are listed in JSA Regulations 1996 reg.31. The agreement must contain: (i) the claimant's name; (ii) unless the claimant is available for any hours at any times, the total number of hours for which he is available for employment and any pattern of availability ("the times at which he is available to take up employment": see reg.7); (iii) any restrictions on availability as permitted by the scheme; (iv) a description of the type of employment being sought; (v) the action the claimant will take to seek employment and to improve the prospects of finding employment; (vi) the start and finish of the "permitted period" in which he is allowed to restrict his availability and jobsearch to his usual occupation and/or his usual rate of remuneration; (vii) a statement of his rights to have a proposed agreement referred to the Secretary State (decision-maker), to have a decision-maker's decision and/or directions reviewed by another decision-maker, and of his right of appeal to a tribunal in respect of the decision and/or direction given on that review; and (viii) the date of the agreement. A copy of the agreement must be given to the claimant (subs.(4)).

It must be the case that, if an agreement that has been entered into by a claimant does not contain one or more of the prescribed requirements, the claimant does not necessarily fail to satisfy the condition of entitlement in s.1(2)(b). Whether that outcome follows would depend on the nature of the requirement concerned and on the circumstances. In the case of most of the prescribed requirements, no doubt in practice the employment officer would decline to enter into the agreement if the claimant had not co-operated so as to allow the necessary matters to be recorded. But if, say, the jobseeker's agreement failed properly to inform the claimant about the rights to have the proposed agreement referred to the Secretary of State, etc. that could not possibly on its own lead to the conclusion that the claimant did not satisfy s.1(2)(b) (see *CH v SSWP (JSA)* [2015] UKUT 373 (AAC); [2016] AACR 28, where Judge Ward found the form of agreement (ES3JP 05/11) in use from 2012 to 2014 in breach of reg.31(g)). The decision in an appeal to the Upper Tribunal (*CJSA/1116/2015* and *1118/2015*) that was thought to raise the issue of whether the form of "claimant commitment" (i.e. in law a jobseeker's agreement) in use from 2014 onwards is affected by the same defect as identified in *CH* in relation to the earlier form did not in the event decide that issue.

1.145 The jobseeker's agreement is an integral part of identifying what steps back to work are appropriate for the claimant and to enable regular and effective monitoring of his activities to that end, reviewing and altering the terms of the agreement as necessary over a period (see White Paper para.4.16, and ss.10 and 11). Note, in particular, that "employment officers" cannot enter into an agreement the terms of which are such that the claimant acting in accordance with them would fail to satisfy either of the key requirements to be available for and actively seeking work, thus placing such officers at the heart of policing these central requirements of the system (subs.(5)). The decision in *PT v SSWP (JSA)* [2015] UKUT 703 (AAC), not in itself of any citable authority as given with the consent of both parties, records an interesting proposition put forward by the Secretary of State. It was accepted that the proper purpose of a jobseeker's agreement is to set out the details of the claimant's jobseeking, not to include "sanctionable activities". Thus, a requirement to attend "skills conditionality for [Universal Jobmatch]/CV workshop" should not have been proposed to become part of a varied jobseeker's agreement. It was accepted that any condition of opening a Universal Jobmatch account should be imposed through a direction under s.19A(2)(c) below. Any requirement to attend a Skills Conditionality Scheme should be imposed through reg.3(7) of the Jobseeker's Allowance (SAPOE) Regulations 2013 (in Part III below).

According to para.5 of Ch.1 of the *Government's response to the Independent review of the operation of Jobseeker's Allowance sanctions validated by the Jobseekers Act 2013* (Cmnd. 8904, July 2014), the "claimant commitment approach" has been rolled out to JSA from October 2013, with the rollout completed in April 2014. It is not clear what this means in relation to old style JSA when there has been no change in the legislation. There is reference in that document to improved claimant understanding of the requirements placed on them and to a new personalised approach to job search, centring on active discussion between advisers and claimants leading to detailed plans of actions, tailored to and owned by individual claimants.

Given that failing to enter into the agreement results in no entitlement to JSA, tribunals may discover that claimants find it difficult to see this as a genuine agreement, freely entered into rather than imposed. That the agreement will contain useful information on the facilities provided by Jobcentre Plus and the standards of service the claimant is entitled to receive under the Jobseeker's Charter (see White Paper para.4.17) is hardly a consolation: this valuable information would presumably have been provided even if, as with UB, the old style JSA scheme lacked the requisite of a jobseeker's agreement as a condition of entitlement to benefit.

1.146 The jobseeker's agreement is supposed not to be a standard pro forma document but one which aims to reflect the particular claimant's circumstances on availability. JSA Regulations 1996 reg.7(2)(b) requires that to be available the claimant must adhere in practice to the pattern of availability (either strictly or by following an even less restrictive pattern) embodied in the jobseeker's agreement unless and until that agreement is varied pursuant to s.10 (*R(JSA)2/07*, para.14). So, in *R(JSA)2/07*, the claimant who had agreed to Saturday working in his jobseeker's agreement, but followed an actual pattern which excluded Saturday, was not protected by reg.7(2) and so was not available. If a claimant is unhappy about the pattern proposed for the agreement, he has a number of choices. First, he can refuse to sign and ask for the agreement to be referred to the Secretary of State, hoping that the Secretary of State will agree with him about its terms and will also backdate the agreement so that the claimant, without benefit until the matter is decided, will not have lost but merely postponed benefit. Alternatively, he can sign under protest and immediately seek a variation of the agreement. But if he does so, he must, if he is to retain benefit pending the variation, adhere to the "agreed" pattern set out in the agreement.

The basic rule on when the agreement comes into effect would appear to be the day it is signed, but that is a deduction from the effect of other rules rather than finding expression in a particular provision. In some cases, no doubt, the claimant and the employment officer will reach ready agreement on the terms of the jobseeker's agreement, which will be signed on the day of claim, and take effect then. Where it is not signed until a date later than the day of claim, JSA Regulations, 1996 reg.35, made pursuant to subs.(11), provides that the agreement is to be automatically backdated to the day of claim, unless the agreement (in reality a proposed agreement) is referred to the Secretary of State (decision-maker) in accordance with subs.(6). Note, though, the possible effect of reg.34 in treating an agreement as having been made, especially in certain circumstances at the beginning of a claim.

The most common situation in which a proposed jobseeker's agreement will be referred to a decision-maker is likely to be where there is a dispute between the parties over the availability and/or actively seeking work aspects of it or over whether it is reasonable to expect the claimant to have to comply with it. In such a situation, the employment officer *must* refer the proposed agreement to a decision-maker if the claimant asks him to do so (subs.(6)). In addition, the employment officer always has power to refer such matters to the decision-maker (subs.(6)), and doubtless will do so particularly where he is unsure about the availability and/or actively seeking work aspects.

In *CJSA/2162/2001,* Commissioner Williams held that: 1.147

"a valid jobseeker's agreement continues in force until it is varied or brought to an end in accordance with the 1995 Act and the Jobseeker's Allowance Regulations. It cannot unilaterally be ignored by the Secretary of State. While in force it is relevant not only to section 1 but also to other parts of the Act including section 7. Section 7 incorporates a test of reasonableness in considering whether someone is actively seeking work for the purposes of section 1. Section 7(1) allows for the possibility that someone can meet the section 1(2)(c) test without taking any step to seek work if that is reasonable. Regulation 18 of the Regulations does not, when read as a whole, preclude that possibility in considering whether the test in section 7(1) is satisfied. The terms of the jobseeker's agreement are relevant to the consideration of the reasonableness of the steps taken by the claimant. I do not decide if the agreement is determinative of that issue" (para.40).

So in an unusual case (the claimant should really have been directed to income support as a person in ill health), where the agreement in force did not effectively require her to take any steps actively to seek work, she was entitled to benefit because of the agreement in force and the fact that she was both available for and actively seeking work. It was reasonable for her to take no active steps as none had been asked for. But in fact she had taken some, had participated in the reviews and had actively found part-time work. These last findings arguably render the Commissioner's suggestion that the s.7(1) test can be satisfied in a week in which no steps are taken unnecessary to the decision itself. It is submitted in the notes to s.7 and to reg.18 of the JSA Regulations 1996 that that suggestion is incompatible with the terms of reg.18(1). The Secretary of State should have taken steps to revise the agreement using s.10, but had not.

If a proposed agreement is referred to a decision-maker, it must, so far as is practicable, be disposed of (determined) within 14 days of the reference (subs.(7)(a)).

The determination must deal with the questions set out in subs.(6), in particular whether it is reasonable to expect the claimant to have to comply with the proposed agreement and may include directions about the terms on which the employment officer is to enter into an agreement with the claimant and about the date on which the agreement, if entered into, takes effect (subs.(7)(b) and (c)), which allows back-dating. The automatic backdating of the effect of an agreement to the date of claim under reg.35 of the JSA Regulations 1996 does not apply where there has been a reference under s.9(6). *CH v SSWP (JSA)*, above, discusses the nature of the proper procedure under s.9(6) and (7) when a claimant is not prepared to accept an initial jobseeker's agreement in the terms proposed by the employment officer. It also criticises some of the administrative guidance in operation at the dates in question there. If there is a reference to the Secretary of State, either at the claimant's request or under the employment officer's discretion, the decision on the reference cannot go beyond determining the questions under s.9(6) and giving directions under s.9(7). In *CH*, it appeared that the decision given by the Secretary of State did not deal with those questions, but went straight to a decision that the claimant was not entitled to JSA because he had not entered into a jobseeker's agreement. That decision had to be set aside for the reference procedure to be followed. There can only be a decision on entitlement once the claimant has had notice of the outcome of the reference and has had the opportunity to consider a proposed agreement prepared in accordance with the determination and any directions. Judge Ward noted in para.39 that the Secretary of State accepted that any physical or mental limitations on a claimant's jobseeking ability should be considered under s.9(6).

In considering whether back-dating is appropriate, JSA Regulations 1996 reg.32 (made under subs.(8)(a)) stipulates that the decision-maker must take into account all relevant matters, including those specifically listed in the regulation (i.e. that list is not exhaustive). The matters so listed are: (i) whether the claimant was reasonable in refusing to accept the proposed agreement; (ii) whether the terms of the agreement which the claimant has indicated, to the decision-maker or the employment officer, that he is prepared to accept, are reasonable; (iii) the fact that the claimant has signified to the decision-maker or the employment officer that he is prepared to accept the proposed agreement; (iv) the date on which, taking account of all the circumstances, the decision-maker considers the claimant was prepared to enter into an agreement the decision-maker considers reasonable; and (v) the fact that the date on which the claimant first had an opportunity to sign a jobseeker's agreement was later than the date of claim. Notification of the decision-maker's determination and any directions given by him will doubtless be given to the employment officer as a matter of the arrangements within the old style JSA administrative structure, and must be given to the claimant under JSA Regulations 1996 reg.33. Any determination of the Secretary of State (decision-maker) under this section is binding (subs.(9)) but not final, because of the possibility of revision and appeal under the DMA arrangements. The right of appeal is created by para.8 of Sch.3 to the Social Security Act 1998.

Generally, a jobseeker's agreement ceases to have effect when the claimant's award of JSA comes to an end (subs.(12)). JSA Regulations 1996 reg.36 prescribes the circumstances in which a jobseeker's agreement shall not so cease to have effect (for example, where a further claim for JSA is made within 14 days of the previous award coming to an end: see reg.36(a)). Note in particular that a mere failure by a claimant to sign a varied jobseeker's agreement directed by the Secretary of State under s.10(6)(b) does not allow the immediate termination of the existing agreement and the consequent ending of entitlement until the claimant has had the 21 days specified under s.10(6)(c) to sign the varied agreement. See the notes to s.10 for further details.

New style JSA

1.148 Note that in those cases and areas where universal credit has come into force, income-based JSA is abolished and replaced by new style JSA (which is contribution-based only). See Pt VI of this book for the legislation relating to new style JSA and for the cases and areas to which it applies.

Variation of jobseeker's agreement

10.—(1) A jobseeker's agreement may be varied, in the prescribed manner, by agreement between the claimant and any employment officer. 1.149

(2) Any agreement to vary a jobseeker's agreement shall be in writing and be signed by both parties.

[[2](2A) Any agreement to vary a jobseeker's agreement may be in electronic form and signed by means of an electronic signature (within the meaning given in section 7(2) of the Electronic Communications Act 2000).]

(3) A copy of the agreement, as varied, shall be given to the claimant.

(4) An employment officer shall not agree to a variation of a jobseeker's agreement, unless, in the officer's opinion, the conditions mentioned in section 1(2)(a) and (c) would continue to be satisfied with respect to the claimant if he were to comply with, or be treated as complying with, the agreement as proposed to be varied.

(5) The employment officer may, and if asked to do so by the claimant shall forthwith, refer a proposed variation of a jobseeker's agreement to [[1]the Secretary of State] for him to determine—

(a) whether, if the claimant concerned were to comply with the agreement as proposed to be varied, he would satisfy—
   (i) the condition mentioned in section 1(2)(a), or
   (ii) the condition mentioned in section 1(2)(c); and
(b) whether it is reasonable to expect the claimant to have to comply with the agreement as proposed to be varied.

(6) [[1]On a reference under subsection (5) the Secretary of State]—

(a) shall, so far as practicable, dispose of it in accordance with this section before the end of the period of 14 days from the date of the reference;
(b) shall give such directions as he considers appropriate as to—
   (i) whether the jobseeker's agreement should be varied, and
   (ii) if so, the terms on which the claimant and the employment officer are to enter into an agreement to vary it;
(c) may bring the jobseeker's agreement to an end where the claimant fails, within a prescribed period, to comply with a direction given under paragraph (b)(ii);
(d) may direct that, if—
   (i) the jobseeker's agreement is varied, and
   (ii) such conditions as he considers appropriate are satisfied,
   the agreement as varied is to be treated as having effect on such date, before it would otherwise have effect, as may be specified in the direction.

(7) Regulations may provide—

(a) for such matters as may be prescribed to be taken into account by [[1]the Secretary of State] in giving a direction under section (6)(b) or (d); and
(b) for such persons as may be prescribed to be notified of—
   (i) any determination of [[1]the Secretary of State] under this section;
   (ii) any direction given by [[1]the Secretary of State] under this section.

(8) [[1] . . .].

AMENDMENTS

1. Social Security Act 1998 Sch.7 para.137 (October 18, 1999).

2. Social Security (Electronic Communications) Order 2011 (SI 2011/1498) art.2(3) (February 1, 2012).

DEFINITIONS

"claimant"—see s.35(1).
"employment officer"—see s.9(13).
"jobseeker's agreement"—see ss.35(1) and 9(1).
"prescribed"—see s.35(1).
"regulations"—*ibid.*

GENERAL NOTE

1.150 This section enables a jobseeker's agreement to be varied, with the aim of ensuring that it reflects the claimant's changing circumstances and the labour market. The section also provides for the mode and manner of decision-making and is amplified by JSA Regulations 1996 regs 37–40.

A jobseeker's agreement can, on the proposal of either the employment officer or the claimant, be varied with the consent of both parties (subs.(1); JSA Regulations 1996 reg.37). An agreement to vary must, like the varied agreement itself, be in writing and signed by both parties (subs.(2); JSA Regulations 1996 reg.37) or in electronic form with electronic signatures (subs.(2A)). The claimant must get a copy of the varied agreement (subs.(3)). An employment officer cannot agree a variation unless satisfied that under its terms the claimant would continue to be available for and actively seeking employment (subs.(4)), once more emphasising the central role for Jobcentre Plus personnel in monitoring those crucial "labour market" conditions of entitlement.

Some cases will be the subject of decisions and directions of decision-makers. The most common situation in which a proposed variation of a jobseeker's agreement will be referred to a decision-maker is likely to be where there is a dispute between the parties over the availability and/or the actively seeking work aspects of it, or over whether it is reasonable to expect the claimant to have to comply with it. In such a situation, the employment officer *must* refer the proposed variation of the agreement to a decision-maker if the claimant asks him to do so (subs.(5)). In addition, the employment officer always has power to refer such matters to the decision-maker (subs.(5), and doubtless will do so particularly where he is unsure about the availability and/or the actively seeking work aspects.

1.151 A decision-maker is, so far as is practicable, to determine the reference within 14 days. He must give such directions as he considers appropriate as to whether the agreement should be varied and if so the terms on which the parties are to agree a varied agreement. Should the claimant fail to do so within 21 days of the direction, the decision-maker can bring the existing jobseeker's agreement to an end, thus disentitling the claimant to old style JSA since s.1(2)(b) requires a jobseeker's agreement to be in force (subs.(6)(a)–(c)). The decision-maker can also backdate the varied agreement (subs.(6)(d)). In giving directions under subs.(6)(b) or (d) the decision-maker must take into account the preference of the claimant if he considers that both the claimant's proposals and those of the employment officer meet the requirements of subs.(5) (the "labour market" conditions and the "reasonableness" requirement) (JSA Regulations 1996 reg.38).

In *HS v SSWP (JSA)* [2015] UKUT 701 (AAC), the claimant refused to sign a new jobseeker's agreement (under the title of a claimant commitment), not being satisfied with its terms (on the basis accepted by Judge Turnbull). The employment officer referred the matter to the Secretary of State, who gave a decision that the claimant was not entitled to old style JSA because he had not entered into a jobseeker's agreement. As agreed by the Secretary of State before the Upper Tribunal, the claimant's refusal to sign the new agreement did not entitle the making of a decision to terminate entitlement. Under s.10(5) and (6)(b) the Secretary of State could only decide on the reference whether the proposed agreement was compatible with the requirements of availability for employment and actively seeking employment and whether it was reasonable to expect the claimant to comply with the proposed terms and give directions about whether the agreement should be varied and the terms on which it was to be entered into. The existing jobseeker's agreement could not be brought to an end under s.10(6)(c) (so ending satisfaction of the condition of entitlement in s.1(2)(b)) until the expiry of the period of 21 days specified under s.10(6)(c) for the claimant to sign the varied agreement.

Commissioner Mesher considered the matter of directions in *R(JSA)2/07*. In the absence of a statutory provision specifying when a varied agreement should be treated as having effect, he thought that in most, if not all, cases a direction needed to be given. As to when the agreement should start, that could be the date of signature or the date the proposal to vary the agreement was made. He thought that where the proposal to vary came from the claimant, then, given the difficult choices faced by a claimant unhappy with the agreement (see commentary to s.9 and JSA Regulations 1996 reg.7(2)), that indicated that the date of the proposal was the more appropriate (see para.30).

Retrospective variation is permissible (*R(JSA)2/07; AT v SSWP (JSA)* [2013] UKUT 073 (AAC), see para.10).

Notification of the decision-maker's determination and any directions given by him will doubtless be given to the employment officer as a matter of the arrangements within the JSA administrative structure, and must be given to the claimant under JSA Regulations 1996 reg.40, made pursuant to subs.(7)(b). A right of appeal against the determination is created by para.8 of Sch.3 to the Social Security Act 1998. **1.152**

A decision-maker can bring a jobseeker's agreement to an end (thus denying benefit) where, within 21 days, a claimant has not agreed the terms of a varied agreement as indicated by the decision-maker. In *CJSA/4435/1998,* Commissioner Levenson was of the view that an appeal against the decision-maker's direction on the terms of the agreement necessarily involved also an appeal against his decision to terminate the agreement (see para.8). In the particular case, dealing only with the type of work for which the claimant should be available, he noted that the relevant standard was that of "reasonable prospects of employment", notwithstanding imposed restrictions, pursuant to JSA Regulations 1996 regs 8 and 10. The tribunal applied a different test of "good prospects" when rejecting his appeal, and so erred in law in imposing on the claimant a higher degree of proof than that stipulated in the regulations.

New style JSA

Note that in those cases and areas where universal credit has come into force, income-based JSA is abolished and replaced by new style JSA (which is contribution-based only). See Pt VI of this book for the legislation relating to new style JSA and for the cases and areas to which it applies. **1.153**

Jobseeker's agreement: reviews and appeals

11.—[1 . . .]. **1.154**

REPEAL

1. Social Security Act 1998 Sch.7 para.138 (October 18, 1999).

Income and capital

Income and capital: general

12.—(1) In relation to a claim for a jobseeker's allowance, the income and capital of a person shall be calculated or estimated in such manner as may be prescribed. **1.155**

(2) A person's income in respect of a week shall be calculated in accordance with prescribed rules.

(3) The rules may provide for the calculation to be made by reference to an average over a period (which need not include the week concerned).

(4) Circumstances may be prescribed in which—

(a) a person is treated as possessing capital or income which he does not possess;
(b) capital or income which a person does possess is to be disregarded;
(c) income is to be treated as capital;
(d) capital is to be treated as income.

DEFINITIONS

"prescribed"—see s.35(1).
"week"—*ibid.*

GENERAL NOTE

1.156 This section is very similar to subss.(3)–(5) of s.136 of the Contributions and Benefits Act and contains extensive powers to prescribe how a claimant's capital and income is to be calculated for the purposes of JSA. See Pt VIII of, and Schs 6, 6A, 7 and 8 to, the JSA Regulations 1996.

See also s.13.

Income and capital: income-based jobseeker's allowance

1.157 **13.**—(1) No person shall be entitled to an income-based jobseeker's allowance if his capital, or a prescribed part of it, exceeds the prescribed amount.

(2) Where a person claiming an income-based jobseeker's allowance is a member of a family, the income and capital of any member of that family shall, except in prescribed circumstances, be treated as the income and capital of the claimant.

[[1](2A) Subsections (1) and (2) do not apply as regards a joint-claim jobseeker's allowance; but a joint-claim couple shall not be entitled to a joint-claim jobseeker's allowance if the couple's capital, or a prescribed part of it, exceeds the prescribed amount.

(2B) Where a joint-claim couple claim a joint-claim jobseeker's allowance—

(a) the couple's income and capital includes the separate income and capital of each of them; and
(b) the income and capital of any other person who is a member of any family of which the couple are members shall, except in prescribed circumstances, be treated as income and capital of the couple.]

(3) Regulations may provide that capital not exceeding the amount prescribed under subsection (1) [[1]or (2A)], but exceeding a prescribed lower amount, shall be treated, to a prescribed extent, as if it were income of a prescribed amount.

AMENDMENT

1. Welfare Reform and Pensions Act 1999 s.59 and Sch.7 para.9 (March 19, 2001).

DEFINITIONS

"claimant"—see s.35(1).
"family"—*ibid.*
"income-based jobseeker's allowance"—see s.1(4).

"joint-claim couple"—*ibid.*
"joint-claim jobseeker's allowance"—*ibid.*
"prescribed"—see s.35(1).
"regulations"—*ibid.*

General Note

The provisions in this section are similar to those in ss.134(1) and 136(1) and (2) of the Contributions and Benefits Act 1992. Note the amendments made on March 19, 2001 relating to the introduction of joint claims for JSA for certain childless couples (see the notes at the beginning of this Act and to s.1(4)). Since February 25, 2008, all childless couples (unless they are exempt) have been required to make a joint claim (see reg.3A of the JSA Regulations 1996). **1.158**

Subsection (1)

The capital limit for income-based JSA was raised to £16,000 for all claimants on April 10, 2006 (JSA Regulations 1996, reg.107). See the 2005 edition of this volume for the different capital limits that applied for most claimants before that date and see the note to s.134(1) of the Contributions and Benefits Act 1992. **1.159**

Subsection (2)

This provides that the general rule for income-based JSA (as for income support) is that all of the family's (as defined in s.35(1)) income and capital is aggregated together and treated as the claimant's. The modifications to this rule for children and young persons were in regs 106 and 109 of the Jobseeker's Allowance Regulations 1996 (see the 2003 edition of this volume for those regulations and the notes to those regulations). However, as a consequence of the removal of amounts for children and young persons from income-based JSA (with effect from April 6, 2004, except in "transitional cases"—see the note to reg.17 of the Income Support Regulations and the note to reg.83 of the JSA Regulations 1996), a child's income and capital will be totally ignored and only a partner's income and capital will count as that of the claimant (see the amended form of reg.88(1) of the JSA Regulations 1996). **1.160**

Subsections (2A) and (2B)

Subsections (1) and (2) do not apply to joint-claim JSA but the effects of subss. (2A) and (2B) is to apply similar rules to those in subss.(1) and (2) to joint-claim JSA. On subs.(2B), see reg.88ZA of the JSA Regulations. **1.161**

Subsection (3)

This enables a similar "tariff income" rule to the one that operates for income support to be applied to income-based (including joint-claim) JSA. Reg.116 of the JSA Regulations 1996 provides for an income to be assumed to be produced from capital between £6,000 and £16,000 (£10,000 and £16,000 in the case of claimants living permanently in a care home, Abbeyfield Home or independent hospital). **1.162**

New style JSA

Note that in those cases and areas where universal credit has come into force, income-based JSA is abolished and replaced by new style JSA (which is contribution-based only). See Pt VI of this book for the legislation relating to new style JSA and for the cases and areas to which it applies. **1.163**

Trade disputes

Trade disputes

14.—(1) Where— **1.164**

(a) there is a stoppage of work which causes a person not to be employed on any day, and

(b) the stoppage is due to a trade dispute at his place of work, that person is not entitled to a jobseeker's allowance for the week which includes that day unless he proves that he is not directly interested in the dispute.

(2) A person who withdraws his labour on any day in furtherance of a trade dispute, but to whom subsection (1) does not apply, is not entitled to a jobseeker's allowance for the week which includes that day.

(3) If a person who is prevented by subsection (1) from being entitled to a jobseeker's allowance proves that during the stoppage—

(a) he became bona fide employed elsewhere;

(b) his employment was terminated by reason of redundancy within the meaning of [[1]section 139 of the Employment Rights Act 1996,] or

(c) he bona fide resumed employment with his employer but subsequently left for a reason other than the trade dispute,

subsection (1) shall be taken to have ceased to apply to him on the occurrence of the event referred to in paragraph (a) or (b) or (as the case may be) the first event referred to in paragraph (c).

(4) In this section "place of work", in relation to any person, means the premises or place at which he was employed.

(5) Where separate branches of work which are commonly carried on as separate businesses in separate premises or at separate places are in any case carried on in separate departments on the same premises or at the same place, each of those departments shall, for the purposes of subsection (4), be deemed to be separate premises or (as the case may be) a separate place.

AMENDMENT

1. Employment Rights Act 1996 Sch.1 para.67(2)(a) (August 22, 1996).

DEFINITIONS

"employment"—see s.35(1) and JSA Regulations 1996 reg.4.
"entitled"—see s.35(1).
"trade dispute"—see s.35(1).
"week"—*ibid.*

GENERAL NOTE

1.165 This section denies entitlement to old style JSA to certain persons affected by or involved in trade disputes in two situations. First, where a stoppage of work due to a trade dispute at the claimant's place of work causes him not to be employed on any day, he will not be entitled to JSA for the week which includes that day, unless either he can establish that he is not directly interested in the dispute or he can invoke one of the escape routes provided by subs.(3) (subs.(1)). The second situation where entitlement is denied throughout a week is where in furtherance of a trade dispute the claimant withdraws his labour on any day in that week, but not in such a way as to be caught by subs.(1) (the first situation of denial of entitlement) (subs.(2)).

In many respects the section replicates the trade dispute disqualification from UB in SSCBA 1992 s.27 and, as noted below, case law interpreting that and its precursor provisions will still be relevant in interpreting this old style JSA provision. There has been some change of terminology without apparent change of meaning (e.g. "place of work" rather than "place of employment"). That one day affected bars title for the whole week rather than just for the day, as would have been the case with UB, is unsurprising; it reflects the change from a daily benefit (UB) to a weekly benefit (JSA). Like the trade dispute disqualification from UB, this provision denies entitlement. Hence weeks ruled out do not form part of a jobseeking period (JSA Regulations 1996 reg.48(3)(e)), but nor do they erode the 182-day maximum period of entitlement to CBJSA founded on a contribution record in a single set of two tax/contribution years (see further notes to ss.2 and 5). This is in marked contrast to the double penalty suffered by the person who, for example, loses his job through misconduct, precluded from payment of JSA by s.19, who not only is denied payment but has the 182-day period eroded by the period of preclusion imposed under that section (see further notes to ss.5 and 19). This differential can to some degree be rationalised on the basis that the role of ss.19 and 19A is to preclude payment to those who are in some way responsible for their own unemployment, whereas, as shown below, the trade dispute preclusion can catch the innocent, and in part the trade dispute preclusion in denying benefit to those affected is said to manifest state neutrality in the dispute, the merits of which should not concern the benefit system.

Subsection (1)

To bring the trade dispute preclusion in subs.(1) into operation, the Secretary of State (decision-maker) must prove on the balance of probabilities that: **1.166**

(1) there was a *trade dispute*;

(2) at the claimant's *place of work*;

(3) which resulted in a *stoppage of work*; and

(4) that stoppage caused the claimant not to be employed on a day.

This adapts for this section the approach to the unemployment benefit trade dispute disqualification set out in *R(U) 17/52(T)*.

Each of these conditions contains terms (highlighted above) whose interpretation is vital to the correct application of the section's denial of entitlement to JSA.

Trade dispute

Determining the existence of a trade dispute seems logically the first task of the adjudicating authorities, because in the absence of a trade dispute the other conditions cannot apply. The basic definition, which is very broad, is now to be found in s.35(1), rather than in the section itself, as was the case in UB, but the definitions are identical. The definition clearly includes strikes, whether official or unofficial (*R(U) 5/59*), lockouts (*R(U) 17/52*) and demarcation disputes (*R(U) 14/64*). There is no requirement that the claimant be a party to the trade dispute: *R(U) 3/69* and see below. It has been held that there can be a trade dispute between an employer and employees of another employer who picket the employer's premises and persuade its employees to strike: *R(U) 1/74*. There is a requirement in the definition of trade dispute in s.35(1) that the dispute concern employment or non-employment of persons or conditions or terms of employment. Disputes outside these parameters are not trade disputes for the purpose of this section. It is now clearly established that a dispute about safety procedures is within the definition: *R(U) 3/71*, *R(U) 5/77* and *R. v National Insurance Commissioner Ex p. Thompson* (1977), reported as an Appendix to *R(U) 5/77*. In *R(U) 5/87* Commissioner Rice held that the words "any dispute . . . which is connected with the employment . . . of any person" are wide enough to include any dispute connected with the manner in which the employment is carried out, and in that case covered the dispute over the employees' "go slow". In most cases establishing the existence of a trade dispute is unlikely to be problematic. But note that in *R(U) 21/59*, para.6, the Commissioner indicated that a dispute between an employer and an employee must have reached "a certain stage of contention before it may properly be termed a [trade] dispute". The Commissioner was clearly satisfied that evidence that the workforce had met to consider their response to their employer's rejection of their claims concerning their terms of employment amounted to a trade dispute and suggested that one may well have existed some time before the meeting took place. **1.167**

It should be noted that in determining the existence of a trade dispute it is no part of the adjudicating authorities' task to make any assessment of the merits of the dispute: *Ex p. Thompson* (cited above) and *R(SSP)1/86.* It may be necessary to make findings of fact about when the trade dispute started and ended, but it should be remembered that the more important dates relate to when the stoppage of work started and ended. This is discussed below. There is a clear distinction to be drawn between a trade dispute and a stoppage of work under the section.

Place of work

1.168 The trade dispute must be at the claimant's place of work as defined in subs.(4). Read with subs.(5) this allows some separation of departments within a range of employment operated by a single employer. It will usually be a straightforward task to identify the premises or place at which the claimant is employed. Obviously each case must be determined on its own facts. How broadly or narrowly the place will be defined will vary according to the circumstances of each case. In *R(U)4/58* the place of employment of an employee loading ships was held to be the whole of the docks.

Where the decision-maker shows on the balance of probabilities a place of work, it will be for the claimant to prove on the balance of probabilities that there are separate branches of work and that the trade dispute is not at his place of work so construed: *R(U)1/70,* at para.14. The escape route in accord with the terms of subs.(4) is complex because the claimant, who may not be best placed to do so, must adduce evidence to show that:

(a) there are separate branches of work; a claimant is unlikely to succeed unless he can show that the branch is engaged in work that is not part of an integrated process of production: *R(U)4/62,* para.7;

(b) the separate branches of work are commonly carried on as separate businesses in separate premises or at separate places; this necessarily involves adducing evidence as to patterns in other similar businesses: *R(U)4/62* and *R(U)1/70,* para.17; and

(c) at his place of employment the branches of work are in fact carried out in separate departments at the same premises or place.

In cases involving such arguments, clear findings of fact are obviously vital. *CU66/1986(T)* affords an illustration. There the claimant successfully appealed her trade dispute disqualification to a Tribunal of Commissioners. She was a colliery canteen worker at Frickley Colliery, laid off during the miner's strike in 1984–1985. The Commissioners held that there was carried on in the canteen a separate branch of work, and one which is commonly carried on as a separate business in separate premises or at a separate place. But was the canteen a separate department? The evidence of the NUM Branch Secretary at the colliery was that the canteen was inside the colliery gates and had been attached to or added to the pit-head baths that had been built in 1937. It was managed by the manageress who was appointed by and answerable to the NCB Catering Manager at Doncaster. While applications for jobs at the canteen would be made to the colliery's personnel manager, the area canteen manager would be responsible for making the appointment. As regards disciplinary matters with respect to canteen workers, again, the area manager would be involved but the colliery manager would also have to be informed. Profits and losses in the canteen did not appear to feature in figures about the profitability of the colliery. The Commissioners, in the light of this evidence, decided that the work carried on in the canteen was a separate branch of work carried on in a separate department on the same premises or at the same place as the colliery. Accordingly, since the trade dispute that caused the stoppage of work was not at the claimant's place of employment she would not be disqualified from benefit. The Commissioners also referred to an Umpire's decision (Case 2185/29, *Umpires Decisions,* Vol.VIII, p.88) under the equivalent provision in s.8(1) of the Unemployment Insurance Act 1920. There, a blacksmith employed in the blacksmiths' department at a colliery, which department did both wagon repairing and general colliery work, was able to rely on the escape route, notwithstanding that only some work in that department was carried on as a separate department from coal-mining.

Stoppage of work

Generally defining a stoppage of work is relatively easy. But defining when it begins may be more problematic and a useful approach may be to adopt the reverse of the principles laid down in the decisions on the ending of stoppages of work discussed below. The starting point will always be to consider the definition given by the Tribunal of Commissioners in *R(U)17/52(T)*: 1.169

> "A stoppage of work must be in the nature of a strike or lockout, that is to say it must be a move in a contest between an employer and his employees, the object of which is that employment shall be resumed on certain conditions."

In *R(U)7/58* it was held that a stoppage of work occurred when 38 production workers out of a total of 90 withdrew their labour. In *R(U)1/87* Commissioner Skinner said that "stoppage of work" means "a situation in which operations are being stopped or hindered otherwise than to a negligible extent" (para.7). There the closure of the furriers' fleshing shop on May 2, 1984, causing a 60 per cent loss of production, resulted in a stoppage from that date. In *R(U)1/65,* following a long line of Commissioners' decisions, it was held that where there was a trade dispute and subsequently the employer indicates that he will never re-employ the strikers, the stoppage of work continues to be due to the trade dispute despite the high improbability that the strikers will be re-employed and despite their acceptance of that position. In effect the disqualification can only end when they become bona fide employed elsewhere or when the stoppage ends. In *R(U)25/57,* the Commissioner adopted the approach taken by the Umpire in 1926 as establishing the principles to be applied in determining when the end of a stoppage of work occurred:

> "A stoppage of work may come to an end without any settlement of the dispute, by the workers returning to work in a body, or by driblets, or by their places being taken by other men. In such cases the stoppage of work comes to an end when the employers have got all the workers they require, that is, when work is no longer being stopped or hindered by the refusal of workers to work on the employer's terms or the refusal of employers to employ the workers on the workers' terms . . . When work is again proceeding normally and is not being held up, either by the men holding back or by circumstances directly resulting from the stoppage of work, the stoppage of work is at an end." (para.6)

This approach was cited with approval in *R(U)1/65.* It is consistent with this approach that, where a dispute had ended but work was needed to industrial plant to carry out repairs necessitated by the stoppage, a lay-off while those repairs were carried out was a part of the stoppage due to the trade dispute: *R. v National Insurance Commissioner Ex p. Dawber* (published as an Appendix to *R(U)9/80*).

The stoppage causes the claimant not to be employed on a day

If the stoppage causes the claimant not to be employed on any day, entitlement to old style JSA is lost for the week including that day (unless one of the escape routes can be invoked), a change reflecting the weekly character of JSA as opposed to the daily benefit structure of UB. 1.170

It has already been noted that the claimant need not be a party to the trade dispute to be caught by the disqualification. A claimant is caught if the stoppage is the effective cause of his not working. So, if enough people stay away from work for a stoppage to occur, all those losing days of employment, whether by their own choice or by force of circumstances, such as picketing or being laid off by the employer, are to be regarded as having lost their employment by reason of the stoppage.

Escape routes

1.171 There are four escape routes for avoiding the preclusive effect of subs.(1): the proviso in the subsection itself and the three exceptions set out in subs.(3).

1.172 *(1) The proviso*: The claimant can avoid the disqualification by proving that he has no direct interest in the trade dispute. In determining what constitutes a direct interest in the trade dispute, it is necessary to look no further than the decision of the House of Lords in *Presho v Insurance Officer* [1984] 1 All E.R. 97 (published as Appendix 2 to *R(U)1/84*), followed by the Court of Appeal in *Cartlidge v Chief Adjudication Officer* [1986] 2 All E.R. 1, appendix to *R(U)5/86*. In *Presho* Lord Brandon said that the words should be given their natural and ordinary meaning, and continued:

> "Where different groups of workers, belonging to different unions, are employed by the same employers at the same place of work and there is a trade dispute between the common employers and one of the unions to which one of the groups of workers belong, those in the other groups of workers belonging to other unions are directly, and not merely indirectly, interested in that trade dispute provided that two conditions are fulfilled. The first condition is that, whatever may be the outcome of the trade dispute, it will be applied by the common employers not only to the group of workers belonging to the one union participating in the dispute, but also to the other groups of workers belonging to the other unions concerned. The second condition is that the application of the outcome of the dispute 'across the board' . . . should come about automatically as a result of one or other of three things: first, a collective agreement which is legally binding; or, second, a collective agreement which is not legally binding; or, third, established industrial custom and practice at the place of work concerned. [These issues involve] a question of fact of a kind which insurance officers, local tribunals and the commissioner, are by reason of their wide knowledge and experience of matters pertaining to industrial relations, exceptionally well qualified to answer." (At 101–102.)

In *Cartlidge,* the Commissioner had found that the miners' dispute concerned both pay and pit closures, and so Mr Cartlidge was directly interested in the trade dispute. It follows that it will be extremely difficult for claimants to take advantage of this escape route. However, the fact that the claimant was at one time directly interested in the trade dispute (and thus then unable to invoke the proviso) does not preclude him from successfully invoking it later during the stoppage should he cease to have a direct interest. The proviso is not invocable once and once only during a stoppage (*R(U)1/87,* para.9, relying on *R(U)5/86(T),* paras 15–28 where a Tribunal of Commissioners disapproved statements to the contrary in *R(U)4/79(T)* because a line of Commissioners' authority running contrary to that relied on in *R(U)4/79(T)* had not been cited or considered in *R(U)4/79(T)*). A claimant, initially directly interested in the trade dispute (and therefore rightly denied benefit), can cease to be so interested and thus claim the benefit of the proviso to conclude the period of denial, where his dismissal by his employer genuinely indicates the employer's intention to sever all relations with him and is not just a tactical manoeuvre in the dispute. In *R(U)1/87* the hindsight available to the Commissioner showed that the claimant's dismissal on the first day of the stoppage was part of plans to trim the size of the workforce and thus a genuine severance of all relations with the claimant rather than a tactical move in the dispute. Accordingly, the claimant was not subject to disqualification after that first day. Of course, were that case being decided now, with respect to old style JSA, the whole week in which that day occurred would be ruled out by subs.(1).

1.173 *(2) Bona fide employment elsewhere (subs.(3)(a))*: If someone caught by the subs.(1) preclusion proves that during the stoppage he became bona fide employed elsewhere, subs.(1) is to be taken to cease to apply to him from the point at which he became so employed elsewhere.

The burden of proof is on the claimant to establish the bona fide nature of the employment. Bona fide means that the employment must not merely be a device to avoid the disqualification; both the employment and the reason for taking it must be genuine (*R(U) 6/74*). There is no objection to the taking of temporary employment so long as it is genuine. It will usually be necessary to show that the relationship with the former employer with whom there was a trade dispute has been permanently severed. So a former boiler-maker who obtained intermittent work in his usual occupation in a different port, but returned to his former employer on the ending of the dispute was held not to have established that he was bona fide employed elsewhere (*R(U)39/56*).

(3) Employment terminated by reason of redundancy (subs.(3)(b)): If someone caught by the subs.(1) preclusion proves that during the stoppage his employment was terminated by reason of redundancy within the meaning of s.139(1) of the Employment Rights Act 1996, subs.(1) is to be taken to have ceased to apply to him from the point of such termination. As to "by reason of redundancy within the meaning of section 139(1)", termination will be by reason of redundancy if it is attributable wholly or mainly to: (a) the fact that the employer has ceased, or intends to cease, to carry on that business in the place where the employee [the JSA claimant] was employed, or (b) the fact that the requirements of that business for employees to carry out work of a particular kind, or for employees to carry out work of a particular kind in the place where [the claimant] was employed, have ceased or diminished or are expected to cease or diminish. 1.174

The precursor of this provision was inserted into the UB trade dispute disqualification scheme, to remove the injustice perceived to exist in the *Cartlidge* case. Mr Cartlidge had volunteered for redundancy prior to the start of the miners' dispute in 1984. Between receiving his notice of redundancy and its taking effect, a stoppage due to a trade dispute at his place of work caused him to not to be employed on some days. He had tried to work and had done so for much of the period but had lost some days' work because of the picketing of his pit. The Court of Appeal reluctantly held that the trade dispute disqualification extended beyond the termination of his employment because the stoppage of work was still continuing (the relevant provision then disqualified "for any day during the stoppage"). The effect of this provision is that subs.(1) can have no preclusive effect beyond the point of termination of employment by reason of redundancy. It is perhaps worth noting that the current formulation of subs.(1) would have worked to benefit someone in Mr Cartlidge's position prior to the termination in that if, despite a stoppage of work, he managed to work throughout the week (not losing a day of employment) he would not be precluded from old style JSA for that week, even though loss of a day's employment due to the stoppage in the preceding and subsequent weeks had precluded title to JSA for those weeks (though see s.1(2)(d) and (e)).

(4) Bona fide resumption of employment and subsequent leaving for another reason (subs. (3)(c)): If someone caught by the subs.(1) preclusion proves that during the stoppage he bona fide resumed employment with his employer, subs.(1) is to be taken to have ceased to apply to him from the point at which he bona fide resumed his employment. 1.175

This is an escape route for the claimant who has withdrawn his labour, subsequently returned to work, but then left it for a reason unconnected with the trade dispute. The reason will usually be something other than leaving his job to take another: subs.(3)(a) would there afford an easier escape route. Bona fide is to be interpreted as in subs.(3)(a). But otherwise it is not easy to see how this provision will work in practice. Does resumption mean that the employment was terminated and re-employment offered, or merely that the claimant returned to work during the trade dispute, or both? There appears to be no case law on the precursor of this provision, so many points await interpretation.

Subsection (2)

This subsection makes it clear that anyone not falling within subs.(1) who withdraws their labour on any day in furtherance of a trade dispute is not entitled to old style JSA for the week which includes that day. It fills a gap in the test in subs.(1)(a) because it 1.176

does not require any stoppage of work to have occurred; nor does it require the trade dispute to be at the claimant's place of employment. As long as the withdrawal of labour is in furtherance of a trade dispute, the preclusion operates. It could require the authorities to draw a distinction between a "withdrawal of labour" and a "lock-out" (*Ogus, Barendt and Wikeley*, p.141), risking an opinion on the merits of the dispute.

Effect on other claimants

1.177 **15.**—(1) Except in prescribed circumstances, subsection (2) applies in relation to a claimant for an income-based jobseeker's allowance where a member of his family ("A") is, or would be, prevented by section 14 from being entitled to a jobseeker's allowance.

(2) For the purposes of calculating the claimant's entitlement to an income based jobseeker's allowance—

(a) any portion of the applicable amount which is included in respect of A shall be disregarded for the period for which this subsection applies to the claimant;

(b) where the claimant and A are a [2 couple], any portion of the applicable amount which is included in respect of them shall be reduced to one half for the period for which this subsection applies to the claimant;

(c) except so far as regulations provide otherwise, there shall be treated as the claimant's income—

(i) any amount which becomes, or would on an application duly made become, available to A in relation to that period by way of repayment of income tax deducted from A's [1 taxable earnings (as defined by section 10 of the Income Tax (Earnings and Pensions) Act 2003 under PAYE regulations]; and

(ii) any other payment which the claimant or any member of his family receives or is entitled to obtain because A is without employment for that period; and

(d) any payment by way of a jobseeker's allowance for that period or any part of it which apart from this paragraph would be made to the claimant—

(i) shall not be made, if the weekly rate of payment ("the rate") would be equal to or less than the prescribed sum; and

(ii) shall be at a weekly rate equal to the difference between the rate and the prescribed sum, if the rate would be more than the prescribed sum.

(3) Where a reduction under subsection (2)(b) would not produce a sum which is a multiple of 5p, the reduction shall be to the nearest lower sum which is such a multiple.

(4) Where A returns to work with the same employer after a period during which subsection (2) applied to the claimant (whether or not his return is before the end of any stoppage of work in relation to which he is, or would be, prevented from being entitled to a jobseeker's allowance), subsection (2) shall cease to apply to the claimant at the commencement of the day on which A returns to work.

(5) In relation to any period of less than a week, subsection (2) shall have effect subject to such modifications as may be prescribed.

(6) Subsections (7) to (9) apply where an order made under section 150 of the Administration Act (annual up-rating of benefits) has the effect of increasing the sum prescribed in regulations made under section 4(5) as the personal allowance for a single person aged not less than 25 ("the personal allowance").

(7) For the sum prescribed in regulations made under subsection (2)(d) there shall be substituted, from the time when the order comes into force, a sum arrived at by increasing the prescribed sum by the percentage by which the personal allowance has been increased by the order.

(8) If the sum arrived at under subsection (7), is not a multiple of 50p—

(a) any remainder of 25p or less shall be disregarded;

(b) any remainder of more than 25p shall be rounded up to the nearest 50p.

(9) The order shall state the sum substituted for the sum prescribed in regulations made under subsection (2)(d).

(10) Nothing in subsection (7) prevents the making of further regulations under subsection (2)(d) varying the prescribed sum.

AMENDMENTS

1. Income Tax (Earnings and Pensions) Act 2003 Sch.6 Pt 2 para.229 (April 6, 2003).

2. Civil Partnership Act 2004 s.254 and Sch.24 para.120 (December 5, 2005).

DEFINITIONS

"applicable amount"—see s.35(1).
"the Administration Act"—*ibid.*
"claimant"—*ibid.*
"couple"—*ibid.*
"employment"—*ibid.* and JSA Regulations 1996 regs 3 and 4.
"family"—see s.35(1).
"income-based jobseeker's allowance"—*ibid.*, and s.1(4).
"prescribed"—see s.35(1).

GENERAL NOTE

Subsection (1)

This provision applies where the partner of an income-based JSA claimant is involved in a trade dispute. Although subs.(1) refers to a member of the claimant's family, the effect of reg.171(b)(i) of the JSA Regulations 1996 is that subs.(2) can only apply to the claimant's partner. Note that benefit will not be affected if the claimant's partner is incapable of work or within the "maternity period" (six weeks before and seven weeks after confinement) (reg.171(b)(ii)), or has limited capability for work (reg.171(b)(iii)). If the *claimant* is involved in a trade dispute see s.14. **1.178**

Note also reg.52(2) of the JSA Regulations 1996, which treats a partner as in remunerative work for seven days beginning on the first day of the stoppage of work or the first day on which the partner withdrew his labour if the claimant was not entitled to income-based JSA when the partner became involved in the dispute. The result is to disentitle the claimant for those days (s.3(1)(e)). The partner is not treated as in remunerative work outside this period (reg.53(g)).

Subsection (2)

This follows the rules for income support in s.126(3)(c) and (5) of the Contributions and Benefits Act 1992. See the notes to s.126. The basic principle is that where the claimant's partner is involved in a trade dispute, no benefit is payable in respect of him (paras (a) and (b)). The "prescribed sum" for the purposes of para.(d) is £40.50 from April 6, 2015 (reg.172 of the JSA Regulations). This sum was not up-rated in April 2016. **1.179**

Subsection (4)

1.180 Subsection (2) ceases to apply from the day the claimant's partner returns to work.

New style JSA

1.181 Note that in those cases and areas where universal credit has come into force, income-based JSA is abolished and replaced by new style JSA (which is contribution-based only). See Pt VI of this book for the legislation relating to new style JSA and for the cases and areas to which it applies.

[[1]Trade disputes: joint-claim couples

1.182 **15A.**—(1) Sections 14 and 15 shall, in relation to a joint-claim couple claiming a joint-claim jobseeker's allowance, apply in accordance with this section.

(2) Where each member of the couple is prevented by section 14 from being entitled to a jobseeker's allowance, the couple are not entitled to a joint-claim jobseeker's allowance.

(3) But where only one member of the couple is prevented by that section from being entitled to a jobseeker's allowance, the couple are not for that reason alone prevented from being entitled to a joint-claim jobseeker's allowance.

(4) Section 15(1) does not have effect in relation to the couple but, except in prescribed circumstances, section 15(2) applies for the purposes of calculating the couple's entitlement to a joint-claim jobseeker's allowance where—

(a) a member of the couple, [[3] . . .]

(b) [[3] . . .]

is, or would be, prevented by section 14 from being entitled to a jobseeker's allowance.

(5) Where section 15(2) applies in relation to the couple by virtue of subsection (4) above, that provision and section 15(4) apply with the following modifications—

(a) references to the claimant are to be taken as references to the couple;

(b) references to "A" are to the person mentioned in subsection (4)(a) or (b) above;

(c) [[3] . . .] and

(d) section 15(2)(c)(ii) has effect as if for "of his family" there were substituted "of any family of which the couple are members".]

AMENDMENTS

1. Welfare Reform and Pensions Act 1999 s.59 and Sch.7 para.10 (March 19, 2001).
2. Civil Partnership Act 2004 s.254 and Sch.24 para.121 (December 5, 2005).
3. Welfare Reform Act 2012 s.147 and Sch.14 Pt 2 (May 8, 2012).

DEFINITIONS

"claimant"—see s.35(1).
"couple"—*ibid.*
"family"—*ibid.*
"joint-claim couple"—see s.1(4).
"joint-claim jobseeker's allowance"—*ibid.*

General Note

This applies the rules in ss.14 and 15 (subject to minor modifications, see subss. (4) and (5)) to joint-claim couples (i.e. since February 25, 2008, all childless couples (unless they are exempt), see reg.3A of the JSA Regulations 1996). **1.183**

New style JSA

Note that in those cases and areas where universal credit has come into force, income-based JSA is abolished and replaced by new style JSA (which is contribution-based only). See Pt VI of this book for the legislation relating to new style JSA and for the cases and areas to which it applies. **1.184**

Persons under 18

Severe hardship

16.—(1) If it appears to the Secretary of State— **1.185**

(a) that a person—
 (i) has reached the age of 16 but not the age of 18;
 (ii) is not entitled to a jobseeker's allowance or to income support; and
 (iii) is registered for training but is not being provided with any training; and
(b) that severe hardship will result to him unless a jobseeker's allowance is paid to him,

the Secretary of State may direct that this section is to apply to him.

(2) A direction may be given so as to have effect for a specified period.

(3) The Secretary of State may revoke a direction if—

(a) it appears to him that there has been a change of circumstances as a result of which failure to receive a jobseeker's allowance need no longer result in severe hardship to the person concerned;
[1(b) it appears to him that the person concerned has, without [2 a good reason]—
 (i) neglected to avail himself of a reasonable opportunity of a place on a training scheme; or
 (ii) after a place on such a scheme has been notified to him by an employment officer as vacant or about to become vacant, refused or failed to apply for it or to accept it when offered to him; or]
(c) he is satisfied that it was given in ignorance of some material fact or was based on a mistake as to some material fact and considers that, but for that ignorance or mistake, he would not have given the direction.

[1(4) In this section—

"employment officer" means an officer of the Secretary of State or such other person as may be designated for the purposes of this section by an order made by the Secretary of State;

"period" includes—
 (a) a period of a determinate length;
 (b) a period defined by reference to the happening of a future event; and
 (c) a period of a determinate length but subject to earlier determination upon the happening of a future event;

"training scheme" has such meaning as may be prescribed.]

AMENDMENTS

1. Social Security Act 1998 s.86(1) and Sch.7 para.139 (October 18, 1999).
2. Welfare Reform Act 2012 s.48 and Sch.7 para.3 (October 22, 2012).

DEFINITION

"training"—see s.35(1) and JSA Regulation 1996 reg.57(1).

GENERAL NOTE

Subsections (1) and (2)

1.186 This provision is similar to the former s.125 of the Contributions and Benefits Act (revoked on October 7, 1996), which dealt with income support severe hardship directions.

Subsection (1) requires that the person under 18 is not entitled to income support or JSA, so the person must fall outside the categories covered in regs 59–61 of the JSA Regulations and not be eligible for income support under reg.4ZA of and Sch.1B to the Income Support Regulations. (He must also not be entitled to contribution-based JSA, but this is very unlikely in the case of a person under 18.) The other main conditions are that the person is registered for, but not receiving, training and that severe hardship will (not may) result if JSA is not paid. The question of whether these conditions are satisfied is for the Secretary of State, and even if they are, there is a discretion whether or not to allow benefit. There is no right of appeal to an appeal tribunal from the Secretary of State's decision.

To claim JSA on the grounds of severe hardship, the person should first register for work and training with the Careers Service where he will be given an ES9 referral form to take to the JobCentre (but see reg.62 of the JSA Regulations for the exceptions to this rule). Staff are instructed that all 16- and 17-year-old claimants should be allowed to make an application for JSA and should not be turned away by the JobCentre. An initial check will be made to see if the young person is eligible for JSA as of right (see regs 59–61 of the JSA Regulations). If not, and the application on the grounds of severe hardship fails at this stage, it will automatically be referred to the Severe Hardship Claims Unit for consideration. The Employment Service has produced detailed guidance on JSA for 16- and 17-year-olds (*Employment Service Guidance, JSA for 16 and 17 year olds*). Chapter 7, which deals with the severe hardship interview, states that the young person should be informed of the need to contact parents, whether or not the young person is living with them, or a third party, in order to verify the information he or she has given. The young person's consent to do this is required, but refusal of permission without good reason may mean that there will not be enough evidence on which to make a direction (although all such potential "nil" decisions still have to go to the Severe Hardship Claims Unit). At the same time no "undue pressure" is to be placed on the young person to give permission. This could be difficult to implement in practice. However, the guidance also states (more flexibly) that evidence from a responsible third party (e.g. a relative, social worker or voluntary worker), either in person, by telephone or in writing, may mean that contact with the young person's parents is not necessary.

1.187 A direction may be made for a definite period (subs.(2)) (usually eight weeks, but this can be varied according to the circumstances). It can be renewed and it may be revoked if any of the conditions in subs.(3) apply. If a direction is made the decision-maker must consider all the other conditions of entitlement.

Note that the three-day waiting period for JSA does not apply if a s.16 direction has been made (reg.46(1) of the JSA Regulations).

Subsection (3)

1.188 Once a direction is made under this section the claimant satisfies s.3(1)(f) (iii). If the claimant ceases to satisfy the other conditions of entitlement, entitlement will cease. The Secretary of State has a general discretion to revoke a direction whenever there is a change of circumstances, which means that severe hardship no longer need follow from non-payment of JSA (para.(a)). This emphasises the strictness of the test under subs.(1). If severe hardship will not definitely follow from the non-payment of JSA subs.(1) cannot operate. It appears that the revocation of the direction may be retrospective from the date of the change of circumstances, and, if there was a failure to disclose facts constituting the change, the overpayment is recoverable under s.71A of the Administration Act. A direction may also be revoked if it was originally given in ignorance of or under a mistake as to a material fact that would have altered the decision on the inevitability of severe hardship (para.(c)). If there was misrepresentation of or failure to disclose that material fact, recovery under s.71A may arise.

In addition, para.(b) allows for revocation of a direction where the person has failed to pursue or refused a training opportunity without good cause ("good cause" for these purposes is not defined, so the existing case law on its meaning will be relevant).

Note that in such a case the sanctions provided for in s.19(5) do not apply (s.20(2)). The young person's "offence" will be dealt with by revocation of the direction, if this is considered appropriate, or by reduction of his JSA under reg.63(1)(b), if this applies. If a direction is revoked the young person can apply for another severe hardship direction to be made but it seems that it will be subject to a 40 per cent reduction (20 per cent if the young person is pregnant or seriously ill) of the appropriate personal allowance under para.1 of Sch.1 to the JSA Regulations for the first two weeks (s.17(3)(a) and reg.63(1)(a)). See the notes to s.17 and reg.63.

Note that the sanctions in s.19(5) also do not apply if a young person who is the subject of a severe hardship direction commits the lesser "misdemeanour" of failing to complete a training course without good cause (s.20(2)). Instead his JSA will be reduced in accordance with s.17 and reg.63 of the JSA Regulations, if applicable. But note that the sanctions in s.19(6) do apply.

New style JSA

Note that in those cases and areas where universal credit has come into force, income-based JSA is abolished and replaced by new style JSA (which is contribution-based only). See Pt VI of this book for the legislation relating to new style JSA and for the cases and areas to which it applies. **1.189**

Reduced payments

17.—(1) Regulations may provide for the amount of an income-based jobseeker's allowance [3 payable in respect of] any young person to whom this section applies to be reduced— **1.190**

(a) in such circumstances;
(b) by such a percentage; and
(c) for such a period.

as may be prescribed.

[2(1A) Regulations may provide for the amount of a joint-claim job-seeker's allowance payable in respect of any joint-claim couple where a member of the couple is a young person to whom this section applies to be reduced—

(a) in such circumstances;
(b) by such a percentage; and
(c) for such a period,

as may be prescribed.]

(2) This section applies to any young person in respect of whom—

(a) a direction is in force under section 16; and
(b) [1 any] of the conditions mentioned in subsection (3) is satisfied.

(3) The conditions are that—

(a) the young person was previously entitled to an income-based jobseeker's allowance and that entitlement ceased by virtue of the revocation of a direction under section 16;

[1(b) he has given up a place on a training scheme, or failed to attend such a scheme on which he has been given a place, and no certificate has been issued to him under subsection (4);

(c) he has lost his place on such a scheme through misconduct.

(4) Where a young person who has given up a place on a training scheme, or failed to attend such a scheme on which he has been given a place—

(a) claims that there was [4 a good reason] for his doing so; and

(b) applies to the Secretary of State for a certificate under this subsection,

the Secretary of State shall, if he is satisfied that there was good cause, issue a certificate to that effect and give a copy of it to the young person.

(5) In this section—

"training scheme" has such meaning as may be prescribed;

"young person" means a person who has reached the age of 16 but not the age of 18.]

AMENDMENTS

1. Social Security Act 1998 s.86(1) and Sch.7 para.140 (October 18, 1999).

2. Welfare Reform and Pensions Act 1999 s.70 and Sch.8 para.29 (November 11, 1999).

3. Welfare Reform and Pensions Act 1999 Sch.7 para.11 (March 19, 2001).

4. Welfare Reform Act 2012 s.48 and Sch.7 para.3 (October 22, 2012).

GENERAL NOTE

1.191 Under this section regulations can provide for JSA that is being paid because a severe hardship direction is in force to be paid at a reduced rate. See reg.63 of the JSA Regulations that has been made under this section. Note that although subs.(3)(a) refers to revocation of a s.16 direction generally, it is only where a direction has been revoked under s.16(3)(b) that a reduction will be applied under reg.63 (see reg.63(1)(a)).

Note the escape-route in para.(4) whereby the Secretary of State can decide that the young person had a good reason for failing to complete the training and issue a certificate to that effect. A decision as to whether or not to issue such a certificate is one against which there is no right of appeal (para.1(b) of Sch.2 to the Social Security Act 1998). See reg.7(24) of the Decisions and Appeals Regulations in relation to supersessions where a sanction has been imposed under reg.63 of the JSA Regulations but the Secretary of State then issues a certificate under s.17(4).

Note also that if a young person who is the subject of a severe hardship direction fails to pursue or refuses a training opportunity without a good reason (so that the direction is liable to be revoked under s.16(3)(b)), or fails to complete a training course without a good reason, or loses his place through misconduct, the sanctions provided for in s.19(5) do not apply (s.20(2)). The young person's "offence" will be dealt with under s.16, or this section and reg.63 of the JSA Regulations, as appropriate. See the notes to reg.63.

New style JSA

1.192 Note that in those cases and areas where universal credit has come into force, income-based JSA is abolished and replaced by new style JSA (which is contribution-based only). See Pt VI of this book for the legislation relating to new style JSA and for the cases and areas to which it applies.

[1 "Work for your benefit" schemes etc.

Schemes for assisting persons to obtain employment: "work for your benefit" schemes etc.

17A.—(1) Regulations may make provision for or in connection with imposing on claimants in prescribed circumstances a requirement to participate in schemes of any prescribed description that are designed to assist them to obtain employment. 1.193

(2) Regulations under this section may, in particular, require participants to undertake work, or work-related activity, during any prescribed period with a view to improving their prospects of obtaining employment.

(3) In subsection (2) "work-related activity", in relation to any person, means activity which makes it more likely that the person will obtain or remain in work or be able to do so.

(4) Regulations under this section may not require a person to participate in a scheme unless the person would (apart from the regulations) be required to meet the jobseeking conditions.

(5) Regulations under this section may, in particular, make provision—

(a) for notifying participants of the requirement to participate in a scheme within subsection (1);

(b) for securing that participants are not required to meet the jobseeking conditions or are not required to meet such of those conditions as are specified in the regulations;

(c) for suspending any jobseeker's agreement to which a person is a party for any period during which the person is a participant;

(d) [2 *Repealed.*]

(e) [2 *Repealed.*]

(f) [2 *Repealed.*]

(6) [2 *Repealed.*]

(7) [2 *Repealed.*]

(8) [2 *Repealed.*]

(9) [2 *Repealed.*]

(10) In this section—

"claimant", in relation to a joint- claim couple claiming a joint- claim jobseeker's allowance, means either or both of the members of the couple;

"the jobseeking conditions" means the conditions set out in section 1(2) (a) to (c);

"participant", in relation to any time, means any person who is required at that time to participate in a scheme within subsection (1).]

AMENDMENTS

1. Welfare Reform Act 2009 s.1 (November 12, 2009).
2. Welfare Reform Act 2012 s.147 Sch.14 Pt 3 (October 22, 2012).

GENERAL NOTE

This provision enables the Secretary of State to make regulations requiring claimants to participate in schemes that are designed to assist them to obtain employment, including requiring them to undertake work or work-related activity (activity which would make it more likely that the participant will obtain or 1.194

remain in work or be able to do so) as part of a "work for your benefit" scheme. Section 20E(3)(a) and (4) allows regulations to provide for any functions of the Secretary of State under regulations under s.17A to be contracted out to any person.

Under the penalty provisions originally in s.17A, benefit was not payable for a period of between one and 26 weeks where a claimant failed without good cause to comply with regulations. Those were replaced with effect from October 22, 2012 by the possibility of a sanction under ss.19 or 19A. A failure without a good reason to participate in a scheme under s.17A(1) can attract a higher-level sanction under s.19(2)(e) but only if the scheme is prescribed for the purposes of s.19. The only scheme so prescribed (in reg.70B of the JSA Regulations 1996) is Mandatory Work Activity (see the MWAS Regulations, below). The relevant potential sanction for other schemes is therefore that under s.19A(2)(b) for failing without a good reason to comply with regulations under s.17A, which requires sanctions of fixed periods of four and 13 weeks for first and second "offences" within a year (see reg.69A of the JSA Regulations 1996).

Section 17A schemes were piloted in limited geographical areas from 2010, to assess their effectiveness (Jobseeker's Allowance (Work for Your Benefit Pilot Scheme) Regulations 2010 (SI 2010/1222), originally operative for three years from November 22, 2010 but revoked on March 1, 2012).

1.195 The other regulations, mainly without geographical limit, made under s.17A are:

- the Jobseeker's Allowance (Mandatory Work Activity Scheme) Regulations 2011 (SI 2011/688) ("the MWAS Regulations");
- the Jobseeker's Allowance (Employment, Skills and Enterprise Scheme) Regulations 2011 (SI 2011/917) ("the ESES Regulations");
- the Jobseeker's Allowance (Schemes for Assisting Persons to Obtain Employment) Regulations 2013 (SI 2013/276) ("the SAPOE Regulations");
- the Jobseeker's Allowance (Supervised Jobsearch Pilot Scheme) Regulations 2014 (SI 2014/1913) (which expired after April 29, 2015 and are not included in Part III below, only in the Supplement to the 2014/15 edition); and
- the Jobseeker's Allowance (18–21 Work Skills Pilot Scheme) Regulations 2014 (SI 2014/3117) (not included in Part III as only operating in limited areas but set out in the Supplement to the 2014/15 edition).

The Jobseekers (Back to Work Schemes) Act 2013 validated retrospectively the ESES Regulations that had been declared ultra vires by the Court of Appeal in *R (Reilly and Wilson) v Secretary of State for Work and Pensions* [2013] EWCA Civ 66; [2013] 1 W.L.R. 2239 on the ground that the regulations failed to describe, rather than merely name, the schemes they purported to bring within s.17A. The Act was passed on the day on which the Secretary of State sought permission to appeal to the Supreme Court. On the day of the Court of Appeal's judgment (February 12, 2013) the ESES Regulations were replaced by the SAPOE Regulations, which set out the details of the schemes that had been named in the ESES Regulations. See the notes to the 2013 Act for discussion of the effect of the decision of the Supreme Court in *Reilly and Wilson* and of the decision of the three-judge panel of the Upper Tribunal in *SSWP v TJ (JSA)* [2015] UKUT 56 (AAC).

The 2013 Act also provided that notices given for the purposes of the ESES Regulations were to be treated as having complied with regs 4(2)(c) and (e) (details of requirements to participate and information about consequences of failure to participate) if fairly minimal conditions were satisfied.

1.196 In *R (Reilly No 2 and Hewstone) v Secretary of State for Work and Pensions* [2014] EWHC 2182 (Admin) Lang J granted a declaration that the 2013 Act was incompatible with art.6 of the ECHR in that its retrospective effect meant that it interfered with the claimants' right to a fair trial. That decision was confirmed by the Court of Appeal in *SSWP v Reilly and Hewstone* and *SSWP v Jeffrey and Bevan* [2016] EWCA Civ 413. See the introductory notes to the 2013 Act for a full discussion.

The 2013 Act also sought to protect the operation of the MWAS Regulations from challenge on the basis that notices given to claimants under reg.4 were invalid in the same way as notices under reg.4 of the ESES Regulations in *Reilly and Wilson*, on which now see the decision of the Supreme Court ([2013] UKSC 68; [2013] 1 A.C. 453). However, the 2013 Act gave no protection to the MWAS Regulations against a vires challenge on the same grounds as in *Reilly and Wilson*. Such a challenge was rejected by Hickinbottom J in *R (Smith) v Secretary of State for Work and Pensions* [2014] EWHC 843 (Admin). He held that there was sufficient description of the scheme to meet the standard required by the Supreme Court. The reasons included that the prescription of the period of the scheme was relevant to its description under s.17A(1) and was not relevant only to subs.(2). That conclusion and reasoning was in essence endorsed by the Court of Appeal on the claimant's appeal ([2015] EWCA Civ 229).

New style JSA

Note that in those cases and areas where universal credit has come into force, income-based JSA is abolished and replaced by new style JSA (which is contribution-based only). See Pt VI of this book for the legislation relating to new style JSA and for the cases and areas to which it applies. **1.197**

Section 17A: supplemental

17B.—(1) For the purposes of, or in connection with, any scheme within section 17A(1) the Secretary of State may— **1.198**

(a) make arrangements (whether or not with other persons) for the provision of facilities;
(b) provide support (by whatever means) for arrangements made by other persons for the provision of facilities;
(c) make payments (by way of fees, grants, loans or otherwise) to persons undertaking the provision of facilities under arrangements within paragraph (a) or (b);
(d) make payments (by way of grants, loans or otherwise) to persons participating in the scheme;
(e) make payments in respect of incidental expenses.

(2) For the purposes of, or in connection with, any scheme within section 17A(1)—

(a) the Scottish Ministers, and
(b) the Welsh Ministers,

may make payments (by way of fees, grants, loans or otherwise) to persons (including the Secretary of State) undertaking the provision of facilities under arrangements within subsection (1)(a) or (b) if the following condition is met.

(3) The condition is that the Scottish Ministers or the Welsh Ministers consider that the facilities are capable of supporting the training in Scotland or Wales of persons for employment.

(4) Unless the Scottish Ministers or Welsh Ministers otherwise specify, the payments may be used by the person to whom they are made for the provision of any of the facilities provided under the arrangements.

(5) In subsections (1) to (4) "facilities" includes services, and any reference to the provision of facilities includes the making of payments to persons participating in the scheme.

(6) The power of the Secretary of State to make an order under section 26 of the Employment Act 1988 (status of trainees etc) includes power to make, in relation to—

(a) persons participating in any scheme within section 17A(1), and
(b) payments received by them by virtue of subsection (1) above,
provision corresponding to any provision which (by virtue of section 26(1) or (2) of that Act) may be made in relation to persons using such facilities, and to such payments received by them, as are mentioned in section 26(1) of that Act.

AMENDMENT

1. Welfare Reform Act 2009 s.1 (November 12, 2009).

DEFINITION

"person"—see Interpretation Act 1978 Sch.1.

GENERAL NOTE

1.199 This contains provisions supplemental to s.17A which relate to the practical operation of the "work for your benefit" schemes prescribed under that section. This section provides support for any contractual arrangements the Secretary of State may make regarding their delivery (e.g. with a non-governmental organisation, including private-sector companies, or for paying transport costs to participants).

New style JSA

1.200 Note that in those cases and areas where universal credit has come into force, income-based JSA is abolished and replaced by new style JSA (which is contribution-based only). See Pt VI of this book for the legislation relating to new style JSA and for the cases and areas to which it applies.

Persons dependent on drugs etc.

Persons dependent on drugs etc.

1.201 **17C.**—[1 . . .]

AMENDMENT

1. Welfare Reform Act 2012 s.60(1) (May 8, 2012).

Recovery of overpayments

1.202 **18.**—*[Omitted. See s.71A of the Social Security Administration Act 1992 in Vol. III.]*

Denial of jobseeker's allowance

[1Higher-level sanctions

1.203 **19.**— (1) The amount of an award of a jobseeker's allowance is to be reduced in accordance with this section in the event of a failure by the claimant which is sanctionable under this section.

(2) It is a failure sanctionable under this section if a claimant—
(a) through misconduct loses employment as an employed earner;
(b) without a good reason voluntarily leaves such employment;
(c) without a good reason refuses or fails to apply for, or accept if offered, a situation in any employment which an employment officer has informed him is vacant or about to become vacant;

(d) without a good reason neglects to avail himself of a reasonable opportunity of employment;
(e) without a good reason fails to participate in any scheme within section 17A(1) which is prescribed for the purposes of this section.

(3) For the purposes of subsection (2)(b), in such circumstances as may be prescribed, including in particular where a person has been dismissed by his employer by reason of redundancy within the meaning of section 139(1) of the Employment Rights Act 1996 after volunteering or agreeing to be so dismissed, a person who might otherwise be treated as having left his employment voluntarily is to be treated as not having left voluntarily.

(4) Regulations are to provide for—
(a) the amount of a reduction under this section;
(b) the period for which such a reduction has effect, not exceeding three years in relation to any failure sanctionable under this section.

(5) Regulations under subsection (4)(b) may in particular provide for the period of a reduction to depend on either or both of the following—
(a) the number of failures by the claimant sanctionable under this section;
(b) the period between such failures.

(6) Regulations may provide—
(a) for cases in which no reduction is to be made under this section;
(b) for a reduction under this section made in relation to an award that is terminated to be applied to any new award made within a prescribed period of the termination.

(7) During any period for which the amount of a joint-claim jobseeker's allowance is reduced under this section by virtue of a failure by one of the claimants which is sanctionable under this section, the allowance is payable to the other member of the couple.

AMENDMENT

1. Welfare Reform Act 2012 s. 46(1) (October 22, 2012).

DEFINITIONS

"a joint-claim jobseeker's allowance"—see s.1(4).
"claimant"—see s.35(1).
"employed earner"—see s.35(1); JSA Regulations 1996 reg.75(4); SSCBA 1992 s.2(1)(a) and 122(1).
"employment"—see s.35(1); JSA Regulations 1996 reg.75(4).
"employment officer"—see s.35(1).
"prescribed"—*ibid.*
"regulations"—*ibid.*

GENERAL NOTE

Subsection (1)

Since 1911, state benefits for unemployment have contained sanctions in respect of voluntary unemployment whether in terms of conduct bringing about a loss of employment or conducing to the continuance of a claimant's unemployment. In the unemployment benefit regime, the sanction of disqualification from benefit for a period was most recently found in SSCBA 1992. Until the October 2012 changes, the previous version of s.19 afforded sanctions by precluding, for varying periods, payment of JSA to which the claimant was otherwise entitled where the claimant fell within the circumstances covered in either subs.(5) or (6) of that section. 1.204

Subsection (5) provided grounds for precluding payment which were concerned with the claimant's failure to comply with a jobseeker's direction issued by an employment officer or with avoidable loss or refusal of a training scheme or employment programme opportunity. The successor to those grounds is not the new s.19, but the new s.19A, dealing with "other sanctions", examined below.

Subsection (6) of the previous version of s.19, essentially echoing the "heads" of disqualification from UB in SSCBA 1992 s.28(1)(a)–(c), provided grounds for precluding payment of JSA which were concerned with the avoidable loss or refusal of employment (e.g. loss of a job through misconduct; voluntarily leaving a job without just cause, etc.). This is the ancestor of this "new" s.19 which deals with the imposition of "higher-level sanctions" (drastic reduction of old style JSA for much longer periods than before) in respect of—with one addition—essentially the same conduct bringing about unemployment or conducing to its continuance, now referred to as "a failure by the claimant sanctionable under this section". What constitutes such a failure is set out in subs.(2).

It cannot be stressed enough that "higher-level sanctions" represent a very much more stringent sanctions regime than those previously applicable. The old UB and early JSA disqualification regime was sometimes justified on the basis of the "causal theory", that the basic purpose was "to provide against the misfortune of unemployment happening against a person's will" (*R(U) 20/64*). So claimants should not be compensated for unemployment caused by their own unreasonable conduct. That was said to be supported by the then maximum length of disqualification of six weeks, said to represent the length of unemployment that could fairly be attributed to the claimant's conduct, rather than the state of the labour market. Although the grounds for sanction under s.19 are much the same, the greatly increased periods of denial of benefit mean that the causal theory can no longer hold water. Sanctions cannot be regarded as anything other than a penalty, even though they are designed to encourage responsible behaviour. As such, it was suggested by Judge Wikeley in *DL v SSWP (JSA)* [2013] UKUT 295 that the legislation on sanctions should be construed strictly and that claimants should be given the benefit of any doubt that might reasonably arise.

Subsection (2)

1.205 This sets out the conduct by the claimant ranking as a failure sanctionable under this section (subs.(1)).

1.206 *Paragraph (a): "through misconduct loses employment as an employed earner"*

"Loses employment": this concept is not confined to dismissal, but can also embrace persons claiming benefit while suspended from work for misconduct (*R(U) 10/71*) and the person who accepts the chance to resign rather than be dismissed as a result of his misconduct (*R(U) 2/76*, where the claimant used a company car without permission to give driving lessons and was found at home in the bath when he should have been out selling). In *CU/056/1989*, Commissioner Heggs, dealing with a situation in which the claimant had been allowed to resign rather than be dismissed, noted in para.7:

> "In Decision *R(U) 17/64* it was held that 'loss of employment' is a more comprehensive phrase than 'leaving voluntarily' because loss of employment may result either from voluntarily leaving or from dismissal. In considering whether employment has been lost through misconduct, therefore, it is not always necessary to determine categorically whether the claimant left voluntarily or was dismissed. In the present case the tribunal, in my view, correctly concluded that the claimant lost his employment through misconduct"

The claimant had been allowed to resign rather than be dismissed after he had been caught eating company products (pies) at his workplace in violation of a general prohibition on eating company products in the production area. He had previously violated this rule and been warned about his conduct. He had also received a final written warning that future misconduct would result in his summary dismissal. Unfortunately, the SSAT decision was erroneous in law because it contained no explanation of why the claimant's admitted conduct constituted misconduct.

"As an employed earner": see s.35(1); JSA Regulations 1996 reg.3; SSCBA 1992 s.2(1)(a). The disqualification does not cover misconduct in self-employment. Nor, if the reasoning in *GP v SSWP (JSA)* [2015] UKUT 476 (AAC); [2016] AACR 14, discussed in the notes to s.7(1) above, is correct, does it cover misconduct in employment outside Great Britain, which would include employment in Northern Ireland.

1.207 According to the then Minister of State Esther McVey (House of Commons written answers April 2, 2014), guidance to Jobcentre Plus staff is that if a JSA claimant leaves a zero hours contract there should be no sanction for misconduct or voluntarily ceasing work. However, it is hard to see the legal basis for such guidance. If a claimant was employed (even if under a zero hours contract) and committed an act of misconduct that led to its loss, that would appear to be a sanctionable failure requiring a reduction of benefit in the absence of any legislative exemption.

"Through misconduct": the loss of employment must be brought about because of the claimant's misconduct. The change from "his misconduct" in SSCBA 1992 s.28(1)(a) to merely "misconduct" in para.(a), as in its immediate predecessor (the "old" s.19(6)(a)), cannot, it is submitted, be read so as to justify penalising a claimant who lost his job through someone else's misconduct. Any such reading would be absurd and unjust and contrary to the aim of penalising "voluntary unemployment".

Authorities directly in point because they deal with the situation where there were several reasons for the loss of employment state that misconduct need not be the sole cause of the loss of employment so long as it is a contributory cause, a necessary element in bringing about the loss (*R(U)1/57; R(U)14/57; CU/34/92*). Suggestions that it must be the main cause in order to ground disqualification read too much into *R(U)20/59,* where the Commissioner's statement that misconduct (trouble with the police) was there the main cause seems to be no more than a finding of fact in that particular case in which the multiple cause point was not really an issue. A Northern Ireland authority (*R8/60(UB)*) requiring that misconduct be the decisive cause cannot stand against British authorities directly in point, being of persuasive authority only.

1.208 *The meaning and scope of misconduct.* "Misconduct" is not statutorily defined. Case law offers such definition as there is. The term has to be interpreted in a common-sense manner and applied with due regard to the circumstances of each case (*R(U)24/56; R(U)8/57,* para.6). It is narrower than unsatisfactory conduct (*124/51(UB)*). Misconduct is "conduct which is causally but not necessarily directly connected with the employment, and having regard to the relationship of employer and employee and the rights and duties of both, can fairly be described as blameworthy, reprehensible and wrong" (*R(U)2/77,* para.15). The Commissioner in *R(U)2/77,* para.6, saw nothing wrong with a tribunal's description of it as an indictment of the claimant's character as an employee. A useful test, particularly where the conduct in question occurred away from work, would be: was the claimant's blameworthy, reprehensible or wrong conduct such as would cause a reasonable employer to dispense with his services on the ground that, having regard to this conduct he was not a fit person to hold that appointment (*R(U)7/57,* para.6).

The act or omission alleged to constitute misconduct need not have been deliberate or intentional, although such might often be the case. Misconduct can consist in carelessness or negligence, but there it is necessary to discriminate between that type and degree of carelessness which may have to be put up with in human affairs, and the more deliberate or serious type of carelessness which justifies withholding benefit because the claimant has lost his employment through his own avoidable fault. In *R(U)8/57* the claimant, a manager of a branch pharmacy, was dismissed for "negligence in the discharge of responsible duties" when a number of cash shortages were discovered over a period of weeks. Serious carelessness could legitimately be inferred and his disqualification was upheld, notwithstanding his acquittal on a charge of embezzlement arising out of the same situation. A claimant who acts on a genuine misunderstanding cannot properly be said to be guilty of misconduct; the behaviour cannot there be described as "blameworthy, reprehensible and wrong" (*CU/122/92,* para.6, citing *R(U)14/56*).

Where the conduct grounding the loss of employment might be regarded as whistleblowing (public interest disclosure) the public interest disclosure provisions in the Employment Act 1999 (ss.43A–43L, 47B and 103) should be considered since the question of whether the disclosure was a protected one is relevant to the question of whether the conduct was blameworthy, reprehensible and wrong. Judge Mesher so held in *AA* v *SSWP (JSA)* [2012] UKUT 100 (AAC); [2012] AACR 42 (see especially paras 10–15). There it had been appropriate for the claimant School Manager to refer concerns about the head teacher's expenses claim to the appropriate LEA officer and probably to the school governors. However, the misconduct found by the disciplinary panel and grounding the dismissal (the "loss of employment") was his disclosure to several other employees to whom, under the legislation, it was not reasonable to disclose the matter. So that, while the tribunal had erred in law by not considering the public interest disclosure provisions, that error was not material.

1.209 This "sanctionable failure" was sometimes referred to as "industrial misconduct", a term denoting that the misconduct must be causally connected with the employment the loss of which is under consideration, rather than requiring its connection with a particular type of employment. Misconduct which occurred before the claimant took up the employment, the loss of which is under consideration but which caused its loss, cannot disqualify him: see *R(U)26/56*, where an accountant was dismissed when his employers learned of a conviction for fraud which occurred before he commenced employment with them. In *R(U)26/56, both* the conduct and its consequences (the criminal conviction) occurred before the employment was taken up. *R(U)1/58*, however, also applies the non-preclusion principle where the conduct occurred before the taking-up of the employment, but the consequences came after its commencement. There a civil engineer and buyer was awaiting trial for certain acts committed before he entered the employment. By agreement with his employer he ceased work pending the result of the trial. On conviction he simply did not return to the employment. Nor, however, was he pressed to do so. The Commissioner held that "acts or omissions occurring before the commencement of the employment do not constitute 'misconduct'" (at para.4), citing *R(U)26/56*, so the only matter remaining was the issue of voluntary leaving without just cause. The leaving was not voluntary: "he merely anticipated a decision by his employers to dispense with his services; he was not altogether a free agent when deciding or agreeing not to attend further at his place of business" (at paras 5 and 6). So, to refer to a case of interest notified to the authors, an SSAT was correct in holding that a van driver, dismissed after conviction of a drink-driving offence and disqualification from driving, could not be disqualified from benefit because the conduct constituting the offence had taken place before he took up the employment in question, even though the conviction came after he had done so.

It may perhaps be arguable that the authority discussed in the previous paragraph depended to an extent on an adoption (whether explicit or implicit) of the "causal theory" of UB disqualifications, that the primary object was not to penalise the claimant, but more to discourage avoidable claims against the fund from which benefit was paid. As it was put in *R(U) 20/64*, the "basic purpose of unemployment benefit is to provide against the misfortune of unemployment happening against a person's will." Thus there was a responsibility on a claimant to do what was reasonable to avoid becoming a burden on the fund. The causal theory was in the past bolstered by the limitation of the period of disqualification to a maximum of six weeks, after which time it was said that the primary cause of continued unemployment was the state of the labour market, rather than the claimant's act of misconduct or leaving employment voluntarily or whatever. Now that the sanctions regime gives every appearance of imposing penalties, with enormously more extensive periods of exclusion from benefit possible, it might be argued that it is irrelevant to whether such penalties are deserved or not that the misconduct occurred before the claimant started the employment that was later lost. However, it is submitted that to constitute misconduct an act still has to be "blameworthy" in the context of the employment relationship and that there cannot be blameworthiness in that sense if the person has not yet taken up the employment in question.

Subject to that, the causal connection with the employment need not be direct (*R(U)2/77*, para.15). The conduct need not have taken place at work or in working hours, though cases where it did would be common. In *R(U)1/71* the Commissioner upheld the disqualification of a local authority parks' gardener dismissed for an act of gross indecency with another man, away from work and out of working hours. The Commissioner said:

> "If a person loses his employment by reason of misconduct which has a sufficient connection with the employment it may not matter that it was committed outside the employment. Common examples are those of the man employed as a motor vehicle driver who loses his licence as a result of his driving outside his employment and is disqualified from driving: there is an obvious link between the misconduct and the work. [See, e.g. *R(U)7/57* and *R(U)24/64*.] Similarly a person who commits offences of dishonesty outside his work may be disqualified, since most employers regard a thief as unsuitable to have about their premises. [See, e.g. *R(U)10/53*.]" (Case references added by annotator.)

Sexual offences outside the employment were said to present considerable difficulty but can rank as misconduct in *special circumstances* where they can be said to have something to do with the employment: **1.210**

> "*The commercial traveller case* [*CU38/51*] is a good instance. The employers may well have thought that there was a real danger that when visiting houses trying to sell ribbons, probably to women who might often be alone in the house, the claimant might attempt some sort of liberties."

The Commissioner further opined that:

> "there are some employments where the employer has a legitimate interest in the conduct of employees even outside the employment. One example may be that of a person who holds a special position, e.g. a schoolteacher. Another may be that of a government department who rightly feel that their employees should maintain a high standard of conduct at all times."

In *R(U)1/71* itself, even though there was no evidence of direct contact with the public in the claimant's job, the Commissioner, in a case he thought close to the line, was not prepared to overturn the tribunal's view that the claimant had lost his employment through misconduct.

Examples of misconduct. Apart from those already noted, instances have been: **1.211** persistent absenteeism without permission (*R(U)22/52*, *R(U)8/61*); unauthorised absence through ill health and/or domestic circumstances when coupled with failure to notify the employer (*R(U)23/58*; *R(U)11/59*); repeated unauthorised absence to seek work more suited to the claimant's state of health in circumstances in which the claimant gave the employer no reasons for his absences and he had received previous warning about his conduct (*R(U)8/61*); overstaying a holiday without permission (*R(U)2/74*; *R(U)11/59*). Theft from fellow workers at a works' social function has been held to be misconduct (*R(U)10/53*). So has offensive behaviour to fellow employees, consisting of obscene language and an element of what would now be termed sexual harassment (suggestive remarks to and, in their presence, about female colleagues) (*R(U)12/56*). By analogy, one would today expect racial abuse and discrimination to be capable of constituting misconduct. Recklessly or knowingly making false allegations about superiors or colleagues can be misconduct, and where a false criminal charge is so laid it would plainly be misconduct (*R(U)24/55*, para.13), but it was not enough to prove misconduct to show that the employee's charge of assault by his supervisor had been dismissed in the magistrates' court (*ibid.*). Refusal to obey a reasonable instruction *in line with the claimant's contract of employment* (e.g. a refusal to work overtime) has been held to be misconduct (*R(U)38/58*), even where obeying the instruction would conflict with trade union policies (*R(U)41/53*). However, disobedience of such an order due to a genuine misunderstanding has been held not to constitute misconduct (*R(U)14/56*), and not every breach of every trivial rule would suffice (*R(U)24/56*). And, of course, the claimant can legitimately refuse to obey instructions not contractually stipulated for without its constituting misconduct (*R(U)9/59; R9/60(UB)*). Where an employee was dismissed for refusing to join a trade union as part of a closed-shop arrangement negotiated after his employment commenced, he did not lose his job through misconduct (*R(U)2/77*).

1.212 *Establishing misconduct, matters of proof and the duties of the statutory authorities; decision-makers, First-tier Tribunals and the Upper Tribunal.* The Secretary of State (decision-maker) bears the onus of proof of establishing misconduct, and it must be clearly proved by the best available evidence. As a general rule, of course, hearsay evidence can be accepted by the statutory authorities, but particularly where a claimant is charged with misconduct and he disputes the facts which are alleged to constitute it, "it is desirable that the most direct evidence of those facts should be adduced, so that the allegations may be properly tested" (*R(U)2/60*, para.7).

Given that decision-makers and tribunals have no powers to force employers to supply information or to compel the attendance of witnesses, it may be difficult to get to the truth of the matter. In some cases the statutory authorities may be able to have regard to what has happened in other legal or disciplinary proceedings arising out of the same situation now said to show misconduct. Where such proceedings are pending one option in difficult cases where the available evidence about the relevant conduct conflicts would be to postpone a decision on the "sanctionable failure" issue until the outcome of such proceedings as are pending is known. There is no obligation to await their outcome (*R(U)10/54* and see *AA v SSWP(JSA)* [2011] AACR 42, above), and one must always keep in view the relationship between those proceedings and the tasks of the tribunals dealing with old style JSA issues.

Another option would be to try to resolve the matter by weighing and comparing the evidence available (e.g. does the tribunal believe the direct evidence given by the claimant it has seen and questioned and how does that compare with the indirect and/or hearsay evidence in any written material from the employer or others which is relied on by the decision-maker) and ultimately, where doubts persist, allow the matter to be settled by application of the rules on onus of proof. It would presumably be open to the decision-maker to revise or supersede the tribunal's decision if new material facts came to light in the course of those other proceedings. The other legal proceedings could be criminal proceedings, court proceedings for breach of contract, or complaints of unfair dismissal heard in industrial tribunals. Disciplinary proceedings may take place before a much wider variety of bodies. An important issue is what is the relationship to the decision-making task of the JSA decision-makers and tribunals, of decisions given by these other bodies on a matter relevant to the claimant's case?

1.213 While in varying degrees decisions given by such bodies certainly can constitute relevant evidence for the statutory authorities, they are not, legally speaking, conclusive of the outcome before the JSA authorities, who are duty bound to make up their own minds as to what constitutes misconduct grounding reduction of benefit, irrespective of the conclusions reached by employers, the courts or disciplinary bodies (*R(U)10/54*, para.6; *R(U)2/74*, para.15). The other proceedings do not deal with the exact issue dealt with by the JSA decision-makers and tribunals. For example, a motoring conviction as a private motorist which did not attract a ban from driving would not necessarily constitute misconduct warranting the disqualification of a lorry-driver who had been sacked by his employer as a result. It would depend on the nature of the conduct constituting the offence: the claimant might be able to show that notwithstanding the conviction his conduct was not "blameworthy" (*R(U)22/64,* para.6). It must be remembered too that the standard of proof of guilt in criminal cases is proof beyond reasonable doubt, a higher standard than that applicable here—proof on the balance of probabilities. So an acquittal on a criminal charge arising out of the conduct now said to constitute misconduct does not necessarily preclude a finding of misconduct. Thus in *R(U)8/57*, where the manager of the branch pharmacy was acquitted of embezzlement in relation to the cash shortages, he nonetheless lost his employment through misconduct since his inadequate supervision of staff amounted to serious carelessness. Similarly, there are important differences between proceedings before First-tier Tribunals on the one hand, and unfair dismissal proceedings in the employment tribunal on the other. In unfair dismissal, while the employee's conduct is relevant, the main issue before the employment tribunal concerns the employer's behaviour in consequence. Before the tribunals dealing with JSA, in contrast, the emphasis is more on the employee's conduct, although that of the employer is also relevant. The issue of loss of employment through misconduct raises issues of what is fair between claimant and the other contributors to the insurance fund and not what is fair as between employer and employee. Commissioners stressed that social security tribunals when dealing with misconduct cases should not express their decisions in such terms as fair or unfair dismissal or proper or improper dismissal. The onus of proof in employment tribunal proceedings may not be the same on issues relevant to the JSA tribunals' task as they are in proceedings before those JSA tribunals. Equally, while the issue before the JSA tribunals is one of substance, the employment tribunal can find a dismissal unfair on procedural grounds. Hence, while the decision of the employment tribunal is conclusive of the matters it had to decide, it does not conclude anything in proceedings before the JSA decision-makers and tribunals authorities, and its findings of fact are not binding on them, even where some of the facts before the employment tribunals are identical with facts relevant to the JSA proceedings:

> "There will, therefore, be cases where a claimant succeeds before an [employment] tribunal on the unfair dismissal question, but the relevant adjudicating authority has decided that disqualification [from benefit] must be imposed by reason of misconduct, and *vice versa*" (per Commissioner Rice in *CU/90/1988,* para.4).

The findings of fact in the employment tribunal are, however, cogent evidence on which JSA decision-makers and tribunals can act (*CU/17/1993*), since it may well be that with both employer and employee present and examined the employment tribunal, a judicial authority presided over by a lawyer, reaching its deliberate findings of fact after due inquiry, is better placed than the JSA decision-makers and tribunals to fully investigate the facts of the matter. But the JSA decision-makers and tribunals are not bound to decide the facts in the same way as the employment tribunal (*R(U)2/74,* paras 14 and 15 and see generally on the relationship between the two sets of proceedings: *R(U)4/78* and *R(U)3/79*).

For similar reasons of ability to obtain and to probe evidence, decisions of the criminal courts on matters relevant to the case before the JSA decision-makers and tribunals are entitled to great respect. Thus where it is clear that a criminal court has decided the identical issue which the claimant needs to reopen before the judicial authorities (First-tier or Upper Tribunal) in order to succeed in his appeal, the decision of that court is likely *in practice* to be dispositive of the issue before those authorities. This is almost certainly so if one follows the view of the Commissioner in *R(U)24/55* that in such a situation, save in exceptional cases, the statutory authorities must treat a conviction by a criminal court as conclusive proof that the act or omission which constitutes the offence was done or made. It is also likely to be so if one prefers to *R(U)24/55* the later view of a Commissioner in a sickness benefit case dealing with a similar issue (*R(S)2/80*). Now see the helpful discussion, not necessary to the decision, in *KL v SSWP (DLA)* [2015] UKUT 222 (AAC), an overpayment recoverability case, of the case law on when it would be found to be an abuse of process for a claimant to seek to argue before a tribunal a point decided against him in the criminal proceedings. It has always been for the person relying on it to prove the fact of a conviction, and it is preferably done through official certification (*R(U)24/64*). In *R(S)2/80* it was said that the initial onus was on the adjudication officer [now Secretary of State/decision-maker] to show that the conviction directly related to points at issue in the appeal, and if that were done the onus passed to the claimant to show on the balance of probabilities that he was nevertheless entitled to the benefit; that is, by analogy in this context, that he did not lose his job through misconduct (e.g. by showing that the true facts were not as found by the court or, if they were, that they do not constitute misconduct).

1.214 Where the decisions of disciplinary bodies (which may well examine a wide range of witnesses) are concerned, it appears that although never binding on the JSA decision-makers and tribunals, they are entitled to an increasing degree of respect the more their proceedings approximate to proceedings in a court of law. Thus a finding by a chief constable after police disciplinary proceedings was cogent evidence that the claimant had committed particular acts (*R(U)10/63*), but a decision by a hospital management committee, the precise reasons for which were not disclosed to the Commissioner, was not so regarded (*R(U)7/61*).

Whether one is concerned with decisions of the courts, of employment tribunals or disciplinary proceedings it is submitted that crucial questions for the JSA decision-makers and tribunals will be: what was the decision; by what sort of body, how, by what process, and on what sort(s) of evidence was the decision made; and how closely does the matter involved in that decision relate to that before the JSA decision-makers and tribunals?

1.215 *Paragraph (b): "without a good reason voluntarily leaves such employment"*

Note at the outset that s.20(3) and JSA Regulations 1996 reg.74 made under it protect from sanction under this head or under that in subs.(2)(d) certain persons who leave employed earner's employment voluntarily and without good reason at any time within the "trial period" (that is, between the beginning of the fifth week and the end of the twelfth week of the employment in question, with some provision to ignore certain weeks). The approach to such cases must be first to consider, in the light of the case law principles elaborated below, whether the claimant voluntarily left without a good reason and, if he did so, then to consider whether s.20(3) and JSA Regulations 1996 reg.74 protect him from preclusion of payment of JSA.

In *CJSA/3304/1999*, Commissioner Levenson considered the case of someone who had left employment A for unspecified reasons, then found employment with employer B, from which he was dismissed, and only then claimed JSA. The tribunal allowed the claimant's appeal against preclusion of payment founded on his having voluntarily left employment A without just cause. Commissioner Levenson upheld the tribunal. A preclusion of payment can only be made where a claim for benefit has been made and only "in respect of the employment immediately preceding the claim" (at para.16). Insofar as *R(U)13/64* might be thought to say otherwise, Commissioner Levenson, drawing support from Commissioner Goodman in para.9 of *CU/64/1994*, declined to follow it.

"*Such employment*". The restriction ("such" referring back to para.(a)) to employed earners' employment means that leaving self-employment cannot ground disqualification under this head. Nor, if the reasoning in *GP v SSWP (JSA)* [2015] UKUT 476 (AAC); [2016] AACR 14, discussed in the notes to s.7(1) above, is correct, can it be grounded by leaving employment outside Great Britain, thus including employment in Northern Ireland.

According to the then Minister of State Esther McVey (House of Commons written answers April 2, 2014), guidance to Jobcentre Plus staff is that if a JSA claimant leaves a zero hours contract there should be no sanction for misconduct or voluntarily ceasing work. However, it is hard to see the legal basis for such guidance. Ceasing such employment would appear to bring the legislation into play, although the terms of the contract might contribute to a good reason for ceasing the employment.

Onus of proof. Those who assert that the claimant left his employment voluntarily must prove it. Once done the onus passes to the claimant to prove that he had "a good reason" for so leaving. In both cases the onus is discharged on the balance of probabilities (*R(U)20/64(T)*). See further, below. 1.216

"Voluntarily leaves": The commonest case of voluntarily leaving will be when the claimant of his own accord handed in his notice or otherwise terminated his contract of employment. Indeed, in many cases there will be no dispute about this aspect of the case; the real issue will be that of 'good reason'. But voluntarily leaving also embraces other means by which employment was lost. So the actors who threatened to leave unless certain demands were met and were then treated by their employers as having given notice left voluntarily (*R(U)33/51*). It is still voluntarily leaving where the employment ends because the employer refuses to accept the claimant's withdrawal of notice (*R(U)27/59*). It can also embrace in limited instances cases where the loss of employment took the form of a dismissal brought about by conduct of the claimant which would inevitably lead to termination of the employment (*R(U)16/52; R(U)2/54, R(U)9/59, R(U)7/74*), but such situations must be looked at with caution and restraint (*R(U)2/77*). Thus, in *R(U)6/52* the claimant's appointment was conditional on her completing a satisfactory medical. She refused to undergo X-ray examination and was given notice. The Commissioner stated as a general rule of unemployment insurance law that if a person deliberately and knowingly acts in a way that makes it necessary for his employer to dismiss him, he may be regarded as having left his employment voluntarily. But another Commissioner later made clear in *R(U)7/74* that "this would normally require a finding that the employee had acted, or was threatening to act, in a manner involving a deliberate repudiation of his contract of employment". So in that case an employee whose written terms of employment made no reference to a requirement to work overtime, did not leave voluntarily when he was dismissed for refusing to work overtime (cf. *R(U)9/59*). Similarly, dismissal of an existing employee for refusal to join a trade union when a closed shop agreement was negotiated was not voluntary leaving (*R(U)2/77*). Nor was dismissal for refusing for good reason to pay a trade union subscription (*R(U)4/51*). Leaving was not voluntary where the claimant who departed had no effective choice but to quit, e.g. because dismissal appeared inevitable (*R(U)1/58:* cf. *R(U)2/76*). In *R(U)1/96*, Commissioner Goodman considered the case of a female nursery assistant who gave her employer four weeks' notice, was prepared to work out those weeks, but whose employer, after an unsuccessful attempt to persuade her to stay on, told her to leave after two days. The Commissioner considered and applied *CU/155/50* and *R(U)2/54* so as to reject the argument that the claimant had not left voluntarily but had been dismissed (and could therefore only be disqualified if misconduct could be proved). He regarded *British Midland Airways v Lewis* [1978] I.C.R. 782 (a decision of the Employment Appeal Tribunal in the context of dismissal under labour legislation) as not laying down "any categorical proposition of law" but as merely being a decision on the facts of that case, and continued: 1.217

> "In my view the ruling in *CU/155/50* and *R(U)2/54* that there is a voluntary leaving applies equally, whether it is a case of an employer not allowing an employee to work out his or her notice or whether it is a case of actual notice to leave given first by the employee, followed by a notice of termination given during the currency of the employee's notice by the employer. In the latter case, once the employee has given in his notice to leave it is a unilateral termination of the employment contract and cannot be withdrawn without the consent of the employer (*Riordan v War Office* [1959] 1 W.L.R. 1046). It follows that in the present case, when the claimant gave her four weeks notice in on Wednesday December 9, 1992 she had

herself terminated the employment and thereby left it voluntarily. Even if what the employer did on Friday December 11, 1992 can be construed as giving in a counter-notice requiring her to leave on that day and not to work out her four weeks notice, that does not, in my view, alter the fact that the effective termination of the employment was a voluntary leaving by the claimant." (At para.12.)

1.218 *Taking early retirement* can constitute voluntarily leaving (*R(U)26/51*, *R(U)20/64*, *R(U)4/70*, *R(U)1/81*). Even where a schoolteacher retired three years early in response to the generalised encouragement to take early retirement offered to teachers in his position by his local education authority, which further certified that his retirement was in the interests of the efficient discharge of the education authority's functions, it was still voluntarily leaving (*Crewe v Social Security Commissioner* [1982] 2 All E.R. 745 CA, published as an Appendix to *R(U)3/81*). However, in *R(U)1/83* the Commissioner distinguished *Crewe* and held that a civil servant who acceded to his employer's specific request that *he* retire early should not be regarded as having left his employment voluntarily. Since these cases were decided, subs.(3) (s.19(7) in previous JSA legislation) has been added to the section, enabling regulations to be made treating someone who might otherwise be regarded as having left his employment voluntarily as not having left voluntarily. Whether this in effect exempts from preclusion under this head a claimant on the *Crewe* side of the line depends on whether in the circumstances of his particular case, including the nature and terms of his early retirement scheme, he can bring himself within the terms of the protection for voluntary redundancy set out in JSA Regulations 1996 reg.71, a matter explored below in the annotations to reg.71. For early retirement cases not saved by that regulation and subsection, the fine distinction between the *Crewe* type of case and those of the type considered in *R(U)1/83* may still be important. In *CSU/22/94*, Commissioner Mitchell applied *R(U)1/83* in favour of a claimant (a principal teacher) who had been pressured by his employers to accept an early retirement package, in a context in which his only alternative was to accept a lower status position (albeit one without loss of income) (being placed on a long-term supply teacher basis). That alternative was one which "a teacher of the claimant's experience and standing could not reasonably be expected to accept" (at para.5). The decision thus stresses the need for tribunals carefully to consider whether the claimant can be said to have left voluntarily before moving on to the "without a good reason" aspect.

In *CU/70/94*, Commissioner Rice made it clear that one cannot base a finding of voluntary leaving without a good reason on the notion that the claimant who left, not considering herself up to the job for medical reasons, ought to have found out more about, or to have known more about, the demands of the job before she accepted it.

1.219 *"Without a good reason"*. There is no definition of "good reason" in the Act, just as there was none of "just cause" in previous legislation dealing with disqualification from benefit or preclusion of payment of JSA. Nor do any of the JSA Regulations 1996 clarify its meaning with respect to this para. (contrast reg.72 with respect to paras (c) and (d), below). Like "just cause" or "good cause" in the previous scheme of sanctions, "good reason" affords the claimant a chance to explain and justify his conduct, whether that be an act or omission. The *Explanatory Memorandum* accompanying the amending regulations stated that "good reason" would be applied in the same way as the predecessor terms, but noted that "in the revised regime regulations will not set out particular circumstances or situations for the Decision Maker leaving him to take into account all reasons considered relevant when determining good reason" (para.7.18). See further *http://www.legislation.gov.uk/uksi/2012/2568/pdfs/uksiem_20122568_en.pdf* [Accessed June 17, 2013].

On that basis, the approach in this annotation (subject to the doubt expressed at the end of the next paragraph) is that court, Commissioners' and Upper Tribunal decisions on "just cause" and "good cause" in UB and previous JSA sanctions regimes are relevant authorities with respect to the interpretation of "good reason". Those decisions avoided laying down hard and fast rules on it for all circumstances, something fully harmonising with the policy intention expressed in the *Explanatory Memorandum*.

"Just cause" was regarded as requiring a balancing of the interests of the claimant with those of the community of fellow contributors to the National Insurance Fund. It was not a matter simply of what is in the best interests of the claimant, or of what is just as between employee and employer, or of what is in the public interest generally. To establish that he did not leave without just cause (that phraseology giving the proper emphasis) the claimant had to show that in leaving he acted reasonably in circumstances that made it just that the burden of his unemployment should be cast on the National Insurance Fund (*Crewe v Social Security Commissioner* [1982] 2 All E.R. 745, per Slade LJ, at 752; per Donaldson LJ, at 750–751, explaining *R(U)20/64(T)*, para.8; per Lord Denning MR, at 749). Was what he did right and reasonable in the context of the risk of unemployment? Was his voluntary leaving such as to create an unreasonable risk of unemployment, bearing in mind that there may be circumstances that leave a person no reasonable alternative but to leave his employment (per Donaldson LJ, at 750)? Establishing just cause may well be a heavier burden than showing "good cause" (per Slade LJ, at 751). In *R(U)4/87*, Commissioner Monroe stated that "the analogy with insurance seems now the paramount criterion of just cause" (para.8). His examination of decisions on the matter led him "to think that in general it is only where circumstances are such that a person has virtually no alternative to leaving voluntarily that he will be found to have had just cause for doing so, rather as a person who throws his baggage overboard to make room in the lifeboat can claim on his baggage insurance" (para.9). There is therefore a faint suggestion in the earlier authority that there may be some difference in the ordinary use of language between "good cause" and "just cause". It may also be arguable that the formula "without a good reason" shifts the focus away from the notion of a balance between the interests of the claimant and those of the community of contributors to the fund from which benefit is paid towards more emphasis on the interests of the claimant. That would make it easier for a claimant to avoid the imposition of a sanction. In *SA v SSWP (JSA)* [2015] UKUT 454 (AAC), a decision on s.19A(2)(c) and failing to carry out a jobseeker's direction, Judge Knowles accepted the Secretary of State's submission that in determining whether a good reason had been shown for the failure all the circumstances should be considered and that the question was whether those circumstances would have caused a reasonable person (with the characteristics of the claimant in question) to act as the claimant did. Expressing the approach in such terms tends to point away from the notion of a balance.

Whether the claimant succeeds in discharging the burden of showing a good reason depends essentially on all the circumstances of the case, including the reasons for leaving and such matters as whether he had another job to go to, whether before he left he had made reasonable inquiries about other work or its prospects, or whether there were in his case good prospects of finding other work. Such elements should not be considered in water-tight compartments (*R(U)20/64(T)*), para.9). The previous claims record is not directly relevant (*ibid.*, para.18). In *R(U)/4/87* Commissioner Monroe, following para.10 of *R(U)3/81* (approved in *Crewe*), ruled as remote from and irrelevant to the just cause issue long-term considerations prayed in aid by the claimant who had "urged that his leaving had in the long run actually benefited the national insurance fund, in that he had made available a vacancy for someone who would otherwise have continued unemployed, and that he was now earning more so that he was paying higher contributions" (at para.10). **1.220**

Such factors had nothing to do with the issue of being forced to leave (*ibid.*). In *CU/048/90*, Commissioner Sanders considered the appeal of a claimant who had, as a result of his employer's attitude, become dissatisfied with his employment and had sought alternative employment by circulating his curriculum vitae to 30 companies. During interviews with Barclays Bank he was given the impression that his application for a particular post would be successful, and he resigned from his employment. In the event he was not offered the other post. Commissioner Sanders considered the correct approach to "just cause" to be that set out in *R(U)4/87* (para.9). He thought that the "circumstances have to be very demanding before a claimant can establish just cause for leaving" (para.3). It seemed to the Commissioner "that in the circumstances of the case the claimant had reason to leave because he thought he was not progressing in his career" but took the view "that the circumstances were not so pressing as to justify his leaving, from an unemployment benefit point of view, before he had secured the job with Barclays Bank even though he had been led to believe that his application for that job would be successful" (*ibid.*). He agreed with the SSAT that the claimant did not have just cause for leaving voluntarily and had to be disqualified.

In some cases, probably rare in practice, an actual promise of immediate suitable new employment (which then falls through after the employment was left or the start of which is delayed) may afford a good reason in the absence of other justificatory circumstances (*R(U)20/64(T)*, para.17; *Crewe*, per Donaldson LJ, para.750). There was no rule of law saying that just cause cannot be established where the claimant leaves without another job to go to. Indeed, in *R(U)20/64(T)* a Tribunal of Commissioners suggested that there could be circumstances in the claimant's personal or domestic life which become so pressing that they justify leaving employment "without regard to the question of other employment" (para.12) and they cited as illustrations *R(U)14/52, R(U)19/52* and *R(U)31/59*, all noted below. Equally, it was clearly established that some feature of the claimant's existing employment may justify leaving it immediately without any regard to the question of other employment (para.11) and here the Commissioners quoted as instances *CU248/49, R(U)15/53, R(U)38/53* and *R(U)18/57*, considered below. But there must be some urgency in the matter and, as regards the latter class of case, the circumstances must be so pressing that it cannot be reasonable to expect the claimant to take such steps as are open to him to resolve before leaving the grievance connected with work through the proper channels of existing grievance procedures. *CU106/1987* makes it clear that a tribunal cannot merely rely on the Secretary of State's (decision-maker's) suggestion that there would be such a grievance procedure in the circumstances of the claimant's employment. It was wrong in law to take account of a suggested grievance procedure to reject the claimant's appeal without having proper findings of fact as to the existence of such a grievance procedure. One would equally have thought that a tribunal should also consider whether any procedure found to exist could cover the claimant's complaint and whether it was reasonable in the circumstances to expect the claimant to have resort to it. A simple desire to change jobs is not usually enough to warrant putting the burden of one's unemployment on the Fund. Nor does moving house without more constitute just cause; it depends on the reasons for the move (*R(U)20/64(T)*, para.15). Rather than approaching the just cause issue from the angle of considering it necessary for the claimant to be assured of suitable alternative employment, unless there were circumstances justifying him in leaving without it (the approach in *R(U)14/52*), the Commissioners in *R(U)20/64(T)* preferred a different perspective. They preferred to look: (1) at whether the reasons for leaving themselves amounted to just cause (i.e. leaving aside the matter of alternative employment or its prospects); and (2) where the reasons did not of themselves establish just cause to then consider whether the "promises or prospects of other employment may be effective as an *additional* factor which may help the claimant establish just cause. For example, where a man *almost* establishes just cause [in relation to, e.g. pressing personal or domestic circumstances] the fact that he has a promise or prospects of other employment may serve to tip the scale in his favour . . . In considering these matters of course the strength of his chances of employment and the gap, if any, likely to occur between the two employments must be taken into account" (para.17).

1.221 The Commissioners stated:

> "that it is impossible to lay down any period of time representing a gap between employments, or any degree of probability of fresh employment which will give an automatic answer to the question whether the claimant has shown just cause for leaving."

They drew:

"a distinction between on the one hand, having suitable employment to go to, as where there is an actual promise of employment, and having only prospects of employment on the other. It may be reasonable to expect a claimant who has only prospects to take some steps before leaving, such as communicating with the employment exchange to see whether his prospects cannot be made more certain."

It is probably true to say that the claimant's chances of establishing a good reason under the current provisions are stronger where there are promises or good prospects of employment, or where the reasons for leaving are in themselves quite strong and he can show efforts made to ascertain job prospects before leaving the old employment.

A number of cases concerning, on the one hand, grievances about existing employment and, on the other, personal or domestic circumstances, can usefully be quoted as *instances* in which just cause was established, and it may be useful to note in contrast a number of examples in each category where it was not. But the importance of looking to the precise circumstances of each and every case cannot be too strongly stressed. Note that whether a given set of facts constitutes a good reason for leaving is a question of mixed fact and law, making it one that the Upper Tribunal can deal with under their jurisdiction to correct errors of law by tribunals (*CU/53/1991*), depending on the nature of the error invoked.

(i) Grievances about work. In *R(U)/15/53* a piece-worker who lost his job when he refused to accept a substantial reduction in earnings thrust on him by his employer had just cause for leaving. In *R(U)38/53* the claimant left after subjection to pressure to join a trade union and was able to establish just cause; it would have been intolerable if he had to remain. In *R(U)18/57* an apprentice ordered to do work clearly outside the scope of his apprenticeship had only the options of doing as he was told or leaving immediately. In choosing the latter he had just cause. It may be now that working under a zero hours contract, especially if it has an exclusivity clause, could contribute towards a good reason for ceasing the employment (and see the guidance mentioned above under "such employment"). But mere failure to get on with colleagues (*R(U)17/54*) or strained relations with one's employer (*R(U)8/74*) has been held not enough. Not feeling oneself capable of the work, where one's employer was satisfied, is unlikely to be enough without clear medical evidence of that fact (*R(U)13/52*), but leaving employment during a probationary period because the claimant considered himself unsuited to the work and that it was unfair to his employer to continue training him was more generously treated in *R(U)3/73*. 1.222

Indeed, in *CU43/87* Commissioner Davenport said that "a person who is experimenting in trying a new line of work should not lightly be penalised if that experiment fails". Persons should be encouraged to try new types of employment where work in their usual field is not available:

"It must be recognised that in such circumstances a person may find that he cannot stay in his employment and it may be that he is reasonable in leaving that employment, whereas a person who had more experience in the field in question would not be held to have acted reasonably if he gave up the employment. Not everyone finds that new and unfamiliar employment is such that she or he can reasonably stay in it". (At para.7.)

CU/90/91 further illustrates that persons who leave employment as unsuitable after a trial period can have just cause for doing so and be protected from preclusion of payment without having to rely on the time-limited "trial period" concept found in s.20(3) and JSA Regulations 1996 reg.74. Commissioner Hallett stated:

"It is clear from the evidence, which I accept, that the claimant took the job with Fords (which would have been permanent) on trial, conditionally on his being able to obtain accommodation in the area. It is well-settled in social security unemployment law that claimants should be encouraged to take jobs on trial and that if, after trial, the job proves unsuitable, they do have just cause for leaving. It is in the interests of the national insurance fund, and of public policy, to encourage persons to obtain employment and not penalise them if, after fair trial, the job proves unsuitable". (At para.10.)

The claimant had just cause for leaving.

There is no such well-settled principle applying to leaving a job taken, not on trial, but as a "stop-gap" pending something better turning up (*R(U) 40/53*; *CJSA/63/2007*, para.15).

1.223 *(ii) Personal or domestic circumstances.* In *R(U) 14/52* the claimant had just cause for leaving his job in order to be with his elderly and sick wife who lived alone. It was not possible for her to move to live with him so as to be near enough to his work. He also thought his chances of employment would be good in his wife's area, but there was little evidence in the case of searching inquiries about those prospects. In *R(U) 19/52* the claimant who left her job to move with her service-man husband to a new posting, likely to be more than short-term, had just cause. Had the posting been short-term, however, she would have had to make inquiries about job prospects in the new area before leaving. See further *R(U) 4/87* and *CU110/1987.* In *CU110/1987* the claimant's service-man husband received telephone notice of posting to Germany on February 14, 1986. He went there on March 1, 1986. On February 14, 1986, the claimant gave the one week's notice required under her contract of employment and ceased work on February 21, claiming benefit the next day. She had to be available to vacate the married quarters in Aldershot from March 1. However, she did not join her husband in Germany until March 25, since repairs were needed to the married quarters there. Commissioner Monroe held that in these circumstances she had just cause for leaving when she did [February 21] rather than later. That, rather than whether she should have left at all, was the real issue in the case, since in the Commissioner's view it could hardly be said that she did not have just cause to leave (whenever she could) to join her husband in Germany. She was not to be disqualified from benefit. Actual entitlement to benefit, however, would turn on the unresolved matter of her availability for work. On this issue of availability in that context, see *R(U) 2/90(T)*. In *R(U) 31/59* the reason for leaving was the move to a new home, too far from the job, because the existing home (two small attic rooms) was wholly unsuitable for his family. By contrast, in *R(U) 6/53* the 21-year-old girl who left her job to move with her rather strict parents to a new area did not have just cause; it was reasonable to expect her to live alone, at least until she could find work in the new area. In *CJSA/2507/2005*, Commissioner Williams applied Commissioner Monroe's statement at para.9 of *R(U) 4/87*, quoted above, to dismiss the 28-year-old claimant's appeal against a tribunal-imposed three week disqualification for voluntary leaving (the decision-maker had imposed eight weeks). He had left to join his fiancée and get married, but had no job to go to. The three-week disqualification represented the period up to the marriage. The Commissioner also noted the need to treat with some caution decisions on this area which are 50 years' old, reflecting a very different job market and attitudes to married women, and given when appeal to the Commissioners covered fact and law.

Leaving for a financial advantage (e.g. to draw a marriage gratuity only payable on resignation (*R(U) 14/55*), or to take early retirement, even where this was encouraged by the employer and might be said to be in the public interest in terms of opening the way for younger teachers and promoting the efficiency of the education service, has been held not to rank as just cause (*Crewe v Social Security Commissioner* [1982] 2 All E.R. 745; *R(U) 26/51*; *R(U) 23/59*; *R(U) 20/64(T)*; *R(U) 4/70*; *R(U) 1/81*; *CU/170/1992* (which is not to be reported), which noted that *CU/95/1989* was either very different or decided against the weight of established authority). However, if "good reason" has different nuances of meaning from "just cause", as discussed above, that might justify more emphasis on what was reasonable in the claimant's own interests. Further, it may be that a different approach is justified where a claimant leaves a job to avoid hardship rather than to pursue extra money (as suggested in *CJSA/1737/2014*, where one of the claimant's arguments was that the cost of travel to and from work was prohibitive).

Subsection (3) and JSA Regulations 1996 reg.71, below, may provide significant assistance for some such claimants by treating them as not having left voluntarily thus obviating the good reason issue.

Paragraph (c)

"Without a good reason refuses or fails to apply . . .. is vacant or about to become vacant": This head of preclusion covers the claimant who has been informed by an "employment officer" that a situation in any employment is vacant or about to become so. The penalty applies where, without a good reason, (i) the claimant has refused to apply for that situation, (ii) has failed to apply for it, or (iii) has refused to accept it when offered. **1.224**

Since para.(c) refers to "any employment", not to "any such employment" (compare para.(b)), it appears that the term covers self-employment as well as employment as an employed earner (the definition of employment in reg.75(4) of the JSA Regulations 1996 applying, since the reg.4 definition does not apply to s.19). However, there must be something that amounts to a "situation", which points towards forms of self-employment that are analogous to employed earner's employment. In *MT v SSWP (JSA)* [2016] UKUT 72 (AAC) doubts were expressed whether registration with an employment agency could fall within para.(c), at least without evidence of some specific vacancy. If the reasoning in *GP v SSWP (JSA)* [2015] UKUT 476 (AAC); [2016] AACR 14, discussed in the notes to s.7(1) above, is correct, only employment in Great Britain can be in issue. If para.(c) is not applicable because there is no situation vacant or about to become vacant, para.(d) should be considered separately (*CJSA/4179/1997* and *MT*), but if that possibility is raised for the first time before a First-tier Tribunal the claimant must be given a fair opportunity to deal with the altered case.

The claimant must have been "informed" of the situation that is vacant or about to become vacant by an employment officer. The previous form of this provision used the term "notified", as had been the case since the 1930s. If there is any difference in meaning it can only be slight, as it had long been accepted that in the nature of things the official doing the notification/informing may have limited information to pass on and that provided that the broad nature of the situation had been made clear there was notification for these purposes (*R(U) 32/52*). In *MT* (above) the Secretary of State referred to "exact details" of a vacancy not having been given, but since in fact no details of anything that could be regarded as a vacancy had been given that phrase cannot be taken as laying down any test. It is then up to claimants to ascertain such further particulars as they require. The informing can be done orally (*CU/40/1987*), although good practice and the potential need for acceptable proof of the information given to the claimant in the light of the principle that the claimant should in sanctions cases be given the benefit of any doubt that might reasonably arise (*DL v SSWP (JSA)* [2013] UKUT 295 (AAC)), must surely point to the need for written or computer records to be kept and to be available to the claimant for reference. In practice something called a Mandatory Employment Notification (MEN) is used.

See the notes to the definition of "employment officer" in s.35(1) for the extension beyond Jobcentre Plus employees for the purpose of subs.(2)(c) to employees of "prime contractors" engaged by the Secretary of State to provide services or facilities in relation to the schemes concerned and employees of "approved subcontractors". The DMG Memos relevant to the two Orders mentioned there that remain in force after April 30, 2015 (now incorporated into the internet version of the DMG) say that an employment officer, including such employees, can inform claimants of reasonable vacancies or employment opportunities, gather evidence to send to decision-makers and make higher-level sanction referrals to a decision-maker if a claimant refuses or fails to comply. They also say that they can "mandate a claimant to attend a job interview". It is not clear what is intended here. For the purposes of subs.(2)(c) it must be implied that a vacancy actually exists or is shortly to exist, but employment officers within the extended meaning given by the Orders in question have no power to give jobseeker's directions under s.19A(2)(a) and (11)(a). So the mandation can only be in the form of a threat of referral for a sanction if the claimant refuses or fails to attend the interview. Such action can properly be regarded as a refusal or failure to apply for the situation that is vacant.

According to the then Minister of State Esther McVey (House of Commons written answers April 2, 2014 and September 1, 2014), guidance to Jobcentre Plus staff is that JSA claimants (in contrast to universal credit claimants) are not to be mandated to apply for vacancies for zero hours contracts, apparently whether there is an exclusivity clause or not. Thus no sanction under s.19(2)(c) should arise from a failure to apply for such a vacancy. If one did, then it would be arguable that the terms of the contract constituted a good reason for failing to apply. See also the prohibition in s.20(1) below of any reduction in benefit for refusing to seek employment in a situation vacant because of a stoppage of work due to a trade dispute.

"Refusal" clearly covers outright rejection of an offer or of the opportunity to apply for the post. Accepting an offer but then telling lies which caused the employer to withdraw it was treated as refusal in a Northern Ireland decision (*R6/50(UB)*). On the meaning of "accept a situation in any employment", see *CSU 7/1995*. The claimant was offered the job of a lampshade maker at a wage of £79 per week, having been informed of the vacancy by the Employment Service. But she changed her mind and did not start the job because the wage was too low to meet her commitments. The tribunal decided that since she did accept the offer of employment, s.28(1)(b) of SSCBA 1992 (whose terms were substantially similar to subs.(2)(c)) did not operate to disqualify her from receiving UB. However, the Commissioner held that although, normally, acceptance of an offer of a situation would be tantamount to accepting the situation it could not have been intended that it would be possible to defeat the operation of s.28(1)(b) by an acceptance in theory but a repudiation in practice. The claimant had not "accepted the situation" within the meaning of s.28(1)(b).

1.225 See also *CJSA 4179/1997* in which the claimant was offered a "trial" as a part-time car washer. The tribunal dealt with the case under the equivalent of subs.(2)(c) but the Commissioner expressed doubt as to whether the "trial" was an offer of a "situation in any employment". The tribunal should have investigated what the trial involved. If that provision did not apply, the equivalent of subs.(2)(d) should then have been considered.

A failure properly to complete an application form can amount to a failure to apply (*CJSA 2692/1999* and see *R(U)32/52*). However, where the applicant disputed the necessity of including a photograph on the employer's application form, contending that it would be accepted without one, the employment officer, without clear information to the contrary from the employer, should have tested the matter by forwarding the form without photograph to see if that indeed was the case. The officer had not done so and, in *CJSA/ 2082/2002* and *CJSA/5415/2002*, Commissioner Rowland allowed the appeal against the sanction imposed.

In *CJSA/4665/2001*, Commissioner Howell held that the "failed to apply" head could not catch someone who had filled in application forms which the Employment Service then refused to pass on because of criticisms of the Employment Service and government training initiatives, on the faith of which he had left his last job and felt badly let down. The Service refused to pass them on because of these criticisms they saw as directed against themselves. Since the forms were otherwise properly completed, and there was no evidence of any intention to spoil his chances or that any employers had been or would be put off by the comments from considering him for employment, it had not been shown that he had "failed to apply" for the posts in question. The Commissioner noted that the claimant might be wise to take the advice of the Employment Service and remove the comments so as to maximise his chances of employment. He noted also that there will be other cases:

> "where the way a claimant completes or spoils a job application will be unsatisfactory and unfit to be put in front of any employer so as to prevent it counting as a genuine application at all, so that he or she will have 'failed to apply': it is all a question of fact." (para.5)

In *CJSA/2931/2003*, Commissioner Howell upheld a tribunal decision disqualifying the claimant for 18 weeks as fully justified on the facts. It had doubted the claimant's credibility in claiming that he had telephoned and been told that the vacancy was filled whereas in fact it had remained open. The sanction imposed was well within the bounds of reasonableness in a case where a long-term claimant was found to have made no real effort to follow up a vacancy notified to him. **1.226**

There is now no requirement that the employment be "suitable", but there is, across all the sub-heads of the paragraph, a saving for "good reason". On "good reason" see the annotation to para.(b), above. Note, however, that JSA Regulations 1996 reg.72, below, stipulates that "good reason" in respect of para.(c) cannot be founded on travel time to and from work of less than an hour and a half each way "unless in view of the health of the person, or any caring responsibilities of his, that time was or is unreasonable".

In the past, however, questions of the suitability of the employment and of "good cause" (now replaced by good reason but intended to operate in the same way) for the refusal or failure to apply, or refusal or failure to accept, tended to intertwine. The case authorities tended not to distinguish between them (see e.g. *R(U)26/52*) to the extent that it almost appeared that the sole basis for "good cause", at least as reflected in reported decisions, was the non-suitability of the employment in the claimant's circumstances.

A general merging of the suitability and good cause heads was evident in the case authorities. The heads focused on such matters as the location of the employment (*R(U)41/51, R(U)34/58*), the claimant's personal and family circumstances (*R(U)13/52, R(U)20/60, R(U)2/77, R2/63(UB)*) and on the terms of the employment. That intertwining of the issues may mean that some issues sometimes characterised as "suitability" issues in the past may still be raised, despite the deletion of "suitable" from the statutory text, as "good reason" issues, save where regulations dictate otherwise.

In *PL v DSD (JSA)* [2015] NI Com 72, the Chief Commissioner for Northern Ireland has approved and applied the obiter suggestion of Judge Ward in *PL v SSWP (JSA)* [2013] UKUT 227 (AAC) (on the pre-October 2012 form of the Great Britain legislation) that, in deciding whether a claimant had good cause for failing to avail himself of a reasonable opportunity of a place on a training scheme or employment programme, a tribunal erred in law, where the circumstances raised the issue, in failing to consider the appropriateness of the particular scheme or programme to the claimant in the light of his skills and experience and previous attendance on any placements. Judge Ward's suggestion had been that the test was whether the claimant had reasonably considered that what was provided would not help him. It seems likely that a similar general approach will be taken to the issue of "good reason" under s.19(2)(c) and the appropriateness of the situation in question, as also suggested in *MT* (above). It may though still need to be sorted out how far the issue turns on the claimant's subjective view, within the bounds of reasonableness, in the light of the information provided at the time, as against a tribunal's view of the appropriateness of the situation in employment. The Chief Commissioner made no comment on the treatment of the claimant's refusal to complete and sign forms with information about criminal convictions and health, that the First-tier Tribunal had found were reasonably required by the training provider as part of its application process for the scheme, as a failure by the claimant to avail himself of a reasonable opportunity of a place on the training scheme.

See as an example of a potential good reason on its own facts (and no more than that), *GR v SSWP (JSA)* [2013] UKUT 645 (AAC), where it was held that a claimant with a genuinely held fear that prevented him going to the town where a course was to take place had good cause (under reg.7 of the Jobseeker's Allowance (Employment, Skills and Enterprise Scheme) Regulations 2011) for failing to participate in the scheme in question. A further example might be that the vacancy was for employment under a zero hours contract (see above).

Paragraph (d)

1.227 *"Without a good reason neglects to avail himself of a reasonable opportunity of employment":* Note at the outset that s.20(3) and JSA Regulations 1996 reg.74 made under it protect from sanction under this head or under that in subs.(2)(b) certain persons who leave employed earner's employment voluntarily and without just cause at any time within the "trial period" (that is, between the beginning of the fifth week and the end of the twelfth week of the employment in question, with some provision to ignore certain weeks). In short, in cases covered by s.20(3) and reg.74, characterising (as one could) the voluntary leaving as a "neglect to avail" will be pointless; those provisions will prevent preclusion.

Since para.(d) refers to "any employment", not to "any such employment" (compare para.(b)), it appears that the term covers self-employment as well as employment as an employed earner (the definition of employment in reg.75(4) of the JSA Regulations 1996 applying, since the reg.4 definition does not apply to s.19). However, there is considerable doubt what might amount to a "reasonable opportunity" outside the familiar context of job as an employee. In that context the judge in *MT v SSWP (JSA)* [2016] UKUT 72 (AAC) cited the DMG guidance (para.34757) that "reasonable" should have its ordinary meaning of sensible or likely, although the examples given of unreasonableness are nowhere near the dividing line. If the reasoning in *GP v SSWP (JSA)* [2015] UKUT 476 (AAC); [2016] AACR 14, discussed in the notes to s.7(1) above, is correct, only employment in Great Britain can be in issue. See also the prohibition in s.20(1) below of any reduction in benefit for refusing to seek employment in a situation vacant because of a stoppage of work due to a trade dispute, which must be taken to apply to this paragraph as much as to para.(c).

This head of sanction overlaps somewhat with para.(c). Preclusion is to be imposed where the claimant has neglected to avail himself of a reasonable opportunity of employment. There is now a saving for "good reason", on which see also the notes to paras (b) and (c), above, and JSA Regulations 1996 reg.72 (noted more fully, and covering this head in the same way as in para.(c)). The submission made in the note to para(c) on the relevance of suitability/good cause case law also applies here, so that decisions like *R(U)2/77* which protected the person, who could have had his old job back if he would, contrary to his convictions, join a trade union, would still be relevant. In *R(U)5/71* an excusing factor was a conscientious objection to a job, connected with religion or morals.

This head of sanction seems designed to cater in part for the person who literally complies with subs.(2)(c) in that he applies for the post, and does not explicitly refuse it, but who behaves in such a way that he would never get it, for example, by turning up at an interview in a dirty or unkempt condition, unwashed and unshaved (*R(U)28/55*). See also s.7(3) and JSA Regulations 1996 reg.18(4) on deeming acts not to count for the purposes of actively seeking work. Neglect to avail will also cover an explicit refusal to take a job or to fulfill a key condition for getting it (e.g. the requirement in Scotland that teachers be registered: *R(U)5/71*).

If para.(c) is not applicable because there is no situation vacant or about to become vacant, para.(d) should be considered separately (*CJSA/4179/1997* and *MT*), but if that possibility is raised for the first time before a First-tier Tribunal, a cautious approach should be taken in the light of the principle in *DL* (see notes to subs.(1)) and the claimant must be given a fair opportunity to deal with the altered case (*MT*).

See the notes to para.(c) above for "good reason" and the relevance of the suitability of the opportunity in question for the particular claimant.

Paragraph (e)

"Without a good reason fails to participate in any scheme within section 17A(1) which is prescribed for the purposes of this section": This is a new head of sanction. On "good reason", including the relevance of the appropriateness of the scheme for the claimant, see the annotation to para.(b), above. Note that JSA Regulations 1996 reg.72 has no application to this head of sanction. On schemes "within s. 17A(1) . . . prescribed for the purposes of this section", see the annotations to s.17A and JSA Regulations 1996 reg.70B. Mandatory Work Activitiy is the only scheme to have been prescribed. **1.228**

See as an example of a potential good reason on its own facts (and no more than that), *GR v SSWP (JSA)* [2013] UKUT 645 (AAC), where it was held that a claimant with a genuinely held fear that prevented him going to the town where a course was to take place had good cause (under reg.7 of the Jobseeker's Allowance (Employment, Skills and Enterprise Scheme) Regulations 2011) for failing to participate in the scheme in question.

See also *SA v SSWP (JSA)* [2015] UKUT 454 (AAC), discussed in the notes to s.19A(2)(c) below, on when turning up late (or some similarly minor infraction of the scheme's requirements) might not amount to a failure to participate in the scheme, regardless of issues of good reason.

Subsection (3)

This enables regulations to provide that certain situations that would otherwise be treated as "voluntarily leaving without a good reason" are not to be so treated. Specifically mentioned is voluntarily agreeing to be dismissed by reason of redundancy. See JSA Regulations 1996 reg. 71. **1.229**

Subsections (5)–(7)

The sanction for a sanctionable failure comes in the form of a reduction of a JSA award (on which see JSA Regulations 1996, new reg.70 (subs.(1)). Basically, this means a reduction of 100 per cent for a single claimant and where each member of a joint-claim couple commits a sanctionable failure, with a lesser reduction where the sanctionable failure is only by one member of such a couple. The greater stringency comes in the increased length of the period for which a sanction can be imposed: broadly speaking, 13 weeks for a first offence; 26 weeks for a second; and 156 weeks (three years) for a third (see JSA Regulations 1996 new reg.69). The principles previousely applying to the fixing of the length of a period of disqualificaton for UB and JSA are thus not applicable to the new regime. Reg.69(6) stipulates when the period of reduction begins. **1.230**

Subsection (6) enables regulations to provide for cases in which no reduction is to be made under s.19. See JSA Regulations 1996 new reg.70A(1). It also enables regulations to provide for a sanction applied to an old style JSA award which has terminated to then be applied to a new JSA award. See JSA Regulations 1996 new reg.70C.

Note in addition that, as before, under s.20 as amended, nothing in s.19 or regulations made under it can authorise reduction merely because the claimant "refuses to seek or accept employment in a situation vacant because of a stoppage of work due to a trade dispute".

New style JSA

Note that in those cases and areas where universal credit has come into force, income-based JSA is abolished and replaced by new style JSA (which is contribution-based only). See Pt VI of this book for the legislation relating to new style JSA and for the cases and areas to which it applies. **1.231**

[[1]Other sanctions

1.232 **19A.**— (1) The amount of an award of a jobseeker's allowance is to be reduced in accordance with this section in the event of a failure by the claimant which is sanctionable under this section.

(2) It is a failure sanctionable under this section if a claimant—

(a) without a good reason fails to comply with regulations under section 8(1) or (1A);

(b) without a good reason fails to comply with regulations under section 17A;

(c) without a good reason refuses or fails to carry out a jobseeker's direction which was reasonable having regard to his circumstances;

(d) without a good reason neglects to avail himself of a reasonable opportunity of a place on a training scheme or employment programme;

(e) without a good reason refuses or fails to apply for, or accept if offered, a place on such a scheme or programme which an employment officer has informed him is vacant or about to become vacant;

(f) without a good reason gives up a place on such a scheme or programme or fails to attend such a scheme or programme having been given a place on it;

(g) through misconduct loses a place on such a scheme or programme.

(3) But a failure is not sanctionable under this section if it is also sanctionable under section 19.

(4) Regulations are to provide for—

(a) the amount of a reduction under this section;

(b) the period for which such a reduction has effect.

(5) Regulations under subsection (4)(b) may provide that a reduction under this section in relation to any failure is to have effect for—

(a) a period continuing until the claimant meets a compliance condition specified by the Secretary of State,

(b) a fixed period not exceeding 26 weeks which is—

(i) specified in the regulations, or

(ii) determined in any case by the Secretary of State, or

(c) a combination of both.

(6) In subsection (5)(a) "compliance condition" means—

(a) a condition that the failure ceases, or

(b) a condition relating to—

(i) future compliance with a jobseeker's direction or any requirement imposed under section 8(1) or (1A) or 17A of this Act, or

(ii) future avoidance of the failures referred to in subsection (2)(d) to (g).

(7) A compliance condition specified under subsection (5)(a) may be—

(a) revoked or varied by the Secretary of State;

(b) notified to the claimant in such manner as the Secretary of State may determine.

(8) The period fixed under subsection (5)(b) may in particular depend on either or both of the following—

(a) the number of failures by the claimant sanctionable under this section;

(b) the period between such failures.

(9) Regulations may provide—
(a) for cases in which no reduction is to be made under this section;
(b) for a reduction under this section made in relation to an award that is terminated to be applied to any new award made within a prescribed period of the termination.

(10) During any period for which the amount of a joint-claim jobseeker's allowance is reduced under this section by virtue of a failure by one of the claimants which is sanctionable under this section, the allowance is payable to the other member of the couple.

(11) In this section—
(a) "jobseeker's direction" means a direction given by an employment officer (in such manner as he thinks fit) with a view to achieving one or both of the following—
 (i) assisting the claimant to find employment;
 (ii) improving the claimant's prospects of being employed;
(b) "training scheme" and "employment programme" have such meaning as may be prescribed.]

AMENDMENT

1. Welfare Reform Act 2012 s.46(1) (October 22, 2012).

DEFINITIONS

"claimant"—see s.35(1).
"employment officer"—*ibid.*
"employment programme"—see JSA Regulations 1996 reg.75(1)(a).
"regulations"—see s.35(1).
"training scheme"—see subs.(11)(b) and JSA Regulations 1996 reg.75(1)(b).
"week"—see JSA Regulations 1996 reg.75(3).

GENERAL NOTE

Subsection (1)

This covers a different set of grounds from those in the new form of s.19 in respect of which failure is sanctionable by a reduction of an old style JSA award. **1.233**

Subsection (2)

The grounds set out in paras (c)–(g) correspond with those set out in the previous s.19(5) but also encompasses two new grounds in subs.(2)(a) and (b). **1.234**

Notions of "without good cause" no longer apply, being replaced by "without a good reason" in paras (a)–(f), on which see the annotation to the new s.19(2)(b), above. JSA Regulations 1996 reg.72 applies only in respect of para.(c). Otherwise what ranks as "good reason" depends on all the circumstances of the case.

Paragraph (a): "without a good reason fails to comply with regulations under section 8(1) or (1A): Sections 8(1) and 8(1A), dealing respectively with single claimants and joint claim couples, require participation in interviews and the provision of information and evidence on availability for and actively seeking employment. See JSA Regulations 1996 regs 23–27. Non-compliance with these provisions is in some circumstances a failure sanctionable under s.19A, but see the complicated relationship with the result of cessation of entitlement discussed in the notes to reg.25.

Paragraph (b): "without a good reason fails to comply with regulations under section 17A": Section 17A enables regulations to provide for or in connection with the imposition on claimants of a requirement to participate in schemes designed to assist them to obtain employment. See the Jobseeker's Allowance (Mandatory Work Activity Scheme) Regulations 2011 (SI 2011/688), the Jobseeker's Allowance (Employment, **1.235**

Skills and Enterprise Scheme) Regulations 2011 (SI 2011/917), the Jobseeker's Allowance (Schemes for Assisting Person to Obtain Employment) Regulations 2013 (SI 2013/276) and the Jobseeker's Allowance (18–21 Work Skills Pilot Scheme) Regulations 2014 (SI 2014/3117) and the annotations to s.17A. Non-compliance with these provisions without a good reason is a failure sanctionable under s.19A.

Paragraph (c): "without a good reason refuses or fails to carry out a jobseeker's direction which was reasonable having regard to his circumstances": This provision constitutes the only statutory authority for the giving of a jobseeker's direction, by making it a sanctionable failure to refuse or fail to carry one out. "Jobseeker's direction" is defined in subs.(11)(a) in fairly wide but not open-ended terms. It must be given by an "employment officer" (defined in s.35(1): see the notes to that definition for discussion, which shows that the extension beyond Jobcentre Plus employees does not apply for the purposes of s.19A(2)(c)). It can be given in whatever manner the employment officer thinks fit. Thus, there is no requirement that the direction be given in writing or in any other permanent form. However, good practice, plus the potential need for acceptable proof of the existence and terms of the direction in the light of the principle that the claimant should in sanctions cases be given the benefit of any doubt that might reasonably arise (*DL v SSWP (JSA)* [2013] UKUT 295 (AAC)), must surely point to the need for written or computer records to be kept and to be available to the claimant for reference. The control comes in the provision that the direction be made with a view to assisting the claimant to find employment or to improving the claimant's prospects of being employed or both. That formulation must require that the direction can objectively be found to have such a purpose, not merely that the particular employment officer subjectively believes that it has. Within that constraint any kind of personal behaviour or activity involving any kind of third party could potentially come within the definition in subs.(11). However, in practice the requirement in subs.(2)(c) that the direction be reasonable before a sanction can be imposed provides a further limit. Claimants faced with directions that they think are unreasonable are nonetheless put in the dilemma that refusing to comply will probably lead to an immediate loss of benefit for at least four weeks (unless they can persuade the employment officer or the Secretary of State on mandatory reconsideration of the unreasonableness), which a successful appeal will not reinstate for many months.

The references to "the claimant" and to having regard to the claimant's circumstances require that the purpose prescribed in subs.(11) must be linked to the particular claimant's employment prospects. In *DM v SSWP (JSA)* [2015] UKUT 67 (AAC), Judge Rowley cited some relevant parts of the DMG as follows:

> "7. Under paragraph 34904 of the [DMG] it is provided that a Jobseeker's Direction should be (amongst other things):
> (1) linked to action to improve the claimant's chances of finding work;
> (2) personalised and appropriate to that individual claimant;
> (3) related to labour market activities.
> 8. It is further provided (under paragraph 34905) that the issue of a Jobseeker's Direction must be tailored to each individual claimant's requirements.
> 9. The [DMG] also provides guidance on certain sessions which are known as Group Information Sessions. Under paragraph 34911 it is said that 'generally a claimant cannot be mandated to attend a Group Information Session. There needs to be a clearly identified and tangible benefit to the individual claimant in terms of improving their employment prospects by attending the session'."

1.236 In *DM*, the claimant, who had been registered unemployed for nearly four years, was issued with a document describing itself as a jobseeker's direction directing him to attend and participate fully in a Group Information Session ["General" at [10] may be a typo] at a specified date, time and place. The reason for the direction was said to be to attend the work programme returnees' information session to improve his chances of employment. It was stated that he would receive additional information to help him look for work, to ensure that he had the correct job goals and improve his CV, although Judge Rowley apparently accepted the claimant's contention that the session was in fact about the sanctions regime. The claimant attended at the right time but was asked to leave the session shortly before the end because he was said to be disrupting it by asking questions and heckling. It was then decided that he was in breach of the direction by failing to participate fully in the session, that the direction was reasonable and that he had not had good reason for failing to comply with the direction, so that he was made subject to a sanction for four weeks. On appeal, the First-tier Tribunal concluded that the jobseeker's direction was reasonable having regard to the claimant's circumstances and confirmed the sanction decision. Judge Rowley held that the tribunal had gone wrong in law by reaching that decision in the absence of any evidence to show why the Group Information Session would have assisted the particular claimant to find employment or to improve his prospects of being employed. Nor was there any evidence to suggest that the conditions in para.34904 were met. She substituted her own decision that the sanction should not have been imposed.

There will inevitably be some overlap between the requirement that the direction be "reasonable, having regard to the claimant's circumstances" and the "good reason" exemption, so that "excusing" factors might be argued as constituting "good reason" for the refusal/failure or as rendering the direction "unreasonable". However, as the circumstances of *DM* (above) show, there may be a discrepancy between what is set out in a direction and what is actually provided to the claimant. The direction itself may be quite reasonable. But what are claimants to do who, having, say, been directed to "participate fully" in a particular course or session, find that it is not in fact directed to their own circumstances or to improving prospects of employment? Can that in itself amount to a good reason for not completing the course or session or should the claimant, having started the course or session, complete it even if under protest or challenge? The approach adopted in *PL v DSD (JSA)* [2015] NI Com 72 by the Chief Commissioner for Northern Ireland, approving and applying the obiter suggestion of Judge Ward in *PL v SSWP (JSA)* [2013] UKUT 227 (AAC) (see notes to para.(d) below) would suggest that the appropriateness of whatever was directed would be relevant.

In *SA v SSWP (JSA)* [2015] UKUT 454 (AAC) the claimant, who had hearing difficulties and wore a hearing aid in one ear, was directed by an employment officer to attend and complete a CV writing course with Learn Direct two days later from 11.15 a.m. to 12.15 p.m. He was given a letter to confirm the time and date. The claimant arrived at 11.25 a.m. and was told that he was too late and so had been deemed to have missed his appointment. He immediately went to the Jobcentre Plus office to rebook an appointment for the course and explained that he had misheard the time for the appointment as 11.50 a.m., the time that he normally signed on. A fixed four-week sanction for failing, without a good reason, to carry out a reasonable jobseeker's direction was imposed. On appeal the claimant said that at the meeting with the employment officer he had not been wearing his hearing aid and that he had not thought to check the time of the appointment on the letter as he genuinely thought that it was the same as his two previous appointments. The First-tier Tribunal regarded it as clear that the direction had been reasonable and that the claimant had failed to comply with it, so that the sole question was whether he had had a good reason for the failure. On that question, the tribunal concluded that, although the error was genuine, that did not in itself give him a good reason and that he had failed to take reasonable steps to confirm the time of the appointment and dismissed his appeal. In setting aside the tribunal's decision and substituting her own decision reversing the imposition of the sanction (as had been suggested by the Secretary of State), Judge Knowles held that the tribunal had erred in law by failing to consider the question of whether the claimant had failed to comply with the direction. In the substituted decision, she concluded that, the claimant not having refused to carry out the direction and taking into account that his error was genuine and that he took immediate steps to rebook, it was disproportionate to treat his late arrival in isolation as amounting to a failure to comply with the direction. That can only be regarded as a determination on the particular facts that does not constitute any sort of precedent to be applied as a matter of law in other cases. The outcome may have reflected an understandable desire in a deserving case to get around the absence of any scope for varying the fixed period of four weeks for a s.19A sanction for a "first offence". However, there could have been nothing unreasonable about a conclusion that arriving 10 minutes after the beginning of a course that only lasted for an hour amounted to a failure to comply with a direction to attend and complete the course, no matter how genuine the error that led to the late arrival.

In discussing whether the tribunal had also approached the question of good reason properly, Judge Knowles accepted the Secretary of State's submission that all the circumstances should be considered and that the question was whether those circumstances would have caused a reasonable person to act as the claimant did, provided that the reasonable person was given the characteristics of the claimant in question. See the notes to s.19(2)(b) above for further discussion of good reason.

Note that JSA Regulations 1996 reg.72 stipulates with respect to this head of sanction that "good reason" cannot be founded on travel time to and from work of less than an hour and a half each way "unless in view of the health of the person, or any caring responsibilities of his, that time was or is unreasonable".

Paragraph (d): "without a good reason neglects to avail himself of a reasonable opportunity of a place on a training scheme or employment programme": Note that in *CJSA/495/2007* and *CJSA/505/2007*, Commissioner May rejected as unarguable the claimant's arguments that the application to him of sanctions for failing to take up a place on an intensive activity period employment programme infringed art.4 ECHR (freedom from slavery or forced labour). Nor was there an arguable case of discrimination. A similar argument for the application of art.4 was comprehensively rejected by the Supreme Court in *R (Reilly and Wilson) v Secretary of State for Work and Pensions* [2013] UKSC 68; [2014] 1 A.C. 453. There is a saving for "good reason".

In *PL v DSD (JSA)* [2015] NI Com 72, the Chief Commissioner for Northern Ireland has approved and applied the obiter suggestion of Judge Ward in *PL v SSWP (JSA)* [2013] UKUT 227 (AAC) (on the pre-October 2012 form of the Great Britain legislation) that in deciding whether a claimant had good cause for failing to avail himself of a reasonable opportunity of a place on a training scheme or employment programme a tribunal erred in law, where the circumstances raised the issue, in failing to consider the appropriateness of the particular scheme or programme to the claimant in the light of his skills and experience and previous attendance on any placements. Judge Ward's suggestion had been that the test was whether the claimant had reasonably considered that what was provided would not help him. It seems likely that a similar general approach will be taken to issues of "good reason" under s.19A(2)(d)–(f). It may though still need to be sorted out how far the issue turns on the claimant's subjective view, within the bounds of reasonableness, in the light of the information provided at the time, as against a tribunal's view of the appropriateness of what was to be provided. The Chief Commissioner made no comment on the treatment of the claimant's refusal to complete and sign forms with information about criminal convictions and health, that the First-tier Tribunal had found were reasonably required by the training provider as part of its application process for the scheme, as a failure by the claimant to avail himself of a reasonable opportunity of a place on the training scheme.

1.237 *Paragraph (e): "without a good reason refuses or fails to apply for, or accept if offered, a place on such a scheme or programme which an employment officer has informed him is vacant or about to become vacant"*: This covers the situation, after an employment officer has informed a claimant of a vacant place on such a scheme or programme, of refusal or failure to apply for such a place or to accept it when offered. There is a saving for "good reason".

Paragraph (f): "without a good reason gives up a place on such a scheme or programme or fails to attend such a scheme or programme having been given a place on it"

R(JSA) 2/06 held that turning up late could rank as "failure to attend". There is a saving for "good reason".

Paragraph (g): "through misconduct loses a place on such a scheme or programme" On the meaning and scope of "misconduct", see the annotation to s.19(2)(a), above. There is no saving for "good reason".

Subsection (3)

A failure under s.19A is not sanctionable under this section if it also sanctionable under the higher level sanctions regime in the "new" s.19. **1.238**

Subsections (4)–(9)

The period for which a sanction can apply is set by regulations made under subs. (4)(b) read with subss.(5)–(8). See JSA Regulations 1996 new reg.69A. Section 19A allows: a fixed period of not more than 26 weeks as set by regulations or determined in a particular case by the Secretary of State; a period (in principle able to be longer that that 26 week maximum) lasting until the claimant complies with a compliance condition set by the Secretary of State (that failure ceases and/or future failures are avoided); or a combination of both (see subs.(5)). However, reg.69A used only a small part of that power. The sanction is of fixed periods of 4 weeks for a first offence and 13 weeks for a second. Regulation 69A(3) stipulates when the period of reduction begins. **1.239**

The amount of the reduction is set, pursuant to subs.(4)(a) by the JSA Regulations 1996 new reg.70 and parallels that with respect to higher-level sanctions. Basically, this means a reduction of 100 per cent for a single claimant and where each member of a joint-claim couple commits a sanctionable failure, with a lesser reduction where the sanctionable failure is only by one member of such a couple.

JSA Regulations 1996 reg.70A(2)–(5) set out circumstances in which no reduction is to be made under s.19A, although those do not remove the status of sanctionable failure (but note reg.69(2)(a) and reg.69A(2)(a)).

Subsection (10)

As regards joint-claim couples where only one of the claimants is subject to a sanction, JSA continues to be paid to the compliant member. **1.240**

New style JSA

Note that in those cases and areas where universal credit has come into force, income-based JSA is abolished and replaced by new style JSA (which is contribution-based only). See Pt VI of this book for the legislation relating to new style JSA and for the cases and areas to which it applies. **1.241**

[1Claimants ceasing to be available for employment etc

19B.— (1) Regulations may make provision for reduction of the amount of an award of a jobseeker's allowance other than a joint-claim jobseeker's allowance if the claimant— **1.242**

(a) was previously entitled to such an allowance or was a member of a couple entitled to a joint-claim jobseeker's allowance, and

(b) ceased to be so entitled by failing to comply with the condition in section 1(2)(a) or (c) (availability for employment and actively seeking employment).

(2) Regulations may make provision for reduction of the amount of a joint-claim jobseeker's allowance if one of the claimants—

(a) was previously entitled to a jobseeker's allowance other than a joint-claim jobseeker's allowance, and

(b) ceased to be so entitled by failing to comply with the condition in section 1(2)(a) or (c).

(3) Regulations may make provision for reduction of the amount of an award of joint-claim jobseeker's allowance if—

(a) the couple were previously entitled to a joint-claim jobseeker's allowance but ceased to be so entitled by either or both of them failing to comply with the condition in section 1(2)(a) or (c), or

(b) either member of the couple was a member of another couple previously entitled to such an allowance and that couple ceased to be so entitled by that person failing to comply with the condition in section 1(2)(a) or (c).

(4) Regulations are to provide for—

(a) the amount of a reduction under this section;

(b) the period for which such a reduction has effect.

(5) The period referred to in subsection (4)(b) must not include any period after the end of the period of 13 weeks beginning with the day on which the claimant's previous entitlement ceased.

(6) Regulations under subsection (4)(b) may in particular provide for the period of a reduction to depend on either or both of the following—

(a) the number of occasions on which a claimant's entitlement has ceased as specified in subsection (1), (2) or (3);

(b) the period between such occasions.

(7) Regulations may provide for a reduction under this section made in relation to an award that is terminated to be applied to any new award made within a prescribed period of the termination.

(8) During any period for which the amount of a joint-claim jobseeker's allowance is reduced under this section by virtue of a failure by one of the claimants to comply with the condition in section 1(2)(a) or (c), the allowance is payable to the other member of the couple.

AMENDMENT

1. Welfare Reform Act 2012 s.46(1) (October 22, 2012).

DEFINITIONS

"a joint-claim jobseeker's allowance"—see s.1(4).
"claimant"— see s.35(1).

GENERAL NOTE

1.243 This section enables regulations to provide for an award of old style JSA to be reduced in respect of a claim for a period not exceeding 13 weeks where a previous JSA entitlement had ended because of failing to be available for or actively seeking employment. Section 19B does not apply when the reason for the termination of the previous award was that there ceased to be a jobseeker's agreement in effect. When a reduction is to apply is set out in JSA Regulations 1996 new reg.69B(1)–(5). The period of reduction is set by paras (6) and (7) of that provision (broadly speaking, four weeks for a first offence and 13 weeks for a second) and its commencement stipulated as the date of claim (reg.69(8)). The amount of reduction is set by JSA Regulations 1996 new reg.70 and parallels that with respect to higher level sanctions. Basically, this means a reduction of 100 per cent for a single claimant and where each member of a joint-claim couple commits a sanctionable failure, with a lesser reduction where the sanctionable failure is only by one member of such a couple.

New style JSA

Note that in those cases and areas where universal credit has come into force, income-based JSA is abolished and replaced by new style JSA (which is contribution-based only). See Pt VI of this book for the legislation relating to new style JSA and for the cases and areas to which it applies. 1.244

[1 Hardship payments

19C.— *(1) Regulations may make provision for the making of payments ("hardship payments") by way of a jobseeker's allowance to a claimant where—* 1.245

(a) the amount of the claimant's award is reduced under sections 19 to 19B, and

(b) the claimant is or will be in hardship.

(2) Regulations under this section may in particular make provision as to—

(a) circumstances in which a claimant is to be treated as being or not being in hardship;

(b) matters to be taken into account in determining whether a claimant is or will be in hardship;

(c) requirements or conditions to be met by a claimant in order to receive hardship payments;

(d) the amount or rate of hardship payments;

(e) the period for which hardship payments may be made;

(f) whether hardship payments are recoverable.]

AMENDMENT

1. Welfare Reform Act 2012 s.46(1) (October 22, 2012).

GENERAL NOTE

It would appear on closer examination that this section is probably not in force. Although s.46 of the Welfare Reform Act 2012 (inserting ss.19–19C) was originally brought into force by art.2(6) of the Welfare Reform Act 2012 (Commencement No.2) Order (SI 2012/1246) as from October 14, 2012, art.2(6) was revoked by art.2(7) of the Welfare Reform Act 2012 (Commencement No.4) Order 2012 (SI 2012/2530). Although art.2(2)(a) of the No.4 Order indeed brought s.46(1) of the Welfare Reform Act 2012 into force on October 22, 2012, its commencement was limited to the "purposes of the substitution of sections 19 to 19B of the Jobseekers Act 1995", thus, on a strict reading, suggesting that s.19C was not included. The text of the "Blue Volumes", however, also incorporates s.19C as in force, as did Westlaw, and the Explanatory Notes to the Welfare Reform Bill which became the 2012 Act clearly envisaged that ss.19–19C would be in force until transfer to universal credit was completely rolled out. Since s.19C only confers rule-making powers (on which see regs 140–146H of the JSA Regulations 1996) enabling the making of hardship payments, no-one is likely to complain about the possible invalidity of those regulations, especially since there appear to be alternative powers to make the regulations in s.20(4) and (6). In view of the dubious situation, the text of s.19C has been included in this volume, but in italics. 1.246

New style JSA

Note that in those cases and areas where universal credit has come into force, income-based JSA is abolished and replaced by new style JSA (which is contribution-based only). See Pt VI of this book for the legislation relating to new style JSA and for the cases and areas to which it applies. 1.247

Exemptions from section 19 [3 and 19A]

1.248 **20.**—(1) Nothing in section 19, or in regulations under that section, shall be taken to [3 authorise reduction] of a jobseeker's allowance merely because the claimant refuses to seek or accept employment in a situation which is vacant in consequence of a stoppage of work due to a trade dispute.

(2) Section [319A] does not apply, in the circumstances mentioned in subsection [3(2)(c) to (g)] of that section, if—

(a) a direction is in force under section 16 with respect to the claimant; and

(b) he has acted in such a way as to risk—

(i) having that direction revoked under subsection (3)(b) of section 16; or

(ii) having the amount of his jobseeker's allowance reduced by virtue of section 17, because [1the condition mentioned in section 17(3)(b) or (c) is satisfied].

(3) Regulations shall make provisions for the purpose of enabling any person of a prescribed description to accept any employed earner's employment without falling within section [319(2)(b) or (d)] should he leave that employment voluntarily and without [3 good reason] at any time during a trial period.

(4) In such circumstances as may be prescribed, an income-based jobseeker's allowance shall be [2payable in respect of] a claimant even though section 19 prevents payment of a jobseeker's allowance to him.

(5) A jobseeker's allowance shall be payable by virtue of subsection (4) only if the claimant has complied with such requirements as to the provision of information as may be prescribed for the purposes of this subsection.

(6) Regulations under subsection (4) may, in particular, provide for a jobseeker's allowance payable by virtue of that subsection to be—

(a) payable at a prescribed rate;

(b) payable for a prescribed period (which may differ from the period fixed under section 19(2) or (3)).

(7) In subsection (3), "trial period" has such meaning as may be prescribed.

(8) Regulations may make provision for determining, for the purposes of this section, the day on which a person's employment is to be regarded as commencing.

AMENDMENTS

1. Social Security Act 1998, Sch.7 para.142 (October 18, 1999).
2. Welfare Reform and Pensions Act 1999 s.70 and Sch.8 para.29 (November 11, 1999).
3. Welfare Reform Act 2012 Sch.7 para.5 (October 22, 2012).

DEFINITIONS

"claimant"—see s.35(1).
"employment"—see s.35(1) and JSA Regulations 1996 reg.4.
"income-based jobseeker's allowance"—see ss.1(4) and 35(1).
"jobseeker's agreement"—see ss.9(1) and 35(1).
"regulations"—see s.35(1).
"trade dispute"—*ibid.*
"trial period"—see JSA Regulations 1996 reg.74(4).

General Note

This section affords a number of exemptions from the preclusive effect of ss.19 and 19A, enabling the making of regulations providing for hardship payments of a reduced rate of IBJSA for those precluded from full old style JSA by ss.19 or 19A. See further JSA Regulations 1996 regs 140–146D. 1.249

Subsection (1)

This provides that nothing in s.19 or regulations made under it can prevent payment of old style JSA merely because the claimant refuses to seek or accept employment vacant in consequence of a stoppage of work due to a trade dispute. On the definition of "trade dispute", see s.35(1) and the notes to s.14(1). On "stoppage of work", see the notes to s.14(1). 1.250

This maintains the traditional "neutral" approach to trade disputes taken in social security law. A claimant is not required to be a strike-breaker and so will not be sanctioned for refusing work that is vacant because of a trade dispute.

Subsection (2)

If a young person who is the subject of a severe hardship direction fails to pursue or refuses a training opportunity without good cause or fails to complete a training course without good cause, or loses his place through misconduct, s.19A(2)(c)–(g) does not apply. The young person's "offence" will be dealt with by revocation of the direction under s.16(3) or reduction in his old style JSA under s.17 as appropriate. See reg.63 of the JSA Regulations 1996. 1.251

Subsections (3), (7) and (8)

This provision and JSA Regulations 1996 reg.74 made under it protect certain persons who leave employment voluntarily without good reason at any time during a trial period from preclusion from JSA under the voluntarily leaving employment without good reason head of s.19(2)(b) or under s.19(2)(d) (neglect to avail oneself of a reasonable opportunity of employment). Regulation 74(4) defines "trial period". See further the annotations to s.19(2)(b) and (d). 1.252

Subsections (4), (5) and (6)

In the past a claimant suspended or disqualified from UB under s.28(1) of the SSCBA 1992, or who would have been so disqualified if otherwise entitled, could (if eligible) receive reduced payments of income support. Now there is no automatic entitlement to reduced income-based JSA where a sanction is imposed under s.19. Benefit will only be paid if hardship can be shown. There can be no hardship payment if the claimant is sanctioned under ss.19A or 19B. 1.253

See regs 140–146H of the JSA Regulations for the rules governing hardship payments and the notes to those regulations.

New style JSA

Note that in those cases and areas where universal credit has come into force, income-based JSA is abolished and replaced by new style JSA (which is contribution-based only). See Pt VI of this book for the legislation relating to new style JSA and for the cases and areas to which it applies. 1.254

[1 Denial or reduction of joint-claim jobseeker's allowance

20A.—[2 . . .] 1.255

Amendments

1. Welfare Reform and Pensions Act 1999 s.59 and Sch.7 para.13 (March 19, 2001).
2. Welfare Reform Act 2012 s.147 and Sch.14 Pt 3 (October 22, 2012).

General Note

1.256 This section, together with s.20B below, made provision corresponding to that made by the former ss.19 and 20 in relation to a joint-claim jobseeker's allowance. For further details see pp.122–123 of Vol.II of the 2012/13 edition. Both sections have now been repealed because the rules for imposing sanctions on joint-claim couples are included in the new ss.19–20.

1.257 [1**20B.**— [2 . . .]

Amendments

1. Welfare Reform and Pensions Act 1999 s.59 and Sch.7 para.13 (March 19, 2001).
2. Welfare Reform Act 2012 s.147 and Sch.14 Pt 3 (October 22, 2012).

General Note

See p.124 of Vol.II of the 2012/2013 edition.

Miscellaneous

[1Contracting out

1.258 **20E.—**(1) *[Not yet in force]*
(2) *[Not yet in force]*
(3) Regulations may provide for any of the following functions of the Secretary of State to be exercisable by, or by employees of, such person (if any) as the Secretary of State may authorise for the purpose—
(a) any function under regulations under section 8, [2 . . .] 17A [2 . . .] [3 . . .], except the making of an excluded decision (see subsection (4));
(b) *[Not yet in force]*
(c) *[Not yet in force]*
(d) *[Not yet in force]*.
(4) Each of the following is an "excluded decision" for the purposes of subsection (3)—
(a) a decision about whether a person has failed to comply with a requirement imposed by regulations under section 8, [2 . . .], [4 . . .] [3 . . .];
(b) a decision about whether a person had good cause for failure to comply with such a requirement;
(c) a decision about not paying or reducing a jobseeker's allowance in consequence of a failure to comply with such a requirement.
(5) Regulations under subsection (3) may provide that a function to which that subsection applies may be exercised—
(a) either wholly or to such extent as the regulations may provide,
(b) either generally or in such cases as the regulations may provide, and
(c) either unconditionally or subject to the fulfilment of such conditions as the regulations may provide.
(6) An authorisation given by virtue of any provision made by or under this section may authorise the exercise of the function concerned—
(a) either wholly or to such extent as may be specified in the authorisation,

(b) either generally or in such cases as may be so specified, and
(c) either unconditionally or subject to the fulfilment of such conditions as may be so specified;

but, in the case of an authorisation given by virtue of regulations under subsection (3), this subsection is subject to the regulations.

(7) An authorisation given by virtue of any provision made by or under this section—

(a) may specify its duration,
(b) may be revoked at any time by the Secretary of State, and
(c) does not prevent the Secretary of State or any other person from exercising the function to which the authorisation relates.

(8) Anything done or omitted to be done by or in relation to an authorised person (or an employee of that person) in, or in connection with, the exercise or purported exercise of the function concerned is to be treated for all purposes as done or omitted to be done by or in relation to the Secretary of State or (as the case may be) an officer of the Secretary of State.

(9) But subsection (8) does not apply—

(a) for the purposes of so much of any contract made between the authorised person and the Secretary of State as relates to the exercise of the function, or
(b) for the purposes of any criminal proceedings brought in respect of anything done by the authorised person (or an employee of that person).

(10) Any decision which an authorised person makes in exercise of a function of the Secretary of State has effect as a decision of the Secretary of State under section 8 of the 1998 Act.

(11) Where—

(a) the authorisation of an authorised person is revoked at any time, and
(b) at the time of the revocation so much of any contract made between the authorised person and the Secretary of State as relates to the exercise of the function is subsisting,

the authorised person is entitled to treat the contract as repudiated by the Secretary of State (and not as frustrated by reason of the revocation).

(12) In this section—

(a) "the 1998 Act" means the Social Security Act 1998;
(b) "authorised person" means a person authorised to exercise any function by virtue of any provision made by or under this section;
(c) references to functions of the Secretary of State under any enactment (including one comprised in regulations) include functions which the Secretary of State has by virtue of the application of section 8(1)(c) of the 1998 Act in relation to the enactment.]

AMENDMENTS

1. Welfare Reform Act 2009 s.32(1) and (2) (March 9, 2011) but only for the purposes of enabling under subss.(3)(a) and (4)–(12) of s.20E the ability to contract out within limits certain of the Secretary of State's functions in regulations made under s.17A. See further the commentary to s.17A.

2. Welfare Reform Act 2012 s.147 and Sch.14 Pt 2 (amending Welfare Reform Act 2009 s.32(2) inserting s.20E) (May 8, 2012).

3. Welfare Reform Act 2012 s.147 and Sch.14 Pt 6 (amending Welfare Reform Act 2009 s.32(2) inserting s.20E) (May 8, 2012).

4. Welfare Reform Act 2012 s.48 and Sch.7 para.16(1) and (2)(c) (amending Welfare Reform Act 2009 s.32(2) inserting s.20E) (October 22, 2012).

GENERAL NOTE

New style JSA

1.259 Note that in those cases and areas where universal credit has come into force, income-based JSA is abolished and replaced by new style JSA (which is contribution-based only). See Pt VI of this book for the legislation relating to new style JSA and for the cases and areas to which it applies.

On contracting out various functions with respect to new style JSA, see s.6L of the new style Jobseekers Act.

Supplementary provisions

1.260 **21.**—Further provisions in relation to a jobseeker's allowance are set out in Schedule 1.

Members of the forces

1.261 **22.**—(1) Regulations may modify any provision of this Act, in such manner as Secretary of State thinks proper, in its application to persons who are or have been members of Her Majesty's forces.

(2) The regulations may, in particular, provide for [[1] section 19(2)(b)] not to apply in relation to a person who is discharged from Her Majesty's forces at his own request.

(3) For the purposes of this section, Her Majesty's forces shall be taken to consist of such establishments and organisations in which persons serve under the control of the Defence Council as may be prescribed.

AMENDMENT

1. Welfare Reform Act 2012 s.48 and Sch.7 para.7 (October 22, 2012).

Recovery of sums in respect of maintenance

1.262 **23.**—(1) Regulations may make provision for the court to have power to make a recovery order against any person where an award of income-based jobseeker's allowance has been made to that person's spouse [[1] or civil partner].

(2) In this section "recovery order" means an order requiring the person against whom it is made to make payments to the Secretary of State or to such other person or persons as the court may determine.

(3) Regulations under this section may make provision for the transfer by the Secretary of State of the right to receive payments under, and to exercise rights in relation to, a recovery order.

(4) Regulations made under this section may, in particular, include provision—

(a) as to the matters to which the court is, or is not, to have regard in determining any application under the regulations; and

(b) as to the enforcement of recovery orders.

(5) In this section, "the court" means—

(a) in relation to England and Wales, [[2] the family court]; and

(b) in relation to Scotland, the sheriff.

AMENDMENTS

1. Civil Partnership Act 2004 s.254 and Sch.24 para.122 (December 5, 2005).

2. Crime and Courts Act 2013 (Family Court: Consequential Provision) Order 2014 (SI 2014/605) art.21(1) (April 22, 2014).

DEFINITIONS

"income-based jobseeker's allowance"—see s.1(4).
"regulations"—see s.35(1).

GENERAL NOTE

This section is concerned with the enforcement of a person's liability to maintain his spouse or civil partner where an award of JSA has been made to that spouse or civil partner (compare s.106 of the Administration Act in relation to income support). It is not known how often these powers to recover such maintenance are in fact used since the child support maintenance system first introduced by the Child Support Act 1991 has been in operation. **1.263**

New style JSA

Note that in those cases and areas where universal credit has come into force, income-based JSA is abolished and replaced by new style JSA (which is contribution-based only). See Pt VI of this book for the legislation relating to new style JSA and for the cases and areas to which it applies. **1.264**

PART II

BACK TO WORK SCHEMES

The back to work bonus

26.—(1) Regulations may make provision for the payment, in prescribed circumstances, of sums to or in respect of persons who are or have been entitled to a Jobseeker's allowance or to income support. **1.265**

(2) A sum payable under the regulations shall be known as "a back to work bonus".

(3) [1 Subject to section 677 of the Income Tax (Earnings and Pensions) Act 2003 (which provides for a back to work bonus not to be taxable)], a back to work bonus shall be treated for all purposes as payable by way of a jobseeker's allowance or (as the case may be) income support.

(4) The regulations may, in particular, provide for—

(a) a back to work bonus to be payable only on the occurrence of a prescribed event;

(b) a bonus not to be payable unless a claim is made before the end of the prescribed period;

(c) the amount of a bonus (subject to any maximum prescribed by virtue of paragraph (g)) to be determined in accordance with the regulations;

(d) enabling amounts to be calculated by reference to periods of entitlement to a jobseeker's allowance and periods of entitlement to income support;

(e) treating a bonus as payable wholly by way of income support or wholly by way of a jobseeker's allowance, in a case where amounts have been calculated in accordance with provision made by virtue of paragraph (d);

(f) keeping persons who may be entitled to a bonus informed of the amounts calculated in accordance with any provision of the regulations made by virtue of paragraph (c);

(g) the amount of a bonus not to exceed a prescribed maximum;

(h) a bonus not to be payable if the amount of the bonus which would otherwise be payable is less than the prescribed minimum;
(i) prescribed periods to be disregarded for prescribed purposes;
(j) a bonus which has been paid to a person to be treated, in prescribed circumstances and for prescribed purposes, as income or capital of his or of any other member of his family;
(k) treating the whole or a prescribed part of an amount which has accrued towards a person's bonus—
 (i) as not having accrued towards his bonus; but
 (ii) as having accrued towards the bonus of another person;
(l) the whole or a prescribed part of a back to work bonus to be payable, in such circumstances as may be prescribed, to such person, other than the person who is or had been entitled to a jobseeker's allowance or to income support, as may be determined in accordance with the regulations.

AMENDMENT

1. Income Tax (Earnings and Pensions) Act 2003 Sch.6 Pt 2 para.230 (April 6, 2003).

DEFINITIONS

"prescribed"—see s.35(1).
"regulations"—*ibid.*

GENERAL NOTE

1.266 The detailed rules relating to the back to work bonus scheme that was introduced on October 7, 1996 were contained in the Social Security (Back to Work Bonus) (No.2) Regulations 1996 (SI 1996/2570) (see the 2004 edition of this volume for those Regulations). The scheme was abolished on October 25, 2004 and the 1996 Regulations were revoked with effect from that date by reg.8 of the Social Security (Back to Work Bonus and Lone Parent Run-on) (Amendment and Revocation) Regulations 2003 (SI 2003/1589), subject to a transitional provision in reg.10. The effect of reg.10 was to continue the 1996 Regulations in force (subject to certain modifications) in order to enable claimants to claim the bonus during a further period. For reg.10 of the 2003 Regulations and the note to that regulation, see the 2008/09 edition of this volume.

The Government's justification for the abolition of the back to work bonus was that evaluation of the scheme had shown that it did not act as an incentive for claimants to take up full-time work and that its complex rules and eligibility criteria had contributed to low levels of awareness of the existence of the scheme. It was replaced by, among other measures, an expansion of the Job Grant scheme (paid under arrangements made under s.2(2) of the Employment and Training Act 1973). From October 2004 the new Job Grant (a one-off payment of £100 or £250) was payable to people who started full-time work after they had been getting certain benefits for at least six months and who satisfied the other qualifying conditions. However, the Job Grant was abolished on April 1, 2013.

New style JSA

1.267 Note that in those cases and areas where universal credit has come into force, income-based JSA is abolished and replaced by new style JSA (which is contribution-based only). See Pt VI of this book for the legislation relating to new style JSA and for the cases and areas to which it applies.

Pilot schemes

29.—(1) Any regulations to which this subsection applies may be made so as to have effect for a specified period not exceeding [3 36 months]. 1.268

(2) Any regulations which, by virtue of subsection (1), are to have effect for a limited period are referred to in this section as "a pilot scheme".

(3) A pilot scheme may provide that its provisions are to apply only in relation to—

(a) one or more specified areas or localities;
(b) one or more specified classes of person;
(c) persons selected—
  (i) by reference to prescribed criteria; or
  (ii) on a sampling basis.

(4) A pilot scheme may make consequential or transitional provision with respect to the cessation of the scheme on the expiry of the specified period.

(5) A pilot scheme ("the previous scheme") may be replaced by a further pilot scheme making the same, or similar, provision (apart from the specified period) to that made by the previous scheme.

(6) Subject to subsection (8), subsection (1) applies to—

(a) regulations made under this Act, other than—
  (i) regulations made under section 4(2) or (5) which have the effect of reducing any age-related amount or applicable amount; or
  (ii) regulations made under section 27;
(b) regulations made under the Administration Act, so far as they relate to a jobseeker's allowance;
(c) regulations made under Part VII of the Benefits Act (income-related benefits), other than any mentioned in subsection (7); and
(d) regulations made under the Administration Act, so far as they relate to income-related benefits payable under Part VII of the Benefits Act.

(7) The regulations referred to in subsection (6)(c) are—

(a) [2 . . .]
(b) [2 . . .]
(c) regulations under section 130(4) of that Act which have the effect of reducing the appropriate maximum housing benefit;
(d) regulations under section 131(10)(a) of that Act which have the effect of reducing the appropriate maximum council tax benefit; and
(e) regulations reducing any of the sums prescribed under section 135(1) of that Act.

(8) Subsection (1) applies only if the regulations are made with a view to ascertaining whether their provisions will, or will be likely to, encourage persons to obtain or remain in work or will, or will be likely to, [3 make it more likely that persons will obtain or remain in work or be able to do so].

AMENDMENTS

1. Tax Credits Act 1999 Sch.1 paras 1 and 6(h) (October 5, 1999).
2. Tax Credits Act 2002 s.60 and Sch.6 (April 8, 2003).
3. Welfare Reform Act 2009 s.28(1) (November 12, 2009).

DEFINITIONS

"the Administration Act"—see s.35(1).
"the Benefits Act"—*ibid.*
"regulations"—*ibid.*

GENERAL NOTE

1.269 This important provision contains the power to "pilot" changes in regulations across particular geographical areas and/or specified categories of claimants for a period of up to (from November 12, 2009) three years (this period can be extended: see subs.(5)). The power can only be exercised in relation to the types of regulations listed in subs.(6) and with a view to assessing whether the proposed changes are likely to encourage people to find or remain in work or make it more likely that they will do so, or be able to do so (subs.(8)). Regulations made under this section are subject to the affirmative resolution procedure (s.37(1)(c)). See the use of this power, as well as that in s.17A(1), in the making of the Jobseeker's Allowance (Supervised Jobsearch Pilot Scheme) Regulations 2014 (SI 2014/1913), set out only in the Supplement to the 2014/15 edition because they cease to have effect on April 30, 2015, and of the Jobseeker's Allowance (18–21 Work Skills Pilot Scheme) Regulations 2014 (SI 2014/3117), also set out only in that Supplement because they only apply to claimants in limited areas of the country and cease to have effect on November 25, 2016.

PART III

MISCELLANEOUS AND SUPPLEMENTAL

Termination of awards

1.270 **31.**—(1) Regulations may make provision allowing, in prescribed circumstances, an award of income support to be brought to an end by [1 the Secretary of State] where the person to whom it was made, or where he is a member of a [3 couple] his partner [2 or the couple], will be entitled to a jobseeker's allowance if the award is brought to an end.

(2) Regulations may make provision allowing, in prescribed circumstances, an award of a jobseeker's allowance to be brought to an end by[1 the Secretary of State] where the person to whom it was made, or where he is a member of a [3 couple] his partner, [2 or where the award was made to a couple a member of the couple,] will be entitled to income support if the award is brought to an end.

(3) In this section "partner" means the other member of the couple concerned.

AMENDMENTS

1. Social Security Act 1998 s.86(1) and Sch.7 para.143 (October 18, 1999).
2. Welfare Reform and Pensions Act 1999 s.59 and Sch.7 para.14 (March 19, 2001).
3. Civil Partnership Act 2004 s.254 and Sch.24 para.123 (December 5, 2005).

DEFINITION

"couple"—see s.35(1).

General Note

New style JSA

Note that in those cases and areas where universal credit has come into force, income-based JSA is abolished and replaced by new style JSA (which is contribution-based only). See Pt VI of this book for the legislation relating to new style JSA and for the cases and areas to which it applies. 1.271

Interpretation

35.—(1) In this Act— 1.272

[2. . .]

"the Administration Act" means the Social Security Administration Act 1992;

"applicable amount" means the applicable amount determined in accordance with regulations under section 4;

"benefit year" has the meaning given by section 2(4);

"the Benefits Act" means the Social Security Contributions and Benefits Act 1992;

"child" means a person under the age 16;

"claimant" means a person who claims a jobseeker's allowance; [3except that in relation to a joint-claim couple claiming a joint-claim jobseeker's allowance it means the couple, or each member of the couple, as the context requires;]

"continental shelf operations" has the same meaning as in section 120 of the Benefits Act;

"contribution-based conditions" means the conditions set out in section 2;

"contribution-based jobseeker's allowance" has the meaning given in section 1(4);

[4 [13 14 "couple" means—

(a) two people who are married to, or civil partners of, each other and are members of the same household; or

(b) two people who are not married to, or civil partners of, each other but are living together as a married couple otherwise than in prescribed circumstances;]]

"employed earner" has the meaning prescribed for the purposes of this Act;

"employment", except in section 7, has the meaning prescribed for the purposes of this Act;

[11 "employment officer", for any purpose of this Act, means an officer of the Secretary of State or such other person as may be designated for that purpose by an order made by the Secretary of State;]

"entitled", in relation to a jobseeker's allowance, is to be construed in accordance with—

(a) the provisions of this Act relating to entitlement; and

(b) [2section 1 of the Administration Act and section 27 of the Social Security Act 1998]

"family" means—

(a) a [5 couple];

(b) a [5 couple] and a member of the same household for whom one of them is, or both are, responsible and who is a child or a person of a prescribed description;

(c) except in prescribed circumstances, a person who is not a member of a [5 couple] and a member of the same household for whom that person is responsible and who is a child or a person of a prescribed description;

[8 "FAS payments" means payments made under the Financial Assistance Scheme Regulations 2005;]

"Great Britain" includes the territorial waters of the United Kingdom adjacent to Great Britain;

"income-based conditions" means the conditions set out in section 3;

"income-based jobseeker's allowance" has the meaning given in section 1(4);

[10 "income-related employment and support allowance" means an income-related allowance under Part 1 of the Welfare Reform Act 2007 (employment and support allowance);]

"jobseeker's agreement" has the meaning given by section 9(1);

[12 "jobseeker's direction" has the meaning given by section 19A;]

"jobseeking period" has the meaning prescribed for the purposes of this Act;

[3"joint-claim couple" and "joint-claim jobseeker's allowance" have the meanings given by section 1(4);]

[6 . . .];

[3 "the nominated member", in relation to a joint-claim couple, shall be construed in accordance with section 3B(4);]

"occupational pension scheme" has the same meaning as it has in the Pension Schemes Act 1993 by virtue of section 1 of that Act;

"pensionable age" has the meaning prescribed for the purposes of this Act;

"pension payments" means—

(a) periodical payments made in relation to a person, under a personal pension scheme or, in connection with the coming to an end of an employment of his, under an occupational pension scheme or a public service pension scheme; and

(b) such other payments as may be prescribed;

"personal pension scheme" means—

(a) a personal pension scheme as defined by section 1 of the Pension Schemes Act 1993;

[9 (b) an annuity contract or trust scheme approved under section 620 or 621 of the Income and Corporation Taxes Act 1988 or a substituted contract within the meaning of section 622(3) of that Act which is treated as having become a registered pension scheme by virtue of paragraph 1(1)(f) of Schedule 36 to the Finance Act 2004; and

(c) a personal pension scheme approved under Chapter 4 of Part 14 of the Income and Corporation Taxes Act 1988 which is treated as having become a registered pension scheme by virtue of paragraph 1(1)(g) of Schedule 36 to the Finance Act 2004;]

[8 "PPF payments" means any payments made in relation to a person—

(a) payable under the pension compensation provisions as specified in section 162(2) of the Pensions Act 2004 or Article 146(2) of the Pensions (Northern Ireland) Order 2005 (the pension compensation provisions); or

(b) payable under section 166 of the Pensions Act 2004 or Article 150 of the Pensions (Northern Ireland) Order 2005 (duty to pay scheme benefits unpaid at assessment date etc.);]

"prescribed" [1, except in section 27 (and in section 36 so far as relating to regulations under section 27),] means specified in or determined in accordance with regulations;

"public service pension scheme" has the same meaning as it has in the Pension Schemes Act 1993 by virtue of section 1 of that Act;

"regulations" [1, except in section 27 (and in section 36 so far as relating to regulations under section 27),] means regulations made by the Secretary of State;

"tax year" means the 12 months beginning with 6th April in any year;

"trade dispute" means any dispute between employers and employees, or between employees and employees, which is connected with the employment or non-employment or the terms of employment or the conditions of employment of any persons, whether employees in the employment of the employer with whom the dispute arises, or not;

"training" has the meaning prescribed for the purposes of this Act and, in relation to prescribed provisions of this Act, if regulations so provide, includes assistance to find training or employment, or to improve a person's prospects of being employed, of such a kind as may be prescribed;

[6 . . .];

"week" means a period of 7 days beginning with a Sunday or such other period of 7 days as may be prescribed;

"work" has the meaning prescribed for the purposes of this Act;

"year", except in the expression "benefit year", means a tax year.

[7 (1A) [13 14 . . .]]

(2) The expressions [10 "limited capability for work"], "linked period", "relevant education" and "remunerative work" are to be read with paragraphs 2, 3, 14 and 1 of Schedule 1.

(3) Subject to any regulations made for the purposes of this subsection, "earnings" is to be construed for the purposes of this Act in accordance with section 3 of the Benefits Act and paragraph 6 of Schedule 1 to this Act.

AMENDMENTS

1. Social Security Contributions (Transfer of Functions, etc.) Act 1999 s.2 and Sch.3 para.62 (April 1, 1999).

2. Social Security Act 1998 Sch.7 para.144 (October 18, 1999).

3. Welfare Reform and Pensions Act 1999 s.59 and Sch.7 para.15 (March 19, 2001).

4. Civil Partnership Act 2004 s.254 and Sch.24 para.124(2) (December 5, 2005).

5. Civil Partnership Act 2004 s.254 and Sch.24 para.124(3) (December 5, 2005).

6. Civil Partnership Act 2004 s.254 and Sch.24 para.124(4) (December 5, 2005).

7. Civil Partnership Act 2004 s.254 and Sch.24 para.124(5) (December 5, 2005).

8. Pensions Act 2004 (PPF Payments and FAS Payments) (Consequential Provisions) Order 2006 (SI 2006/343) art.2 and Sch. Pt 2 para.2(2) (February 14, 2006).

9. Taxation of Pension Schemes (Consequential Amendments) Order 2006 (SI 2006/745) art.12 (April 6, 2006).

10. Welfare Reform Act 2007 s.28(1) and Sch.3 para.12(5) (October 27, 2008).

11. Welfare Reform Act 2012 s.44(5) (June 10, 2012).

12. Welfare Reform Act 2012 s.48 and Sch.7 para.8 (October 22, 2012).

13. Marriage (Same Sex Couples) Act 2013 (Consequential and Contrary Provisions and Scotland) Order 2014 (SI 560/2014) art.2 and Sch.1 para.26 (March 13, 2014).The amendments extend to England and Wales only (see SI 2014/107 art.1(4)).

14. Marriage and Civil Partnership (Scotland) Act 2014 and Civil Partnership Act 2004 (Consequential Provisions and Modifications) Order 2014 (SI 2014/3229) art.29 and Sch.5 para.12 (December 16, 2014). The amendments relate only to

Scotland (see SI 2014/3229 art.3(4)) but are in the same terms as the amendments made in relation to England and Wales by SI 2014/107 (see point 13 above).

General Note

1.273 This section defines certain terms used in the legislation, but leaves some to be construed in accordance with specified paragraphs of Sch.1 and others to be defined through regulations, some of which definitions relate to the whole of the JSA Regulations (see regs 1(3) and 3) and some of which only apply to specified Parts.

"*Child*". The restriction to a person under 16 gives rise to the need to define "young person" in the JSA Regulations to cater for the over-15s (see JSA Regulations 1996 regs 57(1) and 76(1)).

"*Couple*". See the notes to the definition in reg.2(1) of the Income Support Regulations.

"*Employed earner*". See reg.3 of the JSA Regulations.

"*Employment*". This is defined for purposes of "actively seeking employment" in s.7(8) to cover both employed and self-employed earner's employment as those terms are used in SSCBA 1992, but otherwise "employment" has the meaning prescribed in regulations: see JSA Regulations 1996 regs 3, 4 and 75(4).

"*Employment officer*". This is an important definition for many purposes within the old style JSA scheme but in particular for the sanction under s.19A(2)(c) for refusing or failing, without a good reason, to carry out a reasonable jobseeker's direction. Section 19A(11) defines a jobseeker's direction as a direction given by an employment officer with a view to assisting the claimant to find employment, to improving the claimant's prospects of being employed or both. See the notes to s.19A(2)(c) for discussion of those conditions. Other important functions of employment officers include entering into and varying jobseeker's agreements (for which the same definition is provided by s.9(13)) and specifying the time, place and manner of interviews under regs 23 and 23A of the JSA Regulations 1996 and s.8(1). In many places, action by an employment officer forms part of the background (e.g. informing a claimant of a vacancy, failure to apply for which or accept if offered can attract a sanction under s.19(2)(c)). Sometimes action must be approved by an employment officer (e.g. reg.14(1)(a)). Occasionally a determination of an issue of entitlement is to be made by an employment officer, rather than the Secretary of State. Examples are reg.13(6) of the JSA Regulations 1996 (whether a person with caring responsibilities for a child does not have reasonable prospects of securing employment if restricting availability to hours left after fulfilling the caring responsibilities, so as to be exempted from the reasonable prospects test) and reg.17A(3) (whether a claimant may undertake a qualifying course and therefore still be treated as available for employment).

The definition appears to cover any officer of the Secretary of State. Apparently, all Jobcentre Plus employees are regarded as employment officers. It is trickier to pin down just how far the Secretary of State's power to extend the meaning to other persons has in fact been exercised.

The designation of other persons (which can, by virtue of Sch.1 to the Interpretation Act 1978, include corporate and unincorporated associations, such as companies, as well as natural persons) must be made by an order and must be for a purpose of the old style Jobseekers Act 1995. An order under s.9(13) (meaning of employment officer for purposes of jobseeker's agreement) or s.16(4) (meaning for the purposes of hardship payments) falls outside the requirement in s.36(1) for any power under the Act to make orders to be exercisable by statutory instrument. The other provisions mentioned in s.36(1) as exempted no longer exist. However, at the time of writing no orders under ss.9(13) or 16(4) have been identified. Section 36(1A) exempts any order relating to employment officers under s.35(1) from the s.36(1) requirement. Three orders have been made recently but only for the purposes of s.19(2)(c) (see above). They are the Jobseeker's Allowance (Supervised

Jobsearch Pilot Scheme) (Employment Officers) Designation Order 2014 (in force from October 2, 2014 to April 30, 2015), the Jobseeker's Allowance (Community Work Placements) (Employment Officers) Designation Order 2014 (in force from October 27, 2014) and the Jobseeker's Allowance (Work Programme) (Employment Officers) Designation Order 2014 (also in force from October 27, 2014). The Community Work Placements Order relates to the scheme described in reg.3(8A) of the Jobseeker's Allowance (Schemes for Assisting Persons to Obtain Employment) Regulations 2013 and the Work Programme Order relates to the scheme described in reg.3(8). The Orders are deposited in the House of Commons Library and can be accessed on the Parliament website. Their effect is now dealt with in the internet version of the DMG, having previously been the subject of Memos. Each Order designates employees of "prime contractors" and "approved sub-contractors" as employment officers. Prime contractors are organisations specified in a schedule to the Order in question which have been appointed by the Secretary of State to provide services or facilities for the scheme in question. Approved sub-contractors are organisations engaged by a prime contractor to perform its obligations under a relevant contract and which are approved by the Secretary of State.

"Family". The definition is the same as in s.137(1) of the Contributions and Benefits Act 1992. See the notes to that definition. For "person of a prescribed description" see reg.76(1) of the JSA Regulations.

"FAS payments". "PPF payments" (see below) are not available in respect of pension schemes that wound up before April 6, 2005. Payments under the Financial Assistance Regulations are intended to cover defined benefits occupational pension schemes that wound up between January 1997 and April 2005 because of employer insolvency.

"Occupational pension scheme". Section 1(1) of the Pension Schemes Act 1993 (as amended by s.239 of the Pensions Act 2004 with effect from September 22, 2005 in the case of an occupational pension scheme that has its main administration in the UK and with effect from April 6, 2006 in all other cases (see art.2(7) of the Pensions Act 2004 (Commencement No.6, Transitional Provisions and Savings) Order 2005 (SI 2005/1720), and as further amended with effect from November 26, 2007 by reg.2(b) of the Occupational Pension Schemes (EEA States) Regulations 2007 (SI 2007/3014)) defines an "occupational pension scheme" as:

"a pension scheme—

(a) that—

(i) for the purpose of providing benefits to, or in respect of, people with service in employments of a description, or

(ii) for that purpose and also for the purpose of providing benefits to, or in respect of, other people,

is established by, or by persons who include, a person to whom subsection (2) applies when the scheme is established or (as the case may be) to whom that subsection would have applied when the scheme was established had that subsection then been in force, and

(b) that has its main administration in the United Kingdom or outside the EEA states,

or a pension scheme that is prescribed or is of a prescribed description".

Section 1(2)–(5) provides:

"(2) This subsection applies—

(a) where people in employments of the description concerned are employed by someone, to a person who employs such people,

(b) to a person in an employment of that description, and

(c) to a person representing interests of a description framed so as to include—
(i) interests of persons who employ people in employments of the description mentioned in paragraph (a), or
(ii) interests of people in employments of that description.

(3) For the purposes of subsection (2), if a person is in an employment of the description concerned by reason of holding an office (including an elective office) and is entitled to remuneration for holding it, the person responsible for paying the remuneration shall be taken to employ the office-holder.

(4) In the definition in subsection (1) of "occupational pension scheme", the reference to a description includes a description framed by reference to an employment being of any of two or more kinds.

(5) In subsection (1) "pension scheme" (except in the phrases "occupational pension scheme", "personal pension scheme" and "public service pension scheme") means a scheme or other arrangements, comprised in one or more instruments or agreements, having or capable of having effect so as to provide benefits to or in respect of people—
(a) on retirement,
(b) on having reached a particular age, or
(c) on termination of service in an employment."

"Pensionable age". See reg.3 of the JSA Regulations.

"Personal pension scheme". The meaning in s.1(1) of the Pension Schemes Act 1993 (as amended by s.239 of the Pensions Act 2004 with effect from April 6, 2006 (see art.2(7) of the Pensions Act 2004 (Commencement No.6, Transitional Provisions and Savings) Order 2005 (SI 2005/1720), and as further amended with effect from April 6, 2007 by the Finance Act 2007 Sch.27 Pt 3(2) para.1) is

"a pension scheme that—
(a) is not an occupational pension scheme, and
(b) is established by a person within section 154(1) of the Finance Act 2004".

Section 1(5) further provides that "pension scheme" in s.1(1) means "a scheme or other arrangements, comprised in one or more instruments or agreements, having or capable of having effect so as to provide benefits to or in respect of people—
(a) on retirement,
(b) on having reached a particular age, or
(c) on termination of service in an employment."

"PPF payments". The Pension Protection Fund ("PPF") was set up under the Pensions Act 2004 in order to provide protection for members of defined benefits (i.e. normally final salary) occupational pension schemes and in relation to the defined elements of hybrid pension schemes in the event of the employer's insolvency. For the complex provisions see Pt 2 of the Pensions Act 2004.

"Public service pension scheme". A "public service pension scheme" is:

"an occupational pension scheme [as defined above] established by or under an enactment or the Royal prerogative or a Royal charter, being a scheme (a) all the particulars of which are set out in, or in a legislative instrument made under, an enactment, Royal warrant or charter, or (b) which cannot come into force, or be amended, without the scheme or amendment being approved by a Minister of the Crown or government department or by the Scottish Ministers".

The term includes:

"any occupational pension scheme established, with the concurrence of the Treasury, by or with the approval of any Minister of the Crown or established by or with the approval of the Scottish Ministers and any occupational pension scheme prescribed by regulations made by the Secretary of State and the Treasury jointly as being a scheme which ought in their opinion to be treated as a public service pension scheme for the purposes of this Act". (Pension Schemes Act 1993 s.1)

"Training". See reg.57(1) of the JSA Regulations.

New style JSA

Note that in those cases and areas where universal credit has come into force, income-based JSA is abolished and replaced by new style JSA (which is contribution-based only). See Pt VI of this book for the legislation relating to new style JSA and for the cases and areas to which it applies. 1.274

Regulations and orders.

36.—(1) Any power under this Act to make regulations or orders, other than an order under [2 section [3 8(3),] 9(13), 16(4) or 19(10)(a)] shall be exercisable by statutory instrument. 1.275

[7 (1A) Subsection (1) does not apply to an order under section 35(1) in relation to employment officers.]

(2) Any such power may be exercised—

(a) either in relation to all cases to which it extends, or in relation to those cases subject to specified exceptions, or in relation to any specified cases or classes of case;

(b) so as to make, as respects the cases in relation to which it is exercised—

(i) the full provision to which the power extends or any less provision (whether by way of exception or otherwise),

(ii) the same provision for all cases in relation to which it is exercised, or different provision for different cases or different classes of case or different provision as respects the same case or class of case for different purposes of this Act,

(iii) any such provision either unconditionally or subject to any specified condition.

(3) Where any such power is expressed to be exercisable for alternative purposes it may be exercised in relation to the same case for any or all of those purposes.

(4) Any such power includes power—

(a) to make such incidental, supplemental, consequential or transitional provision as appears to the Secretary of State [1 , or (in the case of regulations made by the Treasury) to the Treasury,] to be expedient; and

(b) to provide for a person to exercise a discretion in dealing with any matter.

[4 (4A) Without prejudice to the generality of the provisions of this section—

(a) regulations under section 17A [5 6 . . .] may make different provision for different areas;

(b) regulations under section 17A [5 6 . . .] may make provision which applies only in relation to an area or areas specified in the regulations.]

(5) Any power to make regulations or an order for the purposes of any provision of this Act is without prejudice to any power to make regulations or an order for the purposes of any other provision.

AMENDMENTS

1. Social Security Contributions (Transfer of Functions, etc.) Act 1999 s.2 and Sch.3 para.63 (April 1, 1999).

2. Social Security Act 1998 s.86(1) and Sch.7 para.145 (October 18, 1999 for purposes specified in SI 1999/2860 art.2 and Sch.1).

3. Welfare Reform and Pensions Act 1999 s.70 and Sch.8 para.29(6) (November 11, 1999).

4. Welfare Reform Act 2009 s.1(3) (November 12, 2009).

5. Welfare Reform Act 2009 s.11 and Sch.3 paras 3(1) and (2) (November 12, 2009).

6. Welfare Reform Act 2012 s.147 and Sch.14 Pt. 6 (May 8, 2012).

7. Welfare Reform Act 2012 s.48 and Sch.7 para.9 (October 22, 2012 note that art.2(6) of SI 2012/1246, which originally provided for Sch.7 para.9 to come into force on October 1, 2012 was revoked by SI 2012/2530 art.2(7)).

DEFINITION

"regulations"—see s.35(1).

GENERAL NOTE

1.276 See s.37 for the regulations which require approval by affirmative resolution.

New style JSA

1.277 Note that in those cases and areas where universal credit has come into force, income-based JSA is abolished and replaced by new style JSA (which is contribution-based only). See Pt VI of this book for the legislation relating to new style JSA and for the cases and areas to which it applies.

Parliamentary control

1.278 **37.**—(1) Subsection (2) applies in relation to the following regulations (whether made alone or with other regulations)—

(a) regulations made under, or by virtue of, any provision of this Act other than—
  (i) section 6, 7, 26, 29 or 40,
  (ii) paragraph (b) of the definition of "pension payments" in section 35(1), or
  (iii) paragraph 17 of Schedule 1,

before the date on which jobseeker's allowances first become payable;

[6 (aa) the first regulations to be made under section 6J or 6K;]

[5 (ab) the first regulations to be made under sections 19 to 19C;]

(b) the first regulations to be made under section 26;

(c) regulations made under section [3 . . .] 29, paragraph (b) of the definition of "pension payments" in section 35(1) [1 [4 . . .]] or paragraph [28B or] 17 of Schedule 1.

(2) No regulations to which this subsection applies shall be made unless a draft of the statutory instrument containing the regulations has been laid before Parliament and approved by a resolution of each House.

(3) Any other statutory instrument made under this Act, other than one made under section 41(2), shall be subject to annulment in pursuance of a resolution of either House of Parliament.

AMENDMENTS

1. Welfare Reform Act 2009 s.11 and Sch.3 paras 3(1) and (3) (November 12, 2009).

2. Welfare Reform Act 2009 s.29(2) (January 19, 2012 as SI 2012/68).
3. Welfare Reform Act 2012 s.47 (March 20, 2012).
4. Welfare Reform Act 2012 s.147 and Sch.14 Pt. 6 (May 8, 2012).
5. Welfare Reform Act 2012 s.46(2) (June 10, 2012).
6. Welfare Reform Act 2012 s.49(6) (February 25, 2013).

DEFINITIONS

"pension payments"—see s.35(1).
"regulations"—*ibid.*

GENERAL NOTE

Note in particular that regulations governing availability for, and actively seeking, employment, pilot schemes and requirements for people who are dependent on drugs have to be approved by affirmative resolution (subs.(1)(c)). **1.279**

New style JSA

Note that in those cases and areas where universal credit has come into force, income-based JSA is abolished and replaced by new style JSA (which is contribution-based only). See Pt VI of this book for the legislation relating to new style JSA and for the cases and areas to which it applies. **1.280**

General financial arrangements

38.—*[Omitted as not relevant.]* **1.281**

Provision for Northern Ireland

39.—*[Omitted as not relevant.]* **1.282**

Transitional provisions

40.—(1) The Secretary of State may by regulations make such transitional provision, consequential provision or savings as he considers necessary or expedient for the purposes of or in connection with— **1.283**
(a) the coming into force of any provision of this Act; or
(b) the operation of any enactment repealed or amended by any such provision during any period when the repeal or amendment is not wholly in force;
(2) Regulations under this section may in particular make provision—
(a) for the termination or cancellation of awards of unemployment benefit or income support;
(b) for a person whose award of unemployment benefit or income support has been terminated or cancelled under regulations made by virtue of paragraph (a) to be treated as having been awarded a jobseeker's allowance (a "transitional allowance")—
(i) of such a kind,
(ii) for such period,
(iii) of such an amount, and
(iv) subject to such conditions,
as may be determined in accordance with the regulations;
(c) for a person's continuing entitlement to a transitional allowance to be determined by reference to such provision as may be made by the regulations;

(d) for the termination of an award of a transitional allowance;
(e) for the review of an award of a transitional allowance;
(f) for a contribution-based jobseeker's allowance not to be payable for a prescribed period where a person is disqualified for receiving unemployment benefit;
(g) that days which were days of unemployment for the purposes of entitlement to unemployment benefit, and such other days as may be prescribed, are to be treated as having been days during which a person was, or would have been, entitled to a jobseeker's allowance;
(h) that days which were days of entitlement to unemployment benefit, and such other days as may be prescribed, are to be treated as having been days of entitlement to a contribution-based job-seeker's allowance;
(i) that the rate of a contribution-based transitional allowance is to be calculated by reference to the rate of unemployment benefit paid or payable.

DEFINITIONS

"contribution-based jobseeker's allowance"—see s.1(4).
"prescribed"—see s.35(1).
"regulations"—*ibid.*

GENERAL NOTE

1.284 See the Jobseeker's Allowance (Transitional Provisions) Regulations 1996 (SI 1996/2657) which are consolidating regulations that replaced the Jobseeker's Allowance (Transitional Provisions) Regulations 1995 (SI 1995/3276), as amended, from November 4, 1996. The text and commentary can be found in the 2000 edition of this volume.

Short title, commencement, extent etc.

1.285 **41.**—(1) This Act may be cited as the Jobseekers Act 1995.

(2) Section 39 and this section (apart from subsections (4) and (5)) come into force on the passing of this Act, but otherwise the provisions of this Act come into force on such day as the Secretary of State may by order appoint.

(3) Different days may be appointed for different purposes.

(4) Schedule 2 makes consequential amendments.

(5) The repeals set out in Schedule 3 shall have effect.

(6) Apart from this section, section 39 and paragraphs 11 to 16, 28, 67 and 68 of Schedule 2, this Act does not extend to Northern Ireland.

GENERAL NOTE

Subsections (4) and (5)

1.286 The amendments and repeals effected by, respectively, Schs 2 and 3 have been taken into account in the appropriate places in this book.

SCHEDULE A1

[Repealed by the Welfare Reform Act 2012 s.60(1) with effect from May 8, 2012]

SCHEDULE 1

SUPPLEMENTARY PROVISIONS

Remunerative work

1.287 **1.**—(1) For the purposes of this Act, "remunerative work" has such meaning as may be prescribed.

(2) Regulations may prescribe circumstances in which, for the purposes of this Act—
(a) a person who is not engaged in remunerative work is to be treated as engaged in remunerative work; or
(b) a person who is engaged in remunerative work is to be treated as not engaged in remunerative work.

[6 Limited capability for work

2.—(1) The question whether a person has, or does not have, limited capability for work shall be determined, for the purposes of this Act, in accordance with the provisions of Part 1 of the Welfare Reform Act 2007 (employment and support allowance) [12 or Part 1 of the Welfare Reform Act 2012 (universal credit) as the Secretary of State considers appropriate in the person's case]. **1.288**

(2) References in Part 1 of the Welfare Reform Act 2007 to the purposes of that Part shall be construed, where the provisions of that Part have effect for the purposes of this Act, as references to the purposes of this Act.]

[12 (3) References in Part 1 of the Welfare Reform Act 2012 to the purposes of that Part are to be construed, where the provisions of that Part have effect for the purposes of this Act, as references to the purposes of this Act.]

Linking periods

3.—Regulations may provide— **1.289**
(a) for jobseeking periods which are separated by not more than a prescribed number of weeks to be treated, for purposes of this Act, as one jobseeking period;
(b) for prescribed periods ("linked periods") to be linked, for purposes of this Act, to any jobseeking period.

Waiting days

4.—Except in prescribed circumstances, a person is not entitled to a jobseeker's allowance in respect of a prescribed number of days at the beginning of a jobseeking period. **1.290**

5.—Regulations may make provision in relation to—
(a) entitlement to a jobseeker's allowance, or
(b) the amount payable by way of such an allowance, in respect of any period of less than a week.

Employment protection sums

6.—(1) In relation to any contribution-based jobseeker's allowance, regulations may make provision— **1.291**
(a) for any employment protection sum to be treated as earnings payable by such person, to such person and for such period as may be determined in accordance with the regulations; and
(b) for any such period, so far as it is not a period of employment, to be treated as a period of employment.

(2) In this paragraph "employment protection sum" means—
(a) any sum, or a prescribed part of any sum—
(i) payable, in respect of arrears of pay, under an order for reinstatement or re-engagement made under[1the Employment Rights Act 1996];
(ii) payable, by way of pay, under an order made under that Act for the continuation of a contract of employment;
(iii) payable, by way of remuneration, under a protective award made under section 189 of the Trade Union and Labour Relations (Consolidation) Act 1992; and
(b) any prescribed sum which the regulations provide is to be treated as related to any sum within paragraph (a).

Pension payments

7.—Regulations may make provision, for the purposes of any provision of, or made under, this Act— **1.292**
(a) for such sums by way of pension payments to be disregarded for prescribed purposes;
(b) as to the week in which any pension payments are to be treated as having begun;
(c) for treating, in a case where—
(i) a lump sum is paid to a person in connection with a former employment of his or arrangements are made for a lump sum to be so paid; or

(ii) benefits of any description are made available to a person in connection with a former employment of his or arrangements are made for them to be made so available; or

(iii) pension payments to a person are assigned, reduced or postponed or are made otherwise than weekly,

such payments as being made to that person by way of weekly pension payments as are specified in or determined under the regulations;

(d) for the method of determining whether pension payments are made to a person for any week and their amount.

Exemptions

1.293 **8.**—Regulations may prescribe circumstances in which a person may be entitled to an income-based jobseeker's allowance without—

(a) being available for employment;
(b) having entered into a jobseeker's agreement; or
(c) actively seeking employment.

[4 **8A.**—(1) Regulations may prescribe circumstances in which a joint-claim couple may be entitled to a joint-claim jobseeker's allowance without each member of the couple satisfying all the conditions referred to in section 1(2B)(b).

(2) Regulations may prescribe circumstances in which, and a period for which, a transitional case couple may be entitled to a joint-claim jobseeker's allowance without having jointly made a claim for it.

(3) In sub-paragraph (2)—

(a) "a transitional case couple" means a joint-claim couple a member of which is entitled to an income-based jobseeker's allowance on the coming into force of Schedule 7 to the Welfare Reform and Pensions Act 1999; and
(b) "period" shall be construed in accordance with section 3(3).]

[8 **8B.** —(1) This paragraph applies if domestic violence has been inflicted on or threatened against a person ("V") in prescribed circumstances.

(2) The Secretary of State must exercise the powers to make regulations under sections 6(4) and 7(4) so as to secure that, for an exempt period, V is treated as—

(a) being available for employment; and
(b) actively seeking employment.

(3) If V has not entered into a jobseeker's agreement before the exempt period begins, the Secretary of State must also exercise the power to make regulations under section 9(10) so as to secure that V is treated as having entered into a jobseeker's agreement which is in force for the exempt period.

(4) In this paragraph—

"domestic violence" has such meaning as may be prescribed;

"exempt period" means a period of 13 weeks beginning no later than a prescribed period after the date (or last date) on which the domestic violence was inflicted or threatened.

(5) Regulations may make provision for the purposes of this paragraph prescribing circumstances in which domestic violence is, or is not, to be regarded as being inflicted on or threatened against a person.]

9.—Regulations may provide—

(a) for an income-based jobseeker's allowance to which a person is entitled by virtue of regulations under paragraph 8 [4 or 8A] to be payable at a prescribed rate;
(b) for it to be payable for a prescribed period.

[4 *Continuity of claims and awards: persons ceasing to be a joint-claim couple*

1.294 **9A.**—(1) Regulations may make provision about the entitlement to a jobseeker's allowance of persons ("ex-members") who cease to be members of a joint-claim couple.

(2) Regulations under this paragraph may, in particular, provide—

(a) for treating each or either of the ex-members as having made any claim made by the couple or, alternatively, for any such claim to lapse;
(b) for any award made in respect of the couple to be replaced by an award (a "replacement award") in respect of each or either of the ex-members of the couple or, alternatively, for any such award to lapse.

Continuity of claims and awards: persons again becoming a joint-claim couple

9B.—(1) Regulations may make provision about the entitlement to a jobseeker's allowance of persons ("ex-members") who, having ceased to be members of a joint-claim couple, again become the members of a joint-claim couple. **1.295**

(2) Regulations under this paragraph may, in particular, provide—

(a) for any claim made by the ex-members when they were previously a joint-claim couple to be revived or otherwise given effect as a claim made by the couple;

(b) for any award made in respect of the ex-members when they were previously a joint-claim couple to be restored;

(c) for any such award, or any replacement award (within the meaning of paragraph 9A) made in respect of either of them, to be replaced by an award (a "new award") in respect of the couple.

Continuity of claims and awards: couple becoming a joint-claim couple

9C.—(1) Regulations may make provision about the entitlement to a jobseeker's allowance of persons who become members of a joint-claim couple as a result of the [5 couple] of which they are members becoming a joint-claim couple. **1.296**

(2) Regulations under this paragraph may, in particular, provide—

(a) for any claim made by either member of the couple before the couple became a joint-claim couple to be given effect as a claim made by the couple;

(b) for any award, or any replacement award (within the meaning of paragraph 9A), made in respect of either member of the couple before the couple became a joint-claim couple to be replaced by an award (a "new award") in respect of the couple.

Paragraphs 9A to 9C: supplementary

9D.—(1) Regulations may provide, in relation to any replacement award (within the meaning of paragraph 9A) or new award (within the meaning of paragraph 9B or 9C)— **1.297**

(a) for the award to be of an amount determined in a prescribed manner;

(b) for entitlement to the award to be subject to compliance with prescribed requirements as to the provision of information and evidence.

(2) In paragraphs 9A to 9C and this paragraph—

"award" means an award of a jobseeker's allowance;

"claim" means a claim for a jobseeker's allowance.]

Claims yet to be determined and suspended payments

[4 **10.**—(1) In such circumstances as may be prescribed— **1.298**

(a) a claimant for a jobseeker's allowance other than a joint-claim jobseeker's allowance;

(b) a joint-claim couple claiming a joint-claim jobseeker's allowance; or

(c) a member of such a couple,

may be treated as being entitled to an income-based jobseeker's allowance before his or (as the case may be) the couple's claim for the allowance has been determined.]

(2) In such circumstances as may be prescribed, an income-based jobseeker's allowance shall be [3 payable in respect of]

[4 (a) a claimant for a jobseeker's allowance other than a joint-claim jobseeker's allowance;

(b) a joint-claim couple claiming a joint-claim jobseeker's allowance; or

(c) a member of such a couple,

even though payment to him or (as the case may be) the couple] of a jobseeker's allowance has been suspended by virtue of regulations under [2 section 21(2) of the Social Security Act 1998].

(3) A jobseeker's allowance shall be payable by virtue of sub-paragraph (1) or (2) only if the claimant [4 or (as the case may be) the couple or the member of the couple] has complied with such requirements as to the provision of information as may be prescribed for the purposes of this paragraph.

(4) Regulations may make provision for a jobseeker's allowance payable by virtue of sub-paragraph (1) or (2) to be—

(a) payable at a prescribed rate;

(b) payable for a prescribed period;

(c) treated as being a contribution-based jobseeker's allowance for the purposes of section 5 of this Act.

(5) Regulations may make provision—

(a) for the recovery, by prescribed means and in prescribed circumstances, of the whole or part of any amount paid by virtue of sub-paragraph (1) or (2);

(b) for the whole or part of any amount paid by virtue of sub-paragraph (1) to be treated, if an award is made on the claim referred to there, as having been paid on account of the jobseeker's allowance awarded;

(c) for the whole or part of any amount paid by virtue of sub-paragraph (2) to be treated, if the suspension referred to there is lifted, as having been paid on account of the suspended allowance.

[[9](6) References in sub-paragraphs (1) and (2) to an income-based jobseeker's allowance include a payment by way of such an allowance under section 19C.]

Presence in and absence from Great Britain

1.299 **11.**—(1) Regulations may provide that in prescribed circumstances a claimant who is not in Great Britain may nevertheless be entitled to a contribution-based jobseeker's allowance.

(2) Regulations may make provision for the purposes of this Act as to the circumstances in which a person is to be treated as being or not being in Great Britain.

Households

1.300 **12.**—Regulations may make provision for the purposes of this Act as to the circumstances in which persons are to be treated as being or not being members of the same household.

Responsibility for another person

1.301 **13.**—Regulations may make provision for the purposes of this Act as to the circumstances in which one person is to be treated as responsible or not responsible for another.

Relevant education

1.302 **14.**—Regulations may make provision for the purposes of this Act—

(a) as to what is or is not to be treated as relevant education; and

(b) as to the circumstances in which a person is or is not to be treated as receiving relevant education.

[[10]**14AA.**—For any purpose of this Act regulations may provide for—

(a) circumstances in which a person is to be treated as having or not having a good reason for an act or omission;

(b) matters which are or are not to be taken into account in determining whether a person has a good reason for an act or omission.]

Calculation of periods

1.303 **15.**—Regulations may make provision for calculating periods for any purpose of this Act.

Employment on ships etc.

1.304 **16.**—(1) Regulations may modify any provision of this Act in its application to any person who is, has been, or is to be—

(a) employed on board any ship, vessel, hovercraft or aircraft,

(b) outside Great Britain at any prescribed time or in any prescribed circumstances, or

(c) in prescribed employment in connection with continental shelf operations,

so far as that provision relates to a contribution-based jobseeker's allowance.

(2) The regulations may in particular provide—

(a) for any such provision to apply even though it would not otherwise apply;

(b) for any such provision not to apply even though it would otherwise apply;

(c) for the taking of evidence, in a country or territory outside Great Britain, by a British consular official or other prescribed person;

(d) for enabling payment of the whole, or any part of a contribution-based jobseeker's allowance to be paid to such of the claimant's dependants as may be prescribed.

Additional conditions

17.—Regulations may require additional conditions to be satisfied with respect to the payment of a jobseeker's allowance to any person who is, has been, or is to be, in employment which falls within a prescribed description. 1.305

Benefits Act purposes

18.—Regulations may provide for— 1.306

(a) a jobseeker's allowance;
(b) a contribution-based jobseeker's allowance; or
(c) an income-based jobseeker's allowance,

to be treated, for prescribed purposes of the Benefits Act, as a benefit, or a benefit of a prescribed description.

[[7] *Treatment of information supplied as information relating to social security*

19.—Information supplied in pursuance of any provision made by or under this Act [[11] . . .] shall be taken for all purposes to be information relating to social security.] 1.307

AMENDMENTS

1. Employment Rights Act 1996 Sch.1 para.67(3) (August 22, 1996).
2. Social Security Act 1998 Sch.7 para.146 (October 18, 1999).
3. Welfare Reform and Pensions Act 1999 Sch.8 para.29(7) (October 18, 1999).
4. Welfare Reform and Pensions Act 1999 Sch.7 para.16 (March 19, 2001).
5. Civil Partnership Act 2004 s.254 and Sch.24 Pt 7 para.125 (December 5, 2005).
6. Welfare Reform Act 2007 s.28(1) and Sch.3 para.12(6) (October 27, 2008).
7. Welfare Reform Act 2009 s.34(3) and Sch.3 Pt 1 para.3(4) (January 12, 2010).
8. Welfare Reform Act 2009 s.29(1) (January 19, 2012).
9. Welfare Reform Act 2012 Sch.7 para.10(1), (3) (October 22, 2012).
10. Welfare Reform Act 2012 s.46(3)(b) (June 10, 2012).
11. Welfare Reform Act 2012 s.147 and Sch.14 Pt 6 (May 8, 2012).
12. Universal Credit (Consequential, Supplementary, Incidental and Miscellaneous Provisions) Regulations 2013 (SI 2013/630) reg.10 (April 29, 2013).

DEFINITIONS

"a joint-claim couple"—see s.1(4).
"a joint-claim jobseeker's allowance—*ibid.*
"a transitional case couple"—see para.8A(3).
"the Benefits Act"—see s.35(1).
"contribution-based jobseeker's allowance"—see ss.35(1) and 1(4).
"couple"—see s.35(1).
"employment"—*ibid.*
"employment protection sum"—see para.6(2).
"ex-members"—see paras 9A(1) and 9B(1).
"Great Britain"—see s.35(1).
"income-based jobseeker's allowance"—see ss.35(1) and 1(4).
"jobseeker's agreement"—see ss.35(1) and 9(1).
"jobseeking period"—see s.35(1) and JSA Regulations 1996 reg.47.
"pension payments"—see s.35(1).
"PPF payment"—*ibid.*
"prescribed"—*ibid.*
"regulations"—*ibid.*
"week"—*ibid.*

GENERAL NOTE

Paragraph 1

Where a claimant is engaged in remunerative work, there can be no entitlement to old style JSA (s.1(2)(e)). If only a partner is so engaged, the claimant can still be eligible for CBJSA but not for IBJSA (s.3(1)(e)). This provision enables regulations to define "remunerative work" (in fact setting a threshold of 16 hours for the claimant and 24 hours for a partner). Those regulations can also define situations 1.308

in which, despite not being so engaged, a person is to be treated as if engaged in remunerative work and, conversely, to prescribe situations in which someone who would on the usual rules be regarded as being in remunerative work is to be treated as if he were not. See further JSA Regulations 1996 regs 51–53.

Paragraph 2

1.309 To be entitled to old style JSA, a claimant must not have limited capability for work (s.1(2)(f)). This provision ensures that the assessment of capacity for work is to be determined in accordance with the rules for ESA or universal credit.

Paragraph 3

1.310 This makes provision which benefits those whose unemployment is intermittent, interspersed with, say, periods of employment, of incapacity for work, of training for work or periods when pregnant, by providing, somewhat after the fashion of UB and its notion of "period of interruption of employment" ("PIE"), for the concepts of "linking" and "linked periods" whereby apparently separate jobseeking periods are fused into one and certain periods ("linked periods") do not "break" a jobseeking period.

"Linking", and through it the creation of a single jobseeking period, is important for two reasons: (1) the "waiting days" (see para.4, below) only have to be served once in a jobseeking period; and (2) in determining "the relevant benefit year" for purposes of identifying which tax/contribution years have to be looked at in order to ascertain if the claimant satisfies the contribution-record conditions of entitlement to CBJSA (see further annotation to s.2, above).

A "jobseeking period" is basically any period throughout which the claimant satisfies (or is treated as satisfying) the conditions of entitlement to old style JSA set out in s.1(2)(a)–(c) and (e)–(i): available for employment; a current jobseeker's agreement; actively seeking employment; not in remunerative work; not receiving relevant education; under pensionable age; and in Great Britain (s.35(1); JSA Regulations 1996 reg.47(1)). Where a hardship payment under Pt IX of those Regulations is paid to a claimant who does not satisfy a labour market condition (any of the conditions in s.1(2)(a)–(c): availability; actively seeking; jobseeker's agreement), he is to be treated as satisfying them for purposes of applying the above definition of jobseeking period (JSA Regulations 1996 reg.47(2)). He was also treated as satisfying the conditions in s.1(2)(a)–(c) and (e)–(i) when entitled to JSA under reg.13(3) of the JSA (Transitional) Regulations (JSA Regulations 1996 reg.47(2A)). Certain periods cannot constitute, or be part of, a jobseeking period: (i) any period in which no claim for JSA has been made or treated as made; (ii) any period before the day on which a claim is made or before the earliest date in which good cause for a late claim is shown; (iii) a period caught by the 12-month limit on backdating entitlement under s.1(2) of the SSAA 1992; (iv) a period of disentitlement under JSA Regulations 1996 regs 25 and 26; and (v) any week of disentitlement because the claimant is caught by the trade dispute rule in s.14 (JSA Regulations 1996 reg.47(3)). Note also JSA Regulations 1996 reg.47A on periods of interruption of employment prior to October 7, 1996.

"Linked periods" comprise: (i) any period throughout which the claimant is, or is treated as, incapable of work under Pt XIIA of the SSCBA 1992; (ii) any period throughout which she was entitled to a maternity allowance under s.35 of that Act; (iii) any period throughout which the claimant was engaged in training for which a training allowance is payable; (iv) (but only for contributions-conditions purposes) any period throughout which the claimant was entitled to an invalid care allowance (now "carer's allowance") under s.70 of the SSCBA 1992; (v) a period of attending court in response to a jury summons, which period includes October 6, 1996 and was immediately preceded by a period of entitlement to unemployment benefit; (vi) certain periods of participation in the Employment Option, the Voluntary Sector Option or the Environment Task Force Option of the New Deal and various Intensive Activity Period Programmes; (vii) certain periods of participation in an employment zone programme (JSA Regulations 1996 reg.48(2), (3)).

Two or more jobseeking periods "link" and are treated as one jobseeking period where they are separated by a period comprising only: (i) one of 12 weeks; (ii) a linked period; (iii) a period of not more than 12 weeks falling between any two linked periods or between a jobseeking period and a linked period; and (iv) any period in respect of which the claimant is summoned for jury service and is required to attend court (JSA Regulations 1996 reg.48(1)).

Paragraph 4

UB was a daily benefit payable in respect of a six-day week. Old style JSA is a weekly benefit. Nonetheless, through this provision, as amplified by JSA Regulations 1996 reg.46(2), it deploys the concept of "waiting days", familiar from UB but never part of income support, whereby, despite meeting the other conditions of entitlement to JSA, there is no entitlement to it for a number of days (initially three but extended to seven from October 27, 2014) at the start of a jobseeking period. On "jobseeking period" and the effect of "linking", see notes to para.3, above. Note further that the "waiting days" rule does not apply where the claimant's entitlement to JSA begins within 12 weeks of the ending of his entitlement to income support, incapacity benefit or carer's allowance, nor where the claim for IBJSA has to be determined by reference to s.3(1)(f)(ii), (i.e. the person is 16 or 17, registered for training but is not being provided with any, severe hardship will result to him if JSA is not paid, and the Secretary of State directs that s.16 is to apply to him) (JSA Regulations 1996 reg.46(1)). **1.311**

Paragraph 5

Although old style JSA is a weekly rather than a daily benefit, provision is made through regulations made under this paragraph for entitlement to JSA and the amount payable in respect of a period less than a week. See JSA Regulations 1996 regs 150–155 (regs 150(2), (3) and 152 are the ones relevant to CBJSA). **1.312**

Paragraph 6

This enables regulations to treat as earnings with respect to CBJSA for prescribed periods, certain employment protection sums under the Employment Rights Act 1996 and the Trade Union and Labour Relations (Consolidation) Act 1992 (or treated by regulations as related to those specific sums). It also enables regulations to treat those periods as ones of employment. See JSA Regulations 1996 reg.98(1)(f), (ff), (g) and related regulations on calculating net earnings (reg.99), determining the date on which they are treated for JSA purposes as paid (reg.96), the period over which they are taken into account (reg.94), and a weekly amount (reg.97). **1.313**

Paragraph 7

This enables regulations to deal with the listed aspects of taking into account pension payments. As regards CBJSA, the scheme incorporates the concept of abatement of benefit (even to nil) in respect of pension payments, but extends it to all claimants (not just those 55 or over, as for UB) and raises the weekly amount at which they are to be taken into account to £50 per week. See further notes to s.4(1) and JSA Regulations 1996 reg.81. **1.314**

Paragraphs 8, 8A, and 9

These enable regulations to allow access to reduced rates of income-based JSA for "persons in hardship", both in respect of standard cases and those of joint-claim couples, without having to meet the "labour market" conditions (availability; actively seeking; jobseeker's agreement). See further, JSA Regulations 1996 regs 140–146 (standard cases) and regs 146A–146H (joint-claim couples). In addition, para.8A enables the making of regulations for a "transitional case couple" to be entitled to a joint-claim jobseeker's allowance for a period without having made a claim for it. A "transitional case couple" is a "joint-claim couple" where one member was entitled to income-based JSA when the joint claim changes came into effect (March 19, 2001). JSA Regulations 1996 reg.3F was the product of the exercise of this rule-making power. **1.315**

Paragraph 8B

1.316 This requires the Secretary of State to make regulations under ss.6(4), 7(4) and 9(10) of the Act providing for victims of domestic violence who are claiming a jobseeker's allowance to be treated as available for and actively seeking work for a set 13 week period, and if the claimant has not completed a jobseeker's agreement before the 13 week period begins, to be treated as having entered into a jobseeker's agreement which is in force for the 13 week period. Paragraph 8B enables the regulations to specify the circumstances in which domestic violence must have been inflicted or threatened in order for the exemption to apply, to prescribe the circumstances in which domestic violence is, or is not, to be regarded as having been inflicted or threatened and to define "domestic violence". See reg.14A of the JSA Regulations 1996 inserted by the Jobseeker's Allowance (Domestic Violence) (Amendment) Regulations 2012 (SI 2012/853) with effect from April 23, 2012 and amended, with a new definition of "domestic violence", from October 29, 2013.

Paragraphs 9A–9D

1.317 These rule-making powers deal with matters of continuity where a couple cease to be a joint-claim couple (e.g. because of the birth of a child) (a "replacement award") (para.9A), where a couple again become a joint-claim couple (e.g. because of the death of a child) (para.9B) and where two people newly become one (e.g. because a child has become 16 and left education) (para.9C) (in both cases a "new award"). See further JSA Regulations 1996 regs 3B (ceasing to be a joint-claim couple), 3C (a couple again or newly becoming a joint-claim couple).

Paragraph 10

1.318 This enables regulations to allow access to reduced rate payments of IBJSA for a "person in hardship" before the claim or the joint-claim for JSA has been determined and where payment of JSA has been suspended by virtue of regulations under s.5(1)(n) or (nn) of the SSAA 1992. See further JSA Regulations 1996 regs 140–146 (standard cases) and 146A–146H (joint-claim couples).

Paragraph 11

1.319 Generally, to be entitled to old style JSA, a claimant must be in Great Britain (s.1(2)(i)). Sub-paragraph (1) enables regulations to be made prescribing circumstances in which someone not in Great Britain can nevertheless be entitled to CBJSA. See JSA Regulations 1996 regs 165 and 166. The former effected amendments to reg.11 of the Persons Abroad Regulations (see below). The latter amended the Social Security (Mariners' Benefits) Regulations 1975, which are not reproduced in this book.

Sub-paragraph (2) enables the making of regulations treating a person as being, or as not being, in Great Britain. See JSA Regulations 1996 reg.50, which in the circumstances there set out treats someone temporarily absent from Great Britain as if he were present in Great Britain, thus enabling him to remain eligible for old style JSA while temporarily absent.

Paragraph 12

1.320 This enables the making of regulations to set out when persons are or are not to be regarded for JSA purposes as members of the same household. See reg.78 of the JSA Regulations 1996.

Paragraph 13

1.321 This enables the making of regulations setting out when someone is to be treated as responsible for a child or young person. See reg.77 of the JSA Regulations 1996.

Paragraph 14

1.322 A person cannot be entitled to old style JSA if receiving relevant education (s.1(2)(g)). This paragraph enables regulations to provide for what does and does not constitute relevant education and for when someone is, or is not, to be treated as receiving it. See further JSA Regulations 1996 reg.54, which defines it to cover only full-time education, not being a course of advanced education, which is undertaken by a child or young person. Someone treated as a child for child benefit purposes or who is receiving full-time education as far as the child benefit system is concerned (see SSCBA 1992 s.142), is treated as receiving full-time education for purposes of jobseeker's allowance (JSA Regulations 1996 reg.54(2)). As this exclusion covers persons under 19, the effect of the contribution conditions (the claimant's insurance record) is to make this in practice a hurdle much more relevant to IBJSA than to CBJSA. Those on a full-time course of advanced education, it should be noted, will be excluded from JSA because treated as not available for employment (see s.6 and JSA Regulations 1996 regs 1(3) and 15(a)).

Paragraph 14AA

In many areas of old style JSA involving sanctions "good cause" or "just cause" has been replaced by "good reason". This paragraph enables the making of regulations setting out, for any purposes of the Jobseekers Act 1995, circumstances in which someone is or is not to be treated as having a "good reason" for any act or omission. It also enables regulations to stipulate matters which are or are not to be taken into account in determining whether someone has a "good reason" for an act or omission. See reg.72 of the JSA Regulations 1996, in relation only to ss.19(2)(c) and (d) and 19A(2)(c). **1.323**

Paragraph 16

This enables regulations to modify any provision of this Act, so far as it relates to CBJSA, in its application to those employed on ships, vessels, hovercraft or aircraft, to those outside Great Britain, or to those in prescribed employment in connection with continental shelf operations. See further JSA Regulations 1996 Pt XII (not reproduced in this work), dealing with share fishermen and persons outside Great Britain, including mariners. **1.324**

Paragraph 17

This enables regulations to require additional conditions to be satisfied with respect to payment of old style JSA to those in, or who have been in, or who are to be in, employment of a prescribed description. See further JSA Regulations 1996 Pt XII (not reproduced in this work), dealing with share fishermen and persons outside Great Britain, including mariners. **1.325**

New style JSA

Note that in those cases and areas where universal credit has come into force, income-based JSA is abolished and replaced by new style JSA (which is contribution-based only). See Pt VI of this book for the legislation relating to new style JSA and for the cases and areas to which it applies. **1.326**

State Pension Credit Act 2002

(2002 c.16)

SECTIONS REPRODUCED

State pension credit: entitlement and amount

1. Entitlement. **1.327**

INTRODUCTION AND GENERAL NOTE

1.328 The prime purpose of this Act, embodied in ss.1–17, was to set the framework for the state pension credit that has been available to people aged 60 and over as from

October 6, 2003. The Labour Government elected in 1997 set out its initial proposals in *A New Contract for Welfare: Partnership in Pensions* (Cm.4179, 1998). This led to the introduction of stakeholder pensions under Pt I of the Welfare Reform and Pensions Act 1999, with effect from April 2001, as a new option for private pension provision for those on moderate incomes.

So far as the poorest pensioners were concerned, the Government at that time resisted demands from its own backbenchers and supporters to restore the link between the state retirement pension and increases in average earnings. Instead, the value of income support for pensioners was dramatically increased and that benefit relabelled as the minimum income guarantee (or "MIG") for that client group. This had the effect of increasing the gap between the (higher) MIG entitlement and the (lower) basic state retirement pension respectively for a single pensioner. The disparity increased from £5.75 in April 1998 (when the basic pension represented 92 per cent of the MIG rate) to £22.65 by April 2002 (by which time the basic pension had fallen to 77 per cent of the MIG level). This exacerbated the longstanding problem that pensioners with small amounts of private incomes on top of their state retirement pension saw no benefit from such thrift as any such income is deducted pound-for-pound under income support rules.

The proposal for a pension credit was first canvassed in a DSS consultation paper in November 2000 (DSS, *The Pension Credit: a consultation paper,* Cm.4900), which was followed by the publication of a further paper entitled *The Pension Credit: the government's proposals* (DWP, 2001). The pension credit both continues the previous income support arrangements (or MIG) for pensioners in a modified form and provides some reward for those with small private incomes. Thus the state pension credit comprises two quite distinct elements. The first is the "guarantee credit", which is intended to provide a minimum level of income to those aged 60 or over. This replaces the MIG, the marketing name for income support for pensioners. The second is the "savings credit", which is designed to provide an additional form of income for pensioners from the age of 65 who have low or modest private incomes (e.g. an occupational pension and/or income from savings) in addition to the basic state retirement pension.

Section 1 specifies the common conditions for access to the pension credit, **1.329**
whilst ss.2 and 3 respectively stipulate the extra conditions which must be satisfied in order to qualify for either or both of the guarantee credit and the savings credit. The common conditions for state pension credit in s.1 are that the claimant is in Great Britain and has reached the qualifying age (set at the pensionable age for women). Note also that in *EC v Secretary of State for Work and Pensions* [2010] UKUT 93 (AAC); [2010] AACR 39 it was held that state pension credit is a special non-contributory benefit within art.10a of reg.1408/71 and so is payable only to those living in Great Britain. In addition, s.4 includes a number of exclusions from entitlement to the pension credit and s.5 confirms that a claimant's resources must be aggregated with those of their partner.

The calculation of the guarantee credit entitlement under s.2 essentially works in the same way as the income support scheme. There are, however, two important differences in the substantive rules of entitlement to the guarantee credit when contrasted with those that apply to income support. Income support is not available to those who work for 16 hours or more a week and is subject to an upper capital limit. Neither rule applies to state pension credit.

The savings credit under s.3, comprising the second potential element in the state pension credit, is an entirely novel form of benefit. It works in the opposite way to the traditional means-test which applies for the purposes of income support. Previously a pensioner who had a small private income over and above the state retirement pension saw their MIG or income support reduced pound-for-pound by any such income. In contrast, the savings credit provides a small weekly supplement to reward those with modest savings or private incomes. Section 3 sets out the two extra criteria for the award of the savings credit (in addition to the common rules contained in s.1 for the pension credit as a whole).

As originally enacted in the 2002 Act, the first of these was simply that the claimant (or their partner) was at least 65. This condition was radically altered by the Pensions Act 2014. As from the start date for the new state pension (April 6, 2016), s.3 as amended now provides that the savings credit element of state pension credit is only payable (from the savings credit qualifying age) to those who had already reached pensionable age before that date.

The second is effectively a complicated mathematical formula which is translated into text form. This can only really be understood by following the example provided in the annotation to s.3. Its effect is to provide a small savings credit of up to £13.07 a week at 2016/17 rates for a single pensioner for those with incomes which are just above the MIG level.

1.330 The other important difference from the previous arrangements, at least as the state pension credit scheme was originally enacted, concerns the duration of awards of any pension credit (of either type) and the effects of change in circumstances. Income support is a weekly benefit and any changes in circumstances (e.g. in the amount of an occupational pension) must be reported to the DWP. Where the pension credit is awarded, the Secretary of State had to specify an "assessed income period" (s.6), which will typically be for five years (s.9). The statutory assumption under s.7(4) is that the claimant's income will then remain constant throughout this period, subject to any deemed increases of a foreseeable and regular nature, such as the arrangements for indexation of any occupational or other private pension (e.g. in line with the Retail Price Index); see also s.10. The remarkable effect of these provisions was that where the claimant received a windfall increase during the period of the award, any such increases were disregarded (s.7(5)) and accordingly did not give rise to any obligation to report such a change to the Department. In the event that the pensioner's income fell, a fresh assessment could be applied for (s.8).

However, in the 2013 Spending Round the Government announced the abolition of the assessed income period in state pension credit cases from April 2016, a change effected by the Pensions Act 2014 (ss.28, 29 and Sch.12 paras 88–91). As a result, in future any change in retirement income will need to be reported to the Department when it occurs, triggering a review and a change in benefit award where appropriate.

The remaining provisions of the Act which relate to the state pension credit are of a supplementary nature. Section 11 introduces Sch.1, which applies the social security claims, decisions and appeals procedures to the state pension credit. Section 12 makes special provision for the few polygamous marriages that may fall within the ambit of the new scheme whilst s.13 enables the Secretary of State to make regulations governing transitional arrangements. Section 14 introduces Sch.2, which makes minor and consequential amendments. Sections 15–17 provide definitions of a number of key terms, such as "income" (s.15) and "retirement pension income" (s.16), as well as other general expressions (s.17), but also grant the Secretary of State extensive regulation-making powers to provide further definitions of certain terms. The relevant regulations, also in this volume (see paras 4.1 et seq.), are the State Pension Credit Regulations 2002 (SI 2002/1792), as amended.

The final point to note about the state pension credit is a matter of nomenclature. Throughout the 2002 Act the new benefit is referred to as the *state* pension credit. This formula is required because s.29 of the Welfare Reform and Pensions Act 1999 makes provision for the creation of "pension credits" as a mechanism for effecting pension sharing on divorce. This Act, therefore, could not describe the benefit simply as the pension credit. However, the benefit is known as the *state* pension credit purely for the purposes of statutory drafting. The Department's publicity material describes the benefit as pension credit *simpliciter*. For the reasons explained in the General Note to s.3, the "savings credit", one of the constituent elements in the pension credit, is itself something of a misnomer, as it is not merely a credit on savings. State pension credit has nothing whatsoever to do with the working tax credit and the child tax credit which were introduced in April 2003 by the Tax Credits Act 2002 (see Vol.IV in this series). Those *tax* credits are administered by HRMC; the state pension credit remains firmly in the province of the DWP and its Pension, Disability and Carers Service, the Department's operational arm which now has responsibility for all pensions matters. See further N. Wikeley, "State Pension Credit: completing the pensions jigsaw?" (2004) 11 *Journal of Social Security Law* 12.

Looking to the future, the independent Pensions Commission has pointed out that maintaining the current indexation rules for pension credit and the basic state retirement pension respectively will lead to a steady extension of means-testing of pensioners over time. On the current rules it is estimated that by 2050 over 70 per cent of all pensioners would be subject to means-tested withdrawal of either the state second pension or their private pension income: Pensions Commission, *A New Pension Settlement for the Twenty-First Century – The Second Report of the Pensions Commission* (November 2005), p.142. For more detail see *Pensions: Challenges and Choices – The First Report of the Pensions Commission* (October 2004), pp.224–230. 1.331

Major changes to the state pension regime were made by the Pensions Act 2014, coming into force with effect from April 6, 2016. Pensioners who had already reached state pension age as at that date will continue to be entitled to the state pension under the previous rules. However, 'new' pensioners will now qualify for the new single tier state pension. One of the main principles of the reform was that the new state pension is to be set above the basic level of means-tested support. Thus whereas the standard minimum guarantee under the state pension credit scheme is £155.60 in 2016/17, the starting rate for the new state pension is £155.65.

See also s.142 of the Pensions Act 2008, which enables the Secretary of State to regulations to supply social security information about state pension credit recipients to energy suppliers (or persons providing services to the energy suppliers or the Secretary of State). These provisions also authorise energy suppliers to share their customer information with the Secretary of State or a service provider, so as to enable either the Secretary of State or a third party to match DWP and energy supplier data to identify the relevant state pension credit recipients. The intention is to identify those persons who are eligible for financial assistance towards their electricity bill in accordance with a support scheme established under arrangements made between the Secretary of State and electricity suppliers. See further the Disclosure of State Pension Credit Information (Warm Home Discount) Regulations 2011 (SI 2011/1830).

Commencement

The Act received the Royal Assent on June 25, 2002. Sections 19, 20 and 22 came into effect on that date (s.22(2)). Other provisions come into effect as the Secretary of State may order (s.22(3)). The State Pension Credit Act 2002 (Commencement No.1) Order 2002 (SI 2002/1691 (c.51)) provided that July 2, 2002 was the day appointed for the coming into force of the regulation making powers under ss.1 to 7, 9 and 11–17 (except for certain provisions in s.14). The relevant regulations are the State Pension Credit Regulations 2002 (SI 2002/1792, as amended), which came into force on October 6, 2003. 1.332

The final Commencement Order was the State Pension Credit Act 2002 (Commencement No.5) and Appointed Day Order 2003 (SI 2003/1766 (c.75)). This brought into force on October 6, 2003 all those provisions of the Act which were not already in force and appointed that day as the "appointed day" for the purposes of s.13 of the Act (transitional provisions).

Note also that s.34 and Sch.4 of the Welfare Reform Act 2012 have prospectively amended the 2002 Act to create a new credit within state pension credit to cover housing costs. This is intended to provide support for people who have reached the qualifying age for state pension credit (or for couples where both members have reached the qualifying age) once housing benefit is no longer available following the full introduction of universal credit. In particular, the new s.3A (inserted by Welfare Reform Act 2012 s.34 and Sch.4 paras 1 and 4), sets out the conditions of entitlement to the new housing credit and provides the powers to set out the structure of the housing credit in regulations. There are also a number of consequential amendments. However, these amendments introduced by the Welfare Reform Act 2012 have yet to be brought into force, and so are not included in this edition.

State pension credit: entitlement and amount

Entitlement

1.333 **1.**—(1) A social security benefit to be known as state pension credit shall be payable in accordance with the following provisions of this Act.

(2) A claimant is entitled to state pension credit if—

(a) he is in Great Britain;

(b) he has attained the qualifying age; and

(c) he satisfies—

(i) the condition in section 2(1) (guarantee credit); or

(ii) the conditions in section 3(1) and (2) (savings credit).

(3) A claimant who is entitled to state pension credit is entitled—

(a) to a guarantee credit, calculated in accordance with section 2, if he satisfies the condition in subsection (1) of that section, or

(b) to a savings credit, calculated in accordance with section 3, if he satisfies the conditions in subsections (1) and (2) of that section,

(or to both, if he satisfies both the condition mentioned in paragraph (a) and the conditions mentioned in paragraph (b)).

(4) Subsections (2) and (3) are subject to the following provisions of this Act.

(5) Regulations may make provision for the purposes of this Act—

(a) as to circumstances in which a person is to be treated as being or not being in Great Britain; or

(b) continuing a person's entitlement to state pension credit during periods of temporary absence from Great Britain.

(6) In this Act "the qualifying age" means—

(a) in the case of a woman, pensionable age; or

(b) in the case of a man, the age which is pensionable age in the case of a woman born on the same day as the man.

Definitions

"claimant"—see s.17(1).
"entitled"—*ibid.*
"guarantee credit"—*ibid.*
"pensionable age"—*ibid.*
"the qualifying age"—see subs.(6).
"regulations"—see s.17(1).
"savings credit"—*ibid.*

General Note

1.334 This section sets out the entitlement criteria for the state pension credit. The conditions laid down by this section are the common entitlement rules. These are that the claimant is in Great Britain (subs.(2)(a); see further subs.(5)) and has reached the qualifying age (subs.(2)(b), as defined by subs.(6)). Note also *EC v Secretary of State for Work and Pensions* [2010] UKUT 93 (AAC); [2010] AACR 39, where it was held that state pension credit is a special non-contributory benefit within art.10a of reg.1408/71 which is payable only to those living in Great Britain. In addition, a claimant must satisfy either or both of the additional rules relating to eligibility for the guarantee credit (s.2) and the savings credit (s.3) (see subs.(2)(c)). The guarantee credit replaced the MIG (or, in other words, income support) for the pensioner population. The calculation of the guarantee credit itself works in the same way as the MIG and is designed to bring a pensioner's income up to a minimum threshold, which for 2016/17 is £155.60 for a single claimant and £237.55 for a couple. The savings credit, which may be payable additionally to or independently of the guarantee credit, seeks to provide a reward for those pensioner claimants who have a modest private income over and above the basic state retirement pension. A claimant's entitlement thus comprises either or both such components, depending on which conditions are met (subs.(3)). These requirements are obviously subject to the remaining provisions of the Act (subs.(4)).

Subsection (2)(a)

In *NB v Secretary of State for Work and Pensions (SPC)* [2013] UKUT 266 (AAC), an overpayment appeal, Judge Wright held that living on a British registered boat outside UK territorial waters was not being "in Great Britain" for the purpose of s.1(2)(a) (following *R(IS) 8/06*). However, the claimant will have been in Great Britain for any period that he was either on land in the UK or on his boat when in UK waters, and the tribunal erred in law in not enquiring into this aspect. Remitting the appeal to a new tribunal, the Judge directed it to consider whether the temporary absence rule applied for any period (which provides that a claimant will continue to be entitled to SPC for 13 weeks while not in Great Britain if the period of absence is unlikely to exceed 52 weeks and he continues to satisfy the other conditions of entitlement; see reg.3). **1.335**

Subsection (5)

This power enables regulations to make further provision in respect to the residence requirement. See further State Pension Credit Regulations 2002 (SI 2002/1792) regs 2 and 3, requiring pension credit claimants to be habitually resident, although they may retain their entitlement for up to 13 weeks during a period of temporary absence abroad. **1.336**

Subsection (6)

This definition of "qualifying age" must be read together with the definition of "pensionable age" in s.17(1). Its effect is that the qualifying age for both men and women is the pensionable age for women. From the 1940s until 2010 the state pension age was 65 for men and 60 for women. The Pensions Act 1995 (s.126 and Sch.4) originally provided for the increase from 60 to 65 in the state pension age for women to be phased in over the period from April 2010 to 2020. However, the Coalition Government brought forward the Pensions Act 2011 (see s.1) to accelerate the latter part of this timetable, so that the pensionable age for women will now reach 65 in November 2018. The reason for this change was the overall increase in life expectancy since the timetable was last revised. It had also initially been intended that the equalised pensionable age for men and women would then rise to 66 by April 2020. However, because of concerns expressed about the impact on women born in March 1954, who would see their pensionable age increase by as much as two years as a result, it decided that this should happen over a slightly longer period, with the uniform state pension age reaching 66 in October 2020. See further the report by the House of Commons Work and Pensions Committee, *Communication of state pension age changes*, Seventh Report of 2015/16, HC 899). Note that the Pensions Act 2014 also includes provision to bring forward the increase in the common state pension age to 67 to between 2026 and 2028. **1.337**

The basic requirement under subs.(2)(a) is that a pension credit claimant must have reached this qualifying age; this is also sufficient for entitlement to the guarantee credit under s.2. However, a claimant must actually be 65 (or their partner must be) in order to claim the savings credit (s.3(1)). The Government's justification for this distinction was that "the age of 65 is the first point at which we judge that the savings credit can be fairly and equally paid to ensure that we are not open to legal challenge in respect of gender equality" (Ms M. Eagle MP, Parliamentary Under-Secretary for Work and Pensions, Standing Committee A, col.104). Thus retired single women aged between 60 and 64 may claim the guarantee credit but not the savings credit, even though they may have a small private income. Women of this age who are members of a married or unmarried couple may claim the savings credit if their partner is aged 65 or over, and so may see some benefit from private savings.

In a number of recent decisions the Upper Tribunal has dealt with some of the difficult evidential issues associated with proof of age. In the first, *LS v SSWP (SPC)* [2014] UKUT 249 (AAC), the issue was whether the claimant, the wife of a Gurkha, was born on January 1, 1951 or some other date in 1951. Judge Williams in the Upper Tribunal held that the tribunal had failed to apply the correct standard of proof (balance of probabilities) and to consider all the relevant evidence. Similar issues arose in *SW v SSWP (SPC)* [2016] UKUT 0163 (AAC), where the claimant, who had originally obtained an Ethiopian passport showing her date of birth to be January 1, 1963, subsequently became a naturalized British citizen, her UK passport again showing her date of birth to be January 1, 1963. She later claimed pension credit, stating that her true date of birth was May 23, 1950. The DWP decision-maker and the First-tier Tribunal decided the passport(s) showed the correct date of birth and concluded the claimant was not eligible for pension credit on age grounds. The claimant's explanation, amongst other matters, was that she had obtained her Ethiopian passport at a time when she was travelling to Qatar for domestic work, and had been advised that she would not find employment if she was aged over 30, and so a false date had been used. Judge Hemingway allowed the claimant's appeal and, tasking into account all the evidence, re-made the decision, holding that the claimant had indeed reached the qualifying age. In doing so, Judge Hemingway made the following more general observations:

> "41. . . . There is the question of whether the documents are forgeries, the original tribunal of course thought they were, and I am quite prepared to accept that it is possible to obtain fraudulent documents in Ethiopia just as, of course, it is possible to obtain fraudulent documents, in the right circumstances, I imagine in pretty much every country in the world. There may, of course, be significant variations in the ease with which fraudulent but apparently genuine documents might be obtained. It seems to me that where an allegation of fraud is being made by a party then it will be necessary for the asserting party to prove it to the requisite standard which, here, is a balance of probabilities. Here, though, I cannot see that the respondent did actually submit to the tribunal that the documents were forged. It also seems to me that it will seldom be necessary for a tribunal to reach a definitive view as to whether a document is forged or not. Rather, the inquiry should be directed more as to whether any weight can be attached to the documents provided by a claimant having regard to the evidence as a whole and a claimant's general credibility. There may also be other reasons, irrespective of the veracity of any allegation as to forgery, as to why documents cannot be accorded weight. In this case I have decided, whilst I do not on balance find the appellant to be dishonest, that the documents cannot be accorded weight because of the lack of any evidence and information concerning the existence of or accuracy of record keeping on the part of the church or the relevant government department responsible for issuing birth certificates. So, as it turns out, the documents assist neither the appellant nor the respondent."

Guarantee credit

1.338 **2.**—(1) The condition mentioned in section 1(2)(c)(i) is that the claimant—

(a) has no income; or

(b) has income which does not exceed the appropriate minimum guarantee.

(2) Where the claimant is entitled to a guarantee credit, then—

(a) if he has no income, the guarantee credit shall be the appropriate minimum guarantee; and

(b) if he has income, the guarantee credit shall be the difference between the appropriate minimum guarantee and his income.

(3) The appropriate minimum guarantee shall be the total of—

(a) the standard minimum guarantee; and

(b) such prescribed additional amounts as may be applicable.

(4) The standard minimum guarantee shall be a prescribed amount.

(5) The standard minimum guarantee shall be—

(a) a uniform single amount in the case of every claimant who is a member of a [1 couple]; and

(b) a lower uniform single amount in the case of every claimant who is not a member of [1 a couple].

(6) Regulations may provide that, in prescribed cases, subsection (3) shall have effect with the substitution for the reference in paragraph (a) to the standard minimum guarantee of a reference to a prescribed amount.

(7) Where the claimant is severely disabled, there shall be included among the additional amounts prescribed under subsection (3)(b) an amount in respect of that circumstance.

(8) Where—

(a) the claimant is entitled to an allowance under section 70 of the Contributions and Benefits Act, or

(b) if the claimant is a member of a [1 couple], the other member of the couple is entitled to such an allowance,

there shall be included among the additional amounts prescribed under subsection (3)(b) an amount in respect of that circumstance.

(9) Except for the amount of the standard minimum guarantee, the powers conferred by this section to prescribe amounts include power to prescribe nil as an amount.

Amendment

1. Civil Partnership Act 2004 s.254 and Sch.24 paras 140 and 141 (December 5, 2005).

Definitions

"appropriate minimum guarantee"—see subs.(3) and s.17(1).
"claimant"—see s.17(1).
"Contributions and Benefits Act"—*ibid.*
"entitled"—*ibid.*
"guarantee credit"—*ibid.*
"income"—*ibid.*
"married couple"—*ibid.*
"prescribed"—*ibid.*
"regulations"—*ibid.*
"standard minimum guarantee"—see subss.(4) and (5) and s.17(1).
"unmarried couple"—see s.17(1).

General Note

This section sets out the extra condition (further to the common conditions in s.1) **1.339**
which a pension credit claimant must satisfy in order to be entitled to the guarantee credit (which replaced the MIG, or income support, for pensioners). The extra condition is that the claimant either has no income or has an income which does not exceed the "appropriate minimum guarantee" (subs.(1)). "Income" is defined in accordance with ss.15 and 16 (and see State Pension Credit Regulations 2002 (SI 2002/1792

Pt III)); but note also that the claimant's income is to be aggregated with that of any partner (s.5). The "appropriate minimum guarantee" is equivalent to the applicable amount in the income support scheme. It therefore comprises the "standard minimum guarantee" and other prescribed amounts (subs.(3)). The former is a standard prescribed amount (subss.(4) and (5)) which in 2016/17 is £155.60 for a single person and £237.55 for a couple (State Pension Credit Regulations 2002 (SI 2002/1792) reg.6(1)). The other prescribed amounts mirror the premiums in the income support scheme. Specific provision is made for two particular types of extra prescribed amounts under subs.(3)(b), namely for those who are severely disabled (subs.(7); this is based on SSCBA 1992 s.135(5)) and for those who are entitled to a carer's allowance under SSCBA 1992 s.70 (subs.(8)). The extra amounts under subs.(3)(b) also include other elements, e.g. prescribed sums for owner-occupiers as regards their housing costs (see generally State Pension Credit Regulations 2002 (SI 2002/1792) Schs I and II).

The Secretary of State also has the power to substitute a prescribed amount for the uniform standard minimum guarantee (subs.(6)). This only has effect for the purpose of calculating the appropriate minimum guarantee for that person under subs.(3)(a), which is then based on the prescribed amount plus any other prescribed additional amounts. It does not, therefore, affect the standard minimum guarantee for other purposes in the Act, most notably the assessment of the maximum savings credit under s.3(7). This power has been inserted to enable a different rate to be applied where the claimant (or their partner) remains in hospital for more than 52 weeks. The previous regime provided for "hospital downrating" to apply after six weeks in hospital, but the Government initially increased this period to 13 weeks and then subsequently to 52 weeks by the Social Security (Hospital In-Patients and Miscellaneous Amendments) Regulations 2003 (SI 2003/1195); see now State Pension Credit Regulations 2002 (SI 2002/1792) Sch.III para.2.

The Secretary of State also has the power, taking subss. (6) and (9) together, to prescribe nil as the amount of the standard minimum guarantee in subs.(3)(a). The wording of subs.(9) is not entirely clear, but its import (when read with subs.(6)) appears to be that nil can be prescribed as the amount of the standard minimum guarantee under subs.(3)(a) but not as the rate of the normal standard minimum guarantee under subss.(4) and (5). This enables a nil amount to be specified for prisoners and members of religious orders who are fully maintained by their orders (both being groups who are currently excluded from income support; see now State Pension Credit Regulations 2002 (SI 2002/1792) reg.6(2) and (3) and *Scott v Secretary of State for Work and Pensions* [2011] EWCA Civ 103; [2011] AACR 23).

Three important differences with the rules governing entitlement to income support should be noted. First, there is no provision in the Act for a "16-hour rule" in the state pension credit scheme. Thus, unlike those of working age who claim income support or jobseeker's allowance, pensioners are not disentitled if they work 16 hours or more a week. Secondly, there is no upper capital limit for the pension credit (see further s.15); moreover the deemed rate of return by virtue of the tariff income rule is halved (State Pension Credit Regulations 2002 (SI 2002/1792) reg.15(6)). Finally, the traditional weekly means-test for income support was not originally replicated in the arrangements for the pension credit; instead the typical award was made for an "assessed income period" of five years (see further s.7). However, assessed income periods were abolished by the Pensions Act 2014 with effect from April 2016.

Savings credit

1.340 **3.**—[2 (1) The first of the conditions mentioned in section 1(2)(c)(ii) is that the claimant—

(a) has attained pensionable age before 6 April 2016 and has attained the age of 65 (before, on or after that date), or

(b) is a member of a couple, the other member of which falls within paragraph (a).]

(2) The second of the conditions mentioned in section 1(2)(c)(ii) is that—
(a) the claimant's qualifying income exceeds the savings credit threshold; and
(b) the claimant's income is such that, for the purposes of subsection (3), amount A exceeds amount B.

(3) Where the claimant is entitled to a savings credit, the amount of the savings credit shall be the amount by which amount A exceeds amount B.

(4) For the purposes of subsection (3)—
"amount A" is the smaller of—
(a) the maximum savings credit; and
(b) a prescribed percentage of the amount by which the claimant's qualifying income exceeds the savings credit threshold; and
"amount B" is—
(a) a prescribed percentage of the amount (if any) by which the claimant's income exceeds the appropriate minimum guarantee; or
(b) if there is no such excess, nil.

(5) Where, by virtue of regulations under section 2(6), the claimant's appropriate minimum guarantee does not include the standard minimum guarantee, regulations may provide that the definition of "amount B" in subsection (4) shall have effect with the substitution for the reference in paragraph (a) to the appropriate minimum guarantee of a reference to a prescribed higher amount.

(6) Regulations may make provision as to income which is, and income which is not, to be treated as qualifying income for the purposes of this section.

(7) For the purposes of this section—
"the savings credit threshold" is such amount as may be prescribed;
"the maximum savings credit" is a prescribed percentage of the difference between—
(a) the standard minimum guarantee; and
(b) the savings credit threshold.

(8) Regulations may prescribe descriptions of persons in whose case the maximum savings credit shall be taken to be nil.

AMENDMENTS

1. Civil Partnership Act 2004 s.254 and Sch.24 para.140 (December 5, 2005).
2. Pensions Act 2014 s.23 and Sch.12 Pt.3 para.89 (April 6, 2016).

DEFINITIONS

"appropriate minimum guarantee"—see ss.2(3) and 17(1).
"claimant"—see s.17(1).
"entitled"—*ibid.*
"income"—*ibid.*
"married couple"—*ibid.*
"maximum savings credit"—see subs.(7).
"prescribed"—see s.17(1).
"regulations"—*ibid.*
"savings credit"—*ibid.*
"savings credit threshold"—see subs.(7).
"standard minimum guarantee"—ss.2(4) and (5) and 17(1).
"unmarried couple"—s.17(1).

General Note

1.341 This section sets out the extra conditions (further to the common conditions in s.1) which a pension credit claimant must satisfy in order to be entitled to the savings credit. A claimant may be entitled to the savings credit even if he or she is not entitled to the guarantee credit (s.1(3)). In order to qualify for a savings credit there are two additional requirements that must be satisfied.

The first, as originally enacted, was that the claimant (or their partner) was at least 65. This stood in contrast to the eligibility conditions for guarantee credit, for which the qualifying age was (and remains) the pensionable age for women as specified in the common criteria for pension credit (ss.1(2)(a) and (6)). However, as a result of amendments made by the Pensions Act 2014 (fully in force from April 6, 2016), there is no longer access to the savings credit element for those claimants reaching state pension age on or after that date *unless* they are a member of a couple where the other member reached state pension age before April 6, 2016 (known as "a mixed-age couple"; see further s.3ZA). The policy justification for this change is that whereas the previous basic state pension was set below the level of the standard minimum guarantee in pension credit, the new state pension is set at a level above that threshold, so removing the problem that the savings credit was designed to address. See further the State Pension Credit Regulations 2002 (SI 2002/1792) reg.7A. The policy was first announced in the new state pension green and white papers (DWP, *A State Pension for the 21st Century*, Cm 8053, April 2011, Ch.3 and *The single-tier pension: a simple foundation for saving*, Cm 8528, January 2013, Ch.4).

The second additional condition is more complex. The claimant's "qualifying income" (including that of their partner: see further ss.5, 15 and 16 and State Pension Credit Regulations 2002 (SI 2002/1792) reg.9) must exceed the "savings credit threshold" and must be such that "amount A exceeds Amount B" (subs.(2)), the difference being the amount of savings credit entitlement (subs.(3)). The complexity is the inevitable consequence of the draftsman's attempt to reduce an arithmetical calculation into comprehensible prose. The good news is that this formula does not require the same skills in advanced algebra as did the original child support scheme.

The term "savings credit" is itself something of a misnomer, as will be seen from the examples discussed below. The savings credit is not a credit that is payable simply because a pensioner has savings, e.g. in a bank account. Rather, it is a supplement that is payable to pensioners who have small amounts of private income, whether in the form of an occupational or other private pension or indeed by way of income which is generated from savings.

Note, however, that now the Pensions Act 2014 (Sch.12 para.89) is in force the savings credit element of pension credit will in future only be payable to those who have reached state pension age before April 6, 2016 (however, a younger individual may still qualify in future if they are a member of a couple and their partner qualifies).

Subsection (1)

1.342 See further the annotation to s.1(6). Note also that the words "the age of 65" in subs.(1) will be replaced by the expression "pensionable age" but that this amendment will only take effect from April 6, 2024 (Pensions Act 2007 s.13 and Sch.8 para.44).

Subsections (2)–(4)

1.343 The additional condition in subs.(2) can be understood better if it is broken down into its four constituent terms: qualifying income, the savings credit threshold and amounts A and B respectively, although the component parts of these terms also require further definition.

Qualifying income

1.344 The expression "qualifying income" is further defined by regulations (subs.(6): see State Pension Credit Regulations 2002 (SI 2002/1792) regs 15–18). The claimant's qualifying income includes those elements of their income which arise from contributions to the National Insurance scheme (e.g. the basic state retirement pension and any additional pension such as SERPS) and from their own private provision (e.g. an occupational pension or income from capital). After considerable debate, the government announced that income from work is to be treated in the same way as income from an occupational pension or savings. The term "income" is further defined by ss.15 and 16, and such income must be aggregated with that of any partner (s.5).

Savings credit threshold

The "savings credit threshold" is "such amount as may be prescribed" (subs.(7)). **1.345** This threshold for 2016/17 is £133.82 for a single person and £212.97 for a couple (State Pension Credit Regulations 2002 (SI 2002/1792) reg.7(2)). This means that pensioners whose qualifying income is less than this level, even though they have, e.g. a small occupational pension or income from savings, are unable to claim the savings credit. This is likely to be the case with those women who are not entitled to a full retirement pension because of gaps in their contributions records. Thus these women pensioners may claim the guarantee credit to bring their income up to the appropriate minimum guarantee under s.2, but see no extra benefit for their thrift as their combined income from other sources does not exceed the basic retirement pension.

Furthermore, in the 2010 comprehensive spending review it was announced that the maximum weekly award of savings credit would be frozen in cash terms from April 2011 until April 2014. It was therefore expected to remain at £20.52 for a single person and £27.09 for a couple throughout this period. However, the policy changed with the April 2012 uprating. The standard minimum guarantee (see s.2 above) is required to be raised at least in line with earnings, indicating an increase in the order of 2.8 per cent. In fact, the Government decided to increase the minimum guarantee by 3.9 per cent (e.g. from £137.35 to £142.70 for a single person) and to fund this increase for the poorest pensioners by restricting eligibility to the savings credit. Consequently the savings credit threshold was raised by 8.4 per cent (from £103.15 to £111.80 for a single person and from £164.55 to £178.35 for a couple). Raising the threshold reduces the numbers of pensioners eligible for the savings credit, and at the same time the effect was to reduce the maximum weekly savings credit to £18.54 for a single person and £23.73 for a couple.

The same policy has been adopted in each subsequent annual uprating exercise. Thus for 2015/16 the standard minimum guarantee was increased by 1.9 per cent, above the growth in average earnings (0.6 per cent), to ensure that the poorest pensioners obtain the full value of the increase in their basic state pension. The savings credit thresholds were increased by 5.1 per cent to fund this additional increase in the standard minimum guarantee, so concentrating spending on pensioners at the lower end of the income scale. As a result the maximum savings credit, available to the slightly better off pensioners, has been squeezed further to £13.07 for a single person and £14.75 for a couple for 2016/17.

Amount A

"Amount A" is the *smaller* of the "maximum savings credit" and "a prescribed **1.346** percentage of the amount by which the claimant's qualifying income exceeds the savings credit threshold" (subs.(4)). The "maximum savings credit" is a prescribed percentage (60 per cent: State Pension Credit Regulations 2002 (SI 2002/1792) reg.7(1)(a)) of the difference between the standard minimum guarantee and the savings credit threshold (subs.(7)). By this stage (if not before) the reader of these annotations might appreciate a simple algebraic notation. An example may therefore assist.

For 2016/17 the maximum savings credit is 60 per cent of the difference between the standard minimum guarantee (£155.60 for a single person, £237.55 for a couple) and the savings credit threshold (£133.82 for a single person and £212.97 for a couple). The difference for a single person is thus £21.78, of which 60 per cent is £13.07. For a couple the difference is £24.58, of which 60 per cent is £14.75. The maximum savings credit is accordingly £13.07 for single claimants and £14.75 for couples.

This figure must then be compared with a second figure representing "a prescribed percentage of the amount by which the claimant's qualifying income exceeds the savings credit threshold". In this context the prescribed percentage is also 60 per cent (State Pension Credit Regulations 2002 (SI 2002/1792) reg.7(1)(b)). The savings credit threshold, which used to be aligned with the basic state retirement pension, is now higher and for 2016/17 is £133.82 for a single person and £212.97 for a couple. The "qualifying income" is to be calculated in accordance with ss.15 and 16 and with regulations under subs.(6) (see also above). If a single claimant's qualifying weekly income is £143.82, comprising the basic state retirement pension and a small occupational pension, then this second figure is £6 (being 60 per cent of the difference between £143.82 and £133.82). As £6 is less than £13.07 in this scenario, Amount A is the former, i.e. £6.

Amount B

1.347 Amount B is "a prescribed percentage of the amount (if any) by which the claimant's income exceeds the appropriate minimum guarantee" or, if there is no such excess, nil (subs.(4)). The prescribed percentage in this calculation is 40 per cent in this instance, not 60 per cent (State Pension Credit Regulations 2002 (SI 2002/1792) reg.7(1)(c)). It is also important to note that in this calculation the reference is to the claimant's income, not their *qualifying* income (which may be a lower figure). The appropriate minimum guarantee is defined by s.2(3), and represents the previous minimum income guarantee for pensioners. Let us assume that in the scenario under discussion the claimant's appropriate minimum guarantee consists of the standard minimum guarantee (i.e. there are no extra sums equivalent to further premiums) and is £155.60 in 2016/17. In this example the claimant's income (£143.82) is clearly less than the appropriate minimum guarantee (£155.60) and so amount B must be nil.

In the hypothetical case set out above, amount A is £6 and amount B is nil. We have already established that the claimant's qualifying income (£143.82) exceeds the savings credit threshold (£133.82) and so subs.(2)(a) is met. As amount A exceeds amount B, the requirement in subs.(2)(b) is also satisfied. Assuming that the claimant (or partner) is over 65, this means that both conditions for the award of the savings credit are fulfilled. The amount of the savings credit in such a case is the amount by which amount A exceeds amount B, namely £6 (subs.(3)).

If, however, a single pensioner's total income and qualifying income in 2016/17 is £155.60, e.g. comprising the state retirement pension and an occupational pension, then amount A is £13.07. This figure is both the maximum savings credit, i.e. a figure which is both 60 per cent of the difference between the standard minimum guarantee and the savings credit threshold and 60 per cent of the amount by which this individual's qualifying income exceeds the savings credit threshold. In such a scenario the claimant's income is the same as the appropriate minimum guarantee and so amount B is nil. The excess of amount A over amount B is therefore £13.07 and this sum is payable by way of a savings credit under subs.(3). The pensioner's income is thus £168.67 (retirement pension and occupational pension together with £13.07 savings credit), whereas under the previous arrangements there would have been no entitlement to income support, leaving such a pensioner in the same position as a pensioner claimant whose sole income was the state retirement pension.

Once a pensioner's income starts to exceed the appropriate minimum guarantee, then the way in which amounts A and B are defined is such that the claimant's entitlement to the savings credit is gradually withdrawn as their income increases. A further simple example will suffice. Assume that a single pensioner's total weekly income is £171.60, comprising the state retirement pension and an occupational pension. On these facts amount A is the smaller of the maximum savings credit (£13.07) and 60 per cent of the amount by which the claimant's income (£171.60) exceeds the savings credit threshold (£133.82). The latter figure is £22.67 (60 per cent of the difference, being £37.78). As this obviously is more than £13.07, amount A will be £13.07. Amount B is 40 per cent of the amount by which the claimant's income (and again, for the purposes of exposition, we assume that income and qualifying income are identical) exceeds the appropriate minimum guarantee (i.e. £155.60). The difference between those two figures in this example is £16.00, of which 40 per cent is £6.40. Both the conditions set out in subs.(2) are therefore satisfied, and so the claimant's savings credit is the amount by which amount A (£13.07) exceeds amount B (£6.40), namely £6.67. The claimant, on this scenario, thus has a final income of £178.27; £171.60 by way of retirement pension and occupational pension topped up by £6.67 savings credit). Thus the value of the savings credit will gradually diminish as the claimant's combined income from other sources rises. At 2015/16 rates this meant that no savings credit was payable for a single pensioner with a total income of about £190 a week or more or for a couple whose joint income was about £278 a week or more.

Subsection (5)

Section 2(6) enables the Secretary of State to provide for a different rate for the guarantee credit to be applied in place of the standard minimum guarantee where the claimant (or their partner) remains in hospital for more than 52 weeks. If this same principle were to be carried over into the calculation of the savings credit, the effect would be that amount B would be much higher and might well exceed amount A, which would extinguish any entitlement to the savings credit by virtue of subs.(3). This provision allows regulations to be made to provide for a higher figure to be stipulated in place of the reference to the appropriate minimum guarantee in the definition of amount B. This will reduce amount B and accordingly increase the likelihood that amount A will exceed amount B and so result in the savings credit being payable (State Pension Credit Regulations 2002 (SI 2002/1792) Sch.III para.2). **1.348**

Subsection (8)

This power enables a nil amount to be specified as the maximum savings credit for prisoners and members of religious orders who are fully maintained by their orders. This mirrors the power under s.2(9) and reflects the fact that both groups who are currently excluded from income support (see State Pension Credit Regulations 2002 (SI 2002/1792) reg.7(3)). **1.349**

[1 3ZA Power to limit savings credit for certain mixed-age couples

(1) Regulations may provide that, in prescribed cases, a person who is a member of a mixed-age couple is not entitled to a savings credit. **1.350**

(2) For example, the regulations could provide that a member of a mixed-age couple is not entitled to a savings credit unless—

(a) the person has been awarded a savings credit with effect from a day before 6 April 2016 and was entitled to a savings credit immediately before that date, and

(b) the person remained entitled to state pension credit at all times since the beginning of 6 April 2016.

(3) In this section "mixed-age couple" means a couple (whenever formed) one member of which had attained pensionable age before 6 April 2016 and the other had not.]

AMENDMENT

1. Pensions Act 2014 s.23 and Sch.12 Pt.3 para.90 (July 7, 2015).

DEFINITIONS

"mixed-age couple"—subs.(3).
"couple"—see s.17(1).
"entitled"—*ibid.*
"pensionable age"—*ibid.*

"prescribed"—*ibid.*
"savings credit—*ibid.*

GENERAL NOTE

1.351 The first requirement for entitlement to the savings credit element of pension credit, as originally enacted, was that the claimant (or their partner) was at least 65 (s.3(1)). However, as a result of amendments made by the Pensions Act 2014, there is no longer access to the savings credit element for those claimants reaching state pension age on or after April 6, 2016 unless they are a member of a couple where the other member reached state pension age *before* that date (known as "a mixed-age couple"). This section provides for entitlement to the savings credit to be so restricted and defines what is meant by a "mixed-age couple". The policy justification for this change is that whereas the previous basic state pension was set below the level of the standard minimum guarantee in pension credit, the new state pension is set at a level (just) above that threshold, so removing the problem that the savings credit was designed to address. See further the State Pension Credit Regulations 2002 (SI 2002/1792) reg.7A.

Exclusions

1.352 **4.**—(1) A claimant is not entitled to state pension credit if he is a member of a [1 couple] the other member of which is entitled to state pension credit.

(2) In section 115(1) of the Immigration and Asylum Act 1999 (c.33) (exclusion of certain persons from benefits) in the words preceding paragraph (a), after "Jobseekers Act 1995" insert "or to state pension credit under the State Pension Credit Act 2002".

(3) Where the amount payable by way of state pension credit would (apart from this subsection) be less than a prescribed amount, it shall not be payable except in prescribed circumstances.

AMENDMENT

1. Civil Partnership Act 2004 s.254 and Sch.24 para.140 (December 5, 2005).

DEFINITIONS

"claimant"—see s.17(1).
"entitled"—*ibid.*
"married couple"—*ibid.*
"prescribed"—*ibid.*
"unmarried couple"—*ibid.*

GENERAL NOTE

Subsection (1)

1.353 Only one member of a married or unmarried couple is entitled to the pension credit, so preventing double provision from public funds (subs.(1), modelled on SSCBA 1992 s.134(2)).

Subsection (2)

The general exclusion of persons who are "subject to immigration control" from access to the benefits system is extended to the pension credit scheme (subs.(2); for the limited exceptions to the rule in s.115 of the Immigration and Asylum Act 1999, see the Social Security (Immigration and Asylum) Consequential Amendments Regulations 2000 (SI 2000/636)). On the meaning of "residence" in that context see *CPC/1035/2005.* Commissioner Jacobs held there that "in its ordinary meaning a person does not have to be physically present at a place in order to be resident there. Whether a person is or is not resident in a particular place during a period of physical absence depends on a calculus consisting of the duration and circumstances of the absence" (para.14). On the facts of that case it was held that three prolonged periods of absence in Pakistan— each period being for more than one year—meant that the claimant had not remained "resident" in the United Kingdom.

The concept of a 'person subject to immigration control' may require careful analysis of the basis upon which a person is lawfully in the UK. In *SJ v SSWP (SPC)* [2016] AACR 17 the claimant had originally entered the UK as a sponsored visitor, subject to a maintenance undertaking. She then applied for indefinite leave to remain (ILR) in the UK as a dependant of her adult daughter, who was settled here. The Home Office (HO) refused the application. The First-tier Tribunal (Immigration and Asylum Chamber) allowed her appeal under both the Immigration Rules (para.317) and under art.8 ECHR human rights grounds. The HO then granted the claimant ILR. The DWP refused the claimant's subsequent pension credit claim on the basis that she was still in the UK within five years of the original maintenance undertaking. The Upper Tribunal, distinguishing *R(PC) 109*, rejected the Appellant's argument that she had ILR on art.8 grounds, free of the maintenance undertaking given under the Rules. It followed she was a person subject to immigration control and not entitled to pension credit.

Note that all British citizens have a right of abode under the Immigration Act 1971. As a result, British citizens cannot be regarded as sponsored immigrants or be barred for that reason from access to public funds such as state pension credit (*R(PC) 2/07*).

Subsection (3)

Provision is also made to set a minimum threshold for payment of the pension credit. Entitlement of less than 10 pence a week is not payable, unless it can be combined with another benefit (subs.(3)), modelled on SSCBA 1992 s.134(4); see State Pension Credit Regulations 2002 (SI 2002/1792) reg.13).

Aggregation

Income and capital of claimant, spouse, etc.

5.—Where the claimant is a member of a [1 couple], the income and capital of the other member of the couple shall, except in prescribed circumstances, be treated for the purposes of this Act as income and capital of the claimant. 1.354

AMENDMENT

1. Civil Partnership Act 2004 s.254 and Sch.24 para.140 (December 5, 2005).

DEFINITIONS

"capital"—see s.17(1).
"claimant"—*ibid.*
"income"—*ibid.*
"prescribed"—*ibid.*
"married couple"—*ibid.*
"unmarried couple"—*ibid.*

GENERAL NOTE

This section provides for the aggregation of the income and capital resources of the claimant and his or her partner, irrespective of marital status or sexual orientation. This is in line with standard means-tested benefit principles. Indeed, this 1.355

provision is closely modelled on SSCBA 1992 s.136(1). The definition assumes that the partners are living in the same household. For special cases where persons are treated as either being or not being members of the same household, see State Pension Credit Regulations 2002 (SI 2002/1792) reg.5).

Retirement provision

Duty to specify assessed income period [2 for pre-6 April 2016 awards]

1.356 **6.**—(1) In any case falling within subsection (3) or (4) [2 where the relevant decision takes effect before 6 April 2016], the Secretary of State shall, on the making of the relevant decision, specify a period as the assessed income period, unless prevented by subsection (2).

(2) The Secretary of State is prevented from specifying a period as the assessed income period under subsection (1)—

(a) if the relevant decision takes effect at a time when an assessed income period is in force in the case of the claimant by virtue of a previous application of this section; or

(b) in such other circumstances as may be prescribed.

(3) The first case is where—

(a) the Secretary of State determines the amount of a claimant's income for the purposes of a decision relating to state pension credit;

(b) the decision is a decision under section 8(1), 9 or 10 of the Social Security Act 1998 (c.14) (decisions on claims etc, and decisions revising or superseding decisions);

(c) the decision takes effect on or after—

(i) the day on which the claimant attains the age of 65; or

(ii) if earlier, in a case where the claimant is a member of a [1 couple], the day on which the other member of the couple attains that age; and

(d) the decision is not to the effect that the claimant is not entitled to state pension credit.

(4) The second case is where—

(a) the amount of the claimant's income is determined on, or for the purposes of, an appeal against a decision that the claimant is not entitled to state pension credit;

(b) on the appeal, it is decided that the claimant is entitled to state pension credit; and

(c) the decision takes effect as mentioned in subsection (3)(c).

(5) In this section "the relevant decision" means—

(a) so far as relating to the first case, the decision mentioned in subsection (3)(a);

(b) so far as relating to the second case, the decision on appeal mentioned in subsection (4)(b).

(6) This section is subject to section 9.

(7) This section and sections 7 to 10 shall be construed as one.

AMENDMENTS

1. Civil Partnership Act 2004 s.254 and Sch.24 para.140 (December 5, 2005).
2. Pensions Act 2014 s.28(1) (April 6, 2016).

DEFINITIONS

"assessed income period"—see s.17(1).
"claimant"—*ibid.*
"entitled"—*ibid.*
"income"—*ibid.*
"married couple"—*ibid.*
"prescribed"—*ibid.*
"the relevant decision"—see subs.(5).
"unmarried couple"—see s.17(1).

GENERAL NOTE

When making a decision before April 2016 that a person is entitled to the pension credit, the Secretary of State was required to specify an "assessed income period" in relation to the claimant (subs.(1)). Such a decision could be made in the first instance by the Secretary of State (subs.(3)) or following an appeal (subs.(4)). The Secretary of State was prevented from so doing where an assessed income period was currently in force (subs.(2)(a)). For circumstances prescribed under subs.(2)(b), see State Pension Credit Regulations 2002 (SI 2002/1792) reg.10(1). The significance of the "assessed income period" was that it was used as the basis for a long-term award of the pension credit (see s.7). It should also be noted that this section was subject to s.9 (see subs.(6)), which specifies that the "assessed income period" was normally five years, and that ss.7–10 "shall be construed as one" (subs.(7)). 1.357

Note, however, that now s.28 of the Pensions Act 2014 is in force assessed income periods will be phased out as from April 2016. As a result, any change in retirement income will in future need to be reported to the Department when it occurs, triggering a review and change in benefit award where appropriate. Thus s.28(3) expressly provides that "Regulations under section 9(5) of the State Pension Credit Act 2002 may in particular be made for the purpose of phasing out, on or after 6 April 2016, any remaining assessed income period that is 5 years or shorter than 5 years". See now the amendments to reg.12 of the State Pension Credit Regulations 2002 (SI 2002/1792).

Fixing of claimant's retirement provision for assessed income period

7.—(1) This section applies where, pursuant to section 6(1), the Secretary of State on the making of the relevant decision specifies a period as the assessed income period. 1.358

(2) This section has effect for the purpose of determining, as at any time in the assessed income period—

(a) the claimant's entitlement to state pension credit; or

(b) the amount of state pension credit to which the claimant is entitled.

(3) Where the claimant's income, as determined for the purposes of the relevant decision, includes an amount (the "assessed amount") in respect of an element of the claimant's retirement provision, the amount of that element as at any time in the assessed income period shall be taken to be the assessed amount as for the time being varied in accordance with regulations under subsection (4).

(4) The assessed amount shall be deemed, except in prescribed circumstances—

(a) to increase, or

(b) in the case of income from capital, to increase or decrease,

on such date or dates and by such amounts as may be prescribed.

(5) Where it is determined for the purposes of the relevant decision

that the claimant's income does not include any, or any further, elements of retirement provision, the claimant's income throughout the assessed income period shall be taken not to include those elements.

(6) For the purposes of this Act "retirement provision" means income of any of the following descriptions—

(a) retirement pension income, other than benefit under [2 Part 1 of the Pensions Act 2014 or] the Contributions and Benefits Act;

(b) income from annuity contracts (other than retirement pension income);

(c) income from capital;

and an "element" of a person's retirement provision is income of any of those descriptions from a particular source;

[1 (d) PPF periodic payments.]

(7) For the purposes of this section, regulations may make provision—

(a) for treating income of any particular description as income of another description; or

(b) for treating income from different sources as income from the same source.

(8) Nothing in subsections (3) to (5) prevents the revision under section 9 of the Social Security Act 1998 (c.14) of the relevant decision or of any earlier or later decision under section 10 of that Act.

(9) This section is subject to section 8.

AMENDMENTS

1. Pensions Act 2004 (PPF Payments and FAS Payments) (Consequential Provisions) Order 2006 (SI 2006/343) art.3(1) (February 14, 2006).

2. Pensions Act 2014 s.23 and Sch.12 Pt 1 paras 42 and 43 (April 6, 2016).

DEFINITIONS

"assessed amount"—see subs.(3).
"assessed income period"—see s.17(1).
"capital"—*ibid.*
"claimant"—*ibid.*
"Contributions and Benefits Act"—*ibid.*
"element"—see subs.(6) and s.17(1).
"entitled"—see s.17(1).
"income"—*ibid.*
"regulations"—*ibid.*
"relevant decision"—see s.6(5).
"retirement pension income"—see ss.16 and 17(1).
"retirement provision"—see s.7(6) and s.17(1).

GENERAL NOTE

1.359 This provision is the key to understanding how the pension credit scheme fundamentally differs from other means-tested benefits in terms of the usual requirement to report changes in income during the period of an award. Once the Secretary of State has specified the "assessed income period" under s.6 (which is typically five years: s.9(1)), this has the effect of fixing the "assessed amount" derived from the claimant's "retirement provision" (effectively their income: see subs.(6)) for the duration of that period (subs.(3)). This assessed amount is subject to deemed increases or decreases (reflecting, e.g. the terms of a claimant's pension arrangements, such as a cost-of-living increase) (subs.(4); for further detail on this, see State Pension Credit Regulations 2002 (SI 2002/1792) reg.10(2)–(7)). Any further elements of retirement provision which are acquired at some later date within the assessed income period are then disregarded (subs.(5)). Such changes accordingly need not be reported during the lifetime of the award. Even if the changes deemed under subs.(4) work in favour of the claimant (i.e. their actual increase is more than the deemed increase), the effect of subs.(3) is that there is no overpayment and no need to report the change.

The implications of this radical change were spelt out by Mr Ian McCartney MP, the then Minster for Pensions:

> "Let us be clear about this: if a pensioner wins the lottery in the second week of his or her assessed income period, the increase in capital, be it £10 or £1 million, will not be reflected in the pension credit entitlement until the end of the assessed income period—in four years and 50 weeks' time . . . We can live with ignoring a few individuals' good fortune for the sake of simplification for the overwhelming majority of pensioners". (Standing Committee A, cols 166 and 184.)

But if the claimant actually loses out, in that the deemed increase is more than their actual increase, a new decision can be sought (s.8(1)). The normal powers to effect a revision of an initial decision under s.9 of the SSA 1998 remain in place (subs.(8)).

The Minister's statement to the Standing Committee about the lottery winner was considered by Commissioner Levenson in *CPC/0206/2005*. The claimant disclosed in her claim that she was moving into sheltered accommodation and her house was on the market. An official decided that its value should be disregarded for the time being, but noted that this decision would change in the event of sale. However, the Secretary of State then awarded pension credit for a five-year assessed income period. Later the claimant reported that her house had been sold. Commissioner Levenson observed that the Minister's statement did not cover a case such as this, where the issue was "what the Secretary of State should do if it is known that a large amount of capital is likely to be on its way" (para.10). The Commissioner held that the original decision should be revised for official error and replaced with an award which did not specify an assessed income period ("AIP"). That decision was then subject to supersession for the change of circumstances in the receipt of the proceeds of sale. According to the Commissioner: **1.360**

> "23. It seems to me that the concept of 'error' involves more than merely taking a decision that another decision maker with the same information would not take, but is not limited to (although it includes, subject to the statutory exceptions) a public law or any other error of law. Other than that it is not helpful (and could be misleading) to go beyond the words of the regulation. On the facts of the present case, though, I take the view that no Secretary of State or decision maker acting reasonably could have imposed a 5 year AIP. It was already known that number 8 was up for sale and that it would realise a sum of several tens of thousands of pounds (even if the exact amount was not known) and a view had already been taken that the progress of the sale should be monitored. In these respects the position was very different from that of a lottery winner who, at the time of the decision on the claim, had done no more than buy a ticket."

See also the decision of Commissioner Rowland in *CPC/1928/2005*, discussed in the note to s.9, below.

Fresh determinations increasing claimant's entitlement

8.—(1) Subsections (3) to (5) of section 7 do not prevent the making of fresh determinations as to the elements, or any of the elements, or the amount of any of the elements, of the claimant's retirement provision as at any time during the assessed income period, if— **1.361**

(a) the fresh determinations are for the purpose of making a decision under section 10 of the Social Security Act 1998 (c.14) ("the new decision");

(b) the new decision increases the amount of state pension credit to which the claimant is entitled; and

(c) the increase is in whole or in part the result of the fresh determinations (taken as a whole).

(2) The conditions in paragraphs (b) and (c) of subsection (1) shall be taken to be satisfied if—

(a) the new decision reduces the amount of state pension credit to which the claimant is entitled; but

(b) the reduction is less than it would have been apart from the fresh determinations (taken as a whole).

(3) Where a fresh determination is made by virtue of subsection (1), then, as respects the part of the assessed income period that begins with the day on which the new decision takes effect, subsections (3) to (5) of section 7 shall have effect in accordance with the fresh determination, instead of the determination which it replaces, but as if—

(a) the fresh determination were (and the determination which it replaces were not) a determination for the purposes of the relevant decision;

(b) any assessed amount resulting from the fresh determination were not subject to variation under subsection (4) of that section at any time before the day on which the new decision takes effect; and

(c) the claimant's income, as determined for the purposes of the relevant decision, were constituted accordingly.

DEFINITIONS

"assessed income period"—see ss.9(1) and 17(1).
"claimant"—see s.17(1).
"element"—*ibid.*
"entitled"—*ibid.*
"income"—*ibid.*
"retirement provision"—see ss.7(6) and 17(1).

GENERAL NOTE

1.362 The presumption under s.7 is that the assessment of the claimant's "retirement provision" will remain unchanged during the typical five-year award of pension credit, subject to the usual uprating. However, a fresh determination can be made by way of a supersession decision within the assessed income period to increase the claimant's entitlement. This will not affect the assessed income period (subs.(1)). The assessed income period can also continue where the effect of the supersession decision is to reduce entitlement to the pension credit, but the reduction is less than it would otherwise have been because of the recalculation of some other element of the claimant's income (subs.(2)). Where a supersession decision is made, the remaining elements of the retirement provision are treated as unchanged for the rest of the assessed income period (subs.(3)). See also State Pension Credit Regulations 2002 (SI 2002/1792) reg.11.

Duration of assessed income period

1.363 **9.**—[2 (1) An assessed income period shall (subject to the following subsections) be—

(a) in the case of a claimant who is under the age of 75 on the day on which the relevant decision takes effect, the period of 5 years beginning with that day;

(b) in the case of a claimant who is aged 75 or over on that day, an indefinite period beginning with that day.]

(2) If the Secretary of State considers that the particulars of the claim-ant's retirement provision as determined for the purposes of the relevant decision are not likely, after taking account of any assumed variations under subsection (3), to be typical of the claimant's retirement provision throughout the period of 12 months beginning with the day on which that decision takes effect—

(a) he need not specify a period under section 6(1); and
(b) if he does so, [2 shall specify a period that is shorter than 5 years] (but beginning as mentioned in subsection (1)).

(3) It shall be assumed for the purposes of subsection (2) that the same variations fall to be made in relation to the amount of an element of the claimant's retirement provision as determined for the purposes of the relevant decision as would fall to be made under section 7(4) if an assessed income period were to be specified in accordance with subsection (1).

(4) An assessed income period shall, except in prescribed circumstances, end at any time at which—

(a) the claimant becomes a member of a [1 couple];
(b) the claimant ceases to be a member of a [1 couple];
(c) the claimant attains the age of 65; or
(d) in a case where the claimant is a member of a [1 couple], the other member of the couple attains the age of 65.

(5) Regulations may prescribe further times at which, or circumstances in which, an assessed income period shall end.

[2 (6) Where—

(a) an assessed income period is brought to an end [3 , on or after 6 April 2009 but before 6 April 2014,] by the expiry of a period of 5 years or more, and
(b) the claimant is aged 80 or over at that time,

the assessed income period shall be treated as not ending at that time but, subject to subsection (4) and provision made under subsection (5), as continuing indefinitely.]

AMENDMENTS

1. Civil Partnership Act 2004 s.254 and Sch.24 para.140 (December 5, 2005).
2. Pensions Act 2008 s.105 (April 6, 2009).
3. Pensions Act 2014, s.29(2)(b) (May 14, 2014).

DEFINITIONS

"assessed income period"—see subs.(1) and s.17(1).
"claimant"—see s.17(1).
"element"—*ibid.*
"married couple"—*ibid.*
"prescribed"—*ibid.*
"regulations"—see s.17(1).
"relevant decision"—see s.6(5).
"retirement provision"—see ss.7(6) and 17(1).
"unmarried couple"—see s.17(1).

GENERAL NOTE

The normal rule is that the "assessed income period" for the purposes of an award of the pension credit is five years (subs.(1)). Throughout this period the claimant's "retirement provision" (see s.7), i.e. their standard income during retirement, is **1.364** treated as remaining the same, subject only to uprating in line with inflation. This is in contrast to the requirement that claimants of other means-tested benefits report any changes in income which affect their benefit entitlement. However, if the Secretary of State takes the view that the claimant's retirement provision as assessed is not likely to be typical of their actual income over the next 12 months, a period shorter than five years may be specified (subs.(2)). Foreseeable increases in income on retirement (e.g. in line with inflation) are not treated as making the assessment atypical (subs.(3)). Whatever its initial duration, an assessed income period terminates if the claimant becomes a member of a couple, separates from their partner or reaches 65 (or any partner does so) (subs.(4)). Further circumstances which will result in the termination of an assessed income period, as prescribed under subs.(5), are specified in the State Pension Credit Regulations 2002 (SI 2002/1792) reg.12.

In *CPC/1928/2005* the claimant applied for pension credit, having moved into rented property with her husband and having put their house up for sale. Pension credit was awarded with a seven-year assessed income period and without taking account of the capital value of the house. On April 22, 2004 the claimant's husband moved permanently to a care home. On May 19, 2004 the couple received the proceeds of sale in respect of their former home. The Secretary of State became aware of these facts later made a supersession decision on the basis that the claimant should be treated as a single person from April 22, 2004 and should be regarded as having additional capital representing half the proceeds of sale as from May 19, 2004. The tribunal disallowed the claimant's appeal. Commissioner Rowland, dismissing the claimant's further appeal, held that the tribunal had reached the correct conclusion, albeit for the wrong reasons. On these facts, with sale to be anticipated within a few months, no assessed income period should have been set. Moreover, "Where a substantial sum is expected on an uncertain date, not setting an assessed income period will generally be preferable to setting a short one, in the absence of other considerations such as likely minor variations of other income that the decision-maker considers should be ignored" (para.11). See also the decision of Commissioner Levenson in *CPC/0206/2005*, discussed in the note to s.7, above.

Subsection (5)

1.365 Note that now s.28(3) of the Pensions Act 2014 provides that regulations made under this provision "may in particular be made for the purpose of phasing out, on or after 6 April 2016, any remaining assessed income period that is 5 years or shorter than 5 years."

Subsection (6)

1.366 Subsection (6) was a transitional provision and was originally thought to be necessary only until April 6, 2014. It was therefore repealed from that date by the Pensions Act 2008 (ss.105(6) and 149(2)(c) and (4)). That repeal left some doubt about whether existing assessed income periods under subs.(6) would remain in place after April 6, 2014. Section 29 of the Pensions Act 2014 was therefore enacted to remove the doubt by ensuring that existing indefinite assessed income periods governed by s.9(6) remained in place on or after that date. Section 29(2)(a) accordingly repealed s.105(6) of the Pensions Act 2008 and treated it as never having had effect while s.29(2)(b) amended the restored version of subs.(6) in the terms indicated in the statutory text above.

Effect of variations under section 7(4)

1.367 **10.**—(1) This section applies where—

(a) an assessed income period is in force; and

(b) there is an alteration in an element of the claimant's retirement provision which affects the computation of the amount of state pension credit to which the claimant is entitled.

(2) Where, as a result of the alteration, the amount of state pension credit to which the claimant is entitled is increased or reduced, then, as from the commencing date, the amount of state pension credit payable in the case of the claimant shall be the increased or reduced amount, without any further decision of the Secretary of State (and the award of state pension credit shall have effect accordingly).

(3) Where, notwithstanding the alteration, the claimant continues on and after the commencing date to be entitled to the same amount of state pension credit as before, the award shall continue in force accordingly.

(4) In this section—

"alteration" means a variation in the amount of an element of the claimant's retirement provision in accordance with regulations under section 7(4);

"commencing date", in relation to an alteration, means the date on which the alteration comes into force.

DEFINITIONS

"alteration"—see subs.(4).
"assessed income period"—see s.17(1).
"claimant"—*ibid.*
"commencing date"—see subs.(4).
"element"—see s.17(1).
"entitled"—*ibid.*
"regulations"—*ibid.*
"retirement provision"—*ibid.*

GENERAL NOTE

Section 7(4) provides for the assessed amount of a claimant's retirement provision to be increased or decreased during the assessed income period. This provision deals with the consequences of such a change (subs.(1)). Subsection (2) allows the amount of the pension credit payable to be increased or decreased accordingly without the need for a further decision by the Secretary of State. If the level of the award remains the same, the award continues in force unaffected (subs.(3)). See also State Pension Credit Regulations 2002 (SI 2002/1792) reg.11. **1.368**

Miscellaneous and supplementary

Administration

11.—Schedule 1 shall have effect and in that Schedule— **1.369**

Part 1 makes amendments to Part 1 of the Administration Act (claims for, and payments and general administration of, benefit);

Part 2 makes amendments to Part 1 of the Social Security Act 1998 (c.14) (decisions and appeals); and

Part 3 makes miscellaneous and supplementary provision.

DEFINITION

"the Administration Act"—see s.17(1).

GENERAL NOTE

This section introduces Sch.1 to the Act. This makes amendments to the SSAA 1992 and the SSA 1998 which are designed to apply the normal social security rules for claims, decisions and appeals to the state pension credit scheme. **1.370**

Polygamous marriages

1.371 **12.**—(1) This section applies to any case where—
(a) a person ("the person in question") is a husband or wife by virtue of a marriage entered into under a law which permits polygamy;
(b) either party to the marriage has for the time being any spouse additional to the other party; and
(c) the person in question, the other party to the marriage and the additional spouse are members of the same household.

(2) Regulations under this section may make provision—
(a) as to the entitlement of the person in question to state pension credit;
(b) as to any guarantee credit or savings credit to which that person is entitled;
(c) for prescribing a different amount as the standard minimum guarantee in the case of the person in question;
(d) in a case where the person in question is the claimant, for treating the income and capital of the other party and of the additional spouse as income and capital of the person in question.

(3) Any such regulations may provide—
(a) that prescribed provisions shall apply instead of prescribed provisions of this Act; or
(b) that prescribed provisions of this Act shall not apply or shall apply subject to prescribed modifications or adaptations.

(4) Except in relation to the amount of the standard minimum guarantee, any power to prescribe amounts by virtue of this section includes power to prescribe nil as an amount.

DEFINITIONS

"capital"—see s.17(1).
"claimant"—*ibid.*
"entitled"—*ibid.*
"guarantee credit"—*ibid.*
"income"—*ibid.*
"prescribed"—*ibid.*
"regulations"—*ibid.*
"savings credit"—*ibid.*
"standard minimum guarantee"—*ibid.*

GENERAL NOTE

1.372 This section makes special provision for claimants who are parties to polygamous marriages. See also State Pension Credit Regulations 2002 (SI 2002/1792) reg.8 and Sch.III para.1.

Transitional provisions

1.373 **13.**—(1) The Secretary of State may by regulations make such transitional provision, consequential provision or savings as he considers necessary or expedient for the purposes of, or in connection with—
(a) the coming into force of any of the state pension credit provisions of this Act; or
(b) the operation of any enactment repealed or amended by any of those provisions during any period when the repeal or amendment is not wholly in force.

(2) The provision that may be made by regulations under this section includes in particular—

(a) provision for a person who attains or has attained the qualifying age on or before the appointed day and who immediately before that day is entitled to income support—

(i) to be treated as having been awarded on, and with effect as from, that day state pension credit of an amount specified in or determined in accordance with the regulations; or

(ii) to be treated as having made a claim for state pension credit; and

(b) provision for an assessed income period under section 6 of such length as may be specified in or determined in accordance with the regulations (which may be longer than the maximum period provided for by section 9(1)) to have effect in the case of a person who attains or has attained the qualifying age on or before the appointed day.

(3) In this section—

"the appointed day" means such day as the Secretary of State may by order appoint;

"the state pension credit provisions of this Act" means this Act other than section 18.

DEFINITIONS

"the appointed day"—see subs.(3).
"the qualifying age"—see s.1(6).
"regulations"—see s.17(1).
"the state pension credit provisions of this Act"—see subs.(3).

GENERAL NOTE

This section enables regulations to be made governing the transitional arrangements for the introduction of the pension credit. The scheme came into force on October 6, 2003 (the "appointed day": see State Pension Credit Act 2002 (Commencement No.5) and Appointed Day Order 2003 (SI 2003/1766 (c.75)) and all claims made before October 2004 were backdated to October 2003 (see State Pension Credit (Consequential, Transitional and Miscellaneous Provisions) Regulations 2002 (SI 2002/3019 reg.38(4)). **1.374**

For the text of regs 36–38 and full commentary on reg.38, see the 2012/13 edition of this Volume, paras 4.170–4.173.

Minor and consequential amendments

14.—Schedule 2 (which makes minor and consequential amendments relating to state pension credit) shall have effect. **1.375**

GENERAL NOTE

This section introduces Sch.2 to the Act, which makes a series of minor and consequential amendments to the SSCBA 1992, the SSAA 1992 and other statutes. **1.376**

Interpretation of state pension credit provisions

Income and capital

15.—(1) In this Act "income" means income of any of the following descriptions— **1.377**

(a) earnings;

(b) working tax credit;

(c) retirement pension income;
(d) income from annuity contracts (other than retirement pension income);
(e) prescribed social security benefits (other than retirement pension income and state pension credit);
(f) foreign social security benefits of any prescribed description;
(g) a war disablement pension or war widow's or widower's pension;
(h) a foreign war disablement pension or foreign war widow's or widower's pension;
(i) income from capital;
(j) income of any prescribed description.

(2) Regulations may provide that a person's capital shall be deemed to yield him income at a prescribed rate.

(3) Income and capital shall be calculated or estimated in such manner as may be prescribed.

(4) A person's income in respect of any period shall be calculated in accordance with prescribed rules.

(5) The rules may provide for the calculation to be made by reference to an average over a period (which need not consist of or include the whole or any part of the period concerned).

(6) Circumstances may be prescribed in which—
(a) a person is treated as possessing capital or income which he does not possess;
(b) capital or income which a person does possess is to be disregarded;
(c) income is to be treated as capital; or
(d) capital is to be treated as income.

(7) Subsections (2) to (6) have effect for the purposes of this Act.

DEFINITIONS

"capital"—see s.17(1).
"earnings"—*ibid.*
"foreign social security benefits"—*ibid.*
"foreign war disablement pension"—*ibid.*
"foreign war widow's or widower's pension"—*ibid.*
"income"—see subs.(1).
"prescribed"—see s.17(1).
"regulations"—*ibid.*
"retirement pension income"—see s.16(1).
"social security benefits"—see s.17(1).
"war disablement pension"—*ibid.*
"war widow's or widower's pension"—*ibid.*
"working tax credit"—*ibid.*

GENERAL NOTE

1.378 The term "income" is given a very broad definition in subs.(1) for the purposes of the pension credit scheme. In particular, the Secretary of State has the power under subs.(1)(e) to specify which social security benefits count as income (see State Pension Credit Regulations 2002 (SI 2002/1792) reg.15(1), (3) and (4); and for foreign social security benefits see *ibid.*, reg.15(2)). The Secretary of State may also extend the definition of income to include "income of any prescribed description" (subs.(1)(j)). This latter power has been used to include less commonly found forms of income that some pensioners have (e.g. maintenance payments); see State Pension Credit Regulations 2002 (SI 2002/1792 reg.15(5)). In *R(PC)3/08* the Commissioner ruled that the 2002 Act adopts the ordinary meanings of income and capital.

There is, however, no upper capital limit for the purposes of entitlement to the pension credit. Instead, capital is deemed, by regulations made under subs.(2), to have an assumed rate of return for the purposes of assessing entitlement to both forms of the pension credit. This rate is set at £1 for every £500 (or part thereof) in excess of the threshold of £10,000: see State Pension Credit Regulations 2002 (SI 2002/1792) reg.15(6)–(8). Any capital below this threshold is disregarded. The net result is that pensioners are treated markedly more favourably than those persons of working age in receipt of means-tested benefits, who are subject both to the capital rule and to a harsher tariff income rule on capital below that threshold.

Note that for the purposes of claiming housing benefit, pension credit claimants receiving the guarantee credit have the whole of their capital and income disregarded (see the Housing Benefit (Persons who have attained the qualifying age for state pension credit) Regulations 2006 (SI 2006/214) reg.26). For claimants receiving solely the savings credit, the local authority is required to use the DWP's calculations for claimants' capital and income, see *ibid.*, reg.27. For these reasons it is important that a tribunal reaching a decision on the amount of capital or income in a pension credit case should specify the amount of such capital or income in the Decision Notice.

The extensive powers contained in subss.(3)–(6) replicate those which apply to means-tested benefits by virtue of SSCBA 1992 ss.136(3)–(5). In *R(PC)3/08* the Commissioner observed that the powers in subs.(6) indicate "that income and capital are separate and mutually exclusive categories (even if the boundary line might sometimes be fuzzy)" (para.21).

Retirement pension income

16.—(1) In this Act "retirement pension income" means any of the following— 1.379

[6 (za) a state pension under Part 1 of the Pensions Act 2014 or under any provision in Northern Ireland which corresponds to that Part;]

(a) a Category A or Category B retirement pension payable under sections 43 to 55 of—
 (i) the Contributions and Benefits Act; or
 (ii) the Social Security Contributions and Benefits (Northern Ireland) Act 1992 (c.7);

[7 (b) a shared additional pension payable under—
 (i) section 55A of either of those Acts, or
 (ii) section 55AA of the Contributions and Benefits Act or any corresponding provision under the law of Northern Ireland;]

(c) graduated retirement benefit payable under section 62 of either of those Acts;

(d) a Category C or Category D retirement pension payable under section 78 of either of those Acts;

(e) age addition payable under section 79 of either of those Acts;

(f) income from an occupational pension scheme or a personal pension scheme;

(g) income from an overseas arrangement;

(h) income from a retirement annuity contract;

(i) income from annuities or insurance policies purchased or transferred for the purpose of giving effect to rights under a personal pension scheme or an overseas arrangement;

(j) income from annuities purchased or entered into for the purpose of discharging liability under—
 (i) section 29(1)(b) of the Welfare Reform and Pensions Act 1999 (c.30) (pension credits on divorce); or

(ii) Article 26(1)(b) of the Welfare Reform and Pensions (Northern Ireland) Order 1999 (SI 1999/3147 (NI 11)) (corresponding provision for Northern Ireland).

[1 [5 (k) any sum payable by way of pension under section 5 of the Civil List Act 1837 or section 7 of the Civil List Act 1952;]

[2 (l) any payment, other than a payment ordered by a court or made in settlement of a claim, made by or on behalf of a former employer of a person on account of the early retirement of that person on grounds of ill-health or disability];

[3 (m) any payment made at regular intervals under an equity release scheme];

[4 (n) any payment made under the Financial Assistance Scheme Regulations 2005].

(2) The Secretary of State may by regulations amend subsection (1); and any such regulations may—

(a) add to or vary the descriptions of income for the time being listed in that subsection; or

(b) remove any such description from that subsection.

(3) In this section—

"overseas arrangement" has the meaning given by section 181(1) of the Pension Schemes Act 1993 (c.48);

"retirement annuity contract" means a contract or scheme approved under Chapter 3 of Part 14 of the Income and Corporation Taxes Act 1988 (c.1).

AMENDMENTS

1. State Pension Credit Regulations 2002 (SI 2002/1792) reg.16 (October 6, 2003).

2. State Pension Credit (Consequential, Transitional and Miscellaneous Provisions) (No.2) Regulations 2002 (SI 2002/3197) reg.2 and Sch. para.3 (October 6, 2003).

3. Social Security (Housing Benefit, Council Tax Benefit, State Pension Credit and Miscellaneous Amendments) Regulations 2004 (SI 2004/2327) reg.7(4) (October 4, 2004).

4. State Pension Credit (Amendment) Regulations 2005 (SI 2005/3205) reg.2(3) (December 18, 2005).

5. Sovereign Grant Act 2011 s.14 and Sch.1 para.32 (April 1, 2012).

6. Pensions Act 2014 s.23 and Sch.12 Pt 1 paras.42 and 44 (April 6, 2016).

7. Pensions Act 2014 s.15 and Sch.11 para.15 (April 6, 2016).

DEFINITIONS

"the Contribution and Benefits Act"—see s.17(1).
"occupational pension scheme"—*ibid.*
"overseas arrangement"—see subs.(3).
"personal pension scheme"—*ibid.*
"regulations"—see s.17(1).
"retirement annuity contract"—see subs.(3).

GENERAL NOTE

1.380 This section provides a comprehensive definition of the term "retirement pension income" for the purposes of this Act (subs.(1)). The extensive list includes both social security benefits paid to pensioners as well as various forms of private income received by pensioners. The Secretary of State may by regulations add to, vary or remove any of the descriptions so listed (subs.(2); see further State Pension

Credit Regulations 2002 (SI 2002/1792) reg.16). This power provides the necessary flexibility to accommodate other social security benefits or private financial products for pensioners that may become available in the future. But it also includes the power to remove matters listed in subs.(1).

Judge Williams analysed the definition of "overseas arrangement" in subs.(3) in *SSWP v JK* [2009] UKUT 55 (AAC) and rejected the Secretary of State's argument that all foreign state pensions should necessarily be taken into account for the purposes of the assessed income period. On the facts, the claimant's Irish state pension was an "overseas arrangement" and had therefore to be left out of account. The remedy for the Secretary of State to deal with any perceived unfairness was to set either no assessed income period or a short one. However, reg.6 of the Social Security (Miscellaneous Amendments) (No.2) Regulations 2010 (SI 2010/641) amended the relevant regulations with effect from April 13, 2010 with the intention of reversing the effect of *SSWP v JK*.

Other interpretation provisions

17.—(1) In this Act— **1.381**

"the Administration Act" means the Social Security Administration Act 1992 (c.5);

"assessed income period" shall be construed in accordance with sections 6 and 9;

"appropriate minimum guarantee" shall be construed in accordance with section 2(3);

"capital" shall be construed in accordance with section 15;

"claimant" means a claimant for state pension credit;

"the Contributions and Benefits Act" means the Social Security Contributions and Benefits Act 1992 (c.4);

[5 "couple" means—

(a) two people who are married to, or civil partners of, each other and are members of the same household; or

(b) two people who are not married to, or civil partners of, each other but are living together as a married couple otherwise than in prescribed circumstances;]

"earnings" has the same meaning as in Parts 1 to 5 of the Contributions and Benefits Act (see sections 3(1) and 112, and the definition of "employment" in section 122, of that Act);

"element", in relation to the claimant's retirement provision, shall be construed in accordance with section 7(6);

"entitled", in relation to state pension credit, shall be construed in accordance with—

(a) this Act,

(b) section 1 of the Administration Act (entitlement to be dependent on making of claim, etc.), and

(c) section 27 of the Social Security Act 1998 (c.14) (restrictions on entitlement to benefit in certain cases of error),

(and, in relation to any other benefit within the meaning of section 1 of the Administration Act or section 27 of the Social Security Act 1998, in accordance with that section or (as the case may be) both of those sections in addition to any other conditions relating to that benefit);

"foreign social security benefit" means any benefit, allowance or other payment which is paid under the law of a country outside the United Kingdom and is in the nature of social security;

"foreign war disablement pension" means any retired pay, pension, allowance or similar payment granted by the government of a country outside the United Kingdom—
(a) in respect of disablement arising from forces' service or war injury; or
(b) corresponding in nature to any retired pay or pension to which [1section 641 of the Income Tax (Earnings and Pensions) Act 2003] applies;

"foreign war widow's or widower's pension" means any pension, allowance or similar payment granted to a [2 widow, widower or surviving civil partner] by the government of a country outside the United Kingdom—
(a) in respect of a death due to forces' service or war injury; or
(b) corresponding in nature to a pension or allowance for a [2 widow, widower or surviving civil partner] under any scheme mentioned in [1section 641(1)(e) or (f) of the Income Tax (Earnings and Pensions) Act 2003];

"guarantee credit" shall be construed in accordance with sections 1 and 2;
"income" shall be construed in accordance with section 15;
[2 . . .]
"occupational pension scheme" has the meaning given by section 1 of the Pension Schemes Act 1993 (c.48);
"pensionable age" has the meaning given by the rules in paragraph 1 of Schedule 4 to the Pensions Act 1995 (c.26) (equalisation of pensionable ages for men and women);
"personal pension scheme" means a personal pension scheme—
(a) as defined in section 1 of the Pension Schemes Act 1993; or
(b) as defined in section 1 of the Pension Schemes (Northern Ireland) Act 1993 (c.49);

[4 "PPF periodic payments" means—
(a) any periodic compensation payments made in relation to a person, payable under the pension compensation provisions as specified in section 162(2) of the Pensions Act 2004 or Article 146(2) of the Pensions (Northern Ireland) Order 2005 (the pension compensation provisions); or
(b) any periodic payments made in relation to a person, payable under section 166 of the Pensions Act 2004 or Article 150 of the Pensions (Northern Ireland) Order 2005 (duty to pay scheme benefits unpaid at assessment date etc.);]

"prescribed" means specified in, or determined in accordance with regulations;
"the qualifying age" has the meaning given by section 1(6);
"regulations" means regulations made by the Secretary of State;
"retirement pension income" shall be construed in accordance with section 16;
"retirement provision" shall be construed in accordance with section 7(6);
"savings credit" shall be construed in accordance with sections 1 and 3;
"social security benefits" means benefits payable under the enactments relating to social security in any part of the United Kingdom;
"standard minimum guarantee" shall be construed in accordance with section 2(3) to (5) and (9);
[2 . . .]
"war disablement pension" means—

(a) any retired pay, pension or allowance granted in respect of disablement under powers conferred by or under—
(i) the Air Force (Constitution) Act 1917 (c.51);
(ii) the Personal Injuries (Emergency Provisions) Act 1939 (c.82);
(iii) the Pensions (Navy, Army, Air Force and Mercantile Marine) Act 1939 (c.83);
(iv) the Polish Resettlement Act 1947 (c.19); or
(v) Part 7 or section 151 of the Reserve Forces Act 1980 (c.9); or
(b) without prejudice to paragraph (a), any retired pay or pension to which [[1] any of paragraphs (a) to (f) of section 641(1) of the Income Tax (Earnings and Pensions) Act 2003] applies;

"war widow's or widower's pension" means—
(a) [[2] any widow's, widower's or surviving civil partner's] pension or allowance granted in respect of a death due to service or war injury and payable by virtue of any enactment mentioned in paragraph (a) of the definition of "war disablement pension"; or
(b) a pension or allowance for a [[2] widow, widower or surviving civil partner] granted under any scheme mentioned in [[1]section 641(1) (e) or (f) of the Income Tax (Earnings and Pensions) Act 2003];

"working tax credit" means a working tax credit under the Tax Credits Act 2002 to which a person is entitled whether alone or jointly with another.

[[3](1A) [[5]. . .]

(2) Regulations may make provision for the purposes of this Act—
(a) as to circumstances in which persons are to be treated as being or not being members of the same household;
(b) as to circumstances in which persons are to be treated as being or not being severely disabled.

(3) The following provisions of the Contributions and Benefits Act, namely—
(a) section 172 (references to Great Britain or United Kingdom to include reference to adjacent territorial waters, etc.), and
(b) section 173 (meaning of attaining an age, etc.), shall apply for the purposes of this Act as they apply for the purposes of that Act.

AMENDMENTS

1. Income Tax (Earnings and Pensions) Act 2003 Sch.6 para.263 (October 6, 2003).
2. Civil Partnership Act 2004 s.254 and Sch.24 para.142 (December 5, 2005).
3. Civil Partnership Act 2004 s.254 and Sch.24 para.143 (December 5, 2005).
4. Pensions Act 2004 (PPF Payments and FAS Payments) (Consequential Provisions) Order 2006 (SI 2006/343) art.3(2) (February 14, 2006).
5. Marriage (Same Sex Couples) Act 2013 (Consequential and Contrary Provisions and Scotland) Order 2014 (SI 214/560) art.2 and Sch.1 para.28 (March 13, 2014).

GENERAL NOTE

This is the general definition section for the Act. For definitions of "income" and "retirement pension income", see ss.15 and 16 respectively. 1.382

In *CPC/3891/2004* Commissioner Mesher followed his earlier decision in *CIS/1720/2004* and confirmed that a decision simply that a claimant is "living together as husband and wife" is not in itself a decision which gives rise to a right of appeal. Such a decision is merely a "building block" for an outcome decision which would affect entitlement to benefit and so be capable of appeal under Social Security Act 1998 s.12(1). Accordingly a tribunal has no jurisdiction to make a substantive decision on such a "building block" decision as there is no appeal properly before it.

18.—*[Omitted.]*

[[1] Pilot schemes

1.383 **18A.**—

(1) Any regulations to which this subsection applies may be made so as to have effect for a specified period not exceeding 12 months.

(2) Subject to subsection (3), subsection (1) applies to—

(a) regulations made under this Act, and

(b) regulations made under section 1 or 5 of the Administration Act.

(3) Subsection (1) only applies to regulations if they are made with a view to ascertaining whether their provisions will—

(a) make it more likely that persons who are entitled to claim state pension credit will do so;

(b) make it more likely that persons who are entitled to claim state pension credit will receive it.

(4) Regulations which, by virtue of subsection (1), are to have effect for a limited period are referred to in this section as a "pilot scheme".

(5) A pilot scheme may, in particular—

(a) provide for a relevant provision not to apply, or to apply with modifications, for the purposes of the pilot scheme, and

(b) make different provision for different cases or circumstances.

(6) For the purposes of subsection (5)(a), a "relevant provision" is—

(a) any provision of this Act, and

(b) section 1 of the Administration Act.

(7) A pilot scheme may provide that no account is to be taken of any payment made under the pilot scheme in considering a person's—

(a) liability to tax,

(b) entitlement to benefit under an enactment relating to social security (irrespective of the name or nature of the benefit), or

(c) entitlement to a tax credit.

(8) A pilot scheme may provide that its provisions are to apply only in relation to—

(a) one or more specified areas or localities;

(b) one or more specified classes of person;

(c) persons selected—

(i) by reference to prescribed criteria, or

(ii) on a sampling basis.

(9) A pilot scheme may make consequential or transitional provision with respect to the cessation of the scheme on the expiry of the specified period.

(10) A pilot scheme may be replaced by a further pilot scheme making the same or similar provision.

(11) The power of the Secretary of State to make regulations which, by virtue of this section, are to have effect for a limited period is exercisable only with the consent of the Treasury.]

AMENDMENT

1. Welfare Reform Act 2009 s.27(2) (November 12, 2009).

GENERAL NOTE

This section makes provision for a pilot scheme to test ways in which state pension credit entitlement may be calculated and paid in order to increase the number of eligible persons receiving the credit. See also s.142 of the Pensions Act 2008, which permits data sharing between the Secretary of State and energy suppliers (and see further the Disclosure of State Pension Credit Information (Warm Home Discount) Regulations 2011 (SI 2011/1830)). The relevant pilot scheme has been extended for a further year until March 31, 2016: see the Warm Home Discount (Miscellaneous Amendments) Regulations 2015 (SI 2015/652). 1.384

Regulations and orders

19.—(1) Subject to the following provisions of this section, subsections (1), (2) to (5) and (10) of section 175 of the Contributions and Benefits Act (regulations and orders etc) shall apply in relation to any power conferred on the Secretary of State by any provision of this Act to make regulations or an order as they apply in relation to any power conferred on him by that Act to make regulations or an order, but as if for references to that Act (other than references to specific provisions of it) there were substituted references to this Act. 1.385

(2) A statutory instrument containing (whether alone or with other provisions) the first regulations under—

(a) section 2(3)(b), (4) or (6),
(b) section 3(4), (5), (6), (7) or (8),
(c) section 4(3),
(d) section 12, or
(e) section 15(1)(e), (f) or (j), (2), (3), (4) or (6),

shall not be made unless a draft of the instrument has been laid before, and approved by a resolution of, each House of Parliament.

[1 (2A) A statutory instrument containing regulations which, by virtue of section 18A, are to have effect for a limited period shall not be made unless a draft of the instrument has been laid before, and approved by a resolution of, each House of Parliament.]

(3) A statutory instrument—

(a) which contains regulations under this Act (whether alone or with other provisions), and
(b) which is not subject to any requirement that a draft of the instrument be laid before, and approved by a resolution of, each House of Parliament,

shall be subject to annulment in pursuance of a resolution of either House of Parliament.

AMENDMENT

1. Welfare Reform Act 2009 s.27(3) (November 12, 2009).

DEFINITIONS

"the Contribution and Benefits Act"—see s.17(1).
"regulations"—*ibid.*

GENERAL NOTE

1.386 This section applies the usual regulation-making powers for social security benefits under SSCBA 1992 s.175 to the pension credit scheme (subs.(1)). The first regulations made under the various powers listed in subs.(2) were subject to the affirmative procedure. Other regulations remain subject to the usual negative resolution procedure (subs.(3)).

Financial provisions

1.387 **20.**—(1) There shall be paid out of money provided by Parliament—

(a) any sums payable by way of state pension credit;

(b) any expenditure incurred by the Secretary of State or other government department under or by virtue of this Act; and

(c) any increase attributable to this Act in the sums payable out of money so provided under any other Act.

(2) There shall be paid into the Consolidated Fund any increase attributable to this Act in the sums which under any other Act are payable into that Fund.

Enactments repealed

1.388 **21.**—The enactments specified in Schedule 3 to this Act are repealed to the extent there specified.

GENERAL NOTE

1.389 Schedule 3 to the Act made a small number of minor repeals to existing social security legislation which appeared to be unconnected with the introduction of the pension credit.

Short title, commencement and extent

1.390 **22.**—(1) This Act may be cited as the State Pension Credit Act 2002.

(2) This section and sections 19 and 20 come into force on the passing of this Act.

(3) Except as provided by subsection (2), this Act shall come into force on such day as the Secretary of State may by order appoint; and different days may be so appointed for different purposes.

(4) Any order under this section may make such transitional provision as appears to the Secretary of State to be necessary or expedient in connection with the provisions brought into force by the order.

(5) Any amendment or repeal made by this Act has the same extent as the enactment to which it relates (unless otherwise provided).

(6) Subject to that, this Act extends to England and Wales and Scotland only.

GENERAL NOTE

1.391 For the reasons explained in the Introduction and General Note, although this Act is to be known as the State Pension Credit Act 2002 (subs.(1)), the credit itself is described in official literature as the pension credit. This section (along with ss.19 and 20) came into force on Royal Assent (June 25, 2002) (subs.(2)).

SCHEDULES

Sch.1. to Sch.3. *[Omitted.]* 1.392

Immigration and Asylum Act 1999

(1999 c.33)

Sections Reproduced

Part VI

Support for Asylum-Seekers

Exclusions

Exclusion from benefits

115.—(1) No person is entitled to [10 to universal credit under Part 1 of the Welfare Reform Act 2012] income-based jobseeker's allowance under the Jobseekers Act 1995 [4 or to state pension credit under the State Pension Credit Act 2002] [6 or to income-related allowance under Part 1 of the Welfare Reform Act 2007 (employment and support allowance)] [9 or to personal independence payment] or to— 1.394

(a) attendance allowance,
(b) severe disablement allowance,
(c) [1carer's allowance],
(d) disability living allowance,
(e) income support,
(f) [2. . .]
(g) [2. . .]
(h) a social fund payment,
[7 (ha) health in pregnancy grant;]
(i) child benefit,
(j) housing benefit, [8 . . .]
(k) [8 . . .]

under the Social Security Contributions and Benefits Act 1992 while he is a person to whom this section applies.

(2) [*Omitted*]

(3) This section applies to a person subject to immigration control unless he falls within such category or description, or satisfies such conditions, as may be prescribed.

(4) Regulations under subsection (3) may provide for a person to be treated for prescribed purposes only as not being a person to whom this section applies.

(5) In relation to [7 health in pregnancy grant or] [3 child benefit], "prescribed" means prescribed by regulations made by the Treasury.

(6) In relation to the matters mentioned in subsection (2) (except so far as it relates to [7 health in pregnancy grant or] [3 child benefit]), "prescribed" means prescribed by regulations made by the Department.

(7) Section 175(3) to (5) of the Social Security Contributions and Benefits Act 1992 (supplemental powers in relation to regulations) applies to regulations made by the Secretary of State or the Treasury under subsection (3) as it applies to regulations made under that Act.

(8) Sections 133(2), 171(2) and 172(4) of the Social Security Contributions and Benefits (Northern Ireland) Act 1992 apply to regulations made by the Department under subsection (3) as they apply to regulations made by the Department under that Act.

(9) "A person subject to immigration control" means a person who is not a national of an EEA State and who—

(a) requires leave to enter or remain in the United Kingdom but does not have it;
(b) has leave to enter or remain in the United Kingdom which is subject to a condition that he does not have recourse to public funds;
(c) has leave to enter or remain in the United Kingdom given as a result of a maintenance undertaking; or
(d) has leave to enter or remain in the United Kingdom only as a result of paragraph 17 of Schedule 4.

(10) "Maintenance undertaking", in relation to any person, means a written undertaking given by another person in pursuance of the immigration rules to be responsible for that person's maintenance and accommodation.

AMENDMENTS

1. Regulatory Reform (Carer's Allowance) Order 2002 (SI 2002/1457) art.2(1) and Sch. para.3(c) (April 1, 2003).
2. Tax Credits Act 2002 s.60 and Sch.6 (April 8, 2003).
3. Tax Credits Act 2002 s.51 and Sch.4 paras 20–21 (February 26, 2003).
4. State Pension Credit Act 2002 s.4(2) (October 6, 2003).
5. State Pension Credit Act (Northern Ireland) 2002 s.4(2) (October 6, 2003).
6. Welfare Reform Act 2007 Sch.3 para.19 (October 27, 2008).
7. Health and Social Care Act 2008 s.138 (January 1, 2009).
8. Welfare Reform Act 2012 s.147 and Sch.1 Pt 1 (April 1, 2013).
9. Welfare Reform Act 2012 s.91 and Sch.9 para.44 (April 8, 2013).
10. Welfare Reform Act 2012 s.31 and Sch.2 para.54 (April 29, 2013).

AMENDMENT IN UNIVERSAL CREDIT CASES

In those cases and areas where universal credit has come into force, IBJSA, income-related employment and support allowance and (in most cases) housing benefit are abolished and the references to those benefits in s.115(1) are repealed by Welfare Reform Act 2012 s.147 and Sch.14, Pt 1. For the cases and areas where universal credit has come into force, see Pt IV of Vol.V and the General Note to the JSA Regulations 2013 in Pt VI of this volume.

GENERAL NOTE

1.395 See the notes to reg.21 of the Income Support Regulations and to the Social Security (Immigration and Asylum) Consequential Amendments Regulations 2000.

Paragraph 17 of Sch.4 to the Act was repealed on April 1, 2003 by Sch.9 para.1 of the Nationality, Immigration and Asylum Act 2002 but the reference to the repealed provision in s.115(9)(d) has not itself been repealed. By virtue of s.17(2) of the Interpretation Act 1978, that reference should now be construed as a reference to s.3C(2) of the Immigration Act 1971 which was inserted into that Act by the 2002 Act.

Back-dating of benefits where person recorded as refugee

123.—[2 . . .] 1.396

AMENDMENTS

1. State Pension Credit Act 2002 s.14 and Sch.2 para.42 (October 6, 2003).
2. Asylum and Immigration (Treatment of Claimants, etc.) Act 2004 ss.12(1) and 47 and Sch.4 (June 14, 2007).

GENERAL NOTE

See the note to reg.21ZB of the Income Support Regulations (also revoked on June 14, 2007). In relation to state pension credit, see *CPC/3396/2006* referred to in that note. 1.397

Children (Leaving Care) Act 2000

(2000 C.35)

SECTIONS REPRODUCED

1. Further duties of local authorities towards children whom they are looking after. 1.398
2. Additional functions of local authorities in respect of certain children.
6. Exclusion from benefits.

GENERAL NOTE

The Children (Leaving Care) Act 2000, which came into effect on October 1, 2001, placed new duties on local authorities in connection with the provision of support and assistance to those who are leaving local authority care (i.e. whom the local authority is ceasing to "look after"). The Act replaced the arrangements previously contained in s.24 of the Children Act 1989. Its provisions were amplified in the Children (Leaving Care) (England) Regulations 2001 (SI 2001/2874) and the Children (Leaving Care) (Wales) Regulations 2001 (SI 2001/2189), both of which also came into force on October 1, 2001. 1.399

However, the Children (Leaving Care) (England) Regulations were revoked and partly replaced with effect from April 1, 2011 by the Care Leavers (England) Regulations 2010 (SI 2010/2571). These regulations replace the provisions in the 2001 Regulations relating to relevant children (see below). Provisions relating to eligible children (see below) are now in the Care Planning, Placement and Case Review (England) Regulations 2010 (SI 2010/959) which also came into force on April 1, 2011. See pp.950–952 for the relevant provisions of both these sets of Regulations.

In addition, the Children (Leaving Care) (Wales) Regulations 2001 (SI 2001/2189) were revoked and partly replaced with effect from April 6, 2016 by the Care Leavers (Wales) Regulations 2015 (SI 2015/1820). These Regulations replace the provisions in the 2001 Regulations relating to relevant children who are now referred to as "category 2 young persons". Provisions relating to "category 1 young persons" (previously referred to as eligible children) are now in the Care, Planning, Placement and Case Review (Wales) Regulations 2015 (SI 2015/1818) which also came into force on April 6, 2016. See pp.953–955 for the relevant provisions of both these sets of Regulations.

The Act does not apply to Scotland, with the exception of s.6. It was originally intended that equivalent legislation would be introduced in Scotland in 2002. However, a decision was taken to delay the implementation of the changes in Scotland and the relevant provisions (see the Support and Assistance of Young People Leaving Care (Scotland) Regulations 2003 (SSI 2003/608)) only came into force on April 1, 2004.

The effect of s.6 of the Act is to exclude an "eligible child" (defined in para.19B of Sch.2 to the Children Act 1989, inserted by s.1) or a "relevant child" (defined in s.23A of the 1989 Act, inserted by s.2) from entitlement to income-based JSA, income support and housing benefit. From April 6, 2016, this exclusion also applies to a "category 1 young person" within the meaning of s.104(2) of the Social Services and Well-being (Wales) Act 2014 or a "category 2 young person" within the meaning of s.104(2). Section 6(3) allows regulations to provide for exceptions to this rule: see the Children (Leaving Care) Social Security Benefits Regulations 2001 (SI 2001/3074) (p.955). In addition regulations under s.6(4) can extend the exclusion from these benefits to children who have been looked after by a local authority in Scotland. Such regulations have been made and came into force on April 1, 2004 (see the Children (Leaving Care) Social Security Benefits (Scotland) Regulations 2004 (SI 2004/747)) (p.959).

1.400 Note that s.6(1) has not been amended following the introduction of ESA on October 27, 2008 so as to exclude entitlement to income-related ESA. This would appear to be an oversight as a purported amendment to reg.2(1) of the Children (Leaving Care) Social Security Benefits Regulations 2001 has been made to include a reference to income-related ESA. However, in view of the fact that s.6 has not been amended to exclude an "eligible child" or a "relevant child" from entitlement to ESA, such an amendment to the 2001 Regulations is not necessary (and is ultra vires).

For a discussion of s.6 and of the relevant definitions, see the note to reg.2 of the Children (Leaving Care) Social Security Benefits Regulations 2001 (p.956). See also the note to reg.2 of the Children (Leaving Care) Social Security Benefits (Scotland) Regulations 2004 (p.960).

Further duties of local authorities towards children whom they are looking after

1.401 **1.**—In Part II of Schedule 2 to the Children Act 1989 ("the 1989 Act"), which contains provision as to children being looked after by local authorities, after paragraph 19 insert—

"*Preparation for ceasing to be looked after*

19A.—*[Omitted.]*

19B.—(1) A local authority shall have the following additional functions in relation to an eligible child whom they are looking after.

(2) In sub-paragraph (1) "eligible child" means, subject to subparagraph (3), a child, who—

(a) is aged sixteen or seventeen; and

(b) has been looked after by a local authority [2 or by a local authority in Wales] for a prescribed period, or periods amounting in all to a prescribed period, which began after he reached a prescribed age and ended after he reached the age of sixteen.

(3) The [1 [2 Secretary of State]] may prescribe—

(a) additional categories of eligible children; and
(b) categories of children who are not to be eligible children despite falling within sub-paragraph (2).

(4)–(8) *[Omitted.]*
19C.—*[Omitted.]*."

AMENDMENTS

1. Children and Young Persons Act 2008 Sch.3 para.27(3) (November 13, 2008).
2. Social Services and Well-being (Wales) Act 2014 (Consequential Amendments) Regulations 2016 (SI 2016/413) reg.115 (April 6, 2016).

Additional functions of local authorities in respect of certain children

2.—(1) The 1989 Act is amended as follows. 1.402
(2) *[Omitted.]*
(3) In the heading before section 24, at the end insert "and young persons".
(4) After that heading insert the following new sections—

"The responsible authority and relevant children.

23A.—(1) The responsible local authority shall have the functions set out in section 23B in respect of a relevant child.
(2) In subsection (1) 'relevant child' means (subject to subsection (3)) a child who—

(a) is not being looked after [2 by any local authority in England or by any local authority in Wales];
(b) was, before last ceasing to be looked after, an eligible child for the purposes of paragraph 19B of Schedule 2; and
(c) is aged sixteen or seventeen.

(3) The [1 [2 Secretary of State]] may prescribe—

(a) additional categories of relevant children; and
(b) categories of children who are not to be relevant children despite falling within subsection (2).

(4)–(5) *[Omitted.]*
23B.—*[Omitted.]*
23C.—*[Omitted.]*"

AMENDMENTS

1. Children and Young Persons Act 2008 Sch.3 para.8(2) (November 13, 2008).
2. Social Services and Well-being (Wales) Act 2014 (Consequential Amendments) Regulations 2016 (SI 2016/413) reg.74 (April 6, 2016).

Exclusion from benefits

6.—(1) No person is entitled to income-based jobseeker's allowance under the Jobseekers Act 1995, or to income support or housing benefit under the Social Security Contributions and Benefits Act 1992, while he is a person to whom this section applies. 1.403
(2) Subject to subsection (3), this section applies to—
(a) an eligible child for the purposes of paragraph 19B of Schedule 2 to the Children Act 1989;
(b) a relevant child for the purposes of section 23A of that Act; and
[1 (ba) a category 1 young person within the meaning of section 104 of the Social Services and Well-being (Wales) Act 2014;

(bb) a category 2 young person within the meaning of section 104 of the Social Services and Well-being (Wales) Act 2014;]

(c) any person of a description prescribed in regulations under subsection (4).

(3) The Secretary of State may by regulations provide that this section does not apply to a person who falls within subsection (2)(a) or (b) but who also falls within such category or description, or satisfies such conditions, as may be prescribed in the regulations.

(4) The Secretary of State may make regulations prescribing descriptions of persons who do not fall within subsection (2)(a) or (b) but who—

(a) have been looked after by a local authority in Scotland (within the meaning of section 17(6) of the Children (Scotland) Act 1995); and

(b) otherwise correspond (whether or not exactly) to eligible or relevant children.

(5) The Secretary of State may in regulations make such transitional, consequential and saving provision as he considers necessary or expedient in connection with the coming into force of this section.

(6) Section 175(3) to (5) of the Social Security Contributions and Benefits Act 1992 (supplemental power in relation to regulations) applies to regulations made under this section as it applies to regulations made under that Act.

(7) Powers to make regulations under this section include power to make different provision for different areas.

(8) Powers to make regulations under this section are exercisable by statutory instrument.

(9) No statutory instrument containing regulations under subsection (4) is to be made unless a draft of the instrument has been laid before Parliament and approved by a resolution of each House of Parliament.

(10) A statutory instrument containing regulations under subsection (3) or (5) shall be subject to annulment in pursuance of a resolution of either House of Parliament.

AMENDMENT

1. Social Services and Well-being (Wales) Act 2014 (Consequential Amendments) Regulations 2016 (SI 2016/413) reg.178 (April 6, 2016).

GENERAL NOTE

1.404 Section 104(2) of the Social Services and Well-being (Wales) Act 2014 provides that a category 1 young person is a child who (a) is aged 16 or 17; (b) is being looked after by a local authority; and (c) has been looked after by a local authority or a local authority in England for a specified period, or periods amounting in all to a specified period, which began after the child reached a specified age and ended after the child reached the age of 16. This definition replicates the definition of an "eligible child" in para.19B(2) of Sch.2 to the Children Act 1989). A category 2 young person is a child who (a) is aged 16 or 17; (b) is not being looked after by a local authority or a local authority in England; and (c) immediately before ceasing to be looked after was a category 1 young person. This definition replicates the definition of a "relevant child" in s.23A(2) of the 1989 Act.

Age-Related Payments Act 2004

(2004 c.10)

SECTIONS REPRODUCED

Payments for 2004

1.–6. *[Omitted.]* **1.405**

Future payments

7. Power to provide for payments

General

8. Interpretation
9. Money
10. Extent
11. Citation

General Note

The Age-Related Payments Act 2004 came into force on July 8, 2004 and provides for a one-off payment—made during the winter of 2004—and a general power for the Secretary of State to make "regulations providing for the making of payments by him to persons who have attained the age of 60 years". That power is not limited by any specification of the purposes for which the payment is to be made. It is therefore to be contrasted with the more limited power to make payments "to meet expenses for heating, which appear likely to the Secretary of State to have been or likely to be incurred in cold weather" in s.138(2) of SSCBA 1992 that is used to make cold weather payments and winter fuel payments. **1.406**

The s.7 power has been used twice, once to make a one-off payment during the winter of 2005—see the Age-Related Payments Regulations 2005 (SI 2005/1983) (pp.1246–1252 of Vol.II of the 2007 edition)—and, more recently, to make payments to people who bought a with-profits annuity from the Equitable Life Assurance Society on or before August 31, 1992, and were alive and aged over 60 on March 20, 2013. Such people are not eligible for compensation under the main Equitable Life Payments Scheme.

As it relates to the Equitable Life payments, the function of the Secretary of State under s.7 is exercisable concurrently with the Treasury and a consequential amendment was made to the section to reflect that transfer (see the Transfer of Functions (Age-Related Payments) Order 2013 (SI 2013/1442)). The payments themselves (£5,000 for each "qualifying Equitable Life annuitant" and an additional £5,000 for each such annuitant who was in receipt of SPC on November 1, 2013) are authorised by the Age-Related Payments Regulations 2013 (SI 2013/2980).

Payments to a limited class the policy-holders of a particular mutual Society cannot be described as part of the social security system (even though they are said to be made in recognition of "the particular financial pressures this particular group are under" rather than as compensation for maladministration (see the Explanatory Memorandum to SI 2013/2980)). For that reason, the text of the Order and the Regulations (and the amendment to s.7 made by the former) have not been reproduced. Note, however, **1.407** that—by reg.5 of SI 2013/2980 and s.6 of the Act—no account is to be taken when considering a person's entitlement to benefit under an enactment relating to social security (irrespective of the name or nature of the benefit), or to a tax credit.

The age of 60 years specified in s.7(1) has not been amended to reflect the stepped increase in female pensionable age from April 2010.

Future payments

Power to provide for payments

1.408 **7.**—(1) The Secretary of State may make regulations providing for the making of payments by him to persons who have attained the age of 60 years.

(2) Regulations under subsection (1) may provide for payments to be made—

(a) to persons in a specified class (which may be defined by reference to age or otherwise);
(b) in specified circumstances.

(3) Regulations under subsection (1) may, in particular—

(a) provide for payments to be made only once, at specified times or over a specified period,
(b) provide for exceptions,
(c) apply (with or without modifications) an enactment relating to social security (including, in particular, an enactment relating to claims, payments, evidence, revision of decisions, appeals or recovery of payment in error), and
(d) make different provision for different cases or circumstances.

(4) Regulations under this section—

(a) shall be made by statutory instrument, and
(b) may not be made unless a draft has been laid before and approved by resolution of each House of Parliament.

(5) *[Omitted]*

General

Interpretation

1.409 **8.**—(1) In this Act—

"care home"—

(a) in relation to England and Wales, has the same meaning as that given by section 3 of the Care Standards Act 2000 (c. 14), and
(b) in relation to Scotland, means accommodation provided by a care home service within the meaning of [[1] paragraph 2 of schedule 12 to the Public Services Reform (Scotland) Act 2010 (asp 8)],

"couple" means a man and a woman who share a household and who are, or who live as, husband and wife,

"income—based jobseeker's allowance" has the meaning given by section 1(1) and (4) of the Jobseekers Act 1995 (c. 18),

"income support" means income support under section 124 of the Social Security Contributions and Benefits Act 1992 (c. 4),

"qualifying individual" has the meaning given by section 1,

"the relevant week" has the meaning given by section 1,

"single", in relation to an individual, means not part of a couple, and
"state pension credit" has the meaning given by section 1(1) of the State Pension Credit Act 2002 (c. 16).

(2) The provisions of this Act shall apply, with any necessary modifications, to the parties to a polygamous marriage as if they together formed one couple.

AMENDMENT

1. Public Services Reform (Scotland) Act 2010 (Consequential Modifications of Enactments) Order 2011 (SI 2011/2581) art.2 and Sch.2 para.8 (October 28, 2011).

Money

9.—Expenditure of the Secretary of State under or by virtue of this Act shall be paid out of money provided by Parliament. **1.410**

Extent

10.—This Act shall extend only to— **1.411**
(a) England and Wales, and
(b) Scotland.

Citation

11.—This Act may be cited as the Age-Related Payments Act 2004. **1.412**

Child Support Act 1991

(1991 C.48)

SECTION REPRODUCED

SCHEDULE REPRODUCED

GENERAL NOTE

This book does not deal directly with the system of child support maintenance. For a full treatment, see E. Jacobs, *Child Support: the Legislation*. **1.414**

From its inception the child support legislation provided for certain income-related benefits to be reduced where a parent on benefit failed to cooperate in the process of assessing maintenance from an absent parent (now referred to as a non-resident parent) (see ss.6 and 46 of the Child Support Act 1991). However, s.6 and s.46 were both repealed with effect from July 14, 2008 (see Child Maintenance and Other Payments Act 2008 (c.6) s.15(a) and (b) and s.58 and Sch.8 so far as it relates to the repeal of ss.6 and 46, and the Child Maintenance and Other Payments Act 2008 (Commencement) Order 2008 (SI 2008/1476) (c.67) arts 2(2)(a) and (c) and 2(3)(a) and (c)). Article 2(4) of the Commencement Order provided that the repeal of s.6 did not apply in relation to "existing cases" (i.e. those where immediately before

July 14, 2008 a maintenance calculation was in force or an effective date had been set (art.2(5)). Thus those claimants were still subject to the s.6 compulsion but as s.46 had been repealed they could not be penalised for failing to apply for child support. However, with effect from October 27, 2008 art.3(a) of the Child Maintenance and Other Payments Act 2008 (Commencement No.3 and Transitional and Savings Provisions) Order 2008 (SI 2008/2548) (c.110) brought s.15(a) fully into force and art.4 of that Order provides that "existing cases" are to be treated as if the parent with care had made an application under s.4 of the Child Support Act 1991. The consequence of the repeal of s.46 is that all reduced benefit decisions ceased to have effect on July 14, 2008.

In addition, the original child support scheme ("the 1993 scheme") provided that where an absent parent was on income support or income-based JSA, a deduction could be made from his income support or income-based JSA as a contribution towards child support maintenance. This deduction still applies in cases which have not yet been "converted" to the "new" child support scheme ("the 2003 scheme") introduced by the Child Support, Pensions and Social Security Act 2000 (see below) and since October 6, 2003 and October 27, 2008 has also applied to state pension credit and income-related ESA respectively. (This deduction can also be made from an absent parent's contribution-based JSA/contributory ESA if he would be entitled to income-based JSA/income-related ESA at the same rate but for the fact that he is getting contribution-based JSA/contributory ESA; in addition, deductions for arrears of child support maintenance can be made from contribution-based JSA/contributory ESA in certain circumstances (see further the note to s.43).) There is also provision for the deduction to be made from universal credit (see para.10 of Sch.6 to the Universal Credit, Personal Independence Payment, Jobseeker's Allowance and Employment and Support Allowance (Claims and Payments) Regulations 2013 (SI 2013/380) in Vol.V in this series).

1.415 However, for those cases to which the 2003 scheme applies, a deduction of £5 in respect of the flat rate of child support maintenance can be made from a greatly expanded list of benefits (see further the note to s.43). In relation to the third child support scheme ("the 2012 scheme") (see below) the deduction is £7.

Those parts of the child support legislation relevant to the deduction are included in this book. Readers are referred to the 2002 edition of this volume for the provisions relating to deductions as a contribution towards child maintenance under the 1993 scheme.

On March 3, 2003 the long-delayed changes to the child support scheme introduced by the Child Support, Pensions and Social Security Act 2000 finally came into force (see the Child Support, Pensions and Social Security Act 2000 (Commencement No.12) Order 2003 (SI 2003/192), as amended by the Child Support, Pensions and Social Security Act 2000 (Commencement No.13) Order 2003 (SI 2003/346)). The "new" rules only applied to all new (and non-linking) child support applications (a new application was one with an effective date on or after March 3, 2003); most existing cases were to be "converted" at a future date, although some may transfer earlier. Thus, for example, if after March 3, 2003, a person with a existing child support assessment made a new application for a different child with a different non-resident parent the "new" scheme applied to both applications. For full details of the 2003 scheme and when it applies, see E. Jacobs, *Child Support: the Legislation.*

Further substantial reform to the child support system has been made by the Child Maintenance and Other Payments Act 2008. For the details of this see E. Jacobs, *Child Support: the Legislation.* This third child support scheme ("the 2012 scheme") applied to certain new applications made on or after December 10, 2012 and certain cases linked to those applications. It was extended to certain other new cases on July 29, 2013. It commenced for all other new cases on November 25, 2013 but only started to apply to existing cases in 2014; the Government has stated that it intends to complete this process by 2017.

[1 Applications by those claiming or receiving benefit

6.—[2 . . .]] 1.416

AMENDMENTS

1. Child Support, Pensions and Social Security Act 2000 s.3 (March 3, 2003).
2. Child Maintenance and Other Payments Act 2008 (c.6) s.15(a), s.58 and Sch.8 (July 14, 2008 and October 27, 2008).

Special cases

[1 Recovery of child support maintenance by deduction from benefit

43.—[2 (1) The power of the Secretary of State to make regulations under section 5 of the Social Security Administration Act 1992 by virtue of subsection (1)(p) of that section may be exercised with a view to securing the making of payments in respect of child support maintenance by a non-resident parent. 1.417

(2) The reference in subsection (1) to the making of payments in respect of child support maintenance includes the recovery of—

(a) arrears of child support maintenance, and
(b) fees payable under section 6 of the Child Maintenance and Other Payments Act 2008.]

(3) For the purposes of this section, the benefits to which section 5 of the 1992 Act applies are to be taken as including war disablement pensions and war widows' pensions (within the meaning of section 150 of the Social Security Contributions and Benefits Act 1992 (interpretation)).]

AMENDMENTS

1. Child Support, Pensions and Social Security Act 2000 s.21 (March 3, 2003).
2. Welfare Reform Act 2012 s.139 (February 4, 2014).

DEFINITIONS

"child support maintenance"—see Child Support Act 1991 s.54.
"non-resident parent"—*ibid*.

GENERAL NOTE

The long-delayed changes to the child support scheme introduced by the Child Support, Pensions and Social Security Act 2000 finally came into force on March 3, 2003. The changes were implemented in stages depending on the type of case (see the note at the beginning of the Child Support Act 1991 above). They included the substitution of this section and of Pt I of Sch.1 to the 1991 Act. The new form contained some significant differences from the previous provisions. 1.418

This form of s.43 and para.4 of Pt I of Sch.1 to the 1991 Act apply in those cases to which the "new" child support scheme applies ("the 2003 scheme") (see art.3 of and the Schedule to the Child Support, Pensions and Social Security Act 2000 (Commencement No.12) Order 2003 (SI 2003/192)—broadly these are applications for child support maintenance with an effective date on or after March 3, 2003 and certain cases where there is an existing assessment).

Note that there is now a third child support scheme ("the 2012 scheme"). See the note at the beginning of the Child Support Act 1991 above for when this applies and see further below.

1.419 Note also that s.43 was further amended on February 4, 2014. The main effect of the amendments is to also allow for the recovery by deduction from benefit of fees payable under s.6 of the Child Maintenance and Other Payments Act 2008 by the non-resident parent (subs.(2)(b)).

Under the 2003 scheme, unless the nil rate is applicable, a £5 flat rate of child support maintenance applies for non-resident parents in receipt of certain prescribed benefits (although a different amount may apply under the transitional arrangements when a case converts to the new system). (For when the nil rate is applicable see para.5 of Sch.1 to the 1991 Act and reg.5 of the Child Support (Maintenance Calculations and Special Cases) Regulations 2000 (SI 2001/155) in E. Jacobs, *Child Support: the Legislation.*)

This section, Sch.1 paras 4 and 8 and reg.4 of the Child Support (Maintenance Calculations and Special Cases) Regulations 2000, together with Sch.9B to the Claims and Payments Regulations 1987 (see Vol.III of this series), provide for the deduction of the £5 flat rate from the non-resident parent's benefit and its payment to the parent with care. The deduction will be made if either the non-resident parent or his partner is getting income support, income-based JSA, income-related ESA, state pension credit or universal credit. It is halved if the non-resident parent's partner is also a non-resident parent with a child support maintenance calculation in force. The flat-rate deduction will also be made if the non-resident parent is in receipt of any of the following: contribution-based JSA, contributory ESA, incapacity benefit, severe disablement allowance, retirement pension, carer's allowance, maternity allowance, industrial injuries benefit, bereavement allowance, widowed mother's allowance, widowed parent's allowance, widow's pension, war disablement pension, war widow's or widower's pension, an Armed Forces Compensation Payment, a social security benefit paid by a country other than the UK, or a training allowance (other than work-based learning for young people or, in Scotland, Skillseekers training). In addition, except where income support, income-based JSA, income-related ESA or state pension credit is payable to the non-resident parent or his partner, a deduction of £1 for arrears of child support maintenance can be made from any of those benefits or allowances. A deduction can only be made from one benefit in any one week (para.2(2) of Sch.9B to the Claims and Payment Regulations). No deduction will be made if this would result in less than 10p of the benefit remaining payable (para.2(3) of Sch.9B). Note also that if the non-resident parent is regarded as having "shared care" (i.e. for at least 52 nights in a year), the amount of child support maintenance payable will be nil and no deduction will be made (see para.8(2) of Sch.1 to the 1991 Act). For a discussion of the priority to be given to the flat-rate deduction in relation to other deductions, see the note to reg.35 of the Claims and Payments Regulations in Vol.III of this series.

1.420 Under the 2012 scheme (the third child support scheme—see the note at the beginning of the Child Support Act 1991 as to when this applies), the rules for deductions from benefit were originally the same as under the 2003 scheme (in relation to the 2012 scheme see reg.44 of the Child Support Maintenance Calculations Regulations 2012 (SI 2012/2677) rather than reg.4 of the Child Support (Maintenance Calculations and Special Cases) Regulations 2000). However, from November 25, 2013, the deduction from benefit where maintenance liability has been assessed under the 2012 scheme was increased from £5 to £7. This increased rate does not apply to cases assessed under the 2003 scheme.

There is a right of appeal to a tribunal against a decision to make deductions from benefit in respect of child support maintenance, although there may be little scope for argument if the legislation has been correctly applied.

For the previous form of s.43, Sch.1 para.5(4) and regs 13 and 28 and Schs 4 and 5 of the Child Support (Maintenance Assessments and Special Cases) Regulations 1992, under which (together with para.7A of Sch.9 to the Claims and Payments Regulations 1987 (see Vol.III of this series)) a deduction of £7.40 can be made from the income support, income-based JSA, income-related ESA, or state pension credit of an absent parent (or contribution-based JSA/contributory ESA if the absent parent would be entitled to income-based JSA/income-related ESA at the same rate but for the fact that he is getting contribution-based JSA/contributory ESA, or if the absent parent is getting both contribution-based and income-based JSA/contributory ESA and income-related ESA and his income-based JSA/income-related ESA is insufficient for the deduction to be made: see para.1(1), definition of "specified benefit", and para.1(2) and (3) of Sch.9 to the Claims and Payments Regulations 1987 in Vol.III of this series) as a contribution towards the maintenance of his children, see the 2002 edition of this volume. These provisions still apply for existing cases that have not been converted to the "new" child support scheme (see the note at the beginning of the Child Support Act 1991, above). Note also that in existing cases deductions for arrears of child support maintenance can be made from contribution-based JSA/contributory ESA (even where there would be no entitlement to income-based JSA/income-related ESA) in certain circumstances (see para.7B of Sch.9 to the Claims and Payments Regulations). If the full £7.40 cannot be deducted because other deductions are being made which have a higher priority, £3.70 can be deducted (see paras 7A(4), 8(1) and 9 of Sch.9 to the Claims and Payments Regulations). Contributions towards child maintenance are seventh in priority (out of 10) of the deductions covered by Sch.9.

In *CCS/16904/1996* the Commissioner conducted a detailed analysis of the legislation on deductions in place of child support maintenance. He referred to the fact that s.43(2) allowed regulations to be made for deducting payments in place of child support maintenance from various benefits and reg.28(2) of the Child Support (Maintenance Assessments and Special Cases) Regulations 1992 (SI 1992/1815) (see the 2002 edition of this volume for this regulation) defined the amount of the payments (now see para.4 of Sch.1, together with reg.4(3) of the Child Support (Maintenance Calculations and Special Cases) Regulations) but there was nothing that in so many words imposed an obligation on an absent parent to make such payments. He concluded that the legal basis for liability to make payments in place of child support maintenance was provided by the general duty to maintain a child under s.1 of the 1991 Act. This required the payment of such "maintenance" (not just child support maintenance) as determined in accordance with the provisions of the Act. Thus if it was decided that s.43 applied, this gave rise to a liability on the absent parent to make payment and a corresponding entitlement of the parent with care to receive the amounts deducted by the Secretary of State. The decision was appealed to the Court of Appeal under the name of *Dollar v Child Support Officer*, reported as *R(CS) 7/99*, but there was no specific challenge to the Commissioner's conclusion on this issue. The Court of Appeal proceeded on the basis that there was a liability to make the payments identified in s.43(2). The Commissioner states in *R(CS) 5/05* that he therefore sees no reason to depart from what he said in *CCS/16904/1996*. 1.421

Note also *R. (Plumb) v Secretary of State for Work and Pensions* [2002] EWHC 1125 (Admin), March 22, 2002, unreported (Admin. Ct). The claimant contended that the £5.10 deduction (as it then was) from his JSA made as a contribution towards the maintenance of his child affected the quality and extent of his contact with his daughter and thus was in breach of art.8 of the European Convention on Human Rights (right to family life). The Court accepted that such a deduction was capable of amounting to an interference with an art.8 right but on the facts of this case this was far from being established. Furthermore, any interference with the claimant's right under art.8(1) was justified under art.8(2).

[1 Reduced benefit decisions

46.—[2 . . .]] 1.422

AMENDMENTS

1. Child Support, Pensions and Social Security Act 2000 s.19 (March 3, 2003).
2. Child Maintenance and Other Payments Act 2008 (c.6) s.15(b) s.58 and Sch.8 (July 14, 2008).

SCHEDULE 1 **Section 11**

MAINTENANCE CALCULATIONS

[1 PART I

CALCULATION OF WEEKLY AMOUNT OF CHILD SUPPORT MAINTENANCE

Flat rate

1.423 **4.**—(1) Except in a case falling within sub-paragraph (2), a flat rate of £5 is payable if the nil rate does not apply and—

(a) the non-resident parent's net weekly income is £100 or less; or
(b) he receives any benefit, pension or allowance prescribed for the purposes of this paragraph of this sub-paragraph; or
(c) he or his partner (if any) receives any benefit prescribed for the purposes of this paragraph of this sub-paragraph.

(2) A flat rate of a prescribed amount is payable if the nil rate does not apply and—

(a) the non-resident parent has a partner who is also a non-resident parent;
(b) the partner is a person with respect to whom a maintenance calculation is in force; and
(c) the non-resident parent or his partner receives any benefit prescribed under sub-paragraph (1)(c).

(3) The benefits, pensions and allowances which may be prescribed for the purposes of sub-paragraph (1)(b) include ones paid to the non-resident parent under the law of a place outside the United Kingdom.

[Paras 5 to 7 not reproduced.]

Shared care—flat rate

1.424 **8.**—(1) This paragraph applies only if—

(a) the rate of child support maintenance payable is a flat rate; and
(b) that rate applies because the non-resident parent falls within paragraph 4(1)(b) or (c) or 4(2).

(2) If the care of a qualifying child is shared as mentioned in paragraph 7(2) for at least 52 nights during a prescribed 12-month period, the amount of child support maintenance payable by the non-resident parent to the person with care of that child is nil.]

[The rest of the Schedule has not been reproduced.]

AMENDMENT

1. Child Support, Pensions and Social Security Act 2000 s.1(3) and Sch.1 (March 3, 2003).

GENERAL NOTE

1.425 For those cases to which the 2012 scheme applies, the word "gross" replaces the word "net" in para.4(1)(a) and the words "If the care of a qualifying child is, or is to be shared" replace the words "If the care of a qualifying child is shared" in para.8(2).

Child Support Act 1995

(1995 c. 34)

SECTION REPRODUCED

The child maintenance bonus

10.—[1 . . .] 1.427

AMENDMENT

1. Child Support, Pensions and Social Security Act 2000 s.23 (October 27, 2008).

GENERAL NOTE

With effect from October 27, 2008, s.23 of the Child Support, Pensions and Social Security Act 2000 is brought fully into force by the Child Support, Pensions and Social Security Act 2000 (Commencement No.14) Order 2008 (SI 2008/2545) (c.109) art.4. The effect is that s.10 of the Child Support Act 1995 is repealed in all cases and it will no longer be possible for any person to accrue a child maintenance bonus. Before October 27, 2008 it was still possible for a person to whom the "old" child support scheme applied to accrue a child maintenance bonus. See the 2008/09 edition of this volume for s.10 and the original commencement provisions in relation to its partial repeal and for the Social Security (Child Maintenance Bonus) Regulations 1996 (SI 1996/3195) which contained the detail of the child maintenance bonus scheme. 1.428

The quid pro quo of the abolition of the child maintenance bonus is that all income support, income-based JSA and income-related ESA claimants who are getting child maintenance payments are eligible for the child maintenance disregard. The disregard was initially a partial disregard but from April 12, 2010 any payment of child maintenance is fully disregarded as income (see para.73 of Sch.9 to the Income Support Regulations, para.70 of Sch.7 to the JSA Regulations 1996 and para.60 of Sch.8 to the ESA Regulations 2008 (for the ESA Regulations see Vol.I in this series). For the definition of "child maintenance payments" see sub-para.(2) of the respective paragraph in each of these Regulations.

Jobseekers (Back to Work Schemes) Act 2013

(2013 c.17)

ARRANGEMENT OF SECTIONS

An Act to make provision about the effect of certain provisions relating to participation in a scheme designed to assist persons to obtain employment and about notices relating to participation in such a scheme.[26th March 2013]

GENERAL NOTE

1.430 In *R (Reilly and Wilson) v Secretary of State for Work and Pensions* [2013] EWCA Civ 66; [2013] 1 W.L.R. 2239, the Court of Appeal quashed as unlawful the Jobseeker's Allowance (Employment, Skills and Enterprise Scheme) Regulations 2011 (SI 2011/917) ("the ESES Regulations") under which some of the "Back to Work" schemes operated, because the Secretary of State acted ultra vires in failing to provide sufficient decription of the various schemes in the Regulations to satisfy s.17A(1) of the Jobseekers Act 1995. The Court also held that notices sent to claimants advising them that they were required to take part in a programme within the ESES Scheme did not comply with the requirements of reg.4 of the ESES Regulations. The effect of the decision was that the DWP had no right to impose a sanction on claimants who had failed to meet their requirements. The Court, however, upheld the general policy principle of the employment programmes comprised in the ESES Regulations and also ruled that they did not breach art.4(2) of the ECHR (prohibiting forced or compulsory labour).The Court of Appeal's reasoning was subsequently upheld in substance by the Supreme Court in *R (Reilly and Wilson) v Secretary of State for Work and Pensions* [2013] UKSC 68; [2014] 1 A.C. 453, but because of the retrospective validation of the ESES Regulations by this Act, it was indicated that that would have to be reflected in the order made. It emerges from the judgment of Lang J in *R (Reilly No 2 and Hewstone) v Secretary of State for Work and Pensions* [2014] EWHC 2182 (Admin) that the order was to allow the Secretary of State's appeal on the *ultra vires* point on the basis that the 2013 Act had come into force. The order apparently also allowed the appeal on the point about breach of the notification requirements, which was accepted on behalf of the Secretary of State in *Reilly (No 2)* to have been wrong, so that the declaration in Miss Reilly's favour remained in force.

The DWP on the day of the Court of Appeal's judgment issued the Jobseeker's Allowance (Schemes for Assisting Persons to Obtain Employment) Regulations 2013 (SI 2013/276) ("the SAPOE Regulations"), which came into effect at 18.45 on February 12, 2013 so that sanctions could be applied from the date those new Regulations came into force.

This Act came into force on March 26, 2013, the day on which the Secretary of State sought permission to appeal against the decision of the Court of Appeal in *Reilly and Wilson*, the Bill having been fast-tracked through Parliament. Section 1(14) provides that the ESES Regulations are to be treated as having been revoked by the SAPOE Regulations on the coming into force of the latter.

1.431 This Act is designed retrospectively to validate the impugned ESES Regulations making actions which related to participation in these employment programmes effective, and providing that notices served under those Regulations informing claimants of requirements as to participation, and about consequences of failing to meet requirements, were effective. The provisions affect claimants where sanctions have been applied for failures to comply with the ESES Regulations and cases where the claimant has failed to comply with a requirement of the ESES Regulations but a decision to impose a sanction has not yet been taken. It aims to ensure that any such decisions cannot be challenged on the grounds that the ESES Regulations were invalid or the notices inadequate, notwithstanding the Court of Appeal's judgment, so that benefit sanctions already imposed or to be imposed stand, saving the public purse some £130 million which would otherwise have to be paid to claimants who had been, if the Court of Appeal decision had stood, treated unlawfully. The Act also aims to protect from challenge on the basis of the reasoning in *Reilly and Wilson* about the validity of notices under the Jobseeker's Allowance (Mandatory Work Activity Scheme) Regulations 2011 (SI 2011/688).

The compatibility of the 2013 Act with the ECHR was challenged in *Reilly (No 2)* (above), on the basis that the purported retrospective validation of the ESES Regulations breached the claimants' right to a fair trial under art.6 in relation to the proceedings in existence as at March 26, 2013 (the challenges to Ms Reilly's favourable judgment in the Court of Appeal and to Mr Hewstone's favourable decisions from a First-tier Tribunal against which the Secretary of State had appealed to the Upper Tribunal). Mr Hewstone also had one decision pending and "stockpiled" before the Secretary of State). The only remedy sought by the claimants was a declaration of incompatibility under s.4 of the Human Rights Act 1998, which cannot affect the validity or continuing operation of the provision declared incompatible. At one time, when the staying of other cases to await the outcome of *Reilly (No 2)* was put into operation, it was thought that there was to be a challenge on the basis of European Union law, which could in principle, if successful, have led to a conclusion that the 2013 Act or parts of it had to be disapplied. However, no such challenge was maintained before Lang J.

Lang J granted the declaration of incompatibility with art.6 of the ECHR, having concluded that art.1 of Protocol 1 was not engaged (so that Mr Hewstone could not rely on the ECHR in relation to his stockpiled claim). She had no doubt that the Act had a preclusive retrospective effect on the claimants' pending proceedings. Indeed, she went so far as to say that the Upper Tribunal would be bound in Mr Hewstone's case to allow the Secretary of State's appeal because the only tenable defect in the application of the ESES Regulations in his case had been retrospectively validated. The Judge's view was that there were not the required "compelling grounds of public interest" in order to justify the retrospective interference with the claimants' rights. She rejected the Secretary of State's argument that giving the decision in *Reilly* what was in practice a prospective effect in other cases, through the impact of the 2013 Act, was merely giving effect to the general principle contained in s.27 of the SSA 1998 in relation to decisions of the Upper Tribunal on appeal or of higher courts on further appeal, starkly exposing the misunderstanding of the effect of s.27 involved. If *Reilly and Wilson* is regarded as the test case, s.27 did not prevent its application to the claimant who brought the test case (Ms Reilly), to claimants whose appeals to the First-tier Tribunal or cases before the Upper Tribunal or higher were pending at the date of the test case decision (e.g. Mr Hewstone) or to claimants for whom decisions had been stockpiled under s.25 of the SSA 1998 pending the decision in the test case. Nor could it be accepted that the flaws identified in *Reilly and Wilson* were mere technicalities, that the 2013 Act was restoring the original intentions of Parliament or that the effect was to prevent claimants enjoying an undeserved windfall.

The Secretary of State's appeal against Lang J's decision was heard by the Court of Appeal at the end of November 2015 and judgment was given on April 28, 2016, there having been some post-hearing submissions (*SSWP v Reilly and Hewstone* and *SSWP v Jeffrey and Bevan* [2016] EWCA Civ 413). That appeal was heard at the same time as that of the Secretary of State against the decision of the three-judge panel in February 2015 in *SSWP v TJ (JSA)* [2015] UKUT 56 (AAC), where the cases of three claimants had been selected to attempt to resolve issues left outstanding by *Reilly and Wilson* and *Reilly (No.2)*. There was a detailed description and discussion of the decision in *TJ* in the 2015/16 edition of this volume, which need not now all be repeated here in the light of the Court of Appeal's decision. **1.432**

The three cases before the Upper Tribunal all stemmed from decisions of the Secretary of State, made before the amendment of the ESES Regulations by the Jobseeker's Allowance (Sanctions) (Amendment) Regulations 2012, to impose a sanction of non-payment of JSA on the claimants under reg.8 for having failed without good cause to participate in a scheme under the ESES Regulations (in two cases the Work Programme and in one the Community Action Programme). Regulation 8 as in existence at the time is set out at p.1257 of Vol.II (2012/13 edition). Two tribunals allowed the claimants' appeals on the ground that, following the High Court decision in *Reilly and Wilson*, the notifications requiring participation did not meet the requirements of reg.4. The Secretary of State was given permission to appeal to the Upper Tribunal. The other tribunal disallowed the claimant's appeal without reference to *Reilly and Wilson*.

1.433 The central element of the decision of the majority of the Upper Tribunal (Judges Rowland and Wright; Charles J dissenting on this element) was that the 2013 Act, despite the provision in s.1(1) that the ESES Regulations are to be treated "for all purposes" as made under s.17A of the old style Jobseekers Act 1995, was not to be construed either under ordinary canons of statutory construction or as "read down" under s.3 of the Human Rights Act 1998 so as to be compatible with art.6 of the ECHR, as not applying retrospectively to claimants who had already brought appeals to the First-tier Tribunal prior to March 26, 2013. That conclusion was fairly shortly rejected by the Court of Appeal in *Jeffrey and Bevan*. The Court of Appeal took the view that the phrase "for all purposes" was in essence the beginning and end of the analysis (para.131 of the judgment of the court). It agreed with Charles J in that respect and also in the view that s.27 of the SSA 1998 (the "anti-test-case" rule) played no part in informing the intention underlying the 2013 Act. The Court of Appeal further rejected the argument made for the claimants that s.12(8)(b) of the SSA 1998 (tribunals not to take into account any circumstances not obtaining at the time when the decision appealed against was made) would prevent any First-tier Tribunal that was considering any appeal pending as at March 26, 2013 from giving effect to the 2013 Act because its enactment would, notwithstanding its retrospective effect, constitute a circumstance not obtaining at the date of the sanction decision. The Upper Tribunal had treated this as a separate issue, but counsel for Ms Jeffrey said that the argument was intended to support the construction point. The Court of Appeal held (para.137) that the effect of s.12(8)(b) could not be to nullify subsequent explicitly retrospective legislation that would otherwise govern the tribunal's decision and that the decision in *CAO v McKiernon*, reported as *R(I) 2/94* (extensively discussed by the majority in the Upper Tribunal) was not authority to the contrary, having been concerned with a wholly different question. The Court of Appeal agreed with the conclusion and reasoning in para.175 of the Upper Tribunal's decision to the effect that it would be improper to use the discretion in s.12(2)(a) of the Tribunal, Courts and Enforcement Act 2007 not to set aside a decision of a First-tier Tribunal found to have involved an error of law to avoid a result incompatible with art.6 of the ECHR. To do so would be to ignore the binding effect of the 2013 Act and the fact that even a declaration of incompatibility under s.4 of the Human Rights Act 1998 does not affect the validity or continuing operation of primary legislation.

Since the Court of Appeal took that view of the main parts of the Upper Tribunal decision, the central issue (although it appears in the judgment first) became whether Lang J was right or wrong about incompatibility with art.6 of the ECHR. Following an exhaustive review of the Strasbourg and other authorities it concluded that she had been right. The retrospective provision was, in relation to claimants who had commenced proceedings (appeal or judicial review) prior to March 26, 2013, incompatible with art.6 as designed to influence the judicial determination of those disputes contrary to the *Zielinski* principle (*Zielinski v France* (2001) 31 EHRR 19) as properly understood. There were not the compelling grounds of the general interest to constitute justification for that interference with the right to a fair trial. The Court comprehensively rejected the six grounds, some fairly desperate, to the contrary put forward by the Secretary of State. Very much in brief, it was held that:

(1) it was not necessary that there be an intention to target any particular claimant, but that there is a breach of the *Zielinski* principle if part of the intention is to interfere with the outcome of a class of claims generally, as was plainly the case for the 2013 Act;

(2) although there was no substantive interference with Ms Reilly's access to the court, as she had not been sanctioned, there was in Mr Hewstone's case and it did not matter that he had not in his appeals expressly raised the ground of challenge

to notices that eventually succeeded in the Supreme Court or had other arguable grounds (e.g. good cause) on which he could rely;

(3) and (4) the failures in the ESES Regulations that the 2013 Act was designed to correct retrospectively were not merely technical drafting loopholes; even if the fact that claimants with good cause for failing to participate in a scheme could escape sanction meant that protection from the retrospective effect would go to the undeserving, that did not outweigh the value of protecting the integrity of the judicial process; the financial impact, as only claimants who had commenced proceeding were to be protected, would be limited to about £1.3 million; it did not matter that those in a similar position who had not commenced proceedings would not be protected; and the existence of s.27 of the SSA 1998 assisted the claimants rather than the Secretary of State;

(5) under the heading of justification, the effect of the 2013 Act on existing appeals was not "only incidental"; and

(6) although in places Lang J might have transgressed the principle in art.9 of the Bill of Rights that proceedings in Parliament ought not to be impeached or questioned in any court, there was no such transgression in the Court of Appeal's reasoning.

The Court of Appeal rejected the argument on behalf of Mr Hewstone that claim- **1.434** ants who had been sanctioned under reg.8 of the ESES Regulations before March 26, 2013 but who had not by that date appealed or started other legal proceedings had been deprived of a "possession" under art.1 of Protocol 1 of the ECHR. It appears that that argument was put in two ways: that in any period for which such a claimant satisfied the conditions of entitlement in s.1(2) of the old style Jobseekers Act 1995 the right to receive JSA was a possession and, alternatively, that after the decisions of Foskett J and the Court of Appeal in *Reilly and Wilson*, they had a legitimate expectation of receiving a "repayment" of the JSA withheld during the sanction period which constituted a possession. The Court agreed with Lang J that the first alternative did not work because each sanction decision had the effect that benefit was not payable for a period in the future, so that no possession was ever acquired that was then removed. It may be arguable that that reasoning overlooks the fact that claimants continue to be entitled to old style JSA through a period of a sanction, so that they are deprived of the normal consequence of entitlement, which is that benefit is payable. The Court held that the second alternative did not work under the Strasbourg authority because the claim to "repayment" was not sufficiently supported by settled national case-law as at March 26, 2013 to constitute an asset or possession.

The final issue dealt with in relation to the Upper Tribunal's decision in Mr Bevan's case was its guidance on the so-called prior information requirement (see para.74 of the judgment of the Supreme Court in *Reilly and Wilson*), a failure to comply with which might vitiate the requirement to participate in a scheme. The Upper Tribunal had concluded, in the terms of its own summary in para.13(vi), that in the case of schemes which were mandatory both at the stages of referral onto them and once on them, no basis could be identified on which *meaningful* representations could be made prior to the decision to refer, in the sense of those representations being able to affect the decision to refer. In the 2015/16 edition of this volume there was some criticism of the Upper Tribunal's use of the word "mandatory" in this context.

The Court of Appeal first held that the Upper Tribunal had been right on the particular facts of Mr Bevan's case (where his complaint was that he could not afford the bus fare to attend the appointment given, so needed payment in advance rather than a refund) to find that it would have made no difference to what he would have said to the provider about the fares if he had known about what *The Work Programme Provider Guidance* issued by the DWP said about ability to use transportation.

So far as the Upper Tribunal's general guidance is concerned, the Court said this in para.172 about the submission that the Upper Tribunal had erred in saying that there was no scope for making representations in connection with a decision to refer a claimant to the Work Programme since referral was mandatory:

"We do not believe that that is a fair reading of what the Tribunal said; and if it is properly understood there does not seem to be any dispute of principle between the parties. The Tribunal was not laying down any absolute rule. The Secretary of State's policy, embodied in the guidance, is that referral to the Programme should be automatic (ignoring the specified exceptions) if the criteria are met. All that the Tribunal was doing was to point out that, that being so, any representations would have to address the question why he should depart from the policy; and that it was not easy to see what such representations might be. That seems to us an obvious common sense observation, particularly since referral to the Work Programme does not as such involve any specific obligation: see para.151 above. But it does not mean that there could never be such cases, and indeed para.224 is expressly addressed to that possibility. The Tribunal did not depart from anything that the Supreme Court said in [*Reilly and Wilson*]. It was simply considering its application in the particular circumstances of referral to the Work Programme."

1.435 The Court considered that in the real world application of the prior information duty was unlikely to be important at the point of initial referral to the Work Programme, as claimants were unlikely to object at that stage, before any specific requirements were imposed. Problems were likely to emerge when particular requirements were imposed on claimants that they considered unreasonable or inappropriate. The Upper Tribunal had appeared to say in para.249 of its decision that there was little or no scope for the operation of the duty at that stage. The Court of Appeal says this in paras 177 and 178:

"177. Mr de la Mare [counsel for Mr Bevan] submitted that that is wrong. If it is indeed what the Tribunal meant, we agree. So also does Ms Leventhal [counsel for the Secretary of State], who explicitly accepted in her written submissions that 'the requirements of fairness continue to apply after referral'. In principle, JSA claimants who are required, or who it is proposed should be required, under the Work Programme to participate in a particular activity should have sufficient information to enable them to make meaningful representations about the requirement – for example, that the activity in question is unsuitable for them or that there are practical obstacles to their participation. The fact that participation is mandatory if the requirement is made is beside the point: the whole purpose of the representations, and thus of the claimant having the relevant information to be able to make them, is so that the provider may be persuaded that the requirement should not be made, or should be withdrawn or modified.

178. However we should emphasise that the foregoing is concerned with the position in principle. It is quite another matter whether the Work Programme as operated in fact fails to give claimants such information. The Secretary of State's evidence before the Tribunal was that the relevant guidance in fact provides for them to be very fully informed. We have already referred to the Tribunal's findings about the information given at the referral interview. But it was also the evidence that at the initial interview with the provider post-referral, which is designed to find out how the claimant can be best supported, and in the subsequent inter-actions between claimant and provider claimants are supposed to be given both information and the opportunity to make representations. Whether in any particular case there has nevertheless been a failure to give information necessary to enable the claimant to make meaningful representations will have to be judged on the facts of the particular case. Tribunals will no doubt bear in mind the point made in [*Reilly and Wilson*] that it is important not to be prescriptive about how any necessary information is provided: see para.74 of the judgment of Lord Neuberger and Lord Toulson."

It is understood as at the date of going to press that some of the claimants are still considering whether to apply for permission to appeal to the Supreme Court, possibly depending on the outcome of legal aid applications for claimants not backed by the Child Poverty Action Group. It is difficult to predict whether, in view of the comprehensive rejection of his case on art.6 of the ECHR, the Secretary of State will wish to seek permission to appeal or will be content to accept the limited consequences of the declaration of incompatibility.

There was no challenge in the Court of Appeal to the Upper Tribunal's conclusion that, under reg.7 of the ESES Regulations, to avoid a sanction for failure to participate in a scheme good cause had to be shown within five working days of the claimant's being notified of the failure. Nor was there any challenge to its conclusion that a requirement to give notice under reg.4(2) of the ESES Regulations was met by the provision of a WP05 ("start notification") letter from the Secretary of State, but might be constituted by more than one document (such as, in addition or alternatively, an "opportunity letter" or an "appointment letter" from the scheme provider.

The report required by s.2 was produced by Matthew Oakley in July 2014 (*Independent review of the operation of Jobseeker's Allowance sanctions validated by the Jobseekers Act 2013*) and the government's response is published as Cmnd.8904. An update on improvements to communications was published by the DWP on December 18, 2014. There have been several further official reports on sanctions policy (extending beyond those under s.17A of the old style Jobseekers Act 1995), in particular the House of Commons Work and Pensions Committee, *Benefits Sanctions policy beyond the Oakley Review*, HC 814 2014–15 (March 24, 2015), *Benefit Sanctions: Beyond the Oakley Review: Government Response to the Committee's Fifth Report of Session 2014-15*, HC 557 2015–16 (October 22, 2015) and subsequent letters between the Secretary of State and the chairman of the Committee. There is an excellent summary of this and other literature from many sources as at November 30, 2015 in a House of Commons Debate Pack on Benefit Sanctions produced by the House of Commons Library (CDP-0113). The Scottish Government has also issued a number of updates on benefit sanctions in Scotland.

Regulations and notices requiring participation in a scheme

1.—(1) The 2011 Regulations are to be treated for all purposes as regulations that were made under section 17A of the Jobseekers Act 1995 and other provisions specified in the preamble to the 2011 Regulations and that came into force on the day specified in the 2011 Regulations. 1.436

(2) The Employment, Skills and Enterprise Scheme mentioned in the 2011 Regulations is to be treated as having been, until the coming into force of the 2013 Regulations, a scheme within section 17A(1) of the Jobseekers Act 1995.

(3) The following are to be treated as having been, until the coming into force of the 2013 Regulations, programmes of activities that are part of the Employment, Skills and Enterprise Scheme—

(a) the programmes described in regulation 3(2) to (8) of the 2013 Regulations, and

(b) the programme known as the Community Action Programme,

and references to the scheme are to be read accordingly.

(4) A notice given for the purposes of regulation 4(1) of the 2011 Regulations (requirement to participate and notification) is to be treated as a notice that complied with regulation 4(2)(c) (details of what a person is required to do by way of participation in scheme) if it referred to—

(a) the Employment, Skills and Enterprise Scheme, or

(b) a programme of activities treated under subsection (3) as part of the scheme.

(5) A notice given for the purposes of regulation 4(1) of the 2011

Regulations is to be treated as a notice that complied with regulation 4(2)(e) (information about the consequences of failing to participate) if it described an effect on payments of jobseeker's allowance as a consequence or possible consequence of not participating in the scheme or a programme of activities.

(6) Regulation 4(3) of the 2011 Regulations (notice of changes in what a person is required to do by way of participation in scheme) is to be treated as if at all times—

(a) it required the person in question to be notified only if the changes in the requirements mentioned in regulation 4(2)(c) were such that the details relating to those requirements specified in—

(i) a notice given to the person under regulation 4(1), or

(ii) a notice given to the person under regulation 4(3) on an earlier occasion, were no longer accurate, and

(b) it required the person to be notified only of such changes as made the details inaccurate.

(7) A notice given for the purposes of regulation 4(1) of the Mandatory Work Activity Scheme Regulations is to be treated as a notice that complied with regulation 4(2)(d) (details of what a person is required to do by way of participation in scheme) if it referred to—

(a) the Mandatory Work Activity Scheme, or

(b) a placement described as Mandatory Work Activity.

(8) A notice given for the purposes of regulation 4(1) of the Mandatory Work Activity Scheme Regulations is to be treated as a notice that complied with regulation 4(2)(f) (information about the consequences of failing to participate) if it described an effect on payments of jobseeker's allowance as a consequence or possible consequence of not participating in the scheme or placement.

(9) Regulation 4(3) of the Mandatory Work Activity Scheme Regulations is to be treated as if at all times—

(a) it required the person in question to be notified only if the changes in the requirements mentioned in regulation 4(2)(d) were such that the details relating to those requirements specified in—

(i) a notice given to the person under regulation 4(1), or

(ii) a notice given to the person under regulation 4(3) on an earlier occasion, were no longer accurate, and

(b) it required the person to be notified only of such changes as made the details inaccurate.

(10) The penalty provisions are to be treated (notwithstanding the amendments made by the 2012 Regulations) as having effect after the relevant time as they did before the relevant time, in relation to a failure to comply with the 2011 Regulations or, as the case may be, the Mandatory Work Activity Scheme Regulations that occurred or began to occur before the relevant time

(11) In subsection (10) and this subsection—

"the penalty provisions" means—

(a) in the case of a failure to comply with the 2011 Regulations, the provisions relating to the imposition of a penalty for such a failure that had effect before the relevant time;

(b) in the case of a failure to comply with the Mandatory Work Activity Scheme Regulations, the provisions relating to the imposition of a penalty for such a failure that had effect before the relevant time;

"the relevant time" means the time at which the 2012 Regulations came into force.

(12) A penalty imposed on a person before or after the coming into force of this Act for—

(a) failing to participate in a scheme within section 17A(1) of the Jobseekers Act 1995, or

(b) failing to comply with regulations under section 17A of that Act,

is to be treated as lawfully imposed if the only ground or grounds for treating it as unlawfully imposed is or are removed by subsections (1) to (10).

(13) Subsection (12) does not affect a person's ability to apply for a revision or supersession of, or to appeal against, a decision to impose a penalty by reference to other grounds.

(14) Subject to subsection (10), the 2011 Regulations are to be treated as having been revoked by the 2013 Regulations on the coming into force of the 2013 Regulations.

(15) In this section—

"the 2011 Regulations" means the provisions known as the Jobseeker's Allowance (Employment, Skills and Enterprise Scheme) Regulations 2011 (SI 2011/917);

"the 2012 Regulations" means the Jobseeker's Allowance (Sanctions) (Amendment) Regulations 2012 (S.I. 2012/2568);

"the 2013 Regulations" means the Jobseeker's Allowance (Schemes for Assisting Persons to Obtain Employment) Regulations 2013 (SI 2013/276);

"the Mandatory Work Activity Scheme Regulations" means the Jobseeker's Allowance (Mandatory Work Activity Scheme) Regulations 2011 (SI 2011/688).

Report

2.—(1) The Secretary of State must appoint an independent person to prepare a report on the operation of the provisions relating to the imposition of a penalty during the period of a year beginning with the day on which this Act comes into force, so far as that operation relates to relevant penalties. **1.437**

(2) The person must complete the preparation of the report and send it to the Secretary of State as soon as reasonably practicable after the end of the period mentioned in subsection (1).

(3) On receiving the report, the Secretary of State must lay a copy of it before Parliament.

(4) In this section—

"penalty" means a penalty that may be imposed for—

(a) failing to participate in a scheme within section 17A(1) of the Jobseekers Act 1995, or

(b) failing to comply with regulations under section 17A of that Act;

"relevant penalty" means a penalty that, but for section 1 of this Act, would not be or would not have been lawfully imposed on a person.

Extent, commencement and short title

3.—(1) This Act extends to England and Wales and Scotland. **1.438**

(2) This Act comes into force on the day on which it is passed.

(3) This Act may be cited as the Jobseekers (Back to Work Schemes) Act 2013.

Pensions Act 2014

(2014 c.19)

Section Reproduced

State pension credit: phasing out assessed income periods

1.439 **28.**—(1) In section 6 of the State Pension Credit Act 2002 (duty to specify assessed income period), in subsection (1), after "subsection (3) or (4)" insert "where the relevant decision takes effect before 6 April 2016".

(2) At the end of the heading to that section insert "for pre-6 April 2016 awards".

(3) Regulations under section 9(5) of the State Pension Credit Act 2002 may in particular be made for the purpose of phasing out, on or after 6 April 2016, any remaining assessed income period that is 5 years or shorter than 5 years.

General Note

1.440 See the General Note to the State Pension Credit Act 2002 ss.6 and 9(5).

PART II

INCOME SUPPORT

The Income Support (General) Regulations 1987

(SI 1987/1967) (AS AMENDED)

Made by the Secretary of State under ss.20(1), (3)(d), (4), (9), (11) and (12), 22(1), (2), (4) and (5) to (9), 23(1), (3) and (5), 51(1)(n) and 84(1) of the Social Security Act 1986 and ss.114, 166(1) to (3A) of the Social Security Act 1975

ARRANGEMENT OF REGULATIONS

PART I

GENERAL

PART II

CONDITIONS OF ENTITLEMENT

PART III

MEMBERSHIP OF A FAMILY

PART IV

APPLICABLE AMOUNTS

PART V

INCOME AND CAPITAL

CHAPTER I

GENERAL

CHAPTER II

INCOME

CHAPTER VII

LIABLE RELATIVE PAYMENTS

CHAPTER VIIA

CHILD SUPPORT

CHAPTER VIII

STUDENTS

PART VI

APPLICABLE AMOUNTS AND ASSESSMENT OF INCOME AND CAPITAL IN URGENT CASES

PART VII

CALCULATION OF INCOME SUPPORT FOR PART-WEEKS

SCHEDULES

PART I

GENERAL

Citation and commencement

1. These Regulations may be cited as the Income Support (General) Regulations 1987 and shall come into force on 11th April 1988. 2.2

Interpretation

2.3 **2.**—(1) In these Regulations, unless the context otherwise requires

[88 "the 2012 Act" means the Welfare Reform Act 2012;]

[59 "Abbeyfield Home" means an establishment run by the Abbeyfield Society including all bodies corporate or incorporate which are affiliated to that Society;]

"the Act" means the Social Security Act 1986;

[48 "adoption leave" means a period of absence from work on ordinary or additional adoption leave by virtue of section 75A or 75B of the Employment Rights Act 1996;]

[57 "the Armed Forces and Reserve Forces Compensation Scheme" means the scheme established under section 1(2) of the Armed Forces (Pensions and Compensation) Act 2004;]

[89 "armed forces independence payment" means armed forces independence payment under the Armed Forces and Reserve Forces (Compensation Scheme) Order 2011;]

"attendance allowance" means:—

- (a) an attendance allowance under section 35 of the Social Security Act [SSCBA, s.64];
- (b) an increase of disablement pension under section 61 or 63 of that Act [SSCBA, s.104 or 105];
- (c) a payment under regulations made in exercise of the power conferred by section 159(3)(b) of that Act;
- (d) an increase of an allowance which is payable in respect of constant attendance under section 5 of the Industrial Injuries and Diseases (Old Cases) Act 1975;
- (e) a payment by virtue of articles 14, 15, 16, 43 or 44 of the Personal Injuries (Civilians) Scheme 1983 or any analogous payment; or
- (f) any payment based on need for attendance which is paid as part of a war disablement pension;

[72 "basic rate", where it relates to the rate of tax, has the same meaning as in the Income Tax Act 2007 (see section 989 of that Act)]

[26"the benefit Acts" means the Contributions and Benefits Act [69, the Jobseekers Act 1995 [88 , Part 1 of the Welfare Reform Act [100, Part 4 of the 2012 Act and Part 1 of the Pensions Act 2014]]];]

"benefit week" has the meaning prescribed in paragraph 4 of Schedule 7 to the Social Security (Claims and Payments) Regulations 1987 [4and for the purposes of calculating any payment of income and of regulation 74(2)(a) "benefit week" shall also mean the period of 7 days ending on the day before the first day of the first benefit week following the date of claim or the last day on which income support is paid if it is in payment for less than a week;]

[6"board and lodging accommodation" means—

- (a) accommodation provided to a person or, if he is a member of a family, to him or any other member of his family, for a charge which is inclusive of the provision of that accommodation and at least some cooked or prepared meals which both are cooked or prepared (by a person other than the person to whom the accommodation is provided or a member of his family) and are consumed in that accommodation or associated premises; or

(b) accommodation provided to a person in a hotel, guest house, lodging house or some similar establishment,

except accommodation provided by a close relative of his or of any other member of his family, or other than on a commercial basis;]

[[59]"care home" in England and Wales has the meaning assigned to it by section 3 of the Care Standards Act 2000, and in Scotland means a care home service within the meaning assigned to it by [[81] paragraph 2 of schedule 12 to the Public Services Reform (Scotland) Act 2010];]

[[49]"child tax credit" means a child tax credit under section 8 of the Tax Credits Act 2002;]

[[31]"the Children Order" means the Children (Northern Ireland) Order 1995;]

"claimant" means a person claiming income support;

"close relative" means a parent, parent-in-law, son, son-in-law, daughter, daughter-in-law, step-parent, step-son, step-daughter, brother, sister, [[60] or, if any of the preceding persons is one member of a couple, the other member of that couple]

[[19 70] . . .]

"concessionary payment" means a payment made under arrangements made by the Secretary of State with the consent of the Treasury which is charged either to the National Insurance Fund or to a Departmental Expenditure Vote to which payments of benefit [[71] or tax credits under the benefit Acts or the Tax Credits Act 2002] are charged;

[[19]the "Contributions and Benefits Act" means the Social Security Contributions and Benefits Act 1992;]

[[90] "contribution-based jobseeker's allowance" means an allowance under the Jobseekers Act 1995 as amended by the provisions of Part 1 of Schedule 14 to the 2012 Act that remove references to an income-based allowance, and a contribution-based allowance under the Jobseekers Act 1995 as that Act has effect apart from those provisions;]

[[84] "the Contributions Regulations" means the Social Security (Contributions) Regulations 2001;]

[[69] [[90] "contributory employment and support allowance" means an allowance under Part 1 of the Welfare Reform Act as amended by the provisions of Schedule 3, and Part 1 of Schedule 14, to the 2012 Act that remove references to an income-related allowance, and a contributory allowance under Part 1 of the Welfare Reform Act as that Part has effect apart from those provisions;]]

"co-ownership scheme" means a scheme under which a dwelling is let by a housing association and the tenant, or his personal representative, will, under the terms of the tenancy agreement or of the agreement under which he became a member of the association, be entitled, on his ceasing to be a member and subject to any condition stated in either agreement, to a sum calculated by reference directly or indirectly to the value of the dwelling;

[[60] [[92 94] "couple" means—

(a) two people who are married to, or civil partners of, each other and are members of the same household; or

(b) two people who are not married to, or civil partners of, each other but are living together as a married couple;]]

[[38]"course of study" means any course of study, whether or not it is a sandwich course (within the meaning prescribed in regulation 61(1)) and whether or not a grant is made for attending or undertaking it;]

"Crown tenant" means a person who occupies a dwelling under a tenancy or licence where the interest of the landlord belongs to Her Majesty in right of the Crown or to a government department or is held in trust for Her Majesty for the purposes of a government department, except (in the case of an interest belonging to Her Majesty in right of the Crown) where the interest is under the management of the Crown Estate Commissioners;

[22"date of claim" means the date on which the claimant makes, or is treated as making, a claim for income support for the purposes of regulation 6 of the Social Security (Claims and Payments) Regulations 1987;]

[15"disability living allowance" means a disability living allowance under section 37ZA of the Social Security Act [SSCBA, s.71];

[49 . . .]

"dwelling occupied as the home" means the dwelling together with any garage, garden and outbuildings, normally occupied by the claimant as his home including any premises not so occupied which it is impracticable or unreasonable to sell separately, in particular, in Scotland, any croft land on which the dwelling is situated;

"earnings" has the meaning prescribed in regulation 35 or, as the case may be, 37;

[28 [58. . .]]

[28 [58. . .]]

"employed earner" shall be construed in accordance with section 2(1)(a) of the Social Security Act [SSCBA, s.2(1)*a*];

[4"employment" except for the purposes of section 20(3)(d) of the Act [SSCBA, s.124(1)(d)], includes any trade, business, profession, office or vocation;]

[69 "the Employment and Support Allowance Regulations" means the Employment and Support Allowance Regulations 2008;]

[79 85 . . .]

[37"employment zone" means an area within Great Britain designated for the purposes of section 60 of the Welfare Reform and Pensions Act 1999 and an "employment zone programme" means a programme established for such an area or areas designed to assist claimants for a jobseeker's allowance to obtain sustainable employment;

"employment zone contractor" means a person who is undertaking the provision of facilities in respect of an employment zone programme on behalf of the Secretary of State for Education and Employment;]

[74 "enactment" includes an enactment comprised in, or in an instrument made under, an Act of the Scottish Parliament [91 or the National Assembly for Wales];]

[52[54 . . .]]

[98 "first year of training" means a period of time beginning with a person's first day of training.]

[39"full-time student" has the meaning prescribed in regulation 61(1);]

[57 "a guaranteed income payment" means a payment made under article 14(1)(b) or article 21(1)(a) of the Armed Forces and Reserve Forces (Compensation Scheme) Order 2005;]

[70 "Health Service Act" means the National Health Service Act 2006;

"Health Service (Wales) Act" means the National Health Service (Wales) Act 2006;]

"housing association" has the meaning assigned to it by section 1(1) of the Housing Associations Act 1985;

[30"housing benefit expenditure" means expenditure in respect of which housing benefit is payable as specified in [62 regulation 12(1) of the Housing Benefit Regulations 2006] but does not include any such expenditure in respect of which an amount is applicable under regulation 17(1)(e) or 18(1)(f) (housing costs);]

[35"Immigration and Asylum Act" means the Immigration and Asylum Act 1999;]

[35 . . .]

[69 "income-related employment and support allowance" means an income-related allowance under Part 1 of the Welfare Reform Act (employment and support allowance);]

[59 [78 "independent hospital"—

(a) in England, means a hospital as defined by section 275 of the National Health Service Act 2006 that is not a health service hospital as defined by that section;

(b) in Wales, has the meaning assigned to it by section 2 of the Care Standards Act 2000; and

(c) in Scotland, means an independent healthcare service as defined in [81 section 10F(1)(a) and (b) of the National Health Service (Scotland) Act 1978];]]

[43 68 . . .]

"invalid carriage or other vehicle" means a vehicle propelled by petrol engine or by electric power supplied for use on the road and to be controlled by the occupant;

[38"last day of the course" has the meaning prescribed in regulation 61(1);]

"liable relative" has the meaning prescribed in regulation 54;

[61 "the London Bombings Relief Charitable Fund" means the company limited by guarantee (number 5505072) and registered charity of that name established on 11th July 2005 for the purpose of (amongst other things) relieving sickness, disability or financial need of victims (including families or dependants of victims) of the terrorist attacks carried out in London on 7th July 2005;]

[87 "local welfare provision" means occasional financial or other assistance given by a local authority, the Scottish Ministers or the Welsh Ministers, or a person authorised to exercise any function of, or provide a service to, them, to or in respect of individuals for the purpose of—

(a) meeting, or helping to meet, an immediate short term need—

(i) arising out of an exceptional event, or exceptional circumstances; and

(ii) that requires to be met in order to avoid a risk to the well-being of an individual; or

(b) enabling individuals to establish or maintain a settled home, where those individuals have been or, without the assistance, might otherwise be—

(i) in prison, hospital, a residential care establishment or other institution; or

(ii) homeless or otherwise living an unsettled way of life;]

"lone parent" means a person who has no partner and who is responsible for, and a member of the same household as, a child or young person;

"long tenancy" means a tenancy granted for a term of years certain exceeding twenty one years, whether or not the tenancy is, or may become, terminable before the end of that term by notice given by or to the tenant or by re-entry, forfeiture (or, in Scotland, irritancy) or otherwise and includes a lease for a term fixed by law under a grant with a covenant or obligation for perpetual renewal unless it is a lease by sub-demise from one which is not a long tenancy;

[63 "long-term patient" means a person who—

(a) is a patient within the meaning of regulation 21(3); and

(b) has been such a patient for a continuous period of more than 52 weeks;]

[6 67 . . .]

[79 "the Mandatory Work Activity Scheme" means a scheme within section 17A of the Jobseekers Act 1995, known by that name and provided pursuant to arrangements made by the Secretary of State that is designed to provide work or work-related activity for up to 30 hours per week over a period of four consecutive weeks with a view to assisting claimants to improve their prospects of obtaining employment;]

[22"maternity leave" means a period during which a woman is absent from work because she is pregnant or has given birth to a child, and at the end of which she has a right to return to work either under the terms of her contract of employment or under [66 Part VIII of the Employment Rights Act 1996];]

[75 "MFET Limited" means the company limited by guarantee (number 7121661) of that name, established for the purpose in particular of making payments in accordance with arrangements made with the Secretary of State to persons who have acquired HIV as a result of treatment by the NHS with blood or blood products;]

[71 . . .]

"mobility supplement" means any supplement under [71 article 20 of the Naval, Military and Air Forces Etc. (Disablement and Death) Service Pensions Order 2006] including such a supplement by virtue of any other scheme or order or under Article 25A of the Personal Injuries (Civilians) Scheme 1983;

"net earnings" means such earnings as are calculated in accordance with regulation 36

"net profit" means such profit as is calculated in accordance with regulation 38;

[41"the New Deal options" means the employment programmes specified in regulation 75(1)(a)(ii) of the Jobseeker's Allowance Regulations 1996 and the training scheme specified in regulation 75(1)(b)(ii) of those Regulations;]

"non-dependant" has the meaning prescribed in regulation 3;

"non-dependant deduction" means a deduction that is to be made under regulation 17(*e*) and paragraph [70 18] of Schedule 3;

[59 . . .]

"occupational pension" means any pension or other periodical payment under an occupational pension scheme but does not include any discretionary payment out of a fund established for relieving hardship in particular cases;

"partner" means where a claimant—

(a) is a member of [[60]a couple], the other member of that couple;

(b) is married polygamously to two or more members of his household, any such member;

[[48] [82] "paternity leave" means a period of absence from work on [[96] . . .] paternity leave by virtue of section 80A or 80B of the Employment Rights Act 1996 [[96] . . .]]

"payment" includes a part of a payment;

[[23]"pay period" means the period in respect of which a claimant is, or expects to be, normally paid by his employer, being a week, a fortnight, four weeks, a month or other shorter or longer period as the case may be;]

[[25]"pension fund holder" means with respect to a personal pension scheme or [[64] an occupational pensions scheme], the trustees, managers or scheme administrators, as the case may be, of the scheme [[64] . . .] concerned;]

[[38] "period of study" means the period beginning with the date on which a person starts attending or undertaking a course of study and ending with the last day of the course or such earlier date (if any) such as he finally abandons it or is dismissed from it;]

[[88] "personal independence payment" means personal independence payment under Part 4 of the 2012 Act;]

[[22] [64] "personal pension scheme" means—

(a) a personal pension scheme as defined by section 1 of the Pension Schemes Act 1993;

(b) an annuity contract or trust scheme approved under section 620 or 621 of the Income and Corporation Taxes Act 1988 or a substituted contract within the meaning of section 622(3) of that Act which is treated as having become a registered pension scheme by virtue of paragraph 1(1)(f) of Schedule 36 to the Finance Act 2004;

(c) a personal pension scheme approved under Chapter 4 of Part 14 of the Income and Corporation Taxes Act 1988 which is treated as having become a registered pension scheme by virtue of paragraph 1(1)(g) of Schedule 36 to the Finance Act 2004;]

"policy of life insurance" means any instrument by which the payment of money is assured on death (except death by accident only) or the happening of any contingency dependent on human life, or any instrument evidencing a contract which is subject to payment of premiums for a term dependent on human life;

[[5]"polygamous marriage" means any marriage during the subsistence of which a party to it is married to more than one person and the ceremony of marriage took place under the law of a country which permits polygamy;]

[[44]. . .]

[[74] "public authority" includes any person certain of whose functions are functions of a public nature;]

[16]"qualifying person" means a person in respect of whom payment has been made from the Fund [[21][[56] the Eileen Trust [[75] , MFET Limited] [[61], the Skipton Fund [[80] , the Caxton Foundation] or the London Bombings Relief Charitable Fund]]]

[26. . .]
"relative" means close relative, grand-parent, grand-child, uncle, aunt, nephew or niece;
"relevant enactment" has the meaning prescribed in regulation 16(8)(a);
"remunerative work" has the meaning prescribed in regulation 5;
[59 . . .]
[18[50 . . .]]
[59 . . .]
[25 [64 . . .]]
[101 "Scottish basic rate" means the rate of income tax of that name calculated in accordance with section 6A of the Income Tax Act 2007;
"Scottish taxpayer" has the same meaning as in Chapter 2 of Part 4A of the Scotland Act 1998;]
"self-employed earner" shall be construed in accordance with section 2(1)(b) of the Social Security Act [SSCBA, s.2(1)(b)];
[40 55 "self employment route" means assistance in pursuing self-employed earner's employment whilst participating in—
(a) an employment zone programme; or
(b) a programme provided or other arrangements made pursuant to section 2 of the Employment and Training Act 1973 (functions of the Secretary of State) or section 2 of the Enterprise and New Towns (Scotland) Act 1990 (functions in relation to training for employment etc.)]
[74 [93 . . .]]
[95 "shared parental leave" means leave under section 75E or 75G of the Employment Rights Act 1996;]
"single claimant" means a claimant who neither has a partner nor is a lone parent;
"Social Security Act" means the Social Security Act 1975;
[34"sports award" means an award made by one of the Sports Councils named in section 23(2) of the National Lottery etc. Act 1993 out of sums allocated to it for distribution under that section;]
[66 72 . . .]
[38 . . .]
[37"subsistence allowance" means an allowance which an employment zone contractor has agreed to pay to a person who is participating in an employment zone programme;]
"supplementary benefit" means a supplementary pension or allowance under section 1 or 4 of the Supplementary Benefits Act 1976;
"terminal date" in respect of a claimant means the terminal date in his case for the purpose of regulation 7 of the Child Benefit (General) Regulations 1976;
[80 "the Caxton Foundation" means the charitable trust of that name established on 28th March 2011 out of funds provided by the Secretary of State for the benefit of certain persons suffering from hepatitis C and other persons eligible for payment in accordance with its provisions;]
[21"the Eileen Trust" means the charitable trust of that name established on 29th March 1993 out of funds provided by the Secretary of State for the benefit of persons eligible for payment in accordance with its provisions;]
[16"the Fund" means moneys made available from time to time by the

Secretary of State for the benefit of persons eligible for payment in accordance with the provisions of a scheme established by him on 24th April 1992 or, in Scotland, on 10th April 1992;]

[20 70]

[2 70]

[20 70]

[65 "the Independent Living Fund (2006)" means the Trust of that name established by a deed dated 10th April 2006 and made between the Secretary of State for Work and Pensions of the one part and Margaret Rosemary Cooper, Michael Beresford Boyall and Marie Theresa Martin of the other part;]

[20 70]

[9"the Macfarlane (Special Payments) Trust" means the trust of that name, established on 29th January 1990 partly out of funds provided by the Secretary of State, for the benefit of certain persons suffering from haemophilia;]

[13"the Macfarlane (Special Payments) (No.2) Trust" means the trust of that name, established on 3rd May 1991 partly out of funds provided by the Secretary of State, for the benefit of certain persons suffering from haemophilia and other beneficiaries;]

[1"the Macfarlane Trust" means the charitable trust, established partly out of funds provided by the Secretary of State to the Haemophilia Society, for the relief of poverty or distress among those suffering from haemophilia;]

[56"the Skipton Fund" means the ex-gratia payment scheme administered by the Skipton Fund Limited, incorporated on 25th March 2004, for the benefit of certain persons suffering from hepatitis C and other persons eligible for payment in accordance with the scheme's provisions;]

"training allowance" means an allowance (whether by way of periodical grants or otherwise) payable—

(a) out of public funds by a Government department or by or on behalf of the [12 Secretary of State [99 . . .] [11, [73 Skills Development Scotland,] Scottish Enterprise or Highlands and Islands Enterprise] [42, [83 . . . [77 . . .] [99 . . .] or the [71 Welsh Ministers]];

(b) to a person for his maintenance or in respect of a member of his family; and

(c) for the period, or part of the period, during which he is following a course of training or instruction provided by, or in pursuance of arrangements made with, that department or approved by that department in relation to him or so provided or approved by or on behalf of [12the Secretary of State [99 . . .] [11, [73 Skills Development Scotland,] Scottish Enterprise or Highlands and Islands Enterprise], [42 or the [71 Welsh Ministers]]

but it does not include an allowance paid by any Government department to or in respect of a person by reason of the fact that he is following a course of full-time education [7, other than under arrangements made under section 2 of the Employment and Training Act 1973,] or is training as a teacher;

[90 "universal credit" means universal credit under Part 1 of the 2012 Act;]

[24"voluntary organisation" means a body, other than a public or local authority, the activities of which are carried on otherwise than for profit;]

[45 71 . . .]

[71 "war disablement pension" means any retired pay or pension or allowance payable in respect of disablement under an instrument specified in section 639(2) of the Income Tax (Earnings and Pensions) Act 2003(14);

"war pension" means a war disablement pension, a war widow's pension or a war widower's pension;

"war widow's pension" means any pension or allowance payable to a woman as a widow under an instrument specified in section 639(2) of the Income Tax (Earnings and Pensions) Act 2003 in respect of the death or disablement of any person;

"war widower's pension" means any pension or allowance payable to a man as a widower or to a surviving civil partner under an instrument specified in section 639(2) of the Income Tax (Earnings and Pensions) Act 2003 in respect of the death or disablement of any person;]

[19"water charges" means—

(a) as respects England and Wales, any water and sewerage charges under Chapter 1 of Part V of the Water Act 1991;

(b) as respects Scotland, any water and sewerage charges under Schedule 11 to the Local Government Finance Act 1992;

in so far as such charges are in respect of the dwelling which a person occupies as his home.]

[69 "the Welfare Reform Act" means the Welfare Reform Act 2007;]

[32"welfare to work beneficiary" means a person—

(a) to whom regulation 13A(1) of the Social Security (Incapacity for Work) (General) Regulations 1995 applies; and

(b) who again becomes incapable of work for the purposes of Part XIIA of the Contributions and Benefits Act 1992;]

[49"working tax credit" means a working tax credit under section 10 of the Tax Credits Act 2002;]

[49 . . .]

[23"year of assessment" has the meaning prescribed in section 832(1) of the Income and Corporation Taxes Act 1988;]

"young person" has the meaning prescribed in regulation 14,

[3 "70 . . . [12 . . . youth training]" means—

(a) arrangements made under section 2 of the Employment and Training Act 1973 (functions of the Secretary of State); or

(b) arrangements made by the Secretary of State for persons enlisted in Her Majesty's forces for any special term of service specified in regulations made under section 2 of the Armed Forces Act 1966 (power of Defence Council to make regulations as to engagement of persons in regular forces),

for purposes which include the training of persons who, at the beginning of their training, are under the age of 18.]

[44 (1A) For the purposes of these Regulations, where a person's principal place of residence is a [59 care home, an Abbeyfield Home or an independent hospital and he is temporarily absent from that home or hospital, he shall be regarded as continuing to reside in that home or hospital]—

(a) where he is absent because he is a patient, for the first [51 52] weeks of any such period of absence and for this purpose—

(i) "patient" has the meaning it has in Schedule 7 by virtue of regulation 21(3); and

(ii) periods of absence separated by not more than 28 days shall be treated as a single period of absence equal in duration to all those periods; and

(b) for the first three weeks of any other period of absence.]

[93 (1B) References in these Regulations to a claimant participating as a service user are to—

(a) a person who is being consulted by or on behalf of—

(i) a body which has a statutory duty to provide services in the field of health, social care or social housing; or

(ii) a body which conducts research or undertakes monitoring for the purpose of planning or improving such services,

in their capacity as a user, potential user, carer of a user or person otherwise affected by the provision of those services;

[97 (ab) a person who is being consulted by or on behalf of—

(i) the Secretary of State in relation to any of the Secretary of State's functions in the field of social security or child support or under section 2 of the Employment and Training Act 1973; or

(ii) a body which conducts research or undertakes monitoring for the purpose of planning or improving such functions,

in their capacity as a person affected or potentially affected by the exercise of those functions or the carer of such a person;] or

(b) the carer of a person consulted under [97 sub-paragraphs (a) or (ab)].]

(2) In these Regulations, unless the context otherwise requires, a reference—

(a) to a numbered Part is to the Part of these Regulations bearing that number;

(b) to a numbered regulation or Schedule is to the regulation in or Schedule to these Regulations bearing that number;

(c) in a regulation or Schedule to a numbered paragraph is to the paragraph in that regulation or Schedule bearing that number;

(d) in a paragraph to a lettered or numbered sub-paragraph is to the sub-paragraph in that paragraph bearing that letter or number.

(3) Unless the context requires otherwise, any reference to the claimant's family or, as the case may be, to being a member of his family, shall be construed for the purposes of these Regulations as if it included in relation to a polygamous marriage a reference to any partner and any child or young person who is treated as the responsibility of the claimant or his partner, where that child or young person is a member of the claimant's household.

[29(4) [58 . . .]]

AMENDMENTS

1. Income Support (General) Amendment Regulations 1988 (SI 1988/663) reg.2 (April 11, 1988).

2. Family Credit and Income Support (General) Amendment Regulations 1988 (SI 1988/999) reg.4 (June 9, 1988).

3. Income Support (General) Amendment No.3 Regulations 1988 (SI 1988/1228) reg.2 (August 29, 1988).

4. Income Support (General) Amendment No.4 Regulations 1988 (SI 1988/1445) reg.2 (September 12, 1988).

5. Income Support (General) Amendment No.5 Regulations 1988 (SI 1988/2022) reg.2(*b*) (December 12, 1988).

6. Income Support (General) Amendment No.5 Regulations 1988 (SI 1988/2022) reg.2(*a*) (April 10, 1989).

7. Income Support (General) Amendment No.2 Regulations 1989 (SI 1989/1323) reg.2 (August 21, 1989).

8. Income Support (General) Amendment Regulations 1989 (SI 1989/534) Sch.I para.1 (October 9, 1989).

9. Income-related Benefits Schemes Amendment Regulations 1990 (SI 1990/127) reg.3 (January 31, 1990).

11. Enterprise (Scotland) Consequential Amendments Order 1991 (SI 1991/387) art.9 (April 1, 1991).

12. Income Support (General) Amendment Regulations 1991 (SI 1991/236) reg.2 (April 8, 1991).

13. Income-related Benefits Schemes and Social Security (Recoupment) Amendment Regulations 1991 (SI 1991/1175) reg.5 (May 11, 1991).

15. Disability Living Allowance and Disability Working Allowance (Consequential Provisions) Regulations 1991 (SI 1991/2742) reg.11(2) (April 6, 1992).

16. Income-related Benefits Schemes and Social Security (Recoupment) Amendment Regulations 1992 (SI 1992/1101) reg.6(2) (May 7, 1992).

17. Income-related Benefits Schemes (Miscellaneous Amendments) (No.3) Regulations 1992 (SI 1992/2155) reg.12 (October 5, 1992).

19. Income-related Benefits Schemes (Miscellaneous Amendments) Regulations 1993 (SI 1993/315) reg.3 (April 12, 1993).

20. Social Security Benefits (Miscellaneous Amendments) (No.2) Regulations 1993 (SI 1993/963) reg.2 (April 22, 1993).

21. Income-related Benefits Schemes and Social Security (Recoupment) Amendment Regulations 1993 (SI 1993/1249) reg.4 (May 14, 1993).

22. Income-related Benefits Schemes (Miscellaneous Amendments) (No.4) Regulations 1993 (SI 1993/2119) reg.2 (October 4, 1993).

23. Income-related Benefits Schemes (Miscellaneous Amendments) (No.5) Regulations 1994 (SI 1994/2139) reg.22 (October 3, 1994).

24. Income-related Benefits Schemes (Miscellaneous Amendments) Regulations 1995 (SI 1995/516) reg.17 (April 10, 1995).

25. Income-related Benefits Schemes and Social Security (Claims and Payments) (Miscellaneous Amendments) Regulations 1995 (SI 1995/2303) reg.6(2) (October 2, 1995).

26. Income Support (General) (Jobseeker's Allowance Consequential Amendments) Regulations 1996 (SI 1996/206) reg.2 (October 7, 1996).

28. Income-related Benefits Schemes and Social Fund (Miscellaneous Amendments) Regulations 1996 (SI 1996/1944) reg.13 and Sch. para.1 (October 7, 1996).

29. Income-related Benefits Schemes and Social Fund (Miscellaneous Amendments) Regulations 1996 (SI 1996/1944) reg.13 and Sch. para.2 (October 7, 1996).

30. Income-related Benefits and Jobseeker's Allowance (Miscellaneous Amendments) Regulations 1997 (SI 1997/65) reg.4(1) (April 7, 1997).

31. Social Security (Miscellaneous Amendments) Regulations 1998 (SI 1998/563) reg.5(1) and (2)(e) (April 6, 1998).

32. Social Security (Welfare to Work) Regulations 1998 (SI 1998/2231) reg.13(2) (October 5, 1998).

33. Social Security and Child Support (Tax Credits) Consequential Amendments Regulations 1999 (SI 1999/2566) reg.2(3) and Sch.2 Part III (October 5, 1999).

34. Social Security Amendment (Sports Awards) Regulations 1999 (SI 1999/2165) reg.2(1) and 2(e) (August 23, 1999).

35. Social Security (Immigration and Asylum) Consequential Amendments Regulations 2000 (SI 2000/636) reg.3(2) (April 3, 2000).

37. Social Security Amendment (Employment Zones) Regulations 2000 (SI 2000/724) reg.2 (April 3, 2000).

38. Social Security Amendment (Students) Regulations 2000 (SI 2000/1981) reg.5(1) and (2) (July 31, 2000).

39. Social Security Amendment (Students) Regulations 2000 (SI 2000/1981) reg.5(1) and (2)(b) (July 31, 2000). The new definition was moved to its present—and alphabetically correct—place in the regulation by the Social Security (Students and Income-related Benefits) (No.2) Regulations 2000 (SI 2000/ 2422) reg.4 (October 9, 2000).

40. Social Security Amendment (Employment Zones) (No.2) Regulations 2000 (SI 2000/2910) reg.2(1) and (2) (November 27, 2000).

41. Social Security (Miscellaneous Amendments) Regulations 2001 (SI 2001/ 488) reg.2 (April 9, 2001).

42. Social Security (Miscellaneous Amendments) (No.2) Regulations 2001 (SI 2001/652) reg.2 (March 26, 2001).

43. Social Security Amendment (New Deal) Regulations 2001 (SI 2001/ 1029) reg.15(2) and (3)(c) (April 9, 2001).

44. Social Security Amendment (Residential Care and Nursing Homes) Regulations 2001 (SI 2001/3767) reg.2 and Sch. Pt I para.1 (April 8, 2002).

45. Social Security (Miscellaneous Amendments) Regulations 2002 (SI 2002/ 841) reg.2 (April 8, 2002).

46. Income Support (General) and Jobseeker's Allowance Amendment Regulations 2002 (SI 2002/1411) reg.2 (June 17, 2002).

47. Social Security Amendment (Employment Programme) Regulations 2002 (SI 2002/2314) reg.3(2) (October 14, 2002).

48. Social Security (Paternity and Adoption) Amendment Regulations 2002 (SI 2002/2689) reg.2 (December 8, 2002).

49. Income-related Benefits and Jobseeker's Allowance (Working Tax Credit and Child Tax Credit) (Amendment) Regulations 2002 (SI 2002/2402) reg.2 and Sch.1 para.1 (April 6, 2003).

50. Social Security (Removal of Residential Allowance and Miscellaneous Amendments) Regulations 2003 (SI 2003/1121) reg.2 and Sch.1 (October 6, 2003).

51. Social Security (Hospital In-Patients and Miscellaneous Amendments) Regulations 2003 (SI 2003/1195) reg.3(2) (May 21, 2003).

52. Social Security (Miscellaneous Amendments) (No.2) Regulations 2003 (SI 2003/2279) reg.2(2) (October 1, 2003).

53. Social Security (Miscellaneous Amendments) Regulations 2004) (SI 2004/565) reg.2(2) (April 1, 2004).

54. Social Security (Miscellaneous Amendments) Regulations 2004 (SI 2004/565) reg.2(2) (April 1, 2004).

55. Social Security (Income-Related Benefits Self-Employment Route Amendment) Regulations 2004 (SI 2004/963) reg.2 (May 4, 2004).

56. Social Security (Miscellaneous Amendments) (No.2) Regulations 2004 (SI 2004/1141) reg.2 (May 12, 2004).

57. Social Security (Miscellaneous Amendments) Regulations 2005 (SI 2005/574) reg.2 (April 4, 2005).

58. Social Security (Miscellaneous Amendments) Regulations 2005 (SI 2005/574) reg.3 (April 4, 2005).

59. Social Security (Care Homes and Independent Hospitals) Regulations 2005 (SI 2005/2687) reg.2 and Sch.1 para.1 (October 24, 2005).

60. Civil Partnership (Pensions, Social Security and Child Support) (Consequential, etc. Provisions) Order 2005 (SI 2005/2877) art.2(3) and Sch.3 para.13(2) (December 5, 2005).

61. Income-related Benefits (Amendment) (No.2) Regulations 2005 reg.2 (December 12, 2005).

62. Housing Benefit and Council Tax Benefit (Consequential Provisions) Regulations 2006 (SI 2006/217) reg.5 and Sch.3 para.1 (March 6, 2006).

63. Social Security (Miscellaneous Amendments) Regulations 2007 (SI 2007/719) reg.2(2) (April 9, 2007).

64. Social Security (Miscellaneous Amendments) (No.3) Regulations 2007 (SI 2007/1749) reg.2(2) (July 17, 2007).

65. Independent Living Fund (2006) Order 2007 (SI 2007/2538) reg.2(2) (October 1, 2007).

66. Social Security (Miscellaneous Amendments) (No.5) Regulations 2007 (SI 2007/2618) reg.5(2) (October 1, 2007).

67. Social Security (Miscellaneous Amendments) (No.5) Regulations 2007 (SI 2007/2618) reg.2 and Sch. (October 1, 2007).

68. Social Security (Miscellaneous Amendments) Regulations 2008 (SI 2008/698) reg.2(2) (April 14, 2008).

69. Employment and Support Allowance (Consequential Provisions) (No.2) Regulations 2008 (SI 2008/1554) reg.2(1) and (2) (October 27, 2008).

70. Social Security (Miscellaneous Amendments) (No.6) Regulations 2008 (SI 2008/2767) reg.2(1) and (2) (November 17, 2008).

71. Social Security (Miscellaneous Amendments) (No.7) Regulations 2008 (SI 2008/3157) reg.2(1) and (2) (January 5, 2009).

72. Social Security (Miscellaneous Amendments) Regulations 2009 (SI 2009/583) reg.2(1) and (2) (April 6, 2009).

73. Social Security (Miscellaneous Amendments) Regulations 2009 (SI 2009/583) reg.2(1) and (3) (April 6, 2009).

74. Social Security (Miscellaneous Amendments) (No.4) Regulations 2009 (SI 2009/2655) reg.2(1) and (2) (October 26, 2009).

75. Social Security (Miscellaneous Amendments) (No.2) Regulations 2010 (SI 2010/641) reg.2 (April 6, 2010).

76. Housing and Regeneration Act 2008 (Consequential Provisions) (No.2) Order 2010 art.4 and Sch.1 para.9 (April 1, 2010).

77. Apprenticeships, Skills, Children and Learning Act 2009 (Consequential Amendments to Subordinate Legislation) (England) Order 2010 (SI 2010/1941) reg.3(1) and (2) (September 1, 2010).

78. Health and Social Care Act 2008 (Miscellaneous Consequential Amendments) Order 2010 (SI 2010/1881) regs 2 and 5 (October 1, 2010).

79. Social Security (Miscellaneous Amendments) (No.2) Regulations 2011 (SI 2011/1707) reg.4(2)(a) and (3) (August 5, 2011).

80. Social Security (Miscellaneous Amendments) (No.3) Regulations 2011 (SI 2011/2425) reg.7(1) and (2) (October 31, 2011).

81. Public Services Reform (Scotland) Act 2010 (Consequential Modifications of Enactments) Order 2011 (SI 2011/2581) art.2 and Sch.2 para.14 (October 28, 2011).

82. Social Security (Miscellaneous Amendments) Regulations 2012 (SI 2012/757) reg.3(1) and (2) (April 1, 2012).

83. Young People's Learning Agency Abolition (Consequential Amendments to Subordinate Legislation) (England) Order 2012 (SI 2012/956) reg.3(2) (May 1, 2012).

84. Social Security (Miscellaneous Amendments) (No. 2) Regulations 2012 (SI 2012/2575) reg.2(2) (November 5, 2012).

85. Jobseeker's Allowance (Schemes for Assisting Persons to Obtain Employment) Regulations 2013 (SI 2013/276) reg.13(a) (February 12, 2013).

86. National Treatment Agency (Abolition) and the Health and Social Care Act 2012 (Consequential, Transitional and Saving Provisions) Order 2013 (SI 2013/235) art.9 and Sch.1 para.10(1) and (2) (April 1, 2013).

87. Social Security (Miscellaneous Amendments) Regulations 2013 (SI 2013/443) reg.2(1) and (2) (April 2, 2013).

88. Personal Independence Payment (Supplementary Provisions and Consequential Amendments) Regulations 2013 (SI 2013/388) reg.8 and Sch. para.11(1) and (2) (April 8, 2013).

89. Armed Forces and Reserve Forces Compensation Scheme (Consequential Provisions: Subordinate Legislation) Order 2013 (SI 2013/591) art.7 and Sch. para.4(1) and (2) (April 8, 2013).

90. Universal Credit (Consequential, Supplementary, Incidental and Miscellaneous Provisions) Regulations 2013 (SI 2013/630) reg.28(1) and (2) (April 29, 2013).

91. Social Security (Miscellaneous Amendments) (No.3) Regulations 2013 (SI 2013/2536) reg.4(1) and (2) (October 29,2013).

92. Marriage (Same Sex Couples) Act 2013 (Consequential Provisions) Order 2014 (SI 2014/107) reg.2 and Sch.1 para.9 (March 13, 2014). The amendment extends to England and Wales only (see SI 2014/107 art.1(4)).

93. Social Security (Miscellaneous Amendments) Regulations 2014, (SI 2014/591) reg.2(1) and (2) (April 28, 2014).

94. Marriage and Civil Partnership (Scotland) Act 2014 and Civil Partnership Act 2004 (Consequential Provisions and Modifications) Order 2014 (SI 2014/3229) art.29 and Sch.6 para.5 (December 16, 2014). The amendment relates only to Scotland (see SI 2014/3229 art.3(4)) but is in the same terms as the amendment made in relation to England and Wales by SI 2014/107 (see point 92 above).

95. Shared Parental Leave and Statutory Shared Parental Pay (Consequential Amendments to Subordinate Legislation) Order 2014 (SI 2014/3255) art.5(1) and (2)(b) (December 31, 2014).

96. Shared Parental Leave and Statutory Shared Parental Pay (Consequential Amendments to Subordinate Legislation) Order 2014 (SI 2014/3255) art.5(1) and (2)(a) (April 5, 2015). The amendment is subject to the transitional provision in art.35 of SI 2014/3255, which is reproduced below.

97. Social Security (Miscellaneous Amendments) Regulations 2015 (SI 2015/67) reg.2(1)(a) and (2) (February 23, 2015).

98. Social Security (Members of the Reserve Forces) (Amendment) Regulations 2015 (SI 2015/389) reg.2(1) and (2) (April 6, 2015).

99. Deregulation Act 2015 (Consequential Amendments) Order 2015 (SI 2015/971) art.2 and Sch.3 para.2(1) and (2) (May 26, 2015).

100. Pensions Act 2014 (Consequential, Supplementary and Incidental Amendments) Order 2015 (SI 2015/1985) art.8(1) and (2) (April 6, 2016).

101. Social Security (Scottish Rate of Income Tax etc.) (Amendment) Regulations 2016 (SI 2016/233) reg.2(1) and (2) (April 6, 2016).

Definitions

"dwelling"—see SSCBA s.137(1).
"family"—*ibid.*
"occupational pension scheme"—see PSA s.1.

General Note

The significance of most of these definitions is mentioned in the notes to the regulations in which they occur. A few points are noted here. 2.4

"Armed Forces and Reserve Forces Compensation Scheme": This scheme replaced the War Pensions Scheme ("WPS") for those who suffer injuries, ill health or death due to service in the Armed Forces on or after April 6, 2005. However, the WPS continues to operate for existing beneficiaries and for claims where the cause of the injury, illness or death is due to service before April 6, 2005. Originally the new scheme, as set out in the Armed Forces and Reserve Forces (Compensation Scheme) Order 2005 (SI 2005/439), made three types of payment: tariff based lump sums, regular "guaranteed income payments" and bereavement grants. See the definition of "guaranteed income payment" below which covers payments made 2.5

to the injured person under art.14(1)(b) of the Armed Forces and Reserve Forces (Compensation Scheme) Order 2005 and payments to "a surviving spouse, civil partner or his surviving adult dependant" under art.21(1)(a) of the Order. A "surviving adult dependant" means someone with whom the deceased was "cohabiting as partners in a substantial and exclusive relationship" (see art.22 of and Sch.1 to the Order).

However, the 2005 Order was revoked and replaced, with modifications, by the Armed Forces and Reserve Forces (Compensation Scheme) Order 2011 (SI 2011/517) with effect from May 9, 2011. The amended scheme provides for additional payments, including a supplementary award, a fast payment and a payment for medical expenses. "Guaranteed income payments" are now made under art.15(1)(c) of the 2011 Order or art.29(1)(a) in the case of payments to "a surviving spouse, civil partner or his surviving adult dependant" (s.17(2)(a) and s.23(2) of the Interpretation Act 1978 will apply) . "Surviving adult dependant" is defined in art.30 of, and Sch.1 to, the 2011 Order and is broadly the same definition as in the 2005 Order.

2.6 The £10 disregard that applies to war disablement, war widows and war widowers' pensions paid under the WPS scheme also applies to guarantee income payments (see para.16(cc) of Sch.9). No special provision is made in respect of the lump sum payments but since they are made in respect of personal injury presumably they will be treated in the same way as other personal injury payments (see the disregards in para.15 of Sch.9 and paras 12 and 12A of Sch.10).

The 2011 Order scheme was further amended by the Armed Forces and Reserve Forces (Compensation Scheme) (Amendment) Order 2013 (SI 2013/436) with effect from April 8, 2013. This provides for a new benefit, "armed forces independence payment", which is payable to a person who is entitled to a guaranteed income payment at the rate of at least 50 per cent. An award of armed forces independence payment precludes entitlement to disability living allowance, attendance allowance and personal independence payment. Armed forces independence payment is fully disregarded (see para.76A of Sch.9).

The Armed Forces and Reserved Forces (Compensation Scheme) (Amendment) Order 2014 (SI 2014/412) made further amendments to the 2011 Order on April 7, 2014, as did the Armed Forces and Reserve Forces (Compensation Scheme) (Amendment) Order 2015 (SI 2015/413) on April 6, 2015. These amendments included the uprating of the amount of the armed forces independence payment (not uprated in April 2016).

2.7 *"Armed forces independence payment"*: see under *"Armed Forces and Reserve Forces Compensation Scheme"*.

2.8 "*Board and lodging accommodation*": Since April 1989 there are no special calculations of benefit for claimants in board and lodging accommodation and therefore the definition is of less significance than in the past. Either the accommodation must be in some establishment like a hotel or lodging house or the charge must include the provision of some cooked or prepared meals in the accommodation or associated premises. The requirement in para.(a) that a charge is made for the accommodation has logically to be considered before the exclusion of non-commercial arrangements. In *CSB 1163/1988* the claimant moved with her two children into a house owned by the Jesus Fellowship Church (Baptist), where 17 other people also lived. Meals were provided. The terms of her occupation were that she should put all her income into a "common purse." A basic charge to cover food, accommodation and running costs was set, but any excess of the claimant's income was regarded as a donation to the Church. The Commissioner holds that the claimant was not a boarder because she did not pay a "charge." She was one of a joint community of persons, all sharing their income and outgoings. See also *R. v Sheffield Housing Benefits Review Board Ex p. Smith, Rugby Borough Council Housing Benefits Review Board Ex p. Harrison and Daventry DC Housing Benefits Review Board Ex p. Bodden*, below. Some family arrangements may be of this kind. Similarly, if a person makes a contribution of whatever he can afford week by week to the household expenses, this is probably not a charge. On the other hand, a fixed, but low, amount may require the non-commercial basis exception to be examined. Cases on the meaning of "board" in the Rent Acts (e.g. *Otter v Norman* [1988] 2 All E.R. 897, HL) indicate that merely providing the ingredients will not amount to preparing a meal. This was specifically decided in the supplementary benefit context in *CSB 950/1987*. The argument that getting a packet of cornflakes out of a cupboard constituted preparation was rejected.

If this primary definition is met there is an exclusion either if the accommodation is provided by a close relative (see definition below) of the claimant or any member of his family (see s.137(1)) or if it is provided on other than a commercial basis. Provision by a limited company, of which a close relative of the resident is a director or a shareholder, is not provision by a close relative (*R(SB) 9/89*). In this case the company was formed well before the resident went into the home. It might be different if the company was a mere facade or had been formed for a fraudulent or improper purpose. In *R(IS) 2/91* the claimant became a resident in a nursing home of which his daughter was the sole proprietor. He was actually cared for by the staff employed by his daughter. Nonetheless, his accommodation and meals were "provided" by his daughter. "Provided" means "made available".

What is a commercial basis is unclear, although the *Decision Makers Guide* suggests that the phrase should be interpreted broadly, not simply that a profit has to be made (Ch.24, App.5, paras 49–50). If the charge and the arrangements are as one would expect in a commercial relationship it can clearly be argued that the basis is commercial. The *DMG* considers that if the intention is to cover the cost of food plus a reasonable amount for accommodation, the arrangement should also be regarded as commercial. This approach is confirmed by *CSB 1163/1988* (above), where the tribunal had decided that "commercial basis" contained an element of profit. The Commissioner holds that this was an error of law and that the phrase means a basis that is intended to be more or less self-financing and not provided as part of a quasi "family" setting. On the facts, the lack of the intention to make a profit by the Church did not prevent the basis being commercial, but the "community" nature of the arrangement did. It was probable that if the claimant paid no income in for at least a short time, she would not have been asked to leave. In *R. v Sheffield Housing Benefits Review Board Ex p. Smith, Rugby BC Housing Benefits Review Board Ex p. Harrison and Daventry DC Housing Benefits Review Board Ex p. Bodden* (1996) 28 H.L.R. 36 (housing benefit cases which also concerned the Jesus Fellowship Church) Blackburne J reaches a similar conclusion. In deciding whether an arrangement was on a commercial basis, it was necessary to look at the arrangement as a whole. It was not correct only to consider the amount payable for the accommodation and to ignore the other terms of the agreement. See also *Campbell v (1) South Northamptonshire DC (2) Secretary of State for the Department of Work and Pensions* [2004] EWCA Civ 409, reported as *R(H) 8/04* (the appeal from *CH/5125, CH/5126, CH/5129* and *CH/5130/02*) which again concerned the Jesus Fellowship.

As far as family arrangements are concerned, all the circumstances must be considered. If money has been spent adapting accommodation to a disabled person's needs, this may be relevant. It is not the case, as is often argued by decision-makers, that if a person enters into an arrangement with a friend or a non-close relative it is automatically non-commercial. In *CIS 1951/1991* (confirmed in *R(IS) 17/94* and in *R(IS) 11/98*) whether a family arrangement was on a commercial basis is held to be entirely a question of fact for the tribunal, which has to consider whether it is similar to that which might have been arranged with a paying lodger (see the notes to reg.3). 2.9

See further the notes to reg.9(1)(a) of the Housing Benefit Regulations 2006 in CPAG's *Housing Benefit and Council Tax Benefit Legislation* for the extensive case law on the meaning of "on a commercial basis" in the housing benefit context.

"Care home". The definition in s.3 of the Care Standards Act 2000 reads as follows: 2.10

"**3 Care homes**

(1) For the purposes of this Act, an establishment is a care home if it provides accommodation, together with nursing or personal care, for any of the following persons.

(2) They are—

(a) persons who are or have been ill;

(b) persons who have or have had a mental disorder;

(c) persons who are disabled or infirm;

(d) persons who are or have been dependent on alcohol or drugs.

(3) But an establishment is not a care home if it is—

(a) a hospital;

(b) an independent clinic; or

(c) a children's home,

or if it is of a description excepted by regulations."

In Scotland s.2(3) of the Registration of Care (Scotland) Act 2001 defines a "care home service" as:

"a service which provides accommodation, together with nursing, personal care or personal support, for persons by reason of their vulnerability or need; but the expression does not include—

(a) a hospital;

(b) a public, independent or grant-aided school;

(c) an independent health care service; or

(d) a service excepted from this definition by regulations."

SA v SSWP (IS) [2010] UKUT 345 (AAC) confirms that if an establishment satisfies the conditions in the definition of "care home" then it falls to be treated as a care home even if it is also an educational establishment. Those terms are not mutually exclusive and a care home does not cease to be a care home merely by virtue of fulfilling some other function.

2.11 *"Close relative"*: The words "brother" and "sister" include half-brothers and half-sisters (*R(SB) 22/87*). The same decision confirms that if a child is adopted it becomes the child of its adoptive parents and ceases to have any legal relationship with its natural parents or brothers or sisters. It is legal relationships which are referred to in the definition of "close relative."

From December 5, 2005, references to "step" relationships and "in laws" are to be read as including relationships arising through civil partnership in any provision to which s.246 of the Civil Partnership Act 2004 applies. Section 246 is applied to the definition of "close relative" in reg.2(1) by art.3 of and para.21 of the Schedule to the Civil Partnership Act 2004 (Relationships Arising Through Civil Partnership) Order 2005 (SI 2005/3137).

2.12 *"Couple"*: Whether or not two people are to be treated as a couple for the purposes of IS (and IBJSA) has a number of important consequences. First, if two people are a couple then neither can be a "lone parent", which may mean that neither falls within the "prescribed categories" in Sch.1B. Second, the applicable amount for a couple is less than that for two single claimants. Third, a claimant is excluded from entitlement to income support if her partner (i.e. the other member of the couple) is in remunerative work (see the notes to reg.5) and, fourth, a couple's income and capital are aggregated for the purposes of the means test (see reg.23). Note, however, that a finding that two people are a couple (normally because they are living together as husband and wife) does not, by itself, affect either's right to benefit and it cannot simply be assumed that non-entitlement to benefit will be the automatic consequence of such a finding. In other words, such a determination is merely one step in a chain of reasoning that may eventually lead to the "outcome decision" that the claimant is or is not entitled to benefit but is not itself an outcome decision and therefore cannot be appealed until the outcome decision is taken—see *CIS/1720/2004* and *CPC/3891/2004*.

A new definition of "couple" was introduced on March 13, 2014, the day on which the Marriage (Same Sex Couples) Act 2013 came into force. Two people are now treated as a couple if:

- they married to, or civil partners of, each other and are members of the same household; or if
- they are neither married to, nor civil partners of, each other but are living together as a married couple.

As marriage now includes a same sex marriage, the question of whether two members of the same sex who are not civil partners are "living together as if they were civil partners" (which was the legal test between December 5, 2005 and March 12, 2013: see pp.220–221 of Vol. II of the 2013/2014 edition) no longer arises.

Spouses and civil partners

If two people are legally married, or have formally registered a civil partnership, whether or not they are a couple depends upon whether they are "members of the same household". In *Santos v Santos* [1972] 2 All E.R. 246, 255, it was said that "household" refers to "people held together by a particular kind of tie". According to *R(SB) 4/83*, the concept of a household is a matter of commonsense and common experience. **2.13**

If, in practice, two people each have exclusive occupation of separate accommodation, then they do not live in the same household. But the reverse does not necessarily apply: a single house can contain a number of households. In *CSB/463/1986*, for example, two claimants physically shared one room in a house as well as other facilities, but otherwise lived separately. They were in separate households. Thus a husband and wife can maintain separate households under the same roof. If the couple have decided to live apart in the same house, there can be separate households even if the husband is still maintaining the wife (*CIS/72/1994*). In *CIS/671/1992* the claimant and his wife shared a room in a home for the mentally ill. Both suffered from senile dementia and they did not understand that they were husband and wife. It is held that there must be some communality, something that can be identified as a domestic establishment. Mere presence in the same room did not turn them into a household. It is a question of fact in each case. In *CIS/81/1993* the same Commissioner similarly concludes that a husband and wife (who were not mentally incapacitated) were not members of the same household where they lived in separate rooms in a nursing home, were billed separately and had only limited contact with each other. In *CIS/671/1992* the Commissioner also considers whether the claimant and his wife could be said to be members of some other household (the home as a whole). He refers to the decision of the House of Lords in *Simmons v Pizzey* [1979] A.C. 37 (occupants of a woman's refuge not a single household), and concludes that all the residents of the home were not one household. These decisions are followed in *R(IS) 1/99*, which also concerned a married couple who shared a double room in a residential home (for which they were billed separately). The room was furnished with their own furniture and they had a kettle and a toaster to make breakfast, although they ate their main meals in the communal dining room. They spent much of their time together and were able to wash and dress themselves, apart from needing assistance to get out of the bath. They had entered the home because it was becoming difficult to cope on their own and so they needed someone else to undertake the organisation of their domestic and personal activities. The Commissioner agrees with *CIS/671/1992* that for there to be a "household" there had to be a domestic establishment. This meant two or more people living together as a unit and enjoying a reasonable level of independence and self-sufficiency. If the degree of independence and self-sufficiency fell below a certain level, there was no longer a domestic establishment and therefore no longer a household. The point at which this occurred was a matter for the common sense of the tribunal. The tribunal had correctly concluded in this case that the claimants were not members of the same household.

A person under 16 cannot be a member of a couple (*CFC/7/1992*).

2.14 If a person maintains, and from time to time lives in the same house as, his or her lawful spouse there is an initial presumption that they form a couple.

Difficult issues can arise where one (or both) of the parties might be said to live in more than one place. In *R(SB) 30/83*, the Commissioner holds that the issue is not decided on a week-by-week basis. So where the woman was absent during University terms living in a rented bed-sit, the couple were living together throughout. This principle was implicitly applied in *R(SB) 8/85*. The claimant lived with a Mr G, whose employment brought him to the area and was said to go back to his wife at weekends. The Commissioner holds that a person can only be a member of one couple, and so of one household, at a time. This appears to leave open, to be determined according to the circumstances, whether Mr G was living with the claimant for five days a week and with his wife for two days, or with only one of them. *CIS/11304/1995* explicitly states that there can be two households in these circumstances. Mr K lived with his wife in Zimbabwe for six months of the year and with the claimant in England for the other half of the year. Although Mr K could not simultaneously have two households, he could spend six months of the year in one household and six in another.

Once two people have become a couple (which requires a common household to have been established), reg.16 of the Income Support Regulations (reg.78 of the Jobseeker's Allowance Regulations) treats them as continuing to be members of that household during some periods of temporary absence. Originally, however, the equivalent supplementary benefit regulation had only applied to married couples, not to unmarried ones.

Unmarried partners

2.15 Under what used to be known as the "cohabitation rule", two people who are not married to each other, or civil partners of each other, are treated as a couple for benefit purposes if they are "living together as a married couple", which is the test that replaced the long-standing "living together as husband and wife" test with effect from March 13, 2014. The application of the latter test to individual cases was among the most contentious issues in the whole of social security law. The new test does not reflect any change of social security policy but only the fact that, since the introduction of same sex marriages, it has been possible for two people to be a "married couple" without also being "husband and wife". The case law about the former test will therefore be highly persuasive authority on the interpretation of the current one.

The first point to note is that the income support scheme recognises other ways of living together and has specific rules for determining the entitlement of claimants who live in someone else's household or have someone else living in their household. As Webster J stated in *Robson v Secretary of State for Social Services* [1982] 3 F.L.R. 232, at 236:

> "the legislation provides for three different situations: two persons who are living together being husband and wife is the first; two persons living together as husband and wife is the second; and two persons living together not as husband and wife is the third. It seems to me that where the facts show that there are two persons living together not being husband and wife, then both the second and third situations must be considered."

Thus to show that a couple are living together is only the first step, not the final one, as so often happens in practice (see also, e.g. *Crake v SBC, Butterworth v SBC* [1982] 1 All E.R. 498, 502, SB 38).

There have been a number of Commissioner's decisions on a similar rule in widow's benefit (the test is held to be the same in *R(SB) 17/81* and *R(G) 3/81* and the same principles will apply for the income-related benefits), but the position reached is fairly vague. Early attempts to obtain a judicial definition of "cohabitation" were unsuccessful ("for my part it is so well-known that nothing I could say about it could possibly assist in its interpretation hereafter", Lord Widgery CJ in *R. v S.W. London A.T. Ex p. Barnett*, SB 4). The examination of three main matters is required in deciding if two people are cohabiting: "(1) their relationship in relation to sex: (2) their relationship in relation to money: (3) their general relationship. Although all three are as a rule relevant, no single one of them is necessarily conclusive" (*R(G) 3/71*). In *CIS/87/1993*, however, the Commissioner expresses the view that it is the parties' general relationship that is most important (see below).

In response to criticisms about the operation of the cohabitation rule the Supplementary Benefits Commission produced published guidelines. The last formulation in summary form was in the 1984 edition of the Supplementary Benefits Handbook. A previous form of these guidelines had been approved as "an admirable signpost; the approach cannot be faulted" (Woolf J in *Crake v SBC, Butterworth v SBC*, above) and were found to correspond to the *R(G) 3/71* test in *R(SB) 17/81*. The Handbook said (para.2.13) that the main criteria are: **2.16**

"*1. Members of the same household*
The couple must be living in the same household and neither partner will usually have any other home where they normally live. This implies that the couple live together, apart from absences necessary for employment, visits to relatives, etc.

2. Stability
Living together as husband and wife clearly implies more than an occasional or very brief association. When a couple first live together, it may be clear from the start that the relationship is similar to that of husband and wife (for example, if the woman has taken the man's name and borne his child), but in cases where at the outset the nature of the relationship is less clear it may be right not to regard the couple as living together as husband and wife until it is apparent that a stable relationship has been formed.

3. Financial support
In most husband and wife relationships one would expect to find financial support of one party by the other, or sharing of household expenses, but the absence of any such arrangement does not of itself prove that a couple are not living together.

4. Sexual relationship
Similarly, a sexual relationship is a normal part of a marriage and therefore of living together as husband and wife. But its absence at any particular time does not necessarily prove that a couple are not living as husband and wife.

5. Children
When a couple are caring for a child of their union, there is a strong presumption that they are living together as husband and wife.

6. Public acknowledgment
Whether the couple have represented themselves to other people as husband and wife is relevant. However, many couples living together do not wish to pretend that they are actually married. The fact that they retain their identity publicly as unmarried people does not mean that they cannot be regarded as living together as husband and wife."

The Handbook was wrong to claim that these guidelines had been approved by courts and a Commissioner, for there had been changes in form. The most important, in the paragraph on "sexual relationship", are devastatingly set out by the Commissioner in *R(SB) 35/85*. It was the 1979 version that was approved in *Crake* and *Butterworth* and in *R(SB) 17/81* and that referred to a sexual relationship as an important as well as a normal part of marriage and also noted that the presence of a sexual relationship did not necessarily prove that a couple were living as husband and wife. The 1982 edition added a new sentence: "However, if a couple have never had such a relationship it is most unlikely that they should be regarded as living together as husband and wife." The 1983 edition "watered down" that sentence to suggesting that "it may be wrong" to regard the couple as living together as husband and wife in such circumstances. In the 1984 edition this final sentence disappeared altogether, along with the suggestion that the presence of a sexual relationship does not necessarily prove that a couple are living as husband and wife. In the meantime, the law has remained exactly the same.

However, it is correct to stress that there is no single way by which the issue can be decided in every case. For the criteria tend not to help in making the basic distinction between couples living together as husband and wife and those living together in other ways. As *CIS/87/1993* and *CIS/4156/2006* emphasise, it is important to consider *why* the couple are living together. The issues are now dealt with in Ch.11 of the DMG, where the issues are discussed quite fully and with reference to a range of decisions. It is notable that in para.11108 a sexual relationship is now described as an important part of marriage, and the presence of a sexual relationship is said not to be conclusive in itself of living together as husband and wife.

For a helpful discussion of the practical difficulties of following the "admirable signposts" in individual cases, an account of the developments in the case law in the higher courts since *Crake* and *Butterworth*, and guidance on the importance of also identifying "any relevant features of the emotional relationship between the parties" in order to reduce the extent that the result given by the signposts is equivocal, see the decision of the Upper Tribunal in *PP v Basildon DC (HB)* [2013] UKUT 505 (AAC).

Household

2.17 See the notes under the heading Spouses and Civil Partners, above.

Stability

2.18 Stability of a relationship is only of great weight if the relationship is one like husband and wife. There is no reason why a stable landlady-lodger relationship or flat-sharing relationship should not last for many years (see, for example, *CP/8001/1995*). However, it is sometimes suggested that an element of permanency in a relationship may differentiate it from, say, an employer-housekeeper relationship (e.g. *Campbell v Secretary of State for Social Services* [1983] 4 F.L.R. 138, where the "housekeeper" had sold her furniture and intended to apply for a joint local authority tenancy with the man). This forward-looking approach does make sense. But, as *CP/8001/1995* points out, even if an arrangement has become an established and settled one after some years, it does not follow that it has been on the same footing since the couple first started living together.

Financial support

2.19 The approach to financial support seems to make almost any arrangement point the same way, except a very clearly fixed commercial payment. If one member of the alleged couple pays a lot, s/he is supporting the other. If s/he pays very little, this shows that the relationship is more than a commercial one. This makes it very difficult for parties who are friends, or where the man pays what he can afford, where the proper conclusion may merely be that the two people share a household.

Sexual relationship

2.20 There has been an attempt to decrease reliance on the existence of a sexual relationship, partly in response to criticism of "sex snoopers" and methods of investigation. Officers are now instructed not to initiate questions about sexual relationships and not to seek to inspect sleeping arrangements, but to note statements and evidence presented by the claimant. However, if a rule is to distinguish people living together as husband and wife from people living together in some other way it seems impossible not to give great significance to the nature of the sexual relationship. By playing down its importance, either as being present or absent, the Handbook inevitably shifted the test closer to one which simply tested whether the couple were living together in one household. The Commissioner in *CIS/87/1993* considers that where there has never been a sexual relationship, strong alternative grounds are needed to reach the conclusion that the relationship is akin to that of husband and wife. In his view, the instruction to DSS officers not to ask about the physical aspects of the relationship is inappropriate in an inquisitorial system, and if the information is not volunteered, such questions may have to be asked. But care will need to be taken to prevent any such investigation becoming over-intrusive. In *CSB/150/1985* the Commissioner held that an unmarried couple who refrained on principle from any sexual relationship could not be described as living together as husband and wife. The claimant and his fiancée lived in the same house, but were Mormons. That religion forbids sexual relationships before marriage.

In *CIS/4156/2006*, the Deputy Commissioner considered a situation where the alleged partners had previously cohabited at a different address but had separated because of the man's violent behaviour and had subsequently lived apart for nearly 15 years. He approved as helpful the guidance in Vol.I of the 2006 edition that in such circumstances "it may be proper to test the re-created relationship as if they had not formerly been married (e.g. in relation to the sexual relationship)". The Deputy Commissioner also expressed the view that the expression "living together as husband and wife" did not extend to include a relationship "akin to . . . a so-called open marriage" in which at least one party was free to conduct sexual liaisons with others.

Children and public acknowledgment

The shared care of children, especially children of the couple, and public acknowledgment are obviously important factors. In *R(G) 1/79*, the adoption of the same name on the electoral register was decisive. Other elements might be whether the couple visit relatives or friends, or go on holiday, together. What these points come to is that the so-called "objective facts" of a relationship may be capable of being interpreted either way. This, then, leaves the authorities in a difficulty, although it is clear that the burden of proof (where relevant: see *CIS/317/1994* below) is on the Secretary of State, at least when the rule operates as a disqualification. **2.21**

In two decisions the Divisional Court has stressed the importance of looking at the intention of the parties in explaining the "objective facts". In *Butterworth v SBC*, above, the claimant was disabled following a serious accident, and invited the man, whom she had known for five years, to move into her house, since she was then on her own. The man had his own bedroom, with a lock on the door. He did the cooking and household tasks, and they lived as one household. Woolf J says:

> "If the only reason that [the man] went to that house temporarily was to look after Mrs. Butterworth in her state of illness and, albeit, while doing so, acted in the same way as an attentive husband would behave towards his wife who suffered an illness, this does not amount to living together as husband and wife because it was not the intention of the parties that there should be such a relationship. Looked at without knowing the reason for the man going to live there, it would appear that they were living together as husband and wife, but when the reason was known that would explain those circumstances."

In *Robson's* case (above), the parties were both seriously disabled, needing wheelchairs and invalid cars. They had been friends for a long time before they were widowed. They moved together into a two-bedroom maisonette at their social worker's suggestion. They lived as one household. As so often the SBAT assumed that this was conclusive, and this was an error of law. In order to provide guidance to tribunals, Webster J says that often it is only possible to decide into which category a relationship falls by considering the objective facts, "because usually the intention of the parties is either unascertainable, or, if ascertainable, is not to be regarded as reliable. But if it is established to the satisfaction of the tribunal that the two persons concerned did not intend to live together as husband and wife and still do not intend to do so, in my judgment it would be a very strong case indeed sufficient to justify a decision that they are, or ought to be treated as if they are, husband and wife."

2.22 Although subsequent Divisional Court decisions (e.g. *Kaur v Secretary of State for Social Services* [1982] 3 F.L.R. 237) have not referred to intention as a factor, it has not been rejected either. However, in *R(SB) 17/81* the Commissioner says that Webster J's words are of no real assistance to tribunals. For, he says, it is "the conduct of the person concerned to which regard has to be paid", i.e. "what he or she does or says at the relevant time." If *R(SB) 17/81* is taken as deciding that only the "objective facts" as identified by the Handbook criteria are relevant, and that the intention of the parties is not relevant, it need not be followed as being inconsistent with persuasive decisions of the Divisional Court. If *R(SB) 17/81* is taken as a reminder of the difficulties of establishing intention it is in line with those decisions, although evidence of intention should not be as limited as suggested. On the facts of *R(SB) 17/81* the couple shared a sexual relationship and one household, but said that there was nothing permanent about the relationship. The Commissioner points out that the fact that they did not intend to marry did not mean that they did not intend to live together as though they were married. It is the second view of *R(SB) 17/81* that seems to have been applied in recent Commissioners' decisions, although decision-makers commonly rely on the first view in submissions to tribunals. *CSSB/145/1983* is a decision on facts reminiscent of *Robson's* case. Two disabled people living in a sheltered housing scheme moved into one flat to share living expenses and provide mutual support. At the beginning the housing association running the flats did not have the funds to divide the one bedroom. There was no sexual relationship. The SSAT had decided that the situation was no different from that of a married couple where one partner had a serious disability. The Commissioner holds this to be a wrong approach. A sharing of expenses and mutual support can arise between people of the same sex, or between brother and sister, and does not in itself amount to living together as husband and wife. In *R(SB) 35/85* the claimant was a widow in her seventies. She had taken over the tenancy of her bungalow in 1976, on the death of her brother, with whom she had lived for some years. In 1974, Mr W, who needed care and help, had moved into the household. By August 1984, he was a widower. The claimant did the cooking and there was a sharing of household expenses. The Commissioner holds that the SSAT, in finding the claimant and Mr W to be living together as husband and wife, had failed to see that the existence of a common household was only one ingredient in the decision. He adopts as helpful guidance the approach of Woolf J in *Butterworth* that it is impossible to categorise all the kinds of explanation of why two people were sharing a household, which would mean that the two were not living together as husband and wife. In *CIS/87/1993* the claimant maintained that the only relationship between him and Mrs B, with whom he was living, was that of patient and carer. The Commissioner decides that the SSAT had failed to consider their general relationship and why they were living together. He expresses reservations about the "criteria" relied upon by AOs in cohabitation cases. He points out that Woolf J in *Crake* and *Butterworth* considered it wrong to refer to them as "criteria" and preferred the description "admirable signposts". There was nothing in *R(SB) 17/81* to suggest that only these admirable signposts had to be considered. In the Commissioner's view, the admirable signposts failed to emphasise the significance of the parties' "general relationship". It was arguable that it was the parties' general relationship that was of paramount importance and that their sexual and their financial relationship were only relevant for the light they threw upon the general relationship. The importance of looking at the totality of the parties' relationship and of not simply using the criteria as items on a checklist to be ticked off one by one is emphasised in *CP/8001/1995*. The claimant was a widow who had taken in a lodger. He paid her rent and a contribution towards expenses, but they did not pool resources, even though she had a right to draw cheques on his bank account. As time passed, they became friends, watched TV and ate together and went on holiday together with a group of friends. There was no sexual relationship, but on occasion they went halves on a twin-bedded room when staying in a hotel. The Commissioner decides that even though there were elements in the arrangement that matched those found in a normal marriage, it was equally akin to that of a brother and sister living in the same household, and that the totality of the evidence did not add up to a husband and wife relationship.

Burden of proof

In *CIS/317/1994* the Commissioner decides that the question of onus of proof did not arise where the question of whether the claimant was living together as husband and wife with her alleged partner fell to be determined on an initial claim for income support. What had to be considered was all the relevant facts. He pointed to the duty on the claimant to provide such information as may be required to decide the claim (see reg.7(1) of the Claims and Payments Regulations). The Commissioner also considered that although living together as husband and wife operated as a disqualification for widow's benefit it did not do so for income support. But, with respect, this distinction seems more apparent than real. Even though cohabitation is not an automatic bar in all cases, if the claimant's alleged partner is in remunerative work, or has income or capital that disentitles them to income support, or has himself already claimed income support, the effect of a living together decision will be to disqualify the claimant from income support. Thus it is suggested that the burden of proof (on the decision-maker) may come into play in marginal cases (if the claimant otherwise satisfies the conditions of entitlement to income support), even on initial claims. If benefit is stopped on a revision or supersession on the grounds of alleged cohabitation, the burden of proof will be on the DM. However, as pointed out above, it is often not so much the facts that may be at issue as the interpretation of those facts. Here the intention of the parties and the reason why they are living together may be the deciding factors (and see *CIS/87/1993* above). **2.23**

"Date of claim": See the notes to reg.6 of the Social Security (Claims and Payments) Regulations in Vol.III of this series. **2.24**

"Dwelling occupied as the home": "Home" is no longer defined, but the present definition contains many similarities to that of "home" in the old Supplementary Benefit (Requirements) Regulations and (Resources) Regulations. Instead of referring to accommodation, it refers to a dwelling, but since the definition of "dwelling" in s.137(1) of the Contributions and Benefits Act refers to residential accommodation, there is probably not much difference. The s.137(1) definition does specify that a dwelling can be the whole or part of a building and need not comprise separate and self-contained premises. The dwelling must be normally occupied as the home by the claimant. There is no reference here to the claimant's family, but presumably if the claimant has a family within s.137(1) of the Contributions and Benefits Act, the family's home will normally be his home, although see *CIS 81/1991* below. **2.25**

In *OR v SSWP & Isle of Angelsey CC* [2013] UKUT 65 (AAC) the claimant was not occupying a night shelter as his home, given the very transient nature of his stays there, the fact that he was not allowed to remain there or leave any personal possessions there during the day, and the fact that he had no right to stay there on the following or any given night (if the shelter was full when he arrived he would be turned away). However, as the Upper Tribunal Judge emphasised, this case turned on its own particular facts and did not mean that other users of night shelters (or similar accommodation) are not entitled to housing benefit.

The question whether the reference to "the dwelling" means that only one dwelling at a time can meet the definition or whether in certain circumstances two physically separate buildings may constitute one dwelling has been the subject of several decisions. *R(SB) 30/83* decided that two completely separate units could not constitute one home. However, *R(SB) 10/89* held that two units about 600 yards apart, neither of which on their own could accommodate the assessment unit were one home. The Commissioner relied on some Rent Act cases on when something is let as a separate dwelling (in particular, *Langford Property Co Ltd v Goldrich* [1949] 1 K.B. 511). She took account of the fact that the mode of life of the assessment unit was such that one house was an "extension" or "annexe" of the other, that the two houses were within walking distance of each other, and that neither had been purchased as an investment. In *CIS 299/1992* it was held that a bungalow and an adjoining caravan constituted one dwelling. But in *CIS 81/1991*, where the claimant lived in one house and members of his family slept in another, the second house did not come within the definition in reg.2(1). This was because it was not occupied by the *claimant* as his home. The Commissioner distinguished *R(SB) 10/89* on the grounds that it was decided in relation to what in his view was the significantly different definition of "home" in the Supplementary Benefit Regulations, which referred to ". . . the accommodation . . . normally occupied by the *assessment unit* (emphasis added). . .". On the wording of the definition in reg.2(1), this decision is probably correct where only members of the claimant's family live in the other property. However, where the claimant personally occupies two physically separate properties, there seemed to be no reason why both should not constitute the dwelling normally occupied as his home.

2.26 This has now been confirmed by the Court of Appeal in *Secretary of State for Work and Pensions v Miah* [2003] EWCA Civ 1111; [2003] 4 All E.R. 702, also reported as *R(JSA) 9/03*. The Commissioner in that case had disagreed with *CIS 81/1991* and concluded that a "dwelling occupied as the home" could comprise more than one building. He had directed the new tribunal to have particular regard to para.13 of *R(SB) 10/89* and to consider whether the situation was in effect that of a single home on a split site. Occasional use of the second house by the claimant would not suffice, since the second house also had to be "normally" occupied by the claimant as his home. The Court of Appeal upheld the Commissioner's approach. It took the view that the use of the phrase "dwelling occupied as the home" indicated that the focus should be the functions served by the concept of a dwelling rather than its constituent elements and that function was a place serving as a home for the claimant. Common sense, justice and fairness also supported this approach. If the claimant had been living in one property which was large enough to accommodate him and his family then it would have been disregarded. It could not be fair that he should suffer when the purpose of having two properties was exactly the same. The Court also pointed to the difficulties, if the disregard only applied to one property, of determining which of the properties was to be disregarded in a case where the claimant was occupying both as his home (which, as the Court pointed out, was not the situation in *CIS 81/1991*).

See also *London Borough of Hackney v GA* [2008] UKUT 26 (AAC), reported as *R(H) 5/09*, in which two flats owned by different landlords constituted one dwelling and *Birmingham CC v IB* [2009] UKUT 116 (AAC), in which the additional room rented by a disabled student at university for his carer was held to be part of the dwelling occupied by him.

In *MM v SSWP (IS)* [2012] UKUT 358 (AAC) the claimant was the joint-owner of No.65 with his wife. However, for a number of years the claimant and his wife had stayed at No.16 (his father's house) in order to provide care for his father. The claimant's evidence was that (a) he returned to No.65 every day; (b) he had carried out repairs on No.65; (c) he paid gas and electricity bills in respect of No.65; (d) he kept food at No.65 and occasionally ate snacks there; (e) he kept clothes at both addresses; (f) his bank and insurance statements went to No.65 but other mail was delivered to No.16; and (g) he had not let No.65, in part because he wanted to use the house every day.

Judge Wikeley concluded that the tribunal had not made sufficient findings of fact and had not applied the correct legal test, i.e. whether the claimant normally occupied No.65 as his home, and in particular had not considered the "two properties/one home issue" (see *Miah* and *R(SB) 10/89*). This issue was not confined to the situation where one property alone was not large enough to accommodate the family unit as a whole. The test under the legislation, as interpreted by the case law, was whether or not the claimant himself in effect used No.65 as an annex to No.16 and so had "a single home on a split site". 2.27

The issue in *CH/1786/2005*, a case on the meaning of "dwelling normally occupied as his home" in reg.5(1) of the Housing Benefit Regulations 1987, was whether the claimant, who after his father died stayed with his sister for much of the time, had ceased to occupy his flat as his home. Upholding the tribunal's decision that the claimant's flat remained the dwelling normally occupied as his home, the Commissioner concludes that it is a mistake to try and chop up what is essentially a single factual question into a series of individual tests for particular factors. In his view, identifying a person's "centre of interests" was not a separate test to be applied in determining where a person was truly making his normal home but really an expression of the overall conclusion after looking at all the facts.

In *PJ v SSWP (SPC)* [2014] UKUT 152 (AAC) the claimant was not normally occupying his home when he had gone to live in his daughter's home in order to avoid liability for council tax (and had remained there for three years). His other daughter remained in the family home because she was a student and so was exempt from council tax. The claimant visited at weekends and also stayed there at night for 50 per cent. of the time during a three month period in order to care for his daughter who was ill at that time but this did not mean that he was normally occupying the family home as his home.

Paragraph 3(6) of Sch.3 allows payments to be made for two homes in limited circumstances. 2.28

It also appears that accommodation cannot be normally occupied until some person has actually moved in (*R(SB) 27/84, R(SB) 7/86*), given the special rule created in para.3(7) for periods before anyone moves in. But this raises the question as to what is meant by "moved in" (and see *R(H) 9/05* below). In an unstarred decision, *CIS 4/1990*, the Commissioner doubts the existence of a rule that occupation requires residence. The same point was made in the supplementary benefit context in *CSB 524/1985* (not quoted by the Commissioner) and *CSSB 34/1987*. While it is right that the word used in the legislation is "occupy" and not "reside," it must also be noted that the definition requires not simply occupation, but occupation as the home. This point was the basis of *R(SB) 7/86* also not mentioned in *CIS 4/1990*. However, it is suggested that the issue of what is sufficient to amount to occupation will be one of fact depending on the particular circumstances of the case. Thus, for example in *CH 2521/2002*, a case on the meaning of "dwelling normally occupied as his home" in reg.5(1) of the Housing Benefit Regulations 1987, the Commissioner decided that the claimant did not so occupy a flat when he only slept there a few nights a week while he was decorating it and had not moved in any clothing or possessions (other than a cooker which he did not use and a camp bed).

However, in *R(H) 9/05*, the Deputy Commissioner reached a different conclusion on the facts. The claimant, who was elderly and disabled, entered into a tenancy agreement of a flat near her relatives on February 12, 2004, intending to move in on March 15, 2004 after the flat had been adapted to meet her needs. The work was carried out and her furniture was moved in on March 15, 2004. The claimant gave up her previous accommodation but did not physically go to the flat herself on March 15 because she had been admitted to hospital. Following a rehabilitation period the claimant went to live in the flat on August 9, 2004. The Deputy Commissioner holds that the claimant was normally occupying the flat as her home from March 15, 2004. She was not occupying any other home from that date and the flat had become her new permanent address. The local authority had contended that normal occupation involved physical presence in a property but since the claimant had a physical presence in the shape of her furniture it was difficult to see how she could be said not to have occupied it. As a matter of general law occupation did not require the personal presence of the tenant if the property was under her control and being used by her to store her goods and for no other purpose. The Deputy Commissioner therefore rejected the local authority's submission that it was necessary (but sufficient) for the claimant to spend one night at the property in order to normally occupy it as her home. In his view, if "normally" was intended to refer to some degree of regularity of occupation, far more than one night would be needed. But he did not consider that the word "normally" was directed to any question of length of occupation but was being used to deal with the case where there might be more than one dwelling that was the claimant's home. The local authority had also relied on various references in other parts of reg.5 of the Housing Benefit Regulations 1987 (which contained similar, although not identical, provisions to para.3 of Sch.3) to the claimant moving into the property as inferring that occupation meant physically moving in. But "moving in" was not part of the definition in reg.5(1) (the equivalent of para.3(1)). The subsequent paragraphs modified the general rule in reg.5(1) by spelling out certain circumstances in which a claimant could be treated as occupying a dwelling as her home for housing benefit purposes before she had moved in. But this did not answer the question as to what a claimant had to do in order to "move into" a property. In the Deputy Commissioner's view the claimant in this case had moved into the flat on the date that she removed her furniture from her previous home and moved it into her new flat. A more significant argument in his view was the fact that for the claimant to take advantage of the temporary absence provisions in reg.5(8B) and (8C) (the equivalent of para.3(11) and (12)) she had to be said to intend to *return* to occupy the flat as her home after her stay in hospital. However, the Deputy Commissioner concludes that because she had occupied the flat through the acts of her agents moving her furniture in she could be said to be returning there when she left hospital. Although this strained the use of the word "return", the alternative construction would be to draw an artificial distinction between a person who spent 10 minutes at the property before becoming unwell and a person who became unwell before arriving in person at the property.

2.29 The definition extends to any garden or outbuildings which are occupied as part of the home (like the toilet and coalstore in outbuildings in *R(SB) 13/84* or the "development land" in *R(SB) 27/84* which might have been part of the garden). *CIS 427/1991* holds that the line between a garden and other land occupied with a dwelling is to be drawn according to the view of the ordinary man in the street.

If a building or a garden is occupied as part of the home it does not matter that they could be sold separately. This only comes into play when some buildings or land are not so occupied. Then those premises still count as part of the home if it is impracticable or unreasonable to sell them separately. (Note *C3/99-00(FC) (T)* which draws attention to the different definition in the Northern Ireland legislation.) A potential limit to this extension is exposed by *CSB 965/1986*, where the claimant was a tenant of a council house and owned a half-share in a small-holding two fields away. The small-holding was clearly not occupied as part of the home. The Commissioner holds that the extension could not apply since the home could not be sold and therefore the question of separate sale could not arise. This decision seems dubious, especially since the definition refers by way of example to croft land in Scotland, where the crofter is often only a tenant. Perhaps *CSB 965/1986* can be supported on the basis that if the small-holding was the only premises actually owned by the claimant it could not be unreasonable or impracticable to sell it separately. In *CIS 427/1991* the Commissioner holds that *R(SB) 13/84* was wrong in suggesting that property outside Scotland which is comparable to croft land is to be treated on the same principles. In considering reasonableness and practicability all the circumstances must be considered, including the use to which the premises are put, any profit made from them, etc. (*R(SB) 13/84* and *R(SB) 27/84*). In *CIS 427/1991* the state of health of the claimant's wife was a factor of which account could be taken in assessing whether it was unreasonable to sell land held with the home but not occupied as the home (she was a manic depressive who needed the adjoining fields for therapeutic walking). Medical evidence as to the therapeutic benefit would obviously be highly desirable in these circumstances.

CIS 616/1992 holds that the common parts of a block of flats (e.g. the entrance hall or staircases) do not come within the definition. It is not impracticable or unreasonable to sell such areas separately but quite simply impossible to do so.

"Employed earner": The meaning in s.2(1)(a) of the Contributions and Benefits Act 1992, as amended by the Income Tax (Earnings and Pensions) Act 2003 Sch.6 Pt 2 para.171 with effect from April 6, 2003, and the National Insurance Contributions Act 2014 s.15(1) with effect from May 13, 2014, is "a person who is gainfully employed in Great Britain either under a contract of service, or in an office (including elective office) with earnings." **2.30**

On the tests for deciding whether a person is an employed earner or in self-employment, see *CJSA 4721/2001*.

"A guarantee income payment": See the note to *"the Armed Forces and Reserve Forces Compensation Scheme"* above. **2.31**

"Independent hospital": s.2 of the Care Standards Act 2000 defines an "independent hospital" as a "hospital which is not a health service hospital". In Scotland, an independent healthcare service is defined by s.2(5) of the Regulation of Care (Scotland) Act 2001 as an independent hospital, a private psychiatric hospital, an independent clinic and an independent medical agency (unless it is excepted from that definition by regulations). **2.32**

"Nursing home": The definition of "nursing home" was revoked on October 24, 2005. For the text of, and a note to, the former definition see pp.209 and 221 of Vol.II of the 2005 edition. For the period from October 5, 2005 until its revocation, the definition was modified (in relation to Scotland) by art.2 of, and para.3(1) of the Schedule to, the Mental Health (Care and Treatment) (Scotland) Act 2003 (Modification of Subordinate Legislation) Order 2005 (SSI 2005/445) and, in relation to England and Wales, by art.15 of, and para.3(2) of Sch.2 to, the Mental Health (Care and Treatment) (Scotland) Act 2003 (Consequential Provisions) Order 2005 (SI 2005/2078). The modification consisted of the substitution of the words "an independent health care service within the meaning of section 2(5) of the Regulation of Care (Scotland) Act 2001" for the words "a private hospital within the meaning of section 12 of the Mental Health (Scotland) Act 1984 (private hospitals)". **2.33**

"Occupational pension": Section 1(1) of the Pension Schemes Act 1993 (as amended by s.239 of the Pensions Act 2004 with effect from September 22, 2005 in the case of an occupational pension scheme that has its main administration in the UK and with effect from April 6, 2006 in all other cases (see art.2(7) of the Pensions Act 2004 (Commencement No.6, Transitional Provisions and Savings) Order 2005 (SI 2005/1720), and as further amended with effect from November 26, 2007 by reg.2(b) of the Occupational Pension Schemes (EEA States) Regulations 2007 (SI 2007/3014)) defines an "occupational pension scheme" as **2.34**

"a pension scheme—

(a) that—

(i) for the purpose of providing benefits to, or in respect of, people with service in employments of a description, or

(ii) for that purpose and also for the purpose of providing benefits to, or in respect of, other people,

is established by, or by persons who include, a person to whom subsection (2) applies when the scheme is established or (as the case may be) to whom that subsection would have applied when the scheme was established had that subsection then been in force, and

(b) that has its main administration in the United Kingdom or outside the EEA states,

or a pension scheme that is prescribed or is of a prescribed description".

Section 1(2)–(5) provides:

"(2) This subsection applies—

(a) where people in employments of the description concerned are employed by someone, to a person who employs such people,
(b) to a person in an employment of that description, and
(c) to a person representing interests of a description framed so as to include—

(i) interests of persons who employ people in employments of the description mentioned in paragraph (a), or
(ii) interests of people in employments of that description.

(3) For the purposes of subsection (2), if a person is in an employment of the description concerned by reason of holding an office (including an elective office) and is entitled to remuneration for holding it, the person responsible for paying the remuneration shall be taken to employ the office-holder.
(4) In the definition in subsection (1) of "occupational pension scheme", the reference to a description includes a description framed by reference to an employment being of any of two or more kinds.
(5) In subsection (1) "pension scheme" (except in the phrases "occupational pension scheme", "personal pension scheme" and "public service pension scheme") means a scheme or other arrangements, comprised in one or more instruments or agreements, having or capable of having effect so as to provide benefits to or in respect of people—

(a) on retirement,
(b) on having reached a particular age, or
(c) on termination of service in an employment."

2.35 *"Personal pension scheme"*: The July 16, 2007 amendment to this definition reflects the fact that following the changes made by Pt 4 of the Finance Act 2004 there is no longer any distinction between personal pension schemes for employed and self-employed earners—they are simply referred to as "personal pension schemes". In addition the definition of "retirement annuity contract" has been omitted (see the 2007 edition of this volume for that definition) with effect from the same date as these contracts now come within the definition of "personal pension scheme".

The meaning in s.1(1) of the Pension Schemes Act 1993 (as amended by s.239 of the Pensions Act 2004 with effect from April 6, 2006 (see art.2(7) of the Pensions Act 2004 (Commencement No.6, Transitional Provisions and Savings) Order 2005 (SI 2005/1720), and as further amended with effect from April 6, 2007 by the Finance Act 2007 Sch.27 Pt 3(2) para.1) is

"a pension scheme that—

(a) is not an occupational pension scheme, and
(b) is established by a person within section 154(1) of the Finance Act 2004".

Section 1(5) further provides that "pension scheme" in s.1(1) means "a scheme or other arrangements, comprised in one or more instruments or agreements, having or capable of having effect so as to provide benefits to or in respect of people—

(a) on retirement,
(b) on having reached a particular age, or
(c) on termination of service in an employment."

"Self-employed earner": The meaning in s.2(1)(b) of the Contributions and Benefits Act 1992 is "a person who is gainfully employed in Great Britain otherwise than in employed earner's employment (whether or not he is also employed in such employment)." **2.36**

On the tests for deciding whether a person is an employee or self-employed see *CJSA 4721/2001*.

"Self-employment route": The new form of the definition of *"self-employment route"* is intended to encompass assistance in pursuing self-employed earner's employment while participating in *any* programme provided or other arrangement made under s.2 of the Employment and Training Act 1973 or s.2 of the Enterprise and New Towns (Scotland) Act 1990 (it has been introduced so as to avoid the need to amend the definition each time a new scheme is created). It also covers such assistance while taking part in an employment zone programme (such programmes, which no longer operate, did not come under those provisions but s.60 of the Welfare Reform and Pensions Act 1999). A person who is receiving assistance under the self-employment route is not regarded as being in remunerative work (this was previously achieved by Orders made by the Secretary of State under s.26 of the Employment Act 1988 in relation to individual schemes under s.2 of the 1973 Act but now see the new sub-para.(dd) of reg.6(1) and the amended form of reg.53(bb) of the JSA Regulations 1996). **2.37**

The other main consequence of participating in programmes under the self-employment route is that the normal rules for the treatment of income do not apply to receipts from trading (see reg.23A); such receipts are only to be taken into account as income in accordance with regs 39A–39D. Note the disregards in para.64 of Sch.9 and para.6(3) and (4) and para.52 of Sch.10 and of discretionary payments for those who were participating in an employment zone programme in para.72 of Sch.9 and para.58 of Sch.10.

See also para.13 of Sch.9 which from April 1, 2004 has provided for a single disregard of the various allowances, grants and other payments made under s.2 of the Employment and Training Act 1973 or s.2 of the Enterprise and New Towns (Scotland) Act 1990 to people participating in New Deals and other training and welfare to work schemes. For the capital disregard see para.30 of Sch.10. These disregards have replaced, among other provisions, para.62 of Sch.9 and para.50 of Sch.10 which had previously contained a disregard of top-up grants for people participating in the self-employment route; such grants will now be ignored under the blanket provisions in para.13 of Sch.9 and para.30 of Sch.10.

"The Skipton Fund": This is government-funded and has been set up to make lump sum ex-gratia payments to people (or their dependants if the person died after August 29, 2003) who have contracted hepatitis C from NHS blood, blood products or tissue. Such payments are fully disregarded (see para.39 of Sch.9 for the income disregard and para.22 of Sch.10 for the capital disregard). **2.38**

"The Caxton Foundation": this charitable trust is also government-funded. It was established on March 28, 2011 to provide additional discretionary financial support to people who have been infected with hepatitis C as a result of National Health Service treatment. Payments from the Caxton Foundation are fully disregarded (see para.39 of Sch.9 for the income disregard and para.22 of Sch.10 for the capital disregard). **2.39**

2.40 *"Training allowance"*: *R(IS) 10/98* holds that payments from the European Social Fund can fall within this definition. As part of his part-time course the claimant went on a two-week placement in Brussels and Strasbourg, for which funds were provided by the European Social Fund. The Commissioner decided that this meant that he was in receipt of a training allowance and so could continue to be paid income support during his absence abroad (under reg.4(2)(c)(i) and para.11 of Sch.1 in force at that time; see the 1996 edition of J. Mesher and P. Wood, *Income-Related Benefits: The Legislation*). The payment from the European Social Fund was out of "public funds" administered in the UK by the Department of Employment and so could be said to be made "by or on behalf of the Secretary of State for Employment"; the Secretary of State would also have to have been satisfied that the course, or at least the placement, came within the ambit of the European Social Fund and so could be said to have "approved" the course.

In *R(TC) 1/03* the "training allowance" paid to the claimant was funded from the local authority's budget, not by external funding. It therefore did not fall within the definition in reg.2(1) of the Family Credit Regulations (which paralleled this definition) (see the 2002 edition of this volume for the Family Credit Regulations which were revoked in April 2003).

2.41–2.42 *"Welfare to work beneficiary"*: See the notes to this definition, which was relevant to incapacity for work, in the 2015/16 edition of this volume. The ESA equivalent is a "work or training beneficiary", see para.1(3A)–(3C) and para.15(15) of Sch.6 to the ESA Regulations 2008 in Vol.I of this series.

Paragraph (1B)

2.43 Until April 28, 2014 reg.2(1) included a definition of "service user group." However, that definition has been omitted and replaced by para.(1B). The main effect of the change is to clarify that carers who are paid expenses because the person for whom they care participates as a service user are covered by this provision. Paragraph (1B) was further amended on February 23, 2015 to include claimants who are participating in research conducted by or on behalf of (i) the DWP in connection with its social security, child support or labour market functions, or (ii) a body who undertakes research or monitoring in relation to such functions, as well as those who are research participants in the areas of health, social care and social housing.

2.44 Payment of expenses that result from a "claimant participating as a service user" are disregarded (see para.2A of Sch.9 and the note to that paragraph); reg.35(2)(f) ensures that they do not count as earnings.

Paragraph (3)

2.45 Note that special provision is only made for polygamous marriages. The definition of "family" in s.137(1) of the Contributions and Benefits Act will apply in other situations, e.g. civil partnerships or living together as husband/wife or civil partners.

[1 Disapplication of section 1(1A) of the Administration Act

2.46 **2A.**—Section 1(1A) of the Administration Act (requirement to state national insurance number) shall not apply—

(a) [3 . . .]

(b) to a partner in respect of whom a claim for income support is made or treated as made before [2 5th October 1998].]

[4 (c) to a person who—

(i) is a person in respect of whom a claim for income support is made;

(ii) is subject to immigration control within the meaning of section 115(9)(a) of the Immigration and Asylum Act;
(iii) is not entitled to any income support for the purposes of section 124 of the Contributions and Benefits Act; and
(iv) has not previously been allocated a national insurance number.]

AMENDMENTS

1. Social Security (National Insurance Number Information: Exemption) Regulations 1997 (SI 1997/2676) reg.10 (December 1, 1997).
2. Social Security (National Insurance Number Information: Exemption) (No.2) Regulations 1997 (SI 1997/2814) reg.2 (December 1, 1997).
3. Social Security (Working Tax Credit and Child Tax Credit) (Consequential Amendments) Regulations 2003 (SI 2003 No.455) reg.2 and Sch.1 para.1 (April 6, 2004, except in "transitional cases" and see further the note to reg.17 of the Income Support Regulations).
4. Social Security (National Insurance Number Information: Exemption) Regulations 2009 (SI 2009/471) reg.5 (April 6, 2009).

DEFINITION

"partner"—see reg.2(1).

GENERAL NOTE

Subsection (1A), together with subss.(1B) and (1C), was inserted into s.1 of the Administration Act by s.19 of the Social Security Administration (Fraud) Act 1997 and came into force on December 1, 1997. The effect of these provisions is that where s.1(1)(a) of the Administration Act (no entitlement to benefit unless a claim for it is made) applies, i.e. generally, there will also be no entitlement to benefit unless the claimant provides a national insurance (NI) number, together with information or evidence to show that it is his, *or* provides evidence or information to enable his NI number to be traced, *or* applies for a NI number and provides sufficient information or evidence for one to be allocated to him. This is known colloquially as the "NINO requirement". A P45 or P60 form will be evidence of a person's NI number but these may not always be available; other evidence which shows the person's number should also be sufficient. The NINO requirement applies to both the claimant and any person for whom he is claiming, except in prescribed circumstances (subss.(1A) and (1C)). The effect of reg.2A is that where a claim for income support was made, or treated as made, before October 5, 1998 (but not on or after that date) the national insurance number requirement did not apply to any partner of the claimant. Between December 1, 1997 and April 5, 2004 any child or young person included in the claim was also exempt from the requirement under para.(a). That exemption became unnecessary—and para.(a) was therefore repealed—on April 6, 2004 when support for children and young persons was removed from income support and transferred to child tax credit. See the note to reg.17 for the circumstances in which para.(a) remains in force on a transitional basis. 2.47

Note *CIS 345/2003* which confirms that a decision refusing to allocate an NI number (or alternatively if such a refusal is a determination, not a decision, a decision denying income support on the basis of such a determination) is appealable (*CIS 3692/2001* which decided that a tribunal only had a restricted jurisdiction as regards such a decision not followed). The Commissioner considered that the new tribunal would find the following observations from an officer on behalf of the Secretary of State helpful:

"It is to be hoped that the Secretary of State's representatives in the claimant's local social security office will in the meantime reconsider its refusal to provide to the tribunal the evidence on which its refusal of the claimant's claim under section 1(1B) of the Social Security [Administration Act 1992 was based]. If not, the new tribunal will, in my submission, be at liberty firstly to direct the Secretary of State to produce the evidence in question and secondly, in the event of a refusal to comply with that direction, to consider whether the Secretary of State is thereby seeking to shelter from scrutiny an indefensible decision."

The addition of para.(c) reverses the actual decision of the Court of Appeal in *SSWP v Wilson* [2006] EWCA Civ 882; R(H) 7/06 (see p.226 of Vol.II of the 2008 edition). It applies where:

- the claimant is the partner of a person subject to immigration control (see s.115 Immigration and Asylum Act 1999 and reg.21(3)) and is therefore a special case and entitled to IS at the single person rate only under para.16A(a) of Sch.7, or
- the claimant is a member of a polygamous marriage which includes one or more members who is a person subject to immigration control and is therefore entitled to IS only for him/herself and those members of the marriage who are not subject to immigration control under para.16A(b) of Sch.7.

The effect is that, from April 6, 2009, it is not necessary for the person subject to immigration control to satisfy the NINO requirement unless that person has previously been allocated a national insurance number. Note, however, that the amendment does not affect the reasoning of the Court that "[a]s a matter of ordinary language, benefit is claimed 'in respect of' a person if the benefit claimed is in some way referable to that person, as where the benefit or some component of it is defined or quantified by reference to that person".

Definition of non-dependant

2.48 **3.**—(1) In these Regulations, "non-dependant" means any person, except someone [3 to whom paragraph (2), (2A) or (2B) applies], who normally resides with a claimant [4or with whom a claimant normally resides.]

[3(2) This paragraph applies to—

(a) any member of the claimant's family;

(b) a child or young person who is living with the claimant but who is not a member of his household by virtue of regulation 16 (circumstances in which a person is to be treated as being or not being a member of the household);

(c) a person who lives with the claimant in order to care for him or for the claimant's partner and who is engaged for that purpose by a charitable or [5voluntary organisation] which makes a charge to the claimant or the claimant's partner for the care provided by that person;

(d) the partner of a person to whom sub-paragraph (c) applies.

(2A) This paragraph applies to a person, other than a close relative of the claimant or the claimant's partner,—

(a) who is liable to make payments on a commercial basis to the claimant or the claimant's partner in respect of his occupation of the claimant's dwelling;

(b) to whom the claimant or the claimant's partner is liable to make payments on a commercial basis in respect of his occupation of that person's dwelling;

(c) who is a member of the household of a person to whom sub-paragraph (a) or (b) applies.

(2B) Subject to paragraph (2C), this paragraph applies to—

(a) a person who jointly occupies the claimant's dwelling and who is either—

(i) a co-owner of that dwelling with the claimant or the claimant's partner (whether or not there are other co-owners); or

(ii) jointly liable with the claimant or the claimant's partner to make payments to a landlord in respect of his occupation of that dwelling,

(b) a partner of a person whom sub-paragraph (a) applies.

(2C) Where a person is a close relative of the claimant or the claimant's partner, paragraph (2B) shall apply to him only if the claimant's, or the claimant's partner's, co-ownership, or joint liability to make payments to a landlord in respect of his occupation, of the dwelling arose either before 11th April 1988, or, if later, on or before the date upon which the claimant or the claimant's partner first occupied the dwelling in question.]

(3) [2 . . .].

(4) For the purposes of this regulation a person resides with another only if they share any accommodation except a bathroom, a lavatory or a communal area [1 but not if each person is separately liable to make payments in respect of his occupation of the dwelling to the landlord].

(5) In this regulation "communal area" means any area (other than rooms) of common access (including halls and passageways) and rooms of common use in sheltered accommodation.

AMENDMENTS

1. Income Support (General) Amendment Regulations 1989 (SI 1989/534) reg.2 (April 10, 1989).

2. Income Support (General) Amendment Regulations 1989 (SI 1989/534) Sch.1 para.2 (October 9, 1989).

3. Income Support (General) Amendment No.6 Regulations 1991 (SI 1991/2334) reg.2 (November 11, 1991).

4. Income-related Benefits Schemes (Miscellaneous Amendments) (No.6) Regulations 1994 (SI 1994/3061) reg.2(2) (December 2, 1994).

5. Income-related Benefits Schemes (Miscellaneous Amendments) Regulations 1995 (SI 1995/516) reg.18 (April 10, 1995).

DEFINITIONS

"child"—see SSCBA s.137(1).
"claimant"—see reg.2(1).
"dwelling"—see SSCBA s.137(1).
"family"—*ibid.*
"partner"—see reg.2(1).
"voluntary organisation"—*ibid.*
"young person"—*ibid.*, and reg.14.

General Note

Paragraph (1)

2.49 The definition of "non-dependant" is important for a number of purposes, particularly deductions from housing costs and qualification for the severe disability premium. Its use for different purposes causes difficulties. What might be a sensible test for determining when a contribution towards accommodation costs ought to be assumed from an independent person who shares the claimant's accommodation might be less sensible in determining a severely disabled person's financial needs.

A person who normally resides with the claimant, or with whom the claimant normally resides, (*Chief Adjudication Officer v Bate* [1996] 2 All E.R. 790, HL also reported as *R(IS) 12/96*), unless within the important exceptions in paras (2)–(2C), is a non-dependant.

The December 1994 amendment to para.(1) was the government's immediate (within 48 hours) response to the Court of Appeal's decision in *Bate v Chief Adjudication Officer and Secretary of State for Social Security* on November 30, 1994 (*The Times*, December 12, 1994). Ms Bate was a severely disabled person who lived in her parents' home. The Court of Appeal decided that because her parents were the "householders", in the sense that it was they who jointly occupied the home as tenants, they did not normally reside with *her*, but she normally resided with *them*. Thus they did not come within the definition of non-dependant at all. The Court recognised that this construction did not fit easily with the amendment to reg.3(2)(d) on April 10, 1989 (now recast in para.(2A)), but did not consider that the meaning of the initial regulation could be determined by later amendments. The April 1989 amendment simply showed that the draftsman had assumed that "residing with the claimant" had the meaning which the Court had rejected. However, the House of Lords disagreed, holding that "resides with" meant no more than that the claimant and the other person lived in the same dwelling. It was not limited to the situation where it was the *claimant's* household or dwelling.

2.50 The December 2, 1994 regulations (SI 1994/3061) were introduced without first being referred to the Social Security Advisory Committee. Section 173(1)(a) of the Administration Act permits this if the Secretary of State considers it inexpedient to refer proposed regulations by reason of urgency. The failure to refer these proposed regulations was challenged by Ms Bate (see Welfare Rights Bulletin 125). It was argued that the Court of Appeal had decided that it was Parliament's intention that people in Ms Bate's position should be entitled to a severe disability premium (and therefore it intended that financial provision should be made for this) and so the Secretary of State could not say that it was urgent that payment of the premium should stop. In addition, the Secretary of State should not be allowed to sidestep the consultation procedure, which Parliament clearly considered important, in this way. (See the comment of Hobhouse LJ in *Chief Adjudication Officer v Palfrey* (reported as part of *R(IS) 26/95*) that one reason at least for the consultation procedure is the "remarkable latitude" given to the maker of regulations in the Social Security Acts.) But leave to bring judicial review was refused both by the High Court and the Court of Appeal.

Paragraphs (4) and (5) provide a partial definition of "resides with." In its original form, para.(4) put forward only one necessary, but not on its own sufficient, condition about sharing accommodation. But the general test of para.(1) still had to be satisfied. On "sharing of accommodation" see *CSIS 185/1995* in the note to para. (4). The post-April 1989 form of para.(4) specifically excludes from the definition a situation where co-residents are separately liable to make payments to a landlord. Such a person is already paying for accommodation costs. "Landlord" does not require there to be a tenancy; licensees can come within the exclusion (*CSIS 43/1992*).

Outside this exclusion the arrangement must still come within the general meaning of "residing with" and be the normal situation to come within the definition in para.(1). In *CSIS 100/1993* the claimant's daughter sometimes stayed in her mother's home and used that address for official correspondence. The Commissioner says that where correspondence is sent is a possible indicator that the daughter normally resided with the claimant, but equally, having regard to the other places the daughter stayed, it could be that she had no "fixed abode" (and thus did not normally reside with the claimant). This is further expanded on in *CIS 14850/1996* where the Commissioner states that for a person to be "normally resident" it was necessary for him to have lived in the house concerned, if not permanently, for a sufficient length of time for it to be regarded as his usual abode. The question of normal residence was a practical one to be determined in the light of common sense (see *CSIS 76/1991*). It would be relevant to consider why the residence started, its duration, the relationship, if any, between the people concerned, including its history; the reason why the residence had been taken up and whether it had lasted longer than its original purpose; and whether there was any alternative residence the person could take up. In that case a woman who was previously unknown to the claimant but who may have been his daughter came to live with him on the breakdown of her marriage. The matrimonial proceedings were protracted and she was also waiting for a council house. When the claimant applied for his income support to be reviewed to include a severe disability premium she had been living in his house for nine months. The Commissioner considered that since they had not previously known each other normal residence might take longer to establish and even longer if they were not in fact close relatives. If "the daughter" was waiting for alternative accommodation her residence could be quite lengthy without necessarily becoming normal. Questions such as what steps she had taken to find other accommodation, or with regard to her former matrimonial home, would also need to be investigated. In *CH/4004/2004* a destitute cousin staying temporarily with the claimant was not "normally" residing with her. See also *AM v SSWP* [2011] UKUT 387 (AAC).

Paragraphs (2)–(2C)

These provisions except those who would otherwise count as non-dependants from coming within that category. The exceptions have been through a convoluted series of forms, whose meaning has been a matter of great controversy. The convolutions are traced in previous editions of J. Mesher and P. Wood, *Income-related Benefits: the Legislation*, and great care must be taken in identifying what form of the regulation is in effect at particular dates which may be relevant to outstanding claims and appeals. See *CIS 20034/1997* for a useful summary of the position in relation to each of the periods from October 9, 1989 for a severely disabled claimant living with his family. The House of Lords in *Foster v Chief Adjudication Officer* [1993] A.C. 754; [1993] 1 All E.R. 705 holds that the amendment made on October 9, 1989 (to add the conditions now substantially contained in para.(2B)(a)(i) and (ii)) was not ultra vires on the ground of irrationality. **2.51**

Note that regs 4–6 of the Income Support (General) Amendment No.6 Regulations 1991 provide transitional protection for claimants who were entitled to the severe disability premium before October 21, 1991, by virtue of the pre-November 1991 form of reg.3 (see p.796).

In *R(IS) 17/94* a Tribunal of Commissioners states that tribunals, when considering, for example, a claimant's right to a severe disability premium, should deal with the position from the date of claim down to the date when the issues are finally decided (preferring the approach of *R(IS) 26/95* to that of *CIS 649/1992*, where the Commissioner held that an adjudicating authority should only consider the position as at the date from which benefit is sought). *CIS 649/1992* is also inconsistent with, for example, *R(IS) 13/93* (see the notes to reg.23(2) of the Adjudication Regulations). But in relation to appeals lodged on or after May 21, 1998, note the effect of s.22(8) of the Administration Act inserted by para.3 of Sch.6 to the Social Security Act 1998 where there is a change of circumstances after the date of the decision under appeal, and now see s.12(8)(b) of the 1998

Act. In addition, *R(IS) 17/94* dealt with an argument that once a claimant had acquired a right to a severe disability premium, its removal by subsequent amendment of reg.3(2) was prevented by s.16(1)(c) of the Interpretation Act (protection of acquired rights). Section 16 applies unless the contrary intention appears. The Commissioners hold that the words "shall come into force in relation to a particular claimant" in reg.1(1) of SI 1989/534 (the regulations at issue) indicated that the regulations were intended to apply to existing claimants. A claim made after the regulations came into force would be subject to them without the need for these words. Thus they were clearly intended to provide for existing claimants.

Paragraph (2)

2.52 These four categories excluded from the definition of non-dependant have been in the regulation since 1988 and are relatively straightforward. They cover those who are not sufficiently independent of the claimant to be a non-dependant.

(a) A member of the family. This, by reference to s.137(1) of the Contributions and Benefits Act, covers children and 16–18-year-olds treated as in full time secondary level education as well as partners, but only if members of the same household.

(b) Children who are not members of the family under the operation of the special rules in reg.16.

(c) Certain carers provided at a charge by charities or voluntary bodies, plus the carer's partner.

Paragraph (2A)

2.53 This is a recasting in November 1991 of the previous para.(2)(d)–(db). The difference is that a close relative (defined in reg.2(1)) of the claimant or his partner does not come within para.(2A). Thus, for instance, the parents of a severely disabled person may no longer come within para.(2A). If they are not to be non-dependants from November 1991, they must come within paras (2B) and (2C). Outside the close relative exception, the effect of para.(2A) now is that where the relationship between the claimant (or the claimant's partner) and the other person (or a member of that person's household) is a commercial one, that person is not a non-dependant. No further contribution to accommodation costs is therefore appropriate.

There must be a legal liability (as distinct from a moral or ethical obligation *(CIS 754/1991)*) to make payments for accommodation, i.e. rent or a board and lodging charge, on a commercial basis. The first question is whether there is a liability to pay. It has been held on the pre-November 1991 version of para.(2A) that a severely disabled claimant living with, for example, his parents can be their licensee and therefore liable to pay for his accommodation in the sense that if no payment is made the licence could terminate (*CIS 195/1991*, *CIS 754/1991*). In deciding whether such a liability exists there would need to be findings as to the terms on which a claimant lives in his parents' home, the amount and regularity of the payments and the use made of the claimant's contributions. If the payments go towards rent or a mortgage that would be a stronger case than if they are used for the claimant's own personal needs (*CIS 754/1991*), however, they need not be applied directly to accommodation costs. If the claimant's contributions go into a general fund used for household costs (including accommodation) that will suffice (*R(IS)17/94*). It will then be necessary to conclude on the basis of the relevant findings whether there was an intention to create legal relations. Such an intention can be inferred from a course of conduct (see Scarman LJ in *Horrocks v Forray* [1976] 1 W.L.R. 230 at 239). *CIS 754/1991* holds that this might not be too difficult to infer where an adult member of the family is making regular payments in respect of his occupation. It may be easier to infer where the parents depend on the claimant's contributions because of their own financial circumstances. In his directions to the new SSAT in *CIS 754/1991* the Commissioner concludes:

> "In essence there should be what I might call a broad approach to satisfaction of the condition keeping in mind that the AO has throughout accepted that in [*CIS 195/1991*] it was right to conclude that the claimant [had a liability to make payments in respect of his occupation]. I should have thought that the facts in many of the cases are likely to be essentially indistinguishable from those in [*CIS/195/1991*]."

The facts in *CIS/195/1991* were that the claimant's parents took £20 per week from his benefit. The rest of the money was used for his own needs. The SSAT found that the claimant lived in his parents' house as a licensee and paid them £20 in respect of his occupation of it.

But what of the situation where there can be no contractual liability because one of the parties lacks the capacity to make a contract? In *CIS 195/1991* the claimant was held to be capable of incurring a liability to make payment, despite his mental disability. Under English law the contract was voidable because of his mental disability, not void. However, in Scottish law an "incapax" is not capable of making any personal contract. *R(IS) 17/94* holds that in Scottish cases ATs must first consider whether a claimant is so mentally incapacitated as to be incapax. Although, if this is the case, the doctrine of recompense may well apply to establish a liability on the incapax, so that the result is similar in practical terms to that in *CIS 195/1991* (see 1993 Supplement for fuller discussion of *R(IS) 17/94*, the reported version of *CSIS 28/1992* and *CSIS 40/1992*). The doctrine of recompense is also considered in *CSIS 641/1995*, although on the particular facts of that case (see the summary in the 1998 Supplement to J. Mesher and P. Wood, *Income-related Benefits: the Legislation*) it did not apply. In *CIS 754/1991* the Commissioner expresses the *obiter* view that where a person has no contractual capacity at all, the doctrine of restitution does not seem available to assist claimants in England in the way that recompense can in Scotland. Thus in English cases for mentally disabled claimants it will generally be necessary for there to be a finding of sufficient contractual capacity. On the facts of both *CIS 195/1991* and *CIS 754/1991* the capacity required does not seem to be of a very high order. The claimant in *CIS 754/1991* was found to have sufficient contractual capacity despite having Downs syndrome and needing an appointee to act for her in social security matters.

Since October 1, 1990, the liability to pay has had to be on a commercial basis. 2.54
The words "commercial basis" govern the nature of the liability, not just the quality of the payments made (*R(IS) 17/94*). For a discussion of "commercial basis" see *CSB 1163/1988* and the notes to the definition of "board and lodging accommodation" in reg.2(1). In *CIS 195/1991* (approved in *R(IS) 17/94*) the Commissioner held that the question of whether an arrangement is on a commercial basis was entirely one of fact for the SSAT. What has to be considered is whether the arrangement is the sort that might have been entered into if the parents had taken in a lodger, instead of, in *CIS 195/1991*, their physically and mentally handicapped son. This approach was also expressly approved by another Tribunal of Commissioners in *R(IS) 11/98*. The claimant, who was severely disabled, lived with her parents and paid them £25 per week. The Commissioners emphasise that *CIS 195/1991* had only considered that a commercial arrangement in a family situation was unlikely, not that it was impossible or even improbable. They also confirm that a profit element is not necessary, nor was it relevant whether the family depended financially on the payments or whether they would take any action if the claimant did not pay (although these last two factors were relevant to the question of whether there was a liability to make payments, see *CIS 754/1991*). The Commissioners rejected the AO's contention that in considering the adequacy of the claimant's payments a deduction should be made for the value of the care

provided by the parents, pointing out that reg.3 referred to payments in respect of the *occupation* of the dwelling.

Although there might still be some scope for structuring an informal relationship to get within para.(2A), the requirement of a commercial basis (since October 1, 1990) and the exclusion of close relatives (from November 11, 1991) provide quite a stringent control. Note the transitional protection in regs 4–6 of the Income Support (General) Amendment No.6 Regulations 1991 (see p.796) for claimants entitled to the severe disability premium before October 21, 1991.

Tribunals faced with sorting out severe disability premium entitlement, in particular for the periods October 9, 1989 to September 30, 1990 and October 1, 1990 to November 10, 1991, will need to pay particular regard to the Commissioners' decisions discussed above. There is a useful summary of the position in relation to each of the periods from October 9, 1989 in *CIS 20034/1997*.

Paragraphs (2B)–(2C)

2.55 These provisions replace the previous para.(2)(c) on joint occupiers, and impose a considerably stricter test. The biggest change in November 1991 was to exclude joint occupiers who are close relatives (see reg.2(1)) from the operation of para.(2B) except in restricted circumstances. This is done by para.(2C). If the close relative met the conditions of para.(2B) either before April 11, 1988, or as soon as the claimant or partner moved to the current home, then advantage can be taken of para.(2B). The aim is to exclude arrangements made within a family (in the non-income support sense) designed to take advantage of the definition of a non-dependant. The thinking is that if the arrangement was the basis on which the occupation of the home by the claimant started it is likely to be a genuine one. Existing claimants excluded by this rule may particularly benefit from the transitional protection mentioned above. *CIS 80/1994* rejects the argument that para.(2C) is invalid on the ground that it operates retrospectively. The Commissioner states that para.(2C) imposes a new condition of future eligibility (though with reference to past events). Thus it does not take away any vested right or create any new obligation in regard to events that have already passed.

In *CIS 650/1993* the claimant had been a joint tenant of her home with her husband. When he died in 1990 she became the sole tenant. Later her sister came to live with her and they became joint tenants. The Commissioner rejects the claimant's contention that the previous joint liability of the claimant and her husband meant that para.(2C) was satisfied. In the context of reg.3, para.(2C) only referred to the joint liability of the claimant and the person currently residing with her and not to any other joint liability.

In *CIS 216/1997* the claimant who was in receipt of the severe disability premium gave up the tenancy of her local authority home (with effect from January 22, 1995) and went to live with her daughter and her family. She moved to her daughter's home on January 16, 1995 and became a joint tenant with her of that home on January 23, 1995. During the week from January 16–22, the claimant was moving her belongings from her old home to her new, although she slept at her daughter's home from January 16. The Commissioner decides that the claimant was to be regarded as having "first occupied" her new home when she first normally resided there. It was clear from the evidence that arrangements for the joint tenancy had been made with the local authority before the claimant moved in with her daughter. The move and the creation of the joint tenancy were inextricably linked. In his view the claimant did not finally become an occupier of her new home until January 23, 1995 and so para.(2C) applied.

2.56 The rest of para.(2B) is based on the provisions in force from October 1989. First, there must be joint occupation of the claimant's home. In *CIS 180/1989* the claimant was a single woman in receipt of attendance allowance, severe disablement allowance and income support. She lived with her parents, who owned the house. The Commissioner held that "jointly occupies" is not to be given a technical meaning, but its ordinary meaning. The phrase applies where "persons who normally reside together jointly occupy the premises in the sense of equality of access and use as distinct from a situation where restrictions are imposed in relation to those matters." It did not matter, under the legislation in force at the relevant time, that the claimant did not have any proprietary interest in the house. *CIS 180/1989* (approved by the Tribunal of Commissioners in *R(IS)17/94*) has governed the position, particularly in severe disability premium cases, for the period before October 9, 1989, when amendments to impose the extra conditions now substantially contained in para.(2B)(a)(i) and (ii) were made. Indeed, it has been usual for AOs to concede that for the period before October 9, 1989, parents or other family members are not non-dependants.

It might be objected that the approach of *CIS 180/1989* expanded the exception on joint occupation so far that it excluded everyone who would be caught by the primary definition of a non-dependant. This is not so. People can reside together, but without the equality of access and use stressed by the Commissioner. The House of Lords in the *Foster* case, where it was conceded that the claimant's parents were joint occupiers up to October 9, 1989, expressed similar doubts that the exception, if widely construed, might eat up the rule, but did not reach any authoritative conclusion. In a decision on the equivalent housing benefit provision (*Fullwood v Chesterfield BC, The Times*, June 15, 1993) the Court of Appeal specifically rejected the basis of *CIS 180/1989*, holding that "jointly occupies" is a technical legal phrase, meaning "occupies by right jointly with one or more persons". Thus, joint occupation entails either a joint tenancy or joint liability to make payments under an agreement for occupation. This decision strictly only related to housing benefit, but both the Court of Appeal and the House of Lords in *Bate* (see above) accepted that the phrase should be given the same meaning for the purposes of income support. It connoted a legal relationship and not merely factual co-residence.

From October 9, 1989, it has been specifically provided that one of two extra conditions must be satisfied. One is that the claimant (or partner) is a "co-owner" of the home with the other person (or partner), a concept that can include at least some beneficial owners who are not also legal owners: see *SSWP v HB (SPC)* [2015] UKUT 0389 (AAC). This is unchanged since October 9, 1989. The other condition is that there is joint liability to make payments in respect of the occupation of the home to a landlord. This was changed in November 1991 from the October 9, 1989 form to specify that the payments must be to a landlord. The result is broadly to confirm the outcome of *CIS 299/1990* (discussed in the 1991 edition of J. Mesher and P. Wood, *Income-related Benefits: the Legislation*) and to remove the problem of interpretation addressed in that decision. These conditions narrowed the scope of para.(2B) considerably. Where there is separate, rather than joint, liability a person is deemed not to be residing with the claimant (para.(4)).

Paragraph (3)

The revocation removes the special rule for boarders and hostel-dwellers. **2.57**

Paragraph (4)

2.58 The original form of para.(4) merely meant that if accommodation other than bathroom, lavatory or a communal area was not shared, one person was not "residing with" another. It did not mean that the person was "residing with" the other just because such accommodation was shared. The general test of para.(1) still has to be satisfied. See *R(IS)12/06*, *CSIS/100/1993*, *CIS/14850/1996*, and also *Kadhim v London Borough of Brent Housing Benefit Review Board* (CA, unreported, December 20, 2000) which reaches the same view on the similar provision in reg.3(4) of the Housing Benefit Regulations. Paragraph 4 now also excludes from the definition of non-dependant a person who is separately liable to make payments to the landlord. See *CSIS 43/1992* above. Joint tenants and co-owners (other than close relatives of the claimant or partner) are excluded by para.(2B)(a).

CSIS 185/1995 holds that a person does not share a kitchen with another if it is not used physically by him but only by a third party to prepare food on his behalf. The Commissioner also points out that the issue is whether there is a "sharing of *accommodation*". So deciding whether the claimant shared a room simply because some of her clothes were stored there, would depend on what use, if any, the claimant made of the room, by considering what was stored there, in what, and to what extent, if any, the claimant herself went in and out of the room to deal with her property.

[1Permitted period

2.59 **3A.**—(1) For the purposes of regulation 17(6), [2. . .], paragraph 7(6) of Schedule 3A, paragraph 6(3) of Schedule 3B and paragraphs 4 and 6 of Schedule 8 (applicable amounts, mortgage interest, protected sums and earnings to be disregarded), where a claimant has ceased to be entitled to income support—

(a) because he or his partner becomes engaged in remunerative work the permitted period, [3. . .] shall be 12 weeks; or

(b) for any other reason, the permitted period shall be eight weeks.

(2) [3. . .].

(3) [3. . .].

AMENDMENTS

1. Income Support (General) Amendment No.3 Regulations 1989 (SI 1989/1678) reg.2 (October 9, 1989).

2. Social Security (Income Support, Claims and Payments and Adjudication) Amendment Regulations 1995 (SI 1995/2927) reg.4 (December 12, 1995).

3. Income Support (General) (Jobseeker's Allowance Consequential Amendments) Regulations 1996 (SI 1996/206) reg.3 (October 7, 1996).

GENERAL NOTE

2.60 Regulation 3A provides a definition of the maximum permitted period of break in entitlement for the application of the various provisions set out in para.(1).

The omission of paras (2) and (3) is a consequence of the introduction of jobseeker's allowance on October 7, 1996.

Schedules 3A and 3B were revoked by SI 2006/588 with effect from April 3, 2006. However, para.(1) has not been amended to reflect that change.

PART II

CONDITIONS OF ENTITLEMENT

[1Prescribed categories of person

2.61 **4ZA.**—(1) Subject to the following provisions of this regulation, a person to whom any paragraph of Schedule 1B applies falls within a prescribed category of person for the purposes of section 124(1)(e) of the Contributions and Benefits Act (entitlement to income support).

(2) Paragraph (1) does not apply to a [4 full-time student] during the period of study.

(3) A[4 full-time student] during the period of study falls within a prescribed category of person for the purposes of section 124(1)(e) of the Contributions and Benefits Act only if—

(a) [[11] . . .]
(b) paragraph 1, 2, [[10] . . .] 11, [[10] . . .] [[8] 15A,] or 18 of Schedule 1B applies to him; or
[[7] (c) any other paragraph of Schedule 1B applies to him and—
(i) in the case of a person with a partner, the partner is also a full-time student and either he or his partner is treated as responsible for a child or young person, or
(ii) in any other case, he is treated as responsible for a child or young person,
but this provision applies only for the period of the summer vacation appropriate to his course; [[9] . . .]
[[6] (d) [[9] . . .]]

[[5](3A) Paragraph (1) does not apply to a person to whom section 6 of the Children (Leaving Care) Act 2000 (exclusion from benefits) applies.]

[[2](4) A person who falls within a prescribed category in Schedule 1B for the purposes of this regulation for any day in a benefit week, shall fall within that category for the whole of that week.]

AMENDMENTS

1. Income Support (General) (Jobseeker's Allowance Consequential Amendments) Regulations 1996 (SI 1996/206) reg.4 (October 7, 1996).

2. Income-related Benefits and Jobseeker's Allowance (Amendment) (No.2) Regulations 1997 (SI 1997/2197) reg.5(2) (October 6, 1997).

3. Social Security (Immigration and Asylum) Consequential Amendments Regulations 2000 (SI 2000/636) reg.3(3) (April 3, 2000).

4. Social Security Amendment (Students) Regulations 2000 (SI 2000/1981) reg.5(5) and Sch. (July 31, 2000).

5. Children (Leaving Care) Act 2000 (Commencement No.2 and Consequential Provisions) Order 2001 (SI 2001/3070) art.3(2) and Sch.1 para.(a) (October 1, 2001).

6. Social Security (Adult Learning Option) Amendment Regulations 2006 (SI 2006/2144) reg.2 (September 1, 2006).

7. Social Security (Students Responsible for Children or Young Persons) Amendment Regulations 2008 (SI 2008/1826) reg.2 (July 9, 2008).

8. Social Security (Miscellaneous Amendments) Regulations 2009 (SI 2009/583) reg.2(4) (April 6, 2009).

9. Social Security (Miscellaneous Amendments) (No.4) Regulations 2009 (SI 2009/2655) reg.2(3) (October 26, 2009).

10. Income Support (Prescribed Categories of Person) Regulations 2009 (SI 2009/3152) reg.3(2)(a) and 3(7) (December, 30, 2009). Regulation 3(2)(a) omitted "10," and "12," in reg.4ZA(3)(b) with effect from December 30, 2009 but reg.3(7) provided that this did not apply in the case of a person who was subject to the saving provisions in reg.2(2) of those Regulations. See the 2015/16 edition of this volume for these Regulations and the notes to them.

11. Social Security (Miscellaneous Amendments) (No.3) Regulations 2013 (SI 2013/2536) reg.4(3) (October 29, 2013).

DEFINITIONS

"child"—see SSCBA s.137(1).
"benefit week"—see reg.2(1).
"full-time student"—see reg.61(1).
"partner"—see reg.2(1).
"period of study"—*ibid.*
"young person"—see reg.14.

General Note

Paragraph (1)

2.62 As a consequence of the introduction of JSA on October 7, 1996, the income support scheme had to undergo a fundamental restructuring. Income support was no longer available to people who are claiming benefit because they are unemployed. People who have to be available for, and actively seeking, work as a condition of receiving benefit have to claim JSA. Since October 7, 1996, in order to qualify for income support a person has to fall within a "prescribed category" (see SSCBA s.124(1)(e)). These categories are set out in Sch.1B. When Sch.1B was first introduced the categories broadly resembled most of those in the former Sch.1 (people not required to be available for employment) which was revoked on October 7, 1996, but there were some differences. See the notes to Sch.1B. For the position of full-time students, see paras (2) and (3). Note also para.(3A) (see below).

Schedule 1B provides an exhaustive list of the circumstances in which a person will be entitled to income support. There is no category of analogous circumstances or provision for a reduced rate of benefit on the ground of hardship for people who do not come within these categories (compare the former reg.8(3), see the 1996 edition of J. Mesher and P. Wood, *Income-related Benefits: the Legislation*). Moreover, the provision for hardship payments under JSA is considerably restricted (see regs 140–146 of the JSA Regulations 1996 and the notes to those regulations (regs 146A–146H in the case of joint-claim couples)). Pt VI of the Income Support Regulations, which formerly contained some very limited provision for urgent cases outside the normal scope of the income support rules, was revoked (subject to three savings: see the note to Pt VI) with effect from January 25, 2010.

Note that entitlement to income support and JSA is mutually exclusive, although some people may be eligible for either. Section 124(1)(f) of the Contributions and Benefits Act provides that entitlement to JSA excludes entitlement to income support (any "top-up" to a person's contribution-based JSA will be by way of income-based JSA). Similarly, a person will not be entitled to JSA (contribution- or income-based) if he is entitled to income support (ss.2(1)(d) and 3(1)(b) of the Jobseekers Act). However, there is nothing to prevent a person who qualifies for income support claiming JSA if he also fulfils the conditions of entitlement for JSA. But in most circumstances it will be better for him to claim income support so as to avoid the risk of being "sanctioned" for not complying with the labour market conditions. If the claimant is a member of a couple he will not be entitled to income support if his partner is claiming *income-based* JSA (SSCBA s.124(1)(f)). If his partner is claiming *contribution-based* JSA he will be able to claim income support if he is eligible for this, or his partner (or, from March 19, 2001, he and his partner in the case of most (since February 25, 2008, all, unless exempt) childless couples) can claim income-based JSA. Before October 27, 2008, if the claimant was incapable of work it was better for him to claim income support in order to qualify for the disability premium under para.12(1)(b) of Sch.2 after serving the appropriate waiting period. This was because if the only basis for qualifying for the premium was incapacity for work for 364 days (or 196 days if he was terminally ill), his partner would not be able to get a JSA disability premium for him (see para.14 of Sch.1 to the JSA Regulations 1996). However, following the introduction of ESA on October 27, 2008 *new* claims for income support on the ground of incapacity for work were no longer possible (see further the note to para.7 of Sch.1B in the 2015/16 edition of this volume). Finally, note the "better-off" problem for some claimants as a result of the limit for remunerative work for partners being 24 hours a week from October 7, 1996 (see reg.5(1A) and reg.51(1)(b) JSA Regulations 1996). The consequence of this is that if the claimant's partner is working between 16 and 24 hours a week the couple will have to consider whether they will gain more by claiming working tax credit; see further Vol.IV of this series.

2.63 A further substantial contraction in the number of people covered by income support occurred on October 6, 2003 when the state pension credit scheme commenced. Claimants who have reached "the qualifying age for state pension credit" are not entitled to income support (see s.124(1)(aa) of the Contributions and Benefits Act 1992) and have to claim state pension credit. "The qualifying age for state pension credit" is defined in s.137(1) of the Contributions and Benefits Act 1992—the effect of that definition is that the qualifying age was 60 but from April 2010 it will gradually rise in line with the staged increase in pensionable age for women until it reaches 65 in November 2018 (this equalisation of the state pension age for men and women was previously to have been completed by April 5, 2020 but the timetable for this in the Pensions Act 1995 has been accelerated with effect from April 2016 so that women's state pension age will now be 65 by November 2018; in addition, the increase in state pension age to 66 for both men and women has been brought forward—it will start to rise from 65 in December 2018 to reach 66 by October 2020 (see s.1 of the Pensions Act 2011) and between 2026 and 2028 it will rise to 67 (see s.26 of the Pensions Act 2014)). A claimant whose partner is entitled to (i.e. who has claimed and been awarded) state pension credit is also ineligible (s.124(1)(g) of the 1992 Act). Thus a couple with one member over the qualifying age for state pension credit and the other under that age (who are not already in receipt of state pension credit) can chose to claim either income support (or JSA, or from October 27, 2008, ESA, if eligible) or state pension credit. It will normally be advantageous to claim state pension credit. For an overview of the state pension credit scheme see the Introduction and General Note at the beginning of the State Pension Credit Act 2002.

Note also that with effect from April 6, 2004 when the process of transferring all financial support for children and young persons from income support to child tax credit began, income support has in effect become an "adults only benefit" for many claimants. The transfer of "the child elements" to child tax credit for existing claimants was intended to start in October 2004 but has been repeatedly delayed and it now seems that the transfer process will not take place at all and the situation will be resolved by the abolition of income support and child tax credit and their replacement by universal credit. See further the note to reg.17.

Most recently, the year 2008 saw two substantial changes to the categories of people who can claim income support that will limit eligibility for this benefit still further. The first was the commencement on October 27, 2008 of the ESA scheme, which replaced incapacity benefit, severe disablement allowance and income support on the grounds of incapacity or disability for most (but not all) new claimants. Existing claimants who were receiving income support on the grounds of incapacity or disability continued to be entitled to this, although the process of "migrating" these claimants (and incapacity benefit and severe disablement claimants) to ESA began on a national basis (there had been a pilot in Aberdeen and Burnley from October 2010) on February 28, 2011. See the Employment and Support Allowance (Transitional Provisions, Housing Benefit and Council Tax Benefit) (Existing Awards) (No.2) Regulations 2010 (SI 2010/1907) (as amended) ("the Migration Regulations") in Vol.I of this series, which establish the framework within which most "existing awards" will either be converted to awards of ESA or terminated, and the notes to those Regulations. "Existing award" is defined in para.11 of Sch.4 to the Welfare Reform Act 2007 and covers awards of incapacity benefit, severe disablement allowance and income support under regs 6(4)(a) or 13(2)(b) or (bb), or paras 7(a) or (b), 10, 12 or 13 of Sch.1B. Note that reg.6(4)(a) (disabled workers) was revoked on January 25, 2010 (although there is some transitional protection: see the note to reg.6(4)(a)). In addition, reg.6(4)(a) was not included in the definition of "income support on the grounds of disability" in reg.1(4) of the Employment and Support Allowance (Transitional Provisions) Regulations 2008 (SI 2008/795) (as amended) (see Vol.I of this series for these Regulations). The result is that *claims* (see the notes to the Income Support (Prescribed Categories of Person) Regulations 2009 (SI 2009/3152) in the 2015/16 edition of this volume) under reg.6(4)(a) made in respect of a period on or after October 27, 2008 did not fall within the linking provisions in reg.2(2) of the Transitional Provisions Regulations because they were not claims for income support "on the grounds of disability" and so were treated as claims for ESA. However, a claimant who still has a transitionally protected award of income support under reg.6(4)(a) will be subject to the conversion process. For further details of claimants who (until converted) are still eligible for income support under reg.13(2)(b) or (bb), or paras 7(a) or (b), 10, 12 or 13 of Sch.1B, see the note to the respective provision in the 2015/16 edition of this volume.

2.64 It was intended that the conversion process to ESA would be completed by the end of March 2014 but it is not clear whether this was achieved.

The second significant development was that with effect from November 24, 2008 lone parents with an only or youngest child aged 12 or over were no longer entitled to income support solely on the grounds of being a lone parent (this change was introduced in stages for existing claimants). This was extended to exclude lone parents whose only or youngest child was aged 10 or over from October 26, 2009 and those whose only or youngest child was aged seven or over from October 25, 2010. From May 21, 2012 entitlement to income support solely on the grounds of being a lone parent has been limited to those lone parents whose sole or youngest child is aged under five (although note that since that date any lone parent who is under 18 will be eligible for income support (regardless of the age of her child)). See further the note to para.1 of Sch.1B.

In view of the sustained and continuing reduction in the coverage of the income support scheme, s.9 of the Welfare Reform Act 2009, which made provision for the abolition of income support when "the Secretary of State considers that it is no longer appropriate" for there to be any prescribed categories of people who qualify for income support, came as no great surprise. Section 9 has not been brought into force and has been overtaken by the provisions in the Welfare Reform Act 2012 to introduce a new benefit for working-age claimants—universal credit—which will replace income support, income-based JSA, income-related ESA, housing benefit, working tax credit and child tax credit. It was originally intended that this would be introduced on a national basis from October 2013. However, in the event it was not until April 2016 that new claims were extended to the whole of the country and then only for a restricted category of claimant. See further the note to reg.1 of the JSA Regulations 2013 in Pt VI of this book.

Paragraphs (2) and (3)

2.65 The effect of paras (2) and (3) is to exclude most full-time students (defined in reg.61(1)) from entitlement to income support from the beginning of their course to the end (see the definition of period of study in reg.2(1)).

A full-time student will only be entitled during his/her period of study if s/he is a lone parent whose youngest child is under five, or if s/he is under 18 (regardless of the age of her/his child), a single foster parent, a person who is in non-advanced education and entitled under para.15A of Sch.1B, or a refugee learning English (para.(3)(b); note that para.11 of Sch.1B, also listed in para.(3)(b), is no longer relevant as it applied to disabled full-time students who did not fall under para.7 of the former Sch.1 following its amendment on September 1, 1990).

Until December 30, 2009 para.(3)(b) also included students to whom paras 10 or 12 of Sch.1B applied, although as a consequence of the introduction of ESA, *new* claims for income support on these grounds were no longer possible from October 27, 2008, except in certain circumstances. Paragraph 10 covered students who qualified for the disability or severe disability premium, or had been incapable of work, or treated as incapable of work, or treated as capable of work by virtue of reg.18 of the Incapacity for Work Regulations (disqualification for misconduct, etc.), or entitled to statutory sick pay, for at least 28 weeks (two or more periods separated by not more than eight weeks counted as continuous). Paragraph 12 covered students who were receiving a disabled student's allowance on the grounds of deafness. Both paragraphs were revoked on December 30, 2009, subject to a saving provision. See pp.256–257 of the 2015/16 edition of this volume under "*Consequences of the introduction of ESA*", "*Revocation of paragraphs 10 and 12 on December 30, 2009*" and "*Migration to ESA*" for further details.

2.66 Under the new form of para.(3)(c) (introduced on July 9, 2008 as a consequence of the decision in *CJSA/2663/2006* (see the note to reg.15 of the JSA Regulations 1996) in order to remove the discrimination previously contained in para.(3)(c)), a student who is a single person with responsibility for a child or young person is eligible for income support during the summer vacation on the same basis as a student couple with responsibility for a child or young person. The student (or the claimant for the student couple) must come within one of the categories of people who can claim income support. Similar amendments have been made to reg.15 of the JSA Regulations 1996.

Sub-paragraph (d), which provided for a further category of exempt student to cover a person who was taking part in the "Adult Learning Option" scheme (part of the "New Deal for Skills"), was revoked on October 26, 2009 because that scheme ceased in 2008.

Similarly, sub-para.(a), which covered a full-time student who had limited leave to enter or remain in the UK without recourse to public funds but who was temporarily without funds because remittances from abroad had been interrupted, was revoked on October 29, 2013. This is because entitlement to income support in those circumstances (under reg.2(1) of and para.1 of Pt I of the Schedule to the Social Security (Immigration and Asylum) Consequentional Amendments Regulations 2000 (SI 2000/636)) was abolished with effect from October 29, 2013.

Paragraph (3A)

Section 6 of the Children (Leaving Care) Act 2000 (p.185) excludes certain 16- and 17-year-olds who have been looked after by a local authority in England or Wales on or after October 1, 2001, or by a local authority in Scotland on or after April 1, 2004, from entitlement to income support, income-based JSA and housing benefit. Regulation 2 of the Children (Leaving Care) Social Security Benefits Regulations 2001 (SI 2001/3074) and reg.2 of the Children (Leaving Care) Social Security Benefits (Scotland) Regulations 2004 (SI 2004/747) provide for exceptions to the exclusion from income support and income-based JSA (but not housing benefit). For a discussion of s.6, the relevant definitions and the exceptions, see the notes to reg.2 of the Children (Leaving Care) Social Security Benefits Regulations 2001 (p.956) and to reg.2 of the Children (Leaving Care) Social Security Benefits (Scotland) Regulations 2004 (p.960). **2.67**

Note that s.6(1) of the 2000 Act has not been amended following the introduction of ESA on October 27, 2008 as to exclude entitlement to income-related ESA. This would appear to be an oversight as a purported amendment to reg.2(1) of the Children (Leaving Care) Social Security Benefits Regulations 2001 (SI 2001/3074) has been made to include a reference to income-related ESA. However, in view of the fact that s.6 has not been amended to exclude entitlement to ESA, such an amendment to the 2001 Regulations is not necessary (and is ultra vires).

Note also that reg.2 of the 2001 Regulations has not been amended to take account of the changes in Wales to s.6 made by the Social Services and Well-being (Wales) Act 2014. Thus, as things stand at the moment, the exceptions to the s.6 exclusion do not apply in Wales with effect from April 6, 2014.

Paragraph (4)

This confirms that if a person satisfies any of the paragraphs in Sch.1B on any day in a benefit week, he is treated as doing so for the whole of that week. **2.68**

Temporary absence from Great Britain

4.—(1) Where a claimant is entitled to income support for a period immediately preceding a period of temporary absence from Great Britain, his entitlement to income support [2 shall continue only— **2.69**

(a) in the circumstances specified in paragraph (2), during the first 4 weeks of that period of temporary absence; and

(b) in the circumstances specified in paragraph (3), during the first 8 weeks of that period.]

(2) The circumstances in which a claimant's entitlement to income support is to continue during the first four weeks of a temporary absence from Great Britain are that—

(a) the period of absence is unlikely to exceed 52 weeks; and

(b) while absent from Great Britain, the claimant continues to satisfy the other conditions of entitlement to income support; and

(c) any one of the following conditions apply—

(i) the claimant falls within one or more of the prescribed categories of person listed in Schedule 1B other than paragraphs 7, 15, 20, 21, 24, 25, 26 or 27 of that Schedule; or

(ii) the claimant falls within paragraph 7 of Schedule 1B (persons incapable of work) and his absence from Great Britain is for the sole purpose of receiving treatment from an appropriately qualified person for the incapacity by reason of which he satisfies the conditions of that paragraph; or]

(iii) he is in Northern Ireland; or

(iv) he is a member of a couple and he and his partner are both absent from Great Britain, and a premium referred to in paragraphs 9, [5 9A,] 10, 11 or 13 of Schedule 2 (applicable amounts) is applicable in respect of his partner; [1 or

[3 (v) on the day on which the absence began he had satisfied the provisions of [4 paragraph 7 of Schedule 1B] (persons incapable of work) for a continuous period of not less than—

(aa) 196 days in the case of a claimant who is terminally ill within the meaning of section 30B(4) of the Contributions and Benefits Act, or who is entitled to the highest rate of the care component of disability living allowance[9 , armed forces independence payment] [8 or the enhanced rate of the daily living component of personal independence payment]; or

(bb) 364 days in any other case,

and for this purpose any two or more separate periods separated by a break of not more than 56 days shall be treated as one continuous period.]]

[2 (3) The circumstances in which a claimant's entitlement to income support is to continue during the first 8 weeks of a temporary absence from Great Britain are that—

(a) the period of absence is unlikely to exceed 52 weeks; and

(b) the claimant continues to satisfy the other conditions of entitlement to income support; and

(c) the claimant is, or the claimant and any other member of his family are, accompanying a member of the claimant's family who is a child or young person solely in connection with arrangements made for the treatment of that child or young person for a disease or bodily or mental disablement; and

(d) those arrangements relate to treatment—

(i) outside Great Britain;

(ii) during the period whilst the claimant is, or the claimant and any member of his family are, temporarily absent from Great Britain; and

(iii) by, or under the supervision of, a person appropriately qualified to carry out that treatment.

[6(3A) A claimant's entitlement to income support shall continue during a period of temporary absence from Great Britain if—

(a) he satisfied the conditions of entitlement to income support immediately before the beginning of that period of temporary absence; and

[7(b) that period of temporary absence is for the purpose of the claimant receiving treatment at a hospital or other institution outside Great Britain where the treatment is being provided—

(i) under section 6(2) of the Health Service Act (performance of functions outside England) or section 6(2) of the Health Service (Wales) Act (performance of functions outside Wales);

(ii) pursuant to arrangements made under section 12(1) of the Health Service Act (Secretary of State's arrangements with other bodies), section 10(1) of the Health Service (Wales) Act (Welsh Minister's arrangements with other bodies), paragraph 18 of Schedule 4 to the Health Service Act (joint exercise of functions) or paragraph 18 of Schedule 3 to the Health Service (Wales) Act (joint exercise of functions); or

(iii) under any equivalent provision in Scotland or pursuant to arrangements made under such provision.]]

(4) In paragraphs (2) and (3) "appropriately qualified" means qualified to provide medical treatment, physiotherapy or a form of treatment which is similar to, or related to, either of those forms of treatment.]

AMENDMENTS

1. Income Support (General) Amendment Regulations 1988 (SI 1988/663) reg.3 (April 11, 1988).

2. Income Support (General) Amendment Regulations 1990 (SI 1990/547) reg.3 (April 9, 1990).

3. Disability Working Allowance and Income Support (General) Amendment Regulations 1995 (SI 1995/482) reg.5 (April 13, 1995).

4. Income Support (General) (Jobseeker's Allowance Consequential Amendments) Regulations 1996 (SI 1996/206) reg.5 (October 7, 1996).

5. Income-related Benefits Schemes and Social Fund (Miscellaneous Amendments) Regulations 1996 (SI 1996/1944) reg.6(3) (October 7, 1996).

6. Social Security (Income Support and Jobseeker's Allowance) Amendment Regulations 2004 (SI 2004/1869) reg.2 (October 4, 2004).

7. Social Security (Miscellaneous Amendments) (No.6) Regulations 2008 (SI 2008/2767) reg.2(1) and (3) (November 17, 2008).

8. Personal Independence Payment (Supplementary Provisions and Consequential Amendments) Regulations 2013 (SI 2013/388) reg.8 and Sch. para.11(1) and (3) (April 8, 2013).

9. Armed Forces and Reserve Forces Compensation Scheme (Consequential Provisions: Subordinate Legislation) Order 2013 (SI 2013/591) art.7 and Sch. para.4(1) and (3) (April 8, 2013).

DEFINITIONS

"claimant"—see reg.2(1).
"couple"—*ibid.*
"disability living allowance"—*ibid.*
"partner"—*ibid.*

General Note

2.70 This provision takes over from reg.3 of the old Conditions of Entitlement Regulations a limited right to benefit during the claimant's absence from Great Britain (normally excluded by s.124(1) of the Contributions and Benefits Act; 1986 Act, s.20(3)); see *Perry v Chief Adjudication Officer, The Times*, October 20, 1998, also reported as *R(IS) 4/99*, in the note to s.124(1)). Great Britain means England, Scotland and Wales. If it is the claimant's partner who is temporarily absent, see Sch.7 para.11.

Paragraph (1)

2.71 The absence must be temporary, on the meaning of which see *Chief Adjudication Officer v Ahmed, The Times*, April 6, 1994 (Court of Appeal). In *R. v Social Security Commissioner Ex p. Akbar, The Times*, November 6, 1991, Hodgson J had decided that temporary meant "not permanent". The Court of Appeal in *Ahmed* says that this is wrong, although the decision in *Akbar* itself was correct. However, the Court does agree with Hodgson J that an absence can be temporary, even though the intended date for return remains uncertain. Thus *R(S) 1/85* should not be followed on this point. The Court of Appeal holds that the decision as to whether a person is temporarily absent is one of fact for the adjudicating authority concerned. Relevant factors include the claimant's intention (although this is not decisive) and the length of the absence. If a person initially has the intention of not returning or an intention to stay for some fixed period which goes beyond the temporary (e.g. a matter of years), the absence is not temporary from the outset. In practice, the 52-week period referred to in paras (2)(a) and (3)(a) is likely to be the most important test.

The claimant must have been entitled to income support immediately before the temporary absence. Since the reference is to entitlement, it does not seem that income support must actually have been received. But a claim must have been made for that period before entitlement can arise (Administration Act s.1).

If the conditions set out in para.(2) are met, entitlement at the rate which would have been payable if the claimant had remained in Great Britain, can continue for the first four weeks of the temporary absence. If the conditions of para.(3) are met, entitlement can continue for the first eight weeks of absence. When calculating periods of absence from Great Britain the day of leaving and the day of return are both days on which the person is in Great Britain (see para.070642 of the *Decision Makers Guide* and *R(S) 1/66*).

If the claimant does not satisfy the conditions for continuing entitlement or the four or eight weeks are exhausted, any partner remaining in Great Britain may claim. If the absence is temporary, the couple ought on principle to remain members of the same household (although the effect of reg.16(3)(d) is obscure).

Paragraph (2)

2.72 Sub-paragraphs (a) and (b) are self-explanatory. It is important that all the other conditions of entitlement must continue to be satisfied. The five conditions in sub-para.(c) are alternatives.

Head (i) covers claimants eligible for income support, apart from by reason of incapacity for work (but see (ii) and (v)), secondary education, trade disputes or being a person from abroad.

Some of the conditions which lead to eligibility for income support will obviously continue during absence abroad (e.g. pregnancy) but others may not (e.g. temporarily looking after children, if the children are left behind). Since the October 1993 change in the test of responsibility for a child, a lone parent who goes abroad temporarily without her children should continue to be eligible for income support under para.1 of Sch.1B. This is because reg.15(1) now makes receipt of child benefit the primary test of responsibility. Child benefit can continue to be paid while a claimant is temporarily absent from Great Britain for up to eight weeks. Only if no claim for child benefit has been made is the person with whom the child usually lives treated as responsible under reg.15(2)(a). The matter has to be tested week by week (*CIS 49/1991*). See the 1993 edition of J. Mesher and P. Wood, *Income-related Benefits: the Legislation* for the potential problems for lone parents absent abroad prior to October 4, 1993.

Head (ii) covers incapacity for work, but only subject to these conditions (as applied to incapacity benefit by reg.2(1) of the Social Security (Persons Abroad) Regulations 1975). See *R(S) 2/86* and *R(S) 1/90* for the conditions and head (v). Paragraph (4) defines when the person providing treatment is appropriately qualified. 2.73

Head (iii) is self explanatory.

Head (iv) refers to the pensioner and disability premiums, but only applies to couples who are both abroad. It requires the premium to be "applicable". It is clearly arguable that "applicable" means "ought to be applied", so that entitlement to the premium, even if it is not actually in payment, will do.

Head (v) allows those incapable of work for at least 52 weeks, or 28 weeks if they are terminally ill (i.e. expected to die from a progressive disease within six months) or entitled to the highest rate care component of disability living allowance, the enhanced rate of the daily living component of personal independence payment, or armed forces independence payment, to use the regulation free of the conditions of head (ii). Two or more periods of incapacity count as one continuous period unless there is a break of more than eight weeks. Before April 13, 1995 the minimum period was 28 weeks for all claimants, but it has been increased for most claimants in line with the changes following the introduction of incapacity benefit. For the details of incapacity benefit see Vol.I of this series. Note reg.8(1) of the Income-related Benefits Schemes and Social Security (Claims and Payments) (Miscellaneous Amendments) Regulations 1995 (p.805), which provides that in deciding whether a claimant can satisfy head (v) on or after October 2, 1995, a period of incapacity immediately before April 13, 1995 can count towards the 52 (or 28) weeks, provided it is linked to, or part of, the current period. See also the transitional provision in reg.27(2) of the Income Support (General) (Jobseeker's Allowance Consequential Amendments) Regulations 1996 (p.806) in relation to the October 1996 changes to income support that are a consequence of the introduction of JSA.

Paragraph (3)

The conditions in heads (a) and (b) are the same as in para.(2)(a) and (b). Then the effect of heads (c) and (d) is that where the claimant is accompanying a child or young person in their family abroad for that child or young person to receive treatment, entitlement can continue for eight weeks. The claimant's absence must be solely for that purpose. The treatment must be for a medical condition and be carried out by an appropriately qualified person within the meaning of para.(4). There seems to be no reason why a claimant accompanying a child should be more deserving than a claimant going abroad for treatment for himself. 2.74

Paragraph (3A)

From October 4, 2004 claimants who are temporarily absent from Great Britain in order to receive NHS treatment at a hospital (or similar institution) in another country, and who were entitled to IS immediately before their departure, continue to be so entitled during their absence. 2.75

Persons treated as engaged in remunerative work

5.—(1) Subject to the following provisions of this regulation, for the purposes of section 20(3)(c) of the Act [SSCBA, s.124(1)(*c*)] (conditions of entitlement to income support), remunerative work is work in which a person is engaged, or, where his hours of work fluctuate, he is engaged on 2.76

average, for [6not less than 16 hours] a week being work for which payment is made or which is done in expectation of payment.

[9(1A) In the case of any partner of the claimant paragraph (1) shall have effect as though for the words "16 hours" there were substituted the words "24 hours".]

(2) [8Subject to paragraph (3B),] the number of hours for which a person is engaged in work shall be determined—

(a) where no recognisable cycle has been established in respect of a person's work, by reference to the number of hours or, where those hours are likely to fluctuate, the average of the hours, which he is expected to work in a week;

(b) where the number of hours for which he is engaged fluctuate, by reference to the average of hours worked over—

(i) if there is a recognisable cycle of work, the period of one complete cycle (including, where the cycle involves periods in which the person does no work, those periods but disregarding any other absences);

(ii) in any other case, the period of five weeks immediately before the date of claim or the date [11 on which a superseding decision is made under section 10 (decisions superseding earlier decisions) of the Social Security Act 1998] or such other length of time as may, in the particular case, enable the person's average hours of work to be determined more accurately.

(3) A person shall be treated as engaged in remunerative work during any period for which he is absent from work referred to in paragraph (1) if the absence is either without good cause or by reason of a recognised, customary or other holiday.

[7(3A) A person shall not be treated as engaged in remunerative work on any day on which the person is on maternity leave [14, paternity leave [17, adoption leave or shared parental leave]] or is absent from work because he is ill.]

[8(3B) Where for the purpose of paragraph (2)(b)(i), a person's recognisable cycle of work at a school, other educational establishment or other place of employment is one year and includes periods of school holidays or similar vacations during which he does not work, those periods and any other periods not forming part of such holidays or vacations during which he is not required to work shall be disregarded in establishing the average hours for which he is engaged in work.]

(4) A person who makes a claim and to whom or whose partner section 23 of the Act [SSCBA, s.126] (trade disputes) applies [1or applied] shall, for the period of seven days following the date on which the stoppage of work due to a trade dispute at his or his partner's place of work commenced or, if there is no stoppage, the date on which he or his partner first withdrew his labour in furtherance of a trade dispute, be treated as engaged in remunerative work.

(5) [15 Subject to paragraph (5A), a person], who was or was treated as being, engaged in remunerative work and in respect of that work earnings to which [4 regulation [16 35(1)(b) and (d)]] (earnings of employed earners) applies are [3paid] shall be treated as engaged in remunerative work for the period for which those earnings are taken into account in accordance with Part V.

[15 (5A) Paragraph (5) shall not apply to earnings disregarded under paragraph 1 of Schedule 8 to these regulations.]

[2(6) For the purposes of this regulation, in determining the number of hours in which a person is engaged or treated as engaged in remunerative work, no account shall be taken of any hours in which the person is engaged in an employment or a scheme to which [12. . . regulation 6(1)] (persons not treated as engaged in remunerative work) applies.]

[5(7) For the purposes of paragraphs (1) and (2), in determining the number of hours for which a person is engaged in work, that number shall include any time allowed to that person by his employer for a meal or for refreshment, but only where that person is, or expects to be, paid earnings in respect of that time.]

[13(8)–(10) . . .]

AMENDMENTS

1. Income Support (General) Amendment Regulations 1988 (SI 1988/663) reg.4 (April 11, 1988).

2. Income Support (General) Amendment No.4 Regulations 1988 (SI 1988/1445) reg.3 (September 9, 1988).

3. Income Support (General) Amendment No.5 Regulations 1988 (SI 1988/2022) reg.3 (December 12, 1988).

4. Income Support (General) Amendment No.2 Regulations 1989 (SI 1989/1323) reg.3 (October 9, 1989).

5. Income Support (General) Amendment Regulations 1990 (SI 1990/547) reg.4 (April 9, 1990).

6. Income Support (General) Amendment No.4 Regulations 1991 (SI 1991/1559) reg.3 (April 7, 1992).

7. Income-related Benefits Schemes (Miscellaneous Amendments) (No.4) Regulations 1993 (SI 1993/2119) reg.3 (October 4, 1993).

8. Income-related Benefits Schemes (Miscellaneous Amendments) Regulations 1995 (SI 1995/516) reg.19 (April 10, 1995).

9. Income-related Benefits Schemes and Social Fund (Miscellaneous Amendments) Regulations 1996 (SI 1996/1944) reg.6(4) (October 7, 1996).

10. Social Security (Miscellaneous Amendments) (No.2) Regulations 1999 (SI 1999/2556) reg.2(2) (October 4, 1999).

11. Social Security Act 1998 (Commencement No.12, and Consequential and Transitional Provisions) Order 1999 (SI 1999/3178) art.3(5) and Sch.5 para.1 (November 29, 1999)

12. Social Security (Miscellaneous Amendments) Regulations 2000 (SI 2000/681) reg.2(a) (April 3, 2000).

13. Social Security (Miscellaneous Amendments) Regulations 2001 (SI 2001/488) reg.3 (April 9, 2001).

14. Social Security (Paternity and Adoption) Amendment Regulations 2002 (SI 2002/2689) reg.2 (December 8, 2002).

15. Social Security (Miscellaneous Amendments) (No. 5) Regulations 2007 (SI 2007/2618) reg.5(5) (October 1, 2007).

16. Social Security (Miscellaneous Amendments) Regulations 2008 (SI 2008/698) reg.2(3) (April 14, 2008).

17. Shared Parental Leave and Statutory Shared Parental Pay (Consequential Amendments to Subordinate Legislation) Order 2014 (SI 2014/3255) art.5(1) and (3) (December 31, 2014).

DEFINITIONS

"the Act"—see reg.2(1).
"adoption leave"—*ibid.*
"date of claim"—*ibid.*
"maternity leave"—*ibid.*

"partner"—*ibid.*
"paternity leave"—*ibid.*

General Note

2.77 Under s.124(1)(c) of the SSCBA 1992, and ss.1(2)(e) and 3(1)(e) of the Jobseekers Act 1995, it is a condition of entitlement to income support and income-based JSA that neither the claimant nor her/his partner is in remunerative work. It is also a condition of entitlement to contribution-based JSA that the claimant should not be in remunerative work. Remunerative work is also relevant to the amount of any non-dependant deduction from the claimant's housing costs (see para.18 of Sch.3) and (in transitional cases, see the note to reg.17) to whether the earnings of certain children and young persons are disregarded under para.15 of Sch.8.

The rules governing remunerative work are set out, for income support purposes, in this regulation and reg.6, and, for income-based JSA purposes, in regs 51–53 of the JSA Regulations, which are in similar—though not identical—terms. Since the introduction of JSA on October 7, 1996, the principal rule has been that a claimant (and, where relevant, a non-dependant or a child or young person) is in remunerative work if s/he works for not less than 16 hours a week and the claimant's partner is in remunerative work if s/he works for not less than 24 hours a week (except in those cases where the couple is obliged to make a joint claim for JSA, in which case the 16-hour rule applies to both members because both are claimants). Where the hours of work fluctuate, an average is taken using the rules in para.(2).

In cases (other than joint-claim JSA cases) where the claimant's partner is working between 16 and 24 hours a week, it may be possible for the couple to claim both working tax credit (see Vol.IV) and income support or income-based JSA. In such cases, there is an automatic entitlement to maximum WTC but the claimant's IS or income-based JSA will be reduced pound for pound by the WTC that is paid.

Because income support is normally paid in arrears, the disentitlement applies immediately a person starts remunerative work, regardless of whether wages have been paid or when they will be paid. This situation is specifically mentioned in the Social Fund Guide as one in which a crisis loan might be payable if no other resources are available. The details of the test are therefore important. Note the exceptions in reg.6, brought in by para.(6).

Paragraph (1)

2.78 First note that the test is in terms of work, not employment. Therefore, the precise categorisation of the activities carried out may not be crucial. This is illustrated in two family credit decisions (remunerative work was a qualification for family credit). In *CFC 7/1989* the claimant's husband was working in connection with Moral Re-Armament, a Christian charity, for about 38 hours a week. He received payment by persuading individuals to covenant income to him. He was not employed by Moral Re-Armament or the covenantors, nor did he contract with them on a self-employed basis. But this did not matter, because what he did was undoubtedly work and he was paid for it. In *R(FC) 2/90* both the claimant and her husband were officers of the Salvation Army. It was accepted, following the decision of the Court of Appeal in *Rogers v Booth* [1937] 2 All E.R. 751, that the relationship of officers to the Salvation Army is spiritual, not contractual. Nevertheless, the onerous duties of officers were "work."

Remunerative

2.79 Work is remunerative if payment is made for it, or it is done in the expectation of payment. There is a significant difference from the common law test (on which see *R(FIS) 1/83*), because the mere hope of or desire for payment is not the same as expectation (although note that in *R(IS) 13/99* the Commissioner comments that he did not see any fundamental distinction between "hope of" and "expectation of" payment). Thus in *CFC 3/1989*, the claimant's husband, who regarded himself as a self-employed writer, but who had not sold any manuscripts and did not anticipate any sales in the next six months, was not in remunerative work. The Commissioner puts forward a rule of thumb, not a binding principle, that for work to be done in the expectation of payment some payment must be expected within 26 weeks of the relevant date. This was based partly on the length of a family credit award, but there clearly should be one dividing line between the income support and family credit systems. In *R(IS) 1/93* the Commissioner holds that the guiding principle on when there is an expectation of payment should be common sense and an appreciation of the realities of the situation. The claimant, another writer, had sent several works to publishers, but had had negligible success in selling anything. She was working "on spec", with only the hope of payment, not an expectation. In *Kevin Smith v Chief Adjudication Officer* (*R(IS) 21/95*) the claimant's partner, who was in receipt of an enterprise allowance, wished to establish herself as an agent for pop groups and spent a lot of time building up contacts in the pop music world. The Court of Appeal, having said that the question is really one of fact, distinguishes between work done to set up a business, which is not done in expectation of payment, and work carried out once the business is established, which it would be reasonable to infer was done in expectation of payment. On the facts of that case the claimant's partner was not engaged in remunerative work. On the other side of the line, see *CIS 434/1994* in which a person who had started an estate agent's business and was working without pay until the business became profitable was held to be in remunerative work. In *CIS 929/1995* the two or three hours a freelance musician spent practising each day did not count as hours of work for the purposes of reg.5(1).

In *R(IS) 22/95* the claimant's wife worked in a general shop owned by the two of them. For several months she had worked without pay and had no expectation of receiving any in the future because the business was making a loss. The Commissioner holds that the SSAT had been correct in concluding that on the facts she was not in remunerative work. This decision was upheld by the Court of Appeal in *Chief Adjudication Officer v Ellis* (reported as part of *R(IS) 22/95*). In *Ellis* the Court gives some general guidance on the questions to be considered when deciding whether a person is in remunerative work. In particular, the Court draws a distinction between a person providing a service (such as the claimant carrying on a translation agency in *Perrot v SBC* [1980] 3 All E.R. 110 where the unprofitability of her business was irrelevant) and the position of a retail shop. The Court points out that the price paid for goods sold in a shop is not payment for the work of the salesman, but the price of the goods sold. Thus simply carrying on a retail business did not necessarily mean that a person was in remunerative work (so *CSIS 39/1994* should not be followed on this point). But if the person was not expecting to make any money the question had to be asked why the shop was being kept open. In this case the answer was clear. The claimant's wife was carrying on the business in the hope of disposing of the goodwill. She was not in remunerative work.

In *R(IS) 5/95* the claimant who was both a director and an employee of a small limited company had also worked for some months without pay, due to financial difficulties. The Commissioner states that it was necessary to consider in relation to each week whether he was working in his capacity as an employee or a director (although the functions of a director of a small private company were quite slight (*R(U) 1/93*, para.5)). If this work had been done as an employee it was only remunerative if any payment expected was in that capacity (although reg.42(6) (notional earnings) would also need to be considered). Moreover expectation of payment meant payment for current work. It may be that this is not the case for the self-employed, although the Court of Appeal in *Ellis* states that the question of whether work is done in expectation of payment is to be decided at the time the work is done, not at the end of the year or other accounting period.

If a claimant deliberately arranges to work for no remuneration (and therefore has no expectation of payment) then, unsurprisingly, that work does not qualify as remunerative work. In *CTC 626/2001* a husband went into partnership with his wife. He worked 30 hours a week in the partnership business and she worked **2.80** six. However, in order to save income tax the partners agreed that 100 per cent of the profits was allocated to the wife leaving the husband with no income from the business. The Commissioner upheld the decision of the tribunal that there was no entitlement to WFTC: the wife was in remunerative work but for less than 16 hours a week and the husband, though he worked far more than 16 hours a week, was not in remunerative work at all. As *CTC 626/2001* related to a tax credit the conclusion that the husband was not in remunerative work was to his disadvantage. However, one logical consequence of the decision is the possibility that a similar arrangement could be used by a self-employed claimant who was in fact working for more than 16 hours a week to retain entitlement to IS or income-based JSA. It is suggested that such an arrangement would not in fact be effective because, following the remarks of Millet LJ in *Ellis*, it would be appropriate in such circumstances "to treat the partnership as a single economic unit just as if it were carried on by a sole trader".

The payment must be in return for the work (*R(FIS) 1/86*), but need not derive from an employer. Thus the payments by covenantors in *CFC 7/1989* (see above) counted. So too did the payments from the Salvation Army in *R(FC) 2/90*, although they were not paid under contract and were aimed at providing for the officers' actual needs. There was a distinction from the maintenance grant paid to a student. Provision for actual needs went beyond mere maintenance. A grant is not in return for work (*R(FIS) 1/86*), so that students and trainees (*R(FIS) 1/83*) will still not be said to be in remunerative work. The argument that enterprise allowance is paid in return for work was rejected by the Court of Appeal in *Kevin Smith v Chief Adjudication Officer* (above). The Court holds that it is a payment to enable people to establish themselves in business, not for work. This conclusion was indicated both by the terms of the enterprise allowance scheme and reg.37(1). If receipt of enterprise allowance by itself meant that a person had to be treated as engaged in remunerative work, the inclusion in reg.37(1) of enterprise allowance as earnings was unnecessary since the calculation stage envisaged by reg.37 would never be reached.

A payment in kind will count in the same way as a payment in cash. In *CFC 33/1993* the provision of rent-free accommodation and the payment of gas and electricity bills meant that the claimant's work was done for payment.

Engaged in work

2.81 It is hours during which the person is engaged in work and is paid (or at least expects payment) which are crucial. The calculation is usually relatively easy for employees. Thus in *CIS 3/1989* the claimant's paid one hour lunch break did not count towards the limit. He was not "engaged in" work for that hour. The precise result is reversed from April 1990, by para.(7), but the principle might apply in other situations. *R(FC) 1/92* suggests that where the nature of the job requires a person to work beyond the contractually specified hours, the longer hours count. However, it is not clear just how this translates from the old family credit provision to income support. For the self-employed the test is not of hours costed and charged to a client, but of hours of activities which are essential to the undertaking (*R(FIS) 6/85*). Thus time spent in preparation, research, doing estimates and accounts, travel for the purposes of the undertaking, keeping a shop open, etc. must all count. But activities carried on merely in the hope, rather than expectation, of payment are not remunerative. The actual hours of work must be considered. In *R(IS) 22/95*, although the shop in which the claimant's wife worked was open from 08:30–18:30 Monday to Friday, she only spent three hours a day in it. The rest of the time she was in her home (which was in the same premises), ready to go into the shop if the shop bell rang. The Commissioner expresses the view (without finally deciding the point) that on the particular facts of that case (a small shop with little stock and fewer customers) the hours "on call" may not be hours of work. The decision in *R(IS) 22/95* was upheld by the Court of Appeal in *Chief Adjudication Officer v Ellis* (see above), but the Court of Appeal does not deal with this particular point. But in *R(IS) 13/99* the same Commissioner decides that the time spent by a self-employed minicab driver waiting at the cab office for potential customers (which he was not obliged to do) was work done in expectation of payment. This seems somewhat dubious, in that it was not essential to his work for him to spend that time there. However, the decision was upheld by the Court of Appeal (*Kazantzis v Chief Adjudication Officer*, reported as part of *R(IS) 13/ 99)*. In *R(IS) 12/95* all the hours that a share fisherman was at sea (including those that he was not on watch or was sleeping) counted. The Commissioner referred to *Suffolk CC v Secretary of State for the Environment* [1984] I.C.R. 882 in which the House of Lords had distinguished between a regular fireman required to remain in the station while on duty and a retained fireman free to do as he pleases until called upon. The claimant could not do as he pleased during his rest period. He had to stay on the trawler and could be summoned to assist if, for example, there was a storm. In the *Suffolk* case the House of Lords held that a retained fireman's waiting time could not be taken into account in calculating his contractual hours of employment. The claimant in *R(IS) 13/99* had attempted to rely on this decision but the Commissioner points out that the circumstances were not analogous. The issue under para.(1) was not whether the claimant was employed during his waiting time but whether he was "at work" during that time.

CIS 514/1990 holds that although recipients of enterprise allowance must undertake to work for at least 36 hours a week in their business, that does not mean that they must automatically be treated as doing so for benefit purposes (see *Kevin Smith v Chief Adjudication Officer (R(IS) 21/95)*) above on whether enterprise allowance is paid in return for work).

Paragraphs (2)–(3A)

Where a person works a fixed number of hours, week in, week out, there is no difficulty in applying the weekly limits in para.(1) to his or her claim. Although, what if a person does not work the same hours each week? What, indeed, if there are some weeks in which s/he does no work at all? This is the problem addressed by paras (2)–(3A) and also, for those who work in schools or other places of education and who wish to claim income support (but not JSA) during school holidays, by para.(3B) (see the note on "Term-time only workers" below). 2.82

Although these provisions (and those that preceded them) have been the subject of a considerable number of Commissioners' decisions, consideration of paras (2) to (3A) must now begin with the decision of the Tribunal of Commissioners in *R(JSA) 5/03*, dealing with the equivalent provisions of regs 51 and 52 of the JSA Regulations. The appeals before the Tribunal of Commissioners concerned people who were employees and the principles laid down in its decision must be seen in that context. Other considerations may be relevant in cases where the claimant is "self-employed" (see below).

The Tribunal's starting point was that:

> "11. Defining 'remunerative work' as being work in which someone is engaged for not less than 16 hours a week (24 hours in the case of a claimant's partner) is simple enough. But how do you arrive at the appropriate number of hours when the working hours fluctuate? And how do you deal with those periods during most people's working year, when for some reason or other they are absent from work (and, therefore, not engaged in work at all)?
>
> 12. The first step in any analysis is to recognise that periods when a person does no work fall into various categories. Consideration of regulations 51(2) and 52(1) suggests that the relevant categories are:
>
> (a) periods during which someone is without work because he or she is between jobs,
> (b) periods of no work (other than holidays) during which someone is without work because work is not provided by his or her employer,
> (c) periods during which someone can properly be regarded as being on holiday,
> (d) periods of absence due to sickness and maternity leave.
> (e) periods of unauthorised absence 'without good cause'.

In these appeals, we are not concerned with periods of absence due to sickness or maternity leave, but it is apparent from the terms of regulation 52(1) that a person who is otherwise in remunerative work ceases temporarily to be so engaged during such absences. We are also not concerned with periods of absence without good cause, but it is equally apparent that such absences are to be treated in the same way as holidays."

2.83 The Tribunal's approach to those issues was to look first at whether the person's employment had ended. In doing so, "regard should be had to reality" (at para.25) and not just to the formal legal position:

"22. In our view, the approach taken by decision-makers should be as follows. Where a contract of employment comes to an end at the beginning of what would be a period of absence from work even if the contract continued, the person should be taken still to be in employment if is expected that he or she will resume employment after that period, either because there is some express arrangement, though not necessarily an enforceable contract, or because it is reasonable to assume that a long standing practice of re-employment will continue."

If it is determined that the person is no longer in employment then no question of remunerative work arises. If, on the other hand, the employment relationship is—as a matter of reality—still subsisting, it becomes necessary to decide whether the person is absent from work due to a holiday or for some other reason. This issue is to be decided on the basis that a person is on holiday during those periods of absence for which they are entitled to be paid—either by contract or, from October 1, 1998, under the Working Time Regulations 1998.

The Tribunal continues:

"28. Applying regulation 51(2) [i.e. of the JSA Regulations—equivalent to reg.5(2) of the IS Regulations] is relatively straightforward once it has been established that a person is still engaged in employment and his or her entitlement to holidays has been ascertained. If he works the same number of hours each week when not on holiday, that is the number of hours to be taken into account for the purpose of regulation 51(1). If the number of hours fluctuates, an average is taken. How the average is calculated when there is no cycle of work is determined under regulation 51(2)(b)(ii) [or reg.5(2)(b)(ii)] which allows some discretion as to the period over which the average is to be calculated. Regulation 51(2)(b)(i) [or reg.5(2)(b)(i)] makes more specific provision in a case where there is a recognisable cycle of work."

2.84 Specifically, when there is a recognisable cycle of work of one year the requirement in reg.51(2)(b)(i) [or 5(2)(b)(i)] to calculate the average taking into account "periods in which the person does no work . . . but disregarding other absences" means:

"dividing the total number of hours worked . . . by 52 less the number of weeks of holiday to which the particular claimant is entitled. The result determines whether the person concerned is in remunerative work or not for the whole period of the cycle (*R(IS) 8/95*) so that it is not necessary where there is a cycle to attribute the holiday entitlement to any particular weeks."

The same approach should presumably be adopted to established cycles of work of less than 52 weeks but which include periods in which the person does no work.

On that basis, unpaid "holidays" are "periods in which the person does no work" for the purposes of reg.51(2)(b)(i) [reg.5(2)(b)(i)] and paid holidays and periods of absence through sickness, etc. are "other absences". In cases which pre-date the Working Time Regulations 1998—or to which those Regulations do not apply, see for example *CJSA/4764/2002*—in which the employee has no holiday entitlement, neither the fact that payment of their salary may be spread over the year in equal monthly instalments nor the fact that the rate at which they are paid has been enhanced to reflect the absence of any formal holiday entitlement alters the position that there is no holiday entitlement (although the latter circumstance is relevant to the issue of the claimant's earnings (see para.42)).

In consequence, the Tribunal of Commissioners held that the reasoning in (though not the result of) *R(IS) 15/94* was incorrect and that *R(IS) 7/96* which had followed that reasoning was wrongly decided and should no longer be followed.

For an instructive example of the workings of a complex remunerative work calculation, see *NS v SSWP (IS)* [2015] UKUT 0423 (AAC).

Seasonal workers (other than term-time only workers)

The position of seasonal workers (other than term-time only workers claiming income support—see below) was considered by the Commissioner in *R(JSA) 1/07* and in *CJSA/3832/2006.* 2.85

In the former case, the claimants had, for several years, been able to obtain casual work during the summer season in holiday resorts on the Lincolnshire coast but had been unable to find work during the winter months. The Secretary of State refused their claims for JSA on the basis that they had to be treated as having a cycle of work extending over the whole calendar year. The tribunal rejected that argument and found that they were not in a cycle of work at all during periods when they were not in employment. Confirming that decision, the Commissioner held that whether there was an "expectation" that the claimant would resume his or her employment (i.e. under the test in *R(JSA) 5/03*—see above) was a matter of fact for the tribunal and that "there would need to be some element of mutuality in the arrangement or understanding between employer and employee" before such an "expectation" could be found to exist. The Secretary of State's construction was

> "an attempt to start with the calculation provisions by assuming that the whole year is to be included, and then work backwards to distort the meaning of regulation 51(1) [i.e. of the JSA Regulations and, by implication, also of reg.5(1)] as if it contained a deeming provision making people count as in work when in fact they are not".

The recurrence of an inability to get work at all during the winter months did not turn the whole calendar year into one continuous period of the claimant being "engaged in work" for the purposes of reg.51 so as to be able to call the whole year a recognisable cycle of work. Regulation 51(2) was concerned with the calculation of a numerical average of hours *at* work over a period while a person continues to be *in* work. 2.86

In *CJSA/3832/2006*, the claimant worked as a cleaner during university terms only. At the end of each term his contract of employment was terminated and he and his colleagues were told that if they were interested in re-employment from the beginning of the following term they should contact the facilities manager during the preceding week. The Commissioner stated:

> "As was recently stressed in *CJSA/1390/2006* [now *R(JSA) 1/07*], the real question is whether the person claiming benefit can properly be regarded as being 'in' work at the material time. There must be some sort of continuing relationship between the employer and employee, even if it is not technically a subsisting employment relationship. Unless the circumstances show some commitment to a resumption of the employment relationship by a former worker upon which an employer might reasonably place some reliance, it is difficult to see how a person can be regarded as being in employment between periods of work when his contract of employment has expressly been terminated. It seems to me that there needs to be a 'tacit understanding' or a mutual expectation such as was found in *R(U) 1/66* and *R(U) 8/68*, discussed in *R(JSA) 5/03*. In my judgment, the tribunal erred in apparently not distinguishing between a cycle involving periods of

employment and periods of unemployment and a cycle of employment involving periods of work and periods of no work."

As there was no evidence of any expectation by the employer that the claimant would resume employment, and as it would not be difficult to find other cleaners if he did not apply in the week before the next term, the claimant was not in remunerative work during the vacation.

In the light of the requirement in *R(JSA) 1/07* for the "expectation" to be mutual to both employer and employee, it is suggested that the result should have been the same if the evidence had shown that the claimant did not have an expectation of being re-employed if he were to apply.

Term-time only workers—para. (3B)

2.87 For JSA the position of those who only work during term-time is governed by reg.51(2)(a) and (b) of the JSA Regulations as interpreted by the decision of the Tribunal of Commissioners in *R(JSA) 5/03*. This is because, in *R(JSA) 4/03*, reg.51(2)(c) of the JSA Regulations was held by the same Tribunal to be of no legal effect because it discriminated indirectly against women and could not be objectively justified by reference to factors other than sex. It was therefore inconsistent with EC Directive 79/7 (see Vol.III). However, unlike JSA, income support is not within the material scope of that Directive because it provides protection against poverty rather than against any of the risks listed in art.3 of the Directive—see *Jackson and Cresswell v Chief Adjudication Officer* (C-63/91 and C-64/91) [1992] E.C.R. I-4737 (also reported as an appendix to *R(IS) 10/91*). Therefore reg.5(3B) of the Income Support Regulations (equivalent to reg.52(2)(c)) is unaffected by the decision in *R(JSA) 4/03* and needs to be applied.

In the past the application of reg.5 to term-time-only workers has been a matter of acute controversy and readers are referred to the more detailed historical note at pp.213-219 of Vol.II of the 2000 edition. The law as it relates to income support has, however, now been settled by the decision of the House of Lords in *Chief Adjudication Officer v Stafford and Banks* [2001] UKHL 33, HL, June 28, 2001(also reported as *R(IS) 5/01*).

The issue in *Stafford and Banks* may conveniently be illustrated using the facts of Mr Banks' appeal. He was employed as an assistant for children with special needs at a junior school. During the 38 weeks of term time each year, he worked a regular 20- hour week but during the 14 weeks of the school holidays he did not work at all and was not paid. He had a continuing contract of employment with the same employer and all parties approached the case on the basis that he had a recognisable cycle of work of one year including both term-time and school holidays. It was common ground that in these circumstances, the combined effect of para.(2)(b)(i) and (3B) (which had been introduced to reverse the effect of the decision in *R(IS) 15/94*) was to average Mr Banks' working hours across the cycle but that school holidays had to be disregarded when calculating that average. The effect was that Mr Banks' hours were averaged over term-time only and were accordingly 20 hours a week (20 3 38 4 38) rather than 14.6 hours per week (20 3 38 ÷ 52) which would have been the case if they had been averaged over the whole year including school holidays.

2.88 Up to this point, there was no dispute. What divided the parties and the House of Lords was whether or not—in addition to this averaging process—*the two paragraphs also had the effect of treating Mr Banks as being engaged in remunerative work during the 14 weeks of school holiday when he was not actually working*. In other words, was it possible for Mr Banks to say that he was not engaged in remunerative work at all during those weeks in the cycle which had not been included in the calculation of his average hours?

The majority of the House of Lords (Lord Slynn, Hope and Millet) held that it was not. The disregard in para.(3B) only applied to the calculation of the average number of hours and did not alter the length of the cycle of work. The decision as to whether or not the claimant was engaged in remunerative work was to be applied to the full period of the cycle. The decision is, perhaps, best summarised in the judgment of Lord Millet (at paras 63 and 65):

> "... To my mind the critical point is that paras (2)(b)(i) is not replaced by paragraph (3B) but merely made subject to it. Paragraph 2(b) remains in full force save only to the extent to which it is modified by paragraph (3B). The two paragraphs must be read together. They are both concerned with persons who have a regular cycle of work. Neither of them is concerned with the question when a person is to be treated as being engaged in work, but only with the determination of the average number of hours for which he is engaged in work for the purpose of determining whether the work (in which ex hypothesi he must be treated as being engaged) is remunerative work. Paragraph 2(b)(i) directs that the average number of hours is to be determined by reference to a complete cycle including periods during which he does no work, and there is nothing in paragraph (3B) which modifies this. It does not affect the duration of the cycle or exclude periods during which he does no work. In the case of the present claimant, therefore, the cycle of work remains the complete year . . . and the claimant continues to be treated (by paragraph (2)(b)(i)) as engaged in work throughout the cycle including periods when he does no work. Paragraph (3B) directs that the school holidays are to be disregarded, not for the purpose of determining when a person is to be treated as engaged in work, but merely for the purpose of establishing the average number of hours worked during the cycle."

In the circumstances, the decision of the Commissioner in *CSJSA/395/1998* must be followed in preference to the decisions in *CIS/1118/1997, CIS/3216/1997* and *CJSA/3218/1997* which had held (with Lord Cooke who dissented in *Stafford and Banks*) that para.(3B) restricted the weeks during which a claimant is treated as engaged in remunerative work to those which were included in the averaging calculation. Similarly, the persuasive dissent of Lord Scott (who would have held that neither para.(2) nor para.(3B) had the effect of treating a claimant as being engaged in remunerative work when he was not actually working) cannot be taken as representing the law.

The decision of the majority in *Stafford and Banks* considerably narrows the scope for further dispute about the benefit entitlements of term-time only workers. **2.89** However, it should be noted that para.(3B) (and hence the *Stafford and Banks* ruling) only applies if it is first established that there is a "recognisable cycle of work". In three appeals decided since the decision of the House of Lords in *Stafford and Banks* (*R(JSA) 8/03, CIS/914/1997* and *CJSA/2759/1998*), Commissioner Rowland held that such a cycle had not been established. The Commissioner pointed out that where a person is employed on a casual or relief basis "it may be clear that [he or she] will not work during school holidays *but it may not be clear that he or she will work during the whole of the terms* and for that reason a cycle may not be established" (emphasis added). There may come a time when a pattern of regular employment in practice will establish an annual cycle but in *CIS/914/1997* the Commissioner refused to accept that this had occurred when the claimant had only worked for part of a year before claiming benefit and in *CJSA/2759/1998* he expressed the view that establishing a cycle in practice "is likely to require the completion of two cycles".

It should also be noted that in *Stafford and Banks*, the House of Lords was dealing with a case in which it was not disputed that the employment relationship between the claimant and his employer continued to exist over the holiday period. This issue must now be approached in accordance with *R(JSA) 5/03* (above), i.e. by having regard to the reality of the position rather than a strict analysis of the status of the contract of employment. Even so, there may be cases in which it will not be reasonable to expect that the person will resume employment. In such cases, any recognisable cycle of work that may have been established will be broken with the effect that *Stafford and Banks* no longer applies.

Self-employment

2.90 In the case of a self-employed worker who has periods of work interspersed with periods of no work the position is less clear. Paragraph (1) does not state what is the appropriate period to look at when determining whether a person is engaged in remunerative work. Each case will therefore depend to some extent on its own facts. If, for example, a person carries on a business for six months of the year and does no work in connection with that business for the rest of the year, it must be arguable that the period to be looked at is the six months when his business is dormant and that during that time he is not engaged in work. This was the approach originally taken in the *Decision Makers Guide* (but now see para.20340). However, this is not the conclusion reached by the Commissioner in *CIS 493/1993*. The claimant ran a guest house with a six-month season and did a minimal amount of work during the closed season. The claimant had argued that there were two cycles, or periods, one in which he worked more than 16 hours every week and the second during which he was not engaged in work at all. The Commissioner states that the first question was whether there was a recognisable cycle, and the second was whether the claimant's hours fluctuated within that cycle. The basis of this approach seems to have been that para.(2) is to be used to determine the number of hours for which a person is engaged in work. But para.(2) does not provide a rule for deciding the number of hours worked per week in all cases. It applies in the circumstances described in the opening words of sub-paras (a) and (b) (*R(IS) 8/95*). It is suggested that the first question is what is the appropriate period for deciding whether a claimant is engaged in remunerative work, which will depend on the facts of each case, before going on to consider whether the particular circumstances referred to in para.(2) apply. Note that para.(3B) would not seem to apply to the self-employed.

This approach was confirmed in *Saunderson v Secretary of State for Work and Pensions* [2012] CSIH 102; [2013] AACR 16, which concerned reg.51 of the JSA Regulations (the equivalent of reg.5). The claimant had worked as a self-employed golf caddie in St Andrews in the spring and summer months for a number of years. His authorisation to work as a caddie was withdrawn in October 2007 because the demand for caddies is reduced in the winter. There was no commitment that he would be able to work as a caddie in St Andrews the following or any future year. The Inner House of the Court of Session stated that the notion that a seasonal worker was, by dint of being a seasonal worker, engaged in an annual cycle of work, with the consequence that his hours or earnings fell to be averaged over 12 months, had its origin in the obiter observations in *R(JSA) 1/03* (see para.12). However, the concept of a "recognisable cycle of work" in reg.51(2) only came into play for the purpose of averaging the weekly hours of work *after* the primary question under reg.51(1) as to whether the claimant was "in work" at the time of his claim for JSA had been answered. That primary question was not determined by whether there was a recognisable cycle of work but was a matter of fact, giving "in work" its ordinary meaning. The Secretary of State had accepted this in relation to those who were employees in seasonal work (as held in *R (JSA) 1/07*) but contended that seasonal self-employment was an annual activity. The Court of Session, however, rejected this sharp distinction. While there may be many self-employed trading or professional activities in which the activity continues during an idle period, there are also many seasonally pursued activities, which, while treated as self-employment, are in substance little different from employment. What needed to be considered was the primary question of whether the person was "in work" when his seasonal activity came to an end.

See also *TC v Department for Social Development (JSA)* [2013] NI Com 65 (a decision of a Northern Ireland Commissioner). The claimant was a self-employed eel fisherman on Lough Neagh who claimed JSA following the breakdown of his boat towards the end of the eel fishing season. The Commissioner follows *Sanderson*, rather than the majority in the House of Lords in *Banks* (which was primarily concerned with the calculation of hours of a person in remunerative work and could be distinguished on its facts). The Commissioner considered that in the past the Great Britain Commissioners (as they then were) had taken different approaches to the question of seasonal employment and seasonally-based self-employment but, as stated by the Court of Session (see para.20), there was no textual warrant in the legislative definition of remunerative work for any distinction to be drawn between previously employed or self-employed claimants.

Paragraph (4)

See the notes to s.126 of the Contributions and Benefits Act (1986 Act s.23). **2.91**

Paragraph (5)

Where payments in lieu of remuneration are paid or (within four weeks) holiday pay, the person is treated as in remunerative work for the period covered. See regs 29 and 31. Following the increased disregard of payments made on the termination of full-time employment that was introduced on October 1, 2007 (see para.1 of Sch.8 and the notes to that paragraph), this provision will only apply where a person's employment has been suspended. **2.92**

Paragraph (7)

Paid meal or refreshment breaks count in the calculation of the hours for which a person is engaged in work. **2.93**

Persons not treated as engaged in remunerative work

6.—[10(1)] A person shall not be treated as engaged in [2 remunerative work in so far as—] **2.94**

[3(a) [12. . .]]

(b) he is engaged in child minding in his home;

(c) he is engaged by a charity or [7voluntary organisation [8—],] or is a volunteer where the only payment received by him or due to be paid to him, is a payment which is to be disregarded under regulation 40(2) and paragraph 2 of Schedule 9 (sums to be disregarded in the calculation of income other than earnings) [21 and in this paragraph "volunteer" means a person who is engaged in voluntary work, otherwise than for a relative, where the only payment received, or due to be paid to the person by virtue of being so engaged, is in respect of any expenses reasonably incurred by the person in connection with that work];

(d) he is engaged on a scheme for which a training allowance is being paid; [4 . . .]

[15(dd) he is receiving assistance under the self-employment route;]

(e) [12. . .]

[9(f) [12. . .]]

[6(g) [12. . .]]

[4(h) he is engaged in any one of the employments mentioned in heads (a) to (d) of sub-paragraph (1) of paragraph 7 of Schedule 8 (which relates to persons serving as firemen, in coastal rescue activities etc); [5 . . .]

(j) he is performing his duties as a councillor, and for this purpose "councillor" has the same meaning as in [12section 171F(2) of the Contributions and Benefits Act];] [5 or

(k) he is engaged in caring for a person who is accommodated with him by virtue of arrangements made under any of the provisions referred to in paragraph 26 [7 or in accordance with paragraph 27] of Schedule

9 (sums to be disregarded in the calculation of income other than earnings) and is in receipt of any payment specified in [7those paragraphs].]

(l) *[Omitted]*

[10 (m) he is engaged in an activity in respect of which—

(i) a sports award has been made, or is to be made, to him; and

(ii) no other payment is made or is expected to be made to him]

(2)–(3) [16. . .]

[12 (4) The following persons shall not be treated as engaged in remunerative work—

(a) [20 . . .]

(b) subject to regulation 5(4) and (5) (persons treated as engaged in remunerative work), a person to whom section 126 of the Contributions and Benefits Act (trade disputes) applies or in respect of whom section 124(1) of that Act (conditions of entitlement to income support) has effect as modified by section 127(b) of that Act (effect of return to work);

(c) a person to whom paragraph 4 of Schedule 1B applies;

[17 (d) [20 . . .]]

[13(5) A person shall not be treated as engaged in remunerative work for the period specified in paragraph (6) in so far as—

(a) he or his partner is engaged in work which—

(i) is remunerative work; and

(ii) he, or his partner, is expected to be engaged in remunerative work for a period of no less than five weeks;

(b) he or his partner had, for a continuous period of 26 weeks ending on the day before the day on which he commenced the work referred to in sub-paragraph (a), been entitled to and in receipt of income support [19 , an income-based jobseeker's allowance or an income-related employment and support allowance];

(c) he or his partner had, as at the day before the day on which he commenced the work referred to in sub-paragraph (a), an applicable amount which included—

(i) an amount determined in accordance with Schedule 3 (housing costs) as applicable to him in respect of [18 housing costs which qualify under paragraphs 15 to 17] of that Schedule; [19 . . .]

(ii) an amount determined in accordance with Schedule 2 to the Jobseeker's Allowance Regulations 1996 (housing costs) as applicable to him in respect of [18 housing costs which qualify under paragraphs 14 to 16] of that Schedule; [19 or

(iii) an amount determined in accordance with Schedule 6 to the Employment and Support Allowance Regulations (housing costs) as applicable to him in respect of housing costs which qualify under paragraphs 16 to 18 of that Schedule; and]

(d) he or his partner remain liable to make payments [18 in respect of such housing costs].

(6) A person referred to in paragraph (5) shall not be treated as engaged in remunerative work for—

(a) the period of four weeks commencing with the day on which he was first engaged in the work referred to in sub-paragraph (a) of that paragraph; [16. . .]

(7) In calculating the period of benefit entitlement referred to in paragraph [16. . .] (5)(b), no account shall be taken of entitlement arising by virtue of paragraph [16. . .] (6).

(8) In paragraph (5), a reference to the claimant or his partner being entitled to and in receipt of an income-based jobseeker's allowance or to an amount being applicable to either of them under the Jobseeker's Allowance Regulations 1996 shall include a reference to the claimant and his partner being entitled to, and in receipt of, a joint-claim jobseeker's allowance and to an amount being applicable to that couple under those Regulations.]

AMENDMENTS

1. Income Support (General) Amendment Regulations 1988 (SI 1988/663) reg.5 (April 11, 1988).

2. Income Support (General) Amendment No.4 Regulations 1988 (SI 1988/1445) reg.4 (September 12, 1988).

3. Income Support (General) Amendment No.4 Regulations 1991 (SI 1991/1559) reg.4 (October 7, 1991).

4. Income Support (General) Amendment Regulations 1992 (SI 1992/468) reg.2 (April 6, 1992).

5. Income-related Benefits Schemes (Miscellaneous Amendments) (No.3) Regulations 1992 (SI 1992/2155) reg.13 (October 5, 1992).

6. Social Security Benefits (Miscellaneous Amendments) Regulations 1993 (SI 1993/518) reg.5 (April 1, 1993).

7. Income-related Benefits Schemes (Miscellaneous Amendments) (No.5) Regulations 1994 (SI 1994/2139) reg.23 (October 3, 1994).

8. Income-related Benefits Schemes (Miscellaneous Amendments) Regulations 1995 (SI 1995/516) reg.20 (April 10, 1995).

9. Income Support (General) (Jobseeker's Allowance Consequential Amendments) Regulations 1996 (SI 1996/206) reg.6 (October 7, 1996).

10. Social Security Amendment (Sports Award) Regulations 1999 (SI 1999/2165) reg.6(2) (August 23, 1999).

11. Social Security (Miscellaneous Amendments) (No.2) Regulations 1999 (SI 1999/2556 reg.2(3) (October 4, 1999).

12. Social Security (Miscellaneous Amendments) Regulations 2000 (SI 2000/681) reg.2(b)(i) (April 3, 2000).

13. Social Security (Miscellaneous Amendments) Regulations 2001 (SI 2001/488) reg.4 (April 9, 2001).

14. Social Security Amendment (Residential Care and Nursing Homes) Regulations 2001 (SI 2001/3767) reg.2 and Sch. Pt I para.2 (April 8, 2002).

15. Social Security (Income-Related Benefits Self-Employment Route Amendment) Regulations 2004 (SI 2004/963) reg.3 (May 4, 2004).

16. Social Security (Back to Work Bonus and Lone Parent Run-on) (Amendment and Revocation) Regulations 2003 (SI 2003/1589) reg.2(a) (October 25, 2004).

17. Social Security (Care Homes and Independent Hospitals) Regulations 2005 (SI 2005/2687) reg.2 and Sch.1 para.2 (October 24, 2005).

18. Social Security (Housing Costs and Miscellaneous Amendments) Regulations 2007 (SI 2007/3183) reg.3(2) (December 17, 2007).

19. Employment and Support Allowance (Consequential Provisions) (No.2) Regulations 2008 (SI 2008/1554) reg.2(1) and (3) (October 27, 2008).

20. Social Security (Miscellaneous Amendments) (No.5) Regulations 2009 (SI 2009/3228) reg.4(a)(i) (January 25, 2010).

21. Social Security (Miscellaneous Amendments) (No.2) Regulations 2010 (SI 2010/641) reg.2(1) and (4) (April 6, 2010).

DEFINITIONS

"the Act"—see reg.2(1).
"remunerative work"—*ibid.*
"training allowance"—*ibid.*
"voluntary organisation"—*ibid.*

GENERAL NOTE

2.95 Claimants and their partners must be deemed not to be in remunerative work for the time engaged in these activities, although the "not" could be better placed. The effect is that there is no automatic exclusion from entitlement under s.124(1)(c) of the Contributions and Benefits Act (1986 Act s.20(3)(c)). Any earnings from employment must still be taken into account as income. Most of the categories are self-explanatory.

Paragraph (1)(b) deems a person who is childminding in her own home not to be in remunerative work. However, there is no specific provision in Sch.1B to enable childminders to qualify for income support. If a claimant who is a childminder does not come within any other paragraph of Sch.1B, it may be possible to argue that para.3 applies (looking after a child whose parent is temporarily absent from home). This would be along the lines that a parent who is out at work is absent from home on a temporary basis. Paragraph 3 does not seem to require that the person should be looking after the child all the time; as long as this is done on a regular basis this should suffice.

Under para.(1)(c), para.2 of Sch.9 refers to payments solely of expenses to volunteers or people working for charitable or voluntary bodies. A volunteer is someone who without any legal obligation performs a service for another person without expectation of payment (*R(1S) 12/92*).

2.96 Under para.(1)(d), training allowances are most commonly paid to people on Work Based Learning for Young People (in Scotland "Skillseekers"), which has replaced Youth Training, Modern Apprenticeships, etc.

Under para (1)(dd) those receiving assistance under the "self-employment route" are treated as not being in remunerative work. See the annotation to the definition of "self-employment route" in reg.2(1) and the General Note to reg.39A.

In addition, reg.2(2)(a) of the New Deal (Lone Parents) (Miscellaneous Provisions) Order 2001 (SI 2001/2915), has the effect that from September 13, 2001, top-up payments made to those participating in the self-employment route of the New Deal for Lone Parents and other payments made to assist with the expenses of such participation are to be treated as a training allowance for the purpose of reg.6(1)(d).

2.97 Under para.(1)(j), the definition of "councillor" is—

"(a) in relation to England and Wales, a member of a London borough council, a county council, a district council, a parish or community council, the Common Council of the City of London or the Council of the Isles of Scilly; and

(b) in relation to Scotland, a member of a regional, islands or district council."

Under para.(1)(k) foster parents who receive statutory payments for fostering, or people receiving payments for providing temporary care in their home, are deemed not to be in remunerative work by reason of those payments.

Paragraph (1)(m) provides that a person will be deemed not to be in remunerative work while engaged in activity for which the only payment he is, or will be, receiving is a "sports award" (defined in reg.2(1)). See also reg.37(2)(c) which ensures that the sports award is not treated as self-employed earnings. A sports award is disregarded as income other than earnings under para.69 of Sch.9 except to the extent that it has been made for any of the items listed in para.69(2). There is a similar disregard where the sports award counts as capital (see para.56 of Sch.10) but in this case the disregard only applies for 26 weeks from the date of receipt.

Paragraphs (2) and (3) *Lone-parent run-on*: The "lone-parent run-on" previously established by these paras was abolished on October 25, 2004. For details of the former run-on see p.262 of Vol.II of the 2004 edition. 2.98

Paragraph (4) Until January 25, 2010, para.(4) treated disabled workers (subpara. (a)), certain claimants affected by a trade dispute (subpara.(b)), carers who fall within Sch.1B para.4 (subpara.(c)) and claimants living in care homes, Abbeyfield Homes and independent hospitals (subpara.(d)) as not being in remunerative work. On that date, paras 8 and 9 of Sch.1B (under which people within subparas (a) and (d) automatically fell within a prescribed category for the purposes of s.124(1)(e) of SSCBA) were revoked, as were subparas (a) and (d) themselves. The revocations are part of a broader policy that those who are unable to work fully by reason of a medical condition should claim ESA rather than IS. For further details, see the commentary to Sch.1B.

Those revocations are subject to savings provisions in reg.4 of SI 2009/3228 (below). Those provisions apply where a claimants is entitled to income support for a period including January 24, 2010 (irrespective of when income support was claimed) and falls within subpara.(a) or (d) on that date. In those circumstances, subpara.(a) or (d)—and paras 8 or 9 of Sch.1B—continue to apply to the claimant until they cease to fall within subpara.(a) or (d) or they cease to be entitled to income support, whichever is earlier: see reg.4(3), (4), (7) and (8) of SI 2009/3228.

Paragraphs (5)–(8) *Housing costs run-on*: under paras (5)–(8), some claimants who have been receiving IS, JSA or ESA housing costs are treated as not in remunerative work (and hence still entitled to IS) for the first four weeks of full-time work (i.e., 16 hours for the claimant or 24 for the claimant's partner—see reg.5(1) and (1A)). Before October 25, 2004, those claimants who qualified for the "lone-parent run-on" under the former paras (2) and (3) were potentially entitled to what was then the mortgage interest run-on for two weeks after the end of the two week lone-parent run-on period (under para.6(b)). However, with the abolition of the lone-parent run-on, para.(6)(b) was revoked, so that in all cases the mortgage interest (now housing costs) run-on lasts for the four week period specified in para.(6)(a). To qualify, a claimant (or her/his partner) must have been in receipt of IS, income-based or income-related JSA for a continuous period of at least 26 weeks (not including any earlier run-on periods—see para.(7)) ending on the day before the commencement of full-time work and must have been entitled to housing costs on that day. In addition, the full-time work must be expected to last for a period of at least five weeks. 2.99

During the run-on period, IS is paid at the lower of the weekly amount of housing costs which was payable immediately before the claimant or her/his partner commenced full-time work or the rate of IS, income-related ESA or income-based JSA which was being paid (or would have been paid but for the receipt of a training allowance) in the benefit week before full-time work commenced (see para.19A of Sch.7).

Under para.9A of Sch.1B a person to whom para.(5) applies is in a prescribed category and therefore eligible for IS even if they were previously receiving JSA or ESA.

It is not necessary for a claim to be made to qualify for the mortgage interest (now housing costs) run-on. When the claimant informs the DWP that he or his partner has started full-time work the run-on should be paid automatically.

Meaning of employment

7.—[1. . .] 2.100

AMENDMENT

1. Income Support (General) (Jobseeker's Allowance Consequential Amendments) Regulations 1996 (SI 1996/206) reg.28 and Sch.3 (October 7, 1996).

Persons not required to be available for employment

2.101 **8.**—[1. . .]

AMENDMENT

1. Income Support (General) (Jobseeker's Allowance Consequential Amendments) Regulations 1996 (SI 1996/206) reg.28 and Sch.3 (October 7, 1996).

Persons treated as available for employment

2.102 **9.**—[1. . .]

AMENDMENT

1. Income Support (General) (Jobseeker's Allowance Consequential Amendments) Regulations 1996 (SI 1996/206) reg.28 and Sch.3 (October 7, 1996).

Circumstances in which claimants are not to be treated as available for employment

2.103 **10.**—[1. . .]

AMENDMENT

1. Income Support (General) (Jobseeker's Allowance Consequential Amendments) Regulations 1996 (SI 1996/206) reg.28 and Sch.3 (October 7, 1996).

[1Actively seeking employment

2.104 **10A.**—[2. . .]

AMENDMENTS

1.Income Support (General) Amendment No.2 Regulations 1989 (SI 1989/1323) reg.6 (October 9, 1989).

2. Income Support (General) (Jobseeker's Allowance Consequential Amendments) Regulations 1996 (SI 1996/206) reg.28 and Sch.3 (October 7, 1996).

Registration for employment

2.105 **11.**—[1. . .]

AMENDMENT

1. Income Support (General) (Jobseeker's Allowance Consequential Amendments) Regulations 1996 (SI 1996/206) reg.28 and Sch.3 (October 7, 1996).

[1Relevant Education

2.106 [2 **12.**—For the purposes of these Regulations, a person is to be treated as receiving relevant education if he is a qualifying young person within the meaning of section 142 of the Contributions and Benefits Act (child and qualifying young person).]]

AMENDMENTS

1. Income Support (General) Amendment Regulations 1990 (SI 1990/547) reg.5 (April 9, 1990).

2. Social Security (Young Persons) Amendment Regulations 2006 (SI 2006/718) reg.2(2) (April 10, 2006).

DEFINITIONS

"child"—see SSCBA s.137(1).
"qualifying young person"—see reg.14.

GENERAL NOTE

The general rule under s.124(1)(d) of the Contributions and Benefits Act is that if a claimant is receiving relevant education he is not entitled to income support. Reg.12, which provides when a person is to be treated as receiving relevant education, was recast following the commencement of the Child Benefit Act 2005 on April 10, 2006. The test under reg.12 is now whether the person is a qualifying young person within the meaning of s.142 of the Contributions and Benefits Act 1992 (s.142 was substituted by s.1(2) of the 2005 Act on April 10, 2006). **2.107**

Qualifying young person
The Child Benefit Act 2005 changes the definition of "child" for the purposes of child benefit so that it is now divided into a "child", which means a person under 16, and a "qualifying young person" (see the substituted s.142 of the Contributions and Benefits Act in Vol.IV of this series). A "qualifying young person" is a person who is 16 or over but who has not attained a prescribed age and who satisfies prescribed conditions. Thus the upper age limit for child benefit and the conditions under which child benefit will be paid for a young person aged 16 or over are now all contained in secondary legislation (see regs 3–8 of the Child Benefit (General) Regulations 2006 (SI 2006/223) in Vol.IV). The Government stated that its intention in the first instance was to extend child benefit to young people who were undertaking "approved training" and to 19-year-olds who were completing such training or a course of full-time, non-advanced education; thus the increase in eligibility is relatively modest, at least at this point. **2.108**

The substance of the definition of "qualifying young person" is in reg.3 of the 2006 Child Benefit Regulations. It applies to a person who is: (i) under 20; *and* (ii) undertaking a course of full-time, non-advanced education, which is not provided by virtue of his employment or any office held by him, but which is provided at a school or college, or elsewhere as approved by the Revenue (in the latter case he must have been receiving the approved education before he was 16); *or* (iii) in England (from June 4, 2014), receiving "appropriate full-time education" (commonly referred to as "16–19 study programmes") within s.4 Education and Skills Act 2008, which is not advanced education (see reg.3(2)(ab)(i) which reproduces the definition of "advanced education" in reg.1(3) of the 2006 Child Benefit Regulations), and which is not provided by virtue of his employment or any office held by him (there is no requirement as to where the education is provided); *or* (iv) undertaking approved training that is not provided by means of a contract of employment. "Approved training" covers various training programmes under "arrangements made by the Government" (see the definitions of both these terms in reg.1(3) of the 2006 Regulations). Note that from August 31, 2015 there are no programmes specified for the purposes of the definition of "approved training" in England (sub-para. (a) which used to list these programmes in England was omitted by reg.2(a) of the Child Benefit (General) (Amendment) Regulations 2015 (SI 2015/1512) with effect from August 31, 2015). The Explanatory Memorandum which accompanies SI 2015/1512 appears to take the view that such training will fall within s.4 of the Education and Skills Act 2008 since a study programme under s.4 also includes traineeship. In Scotland approved training includes Employability Fund activity and in Wales it includes Traineeships or Foundation Apprenticeships.

However, note that a person aged 19 can only be a qualifying young person if he began, or was enrolled on, or had been accepted to undertake, the full time education or approved training before he was 19 (although a person who was on such a course/training and has been accepted or enrolled to undertake another such course/training is also included). Furthermore, the new rules did not apply to anyone who became 19 before April 10, 2006; such a person cannot be a "qualifying young person".

2.109 "Full-time education" (defined in reg.1(3) of the 2006 Regulations; the definition is broadly similar to that which applied under the previous child benefit regulations) requires contact hours of at least 12 a week during term-time. *R(F) 1/93* held that "supervised study" (in reg.5 of the Child Benefit Regulations 1976) "would normally be understood to import the presence or close proximity of a teacher or tutor".

A 16–19 year old is not a qualifying person if he is receiving in his own right income support, income-based JSA, incapacity benefit for people disabled in youth, ESA, tax credit or universal credit (reg.8 of the 2006 Regulations).

Ceasing to be a qualifying young person

2.110 A person continues to be a qualifying young person during temporary interruptions, like school holidays, or by reason of illness, etc. When he ceases actually to receive relevant education or approved training he still counts as a qualifying young person (unless he is in remunerative work of 24 hours or more a week and in certain other circumstances) until: (i) in the case of a 16-year-old, the August 31 which follows his 16th birthday (reg.4 of the 2006 Regulations); or (ii) in the case of a person who leaves the education or training before he is 20, the first Sunday on or after the next "terminal date", or, if he reaches 20 before that date, the Sunday on or after his 20th birthday (unless his 20th birthday is on a Monday when he will count as a qualifying person until the Sunday before his birthday). The terminal dates are the last day in February, the last day in May, the last day in August and the last day in November (reg.7 of the 2006 Regulations). The terminal dates are no longer based on school terms as they now also apply to young people who leave approved training. In addition, reg.5 of the 2006 Regulations allows for a twenty week "extension period" for 16- and 17-year-olds who have left education or training (note that "education" and "training" are not defined in this context and so may refer to any kind of education or training) and who are registered for work, education or training, not in remunerative work of 24 hours or more a week and not in receipt of income support, income-based JSA, incapacity benefit for people disabled in youth, ESA, tax credit or universal credit. Provided that a written application for the extension is made within three months of the 16- or17-year-old ceasing education or training, he will continue to count as a qualifying young person during the extension period (or until he reaches 18). Note that this extension period begins on the first day of the week after that in which the 16- or 17-year-old left education or training. Thus it no longer follows on from but runs concurrently with the automatic extension period relevant in his case.

Note that the reg.12 question is one to which the assumption in reg.13(2) of the Decisions and Appeals Regulations 1999 (see Vol.III in this series) applies. If the Secretary of State considers that he does not have all the relevant information or evidence to decide whether the person should count as in relevant education, he will proceed on the basis that the child benefit decision would be adverse to the claimant in the income support sense.

Note also reg.13 and para.15A of Sch.1B which allow certain claimants to receive income support though in relevant education.

Circumstances in which persons in relevant education may be entitled to income support

2.111 **13.**—(1) Notwithstanding that a person is to be treated as receiving relevant education under regulation 12 (relevant education) he shall, if paragraph (2) applies to him and he satisfies the other conditions of entitlement to income support, be entitled to income support.

(2) This paragraph applies to [3a person [7 who [8 (subject to paragraph

(2A))] is a qualifying young person within the meaning of section 142 of the Contributions and Benefits Act (child and qualifying young person)] (hereinafter referred to as an eligible person)] who—

(a) is the parent of a child for whom he is treated as responsible under regulation 15 (circumstances in which a person is to be treated as responsible or not responsible for another) and who is treated as a member of his household under regulation 16 (circumstances in which a person is to be treated as being or not being a member of the household); or

[7 (b) [10 . . .]

(bb) [10 . . .]

(bc) [15 . . .]]

(c) has no parent nor any person acting in the place of his parents; or

[1(d) of necessity has to live away from his [2 parents and any] person acting in the place of his parents because—

(i) he is estranged from his [2 parents and that person]; or

(ii) he is in physical or moral danger; or

(iii) there is a serious risk to his physical or mental health;] or

[4(dd) has ceased to live in accommodation provided for him by a local authority under Part III of the Children Act 1989 (local authority support for children and families) [11 or Part II of the Children (Scotland) Act 1995 (promotion of children's welfare by local authorities and by children's hearings etc.)] [14, or by virtue of any order or warrant made under the Children's Hearings (Scotland) Act 2011,] and is of necessity living away from his parents and any person acting in place of his parents;]

(e) is living away from his parents and any person acting in the place of his parents in a case where his parents are or, as the case may be, that person is unable financially to support him and—

(i) chronically sick or mentally or physically disabled; or

(ii) detained in custody pending trial or sentence upon conviction or under a sentence imposed by a court; or

(iii) prohibited from entering or re-entering Great Britain; or

(f) [6. . .]

(g) [6. . .]

[6(h) is a person to whom paragraph 18 of Schedule 1B (refugees) applies.]

[8 (2A) For the purposes of paragraph (2)—

(a) the eligible person shall be treated as satisfying the condition prescribed in regulation 8 of the Child Benefit (General) Regulations 2006 (child benefit not payable in respect of qualifying young person: other financial support);

(b) where sub-paragraphs (c) to (e) apply, the eligible person shall be treated as satisfying the condition prescribed in regulation 5(2)(e) and (f) of the Child Benefit (General) Regulations 2006 (extension period: 16 and 17 year olds).]

(3) In this regulation—

[5(a) any reference to a person acting in the place of an eligible person's parents includes—

(i) for the purposes of paragraph (2)(c), (d) and (dd), a reference to a local authority or voluntary organisation where the eligible person is being looked after by them under a relevant enactment or where the eligible person is placed by the local authority or voluntary organisation with another person, that other person whether or not a payment is made to him;

(ii) for the purposes of paragraph (2)(e), the person with whom the person is so placed;]

(b) "chronically sick or mentally disabled" means, in relation to a person to whom that expression refers, a person—

(i) in respect of whom the condition specified in paragraph 12(1) of Schedule 2 (additional condition for the higher pensioner and disability premiums) is satisfied; or

(ii) [9 . . .]

(iii) who is substantially and permanently disabled [12 ; or

(iv) who is entitled to an employment and support allowance which includes a work-related activity component or support component [13 or who would be entitled to an employment and support allowance including a work-related activity component but for the application of section 1A of the Welfare Reform Act (duration of contributory allowance)].]

Amendments

1. Family Credit and Income Support (General) Amendment Regulations 1989 (SI 1989/1034) reg.4 (July 10, 1989).

2. Income Support (General) Amendment Regulations 1991 (SI 1991/236) reg.5 (April 8, 1991).

3. Income Support (General) Amendment No.4 Regulations 1991 (SI 1991/1559) reg.6 August 5, 1991).

4. Income Support (General) Amendment Regulations 1992 (SI 1992/468) reg.3 (April 6, 1992).

5. Income Support (General) Amendment Regulations 1992 (SI 1992/468) Sch. para.2 (April 6, 1992).

6. Income Support (General) (Jobseeker's Allowance Consequential Amendments) Regulations 1996 (SI 1996/206) reg.7 (October 7, 1996).

7. Social Security (Young Persons) Amendment Regulations 2006 (SI 2006/718) reg.2(3) (April 10, 2006).

8. Social Security (Miscellaneous Amendments) Regulations 2008 (SI 2008/698) reg.2(4) (April 14, 2008).

9. Social Security (Miscellaneous Amendments) (No.4) Regulations 2009 (SI 2009/2655) reg.2(4) (October 26, 2009).

10. Income Support (Prescribed Categories of Person) Regulations 2009 (SI 2009/3152) reg.2 (December 30, 2009). Regulation 2(1)(a) revoked reg.13(2)(b) and (bb) with effect from December 30, 2009 but this was subject to the saving provisions in reg.2(2). See the 2015/16 edition of this volume for these Regulations and the notes to them.

11. Social Security (Miscellaneous Amendments) (No.2) Regulations 2010 (SI 2010/641 reg.2(5) (April 6, 2010).

12. Social Security (Miscellaneous Amendments) Regulations 2012 (SI 2012/757) reg.14 (April 1, 2012).

13. Employment and Support Allowance (Duration of Contributory Allowance) (Consequential Amendments) Regulations 2012 (SI 2012/913) reg.3(2) (May 1, 2012).

14. Children's Hearings (Scotland) Act 2011 (Consequential and Transitional Provisions and Savings) Order 2013 (SI 2013/1465) art.17(1) and Sch.1 Pt 2 para.12(2) (June 24, 2013).

15. Social Security (Miscellaneous Amendments) (No.3) Regulations 2013 (SI 2013/2536) reg.4(4) (October 29, 2013).

Definitions

"child"—see SSCBA s.137(1).
"relevant enactment"—see reg.2(1) and reg.16(8)(a).

General Note

In the circumstances set out in para.(2) a claimant, if he satisfies the other conditions of entitlement, is entitled to income support, even though he is treated as in relevant education under reg.12. From April 10, 2006 a person counts as in relevant education if he is a "qualifying young person within the meaning of s.142 of the Contributions and Benefits Act" (see further the note to reg.12). Some 19-year-olds now come with the definition of "qualifying young person" as well as certain 16-to 18-year-olds. 2.112

See also para.15A of Sch.1B which extends eligibility for income support to a person who is under 21 and has enrolled on, been accepted for, or is undertaking a course of full-time, non-advanced education, or who reaches the age of 21 while undertaking such a course and who satisfy conditions that are the same as those in para.(2)(c),(d) and (e).

However the effect of regs 2(4) and 8 of the Child Benefit Regulations 2006 (SI 2006/223) (see Vol.IV in this series) is that for a person to be a qualifying young person he must not be in receipt of certain benefits, including income support. Paragraph (2A)(a) therefore provides that a qualifying young person who meets any of the conditions in para.(2) (and is therefore entitled to income support) will be treated as satisfying the condition in reg.8 of the 2006 Regulations.

If a claimant satisfies any of para.(2)(a) to (e), he will be eligible for income support under para.15 of Sch.1B. If he comes within para.(2)(h), he will qualify under para.18.

Paragraph (2)

Sub-paragraph (a): A person of at least 16 who is the parent of a child who is in the same household can claim although in relevant education. 2.113

Sub-paragraphs (b) and (bb): These sub-paragraphs covered a qualifying young person who was entitled to the disability or severe disability premium (sub-para. (b)), or who had been incapable of work, or treated as incapable of work, or treated as capable of work by virtue of reg.18 of the Incapacity for Work Regulations (disqualification for misconduct, etc.), or entitled to statutory sick pay, for at least 28 weeks (two or more periods separated by not more than eight weeks counted as continuous) (sub- para.(bb). However, as a consequence of the introduction of ESA, *new* claims for income support under sub-paras (b) and (bb) were no longer possible from October 27, 2008, except in certain circumstances. Sub-paragraphs (b) and (bb) were then revoked on December 30, 2009, subject to a saving provision. See pp.284–286 of the 2015/16 edition of this volume under "*Consequences of the introduction of ESA*", "*Revocation of sub-paras (b) and (bb) on December 30, 2009*" and "*Migration to ESA*" for further details. 2.114

Sub-paragraph (bc): This covered a qualifying young person who had limited leave to enter or remain in the UK without recourse to public funds but who was temporarily without funds because remittances from abroad had been interrupted. However, sub-para.(bc) was revoked on October 29, 2013 because entitlement to income support in those circumstances (under reg.2(1) of and para.1 of Pt I of the Schedule to the Social Security (Immigration and Asylum) Consequentional Amendments Regulations 2000 (SI 2000/636)) was abolished with effect from October 29, 2013. 2.115

Sub-paragraph (c): A parent presumably means a natural parent or an adoptive parent. A person acting in place of parents may include some informal relation- 2.116

ships, for example, where a child's parents have died and the child is brought up by another member of the family. It did not include, however, the claimant's boyfriend's father in *NP v SSWP* [2009] UKUT 243 (AAC).The claimant was living with her boyfriend at the house of his father. The father provided shelter and some food but took no financial or parental responsibility for her and had not claimed child benefit or child tax credit in respect of her. Judge Wikeley, while accepting that a person acting in place of a parent need not formally hold parental responsibility in relation to the young person, confirms that the person must in practice be acting broadly in a way that a parent would.

If a person is claiming child benefit or child tax credit for the eligible person, this would be a relatively strong factor.

However, a sponsor under the Immigration Act 1971 is not a person acting in place of parents. A sponsor's duties are restricted to the maintenance and accommodation of the dependant without recourse to public funds and there is no responsibility for other aspects of the dependant's life (*R(IS) 9/94*).

2.117 Paragraph (3)(a)(i) specifically includes for this purpose local authorities and voluntary organisations who are looking after children (what used to be known as having them in care) under a relevant enactment (defined in reg.16(8)(a)), and foster parents with whom the eligible person has been placed by *the* local authority or voluntary organisation. Since head (i) refers to eligible persons placed by "the", not "a", local authority or voluntary organisation, it would seem that head (i) only applies where the eligible person is being looked after by the local authority or voluntary organisation under a relevant enactment. In *CIS 447/1994* the claimant was estranged from his parents. A local authority social worker gave him a list of approved accommodation and he went to lodge at an address on the list. The Commissioner decides that "placed" in the second limb of para.(3)(a)(i) referred to placement under the Children Act. But even if it did not, in the Commissioner's view, providing the claimant with a list of approved accommodation did not constitute "placing" him (even in a non-technical sense) with another person. This did not mean that the second limb was redundant. Its purpose was to make clear that where a claimant had been placed with a person by a local authority, it was estrangement, etc., from that person, not from the local authority, that was relevant.

CIS 11766/1996 concerned the position of a claimant who had continued to live with his ex-foster parents after his care order had ended. The Commissioner follows the approach of *CSB 325/1985* and holds that ex-foster parents cease to be acting in place of parents when their fostering contract comes to an end.

Note para.(2A)(b) which deems a 16- or 17-year old who is in the child benefit extension period to satisfy the conditions in reg.5(2)(e) and (f) of the Child Benefit Regulations 2006 (SI 2006/223) (these provisions require that the person responsible for the qualifying young person was entitled to child benefit in respect of him and has applied for payment of this during the child benefit extension period; they are therefore unlikely to be met by a person who comes within sub-para.(c)). This will allow the 16-or 17-year old to remain on income support during the child benefit extension period and avoid the need for him to claim income-based JSA for a short period if there is a gap between his terminal date and his return to education or training.

2.118 *Sub-paragraph (d)*: See sub-para.(c) above for the meaning of parent and of person acting in place of a parent. The 1991 amendment to the effect that the eligible person must be living away from parents *and* substitutes (and see head (i) on estrangement) was described by the DSS as technical. However, this was a change of substance. The previous form referred to living away from or estrangement from parents *or* substitutes. When the Conditions of Entitlement Regulations were in this form, *CSB 677/1983* decided that the eligible person qualified if estranged from his parents even though he was not estranged from a person acting in their place. Now the eligible person has to be living away from or estranged from both. See sub-para.(dd) on eligible persons leaving care.

If the eligible person is within the child benefit extension period note para.(2A) (b) (see the note to sub-para.(c)).

Head (i): The 1989 form of sub-para.(d) is an attempt to provide a test of "genuine estrangement." It is in some respects stricter than the previous form because in addition to showing estrangement, the person in relevant education must also show that as a result, at least partly, of that he has of necessity to live away from his parents and any substitute. It is obviously a matter of judgment when estrangement is serious enough to necessitate that the young person leaves home. There is perhaps some widening in the addition of two extra categories which may lead to a need to leave home. 2.119

Estrangement has "connotations of emotional disharmony" (*R(SB) 2/87, R(IS) 5/05*), although *CH/117/2005* and *CH/3777/2007* (discussed in the note to para.4(b) of Sch.10) take a contrary view. Whether emotional disharmony is a necessary feature may depend on the context but it is suggested that it is relevant in the context of head (i). It seems that estrangement can exist even though financial support is being provided (see, for example, *CIS/11441/1995* below).

In *CIS/4096/2005* the claimant's partner, K, who was aged 16 and in full-time education, had come to live with him after her mother had asked her to leave the family home. The mother did not like the claimant and did not approve of her daughter's pregnancy. The tribunal accepted that K was estranged from her mother but concluded that head (i) did not apply because the alienation was not mutual. The Commissioner reviewed the authorities on estrangement and concluded that there was no requirement of mutuality of feeling for estrangement to exist (as had been suggested by the Commissioner in *CIS/4498/2001*). Disharmony could arise from one person's attitude to another even though the other person might not wish this to be the situation. The position had to be judged from the point of view of the claimant and not from the point of view of the parent(s) or any person acting in place of the parent(s). Since K was estranged from her mother she came within head (i).

CIS 11441/1995 decides that estrangement from a local authority can exist. The claimant, aged 16, was in the care of a local authority but because of her violent and aggressive behaviour in a community home it had been decided that she should live in rented accommodation by herself. She was given help to find suitable accommodation and the authority met her liability for council tax and because income support had been refused provided her with a payment equivalent to her income support entitlement. Her rent was met through housing benefit. The care order remained in place as the claimant wished it to continue for "emotional" reasons. The Commissioner decides that sub-para.(dd) did not apply because the local authority were continuing to provide the claimant with accommodation by supervising and assisting in the arrangements for her rented accommodation (see s.23(2)(f) of the Children Act 1989). But sub-para.(d) did apply. The claimant was "living away" from the local authority because she was living away from the people who represented the authority, i.e. the community home (the terms of reg.13 were clearly intended to reverse *R(SB) 2/87* which had held that it was not possible for a person to live away from a local authority). Further it was "necessary" for her to do this because it had been accepted that it was not possible for the claimant to live in a community home or with foster parents. Moreover she was "estranged" from the local authority because she was estranged from the community home where the local authority had placed her. The fact that she continued to have some contact with and received some assistance from the local authority did not alter the fact of the estrangement. 2.120

See further the decisions on the meaning of "estrangement" discussed in the note to para.4 of Sch.10, although note that the meaning may depend, to some degree at least, on the context (see *CPC/683/2007*).

Head (ii): Under head (ii), the meaning of "physical or moral danger" is again a matter of judgment. It is not a term of art with an established meaning. Obvious points are that a person can be in danger from himself or from others and that a danger can exist before any harm has actually occurred (see *Kelly v Monklands DC* 2.121

1986 S.L.T. 169 on the phrase "at risk of sexual or financial exploitation" in the Code of Guidance on Homelessness). Nor is the danger specified to be immediate, but the test will no doubt be whether the danger is sufficient to necessitate living away from parents or their substitute. The danger does not have to emanate from the pupil's parents. In *R(IS) 9/94* the claimant's parents were in a refugee camp in Ethiopia, having fled there after civil war broke out in Somalia. It is held that he had to live away from his parents in view of the situation in Somalia, as otherwise he was in physical or moral danger; in addition, there was a serious risk to his physical or mental health under head (iii).

2.122 *Head (iii)*: Under head (iii) there is an echo of the "serious risk to health" test of reg.30 of the Supplementary Benefit (Single Payments) Regulations. There was there some dispute about how closely a tribunal had to define the seriousness of the risk (compare *R(SB) 5/81* and *CSB 11/81* with *R(SB) 3/82* and *R(SB) 8/82*). The nature of the risk must no doubt be identified (as the danger must be under head (ii)) and some reason given why it is serious enough to necessitate living away from parents and any substitute. See *R(IS) 9/94* in the notes to head (ii).

2.123 *Sub-paragraph (dd)*: This provision protects the entitlement of eligible persons leaving local authority care who need to live away from their parents and any substitute without the necessity of proving estrangement or moral danger or one of the other conditions in sub-para.(d). See the note to sub-para.(c) for the meaning of parent and person acting in place of a parent.

If the eligible person is within the child benefit extension period note para.(2A)(b) (see the note to sub-para.(c)).

2.124 *Sub-paragraph (e)*: Here the eligible person must be living away from both parents and persons acting in place of parents, and they must be unable to provide financial support. The reason for this inability must be one of those listed. See para.(3)(b) for the definition of chronically sick or mentally or physically disabled. This includes (from April 1, 2012) a person who is entitled to ESA with either the work-related activity component or the support component. It also includes (from May 1, 2012) a person who would have been entitled to ESA with a work-related activity component but for the 365 days' limit on entitlement to contributory ESA for a person who is in the work-related activity group (this limit was introduced by s.1A of the Welfare Reform Act 2007 (inserted into the 2007 Act by s.51 of the Welfare Reform Act 2012 on May 1, 2012)).

See the note to sub-para.(c) for the meaning of parent and person acting in place of a parent.

If the eligible person is within the child benefit extension period note para.(2A)(b) (see the note to sub-para.(c)).

2.125 *Head (iii)*: In *R(IS) 9/94* the claimant's parents who were in a refugee camp in Ethiopia had no leave to enter the UK at the date of the claim. Under s.3 of the Immigration Act 1971 (subject to certain exceptions) all persons who are not British citizens require leave to enter the UK. The claimant's parents were thus prohibited from entering Great Britain.

2.126 *Sub-paragraph (h)*: This is a special case of refugees.

Paragraph (3)(a)

2.127 See the note to para.(2)(c).

[[1]Persons under 18 years

2.128 **13A.**—[[2]. . .],]

AMENDMENTS

1. Income Support (General) Amendment No.3 Regulations 1988 (SI 1988/1228) reg.4 (September 12, 1988).

2. Income Support (General) (Jobseeker's Allowance Consequential Amendments) Regulations 1996 (SI 1996/206) reg.28 and Sch.3 (October 7, 1996).

PART III

MEMBERSHIP OF THE FAMILY

Persons of a prescribed description

14.—(1) Subject to paragraph (2), a person of a prescribed description for the purposes of section 20(11) of the Act [SSCBA, s.137(1)] as it applies to income support (definition of the family) and section 23(1) [[1]and (3)] of the Act [SSCBA, s.126(1) and (3)] is a person [[5] who falls within the definition of qualifying young person in section 142 of the Contributions and Benefits Act (child and qualifying young person)], and in these Regulations such a person is referred to as a "young person". 2.129

[[3] (2) Paragraph (1) shall not apply to a person who is—

(a) [[5] . . .];

(b) entitled to income support or would, but for section 134(2) (provision against dual entitlement of members of family) of the Contributions and Benefits Act, be so entitled; [[6] . . .]

(c) a person to whom section 6 of the Children (Leaving Care) Act 2000 (exclusion from benefits) applies.] [[6] [[7] . . .]

(d) entitled to an employment and support allowance or would, but for paragraph 6(1)(d) of Schedule 1 to the Welfare Reform Act (conditions of entitlement to income-related employment and support allowance), be so entitled [[7] ; or

(e) entitled to universal credit].]

[[4] (3) A person of a prescribed description for the purposes of section 137(1) of the Contributions and Benefits Act as it applies to income support (definition of family) includes a child or young person in respect of whom section 145A of that Act applies for the purposes of entitlement to child benefit but only for the period prescribed under section 145A(1) of that Act.]

AMENDMENTS

1. Income Support (General) Amendment No.4 Regulations 1988 (SI 1988/1445) reg.5 (September 12, 1988).

2. Income Support (General) Amendment Regulation 1990 (SI 1990/547) reg.6 (April 9, 1990).

3. Children (Leaving Care) Act 2000 (Commencement No.2 and Consequential Provisions) Order 2001 (SI 2001/3070) art.3(2) and Sch.1 para.(b) (October 1, 2001).

4. Income-related Benefits and Jobseeker's Allowance (Working Tax Credit and Child Tax Credit) (Amendment) Regulations 2002 (SI 2002/2402) reg.2 and Sch.1 para.2 (April 6, 2003).

5. Social Security (Young Persons) Amendment Regulations 2006 (SI 2006/718), reg.2(4) (April 10, 2006).

6. Employment and Support Allowance (Consequential Provisions) (No.2) Regulations 2008 (SI 2008/1554) reg.2(1) and (4) (October 27, 2008).

7. Universal Credit (Consequential, Supplementary, Incidental and Miscellaneous Provisions) Regulations 2013 (SI 2013/630) reg.28(1) and (3) (April 29, 2013).

DEFINITION

"the Act"—see reg.2(1).

GENERAL NOTE

2.130 For the circumstances in which a person of 16 to 19 is treated as a qualifying young person for child benefit purposes, see reg.12. If such a person could be entitled to income support or ESA in his or her own right (see reg.13) (para.(2)(b) and (d)) or is a 16- or 17-year-old who has been looked after by a local authority in England or Wales on or after October 1, 2001 or a local authority in Scotland on or after April 1, 2004 and is excluded from income support, income-based JSA and housing benefit (see the notes to reg.2 of the Children (Leaving Care) Social Security Benefits Regulations 2001 (SI 2001/3074) (p.956) and to reg.2 of the Children (Leaving Care) Social Security Benefits (Scotland) Regulations 2004 (SI 2004/747) (p.960)) (para.(2)(c)), that person does not come within reg.14. Under s.145A of SSCBA 1992 and reg.20 of the Child Benefit (General) Regulations 2006 (see Vol.I) a claimant who is entitled to child benefit for a child who dies continues to receive that benefit for the following eight weeks or until the end of the week which would have included the qualifying young person's 20th birthday (whichever is the shorter period). Paragraph (3), taken together with the amendment to reg.15(1), has the effect that such a claimant will also continue to get income support in respect of the dead child for the same period.

Circumstances in which a person is to be treated as responsible or not responsible for another

2.131 **15.**—[1(1) Subject to the following provisions of this regulation, a person is to be treated as responsible for a child or young person for whom he is receiving child benefit [2 and this includes a child or young person to whom paragraph (3) of regulation 14 applies].

(1A) In a case where a child ("the first child") is in receipt of child benefit in respect of another child ("the second child"), the person treated as responsible for the first child in accordance with the provisions of this regulation shall also be treated as responsible for the second child.

(2) In the case of a child or young person in respect of whom no person is receiving child benefit, the person who shall be treated as responsible for that child or young person shall be—

(a) except where sub-paragraph (b) applies, the person with whom the child or young person usually lives; or

(b) where only one claim for child benefit has been made in respect of the child or young person, the person who made that claim.]

(3) Where regulation 16(6) (circumstances in which a person is to be treated as being or not being a member of the household) applies in respect of a child or young person, that child or young person shall be treated as the responsibility of the claimant for that part of the week for which he is under that regulation treated as being a member of the claimant's household.

(4) Except where paragraph (3) applies, for the purposes of these Regulations a child or young person shall be treated as the responsibility of only one person in any benefit week and any person other than the one treated as responsible for the child or young person under this regulation shall be treated as not so responsible.

AMENDMENTS

1. Income-related Benefits Schemes (Miscellaneous Amendments) (No.4) Regulations 1993 (SI 1993/2119) reg.5 (October 4, 1993).
2. Income-related Benefits and Jobseeker's Allowance (Working Tax Credit and Child Tax Credit) (Amendment) Regulations 2002 (SI 2002/2402) reg.2 and Sch.1 para.2 (April 6, 2003).

DEFINITIONS

"benefit week"—see reg.2(1).
"child"—see SSCBA s.137(1).
"claimant"—see reg.2(1).
"young person"—*ibid.*, and reg.14.

GENERAL NOTE

Paragraph (1)

This regulation sets out the circumstances in which a person is "responsible" for a child or young person for the purposes of income support. Before April 6, 2004 that question determined whether or not the claimant could claim an applicable amount for the child or young person under regs 17(b) or 18(c) and a family premium under regs 17(c) or 18(d) (because of the definition of "family" in s.137(1) of the Contributions and Benefits Act). Subject to exceptions in transitional cases (as to which see the note to reg.17), income support became an "adults only" benefit on April 6, 2004 with all support for the costs of bringing up children and young persons transferred to child tax credit and regs 17(b) and (c) and 18(c) and (d) were repealed. Regulation 15 has not, however, been repealed, because it continues to be of relevance to the issue of whether or not a claimant is a "lone parent" within para.1 of Sch.1B, for the purposes of housing costs (see Sch.3) and in the transitional cases referred to above. 2.132

The definition of family in s.137(1) of the Contributions and Benefits Act refers to a person being responsible for a child or young person (on which see reg.14). Regulation 15 makes the test of responsibility receipt of child benefit.

In *CIS/2317/2006*, the Commissioner confirmed that the person who is "receiving child benefit" for the purposes of para.(1) is the person who claimed and was awarded that benefit even when that person subsequently paid over a sum equal to the amount of that benefit to another person.

Similarly in *CJSA/2811/2006* a father who (before separating from the mother) had his name on the child benefit book as an alternative payee under reg.34(1) of the Child Benefit and Guardian's Allowance (Administration) Regulations 2003 and who—with the mother's consent—continued to receive child benefit under her claim following the separation was not "receiving child benefit" for the purpose of the equivalent provision of the JSA Regulations. 2.133

In *C2/01–02(IS)(T)*, a Tribunal of Commissioners in Northern Ireland rejected a challenge to the vires of the Northern Ireland equivalent of reg.15(1). The regulation was held not to conflict either with the requirement under art.3 of the Children Order (Northern Ireland) 1995 (equivalent to s.1 of the Children Act 1989) that where a court determines a question with respect to the upbringing of a child, that child's welfare is to be the paramount consideration or with the provisions of the Northern Ireland Act 1998 which apply the European Convention on Human Rights within the province.

Paragraph (1A)

If a child (B) for whom a person (A) is responsible gets child benefit for another child (C), (A) is also treated as responsible for (C). 2.134

Paragraph (2) 2.135

If no one is receiving child benefit for the child, then if one claim only has been made, the person who made that claim is responsible. Otherwise the person responsible is the person with whom the child usually lives. Since para.(4) refers to consideration of responsibility on the basis of benefit weeks, the test of where a child usually lives should be applied week by week and not on some kind of overall assessment on a long-term basis (*CIS 49/1991*). In the vast majority of cases, however, the question of who is responsible for a child for the purposes of income support will now be determined by who is receiving child benefit. The rules for child benefit include methods of establishing priorities between claimants, and a child benefit claimant can agree that someone with lower priority should be paid it.

Paragraphs (3) and (4)

2.136 Paragraph (4) provides that only one person can be treated as responsible for a child in any one benefit week. There is no provision for dividing up income support where a child spends time in different households. The only exceptions are under para.(3), which allows a person to be treated as responsible for a child for the part of the week in which he is in the household, but only where the child is being looked after by a local authority or is in custody (reg.16(6)). The result of the new test is that if someone else is in receipt of child benefit for a child in any one benefit week, an income support claimant cannot be treated as responsible for that child even if the child spends most of, or even all, his time with the claimant. This may provide for even greater administrative simplicity than the previous test of primary responsibility but at a cost of a lack of justice in certain situations.

In this connection note *R. (Chester) v Secretary of State for Social Security* [2001] EWHC (Admin) 1119, HC, December 7, 2001. The claimant and her husband had separated and a contact order provided that the children should reside with her husband during the week in school term times and with the claimant over the weekends and for half of the school holidays. Both the claimant and her husband applied for child benefit. The Secretary of State awarded child benefit to the husband and the claimant applied for judicial review, relying largely on art.8 of the ECHR (right to respect for family life). Collins J held that the Secretary of State had erred in law because he could have made an award which reflected more closely the division of care (for example, a fairer result could have been achieved by awarding the claimant child benefit for one child for the whole period of the school holidays). Collins J also pointed to the power in reg.34 of the Claims and Payments Regulations under which benefit can be paid to a third party on behalf of a beneficiary. However, the question as to the effect that that would have on the claimant's JSA was left open. Although the actual decision in *Chester* remains good law, Collins J's suggestion that payment of child benefit to only one parent in shared care cases might be capable of amounting to a breach of art.8 of the European Convention on Human Rights (or, possibly, arts 8 and 14 taken together) is impossible to reconcile with the decision of the Court of Appeal in *Carson and Reynolds v Secretary of State for Work & Pensions* [2003] EWCA Civ 797. More recently, in CIS/4003/2001 and CIS/1616/2004, two different Commissioners have confirmed that the failure to make split payments of child benefit does not interfere with a claimant's Convention Rights. In *Hockenjos v Secretary of State for Social Security* [2004] EWCA Civ 1749, the Court of Appeal held (on appeal from CJSA/4890/1998) that reg.77(1)–(3) and (5) of the JSA Regulations (equivalent to paras (1)–(2) and (4)) discriminated against men contrary to art.4 of EC Directive 79/7 (see Vol.III) and therefore could not be applied to Mr Hockenjos and, by implication, to any man within the personal scope of that Directive—see further the note to reg.77 of the JSA Regulations. Note, however, that although that decision applies to both income-based and contribution-based JSA—see the earlier decision of the Court of Appeal in the same case (*Hockenjos v Secretary of State for Social Security* [2001] EWCA Civ 624; [2001] 2 C.M.L.R. 51; [2001] I.C.R. 966)—it does not apply to income support because that benefit is not within the material scope of the Directive —see *Jackson and Cresswell v Chief Adjudication Officer* (C–63/91 and C–64/91) [1992] E.C.R. I-4737 (also reported as an appendix to *R(IS) 10/91*).

Although Dir.79/7 does not apply to income support, it could be argued—by analogy with *Hockenjos*—that the link between entitlement to IS and child benefit and the "one child one claimant" rule discriminate unlawfully against men contrary to ECHR art.14 and art.1 of Protocol 1. However, the point is probably academic because it has not been possible to make a fresh claim for the child elements of IS since September 7, 2005 (see the commentary to reg.17 below). If unusual circumstances were to occur in which it might benefit a man to make such a claim, it seems probable that any discrimination would be held to be objectively justified: see the decisions of the Supreme Court on the similar (but not identical) rule for child tax credit in *Humphreys v HMRC* [2012] UKSC 18, [2012] AACR 46 and of the Upper Tribunal on the similar (but not identical) rules for housing benefit and council tax benefit in *Camden LBC v NW and SSWP (HB)* [2011] UKUT 262 (AAC).

Circumstances in which a person is to be treated as being or not being a member of the household

16.—(1) Subject to paragraphs (2) and (5), the claimant and any partner and, where the claimant or his partner is treated as responsible under regulation 15 (circumstances in which a person is to be treated as responsible or not responsible for another) for a child or young person, that child or young person and any child of that child or young person shall be treated as members of the same household [[1]notwithstanding that any of them] [[7]is temporarily living away from the other members of his family]. 2.137

[[7](2) Paragraph (1) shall not apply to a person who is living away from the other members of his family where—

(a) that person does not intend to resume living with the other members of his family; or

(b) his absence from the other members of his family is likely to exceed 52 weeks, unless there are exceptional circumstances (for example the person is in hospital or otherwise has no control over the length of his absence), and the absence is unlikely to be substantially more than 52 weeks.]

(3) Paragraph (1) shall not apply in respect of any member of a couple or of a polygamous marriage where—

(a) one, both or all of them are patients detained in a hospital provided under section 4 of the National Health Service Act 1977 ([[12] high security psychiatric services]) or [[10] section 102 of the National Health Service (Scotland) Act 1978 (state hospitals)]; or

[[9](b) one, both or all of them are—

(i) detained in custody pending trial or sentence upon conviction or under a sentence imposed by a court; or

(ii) on temporary release in accordance with the provisions of the Prison Act 1952 or the Prisons (Scotland) Act 1989;]

(c) [[6]. . .]

(d) the claimant is abroad and does not satisfy the conditions of regulation 4 (temporary absence from Britain); or

(e) one of them is permanently [[11] residing in a care home, an Abbeyfield Home or an independent hospital.]

(4) A child or young person shall not be treated as a member of the claimant's household where he is—

[[5](a) placed with the claimant or his partner by a local authority under section 23(2)(a) of the Children Act 1989 or by a voluntary organisation under section 59(1)(a) of that Act; or

(b) placed with the claimant or his partner prior to adoption; or]

(c) placed for adoption with the claimant or his partner pursuant to a decision under the Adoption Agencies Regulations 1983 or the Adoption Agencies (Scotland) Regulations 1984.

(5) Subject to paragraph (6), paragraph (1) shall not apply to a child or young person who is not living with the claimant[[1] and who]—

(a) [[4]in a case which does not fall within sub-paragraph (aa),] has been continuously absent from Great Britain for a period of more than four weeks commencing—

(i) [[8] subject to paragraph (5A),] where he went abroad before the date of claim for income support, with that date;

(ii) in any other case,[[4]on the day which immediately follows the day] on which he went abroad; or

[[4](aa) where regulation 4(3) or paragraph 11A or 12A of Schedule 7 (temporary absence abroad for the treatment of a child or young person) applies, has been continuously absent from Great Britain for a period of more than eight weeks, that period of eight weeks commencing—

(i) [[8] subject to paragraph (5A),] where he went abroad before the date of the claim for income support, on the date of that claim;

(ii) in any other case, on the day which immediately follows the day on which he went abroad; or]

(b) has been an in-patient or in [[1]accommodation [[11] . . .]] for a continuous period of more than 12 weeks commencing—

(i) [[8] subject to paragraph (5A),] where he became an in-patient or, as the case may be, entered that accommodation, before the date of the claim for income support, with that date; or

(ii) in any other case, with the date on which he became an in-patient or entered that accommodation,

and, in either case, has not been in regular contact with either the claimant or any member of the claimant's household; or

[[5](c) is being looked after by a local authority under a relevant enactment; or

(d) has been placed with a person other than the claimant prior to adoption; or]

(e) has been placed for adoption pursuant to a decision under the Adoption Agencies Regulations 1983 or the Adoption Agencies (Scotland) Regulations 1984; or

(f) is detained in custody pending trial or sentence upon conviction or under a sentence imposed by a court.

[[8](5A) Sub-paragraphs (a)(i), (aa)(i) and (b)(i) of paragraph (5) shall not apply in a case where immediately before the date of claim for income support the claimant was entitled to an income-based jobseeker's allowance.]

(6) A child or young person to whom any of the circumstances mentioned in sub-paragraphs (c) or (f) of paragraph (5) applies shall be treated as being a member of the claimant's household only for that part of any benefit week where that child or young person lives with the claimant.

(7) Where a child or young person for the purposes of attending the educational establishment at which he is receiving relevant education is living with the claimant or his partner and neither one is treated as responsible for that child or young person that child or young person shall be treated

as being a member of the household of the person treated as responsible for him and shall not be treated as a member of the claimant's household.

(8) In this regulation—

[11 (za) "accommodation" means accommodation provided by a local authority in a home owned or managed by that local authority—

(i) under sections 21 to 24 of the National Assistance Act 1948 (provision of accommodation),

(ii) in Scotland, under section 13B or 59 of the Social Work (Scotland) Act 1968 (provision of residential or other establishment), [13 . . .]

(iii) under section 25 of the Mental Health (Care and Treatment) (Scotland) Act 2003 (care and support services etc.), [13 or

(iv) under section 18 or 19 of the Care Act 2014 (duty and power to meet needs for care and support),

where the accommodation is provided for a person whose stay in that accommodation has become other than temporary;]

[5(a) "relevant enactment" means the Army Act 1955, the Social Work (Scotland) Act 1968, the Matrimonial Causes Act 1973, the Adoption (Scotland) Act 1978, the Family Law Act 1986 and the Children Act 1989;]

(b) "voluntary organisation" has the meaning assigned to it in the [5Children Act 1989] or, in Scotland, the Social Work (Scotland) Act 1968.

AMENDMENTS

1. Income Support (General) Amendment Regulations 1988 (SI 1988/663) reg.8 (April 11, 1988).

2. Income Support (General) Amendment Regulations 1989 (SI 1989/534) reg.3 (April 10, 1989).

3. Income Support (General) Amendment Regulations 1989 (SI 1989/534) Sch.1 para.3 (October 9, 1989).

4. Income Support (General) Amendment Regulations 1990 (SI 1990/547) reg.7 (April 9, 1990).

5. Income Support (General) Amendment Regulations 1992 (SI 1992/468) Sch. para.3 (April 6, 1992). *Note:* The previous form (see the 1991 edition) of sub-paras (4)(a) and (b), (5)(c) and (d) and (8)(a) and (b) remains in force in Scotland. The new form was introduced on April 6, 1992, as a consequence of the Children Act 1989.

6. Social Security Benefits (Amendments Consequential Upon the Introduction of Community Care) Regulations 1992 (SI 1992/3147) Sch.1 para.1 (April 1, 1993).

7. Income-related Benefits Schemes (Miscellaneous Amendments) (No.4) Regulations 1993 (SI 1993/2119) reg.6 (October 4, 1993).

8. Income Support (General) (Jobseeker's Allowance Consequential Amendments) Regulations 1996 (SI 1996/206) reg.8 (October 7, 1996).

9. Income-related Benefits Schemes and Social Fund (Miscellaneous Amendments) Regulations 1996 (SI 1996/1944) reg.6(5) (October 7, 1996).

10. Mental Health (Care and Treatment) (Scotland) Act 2003 (Modification of Subordinate Legislation) Order 2005 (SSI 2005/445) art.2 and Sch. para.3(2) (Scotland) and the Mental Health (Care and Treatment) (Scotland) Act 2003 (Consequential Provisions) Order 2005, (SI 2005/2078) art.15 and Sch.3 para.3(3) (England and Wales) (October 5, 2005).

11. Social Security (Care Homes and Independent Hospitals) Regulations 2005 (SI 2005/2687) reg.2 and Sch.1 para.3 (October 24, 2005).

12. Social Security (Miscellaneous Amendments) (No.4) Regulations 2006 (SI 2006/2378) reg.5(2) (October 2, 2006).

13. Care Act 2014 (Consequential Amendments) (Secondary Legislation) Order 2015 (SI 2015/643) art.2 and Sch. para.5(2) (April 1, 2015).

DEFINITIONS

"child"—see SSCBA s.137(1).
"claimant"—see reg.2(1).
"couple"—*ibid.*
"date of claim"—*ibid.*
"dwelling occupied as the home"—*ibid.*
"partner"—see reg.2(1).
"polygamous marriage"—*ibid.*
"young person"—*ibid.*, and reg.14.

GENERAL NOTE

Paragraph (1)

2.138 This provision does two things. The first is to provide that a claimant and partner are deemed to be members of the same household, notwithstanding that they are temporarily apart. Before October 4, 1993, the deeming applied notwithstanding one partner's absence from the dwelling occupied as the home (see below). Since a partner is one of a married or unmarried couple and it is an essential part of the definition of both kinds of couple that the parties should be members of the same household, para.(1) cannot subvert the general meaning of household referred to in the notes to s.137(1) of the Contributions and Benefits Act (see *CIS 671/1992*). Paragraph (1) must only mean that because one partner is temporarily living elsewhere this does not in itself mean that membership of the same household ceases. This means that the exceptions in para.(3) perhaps do not achieve much, but probably indicate that those circumstances do terminate membership of the household.

The other thing done by para.(1) is to deem that where an adult is responsible for a child or young person under reg.15, the child or young person is to be treated as in the same household as the adult, notwithstanding that one of them is temporarily living elsewhere (again, before October 4, 1993, the test was absence from the home). After April 6, 2004, this deeming provision is only of relevance in relation to transitional cases (see the notes to reg.15 and reg.17). There are exceptions in paras (4) and (5).

Thus the test under para.(1) is now one of absence from other members of the family, rather than from the home. *CIS 209/1989* held that the old form of para.(1) only applied if there was a dwelling which could be regarded as the home of both partners. This is no longer required, but it is still necessary for the family to have previously lived as members of the same household. The Commissioner in *CIS 508/1992* seems to have accepted that the home need not have been in this country; how this applies to the new test of absence from other members of the family is not entirely clear. Temporarily is not defined and each case will need to be decided on its particular facts. However, adjudicating authorities still need to investigate whether either of the conditions in para.(2) applies. Note in particular *CIS 13805/1996* in the note to para.(2).

The difficulties which can arise when one member of a couple is living temporarily in a residential care home (or in any of the other types of accommodation listed in para.9 of Sch.7) while the other member continues to live at the couple's home were considered by the Commissioner in *CIS/1544/2001*. In those circumstances, para.9 provides that claimant's applicable amount is to be the higher of the applicable amount to which he would be entitled as a member of the couple or the aggregate of the applicable amounts to which he and his partner would be entitled as a single claimant or (in an appropriate case) as a lone parent. Previous DWP Guidance (now replaced—see *DMG Letter 05/02*) stated that for the purpose of carrying out this calculation, each member of the couple was to be treated as a non-dependent of the other. One consequence of this approach was that—under para.13(2)(a)(ii) of Sch.2—neither partner was entitled to the severe disability premium. The Commissioner held that there was no justification for such an approach. As long as the absence was only temporary, the claimant and his wife remained members of the same household by virtue of reg.16(1). Each therefore remained the partner of the other and could not be each other's non-dependant because of reg.3(2)(a). The notional calculation required by the second alternative in para.9 (which treated the couple as if they were single claimants and therefore did imply that they were to be treated as normally living apart) *only* applied for the purpose of calculating the applicable amount. Applying that approach, the claimant was entitled to have the severe disability premium to which his wife would have been entitled as a single claimant normally living on her own, included in her applicable amount.

Paragraph (2)

Paragraph (1) does not apply where the person living away does not intend to resume living together with the other members of the family or is likely to be away for more than 52 weeks (or longer in exceptional circumstances, provided it is not substantially longer). When either of these conditions applies membership of the same household immediately ceases. **2.139**

In *CIS 13805/1996* the Commissioner points out that the "not" in para.(2)(a) relates to "intend" rather than "resume". This was significant because it was possible for a person to have no intention one way or the other. For example, where a couple had agreed to live apart for a couple of months, and neither had an intention to resume living with the other, but equally neither had an intention not to do so, para.(2)(a) could apply. This interpretation was further supported by the fact that once an intention not to resume living together had been formed, a separation was no longer temporary and so para.(1) ceased to apply in any event; thus para.(2)(a) would serve no function (other perhaps than to provide a partial definition of "temporary") if it was read as only operating when there was an intention not to resume living together. The facts in *CIS 13805/1996* were that the claimant's husband was in Pakistan. He had applied for permission to enter the UK but it had not yet been granted. They intended to resume living together, as long as permission was granted for the claimant's husband to join her. The Commissioner states that the question therefore was whether such intention counted for the purposes of para.(2)(a). *CIS 508/1992* and *CIS 484/1993* had held in relation to para.4(8) of the former Sch.3 (now para.3(10)) that the intention to return must not be a contingent one. In the Commissioner's view the same interpretation applied for the purposes of para.(2)(a), since there was no material distinction between that provision and para.(2)(a). Thus para.(2)(a) applied because the claimant's intention to resume living in the same household as her husband was not an unqualified one. Therefore the fact that the claimant's husband was in remunerative work did not bar her from entitlement to income support.

Paragraph (3)

Paragraph (1) does not apply in these circumstances, as between partners and polygamous marriages. The intention seems to be that the members of the couple or marriage cease to be partners in these circumstances, but para.(3) does not exactly say so. Under sub-para.(b) a person required to live in a bail hostel is not "detained in custody" pending trial (*R(IS) 17/93*); see Sch.7 para.9 as to how his applicable amount is calculated if he is a member of a couple. However, once a person has been charged, he is detained in custody pending trial, even if subsequently no trial takes place (*R(IS) 1/94*). In *Chief Adjudication Officer v Carr, The Times*, June 2, 1994, also reported as *R(IS) 20/95*, the Court of Appeal held that a person on home leave while serving a prison sentence was not "detained in custody" during the leave period. The definition of "prisoner" in reg.21(3) was amended with effect from April 10, 1995, so as to include periods of temporary release, and sub-para.(b) has now been similarly amended with effect from October 7, 1996. **2.140**

Paragraph (4)

2.141 Children or young persons are not to be members of the household of their foster-parents or the people they are placed with for adoption. They therefore cannot be a member of the family.

Paragraph (5)

2.142 Paragraph (1) does not apply to a child or young person who is not living with the claimant when one of heads (a)–(f) applies. Again, the intention seems to be that in these circumstances the child or young person is to be treated as not a member of the household, but para.(5) does not expressly say so. It may be that the general test of membership of the household is relevant. See para.(8) for the meaning of "relevant enactment".

In *Secretary of State for Work & Pensions v Bobezes* [2005] EWCA Civ. 111, CA (Pill & Buxton LJJ and Lord Slynn of Hadley), February 16, 2005 (also reported as *R(IS) 6/05*), the claimant was denied an applicable amount for his 16-year-old step-daughter who was staying temporarily with her grandparents in Portugal. He argued that if he had been British it was probable that the grandparents would have been living in Great Britain with the consequence that para.(5)(a) would not have applied and the general rule in para.(1) would have treated his daughter as continuing to be a member of his household during her temporary absence. The issue before the Commissioner (*CIS/825/2001*) had been whether the fact that income support was a special non-contributory benefit within art.4(2)(a) of Council Regulation 1408/71 (see Vol.III) (and therefore, under art.10a payable "exclusively . . . in accordance with the legislation of" Great Britain), prevented Mr Bobezes from arguing that para.(5)(a) therefore discriminated against him indirectly on the grounds of his Portuguese nationality contrary to art.7 of Council Regulation 1612/68 (see Vol.III). The Commissioner held that it did not but, by the time the case reached the Court of Appeal, it was appreciated that nothing actually turned on this point because, even if Regulation 1408/71 applied to the exclusion of Regulation 1612/68, art.3 of the former Regulation had substantially the same effect as art.7 of the latter.

The issue before the Court of Appeal therefore became whether the jurisprudence of the ECJ required Mr Bobezes to produce detailed statistical evidence, which would not in practice be available, in order to establish discrimination. The Court held that it did not and that, in contrast to the position where discrimination on the ground of sex is alleged, "the Commissioners and the court are entitled to take a broad approach and to find that indirect discrimination is liable to affect a significant number of migrant workers on the ground of nationality without statistical proof being available."

In Mr Bobezes' case, the Court considered that:

> "the proper approach is to compare the children of migrant workers with British children whose families are normally resident here. It is intrinsically likely that significantly more of the former than the latter will be prejudiced by paragraph 16(5) of the Regulation. . . ."

and therefore remitted the appeal to a tribunal to decide the question of whether such discrimination could be justified by the Secretary of State. The Tribunal decided that the discrimination could not be justified and the Secretary of State did not appeal against that decision.

Paragraph (6)

2.143 This provision provides a limited exception to para.(5), allowing a claimant to receive benefit for children or young persons being looked after by a local authority or in custody for the days on which they are in the claimant's home.

Paragraph (7)

2.144 This is a special rule where children live away from home while at school.

PART IV

APPLICABLE AMOUNTS

Applicable amounts

17.—Subject to regulations [8 18 to 22A] [14 . . .] (applicable amounts in other cases and reductions in applicable amounts [14 . . .]), a claimant's weekly applicable amount shall be the aggregate of such of the following amounts as may apply in his case: 2.145

(a) an amount in respect of himself or, if he is a member of a couple, an amount in respect of both of them, determined in accordance with paragraph 1(1), (2) or (3), as the case may be, of Schedule 2;

(b) [11 . . .]

[6 (bb) [10 . . .]]

(c) [11 . . .]

(d) the amount of any premiums which may be applicable to him, determined in accordance with Parts III and IV of Schedule 2 (premiums);

(e) any amounts determined in accordance with Schedule 3 (housing costs) which may be applicable to him in respect of mortgage interest payments or such other housing costs as are prescribed in that Schedule.

[1(f) any amounts determined in accordance with [2paragraphs (2) to (7)].

[2 (g) [13 . . .]]

(2) Where—

(a) a claimant has throughout the period beginning on 11th April 1988 and ending immediately before the coming into force of paragraphs 25 to 28 of Schedule 10 (capital to be disregarded) failed to satisfy the capital condition in section 22(6) of the Act (no entitlement to benefit if capital exceeds prescribed amount); and

(b) as a consequence he is not entitled to any transitional addition, special transitional addition or personal expenses addition under Part II of the Transitional Regulations; and

(c) had those paragraphs been in force on 11th April 1988 he would have satisfied that condition and been entitled to any such addition,

the amount applicable under this paragraph shall, subject to paragraph (3) be equal to the amount of any transitional addition, special transitional addition and personal expenses addition to which he would be entitled under Part II of the Transitional Regulations had he been entitled to any such addition in the week commencing 11th April 1988.

(3) For the purposes of paragraph (2), in determining a claimant's total benefit income in his second benefit week for the purpose of calculating the amount of any transitional addition to which he would have been entitled, no account shall be taken of any payment referred to in paragraph (1)(j) of regulation 9 of the Transitional Regulations (total benefit income) which is made in respect of that week to compensate for the loss of entitlement to income support.

(4) Subject to paragraph (6), where—

(a) the claimant or any member of his family was temporarily absent

from his home in the claimant's first or second benefit week (or both), because he was—
(i) a patient; or
(ii) outside Great Britain for the purpose of receiving treatment for any disease or bodily or mental disablement or for the purpose of accompanying a child or young person who is outside Great Britain for the purpose of receiving such treatment; or
[[12] (iii) in a care home, an Abbeyfield Home or an independent hospital; or]
(iv) in the care of a local authority under a relevant enactment; or
(v) staying with a person who was contributing to his maintenance; and
(b) as a result—
(i) in the claimant's first benefit week his requirements for the purpose of calculating his entitlement to supplementary benefit were increased or reduced or he was not entitled to that benefit; or
(ii) in the claimant's second benefit week his applicable amount was increased or reduced or he was not entitled to income support; and
(c) the period during which his requirements were, or his applicable amount was, increased or reduced, or he was not entitled to benefit, or any one or more of those circumstances existed, did not exceed eight weeks,

the amount applicable under this paragraph (4) shall be equal to the amount determined under paragraph (5).

(5) The amount for the purposes of paragraph (4) shall be an amount equal to the difference between—
(a) the amount that his total benefit income in his first benefit week would have been had he been entitled in respect of that week to supplementary benefit calculated on the basis that he or any member of his family had not been absent from the home; and, if less,
(b) the amount of his total benefit income in the first complete week after the period of temporary absence ends; but for the purpose of calculating his total benefit income in that week—
(i) no account shall be taken of any payment referred to in paragraph (l)(j) of regulation 9 of the Transitional Regulations which is made in respect of that week to compensate for the loss (in whole or in part) of entitlement to income support; and
(ii) if the period of temporary absence ends after the coming into force of paragraph (4), the amount of income support to be taken into account shall, notwithstanding regulation 9(6) of the Transitional Regulations, be calculated as if that paragraph were not in force.

(6) The amount under paragraph (4) shall cease to be applicable to a claimant if he ceases to be entitled to income support for a period exceeding [[4]the permitted period determined in accordance with regulation 3A (permitted period)].

[[4](6A) For the purposes of paragraph (6), where a claimant has ceased to be entitled to income support because he or his partner is participating in arrangements for training made under section 2 of the Employment and Training Act 1973 [[5]or section 2 of the Enterprise and New Towns (Scotland)

Act 1990] or attending a course at an employment rehabilitation centre established under that section [5of the 1993 Act], he shall be treated as if he had been entitled to income support for the period during which he or his partner is participating in such arrangements or attending such a course.]

(7) In this Regulation—

"first benefit week" and "second benefit week" have the meanings given to those expressions in regulations 2(1) of the Transitional Regulations and shall also include the week which would have been the claimant's "first benefit week" or, as the case may be, "second benefit week" had he been entitled to supplementary benefit or, as the case may be, income support in that week;

"total benefit income" has, subject to paragraphs (3) and (5)(b), the same meaning as in regulation 9 of the Transitional Regulations;

"Transitional Regulations" means the Income Support (Transitional Regulations 1987.]

AMENDMENTS

1. Income Support (General) Amendment No.2 Regulations 1988 (SI 1988/910) reg.2 (May 30, 1988).

2. Income Support (General) Amendment No.4 Regulations 1988 (SI 1988/1445) Sch.1 para.11 (April 10, 1989).

3. Income Support (General) Amendment Regulations 1989 (SI 1989/534) Sch.1 para.17 (October 9, 1989).

4. Income Support (General) Amendment No.3 Regulations 1989 (SI 1989/1678) reg.4 (October 9, 1989).

5. Enterprise (Scotland) Consequential Amendments Order 1991 (SI 1991/387) art.2 and 9 (April 1, 1991).

6. Social Security Benefits (Amendments Consequential Upon the Introduction of Community Care) Regulations 1992 (SI 1992/3147) reg.2(1) (April 1, 1993).

7. Income-related Benefits Schemes (Miscellaneous Amendments) (No.4) Regulations 1993 (SI 1993/2119) reg.7 (October 4, 1993).

8. Income Support (General) (Jobseeker's Allowance Consequential Amendments) Regulations 1996 (SI 1996/206) reg.9 (October 7, 1996).

9. Social Security Amendment (Residential Care and Nursing Homes) Regulations 2001 (SI 2001/3767) reg.2 and Sch. Pt I para.3 (April 8, 2002).

10. Social Security (Removal of Residential Allowance and Miscellaneous Amendments) Regulations 2003 (SI 2003/1121) reg.2 and Sch.1 para.2 (October 6, 2003).

11. Social Security (Working Tax Credit and Child Tax Credit) (Consequential Amendments) Regulations 2003 (SI 2003 No.455) reg.2 and Sch.1 para.2 (April 6, 2004, except in "transitional cases" and see further the note to reg.17 of the Income Support Regulations).

12. Social Security (Care Homes and Independent Hospitals) Regulations 2005 (SI 2005/2687) reg.2 and Sch.1 para.4 (October 24, 2005).

13. Social Security (Miscellaneous Amendments) Regulations 2006 (SI 2006/588) reg.2(4) (April 3, 2006).

14. Social Security (Miscellaneous Amendments) (No.5) Regulations 2009 (SI 2009/3228) reg.3(2)(a) (January 25, 2010).

DEFINITIONS

"child"—see SSCBA s.137(1).
"claimant"—see reg.2(1).
"couple"—*ibid.*
"family"—see SSCBA s.137(1).
"young person"—see reg.2(1) and reg.14.

General Note

2.146 Regulation 17 sets out the individual amounts that are aggregated to calculate the applicable amount. Those amounts fall into four categories, namely: (1) personal allowances under reg.17(a); (2) premiums under reg.17(d); (3) housing costs under reg.17(e); and (4) certain transitional amounts under reg.17(2). There are special rules in regs 18, 21, 21AA and 22A and in Sch.7 for particular categories of claimant, including those in polygamous marriages, those detained in prison or hospital, persons from abroad and those appealing against decisions that they are capable of work.

Personal allowances

2.147 Regulation 17(a) establishes a personal allowance for the claimant, either as a single person or as a member of a couple. The amount of the allowance is specified in Sch.2 para.1 and varies according to the age of the claimant and/or any partner and on whether the claimant or partner is responsible for a child.

Before April 6, 2004, reg.17(b) and Sch.2 para.2 provided for a further personal allowance for each child or young person who was a member of the family (see s.137(1) of SSCBA 1992 and regs 14–16). On that date, the "child elements" (see below) of IS were withdrawn for all claimants other than those whom this book describes as "transitional cases", namely:

- those who were in receipt of the child elements on April 6, 2004 and have not subsequently been awarded CTC; and
- those claimants whose families included a child or young person on April 6, 2004, who have not been awarded CTC and who made a new claim for income support or income-based JSA after that date but before September 8, 2005.

See reg.1(2), (3) and (4) of the Social Security (Working Tax Credit and Child Tax Credit) (Consequential Amendments) Regulations 2003 (SI 2003/455), the text of which is analysed below and set out later in this volume.

That withdrawal was the start of a process, under which it was intended that all financial support for children and young persons would be transferred from IS or JSA to child tax credit ("CTC"). However, that process has yet to be completed and, it now seems, never will be. As a result, any claimant who is a transitional case continues to be entitled to the child elements when the applicable amount is calculated.

2.148 What this commentary describes as the "child elements" (and what legislation has taken to describing—incorrectly—as the "child premia") are:

- the additional personal allowance for each child or young person who is a member of the claimant's family (see above);
- the family premium (Sch.2 para.3);
- the enhanced disability premium in respect of a child or young person (Sch.2 para.13A); and
- the disabled child premium (Sch.2 para.14).

The use of the phrase "child premia" to describe those elements is incorrect because a personal allowance for a child or young person is not a "premium" and because, in any event, the plural of "premium" is "premiums", not "premia" (see, e.g. para.12 of Sch.2 to the Income Support Regulations where the correct word is used). The transitional text of Sch.2 paras 3, 13A and 14, and the current rates of the child elements are given in the commentary to Sch.2.

Section 1(3)(d) of the Tax Credits Act 2002 abolishes the child elements. It was originally intended to complete the process of transfer by April 6, 2005 (see art.2(5) of the Tax Credits Act 2002 (Commencement No.4, Transitional and Savings)

Order 2003 (SI 2003/962) which brought s.1(3)(d) into force on that date) but that did not happen. The second target date of December 31, 2006 (SI 2005/1106) was also missed, as was the third target date of December 31, 2008 (SI 2006/3369), the fourth on December 31, 2011 (SI 2008/3151) and the fifth on December 31, 2014 (SI 2011/2910). On July 14, 2014, the Tax Credits Act 2002 (Commencement and Transitional Provisions)(Partial Revocation) Order 2014 (SI 2014/1848) revoked art.2(5) of SI 2003/962 with the result that there is no longer any date fixed for s.1(3)(d) to come into force. It appears (see, e.g. the explanatory note to SI 2014/1848) that it is no longer intended to complete the transfer. IS, JSA and CTC itself are all to be abolished in due course and replaced by universal credit and the current position will eventually be resolved by that abolition or possibly—given the rate at which universal credit is being introduced—by the fact that all the children and young persons for whom transitional cases are responsible, have grown up.

In the meantime, the current position is governed by reg.1(2), (3) and (4) of SI 2003/455 and appears to be as follows:

- for claimants who did not have a child or young person who was a member of their family before April 6, 2004, para.(b) of reg.17 (and also reg.18(b) and paras 2, 14 and the relevant parts of para.13A of Sch.2) was revoked with effect from April 6, 2004 (reg.1(4) of SI 2003/455);

- for claimants who had a child or young person who was a member of their family and who were (or whose partners were) in receipt of CTC prior to April 6, 2004, para.(b) of reg.17 (and also reg.18(b) and paras 2, 14 and the relevant parts of para.13A of Sch.2) was revoked with effect from April 6, 2004 (reg.1(2) of SI 2003/455). From the first day of the first benefit week beginning on or after that date, such claimants are not entitled to the child elements;

- for claimants who have a child or young person who is a member of their family and who were not (and whose partners were not) in receipt of CTC prior to April 6, 2004 but who subsequently became (or whose partners subsequently became) entitled to CTC in respect of a period which precedes that date (i.e. under reg.7 of the Tax Credits (Claims and Notifications) Regulations 2002—see Vol.IV), reg.7 of SI 2003/455 (which provides that, subject to limited disregards, CTC counts as income for income support purposes between April 7, 2003 and April 6, 2004) applies from the first day of the first benefit week beginning on or after the commencement date of the CTC award. (This may mean that there will have been an overpayment for the period before CTC was awarded which, it would seem, would be recoverable under s.74(1) of the Administration Act.) For such claimants, para.(b) of reg.17 (and the other provisions referred to above) are revoked with effect from April 6, 2004 (reg.1(2) of SI 2003/455) with the same consequences as are set out in the previous paragraph;

- for claimants who have a child or young person who is a member of their family and who are in receipt of income support but have not been awarded (and whose partners have not been awarded) CTC as at April 6, 2004 and who do not subsequently become entitled to CTC for a period which begins before that date, para.(b) of reg.17 (and the other provisions referred to above) remain in force until CTC is awarded. They are then revoked with effect from the first day of the first benefit week beginning on or after the day on which the CTC award begins;

- since September 8, 2005, claimants who have a child or young person who is a member of their family but who were not in receipt of income support before April 6, 2004 can no longer make a new claim for income support and be awarded the child elements on that claim (see the amendments to SI 2003/455 by SI 2005/2294 with effect from that date); and

- it is unclear whether such a claimant could have made a new claim for income support between April 7, 2004 and September 7, 2005 and be awarded the child elements on that claim (although the better view is that he or she would have been entitled to do so). For a discussion of this point, which is now of merely historical interest, see pp.275–276 of Vol.II of the 2005 edition.

Until October 5, 2003, claimants living in residential care homes or nursing homes also received a "residential allowance" under para.(bb) (for further details, see pp.486–488 of Vol.II of the 2003 edition). With effect from October 6, 2003, para.(bb) was revoked and residential allowances abolished. All financial help with the costs of care is now provided by local authority social services departments.

Premiums

2.149 The second main category covers premiums. The former family premium under paragraph (c) (payable if the claimant's family included a child or a young person) was also abolished with effect from April 6, 2004 subject to the same transitional provisions.

The other premiums are in Pts III and IV of Sch.2.

Housing Costs

2.150 The third category covers housing costs, set out in Sch.3. Note reg.13(1) of the Decisions and Appeals Regulations 1999 (see Vol.III of this series).

Transitional amounts

2.151 The fourth category, in sub-para.(f), covers transitional protection for a number of groups. Sub-para.(f) first deals with those assisted by paras 25–28 of Sch.10 on disregarded capital, which were inserted from May 30, 1988. The details are in paras (2) and (3). Sub-para.(f) secondly deals with groups who lost out on the ordinary transitional protection because of temporary absence from home around April 11, 1988. Here the details are in paras (4)–(6).

Paragraphs (2) and (3) apply where a person was continuously excluded from entitlement to income support by the capital rule before the additional disregards were added with effect from May 30, 1988. If the person would have satisfied the capital rule on April 11, 1988, if those disregards had been in the regulations and would have been entitled to some transitional protection, then the amount of that protection is applicable from May 30, 1988. There is no statutory provision for filling the gap between April 11 and May 30, but extra-statutory payments were made. The effect of para.(3) is that in doing the calculations of total benefit income in the second benefit week around April 11, any extra-statutory payment is to be ignored.

Paragraphs (4)–(6A): where the calculation of total benefit income in either the first or second benefit week is affected by a person's temporary absence from home (for one of the reasons set out in para.(4)(a)), then the calculation can be done as if the person was still at home. The absence must not exceed eight (or sometimes 12) weeks (para.(4)(c)) and the addition applied will cease if there is a subsequent break in entitlement of more than eight (or sometimes 12) weeks (para.(6)).

Polygamous marriages

2.152 **18.**—[1(1) Subject to paragraph (2) and [9regulations 21] [8 to 22A] [13 . . .] (applicable amounts in other cases and reductions in applicable amounts [13 . . .]), where a claimant is a member of a polygamous marriage his weekly applicable amount shall be the aggregate of such of the following amounts as may apply in his case:

(a) the highest amount applicable to him and one of his partners determined in accordance with paragraph 1(3) of Schedule 2 as if he and that partner were a couple;

(b) an amount equal to the differences between the amounts specified in [8sub-paragraph (3)(d)] [4and (1)(e)] of paragraph 1 of Schedule 2 in respect of each of his other partners;

(c) [11 . . .]

[6 (cc) [10 . . .]]

(d) [11 . . .]

(e) the amount of any premiums which may be applicable to him determined in accordance with Parts III and IV of Schedule 2 (premiums);

(f) any amounts determined in accordance with Schedule 3 (housing costs) which may be applicable to him in respect of mortgage interest payments or such other housing costs as are prescribed in that Schedule.

[2(g) any amount determined in accordance with regulation 17(1)(f) (applicable amounts);]

[3(h) [12 . . .]]

[1(2) In the case of a partner who is aged less than 18, the amount which applies in respect of that partner shall be nil unless—

(a) that partner is treated as responsible for a child, or [8(b) that partner is a person who—

(i) had he not been a member of a polygamous marriage would have qualified for income support under regulation 4ZA; or

(ii) satisfies the requirements of section 3(1)(f)(iii) of the Jobseekers Act 1995 (prescribed circumstances for persons aged 16 but less than 18); or

(iii) is the subject of a direction under section 16 of the Jobseekers Act 1995 (persons under 18: severe hardship).]

AMENDMENTS

1. Income Support (General) Amendment No.3 Regulations 1988 (SI 1988/1228) reg.5 (September 9, 1988).

2. Income Support (General) Amendment No.4 Regulations 1988 (SI 1988/1445) reg.6 (September 9, 1988).

3. Income Support (General) Amendment No.4 Regulations 1988 (SI 1988/1445) Sch.1 para.12 (April 10, 1989).

4. Family Credit and Income Support (General) Amendment Regulations 1989 (SI 1989/1034) reg.5 (July 10, 1989)

5. Income Support (General) Amendment Regulations 1989 (SI 1989/534) Sch.1 para.17 (October 9, 1989).

6. Social Security Benefits (Amendments Consequential Upon the Introduction of Community Care) Regulations 1992 (SI 1992/3147) reg.2(1) (April 1, 1993).

7. Income-related Benefits Schemes (Miscellaneous Amendments) (No.4) Regulations 1993 (SI 1993/2119) reg.8 (October 4, 1993).

8. Income Support (General) (Jobseeker's Allowance Consequential Amendments) Regulations 1996 (SI 1996/206) reg.10 (October 7, 1996).

9. Social Security Amendment (Residential Care and Nursing Homes) Regulations 2001 (SI 2001/3767) reg.2 and Sch. Pt I para.4 (April 8, 2002).

10. Social Security (Removal of Residential Allowance and Miscellaneous Amendments) Regulations 2003 (SI 2003/1121) reg.2 and Sch.1 para.3 (October 6, 2003).

11. Social Security (Working Tax Credit and Child Tax Credit) (Consequential Amendments) Regulations 2003 (SI 2003 No.455) reg.2 and Sch.1 para.3 (April 6, 2004, except in "transitional cases" and see further the note to reg.17 of the Income Support Regulations).

12. Social Security (Miscellaneous Amendments) Regulations 2006 (SI 2006/588) reg.2(4) (April 3, 2006).
13. Social Security (Miscellaneous Amendments) (No.5) Regulations 2009 (SI 2009/3228) reg.3(2)(b) (January 25, 2010).

DEFINITIONS

"the Act"—see reg.2(1).
"child"—see SSCBA s.137(1).
"claimant"—see reg.2(1).
"couple"—*ibid.*
"partner"—*ibid.*
"polygamous marriage"—*ibid.*
"young person"—*ibid.*, and reg.14.

GENERAL NOTE

2.153 Regulation 18 contains special rules for polygamous marriages, but not for other kinds of relationships. There the ordinary living together as husband and wife rule in s.137(1) of the Contributions and Benefits Act (1986 Act s.20(11)) applies.

Applicable amounts for persons in residential care and nursing homes

2.154 **19.**—[1 . . .]

AMENDMENT

1. Social Security Amendment (Residential Care and Nursing Homes) Regulations 2001 (SI 2001/3767) reg.2 and Sch. Pt I para.5 (April 8, 2002).

GENERAL NOTE

2.155 The revocation of reg.19 abolished the system of "preserved rights" for those who were resident in a nursing or residential care home on March 31, 1993 (i.e. immediately before the introduction of care in the community). For details of the operation of that system see pp.255–265 of Vol.II of the 2001 edition.

Applicable amounts for persons on board and lodging accommodation and hostels

2.156 **20.**—[1. . .]

AMENDMENT

1. Income Support (General) Amendment Regulations 1989 (SI 1989/534) Sch.1 para.4 (October 9, 1989).

GENERAL NOTE

2.157 As from October 1989, most hostel-dwellers, unless their accommodation comes within the amended definition of residential accommodation in reg.21(3), are entitled to the ordinary income support personal allowances and premiums and to housing benefit for their accommodation. See Sch.3B for transitional protection from October 1989 and April 1990.

Boarders had already been transferred to a similar system from April 1989. Their transitional protection is under Sch.3A.

Special cases

2.158 **21.**—(1) Subject to [27paragraph (1B)] [21[25regulation 21ZB] (treatment of refugees) and][19regulation 22A] (reductions in applicable amounts) in the case of a person to whom any paragraph in column (1) of Schedule 7 applies (applicable amounts in special cases), the amount included in the claimant's weekly amount in respect of him shall be the amount prescribed in the corresponding paragraph in column (2) of that Schedule [30 . . .].

[6 (1A) [37 . . .]]

[27(1B)[29. . .[28 . . .]]]

(2) [35 . . .]

(3) [18 [31 36 In Schedule 7]

[25. . .]

[25"partner of a person subject to immigration control" means a person—

(i) who is not subject to immigration control within the meaning of section 115(9) of the Immigration and Asylum Act; or

(ii) to whom section 115 of that Act does not apply by virtue of regulation 2 of the Social Security (Immigration and Asylum) Consequential Amendments Regulations 2000; and

(iii) who is a member of a couple and [34 the member's] partner is subject to immigration control within the meaning of section 115(9) of that Act and section 115 of that Act applies to [34 the partner] for the purposes of exclusion from entitlement to income support;]

[14 36 "person from abroad" has the meaning given in regulation 21AA;]

"patient" means a person (other than a prisoner) who is regarded as receiving free in-patient treatment within the meaning of [35 regulation 2(4) and (5) of the Social Security (Hospital In-Patients) Regulations 2005];

[16"prisoner" means a person who—

(a) is detained in custody pending trial or sentence upon conviction or under a sentence imposed by a court; or

(b) is on temporary release in accordance with the provisions of the Prison Act 1952 or the Prisons (Scotland) Act 1989,

other than a person [23 who is detained in hospital under the provisions of the Mental Health Act 1983, or, in Scotland, under the provisions of the [32 Mental Health (Care and Treatment) (Scotland) Act 2003] or the Criminal Procedure (Scotland) Act 1995;]]

[38 (3ZA) In Schedule 7 "person serving a sentence of imprisonment detained in hospital" means a person ("P") who satisfies either of the following conditions.

(3ZB) The first condition is that—

(a) P is being detained under section 45A or 47 of the Mental Health Act 1983 (power of higher courts to direct hospital admission; removal to hospital of persons serving sentences of imprisonment etc.); and

(b) in any case where there is in relation to P a release date within the meaning of section 50(3) of that Act, P is being detained on or before the day which the Secretary of State certifies to be that release date.

(3ZC) The second condition is that P is being detained under—

(a) section 59A of the Criminal Procedure (Scotland) Act 1995 (hospital direction); or

(b) section 136 of the Mental Health (Care and Treatment) (Scotland) Act 2003 (transfer of prisoners for treatment of mental disorder).

[33 . . .]

[18 36 . . .]

[31 36 . . .]

[33 . . .]

(5) A claimant to whom paragraph 19 of Schedule 7 (disability premium) applies shall be entitled to income support for the period in respect of which that paragraph applies to him notwithstanding that his partner was also entitled to income support for that same period.

AMENDMENTS

1. Income Support (General) Amendment No.4 Regulations 1988 (SI 1988/1445) Sch.1 para.1 (April 10, 1989).
2. Income Support (General) Amendment Regulations 1989 (SI 1989/534) Sch.1 para.5 (October 9, 1989).
3. Income Support (General) Amendment Regulations 1990 (SI 1990/547) reg.8 (April 9, 1990).
4. Income Support (General and Transitional) Amendment Regulations 1990 (SI 1990/2324) reg.2 (December 17, 1990).
5. Income Support (General) Amendment Regulations 1991 (SI 1991/236) reg.7 (April 8, 1991).
6. Income Support (General) Amendment (No.3) Regulations 1991 (SI 1991/1033) reg.2 (May 20, 1991).
7. Income Support (General) Amendment (No.5) Regulations 1991 (SI 1991/1656) reg.2 (August 12, 1991).
8. Income-related Benefits Schemes (Miscellaneous Amendments) (No.3) Regulations 1992 (SI 1992/2155) reg.15 (October 5, 1992).
9. Social Security Benefits (Amendments Consequential Upon the Introduction of Community Care) Regulations 1992 (SI 1992/3147) Sch.1 para.3 (April 1, 1993).
10. Social Security Benefits (Miscellaneous Amendments) Regulations 1993 (SI 1993/518) reg.5 (April 1, 1993).
11. Income-related Benefits Schemes (Miscellaneous Amendments) Regulations 1993 (SI 1993/315) reg.4 (April 12, 1993).
12. Income-related Benefits Schemes (Miscellaneous Amendments) (No.4) Regulations 1993 (SI 1993/2119) reg.10 (October 4, 1993).
13. Income-related Benefits Schemes (Miscellaneous Amendments) Regulations 1994 (SI 1994/527) reg.3 (April 11, 1994).
14. Income-related Benefits Schemes (Miscellaneous Amendments) (No.3) Regulations 1994 (SI 1994/1807) reg.4(1) (August 1, 1994).
15. Income-related Benefits Schemes (Miscellaneous Amendments) (No.5) Regulations 1994 (SI 1994/2139) reg.25 (October 3, 1994).
16. Income-related Benefits Schemes (Miscellaneous Amendments) Regulations 1995 (SI 1995/516) reg.21 (April 10, 1995).
17. Social Security (Persons from Abroad) Miscellaneous Amendments Regulations 1996 (SI 1996/30) reg.8(2) (February 5, 1996).
18. Income-related Benefits (Montserrat) Regulations 1996 (SI 1996/2006) reg.4 (August 28, 1996).
19. Income Support (General) (Jobseeker's Allowance Consequential Amendments) Regulations 1996 (SI 1996/206) reg.12 (October 7,1996).
20. Income-related Benefits Schemes and Social Fund (Miscellaneous Amendments) Regulations 1996 (SI 1996/1944) reg.6(6) (October 7, 1996).
21. Income Support and Social Security (Claims and Payments) (Miscellaneous Amendments) Regulations 1996 (SI 1996/2431) reg.2 (October 15, 1996).
22. Income Support (General) Amendment (No.3) Regulations 1996 (SI 1996/2614) reg.2 (November 8, 1996).
23. Social Security (Miscellaneous Amendments) Regulations 1998 (SI 1998/563) reg.8(1) and (2)(c)(i) (April 6, 1998).
24. Social Security (Miscellaneous Amendments) Regulations 1998 (SI 1998/563) reg.18(3) and (4)(c) (April 6, 1998).

25. Social Security (Immigration and Asylum) Consequential Amendments Regulations 2000 (SI 2000/636) reg.3(4)(a) (April 3, 2000).

26. Income-related Benefits and Jobseeker's Allowance (Amendment) Regulations 2000 (SI 2000/979) reg.2 (May 2, 2000).

27. Social Security Amendment (Residential Care and Nursing Homes) Regulations 2001 (SI 2001/3767) reg.2 and Sch. Pt I para.6 (April 8, 2002).

28. Social Security (Removal of Residential Allowance and Miscellaneous Amendments) Regulations 2003 (SI 2003/1121) reg.2 and Sch.1 para.4 (October 6, 2003).

29. Social Security (Third Party Deductions and Miscellaneous Amendments) Regulations 2003 (SI 2003/2325) reg.3 (October 6, 2003).

30. Social Security (Working Tax Credit and Child Tax Credit) (Consequential Amendments) Regulations 2003 (SI 2003 No.455) reg.2 and Sch.1 para.4 (April 6, 2004), except in "transitional cases" and see further the note to reg.17 of the Income Support Regulations.

31. Social Security (Habitual Residence) Amendment Regulations 2004 (SI 2004/1232) reg.3 (May 1, 2004).

32. Mental Health (Care and Treatment) (Scotland) Act 2003 (Modification of Subordinate Legislation) Order 2005 (SSI 2005/445) art.2 and Sch. para.3(3) (Scotland); Mental Health (Care and Treatment) (Scotland) Act 2003 (Consequential Provisions) Order 2005 (SI 2005/2078) art.15 and Sch.2 para.3(4) (England and Wales) (October 5, 2005).

33. Social Security (Care Homes and Independent Hospitals) Regulations 2005 (SI 2005/2687) reg.2 and Sch.1 para.5 (October 24, 2005).

34 Civil Partnership (Pensions, Social Security and Child Support) (Consequential, etc. Provisions) Order 2005 (SI 2005/2877) art.2(3) and Sch.3 para.13(3) (December 5, 2005).

35. Social Security (Hospital In-Patients) Regulations 2005 (SI 2005/3360) reg.4 (April 10, 2006).

36. Social Security (Persons from Abroad) Amendment Regulations 2006 (SI 1026/2006) reg.6(2) (April 30, 2006).

37. Social Security (Miscellaneous Amendments) Regulations 2009 (SI 2009/583) reg.2(1) and (5) (April 6, 2009).

38. Social Security (Persons Serving a Sentence of Imprisonment Detained in Hospital) Regulations 2010 (SI 2010/442) reg.3(1) and (2) (March 25, 2010).

Definitions

"child"—see SSCBA s.137(1).
"claimant"—see reg.2(1).
"local authority"—*ibid.*
"residential care home"—*ibid.*, and reg.19(3).
"young person"—*ibid.*, and reg.14.

General Note

Paragraph (1)

Applicable amounts in special cases are to be as prescribed in Sch.7. Regulation 21ZB was revoked with effect from June 14, 2007. However, the reference to that regulation in para.(1) has yet to be revoked. **2.159**

Claimants without accommodation

Under para.6 of Sch.7 a person "without accommodation" is only entitled to a personal allowance for himself (or the allowance for a couple, if he is a member of a couple). In *R(IS) 23/98* the claimant had lived in his car for approximately two weeks. He was refused a disability premium as part of his income support. The Commissioner decides that a car could not be regarded as accommodation in the **2.160** context of para.6. He approved of the following description of accommodation in para.29503 of the *Adjudication Officer's Guide*: "An effective shelter from the elements which is capable of being heated; and in which the occupants can sit, lie down, cook and eat; and which is reasonably suited for continuous occupation". While there is force in the Commissioner's reasoning in relation to a car, his (obiter) view that an ordinary tent or touring caravan may not constitute accommodation is more surprising (particularly in the light of the AO's concession to the contrary). It is suggested that the AO's distinction between a car as a means of transport and a tent (or caravan) as a means of shelter is correct. In this connection, note also para.17(1)(f) of Sch.3 under which payments in respect of a tent count as allowable housing costs (without any restriction as to the kind of tent).

In *R. (M) v Secretary of State for Work and Pensions* [2008] UKHL 63, (Lords Hope, Rodger, Walker, Mance and Neuberger) rejected an argument that the refusal of premiums to a person without accommodation constituted unlawful discrimination contrary to ECHR, art.14 and art.1 of the First Protocol ("A1P1") on the basis that:

"(a) RJM's claim that he has wrongfully been deprived of disability premium falls, in principle, within the ambit of A1P1, and therefore of article 14;
(b) The discrimination of which RJM claims is based on his homelessness, which is an "other status" for the purposes of article 14;
(c) However, the discrimination of which RJM complains has been justified by the Secretary of State".

The justification put forward by the Secretary of State and accepted by the House was as follows (per Lord Neuberger, with whom all their Lordships agreed):

"50. First, the Secretary of State takes the view that he should encourage the disabled homeless, who are "in a vulnerable position" to seek shelter, and therefore help, rather than rendering it easier, at least in financial terms, for them to remain without accommodation. It appears that 90% of those without accommodation in this country have problems connected with substance abuse and around 45% have mental health problems. Those who are disabled need, or at least would benefit from, accommodation, as indeed is reflected by the fact that they are included among those who are accorded priority need for housing under the Housing Acts (the 1985 Act when disability premium was introduced, and now the 1996 Act). As Mr Johnson [counsel for the Secretary of State] explains, "In the government's view, helping homeless people into accommodation is a much more effective way of helping them than handing out money through the disability premium."

"51. Secondly, the Secretary of State considers that the disabled are less likely to need a supplement if they are without accommodation than if they are not. This view is based on the proposition that, while the disability premium was not precisely calculated by reference to specific needs, much of it would be spent on heating and other household expenses, items which would not be required by someone without accommodation. Mr Johnson says that "claimants in accommodation have a range of expenses and financial pressures related to that accommodation that claimants without accommodation do not have".

The House of Lords also held that the Court of Appeal had not been bound to follow its earlier decision in *Campbell v South Northamptonshire DC* [2004] EWCA Civ 409 that income-related benefits did not constitute "possessions" within A1P1, given the subsequent decision to the contrary by the Grand Chamber of the European Court of Human Rights in *Stec v United Kingdom*.

Members of religious orders

Under para.7 of Sch.7 a claimant "who is a member of and fully maintained by a religious order" has an applicable amount of nil and is therefore not entitled to IS. In *CSPC/677/2007*, the Commissioner considered the position of 12 Carmelite nuns. The monastery in which they lived was "self-maintaining", i.e. the nuns paid all their income into a central account and their living expenses were met from that account. To the extent that a nun's living expenses were less than her contributions to the account, they were met by the contributions of the other nuns. There was no support from the wider Carmelite order and, if its members were unable to support each other, the monastery would have to close. It was held that the legislation did not draw any distinction between self-maintaining, and other, religious communities. Ministerial suggestions to the contrary were "unfortunate". Moreover, as the arrangements for the *maintenance* of the nuns were the same in each case, it was not possible to distinguish between those nuns who had income, and were therefore able to contribute that income to the community were to be ignored for the purpose of deciding whether a claimant was "fully maintained" by a religious order. **2.161**

The issue whether the exclusion from benefit of those who are fully maintained by religious orders amounts to unlawful discrimination contrary to the ECHR has been reconsidered by a three-judge panel of the Upper Tribunal (Walker J, CP, Judges Pacey and Jacobs) following the decision of the House of Lords in *M* (see above). (The issue had been considered in *CSPC/677/2007* but, at that time, the Commissioner was bound by the decisions of the Court of Appeal in the *Campbell* case and *M* ([2007] EWCA Civ 614) that that income-related benefits did not constitute "possessions" within A1P1: see above under *Claimants without accommodation*.) The Upper Tribunal held that the claimants were not "victims" within s.7(1) of the Human Rights Act 1998 because the discriminatory effect of the exclusion could be removed without conferring any advantage on them. As proceedings under the Act may only be brought by a "victim", it was unnecessary to consider any other Human Rights issues.

Temporarily separated couples

On para.9 of Sch.7 see *CIS 1544/2001* in the notes to reg.16(1). **2.162**

Paragraph (1A)

Until it was revoked on April 6, 2009, this provision provided that, except where the particular paragraph of Sch.7 expressly allows the payment of a premium, a person whose entitlement falls under Sch.7 does not qualify for the severe disability premium. **2.163**

The effect of the revocation is not entirely clear. If para.(1A) ever performed a function, revocation would mean that some special cases have become entitled to a severe disability premium even though no such entitlement is conferred by Sch.7. However, the better view is that para.(1A) was always otiose. Regulations 17 and 18 are expressly subject to reg.21 and para.(1) makes it clear that for all special cases, the applicable amount "shall be" the amount specified in Sch.7 (i.e. that amount and no other).

Paragraph (3)

This paragraph contains some important definitions for Sch.7, which are also referred to in other parts of the Regulations. **2.164**

"Partner of a person subject to immigration control"

For a discussion of "person subject to immigration control" see the notes to the Social Security (Immigration and Asylum) Consequential Amendments Regulations 2000 (SI 2000/636). In *CIS 1159/2004*, the claimant had been entitled to the severe disability premium under para.13(2)(a) of Sch.2. Subsequently his wife, who was a person subject to immigration control, came to live with him and **2.165** he therefore became a "partner of a person subject to immigration control". The consequence was that whilst he retained his own personal allowance, he could not claim for his wife because, under para.16A of Sch.7, her personal allowance was nil. Ms Commissioner Fellner held that despite this circumstance, his wife was still the claimant's "partner" as defined by reg.2(1) with the effect that—as she herself was not entitled to the severe disability premium—para.13(2)(b) of Sch.2 disentitled the claimant to the premium. The Commissioner also rejected the claimant's argument that the SDP provisions were ultra vires.

"Patient"

2.166 See the commentary to the Social Security (Hospital In-Patients) Regulations 2005 in Vol.I.

"Prisoner"

2.167 A person is detained in custody pending trial once he has been charged. It does not matter that in fact no trial takes place because the proceedings are discontinued. For the period he was in custody he was a prisoner (*R(IS) 1/94*). However, a person required to live in a bail hostel is not detained in custody pending trial (*R(IS) 17/93*); see Sch.7 para.9 as to how his applicable amount is calculated if he is a member of a couple.

Sub-paragraph (b) of the definition has been added to reverse the effect of *Chief Adjudication Officer v Carr, The Times*, June 2, 1994, also reported as *R(IS) 20/95*. A person on temporary release will now continue to count as a prisoner and will not be eligible for income support.

For the rules regarding prisoners who are detained in hospital under the Mental Health Act 1983, the Criminal Procedure (Scotland) Act 1995 or the Mental Health (Care and Treatment) (Scotland) Act 2003, see *Person serving a sentence of imprisonment detained in hospital* below.

Person serving a sentence of imprisonment detained in hospital

2.168 Paragraphs (3ZA)–(3ZC) were introduced to reverse the decision of the Court of Appeal (Waller, Carnwath and Patten LJJ) in *R(RD & PM) v SSWP* [2010] EWCA Civ 18. In that case, the appellants were "post-tariff lifers", i.e. prisoners serving a mandatory term of life imprisonment whose "tariff" sentences had expired but who had not been released on licence. By the time under consideration, they had been transferred to psychiatric hospitals under s.47 of the Mental Health Act 1983 and were prevented from applying to the Parole Board for release. Under the previous version of Sch.7 para.(2A), a s.47 patient had an applicable amount of nil "but not if his detention continues after . . . *the earliest date on which he could have been released* in respect of, or from, the prison sentence if he had not been detained in hospital" (emphasis added). The Court of Appeal held that, in relation to those serving a life sentence, the italicised words referred to the date on which the prisoner's tariff expired and the Parole Board was first able to direct release and not, as the High Court had held ([2008] EWHC 2635 (Admin), para.48), the first date on which the prisoner was entitled to be released (which in the case of a prisoner serving a life sentence was never). The effect was that a post-tariff lifer who was compulsorily removed to a hospital under s.47 became eligible for income support at the normal rate applicable to him as soon as his tariff expired. The amendments from March 25, 2010, reverse that result by amending para.2A of Sch.7 to create a new category of *Person serving a sentence of imprisonment detained in hospital* with an applicable amount of nil. Paragraphs (3ZA)–(3ZC) then define that category in terms which include any claimant who is detained in hospital under either s.45A or s.47 of the Mental Health Act until his or her "release date" as defined by s.50(3) of that Act. That section is in the following terms:

> "(3) In this section, references to a person's release date are to the day (if any) on which he would be entitled to be released (whether unconditionally or

on licence) from any prison or other institution in which he might have been detained if the transfer direction had not been given; and in determining that day there shall be disregarded—

(a) any powers that would be exercisable by the Parole Board if he were detained in such a prison or other institution, and
(b) any practice of the Secretary of State in relation to the early release under discretionary powers of persons detained in such a prison or other institution."

As prisoners serving a life sentence are never "entitled" to be released, the effect is to exclude them from entitlement to IS while they are detained in hospital.

Note, finally, that in *R(EM) v SSWP* [2010] EWCA Civ 18 (which was heard together with *RD & PM*) the Court of Appeal rejected an argument that to exclude those detained under ss.45A and 47 (who are detained in hospital in addition to a prison sentence) from benefit that was payable to claimants detained under s.37 (who are detained in hospital instead of a prison sentence) constituted unlawful discrimination contrary to art.14 of, and art.1 of the First Protocol to, ECHR taken together. Neither does the introduction of the exclusion with effect from April 10, 2006 (in the Social Security (Hospital In-Patients) Regulations 2005) amount to the deprivation of a possession contrary to art.1 of the First Protocol taken on its own: see *JB v SSWP (IS)* [2010] UKUT 263 (AAC).

[1 Special cases: supplemental—persons from abroad

21AA.—(1) "Person from abroad" means, subject to the following provisions of this regulation, a claimant who is not habitually resident in the United Kingdom, the Channel Islands, the Isle of Man or the Republic of Ireland. 2.169

(2) No claimant shall be treated as habitually resident in the United Kingdom, the Channel Islands, the Isle of Man or the Republic of Ireland unless he has a right to reside in (as the case may be) the United Kingdom, the Channel Islands, the Isle of Man or the Republic of Ireland other than a right to reside which falls within paragraph (3).

(3) A right to reside falls within this paragraph if it is one which exists by virtue of, or in accordance with, one or more of the following—

(a) regulation 13 of the Immigration (European Economic Area) Regulations 2006;
(b) regulation 14 of those Regulations, but only in a case where the right exists under that regulation because the claimant is—
    (i) a jobseeker for the purpose of the definition of "qualified person" in regulation 6(1) of those Regulations, or
    (ii) a family member (within the meaning of regulation 7 of those Regulations) of such a jobseeker;
[7 (bb) regulation 15A(1) of those Regulations(8), but only in a case where the right exists under that regulation because the claimant satisfies the criteria in regulation 15A(4A) of those Regulations;]
(c) Article 6 of Council Directive No.2004/38/EC; [7 . . .]
(d) Article 39 of the Treaty establishing the European Community (in a case where the claimant is a person seeking work in the United Kingdom, the Channel Islands, the Isle of Man or the Republic of Ireland). [7 ; or
(e) Article 20 of the Treaty on the Functioning of the European Union (in a case where the right to reside arises because a British citizen would otherwise be deprived of the genuine enjoyment of the substance of their rights as a European Union citizen).]

(4) A claimant is not a person from abroad if he is—

[10 (za) a qualified person for the purposes of regulation 6 of the Immigration (European Economic Area) Regulations 2006 as a worker or a self-employed person;

(zb) a family member of a person referred to in sub-paragraph (za) within the meaning of regulation 7(1)(a), (b) or (c) of those Regulations;

(zc) a person who has a right to reside permanently in the United Kingdom by virtue of regulation 15(1)(c), (d) or (e) of those Regulations;]

(g) a refugee within the definition in Article 1 of the Convention relating to the Status of Refugees done at Geneva on 28th July 1951, as extended by Article 1(2) of the Protocol relating to the Status of Refugees done at New York on 31st January 1967;

[3 [9 (h) a person who has been granted leave or who is deemed to have been granted leave outside the rules made under section 3(2) of the Immigration Act 1971 where that leave is—

(i) discretionary leave to enter or remain in the United Kingdom;

(ii) leave to remain under the Destitution Domestic Violence concession; or

(iii) leave deemed to have been granted by virtue of regulation 3 of the Displaced Persons (Temporary Protection) Regulations 2005;]

(hh) a person who has humanitarian protection granted under those rules;] [9 or]

(i) a person who is not a person subject to immigration control within the meaning of section 115(9) of the Immigration and Asylum Act and who is in the United Kingdom as a result of his deportation, expulsion or other removal by compulsion of law from another country to the United Kingdom; [5. . .] [9 . . .]

AMENDMENTS

1. Social Security (Persons from Abroad) Amendment Regulations 2006 (SI 1026/2006) reg.6(3) (April 30, 2006).

2. Social Security (Lebanon) Amendment Regulations 2006 (SI 2006/1981) reg.2 (July 25, 2006). The amendment ceased to have effect from January 31, 2007.

3. Social Security (Persons from Abroad) Amendment (No.2) Regulations 2006 (SI 2006/2528) reg.2 (October 9, 2006).

4. Social Security (Bulgaria and Romania) Amendment Regulations 2006 (SI 2006/3341) reg.2 (January 1, 2007).

5. Social Security (Habitual Residence) (Amendment) Regulations 2009 (SI 2009/362) reg.2 (March 18, 2009).

6. Social Security (Miscellaneous Amendments) (No.3) Regulations 2011 (SI 2011/2425) reg.7(1) and (3) (October 31, 2011).

7. Social Security (Habitual Residence) (Amendment) Regulations 2012 (SI 2012/2587) reg.2 (November 8, 2012).

8. Social Security (Croatia) Amendment Regulations 2013 (SI 2013/1474) reg.2 (July 1, 2013).

9. Social Security (Miscellaneous Amendments) (No.3) Regulations 2013 (SI 2013/2536) reg.4(1) and (5) (October 29, 2013).

10. Social Security (Habitual Residence) (Amendment) Regulations 2014 (SI 2014/902) reg.2(1) (May 31, 2014).

GENERAL NOTE 2.170

Structure of this Note

The structure of this lengthy note is as follows:

Introduction and historical background

2.171 Claimants who are "persons from abroad" as defined in reg.21AA, reg.85A of the JSA Regulations and reg.70 of the ESA Regulations are not entitled to IS, JSA or ESA. This is because they are treated as a special case with an applicable amount of nil (see para.17 of Sch.7, para.14 of Sch.5 to the JSA Regulations and para.11 of Sch.5 to the ESA Regulations). For SPC and universal credit, the same result is achieved by treating such claimants as "not in Great Britain" (see reg.2 of the SPC Regulations and reg.9 of the Universal Credit Regulations) and, therefore, as failing to satisfy the conditions of entitlement in, respectively, s.1(2)(a) of SPCA 2002 and s.4(1)(c) of WRA 2012.

From the introduction of the IS and HB Schemes in April 1988 until the Immigration and Asylum Act 1999 came into force on April 3, 2000, the exclusion of "persons from abroad" from benefit was the principal mechanism for denying income-related benefits to those claimants who were considered to have insufficiently close links with Great Britain. The approach was extended to community charge benefit when that benefit was introduced on April 1, 1990 and then to CTB, JSA and ESA when they were introduced on April 1, 1993, October 7, 1996 and October 27, 2008 respectively.

Originally, the definition of "person from abroad" was in para.(3) of reg.21. It was a wide definition and encompassed, broadly, all those who did not have leave to enter or remain in the UK or whose leave had been granted on a sponsorship undertaking or was conditional upon not having recourse to public funds (see pp.164–167 of the 1999 edition of J. Mesher and P. Wood, *Income-related Benefits: the Legislation* for further details).

2.172 That definition was widened on August 1, 1994 by the introduction of the "habitual residence test". That test was aimed principally at EEA nationals (although it affects many others) but EC law prohibiting discrimination against the citizens of other Member States meant that, to be valid, it had to apply to British citizens as well. One of the results of the change was therefore that, for the first time, a British citizen could be excluded from income-related benefits as a "person from abroad".

In the early days of the test there were a number of challenges to its validity both on the grounds that it was ultra vires s.124(1) of the Contributions and Benefits Act and as being unlawful under EC law. However, these challenges were all unsuccessful (see pp.290–291 of the 1999 edition of J. Mesher and P. Wood, *Income-related Benefits: the Legislation*).

More recently, in *Couronne v Crawley BC and Secretary of State for Work and Pensions* [2007] EWCA Civ 1086, the Court of Appeal held that the test did not discriminate unlawfully against British Citizens from the Chagos Islands in comparison with British Citizens of Irish ethnic or national origin either under the Race Relations Act 1976 or art.14 and art.8 and or art.1 First Protocol ECHR. In that case, the appellants had been unlawfully prevented by the British government from returning to their homeland but the Court held that it was not irrational for the habitual residence test to be applied to them.

With effect from April 3, 2000, the definition of "person from abroad" was narrowed to such an extent that only the habitual residence test remained. Most claimants who had previously fallen within other heads of the definition were re-categorised as "persons subject to immigration control" and excluded from income-related benefits by s.115 of the Immigration and Asylum Act 1999. **2.173**

On May 1, 2004, 10 additional countries joined the EU and the habitual residence test was supplemented by the introduction (as reg.21(3G), reg.85(4B) to the JSA Regulations and reg.2(2) of the SPC Regulations) of the "right to reside" test. The test was also applied to child benefit and child tax credit by amendments to reg.23 of the Child Benefit Regulations and reg.3 of the Tax Credits (Residence) Regulations 2003 reg.3.

In addition, the Accession (Immigration and Worker Registration) Regulations 2004 (SI 2004/1219) ("the A8 Regulations") established a registration scheme which imposed greater restrictions on the rights of "A8 Nationals" (see below) to reside in the UK as workers or workseekers than applied to the nationals of other member States.

From that point on, EEA nationals who did not have a legal right to reside—very broadly, those who had never been, or (in certain circumstances) were no longer, economically active and were not the family members of people who were, or had been, economically active—ceased to be regarded as habitually resident unless they had the benefit of transitional protection, and stood no chance of becoming habitually resident in the future, irrespective of their intentions and the length of time for which they had actually lived in the UK. **2.174**

On April 30, 2006, Directive 2004/38 ("the Citizenship Directive"—see Vol.III) came into force and repealed the previous Directives upon which EC immigration law had been based. The Citizenship Directive is implemented in UK domestic law by the Immigration (European Economic Area) Regulations 2006 ("the 2006 Regulations"). Those parts of the 2006 Regulations that are relevant to entitlement to social security benefits are reproduced later in this volume.

On the same day, the right to reside test was revised to reflect the new EU Law and the definition of "person from abroad" was removed from reg.21 to reg.21AA (and from reg.85 to reg.85A of the JSA Regulations).

On January 1, 2007, Bulgaria and Romania joined the EU and the Accession (Immigration and Worker Authorisation) Regulations 2006 (SI 2006/3317) ("the A2 Regulations") (see below) established an authorisation scheme which restricted the rights of "A2 nationals" (see below) to reside in the UK as workers or workseekers. With effect from the same day, the right to reside test was further amended. **2.175**

On either May 1, 2009 or May 1, 2011 (see the discussion of *TG v SSWP (PC)* [2015] UKUT 50 (AAC) under the heading, *The A8 Regulations*, below), the A8 states became full members of the EU and their nationals ceased to be subject to additional restrictions on their right to reside in the UK (i.e. over and above those that apply to the nationals of other EU states) from that date. Whether previous periods of residence were lawful under the former A8 Scheme remains relevant to whether an A8 national has acquired a permanent right of residence (see reg.7A of the 2006 Regulations).

On July 1, 2013, Croatia joined the EU and the Accession of Croatia (Immigration and Worker Authorisation) Regulations 2013 (SI 2013 No.1460) (see below) established a further authorisation scheme which restricted the rights of Croatian nationals to reside in the UK as workers or workseekers (see below), along similar lines to the A2 scheme.

2.176 On January 1, 2014, Bulgaria and Romania became full members of the EU and their nationals ceased to be subject to additional restrictions on their right to reside in the UK (i.e. over and above those that apply to the nationals of other EU states) from that date. Whether previous periods of residence were lawful under the former A8 Scheme remains relevant to whether an A8 national has acquired a permanent right of residence (see reg.7B of the 2006 Regulations).

Also on January 1, 2014, the habitual residence test for jobseeker's allowance was amended to include an additional requirement that the claimant should have been living in the Common Travel Area for the past three months.

Decisions of the courts and the Upper Tribunal

2.177 The habitual residence test applies to all the income-related benefits (and also in other areas of the law such as the homelessness provisions made under s.185 of the Housing Act 1996). Decisions by a court, the Upper Tribunal, or the former social security and child support commissioners about whether a claimant is person from abroad for the purposes of a particular benefit (or for the purposes of housing law) may therefore also be relevant in other cases concerning different benefits.

The concept of habitual residence is used in the child support scheme as the criterion for deciding whether the Secretary of State for Work and Pensions has jurisdiction to make a maintenance calculation (see s.44 of the Child Support Act 1991 and, e.g. *R(CS) 5/96)*. It is also sometimes used in family law as a test of whether a court in the UK has jurisdiction over a particular dispute. As will be seen, family law cases have played an important role in the interpretation of the habitual residence test in social security law. However, it is suggested that caution is necessary when applying decisions where the issue is one of jurisdiction to social security disputes where the issue is entitlement to publicly-funded benefits. The considerations that would make it desirable for a UK court to assume jurisdiction over, say, an international child abduction case, are not necessarily relevant to the benefit rights of the parents in that case. It follows that different factors will be important in reaching a conclusion on habitual residence, depending on the context: see *R(IS) 2/00*.

Overview

2.178 Given that background, the framework of the law is now as follows:

(1) under s.115(1) and (3) of the Immigration and Asylum Act 1999, a "person subject to immigration control" is not entitled to a wide range of benefits including income support, income-based jobseeker's allowance, income-related ESA, state pension credit, universal credit and social fund payments;

(2) this general rule is subject to the limited exceptions that are set out in the Social Security (Immigration and Asylum) Consequential Amendments Regulations 2000 (SI 2000/636—see below);

(3) even if a claimant is not a "person subject to immigration control" he may nevertheless be a "person from abroad" if he is not habitually resident in the Common Travel Area ("CTA") (i.e. the UK, Channel Islands, Isle of Man and Republic of Ireland). This includes British and Irish nationals; and

(4) claimants who are nationals of EEA countries (other than the UK and the Republic of Ireland), or of Switzerland, only satisfy the habitual residence test if they have a "right to reside" in the CTA—see reg.21AA(2). That is so even though an EEA national can never be a person subject to immigration control (see the definition in s.115(9): *CIS/3762/2006*, para.5 can be read as suggesting the contrary but *Ismail and Abdi v London Borough of Barnet* [2006] EWCA Civ 383 on which the Deputy Commissioner relied was concerned with a different definition of "person subject to immigration control" in s.13(2) of the Asylum and Immigration Act 1996 which, unlike s.115(9), did not exclude EEA nationals).

For a more detailed discussion of points (1) and (2) above, see the notes to SI 2000/636.

Subject to what is said about the burden of proof in *Kerr v Department for Social Development* [2004] UKHL 23 (*R 1/04 (SF)*), it is for the Secretary of State to prove that a claimant is not habitually resident, rather than for the claimant to show that he is, although it is preferable to resolve any doubts by enquiring further into the facts rather than relying on the burden of proof—see *R(IS) 6/96*.

Structure of the habitual residence test

The habitual residence test is established by para.(1). Unless they fall within one of the exempted groups in para.(4), claimants who are not subject to immigration control may nevertheless be refused benefit unless they are "habitually resident" in the Common Travel Area of the UK, Channel Islands, Isle of Man or Republic of Ireland (see s.1(3) of the Immigration Act 1971 and r.15 of the Immigration Rules). This includes UK nationals and nationals of other EEA states. **2.179**

A preliminary reading of reg.21AA (and reg.85A of the JSA Regulations and reg.70 of the ESA Regulations) would suggest that the habitual residence test has the following formal structure:

(1) Is the claimant exempt from the test under para.(4)?

A claimant who falls into any of the categories listed in para.(4) is deemed not to be a person from abroad and is therefore exempt from both the habitual residence and right to reside tests.

(2) If not, does the claimant have a right to reside?

Under para.(2), a claimant cannot be habitually resident—and is therefore a person from abroad—unless s/he has a right to reside in the CTA. Not every right to reside counts for this purpose: those listed in para.(3) are disregarded.

(3) If so, is the claimant habitually resident in the CTA under para.(1)?

That is not, however, how habitual residence and right to reside issues actually present themselves. In practice the most important question is *whether the claimant is—or is the family member of—an EEA (or Swiss) national.*

If so, then the DWP will first consider whether s/he has a right to reside in the CTA. Although there are a number of important exceptions (notably certain British nationals), most EEA nationals (and their family members) who do have a right to reside will fall within one of the categories in para.(4)(a)–(f) and in such cases it will not be necessary to consider actual habitual residence at all. A decision to refuse benefit will therefore usually be expressed in terms of the right to reside, or for JSA since January 1, 2014, in terms of the three-months test: see below. **2.180**

If not, then—for the reasons given below—the right to reside test will have no practical effect. Any claimant without EEA connections who does not have a right to reside will, in practice, have been excluded from benefit as a person subject to immigration control before any question of habitual residence can arise. Therefore only paras (1) and (4)(g)–(j) need to be considered and a decision to refuse benefit will be expressed in terms that the claimant is neither habitually resident nor exempt from the habitual residence test.

EEA and Swiss nationals and their family members—the right to reside

Consequences of the EU referendum

On June 23, 2016, the UK voted in a referendum to leave the EU. However, that vote has no immediate legal effect. The UK will remain a full member of the EU (and therefore the law set out below will continue to apply) until either the process established by art.50 TEU has run its course, or—much less probably—the UK parliament unilaterally repeals the European Communities Act 1972. The negotiations under art.50 are likely to take at least two years and, at the time of going to press, the formal notice that is necessary to begin those negotiations, has yet to be given. **2.180A**

Introduction

2.181 The right to reside test was first introduced on May 1, 2004. Under what is now para.(2) (formerly reg.21(3G)), no person "shall be treated as habitually resident" in the CTA unless s/he has a "right to reside there".

Although, conceptually, the "right to reside" test applies to all claimants, in practical terms it will only affect nationals of the EEA states and their family members (including, in exceptional cases, the parents of British children: see below under the heading: *Parents of British children: Zambrano*). This is because non-EEA nationals will either have a right of abode in the UK, in which case, they will obviously also have a right to reside here; or they will have some type of leave to remain here, in which case, they will have a right to reside here for the duration of that leave, and any extension of it (although they will not necessarily be entitled to income-related benefits); or they will be illegal entrants or overstayers, in which case they are already excluded from benefit as persons subject to immigration control so that the additional requirement that they have should have the right to reside before being entitled to benefit has no practical effect.

By contrast, under s.7 of the Immigration Act 1988, EEA nationals do not usually require leave to enter or remain in the UK and, in principle, "must be admitted to the United Kingdom if [they produce], on arrival, a valid national identity card or passport issued by an EEA state" (see reg.11 of the 2006 Regulations)). It is therefore possible for EEA nationals to be admitted to the UK who have no legal right to reside here: whether or not they have such a right depends on EU Law.

Who are EEA nationals?

2.182 The EEA consists of the 28 EU countries (namely Austria, Belgium, Bulgaria, Croatia, Cyprus, the Czech Republic, Denmark, Estonia, Finland, France, Germany, Greece, Hungary, Ireland, Italy, Latvia, Lithuania, Luxembourg, Malta, the Netherlands, Poland, Portugal, Romania, Slovakia, Slovenia, Spain, Sweden and the UK) together with Norway, Liechtenstein and Iceland.

Croatia, which joined the EU on July 1, 2013 is not yet a full member for the purposes of free movement of workers and, therefore, the rights of its nationals to reside in the UK as workers or workseekers are more restricted than for nationals of the other 26 Member States.

As with the current rules for Croatian nationals, the rights of A8 nationals (i.e. nationals of the Czech Republic, Estonia, Hungary, Latvia, Lithuania, Poland, Slovakia and Slovenia, which joined the EU on May 1, 2004) and of A2 nationals (i.e. nationals of Bulgaria and Romania) to reside in the UK as workers or workseekers were once more restricted than for nationals of most other Member States. The A8 restrictions applied from May 1, 2004 until either April 30, 2009 or April 30, 2011 (see the discussion of *TG v SSWP (PC)* [2015] UKUT 50 (AAC) under the heading, *The A8 Regulations*, below) and the A2 restrictions applied from January 1, 2007 to December 31. 2013. The former restrictions remain relevant to the question whether the residence of an A8 or A2 national during those periods counts towards the acquisition of a permanent right of residence.

The rights of Croatian, A8 and A2 nationals are considered in more detail below.

British nationals

2.183 British nationals have a right of abode in the UK (see s.2(1)(a) of the Immigration Act 1971 and *R(PC)2/07*) and therefore automatically have a right to reside in the CTA.

In some circumstances—for example, the treatment of family members—EU Law is more favourable to the nationals of other Member States than domestic UK law is to British nationals. In such circumstances, British nationals cannot rely upon their status as EU citizens to obtain the more favourable treatment unless the unfavourable treatment is the consequence of having exercised an EU right, such as the rights to freedom of movement or establishment.

For similar reasons, British nationals who have not exercised any EU right are subject to the habitual residence test as it applies to non-EEA nationals (see below) because they cannot take advantage of the exemptions in para.(4)(a)–(e).

For the position of British nationals who are also nationals of another EEA State see the discussion of the *McCarthy* case under the heading , *The personal scope of the Citizenship Directive* below. 2.184

For the rights of non-British nationals who are parents of British children, see the discussion under the heading "*Parents of British children: Zambrano*" below.

Irish and Island Nationals

Ireland, the Channel Islands and the Isle of Man are part of the CTA and their nationals automatically have a right to reside in the UK. However, the Channel Islands and the Isle of Man are not part of the EU or the EEA (see *SSWP v JG (RP)* [2013] UKUT 0300 (AAC), para.34) and their nationals are subject to the habitual residence test as it applies to non-EEA nationals (see below). The exemptions in para.(4)(a)–(e) cannot apply to them. There are reciprocal agreements between the UK and the Isle of Man (SI 2016/187) and Jersey and Guernsey (SI 1994/2802). 2.185

As Ireland is a member of the EU, Irish nationals in the UK may well be exercising EU rights and therefore have a right to reside under EU law in addition to their rights under domestic UK law. Therefore, even though Irish nationals have a right to reside, it may be to their advantage to establish that they fall within one of the EU categories in para.(4)(a)–(e) in order to obtain exemption from the habitual residence test. Those Irish nationals who are unable to establish such an exemption will be subject to the habitual residence test as it applies to non-EEA nationals.

The special treatment accorded by the UK to Irish nationals, but not accorded to citizens of other member States, which might otherwise be thought to be contrary to the various prohibitions in EU law against discrimination on the ground of nationality, is lawful because the provision for Irish citizens is protected by art.2 of the Protocol on the Common Travel Area (Protocol 20 annexed to the TFEU and TEU). That article states that the United Kingdom and Ireland "may continue to make arrangements between themselves relating to the movement of persons between their territories" and provides that nothing in articles 26 and 77 TFEU or in any other provision of that Treaty or the TEU or in any other measure adopted under them shall affect any such arrangements": see *Patmalniece v SSWP* [2011] UKSC 11, paras 54-61.

Complications sometimes arise because, before January 1, 2005, the domestic law of the Republic of Ireland entitled anyone born on the island of Ireland (i.e. including Northern Ireland) to Irish citizenship, irrespective of the nationality of their parents or the existence of any other connection with the Republic. In particular, non-EEA nationals have sometimes arranged for a child to be born in Northern Ireland (or in the Republic) so as to obtain a right to reside in the UK by virtue of that child's Irish citizenship. It is clear from *Zhu and Chen v Home Secretary* (C–200/02) (ECJ) that this stratagem will sometimes work as far as immigration law is concerned. But its success depends upon the parents and child being self-sufficient and having health insurance (see *W(China) v Home Secretary* [2006] EWCA Civ 1494) and it will therefore be of limited efficacy in establishing a right to reside for the purpose of entitlement to income-related benefits. 2.186

The 2006 Regulations were amended with effect from July 16, 2012 by SI 2012/1547 to implement the Citizenship Directive as interpreted in *Chen*.

Gibraltar

The status of Gibraltar was explained by Upper Tribunal Judge White in *SSWP v JG (RP)* (above) as follows: 2.187

> "29. Gibraltar was ceded in perpetuity by Spain to Great Britain under the Treaty of Utrecht 1713. It is a British Crown Colony. It is not part of the United Kingdom. This separate status is recognized under national law, international law and European Union law.
>
> 30. In Case C-145/04 *Spain v United Kingdom* [2006] ECR I-7917, the Court of Justice described the status of Gibraltar as follows:

"19. In Community law, Gibraltar is a European territory for whose external relations a Member State is responsible within the meaning of Article 299(4) EC and to which the provisions of the EC Treaty apply. The Act concerning the conditions of accession of the Kingdom of Denmark, Ireland and the United Kingdom of Great Britain and Northern Ireland and the adjustments to the Treaties (OJ 1972 L 73, p.14) provides, however, that certain parts of the Treaty are not to apply to Gibraltar.

31. European Union law on citizenship of the Union and the free movement of persons applies to Gibraltar.

32. The Family Allowances, National Insurance and Industrial Injuries (Gibraltar) Order 1974 (SI 1974 No 555) ("the Gibraltar Order") provides:

1 Any reference in the following paragraphs to a territory shall be construed as a reference to the territory of the United Kingdom or Gibraltar or both as the case may be and any reference to a child shall be construed as a reference to any person for whom family allowances are payable under the legislation in question.

2(a) Any person shall have the same rights and liabilities in relation to social security other than family allowances, as he would have had if the United Kingdom and Gibraltar had been separate Member States of the European Economic Community.

(b) For the purpose of giving effect to paragraph (a) above the same procedures shall so far as is practicable be adopted in relation to the person and benefit concerned as would have been applicable had the United Kingdom and Gibraltar been such separate Member States."

Nationals of Norway, Iceland and Liechtenstein

2.188 Nationals of the three EEA states that are not EU members enjoy the same rights as EU citizens by virtue of the EEA Treaty (also known as the "Oporto Agreement"): see *Ullusow v Secretary of State for Work and Pensions* [2007] EWCA Civ 657 (July 5, 2007, CA, Sir Andrew Morritt C, Lloyd and Moses LJJ) overturning *CPC/2920/2005* in which a Tribunal of Commissioners held that, on a true interpretation of the Oporto Agreement, Directive 90/364 only conferred a right to reside on those (non-EU) EEA nationals who are seeking to exercise a right of establishment (i.e. to set up a business in the UK).

The 2006 Regulations do not distinguish between EEA nationals who are EU citizens and those who are not. The exemptions in sub-paras (za)–(f) of para.(4) apply to nationals of Iceland, Liechtenstein and Norway, and to their family members (as defined by art.2 of the Citizenship Directive), as if they were EU nationals (see reg.10(e) of SI 1026/2006 and ss.17(2) and 23 of the Interpretation Act 1978).

Swiss nationals

2.189 Switzerland is not a member of either the EU or the EEA. However, since June 1, 2002, Swiss nationals have had rights of residence in Britain that are similar to those enjoyed by EEA nationals. Those rights are conferred by the Luxembourg Agreement (*Agreement between the European Community and its Member States, of the one part, and the Swiss Confederation, of the other, on the Free Movement of Persons,* Luxembourg, June 21, 1999, Cmnd. 5639).

Before April 30, 2006, that agreement was implemented as a matter of domestic law by the Immigration (Swiss Free Movement of Persons) (No.3) Regulations 2002 (SI 2002/1241). From that date, SI 2002/1241 was revoked and reg.2(1) of the 2006 Regulations deemed Switzerland to be an EEA state, even though it is not actually one. In addition, the exemptions in sub-paras (za)–(f) of para.(4) apply to Swiss nationals, and to their family members (as defined by art.2 of the Citizenship Directive), as if they were EU nationals (see reg.10(e) of SI 2006/1026 and ss.17(2) and 23 of the Interpretation Act 1978).

The effect is that Swiss nationals have the full range of rights conferred on EEA nationals by the 2006 Regulations.

Switzerland is also a party to the European Social Charter (see immediately below), but that Charter does not confer any additional right to reside on Swiss nationals.

Turkish nationals and nationals of the Former Yugoslav Republic of Macedonia

Although not EEA States, Turkey has ratified the European Convention on Social and Medical Assistance ("the ECSMA Agreement") and the European Social Charter, and the Former Yugoslav Republic of Macedonia has ratified the Social Charter. In some circumstances, this will have the effect that Turkish and Macedonian nationals are not excluded from benefit as "persons subject to immigration control"(see the commentary to SI 2000/636 below). However, the right to reside and habitual residence tests remain applicable *(CH/2321/2007)* and neither the ECSMA Agreement nor the Social Charter confers any direct right of residence or right to benefit: see *Yesilov v London Borough of Camden and SSWP* [2009] EWCA Civ 415 (R(H) 7/09. This is because, as the Commissioner pointed out at para.6 of *CIS/1773/2007*, the ECSMA Agreement "requires the Contracting Powers to enact legislation conferring rights to benefit but it does not confer those rights itself. In the United Kingdom, it is for Parliament to give effect to ECSMA through domestic legislation" (see also para.24 of *CJSA/4705/1999*, *CIS/259/2008* and paras 27–40 of the decision of the Court of Appeal in *Abdirahman* v *Secretary of State for Work and Pensions* [2007] EWCA Civ 657). Therefore, it is not possible for an ECSMA national who is not also an EEA national to assert in the domestic courts of the UK that legislation breaches the UK's international obligations under ECSMA: s/he can only rely on the rights conferred by domestic law. The same is true of the Social Charter (*Abdirahman*, para.39). **2.190**

The right to reside from April 30, 2006

The Citizenship Directive

The phrase "right to reside" is not defined in social security legislation and whether or not a claimant has such a right therefore falls to be determined by the ordinary rules of immigration law and, in particular, EU Law. **2.191**

That law changed with effect from April 30, 2004 when Directive 2004/38 (the "Citi zenship Directive") came into force and it is therefore necessary to ascertain the period with which one is dealing in order to know which law to apply. This note will concentrate on the law in force from April 30, 2006. Readers are referred to pp.298-306 of Vol.II of the 2006 edition, and to the Updating Material for those pages in the Supplement to that edition, for a full discussion of the law as it stood before April 30, 2006.

The purpose of the Citizenship Directive is to extend the rights of EU citizens. Therefore, arguments suggesting that the rights it confers are less extensive than those conferred by the former law need to be treated with caution. As the ECJ held in *Metock v Minister for Justice, Equality and Law Reform* (C-127/08) at para.59:

> "As is apparent from recital 3 in the preamble to Directive 2004/38, it aims in particular to 'strengthen the right of free movement and residence of all Union citizens', so that Union citizens cannot derive less rights from that directive than from the instruments of secondary legislation which it amends or repeals."

The only exception to this principle in UK law occurred in the decision of the Court of Appeal in *State for Work and Pensions v Elmi* [2011] EWCA Civ 1403 (see below). However the principle appears to have been ignored rather than disapplied in that case. **2.192**

The changes in EU Law from April 30, 2006 were reflected by amendments to domestic social security law and, in particular, the introduction of reg.21AA and of reg.85A of the JSA Regulations, and the substitution of a new reg.2 in the SPC Regulations.

The most important conceptual change in the domestic law is that, whereas, before April 30, 2006, any right of residence was sufficient to satisfy the right to reside test, it is now necessary to ask whether the *particular* right of residence enjoyed by the claimant counts for the purpose of the *particular* benefit that s/he has claimed (see para.(3) of each of those Regulations). For example, the initial right of residence (see below) does not count for the purposes of any income-related benefit and the extended right of residence enjoyed by workseekers only counts for the purposes of JSA.

The personal scope of the Citizenship Directive

2.193 By art.3(1) of the Citizenship Directive, it applies to all EU citizens "who move to or reside in a Member State other than that of which they are a national, and to their family members … who accompany or join them". For the definition of "family members", see below.

It follows that, whatever rights they may have under the EU Treaties, EU citizens do not have rights *under the Citizenship Directive* against the Member States of which they are nationals unless they have exercised their rights to freedom of movement to live in another EU state.

The leading case on this point is *McCarthy v Secretary of State for the Home Department* (C-434/09). Mrs McCarthy was a dual British/Irish citizen who was born in, and had always lived in, the UK. She was in receipt of social security benefits. She married a Jamaican citizen who did not have leave to remain in the UK. She then obtained an Irish passport and she and her husband applied for a residence permit and a residence document as, respectively, an EU citizen and the family member of an EU citizen. Those applications were refused, on the basis that Mrs McCarthy was not a qualifying person (see below). On appeal, the Supreme Court referred the following question to the ECJ for a preliminary ruling:

> "1. Is a person of dual Irish and United Kingdom nationality who has resided in the United Kingdom for her entire life a "beneficiary" within the meaning of Article 3 of [the Citizenship Directive]?"

The ECJ reformulated that question and answered as follows:

> "— Article 3(1) of [the Citizenship Directive] must be interpreted as meaning that that directive is not applicable to a Union citizen who has never exercised his right of free movement, who has always resided in a Member State of which he is a national and who is also a national of another Member State."

Note, however, that the Citizenship Directive is not the only source of rights of residence. Such rights can arise directly under arts 20, 21 and 45 of TFEU, under EU Regulations (particularly, Regulation 492/2011, formerly Regulation 1612/68) and under the domestic law of the UK. Such rights do not necessarily depend upon the exercise by the EU citizen of his or her free movement rights. In particular:

- An EU citizen who has never exercised his/her rights of free movement, who has always resided in a Member State of which s/he is a national may , exceptionally, derive rights against such a Member State under art.21 TFEU where the application of measures by that Member State would have the effect of depriving him or her of "the genuine enjoyment of the substance of the rights conferred by virtue of his [or her] status as a Union citizen or of impeding the exercise of his [or her] right of free movement and residence within the territory of the Member States: see the discussion of *Zambrano* below.

- Until October 15, 2012, a British citizen who is a dual national of of another EU State was able to derive rights from his or her other nationality under domestic UK law (i.e. the 2006 Regulations) where those Regulations were more favourable to him or her than EU law would be (see the decisions of the Upper Tribunal in *SSWP v AA* [2009] UKUT 249 (AAC) and *HG v SSWP (SPC)* [2011] UKUT 382 (AAC). However, from October 16, 2012, the 2006 Regulations were amended by SI 2012/1547 to reflect the Citizenship Directive as interpreted in *McCarthy*. The changes, which effectively reverse the decisions of the Upper Tribunal referred to above, are subject to transitional protection set out in Sch.3 to the amending regulations: see the commentary to reg.2 of the 2006 Regulations (below).

"Residence" and "lawful presence"

Lawful presence is not the same as a right of residence. A claimant who is lawfully present in the UK (i.e. who has been admitted under the right of entry in reg.11 of the 2006 Regulations, is in fact present in the UK, and would have an immediate right of re-entry if ever removed) does not ipso facto have a right to reside (see *Abdirahman* and *Ulluslow*). **2.194**

Whether a claimant is lawfully present in the UK is, however, relevant for other social security purposes (see, in particular, the commentary on the ECSMA Agreement and the European Social Charter in the General Note to SI 2000/636).

Residence permits and registration cards

As the law stood before April 30, 2006, the Home Secretary was required by reg.15 of the Immigration (European Economic Area) Regulations 2000 ("the 2000 Regulations") (subject to certain exceptions) to issue a residence permit to any "qualified person" (see below) and to the family members of any qualified person who were themselves EEA nationals who made the necessary application and supplied the required evidence of their status. With effect from that date, residence permits were abolished and replaced by registration cards issued under reg.16 of the 2006 Regulations. Transitional provisions in Sch.4 to the 2006 Regulations had the effect that residence permits issued before April 30, 2006 should thereafter be treated as if they were registration cards. **2.195**

It was well-established that it was not necessary for an EEA national to hold a residence permit in order to exercise rights of residence under EEA law. But the effect of a permit where one was issued has been a matter of controversy.

On one view a residence permit "was what it purported to be and conferred on the person to whom it had been issued a right of residence in the United Kingdom that was effective until the permit expired or was revoked." (per Judge Rowland in *SSWP v EM and KN* [2009] UKUT 44 (AAC)).

The other view was expressed by Mr Commissioner Jacobs in *CPC/3588/2006* and *CIS/865/2008*, namely that residence permits were procedural only. They were evidence of the rights possessed by the person to whom they were issued but did not confer any such rights. **2.196**

The issue has now been resolved by the ECJ in *Dias v Secretary of State for Work and Pensions* (C-325/09) [2012] AACR 36. The court held, confirming the provisional view expressed by the Court of Appeal (*Secretary of State for Work and Pensions v Dias* [2009] EWCA Civ 807), that the mere possession of a residence permit did not make the claimant's residence "legal" for the purposes of art.16(1) of the Citizenship Directive. The ECJ's formal answer to the question referred by the Court of Appeal was that:

> "– periods of residence completed before 30 April 2006 on the basis solely of a residence permit validly issued pursuant to Directive 68/360, without the conditions governing entitlement to any right of residence having been satisfied, cannot be regarded as having been completed legally for the purposes of the acquisition of the right of permanent residence under Article 16(1) of Directive 2004/38"

and its reasoning is summarised succinctly at para.54 of its judgment:

> ". . . the declaratory character of residence permits means that those permits merely certify that a right already exists. Consequently, just as such a declaratory character means that a citizen's residence may not be regarded as illegal, within the meaning of European Union law, solely on the ground that he does not hold a residence permit, it precludes a Union citizen's residence from being regarded as legal, within the meaning of European Union law, solely on the ground that such a permit was validly issued to him."

In *EM and KN* above, it was held that, whatever the position may have been before April 30, 2006, a registration card issued on or after that date (or a residence permit treated as a registration card under Sch.4 to the 2006 Regulations) merely shows that the holder had a right of residence at the time it was issued. See also *MD v SSWP (SPC)* [2016] UKUT 0319 (AAC).

A registration certificate does not have retrospective effect (*CIS/4237/2007*, para.9).

Meaning of "right to reside"

2.197 EU law affecting social security is covered in more detail in Vol.III. For present purposes, the starting point must be that under art.20 of the Treaty on the Functioning of the European Union ("TFEU") (formerly art.17 of the EC Treaty ("TEC")) "[e]very person holding the nationality of a Member State shall be a citizen of the Union" and that, under art.21 (ex-art.18 TEC).

> "1. Every citizen of the Union shall have the right to move and reside freely within the territory of the Member States, subject to the limitations and conditions laid down in this Treaty and by the measures adopted to give it effect. . . ."

The "limitations and conditions" authorised by art.20(1) are now contained in the Citizenship Directive. In particular, the Directive provides (art.7(1)(b), (c) and (2)) that, in relation to the extended right to reside (see below), the residence rights of the economically inactive are to be subject to their having "sufficient resources for themselves and their family members not to become a burden on the social assistance system of the host Member State during their period of residence and. . . comprehensive sickness insurance cover in the host Member State."

It is also of potential relevance that, under art.18 (ex-art.12 TEC):

> "Within the scope of application of this Treaty, and without prejudice to any special provisions contained therein, any discrimination on grounds of nationality shall be prohibited"

and that, under art.45 (ex-art.39 TEC):

> "1. Freedom of movement for workers shall be secured within the Community.
> 2. Such freedom of movement shall entail the abolition of any discrimination based on nationality between workers of the Member States as regards employment, remuneration and other conditions of work and employment.
> 3. It shall entail the right, subject to limitations justified on grounds of public policy, public security or public health:
> . . .
> (c) to stay in a Member State for the purpose of employment in accordance with the provisions governing the employment of nationals of that State laid down by law, regulation or administrative action;
> (d) to remain in the territory of a Member State after having been employed in that State, subject to conditions which shall be embodied in implementing regulations to be drawn up by the Commission."

2.198 Although it is sometimes possible for EU citizens to rely directly on rights conferred by the Treaty, it is normally regarded as establishing the general principles on which the EU is based, and which are then given practical effect through being implemented by Directives and Regulations. From April 30, 2006, the relevant provisions are the Citizenship Directive, Regulation 492/2011 (formerly Regulation 1612/68) and Regulation (EC) No.883/2004 (which replaced Regulation (EEC) No. 1408/71). The relevant parts of those provisions are set out in Vol.III.

The Citizenship Directive has been implemented in the domestic legislation of the UK by the 2006 Regulations, the relevant parts of which are reproduced later in this volume. In this section of this note, references to numbered regulations are to the 2006 Regulations).

It is convenient to consider first the general position of EEA nationals under those Regulations (although it is important to remember that a right to reside can arise in other circumstances as well—see *CIS/3573/2005*, para.34); then, secondly, the position of the primary carers of the children of migrant workers who are in education in the UK; then, thirdly, the rights of non-British parents of British children; and, fourthly, the special rules that apply to A2 nationals (and applied to A8 nationals before May 2009 (or, possibly, May 2011 (see the discussion of *TG v SSWP (PC)* [2015] UKUT 50 (AAC) under the heading, *The A8 Regulations*, below)); and, finally, to consider whether the right to reside test is generally compatible with EU Law.

Initial right of residence

Regulation 13(1) and (2) implements art.6 of the Citizenship Directive. It permits EEA nationals, and their non-EEA national family members, to reside in the UK for up to three months for any reason. That right is subject to reg.13(3)(b) (implementing art.14 of the Citizenship Directive) and therefore ceases if either the EEA national or the family member "becomes an unreasonable burden on the social assistance system of the United Kingdom". **2.199**

Rights of residence under the Citizenship Directive normally carry with them the right to equal treatment under art.24. However, the right to equal treatment that accompanies the initial right of residence is subject to a derogation in art.24(2) which states that "the host Member State shall not be obliged to confer entitlement to social assistance during the first three months of residence". In *Vestische Arbeit Jobcenter Kreis Recklinghausen v Garcia-Nieto* (C-299/14), the CJEU confirmed that neither art.24, nor the principle of equality of treatment in art.4 of Regulation (EC) No 883/2004, prevented Member States from excluding those whose only right of residence arose under art.6 of the Citizenship Directive from entitlement to special non-contributory cash benefits (see art.70(2) of Regulation No 883/2004) which also constitute "social assistance" within the meaning of art.24(2). In such circumstances, (following *Alimanovic* (C-67/14) and distinguishing (or, more probably, not following) *Brey* (C-140/12): see further below) it was unnecessary to carry out an individual assessment of the circumstances of the person concerned.

In accordance with that derogation, reg.21AA(3)(a) and (c) of the IS Regulations, reg.85A(3) of the JSA Regulations, reg.70(a) and (c) of the ESA Regulations, and reg.2(3)(a) and (c) of the SPC Regulations provide that the initial right of residence does not qualify a claimant to any of those benefits. It is therefore unnecessary to consider the initial right of residence further.

Extended right of residence

Regulation14 implements art.7 of the Citizenship Directive. It establishes an extended right of residence for three categories of people: **2.200**

- qualified persons (reg.14(1));
- family members of qualified persons or of EEA nationals with a permanent right of residence (reg.14(2)); and
- family members who have retained the right of residence (reg.14(3)).

Note that, where an extended right of residence exists, it does so *in addition* to any initial or permanent right of residence that may exist during the same period (see reg.14(4)).

Qualified persons

The "qualified persons" who have the right to reside under reg.14(1) are specified in reg.6(1). To qualify, a person must be an EEA national and in the UK as a "jobseeker", a worker, a self-employed person, a self-sufficient person, or a student. **2.201**

British nationals are not EEA nationals for the purposes of the 2006 Regulations (see the definition of that phrase in reg.2(1)). From October 16, 2012, they can only be "qualified persons" if they benefit from the transitional provisions in Sch.3 to SI 2012/1547 (see the commentary to reg.2 of the 2006 Regulations later in this volume).

Workers and workseekers/jobseekers: nomenclature

2.202 The most significant impediment to understanding this important aspect of the right to reside, is the confusing and inconsistent use of the words listed in the heading above, both in legislation and judicially. Specifically, there are inconsistencies in the use of language:

- between the law as it has been since April 30, 2006 and as it was before that date;
- between the Citizenship Directive and the 2006 Regulations that implement it;
- between the 2006 Regulations and the Social Security (Persons from Abroad) Amendment Regulations 2006, which prescribe what consequences the 2006 Regulations have for entitlement to income-related benefits; and
- between the use of the word "jobseeker" in the 2006 Regulations and the normal use of that word in social security law.

As was said in *Martinez Sala* (at para.32):

> ". . . a person who, for a certain period of time, performs services for and under the direction of another person in return for which he receives remuneration must be considered to be a worker. Once the employment relationship has ended, the person concerned as a rule loses his status of worker, although that status may produce certain effects after the relationship has ended, and a person who is genuinely seeking work must also be classified as a worker".

The use of a single word to describe those who are working in the UK, those who have worked in the UK but are not doing so at present, and those who may never have worked in the UK but are genuinely seeking to do so, does not promote clarity in what is already a difficult area.

2.203 This note will suggest that, for the purposes of the right to reside, the law is best understood if a clear distinction is drawn between a "worker"; "a person who has retained the status of a worker"; and a "workseeker" (see the discussion of this issue at paras 8–10 of *CJSA/1475/2006*). It would also be preferable not to use the word "jobseeker" at all in this context, but the use of the term in the 2006 Regulations and reg.21AA(3) means that it will be impossible to avoid altogether. It is accepted that analysing the law in this way involves a departure from the legislative and judicial language. The inconsistencies in that language make such a departure inevitable.

The system of nomenclature suggested in the preceding paragraph has been questioned by the Upper Tribunal. In *SSWP v A* [2009] UKUT 35 (AAC), the judge stated:

> "7. Accurate terminology to convey appropriately delineated concepts is a valuable aid to precision of legal analysis. The editor of the relevant provisions in Social Security Legislation: Volume II has drawn a distinction between a jobseeker (someone who comes to a country to look for work) and a workseeker (someone who has worked and is now looking for work again). Tribunals have adopted that terminology. I have chosen not to for three reasons. First, it is not the language used by the legislation. Second, it is not comprehensive of all the possibilities. A person may decide to look for work in a host State after (i) entering for other reasons or (ii) having worked and then left the labour market. Third, it may conceal the similarity, if not unity, of the relevant legal analysis."

In an earlier version of the decision, the judge explained that the similarity or unity of the legal analysis of those looking for work in a host Member State, might be concealed because that analysis "depends on whether the person is in the labour market."

The learned judge is correct that, where a claimant is not actually working, the crucial question is whether s/he is in the labour market. However, it is apparent from the quoted passage, that previous editions cannot have been sufficiently clear about the point being made. That point was not to draw a distinction between "work-seekers" and "jobseekers". It is agreed that, as defined in the 2006 Regulations (at least until December 31, 2013), "jobseeker" is synonymous with "workseeker" as that term has previously been understood in EU Law). Rather, it was to adopt a nomenclature that, so far as possible, avoids the use of "jobseeker" altogether. That is considered desirable in order to avoid the confusion that regularly occurs because, historically, "jobseeker" has been used in a domestic UK context as a semi-colloquial shorthand for "a person claiming jobseeker's allowance". Further confusion is caused by the fact that the Citizenship Directive appears to use the term in a sense similar to the colloquial meaning in art.7(3)(b) and (c) but to mean "workseeker" in the narrower EC sense in the Preamble (e.g. in Recital (16)). Unless different terms are used to denote the UK and EC concepts, there is a risk that decision makers and tribunals will treat everyone who is a "jobseeker" in the colloquial UK sense as being "jobseekers" for the purposes of the 2006 Regulations (when they may in fact be "workers" or "persons who have retained the status of workers") and thereby refuse benefit entitlements that are lawfully due. 2.204

The distinction between those senses of "jobseeker" could, of course, be retained by the use of appropriate suffixes. But it is felt that "workseeker" (a term with a long pedigree in EU Law before April 30, 2006) is more elegant and easily understood than, for example, "jobseeker_{EU}".

Therefore, this commentary will persist in using the terms as follows:

"worker" is used for people who are currently employed (in effective and genuine work);

"person who retains the status of worker" is used for people who are not currently employed but who have previously been workers and have continued to have that status by being temporarily incapable of work, or being in duly recorded involuntary unemployment, or (in certain cases) being in vocational training (see art.7(3) of the Citizenship Directive and reg.6(2) of the 2006 Regulations).

"workseeker" will be used not for "someone who has worked and is now looking for work again" but for someone who is looking for work either without having previously been in effective and genuine work in the UK or, if they have previously been in such work, without having retained worker status; and

"jobseeker" will not be used at all unless it is unavoidable.

On that basis, the people in examples (i) and (ii) given by the judge in the quoted passage are both "workseekers".

Workers 2.205

Workers have an extended right to reside under reg.6(1)(b) of the 2006 Regulations that counts for the purposes of entitlement to all income-related benefits and are exempt from the habitual residence test under reg.21AA(4)(a) and the equivalent provisions of the JSA Regulations, the SPC Regulations, the ESA Regulations 2008 and the Universal Credit Regulations

A worker is defined by reg.4(1)(a) of the 2006 Regulations as being "a worker within the meaning of Article 39 of the Treaty establishing the European Community [now art.45 TFEU]". That is not as informative as it appears because neither that Treaty nor the measures that have implemented it (including the

Citizenship Directive) include a definition of the term "worker" and case law makes it clear that it means different things in different contexts and sometimes even in different parts of the same Regulation (see *Martinez Sala v Freistaat Bayern* (C–85/96); *Collins v Secretary of State for Work and Pensions* (C–138/02) [2005] Q.B. 145 (reported as *R(JSA) 3/06* and *CJSA/1475/2006*). However, the reference to art.39 TEC in reg.4(1)(a) does make it clear that the word is to be interpreted in accordance with EU law and hence in accordance with the established case law of the ECJ. A number of principles can be derived from those cases:

- The term "worker" has a Community meaning and may not be defined by reference to the national laws of Member States (*Hoekstra (née Unger) v Bestuur der Bedrijfsvereniging voor Detailhandel en Ambachten* (C–75/63) [1964] E.C.R. 177).
- As a concept that defines the field of application of one of the fundamental freedoms guaranteed by the Treaty, it may not be interpreted restrictively (*Levin v Staatssecretaris van Justitie* (C–53/81) [1982] E.C.R. 1035).
- The term applies to those who, broadly speaking, are employees rather than self-employed. For these purposes "the essential characteristic of an employment relationship is that for a certain period a person performs services for and under the direction of another person in return for which he receives remuneration" (*Raulin v Minister Van Onderwijs en Wetenschappen* (C–357/89)[1992] E.C.R. I-1027, at para.10). However, the existence of a legally-binding employment relationship is not conclusive of whether the employee is a worker (*Bettray v Staatssecretaris Van Justitie* (C–344/87) [1989] E.C.R. 1621).
- The requirement that a "worker" should receive remuneration means that voluntary activity is not "work" for these purposes (*CIS/868/2008* and *CIS/1837/2006*). Similarly, a person who receives carer's allowance for caring for a severely disabled person is not providing services for remuneration and so is not a worker for the purposes of art.7(1)(a) of the Citizenship Directive: see *JR v SSWP (IS)* and *JR v Leeds CC (HB)* [2014] UKUT 154 (AAC).
- The concept extends to part-time workers but only to the extent that the work undertaken is "effective and genuine . . . to the exclusion of activities on such a small scale as to be regarded as purely marginal and ancillary" (*Levin*, para.17).
- As long as the work undertaken, is "effective and genuine" in this sense, it is irrelevant whether it "yields an income lower than that which, in the [host] state, is considered as the minimum required for subsistence, whether that person supplements the income from his activity as an employed person with other income so as to arrive at that minimum or is satisfied with means of support lower than the said minimum" (*Levin*, para.18). Moreover, "where a national of a Member State pursues within the territory of another Member State by way of employment activities which may in themselves be regarded as effective and genuine work, the fact that he claims financial assistance payable out of the public funds of the latter Member State in order to supplement the income he receives from those activities does not exclude him from the provisions of community law relating to freedom of movement for workers" (*Kempf v Staatssecretaris Van Justitie* (C–139/85) [1986] E.C.R. 1741 (formal ruling of the Court)).
- The motives which may have prompted the worker to seek employment in another Member State are irrelevant provided s/he pursues, or wishes to pursue, an effective and genuine activity (*Levin*, para.23).
- In assessing whether a person is a worker, account should be taken of all the occupational activities s/he has undertaken in the host State (although activities pursued in other Member States do not count) (*Raulin*). In principle,

there seems to be no reason why this should not include work done during a claimant's previous stay in the UK (even if on this occasion the person has not yet obtained employment) although this will depend on the length of time which has passed since the previous stay, the circumstances in which that employment came to an end, and the extent to which it can be said that the work now sought is connected to the work previously undertaken—see also the discussion of *Collins*, below.

Whether work undertaken by a particular claimant is, on the facts, "effective and genuine" within the case law of the ECJ is a matter for the national courts (i.e. the First-tier Tribunal and, on appeal, the Upper Tribunal) (*Levin*, para.13). Traditionally, Until recently, the "effective and genuine" test was thought to present a low threshold. It excluded cases of abuse (i.e. relationships not really entered into for the purpose of pursuing economic activity but for the sole purpose of obtaining some other advantage: see the Advocate General in *Raulin*, para.9) and cases in which the work undertaken was not really economic activity at all (such as the rehabilitative work in *Bettray*) or "if it is done pursuant to some other relationship between the parties which is not an employment relationship, as where a lodger performs some small task for his landlord as part of the terms of his tenancy" (see the decision of the Court of Appeal in *Barry v London Borough of Southwark* [2008] EWCA Civ 1440, para.20). Although the duration of the work is a relevant factor (*Raulin*), work undertaken for very short periods and for a very few hours a week has been held to qualify. For example, in *R(IS) 12/98* an au pair who had worked for five weeks (being paid £35 for a 13-hour week, plus free board and lodging) was held to be a worker.

However, there was a difference of opinion between Commissioners over whether, for work to be effective and genuine, the claimant's hours of work and earnings (or, in the case of a work seeker, the prospective hours of work and earnings) had to be such that s/he was not eligible to claim social assistance. In *CH/3314/2005* and *CIS/3315/2005*, Mr Commissioner Rowland held that, as Member States may insist that nationals of other states residing in their territory do not become a burden on their social assistance systems (*Trojani v Centre public d'aide sociale de Bruxelles (*C–456/02) [2004] E.C.R. I-7573), the claimant's hours of work and earnings had to be sufficient to remove entitlement to IS or income-based JSA, and to pay those housing costs that would be covered by housing benefit (i.e. the "eligible rent" calculated in accordance with the determinations made by the Rent Officer), in order to be "effective". Readers are referred to pp.312–313 of Vol.II of the 2010/11 edition for a discussion of *CH/3314/2005* and *CIS/3315/2005*, including the various ways in which it was qualified and details of the decisions that followed it and disagreed with it. The current position is that, in *SS v Slough BC* [2011] UKUT 128 (AAC), Judge Rowland has re-considered the issue in the light of subsequent decisions of the Court of Appeal and the ECJ and has accepted that, whilst the level of the claimant's hours and earnings are a relevant factor, the decision cannot be taken on a formulaic basis (including the formulaic basis proposed in *CH/3314/2005* and *CIS/3315/2005*): **2.206**

"25. I am prepared to accept that a formulaic approach is apt to raise as many questions as it answers. However, I do not accept that no regard can be had to matters outside the employment relationship when determining whether a person is a worker for the purpose of obtaining a right of residence. In *Trojani*, the Advocate General pointed out that there is no obligation of member states to provide social assistance to those without a right of residence and it was held that Member States can require of nationals of other states who wish to reside within their territory that they have sufficient resources to avoid becoming a burden on their social assistance systems during their period of residence. It is true that, as [counsel for the appellant] submits, in both that case and in *Grzelczyk v. Centre public d'aide sociale d'Ottignes-Louvain-la-Neuve* (Case C-184/99) [2001] E.C.R. I-6193, the Court was concerned with people who were not economically active. However, Article 39 of the Treaty guaranteed freedom of movement for workers and not for those

who intended to be reliant on social assistance and it seems to me that it is perfectly proper in the present context to consider whether work is "marginal" having regard to the extent of a person's need or intention to claim social assistance while accepting that a need or intention to claim social assistance cannot be conclusive.
26. I therefore prefer the approach suggested by [counsel for the Secretary of State] of simply considering what is proportionate. It is fair and gives effect to one of the overarching principles of Community law. Moreover, proportionality is an approach that enables all possibly relevant matters to be taken into consideration. . . ."

The issue of sufficiency of earnings has also been considered by the ECJ in *Vatsouras and Koupatantze v Arbeitsgemeinschaft (ARGE) Nürnberg 900* (C-22/08 and C-23/08) and *Hava Genc v Land Berlin (*C-14/09). In the former case, the Court stated:

"27. Neither the origin of the funds from which the remuneration is paid nor the limited amount of that remuneration can have any consequence in regard to whether or not the person is a 'worker' for the purposes of Community law (see Case 344/87 *Bettray* [1989] E.C.R 1621, paragraph 15, and Case C-10/05 *Mattern and Cikotic* [2006] E.C.R. I-3145, paragraph 22).
28 The fact that the income from employment is lower than the minimum required for subsistence does not prevent the person in such employment from being regarded as a 'worker' within the meaning of Article 39 EC (see Case 53/81 *Levin* [1982] E.C.R. 1035, paragraphs 15 and 16, and Case C-317/93 *Nolte* [1995] E.C.R. I-4625, paragraph 19), even if the person in question seeks to supplement that remuneration by other means of subsistence such as financial assistance drawn from the public funds of the State in which he resides (see Case 139/85 *Kempf* [1986] E.C.R. 1741, paragraph 14)."

In the latter, it reiterated that:

"20 Neither the origin of the funds from which the remuneration is paid nor the limited amount of that remuneration, nor indeed the fact that the person in question seeks to supplement that remuneration by other means of subsistence such as financial assistance drawn from the public funds of the State in which he resides, can have any consequence in regard to whether or not the person is a 'worker' for the purposes of European Union law (see, to that effect, Case 139/85 *Kempf* [1986] E.C.R. 1741, paragraph 14; Case 344/87 *Bettray* [1989] E.C.R. 1621, paragraph 15; and Case C-10/05 *Matternand Cikotic* [2006] E.C.R. I-3145, paragraph 22)."

In *CJSA/3066/2007*, the Commissioner held that, in JSA cases, the right to reside test does not usually impose a greater hurdle for EU citizens than is imposed by the Jobseekers Act. However, in *CIS/2364/2006*, he recanted on the grounds that "some people may be available for work and be actively seeking employment but not have a genuine chance of being engaged because, for instance, they have an insufficient command of English or Welsh for the type of job they are seeking or, perhaps, they have settled in an area where there is a particularly high level of unemployment and a dearth of jobs so that the requirement to have a genuine chance of being engaged can be an additional hurdle". However, it was not usually appropriate to treat the right to reside test as a preliminary issue in JSA cases.

2.207 In *CSIS/467/2007*, the Commissioner held that the claimant's physical incapacity to do the work she had undertaken and the fact that she had been dismissed from it after a short period were relevant to the issue of whether the work was genuine and effective.

The issue of when a workseeker becomes a worker was considered by the Upper Tribunal in *NE v SSWP* [2009] UKUT 38 (AAC). The claimant had worked for 15 hours in December 2004 and (possibly) for three weeks for an agency in January 2005 before claiming IS in July 2005. Judge Rowland stated:

"9. The issue in a case like the present may be said to be whether the claimant has genuinely and effectively (to borrow that phrase from its usual context) become a worker rather than a workseeker. I do not accept [counsel for the claimant]'s submission that agency work is by its nature ancillary and insufficient to confer on a claimant the status of worker. Although agency work is often temporary and for short periods, it is not necessarily so. However, I do accept that a distinction is to be drawn between temporary employment for a short period and indefinite employment that has been curtailed prematurely. Where work is undertaken for what is expected from the outset to be for a very short period and is known to be temporary, the person concerned is obliged to keep looking for work and often he or she cannot realistically be said to have become established in work and to have ceased to be a workseeker. It does not follow that all agency workers always remain workseekers. Where short periods of temporary work are not separated by longer periods of no work, it will often be appropriate to regard the person concerned as having become a worker rather than a workseeker. There will be cases where work that is temporarily is nonetheless for a prolonged period or where there is a high likelihood of further work being obtained and, in particular, many agency workers will be able to show that the agency has regularly found them work albeit for short periods and they have, for practical purposes, become established members of the national workforce. On the other hand, where a person has worked only intermittently for very short periods, as in CIS/1793/2007, the claimant is more likely to have remained a workseeker because the work performed has been marginal. The case-law shows that whether work is marginal is a matter of judgement on the facts of each case. In *Ninni-Orasche v Bundesminister für Wissenschaft, Verkehr und Kunst* (C-413/01) [2003] E.C.R. I-13187, the Court did not rule out the possibility that work under a fixed-term contract for two and a half months might be marginal and ancillary."

The duration of work was also an issue in *Barry*, in which a citizen of the Netherlands was held to be a worker on the basis of having done two weeks' work as a steward at the All England Tennis Championships at Wimbledon for which he was paid £789.86 net. See, however, the comments of Judge Rowland, *NE v SSWP*, at para.8. **2.208**

An employee undertaking genuine and effective work is a worker for the purposes of the Citizenship Directive even if employed under a contract that is performed illegally (e.g. because the employer does not account to HMRC for the PAYE and national insurance contributions due on the employee's wages): see *JA v SSWP (ESA)* [2012] UKUT 122 (AAC) (*CE/2190/2011*), paras 15–20. Similarly, undeclared work by a person claiming benefit can still be genuine and effective, see *Barry* at paras 28, 31 and 45 and *NE v SSWP* at para.4.

Minimum earnings threshold

Although there has been no change in the law governing whether work is effective and genuine, there was a change in the administrative practice followed by the DWP when deciding that issue with effect from March 1, 2014. The change is set out in DMG Memo 1/14 which establishes a "Minimum Earnings Threshold". The DWP will now accept that claimants who have had average gross earnings of at least the primary earnings threshold for national insurance contributions (£153 pw in 2014/15 and £155 pw in 2015/16 and 2016/17) for the three months before the claim are (or were) in effective and genuine work, without making further enquiries. The circumstances of claimants who do not meet that threshold, or have not done so for a continuous period of three months before the claim, will be investigated in more detail. **2.209**

Contrary to the way in which the change has been misrepresented in the press, the law does not require that a claimant must earn at least £155 pw before s/he can be accepted as being in effective and genuine work.

Persons who retain the status of worker

The rules about retaining worker status relate to people who do not have subsisting contracts of employment. Those who are still employed, even though, temporarily, they are not actually working because of illness or pregnancy, continue to be **2.210** "workers" and therefore do not need to rely on the rules (see *CS v SSWP* [2009] UKUT 16 (AAC) and *CIS/185/2008*, para.8).

Although the Citizenship Directive and the 2006 Regulations contain detailed rules about the circumstances in which worker status is retained, the underlying principle by which those rules should be interpreted is whether the former worker continues to be in the labour market. As was explained by the Commissioner in *CIS/3789/2006* (at para.8):

> ". . . It may seem harsh, but the status of a "worker" is accorded only to those actually engaged in economic activity in the labour market or as self-employed persons at the material time. Accepting that this description can extend to those temporarily unable to be at their work because of illness or accident, or an involuntary spell of unemployment, it is still not apt to include a person who has withdrawn from employment voluntarily and has been and remains economically inactive, neither in work nor seeking it: albeit for entirely proper and understandable practical reasons such as having had to take a break from the world of work because of the breakdown of a relationship and the continuing family responsibilities of having a young child under school age to look after and another one on the way"

See also the observations of the Court of Appeal to similar effect at paras 21 and 22 of *SSWP v Dias.*

2.211 Former workers who retain that status are treated as workers by the 2006 Regulations and therefore have an extended right of residence under reg.6(1)(b) of those Regulations. They are also exempt from the habitual residence test (see reg.21AA(4)(c), reg.85A(4) of the JSA Regulations, reg.2(4)(c) of the SPC Regulations, reg.70(4)(c) of the ESA Regulations 2008 and reg.9(4)(a) of the Universal Credit Regulations).

Whether worker status has been retained can involve a detailed analysis of the facts of the case. Tribunals need to investigate the issues and make proper findings of fact (see *SSWP v IR* [2009] UKUT 11 (AAC)).

In domestic UK law, the question is governed by reg.6(2), (2A) and (5)–(7) of the 2006 Regulations (see below), which implements art.7(3) of the Citizenship Directive.

Temporarily unable to work

2.212 Under reg.6(2)(a), a person who is no longer working retains worker status if "he is temporarily unable to work as the result of an illness or accident".

Inability to work is a concept of EU law and must be interpreted the same way throughout the EU (*CIS/4304/2007*). It therefore does not depend upon the domestic legislation governing incapacity benefits in the individual Member States. The Commissioner stated (at para.35):

> "The context provides some guidance. It ensures continuity of worker status for someone who would otherwise be employed or looking for work. That employment or search for employment provides the touchstone against which the claimant's disabilities must be judged. The question is: can she fairly be described as unable to do the work she was doing or the sort of work that she was seeking?"

The meaning of "temporarily" was considered by the Commissioner in *CIS/3890/2005*.The Tribunal had taken the view that a temporary incapacity was one "which had a certainty of recovery". The Commissioner stated:

> "5 . . . . The tribunal was entitled to take the view that the condition from which the claimant was suffering was a permanent one. However, it does not follow that incapacity was not temporary, if the claimant was to be regarded as incapable of work at all. The fact that the claimant had returned to work was sufficient to show that the condition was not one that would permanently incapacitate the claimant in respect of all work. (Although the return to work was after the

date of the Secretary of State's decision, it was evidence that could be taken into account in considering what could have been anticipated at the date of that decision.) However, it is reasonable to consider a person to be incapable of work for a period after he or she has become incapable of following previous employment, even if there is other work that he or she might undertake. Moreover, the British system in respect of incapacity benefit deems a person to be incapable of work for benefit purposes if a personal capability assessment is satisfied and also pending such an assessment. Such a person may not actually be incapable of work and may be looking for a job. If such a person is not to be treated as incapable of work for the purposes of the 2000 Regulations, there would arise the question whether that person should be treated as a workseeker instead. However, there are practical difficulties in treating a person who is entitled to benefit on the basis of incapacity as a workseeker, not the least of which is arranging for registration as being available for work. There is therefore much to be said for what appears to be implied in the Secretary of State's submission, which is that a person should be treated as incapable of work if entitled to benefits on that basis.

6. It seems to me that the tribunal erred in assuming that because the claimant may have had a permanent disability, she was necessarily permanently incapable of work or, alternatively, in failing to consider whether she was a workseeker if she was not incapable of work. I therefore set aside the tribunal's decision and I accept the Secretary of State's suggestion that I should find that the claimant was temporarily incapable of work. . . ."

In *Secretary of State for the Home Department v FB* [2010] UKUT 447 (IAC), a two-judge-panel of the Upper Tribunal held that a "temporary" incapacity is one that is not "permanent". See also the decisions of the Court of Appeal in *De Brito v Secretary of State for the Home Department* [2012] EWCA Civ 709 (at para.33), *Konodyba v Royal Borough of Kensington & Chelsea* [2012] EWCA Civ 982 (at paras 18–23) and in *Samin v City of Westminster* [2012] EWCA Civ 1468 where the relevant law was summarised as follows (at para.31): **2.213**

"Temporary is to be contrasted with permanent. The question is one of fact in every case; plainly the circumstances which will fall to be examined will vary infinitely. It will generally be helpful to ask whether there is or is not a realistic prospect of a return to work. It will generally not be helpful to ask if the interruption is indefinite; an indefinite absence from work may well not be temporary, but it might be, for example if an injured man is awaiting surgery which can be expected to restore him to fitness to work, but the date when it will be available is uncertain".

The temporary incapacity for work must be the result of an illness or accident suffered by the EEA national and not, for example, the illness of a dependent child—*CIS/3182/2005*.

Pregnancy

The position of pregnant women requires particular mention here. **2.214**

Some pregnant women who are EEA nationals will be entitled to benefits that are not subject to the right to reside test or because they satisfy that test:

- A woman who has worked may have an entitlement to statutory maternity pay, maternity allowance or, in some very limited circumstances, incapacity benefit (none of which depends on her having a right to reside).
- A woman who still has a contract of employment but takes time off to give birth will still be a "worker" (in the same way as a person who takes leave for other reasons) and will therefore not need to show that she has "retained" that status (see *CIS/185/2008* at para.8 and *CIS/4237/2007* in which an A8 national was held to be legally working while on maternity leave).

However, for other women a problem arises because of the conditions of entitlement for IS, JSA and ESA under domestic law. Under para.14 of Sch.1B, a woman falls within a prescribed category if she is "incapable of work by reason of pregnancy" and also during the period from eleven weeks before the expected week of confinement until seven weeks after the end of the pregnancy. Women in this category may claim IS but, subject to what is said below, may also claim JSA if they can satisfy the labour market conditions. Regulations 20(d) and (f) of the ESA Regulations (see Vol.I) treat pregnant women as having limited capability for work either if working would endanger their health or the health of the unborn child or (in the case of women with no entitlement to statutory maternity pay or maternity allowance) from the sixth week before the expected week of confinement and the fourteenth day after the actual date of confinement. A woman who is treated as having limited capability for work may not claim JSA and, if she is to be entitled to an income-related benefit at all, must claim either IS or ESA.

2.215 But many pregnant women who are EEA nationals will be unable to make such a claim. Those who have never worked in the UK (or have worked but since withdrawn from the labour-market) will, at most, have a right to reside as a workseeker (in the narrow sense described below) and that right does not count for the purposes of IS or ESA. Women who have worked in the UK but who give up their jobs because of their pregnancies, or those who—when they became pregnant—were involuntarily unemployed (see below) and claiming JSA as a person who had retained worker status, need to rely on art.7 of the Citizenship Directive or reg.6(2)(a). In the past, they could not always do so. In an individual case a pregnant woman might be suffering from an illness by reason of her pregnancy (see *CIS/731/2007*) but pregnancy per se is not an "illness or accident" (*CIS/4010/2006* and the judgment of the ECJ in *Saint Prix* (below) at paras 29–30). The question therefore arises whether a woman who gives up employment (or the search for employment in cases where she was previously retaining worker status on the basis of involuntary unemployment) can retain (or continue to retain) worker status simply by virtue of being pregnant.

It can now be said that the answer to that question is yes. In *Saint Prix v Secretary of State for Work and Pensions* (C-507/12) [2014] AACR 18, the claimant was a French national who had worked until she was nearly six months pregnant but then gave up because the demands of her job had become too strenuous for her. She spent about a week looking for less strenuous work and then, at the beginning of the 11th week before her expected date of confinement, she claimed income support. She returned to work three months after the premature birth of her child.

The Secretary of State refused her income support claim on the ground that she had no longer retained worker status. An appeal tribunal upheld her appeal against that decision. However, the Upper Tribunal (*JS v SSWP (IS)* [2010] UKUT 131 (AAC) upheld the Secretary of State's appeal as did the Court of Appeal (*JS v Secretary of State for Work and Pensions* [2011] EWCA Civ 806, [2012] AACR 7). The claimant then appealed to the Supreme Court, which referred the following questions to the CJEU (see *Saint Prix v Secretary of State for Work and Pensions* [2012] UKSC 49):

> "1. Is the right of residence conferred upon a 'worker' in Article 7 of the Citizenship Directive to be interpreted as applying only to those (i) in an existing employment relationship, (ii) (at least in some circumstances) seeking work, or (iii) covered by the extensions in article 7(3), or is the Article to be interpreted as not precluding the recognition of further persons who remain 'workers' for this purpose?
> 2. (i) If the latter, does it extend to a woman who reasonably gives up work, or seeking work, because of the physical constraints of the late stages of pregnancy (and the aftermath of childbirth)?
> (ii) If so, is she entitled to the benefit of the national law's definition of when it is reasonable for her to do so?"

2.216 The CJEU answered those questions by ruling that:

"Article 45 TFEU must be interpreted as meaning that a woman who gives up work, or seeking work, because of the physical constraints of the late stages of pregnancy and the aftermath of childbirth retains the status of 'worker', within the meaning of that article, provided she returns to work or finds another job within a reasonable period after the birth of her child."

The Court's reasoning is set out at paras 38–46 of its judgment:

"38 . . . it cannot be argued, contrary to what the United Kingdom Government contends, that Article 7(3) of [the Citizenship] Directive lists exhaustively the circumstances in which a migrant worker who is no longer in an employment relationship may nevertheless continue to benefit from that status.
39 In the present case, . . . Ms Saint Prix was employed in the territory of the United Kingdom before giving up work, less than three months before the birth of her child, because of the physical constraints of the late stages of pregnancy and the immediate aftermath of childbirth. She returned to work three months after the birth of her child, without having left the territory of that Member State during the period of interruption of her professional activity.
40 The fact that such constraints require a woman to give up work during the period needed for recovery does not, in principle, deprive her of the status of 'worker' within the meaning Article 45 TFEU.
41 The fact that she was not actually available on the employment market of the host Member State for a few months does not mean that she has ceased to belong to that market during that period, provided she returns to work or finds another job within a reasonable period after confinement . . ..
42 In order to determine whether the period that has elapsed between childbirth and starting work again may be regarded as reasonable, the national court concerned should take account of all the specific circumstances of the case in the main proceedings and the applicable national rules on the duration of maternity leave, in accordance with Article 8 of Council Directive 92/85/EEC of 19 October 1992 on the introduction of measures to encourage improvements in the safety and health at work of pregnant workers and workers who have recently given birth or are breastfeeding . . ..
43 The approach adopted in paragraph 41 of the present judgment is consistent with the objective pursued by Article 45 TFEU of enabling a worker to move freely within the territory of the other Member States and to stay there for the purpose of employment . . ..
44 As the Commission contends, a Union citizen would be deterred from exercising her right to freedom of movement if, in the event that she was pregnant in the host State and gave up work as a result, if only for a short period, she risked losing her status as a worker in that State.
45 Furthermore, it must be pointed out that EU law guarantees special protection for women in connection with maternity. In that regard, it should be noted that Article 16(3) of [the Citizenship] Directive provides, for the purpose of calculating the continuous period of five years of residence in the host Member State allowing Union citizens to acquire the right of permanent residence in that territory, that the continuity of that residence is not affected, inter alia, by an absence of a maximum of 12 consecutive months for important reasons such as pregnancy and childbirth.
46 If, by virtue of that protection, an absence for an important event such as pregnancy or childbirth does not affect the continuity of the five years of residence in the host Member State required for the granting of that right of residence, the physical constraints of the late stages of pregnancy and the immediate aftermath of childbirth, which require a woman to give up work temporarily, cannot, a fortiori, result in that woman losing her status as a worker."

Tribunals must therefore assess whether the woman has claimed IS or ESA because she gave up work, or seeking work, because of the physical constraints of the late stages of pregnancy and the aftermath of childbirth and, if so, whether—taking into account paras 40–42 of the judgment—she remains in the labour market. In *SSWP v SFF, ADR v SSWP, CS v LB Barnet & SSWP* [2015] UKUT 502, the Upper Tribunal considered a number of legal and practical issues arising from that assessment namely:

(a) What is the nature of the *Saint Prix* right: in particular, is it a right to be assessed prospectively or retrospectively?
(b) To whom is the *Saint Prix* right available?
(c) When does a *Saint Prix* right start?
(d) How long does the "reasonable period" last?
(e) Does a woman have to return to work (or find another job) or will a return to seeking work suffice?
(f) Can a *Saint Prix* right contribute to the period of time necessary to acquire the right of permanent residence under art.16 of Directive 2004/38?

Judge Ward answered those questions as follows:

(a) The *Saint Prix* right is to be assessed prospectively. The proviso in para.41 of the CJEU's judgment—namely that in order to retain worker status a formerly-pregnant woman should "[return] to work or find another job within a reasonable period after confinement"—did not create "a condition precedent to the [*Saint Prix*] right coming into existence, which would have the consequence that the existence of the right could only be assessed retrospectively, but . . . a condition subsequent for terminating it where it is not met . . .". The issue was "primarily one of the woman's intention, but subject to the special protection conferred by the CJEU's judgment". Approaching it in that way "means that a woman is protected by her worker status until such time, not exceeding the end of the "reasonable period" contemplated by para.47 of *Saint-Prix*, as she by her words or actions shows an intention not to be part of the employment market": see para.22 of *SFF*. This approach avoids the potential problem with s.12(8)(b) of the Social Security Act 1998, i.e. that any return to work will often occur after the date of the decision under appeal.
(b) As is implicit in the CJEU's decision itself—and as was not in dispute in before the Upper Tribunal—the *Saint Prix* right is available to women who have exercised the right of freedom of movement for workers and have been employed in a Member State other than that of their residence and to those who by meeting the conditions of Article 7(3) retain worker status while looking for work. It has yet to be decided whether a "jobseeker" in the EU sense—i.e., a woman who has never previously worked in the UK or who, having worked in the UK, has left the labour market but is now seeking work—can avail herself of the right. That is because none of the claimants in *SFF* fell within that category.
(c) Judge Ward ruled that "the 11th week before the expected date of childbirth which appears as the earliest permitted commencement of a maternity pay period and for payment of maternity allowance and, more importantly, as the start of the period when a claimant for income support fulfils, without more, the requirement to fall within a "prescribed category" of person . . . provides a convenient yardstick by which to assess whether the test is fulfilled but one that is capable of being displaced in particular cases".
(d) Contrary to the guidance issued by the Secretary of State in DMG Memo 25/14—which had advised decision makers that the maximum reasonable period was the 26 weeks during which a woman is entitled to ordinary maternity leave—Judge Ward ruled that the reasonable period is to be determined taking account of the 52-week period covered by the rights to ordinary and additional maternity leave and of the circumstances of the particular case: see para.35. He added:

> "As a matter of practice rather than of law, it seems likely that it will be an unusual case in which the period is other than the 52 week period".

(e) A return to seeking work will suffice. Judge Ward accepted (at para.39) a submission from the Secretary of State, that:

> "if a woman with rights under Article 7(3)(b) or (c) had to find a job within the reasonable period after childbirth rather than merely returning to qualifying work seeking, then she would have to do more as the result of leaving the labour market temporarily because of pregnancy and the aftermath of childbirth than if she had remained as a person with retained worker status under Article 7(3)(b) or (c)."

The same was true of a woman who was in employment at the beginning of the reasonable period but whose job had come to an end during that period (para.40). The reference in the CJEU's judgment to a condition that a woman "returns to work or finds another job" could be explained by the fact that that is what had happened on the facts of *Saint Prix* (para.41).

(f) The *Saint Prix* right does count towards the continuous period of legal residence necessary to acquire the right of permanent residence. The Secretary of State did not dispute that in *SFF* and therefore the reason why it is so is not explained. It is because a woman exercising the *Saint Prix* right retains worker status while she does so. Therefore, that period counts towards the qualifying residence period for the permanent right of residence in the same way as any other period of residence as a retained-status worker.

Note that receipt of maternity allowance does not lead to a woman automatically abandoning her worker status: see *Secretary of State for Work and Pensions v MM (IS)* [2015] UKUT 0128 (AAC), para.57.

Where a pregnant woman is wrongly advised to claim IS or ESA rather than JSA, see the discussion below.

Involuntary unemployment

The provisions on involuntary unemployment in reg.6 of the 2006 Regulations purport to implement art.7(3)(b)–(d) of the Citizenship Directive. Until December 31, 2013, they were more generous to claimants than art.7(3) strictly required. However, the provisions were substantially amended with effect from January 1, 2014, July 1, 2014 and November 10, 2014 and there must now be a question as to whether they are more restrictive than art.7(3) permits. 2.217

For the position until December 31, 2013, see pp.321–325 of Vol.II of the 2013/14 edition. The position from January 1, 2014 to June 30, 2014 is set out at p.329 of Vol.II of the 2014/15 edition. From July 1, 2014, the domestic law of the UK is as follows.

Under reg.6, EEA nationals who have ceased to be workers retain worker status if they are in duly recorded involuntary unemployment provided they have registered as a jobseeker with the relevant employment office and satisfy two conditions, namely Condition A and Condition B.

Condition A is that they either entered the United Kingdom in order to seek employment, or are present in the United Kingdom seeking employment, immediately after enjoying a right to reside as a worker, a self-employed person, a self-sufficient person, or as a student: see reg.6(5). When applying the "immediately after" test, "any period during which worker status was retained" is disregarded. 2.218

Condition B is that they "can provide evidence that [they are] seeking employment and [have] a genuine chance of being engaged": see reg.6(6).

Under reg.6(2)(ba) and (2A), EEA nationals who have been employed in the UK for less than a year, cannot retain worker status for longer than six months.

Under reg.6(2)(b) and (7), EEA nationals who have been employed in the UK for at least a year may retain the status of worker for longer than six months but only if they can provide "compelling evidence" that they are continuing to seek employment and have a genuine chance of being engaged. 2.219

The requirement in reg.6(7) for claimants to provide "compelling evidence" that they are continuing to seek employment and have a genuine chance of being engaged sounds as if it is more onerous than the requirement in reg.6(6) to provide "evidence" of those matters. However, it is doubted whether that is in fact the case. The general rule in civil law is that those under the burden of proving the existence of a state of affairs must do so "on a balance of probabilities": that is they must establish that it is more probable than not that the facts are as they say. That is done by producing evidence, and the evidence produced is compelling if, on balance, it satisfies that standard. There is no indication in reg.6 that the standard of proof has been changed. Therefore, it is suggested that all a claimant has to show is that on the evidence as a whole it is more likely than not that s/he has a genuine chance of being engaged: see *KS v SSWP (JSA)* [2016] UKUT 0269 (AAC) in which a similar conclusion is reached under the law of Scotland. On that basis, the word "compelling" is otiose. The alternative appears to be that the requirement in reg.6(6) to provide "evidence" rather than "compelling evidence" is satisfied by providing any evidence at all even if it is unpersuasive and does not satisfy the decision maker on a balance of probabilities. Which would be absurd.

EEA nationals who cease to retain worker status under the six months rule but remain in the UK and continue to seek work will become "jobseekers" (see below) if they continue to satisfy Condition A (as they inevitably will), and Condition B and (where relevant) an additional condition ("Condition C").

2.220 In *Jobcenter Berlin Neukölln v Alimanovic* (C-67/14), the Bundessozialgericht (the German Federal Social Court) referred a number of questions on the issue of whether a German law that excludes:

> "foreign nationals whose right of residence arises solely out of the search for employment and their family members"

from entitlement to *Grundsicherung*, (a benefit making basic provision for jobseekers) is compatible with EU law.

Ms Alimanovic and her children were Swedish nationals (although the children had been born in Germany). They left Germany in 1999 and re-entered in June 2010. Ms Alimanovic and her eldest daughter worked for less than a year in short-term jobs or under employment-promotion measures but, according to the findings of the Berlin Social Court—by which the Federal Social Court was bound—no longer retained worker status and therefore fell within the words quoted above.

On September 15, 2015, the Grand Chamber of the CJEU ruled that:

> "Article 24 of [the Citizenship Directive] and Article 4 of [Regulation (EC) No 883/2004], must be interpreted as not precluding legislation of a Member State under which nationals of other Member States who are in a situation such as that referred to in Article 14(4)(b) of that directive are excluded from entitlement to certain 'special non-contributory cash benefits' within the meaning of Article 70(2) of Regulation No 883/2004, which also constitute 'social assistance' within the meaning of Article 24(2) of Directive 2004/38, although those benefits are granted to nationals of the Member State concerned who are in the same situation."

In plain English, this means that Member States may discriminate against those whose only right of residence is as a jobseeker (*i.e.* in the narrow EU sense) by refusing them social assistance in circumstances in which it would be granted to their own nationals. Thus, the UK's refusal to pay IS, ESA and HB to jobseekers is probably lawful. It is not, however, clear that this aspect of *Alimanovic* has any further consequences for UK benefits. The Court was careful to distinguish between social assistance and benefits intended to facilitate integration into the labour market. Putting it at its lowest, it is arguable the JSA falls into the latter category.

The meaning of "voluntary" (and hence "involuntary") unemployment was considered by the Commissioner in *CIS/3315/2005*. Following *R(IS) 12/98*, he held that the term.

"Must be regarded as focussing on the question whether the claimant is still in the labour market rather than on the circumstances in which he or she ceased to be employed, although the latter may be relevant as evidence as to whether the clamant is still genuinely in the labour market".

It was therefore unnecessary for the claimant to argue that she was forced to give up her job by her circumstances and therefore did not give it up voluntarily and, depending on those circumstances—for example, if she were unable to work or be available for work because of childcare responsibilities—such an argument would be detrimental to her case.

"Duly recorded" and "registered as a jobseeker": The Commissioner in *CIS/3315/2005* also considered the requirement (in the 2000 Regulations) that such unemployment should be "duly recorded by the relevant employment office" and accepted a concession from the Secretary of State that the requirement was met by an income support claimant who declared that s/he was seeking work at the first opportunity (in this case in answer to a question on the "Right To Reside Stencil"). The Commissioner left open the question of whether an income support claimant who was in fact looking for work but, for some reason, answered "no" to that question would nevertheless meet the requirement. **2.221**

The position from April 30, 2006 was less clear but has now been clarified. From that date, it was no longer sufficient for claimants to be in "duly recorded involuntary unemployment": they also had to have "registered as a job-seeker with the relevant employment office" (7(3)(b) and (c) of the Citizenship Directive and reg.6(2)(b) of the 2006 Regulations). In *CIS/3799/2007* (at paras 17 and 18) and *CIS/184/2008*, the Secretary of State did not repeat the concession that had been made in *CIS/3315/2005*. The Commissioner held that, in order to satisfy the additional requirement of registration as a jobseeker with the relevant employment office, a claimant must claim JSA rather than IS. However, in *SSWP v FE* [2009] UKUT 287 (AAC) a three-judge panel decided (by a majority, Walker J, CP, and Judge Ward, Judge Howell QC dissenting) that claiming JSA or registering for NI credits were not the only means of "registering as a jobseeker". Summarising its conclusions, the majority stated:

"29. We conclude that the Secretary of State has not shown that the UK has defined specific mechanisms as being the only ways in which an individual can, for the purposes of Article 7(3)(c) "register as a jobseeker with the relevant employment office". That being so, the tribunal was entitled to hold that the Secretary of State's factual concessions meant that the claimant succeeded in her appeal. In summary:

a. What the Directive contemplates is that a claimant has done what is needed in order to have his or her name recorded as looking for work by the relevant employment office
b. Whether or not this has been done is a question of fact
c. There is no rule of law that such registration can be effected only by way of registering for jobseeker's allowance or national insurance credits, less still only by successfully claiming one or other of those benefits
d. Nor was there at the material time an administrative practice to that effect (even assuming—without deciding—that to be a lawful way of implementing the Directive)
e. Successfully claiming jobseeker's allowance or national insurance credits will no doubt provide sufficient evidence to satisfy Article 7(3)(c); but
f. Those who are able to show not merely that they were seeking work, but that they had done what is needed in order to have their name recorded as looking for work by the relevant employment office—will meet the registration requirement of Article 7(3)(c).
g. It being conceded that the claimant had stated on the Habitual Residence

> Test documents that she was seeking work and that the extent of the work being sought was sufficient, it follows that she met the relevant test."

Therefore, the claimant who (as the Secretary of State conceded, the relevant documents having been lost) had ticked the "Yes" box on the HRT2 form in response to the question "Are you looking for work in the UK?" and was actually seeking work retained her former worker status. The decision of the majority of the Upper Tribunal in *SSWP v FE* was subsequently upheld by the Court of Appeal in *Secretary of State for Work and Pensions v Elmi* [2011] EWCA Civ 1403, [2012] AACR 22.

2.222 This issue highlights the unfortunate consequences that can flow from the use of the word "jobseeker" to denote what the French text of the Citizenship Directive describes as a *demandeur d'emploi* and what this note describes as a "workseeker": see above. If the English text had required those who wished to retain worker status to register "as a workseeker" with the relevant employment office, no one would have thought that requirement necessarily involved making a claim for JSA.

The decision in *FE* means that former workers who retain worker status may be entitled to claim IS. However, they would be much better advised to claim JSA. The risk with claiming IS is that the efforts of IS claimants' to find work are not actively monitored by the Department. It will therefore be up to them to prove that they satisfy Conditions A and B (above) and (where relevant) Condition C (below). If they are unable to do so, they will be classed as workseekers, and therefore not entitled to IS.

Participation in a work-focused interview by an IS claimant does not amount to or involve registration for work: see *SSWP v ZW* [2009] UKUT 25 (AAC). The decision was doubted by Maurice Kay LJ in *Elmi* (at para.20) but has not been overruled and remains binding, at least on the First-tier Tribunal.

2.223 Two further issues arise. The first is whether, in order to satisfy the requirement of registration, the claim for JSA (or IS) must be made immediately after the cessation of employment. The second concerns the position of the, mostly female, claimants who are wrongly advised by the DWP to claim IS or ESA rather than JSA.

The first issue was considered by the Commissioner in *CIS/1934/2006* (at para.8) and *CIS/0519/2007* and by the Upper Tribunal in *SSWP v IR (IS)* [2009] UKUT 11 (AAC), *SSWP v MK (IS)* [2013] UKUT 163 (AAC) and *VP v SSWP (JSA)* [2014] UKUT 32 (AAC), [2014] AACR 25. In *IR*, the judge stated (at para.15):

> "There is still a question of the speed with which the claim must be made. A gap between becoming involuntarily unemployed and claiming jobseeker's allowance is not necessarily fatal. Whether it is significant or not will depend on the length of the gap and the reasons for it. Put into the legal terms of EC analysis, the question is whether the gap shows that the claimant has withdrawn from the labour market. A claimant may take a few days to think about the future or to rest after a stressful period leading to redundancy. That may be consistent with remaining in the labour market. In contrast, a claimant who decides to spend six months backpacking in the Australian outback before looking for work has clearly left the labour market for the time being. The tribunal must investigate this issue at the rehearing."

However, *IR* was a decision on the pre-Directive law under which it was only necessary for claimants to establish that they were in duly-recorded involuntary unemployment. The Upper Tribunal has decided that, because the Citizenship Directive introduced an additional requirement that a claimant should be "registered as a jobseeker with the relevant unemployment office", the appropriate test is now whether there has been "undue delay" in so registering (*VP*, at paras 51–57, following *MK*, para.69).

2.224 The law as stated in *VP* and *MK* is problematic. The concept of "undue delay" is not found in the Citizenship Directive or the 2006 Regulations. Further, the basis for the conclusion that *IR* does not apply after the Citizenship Directive came into force appears to be the decision of the Court of Appeal in *Elmi*. In that case, the majority of the Upper Tribunal had concluded that words requiring registration "as a jobseeker with the relevant employment office" did not add anything to the pre-April 2006 law. A clear majority of the Court (Moses LJ, at para.26 and Baron J, at para.29) held that that conclusion was incorrect and that registration as a jobseeker was an additional requirement. However, the majority decision of the Upper Tribunal was based on the authority of the ECJ in *Metock* that "Union citizens cannot derive less rights from that directive than from the instruments of secondary legislation which it amends or repeals" (see above). It is implicit in the Court of Appeal decision that the majority of the Upper Tribunal was wrong to follow *Metock*. However, no explanation is given why that is the case: *Metock* is not even mentioned either in the Court of Appeal decision or in the minority decision of the Upper Tribunal with which, on this point, the Court of Appeal agreed.

What amounts to undue delay will depend heavily on the facts of individual cases. However, in *SSWP v MM (IS)* [2015] UKUT 128 (AAC) the Upper Tribunal held that a delay of five weeks did not amount to undue delay where the claimant did not claim JSA while she waited to see if she would get more work from her agency and made a claim promptly as soon as it became apparent that there was no further work. Also, in *FT v (1) LB of Islington and (2) SSWP (HB)* [2015] UKUT 121 (AAC)) the Secretary of State and the local authority accepted that the same was true of a delay of six weeks where the claimant had previously obtained jobs quickly, had savings to tide her over and had provided specific details of her steps to find work during the period between the end of her previous employment and her registration as a jobseeker.

As to the second issue, EEA nationals who are looking for work in the UK would always have been well-advised to claim JSA rather than IS. But people are not always well-advised. In particular, lone parents, and women in the late stages of pregnancy (see above), are often advised to claim IS rather than JSA. As pointed out in *SSWP v CA* [2009] UKUT 169 (AAC) —and contrary to the view stated in previous editions—it will usually be incorrect for Jobcentre staff to advise lone parents and pregnant women to claim income support rather than jobseeker's allowance, even if they are CTA nationals. As the Judge explained:

> "18. In cases where the claimant is a British or Irish citizen, or has leave to remain in the UK, there may be circumstances in which it is correct for Jobcentre staff to advise a lone parent who is receiving jobseeker's allowance to cease her jobsearch and claim income support instead.
>
> 19. However, such cases are likely to be few and far between because:
>
> (a) even if the lone parent would be entitled to income support, ceasing to sign on may affect her eventual entitlement to retirement pension by making her ineligible for unemployment credits under regulation 8A of the Social Security (Credits) Regulations 1975 and forcing her instead to rely upon the less advantageous rules for home responsibilities protection; and
>
> (b) in any event, it is government policy that lone parents should be encouraged and assisted to seek work.
>
> 20. In cases where the right to reside is an issue, such advice will almost always be incorrect. The structure of the right to reside test means that a lone parent who is an EEA national (other than a citizen of the United Kingdom or Ireland) will only be entitled to income support if they have acquired a permanent right of residence or are the separated (but not divorced) spouse of another EEA national who has right to reside in the UK."

If the EEA national has never been on JSA and is wrongly advised to claim IS, the only remedy is to seek compensation either under the Department's *Financial Redress for Maladministration* scheme (details of which can be found on its website) or, less easily, through the courts as damages for negligent misstatement. However, where the claimant was already on JSA and has been wrongly advised to cease claiming that benefit and claim IS instead, s/he should appeal against the decision to terminate the JSA claim (which will often not have been notified expressly) as well as the refusal of IS (see *CIS/571/2007*, para.5 and *CIS/4144/2007*, paras 29-32). Note that an extension of time may be necessary. The claimant should argue that s/he did not give informed consent to the withdrawal of the JSA award. In addition, the power to supersede a decision awarding benefit is just that, a power not a duty. Claimants should argue that for the Secretary of State to exercise that power so as to disadvantage a claimant for having relied on the advice of his own staff would be an abuse of power contrary to the principle in *CIS/6249/1999* (see *CIS/4144/2007*, para.32).

Vocational Training

2.225 In *SSWP v EM* [2009] UKUT [2009] UKUT 146 (AAC), Judge Rowland held (at para.10) that reg.6(2)(c) of the 2006 Regulations gives effect to art.7(3)(d) of Directive, which in turn codifies the effects of *Lair* and *Raulin*. It applies:

> ". . . Only where a person has to retrain in order to find work reasonably equivalent to his or her former employment. Like regulation 6(2)(b), it does not look back at the circumstances in which the person has become unemployed, although that may be part of the background; it is concerned with the situation where a person cannot reasonably be expected to be in the labour market because there is no appropriate market. That is not the case here. Jobs in education have obvious attractions for parents with young children, but the claimant in the present case could have looked for work equivalent to her former employment."

The claimant, who had worked in a chicken processing factory and had left to train as a teaching assistant, was therefore not "involuntarily unemployed" within reg.6(2)(c) and could not rely upon reg.6(2)(d) because her training was not "related to [her] previous employment".

"Workseekers" and "Jobseekers"

2.226 Regulations 6(1)(a) and 14 of the 2006 Regulations grant an extended right of residence to "a jobseeker". That right is not conferred by the Citizenship Directive but is derived directly from art.45 TFEU (ex-art.39 TEC) (see *R. v Immigration Appeal Tribunal Ex p. Antonissen* (C–292/89) [1991] E.C.R. I-745).

The use of the word "jobseeker" in reg.6(1)(a) is ambiguous and confusing. The term may be neutral from the point of view of immigration law, but as a matter of social security law it has acquired the colloquial meaning of a person who claims jobseeker's allowance or, at least, signs on at a Jobcentre in order to receive national insurance credits.

It is very important to appreciate that that is not the sense in which the word is used here.

Following the terminology used in this note, there are three categories of people who may claim JSA, namely:

- Workers

  Part-time workers in effective and genuine work may sign on to look for full-time work and to supplement their part-time earnings from benefit. Such people are workers.

- Persons who retain the status of workers

  People who are no longer working but are involuntarily unemployed and still in the labour market in the sense described above. In most cases, such people usually enjoy the same rights as workers.

- Workseekers

People who have not previously worked in the UK, or who have done so but no longer retain worker status, will be what UK legislation implementing EU law has previously called "workseekers" (see, e.g. reg.4 of SI 2004/1219, below). Such people are not workers (at least in the terminology used by this note, although some decisions of the ECJ unhelpfully describe them as such).

Since July 1, 2014, "jobseeker" is defined for the purposes of the 2006 Regulations by reg.62(4) as "a person who satisfies conditions A, and B and, where relevant, C". Conditions A and B are described above in the discussion of retention of worker status.

Condition C is that "the person has had a period of absence from the United Kingdom" (see reg.6(10) of the 2006 Regulations). In addition, where Condition C applies, Condition B must be read as if it said "compelling evidence" rather than "evidence": see reg.6(11).

By reg.6(9), Condition C applies:

"where the person concerned has, previously, enjoyed a right to reside under [regulation 6] as a result of satisfying conditions A and B—

(a) in the case of a person to whom paragraph (2)(b) or (ba) applied, for at least 6 months; or

(b) in the case of a jobseeker for at least 91 days in total

unless the person concerned has, since enjoying the above right to reside, been continuously absent from the United Kingdom for at least 12 months."

The length of the period of absence is not specified. In particular, reg.6(9) does not say that the period of absence must be at least 12 months. It only says that Condition C does not apply at all where there has been a continuous absence for 12 months or more.

A period of absence of more than three months may have the effect that the claimant will not be entitled to JSA immediately on return to the UK: see the discussion on below under the heading, The additional "three-months" requirement for jobseeker's allowance.

The figure of 91 days in reg.6(9) replaced the former figure of 182 days which had effect from July 1, 2014 to November 9, 2014 (both dates included).

The rights enjoyed by workers and persons who retain that status are greater than those enjoyed by those who can only establish a right to reside under reg.6(1)(a).

Specifically:

- The extended right of residence conferred on a workseeker, and on the family members of a workseeker, only counts for the purposes of JSA, not IS, ESA or SPC (see reg.21AA(3)(b) and (d) of the IS Regulations, reg.70(3)(b) of the ESA Regulations and reg.2(3)(b) and (d) of the SPC Regulations): a person whose only right to reside is as a workseeker or as the family member of a workseeker, must claim JSA.

- Those who retain worker status on the basis of involuntary unemployment can continue to do so during a subsequent period when they are temporarily unable to work (and vice versa). If a workseeker becomes too ill to work, s/he immediately loses her right to income-related benefits because s/he will almost certainly cease to be a workseeker and, in any event, a right of residence as a workseeker does not count for ESA.

- Workseekers with a right of residence are not exempted from the habitual residence test by reg.85A(4) of the JSA Regulations. In addition to having a right to reside, they must also be actually habitually resident in the sense explained in the *Collins* case (see below) and satisfy the additional requirements introduced into the habitual residence test for JSA with effect from January 1, 2014.

- Finally, those whose only right to reside is as a jobseeker ceased to be entitled to housing benefit with effect from April 1, 2014 (see the amendments made to reg. 10(3B) of the Housing Benefit Regulations 2006 by reg.2 of the Housing Benefit (Habitual Residence) Amendment Regulations 2014 (SI 2014/539)).

For those reasons, those considering the right to reside in the context of a claimant who is looking for work should not assume that s/he is a "jobseeker" for the purposes of reg.6(1)(a) without first considering whether s/he is a worker or a person who has retained the status of worker.

To qualify as a workseeker it is necessary to be seeking work that is "effective and genuine" in the sense described above and to have a "genuine chance" or "reasonable prospects" of securing such work. As workseekers can only claim JSA, this can be tested through the same "labour market" conditions that are applied to claimants under domestic British law.

The decision in SSWP v RR (IS)

2.227 Previous editions drew attention to the fact that unnecessarily broad language in the decision of a Three-Judge Panel in *SSWP v RR (IS)* [2013] UKUT 21 (AAC) seemed to have blurred the distinction between "workers" and "jobseekers" (in the EU sense of the latter term) by suggesting that anyone who could bring themselves within art.39 TEC (which would include *Antonissen* jobseekers) are thereby workers for the purposes of art.7(1)(a) of the Citizenship Directive: for more details, see pp.344–345 of Vol.II of the 2015/16 edition. However, *RO v SSWP (JSA)* [2015] UKUT 533 (AAC), confirms that *RR* is not authority for that proposition. *RR* remains authority that a national of another EEA state who comes to the UK in order to take up an offer of employment but has not yet been able to take it up for medical reasons and has therefore never worked in the UK, she has a right to reside under art.39(3)(a) and (b) TEC (now art.45 TFEU) as the holder of a job offer—at least while the job offer was being kept open for her—and so was a worker for the purposes of art.7(1)(a) of the Citizenship Directive.

Pre-accession work

2.228 In *CIS/1833/2006*, the Commissioner held, applying the decision of the ECJ in Case C-171/91 *Tsiotras v Landeshauptstadt Stuttgart*, that work undertaken by a Maltese national in the UK before Malta acceded to the EU on May 1, 2004 did not count for the purposes of the predecessor to reg.6(2). However, that position may need to be reconsidered following the more recent decision of the ECJ in *Ziolkowski and Szeja* (see below).

Self-employed persons

2.229 For the purposes of the 2006 Regulations, "self-employed person" is defined by reg.4(1)(b) as "a person who establishes himself in order to pursue activity as a self-employed person in accordance with Article 43 of the Treaty establishing the European Community".

That definition is narrower than the equivalent definition in the 2000 Regulations, which included the words "or who seeks to do so" at the end. It follows that to have an extended right of residence as a self-employed person it is not sufficient to arrive in the UK with the wish to establish oneself. It is necessary to have taken active steps to pursue self-employment. This accords with the previous law; see *R(IS) 6/00*, at para.31 (a case on the former Directive 73/148). Exactly what steps will suffice to give rise to the extended right of residence will depend upon the particular circumstances of individual cases.

RM v SSWP (IS) [2014] UKUT 0401 (AAC), [2015] AACR 11 contains guidance on the concept of self-employment in EU law.

It is not necessary to register as self-employed with HMRC in order to have a right to reside as a self-employed person (see *SSWP v IM-M* [2009] UKUT 71 (AAC)). However, registration with HMRC is evidence of self-employed status.

The Upper Tribunal has decided that, as is the case for work as an employee, activity as a self-employed person must be "genuine and effective", rather than "marginal or ancillary" in order to give rise to a right of residence (see *Bristol CC v FV (HB)* [2011] UKUT 494 (AAC) (*CH/2859/2011*), in which Judge Rowland upheld a decision of the First-tier Tribunal that the activities of a *Big Issue* seller were genuine and effective and amounted to self-employment). The authority cited for that proposition, namely *Jany v Staatssecretarie van Justitie* (C-268/99), at para.33 is equivocal, as are the authorities from which *Jany* is itself derived: see *Deliège v Ligue Francophone de Judo* (C-56/91 and C-191/97), at paras 52–55 and *Steymann v Staatssecretaris van Justitie* (C-196/87), at paras 14–15, but it is suggested that *Bristol City Council* is correctly decided on the point. For a case in which self-employed work was held by the Upper Tribunal not to be effective and genuine, see *SSWP v HH (SPC)* [2015] UKUT 0583 (AAC).

Note that fostering is not self-employment (see *SSWP v SY (IS)* [2012] UKUT 233 (AAC), at paras 10–11). Similarly, a person who receives carer's allowance for caring for a severely disabled person is not providing services for remuneration and so is not a self-employed person for the purposes of art.7(1)(a) of the Citizenship Directive: see *JR v SSWP (IS) and JR v Leeds CC (HB)* [2014] UKUT 154 (AAC).

A person who has ceased self-employment because they are temporarily incapable of work retains the status of a "self-employed person" in the same way as a worker (see above and art.7(3)(a) of the Citizenship Directive).

However, a formerly self-employed person does not retain self-employed status during periods of involuntary unemployment: see *SSWP v RK* [2009] UKUT (AAC) 209, in which Judge Rowland held that arts 7(3)(b)–(d) of the Citizenship Directive do not apply to self-employed persons. The judge stated:

> "11. However, I am not persuaded that the draftsman of the 2006 Regulations did misconstrue the Directive. It seems to me that sub paragraphs (b), (c) and (d) do apply only to former workers and not to those formerly self-employed. It would be surprising if the rights of self-employed persons had been aligned to those of workers without any indication of an intention to do so being included in the lengthy preamble to the Directive. That makes sense of the use of the words 'retained' and 'retention' in subparagraphs (c) and (d). Moreover, it is plain that job-seeking for the purposes of subparagraphs (b) and (c) must relate to a preparedness to take up offers of employment as a worker made through an employment office and not merely opportunities for establishment as a self-employed person with which such offices do not generally deal. It is difficult to see why a self-employed person should retain that status while looking for employment as a worker. There is no right of residence for the purpose of becoming established as a provider of services.
>
> 12. It is also, of course, difficult to see why a person who ceases to be self-employed but who seeks employment as a worker should not retain a right of residence. I am quite satisfied that such a person does ordinarily retain a right of residence because it would be quite inconsistent with Article 15(4)(b) of the Directive not to do recognise such a right. There is no reason why a person who was formerly self-employed in a member State should have fewer rights than a person who has never worked in that State at all. Whether the word 'entered' in Article 15(4)(b) must be read as 'is in' or whether it is necessary to recognise the right of residence as existing under Article 18 of the EC Treaty outside the Directive does not matter. What, however, is clear is that the right of residence is held by virtue of the person's current status as a person seeking employment as a worker, rather than his or her former status as a self-employed person."

As the claimant in *RK* was an A8 national, and as the period in question was before the date on which the former restrictions on the rights of A8 nationals ceased to apply, the fact that his right to reside was as a workseeker, rather than as a person who retained the status of a self-employed person, meant that he was excluded from benefit by reg.5(2) of the former A8 Regulations.

The same view was taken by the High Court in *R. (Tilianu) v Social Fund Inspector and Secretary of State for Work and Pensions* [2010] EWHC 213 (Admin) and by the Court of Appeal in *R. (Tilianu) v Secretary of State for Work and Pensions* [2010] EWCA Civ 1397.

However, the issue whether a formerly self-employed person has to retain self-employed status only arises if that person has actually ceased to be self-employed. That is a question of fact in each case: see the decisions of the Upper Tribunal in *RJ v SSWP (JSA)* [2011] UKUT 477 (AAC), [2012] AACR 12; *SSWP v AL (JSA)* [2010] UKUT 451 (AAC) and *SSWP v JS* [2010] UKUT 240 (AAC). In the last of those cases, Judge Jacobs stated (at para.5):

> "5. I do not accept that a claimant who is for the moment doing no work is necessarily no longer self-employed. There will commonly be periods in a person's self-employment when no work is done. Weekends and holiday periods are obvious examples. There may also be periods when there is no work to do. The concept of self-employment encompasses periods of both feast and famine. During the latter, the person may be engaged in a variety of tasks that are properly seen as part of continuing self-employment: administrative work, such as maintaining the accounts; in marketing to generate more work; or developing the business in new directions. Self-employment is not confined to periods of actual work. It includes natural periods of rest and the vicissitudes of business life. This does not mean that self-employment survives regardless of how little work arrives. It does mean that the issue can only be decided in the context of the facts at any particular time. The amount of work is one factor. Whether the claimant is taking any other steps in the course of self-employment is also relevant. The claimant's motives and intentions must also be taken into account, although they will not necessarily be decisive."

Self-sufficient persons

2.230 "Self-sufficient person" is defined by reg.4(1)(c) as meaning a person with comprehensive sickness cover in the UK, "who has sufficient resources not to become a burden on the social assistance system of the United Kingdom during his period of residence".

The decision of the ECJ in *Pensionsversicherungsanstalt v Brey* (C-140/12) holds (at para.61) that "social assistance":

> "must be interpreted as covering all assistance introduced by the public authorities, whether at national, regional or local level, that can be claimed by an individual who does not have resources sufficient to meet his own basic needs and the needs of his family and who, by reason of that fact, may become a burden on the public finances of the host Member State during his period of residence which could have consequences for the overall level of assistance which may be granted by that State"

Further, the fact that a benefit is a special non-contributory cash benefit for the purposes of Regulation (EC) 883/2004 does not prevent its being social assistance for the purposes of art.7(1)(b) of the Citizenship Directive (*ibid.*, at para.58). In *Brey*, an Austrian benefit called the *Ausgleichzulage* (compensatory supplement), which appears to be similar to state pension credit was held (at para.62) to be social assistance. Housing benefit and the former council tax benefit are also social assistance *SG v Tameside MBC (HB)* [2010] UKUT 243 (AAC), at para.50. However, tax credits may not be (see *R (A, B and C) v Secretary of State for the Home Department* [2013] EWHC 1272, at para.46, although the observations were made when granting permission to apply for judicial review and are therefore not binding).

The person's resources are "sufficient" if (taking into account the resources of any relevant family member) they exceed the maximum level of resources which a British citizen and his family members may possess if he is to become eligible for social assistance under the United Kingdom benefit system; or, if that is not the case, it appears those resources should be regarded as sufficient "taking into account the personal situation of the person concerned and, where applicable, any family members" (see reg.4(4)).

If a person "has" sufficient resources then, with one exception, the origin of those resources is irrelevant. So, for example, where accommodation is made available to a claimant by a third party, the claimant "is in principle entitled to have that taken into account towards determining the sufficiency of their resources" (*SG v Tameside MBC* (HB) [2010] UKUT 243 (AAC), at paras 51–52, following the decision of the ECJ in *Commission v Kingdom of Belgium* (C-408/03). This includes the earnings of a spouse or partner who is a third-country national: see *Singh v Minister for Justice and Equality* (C-218/14).

The exception is that a person who has earnings, but who is nevertheless not a worker, cannot rely upon those earnings to establish self-sufficiency (*VP v SSWP (JSA)* [2014] UKUT 32 (AAC), at para.92, agreeing with the Chief Commissioner for Northern Ireland in *AS v HMRC (CB)* [2013] NICom 15 at para.110 and with the former Asylum and Immigration Tribunal in *MA (EU national; self-sufficiency; lawful employment) Bangladesh* [2006] UKAIT 00090, at para.44).

It will often seem self-evident that a person who has been driven by circumstances to claim an income-related benefit, no longer satisfies that definition of a "self-sufficient person". However, the decision in *Brey* means that that consequence does not follow automatically. There may be cases in which a person can assert that, although they are without resources at present, they should still be regarded as self-sufficient because their claim for benefit does not represent a burden on the social assistance system of the United Kingdom. The reasoning underlying that conclusion is stated at paras 63–78 of *Brey*:

> "63. . . . the fact that a national of another Member State who is not economically active may be eligible, in light of his low pension, to receive [a social assistance] benefit could be an indication that that national does not have sufficient resources to avoid becoming an unreasonable burden on the social assistance system of the host Member State for the purposes of Article 7(1)(b) of [the Citizenship] Directive . . ..
>
> 64. However, the competent national authorities cannot draw such conclusions without first carrying out an overall assessment of the specific burden which granting that benefit would place on the national social assistance system as a whole, by reference to the personal circumstances characterising the individual situation of the person concerned.
>
> 65. First, it should be pointed out that there is nothing in [the Citizenship] Directive . . . to preclude nationals of other Member States from receiving social security benefits in the host Member State . . ..
>
> 66. On the contrary, several provisions of that directive specifically state that those nationals may receive such benefits. Thus, as the Commission has rightly pointed out, the very wording of Article 24(2) of that directive shows that it is only during the first three months of residence that, by way of derogation from the principle of equal treatment set out in Article 24(1), the host Member State is not to be under an obligation to confer entitlement to social assistance on Union citizens who do not or no longer have worker status. In addition, Article 14(3) of that directive provides that an expulsion measure is not to be the automatic consequence of recourse to the social assistance system of the host Member State by a Union citizen or a member of his family.
>
> 67. Second, it should be noted that the first sentence of Article 8(4) of [the Citizenship] Directive . . . expressly states that Member States may not lay down a fixed amount which they will regard as 'sufficient resources', but must take into account the personal situation of the person concerned. Moreover, under the second sentence of Article 8(4), the amount ultimately regarded as indicating sufficient resources may not be higher than the threshold below which nationals of the host Member State become eligible for social assistance, or, where that

criterion is not applicable, higher than the minimum social security pension paid by the host Member State.

68. It follows that, although Member States may indicate a certain sum as a reference amount, they may not impose a minimum income level below which it will be presumed that the person concerned does not have sufficient resources, irrespective of a specific examination of the situation of each person concerned . . . .

69. Furthermore, it is clear from recital 16 in the preamble to [the Citizenship] Directive 2004/38 that, in order to determine whether a person receiving social assistance has become an unreasonable burden on its social assistance system, the host Member State should, before adopting an expulsion measure, examine whether the person concerned is experiencing temporary difficulties and take into account the duration of residence of the person concerned, his personal circumstances, and the amount of aid which has been granted to him.

70. Lastly, it should be borne in mind that, since the right to freedom of movement is – as a fundamental principle of EU law – the general rule, the conditions laid down in Article 7(1)(b) of [the Citizenship] Directive . . . must be construed narrowly . . . and in compliance with the limits imposed by EU law and the principle of proportionality . . ..

71. In addition, the margin for manoeuvre which the Member States are recognised as having must not be used by them in a manner which would compromise attainment of the objective of [the Citizenship] Directive . . ., which is, inter alia, to facilitate and strengthen the exercise of Union citizens' primary right to move and reside freely within the territory of the Member States, and the practical effectiveness of that directive . . ..

72. By making the right of residence for a period of longer than three months conditional upon the person concerned not becoming an 'unreasonable' burden on the social assistance 'system' of the host Member State, Article 7(1)(b) of [the Citizenship] Directive . . ., interpreted in the light of recital 10 to that directive, means that the competent national authorities have the power to assess, taking into account a range of factors in the light of the principle of proportionality, whether the grant of a social security benefit could place a burden on that Member State's social assistance system as a whole. [The Citizenship] Directive . . . thus recognises a certain degree of financial solidarity between nationals of a host Member State and nationals of other Member States, particularly if the difficulties which a beneficiary of the right of residence encounters are temporary . . . .

. . .

75. It can be seen from paragraphs 64 to 72 above that the mere fact that a national of a Member State receives social assistance is not sufficient to show that he constitutes an unreasonable burden on the social assistance system of the host Member State.

76. As regards the legislation at issue in the main proceedings, it is clear from the explanation provided by the Austrian Government at the hearing that, although the amount of the compensatory supplement depends on the financial situation of the person concerned as measured against the reference amount fixed for granting that supplement, the mere fact that a national of another Member State who is not economically active has applied for that benefit is sufficient to preclude that national from receiving it, regardless of the duration of residence, the amount of the benefit and the period for which it is available, that is to say, regardless of the burden which that benefit places on the host Member State's social assistance system as a whole.

77. Such a mechanism, whereby nationals of other Member States who are not economically active are automatically barred by the host Member State from receiving a particular social security benefit, even for the period following the first three months of residence referred to in Article 24(2) of the Citizenship Directive . . ., does not enable the competent authorities of the host Member State. . . to

carry out – in accordance with the requirements under, inter alia, Articles 7(1)(b) and 8(4) of that directive and the principle of proportionality – an overall assessment of the specific burden which granting that benefit would place on the social assistance system as a whole by reference to the personal circumstances characterising the individual situation of the person concerned.

78. In particular, in a case such as that before the referring court, it is important that the competent authorities of the host Member State are able, when examining the application of a Union citizen who is not economically active and is in Mr Brey's position, to take into account, inter alia, the following: the amount and the regularity of the income which he receives; the fact that those factors have led those authorities to issue him with a certificate of residence; and the period during which the benefit applied for is likely to be granted to him. In addition, in order to ascertain more precisely the extent of the burden which that grant would place on the national social assistance system, it may be relevant, as the Commission argued at the hearing, to determine the proportion of the beneficiaries of that benefit who are Union citizens in receipt of a retirement pension in another Member State."

Brey was considered by the Upper Tribunal in *VP v SSWP (JSA)* [2014] UKUT 32 (AAC). For the reasons given at [71]-[79] of his decision, Judge Ward held that "*Brey* is concerned with what follows where a right of residence has arisen in the first place": it does not operate to confer a right of residence on a claimant who has not previously had such a right. 2.231

Judge Ward also expressed the view (at para.84) that the requirement for a person to have sufficient resources not to become a burden on the social assistance system of the United Kingdom "during his period of residence" meant that:

> "a person wishing to assert self-sufficiency at the beginning of a five year period (with a view to subsequent permanent residence) would have to point to "resources" to see them through five years. . . . [i]t may often be the case . . . that consideration is only given to the topic at the end of the five year period when a right of permanent residence is asserted (whether as part of a benefit claim or otherwise). . . . In my view the question, whenever asked, remains: was the person at the beginning of year 1 – and in principle at any other times in the period – able to show sufficient resources to meet the test? I do not accept that a person who could not meet the test on that basis could simply lie low for five years and through a combination of luck and an unusually frugal lifestyle avoid being any kind of burden to the social assistance system and then argue that they have retrospectively shown that they had throughout had the resources to be self-sufficient."

Comprehensive sickness insurance

SG v Tameside MBC (HB) [2010] UKUT 243 (AAC) also considered the requirement for "comprehensive sickness insurance". In that appeal, the claimant, a Polish national who had been living in Sweden for many years and was receiving Swedish invalidity benefit in the UK under the provisions of the former Regulation (EEC) No.1408/71. The Upper Tribunal accepted a concession from the Secretary of State that the claimant could rely on the UK's right to the reimbursement of healthcare costs under arts 27–34 of that Regulation and art.95 of Regulation (EEC) No. 574/72 as meeting the requirement for comprehensive sickness insurance. However, in *SSWP v HH (SPC)* [2015] UKUT 0583 (AAC), it was emphasised that, under art.28a of Regulation 1408/71 the Member State competent in respect of pensions was only responsible for the costs of healthcare "to the extent that the pensioner and members of his family would have been entitled to such benefits under the legislation [of that Member State] if they resided in the territory of [that] Member State". Whether a claimant and her/his family members would have been so entitled was a question of foreign law that had to be proved by evidence: see paras 5–6 of *HH*. 2.232

The right to free medical treatment under the National Health Service does not amount to comprehensive sickness insurance (see *Ahmad v Secretary of State for the Home Department* [2014] EWCA Civ 988; *FK (Kenya) v Secretary of State for the Home Department* [2010] EWCA Civ 1302; *W (China) and X (China) v Secretary of State for the Home Department* [2006] EWCA Civ 1494 and *VP v SSWP (JSA)* [2014] UKUT 32 (AAC), at paras 98–105). It follows from the decision in *Ahmad* that the observations made by Judge Rowland in *SSWP v SW (IS)* [2011] UKUT 508 (AAC), at para.20 and by the Chief Commissioner of Northern Ireland in *AS v HMRC (CB)*, at para.128 (xi) and (xii), do not correctly state the law.

Whether a person has comprehensive sickness insurance is judged as at the time under consideration. It is not possible to look at the matter retrospectively where the claimant did not in fact require to use the NHS and then argue that it is not proportionate that he be required to have comprehensive medical insurance: see *KS v SSWP (JSA)* [2016] UKUT 0269 (AAC).

Students

2.233 The students who have a right of residence are those who are "enrolled, for the principal purpose of following a course of study (including vocational training), at a public or private establishment which is … financed from public funds; or … otherwise recognised by the Secretary of State as an establishment which has been accredited for the purpose of providing such courses or training within the law or administrative practice of the part of the United Kingdom in which the establishment is located;" (see the definition of "student" in reg.4(1)(c)).

It is necessary for students to make a declaration to the Secretary of State (or satisfy him in some other manner) that they have sufficient resources to avoid them (and any family members) becoming a burden on the social assistance system of the United Kingdom (see reg.4(1)(d)). For the level of resources that is sufficient and the approach to be taken where a student claims an income-related benefit, see the note on "self-sufficient persons" (above). It is also necessary for students to have comprehensive sickness insurance cover in the United Kingdom. From April 6, 2015 such insurance must cover family members as well as the student (see the amendment to reg.4(2) and (3) by reg.4 of SI 2015/694).

In *CIS/419/2007*, the Commissioner held that a Polish single parent intercalating student who is not looking for work does not have a right of residence under the former Directive 93/96/EEC.

Family members and extended family members

Family members

2.234 Under reg.14(2), the "family members" of a qualified person and of a person with a permanent right of residence have an extended right of residence in the UK. In addition, some people are categorised as "extended family members" of a qualified person and are treated as family members with a right of residence for as long as they continue to fall within that category.

In *CIS/1685/2007*, the Commissioner held that, in an appropriate case, a tribunal must consider whether the claimant has a right of residence as a family member of a qualified person as well as considering his/her rights as a qualified person. See also *CIS/2431/2006*.

"Family member" is defined by reg.7. Except where the qualified person only has a right of residence as a student, the phrase means the qualified person's spouse or civil partner, the "direct descendants" (i.e. children, grandchildren, etc.) of the qualified person (or of the spouse or civil partner) who are either their dependants or are under the age of 21, and "dependant direct relatives in the ascending line", i.e. parents and grandparents, etc. of the qualified person (or of the spouse or civil partner). Where the qualified person's sole right of residence is as a student, only the qualified person's spouse or civil partner and their dependent children count as "family members" after the initial period of three months has expired.

2.235 Note that "spouse" in this context does not include a party to a UK same sex marriage under the Marriage (Same Sex Couples) Act 2013: see the Marriage (Same Sex Couples) Act 2013 (Consequential and Contrary provisions and Scotland) Order 2014 (SI 2014/560) art.3 and Sch.2 Pt 2. The phrase "EU instruments" used in that Schedule is defined in Sch.1 to the European Communities Act 1972 (as amended) as "any instrument issued by an EU institution". However, a party to a same sex marriage might nevertheless be a "family member" within art.2(2)(b) of the Citizenship Directive, (i.e. the provision that treats civil partners as family members).

Under reg.11 of the 2006 Regulations, family members of EEA nationals who are not themselves EEA nationals and who do not hold a residence card issued by the UK under art.10 of the Citizenship Directive must obtain a document called an "EEA family permit" (see reg.12) before travelling to the UK. However, in *McCarthy v Secretary of State for the Home Department* (C-202/13), the Grand Chamber of the ECJ ruled that this additional requirement was contrary to the Citizenship Directive in cases where the family member holds a residence card issued by another Member State. The definition of "a qualifying EEA State residence card" in reg.2(1) of the 2006 Regulations has been amended with effect from April 6, 2015 to give effect to the Court's judgment.

The requirement that certain family members should be "dependent" on the EEA national or his/her spouse has been considered by the Court of Appeal in *Jeleniewicz v SSWP* [2008] EWCA Civ 1163 reported as *R(1S)3/09* and by the Commissioner in *CIS/2100/2007* and *CPC/1433/2008*.

In *Jeleniewicz*, the Court upheld a finding by the Commissioner (in *CIS/1545/2007*) that (under the law as it stood before April 30, 2006) where a student had contact with his daughter twice a week and made irregular payments towards her maintenance averaging £10 per week, the daughter did not have a right to reside as his dependent child (and the daughter's mother did not have a right to reside as the daughter's primary carer). It was not enough that there should be some emotional dependency. There must be material support which, though not necessarily financial, must provide for or contribute towards, the basic necessities of life 2.236

In *CIS/2100/2007*, the Commissioner reviewed the ECJ caselaw (*Centre Public D'Aide Sociale de Courcelles v Lebon* (C–316/85) [1987] E.C.R. 2811, *Chen v Secretary of State for the Home Department* (C–200/02) [2005] Q.B. 325 and *Jia v Migrationsverket* (C–1/050) [2007] Q.B. 545) and concluded as follows:

"44. In summary, the case law is authority for these propositions:

- A person is only dependent who actually receives support from another.
- There need be no right to that support and it is irrelevant that there are alternative sources of support available.
- That support must be material, although not necessarily financial, and must provide for, or contribute towards, the basic necessities of life."

In *Pedro v SSWP* [2009] EWCA Civ 1358, the Court of Appeal (Mummery, Sullivan and Goldring LJJ) (an appeal from the decision of the Deputy Commissioner in *CPC/1433/2008*) considered whether, to be dependent, the family member had to prove that they needed the support of the EEA national or their spouse *in the country of origin* rather than in the host Member State. In *Jia* the Grand Chamber of the ECJ held that dependence in the country of origin was required for the purposes of the former Directive 73/148 on the freedom of establishment and provision of services. However, the Court—in reliance on *Metock* (see above)—confined the application of *Jia* to cases arising under the pre-April 30, 2006 law. Therefore it was only necessary for Mrs Pedro to prove that she was dependent on her son in the United Kingdom in order to be a "dependent direct relative in the ascending line" for the purposes of art.2(2)(d) of the Citizenship Directive. Giving the judgment of the Court, Goldring LJ stated:

"67. Article 2(2) [i.e., of the Citizenship Directive] does not specify when the dependency has to have arisen. Neither does it require that the relative must be dependent in the country of origin. Article 3(2)(a), on the other hand, requires actual dependency at a particular time and place. That difference, as I have said, is reflected by Article 8(5)(d) as compared with 8(5)(e). It cannot be an accident of drafting. It contemplates, as it seems to me, that where in an Article 2(2)(d) case reliance is placed on dependency, it can be proved by a document from the host state without input from the state of origin. Taking Article 2(2)(d) together with Article 8(5)(d) suggests that dependency in the state of origin need not be proved for family members. It is sufficient if, as is alleged here, the dependency arises in the host state."

2.237 The authority of *Pedro* may be somewhat compromised because it does not refer to the decision of the Court of Appeal (Sullivan, Ward and Etherton LJJ) in *SM (India) v Entry Clearance Officer* [2009] EWCA Civ 1426 which was given approximately two weeks earlier. In *SM (India),* the Court applied *Jia* to a post-April 30, 2006 case: the appeal was stated to be against the refusal to issue the appellants with "EEA family permits under Regulation 12 of the Immigration (European Economic Area) Regulations 2006". The decision in *SM (India)* was given after the hearing in *Pedro* but before judgment in that case was handed down. However, it cannot be that the Court in *SM (India)* was unaware of the issue in *Pedro* because Sullivan LJ was a member of both panels. The decisions can be reconciled on the basis that *SM (India)* was about entry clearance and therefore inevitably involved people who had yet to come to the UK. In such circumstances, the only type of dependence that could arise was dependence in the country of origin, so that the possibility or reliance on dependence in the UK did not arise. The aspect of *Jia* that was in issue in *SM (India)* was whether dependence had to arise as a matter of necessity or whether it could be a matter of choice. Therefore the Court in *SM (India)* was not dealing with the issue that had to be considered in *Pedro* and which led the Court in that case to confine the operation of *Jia* to circumstances arising before April 30, 2006.

VN (EEA rights – dependency) Macedonia [2010] UKUT 380 (IAC) confirms that the decision in *Pedro* applies to family members who are dependent direct relatives as defined by art.2(2)(d) of the Citizenship Directive but not extended family members ("other family members" as defined by art.3.2(a) of the Directive). To establish a right of residence the extended family members are required to show both dependence in the country from which they have come and dependence in the UK.

Dependency is a question of fact. If one person is in fact dependent on another, the reasons why that is so are irrelevant. *Entry Clearance Officer, Manila v Lim (EEA—dependency)* [2013] UKUT 437 (IAC) concerned a Malaysian citizen, aged 60, who owned a three-bedroom house in Malaysia (valued at £80,000) and had savings of approximately £55,000 in an Employers Provident Fund based on her past employment, which she was entitled to withdraw. However, she wished to leave her savings and her house to her children and grandchildren and so relied on remittances from her daughter, who was married to a Finnish national working in the UK. Judge Storey confirms that, subject to there being no abuse of rights, the jurisprudence of the Court of Justice allows for dependency of choice and that there was no discernible reason why this should not include dependency of choice in the form of choosing not to live off savings. Similarly in *Reyes v Migrationsverket* (C-423/12) the ECJ confirmed that there was no need to determine the reasons for the dependence. Ms Reyes was a Philippines citizen born in 1987 who moved to Sweden in March 2011 to join her mother who was married to a Norwegian. Her mother had moved to Germany to work when she was three years old and had regularly sent money to support her family in the Philippines. The Court ruled that Ms Reyes did not have to show that she had tried to find work or subsistence support in the Philippines in order to establish her dependency, nor did the fact that Ms Reyes was well placed to obtain employment and intended to start work affect the interpretation of dependency. The ECJ did refer to the fact that following *Jia* it was necessary for Ms Reyes to have been dependent in the country from which she had come (cf. *Pedro* above). However, on the facts, Ms Reyes was dependent in the Philippines so the point cannot have been essential to the Court's reasoning.

Pedro also clarifies an ambiguity in the drafting of reg.2(4)(d) of the SPC Regulations (and reg.21AA(4)(d) of the IS Regulations, reg.85A(4)(d) of the JSA Regulations and reg.70(4)(d) of the ESA Regulations). The regulation refers to a "family member of a person referred to in sub-paragraph (a), (b) or (c) within the meaning of Article 2 of [the] Directive". That is a reference to reg.2(4)(a), (b) or (c) of the SPC Regulations, not to art.2(2)(a), (b) or (c) of the Directive. The reference to "Article 2" is included to qualify the words "family member". The references to reg.2(4)(a), (b) or (c) are there to identify the person of whom the claimant must be a family member in order to fall within reg.2(4)(d). **2.238**

Note that, even in those categories of family member where dependence on the qualified person forms part of the definition, it is not necessary for the family member to live in the same household as the qualified person in order to have a right of residence. This is important because family breakdown will often be the reason the family member claims an income-related benefit.

The spouse of a qualified person retains that status until finally divorced (*Diatta v Land Berlin* (C–267/83) [1985] E.C.R. 567). By the same reasoning, the civil partner of a qualified person should retain that status until the partnership is finally dissolved. For the circumstances in which the former spouse or civil partner of a qualified person can retain a right of residence in the UK following divorce or dissolution of the partnership, see below under the heading, *Family members who have retained the right of residence.*

Extended family members

Extended family member is defined by reg.8, which implements art.3 of the Citizenship Directive. **2.239**

In *Soares v Secretary of State for the Home Department* [2013] EWCA Civ 575 the Court of Appeal held that reg.8(2)(a) and (c) require dependence on, or household membership of, the EEA national him/herself. Dependence on, or household membership of, the EEA national's spouse or civil partner does not count for this purpose.

It is not necessary for the relative to establish the prior and present connection with the EEA national in the same capacity. So, for example, a relative who was a member of the EEA national's household (but not a dependant) before coming to the UK and is now dependant on the EEA national (but not a household member) within the UK satisfies the definition (see *Dauhoo (EEA Regulations—reg.8(2))* [2012] UKUT 79 (IAC)). However, it is necessary that the situation of dependence (or household membership) must have existed "in the country from which the family member concerned comes" and must have done so "at the very least at the time when [the extended family member] applies to join the Union citizen on whom he is dependent": see paras 32–35 of the decision of the ECJ in *Secretary of State for the Home Department v Rahman* (C-83/11). See also *CIS/612/2008* and *AP and FP (Citizens Directive Article 3(2); discretion; dependence) India* [2007] UKAIT 48.

"Durability" was considered by the Commissioner in *CIS/612/2008.* It was stated that: **2.240**

> "36. 'Durable' has an element of ambiguity. It may mean that it has lasted or that it is capable of lasting. Too much should not be made of this. If the focus is on the past, the length of time for which the partnership has survived will not be the only factor that is relevant. The circumstances will be as important as the duration of the relationship. Survival in times of wealth, health and good fortune is less an indication of durability than survival in terms of poverty, poor health and misfortune. And if the focus in on the present and future, the fact that it has lasted may, depending on the circumstances, be very good evidence that it is and will remain durable.
> 37. 'Durable' governs the relationship, not the partnership. However, the rela-

tionship has to be with the partner. It may, and usually will, have existed before the couple became partners and evidence of the relationship at that time is relevant to its durability.

38. Subject to these points, the durability of a relationship is an issue of fact."

Extended family members are treated as family members for as long as they satisfy the criteria in reg.8 and also hold a valid EEA family permit, a registration certificate or a residence card (see reg.7(3)). A permit, certificate or card is required because art.3(2) of the Citizenship Directive does not confer a right of residence on extended family member but only imposes an obligation on Member States to "facilitate entry and residence" in accordance with their national legislation. The right only exists if the host state grants it. The issue of a family permit, registration certificate or residence card is the mechanism by which the UK grants the right (see *CIS/612/2008*).

That has now been confirmed (subject to the caveats set out below) by the Grand Chamber of the ECJ in *Rahman*. The Court ruled that:

"1. On a proper construction of Article 3(2) of [the Citizenship Directive]:

- the Member States are not required to grant every application for entry or residence submitted by family members of a Union citizen who do not fall under the definition in Article 2(2) of that directive, even if they show, in accordance with Article 10(2) thereof, that they are dependants of that citizen;
- it is, however, incumbent upon the Member States to ensure that their legislation contains criteria which enable those persons to obtain a decision on their application for entry and residence that is founded on an extensive examination of their personal circumstances and, in the event of refusal, is justified by reasons;
- the Member States have a wide discretion when selecting those criteria, but the criteria must be consistent with the normal meaning of the term 'facilitate' and of the words relating to dependence used in Article 3(2) and must not deprive that provision of its effectiveness; and
- every applicant is entitled to a judicial review of whether the national legislation and its application satisfy those conditions."

Family members and extended family members who are EEA nationals can become qualified persons in their own right by, for example, looking for or accepting work.

Family members who have retained the right of residence

2.241 Under reg.14(3) of the 2006 Regulations, a "family member who has retained the right of residence" has an extended right of residence in the UK for as long as s/he retains that status.

"Family member who has retained the right of residence" is defined by reg.10. The phrase means a person—other than a person with a right of permanent residence (see reg.10(8))—who falls into one or more of the following categories:

- Family members of a qualified person, or of an EEA national with a permanent right residence, who has died, who have resided in the UK in accordance with the 2006 Regulations for at least a year immediately before the death. This category only applies where:
    - the person seeking to retain the right of residence is not an EEA national, but would qualify as a worker, a self-employed person or a self-sufficient person if s/he were; or
    - is the family member of a person who meets those criteria.
- Direct descendants of a qualified person, or of an EEA national with a permanent right residence, who has died or ceased to live in the UK (or of the spouse or civil partner of such a qualified person) who were attending an educational course (within the scope of art.12 of Regulation 1612/68 (now art.10 of

regulation 492/2011) in the UK immediately before the qualified person died or ceased to live in the UK and who continue to attend such a course.

- Parents who have custody of a child who satisfies the conditions in the previous bullet point.
- Former spouses or civil partners of a qualified person, or of an EEA national with a permanent right residence (a "former spouse or partner"), who were residing in the UK on the date when the marriage or civil partnership came to an end, where either:
  - the marriage or civil partnership had lasted for at least three years before the commencement of the legal proceedings to terminate it and the parties had both resided in the UK for at least one year during its duration. The decisions of the CJEU in *Singh v Minister for Justice and Equality* (C-218/14) and *Secretary of State for the Home Department v NA* (C-115/15) hold that art.13(2) of the Citizenship Directive (which is implemented by reg.10) only applies where the former spouse or partner was still resident in the host Member State at the time when the divorce proceedings (or proceedings to terminate the civil partnership) were commenced;
  - the former spouse or partner has custody of a child of the qualified person, or of the EEA national with a permanent right residence, or a right of access to such a child that, by court order, can only take place in the UK; or
  - there are "particularly difficult circumstances" that warrant the former spouse or partner continuing to have a right of residence in the UK. The example that is given is where the former spouse or partner or another family member has "been a victim of domestic violence while the marriage or civil partnership was subsisting"

  This category only applies where:

  - the person seeking to retain the right of residence is not an EEA national, but would qualify as a worker, a self-employed person or a self-sufficient person if s/he were; or
  - is the family member of a person who meets those criteria.

Residence in the UK before April 30, 2006 counts as residence in accordance with the 2006 Regulations if it was in accordance with the 2000 Regulations (see Sch.4 para.6 to the 2006 Regulations). 2.242

For the date on which a marriage or civil partnership ends, see the note on "family member" above.

Note, finally, that where the qualified person from whom the reg.14(3) right is derived was a jobseeker (i.e. in the narrow EU sense) then that right does not count for the purposes of IS by virtue of reg.21AA(3)(b)(ii) of the IS Regulations: see *SSWP v SS (IS)* [2016] UKUT 110 AAC. The same will be true of the identically-worded provisions governing HB, SPC, and old style ESA.

Permanent right of residence

Regulation 15 implements arts 16 and 17 of the Citizenship Directive. It establishes a permanent right of residence for five categories of people: 2.243

- EEA nationals who have "resided in the UK in accordance with [the 2006] regulations for a continuous period of five years";
- family members of an EEA national who have resided in the UK with the EEA national "in accordance with [the 2006 Regulations] for a continuous period of five years.

  This category only applies where the family member is not an EEA national him or herself: otherwise there would be a permanent right of residence because of the previous category;

- a "worker or self-employed person who has ceased activity" and the family members of such a person;
- (in certain circumstances) family members of workers or self-employed persons who have died; and
- (in certain circumstances) people who were formerly "family members who ha[d] retained the right of residence".

Residence "in accordance with" the 2006 Regulations includes certain types of residence before April 30, 2006 including residence under the 2000 Regulations, and before October 2, 2000 in accordance the Immigration (European Economic Area) Order 1994 (see the discussion below and Sch.4 para.6(1) and (2) of the 2006 Regulations as amended by reg.2 and Sch.1 para.25 of SI 2012/1547 with effect from July 16, 2012).

Those whose right of residence arises under art.17 (i.e. those who fall within the last three of the five categories set out above) are exempt from the habitual residence test (and therefore also from the right to reside test) under reg.21AA(4)(e) of the IS Regulations, reg.85A(4)(e) of the JSA Regulations, reg.2(4)(e) of the SPC Regulations and reg.70(4)(e) of the ESA Regulations.Those whose right arises under art.16 are not automatically exempt but will almost inevitably have been living in the UK for considerably longer than would be required to become actually habitually resident.

Legal residence—Ziolkowski and Szeja

2.244 The question of what type or types of residence can form the basis of a permanent right to reside under art.16 of the Citizenship Directive has been an area of considerable legal uncertainty (see pp.334-340 of Vol.II of 2011/12 edition).

The problem arose because although reg.15 requires that the period of five years' continuous residence should have been "in accordance with" the 2006 Regulations, art.16 merely provides that the EEA national should have "resided legally" for that period. As it is possible for EEA national to reside legally in the UK without such residence being in accordance with the 2006 Regulations, it was unclear whether reg.15 correctly implemented art.16 and, if not, what other types of lawful residence would give rise to the permanent right.

However, the law has now been clarified—at least in relation to this point—by the decision of the Grand Chamber of the ECJ in *Tomasz Ziolkowski v Land Berlin* and *Barbara Szeja, Maria-Magdalena Szeja, Marlon Szeja v Land Berlin* (C-424/10 and C-425/10). In the light of that decision, it now appears that reg.15 not only fully implements art.16 but—at least as regards the rights of workseekers—may be more generous to certain EEA nationals than art.16 strictly requires.

2.245 In *Ziolkowski* and *Szeja*, the appellants in the proceedings before the Bundesverwaltungsgericht (the German Federal Administrative Court) were Polish nationals who had lived in Germany since 1989 and 1988 respectively. At that time, Poland had not acceded to the EU and both were granted residence permits on humanitarian grounds under German domestic law. Although Mr Ziolkowski (at least) had worked in Germany in the past, by the time Poland acceded to the EU on May 1, 2004, neither was in employment or had sufficient resources to support him- or herself economically so as not to be a burden on the German social assistance system.

In 2005, both applied to the State of Berlin to extend their residence permits under German domestic law or to issue a residence permit under EU law. Those applications were refused on the basis that the applicants were unable to support themselves financially and did not have a right of residence under EU law. Mr Ziolkowski and Mrs Szeja appealed and it was ultimately argued on their behalf that they had resided legally in Germany under German domestic law (i.e. by virtue of the residence permits) for a continuous period in excess of five years before Poland acceded to the EU and that—following the principle in *Lassal* (see below)—each acquired a right of permanent residence under art.16 when the Citizenship Directive came into force on April 30, 2006.

The Bundesverwaltungsgericht took the view that residence which was lawful under national law alone did not amount to legal residence for the purposes of art.16. It nevertheless referred the following questions to the ECJ:

"1. Is the first sentence of Article 16(1) of Directive 2004/38 to be interpreted as conferring on Union citizens who have resided legally for more than five years in the territory of a Member State on the basis of national law alone, but who did not during that period fulfil the conditions laid down in Article 7(1) of Directive 2004/38, a right of permanent residence in that Member State?

2. Are periods of residence by Union citizens in the host Member State which took place before the accession of their Member State of origin to the European Union also to be counted towards the period of lawful residence under Article 16(1) of Directive 2004/38?"

The ECJ answered those questions as follows: **2.246**

"1. Article 16(1) of [the Citizenship] Directive ... must be interpreted as meaning that a Union citizen who has been resident for more than five years in the territory of the host Member State on the sole basis of the national law of that Member State cannot be regarded as having acquired the right of permanent residence under that provision if, during that period of residence, he did not satisfy the conditions laid down in Article 7(1) of the directive.

2. Periods of residence completed by a national of a non-Member State in the territory of Member State before the accession of the non-Member State to the European Union must, in the absence of specific provisions in the Act of Accession, be taken into account for the purpose of the acquisition of the right of permanent residence under Article 16(1) of Directive 2004/38, provided those periods were completed in compliance with the conditions laid down in Article 7(1) of the directive."

It follows that *Lekpo-Bozua v Hackney LBC* [2010] EWCA Civ 909 and *Okafor v Secretary of State for the Home Department* [2011] EWCA Civ 499 are correctly decided. It also follows that previously binding UK authority to the effect that pre-accession residence cannot count towards the five-year period (including *GN (EEA Regulations: Five years' residence) Hungary* [2007] UKAIT 00073 and *CPC/3764/2007,* at para.18) must now be read in the light of the decision in *Ziolkowski* and *Szeja*.

The Court's reasoning on the first question is set out in paras 31–51 of its judgment as follows:

- Article 16 made no express reference to the law of the Member States for the purpose of determining how the phrase "resided legally" was to be interpreted, that phrase must be regarded "as designating an autonomous concept of EU law which must be interpreted in a uniform manner throughout the Member States" (paras 31–33).

- As the Citizenship Directive contained no definition of that phrase, its meaning must be determined by considering, among other things, the context in which it occurs and the purposes of the rules of which it forms part. The aim of the Directive was to facilitate and strengthen the exercise of each EU citizen's right to move and reside freely within the territory of the Member States by providing a single legislative act codifying and revising the instruments of EU law which preceded the Citizenship Directive. But the subject matter of the Citizenship Directive, as was apparent from art.1(a) and (b), concerned the conditions governing the exercise of that right and the right of permanent residence (paras 34–37).

- The Citizenship Directive introduced a gradual system as regards the right of residence in a host Member State (para.38).

- First, for periods of residence of up to three months, art.6 limits the conditions and formalities of the right of residence to the requirement to hold a valid identity card or passport and the requirement, under art.14(1), for the EU citizen and any family members not to become an unreasonable burden on the social assistance system of the host Member State (para.39).
- Then, for periods of residence of longer than three months, the right is subject to the conditions set out in art.7(1) and, under art.14(2), is retained only if the EU citizen and any family members satisfy those conditions. Recital 10 in the preamble to the Citizenship Directive in particular showed that those conditions are intended, inter alia, to prevent nationals of other Member States becoming an unreasonable burden on the social assistance system of the host Member State (para.40).
- Finally, EU citizens acquire the right of permanent residence after residing legally for a continuous period of five years in the host Member State and that that right is not subject to the conditions referred to above. Recital 17 in the preamble states that such a right of should be laid down for all EU citizens and their family members who have resided in the host Member State 'in compliance with the conditions laid down in this Directive' during a continuous period of five years without becoming subject to an expulsion measure. The *travaux préparatoires* showed that the relevant part of recital 17 was included "in order to clarify the content of the term "legal residence"" for the purpose of art.16(1) (paras 41–42).
- Further the Citizenship Directive stated explicitly that, to acquire a permanent right of residence, family members of an EU citizen who retain a right of residence following the death of the EU citizen; or his or her departure from the host State; or following divorce, annulment of marriage or the termination of a registered partnership must satisfy the conditions in art.7(1) (see arts 12, 13 and 18) (paras 43–44).
- It follows that "resided legally" in art.16(1) of the Citizenship Directive should be construed as meaning residence which complies with the conditions laid down in the Directive, in particular those set out in art.7(1). Consequently, a period of residence which complies with the law of a Member State but does not satisfy the conditions in art.7(1) cannot be regarded as a 'legal' period of residence within the meaning of art.16(1) (paras 45–47).
- Article 37 of the Citizenship Directive does not affect that analysis.It simply provides that the Directive does not preclude the laws of the Member States from introducing provisions that are more favourable than those established by the Directive. That does not mean that such provisions must be incorporated into the system introduced by the Citizenship Directive. It is for each Member State to decide not only whether it will introduce more favourable provision but also the conditions to which the more favourable rules are subject and, in particular, the legal consequences of a right of residence granted on the basis of national law alone (paras 47–50).

On the second question (i.e. that concerning pre-accession residence), the Court reasoned that, on the Accession of a new Member State, the principle is that EU law applies to that State in full from the outset unless there are express derogations which establish transitional provisions. Nationals of any Member State may rely on EU law as regards the present effects of circumstances which existed previously including circumstances which arose before the accession of a Member State to the EU (e.g. *Saldanha and MTS* (C-122/96) [1997] E.C.R. I-5325, para.14; *Österreichischer Gewerkschaftsbund* (C-195/98) [2000] E.C.R. I-10497, para.55; and *Duchon* (C-290/00) [2002] E.C.R. I-3567, [44]). As there are no transitional provisions that are relevant to the question, art.16(1) can be applied to the present and future effects of situations arising before the accession of the Member State of which the EU citizen is a national to the EU. Although periods of residence completed in the territory of the host Member State by a national of another State before the accession of the latter State to the EU do not fall within the scope of EU law but solely within the domestic law of the host Member State, provided the person concerned can demonstrate that such periods were completed in compliance with the conditions laid down in art.7(1) of Directive, taking such periods into account from the date of accession of the Member State of nationality to the EU does not give retroactive effect to art.16, but simply gives present effect to situations which arose before the date of transposition of that Directive.

Residence from April 30, 2006

Following *Ziolkowski* and *Szeja*, the position as regards residence for periods from April 30, 2006 (when the Citizenship Directive came into force) may be summarised as follows. 2.247

Such residence is 'legal' for the purposes of art.16(1)—and therefore counts towards the acquisition of a right of permanent residence—only if the person whose residence is under consideration satisfies the conditions in art.7(1) of the Citizenship Directive (i.e. if that person is a worker (or has retained that status), self-employed (or has retained that status), self-sufficient, a student or a family member of someone who falls into those categories).

Therefore, residence that is lawful solely by virtue of rights enjoyed:

- as a workseeker (i.e. under art.45 TFEU (ex-art.39 TEC): see *R. v IAT Ex p. Antonissen* (C-292/89));
- as the child of a migrant worker or former migrant worker who has established him- or herself in education (i.e. under art.10 of Regulation 492/2011 (formerly art.12 of Regulation 1612/68) or as the primary carer of such a child (i.e. under the principles established in *Ibrahim* and *Teixeira*). See further *Okafor*, para.31;
- under arts 20 and 21 TFEU (including the rights enjoyed by some parents of British children under the principle established in *Zambrano*: see below); or
- (to the extent that the resident does not satisfy the conditions in art.7(1)) under the domestic law of the UK

is **not** "legal" for the purposes of art.16(1) and does **not** count towards the acquisition of a right of permanent residence.

In *Ziolkowski* and *Szeja* none of the applicants had any of the rights of residence listed immediately above. Thus the question of whether residence pursuant to such rights is "legal" for the purposes of art.16 was not strictly before the Court. However, it has now been confirmed by the ECJ in paras 32–48 of *Alarape and Tijani v Secretary of State for the Home Department* (C–529/11) that: 2.248

> "Periods of residence in a host Member State which are completed by family members of a Union citizen who are not nationals of a Member State solely on the basis of Article 12 of Regulation No 1612/68, as amended by Directive 2004/38, where the conditions laid down for entitlement to a right of residence under that directive are not satisfied, may not be taken into consideration for the purposes of acquisition by those family members of a right of permanent residence under that directive."

The 2006 Regulations were amended with effect from July 16, 2012 by the introduction of the new concept of a "derivative right of residence" in reg.15A and the exclusion of residence pursuant to a derivative right for the purposes of the permanent right to reside by the insertion of para.(1A) into reg.15. The effect is to codify this aspect of *Ziolkowski* and *Szeja* as summarised in the last three of the four bullet points above.

However, although residence as a workseeker does not count towards the acquisition of a permanent right of residence under *EU* law, it may count towards the acquisition of such a right under the more favourable provisions of UK domestic law, namely reg.15 of the 2006 Regulations: see below. The more favourable provisions of reg.15 apply only to residence as a workseeker and not to residence in any of the other capacities listed above.

Residence before April 30, 2006

2.249 As is apparent from the Court's answer to the second question in *Ziolkowski* and *Szeja*, it is also possible for certain types of residence during periods before the Citizenship Directive came into force on April 30, 2006 to count towards the acquisition of the right of permanent residence after that date.

Where the member State of nationality was a member of the EU at the time when the claimant was resident in the UK, the decision of the ECJ in *Secretary of State for Work and Pensions v Lassal* (C-162/09) holds that pre-Directive residence will count towards the five-year period, if it is "in accordance with earlier European Union law instruments". In *Alarape and Tijani v Secretary of State for the Home Department,* the ECJ confirmed that that phrase only refers to the instruments that were repealed by, and consolidated in, the Citizenship Directive and does not include instruments, such as art.12 of Regulation 1612/68 (now art.10 of Regulation 492/2011), which are unaffected by the Citizenship Directive.

Where the Member State of nationality was not a member of the EU at the time when the claimant was resident in the UK, *Ziolkowski* and *Szeja* holds that—in the absence of specific provisions in the Act of Accession—pre-Directive residence counts towards the five-year period if it was "in compliance with the conditions laid down in Article 7(1) of the [Directive]". Previously binding UK authority to the effect that pre-accession residence cannot count towards the five-year period (including *R(IS) 3/08* and *CPC/3764/2007*) should no longer be followed.

2.250 This aspect of the decision in *Ziolkowski* and *Szeja* raises two further issues:

- First, there is the obvious conceptual problem about how residence can have been "in compliance with" the conditions in art.7(1) at a time when that provision was not in force and the resident's state of nationality was not even a member of the EU. The answer to that problem can be found in the Court's insistence that it was not applying Art.16 retrospectively but rather giving present and future effect to circumstances which had arisen in the past. Articles 7(1) and 16(1) exist now. Although the Citizenship Directive as a whole may only affect those who are "beneficiaries" as defined by art.3(1), none of the, relatively well-established, criteria for establishing whether the conditions in art.7(1) are satisfied require that the person to whom they are applied should be an EU citizen at the relevant time. If, for example, it is possible to conclude that a Polish national was a self-employed person in May 2004, there is no reason why one cannot also conclude that she was a self-employed person during the previous month, or year, or years and therefore say that, during that period, she satisfied the condition that is now laid down in art.7(1)(a). Analysed in that way, the difficulties are likely to be evidential rather than conceptual.

- However, that analysis leads to the second issue, namely that the narrow criteria for establishing whether the conditions in art.7(1) are satisfied do not require that the residence or work under consideration must also have been legal under the domestic law of the host state at the time. Suppose that the same Polish national referred to in the previous bullet point entered the UK illegally in March 2001 and worked here illegally on a self-employed basis for a continuous period ending after April 2006. Presumably she did not acquire a permanent right of residence as soon as the Citizenship Directive came into force on April 30, 2006, but nothing in *Ziolkowski* and *Szeja* actually says otherwise. The contrary outcome could, perhaps, be achieved by holding that a person in that position was not resident at all but only present, so that even if her activities would otherwise bring her within art.7(1), there would still be no "residence" for the purposes of art.16. Some support for that approach can be found in *R(IS) 3/08* which holds that temporary admission as an asylum seeker does not amount to a right of residence and *SSWP v LS (IS)* [2012] UKUT 207 (AAC).

Schedule 4 para.6 of the 2006 Regulations has been amended with effect from July 16, 2012 to codify what was said in *Ziolkowski and Szeja* about pre-accession residence. New para.6(3)(a) makes the codified right conditional on the person concerned having had leave to enter or remain in the UK at the relevant time. Note also that the codification in the new para.6(3)(b) refers to residence "in accordance with these Regulations" and will therefore include jobseekers in addition to people who come within art.7 of the Citizenship Directive.

Loss of the Lassal right

Once the inchoate permanent right of residence conferred by *Lassal* has accrued, it can potentially be lost by: 2.251

- a period of absence from the UK (see *Lassal,* paras 56–58); or
- a period of residence in the UK that was not legal (i.e. in the sense that it was not "in accordance with earlier European Union law instruments") (see *Secretary of State for the Home Department v Dias* (C-325/09), paras 62–66); between the date on which the five years' continuous residence was completed and April 30, 2006.

Although there is no ECJ authority on the point, it seems probable that the inchoate right of permanent residence based on pre-Directive, pre-accession, residence that was recognised in *Ziolkowski* and *Szeja,* will be lost in the same circumstances as the *Lassal* right.

That conclusion in *Lassal* that the inchoate right can be lost through absence from the UK is unexceptionable. As the Court rightly points out, any other interpretation would have required Member States "to grant the right of permanent residence . . . even in cases of prolonged absences which [called] into question the link between the person concerned and the host Member State".

However, the rule was extended by analogy in *Dias* to cover situations in which a concluded period of five years' lawful residence before April 30. 2006 is followed by a period of residence for which there is no legal basis. The Court ruled that: 2.252

"– periods of residence of less than two consecutive years, completed on the basis solely of a residence permit validly issued pursuant to Directive 68/360, without the conditions governing entitlement to a right of residence having been satisfied, which occurred before 30 April 2006 and after a continuous period of five years' legal residence completed prior to that date, are not such as to affect the acquisition of the right of permanent residence under Article 16(1) of Directive 2004/38."

The ECJ's justification for that ruling was that:

"64. . . . it should be noted, as the Advocate General has stated in points 106 and 107 of her Opinion, that the integration objective which lies behind the acquisition of the right of permanent residence laid down in Article 16(1) of Directive 2004/38 is based not only on territorial and time factors but also on qualitative elements, relating to the level of integration in the host Member State.

65. As the situations are comparable, it follows that the rule laid down in Article 16(4) of Directive 2004/38 must also be applied by analogy to periods in the host Member State completed on the basis solely of a residence permit validly issued under Directive 68/360, without the conditions governing entitlement to

a right of residence of any kind having been satisfied, which occurred before 30 April 2006 and after a continuous period of five years' legal residence completed prior to that date."

The analogy drawn by the ECJ is false or, at any rate, is not inevitably true. Leaving a country for a period of two consecutive years obviously reduces one's level of integration in that country. The same cannot be said of Mrs Dias's decision to remain in the country but to spend time looking after her child instead of working, even if that decision meant that she left the labour market for a period. On the contrary, the process of raising a child in the UK probably increases one's level of integration in British society. One could go further. It is arguable that even claiming UK social security benefits involves being integrated in Britain: the process necessitates interacting with institutions of the state and involves doing something that almost every UK citizen will do at some time during his or her life. Finally, as it stands the analogy proves too much. It is being asserted that two years of economic inactivity is to be equated with two years' absence from the host State, but if that were the case before April 30, 2006 it is equally the case after that date. If, therefore, the analogy were correct, the implication would be that those who acquired a permanent right of residence after April 30, 2006 should be deprived of that right after two years of economic inactivity in the same way as they would be after two years' absence.

The passages from the Advocate General's opinion in *Dias* (to which the Court refers) explain the analogy on a slightly different basis:

"106. First, the integration objective which lies behind Article 16 of the directive is based not only on territorial and time factors but also on qualitative elements. It therefore seems to me quite possible that unlawful conduct of a Union citizen may diminish his integration in the host State from a qualitative point of view. In so far as a Union citizen, following a period of legal residence in the host Member State, remains without a right of residence based on European Union law or national law in the host Member State, and the national authorities do not grant leave to remain, that can clearly in my view be taken into account from the perspective of integration.

107. Second, the principle of equal treatment also supports that point of view. A Union citizen who complies with the law, who did not remain unlawfully contrary to the wishes of the host Member State in that State, would not be entitled to a right of permanent residence on 30 April 2006 following absence for more than two years, pursuant to Article 16(4) of Directive 2004/38. It does not seem justified to reward a Union citizen who does not comply with the law."

2.253 At least in the UK, the premise on which those passages are based is incorrect. An EEA national who stays in the UK after a positive right of residence comes to an end is *not* acting unlawfully. S/he commits no criminal offence; remains lawfully present here; is not, without more, subject to removal; and, if removed, would have an immediate right of re-entry. Even if it is the case that "unlawful conduct" can diminish the level of integration, no unlawful conduct occurs in these circumstances. For that reason, treating a period of lawful presence after the acquisition of an inchoate right of residence as neutral, rather than as potentially preventing the right from crystallising, would not involve "rewarding" a Union citizen who does not comply with the law.

The 2006 Regulations were amended with effect from July 16, 2012 by (SI 2012/1547) to reflect the Directive as interpreted in *Dias*. The amended Regulations provide for the automatic loss of the *Lassal* right after two years' residence that is not in accordance with the Regulations.

The position of workseekers and their family members under UK domestic law

2.254 As noted above, workseekers do not satisfy the conditions in art.7(1) of the Citizenship Directive and therefore, under EU law as declared in *Ziolkowski* and

Szeja, residence as a workseeker—though lawful by virtue of art.45 TFEU—does not count towards the acquisition of the permanent right of residence under art.16(1). The same is true of residence as the family member of a workseeker.

However, domestic UK law is more favourable to workseekers and their family members. From April 30, 2006, reg.6 of the 2006 Regulations have included "jobseekers" (i.e. those whom this note describes as workseekers: see above) as "qualified persons". They therefore have an extended right of residence under reg.14. The consequence is that residence as a workseeker, or as the family member of a workseeker, is "in accordance with these regulations" for the purposes of reg. 15(1) so that if it lasts for a continuous period of five years—or, more probably, forms part of a continuous period of five years throughout which the claimant was a qualified person for a number of different reasons (or a family member of such a person)—the claimant will acquire a permanent right of residence by virtue of that regulation.

The definition of "jobseeker" in reg.6(4) of the 2006 Regulations does not contain any requirement to *register* as a jobseeker. Therefore, it is suggested that periods during which a claimant can show that s/he was seeking employment and had a genuine chance of being engaged will count towards the five-year period even if s/he was not claiming JSA or jobseeking credits.

Regulation 5 of the 2000 Regulations, did not expressly include "workseekers" in the definition of "qualified person". However, "workers" were so included and "worker" was defined as meaning "a worker within the meaning of Article 39 of the EC Treaty". "Worker" in art.39 TEC (now art.45 TFEU) has a wider meaning than it has in art.7 of the Citizenship Directive. A workseeker who would have been treated as "worker" under art.39 was therefore a qualified person with a right of residence under reg.14(1). Family members of such a workseeker had a right of residence under reg.14(2). As already noted, the types of residence before April 30, 2006 specified in para.6 of Sch.4 to the 2006 Regulations count towards the five-year period in reg.15.

Continuity of residence

Continuity of residence is governed by reg.3 and art.16(3). These provide that continuity is not affected by absence on military service, absences for any reason that do not in total exceed six months in any year or by a single absence of no more than 12 months "for an important reason such as pregnancy and childbirth, serious illness, study or vocational training or an overseas posting". **2.255**

As is clear from the quoted words, that list is not exhaustive. In *Babajanov v Secretary of State for the Home Department (Continuity of residence – Immigration (EEA) Regulations 2006)* [2013] UKUT 513 (IAC), the Upper Tribunal held that when deciding whether absence for a non-listed reason falls within art.16(3), the purpose of the absence needs to be considered and should involve compelling events and/or an activity linked to the exercise of Treaty rights in the UK.

Although absences within art.16(3) do not break continuity of residence, it has previously been unclear whether the period of absence counts towards the five-year period. In *CIS/2258/2008,* para.17, the Commissioner held that it did not. However, in *Idezuna (EEA—permanent residence) Nigeria* [2011] UKUT 474 (IAC) the Immigration Appeals Chamber of the Upper Tribunal held—without expressly addressing the point or being referred to *CIS/2258/2008*—that the appellant had acquired a permanent right of residence through a period of five years' continuous residence beginning on April 23, 2004 and ending on April 23, 2009 even though there was evidence that he had been absent from the UK for two periods including one from October 29, 2006 to December 17, 2006.

Previous editions have suggested that the reasoned decision of the Commissioner in CIS/2258/2008 should be followed in preference to *Idezuna.* However, the weight of authority now favours the opposite conclusion. In *Babajanov* (above), a two-judge panel of the Immigration Appeals Chamber of the Upper Tribunal held that the right of permanent residence is capable of being established whilst a national of a Member State or a family member of that national is outside the host country. If that is correct, it follows that periods of absence within art.16(3) do count towards the five-year period.

Imprisonment

2.256 Any period during which an EEA national is serving a sentence of imprisonment in this country is not to be included when calculating whether he has resided in the United Kingdom for a continuous period and breaks continuity of residence so that a the person must reside lawfully for five years after his or her release from prison before acquiring a permanent right of residence: *Onuekwere v Secretary of State for the Home Department* (C-378/12); *Secretary of State for the Home Department v MG* (Case C-400/12), *HR (Portugal) v Secretary of State for the Home Office* [2009] EWCA Civ 371; *Carvalho v Secretary of State for the Home Department* [2010] EWCA Civ 1406; *Jarusevicius (EEA Reg 21—effect of imprisonment)* [2012] UKUT 00120 (IAC) and *SO (imprisonment breaks continuity of residence) Nigeria* [2011] UKUT 164 (IAC).

However, an EEA national does not cease to be a qualified person as a result of being detained in a hospital pursuant to an order of the court under the Mental Health Act 1983, having not been convicted of any criminal offence: *JO (qualified person—hospital order—effect) Slovakia* [2012] UKUT 00237(IAC).

Worker or self-employed person who has ceased activity

2.257 *Worker or self-employed person who has ceased activity* is defined by reg.5.

Family members of a worker or self-employed person who has ceased activity also have a permanent right of residence (see reg.15(1)(d)).

There is conflicting authority at Upper Tribunal level on the issue of whether, to qualify for a permanent right of residence on the basis of terminating activity in the UK as a worker or self-employed person as a result of permanent incapacity for work following two years' continuous residence in the UK (i.e. under reg.5(3)(b)), the residence must have been legal residence or whether actual residence will suffice. In *ID v SSWP (IS)* [2011] UKUT 401 (AAC) Judge Jacobs held that legal residence was necessary. However, in *TG v SSWP (PC)* [2015] UKUT 0050 (AAC) Judge Ward declined (at paras 65–67) to follow *ID*. The Secretary of State has appealed to the Court of Appeal (sub nom. *Secretary of State for Work and Pensions v Gubeladze*) against the Upper Tribunal's decision and the appeal is listed to be heard on February 7 or 8, 2017.

Family members of workers or self-employed persons who have died

2.258 Under reg.15(1)(e), a family member of a worker or self-employed person who has died has a permanent right of residence where the family member resided with the deceased person immediately before his or her death, and either:

- the deceased person had resided continuously in the UK for at least two years immediately before his death; or
- the death was the result of an accident at work or an occupational disease.

Family member who has retained the right of residence

2.259 A person who has lived in the UK in accordance with the 2006 Regulations for a continuous period of five years acquires a permanent right of residence if, at the end of that period, s/he is a *family member who has retained the right of residence* (see reg.15(1)(f)).

In practice, this category only affects non-EEA nationals: an EEA national who had lived in the UK in accordance with the 2006 Regulations for a continuous period of five years would acquire a permanent right of residence under reg.15(1)(a), irrespective of whether s/he was a family member who has retained the right of residence.

For the definition of "family member who has retained the right of residence" see under *Extended right of residence* (above). One consequence of that definition is that (despite reg.14(4)) the permanent right of residence conferred by reg.15(1)(f) replaces rather than supplements the extended right of residence granted by reg.14(3). Under reg.10(8), the acquisition of the permanent right of residence brings an end to the person's former status as a family member who has retained the right of residence; by ceasing to hold that status, the person loses his or her former rights under reg.14(3).

That change meant that, as a person with a permanent right of residence, the former family member who has retained the right of residence becomes exempt from the habitual residence test (and right to reside test) under the regulations cited above.

Rights to reside of children in education and their principal carers: Baumbast, Ibrahim and Teixeira

In some cases, a claimant who is the primary carer for children in education will have a right to reside that is derived from the rights of those children under art.10 of Regulation 492/2011 (formerly art.12 of Regulation 1612/68). **2.260**

Article 10 states:

> "The children of a national of a Member State who is or has been employed in the territory of another Member State shall be admitted to that State's general educational, apprenticeship and vocational training courses under the same conditions as the nationals of that State, if such children are residing in its territory.
>
> Member States shall encourage all efforts to enable such children to attend these courses under the best possible conditions".

In *Baumbast v Secretary of State for the Home Department* (C–413/99) [2002] E.C.R. I-7091, Mrs Baumbast was a Colombian national married to a German national who was exercising his rights as a migrant worker in the UK and the couple's children went to school here. Subsequently, Mr Baumbast left to work outside the EEA and the Home Secretary refused to renew the residence documents of Mrs Baumbast and the children. She appealed against that decision and, in due course, the Immigration Appeal Tribunal referred the case to the ECJ. The Court found as follows:

> "68. First, Article 12 of Regulation No 1612/68 [now art.10 of Regulation 492/2011] and the rights which flow from it must be interpreted in the context of the structure and purpose of that regulation. It is apparent from the provisions of the regulation, taken as a whole, that in order to facilitate the movement of members of workers' families the Council took into account, first, the importance for the worker, from a human point of view, of having his entire family with him and, secondly, the importance, from all points of view, of the integration of the worker and his family into the host Member State without any difference in treatment in relation to nationals of that State (see, to that effect, Case 249/86 *Commission v Germany* [1989] E.C.R. 1263, paragraph 11)
>
> 69. As is clear from the answer to the first question, Article 12 of Regulation No 1612/68 seeks in particular to ensure that children of a Community worker can, even if he has ceased to pursue the activity of an employed person in the host Member State, undertake and, where appropriate, complete their education in that Member State
>
> 70. Second, according to the case-law of the Court, just like the status of migrant worker itself, the rights enjoyed by members of a Community worker's family under Regulation No 1612/68 can, in certain circumstances, continue to exist even after the employment relationship has ended (see, to that effect, *Echternach and Moritz*, paragraph 21, and Case C-85/96 *Martínez Sala* [1998] E.C.R. I-2691, paragraph 32)
>
> 71. In circumstances such as those of the main proceedings, where the children enjoy, under Article 12 of Regulation No 1612/68, the right to continue their education in the host Member State although the parents who are their carers are at risk of losing their rights of residence as a result, in one case, of a divorce from the migrant worker and, in the other case, of the fact that the parent who pursued the activity of an employed person in the host Member State as a migrant worker has ceased to work there, it is clear that if those parents were refused the right to remain in the host

Member State during the period of their children's education that might deprive those children of a right which is granted to them by the Community legislature
72. Moreover, in accordance with the case-law of the Court, Regulation No 1612/68 must be interpreted in the light of the requirement of respect for family life laid down in Article 8 of the European Convention. That requirement is one of the fundamental rights which, according to settled case-law, are recognised by Community law (see *Commission v Germany*, cited above, paragraph 10)
73. The right conferred by Article 12 of Regulation No 1612/68 on the child of a migrant worker to pursue, under the best possible conditions, his education in the host Member State necessarily implies that that child has the right to be accompanied by the person who is his primary carer and, accordingly, that that person is able to reside with him in that Member State during his studies. To refuse to grant permission to remain to a parent who is the primary carer of the child exercising his right to pursue his studies in the host Member State infringes that right
74. As to the Commission's argument to the effect that a right of residence cannot be derived from Article 12 of Regulation No 1612/68 in favour of a person who is not the child of a migrant worker, on the ground that possession of that status is a sine qua non of any right under that provision, having regard to its context and the objectives pursued by Regulation No 1612/68 and in particular Article 12 thereof, that provision cannot be interpreted restrictively (see, to that effect, *Diatta*, paragraph 17) and must not, under any circumstances, be rendered ineffective
75. In the light of the foregoing, the answer to the second question must be that where children have the right to reside in a host Member State in order to attend general educational courses pursuant to Article 12 of Regulation No 1612/68, that provision must be interpreted as entitling the parent who is the primary carer of those children, irrespective of his nationality, to reside with them in order to facilitate the exercise of that right notwithstanding the fact that the parents have meanwhile divorced or that the parent who has the status of citizen of the European Union has ceased to be a migrant worker in the host Member State".

2.261 To avoid confusion, it should perhaps be added that the discussion of *Baumbast* by the Court of Appeal in *Abdirahman* concerned the claim of *Mr* Baumbast to have a right to reside under art.20 TFEU (ex-art.18 TEC) and not Mrs Baumbast's derived right to reside as the primary carer of her children.

Previous editions of this work have noted that the precise application of *Baumbast* in the field of income-related benefits was hotly disputed in the past. However, that dispute was ended by the decisions of the Grand Chamber of the ECJ, in *Ibrahim v London Borough of Harrow* (C-310/08) and *Teixeira v London Borough of Lambeth* (C-480/08).

In *Ibrahim*, the Court held that:

"In circumstances such as those of the main proceedings, the children of a national of a Member State who works or has worked in the host Member State and the parent who is their primary carer can claim a right of residence in the latter State on the sole basis of Article 12 of Regulation (EEC) No 1612/68 of the Council of 15 October 1968 on freedom of movement for workers within the Community, as amended by Council Regulation (EEC) No 2434/92 of 27 July 1992 [now art.10 of Regulation 492/2011], without such a right being conditional on their having sufficient resources and comprehensive sickness insurance cover in that State."

2.262 In *Teixeira*, it held:

"1. A national of a Member State who was employed in another Member State in which his or her child is in education can, in circumstances such as those of the main proceedings, claim, in the capacity of primary carer for that child, a right of residence in the host Member State on the sole basis of Article 12 of Regulation

(EEC) No 1612/68 of the Council of 15 October 1968 on freedom of movement for workers within the Community, as amended by Council Regulation (EEC) No 2434/92 of 27 July 1992 [now art.10 of Regulation 492/2011], without being required to satisfy the conditions laid down in [the Citizenship Directive].
2. The right of residence in the host Member State of the parent who is the primary carer of a child exercising the right to pursue his or her education in accordance with Article 12 of Regulation No 1612/68 is not conditional on that parent having sufficient resources not to become a burden on the social assistance system of that Member State during the period of residence and having comprehensive sickness insurance cover there.
3. The right of residence in the host Member State of the parent who is the primary carer for a child of a migrant worker, where that child is in education in that State, is not conditional on one of the child's parents having worked as a migrant worker in that Member State on the date on which the child started in education.
4. The right of residence in the host Member State of the parent who is the primary carer for a child of a migrant worker, where that child is in education in that State, ends when the child reaches the age of majority, unless the child continues to need the presence and care of that parent in order to be able to pursue and complete his or her education."

The scope of the two decisions is far-reaching and so comprehensive that, while factual issues may arise about, e.g. whether a child's parent is or was a "worker" and the identity of the child's primary carer, there is little scope for further argument about the law. The UK Government has issued guidance (Memo DMG 30/10, now consolidated at para.071254 of the *Decision Makers Guide*) accepting that:

"A claimant to IS, ESA(IR), JSA(IB) or SPC will have a right to reside in GB under Article 12 of Regulation (EEC) 1612/68 if, at the date of claim to that benefit

1. the claimant is the parent (or step parent) and primary carer of a child ...and
2. the claimant or the child's other parent is a citizen of another EEA State or Switzerland ... and
3. that person is working or has worked as an employed person in the UK... and
4. that child of the migrant worker was installed (or born) in the UK and had entered general education in the UK whilst the migrant worker also lived in the UK ... and
5. that child is still in general education in the UK and is under 18."

It is not necessary for there ever to have been a period when the child was in education and, at the same time, one of the parents was a "worker". The Secretary of State previously took a different view but now accepts this position: see Memo DMG 21/12.

Neither is it necessary for the migrant worker parent still to have been living in the UK when the child entered education. In *Secretary of State for the Home Department v NA* (C-115/15), the CJEU held that: **2.263**

"Article 12 of Regulation (EEC) No 1612/68 [now art.10 of Regulation 492/2011] ... must be interpreted as meaning that a child and a parent who is a third-country national and who has sole custody of that child qualify for a right of residence in the host Member State, under that provision, in a situation ... where the other parent is a Union citizen and worked in that Member State, but ceased to reside there before the child began to attend school in that Member State."

The effect of this aspect of the decision in *NA* is that the requirement in reg.15A(3)(c) of the 2006 Regulations that the child "was in education [in the UK] at a time when the EEA national parent was in the United Kingdom" is too restrictive and is inconsistent with art.10 of Regulation 492/2011 which is directly effective EU law.

The *Teixeira* principle includes a child who has resided since birth in the Member State in which their father or mother is or was employed (see *Teixeira* at para.45).

However, the child must be a child of the migrant worker or his/her spouse. Thus art.10 does not apply to a third country national child who is not a child of the migrant worker father and whose third country national mother had only co-habited with the migrant worker (see *ONAFTS v Ahmed* (C–45/12) and *IP v SSWP (IS)* [2015]UKUT0691(AAC)). Neither does it apply where the only migrant worker is the child's grandparent (see *JS v SSWP (ESA)* [2016] UKUT 0314 (AAC)).

2.264 Note also that self-employment does not count as being "employed" for the purposes of art.10. For the child in education to have a right of residence, one of his/her parents must be working—or have worked—in the UK as an employee: see *Czop and Punakova v Secretary of State for Work and Pensions* (C-147/11 and C-148/11) and *RM v SSWP (IS)* [2014] UKUT 0401 (AAC), [2015] AACR 11.

The Secretary of State's view that the age of majority for these purposes is 18 is also now clearly incorrect. The better view has always been that there is no age absolute age limit for the purposes of art.10 and that a person remains a "child" for those purposes for as long as is necessary for him or her to complete his or her studies, irrespective of whether s/he remains dependent on his or her parents. In *Landesamt für Ausbildungsförderung Nordrhein-Westfalen v Gaal* (C-7/94) the Court stated:

> "24. Secondly, as the Court has consistently held (C-389/87 and C-390/87) *Echternach and Moritz v Netherlands Minister for Education and Science* [1989] ECR 723, paras 29 and 30), the principle of equal treatment set out in Article 12 of the Regulation extends to all forms of education, whether vocational or general, including university courses. The same principle requires that the child of a migrant worker be able to continue his studies in order to complete his education successfully.
>
> 25. Consequently, Article 12 of the Regulation also encompasses financial assistance for those students who are already at an advanced stage in their education, even if they are already 21 years of age or older and are no longer dependants of their parents. Accordingly, to make the application of Article 12 subject to an age-limit or to the status of dependent child would conflict not only with the letter of that provision, but also with its spirit."

That has now been confirmed by the ECJ in *Alarape and Tijani v Secretary of State for the Home Department* (C-529/11). First the Court notes (at para.24) that:

> "reaching the age of majority has no direct effect on the rights conferred on a child by Article 12 of Regulation No 1612/68, as interpreted by the Court, given that, having regard to their subject-matter and purpose, both the right of access to education under that article and the child's associated right of residence continue until the child has completed his or her education"

and (at para.25) that:

> "according to the Court's settled case-law, the scope of Article 12 of Regulation No 1612/68 extends also to higher education, the date on which a child completes his or her education may lie after reaching the age of majority."

It goes on to rule that:

> "The parent of a child who has attained the age of majority and who has obtained access to education on the basis of Article 12 of [Regulation (EEC) No 1612/68], may continue to have a derived right of residence under that article if that child remains in need of the presence and care of that parent in order to be able to continue and to complete his or her education, which it is for the referring court to assess, taking into account all the circumstances of the case before it."

At para.30, the court accepts that:

> "... determining whether an adult child does or does not continue to need the presence and care of his parent in order to pursue and complete his education is a

question of fact that falls to be resolved by the national courts. In that regard, the national courts may take into account the particular circumstances and features of the main proceedings which might indicate that the need was genuine, such as, *inter alia*, the age of the child, whether the child is residing in the family home or whether the child needs financial or emotional support from the parent in order to be able to continue and to complete his education."

"Child" for the purposes of art.10 of Regulation 492/2011 includes "step-child": see *Alarape (Article 12, EC Reg 1612/68) Nigeria* [2011] UKUT 00413(IAC), paras 28–29. Article 10 applies even if the child is British. *SSWP v RR (IS)* [2013] UKUT 21 (AAC) a decision of a three-judge-panel overruling *SSWP v SW (IS)* [2011] UKUT 508 (AAC) ([17]) on this point. In *Shabani (EEA—jobseekers; nursery education)* [2013] UKUT 00315 (IAC) the Home Secretary conceded, that the exclusion by reg.15A(6) of the 2006 Regulations of those in "nursery education" from the derived right of residence conferred by that section does not apply to those in reception class education within a primary school: see para.61 of the decision. 2.265

In England (but not necessarily other parts of the UK) the right under art.10 "arises when a child enters compulsory education at around the age of 5" (see *SSWP v IM (IS)* [2011] UKUT 231 (AAC))

In *MA v Department for Social Development (JSA)* [2011] NICom 205, a Northern Ireland Commissioner accepted a concession by the Department for Social Development that the claimant also had a right to reside where it was his wife who was the primary carer of the child in education. Although the claimant in this case was married, it would certainly seem arguable that this should also apply where the claimant and his/her partner are not married. 2.266

In *SSWP v JS (IS)* [2010] UKUT 347 (AAC), the Upper Tribunal held that an A8 national who had worked lawfully in the UK but had not completed 12 months' registered employment under the law as it stood under the A8 Regulations could assert a right to reside as the primary carer of her child in education. By implication the same is true of Croatian nationals who have been authorised workers and was true of Bulgarian and Romanian nationals who were authorised workers under the law as it stood between January 1, 2007 and December 31, 2013.

The right of residence recognised in *Ibrahim* and *Teixeira* does not give rise to a right of permanent residence under art.16 of the Citizenship Directive: *Ziolkowski and Szeja, Alarape* and *Okafor* (above) (the last paras 31 and 32).

The 2006 Regulations were amended by the introduction of a new reg.15A with effect from July 16, 2012 by SI 2012/1547 to reflect EU law as interpreted in *Ibrahim* and *Teixeira*. The amended regulations reflect the view of the Secretary of State that the *Teixeira* rights of the primary carer only persist while the child who has installed him or herself in education is under the age of 18. For the reasons given above, the better view is that there is no such age limit.

Parents of British children: Zambrano

With effect from November 8, 2012, reg.21AA, and the equivalent regulations in the JSA Regulations, the SPC Regulations and the ESA Regulations, were amended by the insertion of a new sub-paragraph in para.(3) which excludes rights of residence arising under art.20 TFEU "in a case where the right to reside arises because a British citizen would otherwise be deprived of the genuine enjoyment of the substance of their rights as an EU citizen". Similar amendments were made to the right to reside tests for child benefit and child tax credit. Subject to one caveat, the consequence is that the *Zambrano* right discussed below is not a right of residence that count for the purposes of any UK benefit. This section therefore only applies to claims for periods before November 8, 2012 and is included because there remains the possibility that the issue will be considered by the Supreme Court and because there will still be appeals in the system which relate to such periods. 2.267

The caveat is that the *Zambrano* principle may itself invalidate the November 2012 amendments in an individual case because the denial of income-related benefits to the parents of an EU citizen child may in practice lead to the child's having to leave the territory of the Union in the same way as the denial of a right of residence to the parents would have that effect. A challenge to the amendments failed in *R (HC) v Secretary of State for Work and Pensions* [2013] EWHC 3874 and also before the Court of Appeal in *Sanneh v Secretary of State for Work and Pensions, Scott v London Borough of Croydon, Birmingham CC v Merali,* and *R (on the application of HC) v Oldham Council* [2015] EWCA Civ 49 (see below). However, the claimant in *HC* has been granted funding by the Legal Aid Agency to petition the Supreme Court for permission to appeal against the decision of the Court of Appeal.

The decision of the Grand Chamber of the ECJ in *Zambrano v Office national de l'emploi (ONEm)* (C-34/09) means that at least some non-British parents of dependent minor British children have a right of residence in the UK under EU law.

2.268 In that case, the Colombian father of minor children who had Belgian nationality and were therefore EU citizens, was refused Belgian unemployment benefit on the basis that he did not have a right of residence in Belgium or a work permit. The ECJ held that:

> "Article 20 TFEU [which confers the status of citizen of the Union on every person holding the nationality of a member State] is to be interpreted as meaning that it precludes a Member State from refusing a third country national upon whom his minor children, who are European Union citizens, are dependent, a right of residence in the Member State of residence and nationality of those children, and from refusing to grant a work permit to that third country national, in so far as such decisions deprive those children of the genuine enjoyment of the substance of the rights attaching to the status of European Union citizen."

It is important to understand that the Citizenship Directive does not apply in this situation. Article 3(1) of that Directive applies to "all Union citizens who move to or reside in a Member State other than that of which they are a national, and to their family members . . .". The EEA nationals in *Zambrano* (i.e. the children) had not moved to another Member State and were therefore outside the personal scope of the Citizenship Directive. However, they had rights as EU citizens directly under art.20 TFEU and their parents' derived rights of residence from them.

The decision is an extension of the Court's previous case law which had only recognised the existence of a derived right of residence for parents where the child is covered by appropriate sickness insurance and is in the care of a parent who is a third-country national having sufficient resources for that minor not to become a burden on the public finances of the host Member State. In *Zambrano,* the issue was whether the non-EEA father was entitled to Belgian unemployment benefit so there is no longer any room for the argument that the family has to be self-sufficient to benefit from art.20

2.269 The Court's ruling in *Zambrano* is expressed in terms that refer to third country nationals. It was unclear whether this is because the principle established by the decision only applies to the third country national parents of minor EU citizens or whether it is expressed in that way simply because the parents in that case happened to be third country nationals.

The rights of the Zambrano children as EU citizens were said to be impaired because:

> "... [i]t must be assumed that ... a refusal [to grant a right of residence] would lead to a situation where those children, citizens of the Union, would have to leave the territory of the Union in order to accompany their parents... . In those circumstances, those citizens of the Union would, as a result, be unable to exercise the substance of the rights conferred on them by virtue of their status as citizens of the Union".

That gave rise to three questions:

- Did the Court's use of the word "assumed" mean that, at least where both parents are third-country nationals, it was unnecessary to enquire in each individual case whether the EU citizen children "would have to leave the territory of the Union in order to accompany their parents"?

- Does the *Zambrano* principle also apply when a British child has at least one EU national parent (and could therefore live with that parent elsewhere in the EU without being compelled to leave the territory of the Union as a whole)?
- (Closely linked to the previous question) what, if any, other rights are "conferred on [EU citizen children] by virtue of their status as citizens of the Union"? In particular, are the rights conferred by the Charter of Fundamental Rights of the European Union relevant in this context?

As a matter of domestic UK law, the answer to all those questions may now be found in the decision of the Court of Appeal in *Harrison and AB v Secretary of State for the Home Department* [2012] EWCA Civ 1736. That decision is binding authority that: 2.270

> "... there is really no basis for asserting that it is arguable in the light of the authorities that the *Zambrano* principle extends to cover anything short of a situation where the EU citizen is forced to leave the territory of the EU. If the EU citizen, be it child or wife, would not in practice be compelled to leave the country if the non-EU family member were to be refused the right of residence, there is in my view nothing in these authorities to suggest that EU law is engaged. Article 8 Convention rights may then come into the picture to protect family life as the Court recognised in *Dereci*, but that is an entirely distinct area of protection."

The decision of the ECJ in *Ymeraga v Ministre du Travail, de l'Emploi et de l'Immigration* (C-87/12, at paras 40–43 is to similar effect).

Mr Harrison applied for permission to appeal to the Supreme Court. However, permission was refused on June 6, 2013.

In the light of *Harrison*, the answers to the three questions raised above are as follows: 2.271

- *"Assumed"*

  The Court of Appeal's insistence that the EU citizen must be compelled to leave the territory of the EU "in practice" does not leave any room for that outcome to be assumed on the basis of what the ECJ said in *Zambrano*. The actual consequences of the refusal of a right to reside to the parents will need to be investigated in each individual case.

  This approach was also taken by the ECJ in *O and S v Maahanmuuttovirasto* (C-356 and C-357/11, paras 49–57). In those cases both parents were third country nationals but one had a permanent right to reside in Finland. The ECJ stated that it was for the national court to establish, having regard to all the circumstances, whether the refusal of a residence permit to the other parent would entail for the Finnish child concerned a denial of the genuine enjoyment of the substance of the child's rights as an EU citizen.

  The rights of "Zambrano carers", i.e. non-EU citizens responsible for the care of an EU citizen child, were also considered by the Court of Appeal in *Sanneh v Secretary of State for Work and Pensions, Scott v London Borough of Croydon, Birmingham CC v Merali,* and *R (on the application of HC) v Oldham Council* [2015] EWCA Civ 49. The two main issues considered by the Court were: (1) when does the status of a *Zambrano* carer arise? (2) Does it confer any right to social benefits? (see Arden LJ, para.22).

  As to the first issue, the Court held that the status arises on the "First Date", namely, the date on which the carer ceases to be subject to "prohibited national measures" which would deprive the EU citizen child of the genuine enjoyment of the substance of his or her EU citizenship rights by having to move out of the EU, rather than on the "last date", when such measures are actually taken or imminent. The result is that *Zambrano* carers were entitled to income-related benefits until November 8, 2012, even if they were not under an imminent threat of removal.

However, the Court also held that *Zambrano* carers are not entitled to the same level of payments of social assistance as is required by EU law to be paid to EU citizens lawfully who are lawfully in the United Kingdom. Their only right is to be paid "such amount as will enable them to support themselves in order to be the carer for the EU citizen child within the EU" and as long as that "basic support test" is met, the entitlement of *Zambrano* carers to social assistance was entirely a matter of domestic law. In particular, *Zambrano* carers cannot derive an equal entitlement to social benefits by virtue of the EU principle of nationality non-discrimination because, by definition, they are not EU citizens and (at para.29):

> "29. Only EU citizens can rely on the nationality non-discrimination principle. Furthermore, EU law has no application when a member state treats some people within its jurisdiction less favourably than others (so-called "reverse discrimination"). The only restrictions are those imposed by the national law, which, in the case of the UK, incorporates Article 14 of the [European] Convention [on Human Rights]."

Article 14 was not infringed in this case because the UK Government's policy reasons for distinguishing between *Zambrano* carers and others were not manifestly without foundation (see paras 115–116).

Overall, on the evidence available to the Court of Appeal, it was not in a position to determine that the basic support test is not met by the domestic law of the UK as amended from November 8, 2012. The UK government relies on the duty imposed on local authorities by s.17 of the Children Act 1989 to provide support to children in need as being adequate to satisfy the test.

The claimant in *R. (on the application of HC) v Oldham Council* was granted permission to appeal to the Supreme Court on March 7, 2016 (Case ID UKSC 2015/0215). At the time of going to press, no date had been fixed for the hearing of the appeal.

- *EU national parents*

The decision in *Maahanmuuttovirasto* makes it clear that the *Zambrano* principle can apply to a British child who has a parent who is not a third-country national. However, the application of the principle will be subject to the same case by case enquiry into whether a refusal of a right of residence to a non-British parent (of whatever nationality) will mean "in practice" that the British EU citizen child will be compelled to leave the territory of the EU. That will be difficult to establish where the child has a parent who is an EU national and the child could live with that parent in Britain or another Member State see, e.g. *Alopka, Mondoulou and Mondoulou v Ministre du Travail, de l'Emploi et de l'Immigration* (C86/12, at paras 33–35).

- *Other rights of EU citizens*

Even if the rights which attach to EU citizenship are more extensive than the right not to be compelled to leave the territory of the Union, the decision in *Harrison* means that those rights are not engaged in this context. See also *Iida v Stadt Ulm* (C-40/11) and *Ymerga* (above).

However, in *Secretary of State for the Home Department v NA (Pakistan)* [2015] EWCA Civ 140, the Court of Appeal has referred the following questions to the CJEU:

"(1) Does an EU citizen have a right to reside in a host member state under Articles 20 and 21 of the TFEU in circumstances where the only state within the EU in which the citizen is entitled to reside is his state of nationality, but there is a finding of fact by a competent tribunal that the removal of the citizen from the host member state to his state of nationality would breach his rights under Article 8 of the ECHR or Article 7 of the Charter?

(2) If the EU citizen in (1) (above) is a child, does the parent having sole care of that child have a derived right of residence in the host member state if the child would have to accompany the parent on removal of the parent from the host member state?"

In *Secretary of State for the Home Department v NA* (C-115/15), the CJEU answered those questions as follows:

> "3. Article 20 TFEU must be interpreted as meaning that it does not confer a right of residence in the host Member State either on a minor Union citizen, who has resided since birth in that Member State but is not a national of that State, or on a parent who is a third-county national and who has sole custody of that minor, where they qualify for a right of residence in that Member State under a provision of secondary EU law.
>
> Article 21 TFEU must be interpreted as meaning that that it confers on that minor Union citizen a right of residence in the host Member State, provided that that citizen satisfies the conditions set out in Article 7(1) of Directive 2004/38, which it is for the referring court to determine. If so, that same provision allows the parent who is the primary carer of that Union citizen to reside with that citizen in the host Member State."

The special position of A8 and A2 nationals

Introduction

The Treaties under which Croatia and the A2 and A8 states (see above for details of the countries that fall within those categories) joined the EU permitted the existing Member States to derogate for a limited transitional period from the rights of Croatian, A2 and A8 nationals to freedom of movement as workers (for further details see the commentary to art.45 TFEU (ex-art.39 TEC) in Vol.III). That transitional period ended on April 30, 2009 (or, possibly, April 30, 2011 (see the discussion of *TG v SSWP (PC)* [2015] UKUT 50 (AAC) under the heading, *The A8 Regulations*, below)) for the A8 states and on December 31, 2013 for the A2 states. 2.272

The UK exercised the powers conferred by the derogations to make the A8 Regulations, the A2 Regulations and the Accession of Croatia (Immigration and Worker Authorisation) Regulations 2013 ("the Croatia Regulations"). The House of Lords has held that the A8 Regulations represented a proportionate and lawful exercise of the those powers (see the discussion of *Zalewska v Department for Social Development* below) and it seems probable that the same conclusion would be reached in relation to the A2 Regulations and the Croatia Regulations, were they to be challenged.

When considering the position of Croatian nationals (and the former position of A2 and A8 nationals) under those Regulations, it is important to begin from the premise that Croatian, A2 and A8 nationals are Citizens of the Union, and have the same rights under EU law as the nationals of other Member States unless some provision of EU law removes or restricts those rights either expressly or by implication. In particular, the provisions considered below only affect the rights of Croatian (and only affected the rights of A2 and A8) nationals as workers and workseekers:

the rights of A2 nationals to reside in the UK as, for example, self-employed persons are unaffected (as were the rights of A2 and A8 nationals) see *CIS/1042/2008*.

As EEA nationals who are not in work often claim JSA, it should be noted that it is only income-based JSA that is subject to the right to reside test. Contribution-based JSA is not subject to that test and, where an EEA national claimant last worked in the United Kingdom, s/he may be entitled to rely upon periods of insurance, employment or residence in other member States (including Croatia and the A2 and A8 states) to acquire entitlement to contribution-based JSA (see art.61 of Regulation 883/2004 (see Vol.III) or art.67 of the former Regulation (EEC) 1408/71 (Vol.III of the 2009/2010 edition)).

The Croatia Regulations and the A2 Regulations

2.273 The text of these Regulations is set out in full later in this volume. The regime which the Regulations impose on Croatian nationals is, and on Bulgarian and Romanian nationals was, one of prior authorisation (as opposed to the regime of registration which was imposed on A8 nationals). If an Croatian national is, or an A2 national was, "subject to worker authorisation", then s/he must obtain an authorisation document from the Home Office before starting work. Authorisation is only likely to be granted if the worker wishes to come to the UK to undertake approved employment in certain sectors of agriculture or industry..

Croatian nationals who are, and A2 nationals who were, "subject to worker authorisation" only count as "workers" for the purpose of the 2006 Regulations if they hold the necessary authorisation and are working in accordance with it. If they are not working but only seeking employment, they do not have a right to reside as workseekers. If they cease to work, they cease to have a right to reside, even if they are involuntarily unemployed.

Not every Croatian national needs authorisation in order to work in the UK. This depends upon whether they are an "accession state national subject to worker authorisation" as defined in reg.2. That definition contains a long list of exceptions. The principal excepted categories are:

- those who had unconditional leave to enter or remain in the UK before July 1, 2013. Those advising claimants should (in appropriate cases) make enquiries about their pre-accession immigration status;
- those who have been legally working in the UK (whether before or after June 30, 2013) for a continuous period of at least 12 months. Interruptions of up to 30 days do not affect continuity;
- those who are dual nationals of other EEA states;
- those who are the spouse or civil partner of a UK national or a person settled in the UK;
- (in most cases) those who are family members of non-UK EEA nationals with the right to reside;
- those who are "highly skilled persons" as defined by reg.3. People in this category would have been granted a work permit under the Immigration Act 1971 before Croatia became a EU member. They should be able to produce a registration certificate stating that they have "unconditional access to the United Kingdom labour market"; and
- those who are "posted workers" (i.e. those working in the UK for non-UK EEA employers).

Similar rules applied to Bulgarian and Romanian nationals under the A2 Regulations.

As the Croatian and A2 schemes are schemes of authorisation rather than registration, the difficulties which have been experienced in relation to the A8 scheme over the calculation of the 12-month period do not normally occur.

The A8 Regulations

The A8 Regulations have largely been revoked. The text immediately before revocation is set out at pp.792–798 of Vol.II of the 2011/2012 edition. This commentary has been retained in the current edition because it remains relevant to whether past periods of residence by A8 nationals count towards the acquisition of the permanent right of residence. 2.274

It is relevant to that issue that, in *TG v SSWP (PC)* [2015] UKUT 50 (AAC), the Upper Tribunal has held that the two-year extension of the A8 accession period from May 1, 2009 to April 30, 2011 by the Accession (Immigration and Worker Registration) (Amendment) Regulations 2009 (SI 2009/892) was not compatible with EU law because it was not a proportionate exercise of the UK's powers under the Treaty of Accession. The provisions of SI 2009/892 therefore had to be disapplied, with the consequence that the rights of A8 nationals to reside in the UK as workers or jobseekers were the same as for other EU citizens (other than A2 nationals) and were no longer subject to restriction. In practical terms this means that, between May 1, 2009 and April 30, 2011:

- an A8 national who was in unregistered work had a right of residence as a worker;
- A8 nationals who were temporarily incapable of work or involuntarily unemployed retained worker status; and
- A8 nationals who had not previously worked in the UK (or had not retained their former worker status) but were looking for work here had a right to reside in the same way as other EEA nationals.

The Secretary of State has appealed to the Court of Appeal (sub nom. *Secretary of State for Work and Pensions v Gubeladze*) against the Upper Tribunal's decision and the appeal is listed to be heard on February 7 or 8, 2017.

It is important to emphasise again that the A8 Regulations only affect the rights of A8 nationals as *workers* and *workseekers* and do not affect the self-employed. The scheme of the Regulations was to derogate from art.45 TFEU (ex-art.39 TEC), the Citizenship Directive and parts of the former Regulation 1612/68 by requiring (reg.7) most A8 nationals to register with the Home Office (under reg.8) in order to work lawfully in the UK. The 2006 Regulations were modified (by reg.5) so that an A8 national was only a "worker", i.e. with the right to reside, during periods in which s/he was actually working in accordance with the registration scheme. During such periods, the A8 national was exempt from the habitual residence test and the right to reside test under reg.21AA(4)(f) of the Income Support Regulations, reg.85A(4)(f) of the JSA Regulations and reg.2(4)(f) of the SPC Regulations and reg.70(4)(f) of the ESA Regulations. By reg.6 a workseeker from an A8 country who would be required to register if s/he were to find employment did not have a right to reside other than as a self-sufficient person. The effect was that affected A8 nationals could not receive benefits while first looking for work in the UK. If they found a job and registered with the Home Office in accordance with the rules of the registration scheme, they might receive any in-work benefits to which they were otherwise entitled while employed (including periods of sickness or maternity leave during which the contract of employment subsists, see *CJSA/1459/2008* and *CIS/4237/2008*) but were not entitled to income-related benefits if, for any reason, they ceased employment before they had worked continuously for 12 months (reg.2(4)).

The following A8 nationals were permitted to work (i.e. as "workers") without registering with the Home Office and enjoyed the full rights enjoyed by other EEA nationals (reg.2(2)–(6)):

- those who, on April 30, 2004, had leave to enter or remain in the UK that was not subject to an condition restricting their employment. The Department does not appear to ask routinely about a claimant's pre-accession immigration status and it will therefore be important for those advising claimants to make such enquiries;

- those who were working legally in the UK on April 30, 2004 and who had been so working without interruption throughout the preceding 12 months;
- those who have worked legally in the UK without interruption for a period of 12 months falling partly or wholly after April 30, 2004;
- those who are also nationals of the UK, another EEA state that is not an A8 state or of Switzerland;
- those who are "posted workers" (i.e. workers in the UK for employers that are not established here); and
- those who are family members of (non-A8) EEA or Swiss nationals who are in the UK as workers or self-sufficient persons, retired persons or students.

2.275 When deciding whether claimants had worked for 12 months without interruption, up to 30 days on which they were not working could be ignored as long as they were working at the beginning and end of the period.

A particular problem arose with the calculation of the 12 month period because the A8 Regulations required decision-makers to know when an application for registration had been received by the Home Office. Unhelpfully, the Registration Card issued by the Home Office did not record that information and, on occasions at least, the Department did not make the necessary enquiries of the Home Office. The guidance from the Commissioner and the Upper Tribunal on how the First-tier Tribunal should deal with appeals in which there is no evidence on this crucial point is equivocal. *CJSA/968/2008* decides that in some cases, it may be an error of law for a tribunal to rely upon the oral evidence of A8 nationals about when they applied for registration rather than adjourn to obtain confirmation via the Secretary of State. By contrast, *SSWP v ZA* [2009] UKUT 294 places the burden on the Secretary of State. Judge Ward stated:

> "73. It is appropriate to say a word about the provision of evidence in cases of this type. As Baroness Hale put it at para.62 in *Kerr v Department for Social Development* [2004] UKHL 23; [2004] 1 WLR 1372:
> '62. What emerges from all this is a co-operative process of investigation in which both the claimant and the department play their part. The department is the one which knows what questions it needs to ask and what information it needs to have in order to determine whether the conditions of entitlement have been met. The claimant is the one who generally speaking can and must supply that information. But where the information is available to the department rather than the claimant, then the department must take the necessary steps to enable it to be traced.'
>
> It is clear to me from the present proceedings that the Department for Work and Pensions can, as one would expect, readily get details of when a person's application for a worker registration certificate was made from the Home Office. By contrast, I have noted above that nowhere does the attention of claimants appear to have been brought to any need to make a copy of the application papers and to retain it even once the certificate has been received. Absent any express instruction, I would generally regard it as unreasonable to expect them to have done so. I would anticipate therefore that in most cases, applying the principles of *Kerr* will result in the Department for Work and Pensions having to obtain the relevant details of a person's application from the Home Office and to include them in tribunal bundles.If it does not do so initially, whether or not to permit it to do so subsequently and to allow an adjournment for the purpose will be a matter for the discretion of the tribunal, to the exercise of which the existence of the guidance provided by this paragraph might be thought relevant."

It is suggested that Judge Ward is clearly correct and that *CJSA/968/2008* is wrongly decided.

There was also an issue as to whether, once issued, a Registration Certificate or Card had retrospective effect to the date on which the employment to which it relates began. In *SSWP v ZA* and *MS v SSWP (JSA)* [2011] UKUT 452 (AAC), Judge Ward held that it did not. That decision has now been confirmed by the Court of Appeal *sub nom. Szpak v Secretary of State for Work and Pensions* [2013] EWCA Civ 46. It is understood that the decision will not be appealed further. 2.276

An A8 national who had been self-employed for over 12 months could not thereby avoid being an accession State worker requiring registration if s/he ceased trading and became a jobseeker, even if the self-employment was registered with HMRC for tax and national insurance purposes: see *SSWP v RK* [2009] UKUT 209 (AAC), para.15. However, a self-employed A8 national who was temporarily incapable of work retained a right of residence under reg.6(3) of the 2006 Regulations even though, by virtue of reg.5(3) of the A8 Regulations, an A8 national who is a worker does not retain worker status under reg.6(2)(a) in the same circumstances: *ibid.* Judge Rowland suggests that the difference in treatment:

> "May be explicable on the basis that a worker will often be entitled to sick leave and will retain a right of residence while on such leave without the need to rely on regulation 6(2)(a) of the 2006 Regulations and without therefore falling foul of the derogation (see *CIS/4237/2007*)".

Compatibility of the right to reside test with EU law

In the past, it has been controversial whether the right to reside test, both as it affects A8 and A2 nationals, and as it affects some economically-inactive nationals of all Member States, is fully in accordance with EU law. However, that controversy has—at least for the time being—been put to rest by the decisions of the Court of Appeal of England and Wales in *Abdirahman* (above) and Kaczmarek v SSWP [2008] EWCA Civ 1310; (*R(IS) 5/09*) (on appeal from CIS/2358/2006), of the House of Lords in *Zalewska v Department for Social Development* [2008] UKHL 67, *R 1/09(IS)*, and by the decisions of the Supreme Court in *Patmalniece v SSWP* [2011] UKSC 11 and *Mirga v Secretary of State for Work and Pensions* [2016] UKSC 1. 2.277

Abdirahman was the appeal against the decisions of the Tribunal of Commissioners in *CIS/3573/2005* and *CH/2484/2005*. The challenge was effectively to the right to reside test as a whole. Mrs Abdirahman was a Swedish national who, at the time under consideration had not been economically active in the UK and did not have a right to reside under the Citizenship Directive or the 2006 Regulations. She argued that she had a right to reside as a citizen of the European Union under art.21 TFEU (ex-art.18 TEC) and that the right to reside test discriminated against her on the grounds of nationality contrary to art.18 TFEU (ex-art.12 TEC). Both those arguments were rejected. Her art.21 (ex-art.18) right was "subject to the limitations and conditions laid down in [the] Treaty and by the measures adopted to give it effect" and on the authority of the *Trojani* case (above) and of a number of previous Court of Appeal decisions, including *W (China) v Secretary of State for the Home Department* (above), that article did not confer a right of residence in circumstances where the limitations imposed by the relevant Directive (in that case Directive 90/364) were not satisfied. Although the right to reside test was discriminatory, that discrimination was not "within the scope of application of the Treaty" because art.12 did not extend to cases in which there was no right to reside under either the Treaty or the relevant domestic law. Moreover, even if art.12 were engaged, the discrimination was in any event justified by the need to prevent benefit tourism and as an aspect of immigration control.

In *Kaczmarek*, the claimant had been economically active for a period of three years in the past but was no longer so. She relied on a passage from the judgment in *Trojani* (at para.43) in submitting that "a citizen of the Union who is not economically active may rely on Article 12 EC [now art.18 TFEU] where he has been lawfully resident in the host Member State *for a certain time* or possesses a residence permit" (emphasis added). However, the Court decided that "the reference to 'a certain time' is a reference to specific qualifying periods which give rise to an express right of residence".

2.278 *Zalewska* was about the validity of one aspect of the former registration scheme for A8 nationals (and, by implication, the equivalent provisions of the former authorisation scheme for A2 nationals and the current authorisation scheme for Croatian nationals). Specifically, it concerned the position of an A8 (or A2) national who worked lawfully in the UK but became involuntarily unemployed or temporarily incapable of work before completing 12 months' lawful work. Any other EEA national would be regarded in those circumstances as a "person retaining the status of worker" with an entitlement to benefit. However, the effect of the former A8 Regulations was that an A8 national in that position was treated as a 'workseeker' with no such entitlement. By the time the appeal reached the House of Lords, the issue was whether that treatment amounted to the unlawful denial of a social advantage that was available to UK nationals (i.e. contrary to art.7(2) of the former Regulation 1612/68). This, in turn depended on whether the exclusion from benefit was a proportionate exercise of the authority given by the relevant derogation in the Treaty of Accession. Although that derogation did not mention art.7 of Regulation 1612/68, it was not necessary to do so because, if the A8 scheme was proportionate, an A8 national who did not comply with it was not a worker for the purposes of art.7 and was therefore not entitled to its protection. Their Lordships decided by a majority (Lords Hope, Carswell and Brown, Baroness Hale and Lord Neuberger dissenting) that the A8 scheme was compatible with the EU law principle of proportionality. See also in this context the decision of the Court of Appeal in England and Wales in *R. (D) v Secretary of State for Work and Pensions* [2004] EWCA Civ 1468 (October 11, 2004, CA, Mummery and Kay LJJ) and *CIS/3232/2006.*

Patmalniece was concerned with the application of the "Equality of Treatment" provisions of art.3 of the former Regulation 1408/71 to the claimant's claim for SPC. In that case, the claimant was within the personal scope of the Regulation and SPC was within the material scope. It therefore could not be said, as had been held in *Abdirahman*, that the subject matter of the appeal was not within the scope of the anti-discrimination provision in question. Relying on the decision of the ECJ in *Bressol v Gouvernement de la Communauté Française* (C-73/08), the Supreme Court held unanimously that the right to reside test was indirectly rather than directly discriminatory. Regulation 2 of the SPC Regulations was said to impose:

> "a composite test, one element of which [i.e., the right to reside test] could be satisfied by a- person who was not a national of the host Member State only if he met certain additional conditions but which every national of the host member state would automatically satisfy"

and that the effect of the conditions in that regulation (i.e. both the right to reside test and the habitual residence test) had to be looked at cumulatively. It was not directly discriminatory on grounds of nationality but, as it put nationals of other member States at a particular disadvantage, it was indirectly discriminatory and needed to be justified. By a majority (Lord Walker dissenting), it found that discrimination to be justified by:

> "the principle that those who are entitled to claim social assistance in the host Member State should have achieved a genuine economic tie with it or a sufficient degree of social integration as a pre-condition for entitlement to it"

and that justification was not undermined by the more favourable treatment accorded by the UK to Irish nationals because of art.2 of Protocol 20 to the TFEU and TEU (the Protocol on the Common Travel Area, see above).

The decision in *Patmalniece* applies to child benefit and child tax credit as it does to other social security benefits. In *AS v HMRC (CB)* [2013] NICom 15, the Chief Commissioner of Northern Ireland distinguished *Patmalniece* and held that the right to reside test in reg.27(3) of the Child Benefit (General) Regulations 2006 (i.e. of the Northern Ireland regulations which is equivalent to reg.23(4) of the GB regulations) is unlawfully discriminatory on the grounds of nationality contrary to art.3 of Regulation 1408/71. However, the Court of Appeal in Northern Ireland allowed HMRC's appeal (*HM Revenue & Customs v Spiridonova* [2014] NICA 63) and confirmed the validity of the test.

That leaves the question of whether it is possible to derive a right of residence directly from art.21(1) TFEU (ex-art.18(1) TEC) in circumstances where no such right is expressly conferred by the Citizenship Directive or the Regulations. In *Kaczmarek*, the Court followed the approach adopted by the Commissioner in that case (*CIS/2538/2006*), namely that there is no direct right of residence under art.21 unless the denial of such a right would offend the general principles of community law and, in particular, the principle of proportionality. In such cases, there may be a freestanding right of residence under art.21(1). However, Directive 2004/38/EC provides the benchmark for proportionality (even in cases arising before that Directive came into force) and art.21(1) cannot be interpreted so as to confer rights that go beyond the Citizenship Directive except where it can be shown that there is a lacuna in the Directive. The circumstances in which it is permissible to conclude that there is such a lacuna were considered further by the Upper Tribunal in *RM v SSWP (IS)* [2010] UKUT 238 (AAC). **2.279**

In *CIS/599/2007* and *CPC/3764/2007*, however, the commissioner analysed the issue of proportionality as merging "with the issue of whether the claimant's reliance on social assistance is sufficient to become a burden". The Commissioner held (*CPC/3764/2007*, at para.44) that "[p]roportionality requires me to ask whether excluding the claimant from a right to reside is reasonably necessary to protect the social assistance system". In the light of *Kaczmarek* and, in particular, its emphasis on the "lacuna-filling" role played by art.18 (see para.20), these two decisions can no longer be followed without reservation. For examples of post-*Kaczmarek* decisions on proportionality see *SSWP v DWP* [2009] UKUT 17 (AAC), *SSWP v IM-M* [2009] UKUT 71 (AAC) and *SSWP v CA* [2009] UKUT 169 (AAC) Cases in which a right to reside is conferred on the basis that it is disproportionate to apply the normal rules will be exceptional. For an example, see *R(IS) 4/09*.

More recently, the issue of proportionality has been considered again by the Supreme Court in *Mirga v Secretary of State for Work and Pensions*. The claimant was a Polish national who had come to the UK in 1998 at the age of 10 with her parents and siblings. The family went back to Poland in 2002 but returned to the UK in June 2004. After completing her education, the claimant started work in April 2005. Her first period of work of seven months was registered under the former worker registration scheme for A8 nationals but the two subsequent short periods were not. She left home in June 2006, having fallen out with her father because she was pregnant (her mother had died in October 2004). Her claim for income support made in August 2006 was refused on the ground that she did not have a right to reside. The Court of Appeal ([2012] EWCA Civ 1952) rejected the argument that in these circumstances the refusal of income support was disproportionate and therefore offensive to EU law. The Court relied, firstly, on *Zalewska* and, secondly, on the distinction drawn in, at para.5 of *Kaczmarek* between lawful presence and right to reside. The protection of the claimant's fundamental rights did not require that she be accorded a right of residence. She was lawfully present, and if the Home Office decided to remove her, would have a right of appeal against that decision and be able to raise any argument based on fundamental rights arising out of EU law or art.8 ECHR at that point.

On further appeal, the Supreme Court upheld the decision of the Court of Appeal. On the issue of proportionality, the Court decided, following the judgments of the CJEU in *Dano v Jobcenter Leipzig* (C-333/13) and *Jobcenter Berlin Neukölln v Alimanovic* (Case C-67/14), that the provisions of Directive 2004/38/EC "guarantees a significant level of legal certainty and transparency in the context of the award of social assistance by way of basic provision while complying with the principle of proportionality" so that an examination of proportionality in the context of an individual case was not necessary, except (possibly) in exceptional cases, of which Ms Mirga's case was not one.

In *Pensionsversicherungsanstalt v Brey* (Case C-140/12) (see above) the CJEU had held that (in the circumstances of that case) it was necessary for a host member States to carry out individual assessment of whether allowing a claim for social assistance by a national of another EEA State would amount to a burden on the social assistance system of the host member State before it could refuse that claim (see pp.348–50 of the main volume). Taken together with the judgments in *Dano*, and *Alimanovic*, the Supreme Court's judgment in *Mirga* raises the issue—which will need to be explored in other cases—of whether any circumstances remain in which the *Brey* requirement continues to apply.

2.280 The UK case law which holds that there is no general right for EEA nationals who are not economically active to reside in a Member State of which they are not a national is reinforced by the Grand Chamber of the ECJ in *Dano v Jobcenter Leipzig* (C-333/13). The court ruled that:

> "Article 24(1) of Directive 2004/38/EC . . ., read in conjunction with Article 7(1)(b) thereof, and Article 4 of Regulation No 883/2004, . . . must be interpreted as not precluding legislation of a Member State under which nationals of other Member States are excluded from entitlement to certain 'special non-contributory cash benefits' within the meaning of Article 70(2) of Regulation No 883/2004, although those benefits are granted to nationals of the host Member State who are in the same situation, in so far as those nationals of other Member States do not have a right of residence under Directive 2004/38 in the host Member State."

The Court's decision received considerable publicity in the UK but does not actually change the law as it was previously understood: economically inactive EEA nationals who are without sufficient resources do not have a right to reside and so are not entitled to social assistance.

European Commission's challenges to the right to reside test

2.281 On September 29, 2011, the European Commission announced that it had requested the UK to stop the application of the right to reside test on the basis that the test contravenes EU law as it indirectly discriminates against non-UK nationals coming from other EU Member States. The request takes the form of a "reasoned opinion" under EU infringement procedure. The UK was given two months to inform the Commission of measures it has taken to bring its legislation into line with EU law. Otherwise, it was open to the Commission decide to refer the UK to the ECJ. The DWP issued an Urgent Bulletin (U5/2011) to decision makers stating that the UK would be responding to the Commission's points and that decision makers should continue to make right to reside decisions as normal.

On April 26, 2012, the European Commission issued a further reasoned opinion to the effect that:

- The Citizenship Directive guarantees that non-EU family members of EU citizens who hold a valid residence card issued by one EU country can travel together with EU citizens within the European Union without an entry visa. The UK laws do not grant this important right which lies at the heart of free movement.
- The United Kingdom does not allow extended family members of EU citizens to apply to have their residence in the UK considered under EU law

when they were lawfully residing in the UK before the arrival to the UK of the EU citizen on whom they are dependent.

- Under the Citizenship Directive, EU citizens who settle in another EU country but do not work there may be required to have sufficient resources and sickness insurance. The United Kingdom, however, does not consider entitlement to treatment by the UK public healthcare scheme (NHS) as sufficient. This breaches EU law.
- Finally, the United Kingdom does not issue workers from Romania and Bulgaria during the first 12 months with the same residence documents as workers from other EU Member States. While EU law allows the United Kingdom to temporarily keep in place a work-permit scheme for workers from Bulgaria and Romania, those who have a work permit have the same right to reside as other EU workers and must be issued the corresponding residence documents.

The deadline for the UK to respond to the reasoned opinion expired on June 29, 2012.

On May 30, 2013 the Commission announced that, since no measures had been taken by the UK Government to end the discrimination notified in September 2011, it had decided to refer the UK to the European Court. The reference to the Court (*Commission v United Kingdom* (C-308/14)) was actually made on June 27, 2014, nearly three years later. The Commission claimed that the Court should declare that the UK has failed to comply with its obligations under Regulation (EC) No 883/2004, by requiring that a claimant for child benefit or child tax credit should have a right to reside in the UK. It will be observed that this is very much more narrow that the original reasoned grounds of challenge.

On June 14, 2016, the CJEU dismissed the action in its entirety. 2.282

First, it held that child benefit and child tax credit were social security benefits, not social assistance or special non-contributory cash benefits (paras.54–61).

Next, it accepted the submissions of the United Kingdom that art.11(3)(e) of Regulation No. 883/2004 (upon which the Commission relied) sets out a "conflict rule" for determining the national legislation applicable to payment of the social security benefits listed in art.3(1) of the Regulation. It is intended not only to prevent the concurrent application of a number of national legislative systems to a given situation and the complications which may ensue, but also to ensure that persons covered by that regulation are not left without social security cover because there is no legislation which is applicable to them. However, it is not intended to lay down the conditions creating the right to social security benefits: that is for the legislation of each Member State (paras 63–65).

Thirdly, the Court held (following *Brey* and *Dano*) that there is nothing in principle to prevent the grant of social benefits to Union citizens who are not economically active being made subject to the substantive condition that those citizens meet the necessary requirements for possessing a right to reside lawfully in the host Member State (paras 68 and 75).

Finally, the Court held that such a condition amounts to indirect discrimination, but will be justified if it is appropriate for securing the attainment of a legitimate objective and does not go beyond what is necessary to attain that objective (paras 76 and 79). The need to protect the finances of the host Member State was capable in principle of providing such justification and the way in which the United Kingdom had implemented the right to reside test for child benefit and child tax credit had not been shown to be disproportionate. In particular, the Commission had failed to establish that it amounted to the systematic verification of the lawfulness of the residence of EU citizens, contrary to art.14(2) of the Citizenship Directive.

Transitional protection

2.283 Note, finally, that reg.6 of the Social Security (Habitual Residence) Amendment Regulations 2004 (reproduced later in this volume) establishes transitional protection from the right to reside test. That protection applies to those who were entitled (or who subsequently proved to have been entitled) to one of five "specified benefits" (income support, JSA, state pension credit, housing benefit and council tax benefit) on April 30, 2004 (see *CIS/1138/2006*). The transitional protection continues until the day on which the claimant is no longer entitled to any of those benefits.

With effect from October 31, 2011, reg.6 was amended by reg.17 of SI 2011/2425 to include ESA in the list of specified benefits. Thus a claimant who moves from, e.g. IS or IBJSA to IRESA can retain the transitional protection, provided his/her entitlement to ESA (including any linked entitlement to ESA) is continuous with entitlement to any of the specified benefits and that entitlement included April 30, 2004.

CIS/1096/2007 and *CIS/352/2008* hold that the transitional protection only applies to the claimant who was entitled to benefit on April 30, 2004 and not to another member of the same family who was covered by the claim on that date and subsequently makes a claim in his or her own right. That rule does not infringe Convention Rights.

A modified form of reg.6 applies where the claimant is entitled to ESA by virtue of a conversion decision under the ESA (Transitional Provisions, Housing Benefit and Council Tax Benefit) (Existing Awards) (No.2) Regulations 2010 (SI 2010/1907) (as amended), or is treated as having limited capability for work under reg.30 of the ESA Regulations while appealing against such a conversion decision. In a conversion case it is only necessary for the person's entitlement to any of the specified benefits to have been continuous with entitlement to the same or another specified benefit for a period that included April 30, 2004 immediately before the effective date of the conversion decision. The effect would seem to be that in a conversion case the transitional protection will continue if a linked ESA claim is made (i.e. one that is separated by 12 weeks or less) even if there was no entitlement to any of the specified benefits in those 12 weeks.

Habitual residence

2.284 Unless they are exempt under para.(4)(g)–(j), the following claimants must satisfy the habitual residence test in para.1:

- British nationals who have recently spent time outside the CTA in circumstances that do not engage their rights to free movement under EC law;
- nationals of the Channel Islands or the Isle of Man who have recently spent time outside the CTA;
- EEA nationals and their family members who have a right to reside but who do not fall within para.(4)(a)–(f); and
- nationals of non-EEA states who are not family members of EEA nationals.

Who is exempt?

2.285 The following are deemed not to be persons from abroad and are therefore exempt from the habitual residence test:

- Refugees, and those who—outside the Immigration Rules—have been granted humanitarian protection or exceptional leave to enter, or to remain in, the UK are deemed not to be persons from abroad: see sub-paras (g)–(hh).

  In *R(IS) 9/98* the Commissioner confirms that a person counts as a refugee entitled to the protection of the 1951 Convention from the time he fulfils the criteria contained in the definition in the Convention. It is not necessary for his status as a refugee to have been recognised by the Home Office. Such recognition does not make the person a refugee but merely declares him one.
- People who have been deported, expelled or otherwise compulsorily removed from another country to the UK: see sub-para.(i). The exemption does not apply to those who are "persons subject to immigration control"—see the overview above.

- (For the period from August 28, 1996 to October 28, 2013) people from Montserrat who came to Great Britain after November 1, 1995 following the volcanic eruption in that territory: see the former sub-para.(j) (p.299 of Vol. II of the 2013/2014 edition).
- (For the period from July 25, 2006 to January 31, 2007 only) people from Lebanon who came to Great Britain on or after July 12, 2006 because of the armed conflict there: see sub-para.(k), temporarily inserted by the Social Security (Lebanon) Amendment Regulations 2006 (SI 2006/1981) as follows:

  "(k) a person in Great Britain who left Lebanon on or after 12th July 2006 because of the armed conflict there."

Habitual residence: overview

The requirement to be habitually resident only applies to the claimant, not to a partner or dependant. **2.286**

"Habitual residence" is not defined in the regulation but case law since 1994 has established that, except in cases where EU citizens are exercising their rights as migrant workers (see *Swaddling*, below), to be habitually resident in the CTA, a claimant must:

- have a settled intention to reside here; and
- have been "[resident] in fact for a period that shows that the residence has become 'habitual' and . . . will or is likely to continue to be habitual".

See *Nessa v Chief Adjudication Officer* [1999] 1 W.L.R. 1937; [1999] 4 All E.R. 677, HL (also reported as *R(IS) 2/00*). Whether that legal test is satisfied so that a person is habitually resident is a question of fact to be decided by reference to all the circumstances in each case (*Re J*).

The period of residence that is necessary is usually referred to as the "appreciable period" in accordance with the use of that phrase by Lord Bridge of Harwich in *Re J (A Minor) (Abduction: Custody Rights)* [1990] 2 A.C. 562; [1990] 2 All E.R. 961, HL: **2.287**

> "In considering this issue it seems to me to be helpful to deal first with a number of preliminary points. The first point is that the expression 'habitually resident' . . . is nowhere defined. It follows, I think, that the expression is not to be treated as a term of art with some special meaning, but is rather to be understood according to the ordinary and natural meaning of the two words which it contains. The second point is that the question whether a person is or is not habitually resident in a specified country is a question of fact to be decided by reference to all the circumstances of any particular case. The third point is that there is a significant difference between a person ceasing to be habitually resident in country A, and his subsequently becoming habitually resident in country B. A person may cease to be habitually resident in country A in a single day if he or she leaves it with a settled intention not to return to it but to take up long-term residence in country B instead. Such a person cannot, however, become habitually resident in country B in a single day. An appreciable period of time and a settled intention will be necessary to enable him or her to become so. During that appreciable period of time the person will have ceased to be habitually resident in country A but not yet have become habitually resident in country B. The fourth point is that, where a child of J.'s age is in the sole lawful custody of the mother, his situation with regard to habitual residence will necessarily be the same as hers."

Habitual residence is not the same as domicile (*R(U)8/88*). It is possible to be habitually resident in more than one country although it is unusual (*R(IS) 2/00*, para.20); it is also possible to be habitually resident in none.

Habitual residence can continue during absences of long or short duration.

"Settled intention" and "appreciable period of time"

2.288 The two limbs of the habitual residence test, a settled intention and an appreciable period of time, are difficult to analyse separately. This is because the two are closely linked: the overall question is whether "in all the circumstances, including the settledness of the person's intentions as to residence, the residence has continued for a sufficient period for it to be said to be habitual" (*R(IS) 2/00*). So, if there is a doubt about the claimant's intention to reside in the UK, it may require a longer period of residence to resolve that doubt. Similarly, where a person's circumstances are such that s/he clearly intends to make a home in the UK, it may be possible to say that s/he has become habitually resident after a relatively short period of time. There is thus no minimum "appreciable period": the length of the period required will depend upon all the circumstances of the individual case.

The intention to reside here does not need to be permanent or indefinite. It can be for a limited period. To be resident a person had to be seen to be making a "genuine home for the time being" here but it need not be his only home or a permanent one (*R(IS) 6/96*). (Actual residence in two places is perfectly possible: *R(IS) 9/99.*) Some of the relevant factors in judging intention will include the reason for coming (or returning) here, the location of his/her possessions and family, where s/he has previously worked, the length and purpose of any absence from the UK, etc.

If the claimant's intention is conditional, e.g. on benefit being awarded, this is not a settled intention to stay (*CIS/12703/1996*).

2.289 The leading case on the requirement for an appreciable period is the decision of the House of Lords in *Nessa* [1999] 1 W.L.R. 1937. Mrs Nessa came to the UK in August 1994, aged 55. She had previously lived all her life in Bangladesh. Her father-in-law, in whose house she had been living, had died and she had come to the UK for the emotional support of her late husband's brother and his family. Her husband had lived and worked in the UK until his death in 1975 and she had a right of abode here. She claimed income support in September 1994.

The Commissioner (*R(IS) 2/00*) and a majority of the Court of Appeal followed *Re J* and held that in order to establish habitual residence it was necessary for a claimant not only to have been in the UK voluntarily, and for settled purposes, but also to have fulfilled those conditions for an appreciable period of time. However, the CA considered that the appreciable period need not be particularly long. The dissenting judge (Thorpe LJ) considered that Lord Brandon's comments in *Re J* were clearly obiter and that an appreciable period was not an essential ingredient of habitual residence. In his view the adjective "habitual" ensured that "the connection [to the country] is not transitory or temporary but enduring and the necessary durability can be judged prospectively in exceptional cases".

Mrs Nessa appealed again to the House of Lords which unanimously upheld the majority in the Court of Appeal. Lord Slynn of Hadley, with whom all the other judges agreed, reviewed the authorities discussed above and stated:

> "With the guidance of these cases it seems to me plain that as a matter of ordinary language a person is not habitually resident in any country unless he has taken up residence and lived there for a period. . . . If Parliament had intended that a person seeking to enter the United Kingdom or such a person declaring his intention to settle here is to have income support on arrival, it could have said so. It seems to me impossible to accept the argument at one time advanced that a person who has never been here before who says on landing, 'I intend to settle in the United Kingdom' and who is fully believed is automatically a person who is habitually resident here. Nor is it enough to say I am going to live at X or with Y. He must show residence in fact for a period which shows that the residence has become 'habitual' and, as I see it, will or is likely to continue to be habitual."

Lord Slynn did accept that there might be "special cases where the person concerned is not coming here for the first time, but is resuming an habitual residence previously had . . . On such facts the Adjudication Officer may or of course may not be satisfied that the previous habitual residence has been resumed. This position is quite different from that of someone coming to the United Kingdom for the first time." Although *Swaddling* (see below) was cited by Lord Slynn as one example of this type of case the exception seems to be considerably narrower than the principle of Community law established by that case, namely that the length of residence in a Member State could not be regarded as an intrinsic element of the concept of habitual residence where a claimant comes within Regulation 1408/71. Lord Slynn appears to be saying no more than that in some cases it will be possible to say on the facts that a returning resident is merely resuming a habitual residence which has already been established. The reference to the possibility that the AO (now decision-maker) "may not be satisfied" clearly indicates that this will not always be the case and that some returning residents will need to re-establish habitual residence by living in the CTA for a period of time.

How long is the appreciable period?

Lord Slynn's opinion also contains interesting observations on how long the appreciable period of time should be. Whilst recognising that the period is not fixed and "may be longer where there are doubts", he also stated that "it may be short" and quoted with approval the statement of Butler Sloss LJ in *Re F (A Minor) (Child Abduction)* [1994] F.L.R. 548, at 555 that "A month can be . . . an appreciable period of time". He also agreed with the Commissioner that there were factors which indicated that habitual residence had been established in Mrs Nessa's case, "even by the date of the tribunal hearing *or as I see it, even earlier*" (emphasis added). At the date of her tribunal hearing on December 6, 1994, Mrs Nessa had been in the UK for 15 weeks. **2.290**

It must be stressed that the House of Lords clearly regarded this issue as one to be determined by tribunals on the facts of individual cases; however the view of the Commissioner in *R(IS) 6/96* that the establishment of habitual residence would normally require residence of at least some months must now be read in the light of Lord Slynn's comments.

As the issue of what is an "appreciable period" is one of fact and degree, and the decisions highlighted by Commissioners for wider circulation normally concern issues of law, there are few public examples of how the Commissioners approach that issue when exercising their discretion under s.14(8)(a) of SSA 1998. However, post-*Nessa* examples can be found in *CIS/1304/1997* and *CJSA/5394/1998* and in *CIS/376/2002*, all of which involved returning residents.

In the former decision, guidance was given that in a typical case tribunals should conduct a three-stage enquiry into: (i) the circumstances in which the claimant's earlier habitual residence was lost; (ii) the links between the claimant and the UK while abroad; and (iii) the circumstances of his return to the UK. So, for example, if the claimant's departure from the UK was temporary (albeit long-term) or conditional or if habitual residence was lost only as a result of events which occurred after the claimant's departure, those would be factors favouring a resumption of habitual residence immediately on return. On the facts of those appeals, the Commissioner held that the claimants, both British nationals who—as was accepted—had previously been habitually resident here, but had lost that habitual residence during an extended period of absence abroad, nevertheless resumed their previous habitual residence on the very day of their return to Britain. The relevant extracts from *CIS/1304/1997* and *CJSA/5394/1998* were reissued as an Appendix to *CIS/4474/2003* (see below). **2.291**

By contrast the claimant in *CIS/376/2002*, a naturalised British citizen who had worked in Britain for many years but had spent no more than 11 months here in the five years before the claims for benefit which were under consideration, was held not to have become habitually resident immediately. Commissioner Howell Q.C. accepted the tribunal's finding that although the claimant had been habitually resident in the past he had ceased to be so over that five-year period, but rejected the tribunal's doubts about whether he had a settled intention to remain here. On that basis, the Commissioner held that the claimant had not been resident for an appreciable period of time when his claim for IS was made (some three days after his arrival) but had become habitually resident by the date of the decision on that claim approximately five weeks later. In reaching his decision the Commissioner denied the possibility that a claimant who had lost his or her habitual residence could resume it immediately without first being present for an appreciable period of time. He stated (at para.12):

> "Everything therefore depends on what counts as an 'appreciable period' of resumed residence in this context so that his residence in the United Kingdom can be said to have become established as habitual . . . As has been said many times in the cases where judges from the House of Lords down to more humble levels have had to struggle with the meaning of this expression, this is ultimately a question of fact and degree, depending on the individual circumstances of each case, and there are no hard and fast rules to apply. For a returning citizen of this country coming back to live here again after a period of residence overseas . . . the period may be short: as little as a month or so. But it is not zero or minimal, since even a returning expatriate may change his plans again and there is therefore at least some space of time after actual arrival when one simply has to wait and see."

The issue of the length of the appreciable period was also considered by the Commissioner in *CIS/4474/2003*. The Commissioner also noted that the approach taken by Commissioners to that issue had developed since *R(IS) 6/96* and gave the following guidance:

> "19. What is an appreciable period depends on the circumstances of the particular case. But I agree with the Secretary of State that in the general run of cases the period will lie between one and three months. *I would certainly require cogent reasons from a tribunal to support a decision that a significantly longer period was required*" (emphasis added).

2.292 In *R(IS) 7/06*, the Commissioner indicated his broad agreement with *CIS/ 4474/2003*:

> "I am content to accept that, where a claimant is likely to remain in the United Kingdom permanently or for a substantial period of time, the conventional period that must have elapsed between his arrival and his establishing habitual residence is between one month and three months. However, those are not rigid limits. In an exceptional case, a person with a right of abode in the United Kingdom who, although not falling within the scope of regulation 21(3)(d), has been forced to flee another country and is nonetheless able to show a settled intention to remain in the United Kingdom might be accepted as habitually resident after less than a month of residence. Perhaps less exceptionally, a person with no ties to the United Kingdom and making no effort to become established here despite a vague intention to remain might be found not to be habitually resident in the United Kingdom until considerably longer than three months had elapsed."

However, disagreement with that approach was expressed in *CIS/1972/2003* (at para.14):

> "I comment only that I have seen tribunals decide on shorter periods than a month and longer periods than three months without being appealed, or appealed successfully. Too much should not be read into the facts of individual decisions or, I suggest, trends in the small number of—usually difficult—cases that Commissioners come to decide on the facts. It does not help when Commissioners' decisions are used to play a forensic game (for it is no more than that) of finding the longest, or the shortest, period endorsed by a Commissioner and then claiming some general rule from it. Parliament could have set a specific time limit. It did not. Advisors cannot seek certainty where it does not exist."

That disagreement was echoed by the Tribunal of Commissioners in *CIS/2559/2005*. The Commissioners stated that:

"The relevant period of residence required to support evidence of intention is not, in our view, something which can be reduced to a tariff. In so far as the decision of Mr Commissioner Jacobs in *CIS/4474/2003* can be interpreted to the contrary, we take a different view."

It is suggested that the approach in *CIS/4474/2003* and *R(IS) 7/06* (a reported decision that was subsequently upheld by the Court of Appeal) is to be preferred. Although it is accepted that no two cases are identical and that the decision must always be one of fact and degree in an individual case, justice as between claimants in similar situations requires that there should be some consistency in decision-making: that the appreciable periods of time required by different decision makers, tribunals and Commissioners should at least be "in the same ball park". In the early days of the test, the periods chosen varied wildly from case to case: at that time, many decision-makers—and some tribunals—would have required an appreciable period of at least a year and sometimes more on the facts of *Nessa*, whereas the Commissioner and Lord Slynn considered that Mrs Nessa had become habitually resident in approximately three months or less. In such circumstances, recognising the existence of a conventional period does not involve the imposition of a tariff as long as the period is applied flexibly in each individual case. As Commissioner Jacobs has subsequently said (in *CJSA/1223/2006* and *CJSA/1224/2006*): **2.293**

"I respectfully agree with the Tribunal of Commissioners in *CIS/2559/2005* . . . that: 'The relevant period of residence required to support evidence of intention is not, in our view, something which can be reduced to a tariff.' I do not understand why the Tribunal thought that my comments might be interpreted as setting a tariff and counsel could not suggest how they might have been so understood. I remain of the view that for most cases an appreciable period is likely to be between one and three months. [Counsel for the Secretary of State] told me that that was the experience of decision-makers and he was not instructed to argue otherwise".

It is suggested that Commissioner Jacobs was surely correct to express the point in *CIS/4474/2003* as being about reasoning: a tribunal may be justified in giving a decision that is outside the normal range of decisions given by tribunals generally, but if so, it should be prepared to explain why.

For an analysis of the process involved in fixing an appreciable period, see *CJSA/1223/2006* and *CJSA/1224/2006*. That decision emphasises the importance of looking at the steps taken by the claimant to integrate him- or herself into the UK during that period.

Viability

Another issue that has vexed the application of the habitual residence test over the years is that of viability. The starting point is *R(IS) 6/96*, the first Commissioner's decision on the habitual residence test. The Commissioner in that case held that the "appreciable period of time" should be a period which showed "a settled and viable pattern of living here as a resident". Thus the practicality of a person's arrangements for residence had to be considered. In determining whether the plans were viable, the possibility of claiming income support had to be left out of account (although this did not mean that there must be no conceivable circumstances in which a person might need to resort to income support). In reliance on that decision, some decision-makers and tribunals took the view that many people from abroad could never become habitually resident because the mere fact that they had claimed income support showed that their residence was not viable in the sense required by the Commissioner. The requirement of viability certainly contributed towards the phenomenon of very long appreciable periods in the early days of the test that has been referred to above. **2.294**

However, the law has developed since *R(IS) 6/96*. The Commissioner in *Nessa* (*R(IS) 2/00*) disagreed with *R(IS) 6/96* to the extent that the viability of a person's residence in the UK, either generally or with or without assistance from public funds, was only one relevant factor among others, to be given the appropriate weight according to the circumstances. In his view *R(IS) 6/96* should not be read as imposing an additional condition that only residence without resort to IS or public assistance was relevant to the *Re J* test.

The approach that whether the claimant's residence in the UK is viable without recourse to public funds is only one factor and not by itself decisive was followed in *CIS/1459/1996* and *CIS/16097/1996*. And in *CIS/4474/2003*, the Commissioner warns against the danger of overemphasising viability as a factor:

> "16. The danger of overemphasising viability is this. A claimant needs to establish habitual residence in order to claim an income-related benefit. A claim would not be necessary if the claimant has a guaranteed source of funds sufficient for survival. The danger is that the only claimants who can establish habitual residence will be those who have sufficient access to funds not to need it. That cannot be right. Habitual residence is a test of entitlement, not a bar to entitlement. It must be applied in a way that allows for the possibility of a claimant establishing both habitual residence and an entitlement to income support."

Habitual residence and EEA nationals

2.295 As explained above, for many EEA nationals, the habitual residence test is irrelevant. If they satisfy the right to reside test, then in most cases they are exempt from the habitual residence test. If they do not satisfy the right to reside test then they are not habitually resident for that reason. But there are a few categories of EEA nationals with the right to reside, in particular those nationals whose only right to reside is as a workseeker, who are not exempt from the habitual residence test and must therefore actually be habitually resident in order to receive benefit.

The habitual residence test differs in its application to some EEA nationals:

- Claimants who have been absent from the UK as migrant workers within the EEA can become habitually resident here immediately on their return and without first living here for an appreciable period of time (see *Swaddling v Adjudication Officer* (C–90/97), reported as *R(IS) 6/99*);
- For EEA workseekers who have not previously worked in the UK, the requirement for an appreciable period of residence must be applied having regard to the principles established in *Collins v Secretary of State for Work and Pensions* ((C–138/02) in the ECJ and [2006] EWCA Civ 376 in the Court of Appeal, both reported as *R(JSA) 3/06*).

Swaddling

2.296 Mr Swaddling was a British national who, until he was 23, had lived and worked in the UK. From 1980–1994 for the majority of the time he worked in France. In late 1994 he was made redundant. After failing to find further employment in France, he returned to the UK in January 1995 to live with his brother and in order to obtain work here. His claim for IS was made on January 9, 1995 (i.e. at a time when IS was a benefit claimed by workseekers as well as those currently entitled) and was refused on the ground that he was not habitually resident in the UK.

The Commissioner held that the appropriate appreciable period in all the circumstances was eight weeks from the date of his return to the UK. Under the terms of purely domestic law the claimant was thus not entitled to income support for the period January 9 through March 3, 1995. The Commissioner rejected an argument put forward by the claimant that under art.10a(2) of Regulation 1408/71 he could rely on his period of residence in France to satisfy the habitual residence condition. The Commissioner decided that art.10a(2) did not assist the claimant since the habitual residence test did not make entitlement to IS subject to completion of a period of employment, self-employment or residence (note that in Regulation 1408/71 "residence" means "habitual residence": art.1(h)) but went to whether habitual residence had been established initially.

But the Commissioner did refer to the ECJ the question whether the application of a habitual residence test (involving the requirement of an appreciable period of residence) to a person who had exercised his right to freedom of movement and had worked and been habitually resident in another Member State and then returned to the UK to seek work infringed art.48 of the Treaty of Rome. It was contended on behalf of the claimant that the test had the effect of deterring a person from exercising his Community rights since he had been made worse off by its application than if he had worked throughout in the UK. For the AO it was submitted that the principle in art.48 did not extend to conditions for acquiring entitlement to a non-contributory benefit like income support.

However, the ECJ did not answer the question as to whether there had been an infringement of art.48 since it considered that the case could be dealt with under Regulation 1408/71. It was accepted that Mr Swaddling was a person covered by Regulation 1408/71 (as an employed person he had been subject to both the British and French social security schemes). Article 10a(1) provides that a person to whom the Regulation applies is to be granted certain special non-contributory benefits (which include IS) in the territory of the Member State in which s/he resides. "Reside" means "habitually reside": art.1(h). The Court stated that, in deciding where a person habitually resided, account had to be taken in particular of his/her family situation; the reasons which had led him/her to move; the length and continuity of his/her residence; the fact (where this was the case) that s/he was in stable employment; and his/her intention as it appeared from all the circumstances. However, the Court also held that the length of residence in the Member State in which payment of benefit was sought could not be regarded as an intrinsic element of the concept of residence within the meaning of art.10a. **2.297**

The result of the ECJ's judgment would thus seem to be that a person covered by Regulation 1408/71 can be habitually resident in a Member State for the purposes of art.10a on the day of arrival if the circumstances as a whole, including the other factors referred to by the Court, lead to that conclusion. The Community meaning of "habitually resident" therefore differs from the interpretation that currently applies in a domestic context.

One question that arises is to whom does the ECJ's judgment apply? Clearly it covers returning British nationals who come within the scope of Regulation 1408/71 and, it is difficult to see how non-British EEA nationals in a similar position could be excluded without breaching art.7 of Regulation 1612/68.

For a detailed discussion of the personal scope of Regulation 1408/71 see *R(IS) 1/06*. The Commissioner in *R(IS) 1/06* also decided that—at least in the circumstances of that case—the habitual residence test did not discriminate against the claimant on the grounds of her nationality contrary to art.12 of the EC Treaty (see Vol.III) because even if that article were otherwise applicable, any discriminatory effect was objectively justified as a way of ensuring that a national of another Member State had a sufficient link to UK society (see also the decision of the ECJ in *R. (on the application of Bidar) v London Borough of Ealing* (C–209/03) [2005] E.C.R. I-2119.

Collins

Where the benefit claimed is JSA and the claimant is an EEA national, the habitual residence test must now be applied in accordance with the decision of the European Court of Justice in *Collins v Secretary of State for Work and Pensions* (C–138/02) [2005] Q.B. 145 (ECJ, March 23, 2004) and the subsequent decisions of Commissioner Mesher in *CJSA/4065/1999* and the Court of Appeal [2006] EWCA Civ 376 (*R(JSA) 3/06*). Mr Collins was born and brought up in the USA and had American citizenship. He spent one semester studying in the UK in 1978 and had also spent 10 months doing part-time and casual work in London between 1980 and 1981. During that period he acquired Irish nationality. Since 1981 he had worked in the US and Africa but had not worked in the UK. In 1998 he returned to the UK for settlement and, on June 8, 1998, claimed JSA while he looked for work. On July 1, 1998 an adjudication officer decided that he was not habitually resident. Mr Collins' appeal against that decision was referred to the ECJ by the **2.298**

Commissioner. The Court held that the work which Mr Collins had done in the UK in 1980 and 1981 was not sufficiently closely connected to the work he was seeking in 1998 for him to have retained his former status as a "worker" and that he therefore was in the same position—from an EU/EEA law point of view—as someone who had never worked in the UK. On that basis the Court held that:

- Mr Collins was not a "worker" for the purposes of Title II of Part I of Regulation 1612/68; and
- Directive 68/630 only accords rights of residence to those already in employment and therefore Mr Collins did not have a right of residence under that provision.

Up to this point, the decision of the Court breaks no new ground. However, in its answer to the third question referred to it, the Court went on to hold that in the light of the establishment (by the Maastricht Treaty) of EU citizenship and of its previous decision in *Grzelczyk v Belgium* (C–184/99) [2005] E.C.R. I-6193, it was no longer possible to exclude from the scope of art.39(2) of the Treaty (now art.45(2) TFEU)—which abolishes discrimination based on nationality between workers of the Member States as regards employment, remuneration and other conditions of work and employment (see Vol.III)—a benefit of a financial nature intended to facilitate access to employment in the labour market of a Member State. As the habitual residence test could more easily be met by UK nationals, it disadvantaged nationals of other Member States who had exercised their rights of movement to seek employment and could only be justified if it was based on objective considerations which were independent of the nationality of the persons concerned and proportionate to the legitimate aim of the national provisions. Although Member States were entitled to ensure that there was a genuine link between the person seeking work and the employment market of that State before granting an allowance such as JSA, and although that link might be determined by the fact that the claimant had genuinely sought work in the Member State in question for a reasonable period, a residence requirement could not, if it was to be proportionate, go beyond what was necessary to obtain the objective of ensuring such a link:

> "More specifically, its application by the national authorities must rest on clear criteria known in advance and provision must be made for the possibility of a means of redress of a judicial nature. In any event, if compliance with the requirement demands a period of residence, the period must not exceed what is necessary in order for the national authorities to be able to satisfy themselves that the person concerned is genuinely seeking work in the employment market of the host Member State."

Mr Collins' appeal therefore returned to the Commissioner to decide the issue of justification in accordance with the ruling of the Court. The Commissioner rejected the submissions of counsel for Mr Collins (which were along similar lines to the views expressed in a previous edition) that the answer to the question of whether the claimant was genuinely seeking work was provided by the satisfaction of the other conditions of entitlement to JSA so that there was no justifiable role left for a habitual residence test, or that, in the alternative, the habitual residence test as established by reg.85 and interpreted by the courts (including the ECJ) did not "rest on clear criteria known in advance" as the ECJ had required. Rather:

> "The application of the residence requirement embodied in the habitual residence test in the JSA legislation and in Article 10a of Regulation 1408/71 is, subject to the proviso mentioned below, justified by objective considerations independent of the nationality of the claimant and proportionate to the legitimate aim in the making of the JSA legislation. The requirement meets the conditions as to proportionality set out in paragraph 72 of the ECJ's judgment in relation to the legitimate aim of establishing that a real or genuine link exists between a

claimant and the UK employment market, such as by being satisfied of the genuineness of the claimant's search for work in that employment market."

The proviso referred to is that if, on any day, the answer to the question "has the point been reached on that day that the relevant national authority has become satisfied of the genuineness of the claimant's search for work [in the sense referred to in the next paragraph]?" is answered yes, the result of the normal habitual residence test can no longer be applied in his case. **2.299**

An important part of the Commissioner's decision is that, for the purpose of assessing whether the habitual residence test is proportional, the genuineness of the claimant's search for work is not established on the basis that s/he satisfies the labour market conditions for entitlement to JSA for a particular week:

> "32. I leave aside for the moment what was said in paragraph 72 of the ECJ's judgment about proportionality, clear criteria and means of redress. The crucial sentence is then this: 'In any event, if compliance with the [residence] requirement demands a period of residence, the period must not exceed what is necessary in order for the national authorities to be able to satisfy themselves that the person concerned is genuinely seeking work in the employment market of the host Member State.'
> 33. First, I have no doubt that that sentence does not have the effect that the sole legitimate question to be asked is whether the claimant was genuinely seeking work on any particular day, in the sense merely of taking active and appropriate steps to seek suitable work. The relevant legitimate aim in making the JSA legislation, as identified by the ECJ, is the wish to ensure that there is a genuine link (or in other words a real link) between the claimant and the UK employment market. That is the aim in relation to which proportionality must be tested.
> 34. Then, paragraph 69 of the judgment spells out that in pursuance of that aim it is legitimate to award benefit only after it has been possible to establish that such a link exists. And it is plainly accepted in paragraphs 69 and 70 that it is legitimate only to accept that there is such a link at any particular date if there has previously been some sufficiently concrete expression of a connection with the UK employment market. It also seems to me that the notion of a genuine link or a real link carries with it a sense that the link has to have some concrete expression. In that context, I conclude that the pivotal part of the final sentence of paragraph 72 is the reference to what period of residence is necessary for the national authorities to be able to satisfy themselves that the claimant is genuinely seeking work. To be consistent with what has been said earlier, it must be legitimate for the national authorities to say that they are not able to satisfy themselves about the genuineness of a search for work until a proper search has continued for some period. A person may actually take steps to search for work on a particular day and actually have on that day an intention to continue to search diligently for suitable vacancies, but national authorities can legitimately say that they have not been satisfied that the search is genuine until they have seen that the search has been sustained, and in a sufficiently diligent and well directed form, for some period. The condition of proportionality laid down by the final sentence of paragraph 72 is thus that a residence requirement, in principle appropriate, cannot be applied to deny entitlement to benefit beyond the date at which the relevant national authority has become satisfied of the genuineness of the claimant's search for work."

Applying those principles to Mr Collins' appeal the Commissioner held that Mr Collins had not been habitually resident from June 8, 1998 to July 1, 1998 and, on the assumption that *R(IS) 7/06* was correctly decided (as to which see the commentary under the heading *"Habitual residence" and "down to the date of decision"*' below), would not have become so by July 31, 1998, shortly after which, Mr Collins found work.

The Court of Appeal dismissed Mr Collins' appeal against the Commissioner's decision. The reasoning of Jonathan Parker LJ, who gave the judgment of the court, **2.300** mirrors that of the Commissioner except in relation to the proviso referred to above. On that point, he stated:

> "86. The effect of the Commissioner's proviso, as I understand it, is that although the habitual residence test is to be applied in the ordinary way, it cannot be justified as laying down the sole test for establishing the existence of the requisite 'genuine link' between an applicant for JSA and the UK market; so that if the decision-maker can be satisfied on other grounds that such a link has been established, then the habitual residence requirement must fall away.
> 87. With respect to the Commissioner, I cannot see any basis in Community law for the introduction of such a proviso. Certainly, as I read the ECJ's judgments in this case and in *Swaddling*, there is nothing in those judgments which suggests the need for such a proviso. In my judgment the correct analysis is that under Community law it is a matter for the national legislature whether to require the existence of a 'genuine link' and (if so) to prescribe how that link may be established; and that the prescription of a habitual residence test for that purpose is both legitimate and justified. Had the ECJ taken a contrary view, I would have expected it to say so: the more so because, as I have already pointed out (see paragraph 81 above), the discussion which follows paragraph 66 of its judgment is clearly directed specifically at the habitual residence requirement prescribed by regulation 85(4), rather at the general concept of a residence requirement.
> 88. Accordingly I respectfully conclude that the Commissioner was in error in concluding that in order to render the habitual residence requirement compatible with Community law it was necessary to introduce the proviso in question; and that on the proper interpretation of the ECJ's judgment in this case a habitual residence test *simpliciter* as a means of establishing the requisite 'genuine link' between an applicant for JSA and the UK employment market is fully compatible with Community law."

The problem faced by decision makers and tribunals who must apply the Court of Appeal's approach (and the problem that the Commissioner's proviso was intended to help them address) is that the length of an appreciable period of time is a question of judgment to be made taking into account all the circumstances of the individual case. If the purpose of the test as applied to EEA nationals is that a Member State is entitled to require a genuine link between the person seeking work and its employment market before granting an allowance such as JSA, then whether or not a link has been forged must be a circumstance to be taken into account when fixing the length of the appreciable period. The question that divides the Court of Appeal and the Commissioner is whether it is possible to decide in an individual case that the genuine link exists but that the claimant has nevertheless not been resident for an appreciable period of time, and is therefore not habitually resident. On the approach required by the Court of Appeal such a decision is at least theoretically possible because the habitual residence test *simpliciter* satisfies EU law. However, it is difficult to think of circumstances in which such a decision would in fact be appropriate. If a genuine link with the UK employment market exists in an individual case, that is likely to be a compelling factor in favour of the conclusion that the claimant has been present for an appreciable period of time and has become habitually resident in the UK. On that basis, there is little practical difference between the approaches of the Court of Appeal and the Commissioner and the Commissioner's proviso, though not part of the legal test in the light of the Court of Appeal's decision, is a useful reminder to tribunals of the importance of the existence of the genuine link with the UK employment market as a factor in habitual residence decisions involving UK nationals.

The additional "three-months" requirement for jobseeker's allowance

2.301 From January 1, 2014, reg.85A of the Jobseeker's Allowance Regulations 1996 was amended to provide (in para.(2)(a)) that no claimant shall be treated as habitually resident in the United Kingdom, the Channel Islands, the Isle of Man or the

Republic of Ireland unless s/he has been living in any of those places for the past three months. That "three-months" requirement was subsequently applied to child benefit and child tax credit with effect from July 1, 2014 by the Child Benefit (General) and the Tax Credits (Residence) (Amendment) Regulations 2014 (SI 2014/1511), subject to a number of exceptions: see further Vol.IV. For those affected, the requirement applies even if they have a right of residence and would satisfy the habitual residence test on the "settled intention" and "appreciable period of time" tests.

Not all those claiming JSA are affected. Although the drafting could be clearer—and, in particular, could say in as many words that reg.85A(2) is subject to reg.85A(4)—that is the effect of the regulation taken as a whole. It is categorically stated that a person who falls within para.(4) "is not a person from abroad". Under para.(1), the habitual residence test is a mechanism for determining whether a person is a "person from abroad". There is therefore no need to apply it in cases where it is known that the person is not a person from abroad because para.(4) says so. The "three-months" and right to reside tests are part of the habitual residence test and are therefore subject to para.(4) for the same reason.

The three-month requirement is that the claimant must have been "living in" the Common Travel Area for "the past three months". The use of "living in" rather than "residing in" suggests a factual rather than legal test. A JSA claimant who has in fact been living in the UK for the past three months (and who has become habitually resident as a mater of fact) but who only acquired a right of residence on the day when he first claims JSA appears to satisfy the test.

"Living in" is also to be distinguished from "present in". Whether a period of absence abroad has the effect that the claimant is no longer "living in" the CTA on his/her return will be a question of fact for decision makers and tribunals to decide taking into account all the circumstances of the case. **2.302**

It is only necessary for the claimant to have been living in the CTA for three months. It is not a requirement that s/he should have been seeking work during that period. The fact that the three-month period is not connected in any way with the employment market is likely to raise issues of EU law (see below).

The requirement is not that the claimant should have been living in the CTA for an *initial* period of three months, but rather that s/he should have been so living for *the past* three months. In other words the test is continuous. However long the claimant may have been living in the CTA, if at any time it can be said that s/he has not been doing so for the past three months, then s/he ceases to be habitually resident and becomes a person from abroad. Even a very brief period during which the claimant is not "living in" the CTA means that s/he must live here for a further period of three months before becoming entitled to benefit again. However, note the transitional protection in reg.3 of SI 2013/2196 (reproduced later in this volume) under which the three-months test does not apply "in relation to a claim for a jobseeker's allowance which is made or treated as made before" January 1, 2014.

The three-months test affects JSA claimants of all nationalities—including British citizens—unless they are exempt under para.(4). However, issues arise in its application to EEA nationals who have exercised their rights to freedom of movement. **2.303**

In the particular case of returning residents, it is difficult to reconcile the test with EU law as established in *Swaddling* (above). The ECJ in that case stated that the length of residence in the Member State in which payment of benefit was sought could *not* be regarded as an intrinsic element of habitual residence.

More generally, it will have to be decided whether the "habitual residence test *simpliciter*" continues to comply with EU law—as it was previously held to do in *Collins*—now that it effectively includes inflexible rules that a genuine link with the UK employment market cannot be established without having lived in the UK for at least three months and that, once established, such a link is invariably lost by ceasing to live in the UK.

Habitual residence and "down to the date of decision"

2.304 Until May 23, 2007, it was possible to make an advance award of benefit where the a claimant failed the habitual residence test because s/he had not been resident for an appreciable period of time by the date of the Secretary of State's decision, but it was likely that habitual residence would be established within three months (see *Secretary of State for Work and Pensions v Bhakta* [2006] EWCA Civ 65, reported as *R(IS) 7/06*).

However, the *Bhakta* case has now been reversed by legislation. For the position where the Secretary of State's decision was made before May 23, 2007, see pp.317–318 of Vol.II of the 2007 edition.

[1 Treatment of refugees

2.305 [2 **21ZB.**—[1. . .]]

AMENDMENTS

1. Asylum and Immigration (Treatment of Claimants, etc.) Act 2004 (c.19) s.12(2)(a)(i) (June 14, 2007).
2. Social Security (Immigration and Asylum) Consequential Amendments Regulations 2000 (SI 2000/636) reg.3 (5) (April 3, 2000).
3. Social Security (Working Tax Credit and Child Tax Credit) (Consequential Amendments) Regulations 2003 (SI 2003/455) reg.2 and Sch.1 para.5 (April 6, 2004), except in "transitional cases" and see further the note to reg.17 of the Income Support Regulations.

GENERAL NOTE

2.306 Backdated payments of income support to refugees under reg.21ZB and the former s.123 of the Immigration and Asylum Act 1999 have been abolished and replaced with discretionary "refugee integration loans" under s.13 of the Asylum and Immigration (Treatment of Claimants, etc.) Act 2004 (c.19) and the Integration Loans for Refugees and Others Regulations 2007 (SI 2007/1598).

By art.2(3) of the Asylum and Immigration (Treatment of Claimants, etc.) Act 2004 (Commencement No.7 and Transitional Provisions) Order 2007 (SI 2007/1602), the revocation of reg.21ZB "shall not apply to a person who is recorded as a refugee on or before 14th June 2007". For those purposes a person is recorded as a refugee on the day on which the Home Secretary notifies him that he has been recognised as a refugee and granted asylum in the UK (see art.2(4)).

For the text of, and commentary on, the former reg.21ZB see pp.318-320 of Vol. II of the 2007 edition. Note that *Tkachuk v Secretary of State for Work and Pensions* (which is referred to in that commentary) has now been reported as *R(IS) 3/07*.

2.307 The revocation of reg.21ZB did not offend against EU law or infringe the ECHR. Article 28 of Directive 2004/83/EC (the "Qualification Directive") does not require the UK to provide income support to a refugee for the period prior to the decision recognising refugee status even once such a decision has been made, and if the removal of the backdating rule did discriminate against the appellant (pursuant to art.14 of the European Convention on Human Rights when read with art.1 of the First Protocol to that Convention) it is justified: see the decision of the Court of Appeal in *Blakesley v Secretary of State for Work and Pensions* [2015] EWCA Civ 141, [2015] AACR 17, upholding the decision of the three-judge panel of the Upper Tribunal in *HB v Secretary of State for Work and Pensions (IS)* [2013] UKUT 433 (AAC).

No provision equivalent to reg.21ZB was ever made in relation to SPC. The effect was that between October 6, 2003 and June 13, 2007 backdated benefit was available to refugees under the age of 60 but not to those who were 60 or over (60 being the qualifying age for SPC at the time). In *CPC/3396/2006*, the Commissioner held that, even if that situation amounted to unlawful discrimination on the grounds of age contrary to art.14 ECHR (and no ruling was made on that point), the Human Rights Act 1998 did not permit him to remedy that discrimination.

[[1]Reductions in applicable amounts in certain cases of failure to attend courses 2.308

21A.—[[2] . .].]

AMENDMENTS

1. Income Support (General and Transitional) Amendment Regulations 1990 (SI 1990/2324) reg.3 (December 17, 1990).
2. Income Support (General) (Jobseeker's Allowance Consequential Amendments) Regulations 1996 (SI 1996/206) reg.28 and Sch.3 (October 7, 1996).

[Reductions in applicable amounts in certain cases of actual or notional unemployment benefit disqualification

22.—[[1]. . .] 2.309

AMENDMENT

1. Income Support (General) (Jobseeker's Allowance Consequential Amendments) Regulations 1996 (SI 1996/206) reg.28 and Sch.3 (October 7, 1996).

[[1]Reduction in applicable amount where the claimant is appealing against a decision [[2] which embodies a determination] that he is not incapable of work

22A.—(1) Subject to paragraph (3), where a claimant falls within paragraph 25 of Schedule 1B (persons appealing against a decision [[2]which embodies a determination] that they are not incapable of work under the [[3]personal capability assessment]), and none of the other paragraphs of that Schedule applies to him, his applicable amount shall be reduced by a sum equivalent to 20 per cent, of the following amount— 2.310

(a) in the case of a person to whom regulation 17 or 18 or paragraphs 6, 9 to 12 [[6] . . .] of Schedule 7 applies—
 (i) where he is a single claimant aged less than 18 or a member of a couple or a polygamous marriage where all the members, in either case, are less than 18, the amount specified in paragraph 1(1)(a), (b) or (c), as the case may be, of Schedule 2 (applicable amounts);
 (ii) where he is a single claimant aged not less than 18 but less than 25 or a member of a couple or a polygamous marriage where one member is aged not less than 18 but less than 25 and the other member, or in the case of a polygamous marriage each other member, is a person under 18 who—
  (aa) does not qualify for income support under regulation 4ZA, or who would not so qualify if he were to make a claim; and
  (bb) does not satisfy the requirements of section 3(1)(f)(iii) of the Jobseekers Act 1995 (prescribed circumstances for persons aged 16 but less than 18); and
  (cc) is not the subject of a direction under section 16 of the Jobseekers Act 1995 (persons under 18: severe hardship),
 the amount specified in paragraph 1(1)(d) of that Schedule;
 (iii) where he is a single claimant aged not less than 25 or a member of a couple or a polygamous marriage (other than a member of a couple or a polygamous marriage to whom head (ii) of this sub-paragraph applies) at least one of whom is aged not less than 18, the amount specified in paragraph 1(1)(e) of that Schedule;

(b) [5. . .].

(2) A reduction under paragraph (1) shall, if it is not a multiple of 5p, be rounded to the nearest such multiple or, if it is a multiple of 2.5p but not of 5p, to the next lower multiple of 5p.

(3) Paragraph (1) shall not apply to a claimant who is appealing against a decision [2which embodies a determination] that he is not incapable of work under the [3personal capability assessment] where that [2determination] was [4the first determination made in accordance with, the all work test before 3rd April 2000 or, after that date, the personal capability assessment, in relation to the claimant], and the claimant was, immediately prior to 13th April 1995, either—

(a) in receipt of invalidity pension under Part II of the Contributions and Benefits Act as then in force, or severe disablement allowance; or

(b) incapable of work in accordance with paragraph 5 of Schedule 1 as in force on 12th April 1995 and had been so for a continuous period of 28 weeks.]

AMENDMENTS

1. Income Support (General) (Jobseeker's Allowance Consequential Amendments) Regulations 1996 (SI 1996/206) reg.13 (October 7, 1996).

2. Social Security Act 1998 (Commencement No.9 and Savings and Consequential and Transitional Provisions) Order 1999 (SI 1999/2422 (C.61)) art.3(7) and Sch.6 para.1 (September 6, 1999).

3. Social Security (Incapacity for Work) Miscellaneous Amendments Regulations 1999 (SI 1999/3109) reg.6 (April 3, 2000).

4. Social Security (Incapacity) Miscellaneous Amendments Regulations 2000 (SI 2000/590) reg.5 (April 3, 2000).

5. Social Security Amendment (Residential Care and Nursing Homes) Regulations 2001 (SI 2001/3767) reg.2(1) and Pt I of Sch. para.7 (April 8, 2002).

6. Social Security (Miscellaneous Amendments) (No.5) Regulations 2007 (SI 2007/2618) reg.5(4) (October 1, 2007).

DEFINITION

"personal capability assessment"—SSCBA s.171C and Incapacity for Work Regulations reg.24.

GENERAL NOTE

2.311 This regulation is no longer of any practical application because it relates to the old incapacity for work regime. However, it has not been formally revoked and so is being retained, together with the note to it.

Paragraphs (1) and (2) of this regulation replace the provisions formerly in regs 8(2A) and 22 (now revoked). Paragraph (3) repeats the transitional protection in reg.19(5) of the Disability Working Allowance and Income Support (General) Amendment Regulations 1995 (see p.801).

The regulation applies where a claimant is appealing against a decision that he is fit for work on the basis of the "personal capability assessment" (which replaced the "all work test" from April 3, 2000) and so is eligible for income support under para.25 of Sch.1B (and does not qualify under any of the other paragraphs in Sch.1B). See the 2010/11 edition of Vol.I of this series for full details of the personal capability assessment and when it applies. A claimant will be eligible for income support under para.25 until the appeal is determined (which means the final determination of the appeal, e.g. if it is taken to the Social Security Commissioner (now Upper Tribunal), confirmed in *CIS 2654/1999*, see further the notes to para.25 of Sch.1B). However, his income support will be reduced by

20 per cent of the appropriate personal allowance for a single claimant of his age (para.(1)). If the appeal is successful the reduction will be repaid—see further the note to paras 24–25 of Sch.1B. (Paragraph (3) allowed full income support to be paid where the claimant had appealed after failing his first all work test or personal capability assessment if he had been incapable of work for 28 weeks or in receipt of invalidity benefit or severe disablement allowance immediately before April 13, 1995. Note also reg.27(3) of the Income Support (General) (Jobseeker's Allowance Consequential Amendments) Regulations 1996 which provided for the reduction under para.(1) not to apply to people covered by reg.19(5) of the Disability Working Allowance and Income Support (General) Amendment Regulations 1995 as originally made (see the notes to reg.19(5) and (6) of those Regulations).)

In order to receive full benefit the person will have to sign on as available for work and claim JSA while waiting for his appeal to be decided (or after the introduction of ESA on October 27, 2008 he could consider claiming ESA). The fact that a person has been available for employment will not prejudice the appeal about incapacity as it will be a change of circumstances that has occurred after the date of decision under appeal (s.12(8)(b), SSA 1998). See further the notes to para.25 of Sch.1B.

In *Smyth* (High Court of Northern Ireland, July 6, 2001) it was argued that the **2.312**
reduction under the equivalent Northern Ireland provision to para.(1) constituted "an impermissible clog" on the exercise of the right to appeal and was therefore a violation of art.6 of the European Convention on Human Rights. However, this was rejected by Kerr J. In his view, the reduction was "a proportionate means of discouraging unmeritorious or frivolous appeals" and was not such a disincentive that it destroyed the essence of the right to appeal. He considered that a claimant's art.6 rights were "sufficiently safeguarded by the existence of the right of appeal, the availability of income support (albeit at a reduced level) while the appeal is pending, and the backdated repayment of the full amount on a successful outcome for the appeal".

Note that following the introduction of ESA on October 27, 2008 most *new* claims for benefit on the basis of incapacity for work made on or after that date will be treated as claims for ESA. See further the note to para.7 of Sch.1B in the 2015/16 edition of this volume.

[1 Period for which applicable amount is to be calculated where person not excluded from income support under section 115 of the Immigration and Asylum Act 1999

22B.—[2 . . .]] **2.313**

AMENDMENTS

1. Social Security (Miscellaneous Amendments) (No.5) Regulations 2009 (SI 2009/3228) reg.3(2)(c) (January 25, 2010).
2. Social Security (Miscellaneous Amendments) (No.3) Regulations 2013 (SI 2013/2536) reg.4(1) and (6) (October 29, 2013).

GENERAL NOTE

Until its revocation, reg.22B (taken together with reg.2 of, and para.1 of Pt 1 **2.314**
of the Schedule to, the Social Security (Immigration and Asylum) Consequential Amendments Regulations 2000 (SI 2000/636), which was also revoked with effect from October 29, 2009) allowed claimants with limited leave to enter or remain in the UK subject to a condition that they do not have recourse to public funds, to receive income support in some circumstances where they were temporarily without funds because remittances to them from abroad had been disrupted. Such people would otherwise have been—and are now—excluded from benefit under s.115 of the Immigration and Asylum Act 1999 as persons subject to immigration control.

For commentary on the law as it stood before October 29, 2013, see pp.375, 800–801 and 809–810 of Vol.II of the 2013/14 edition.

PART V

INCOME AND CAPITAL

Chapter I

General

Calculation of income and capital of members of claimant's family and of a polygamous marriage

2.315 **23.**—(1) [3Subject to paragraph (4), the income and capital of a claimant's partner which by virtue of section 136(1) of the Contributions and Benefits Act] is to be treated as income and capital of the claimant, shall be calculated in accordance with the following provisions of this Part in like manner as for the claimant; and any reference to the "claimant" shall, except where the context otherwise requires, be construed, for the purposes of this Part, as if it were a reference to his partner [3. . .].

[3(2) Subject to the following provisions of this Part, the income paid to, or in respect of, and capital of, a child or young person who is a member of the claimant's family shall not be treated as the income or capital of the claimant.]

(3) [1Subject to paragraph (5)] where a claimant or the partner of a claimant is married polygamously to two or more members of his household—

(a) the claimant shall be treated as possessing capital and income belonging to each such member [3. . .]; and

(b) the income and capital of that member [3. . .] shall be calculated in accordance with the following provisions of this Part in like manner as for the claimant [3. . .].

[1(4) Where at least one member of a couple is aged less than 18 and the applicable amount of the couple falls to be determined under [2paragraphs 1(3)(b), (c), (f) or (g)] of Schedule 2 (applicable amounts), the income of the claimant's partner shall not be treated as the income of the claimant to the extent that—

(a) in the case of a couple where both members are aged less than 18, the amount specified in paragraph 1(3)(a) of that Schedule exceeds the amount specified in [2paragraph 1(3)(c)] of that Schedule; and

(b) in the case of a couple where only one member is aged less than 18, the amount specified in paragraph 1(3)(d) of that Schedule exceeds the amount which applies in that case which is specified in [2paragraph 1(3)(f) or (g)] of that Schedule.

(5) Where a member of a polygamous marriage is a partner aged less than 18 and the amount which applies in respect of him under regulation 18(2) (polygamous marriages) is nil, the claimant shall not be treated as possessing the income of that partner to the extent that an amount in respect of him would have been included in the applicable amount if he had fallen within the circumstances set out in regulation 18(2)(a) or (b).]

AMENDMENTS

1. Income Support (General) Amendment No.3 Regulations 1988 (SI 1988/1228) reg.6 (September 12, 1988).

2. Income Support (General) (Jobseeker's Allowance Consequential Amendments) Regulations 1996 (SI 1996/206) reg.14 (October 7, 1996).
3. Social Security (Working Tax Credit and Child Tax Credit) (Consequential Amendments) Regulations 2003 (SI 2003/455) reg.2 and Sch.1 para.6 (April 6, 2004, except in "transitional cases" and see further the note to reg.17 of the Income Support Regulations).

DEFINITIONS

"child"—see SSCBA s.137(1).
"claimant"—see reg.2(1).
"family"—see SSCBA s.137(1).
"partner"—see reg.2(1).
"polygamous marriage"—*ibid.*
"young person"—*ibid.*, and reg.14.

GENERAL NOTE

Distinction between capital and income

Resources are to be either capital or income. There is nothing in between. On this see *R(IS) 9/08* below, which also confirms that advance payments (in that case made by a local authority to a foster parent) could not be taken into account, as either income or capital, before the period to which they related. 2.316

The distinction between capital and income is one which has given a good deal of trouble in the past, and in many other legal contexts. There is no attempt at any general definition in the Regulations, although see regs 35, 41 and 48. The approach tends to be that around the borderlines a decision can go either way, and it is only if a decision is completely unreasonable that it embodies an error of law (*R. v W. London SBAT Ex p. Taylor* [1975] 2 All E. R. 790). But ultimately the question is one of law (see *Lillystone v SBC* [1982] 3 F.L.R. 52, CA). However, note *CIS 2537/1997* in which the Commissioner queries whether the question is one of law. He points to *Gallagher v Jones* [1994] Ch. 107, CA and *Herbert Smith v Honour* [1999] S.T.C. 173 as authority for the proposition that for income tax and similar purposes the principal guide to whether something is income or capital is by reference to accounting principles. See also *CIS 5481/1997* below.

So far as general principle goes it has been said that the "essential feature of receipts by way of income is that they display an element of periodic recurrence. Income cannot include ad hoc receipts." (Bridge J in *R. v Supplementary Benefits Commission Ex p. Singer* [1973] 1 W.L.R. 713). This links the notion of recurrence (which may only be expected in the future) with the notion of a period to which the income is linked. Similar notions are applied by the Commissioner in *R(SB) 29/85* where the issue was the proper treatment of a £15 loan made to a striking miner by a local authority Social Work Department to meet arrears on hire purchase agreements. The Commissioner holds that this was a capital payment, since it was a "one-off" advance and there was no evidence that it was one of a series of payments. Earlier he had referred to income payments normally bearing a readily identifiable relationship with a period. However, periodic recurrence alone is not enough. The nature of the obligation (if any) under which a payment is made must be looked at. As the Court of Appeal put it in *Minter v Kingston Upon Hull CC* and *Potter v Secretary of State for Work and Pensions* [2011] EWCA Civ 1155; [2012] AACR 21, the "first task is to determine the true characteristics of the payment in the hands of the recipient" (see *R. v National Insurance Commissioner Ex p. Stratton* [1979] I.C.R. 209). In determining the true characteristic of the payment (i.e. its substantive nature and purpose), the label that the parties attach to it is irrelevant.

A capital payment may be made by instalments. Then in general each instalment is a capital payment, so that reg.41 is necessary. The general rule is supported by the Court of Appeal in *Lillystone v SBC* where the purchase price of a house was to be paid in monthly instalments over 10 years. It was agreed that each £70 instalment, when it was paid, was capital, not income. 2.317

See also *CIS 5481/1997* which concerned the assets of a business partnership. The Commissioner emphasised that some of the assets would be income, not capital; the distinction was to be drawn in accordance with accounting practice. This provided that the key principle was what the expenditure was calculated to effect from a practical and business point of view, and the same also applied to receipts (see *CIR v Wattie* [1998] S.T.C. 1160).

A similar approach was taken by the Court of Appeal in *Morrell v Secretary of State for Work and Pensions* [2003] EWCA Civ 526, reported as *R(IS) 6/03*. Following her divorce, the claimant had been receiving regular sums of money from her mother, either paid to her to help her pay her rent and other living expenses, or paid directly to her landlord in respect of her rent. It was not in dispute that the payments were made to the claimant by way of loan, although the repayment terms were quite vague, the mother merely expecting reimbursement gradually as her daughter's problems decreased. The claimant argued that because the payments made by her mother were a loan, they were not income payments but should have been treated as capital. However, the Court rejected this argument. Referring to *Chief Adjudication Officer v Leeves*, CA, reported as *R(IS) 5/99* (see the note to reg.40), it said that the word "income" was to be given its ordinary and natural meaning. There was no general principle (in tax cases or elsewhere) that loans should be treated as capital rather than income. (On this see also *R(H) 8/08*.) The regular monthly receipts from her mother clearly had the character of income. The Court agreed with *Leeves* that a sum received under a certain and immediate obligation to repay did not amount to income. However, there was no such obligation in this case and so the payments counted as income.

2.318 See also *KW v Lancaster CC & SSWP (HB)* [2011] UKUT 266 (AAC) in which a large payment of arrears of child support accrued over many years was income, not capital.

DN v Leicester CC (HB) [2010] UKUT 253 (AAC) discusses the nature of annuity payments. In that case the claimant's annual annuity payment, which was derived from a personal pension plan and was subject to income tax, counted as income to be attributed over the whole year. In any event, however, reg.41(2) of the Housing Benefit Regulations 2006 (which is in the same terms as reg.41(2)) was there to ensure that all annuity payments, whatever their complexion, were taken into account as income.

In *EM v LB Waltham Forest* [2009] UKUT 245 (AAC) the issue was whether the two payments that the claimant had received for resolution of a potential claim against his employer under the Part-time Workers (Prevention of Less Favourable Treatment) Regulations 2000 (SI 2000/1551) ("the PTWR 2000") were capital or income for the purposes of his housing benefit claim. It had been contended that the payments were income by way of earnings in the form of arrears of bonus payments. The payments had been calculated on the basis of the weekly bonus payments that the claimant would have received over a three year period had the provisions governing full-time drivers been applied to part-time drivers by his employer; moreover the payments had been treated as income for PAYE purposes. Judge Wikeley concluded, however, that the payments were capital. He did not attach much weight to the way the payments had been treated for tax purposes (it was unclear if any thought had been given to this matter), nor did the method of calculation of the payments prevent them from being capital payments by way of settlement for a breach of the PTWR 2000. Had the matter gone to an employment tribunal there was no guarantee that the amount awarded would have been based simply on the bonus payments that had been denied, since the ultimate criterion under the PTWR 2000 was "just and equitable" compensation. On that basis this case could be distinguished from *CIS/590/1993* (see the notes to reg.35(1)) where the compensation was directly referable to a loss of earnings caused by an act of sex discrimination; in addition the payment in that case covered only five weeks, not three years. Furthermore, the claimant had no absolute contractual right to the bonus payments under the PTWR 2000 because the PTWR 2000 did not operate by way of implying a statutory term into his contract that he was automatically entitled to all the benefits enjoyed by full-time workers (contrast the position under the equal pay legislation). Finally, although there was no actual litigation, there had been a long-running dispute over this issue and the claimant had signed a compromise agreement. The consequence was that the correct analysis was that the two payments were by way of settlement of a potential (and highly probable) legal liability under the PTWR 2000 and counted as capital.

SSWP v JP (JSA) [2010] UKUT 90 (AAC), on the other hand, concerned a payment made as part of an offer of settlement under the Equal Pay Act 1970. The claimant's employer paid her 10 per cent of the offer on the basis that if she accepted the offer she would be paid the remaining 90 per cent, but if she did not, she could retain the 10 per cent but it would be treated as paid on account of any award that might be made by an employment tribunal. The claimant kept the payment but did not sign the agreement. Judge Jacobs states that under social security caselaw the classification of a payment depends on what the payment is made for. Is it for loss of a capital asset, such as a job or a right to bring proceedings, or is it for loss of income, past or future? The essence of any claim by the claimant would be for the amount she would have been paid if her employer had honoured the equality clause that was part of her contract of employment by virtue of the Equal Pay Act. The fact that these earnings would be paid later and as a lump sum did not change their essential nature. This was in contrast to the nature of the award in a part-time workers case, as analysed in *EM v LB Waltham Forest*. And if the payment awarded by an employment tribunal would be income, so must a payment on account of that award. **2.319**

Kingston upon Hull CC v DLM (HB) [2010] UKUT 234 (AAC) also concerned a compensation payment received by the claimant in settlement of a potential equal pay claim. The actual sum had been calculated using average comparators over the period when the claimant had been paid less than she should have been paid. Judge Howell decides that the payment was clearly earnings (agreeing with *SSWP v JP* on this point). He disagreed, however, with the distinction endorsed in that case that had been made in *EM v LB Waltham Forest* between equal pay settlements and those under the Part-time Workers (Prevention of Less Favourable Treatment) Regulations 2000. In Judge Howell's view there was no material distinction between the two types of payment as both were "catch-up redress for past failure to recognise the existence of claims to equal treatment in the matter of remuneration". Thus both counted as income.

The claimants in *SSWP v JP* and *Kingston upon Hull CC v DLM* appealed to the Court of Appeal. However, their appeals were dismissed in *Minter v Kingston Upon Hull CC* and *Potter v Secretary of State for Work and Pensions* [2011] EWCA Civ 1155; [2012] AACR 21. Thomas LJ, who gave the judgment of the court, stated that the first task was "to determine the true characteristic of the payment in the hands of the recipient" (see *R. v National Insurance Commissioner Ex p. Stratton* [1979] I.C.R. 209). In determining the true characteristic of the payment, the label that the parties attach to it is irrelevant. Nor does it matter whether the payment is made as a lump sum or as a series of periodic payments. The size of the payment is also irrelevant, as is the fact that the sum may have accumulated over a prolonged period. The payments that the two claimants had received were compensation for the lower wages that had been paid in breach of equal pay provisions and as such were compensation for past lost income. Since the payments were payments of income that should have been paid as wages, they fell to be treated as earnings. Note that the Court was referred to the decision in *EM v LB Waltham Forest* but did not find it necessary to pass comment on it.

The metamorphosis of income into capital

In *R(SB) 2/83* the Tribunal of Commissioners says "In most cases capital resources arise out of income resources. They represent savings out of past earnings. However, before they undergo the metamorphosis from income to capital all relevant debts, including, in particular, tax liabilities, are first deducted." In *R(SB) 35/83* the Commissioner holds that accumulated earnings will not become capital until all relevant liabilities are deducted. Since the "relevant liabilities" seems to mean the deductions appropriate under the benefit legislation, presumably it is only the categories mentioned in reg.36(3), if not already deducted, which can be **2.320** considered, plus, it seems, expenses necessarily incurred in obtaining the earnings (*R(FC) 1/90* and *R(IS) 16/93*—see the note to reg.36(3)). *CIS 563/1991* decides that such expenses are not deductible in the case of income other than earnings (see the note to reg.40(1)). There is no provision for deducting amounts which are to be used for ordinary current expenditure (*R(IS) 3/93*).

R(IS) 3/93 also confirms that a payment does not metamorphose into capital until the end of the period to which it is attributed as income. Thus, for example, payment of a month's salary, attributable for a forward period of a month from the date it was due to be paid, would retain its character as income until the end of that period. This principle should apply to other forms of income as it does to earnings. Thus if, for instance, arrears of a social security benefit are paid, then any amount of those arrears left after the end of the period to which the benefit is properly attributed as income comes into the category of capital. *R(SB) 4/89*, holding arrears of special hardship allowance to be income, did not deal with this point.

However, in *CIS/515/2006* the Commissioner takes a rather different approach. He rejects the proposition that saved benefit left over at the end of each month becomes capital. He considered that a longer view had to be taken, possibly by looking at the situation after a year in line with the position of arrears of benefit (see further below). In his view if income accumulates in an account for a specific reason (e.g. saving for a trip abroad) it would not be capital. Although, if it accumulates from one year to the next and the claimant has no specific plans to spend it, it will at some point become capital. At what point is a question of fact. The Commissioner also considered that the type of account into which the money was paid was relevant. If it was paid into an account from which it could not be withdrawn without a penalty in the short term, it could become capital on payment in. The Commissioner further accepted the Secretary of State's submission that arrears of benefit did not become capital until 52 weeks after payment. This was on the basis that para.7(1) of Sch.10 provides that arrears or concessionary payments of benefit are excluded from capital for 52 weeks from receipt. However, with respect, this appears to conflate the issue of whether an item is capital or not with the separate question of whether it is disregarded as capital under any of the provisions in Sch.10. The fact that arrears of benefit are ignored as capital for 52 weeks from receipt does not mean that they cannot be capital for any of that period; if this was the case there would be nothing for para.7(1) of Sch.10 to bite on. (As *CH/1561/2005* states, the fact that arrears (in that case of working families' tax credit) are paid late and in a lump sum does not change the nature of the payment from being one of income, to be taken into account over the period that the payment would have been received if it had been paid on time; however at the end of the week to which the payment relates each payment then metamorphoses into capital and the capital disregard of arrears of benefit applies.) Furthermore, the Commissioner's approach in *CIS/515/2006* to accumulated income raises difficulties. If income that is being saved for a specific purpose retains its character as income, how is that income to be treated? Take the example of incapacity benefit. Since it will have already been taken into account under the rules for attribution of income other than earnings in regs 29 and 31, it would clearly be unfair for it to be taken into account over a further period. Yet there is no provision in Sch.9 for ignoring such saved "income"—since savings are traditionally taken into account as capital. The root of the problem, which was perhaps the issue that the Commissioner was attempting to address, is that it is only liabilities that are secured on capital that can be deducted; there is no provision for deducting, for example, money that is being saved for future bills.

2.321 The conflict between *R(IS) 3/93* and *CIS/515/2006* was considered in *R(IS) 9/08*. The Commissioner states:

> "I prefer the authority of *R(IS) 3/93* for these reasons. First, it is a reported decision, which shows that the majority of the Commissioners at the time considered that it was at least broadly correct. Second, I consider that its reasoning is sound. Given that a resource has to be either income or capital, it must become capital

when it is no longer income. Mr Williams did not deal with that point. Third and particularly relevant to this case, the income support legislation failed to carry forward an express provision in supplementary benefit law that disregarded savings made out of income in order to meet personal living expenses and the expenses of the home. (It is quoted in *R(IS) 3/93* at paragraph 24.) Income support replaced supplementary benefit in April 1988 and was, of course, a new benefit. However, there is sufficient continuity in the income and capital provisions of the two schemes to make it significant that no equivalent disregard was adopted in income support. Fourth, the approach in *CIS/515/2006* draws on the Commissioner's experience in business and tax. In those contexts, it may be appropriate to identify capital on an annual basis. However, income support is a weekly benefit and a much shorter timescale is appropriate. The timescale fixed by *R(IS) 3/93* is consistent with the allocation of income to a particular period."

But note that the "metamorphosis" principle does not apply to self-employed earnings, as held by the Commissioner in *CIS/2467/2003* (although he confirmed that it did apply to income other than earnings, such as incapacity benefit and disability living allowance which were in issue in that case, as well as earnings from employment). This was because the calculation of earnings from self-employment did not turn on when particular receipts came in but was, under reg.30(1), to be calculated as average weekly earnings (net profit, subject to deductions for income tax and social security) over a period of normally a year. Those average weekly earnings are then taken into account for income support purposes for an equivalent period into the future. There was therefore no period of attribution to be attached to any particular business receipt and the basis of the *R(IS) 3/93* principle did not exist. In the Commissioner's view it would be artificial and wrong to regard all business receipts as retaining the character of income until the expiry of the period for which earnings calculated over the whole period were taken into account. Instead the protection for self-employed earners in relation to the capital rules lay in the disregard of the value of business assets under para.6 of Sch.10. The Commissioner also held that the *R(IS) 3/93* principle did not apply to self-employed earnings covered by the special attribution rule in reg.30(2) (royalties, etc.). The claimant in *CIS/2467/2003* was a self-employed author who received advances on contracting to write a book and subsequent royalties on sales. His claim for income support was refused on the ground that he had capital in excess of the prescribed limit. The Commissioner rejected his argument that money paid by way of advances was not legally owned by him because the advances were repayable if he did not fulfill the contract. In his view the advances fully belonged to the claimant as soon as they were received. The Commissioner further concluded that the claimant's business receipts had the character of capital as soon as they were paid to him and that the disregard of business assets in para.6 of Sch.10 did not apply (for further discussion of this case see the note to reg.30 and the note to para.6 of Sch.10).

R(PC) 3/08 rejects the Secretary of State's argument that "capital" has a special meaning in the state pension credit scheme and the "metamorphosis" principle did not apply. The general rule as stated in *R(IS) 3/93* applied, despite the absence of an equivalent provision to reg.29(2)(a) in the State Pension Credit Regulations.

What constitutes income?

On the meaning of "income" see *R(IS) 4/01*. The Commissioner decides, applying *Leeves* (see the note to reg.40), that the part of the claimant's occupational pension that was being paid to his former wife under an attachment of earnings order did not count as his income for the purposes of income support. He concluded that in the absence of a statutory definition, income meant "money paid regularly to the recipient or to his order but not money which is being paid and which he cannot prevent from being paid directly to a third party instead of him". The Commissioner also held that the notional income rule in reg.42(4)(a) did not apply: see the note to reg.42(4)(a). In *CH/1672/2007* the half of the claimant's 2.322

pension that he was required to pay to his wife under the terms of a court order following a judicial separation did not count as his income. However, income subject to a direction which could be revoked at any time (in that case a pension signed over by a nun to a religious order under a deed of trust) remained the claimant's income (*C 10/06–07(IS)*, a Northern Ireland decision). So did the half of his annuities that the claimant in *CH/1076/2008* voluntarily paid to his wife from whom he was separated. In that case the Commissioner drew attention to the "further problem" that would need to be considered if the annuities were retirement annuity pensions in connection with a former employment, namely the conditions in s.91 of the Pension Schemes Act 1995 for assignment of such an annuity.

In addition see *CIS 5479/1997* in which an overpayment of an occupational pension was being recovered by the Italian authorities by withholding the monthly payments of the pension. The Commissioner refers to *Leeves* as confirming his own view that in the general context of the income support scheme income to be taken into account is income that is actually paid to a claimant. If a claimant who has not actually received income is to be treated as having that income, that has to be achieved by a specific provision in the legislation. In *R(IS) 4/02* the same Commissioner applies this approach to conclude, contrary to the view taken in *CIS 212/1989*, para.9 (and followed with some hesitation in *CIS 295/1994*), that payments of the claimant's husband's annuity which had vested in his trustee in bankruptcy under s.306 of the Insolvency Act 1986 were not part of his income (and thus not part of the claimant's income) for the purposes of income support. See also *R(IS) 2/03*, which agrees with *R(IS) 4/02* (on the basis of the principle in *Re Landau* [1998] Ch. 223, affirmed in *Krasner v Dennison* [2001] Ch. 76) that *CIS 212/1989* should no longer be followed. Thus the payments under the claimant's self-employed pension annuity that were being applied entirely for the benefit of his creditors were not his actual income (see the note to reg.42(4) and (4ZA) for the position in relation to notional income). Note that the law has now changed on the exclusion of pension rights from a bankrupt's estate (Welfare Reform and Pensions Act 1999 s.11), but only for bankruptcy orders made on or after May 29, 2000. Regulation 42(4) and (4ZA) were also amended on November 9, 1999 to make specific provision for pensions paid to third parties (see the note to reg.42(4) and (4ZA) and in particular *R(IS) 4/01* discussed in that note). The general principle of the meaning of "income", however, will remain of significance.

The question has also arisen in relation to overpaid working tax credit. *CIS/647/2007* points out that the Court of Appeal in *Leeves* had made it clear the demand for repayment and the immediate obligation it gave rise to only affected the claimant's grant income that was to be attributed to the future. It did not have retrospective effect so as to remove the quality of income from the part of the grant that had already been attributed. The key date was the date of the demand for repayment. So up to the date that the Revenue decided that the claimant had to repay her working tax credit it counted as her income. This is confirmed by the same Upper Tribunal Judge in *CC v SSWP* [2009] UKUT 280 (AAC). The claimant's award of JSA had been reduced to take account of the working tax credit that he was being (wrongly) paid. Subsequently a decision was made retrospectively terminating his working tax credit. This provided grounds for a supersession of the decision awarding JSA so as to increase the amount payable. The claimant's appeal was treated as both an appeal against the decision awarding JSA at a reduced rate and the supersession decision. This did not, however, assist the claimant. This was because: (i) the removal of the working tax credit was not a circumstance obtaining at the date of the decision awarding JSA (at the date of that decision the claimant was receiving working tax credit) and so could not be taken into account by virtue of s.12(8)(b) SSA 1998; (ii) under reg.7(2) of the Decisions and Appeals Regulations the supersession decision took effect on the date the change occurred, i.e. the date HMRC made the change to the working tax credit award, not the date from which that change had effect. Judge Jacobs acknowledges that this meant that the claimant lost both part of his JSA and the tax credit but he could see no way to avoid this effect.

However, in *CIS/1813/2007* the Commissioner holds that payments of working tax credit made after the claimant had notified the Revenue that she had ceased work and had asked for the payments to stop did not count as income. Although, if that was wrong, the payments were voluntary payments which were to be disregarded under para.15(5A)(b) of Sch.9. Once the claimant had made proper disclosure, and even more so where she had asked not to be paid, it was entirely a matter for the Revenue whether to continue payment. The Commissioner distinguishes *CIS/647/2007* on the basis that the claimant in that case had not informed the Revenue of her change of circumstances. The Revenue had therefore continued to be under an obligation to make the payments and there was no question of the payments being voluntary. Similarly in *Leeves* there was no suggestion that the claimant had told the local authority before the grant was paid that it should not pay him or that there were grounds for revoking the award and so the question of whether the payments were voluntary had not arisen. **2.323**

For a discussion of the meaning of "voluntary payment" see the notes to para.15 of Sch.9; note in particular *R(H) 5/05* which held that the loans in that case which had not created any legally enforceable rights or obligations and for which the lender had not obtained anything in return were voluntary payments. Thus loans made at regular intervals which do count as income because they do not satisfy the *Leeves* test of a certain and immediate obligation to repay may nevertheless be disregarded under para.15(5A)(b) of Sch.9, depending on the circumstances of the loan. If the loan is a one-off or the loans are irregular, note reg.48(9) which treats irregular voluntary payments as capital.

R(H) 5/05 also considered the position in relation to bank overdrafts. The Commissioner referred to the fact that the standard terms of a bank overdraft were that it was repayable on demand, although the demand might not be made while the amount stayed within an agreed limit. Those terms brought the repayment obligation within the *Leeves* principle. The obligation was certain, as the amount overdrawn could be identified day by day, and was immediate, even though the bank choose not to enforce the immediate obligation. Thus the resources provided by the use of the claimant's overdraft facility did not amount to income. The Commissioner commented that that result was also in accord with the ordinary and natural meaning of "income". One would not naturally speak of a person having an income from incurring expenditure and running up an overdraft. (Note that the Commissioner did not refer to the Court of Appeal's decision in *R. v West Dorset DC Ex p. Poupard* [1998] 28 R.V.R. 40 which had held that borrowings by way of a bank overdraft secured by capital and used for living expenses constituted income for the purposes of the housing benefit scheme as it then existed. But arguably this decision is no longer pertinent, bearing in mind that it concerned the former housing benefit scheme, and in the light of *Leeves*. And see *AR v Bradford Metropolitan DC* [2008] UKUT 30 (AAC), reported as *R(H) 6/09*, in which the Upper Tribunal Judge states that *Poupard* never stood for any rigid rule that loans have to count as income and that the decision was not relevant to the current housing benefit and council tax benefit schemes, and should be confined to a historical footnote at most.) The Commissioner left open the question of whether the same would apply to credit cards, although he did refer to *CH/3393/2003* in which it was accepted that the juggling of credit card balances, where there was no immediate liability to repay beyond the minimum monthly payment, created a regular funding facility to be taken into account as income; however in the circumstances of the case before him there was no need to decide whether or not *CH/3393/2003* was correctly decided or whether it depended on its particular facts. But note *R(H) 8/08* in which the Commissioner does voice his opinion that *CH/3393/2003* was wrong to treat credit card payments as income.

SH v SSWP [2008] UKUT 21 (AAC) concerned the weekly sums which the claimant was allowed to withdraw for living expenses from his bank account which was subject to a restraint order under s.77 of the Criminal Justice Act 1988. It is held that these sums were not income at the time of withdrawal but remained capital. Furthermore there was nothing in the JSA Regulations 1996 (or the equivalent provisions in the Income Support Regulations) which treated these payments of **2.324** capital as income. They were not capital payable by instalments within the meaning of reg.104(1) of the JSA Regulations 1996 (the equivalent of reg.41(1)) as this provision only applied if there was a contractual or other obligation on the part of some other person to pay a capital sum to the claimant by instalments.

Drawings from a partnership (or a business) are not income other than earnings, nor are they earnings from self-employment (*AR v Bradford Metropolitan DC* [2008] UKUT 30 (AAC), reported as *R(H) 6/09*).

Paragraphs (1) and (2)

2.325 These provisions contain the basic rule on the aggregation of resources. With effect from April 6, 2004 (except in "transitional cases"—see the note to reg.17), only the income and capital of the claimant's partner is treated as the claimant's. Note that the definition of partner refers on to a couple, also defined in reg.2(1) (and see para.(3) for polygamous marriages). It is an essential part of the definition of couple that the parties should be members of the same household, so that reg.16 may also be relevant. There are special rules for couples where at least one member is under 18 (paras (4) and (5)).

Under the form of reg.23 in force before April 6, 2004 (the old form continues to apply for "transitional cases"—see the note to reg.17) the income (but not the capital) of a child or young person who was a member of the clamaint's family was aggregated with the claimant's (see the 2003 edition of this volume for the old form of reg.23 and the notes to that regulation for further details of the former rules relating to treatment of a child or young person's income and capital). However, with effect from April 6, 2004 (except in "transitional cases"—see the note to reg.17) amounts for children and young persons have been removed from the income support scheme; financial assistance to help with the cost of bringing up a child or young person is now to be provided through the child tax credit system, see Vol.IV of this series. As a consequence the new form of para.(2) provides that income paid to, or in respect of, and the capital of, a child or young person does not count as that of the claimant. Note the new disregards of child benefit and child tax credit (see para.5B of Sch.9) (for income support claimants who had an award of child tax credit before April 6, 2004 see reg.7 of the Social Security (Working Tax Credit and Child Tax Credit) (Consequential Amendments) Regulations 2003 (SI 2003/455) (as amended) on p.812 and the notes to that regulation).

References to "the claimant" in the following regulations are to be treated as references to any partner. However, see *R(IS) 3/03* discussed in the note to para.12 of Sch.10.

Paragraph (4)

2.326 This paragraph applies where a couple receives less than the ordinary couple's rate of personal allowance because of the ineligibility of one partner who is under 18 (this is the effect of the reference to para.1(3)(b), (c), (f) and (g) of Sch.2). The income of the ineligible partner is not treated as the claimant's except to the extent that it exceeds the difference between the reduced rate of personal allowance and the ordinary rate. The aggregation of capital is not affected.

Paragraph (5)

2.327 This makes similar provision for polygamous marriages.

[1 Income of participants in the self-employment route [2 . . .]

2.328 **23A.**—Chapters II, III, IV, V, VII and VIIA of this Part and regulations 62 to 66A, 68 and 69 shall not apply to any income which is to be calculated in accordance with Chapter IVA of this Part (participants in the self-employment route [2 . . .]).]

AMENDMENTS

1. Social Security (Miscellaneous Amendments) (No.4) Regulations 1998 (SI 1998/1174) reg.6(2) (June 1, 1998).
2. Social Security Amendment (Employment Zones) (No.2) Regulations 2000 (SI 2000/2910) reg.5(1)(a) (November 27, 2000).

DEFINITION

"self-employment route"—see reg.2(1).

GENERAL NOTE

Regulation 23A takes any gross receipts from trading while on the "self-employment route" out of the categories of earnings, self-employed earnings and income other than earnings for the purposes of any claim for income support. The rules for liable relative payments and student income (except reg.67) also do not apply. Any such receipts may only be taken into account in accordance with regs 39A–39D. For the definition of the "self-employment route", see reg.2(1). **2.329**

Treatment of charitable or voluntary payments

24.—[1. . .] **2.330**

AMENDMENT

1. Income Support (General) Amendment No.5 Regulations 1988 (SI 1988/2022) reg.5 (December 12, 1988).

[2 [4 . . .]] liable relative payments

25.—Regulations 29 to [142], 46 to 52 and Chapter VIII of this Part shall not apply to any payment which is to be calculated in accordance with Chapter VII thereof ([3 [5 . . .] liable relative payments]). **2.331**

AMENDMENTS

1. Social Security (Working Tax Credit and Child Tax Credit) (Consequential Amendments) Regulations 2003 (SI 2003/455) reg.2 and Sch.1 para.7 (April 6, 2004, except in "transitional cases" and see further the note to reg.17 of the Income Support Regulations).
2. Social Security (Child Maintenance Amendments) Regulations 2008 (SI 2008/2111) reg.2(2)(a) (October 27, 2008).
3. Social Security (Child Maintenance Amendments) Regulations 2008 (SI 2008/2111) reg.2(3) (October 27, 2008).
4. Social Security (Miscellaneous Amendments) (No.4) Regulations 2009 (SI 2009/2655) reg.2(5) (April 12, 2010).
5. Social Security (Miscellaneous Amendments) (No.4) Regulations 2009 (SI 2009/2655) reg.2(6) (April 12, 2010).

[1Child support

25A.—[2. . .]] **2.332**

AMENDMENTS

1. Social Security (Miscellaneous Provisions) Amendment Regulations 1993 (SI 1993/846) reg.2 (April 19, 1993).
2. Social Security (Child Maintenance Amendments) Regulations 2008 (SI 2008/2111) reg.2(4)(a) (October 27, 2008).

Calculation of income and capital of students

2.333 **26.**—The provisions of Chapters II to VI of this Part (income and capital) shall [1 have effect in relation to students and their partners subject to the modifications set out in Chapter VIII thereof (students)].

AMENDMENT

1. Income Support (General) Amendment Regulations 2001 (SI 2001/721) reg.2(a) (March 29, 2001).

DEFINITIONS

"partner"—see reg.2(1).
"student"—*ibid.*, and reg.61(1).

[1Rounding of fractions

2.334 **27.**—Where any calculation under this Part results in a fraction of a penny that fraction shall, if it would be to the claimant's advantage, be treated as a penny, otherwise it shall be disregarded.]

AMENDMENT

1. Income Support (General) Amendment Regulations 1988 (SI 1988/663) reg.13 (April 11, 1988).

CHAPTER II

INCOME

Calculation of income

2.335 **28.**—(1) For the purposes of section 20(3) of the Act [SSCBA, s.124(1)] (conditions of entitlement to income support), the income of a claimant shall be calculated on a weekly basis—

(a) by determining in accordance with this Part, other than Chapter VI, the weekly amount of his income; and
(b) by adding to that amount the weekly income calculated under regulation 53 (calculation of tariff income from capital).

[1(2) For the purposes of paragraph (1) "income" includes capital treated as income under regulations 41 (capital treated as income) and income which a claimant is treated as possessing under regulation 42 (notional income).]

AMENDMENT

1. Income Support (General) Amendment No.4 Regulations 1991 (SI 1991/1559) reg.7 (October 7, 1991).

DEFINITIONS

"the Act"—see reg.2(1).
"claimant"—*ibid.*

GENERAL NOTE

2.336 Regulation 28 simply confirms that all resources which would come under the description of income, including resources specifically treated as earnings or income, are to be taken into account in the income calculation.

Calculation of earnings derived from employed earner's employment and income other than earnings

29.—(1) [1. . .] Earnings derived from employment as an employed earner and income which does not consist of earnings shall be taken into account over a period determined in accordance with the following paragraphs and at a weekly amount determined in accordance with regulation 32 (calculation of weekly amount of income). 2.337

(2) Subject to [4the following provisions of this regulation], the period over which a payment is to be taken into account shall be—

[9 (a) where the payment is monthly, a period equal to the number of weeks from the date on which the payment is treated as paid to the date immediately before the date on which the next monthly payment would have been so treated as paid whether or not the next monthly payment is actually paid;

(aa) where the payment is in respect of a period which is not monthly, a period equal to the length of the period for which payment is made;]

(b) in any other case, a period equal to such number of weeks as is equal to the number obtained (and any fraction shall be treated as a corresponding fraction of a week) by dividing the net earnings, or in the case of income which does not consist of earnings, the amount of that income [3less any amount paid by way of tax on that income which is disregarded under paragraph 1 of Schedule 9 (income other than earnings to be disregarded)] by the amount of income support which would be payable had the payment not been made plus an amount equal to the total of the sums which would fall to be disregarded from that payment under Schedule 8 [3(earnings to be disregarded) or, as the case may be, any paragraph of Schedule 9 other than paragraph 1 of that Schedule,] as is appropriate in the claimant's case;

and that period shall begin on the date on which the payment is treated as paid under regulation 31 (date on which income is treated as paid).

[4(2A) The period over which a Career Development Loan, which is paid pursuant to section 2 of the Employment and Training Act 1973, shall be taken into account shall be the period of education and training intended to be supported by that loan.

(2B) Where grant income as defined in Chapter VIII of this Part has been paid to a person who ceases to be a [8 full-time student] before the end of the period in respect of which that income is payable and, as a consequence, the whole or part of that income falls to be repaid by that person, that income shall be taken into account over the period beginning on the date on which that income is treated as paid under regulation 31 and ending—

(a) on the date on which repayment is made in full; or

[5(aa) where the grant is paid in instalments, on the day before the next instalment would have been paid had the claimant remained a [8 full-time student]; or]

(b) on the last date of the academic term or vacation during which that person ceased to be a [8 full-time student],

whichever shall first occur.]

[11 [12 (2C)(a) This paragraph applies where earnings are derived by a claimant as a member of a reserve force prescribed in Part 1 of Schedule 6 to the Contributions Regulations—

(i) in respect of a period of annual continuous training for a maximum of 15 days in any calendar year; or
(ii) in respect of training in the claimant's first year of training as a member of a reserve force for a maximum of 43 days in that year.

(b) Earnings, whether paid to the claimant alone or together with other earnings derived from the same source, are to be taken into account—
(i) in the case of a period of training which lasts for the number of days listed in column 1 of the table in sub-paragraph (c), over a period of time which is equal to the number of days set out in the corresponding row in column 2 of that table; or
(ii) in any other case, over a period of time which is equal to the number of days of the training period.

(c) This is the table referred to in sub-paragraph (b)(i)—

Column 1 *Period of training in days*	*Column 2* *Period of time over which earnings are to be taken into account in days*
8 to 10	7
15 to 17	14
22 to 24	21
29 to 31	28
36 to 38	35
43	42]

(2D) The period over which earnings to which paragraph (2C) applies are to be taken into account shall begin on the date on which the payment is treated as paid under regulation 31.]

(3) Where earnings not of the same kind are derived from the same source and the periods in respect of which those earnings would, but for this paragraph, fall to be taken into account—
(a) overlap, wholly or partly, those earnings shall be taken into account over a period equal to the aggregate length of those periods;
(b) and that period shall begin with the earliest date on which any part of those earnings would otherwise be treated as paid under regulation 31 (date on which income is treated as paid).

[[2](4) In a case to which paragraph (3) applies, earnings under regulation 35 (earnings of employed earners) shall be taken into account in the following order of priority—
(a) earnings normally derived from the employment;
(b) any payment to which paragraph (1)(b) or (c) of that regulation applies;
(c) any payment to which paragraph (1)(i) of that regulation applies;
(d) any payment to which paragraph (1)(d) of that regulation applies.]

[[1](4A) Where earnings to which regulation 35(1)(b) to (d) (earnings of employed earners) applies are paid in respect of part of a day, those earnings shall be taken into account over a period equal to a day.]

[[2](4B) [[10]. . .]

(4C) Any earnings to which regulation 35(1)(i)(ii) applies which are paid in respect of or on the termination of part-time employment, shall be taken into account over a period equal to one week.

(4D) In this regulation—

(a) "part-time employment" means employment in which a person is not to be treated as engaged in remunerative work under regulation 5 or [[6]6(1)[[7] and (4)]] (persons treated, or not treated, as engaged in remunerative work);

(b) [[10]. . .].]

(5) For the purposes of this regulation the claimant's earnings and income which does not consist of earnings shall be calculated in accordance with Chapters III and V respectively of this Part.

AMENDMENTS

1. Income Support (General) Amendment No.5 Regulations 1988 (SI 1988/2022) reg.7 (December 12, 1988).
2. Income Support (General) Amendment No.2 Regulations 1989 (SI 1989/1323) reg.9 (October 9, 1989).
3. Income Support (General) Amendment Regulations 1990 (SI 1990/547) reg.10 (April 9, 1990).
4. Income-related Benefits and Jobseeker's Allowance (Miscellaneous Amendments) Regulations 1997 (SI 1997/65) reg.5 (April 7, 1997).
5. Social Security (Miscellaneous Amendments) Regulations 1998 (SI 1998/563) reg.12 (April 6, 1998).
6. Social Security (Miscellaneous Amendments) (No.2) Regulations 1999 (SI 1999/2556) reg.2(4) (October 4, 1999).
7. Social Security (Miscellaneous Amendments) Regulations 2000 (SI 2000/681) reg.2(c) (April 3, 2000).
8. Social Security Amendment (Students) Regulations 2000 (SI 2000/1981) reg.5(5) and Sch. (July 31, 2000).
9. Social Security (Miscellaneous Amendments) Regulations 2008 (SI 2008/698) reg.2(5)(a) (April 14, 2008).
10. Social Security (Miscellaneous Amendments) Regulations 2008 (SI 2008/698) reg.2(5)(b) (April 14, 2008).
11. Social Security (Miscellaneous Amendments) (No.2) Regulations 2012 (SI 2012/2575) reg.2(3) (November 5, 2012).
12. Social Security (Members of the Reserve Forces) (Amendment) Regulations 2015 (SI 2015/389) reg.2(3) (April 6, 2015).

DEFINITIONS

"claimant"—see reg.2(1) and reg.23(1).
"employed earner"—see reg.2(1).
"first year of training"—*ibid.*
"full-time student"—see reg.61(1).
"grant income"—*ibid.*

GENERAL NOTE

Paragraphs (1)–(2)

This regulation applies to the earnings of employees and income other than earnings. Thus it covers other social security benefits. Earnings from self-employment are dealt with in reg.30. It defines the period over which income is to be taken into account and the date on which that period starts. The general rule is set out in para.(2). **2.338**

The first part of para.(2) covers payments that are made in respect of a period. The new form of para.(2)(a) and the new para.(2)(aa), introduced on April 14,

2008, distinguish between monthly and other payments. To avoid the need to reassess monthly income each month (because the length of a month varies), payments in respect of a month will be taken into account for a period equal to the number of weeks from the date on which the payment is treated as paid (see reg.31) to the date immediately before the date on which the next monthly payment would be treated as paid (even if it is not so paid).

The *Decision Makers Guide* gives the following example of the effect of the new provision:

> J claims income support because he is absent from work due to illness. His benefit week ending day is a Monday.
> His employer pays him on the last day of each month. On March 31, 2008 (a Monday) J receives three weeks' statutory sick pay of £217.65 (£72.55 × 3). The payment is taken into account for one month at the weekly rate of £50.22 (£217.65 × 12 ÷ 52).
> The weekly amount is taken into account for the following five benefit weeks ending on March 31, April 7, April 14, April 21 and April 28 at the rate of £50.22 per week.
> J's next payment from his employer would be due to be paid on April 30 and the weekly amount would be taken into account for the benefit weeks ending May 5, May 12, May 19 and May 26.

2.339 If the payment is made in respect of a period which is other than monthly, it is taken into account for an equal period. Thus a fortnight's unemployment benefit is to be taken into account for a fortnight (*R(SB) 17/82*) and an annual covenant for a year (*R(SB) 25/86*, but see Chapter VIII for students).

There will be problems in determining the period in respect of which a payment is made in some cases. For instance, is holiday pay in terms of days, to be attributed to each of the seven days in a week (as done in *R(SB) 11/85* and *CSB 1004/1988*), or is it in terms of weeks, so that only five days' worth is attributed to each week? The Commissioner in *R(JSA) 1/06* adopts the former approach, preferring *CJSA/3438/1998* to *CJSA/4508/1998* (the latter decision had accepted that holiday pay should be attributed on the basis of "working days"). The claimant who had been contracted to work a three-day week was paid 11.115 days holiday pay on the termination of his employment. The Commissioner holds that he was by virtue of that holiday pay (which counted as earnings: see reg.98(1)(c) of the JSA Regulations 1996) to be treated as being in remunerative work (see reg.52(3) of the JSA Regulations 1996) for 12 days (see reg.94(5) of the JSA Regulations 1996, the equivalent of para.(4A) where earnings are paid in respect of part of a day), namely from November 28 to December 9, 2002, and not for four weeks as the tribunal had decided. (Note that under the new form of para.1 of Sch.8 introduced on October 1, 2007, such holiday pay would now be disregarded.) A further example could be that of a supply teacher who works for a varying number of days in each month and is paid at the end of the month. Is that payment in respect of the month or in respect of the number of days worked? Much will turn on the precise contractual situation and the terms used by the parties, as confirmed by *R(IS) 3/93*. Decisions on the former reg.7(1)(g) of the Social Security (Unemployment, Sickness and Invalidity Benefit) Regulations 1983 (like *R(U) 3/84*) may be helpful.

The question in relation to supply teachers was specifically considered in *R(IS) 10/95*. The claimant had worked as a supply teacher for five days in the month of June. She was paid for work done in a month at the end of the following month. The Commissioner accepts that the claimant's contract with the local education authority was on a daily basis (see *R(U) 2/87*). However, he rejected her argument that the period for which payment was made was five days. He holds that since she was employed on a daily basis, she was in fact paid for five different periods in June. Paragraph (2)(a) clearly only envisaged payment in respect of a single period, since neither para.(2) nor reg.32(1) could operate satisfactorily if a single payment could be in respect of two or more periods. Thus the payment for the days worked in a particular month had to be attributed to the period of a month. *R(IS) 10/95* is followed with some reluctance in *CIS 167/1992*. The result of this approach is that the period is determined by the employer's administrative arrangements for payment, rather than the terms of the employment. But it is surely arguable that the period in respect of which the payment was payable was one day. The terms of the claimant's employment were that she was paid £42.23 per session (i.e. day). The Commissioner's approach equates the period in respect of which a payment is *payable* with the period for which payment is *due to be made*, which is not necessarily the same. Moreover, the Commissioner does not seem to have taken account of the fact that "payment" can include part of a payment (see reg.2(1)). Thus some of the operational difficulties referred to by the Commissioner could be overcome by dividing the claimant's monthly payment by the number of days worked in that month and attributing this on a daily basis. However, this does not deal with the point that all the payments would be due on one day. If the payments were due before the date of the claim, reg.31(1)(a) would apply to attribute them all to that day; if they were paid during a claim see reg.32(5) and reg.31(1)(b). See also para.13 of Sch.8.

Despite the fact that "there appeared to be some force in this criticism", *R(IS) 10/95* is applied in *CIS/3737/2003*. The claimant, who worked three days a week, was paid in arrears on the 25th of each month. When she became ill her employer paid her statutory sick pay on a monthly basis. In calculating her entitlement to income support the Department took the monthly figure of SSP that her employer had paid her, multiplied that by 12 and then divided it by 52, and used the resulting figure in their assessment, rather than the standard weekly rate of SSP. As a consequence, the income figure it arrived at was some £10 above the actual weekly rate of SSP. Despite his initial doubts the Deputy Commissioner concludes that the SSP had been correctly attributed. *R(IS) 10/95* had made clear that a payment which is for days worked in a particular month is "payable in respect of that month" and that the period referred to in para.(2) had to be a single period. That decision had been followed and applied in *R(JSA) 2/03* and *CIS/2654/2000* and was therefore an established precedent which had stood the test of time. It was not possible to distinguish *R(IS) 10/95* on the facts because the claimant was paid monthly and the regulations prescribed how income was to be calculated for the purposes of income support when a claimant was paid monthly. 2.340

However, *R(IS) 10/95* is not followed in *CG/607/2008*, a decision which concerned the calculation of earnings for the purposes of carer's allowance.

If the payment is not in respect of a period then there is a mechanical rule in para.(2)(b) spreading it at the rate of income support which would otherwise be payable, taking account of any disregards. See *SSWP v JP (JSA)* [2010] UKUT 90 (AAC) (discussed in the notes to reg.31(1)) which concerned a payment made as part of an offer of settlement under the Equal Pay Act 1970. It was held that the payment was not in respect of a period and so came within reg.94(2)(b) of the JSA Regulations (the equivalent of para.(2)(b)). The appeal against this decision, which was dismissed by the Court of Appeal (*Minter v Kingston Upon Hull CC* and *Potter v Secretary of State for Work and Pensions* [2011] EWCA Civ 1155; [2012] AACR 21) did not deal with this point.

Once the period is fixed, it begins on the date specified in reg.31.

Paragraph (2A)

This relates to Career Development Loans. 2.341

Paragraph (2B)

Paragraph (2B), in force from April 7, 1997, concerns the situation where a person is due to repay part or all of a student grant because he leaves or is dismissed from his course before it finishes. Note *CIS 4201/2003* which confirms that para.(2B) has no application if the claimant has already left the course by the time the 2.342

grant (or instalment of the grant) is paid (see further below). If para.(2B) does apply, the grant income (defined in reg.61(1)) will be taken into account from the date it is treated as paid under reg.31 until full repayment has been made, or, where the grant is paid in instalments, the day before the next instalment would be due, or the last day of the term or vacation in which the person ceases to be a full-time student, whichever is earlier. See reg.32(6A) for calculation of the weekly amount to be taken into account and note reg.40(3B). Paragraph (2B) thus confirms the effect of the decision in *CIS 5185/1995*. The claimant who had been a full-time student left his course and claimed income support on January 10, 1994. The education authority did not inform him of the amount of the grant he had to repay until March 20, 1994. The Commissioner holds that the claimant was not entitled to income support because until the grant was repaid it was income that remained available to the claimant and had to be taken into account (see *R. v Bolton SBAT Ex p. Fordham* [1981] 1 All E.R. 50 and *CSB 1408/1988*) and it exceeded his applicable amount. Moreover, once the claimant had ceased to be a student, the disregards in reg.62 did not apply (but now see reg.32(6A)). The Commissioner rejects the argument that the grant income could be disregarded under the principle in *Barclays Bank v Quistclose Investments Ltd* [1970] A.C. 567. That principle did not apply because the education authority retained no beneficial interest in the grant. They merely reserved the right to demand repayment of a sum calculated in accordance with how much of the relevant term had expired when the claimant ceased to be a student.

However, in *CIS 12263/1996* the Commissioner took the view that as soon as a student had abandoned his course and an obligation to repay the balance of his grant to the education authority arose, he held the money on constructive trust for the authority. Thus in assessing the claimant's entitlement to income support the repayable balance of the grant was not to be taken into account as his income. The Commissioner in *CIS 12263/1996* considered that the *Quistclose* case was concerned with a "purpose trust" (i.e. where a grant or loan was impressed with a particular purpose from the beginning), whereas in this situation a constructive trust had arisen because the grant had been paid on the condition that the claimant continued to be a student. He also distinguished the Court of Appeal's decision in *Fordham* on the ground that in that case there had been uncertainty as to the obligation to repay (there was none here). Moreover, an alternative approach was that once the balance of the grant became repayable it could no longer be regarded as the claimant's income at all (see para.9(7) of *R(SB) 20/83*).

Leave to appeal against the decision in *CIS 5185/1995* was granted by the Court of Appeal but the appeal was not pursued for financial reasons. However, an appeal was brought by the Department against the decision in *CIS 12263/1996* (*Chief Adjudication Officer v Leeves*, reported as *R(IS) 5/99*). It was conceded on behalf of the claimant that there was no constructive trust in these circumstances, since no proprietary right had been retained by the education authority, nor had any fiduciary obligation been created. However, the Court of Appeal held that money that the claimant was under a "certain and immediate liability" to repay did not amount to income. Thus once the claimant had received a request for immediate repayment of a specified sum from the local education authority the grant ceased to count as his income (although it fell to be treated as such until that time, even though he had abandoned his course). The Court distinguished its decision in *Fordham* as the liability to repay in that case had been uncertain. The Court's approach in *Leeves* was affirmed in *Morrell v Secretary of State for Work and Pensions* [2003] EWCA Civ 526, reported as *R(IS) 6/03* (see the note to reg.23).

2.343 Thus in relation to periods before April 7, 1997, the repayable balance of a grant will not count as a claimant's income from the date that the liability to repay has "crystallised" (*Leeves*). As regards periods after April 6, 1997, para.(2B) will apply. However, it is suggested that this is subject to the preliminary question of whether the repayable grant counts as the claimant's income at all. If it does not do so because there is a "certain and immediate" liability to repay, it is arguable that para.(2B) will not (or will cease to) apply. This is because neither para.(2B), nor reg.40(3B) or reg.32(6A), would seem to have the effect of deeming the grant to be income but simply provide for the period over which the grant is to be taken into account *if* it does count as income, and the method of calculating that income. Compare the wording of the former reg.40(3A) (in force until August 1, 2001; see *Social Security Legislation 2001*, Vol.II, p.337) (treatment of student loans where a claimant has ceased to be a full-time student): this required "a sum equal to the weekly amount" to be taken into account as income.

Where para.(2B) is applicable (for example, where repayment is not required immediately, or the amount of the repayment has not been calculated), note that the disregards for grant income in reg.62 will apply (reg.32(6A)); see also reg.40(3B).

Note that para.(2B) will not apply if the claimant has already ceased to be a full-time student by the time the grant (or the instalment of the grant) is paid (*CIS 4201/2003*). In *CIS 4201/2003* the question of whether the third instalment of the claimant's dependants' grant for the year 2000/1 which had been paid to her after she left her course was income for the purposes of her income support claim therefore had to be determined in accordance with *Leeves*. The Commissioner analyses the relevant provisions of the Education (Student Support) Regulations 2000 and concludes that on the facts of that case there was no obligation to repay an ascertained amount until the request for repayment had been made by the Student Loan Company (which was almost a year later). The instalment therefore fell to be taken into account as income until the middle of June 2001 (presumably under reg.40(3AA) although the Commissioner does not refer to this provision).

Any grant or covenant income or student loan left over at the end of the person's course is disregarded as income (see para.61 of Sch.9).

Paragraphs (2C) and (2D)

Paragraph (2C), as substituted from April 6, 2015, provides that where a claimant (or any partner, see reg.23(1)) has earnings as a member of a reserve force from training (i) for a maximum of 43 days in the claimant's first year of training (see the definition of "first year of training" in reg.2(1)); *or* (ii) for a maximum of 15 days' annual continuous training in any calendar year, the earnings will be taken into account, where the training lasts for the number of days listed in column 1 of the table in sub-para.(c), for the number of days listed in column 2 of the table, or in any other case, for the number of days that the training lasts. The intention of the table in sub-para.(c) is apparently to ensure that claimants who undertake reservist training do not lose a disproportionate amount of benefit when training extends into a new benefit week for three days or less. The period begins on the date that the earnings are treated as paid under reg.31 (para.(2D)). Such earnings are disregarded to the extent that they would have the effect of reducing income support entitlement to less than 10p per week (see the disregard in para.15A of Sch.8). 2.344

Paragraphs (3) and (4)

Paragraph (3) establishes an exception in the case of earnings only, to the rule about the date from which a payment is to be taken into account. It is to deal mainly with the situation on the termination of employment when a claimant may be entitled to regular earnings, week in hand payments, pay in lieu of notice or compensation for breach of contract and holiday pay. The effect is that each payment which is not disregarded (Sch.8 paras 1–2) is to be taken into account for the appropriate period, and the periods are to be put together consecutively. Then the aggregate period starts on the earliest date which would be fixed for any of the periods under reg.31. Note that para.(3) only applies where the earnings are of different kinds, and derive from the same source. Thus it would not apply to payments from different employers. 2.345

Paragraph (4) deals with the order in which payments in lieu of notice, compensation payments and holiday pay are to be taken into account in conjunction with ordinary earnings.

Note that these provisions will be of less relevance following the increased disregard of payments made on the termination of full-time employment introduced on October 1, 2007 (see para.1 of Sch.8 and the notes to that paragraph). However they will still apply where part-time work ends while the claimant is claiming income support or where full-time employment has been suspended.

Paragraph (4A)

2.346 If these earnings are paid in respect of a part of a day they are taken into account for a day.

Paragraph (4C)

2.347 See the notes to reg.35(1)(i). Where a payment of compensation (defined in reg.35(3)(a)) is made on the termination of part-time employment (para.(4D)(a) and reg.35(3)(c)) it is to be taken into account for one week. See also reg.32(7).

Note however that earnings under reg.35(1)(i)(ii) paid on the cessation of part-time employment (whether or not the employment has terminated) are disregarded, except in the case of part-time work which ends while the claimant is claiming income support: see para.2 of Sch.8 and the notes to that paragraph.

Calculation of earnings of self-employed earners

2.348 **30.**—(1) Except where paragraph (2) applies, where a claimant's income consists of earnings from employment as a self-employed earner the weekly amount of his earnings shall be determined by reference to his average weekly earnings from that employment—

(a) over a period of[[1]one year]; or

(b) where the claimant has recently become engaged in that employment or there has been a change which is likely to affect the normal pattern of business, over such other period [[1]. . .] as may, in any particular case, enable the weekly amount of his earnings to be determined more accurately.

(2) Where the claimant's earnings consist of [[2] any items to which paragraph (2A) applies] those earnings shall be taken into account over a period equal to such number of weeks as is equal to the number obtained (and any fraction shall be treated as a corresponding fraction of a week) by dividing the earnings by the amount of income support which would be payable had the payment not been made plus an amount equal to the total of the sums which would fall to be disregarded from the payment under Schedule 8 (earnings to be disregarded) as is appropriate in the claimant's case.

[[2] [[3] (2A) This paragraph applies to—

(a) royalties or other sums paid as a consideration for the use of, or the right to use, any copyright, design, patent or trade mark; or

(b) any payment in respect of any—

(i) book registered under the Public Lending Right Scheme 1982; or

(ii) work made under any international public lending right scheme that is analogous to the Public Lending Right Scheme 1982,

where the claimant is the first owner of the copyright, design, patent or trade mark, or an original contributor to the book or work concerned.]]

(3) For the purposes of this regulation the claimant's earnings shall be calculated in accordance with Chapter IV of this Part.

AMENDMENTS

1. Income-related Benefits Schemes (Miscellaneous Amendments) (No.4) Regulations 1993 (SI 1993/2119) reg.11 (October 4, 1993).
2. Social Security (Miscellaneous Amendments) Regulations 2008 (SI 2008/698) reg.2(6) (April 7, 2008).
3. Social Security (Miscellaneous Amendments) Regulations 2009 (SI 2009/583) reg.2(6) (April 6, 2009).

DEFINITIONS

"claimant"—see reg.2(1) and reg.23(1).
"self-employed earner"—see reg.2(1).

GENERAL NOTE

Regulation 30 applies to earnings from self-employment. A person is a self-employed earner if he is in "gainful employment", other than employed earner's employment (SSCBA s.2(1)(b), imported by reg.2(1)). **2.349**

For a discussion of the previous case law as to whether a person is in "gainful employment", see the notes to this regulation in the 2012/13 edition of this volume. However, that case law needs to be read in the light of the Court of Session's decision in *Saunderson v Secretary of State for Work and Pensions* [2012] CSIH 102; [2013] AACR 16 (see the notes to reg.5 under the heading "*Self-employment*"). The claimant in *Saunderson* had worked as a self-employed golf caddie in St Andrews in the spring and summer months for a number of years. The Court of Session rejects the contention that there is a sharp distinction between those who work seasonally as employees and those who are in seasonal self-employment. The notion had grown up that those who were in seasonal self-employment were likely to be in an annual cycle of work (although this did not apply to employees—see *R(JSA) 1/07*). The primary question, however, under reg.51(1) of the JSA Regulations 1996 (the equivalent of reg.5) for both employees and the self-employed was whether the person was "in work" at the time of the claim. This was a matter of fact, giving "in work" its ordinary meaning. The fact that a person had previously, even repeatedly, been engaged in an activity for part of the year did not mean that he had chosen to treat that part-time activity as an enduring annual activity with the rest of the year being fallow. The concept of a recognisable cycle of work in reg.51(2) was only for the purpose of averaging the hours of work and did not come into play until *after* the primary question of whether the person was "in work" at the end of his seasonal activity had been determined. *Saunderson* is followed in *TC v Department for Social Development (JSA)* [2013] NI Com 65 (a decision of a Northern Ireland Commissioner)—see the note to reg.5 under the heading "*Self-employment*".

Although *Saunderson* concerned a seasonal worker who was self-employed, its approach will also apply to those who are in non-seasonal self-employment (and in effect removes the distinction that was sometimes drawn in the previous case law between the two--see, for example, *JC v SSWP* [2008] UKUT 40 (AAC), reported as *R(JSA) 1/09*).

Thus the first question that has to be determined is whether the person is "in work" at the date of the claim. This will depend on whether the person's self-employment has ceased or whether it is continuing. This is a question of fact and will depend on the person's current and prospective activities and intentions (see *CIS/166/1994* for a list of factors for considering this). However, other factors may be relevant. For example, in *Saunderson* the fact that the claimant was no longer authorised to work as a caddie seemed to be an important factor. In *TC v Department for Social Development (JSA)*, which concerned a self-employed eel fisherman, the fact that the claimant was unable to pursue self-employment as an eel fisherman between January 8 and May 1 of each year, due to legislation governing the duration of the eel fishery season meant that he was not gainfully employed during that period. He **2.350** was also not gainfully employed during October, November and December and the first week in January when he did not fish because it was not economical to do so. In addition, in the year in question when he had to stop fishing in August because the gearbox on his boat had ceased to function and he could not afford a replacement, he was not gainfully employed (and from that date onwards he had no income). The eel fisherman in *TC* had indicated that he intended to resume self-employment the following May. However, in the Commissioner's view, just as ceasing employment did not indicate an intention to permanently retire from employment but merely an end to a particular job, it was possible to cease self-employment with the intention of resumption at a later date.

If the self-employment has ended, the earnings disregard in para.3 of Sch.8 (para.4 of Sch.6 to the JSA Regulations 1996) will apply. If it has not, the attribution of the person's earnings will need to be considered under this regulation.

Attribution of earnings

2.351 As already stated, if the self-employment has ceased, earnings from that self-employment are ignored (para.3 of Sch.8). But note that this does not apply to royalty, copyright or public lending rights payments. For the treatment of those payments, see below. Note also the disregard of business assets in para.6 of Sch.10 and see *CIS/2467/2003* below.

Otherwise the earnings (calculated under regs 37–39) are generally to be averaged over a period of one year. The view previously expressed in this book was that it did not seem necessary that the period immediately precedes the benefit week in question and that any one-year period—normally the last year for which accounts are available—will do. However, *GM v SSWP (JSA)* [2010] UKUT 221 (AAC); [2011] AACR 9 concludes that the relevant year is the year ending with the first week of the claim. The alternative period under para.(1)(b) can only be chosen if there has been a change likely to affect the normal pattern of business or if the self-employment has recently started. In *CIS 166/1994* the Commissioner accepts that where such a change had produced, or was likely to produce, a substantial reduction in the claimant's earnings, it was appropriate for the period to start from the date of the change (with the likely result that no earnings fell to be taken into account). See also *CIS 14409/1996*. Note also the more general exception hidden in reg.38(10), which allows the amount of any item of income or expenditure to be calculated over a different period if that will produce a more accurate figure.

Paragraphs (2) and (2A) supply a special rule for payments of royalties or for copyright or public lending rights payments, which are to be spread in the same way as income of an employee not in respect of a period (reg.29(2)(b)). *CIS/731/2008* confirms that before specific provision for the treatment of public lending rights payments was made on April 7, 2008 such payments counted as earnings from self-employment under the general rule in para.(1). The April 2009 form of para.(2A) includes payments from abroad that are analogous to public lending rights payments.

2.352 *CIS/2467/2003* concerned a self-employed author who received advances on contracting to write a book and subsequent royalties on sales above the amount of the advance. However, he had not been able to undertake any writing for some months due to illness, although he intended to resume this activity as soon as he had recovered. His income support claim was refused on the ground that he had capital above the prescribed limit. The Commissioner rejected his argument that money paid by way of advances was not legally owned by him because the advances were repayable if he did not fulfill the contract. In his view the advances fully belonged to the claimant as soon as they were received. The Commissioner then went on to consider whether the principle in *R(IS) 3/93* that a payment does not metamorphose into capital until the end of the period to which it is attributed as income applied to self-employed earnings. He concluded that it did not. This was because the calculation of earnings from self-employment did not turn on when particular receipts came in but was, under para.(1), to be calculated as average weekly earnings (net profit, subject to deductions for income tax and social security) over a period of normally a year. Those average weekly earnings were then taken into account for an equivalent period into the future. There was therefore no period of attribution to be attached to any particular business receipt and the basis of the *R(IS) 3/93* principle did not exist. In the Commissioner's view it would be artificial and wrong to regard all business receipts as retaining the character of income until the expiry of the period for which earnings calculated over the whole period were taken into account. Instead the protection for self-employed earners in relation to the capital rules lay in the disregard of the value of business assets under para.6 of Sch.10. The Commissioner also held that the fact that para.(2) did provide a special rule for the attribution of the kind of self-employed earnings in issue in this case did not make a difference in relation to capital. First, there was still the protection of the disregard in para.6 of Sch.10. Secondly, the attribution rule in para.(2) (which was very difficult to apply) was an artificial one, not linked to any assessment of the period in respect of which any particular payment was made. The rationale for the operation of the *R(IS) 3/93* principle was therefore also missing in relation to these types of self-employed earnings. The Commissioner accordingly concluded that the claimant's business receipts had the character of capital as soon as they were paid to him (although he did accept that payments of VAT which the claimant had a liability to pay over to Customs and Excise did not form part of his capital). The Commissioner finally considered whether the disregard in para.6 applied but decided that it did not (see further the note to para.6 of Sch.10).

Note that the profit simply derived from a capital asset is not earnings, which must be derived from some employment or occupation. See *R(U) 3/77*. Thus, it is suggested that making a profit from one's own portfolio of shares on the stock market would probably not be self-employment. Note also *R(FC) 2/92* and the other decisions in the note to para.6 of Sch.10 on the question of whether ownership of a tenanted house is a business.

Date on which income is treated as paid

31.—(1) Except where paragraph [8 (2) [9applies]], a payment of income to which regulation 29 (calculation of earnings derived from employed earner's employment and income other than earnings) applies shall be treated as paid— 2.353

(a) in the case of a payment which is due to be paid before the first benefit week pursuant to the claim, on the date on which it is due to be paid;

(b) in any other case, on the first day of the benefit week in which it is due to be paid or the first succeeding benefit week in which it is practicable to take it into account.

(2) Income support, [4jobseeker's allowance], [2maternity allowance,] [3short-term or long term incapacity benefit], [7 severe disablement allowance [10, employment and support allowance or universal credit]] [3. . .], shall be treated as paid [10 on any day] in respect of which [1it is payable].

[5[6(3) [9. . .]]]

[8(4) [9. . .]]

Amendments

1. Income Support (General) Amendment Regulations 1988 (SI 1988/663) reg.14 (April 11, 1988).

2. Income Support (General) Amendment No.4 Regulations 1988 (SI 1988/1445) reg.8 (September 12, 1988).

3. Disability Working Allowance and Income Support (General) Amendment Regulations 1995 (SI 1995/482) reg.10 (April 13, 1995).

4. Income Support (General) (Jobseeker's Allowance Consequential Amendments) Regulations 1996 (SI 1996/206) reg.15 (October 7, 1996).

5. Social Security (Miscellaneous Amendments) Regulations 2000 (SI 2000/681) reg.3(1) (April 3, 2000).
6. Social Security (Working Tax Credit and Child Tax Credit) (Consequential Amendments) (No.3) Regulations 2003 (SI 2003/1731) reg.2(2) (August 8, 2003).
7. Employment and Support Allowance (Consequential Provisions) (No.2) Regulations 2008 (SI 2008/1554) reg.2(5) (October 27, 2008).
8. Social Security (Miscellaneous Amendments) (No.6) Regulations 2008 (SI 2008/2767) reg.2(4) (November 17, 2008).
9. Social Security (Miscellaneous Amendments) Regulations 2011 (SI 2011/674) reg.3(2) (April 11, 2011).
10. Universal Credit (Consequential, Supplementary, Incidental and Miscellaneous Provisions) Regulations 2013 (SI 2013/630) reg.28(4) (April 29, 2013).

Definitions

"benefit week"—see reg.2(1).
"child tax credit"—*ibid.*
"working tax credit"—*ibid.*

General Note

Paragraph (1)

2.354 This provision applies to determine when the period of attribution of earnings from employment and income (other than the benefits specified in para.(2)) fixed in reg.29 begins. The crucial date is that on which the payment is due to be paid. This date may well be different from the date of actual payment. Legal obligations must be considered, e.g. the terms of a contract of employment *(R(SB) 33/83)*. If a claimant's contract of employment is terminated without due notice any deferred holiday pay and wages withheld under week-in-hand arrangements are due immediately. So are any agreed payments in lieu of notice *(R(SB) 23/84* and *R(SB) 11/85)*. Note the operation of reg.29(3) and (4) when different kinds of earnings are received for overlapping periods.

For an example of a case where payment was not due to be made when the claimant was laid off, see *CJSA/4261/2003*. The claimant was a "core casual" dock worker who was laid off and claimed JSA the next day. His employers said that six days' holiday pay was due to him and a decision-maker therefore treated him as in remunerative work for that period. However, evidence was provided by his union which confirmed that as a core casual worker his employment was not terminated when he was laid off. He could chose, but was not obliged, to take his holiday when he was laid off. Furthermore, if he did not take his holiday when laid off (or by agreement at other times), he could not receive payment for any accrued holiday entitlement until more than four weeks after the termination or interruption of his employment. Thus the terms of his contract clearly showed that no holiday pay was due when he was laid off and he was entitled to JSA from the day he claimed, subject to the then three waiting days rule.

If the payment is due before the first week pursuant to the claim (on which see Sch.7 to the Claims and Payments Regulations), it is treated as paid on the date it is due. This date then starts the period under reg.29. In other cases the payment is treated as paid on the first day of the benefit week in which it is due (or the next week if the main rule is impracticable).

2.355 In *CIS 590/1993* the claimant had been dismissed from her employment in April 1991 because she was pregnant. In June 1992 she was awarded compensation by an industrial tribunal under the Sex Discrimination Act 1975 which included one month's loss of earnings. The tribunal had deducted the income support paid to the claimant for the month after her dismissal. It is held that the loss of earnings element of the award was to be taken into account as earnings under reg.35 (see the notes to reg.35). For the purpose of reg.31(1), the date on which it was due to be paid was the date when the lost earnings were due to be paid, not when the award was made. This was because the award was to be regarded as a payment in lieu of remuneration and the purpose of the sex discrimination legislation was to put the claimant in the position she would have been if the employer had not acted unlawfully. If the payment was treated as due at the date of the award this could produce unfairness. The result was that the earnings were to be attributed to a period of one month in April/May 1991 and she was to be treated as in remunerative work for that period. However, the income support that had been paid to the claimant for that period was not recoverable as there had been no failure to disclose or misrepresentation. It had in any event been recouped.

SSWP v JP (JSA) [2010] UKUT 90 (AAC), however, disagrees with *CIS/590/1993* on the basis that it confuses the payment with what the payment was compensation for. *SSWP v JP* concerned a payment made as part of an offer of settlement under the Equal Pay Act 1970 which was held to be earnings (see further the notes to reg.23 under "*Distinction between capital and income*"). In relation to the attribution of the payment, Judge Jacobs states that it was not a late payment of money that was due earlier (although it would have been due earlier if the employer had honoured the equality clause in the claimant's contract). Nor was the payment made in respect of a period. At most it was a payment on account of an amount that would be *calculated* by reference to a period. He concluded that as the payment was not in respect of a period it fell within reg.94(2)(b) of the JSA Regulations 1996 (the equivalent provision to reg.29(2)(b)) with the result that the claimant was deprived of JSA for the number of weeks calculated in accordance with that provision. In relation to reg.96 (the equivalent of reg. 31), in his view the payment was never due to be paid at all but was simply paid into the claimant's bank account. He therefore found that it fell within reg.96(1)(b) (the equivalent of para.(1)(b)) to be treated as paid in the first benefit week in which it was practicable to take it into account after payment. Judge Jacobs states:

> "The '*first succeeding* benefit week' actually reads as the first week after 'the benefit week in which [it] is due to be paid'. On that reading regulation 96 would not apply and the payment would never be treated as being paid. That would be absurd. That can, and must, be avoided by reading 'first succeeding' as the first week after the actual date of payment. Practicability is determined by when the decision-maker is able to take the amount into account for the purposes of the calculations that lead to entitlement. In this case, that was the week following payment."

It is not entirely clear (to me) why Judge Jacobs found that the payment was never due to be paid because the letter concerning the payment on account of the offer of settlement stated that it would be paid in the claimant's December salary. Was it not therefore due to be paid on the claimant's December pay date?

The appeal against this decision, which was dismissed by the Court of Appeal (*Minter v Kingston Upon Hull CC* and *Potter v Secretary of State for Work and Pensions* [2011] EWCA Civ 1155; [2012] AACR 21) did not deal with this point.

Paragraph (2)

It seems that the effect of para.(2) is that all these benefits are treated as paid on a daily basis. This is made clearer by the April 2013 amendment. A proportion of the weekly rate is treated as paid for each day covered by the entitlement. This should avoid overlaps of the kind revealed in *R(SB) 15/82*. See regs 75(b) and 32(4). **2.356**

Paragraphs (3) and (4)

These paragraphs, which provided rules for attributing an award of working tax credit or the working tax credit four week run-on (see reg.7D of the Working Tax Credit (Entitlement and Maximum Rate) Regulations 2002 (SI 2002/2005) in Vol. IV of this series for the working tax credit run-on) respectively, have been omitted with effect from April 11, 2011. The effect is that the date that the period of attribution of working tax credit fixed under reg.29 begins will be the same as for other types of income (see para.(1)). **2.357**

Calculation of weekly amount of income

2.358 **32.**—(1) For the purposes of regulation 29 (calculation of earnings derived from employed earner's employment and income other than earnings) [9[10. . .]], subject to [3paragraphs (2) to (7)][1. . .], where the period in respect of which a payment [9 of income or tax credit] is made—

(a) does not exceed a week, the weekly amount shall be the amount of that payment;

(b) exceeds a week, the weekly amount shall be determined—

(i) in a case where that period is a month, by multiplying the amount of the payment by 12 and dividing the product by 52;

(ii) in a case where that period is three months, by multiplying the amount of the payment by 4 and dividing the product by 52;

[9 (iii) in a case where that period is a year and the payment is an award of working tax credit, by dividing the payment by the number of days in the year and multiplying the result by 7;

(iiia) in a case where that period is a year and the payment is income other than an award of working tax credit, by dividing the amount of the payment by 52;]

(iv) in any other case by multiplying the amount of the payment by 7 and dividing the product by the number equal to the number of days in the period in respect of which it is made.

(2) Where a payment for a period not exceeding a week is treated under regulation 31(1)(a) (date on which income is treated as paid) as paid before the first benefit week and a part is to be taken into account for some days only in that week (the relevant days), the amount to be taken into account for the relevant days shall be calculated by multiplying the amount of the payment by the number equal to the number of relevant days and dividing the product by the number of days in the period in respect of which it is made.

(3) Where a payment is in respect of a period equal to or in excess of a week and a part thereof is to be taken into account for some days only in a benefit week (the relevant days), the amount to be taken into account for the relevant days shall, except where paragraph (4) applies, be calculated by multiplying the amount of the payment by the number equal to the number of relevant days and dividing the product by the number of days in the period in respect of which it is made.

(4) In the case of a payment of—

(a) [5. . .] [2maternity allowance], [4short-term or long-term incapacity benefit], or severe disablement allowance [4. . .], the amount to be taken into account for the relevant days shall be the amount of benefit [1payable] in respect of those days;

(b) income support [5[8, jobseeker's allowance or employment and support allowance]], the amount to be taken into account for the relevant days shall be calculated by multiplying the weekly amount of the benefit by the number of relevant days and dividing the product by seven.

(5) Except in the case of a payment which it has not been practicable to treat under regulation 31(1)(b) as paid on the first day of the benefit week in which it is due to be paid, where a payment of income from a particular source is or has been paid regularly and that payment falls to be taken into account in the same benefit week as a payment of the same kind and from the same source, the amount of that income to be taken into account in any one benefit

week shall not exceed the weekly amount determined under paragraph (1)(a) or (b), as the case may be, of the payment which under regulation 31(1)(b) (date on which income is treated as paid) is treated as paid first.

(6) Where the amount of the claimant's income fluctuates and has changed more than once, or a claimant's regular pattern of work is such that he does not work every week, the foregoing paragraphs may be modified so that the weekly amount of his income is determined by reference to his average weekly income—

(a) if there is a recognisable cycle of work, over the period of one complete cycle (including, where the cycle involves periods in which the claimant does no work, those periods but disregarding any other absences);

(b) in any other case, over a period of five weeks or such other period as may, in the particular case, enable the claimant's average weekly income to be determined more accurately.

[6(6A) Where income is taken into account under paragraph (2B) of regulation 29 over the period specified in that paragraph, the amount of that income to be taken into account in respect of any week in that period shall be an amount equal to the amount of that income which would have been taken into account under regulation 62 had the person to whom that income was paid not ceased to be a[7 full-time student].]

[3(7) Where any payment of earnings is taken into account under paragraph (4C) of regulation 29 (calculation of earnings derived from employed earner's employment and income other than earnings), over the period specified in that paragraph, the amount to be taken into account shall be equal to the amount of the payment.]

AMENDMENTS

1. Income Support (General) Amendment Regulations 1988 (SI 1988/663) reg.15 (April 11, 1988).

2. Income Support (General) Amendment Regulations 1988 (SI 1988/1445) reg.8 (September 12, 1988).

3. Income Support (General) Amendment No.2 Regulations 1989 (SI 1989/1323) reg.10 (October 9, 1989).

4. Disability Working Allowance and Income Support (General) Amendment Regulations 1995 (SI 1995/482) reg.11 (April 13, 1995).

5. Income Support (General) (Jobseeker's Allowance Consequential Amendments) Regulations 1996 (SI 1996/206) reg.16 (October 7, 1996).

6. Income-related Benefits and Jobseeker's Allowance (Miscellaneous Amendments) Regulations 1997 (SI 1997/65) reg.6 (April 7, 1997).

7. Social Security Amendment (Students) Regulations 2000 (SI 2000/1981) reg.5(5) and Sch. (July 31, 2000).

8. Employment and Support Allowance (Consequential Provisions) (No.2) Regulations 2008 (SI 2008/1554) reg.2(6) (October 27, 2008).

9. Social Security (Miscellaneous Amendments) (No.6) Regulations 2008 (SI 2008/2767) reg.2(5) (November 17, 2008).

10. Social Security (Miscellaneous Amendments) Regulations 2011 (SI 2011/674) reg.3(3) (April 11, 2011).

DEFINITIONS

"benefit week"—see reg.2(1).
"claimant"—*ibid.*, and reg.23(1).
"full-time student"—see reg.61(1).

GENERAL NOTE

Paragraph(1)

2.359 This provision gives a straightforward method of converting payments to be taken into account for various periods to a weekly equivalent. Regulation 75 deals with the calculation for part-weeks of entitlement.

The new form of sub-para.(b)(iii), in force from November 17, 2008, has been introduced to reflect the fact that the benefit computer systems have been designed to produce a daily rate of working tax credit, which is then multiplied by seven to arrive at a weekly rate. This results in a slightly different weekly amount of working tax credit than by dividing the annual award by 52. Therefore, in order to reflect the computer process (which apparently results in a very small gain for claimants), the new form of sub-para.(b)(iii) contains a separate rule where the income to be taken into account is working tax credit.

Paragraphs (2)–(4)

2.360 These provisions establish the rules where the period for which a payment is to be taken into account under regs 29 and 31 does not coincide with a benefit week and some odd days ("the relevant days") come into a benefit week.

Paragraph (5)

2.361 There are two different rules, according to whether two payments from the same regular source fall to the same benefit week because of the rules of attribution or because of the operation of reg.31(1)(b). The general rule is the first one, under which the maximum amount to be taken into account in the benefit week is the weekly amount of the payment due first. The *Decision Makers Guide* (para.25081) gives an example of how this could arise. A claimant has been receiving statutory sick pay from his employer every two weeks on a Friday. He receives a payment for two weeks on May 15, 2009. This is attributed to the period May 15 to May 28 inclusive. The claimant is to return to work on June 1 and receives a final payment of two weeks' sick pay on May 26. The decision-maker treats this as paid on May 22 for the period May 22 to June 4. For the income support benefit week from May 22 to May 28 the amount of sick pay to be taken into account is limited to the weekly amount of the payment made on May 15. There is an exception to this rule in that if the first payment was due to be paid before the date of claim it is to be disregarded (Sch.8 para.13 and Sch.9 para.35). Then there will no longer be an overlap. The second rule applies where under reg.31(1)(b) it has not been practicable to take a payment into account in the benefit week in which it was due to be paid. The payment then is taken into account in the first practicable benefit week. In this situation both payments can be taken into account in the same week, although each payment can have the appropriate disregard applied (Sch.8 para.10 and Sch.9 para.37). The disregards in para.13 of Sch.8 and para.35 of Sch.9 (see above) may also apply.

Paragraph (6)

2.362 This paragraph is oddly placed because it only allows the preceding paragraphs to be modified, not any of the other regulations on the calculation or attribution of income.

In *MC v SSWP (IS)* [2013] UKUT 384 (AAC) the claimant worked as a football steward every other week when the club played at home. He received a payment for two home cup matches which for reasons that were not entirely clear the tribunal treated as an exceptional payment outside the normal pattern. The claimant argued that the payment should be treated as part of his 52-week cycle of work for the club and that his earnings should be averaged over 52 weeks under para.(6)(a).

Judge Wright points out that para.(6) mirrors reg.5(2)(b), albeit in the context of the income earned rather than hours of work. Thus in deciding whether the claimant did have a recognisable cycle of work, the caselaw under reg.5(2)(b), and the equivalent JSA provision, reg.51(2)(b), should be applied, in particular *R(JSA) 5/03* and *R(JSA) 1/07* (see the notes to reg.5(2)–(3A) for a discussion of these cases).

Judge Wright remitted the appeal to a fresh tribunal for it to decide whether the claimant did have a recognisable cycle of work, having regard to the nature of his agreement with the football club to work as a steward, how the off-season was treated, and whether he had to reapply (and if so, how) for the job of steward each August. (There was also the question of whether a six month period during which the claimant had not worked that year had broken any recognisable cycle.) The more casual the claimant's working relationship with the club was, the less likely it may be that he was in a recognisable cycle of work. The Secretary of State had accepted that para.(6) could apply in this case on the basis that the claimant's income fluctuated and had changed more than once. The new tribunal would therefore need to decide whether either para.(6)(a) or (b) applied (if neither applied, it would seem that para.(1) could not be modified and would apply to the payment). Judge Wright concluded by observing that this appeal had proceeded on the basis that the claimant was an employee (rather than self-employed)—if the claimant was self-employed, para.(6) would of course not apply.

Paragraph (6A)

Regulation 29(2B) deals with the period over which a student grant is to be taken into account in the case of a person who has left or been dismissed from his course before it finishes and so has to repay part or all of his grant. Paragraph (6A) provides that where reg.29(2B) applies, the weekly amount of the income to be taken into account is to be calculated in accordance with reg.62. This means that the grant income will be apportioned over the period of study (i.e. from the beginning of the academic year to the day before the summer vacation), except for those elements which are apportioned over 52 weeks, and the disregards in reg.62(2), (2A) and (2B) will apply. See further reg.62 and the notes to that regulation. See also reg.40(3B) which provides that the amount of the grant income to be taken into account is to be calculated on the basis that none of it has been repaid. However, note *Chief Adjudication Officer v Leeves* reported as *R(IS) 5/99*) in the notes to reg.29(2B) and the argument discussed in those notes as to when reg.29(2B) applies. **2.363**

Any grant or covenant income or student loan left over at the end of the person's course is disregarded as income (see para.61 of Sch.9).

Paragraph (7)

Where a payment of compensation (reg.35(3)(a)) is made on the termination of part-time employment (reg.29(4D)(a) and reg.35(3)(c)) it is taken into account for a week (reg.29(4C)). This provision confirms that the whole payment is taken into account for that week. Note the disregard in para.2 of Sch.8. **2.364**

Weekly amount of charitable or voluntary payment

33.—(1)[[1] . . .] **2.365**

AMENDMENT

1. Income Support (General) Amendment No.5 Regulations 1988 (SI 1988/2022) reg.8 (December 12, 1988).

Incomplete weeks of benefit

34.—[[1] . . .] **2.366**

AMENDMENT

1. Income Support (General) Amendment Regulations 1988 (SI 1988/663) reg.16 (April 11. 1988).

CHAPTER III

EMPLOYED EARNERS

Earnings of employed earners

2.367 **35.**—(1) [2Subject to paragraphs (2) and (3),] "earnings" means in the case of employment as an employed earner, any remuneration or profit derived from that employment and includes—

(a) any bonus or commission;

(b) any payment in lieu of remuneration except any periodic sum paid to a claimant on account of the termination of his employment by reason of redundancy;

(c) any payment in lieu of notice [2. . .];

(d) any holiday pay except any payable more than four weeks after the termination or interruption of employment but this exception shall not apply to a claimant to whom [1section 23 of the Act [SSCBA, s.126] (trade disputes) applies or in respect of whom section 20(3) of the Act [SSCBA, s.124(1)] (conditions of entitlement to income support) has effect as modified by section 23A(*b*) of the Act [SSCBA, s.127(b)] (effect to return to work)];

(e) any payment by way of a retainer;

(f) any payment made by the claimant's employer in respect of expenses not wholly, exclusively and necessarily incurred in the performance of the duties of the employment, including any payment made by the claimant's employer in respect of—

(i) travelling expenses incurred by the claimant between his home and place of employment;

(ii) expenses incurred by the claimant under arrangements made for the care of a member of his family owing to the claimant's absence from home;

(g) any award of compensation made under section [11112(4) or 117(3)(a) of the Employment Rights Act 1996 (the remedies: orders and compensation, enforcement of order and compensation)];

[11(gg) any payment or remuneration made under section 28, 34, 64, 68 or 70 of the Employment Rights Act 1996 (right to guarantee payments, remuneration on suspension on medical or maternity grounds, complaints to employment tribunals);]

(h) any such sum as is referred to in section [11 112(3) of the Contributions and Benefits Act [(certain sums to be earnings for social security purposes).

[2(i) where—

(i) [12 . . .]

(ii) a payment of compensation is made in respect of employment which is part-time, the amount of the compensation.]

[6(j) the amount of any payment by way of a non-cash voucher which has been taken into account in the computation of a person's earnings in accordance with [10 Part 5 of Schedule 3 to the Social Security (Contributions) Regulations 2001].]

[2(1A) [12 . . .].]

(2) "Earnings" shall not include—

(a) [6 Subject to paragraph (2A),] any payment in kind;

(b) any remuneration paid by or on behalf of an employer to the claimant [4in respect of a period throughout which the claimant is on maternity leave [9, paternity leave [15, adoption leave or shared parental leave]] or is absent from work because he is ill];
(c) any payment in respect of expenses wholly, exclusively and necessarily incurred in the performance of the duties of the employment;
(d) any occupational pension.
[5(e) any lump sum payment made under the Iron and Steel Re-adaptation Benefits Scheme].
[13(f) any payment in respect of expenses arising out of the [14 claimant participating as a service user].]

[6(2A) Paragraph (2)(a) shall not apply in respect of any non-cash voucher referred to in paragraph (1)(j).]

[2(3) In this regulation—
(a) "compensation" means any payment made in respect of or on the termination of employment in a case where a person has not received or received only part of a payment in lieu of notice due or which would have been due to him had he not waived his right to receive it, other than—
 (i) any payment specified in paragraph (1)(a) to (h);
 (ii) any payment specified in paragraph (2)(a) to [5(e)];
 (iii) any redundancy payment within the meaning of section [11135(1) of the Employment Rights Act 1996], and
 (iv) any refund of contributions to which that person was entitled under an occupational pension scheme within the meaning of section 66(1) of the Social Security Pensions Act 1975;
 [3(v) any compensation payable by virtue of section 173 or section 178(3) or (4) of the Education Reform Act 1988;]
(b) [12 . . .];
(c) "part-time employment" means employment in which a person is not to be treated as engaged in remunerative work under regulation 5 or [7 6(1) [8 and (4)]] (persons treated, or not treated, as engaged in remunerative work).]

AMENDMENTS

1. Income Support (General) Amendment Regulations 1988 (SI 1988/663) reg.17 (April 11, 1988).
2. Income Support (General) Amendment No.2 Regulations 1989 (SI 1989/1323) reg.11 (October 9, 1989).
3. Education (Inner London Education Authority) (Transitional and Supplementary Provisions) (No.2) Order 1990 (SI 1990/774) art.2 (April 1, 1990).
4. Income-related Benefits Schemes (Miscellaneous Amendments) (No.4) Regulations 1993 (SI 1993/2119) reg.12 (October 4, 1993).
5. Social Security (Miscellaneous Amendments) Regulations 1997 (SI 1997/454) reg.7 (April 7, 1997).
6. Social Security Amendment (Non-Cash Vouchers) Regulations 1999 (SI 1999/1509) reg.2(5) (July 1, 1999).
7. Social Security (Miscellaneous Amendments) (No.2) Regulations 1999 (SI 1999/2556) reg.2(4) (October 4, 1999).
8. Social Security (Miscellaneous Amendments) Regulations 2000 (SI 2000/681) reg.2(c) (April 3, 2000).
9. Social Security (Paternity and Adoption) Amendment Regulations 2002 (SI 2002/2689) reg.2(4) (December 8, 2002).

10. Social Security (Miscellaneous Amendments) (No.4) Regulations 2006 (SI 2006/2378) reg.5(3) (October 2, 2006).

11. Social Security (Miscellaneous Amendments) (No. 5) Regulations 2007 (SI 2007/2618) reg.5(6) (October 1, 2007).

12. Social Security (Miscellaneous Amendments) Regulations 2008 (SI 2008/698) reg.2(7) (April 14, 2008).

13. Social Security (Miscellaneous Amendments) (No.4) Regulations 2009 (SI 2009/2655) reg.2(7) (October 26, 2009).

14. Social Security (Miscellaneous Amendments) Regulations 2014 (SI 2014/591) reg.2(3) (April 28, 2014).

15. Shared Parental Leave and Statutory Shared Parental Pay (Consequential Amendments to Subordinate Legislation) Order 2014 (SI 2014/3255) art.5(4) (December 31, 2014).

Definitions

"the Act"—see reg.2(1).
"adoption leave"—*ibid.*
"claimant"—*ibid.*, reg.23(1).
"claimant participating as a service user"—see reg.2(1B).
"employed earner"—see reg.2(1).
"family"—see SSCBA s.137(1).
"maternity leave"—see reg.2(1).
"occupational pension"—*ibid.*
"paternity leave"—*ibid.*
"shared parental leave"—*ibid.*

General Note

2.368 Regulation 35 applies to earnings from employment as an employed earner. See the definition of "employed earner" in reg.2(1). On the tests for deciding whether a person is an employed earner or in self-employment, see *CJSA 4721/2001*.

The category of office-holder includes holders of elective office, such as local councillors. Some payments made to councillors (e.g. for travelling expenses and subsistence allowances: *CIS 89/1989*) will be excluded under para.(2)(c), but attendance allowances, which are not paid to meet specific expenses, count as earnings (*R(IS) 6/92*). *CIS 77/1993* decides that basic allowances are also earnings, but applies the disregard in para.(2)(c), reg.40(4) (now reg.40(4)(a)) and Sch.9 para.3. The purpose of the basic allowance is to compensate the councillor for his time and to cover the expenses incurred in the execution of his duties. The expenses may, as in that case, absorb the total allowance. The Commissioner points out that since March 18, 1992, basic allowances had been disregarded for the purposes of the former reg.7(1)(g)(i) of the Social Security (Unemployment, Sickness and Invalidity Benefit) Regulations 1983. The allowance was therefore treated differently depending on whether unemployment benefit or income support was claimed. However, its treatment under JSA is the same as for income support. See also *CJSA/2396/2002* and *SS v SSWP (JSA)* [2013] UKUT 233 (AAC).

Similarly, although payments of expenses to claimants participating as a service user (see reg.2(1B) for those to whom this refers) do not count as earnings (see para.(2)(f)) and are disregarded as income (see para.2A of Sch.9), any payment for taking part in a service user group (e.g. for attending meetings) will be taken into account as earnings. The notional income rules, however, do not apply (see reg.42(8ZA)).

2.369 See also the notes to reg.36(3) for discussion of the application of the principle of *Parsons v Hogg* [1985] 2 All E.R. 897, CA to the meaning of "gross earnings". This allows the deduction from earnings of necessary, etc., expenses incurred by the employee.

Note in addition *R(TC) 2/03* discussed below which concerned deductions for previously overpaid salary.

See Sch.8 for earnings that are disregarded. Note that the disregard that applies to payments made on the termination of full-time employment (i.e. 16 hours or more per week in the case of the claimant, 24 hours or more per week for a partner) was significantly extended with effect from October 1, 2007. See the new form of para.1 of Sch.8 and the notes to that paragraph.

CIS/1068/2006 holds that payments made to the claimant by his wife (from money she received from the local authority under s.57 of the Health and Social Care Act 2001) in consideration of the care services he provided to her were "earnings" and fell to be taken into account in calculating his income support. It did not matter whether the claimant was to be regarded as an employed or self-employed earner for these purposes—the issue was whether the claimant had been engaged by his wife to provide care services for reward, which on the facts of the case was the only possible inference. The Commissioner rejected the claimant's argument that the payments by his wife should be disregarded under para.58 of Sch.9 (see further the note to para.58). The claimant appealed to the Court of Appeal against this decision but his appeal was dismissed (*Casewell v Secretary of State for Work and Pensions* [2008] EWCA Civ 524, reported as *R(IS) 7/08*). The claimant contended that s.136 of the Contributions and Benefits Act requires that payments made to a member of the family are counted when they come into the family, and if at that point they are disregarded, they cannot be counted again if they are transferred from one member of the family to another. However the Court agreed with the Commissioner that the payments to the claimant by his wife were earnings in respect of the care he provided and in the claimant's hands they became his income under s.136(1). It should be noted that the payments to the claimant's wife in this case were made on the basis that she was instructed to pay the claimant the appropriate sum each week against a payslip. There was therefore a specific obligation for the claimant's wife to deal with the payments in a particular way, which had the result that the money paid to her husband was treated as earnings. Thus this was a somewhat different situation from the more usual informal transfer of resources between family members.

Paragraph (1)

This paragraph first provides a general definition of earnings from employment as an employee—any remuneration or profit derived from that employment—and then deems certain payments to be earnings. Paragraph (2) provides a number of exceptions and Sch.8 lists items which would otherwise count as earnings which are to be disregarded. See in particular paras 1 to 2 which concern the earnings that are ignored on the termination of employment or where hours of work are reduced (possibly to nil). The disregard that applies to payments made on the termination of full-time employment (i.e. 16 hours or more per week in the case of the claimant, 24 hours or more per week for a partner) was significantly extended with effect from October 1, 2007. See the new form of para.1 of Sch.8 and the notes to that paragraph. **2.370**

The general test covers straightforward wages or salary, but can extend to other remuneration derived from employment. According to *R(SB) 21/86*, these are wide words, which mean "having their origin in." Thus if it had been necessary to decide whether a compensatory award for unfair dismissal by an Industrial Tribunal was derived from employment, the Commissioner would have held that it did. *R(SB) 21/86* is followed in *CIS 590/1993*, which concerned the loss of earnings element in a compensation award for sex discrimination. In *Minter v Kingston Upon Hull CC* and *Potter v Secretary of State for Work and Pensions* [2011] EWCA Civ 1155; [2012] AACR 21 the Court of Appeal held that payments in settlement of potential equal pay claims were "remuneration" within reg.35(1) of the Housing Benefit Regulations 2006 and reg.98(1) of the JSA Regulations 1996 (the equivalents of para.(1)), or, if not, were payments "in lieu of remuneration" within the equivalent housing benefit and JSA provisions of para.(1)(b). Note, however, that in *EM v LB Waltham Forest* [2009] UKUT 245 (AAC) the two payments that the claimant received by way of settlement of a potential claim against his employer under the Part-time Workers (Prevention of Less Favourable Treatment) Regulations 2000 (SI

2000/1551) did not come within reg.35(1) of the Housing Benefit Regulations 2006 (the equivalent housing benefit provision to para.(1)) but counted as capital (see the notes to reg.23 under "*Distinction between capital and income*" for further discussion of *Minter and Potter*, and the Upper Tribunal decisions that were under appeal in that case, and *EM v Waltham Forest LBC*).

Payments to a NCB employee in lieu of concessionary coal constituted remuneration derived from employment (*R(SB) 2/86*).

2.371 Tips and gratuities would be an example of payments from third parties which are nonetheless derived from employment (see Williams, *Social Security Taxation*, paras 4.21–4.22 for discussion of the income tax cases).

See also *CH 2387/2002*, a case on the then equivalent council tax benefit provision (reg.19(1) of the Council Tax Benefit Regulations). The company accounts showed that the claimant had drawn £6,400 for the year 1999/2000, whereas he had actually received less than half that amount, the remainder having been loaned by him to the company. The Commissioner rejects the claimant's contention that only the amount he received constituted earnings and confirms that for the purpose of council tax benefit his earnings were £6,400. But the repayment of a loan by a company to a director is not a profit derived from employment (*CCS 3671/2002*). The Commissioner in *CCS 3671/2002* refers to *Shilton v Wilmshurst (Inspector of Taxes)* [1991] 1 A.C. 684 in which the House of Lords stated that an emolument was not "from" employment if it was not paid as a reward for past services or as an inducement to enter into employment and provide future services. It was not enough on its own that the payment came from the employer. See also *CCS/3387/2006* (withdrawals from a director's current account were capital, not income).

Note *R(TC) 2/03* which concerned the meaning of "earnings" in reg.19(1) of the Family Credit Regulations (the working families' tax credit equivalent of this provision—see the 2002 edition of this volume for these Regulations). The claimant's partner's employer had made deductions from his current salary in order to recover an earlier overpayment. His payslips showed his "gross for tax" figure as £76 less than his usual salary. The Commissioner held that his gross earnings for the months the deduction was made was the reduced figure. The most likely analysis was that there had been a consensual variation of the contract of employment for those months, making the lower figure the remuneration or profit derived from that employment. In so doing the Commissioner declined to follow *CCS 4378/2001* (a child support case) which had also concerned an overpayment by the employer that was being recovered by deductions from current salary. The Commissioner in *CCS 4378/2001* held that the whole of the absent parent's salary before deductions counted as "earnings". However, he suggested that the solution to the apparent unfairness of that conclusion lay in the fact that an overpayment of salary paid by mistake and to which the person was not entitled was not "earnings" at the time it was made because it was not "remuneration or profit *derived from* . . . employment". He therefore directed the new tribunal to consider whether it had jurisdiction to go back to the period of the overpayment and alter the maintenance assessment. The Commissioner in *R(TC) 2/03*, however, did not see why the overpayment was not derived from employment at least for any period before the mistake was identified and recovery required by the employer. He therefore preferred his own approach. Certainly the solution adopted in *R(TC) 2/03* has the merit of focusing on the earnings that are actually being received for the period in question and avoids the need to attempt to revisit earlier periods in a claim.

The particular categories in sub-paras (a)–(j) are deemed to be earnings, whether they would in general count as earnings or not (*R(SB) 21/86*). Only a few categories require comment.

2.372 *Sub-paragraph (b)*: A payment in lieu of remuneration will in its nature be an income payment. Capital payments (e.g. for the loss of the job itself) are excluded. *R(SB) 21/86* held that a compensatory award for unfair dismissal made by an industrial tribunal (now an employment tribunal) was a payment in lieu of remuneration, to be taken into account for the number of weeks specified in the award. Such an award is now expressly included in sub-para.(g) and so will fall to be taken into account on the termination of full-time employment, although since October 1, 2007 payments under sub-para.(b) on the termination of full-time employment have been disregarded (see para.1 of Sch.8 and the notes to that paragraph).

In *CIS/590/1993* the claimant's award of compensation under the Sex Discrimination Act included amounts for injured feelings, the loss of a tax rebate and one month's loss of earnings. It was accepted that the first two items counted as capital. The Commissioner follows *R(SB) 21/86* and holds that the loss of earnings element fell to be treated as earnings under sub-para.(b). There was no reason for drawing a distinction between a compensatory award for unfair dismissal and that part of a sex discrimination award that was for loss of earnings. The fact that only the former was referred to in sub-para.(g) did not imply that the loss of earnings elements in sex (or race) discrimination awards (or indeed awards made by county courts for breach of employment contracts) were excluded from para.(1), since the categories listed in sub-paras (a)–(i) were only included as examples. See the notes to reg.31(1) as to when the earnings were treated as due to be paid. However, the fact that the loss of earnings element in such awards comes within sub-para.(b), rather than sub-para.(g), means that from October 1, 2007 it will be disregarded (except where it is awarded in respect of employment which has been suspended or part-time work where the claimant was claiming income support, see paras 1–2 of Sch.8 and the notes to those paragraphs).

See also *Minter v Kingston Upon Hull CC* and *Potter v Secretary of State for Work and Pensions* [2011] EWCA Civ 1155; [2012] AACR 21 in which payments in settlement of potential claims under the Equal Pay Act 1970 counted as earnings. In contrast note *EM v LB Waltham Forest* [2009] UKUT 245 (AAC) which holds that the two payments that the claimant received by way of settlement of a potential claim against his employer under the Part-time Workers (Prevention of Less Favourable Treatment) Regulations 2000 (SI 2000/1551) were capital (for a discussion of these decisions see the notes to reg.23 under "*Distinction between capital and income*").

Sub-paragraph (c): This sub-paragraph is now confined to payments in lieu of notice, whether full or partial. Presumably, it covers payments expressly in lieu of notice (see *CIS 400/1994*). "Global" payments will fall under sub-para.(i). Note that from October 1, 2007 earnings received under this sub-paragraph are disregarded (except in the case of part-time work which ends while the claimant is claiming income support: see paras 1–2 of Sch.8 and the notes to those paragraphs). **2.373**

Sub-paragraph (d): Holiday pay which is payable (i.e due to be paid, not received or paid: *R(SB) 15/82, R(SB) 33/83, R(SB) 11/85*) within four weeks of termination or interruption of employment counts as earnings. In cases of termination holiday pay will be due immediately, unless the contract of employment expressly provides otherwise. Therefore, whenever it is paid (and presumably it cannot count until it is actually paid) it will count as earnings to be taken into account for the benefit week in which it was due to be paid. Then s.74 of the Administration Act might come into play. If employment is merely interrupted it is more likely that holiday pay will not be payable immediately. Note that from October 1, 2007 earnings received under this sub-paragraph are disregarded (except in the case of employment which has been suspended or where the holiday pay is paid in connection with part-time work undertaken while the claimant is claiming income support: see paras 1–2 of Sch.8 and the notes to those paragraphs). **2.374**

Holiday pay outside this sub-paragraph is capital (reg.48(3)).

CIS 894/1994 holds that for a payment to be holiday pay there has to be entitlement to holidays under the contract of employment. The claimant worked on a North Sea oil rig. His contract of employment provided that there was no entitlement to holidays but that he would accrue 42 hours vacation pay per quarter. He could ask for this pay at any time and payment would be made at the end of the quarter. On the termination of his employment he was paid 100 days accrued vacation pay. The Commissioner decides that the vacation pay was not holiday pay in the ordinary sense of the word. It had nothing to do with the taking of holidays but was in reality compensation for the fact that there was no holiday entitlement. The consequence was that it fell to be disregarded under what was then para.1(a)(ii) (now para.1(1)(a)) of Sch.8.

2.375 *Sub-paragraph (e)*: *R(IS) 9/95* decides that a guarantee payment under s.12 of the Employment Protection (Consolidation) Act 1978 is a payment by way of a retainer. Presumably the same will apply to guarantee payments under the current provision, s.28 of the Employment Rights Act 1996.

See also the payments included under sub-para.(gg).

Note the amendments made to paras 1 and 2 of Sch.8 on October 26, 2009 which confirm that the disregards in those paragraphs do not apply to payments in the nature of a retainer (i.e. guarantee payments under s.28 of the Employment Rights Act 1996, and the right to remuneration while suspended on medical grounds under s.64 or while suspended on maternity grounds under s.68, together with awards under s.34 or 70, of that Act), as well as payments by way of a retainer.

2.376 *Sub-paragraph (f)*: The conditions here are in line with those under which expenses are deductible from earnings for income tax purposes. Payment for all items beyond those solely necessary for *the performance of* the duties of the employment are caught. It is not enough if the expenses are incurred in order to enable the person to perform those duties (*Smith v Abbott* [1994] 1 All E.R. 673). The express mention of the expenses of travel to and from work and of looking after a family member merely spells this out. (On child care expenses see *Jackson and Cresswell v Chief Adjudication Officer* (C-63/91 and C-64/91) [1992] E.C.R. I-4737, also reported as Appendix 2 to *R(IS) 10/91*, and *R(FC) 2/98 (Meyers)*, in the notes to reg.36(3).) The reimbursement of a local councillor's home telephone expenses in *CIS 38/1989* is an example. On the evidence, the expenses were necessarily incurred, but not wholly or exclusively, in the performance of his duties as a councillor. On other evidence, such expenses could be apportioned between personal and employment purposes (cf. *R(FC) 1/91, CFC 26/1989* and *R(FIS) 13/91* on reg.38(3)). See also *CFC 836/1995* in the notes to reg.38(11) on apportionment of expenses between earnings as an employee and from self-employment. There is helpful guidance in *R(FIS) 4/85*.

CIS 89/1989 holds that travel and subsistence allowances paid to a local councillor, which included travel from home to the place of employment, were for necessary etc. expenses, because a councillor's home is also a place of employment. *R(IS) 6/92* confirms this result, because under s.174(1) of the Local Government Act 1972 payments of travelling and subsistence allowances can only be made where the expenses have been necessarily incurred for the performance of any duty as a councillor. Therefore, such a payment must fall outside sub-para.(f) and within para.(2)(c).

In *CH/1330/2008* the claimant was a care worker who travelled to her clients from her home. The Commissioner finds that in these circumstances she did not have a place of employment within the meaning of reg.35(1)(f)(i) of the Housing Benefit Regulations 2006 (which is the equivalent of sub-para.(f)(i)) and that all her travel expenses from the moment she left home did not count as earnings.

2.377 But in *SS v St Edmundsbury BC (HB)* [2014] UKUT 172 (AAC) the travel allowance paid to the claimant following her employer's relocation which substantially increased the distance she had to travel to work (which was taxable) was earnings.

See also the notes to reg.36(3).

2.378 *Sub-para.(g)*: Awards of compensation which come under this sub-paragraph, including "out of court" settlement payments, are taken into account on the termination of full-time employment (see para.1 of Sch.8 and the notes to that paragraph).

2.379 *Sub-paragraph (gg)*: Section 28 of the Employment Rights Act 1996 provides a right to guarantee payments, s.64, a right to remuneration on suspension on medical grounds, and s.68, a right to remuneration on suspension on maternity grounds. Section 34 provides for a complaint to an employment tribunal in respect of an employer's failure to pay guarantee payments and s.70 for a complaint to an employment tribunal in respect of an employer's failure to pay under s.64 or 68.

Note the amendments made to paras 1 and 2 of Sch.8 on October 26, 2009 which have the effect that the disregards in those paragraphs do not apply to any of these payments.

Sub-paragraph (h): The sums referred to in s.112(3) of the Contributions and Benefits Act are arrears of pay under an order for reinstatement or re-engagement under the Employment Rights Act 1996; a sum payable under an award for the continuation of a contract of employment; and remuneration under a protective award. Such payments, including "out of court" settlement payments, are taken into account on the termination of full-time employment (see para.1 of Sch.8 and the notes to that paragraph). **2.380**

Sub-paragraph (i): There was a significant change in 1989 in the treatment of lump sum payments made on the termination of employment, which was designed to simplify decision-making. It was along similar lines to the change in the UB rules, but introduced several differences. In *CIS 400/1994* the Commissioner drew attention to the different ways that termination payments at the end of a period of employment were treated by the income support and unemployment benefit legislation. In particular, the definition of "compensation" was not the same (e.g. for unemployment benefit purposes "compensation" could include payments in lieu of notice; for income support it did not). For the position under JSA, see reg.98(1)(b) and (3) of the JSA Regulations 1996. **2.381**

There were separate provisions depending whether it was full-time or part-time employment which was terminated. See para.(3)(c) and reg.29(4D)(a) which adopts the test of remunerative work in regs 5 and 6(1) and (4) for the dividing line.

However, since April 14, 2008, the provisions relating to compensation payments only apply where part-time employment is terminated (see the amendment to para.(1)(i)). This is because the provisions were considered to be obsolete in relation to full-time employment following the increased disregard of payments made on the termination of full-time employment that was introduced on October 1, 2007 (see para.1 of Sch.8 and the notes to that paragraph). Where a compensation payment is made in respect of part-time employment that ceases before the claim for income support is made (whether or not the employment has terminated), it will continue to be ignored, as was the case before October 1, 2007 (see para.2 of Sch.8). However, a compensation payment will be taken into account in the case of part-time work which ends while the claimant is claiming income support: see the note to para.2 of Sch.8. The whole payment is taken into account in one week (reg.29(4C)), generally the week in which it is due to be paid (reg.31).

"Compensation" is defined in para.(3)(a). First, the person must not have received a payment in lieu of all the notice to which he was legally entitled. If this has happened, no other payment can be "compensation" within sub-para.(i) (confirmed in *CIS 400/1994*). Second, all the payments already counted as earnings by para.(1)(a) to (h) or excluded from that category by para.(2), refunds of pension contributions and "any redundancy payment within the meaning of s.135(1) of the Employment Rights Act 1996" are excluded. On the meaning of "any redundancy payment . . .", see *CJSA 82/1998* (which concerned the same phrase in reg.98(2)(f) of the JSA Regulations 1996). In the Commissioner's view, a payment "within the meaning of . . ." was wider than a payment "made under . . .". He concludes that the exemption under reg.98(2)(f) applied to all payments genuinely made in lieu of a redundancy payment up to the level of entitlement that would arise under the statutory duty to make a redundancy payment (now contained in s.135 of the Employment Rights Act 1996). The same should apply to the exclusion under para.(3)(a)(iii). **2.382**

Other payments made in respect of or on the termination of employment count as compensation. It does not particularly matter what the employer calls the payment, providing that it is connected to the termination (cf. *R(U) 4/92* and *R(U) 5/92*), so that merely calling the payment a capital payment (e.g. for loss of the job as a capital asset) does not take it outside sub-para.(i). The main categories will be payments from employers which are not precisely categorised (e.g. the ubiquitous "ex gratia" payment) and payments made in settlement of claims for unfair or wrongful dismissal (providing that a payment in lieu of full notice has not already been paid). But a payment solely in relation to racial discrimination during employment is not within the definition (*CU 88/1991*).

Note that although payments made on the termination of employment such as statutory redundancy payments, and (unless they count as "compensation" payments—see above) contractual redundancy payments and ex gratia payments are not earnings, they will count as capital. Periodic sums paid on account of the termination of employment due to redundancy do not count as earnings under para.(1)(b) but will be income other than earnings (or possibly capital payable by instalments, depending on the circumstances).

2.383 *Sub-paragraph (j)*: The effect of this sub-paragraph, together with para.(2A), is that non-cash vouchers liable for Class 1 national insurance contributions will be treated as earnings. This does not apply to non-cash vouchers that are not taken into account for national insurance purposes. As payments in kind they will count as other income (see reg.40(4)(a)) but note the disregard in para.21 of Sch.9.

Note that reg.2(2) of the Social Security Amendment (Non-Cash Vouchers) Regulations 1999 (SI 1999/1509) provides that where a claimant has an existing award of income support (or JSA) on June 30, 1999, sub-para.(j) and para.(2A) will not operate until the date that the first decision on review of that award after June 30, 1999 takes effect.

Paragraph (2)

2.384 These amounts—payments in kind, sick, maternity, paternity, shared parental or adoption leave pay, reimbursement of necessary expenses, payments of expenses that result from "a claimant participating as a service user" (see reg.2(1B) for those to whom this refers) and occupational pensions—are not earnings, but do count as other income (reg.40(4)(a)). It is apparently intended that lump sum payments covered by subpara.(e) should count as capital (as their nature would indicate), although reg.40(4) (now reg.40(4)(a)) has not also been amended. But note that income in kind is disregarded (Sch.9 para.21); so are payments of necessary expenses (Sch.9 para.3) and payments of expenses in respect of a claimant participating as a service user (Sch.9 para.2A). Deductions from contractual or statutory sick, maternity, paternity, shared parental or adoption leave pay for Class 1 NI contributions and one-half of any contribution by the claimant to an occupational or personal pension scheme are disregarded under paras 4 and 4A of Sch.9. There is no provision for the disregard of ill-health payments or occupational pensions (confirmed in *CIS 6/1989*). If a person is remunerated by payments in kind, there is the possibility of notional earnings being attributed to the person under reg.42(6). However, the notional income rules are specifically excluded in the case of expenses *and* earnings as a result of a claimant participating as a service user (see reg.42(2)(ga) and (8ZA)).

See the notes to para.(1)(f) for what are necessary, etc. expenses. In a decision on the equivalent provision in the Family Credit Regulations (reg.19(2)), the Commissioner suggested that its effect is that expenditure by the employee on necessary etc. expenses is to be deducted from the amount of his earnings (*CFC 2/1989*). This does not seem to be consistent with the pattern of reg.35, which is otherwise concerned with payments to the employee, and is rejected in *R(FC) 1/90*, *R(IS) 16/93* and *CIS 77/1993*. See the notes to reg.19(2) of the Family Credit Regulations in the 2002 edition of this volume for full discussion of the point. The payment can be by way of reimbursement to the employee for expenses initially met by him (*CIS 77/1993*). But the application of the principle of *Parsons v Hogg* to the meaning of "gross earnings" in reg.36 will, it seems, permit the deduction from earnings of necessary, etc. expenses incurred by the employee. See the notes to reg.36(3). *CJSA 2402/2003* confirms that a trade union subscription is not deductible as such an expense and that this does not infringe art.11 ECHR (right of assembly and association).

CIS 4317/1997 has highlighted an anomaly in the legislation that results from sick or maternity pay, etc. not being treated as earnings. The claimant stopped work in September 1996 because of illness. He was paid four weeks' statutory and contractual sick pay on October 31, 1996 and his contract of employment was terminated on the same day. He claimed income support on November 1 but was treated as having income for four weeks from October 31 under regs 29(1) and (2) and 31(1). The Commissioner confirmed that this was correct. Although final earnings were disregarded under para.1 of Sch.8, there was no equivalent disregard in Sch.9 (or elsewhere) to enable final payments of sick pay to be ignored. He rejected the argument that reg.29(2) was ultra vires. This argument was renewed before the Court of Appeal but was dismissed (*Owen v Chief Adjudication Officer*, April 29, 1999). The claimant had contended that the power in s.136(5)(a) (person can be treated as possessing income or capital which he does not possess) did not apply where the person in fact possessed the income; it therefore did not authorise a provision treating income received by the claimant at one time as available to him at another time. In addition, reg.29(2) was outside the power in s.136(3) (income to be calculated or estimated in prescribed manner). It was contended that simply shifting income from one period to another was neither "calculation" nor "estimation". But the Court of Appeal held that reg.29(2) was within the power in s.136(5)(a). A deeming provision by its very nature had the effect of treating a fact or state of affairs as existing for a stated purpose when that fact or state of affairs did not in truth exist. Section 136(5)(a) was sufficiently widely framed to authorize a provision that spread or apportioned income to a stated period. The Court also rejected the contention that reg.29(2) was ultra vires on the ground of irrationality. However, the Court of Appeal (like the Commissioner and the tribunal) expressed disquiet at the anomalous result arising from the different treatment of sick pay and final earnings and voiced the hope that the operation of the regulations in these circumstances would be reconsidered. But this has not occurred despite the increased disregard of payments made on the termination of full-time employment introduced on October 1, 2007 (see para.1 of Sch.8 and the notes to that paragraph).

Calculation of net earnings of employed earners

36.—(1) For the purposes of regulation 29 (calculation of earnings of employed earners) the earnings of a claimant derived from employment as an employed earner to be taken into account shall, subject to paragraph (2), be his net earnings. **2.385**

(2) There shall be disregarded from a claimant's net earnings, any sum specified in paragraphs 1 to 13 [[2][[3] or 15A]] of Schedule 8.

(3) For the purposes of paragraph (1) net earnings shall be calculated by taking into account the gross earnings of the claimant from that employment less—

(a) any amount deducted from those earnings by way of—
  (i) income tax;
  (ii) primary Class 1 contributions under the Social Security Act; and

(b) one-half of any sum paid by the claimant [[1]in respect of a pay period] by way of a contribution towards an occupational or personal pension scheme.

AMENDMENTS

1. Income-related Benefits Schemes (Miscellaneous Amendments) (No.5) Regulations 1994 (SI 1994/2139) reg.26 (October 3, 1994).
2. Social Security (Miscellaneous Amendments) (No.2) Regulations 1999 (SI 1999/2556) reg.2(5) (October 4, 1999).
3. Social Security (Back to Work Bonus and Lone Parent Run-on) (Amendment and Revocation) Regulations 2003 (SI 2003/1589) reg.2(b) (October 25, 2004).

DEFINITIONS

"claimant"—see reg.2(1) and reg.23(1).
"employed earner"—see reg.2(1).
"occupational pension scheme"—see Pension Schemes Act 1993 s.1.
"pay period"—see reg.2(1).
"personal pension scheme"—*ibid.*
"Social Security Act"—*ibid.*

GENERAL NOTE

Paragraph (1)

2.386 Earnings defined in reg.35 are to be converted to net earnings before being taken into account. This is to be done according to para.(3).

Paragraph (2)

2.387 After the conversion to net earnings has been carried out, the amounts specified in paras 1–13 or 15A of Sch.8 are to be disregarded. (Paragraph 2 has not been updated to include a reference to para.15C of Sch.8.) For the position relating to earnings of a child or young person see the note to para.14 of Sch.8.

Paragraph (3)

2.388 Only this limited list of deductions for payments made by the employee may be made from gross earnings. Nothing is to be deducted for travel costs (see *CJSA 4721/2001*), child care expenses or meals at work. This leads to a much simpler calculation than under supplementary benefit. The compensation was an increase in the basic disregard from its previous £4–£5.

R(FC) 1/90 holds that if the employee makes contributions to both an occupational and a personal pension scheme, half of both contributions can be deducted. See also *R(CS) 3/00* which decides that half of the contributions made under retirement annuity contracts by employed earners were to be deducted from gross earnings under para.1(3)(c) of Sch.1 to the Child Support (Maintenance Assessments and Special Cases) Regulations 1992. Such contracts came within the meaning of "personal pension scheme" for employed earners. The same definition of "personal pension scheme" was used for income support (see reg.2(1)) and the Commissioner's reasoning should apply to deductions under para.(3)(b). Now note that following the changes made by Pt 4 of the Finance Act 2004 retirement annuity contracts come within the definition of "personal pension scheme" (see further the notes to "*personal pension scheme*" in reg.2(1)).

There was, however, some doubt about the meaning of "gross earnings." In *R(FC) 1/90* the Commissioner refers to the principle adopted by the Court of Appeal in *Parsons v Hogg* [1985] 2 All E.R. 897, appendix to *R(FIS) 4/85*, and by the Commissioner in *R(FIS) 4/85*, that "earnings," even associated with the word "gross," in the Family Income Supplements (General) Regulations 1980 meant not the remuneration actually received, but the receipts after payment of expenses wholly and necessarily incurred in the course of winning those receipts. He applies this principle to the equivalent provision to reg.36 in the Family Credit Regulations (reg.20) (see the 2002 edition of this volume for the Family Credit Regulations) and holds that expenses necessarily wholly and exclusively incurred by the employee in the performance of the duties of employment are to be deducted from the gross receipts to produce a figure of gross earnings. The same Commissioner applies the principle to income other than earnings in *CIS 25/1989*, but this has not been followed in *CIS 563/1991* and *R(IS) 13/01* (see the note to reg.40(1)). In *R(FC) 1/90*, the claimant's expenditure on work equipment might be deducted, but not child-care expenses (*R(FIS) 2/88*).

The wording of reg.36 is not the same as was considered in *Parsons v Hogg*, so that there was some doubt about the application of the principle. In *R(IS) 6/92* the Commissioner held that an attendance allowance paid to a local councillor had to be taken into account as earnings, subject only to the £5 disregard, although the councillor incurred necessary, etc. expenses on such things as stationery and telephone calls. However, the Commissioner referred only to reg.35 and not to reg.36 or any of the decisions cited in the previous paragraph. In *CIS 77/1993*, which concerned a local councillor's basic allowance, the same Commissioner considered that *Parsons v Hogg* did not apply, but decided that the allowance fell within reg.35(2)(c). However, the application of *Parsons v Hogg* does produce a result where only resources actually available to the person are counted. It is also the approach taken in para.26016 of the *Decision Makers Guide*. *R(IS) 16/93* has now expressly decided that the principle of *Parsons v Hogg* applies to reg.36. This has been followed in *CIS 507/1994*. 2.389

Parsons v Hogg has also been applied to "gross earnings" in para.1(3) of Sch.I to the Child Support (Maintenance Assessments and Special Cases) Regulations 1992 (SI 1992/1815) in *R(CS) 2/96*. Moreover, *CCS 3882/1997* has held that the principle of *Parsons v Hogg* is not restricted to expenses wholly, exclusively and necessarily incurred in the performance of the duties of the employment but can extend to subscriptions to professional bodies or learned societies which are tax-deductible under s.201 of the Income and Corporation Taxes Act 1988, provided that they have to be incurred in order to win the earnings in question. *CJSA 2402/2003* confirms that this would not apply to a trade union subscription since there was (as far as the Commissioner was aware) no specific provision of the income tax legislation under which the union subscription would be deductible in computing the amount of income for income tax purposes.

See also *CCS 318/1995* which decided that an armed forces "local overseas allowance" could be deducted on the ground that it covered the special expenses of working abroad, whereas a lodgings allowance for those stationed in the UK was not allowable (*CCS 5352/1995*). Rent allowances for police officers would seem not to be a deductible expense (*R(CS) 2/99*, *CCS 101/1994* and *R(CS) 10/98*, although *CCS 12769/1996* is to the contrary. See also *CCS 2561/1998* which "entirely agrees" with the approach taken in *R(CS) 2/99*.

In calculating the amount of necessary, etc. expenses to be deducted the principle established in *R(FC) 1/91*, *CFC 26/1989* and *R(IS) 13/91* should be applied. That is that if items have a dual private and work use, and that use can be apportioned on a time basis, the appropriate proportion should be deducted. See the note to reg.38(3). See also *CFC 836/1995* in the notes to reg.38(11) on apportionment of expenses between two employments. 2.390

In *R(IS) 10/91*, a challenge to the inability to deduct child-care expenses from earnings as being discriminatory and therefore contrary to EC Directive 79/7 was rejected. On appeal, the Court of Appeal referred the question whether supplementary benefit and/or income support fall within art.3 of the Directive to the European Court of Justice (*Cresswell v Chief Adjudication Officer*, *Jackson v Chief Adjudication Officer*, reported as Appendix 1 to *R(IS) 10/91*).

A similar question in relation to housing benefit had been referred by the Divisional Court in *R. v Secretary of State for Social Security Ex p. Smithson* (June 26, 1990). The Advocate General's opinion in *Smithson* (delivered on November 20, 1991) was that the provisions on higher pensioner premium were part of the statutory scheme protecting against the risks of invalidity and old age, so that they came within art.3. The ECJ (February 4, 1992) (C-243/90) disagreed, finding that the higher pensioner premium was an inseparable part of the whole scheme of housing benefit, which was intended to compensate for the fact that the beneficiary's income was insufficient to meet housing costs and not to provide protection against one of the risks specified in art.3(1) (e.g. sickness, invalidity, old age). Although criteria concerning protection against old age and sickness were part of the criteria for determining the level against which the beneficiary's income was tested, that did not affect the purpose of the whole scheme.

2.391 Once that decision had been made, the ECJ's decision in *Cresswell and Jackson* (July 16, 1992) [1992] E.C.R. I-4737; [1993] 3 All E.R. 265, also reported as Appendix 2 to *R(IS) 10/91*, followed fairly inevitably. Benefits such as supplementary benefit and income support could be granted in a variety of personal situations to persons whose means are insufficient to meet their needs as defined by statute. Therefore, they did not come within art.3(1) of the Directive. In the particular cases the claimants' theoretical needs were set independently of any consideration of any of the risks specified in art.3(1). Nor did the fact that the conditions of entitlement to a benefit affected a single parent's ability to take up access to vocational training or part-time employment bring that benefit within EC Directive 76/207 on equal treatment for men and women as regards access to employment, vocational training and promotion, and working conditions. Benefit schemes only come within Directive 76/207 if their subject matter is access to employment, etc. or working conditions.

These decisions seem to rule out challenges to the income support scheme under either Directive, as accepted in *CIS 8/1990* and *CIS 375/1990.* (But the position is different under JSA. In *Hockenjos v Secretary of State;* [2001] EWCA Civ 624; [2001] 2 C.M.L.R. 51; [2001] I.C.R. 966, also reported as *R(JSA) 1/05*, the Court of Appeal held that the Jobseekers Act 1995 had set up a unitary statutory scheme to provide against the risk of unemployment which was covered by art.3(1)(a) of EC Directive 79/7. The result is that both contribution-based and income-based JSA are within the scope of Directive 79/7.)

However, the possibility of a challenge to the family credit scheme (now abolished) under Directive 76/207 remained. Family credit similarly did not, until October 4, 1994, permit the offsetting of any child care expenses against earnings. In *R(FC) 2/98 (Meyers)*, the claimant argued that the family credit rule before October 4, 1994, was discriminatory and in breach of Directive 76/207. The contention was that since the main purpose of family credit was to supplement the income of low-paid workers, family credit was directly concerned with access to employment and/or working conditions. The Commissioner referred the question as to whether family credit was covered by Directive 76/207 to the ECJ. On July 13, 1995 the ECJ (*Meyers v Adjudication Officer* (C-116/94) [1995] All E.R.(EC) 705, also reported as *R(FC) 2/98*) held that family credit was concerned with both access to employment and working conditions and so fell within the scope of Directive 76/207. The case then went back to the Commissioner for him to consider whether the family credit rules did indirectly discriminate against women and, if so, whether this was objectively justifiable. The Commissioner accepted that the absence of a child care costs disregard had a disparate impact on women but found that this discrimination was objectively justified and so the family credit rules were compatible with Directive 76/207.

Chapter IV

Self-Employed Earners

Earnings of self-employed earners

2.392 **37.**—(1) Subject to paragraph (2), "earnings", in the case of employment as a self-employed earner, means the gross receipts of the employment and shall include any allowance paid under section 2 of the Employment and Training Act 1973 [[1]or section 2 of the Enterprise and New Towns

(Scotland) Act 1990] to the claimant for the purpose of assisting him in carrying on his business.

[[2](2) "Earnings" shall not include—

(a) where a claimant is involved in providing board and lodging accommodation for which a charge is payable, any payment by way of such a charge;

[[3](b) any payment to which paragraph 26 or 27 of Schedule 9 refers (payments in respect of a person accommodated with the claimant under an arrangement made by a local authority or voluntary organisation and payments made to the claimant by a health authority, local authority or voluntary organisation in respect of persons temporarily in the claimant's care).]]

[[4](c) any sports award.]

AMENDMENTS

1. Enterprise (Scotland) Consequential Amendments Order 1991 (SI 1991/ 387) art.2 (April 1, 1991).

2. Income-related Benefits Schemes (Miscellaneous Amendments) (No.3) Regulations 1992 (SI 1992/2155) reg.16 (October 5, 1992).

3. Income-related Benefits Schemes (Miscellaneous Amendments) (No.5) Regulations 1994 (SI 1994/2139) reg.27 (October 3, 1994).

4. Social Security Amendment (Sports Awards) Regulations 1999 (SI 1999/ 2165) reg.6(3) (August 23, 1999).

DEFINITIONS

"board and lodging accommodation"—see reg.2(1).
"claimant"—see reg.2(1) and reg.23(1).
"self-employed earner"—see reg.2(1).
"sports award"—*ibid.*
"voluntary organisation"—*ibid.*

GENERAL NOTE

Paragraph (1)

On the tests for deciding whether a person is an employee or self-employed, see *CJSA 4721/2001*. **2.393**

The starting point for the self-employed is the figure of gross receipts, to be reduced to net profits under reg.38.

In *CFC 4/1991*, the claimant's husband had recently started a construction business. He received a loan of £5,500 from a relative and made part repayment of £4,000 not long afterwards. The Department and the Tribunal treated the loan as part of the "gross receipts" of the self-employment. The repayment could not be deducted from the gross receipts because of reg.22(5)(a) of the Family Credit Regulations (the equivalent of reg.38(5)(a) below). (See the 2002 edition of this volume for the Family Credit Regulations.) The result was that the net profit so calculated took the claimant above family credit level. The Commissioner found that the loan was a capital receipt, but concluded that the words of reg.21(1) of the Family Credit Regulations (the equivalent of reg.37(1)) were unambiguous and included capital receipts. On appeal under the name of *Kostanczwk*, an order of the Registrar of the Court of Appeal (dated August 21, 1992) allowed the appeal by consent and directed that capital receipts not generated by a claimant's business do not form part of the gross receipts of that employment for the purposes of reg.21 of the Family Credit Regulations. As *R(FC) 1/97* confirmed, since that direction was contained in an Order made by consent and without argument it was not binding on anyone other than the parties to the Order and the tribunal to whom the direction was made. But as the decision in *CFC 4/1991* had been set aside by the Court of Appeal, *CFC 24/1989* remained at that time the only authoritative Commissioner's decision on the point. In *CFC 24/1989* it was held that a grant of £900 from the Prince's Youth Business Trust to assist in the setting up of a business was not part of the gross receipts. The Commissioner focuses on the bizarre consequences if a capital receipt has to count as part of the gross receipts, when capital expenditure cannot be deducted from the gross receipts. The approach of *CFC 24/1989* was to be preferred as a matter of principle. In *CFC 23/1991* a legacy used to keep the claimant's business afloat was not a receipt of the business. The argument that since reg.37 is placed within the income section of the regulations, gross receipts must mean "revenue receipts" and exclude loans or receipts from the sale of capital assets, etc. did seem to be a convincing one. This has now been confirmed by *R(FC) 1/97*. In a comprehensive decision the Commissioner holds that neither a loan for business purposes nor the proceeds of sale of capital assets (in that case a car and a computer printer) form part of the gross receipts of the employment for the purposes of reg.21 of the Family Credit Regulations (the equivalent of reg.37).

Paragraph (2)

2.394 *CIS 55/1989* decided that the predecessor of sub-para.(a), which referred to a claimant "employed" in providing board and lodging accommodation (defined in reg.2(1)), applied whenever the claimant made a charge for providing the accommodation. It was not necessary for the claimant to provide it by way of business. The substitution of the word "involved" reinforces this conclusion. The payments received count as income under reg.40(4)(a), but subject to disregards.

Equally sub-para.(a) will apply where the claimant is engaged in a board and lodging business. In *CIS 521/2002* the claimant was one of four partners who ran a hotel providing board and lodging accommodation for the homeless. The consequence of sub-para.(a) was that rather than her share of the net partnership profits (after deducting income tax, NI contributions and half of any pension contributions) falling under reg.38(1)(b), the gross amount of the receipts from the tenants had to be taken into account under reg.40(4)(a), subject to any disregard in Sch.9. As the claimant lived in the hotel (and on the basis that she was to be regarded as living in the whole hotel as her home) para.20 of Sch.9 applied. The issue was how the claimant's income was to be calculated. The tribunal applied the disregard under para.20(b) to the total of the receipts from the boarders and then divided by four to obtain the claimant's share. The result of this calculation was that the claimant was not entitled to income support because her income exceeded her applicable amount. However, the Commissioner concluded that the disregard under para.20(b) fell to be applied *after* the claimant's gross income had been calculated. Her gross income was her partnership share, not the total of the board and lodging charges. Furthermore, as para.20 made no provision for partnerships or for taking into account only a proportion of the number of boarders, the disregard to be set against the claimant's quarter share under para.20(b) was £20 plus 50 per cent of any excess for each of the 16 boarders. On this basis, the claimant had no income to be taken into account for the purpose of income support.

Sub-paragraph (b) applies to payments to foster-parents and to people for providing temporary care in their home. Those payments are disregarded as income other than earnings under paras 26 and 27 of Sch.9. Sub-paragraph (b) ensures that they are not treated as earnings. See also reg.6(1)(k).

2.395 On sub-para.(c), see reg.6(1)(m) and the note to that provision. See also the disregards in para.69 of Sch.9 and para.56 of Sch.10.

Note also *CIS/1068/2006* which holds that payments made to the claimant by his wife (from money she received from the local authority under s.57 of the Health and Social Care Act 2001) in consideration of the care services he provided to her were "earnings" and fell to be taken into account in calculating his income support. It did not matter whether the claimant was to be regarded as an employed or self-employed earner for these purposes—the issue was whether the claimant had been engaged by his wife to provide care services for reward, which on the facts of the case was the only possible inference. The Commissioner rejected the claimant's argument that the payments by his wife should be disregarded under para.58 of Sch.9 (see further the note to para.58). The claimant appealed to the Court of Appeal against this decision but his appeal was dismissed (*Casewell v Secretary of State for Work and Pensions* 2008 EWCA Civ 210, reported as *R(IS) 7/08*). The claimant contended that s.136 of the Contributions and Benefits Act requires that payments made to a member of the family are counted when they come into the family, and if at that point they are disregarded, they cannot be counted again if they are transferred from one member of the family to another. However the Court agreed with the Commissioner that the payments to the claimant by his wife were earnings in respect of the care he provided and in the claimant's hands they became his income under s.136(1). It should be noted that the payments to the claimant's wife in this case were made on the basis that she was instructed to pay the claimant the appropriate sum each week against a payslip. There was therefore a specific obligation for the claimant's wife to deal with the payments in a particular way, which had the result that the money paid to her husband was treated as earnings. Thus this was a somewhat different situation from the more usual informal transfer of resources between family members.

Calculation of net profit of self-employed earners

38.—(1) For the purposes of regulation 30 (calculation of earnings of self-employed earners), the earnings of a claimant to be taken into account shall be— **2.396**

(a) in the case of a self-employed earner who is engaged in employment on his own account, the net profit derived from that employment;

(b) in the case of a self-employed earner whose employment is carried on in partnership or is that of a share fisherman within the meaning of the Social Security (Mariners' Benefits) Regulations 1975, his share of the net profit derived from that employment less—

(i) an amount in respect of income tax and of social security contributions payable under the Social Security Act [SSCBA] calculated in accordance with regulation 39 (deduction of tax and contributions for self-employed earners); and

(ii) [[1]one half of any premium paid [[2]in the period that is relevant under regulation 30] in respect of [[7] . . .] a personal pension scheme].

(2) There shall be disregarded from a claimant's net profit any sum, where applicable, specified in paragraphs 1 to 13 [[4] [[6] . . .]] of Schedule 8.

(3) For the purposes of paragraph (1)(a) the net profit of the employment shall, except where paragraph (9) applies, be calculated by taking into account the earnings of the employment over the period determined under regulation 30 (calculation of earnings of self-employed earners) less—

(a) subject to paragraphs (5) to (7), any expenses wholly and exclusively defrayed in that period for the purposes of that employment;

(b) an amount in respect of—

(i) income tax; and

(ii) social security contributions payable under the Social Security Act [SSCBA], calculated in accordance with regulation 39 (deduction of tax and contributions for self-employed earners); and

(c) [[1]one half of any premium paid [[2] in the period that is relevant under regulation 30] in respect of [[7] . . .] a personal pension scheme].

(4) For the purposes of paragraph (1)(b), the net profit of the employment shall be calculated by taking into account the earnings of the employment over the period determined under regulation 30 less, subject to paragraphs (5) to (7), any expenses wholly and exclusively defrayed in that period for the purposes of that employment.

(5) Subject to paragraph (6), no deduction shall be made under paragraph (3)(a) or (4) in respect of—

(a) any capital expenditure;

(b) the depreciation of any capital asset;

(c) any sum employed or intended to be employed in the setting up or expansion of the employment;

(d) any loss incurred before the beginning of the period determined under regulation 30 (calculation of earnings of self-employed earners);

(e) the repayment of capital on any loan taken out for the purposes of the employment;

(f) any expenses incurred in providing business entertainment.

(6) A deduction shall be made under paragraph (3)(a) or (4) in respect of the repayment of capital on any loan used for—

(a) the replacement in the course of business of equipment or machinery; and

(b) the repair of an existing business asset except to the extent that any sum is payable under an insurance policy for its repair.

(7) [[5]The Secretary of State] shall refuse to make a deduction in respect of any expenses under paragraph (3)(a) or (4) where he is not satisfied that the expense has been defrayed or, having regard to the nature of the expense and its amount, that it has been reasonably incurred.

(8) For the avoidance of doubt—

(a) a deduction shall not be made under paragraph (3)(a) or (4) in respect of any sum unless it has been expended for the purposes of the business;

(b) a deduction shall be made thereunder in respect of—

(i) the excess of any VAT paid over VAT received in the period determined under regulation 30 (calculation of earnings of self-employed earners);

(ii) any income expended in the repair of an existing asset except to the extent that any sum is payable under an insurance policy for its repair;

(iii) any payment of interest on a loan taken out for the purposes of the employment.

(9) Where a claimant is engaged in employment as a child minder the net profit of the employment shall be one-third of the earnings of that employment, less—

(a) an amount in respect of—

(i) income tax; and

(ii) social security contributions payable under the Social Security Act [SSCBA],

calculated in accordance with regulation 39 (deduction of tax and contributions for self-employed); and

(b) [[1]one half of any premium paid in respect of [[7] . . .] a personal pension scheme].

(10) Notwithstanding regulation 30 (calculation of earnings of self-employed earners) and the foregoing paragraphs, [[5]the Secretary of State] may assess any item of a claimant's income or expenditure over a period other than that determined under regulation 30 as may, in the particular case, enable the weekly amount of that item of income or expenditure to be determined more accurately.

(11) For the avoidance of doubt where a claimant is engaged in employment as a self-employed earner and he is also engaged in one or more other employments as a self-employed or employed earner any loss incurred in any one of his employments shall not be offset against his earnings in any other of his employments.

(12) [[3]. . .].

AMENDMENTS

1. Income-related Benefits Schemes (Miscellaneous Amendments) (No.4) Regulations 1993 (SI 1993/2119) reg.13 (October 4, 1993).

2. Income-related Benefits Schemes (Miscellaneous Amendments) (No.5) Regulations 1994 (SI 1994/2139) reg.28 (October 3, 1994).

3. Income-related Benefits Schemes and Social Security (Claims and Payments) (Miscellaneous Amendments) Regulations 1995 (SI 1995/2303) reg.6(3) (October 2, 1995).

4. Social Security (Miscellaneous Amendments) (No.2) Regulations 1999 (SI 1999/2556) reg.2(6) (October 4, 1999).

5. Social Security Act 1998 (Commencement No.12 and Consequential and Transitional Provisions) Order 1999 (SI 1999/3178 (C.81)) art.3(5) and Sch.5 para.2 (November 29, 1999).

6. Social Security (Back to Work Bonus and Lone Parent Run-on) (Amendment and Revocation) Regulations 2003 (SI 2003/1589) reg.2(c) (October 25, 2004).

7. Social Security (Miscellaneous Amendments) (No.3) Regulations 2007 (SI 2007/1749) reg.2(3) (July 16, 2007).

DEFINITIONS

"claimant"—see reg.2(1) and reg.23(1).
"personal pension scheme"—see reg.2(1).
"self-employed earner"—*ibid.*
"Social Security Act"—*ibid.*

GENERAL NOTE

The structure is as follows: **2.397**

(1) General rule.
(2) Disregards.
(3) Net profit of sole traders.
(4) Net profit of partners and share fishermen.
(5) Deductions are not allowed.
(6) Deductions allowed.
(7) Tests for (3), (4) and (6).
(8) Tests for (3), (4) and (6).
(9) Child minders.
(10) Period of calculation to be adjusted.
(11) Two employments.

Paragraph (1)

2.398 This provision sets up two categories—

(a) those in employment on their own account ("sole traders"), and

(b) partners and share fishermen.

For both, the earnings to be taken into account under reg.30 are to be net profits. Under (b) the deductions for income tax, social security contributions and personal pension (see reg.2(1)) premiums are put under para.(1). For (a), these appear in para.(3).

A "net profit" of a business cannot be less than nil (*R(FC) 1/93* [10], *R(H) 5/08*). See further the note to para.11.

Drawings are not earnings from self-employment because para.(1) confines earnings to the net profit of the employment, or in the case of a partnership to the person's share of the net profit. Nor are drawings to be taken into account as other income (*AR v Bradford Metropolitan DC* [2008] UKUT 30 (AAC), reported as *R(H) 6/09*).

Paragraph (2)

2.399 See the notes to reg.36(2). The difference is that para.(2) does not refer to the disregard in para.15A of Sch.8 as this is not relevant to self-employed earnings.

Paragraph (3)

2.400 For sole traders apart from child minders (para.(9)) the starting point in calculating net profit under para.(1) is earnings, i.e. gross receipts (see notes to reg.37(1) on the meaning of gross receipts). From that are deducted expenses. Any expenses wholly and exclusively defrayed may be deducted providing that they are reasonably incurred (para.(7)) and the rules of paras (5) and (6) are applied. The expenses must have been actually defrayed, so that unpaid liabilities cannot be deducted (*CIS 212/1988*). The difference between opening and closing stock is not an expense that has been defrayed in the accounting period (*SSWP v SK* [2014] UKUT 12 (AAC)).

There has been considerable doubt about whether the cost of items which have a dual use, for business and private purposes, can be apportioned. *The Adjudication Officer's Guide* originally suggested that the cost of telephone calls, units of gas or electricity consumption and petrol could be apportioned (because consumption can be identified as for business or private purposes), but not, for instance, standing charges or road fund tax or insurance for a car. In a series of appeals heard together, the Commissioner convincingly demolished this approach (*R(FC) 1/91, CFC 26/1989* and *R(IS) 13/91*). He holds that where expenses can be apportioned on a time basis, this can identify the amount wholly and exclusively defrayed on business expenses. There remain some expenses, like the cost of lunches for clients, which are not capable of apportionment. The Commissioner also holds that the apportionment made by the Inspector of Taxes is cogent evidence of the amounts wholly and exclusively incurred for the purposes of the business, which should be accepted in the absence of evidence to the contrary. The *Adjudication Officer's Guide* was subsequently amended to reflect this decision. Now see para.26029 of the *Decision Makers Guide*. See also *CFC 836/1995* in the note to para.(11).

The standard deductions for tax and social security contributions (see reg.39) and personal pension (see reg.2(1)) premiums are made.

Paragraph (4)

2.401 For partners and share fishermen the calculation is effectively the same apart from the standard deductions already in para.(1)(b).

Paragraph (5)

2.402 No deductions are allowed for these items, many of which will appear in profit and loss accounts. But see para.(6) for exceptions to (e).

Paragraph (6)

Deductions can be made for the repayment of capital on loans for these repairs or replacements. The interest on such a loan will be an allowable expense under the general test (and see para.(8)(b)(iii)). **2.403**

R(H) 5/07, which concerned reg.31(6) of the Housing Benefit Regulations 1987 (the equivalent of para.(6)), holds that a car is capable of being "equipment" or "machinery" and therefore repayments of capital on a loan used to replace the car in the course of business were deductible. The Commissioner applied the principle in *R(FC) 1/91* (apportionment of expenses between business and personal use) to the capital (and interest—see paras (3)(a) and (8)(b)(iii)) repayments on the loan.

Paragraph (7)

This provision confirms that an expense must have been actually paid out (*CIS 212/1988*), and imposes a general test of reasonableness. **2.404**

Paragraph (8)

The test of business purpose merely confirms the general requirement under paras (3) and (4). It is useful to have the categories in (b) expressly confirmed. **2.405**

Paragraph (9)

For child-minders the simple rule of taking profit as one third of gross receipts is used. The standard deductions are then made. Child-minders who work at home are treated as not in remunerative work (reg.6(1)(b)). See the note to reg.6(1)(b). **2.406**

Paragraph (10)

This provision gives a very general power to average items over different periods from that set in reg.30, where the basic rule is to take the previous one year. **2.407**

Paragraph (11)

R(FC) 1/93 applies the principle that a loss in one employment cannot be set off against a profit or earnings in another separate employment. The claimant ran a sub-post office and a shop in the same premises. The Commissioner decides that carrying out the office of sub-postmistress was employment as an employed earner, while running the shop was employment as a self-employed earner. The loss made by the shop could not be set off against the claimant's earnings as a sub-postmistress. *CFC 836/1995* concerned similar facts. However, the Commissioner went on to consider the apportionment of expenses between the two employments. Applying by analogy *R(FC) 1/91* (apportionment of expenses between business and personal use), he held that expenses which were not solely attributable to the shop could be apportioned between the shop and the claimant's husband's employment as a sub-postmaster. The basis of the apportionment in that case was 75 per cent to the post office and 25 per cent to the shop, since the primary reason most customers visited the premises was for the post office services. Thus 75 per cent of the expenses relating to the general running of the premises and the two activities and the repayments on a loan to acquire the post office and shop could be deducted from the earnings as a sub-postmaster, as the Commissioner accepted that these had been wholly, exclusively and necessarily incurred in the performance of the duties of sub-postmaster (see *R(FC) 1/90*, applying *Parsons v Hogg*). See also *CFC 4238/1997*. **2.408**

CPC/3373/2007 also confirms that under the equivalent state pension credit provision (see reg.17B of the State Pension Credit Regulations, which applies as modified reg.13 of the Social Security Benefit (Computation of Earnings) Regulations 1996 (SI 1996/2745)) the loss from the claimant's self-employment could not be offset against his other income (retirement pension and an annuity). The Commissioner rejects the claimant's argument that because reg.13(12) (the equivalent of para. (11)) specifies particular circumstances in which losses may not be offset the implication was that in other circumstances offsetting of losses was possible. Regulation

13(12) (like para.(11)) stated that it had been made for the avoidance of doubt, that is, it was intended merely to clarify the law as it would exist even if the regulation had not been made. The calculation of state pension credit (like income support) was governed by a statutory scheme and in the absence of a regulation positively requiring an offset, either expressly or by necessary implication, that offset was not permitted. The Revenue permitted the offset of a loss from self-employment against other income because it was required to do this (for the current provision see s.64 of the Income Tax Act 2007) but the rules for state pension credit did not contain any equivalent provision.

In *R(H) 5/08* (which concerned reg.22 of the Council Tax Benefit Regulations 1992, the then equivalent council tax benefit regulation of reg.38) the claimant argued that the loss in his business should be deducted from his wife's earnings from her part-time employment (not in his business). The Commissioner accepted that reg.22(10) (the equivalent of para.(11)) did not apply because this only applied where the *claimant* was engaged in two or more employments. However, reg.22(1) (the equivalent of para.(1)) spoke of "net *profit*". A "net *profit*" of a business could not be less than nil (see also para.10 of *R(FC) 1/93* in which the Commissioner took the same approach). There was thus nothing to deduct.

Deduction of tax and contributions for self-employed earners

2.409 **39.**—(1) The amount to be deducted in respect of income tax under regulation 38(1)(b)(i), (3)(b)(i) or (9)(a)(i) (calculation of net profit of self-employed earners) shall be calculated on the basis of the amount of chargeable income and as if that income were assessable to income tax at [1 [6. . .] the basic rate [8 , or in the case of a Scottish taxpayer, the Scottish basic rate,] of tax] less only the [8 personal reliefs to which the claimant is entitled under Chapters 2, 3 and 3A of Part 3 of the Income Tax Act 2007 as are] appropriate to his circumstances; but, if the period determined under regulation 30 (calculation of earnings of self-employed earners) is less than a year, [1the earnings to which the [5 [6 basic] rate] [8 , or the Scottish basic rate,] [3. . .] of tax is to be applied and] the amount of the [4 [8 personal reliefs]] deductible under this paragraph shall be calculated on a pro rata basis.

(2) The amount to be deducted in respect of social security contributions under regulation 38(1)(b)(i), (3)(b)(ii) or (9)(a)(ii) shall be the total of—

[2(a) the amount of Class 2 contributions payable under section [7 11(2)] or, as the case may be, [7 11(8)] of the Contributions and Benefits Act at the rate applicable at the date of claim except where the claimant's chargeable income is less than the amount specified in section 11(4) of that Act ([7 small profits threshold]) for the tax year in which the date of claim falls; but if the assessment period is less than a year, the amount specified for that tax year shall be reduced pro rata; and

(b) the amount of Class 4 contributions (if any) which would be payable under section 15 of that Act (Class 4 contributions recoverable under the Income Tax Acts) at the percentage rate applicable at the date of claim on so much of the chargeable income as exceeds the lower limit but does not exceed the upper limit of profits and gains applicable for the tax year in which the date of claim falls; but if the assessment period is less than a year, those limits shall be reduced pro rata.]

(3) In this regulation "chargeable income" means—

(a) except where sub-paragraph (b) applies, the earnings derived from the employment less any expenses deducted under paragraph (3)(a) or, as the case may be, (4) of regulation 38;

(b) in the case of employment as a child minder, one-third of the earnings of that employment.

AMENDMENTS

1. Income-related Benefits Schemes (Miscellaneous Amendments) (No.3) Regulations 1992 (SI 1992/2155) reg.17 (October 5, 1992).
2. Income-related Benefits Schemes (Miscellaneous Amendments) (No.4) Regulations 1993 (SI 1993/2119) reg.14 (October 4, 1993).
3. Income-related Benefits Schemes (Miscellaneous Amendments) (No.5) Regulations 1994 (SI 1994/2139) reg.29 (October 3, 1994).
4. Social Security (Miscellaneous Amendments) (No.3) Regulations 2007 (SI 2007/1749) reg.2(4) (July 16, 2007).
5. Social Security (Miscellaneous Amendments) (No.5) Regulations 2007 (SI 2007/2618) reg.5(7) (October 1, 2007).
6. Social Security (Miscellaneous Amendments) Regulations 2009 (SI 2009/583) reg.2(7) (April 6, 2009).
7. Social Security (Miscellaneous Amendments No.2) Regulations 2015 (SI 2015/478) reg.27 (April 6, 2015).
8. Social Security (Scottish Rate of Income Tax etc.) (Amendment) Regulations 2016 (SI 2016/233) reg. 2(3) (April 6, 2016).

DEFINITIONS

"claimant"—see reg.2(1) and reg.23(1).
"date of claim"—see reg.2(1).
"Scottish basic rate"—*ibid.*
"Scottish taxpayer"—*ibid.*
"Social Security Act"—*ibid.*
"starting rate"—*ibid.*

GENERAL NOTE

Paragraph (1)

The deduction for income tax from the amount of earnings calculated under reg.38 is to be made by applying the basic rate of tax (from April 6, 2008 the basic rate has been reduced to 20 per cent) or the Scottish basic rate, in the case of a Scottish taxpayer, and the personal relief as a single or married person. This figure may well be higher than the actual tax payable. 2.410

Paragraph (2)

Deductions are made for the Class 2 and Class 4 national insurance contributions payable on the amount calculated under reg.38. 2.411

[1 Chapter IVA

Participants in the Self-Employment Route [3 . . .]

Interpretation

39A.—In this Chapter— 2.412

"[2 . . .]

"special account" means, where a person was carrying on a commercial activity in respect of which assistance is received under the self-employment route, the account into which the gross receipts from that activity were payable during the period in respect of which such assistance was received.]

Amendments

1. Social Security (Miscellaneous Amendments) (No.4) Regulations 1998 (SI 1998/1174) reg.6(3) (June 1, 1998).
2. Social Security Amendment (Employment Zones) (No.2) Regulations 2000 (SI 2000/2910) reg.5(1)(b) (November 27, 2000).
3. Social Security Amendment (Employment Zones) (No.2) Regulations 2000 (SI 2000/2910) reg.5(1)(c) (November 27, 2000).

Definition

"self-employment route"—see reg.2(1).

General Note

2.413 Regulations 39A–39D are the same in substance as regs 102A–102D of the JSA Regulations (apart from necessary differences in cross-references). They apply to the income from "test-trading" of people who have taken part in the "self-employment route" (defined in reg.2(1)). See the notes to reg.102C of the JSA Regulations 1996.

See also reg.23A, the effect of which is that the normal rules for the treatment of income do not apply to receipts from trading while on the self-employment route; such receipts are only to be taken into account as income in accordance with regs 39A–39D.

Note the disregards in para.64 of Sch.9 and para.6(3) and (4) and para.52 of Sch.10.

[1 Treatment of gross receipts of participants in the self-employment route [2 . . .]

2.414 **39B.**—The gross receipts of a commercial activity carried on by a person in respect of which assistance is received under the self-employment route, shall be taken into account in accordance with the following provisions of this Chapter.]

Amendments

1. Social Security (Miscellaneous Amendments) (No.4) Regulations 1998 (SI 1998/1174) reg.6(3) (June 1, 1998).
2. Social Security Amendment (Employment Zones) (No.2) Regulations 2000 (SI 2000/2910) reg.5(1)(c) (November 27, 2000).

Definition

"self-employment route"—see reg.2(1).

General Note

2.415 See the note to reg.39A.

[1 Calculation of income of participants in the self-employment route [2. . .]

2.416 **39C.**—(1) The income of a person who has received assistance under the self-employment route shall be calculated by taking into account the whole of the monies in the special account at the end of the last day upon which such assistance was received and deducting from those monies—

(a) an amount in respect of income tax calculated in accordance with regulation 39D (deduction in respect of tax for participants in the self-employment route [2 . . .]); and

(b) any sum to which paragraph (4) refers.

(2) Income calculated pursuant to paragraph (1) shall be apportioned equally over a period which starts on the date the income is treated as paid under paragraph (3) and is equal in length to the period beginning with the day upon which assistance was first received under the self-employment route and ending on the last day upon which such assistance was received.

(3) Income calculated pursuant to paragraph (1) shall be treated as paid—

(a) in the case where it is due to be paid before the first benefit week in respect of which the participant or his partner first claims income support following the last day upon which assistance was received under the self-employment route, on the day in the week in which it is due to be paid which corresponds to the first day of the benefit week;

(b) in any other case, on the first day of the benefit week in which it is due to be paid.

(4) This paragraph refers, where applicable in each benefit week in respect of which income calculated pursuant to paragraph (1) is taken into account pursuant to paragraphs (2) and (3), to the sums which would have been disregarded under paragraphs 4 to 6B and 9 of Schedule 8 had the income been earnings.]

AMENDMENTS

1. Social Security (Miscellaneous Amendments) (No.4) Regulations 1998 (SI 1998/1174) reg.6(3) (June 1, 1998).

2. Social Security Amendment (Employment Zones) (No.2) Regulations 2000 (SI 2000/2910) reg.5(1)(c) (November 27, 2000).

DEFINITION

"self-employment route"—see reg.2(1).

GENERAL NOTE

See the note to reg.39A. 2.417

[1Deduction in respect of tax for participants in the self-employment route [2. . .]

39D.—(1) The amount to be deducted in respect of income tax under regulation 39C(1)(a) (calculation of income of participants in the self-employment route [2. . .]) in respect of the period determined under regulation 39C(2) shall be calculated as if— 2.418

(a) the chargeable income is the only income chargeable to tax:

[3[6(b) the personal reliefs applicable to the person receiving assistance under the self-employment route under Chapters 2, 3 and 3A of Part 3 of the Income Tax Act 2007 are allowable against that income;]]

(c) the rate at which the chargeable income less the personal [6 reliefs] is assessable to income tax is [5. . .] the basic rate [6, or in the case of a Scottish tax payer, the Scottish basic rate,] of tax.

(2) For the purpose of paragraph (1), the [4 [5 basic] rate] [6, or the

Scottish basic rate,] of tax to be applied and the amount of the [3 [6 personal reliefs]] deductible shall, where the period determined under regulation 39C(2) is less than a year, be calculated on a pro rata basis.

(3) In this regulation, "chargeable income" means the monies in the special account at the end of the last day upon which assistance was received under the self-employment route.]

AMENDMENTS

1. Social Security (Miscellaneous Amendments) (No.4) Regulations 1998 (SI 1998/1174) reg.6(3) (June 1, 1998).
2. Social Security Amendment (Employment Zones) (No.2) Regulations 2000 (SI 2000/2910) reg.5(1)(c) (November 27, 2000).
3. Social Security (Miscellaneous Amendments) (No.3) Regulations 2007 (SI 2007/1749) reg.2(5) (July 16, 2007).
4. Social Security (Miscellaneous Amendments) (No.5) Regulations 2007 (SI 2007/2618) reg.5(8) (October 1, 2007).
5. Social Security (Miscellaneous Amendments) Regulations 2009 (SI 2009/583) reg.2(8) (April 6, 2009).
6. Social Security (Scottish Rate of Income Tax etc.) (Amendment) Regulations 2016 (SI 2016/233) reg. 2(4) (April 6, 2016).

DEFINITIONS

"Scottish basic rate"—see reg.2(1).
"Scottish taxpayer"—*ibid.*
"self-employment route"—*ibid.*
"starting rate"—*ibid.*

GENERAL NOTE

2.419 See the note to reg.39A.

Chapter V

Other Income

Calculation of income other than earnings

2.420 **40.**—(1) For the purposes of regulation 29 (calculation of income other than earnings) [13[14. . .]] the income of a claimant which does not consist of earnings to be taken into account shall, subject to [6paragraphs (2) to (3B)], be his gross income and any capital treated as income under [10regulation 41 (capital treated as income)].

(2) There shall be disregarded from the calculation of a claimant's gross income under paragraph (1), any sum, where applicable, specified in Schedule 9.

(3) Where the payment of any benefit under the benefit Acts is subject to any deduction by way of recovery the amount to be taken into account under paragraph (1) shall be the gross amount payable.

[9 (3A) [11 Paragraphs (3AA) and (3AAA) apply] where—

(a) a relevant payment has been made to a person in an academic year; and
(b) that person abandons, or is dismissed from, his course of study before the payment to him of the final instalment of the relevant payment.

(3AA) [11 Where a relevant payment is made quarterly, the] amount of a relevant payment to be taken into account for the assessment period for the purposes of paragraph (1) in respect of a person to whom paragraph (3A) applies, shall be calculated by applying the formula—

$$\frac{A - (B \times C)}{D}$$

where—

A = the total amount of the relevant payment which that person would have received had he remained a student until the last day of the academic term in which he abandoned, or was dismissed from, his course, less any deduction under regulation 66A(5);

B = the number of benefit weeks from the benefit week immediately following that which includes the first day of that academic year to the benefit week immediately before that which includes the day on which the person abandoned, or was dismissed from, his course;

C = the weekly amount of the relevant payment, before the application of the £10 disregard, which would have been taken into account as income under regulation 66A(2) had the person not abandoned or been dismissed from, his course and, in the case of a person who was not entitled to income support immediately before he abandoned or was dismissed from his course, had that person, at that time, been entitled to income support;

D = the number of benefit weeks in the assessment period.

[11 (3AAA) Where a relevant payment is made by two or more instalments in a quarter, the amount of a relevant payment to be taken into account for the assessment period for the purposes of paragraph (1) in respect of a person to whom paragraph (3A) applies, shall be calculated by applying the formula in paragraph (3AA) but as if—

A = the total amount of relevant payments which that person received, or would have received, from the first day of the academic year to the day the person abandoned the course, or was dismissed from it, less any deduction under regulation 66A(5).]

(3AB) [11 In this regulation]—

"academic year" and "student loan" shall have the same meanings as for the purposes of Chapter VIII of this Part;

[11 "assessment period" means—

(a) in a case where a relevant payment is made quarterly, the period beginning with the benefit week which includes the day on which the person abandoned, or was dismissed from, his course and ending with the benefit week which includes the last day of the last quarter for which an instalment of the relevant payment was payable to that person;

(b) in a case where the relevant payment is made by two or more instalments in a quarter, the period beginning with the benefit week which includes the day on which the person abandoned, or was dismissed from, his course and ending with the benefit week which includes—

(i) the day immediately before the day on which the next instalment of the relevant payment would have been due had the payments continued; or

(ii) the last day of the last quarter for which an instalment of the relevant payment was payable to that person,

whichever of those dates is earlier;]

[11 "quarter" in relation to an assessment period means a period in that year beginning on—

(a) 1st January and ending on 31st March;
(b) 1st April and ending on 30th June;
(c) 1st July and ending on 31st August; or
(d) 1st September and ending on 31st December;]

"relevant payment" means either a student loan or an amount intended for the maintenance of dependants referred to in regulation 62(3B) or both.]

[4(3B) In the case of income to which regulation 29(2B) applies (calculation of income of former students), the amount of income to be taken into account for the purposes of paragraph (1) shall be the amount of that income calculated in accordance with regulation 32(6A) and on the basis that none of that income has been repaid.]

(4) [7Subject to paragraph (5)] for the avoidance of doubt there shall be included as income to be taken into account under paragraph (1)

[7(a) any payment to which regulation 35(2) or 37(2) (payments not earnings) applies; or
(b) in the case of a claimant who is receiving support provided under section 95 or 98 of the Immigration and Asylum Act including support provided by virtue of regulations made under Schedule 9 to that Act, the amount of such support provided in respect of essential living needs of the claimant and his [10 partner] (if any) as is specified in regulations made under paragraph 3 of Schedule 8 to the Immigration and Asylum Act;

(5) In the case of a claimant who is the partner of a person subject to immigration control and whose partner is receiving support provided under section 95 or 98 of the Immigration and Asylum Act including support provided by virtue of regulations made under Schedule 9 to that Act, there shall not be included as income to be taken into account under paragraph (1) the amount of support provided in respect of essential living needs of the partner of the claimant and his dependants (if any) as is specified in regulations made under paragraph 3 of Schedule 8 to the Immigration and Asylum Act.]

[12 (6) Where the claimant—

(a) is a member of a couple;
(b) his partner is receiving a contributory employment and support allowance; and
(c) that benefit has been reduced under regulation 63 of the Employment and Support Allowance Regulations [15 or section 11J of the Welfare Reform Act as the case may be],

the amount of that benefit to be taken into account is the amount as if it had not been so reduced.]

AMENDMENTS

1. Income Support (General) Amendment No.5 Regulations 1988 (SI 1988/2022) reg.9 (December 12, 1988).

2. Social Security Benefits (Student Loans and Miscellaneous Amendments) Regulations 1990 (SI 1990/1549) reg.5(4) (September 1, 1990).

3. Income Support (General) Amendment Regulations 1991 (SI 1991/236) reg.9 (March 13, 1991).

4. Income-related Benefits and Jobseeker's Allowance (Miscellaneous Amendments) Regulations 1997 (SI 1997/65) reg.7 (April 7, 1997).

5. Income-related Benefits and Jobseeker's Allowance (Amendment) (No.2) Regulations 1997 (SI 1997/2197) reg.5(3) (October 6, 1997).

6. Social Security (Miscellaneous Amendments) Regulations 1998 (SI 1998/563) reg.13(1)(a) (April 6, 1998).

7. Social Security (Immigration and Asylum) Consequential Amendments Regulations 2000 (SI 2000/636) reg.3(6) (April 3, 2000).

8. Social Security Amendment (Students) Regulations 2000 (SI 2000/1981) reg.5(5) and Sch. (July 31, 2000).

9. Social Security Amendment (Students and Income-related Benefits) Regulations 2001 (SI 2001/2319) reg.5(1) (August 1, 2001).

10. Social Security (Working Tax Credit and Child Tax Credit) (Consequential Amendments) Regulations 2003 (SI 2003/455) reg.2 and Sch.1 para.8 (April 6, 2004, except in "transitional cases" and see further the note to reg.17 of the Income Support Regulations).

11. Social Security (Students and Miscellaneous Amendments) Regulations 2008 (SI 2008/1599) reg.2(2) (September 1, 2008, or if the student's period of study begins between August 1 and August 31, 2008, the first day of the period).

12. Employment and Support Allowance (Consequential Provisions) (No.2) Regulations 2008 (SI 2008/1554) reg.2(7) (October 27, 2008).

13. Social Security (Miscellaneous Amendments) (No.4) Regulations 2009 (SI 2009/2655) reg.2(8) (October 26, 2009).

14. Social Security (Miscellaneous Amendments) Regulations 2011 (SI 2011/674) reg.3(4) (April 11, 2011).

15. Universal Credit (Consequential, Supplementary, Incidental and Miscellaneous Provisions) Regulations 2013 (SI 2013/630) reg.28(5) (April 29, 2013).

DEFINITIONS

"academic year"—see reg.61(1).
"benefit Acts"—see reg.2(1).
"benefit week"—*ibid.*
"claimant"—see reg.2(1) and reg.23(1).
"full-time student"—see reg.2(1) and reg.61(1).
"Immigration and Asylum Act"—see reg.2(1).
"partner of a person subject to immigration control"—see reg.21(3).
"student"—see reg.61(1).
"student loan"—*ibid.*
"Welfare Reform Act"—see reg.2(1).

GENERAL NOTE

Paragraph (1)

This paragraph mainly confirms that all forms of income other than earnings fall into this category, and provides that the gross amount is to be taken into account. **2.421**

Is it the claimant's or partner's income?

The first point is that the income must of course be the claimant's (or his partner's—as a consequence of the removal of amounts for children and young persons from income support (with effect from April 6, 2004, except in "transitional cases"—see the note to reg.17) the income of a child or young person who is a member of the claimant's family is no longer aggregated with the claimant's—see further the note to reg.23). **2.422**

A loan can constitute income (*R(SB) 20/83, R(SB) 7/88, Morrell v Secretary of*

State for Work and Pensions [2003] EWCA Civ 526, reported as *R(IS) 6/03*, *R(JSA) 4/04* (student loan paid (whether properly or otherwise) to part-time student), *R(H)1/05* (wrongly obtained benefit), *R(H) 8/08*). However, note the disregard of regular voluntary payments in para.15(5A)(b) of Sch.9 (see the notes to para.15 of Sch.9). A loan may be a voluntary payment, depending on the circumstances of the loan (*R(H) 5/05*); if the loans are irregular, see reg.48(9) which treats irregular voluntary payments as capital.

However, money that a claimant is under a "certain and immediate liability" to repay does not amount to income after the date of the demand for repayment (see *Chief Adjudication Officer v Leeves*, reported as *R(IS) 5/99*) in the notes to reg.29(2B)). Thus resources provided by the use of an overdraft facility do not amount to income since the standard terms of a bank overdraft are that it is repayable on demand, even though that demand may not be made while the amount stays within an agreed limit (*R(H) 5/05*—see further the note to reg.23 under "*What constitutes income*" and the discussion in that note as to whether the same applies to credit cards).

2.423 See also *R(IS) 4/01* which decides, applying *Leeves*, that the part of the claimant's occupational pension that was being paid to his former wife under an attachment of earnings order did not count as his income for the purposes of income support. The notional income rule in reg.42(4)(a) also did not apply: see the note to reg.42(4)(a). A similar approach was taken in *CIS 5479/1997* (where an overpayment of an occupational pension was being recovered by the Italian authorities by withholding the monthly payments of the pension) and in *R(IS) 4/02* (both decided by the same Commissioner). In *R(IS) 4/02* the Commissioner decides, contrary to the view taken in *CIS 212/1989*, para.9 (and followed with some hesitation in *CIS 295/1994*), that payments of the claimant's husband's annuity which had vested in his trustee in bankruptcy under s.306 of the Insolvency Act 1986 were not part of his income (and thus not part of the claimant's income) for the purposes of income support. In his view, in the general context of the income support scheme income to be taken into account is income that is actually paid to a claimant. Note also *R(IS) 2/03*, that concerned payments under the claimant's self-employed pension annuity that were being applied for the benefit of his creditors, which agrees with *R(IS) 4/02*. In *CH/1672/2007* the half of the claimant's pension that he was required to pay to his wife under the terms of a court order following a judicial separation did not count as his income. But income subject to a direction which could be revoked at any time (in that case, a pension signed over by a nun to a religious order under a deed of trust) remained the claimant's income (*C 10/06–07(IS)*, a Northern Ireland decision). So did the half of his annuities that the claimant in *CH/1076/2008* voluntarily paid to his wife from whom he was separated. See further the notes to reg.23 under "*What constitutes income*".

The issue has also arisen in relation to overpaid working tax credit. C*IS/647/2007* holds that up to the date that the Revenue decided that the claimant had to repay her working tax credit it counted as her income, as the *Leeves* principle only applied to income after the date of the demand for repayment. It did not have retrospective effect so as to remove the quality of income from the working tax credit that had already been attributed. This is confirmed by the same Upper Tribunal Judge in *CC v SSWP* [2009] UKUT 280 (AAC) (see further the notes to reg.23 under "*What constitutes income*"). However, in *CIS/1813/2007* the Commissioner holds that payments of working tax credit made after the claimant had notified the Revenue that she had ceased work and had asked for the payments to stop did not count as income. But if that was wrong, the payments were voluntary payments which were to be disregarded under para.15(5A)(b) of Sch.9 (see further the notes to reg.23 under "*What constitutes income*").

In *SH v SSWP* [2008] UKUT 21 (AAC) the weekly sums that the claimant was allowed to withdraw for living expenses from his bank account which was subject to a restraint order under s.77 of the Criminal Justice Act 1988 were not income;

furthermore there was nothing in the JSA Regulations 1996 (or the equivalent provisions in the Income Support Regulations) which treated these payments of capital as income.

Note also *AR v Bradford MDC* [2008] UKUT 30 (AAC), reported as *R(H) 6/09*, which holds that drawings from a partnership (or a business) are not income other than earnings (nor are they earnings from self-employment).

Meaning of "gross income"

Secondly, the amount of the gross income has to be calculated. *CIS 25/1989* held that, applying the principle of *Parsons v Hogg* [1985] 2 All E.R. 897, appendix to *R(FIS) 4/85*, expenditure necessary to produce the income is to be deducted to produce a figure of gross income. The claimant was entitled to £21.60 per month sickness benefit from the Ideal Benefit Society only while he continued to pay £60 annual payment to the Society. The monthly equivalent (£5) was to be deducted from the £21.60. However, in *CIS 563/1991* the Commissioner disagrees with *CIS 25/1989* and holds that gross income in para.(1) means without any deduction of the expenses incurred in gaining that income, except to the extent expressly allowed by Sch.9. He considers that the various provisions in Sch.9 relating to deduction of expenses incurred by the claimant would not be necessary if "gross income" meant income after deducting the expenses of obtaining it. In his view *CIS 25/1989*, in applying *Parsons v Hogg* in this context, had not paid sufficient regard to the fact that that case was concerned with earnings of employed earners and involved different statutory provisions. The phrase "gross income" was an equivocal one, as indicated by the Court of Appeal's decision in *Parsons v Hogg*, and the statutory context had to be considered. The principle of *Parsons v Hogg* had been applied to earnings in *R(FC) 1/90* and *R(IS) 16/93*, (but apparently not to attendance and basic allowances paid to councillors, which are counted as earnings, in *R(IS) 6/92* and *CIS 77/1993*). (On the application of *Parsons v Hogg* to the meaning of "gross earnings", see further the notes to reg.36(3).) The Commissioner in *CIS 563/1991* considered that the statutory context of earnings of employed earners and income other than earnings was sufficiently different not to necessitate a uniform approach to the deduction of expenses. 2.424

This question was considered again in *R(IS) 13/01*. The Commissioner opined that arguably the principle in *Parsons v Hogg* should apply to income other than earnings in the light of the fact that so few of the paragraphs in Sch.9 were concerned with expenses. However, he followed *CIS 563/1991* rather than *CIS 25/1989* on the basis of *Colchester Estates (Cardiff) v Carlton Industries Plc* [1986] Ch. 80. In that case Nourse LJ had said that where there were two conflicting decisions of equal status and the earlier decision was fully considered in the later decision, the later decision should be followed unless the Judge was convinced that the later decision was wrong because, for instance, some binding or persuasive authority had not been cited in either of the two cases. The Commissioner considered that the same approach should be applied by Commissioners and therefore followed *CIS 563/1991* which had considered *CIS 25/1989* in detail and not followed it.

But on the issue of precedent, note *R(IS) 9/08* in which the Commissioner points out that *Colchester* had been disapproved in *Re Taylor (a bankrupt)* [2007] Ch.150. Thus a later decision of a Commissioner was not necessarily to be followed in preference to an earlier one but the question of which decision to follow had to be determined on the merits.

Certain kinds of income are disregarded under Sch.9 (para.(2)). With the revocation of reg.24 there is now no special rule for charitable or voluntary payments, but note the now total disregard of these payments in para.15 of Sch.9. Note also reg.48 on income treated as capital.

Benefit income

2.425 A major form of income for income support claimants will be from other social security benefits. All benefits of an income nature (presumably benefits like bereavement payment continue to be treated as capital although there is now no classification in the regulations (cf. *R(SB) 4/89*)) count in full as income unless disregarded under Sch.9. Benefits disregarded include housing benefit (para.5), the mobility component of disability living allowance, the mobility component of personal independence payment, and mobility supplement (paras 6 and 8), attendance allowance, the care component of disability living allowance and the daily living component of personal independence payment (para.9), armed forces independence payment (para.76A), social fund payments (para.31), local welfare provision (para.31A), payments under local council tax reduction schemes (para.46) and guardian's allowance (para.5A). In addition, with effect from April 6, 2004 (except in "transitional cases"—see the note to reg.17) child benefit and child tax credit are ignored (para.5B) (for income support claimants who had an award of child tax credit before April 6, 2004 see reg.7 of the Social Security (Working Tax Credit and Child Tax Credit) (Consequential Amendments) Regulations 2003 (SI 2003/455) (as amended) on p.812 and the notes to that regulation).

Benefits which count as income are income whether they are paid on time or in the form of arrears (*R(SB) 4/89*). Then reg.31 defines the date on which the income is treated as paid. The fact that there is a partial disregard of some kinds of benefit arrears as capital in para.7 of Sch.10 does not affect this conclusion. This is because the conclusion, and *R(SB) 4/89*, must be subject to the principle of *R(SB) 2/83* and *R(SB) 35/83* that at some point accumulated income turns into capital. The sensible approach would be that if any amount of income is still possessed after the end of the period to which it is properly attributed as income under regs 29 and 31, then it becomes capital, subject to the deduction of relevant liabilities under *R(SB) 2/83* and *R(SB) 35/83*. See *R(IS) 3/93*. Thus there is still something for para.7 of Sch.10 to bite on. However, note *CIS/515/2006* discussed in the note to reg.23 in which the Commissioner takes a rather different approach.

Paragraph (2)

2.426 This paragraph authorises the disregards in Sch.9. See *CIS 563/1991* discussed in the note to para.22 of Sch.9 and *CIS 82/1993* and *CIS 13059/1996* in the notes to paras 19 and 30 where more than one disregard applies. *CIS 683/1993* confirms that income can only be disregarded to the extent allowed for by Sch.9. Therefore, no deduction could be made for the maintenance payments made by the claimant, whether under a court order or otherwise, or for his insurance premiums, in calculating his income. But see *R(IS) 4/01* (and also note the other decisions discussed above). If the maintenance payments are made under an attachment of earnings order rather than by the claimant out of his own income they will not count as his income. However, the deprivation of income rule in reg.42(1) might be applicable if the claimant has deliberately provoked an attachment of earnings order in order to secure benefit.

Paragraph (3)

2.427 If deductions are made from social security benefits for recovery of overpayments or social fund loans the gross amount of benefit is used in the calculation of income support. A deduction for child support maintenance is a deduction by way of recovery for the purposes of para.(3) (and reg.103(3) of the JSA Regulations 1996) (Social Security (Claims and Payments) Regulations 1987 Sch.9B para.8, see Vol.III in this series).

R(H) 2/09 confirms that if incapacity benefit is being reduced due to receipt of an occupational pension this is not a "deduction by way of recovery" for the purposes of para.(3). The income to be taken into account is the net amount of the incapacity benefit that the claimant actually receives.

Paragraphs (3A)–(3AB)

Paragraphs (3A)–(3AB) contain precise rules for calculating the amount of a student loan and/or any non-repayable amount for dependants to be taken into account as income where a student abandons or is dismissed from his course. Note the definitions in para.(3AB) and see the notes to reg.66A for a discussion of the current system for student support. For an example of how the provisions in paras (3A)–(3AB) work in practice see Annex D to HB/CTB Circular A31/2001. Note that the calculation can result in a nil income figure, depending on the point in the term at which the student abandoned or was dismissed from his course. The amendments made on September 1, 2008 clarify how student loans paid by two or more instalments in a quarter are to be taken into account when a student abandons or is dismissed from his course. **2.428**

If the former student repays the loan this does not constitute a change of circumstances so as to provide grounds for supersession (see reg.6(6)(a) of the Decisions and Appeals Regulations 1999 in Vol.III of this series). The intention is that the amount calculated under para.(3AA) should still be taken into account as income. However the guidance to decision-makers does state that if the Student Loan Company demands immediate repayment (e.g. because the loan instalment should not have been paid because the student had abandoned or been dismissed from the course), no loan income should be taken into account from the date that demand is made (see DMG Memo, Vol.6 02/01, paras 17–18). This is on the basis that the student is under a "certain and immediate liability" to repay the loan and so it should not be treated as his income (see *Chief Adjudication Officer v Leeves*, reported as *R(IS) 5/99*, discussed in the notes to reg.29(2B)). But this would not apply if the former student voluntarily repaid the loan, as confirmed in *CJSA 549/2003*. The Commissioner considered that the particularly harsh effect of these provisions in such circumstances where no account was taken of any repayment and it was simply assumed that the loan could still be used for living expenses merited the attention of the Secretary of State (but so far the Commissioner's suggestion remains unheeded).

Note para.61 of Sch.9 under which any part of a student loan or grant left over at the end of a course is ignored.

See also para.(3B).

Paragraph (3B)

See the notes to regs 29(2B) and 32(6A). But note *Chief Adjudication Officer v Leeves*, reported as *R(IS) 5/99*) and the argument discussed in the notes to reg.29(2B) as to when that provision applies. **2.429**

Note also para.61 of Sch.9 under which any grant or covenant income or student loan left over at the end of the person's course is disregarded.

Paragraph (4)(a)

These amounts, which do not count as earnings, do count as other income. However, note the disregards in paras 1, 2A, 3, 4, 4A, 18, 20, 21, 26, 27 and 69 of Sch.9. See also *CIS 521/2002* discussed in the note to reg.37(2). **2.430**

Paragraphs (4)(b) and (5)

See the notes to reg.21(3). **2.431**

Capital treated as income

41.—[8(1) Capital which is payable by instalments which are outstanding on— **2.432**

(a) the first day in respect of which income support is payable or the date of the determination of the claim, whichever is earlier; or

(b) in the case of a supersession, the date of that supersession,
shall be treated as income if the aggregate of the instalments outstanding and the amount of the claimant's capital otherwise calculated in accordance with Chapter VI of this Part exceeds [[13] . . .] £16,000.]

(2) Any payment received under an annuity shall be treated as income.

(3) [[12]. . .]

[[2](4) In the case of a person to whom section 20(3) of the Act [SSCBA, s.124(1)] (conditions of entitlement to income support) has effect as modified by section 23A(b) of that Act [SSCBA, s.127(b)] (effect of return to work), any amount by way of repayment of income tax deducted from his emoluments in pursuance of section 203 of the Income and Corporation Taxes Act 1988, shall be treated as income.]

[[4](5) Any earnings to the extent that they are not a payment of income shall be treated as income.]

[[7](6) Any Career Development Loan paid pursuant to section 2 of the Employment and Training Act 1973 shall be treated as income.]

[[11](7) Where an agreement or court order provides that payments shall be made to the claimant in consequence of any personal injury to the claimant and that such payments are to be made, wholly or partly, by way of periodical payments, any such periodical payments received by the claimant (but not a payment which is treated as capital by virtue of this Part), shall be treated as income.]

AMENDMENTS

1. Income Support (General) Amendment Regulations 1988 (SI 1988/663) reg.18 (April 11, 1988).

2. Income Support (General) Amendment No.4 Regulations 1988 (SI 1988/1445) reg.9 (September 12, 1988).

3. Family Credit and Income Support (General) Amendment Regulations 1989 (SI 1989/104) reg.7 (July 10, 1989).

4. Income Support (General) Amendment No.2 Regulations 1989 (SI 1989/1323) reg.13 (October 9, 1989).

5. Income-related Benefits (Miscellaneous Amendments) Regulations 1990 (SI 1990/671) reg.5 (April 9, 1990).

6. Income Support (General) Amendment Regulations 1992 (SI 1992/468) Sch. para.4 (April 6, 1992).

7. Income-related Benefits and Jobseeker's Allowance (Miscellaneous Amendments) Regulations 1997 (SI 1997/65) reg.3 (April 7, 1997).

8. Social Security Act 1998 (Commencement No.12 and Consequential and Transitional Provisions) Order 1999 (SI 1999/3178 (C.81)) art.3(5) and Sch.5 para.3 (November 29, 1999)

9. Social Security Amendment (Capital Limits and Earnings Disregards) Regulations 2000 (SI 2000/2545) reg.2(1)(a) (April 9, 2001).

10. Children (Leaving Care) Act 2000 (Commencement No.2 and Consequential Provisions) Order 2001 (SI 2001/3070) art.3(2) and Sch.1 para.(c) (October 1, 2001).

11. Social Security Amendment (Personal Injury Payments) Regulations 2002 (SI 2002/2442) reg.2 (October 28, 2002).

12. Social Security (Working Tax Credit and Child Tax Credit) (Consequential Amendments) Regulations 2003 (SI 2003/455) reg.2 and Sch.1 para.9 (April 6, 2004, except in "transitional cases" and see further the note to reg.17 of the Income Support Regulations).

13. Social Security (Miscellaneous Amendments) (No.2) Regulations 2005 (SI 2005/2465) reg.2(2) (April 10, 2006).

Definitions

"the Act"—see reg.2(1).
"claimant"—*ibid.*

General Note

Paragraph (1)

The value of the right to receive any outstanding instalments of capital payable by instalments is disregarded (Sch.10 para.16). See the notes to reg.23 on the line between capital and income. Normally each instalment, when it is paid, would add to the claimant's capital (*Lillystone v SBC* [1982] 3 F.L.R. 52). The literal efect of para.(1) is that if the amount of the instalments outstanding plus the claimant's (including partner's: reg.23) other capital comes to more than £16,000 (which has been the increased upper capital limit for income support (and income-based JSA) since April 10, 2006), the whole amount outstanding is to be treated as income. What para.(1) does not say is what this means. A capital sum cannot simply be treated as income. The common sense rule would be that each instalment, when paid, was treated as a payment of income (as suggested in paras 28532 and 28536 of the *Decision Makers Guide*), but this is not expressed in para.(1). For an example of where the rule in para.(1) applied see *R(IS) 7/98* in the notes to para.15 of Sch.10 and see *R(IS) 10/01* referred to in the note to para.(2). 2.433

Weekly sums that the claimant was allowed to withdraw for living expenses from his bank account which was subject to a restraint order under s.77 of the Criminal Justice Act 1988 were not capital payable by instalments. Regulation 104(1) of the JSA Regulations 1996 (the equivalent of para.(1)) only applied if there was a contractual or other obligation on the part of some other person to pay a capital sum to the claimant by instalments (*SH v SSWP* [2008] UKUT 21 (AAC)).

Paragraph (2)

The value of the right to receive income under an annuity is disregarded as capital (Sch.10 para.11). The income under some "home income" schemes is disregarded under para.17 of Sch.9. 2.434

The general rule, however, is that payments under an annuity count as income. See *DN v Leicester CC (HB)* [2010] UKUT 235 (AAC) which discusses the nature of annuity payments.

In *R(IS) 10/01* part of the claimant's damages award following a road traffic accident was in the form of two structured settlement annuities. The monthly annuity payments were used for the claimant's substantial care needs. However, as these fell squarely within para.(2) they counted as income with the result that the claimant was not entitled to income support. The Commissioner also accepted that they came within para.(1). The claimant appealed but the Court of Appeal dismissed the appeal and upheld the decision of the Commissioner (*Beattie v Secretary of State for Social Security*, reported as part of *R(IS) 10/01*).

However, the problem highlighted by *Beattie* was ameliorated by the introduction of a disregard for regular payments from annuities purchased from funds derived from personal injury awards to claimants on October 28, 2002 (see the previous form of para.15 of Sch.9 in the 2006 edition of this volume). The disregard in para.15 of Sch.9 was changed to a total disregard on October 2, 2006.

Paragraph (3)

This paragraph was omitted with effect from April 6, 2004 by reg.2 of and para.9 of Sch.1 to the Social Security (Working Tax Credit and Child Tax Credit) (Consequential Amendments) Regulations 2003 (SI 2003/455), except in "transitional cases" (i.e. those cases in which the claimant is still receiving amounts for his children in his income support—see further the note to reg.17). For "transitional cases" para.(3) continues in force (see the 2003 edition of this volume for this provision). With effect from May 12, 2004, reg.5 of the Social Security 2.435

(Miscellaneous Amendments) (No.2) Regulations 2004 (SI 2004/1141) substituted the words "section 12 of the Social Work (Scotland) Act 1968 or sections 29 or 30 of the Children (Scotland) Act 1995" for the words "section 12, 24 or 26 of the Social Work (Scotland) Act 1968" in para.(3). The effect of this amendment is simply to update the references to the Scottish legislation referred to in para.(3).

Paragraph (4)

2.436 In trade dispute cases repayments of PAYE tax, normally capital, are to be treated as income.

Paragraph (5)

2.437 This seems merely to confirm that sums which are defined as earnings in reg.35 which might under the general law be categorised as capital are income.

Paragraph (6)

2.438 This treats Career Development Loans, which are provided in order to help adults pay for vocational education or training, as income. However, the income will be disregarded under para.13 of Sch.9 (replacing the previous disregards in paras 59 and 60 of Sch.9 which were revoked on April 1, 2004), except any part of the loan that was intended to meet the cost of food, ordinary clothing or footwear, household fuel, rent for which housing benefit is payable, housing costs met by income support, council tax or water charges during the period of training or education. On "ordinary clothing or footwear" see paras 28671–2 of the *Decision Makers Guide*. In addition, any part of the loan left over at the end of the course is ignored.

For treatment of career development loans before these rules were introduced on April 7, 1997, see *CIS 507/1997*.

Paragraph (7)

2.439 See the note to para.(2) above. Paragraph (7) provides that any periodical payments paid under an agreement or court order to a claimant in consequence of personal injury to him, other than payments that are treated as capital (see reg.48(4)), count as income. However, from October 2, 2006, such payments are totally ignored under para.15 of Sch.9. Note also that since the amendments to reg.48(4) on October 2, 2006, not only capital disregarded under para.12 (trusts of personal injury compensation) but also capital disregarded under paras 44 and 45 (funds held in court derived from compensation for personal injury or the death of a parent) are excepted from the rule in reg.48(4); thus regular payments from such sources will count as income in the normal way (and be disregarded under para.15 of Sch.9).

Notional income

2.440 **42.**—[77 (1) A claimant is to be treated as possessing income of which the claimant has deprived themselves for the purpose of securing entitlement to income support or increasing the amount of that benefit, or for the purpose of securing entitlement to, or increasing the amount of a jobseeker's allowance or an employment and support allowance.]

(2) Except in the case of—

(a) a discretionary trust;

(b) a trust derived from a payment made in consequence of a personal injury;

[23(c) jobseeker's allowance; or]

[25(d) [51. . .]]

[8(e) [48 working tax credit];

(f) [49 child tax credit],]

[20(g) a personal pension scheme [59, occupational pension scheme]

[63 [65 . . .] or a payment made by the Board of the Pension Protection Fund] where the claimant [74 has not attained the qualifying age for state pension credit],]

[72(ga) any sum to which paragraph (8ZA) applies;]

[24(h) [54. . .]] [26 or

[64 (i) any sum to which paragraph 44(2)(a) of Schedule 10 (capital to be disregarded) applies which is administered in the way referred to in paragraph 44(1)(a);

(ia) any sum to which paragraph 45(a) of Schedule 10 refers; or]

[30 (j) rehabilitation allowance made under section 2 of the Employment and Training Act 1973],

income which would become available to the claimant upon application being made but which has not been acquired by him shall be treated as possessed by him but only from the date on which [1it could be expected to be acquired were an application made.]

[20 [60 (2ZA) A claimant who has attained the [74 qualifying age for state pension credit] shall be treated as possessing—

(a) the amount of any income from an occupational pension scheme, [63 a personal pension scheme [65 . . .] or the Board of the Pension Protection Fund]—

(i) for which no claim has been made, and

(ii) to which he might expect to be entitled if a claim for it were made;

(b) income from an occupational pension scheme which the claimant elected to defer,

but only from the date on which it could be expected to be acquired were an application for it to be made.

[65 (2A) This paragraph applies where a person [74 who has attained the qualifying age for state pension credit]—

(a) is entitled to money purchase benefits under an occupational pension scheme or a personal pension scheme;

(b) fails to purchase an annuity with the funds available in that scheme; and

(c) either—

(i) defers in whole or in part the payment of any income which would have been payable to him by his pension fund holder, or

(ii) fails to take any necessary action to secure that the whole of any income which would be payable to him by his pension fund holder upon his applying for it, is so paid, or

(iii) income withdrawal is not available to him under that scheme.

(2AA) Where paragraph (2A) applies, the amount of any income foregone shall be treated as possessed by that person, but only from the date on which it could be expected to be acquired were an application for it to be made.]]

(2B) The amount of any income foregone in a case [65 where paragraph (2A)(c)(i) or (ii)] applies shall be the maximum amount of income which may be withdrawn from the fund and shall be determined by the [39 Secretary of State] who shall take account of information provided by the pension fund holder in accordance with regulation 7(5) of the Social Security (Claims and Payments) Regulations 1987.

(2C) The amount of any income foregone in a case [65 where paragraph (2A)(c)(iii)] applies shall be the income that the [50 person] could have received without purchasing an annuity had the funds held under the [61 relevant occupational or personal pension scheme] [65 . . .] been held [61 under a scheme] where income withdrawal was available and shall be determined in the manner specified in paragraph (2B).]

[62 (2CA) In paragraph (2A), "money purchase benefits" has the meaning it has in the Pension Schemes Act 1993.]

[25(2D) [51 . . .]]

(3) Except in the case of a discretionary trust, or a trust derived from a payment made in consequence of a personal injury, any income which is due to be paid to the claimant but—

(a) has not been paid to him;
(b) is not a payment prescribed in regulation [448 or 9] of the Social Security (Payments on Account, Overpayment and Recovery) Regulations [44 1988] (duplication and prescribed payments or maintenance payments) and not made on or before the date prescribed in relation to it,

shall [10except for any amount to which paragraph (3A) [41, (3B) or (3C)] applies] be treated as possessed by the claimant.

[10(3A) This paragraph applies to an amount which is due to be paid to the claimant under an occupational pension scheme but which is not paid because the trustees or managers of the scheme have suspended or ceased payments [13. . .] due to an insufficiency of resources.

(3B) This paragraph applies to any amount by which a payment made to the claimant from an occupational pension scheme falls short of the payment to which he was due under the scheme where the shortfall arises because the trustees or managers of the scheme have insufficient resources available to meet in full the scheme's liabilities [13. . .].]

[41(3C) This paragraph applies to any earnings which are due to an employed earner on the termination of his employment by reason of redundancy but which have not been paid to him.]

[2(4) [32 Any payment of income, other than a payment of income specified in paragraph (4ZA)], made—

(a) to a third party in respect of a single claimant or [51 his partner] (but not a member of the third party's family) shall be treated—
    (i) in a case where the payment is derived from a payment of any benefit under the benefit Acts,[53 a payment from the Armed Forces and Reserve Forces Compensation Scheme,] a war disablement pension [21, war widow's pension [47 or war widower's pension] or a pension payable to a person as a [58 widow, widower or surviving civil partner] under [70. . .] any power of Her Majesty otherwise than under an enactment to make provision about pensions for or in respect of persons who have been disabled or have died in consequence of service as members of the armed forces of the Crown,] as possessed by that single claimant, if it is paid to him, [51 or by his partner, if it is paid to his partner];
    [36(ia) in a case where that payment is a payment of an occupational pension [63, a pension or other periodical payment made under a personal pension scheme or a payment made by the Board of the Pension Protection Fund], as possessed by that single claimant or, as the case may be, by [51 the claimant's partner];]
    (ii) in any other case, as possessed by that single claimant [51 or his partner] to the extent that it is used for the food, ordinary clothing or footwear, household fuel, rent [55. . .] for which

housing benefit is payable, [16or] [7. . .] any housing costs to the extent that they are met under regulations 17(1)(e) or 18(1)(f) (housing costs) [16. . .] [4. . .] [3. . .] [4. . .], of that single claimant or, as the case may be, [51 of his partner] [7, or is used for any [12council tax] or water charges for which that claimant or [51 partner is liable]];

[51 (b) to a single claimant or his partner in respect of a third party (but not in respect of another member of his family) shall be treated as possessed by that single claimant or, as the case may be, his partner, to the extent that it is kept or used by him or used by or on behalf of his partner;]

but, except where sub-paragraph (a)(i) applies and in the case of a person to whom section 23 of the Act [SSCBA, s.126] (trade disputes) applies, this paragraph shall not apply to any payment in kind [56 to the third party].]

[32 (4ZA) Paragraph (4) shall not apply in respect of a payment of income made—

(a) under [75 or by] the Macfarlane Trust, the Macfarlane (Special Payments) Trust, the Macfarlane (Special Payments) (No.2) Trust, the Fund, the Eileen Trust [73, MFET Limited] [78 , the Skipton Fund, the Caxton Foundation] or the Independent Living [68 Fund (2006)];

(b) pursuant to section 19(1)(a) of the Coal Industry Act 1994 (concessionary coal); or

(c) pursuant to section 2 of the Employment and Training Act 1973 in respect of a person's participation—

(i) in an employment programme specified in regulations 75(1)(a)(ii) of the Jobseeker's Allowance Regulations 1996;

(ii) in a training scheme specified in regulation 75(1)(b)(ii) of those Regulations; or

[45 (iia) in the Intensive Activity Period specified in regulation 75(1)(a)(iv) of those Regulations [67 . . .]; or]

(iii) in a qualifying course within the meaning specified in regulation 17A(7) of those Regulations.]

(iv) [*Omitted.*]

[76(ca) in respect of a person's participation in [79 a scheme prescribed in regulation 3 of the Jobseeker's Allowance (Schemes for Assisting Persons to Obtain Employment) Regulations 2013] or the Mandatory Work Activity Scheme; or]

[37(d) under an occupational pension scheme [63, in respect of a pension or other periodical payment made under a personal pension scheme or a payment made by the Board of the Pension Protection Fund] where—

(i) a bankruptcy order has been made in respect of the person in respect of whom the payment has been made or, in Scotland, the estate of that person is subject to sequestration or a judicial factor has been appointed on that person's estate under section 41 of the Solicitors (Scotland) Act 1980;

(ii) the payment is made to the trustee in bankruptcy or any other person acting on behalf of the creditors; and

(iii) the person referred to in (i) and [51 his partner (if any)] does not possess, or is not treated as possessing, any other income apart from that payment.]

[16(4A) Where the claimant [57 resides in a care home, an Abbeyfield Home or an independent hospital, or is temporarily absent from such a home or hospital], any payment made by a person other than the claimant or a member of his family in respect of some or all of the cost of maintaining the claimant [51 or his partner in that home [69 or hospital] shall be treated as possessed by the claimant or his partner].]

(5) Where a claimant's earnings are not ascertainable at the time of the determination of the claim or of any [40 revision or supersession the Secretary of State] shall treat the claimant as possessing such earnings as is reasonable in the circumstances of the case having regard to the number of hours worked and the earnings paid for comparable employment in the area.

[43(5A) Where the amount of a subsistence allowance paid to a claimant in a benefit week is less than the amount of income-based jobseeker's allowance that person would have received in that benefit week had it been payable to him, less 50p, he shall be treated as possessing the amount which is equal to the amount of income-based jobseeker's allowance which he would have received in that week, less 50p.]

(6) [33Subject to paragraph (6A),] where—

(a) a claimant performs a service for another person; and

(b) that person makes no payment of earnings or pays less than that paid for a comparable employment in the area,

the [39Secretary of State] shall treat the claimant as possessing such earnings (if any) as is reasonable for that employment unless the claimant satisfies him that the means of that person are insufficient for him to pay or to pay more for the service [33. . .].

[33(6A) Paragraph (6) shall not apply—

(a) to a claimant who is engaged by a charitable or voluntary organisation or who is a volunteer if the [38Secretary of State] is satisfied in any of those cases that it is reasonable for him to provide the service free of charge;

[42(b) in a case where the service is performed in connection with—

(i) the claimant's participation in an employment or training programme in accordance with regulation 19(1)(q) of the Jobseeker's Allowance Regulations 1996 ,[46, other than where the service is performed in connection with the claimant's participation in the Intensive Activity Period specified in regulation 75(1)(a)(iv) of those Regulations [67 . . .]]; or

(ii) the claimant's or the claimant's partner's participation in an employment or training programme as defined in regulation 19(3) of those Regulations for which a training allowance is not payable or, where such an allowance is payable, it is payable for the sole purpose of reimbursement of travelling or meal expenses to the person participating in that programme; or]

(c) to a claimant who is engaged in work experience whilst participating in—

(i) the New Deal for Lone Parents; or

(ii) a scheme which has been approved by the Secretary of State as supporting the objectives of the New Deal for Lone Parents [66; or

(d) to a claimant who is participating in a work placement approved by the Secretary of State (or a person providing services to the Secretary of State) before the placement starts.

(6AA) In paragraph (6A)(d) "work placement" means practical work experience which is not undertaken in expectation of payment.]

[52. . .].

(6B) [52. . .]

(6C) [52. . .]]

(6D) [*Omitted.*]

(7) Where a claimant is treated as possessing any income under any of [31 paragraphs (1) to (4A)] the foregoing provisions of this Part shall apply for the purposes of calculating the amount of that income as if a payment had actually been made and as if it were actual income which he does possess.

(8) Where a claimant is treated as possessing any earnings under paragraph (5) or (6) the foregoing provisions of this Part shall apply for the purposes of calculating the amount of those earnings as if a payment had actually been made and as if they were actual earnings which he does possess except that paragraph (3) of regulation 36 (calculation of net earnings of employed earners) shall not apply and his net earnings shall be calculated by taking into account the earnings which he is treated as possessing, less—

(a) an amount in respect of income tax equivalent to an amount calculated by applying to those earnings [11 [71. . .] the basic rate [81, or in the case of a Scottish taxpayer, the Scottish basic rate,] of tax] in the year of assessment less only the [81 personal reliefs to which the claimant is entitled under Chapters 2, 3 and 3A of Part 3 of the Income Tax Act 2007 as are] appropriate to his circumstances; but, if the period over which those earnings are to be taken into account is less than a year, [11the earnings to which the [66 [71 basic] rate] [81, or the Scottish basic rate,] [18. . .] of tax is to be applied and] the amount of the [65 [81 personal reliefs]] deductible under this paragraph shall be calculated on a pro rata basis;

[16(b) where the weekly amount of those earnings equals or exceeds the lower earnings limit, an amount representing primary Class 1 contributions under the Contributions and Benefits Act, calculated by applying to those earnings the initial and main primary percentages in accordance with sections 8(1) (a) and (b) of that Act; and]

(c) one-half of any sum payable by the claimant [17in respect of a pay period] by way of a contribution towards an occupational or personal pension scheme.

[72 (8ZA) Paragraphs (1), (2), (3), (4), (5) and (6) shall not apply in respect of any amount of income other than earnings, or earnings derived from employment as an employed earner, arising out of the [80 claimant participating as a service user].]

[10(8A) In paragraphs (3A) and (3B) the expression "resources" has the same meaning as in the Social Security Pensions Act 1975 by virtue of section 66(1) of that Act.]

[2(9) In paragraph (4) the expression "ordinary clothing or footwear" means clothing or footwear for normal daily use, but does not include school uniforms, or clothing or footwear used solely for sporting activities.]

AMENDMENTS

1. Income Support (General) Amendment Regulations 1988 (SI 1988/663) reg.19 (April 11, 1988).

2. Income Support (General) Amendment (No.4) Regulations 1988 (SI 1988/1445) reg.10 (September 12, 1988).

3. Income Support (General) Amendment (No.4) Regulations 1988 (SI 1988/1445) Sch.1 para.4 (April 10, 1989).

4. Income Support (General) Amendment Regulations 1989 (SI 1989/534) Sch.1 para.7 (October 9, 1989).

5. Income-related Benefits Schemes Amendment Regulations 1990 (SI 1990/127) reg.3 (January 31, 1990).

6. Income-related Benefits Schemes and Social Security (Recoupment) Amendment Regulations 1991 (SI 1991/1175) reg.5 (May 11, 1991).

7. Income Support (General) Amendment No.4 Regulations 1991 (SI 1991/1559) reg.8 (October 7, 1991).

8. Income Support (General) Amendment Regulations 1992 (SI 1992/468) reg.4 (April 6, 1992).

9. Income-related Benefits Schemes and Social Security (Recoupment) Amendment Regulations 1992 (SI 1992/1101) reg.6 (May 7, 1992).

10. Income Support (General) Amendment (No.2) Regulations 1992 (SI 1992/1198) reg.2 (May 22, 1992).

11. Income-related Benefits Schemes (Miscellaneous Amendments) (No.3) Regulations 1992 (SI 1992/2155) reg.18 (October 5, 1992).

12. Income-related Benefits Schemes (Miscellaneous Amendments) Regulations 1993 (SI 1993/315) Sch. para.2 (April 1, 1993).

13. Income-related Benefits Schemes (Miscellaneous Amendments) Regulations 1993 (SI 1993/315) reg.6 (April 12, 1993).

14. Social Security Benefits (Miscellaneous Amendments) (No.2) Regulations 1993 (SI 1993/963) reg.2(3) (April 22, 1993).

15. Income-related Benefits Schemes and Social Security (Recoupement) Amendment Regulations 1993 (SI 1993/1249) reg.4(3) (May 14, 1993).

16. Income-related Benefits Schemes (Miscellaneous Amendments) Regulations 1994 (SI 1994/527) reg.4 (April 11, 1994).

17. Income-related Benefits Schemes (Miscellaneous Amendments) (No.5) Regulations 1994 (SI 1994/2139) reg.26 (October 3, 1994).

18. Income-related Benefits Schemes (Miscellaneous Amendments) (No.5) Regulations 1994 (SI 1994/2139) reg.29 (October 3, 1994).

19. Income-related Benefits Schemes (Miscellaneous Amendments) Regulations 1995 (SI 1995/516) reg.22 (April 10, 1995).

20. Income-related Benefits Schemes and Social Security (Claims and Payments) (Miscellaneous Amendments) Regulations 1995 (SI 1995/2303) reg.6(4) (October 2, 1995).

21. Income-related Benefits Schemes Amendment (No.2) Regulations 1995 (SI 1995/2792) reg.6(2) (October 28, 1995).

22. Income-related Benefits Schemes (Widows' etc. Pensions Disregards) Amendment Regulations 1995 (SI 1995/3282) reg.2 (December 20, 1995).

23. Income Support (General) (Jobseeker's Allowance Consequential Amendments) Regulations 1996 (SI 1996/206) reg.17 (October 7, 1996).

24. Income-related Benefits Schemes and Social Fund (Miscellaneous Amendments) Regulations 1996 (SI 1996/1944) reg.13 and Sch. para.3 (October 7, 1996).

25. Child Benefit, Child Support and Social Security (Miscellaneous Amendments) Regulations 1996 (SI 1996/1803) reg.37 (April 7, 1997).

26. Income-related Benefits and Jobseeker's Allowance (Amendment) (No.2) Regulations 1997 (SI 1997/2197) reg.5(4) (October 6, 1997).

27. Income-related Benefits and Jobseeker's Allowance (Amendment) (No.2) Regulations 1997 (SI 1997/2197) reg.7(3) and (4)(e) (October 6, 1997).

28. Social Security Amendment (New Deal) Regulations 1997 (SI 1997/ 2863) reg.17(1) and (2)(e) (January 5, 1998).

29. Social Security Amendment (New Deal) Regulations 1997 (SI 1997/ 2863) reg.17(3) and (4)(e) (January 5, 1998).

30. Social Security (Miscellaneous Amendments) Regulations 1998 (SI 1998/563) reg.6(1) and (2)(e) (April 6, 1998).

31. Social Security (Miscellaneous Amendments) Regulations 1998 (SI 1998/563) reg.13(1)(b) (April 6, 1998).
32. Social Security Amendment (New Deal) (No.2) Regulations 1998 (SI 1998/2117) reg.2(2) (September 24, 1998).
33. Income Support (General) Amendment Regulations 1999 (SI 1999/ 2554) reg.2(2)(a) and (b) (October 4, 1999).
34. Social Security and Child Support (Tax Credits) Consequential Amendments Regulations 1999 (SI 1999/2566) reg.2(1) and Sch.2 Pt I (October 5, 1999).
35. Social Security and Child Support (Tax Credits) Consequential Amendments Regulations 1999 (SI 1999/2566) reg.2(2) and Sch.2 Pt II (October 5, 1999).
36. Social Security Amendment (Notional Income and Capital) Regulations 1999 (SI 1999/2640) reg.2(1)(a) (November 15, 1999).
37. Social Security Amendment (Notional Income and Capital) Regulations 1999 (SI 1999/2640) reg.2(3)(c) (November 15, 1999).
38. Income Support (General) Amendment Regulations 1999 (SI 1999/ 2554) reg.2(2)(c) (November 29, 1999).
39. Social Security Act 1998 (Commencement No.12 and Consequential and Transitional Provisions) Order 1999 (SI 1999/3178 (C.81)) art.3(5) and Sch.5 para.4(a) (November 29, 1999).
40. Social Security Act 1998 (Commencement No.12 and Consequential and Transitional Provisions) Order 1999 (SI 1999/3178 (C.81)) art.3(5) and Sch.5 para.4(b) (November 29, 1999).
41. Income Support (General) and Jobseeker's Allowance Amendment (No.2) Regulations 1999 (SI 1999/3324) reg.2 (January 7, 2000).
42. Social Security (Approved Work) Regulations 2000 (SI 2000/678) reg.2(2) (April 3, 2000).
43. Social Security Amendment (Employment Zones) Regulations 2000 (SI 2000/724) reg.3(1) (April 3, 2000).
44. Social Security (Miscellaneous Amendments) (No.3) Regulations 2001 (SI 2001/859) reg.3(2) (April 9, 2001).
45. Social Security Amendment (New Deal) Regulations 2001 (SI 2001/ 1029) reg.15(4) and (5)(c) (April 9, 2001).
46. Social Security Amendment (New Deal) Regulations 2001 (SI 2001/ 1029) reg.15(6) and (7)(c) (April 9, 2001).
47. Social Security (Miscellaneous Amendments) Regulations 2002 (SI 2002/841) reg.2(2) (April 8, 2002).
48. Social Security (Working Tax Credit and Child Tax Credit) (Consequential Amendments) Regulations 2003 (SI 2003/455) reg.2 and Sch.1 para.10(b) (April 7, 2003).
49. Social Security (Working Tax Credit and Child Tax Credit) (Consequential Amendments) Regulations 2003 (SI 2003/455) reg.2 and Sch.1 para.10(c) (April 7, 2003).
50. State Pension Credit (Consequential, Transitional and Miscellaneous Provisions) Regulations 2002 (SI 2002/3019) reg.29(2) (October 6, 2003).
51. Social Security (Working Tax Credit and Child Tax Credit) (Consequential Amendments) Regulations 2003 (SI 2003/455) reg.2 and Sch.1 para.10 (except sub-paras (b) and (c)) (April 6, 2004, except in "transitional cases" and see further the note to reg.17 of the Income Support Regulations).
52. Social Security (Miscellaneous Amendments) (No.3) Regulations 2004 (SI 2004/2308) reg.5(2) (October 4, 2004).
53. Social Security (Miscellaneous Amendments) Regulations 2005 (SI 2005/574) reg.2(5) (April 4, 2005).
54. Social Security (Miscellaneous Amendments) Regulations 2005 (SI 2005/574) reg.3(3)(a) (April 4, 2005).
55. Social Security (Miscellaneous Amendments) Regulations 2005 (SI 2005/574) reg.3(3)(b) (April 4, 2005).
56. Social Security (Miscellaneous Amendments) (No.2) Regulations 2005 (SI 2005/2465) reg.2(3)(e) (October 3, 2005).

57. Social Security (Care Homes and Independent Hospitals) Regulations 2005 (SI 2005/2687) reg.2 and Sch.1 para.6 (October 24, 2005).
58. Social Security (Civil Partnership) (Consequential Amendments) Regulations 2005 (SI 2005/2878) reg.4(2) (December 5, 2005).
59. Social Security (Miscellaneous Amendments) (No.2) Regulations 2005 (SI 2005/2465) reg.2(3)(a) (April 6, 2006).
60. Social Security (Miscellaneous Amendments) (No.2) Regulations 2005 (SI 2005/2465) reg.2(3)(b) (April 6, 2006).
61. Social Security (Miscellaneous Amendments) (No.2) Regulations 2005 (SI 2005/2465) reg.2(3)(c) (April 6, 2006).
62. Social Security (Miscellaneous Amendments) (No.2) Regulations 2005 (SI 2005/2465) reg.2(3)(d) (April 6, 2006).
63. Social Security (Miscellaneous Amendments) Regulations 2006 (SI 2006/588) reg.2(2) (April 6, 2006).
64. Social Security (Miscellaneous Amendments) Regulations 2007 (SI 2007/719) reg.2(3) (April 2, 2007).
65. Social Security (Miscellaneous Amendments) (No.3) Regulations 2007 (SI 2007/1749) reg.2(6) (July 16, 2007).
66. Social Security (Miscellaneous Amendments) (No.5) Regulations 2007 (SI 2007/2618) reg.5(9) (October 1, 2007).
67. Social Security (Miscellaneous Amendments) Regulations 2008 (SI 2008/698) reg.2(7)(a) (April 14, 2008).
68. Social Security (Miscellaneous Amendments) (No.6) Regulations 2008 (SI 2008/2767) reg.2(6) (November 17, 2008).
69. Social Security (Miscellaneous Amendments) (No.6) Regulations 2008 (SI 2008/2767) reg.2(7) (November 17, 2008).
70. Social Security (Miscellaneous Amendments) (No.7) Regulations 2008 (SI 2008/3157) reg.2(4) (January 5, 2009).
71. Social Security (Miscellaneous Amendments) Regulations 2009 (SI 2009/583) reg.2(7) (April 6, 2009).
72. Social Security (Miscellaneous Amendments) (No.4) Regulations 2009 (SI 2009/2655) reg.2(9) (October 26, 2009).
73. Social Security (Miscellaneous Amendments) (No.2) Regulations 2010 (SI 2010/641) reg.2(3)(b) (April 6, 2010).
74. Social Security (Miscellaneous Amendments) (No.2) Regulations 2010 (SI 2010/641) reg.2(6) (April 6, 2010).
75. Social Security (Miscellaneous Amendments) (No.2) Regulations 2010 (SI 2010/641) reg.2(7)(a) (April 6, 2010).
76. Social Security (Miscellaneous Amendments) (No.2) Regulations 2011 (SI 2011/1707) reg.4(4)(a) and (5) (August 5, 2011).
77. Social Security (Miscellaneous Amendments) (No.3) Regulations 2011 (SI 2011/2425) reg.7(4) (October 31, 2011).
78. Social Security (Miscellaneous Amendments) (No.3) Regulations 2011 (SI 2011/2425) reg.7(5) (October 31, 2011).
79. Jobseeker's Allowance (Schemes for Assisting Persons to Obtain Employment) Regulations 2013 (SI 2013/276) reg.13(b) (February 12, 2013).
80. Social Security (Miscellaneous Amendments) Regulations 2014 (SI 2014/591) reg.2(4) (April 28, 2014).
81. Social Security (Scottish Rate of Income Tax etc.) (Amendment) Regulations 2016 (SI 2016/233) reg. 2(5) (April 6, 2016).

Definitions

"Abbeyfield Home"—see reg.2(1).
"the Act"—*ibid.*
"the Armed Forces and Reserve Forces Compensation Scheme"—*ibid.*
"benefit Acts"—*ibid.*

"care home"—*ibid.*
"child tax credit"—*ibid.*
"claimant"—see reg.2(1), reg.23(1).
"claimant participating as a service user"—see reg.2(1B).
"earnings"—see reg.2(1).
"family"—see SSCBA s.137(1).
"independent hospital"—see reg.2(1).
"Intensive Activity Period for 50 plus"—*ibid.*
"the Mandatory Work Activity Scheme"—*ibid.*
"MFET Limited"—*ibid.*
"occupational pension"—*ibid.*
"partner"—*ibid.*
"pay period"—*ibid.*
"payment"—*ibid.*
"pension fund holder"—*ibid.*
"personal pension scheme"—*ibid.*
"qualifying age for state pension credit"—see SSCBA s.137(1).
"Scottish basic rate"—see reg.2(1).
"Scottish taxpayer"—*ibid.*
"single claimant"—*ibid.*
"Social Security Act"—*ibid.*
"subsistence allowance"—*ibid.*
"the Caxton Foundation"—*ibid.*
"the Eileen Trust"—*ibid.*
"the Fund"—*ibid.*
"the Independent Living Fund (2006)"—*ibid.*
"the Macfarlane (Special Payments) Trust"—*ibid.*
"the Macfarlane (Special Payments) (No.2) Trust"—*ibid.*
"the Macfarlane Trust"—*ibid.*
"the Skipton Fund"—*ibid.*
"training allowance"—*ibid.*
"voluntary organisation"—*ibid.*
"war widow's pension"—*ibid.*
"war widower's pension"—*ibid.*
"water charges"—*ibid.*
"working tax credit"—*ibid.*
"year of assessment"—*ibid.*

General Note

The structure is as follows: **2.441**

(1) Deprivation of income.

(2)–(2CA) Income available on application.

(3) Income due.

(3A) and (3B) Income from occupational pension schemes not paid.

(3C) Unpaid earnings due on termination of employment by reason of redundancy.

(4)–(4A) Third parties.

(5) Earnings not ascertainable.

(5A) Subsistence allowances paid to people participating in employment zone programmes.

(6)–(6A) Underpaid services.

(7) Calculation.

(8) Deductions.

(8A) and (9) Definitions.

Paragraph (1)

2.442 See notes to reg.51(1). A social security benefit is "income" which a claimant may be treated as still possessing under para.(1) (*CSIS 57/1992*). But a refusal to take up an offer of employment would not be a deprivation of income (*CCS 7967/1995*), although leaving a job may be depending on the circumstances (*CCS/4056/2004*) (both cases decided under the child support legislation).

Note that until October 31, 2011, para.(1) only applied if the deprivation had been for the purpose of securing entitlement to, or increasing the amount of, income support. The question could therefore have arisen on a claimant transferring from income support to JSA, or ESA, as to whether a deprivation which had only been for the purposes of income support could be caught by the corresponding rule under JSA (reg.105(1) of the JSA Regulations 1996) or the equivalent ESA regulation (reg.106(1) of the ESA Regulations 2008—see Vol.1 in this series). Before October 31, 2011 reg.105(1) of the JSA Regulations applied if a person had deprived himself of income in order to secure entitlement to, or increase the amount of, JSA *or income support*. Regulation 106(1) of the ESA Regulations, however, applied if the deprivation had been for the purpose of securing entitlement to, or increasing the amount of, ESA, *income support or JSA*. Neither para.(1) nor reg.105(1) of the JSA Regulations were amended when ESA was introduced (similarly para.(1) had not been amended when JSA was introduced).

Paragraph (1) has, however, been amended with effect from October 31, 2011 so that it now applies if the person has deprived himself of income in order to secure entitlement to, or increase the amount of, income support, JSA or ESA. A similar amendment has been made to reg.105(1) of the JSA Regulations, so that it now also applies if the deprivation was for the purpose of securing entitlement to, or increasing the amount of, ESA.

2.443 According to the Explanatory Memorandum which accompanied the SI that made these amendments, the purpose of this "minor" change is so that it covers people who deprive themselves of income whilst claiming ESA and then move across to income support or JSA. The need for these amendments was apparently overlooked when ESA was introduced. However, the need for an amendment to para.(1) had also been overlooked when JSA was introduced in 1995. Furthermore, the change to para.(1) could have a significant effect in certain cases because a deprivation of income now counts for the purposes of all three benefits. Paragraph (1) arguably would not previously have applied where a claimant had deprived himself of income for the purposes of securing or increasing entitlement to ESA or JSA and then claimed income support. Equally reg.105(1) of the JSA Regulations would not have bitten if the deprivation had been for the purpose of securing, or increasing, entitlement to ESA.

Note that the income support deprivation of capital rule (reg.51(1)) has not been amended; it continues to apply only where the deprivation was for the purposes of securing entitlement to, or increasing the amount of, income support. The JSA deprivation of capital rule (reg.113(1) of the JSA Regulations 1996) has also not been amended and only applies where the deprivation was for the purpose of securing, or increasing, entitlement to JSA or income support.

Paragraph (2)(a)–(f)

2.444 See notes to reg.51(2). There are some extra excluded categories here. The fact that a number of social security benefits are excluded suggests that social security benefits generally are caught by the rule. It is not at all clear that such benefits "would become available upon application being made" if an award has not already been made. Stages of the gathering of evidence and a decision by a decision-maker are necessary before a claimant becomes entitled to payment. The words "would become" may be broad enough to cover that process, but that could only be the case where entitlement is straightforward. See *CIS 16271/1996*. The income available to be acquired by the claimant must be for his own benefit (and not, for example, rent under a sub-lease that had to be paid straight over to the head landlord) (*CIS 15052/1996*).

Note the exclusion of working tax credit (para.(2)(e)). Its various predecessors, working families' tax credit, disabled person's tax credit, family credit and disability working allowance had similarly been exempted. Child tax credit is also excluded (para.(2)(f)). Paragraph (2)(d) and para.(2D) (which exempted the additional amount of child benefit for a lone parent (if any)) were revoked with effect from April 6, 2004 (except in "transitional cases"—see the note to reg.17) as part of the amendments consequential on the removal of amounts for children and young persons from income support.

Paragraph (2)(g) and paras (2ZA)–(2CA)

Under para.(2)(g) income available on request from an occupational or a personal pension scheme (see reg.2(1)), or from the Board of the Pension Protection Fund ("PPF") is exempt from the notional income rules until a person reaches the qualifying age for state pension credit (defined in s.137(1) of the Contributions and Benefits Act 1992—the effect of that definition is that the qualifying age was 60 but from April 2010 it will gradually rise in line with the staged increase in pensionable age for women until it reaches 65 in November 2018. This equalisation of the state pension age for men and women was previously to have been completed by April 5, 2020 but the timetable for this in the Pensions Act 1995 has been accelerated with effect from April 2016 so that women's state pension age will now be 65 by November 2018; in addition, the increase in state pension age to 66 for both men and women has been brought forward—it will start to rise from 65 in December 2018 to reach 66 by October 2020 (see s.1 of the Pensions Act 2011, and between 2026 and 2028 it will rise to 67 (see s.26 of the Pensions Act 2014)). Occupational pensions have been included in this exemption from April 6, 2006 because, as a result of changes to income tax legislation made by the Finance Act 2004, which take effect on April 6, 2006, there is more scope for taking occupational pensions early (and for deferring entitlement). Payments from the PPF, which has been set up under the Pensions Act 2004 to provide protection for members of an occupational pension scheme in the event of their employer's insolvency, have also been included from this date as the earliest date such payments could be made is April 6, 2006. **2.445**

If after reaching the qualifying age for state pension credit the "claimant" fails to claim income due from an occupational or personal pension scheme or the PPF, or elects to defer income from an occupational pension scheme, they will be treated as having that income (para.(2ZA)). Further, para.(2A) provides that if a person who has reached the qualifying age for state pension credit and who is entitled to "money purchase benefits" (defined in para.(2CA)) under an occupational or personal pension scheme, fails to purchase an annuity with the money available from, and (if this is an option) does not draw the income from, any such pension fund, he will be assumed to have an amount of income determined in accordance with para.(2B) or (2C). The meaning of "money purchase benefits" in the Pensions Schemes Act 1993 is "in relation to a member of a personal or occupational pension scheme or the widow or widower of a member of such a scheme, . . . benefits the rate or amount of which is calculated by reference to a payment or payments made by the member or by any other person in respect of the member and which are not average salary benefits" (see s.181 of the 1993 Act). At first sight these provisions would not seem of particular relevance to income support since a person who has reached the qualifying age for state pension credit is not entitled to income support (s.124(1)(aa) of the 1992 Act). However, a claimant who has not yet reached the qualifying age for state pension credit may have a partner who has done so and who is entitled to income from an occupational or personal pension scheme or the PPF and thus these provisions could apply. But note that para.(2ZA) refers to a "claimant who has attained the qualifying age for state pension credit". It is not entirely clear why the draftsman has chosen to use the word "claimant" in this paragraph (which may be contrasted with para.(2A) which refers to a "person has attained the qualifying age for state pension credit"). However, presumably the draftsman is relying on reg.23(1) which provides that a reference to the "claimant" in this Part of the regulations is to be treated as a reference to any partner.

BRG v SSWP (SPC) [2014] UKUT 246 (AAC), which concerned reg.18(2)–(5) of the State Pension Credit Regulations, the equivalent of paras (2A)–(2CA), holds that these provisions apply where a beneficiary has attained the age at which he could request that benefits under the scheme be made available to him, even though he has not yet reached the retirement age which he originally selected. This is the case even if the consequences of such a request are financially disadvantageous to the claimant.

2.446 No notional capital will be assumed (see reg.51(2)(d) and (da)), although in the case of an occupational pension or a PPF payment this only applies if the claimant has not reached the qualifying age for state pension credit (see reg.51(2)(da)). It is understood that the exemption under reg.51(2)(d) is not limited to claimants under the qualifying age for state pension credit because it would not be possible to predict in the case of a personal pension scheme how much capital a person might chose to take (and thus could be treated as having) from the scheme, whereas in relation to an occupational pension scheme there will be a default provision that can form the basis for the attribution of notional capital to the claimant under this rule.

In addition, the actual capital value of any funds held in a personal pension scheme is disregarded (para.23A of Sch.10); the value of the right to receive an occupational or personal pension is also ignored (para.23 of Sch.10). Note also the provisions in regs 7 and 32 of the Claims and Payments Regulations relating to the provision of information by pension fund holders (see Vol.III of this series).

For an illustration of the operation of the provisions in paras (2A)–(2C) in their then form, see *CIS 4080/2001*. In *CIS 4501/2002* para.(2A) applied even though the claimant was not drawing on her pension because it was a pension mortgage which she needed to retain in order to pay her mortgage. The argument that para.(2A) contravenes art.14, when read with art.1 of Protocol 1, ECHR because it interferes with a claimant's ability to leave funds in a pension scheme to accumulate was rejected in *R(IS) 12/04*. The Commissioner holds that even if art.1 of Protocol 1 (or art.8) was engaged for the purposes of art.14 (which had not been established), the claimant had not shown a sufficient basis of comparison of his position with that of a woman for art.14 to be invoked.

Paragraph (2)(i)–(j)

2.447 On para.(2)(i) and (ia), see the notes to paras 44 and 45 of Sch.10.

The purpose of para.(2)(j) was to enable a claimant who was on a full-time rehabilitation course and so eligible for rehabilitation allowance from the DfEE to choose whether to claim the allowance or remain on income support. Rehabilitation courses are designed to assist people who have been incapable of work for a prolonged period to return to the labour market. If a person claims the allowance he is treated as capable of work and so would cease to be entitled to income support on the ground of incapacity for work (although he could claim JSA). From October 27, 2008 new claims for income support on the grounds of incapacity for work are not generally possible.

Paragraph (3)

2.448 Sub-paragraph (b) excludes almost all social security benefits from the operation of this paragraph (although abandoning entitlement might be a deprivation of income under para.(1)). The other exclusions are of income due, but not paid, under discretionary trusts and trusts of personal injury compensation, entitlements under occupational pension schemes covered by paras (3A) and (3B) and earnings due but not paid where employment has ended due to redundancy (para.(3C)).

Outside these exclusions if income is due, i.e. legally due, it is to be treated as possessed by the claimant, and as income. The value of a debt would normally be a capital asset. Note that there is no discretion. An example would be of wages legally due but not paid but note the effect of para.(3C) where earnings are due but not paid on the termination of employment by reason of redundancy. However, the income that is due to be paid must be payable to the claimant for his own benefit (and not, for example, rent under a sub-lease that has to be paid straight over to the head landlord) (*CIS 15052/1996*).

Paragraphs (3A) and (3B)

Where a payment due from an occupational pension scheme is either not made or is not made in full because of a deficiency in the scheme's resources (defined in para.(8A)) the amount not paid does not fall within para.(3). The original form of the provisions applied only where the scheme stopped making payments to members of the scheme. The amendment puts beyond doubt that if payments to relatives or dependants of members are stopped, para.(3) does not apply. **2.449**

Paragraph (3C)

For the definition of earnings see reg.35. The intention is that when the earnings are paid any benefit that would not have been paid if the earnings had been paid at the right time will be recovered (see SSAA s.74 and Overpayments Regulations reg.7). **2.450**

Paragraphs (4) and (4ZA)

See the notes to reg.51(3) and (3A). **2.451**

In *R(FC) 4/98* (which concerned the similar provision in the Family Credit Regulations (reg.26(3)); see the 2002 edition of this volume for the Family Credit Regulations) the claimant's husband, from whom she was separated, was paying the mortgage payments on her home. They were joint owners of the property. The Commissioner held that only one half of the payments should be regarded as her notional income. Although the claimant and her husband were jointly and severally liable to the lender for the repayment of the mortgage, as between themselves they were each only responsible for repaying one half.

The words "to the third party" were added to the end of para.(4) on October 3, 2005 in order to close a potential loophole in the notional income rules revealed by the decision in *CJSA/3411/1998.*

In *CJSA 3411/1998* the claimant was on a one year residential training course. He was in receipt of an adult education bursary, part of which was paid directly to the college. The Commissioner decided that no notional income was to be attributed to the claimant under reg.105(10)(a)(ii) of the JSA Regulations 1996 (the equivalent of para.(4)(a)(ii)). Of the listed items only "food" was covered by the payment to the college (the power supplies used in the college did not constitute "household fuel"). But this was not caught by reg.105(10)(a)(ii) as the food provided by the college was a "payment in kind". These words referred to any payment to, or income of, the claimant in kind as well as any payment to the third party in kind. However, since many payments to third parties will result in the claimant receiving goods or services, it was felt that this could defeat the purpose of the "payments to third parties" rule because such payments would fall to be disregarded as payments in kind. Paragraph (4) (and reg.105(10) of the JSA Regulations) have therefore been amended to make it clear that the exemption for payments in kind only applies if the payment in kind is to the third party. See also the amendments to para.21 of Sch.9 and para.22 of Sch.7 to the JSA Regulations 1996 the effect of which is that income in kind disregarded under those provisions does not include a payment to a third party which is used by the third party to provide benefits in kind to the claimant. **2.452**

Note also *SA v SSWP (IS)* [2010] UKUT 345 (AAC); [2011] AACR 16 in the note to para.(4A) below.

R(IS) 4/01 considers the effect of head (ia) inserted into para.(4)(a) with effect from November 15, 1999 (note also para.(4ZA)(d) inserted at the same time). In that case virtually all of the claimant's occupational pension was paid over to his former wife under an attachment of earnings order. The Commissioner points out that before November 15, 1999 the effect of head (ii) was that payments of occupational pensions to third parties would be treated as the claimant's income only to the extent that the payments had been used for the support of the claimant. After that date head (ia) removed that limitation but it was still necessary to consider if the payments were made "in respect of" the claimant. In the Commissioner's view, the context of all three provisions in para.(4)(a) indicated that the payments caught by head (ia) were restricted to those payments which were made for the support of the claimant so as to reduce the need for him to be supported by income support. The payments in this case did nothing to support the claimant. The consequence was that the payments did not count as the claimant's income either before or after November 15, 1999. *R(IS) 2/03* agrees as to the effect of the phrase "in respect of" in the opening part of para.(4)(a). The result in that case was that payments under the claimant's self-employed pension annuity that were being applied entirely for the benefit of his creditors did not count as notional income (see further the note to reg.23 as to whether such payments count as actual income). *R(IS) 4/02* further refers to these somewhat problematic provisions, pointing out that even if heads (i) and (ii) of para.(4ZA)(d) are satisfied, head (iii) will not be if the claimant (or any member of his family, from April 6, 2004 (except in "transitional cases"—see the note to reg.17) only his partner) has, or is treated as having, any other income.

Paragraph (4A)

2.453 Where the claimant lives in a care home, an Abbeyfield Home or an independent hospital (for the definition of these terms see reg.2(1)), any payment made by a third party towards the cost of the claimant's or any partner's fees counts as the claimant's income (before April 6, 2004 the old form of this paragraph also applied to the cost of any other member of the claimant's family's fees—the old form remains in existence for "transitional cases"—see the note to reg.17). However, under paras 15, 30, 30A and 66 of Sch.9 certain payments to people in such accommodation are disregarded. "Person" in para.(4A) will include a local authority (Sch.1 to the Interpretation Act 1978).

In *SA v SSWP (IS)* [2010] UKUT 345 (AAC); [2011] AACR 16 the claimant, who had learning difficulties, attended a residential college, the cost of which was funded, inter alia, by his local authority. The issue was whether part of the local authority's payment towards his college fees counted as notional income in respect of meals under para.(4)(a)(ii) or whether it fell within para.(4A), in which case it would be disregarded under para.66 of Sch.9. This hinged on whether the residential college was a care home. Judge Wikeley confirms that if an establishment satisfies the conditions in the definition of "care home" (see reg.2(1)), it falls to be treated as a care home even if it was also an educational establishment. The terms are not mutually exclusive. The consequence was that the payment in respect of meals counted as the claimant's notional income under para.(4A) but was then disregarded under para.66.

Paragraph (5)

2.454 This is a very general discretion. The decision-maker (or tribunal) must have regard to the number of hours worked and the going rate locally for comparable employment in deciding what is reasonable, but is not prevented from considering all relevant circumstances (*R(SB) 25/83, R(SB) 15/86, R(SB) 6/88*).

Paragraph (5A)

2.455 This concerns claimants who are participating in an "employment zone" (defined in reg.2(1)) programme established under s.60 of the Welfare Reform and Pensions Act 1999 and being paid a "subsistence allowance" (reg.2(1)). The aim is that the subsistence allowance will be taken into account as income at the time it is due to be paid (see reg.105(11A) of the JSA Regulations 1996 for the income-based JSA provision). Note the corresponding disregard in para.71 of Sch.9 (para.68 of Sch.7 to the JSA Regulations 1996) where the amount of a subsistence allowance exceeds the amount of income-based JSA that the person would have received. Any arrears of a subsistence allowance paid as a lump sum are treated as capital (reg.48(12); JSA Regulations 1996 reg.110(11)) and ignored for 52 weeks from the date of receipt (para.59 of Sch.10; JSA Regulations 1996 para.54 of Sch.8). Any discretionary payment from an "employment zone contractor" (defined in reg.2(1)) is also disregarded, but if the payment counts as capital only for 52 weeks from the date of receipt (see para.72 of Sch.9 and para.58 of Sch.10; JSA Regulations 1996, para.69 of Sch.7 and para.53 of Sch.8).

From September 1, 2011 employment zone programmes are no longer in operation.

Paragraphs (6)–(6A)

These paragraphs are concerned with what is commonly referred to as the "notional earnings" rule. Paragraph (6) was restructured in October 1999 so that it only contains the basic rule while the specific exceptions are now in para.(6A). Paragraph (6A)(a) and (b)(i) are simply a reordering of the exceptions that were previously set out in para.(6) itself but paras (6A)(c) and (b)(ii) (the latter was added on April 3, 2000) are new. In addition a further exception was introduced on October 1, 2007 (see para.(6A)(d)). **2.456**

Paragraph (6)

If the two conditions in sub-paras (a) and (b) are met there is no discretion whether or not to apply the rule, unless the claimant comes within the proviso in para.(6) itself or one of the exceptions in para.(6A). However, the application of both the rule and the exception in para.(6A)(a) involve a number of value judgments (e.g. in relation to "comparable employment", what earnings (if any) are "reasonable" to treat the claimant as possessing and whether it is "reasonable" for the claimant to provide the service free of charge if he is a volunteer or working for a charitable or voluntary body). See *CIS 2916/1997* in which the claimant was spending time in her mother's shop to keep her mother company following recent bereavements. The Commissioner says that whether this amounted to a "service" was a question of fact and degree, having regard, inter alia, to the effort and time put in (see *Clear v Smith* [1981] 1 W.L.R. 399) but in particular to the advantage derived by the mother. If the help given was substantial, the claimant was providing a service. However, when deciding whether it was reasonable for her to provide this service free of charge, it was necessary to consider whether what the claimant was doing amounted to "work". **2.457**

In *R(SB) 3/92* (on the supplementary benefit predecessor of this provision) the Commissioner held that the rule applied where a mother provided services to her disabled adult son out of love and affection. On appeal in *Sharrock v Chief Adjudication Officer* (March 26, 1991; appendix to *R(SB) 3/92*) the Court of Appeal agreed that such relationships came within the old provision, providing that the service provided was of a character for which an employer would be prepared to pay. In *CIS 93/1991* the Commissioner holds that the principle of *Sharrock* applies to reg.42(6), which thus covers services provided within informal family relationships without any contract. Under supplementary benefit there was no proviso exempting volunteers, etc. at the time. Now unpaid carers can be defined as volunteers (*CIS 93/1991*), so that there is a discretion not to apply the rule (see below). In *CIS 422/1992* (which again concerned Mrs Sharrock), the Commissioner held that she was a volunteer and that it was reasonable for her to provide her services free. The evidence was that her son made a substantial contribution to the household expenses. If she were to charge for her services the whole basis of the arrangement between them would have to change, which could have a deleterious effect on their relationship. (However, the part of the son's contribution that was not in respect of *his* living and accommodation costs could not be disregarded under para.18 of Sch.9.) It is difficult to see how in most cases it can be unreasonable for carers to look after a relative without payment. This is acknowledged by paras 26200–1 of the *Decision Makers Guide* which also lists factors to be considered in cases of doubt which are broadly in line with those suggested in *CIS 93/1991* (see below).

Under sub-para.(b) the "employer" must either make no payment or pay less than is paid for comparable employment in the area. Since the amount of notional earnings is set according to what is reasonable for that comparable employment, it seems that some comparable employment must exist in all cases.

2.458 Some of the points made in *R(SB) 13/86* on the previous supplementary benefit provision also apply to para.(6). It is necessary to identify the employer for whom the services were provided. "Person" includes a company or other corporate employer (Interpretation Act 1978). Thus in *R(IS) 5/95* where the claimant, who was an employee and director of a small company, was working unpaid because of the company's financial difficulties, and *CSJSA/23/2006* which concerned the sole director and majority shareholder of an unlimited company who was not paid for his part-time work for the company, it was necessary to consider whether para.(6) applied. See also *CCS 4912/1998* which holds that a similar child support rule applied where a person provided his services through a personal service company that he had set up himself and which was paying him a very low hourly rate.

Particulars of the services provided and any payments made must be ascertained. See *CIS 701/1994* on the factors to consider when assessing comparable employment (the claimant in that case was again a carer) and the amount of notional earnings. In *CSJSA/23/2006* the tribunal had erred in simply adopting the decision-maker's use of the national minimum wage as the appropriate comparator for deciding the amount of the claimant's notional earnings. The test was what was paid for a comparable employment in the area and so relevant findings of fact needed to be made to establish local comparable earnings. In addition, in a case such as this where there was no actual or implied contract, the period over which the earnings were payable and when they were due to be paid also had to be established in accordance with what were the likely terms of employment in a similar job in the area.

It was suggested in earlier editions of the predecessor of this book that although payments of earnings in kind are disregarded in the calculation of income (reg.35(2)(a) and Sch.9 para.21), payments in kind should be considered in testing whether a claimant is paid at all or is paid less than the rate for comparable employment. However, *CIS 11482/1995* decides that this is not correct. The claimant's wife worked as a shop assistant for 12 hours a week for which she was paid £5 in cash and took goods to the value of £36 from the shelves. The Commissioner, after deciding that earnings in para.(6) meant earnings as defined in regs 35 or 37 (see reg.2(1)), holds that since earnings in kind were ignored when considering whether any payment at all of earnings had been made, this must also be the case when deciding whether a person was paid less than the rate for comparable employment. Thus in considering whether the claimant's wife was paid less than the rate for comparable employment, the £36 that she received in goods was to be left out of account. But to avoid unfair double counting it was necessary to deduct any cash payments in the calculation of her notional earnings under para.(6). This was permissible because para.(6) allowed the amount of earnings which would be paid for comparable employment to be adjusted where circumstances made it reasonable. However, it would not be "reasonable" to deduct the earnings in kind because that did not involve a double counting as the actual value of the earnings in kind was disregarded.

The claimant can then escape if he proves (on the balance of probabilities) that the person to whom he has provided the services has insufficient means to pay more. This could well cause difficulties for claimants reluctant to make embarrassing enquiries. But there is an interest in preventing employers from economising at the expense of the income support budget. The Court of Appeal in *Sharrock v Chief Adjudication Officer* suggests that "means" refers simply to monetary resources and is a matter of broad judgment. No automatic test of ignoring certain benefits or regarding an income above income support level as available should be adopted. In *CIS 93/1991*, the claimant looked after his elderly and severely disabled father, but declined to give any information about the father's means. The Commissioner confirms that in such circumstances the basic rule of para.(6) must be applied, but subject to the exception for volunteers.

Paragraph (6A)

Paragraph (6A) specifies five situations in which the rule in para.(6) will not apply. First, sub-para.(a) allows volunteers or those engaged by charities or voluntary organisations not to have any notional earnings if it is reasonable for them to provide their services free of charge. Volunteer in this context means someone who without any legal obligation performs a service for another person without expectation of payment (*R(IS) 12/92*). Thus, it would seem that if any payment is made to the claimant, the proviso cannot apply. The Commissioner in *CIS 93/1991* holds that the means of the "employer" is a factor here, but other factors are relevant too. *CSJSA/23/2006* emphasises that all the circumstances, not just the means of the employer, must be considered. There could be other factors making it reasonable for the claimant, who was the sole director and majority shareholder of an unlimited company who was not paid for his part-time work for the company, to undertake such gratuitous work, quite separate from the finances of the business. **2.459**

It may be more reasonable for close relatives to provide services free of charge than for others to do so. The basis on which the arrangement was made, the expectations of the family members concerned, the housing arrangements and the reason why the carer gave up any paid work might need to be considered. Anomalies like the loss of invalid care allowance (now carer's allowance) if the carer accepted payment should be considered. So should the question of what alternatives would be available if the relative ceased to provide the care. If there was no realistic alternative to the relative continuing to provide the care and the person would not agree to make any payment, that would point to it being reasonable for the claimant to provide the services free of charge (*CIS 701/1994*). In *CIS 93/1991* the tribunal went wrong in not properly considering their discretion under the exception and concentrating on the legitimate inference that the "employer" could afford to pay the going rate. In *CIS 701/1994* the Commissioner expresses the view that if a person had substantial resources that were genuinely surplus to requirements, that would be different from the situation, for example, of a person saving towards the costs of future residential care. It should be noted that the test is whether it is reasonable for the person to provide his services free of charge, rather than whether it is reasonable for payment not to be made for the service, although this is a factor (*CIS 147/1993*). If the claimant was receiving training while, or by doing, the work, this may be relevant (*R(IS) 12/92*).

In *CIS 93/1991* the Commissioner points out that the aim of the rule is clearly to prevent an employer who has the means to pay the going rate profiting at the expense of the public purse. If, therefore, a claimant volunteers to undertake painting work (as in *CIS 147/1993*), which otherwise would have remained undone, there is no element of financial profit to the employer in the claimant doing the work. If, however, the employer would have paid the claimant if he had not said he did not wish to be paid, it may be concluded that it was not reasonable for the claimant to offer his services free of charge.

Secondly, para.(6A)(b)(i) covers the situation where a person is on an employment programme or training scheme for three or more days in any benefit week and is not paid a training allowance. Sub-paragraph (b)(i) ensures that a person who is on such a programme or scheme will not be treated as possessing notional earnings by virtue of providing a service for which he is not being paid. (For income support purposes this provision will usually only be relevant to the claimant's partner rather than the claimant himself.) The third exception in para.(6A)(b)(ii) prevents the attribution of notional earnings where the claimant, or his partner, is taking part in an employment or training programme of any length, for which no training allowance, or one that only reimburses travelling or meal expenses, is payable. **2.460**

The fourth exclusion from the notional earnings rule applies to lone parents who are on work experience while participating in the New Deal for Lone Parents (no longer in operation) or a similar scheme (para.(6A)(c)). The exemption originally only lasted for up to 150 hours, or six months, work with the same employer, but the October 2004 amendments meant that this exemption applied without limit.

The fifth (and new from October 1, 2007) exception provides that a claimant is not to be treated as having notional earnings if he is undertaking an unpaid work placement (defined in para.(6AA)); the work placement must have been approved by the Secretary of State before it started.

Paragraphs (7)–(8)

2.461 If notional income counts it is to be calculated as though it was actual income. Notional deductions are to be made from earnings to get a net figure.

Paragraph (8ZA)

2.462 The effect of this paragraph is that the notional income rules do not apply to either payments of expenses or earnings as a result of a "claimant participating as a service user" (see reg.2(1B) for those to whom this refers). Note that actual payments of such expenses are not earnings (see reg.35(2)(f)) and are disregarded as income (Sch.9 para.2A). However, earnings that result from a claimant participating as a service user other than expenses (e.g. for attending a meeting) will be taken into account in the normal way, subject to the appropriate disregard.

Paragraph (9)

2.463 The examples given in paras 28671–2 of the *Decision Makers Guide* suggest that football boots are not for "normal daily use", and that when applying the test of "for normal daily use" the wide needs of all claimants should be considered.

Notional earnings of seasonal workers

2.464 **43.**—[1. . .].

AMENDMENT

1. Income Support (General) Amendment No.2 Regulations 1989 (SI 1989/1323) reg.14 (October 9, 1989).

GENERAL NOTE

2.465 When the special rules for seasonal workers were removed from the unemployment benefit scheme this was consequently also done for income support.

Modifications in respect of children and young persons

2.466 **44.**—[1. . .]

AMENDMENT

1. Social Security (Working Tax Credit and Child Tax Credit) (Consequential Amendments) Regulations 2003 (SI 2003/455) reg.2 and Sch.1 para.11 (April 6, 2004, except in "transitional cases" and see further the note to reg.17 of the Income Support Regulations).

GENERAL NOTE

2.467 This regulation contained the special rules for treatment of the income of a child or young person who was a member of the claimant's family (see the 2003 edition of this volume for this regulation and the notes to it). However, with effect from April 6, 2004 (except in "transitional cases"—see the note to reg.17) amounts for children and young persons have been removed from the income support scheme; financial assistance to help with the cost of bringing up a child or young person is now to be provided through the child tax credit system, see Vol.IV of this series. As a consequence, the income of a child or young person is no longer aggregated with the claimant's (see the new form of reg.23 and the notes to that regulation) and therefore most of the modifications made by reg.44 are no longer needed (but see below). Regulation 44 does however remain in force for "transitional cases"—see the note to reg.17.

For income support claimants who had an award of child tax credit before April 6, 2004 see reg.7 of the Social Security (Working Tax Credit and Child Tax Credit) (Consequential Amendments) Regulations 2003 (SI 2003/455) (as amended) on p.812 and the notes to that regulation.

Paragraph (2) of reg.44 was concerned with payments to residential schools for a child's or young person's maintenance. Since there is a continuing need to make provision for such payments, a new disregard (see para.25A of Sch.9) has been introduced with effect from April 6, 2004 (except in "transitional cases"—see the note to reg.17). This provides that payments to a boarding school for the maintenance of a child or young person who is a member of the claimant's family made by a third party or out of funds provided by a third party are ignored in full.

Chapter VI

Capital

[1 Capital limit

45.—For the purposes of section 134(1) of the Contributions and Benefits Act as it applies to income support (no entitlement to benefit if capital exceeds prescribed amount), the prescribed amount is £16,000.] **2.468**

AMENDMENT

1. Social Security (Miscellaneous Amendments) (No.2) Regulations 2005 (SI 2005/2465) reg.2(4) (April 10, 2006).

GENERAL NOTE

Under s.134(1) of the Contributions and Benefits Act there is no entitlement to income support if the claimant's capital exceeds the prescribed amount. From April 10, 2006 this is £16,000 for all claimants, thus bringing the limit into line with that which applies for housing benefit and until the abolition of council tax benefit on April 1, 2013 applied for that benefit. In addition, the amount above which the tariff income rule applies has been increased to £6,000, except in the case of residents in a care home, Abbeyfield Home or independent hospital, for whom the tariff income rule will continue to apply only to capital above £10,000 (see reg.53). **2.469**

The capital of a claimant's partner is aggregated with the claimant's (reg.23(1)), but not that of children or young persons (reg.23(2), replacing the rule formerly in reg.47 with effect from April 6, 2004, except for "transitional cases"—see the note to reg.17).

In *CIS 127/1993* the Commissioner raises the question of where the burden of proof lies when considering whether the capital rule is satisfied. The Tribunal of Commissioners in *CIS 417/1992* (reported as part of *R(IS) 26/95*) treat this as part of what the claimant has to prove in showing entitlement to income support. However, the argument that the capital rule operates as an exception to the conditions of basic entitlement does not appear to have been put. See sidenote to s.134 which is entitled

"Exclusions from benefit". But once it has been shown that the claimant possesses an item of capital, it is for him to prove that one of the disregards in Sch.10 applies (*CIS 240/1992*). Similarly, once it has been established that the claimant is the legal owner of a property, the burden is on her to show that she does not have any or all of the beneficial interest (*CIS 30/1993*). These decisions, however, need to be read in the light of the House of Lords' judgment in *Kerr v Department of Social Development for Northern Ireland* [2004] UKHL 23; [2004] 4 All E.R. 385, also reported as an appendix to *RI/04(SF)*, in which Baroness Hale emphasised that the process of adjudication for social security benefits is a co-operative one in which both the Department and the claimant should play their part and that normally it ought not to be necessary to resort to more formal concepts such as the burden of proof. In *MB v Royal Borough of Kensington & Chelsea (HB)* [2011] UKUT 321 (AAC) the claimant relied on *Chichester DC v B and SSWP* [2009] UKUT 34 (AAC) in which it was stated that it was for the Council to show that the claimant had a beneficial interest in the capital at issue (see para.28). Judge Wikeley, however, considered that the answer to this lay in the point made by Baroness Hale in *Kerr* that it was for each party (claimant or department) to provide such information as they reasonably can. The claimant in *MB v RB Kensington & Chelsea* was the one who had exclusive knowledge about the purchase of the property in issue and the mortgage payments and thus it was her responsibility to marshal what evidence she could to show that, although she was the legal owner, she was not the sole beneficial owner of the property.

Calculation of capital

2.470 **46.**—(1) For the purposes of Part II of the Act [SSCBA, Part VII] as it applies to income support, the capital of a claimant to be taken into account shall, subject to paragraph (2), be the whole of his capital calculated in accordance with this Part and any income treated as capital under [1regulation 48 (income treated as capital)].

(2) There shall be disregarded from the calculation of a claimant's capital under paragraph (1) any capital, where applicable, specified in Schedule 10.

AMENDMENT

1. Income Support (General) Amendment No.5 Regulations 1988 (SI 1988/2022) reg.10 (December 12, 1988).

DEFINITIONS

"the Act"—see reg.2(1).
"claimant"—*ibid.*, and reg.23(1).

GENERAL NOTE

2.471 All the claimant's (and partner's) capital, both actual and notional, counts towards the £16,000 limit, subject to the disregards in Sch.10. The disregards are to be applied before the value or the amount of the capital is calculated (*Guildford BC v MW (HB)* [2014] UKUT 49 (AAC), a case on the equivalent housing benefit provision). In *R(IS) 15/96* the Commissioner considers that claimants should be advised by the Benefits Agency of the existence of the disregards so that they can take advantage of them (the claimant had received a criminal injuries compensation award so that the trust disregard in para.12 of Sch.10 could have been relevant).

Distinguishing between actual and notional capital

2.472 *AB v SSWP and Canterbury CC (IS and HB)* [2014] UKUT 212 (AAC) emphasises the importance of decision-makers and tribunals making a clear distinction in their findings of fact as to whether the claimant has *actual* or *notional* capital. If it is found that the claimant has *actual* capital over £16,000, there will usually be no entitlement to income support. If the claimant shows that he possesses capital of less than £16,000, because some of it has been spent or otherwise disposed of, it is usually necessary to consider whether he should be treated as possessing *notional* capital (see reg.51(1) and the notes to that regulation). In this case the claimant's wife had received an inheritance. The burden therefore shifted to the claimant to show that his wife no longer possessed that capital. See *R(SB) 38/85* where Commissioner Hallett held at para.18:

> "The claimant says that he expended this sum of £18,700 in repaying loans. It is for him to prove that this is so. Failing a satisfactory account of the way in which the money has been disposed of, it will be open to the tribunal, and a natural conclusion, to find that the claimant still has, in some form or other, that resource and consequently to conclude that his actual resources are above the prescribed limit."

The tribunal's statement of reasons in *AB* concluded that the claimant "should be deemed to still have, through his partner, capital in excess of £16,000". Judge Wikeley held that the ambiguity inherent in the use of the word "deemed" (or "treated") meant that it was not sufficiently clear whether the tribunal had found that the claimant, through his wife, still had the capital from the inheritance in some form or whether he had deprived himself of it for the purpose of obtaining benefit such as to be fixed with notional capital. In addition, the tribunal had failed to adequately explain why it did not accept the claimant's wife's explanation. In relation to this issue Judge Wikeley emphasises the importance of having a sound evidential basis for an adverse credibility finding against a claimant.

Actual capital

There is a good deal of law on actual capital. 2.473

The first condition is of course that the capital resource is the claimant's or his partner's. This is not as simple as it sounds.

In *CIS 634/1992* the claimant was made bankrupt on November 29, 1990. However, his trustee in bankruptcy was not appointed until April 1991. Between November 29 and December 28, 1990, when he claimed income support the claimant divested himself of most of his capital. Under the Insolvency Act 1986 (subject to certain exceptions) a bankrupt's property does not vest in his trustee in bankruptcy on the making of a bankruptcy order, but only when the trustee is appointed. The appointment does not have retrospective effect. It is held that since he had failed to give a satisfactory account of how he had disposed of his capital he was to be treated as still possessing it (*R(SB) 38/85* referred to in the notes to reg.51(1)). Thus the claimant was not entitled to income support prior to the appointment of the trustee in bankruptcy because until then he possessed actual capital over the income support limit.

KS v SSWP (JSA) [2009] UKUT 122 (AAC); [2010] AACR 3, however, disagrees with *CIS/634/1992*. Judge Mark points out that a person cannot realise or use any part of his capital after a bankruptcy order has been made and that, subject to any order of the court, it will vest in his trustee in due course. Whether the capital remained the claimant's with a nil value or whether it ceased to be his capital at all (on which Judge Mark did not reach any firm conclusion), the result was that the claimant had no capital, or no capital of any value, after the bankruptcy order had been made. 2.474

In *SH v SSWP* [2008] UKUT 21 (AAC) Judge Turnbull also does not reach a final conclusion as to whether money in a bank account or other property that is subject to a restraint order under s.77 of the Criminal Justice Act 1988 (now the Proceeds of Crime Act 2002) or a freezing order ceases to be the claimant's capital. He was inclined to think that such assets remained the claimant's capital. However, their market value would be nil since the claimant was prohibited by court order from disposing of them. *CS v Chelmsford BC* [2014] UKUT 518 (AAC) takes the same view as *SH* but again without reaching a final conclusion on the point. In *CS*, which concerned assets subject to a restraint order under the Proceeds of Crime Act

2002, Judge Markus points out that not only is a restraint order under the Proceeds of Crime Act 2002 not expressed to deprive a person of his interest in the property but also the terminology of the Act consistently presupposes that the person retains his interest in property that is subject to a restraint order. Its market value, however, would be nil.

See also *CIS 1189/2003* which concerned a claimant who was the sole residuary beneficiary under her mother's will. The estate had remained unadministered for several years so that her mother's property had not actually vested in the claimant. However, the property counted as the claimant's actual capital for the purposes of income support since, subject only to the formalities needed to perfect her title, she had for all practical purposes an entitlement in respect of the property that was equivalent to full beneficial ownership.

2.475 *R(IS) 9/04* confirms that assets being administered on a patient's behalf either at the Court of Protection or by his or her receiver remain the patient's assets which have to be valued at their current market value (see reg.49) (following *CIS 7127/1995*). Such assets are held under a "bare trust" with the entire beneficial ownership remaining with the patient. The fact that the Court had discretionary powers of *control* over the management of the patient's property for his or her benefit did not mean that the patient's beneficial *ownership* had ceased.

However, capital that a claimant is under a "certain and immediate liability" to repay at the moment of its receipt by, or attribution to, the claimant, will not count as his capital (*CIS/2287/2008*). In *CIS/2287/2008* the Commissioner decides that the principle in *Chief Adjudication Officer v Leeves*, reported as *R(IS) 5/99* (see the note to reg.29(2B)) does apply to capital as well as income. However, it only applies at the moment of receipt or attribution and is relevant only to the issue of whether money or an asset should be classified as the claimant's capital. *Leeves* does not apply if the liability to repay arises after something has become capital in the claimant's hands. That issue continues to be governed by the principle in *R(SB) 2/83* that in calculating capital liabilities are not to be deducted, except those expressly provided for in the legislation. See also *JH v SSWP* [2009] UKUT 1 (AAC) which explains that *Leeves* only operates where, outside trust relationships, there is a certain obligation of immediate repayment or return of the asset to the transferor. It does not bite where the claimant is under some liability to a third party.

Beneficial ownership

2.476 The mere fact that an asset or a bank or building society account is in the claimant's name alone does not mean that it belongs to the claimant. It is the "beneficial ownership" which matters. The claimant may hold the asset under a trust which means that he cannot simply treat the asset as his, but must treat it as if it belonged to the beneficiary or beneficiaries under the trust. It is they who are "beneficially entitled." A trustee may also be a beneficiary, in which case the rule in reg.52 may come into play, or may have no beneficial interest at all (see further below under "*Claimant holding as trustee*").

These issues often arise in the context of attributing the beneficial ownership of former matrimonial assets. One example where the first situation applied is *R(IS) 2/93*. The claimant had a building society account in her sole name, which she had had since before her marriage. Her husband deposited the bulk of the money in it, including his salary. On their separation, the AO and the SSAT treated the entire amount in the account as part of the claimant's capital. The Commissioner holds that she was not solely beneficially entitled to the money so that reg.52 had to operate. There is helpful guidance on the limited circumstances in which the "presumption of advancement" (i.e. that when a husband puts an asset into his wife's name he intends to make an outright gift of it) will operate in modern circumstances. (Note that the presumption of advancement is due to be abolished by s.199 of the Equality Act 2010 but this section has not yet come into force.) And see *CIS 982/2002* (which concerns the valuation of a share in a frozen joint bank account) in the notes to reg.52. Note also *R(IS) 10/99* below. In *CIS 553/1991* where a house was in the husband's sole name it is held that its valuation should take into account the wife's statutory right of occupation under the Matrimonial Homes Act 1967. See also *R(IS) 1/97*, in the note to para.5 of Sch.10.

In most cases of spouses, in whoever's name the asset is, there will be some degree of joint ownership. But if an asset is in the sole name of one, arguably the other should not be treated as having a half share under reg.52 until it has been established that s/he does own at least part of it. On this see *R(IS) 1/03* which holds that a person's right to seek a lump sum payment or property transfer order under the Matrimonial Causes Act 1973 is not a capital asset. Moreover, *CIS 984/2002* should also be noted in this context. This holds that money held by the claimant's solicitor pending quantification of the statutory charge to the Legal Services Commission under s.10(7) of the Access to Justice Act 1999 was not part of the claimant's capital. Until that quantification had been carried out, it was not possible to identify any particular amount as the claimant's capital. Another way of looking at it was to treat the statutory charge as an incumbrance for the purpose of reg.49(a)(ii) (see *CIS 368/1993*). Nor was any part of the money available to the claimant on application for the purposes of reg.51(2).

In *LC v Bournemouth Borough Council (HB)* [2016] UKUT 175 (AAC), discussed in the note to reg.51(2), Judge White applies reg.49(2) of the Housing Benefit Regulations 2006 (the equivalent of reg.51(2)) in a case where the proceeds of sale of a former matrimonial home were being held in a solicitors' client account until the claimant's partner and his ex-wife agreed how the sum was to be split or the issue was resolved by a court order. In his view the value of the capital prior to agreement or an order of the court would be minimal.

Claimant holding as trustee

In relation to trusts of land, *SB v SSWP (IS)* [2012] UKUT 252 (AAC) is a useful reminder that s.53(1)(b) of the Law of Property Act 1925 only requires a trust relating to land to be *evidenced* in writing. Absence of writing makes the trust unenforceable but not void (*Gardner v Rowe* [1828] 5 Russ. 258). The tribunal had found that there was no trust of the property in question because there was no trust deed. This error of law had led the tribunal to fail to investigate and make findings on whether there had been a declaration of trust, whether the scope of the trust was certain, the subject matter of the trust, the objects/persons intended to benefit from any such trust and (in the absence of any documentation) whether the surrounding circumstances were consistent with the existence of a trust in order to decide whether there was an implied, resulting or constructive trust. 2.477

There have been many cases in which the issue was whether the claimant was holding as trustee and therefore had no beneficial interest.

In *R(SB) 49/83* the claimant had bought a house, but said that this was on behalf of his son, who was paying off the loan. The Commissioner held that if this could be established, the claimant would hold the house on a resulting trust for his son. It would not then be part of his capital resources. See *CSB 200/1985* (applying *Cowcher v Cowcher* [1972] 1 W.L.R. 425) for the position where another person provides part of the money. In *R(SB) 53/83* the claimant's son had paid him £2,850 to be used for a holiday in India. The claimant died without taking the holiday or declaring the existence of the money to the DHSS. The Commissioner, applying the principle of *Barclays Bank Ltd v Quistclose Investments Ltd* [1970] A.C. 567, held that there was a trust to return the money to the son if the primary purpose of the loan was not carried out. Since the Commissioner held that there had been no overpayment while the claimant was alive, this must mean that the claimant held the money on trust to use it for the specified purpose or to return it. It was not part of the claimant's resources. This is an important decision, which overtakes some of the reasoning of *R(SB) 14/81* (see below). The actual decision in *R(SB) 53/83* was reversed (by consent) by the Court of Appeal, because the Commissioner had differed from the appeal tribunal on a point of pure fact. *R(SB) 1/85* holds that this does not affect its authority on the issue of principle. In *R(SB) 1/85*, the claimant's mother-in-law had some years previously provided the money for the purchase of the lease of a holiday chalet for the use of the claimant's mentally handicapped son, Keith. The lease was in the claimant's name and its current value was probably about £5,000. The AO's initial statement of the facts was that the mother-in-law had bought the chalet in the claimant's name. The Commissioner holds that this would give rise to a presumption of a resulting trust in her favour, so that the claimant would have no beneficial interest in the chalet—nothing he could sell. The presumption could be rebutted if in fact the mother-in-law had made an outright gift to the claimant, or to Keith. In the second case the claimant again would have no beneficial interest. In the first, he would be caught, for even if he had said that he intended to use the chalet purely for Keith, he had not made the necessary written declaration of trust (Law of Property Act 1925 s.53). Another possibility was that the mother-in-law had made a gift to the claimant subject to an express (but unwritten) trust in favour of Keith, when again the claimant clearly would not be the beneficial owner. This is a very instructive decision, which will give valuable guidance in sorting out many family-type arrangements. *CIS 30/1993* also sets out helpful guidance on the points to consider when deciding whether a resulting trust has been created. The claimant had purchased her flat with the proceeds of sale of her previous home. She had bought that home as a sitting tenant with the aid of a loan, the repayments on which had been made by her children. The Commissioner states that the children's contributions indicated a resulting trust in their favour in the beneficial interest in the house in proportion to their and the claimant's contributions to the purchase price. If the claimant had, as a sitting tenant, received a discount on the price, that would be treated as a contribution. The resulting trust would transfer to the flat on the sale of the house. However, the presumption of a resulting trust created by the children's contributions could be rebutted by proof of the purchasers' true intentions, e.g. that an outright gift was, or different beneficial interests under the trust than those created by the presumption were, intended.

2.478 The *Quistclose* principle was re-affirmed in *R(SB) 12/86*, where £2,000 was lent to the claimant on condition that she did not touch the capital amount, but only took the interest, and repaid the £2,000 on demand. The £2,000 was not part of her capital, never having been at her disposal. The Commissioner in *CSB 975/1985* was prepared to apply the principle to a loan on mortgage from a Building Society for property renovation. But it would have to be found that the loan was made for no other purpose and was to be recoverable by the Building Society if for any reason the renovations could not be carried out. See also *YH v SSWP (IS)* [2015] UKUT 85 (AAC) in which the claimant raised a loan on his property and gave the money to his sons to establish a business. The sons used the money to set up the business and made the repayments on the loan. The *Quistclose* principle did not apply because there was no evidence to suggest that the lender had advanced the money on the condition that it was only to be used to establish the business. A borrower does not create a trust in favour of the lender simply by having his own clear intention as to the application of the money. The Secretary of State had decided that the claimant, by giving the money to his sons, had deprived himself of the capital and so was to be treated as still possessing it under reg.51. However, what needed to be considered (and which had not been) was the claimant's purpose in giving the money to his sons. See the discussion under the heading "*(ii) The test for purpose*" in the notes to reg.51.

CIS/5185/1995 decides that the decision in *Quistclose* did not apply to a student grant which the claimant became liable to repay to the education authority when he left his course early (for the treatment of student grants in these circumstances now see reg.29(2B) but note the argument discussed in the notes to reg.29(2B) as to when that provision applies). The Commissioner holds that the grant was income that remained available to him until it was repaid to the authority (see *R. v Bolton SBAT Ex p. Fordham* [1981] 1 All E.R. 50 and *CSB 1408/1988*). It could not be disregarded under the *Quistclose* principle because the education authority retained no beneficial interest in the grant. The authority merely reserved the right to demand repayment of a sum calculated according to the unexpired balance of the relevant term when the person ceased to be a student. But in *CIS 12263/1996* the Commissioner took the view that as soon as a student had abandoned his course and an obligation to repay the balance of his grant to the education authority arose, he held the money on constructive trust for the authority. The Commissioner in *CIS 12263/1996* considered that the *Quistclose* case was concerned with a "purpose trust" (i.e. where a grant or loan was impressed with a particular purpose from the beginning), whereas in this situation a constructive trust had arisen because the grant had been paid on the condition that the claimant continued to be a student. An appeal was brought against this decision by the Department (*Chief Adjudication Officer v Leeves*, reported as *R(IS) 5/99*). It was conceded on behalf of the claimant that there was no constructive trust in these circumstances, since no proprietary right had been retained by the education authority, nor had any fiduciary obligation been created. However, the Court of Appeal held that money that the claimant was under a "certain and immediate liability" to repay did not amount to income. Thus once the claimant had received a request for immediate repayment of a specified sum from the local education authority the grant ceased to count as his income (although it fell to be treated as such until that time, even though he had abandoned his course). The Court distinguished its decision in *Fordham* as the liability to repay in that case had been uncertain. In *CIS/2287/2008* the Commissioner decides that the same principle does apply to capital but it only applies at the moment of receipt by, or attribution to, the claimant and is relevant only to the issue of whether money or an asset should be classified as the claimant's capital. For further discussion of *CIS/2287/2008* see above under the heading "*Actual capital*".

The dangers and difficulties of *Quistclose* are further pointed out in *CSB 1137/1985*, particularly where family transactions are concerned. If a gift or loan is made with a particular motive, the whole sum becomes part of the recipient's resources. The intention to impose a trust must appear expressly (as in *R(SB) 12/86*) or by implication from the circumstances. Perhaps it is easier to prove (e.g. by contemporaneous documents) such an intention in business transactions. Often such evidence will be lacking in domestic situations, but the issue is one of proof, as is shown in *R(IS) 1/90*. There, the claimant established a building society account in his own name which was to be used solely to finance his son's medical education. He executed no documents about the account. It was argued that there was sufficient evidence of a declaration of trust over the account, but the Commissioner holds that the claimant had not unequivocally renounced his beneficial interest in the sum in the account. Although he had earmarked the money for the son's education, the situation was like an uncompleted gift and there was insufficient evidence of a declaration of trust. There is a thin line between an outright gift or loan, and one subject to an implied trust. In *R(IS) 5/98* where the claimant had transferred her flat to her daughter partly on the condition that her daughter looked after her, it is held that the gift failed when this condition was not fulfilled and the daughter held the flat on trust for her mother. An appeal against this decision was dismissed by the Court of Appeal (*Ellis v Chief Adjudication Officer*, reported as part of *R(IS) 5/98*). The claimant had argued that the condition was void for uncertainty but this was rejected by the Court. 2.479

The furthest extension so far of the *Quistclose* principle is in *CFC 21/1989*. The claimant's father paid her each month an amount to meet her mortgage obligation to a building society. The Commissioner accepts that the money was impressed with a trust that it should be used only for that purpose and did not form part of her capital. The extension is that the purpose was to meet expenditure on an item which could be covered by income support.

In *R(IS) 9/08* payments of a boarding-out allowance which the foster parent had saved up over the years were not held on trust for the children in her care. However, *MC v SSWP (IS)* [2015] UKUT 600 (AAC) reaches the opposite conclusion where the claimant had saved up her daughters' disability living allowance in an account in the claimant's name. A tribunal accepted that in relation to an earlier period the claimant was holding the money on trust for her daughters. However, when she used a substantial part of the money to meet rent arrears, the tribunal considered that this suggested that what was previously held on trust had been subsequently "converted" into the claimant's capital by her actions. Judge Wikeley holds, however, that this was wrong in law. Firstly, as the claimant had been made an appointee by DWP to act on behalf of her daughters in benefit matters, she was acting as a *de facto* trustee. Secondly, this was an obvious example of an informal trust over money, created without any legal formalities. Thirdly, paying off rent arrears helped to keep a roof over the daughters' heads and was a perfectly reasonable use of their savings, consistent with the purposes of the trust.

2.480 It will sometimes be the case that the claimant's explanation as to why she is holding capital for someone else may involve some unlawful purpose, *e.g.* in order to conceal assets from the Revenue. In *MC v SSWP* [2010] UKUT 29 (AAC) the claimant had purchased a house for £26,000 in her own name. The money had come from her bank account. She asserted that £14,000 of the £26,000 had been paid into her account by her husband by way of a gift for their son and the remaining £12,000 was her son's money which had been paid into her bank account because he had no bank account of his own. The tribunal found that the only explanation for her son providing the £12,000 was to "deny monies obtained illicitly to the revenue or that the sums were obtained from some illegal sources" and that as a consequence her son was estopped from denying that the capital belonged to the claimant. Judge Turnbull points out, however, that this was wrong in law. As the House of Lords held in *Tinsley v Milligan* [1993] 3 All E.R. 65; [1994] 1 A.C. 340, the principle that prevents a person putting forward evidence of his own wrongdoing in order to establish a resulting trust in his favour only applies where the person needs to put forward that evidence in order to *rebut* the presumption of advancement or of resulting trust. It does not apply where the person does not need to assert the illegality and only needs to show that he paid or contributed to the purchase price. In this case the claimant's son would be able to rely on the presumption of resulting trust without asserting any illegality. The question therefore was, in so far as it was accepted that the money was provided by her son, whether there was a resulting trust in his favour or whether he had intended to make a gift to the claimant.

For another example of money paid into a mother's bank account potentially being held on resulting trust for her daughter see *DL v Southampton CC (CTB)* [2010] UKUT 453 (AAC).

See also *CH/2233/2007* in which the claimant opened a bank account with money which he said represented money left to his sons by their late aunt. The tribunal failed to make a clear finding as to whether the money belonged to the claimant's sons or whether it came from another source. If it did belong to the claimant's sons, this would give rise to a bare trust. As the money was held in an ordinary account which the claimant was able to operate and use himself (as he had done on three occasions), the burden was on him to show that the money was held for his sons.

DF v Secretary of State (ESA) [2015] UKUT 611 (AAC) concerns the question of whether a claimant can argue that he is not the beneficial owner of the funds in an Individual Savings Account (ISA) that is in his name. One of the conditions for an ISA account is that money invested in the account is in the beneficial ownership of the account holder (see reg.4(6) of the Individual Savings Account Regulations 1998 (SI 1998/1870) (ISA Regulations 1998)).

The claimant maintained that the money in his ISA account really belonged to his daughter. His daughter confirmed this, stating that the ISA was designed to keep her money away from an unreliable partner.

The Secretary of State argued that a person in whose name an ISA is held has to be regarded as the beneficial owner of the money in the account, relying on the decision in *CIS/2836/2006*. While *CIS/2836/2006* concerned the Personal Equity

Plan Regulations 1989 (SI 1989/469), the ISA Regulations 1998 were said to be identical.

Judge Mitchell, however, concludes that *CIS/2836/2006* is restricted to "presumption of advancement" cases, i.e. cases in which the money is given by someone standing in loco parentis to a child, or by a husband to a wife, where there is a presumption that a gift was intended (note that the presumption of advancement is due to be abolished by s.199 of the Equality Act 2010 but this section has not yet come into force). To the extent that *CIS/2836/2006* could be read as going further, in his view it was not consistent with the House of Lords' decision in *Tinsley v Milligan* [1994] 1 A.C. 34.

He also holds that *CIS/2836/2006* did not decide that ISA-type legislation operates to extinguish beneficial interests of third parties in ISA deposits. Neither the ISA Regulations 1998 nor the enabling power under which they were made (s.333(2) Income and Corporation Taxes Act 1988) had the effect of altering existing rights in relation to property. The legislation was only concerned with creating a special account with special tax advantages.

Judge Mitchell then goes on to reject the Secretary of State's argument that the law of illegality meant that, as a matter of public policy, a claimant could not rely on a beneficial interest that he had previously denied. This was inconsistent with the Supreme Court's decision in *Hounga v Allen* [2014] UKSC 47; [2014] 1 WLR 2889 and the Court of Appeal's decision in *R. (Best) v Secretary of State for Justice* (Rev 1) [2015] EWCA Civ 17. In his view it was better for a First-tier Tribunal in an ISA case to ignore the role that may or may not be played by the law of illegality and to simply focus on whether it accepted that the beneficial interest in the funds lay elsewhere.

He does, however, point out the risks that a claimant runs if he argues that a third party has a beneficial interest in the sums deposited in an ISA, namely, conceding that any ISA tax reliefs were improperly awarded and the possibility of criminal proceedings for a tax offence under s.106A of the Taxes Management Act 1970 (see para.17 of the decision).

For the position under Scots law see *R(IS) 10/99*. The claimant agreed that he **2.481**
would pay his former wife (from whom he was separated) £22,250, representing a share of his pension. When he claimed income support, the claimant had £15,500 in his bank account which he said he was holding for his wife. The Commissioner decides that the £15,500 was not subject to a trust. This was because there had been no delivery of the subject of the trust, nor any satisfactory equivalent to delivery, "so as to achieve irrevocable divestiture of the truster and investiture of the trustee in the trust estate", as required by Scots law (see *Clark Taylor & Co Ltd v Quality Site Development (Edinburgh) Ltd* 1981 S.C. 11). There was no separate bank account and had been no clear indication to the claimant's wife that the money was held on trust for her. In addition, the Requirements of Writing (Scotland) Act 1995 required the trust to be proved in writing and the signature of the grantor. This had not been done here. The Commissioner also decided that the money could not be regarded as matrimonial property for the purposes of the Family Law (Scotland) Act 1995, since the claimant's severance package (which was being used to pay his wife) only came into existence after the parties ceased to cohabit and thus did not satisfy the definition of matrimonial property in s.10(3) and (4) of the Act. It was also clear that the claimant was not holding the sum as his wife's agent as there was no evidence of her consent to this. Finally, there was no "incumbrance" within the meaning of reg.49(a)(ii) preventing the claimant disposing of the money. The consequence was that the £15,500 counted as the claimant's capital. (*Note*: as (1999) 6 J.S.S.L. D41 points out, the outcome of this case is in fact unlikely to have been different if the principles of trust law in England and Wales had been applied.)

For a further case which considered whether a trust had been validly constituted for the purposes of Scots law, see *CSIS/639/2006*.

JK v SSWP (JSA) [2010] UKUT 437 (AAC); [2011] AACR 26 holds, however, that by asking whether there was a trust the tribunal had posed the wrong question.

It should have considered whether the presumption of ownership had been rebutted under Scots law. The claimant had contended that some of the money in his and his wife's joint account belonged to his mother-in-law. Applying the principle in *Cairns v Davidson* 1913 S.C. 1053, the tribunal should have considered, by way of such written or oral evidence available to it that it accepted, whether the presumption in favour of all the money in the joint account belonging to the claimant and his wife had been rebutted, so as to establish whether or not some of it belonged to his mother-in law.

2.482 *CIS/213/2004* and *CIS/214/2004* concerned the applicability of French law. A property in France had been purchased in the name of the claimant but the purchase price and renovation costs had been met by Ms V. Ms V was not the claimant's partner but they had a son and the purpose of putting the property in the claimant's name was so that their son and not Ms V's other children would inherit it (under French law all five of Ms V's children would otherwise have been entitled to an interest in the property). On the same day that the property was purchased the claimant executed a holograph will bequeathing a "usufruct" (the French equivalent of a life interest) in the property to Ms V. Applying the Recognition of Trusts Act 1987, which implements the Hague Convention of 1986 on the law applicable to trusts and their recognition, the Commissioner concludes that French law was the applicable law. But since French law does not recognise the concept of a trust, it followed that there was no resulting or constructive trust in favour of Ms V (although in the Commissioner's view if English law had been applicable the facts would have given rise to such a trust). The Commissioner directed the Secretary of State to obtain a further opinion as to the remedies available under French law to Ms V if the claimant decided to treat the property as his own, but after receiving this concluded that there was no reason under French law or otherwise why the value of the property should not be included in the claimant's capital. The claimant appealed against this decision to the Court of Appeal but the appeal was dismissed (*Martin v Secretary of State for Work and Pensions* [2009] EWCA Civ 1289; [2010] AACR 9).

It will be an error of law if a tribunal fails to consider the question of the applicable law in relation to property abroad (*MB v Royal Borough of Kensington & Chelsea (HB)* [2011] UKUT 321 (AAC)). The claimant in *MB v RB Kensington & Chelsea* was an Irish national, who had, while domiciled and resident in Ireland, bought a property in Ireland with the assistance of a mortgage from an Irish bank. In those circumstances it was difficult to see how the applicable law could be other than Irish law but the tribunal had not referred to this issue at all, nor had it sought any evidence as to the nature and content of Irish law and the Irish law of trusts (foreign law is a question of fact (see *R(G) 2/00*, at para.20)).

Note also the doctrine of secret trusts, under which a person, who receives property under an intestacy when the deceased refrained from making a will in reliance on that person's promise to carry out his expressed intentions, holds the property on trust to carry out those intentions (*CSB 989/1985*). The doctrine also applies to property left by will where on the face of the will the property has been left to A but this is on the understanding that he is merely a trustee of it in favour of B.

2.483 For an example of where there may have been a secret trust, see *GK v SSWP (JSA)* [2012] UKUT 115 (AAC). In that case the claimant had inherited money from her aunt which she understood from conversations with her aunt was to be shared between her five children and herself. She used the money to purchase some land, which although in her sole name, she regarded as belonging to all six of them. Judge Mark held that the tribunal had erred in not considering whether there was a secret trust.

Another example of the legal owner having nothing to sell is *R(SB) 23/85*. The claimant's wife in a home-made and legally ineffective deed of gift purported to give an uninhabitable property to her son. He, as intended, carried out the works to make it habitable. The Commissioner holds that although a court will not normally "complete" such an "uncompleted gift" in favour of someone who has not given valuable consideration, one of the situations in which a transfer of the property will be ordered is where the intended recipient is induced to believe that he has or will have an interest in the property and acts on that belief to his detriment. Thus in the meantime the claimant's wife held the property merely as a "bare trustee" and could not lawfully transfer it to anyone but the son. There is discussion of what kind of action might give rise to the right to complete the gift in *R(SB) 7/87*. See also *CIS 807/1991* on proprietary estoppel.

Choses in action

There is also a remarkable range of interests in property which do have a present market value and so are actual capital resources. These are usually things in action (or choses in action), rights to sue for something. Debts, even where they are not due to be paid for some time, are things in action which can be sold. A good example is *R(SB) 31/83* where the claimant in selling a house allowed the purchaser a mortgage of £4,000, to be redeemed in six months. The debt conferred a right to sue and had to be valued at what could be obtained on the open market. In *CJSA 204/2002* the claimant had lent her son £8,500 for the deposit on a flat. The Commissioner holds that the legal debt owed by the son to the claimant had to be valued in order to decide whether the claimant had actual capital in excess of £8,000 (which was then the prescribed limit). The terms of the loan, including the rate of any interest and whether there was any security for the loan, as well as the terms of repayment, were clearly relevant to this valuation. Once the value of the loan had been determined, the question of deprivation of capital then had to be considered. To the extent that the value of the loan was less than £8,500, to that extent the claimant had deprived herself of capital. However, on the facts the Commissioner found that the claimant had not deprived herself of the capital for the purpose of securing entitlement to, or increasing the amount of, jobseeker's allowance (see further the note to reg.51(1)). See also *JC v SSWP* [2009] UKUT 22 (AAC) which points out that the value of the loan will depend on whether it is likely to be recoverable. If the claimant had lent the money with no expectation of getting it back he had in effect reduced the value of the *chose in action* to nil. The issue of deprivation of capital then arose. *R 2/09(IS)*, a Northern Ireland decision, gives further guidance on the approach to choses in action and their value. 2.484

In *GS v Department for Social Development (IS)* [2012] NI Com 284 (another Northern Ireland decision) the claimant agreed in June 2004 to buy a house (not yet built) from Mr McK in return for the transfer of ownership of the claimant's present house, plus £33,000. The £33,000 was paid by cheque in August 2006. However, the building work was delayed due to the illness of Mr McK's brother and the house was only eventually built during 2009. But by March 2010 (the date of the decision under appeal) the agreement still had not been fulfilled due to difficulties with Mr McK's title to the land. Mr McK accepted that the £33,000 deposit would be returned if these difficulties could not be resolved. Commissioner Stockman points out that a chose in action can only arise upon breach of contract, or possibly frustration of contract; the mere existence of the contract did not give rise to the right to sue. The difficulty was determining whether there had been a breach of contract and in identifying when that occurred. In the circumstances of this case, where there was no date for the completion of the contract and the delay in completing the building work had been waived by the claimant because of the personal friendship between Mr McK and himself, the claimant would not have had a strong case for breach of contract for unreasonable delay. This would have a resultant effect on the value of the chose in action, for which there was unlikely to be a ready market. The Commissioner decides that the value of the chose in action was nil from August 2006 and £3,000 from November 2008 up to March 2010.

Similarly, a life interest in a trust fund is a present asset which can be sold and has a market value (*R(SB) 2/84, R(SB) 43/84, R(SB) 15/86* and *R(SB) 13/87*). The practical effect is reversed by para.13 of Sch.10. An action for breach of fiduciary duty against an attorney appointed under the Enduring Powers of Attorney Act 1985 who had used the claimant's capital to repay her own debts also constitutes actual capital; so too would a claim against the attorney for misapplication of capital on the ground that she had made gifts outside the circumstances sanctioned by s.3(5) of the 1985 Act (this allows an attorney to make gifts (to herself or others) "provided that the value of each such gift is not unreasonable having regard to all the circumstances and in particular the size of the donor's estate") (*R(IS) 17/98*).

Bank or building society accounts

2.485 A more direct way of holding capital is in a bank or building society account. In *CSB 296/1985* the claimant's solicitor received £12,000 damages on behalf of the claimant and placed the money on deposit, presumably in the solicitor's client account. The Commissioner held that the £12,000 was an actual resource of the claimant, on the basis that there was no difference in principle between monies being held by a solicitor on behalf of a client and monies held by a bank or building society on behalf of a customer. This decision was upheld by the Court of Appeal in *Thomas v Chief Adjudication Officer* (reported as *R(SB) 17/87*). Russell LJ says "the possession of this money by the solicitors as the agent for the claimant was, in every sense of the term, possession by the claimant."

However, note *CIS 984/2002* which holds that money held by the claimant's solicitor pending quantification of the statutory charge to the Legal Services Commission under s.10(7) of the Access to Justice Act 1999 was not part of the claimant's capital. Until that quantification had been carried out, it was not possible to identify any particular amount as the claimant's capital. Another way of looking at it was to treat the statutory charge as an incumbrance for the purpose of reg.49(a)(ii) (see *CIS 368/1993*). Nor was any part of the money available to the claimant on application for the purposes of reg.51(2).

See also *LC v Bournemouth Borough Council (HB)* [2016] UKUT 175 (AAC), discussed in the notes to reg.51(2), where the proceeds of sale of a former matrimonial home were being held in a solicitors' client account until the claimant's partner and his ex-wife could agree how the sum was to be split or the issue was resolved by a court order. In Judge White's view the value of the capital prior to agreement or an order of the court would be minimal.

The approach taken in *Thomas* seems to involve valuing the amount of money directly, not as a technical chose in action. However, the importance of the legal relationship between a bank and a customer being one of debtor and creditor was revealed in *CSB 598/1987*. A large cheque was paid into the claimant's wife's bank account on October 9, 1987. The amount was credited to her account on that date, but the cheque was not cleared until October 15. The bank's paying-in slips reserved the bank's right to "postpone payment of cheques drawn against uncleared effects which may have been credited to the account." The effect was that the bank did not accept the relationship of debtor and creditor on the mere paying in of a cheque. Thus the amount did not become part of the claimant's actual resources until October 15. A person who deliberately refrains from paying in a cheque may be fixed with notional capital under reg.51.

CIS/255/2005 concerned the effect on capital of the issue of a cheque. The Commissioner holds that the claimant's capital was reduced from the date that the cheque was issued (this would not apply if the cheque was postdated). After that time she could not honestly withdraw money from her bank account so as to leave insufficient funds to meet the cheque.

In *R(IS) 15/96* the Commissioner confirms that money in a building society or bank (or solicitor's client) account is an actual resource in the form of a chose in action. It is not, as the SSAT had decided, held in trust. If the money is in an account from which it can be withdrawn at any time, its value is the credit balance (less any penalties for early withdrawal, etc.). But if the money cannot be withdrawn for a specified term the value will be less (although the notional capital rules may come into play in respect of the difference in value: *CIS 494/1990;* see also *CIS 2208/2003*).

Interests in trusts

2.486 The nature of interests in capital under trusts gives rise to several problems. It is clear that a person may have an absolute vested interest under a trust, although payment is deferred, e.g. until the age of 21. This was the case in *R(SB) 26/86*, where the resource was held to be the person's share of the fund. However, an interest may be contingent on reaching a particular age. This appears to have been one of the assumptions on which the Court of Appeal decided the unsatisfactory case of *Peters v Chief Adjudication Officer, R(SB) 3/89*. It was conceded that sums were held on trust to be paid over to each of three sisters on attaining the age of 18, with the power to advance up to 50 per cent of the capital before then. In the end, the Court of Appeal accepted the valuation of half of the full value for each sister under 18. The precise finding may depend on the supplementary benefit rule on discretionary trusts, which has not been translated into the income support legislation. But some statements about the general market value of such interests are made. May LJ says "in an appropriate market a discretionary entitlement of up to 50 per cent now and at least 50 per cent in, say, six months in a given case, or three to four years in another, could well be said to have a value greater than 50 per cent of the capital value of the trust." This clearly supports the view that a contingent interest has a market value and so is actual capital. See also *CTC 4713/2002* which concerned a similar trust in favour of the claimant's son to that in *Peters* (although in this case the trustees had power to advance the whole of the fund). The Commissioner notes that in *Peters* the Court of Appeal had accepted the valuation agreed by the parties without argument. He acknowledged that each case must turn on its facts and that valuation of different interests would differ depending on such factors as the nature of the underlying investments (there was evidence in this case that due to lack of investor confidence the market value of the fund was much diminished); in addition in this case, unlike *Peters*, the whole of the fund could be advanced. However, he concluded that the Court of Appeal's approach in *Peters* led to a valuation of the claimant's son's equitable interest as being more or less equal to the whole net value of the trust fund (less 10 per cent for the expenses of sale).

All interests which can be sold or borrowed against will need to be considered. However, in the case of an interest under a discretionary trust, the DWP will normally only take payments of capital (or income) into account when they are actually made.

In *R(IS) 9/04* it was argued that funds held by the Court of Protection were analogous to those held by a discretionary trustee. Since neither the claimant nor her receiver could insist on the Court releasing any part of the funds it was contended that the market value of the claimant's actual interest was so small as to be negligible. However, the Commissioner followed *CIS 7127/1995* in holding that the entire beneficial interest in the funds administered by the Court remained with the claimant to whom alone they belonged. The fact the Court had discretionary powers of *control* over the management of a patient's property for his or her benefit did not mean that the patient's beneficial *ownership* had ceased. The funds therefore had to be valued at their current market value, less any appropriate allowance for sale expenses, in the normal way (see reg.49).

Realisation of assets

R(SB) 18/83 stresses that there are more ways of realising assets than sale. In particular, assets can be charged to secure a loan which can be used to meet requirements. In that case the asset was a minority shareholding in a family company. The Commissioner says that only a person prepared to lend money without security would do so in such circumstances. The articles of association of the company provided that if a shareholder wanted to sell shares they were to be offered to the existing shareholders at the fair value fixed by the auditors. The Commissioner holds that the regulations do not require assets to be valued at a figure higher than anything the person would realise on them, i.e. the auditor's fair value. This is in line with the purpose of the capital cut-off that a claimant can draw on resources until they fall below the limit. 2.487

This approach to valuation can usefully deal with unrealisable assets. See the notes to reg.49. However, it is no part of the definition of capital that it should be immediately realisable, although its market value may be affected by such factors. It thus remains possible (especially in circumstances like those imposed by reg.52

below) for a claimant to be fixed with a large amount of capital which is not available to him.

Deduction of liabilities

2.488 The general rule is that the whole of a capital resource is to be taken into account. Liabilities are not to be deducted from the value (*R(SB) 2/83*). Otherwise, it is only if a debt is secured on the capital asset that it can be deducted, at the stage specificially required by reg.49 or 50 (*R(IS) 21/93*). See the notes to reg.49 and note *JRL v SSWP (JSA)* [2011] UKUT 63 (AAC); [2011] AACR 30. In *JRL v SSWP* the claimant had three accounts with the same bank, of which one was in credit, one was overdrawn and one had a nil balance. The three-judge panel pointed out that this meant that the claimant was both a creditor and a debtor of the same body. Under the bank's terms and conditions, the bank had a contractual right to debit at any time any of a customer's accounts which were in credit with sums sufficient to clear the customer's indebtedness to the bank. This created what was effectively a charge on the customer's credit balance(s). The market value of the account that was in credit was therefore its net value after deduction of the amount of the claimant's overdraft on his other account.

Disregard of capital of child or young person

2.489 **47.**—[1. . .].

AMENDMENT

1. Social Security (Working Tax Credit and Child Tax Credit) (Consequential Amendments) Regulations 2003 (SI 2003/455) reg.2 and Sch.1 para.11 (April 6, 2004, except in "transitional cases" and see further the note to reg.17 of the Income Support Regulations).

GENERAL NOTE

2.490 This regulation provided that the capital of a child or young person who was a member of the claimant's family was not to be treated as the claimant's (see the 2003 edition of this volume for this regulation and the notes to it). However, with effect from April 6, 2004 (except in "transitional cases"—see the note to reg.17) amounts for children and young persons have been removed from the income support scheme; financial assistance to help with the cost of bringing up a child or young person is now to be provided through the child tax credit system, see Vol.IV of this series. As a consequence, under the new form of reg.23 (in force from April 6, 2004, except for "transitional cases"—see the note to reg.17) neither the income nor the capital of a child or young person counts as the claimant's (see the new form of reg.23(2) and the notes to that regulation). This regulation has therefore been revoked. It does however, remain in force for "transitional cases"—see the note to reg.17.

For income support claimants who had an award of child tax credit before April 6, 2004 see reg.7 of the Social Security (Working Tax Credit and Child Tax Credit) (Consequential Amendments) Regulations 2003 (SI 2003/455) (as amended) on p.812 and the notes to that regulation.

Income treated as capital

2.491 **48.**—(1) Any [2. . .] bounty derived from employment to which paragraph 7 of Schedule 8 applies [2and paid at intervals of at least one year] shall be treated as capital.

(2) Except in the case of an amount to which section 23(5)(a)(ii) of the Act [SSCBA, s.126(5)(a)(ii)] (refund of tax in trade dispute cases) [2or regulation 41(4) (capital treated as income)] applies, any amount by way of a refund of income tax deducted from profit or emoluments chargeable to income tax under Schedule D or E shall be treated as capital.

(3) Any holiday pay which is not earnings under regulation 35(1)(d) (earnings of employed earners) shall be treated as capital.

(4) Except any income derived from capital disregarded under paragraph 1, 2, 4, 6, [3 12 [14 25 to 28, 44 or 45] of Schedule 10, any income derived from capital shall be treated as capital but only from the date it is normally due to be credited to the claimant's account.

(5) Subject to paragraph (6), in the case of employment as an employed earner, any advance of earnings or any loan made by the claimant's employer shall be treated as capital.

[1 (6) Paragraph (5) shall not apply to a person to whom section 23 of the Act [SSCBA, s.126] (trade disputes) applies or in respect of whom section 20(3) of the Act [SSCBA, s.124(1)] (conditions of entitlement to income support) has effect as modified by section 23A(b) [SSCBA, s.127(b)] (effect of return to work).]

(7) Any payment under section 30 of the Prison Act 1952 (payments for discharged prisoners) or allowance under section 17 of the Prisons (Scotland) Act 1952 (allowances to prisoners on discharge) shall be treated as capital.

[11 (8) [13 . . .]

(8A) [13 . . .].]

[3 (9) Any charitable or voluntary payment which is not made or not due to be made at regular intervals, other than one to which paragraph (10) applies, shall be treated as capital.

(10) This paragraph applies to a payment—

(a) which is made to a person to whom section 23 of the Act [SSCBA, s.126] (trade disputes) applies or in respect of whom section 20(3) of the Act [SSCBA, s.124(1)] (conditions of entitlement to income support) has effect as modified by section 23A(b) of the Act [SSCBA, s.127(b)] (effect of return to work) [13 or to the partner] of such a person;

(b) [13 . . .].]

(c) which is made under [18 or by] the Macfarlane Trust[5, or the Macfarlane (Special Payments) Trust][6, the Macfarlane (Special Payments) (No.2) Trust][8, the Fund][10, the Eileen Trust] [17 , MFET Limited] [19 , the Skipton Fund, the Caxton Foundation] or [9 the Independent Living [16 Fund (2006)]].]

[4 (11) [15 . . .].]

[12 (12) Any arrears of subsistence allowance which are paid to a claimant as a lump sum shall be treated as capital.]

AMENDMENTS

1. Income Support (General) Amendment Regulations 1988 (SI 1988/663) reg.21 (April 11, 1988).

2. Income Support (General) Amendment No.4 Regulations 1988 (SI 1988/1445) reg.11 (September 12, 1988).

3. Income Support (General) Amendment No.5 Regulations 1988 (SI 1988/2022) reg.11 (December 12, 1988).

4. Income Support (General) Amendment No.2 Regulations 1989 (SI 1989/1323) reg.15 (October 9, 1989).

5. Income-related Benefits Schemes Amendment Regulations 1990 (SI 1990/127) reg.33 (January 31, 1990).

6. Income-related Benefits Schemes and Social Security (Recoupment) Amendment Regulations 1991 (SI 1991/1175) reg.5 (May 11, 1991).

7. Income Support (General) Amendment Regulations 1992 (SI 1992/468) Sch. para.5 (April 6, 1992).

8. Income-related Benefits Schemes and Social Security (Recoupment) Amendment Regulations 1992 (SI 1992/1101) reg.6 (May 7, 1992).

9. Social Security Benefits (Miscellaneous Amendments) (No.2) Regulations 1993 (SI 1993/963) reg.2(3) (April 22, 1993).

10. Income-related Benefits Schemes and Social Security (Recoupment) Amendment Regulations 1993 (SI 1993/1249) reg.4(3) (May 14, 1993).

11. Social Security (Miscellaneous Amendments) Regulations 1998 (SI 1998/563) reg.4(1) (April 6, 1998).

12. Social Security Amendment (Employment Zones) Regulations 2000 (SI 2000/724) reg.3(2) (April 3, 2000).

13. Social Security (Working Tax Credit and Child Tax Credit) (Consequential Amendments) Regulations 2003 (SI 2003/455) reg.2 and Sch.1 para.12 (April 6, 2004, except in "transitional cases" and see further the note to reg.17 of the Income Support Regulations).

14. Social Security (Miscellaneous Amendments) (No.4) Regulations 2006 (SI 2006/2378) reg.5(4) (October 2, 2006).

15. Social Security (Miscellaneous Amendments) Regulations 2008 (SI 2008/698) reg.2(9) (April 14, 2008).

16. Social Security (Miscellaneous Amendments) (No.6) Regulations 2008 (SI 2008/2767) reg.2(6) (November 17, 2008).

17. Social Security (Miscellaneous Amendments) (No.2) Regulations 2010 (SI 2010/641 reg.2(3)(c) (April 6, 2010).

18. Social Security (Miscellaneous Amendments) (No.2) Regulations 2010 (SI 2010/641 reg.2(7)(b) (April 6, 2010).

19. Social Security (Miscellaneous Amendments) (No.3) Regulations 2011 (SI 2011/2425) reg.7(5) (October 31, 2011).

DEFINITIONS

"the Act"—see reg.2(1).
"claimant"—see SSCBA s.137(1) and reg.23(1).
"employed earner"—see reg.2(1).
"MFET Limited"—*ibid.*
"subsistence allowance"—*ibid.*
"the Eileen Trust"—*ibid.*
"the Fund"—*ibid.*
"the Independent Living Funds"—*ibid.*
"the Macfarlane (Special Payments) Trust"—*ibid.*
"the Macfarlane (Special Payments) (No.2) Trust"—*ibid.*
"the Macfarlane Trust"—*ibid.*

GENERAL NOTE

2.492 Most of these categories deemed to be capital are self-explanatory. They are then disregarded as income (Sch.9 para.32).

Paragraph (4)

2.493 The general rule is that the income from capital is not to be treated as income, but is added to the capital when it is credited. The excepted cases are premises and business assets plus trusts of personal injury compensation, and from October 2, 2006, funds held in court that derive from damages for personal injury or compensation for the death of a parent. But in the case of such court funds or trusts for personal injury compensation, income is (from October 2, 2006) totally disregarded (see para.15 of Sch.9).

For the rule in para.(4) to apply, the income must be derived from some capital asset of the claimant (*CIS 25/ 1989*). A 12-month assured shorthold tenancy is not a capital asset and income from the subletting of rooms is not "derived from" the tenancy (*CIS 82/1993*).

The income covered by this provision is disregarded as income (Sch.9 para.22), but remember that capital over £6,000 (£10,000 for claimants living permanently in a care home, Abbeyfield Home or independent hospital) is deemed to produce a tariff income under reg.53.

In *CIS 563/1991* the Commissioner considers that the effect of para.(4) is to treat a payment of income as capital for the same length of time as it would have been taken into account as income. So, for example, a payment of a month's rent from a property let out to tenants counts as capital for a month from the date that the claimant is due to receive it. After that, reg.48(4) ceases to have effect. Money spent during that month cannot form part of the claimant's actual capital at the end of the month (subject to the possible effect of the notional capital rule in reg.51(1)). Although saved-up income only metamorphoses into capital after deducting all relevant debts (see the notes to reg.23), the Commissioner considers that where para.(4) has effected a statutory metamorphosis, any unspent money at the end of the period covered by para.(4) continues to count as capital; it does not change into income and then immediately back into capital. Thus any outstanding debts will only reduce the amount of the capital if they are secured on the capital itself (reg.49(a)(ii)). *CIS 563/1991* also deals with the situation where more than one disregard in Sch.10 could apply. If a property was disregarded under para.26 (taking steps to dispose of premises) the rental income from it would count as income and would only be ignored to the extent allowed for by para.22(2) of Sch.9. But if the property was let by the claimant and the para.5 disregard also applied (as was possible under the form of para.5 in force before October 2, 1995: see the 1995 edition of J. Mesher and P. Wood, *Income-related Benefits: the Legislation*) the rental income would count as capital. The Commissioner concludes that considering reg.48(4) and para.22 of Sch.9 together, the primary rule was that income derived from capital was to be treated as capital. The disregard in para.5 therefore took precedence, and the rental income counted as capital, even during periods when the property could also be disregarded under one or more of the provisions listed in paras 22 and (4). Note that under the new form of para.5 a property let to tenants by the claimant is no longer disregarded (see the note to para.5); the rent will still generally count as capital under the normal rule in para.(4) (unless one of the exceptions applies).

Paragraphs (8) and (8A)

These paragraphs provided that arrears of payments made by local authorities in Great Britain (para.(8)) and authorities in Northern Ireland (para.(8A)) towards the maintenance of children were treated as capital, but arguably they were capital in any event. For the disregard of current payments see para.25(1)(ba)–(d) of Sch.9. With effect from April 6, 2004 (except in "transitional cases"—see the note to reg.17) amounts for children and young persons have been removed from the income support scheme; financial assistance to help with the cost of bringing up a child or young person is now to be provided through the child tax credit system, see Vol.IV of this series. The revocation of paras (8) and (8A) is another of the consequential changes that apply from April 6, 2004 (except in "transitional cases"—see the note to reg.17) as a result of income support becoming an "adults only" benefit. **2.494**

Paragraphs (9) and (10)

Regulations 24 and 33 on charitable or voluntary payments were revoked from December 1988. See the notes to para.15 of Sch.9 for the meaning of "charitable" and "voluntary." The general rule in para.(9) is that such payments not made or due to be made at regular intervals are to be treated as capital. This rule does not apply to the three (now two) kinds of payments set out in para.(10). However, there is nothing to say how such payments are to be treated. Presumably they must be treated as capital or income according to general legal principles (on which see the notes to reg.23). Similarly, there is nothing expressly to say how payments which are made or due to be made regularly are to be treated, but no doubt they will usually have the character of income. **2.495**

In *CJSA/2336/2005* the claimant ceased work on September 3, 2004 and claimed JSA. Her mother lent her £200 to pay her rent on October 1, 2004, the agreement being that the money would be repaid on October 31, 2004. However, as no decision had been made on the claimant's claim for JSA she lent her a further £200 for the rent due on November 1, 2004. The claimant's claim for JSA was refused on November 11, 2004 on the grounds that her income (i.e. the £200 a month loan from her mother) exceeded her applicable amount. Her mother made a third payment for the rent due on December 1, 2004 but refused to make any further payments.

The Commissioner rejected the contention that the loans could be regarded as not part of the claimant's income under the principle in *Leeves v Adjudication Officer*, reported as *R(IS) 5/99* and *Morrell v Secretary of State for Work and Pensions*, reported as *R(IS) 6/03*. This was because on the facts there was no intention to create legal relations and so it could not be said that the claimant was under a legal obligation to repay, let alone a certain and immediate obligation.

2.496 He considered whether the loan payments should be treated as capital, since the first payment was clearly intended to be a one-off when it was made. But did the character of the payments change after the second payment was made? The Commissioner did not reach a decision on this but instead went on to consider, if the loan payments were income, the effect of reg.110(9) of the JSA Regulations 1996 (the equivalent of para.(9)) in these circumstances.

He concludes that the loans were a voluntary payment and that, looking at the position at the date of the decision under appeal when only two payments had been made, the condition that the payments were not made at regular intervals was met. At that point there had not been payments at intervals in the plural and moreover the hope was that JSA and housing benefit would finally be awarded in time for the claimant to pay the December rent payment herself. The result was that the loan payments were to be treated as capital under reg.110(9) and the claimant was entitled to JSA on the basis that her income was nil.

Note that since October 2, 2006 voluntary payments (such as the loans in *CJSA/2336/2005*) which *are* made at regular intervals and so are not treated as capital under para.(9) have been totally disregarded (see para.15(5A)(b) of Sch.9).

Paragraph (12)

2.497 "Subsistence allowances" (reg.2(1)) are paid to claimants participating in an "employment zone" (defined in reg.2(1)) programme. Any arrears paid as a lump sum are treated as capital and ignored for 52 weeks from the date of receipt (para.59 of Sch.10). See further the note to reg.42(5A). From September 1, 2011 employment zone programmes are no longer in operation.

[1 Calculation of capital in the United Kingdom

2.498 **49.**—Capital which a claimant possesses in the United Kingdom shall be calculated at its current market or surrender value less—

(a) where there would be expenses attributable to sale, 10 per cent; and
(b) the amount of any incumbrance secured on it.]

AMENDMENT

1. Social Security (Miscellaneous Amendments) (No.5) Regulations 2007 (SI 2007/2618) reg.5(10) (October 1, 2007).

DEFINITION

"claimant"—see reg.2(1) and reg.23(1).

GENERAL NOTE

2.499 The new form of reg.49 introduced on October 1, 2007 no longer contains any special provision for the valuation of National Savings Certificates (valuations of National Savings and Investments were previously uprated annually on July 1 but this no longer happens). See *CIS/1733/2008* on the valuation of National Savings

Certificates under the previous rule. Under the new form of reg.49 National Savings Certificates will be valued in the same way as other capital.

The general rule is that the market value of the asset is to be taken. The surrender value will be taken if appropriate (although the surrender value of life insurance policies and of annuities is totally disregarded (Sch.10 paras 15 and 11)). The value at this stage does not take account of any incumbrances secured on the assets, since those come in under para.(b) (*R(IS) 21/93*).

In *R(SB) 57/83* and *R(SB) 6/84* the test taken is the price that would be commanded between a willing buyer and a willing seller at a particular date. In *R(SB) 6/84* it is stressed that in the case of a house it is vital to know the nature and extent of the interest being valued. Also, since what is required is a current market value, the Commissioner holds that an estate agent's figure for a quick sale was closer to the proper approach than the District Valuer's figure for a sale within three months. All the circumstances must be taken into account in making the valuation. In *CIS 553/1991* it is held that in valuing a former matrimonial home the wife's statutory right of occupation under the Matrimonial Homes Act 1967 has to be taken into account. See further the decisions discussed under "*Valuation under reg.52*" in the notes to reg.52.

Similarly, if personal possessions are being valued, it is what the possessions could be sold for which counts, not simply what was paid for them (*CIS 494/1990, CIS 2208/2003*). See also *JJ v SSWP (IS)* [2012] UKUT 253 (AAC) which points out that where a sale of a chattel is by auction there are buyer's premiums added as well as seller's commission and that this could result in the seller being treated as having much more capital than he would realise on a sale. In the Judge's view this was not the object of the regulations and the valuation had to be based on the standard test of what the claimant could expect to realise on a transaction between a willing seller and a willing buyer. **2.500**

Sometimes a detailed valuation is not necessary, such as where the value of an asset is on any basis clearly over the prescribed (which since April 10, 2006 has been £16,000) limit (*CIS/40/1989*).

Shares

It is accepted that the test of the willing buyer and the willing seller is the starting point for the valuation of shares (*R(SB) 57/83, R(SB) 12/89* and *R(IS) 2/90*). The latter case emphasises that in the income support context the value must be determined on the basis of a very quick sale, so that the hypothetical willing seller would be at a corresponding disadvantage. In the case of private companies there is often a provision in the articles of association that a shareholder wishing to sell must first offer the shares to other shareholders at a "fair value" fixed by the auditors (this was the case in *R(SB) 18/83* and *R(IS) 2/90*). Then the value of the shares ought not to be higher than the fair value, but for income support purposes may well be less. The possible complications are set out in *CSB 488/1982* (quoted with approval in *R(SB) 12/89* and *R(IS) 2/90*). In *R(IS) 8/92* it is suggested that the market value is what a purchaser would pay for the shares subject to the same restriction. Whether the shareholding gives a minority, equal or controlling interest is particularly significant. All the circumstances of the share structure of the company must be considered. For instance, in *R(SB) 12/89* shares could only be sold with the consent of the directors, which it was indicated would not be forthcoming. It seems to be agreed that valuation according to Revenue methods is not appropriate (*R(SB) 18/83* and *R(IS) 2/90*), although it is suggested in *R(SB) 12/89* that the Revenue Shares Valuation Division might be able to assist tribunals. It is not known if this is so. What is absolutely clear is that the total value of the company's shareholding cannot simply be divided in proportion to the claimant's holding (*R(SB) 18/83*). **2.501**

However, in the case of shares in companies quoted on the London Stock Exchange the Revenue method of valuation should be used (*R(IS) 18/95*). This involves looking at all the transactions relating to the relevant share during the previous day, taking the lowest figure and adding to this a quarter of the difference between the lowest and the highest figure. The Commissioner considered that decision-makers could use the valuation quoted in newspapers (which is the mean between the best bid and best offer price at the close of business the previous day) to obtain approximate valuations. However, where a completely accurate valuation was essential, the Revenue method would need to be adopted. See also *DW v SSWP (JSA)* [2012] UKUT 478 (AAC).

Valuation affected by difficulties in realisation

2.502 The proper approach to valuation can usefully deal with unrealisable assets. Sometimes their market value will be nil (e.g. a potential interest under a discretionary trust: R(SB) 25/83; assets that are subject to a restraint or freezing order: SH v SSWP [2008] UKUT 21 (AAC); *CS v Chelmsford BC* [2014] UKUT 518 (AAC)); sometimes it will be very heavily discounted. However, if the asset will be realisable after a time, it may have a current value. The claimant may be able to sell an option to purchase the asset in the future (see *R(IS) 8/92*) or borrow, using the asset as security. But the valuation must reflect the fact that the asset is not immediately realisable. In *R(IS) 4/96* the claimant had on his divorce transferred his interest in the former matrimonial home to his wife in return for a charge on the property which could only be enforced if she died, remarried or cohabited for more than six months. The claimant's former wife was 46 and in good health. A discount had to be applied to the present day value of the charge to reflect the fact that it might not be realisable for as long as 40 years or more; consequently it was unlikely to be worth more than £3,000. See also *CIS 982/2002* in which the Commissioner sets out a number of detailed questions that had to be considered when valuing the claimant's share (if any) in a joint bank account that had been frozen following the claimant's separation from her husband. And note *LC v Bournemouth Borough Council (HB)* [2016] UKUT 175 (AAC), discussed in the notes to reg.51(2) and reg.52.

In *JC-W v Wirral MBC (HB)* [2011] UKUT 501 (AAC) Judge Mark concluded that nobody would be willing to purchase (for more than a nominal amount) the claimant's beneficial interest pending divorce in two heavily mortgaged properties, one of which was only partly built, in respect of which the claimant's parents-in-law claimed an interest in the proceeds of sale, and which the claimant's husband was unwilling to sell.

As the Tribunal of Commissioners in *R(SB) 45/83* point out, the market value (in this case of an interest in an entire trust fund) must reflect the outlay the purchaser would expect to incur in obtaining transfer of the assets and the profit he would expect as an inducement to purchase. If there might be some legal difficulty in obtaining the underlying asset (as there might have been in *R(SB) 21/83* and in *R(IS) 13/95*) where shares were held in the names of the claimant's children) this must be taken into account.

See also *MB v Wychavon DC (HB)* [2013] UKUT 67 (AAC) which concerned the valuation of the claimant's beneficial interest under a declaration of trust made by his mother in relation to a property held in the mother's name. The claimant had contributed 10 per cent towards the purchase price. In the absence of a family member willing to purchase the claimant's share, Judge Mark finds that the market value of the claimant's interest was substantially less than the amount of his contribution to the purchase price (he decided it was less than half that amount). However, it was possible that there would be no market at all for the claimant's share, in which case its value would be nil.

Where the property is jointly owned, see the decisions discussed under "*Valuation under reg.52*" in the notes to reg.52.

Deductions from market value

2.503 The general rule is that the whole of a capital resource is to be taken into account. Liabilities are not to be deducted from the value (*R(SB) 2/83*). It is only where a debt is secured on the capital asset that it is deducted under para.(b).

In this connection, note *JRL v SSWP (JSA)* [2011] UKUT 63 (AAC); [2011] AACR 30. In *JRL v SSWP* the claimant had three accounts with the same bank, of which one was in credit, one was overdrawn and one had a nil balance. The Three-Judge Panel pointed out that this meant that the claimant was both a creditor and a debtor of the same body. Under the bank's terms and conditions, the bank had a contractual right to debit at any time any of a customer's accounts which were in credit with sums sufficient to clear the customer's indebtedness to the bank. This created what was effectively a charge on the customer's credit balance(s). The market value of the account that was in credit was therefore its net value after deduction of the amount of the claimant's overdraft on his other account.

The first deduction to be made is a standard 10 per cent if there would be any expenses attributable to sale, as there almost always will be. The second is the amount of any incumbrance secured on the asset. There is particularly full and helpful guidance on the nature of incumbrances on real property and the evidence which should be examined in *R(IS) 21/93*, and see below. In *R(IS) 10/99* the Commissioner points out that the word "incumbrance" is unknown to the law of Scotland, but goes on to interpret what is now para.(b) as meaning that there must be something attached to the capital in question that prevents the claimant from disposing of it.

The standard case of a debt being secured on a capital asset is a house that is mortgaged. The amount of capital outstanding will be deducted from the market value of the house. In *R(SB) 14/81* (see Sch.10 para.8) the claimant had been lent £5,000 for work on his bungalow, which was mortgaged to secure the debt. He had £3,430 left. Although he was obliged to make monthly repayments this liability could not be deducted from the £3,430, for the debt was not secured on the money. However, the principle of *R(SB) 53/83* (see the notes to reg.46) would make the money not part of the claimant's resources. In *JH v SSWP* [2009] UKUT 1 (AAC) the site owner's commission payable on the sale of a beach hut was not "an incumbrance secured on" the hut but a personal contractual obligation on the seller which could not be enforced against the asset itself. 2.504

In *R(SB) 18/83* the Commissioner says that personal property such as shares (or money) can be charged by a contract for valuable consideration (e.g. a loan) without any writing or the handing over of any title documents. But this is not the case in Scots law (*R(SB) 5/88*). In *R(IS) 18/95* the claimant's brokers had a lien on his shares for the cost of acquisition and their commission which fell to be offset against the value of the shares. *CIS 368/1993* concerned money held under a solicitor's undertaking. £40,000 of the proceeds of sale of the claimant's house was retained by his solicitors in pursuance of an undertaking to his bank given because of a previous charge on the property. The Commissioner decides that the undertaking was an incumbrance within what is now para.(b). It was the equivalent of a pledge or lien and was secured on the proceeds of sale. Thus the £40,000 did not count as part of the claimant's resources. See also *CIS 984/2002* which concerned money held by the claimant's solicitor pending quantification of the statutory charge to the Legal Services Commission under s.10(7) of the Access to Justice Act 1999. The Commissioner holds that this was not part of the claimant's capital until the charge had been quantified as until then it was not possible to identify any particular amount as the claimant's capital. He added that another way of looking at it was to treat the statutory charge as an incumbrance for the purpose of what is now para.(b).

In *R(IS) 5/98* the claimant transferred her flat to her daughter on the understanding that the daughter would care for her in the flat and pay off the mortgage. The daughter complied with the second condition, but evicted her mother from the flat. The Commissioner decides that the gift of the flat to the daughter had been subject to the condition that she looked after her mother. As that condition had not been fulfilled, the gift failed and the daughter held the property on trust for the claimant. In valuing the claimant's interest, the mortgage was to be deducted because the daughter was to be treated as subrogated to the rights of the mortgagee. In addition, the costs of the litigation to recover the property from the daughter also fell to be deducted. The claimant appealed against this decision to the Court of Appeal but her appeal was dismissed (*Ellis v Chief Adjudication Officer*, reported as part of *R(IS) 5/98*).

Calculation of capital outside the United Kingdom

2.505 **50.**—Capital which a claimant possesses in a country outside the United Kingdom shall be calculated—

(a) in a case in which there is no prohibition in that country against the transfer to the United Kingdom of an amount equal to its current market or surrender value in that country, at that value;

(b) in a case where there is such a prohibition, at the price which it would realise if sold in the United Kingdom to a willing buyer,

less, where there would be expenses attributable to sale, 10 per cent. and the amount of any incumbrance secured on it.

DEFINITION

"claimant"—see reg.2(1) and reg.23(1).

GENERAL NOTE

2.506 There had been problems under supplementary benefit in valuing overseas assets. Now the standard rules about the deduction of 10 per cent. for sale expenses and the deduction of the amount of any incumbrance secured on the asset apply. But then there are two separate situations. Under para.(a), if there is no prohibition in the country where the asset is located against transferring to the UK an amount of money equal to the asset's value in that country, the market value there is the test. *CH 4972/2002* confirms that under para.(a) it is the local market value that is taken, not the value that could be obtained by marketing the asset in the UK. If there are merely restrictions or delays in transfer this does not seem to come within para.(a). If there is such a prohibition, under para.(b) the value is the market value in the UK.

Notional capital

2.507 **51.**—(1) A claimant shall be treated as possessing capital of which he has deprived himself for the purpose of securing entitlement to income support or increasing the amount of that benefit [6 except—

(a) where that capital is derived from a payment made in consequence of any personal injury and is placed on trust for the benefit of the claimant; or

(b) to the extent that the capital which he is treated as possessing is reduced in accordance with regulation 51A (diminishing notional capital rule)] [15or

[31(c) any sum to which paragraph 44(2)(a) of Schedule 10 (capital to be disregarded) applies which is administered in the way referred to in paragraph 44(1)(a);

(d) any sum to which paragraph 45(a) of Schedule 10 refers.]]

(2) Except in the case of—

(a) a discretionary trust;

(b) a trust derived from a payment made in consequence of a personal injury; or

(c) any loan which would be obtainable if secured against capital disregarded under Schedule 10, [13 or

(d) a personal pension scheme [33 . . .],] [15 or

[29 (da) an occupational pension scheme [30 or a payment made by the Board of the Pension Protection Fund] where the claimant [39 has not attained the qualifying age for state pension credit]; or]

[32 (e) any sum to which paragraph 44(2)(a) of Schedule 10 (capital to be disregarded) applies which is administered in the way referred to in paragraph 44(1)(a); or

(f) any sum to which paragraph 45(a) of Schedule 10 refers,]]

any capital which would become available to the claimant upon application being made but which has not been acquired by him shall be treated as possessed by him but only from the date on which [1 it could be expected to be acquired were an application made.]

[2(3) [17 Any payment of capital, other than a payment of capital specified in paragraph (3A)], made—

(a) to a third party in respect of a single claimant or [23 his partner] (but not a member of the third party's family) shall be treated—

(i) in a case where that payment is derived from a payment of any benefit under the benefit Acts, [25 a payment from the Armed Forces and Reserve Forces Compensation Scheme,] a war disablement pension [14, war widow's pension [22 or war widower's pension] or a pension payable to a person as a [27 widow, widower or surviving civil partner] under [36 . . .] any power of Her Majesty otherwise than under an enactment to make provision about pensions for or in respect of persons who have been disabled or who have died in consequence of service as members of the armed forces of the Crown,] as possessed by that single claimant, if it is paid to him, [23 or by his partner, if it is paid to his partner];

[18(ia) in a case where that payment is a payment of an occupational pension or [30, a pension or other periodical payment made under a personal pension scheme or a payment made by the Board of the Pension Protection Fund], as possessed by that single claimant or, as the case may be, by [23 the claimant's partner];]

(ii) in any other case, as possessed by that single claimant [23 or his partner] to the extent that it is used for the food, ordinary clothing or footwear, household fuel, rent [26. . .] for which housing benefit [21 is payable or] [8. . .] any housing costs to the extent that they are met under regulation 17(1)(e) and 18(1)(f) (housing costs) [21 . . .] of that single claimant or, as the case may be, [23 of his partner] [8, or is used for any [10council tax] or water charges for which that claimant or [23 partner is liable]];

[23 (b) to a single claimant or his partner in respect of a third party (but not in respect of another member of his family) shall be treated as possessed by that single claimant or, as the case may be, his partner, to the extent that it is kept or used by him or used by or on behalf of his partner.]].

[17(3A) Paragraph (3) shall not apply in respect of a payment of capital made—

(a) under [38 or by] the Macfarlane Trust, the Macfarlane (Special Payments) Trust, the Macfarlane (Special Payments) (No.2) Trust, the Fund, the Eileen Trust [37 , MFET Limited] [24, the Independent Living [35 Fund (2006)] [28, the Skipton Fund [41, the Caxton Foundation] or the London Bombings Relief Charitable Fund]];

(b) pursuant to section 2 of the Employment and Training Act 1973 in respect of a person's participation—

(i) in an employment programme specified in regulation 75(1)(a)(ii) of the Jobseeker's Allowance Regulations 1996;

(ii) in a training scheme specified in regulation 75(1)(b)(ii) of those Regulations; or

[20(iia) in the Intensive Activity Period specified in regulation 75(1)(a)(iv) of those Regulations [34 . . .]; or]

(iii) in a qualifying course within the meaning specified in regulation 17A(7) of those Regulations.]

(iv) [*Omitted.*]

[40(ba) in respect of a person's participation in [42 a scheme prescribed in regulation 3 of the Jobseeker's Allowance (Schemes for Assisting Persons to Obtain Employment) Regulations 2013] or the Mandatory Work Activity Scheme;]

[19(c) under an occupational pension scheme [30, in respect of a pension or other periodical payment made under a personal pension scheme or a payment made by the Board of the Pension Protection Fund] where—

(i) a bankruptcy order has been made in respect of the person in respect of whom the payment has been made or, in Scotland, the estate of that person is subject to sequestration or a judicial factor has been appointed on that person's estate under section 41 of the Solicitors (Scotland) Act 1980;

(ii) the payment is made to the trustee in bankruptcy or any other person acting on behalf of the creditors; and

(iii) the person referred to in (i) and [23 his partner (if any)] does not possess, or is not treated as possessing, any other income apart from that payment.]

(4) Where a claimant stands in relation to a company in a position analogous to that of a sole owner or partner in the business of that company, he shall be treated as if he were such sole owner or partner and in such a case—

(a) the value of his holding in that company shall, notwithstanding regulation 46 (calculation of capital), be disregarded; and

(b) he shall, subject to paragraph (5), be treated as possessing an amount of capital equal to the value or, as the case may be, his share of the value of the capital of that company and the foregoing provisions of this Chapter shall apply for the purposes of calculating that amount as if it were actual capital which he does possess.

(5) For so long as the claimant undertakes activities in the course of the business of the company, the amount which he is treated as possessing under paragraph (4) shall be disregarded.

(6) Where a claimant is treated as possessing capital under any of paragraphs (1) to (4), the foregoing provisions of this Chapter shall apply for the purposes of calculating its amount as if it were actual capital which he does possess.

[1(7) For the avoidance of doubt a claimant is to be treated as possessing capital under paragraph (1) only if the capital of which he has deprived himself is actual capital.]

[2(8) In paragraph (3) the expression "ordinary clothing or footwear" means clothing or footwear for normal daily use, but does not include school uniforms, or clothing or footwear used solely for sporting activities].

AMENDMENTS

1. Income Support (General) Amendment Regulations 1988 (SI 1988/663) reg.22 (April 11, 1988).
2. Income Support (General) Amendment No.4 Regulations 1988 (SI 1988/1445) reg.12 (September 12, 1988).
3. Income Support (General) Amendment No.4 Regulations (SI 1988/1445) Sch.1 para.4 (April 10, 1989).
4. Income Support (General) Amendment Regulations 1989 (SI 1989/534) Sch.1 para.7 (October 9, 1989).
5. Income-related Benefits Schemes Amendment Regulations 1990 (SI 1990/127) reg.3 (January 31, 1990).
6. Income Support (General) Amendment No.3 Regulations 1990 (SI 1990/1776) reg.5 (October 1, 1990).
7. Income-related Benefits Schemes and Social Security (Recoupment) Amendment Regulations 1991 (SI 1991/1175) reg.5 (May 11, 1991).
8. Income Support (General) Amendment No.4 Regulations 1991 (SI 1991/1559) reg.8 (August 5, 1991).
9. Income-related Benefits Schemes and Social Security (Recoupment) Amendment Regulations 1992 (SI 1992/1101) reg.6 (May 7, 1992).
10. Income-related Benefits Schemes (Miscellaneous Amendments) Regulations 1993 (SI 993/315) Sch. para.3 (April 1, 1993).
11. Social Security Benefits (Miscellaneous Amendments) (No.2) Regulations 1993 (SI 1993/963) reg.2(3) (April 22, 1993).
12. Income-related Benefits Schemes and Social Security (Recoupment) Amendment Regulations 1993 (SI 1993/1249) reg.4(3) (May 14, 1993).
13. Income-related Benefits Schemes and Social Security (Claims and Payments) (Miscellaneous Amendments) Regulations 1995 (SI 1995/2303) reg.6(5) (October 2, 1995).
14. Income-related Benefits and Jobseeker's Allowance (Miscellaneous Amendments) Regulations 1997 (SI 1997/65) reg.9 (April 7, 1997).
15. Income-related Benefits and Jobseeker's Allowance (Amendment) (No.2) Regulations 1997 (SI 1997/2197) reg.5(4) (October 6, 1997).
16. Social Security Amendment (New Deal) Regulations 1997 (SI 1997/2863) reg.17(5) and (6)(e) (January 5, 1998).
17. Social Security Amendment (New Deal) (No.2) Regulations 1998 (SI 1998/2117) reg.3(2) and (3)(c) (September 24, 1998).
18. Social Security Amendment (Notional Income and Capital) Regulations 1999 (SI 1999/2640) reg.2(1)(a) (November 15, 1999).
19. Social Security Amendment (Notional Income and Capital) Regulations 1999 (SI 1999/2640) reg.2(3)(c) (November 15, 1999).
20. Social Security Amendment (New Deal) Regulations 2001 (SI 2001/1029) reg.15(8) and (9)(c) (April 9, 2001).
21. Social Security Amendment (Residential Care and Nursing Homes) Regulations 2001 (SI 2001/3767) reg.2(1) and Pt I of Sch. para.8 (April 8, 2002).
22. Social Security (Miscellaneous Amendments) Regulations 2002 (SI 2002/841) reg.2(3) (April 8, 2002).
23. Social Security (Working Tax Credit and Child Tax Credit) (Consequential Amendments) Regulations 2003 (SI 2003/455) reg.2 and Sch.1 para.13 (April 6, 2004, except in "transitional cases" and see further the note to reg.17 of the Income Support Regulations).
24. Social Security (Miscellaneous Amendments) (No.3) Regulations 2004 (SI 2004/2308) reg.3(1) and (2)(a) (October 4, 2004).
25. Social Security (Miscellaneous Amendments) Regulations 2005 (SI 2005/574) reg.2(5) (April 4, 2005).
26. Social Security (Miscellaneous Amendments) Regulations 2005 (SI 2005/574) reg.3(4) (April 4, 2005).

27. Social Security (Civil Partnership) (Consequential Amendments) Regulations 2005 (SI 2005/2878) reg.4(3) (December 5, 2005).

28. Income-related Benefits (Amendment) (No.2) Regulations 2005 (SI 2005/3391) reg.2(3) (December 12, 2005).

29. Social Security (Miscellaneous Amendments) (No.2) Regulations 2005 (SI 2005/2465) reg.2(5) (April 6, 2006).

30. Social Security (Miscellaneous Amendments) Regulations 2006 (SI 2006/588) reg.2(3) (April 6, 2006).

31. Social Security (Miscellaneous Amendments) Regulations 2007 (SI 2007/719) reg.2(4)(a) (April 2, 2007).

32. Social Security (Miscellaneous Amendments) Regulations 2007 (SI 2007/719) reg.2(4)(b) (April 2, 2007).

33. Social Security (Miscellaneous Amendments) (No.3) Regulations 2007 (SI 2007/1749) reg.2(7) (July 16, 2007).

34. Social Security (Miscellaneous Amendments) Regulations 2008 (SI 2008/698) reg.2(7)(b) (April 14, 2008).

35. Social Security (Miscellaneous Amendments) (No.6) Regulations 2008 (SI 2008/2767) reg.2(6) (November 17, 2008).

36. Social Security (Miscellaneous Amendments) (No.7) Regulations 2008 (SI 2008/3157) reg.2(4) (January 5, 2009).

37. Social Security (Miscellaneous Amendments) (No.2) Regulations 2010 (SI 2010/641) reg.2(3)(d) (April 6, 2010).

38. Social Security (Miscellaneous Amendments) (No.2) Regulations 2010 (SI 2010/641) reg.2(7)(c) (April 6, 2010).

39. Social Security (Miscellaneous Amendments) (No.2) Regulations 2010 (SI 2010/641) reg.2(8) (April 6, 2010).

40. Social Security (Miscellaneous Amendments) (No.2) Regulations 2011 (SI 2011/1707) reg.4(6)(a) and (7) (August 5, 2011).

41. Social Security (Miscellaneous Amendments) (No.3) Regulations 2011 (SI 2011/2425) reg.7(6) (October 31, 2011).

42. Jobseeker's Allowance (Schemes for Assisting Persons to Obtain Employment) Regulations 2013 (SI 2013/276) reg.13(b) (February 12, 2013).

DEFINITIONS

"the Armed Forces and Reserve Forces Compensation Scheme"—see reg.2(1).
"the benefit Acts"—*ibid.*
"claimant"—see reg.2(1) and reg.23(1).
"family"—see SSCBA s.137(1).
"Intensive Activity Period for 50 plus"—see reg.2(1).
"the London Bombings Relief Charitable Fund"—*ibid.*
"the Mandatory Work Activity Scheme"—*ibid.*
"MFET Limited"—*ibid.*
"occupational pension"—*ibid.*
"payment"—*ibid.*
"personal pension scheme"—*ibid.*
"the Caxton Foundation"—*ibid.*
"the Eileen Trust"—*ibid.*
"the Fund"—*ibid.*
"the Independent Living Funds"—see reg.2(1).
"the Macfarlane (Special Payments) Trust"—*ibid.*
"the Macfarlane (Special Payments) (No.2) Trust"—*ibid.*
"the Macfarlane Trust"—*ibid.*
"the Skipton Fund"—*ibid.*
"water charges"—see reg.2(1).

General Note

See the note at the beginning of the annotation to reg.46 on distinguishing between actual and notional capital , and see below, under "*Deprivation*". 2.508

Paragraph (1)

In order for para.(1) to apply, only two elements must be proved by the decision-maker—that the person has deprived himself of actual capital (see para.(7)) and that his purpose was to secure entitlement to or increase the amount of income support. It is clear that the principles applied to these questions for supplementary benefit purposes are to be applied to para.(1) (*CIS 24/1988, CIS 40/1989* and *R(IS) 1/91*, although the first decision is in error in failing to note the crucial difference identified in the next sentence). There is now no discretion (the regulation says "shall," not "may"). This was thought to give rise to the problems mentioned at the end of the note to this paragraph under "*Diminishing capital*". These problems led to the insertion of reg.51A, applying a diminishing capital rule. Capital subject to that rule is excluded from reg.51(1) by sub-para.(b). 2.509

Sub-paragraph (a) excludes the operation of reg.51(1) where money derived from compensation for personal injury is placed on trust for the claimant. Sub-paragraphs (c) and (d) do the same in respect of funds held in court on behalf of a person that derive from damages for personal injury to that person. See also the notes to para.12 and paras 44–45 of Sch.10.

Note *CIS/2540/2004* which confirms that a finding by a tribunal that a claimant is to be treated as having notional capital is not binding in relation to a subsequent claim. Section 17 of the Social Security Act 1998 draws a distinction between a decision which by s.17(1) is made "final" and a finding of fact necessary to the decision which under s.17(2) is only conclusive for the purpose of further decisions to the extent that regulations so provide; no regulations providing for any such conclusive effect have been made in this context. A subsequent tribunal hearing an appeal against the refusal of income support when the claimant made a further claim was not therefore bound by the previous tribunal's finding on the issue of deprivation of capital but could consider the issue afresh.

Deprivation

Here the onus of proof is complicated by the relationship with the claimant's actual capital. Once it is shown that a person did possess, or received, an asset, the burden shifts to him to show that it has ceased to be a part of his actual capital, to be valued under reg.49 (*R(SB) 38/85*). Therefore, para.(1) can only come into play after these two stages have been passed, with the second stage depending on the claimant. If he cannot satisfactorily account for the way in which an asset or a sum of money which he says he no longer has was disposed of, the proper conclusion is that it remains a part of his actual capital. But if there is evidence as to where the money has gone, as there was in *WR v SSWP (IS)* [2012] UKUT 127 (AAC) where the claimant had made payments to each of her parents, the fact that the tribunal did not accept the claimant's explanations for the payments did not mean that the money remained the claimant's actual capital. Instead the claimant was to be treated as having notional capital and the diminishing capital rule in reg.51A applied from the date of the payments to her parents. 2.510

In *CIS 634/1992* the claimant was made bankrupt on November 29, 1990. Between November 29 and December 28, 1990, when he claimed income support the claimant divested himself of most of his capital. His trustee in bankruptcy was not appointed until April 1991. Under the Insolvency Act 1986 (subject to certain exceptions) a bankrupt's property does not vest in his trustee on the making of a bankruptcy order but only when the trustee is appointed. However, s.284 of the Insolvency Act 1986 makes any disposal of property or payment by a bankrupt between the presentation of a bankruptcy petition and the vesting of his estate in his trustee void (except with the consent or later ratification of the court). The claimant could not therefore in law deprive himself of any resources from November

29, onwards and para.(1) could not apply. However, since he had failed to give a satisfactory account of how he had disposed of his capital, he was to be treated as still possessing it (*R(SB) 38/85*). Thus he was not entitled to income support prior to the appointment of the trustee in bankruptcy because until then he possessed actual capital over the income support limit. See however *KS v SSWP (JSA)* [2009] UKUT 122 (AAC); [2010] AACR 3 in which Judge Mark agrees that the effect of s.284 of the Insolvency Act is that reg.51(1) cannot apply but disagrees that a bankrupt's capital remains his capital until the appointment of the trustee in bankruptcy. Judge Mark points out that a bankrupt cannot realise or use any part of his capital after a bankruptcy order has been made and that, subject to any order of the court, it will vest in his trustee in due course. Whether the capital remains his capital with a nil value or whether it ceases to be his capital at all (on which the Judge did not reach any firm conclusion), the result was that the claimant in that case had no capital, or no capital of any value, after the bankruptcy order had been made.

It is suggested, however, that *R(SB) 38/85* should not be taken as sanctifying the Department's common practice of requiring a claimant to produce receipts to substantiate his expenditure and of automatically treating him as still having the balance of his capital not covered by receipts. As the Commissioner in *CIS/515/2006* points out, it is inherently improbable that a claimant will be able to produce receipts for day to day expenditure, particularly in relation to a period sometimes several years in the past. The claimant should be asked to produce what records he does have and can be asked to explain any large or unusual payments. But to demand actual receipts for all expenditure, however small, particularly over a lengthy period is not reasonable. General conclusions should be drawn on the basis of the claimant's oral evidence and the documentary evidence that is available.

2.511 See also *KW v SSWP* [2012] UKUT 350 (AAC) in which lack of receipts for the claimant's alleged expenditure on sexual services was understandable, given the nature of that expenditure. The question as to whether this expenditure took place, and if so, how much, therefore came down to a question of credibility.

"Deprive" is an ordinary English word and is not to be given any special legal definition (*R(SB) 38/85, R(SB) 40/85*). The result is that a person deprives himself of a resource if he ceases to possess it, regardless of the reason for doing so or the fact that he receives some other resource in return. This is the clear assumption in *R(SB) 38/85* and is expressly decided in *R(SB) 40/85*. That decision holds that the approach in the *S Manual* (para.6042—set out on p.177 of the 2nd edition of J. Mesher, CPAG's *Supplementary Benefit and Family Income Supplement: the Legislation* (1985)), that a person had not deprived himself of a resource if he spent money or changed it into another form which is still available to him, was wrong. The effect is to put the main emphasis on the purpose of the deprivation.

However, this raises the question of the interaction of reg.51(1) with para.10 of Sch.10. Under para.10 the value of personal possessions is disregarded except those that have been acquired with the intention of reducing capital so as to gain entitlement to income support. This interaction was discussed in *CIS 494/1990* and has now been further explored in *R(IS) 8/04*. Both cases concerned the use of capital to buy a vehicle, for the purpose of securing entitlement to income support. In *CIS 494/1990* the Commissioner points out that the value of the vehicle will be considerably less than the purchase price and treats only this "depreciation" as notional capital under reg.51(1). He proceeded on the assumption that there was an immediate depreciation of £1,000. The Commissioner in *R(IS) 8/04* agrees that where capital is used, for a purpose caught by reg.51(1), to buy personal possessions, the value of the assets as actual capital must be taken into account in calculating the amount of notional capital under reg.51(1). It would be unfair to treat a claimant as still having all the capital used to buy the possessions and also as having the market value of the possessions. He acknowledges that the mechanism for reaching this result was not entirely clear as reg.51(1) and the exception in para.10 of Sch.10 appear to operate independently. However, he was satisfied that the general principle that actual capital should be looked at before notional capital supported the approach taken in *CIS 494/1990*. But he did not agree with *CIS 494/1990* that as the value of the car further depreciated over time there was a corresponding increase in the claimant's notional capital. The amount of the capital of which the claimant had deprived himself had to be fixed at the date of the deprivation, since it was only that amount to which the prohibited purpose in reg.51(1) could be attached. Any future depreciation could only fairly be said to result from the operation of the market and not from the claimant's original purpose to gain entitlement to benefit. The Commissioner added that the same principles would apply to other factors which resulted in a difference between the amount of capital spent on an asset and the amount to be taken into account for the asset as actual capital (e.g. the effect of expenses that would be incurred in selling the asset). See also under *Diminishing capital*, below.

2.512 It is arguable that a person cannot deprive himself of something which he has never possessed, but it may be that a deliberate failure to acquire an asset is also a deprivation. In *CSB 598/1987* it is suggested that a deliberate failure to pay a cheque into a bank account could be a deprivation. See also *CIS 1586/1997* which states that a sale at a known undervalue and the release of a debtor from a debt were capable of amounting to deprivation. However, a person does not deprive herself of an asset by failing to seek a lump sum payment or property transfer order under the Matrimonial Causes Act 1973, since the right to make an application under the Act is not a capital asset (*R(IS) 1/03*). Moreover, even if this had constituted deprivation, the claimant's reasons for not bringing proceedings (which included, inter alia, fear of her abusive husband) clearly indicated that her purpose had not been to secure entitlement to income support.

R(IS) 7/07 decides that the rule in para.(1) can apply to deprivations made by someone who only later becomes the claimant's partner. About a year before she became the claimant's partner Ms H, who was unemployed and who had been in receipt of JSA, sold her house. She used the proceeds of sale to, among other things, repay her daughter's debts of £30,000 (incurred when the daughter was a student) and to take her family on holiday. The tribunal found that in disposing of her capital Ms H had acted with the purpose of securing entitlement to income support. The Commissioner considered that this conclusion was one that was open to the tribunal to make on the evidence before it. He then went on to decide that the claimant was caught by the rule in para.(1) even though Ms H was not his partner at the time of the deprivation.

In his view the combined effect of s.134(1) and the enabling provision in s.136(5)(a) of the Contributions and Benefits Act is to treat a partner's deprivation of capital as a deprivation of the claimant, even though they were not a couple at the time. The focus of reg.51(1) is on the purpose of a past disposal but reg.51(1) operates at the time when entitlement is in issue so the reference to the claimant (which by virtue of reg.23(1) includes a reference to his partner) is a reference to the person's status at that time. The Comissioner states:

> "Both in aggregating the capital of the members of a family and in taking account of notional capital, the legislation fulfils an anti-avoidance function. If notional capital were not aggregated, a future partner could dispose of capital before coming to live with the claimant or couples could separate in order to dispose of capital before reuniting. . . . The notional capital rule will only apply to a future partner where there has been conduct that is related to future entitlement to benefit either for the person alone or as a member of a family. That will limit the circumstances in which the rule applies and restrict it to those cases in which a course of conduct has been directed at future benefit entitlement."

2.513 The Commissioner further held that although he was prepared to assume that art.8 ECHR was engaged in respect of both the claimant's family life and home the interference was authorised by art.8(2).

Although it is not made explicit in the decision, it would seem that the Commissioner (and the tribunal) must have taken the view that Ms H was at least contemplating becoming the claimant's partner at the time of the disposals because otherwise there was no basis for the finding that Ms H had deprived herself of capital for the purpose of securing entitlement to *income support* (there is no indication that as a single person she would qualify for income support since before she received the proceeds of sale of her house she had been in receipt of JSA). Under para.(1) the deprivation has to be for the purpose of securing entitlement to income support; contrast the position under the corresponding JSA regulation (reg.113(1) of the JSA Regulations 1996) which applies if the person has deprived herself of capital in order to secure entitlement to or increase the amount of JSA *or* income support. It is suggested that the decision should therefore be limited to such circumstances, that is where the parties may become a couple in the future. Moreover, this would seem to be in line with the Commissioner's view of when the rule will apply to a future partner (see above).

The decision in *R(IS) 7/07* was a refusal of leave to appeal by the Commissioner. The claimant applied for judicial review of the Commissioner's decision but his application was dismissed (*R. (on the application of Hook) v Social Security Commissioner and Secretary of State for Work and Pensions* [2007] EWHC 1705 (Admin) reported as part of *R(IS) 7/07*).

If the claimant's attorney appointed under the Enduring Powers of Attorney Act 1985 repays a loan or makes gifts of the claimant's capital this may amount to deprivation by the claimant, since the attorney is the agent of the claimant (*CIS 12403/1991*). In that case there was a question as to whether the loan was the responsibility of the claimant or the attorney and whether the gifts were allowable under s.3(5) of the 1985 Act which permits the making of gifts "provided that the value of each such gift is not unreasonable having regard to all the circumstances and in particular the size of the donor's estate". The Commissioner states that the new tribunal would have to consider whether the payments were properly made; if not, there would be a claim against the attorney which would constitute actual capital; if they were properly made the question of deprivation would have to be considered.

Purpose

(i) Knowledge of the capital limit

2.514 *CIS/124/1990* held that it must be proved that the person actually knew of the capital limit rule, otherwise the necessary deliberate intention to obtain benefit could not have been present. It is not enough that the person ought to have known of the rule. The crunch comes, and the resolution with the approach in *R(SB) 40/85* (where it was suggested that the existence of some limit might be said to be common knowledge), in the assessment of the evidence about the person's knowledge. The Commissioner stresses that the person's whole background must be considered, including experience of the social security system and advice which is likely to have been received from the family and elsewhere. The burden of proof is on the Secretary of State, but in some circumstances a person's assertion that they did not know of the rule will not be credible. In *CIS/124/1990* itself the claimant was illiterate and spoke and understood only Gujerati. The Commissioner says that this should put her in no better or worse situation than a literate claimant whose mother tongue was English, but that the possibility of misunderstandings in interpretation should be considered. *CIS/124/1990* is followed in *R(SB) 12/91*, where the necessity of a positive finding of fact, based on sufficient evidence, that the person knew of the capital limit is stressed. Evidence that the person had been in receipt of supplementary benefit or income support for some years was not in itself enough. But information which the person has received, together with his educational standing and other factors, will be material in deciding whether actual knowledge exists or not. *CIS/30/1993* similarly holds that it is not possible to infer actual knowledge of the capital limit simply from the claimant signing a claim form which contained that information. The claimant was partially sighted and had not completed the claim form herself but merely signed it. It was necessary for the tribunal to indicate what evidence satisfied it that the claimant did know of the capital limit.

Where a claimant has not previously claimed a means-tested benefit, nor made any inquiry about the conditions of entitlement, nor had any dealings with benefits, a specific finding that he knew of the capital limit is required (*LBC Waltham Forest v TM* [2009] UKUT 96 (AAC)).

(ii) The test for "purpose"

The decision-maker has to show that the person's purpose is one of those mentioned in para.(1). There is unlikely to be direct evidence of purpose (although there might be contemporary letters or documents), so that primary facts must be found from which an inference as to purpose can be drawn (*CSB 200/1985, R(SB) 40/85*). 2.515

The view put forward in *CSB 28/81* that the test is of the person's predominant purpose, is rejected in *R(SB) 38/85* and *R(SB) 40/85*. In *R(SB) 38/85* it was suggested that it was enough that a subsidiary purpose was to obtain supplementary benefit. In *R(SB) 40/85* the Commissioner says that this must be a "significant operative purpose." If the obtaining of benefit was a foreseeable consequence of the transaction then, in the absence of other evidence, it could be concluded that this was the person's purpose. This would exclude some cases caught by the width of the approach to deprivation, e.g. where a resource is converted into another form in which it is still taken into account. For then there would be no effect on eligibility for benefit. But beyond that situation there remain great difficulties. The Commissioners mention a number of relevant factors, e.g. whether the deprivation was a gift or in return for a service, the personal circumstances of the person (e.g. age, state of health, employment prospects, needs), whether a creditor was pressing for repayment of a loan. It must be an issue of fact when these other factors indicate that the reasonably foreseeable consequence of obtaining benefit was not a significant operative factor. A tribunal is not entitled to infer that the claimant had the relevant purpose simply from rash and excessive expenditure with some knowledge of some sort of capital limit—it has to go further and consider whether on its assessment of the claimant's character and thinking this is what happened (*CH/264/2006*, a case on the equivalent housing benefit provision). As *R(H) 1/06* (another case on the equivalent housing benefit provision) confirms, the test is a subjective one, which depends upon the evidence about the particular claimant in question (the claimant in that case was a schizophrenic whose mental state was such that he was unlikely to fully appreciate the implications of his behaviour and had limited capacity to plan for the future). See also *KW v SSWP (IS)* [2012] UKUT 350 (AAC) in which the claimant spent £40 to £100 a day of his inheritance on "one or two females out of four doing some fetish things for me". The claimant had a personality disorder and may not have appreciated the potential implications of his behaviour.

R(H) 1/06 is followed in *CIS/218/2005*. The claimant in *CIS/218/2005* had made large gifts to her children from the proceeds of the sale of her former matrimonial home. The Commissioner states that whether a gift is reasonable or prudent, although relevant, does not answer the question of whether it was made for the purpose of securing or increasing entitlement to income support. The test is not one of reasonableness or prudence but what has to be considered is the claimant's purpose. On the other hand, in *CJSA/1425/2004* the fact that it was reasonable for the claimant to pay his credit card debts in order to avoid further liability for interest led to the conclusion that this had not been done for the purpose of obtaining or increasing entitlement to income-based JSA (*CJSA/1425/2004* is discussed further below).

The length of time since the disposal of the capital may be relevant (*CIS 264/1989*). 2.516

Where the claimant had been warned about the consequences of a transaction by the local DSS office (i.e. that reg.51(1) would be applied) and still went ahead, this showed that he could not have as any part of his purpose securing of entitlement, or continued entitlement, to income support (*CIS 621/1991*).

The effect of DWP advice on the claimant's intention is further considered in *LH v SSWP (IS)* [2014] UKUT 60 (AAC). The claimant received £54,000 from an endowment policy. She did not inform the DWP at the time because she thought that since the policy had been set up to pay the mortgage it did not count as capital. However, she was not required to use the money to pay off her mortgage and so she used part of it to pay other debts which charged a higher rate of interest. When she was later visited by a DWP officer, she sought advice from him about the impact on her income support entitlement of using the proceeds from the policy to pay off her debts before meeting her mortgage liability. He informed her that it was reasonable and acceptable to pay off outstanding loans and debts before using the remainder to pay off part of the mortgage, as long as she did not spend the money on, for example, exotic holidays. The officer did not advise the claimant that she would be able to secure entitlement to income support if she used the remaining excess capital in the way she was doing, nor was this the advice sought by the claimant. After the visit she continued to use the proceeds of the policy to pay her debts before paying off part of the mortgage.

2.517 Judge Wright emphasises that the effect of the advice depends on precisely what advice is sought, and given, and its context. He disagrees with the obiter remarks made in *CIS/307/1992* that advice given would of itself nullify any finding of adverse intention under para.(1) and thus insulate a claimant from being caught by para.(1). In his view (again obiter), if a claimant sought advice from the DWP in relation to disposal of capital, e.g. an inheritance, and was wrongly advised that it would not affect his entitlement, arguably securing or retaining entitlement to income support would have been the significant operative purpose behind the disposal of the capital. On the other hand, if the claimant was being taken to court over debts, the advice given would not change the position that staying on benefit was not a "significant operative purpose", the main motivation being to pay the debts.

Judge Wright concluded that the claimant's disposal of the capital after the DWP visit was not made with the "significant operative purpose" of securing entitlement to income support. In his view, it was reasonable for the claimant to use the proceeds of the policy to pay debts which she could not meet in any other way and which would avoid greater indebtedness than if they had not been paid off. These were actions she had taken before the DWP officer's visit and planned to take after the visit, regardless of the consequences for her entitlement to income support, albeit that the remarks of the visiting officer reassured her that taking such steps was appropriate and either would not, or was unlikely to, affect her entitlement to income support. The tribunal had erred by failing to adequately investigate the effect of the DWP's advice and by focusing on whether the debts were immediately repayable, rather than the reasons *why* the claimant used the proceeds of the policy in the way that she did.

In effect, the test seems to be whether the person would have carried out the transaction at the same time if there had been no effect on eligibility for benefit. Similarly, where the transaction had no effect on the claimant's entitlement, as in *CJSA/3937/2002* where the property transferred was the house in which the claimant was living (which was therefore disregarded under para.1 of Sch.8 to the JSA Regulations 1996), an intention to secure entitlement to income-based JSA was not shown. The onus of proof on the Secretary of State may come into play in marginal cases.

2.518 A number of other decisions have firmed up the principles to be applied.

The Commissioner in *R(SB) 9/91* stresses that a positive intention to obtain benefit must be shown to be a significant operative purpose. It is not enough for the AO merely to prove that the obtaining of benefit was a natural consequence of the transaction in question. The claimant had transferred her former home to her two daughters. Evidence was given that her sole intention was to make a gift to her daughters, as she intended to leave the property to them in her will and it was no longer of any use to her (she being permanently in need of residential nursing care). The Commissioner notes that this did not explain why the transfer was made when it was, why the proceeds of sale of the property would not have been of use to the claimant and what she thought she would live on if she gave the property away. She had been in receipt of supplementary benefit for several years. On the evidence the obtaining of benefit was a significant operative purpose. As *CJSA 1395/2002* confirms, *R(SB) 9/91* thus endorses the attribution of an intention to a claimant by implication from all the circumstances but the conclusion must be in terms of the claimant's purpose, not in terms of the natural consequences of the transaction in question. See *R(H) 1/06* (applied in *CIS/218/2005*) referred to above, which reiterates that it is necessary for a tribunal to determine the claimant's actual (i.e. subjective) intention.

In *CIS 242/1993*, another case where the claimant had gone into residential care, the Commissioner reaches the opposite conclusion on the facts to that in *R(SB) 9/91*. The claimant's son had cared for his mother for 15 years. When she went into a residential care home, she gave her share of the proceeds of sale of their jointly owned home to her son to be used towards the purchase of his flat. The Commissioner accepts that she had relinquished her share in gratitude to her son and not to secure income support.

In *R(IS) 13/94* the claimant's capital was in excess of the statutory limit when he purchased his council house. The deposit used up enough of his capital to bring him below the limit. It was necessary to consider whether para.(1) applied to this use of the capital since the claimant was apparently dependent on income support to meet the mortgage interest. But in *R(IS) 15/96* using a criminal injuries compensation award to pay off part of a mortgage was not caught by para.(1). The SSAT had found that the claimant's purpose had been to secure his future and to reduce the burden on the DSS for his mortgage payments. This was a matter for the judgment of the tribunal. 2.519

A further example is *CJSA 204/2002.* The claimant had agreed to provide the deposit for a flat that she and her son would buy. In the event the claimant did not move into the new flat with her son and his girlfriend because of a disagreement but she still lent her son the deposit. The claimant did correspond with her solicitor about obtaining security for the loan but no formal agreement or legal charge was entered into. The Commissioner holds that the claimant clearly had reasons for keeping her promise to lend the deposit (for example, so as not to let her son down or sour relations further) and in his view there had been no deprivation within reg.51(1). See also *R(IS) 1/03* above.

In *CIS 109/1994* and *CIS 112/1994* the claimants had used their capital to purchase an annuity and a life insurance policy respectively. In *CIS 109/1994* the claimant was both physically and mentally frail and lived in a nursing home. The tribunal found that at the material time she had no knowledge of the income support capital and deprivation of capital rules, and entered into the transaction on her son's advice, who considered that this was the best use of her capital to enable her to stay in the nursing home. The Commissioner holds that the tribunal had not erred in concluding that she had not purchased the annuity in order to obtain income support. In *CIS 112/1994* the Commissioner decides that para.(1) did apply, but that para.15 of Sch.10 applied to disregard the life policy. The Commissioner also deals with "double counting" of notional and actual capital (see below under "*Diminishing capital*"). See also *R(IS) 7/98* where capital had been used to purchase an "investment bond". The Commissioner decides that the bond fell within the definition of "policy of life insurance" in reg.2(1) and so could be disregarded under para.15 of Sch.10. But the claimant's intention at the time of the investment had to be considered to see whether para.(1) applied.

In *R(SB) 12/91* Commissioner Rice held that if capital is used to repay debts which are immediately repayable, then that could not be said to be for the purpose of obtaining benefit (see para.13). In *R(SB) 12/91* there were doubts whether the alleged debts, to members of the family, were legally enforceable debts and whether they were owed by the claimant personally. But the fact that a debt is not legally enforceable and/or immediately repayable does not mean that repayment of it must be for the purpose of securing income support. As *CJSA 1395/2002* points out, what the Commissioner said in *R(SB) 12/91,* at para.14 was that in such circumstances "the question will arise" of whether the securing of benefit or an increased amount was a significant operative purpose. It is still necessary to consider the claimant's purpose in repaying the debt (*CIS 2627/1995, Jones v Secretary of State for Work and Pensions* [2003] EWCA Civ 964). In *Jones* the Court of Appeal emphasises that the issue as to whether or not repayment of a debt was for the purpose of obtaining income support was a question of fact to be determined according to the circumstances in each case. Thus, even if a debt was not immediately repayable, this did not necessarily mean that its repayment was made in order to obtain income support. Conversely (and more rarely) there could be cases where repayment of an immediately repayable debt was for the purpose of securing entitlement to income support—an example might be where the debtor thought the creditor would not call in the debt for some time but still made immediate repayment. It was a question of fact in each case. *London Borough of* 2.520

Waltham Forest v TM [2009] UKUT 96 (AAC) recognises that a claimant's financial predicament and possible insolvency may alone be the reason for the repayment.

The facts in *Jones* were unusual. The claimant and her husband had sold some land and used the money to pay off a number of their many debts. One of those debts was for £17,000 which was owed to a friend, Mr S. The claimant's husband and Mr S came to an arrangement whereby the claimant purchased a BMW car for £13,500 as security for this debt. The car was to be Mr S's property but he allowed the claimant and her husband full use of it on the basis that they paid all the running costs. The issue was whether the claimant's significant operative purpose in entering into this arrangement was the retention of entitlement to income support.

2.521 The Court of Appeal held that since the tribunal had accepted that the car belonged to Mr S, the effect of the transaction had been that the debt to Mr S had been repaid. The fact that Mr S was content for the money to be used to buy him a car was irrelevant, as was the fact that Mr S was content for the claimant and her husband to use the car. On the facts Mr S had been pressing for repayment of the debt and so the claimant had not deprived herself of capital for the purpose of securing entitlement to income support. However, even if the true position was that the claimant had not repaid Mr S and the car was hers, it was subject to a charge by way of security in favour of Mr S for £17,000 and so under reg.49(a)(ii) the charge had to be deducted from the value of the car (with the result that its value was nil). It could not be said that in creating the charge on the car the claimant had deprived herself of capital for the purpose of securing entitlement to income support since clearly this was the only way the claimant could secure use of the car and if the arrangement had not been made the claimant and her husband would have had to repay the £17,000 loan.

The question of whether a claimant who has used capital to repay debts is caught by para.(1) and in particular to what extent does it matter that the creditor is not pressing for payment, was revisited in *VW v SSWP (IS)* [2015] UKUT 51 (AAC); [2015] AACR 39. The claimant had repaid her ex-partner £7,000 on the same day that she had been visited by a DWP compliance officer. She later supplied more details about the loan, together with a letter from her ex-partner stating that he had asked for the money to be returned because he himself had debts and his working hours had been reduced and there was a chance that he would lose his job altogether. Judge Rowland stated:

> "11. It is quite common for it to be argued that a debt is not immediately repayable if the creditor is not pressing for payment. However, it is clear from both *R(SB) 12/91* and from what Dyson LJ said in *Jones* that that is not terminologically accurate. All debts are immediately repayable unless there is a mutual agreement to the contrary, as in the examples given by Mr Commissioner Rice in paragraph 14 of *R(SB) 12/91*. On the other hand, as Dyson LJ makes clear, even where a debt is immediately repayable, a debtor who believes that the creditor will not call it in for some time is in the same position vis-à-vis regulation 51 as he or she would be if the debt were not immediately repayable.
>
> 12. Moreover, Dyson LJ also makes it clear that the fact that a debt *is not* immediately repayable or a creditor *is not* calling in an immediately repayable debt, is not decisive against the claimant for the purpose of regulation 51. Schiemann LJ mentioned the person who pays off a bank overdraft. In *CJSA/1425/2004*, I considered the position of a person who had paid off credit card debts and held that the payment had not been for the purpose of obtaining income-related jobseeker's allowance.
>
> 13. But, what if a creditor *is* calling for repayment of an immediately repayable debt? It is clear from the Court of Appeal's decision that it is a question of fact whether a claimant paying such a debt thereby deprives himself or herself of capital for the purpose of securing entitlement to income support or increasing the amount of that benefit, rather than it being an inevitable legal consequence that that is not the purpose of the deprivation. To that extent, the Court disagreed with Mr Commissioner Rice. However, this disagreement may be more one of

legal theory than of practical significance. Dyson LJ said that "the fact-finder will not usually conclude that, in making the payment, the debtor's purpose was to secure an entitlement to income support, rather than simply to repay the debt" and none of the Judges suggested any circumstance in which it would be reasonable to say that a person who had no choice but to repay a debt was caught by regulation 51(1) as a result of the repayment."

Judge Rowland concluded that, although the compliance officer's visit may have precipitated the repayment of the loan, the debt had to be paid and the claimant had no *legitimate* choice but to repay it immediately; the repayment had not therefore been made for the purpose of obtaining income support.

CJSA/1425/2004, referred to in *VW v SSWP*, had concerned payment of credit card debts. The claimant had been made redundant and claimed JSA three months later. His claim was initially processed as a claim for contribution-based JSA only but was later "reviewed" and income-based JSA was awarded from the date of the initial claim. Between the date of the initial claim and the application for "review" the claimant paid £6,000 to three credit card accounts and £3,000 to his mother. The Commissioner accepts that the timing of the payments indicated that the claimant knew that this would reduce his capital to a level that would entitle him to benefit and that this was one purpose of the payments. However it did not follow that the claimant did not intend to pay the credit card bills in order to settle his debts and avoid the interest that would otherwise be charged on them. If the claimant had mixed motives, the question whether the purpose of obtaining benefit was a significant operative purpose had to be determined by deciding whether it was reasonable for the claimant to act in the way that he did. In the Commissioner's view, the threat of having to make high-interest payments was just as capable of making it reasonable to pay a debt as the threat of enforcement of a liability to pay. He considered that any other view would be contrary to public policy as expressed in s.94 of the Consumer Credit Act 1974 which entitles a debtor under a regulated consumer credit agreement to discharge his indebtedness at any time. The plain purpose of that provision was to allow a debtor to escape further interest payments. The Commissioner commented that it "would be anomalous if the benefit system were to require people to incur additional liability for interest. I can see no reason why the benefit system should treat differently a person who has just cleared his debts to avoid them growing and a person who never had any debts". He therefore concluded that payment of the credit cards debts was reasonable and was for the purpose of avoiding further substantial liabilities for interest payments and not for the purpose of obtaining or increasing entitlement to income-based JSA. However, the Commissioner did not find it reasonable for the claimant to have repaid his mother (the appellant's own evidence to the tribunal had been that "[i]t wasn't a loan but I felt obliged to give it back when she asked") and that this had been done for the purpose of increasing entitlement to income-based JSA.

However, in *CH/264/2006* the Commissioner disagrees with the approach of *CJSA/1425/2004* because in his view it "erroneously converts an evidentiary factor of reasonableness into a legal test and a subjective test of purpose into an objective test of reasonableness". Certainly as other decisions, for example *R(H) 1/06* and *CIS/218/2005*, have emphasised, correctly it is suggested, the test is one of the claimant's purpose, rather than whether the disposal/expenditure was reasonable or prudent, although reasonableness is a relevant factor. To the extent, therefore, that the Commissioner in *CJSA/1425/2004* considered that the reasonableness of the claimant's actions was determinative, his decision would seem to be out of step with the other authorities. He has, however, reiterated his view in *JM v SSWP* [2009] UKUT 145 (AAC). It was from the test of reasonableness of the expenditure that one inferred whether the claimant intended to gain entitlement to benefit or merely knew that that would be the consequence of the expenditure. A person who knows of the capital limit must be taken to realise that benefit may be payable if he disposes of capital above that limit and to intend that consequence if the expenditure was unreasonable. 2.522

SH v London Borough of Tower Hamlets (HB) [2011] UKUT 500 (AAC), however, agrees with the criticism of *CJSA/1425/2004* in *CH/264/2006*. In *SH v LB Tower Hamlets* Judge Mark also disagrees with Judge Rowland's comments in *JM v SSWP*. In his view, such presumed intention is not the same as purpose. A person may act unreasonably in a way that could foreseeably lead to impoverishment but that did not mean that she acted "for the purpose of securing entitlement" to benefit. Making an unreasonable judgment or simply not thinking about the consequences did not mean that the person had acted for the purpose of obtaining benefit. The obtaining of benefit had to be a positive part of the person's planning.

CIS 40/1989 provides an interesting example on its facts of the securing or increase of benefit not being a significant operative purpose. The claimant had been on supplementary benefit and then income support since 1978. Her father died intestate. The estate consisted almost entirely of a house in which the claimant's sister had lived with the father. The claimant and her sister were the sole beneficiaries of the estate. Legal proceedings had to be taken to enforce a sale of the house. In March 1988 the claimant received £38,000 net of costs, which her solicitor divided equally between the claimant, her son, her daughter and her grand-daughter. After repaying a number of debts and buying a secondhand car, the amount possessed by the claimant quickly fell below £6,000. The tribunal found that she should be treated as still possessing the amounts given to her children and grandchild. The Commissioner, having heard the claimant give evidence and be cross-examined, accepted that her purpose was to carry out her father's wishes, which were that the house should be used to provide for his grandchildren and great-grandchildren. She had originally intended to take nothing, but had been encouraged by her children to take a quarter share. She knew of the capital limit, but did not know of the effect her actions would have on her benefit entitlement. On these particular facts, the Commissioner found that para.(1) did not apply. See also *CJSA 1395/2002* in which the claimant considered herself under a moral obligation to give £10,000 to her mother, brother and sister after her grandmother had made the claimant the sole beneficiary under her will, allegedly to spite the rest of the family.

2.523 In many cases of alleged deprivation of capital there will have been a course of spending, often on various items, and sometimes over a considerable period of time. In *R(H) 1/06* (a case on the equivalent housing benefit provision), the Commissioner emphasises the need to go through all the various items of expenditure, taking account of any explanations put forward by the claimant, and to reach a specific determination as to: (i) what amounts (if any) represent deprivation of capital in excess of a reasonable level of general expenditure in the claimant's circumstances; and as regards *those* (ii) what had been the claimant's purpose at the time and whether this included an intention to obtain benefit. The tribunal had erred in simply expressing its decision in generalised terms without attempting to analyse the movements on the claimant's account during the relevant period. *CIS/1775/2007* makes the same point. The tribunal had been wrong to treat all payments as having been made with the same motivation but should have considered each type of expenditure separately when applying the significant operative purpose test.

There may be a problem in the transfer from the corresponding supplementary benefit regulation (Resources Regulations reg.4(1)). Regulation 51(1) only mentions income support. What if a person deprived himself of capital in December 1987, thinking only of supplementary benefit. On a claim for income support, can he be caught by reg.51(1)? In *CIS 259/1990* (which was to be reported as *R(IS) 8/91*, but was withdrawn from reporting) the Commissioner accepts that the purpose must be to secure or increase income support, but held that the claimant in March 1987 knew enough about the effect of depleting her resources on her means-tested benefit for her purpose to satisfy reg.51(1). The Commissioner found that the claimant was aware that the existing means-tested benefit was to be replaced by another means-tested benefit (although the evidential basis for this finding does not appear). There was an appeal to the Court of Appeal, but the decision was set aside by consent. In *R(IS) 14/93* the Commissioner does not accept the reliance in *CIS 259/1990* on the enactment of the Social Security Act 1986 well before the income support scheme came into operation. He holds that a provision of a statute has no legal existence until it comes into force. Therefore, when in that case the claimant in November/December 1987, divested himself of capital he could not have done it with the intention of obtaining income support, because at that time it did not exist. Nor can the words "income support" be taken to refer to means-tested benefits which previously went under the name of supplementary benefit. This approach has the merit of not making the result depend on the vagaries of the particular claimant's advance knowledge of the nature of the income support reforms in April 1988.

Note that the corresponding regulation under JSA (reg.113(1) of the JSA Regulations 1996) applies if a person has deprived himself of capital in order to secure entitlement to or increase the amount of JSA *or income support*. That avoids the question that might otherwise have arisen on a claimant transferring from income support to JSA as to whether a deprivation which had only been for the purposes of income support could be caught by reg.113(1). Similarly the ESA deprivation rule (reg.115(1) of the ESA Regulations 2008—see Vol.I in this series) applies if a person has deprived himself of capital in order to secure entitlement to, or increase the amount of, ESA *or income support or JSA*. But para.(1) has not been amended along those lines. Note, however, that reg.42(1) has been amended (but only from October 31, 2011) so that it now applies if a person has deprived himself of income in order to secure entitlement to, or increase the amount of, income support, *JSA or ESA*.

Effect of bankrupty on the notional capital rule

In *London Borough of Waltham Forest v TM* [2009] UKUT 96 (AAC) the claimant used the proceeds of sale of a property to repay loans to three family members three months before he was made bankrupt. The issue was whether any resulting notional capital that the claimant was found to have for the purposes of his housing benefit claim was part of his estate as a bankrupt. It is held that since by definition the claimant does not possess the capital but is only deemed to do so for the purposes of entitlement to benefit, notional capital is not part of a bankrupt's estate as defined in the Insolvency Act 1986. Thus the application of the notional capital rule was not affected by the claimant's bankruptcy. *KS v SSWP(JSA)* [2009] UKUT 122 (AAC); [2010] AACR 3 agrees with *London Borough of Waltham Forrest v TM* where the deprivation occurs before a bankruptcy order is made. After the making of the order, however, a claimant cannot deprive himself of capital for the purposes of para.(1) (see under *"Deprivation"* at the beginning of this note). Judge Mark goes on to suggest that if a claimant presents a petition, or possibly fails to resist a petition presented by a creditor, and is declared bankrupt as a result, he may be found to have deprived himself of capital if he has taken this step (or not opposed the petition) for the purpose of securing entitlement to benefit. The capital he would have deprived himself of would be the capital he was entitled to after taking into account what he would have to pay to avoid bankruptcy. This is unlikely to be much in most circumstances. 2.524

Diminishing capital

There were problems from the removal of discretion in the shift to income support. Under the Supplementary Benefit (Resources) Regulations this was used in particular for two purposes. One was to avoid double counting with the rule about personal possessions, now contained in para.10 of Sch.10. The value of personal possessions is not disregarded if they were acquired with the intention of reducing capital so as to gain entitlement to benefit. With no discretion at either end a claimant could have the market value of the possessions counted as part of his actual capital and the money he spent on them counted as notional capital under this paragraph. The Commissioner in *CIS 494/1990* avoided this problem by treating only the shortfall between the market value of the personal possessions from time to time and the purchase price (the "depreciation") as the notional capital to be imputed under reg.51(1). This is followed in part in *R(IS)8/04*. The Commissioner 2.525

in *R(IS)8/04* agrees that only the shortfall should be treated as notional capital but does not agree that the notional capital should be deemed to increase over time in line with the reduction in the market value of the asset. In his view the amount of the capital of which the claimant had deprived himself had to be fixed at the date of the deprivation, since it was only that amount to which the prohibited purpose in reg.51(1) could be attached. Any future depreciation could only fairly be said to result from the operation of the market and not from the claimant's original purpose to gain entitlement to benefit. It would also seem to be difficult to combine such an increase with the diminishing capital rule under reg.51A.

In *CIS 112/1994* the Commissioner had also recognised the gross unfairness to a claimant if she were to be penalised twice because of the lack of discretion in reg.51(1). In the Commissioner's view this was not the intention of the regulation. But in that case double counting did not arise. The claimant had purchased a life insurance policy with a legacy. Although she was to be treated as still possessing the notional capital by virtue of reg.51(1), the actual capital (the life policy) could be disregarded under para.15 of Sch.10.

The second problem for which the use of discretion was useful was that it was unfair to fix a claimant with an amount of notional capital for eternity. If he had still had the capital and not been entitled to benefit, he would have had to use up the capital for living expenses. Thus the figure of notional capital could be reduced by the equivalent of the weekly benefit lost by the capital counting (*R(SB) 38/85, R(SB) 40/85*). There had seemed no possibility of such a process applying to reg.51(1) until the decision of the Tribunal of Commissioners in *R(IS) 1/91*. The Tribunal concluded that the diminishing capital rule did apply. This is because para.(6) provides that regs 45–50 apply to the calculation of notional capital as if it was actual capital. If a claimant has capital over the prescribed limit, reasonable expenditure on living and other sensible expenses (not necessarily limited to income support rates) will reduce the amount of capital until it falls below the limit. He will then be entitled to income support. The same situation is held to apply where it is notional capital, rather than actual, which is held initially. The decision is wrong in principle, because if actual capital is held, the actual amount, reduced by any expenditure, must be considered week by week. This is not a consequence of any of regs 45–50 and there is no analogy with the notional reduction of notional capital. Paragraph (6) is primarily concerned with the calculation of the market value of assets. Nonetheless, *R(IS) 1/91* must be followed in relation to weeks before October 1, 1990.

With effect from October 1, 1990, reg.51A provides an express diminishing notional capital rule. *R(IS) 9/92* decides that while the principles of *R(IS) 1/91* apply up to that date, they do not apply thereafter. They are superseded by the rules laid down in reg.51A. See also *CIS 3268/2002*, discussed in the notes to reg.51A, as to the date when the rule in reg.51A comes into play and as to the position before that rule operates. *R(IS)8/04* confirms that reg.51A only applies if the claimant is not entitled to income support or entitled to a reduced amount of income support because of notional capital; it does not operate if for example his actual capital exceeds the prescribed limit (see further the notes to reg.51A). In that case his actual capital can reduce by the amount of his expenditure, using inferences in the fact-finding process if necessary (*CIS/2287/2008*).

Paragraph (2)

2.526 It is not at all clear what sort of capital would be caught by this rule. It must be available simply on application, with no other conditions, but not amount to actual capital (cf. *R(SB) 26/86* and *R(SB) 17/87*). Examples might be money held in court which would be released on application or arrears of employer's sick pay which needed to be applied for. Note the exclusions. Although discretionary trusts are specifically excluded, a potential beneficiary would not seem to be caught by para.(2) anyway. More than an application is needed for payment to be made: the discretion has to be exercised. On sub-paras (d) and (da) see the note to reg.42(2)(g) and (2ZA)–(2CA). On sub-paras (e) and (f) see the notes to paras 44 and 45 of Sch.10.

In *LC v Bournemouth Borough Council (HB)* [2016] UKUT 175 (AAC) Judge White applies reg.49(2) of the Housing Benefit Regulations 2006 (the equivalent of para.(2)) in a case where the proceeds of sale of a former matrimonial home were being held in a solicitors' client account until the claimant's partner and his ex-wife agreed how the sum was to be split. The claimant stated that it would be necessary to go to court to reach a settlement and that was likely to take between eight months and a year. The local authority had jumped the gun by treating the claimant as having capital in excess of £16,000 from the date that the proceeds of sale were placed in the client account. The local authority should make an assessment of the likely period it would take for a Financial Dispute Resolution hearing to be concluded and advise the claimant that the local authority would regard her as having capital above £16,000 from that date. Judge White also held that reg.51 of the Housing Benefit Regulations (the equivalent of reg.52) did not apply in these circumstances (see the notes to reg.52).

Paragraphs (3) and (3A)

Note that if the conditions are met, there is no discretion whether or not to apply para.(3). In this respect, as in others, *R(SB) 6/88* would be decided differently under income support. **2.527**

Paragraph (3)(a) applies where payments are made to a third party in respect of the claimant or any partner. (The form of this provision in force before April 6, 2004, and which remains in force for "transitional cases"—see the note to reg.17, also applied if payments were made to a third party in respect of any child or young person who was a member of the claimant's family. However, with effect from April 6, 2004 (except in "transitional cases"—see the note to reg.17) amounts for children and young persons were removed from the income support scheme (financial support for children and young persons was from then on to be provided through the child tax credit system, see Vol. IV in this series) and income support became in effect an "adults only" benefit. Thus the current form of para.(3)(a) only applies to payments made to a third party in respect of the claimant or his partner, if any.)

If the payment is derived from a benefit or pension listed in head (i) it counts as the claimant's. From November 15, 1999 this also applies to a payment from an occupational or personal pension (head (ia)), but not if the payment is made to the trustee in bankruptcy (or other person acting on the creditors' behalf) of a person who is bankrupt (or the subject of sequestration) and he (and his partner (before April 6, 2004, and still in "transitional cases"—see the note to reg.17, his family)) has no other actual or notional income (para.(3A)(c)). See *R(IS) 4/01* in the note to reg.42(4) and (4ZA) on the effect of head (ia). From April 6, 2006 head (ia) and para.(3A)(c) also apply to payments from the Pension Protection Fund ("PPF"). The PPF has been set up under the Pensions Act 2004 to provide protection for members of an occupational pension scheme in the event of their employer's insolvency.

In other cases the payment counts as the claimant's in so far as it is actually used for food, ordinary clothing or footwear, fuel, housing costs met by income support or housing benefit, council tax or water charges (head (ii)). "Ordinary clothing or footwear" is defined in para.(8). Paragraph 29867 of the *Decision Makers Guide* suggests that wellington boots are not for "normal daily use", nor are special shoes needed because of a disability (as these are not worn by people in general on a daily basis). **2.528**

If the payment is used for items or costs other than those listed in head (ii), it does not form part of the claimant's capital. However, *CJSA 1458/2002* holds that the exclusion from capital in head (ii) will not apply and money used for other items or costs will count as the claimant's if the money is paid to a third party at the claimant's own direction. The facts in *CJSA 1458/2002* were that the claimant had devised a scheme whereby rent from his tenant was paid into a particular account to be used "(either directly or indirectly) in respect of any of the landlords costs relating to the premises and (either directly or indirectly) in respect of any of the landlords mortgage capital repayments". The account into which the money was paid was a PEP (which the claimant had tried to open in the name of his mortgagee but had found this to be impossible in law). The Commissioner confirms the tribunal's decision that the claimant's deliberate failure to acquire an asset was a deprivation caught by para.(1). The claimant also contended that the payments into the PEP were excluded from his capital under head (ii) because they were being used for capital repayments on his mortgage. However, the tribunal had rejected this argument on the ground that the payments were not made to a third party but into an investment vehicle that was beneficially owned by the claimant. The Commissioner agreed with that analysis but stated that he would also reach the same result by another route, namely that the money was paid to the third party at the claimant's own direction and therefore the exclusion from capital in para.(3)(a) was not applicable. However, with respect to the Commissioner, it is suggested that there is nothing in the wording of para.(3)(a) that requires such an interpretation. Furthermore, it would seem to depart from the approach previously taken to this provision (and its income counterpart in reg.42(4)(a)(ii)), since it has long been recognised that the rules about payments to third parties do allow for some "benefit planning", as a means of meeting expenditure that is not covered by income support.

The operation of para.(3)(b) is clear. In these circumstances the payment would not form part of the claimant's actual capital in view of the obligation to use it for a third party.

Paragraph (3) does not apply to payments from the listed Trusts and Funds, nor to payments made in respect of an 18–25 year-old on a "New Deal" option or a person in the Intensive Activity Period (IAP) of the New Deal (these schemes are no longer offered), nor to payments to a person aged 25 or over who is undertaking a "qualifying course" (see the note to reg.17A of the JSA Regulations 1996), or a person who is participating in the Mandatory Work Activity Scheme or a scheme listed in reg.3 of the Jobseeker's Allowance (Schemes for Assisting Persons to Obtain Employment) Regulations 2013 (para.(3A)). For the equivalent notional income disregard see reg.42(4ZA).

Paragraphs (4) and (5)

2.529 These two paragraphs establish an artificial method of dealing with one person companies or similar. The basic legal position is that if there is a company, the shareholders' assets are the value of the shares, not the value of the company's assets (*R(SB) 57/83*). But under para.(4), if the claimant is in a position analogous to a sole owner or partner in the business of the company (on which, see *R(IS) 8/92*), the value of his shareholding is disregarded, and he is treated as possessing a proportionate share of the capital of the company. The value is the net worth of the company's total assets taken together (*R(IS) 13/93*). The value of one particular asset within the total is not relevant in itself. However, as long as the claimant undertakes activities in the course of the business of the company, the amount produced by para.(4) is disregarded (para.(5)). Temporary interruptions in activity (e.g. holidays, short-term sickness) ought not to prevent para.(5) from applying. It is accepted in *R(IS) 13/93* that any activities which are more than de minimis satisfy para.(4). See also *R(IS) 14/98* discussed in the note to para.6 of Sch.10.

Paragraph (6)

2.530 One of the effects of para.(6) is that the disregards in Sch.10 can apply to notional capital. However, *CIS 30/1993* decides that the disregard in para.26 of Sch.10 (taking steps to dispose of premises) could not apply where the claimant had already disposed of the capital so as to trigger para.(1). Paragraph (6) did not provide any authority for altering the provisions of Sch.10 which could only apply where their conditions were met. This is a different view from that taken in some other decisions. See the note to para.26 of Sch.10.

CIS 231/1991 confirms that it is not necessary for the disregard under Sch.10 to have been applicable before the claimant deprived himself of the capital. The claimant had transferred his former home to his parents who were both over 60. When he claimed income support his parents were living in the home. The

Commissioner holds that the former home fell to be disregarded under para.4(a) of Sch.10; the disregard in para.4 applied to notional, as well as actual, capital.

Paragraph (7)

The capital of which a person has deprived himself must be actual capital. In *CIS 240/1992* and *CIS 30/1993* the Commissioner raises the question (without expressing a conclusion) as to whether para.(1) can apply when a claimant is deemed to possess an equal share in a capital asset under reg.52. In *CIS 240/1992* the claimant had a quarter share in a property, but the effect of reg.52 was to treat him as having a halfshare. The claimant's parents (his mother owned the other three-quarters of the property) then bought his share for £5,000, out of which he repaid them loans of £3,883. The Commissioner points out that as reg.52 operated to treat the claimant as having a notional equal share in the property, his actual share should not also count, since otherwise there would be double counting. Therefore, when he sold his actual share to his parents, was there no disposal of *actual* capital at all, or no disposal to the extent that his notional share exceeded his actual share? Paragraph 29809 of the *Decision Makers Guide* assumes that the rule in para.(1) can only apply to the claimant's actual share of the capital, even though the effect of reg.52 is to deem him to own a larger share. But this does not entirely deal with the Commissioner's point. In fact in *CIS 240/1992*, since the property was subject to a tenancy, even if under para.(1) the claimant was treated as still possessing his actual interest, the disregard in para.5 of Sch.10 (as in force at that time) would result in him having no capital. The new tribunal would also have to consider whether para.(1) applied when the claimant repaid the loans (see *R(SB) 12/91* above). 2.531

[[1]Diminishing notional capital rule

51A.—(1) Where a claimant is treated as possessing capital under regulation 51(1) (notional capital), the amount which he is treated as possessing— 2.532

(a) in the case of a week that is subsequent to—

(i) the relevant week in respect of which the conditions set out in paragraph (2) are satisfied, or

(ii) a week which follows that relevant week and which satisfies those conditions,

shall be reduced by an amount determined under paragraph (2);

(b) in the case of a week in respect of which paragraph (1)(a) does not apply but where—

(i) that week is a week subsequent to the relevant week, and

(ii) that relevant week is a week in which the condition in paragraph (3) is satisfied,

shall be reduced by the amount determined under paragraph (3).

(2) This paragraph applies to a benefit week or part week where the claimant satisfies the conditions that—

(a) he is in receipt of income support; and

(b) but for regulation 51(1), he would have received an additional amount of income support in that benefit week or, as the case may be, that part week;

and in such a case, the amount of the reduction for the purposes of paragraph (1)(a) shall be equal to that additional amount.

(3) Subject to paragraph (4), for the purposes of paragraph (1)(b) the condition is that the claimant would have been entitled to income support in the relevant week, but for regulation 51(1), and in such a case the amount of the reduction shall be equal to the aggregate of—

(a) the amount of income support to which the claimant would have been entitled in the relevant week but for regulation 51(1); and for the purposes of this sub-paragraph if the relevant week is a part-week that amount shall be determined by dividing the amount of income support to which he would have been so entitled by the number equal to the number of days in the part-week and multiplying the quotient by 7;

(b) the amount of housing benefit (if any) equal to the difference between his maximum housing benefit and the amount (if any) of housing benefit which he is awarded in respect of the benefit week, within the meaning of regulation 2(1) of [4 the Housing Benefit Regulations 2006] (interpretation), which includes the last day of the relevant week;

(c) [6 . . .]

[2(d) the amount of council tax benefit (if any) equal to the difference between his maximum council tax benefit and the amount (if any) of council tax benefit which he is awarded in respect of the benefit week which includes the last day of the relevant week, and for this purpose "benefit week" [7 means a period of 7 consecutive days beginning on a Monday and ending on a Sunday].]

(4) The amount determined under paragraph (3) shall be redetermined under that paragraph if the claimant makes a further claim for income support and the conditions in paragraph (5) are satisfied, and in such a case—

(a) sub-paragraphs [3(a) to (d)] of paragraph (3) shall apply as if for the words "relevant week" there were substituted the words "relevant subsequent week"; and

(b) subject to paragraph (6), the amount as re-determined shall have effect from the first week following the relevant subsequent week in question.

(5) The conditions are that—

(a) a further claim is made 26 or more weeks after—

(i) the date on which the claimant made a claim for income support in respect of which he was first treated as possessing the capital in question under regulation 51(1); or

(ii) in a case where there has been at least one re-determination in accordance with paragraph (4), the date on which he last made a claim for income support which resulted in the weekly amount being re-determined; or

(iii) the date on which he last ceased to be in receipt of income support;

whichever last occurred; and

(b) the claimant would have been entitled to income support but for regulation 51(1).

(6) The amount as re-determined pursuant to paragraph (4) shall not have effect if it is less than the amount which applied in that case immediately before the re-determination and in such a case the higher amount shall continue to have effect.

(7) For the purpose of this regulation—

(a) "part-week" means a period to which sub-section (1A) of section 21 of the Act [SSCBA, s.124(5)] (amount etc. of income support) applies;

(b) "relevant week" means the benefit week or part-week in which the capital in question of which the claimant has deprived himself within the meaning of regulation 51(1)—

(i) was first taken into account for the purpose of determining his entitlement to income support; or

(ii) was taken into account on a subsequent occasion for the purpose of determining or re-determining his entitlement to income support on that subsequent occasion and that determination or re-determination resulted in his beginning to receive, or ceasing to receive, income support;

and where more than one benefit week or part-week is identified by reference to heads (i) and (ii) of this sub-paragraph the later or latest such benefit week or, as the case may be, the later or latest such part-week;

(c) "relevant subsequent week" means the benefit week or part-week which includes the day on which the further claim or, if more than one further claim has been made, the last such claim was made.]

AMENDMENTS

1. Income Support (General) Amendment No.3 Regulations 1990 (SI 1990/1776) reg.6 (October 1, 1990).
2. Income-related Benefits Schemes (Miscellaneous Amendments) Regulations 1993 (SI 1993/315) Sch. para.4 (April 1, 1993).
3. Social Security (Miscellaneous Amendments) (No.3) Regulations 2001 (SI 2001/859) reg.6(2) (April 9, 2001).
4. Housing Benefit and Council Tax Benefit (Consequential Provisions) Regulations 2006 (SI 2006/217) reg.5 and Sch.2 para.1(3) (March 6, 2006).
5. Housing Benefit and Council Tax Benefit (Consequential Provisions) Regulations 2006 (SI 2006/217) reg.5 and Sch.2 para.1(4) (March 6, 2006).
6. Social Security (Miscellaneous Amendments) (No.6) Regulations 2008 (SI 2008/2767) reg.2(8) (November 17, 2008).
7. Council Tax Benefit Abolition (Consequential Provision) Regulations 2013 (SI 2013/458) reg.4 and Sch.2 para.1 (April 1, 2013).

DEFINITIONS

"benefit week"—see reg.2(1).
"claimant"—*ibid.*

GENERAL NOTE

See the note to reg.51(1) for the general background. Regulation 51A provides for the reduction of the amount of notional capital fixed by reg.51(1). If the amount of notional capital remaining is not sufficient to remove entitlement to income support altogether, it is to be treated as reducing each week by the amount by which income support would be increased if it did not exist at all (paras (1)(a) and (2)). If the amount does remove entitlement it is to be treated as reducing each week by the amount of income support the person would receive if the notional capital had not been fixed plus the proportion of rent and council tax not met by housing benefit or council tax benefit (paras (1)(b) and (3)). There are complicated provisions for redetermination and recalculation. 2.533

Note that the reduction required by reg.51A does not start to operate until there is a week in which the claimant either would have been in receipt of income support (para.(3)) or would have been in receipt of an increased amount of income support (para.(2)) *but for* reg.51(1). Thus in *R(IS)8/04*, where the claimant had used capital to purchase a car for the purpose of securing entitlement to income support and it seemed likely that the value of the car (once this was established) would result in his actual capital exceeding the then prescribed limit of £8,000, reg.51A did not apply to reduce his notional capital. This was because it could not be said that "but for" the notional capital he would have been in receipt of income support.

The inter-relationship of this regulation, which ties the reduction in notional capital very much to income support rates, and *R(IS) 1/91* is of considerable difficulty. The Tribunal of Commissioners' diminishing capital rule works on reasonable expenditure not necessarily limited to income support rates. Could a claimant take the benefit of this more generous rule, or had its implication from the regulations been destroyed by the introduction of this express provision? *R(IS) 9/92* holds that the second alternative is correct.

Another pertinent issue is the date from which the diminishing notional capital rule applies. If reg.51A only operates from the date of the claim for income support, as its terms imply and as *CIS 3268/2002* confirms, it would seem unfair for some equivalent diminishing notional capital rule not to apply to amounts of notional capital during any gap between the date of the intentional deprivation and the claim for income support. This point is considered in *CIS 3268/2002*. However, the Commissioner concludes that in many cases it is a "red herring". This is because expenses such as living and household expenses which could be taken into account in applying a diminishing notional capital rule will often have already been taken into account in calculating the amount of actual capital of which a claimant deprived himself. If such expenses have already been taken into account there is no justification for making any further deduction from the amount of the notional capital. The Commissioner recognises that there may be a problem where a claimant has deprived himself of the entire amount of his actual capital in one transaction and then does not claim income support for some time. However, this did not arise on the facts of the case before him.

Capital jointly held

2.534 **52.**—Except where a claimant possesses capital which is disregarded under regulation 51(4) (notional capital), where a claimant and one or more persons are beneficially entitled in possession to any capital asset they shall be treated as if each of them were entitled in possession [[1]to the whole beneficial interest therein in an equal share and the foregoing provisions of this Chapter shall apply for the purposes of calculating the amount of capital which the claimant is treated as possessing as if it were actual capital which the claimant does possess.]

Amendment

1. Social Security Amendment (Capital) Regulations 1998 (SI 1998/2250) reg.2 (October 12, 1998).

Definition

"claimant"—see reg.2(1) and reg.23(1).

General Note

2.535 This regulation was amended on October 12, 1998 following the decision in *CIS 15936/1996, CIS 263/1997* and *CIS 3283/1997* (see the common Appendix). In that decision the Commissioner held that the October 1995 amendment to the regulation was ultra vires (see also *CIS 2575/1997* below). The October 1995 amendment had provided that the value of a claimant's actual or deemed share of jointly-owned capital was to be calculated by dividing the net value of the capital as a whole by the number of co-owners. The aim of that amendment had been to reverse the effect of the Court of Appeal's decision in *Chief Adjudication Officer v Palfrey and others,* reported as part of *R(IS) 26/95* (see below). See the 1998 edition of J. Mesher and P. Wood, *Income-related Benefits: the Legislation* for the October 1995 form of reg.52. The Government decided not to appeal against the decision in *CIS 15936/1996, CIS 263/1997* and *CIS 3283/1997* but (somewhat unusually) to restore the form of the regulation that existed before October 2, 1995. A similar amendment was made to the JSA Regulations 1996, the Family Credit Regulations and Disability Working

Allowance Regulations (both now revoked), the Housing Benefit Regulations and the Council Tax Benefit Regulations.

The result, broadly, is that there is no double "deeming" under this regulation. The first "deeming" remains, i.e. joint owners are still deemed to have equal shares in the property (although see the Court of Appeal's decision in *Hourigan* under "*Scope of the rule*" below for the limited meaning of joint-owner in this context). But the second, that the value of the share was to be "deemed" by reference to the value of the property as a whole, does not. Thus instead of attributing what could be a totally artificial value to the deemed (or actual) share, it will, following *Palfrey*, have to be given its true market value. This, together with the Court of Appeal's decision in *Hourigan*, will have the effect of mitigating the worst effects of this rule in certain cases but it will still have arbitrary and unfair consequences for some claimants.

The basis of the Commissioner's decision in *CIS 15936/1996*, *CIS 263/1997* and *CIS 3283/1997* was that the October 1995 amendment was outside the powers in s.136(3) and (5)(a) of the Contributions and Benefits Act 1992. He held that the power in s.136(3) to provide for the calculation or estimation of capital did not allow assets to be valued in a way that had no relationship to their actual value. In addition, s.136(5)(a) did not authorise the amendment because the amendment was concerned with valuation, not the actual capital or income which a person did or did not possess. In *CIS 2575/1997* the Commissioner confirms that his decision in *CIS 15936/1996*, *CIS 263/1997* and *CIS 3283/1997* equally applies to land outside the UK and to all forms of co-ownership.

The decision in *CIS 15936/1996*, *CIS 263/1997* and *CIS 3283/1997* was given on May 21, 1998. The guidance to AOs on the effect of this decision expressed the view that it could not be applied for any period before May 21, 1998 because of s.69 of the Administration Act 1992 (the "anti-test case rule"). However, it is by no means certain that s.69 was applicable in cases of ultra vires regulations. There is indeed provision for this in s.27(5) of the Social Security Act 1998 (which has replaced s.69) but s.69 was silent on the matter. Given the nature of ultra vires declarations, it is certainly arguable that in the absence of an express provision, s.69 did not apply in this situation. The Commissioner in *CIS 2575/1997* refers to but does not rule on this question, although he does draw attention to *CA 73/1994* which apparently held that s.69 did bite on an ultra vires decision by a Commissioner. **2.536**

As has been suggested to me by Nick Wikeley, there was another complication arising out of the Government's decision to restore the pre-October 1995 form of reg.52. Because JSA was not introduced until October 7, 1996, there was no pre-October 1995 formulation to which the parallel JSA provision (reg.115 of the JSA Regulations) could revert. Since the effect of the decision in *CIS 15936/1996*, *CIS 263/1997* and *CIS 3283/1997* was to remove the last part of reg.115, it followed that there was no sensible provision dealing with the valuation of jointly-owned assets for the purposes of JSA at least from May 21, 1998 (and possibly from the commencement of the JSA scheme if an ultra vires decision was not caught by s.69) until the 1998 amendment came into force on October 12, 1998.

The validity of reg.52 had also been challenged before the Tribunal of Commissioners in *R(IS) 26/95 (Palfrey)* on the ground of irrationality. But the Commissioners held, given their ruling on valuation under reg.52, that irrationality had not been made out and that reg.52 was validly made. The Court of Appeal in *Palfrey* did not express a view as to whether reg.52 was invalid, as this argument only became relevant if the CAO's construction of reg.52 was correct; nor did the Court of Appeal in *Hourigan*.

Scope of the rule

Previous editions of J. Mesher and P. Wood, *Income-related Benefits: the Legislation* have described this regulation as containing an extraordinary rule (a view endorsed in *CIS 408/1990*). In *CIS 807/1991* the rule is described as draconian. In the words of Brooke LJ in *Hourigan* (see below): "The intention of this statutory scheme is that people should be expected to dip into their capital rather than be reliant on the state **2.537** for income support. Why should Parliament have expected people to dip into capital which they did not in fact possess?" Shared interests in assets had caused difficult problems of valuation under supplementary benefit. The intention of reg.52 was to provide a solution which is simple to apply, but the conceptual difficulties posed are formidable.

The intended effect of reg.52 is that except in the case of deemed ownership of a company's assets under reg.51(4), if the claimant has any share of the beneficial interest (i.e. the right to dispose of something) in an asset he is treated as having an equal share in the interest, regardless of the legal and equitable position. ("In possession" means that ownership is enjoyed at present, rather than on the happening of some event in the future.) Thus if a person has a 10 per cent interest in a house, and another person has a 90 per cent interest, each is treated as having a 50 per cent. interest. There are many situations in which such a division might occur. The same could apply to, say, joint bank accounts or Building Society accounts. The result could easily be, in conjunction with the rules on disregards in Sch.10, that a claimant is fixed with capital assets which he is not legally entitled to at all, let alone able to realise immediately. Normally the claimant's "remedy" for the artificial effects of reg.52 would be to dispose of his share in the asset, when he will receive an amount appropriate to his actual legal share. But this will not always be possible. The deprivation rule in reg.51(1) should not apply in these circumstances: see reg.51(7) and the note to that paragraph and para.29809 of the *Decision Makers Guide*.

However, doubt as to the ambit of reg.52 was raised as a result of the decision in *CIS 7097/1995*. The claimant's husband went to live in a nursing home on a permanent basis. In order to help finance the cost of this, £7,000 National Savings belonging to him was cashed in and paid into their joint bank account. It was never intended that this should thereby become part of the joint money in the account; it had simply been paid into the account so that the nursing home fees could be paid by direct debit. A separate tally was kept of this money which had been declared as the husband's own money for the purposes of his application to the local authority for help with the nursing home fees. The AO treated the claimant as entitled to half of the balance in the joint account (including her husband's National Savings) which when added to her other capital meant that she did not qualify for income support. However, the Commissioner holds that reg.52 did not apply to her husband's National Savings. Regulation 52 only operated where property was held in joint beneficial ownership because it was only then that two or more people were "beneficially entitled in possession" to a given capital asset. Regulation 52 was needed because of the special nature of joint beneficial ownership and deemed a joint beneficial owner to have the equal share that he would by law have if the joint ownership was severed. But cases where property was held in undivided shares fell outside reg.52 because under such an arrangement each co-owner was beneficially and individually entitled to his own share of the actual capital. His share was a different asset from the shares belonging to the others; and in contrast to the joint right of a joint owner was an asset which was separately disposable by him. On the facts of this case, there was clear evidence that the normal presumption of joint beneficial ownership between a husband and wife operating a joint bank account did not apply. It was obviously intended that the balance of the husband's National Savings was to remain his sole property and that it had merely been paid into the joint account for convenience. The consequence was that the claimant was entitled to income support as her capital did not include any of her husband's National Savings. See also *JK v SSWP (JSA)* [2010] UKUT 437 (AAC); [2011] AACR 26 in the note to reg.46 under "*Claimant holding as trustee*".

2.538 The question whether reg.52 also applies to deem actual unequal shares in a capital asset to be equal shares was, as the Commissioner in *CIS 7097/1995* points out, expressly reserved by the Tribunal of Commissioners in *CIS 417/1992*, reported as part of *R(IS) 26/95*, and there was no argument on the point before the Court of Appeal. But it was considered, albeit briefly, in *CIS 240/1992*. In that case the claimant and his mother were tenants in common of a property, the claimant's share being one quarter. The Commissioner accepted that a situation where a claimant had an unequal share of the beneficial interest fell within the scope of reg.52, so that the claimant was to be treated as having a half-share in the property. See also *CIS 127/1993*. Moreover, in *CIS 15936/1996*, *CIS 263/1997* and *CIS 3283/1997* the Commissioner expressly dissents from any general statement in *CIS 7097/1995* that reg.52 was confined to joint tenancies. In his view, reg.52 applied to all kinds of co-ownership, including joint tenancies and tenancies in common. He repeats this view in *CIS 2575/1997*.

Clearly the policy intention is that reg.52 has effect beyond the fairly limited role of deeming a person to have an equal share of a capital asset that is in joint beneficial ownership. However, the Secretary of State's contention that reg.52 does also apply to tenancies in common was unanimously rejected by the Court of Appeal in *Hourigan v Secretary of State for Work and Pensions* [2002] EWCA Civ 1890, reported as *R(IS) 4/03* (which was the appeal from *CIS 5906/1999*). The claimant had purchased her home from the local authority with the help of her son who contributed five-sixths of the purchase price. When she went into a residential care home her income support was stopped on the basis that she had capital in excess of the prescribed limit because she was deemed to be the beneficial owner of half the house under reg.52.

Brooke LJ accepted that the language of reg.52 lent itself naturally to the situation in which two or more people were jointly entitled to the equitable interest in the same capital asset since they did not each possess a separate share in the equitable interest. In that situation the effect of reg.52 was to treat the joint tenancy as severed and to deem the claimant as having an equal share (with the other joint tenants) of the whole beneficial interest. However, in relation to tenancies in common, there was no need for such a deemed severing as the beneficial interest that a tenant in common owned was a separately disposable asset. It was a misuse of language to say that the claimant and her son were beneficially entitled to the house within the meaning of reg.52 as they were not. To interpret the provision in the way contended for by the Secretary of State would require very much clearer words. The Court acknowledged that a crude deeming of equal apportionment where property is jointly-owned could produce unjust results, not only against claimants but also in some cases in their favour, as it could in the case of a tenancy in common. Its approach therefore was to restrict the manifest unfairness that could result from reg.52 to the situation where its wording clearly did apply, that is in relation to property held in joint beneficial ownership. The consequence was that it was the claimant's one sixth share that fell to be valued with the result that she did not have capital in excess of the prescribed limit.

The Secretary of State decided not to apply for leave to appeal to the House of Lords against the decision in *Hourigan*. Thus the consequence is that it has now been authoritively established that reg.52 only applies to property held under a joint tenancy, not a tenancy in common. **2.539**

Note that reg.52 only applies where the beneficial interest is jointly-owned. It does not apply merely because there is a separation between legal and beneficial interests, for instance where one person holds assets on trust for another. But if an interest in a trust fund is jointly-owned, then reg.52 may apply.

Former matrimonial assets

Thus reg.52 was held to apply in *R(IS)2/93*, where a building society account in the claimant's sole name was in fact a joint asset of herself and her (separated) husband. She had to be treated as possessing half of the amount in the account, regardless of how it might be dealt with in matrimonial proceedings. But it is arguable that in the case of assets that are the subject of matrimonial (or other) dispute, reg.52 should not apply and their value should be disregarded, until ownership is resolved. See *Welfare Rights Bulletin* 108 p.5, referring to *CIS 298/1989* (a decision given without reasons). This should apply whether or not a couple were married. However, note *CIS 982/2002* which states that there is no general rule that property which is frozen or the subject of a dispute is to be disregarded or taken as having no **2.540** value. The claimant and her husband, from whom she was separated, had a savings account in their joint names. The account was subject to a "matrimonial difficulties stop", the effect of which was that the claimant had no access to the funds without her husband's consent or an order from the court. The decision sets out a number of detailed questions that had to be considered in deciding whether the funds in the account were part of the claimant's capital and, if so, how her share was to be valued.

But in *LC v Bournemouth Borough Council (HB)* [2016] UKUT 175 (AAC) Judge White holds that reg.51 of the Housing Benefit Regulations 2006 (the equivalent of reg.52) does not apply to the proceeds of sale held by a solicitor in a client account which could only be distributed with the agreement of the parties, or in accordance with an order of the court. This was because it could not be said that such funds constituted a capital assert to which the two parties were "beneficially entitled in possession". Judge White had doubts as to whether reg.51 applied to disputed matrimonial property at all.

Where the claimant has no legal title, joint or otherwise, to a property, but only an equitable interest by virtue of the Matrimonial Causes Act 1973 which she could realise in divorce or judicial separation proceedings, this is not a capital asset (*R(IS) 1/03*). And note *R(IS) 1/97*, discussed in the note to para.5 of Sch.10, which decided that the claimant's wife, who had remained living in the former matrimonial home of which he was the sole legal owner, was a tenant for life under a constructive trust and so his interest could be disregarded under para.5.

Valuation under regulation 52

2.541 The restoration of reg.52 to its original form on October 12, 1998 means that it is the deemed equal share that has to be valued, *not* the proportionate share of the overall value that has to be taken (see the Court of Appeal's decision in *Chief Adjudication Officer v Palfrey*, reported as part of *R(IS) 26/95*, which had upheld the Tribunal of Commissioners' decisions in *CIS 391/1992* and *CIS 417/1992* (reported as part of *R(IS) 26/95*). The Tribunal of Commissioners gave detailed guidance as to the basis of a proper valuation of such a share (*CIS 391/1992*, paras 53 and 54). In both *CIS 391/1992* and *CIS 417/1992* ownership was shared with relatives who were unable or unwilling to sell the property or buy the claimant's interest. The Commissioners recognised, as did the Court of Appeal, that the market value in such cases may well be nil.

See J. Mesher and P. Wood, *Income-related Benefits: the Legislation* (1995) for a summary of the Tribunal of Commissioners' decision and the Court of Appeal's decision in *Palfrey*. See also *CIS 413/1992* which notes the differences that arise from the law of property in Scotland. In *Palfrey* the Tribunal of Commissioners state that the SSAT should have exercised its inquisitorial jurisdiction to call for the documents under which the property was acquired in order to sort out the beneficial ownership. But in *CIS 127/1993* the Commissioner did not find this necessary, since it was not disputed that the house had been conveyed into the names of the claimant and her daughter, and the method of valuation was the same whether the claimant and her daughter actually had equal shares or were deemed to do so by reg.52.

Note *R(IS) 3/96* which contains a useful discussion as to whether the District Valuer's opinion supplied in that case met the requirements of *CIS 391/1992*. The guidance to decision makers suggests that they should obtain an expert opinion on the market value of a deemed share in land/premises. In a case where the other owners will not buy the share or agree to a sale of the asset as a whole, the guidance states that the valuer should not simply assume that a court would order a sale but must consider the particular circumstances and take into account legal costs, length of time to obtain possession, etc. The guidance also says that the expert would need to explain whether on the facts of the case there was any market for the deemed share and indicate how the value of the deemed share had been calculated.

2.542 However, in practice, it seems that the valuations obtained do not always meet such criteria (as noted in *CIS 3197/2003*, see below). See, for example, *R(JSA)*

1/02 which was concerned with valuing the claimant's interest in his former matrimonial home. His wife, from whom he was separated and who was in ill-health, continued to live there with their daughter, who had learning difficulties. The valuation obtained by the Jobcentre on a standard form (A64A/LA1) gave the open market value as £30,000 and the claimant's deemed undivided share as £9,200. No reasons were given for this conclusion. The property was leasehold but there was no evidence as to the remaining term of the lease, or as to the condition of the property. There was also no evidence as to the age of the daughter and no consideration as to whether a court would order a sale (which seemed very unlikely, given the purpose for which the property had been acquired and the purpose for which it was being used). The Commissioner, referring to *CIS 191/1994*, holds that there was no evidence that the claimant's capital exceeded the then prescribed limit of £8,000. He stated that everything depended on the facts and the evidence before the tribunal. In this case the valuation evidence was so unsatisfactory as to be worthless. He set out the following guidance on valuation:

> "13. Proper valuation evidence should include details of the valuer's expertise, the basis on which he or she holds him or herself out as able to give expert evidence in relation to the property in question. Where it is the sale of a share in a property which is in issue, the evidence should deal with the valuer's experience in relation to such shares, and their sale. The property, and any leasehold interest, should be described in sufficient detail, including details of the length of any lease, of any special terms in it, and of the location, size and condition of the property, to show that the factors relevant to its value have been taken into account, and the reasons for the conclusion as to the value should be given. A similar approach should be applied to a share of a property, and an explanation should be given of the factors identified as relevant to the valuation, and how they affect it. The expert should also give evidence of any comparables identified, or of other reasons why it is concluded that the share could be sold at any particular price. If there is no evidence of actual sales of such interests, an acceptable explanation of the absence of such evidence should be given.
> 14. I appreciate that, in cases of this kind, this will on occasions be a counsel of perfection which cannot be realised. Where a valuer does not have relevant information, and proceeds upon assumptions, the report should state what is missing, and should also state the assumptions upon which it is based. This will normally give the claimant the opportunity to correct any mistaken assumptions or other errors of fact in the report."

See also *JC-W v Wirral Metropolitan BC(HB)* [2011] UKUT 501 (AAC), paras 13–18, for Judge Mark's critical comments in relation to the District Valuer's valuation in that case, and *MN v LB Hillingdon (HB)* [2014] UKUT 427 (AAC) and *PE v SSWP (SPC)* [2014] UKUT 387 (AAC) noted below.

It will not always be the case that a deemed equal share in a property will be of minimal value, even if the other co-owners are unwilling to sell. As *Wilkinson v Chief Adjudication Officer*, CA, March 24, 2000, reported as *R(IS) 1/01*, illustrates, the purposes for which the joint ownership was established will need to be scrutinised in order to assess whether a court would order a sale. In *Wilkinson* the claimant's mother had died, leaving her home to the claimant and her brother "to do with as they wish". It was accepted that the mother had expressed the hope that the claimant's brother would live in the house with his son when his divorce proceedings in Australia were resolved (although there was nothing in the will to this effect). The claimant contended that the capital value of her half share in the property was of a nominal value only because her brother was unwilling to leave the property and unwilling to sell his share in it. She maintained that a court would not order a sale under s.30 of the Law of Property Act 1925 (repealed with effect from January 1, 1998 and replaced by ss.14 and 15 of the Trusts of Land and Appointment of Trustees Act 1996). But the Court of Appeal, by a majority (Mummery and

Potter LJJ), disagreed. This was not a case like *Palfrey* where property had been acquired by joint owners for a collateral purpose (e.g. for them to live in as long as they wished) and that purpose would be defeated by ordering a sale. On the contrary, this was a case where an order for sale would enable the claimant's mother's wishes, as expressed in her will, to be carried out. Her brother's unwillingness to sell or pay the claimant for the value of her share was in fact having the effect of defeating that testamentary purpose. Evans LJ, however, took the opposite view. He considered that the claimant's share should be valued on the basis that a sale would not be ordered because this would defeat the mother's wish that her son and grandson be allowed to live in the property. As this case illustrates, much will depend on the circumstances in a particular case (and the view that is taken of those circumstances).

2.543 The issue was again revisited in *CIS 3197/2003*. The claimant jointly owned a house with her daughter, the daughter having a two-thirds share. The claimant went into a nursing home, leaving the house in the occupation of her daughter and the daughter's disabled child. The daughter would not agree to a sale of the house nor was she willing to buy out the claimant's share. It semed unlikely that a court would order a sale. In view of the Secretary of State's failure to provide proper evidence of the value of the claimant's share the Commissioner found that the value of the claimant's interest was nil. However, he added that tribunals should not approach the matter in this way. If the evidence was incomplete they should adjourn with directions as to the ways in which the evidence should be supplemented and should not decide the case on the burden of proof. Clearly where there has been no attempt to obtain any valuation evidence this should apply. However, if such attempts have been made and the evidence remains inadequate, it is suggested that the burden of proof may need to come into play (and indeed this was the approach taken in both *R(IS) 3/96* and *CIS 417/1992*). For example, in *R(IS) 3/96* it was held that grounds for revising the claimant's award had not been shown in the light of the deficiences in the District Valuer's report.

Despite the above caselaw, examples continue to crop up of a claimant's share in a property being wrongly valued as a proportion of the whole, rather than the claimant's actual or deemed share being properly valued, taking into account all the relevant circumstances. See, for instance, *R(IS) 5/07* and *AM v SSWP* [2010] UKUT 134 (AAC).

As indeed do cases involving valuation evidence from the District Valuer. For a further example of a case where the valuation evidence from the District Valuer was wholly inadequate and the tribunal had erred in law in relying on it, see *MN v London Borough of Hillingdon (HB)* [2014] UKUT 427 (AAC). The claimant had been living in the jointly-owned matrimonial home with his wife, who had serious mental health problems, and their severely disabled son. However, it became necessary for the claimant and his son to leave, due to deterioration in his wife's health. Judge Ovey, after noting that the District Valuer appeared to have arrived at her valuation by halving the total value of the property and deducting just under 1 per cent, despite having been given details of the circumstances of the case, stated:

> "32. . . . As a matter of common sense, it seems unlikely in the extreme that a purchaser would pay just under half the vacant possession value of a property for a half interest which would not enable him to occupy the property without first obtaining some form of court order against a defendant suffering from paranoid schizophrenia who was in occupation of a former matrimonial home, bought for the purpose of being a home, and who might be entitled to a property adjustment order. . . ."

2.544 See also *PE v SSWP (SPC)* [2014] UKUT 387 (AAC) which concerned the value of the claimant's interest in his former home, which remained occupied by his wife, son and step-son (the step-son had mental health problems). The District Valuer's valuation was based on an assumption that there had been a hypothetical application under the Trusts of Land and Appointment of Trustees Act 1996. The Secretary of State argued that in the circumstances of the case the District Valuer's assumption was unrealistic. Although no divorce proceedings were in place at the time, any application under the 1996 Act would be likely to generate such proceedings by the other party who was likely to obtain a more favourable outcome under the Matrimonial Causes Act 1973. Judge Jacobs accepted that the evidence relied on by the tribunal as to valuation was therefore flawed and decided, with the consent of the Secretary of State, that there were no grounds to supersede the decision awarding state pension credit.

Note the increased upper and lower capital limits for income support (and income-based JSA) from April 10, 2006. The upper capital limit is now £16,000 for all claimants (see reg.45). The lower capital limit is £6,000, except for claimants living permanently in a care home, Abbeyfield Home or independent hospital when it is £10,000 (see reg.53).

Calculation of tariff income from capital

53.—(1) [3Except where the circumstances prescribed in paragraph [10 . . .] (1B) apply to the claimant,] where the claimant's capital calculated in accordance with this Part exceeds [10 £6,000] it shall be treated as equivalent to a weekly income of £1 for each complete £250 in excess of [10 £6,000] but not exceeding [10 £16,000]. 2.545

[6 (IZA) [10 . . .]]

[3(1A) Where the circumstances prescribed in paragraph (1B) apply to the claimant and that claimant's capital calculated in accordance with this Part exceeds £10,000, it shall be treated as equivalent to a weekly income of £1 for each complete £250 in excess of £10,000 but not exceeding £16,000.

(1B) For the purposes of paragraph (1A) [10 . . .], the prescribed circumstances are that the claimant lives permanently in—

[9 (a) a care home or an independent hospital;

(b) an Abbeyfield Home;]

(c) accommodation provided under section 3 of, and Part II of the Schedule to, the Polish Resettlement Act 1947 (provision of accommodation in camps) where the claimant requires personal care [5 by reason of old age, disablement, past or present dependence on alcohol or drugs, past or present mental disorder or a terminal illness and the care is provided in the home].

[4(d) [9 . . .].]

(1C) For the purposes of paragraph (1B), a claimant shall be treated as living permanently in such home [9, hospital] or accommodation where he is absent—

(a) from a home [9, hospital] or accommodation referred to in sub-paragraph [4(a) [9 or (b)]] of paragraph (1B)—

(i) [7 . . .] in the case of a person over pensionable age, for a period not exceeding 52 weeks, and

(ii) in any other case, for a period not exceeding 13 weeks;

(b) from accommodation referred to in sub-paragraph (c) of paragraph (1B), where the claimant, with the agreement of the manager of the accommodation, intends to return to the accommodation in due course.]

(2) Notwithstanding [3paragraphs (1) [10 . . .] and (1A)], where any part of the excess is not a complete £250 that part shall be treated as equivalent to a weekly income of £1.

(3) For the purposes of [3paragraphs (1) [10 . . .] and (1A)], capital includes any income treated as capital under regulations [1 . . .] 48 and

60 ([1 . . .] income treated as capital and liable relative payments treated as capital).

[3(4) [9 . . .].]

AMENDMENTS

1. Income Support (General) Amendment No.5 Regulations 1988 (SI 1988/2022) reg.13 (December 12, 1988).

2. Income-Related Benefits (Miscellaneous Amendments) Regulations 1990 (SI 1990/671) reg.5 (April 9, 1990).

3. Income-related Benefits Schemes (Miscellaneous Amendments) Regulations 1996 (SI 1996/462) reg.12(1) (April 8, 1996).

4. Income-related Benefits and Jobseeker's Allowance (Miscellaneous Amendments) Regulations Regulations 1997 (SI 1997/65) reg.8 (April 7, 1997).

5. Income-related Benefits and Jobseeker's Allowance (Amendment) (No.2) Regulations 1997 (SI 1997/2197) reg.7(5) and (6)(a) (October 6, 1997).

6. Social Security Amendment (Capital Limits and Earnings Disregards) Regulations 2000 (SI 2000/2545) reg.2(1)(c) (April 9, 2001).

7. Social Security Amendment (Residential Care and Nursing Homes) Regulations 2001 (SI 2001/3767) reg.2(1) and Pt I of Sch. para.9 (April 8, 2002).

8. State Pension Credit (Consequential, Transitional and Miscellaneous Provisions) Regulations 2002 (SI 2002/3019) reg.29(3) (October 6, 2003).

9. Social Security (Care Homes and Independent Hospitals) Regulations 2005 (SI 2005/2687) reg.2 and Sch.1 para.7 (October 24, 2005).

10. Social Security (Miscellaneous Amendments) (No.2) Regulations 2005 (SI 2005/2465) reg.2(6) (April 10, 2006).

DEFINITIONS

"Abbeyfield Home"—see reg.2(1).
"care home"—*ibid.*
"claimant"—*ibid.*, and reg.23(1).
"independent hospital"—see reg.2(1).

GENERAL NOTE

2.546 On April 10, 2006 the overall capital limit for income support was raised to £16,000 for all claimants (reg.45) and the amount above which the tariff income rule applies was increased to £6,000 (para.(1)), except for claimants who live permanently in a care home, Abbeyfield Home or independent hospital (for the definitions of these terms see reg.2(1)) or a Polish resettlement home (para.(1B)). For these claimants the tariff income rule will continue to apply only to capital above £10,000 (para.(1A)). See the 2005 edition of this volume for the different upper capital limits that applied before April 10, 2006.

The effect of paras (1), (1A) and (2) is that if the claimant and partner (if any) have capital over £6,000 (£10,000 for claimants within para.(1B)) but not over £16,000, it is treated as producing an income of £1 per week for each complete £250 between the limits, and £1 per week for any odd amount left over. Thus if a claimant (other than one to whom para.(1B) applies) has exactly £9,000, that is treated as producing £12 per week. If he has £7,001, that is treated as producing £5 per week. The actual income from most forms of capital is disregarded under para.22 of Sch.9.

Paragraph (1B)

2.547 See the definitions of "Abbeyfield Home", "care home" and "independent hospital" in reg.2(1) and the notes to those definitions.

Paragraph (1C)

This deals with periods of temporary absence from the accommodation for claimants covered by para.(1B). 2.548

Chapter VII

[6 [8 . . .] Liable Relative Payments]

Interpretation

54.—In this Chapter, unless the context otherwise requires— 2.549

[7 [9 . . .]

"claimant" includes a young claimant;

[7 "claimant's family" shall be construed in accordance with section 137 of the Contributions and Benefits Act 1992 (interpretation of part 7 and supplementary provisions);]

[7 "housing costs" means those costs which may be met under regulation 17(1)(e) or 18(1)(f) (housing costs);]

"liable relative" means—

(a) a spouse [3, former spouse, civil partner or former civil partner] of a claimant or of a member of the claimant's family;

(b) a parent of a child or young person who is a member of the claimant's family or of a young claimant;

(c) a person who has not been adjudged to be the father of a child or young person who is a member of the claimant's family or of a young claimant where that person is contributing towards the maintenance of that child, young person or young claimant and by reason of that contribution he may reasonably be treated as the father of that child, young person or young claimant;

(d) a person liable to maintain another person [7 in the circumstances set out in section 78(6)(c) of the Social Security Administration Act 1992 (liability to maintain another person)] where the latter is the claimant or a member of the claimant's family,

and, in this definition, a reference to a child's, young person's or young claimant's parent includes any person in relation to whom the child, young person or young claimant was treated as a child or a member of the family;

[7 "ordinary clothing and footwear" means clothing and footwear for normal daily use but does not include school uniforms;]

"payment" means a periodical payment or any other payment made by or derived from a liable relative [7 . . .] but it does not include any payment—

(a) arising from a disposition of property made in contemplation of, or as a consequence of—

(i) an agreement to separate; or

(ii) any proceedings for judicial separation, divorce or nullity of marriage; [4 or

(iii) any proceedings for separation, dissolution or nullity in relation to a civil partnership;]

(b) made after the death of the liable relative;

(c) made by way of a gift but not in aggregate or otherwise exceeding £250 in the period of 52 weeks beginning with the date on which the payment, or if there is more than one such payment the first payment, is made; and, in the case of a claimant who continues to be in receipt of income support at the end of the period of 52 weeks, this provision shall continue to apply thereafter with the modification that any subsequent period of 52 weeks shall begin with the first day of the benefit week in which the first payment is made after the end of the previous period of 52 weeks;

(d) [2 . . .]

[7 (e) made to a third party, or in respect of a third party, unless the payment is—

(i) in relation to the claimant or the claimant's [9 partner or is made or derived from a person falling within sub-paragraph (d) of the definition of liable relative]; and

(ii) [10 . . .] in respect of food, ordinary clothing or footwear, fuel, [10 rent for which housing benefit is payable, housing costs to the extent that they are met under regulation 17(1)(e) or 18(1))(f) (housing costs),] council tax or water charges;]

(f) in kind;

(g) to, or in respect of, a child or young person who is to be treated as not being a member of the claimant's household under regulation 16 (circumstances in which a person is to be treated as being or not being a member of the same household);

(h) which is not a periodical payment, to the extent that any amount of that payment—

(i) has already been taken into account under this Part by virtue of a previous claim or determination; or

(ii) has been recovered under section 27(1) of the Act [SSAA, s.74(1)] (prevention of duplication of payments) or is currently being recovered; or

(iii) at the time the determination is made, has been used by the claimant except where he has deprived himself of that amount for the purpose of securing entitlement to income support or increasing the amount of that benefit;

[9 (i) to which paragraph 73 of Schedule 9 (sums to be disregarded in the calculation of income other than earnings) applies.]

"periodical payment" means—

(a) a payment which is made or is due to be made at regular intervals [7 . . .];

(b) in a case where the liable relative has established a pattern of making payments at regular intervals, any such payment;

(c) any payment [7[9. . .] that does not exceed] the amount of income support payable had that payment not been made;

(d) any payment representing a commutation of payments to which sub-paragraphs (a) or (b) of this definition applies whether made in arrears or in advance,

but does not include a payment due to be made before the first benefit week pursuant to the claim which is not so made;

"young claimant" means a person aged 16 or over but under [5 20] who makes a claim for income support.

AMENDMENTS

1. Income Support (General) Amendment Regulations 1988 (SI 1988/663) reg.23 (April 11, 1988).

2. Social Security (Working Tax Credit and Child Tax Credit) (Consequential Amendments) Regulations 2003 (SI 2003/455) reg.2 and Sch.1 para.14 (April 6, 2004, except in "transitional cases" and see further the note to reg.17 of the Income Support Regulations).

3. Civil Partnership (Pensions, Social Security and Child Support) (Consequential, etc. Provisions) Order 2005 (SI 2005/2877) art.2(3) and Sch.3 para.13(4)(a) (December 5, 2005).

4. Civil Partnership (Pensions, Social Security and Child Support) (Consequential, etc. Provisions) Order 2005 (SI 2005/2877) art.2(3) and Sch.3 para.13(4)(b) (December 5, 2005).

5. Social Security (Young Persons) Amendment Regulations 2006 (SI 2006/718) reg.2(5) (April 10, 2006).

6. Social Security (Child Maintenance Amendments) Regulations 2008 (SI 2008/2111) reg.2(5) (October 27, 2008).

7. Social Security (Child Maintenance Amendments) Regulations 2008 (SI 2008/2111) reg.2(6) (October 27, 2008).

8. Social Security (Miscellaneous Amendments) (No.4) Regulations 2009 (SI 2009/2655) reg.2(6) (April 12, 2010).

9. Social Security (Miscellaneous Amendments) (No.4) Regulations 2009 (SI 2009/2655) reg.2(10) (April 12, 2010).

10. Social Security (Miscellaneous Amendments) Regulations 2013 (SI 2013/443) reg.2(3) (April 2, 2013).

DEFINITIONS

"the Act"—see reg.2(1).
"benefit week"—*ibid.*
"child"—see SSCBA s.137(1).
"claimant"—see reg.2(1) and reg.23(1).
"family"—see SSCBA s.137(1).
"young person"—see reg.2(1) and reg.14.

GENERAL NOTE

From October 27, 2008 regs 60A–60D which contained separate rules for the treatment of child support maintenance were omitted. Thereafter all liable relative and child maintenance payments were taken into account in accordance with this Chapter. However, as a consequence of the fact that payments of child maintenance payments are fully disregarded as income from April 12, 2010 (see para.73 of Sch.9), the special rules for the treatment of child maintenance have also been omitted from that date and this Chapter again only deals with liable relative payments. For the definition of "child maintenance" see para.73(2) of Sch.9. It would seem that a lump sum payment of child maintenance will count as capital. **2.550**

"Liable relative"

Note that the definition for these purposes is not restricted to those who are obliged to maintain others under s.78(6)(c) of the Administration Act, but includes in particular, a former spouse (and from December 5, 2005) a civil partner or former civil partner, and a person who may reasonably be treated as the father of a child (by reason of contributing to the maintenance of the child). **2.551**

"Payment"

The general definition is wide, but from October 27, 2008 no longer includes payments not yet acquired which would be made on application. The general cat- **2.552** egory of "payment" is divided into "periodical payments" (further defined below) and "other payments". This division is important in the following regulations.

The list of exceptions is also very important—

(a) A payment arising from a disposition of property made in connection with an agreement to separate or matrimonial or civil partnership proceedings is not a liable relative payment (LRP). There had been great problems in construing the similar, but not identical, supplementary benefit provision, in particular in deciding when a payment "resulted from" a disposition of property. Although the words here are "arising from," the authoritative settlement of the supplementary benefit problem in *R(SB) 1/89* should apply. The claimant received a payment of £2,500 from her ex-husband pursuant to a county court order. This was a consent order made on the basis that the claimant gave up any claims against her ex-husband's houses. The Tribunal of Commissioners holds that there must be a chain of causation, however short, between the disposition and the payment, and that the prior disposition does not have to be by way of sale. Where a payment is made in discharge of a claimant's proprietary interest (or a claim to such an interest) it results from a disposition of property. Where it is made in discharge of maintenance obligations the payment stands alone and does not result from a disposition. *R(SB) 1/89* approves the result of *CSB 1160/1986* where a husband and wife had a joint building society account. On their separation they agreed to split the account and as a result the husband paid £2,500 to the wife, who was receiving supplementary benefit. It was held that the building society account was "property" and that the agreement to split it was a "disposition." The payment then resulted from a disposition of property. It was not a LRP, and had to be dealt with under the ordinary rules on resources.

(b) Payments made after the liable relative's death are not LRPs.

(c) Gifts up to £250 in 52 weeks do not count as LRPs. In view of para.(f), para.(c) must apply to gifts of money or property.

(d) This paragraph, which was revoked on April 6, 2004 (except in "transitional cases"—see the note to reg.17), excluded payments to which reg.44(2) (payments to residential schools for a child's or young person's maintenance) applied (reg.44(2) was also revoked with effect from April 6, 2004, except in "transitional cases"—see reg.17; see the 2003 edition of this volume for reg.44 and the notes to that regulation). The revocation of reg.44, and in turn this paragraph, are part of the consequential changes that apply from April 6, 2004 (except in "transitional cases"—see the note to reg.17) because of the removal of amounts for children and young persons from the income support scheme; financial assistance to help with the cost of bringing up a child or young person is now to be provided through the child tax credit system, see Vol.IV of this series.

    Note that a new disregard has been introduced in place of the provisions formerly in reg.44(2) (see para.25A of Sch.9). Note also para.(e).

(e) Under the new form of para.(e) (substituted on October 27, 2008) payments from liable relatives to third parties in respect of the claimant or the claimant's family only count as liable relative payments if the payment is for the items listed in sub-para.(ii). The same applies if the payment is to the claimant or a member of the claimant's family for a third party. The test of reasonableness under the old form of para.(e) has gone. The April 12, 2010 amendment which replaces a reference to the claimant's family with a reference to the claimant's partner reflects the fact that payments of child maintenance are fully disregarded as income from that date (see para.73 of Sch.9).

The effect of the April 2, 2013 amendment is that third party payments for rent or housing costs are only taken into account where the payment is for rent for which housing benefit is payable or housing costs met by income support. The policy intention is that such payments should only count if they are in respect of items covered by benefit.

(f) Payments in kind are not LRPs. This could be an important factor in benefit planning.

(g) Payments to or in respect of a child or young person who would otherwise be a member of the claimant's household, but is treated as not being in the household by reg.16, do not count as LRPs. See reg.51(3).

(h) Where an "other payment" is being considered, its amount is to be reduced if any of the three categories listed apply. Category (iii) is likely to be particularly important where there is a significant gap between the date of receipt of the payment in question and the date on which the claim for income support is determined. See the notes to reg.51(1) for the difficulties of deciding when a claimant's purpose is to secure or increase entitlement to income support.

(i) From April 12, 2010, all payments of child maintenance are fully disregarded as income under para.73 of Sch.9.

"Periodical payment"

This definition is also wide, as the four categories are alternatives. 2.553

Sub-paras (a) and (b) are relatively straightforward, covering the standard cases where payments are due to be made at regular intervals or a regular pattern has been established.

The effect of sub-para.(d) is that a payment of arrears of payments under (a) and (b), or a payment in advance, also counts as a periodical payment (subject to the final exception). If, however, a regular pattern of payments has ceased to exist and there is no court order or agreement to make regular payments, such a payment cannot be a commutation of payments under sub-paras (a) or (b) (*Bolstridge v Chief Adjudication Officer* [1993] 2 F.L.R. 657. It will be a matter of fact in each case by what date a regular pattern of payments ceases to exist. The facts in *Bolstridge* were that the claimant's ex-husband paid her maintenance of £40 per week on a voluntary basis up to July 31, 1986. He was then made redundant and ceased making payments. In September 1987 her ex-husband made her a payment of £10,500 "in lieu of future maintenance". In July 1988, she claimed income support. The Court of Appeal held that, in the absence of any subsisting contract or outstanding liability, it could not be said that by September 1987, there was an agreement for maintenance of any particular sum or any pattern of regular payment. Therefore, the £10,500 was not a periodical payment. It was an "other payment", to be taken into account under reg.57. Any part of the total amount which fell outside the definition of "payment" (above) would not be taken into consideration at all. In particular, amounts which the claimant had already spent for "legitimate" purposes would be excluded under sub-para.(h)(iii) of the definition.

The intention of sub-para.(c) seems to be that relatively small payments (i.e. up to the amount of one week's income support) are to be treated as periodical payments. 2.554

The final exception is crucial to the working of the LRP system. If a payment was due to be made before the first benefit week, pursuant to the claim, but is paid in or after that benefit week, it is an "other payment," not a periodical payment. Thus the treatment of arrears will vary according to whether the claimant was or was not in receipt of benefit during the period to which the arrears relate (on which see *McCorquodale v Chief Adjudication Officer*, reported as *R(SB) 1/88*).

Treatment of [2[4 . . .]] liable relative payments

2.555 **55.**—[1Subject to regulation 55A] [5 . . . [3. . .]] a payment shall—

(a) to the extent that it is not a payment of income, be treated as income;
(b) be taken into account in accordance with the following provisions of this Chapter.

AMENDMENTS

1. Social Security Benefits (Maintenance Payments and Consequential Amendments) Regulations 1996 (SI 1996/940) reg.6(2) (April 19, 1996).
2. Social Security (Child Maintenance Amendments) Regulations 2008 (SI 2008/2111) reg.2(2)(b) (October 27, 2008).
3. Social Security (Child Maintenance Amendments) Regulations 2008 (SI 2008/2111) reg.2(7) (October 27, 2008).
4. Social Security (Miscellaneous Amendments) (No.4) Regulations 2009 (SI 2009/2655) reg.2(5) (April 12, 2010).
5. Social Security (Miscellaneous Amendments) (No.4) Regulations 2009 (SI 2009/2655) reg.2(11) (April 12, 2010).

DEFINITION

"payment"—see reg.54.

GENERAL NOTE

2.556 From April 12, 2010 reg.55 only applies to liable relative payments since all payments of child maintenance are fully disregarded from that date (see para.73 of Sch.9). The effect of reg.55 is that, subject to reg.55A, all liable relative payments that fall within reg.54 will be treated as and taken into account as income in accordance with regs 56–59.

[1Disregard of payments treated as not relevant income

2.557 **55A.**—Where the Secretary of State treats any payment as not being relevant income for the purposes of section 74A of the Social Security Administration Act 1992 (payment of benefit where maintenance payments collected by Secretary of State), that payment shall be disregarded in calculating a claimant's income.]

AMENDMENT

1. Social Security Benefits (Maintenance Payments and Consequential Amendments) Regulations 1996 (SI 1996/940) reg.6(3) (April 19, 1996).

DEFINITIONS

"payment"—see reg.54.
"relevant income"—see reg.2(c), Social Security Benefits (Maintenance Payments and Consequential Amendments) Regulations 1996 (p.949).

GENERAL NOTE

2.558 See the note to s.74A of the Administration Act in Vol.III of this series.

Period over which periodical payments are to be taken into account

2.559 **56.**—(1) The period over which a periodical payment is to be taken into account shall be—

(a) in a case where the payment is made at regular intervals, a period equal to the length of that interval;
(b) in a case where the payment is due to be made at regular intervals but is not so made, such number of weeks as is equal to the number (and any fraction shall be treated as a corresponding fraction of a week) obtained by dividing the amount of that payment by the weekly amount of that periodical payment as calculated in accordance with regulation 58(4) (calculation of the weekly amount of a liable relative payment);
(c) in any other case, a period equal to a week.

(2) The period under paragraph (1) shall begin on the date on which the payment is treated as paid under regulation 59 (date on which a liable relative payment is to be treated as paid).

DEFINITION

"periodical payment"—see reg.54.

GENERAL NOTE

If a periodical payment is actually paid at regular intervals, it is to be taken into account for the length of the interval. If it is due to be paid regularly but is not, each payment is spread at the weekly rate of proper payment. In other cases (e.g. some payments within sub-para.(c) of the definition of periodical payment) the payment is taken into account for a week. 2.560

The application of reg.56 to payments under sub-para.(d) of the definition of periodical payment is not straightforward. In *Bolstridge v Chief Adjudication Officer* [1993] 2 F.L.R. 657 it was accepted that reg.56(1)(b) can be given a sensible meaning only if the word "payment" in that regulation sometimes applies to the commutated payment and sometimes to the payment that was due to be made at regular intervals.

Payments are taken into account from the date on which they are treated as paid under reg.59.

[1 Period over which payments other than periodical payments are to be taken into account

57.—(1) The period over which a payment other than a periodical payment (a "non-periodical payment") is to be taken account shall be determined as follows. 2.561

(2) Except in a case where paragraph (4) applies, the number of weeks over which a non-periodical payment is to be taken into account shall be equal to the number obtained by dividing that payment by the amount referred to in paragraph (3).

(3) The amount is the aggregate of £2 and—

(a) the amount of income support that would be payable had no payment been made [2 . . .]
(b) [2 . . .].

(4) This paragraph applies in a case where a liable relative makes a periodical payment and a non-periodical payment concurrently and the weekly amount of the periodical payment (as calculated in accordance with regulation 58) is less than B.

(5) In a case where paragraph (4) applies, the non-periodical payment shall, subject to paragraphs (6) and (7), be taken into account over a period

of the number of weeks equal to the number obtained by applying the formula—

$$\frac{A}{B-C}$$

(6) If the liable relative ceases to make periodical payments, the balance (if any) of the non-periodical payment shall be taken into account over the number of weeks equal to the number obtained by dividing that balance by the amount referred to in paragraph (3).

(7) If the amount of any subsequent periodical payment varies, the balance (if any) of the non-periodical payment shall be taken into account over a period of the number of weeks equal to the number obtained by applying the formula—

$$\frac{D}{B-E}$$

(8) The period under paragraph (2) or (4) shall begin on the date on which the payment is treated as paid under regulation 59 (date on which a liable relative payment is treated as paid) and the period under paragraph (6) and (7) shall begin on the first day of the benefit week in which the cessation or variation of the periodical payment occurred.

(9) Any fraction which arises by applying a calculation or formula referred to in this regulation shall be treated as a corresponding fraction of a week.

(10) In paragraphs (4) to (7)—

A = the amount of the non-periodical payment;

B = the aggregate of £2 and the amount of income support that would be payable had the periodical payment not been made [2 . . .];

C = the weekly amount of the periodical payment;

D = the balance (if any) of the non-periodical payment;

E = the weekly amount of any subsequent periodical payment.]

AMENDMENTS

1. Social Security (Child Maintenance Amendments) Regulations 2008 (SI 2008/2111) reg.2(8) (October 27, 2008).

2. Social Security (Miscellaneous Amendments) (No.4) Regulations 2009 (SI 2009/2655) reg.2(12) (April 12, 2010).

DEFINITIONS

"benefit week"—see reg.2(1).
"liable relative"—see reg.54.
"payment"—*ibid.*
"periodical payment"—*ibid.*

GENERAL NOTE

2.562 This regulation deals with payments other than periodical payments (referred to in this regulation as "non-periodical payments"). The amendments made on April 12, 2010 reflect the fact that there is now a total disregard of child maintenance payments (see para.73 of Sch.9) and so this regulation once again only deals with liable relative payments. The basic rule under paras (2) and (3) is to spread non-periodical payments at the rate of income support that would have been payable if the payment had not been made, plus £2. Paragraphs (4)–(5) modify this rule where the non-periodical payment is in addition to periodical payments so as to spread the non-periodical payment at the rate of the difference between the amount identified under para.(3) and the periodical payment, as long as the periodical payments continue to be made. If the periodical payments cease, the balance of the non-periodical payment will be taken into account in accordance with paras (2) and (3) (see para.(6)). Paragraph (7) provides for an adaptation of the formula in para.(5) if the amount of any subsequent periodical payment varies. See para.(8) for when the period calculated under paras (2), (4), (6) or (7) begins and reg.58(5) for the weekly amount to be taken into account.

Note that the pre-April 6, 2004 form of this regulation which had been retained for "transitional cases" (i.e. where the claimant remains entitled to the child elements in income support and has not transferred to child tax credit, see further the note to reg.17) was omitted on October 27, 2008 (see reg.4 of the Social Security (Child Maintenance Amendments) Regulations 2008 (SI 2008/2111)).

Calculation of the weekly amount of a [1[2 . . .]] liable relative payment

58.—(1) Where a periodical payment is made or is due to be made at intervals of one week, the weekly amount shall be the amount of that payment. 2.563

(2) Where a periodical payment is made or is due to be made at intervals greater than one week and those intervals are monthly, the weekly amount shall be determined by multiplying the amount of the payment by 12 and dividing the product by 52.

(3) Where a periodical payment is made or is due to be made at intervals and those intervals are neither weekly nor monthly, the weekly amount shall be determined by dividing that payment by the number equal to the number of weeks (including any part of a week) in that interval.

(4) Where a payment is made and that payment represents a commutation of periodical payments whether in arrears or in advance, the weekly amount shall be the weekly amount of the individual periodical payments so commutated, as calculated under paragraphs (1) to (3) as is appropriate.

(5) The weekly amount of a payment to which regulation 57 applies (period over which payments other than periodical payments are to be taken into account) shall be equal to the amount of the divisor used in calculating the period over which the payment or, as the case may be, the balance is to be taken into account.

AMENDMENTS

1. Social Security (Child Maintenance Amendments) Regulations 2008 (SI 2008/2111) reg.2(2)(c) (October 27, 2008).

2. Social Security (Miscellaneous Amendments) (No.4) Regulations 2009 (SI 2009/2655) reg.2(5) (April 12, 2010).

DEFINITIONS

"payment"—see reg.54.
"periodical payment"—*ibid.*

GENERAL NOTE

2.564 The weekly rate of periodical payments is normally calculated by dividing the payment into weekly bits depending on the intervals between payment dates (paras (1)–(3)). For a commutation of periodical payments, whether in arrears or in advance (which itself comes within the definition of periodical payment), the weekly rate is the appropriate one for the recurring payments.

Date on which a [1[2 . . .]] liable relative payment is to be treated as paid

2.565 **59.**—(1) A periodical payment is to be treated as paid—

(a) in the case of a payment which is due to be made before the first benefit week pursuant to the claim, on the day in the week in which it is to be paid which corresponds to the first day of the benefit week;

(b) in any other case, on the first day of the benefit week in which it is due to be paid unless, having regard to the manner in which income support is due to be paid in the particular case, it would be more practicable to treat it as paid on the first day of a subsequent benefit week.

(2) Subject to paragraph (3), any other payment shall be treated as paid—

(a) in the case of a payment which is made before the first benefit week pursuant to the claim, on the day in the week in which it is paid which corresponds to the first day of the benefit week;

(b) in any other case, on the first day of the benefit week in which it is paid unless, having regard to the manner in which income support is due to be paid in the particular case, it would be more practicable to treat it as paid on the first day of a subsequent benefit week.

(3) Any other payment paid on a date which falls within the period in respect of which a previous payment is taken into account, not being a periodical payment, is to be treated as paid on the first day following the end of that period.

AMENDMENTS

1. Social Security (Child Maintenance Amendments) Regulations 2008 (SI 2008/2111) reg.2(2)(d) (October 27, 2008).
2. Social Security (Miscellaneous Amendments) (No.4) Regulations 2009 (SI 2009/2655) reg.2(5) (April 12, 2010).

DEFINITIONS

"benefit week"—see reg.2(1).
"payment"—see reg.54.
"periodical payment"—*ibid.*

GENERAL NOTE

Paragraph (1)

2.566 This provision effectively applies the ordinary rule for income (see reg.31) to periodical payments. Under sub-para.(a) for the payment still to be a periodical payment it must have been paid as well as been due before the first benefit week pursuant to the claim. Once the benefit week is determined under para.4 of Sch.7 to the Claims and Payments Regulations, prior weeks can be counted off and payments attributed to the first day of each week. Under sub-para.(b), for other periodical payments (which can include many payments of arrears) the crucial thing is the benefit week in which the payment is due, or, if it would be more practicable, a subsequent week. A payment of arrears within the definition of a periodical payment may well have been due in a large number of past weeks, for which benefit has already been paid on the assumption that no LRP had been received. This would seem to trigger the application of s.74(1) of the Administration Act (1986 Act s.27(1)). Paragraph 28834 of the *Decision Makers Guide* suggests that in such circumstances it is more practicable to take the payment into account from the next benefit week in which the amount of benefit can be adjusted, although the *Guide* does not really face the problem of payments of arrears. If continuing periodical payments are being made, the spreading of a payment of arrears over future benefit weeks could lead to more than one periodical payment being taken into account in the same benefit week. Whether this leaves the claimant better off than if recovery under s.74(1) had been triggered depends on the levels of payment in relation to income support entitlement. It is not at all clear that this solution is "more practicable" than spreading the payment of arrears over the past period to which the arrears related. The latter solution, with the recovery of any overpayment under s.74(1), may be better.

Paragraph (2)

This provision applies to all "other payments", including payments of arrears identified in the final exception to the definition of "periodical payment". Here it is the date of actual payment, rather than the date on which payment is due, which is crucial. Sub-paragraph (a) applies to payments made before the first benefit week pursuant to the claim. Sub-paragraph (b) applies in all other cases, and allows attribution to a later benefit week than that of payment if that is more practicable. **2.567**

The result for payments of arrears relating to a period before entitlement to benefit, is that the payment is treated as income to be spread at the rate identified in reg.58 from the date of actual payment. This reverses the result of *McCorquodale v Chief Adjudication Officer* (reported as *R(SB) 1/88*). If this results in one "other payment" being attributed to a benefit week to which another "other payment" has already been attributed, the attribution of the later payment is deferred until the first one runs out (para.(3)).

Liable relative payments to be treated as capital

60.—[1 . . .] **2.568**

AMENDMENT

1. Social Security (Child Maintenance Amendments) Regulations 2008 (SI 2008/2111) reg.2(4)(b) (October 27, 2008).

[1Chapter VIIA

Child Support

Interpretation

60A.—[2 . . .]] **2.569**

AMENDMENTS

1. Social Security (Miscellaneous Provisions) Amendment Regulations 1993 (SI 1993/846) reg.3 (April 19, 1993).

2. Social Security (Child Maintenance Amendments) Regulations 2008 (SI 2008/2111) reg.2(4)(c) (October 27, 2008).

[1Treatment of child support maintenance

2.570 **60B.**—[2 . . .]]

AMENDMENTS

1. Social Security (Miscellaneous Provisions) Amendment Regulations 1993 (SI 1993/846) reg.3 (April 19, 1993).
2. Social Security (Child Maintenance Amendments) Regulations 2008 (SI 2008/2111) reg.2(4)(c) (October 27, 2008).

[1Calculation of the weekly amount of payments of child support maintenance

2.571 **60C.**— [2 . . .]]

AMENDMENTS

1. Social Security (Miscellaneous Provisions) Amendment Regulations 1993 (SI 1993/846) reg.3 (April 19, 1993).
2. Social Security (Child Maintenance Amendments) Regulations 2008 (SI 2008/2111) reg.2(4)(c) (October 27, 2008).

[1Date on which child support maintenance is to be treated as paid

2.572 **60D.**— [2 . . .]]

AMENDMENTS

1. Social Security (Miscellaneous Provisions) Amendment Regulations 1993 (SI 1993/846) reg.3 (April 19, 1993).
2. Social Security (Child Maintenance Amendments) Regulations 2008 (SI 2008/2111) reg.2(4)(c) (October 27, 2008).

[1Disregard of payments treated as not relevant income

2.573 **60E.**—[2 . . .]]

AMENDMENTS

1. Social Security Benefits (Maintenance Payments and Consequential Amendments) Regulations 1996 (SI 1996/940) reg.6(5) (April 19, 1996).
2. Social Security (Child Maintenance Amendments) Regulations 2008 (SI 2008/2111) reg.2(4)(c) (October 27, 2008).

Chapter VIII

[15 Students]

Interpretation

2.574 **61.**—[12(1)] In this Chapter, unless the context otherwise requires—

[18 "academic year" means the period of twelve months beginning on 1st January, 1st April, 1st July or 1st September according to whether the course in question begins in the winter, the spring, the summer or the autumn respectively but if students are required to begin attending the course during August or September and to continue attending through the autumn, the academic year of the course shall be considered to begin in the autumn rather than the summer;]

[[13] "access funds" means—

(a) grants made under section [[28] 68] of the Further and Higher Education Act 1992 [[28] . . .] [[18] for the purpose of providing funds on a discretionary basis to be paid to students];

(b) grants made under sections 73(a) and (c) and 74(1) of the Education (Scotland) Act 1980; [[18]. . .]

(c) grants made under Article 30 of the Education and Libraries (Northern Ireland) Order 1993, or grants, or grants loans or other payments made under Article 5 of the Further Education (Northern Ireland) Order 1997 in each case being grants, or loans or other payments as the case may be, made for the purpose of assisting students in financial difficulties;] [[18] [[20] . . .]

(d) discretionary payments, known as "learner support funds", which are made available to students in further education by institutions out of funds provided by the [[31] [[32] Secretary of State under section 14 of the Education Act 2002] or [[33] . . .] under sections 100 and 101 of [[32] the Apprenticeships, Skills, Children and Learning Act 2009]];] [[20] or

(e) Financial Contingency Funds made available by the [[26]Welsh Ministers];]

[[8]"college of further education" means a college of further education within the meaning of Part I of the Further and Higher Education (Scotland) Act 1992;]

[[8] [[27] "contribution" means—

(a) any contribution in respect of the income of a student or any person which the Secretary of State, the Scottish Ministers or an education authority takes into account in ascertaining the amount of a student's grant or student loan; or

(b) any sums, which in determining the amount of a student's allowance or bursary in Scotland under the Education (Scotland) Act 1980, the Scottish Ministers or education authority takes into account being sums which the Scottish Ministers or education authority consider that it is reasonable for the following persons to contribute towards the holder's expenses—

  (i) the holder of the allowance or bursary;

  (ii) the holder's parents;

  (iii) the holder's parent's spouse, civil partner or person ordinarily living with the holder's parent as if he or she were the spouse or civil partner of that parent; or

  (iv) the holder's spouse or civil partner;]]

[[8]"course of advanced education" means—

(a) a course leading to a postgraduate degree or comparable qualification, a first degree or comparable qualification, a diploma of higher education or a higher national diploma; or

(b) any other course which is of a standard above advanced GNVQ or equivalent, including a course which is of a standard above a general certificate of education (advanced level), [[21] a Scottish national qualification (higher or advanced higher)];]

"covenant income" means the income [8. . .] payable to a student under a Deed of Covenant by a person whose income is, or is likely to be, taken into account in assessing the student's grant or award;

"education authority" means a government department, [30 a local authority as defined in section 579 of the Education Act 1996 (interpretation)], [8a local education authority as defined in section 123 of the Local Government (Scotland) Act 1973], an education and library board established under Article 3 of the Education and Libraries (Northern Ireland) Order 1986, any body which is a research council for the purposes of the Science and Technology Act 1965 or any analogous government department, authority, board or body, of the Channel Islands, Isle of Man or any other country outside Great Britain;

[16 . . .]

[8"full-time course of advanced education" means a course of advanced education which is [12 . . .]—

(a) [12 . . .] a full-time course of study which is not funded in whole or in part by [17 the [31[32 Secretary of State under section 14 of the Education Act 2002] [33 or under section 100 of the Apprenticeships, Skills, Children and Learning Act 2009]] or by the [23[26 Welsh Ministers]]] or a full-time course of study which is not funded in whole or in part by the [19Scottish Ministers] at a college of further education or a full-time course of study which is a course of higher education and is funded in whole or in part by the [19Scottish Ministers];

[17(b) a course of study that is funded in whole or in part by the [31[32 Secretary of State under section 14 of the Education Act 2002] [33 or under section 100 of the Apprenticeships, Skills, Children and Learning Act 2009]] or by the [23[26 Welsh Ministers]] if it involves more than 16 guided learning hours per week for the student in question, according to the number of guided learning hours per week for that student set out—

[31 (i) in the case of a course funded by the [32 Secretary of State [33 . . .]], in the student's learning agreement signed on behalf of the establishment which is funded by [33 the Secretary of State] for the delivery of that course; or]

(ii) in the case of a course funded by the [23[26 Welsh Ministers]], in a document signed on behalf of the establishment which is funded by that Council for the delivery of that course; or]

(c) [12 . . .] a course of study (not being higher education) which is funded in whole or in part by the [19Scottish Ministers] at a college of further education if it involves—

(i) more than 16 hours per week of classroom-based or workshop-based programmed learning under the direct guidance of teaching staff according to the number of hours set out in a document signed on behalf of the college; or

(ii) 16 hours or less per week of classroom-based or workshop-based programmed learning under the direct guidance of teaching staff and it involves additional hours using structured learning packages supported by the teaching staff where the combined total of hours exceeds 21 per week, according to the number of hours set out in a document signed on behalf of the college;]

[8"full-time course of study" means a full-time course of study which—
(a) is not funded in whole or in part by [16 the [31 [32 Secretary of State under section 14 of the Education Act 2002] [33 or under section 100 of the Apprenticeships, Skills, Children and Learning Act 2009]] or by the [23 [26 Welsh Ministers]]] or a full-time course of study which is not funded in whole or in part by the [19Scottish Ministers] at a college of further education or a full-time course of study which is a course of higher education and is funded in whole or in part by the [19Scottish Ministers];
[16 (b) a course of study which is funded in whole or in part by the [31 [32 Secretary of State under section 14 of the Education Act 2002] [33 or under section 100 of the Apprenticeships, Skills, Children and Learning Act 2009]] or by the [23 [26 Welsh Ministers]] if it involves more than 16 guided learning hours per week for the student in question, according to the number of guided learning hours per week for that student set out—
[31 (i) in the case of a course funded by the [32 Secretary of State [33. . .]], in the student's learning agreement signed on behalf of the establishment which is funded by [33 the Secretary of State] for the delivery of that course; or]
(ii) in the case of a course funded by the [23 [26 Welsh Ministers]], in a document signed on behalf of the establishment which is funded by that Council for the delivery of that course; or]
(c) is not higher education and is funded in whole or in part by the [19Scottish Ministers] at a college of further education if it involves—
(i) more than 16 hours per week of classroom-based or workshop-based programmed learning under the direct guidance of teaching staff according to the number of hours set out in a document signed on behalf of the college; or
(ii) 16 hours or less per week of classroom-based or workshop-based programmed learning under the direct guidance of teaching staff and it involves additional hours using structured learning packages supported by the teaching staff where the combined total of hours exceeds 21 per week, according to the number of hours set out in a document signed on behalf of the college;]

[12 "full-time student" [24 means a person who is not a qualifying young person or child within the meaning of section 142 of the Contributions and Benefits Act (child and qualifying young person) and] who is—
(a) aged less than 19 and is attending or undertaking a full-time course of advanced education;
(b) aged 19 or over but under pensionable age and is attending or undertaking a full-time course of study at an educational establishment; or
(c) on a sandwich course;]

[13 "grant" (except in the definition of "access funds") means any kind of educational grant or award and includes any scholarship, studentship, exhibition, allowance or bursary but does not include a payment from access funds [21 or any payment to which paragraph 11 of Schedule 9 or paragraph 63 of Schedule 10 applies];]

"grant income" means—

(a) any income by way of a grant;

(b) in the case of a student other than one to whom sub-paragraph (c) refers, any contribution which has been assessed whether or not it has been paid;

(c) in the case of a student to whom [9 paragraph 1, 2 [29 *10*,] 11 [27, [29 *12*] or 15A of Schedule 1B] applies (lone parent, disabled student or persons in education)], any contribution which has been assessed and which has been paid;

and any such contribution which is paid by way of a covenant shall be treated as part of the student's grant income;

[8"higher education" means higher education within the meaning of Part II of the Further and Higher Education (Scotland) Act 1992;]

[3"last day of the course" means the date on which the last day of the final academic term falls in respect of the course in which the student is enrolled;]

"period of study" means—

(a) in the case of a course of study for one year or less, the period beginning with the start of the course [3and ending with the last day of the course];

(b) in the case of a course of study for more than one year, in the first or, as the case may be, any subsequent year of the course, [3other than the final year of the course,] the period beginning with the start of the course or, as the case may be, that year's start and ending with either—

[14 (i) the day before the start of the next year of the course in a case where the student's grant or loan is assessed at a rate appropriate to his studying throughout the year or, if he does not have a grant or loan, where a loan would have been assessed at such a rate had he had one; or]

(ii) in any other case the day before the start of the normal summer vacation appropriate to his course;

[3 (c) in the final year of a course of study of more than one year, the period beginning with that year's start and ending with the last day of the course;]

[20 "periods of experience" means periods of work experience which form part of a sandwich course;]

[13[25 "sandwich course" has the meaning prescribed in regulation 2(9) of the Education (Student Support) Regulations 2008, regulation 4(2) of the Education (Student Loans) (Scotland) Regulations 2007, regulation 2(8) of the Education (Student Support) Regulations (Northern Ireland) 2007;]]

[8"standard maintenance grant" means—

(a) except where paragraph (b) or (c) applies, in the case of a student attending [12 or undertaking] a course of study at the University of London or an establishment within the area comprising the City of London and the Metropolitan Police District, the amount specified for the time being in paragraph 2(2)(a) of Schedule 2 to the Education (Mandatory Awards) Regulations 1995 ("the 1995 Regulations") for such a student;

(b) except where paragraph (c) applies, in the case of a student residing at his parents' home, the amount specified in paragraph 3(2) thereof;

[18 (c) in the case of a student receiving an allowance or bursary under the Education (Scotland) Act 1980, the amount of money specified as the "standard maintenance allowance" for the relevant year appropriate for the student set out in the Student Support in Scotland Guide issued by the Student Awards Agency for Scotland, or its nearest equivalent in the case of a bursary provided by a college of further education or a local education authority [25 . . .];]

(d) in any other case, the amount specified in paragraph 2(2) of Schedule 2 to the 1995 Regulations other than in sub paragraph (a) or (b) thereof;]

[12 "student" means a person, other than a person in receipt of a training allowance, who is attending or undertaking a course of study at an educational establishment;]

[11"student loan" means a loan towards a student's maintenance pursuant to any regulations made under section 22 of the Teaching and Higher Education Act 1998, section 73 of the Education (Scotland) Act 1980 or Article 3 of the Education (Student Support) (Northern Ireland) Order 1998 [18 and shall include, in Scotland, a young student's bursary paid under regulation 4(1)(c) of the Students' Allowances (Scotland) Regulations 1999];

[18. . .]

[12 (2) For the purposes of the definition of "full-time student" in paragraph (1), a person shall be regarded as attending or, as the case may be, undertaking a full-time course of study, a full-time course of advanced education or as being on a sandwich course—

(a) subject to paragraph (3), in the case of a person attending or undertaking a part of a modular course that would be a full-time course of study for the purposes of this Part, for the period beginning on the day on which that part of the course starts and ending—
   (i) on the last day on which he is registered with the educational establishment as attending or undertaking that part as a full-time course of study; or
   (ii) on such earlier date (if any) as he finally abandons the course or is dismissed from it;

(b) in any other case, throughout the period beginning on the date on which he starts attending or undertaking the course and ending on the last day of the course or on such earlier date (if any) as he finally abandons it or is dismissed from it.

(3) For the purpose of sub-paragraph (a) of paragraph (2), the period referred to in that sub-paragraph shall include—

(a) where a person has failed examinations or has failed to successfully complete a module relating to a period when he was attending or undertaking a part of the course as a full-time course of study, any period in respect of which he attends or undertakes the course for the purpose of retaking those examinations or that module;

(b) any period of vacation within the period specified in that paragraph or immediately following that period except where the person has registered with the educational establishment to attend or undertake the final module in the course and the vacation immediately follows the last day on which he is required to attend or undertake the course.

(4) In paragraphs (2), "modular course" means a course of study which consists of two or more modules, the successful completion of a specified

number of which is required before a person is considered by the educational establishment to have completed the course.]

AMENDMENTS

1. Income Support (General) Amendments No.5 Regulations 1988 (SI 1988/2022) reg.14 (December 12, 1988).
2. Social Security Benefits (Student Loans and Miscellaneous Amendments) Regulations 1990 (SI 1990/1549) reg.5(5) (September 1, 1990).
3. Income Support (General) Amendment No.4 Regulations 1991 (SI 1991/1559) reg.10 (August 5, 1991).
4. Income Support (General) Amendment Regulations 1992 (SI 1992/468) reg.5 (April 6, 1992).
5. Income-related Benefits Schemes (Miscellaneous Amendments) (No.3) Regulations 1992 (SI 1992/2155) reg.19 (October 5, 1992).
6. Income-related Benefits Schemes (Miscellaneous Amendments) (No.4) Regulations 1993 (SI 1993/2119) reg.16 (October 4, 1993).
7. Social Security Benefits (Miscellaneous Amendments) Regulations 1995 (SI 1995/1742) reg.2 (August 1, 1995).
8. Income-related Benefits Schemes and Social Fund (Miscellaneous Amendments) Regulations 1996 (SI 1996/1944) reg.6(8) (October 7, 1996).
9. Income-related Benefits and Jobseeker's Allowance (Amendment) (No.2) Regulations 1997 (SI 1997/2197) reg.5(5) (October 6, 1997).
10. Social Security (Miscellaneous Amendments) Regulations 1998 (SI 1998/563) reg.4(1) and (2)(e) (April 6, 1998).
11. Social Security Amendment (Students) Regulations 1999 (SI 1999/1935) reg.3(2) (August 30, 1999, or if the student's period of study begins between August 1 and 29, 1999, the first day of the period).
12. Social Security Amendment (Students) Regulations 2000 (SI 2000/1981) reg.5(3) (July 31, 2000).
13. Social Security Amendment (Students and Income-related Benefits) Regulations 2000 (SI 2000/1922) reg.2(2) (August 28, 2000, or if the student's period of study begins between August 1 and 27, 2000, the first day of the period).
14. Social Security Amendment (Students and Income-related Benefits) Regulations 2000 (SI 2000/1922) reg.2(3) (August 28, 2000, or if the student's period of study begins between August 1 and 27, 2000, the first day of the period).
15. Income Support (General) Amendment Regulations 2001 (SI 2001/721) reg.2(b) (March 29, 2001).
16. Social Security (Miscellaneous Amendments) (No.2) Regulations 2001 (SI 2001/652) reg.3(1) and (2)(c) (April 1, 2001).
17. Social Security (Miscellaneous Amendments) (No.2) Regulations 2001 (SI 2001/652) reg.3(3) (April 1, 2001).
18. Social Security Amendment (Students and Income-related Benefits) Regulations 2001 (SI 2001/2319) reg.2(1) and (2)(c) (August 1, 2001).
19. Social Security Amendment (Students and Income-related Benefits) Regulations 2001 (SI 2001/2319) reg.2(3) (August 1, 2001).
20. Social Security Amendment (Students and Income-related Benefits) Regulations 2002 (SI 2002/1589) reg.2(1) (August 1, 2002).
21. Social Security (Students and Income-related Benefits) Amendment Regulations 2004 (SI 2004/1708) reg.5(1) (September 1, 2004, or if the student's period of study begins between August 1 and August 31, 2004, the first day of the period).
22. Civil Partnership (Pensions, Social Security and Child Support) (Consequential, etc. Provisions) Order 2005 (SI 2005/2877) art.2(3) and Sch.3 para.13(5) (December 5, 2005).

23. National Council for Education and Training for Wales (Transfer of Functions to the National Assembly for Wales and Abolition) Order 2005 (SI 2005/3238 (W.243)) art.9(2) and Sch.2 para.1(1) (April 1, 2006).
24. Social Security (Young Persons) Amendment Regulations 2006 (SI 2006/718) reg.2(6) (April 10, 2006).
25. Social Security (Miscellaneous Amendments) (No.6) Regulations 2008 (SI 2008/2767) reg.2(9) (November 17, 2008).
26. Social Security (Miscellaneous Amendments) (No.7) Regulations 2008 (SI 2008/3157) reg.2(5) (January 5, 2009).
27. Social Security (Miscellaneous Amendments) Regulations 2009 (SI 2009/583) reg.2(9) (April 6, 2009).
28. Social Security (Miscellaneous Amendments) (No.4) Regulations 2009 (SI 2009/2655) reg.2(13) (October 26, 2009).
29. Income Support (Prescribed Categories of Person) Regulations 2009 (SI 2009/3152) reg.3(2)(c) and 3(7) (December, 30, 2009). Regulation 3(2)(c) omits "10," and "12" in para.(c) of the definition of "grant income " with effect from December 30, 2009 but reg.3(7) provides that this does not apply in the case of a person who is subject to the saving provisions in reg.2(2) of those Regulations.
30. Local Education Authorities and Children's Services Authorities (Integration of Functions) (Local and Subordinate Legislation) Order 2010 (SI 2010/1172) art.5 and Sch.3 para.13 (May 5, 2010).
31. Apprenticeships, Skills, Children and Learning Act 2009 (Consequential Amendments to Subordinate Legislation) (England) Order 2010 (SI 2010/1941) art.3(3) (September 1, 2010).
32. Young People's Learning Agency Abolition (Consequential Amendments to Subordinate Legislation) (England) Order 2012 (SI 2012/956) art.3(3) (May 1, 2012).
33. Deregulation Act 2015 (Consequential Amendments) Order 2015 (SI 2015/971) art.2 and Sch.3 para.2(3) (May 26, 2015).

DEFINITIONS

"training allowance"—see reg.2(1).
"course of study"—*ibid.*

GENERAL NOTE

"Academic year"

This definition is important for the purposes of calculating student loan income. "Academic year" means a period of 12 months beginning on January 1, April 1, July 1 or September 1, depending on whether the course in question starts in the winter, the spring, the summer or the autumn respectively. For students who begin their course in August or September and continue to attend during the autumn (i.e. for most students) the academic year is treated as starting in the autumn—i.e. on September 1. **2.575**

"Grant"

R(SB) 20/83 decided that "award" included a loan. However, in *R(IS) 16/95* the Commissioner disagrees with *R(SB) 20/83*. In his view, "award", if given its everyday meaning, particularly in the context of academic grants and awards, implied an outright gift with no liability to repay. Thus the education loan received by the claimant's partner from the Norwegian Government did not fall within reg.61, but was to be taken into account as income under reg.40 (see *R(SB) 7/88*). Regulation 66A (concerning the student loan scheme in its then form) had been introduced simply for the removal of doubt and did not indicate that, without it, loans would not count as income. *R(JSA) 4/04* confirms that a student loan paid to **2.576** a part-time student (whether properly paid under the student loan scheme or not) constituted income for the purposes of income-based JSA (the same would apply for income support), to be taken into account over the period of the academic year in respect of which it was paid; furthermore the claimant was not entitled to the benefit of the disregards in reg.136 of the JSA Regulations 1996 (reg.66A of the Income Support Regulations) because this only applied to full-time students.

The September 2004 amendment ensures that education maintenance allowances (EMAs) are excluded from the definition of grant. EMAs (which now only apply in Wales and Scotland) are fully disregarded (see para.11 of Sch.9 for the income disregard and para.63 of Sch.10 for the capital disregard). In England, from September 2011, EMAs have been replaced by payments from the "16–19 Bursary Fund"; payments from this Fund are also disregarded under para.11 of Sch.9 and para.63 of Sch.10.

"Grant income"

2.577 Note that in most cases a contribution (e.g. from a parent) is included whether paid or not.

Where a person is due to repay part or all of a student grant because he leaves or is dismissed from his course before it finishes, see regs 29(2B), 32(6A) and 40(3B). However, note *Chief Adjudication Officer v Leeves* reported as *R(IS) 5/99*) in the notes to reg.29(2B) and the argument discussed in those notes as to when reg.29(2B) applies. Note also para.61 of Sch.9 under which any grant (or covenant income or student loan or contribution) left over at the end of a person's course is ignored.

"Student" and "Full-time student"

2.578 On July 31, 2000 the existing definition of "student" was substituted and a new definition of "full-time student" was inserted. The latter definition needs to be read in conjunction with paras (2)–(4) which expand upon it.

The aim of these new definitions is to reinforce the Government's policy intention that a full-time student should count as such throughout the duration of his course until he completes or is finally dismissed from or finally abandons it (but note the new provisions relating to "modular courses" (defined in para.(4)) in paras (2)(a) and (3)). It had been felt necessary to introduce these changes following the Court of Appeal's decisions in *Clarke and Faul* and *Webber* (see below). The Government's original proposals for change (first mooted in March 1998) were more extensive and were roundly rejected by the Social Security Advisory Committee (SSAC) in their report submitted in May 1998 (for SSAC's report and the Government's statement in reply see Cmnd. 4739 (2000)). SSAC's primary recommendation was that the proposed amendments should be withdrawn and replaced by regulations designed "to provide safety net support for people who are not currently engaged in full-time studies—either through social security (subject to the normal conditions of entitlement) or mandatory grants". Not surprisingly this did not find favour with the Government, although the Secretary of State's reply to SSAC's report did acknowledge "the need to ensure that the interaction of legislation underpinning [the Government's] overall policy on full-time students does not result in individual students being denied financial support in certain circumstances". Thus the final version of the amendments to the JSA Regulations 1996 includes a provision enabling those full-time students who interrupted their studies because of illness or caring responsibilities but who have now recovered or whose caring responsibilities have ceased to claim JSA. They will be eligible until the earlier of the day before they rejoin their course or the day before the start of their next academic year, provided that they do not qualify for a student grant or loan in this period (see reg.1(3D) and (3E) of the JSA Regulations 1996). (A similar provision was also introduced into the Housing Benefit and Council Tax Benefit Regulations). The Government did not, however, accept one of SSAC's other recommendations, namely, that lone parents students who had completed a substantial part of their full-time course should continue to be eligible for benefit after their youngest child reached 16. The response that "the Government believes that it is reasonable to expect a lone parent who wishes to study full-time to undertake and complete a course of full-time study before the youngest child reaches the age of 16" is not a particularly helpful one.

Note that the definitions of "student" and "full-time student" now encompass a person who is "undertaking" as well as "attending" a course. The stated purpose of the inclusion of the word "undertaking" is to indicate that it is not necessary for the person to be physically present at the relevant educational establishment in order to count as a student.

"Full-time student"

The definition of full-time student is important not just for the purposes of this Chapter of the Regulations, but also because it feeds back in through the additional definition of "period of study" in reg.2(1) to remove most full-time students' entitlement (see reg.4ZA(2) and (3)). Note that those in receipt of a training allowance are excluded from the definition of student and hence full-time student. Further, from April 10, 2006 a person who is a "qualifying young person within the meaning of s.142 of the Contributions and Benefits Act 1992" is also excluded (see below). **2.579**

Besides those on sandwich courses (see the definition of sandwich course later in para.(1)), there are two categories, depending on whether the person is under 19 or not. A person under 19 is a full-time student if attending or undertaking a full-time course of advanced education. Advanced education is defined earlier in para.(1).

A person of 19 or over (but under pensionable age) is a full-time student if attending or undertaking a full-time course of study at an educational establishment. It does not have to be any particular level. However, following the introduction of the new rules for child benefit on April 10, 2006, a person aged 19 who "falls within the definition of qualifying young person in s.142 of the Contributions and Benefits Act" can be in relevant education (see reg.12 and the notes to that regulation). An exception has therefore been added to the definition of full-time student for qualifying young persons.

"Course of study at an educational establishment"

The reference in the definition of full-time student (and student) is to a course of study, rather than of education, as it was in the Supplementary Benefit (Conditions of Entitlement) Regulations. This probably makes little difference, although it makes it harder to argue that students pursuing degrees purely by research, with no coursework, are not "attending" a course (see (*R(SB) 26/82*), but pursuing or following it. (Now that the reference is to "attending or undertaking" a course, this argument is no longer open.) **2.580**

R(SB) 25/87 decides that a pupil barrister is not a student because pupillage is not a course of education, but an assimilation of specific vocational skills by attending on the pupil master. Presumably, a pupil barrister would be said not to be attending a "course of study" (the phrase here) either. *CIS 50/1990* suggests that this approach is not lightly to be extended to other circumstances. The claimant was attending an intensive shorthand and typing course at a commercial training centre. There was little difficulty in deciding that this was a full-time course. The Commissioner holds that since there was active tuition, the claimant was engaged in study, regardless of the technical nature of the skills studied. The centre was within the ordinary meaning of "educational establishment." In *R(IS) 5/97* a person attending the Bar Vocational Course at the Council of Legal Education was a student. *R(SB) 25/87* was clearly distinguishable. See also *CIS 450/1997* which decides that a Project 2000 student nurse came within the definition of "student".

On the meaning of "course", see *R(IS) 1/96*. The claimant was training to be an architect. He had obtained his degree and had to find a year's placement with a firm before undertaking a further two years' study (to be followed by a further year's practical experience) in order to complete his professional training. The Commissioner holds that he was not a student during the year "out". In the Commissioner's view, a course was a "unified sequence of study, tuition and/or practical training . . .

intended to lead to one or more qualifications obtained on its completion". So if a profession required more than one qualification for which colleges did not provide a single sequence of tuition and/or experience, the person was not engaged on one continuous "course" throughout, but completed one "course" before moving onto another. Thus para.(a) of the then definition (see the 1995 edition of J. Mesher and P. Wood, *Income-related Benefits: the Legislation*) of student did not apply to him. Paragraph (b) also did not apply as the claimant was not on a "sandwich course", since any periods of outside practical experience were not "associated with" his full-time study within the meaning of the Education (Mandatory Awards) Regulations. See also *CIS 576/1994* in which the Commissioner similarly decides that the course is the whole course leading to the qualification and not a separate course each year. Note that a student who passes resits after a year's absence from his course is rejoining the same, not a different, course (*O'Connor v Chief Adjudication Officer* [1999] All E.R.(D) 220 (see below)).

On the other hand, *R(JSA) 2/02* holds that where the course of training is separated from the course of examinations it is only the course of training that constitutes the course of study, not the course of examinations, nor some sort of amalgam of both. Thus where a University provided a course of training to prepare the claimant for a course of examinations set and marked by an outside professional institute, the claimant could abandon the University course and cease to be a student for the purposes of JSA, while still being able to pursue his professional qualification.

"Full-time course"

2.581 The question whether the course is full- or part-time is clearly important, since the exclusion from income support does not apply to part-time students who may be eligible for benefit if they fall within any of the categories in Sch.1B.

Note that it is the course which has to be full-time, rather than the claimant's hours of attendance on it (see *R(SB) 40/83, R(SB) 41/83, CSB 176/1987*). If a non-modular course (see below for the position of modular courses under the new rules introduced on July 31, 2000) is full-time, the effect of para.(2)(b) is that the definition of full-time student applies for the entire length of the course, unless the student finally abandons the course or is dismissed from it (see further below). Note *CIS 368/1992* which decided that a student who exercised the option of working in France for a year as part of her course remained a student throughout her four-year course. Her course was continuing, even if in a different form.

Although the distinction between full- and part-time courses is a crucial one, there continues to be no definition of "full-time course", with the exception of certain courses that are referred to in sub-paras (b) and (c) of the definitions of "full-time course of study" and "full-time course of advanced education". In England and Wales, for courses funded totally or partly by the Secretary of State under s.14 of the Education Act 2002 or the Welsh Ministers, the cut-off for a full-time course is 16 or more "guided learning hours" each week. The number of a person's "guided learning hours" will be set out in his learning agreement with his college (in Wales referred to simply as a document). Guided learning hours are "hours when a member of staff is present to guide learning on a programme including lectures, tutorials and supervised study", as opposed to time spent in private study (*Decision Makers Guide*, para.30077). Note the different definitions that apply in Scotland.

2.582 But for courses which are not so funded, whether or not a course is full-time remains to be determined by the circumstances in each case. The educational establishment's description of the course is not conclusive but should be accepted unless challenged by pertinent evidence (*R(SB) 40/83; R(SB) 41/83*). An example of such evidence could be that the claimant is exempt from certain course requirements (*CG/3189/2004*).

In *CIS 152/1994* the Commissioner recognised that recent developments in education, and in particular the advent of modular courses, have blurred the distinction between full-time and part-time courses, and that what is in essence the same course can often be accessed on either a full-time or a part-time basis. The claimant had begun a full-time course in 1992, studying 21 and three-quarters hours a week. In 1993 he reduced the number of modules he was taking from seven to five, so that his hours of study became 15 a week. The Commissioner states that it is no longer sufficient just to look at the course. The overall circumstances (e.g. the hours of study, number of modules, length of time it would take to obtain the qualification on the basis of five as opposed to seven modules at a time, correspondence from the college, fees payable and any relevant information in the college prospectus) therefore had to be examined to ascertain whether the course the claimant was *currently* attending was full or part-time. (But note that it now seems clear that whether a non-modular course is full-time is to be determined by the nature of the course at its start, not according to later changes, see *O'Connor* and *R(IS) 1/00* below. For the position of modular courses under the new rules introduced on July 31, 2000, see below.)

A similar approach was taken in *CIS 576/1994*. The claimant's modular degree course could be undertaken on a full-time or part-time basis. He attended on a full-time basis for the first year and then changed to part-time. He became full-time again for the last two terms of the third year. The Commissioner states that para.(a) of the then definition of "student" (see the 1995 edition of J. Mesher and P. Wood, *Income-related Benefits: the Legislation*) did not have the effect of turning a course, attendance on which was on a part-time basis, into a full-time course. Whether a person was, or was not, attending a full-time course depended on the facts at the material time. The factors suggested in *CIS 152/1994* were relevant; whether the person had a local authority grant or student loan might also be pertinent since these were not available to part-time students (see the Education (Mandatory Awards) Regulations). The claimant was not a student (as then defined) when he was attending part-time.

An appeal against this decision was dismissed by the Court of Appeal (*Chief Adjudication Officer v Webber* [1997] 4 All E.R. 274, also reported as *R(IS) 15/98*, but for differing reasons. Hobhouse LJ stated that the definition of "course of study" presupposes that it is possible at the outset to categorise a course as full-time or part-time and that the same categorisation will apply from the start to the end of the course. However, that assumption did not accord with the practice of many educational institutions. Many courses allowed students the option of attending on a full- or part-time basis at different stages of the course, as was the case in this appeal. The consequence was that the claimant had *never* been a student (as then defined) because the course on which he was enrolled did not require full-time attendance and so could not be described as full-time. Such an interpretation clearly had significant implications and went considerably beyond that of the Commissioner. Evans LJ held that the deeming provision in para.(a) of the then definition of "student" could not be relied upon to confer the status of student when this did not in fact exist. In his view, if interpreted in that way the provision created "an anomalous class of people left to destitution without state support of any kind" and he would require "express words of the utmost clarity to persuade [him] that Parliament intended to produce that disgraceful result". Peter Gibson LJ's judgment was based on the fact that the definition of "student" at the time in question included the words "throughout any period of term or vacation within it" (which phrase was omitted from August 1, 1995 following the Court of Appeal's decision in *Clarke and Faul*, see below). **2.583**

The result of these differing approaches was that the position was somewhat unclear. However in *O'Connor v Chief Adjudication Officer* [1999] All E.R.(D) 220, also reported as *R(IS) 7/99*, the judges who were in the majority agreed with Hobhouse LJ that the status of student (as then defined) was determined by the nature of the course at its beginning and distinguished their own decision from that in *Webber* on that basis. Auld LJ stated that in Mr O'Connor's case his course was a full-time three year course, with no provision for part-time or modular or other flexible arrangements. Although he had been allowed a year's break in order to re-take exams that he had failed, this was not an option of the course when he started it. But if at its start a course could be followed full- or part-time according to the student's preference, the position was different for the reasons given by Hobhouse LJ in *Webber*.

The consequence therefore seemed to be that a claimant on a course that could not be characterised as full-time at the outset because he could study full- or part-time for different periods of it would not come within the definition of "student" (as then defined). This was confirmed by *R(IS) 1/00*.

2.584 In *R(IS) 1/00* the claimant was undertaking a BTEC National Diploma course. When she claimed income support she was studying for 20 hours a week. The college stated that they did not designate courses as full-time or part-time, as students were able to take separate modules to build towards a final qualification. The Commissioner concluded that the express approval by Auld and Swinton LJJ in *O'Connor* of the view taken by Hobhouse LJ in *Webber* had been necessary to the decision in *O'Connor* and so authoritatively established the position. Thus the fundamental question was how the course was characterised at its outset. As Hobhouse LJ had stated, a course that did not have a fixed and determined character at its commencement and which could be followed on a full-time or part-time basis was not a full-time course. Moreover, in the Commissioner's view it inevitably followed from this approach that the result would be the same even if the claimant's actual attendance throughout had been on a full-time basis.

To determine whether the claimant's course should be treated as full-time, the Commissioner suggested that information would be needed about such matters as the structure of the course (modular or otherwise), the length of time over which it could be completed, whether a student was committed to any particular structure on initial registration and whether it was possible to change from full-time to part-time attendance or vice versa within the same course.

C5/98 (JSA) (a decision of a Northern Ireland Commissioner) also accepted that it was the nature of the course, as determined at the outset, that was relevant, as did *CJSA/836/1998*, although this was not the primary ground of the Commissioner's decision (see further below).

2.585 The Commissioner in *C5/98(JSA)* granted the claimant leave to appeal to the Court of Appeal in Northern Ireland but the appeal was dismissed (*McComb v Department for Social Development*, Northern Ireland Court of Appeal, reported as *R 1/01 (JSA)*). The claimant contended that the tribunal and the Commissioner, in classifying his course as full-time, had failed to take account of its modular nature. The Court agreed that a modular course was not readily distinguishable from a mixed mode one (the university concerned did not classify any course as mixed mode). It then continued: "The critical matter, however, is whether [the claimant] started out on a course of full-time study, even if he had the option of converting at a later stage to part-time by reducing the number of modules." But with respect to the Northern Ireland Court of Appeal this does not seem to fully accord with the approach of Hobhouse LJ in *Webber* (which has been followed in subsequent British cases, see above). If a claimant has the option of changing to studying on a part-time basis, how can it be said that the course requires full-time attendance, or that it has a fixed and determined character at its commencement? If it does not, then applying Hobhouse LJ's approach, it cannot be characterised as full-time at its outset.

On its facts, however, the decision in *McComb* that the claimant's course was full-time would seem correct. Mr McComb had enrolled on a full-time degree course for which he received an education authority grant for the first three years. When he failed to complete the final year's requirements he was allowed to register as an "examination only" student for a fourth year but he remained on the full-time course on which he had originally enrolled. Now see the new rules for modular courses introduced on July 31, 2000, although on the facts of Mr McComb's case the outcome is likely to be the same (see para.(3)(a)).

"Modular courses"

New rules were introduced on July 31, 2000 which were intended to clarify the position of modular courses. "Modular course" is defined in para.(4). To come within para.(4) a course must simply consist of two or more modules, the successful completion of a specific number of which is required in order for a student to finish the course. **2.586**

A person attending or undertaking part of a modular course which would be classified as a full-time course will be treated as a full-time student for the period from the day that part of the course begins until the last day he is registered as attending or undertaking that part as a full-time course (subject to earlier final abandonment or dismissal) (para.(2)(a)). This includes any vacation in that period, or immediately following that part of the course, unless the vacation follows the last day on which he is required to attend or undertake the course (para.(3)(b)). It also includes any period that the person attends or undertakes the course in order to retake examinations or a module that he had previously taken on a full-time basis. It seems that this will apply even if the person is now registered as a part-time student.

It will be a question of fact whether a person is attending or undertaking a part of a modular course that counts as a full-time course. Relevant evidence might include the university or college's regulations and registration procedures, the course regulations and course handbook and any other relevant information given to the student about his status. As stated above, the educational establishment's description is not conclusive but should be accepted unless challenged by pertinent evidence (*R(SB) 40/83; R(SB) 41/83*). It should be noted, however, that not all modular courses allow the option of full-time or part-time attendance. Some universities and colleges do not have mixed mode courses but only offer separate full-time and part-time courses, even though the courses are classed as modular. Disputes about whether the part of the modular course (or indeed the whole of the course) that the person is attending or undertaking counts as a full-time course may therefore still continue. If the modular course is a full-time course throughout it would seem to come within sub-para.(a) of para.(2) but may also be covered by sub-para.(b).

However, the importance of these new rules is that for modular courses the deeming of full-time student status only operates during the periods prescribed in paras (2) and (3). It does not apply outside these periods if the student's status has changed to part-time. A student on a part of a modular course which is not classed as full-time and who is not caught by para.(3) may thus be able to claim income support or JSA if he satisfies the normal condition of entitlement for one of these benefits.

"Attending or undertaking [a course] . . . finally abandons . . . or is dismissed from it"

The deeming provision, whereby a person whose non-modular course is full-time (as determined at its start, see above under "*Full-time course*") will count as a full-time student until the last day of the course or until he finally abandons or is dismissed from it is now contained in para.(2)(b). Note the separate deeming provision for those on a part of a modular course that is classed as full-time in para.(2)(a) (and note paras (3) and (4); see above for a discussion of these new rules for modular courses). **2.587**

The predecessor of para.(2)(b) (para.(a) of the former definition of "student", see the 2000 edition of this book, and see the 1995 edition of J. Mesher and P. Wood, *Income-related Benefits: the Legislation* for the form of para.(a) that was in force before August 1, 1995) came under close scrutiny in several cases, notably *Chief Adjudication Officer and Secretary of State for Social Security v Clarke and Faul* [1995] E.L.R. 259, *CIS 15594/1996* (appealed to the Court of Appeal as *O'Connor v Chief Adjudication Officer* [1999] All. E.R.(D) 220, also reported as *R(IS) 7/99*), *CIS 13986/1996* and *CIS 14255/1996*. For a discussion of these decisions see the 2000 edition of this book (pp.405–6). Note that one of the points decided in those cases, namely that "abandon" in this context meant "abandon permanently" has now received statutory endorsement in para.(2). Dismissal similarly means final dismissal (*CIS 15594/1996*). Note also *Driver v Chief Adjudication Officer* (Court of Appeal, December 12, 1996, reported as *R(IS) 6/97*) which held that a student on a sandwich course whose industrial placement ended prematurely nevertheless remained a student throughout the period of her intended placement.

As a result of those decisions, it seems fairly clearly established that a person whose non-modular course is full-time (as determined at its outset) will count as a full-time student until the last day of the course (subject to any earlier final abandonment or dismissal), regardless of non-attendance on the course for whatever reason. (But see above for the position of modular courses.) See also *MS v SSWP* [2009] UKUT 9 (AAC) which holds that the denial of JSA to a student who is not attending college for a year while he resits exams externally is not contrary to art.14, read with art.1 Prot.1 of the ECHR.

One other point should be made. Paragraph (2)(b) refers to "the course" that the full-time student is attending or undertaking. So if a student does finally abandon his full-time, non-modular course and then starts a separate part-time course he should not be caught by the deeming provision. In this connection it is interesting to note that para.12 of the Secretary of State's response to SSAC's report on the amendment regulations introduced on July 31, 2000 (Cmnd. 4739 (2000), see above under *"Student"* and *"Full-time Student"*) seems to accept that those changing from full-time to part-time courses are abandoning one course before starting another. Note, however, that this would not appear to assist a claimant who is not attending his course because he has failed exams and is only permitted to return if and when he successfully passes the resits. Although *CIS 13986/1996* decided that a claimant in that situation had been dismissed from his *original* course and if he passed the resit examinations a year later would be joining a *different* course, this was not followed in *CIS 15594/1996* (*O'Connor*). The Commissioner's view in *CIS 15594/1996* was that if a person was readmitted after an interval to follow essentially the same programme, that person was returning to the same course. On appeal the Court of Appeal in *O'Connor* decided the substantive issue in *CIS 13986/1996* against the claimant (for further discussion see pp.405–6 of the 2000 edition of this volume). See also MS v SSWP [2009] UKUT 9 (AAC) above.

2.588 Until October 27, 2008 a full-time student who had been incapable of work for 28 weeks (or who qualified for a disability or severe disability premium or was receiving a disabled student's allowance on the grounds of deafness) was eligible for income support (reg.4ZA(3)(b) and paras 10 and 12 of Sch.1B). However, following the introduction of ESA on October 27, 2008, new claims for income support on these grounds were no longer possible, except in certain circumstances. Thus from October 27, 2008 full-time students who are sick or disabled and are making a new claim have to claim ESA. However they will not qualify for income-related ESA unless they are entitled to disability living allowance ("DLA") (at any rate), personal independence payment ("PIP") (at any rate) or armed forces independence payment—see further para.6(1)(g) of Sch.1 to the Welfare Reform Act 2007 and regs 14–18 of the ESA Regulations 2008 in Vol.I of this series and the notes to those provisions. But a student who had an award of income support under paras 10 or 12 of Sch.1B when "migrated" to ESA will still be able to get ESA while a student, even though he is not entitled to DLA, PIP or armed forces independence payment (see Sch.1 para.2 and Sch.2 para.2 of the Employment and Support Allowance (Transitional Provisions, Housing Benefit and Council Tax Benefit) (Existing Awards) (No.2) Regulations 2010 (SI 2010/1907) (as amended) ("the Migration Regulations") also in Vol.1 of this series).

A further change took place on December 30, 2009 in relation to a student's eligibility for income support when paras 10 and 12 of Sch.1B were revoked, subject to a saving provision. See further the notes to reg.61 on pp.554–555 of the 2015/16 edition of this volume.

2.589 Note also that from July 31, 2000, a full-time student who has taken time out of his course with the consent of his university or college because of illness or caring responsibilities, and who has now recovered or whose caring responsibilities have ended, can claim JSA until the day before he rejoins his course or the first day of the following academic year, whichever is the earlier, provided that he is not eligible for a grant or student loan during this period (see reg.1(3D) and (3E) of the JSA Regulations 1996). Note that caring responsibilities in this context is not defined. For the position of pregnant students and JSA, see *Secretary of State for Social Security v Walter* [2001] EWCA Civ 1913, reported as *R(JSA) 3/02* (which overturned the decision in *CJSA 1920/1999*) and *CM v SSWP* [2009] UKUT 43 (AAC), reported as *R(IS) 7/09*, discussed in the notes to reg.130 of the JSA Regulations 1996. A pregnant student is excluded from income support (see reg.4ZA and Sch.1B; para.14 of Sch.1B which covers pregnant women is not one of the paragraphs applied to students by reg.4ZA(3)(b)). But once the child is born the student may be eligible under reg.4ZA(3)(b) and para.1 of Sch.1B if she is a lone parent. See further the note to reg.130 of the JSA Regulations.

Differences between income support and JSA definition

The definitions applying to full-time students under the JSA Regulations take a slightly different form (see the notes to reg.130 of the JSA Regulations 1996). **2.590**

Since the amendments made to both the Income Support and the JSA Regulations on July 31, 2000 by SI 2000 No.1981 the differences are less marked. However, in *CJSA 836/1998* (a decision on the pre-July 31, 2000 form) the Commissioner took the view that the differences between the then form of the JSA and income support definitions had a material effect. This was because for the purposes of JSA the provision deeming a person who had started a course to be attending or undertaking it until the last day of the course (or earlier abandonment or dismissal) was contained in the definition of "course of study" in reg.1(3) of the JSA Regulations 1996. Under income support the deeming provision was in the definition of "student" in reg.61. This defined a student as someone who was attending a full-time course and provided that a person who had started on "such a course" (i.e. a full-time course) was to be treated as attending it until the last day of the course or earlier abandonment or dismissal. The deeming under the definition of "course of study" in reg.1(3), on the other hand, did not necessarily refer to a full-time course. In the Commissioner's view, therefore, there was nothing in the JSA Regulations that required a person who had started a course on a full-time basis but changed to part-time to be treated as continuing to be a full-time student. Whether the course was full- or part-time was to be determined by looking at the situation at the time in question. But this approach was not followed in *C5/98 (JSA)*. The Commissioner in that case considered that the "it" in the definition of "course of study" in reg.1(3) referred to the course started. The fact that the "deeming" under JSA was contained in the definition of "course of study" rather than the definition of "student" was not material. This point was not dealt with by the Northern Ireland Court of Appeal in the appeal against *C5/98 (JSA)* (*McComb v Department for Social Development*, reported as *R 1/01 (JSA)*); see above).

But since the insertion of paras (3A)–(3C) into reg.1 of the JSA Regulations 1996 (which provisions parallel paras (2)–(4)) with effect from July 31, 2000 the Commissioner's reasoning in *CJSA 836/1998* no longer applies. This is because the deeming of full-time student status for the entire length of a course (subject to earlier final abandonment or dismissal) is now contained in reg.1(3A)(b) of the JSA Regulations, rather than the definition of "course of study" in reg.1(3).

Note also paras (3D) and (3E) of reg.1 of the JSA Regulations 1996 (see the notes to reg.130 of the JSA Regulations). There is no equivalent to these provisions in the Income Support Regulations.

Summary

The position for non-modular courses may thus be summarised as follows. Whether or not a person comes within the definition of "full-time student" depends on the nature of his course, as determined at its outset. If the course is not full-time so that the definition of full-time student does not apply, the fact that the person **2.591** attends the course on a full-time basis throughout would seem to be immaterial (see *CIS 12823/1996*). On the other hand, if the person's course is classified as full-time at its beginning, he will count as a student for the duration of his course (subject to earlier abandonment or dismissal), regardless of his actual mode of attendance on the course.

If the course is a modular one (as defined in para.(4)), the rules in paras (2) and (3) will apply (see above under *"Modular courses"*). Under para.(2)(a), it will be a question of fact whether a student is attending or undertaking a part of a modular course that would be classified as a full-time course. If a modular course is a full-time course throughout it would seem to come within sub-para.(a) of para.(2) but may also be covered by sub-para.(b). However, the importance of these new rules is that for modular courses the deeming of full-time student status only operates during the periods prescribed in paras (2) and (3). It does not apply outside these periods if the student's status has changed to part-time. A student on a part of a modular course which is not classed as full-time and who is not caught by para.(3) may thus be able to claim income support or JSA if he satisfies the normal conditions of entitlement for one of these benefits.

As readers will be aware, the Human Rights Act 1998 came into force on October 2, 2000 (see Vol.III of this series). The claimant in *O'Connor* had relied on the right to education in art.2 of the First Protocol to the European Convention on Human Rights in support of his argument on irrationality. However, Auld LJ considered that there was no potential breach of the right to education. This was because, firstly, there were rulings of inadmissibility by the European Commission of Human Rights suggesting that art.2 was concerned primarily with school, not higher, education (although now see *R. (Douglas) v North Tyneside and Metropolitan Borough Council* [2003] EWCA Civ 1847 in which the Court of Appeal held that tertiary or higher education fell within the meaning of "education" in art.2). Secondly, art.2 did not require the state to subsidise a student in his exercise of his right to avail himself of education which it provided (see further *Douglas*). For further challenges to the treatment of students in social security legislation both under EC Directive 79/7 and the Human Rights Act, see *Secretary of State for Social Security v Walter* [2001] EWCA Civ 1913, reported as *R(JSA) 3/02*, and *CM v SSWP* [2009] UKUT 43 (AAC), reported as *R(IS) 7/09*, (discussed in the note to reg.130 of the JSA Regulations 1996) and *CJSA/2663/2006* (in the note to reg.15(a) of those Regulations).

"Student loan"

2.592 Note *CIS/3734/2004* which confirms that since a claimant does not count as a student until he starts a course, in apportioning his loan income under reg.66A any loan income should be ignored until the beginning of the first term (despite the provision in reg.66A(2)(c)). The Commissioner accepted the Secretary of State's submission that "a student loan can only have an existence for the purposes of the Income Support (General) Regulations 1987 where it is for the maintenance of a student. Until the claimant starts to attend or undertake the course of study . . . [he] is not a student. Until [he] is a student, whatever the point in its administrative path [his] student loan application has reached, it cannot meet the definition of student loan herein and so does not fall to be taken into account as income."

Calculation of grant income

2.593 **62.**—(1) The amount of a student's grant income to be taken into account shall, subject to [3paragraphs [7(2) and (2A)]], be the whole of his grant income.

(2) There shall be disregarded from the amount of a student's grant income any payment—

(a) intended to meet tuition fees or examination fees;

(b) [4. . .]

(c) intended to meet additional expenditure incurred by a disabled student in respect of his attendance on a course;
(d) intended to meet additional expenditure connected with term time residential study away from the student's educational establishment;
(e) on account of the student maintaining a home at a place other than that at which he resides during his course but only to the extent that his rent [20. . .] is not met by housing benefit;
(f) on account of any other person but only if that person is residing outside of the United Kingdom and there is no applicable amount in respect of him;
(g) intended to meet the cost of books and equipment [4. . .] [6. . .];
(h) intended to meet travel expenses incurred as a result of his attendance on the course.
[18(i) intended for the maintenance [19. . .] of a child dependant.]
[19 (j) intended for the child care costs of a child dependant.]
[25 (k) of higher education bursary for care leavers made under Part III of the Children Act 1989.]

[6(2A) Where a student does not have a student loan and is not treated as possessing such a loan, there shall be excluded from the student's grant income—
(a) the sum of [23[26 £303] per academic year] in respect of travel costs; and
[12(b) the sum of [24[27 £390] per academic year] towards the costs of books and equipment,]
whether or not any such costs are incurred.]
[13[18 (2B) [21[22. . .]]]]

(3) [9 Subject to paragraph (3B), a student's grant income except any amount intended for the maintenance of [18 adult] dependants under Part III of Schedule 2 to the Education (Mandatory Awards) Regulations 1999 [18 . . .]] shall be apportioned—
(a) subject to paragraph (4), in a case where it is attributable to the period of study, equally between the weeks [16 in the period beginning with the benefit week, the first day of which coincides with, or immediately follows, the first day of the period of study and ending with the benefit week, the last day of which coincides with, or immediately precedes, the last day of the period of study];
(b) in any other case, equally between the weeks in the period [16 beginning with the benefit week, the first day of which coincides with, or immediately follows, the first day of the period for which it is payable and ending with the benefit week, the last day of which coincides with, or immediately precedes, the last day of the period for which it is payable].

[1(3A) [14 Any grant in respect of [18 an adult dependant] paid under section 63(6) of the Health Services and Public Health Act 1968 (grants in respect of the provision of instruction to officers of hospital authorities) and] any amount intended for the maintenance of [18 an adult dependant] under the provisions referred to in paragraph (3) shall be apportioned equally over a period of 52 weeks or, if there are 53 benefit weeks (including part-weeks) in the year, 53.]

[10 (3B) [16 In a case where a student is in receipt of a student loan or where he could have acquired a student loan by taking reasonable steps but had not done so,] any amount intended for the maintenance of [18 an adult dependant] under provisions other than those referred to in paragraph (3) shall be apportioned over the same period as the student's loan is apportioned or [16, as the case may be, would have been apportioned].]

(4) In the case of a student on a sandwich course, any periods of experience within the period of study shall be excluded and the student's grant income shall be apportioned equally between [16 the weeks in the period beginning with the benefit week, the first day of which immediately follows the last day of the period of experience and ending with the benefit week, the last day of which coincides with, or immediately precedes, the last day of the period of study].

AMENDMENTS

1. Income Support (General) Amendment Regulations 1988 (SI 1988/663) reg.24 (April 11, 1988).

2. Income Support (General) Amendment Regulations 1992 (SI 1992/468) reg.5 (April 6, 1992).

3. Income-related Benefits Schemes (Miscellaneous Amendments) (No.3) Regulations 1992 (SI 1992/2155) reg.20 (October 5, 1992).

4. Income-related Benefits Schemes and Social Fund (Miscellaneous Amendments) Regulations 1996 (SI 1996/1944) reg.6(9) (October 7, 1996).

5. Social Security (Student Amounts Amendment) Regulations 1998 (SI 1998/1379) reg.2 (August 31, 1998, or if the student's period of study begins between August 1, and 30, 1998, the first day of the period).

6. Social Security Amendment (Students) Regulations 1999 (SI 1999/1935) reg.3(3) (August 30, 1999, or if the student's period of study begins between August 1 and 29, 1999, the first day of the period).

7. Social Security Amendment (Students and Income-related Benefits) Regulations 2000 (SI 2000/1922) reg.2(4)(a) (August 28, 2000, or if the student's period of study begins between August 1 and 27, 2000, the first day of the period).

8. Social Security Amendment (Students and Income-related Benefits) Regulations 2000 (SI 2000/1922) reg.2(4)(b) (August 28, 2000, or if the student's period of study begins between August 1 and 27, 2000, the first day of the period).

9. Social Security Amendment (Students and Income-related Benefits) Regulations 2000 (SI 2000/1922) reg.2(4)(d) (August 28, 2000, or if the student's period of study begins between August 1 and 27, 2000, the first day of the period).

10. Social Security Amendment (Students and Income-related Benefits) Regulations 2000 (SI 2000/1922) reg.2(4)(e) (August 28, 2000, or if the student's period of study begins between August 1 and 27, 2000, the first day of the period).

11. Social Security Amendment (Students and Income-related Benefits) Regulations 2001 (SI 2001/2319) reg.3(1) and (3)(c) (August 27, 2001, or if the student's period of study begins between August 1 and 26, 2001, the first day of the period).

12. Social Security Amendment (Students and Income-related Benefits) Regulations 2001 (SI 2001/2319) reg.3(2) and (3)(c) (August 27, 2001, or if the student's period of study begins between August 1 and 26, 2001, the first day of the period).

13. Social Security Amendment (Students and Income-related Benefits) Regulations 2001 (SI 2001/2319) reg.3(4) (August 27, 2001, or if the student's period of study begins between August 1 and 26, 2001, the first day of the period).

14. Social Security Amendment (Students and Income-related Benefits) Regulations 2001 (SI 2001/2319) reg.6 (August 27, 2001, or if the student's period of study begins between August 1 and 26, 2001, the first day of the period).

15. Social Security Amendment (Students and Income-related Benefits) Regulations 2002 (SI 2002/1589) reg.3 (August 26, 2002, or if the student's period of study begins between August 1 and 25, 2002, the first day of the period).

16. Social Security Amendment (Students and Income-related Benefits) Regulations 2002 (SI 2002/1589) reg.4 (August 26, 2002, or if the student's period of study begins between August 1 and 25, 2002, the first day of the period).

17. Social Security Amendment (Students and Income-related Benefits) (No.2) Regulations 2002 (SI 2002/2207) reg.2 (September 2, 2002).

18. Social Security (Working Tax Credit and Child Tax Credit) (Consequential Amendments) Regulations 2003 (SI 2003/455) reg.2 and Sch.1 para.16 (April 6, 2004, except in transitional cases and see further the note to reg.17 of the Income Support Regulations), as amended by Social Security (Working Tax Credit and Child Tax Credit) (Consequential Amendments) (No.3) Regulations 2003 (SI 2003/1731) (August 8, 2003).

19. Social Security (Students and Income-related Benefits) Amendment Regulations 2004 (SI 2004/1708) reg.3(3) (September 1, 2004, or if the student's period of study begins between August 1 and August 31, 2004, the first day of the period).

20. Social Security (Miscellaneous Amendments) Regulations 2005 (SI 2005/574) reg.3(4) (April 4, 2005).

21. Social Security (Students and Income-related Benefits) Amendment Regulations 2005 (SI 2005/1807) reg.2(6) (September 1, 2005, or if the student's period of study begins between August 1 and August 31, 2005, the first day of the period).

22. Social Security (Students and Income-related Benefits) Amendment Regulations 2006 (SI 2006/1752) regs 4(3) and 6 (September 1, 2006, or if the student's period of study begins between August 1 and August 31, 2006, the first day of the period).

23. Social Security (Students and Income-related Benefits) Amendment Regulations 2007 (SI 2007/1632) reg.2(2)(a) (September 1, 2007, or if the student's period of study begins between August 1 and August 31, 2007, the first day of the period).

24. Social Security (Students and Income-related Benefits) Amendment Regulations 2007 (SI 2007/1632) reg.2(2)(b) (September 1, 2007, or if the student's period of study begins between August 1 and August 31, 2007, the first day of the period).

25. Social Security (Miscellaneous Amendments) Regulations 2009 (SI 2009/583) reg.2(10) (April 6, 2009).

26. Social Security (Students and Miscellaneous Amendments) Regulations 2009 (SI 2009/1575) reg.2(2) and (4)(a) (September 1, 2009, or if the student's period of study begins between August 1 and August 31, 2009, the first day of the period).

27. Social Security (Students and Miscellaneous Amendments) Regulations 2009 (SI 2009/1575) reg.2(3) and (4)(a) (September 1, 2009, or if the student's period of study begins between August 1 and August 31, 2009, the first day of the period).

Definitions

"grant"—see reg.61(1).
"grant income"—*ibid.*
"period of study"—*ibid.*
"periods of experience"—*ibid.*
"sandwich course"—*ibid.*
"student"—*ibid.*
"student loan"—*ibid.*

General Note

For students who started their course in or after the 1998/99 academic year, the main source of financial help is the student loan system (see the note to reg.66A). However, they may also be eligible for various additional allowances, which may be paid as grants (for example, if they have a child or a disability). Some of these grants will come under the rules in this regulation. **2.594**

Paragraph (2)

2.595 A student's grant is first to be subject to the disregards listed in paras (2)–(2A). Note that from August 30, 1999 the disregard in para.(2A) only applies if the student does not, and is not deemed to, have a student loan (defined in reg.61(1)): see reg.66A. The disregards referred to in para.(2A) will normally be applied to the student loan (see reg.66A(5)).

The disregard in para.(2)(i) is a general disregard of any payment intended for the maintenance of a child and that in para.(2)(j) is a general disregard of any payment intended for child care costs. They replaced the various disregards for students with child care responsibilities previously contained in para.(2B). Paragraph (2B) had gone through a number of forms and parts of the penultimate form of it remained in force in "transitional cases" (i.e. those cases in which the claimant is still receiving amounts for his children in his income support—see the notes to reg.17) but the one remaining sub-para.that was still in force for transitional cases (sub-para.(e)) was omitted on September 1, 2006 (or if the student's period of study began between August 1 and 31, 2006, on the first day of the period) by reg.4(3) of the Social Security (Students and Income-related Benefits) Amendment Regulations 2006 (SI 2006/1752) (see further the notes to this regulation in the 2006 edition of this volume and in the 2006/2007 Supplement to this series).

In *CIS 91/1994* the claimant argued that the disregard for books in para.(2)(g) should be apportioned over 52 weeks. It would then reduce the dependants and mature student elements of her grant that were taken into account in calculating her income support during the summer vacation. But the Commissioner holds that the deduction in sub-para.(g) could only be applied to the basic maintenance grant, as this was clearly the part of the grant which contained provision for books.

2.596 *R(IS) 7/95* confirms that it is the intention of the grant-making authority, not of the student, that counts under sub-para.(h). *R(IS) 16/95* similarly holds that in the case of the disregard for tuition fees under sub-para.(a), it is the intention of the provider of the payment that has to be considered. The fact that the claimant's partner spent all his grants from the Norwegian Government on tuition fees was irrelevant. Presumably the same approach would also be applied to the disregards in sub-paras (c), (d), (g), (i) and (j).

In *SB v Oxford CC (HB)* [2014] UKUT 166 (AAC) Judge Rowland takes the view that "to meet tuition fees" in reg.59(2)(a) of the Housing Benefit Regulations 2006 (the equivalent of sub-para.(a)) should be interpreted broadly so as to include repayment of a loan which had been used to pay tuition fees. However, the evidence in this case suggested that the claimant's bursary was intended to be used for living costs rather than tuition fees and so the repayment of the fee loan from the bursary was not covered by sub-para.(a). But that did not prevent part of that bursary being disregarded for other course-related costs, such as books and equipment and travel costs, since "living costs" may include course-related costs. On the facts Judge Rowland concluded that the minimum amount of the bursary—£305 in 2007–2008—should be excluded from the claimant's grant income as the claimant could legitimately expect this in accordance with published Government policy, including DWP guidance to decision makers, at the time.

Paragraphs (3)–(4)

2.597 A grant is normally apportioned over the weeks of the period of study, i.e. from the beginning of the academic year to the day before the summer vacation (para.(3)(a)). (The August 2002 amendment to para.(3)(a) is to ensure that the grant income is attributed to complete benefit weeks; see the similar amendments to paras (3)(b) and (4)).

Elements of the grant for mature students or dependants under the Mandatory Awards Regulations were apportioned over 52 weeks, but only while the person remained a student. *CIS 7/1988* holds that these elements of grant would ordinarily be attributable to the same period as the maintenance grant under the Mandatory Awards Regulations. *CIS 7/1988* is followed (with some reservation) in *R(IS) 1/96*, where the Commissioner points out that under reg.15(1) of the Mandatory Awards Regulations an award comes to an end on the expiry of the course. This supported the conclusion that in the final year the dependants and mature student elements were, like the ordinary maintenance grant, to be treated as payable for the period up to the day before the summer vacation. After that date the person was no longer a student and reg.62 no longer applied. A grant or bursary for dependants paid to NHS-funded students is also apportioned over 52 weeks (para.(3A)). In relation to social work bursaries, see *SSWP v LB* [2009] UKUT 117 (AAC). The tribunal decided that because it was paid by three termly instalments (which was the only evidence before it) the bursary was to be taken into account during the claimant's period of study (43 weeks) under para.(3)(a). However, further evidence produced by the Secretary of State before the Upper Tribunal indicated that in other cases it might be appropriate to take a similar bursary into account over a 52-week period under para.(3)(b).

In *R(IS) 15/95* the claimant claimed income support for the summer vacation at the end of the first year of her course. Her grant included a dependants allowance and a single parent's allowance. The Commissioner decides that the single parent element had to be apportioned over 52 weeks. This was because the single parent's allowance was provided for in Sch.4 to the Mandatory Awards Regulations. The effect of Sch.4 was to increase in certain circumstances the amount awarded under Pt III of Sch.2 for the maintenance of dependants. Sch.4 on its own awarded nothing. Thus the single parent's allowance was in fact merely an increase of the amount intended for the maintenance of dependants and so fell to be apportioned in accord with para.(3A). Even if this was not the case, the allowance had to be apportioned equally between the weeks in the period in respect of which it was payable (para.(3)(b)). That period was 52 weeks (see paras 12(1) and 20 of Sch.2 to the Mandatory Awards Regulations).

However, if the student's course started on or after September 1, 1998 (August 1, 1998 for Scotland) the grant for dependants is taken into account for the same period as the student loan (this used to apply even if the claimant did not have a student loan but from August 2002 it only applies if the student has received such a loan or could get one by taking reasonable steps) (para.(3B)). This is because under the system for student support introduced from the start of the 1998/1999 academic year (see further the note to reg.66A), the non-repayable dependants element is payable on the same basis as the student loan. **2.598**

Note that from September 1, 2003 grants for dependants have only been payable in respect of certain adult dependants or a spouse (Education (Student Support) (No.2) Regulations 2002 (SI 2002/3200) reg.15; the same applied to grants under the Education (Mandatory Awards) Regulations, see para.13(1) of Sch.2 to the 2003 Regulations (SI 2003/1994). "Partner" later replaced spouse and subsequently included, among others, a civil partner. Students with children are expected to apply for child tax credit for help with their costs

In addition, paras (3), (3A) and (3B) were amended with effect from April 6, 2004 (except in "transitional cases"—see reg.17) so that they only refer to grants in respect of adult dependants. This is as a consequence of the removal of amounts for children and young persons from the income support scheme with effect from April 6, 2004 (except in "transitional cases"). Financial assistance to help with the cost of bringing up a child or young person is to be provided through the child tax credit system, see Vol.IV of this series. The old form of these provisions (see the 2003 edition of this volume) continues in force for "transitional cases"—see the note to reg.17.

The current provisions (as at April 2016) for support for students are in the Education (Student Support) Regulations 2011 (SI 2011/1986), as amended. Among the amending regulations note in particular the Educational (Student Support) (Amendment) Regulations 2015 (SI 2015/1951) which came into force on December 23, 2015. Regulation 57 and the Schedule to the Regulations contain the rates for student support in respect of an academic year beginning on or after August 1, 2016. See also the Education (Student Support) (Amendment) **2.599**

Regulations 2016 (SI 2016/270) (in force from March 25, 2016 and which apply in respect of an academic year beginning on or after August 1, 2016), the main effect of which is to increase the residence condition for a student who is an EU national (but not a UK national) from three to five years preceding the start of the course for which s/he seeks support.

Subject to reg.62, a student's grant will be taken into account as income under reg.40. Thus any relevant disregards in Sch.9 will apply (*R(IS) 16/95*).

For the disregard of any grant (or covenant income, student loan or contribution) left over after a student has completed his course, see para.61 of Sch.9.

Calculation of covenant income where a contribution is assessed

2.600 **63.**—(1) Where a student is in receipt of income by way of a grant during a period of study and a contribution has been assessed, the amount of his covenant income to be taken into account for that period and any summer vacation immediately following shall be the whole amount of his covenant income less, subject to paragraph (3), the amount of the contribution.

(2) The weekly amount of the student's covenant income shall be determined—

(a) by dividing the amount of income which falls to be taken into account under paragraph (1) by 52 or, if there are 53 benefit weeks (including part weeks) in the year, 53; and

(b) by disregarding from the resulting amount, £5.

(3) For the purposes of paragraph (1), the contribution shall be treated as increased by the amount, if any, by which the amount excluded under [[1]regulation 62(2)(h) (calculation of grant income) falls short of the amount for the time being specified in paragraph 7(4)(i) of Schedule 2 to the Education (Mandatory Awards) Regulations 1991 (travel expenditure).]

AMENDMENT

1. Income Support (General) Amendment Regulations 1992 (SI 1992/468) reg.5 (April 6, 1992).

DEFINITIONS

"benefit week"—see reg.2(1).
"contribution"—see reg.61(1).
"covenant income"—*ibid.*
"grant"—*ibid.*
"period of study"—*ibid.*
"student"—*ibid.*

GENERAL NOTE

2.601 Although the number of covenants dropped away following the 1988 Budget, some existing covenants may have continued running, perhaps at inadequate levels.

If a student has a grant, with a parental contribution assessed, covenant income is only taken into account to the extent that it exceeds the assessed contribution (plus any addition under para.(3)). The definition of covenant income in reg.61 confines it to the payment net of tax. Any excess is spread over the whole year, with a £5 per week disregard.

Covenant income where no grant income or no contribution is assessed

2.602 **64.**—(1) Where a student is not in receipt of income by way of a grant the amount of his covenant income shall be calculated as follows—

(a) any sums intended for any expenditure specified in regulation 62(2)(a) to (f), (calculation of grant income) necessary as a result of his attendance on the course, shall be disregarded;

(b) any covenant income, up to the amount of the standard maintenance grant, which is not so disregarded, shall be apportioned equally between the weeks of the period of study and there shall be disregarded from the covenant income to be so apportioned the amount which would have been disregarded under [[1]regulation 62(2)(g) and (h) and (2A)] (calculation of grant income) had the student been in receipt of the standard maintenance grant;

(c) the balance, if any, shall be divided by 52 or, if there are 53 benefit weeks (including part weeks) in the year, 53 and treated as weekly income of which £5 shall be disregarded.

(2) Where a student is in receipt of income by way of a grant and no contribution has been assessed, the amount of his covenant income shall be calculated in accordance with sub-paragraphs (a) to (c) of paragraph (1), except that—

(a) the value of the standard maintenance grant shall be abated by the amount of his grant income less an amount equal to the amount of any sums disregarded under regulation 62(2)(a) to (f); and

(b) the amount to be disregarded under paragraph (1)(b) shall be abated by an amount equal to the amount of any sums disregarded under [[1]regulation 62(2)(g) and (h) and (2A)].

AMENDMENT

1. Income Support (General) Amendment Regulations 1992 (SI 1992/468) reg.5 (April 6, 1992).

DEFINITIONS

"benefit week"—see reg.2(1).
"contribution"—see reg.61(1).
"covenant income"—*ibid.*
"grant"—*ibid.*
"grant income"—*ibid.*
"student"—*ibid.*

GENERAL NOTE

Paragraph (1)

If the student has no grant, first any sums earmarked for things listed in reg.62(2)(a)–(f) are excluded. Then the amount of covenant income up to the rate of the standard maintenance grant (less the items specified above) is spread over the weeks of the period of study, disregarding items specified in reg.62(2)(g) and (h) and (2A). Then any excess is spread over the whole year with a £5 p.w. disregard. **2.603**

Paragraph (2)

If the student has a grant with no parental contribution, the effect is to spread the covenant income, after topping up any deficiency from the standard maintenance grant, over the whole year, as in para.(1). **2.604**

Relationship with amounts to be disregarded under Schedule 9

65.—No part of a student's convenant income or grant income shall be disregarded under paragraph 15 of Schedule 9 (charitable and voluntary payments) [[3] . . .]. **2.605**

AMENDMENTS

1. Income Support (General) Amendment Regulations 1990 (SI 1990/547) reg.14 (April 9, 1990).

2. Income-related Benefits Schemes (Miscellaneous Amendments) Regulations 1996 (SI 1996/462) reg.8 (April 8, 1996).

3. Social Security (Miscellaneous Amendments) (No.4) Regulations 2006 (SI 2006/2378) reg.5(5) (October 2, 2006).

DEFINITIONS

"covenant income"—see reg.61(1).
"grant income"—*ibid.*
"student"—*ibid.*

Other amounts to be disregarded

2.606 **66.**—(1) For the purposes of ascertaining income [1other than grant income, covenant income and loans treated as income in accordance with regulation 66A], any amounts intended for any expenditure specified in regulation 62(2) (calculation of grant income) necessary as a result of his attendance on the course shall be disregarded but only if, and to the extent that, the necessary expenditure exceeds or is likely to exceed the amount of the sums disregarded under regulation 62(2) [1and (2A)], 63(3) [2, 64(1) (a) or (b) and 66A(5) (calculation of grant income, covenant income and treatment of student loans)] on like expenditure.

(2) Where a claim is made in respect of any period in the normal summer vacation and any income is payable under a Deed of Convenant which commences or takes effect after the first day of that vacation, that income shall be disregarded.

AMENDMENTS

1. Income-related Benefits Schemes (Miscellaneous Amendments) Regulations 1994 (SI 1994/527) reg.5 (April 11, 1994).

2. Social Security Amendment (Students) Regulations 1999 (SI 1999/1935) reg.3(4) (August 30, 1999, or if the student's period of study begins between August 1 and 29, 1999, the first day of the period).

DEFINITIONS

"covenant income"—see reg.61(1).
"grant income"—*ibid.*
"student loan"—*ibid.*

GENERAL NOTE

2.607 Paragraph (2) will not be of any practical effect, because new covenants are unlikely to be made now that the tax advantages have been removed in the 1988 Budget.

[1Treatment of student loans

2.608 **66A.**—[6(1) A student loan shall be treated as income [13. . .].

(1A) [13. . .].

(2) In calculating the weekly amount of the loan to be taken into account as income—

[10(a) in respect of a course that is of a single academic year's duration or less, a loan which is payable in respect of that period shall be apportioned equally between the weeks in the period beginning with—
(i) except in a case where (ii) below applies, the benefit week, the first day of which coincides with, or immediately follows, the first day of the single academic year;
(ii) where the student is required to start attending the course in August or where the course is of less than an academic year's duration, the benefit week, the first day of which coincides with, or immediately follows, the first day of the course,
and ending with the benefit week, the last day of which coincides with, or immediately precedes, the last day of the course;]
[9(aa) in respect of an academic year of a course which starts other than on 1st September, a loan which is payable in respect of that academic year shall be apportioned equally between the weeks in the period beginning with the benefit week [10 , the first day of which coincides with, or immediately follows, the first day of that academic year and ending with the benefit week, the last day of which coincides with, or immediately precedes,] the last day of that academic year but excluding any benefit weeks falling entirely within the quarter during which, in the opinion of the Secretary of State, the longest of any vacation is taken and for the purposes of this sub-paragraph, "quarter" shall have the same meaning as for the purposes of the Education (Student Support) Regulations 2001;]
(b) in respect of the final academic year of a course (not being a course of a single year's duration), a loan, which is payable in respect of that final academic year shall be apportioned equally between the weeks in the period beginning with [10. . .]—
[10 (i) except in a case where (ii) below applies, the benefit week, the first day of which coincides with, or immediately follows, the first day of that academic year;
(ii) where the final academic year starts on 1st September, the benefit week, the first day of which coincides with, or immediately follows, the earlier of 1st September or the first day of the autumn term;]
and ending with [10 the benefit week, the last day of which coincides with, or immediately precedes,] the last day of the course;
(c) in any other case, the loan shall be apportioned equally between the weeks in the period beginning with the earlier of—
(i) the first day of the first benefit week in September; or
[10 (ii) the benefit week, the first day of which coincides with, or immediately follows, the first day of the autumn term,]
and ending with [10 the benefit week, the last day of which coincides with, or immediately precedes, the last day of June],
and, in all cases, from the weekly amount so apportioned there shall be disregarded £10.]

[5(3) A student shall be treated as possessing a student loan in respect of an academic year where—
(a) a student loan has been made to him in respect of that year; or
(b) he could acquire such a loan in respect of that year by taking reasonable steps to do so.
(4) Where a student is treated as possessing a student loan under

paragraph (3), the amount of the student loan to be taken into account as income shall be, subject to paragraph (5)—

(a) in the case of a student to whom a student loan is made in respect of an academic year, a sum equal to the maximum student loan he is able to acquire in respect of that year by taking reasonable steps to do so and either—

(i) in the case of a student other than one to whom head (ii) refers, any contribution whether or not it has been paid to him; or

(ii) in the case of a student to whom paragraph 1, 2, [17 *10*,] 11 [14 , [17 *12*] or 15A of Schedule 1B applies (lone parent, disabled student or persons in education)], any contribution which has actually been paid to him;

(b) in the case of a student to whom a student loan is not made in respect of an academic year, the maximum student loan that would be made to the student if—

(i) he took all reasonable steps to obtain the maximum student loan he is able to acquire in respect of that year; and

(ii) no deduction in that loan was made by virtue of the application of a means test.

(5) There shall be deducted from the amount of income taken into account under paragraph (4)—

(a) the sum of [11[15£303] per academic year] in respect of travel costs; and,

[8(b) the sum of [12[16£390] per academic year] towards the costs of books and equipment,]

whether or not any such costs are incurred.]]

AMENDMENTS

1. Social Security Benefits (Student Loans and Miscellaneous Amendments) Regulations 1990 (SI 1990/1549) reg.5(7) (September 1, 1990).

2. Income Support (General) Amendment Regulations 1991 (SI 1991/236) reg.9 (March 13, 1991).

3. Income Support (General) Amendment No.4 Regulations 1991 (SI 1991/1559) reg.12 (August 5, 1991).

4. Income-related Benefits Schemes (Miscellaneous Amendments) Regulations 1996 (SI 1996/462) reg.9 (April 8, 1996).

5. Social Security Amendment (Students) Regulations 1999 (SI 1999/1935) reg.3(5) (August 30, 1999, or if the student's period of study begins between August 1 and 29, 1999, the first day of the period).

6. Social Security Amendment (Students and Income-related Benefits) Regulations 2000 (SI 2000/1922) reg.2(5) (August 28, 2000, or if the student's period of study begins between August 1 and 27, 2000, the first day of the period).

7. Social Security Amendment (Students and Income-related Benefits) Regulations 2001 (SI 2001/2319) regs 3(1) and (3)(c) (August 27, 2001, or if the student's period of study begins between August 1 and 26, 2001, the first day of the period).

8. Social Security Amendment (Students and Income-related Benefits) Regulations 2001 (SI 2001/2319) reg.3(2) and (3)(c) (August 27, 2001, or if the student's period of study begins between August 1 and 26, 2001, the first day of the period).

9. Social Security Amendment (Students and Income-related Benefits) Regulations 2001 (SI 2001/2319) reg.4 (August 27, 2001, or if the student's period of study begins between August 1 and 26, 2001, the first day of the period).

10. Social Security Amendment (Students and Income-related Benefits) Regulations 2002 (SI 2002/1589) reg.5 (August 26, 2002, or if the student's period of study begins between August 1 and 25, 2002, the first day of the period).

11. Social Security (Students and Income-related Benefits) Amendment Regulations 2007 (SI 2007/1632) reg.2(3)(a) (September 1, 2007, or if the student's period of study begins between August 1 and August 31, 2007, the first day of the period).

12. Social Security (Students and Income-related Benefits) Amendment Regulations 2007 (SI 2007/1632) reg.2(3)(b) (September 1, 2007, or if the student's period of study begins between August 1 and August 31, 2007, the first day of the period).

13. Social Security (Miscellaneous Amendments) (No.6) Regulations 2008 (SI 2008/2767) reg.2(10) (November 17, 2008).

14. Social Security (Miscellaneous Amendments) Regulations 2009 (SI 2009/583) reg.2(11) (April 6, 2009).

15. Social Security (Students and Miscellaneous Amendments) Regulations 2009 (SI 2009/1575) reg.2(2) and (4)(a) (September 1, 2009, or if the student's period of study begins between August 1 and August 31, 2009, the first day of the period).

16. Social Security (Students and Miscellaneous Amendments) Regulations 2009 (SI 2009/1575) reg.2(3) and (4)(a) (September 1, 2009, or if the student's period of study begins between August 1 and August 31, 2009, the first day of the period).

17. Income Support (Prescribed Categories of Person) Regulations 2009 (SI 2009/3152) reg.3(2)(d) and 3(7) (December, 30, 2009). Regulation 3(2)(d) omitted "10," and "12" in reg.66A(4)(a)(ii) with effect from December 30, 2009 but reg.3(7) provided that this did not apply in the case of a person who was subject to the saving provisions in reg.2(2) of those Regulations. See the 2015/16 edition of this volume for these Regulations and the notes to them.

DEFINITIONS

"academic year"—see reg.61(1).
"benefit week"—see reg.2(1).
"last day of the course"—see reg.61(1).
"student"—*ibid.*
"student loan"—*ibid.*
"year"—*ibid.*

GENERAL NOTE

The changes made to this regulation on August 30, 1999, and the further changes made on August 28, 2000, reflected the introduction of the "new" system for student support from the start of the 1998/1999 academic year. The previous system of grants and non-means-tested loans continued for "existing" students (i.e. broadly those who started their course before September 1, 1998 (August 1, 1998 for Scotland)). However, "new" students received financial support by way of a loan. **2.609**

The basic rule is that if a student is, exceptionally, entitled to income support, the amount of the maximum student loan (defined in reg.61(1)) that he would be entitled to if he applied for it is treated as income, whether he actually applies for the loan or not. The amount of the student loan taken into account will include any assessed contribution, but in the case of lone parent or disabled students or students who are in non-advanced education and entitled under para.15A of Sch.1B only to the extent that any such contribution has actually been paid (para.(4)(a)). However, if no loan has been applied for, the amount treated as income will be the maximum student loan without any deduction for unpaid contributions (para.(4)(b)). A deduction of £303 for travel costs and £390 for books and equipment will be made (para.(5)). Note that the amount of the travel disregard is now specified in the regulations as the DfEE have introduced one unified figure for travel costs rather than having differing amounts for those living in the parental home and elsewhere.

The income so calculated is then apportioned in accordance with the rules in para.(2), with a £10 disregard. Note the definition of "academic year" in reg.61(1). If the student is required to start attending his course during August or September (as will usually be the case) and to continue attending through the autumn, the academic year of the course will be the 12 months starting on September 1. Loans payable for courses of one year's duration or less, or for the final year of a course, are covered by sub-paras (a) and (b) respectively; sub-para.(aa) deals with courses in which the academic year starts other than in the autumn; and sub-para.(c) applies in other cases. The purpose of the amendments made to para.(2) in August 2002 is to ensure that a student loan is apportioned over and attributed to complete benefit weeks.

2.610 Under sub-para.(c), the loan is apportioned over the period from the first benefit week in September, or the benefit week, the first day of which coincides with, or immediately follows, the beginning of the autumn term (whichever is the earlier), to the benefit week, the last day of which coincides with, or immediately precedes the last day of June. In the first year of a course the effect of this rule could be to attribute loan income to a period before the actual start of the claimant's course. But since a claimant does not count as a student until he starts a course, it is suggested that any loan income should be ignored until the beginning of the term. This has now been confirmed by *CIS/3734/2004*. The Commissioner accepted the Secretary of State's submission that "a student loan can only have an existence for the purposes of the Income Support (General) Regulations 1987 where it is for the maintenance of a student. Until the claimant starts to attend or undertake the course of study . . . she is not a student. Until she is a student, whatever the point in its administrative path her student loan application has reached, it cannot meet the definition of student loan herein and so does not fall to be taken into account as income."

In the final year of the course the period that the loan income is taken into account starts from the benefit week, the first day of which coincides with, or immediately follows, the earlier of September 1 or the first day of the autumn term in a case where the final year begins on September 1; otherwise it starts from the benefit week, the first day of which coincides with, or immediately follows, the first day of that final year. It ends with the benefit week which coincides with, or immediately precedes, the last day of the course (sub-para.(b)).

In the case of courses of one year's duration or less, the period over which the loan is apportioned starts from the benefit week which coincides with, or immediately precedes, the first day of the course in a case where the course begins in August or is for less than one academic year; otherwise it starts from the benefit week, the first day of which coincides with, or immediately follows, the first day of the academic year. It ends with the benefit week, the last day of which coincides with, or immediately precedes, the last day of the course (sub-para.(a)).

2.611 Where the academic year starts other than in the autumn, the loan is apportioned over the period which begins with the benefit week, the first day of which coincides with, or immediately follows, the first day of that academic year and ends with the benefit week, the last day of which coincides with, or immediately precedes, the last day of that academic year but excluding any complete benefit weeks within the "quarter" during which the longest vacation falls (sub-para.(aa)). A quarter is one of the periods from January 1 to March 31, April 1 to June 30, July 1 to August 31 and September 1 to December 31 (see the Education (Student Support) Regulations 2011 (SI 2011/1986), as amended, which contain the current (as at April 2016) provisions for support for students).

For the apportionment of student loans under the previous form of para.(2) (in force until August 28, 2000), see the note to reg.66(2) in the 2000 edition of this volume.

See reg.40(3A)–(3B) for the position where a student ends the course prematurely.

2.612 For the disregard of any student loan (grant or covenant income or contribution) left over after the student has completed his course, see para.61 of Sch.9.

Note also *R(IS) 16/95* and *R(JSA) 4/04*, referred to in the note to "grant" in reg.61. *R(JSA) 4/04* confirms that reg.136 of the JSA Regulations 1996 (which is the equivalent of reg.66A) only applies to loans paid to full-time students; thus the student loan paid to the claimant who was a part-time student fell to be taken into account in full without any disregards.

For the treatment of access funds see regs 66B and 68(2) and (3).

[1 Treatment of payments from access funds

66B.—(1) This regulation applies to payments from access funds that are not payments to which regulation 68(2) or (3) (income treated as capital) applies. 2.613

(2) A payment from access funds, other than a payment to which paragraph (3) of this regulation applies, shall be disregarded as income.

(3) Subject to paragraph (4) of this regulation and paragraph 36 of Schedule 9, any payments from access funds which are intended and used for food, ordinary clothing or footwear [4 . . .], household fuel, rent for which housing benefit is payable [2 or any housing costs] to the extent that they are met under regulation 17(1)(e) or 18(1)(f) (housing costs) [2 . . .], of a single claimant or, as the case may be, of [3 his partner], and any payments from access funds that are used for any council tax or water charges for which that claimant or [3 partner is liable] shall be disregarded as income to the extent of £20 per week.

[4 (3A) In paragraph (3) "ordinary clothing or footwear" means clothing or footwear for normal daily use, but it does not include—

(a) school uniforms, or

(b) clothing or footwear used solely for sporting activities.]

(4) Where a payment from access funds is made—

(a) on or after 1st September or the first day of the course, whichever first occurs, but before receipt of any student loan in respect of that year and that payment is intended for the purpose of bridging the period until receipt of the student loan; or

(b) before the first day of the course to a person in anticipation of that person becoming a student,

that payment shall be disregarded as income.]

AMENDMENTS

1. Social Security Amendment (Students and Income-related Benefits) Regulations 2000 (SI 2000/1922) reg.2(6) (August 28, 2000, or if the student's period of study begins between August 1 and 27, 2000, the first day of the period).

2. Social Security Amendment (Residential Care and Nursing Homes) Regulations 2001 (SI 2001/3767) reg.2(1) and Pt I of Sch. para.10 (April 8, 2002).

3. Social Security (Working Tax Credit and Child Tax Credit) (Consequential Amendments) Regulations 2003 (SI 2003/455) reg.2 and Sch.1 para.17 (April 6, 2004, except in "transitional cases" and see further the note to reg.17 of the Income Support Regulations).

4. Social Security (Miscellaneous Amendments) Regulations 2007 (SI 2007/719) reg.2(5) (April 2, 2007).

DEFINITIONS

"access funds"—see reg.61(1).
"claimant"—see reg.2(1).
"payment"—*ibid.*
"single claimant"—*ibid.*
"student"—see reg.61(1).
"student loan"—*ibid.*

GENERAL NOTE

2.614 Regulation 66B and the new paras (2) and (3) of reg.68 (added with effect from August 28, 2000) are concerned with the treatment of payments from access funds (defined in reg.61(1)). These funds are administered by individual colleges and universities. An access fund payment (for the definition of "payment" see reg.2(1)) that is paid as a single lump sum will be treated as capital (reg.68(2)). If such a payment of capital is intended and used for items other than food, ordinary clothing or footwear (defined in reg.68(4)), fuel, housing costs met by income support or housing benefit, council tax or water charges, it is disregarded for 52 weeks from the date of payment (reg.68(3)). Other payments from access funds are ignored as income unless they are intended and used for food, ordinary clothing or footwear (defined in para.(3A)), fuel, housing costs met by income support or housing benefit, council tax or water charges, in which case a disregard of up to £20 applies (this is subject to the overall limit of £20 for this and other payments in para.36 of Sch.9) (reg.66B(2) and (3)). But even if the payment is to cover the cost of food, etc. it will be totally ignored as income if it is intended to bridge a gap before the start of a course or receipt of a student loan (reg.66B(4)).

Note that the amendments made to this regulation (and to reg.68) with effect from April 6, 2004 (except in "transitional cases"—see the note to reg.17) are as a consequence of the removal of amounts for children and young persons from the income support scheme with effect from April 6, 2004 (except in "transitional cases"). Financial assistance to help with the cost of bringing up a child or young person is now to be provided through the child tax credit system, see Vol.IV of this series, and income support has in effect become an "adults only" benefit. The old form of this regulation (see the 2003 edition of this volume) continues in force for "transitional cases"—see the note to reg.17.

[1 Treatment of fee loans

2.615 **66C.**—A loan for fees, known as a fee loan or a fee contribution loan, made pursuant to regulations made under Article 3 of the Education (Student Support) (Northern Ireland) Order 1998, section 22 of the Teaching and Higher Education Act 1998 or section 73(f) of the Education (Scotland) Act 1980, shall be disregarded as income.]

AMENDMENT

1. Social Security (Students and Income-related Benefits) Amendment Regulations 2006 (SI 2006/1752) reg.4(4) (September 1, 2006, or if the student's period of study begins between August 1 and August 31, 2006, the first day of the period).

GENERAL NOTE

2.616 Fee loans and fee-contribution loans have been introduced as part of the student support system from the beginning of the academic year in 2006. Any such loan for tuition fees is to be disregarded.

Disregard of contribution

2.617 **67.**—Where the claimant or his partner is a student and [1, for the purposes of assessing a contribution to the student's grant [2or student loan], the other partner's income has been taken into account, an account equal to that contribution shall be disregarded for the purposes of assessing that other partner's income.]

AMENDMENTS

1. Income-related Benefits Schemes (Miscellaneous Amendments) Regulations 1996 (SI 1996/462) reg.10 (April 8, 1996).
2. Social Security Amendment (Students) Regulations 1999 (SI 1999/1935) reg.3(6) (August 30, 1999, or if the student's period of study begins between August 1 and 29, 1999, the first day of the period).

DEFINITIONS

"claimant"—see reg.2(1) and reg.23(1).
"contribution"—see reg.61(1).
"grant"—*ibid.*
"partner"—see reg.2(1).
"student"—see reg.61(1).
"student loan"—*ibid.*

Further disregard of student's income

67A.—Where any part of a student's income has already been taken into account for the purposes of assessing his entitlement to a grant [2 or student loan], the amount taken into account shall be disregarded in assessing that student's income.] **2.618**

AMENDMENTS

1. Social Security (Miscellaneous Amendments) Regulations 1998 (SI 1998/563) reg.4(3) and (4)(e) (April 6, 1998),
2. Social Security Amendment (Students) Regulations 1999 (SI 1999/1935) reg.3(7) (August 30, 1999, or if the student's period of study begins between August 1 and 29, 1999, the first day of the period).

DEFINITIONS

"grant"—see reg.61(1).
"student"—*ibid.*
"student loan"—*ibid.*

Income treated as capital

68.—[1(1)] Any amount by way of a refund of tax deducted from a student's income shall be treated as capital. **2.619**

[1 (2) An amount paid from access funds as a single lump sum shall be treated as capital.

(3) An amount paid from access funds as a single lump sum which is intended and used for an item other than food, ordinary clothing or foot-wear [4 . . .], household fuel, rent for which housing benefit is payable, [2 or any housing costs] to the extent that they are met under regulation 17(1)(e) or 18(1)(f) (housing costs) [2 . . .], of a single claimant or, as the case may be, of [3 his partner], or which is used for an item other than any council tax or water charges for which that claimant or [3 partner is liable] shall be disregarded as capital but only for a period of 52 weeks from the date of the payment.]

[4 (4) In paragraph (3) "ordinary clothing or footwear" means clothing or footwear for normal daily use, but it does not include—

(a) school uniforms, or
(b) clothing or footwear used solely for sporting activities.]

Amendments

1. Social Security Amendment (Students and Income-related Benefits) Regulations 2000 (SI 2000/1922) reg.2(7) (August 28, 2000, or if the student's period of study begins between August 1 and 27, 2000, the first day of the period).

2. Social Security Amendment (Residential Care and Nursing Homes) Regulations 2001 (SI 2001/3767) reg.2(1) and Pt I of Sch. para.11 (April 8, 2002).

3. Social Security (Working Tax Credit and Child Tax Credit) (Consequential Amendments) Regulations 2003 (SI 2003/455) reg.2 and Sch.1 para.17 (April 6, 2004, except in "transitional cases" and see further the note to reg.17 of the Income Support Regulations.

4. Social Security (Miscellaneous Amendments) Regulations 2007 (SI 2007/719) reg.2(6) (April 2, 2007).

Definitions

"access funds"—see reg.61(1).
"claimant"—see reg.2(1).
"payment"—*ibid.*
"single claimant"—*ibid.*
"student"—see reg.61(1).

General Note

2.620 On paras (2)–(4), see the note to reg.66A.

Disregard of changes occurring during summer vacation

2.621 **69.**—In calculating a student's income [1 there shall be disregarded] any change in the standard maintenance grant occurring in the recognised summer vacation appropriate to the student's course, if that vacation does not from part of his period of study, from the date on which the change occurred up to the end of that vacation.

Amendment

1. Social Security Act 1998 (Commencement No.12 and Consequential and Transitional Provisions) Order 1999 (SI 1999/3178 (C.81)) art.3(5) and Sch.5 para.7 (November 29, 1999).

Definitions

"period of study"—see reg.61(1).
"standard maintenance grant"—*ibid.*
"student"—*ibid.*

Part VI

Urgent Cases

General Note

2.622 For a detailed commentary on urgent cases payments, see pp.497–509 of Vol.II of the 2009/10 edition. In summary, Pt VI (regs 70–72), provided for payments of IS at a reduced (90 per cent) "urgent cases" rate to:

- certain claimants who were treated as possessing notional income under reg.42(3);

- claimants who would otherwise be persons subject to immigration control but who are excluded from s.115 of the Immigration and Asylum Act 1999 by reg.2 of, and Sch.1 Pt 1 paras 3 and 4 to, the Social Security (Immigration and Asylum) Regulations 2000 (SI 2000/636); and

- (by virtue of the savings provision in reg.12(3)–(5) of SI 2000/636) certain asylum seekers whose claim for asylum was made on or before April 2, 2000.)

Part VI was revoked by the Social Security (Miscellaneous Amendments) (No.5) Regulations 2009 (SI 2009/3228) reg.2 with effect from January 25, 2010. That revocation was subject to three savings.

The first saving covers any person to whom reg.70(2)(b) applied (i.e. who was treated as possessing notional income) on January 24, 2010: see reg.2(2) of SI 2009/3228 (below).

The second saving covers any person who, on the same date, fell within Sch.1 Pt 1 para.1 of SI 2000/636. That paragraph relates to claimants with limited leave to enter or remain in the UK (and who, but for that paragraph and reg.2 of SI 2000/636 would have been persons subject to immigration control) and who are temporarily without funds because remittances to them from abroad had been disrupted. The savings provision applies for a period of 42 days—or a number of periods not exceeding 42 days in total—within the same period of leave or until the claimant ceases to fall within para.1 of the Schedule: see reg.2(3) of SI 2009/3228 (below). Claimants who first fell within Sch.1 Pt 1 para.1 of SI 2000/636 after January 24, 2010, but before October 29, 2013, could claim income support at the full rate, rather than the urgent cases rate. Once again entitlement lasted for a maximum period of 42 days—or a number of periods not exceeding 42 days in total—within the same period of leave. However, Sch.1 Pt 1 para.1 and reg.22B were both revoked with effect from October 29, 2013: see respectively below and above. **2.623**

The third saving relates to pre-April 3, 2000 asylum seekers. It is possible that by the date on Pt VI was revoked, nearly 10 years later, everyone who had claimed asylum on or before April 2, 2000, had either abandoned that claim or had it granted or refused. Such people would have ceased to be an asylum seeker by virtue of reg.12(5) of SI 2000/636(see pp.501–502 of Vol.II of the 2009–2010 edition). If that is correct, then it may be that no-one was actually receiving urgent cases payments under reg.12(3) of SI 2000/636 when that provision was reversed. However, if there were any such people, they became entitled to income support at the full rate rather than the urgent cases rate until such time as reg.12(5) applies to them: (see Sch.1B para.21 (below) and reg.2(5) of SI 2000/636 (below).

[1PART VII

CALCULATION OF INCOME SUPPORT FOR PART-WEEKS

Amount of income support payable

73.—(1) Subject to regulations 75 (modifications in income) and 76 (reduction in certain cases), where a claimant is entitled to income support for a period (referred to in this Part as a part-week) to which subsection (1A) of section 21 of the Act [SSCBA, s.124(5)] (amount etc. of income-related benefit) applies, the amount of income support payable shall, except **2.624**

where paragraph (2) applies, be calculated in accordance with the following formulae—

(a) if the claimant has no income, $\frac{N \times A}{7}$;

(b) if the claimant has income, $\frac{N \times (A - I)}{7} - B$.

(2) [6. . .]

(3) In this Regulation—

"A", [6. . .] means the claimant's weekly applicable amount in the relevant week;

"B" means the amount of any income support, [5jobseeker's allowance], [2maternity allowance,] [4short-term or long-term incapacity benefit], or [7 severe disablement allowance or employment and support allowance] payable in respect of any day in the part-week;

"I" means his weekly income in the relevant week less B;

"N" means the number of days in the part-week;

"relevant week" means the period of 7 days determined in accordance with regulation 74.

(4) and (5) [6. . .]

AMENDMENTS

1. Income Support (General) Amendment Regulations 1988 (SI 1988/663) reg.27 (April 11, 1988).

2. Income Support (General) Amendment No.4 Regulations 1988 (SI 1988/1445) reg.17 (September 12, 1988).

4. Disability Working Allowance and Income Support (General) Amendment Regulations 1995 (SI 1995/482) reg.12 (April 13, 1995).

5. Income Support (General) (Jobseeker's Allowance Consequential Amendments) Regulations 1996 (SI 1996/206) reg.19 (October 7, 1996).

6. Social Security Amendment (Residential Care and Nursing Homes) Regulations 2001 (SI 2001/3767) reg.2 and Sch. Pt I para.13 (April 8, 2002).

7. Employment and Support Allowance (Consequential Provisions) (No.2) Regulations 2008 (SI 2008/1554) reg.2(1) and (9) (October 27, 2008).

DEFINITIONS

"the Act"—see reg.2(1).
"claimant"—*ibid.*

GENERAL NOTE

2.625 Although the rules set out in regs 73–77 do look very complex, they set out a relatively straightforward method of calculating benefit for part-weeks. See *CIS 706/1997* for an exposition of how these rules operate.

[1Relevant week

2.626 **74.**—(1) Where the part-week—

(a) is the whole period for which income support is payable or occurs at the beginning of the claim, the relevant week is the period of 7 days ending on the last day of that part-week; or

(b) occurs at the end of the claim, the relevant week is the period of 7 days beginning on the first day of that part-week.

(2) Where during the currency of a claim the claimant makes a claim

for a relevant social security benefit within the meaning of paragraph 4 of Schedule 7 to the Social Security (Claims and Payments) Regulations 1987 and as a result his benefit week changes, for the purpose of calculating the amount of income support payable—

(a) for the part-week beginning on the day after his last complete benefit week before the date from which he makes a claim for the relevant social security benefit and ending immediately before that date, the relevant week is the period of 7 days beginning on the day after his last complete benefit week (the first relevant week);

(b) for the part-week beginning on the date from which he makes a claim for the relevant social security benefit and ending immediately before the start of his next benefit week after the date of that claim, the relevant week is the period of 7 days ending immediately before the start of his next benefit week (the second relevant week).

(3) Where during the currency of a claim the claimant's benefit week changes at the direction of the Secretary of State under paragraph 3 of Schedule 7 to the Social Security (Claims and Payments) Regulations 1987, for the purpose of calculating the amount of income support payable for the part-week beginning on the day after his last complete benefit week before the change and ending immediately before the change, the relevant week is the period of 7 days beginning on the day after the last complete benefit week.]

AMENDMENT

1. Income Support (General) Amendment Regulations 1988 (SI 1988/663) reg.27 (April 11, 1988).

DEFINITIONS

"benefit week"—see reg.2(1).
"claimant"—*ibid.*

[1Modifications in the calculation of income

75.—For the purposes of regulation 73 (amount of income support payable for part-weeks), a claimant's income and the income of any person which the claimant is treated as possessing under section 22(5) of the Act [SSCBA, s.136(1)] or regulation 23(3) shall be calculated in accordance with Part V and, where applicable, VI subject to the following modifications— **2.627**

(a) any income which is due to be paid in the relevant week shall be treated as paid on the first day of that week;

(b) any income support, [4jobseeker's allowance], [2maternity allowance,] [3short-term or long-term incapacity benefit], [5 severe disablement allowance [6 , employment and support allowance or universal credit]] [3. . .] payable in the relevant week but not in respect of any day in the part-week shall be disregarded;

(c) where the part-week occurs at the end of the claim, any income or any change in the amount of income of the same kind which is first payable within the relevant week but not on any day in the part-week shall be disregarded;

(d) where the part-week occurs immediately after a period in which a person was treated as engaged in remunerative work) under regulation 5(5) (persons treated as engaged in remunerative work) any earnings which are taken into account for the purposes of determining that period shall be disregarded;

(e) where regulation 74(2) (relevant week) applies, any payment of income which—

(i) is the final payment in a series of payments of the same kind or, if there has been an interruption in such payments, the last one before the interruption;

(ii) is payable in respect of a period not exceeding a week; and

(iii) is due to be paid on a day which falls within both the first and second relevant weeks,

shall be taken into account in either the first relevant week or, if it is impracticable to take it into account in that week, in the second relevant week; but this paragraph shall not apply to a payment of income support, [4jobseeker's allowance], [2maternity allowance,] [3short-term or long-term incapacity benefit] [5 severe disablement allowance or employment and support allowance], [3. . .];

(f) where regulation 74(2) applies, any payment of income which—

(i) is the final payment in a series of payments of the same kind or, if there has been an interruption in such payments, the last one before the interruption;

(ii) is payable in respect of a period exceeding a week but not exceeding 2 weeks; and

(iii) is due to be paid on a day which falls within both the first and second relevant weeks,

shall be disregarded; but this sub-paragraph shall not apply to a payment of income support, [4jobseeker's allowance], [2maternity allowance,] [3short-term or long term incapacity benefit], [5 severe disablement allowance or employment and support allowance] [3. . .]

(g) where regulation 74(2) applies, if the weekly amount of any income which is due to be paid on a day which falls within both the first and second relevant weeks is more than the weekly amount of income of the same kind due to be paid in the last complete benefit week, the excess shall be disregarded;

(h) where only part of the weekly amount of income is taken into account in the relevant week, the balance shall be disregarded.]

AMENDMENTS

1. Income Support (General) Amendment Regulations 1988 (SI 1988/663) reg.27 (April 11, 1988).

2. Income Support (General) Amendment No.4 Regulations 1988 (SI 1988/1445) reg.17 (September 12, 1988).

3. Disability Working Allowance and Income support (General) Amendment Regulations 1995 (SI 1995/482) reg.13 (April 13, 1995).

4. Income Support (General) (Jobseeker's Allowance Consequential Amendments) Regulations 1996 (SI 1996/206) reg.20 (October 7, 1996).

5. Employment and Support Allowance (Consequential Provisions) (No.2) Regulations 2008 (SI 2008/1554) reg.2(1) and (10) (October 27, 2008).

6. Universal Credit (Consequential, Supplementary, Incidental and Miscellaneous Provisions) Regulations 2013 (SI 2013/630) reg.28(1) and (6) (April 29, 2013).

DEFINITIONS

"claimant"—see reg.2(1).
"Social Security Act"—*ibid.*

[1Reduction in certain cases

76.—There shall be deducted from the amount of income support which would, but for this regulation, be payable for a part-week— 2.628

(a) [2 in the case of a claimant to whom regulation 22A (reduction in applicable amount where the claimant is appealing against a decision [3 which embodies a determination] that he is not incapable of work) applies], the proportion of the relevant amount specified therein appropriate to the number of days in the part-week;

(b) where regulation 75(f) (modifications in the calculation of income) applies, one-half of the amount disregarded under regulation 75(f) less the weekly amount of any disregard under Schedule 8 or 9 appropriate to that payment.]

AMENDMENTS

1. Income Support (General) Amendment Regulations 1988 (SI 1988/663) reg.27 (April 11, 1988).
2. Income Support (General) (Jobseeker's Allowance Consequential Amendments) Regulations 1996 (SI 1996/206) reg.21 (October 7, 1996).
3. Social Security Act 1998 (Commencement No.9 and Savings and Consequential and Transitional Provisions) Order 1999 (SI 1999/2422) art.3(7) and Sch.6 para.2.

DEFINITION

"claimant"—see reg.2(1).

[1Modification of section 23(5) of the Act [SSCBA, s.126(5)]

77.—Where income support is payable for a part-week, section 23(5) of the Act [SSCBA, s.126(5)] (trade disputes) shall have effect as if the following paragraph were substituted for paragraph (b)— 2.629

"(b) any payment by way of income support for a part-week which apart from this paragraph would be made to him, or to a person whose applicable amount if aggregated with his—

(i) shall not be made if the payment for the part-week is equal to or less than the proportion of the relevant sum appropriate to the number of days in the part-week; or
(ii) if it is more than that proportion, shall be made at a rate equal to the difference."

AMENDMENT

1. Income Support (General) Amendment Regulations 1988 (SI 1988/663) reg.27 (April 11, 1988).

DEFINITION

"the Act"—see reg.2(1).

SCHEDULES

SCHEDULE 1

2.630 *[Revoked by the Income Support (General) (Jobseeker's Allowance Consequential Amendments) Regulations 1996 (SI 1996/206), reg.28 and Sch.3 with effect from October 7, 1996.]*

SCHEDULE 1A

2.631 *[Revoked by the Income Support (General) (Jobseeker's Allowance Consequential Amendments) Regulations 1996 (SI 1996/206), reg.28 and Sch.3 with effect from October 7, 1996.]*

[1 SCHEDULE 1B **Regulation 4ZA**

PRESCRIBED CATEGORIES OF PERSON

2.632 **[32[36[46[52 Lone Parents**

1.—(1) A lone parent who is responsible for, and a member of the same household as-

(a) a single child aged under 5, or

(b) more than one child where the youngest is aged under 5.

(2) A lone parent who is under the age of 18.]]]]

Single persons looking after foster children

2.633 [55 **2.**—A single claimant or a lone parent with whom a child is placed—

(a) by a local authority or voluntary organisation within the meaning of the Children Act 1989;

(b) by a local authority or voluntary organisation within the meaning of the Children (Scotland) Act 1995;

(c) by virtue of any order or warrant made under the Children's Hearings (Scotland) Act 2011.]

[38 Single persons looking after children placed with them prior to adoption

2.634 **2A.**—A single claimant or a lone parent with whom a child is placed for adoption by an adoption agency within the meaning of the Adoption and Children Act 2002 or the Adoption and Children (Scotland) Act 2007.]

Persons temporarily looking after another person

2.635 **3.**—A person who is—

(a) looking after a child because the parent of that child or the person who usually looks after him is [35 temporarily] ill or is temporarily absent from his home; or

(b) looking after a member of his family who is temporarily ill.

Persons caring for another person

2.636 **4.**—A person (the carer)—

(a) who is regularly and substantially engaged in caring for another person if—

(i) the person being cared for is in receipt of attendance allowance [2. . .] [53 [54, armed forces independence payment, the care component of disability living allowance at the highest or middle rate prescribed in accordance with section 72(3) of the Contributions and Benefits Act] or the daily living component of personal independence payment at the standard or enhanced rate in accordance with section 78(3) of the 2012 Act]; or

(ii) the person being cared for has claimed attendance allowance [2. . .] but only for the period up to the date of determination of that claim, or the period of 26 weeks from the date of that claim, whichever date is the earlier; or

[2(iia) the person being cared for has claimed attendance allowance in accordance with section 65(6)(a) of the Contributions and Benefits Act (claims in advance of entitlement), an award has been made in respect of that claim under section 65(6)(b) of that Act and, where the period for which the award is payable has begun, that person in receipt of the allowance;] [16 or]

(iii) the person being cared for has claimed entitlement to a disability living allowance [54, armed forces independence payment] [53or personal independence payment] but only for the period up to the date of determination of that claim, or the period of 26 weeks from the date of that claim, whichever date is the earlier; or

[2(iiia) the person being cared for has claimed entitlement to the care component of a disability living allowance in accordance with regulation 13A of the Social Security (Claims and Payments) Regulations 1987 (advance claims and awards), an award at the highest or middle rate has been made in respect of that claim and, where the period for which the award is payable has begun, that person is in receipt of the allowance;] [53 ; or

(iv) the person being cared for has claimed entitlement to the daily living component of personal independence payment in accordance with regulation 33 of the Universal Credit, Personal Independence Payment, Jobseeker's Allowance and Employment and Support Allowance (Claims and Payments) Regulations 2013 (advance claim for and award of personal independence payment), an award at the standard or enhanced rate has been made in respect of that claim and, where the period for which the award is payable has begun, that person is in receipt of the payment;]

(b) who is engaged in caring for another person and [10who is both entitled to, and in receipt of,] [18 a carer's allowance] [17 or would be in receipt of that allowance but for the application of a restriction under section [44 6B or] 7 of the Social Security Fraud Act 2001 (loss of benefit provisions)].

5.—A person to whom paragraph 4 applied, but only for a period of 8 weeks from the date on which that paragraph ceased to apply to him.

6.—A person who, had he previously made a claim for income support, would have fulfilled the conditions of paragraph 4, but only for a period of 8 weeks from the date on which he ceased to fulfil those conditions.

[41 Persons treated as capable of work and persons entitled to statutory sick pay] **2.637**

7.—A person who—

[40 (a) [40 ...]

(b) [40 ...]

(c) is treated as capable of work by virtue of regulations made under section 171E(1) of [47the Contributions and Benefits Act] (disqualification etc); or

(d) is entitled to statutory sick pay.

Disabled workers **2.638**

8.—[43 . . .]

Persons in employment living in residential care homes, nursing homes or residential accommodation **2.639**

9.—[43 . . .]

[15 Persons who have commenced remunerative work **2.640**

9A.—A person to whom regulation 6(5) (persons not treated as engaged in remunerative work) applies.]

Disabled students **2.641**

10.—[40 . . .]

11.—A person who is a [11 full-time student] and who—

(a) immediately before 1st September 1990 was in receipt of income support by virtue of paragraph 7 of Schedule 1 as then in force; or

(b) on or after that date makes a claim for income support and at a time during the period of 18 months immediately preceding the date of that claim was in receipt of income support either by virtue of that paragraph or regulation 13(2)(b),

but this paragraph shall not apply where for a continuous period of 18 months or more the person has not been in receipt of income support.

Deaf students

12.—[40 . . .] **2.642**

Blind persons

13.—[40 . . .] **2.643**

Pregnancy

14.—A woman who— **2.644**

(a) is incapable of work by reason of pregnancy; or

(b) is or has been pregnant but only for the period commencing 11 weeks before her expected week of confinement and ending [48. . .] [19 fifteen weeks after the date on which her pregnancy ends [48 . . .]].

[6Parental leave

2.645 **14A.**—(1) A person who is—

(a) entitled to, and taking, parental leave by virtue of Part III of the Maternity and Parental Leave etc. Regulations 1999 in respect of a child who is a member of his household; and

(b) not entitled to any remuneration from his employer in respect of that leave for the period to which his claim for income support relates; and

(c) entitled [22. . .] [21 working tax credit, child tax credit payable at a rate higher than the family element,] housing benefit or council tax benefit on the day before that leave begins.

(2) In this paragraph "remuneration" means payment of any kind [21 and "family element" means in a case where any child in respect of whom child tax credit is payable is under the age of one year, the amount specified in regulation 7(3)(a) of the Child Tax Credit Regulations 2002 or in any other case, the amount specified in regulation 7(3)(b) of those Regulations] [22 but subject in any case to calculations of those amounts made in accordance with the Tax Credits (Income Thresholds and Determination of Rates) Regulations 2002.]]

[20Paternity Leave

2.646 **14B.**— (1) A person who is entitled to, and is taking, [49 [56 . . .] paternity leave by virtue of section 80A or 80B of the Employment Rights Act 1996] and who satisfies either or both of the conditions set out in sub-paragraph (2) below.

(2) The conditions for the purposes of sub-paragraph (1) are—

(a) he is not entitled to [49 [56 . . .] statutory paternity pay] by virtue of Part 12ZA of the Contributions and Benefits Act, or to any remuneration from his employer in respect of that leave for the period to which his claim for income support relates;

(b) he is entitled to [22. . .] [21 working tax credit, child tax credit payable at a rate higher than the family element,] housing benefit or council tax benefit on the day before that leave begins.

(3) In this paragraph "remuneration" means payment of any kind [21 and "family element" means in a case where any child in respect of whom child tax credit is payable is under the age of one year, the amount specified in regulation 7(3)(a) of the Child Tax Credit Regulations 2002 or in any other case, the amount specified in regulation 7(3)(b) of those Regulations] [22 but subject in any case to calculations of those amounts made in accordance with the Tax Credits (Income Thresholds and Determination of Rates) Regulations 2002.]]

Persons in education

2.647 **15.**—A person to whom any provision of regulation 13(2)(a) to (e) (persons receiving relevant education who are parents, [27 disabled persons, persons with limited leave to enter or remain], orphans and persons estranged from their parents or guardian) applies.

[35[39[50 Certain persons who have enrolled on, been accepted for or are undertaking full-time, non-advanced education]]

2.648 **15A.**— [50 (1) A person ("P") who satisfies the following conditions.

(2) The first condition is that P has enrolled on, been accepted for or is undertaking a course of full-time, non-advanced education.

(3) The second condition is that P is –

(a) under the age of 21; or

(b) 21 and attained that age whilst undertaking a course of full-time, non-advanced education.

(4) The third condition is that –

(a) P has no parent;

(b) of necessity P has to live away from P's parents because –

(i) P is estranged from P's parents,

(ii) P is in physical or moral danger, or

(iii) there is a serious risk to P's physical or mental health; or

(c) P is living away from P's parents because they are unable to support P financially and are –

(i) chronically sick or mentally or physically disabled,

(ii) detained in custody pending trial or sentencing upon conviction or under a sentence imposed by a court, or

(iii) prohibited from entering or re-entering Great Britain.]

(5) [50 . . .]

(6) In this paragraph—
"chronically sick or mentally or physically disabled" has the meaning given in regulation 13(3)(b);
[[50] "course of full-time, non-advanced education" means a course of full-time education which is not a course of advanced education and which is not provided to P by virtue of P's employment or any office held by P, which is –
(a) provided at a school or college, or
(b) provided elsewhere but is approved by the Secretary of State as being such a course,
and for this purpose, "course of advanced education" has the same meaning as in regulation 61(1)];
"parent" includes a person acting in place of a parent which—
(a) for the purposes of sub-paragraph (5)(a) and (b) has the meaning given in regulation 13(3)(a)(i), and
(b) for the purposes of sub-paragraph (5)(c), has the meaning given in regulation 13(3)(a)(ii).]

Certain persons aged 50 who have not been in remunerative work for 10 years

16.—[[28] . . .] 2.649

[[14] Certain persons aged between 55 and 60 whose spouse has died

16A.—[[26] . . .]] 2.650

Persons aged 60 or over

17.—[[23]. . .] 2.651

Refugees

18.—A person who is a refugee within the definition in Article 1 of the Convention relating to the Status of Refugees done at Geneva on 28th July 1951 as extended by Article 1(2) of the Protocol relating to the Status of Refugees done at New York on 31st January 1967 and who— 2.652
(a) is attending for more than 15 hours a week a course for the purpose of learning English so that he may obtain employment; and
(b) on the date on which that course commenced, had been in Great Britain for not more than 12 months.
but only for a period not exceeding nine months.

[[8]**18A.**—[[30] . . .]]

[[29] Persons required to attend court or tribunal

19.—(1) A person who is required to attend a court or tribunal as a justice of the peace, a party to any proceedings, a witness or a juror. 2.653

(2) In this paragraph, "tribunal" means any tribunal listed in Schedule 1 to the Tribunals and Inquiries Act 1992.]

Persons affected by a trade dispute

20.—A person to whom section 126 of the Contributions and Benefits Act (trade disputes) applies or in respect of whom section 124(1) of the Act (conditions of entitlement to income support) has effect as modified by section 127(b) of the Act (effect of return to work). 2.654

[[42] Persons from abroad

21.—A person not excluded from entitlement to income support under section 115 of the Immigration and Asylum Act 1999 by virtue of regulation 2 of the Social Security (Immigration and Asylum) Consequential Amendments Regulations 2000 except for a person to whom paragraphs 2, 3 and 4 of Part 1 of the Schedule to those Regulations applies.] 2.655

Persons in custody

22.—A person remanded in, or committed in, custody for trial or for sentencing. 2.656

Member of couple looking after children while other member temporarily abroad

23.—A person who is a member of a couple and who is treated as responsible for a child who is a member of his household where the other member of that couple is temporarily not present in the United Kingdom. 2.657

Persons appealing against a decision [[4] which embodies a determination] that they are not incapable of work

24.—A person— 2.658
(a) in respect of whom it has been determined for the purposes of section 171B of the Contributions and Benefits Act (the own occupation test) that he is not incapable of work; and

(b) whose medical practitioner continues to supply evidence of his incapacity for work in accordance with regulation 2 of the Social Security (Medical Evidence) Regulations 1976 (evidence of incapacity for work); and

(c) who has made and is pursuing an appeal against the [4 decision which embodies a] determination that he is not so incapable.

but only for the period prior to the determination of his appeal.

25.—A person—

(a) in respect of whom it has been determined for the purposes of section 171C of the Contributions and Benefits Act ([7 personal capability assessment]) that he is not incapable of work; and

(b) who has made and is pursuing an appeal against the [4 decision which embodies a] determination that he is not so incapable.

but only for the period [24 beginning with the date on which that determination takes effect until] the determination of his appeal.

26.—[31. . .]

27.—[31. . .]

[27 Persons engaged in training]

2.659 **28.**—A person who is [27 not a qualifying young person or child within the meaning of section 142 of the Contributions and Benefits Act (child and qualifying young person) and who is] engaged in training, and for this purpose "training" means training for which persons aged under 18 are eligible and for which persons aged 18 to 24 may be eligible [13 secured by the [45 [51 Secretary of State] [57 . . .]] the Chief or by the [25 [33 Welsh Ministers]]] and, in Scotland, directly or indirectly by a Local Enterprise Company pursuant to its arrangement with, as the case may be, [34 Skills Development Scotland,] Scottish Enterprise or Highlands and Islands Enterprise (whether that arrangement is known as an Operating Contract or by any other name).]

AMENDMENTS

1. Income Support (General) (Jobseeker's Allowance Consequential Amendments) Regulations 1996 (SI 1996/206) reg.22 and Sch.1 (October 7, 1996).

2. Jobseeker's Allowance and Income Support (General) (Amendment) Regulations 1996 (SI 1996/1517) reg.33 (October 7, 1996).

3. Social Security and Child Support (Miscellaneous Amendments) Regulations 1997 (SI 1997/827) reg.5 (April 7, 1997).

4. Social Security Act 1998 (Commencement No.9 and Savings and Consequential and Transitional Provisions) Order 1999 (SI 1999/2422 (C.61)) art.3(7) and Sch.6 para.3 (September 6, 1999).

5. Social Security (Miscellaneous Amendments) (No.2) Regulations 1999 (SI 1999/2556) reg.2(7) (October 4, 1999).

6. Income Support (General) Amendment (No.2) Regulations 1999 (SI 1999/3329) reg.2 (January 5, 2000).

7. Social Security (Incapacity for Work) Miscellaneous Amendments Regulations 1999 (SI 1999/3109) reg.6 (April 3, 2000).

8. Social Security (Immigration and Asylum) Consequential Amendments Regulations 2000 (SI 2000/636) reg.3(9) (April 3, 2000).

9. Social Security (Miscellaneous Amendments) Regulations 2000 (SI 2000/681) reg.2(d) (April 3, 2000).

10. Social Security (Miscellaneous Amendments) Regulations 2000 (SI 2000/681) reg.4(1) (April 3, 2000).

11. Social Security Amendment (Students) Regulations 2000 (SI 2000/1981) reg.5(5) and Sch. (July 31, 2000).

12. Social Security Amendment (Students and Income-related Benefits) Regulations 2000 (SI 2000/1922) reg.2(8) (August 28, 2000, or if the student's period of study begins between August 1 and 27, 2000, the first day of the period).

13. Social Security (Miscellaneous Amendments) (No.2) Regulations 2001 (SI 2001/652) reg.4 (March 26, 2001).

14. Social Security Amendment (Bereavement Benefits) Regulations 2000 (SI 2000/2239) reg.2(2) (April 9, 2001).

15. Social Security (Miscellaneous Amendments) Regulations 2001 (SI 2001/488) reg.5 (April 9, 2001).

16. Social Security (Miscellaneous Amendments) (No.3) Regulations 2001 (SI 2001/859) reg.3(4) (April 9, 2001).

17. Social Security (Loss of Benefit) (Consequential Amendments) Regulations 2002 (SI 2002/490) reg.4 (April 1, 2002).

18. Social Security Amendment (Carer's Allowance) Regulations 2002 (SI 2002/2497) reg.3 and Sch.2 (April 1, 2003).

19. Social Security (Paternity and Adoption) Amendment Regulations 2002 (SI 2002/2689) reg.2(5)(a) (November 24, 2002).

20. Social Security (Paternity and Adoption) Amendment Regulations 2002 (SI 2002/2689) reg.2(5)(b) (December 8, 2002).

21. Social Security (Working Tax Credit and Child Tax Credit) (Consequential Amendments) Regulations 2003 (SI 2003/455) reg.2 and Sch.1 para.19 (April 7, 2003).

22. Social Security (Working Tax Credit and Child Tax Credit) (Consequential Amendments) (No.3) Regulations 2003 (SI 2003/1731) reg.2(3) (August 8, 2003).

23. State Pension Credit (Consequential, Transitional and Miscellaneous Provisions) Regulations 2002 (SI 2002/3019) reg.29(4) (October 6, 2003).

24. Social Security Child Support and Tax Credits (Miscellaneous Amendments) Regulations 2005 (SI 2005/337) reg.6 (March 18, 2005).

25. National Council for Education and Training for Wales (Transfer of Functions to the National Assembly for Wales and Abolition) Order 2005 (SI 2005/3238 (W.243)) art.9(2) and Sch.2 para.1(2) (April 1, 2006).

26. Social Security (Miscellaneous Amendments) Regulations 2006 (SI 2006/588) reg.2(4)(d) (April 10, 2006).

27. Social Security (Young Persons) Amendment Regulations 2006 (SI 2006/718) reg.2(7) (April 10, 2006).

28. Social Security (Miscellaneous Amendments) (No.4) Regulations 2006 (SI 2006/2378) reg.5(6) (October 7, 2006).

29. Social Security (Income Support and Jobseeker's Allowance) Amendment Regulations 2006 (SI 2006/1402) reg.3 (May 30, 2006).

30. Asylum and Immigration (Treatment of Claimants, etc.) Act 2004 (c.19) s.12(2)(a)(ii) (June 14, 2007).

31. Social Security (Miscellaneous Amendments) Regulations 2008 (SI 2008/698) reg.2(11) (April 14, 2008).

32. Social Security (Lone Parents and Miscellaneous Amendments) Regulations 2008 (SI 2008/3051) reg.2 (November 24, 2008).

33. Social Security (Miscellaneous Amendments) (No.7) Regulations 2008 (SI 2008/3157) reg.2(6) (January 5, 2009).

34. Social Security (Miscellaneous Amendments) Regulations 2009 (SI 2009/583) reg.2(3) (April 6, 2009).

35. Social Security (Miscellaneous Amendments) Regulations 2009 (SI 2009/583) reg.2(12) (April 6, 2009).

36. Social Security (Lone Parents and Miscellaneous Amendments) Regulations 2008 (SI 2008/3051) reg.3 (October 26, 2009).

37. Social Security (Miscellaneous Amendments) (No.4) Regulations 2009 (SI 2009/2655) reg.2(14)(a) (October 26, 2009).

38. Social Security (Miscellaneous Amendments) (No.4) Regulations 2009 (SI 2009/2655) reg.2(14)(b) (October 26, 2009).

39. Social Security (Miscellaneous Amendments) (No.4) Regulations 2009 (SI 2009/2655) reg.2(14)(c) (October 26, 2009).

40. Income Support (Prescribed Categories of Person) Regulations 2009 (SI 2009/3152) reg.2 (December, 30, 2009). Regulation 2(1)(b) revoked paras 7(a) and (b), 10, 12 and 13 with effect from December 30, 2009 but this was subject to the saving provisions in reg.2(2). See the 2015/16 edition of this volume for these Regulations and the notes to them.

41. Income Support (Prescribed Categories of Person) Regulations 2009 (SI 2009/3152) reg.3(2)(e) and 3(7) (December, 30, 2009). Regulation 3(2)(e) substitutes a new heading for the existing heading to para.7 with effect from December 30, 2009 but reg.3(7) provides that this does not apply in the case of a person who is subject to the saving provisions in reg.2(2) of those Regulations. For this reason the heading is in italics.

42. Social Security (Miscellaneous Amendments) (No .5) Regulations 2009 (SI 2009/3228) reg.3(2)(d) (January 25, 2010).

43. Social Security (Miscellaneous Amendments) (No. 5) Regulations 2009 (SI 2009/3228) reg.4(1)(a)(ii) (January 25, 2010).

44. Social Security (Loss of Benefit) Amendment Regulations 2010 (SI 2010/1160) reg.10(2) (April 1, 2010).

45. Apprenticeships, Skills, Children and Learning Act 2009 (Consequential Amendments to Subordinate Legislation) (England) Order 2010 (SI 2010/1941) art.3(4) (September 1, 2010).

46. Social Security (Lone Parents and Miscellaneous Amendments) Regulations 2008 (SI 2008/3051) reg.4 (October 25, 2010).

47. Social Security (Miscellaneous Amendments) (No. 5) Regulations 2010 (SI 2010/2429) reg.2(2)(a) (November 1, 2010).

48. Social Security (Miscellaneous Amendments) (No. 5) Regulations 2010 (SI 2010/2429) reg.2(2)(b) (November 1, 2010).

49. Social Security (Miscellaneous Amendments) Regulations 2012 (SI 2012/757) reg.3(3) (April 1, 2012).

50. Social Security (Miscellaneous Amendments) Regulations 2012 (SI 2012/757) reg.11 (April 1, 2012).

51. Young People's Learning Agency Abolition (Consequential Amendments to Subordinate Legislation) (England) Order 2012 (SI 2012/956) art.3(4) (May 1, 2012).

52. Social Security (Lone Parents and Miscellaneous Amendments) Regulations 2012 (SI 2012/874) reg.2 (May 21, 2012).

53. Personal Independence Payment (Supplementary Provisions and Consequential Amendments) Regulations 2013 (SI 2013/388) reg.8 and Sch. Pt 2 para.11(4) (April 8, 2013).

54. Armed Forces and Reserve Forces Compensation Scheme (Consequential Provisions: Subordinate Legislation) Order 2013 (SI 2013/591) art.7 and Sch. para.4(4) (April 8, 2013).

55. Children's Hearings (Scotland) Act 2011 (Consequential and Transitional Provisions and Savings) Order 2013 (SI 2013/1465) art.17(1) and Sch.1 Pt 2 para.12(3) (June 24, 2013).

56. Shared Parental Leave and Statutory Shared Parental Pay (Consequential Amendments to Subordinate Legislation) Order 2014 (SI 2014/3255) art.5(5) (April 5, 2015).

57. Deregulation Act 2015 (Consequential Amendments) Order 2015 (SI 2015/971) art.2 and Sch.3 para.2(4) (May 26, 2015).

DEFINITIONS

"adoption leave"—see reg.2(1).
"armed forces independence payment"—*ibid.*
"attendance allowance"—*ibid.*
"child"—see SSCBA s.137(1).
"disability living allowance"—see reg.2(1).
"full-time student"—*ibid.*, reg.61(1).
"lone parent"—see reg.2(1).
"maternity leave"—*ibid.*
"paternity leave"—*ibid.*
"payment"—*ibid.*
"personal capability assessment"—SSCBA s.171C and Incapacity for Work Regulations reg.24.

"personal independence payment" —see reg.2(1).
"single claimant"—*ibid.*
"student"—*ibid.*, reg.61(1).
"voluntary organisation"—see reg.2(1).

General Note

As a consequence of the introduction of JSA on October 7, 1996, the income support scheme had to undergo a fundamental restructuring. Income support was no longer available to people who are claiming benefit because they are unemployed. People who have to be available for, and actively seeking, work as a condition of receiving benefit have to claim JSA. Since October 7, 1996, in order to qualify for income support a person has to fall within a "prescribed category" (see SSCBA s.124(1)(e) and reg.4ZA). Schedule 1B sets out these categories. **2.660**

See the notes to reg.4ZA for discussion of the position of claimants who may be able to claim either income support or JSA; note also that the raising of the limit for remunerative work for partners to 24 hours a week from October 7, 1996 meant that some couples have to decide whether they will gain more by claiming working tax credit.

When Sch.1B was first introduced the categories broadly resembled most of those in the former Sch.1 (people not required to be available for employment) (revoked on October 7, 1996), but there were some differences. There was no equivalent to paras 12 (Open University students attending a residential course), 18 (discharged prisoners) or 23 (persons taking child abroad for medical treatment) of the former Sch.1. But if people in these circumstances claim JSA they will be treated as available for work (see sub-paras (f), (h) and (c) respectively of reg.14(1) of the JSA Regulations 1996). See the note to para.28 for people in receipt of a training allowance.

Schedule 1B provides an exhaustive list of the circumstances in which a person will be entitled to income support. There is no category of analogous circumstances or provision for a reduced rate of benefit on the ground of hardship for people who do not come within these categories (compare the former reg.8(3), see the 1996 edition of J. Mesher and P. Wood, *Income-related Benefits: the Legislation*). Moreover, the provision for hardship payments under JSA is considerably restricted (see regs 140–146 (regs 146A–146H in the case of joint-claim couples) of the JSA Regulations 1996 and the notes to those regulations). Part VI of the Income Support Regulations, which formerly contained some very limited provision for urgent cases outside the normal scope of the income support rules, was revoked (subject to three savings: see the note to Pt VI) with effect from January 25, 2010. **2.661**

See the notes to reg.4ZA(1) for the subsequent major contraction in the coverage of the income support scheme that is a consequence of:

- on October 6, 2003 the introduction of state pension credit;
- starting from April 6, 2004 the removal of amounts for children and young persons from income support (except in "transitional cases"—see the note to reg.17);
- starting from November 24, 2008 the staged reduction of lone parents' entitlement to income support (see the note to para.1 below);
- on October 27, 2008 the introduction of ESA (see the notes to paras 7, 10, 12 and 13 below); and
- from February 28, 2011 the migration of claimants in receipt of income support on the grounds of incapacity or disability to ESA. It was intended that the conversion process to ESA would be completed by the end of March 2014 but it is not clear whether this was achieved.

Paragraph 1

See reg.15 for responsibility for a child and reg.16 for membership of the household. *CIS/43/2008* confirms that whether a person is "responsible for a child" is governed by reg.15. It is not sufficient for the purposes of para.1 that the claimant is **2.662** caring for the child. However, para.3 may apply, depending on the circumstances. See further the note to para.3.

Before November 24, 2008 para.1 applied if a lone parent was responsible for a child (i.e. a person under 16) who was a member of her household. From that date, however, the staged reduction in the entitlement of lone parents under para.1 began. Subject to phasing-in provisions, from November 24, 2008 para.1 only applied if a lone parent was responsible for a sole or youngest child aged under 12; from October 26, 2009 only those lone parents with a sole or youngest child under 10 qualified; from October 25, 2010 the sole or youngest child had to be under seven; and from May 21, 2012 entitlement under para.1 has been limited to lone parents whose sole or youngest child is aged under five. Note subs.(1A) inserted into s.124 of the Contributions and Benefits Act on May 21, 2012 which provides that regulations must provide for income support to be available to a lone parent who has a child under five. Thus any further reduction in entitlement under para.1 will require an amendment to s.124(1A).

Note the additional change from May 21, 2012 which provides that a lone parent will be eligible for income support if she is under the age of 18 (regardless of the age of her child) (sub-para.(2)).

VL v SSWP (IS) [2011] UKUT 227 (AAC); [2012] AACR 10 holds that the reduced entitlement for lone parents, although indirectly discriminatory against women, was not in breach of art.14, read with art.1 Prot.1, ECHR because it was well within the wide margin of appreciation that the state has in the implementation of social policy and in economic matters. The claimant had also contended that the amending legislation was ultra vires s.7 of the Education Act 1996 because it prevented a lone parent from exercising the right to educate her children at home. Judge Levenson, however, rejected this argument, pointing out that s.7 does not confer a right to home educate but creates a duty to secure education (which may be fulfilled by home education). Permission to appeal against this decision was refused by the Court of Appeal on the papers on March 30, 2012.

Phasing-in provisions

2.663 In relation to the reductions in entitlement for lone parents which took effect on November 24, 2008, October 26, 2009 and October 25, 2010, there were special phasing-in provisions that applied to certain claimants who had an existing entitlement under para.1 at the respective date (and to whom no other paragraph in Sch.1B applied) (see the Schedule to the Social Security (Lone Parents and Miscellaneous Amendments) Regulations 2008 (SI 2008/3051)). These provisions did not, or ceased to, apply if the lone parent made a further claim for income support or while the transitional provisions for certain full-time students and full-time participants in the New Deal for Lone Parents in reg.13 of the 2008 Regulations applied to the claimant. For the effect of these phasing-in provisions see the notes to para.1 of Sch.1B in the 2009/10 edition of this volume; for reg.13 of the 2008 Regulations see the 2012/13 edition of this volume.

There were similar phasing-in provisions for certain claimants who were aged 18 or over and had an existing entitlement under para.1 immediately before May 21, 2012, and to whom no other paragraph in Sch.1B applied (see the Schedule to the Social Security (Lone Parents and Miscellaneous Amendments) Regulations 2012 (SI 2012/874)). Again these provisions did not, or ceased to, apply if the lone parent made a further claim for income support or while the transitional provisions for certain full-time students and those undertaking a full-time course of training or instruction under arrangements made, or approved, by the Secretary of State applied to the claimant.

For the effect of these phasing-in provisions, see the notes to para.1 of Sch.1B in the 2014/15 edition of this volume.

Transitional Provisions

2.664 As was the case under the 2008 Regulations (see the note to para.1 of Sch.1B in the 2012/13 edition of this volume), there is transitional protection for certain lone parents. The transitional protection under the 2012 Regulations applies to lone parents who: (i) immediately before May 21, 2012 were entitled to income support solely on the grounds of being a lone parent (and to whom no other paragraph in Sch.1B applies); (ii) immediately before, on and after May 21, 2012 are full-time students or undertaking a full-time course of training or instruction under arrangements made, or approved, by the Secretary of State; and (iii) on and after May 21, 2012 have an only or youngest child aged five or over (see reg.7 of the Social Security (Lone Parents and Miscellaneous Amendments) Regulations 2012 (SI 2012/874) (p.827)).

The transitional protection does not apply (or ceases to apply) if the lone parent makes a further claim for income support on or after May 21, 2012.

A claimant to whom reg.7 applies will continue to be entitled to income support until the date she ceases attending the course or the date that her only or youngest child reaches the age at which her income support entitlement would have ended under the rules in force when she started her course, whichever is the earlier. The claimant will continue to be required to take part in work-focused interviews while reg.7 applies.

Requirement to take part in work-focused interviews

Since April 5, 2004 the requirement to attend work-focused interviews ("WFIs") **2.665**
has applied to all lone parents aged 18 or over and under 60 who are responsible for a child in their household and who are not subject to the Jobcentre Plus scheme (see the Social Security (Work-focused Interviews for Lone Parents) and Miscellaneous Amendments Regulations 2000 (SI 2000/1926) (as amended) in Vol.III of this series. Note that from April 6, 2010 the upper age limit has changed from "60" to "pensionable age" as a consequence of the staged equalisation of state pension age. This equalisation was to have taken place between April 6, 2010 and April 5, 2020 but the timetable for this in the Pensions Act 1995 has been accelerated with effect from April 2016 so that women's state pension age will now be 65 by November 2018; in addition, the increase in state pension age to 66 for both men and women has been brought forward—it will start to rise from 65 in December 2018 to reach 66 by October 2020 (see s.1 of the Pensions Act 2011, and between 2026 and 2028 it will rise to 67 (see s.26 of the Pensions Act 2014)). For the purposes of the 2000 Regulations and the Social Security (Jobcentre Plus Interviews) Regulations 2002 (SI 2002/1703) (as amended) (see Vol.III) "pensionable age" in the case of men born before April 6, 1955 is the age when a woman born on the same day as the man would attain that age.

A further amendment to the 2000 and 2002 Regulations was made on October 31, 2011 so that a lone parent who has a youngest child under one will not be required to attend a WFI (see reg.2(6)(b) of the Social Security (Work-focused Interviews for Lone Parents and Partners) (Amendment) Regulations 2011 (SI 2011/2428), which amends reg.4 of the 2000 Regulations and reg.3(9)(b) of the same Regulations which amends reg.8 of the 2002 Regulations). In addition, reg.7 of the 2000 Regulations was amended by reg.2(8) of the 2011 Regulations on October 31, 2011 so that under those regulations a lone parent who fails to take part in her initial WFI without good cause is no longer treated as not having made a claim for income support but instead will be subject to the same sanction that applies for failing to take part in subsequent WFIs.

Lone parents who were entitled to income support *solely* on the grounds of being a lone parent were required to take part in a WFI every 13 weeks under either the lone parents WFI scheme or the Jobcentre Plus scheme. From October 31, 2011 such a lone parent had to attend quarterly WFIs if she had a child of four, five or six—this change was made in anticipation of the lowering of the age threshold of the only or youngest child to under five that was due to come into force on May 21, 2012. From May 21, 2012 such a lone parent had to attend quarterly WFIs if she had a sole or youngest child aged four.

Since April 28, 2014 the requirement to take part in a WFI applies to such a lone **2.666** parent whose only or youngest child is aged between one and four years and WFIs for such claimants will no longer take place at set intervals but their timing is to be at the discretion of the employment adviser. In addition, the requirement for such claimants to attend WFIs can no longer be waived but can still be deferred.

A lone parent who fails to take part in a WFI and who does not show good cause before the end of five working days following the date on which the Secretary of State gave notice of the failure (the five days can be extended to one month if the claimant provides new facts which could not reasonably have been provided within the five days) will be subject to a sanction. See reg.7(5) of the 2000 Regulations and reg.14 of the 2002 Regulations for a non-exclusive list of matters to be taken into account when determining whether the lone parent has shown good cause.

The sanction is that the lone parent's income support is reduced by 20 per cent of the applicable amount for a single claimant aged not less than 25 for the first failure, and for every subsequent failure (provided that it is not reduced below 10p). But no reduction will be made if a previous sanction under regs 7(3) and 8 of the 2000 Regulations, reg.12(2)(c) of the 2002 Regulations or reg.8(1) and (2) of the Income Support (Work-Related Activity) and Miscellaneous Amendments Regulations 2014 (see below) has been imposed in the two-week period before the date of the current failure. The sanction applies until the first day of the benefit week in which the claimant satisfies a "compliance condition" (i.e. a requirement to take part in a WFI or to undertake work-related activity (see below)).

Requirement for lone parents on income support to undertake work-related activity

2.667 From April 28, 2014 a lone parent who is entitled to income support solely on the grounds of being a lone parent and whose only or youngest child is aged three or four can also be required to undertake work-related activity as a condition of continuing to receive the full amount of income support (see Pt 2 of the Income Support (Work-Related Activity) and Miscellaneous Amendments Regulations 2014 (SI 2014/1097) (p.830)).

"Work-related activity" is "activity which makes it more likely that the person will obtain or remain in work or be able to do so" (see s.2D(9)(d) SSAA 1992 in Vol.III of this series). The work-related activity that the lone parent is to carry out has to be notified in a written action plan, must be reasonable, having regard to her/his circumstances, and cannot include a requirement to apply for a job or undertake work (regs 2(3) and 3 of the 2014 Regulations). A requirement to undertake work-related activity can be deferred where it would be unreasonable to require the person to undertake it at, or by, that time (reg.4 of the 2014 Regulations).

The lone parent has to be available to undertake such work-related activity during her/his child's normal school hours or during any period when the child is in the care of a person over 18 (other than any form of health care for the child) but can otherwise restrict the times that s/he is available to undertake work-related activity (reg.10 of the 2014 Regulations).

2.668 If a lone parent fails to undertake the required work-related activity and does not show good cause for the failure before the end of five working days beginning with the date on which the Secretary of State gave notice of the failure (the five days can be extended to one month if new facts are provided which could not reasonably have been provided within the five days) s/he will be subject to a sanction (regs 6 and 8 of the 2014 Regulations). See reg.7 of the 2014 Regulations for a non-exclusive list of matters to be taken into account when determining whether the lone parent has shown good cause.

The sanction is that the lone parent's income support is reduced by 20 per cent of the applicable amount for a single claimant aged not less than 25 for the first failure, and for every subsequent failure (provided that it is not reduced below 10p). But no reduction will be made if a previous sanction under reg.8(1) and (2) of the 2014 Regulations, regs 7(3) and 8 of the 2000 Regulations or reg.12(2)(c) of the 2002 Regulations has been imposed in the two week period before the date of the current failure. The sanction applies until the lone parent is no longer required to carry out work-related activity or the first day of the benefit week in which s/he satisfies a "compliance condition" (i.e. a requirement to undertake work-related activity or take part in a WFI), whichever is earlier.

Following the Supreme Court's decision in *R (Reilly and Wilson) v Secretary of State for Work and Pensions* [2013] UKSC 68; [2014] AACR 9 (see in particular para.74), a lone parent may be able to argue that a sanction should not be imposed if she has not been given sufficient information about the work-related activity she will be required to undertake in order to make "informed and meaningful" representations before the requirement is imposed (see further pp.209–210).

JSA and ESA claims by lone parents

Lone parents who are no longer eligible for income support will have to claim JSA (or ESA if they have limited capability for work). In recognition of the fact that "lone parents, parents and others with caring responsibilities for a child face circumstances that need special consideration" (to quote DMG Memo 45/08), when the reduction in entitlement to income support for lone parents was first introduced, amendments were made to the JSA rules governing availability for and actively seeking employment, good cause for refusing to carry out a jobseeker's direction or take up an offer of employment, and just cause for leaving a job voluntarily, in order to introduce "additional flexibilities". See regs 5, 13, 14, 19 and 72 of the JSA Regulations 1996 and the notes to those Regulations. In addition, on April 26, 2010 a new reg.13A was inserted into the JSA Regulations 1996 by the JSA (Lone Parents) (Availability for Work) Regulations 2010 (SI 2010/837) which allows a lone parent who is responsible for, and a member of the same household as, a child aged under 13 to restrict her availability for work to the child's normal school hours. **2.669**

A further amendment was made to the JSA Regulations 1996 on May 21, 2012 when the age threshold for the only or youngest child was reduced to under five. A new reg.17B was inserted to treat as available for employment, and a new reg.21B to treat as actively seeking employment, a lone parent whose sole or youngest child is aged five but who has not yet started (and who is not yet required by law to start) full-time education, where it would be unreasonable for the lone parent to make other arrangements for the care of the child.

Finally note that if a lone parent's income support included the disability premium when it came to an end under para.1, and she became entitled to ESA within 12 weeks of income support ceasing, her ESA will include the work-related activity or support component even though the ESA assessment period has not ended (see reg.7 of the ESA Regulations 2008 in Vol.1 in this series).

Paragraph 2

Special provision is necessary for foster children because they are not members of the foster-parent's household (reg.16(4)). **2.670**

JS v SSWP (IS) [2015] UKUT 306 (AAC); [2016] AACR 13 discusses the meaning of "placed" in para.2. It concludes that "placed" within the meaning of the Children Act 1989 meant that the claimant must actually have a child living with her, or accommodated by her, in discharge of the local authority's functions under that Act. Paragraph 2 therefore did not apply when the claimant did not have a child staying with her, even though she continued to be on call as a foster carer, had a day care child and was providing support to other foster carers.

Paragraph 2A

With effect from October 26, 2009 a single claimant or a lone parent with whom a child is placed for adoption by an adoption agency prior to adoption can qualify for income support. Again, special provision is needed because such a child is not a member of the claimant's household (reg.16(4)). **2.671**

Paragraph 3

2.672 This covers a person who is looking after a child (i.e. a person under 16: s.137(1) SSCBA) because his parent or the person who usually looks after him is (from April 6, 2009) temporarily ill or temporarily absent (sub-para.(a)); or who is looking after a member of the family (SSCBA s.137(1)) who is temporarily ill (sub-para.(b)).

The April 2009 amendment to para.3(a) so that it only applies where the parent of the child or the person who usually looks after him is *temporarily* ill reverses the effect of the decision in *R(IS) 11/08*. In that case the Commissioner had pointed out that it was only under sub-para.(b) that the illness of the other person (in that case the member of the family) must be temporary; under sub-para.(a) (in its then form) the illness of the parent or the person who usually looked after the child need not be. He therefore concluded that para.3 did not require that the claimant was only looking after the other person temporarily. The April 2009 amendment restores the policy intention.

In *CIS 866/2004* the claimant argued that she came within para.3(a) because her husband was unable to look after their young child due to his alcohol problems. The child had a long-term disability. However, the Deputy Commissioner holds that for para.3(a) to apply either the parent of the child who usually looked after the child or some other person who usually looked after the child had to be ill or temporarily absent. In his view it was only if read in this way that the use of the term "the parent" in para.3(a) rather than "a parent" made sense. On the facts it was the claimant who usually looked after the child, not her husband. Furthermore, para.3(b) did not apply. This was because the child was not temporarily ill but had a long-term disability and the claimant was not looking after her husband. Since the husband could not claim because his application for asylum had been refused the consequence was that the claimant had no obvious means of state financial support other than child benefit.

2.673 *CIS/4312/2007* also concerned a claimant who was looking after her husband who had no recourse to public funds and who was ill. He had kidney problems and underwent renal dialysis three times a week. He was on the waiting list for a kidney transplant and had been for three years. The Commissioner points out that it is possible for a person to have a permanent condition but not be ill except at particular times and that it did not necessarily follow that an *illness* could not be temporary because a *condition* would require long term treatment. It was common for people who need dialysis to feel better at times and worse at others. There was no doubt on the facts that the claimant was looking after her husband. Paragraph 3(b) therefore applied.

See also the note to reg.6(1)(b) on childminders.

Paragraphs 4–6

2.674 There is no requirement that alternative arrangements cannot be made. Under para.4(a) the fact of being substantially and regularly engaged in providing care for someone who receives or has been awarded attendance allowance, one of the two higher care components of disability living allowance, the daily living component of personal independence payment or armed forces independence payment, or who is waiting for a decision on entitlement is enough. In the last case, entitlement to income support under para.4(a) lasts for up to 26 weeks from the date of the claim for attendance allowance, disability living allowance, personal independence payment or armed forces independence payment, or until it is decided, whichever is the earlier.

For carer's allowance purposes "substantial" is 35 hours a week but *R(IS) 8/02* confirms that there is no such minimum requirement in order for para.4(a) to apply. Under para.4(a) it is simply a question of fact, having regard to the nature and amount of care provided, whether the claimant is "regularly and substantially engaged in caring". The Commissioner in *CSIS 1081/2001* also holds that care covers assistance or supervision arising out of the disabled person's needs and therefore will include domestic tasks that the person is unable to carry out themselves because of their disability, even if such tasks are not carried out in the person's presence. But it would not include travelling time to the person's home in order to provide the care as this is not in itself assistance to the disabled person. On the facts the claimant who went to her parents' home three times each weekday and provided care for 25–30 hours a week fell within para.4(a). It was irrelevant that she was also looking after her daughter (following a back injury) and her granddaughter.

Paragraph 4(b) covers anyone entitled to and in receipt of carer's allowance (or who would be but for the application of a sanction under s.7 of the Social Security Fraud Act 2001 (see Vol.III in this series)).

The effect of paras 5 and 6 is that the carer can qualify for income support in the eight weeks after ceasing to meet the conditions in para.4.

Paragraph 7

Paragraph 7 used to cover people who are incapable of work. However, from October 27, 2008, as a consequence of the start of the ESA scheme, *new* claims for income support under para.7(a) or (b) on the ground of incapacity or deemed incapacity for work were no longer possible, except in certain circumstances (see reg.2(2)(b)–(d) of the Employment and Support Allowance (Transitional Provisions) Regulations 2008 (SI 2008/795) (as amended) in Vol.I of this series for those circumstances). 2.675

Sub-paragraphs (a) and (b) of para.7 were then revoked with effect from December 30, 2009, subject to a savings provision for certain claimants (see the Income Support (Prescribed Categories of Person) Regulations 2009 (SI 2009/3152) at p.823 in the 2015/16 edition of this volume).

See the 2015/16 edition of this volume, pp.592–597, for details of who was previously covered by para.7(a) and (b) and for the consequences of the introduction of ESA and the revocation of para.7(a) and (b). See also under "*Migration to ESA*" on p.596 of the 2015/16 edition of this volume for the reassessment of claimants with existing awards of incapacity benefit, severe disablement allowance and/or income support on the grounds of incapacity or disability.

Sub-paragraphs (c) and (d) of para.7, however, remain in force. Sub-paragraph (c) covers people who are treated as capable of work under regulations made under s.171E(1) of the Social Security Contributions and Benefits Act 1992 (disqualification, etc.). The relevant regulation is reg.18 of the Social Security (Incapacity for Work) Regulations 1995 (SI 1995/311)—see the 2010/11 edition of Vol.I in this series for these provisions. As this relates to the incapacity for work scheme, it seems likely that sub-para.(c) will rarely, if ever, be applicable. Sub-paragraph (d), however, remains applicable as it covers people who are entitled to statutory sick pay.

"Fit notes, not sick notes"

Note also the amendments made to reg.2 of the Social Security (Medical Evidence Regulations) 1976 (SI 1976/615) on April 6, 2010 (see Vol.III of this series). These change the format of medical certificates and the rules for their completion to allow a doctor to consider not only whether the person is unfit for work but also whether he may be able to work with appropriate support if available. The Med 3 and Med 5 certificates are replaced by a new single certificate called "Statement of Fitness for Work" on which doctors are encouraged to provide more information on the functional effects of the person's condition and to suggest options that would facilitate a return to work, such as a phased return to work, altered hours, amended duties and workplace adaptations. Where the advice does not result in a return to work, the DWP's guidance to doctors ("*Statement of Fitness for Work: A Guide for General Practitioners and other doctors*" (February 2010)) stated that the person will be treated as if the doctor had advised that he was not fit for work. Furthermore, since reg.2(1) of the Medical Evidence Regulations (as amended) only requires the production of a "statement given by a doctor in accordance with the rules set out in Part 1 of Schedule 1 to these Regulations" as evidence of incapacity or limited capability for work, this would seem to include a statement that the claimant may be fit for work (as well as a statement that he is not fit for work). The new form of certificate may therefore have little effect on the payment of benefit. 2.676

Paragraphs 8 and 9

2.677 These paragraphs were revoked on January 25, 2010. Paragraph 8 covered a person to whom reg.6(4)(a) applied (disabled workers) and para.9 a person to whom reg.6(4)(d) applied (people in employment living in care homes, etc.). Regulation 6(4)(a) and (d) had treated such people as not engaged in remunerative work. See the 2009/10 edition of this volume for these provisions. According to the Explanatory Memorandum which accompanied the Social Security (Miscellaneous Amendments) (No.5) Regulations 2009 (SI 2009/3228), which abolished these provisions, they had "become obsolete, and the current more generous ESA and WTC regimes ensure the right level of support for this client group". The Memorandum also states that very few claimants currently receive benefit under these provisions. One wonders, however, if this was at least partly due to the fact that the necessary investigation in order to determine whether para.8 applied was not always carried out (for an analysis of reg.6(4)(a) and para.8 and when they were applicable see in particular *R(IS) 10/05* discussed in the notes to paras 7 and 8 of Sch.1B in the 2009/10 edition of this volume). *R(IS) 10/05* will still be of relevance where, e.g. there was an alleged overpayment of income support before January 25, 2010 because a person had failed to report that he was doing some work but the question as to whether he may have been eligible for income support as a disabled worker under para.8 has not been (fully) considered.

There is transitional protection for claimants to whom either of these paragraphs applied on January 24, 2010 which continues until the claimant ceases to fall within the relevant paragraph or ceases to be entitled to income support, whichever is the earlier (see reg.4 of the Social Security (Miscellaneous Amendments) (No.5) Regulations 2009 (SI 2009/3228) on p.826).

Paragraph 9A

2.678 See the notes to reg.6(5)–(8).

Paragraphs 10–12

2.679 Paragraphs 10 and 12 covered full-time students (defined in reg.61) who contrary to the normal rule could claim income support.

Paragraph 10 applied to a full-time student who qualified for the disability or severe disability premium or who had been incapable of work, or treated as incapable of work, or treated as capable of work by virtue of reg.18 of the Incapacity for Work Regulations (disqualification for misconduct, etc.) (see the 2010/11 edition of Vol.I in this series for these Regulations), or entitled to statutory sick pay, for at least 28 weeks (two or more periods of incapacity counted as one continuous period unless there was a break of more than eight weeks).

Paragraph 12 applied to full-time students who were within the definition of "deaf" for one of the listed grant purposes.

These paragraphs were revoked on December 30, 2009, subject to a saving provision. See under *"Introduction of ESA"*, *"Revocation of paras 10 and 12 on December 30, 2009"* and *"Migration to ESA"* on p.598 of the 2015/16 edition of this volume for further details.

Paragraph 11 continued to protect disabled full-time students who no longer fell under para.7 of the former Sch.1 following its amendment on September 1, 1990. See *CIS 276/1989* on the pre-September 1990 form of para.7, which held that in asking whether the student was unlikely to obtain employment within a reasonable period of time, the period started with the date of claim, not with the end of the course. It is no longer of any application.

Paragraph 13

2.680 Paragraph 13 covered people who were registered as blind and for 28 weeks after they ceased to be registered if they regained their sight. Paragraph 13 was revoked on December 30, 2009, subject to a saving provision. See under *"Introduction of*

ESA", "Revocation of para.13 on December 30, 2009" and *"Migration to ESA"* on p.599 of the 2015/16 edition of this volume for further details.

Paragraph 14

Sub-paragraph (a) covers a person who is incapable of work because of pregnancy and sub-para.(b) applies for 11 weeks before the expected week of confinement plus 15 weeks after the pregnancy ends. In *CIS 542/2001* the issue was the relationship, if any, between sub-para.(a) and para.7. Paragraph 7 covered, inter alia, a person who was incapable of work or treated as incapable of work in accordance with Pt XIIA SSCBA 1992 or regulations made thereunder. Those regulations included reg.14 of the Incapacity for Work (General) Regulations 1995, the effect of which was that a pregnant woman was to be treated as incapable of work during any period when, because of her pregnancy, there was a serious risk to her health or that of the unborn child if she continued to work. Sub-paragraph (a), on the other hand, simply requires the woman to be incapable of work due to her pregnancy. The Secretary of State argued that sub-para.(a) had to be read as incorporating the stricter test in reg.14(a). The Commissioner, however, holds that sub-para.(a) stands alone. In his view, if it had been intended that sub-para.(a) was to incorporate the reg.14(a) test, this could have been expressly stated. Furthermore, the provision in para.14 had been included in the Income Support Regulations since they first came into force in 1987 (it had formerly appeared as para.9 of Sch.1). This was several years before the introduction of incapacity benefit and thus supported the conclusion that sub-para.(a) was free-standing and not dependent on any other provision dealing with incapacity. The Secretary of State had relied on s.171A(1) SSCBA 1992 which provides that whether a person is capable or incapable of work is to be determined in accordance with Pt XIIA of the Act (thus including reg.14(a)). In the Commissioner's opinion, however, s.171A(1) had to be read subject to the later provisions of the Jobseekers Act 1995 and associated regulations (including s.124(1)(e) SSCBA, inserted by the 1995 Act, which provides that a person is entitled to income support if they fall into a prescribed category, and s.40 of the 1995 Act which authorises the making of transitional, consequential and saving provisions). The result is that sub-para.(a) applies to any woman who is incapable of work by reason of pregnancy. **2.681**

Paragraph 14A

This covers a member of a couple who is on unpaid parental leave to care for a child who is a member of his household (lone parents with a child under five are already eligible for income support, as are couples where one member is ill or temporarily absent, see paras 1, 3, and 23). The right to claim parental leave first came into effect on December 15, 1999 (for details see the Maternity and Parental Leave etc. Regulations 1999 (SI 1999/3312)). To come within para.14A the person must have been entitled to working tax credit, child tax credit (CTC) payable at a rate higher than the family element (at April 2003 rates (not increased in April 2004, April 2005, April 2006, April 2007, April 2008, April 2009 or April 2010) this was £1,090 where any child for whom CTC was payable was under one year old and £545 in any other case; from April 2011 it is £545 in all cases (not increased in April 2012, April 2013, April 2014, April 2015 or April 2016)), housing benefit or council tax benefit immediately before the leave began. (Note that para.14A has not been updated to reflect the fact that council tax benefit was abolished on April 1, 2013.) Note also that the claimant must not be getting any kind of payment from his employer during the parental leave (sub-para.(1)(b) and (2)). **2.682**

Paragraph 14B

This applies to a person who is entitled to and is on paternity leave and who: (i) is not entitled to statutory paternity pay or any other pay from his employer in respect of the paternity leave *or* (ii) was entitled to working tax credit, child tax credit (CTC) payable at a rate higher than the family element (at April 2003 rates (not increased in April 2004, April 2005, April 2006, April 2007, April 2008, April **2.683**

2009 or April 2010) this was £1,090 where any child for whom CTC was payable was under one year old and £545 in any other case; from April 2011 it is £545 in all cases (not increased in April 2012, April 2013, April 2014, April 2015 or April 2016)), housing benefit or council tax benefit immediately before the paternity leave began. (Note that para.14B has not been updated to reflect the fact that council tax benefit was abolished on April 1, 2013.)

The new rights to paternity leave and adoption leave introduced by the Employment Act 2002 applied where the expected week of confinement or birth was on or after April 6, 2003 (in the case of adoption leave and paternity leave for adopters this applied where a child was either matched or placed for adoption on or after April 6, 2003 (Paternity and Adoption Leave Regulations 2002 (SI 2002/2788 reg.3)). Such rights were further extended by the Work and Families Act 2006, which introduced additional paternity leave (of up to 26 weeks) from April 3, 2011.

Part 7 of the Children and Families Act 2014 makes provision for shared parental leave and statutory shared parental pay in place of additional paternity leave and additional statutory paternity pay. These new entitlements apply where the expected week of childbirth starts on or after April 5, 2015 or the adoption placement occurs on or after that date. As a consequence, from April 5, 2015 "ordinary paternity leave" and "ordinary statutory paternity pay" have become just "paternity leave" and "statutory paternity pay".

Paragraph 15

2.684 Since October 7, 1996 the lower age limit for income support is now 16 in all cases (SSCBA s.124(1)(a)). However, the exclusion for those who are treated as receiving relevant education (see reg.12 and the notes to that regulation) remains, except for those who fall within reg.13(2). This paragraph enables "qualifying young people" covered by reg.13(2)(a)–(e) to claim income support; a "qualifying young person" to whom reg.13(2)(h) applies will be eligible under para.18. See the notes to reg.13 for the circumstances in which reg.13(2) applies.

Paragraph 15A

2.685 A "qualifying young person" who comes within reg.13(2)(a)–(e) is eligible for income support under para.15 even though he is in full-time, non-advanced education. However, it is part of the definition of "qualifying young person" that the person is under 20. Paragraph 15A was therefore introduced on April 6, 2009 to extend eligibility for income support to 20-year-olds in full-time, non-advanced education (defined in sub-para.(6)) who meet conditions which are the same as those in reg.13(2)(c), (d) and (e), provided that they were accepted to attend, enrolled on, or began the course before reaching the age of 19.

With effect from April 1, 2012 para.15A has been extended so that it is no longer a requirement that the person was accepted to attend, enrolled on, or began the course before becoming 19. It is now sufficient if this occurred while he was under the age of 21. In addition, para.15A also applies to a person who reaches the age of 21 while undertaking a course of full-time, non-advanced education. This will enable such a person to finish his course, even though he is aged 21 (or over). The definition of "course of full-time, non-advanced education" has also been clarified to make clear that it applies provided that the course is not a course of advanced education, as defined in reg.61(1).

Note that the references in the definition of "parent" in sub-para.(6) have not been updated and still refer to sub-paragraph (5)(a), (b) and (c). Following the April 2012 amendments, the provisions that were in sub-para.(5) are now in sub-para.(4). The Interpretation Act 1978 ss.17(2)(a) and 23(1) will apply.

Paragraph 16

2.686 This paragraph was revoked with effect from October 7, 2006 because it only applied to people who were aged 50 or over on October 6, 1996. By October 7, 2006 such a person would be 60 or over and therefore would have reached the qualifying age for state pension credit (which was 60 at that time) and so would no longer be entitled to income support (SSCBA s.124(1)(aa)).

Paragraph 16A

This provision was a transitional provision introduced as part of the new system of bereavement benefits that came into effect on April 9, 2001 (see the 2005 edition of this volume for the details of this provision). It ceased to have effect on April 10, 2006 and has been revoked. **2.687**

Paragraph 18A

Paragraph 18A covered asylum seekers who were allowed under reg.21ZB to claim income support retrospectively if their refugee status was subsequently recognised by the IND. It was revoked on June 14, 2007 (as was reg.21ZB). However under art.2(3) of the Asylum and Immigration (Treatment of Claimants, etc.) Act 2004 (Commencement No.7 and Transitional Provisions) Order 2007 the revocation of para.18A does not apply in the case of a person who is recorded as a refugee on or before June 14, 2007. For these purposes a person is recorded as a refugee on the day that the Secretary of State notifies him that he has been recognised as a refugee (art.2(4) of the Order). **2.688**

For people recorded as refugees or granted humanitarian protection after June 14, 2007 there is a new system of "refugee integration loans" under s.13 of the 2004 Act (as amended by s.45 of the Immigration, Asylum and Nationality Act 2006). Decisions in relation to these loans are made by the Home Office Border and Immigration Agency. See further the Integration Loans for Refugees and Others Regulations 2007 (SI 2007/1598) and the Social Security (Claims and Payments) Amendment (No.2) Regulations 2007 (SI 2007/1866) (the latter amends Sch.9 to the Claims and Payments Regulations to allow for deductions to repay integration loans—see Vol.III in this series).

Paragraph 19

The previous form of para.19 only applied to a person who had to attend court as a justice of the peace, a party to any proceedings, a witness or a juror. From May 30, 2006 this has been extended so that para.19 now also applies where a person is required to attend a tribunal in a relevant capacity. **2.689**

Paragraph 21

A new form of this paragraph was introduced on January 25, 2010 as a consequence of the revocation of Pt VI (Urgent Cases) of the Income Support Regulations on that date (see the General Note to Pt VI). Claimants who first fell within reg.2(1) of and para.1 of Pt I of the Schedule to the Social Security (Immigration and Asylum) Consequential Amendments Regulations 2000 (SI 2000/636) after January 24, 2010 could claim income support at the full rate (as opposed to the urgent cases rate) under reg.22B. Paragraph 1 of Pt I of the Schedule to the 2000 Regulations related to claimants with limited leave to enter or remain in the UK (and who, but for that paragraph and reg.2 of the 2000 Regulations, would have been persons subject to immigration control) and who were temporarily without funds because remittances to them from abroad had been disrupted. Entitlement to income support lasted for a maximum of 42 days—or a number of periods not exceeding 42 days in total—within the same period of leave. **2.690**

Paragraph 1 of Pt I of the Schedule to the 2000 Regulations was revoked with effect from October 29, 2013 by reg.9(3) of the Social Security (Miscellaneous Amendments) (No.3) Regulations 2013 (SI 2013/2536) on the basis that the provision was rarely used because people could use credit cards, etc. to tide them over. Regulation 22B (together with other income support provisions that involved entitlement under para.1 of Pt I of the Schedule to the 2000 Regulations) was also revoked. Paragraph 21, however, has not been revoked because it concerns possible entitlement to income support under reg.2 of the 2000 Regulations as a whole (see reg.2(4) and (5)) and is not restricted to entitlement under reg.2(1).

Paragraph 22

2.691 A person required to live in a bail hostel is not "detained in custody" (*R(IS) 17/93*; note the effect of Sch.7 para.9, if a person in a bail hostel is a member of a couple). However, once a person has been charged, he is detained in custody pending trial, even if subsequently no trial takes place (*R(IS) 1/94*). See the notes to "prisoner" in reg.21(3). The definition of prisoner was amended from April 10, 1995 to reverse the effect of *Chief Adjudication Officer v Carr* (reported as *R(IS) 20/95*) which held that a person serving a prison sentence was not "in custody" while on home leave.

Paragraph 23

2.692 Someone in this situation could not come within para.1 because they would not be a lone parent while the absence of the partner was only temporary, but clearly deserves the same treatment in these circumstances.

Paragraphs 24–25

2.693 These paragraphs are no longer of any practical application because they relate to the old incapacity for work regime. However, they have not been formally revoked and so are being retained, together with the note to them.

Paragraphs 24 and 25 cover those who are appealing against a decision that they are capable of work under the "own occupation test" (para.24) or the personal capability assessment" (para.25). See the 2010/11 edition of Vol.I of this series for full details of these tests and when they apply.

Under para.24, if the claimant's own doctor continues to certify that he is incapable of work while he is pursuing an appeal against the incapacity decision, he will be eligible for income support pending the determination of the appeal. This means the final determination of the appeal, e.g. if it is taken to the Social Security Commissioner, confirmed in *CIS 2654/1999*. The person does not have to have been in receipt of income support before the incapacity decision was made. If para.24 applies full income support is payable (compare para.25).

2.694 If the claimant is appealing against capacity for work on the basis of the personal capability assessment, there is no requirement under para.25 for him to continue to submit medical certificates from his own doctor. This is because they are no longer required once the personal capability assessment has been applied. Again it is not necessary for the person to have been in receipt of income support before the incapacity decision was made. But if para.25 applies, the claimant's income support is reduced by 20 per cent of the appropriate personal allowance for a single claimant of his age until the appeal is determined (reg.22A), unless he is appealing after failing his first all work test or personal capability assessment and immediately before April 13, 1995 he had been incapable of work for 28 weeks or in receipt of invalidity benefit or severe disablement allowance (reg.22A(3); and see the transitional protection in reg.27(3) of the Income Support (General) (Jobseeker's Allowance Consequential Amendments) Regulations 1996 referred to in the note to reg.22A(3)). (If the appeal is successful, the reduction will be repaid.) See above for when an appeal is determined.

In order to receive full benefit, a claimant who is appealing against a failure to satisfy the personal capability assessment will have to sign on as available for work and claim JSA (unless any of the other paragraphs of Sch.1B apply; after the introduction of ESA on October 27, 2008 he could also consider claiming ESA). This could place the claimant in a dilemma if he is maintaining that he is unable to work. The best course may be for him to say to the Job Centre that he has been found capable of work and that he will accept any suitable work having regard to his limitations (see reg.13(3) of the JSA Regulations 1996). However, the fact that he has claimed JSA will not prejudice the appeal about incapacity as it will postdate the decision under appeal (s.12(8)(a) SSA 1998).

It will be noted that both paras 24 and 25 refer to a person who "has made and is pursuing an appeal" against an incapacity decision. There will usually be a gap between the date that the incapacity decision takes effect and the date the appeal is lodged. Can paras 24 or 25 apply during this gap? According to the Commissioner in *CIS 2075/2002* the legislation implies that benefit will be paid in respect of the period between such a decision being given and an appeal being brought, at least if the appeal is not late or is admitted despite its lateness (and moreover this also applied where an appeal had been rejected as not duly made but was later reinstated as had occurred in the case before him). He therefore agreed with the Secretary of State that the claimant had remained entitled to income support ever since the decision was made that he was not incapable of work. However, the difficulty was the procedural hurdles created by the Social Security Act 1998 and the Decisions and Appeals Regulations 1999. The question was, if lodging an appeal or having one reinstated retrospectively did affect entitlement to income support, what was the ground for backdating an income support claim or for revision or supersession and from what date was the supersession, if supersession was appropriate, effective? The Commissioner found a solution to this dilemma on the facts of the case before him but suggested that amendments to the Decisions and Appeals Regulations may be needed to adequately cater for decision-making under paras 24–25.

However, in *R(IS)2/05* the Commissioner disagreed with *CIS/2075/2002* as in his view the legislation contained no such implication. He held that there was no entitlement to income support under para.25 in the period between the date of the decision that supersedes the award of benefit on the ground that the person is not incapable of work and the date of the appeal against that decision. On the Commissioner's reasoning the same would apply in relation to para.24. **2.695**

The problems highlighted by these decisions lead to the amendment made to para.25 with effect from March 18, 2005. This provides that para.25 applies from the date that the determination that the claimant is not incapable of work takes effect. Associated amendments were also made to the Decisions and Appeals Regulations 1999 (see Vol.III of this series). Two new provisions were introduced into reg.3 of those regulations: reg.3(7C) which allows for revision of a decision to terminate income support entitlement where that entitlement was ended because the claimant was found capable of work and he appeals that decision (reg.3(7C) was further amended on April 10, 2006 to allow for revision of the income support decision where the incapacity determination is revised); and reg.3(7B) which provides that where the appeal against the incapacity decision is successful (or, from April 10, 2006, lapses) the decision to award reduced rate income support under reg.22A can be revised (in practice this has happened and the reduction has been repaid even in the absence of such an express provision). A further provision (reg.3(7F)), introduced on April 10, 2006, allows for revision of a decision to remove the disability premium (in a case where a claimant found capable of work had remained entitled to income support on another ground) and the claimant's appeal against the incapacity decision is subsequently successful or the incapacity decision is revised. In addition a new reg.6(2)(n) deals with the situation where income support has been disallowed as a result of the incapacity decision and the claimant appeals against that disallowance (as well as the incapacity decision). In the past, if the appeal against the income support disallowance was heard before the appeal against the incapacity decision (and assuming that the claimant did not qualify for income support on any other ground), the tribunal would (unless it adjourned that appeal pending the outcome of the incapacity appeal) be bound to uphold the disallowance decision. If the incapacity appeal subsequently succeeded, there was no provision that enabled the first tribunal's decision upholding the income support disallowance to be revised. However, reg.6(2)(n) of the 1999 Regulations now provides for supersession of the first tribunal's decision in these circumstances; in addition a new reg.7(34) provides that such a supersession takes effect from the date that income support was terminated as a result of the decision that the person was not incapable of work.

See *CIS/2445/2005* in the note to para.7 which highlights the problems that can occur in cases where a person who has been treated as capable of work because he failed to return the incapacity for work questionnaire (IB50) makes a (further) claim for income support which is refused and his appeal against the incapacity decision subsequently succeeds (note that paras 24 and 25 only apply while a person is appealing against a decision that he has failed the own occupation test/personal capability assessment; they do not apply in the case of a claimant who has been treated as capable of work because he has failed to return the IB50 (or attend a medical examination)).

Paragraph 28

2.696 Paragraph 11 of the former Sch.1 applied to a person in receipt of a training allowance. Paragraph 28 only covers a person under 25 who is on a training course provided by the Secretary of State, the Welsh Ministers, or, in Scotland, by a local enterprise company. However, under reg.170 of the JSA Regulations 1996 a person in receipt of a training allowance (in respect of training *other* than that covered by para.28) may qualify for income-based JSA without having to be available for, or actively seek, employment or enter into a jobseeker's agreement.

Note that as a result of the new child benefit rules introduced on April 10, 2006, a person under 20 who is on "approved training" can come within the definition of "qualifying young person within the meaning of s.142 of the Contributions and Benefits Act" and so count as in relevant education (see reg.12 and the notes to that regulation). This paragraph has therefore been amended with effect from April 10, 2006 to exclude a qualifying young person or child.

SCHEDULE 2 **Regulations 17 [3 (1)] and 18**

Applicable Amounts

[35Part I

Personal Allowances

2.697 1.—The weekly amounts specified in column (2) below in respect of each person or couple specified in column (1) shall be the weekly amounts specified for the purposes of regulations 17(1) and 18(1) (applicable amounts and polygamous marriages).

Column (1)	*Column (2)*
Person or Couple	*Amount*
(1) Single claimant aged—	
(a) except where head (b) or (c) of this sub-paragraph applies, less than 18;	(1)(a) [78 £57.90];
[28(b) less than 18 who falls within any of the circumstances specified in paragraph 1A;]	(b) [78 £57.90];
(c) less than 18 who satisfies the condition in [65 paragraph 11(1)(a)]	(c) [78 £57.90];
(d) not less than 18 but less than 25;	(d) [78 £57.90];
(e) not less than 25.	(e) [78 £73.10].
(2) Lone parent aged—	(2)
(a) except where head (b) or (c) of this sub-paragraph applies, less than 18;	(a) [78 £57.90];
[28(b) less than 18 who falls within any of the circumstances specified in paragraph 1A;]	(b) [78 £57.90];
(c) less than 18 who satisfies the condition in [65 paragraph 11(1)(a)]	(c) [78 £57.90];
(d) not less than 18.	(d) [78 £73.10].

Column (1)	*Column (2)*
Person or Couple	*Amount*
[28(3) Couple—	(3)
(a) where both members are aged less than 18 and— (i) at least one of them is treated as responsible for a child; or (ii) had they not been members of a couple, each would have qualified for income support under regulation 4ZA [71 or income-related employment and support allowance]; or (iii) the claimant's partner satisfies the requirement of section 3(1)(f)(iii) of the Jobseekers Act 1995 (prescribed circumstances for persons aged 16 but less than 18); or (iv) there is in force in respect of the claimant's partner a direction under section 16 of the Jobseekers Act 1995 (persons under 18: severe hardship);	(a) [78 £87.50];
(b) where both members are aged less than 18 and head (a) does not apply but one member of the couple falls within any of the circumstances specified in paragraph 1A;	(b) [78 £57.90];
(c) where both members are aged less than 18 and heads (a) and (b) do not apply;	(c) [78 £57.90];
(d) where both members are aged not less than 18;	(d) [78 £114.85];
(e) where one member is aged not less than 18 and the other member is a person under 18 who— (i) qualifies for income support under regulation 4ZA [71 or income-related employment and support allowance], or who would so qualify if he were not a member of a couple; or (ii) satisfies the requirements of section 3(1)(f)(iii) of the Jobseekers Act 1995 (prescribed circumstances for persons aged 16 but less than 18); or (iii) is the subject of a direction under section 16 of the Jobseekers Act 1995 (persons under 18: severe hardship);	(e) [78 £114.85];
(f) where the claimant is aged not less than 18 but less than 25 and his partner is a person under 18 who— (i) would not qualify for income support under regulation 4ZA [71 or income-related employment and support allowance] if he were not a member of a couple; and (ii) does not satisfy the requirements of section 3(1)(f)(iii) of the Jobseekers Act 1995 (prescribed circumstances for persons aged 16 but less than 18); and (iii) is not the subject of a direction under section 16 of the Jobseekers Act 1995 (persons under 18: severe hardship);	(f) [78 £57.90];
(g) where the claimant is aged not less than 25 and his partner is a person under 18 who— (i) would not qualify for income support under regulation 4ZA [71 or income-related employment and support allowance] if he were not a member of a couple; and (ii does not satisfy the requirements of section 3(1)(f)(iii) of the Jobseekers Act 1995 (prescribed circumstances for persons aged 16 but less than 18); and (iii) is not the subject of a direction under section 16 of the Jobseekers Act 1995 (persons under 18: severe hardship).]]	(g) [78 £73.10].

[28 **1A.**—(1) The circumstances referred to in paragraph 1 are that— **2.698**

(a) the person has no parents nor any person acting in the place of his parents;

(b) the person—

(i) is not living with his parents nor any person acting in the place of his parents; and
(ii) in England and Wales, was being looked after by a local authority pursuant to a relevant enactment who placed him with some person other than a close relative of his; or in Scotland, was in the care of a local authority under a relevant enactment and whilst in that care was not living with his parents or any close relative, or was in custody in any institution to which the Prison Act 1952 or the Prisons (Scotland) Act 1989 applied immediately before he attained the age of 16;

(c) the person is in accommodation which is other than his parental home, and which is other than the home of a person acting in the place of his parents, who entered that accommodation—
(i) as part of a programme of rehabilitation or resettlement, that programme being under the supervision of the probation service or a local authority; or
(ii) in order to avoid physical or sexual abuse; or
(iii) because of a mental or physical handicap or illness and needs such accommodation because of his handicap or illness;

(d) the person is living away from his parents and any person who is acting in the place of his parents in a case where his parents are or, as the case may be, that person is, unable financially to support him and his parents are, or that person is—
(i) chronically sick or mentally or physically disabled; or
(ii) detained in custody pending trial or sentence upon conviction or under sentence imposed by a court; of
(iii) prohibited from entering or re-entering Great Britain; or

(e) the person of necessity has to live away from his parents and any person acting in the place of his parents because—
(i) he is estranged from his parents and that person; or
(ii) he is in physical or moral danger; or
(iii) there is a serious risk to his physical or mental health.

(2) In this paragraph—
(a) "chronically sick or mentally or physically disabled" has the same meaning it has in regulation 13(3)(b) (circumstances in which persons in relevant education are to be entitled to income support);
(b) in England and Wales, any reference to a person acting in place of a person's parents includes a reference to—
(i) where the person is being looked after by a local authority or voluntary organisation who place him with a family, a relative of his, or some other suitable person, the person with whom the person is placed, whether or not any payment is made to him in connection with the placement; or
(ii) in any other case, any person with parental responsibility for the child, and for this purpose "parental responsibility" has the meaning it has in the Children Act 1989 by virtue of section 3 of that Act;
(c) in Scotland, any reference to a person acting in place of a person's parents includes a reference to a local authority or voluntary organisation where the person is in their care under a relevant enactment, or to a person with whom the person is boarded out by a local authority or voluntary organisation whether or not any payment is made by them.]

2.699 [35 **2.**—[59 . . .]]

2.700 [17 **2A.**—[55 . . .]]

PART II

Regulations 17[3(1)(c)
[3and 18(1)](d)

Family Premium

2.701 **3.**—[59 . . .]

PART III

Regulations 17[3(1)](d)
[3and 18(1)](e)

Premiums

2.702 **4.**—Except as provided in paragraph 5, the weekly premiums specified in Part IV of this Schedule shall, for the purposes of regulations 17[3(1)](d)[3 and 18(1)](e), be applicable to a claimant who satisfies the condition specified in [42paragraphs 8A] [10 to 14ZA] in respect of that premium.

5.—Subject to paragraph 6, where a claimant satisfies the conditions in respect of more than one premium in this Part of this Schedule, only one premium shall be applicable to him and, if they are different amounts, the higher or highest amount shall apply.

[58 **6.**—(1) Subject to sub-paragraph (2), the following premiums, namely—

(a) a severe disability to which paragraph 13 applies;
(b) an enhanced disability premium to which paragraph 13A applies;
(c) [59 . . .]; and
(d) a carer premium to which paragraph 14ZA applies,

may be applicable in addition to any other premium that may apply under this Schedule.

(2) An enhanced disability premium in respect of a person shall not be applicable in addition to—

(a) a pensioner premium under paragraph 9 or 9A; or
(b) a higher pension premium under paragraph 10.]

7.—[10(1) Subject to sub-paragraph (2)] for the purposes of this Part of this Schedule, once a premium is applicable to a claimant under this Part, a person shall be treated as being in receipt of any benefit—

(a) in the case of a benefit to which the Social Security (Overlapping Benefits) Regulations 1979 applies, for any period during which, apart from the provisions of those Regulations, he would be in receipt of that benefit; and
(b) for any period spent by a claimant in undertaking a course of training or instruction provided or approved by the [12 Secretary of State [68 . . .]] under section 2 of the Employment and Training Act 1973 [11, or by [69 Skills Development Scotland,] Scottish Enterprise or Highlands and Islands Enterprise under section 2 of the Enterprise and New Towns (Scotland) Act 1990,] [7or for any period during which he is in receipt of a training allowance].

[10(2) For the purposes of the carer premium under paragraph 14ZA, a person shall be treated as being in receipt of [49 carer's allowance] by virtue of sub-paragraph (1)(a) only if and for so long as the person in respect of whose care the allowance has been claimed remains in receipt of attendance allowance [15 , [75 . . .] the care component of disability living allowance at the highest or middle rate prescribed in accordance with section 37ZB(3) of the Social Security Act [SSCBA, s.72(3)]] [75 or the daily living component of personal independence payment at the standard or enhanced rate in accordance with section 78(3) of the 2012 Act] [76 or armed forces independence payment].]

Lone Parent Premium

8.—[29. . .]. 2.703

[42 Bereavement Premium

8A.—[67 . . .]] 2.704

[Pensioner premium for persons under 75

[54 **9.**—The condition is that the claimant has a partner aged [70 not less than the qualifying age for state pension credit] but less than 75.] 2.705

Pensioner premium for persons 75 and over

[54 **9A.**—The condition is that the claimant has a partner aged not less than 75 but less than 80.]] 2.706

Higher Pensioner Premium

10.—[54 (1) [65 Subject to sub-paragraph (6), the] condition is that— 2.707

(a) the claimant's partner is aged not less than 80; or
(b) the claimant's partner is aged less than 80 but [70 not less than the qualifying age for state pension credit] and either—
  (i) the additional condition specified in [58 paragraph 12(1)(a), (c) or (d)] is satisfied; or
  (ii) the claimant was entitled to, or was treated as being in receipt of, income support and—
    (aa) the disability premium was or, as the case may be, would have been, applicable to him in respect of a benefit week within eight weeks of [70 the day his partner attained the qualifying age for state pension credit]; and
    (bb) he has, subject to sub-paragraph (3), remained continuously entitled to income support since his partner attained [70 the qualifying age for state pension credit].

(2) . . .]

(3) For the purposes of this paragraph and paragraph 12—

(a) once the higher pensioner premium is applicable to a claimant, if he then ceases, for a period of eight weeks or less, to be entitled to [41or treated as entitled to] income support, he shall, on becoming re-entitled to income support, thereafter be treated as having been continuously entitled thereto;

(b) in so far as [54 sub-paragraph (1)(b)(ii) is] concerned, if a claimant ceases to be entitled to [41or treated as entitled to] income support for a period not exceeding eight weeks which includes [70 the day his partner attained the qualifying age for state pension credit], he shall, on becoming re-entitled to income support, thereafter be treated as having been continuously entitled thereto.

[33(4) In the case of a claimant who is a welfare to work beneficiary, references in sub-paragraphs (1)(b)(ii) [65 . . .] and (3)(b) to a period of 8 weeks shall be treated as references to a period of [64 104 weeks].]

[41 (5) For the purposes of this paragraph, a claimant shall be treated as having been entitled to and in receipt of income support throughout any period which comprises only days on which he was participating in an employment zone programme and was not entitled to income support because, as a consequence of his participation in that programme, he was engaged in remunerative work or had income in excess of his applicable amount as prescribed in Part IV.]

[65 (6) The condition is not satisfied if the claimant's partner to whom sub-paragraph (1) refers is a long-term patient.]

Disability Premium

2.708 **11.**—[65 —(1) Subject to sub-paragraph (2), the] condition is that—

(a) where the claimant is a single claimant or a lone parent, [54 . . .] the additional condition specified in paragraph 12 is satisfied; or

(b) where the claimant has a partner, either—

[54 (i) the claimant satisfies the additional condition specified in paragraph [58 12(1)(a), (b), (c) or (d)]; or]

(ii) his partner [70 has not attained the qualifying age for state pension credit] and the additional condition specified in [58 paragraph 12(1)(a), (c) or (d)] is satisfied by his partner.

[65 (2) The condition is not satisfied if—

(a) the claimant is a single claimant or a lone parent and (in either case) is a long-term patient;

(b) the claimant is a member of a couple or polygamous marriage and each member of the couple or polygamous marriage is a long-term patient; or

(c) the claimant is a member of a couple or a polygamous marriage and a member of that couple or polygamous marriage is—

(i) a long-term patient; and

(ii) the only member of the couple or polygamous marriage to whom sub-paragraph (1)(b) refers.]

Additional condition for the Higher Pensioner and Disability Premiums

2.709 **12.**—(1) Subject to sub-paragraph (2) and paragraph 7 the additional condition referred to in paragraphs 10 and 11 is that either—

(a) the claimant or, as the case may be, his partner—

(i) is in receipt of one or more of the following benefits: attendance allowance, [15disability living allowance, [76 armed forces independence payment,] [75 personal independence payment,] [50 the disability element or the severe disability element of working tax credit as specified in regulation 20(1)(b) and (f) of the Working Tax Credit (Entitlement and Maximum Rate) Regulations 2002], mobility supplement, [25long-term incapacity benefit] under [22Part II of the Contributions and Benefits Act or severe disablement allowance under Part III of that Act] [1but, in the case of [25long-term incapacity benefit] or severe disablement allowance only where it is paid in respect of him]; or

(ii) is provided by the Secretary of State with an invalid carriage or other vehicle under section 5(2) of the National Health Service Act 1977 (other services) or, in Scotland, under section 46 of the National Health Service (Scotland) Act 1978 (provision of vehicles) or receives payments by way of grant from the Secretary of State under paragraph 2 of Schedule 2 to that 1977 Act (additional provisions as to vehicles) or, in Scotland, under that section 46; or

[77 (iii) is certified as severely sight impaired or blind by a consultant ophthalmologist; or]

[26(b) the claimant—

(i) is entitled to statutory sick pay or [27is, or is treated as, incapable of work,] in accordance with the provisions of Part XIIA of the Contributions and Benefits Act and the regulations made thereunder (incapacity for work), and

(ii) has been so entitled or so incapable [27, or has been treated as so incapable,] for a continuous period of not less than—

(aa) 196 days in the case of a claimant who is terminally ill within the meaning of section 30B(4) of the Contributions and Benefits Act; or

(bb) [63 subject to [65 paragraph 2A] of Schedule 7] 364 days in any other case; and for these purposes any two or more periods of entitlement or incapacity separated by a break of not more than 56 days shall be treated as one continuous period; or]

[54 (c) the claimant's partner was in receipt of long-term incapacity benefit under Part II of the Contributions and Benefits Act when entitlement to that benefit ceased on account of the payment of a retirement pension under that Act [81 or a state pension under Part 1 of the Pensions Act 2014] and—

(i) the claimant has since remained continuously entitled to income support;

(ii) the higher pensioner premium or disability premium has been applicable to the claimant; and

(iii) the partner is still alive;

(d) except where paragraph [63 2A [65 . . .]] of Schedule 7 (patients) applies, the claimant or, as the case may be, his partner was in receipt of attendance allowance [75 , disability living allowance or personal independence payment]—

(i) but payment of that benefit has been suspended under the [60 Social Security (Attendance Allowance) Regulations 1991 [75 , the Social Security (Disability Living Allowance) Regulations 1991 or regulations made under section 86(1) (hospital in-patients) of the 2012 Act]] or otherwise abated as a consequence of the claimant or his partner becoming a patient within the meaning of regulation 21(3); and

(ii) a higher pensioner premium or disability premium has been applicable to the claimant.]

[34(1A) In the case of a claimant who is a welfare to work beneficiary, the reference in sub-paragraph (1)(b) to a period of 56 days shall be treated as a reference to a period of [64 104 weeks].]

[77 (2) For the purposes of sub-paragraph (1)(a)(iii), a person who has ceased to be certified as severely sight impaired or blind on regaining his eyesight shall nevertheless be treated as severely sight impaired or blind, as the case may be, and as satisfying the additional condition set out in that sub-paragraph for a period of 28 weeks following the date on which he ceased to be so certified.]

(3) [26 . . .]

(4) For the purpose of [58 sub-paragraph (1)(c) and (d)], once the higher pensioner premium is applicable to the claimant by virtue of his satisfying the condition specified in that provision, if he then ceases, for a period of eight weeks or less, to be entitled to income support, he shall on again becoming so entitled to income support, immediately thereafter be treated as satisfying the condition in [58 sub-paragraph (1)(c) and (d)].

[4(5) For the purposes of sub-paragraph (1)(b), once the disability premium is applicable to a claimant by virtue of his satisfying the additional condition specified in that provision, he shall continue to be treated as satisfying that condition for any period spent by him in undertaking a course of training provided under section 2 of the Employment and Training Act 1973 [7or for any period during which he is in receipt of a training allowance].]

[25(6) For the purposes of [58 sub-paragraph (1)(a)(i) and (c)], a reference to a person in receipt of long-term incapacity benefit includes a person in receipt of short-term incapacity benefit at a rate equal to the long-term rate by virtue of section 30B(4)(a) of the Contributions and Benefits Act (short-term incapacity benefit for a person who is terminally ill), or who would be or would have been in receipt of short-term incapacity benefit at such a rate but for the fact that the rate of short-term incapacity benefit already payable to him is or was equal to or greater than the long-term rate.]

[40 [61 . . .]]

Severe Disability Premium

13.—(1) The condition is that the claimant is a severely disabled person. **2.710**

(2) For the purposes of sub-paragraph (1), a claimant shall be treated as being a severely disabled person if, and only if—

(a) in the case of a single claimant[[19], a lone parent or a claimant who is treated as having no partner in consequence of sub-paragraph (2A)]—

(i) he is in receipt of attendance allowance [[15][[75] . . .] the care component of disability living allowance at the highest or middle rate prescribed in accordance with section 37ZB(3) of the Social Security Act [SSCBA, s.72(3)]] [[75] or the daily living component of personal independence payment at the standard or enhanced rate in accordance with section 78(3) of the 2012 Act] [[76] or armed forces independence payment], and

(ii) subject to sub-paragraph (3), he has no non-dependants aged 18 or over [[23]normally residing with him or with whom he is normally residing,] and

(iii) [[41]no person is entitled to, and in receipt of, [[49] a carer's allowance] under section 70 of the Contributions and Benefits Act [[80] or has an award of universal credit which includes the carer element] in respect of caring for him;]

(b) [[42] in the case of a claimant who] has a partner—

(i) he is in receipt of attendance allowance [[15], [[75] . . .] the care component of disability living allowance at the highest or middle rate prescribed in accordance with section 37ZB(3) of the Social Security Act [SSCBA, s.72(3)]] [[75] or the daily living component of personal independence payment at the standard or enhanced rate in accordance with section 78(3) of the 2012 Act] [[76] or armed forces independence payment]; and

(ii) his partner is also in receipt of such an allowance or, if he is a member of a polygamous marriage, all the partners of that marriage are in receipt thereof; and

(iii) subject to sub-paragraph (3), he has no non-dependants aged 18 or over [[23]normally residing with him or with whom he is normally residing,]

and either [[41]a person is entitled to, and in receipt of, [[49] a carer's allowance] [[80] or has an award of universal credit which includes the carer element] in respect of caring for only one of the couple or, in the case of a polygamous marriage, for one or more but not all the partners of the marriage or, as the case may be, no person is entitled to, and in receipt of, such an allowance] [[80] or has such an award of universal credit] in respect of caring for either member of the couple or any partner of the polygamous marriage.

[[19](2A) Where a claimant has a partner who does not satisfy the condition in sub-paragraph (2)(b)(ii), and that partner is [[77] severely sight impaired or blind or treated as severely sight impaired or blind] within the meaning of paragraph 12(1)(a)(iii) and (2), that partner shall be treated for the purposes of sub-paragraph (2) as if he were not a partner of the claimant.]

(3) For the purposes of sub-paragraph (2)(a)(ii) and (2)(b)(iii) no account shall be taken of—

(a) a person receiving attendance allowance [[15], [[75] . . .] the care component of disability living allowance at the highest or middle rate prescribed in accordance with section 37ZB(3) of the Social Security Act [SSCBA, s.72(3)]] [[75] or the daily living component of personal independence payment at the standard or enhanced rate in accordance with section 78(3) of the 2012 Act] [[76] or armed forces independence payment]; or

(b) [[21]. . .]

(c) subject to sub-paragraph (4), a person who joins the claimant's household for the first time in order to care for the claimant or his partner and immediately before so joining the claimant or his partner was treated as a severely disabled person; [[19] or

(d) a person who is [[77] severely sight impaired or blind or treated as severely sight impaired or blind] within the meaning of paragraph 12(1)(a)(iii) and (2).]

[[1](3A) For the purposes of sub-paragraph (2)(b) a person shall be treated [[41] . . .]

(a) [[41] as being in receipt of] attendance allowance[[15], or the care component of disability living allowance at the highest or middle rate prescribed in accordance with section 37ZB(3) of the Social Security Act [SSCBA, s.72(3)]] if he would, but for his being a patient for a period exceeding 28 days, be so in receipt;

(b) [[41] as being entitled to and in receipt of [[49] a carer's allowance] [[80] or having an award of universal credit which includes the carer element] if he would, but for the person for whom he was caring being a patient in hospital for a period exceeding 28 days, be so entitled and in receipt [[80] of carer's allowance or have such an award of universal credit].]]

[[75] (c) as being in receipt of the daily living component of personal independence payment at the standard or enhanced rate in accordance with section 78(3) of the 2012 Act if he would, but for a suspension of benefit in accordance with regulations under section

86(1) (hospital in-patients) of the 2012 Act, be so in receipt.]

[22(3ZA) For the purposes of sub-paragraph (2)(a)(iii) and (2)(b), no account shall be taken of an award of [49 a carer's allowance] [80 or universal credit which includes the carer element] to the extent that payment of such an award is back-dated for a period before [66 the date on which the award is first paid].]

(4) Sub-paragraph (3)(c) shall apply only for the first 12 weeks following the date on which the person to whom that provision applies first joins the claimant's household.

[45 (5) In sub-paragraph (2)(a)(iii) and (b), references to a person being in receipt of [49 a carer's allowance] [80 or as having an award of universal credit which includes the carer element] shall include references to a person who would have been in receipt of that allowance [80 or had such an award] but for the application of a restriction under section [72 6B or] 7 of the Social Security Fraud Act 2001 (loss of benefit provisions).]

[80 (6) For the purposes of this paragraph, a person has an award of universal credit which includes the carer element if the person has an award of universal credit which includes an amount which is the carer element under regulation 29 of the Universal Credit Regulations 2013.]

[43 Enhanced disability premium

13A.— [75 76 (1) Subject to sub-paragraph (2), the condition is that— **2.711**

(a) the claimant; or

(b) the claimant's partner, if any, who has not attained the qualifying age for state pension credit,

is a person to whom sub-paragraph (1ZA) applies.

(1ZA) This sub-paragraph applies to the person mentioned in sub-paragraph (1) where—

(a) armed forces independence payment is payable to that person;

(b) the care component of disability living allowance is, or would, but for a suspension of benefit in accordance with regulations under section 113(2) of the Contributions and Benefits Act or but for an abatement as a consequence of hospitalization, be payable to that person at the highest rate prescribed under section 72(3) of that Act; or

(c) the daily living component of personal independence payment is, or would, but for regulations made under section 86(1) (hospital in-patients) of the 2012 Act, be payable to that person at the enhanced rate in accordance with section 78(2) of that Act.]

[73 (1A) Where the condition in sub-paragraph (1) ceases to be satisfied because of the death of a child or young person, the condition is that the claimant [74 or partner] is entitled to child benefit in respect of that person under section 145A of the Contributions and Benefits Act (entitlement after death of child or qualifying young person).]

[65 (2) The condition is not satisfied if the person to whom sub-paragraph (1) refers is—

(a) [50 . . .]

(b) a single claimant or a lone parent and (in either case) is a long-term patient;

(c) a member of a couple or polygamous marriage and each member of the couple or polygamous marriage is a long-term patient; or

(d) a member of a couple or polygamous marriage who—

(i) is a long-term patient; and

(ii) is the only member of the couple or polygamous marriage to whom sub-paragraph (1) refers.]

Disabled Child Premium

14.—[59 . . . 65] **2.712**

[10Carer premium

14ZA.—(1) [13Subject to sub-paragraphs (3) and (4),] the condition is that the claimant or his partner is, or both of them are, [41 entitled to [49 a carer's allowance] under section 70 of the Contributions and Benefits Act] **2.713**

(2) [57 . . .]

[41 [48 (3) Where a carer premium is awarded but—

(a) the person in respect of whose care the [49 carer's allowance] has been awarded dies; or

(b) in any other case the person in respect of whom a carer premium has been awarded ceases to be entitled [57 . . .] to [49 a carer's allowance],

the condition for the award of the premium shall be treated as satisfied for a period of eight weeks from the relevant date specified in sub-paragraph (3A) below.

(3A) The relevant date for the purposes of sub-paragraph (3) above shall be—
(a) [57 where sub-paragraph (3)(a) applies,] the Sunday following the death of the person in respect of whose care [49 a carer's allowance] has been awarded or the date of death if the death occurred on a Sunday;
(b) [57 . . .]
(c) in any other case, the date on which the person who has been entitled to [46 a carer's allowance] ceases to be entitled to that allowance.]

(4) Where a person who has been entitled to an invalid care allowance ceases to be entitled to that allowance and makes a claim for income support, the condition for the award of the carer premium shall be treated as satisfied for a period of eight weeks from the date on which—
[48(a) the person in respect of whose care the [49 carer's allowance] has been awarded dies;
(b) [57 . . .]
[57 (c) in any other case, the person who has been entitled to a carer's allowance ceased to be entitled to that allowance.]]

[3Persons in receipt of concessionary payments

2.714 **14A.**—For the purpose of determining whether a premium is applicable to a person [12 under paragraphs 12 to 14ZA], any concessionary payment made to compensate that person for the non-payment of any benefit mentioned in those paragraphs shall be treated as if it were a payment of that benefit.]

[8Person in receipt of benefit

2.715 **14B.**—For the purposes of this Part of this Schedule, a person shall be regarded as being in receipt of any benefit if, and only if, it is paid in respect of him and shall be so regarded only for any period in respect of which that benefit is paid.]

[37 PART IV

2.716 *Weekly Amounts of Premiums Specified in Part III*

Column (1)	*Column (2)*
Premium	*Amount*
15.—(1) [29. . .]	(1) [29. . .].
[42(1A) [67 . . .]]	[42 (1A) [67 . . .]]
[54 (2) Pensioner premium for persons to whom paragraph 9 applies.	(2) [54. . .] [82 £122.70].
(2A) Pensioner premium for persons to whom paragraph 9A applies.	(2A) [54. . .] [82 £122.70].
(3) Higher pensioner premium for persons to whom paragraph 10 applies.]	(3) [54. . .] [82 £122.70].
(4) Disability Premium—	(4)
(a) where the claimant satisfies the condition in [65 paragraph 11(1)(a)];	(a) [79 £32.25];
(b) where the claimant satisfies the condition in [65 paragraph 11(1)(b)].	(b) [79 £45.95].
(5) Severe Disability Premium—	(5)
(a) where the claimant satisfies the condition in paragraph 13(2)(a);	(a) [79 £61.85];
(b) where the claimant satisfies the condition in paragraph 13(2)(b).	(b)
(i) if there is someone in receipt of [49 a carer's allowance] or if he or any partner satisfies that condition only by virtue of paragraph 13(3A);	(i) [79 £61.85];
(ii) if on-one is in receipt of such an allowance.	(ii) [79 £123.70].

Column (1)	Column (2)
Premium	*Amount*
(6) [59 . . .]	(6) [59 . . .]
(7) Carer Premium—	(7) [79 £34.60] in respect of each person who satisfied the condition specified in paragraph 14ZA.]
[43 (8) Enhanced disability premium where the conditions in paragraph 13A are satisifed—	(8) (a) [59 . . .] (b) [79 £15.75] in respect of each person who is neither— (i) a child or young person; nor (ii) a member of a couple or a polygamous marriage, in respect of whom the conditions specified in paragraph 13A are satisfied: (c) [79 £22.60] where the claimant is a member of a couple or a polygamous marriage and the conditions specified in paragraph 13A are satisfied in respect of a member of that couple or polygamous marriage.]

PART V

Rounding of Fractions

16.—Where income support is awarded for a period which is not a complete benefit week and the applicable amount in respect of that period results in an amount which includes a fraction of a penny that fraction shall be treated as a penny. **2.717**

AMENDMENTS

1. Income Support (General) Amendment Regulations 1988 (SI 1988/663) reg.29 (April 11, 1988).

2. Income Support (General) Amendment No.3 Regulations 1988 (SI 1988/1228) reg.9 (September 12, 1988).

3. Income Support (General) Amendment No.4 Regulations 1988 (SI 1988/1445) reg.19 (September 12, 1988).

4. Income Support (General) Amendment No.5 Regulations 1988 (SI 1988/2022) reg.17(*b*) (December 12, 1988).

5. Income Support (General) Amendment No.5 Regulations 1988 (SI 1988/2022) reg.17(*a*) (April 10, 1989).

6. Income Support (General) Amendment Regulations 1989 (SI 1989/534) reg.5 (October 9, 1989).

7. Income Support (General) Amendment No.3 Regulations 1989 (SI 1989/1678) reg.6 (October 9, 1989).

8. Income Support (General) Amendment Regulations 1990 (SI 1990/547) reg.17 (April 9, 1990).

9. Income Support (General) Amendment No.2 Regulations 1990 (SI 1990/1168) reg.2 (July 2, 1990).

10. Income Support (General) Amendment No.3 Regulations 1990 (SI 1990/1776) reg.8 (October 1, 1990).

11. Enterprise (Scotland) Consequential Amendments Order 1991 (SI 1991/3870 art.9 (April, 1991).

12. Income Support (General) Amendment Regulations 1991 (SI 1991/236) reg.2 (April 8, 1991).

13. Income Support (General) Amendment No.4 Regulations 1991 (SI 1991/236) reg.15 (August 5, 1991).

14. Income Support (General) Amendment No.4) Regulations 1991 (SI 1991/1559) reg.15 (October 7, 1991).

15. Disability Living Allowance and Disability Working Allowance (Consequential Provisions) Regulations 1991 (SI 1991/2742) reg.11(4) (April 6, 1992).

16. Income Support (General) Amendment Regulations 1992 (SI 1992/468) reg.6 (April 6, 1992).

17. Social Security Benefits (Amendments Consequential Upon the Introduction of community Care) Regulations 1992 (SI 1992/3147) reg.2 (April 1, 1993).

18. Social Security Benefits (Miscellaneous Amendments) Regulations 1993 (SI 1993/518) reg.5 (April 1, 1993).

19. Income-related Benefits Schemes (Miscellaneous Amendments) (No.2) Regulations 1993 (SI 1993/1150) reg.3 (May 25, 1993).

[20.]

21. Income-related Benefits Schemes (Miscellaneous Amendments) (No.4) Regulations 1993 (SI 1993/2119) reg.18 (October 4, 1993).

22. Income-related Benefits Schemes (Miscellaneous Amendments) (No.5) Regulations 1994 (SI 1994/2139) reg.30 (October 3, 1994).

23. Income-related Benefits Schemes (Miscellaneous Amendments) (No.6) Regulations 1994 (SI 1994/3061) reg.2(3) (December 2, 1994).

24. Income-related Benefits Schemes (Miscellaneous Amendments) Regulations 1995 (SI 1995/516) reg.24 (April 10, 1995).

25. Disability Working Allowance and Income Support (General) Amendment Regulations 1995 (SI 1995/482) reg.16 (April 13, 1995).

26. Disability Working Allowance and Income Support (General) Amendment Regulations 1995 (SI 1995/482) reg.17 (April 13, 1995).

27. Income-related Benefits Schemes and Social Security (Claims and Payments) (Miscellaneous Amendments) Regulations 1995 (SI 1995/2303) reg.6(8) (October 2, 1995).

28. Income Support (General) (Jobseeker's Allowance Consequential Amendments) Regulations 1996 (SI 1996/206) reg.23 and Sch.2 (October 7, 1996).

29. Child Benefit, Child Support and Social Security (Miscellaneous Amendments) Regulations 1996 (SI 1996/1803) reg.39 (April 7, 1997).

30. Income-related Benefits and Jobseeker's Allowance (Personal Allowances

for Children and Young Persons) (Amendment) Regulations 1996 (SI 1996/2545) reg.2 (April 7, 1997).

31. Income-related Benefits and Jobseeker's Allowance (Amendment) (No.2) Regulations 1997 (SI 1997/2197) regs 7(5) and (6)(a) (October 6, 1997).

32. Social Security Amendment (Lone Parents) Regulations 1998 (SI 1998/766) reg.12 (April 6, 1998).

33. Social Security (Welfare to Work) Regulations 1998 (SI 1998/2231) reg.13(3)(a) (October 5, 1998).

34. Social Security (Welfare to Work) Regulations 1998 (SI 1998/2231) reg.13(3)(b) (October 5, 1998).

35. Social Security Benefits Up-rating Order 1999 (SI 1999/264) art.18(3) and Sch.4 (April 12, 1999).

36. Social Security Benefits Up-rating Order 1999 (SI 1999/264) art.18(4)(b) (April 12, 1999).

37. Social Security Benefits Up-rating Order 1999 (SI 1999/264) art.18(5) and Sch.5 (April 12, 1999).

38. Social Security Amendment (Personal Allowances for Children and Young Persons) Regulations 1999 (SI 1999/2555) reg.2(1)(b) and (2)(April 10, 2000).

39. Social Security and Child Support (Tax Credits) Consequential Amendments Regulations 1999 (SI 1999/2566) reg.2(2) and Sch.2 Pt II (October 5, 1999).

40. Social Security (Miscellaneous Amendments) (No.2) Regulations 1999 (SI 1999/2556) reg.2(8) (October 4, 1999).

41. Social Security (Miscellaneous Amendments) Regulations 2000 (SI 2000/681) reg.4 (April 3, 2000).

42. Social Security Amendment (Bereavement Benefits) Regulations 2000 (SI 2000/2239) reg.2(3) (April 9, 2001).

43. Social Security Amendment (Enhanced Disability Premium) Regulations 2000 (SI 2629) reg.2(c) (April 9, 2001).

44. Social Security Amendment (Residential Care and Nursing Homes) Regulations 2001 (SI 2001/3767) reg.2 and Sch. Pt I para.14 (April 8, 2002).

45. Social Security (Loss of Benefit) (Consequential Amendments) Regulations 2002 (SI 2002/490) reg.2 (April 1, 2002).

46. Social Security Amendment (Residential Care and Nursing Homes) Regulations 2001 (SI 2001/3767) reg.2 and Sch. Pt I para.14 (as amended by Social Security Amendment (Residential Care and Nursing Homes) Regulations 2002 (SI 2002/398) reg.4(2)) (April 8, 2002).

47. Social Security Amendment (Personal Allowances for Children and Young Persons) Regulations 2002 (SI 2002/2019) reg.2 (October 14, 2002).

48. Social Security Amendment (Carer Premium) Regulations 2002 (SI 2002/2020) reg.2 (October 28, 2002).

49. Social Security Amendment (Carer's allowance) Regulations 2002 (SI 2002/2497) reg.3 and Sch.2 (April 1, 2003).

50. Social Security (Working Tax Credit and Child Tax Credit) (Consequential Amendments) Regulations 2003 (SI 2003/455) regs 1(5) and 2 and Sch.1 para.20(b) (April 7, 2003).

51. Social Security Benefits Up-Rating Order 2003 (SI 2003/526) art.17(3) and Sch.2 (April 7, 2003).

52. Social Security Benefits Up-Rating Order 2003 (SI 2003/526) art.17(5) and Sch.3 (April 7, 2003).

53. Social Security Benefits Up-Rating Order 2003 (SI 2003/526) art.17(4) (April 7, 2003).

54. State Pension Credit (Consequential, Transitional and Miscellaneous Provisions) Regulations 2002 (SI 2002/3019) reg.29(5) (October 6, 2003).

55. Social Security (Removal of Residential Allowance and Miscellaneous Amendments) Regulations 2003 (SI 2003/1121) reg.2 and Sch.1 para.6 (October 6, 2003).

56. Social Security (Hospital In-Patients and Miscellaneous Amendments) Regulations 2003 (SI 2003/1195) reg.3 (May 21, 2003).

57. Social Security (Miscellaneous Amendments) (No.2) Regulations 2003 (SI 2003/2279 reg.2(3) (October 1, 2003).

58. Income Support (General) Amendment Regulations 2003 (SI 2003/2379) reg.2 (October 6, 2003).

59. Social Security (Working Tax Credit and Child Tax Credit) (Consequential Amendments) Regulations 2003 (SI 2003/455) reg.2 and Sch.1 para.20 (April 6, 2004, except in "transitional cases" and see further the note to reg.17 of the Income Support Regulations).

60. Social Security (Miscellaneous Amendments) (No.2) Regulations 2004 (SI 2004/1141) reg.6 (May 12, 2004).

61. Social Security (Back to Work Bonus and Lone Parent Run-on) (Amendment and Revocation) Regulations 2003 (SI 2003/1589) reg.2(d) (October 25, 2004).

62. Civil Partnership (Pensions, Social Security and Child Support) (Consequential, etc. Provisions) Order 2005 (SI 2005/2877) art.2(3) and Sch.3 para.13(3) (December 5, 2005).

63. Social Security (Hospital In-Patients) Regulations 2005 (SI 2005/3360) reg.4 (April 10, 2006).

64. Social Security (Miscellaneous Amendments) (No.4) Regulations 2006 (SI 2006/2378) reg.5(7) (October 2, 2006).

65. Social Security (Miscellaneous Amendments) Regulations 2007 (SI 2007/719) reg.2(7) (April 9, 2007). As it relates to paras 13A(2)(a) and 14, the amendment only affects "transitional cases". See further the note to reg.17 of the Income Support Regulations and the commentary below.

66. Social Security (Miscellaneous Amendments) Regulations 2007 (SI 2007/719) reg.2(7)(e) (April 2, 2007).

67. Social Security (Miscellaneous Amendments) (No. 5) Regulations 2007 (SI 2007/2618) reg.2 and Sch. (October 1, 2007).

68. Social Security (Miscellaneous Amendments) Regulations 2008 (SI 2008/698) reg.2(12) (April 14. 2008).

69. Social Security (Miscellaneous Amendments) Regulations 2009 (SI 2009/583) reg.2(1) and (3) (April 6, 2009).

70. Social Security (Equalisation of State Pension Age) Regulations 2009 (SI 2009/1488) reg.3 (April 6, 2010).

71. Social Security (Miscellaneous Amendments) (No.2) Regulations 2010 (SI 2010/641) reg.2(1) and (9) (April 13, 2010).

72. Social Security (Loss of Benefit) Amendment Regulations 2010 (SI 2010/1160) reg.10(1) and (3) (April 1, 2010).

73. Social Security (Miscellaneous Amendments) Regulations 2011 (SI 2011/674) reg.3(5) (April 11, 2011).

74. Social Security (Miscellaneous Amendments) (No. 3) Regulations 2011 (SI 2011/2425) reg.7(1) and (7) (October 31, 2011).

75. Personal Independence Payment (Supplementary Provisions and Consequential Amendments) Regulations 2013 (SI 2013/388) reg.8 and Sch. para.11(1) and (5) (April 8, 2013).

76. Armed Forces and Reserve Forces Compensation Scheme (Consequential Provisions: Subordinate Legislation) Order 2013 (SI 2013/591) art.7 and Sch. para.4(1) and (5) (April 8, 2013).

77. Universal Credit and Miscellaneous Amendments (No.2) Regulations 2014 (SI 2014/2888) reg.3(2)(a) (November 26, 2014).

78. Welfare Benefits Up-rating Order 2015 (SI 2015/30) art.6 and Sch.1 (April 6, 2015).

79. Social Security Benefits Up-rating Order 2015 (SI 2015/457) art.14(5) and Sch.3 (April 6, 2015).

80. Universal Credit and Miscellaneous Amendments Regulations 2015 (SI 2015/1754) reg.14 (October 28, 2015).

81. Pensions Act 2014 (Consequential, Supplementary and Incidental Amendments) Order 2015 (SI 2015/1985) art.8(1) and (3) (April 6, 2016).

82 Social Security Benefits (Adjustment of Amounts and Thresholds) Regulations 2016 (SI 2016/242) reg.2(1) and (2) (April 11, 2016).

DEFINITIONS

"attendance allowance"—see reg.2(1).
"benefit week"—*ibid.*
"child"—see SSCBA s.137(1).
"claimant"—see reg.2(1).
"close relative"—*ibid.*
"couple"—*ibid.*
"disability living allowance"—*ibid.*
"family"—see SSCBA s.137(1).
"invalid carriage or other vehicle"—see reg.2(1).
"lone parent"—*ibid.*
"mobility supplement"—*ibid.*
"non-dependent"—see reg.3.
"partner"—see reg.2(1).
"polygamous marriage"—*ibid.*
"preserved right"—see reg.2(1) and reg.19.
"single claimant"—see reg.2(1).
"Social Security Act"—*ibid.*
"welfare to work beneficiary"—*ibid.*
"young person"—*ibid.*, reg.14.

GENERAL NOTE

Updating

Most of the amounts specified in paras 1 and 15 have applied from April 6, 2015. **2.217A** In the past, they would have been up-rated each year under s.150(1)(h) SSAA 1992. However, on March 16, 2016, s.11 and Sch.1 of the Welfare Reform and Work Act 2016 came into force. As a result, all the amounts specified in para.1 (Sch.1 para.1(a)) are frozen at their 2015/16 levels for four tax years (i.e. until April 6, 2020). The amounts of the pensioner premiums and higher pensioner premium in para.15 were up-rated by approximately 5.8 per cent (from £116.00 per week to £122.70 per week) with effect from April 11, 2016 as a consequence of the so-called "triple lock" under which the state pension increases each year by the higher of inflation, the increase in average earnings or 2.5 per cent. The other amounts in para.15 are not subject to the four-year freeze. However, they were not up-rated for 2016/17 as the Secretary of State decided that they had maintained their value in relation to prices as measured by the Consumer Prices Index over the 12-month period ending September 2015 (which had showed negative inflation of 0.1 per cent): see para.4.2 of the Explanatory Memorandum to SI 2016/230.

Personal Allowances

Paragraph 1

This paragraph was amended (and para.1A was introduced) in October 1996 as **2.718** a consequence of the changes to income support following the introduction of JSA.

The lower age limit for income support is now 16 (SSCBA s.124(1)(a)) but a person is only eligible if he falls into one of the categories prescribed by reg.4ZA and Sch.1B (s.124(1)(e)). (Note too that a person aged 16–18 in relevant education is still only entitled to income support in certain circumstances (s.124(1)(d) and reg.13)). However, the age-break of 18 remains significant as regards the rate of the personal allowance (and so the immense complexity of sub-para.(3) is retained), with another very significant break at 25 for single claimants.

For couples, where both partners are aged less than 18, the lower couple rate is only paid if either a child is a member of the family, or both partners are eligible for income support, or the non-claiming partner is either eligible for JSA or the subject of a severe hardship direction under s.16 of the Jobseekers Act 1995 (sub-para.(3)(a)). If this does not apply but one member of the couple comes within para.1A (person living away from parents and anyone acting in place of parents in specified circumstances), the personal allowance is the same as the higher rate for a single claimant under 18 (sub-para.(3)(b)), but otherwise only the equivalent of the lower rate for a single claimant under 18 is paid (sub-para.(3)(c)). Where one partner is 18 or over and the other is under 18, the higher couple rate is only paid if the partner under 18 is eligible for income support or income-based JSA or the subject of a JSA severe hardship direction (sub-para.(3)(e)). If this is not the case, the personal allowance is the same as for a single claimant (sub-para.(3)(f)), with another age-break at 25 (sub-para.(3)(g)).

2.719 The crucial age for lone parents is 18 (sub-para.(2)(d)). Lone parents of 16 and 17 are always eligible (para.1 of Sch.1B) but are paid at a higher rate if they fall within para.1A (person living away from parents and any substitute in certain circumstances) or qualify for a disability premium (sub-para.(2)(b) and (c)).

Single claimants under 18 qualify for the 18–24-year-old rate if they fall within para.1A (sub-para.(1)(b)) or qualify for a disability premium (sub-para.(1)(c)). But for single claimants there is another very significant break at the age of 25 (para.1(1)(e)). This is connected to the absence of any distinction in the personal allowances between householders and non-householders. Instead, the assumptions are made that most single people of 25 and over are responsible for their own households and that most single people under 25 are not responsible for independent households, typically living with parents. Thus a higher rate is paid to those of 25. Both these assumptions are correct, looking at the entire age-groups involved, but clearly have no direct applicability to the needs and circumstances of individuals. Young single claimants were one of the losing groups in the 1988 reforms.

In *Reynolds v Secretary of State for Work & Pensions* [2002] EWHC 426 (Admin), Q.B.D. (Wilson J), (March 7, 2002) a challenge to the lower rates for those under 25 on the basis that they infringed various provisions of the European Convention on Human Rights (including art.14 and art.1 of the First Protocol taken together) was rejected. That decision was upheld by the Court of Appeal and by the House of Lords in *Carson and Reynolds v Secretary of State for Work and Pensions* ([2003] EWCA Civ 797 (CA), [2005] UKHL 37 (HL)).

See Sch.7 for special cases, such as hospital patients. From April 1989 there are no special rules for people in board and lodging accommodation and from October 1989 no special rules for residents in most hostels. Special rules for the residents of residential care and nursing homes were abolished on October 6, 2003. For details of the position before that date, see pp.486–488 of Vol.II of the 2003 edition.

Paragraph 1A

2.720 This paragraph lists those categories of 16- and 17-year-olds who qualify for the higher rate of personal allowance under para.1(1)(b), (2)(b) and (3)(b). The categories replicate those formerly in paras 6–9A of Pt II of Sch.1A (Sch.1A was revoked on October 7, 1996 as a consequence of the changes to income support following the introduction of JSA).

See sub-para.(2) for definitions. On heads (a), (d) and (e) of sub-para.(1), see the notes to reg.13(2)(c), (e) and (d) respectively. Head (b) is similar to reg.13(2)(dd) but there are some important differences in the wording. Those covered by head (c) are expected to be particularly vulnerable.

Paragraph 2

2.721 Personal allowances for dependant children and young persons were abolished with effect from April 6, 2004. Except in transitional cases (as to which see the note to reg.17), financial help with the cost of supporting and bringing up a child or young person is now provided through child tax credit (see Vol.IV). For details of the position before April 6, 2004, see p.486 of Vol.II of the 2003 edition. In transitional cases the personal allowance for a child or young person was increased to £66.90 from the beginning of the first benefit week after April 6, 2015 by art.14(3) and Sch.2 to the Social Security Benefits Up-rating Order 2015 (SI 2015/457).

Paragraph 2A

The system of special payments of IS, known as "residential allowances", to people in private or voluntary sector residential care or nursing homes were abolished with effect from October 6, 2003. For details of the position before that date, see pp.486–488 of Vol.II of the 2003 edition. 2.722

Premiums

Paragraph 3

The family premium was also abolished with effect from April 6, 2004. For details of the position before April 6, 2004, see pp.488–489 of Vol.II of the 2003 edition and see the note to reg.17 for details of the transitional provisions. For those still entitled to the premium on a transitional basis, the text of para.3 is as follows: 2.723

"3.—(1) The weekly amount for the purposes of regulations 17(1)(c) and 18(1)(d) in respect of a family of which at least one member is a child or young person shall be—

(a) where the claimant is a lone parent to whom the conditions in both sub-paragraphs (2) and (3) apply and no premium is applicable under paragraph 9, 9A, 10 or 11, £117.45

(b) in any other case, £17.45.

(2) The first condition for the purposes of sub-paragraph (1)(a) is that the claimant—

(a) was both a lone parent and entitled to income support on 5th April 1998; or

(b) does not come within head (a) above but—

(i) was both a lone parent and entitled to income support on any day during the period of 12 weeks ending on 5th April 1998;

(ii) was both a lone parent and entitled to income support on any day during the period of 12 weeks commencing on 6th April 1998; and

(iii) the last day in respect of which (i) above applied was no more than 12 weeks before the first day in respect of which (ii) above applied.

(3) The second condition for the purposes of sub-paragraph (1)(a) is that as from the appropriate date specified in sub-paragraph (4), the claimant has continued, subject to sub-paragraph (5), to be both a lone parent and entitled to income support.

(4) The appropriate date for the purposes of sub-paragraph (3) is—

(a) in a case to which sub-paragraph (2)(a) applies, 6th April 1998;

(b) in a case to which sub-paragraph (2)(b) applies, the first day in respect of which sub-paragraph (2)(b)(ii) applied.

(5) For the purposes of sub-paragraph (3), where the claimant has ceased, for any period of 12 weeks or less, to be—

(a) a lone parent; or

(b) entitled to income support; or

(c) both a lone parent and entitled to income support,

the claimant shall be treated, on again becoming both a lone parent and entitled to income support, as having continued to be both a lone parent and entitled to income support throughout that period.

(6) In determining whether the conditions in sub-paragraphs (2) and (3) apply, entitlement to an income-based jobseeker's allowance shall be treated as entitlement to income support for the purposes of any requirement that a person is entitled to income support.

(7) For the purposes of this paragraph, a claimant shall be treated as having been

entitled to income support throughout any period which comprises only days on which he was participating in an employment zone programme and was not entitled to income support because, as a consequence of his participation in that programme, he was engaged in remunerative work or had income in excess of his applicable amount as prescribed in Part IV."

The rate of the premium (which had not been increased in April 2011, April 2012 or April 2013) was increased by 5 pence to £17.45 from the beginning of the first benefit week after April 7, 2014 by art.14(4) of the Social Security Benefits Up-rating Order 2014 (SI 2014/516). It was not further increased in April 2015 (see 14(4) of the Social Security Benefits Up-rating Order 2015 (SI 2015/457).

Paragraphs 4–7

2.724 These provisions establish the general framework for the other premiums, in paras 9–14. Paragraph 4 provides that in each case the premium is applicable to the claimant, although the condition will sometimes relate to the claimant's partner and, in the cases of the pensioner, enhanced pensioner and higher pensioner premiums, can only relate to, the claimant's partner since—with effect from October 6, 2003—people aged 60 or over can no longer be the claimant for income support (see note to s.124(1)(aa) of the Contributions and Benefits Act). The general rule is that only one of these premiums is applicable. If the claimant satisfies the conditions for more than one, the highest is applicable (para.5). However, a number of exceptions appear in para.6. The severe disability premium is allowed in addition to any other premium, as is the carer premium; so too is the enhanced disability premium in some cases.

Many of the conditions for premiums are based on the receipt of other social security benefits. Paragraph 7(1) deals with two situations where, once a premium has been allowed, the person concerned ceases actually to receive the other benefit. It allows entitlement to the premium to continue if the person has only ceased to receive the relevant benefit because of another, overlapping, benefit or is on a government training course or in receipt of a training allowance (the main example being Work Based Learning for Young People, which has replaced Youth Training and other training provision focussed on 16–17-year-olds). See para.14B on the meaning of receipt of benefit.

Under para.7(2), the above rules do not allow the carer premium to continue unless the person cared for continues to receive attendance allowance or one of the two higher rates of the care component of disability living allowance.

Paragraph 8A

2.725 The bereavement premium was introduced with effect from April 9, 2001 as part of the overall reforms of the former widow's benefits. By reg.6 of the Social Security Amendment (Bereavement Benefits) Regulations 2000 (SI 2000/2239), the premium ceased to apply from April 10, 2006. For further details see pp.527–8 of the 2007 edition.

Paragraphs 9 and 9A

2.726 These provisions, together with the increases in the higher pensioner premium under para.15(3), implemented the Government's commitment to give increased help to needy pensioners in October 1989. The ordinary pensioner premium under para.9 was limited to people aged 60–74. Paragraph 9A provided a separate premium for those aged 75–79, with a small differential over the ordinary pensioner premium. The effect of reg.14(1D) of the Transitional Regulations was that these increases did not affect any transitional addition in payment. Although from April 2001 the differential has been removed. From October 6, 2003, the premium can only be paid where a claimant who has not reached the qualifying age for state pension credit has a partner who has reached that age (or, in the case of the enhanced pensioner premium, is 75 or older) and who is not entitled to state pension credit. Many couples in this position will be better off by claiming state pension credit and the importance of the pensioner premium and enhanced pensioner premium is therefore likely to decline.

Paragraph 10

From October 6, 2003, the first qualification for the HPP is that the claimant's partner is aged 80 or over. If that is not satisfied, there are another two alternatives, provided that the claimant's partner has reached the qualifying age for state pension credit. The first is that the claimant's partner satisfies the disability test in para.12(1)(a), (c), or (d). The second is that the claimant was entitled to, or treated as entitled to, the income support disability premium within eight weeks of the day on which the partner reached the qualifying age for state pension credit and has remained continuously entitled to income support since that birthday. The requirement that the disability premium was, or would have been applicable to the claimant presumably now means applicable in respect of his or her partner rather than in his or her own right, although sub-para.(1)(b)(ii)(aa) does not actually spell that out. Further, *CIS 458/1992* decides that a premium is not "applicable" unless it actually forms part of the claimant's applicable amount (but see *CIS 11293/1996* in the notes to para.12). 2.727

The second alternative is subject to a number of extensions which may assist claimants:

- first, entitlement to income-based JSA is treated as entitlement to income support—see reg.32 of the Income Support (General) (Jobseeker's Allowance Consequential Amendments) Regulations 1996;
- secondly, sub-para.(5) treats claimants who were participating in an employment zone programme and who were not entitled to income support because, as a result of that participation, they were in remunerative work (see regs 5 and 6) or had income in excess of their applicable amounts as being entitled to income support;
- thirdly, claimants who cease to be entitled to income support for a period of up to eight weeks which includes the day on which the partner reaches the qualifying age for state pension credit are treated by sub-para.(3)(b) as having been continuously entitled to income support when they become re-entitled. Whilst an eight week linking period is better than no linking period at all, this rule is entirely arbitrary. There are many circumstances in which a claimant might cease to be entitled to income support at the time his or her partner reaches the qualifying age for state pension credit (for example, receipt of capital from the proceeds of an endowment or retirement annuity policy or an occupational pension) which have nothing to do with the future disability needs of the claimant's partner;
- fourthly, if the claimant is a "welfare to work beneficiary" (as defined in reg.2(1)) the eight week period is extended to 104 weeks by sub-para.(4); and
- finally, sub-para.(3)(a) provides that once a claimant has become entitled to the HPP, breaks in entitlement to income support of up to eight weeks will not affect entitlement to the premium, despite the concluding words of sub-para.(1)(b)(ii).

Paragraph 11

The qualification for the DP can be for the claimant personally to satisfy one of the conditions in para.12. If it is the claimant's partner who might qualify, then only para.12(1)(a), (c) or (d), not (b), will do. If the condition is to be satisfied by the claimant's *partner*, s/he must be under 60. If s/he is over 60 then there will be entitlement to the HPP under para.10(1)(b)(i). Following the introduction of state pension credit on October 6, 2003, all income support claimants must be under 60 (see notes to s.124(1)(aa) of the Contributions and Benefits Act). 2.728

Paragraph 12

2.729 Sub-paragraph (1) prescribes four alternative conditions for HPP and DP. Heads (a) and (d) may be satisfied by either the claimant or his or her partner, head (b) may only be satisfied by the claimant. Head (c) contains some criteria which must be satisfied by the claimant's partner and some which must be satisfied by the claimant. As far as possible the conditions are made to depend on decisions already taken by other authorities, so that decision-making here should be routine.

Head (a) applies to receipt of the benefits listed in head (i), provision of or grant towards an invalid carriage, or being registered blind. From April 1990, para.14B defines receipt of benefit in terms of payment, reversing the effect of *R(SB) 12/87*. Long-term incapacity benefit requires 52 weeks of incapacity for work, and has a contribution test. (Previously invalidity pension required only 28 weeks of incapacity.) Note sub-para.(6), the effect of which is to treat a person who is terminally ill as in receipt of long-term incapacity benefit after 28 weeks. Severe disablement allowance is non-contributory, but has an additional (and tough) test of disablement. The extension to all levels of disability living allowance brought in some previously excluded claimants. See sub-para.(2) for blindness, and the notes to para.13 of Sch.1B.

Entitlement to HPP is affected by the discriminatory age limit for claims for long-term incapacity benefit (previously invalidity benefit) that results from the UK's different pensionable ages for men and women (i.e. 65 for men, between 60 and 65 for women (depending when they were born); full equalisation of pensionable age will not be achieved until November, 2018) (but see *CIB 13368/1998* below where the entitlement to incapacity benefit derives from an industrial injury or a prescribed industrial disease). (As a result of the ECJ's decision in *Secretary of State for Social Security v Thomas* [1993] E.C.R. I-1247, [1993] 4 All E.R. 556, also reported as *R(G) 2/94*, the discriminatory age limit for initial claims for severe disablement allowance was finally changed on October 28, 1994 (see Social Security (Severe Disablement Allowance and Invalid Care Allowance) Amendment Regulations 1994 (SI 1994/2556)). In *Secretary of State for Social Security and Chief Adjudication Officer v Graham* (C-92/94), [1995] 3 C.M.L.R. 169, [1995] All E.R. (EC) 865, also reported as *R(S) 2/95*) the ECJ held that the different treatment of men and women in relation to invalidity benefit was not in breach of EC Directive 79/7 on equal treatment for men and women in matters of social security. The discrimination in the rules for invalidity benefit was permitted under art.7(1)(a) of the Directive as it was "necessarily and objectively linked" to the UK's different pension ages (see *Thomas*). The Court's reasoning is scanty (compare the Advocate General's Opinion delivered on June 15, 1995). But the judgment has put an end to the argument that a discriminatory link to pensionable age for *contributory* (as opposed to non-contributory: see *Thomas*) benefits is unlawful. See the 1995 edition of J. Mesher and P. Wood, *Income-related Benefits: the Legislation* for further details of *Graham* (and associated issues) and related European case law on the scope of Directive 79/7. Long-term incapacity benefit is not payable to people over pensionable age (the transitional protection given to those who were over pensionable age before April 13, 1995 having expired). The consequence of the ECJ's judgment in *Graham* is that this discrimination against women (and its effect on entitlement to HPP) remains (until the pensionable age differential is finally abolished). Note, however, that in *CIB 13368/1996* Commissioner Levenson held that for women who were getting invalidity benefit because of industrial injury or prescribed disease, and who transferred to transitional incapacity benefit (being deemed to satisfy the contribution conditions), the discriminatory age limit was unlawful. Regulation 17(4) of the Social Security (Incapacity Benefit) (Transitional) Regulations 1995) fell on the *Thomas*, rather than the *Graham* side of the line. But Commissioner Levenson's decision was, by concession, reversed by the Court of Appeal in *CAO v Rowlands* on June 27, 2000, following the ECJ's decision in *Hepple*.

2.730 The current form of head (b) is a consequence of the changes associated with the introduction of incapacity benefit (which replaced sickness benefit and invalidity benefit from April 13, 1995). It is no longer linked to what is now para.7 of Sch.1B (see the 1994 edition of J. Mesher and P. Wood, *Income-related Benefits: the Legislation* for notes on the previous form of head (b)), although it employs the same criteria as heads (a), (b) and (d) of para.7. See the notes to para.7 of Sch.1B. The test must now be satisfied for a continuous period of at least 52 weeks before a disability or higher pensioner premium can be awarded under head (b), unless the claimant is terminally ill when the period is 28 weeks. Two or more periods separated by not more than eight weeks (from October 5, 1998, 104 weeks in the case of a "welfare to work beneficiary" (sub-para.(1A)); see the notes to reg.2(1) for when a person counts as a welfare to work beneficiary) count as one continuous period. A person is defined as terminally ill if he is expected to die from a progressive disease within six months. If the person has been incapable of work (or entitled to statutory sick pay) for 28 weeks by the time a decision-maker decides he is terminally ill, head (b) will immediately apply. Before April 13,1995 the qualifying period under head (b) was 28 weeks. There is some transitional protection, see below. In the case of a couple, head (b) can only be satisfied by the claimant.

A person is entitled to statutory sick pay from the first day of incapacity (even though it is not paid for the first three "waiting days"). Otherwise it is only days on which it is accepted that the claimant is, or is to be treated as, incapable of work in accordance with the rules for determining incapacity for work (see Vol.I of this series) that count. A claimant does not have to be in receipt of income support during the qualifying period, so if a person has been incapable of work for 52 weeks before claiming income support head (b) will immediately apply.

Any days when the claimant is treated as capable of work under the incapacity rules (see Vol.I of this series) will not count, but note the linking rule. A person may be treated as capable of work for a maximum of 6 weeks under reg.18 of the Social Security (Incapacity for Work) (General) Regulations; or indefinitely in other cases. Thus the effect of a decision to treat a claimant as capable of work may (depending on the circumstances) only result in that period not counting towards establishing entitlement to a disability or higher pensioner premium, rather than necessitate a return to square one. If the claimant has already been awarded a premium it will not be payable while he is treated as capable of work. But if this is for eight weeks or less it will apply again immediately after the break. Note also the 52-week linking rule from October 5, 1998 for a claimant who is a "welfare to work beneficiary" (see reg.2(1) and the notes to that regulation).

Note *CIS 15611/1996* which decides that a claimant who had been entitled to a **2.731**
disability premium before going into prison and who continued to be incapable of work while in prison did not have to re-serve the 52-week qualifying period on his release. Although days of disqualification from incapacity benefit during a period of imprisonment did not count as days of incapacity for work under reg.4(1)(b) of the Incapacity Benefit Regulations 1994, this only applied for the purposes of incapacity benefit. The Incapacity for Work (General) Regulations 1995 contained no such provision and so subject to the claimant providing evidence of his incapacity for work throughout his period in prison he was entitled to a disability premium when he reclaimed income support on his release.

If a claimant makes a late claim for a benefit on the grounds of incapacity for work, the days on which it is accepted that he was, or was to be treated as, incapable of work should count under head (b). It does not matter that there is no entitlement to the benefit because the claim is late. See *R(IS) 8/93* (but note the amendments to reg.2(1) of the Social Security (Medical Evidence) Regulations 1976 (SI 1976/615) from April 13, 1995).

In *CIS/2699/2001* Commissioner Mesher considered whether the requirement that a claimant should have been incapable of work for a continuous period of 364 days (or 196 days if terminally ill) could be satisfied on the basis of retrospective medical evidence. He concluded that this was permitted by reg.28(2)(a) of the Social Security (Incapacity for Work) (General) Regulations 1995 and reg.2(1)(d) of the Social Security (Medical Evidence) Regulations 1976. However, by virtue of s.12(8)(b) of the Social Security Act 1998 (which prohibits a tribunal from considering circumstances arising after the date of the decision under appeal), such medical evidence had to be provided *before* the date of the Secretary of State's decision. This was because under reg.28(2)(a), the production of medical evidence was *itself* a circumstance relevant to the claimant's entitlement and not merely evidence related to some relevant circumstance. In so holding, Commissioner Mesher differed from the decision of Commissioner Rowland in *CIS/4772/2000* in which the point about s.12(8)(b) had not been raised.

2.732 There is transitional protection for claimants entitled to a disability premium on April 12, 1995 under head (b) as then in force. See reg.19(2) to (4) of the Disability Working Allowance and Income Support (General) Amendment Regulations 1995 (p.799). The premium will continue to be paid as long as they remain incapable of work (in accordance with the new rules, including the transitional protection). Note the linking rule. In addition, any period immediately before April 13, 1995 during which a claimant satisfied para.5 of Sch.1 as then in force (see the 1994 edition of J. Mesher and P. Wood, *Income-related Benefits: the Legislation*) counts towards the qualifying period under head (b).

Heads (c) and (d) apply where receipt of some benefits specified in (a) only ceased because of age limits or going into hospital. The claimant has to remain continuously entitled to income support (or income-based JSA: reg.32 of the Income Support (General) (Jobseeker's Allowance Consequential Amendments) Regulations 1996 (see p.805) under which entitlement to income-based JSA counts as entitlement to income support for the purpose of satisfying any condition that the person is or has been entitled to income support) and if it is his partner who has ceased to receive long-term incapacity benefit she must still be alive. Note the linking rule in sub-para.(4). Note also sub-para.(6) in relation to incapacity benefit, the effect of which is to treat a person who is terminally ill as in receipt of long-term incapacity benefit after 28 weeks. There is transitional protection for claimants entitled to a higher pensioner premium under the old form of head (c)(i) at any time in the eight weeks before April 12, 1995 (i.e. those who transferred to retirement pension from invalidity benefit): see reg.20(4) of the Disability Working Allowance and Income Support (General) Amendment Regulations 1995 (p.800).

CIS 587/1990 exposes a gap in the legislation which has not yet been closed. The claimant transferred from invalidity benefit to retirement pension in 1982. He could not qualify under the old form of head (c) because he had not been continuously entitled to income support since the transfer. If he had delayed the transfer until after April 10, 1988, he would have qualified. The extent of his need at the relevant date (April 1990) was identical under either alternative. See sub-para.(4) for linking rules. Another gap is highlighted by *CIS 458/1992* which holds that the condition that a premium has been applicable requires that it should have been part of the claimant's applicable amount. So where a claimant had been in a residential care home he could not use head (c), because Sch.4 has no provision for premiums. But see *CIS 11293/1996* in the notes to para.4(6) of Sch.3 where the Commissioner holds that housing costs were "applicable" under para.5A(3) of the former Sch.3 if they were potentially applicable.

Paragraph 13

2.733 The presence of this category is required by s.22(3) of the 1986 Act, now s.135(5) of the Contributions and Benefits Act. The concern which prompted the inclusion of that subsection was that a severely disabled claimant on supplementary benefit might be getting high additional requirements for a range of extra needs (e.g. heating, laundry, diet, wear and tear on clothes, etc.), which the ordinary disability premium would go nowhere near matching. However, the conditions for the severe disability premium (SDP) are so tight that very few will qualify. The Independent Living Fund was set up to provide further cash help to the very severely disabled, but its budget was usually fully spent part way through its financial year. The

Fund was suspended in 1992. On April 1, 1993, it was replaced by two funds, the Independent Living (Extension) Fund which took over payments to existing beneficiaries and the Independent Living (1993) Fund for new applications.

First note that the SDP can only apply to the claimant, not to his partner. But since a couple has a free choice as to which of them should be the claimant (Claims and Payments Regulations reg.4) this should not be a problem.

If the claimant has no partner, he first must either be in receipt of one of the two higher rates of the care component of disability living allowance, or of either rate of the daily living component of personal independence payment, or of armed forces independence payment: see sub-para.(2)(a)(i)). That sub-paragraph also contemplates that a claimant might qualify for the premium through entitlement to attendance allowance. However, that appears to be a historical anomaly: anyone entitled to attendance allowance will have attained the qualifying age for state pension credit and therefore be disentitled to IS altogether by SSCBA 1992 s.124(1)(aa). Then there must be no non-dependants of 18 or over residing with him (sub-para. (2)(a)(ii)). The addition of the words "with whom he is normally residing" from December 2, 1994 is to reverse the effect of the Court of Appeal's decision in *Bate v Chief Adjudication Officer and Secretary of State for Social Security* [1995] 3 F.C.R. 145; *The Times*, December 12, 1994 (subsequently overturned by the House of Lords [1996] 1 W.L.R. 814: see the notes to reg.3).

The fact that the non-dependant is not lawfully resident in the UK does not prevent him or her from "normally residing" with the claimant. For the purposes of para.(2), whether one person "normally resides with" another is a purely factual question of their living arrangements and involves no judgment on the quality of his or her residence: see *ST v SSWP* [2009] UKUT 269 (AAC). In that case, Upper Tribunal Judge Jacobs explained the structure of para.13 as follows: 2.734

> "22. In the narrow context of paragraph 13, the emphasis is on a person who is living with the claimant and who is, therefore, able to provide some care for the claimant. The exclusion in paragraph 13(2)(a)(ii) is integral to the scope of the premium. It is reserved for claimants who (i) are disabled and (ii) have nobody available to provide care for them. (i) is shown by an appropriate award of a disability living allowance or an attendance allowance. (ii) is shown by the absence of an award of carer's allowance and of anyone resident with the claimant to help. Paragraph 13(3)(c) and (4) provides what Mr Brown conveniently called a bedding-in period. This allows a carer to move in with the claimant for a period of 12 weeks in order to see if the relationship works before the premium is removed."

The effect of sub-para.(3) is that adults in receipt of attendance allowance or one of the two higher rates of care component of disability living allowance or who are registered as blind or treated as blind or carers for the first 12 weeks of residence do not count for this purpose. "Non-dependant" is defined in reg.3. See the notes to that regulation for the intricacies of the definition. Care must be taken to apply the particular form of reg.3 in force at the relevant time. The current version makes it very diffcult for the parents, or other "close relatives", with whom an adult claimant is living not to be regarded as non-dependants. In *R(IS)12/06* the Commissioner holds that the refusal of the SDP to a claimant who lives with a close relative on a commercial basis in circumstances (i.e. where it would be paid if the claimant lived on the same terms with someone who was not a close relative) did not amount to unlawful discrimination contrary to art.14 of the ECHR. Finally, no one must be receiving carer's allowance (formerly invalid care allowance (ICA)) or the carer element of universal credit for caring for the claimant (sub-para.(2)(a)(iii)). Sub-para.(3ZA) provides that where an award of carer's allowance or the carer element of UC is made which includes arrears, entitlement to the SDP only ceases from the date the award of is actually made. So such an award does not lead to an overpayment of the SDP. This reverses the decision of the Commissioner in *R(IS) 14/94*.

If the claimant has a partner, the assumption is that the partner can care for the claimant. So there is an additional qualification that the partner is also in receipt of a qualifying allowance (sub-para.(2)(b)(ii)) or, if not, is registered as blind or treated as blind (sub-para.(2A)). There must be no eligible non-dependants in residence (see above), and at least one of the couple must not have a carer receiving carer's allowance or the carer element of universal credit.

2.735 In *R(IS) 22/93* and a number of associated appeals, the Commissioner held that sub-para.(2)(a)(ii) and (iii) were not validly made, since s.22(4) of the Social Security Act 1986 (now s.135(6) of the Contributions and Benefits Act) only gave power to prescribe conditions relating to a claimant's disability. Section 22(3) (SSSCBA s.135(5)) requires a severely disabled person's applicable amount to include a special premium. Heads (ii) and (iii) are concerned with the presence of others in the household and the benefit entitlement of other people, which are not connected to the claimant's disability. This cogently argued decision was reversed by the Court of Appeal in *Chief Adjudication Officer v Foster* [1992] Q.B. 31; [1991] 3 All E.R. 846, which held by a majority that the provisions were valid. The House of Lords confirmed this part of the Court of Appeal's decision (*Foster v Chief Adjudication Officer* [1993] A.C. 754, [1993] 1 All E.R. 705, also reported as part of *R(IS) 22/93*). Therefore, the full conditions of para.13 must be applied at all points of its history. See the notes to s.135 of the Contributions and Benefits Act for more details, and see Vol.III of this series for the power of the Social Security Commissioners and others to determine whether regulations have been validly made.

The premium is high, since it is in addition to DP or HPP (para.6(1)). For a claimant without a partner it is £61.85. For a couple (where both partners have to qualify) it is £61.85 for each of them who does not have a carer with carer's allowance (para.15(5)).

It was argued in *Rider v Chief Adjudication Officer*, reported as *R(IS) 10/94*, that for periods before April 1990, (when para.14B was introduced) where a lone parent received attendance allowance in respect of a child under 16, para.13(2)(a)(i) was satisfied. Regulation 6(4) of the Social Security (Attendance Allowance) (No.2) Regulations 1975 made the parent entitled to the attendance allowance in these circumstances. But if the parent, and not the child, were treated as in receipt of attendance allowance, that would mean that a child could never have satisfied the conditions of para.14(b) on the DCP. *R(IS) 10/94* decides that in the context of para.14(b) a child is in receipt of attendance allowance when the child satisfies the prescribed conditions and the meaning must be the same in para.13(2)(a)(i). The introduction of para.14B in April 1990, providing that a person is to be regarded as in receipt of any benefit only where it is paid in respect of that person was to clarify the law, not to change it. The decision in *R(IS) 10/94* was confirmed by the Court of Appeal which held that on an overall comparison of the words "in receipt of" in paras 13(2)(a)(i) and 14(b) (and also para.12(1)(a)(i) in relation to the disability premium), it could be seen that the words were not to be read just as they stood but as importing the additional requirement that the attendance allowance should be payable in respect of the recipient's own needs. Paragraph 13 (and para.12) was concerned only with the needs of claimants and their partners; para.14 only with the needs of children and young persons.

Note that entitlement to a severe disability premium is a question to which the assumption in reg.13(2) of the Decisions and Appeals Regulations 1999 applies (relevant information not in possession of decision-maker deemed to be adverse to claimant).

Paragraph 13A

2.736 With effect from April 9, 2001, this paragraph establishes an enhanced disability premium for claimants who (or whose partners or, in transitional cases (see the note to reg.17), family members) have not reached the qualifying age for state pension credit and are entitled to the highest rate of the care component of disability living allowance. By para.6(2) above the premium may be paid in addition to any other premium except the pensioner, enhanced pensioner and higher pensioner premiums payable under paras 9, 9A and 10.

In transitional cases, the text of sub-para.(1)(b) reads as follows:

"(b) a member of the claimant's family who is aged less than 60."

and sub-para.(2)(a) remains in force in the following terms:

"(2) The condition is not satisfied if the person to whom sub-paragraph (1) refers is—

(a) a child or young person—

(i) whose capital if calculated in accordance with Part 5 of these Regulations in like manner as for the claimant, except as provided in regulation 44(1), would exceed £3,000; or

(ii) who is a long-term patient;"

The premium is payable for the first 52 weeks of any stay in a hospital or similar institution even if payment of disability living allowance has been suspended because of the hospitalisation. If the claimant is a member of a couple or a polygamous marriage, the premium is payable unless both members of the couple or all members of the marriage have been hospitalised for 52 weeks.

In transitional cases, the enhanced disability premium for a child was increased to £24.43 from the beginning of the first benefit week after April 6, 2015 by art.14(5) and Sch.3 to the Social Security Benefits Up-rating Order 2015 (SI 2015/457).

Paragraph 14

Except in transitional cases (as to which see the note to reg.17), the disabled child premium was abolished with effect from April 6, 2004. For details of the position before that date, see p.496 of Vol.II of the 2003 edition. In transitional cases the disabled child premium was increased to £60.06 from the beginning of the first benefit week after April 6, 2015 by art.14(5) of, and Sch.3 to, the Social Security Benefits Up-rating Order 2015 (SI 2015/457). The transitional text of para.14 (as substituted with effect from April 9, 2007 by reg.2(7)(g) of SI 2007/719 and amended with effect from April 11, 2011 by reg.3(5) of SI 2011/674, with effect from April 8, 2013 by reg.8 and Sch. para.11(5)(d) of SI 2013/388 and reg.7 and Sch. para.4(5)(e) of SI SI 2013/591, with effect from April 28, 2014 by reg.2(1) and (5) of SI 2014/591, and with effect from November 26, 2014 by reg.3(2)(a)(iii) of SI 2014/2888) is as follows: 2.737

"Disabled Child Premium

14.—(1) Subject to sub-paragraph (2), the condition is that where the child or young person for whom the claimant or a partner of his is responsible and who is a member of the claimant's household is—

(a) in receipt of disability living allowance or is no longer in receipt of that allowance because he is a patient provided that the child or young person continues to be a member of the family; [. . .]

(b) [severely sight impaired or blind or treated as severely sight impaired or blind] within the meaning of paragraph 12(1)(a)(iii) and (2)[; or

(c) a child or young person in respect of whom section 145A of the Contributions and Benefits Act (entitlement after death of child or qualifying young person) applies for the purposes of entitlement to child benefit but only for the period prescribed under that section, and in respect of whom a disabled child premium was included in the claimant's applicable amount immediately before the death of that child or young person, or ceased to be included in the claimant's applicable amount because of that child or young person's death] [; or

(d) a young person who is in receipt of personal independence payment or who would, but for regulations made under section 86(1) (hospital in-patients) of the 2012 Act, be so in receipt provided that the young person continues to be a member of the family] [; or

(e) in receipt of armed forces independence payment.]

(2) The condition [in sub-paragraph (1)(a) [, (b), (d) or (e)]] is not satisfied in respect of a child or young person —

(a) whose capital, if calculated in accordance with Part.5 of these Regulations in like manner as for the claimant, except as provided in regulation 44(1), would exceed £3,000; or

(b) who is a long-term patient."

Paragraph 14ZA

2.738 The carer premium (CP) is part of the Government's shift of resources amongst the disabled. It goes to a person who is entitled to carer's allowance. The CP may encourage the claiming of carer's allowance (formerly called "invalid care allowance" ("ICA")) against which must be balanced the possible loss of SDP for the disabled person being cared for. See *R(IS) 14/94* above and para.13(3ZA). Under sub-paras (3) and (4) entitlement to the premium continues for eight weeks after ceasing to receive carer's allowance. In cases where carer's allowance is not payable because of the overlapping benefits rules, one of the conditions of entitlement is that the claim for carer's allowance should have been made on or after October 1, 1990. Whether this means the original claim or can also encompass any later claim is not entirely clear. DWP Policy is now that those who established an underlying entitlement to ICA (as it then was) before October 1, 1990 can be paid the premium with effect from April 3, 2000 (see Memo DMG JSA/IS 32). For the legal basis for the advice given in the Memo see *CIS/367/2003*.

Paragraph 14ZA (as it was worded in July 1999) was considered by Commissioner Jacobs in *CIS 4267/2001*. In that case, the claimant had been entitled to ICA and hence—under sub-para.(1)—to a carer permium (CP) immediately before he reached the age of 65. He then ceased to receive ICA because of the operation of the Overlapping Benefits Regulations (i.e. presumably because he had begun to receive his state retirement pension) but nevertheless continued to be *treated as* receiving that benefit—and therefore to be entitled to the CP—under sub-para.(2), as then in force. Subsequently, the person for whom he was caring ceased to be entitled to disability living allowance ("DLA"). If the Overlapping Benefits Regulations had not applied, the claimant would have continued to be entitled to ICA even though he was no longer caring for a severely disabled person (see SSCBA 1992 s.70(6) and reg.11 of the Invalid Care Allowance Regulations) and would therefore have continued to be entitled to a CP under sub-para.(1). However, sub-para.(2) provided that a person who was not *actually* in receipt of ICA could only be *treated as* in receipt of that benefit for as long as the person cared for was in receipt of attendance allowance or the middle or highest rates of the care component of DLA. The Commissioner rejected the argument by the claimant's representative that the income support legislation was in conflict with the ICA legislation and that the latter should be given priority. The legislation simply established different rules for different benefits and there was nothing inconsistent in providing differently for the carer premium and for ICA itself.

The wording of para.14ZA has been clarified by the amendments made by SI 2002/2020 with effect from October 28, 2002.

Paragraph 14A

2.739 In paras 12–14ZA receipt of a concessionary (i.e. extra-statutory) payment to compensate for non-payment of a benefit is to be equated with actual payment of that benefit.

Paragraph 14B

2.740 This important definition of receipt of benefit in terms of payment, not entitlement, reverses the effect of *R(SB) 12/87*. It makes for a further simplification of decision-making. It also ended the argument that it was the parent of a child under 16 who qualified for attendance allowance who received the benefit. See the note to para.13.

[1SCHEDULE 3 **Regulations 17(1)(e) and 18(1)(f)**

HOUSING COSTS

Housing costs

1.—(1) Subject to the following provisions of this Schedule, the housing costs applicable to a claimant are those costs— **2.741**

(a) which he or, where he is a member of a family, he or any member of that family is, in accordance with paragraph 2, liable to meet in respect of the dwelling occupied as the home which he or any other member of his family is treated as occupying, and

(b) which qualify under paragraphs 15 to 17.

(2) In this Schedule—

"housing costs" means those costs to which sub-paragraph (1) refers;

[74 . . .]

[74 . . .]

"standard rate" means the rate for the time being [26 determined in accordance with] paragraph 12.

(3) For the purposes of this Schedule a disabled person is a person—

(a) in respect of whom a disability premium, a disabled child premium, a pensioner premium for persons aged 75 or over or a higher pensioner premium is included in his applicable amount or the applicable amount of a person living with him; or

(b) [2. . .] who, had he in fact been entitled to income support, would have had included in his applicable amount a disability premium, a disabled child premium, a pensioner premium for persons aged 75 or over or a higher pensioner premium [38 ; or

(c) who is disabled or severely disabled for the purposes of section 9(6) (maximum rate) of the Tax Credits Act 2002.]

[49 [65(d) who-

(i) is in receipt of an employment and support allowance which includes an amount under section 2(2) or (3) or 4(4) or (5) of the Welfare Reform Act (components); or

(ii) would be entitled to an employment and support allowance including an amount of a work-related activity component under section 2(3) of that Act (amount of contributory allowance: work-related activity component), but for the application of section 1A of the Act (duration of contributory allowance)]] [70 ; or

(e) who is entitled to an award of universal credit the calculation of which includes an amount under regulation 27(1) of the Universal Credit Regulations 2013 in respect of the fact that he has limited capability for work or limited capability for work and work-related activity, or would include such an amount but for regulation 27(4) or 29(4) of those Regulations].

(4) For the purposes of sub-paragraph (3), a person shall not cease to be a disabled person on account of his being disqualified for receiving benefit or treated as capable of work by virtue of the operation of section 171E of the Contributions and Benefits Act (incapacity for work, disqualification etc.) [49 or disqualified for receiving employment and support allowance or treated as not having limited capability for work in accordance with regulations made under section 18 of the Welfare Reform Act (disqualification)].

[6 [44 Previous entitlement to income-based jobseeker's allowance [49, income-related employment and support allowance] or state pension credit]

1A.—(1) Where a claimant or his partner was in receipt of or was treated as being in receipt of income-based jobseeker's allowance [49 or income-related employment and support allowance] not more than 12 weeks before one of them becomes entitled to income support or, where the claimant or his partner is a person to whom paragraph 14(2) or (8) (linking rules) refers, not more than 26 weeks before becoming so entitled and— **2.742**

(a) the applicable amount for that allowance included an amount in respect of housing costs under [44 paragraphs 14 to 16] of Schedule 2 to the Jobseeker's Allowance Regulations 1996 [49 or paragraphs 16 to 18 of Schedule 6 to the Employment and Support Allowance Regulations]; and

(b) the circumstances affecting the calculation of those housing costs remain unchanged since the last calculation of those costs,

the applicable amount in respect of housing costs for income support shall be the applicable amount in respect of those costs current when entitlement to income-based jobseeker's allowance [49 or income-related employment and support allowance] was last determined.

[44 (1A) Where a claimant or his partner was in receipt of state pension credit not more than 12 weeks before one of them becomes entitled to income support or, where the claimant or his partner is a person to whom paragraph 14(2) or (8) (linking rules) refers, not more than 26 weeks before becoming so entitled, and—

(a) the appropriate minimum guarantee included an amount in respect of housing costs under paragraphs 11 to 13 of Schedule II to the State Pension Credit Regulations 2002; and

(b) the circumstances affecting the calculation of those housing costs remain unchanged since the last calculation of those costs,

the applicable amount in respect of housing costs for income support shall be the amount applicable in respect of those costs current when entitlement to state pension credit was last determined.]

(2) Where, in the period since housing costs were last calculated for income-based jobseeker's allowance [49 or income-related employment and support allowance] [44 or (as the case may be) state pension credit], there has been a change of circumstances, other than a reduction in the amount of an outstanding loan, which increases or reduces those costs, the amount to be met under this Schedule shall, for the purposes of the claim for income support, be recalculated so as to take account of that change.]

Circumstances in which a person is liable to meet housing costs

2.743 **2.**—(1) A person is liable to meet housing costs where—

(a) the liability falls upon him or his partner but not where the liability is to a member of the same household as the person on whom the liability falls;

(b) because the person liable to meet the housing costs is not meeting them, the claimant has to meet those costs in order to continue to live in the dwelling occupied as the home and it is reasonable in all the circumstances to treat the claimant as liable to meet those costs;

(c) he in practice shares the housing costs with other members of the household none of whom are close relatives either of the claimant or his partner, and

(i) one or more of those members is liable to meet those costs, and

(ii) it is reasonable in the circumstances to treat him as sharing responsibility.

(2) Where any one or more, but not all, members of the claimant's family are affected by a trade dispute, the housing costs shall be treated as wholly the responsibility of those members of the family not so affected.

Circumstances in which a person is to be treated as occupying a dwelling as his home

2.744 **3.**—(1) Subject to the following provisions of this paragraph, a person shall be treated as occupying as his home the dwelling normally occupied as his home by himself or, if he is a member of a family, by himself and his family and he shall not be treated as occupying any other dwelling as his home.

(2) In determining whether a dwelling is the dwelling normally occupied as the claimant's home for the purposes of sub-paragraph (1) regard shall be had to any other dwelling occupied by the claimant or by him and his family whether or not that other dwelling is in Great Britain.

(3) Subject to sub-paragraph (4), where a single claimant or a lone parent is a [15 full-time student] or is on a training course and is liable to make payments (including payments of mortgage interest or, in Scotland, payments under heritable securities or, in either case, analogous payments) in respect of either (but not both) the dwelling which he occupies for the purpose of attending his course of study or his training course or, as the case may be, the dwelling which he occupies when not attending his course, he shall be treated as occupying as his home the dwelling in respect of which he is liable to make payments.

(4) A full-time student shall not be treated as occupying a dwelling as his home for any week of absence from it, other than an absence occasioned by the need to enter hospital for treatment, outside the period of study, if the main purpose of his occupation during the period of study would be to facilitate attendance on his course.

(5) Where a claimant has been required to move into temporary accommodation by

reason of essential repairs being carried out to the dwelling normally occupied as his home and he is liable to make payments (including payments of mortgage interest or, in Scotland, payments under heritable securities or, in either case, analogous payments) in respect of either (but not both) the dwelling normally occupied or the temporary accommodation, he shall be treated as occupying as his home the dwelling in respect of which he is liable to make those payments.

(6) Where a person is liable to make payments in respect of two (but not more than two) dwellings, he shall be treated as occupying both dwellings as his home only—

(a) where he has left and remains absent from the former dwelling occupied as the home through fear of violence in that dwelling or by a former member of his family and it is reasonable that housing costs should be met in respect of both his former dwelling and his present dwelling occupied as the home; or

(b) in the case of a couple or a member of a polygamous marriage where a partner is [15] full-time student] or is on a training course and it is unavoidable that he or they should occupy two separate dwellings and reasonable that housing costs should be met in respect of both dwellings; or

(c) in the case where a person has moved into a new dwelling occupied as the home, except where sub-paragraph (5) applies, for a period not exceeding four benefit weeks [[43] from the first day of the benefit week in which the move occurs] if his liability to make payments in respect of two dwellings is unavoidable.

(7) Where—

(a) a person has moved into a dwelling and was liable to make payments in respect of that dwelling before moving in, and

(b) he had claimed income support before moving in and either that claim has not yet been determined or it has been determined but an amount has not been included under this Schedule and if the claim has been refused a further claim has been made within four weeks of the date on which the claimant moved into the new dwelling occupied as the home; and

(c) the delay in moving into the dwelling in respect of which there was liability to make payments before moving in was reasonable and—

(i) that delay was necessary in order to adapt the dwelling to meet the disablement needs of the claimant or any member of his family; or

[[39] (ii) the move was delayed pending [[66] local welfare provision or] the outcome of an application under Part 8 of the Contributions and Benefits Act for a social fund payment to meet a need arising out of the move or in connection with setting up the home in the dwelling, and—

(aa) a member of the claimant's family is aged five or under,

(bb) the claimant's applicable amount includes a premium under paragraph 9, 9A, 10, 11, 13 or 14 of Schedule 2 (applicable amounts), or

(cc) a child tax credit is paid for a member of the claimant's family who is disabled or severely disabled for the purposes of section 9(6) (maximum rate) of the Tax Credits Act 2002; or]

(iii) the person became liable to make payments in respect of the dwelling while he was a patient or was in residential accommodation,

he shall be treated as occupying the dwelling as his home for any period not exceeding four weeks immediately prior to the date on which he moved into the dwelling and in respect of which he was liable to make payments.

(8) This sub-paragraph applies to a person who enters residential accommodation—

(a) for the purpose of ascertaining whether the accommodation suits his needs; and

(b) with the intention of returning to the dwelling which he normally occupies as his home should, in the event, the residential accommodation prove not to suit his needs,

and while in the accommodation, the part of the dwelling which he normally occupies as his home is not let, or as the case may be, sub-let to another person.

(9) A person to whom sub-paragraph (8) applies shall be treated as occupying the dwelling he normally occupies as his home during any period (commencing with the day he enters the accommodation) not exceeding 13 weeks in which the person is resident in the accommodation, but only in so far as the total absence from the dwelling does not exceed 52 weeks.

(10) A person, other than a person to whom sub-paragraph (11) applies, shall be treated as occupying a dwelling as his home throughout any period of absence not exceeding 13 weeks, if, and only if—

(a) he intends to return to occupy the dwelling as his home; and

(b) the part of the dwelling normally occupied by him has not been let or, as the case may be, sub-let to another person; and

(c) the period of absence is unlikely to exceed 13 weeks.

(11) This sub-paragraph applies to a person whose absence from the dwelling he normally occupies as his home is temporary and—

(a) he intends to return to occupy the dwelling as his home; and

(b) while the part of the dwelling which is normally occupied by him has not been let or, as the case may be, sub-let; and

(c) he is—

[30 (i) detained in custody on remand pending trial or, as a condition of bail, required to reside—

(aa) in a dwelling, other than the dwelling he occupies as his home; or

(bb) in premises approved under [53 section 13 of the Offender Management Act 2007],

or, detained pending sentence upon conviction, or]

(ii) resident in a hospital or similar institution as a patient, or

(iii) undergoing or, as the case may be, his partner or his dependent child is undergoing, in the United Kingdom or elsewhere, medical treatment, or medically approved convalescence, in accommodation other than residential accommodation, or

(iv) following, in the United Kingdom or elsewhere, a training course, or

(v) undertaking medically approved care of a person residing in the United Kingdom or elsewhere, or

(vi) undertaking the care of a child whose parent or guardian is temporarily absent from the dwelling normally occupied by that parent or guardian for the purpose of receiving medically approved care or medical treatment, or

(vii) a person who is, whether in the United Kingdom or elsewhere, receiving medically approved care provided in accommodation other than residential accommodation, or

(viii) a [15 full-time student] to whom sub-paragraph (3) or (6)(b) does not apply, or

(ix) a person other than a person to whom sub-paragraph (8) applies, who is receiving care provided in residential accommodation; or

(x) a person to whom sub-paragraph (6)(a) does not apply and who has left the dwelling he occupies as his home through fear of violence in that dwelling [2, or by a person] who was formerly a member of his family; and

(d) the period of his absence is unlikely to exceed a period of 52 weeks or, in exceptional circumstances, is unlikely substantially to exceed that period.

(12) A person to whom sub-paragraph (11) applies is to be treated as occupying the dwelling he normally occupies as his home during any period of absence not exceeding 52 weeks beginning with the first day of that absence.

(13) In this paragraph—

(a) "medically approved" means certified by a medical practitioner;

(b) "patient" means a person who is undergoing medical or other treatment as an in-patient in a hospital or similar institution;

[56 (ba) "period of study" has the meaning given in regulation 61(1) (interpretation);]

[32 (c) "residential accommodation" means accommodation which is a care home, an Abbeyfield Home or an independent hospital;]

(d) "training course" means such a course of training or instruction provided wholly or partly by or on behalf of or in pursuance of arrangements made with, or approved by or on behalf of, [55 Skills Devolopment Scotland,] Scottish Enterprise, Highlands and Islands Enterprise, a government department or the Secretary of State.

Housing costs not met

2.745 **4.**—(1) No amount may be met under the provisions of this Schedule—

(a) in respect of housing benefit expenditure; or

(b) where the claimant is [32 living in care home, an Abbeyfield Home or an independent hospital except where he is living in such a home or hospital] during a temporary absence from the dwelling he occupies as his home and in so far as they relate totemporary absences, the provisions of paragraph 3(8) to (12) apply to him during that absence.

(2) Subject to the following provisions of this paragraph, loans which, apart from this paragraph qualify under paragraph 15 shall not so qualify where the loan was incurred during the relevant period and was incurred—

(a) after 1st October 1995, or

(b) after 2nd May 1994 and the housing costs applicable to that loan were not met by virtue of the former paragraph 5A of this Schedule in any one or more of the 26 weeks preceding 2nd October 1995, or

(c) subject to sub-paragraph (3), in the 26 weeks preceding 2nd October 1995 by a person—
(i) who was not at that time entitled to income support; and
(ii) who becomes, or whose partner becomes entitled to income support after 1st October 1995 and that entitlement is within 26 weeks of an earlier entitlement to income support for the claimant or his partner.

(3) Sub-paragraph (2)(c) shall not apply in respect of a loan where the claimant has interest payments on that loan met without restrictions under an award of income support in respect of a period commencing before 2nd October 1995.

[2(4) The "relevant period" for the purposes of this paragraph is any period during which the person to whom the loan was made—
(a) is entitled to income support [49 or income-related employment and support allowance], or
(b) is living as a member of a family one of whom is entitled to income support [49 or income-related employment and support allowance],
together with any linked period, that is to say a period falling between two such periods of entitlement to income support [49 or income-related employment and support allowance] separated by not more than 26 weeks.]

[7(4A) For the purposes of sub-paragraph (4), a person shall be treated as entitled to income support during any period when he or his partner was not so entitled because—
(a) that person or his partner was participating in an employment programme specified in regulation 75(1)(a)(ii) of the Jobseeker's Allowance Regulations 1996 [19, in the Intensive Activity Period specified in regulation 75(1)(a)(iv) of those Regulations [47 . . .]]; and
(b) in consequence of such participation that person or his partner was engaged in remunerative work or had an income [61equal to or] in excess of the claimant's applicable amount as prescribed in Part IV.]

[45 (4B) A person treated by virtue of paragraph 14 as being in receipt of income support for the purposes of this Schedule is not to be treated as entitled to income support for the purposes of sub-paragraph (4).]

(5) For the purposes of sub-paragraph (4)—
(a) any week in the period of 26 weeks ending on 1st October 1995 on which there arose an entitlement to income support such as is mentioned in that sub-paragraph shall be taken into account in determining when the relevant period commences; and
(b) two or more periods of entitlement and any intervening linked periods shall together form a single relevant period.

(6) Where the loan to which sub-paragraph (2) refers has been applied—
(a) for paying off an earlier loan, and that earlier loan qualified under paragraph 15 [4during the relevant period]; or
[4(b) to finance the purchase of a property where an earlier loan, which qualified under paragraph 15 or 16 during the relevant period in respect of another property, is paid off (in whole or in part) with monies received from the sale of that property;]
then the amount of the loan to which sub-paragraph (2) applies is the amount (if any) by which the new loan exceeds the earlier loan.

(7) Notwithstanding the preceding provisions of this paragraph, housing costs shall be met in any case where a claimant satisfies any of the conditions specified in sub-paragraphs (8) to (11) below, but—
(a) those costs shall be subject to any additional limitations imposed by the sub-paragraph; and
(b) where the claimant satisfies the conditions in more than one of these sub-paragraphs, only one sub-paragraph shall apply in his case and the one that applies shall be the one most favourable to him.

(8) The conditions specified in this sub-paragraph are that—
(a) during the relevant period the claimant or a member of his family acquires an interest ("the relevant interest") in a dwelling which he then occupies or continues to occupy, as his home; and
(b) in the week preceding the week in which the relevant interest was acquired, housing benefit was payable to the claimant or a member of his family;
so however that the amount to be met by way of [2. . .] housing costs shall initially not exceed the aggregate of—
(i) the housing benefit payable in the week mentioned at sub-paragraph (8)(b); and
(ii) any amount included in the applicable amount of the claimant or a member of his family in accordance with regulation 17(1)(e) or 18(1)(f) in that week;

and shall be increased subsequently only to the extent that it is necessary to take account of any increase, arising after the date of the acquisition, in the standard rate or in any housing costs which qualify under paragraph 17 (other housing costs).

(9) The condition specified in this sub-paragraph is that the loan was taken out, or an existing loan increased, to acquire alternative accommodation more suited to the special needs of a disabled person than the accommodation which was occupied before the acquisition by the claimant.

(10) The conditions specified in this sub-paragraph are that—

(a) the loan commitment increased in consequence of the disposal of the dwelling occupied as the home and the acquisition of an alternative such dwelling; and

(b) the change of dwelling was made solely by reason of the need to provide separate sleeping accommodation for [53 persons] of different sexes aged 10 or over [53 but under the age of 20 who live with the claimant and for whom the claimant or the claimant's partner is responsible].

(11) The conditions specified in this sub-paragraph are that—

(a) during the relevant period the claimant or a member of his family acquires an interest ("the relevant interest") in a dwelling which he then occupies as his home; and

(b) in the week preceding the week in which the relevant interest was acquired, the applicable amount of the claimant or a member of his family included an amount determined by reference to paragraph 17 and did not include any amount specified in paragraph 15 or paragraph 16;

so however that the amount to be met [2by way of housing costs] shall initially not exceed the amount so determined, and shall be increased subsequently only to the extent that it is necessary to take account of any increase, arising after the date of acquisition, in the standard rate or in any housing costs which qualify under paragraph 17 (other housing costs).

(12) The following provisions of this Schedule shall have effect subject to the provisions of this paragraph.

Apportionment of housing costs

2.746 **5.**—(1) Where the dwelling occupied as the home is a composite hereditament and—

(a) before 1st April 1990 for the purposes of section 48(5) of the General Rate Act 1967 (reduction of rates on dwellings), it appeared to a rating authority or it was determined in pursuance of subsection (6) of section 48 of that Act that the hereditament, including the dwelling occupied as the home, was a mixed hereditament and that only a proportion of the rateable value of the hereditament was attributable to use for the purpose of a private dwelling; or

(b) in Scotland, before 1st April 1989 an assessor acting pursuant to section 45(1) of the Water (Scotland) Act 1980 (provision as to valuation roll) has apportioned the net annual value of the premises including the dwelling occupied as the home between the part occupied as a dwelling and the remainder,

the amounts applicable under this Schedule shall be such proportion of the amounts applicable in respect of the hereditament or premises as a whole as is equal to the proportion of the rateable value of the hereditament attributable to the part of the hereditament used for the purposes of a private tenancy or, in Scotland, the proportion of the net annual value of the premises apportioned to the part occupied as a dwelling house.

(2) Subject to sub-paragraph (1) and the following provisions of this paragraph, where the dwelling occupied as the home is a composite hereditament, the amount applicable under this Schedule shall be the relevant fraction of the amount which would otherwise be applicable under this Schedule in respect of the dwelling occupied as the home.

(3) For the purposes of sub-paragraph (2), the relevant fraction shall be obtained in accordance with the formula—

$$\frac{A}{A+B}$$

where—

"A" is the current market value of the claimant's interest in that part of the composite hereditament which is domestic property within the meaning of section 66 of the Act of 1988;

"B" is the current market value of the claimant's interest in that part of the composite hereditament which is not domestic property within that section.

(4) In this paragraph—

"composite hereditament" means—
(a) as respects England and Wales, any hereditament which is shown as a composite hereditament in a local non-domestic rating list;
(b) as respects Scotland, any lands and heritages entered in the valuation roll which are part residential subjects within the meaning of section 26(1) of the Act of 1987;
"local non-domestic rating list" means a list compiled and maintained under section 41(1) of the Act of 1988;
"the Act of 1987" means the Abolition of Domestic Rates Etc. (Scotland) Act 1987;
"the Act of 1988" means the Local Government Finance Act 1988.

(5) Where responsibility for expenditure which relates to housing costs met under this Schedule is shared, the amounts applicable shall be calculated by reference to the appropriate proportion of that expenditure for which the claimant is responsible.

Existing housing costs
6.—[74 . . .] 2.747

Transitional Protection
7.—[74 . . .] 2.748

[74 Housing costs]
8.—(1) Subject to the provisions of this Schedule, the [74 . . .] housing costs to be met in any particular case are— 2.749
(a) where the claimant has been [2entitled to] income support for a continuous period of 39 weeks or more, an amount—
(i) determined in the manner set out in paragraph 10 by applying the standard rate to the eligible capital for the time being owing in connection with a loan which qualifies under paragraph 15 or 16; and
(ii) equal to any payments which qualify under paragraph 17(1)(a) to (c);
(b) in any other case, nil.

[2(1A) For the purposes of sub-paragraph (1) [6 and subject to sub-paragraph (1B),] the eligible capital for the time being owing shall be determined on the date the [74 . . .] housing costs are first met and thereafter on each anniversary of that date.]

[6(1B) Where a claimant or his partner ceases to be in receipt of or treated as being in receipt of income-based jobseeker's allowance [25 [49 , state pension credit or income-related employment and support allowance]] and one of them becomes entitled to income support in a case to which paragraph 1A applies, the eligible capital for the time being owning shall be recalculated on each anniversary of the date on which the housing costs were first met for whichever of the benefits concerned the claimant or his partner was first entitled.]

(2) [74 . . .]
(3) [74 . . .]
(4) [74 . . .]
(5) [74 . . .]

General exclusions from [74 paragraph 8]
9.—(1) [74 Paragraph 8] shall not apply where— 2.750
[25 (a) the claimant's partner has attained the qualifying age for state pension credit;]
(b) the housing costs are payments—
(i) under a co-ownership agreement;
(ii) under or relating to a tenancy or licence of a Crown tenant; or
(iii) where the dwelling occupied as the home is a tent, in respect of the tent and the site on which it stands.

(2) In a case falling within sub-paragraph (1), the housing costs to be met are—
(a) where head (a) of sub-paragraph (1) applies, an amount—
(i) determined in the manner set out in paragraph 10 by applying the standard rate to the eligible capital for the time being owing in connection with a loan which qualifies under paragraph 15 or 16; and
(ii) equal to the payments which qualify under paragraph 17;
(b) where head (b) of sub-paragraph (1) applies, an amount equal to the payments which qualify under paragraph 17(1)(d) to (f).

[20 The calculation for loans

2.751 **10.**—(1) The weekly amount of [74 housing costs] to be met under this Schedule in respect of a loan which qualifies under paragraph 15 or 16 shall be calculated by applying the formula:—

$$\frac{(A \times B)}{52}$$

where—

A = the amount of the loan which qualifies under paragraph 15 or 16;
B = the standard rate for the time being [27 applicable in respect of that loan].]

General provisions applying to [74 . . .] housing costs

2.752 **11.**—(1) [2 . . .]

(2) [74 . . .]

(3) [74 . . .]

(4) Where for the time being a loan exceeds, or in a case where more than one loan is to be taken into account, the aggregate of those loans exceeds the appropriate amount specified in sub-paragraph (5), then the amount of the loan or, as the case may be, the aggregate amount of those loans, shall for the purposes of this Schedule, be the appropriate amount.

(5) Subject to the following provisions of this paragraph, the appropriate amount is £100,000.

(6) Where a person is treated under paragraph 3(6) (payments in respect of two dwellings) as occupying two dwellings as his home, then the restrictions imposed by subparagraph (4) shall be applied separately to the loans for each dwelling.

(7) In a case to which paragraph 5 (apportionment of housing costs) applies, the appropriate amount for the purposes of sub-paragraph (4) shall be the lower of—

(a) a sum determined by applying the formula—
$P \times Q$, where—
P = the relevant fraction for the purposes of paragraph 5, and
Q = the amount or, as the case may be, the aggregate amount for the time being of any loan or loans which qualify under this Schedule; or

(b) the sum for the time being specified in sub-paragraph (5).

(8) In a case to which paragraph 15(3) or 16(3) (loans which qualify in part only) applies, the appropriate amount for the purposes of sub-paragraph (4) shall be the lower of—

(a) a sum representing for the time being the part of the loan applied for the purposes specified in paragraph 15(1) or (as the case may be) paragraph 16(1); or

(b) the sum for the time being specified in sub-paragraph (5).

(9) In the case of any loan to which paragraph 16(2)(k) (loan taken out and used for the purpose of adapting a dwelling for the special needs of a disabled person) applies the whole of the loan, to the extent that it remains unpaid, shall be disregarded in determining whether the amount for the time being specified in sub-paragraph (5) is exceeded.

[2(10) Where in any case the amount for the time being specified for the purposes of sub-paragraph (5) is exceeded and there are two or more loans to be taken into account under either or both paragraphs 15 and 16, then the amount of eligible interest in respect of each of those loans to the extent that the loans remain outstanding shall be determined as if each loan had been reduced to a sum equal to the qualifying portion of that loan.

(11) For the purposes of sub-paragraph (10), the qualifying portion of a loan shall be determined by applying the following formula—

$$R \times \frac{S}{T}$$

where—

R = the amount for the time being specified for the purposes of sub-paragraph (4);
S = the amount of the outstanding loan to be taken into account;
T = the aggregate of all outstanding loans to be taken into account under paragraphs 15 and 16.]

The standard rate

12.—[28(1) The standard rate is the rate of interest applicable per annum to a loan which qualifies under this Schedule. 2.753

[60 (2) Subject to the following provisions of this paragraph, the standard rate is to be the average mortgage rate published by the Bank of England in August 2010.

(2A) The standard rate is to be varied each time that sub-paragraph (2B) applies.

(2B) This sub-paragraph applies when, on any reference day, the Bank of England publishes an average mortgage rate which differs by [72 0.5 percentage points] or more from the standard rate that applies on that reference day (whether by virtue of sub-paragraph (2) or of a previous application of this sub-paragraph).

(2C) The average mortgage rate published on that reference day then becomes the new standard rate in accordance with sub-paragraph (2D).

(2D) Any variation in the standard rate by virtue of sub-paragraphs (2A) to (2C) comes into effect—

(a) for the purposes of sub-paragraph (2B) (in consequence of its first and any subsequent application), on the day after the reference day referred to in sub-paragraph (2C);

(b) for the purpose of calculating the weekly amount of housing costs to be met under this Schedule, on the day specified by the Secretary of State.

(2E) In this paragraph—

"average mortgage rate" means the effective interest rate (non-seasonally adjusted) of United Kingdom resident banks and building societies for loans to households secured on dwellings published by the Bank of England in respect of the most recent period for that rate specified at the time of publication;

"reference day" means any day falling after 1st October 2010.]

(3) [52. . .]
(4) [46 . . .]
(5) [46 . . .]
(6) [46 . . .].]

Excessive Housing Costs

13.—(1) Housing costs which, apart from this paragraph, fall to be met under this Schedule shall be met only to the extent specified in sub-paragraph (3) where— 2.754

(a) the dwelling occupied as the home, excluding any part which is let, is larger than is required by the claimant and his family and any child or young person to whom regulation 16(4) applies (foster children) and any other non-dependants having regard, in particular, to suitable alternative accommodation occupied by a household of the same size; or

(b) the immediate area in which the dwelling occupied as the home is located is more expensive than other areas in which suitable alternative accommodation exists; or

(c) the outgoings of the dwelling occupied as the home which are met under paragraphs 15 to 17 are higher than the outgoings of suitable alternative accommodation in the area.

(2) For the purposes of heads (a) to (c) of sub-paragraph (1), no regard shall be had to the capital value of the dwelling occupied as the home.

(3) Subject to the following provisions of this paragraph, the amount of the loan which falls to be met shall be restricted and the excess over the amounts which the claimant would need to obtain suitable alternative accommodation shall not be allowed.

(4) Where, having regard to the relevant factors, it is not reasonable to expect the claimant and his family to seek alternative cheaper accommodation, no restriction shall be made under sub-paragraph (3).

(5) In sub-paragraph (4) "the relevant factors" are—

(a) the availability of suitable accommodation and the level of housing costs in the area; and

(b) the circumstances of the family including in particular the age and state of health of its members, the employment prospects of the claimant and, where a change in accommodation is likely to result in a change of school, the effect on the education of any child or young person who is a member of his family, or any child or young person who is not treated as part of his family by virtue of regulation 16(4) (foster children).

[13(6) Where sub-paragraph (4) does not apply and the claimant (or other member of the family) was able to meet the financial commitments for the dwelling occupied as the home when these were entered into, no restriction shall be made under this paragraph during the 26 weeks immediately following the date on which—

(a) the claimant became entitled to income support where the claimant's housing costs fell within one of the cases in sub-paragraph (1) on that date; or

(b) a decision took effect which was made under section 10 (decisions superseding earlier decisions) of the Social Security Act 1998 on the ground that the claimant's housing costs fell within one of the cases in sub-paragraph (1),

nor during the next 26 weeks if and so long as the claimant uses his best endeavours to obtain cheaper accommodation.]

(7) For the purposes of calculating any period of 26 weeks referred to in sub-paragraph (6), and for those purposes only, a person shall be treated as entitled to income support for any period of 12 weeks or less in respect of which he was not in receipt of income support and which fell immediately between periods in respect of which he was in receipt thereof.

(8) Any period in respect of which—

(a) income support was paid to a person, and

(b) it was subsequently determined [[13]. . .] that he was not entitled to income support for that period,

shall be treated for the purposes of sub-paragraph (7) as a period in respect of which he was not in receipt of income support.

(9) Heads (c) to (f) of sub-paragraph (1) of paragraph 14 shall apply to sub-paragraph (7) as they apply to [[74] paragraph 8] but with the modification that the words "Subject to sub-paragraph (2)" were omitted and references to "the claimant" were references to the person mentioned in sub-paragraph (7).

Linking rule

2.755 **14.**—(1) [[62]. . .] for the purposes of this Schedule—

(a) a person shall be treated as being in receipt of income support during the following periods—

(i) any period in respect of which it was subsequently [[13]determined] that he was entitled to income support; and

(ii) any period of 12 weeks or less [[16] or, as the case may be, 52 weeks or less,] in respect of which he was not in receipt of income support and which fell immediately between periods in respect of which

[[4](aa) he was, or was treated as being, in receipt of income support,

(bb) he was treated as entitled to income support for the purpose of subparagraph (5) or (5A), or

(cc) (i) above applies;]

(b) a person shall be treated as not being in receipt of income support during any period other than a period to which (a)(ii) above applies in respect of which it is subsequently [[13]determined] that he was not so entitled;

(c) where—

(i) the claimant was a member of a couple or a polygamous marriage; and

(ii) his partner was, in respect of a past period, in receipt of income support for himself and the claimant; and

(iii) the claimant is no longer a member of that couple or polygamous marriage; and

(iv) the claimant made his claim for income support within twelve weeks [[16] or, as the case may be, 52 weeks,] of ceasing to be a member of that couple or polygamous marriage,

he shall be treated as having been in receipt of income support for the same period as his former partner had been or had been treated, for the purposes of this Schedule, as having been;

(d) where the claimant's partner's applicable amount was determined in accordance with paragraph 1(1) (single claimant) or paragraph 1(2) (lone parent) of Schedule 2 (applicable amounts) in respect of a past period, provided that the claim was made within twelve weeks [[16] or, as the case may be, 52 weeks,] of the claimant and his partner becoming one of a couple or polygamous marriage, the claimant shall be treated as having been in receipt of income support for the same period as his partner had been or had been treated, for the purposes of this Schedule, as having been;

(e) where the claimant is a member of a couple or a polygamous marriage and his partner was, in respect of a past period, in receipt of income support for himself and the claimant, and the claimant has begun to receive income support as a result of an election by the members of the couple or polygamous marriage, he shall be treated as having been in receipt of income support for the same period as his partner had been or had been treated, for the purposes of this Schedule, as having been;

[7(ee) where the claimant—
(i) is a member of a couple or a polygamous marriage and the claimant's partner was, immediately before the participation by any member of that couple or polygamous marriage in an employment programme specified in regulation 75(1)(a)(ii) of the Jobseeker's Allowance Regulations 1996 [19, in the Intensive Activity Period specified in regulation 75(1)(a)(iv) of those Regulations [47 . . .]], in receipt of income support and his applicable amount included an amount for the couple or for the partners of the polygamous marriage; and
(ii) has, immediately after that participation in that programme, begun to receive income support as a result of an election under regulation 4(3) of the Social Security (Claims and Payments) Regulations 1987 by the members of the couple or polygamous marriage,

the claimant shall be treated as having been in receipt of income support for the same period as his partner had been or had been treated, for the purposes of this Schedule, as having been;]

(f) where—
(i) the claimant was a member of a family of a person (not being a former partner) entitled to income support and at least one other member of that family was a child or young person; and
(ii) the claimant becomes a member of another family which includes that child or young person; and
(iii) the claimant made his claim for income support within 12 weeks 1996[16 or, as the case may be, 52 weeks,] of the date on which the person entitled to income support mentioned in (i) above ceased to be so entitled,

the claimant shall be treated as being in receipt of income support for the same period as that person had been or had been treated, for the purposes of this Schedule, as having been.

(2) [63 . . .]

(3) For the purposes of this Schedule, where a claimant has ceased to be entitled to income support because he or his partner is participating in arrangements for training made under section 2 of the Employment and Training Act 1973 or attending a course at an employment rehabilitation centre established under that section [53 or under the Enterprise and New Towns (Scotland) Act 1990], he shall be treated as if he had been in receipt of income support for the period during which he or his partner was participating in such arrangements or attending such a course.

[7(3ZA) For the purposes of this Schedule, a claimant who has ceased to be entitled to income support because—
(a) that claimant or his partner was participating in an employment programme specified in reglation 75(1)(a)(ii) of the Jobseeker's Allowance Regulations 1996 [19, in the Intensive Activity Period specified in regulation 75(1)(a)(iv) of those Regulations [48 . . .]] [14or in an employment zone scheme]; and
(b) in consequence of such participation the claimant or his partner was engaged in remunerative work or had an income in excess of the claimant's applicable amount as prescribed in Part IV,

shall be treated as if he had been in receipt of income support for the period during which he or his partner was participating in that programme [19or activity].]

[2(3A) Where, for the purposes of sub-paragraphs [7(1), (3) and (3ZA)], a person is treated as being in receipt of income support, for a certain period, he shall [12, subject to sub-paragraph (3AA),] be treated as being entitled to income support for the same period.]

[12(3AA) Where the appropriate amount of a loan exceeds the amount specified in paragraph 11(5), sub-paragraph (3A) shall not apply except—
(a) for the purposes of paragraph [74 . . .] 8(1); or
(b) where a person has ceased to be in receipt of income support for a period of [42 104] weeks or less because he or his partner is a welfare to work beneficiary.]

[7(3B) For the purposes of this Schedule, in determining whether a person is entitled to or to be treated as entitled to income support, entitlement to a contribution-based jobseeker's allowance immediately before a period during which that person or his partner is participating in an employment programme specified in regulation 75(1)(a)(ii) of the Jobseeker's Allowance Regulations 1996 [19, in the Intensive Activity Period specified in regulation 75(1)(a)(iv) of those Regulations [47 . . .]] shall be treated as entitlement to income support for the purposes of any requirement that a person is, or has been, entitled to income support for any period of time.]

(4) For the purposes of this Schedule, sub-paragraph (5) applies where a person is not entitled to income support by reason only that he has—

(a) capital exceeding [36£16,000]; or
(b) income [61equal to or] exceeding the applicable amount which applies in his case, or
(c) both capital exceeding [36£16,000] and income exceeding the applicable amount which applies in his case.

(5) A person to whom sub-paragraph (4) applies shall be treated as entitled to income support throughout any period of not [2more] than 39 weeks which comprises only days—
(a) on which he is entitled to unemployment benefit, [3a contribution-based jobseeker's allowance,] statutory sick pay [49 , incapacity benefit or contributory employment and support allowance]; or
(b) on which he is, although not entitled to any of the benefits mentioned in head (a) above, entitled to be credited with earnings equal to the lower earnings limit for the time being in force in accordance with [11regulation 8A or 8B] of the Social Security (Credits) Regulations 1975; or
(c) in respect of which the claimant is treated as being in receipt of income support.

[2(5A) Subject to sub-paragraph (5B), a person to whom sub-paragraph (4) applies and who is either a person to whom [3paragraph 4 or 5 of Schedule 1B (persons caring for another person) applies] or a lone parent shall, for the purposes of this Schedule, be treated as entitled to income support throughout any period of not more than 39 weeks following the refusal of a claim for income support made by or on behalf of that person.

(5B) Sub-paragraph (5A) shall not apply in relation to a person mentioned in that sub-paragraph who, during the period referred to in that sub-paragraph—
(a) is engaged in, or is treated as engaged in, remunerative work or whose partner is engaged in, or is treated as engaged in, remunerative work;
[3(b) is a [15 full-time student], other than one who would qualify for income support under regulation 4ZA(3) (prescribed categories of person);]
(c) is temporarily absent from Great Britain, other than in the circumstances specified in regulation 4(2) and (3)(c) (temporary absence from Great Britain).]

(6) In a case where—
(a) [2sub-paragraphs (5) and (5A) apply] solely by virtue of sub-paragraph (4)(b); and
(b) the claimant's income includes payments under a policy taken out to insure against the risk that the policy holder is unable to meet any loan or payment which qualifies under paragraphs 15 to 17,

[2sub-paragraphs (5) and (5A)] shall have effect as if for the words "throughout any period of not [2more] than 39 weeks" there shall be substituted the words "throughout any period that payments made in accordance with the terms of the policy".

(7) [2. . .]

(8) This sub-paragraph applies—
(a) to a person who claims income support, or in respect of whom income support is claimed, and who—
(i) received payments under a policy of insurance taken out to insure against loss of employment, and those payments are exhausted; and
(ii) had a previous award of income support where the applicable amount included an amount by way of housing costs; and
(b) where the period in respect of which the previous award of income support was payable ended not more than 26 weeks before the date the claim was made.

(9) Where sub-paragraph (8) applies, in determining—
(a) [74 . . .]
(b) for the purposes of paragraph 8(1) whether a claimant has been [2entitled to] income support for a continuous period of 39 weeks or more,

any week falling between the date of the termination of the previous award and the date of the new claim shall be ignored.

[10(10) In the case of a person who is a welfare to work beneficiary, the references in sub-paragraphs (1)(a)(ii), [17 (1)(c)(iv),] (1)(d) and (1)(f)(iii) to a period of 12 weeks shall be treated as references to a period of [42 104] weeks.]

[18 (11) For the purposes of sub-paragraph (1)(a)(ii), (1)(c)(iv), (1)(d) and (1)(f)(iii), the relevant period shall be—
(a) 52 weeks in the case of a person to whom sub-paragraph (12) applies;
(b) subject to sub-paragraph (10), 12 weeks in any other case.

(12) This sub-paragraph applies, subject to sub-paragraph (13), in the case of a person who, on or after 9th April 2001, has ceased to be entitled to income support because he or his partner—
(a) has commenced employment as an employed earner or as a self-employed earner or has increased the hours in which he is engaged in such employment;

(b) is taking active steps to establish himself in employment as an employed earner or as a self-employed earner under any scheme for assisting persons to become so employed which is mentioned in regulation 19(1)(r)(i) to (iii) of the Jobseeker's Allowance Regulations 1996; or

(c) is participating in—

(i) a New Deal option;

(ii) an employment zone programme; or

(iii) the self-employment route; [19 or

(iv) the Intensive Activity Period specified in regulation 75(1)(a)(iv) of the Jobseeker's Allowance Regulations 1996 [47 . . .],]

and, as a consequence, he or his partner was engaged in remunerative work or had income [61 equal to or] in excess of the applicable amount as prescribed in Part IV.

(13) Sub-paragraph (12) shall only apply to the extent that immediately before the day on which the person ceased to be entitled to income support, his housing costs were being met in accordance with paragraph [74 . . .] 8(1)(a) or would have been so met but for any non-dependant deduction under paragraph 18.]

[25 (14) For the purpose of determining whether the linking rules set out in this paragraph apply in a case where a claimant's former partner was entitled to state pension credit, any reference to income support in this Schedule shall be taken to include also a reference to state pension credit.]

[49 (15) For the purpose of determining whether the linking rules set out in this paragraph apply in a case where [50 a claimant, a claimant's partner or] a claimant's former partner was entitled to income-related employment and support allowance, any reference to income support in this Schedule shall be taken to include also a reference to income-related employment and support allowance.]

Loans on residential property

15.—(1) A loan qualifies under this paragraph where the loan was taken out to defray monies applied for any of the following purposes— **2.756**

(a) acquiring an interest in the dwelling occupied as the home; or

(b) paying off another loan to the extent that the other loan would have qualified under head (a) above had the loan not been paid off.

(2) For the purposes of this paragraph, references to a loan include also a reference to money borrowed under a hire purchase agreement for any purpose specified in heads (a) and (b) of sub-paragraph (1) above.

(3) Where a loan is applied only in part for the purposes specified in heads (a) and (b) of sub-paragraph (1), only that portion of the loan which is applied for that purpose shall qualify under this paragraph.

Loans for repairs and improvements to the dwelling occupied as the home

16.—(1) A loan qualifies under this paragraph where the loan was taken out, with or without security, for the purpose of— **2.757**

(a) carrying out repairs and improvements to the dwelling occupied as the home;

(b) paying any service charge imposed to meet the cost of repairs and improvements to the dwelling occupied as the home;

(c) paying off another loan to the extent that the other loan would have qualified under head (a) or (b) of this sub-paragraph had the loan not been paid off,

and the loan was used for that purpose, or is used for that purpose within 6 months of the date of receipt or such further period as may be reasonable in the particular circumstances of the case.

(2) In sub-paragraph (1) "repairs and improvements" means any of the following measures undertaken with a view to maintaining the fitness of the dwelling for human habitation or, where the dwelling forms part of a building, any part of the building containing that dwelling—

(a) provision of a fixed bath, shower, wash basin, sink or lavatory, and necessary associated plumbing, including the provision of hot water not connected to a central heating system;

(b) repairs to existing heating systems;

(c) damp proof measures;

(d) provision of ventilation and natural lighting;

(e) provision of drainage facilities;

(f) provision of facilities for preparing and cooking food;

(g) provision of insulation of the dwelling occupied as the home;

(h) provision of electric lighting and sockets;

(i) provision of storage facilities for fuel or refuse;
(j) repairs of unsafe structural defects;
(k) adapting a dwelling for the special needs of a disabled person; or
(l) provision of separate sleeping accommodation for [53 persons] of different sexes aged 10 or over [53 but under the age of 20 who live with the claimant and for whom the claimant or the claimant's partner is responsible].

(3) Where a loan is applied only in part for the purposes specified in sub-paragraph (1), only that portion of the loan which is applied for that purpose shall qualify under this paragraph.

Other housing costs

2.758 **17.**—(1) Subject to the deduction specified in sub-paragraph (2) and the reductions applicable in sub-paragraph (5), there shall be met under this paragraph the amounts, calculated on a weekly basis, in respect of the following housing costs—
(a) payments by way of rent or ground rent relating to a long tenancy [41 . . .];
(b) service charges;
(c) payments by way of rentcharge within the meaning of section 1 of the Rentcharges Act 1977;
(d) payments under a co-ownership scheme;
(e) payments under or relating to a tenancy or licence of a Crown tenant;
(f) where the dwelling occupied as the home is a tent, payments in respect of the tent and the site on which it stands.

(2) Subject to sub-paragraph (3), the deductions to be made from the weekly amounts to be met under this paragraph are—
(a) where the costs are inclusive of any of the items mentioned in [33 paragraph 6(2) of Schedule 1 to the Housing Benefit Regulations 2006] (payment in respect of fuel charges), the deductions prescribed in that paragraph unless the claimant provides evidence on which the actual or approximate amount of the service charge for fuel may be estimated, in which case the estimated amount;
(b) where the costs are inclusive of ineligible service charges within the meaning of [34 paragraph 1 of Schedule 1 to the Housing Benefit Regulations 2006] (ineligible service charges) the amounts attributable to those ineligible service charges or where that amount is not separated from or separately identified within the housing costs to be met under this paragraph, such part of the payments made in respect of those housing costs which are fairly attributable to the provision of those ineligible services having regard to the costs of comparable services;
(c) any amount for repairs and improvements, and for this purpose the expression "repairs and improvements" has the same meaning it has in paragraph 16(2).

(3) Where arrangements are made for the housing costs, which are met under this paragraph and which are normally paid for a period of 52 weeks, to be paid instead for a period of 53 weeks, or to be paid irregularly, or so that no such costs are payable or collected in certain periods, or so that the costs for different periods in the year are of different amounts, the weekly amount shall be the amount payable for the year divided by 52.

(4) Where the claimant or a member of his family—
(a) pays for reasonable repairs or redecorations to be carried out to the dwelling they occupy; and
(b) that work was not the responsibility of the claimant or any member of his family; and
(c) in consequence of that work being done, the costs which are normally met under this paragraph are waived,

then those costs shall, or a period not exceeding 8 weeks, be treated as payable.

(5) Where in England and Wales an amount calculated on a weekly basis in respect of housing costs specified in sub-paragraph (1)(e) (Crown tenants) includes water charges, that amount shall be reduced—
(a) where the amount payable in respect of water charges is known, by that amount;
(b) in any other case, by the amount which would be the likely weekly water charge had the property not been occupied by a Crown tenant.

Non-dependant deductions

2.759 **18.**—(1) Subject to the following provisions of this paragraph, the following deductions from the amount to be met under the preceding paragraphs of this Schedule in respect of housing costs shall be made—
[31(a) in respect of a non-dependant aged 18 or over who is engaged in any remunerative work, [75£94.50];

(b) in respect of a non-dependant aged 18 or over to whom paragraph (a) does not apply, [75£14.65].]

(2) In the case of a non-dependant aged 18 or over to whom sub-paragraph (1)(a) applies because he is in [2remunerative] work, where the claimant satisfies the [13Secretary of State] that the non-dependant's gross weekly income is—

(a) less than [75£133.00], the deduction to be made under this paragraph shall be the deduction specified in sub-paragraph (1)(b);
(b) not less than [75£133.00] but less than [75£195.00], the deduction to be made under this paragraph shall be [75£33.65];
(c) not less than [75£195.00] but less than [75£253.00], the deduction to be made under this paragraph shall be [75£46.20];
(d) not less than [75£253.00] but less than [75£338.00], the deduction to be made under this paragraph shall be [75£75.60];
(e) not less than [75£338.00] but less than [75£420.00], the deduction to be made under this paragraph shall be [75£86.10]].

(3) Only one deduction shall be made under this paragraph in respect of a couple or, as the case may be, the members of a polygamous marriage, and where, but for this sub-paragraph, the amount that would fall to be deducted in respect of one member of a couple or polygamous marriage is higher than the amount (if any) that would fall to be deducted in respect of the other, or any other, member, the higher amount shall be deducted.

(4) In applying the provisions of sub-paragraph (2) in the case of a couple or, as the case may be, a polygamous marriage, regard shall be had, for the purpose of sub-paragraph (2), to the couple's or, as the case may be, all the members of the polygamous marriage's, joint weekly income.

(5) Where a person is a non-dependant in respect of more than one joint occupier of a dwelling (except where the joint occupiers are a couple or members of a polygamous marriage), the deduction in respect of that non-dependant shall be apportioned between the joint occupiers (the amount so apportioned being rounded to the nearest penny) having regard to the number of joint occupiers and the proportion of the housing costs in respect of the dwelling occupied as the home payable by each of them.

(6) No deduction shall be made in respect of any non-dependants occupying the dwelling occupied as the home of the claimant, if the claimant or any partner of his is—

(a) [73 severely sight impaired or blind or treated as severely sight impaired or blind] by virtue of paragraph 12 of Schedule 2 (additional condition for the higher pensioner and disability premiums); or
(b) receiving in respect of himself either—
    (i) an attendance allowance; [68. . .]
    (ii) the care component of the disability living allowance [68 ; [69 . . .]
    (iii) the daily living component of personal independence payment] [69 or
    (iv) armed forces independence payment].

(7) No deduction shall be made in respect of a non-dependant—

(a) if, although he resides with the claimant, it appears to the [13 Secretary of State] that the dwelling occupied as his home is normally elsewhere; or
(b) if he is in receipt of a training allowance paid in connection with [53 youth training] established under section 2 of the Employment and Training Act 1973 or section 2 of the Enterprise and New Towns (Scotland) Act 1990; or
(c) if he is a full-time student during a period of study or, if he is not in remunerative work, during a recognised summer vacation appropriate to his course; or
(d) if he is aged under 25 and in receipt of income support [5or an income-based jobseeker's allowance]; or
(e) in respect of whom a deduction in the calculation of a rent rebate or allowance falls to be made under [35 regulation 74 of the Housing Benefit Regulations 2006] (non-dependant deductions); or
(f) to whom, but for paragraph (2C) of regulation 3 (definition of non-dependant) paragraph (2B) of that regulation would apply; or
(g) if he is not residing with the claimant because he has been a patient for a period in excess of [24 52] weeks, or is a prisoner, and for these purposes—
    [37 (i) "patient" has the meaning given in paragraph 3(13)(b) and "prisoner" has the meaning given in regulation 21(3); and
    (ii) in calculating a period of 52 weeks as a patient, any two or more distinct periods separated by one or more intervals each not exceeding 28 days shall be treated as a single period; or]

[31(h) if he is in receipt of state pension credit.]

[49 (i) he is aged less than 25 and is in receipt of [67 income–related] employment and support allowance which does not include an amount under section [51 . . .] 4(4) or (5) of the Welfare Reform Act (components)] [71 ;or

(j) if he is aged less than 25 and is entitled to an award of universal credit which is calculated on the basis that he does not have any earned income].

(8) In the case of a non-dependant to whom sub-paragraph (2) applies because he is in [2remunerative] work, there shall be disregarded from his gross income—

(a) any attendance allowance [68 , disability living allowance or personal independence payment] [69 or armed forces independence payment] received by him;

(b) any payment made under [58 or by] the Macfarlane Trust, the Macfarlane (Special Payments) Trust, the Macfarlane (Special Payments) (No.2) Trust, the Fund, the Eileen Trust [57, MFET Limited] [64, the Skipton Fund, the Caxton Foundation] or the Independent Living [52 Fund (2006)] which, had his income fallen to be calculated under regulation 40 (calculation of income other than earnings), would have been disregarded under paragraph 21 of Schedule 9 (income in kind); and

(c) any payment which, had his income fallen to be calculated under regulation 40 would have been disregarded under paragraph 39 of Schedule 9 (payments made under certain trusts and certain other payments).

[71 (9) For the purposes of sub-paragraph (7)(j), "earned income" has the meaning given in regulation 52 of the Universal Credit Regulations 2013.]

Rounding of fractions

2.760 **19.**—Where any calculation made under this Schedule results in a fraction of a penny, that fraction shall be treated as a penny.]

AMENDMENTS

1. Social Security (Income Support and Claims and Payments) Amendment Regulations 1995 (SI 1995/1613) reg.2 and Sch.1 (October 2, 1995).

2. Social Security (Income Support, Claims and Payments and Adjudication) Amendment Regulations 1995 (SI 1995/2927) reg.5 (December 12, 1995).

3. Income Support (General) (Jobseeker's Allowance Consequential Amendments) Regulations 1996 (SI 1996/206) reg.24 (October 7, 1996).

4. Income-related Benefits Schemes and Social Fund (Miscellaneous Amendments) Regulations 1996 (SI 1996/1944) reg.6(10) (October 7, 1996).

5. Social Security and Child Support (Miscellaneous Amendments) Regulations 1997 (SI 1997/827) reg.6 (April 7, 1997).

6. Social Security (Miscellaneous Amendments) (No.4) Regulations 1997 (SI 1997/2305) reg.2 (October 22, 1997).

7. Social Security Amendment (New Deal) Regulations 1997 (SI 1997/2863) reg.16 (January 5, 1998).

8. Social Security (Non-Dependant Deductions) Regulations 1996 (SI 1996/2518) reg.4 (April 6, 1998).

9. Social Security (Welfare to Work) Regulations 1998 (SI 1998/2231) reg.13(4)(a) (October 5, 1998).

10. Social Security (Welfare to Work) Regulations 1998 (SI 1998/2231) reg.13(4)(b) (October 5, 1998).

11. Social Security Benefits (Miscellaneous Amendments) Regulations 1999 (SI 1999/714) reg.3 (April 5, 1999).

12. Income Support (General) and Jobseeker's Allowance Amendment Regulations 1999 (SI 1999/1921) reg.2(1) (August 2, 1999).

13. Social Security Act 1998 (Commencement No.12 and Consequential and Transitional Provisions) Order 1999 (SI 1999/3178 (C.81)) art.3(5) and Sch.5 para.9 (November 29, 1999)

14. Social Security Amendment (Employment Zones) Regulations 2000 (SI 2000/724) reg.4(3)(c) (April 3, 2000).

15. Social Security Amendment (Students) Regulations 2000 (SI 2000/1981) reg.5(5) and Sch. (July 31, 2000).

16. Social Security (Miscellaneous Amendments) Regulations 2001 (SI 2001/488) reg.6(a) (April 9, 2001).

17. Social Security (Miscellaneous Amendments) Regulations 2001 (SI 2001/488) reg.6(b) (April 9, 2001).

18. Social Security (Miscellaneous Amendments) Regulations 2001 (SI 2001/488) reg.6(c) (April 9, 2001).

19. Social Security Amendment (New Deal) Regulations 2001 (SI 2001/ 1029) reg.14 (April 9, 2001).

20. Income Support (General) and Jobseeker's Allowance Amendment Regulations 2001 (SI 2001/3651) reg.2(1) (December 10, 2001).

21. Social Security Amendment (Residential Care and Nursing Homes) Regulations 2001 (SI 2001/3767) reg.2(1) and Pt I of Sch. para.15 (April 8, 2002).

22. Social Security (Miscellaneous Amendments) Regulations 2002 (SI 2002/841) reg.6 (April 8, 2002).

23. Child Support (Consequential Amendments and Transitional Provisions) Regulations 2001 (SI 2001/158) reg.6(3) (in force in relation to any particular case on the day on which s.1 of the Child Support, Pensions and Social Security Act 2000 comes into force in relation to that type of case).

24. Social Security (Hospital In-Patients and Miscellaneous Amendments) Regulations 2003 (SI 2003/1195) reg.3(4) (May 21, 2003).

25. State Pension Credit (Consequential, Transitional and Miscellaneous Provisions) Regulations 2002 (SI 2002/3019) reg.29(6) (October 6, 2003).

26. Social Security (Housing Costs Amendments) Regulations 2004 (SI 2004/2825) reg.2(2) (November 28, 2004).

27. Social Security (Housing Costs Amendments) Regulations 2004 (SI 2004/2825) reg.2(3) (November 28, 2004).

28. Social Security (Housing Costs Amendments) Regulations 2004 (SI 2004/2825) reg.2(4) (November 28, 2004).

29. Social Security (Housing Costs Amendments) Regulations 2004 (SI 2004/2825) reg.2(5) (November 28, 2004).

30. Social Security (Housing Benefit, Council Tax Benefit, State Pension Credit and Miscellaneous Amendments) Regulations 2004 (SI 2004/2327) reg.5(a) (April 4, 2005).

31. Social Security (Housing Benefit, Council Tax Benefit, State Pension Credit and Miscellaneous Amendments) Regulations 2004 (SI 2004/2327) reg.5(b) (April 4, 2005).

32. Social Security (Care Homes and Independent Hospitals) Regulations 2005 (SI 2005/2687) reg.2 and Sch.1 para.8 (October 24, 2005).

33. Housing Benefit and Council Tax Benefit (Consequential Provisions) Regulations 2006 (SI 2006/217) reg.5 and Sch.2 para.1(5)(a) (March 6, 2006).

34. Housing Benefit and Council Tax Benefit (Consequential Provisions) Regulations 2006 (SI 2006/217) reg.5 and Sch.2 para.1(5)(b) (March 6, 2006).

35. Housing Benefit and Council Tax Benefit (Consequential Provisions) Regulations 2006 (SI 2006/217) reg.5 and Sch.2 para.1(5)(c) (March 6, 2006).

36. Social Security (Miscellaneous Amendments) (No.2) Regulations 2005 (SI 2005/2465) reg.2(7) (April 10, 2006).

37. Social Security (Hospital In-Patients) Regulations 2005 (SI 2005/3360) reg.4(4) (April 10, 2006).

38. Social Security (Miscellaneous Amendments) (No.4) Regulations 2006 (SI 2006/2378) reg.5(8)(a) (October 2, 2006).

39. Social Security (Miscellaneous Amendments) (No.4) Regulations 2006 (SI 2006/2378) reg.5(8)(b) (October 2, 2006).

40. Social Security (Miscellaneous Amendments) (No.4) Regulations 2006 (SI 2006/2378) reg.5(8)(c) (October 2, 2006).

41. Social Security (Miscellaneous Amendments) (No.4) Regulations 2006 (SI 2006/2378) reg.5(8)(d) (October 2, 2006).

42. Social Security (Miscellaneous Amendments) (No.4) Regulations 2006 (SI 2006/2378) reg.5(7)(b) (October 9, 2006).
43. Social Security (Miscellaneous Amendments) (No.5) Regulations 2006 (SI 2006/3274) reg.2 (January 8, 2007).
44. Social Security (Housing Costs and Miscellaneous Amendments) Regulations 2007 (SI 2007/3183) reg.3(3)(a) (December 17, 2007).
45. Social Security (Housing Costs and Miscellaneous Amendments) Regulations 2007 (SI 2007/3183) reg.3(3)(b) (December 17, 2007).
46. Social Security (Housing Costs and Miscellaneous Amendments) Regulations 2007 (SI 2007/3183) reg.3(3)(c) (December 17, 2007).
47. Social Security (Miscellaneous Amendments) Regulations 2008 (SI 2008/698) reg.2(8)(c) (April 14, 2008).
48. Social Security (Miscellaneous Amendments) Regulations 2008 (SI 2008/698) reg.2(13) (April 14, 2008).
49. Employment and Support Allowance (Consequential Provisions) (No.2) Regulations 2008 (SI 2008/1554) reg.2(11) (October 27, 2008).
50. Employment and Support Allowance (Miscellaneous Amendments) Regulations 2008 (SI 2008/2428) reg.41(2)(a) (October 27, 2008).
51. Employment and Support Allowance (Miscellaneous Amendments) Regulations 2008 (SI 2008/2428) reg.41(2)(b) (October 27, 2008).
52. Social Security (Miscellaneous Amendments) (No.6) Regulations 2008 (SI 2008/2767) reg.2(6) (November 17, 2008).
53. Social Security (Miscellaneous Amendments) (No.6) Regulations 2008 (SI 2008/2767) reg.2(11) (November 17, 2008).
54. Social Security (Housing Costs Special Arrangements) (Amendment and Modification) Regulations 2008 (SI 2008/3195) reg.2(1)(b) and (2) (January 5, 2009).
55. Social Security (Miscellaneous Amendments) Regulations 2009 (SI 2009/583) reg.2(3) (April 6, 2009).
56. Social Security (Miscellaneous Amendments) (No.4) Regulations 2009 (SI 2009/2655) reg.2(15)(a) (October 26, 2009).
57. Social Security (Miscellaneous Amendments) (No.2) Regulations 2010 (SI 2010/641) reg.2(3)(e) (April 6, 2010).
58. Social Security (Miscellaneous Amendments) (No.2) Regulations 2010 (SI 2010/641) reg.2(7)(d) (April 6, 2010).
59. Social Security (Miscellaneous Amendments) (No.4) Regulations 2009 (SI 2009/2655) reg.2(15)(b) (April 12, 2010).
60. Social Security (Housing Costs) (Standard Interest Rate) Amendment Regulations 2010 (SI 2011/1811) reg.2(1)(a) and (2) (October 1, 2010).
61. Social Security (Miscellaneous Amendments) Regulations 2011 (SI 2011/674) reg.3(6)(a) (April 11, 2011).
62. Social Security (Miscellaneous Amendments) Regulations 2011 (SI 2011/674) reg.3(6)(b) (April 11, 2011).
63. Social Security (Miscellaneous Amendments) Regulations 2011 (SI 2011/674) reg.3(6)(c) (April 11, 2011).
64. Social Security (Miscellaneous Amendments) (No.3) Regulations 2011 (SI 2011/2425) reg.7(5) (October 31, 2011).
65. Employment and Support Allowance (Duration of Contributory Allowance) (Consequential Amendments) Regulations 2012 (SI 2012/913) reg.3(3) (May 1, 2012).
66. Social Security (Miscellaneous Amendments) Regulations 2013 (SI 2013/443) reg.2(4)(a) (April 2, 2013).
67. Social Security (Miscellaneous Amendments) Regulations 2013 (SI 2013/443) reg.2(4)(b) (April 2, 2013).
68. Personal Independence Payment (Supplementary Provisions and Consequential Amendments) Regulations 2013 (SI 2013/388) reg. 8 and Sch. Pt 2 para.11(6) (April 8, 2013).
69. Armed Forces and Reserve Forces Compensation Scheme (Consequential

Provisions: Subordinate Legislation) Order 2013 (SI 2013/591) art.7 and Sch. para.4(6) (April 8, 2013).

70. Universal Credit (Consequential, Supplementary, Incidental and Miscellaneous Provisions) Regulations 2013 (SI 2013/630) reg.28(7)(a) (April 29, 2013).

71. Universal Credit (Consequential, Supplementary, Incidental and Miscellaneous Provisions) Regulations 2013 (SI 2013/630) reg.28(7)(b) (April 29, 2013).

72. Social Security (Miscellaneous Amendments) Regulations 2014 (SI 2014/591) reg.2(6) (April 28, 2014).

73. Universal Credit and Miscellaneous Amendments (No.2) Regulations 2014 (SI 2014/2888) reg.3(2)(b) (November 26, 2014).

74. Social Security (Housing Costs Amendments) Regulations 2015 (SI 2015/1647) reg.2(2) (April 1, 2016).

75. Social Security Benefits (Adjustment of Amounts and Thresholds) Regulations 2016 (SI 2016/242) reg.2(3) (April 11, 2016).

DEFINITIONS

"Abbeyfield Home"—see reg.2(1).
"armed forces independence payment"—*ibid.*
"attendance allowance"—*ibid.*
"benefit week"—*ibid.*
"care home"—*ibid.*
"claimant"—*ibid.*
"close relative"—*ibid.*
"couple"—*ibid.*
"course of study"—*ibid.*
"co-ownership scheme"—*ibid.*
"Crown tenant"—*ibid.*
"disability living allowance"—*ibid.*
"dwelling occupied as the home"—*ibid.*
"employment zone"—*ibid.*
"family"—see SSCBA s.137(1).
"full-time student"—see reg.61(1).
"housing benefit expenditure"—see reg.2(1).
"independent hospital"—*ibid.*
"Intensive Activity Period for 50 plus"—*ibid.*
"local welfare provision" —*ibid.*
"lone parent"—*ibid.*
"MFET Limited"—*ibid.*
"non-dependant"—see reg.3.
"partner"—see reg.2(1).
"period of study"—*ibid.*
"personal independence payment"—*ibid.*
"polygamous marriage"—*ibid.*
"remunerative work"—see reg.5.
"self-employment route"—see reg.2(1).
"single claimant"—*ibid.*
"the Caxton Foundation"—*ibid.*
"the Eileen Trust"—*ibid.*
"the Fund"—*ibid.*
"the Independent Living Funds"—*ibid.*
"the Macfarlane (Special Payments) Trust"—*ibid.*
"the Macfarlane (Special Payments) (No.2) Trust"—*ibid.*
"the Macfarlane Trust"—*ibid.*
"the Skipton Fund"—*ibid.*
"training allowance"—*ibid.*

"universal credit"—*ibid.*
"water charges"—*ibid.*
"Welfare Reform Act"—*ibid.*
"welfare to work beneficiary"—*ibid.*
"year of assessment"—*ibid.*

GENERAL NOTE

Introduction

2.761 A new Sch.3 came into force on October 2, 1995 which introduced major changes to the rules for payment of housing costs by income support. See the notes to Sch.3 in the 1995 edition of J. Mesher and P. Wood, *Income-related Benefits: the Legislation* for details of the previous rules. See also the associated changes to paras 29 and 30 of Sch.9, and Schs 9 and 9A of the Claims and Payments Regulations. Note reg.5(2) of the Social Security (Income Support and Claims and Payments) Amendment Regulations 1995 which preserves the operation of previous saving provisions (see p.804).

The new rules placed further substantial limits on the housing costs that will be met by income support. Since August 1993 this had been increasingly restricted. The upper ceiling for loans, first introduced on August 2, 1993, had been reduced twice and since April 10, 1995 has remained at £100,000 (but note that with effect from January 5, 2009 it has been raised to £200,000 for certain claimants—see below under "*Modifications to the waiting periods and the cap on loans for certain claimants from January 5, 2009*" and "*Further modifications from January 5, 2010*"). Since May 2, 1994, interest on loans taken out or increased while a person was entitled to income support (or caught by the 26 weeks linking rule), which increased his housing costs, had not been met, subject to certain exceptions (note that from October 2, 1995 this rule only applies to loans taken out for house purchase and not those for repairs and improvements). These limits were in addition to those applying to tenants buying their own homes and the rules concerning excessive housing costs. All these provisions were retained (although there was no longer a separate rule for tenants who buy their own homes, to whom para.4(8) will now apply). However, the new restrictions signified a more fundamental change of approach to the meeting of housing costs by income support.

The main new departure was that no mortgage interest (nor some other housing costs—see below) was to be paid at all for certain periods which varied according to whether the loan or other agreement existed before October 2, 1995 (for the position of replacement loans see below). Interest was also generally to be payable at a set rate rather than at the actual rate charged. Interest on arrears of interest (previously payable in limited circumstances, e.g. on arrears which accrued during the first 16 weeks of a claim) was no longer to be met, nor was interest on loans for non-approved purposes for separated partners. In addition, the loans for repairs and improvements that qualify were further restricted. There was some transitional protection for existing claimants. In addition *all* payments of loan interest were now to be made directly to lenders who participate in the mortgage interest direct scheme; previously such loan interest payments were paid to claimants during the 50 per cent period (see the amendment to para.2 of Sch.9A to the Claims and Payments Regulations).

2.762 These changes were introduced as part of the Government's long-term aim of replacing state support with private insurance where possible. According to the Social Security Advisory Committee's (SSAC) report on the proposals (Cmnd. 2905(1995)), about 10 per cent of all home buyers then had mortgage payment protection insurance (para.16). The DSS's Memorandum to SSAC also referred to the need to simplify the calculation of housing costs (which were responsible for 13.1 per cent of all income support errors in the period April to December 1994). But the Memorandum acknowledged that the introduction of a set rate of interest was also part of a clear policy that the state would not, even in the long-term, take full responsibility for borrowers' commitments (para.36). SSAC recommended that the changes, in particular for existing borrowers, be postponed until April 1996 and made a number of other proposals to mitigate the effect of the new scheme. However, most of the recommendations were rejected. In reply to SSAC, the Government stated that the shift to private insurance for payment of mortgage interest was primarily directed at new loans (i.e. those taken out after October 1, 1995). In the Government's view the changes did not increase the need for mortgage insurance for existing borrowers, because most mortgage protection policies do not cover the first two months (under the new rules the waiting period for existing borrowers was eight weeks). But this ignored other important features of the new rules (such as 50 per cent only for the next 18 weeks, interest to be paid at the standard rate, etc.) which also had a major impact on existing borrowers. The concessions made by the Government in response to the widespread criticism of the new restrictions were very limited. Where concessions were made, for example in relation to carers, this generally only resulted in the existing borrower rule being applied, rather than complete exemption from the changes.

In *CIS 16769/1996* the Commissioner rejects the contention that the amending regulations substituting the new Sch.3 were ultra vires. In that case the claimant was not entitled to income support on October 1, 1995; he simply had an expectation that if the regulations and any other relevant circumstances did not change, he would be entitled to income support on a new claim made on or after November 7, 1995. In those circumstances there was no question of any accrued right being interfered with by the revocation of the former Sch.3.

In addition, from October 7, 1996, the effect of reg.32 of the Income Support (General) (Jobseeker's Allowance Consequential Amendments) Regulations 1996 (see p.807) should be noted. This provides that entitlement to income-based JSA counts as entitlement to income support for the purpose of satisfying any condition that the person is or has been entitled to income support for any period of time. It also has the same effect where the requirement is that the person is or has been treated as being in receipt of income support. This is obviously important for claimants transferring from JSA to income support. See para.18 of Sch.2 to the JSA Regulations 1996 where the transfer is the other way round. Note also para.1A, introduced on October 22, 1997.

Since October 6, 2003 when the state pension credit scheme commenced, claimants who have reached "the qualifying age for state pension credit" are not entitled to income support (see s.124(1)(aa) of the Contributions and Benefits Act 1992) and have to claim state pension credit. "The qualifying age for state pension credit" is defined in s.137(1) of the Contributions and Benefits Act 1992—the effect of that definition is that the qualifying age was 60 but from April 2010 it will gradually rise in line with the staged increase in pensionable age for women until it reaches 65 in November 2018 (this equalisation of the state pension age for men and women was previously to have been completed by April 5, 2020 but the timetable for this in the Pensions Act 1995 has been accelerated with effect from April 2016 so that women's state pension age will now be 65 by November 2018; in addition, the increase in state pension age to 66 for both men and women has been brought forward—it will start to rise from 65 in December 2018 to reach 66 by October 2020 (see s.1 of the Pensions Act 2011) and between 2026 and 2028 it will rise to 67 (see s.26 of the Pensions Act 2014)). A claimant whose partner is *entitled* to state pension credit is also ineligible (s.124(1)(g) of the 1992 Act). For an overview of the state pension credit scheme see the Introduction and General Note at the beginning of the State Pension Credit Act 2002. There are no waiting periods for housing costs for state pension credit claimants (as there were not for income support claimants who, or whose partner, were aged 60 or over (see the previous form of para.9(1)(a) of this Schedule in the 2003 edition of this volume)). However, for claimants whose former partners were entitled to state pension credit and who transfer to income support note the effect of the linking rule in para.14(14) which was added with effect from October 6, 2003. **2.763**

See also the further linking rule in para.14(15) that has been inserted as a consequence of the introduction of ESA on October 27, 2008. This is important for claimants transferring from ESA to income support. See para.20 of Sch.6 to the ESA Regulations 2008 in Vol.I of this series where the transfer is the other way round.

Modifications to the waiting periods and the cap on loans for certain claimants from January 5, 2009

2.764 For certain claimants the waiting periods for existing and new housing costs were changed (broadly to 13 weeks) and the ceiling on loans was increased from £100,000 to £200,000 with effect from January 5, 2009 by the Social Security (Housing Costs Special Arrangements) (Amendment and Modification) Regulations 2008 (SI 2008/3195) (see p.816 for these Regulations, which were themselves amended on January 5, 2010, see further below). These modifications apply for the purposes of income support, old style JSA and old style ESA. In addition, in the case of old style JSA only, housing costs in respect of eligible loans will only be payable for two years. According to the Explanatory Memorandum which accompanied the Regulations, the modifications had been made in order to provide help more quickly to home-owners in the current economic climate. They were intended to be temporary measures, to be reviewed once the housing market recovered.

As already stated, the changes do not apply to all claimants. Broadly the claimants affected by the new rules are those entitled to income support (or old style JSA or old style ESA) on January 4, 2009 who are serving a waiting period for "full" housing costs or those who make a new claim for income support (or old style JSA or old style ESA) on or after January 5, 2009, or a repeat claim that does not link to an earlier claim (other than a claim under which they were entitled to income support (or old style JSA or old style ESA) on January 4, 2009 *and* in relation to which the modified rules for housing costs applied). Claimants who do not fall within the new rules will continue to be subject to the old rules, that is they will continue to have to satisfy the longer waiting periods and for them the limit on eligible loans will remain at £100,000. However, the two-year time limit for JSA housing costs in respect of eligible loans will also not apply.

Note that the new rules were further modified on January 5, 2010 (see further below).

Claimants entitled to income support/old style JSA/old style ESA on January 4, 2009

2.765 Under Pt 2 of the 2008 Regulations, for claimants who are *entitled* to income support (or old style JSA or old style ESA) on January 4, 2009 (note that the intention is that this therefore does not include claimants who are serving their waiting period for housing costs but are not actually entitled to income support (or old style JSA or old style ESA)) *and:*

(i) whose housing costs in the benefit week including January 4, 2009 would otherwise be nil because they had not yet completed the 26-week qualifying period for "existing" housing costs or the 39-week qualifying period for "new" housing costs; *or*

(ii) who are entitled to have 50 per cent of their housing costs met because they have been entitled to income support (or old style JSA or old style ESA) for a continuous period (which includes January 4, 2009) of at least eight, but less than 26, weeks;

the Income Support Regulations are modified as follows (similar modifications are made to the JSA Regulations 1996 and the ESA Regulations 2008 (for the latter see Vol.I in this series)):

- the waiting period for both new and existing housing costs to be met "in full" is reduced to 13 weeks;
- the capital limit for loans is increased from £100,000 to £200,000 (note that the effect of para.7(b) of the 2008 Regulations is that this increased

limit will not apply to a claimant who is entitled to 50 per cent of the interest on his loan until he qualifies for "full" housing costs under these modified rules); and

- in the case of JSA only, housing costs in respect of eligible loans will only be payable for two years. Note that in calculating this two-year period any week in which the limit for the claimant's loan(s) was £100,000 (i.e. in which the old limit still applied) is ignored. Moreover, the two-year limit does not apply where the claimant, partner or other member of a joint-claim couple was previously entitled to income support or old style ESA and became entitled to old style JSA within 12 weeks of that entitlement ceasing (but see below). However, apart from these provisions, it seems that in calculating the two-year period the normal linking rules will apply.

  For JSA claimants who were receiving housing costs as part of their JSA before they started remunerative work, the four-week housing costs run-on is paid as income support (see reg.6(5)–(6), para.9A of Sch.1B and para.19A of Sch.7). It was not the policy intention that such an income support entitlement should led to exemption from the two-year limit. A further amendment was therefore made to reg.6 of the 2008 Regulations on October 31, 2011 (reg.6 modifies Sch.2 to the JSA Regulations in relation to claimants to whom Pt 2 of the 2008 Regulations apply, in particular by inserting para.4A into Sch.2—the amendment inserts a new sub-para.(4) into para.4A). The effect of the amendment is that a JSA claimant will not be exempt from the two-year limit if the income support he was receiving no more than 12 weeks before his JSA entitlement started was the four-week housing costs run-on following a previous entitlement to JSA.

Note that if the person makes a further claim to income support (or old style JSA or old style ESA), or to another of these benefits, after January 4, 2009, the modifications under Pt 2 of the Regulations cease to apply but the modifications under Pt 3 will do so—see below.

Claimants who claim income support/old style JSA/old style ESA after January 4, 2009

Under Pt 3 of the 2008 Regulations, for claimants who claim income support (or old style JSA or old style ESA) after January 4, 2009 *and*: 2.766

(i) who fell within the provisions under Pt 2 of the Regulations at any time;

(ii) whose entitlement to income support (or old style JSA or old style ESA) after January 4, 2009 (including any previous entitlement after January 4, 2009) was not immediately preceded by a "linked period" (i.e. a period when the claimant was treated as in receipt of income support (or old style JSA or old style ESA) under para.14 of Sch.3 to the Income Support Regulations (or para.13 of Sch.2 to the JSA Regulations 1996 or para.15 of Sch.6 to the ESA Regulations 2008); *or*

(iii) who, or whose partner (or other member of a joint-claim couple), was receiving state pension credit with housing costs and whose entitlement to income support (or old style JSA or old style ESA) after January 4, 2009 (including any previous entitlement after January 4, 2009) began more than 12 weeks after state pension credit with housing costs ceased (26 weeks where the linking rules apply because of (up to April 11, 2011) a lower child support maintenance assessment, or because of payments from a policy to insure against loss of employment ceasing);

the Income Support Regulations are modified as follows (similar modifications are made to the JSA Regulations 1996 and the ESA Regulations 2008 (for the latter see Vol.I in this series)):

- the distinction between "existing housing costs" and "new housing costs" is removed and a single waiting period of 13 weeks for housing costs replaces the previous different waiting periods;
- the capital limit for loans is increased from £100,000 to £200,000; and
- in the case of JSA only, housing costs in respect of eligible loans will only be payable for two years (in this case the two-year period only starts to run if it was not immediately preceded by a linked period). Note that in calculating the two-year period any week in which the limit for the claimant's loan(s) was £100,000 (i.e. in which the old limit still applied) is ignored. Moreover the two-year limit does not apply where the claimant, partner or other member of a joint-claim couple was previously entitled to income support or old style ESA and became entitled to old style JSA within 12 weeks of that entitlement ceasing (but see below). However, apart from these provisions, it seems that in calculating the two-year period the normal linking rules will apply.

  For JSA claimants who were receiving housing costs as part of their JSA before they started remunerative work, the four-week housing costs run-on is paid as income support (see reg.6(5)–(6), para.9A of Sch.1B and para.19A of Sch.7). It was not the policy intention that such an income support entitlement should led to exemption from the two-year limit. A further amendment was therefore made to reg.11 of the 2008 Regulations on October 31, 2011 (reg.11 modifies Sch.2 to the JSA Regulations in relation to claimants to whom Pt 3 of the 2008 Regulations apply, in particular by inserting para.4A into Sch.2—the amendment inserts a new sub-para.(7) into para.4A). The effect of the amendment is that a JSA claimant will not be exempt from the two-year limit if the income support he was receiving no more than 12 weeks before his JSA entitlement started was the four-week housing costs run-on following a previous entitlement to JSA.

Note that the January 2009 modified rules only apply to claimants as set out above. Thus they do not apply to claimants who after January 4, 2009 make a claim to income support (or old style JSA or old style ESA), or a claim for another of these benefits, which is immediately preceded by a linked period. But as DMG Memo 1/09 suggests, if there is no gap between the claims, and so no linked period, the claimant can fall within, and indeed may immediately benefit from, the modified rules (but see below under "*Further modifications from January 5, 2010*").

The January 2009 modified rules (at least under Pt 2 and reg.8(3)–(5) of Pt 3) also only apply to claimants who are *entitled* to income support (or old style JSA or old style ESA) (it is not entirely clear whether a claimant who falls within reg.8(2) of Pt 3 (i.e. a claimant to whom Pt 2 of the Regulations has applied at any time) has to be entitled on a claim made after January 4, 2009). The apparent intention is that a person who, e.g. is in receipt of incapacity benefit which exceeds his income support applicable amount until housing costs are included, will not benefit from these new rules but will remain subject to the old ones. However, note that the definition of "relevant benefit" in reg.1(4) of the Regulations refers to "an employment and support allowance" or "a jobseeker's allowance", not "income-related ESA", or "income-based JSA". Entitlement to contributory ESA or contribution-based JSA will therefore count as entitlement to a relevant benefit for the purposes of the application of the modifications made by these Regulations.

Claimants whose "full" housing costs are already being met on January 5, 2009 will continue to fall under the old rules, including the £100,000 limit.

State pension credit claimants

2.767 Under Pt 4 of the 2008 Regulations, the increased capital limit for eligible loans will also apply to state pension credit but only where the claimant or his partner was entitled to housing costs under the modified provisions in Pts 2 or 3 of the

Regulations and the claimant becomes entitled to state pension credit within 12 weeks of that entitlement ending.

Further modifications from January 5, 2010

2.768 The Social Security (Housing Costs Special Arrangements) (Amendment and Modification) Regulations 2008 (SI 2008/3195) ("the principal Regulations") were amended by the Social Security (Housing Costs Special Arrangements) (Amendment) Regulations 2009 (SI 2009/3257) on January 5, 2010 (see p.816 for the principal Regulations, as amended). According to the Explanatory Memorandum which accompanies the 2009 Regulations, the purpose of the amendments is that from January 5, 2010:

- the modified rules *will* apply to claimants who are not entitled to income support, old style JSA or old style ESA in their waiting period because their income (other than from a relevant benefit) exceeds their applicable amount. The Explanatory Memorandum states that claimants who were excluded from the modified rules before January 5, 2010 because they were not entitled to benefit during their waiting period may be eligible for assistance under an extra-statutory scheme;
- claimants who move, from, e.g. income support to old style JSA or old style ESA, or who make a repeat claim, without a gap between claims, whose previous claim did not fall under the modified rules, cannot benefit from these rules on their new claim; and
- in the case of JSA, a further two years' payment of housing costs will only be possible where there is a break in claim to which the housing costs linking rules do not apply.

The 2009 Regulations substitute a new reg.8, the effect of which is that from January 5, 2010 the modified rules (under Pt 3) will apply in the case of a claimant who claims income support, old style JSA or old style ESA after January 4, 2009 if he satisfies any of the following conditions:

(i) Pt 2 of the principal Regulations applied to him at any time;

(ii) Pt 3 (as it has effect after January 4, 2010) applied in relation to a previous award;

(iii) he or his partner has not been awarded income support, old style JSA or old style ESA as a result of an earlier claim, is not in receipt of state pension credit, and he does not fall to be treated under a linking rule (i.e. a provision in para.14 of Sch.3 to the Income Support Regulations, para.13 of Sch.2 to the JSA Regulations 1996 or para.15 of Sch.6 to the ESA Regulations 2008; for the latter see Vol.I of this series) as being in continuous receipt of income support, old style JSA or old style ESA for a period that includes January 4, 2009 and ends immediately before the claim is made or treated as made;

(iv) the claimant was not in receipt of income support, old style JSA or old style ESA immediately before the claim was made or treated as made, neither he nor his partner was getting state pension credit, he or his partner was awarded income support, old style JSA or old style ESA as a result of an earlier claim but he does not fall to be treated under a linking rule as being in continuous receipt of income support, old style JSA or old style ESA during the period between the end of the last earlier award and the date on which the claim is made or treated as made; *or*

(v) the claimant or his partner was receiving state pension credit with housing costs and the entitlement to income support (or old style JSA or old style ESA) on a claim made or treated as made after January 4, 2009 began more than 12 weeks after state pension credit with housing costs ceased (26 weeks where the linking rules apply because of (up to April 11, 2011) a lower child support maintenance assessment, or because of payments from an insurance policy ceasing).

Note that where there is more than one claim for income support, old style JSA or old style ESA after January 4, 2009, the modified rules will apply where any claim made after that date meets one of the conditions in (i)–(v) above. But see below under "*Waiting period for new claims made on or after April 1, 2016*".

See DMG Memo 43/09 which explains how these modified rules are intended to work and gives a number of examples of their application.

Waiting period for new claims made on or after April 1, 2016

2.769 Further changes have been made to the rules for waiting periods with effect from April 1, 2016. For new claims for income support, old style JSA and old style ESA made on or after April 1, 2016 (which do not link to a previous claim) the distinction between "new" and "existing" housing costs is abolished and there is only one waiting period of 39 weeks. See the amendments made to this Schedule (and to Sch.2 to the JSA Regulations 1996 and Sch.6 to the ESA Regulations 2008 (for the latter see Vol.I in this series)) by the Social Security (Housing Costs Amendments) Regulations 2015 (SI 2015/1647) with effect from April 1, 2016. This is subject to a saving provision (see p.824), and see below.

In addition, the provisions in the Social Security (Housing Costs Special Arrangements) (Amendment and Modification) Regulations 2008 (as amended) that reduced the waiting period to 13 weeks for certain claimants are revoked, subject to the same saving provision (see p.824)

The effect of the saving provision is that for those claimants who are entitled, or treated as entitled, to income support, old style JSA or old style ESA for a continuous period which includes March 31, 2016, the form of Sch.3, Sch.2 to the JSA Regulations 1996 and Sch.6 to the ESA Regulations 2008 that was in force before the April 1, 2016 amendments, as modified by the 2008 Special Arrangements Regulations (as amended), continues to have effect. So for claimants who are in a waiting period on March 31, 2016 to whom the 2008 Special Arrangements Regulations (as amended) apply, the waiting period for housing costs remains 13 weeks. For claimants who are in a waiting period on March 31, 2016 to whom the 2008 Special Arrangements Regulations (as amended) do not apply, but whose housing costs are, or count as, "existing housing costs" (see the 2015/16 edition of this volume for what constituted "existing housing costs" and the rules that applied to such costs), the waiting period for "full" housing costs to be payable remains 26 weeks.

The saving provision also applies to universal credit—see Vol.V in this series for this provision as it applies to universal credit.

The Explanatory Memorandum which accompanies the amending Regulations states that the 13 week waiting period was part of a package of temporary measures intended to support homeowners and the housing industry during the recession. However, "[a]s the housing and labour markets have now recovered, the Government has decided that it is the right time to re-introduce a 39 week waiting period for new claims". However, the 39 week waiting period did not apply to all claims before the introduction of the 13 week waiting period for certain claimants by the Social Security (Housing Costs Special Arrangements) (Amendment and Modification) Regulations 2008. If the claimant's housing costs counted as "existing housing costs", a shorter waiting period (no housing costs for the first eight weeks and 50 per cent for the next 18 weeks) applied (see the 2015/16 edition of this volume for the definition of "existing housing costs" and para.6 (existing housing costs), both revoked with effect from April 1, 2016). Moreover, even if the claimant's housing costs counted as "new housing costs", para.8(2)–(5) treated them as existing housing costs in certain circumstances (see the 2015/16 edition of this volume for the definition of "new housing costs" and para.8(2)-(5), both revoked with effect from April 1, 2016). Paragraph 8(2)–(5) covered claimants who were eligible for income support as carers, were in custody pending trial or sentence, had been refused payment under a mortgage protection policy because of a pre-existing medical condition or HIV or who were lone parents who had claimed due to the death of, or being abandoned by, a partner (in the case of a lone parent this ceased to apply if she became a member of a couple again). From April 1, 2016 new claimants (who do not come within the saving provision (see p.824)) whose housing costs may previously have counted, or been treated, as existing housing costs will have to serve a 39 week waiting period.

Note that the other modifications made by the 2008 Regulations, that is, the increased ceiling for loans of £200,000 and the two year limit on the payment of housing costs in respect of eligible loans in the case of old style JSA, continue for those claimants to whom 2008 Regulations (as amended) apply, as does the modification relating to claimants of state pension credit.

Note also that para.7 of this Schedule (which provided transitional protection on the introduction of the October 1995 changes to housing costs) has been revoked by SI 2015/1647. For the details of this transitional protection, see the 2015/16 edition of this volume. However, note that the additional transitional protection for existing claimants in reg.3 of the Income Support (General) Amendment and Transitional Regulations 1995 (see p.804) remains—see the note to para.7.

Paragraph 1—Housing costs

To be entitled to a sum for housing costs, the claimant, or another member of the family, must be liable to meet any of those costs on the home which are eligible under paras 15–17. Paragraph 2 deals with when a person is "liable to meet" housing costs. Whether a person is occupying a dwelling as his home is essentially a question of fact (*CIS 480/1992*). 2.770

CIS 636/1992 (confirmed by the Court of Appeal in *Brain v Chief Adjudication Officer*, December 2, 1993) held in relation to the previous form of Sch.3 that an amount for housing costs was limited to what the claimant was actually required to pay. Under the terms of her mortgage the claimant was not liable to pay any capital or interest so long as the amount outstanding (including accrued interest) did not exceed 75 per cent of the value of the mortgaged property. She was not entitled to an amount for mortgage interest while she was not liable to pay it. The reasoning in that case would also seem to apply to the current form of Sch.3, despite the differences in the wording. See also *R(IS) 19/95* in the note to para.2(a).

Housing costs are limited to those specified in paras 15–17. To be doubly sure, para.4(1) excludes housing benefit expenditure and also provides that if a person is in a residential care or nursing home, no housing costs can usually be paid. But if the person is temporarily absent from his home, see para.3(8)–(12) as to when housing costs for that dwelling can continue to be met although the person is in the residential care home, etc.

The categories in paras 15–17 are the same as those listed in para.1 of the former Sch.3 (but note the reduced eligibility of loans for repairs and improvements: see para.16). As far as mortgage interest, payments under a hire-purchase agreement and interest on loans for repairs and improvements are concerned, the question is no longer whether the interest is eligible, but whether the loan qualifies (see paras 15 and 16). Presumably this is at least partly the consequence of introducing a standard rate of interest (see para.12). It also means that the kind of situation dealt with in *R(IS) 11/95* (where the question was whether interest on a replacement loan was eligible where the original loan had been interest free—see p.264 of J. Mesher and P. Wood, *Income-related Benefits: the Legislation* (1995)) will no longer be an issue. 2.771

In *RV v SSWP (IS)* [2013] UKUT 273 (AAC) it was argued that, since the question was now whether the loan qualifies, not whether the interest is eligible, the capital repayments of £100 per month on an interest-free loan to the claimant to assist with the purchase of his home qualified under para.15. Judge West, however, holds that Sch.3 has to be construed in the light of reg.17(1)(e) which limits the scope of housing costs to "mortgage interest payments or such other housing costs as are prescribed in [Schedule 3]". Regulation 17(1)(e) was not amended when the new form of Sch.3 was introduced in October 1995 and capital payments do not fall within its scope.

Note the restrictions on loans that will be met in paras 4(2)–(12), 11(4)–(11) and 13.

Note also reg.13(1) of the Decisions and Appeals Regulations 1999 (see Vol.III of this series) which provides that if the Secretary of State considers that he does not have all the relevant information or evidence to decide what housing costs to award, the claim will be decided on the basis of those housing costs that can immediately be awarded.

Definitions

2.772 As a consequence of the introduction of one waiting period of 39 weeks for housing costs for new claims made on or after April 1, 2016 (subject to a saving provision—see under "*Waiting period for new claims made on or after April 1, 2016*" above), the definitions of "existing housing costs" and "new housing costs" are no longer needed and so have been omitted. See the 2015/16 edition of this volume for these definitions and the notes to those definitions.

2.773 Paragraph 1 defines who is a "disabled person" for the purposes of Sch.3 (*CIS/13661/1996* confirms that this is an exhaustive definition). A person counts as disabled if he qualifies for, or would do so if entitled to income support (including periods when he is disqualified from receiving benefit or treated as capable of work by virtue of regulations made under s.171E SSCBA), one of the listed premiums. This list includes the disabled child premium. However, due to the transfer to tax credits of financial support for children and the consequential abolition of the "child elements" in income support, including the disabled child premium (except in "transitional cases"—see the notes to reg.17), the definition was updated to also cover a person who satisfies the conditions for the disabled or severely disabled child elements of child tax credit (for these conditions see reg.8 of the Child Tax Credit Regulations 2002 (SI 2002/2008) in Vol.IV of this series).

From October 27, 2008, following the introduction of ESA, a person also counts as disabled if he is in receipt of the work-related activity component or support component of ESA (including periods when he is disqualified from receiving benefit or treated as having limited capability for work by virtue of regulations made under s.18 WRA 2007).

2.774 From May 1, 2012 this includes a person who would have been entitled to ESA with a work-related activity component but for the 365 days' limit on entitlement to contributory ESA for a person who is in the work-related activity group that was introduced by s.1A of the Welfare Reform Act 2007. Section 1A was inserted into the 2007 Act by s.51 of the Welfare Reform Act 2012 and came into force on May 1, 2012 (see art.2(2)(a) of the Welfare Reform Act 2012 (Commencement No.1) Order 2012 (SI 2012/863) which brought s.51 of the 2012 Act into force on May 1, 2012).

An additional category has been added from April 29, 2013 to take account of the commencement of universal credit. A person will count as "disabled" if he has an award of universal credit which includes a limited capability for work element or a limited capability for work and work-related activity element, or, in the case of a limited capability for work element, would do so but for the fact that the person satisfies the conditions for a carer element, or, in the case of joint claimants, would do so but for the fact that only one limited capability for work (or limited capability for work and work-related activity) element can be included even if both joint claimants meet the conditions for such an element (or elements).

Paragraph 1A—previous entitlement to income-based JSA or state pension credit

The effect of this provision is that a claimant who moves from income-based JSA, income-related ESA or state pension credit to income support within a linked period (normally 12 weeks but 26 weeks if para.14(8) applies) will receive the same amount for housing costs on any eligible loan as he did under JSA, ESA or state pension credit. The same will apply if it is the claimant's partner who was, or was treated as, getting income-based JSA, income-related ESA or state pension credit or who becomes entitled to income support. But if there has been a change in circumstances (other than a reduction in the amount of the loan), the housing costs will be recalculated. There is a parallel provision in para.1A of Sch.2 to the JSA Regulations 1996 that has the same result where the move is from income support, income-related ESA or state pension credit to income-based JSA. For the ESA provision where the move is from income support, income-based JSA or state pension credit to income-related ESA, see para.3 of Sch.6 to the ESA Regulations 2008 in Vol.I of this series, and for the state pension credit provision where the move is from income support, income-based JSA or income-related ESA to state pension credit, see para.7(4A)-(5) of Sch.II to the State Pension Credit Regulations. See also para.8(1B) under which the anniversary date for the recalculation of the eligible capital in these circumstances will be the date that the claimant or his partner was first entitled to housing costs under any of the four benefits. 2.775

Paragraph 2—liability to meet housing costs

Paragraph 2 defines when a person is "liable to meet housing costs". Three situations are specified, to satisfy para.1(1): 2.776

(A) Where the claimant, or any partner, has a liability for housing costs, it must not be to a member of the same household. See *R(SB) 13/82*, *R(SB) 4/83*, *CSB 145/1984* and *CSB 463/1986*, and the notes to s.137(1) of the Contributions and Benefits Act 1992.

Where a separated spouse or cohabitee has a joint mortgage with the former partner who has left the home, normally the liability for the mortgage will be a joint and several one (although each case will depend on the exact terms of the mortgage deed or loan agreement). This means that each party will be legally liable for the whole payment. *R(IS) 4/00* confirms that a claimant in this situation where the other party is not paying his share is therefore entitled to housing costs for the total payment. Even if each party is liable separately for a defined share of the payment, then the claimant will in most circumstances of separation be treated as responsible for the other party's share under sub-para.(b), if the other party is not paying this. But if the claimant is only paying half the mortgage interest (even though she is jointly and severally liable), because payments for the other half are being made by someone else, the amount of her housing costs will be restricted to what she actually pays (*R(IS) 19/95*, and see *CIS 636/1992* in the note to para.1). See para.5(5).

(B) This may apply, e.g. in the case of separated couples. It must be reasonable in all the circumstances to treat the claimant as liable where the person liable is not paying the housing costs, which will probably be the case for most separated couples.

It would not seem to be necessary for the claimant to have continuously lived in the home since the person liable to meet the housing costs failed to meet, or stopped meeting, them. What is required is that the claimant is living in the home and has to meet the housing costs in order to continue to do so when she claims income support. See *Ewens v Secretary of State for Social Security*, reported as *R(IS) 8/01*, which holds that the phrase "in order to continue living in the dwelling occupied as the home" in para.7(7) of the former Sch.3 (loans for non-approved purposes) did not require that the claimant had continuously lived in the home since her former partner had left.

An example of where the predecessor of para.(1)(b) was applied is *R(IS) 12/94*. The claimant lived with her daughter and grandson. Her daughter had a mortgage on their home. Following the death of her daughter the claimant applied for income support. The daughter's will left the property in trust for her son until he reached 21 (he was then aged seven). The Commissioner holds that "the person" liable can include an incorporeal person such as the estate of a deceased person. The daughter's estate was liable to pay the mortgage but was not doing so. It was reasonable to treat the claimant as liable for the mortgage interest. See also *R(H)5/05* on reg.6(1)(c) of the Housing Benefit Regulations 1987 which contained a similar provision to head (b). The Commissioner holds that "person" in reg.6(1)(c) could include a "body of persons corporate or unincorporate" (see s.5 of and Sch.1 to the Interpretation Act 1978). Thus the operation of the provision in reg.6(1)(c) was not excluded by reason only of the fact that it was a limited company who had the legal liability to pay rent under the tenancy agreement (and was not meeting it).

In *CIS 14/1993* the claimant lived with her daughter in a home in their joint names. The daughter took out a hire purchase agreement for a central heating boiler and a cooker. The claimant reimbursed her daughter for half of the hire purchase payments. The claimant argued that she could bring herself within sub-para.(1)(b) because there was a possibility that if the payments were not made, British Gas would apply for a charging order on the home under the Charging Orders Act 1979. The Commissioner holds that for sub-para.(1)(b) to apply, there had to be an immediate threat to the continued occupation of the home, not a theoretical possibility of this in the future. On its particular facts this decision would seem to be correct (the daughter was in fact making the payments). But it is suggested that importing a requirement of an immediate threat to possession into sub-para.(1)(b) is not justified by the wording of the provision and so this decision should be restricted to its particular circumstances.

However, *SSWP v DP* [2009] UKUT 225 (AAC), a case on the equivalent state pension credit provision, agrees with *CIS/14/1993* that there has to be an immediate threat to the continued occupation of the home. In *SSWP v DP* the claimant and her husband had purchased and mortgaged a property in their son's name because they wished to provide for his future (he was disabled and had learning difficulties). They had undertaken responsibility for paying the mortgage on behalf of their son. In the view of Judge Lane this arrangement had the effect of paying housing costs by proxy to a person who might not have been so entitled. It was not just a matter of finding that, because A, who is liable to pay the mortgage is not doing so, then B who lives there, must do so in order to remain living there. It had to be reasonable to treat the claimant as liable to meet the housing costs. Judge Lane remitted the appeal to another tribunal to explore further whether the circumstances fell within the rule in *CIS/14/1993*. Again, however, it is suggested that what has to be applied is the wording in sub-para.(1)(b) (in this case its state pension credit equivalent) and that importing a requirement of an immediate threat to possession is not justified by that wording. If the son's earning capacity was such that he was unable to meet the mortgage payments and the parents did not have the resources to do so, it was likely (sooner or later) that there would be a threat to possession of the home. As the parents were unable to obtain a mortgage in their own names because of their ages, it would not seem unreasonable for them to have entered into this arrangement in order to provide a home for themselves and their son. The facts of this case, even without further investigation, would therefore seem somewhat different from those in *CIS/14/1993* where the likelihood of British Gas applying for a charging order may well have been a theoretical possibility in the future (particularly as the daughter was in fact making the hire-purchase payments). It is also of note that the claimant in *SSWP v DP* had in fact been allowed housing costs on a previous property in the same circumstances. *AH v SSWP (IS)* [2010] UKUT 353 (AAC) expresses the view that the concept of an immediate threat has some use as a means of stressing the significance of the words "has to" in sub-para.(1)(b) but that care needed to be taken not to overstate the necessity of the immediacy of the threat.

(C) Only sharing with another member of the same household will do, but see the definition of close relative. This enables sharers to get their proportionate share of housing costs. See para.5(5).

Paragraph 3—occupying a dwelling as the home

Generally a claimant can only have one home—the one normally occupied (sub-paras (1) and (2)), although in some circumstances two separate units of accommodation may constitute one dwelling (see notes to reg.2(1)). *R(SB) 7/86* holds that premises cannot be "normally occupied as the home" if the claimant has never actually resided in them. However, doubts were expressed about this rule in *CSB/524/1985* and *CIS/4/1990* and it is suggested that the issue will be one of fact in each case. See *CH/2521/2002* and *R(H) 9/05* (which concerned reg.5(1) of the Housing Benefit Regulations 1987, the equivalent provision to sub-para.(1)) and the other cases referred to in the note to the definition of "*dwelling occupied as the home*" in reg.2(1) for further discussion of this question. **2.777**

Sub-paragraphs (3) and (4): These give special rules for choosing the home of full-time students (defined in reg.61(1)) with a term-time and a vacation base. **2.778**

Note para.3(13)(ba), inserted on October 26, 2009, which provides that "period of study" in para.3 has the meaning given in reg.61(1). This is because there are two definitions of "period of study" in the Income Support Regulations. The other definition is in reg.2(1) and is of general application, whereas the reg.61(1) definition applies for the purposes of Ch.VIII (*Students*) of Pt V of the Regulations. Applying the definition in reg.2(1) to para.3(4) has the effect that a student can never be outside his period of study, hence the insertion of para.3(13)(ba).

Sub-paragraph (5): This covers moving into temporary accommodation while repairs are done. There is no limit in sub-para.(5) itself as to how long it can apply. *CIS 719/1994* rejects the argument that para.4(8) of the former Sch.3 (now para.3(10)) applied to restrict the operation of sub-para.(5). The claimant's house had been declared unfit for human habitation in 1989 and he had moved into rented accommodation while the repairs were carried out. These had still not been completed when he claimed income support in December 1992. The Commissioner holds that once the SSAT had found that the claimant was to be treated as occupying the house as his home by virtue of sub-para.(5) they had been right to ignore the fact that he had been absent from that home for more than 52 weeks (which was the limit for temporary absences under paragraph 4(8)). Paragraph 4(8) provided an alternative basis to the bases provided by the other sub-paragraphs for treating a claimant as occupying a dwelling as his home while temporarily absent from it. In taking this approach the Commissioner does not follow *CIS 252/1994* which had reached the opposite conclusion. It is suggested that the construction adopted in *CIS 719/1994* is to be preferred, since the former sub-paras (3)–(8) (now sub-paras (3)–(12)) do seem to deal with specific and distinct situations. The reasoning in *CIS 719/1994* will also apply to para.3 which has a similar structure to that of the former para.4. **2.779**

Although the wording of para.3(10) is different from para.4(8) it is not materially different in relation to this issue. There is also an additional argument, which supports the conclusion of *CIS 719/1994*, although not all its reasoning. Where sub-para.(5) applies, its effect is to define which dwelling a claimant is to be treated as occupying. So long as the same situation prevails, the claimant is not to be treated as absent from that dwelling. Therefore sub-paras (10) and (11) simply do not bite in these circumstances.

In some circumstances payments will be made for two homes. The limit in para.11(5) will be applied separately to each home (para.11(6)).

2.780 *Sub-paragraph (6)*: This allows payments in three cases where there is an overlap of liability. *R(SB) 7/86* decides that there must be a liability at both the "outgoing" end and the "ingoing" end. It was suggested that a legal liability at the outgoing end might not be necessary, but *CSSB 564/1987* decides that the liability in respect of the old home had to constitute a responsibility for housing expenditure within reg.14 of the Requirements Regulations. It was argued there that the claimant was liable to make payments to her father as a licensee, but she could not be responsible under reg.14 because the payment was to another member of the same household (differing from *CSB 865/1986*).

It is not clear how these principles might apply under the rules for income support. Paragraph 2 deals with liability (including in sub-para.(1)(a) an exclusion of liability to a member of the same household), but only for housing costs. Items which count as housing costs are those which qualify under paras 15–17 (see para.1(1) and (2)) and do not include ordinary rent or payments as a licensee to occupy a dwelling. A straightforward application of *CSSB 564/1987* would conclude that there could be no overlap of liability if there was only an obligation to make these kinds of payments at the ingoing end. However, it is necessary to look at the problem to which sub-para.(6) is directed. This is that the "new home" would not ordinarily count as "the dwelling occupied as the home" when the claimant had not moved in, or the family more regularly lived elsewhere (reg.2(1), sub-para.(1), *R(SB) 7/86*). Sub-paragraph (6) is to enable the "new home" to be treated as occupied as the home. In the circumstances it does not seem to matter that the liability in respect of the "old home" was not one included as a housing cost, provided that there was a true liability. But the reference in sub-para.(6)(a) and (b) to meeting two lots of housing costs and the definition of "housing costs" in para.1(2) raise doubts. See sub-para.(7).

Of the three cases covered, one is fear of violence in the former home or by a former member of the family. This can continue as long as reasonable. The fear of violence leading to the claimant leaving the former home has to be directed against the claimant, not caused by him (*CIS 339/1993*). The second is where one of a couple is a full-time student or on a training course and the double expenditure is unavoidable. This can also continue as long as reasonable. The third is an unavoidable overlap of liability on moving home. What is unavoidable is a matter of fact. This can last for a maximum of four weeks, starting from the first day of the benefit week in which the moves occurs.

2.781 *CIS 543/1993* contains some useful guidance as to when head (a) will apply, although its particular facts were highly unusual. The claimant was a former police officer who had been convicted of conspiracy to murder but whose release was later ordered by the Home Secretary. On his release he went to live with his wife in a rented flat. They also owned a house in another part of the country which was let to tenants on an assured shorthold tenancy. The claimant had left this house through fear of violence from gangsters when he was on bail pending trial. The Commissioner points out that head (a) is not restricted to domestic violence and can apply in any case where one of the reasons for the claimant leaving the home was fear of violence in that home. It did not matter if in addition there was a fear of violence in places other than the home. But a fear of violence outside the home, even if in the vicinity of the home, would not suffice. Furthermore, the relevant leaving was the last one before the week to which head (a) might apply. Leaving in this context meant the ending of normal occupation of the home; it should be interpreted broadly as the circumstances of the departure might well be confused and distressing. Moreover, if a person had left, and was currently absent from, a home through fear of violence there, he *remained* absent for that reason, even if during an intervening period the absence was for a different reason (in this case imprisonment).

Although the claimant in this case was liable to make payments for two dwellings he did not have two lots of income support housing costs as his current accommodation was rented. The Commissioner states that in these circumstances the test in head (a) had to be interpreted as asking whether it was reasonable to meet housing costs for the former dwelling when another dwelling was currently occupied as the person's home. The question of reasonableness had to be determined at the date when the adjudicating authority was considering the issue (although what it was reasonable for the claimant to have done at the time could be relevant in deciding this question), and in the light of all the circumstances. These could include among other factors the length of absence, whether it was reasonable to expect the person to take steps to end the liability in respect of the former home (e.g. whether there was a hope of resuming occupation, whether it was practicable to end the liability, his current financial situation and means of support), and the extent to which the liability was in practice being met otherwise than through income support (in this case from the tenants' rent). The conclusion might be different in relation to different weeks.

Sub-paragraph (7): This is an important provision allowing a person in certain circumstances to be treated as occupying a dwelling as his home for up to four weeks before moving in. This may fill in some of the gaps in sub-para.(6). The decision can only be made once the claimant has moved in. Then the claimant can be treated as occupying the dwelling for up to four weeks before the date of the move. The delay in moving while there was a liability to make payments must have been reasonable and fall into one of the three categories set out in sub-para.(7)(c). The categories cover: (i) delay necessary for adaptations for disablement needs; (ii) delay waiting for "local welfare provision" (defined in reg.2(1) and see below) or while a social fund application is determined and a member of the family is aged under six, or is disabled (see para.1(3) and (4)), or the claimant's partner has reached "the qualifying age for state pension credit" (see below); or (iii) the move is from being a patient or in residential accommodation (see sub-para.(13)). 2.782

"The qualifying age for state pension credit" was 60 but from April 2010 has gradually risen in line with the staged increase in pensionable age for women until it reaches 65 in November 2018; note also that state pension age is to be increased to 66 for both men and women—this will start to rise from 65 in December 2018 to reach 66 by October 2020 (see s.1 of the Pensions Act 2011); between 2026 and 2028 it will rise to 67 (see s.26 of the Pensions Act 2014).

"Local welfare provision" is financial or other assistance under local schemes set up by the local authority (at the local authority's discretion) (in England) or by the devolved administrations (in Wales and Scotland). It replaces social fund community care grants and crisis loans which were abolished in April 2013.

On sub-para.(7)(c)(i) (delay necessary to adapt a dwelling to meet disablement needs), see *R (on the application of Mahmoudi) v London Borough of Lewisham* [2014] EWCA Civ 284; [2014] AACR 14 (which concerned reg.7(8)(c)(i) of the Housing Benefit Regulations 2006, the equivalent of sub-para.(7)(c)(i)). The claimant required kidney dialysis three times a week. He was living in damp accommodation which made it impossible for him to receive home dialysis. He was offered new accommodation, which he had to accept straight away, but could not move into it for three weeks, partly because it had to be cleaned and redecorated to minimise the risk of infection. His claim for housing benefit for his new home was refused on the ground that redecoration did not amount to "adapting" a dwelling to meet disablement needs, as held in *R(H) 4/07*. *R(H) 4/07* (followed in *Bury Metropolitan BC v* 2.783

DC (HB) [2011] UKUT 43 (AAC) and by Judge Mesher in this case, even though, if free from authority, he might have taken a different approach) had decided that "adapt" entailed a change to the fabric or structure of the dwelling and so did not encompass furnishing, carpeting or decorating. The Court of Appeal, however, after pointing out that the Oxford English Dictionary considers "adapt" to be synonymous with, among other things: "fit, adjust, make suitable (to or for)", stated:

> "[the] hypothesis [of reg.7(8)(c)(i)] is that something may have to be done in the dwelling "to meet the disablement needs" of the claimant or any member of his family . . . [it cannot] have been intended to exclude a disabled person who is kept out for two weeks while the dwelling is being decorated "to meet his disablement needs" but to include one who is kept out for the same period of time while the bathroom and kitchen are being refitted "to meet his disablement needs". Such a differentiation would lack a rational basis."

The question to be asked, therefore, is whether the process which the dwelling has undergone is a change that makes it more suitable for the needs of the disabled person.

Note that *Bury Metropolitan BC v DC (HB)* confirms that "disablement" in head (c)(i) includes both physical and mental disablement and "necessary" means reasonably required, rather than essential.

2.784 On the meaning of "moving in", see *R(H) 9/05*, discussed in the note to the definition of "*dwelling occupied as the home*" in reg.2(1). The Deputy Commissioner concluded that the claimant had moved in for the purposes of reg.5(6) of the Housing Benefit Regulations 1987 (the equivalent provision to sub-para.(7)) when through her agents she had removed all her furniture from her previous home and moved it into her new flat, even though she was not physically present because she was in hospital.

See para.6(6) of Sch.7 to the Claims and Payments Regulations.

2.785 *Sub-paragraphs (8)–(12)*: These deal with temporary absences from home. See also the definitions in sub-para.(13).

The primary rule is in sub-para.(10). Sub-paragraphs (11) and (12) deal with absences in special cases and there is a separate provision for absences due to trial periods in residential accommodation (sub-paras (8) and (9)).

If the reason for the absence changes, the rule governing absence for the latest reason will apply. The intention is that the absence will count from the first day the person left his own home, not the date the reason changed, except where the special rule for trial periods in residential accommodation applies.

2.786 *KdeS v London Borough of Camden (HB)* [2011] UKUT 457 (AAC), a case on the equivalent housing benefit provision, confirms that the temporary absence begins on and includes the day of departure (see also *CSH/499/2006, CH/2638/2006* and *CH/1237/2004*). Conversely, the day of return is to be excluded.

There are no linking rules for any of these provisions (see *R. v Penwith District Council Housing Benefit Review Board Ex p. Burt* (1990) 22 H.L.R. 292 on the equivalent housing benefit provisions). This means that provided the person returns to his own home for a period, he can be treated as occupying his own home for repeated 13 or, as the case may be, 52-week absences. As the rules do not specify any length of time for which the person must return to his own home, presumably a very short period (24 hours?) will suffice.

SK v South Hams DC [2010] UKUT 129 (AAC); [2010] AACR 40 concerned a student who was absent from his parental home to live in a hall of residence for terms of less than 13 weeks. Judge Mesher holds that for the purposes of reg.7(13), (16) and (17) of the Housing Benefit Regulations 2006 (the equivalent of sub-paras (10)–(12)) there is no underlying test of what is the normal home. If the conditions in these provisions are met, the person is deemed to occupy the dwelling as the home, cutting through the ordinary test of normal occupation in reg.7(1) (the equivalent of sub-para.(1)). Judge Mesher therefore did not entirely agree with the analysis accepted by Judge Williams in *Stroud DC v JG* [2009] UKUT 67 (AAC), reported as *R(H) 8/09*, (referred to below under "*Absences for certain reasons*") that the fundamental question was whether the student "normally occupied" the claimant's home as his home. However, this did not mean that he considered that the result in that case was wrong.

See also *LES v Horsham DC (HB)* [2013] UKUT 494 (AAC) (which also concerned reg.7(1), (13) and (16)–(17) of the Housing Benefit Regulations 2006). This applies para.19 of *R(H) 9/05* in holding that where a claimant is temporarily absent from the dwelling that she normally occupies as her home, she can only be treated as continuing to occupy that dwelling as her home if, and so long as, one of the provisions in reg.7 relating to temporary absences applies, but not otherwise. **2.787**

SK v South Hams DC also confirms that reg.7 can apply where the question of occupation by persons other than claimants is in issue. This will also hold good for para.3.

Absences for up to 13 weeks

Under sub-para.(10) a person is to be treated as occupying the home during any absence of up to 13 weeks. All three of heads (a)–(c) have to be satisfied (see the Northern Ireland decision *R1/91(IS)* and *R(IS) 17/93*). *CIS 613/1997* confirms that as long as all three conditions are satisfied a claimant will be entitled to the benefit of the rule for the first 13 weeks' absence, even if in the event his absence extends beyond that period. This decision also holds that although there is a difference in wording between the previous provision (para.4(8) of the former Sch.3) and sub-para.(10), their effect is the same. *CIS 508/1992* and *CIS 484/1993* hold that the intention to return in head (a) must be an unqualified one. It is not enough for the intention to be contingent on the outcome of an event (such as a partner's admission into the UK: *CIS 508/1992*, or the obtaining of employment: *CIS 484/1993*). A desire or wish to return is not sufficient; objectively return must be a realistic possibility (*CSHB/405/2005*). The same should apply to sub-para.(11) (see below). On the meaning of "return", see *R(H) 9/05*, discussed in the note to the definition of *"dwelling occupied as the home"* in reg.2(1). **2.788**

However, if the absence is likely to exceed 13 weeks, the person is not treated as occupying the home from the outset. Thus in *Torbay BC v RF (HB)* [2010] UKUT 7 (AAC); [2010] AACR 26 where the claimant's sentence following his conviction meant that he was likely to be in prison for 14–17 weeks, reg.7(13) of the Housing Benefit Regulations 2006 (the equivalent of sub-para.(10)) did not apply. Sub-para.(10) does not have the added degree of flexibility that sub-para.(11)(d), which refers to an absence "unlikely to exceed a period of 52 weeks or, in exceptional circumstances, [. . .] unlikely substantially to exceed that period", contains.

In *CB v Liverpool CC (HB)* [2015] UKUT 359 (AAC) the claimant was sentenced to prison on Wednesday February 26, 2014 and her Home Detention Curfew date (on which date she was released) was Thursday May 29, 2014. She was required to stay at her parents' home during the curfew hours but was in her own home throughout the day. It was accepted that she was no longer absent from her home from the date of her release on curfew. However, as she had been absent for 13 weeks and one day, reg.7(13) of the Housing Benefit Regulations 2006 did not assist her (the absence begins on and includes the day of departure, although the day of return is excluded (see *KdeS v London Borough of Camden (HB)* [2011] UKUT 457 (AAC) above)).

Absences for certain reasons

Sub-paragraphs (11) and (12) deal with absences for particular reasons. See *Torbay BC v RF (HB)* [2010] UKUT 7 (AAC); [2010] AACR 26 (a case on the equivalent housing benefit provision) which confirms that there must be a causal link between the reason for the absence from home and being within one of the specified categories of claimant in sub-para.(11)(c). Thus a claimant who was **2.789** serving a prison sentence following his conviction did not come within head (c)(iii) on the basis that he was receiving treatment for his Crohn's disease while in prison. This was because there was no connection between the reason for his absence and his undergoing medical treatment.

The people who can be treated as occupying the home during temporary absences of up to 52 weeks are listed in sub-para.(11)(c). They are: people remanded in custody pending trial or sentence, and those required as a condition of bail to live at an address away from "home" or in a bail hostel; patients; people (or whose partner, or dependant child, is) undergoing medical treatment or medically approved convalescence in the UK, or abroad (but not in residential accommodation (defined in sub-para.(13)(c))); people providing or receiving (but not in residential accommodation) medically approved care in the UK or abroad; people caring for a child whose parent or guardian is temporarily away from home in order to receive medical treatment or medically approved care; people in residential accommodation, other than on a trial basis; people on a training course (defined in sub-para.(13)(d)) in the UK or abroad; people in fear of violence who are not covered by sub-para.(6)(a); full-time students not covered by sub-paras (3) or (6)(b).

In relation to students, see *Stroud DC v JG* [2009] UKUT 67 (AAC), reported as *R(H)8/09*, which applies the equivalent housing benefit provision to head (c)(viii) and decides that a full-time student may still be normally residing with his parents (and thus a non-dependant) even though he is living in student accommodation during the term-time. However, note the analysis of sub-paras (10)–(12) in *SK v South Hams DC* discussed above, and see also *LES v Horsham DC (HB)*.

2.790 Several of the categories refer to "medically approved" care (or convalescence: head (iii)), which is defined in sub-para.(13)(a). According to DSS guidance, some kind of corroboration from a doctor (or nurse) will do, not necessarily in the form of a medical certificate or "fit note". There does not seem to be any restriction on who can provide the care.

A person in one of the categories in head (c) must also satisfy the conditions in heads (a), (b) and (d). Heads (a) and (b) are the same as heads (a) and (b) in sub-para.(10), except that the use of the word "while" in head (b) confirms that if there has been a letting, the person can satisfy sub-para.(11) when it terminates. On head (a), see *CIS 508/1992* and *CIS 484/1993* above. Under head (d), sub-para.(12) can apply where the absence is unlikely substantially to exceed 52 weeks and there are exceptional circumstances. Presumably a stay in hospital or other circumstances over which the person has no control (which were previously given as examples under the pre-April 1995 rule) should qualify.

In relation to head (d), see *CH 1237/2004* which concerned a claimant who was temporarily absent from her home through fear of violence. The Commissioner decides that the question of whether the absence is unlikely to exceed 52 weeks, or in exceptional circumstances unlikely to substantially exceed that period, in reg.5(8B)(d) of the Housing Benefit Regulations 1987 (the equivalent of head (d)) had to be assessed at the date the claimant left her home. Furthermore, whether she continued to satisfy the conditions in reg.5(8B) had to be judged on a week by week basis. The question whether the absence was unlikely to be longer than 52 weeks had to be assessed objectively; the claimant's belief was a factor in deciding, but was not determinative of, this issue.

2.791 *MR v Bournemouth BC (HB)* [2011] UKUT 284 (AAC) holds that reg.7(16)(c)(i) of the Housing Benefit Regulations 2006 (the equivalent of para.3(11)(c)(i)) applies to a person who has been remanded in custody pending trial or detained pending sentence, even if the person is simultaneously serving another prison sentence.

In *R. (Waite) v Hammersmith and Fulham LBC and Secretary of State for Social Security* [2002] EWCA Civ 482, a case on reg.5(8), (8B) and (8C) of the Housing Benefit Regulations 1987 (the equivalent of sub-paras (10)–(12)), the issue was whether the fact that the claimant, who had been released on licence from a sentence of detention at Her Majesty's Pleasure and then recalled to prison, was only entitled to 13 weeks' housing benefit, whereas a person held on remand awaiting trial (or sentence following conviction) was entitled for 52 weeks, violated art.14 ECHR taken with either art.8 or art.1 of Protocol 1. The Court of Appeal dismissed the appeal, holding that the claimant's position was not analogous to that of an unconvicted prisoner (or indeed a convicted prisoner held on remand awaiting sentence). He had been convicted and sentenced whereas an unconvicted person on remand had the presumption of innocence in his favour. Further, in the case of a convicted prisoner on remand he might only have been convicted of a relatively minor offence and not receive a long sentence. But even if this was wrong, the Court accepted that the discrimination between the two groups was justified.

See also *CH 4574/2003* which held that the then form of reg.5(8B)(c)(i) of the Housing Benefit Regulations 1987 (the equivalent of the then form of sub-para.(11)(c)(i)) did treat a person required as a condition of bail to live at a specified address away from "home" differently from a person who was required to live in a bail hostel but concluded that the difference in treatment was within the margin of judgment that was allowed to the legislature and so there was no breach of ECHR. Leave to appeal to the Court of Appeal was granted by the Commissioner on May 25, 2004 (under the name of *Walsh v Peterborough CC and Secretary of State for Work and Pensions*) but the appeal was dismissed by consent on February 11, 2005. However, the new form of sub-para.(11)(c)(i) introduced with effect from April 4, 2005 removed this discrimination (reg.5(8B)(d) of the Housing Benefit Regulations 1987 was similarly amended). The new form applies to a person who is required as a condition of bail to live at an address away from his home (sub-head (aa)) as well as a person required to live in a bail hostel (sub-head (bb)).

In *Obrey v Secretary of State for Work and Pensions* [2013] EWCA Civ 1584, a case on reg.7(16)–(17) of the Housing Benefit Regulations 2006 (the equivalent of sub-paras (11)–(12)), the claimants had been detained in hospital under s.3 of the Mental Health Act 1983 for more than 52 weeks. They contended that the 52 weeks' rule for the payment of housing benefit in reg.7(16)(c)(ii) and (17) unlawfully discriminated against them as mental health patients, and in particular as mental health patients detained under s.3, because detained mental health patients are more likely than other hospital patients to be resident in hospital for more than 52 weeks. The Court of Appeal, however, confirmed the decision of Judge Lloyd-Davies in *SSWP and Warwick DC v WO, JS and JS (CTB)* [2012] UKUT 489 (AAC) that, although the 52 weeks' rule did indirectly discriminate against the mentally ill in breach of art.14, read with art.1 Prot. 1, ECHR, the discrimination was justified as it did not meet the "manifestly without reasonable foundation" test (see *Humphreys v Revenue and Customs Commissioners* [2012] UKSC 18; [2012] AACR 46). The Court of Appeal found that there was no error of law in the Upper Tribunal's decision, emphasising that: 2.792

> "18. . . . the question whether the indirectly discriminatory effect of a particular rule in the benefits system because it does not distinguish between mental patients and other patients in hospital, is, or is not, "manifestly without reasonable foundation" is . . . precisely the kind of issue that is best left for evaluation and judgment by a specialist appellate tribunal with a particular expertise in the field of social security law. . . ."

Absences for trial period in residential accommodation

Sub-paragraphs (8) and (9) apply where a person has gone into residential accommodation (defined in sub-para.(13)(c)) for a trial period with the intention of returning to his own home if the accommodation proves unsuitable. If the person has entered the home for the purpose of, e.g. respite care, or convalescence, the 52 weeks rule, not this one, should apply (see sub-para.(11)(c)(ix)). There will obviously be some grey areas here; as was pointed out to SSAC in the course of their consultation on these rules, the reason given for entry into 2.793

a residential home may well vary depending on who is asked. Note that, in this case, unlike absences covered by sub-paras (10) and (11), the person does not have to intend to return home within a specified period. He will be treated as occupying his home during the first 13 weeks of the absence, starting with the day he first goes into the residential accommodation (not the date his absence from home begins) even if it is likely at the outset that he will be away for longer. Furthermore, in *Secretary of State for Work and Pensions v Selby DC* [2006] EWCA Civ 721, reported as *R(H) 4/06*, a case on reg.5(7B) and (7C) of the Housing Benefit Regulations 1987 (the equivalent of sub-paras (8) and (9)), the Court of Appeal held that, provided that an intention to return home if the care home proves unsuitable is present at the time the claimant enters the care home, if he then decides not to return and gives notice to quit his old home, he can still be treated as occupying his old home under the deeming provision in reg.5(7C) (the equivalent of sub-para.(9)) until the end of the 13-week period or the expiry of the notice to quit, whichever is the shorter. There is no limit on the number of times sub-paras (8) and (9) can apply, so a person will be able to try out different homes. But the 13 weeks is subject to a maximum of 52 weeks for that period of absence. So, for example, if the person has been in hospital for 40 weeks before going into a residential home for a trial period, he will only be treated as occupying his own home for a further 12 weeks.

Paragraph 4—housing costs not met

2.794 *Sub-paragraph (1)*: This excludes housing benefit expenditure and payment of housing costs if a person is in a care home, Abbeyfield Home or independent hospital (for the definitions of these terms see reg.2(1)). But if the person in a care home, Abbeyfield Home or independent hospital is only temporarily absent from his home see para.3(8)–(12) as to when he can continue to receive housing costs for his home.

Sub-paragraphs (2)–(12) contain the restriction on payment of interest on loans taken out while income support, or, from October 7, 1996, income-based JSA (see reg.32 of the Income Support (General) (Jobseeker's Allowance Consequential Amendments) Regulations 1996, p.807), or, from October 27, 2008, income-related ESA is being claimed (or a person is caught by the linking rule; from October 6, 2003 note the effect of para.14(14) where the claimant's former partner was entitled to state pension credit) which was first introduced on May 2, 1994 (see para.5A of the former Sch.3). It stemmed from the Government's concern about possible "upmarketing" at the expense of the benefit system, although no figures were produced as to the numbers of people said to have been exploiting income support by taking on bigger mortgages while on benefit. There may be many reasons why a claimant needs to take out or increase a loan while in receipt of income support (or income-based JSA or income-related ESA) which have nothing to do with "upmarketing". Some, but by no means all, of these are catered for by the limited exceptions in sub-paras (8)–(11). Furthermore, as the Social Security Advisory Committee pointed out (Cmnd. 2537(1994)), "not only has it been Government policy to encourage home ownership, but . . . the rented sector is unable to meet the demands placed on it".

Note the similar rules for state pension credit (see para.5 of Sch.2 to the State Pension Credit Regulations).

2.795 *Sub-paragraph (2)*: This provision contains the basic rule. Note that the restriction now only applies to loans (or money borrowed under a hire purchase agreement) for house purchase. Before October 2, 1995 it also applied to *some* loans for repairs and improvements. (See *CIS 14141/1996* which decides that para.5A of the former Sch.3 was not invalid on the ground of irrationality, even though it had the unfair and absurd result of treating claimants with identical needs for housing costs differently. The Commissioner holds that para.5A did prevent claimants with no previous housing costs for loan interest from receiving housing costs for new loans for repairs and improvements, but not claimants who had been receiving housing costs for loan interest.)

Sub-paragraph (2) states that a loan for house purchase will not be eligible if it has been incurred during "the relevant period" (see sub-paras (4)–(5)), and: (i) after October 1, 1995, (ii) after May 2, 1994 and the loan interest was not met under the former para.5A in the 26 weeks before October 2, 1995, or (iii) between April 3, and October 1, 1995 when the person was not entitled to income support but he or his partner became entitled after October 1, 1995 and was entitled within the previous 26 weeks, unless interest on the loan was being met before October 2, 1995 (see sub-para.(3)). (The purpose of heads (b) and (c) of sub-para.(2) is presumably to catch loans which might otherwise escape restriction because the new form of Sch.3 was not retrospective.) But in the case of replacement loans the restriction will only apply to the extent of any increase in the amount loaned (see sub-para.(6)).

When is a loan incurred in this context? For example, if a further advance is added to a person's existing mortgage does this constitute incurring a loan, or is it merely increasing a loan that has already been incurred? (It may be that it is the former that is intended; cf. sub-para.(6) which catches increases in the amount borrowed in the case of replacement loans.) Will the restriction apply where the terms of an existing mortgage are varied rather than a new agreement entered into (as may happen, e.g. where a couple separate and one member takes over the whole mortgage for which they were previously jointly and severally liable)? In those circumstances it would certainly seem arguable that the loan was incurred when the mortgage was first taken out, not when its terms were changed. It should also be noted that it is the date that the loan was incurred that counts, not the date that the person became liable to meet (see para.2) the housing costs.

The question when a loan is incurred within the meaning of sub-para.(2) was one **2.796**
of the issues in *Secretary of State for Work and Pensions v Mohammed* [2011] EWCA Civ 1358; [2012] AACR 29 (see below under the note to para.15). The Court rejected the argument that a loan could in some circumstances be "taken out" for the purposes of para.15(1) at a different time from when it was "incurred" for the purposes of sub-para.(2).

In *R(IS) 5/01* the Commissioner applies *CIS 2978/1995* in holding that where a claimant came under a legal obligation to pay for a property (as would happen when contracts were exchanged) and the only practical way of doing so was to take up the offer of a loan, in reliance on which the obligation was undertaken, the loan had been incurred at the time that legal obligation arose. Thus since the completion of the purchase of the new property was on May 10, 1994, it was likely that contracts had been exchanged (and the loan incurred) before the restriction on loans taken out while on income support came into force on May 2, 1994. (But apparently exchange and completion did in fact take place on the same day; the claimant appealed to the Court of Appeal on another point, but his appeal was dismissed (*Saleem v Secretary of State for Social Security*, reported as part of *R(IS) 5/01*), see the note to sub-para.(10) below.)

The restriction only applies to loans taken out by the claimant or a member of his family during the claimant's current entitlement to income support or income-related ESA or a period of non-entitlement included in "the relevant period" by the operation of sub-para.(4). Note sub-paras (4A) and (5). Note also reg.32 of the Income Support (General) (Jobseeker's Allowance Consequential Amendments) Regulations 1996 (see p.807), the effect of which is that entitlement to income-based JSA will count as entitlement to income support. Although sub-para.(2) does not specifically limit the period during which the loan will not qualify to the claimant's current claim (and any linked period), it is understood that this is the intention. Sub-paragraph (2) does refer to "the" (not "a") relevant period. Moreover, any other interpretation would have a draconian effect. Thus if entitlement to income support/income-related ESA/income-based JSA ceases for more than 26 weeks, the claimant should be paid the full amount of his loan interest (at the standard rate: see para.12) if he makes a further claim (subject to the waiting period (para.8(1)) and the ceiling on loans (para.11(5)). In addition loans taken out *before* a claimant or his partner claimed income support, income-related ESA or income-based JSA are not caught (subject to the 26-week linking rule). However, note CPC/3226/2005, a case on para.5(4) of Sch.II to the State Pension Credit Regulations (the equivalent of sub-para.(4)), which holds that a loan was incurred during the relevant period where state pension credit was retrospectively awarded to include the date that the loan was taken out, even though it had been taken out before the claim for state pension credit was made. *CPC/3226/2005* is applied in *CIS/88/2008* (by the same Commissioner) and *CPC/3992/2007*. There are exceptions in sub-paras (7)–(11).

2.797 *Sub-paragraphs (4) and (5)*: Periods of entitlement to income support, income-related ESA (or income-based JSA: reg.32 of the Income Support (General) (Jobseeker's Allowance Consequential Amendments) Regulations 1996, see p.807, assuming that this rule can be interpreted as a "requirement" that the person is, or has been, entitled to income support: see reg.32(a)) separated by 26 weeks or less are treated as continuous for the purposes of sub-para.(2). So a loan taken out during a period of 26 weeks or less that falls between two periods of entitlement to income support/income-related ESA/income-based JSA will be subject to the restriction. The 26 weeks is much more stringent than the normal linking rule (now 12 weeks: see para.14(1)). There is also no provision for the restriction to cease to apply if there is a major change of circumstances.

R(IS) 2/09 rejects the argument that a loan was not incurred in a relevant period in a case where the claimant had reclaimed income support within 26 weeks but because of other income was not entitled unless housing costs were added to his applicable amount. The Commissioner held that in order to apply sub-para.(4) sensibly it had to be read as if it began:

> "The 'relevant period' for the purposes of this paragraph is any period during which the person to whom the loan was made (a) is *or would but for paragraph (2) above be* entitled to income support".

However, a period in respect of which a previous claim had been made but disallowed was not a period of "entitlement". Therefore the claimant was not caught by para.4 when he made a further fresh claim more than 26 weeks after his original entitlement to income support had ended. The Commissioner confirms that it was necessary (and sufficient) for the claimant to make a fresh claim for income support after the 26-week gap had elapsed.

Note sub-para.(4B) which clarifies that if a person is treated as being in receipt of income support by virtue of the linking rules in para.14, this does not mean that he is to be treated as entitled to income support for the purposes of sub-para.(4).

2.798 The effect of sub-para.(4) is that if a couple who are entitled to income support, income-related ESA or income-based JSA separate, the restriction will also apply to the partner who was not the claimant if s/he claims income support, income-related ESA or income-based JSA within 26 weeks.

See also sub-para.(4A), the effect of which is that any period which the claimant or his partner spent on a New Deal option for 18–24-year-olds or in the Intensive Activity Period (note that these schemes are no longer offered), during which he (or his partner) was in remunerative work or had an income that was too high to qualify for income support counts as part of the relevant period. Thus even though the claimant (or his partner) may not have been entitled to income support (or income-based JSA) for 26 weeks because the claimant (or his partner) was taking part in this kind of New Deal option, or activity, this will not break the running of any relevant period for the purposes of sub-para.(4).

2.799 *Sub-paragraph (6)*: This will cover the situation where a person moves, or remortgages his home, when only the increase in the amount loaned will be caught by sub-para.(2). Under head (a) the replaced loan must have qualified under para.15 during the relevant period (defined in sub-para.(4); note para.(4A)). The inclusion of the words "during the relevant period" from October 7, 1996 is significant, since sub-para.(2) treats a loan that would otherwise qualify under para.15 because of its purpose as not doing so if it was incurred during the relevant period and at any of the times specified in sub-para.(2). Head (b) was also amended on October 7, 1996. The previous form (see the 1996 edition of J. Mesher and P. Wood, *Income-related Benefits: the Legislation*) was potentially quite wide as it merely required that a previous loan (or loans: ss.6(c) and 23(1) of the Interpretation Act 1978) that was secured on another property had been wholly or partly repaid. So it seemed that the earlier loan could, for example, have been for business purposes, or one that was not eligible under sub-para.(2). But under the new form the loan that has been repaid has to be one that qualified under paras 15 or 16 during the relevant period (although there is no requirement that it was a secured loan). It does not seem to be necessary for the repaying of the earlier loan and the taking out of the new to be connected in time. See *R(IS) 20/98* which confirms that the fact that there was a gap (of over two years) between paying off the old mortgage and taking out the new larger one did not remove the claimant's entitlement to housing costs to the extent met on the original mortgage. This was a decision on para.5A(3) of the former Sch.3 (see J. Mesher and P. Wood, *Income-related Benefits: the Legislation* (1995 edition)) but the position should be the same under sub-para.(6). Under the former para.5A(3) and (7), if the claimant (or a member of the family) received housing benefit during the gap, it seemed that interest payments could be restricted to the amount of housing benefit payable in the intervening period, even if the second home was cheaper than the first. But this will not be the case under sub-para.(6). If there is no increase (or even a decrease) in the amount of the claimant's new loan, the restriction will not apply, whether or not the claimant receives housing benefit in the intervening period. Sub-paragraph (8) may, however, come into play in cases where sub-para.(2) does bite and the claimant received housing benefit during the gap.

In *AH v SSWP (IS)* [2010] UKUT 353 (AAC) the claimant's husband had taken out a mortgage to purchase their home in his sole name. After he left she claimed income support and then took out a mortgage that was used to repay her husband's mortgage. Judge Ovey points out that para.15 is concerned solely with the purpose for which the loan was taken out. It does not contain any requirement as to the person by whom the loan was taken out or that housing costs were payable in respect of the loan. The result was that the claimant was entitled to housing costs under sub-para.(6)(a) to the extent that her loan was used to discharge the part of her husband's mortgage that had been taken out to purchase the home.

Thus the effect of sub-para.(6) would seem to be that if a couple who are in receipt of income support, income-related ESA or income-based JSA separate, and the former home is sold each partner will be entitled to interest on a loan up to the previous amount (i.e. each would receive interest on a £30,000 loan if that was the amount of the loan they had as a couple). *CIS 11293/1995* decides that this was the position under the previous rule in para.5A(3) of the former Sch.3. The claimant was jointly and severally liable with her ex-husband for a mortgage of £18,000 on the home in which she lived. She was awarded housing costs on £9,000 only. She then sold that house and moved to a new home which she purchased with a mortgage of £18,000 (the old mortgage having been paid off). The Commissioner holds that she was entitled to interest on £18,000 because the "new liability" under para.5A(3) did not exceed the "former liability". It was the claimant's legal liability that was material, not what had actually been paid as income support housing costs, and she had potentially been liable for all the interest on the original mortgage. The Commissioner disagrees with *CIS 5353/1995* which considered that housing costs were only "applicable" under para.5A(3) if they had actually been met; in his view "applicable" in para.5A(3) meant "potentially applicable". The comparison in sub-para.(6) is between the amount of the old and new *loans*, which wording would seem to achieve the same result as in *CIS 11293/1995*. But if one member of the couple buys a new property without the former matrimonial home being sold, sub-para.(2) will apply and the loan will not be eligible (unless it involved some remortgaging and so sub-para.(6)(a) applies). A new (or increased, but see the note to sub-para.

(2) for discussion of when a loan is incurred) loan to buy out the other partner's share will not be met if it is taken out during the relevant period. If the couple were not in receipt of income support (or income-based JSA or income-related ESA), the restriction will not apply if the loan for the new property, or to buy out the other partner's share, is taken out before a claim for income support (or income-based JSA or income-related ESA) is made (subject to the 26-week linking rule and any backdating of the income support (or income-based JSA or income-related ESA) award: see *CPC/3226/2005*, *CIS/88/2008* and *CPC/3992/2007* referred to above.

2.800 *Sub-paragraph (8)*: A person receiving housing benefit who buys a home will be paid housing costs but only up to the level of the housing benefit payable in the week before the purchase, together with any amount for housing costs that he was being paid that week. *CIS 4712/2002* holds that "payable" in sub-para.(b)(i) referred to entitlement, rather than to the amount actually paid in the week before the purchase. However, the Commissioner added that it was not for the tribunal to determine the level of entitlement but it was for the parties to produce evidence of the correct figure to the tribunal.

Sub-paragraph (8) covers tenants who buy their own homes as well as those receiving housing benefit who move into owner occupation. There can be an increase in the restricted level equivalent to any subsequent increase in the standard rate (*not* the claimant's actual rate) or in housing costs that are eligible under para.17. But there is no provision for subsequent reductions. So if the standard rate is later lowered or the para.17 housing costs reduce, a claimant can continue to enjoy the partial relief from restriction due to the previous increase (*R(IS) 8/94*). If the housing costs fall below the restricted level the amount payable will be the lower figure (*R(IS) 8/94*).

No reference is made to loans under para.16. Does this mean that if sub-para.(8) applies, no payment will be made for loans for repairs and improvements? This would seem unfair and also illogical in view of the exclusion of para.16 loans from the restriction in sub-para.(2). It is understood that it is not the DSS's intention to preclude payment for loans for repairs and improvements taken out by people covered by sub-para.(8) (or sub-para.(11) where the same point arises). The DSS take the view that because sub-para.(2) only relates to para.15 loans these provisions do not affect para.16 loans at all.

2.801 *Sub-paragraph (9)*: If the loan is taken out, or increased, to acquire a home to meet the needs of a disabled person, this is exempt from restriction under sub-para.(2) (although the excessive housing costs rule (para.13) and the ceiling on loans in para.11(5) could, depending on the amount of the loan, apply). See para.1(3) and (4) for who counts as a disabled person. This provision should cover people wanting to move into sheltered accommodation. Note that the new accommodation only has to be more suited to the needs of the disabled person; there is no requirement that it has been specifically adapted for that person's needs (*CIS 16250/1996*). The disabled person does not have to be a member of the claimant's family, or to have previously lived with the claimant. However, he does have to qualify as a disabled person at the time the loan is taken out (*R(IS) 20/98*).

The scope of this provision is discussed in *CIS/14551/1996*, and again more recently in *R(IS) 12/08* (see para.47 of that decision for a useful summary of the authorities on the test in sub-para.(9)). In *CIS/14551/1996* the Commissioner points out that the fact that new accommodation is more suited to the special needs of the disabled person only has to be a reason for its acquisition, not the sole or predominant reason; moreover, the test is whether the new accommodation is more suited, not whether it was reasonable to acquire it. Further, the person's overall mental and physical condition had to be taken into account, not just the condition that triggered the application of the definition of "disabled person". But the person's needs had to stem from a specific disease or bodily or mental disablement to count under this paragraph. The claimant had contended that part of the reason for moving was to alleviate mental stress caused by financial worries. The Commissioner accepts that, for example, moving to smaller or more compact accommodation that is less expensive to heat, or to accommodation that is nearer to a person who can look after the claimant so as to reduce that person's travelling expenses, could come within this provision. But it was the accommodation itself that had to be more suited, not the terms of its acquisition, so moving simply in order to reduce mortgage liability, or so as to take advantage of the exemption from restriction under this provision, would not be covered. Nor was moving so that the claimant, his wife and daughter were no longer living in his son's house on a grace and favour basis (*MA v SSWP (SPC)* [2013] UKUT 593 (AAC) (a case on the equivalent state pension credit provision)). The move did not render the new accommodation "more suited to the special needs of a disabled person", as the psychological benefits of a move to a home of one's own are not restricted to disabled people but are universal. However, wider social issues, such as better access to local health care services or closer proximity to family members providing care and support may make the accommodation more suitable (see *CIS/16250/1996*).

In *CIS/3382/2006* sub-para.(9) did not apply where the move was to suit the broader needs of the household generally rather than those of the disabled person; the new house was in fact impossible for him to live in until extensive work had been carried out to put it in a fit condition.

In *CIS 3295/2003* the claimant had moved to the property over a year before she **2.802**
acquired ownership of it. The Commissioner points out that there are no time limits in sub-para.(9), and in particular no requirement of immediacy linking the time of acquisition, the time the loan is taken out, and the time the claimant moves to the property. He states that what is required for sub-para.(9) to apply is: (i) that alternative accommodation is acquired; (ii) that it is more suited to the special needs of the disabled person than the accommodation occupied by that person before the acquisition; and (iii) that the loan was taken out to acquire the accommodation. Thus whether sub-para.(9) applies is ultimately a matter of fact.

In *Ahmed v Secretary of State for Work and Pensions* [2011] EWCA Civ 1186; [2012] AACR 23 the tribunal had relied on *CIS/3295/2003*, in the words of the Court of Appeal to "almost [ignore] the need for any connection between the move, the loan and the acquisition at all". The facts in *Ahmed* were that the claimant, whose son was severely disabled, had moved to her current home in 2001, having previously lived in Old Trafford. After renting the property for six years, in 2007, while in receipt of income support, she purchased it with the aid of an interest only mortgage. It was accepted that her current home was more suited to her son's special needs than the house in which she had lived in Old Trafford. The tribunal decided that the fact that the claimant had occupied the property for some six years before she acquired it did not prevent the application of sub-para.(9). However, Judge Lloyd-Davies overturned the tribunal's decision, stating:

> "I accept that the acquisition, loan and move do not need to be contemporaneous but there does, however, in my judgment have to be a link between them ... in truth what happened in the present case was not that the loan was taken out for the acquisition of alternative more suitable accommodation but that the loan was taken out for the purposes of the acquisition of the existing, already suitable, accommodation."

The Court of Appeal agreed with Judge Lloyd-Davies. While there may be cases where there is a gap between leaving the first accommodation and the acquisition of the more suitable accommodation that do fall within sub-para.(9), the Court considered that what the Commissioner had said in *CIS/3295/2003* should be approached with considerable care. It was necessary on a true construction of the paragraph to find some link between the move, the loan and the acquisition. The required link did not exist in this case.

2.803 Thus *CIS/3295/2003* may still apply, depending on the facts of a particular case, but only if the necessary link is shown.

What if there is simply a gap before the move to the new property (rather than between the move to, and the acquisition of, the new property)? In *MA v SSWP (SPC)* [2013] UKUT 593 (AAC) the claimant, his wife and daughter (all of whom fell within the definition of "disabled person") had lived in his son's house for 22 months before purchasing a new home in the same street as the son's house. The accommodation in the new property was physically much the same as in the son's house. It was argued that the correct comparator was the property in which the claimant had lived before moving in with his son (it had originally been intended he would live with his son on a temporary basis only). Judge Gray, however, holds that a gap of 22 months between leaving the comparator property and the acquisition of the new home was too long for the purposes of para.5(10) of Sch.II to the State Pension Credit Regulations 2002 (the equivalent of sub-para.(9)). The correct comparator was therefore the son's house and the test in para.5(10) was not met. But it will depend on the facts and in other circumstances a temporary move to intermediate accommodation may not preclude the application of sub-para.(9) (as Judge Gray herself states).

Sub-paragraph (9) only applies to loans to purchase a home. A loan taken out to adapt a home to meet the needs of a disabled person will be eligible under para.16 (see para.16(2)(k) and note para.11(9)).

The fact that sub-para.(9) only applies where the claimant *acquires* alternative accommodation more suited to the needs of a disabled person and not where the claimant does not move because of the state of health of the disabled person but remortgages to buy out her ex-husband is not contrary to art.14, read with art.1 Prot.1 of the ECHR (*CL v SSWP (IS)* [2015] UKUT 259 (AAC)—see further the note to para.15).

2.804 *Sub-paragraph (10)*: Increased loans taken out because of a need to move to provide separate sleeping accommodation for people of different sexes aged 10 or over but under 20 who live with the claimant and for whom the claimant or the claimant's partner is responsible (for the meaning of "responsible"—see reg.15) are exempt (although the ceiling on loans in para.11(5) and the excessive housing costs rule (para.13) could apply). Note the change in wording from November 17, 2008. Before that date the exemption only applied in the case of a need to move in order to provide separate sleeping accommodation for male and female *children* aged 10 or over who were members of the claimant's family. As a child is a person under 16 (see s.137 SSCBA), this was ambiguous because a family could include a "qualifying young person" (i.e. a person up to the age of 20). It had prompted the Commissioner in *CIS/1390/2007* to comment that it might be necessary for "child" in sub-para.(10)(b) to be given a broader meaning than a person under 16. It seems that heed was taken of that comment.

See *CIS 14657/1996* in which the Commissioner points out that the need to provide separate sleeping accommodation for people of different sexes aged 10 or over may exist before all the people involved reach 10. Action may have to be taken earlier to secure that result by the time those people become 10. However, where the move was more than five years before the relevant person became 10 it could not be said that the need to provide separate sleeping accommodation currently existed; in addition the need was too remote to say that it was the sole reason for the move (*CIS/1390/2007*). On the issue of the timing of the loan see further the decisions discussed in the note to para.16(2) under "*Separate sleeping accommodation*".

CIS/1068/2003 emphasises that there must be a need for separate accommodation. *R(IS) 5/01* considered the meaning of the phrase "solely by reason of" in sub-para.(10)(b). In the Commissioner's view, providing separate sleeping accommodation for older children of opposite sexes was not likely to be the only reason but one of a number of reasons for choosing the particular new home. It was therefore necessary to look primarily at the reasons for moving. However, the tribunal in that case had been entitled to conclude that the main reason for moving was to acquire space generally. The claimant's appeal against this decision was dismissed (*Saleem v Secretary of State for Social Security*, reported as part of *R(IS) 5/01*). The Court agreed with the Commissioner that it was necessary to focus on the reason for the change of home. Paragraph (10)(b) would not apply if the operative reason for the change was other than to provide separate sleeping accommodation for people of different sexes aged 10 or over. However, the Court did accept that if this was the sole reason for the change, the fact that the new home brought other advantages would not prevent para.(10)(b) from applying. The Court also rejected an argument that the provision was ultra vires on the ground of irrationality.

Sub-paragraph (11): Claimants who were only receiving para.17 housing costs before they purchased their home will have their loan interest met up to the level of their previous housing costs. The rule is similar to that for claimants previously in receipt of housing benefit in sub-para.(8). The restricted level can be increased for subsequent increases in the standard rate or in para.17 housing costs (see the notes to sub-para.(8)). **2.805**

Sub-paragraph (12): This reads "The following provisions of this Schedule shall have effect subject to the provisions of this paragraph". *R(IS) 1/07* confirms that this does not have the effect that the restrictions on meeting housing costs contained in subsequent paragraphs of Sch.3, e.g. the £100,000 ceiling in para.11(5), do not apply in a case where the claimant falls within any of the provisions in sub-paras (8)–(11). As *CIS/5327/1998* had explained, those sub-paragraphs contain exceptions to the normal exclusion under para.(2) of loans taken out by a person while entitled to income support (or income-related ESA or income-based JSA) or caught by the linking rule. They are not concerned with defining or quantifying the amount of housing costs to be met in those special cases, which is dealt with under the normal rules for computation to be found elsewhere in the Schedule. That is made clear by the reference in sub-para.(7) (which introduces the provisions in sub-paras (8)–(11)) to "additional limitations". In other words, any special limitations imposed by sub-paras (8)–(11) are to be in addition to whatever limitations otherwise apply in any case in determining the amount of housing costs allowable. **2.806**

Paragraph 5—Apportionment of housing costs

Sub-paragraph (1): This allows the expenditure on premises used for mixed purposes (e.g. business and domestic) to be apportioned and the part attributable to a private dwelling met (subject to the limit in para.11(7)). Where the "composite hereditament" existed before the community charge came into force the apportionment follows the rateable value of each part of the premises (sub-para.(1)). Where the composite hereditament comes into existence after the advent of the community charge, the apportionment is to follow the current market value of each part (sub-paras (2)–(4)) **2.807**

On the application of sub-paras (1) and (2) see *CIS 2024/1998.*

Sub-paragraph (5): In *R(IS) 19/95* the Commissioner holds that "responsible" at the end of sub-para.(5) did not mean legally responsible (as it did elsewhere in the Schedule), but referred to the proportion of the shared responsibility that a claimant was actually paying. The claimant was jointly and severally liable with her ex-husband under the terms of the mortgage but only paid half the mortgage interest. She was only entitled to housing costs for the amount she actually paid. **2.808**

Where para.5 applies, the effect of para.11(7) is that the ceiling on loans is applied to the eligible part of the loan.

Paragraph 6—Existing housing costs

2.809 Paragraph 6 was omitted with effect from April 1, 2016 due to the introduction of a single waiting period for housing costs of 39 weeks for new claims made on or after April 1, 2016 (subject to a saving provision—see under "*Waiting period for new claims made on or after April 1, 2016*" above). As a consequence, the distinction between "existing housing costs" and "new housing costs" was abolished for such claims.

See the notes to para.6 in the 2015/16 edition of this volume for the details of this provision and when it applied.

Paragraph 7—Transitional protection

2.810 Paragraph 7, which provided transitional protection on the introduction of the October 1995 changes to housing costs, was omitted with effect from April 1, 2016. See the notes to para.7 in the 2015/16 edition of this volume for the details of this provision and when it applied.

Further transitional protection

2.811 However, the additional transitional protection for existing (i.e. as at October 1, 1995) claimants in reg.3 of the Income Support (General) Amendment and Transitional Regulations 1995 (see p.804) remains. Interest on arrears of interest, on loans for non-approved purposes or for repairs and improvements that are no longer eligible that was included in a claimant's applicable amount for income support on October 1, 1995 will continue to be met for as long as the claimant continues to satisfy the conditions of paras 7(6), 7(7) or 8(1)(a) of the former Sch.3 (see the 1995 edition of J. Mesher and P. Wood, *Income-related Benefits: the Legislation*) and be in, or treated as in, receipt of income support (and/or, from October 7, 1996, income-based JSA: reg.32 of the Income Support (General) (Jobseeker's Allowance Consequential Amendments) Regulations 1996, see p.807). Note reg.3(3) which provides that only the linking rules in para.14(1)(a), (c) and (e) will apply in these cases. Since the effect of reg.3(2) is to treat these three categories as eligible housing costs under para.15 or 16, the protection in reg.3 operates separately from the transitional protection in para.7 (which was revoked on April 1, 2016) and is not affected by it.

In *Ewens v Secretary of State for Social Security*, reported as *R(IS) 8/01*, the Court held (disagreeing with the Commissioner) that under para.7(7) of the former Sch.3 it was not necessary for the claimant: (i) to have been occupying the dwelling as her home when the non-approved loan was first secured on the dwelling (agreeing with *CIS 450/1993*), or (ii) to have continuously lived in the home after her partner had left. What was required for para.7(7) to apply was that: (a) a non-approved loan, e.g. for business purposes) had been secured on the home (it was immaterial whether either the claimant or her partner were living there at the time); (b) the former partner had lived in the dwelling at some point but had since left; (c) the former partner was not meeting the interest on the loan; and (d) that the claimant was living there when she claimed income support and had to meet the loan in order to continue doing so.

On para.7(6) of the former Sch.3, which allowed interest on arrears of interest to be met in certain circumstances, note *CIS 8166/1995*. The Commissioner decides that for the former para.7(6)(c) to apply it was not necessary for the mortgage to specifically stipulate that the liability to make payments had been deferred for at least two years. It was sufficient for the terms of the mortgage to result in there being a deferral period of at least two years.

2.812 *CSIS 162/1996* deals with the relationship between the transitional protection in para.7 (revoked on April 1, 2016) and in reg.3 and the question whether the claimant had an applicable amount for housing costs in the week including October 1, 1995. The claimant had been in receipt of income support, including an amount for interest on a loan for repairs and improvements under para.8 of the former Sch.3, until September 20, 1995. He then obtained work but reclaimed income support on

October 23, 1995 when his employment ended. His housing costs were calculated under para.16 which resulted in a lower award than on his original claim. But the Commissioner holds that reg.3 applied so that the claimant was entitled to have his housing costs met in accordance with the former para.8. The Commissioner's reasoning was as follows. The claimant fell to be treated as in receipt of income support during the period September 20 to October 23, 1995 under the linking rule in para.14(1)(a)(ii). Since he was to be treated as being in receipt of income support he must also be regarded as being entitled to income support. Consequently he had a "benefit week" in each of the weeks in the gap in his income support claim within the meaning of para.4 of Sch.7 to the Claims and Payments Regulations (see the definition of "benefit week" in reg.2(1)) because he was sufficiently "entitled" to a social security benefit. He also had an applicable amount in those weeks because if a person is to be treated as entitled to, and in receipt of, income support in any particular week, his applicable amount can be ascertained in accordance with Pt IV in the normal way. The Commissioner also considered that the transitional protection in reg.3 applied in this case, rather than that in para.7. This was because reg.3 dealt with the particular situation at issue in this case, whereas para.7 was a general provision and operated only where no specific provision applied. The result was that the claimant's income support was not subject to diminution of any "add back" which would have been the case if para.7 had applied. Instead his housing costs would continue to be met in accordance with the former para.8 as long as he remained in, or treated as in, receipt of income support. The Department appealed against this decision to the Court of Session but the appeal was later withdrawn.

Note also the transitional protection in relation to housing costs for claimants transferring from income support to JSA in reg.87(4)–(6) of and para.18 of Sch.2 to the JSA Regulations 1996. For the transitional protection in relation to housing costs for claimants transferring from income support (or income-based JSA or state pension credit) to income-related ESA, see paras 12(11)–(12) and 20 of Sch.6 to the ESA Regulations 2008 in Vol.1 in this series.

Paragraph 8—Housing costs

Note the restriction on house purchase loans incurred while entitled to income support, income-related ESA or income-based JSA (see reg.32 of the Income Support (General) (Jobseeker's Allowance Consequential Amendments) Regulations 1996 (p.807)), or while a person is caught by the linking rule in para.4(2)–(12) as well as the limits imposed under paras 11(5) and 13. In relation to the cap on loans in para.11(5) note the increased limit that has been introduced for certain claimants by the Social Security (Housing Costs Special Arrangements) (Amendment and Modification) Regulations 2008 (SI 2008/3195), as amended by the Social Security (Housing Costs Special Arrangements) (Amendment) Regulations 2009 (SI 2009/3257) (see the note on these Regulations under "*Modifications to the waiting periods and the cap on loans for certain claimants from January 5, 2009*" and "*Further Modifications from January 5, 2010*" above). 2.813

Before April 1, 2016 the modifications made by the 2008 Special Arrangements Regulations, as amended, included a single waiting period for housing costs of 13 weeks. However, the parts of those Regulations that related to the waiting period were revoked on April 1, 2016, subject to a saving provision—see under "*Waiting period for new claims made on or after April 1, 2016*" above. In addition, this Schedule (and Sch.2 to the JSA Regulations 1996 and Sch. 6 to the ESA Regulations 2008) were amended with effect from April 1, 2016 to remove the distinction between "existing" and "new" housing costs and to provide for a single waiting period for housing costs of 39 weeks for new claims made on or after April 1, 2016, subject to the same saving provision—see under "*Waiting periods for new claims made on or after April 1, 2016*" above. 2.814

Sub-paragraphs (1), (1A) and (1B): With effect from April 1, 2016 housing costs (defined in para.1(2)) on new claims are not met until the claimant has been enti- 2.815

tled to income support (and/or income-based JSA: reg.32 of the Income Support (General) (Jobseeker's Allowance Consequential Amendments) Regulations 1996, see p.807) for 39 weeks (but see the exceptions from waiting period in para.9). Note the linking rules in para.14 and in particular the effect of para.14(14) where the claimant's former partner was entitled to state pension credit, and para.14(15) where the claimant, his partner or his former partner was entitled to income-related ESA.

Note in addition that the April 1, 2016 amendments do not apply if the claimant falls within the saving provision—see under "*Waiting period for new claims made on or after April 1, 2016*" above).

The qualifying period recommences each time a fresh claim for income support is made (subject to the linking rules in para.14 — *R(IS) 2/94*).

CJSA/125/2004 held that the waiting periods for housing costs are not in breach of the ECHR.

Amount of housing costs payable

2.816 To calculate the amount of housing costs that are payable under para.8, for loans that qualify under paras 15 or 16 the standard rate (see para.12) is applied to the eligible capital owing for the time being (sub-para.(1)(a)(i)). To this are added the actual payments due for any housing costs in para.17(1)(a)–(c) (i.e. ground rent, service charges and rentcharges) (sub-para.(1)(a)(ii)).

"Eligible capital" is not defined, but see paras 4(2)–(12), 11(4)–(9) and 13 for the limits on loans that will be met. What does "eligible capital for the time being owing" mean? Does it just mean the original amount of the loan less any that has been repaid, or could it include an increase in that capital, due, for example, to capitalised interest? The terms of the claimant's mortgage may be relevant here. See, for example, *CIS 146/1993*, where the claimant's mortgage repayments were adjusted annually. Any arrears due to changes in interest rates during the year were capitalised, divided into 12 and added to the monthly instalments for the following year. The Commissioner holds that the capitalised interest was not arrears but part of the interest payable in the following year. Thus it qualified as eligible interest. However, the interest on the capitalised interest was to be treated as arrears and so was not payable. A similar distinction may be relevant to the question of what is the eligible capital owing for the time being, depending on the terms of the mortgage. In *CIS 141/1993* the Commissioner confirmed that for interest to qualify as eligible interest under the former para.7(3), any increase in the capital owing on the loan had to be for the purpose of acquiring an interest in the home. *CJSA 888/1999* similarly so decides in relation to the current provisions. The claimant's mortgage agreement allowed payment of a proportion of the chargeable interest to be delayed for 10 years. At the end of the 10 years the accumulated deferred interest was added to his outstanding loan and interest charged on the new balance. The Commissioner confirmed that interest attributable to the capitalised deferred interest could not be met. *CPC/3322/2007* (a case on the equivalent state pension credit provisions) concerned similar facts. As *R(IS) 14/01* had put it, the deferred interest arrangement under the terms of the claimant's mortgage enabled her to afford to buy her home but no interest in the home was acquired by means of it. Thus only the amount of her original loan qualified. For *R(IS) 14/01* see the note to para.15(1).

Note that the amount of eligible capital will be recalculated only once a year (sub-paras (1A) and (1B)). See also reg.7(14) of the Decisions and Appeals Regulations 1999 which provides that a supersession due to a reduction in eligible capital will only have effect on the next anniversary of the date the claimant's housing costs were first met. Since reg.7(14) only applies to *reductions* in the outstanding capital, arguably a supersession due to any eligible increase should take effect in the normal way (despite sub-paras (1A) and (1B)). Indeed this is the approach taken in the *Decision Makers Guide* (see para.23506).

2.817 See the notes to paras 15 and 16 for which loans are eligible.

The formula for determining the weekly amount of loan interest payable is in para.10. Interest is only met when the claimant is actually required to pay it (*CIS 636/1992 (Brain)* and *CIS 743/1993* referred to in the notes to para.1).

Only interest is covered, not the capital element in loan repayments. There are a number of ways round this deficiency. First, the lender may be prepared to accept repayments of interest only. Secondly, if the claimant sub-lets part of the home, the first £20 is disregarded (Sch.9 para.19). See also *CIS 13059/1996* referred to below. Contributions to living or accommodation expenses by someone who normally resides with the claimant are disregarded entirely (Sch.9 para.18) (but see para.18 of this Schedule). See also para.20 of Sch.9 for the disregard of board and lodging payments. Payments from others to meet capital repayments (or interest not met by income support or premiums on a mortgage protection or buildings insurance policy) are disregarded (Sch.9 para.30). See *CIS 13059/1996* in the note to para.30 of Sch.9 which decides (contrary to the view expressed in *CIS 82/1993*) that the disregard in para.30(1) can apply to payments made by a tenant (or licensee) of the claimant who lives in his home. Payments from liable relatives would not be disregarded (reg.54). Payments from mortgage protection policies are disregarded to the extent that they cover capital repayments (or interest on a qualifying loan that is not met by income support or the premiums on a mortgage protection or buildings insurance policy) (Sch.9 para.29). See also *R(IS) 13/01* in the note to para.30 of Sch.9.

The cost of premiums on insurance policies connected with the loan is also not met (*R(SB) 46/83*).

Sub-paragraphs (2)–(5) These paragraphs were omitted with effect from April 1, 2016, subject to a saving provision—see under "*Waiting period for new claims made on or after April 1, 2016*" above. See the 2015/16 edition of this volume for these paragraphs and the notes to those paragraphs. **2.818**

Paragraph 9—exclusions from para.8

This paragraph does two things. First, it provides for exemption for certain claimants from the waiting period in para.8 so that housing costs will be met from the start of the claim (sub-paras (1)(a) and (2)(a)). Before April 1, 2016 the exemption also applied to the waiting period under para.6, but para.6 was revoked on April 1, 2016, subject to a saving provision (see p.824). **2.819**

Before October 6, 2003 sub-para.(1)(a) applied to a claimant who or whose partner was aged 60 or over. However from October 6, 2003 it only applies to a claimant whose partner has attained the qualifying age for state pension credit (defined in s.137(1) of the Contributions and Benefits Act 1992—the effect of that definition is that the qualifying age was 60 but from April 2010 it will gradually rise in line with the staged increase in pensionable age for women until it reaches 65 in November 2018 (this equalisation of the state pension age for men and women was previously to have been completed by April 5, 2020 but the timetable for this in the Pensions Act 1995 has been accelerated with effect from April 2016 so that women's state pension age will now be 65 by November 2018; in addition, the increase in state pension age to 66 for both men and women has been brought forward—it will start to rise from 65 in December 2018 to reach 66 by October 2020, see s.1 of the Pensions Act 2011, and between 2026 and 2028 it will rise to 67 (see s.26 of the Pensions Act 2014)). This is because a person who has reached the qualifying age for state pension credit or whose partner is entitled to state pension credit is not entitled to income support (SSCBA s.124(1)(aa) and (g)).

Secondly, it also disapplies the waiting period under para.8 in relation to housing costs covered by para.17(1)(d)–(f), i.e. payments under a co-ownership scheme, by a Crown tenant or in respect of a tent, so that these are also met from the start of a claim for income support (sub-paras (1)(b) and (2)(b)). Before April 1, 2016 the waiting period under para.6 was also disapplied in relation to these housing costs but para.6 was revoked on April 1, 2016, subject to a saving provision (see p.824).

Note the restriction on house purchase loans incurred while entitled to income support, income-related ESA or income-based JSA (see reg.32 of the

Income Support (General) (Jobseeker's Allowance Consequential Amendments) Regulations 1996 (p.807)), or while a person is caught by the linking rule in para.4(2)–(12) as well as the limits imposed under paras 11(5) and 13. In relation to the cap on loans in para.11(5) note the increased limit that has been introduced for certain claimants by the Social Security (Housing Costs Special Arrangements) (Amendment and ModiWcation) Regulations 2008 (SI 2008/3195), as amended by the Social Security (Housing Costs Special Arrangements) (Amendment) Regulations 2009 (SI 2009/3257) (see the note on these Regulations under "*ModiWcations to the waiting periods and the cap on loans for certain claimants from January 5, 2009*" and "Further Modifications from January 5, 2010" above).

Paragraph 10—calculation for loans

2.820 This contains the formula (referred to in paras 6(1)(a)(i) and 8(1)(a)(i) (from April 1, 2016, para.8(1)(a)(i) only, due to the revocation of para.6, subject to a saving provision—see under "*Waiting period for new claims made on or after April 1, 2016*" above)) for calculating the weekly amount of interest that will be met on a qualifying loan. Presumably "A" is only intended to refer to the amount of a loan that qualifies under paras 15 or 16 to the extent that it comprises eligible capital, although para.10 does not actually say that. The current form of para.10 was introduced to reflect the abolition of MIRAS (mortgage interest relief at source) in April 2000.

Paragraph 11—general provisions applying to housing costs

2.821 *Sub-paragraphs (2) and (3)*: These paragraphs were omitted with effect from April 1, 2016, subject to a saving provision—see under "*Waiting period for new claims made on or after April 1, 2016*" above. See the 2015/16 edition of this volume for these sub-paragraphs and the note to sub-para.(2).

Ceiling on loans

2.822 Sub-paragraphs (4)–(11) contain the provisions first introduced in August 1993 relating to the ceiling on loans (see the notes to para.7(6B)–(6F) of the former Sch.3 in the 1995 edition of J. Mesher and P. Wood, *Income-related Benefits: the Legislation*). For SSAC's report on these changes see Cm. 2272. Sub-paras (4) and (5) provide that there is an absolute limit on the size of loans that can be taken into account in calculating housing costs. The current limit under sub-para.(5) is £100,000 but with effect from January 5, 2009 this has been increased to £200,000 for certain claimants by the Social Security (Housing Costs Special Arrangements) (Amendment and Modification) Regulations 2008 (SI 2008/3195), as amended by the Social Security (Housing Costs Special Arrangements) (Amendment) Regulations 2009 (SI 2009/3257) (see the note on these Regulations under "*Modifications to the waiting periods and the cap on loans for certain claimants from January 5, 2009*" and "*Further Modifications from January 5, 2010*" above).

CIS/4230/2002 holds that the £100,000 cap on loans was not *ultra vires* nor in breach of ECHR. The Commissioner found that the imposition of a ceiling did come within the ambit of art.8 but concluded that there had not been a breach of art.8, or art.8 in conjunction with art.14.

If there is more than one loan, all qualifying loans (except any loan taken out to adapt a home for disablement needs (sub-para.(9)) are aggregated and the total amount outstanding is subject to the ceiling (sub-para.(4)). Sub-paragraph (10) provides that the restriction is to be applied proportionately to each loan where the total outstanding exceeds the ceiling. If a claimant qualifies for loan interest for two homes the limit is applied separately to the loans for each home (sub-para.(6)). If only a proportion of the loan is for a qualifying purpose, or the property is used for mixed purposes (e.g. business and domestic), the limit is applied to the proportion of the loan covered by income support (sub-paras (7) and (8)).

2.823 If the loan was "to adapt a dwelling" for the needs of a disabled person, that loan is ignored in calculating whether the limit on loans in sub-para.(5) (as modified by the Social Security (Housing Costs Special Arrangements) (Amendment and Modification) Regulations 2008, as amended (see above)) is exceeded (sub-para. (9)). For when a person counts as disabled see para.1(3) and (4). The disabled person does not have to be a member of the claimant's family. "Adapt a dwelling" is not defined, but following the Court of Appeal's decision in *R (on the application of Mahmoudi) v London Borough of Lewisham* [2014] EWCA Civ 284; [2014] AACR 14 means whether the process which the dwelling has undergone is a change that makes it more suitable for the needs of the disabled person (see further the note to para.3(7)(c)(i) above).

The limit on loans was £150,000 from August 2, 1993 until April 10, 1994, £125,000 from April 11, 1994 to April 9, 1995 and has been £100,000 since April 10, 1995. The rules applied to loans taken out before, as well as those taken out or increased after, these dates, but there was transitional protection for existing claimants (see reg.4 of the Income Support (General) Amendment No.3 Regulations 1993 (p.800) and reg.28 of the Income-related Benefits Schemes (Miscellaneous Amendments) Regulations 1995 (p.803)). The effect of this is that there is no limit on the existing loans of claimants entitled to income support on August 2, 1993 (or who were treated as entitled by virtue of the linking rules) while their entitlement continues; for claimants who did not qualify for this protection but who were entitled, or treated as entitled, to income support on April 11, 1994, the ceiling on their existing loans is £150,000 while they remain entitled to income support (reg.4). There was similar transitional protection in connection with the reduction of the limit to £100,000 from April 10, 1995 (reg.28). *CIS 12885/1996* confirms that the claimant's entitlement to income support must be continuous; the protection is lost if it ceases for even a single day. (But see the note to para.14(3AA) where the claimant or his partner is a "welfare to work beneficiary".) Note that reg.5(2) of the amending regulations preserves the operation of the respective saving provisions (see the Social Security (Income Support and Claims and Payments) Amendment Regulations 1995 (p.804)). Note also reg.32 of the Income Support (General) (Jobseeker's Allowance Consequential Amendments) Regulations 1996 (see p.807) under which entitlement to income-based JSA counts for the purpose of satisfying a condition that the person is entitled to income support, and the linking rules in para.14, in particular the effect of para.14(14) where the claimant's former partner was entitled to state pension credit and para.14(15) where the claimant, his partner or his former partner was entitled to income-related ESA.

The ceiling on loans is in addition to the rules on "excessive" housing costs (see para.13) and the restriction on house purchase loans incurred while entitled to income support, income-related ESA or income-based JSA (see reg.32 of the Income Support (General) (Jobseeker's Allowance Consequential Amendments) Regulations 1996 (p.807)), or while a person is caught by the linking rule (see para.4(2)–(12)). Note that the disregard in para.29 of Sch.9 of payments from mortgage protection policies includes any interest payment on a qualifying loan that is not met by income support; see also the disregard in para.30(1)(b) of Sch.9 and *CIS 13059/1996* in the note to that paragraph.

Paragraph 12—standard rate

Interest on eligible loans is paid at the "standard rate". **2.824**

From October 1, 2010 the previous fixed standard interest rate of 6.08 per cent (see further the 2010/11 edition of this volume) has been replaced with a rate based on the "average mortgage rate" (defined in sub-para.(2E)) published by the Bank of England. According to the Explanatory Memorandum which accompanies the SI which introduced this change, the average mortgage rate is based on information from approximately 30 banks and building societies, representing more than 75 per cent of mortgage business, and is a weighted average of all existing loans to households secured on dwellings from banks and building societies in the sample.

Initially the standard interest rate from October 1, 2010 was set at the average mortgage rate in August 2010 (see sub-para.(2)). The average mortgage rate in August 2010 was 3.63 per cent which was considerably lower than the previous fixed rate of 6.08 per cent. It remained at 3.63 per cent from October 1, 2010 until July 6, 2015 when it reduced to 3.12 per cent. It continues (in July 2016) to be the same rate.

Changes in the standard interest rate will only be triggered when the average mortgage rate and the standard interest rate differ by 0.5 percentage points or more (see sub-para.(2B)). Until April 28, 2014 the trigger point was a difference of "0.5 per cent" or more. Such a percentage (or relative) change is more generous than a percentage points change (which is the arithmetic difference between the two percentages). This was not the policy intention and so sub-para.(2B) has been amended so that a change in the standard interest rate will only be triggered by a difference of at least 0.5 percentage points. The consequence is that the October 2010 standard interest rate of 3.63 per cent has only been adjusted when the average mortgage rate reduced by at least 0.5 percentage points (which was not until April 2015).

2.825 When a decrease or increase of 0.5 percentage points or more in the average mortgage rate occurs, that decreased or increased average mortgage rate becomes the new standard rate but this will only take effect for the purpose of calculating the weekly amount of a claimant's housing costs on a day specified by the Secretary of State (see sub-para.(2D)). It apparently takes five to six weeks to amend the standard rate in the Department's computer systems and thus to implement a change to benefit awards (para.7.4 of the Explanatory Memorandum).

A footnote to the SI states that any new standard interest rate, and the day specified by the Secretary of State as the day on which it comes into effect, will be published on the Directgov website.

In *CJSA 232/2003* the claimant contended that the standard interest rate was in violation of art.14 of ECHR when read with either art.8 or art.1 of Protocol 1. The Commissioner was prepared to accept that the standard interest rate might come within the ambit of art.8 but found that discrimination had not been established and moreover that the standard interest rate was a proportionate response to legitimate aims.

Paragraph 13—excessive housing costs

2.826 This restricts the housing costs that will be met where the accommodation is too large or expensive. These limits are in addition to the ceiling on loans (para.11(4)–(11)), and the restriction on house purchase loans incurred while the claimant is entitled to income support, income-related ESA or income-based JSA (see reg.32 of the Income Support (General) (Jobseeker's Allowance Consequential Amendments) Regulations 1996 (p.807)), or caught by the linking rule in para.4(2)–(12). In relation to the cap on loans in para.11(5) note the increased limit that has been introduced for certain claimants by the Social Security (Housing Costs Special Arrangements) (Amendment and Modification) Regulations 2008 (SI 2008/3195), as amended by the Social Security (Housing Costs Special Arrangements) (Amendment) Regulations 2009 (SI 2009/3257) (see the note on these Regulations under "*Modifications to the waiting periods and the cap on loans for certain claimants from January 5, 2009*" and "*Further Modifications from January 5, 2010*" above).

2.827 *Sub-paragraph (1)*: This does not specifically provide for any deduction for the presence of a non-dependant to be made first, before deciding whether the level of housing costs is excessive. But since sub-para.(1) refers to housing costs that fall to be met under this Schedule, this indicates that it is the amount of housing costs net of deductions (and restrictions) that is the relevant figure.

There are three sets of circumstances in which a restriction can be applied. The first is that the home is unnecessarily large for the claimant's family, including any foster children and non-dependants living in the household. An absolutely literal reading of the provision would lead to the result that it does not apply to a single claimant, who does not have a family. *CIS 104/1991* decides that the words must be read as "the claimant and his family (if any)." Any part of the home which is let is ignored in assessing the size of the accommodation against the needs of its occupants. At base is an issue of opinion about what is unnecessarily large. Some common situations caught by this provision (e.g. a married couple whose children have left home, or a deserted spouse) may escape under sub-para.(4) or (6).

The second set of circumstances, under head (b), is that the immediate area of the home is more expensive than other areas in which suitable alternative accommodation is available. It is not at all clear how restricted the immediate area might be, but it will probably be more limited than the area under (c). *CSB 1016/1982* suggests that the delimitation of an area is likely to be within the knowledge of tribunals. It must be possible also to identify another cheaper area (using the *CSB 1016/1982* definition) in which suitable alternative accommodation exists. The condition of suitability will limit the distance within which other areas can be sought (*R(IS) 12/91*).

Finally, under head (c), there is a restriction if the outgoings of the home are higher than for suitable alternative accommodation in the area (not the immediate area). In *CSB 1016/1982* (in relation to an earlier formulation of this rule) "area" was said to connote "something more confined, restricted and more compact than a locality or district. It might consist of dwelling houses or flats contiguous to a road or a number of roads, refer to a neighbourhood or even to a large block of flats. It is not capable of precise definition." This approach was commended for the purposes of sub-para.(1) in *CIS 34/1989* and *R(IS) 12/91*. **2.828**

If sub-para.(1) applies, sub-para.(3) provides that the "amount of the loan" shall be restricted and the excess expenditure over that for a home of suitable size or expense will not be met. The purpose of the reference to "the amount of *the loan*" is not entirely clear, since sub-para.(1) applies to any housing costs met under Sch.3, not just qualifying loans. Sub-paragraphs (4) and (6) contain exceptions to the operation of sub-paras (1) and (3).

R(IS) 9/91 decides that sub-paras (1) and (3) operate in the same way as *R(SB) 6/89* decided that the old reg.21 of the Requirements Regulations did. The excess is not the difference between the actual expenditure and the maximum that would be allowed for a family of similar size in a home of the necessary size or in an acceptably cheaper area. The excess is the difference between the actual expenditure and the housing costs which would be incurred by the claimant in the alternative accommodation. On the facts of *R(IS) 9/91*, the net proceeds of sale of the existing home would have completely covered the cost of acquiring alternative accommodation, so that there would be no income support housing costs. Thus the entire actual expenditure was "excess".

Note also *CJSA 2683/2002*. This holds that in considering the amount of a loan that the claimant would need to obtain alternative cheaper accommodation under sub-para.(3), unsecured loans that became repayable on the sale of the existing home could be taken into account when calculating the net proceeds of sale of that home which could be put towards the alternative accommodation.

Sub-paragraph (4): If it is not reasonable to expect the claimant to seek alternative cheaper accommodation, no restriction is to be made at all. It must already have been determined under sub-para.(1) that cheaper alternative accommodation which is suitable exists. All the relevant factors set out in sub-para.(5) must be considered. **2.829**

Under head (a) the availability of suitable accommodation must be judged objectively (*R(SB) 7/89* and *R(IS) 10/93*). The particular circumstances of the claimant and his family are taken into account under head (b). The reference in head (a) to area is particularly obscure. Does it mean the area in which the home is situated or can it include another area in which suitable accommodation is available? In *CSB 1016/1982* it is suggested that it only governs the level of housing costs, not the availability of suitable accommodation, but it seems to be assumed in *R(SB) 7/89* that it governs both matters.

2.830 *Sub-paragraph (5)(b)*: This brings in all the relevant circumstances, not just those mentioned (*R(SB) 6/89, R(SB) 7/89* and *R(IS) 10/93*). One relevant factor mentioned in *CSB 1016/1982* was that the home had only just come into the claimant's occupation in matrimonial proceedings. In *CSB 617/1988* the claimant was assured by the manager of the local DSS office before she moved from a house with a mortgage of £25,000 to a house with a mortgage of £69,890 that the full interest on the new mortgage would be met by supplementary benefit. Although such an assurance could not bind the Department by creating an estoppel (*R(SB) 14/88*) it was one of the circumstances to be considered. (*CSB 617/1988* is reported as *R(SB) 14/89* but it is the unreported version that should be referred to, as the reported decision omits the last three paragraphs which are the relevant ones here.)

Financial hardship is also a relevant factor. In *R(SB) 6/89* the invidious financial position the claimant would be put in if she were forced to sell the home in which she had lived for many years before its renovation was complete was relevant. As was the claimant's inability to find a buyer because of the stagnant housing market (*CIS 347/1992*). In that case the claimant had been advised of a price range for selling his home and would suffer financial hardship if forced to sell below that price. In *CIS 434/1992* the not uncommon problem of a negative equity was relevant. A further factor mentioned in *R(SB) 7/89* was that if the claimant sold his home, his lenders would not be prepared to lend to him again, but if the proceeds of sale were not put to purchasing another house, the capital would disentitle him from benefit. Thus rented accommodation may not be a straightforward alternative. *R(IS) 10/93* holds that the inability of the claimant to obtain suitable accommodation is a relevant factor. As in that case, that inability may stem from the fact that the claimant is unable to sell his existing home, despite making all reasonable efforts to do so.

2.831 *Sub-paragraph (6)*: If the restriction is not removed completely under sub-para. (4) there can be a limited exemption here. If the claimant (or a member of the family) was able to meet the financial commitments for the home when they were first entered into, there is to be no restriction under this paragraph (but the ceiling in para.11(5) may apply; note the increase in the ceiling that has been introduced for certain claimants by the Social Security (Housing Costs Special Arrangements) (Amendment and Modification) Regulations 2008 (SI 2008/3195), as amended by the Social Security (Housing Costs Special Arrangements) (Amendment) Regulations 2009 (SI 2009/3257) (see the note on these Regulations under "*Modifications to the waiting periods and the cap on loans for certain claimants from January 5, 2009*" and "*Further Modifications from January 5, 2010*" above)) for the first six months on income support (and/or income-based JSA: reg.32 of the Income Support (General) (Jobseeker's Allowance Consequential Amendments) Regulations 1996, see p.807) or from the date on which the housing costs are determined on a supersession to be excessive. (Note that sub-para.(6)(a) has not been amended so that it also refers to income-related ESA.) This should include a person who was a member of the family when the mortgage was taken on (e.g. where a couple have separated). The exemption can be extended for up to another six months so long as the claimant uses his best endeavours to obtain cheaper accommodation. What are the best endeavours is an issue of fact. *R(SB) 7/89* holds that a claimant can only be penalised for failing to use his best endeavours if he has been given some advance notice of the necessity to do so. In *R(IS) 13/92* the claimant's housing costs were restricted from the beginning of the claim to £146.85 a week, the amount appropriate to interest on a capital sum of £110,000. At the time the capital and accrued unpaid interest amounted to £696,063.44. The Commissioner agreed that a restriction under sub-paras (1) and (3) was indicated, but on the evidence the claimant was able to meet the financial commitments for the dwelling at the time the mortgage was obtained. Therefore the absence of restriction for the first six months under sub-para.(6) was mandatory. The Commissioner did however consider that the initial improper restriction operated as a notice of the intention to restrict housing costs after the six months under

R(SB) 7/89. The Court of Appeal in *Secretary of State for Social Security v Julien*, reported as *R(IS) 13/92*, confirmed the Commissioner's decision, saying that the issue is ability to meet the financial commitments, not prudence.

In *CIS 104/1991* the Commissioner takes the approach of *R(SB) 7/89* a little further. He holds that if the claimant could afford the housing commitments when he took them on there cannot be a restriction until there has been an explicit notice in a decision that there may be a restriction in six months' time. The sub-para.(6) meter has to be started explicitly and it has to run for six months. In *CIS 104/1991* only two months notice was given. The claimant had to be allowed another four months and then the question of using best endeavours to obtain cheaper accommodation had to be explored.

In *CIS 3163/1997* the claimant contended that because there would have to be what was then a review (now a supersession) at the end of any exemption period under sub-para.(6), this meant that on that review a new automatic 26 weeks' exemption from restriction would have to be allowed (with a possible extension for an extra 26 weeks), and so on, on a rolling basis. However, the Commissioner holds that the reference to review in the then form of sub-para.(6) was to the review which first started the sub-para.(6) clock running within any period of income support entitlement. The maximum period for the application of sub-para.(6) was thus 52 weeks from the date of that review (or from the start of entitlement if sub-para.(6) was applied immediately on the award of entitlement). To allow a new automatic 26-week period to start on any review would undermine the manifest purpose of sub-para.(6). However, where after a restriction had been imposed, a decision was made (e.g. that sub-para.(4) applied or that the conditions of sub-para.(1) were no longer met) which had the effect of lifting that restriction, but later still it was decided that a restriction should be made, then the review (now supersession) decision reimposing the restriction *did* trigger the operation of sub-para.(6) (*CJSA 2536/2000*).

Sub-paragraphs (7)–(9): A person can now only requalify for the deferment of a restriction under sub-para.(6) if there is a break in entitlement to income support of more than 12 weeks. Note that the linking rules in para.14(1)(c)–(f) apply. **2.832**

Paragraph 14—linking rules

These rules are particularly important for the waiting periods for housing costs, but apply throughout the Schedule. From April 1, 2016 there is only one waiting period of 39 weeks under para.8, following the revocation on April 1, 2016 of para.6, but note that this is subject to a saving provision—see under "*Waiting period for new claims made on or after April 1, 2016*" above. The provisions of the Social Security (Housing Costs Special Arrangements) (Amendment and Modification) Regulations 2008 (as amended) (see p.816) that related to the modification of the waiting periods for certain claimants were also revoked on April 1, 2016 but again this is subject to the same saving provision. See the note on these Regulations under "*Modifications to the waiting periods and the cap on loans for certain claimants from January 5, 2009*" and "*Further Modifications from January 5, 2010*" above. **2.833**

The basic linking period is 12 weeks but note the extended linking periods of 52 weeks where sub-paras (11)–(13) apply and 104 weeks (increased from 52 weeks with effect from October 9, 2006) in the case of a welfare to work beneficiary (see sub-para.(10)). See the notes to those paragraphs.

Regulation 32 of the Income Support (General) (Jobseeker's Allowance Consequential Amendments) Regulations 1996 (see p.807) should also be noted. This provides that entitlement to income-based JSA counts as entitlement to income support for the purpose of satisfying any condition that the person is or has been entitled to income support for any period of time. It also has the same effect where the requirement is that the person is or has been treated as being in receipt of income support. See para.18(1)(c) of Sch.2 to the JSA Regulations for the converse provision under the JSA rules. Where the claimant's former partner was entitled to state pension credit, see sub-para.(14), inserted with effect from October

6, 2003. See also sub-para.(15), inserted with effect from October 27, 2008, where the claimant, his partner or his former partner was entitled to income-related ESA.

Note also the linking rules in sub-para.(1)(ee) and sub-paras (3ZA) and (3B) introduced on January 5, 1998 as a consequence of the "New Deal". The intention is that time spent on a New Deal option should not put claimants at a disadvantage in terms of qualifying for housing costs. Thus under sub-para.(3ZA) a claimant is deemed to be in receipt of income support during any period that he stops getting income support because he or his partner is on a New Deal option, or (from April 3, 2000) an employment zone (defined in reg.2(1)) scheme, or (from April 9, 2001) in the Intensive Activity Period, that results in him (or his partner) being in remunerative work or having an income that is too high to qualify for income support. In addition, sub-para.(1)(ee) treats a claimant as in receipt of income support for the same period that his partner was in receipt, or treated as in receipt, of income support where the claimant is awarded income support for the couple immediately after either of them has been taking part in a New Deal option or the Intensive Activity Period and immediately before this his partner had been getting income support for the couple. See also sub-para.(3B) which treats any period of entitlement to contribution-based JSA immediately before a person or his partner took part in a New Deal option or the Intensive Activity Period as a period of entitlement to income support. (Note that these programmes have ceased to operate and that reg.75(1)(a) of the JSA Regulations 1996 was recast on October 22, 2012 so that it simply refers to "an employment programme".) Similar provisions were inserted into Sch.2 to the JSA Regulations 1996 (see para.13(1)(ee) and (3A) of Sch.2; an equivalent of sub-para.(3B) was obviously not needed).

2.834 *Sub-paragraph (3A)*: The waiting periods in paras 6 and 8 (note that para.6 was revoked on April 1, 2016, subject to a saving provision—see under "*Waiting period for new claims made on or after April 1, 2016*" above) talk in terms of entitlement to income support but the linking rules in sub-paras (1)–(3ZA) refer to deemed receipt of income support. Sub-paragraph (3A) states that deemed receipt for the purposes of sub-paras (1), (3) and (3ZA) counts as deemed entitlement, to confirm that these linking rules apply to the waiting periods (from April 1, 2016, waiting period).

2.835 *Sub-paragraph (3AA)*: Sub-paragraph (3AA), inserted with effect from August 2, 1999, was considered necessary because the DSS had received advice that the effect of para.14 (since December 12, 1995) had been to provide a linking rule for the payment of interest on loans above the £100,000 ceiling in para.11(5) (although see *CIS 12885/1996* in the note to para.11). The purpose of sub-para.(3AA) is to reaffirm the policy intention that *any* break in claim (however short) will result in the loss of transitional protection for payment of interest on loans above the ceiling. There is an exception for welfare to work beneficiaries (see above) for whom the right to this transitional protection is preserved during their 104-week linking period. A similar amendment has been made to para.13 of Sch.2 to the JSA Regulations 1996.

2.836 *Sub-paragraphs (4)–(9)*: These were new in October and December 1995 and are intended to assist claimants in satisfying their waiting period. Note also sub-para.(3B) (see above). Sub-paragraphs (4), (5), (5A) and (5B) provide that a person who is not entitled to income support only because s/he has too much capital and/or income will be treated as so entitled for any period (or periods: Interpretation Act 1978 s.6) of up to 39 weeks during which s/he is entitled to unemployment benefit, contribution-based JSA, statutory sick pay, contributory ESA or incapacity benefit (or credits), eligible for income support as a carer, a lone parent, or treated as in receipt of income support (and/or income-based JSA: reg.32 of the Income Support (General) (Jobseeker's Allowance Consequential Amendments) Regulations 1996, see p.807). Note that for these provisions to apply the person must not be entitled to income support by reason *only* that he has too much income and/or capital. In *CIS 621/2004* the claimant who was in receipt of incapacity benefit was paid contractual sick pay by his employer until his employment was terminated with three months pay in lieu of notice. Although he was not treated as in remunerative work while he was absent from work while ill (see reg.5(3A)), the effect of reg.5(5) was to treat him as in remunerative work during the three-month notice period. The consequence was that he ceased to fall within sub-para.(4) during the 13-week notice period (and could not take advantage of the linking rule in sub-para.(1)(a)(ii) because the notice period was more than 12 weeks).

Further note that a lone parent includes a person who is responsible only for a young person (i.e. aged 16–19) (see reg.2(1)). (But since such a lone parent will not be eligible for income support under para.1 of Sch.1B, she will have to satisfy one of the other paragraphs in Sch.1B in order to come within para.(4).) In the case of carers and lone parents covered by sub-para.(5A) it is necessary for a claim for income support to have been made, the refusal of which fixes the start of the deemed entitlement. The absence of such a requirement in sub-para.(5) would seem to imply that it is not necessary for a claim to have been made for a person to benefit from this provision. This was confirmed by *CJSA 4613/2001*. The Commissioner holds that the words "not entitled . . . by reason only of his income" in para.13(5) of Sch.2 to the JSA Regulations 1996 (the equivalent of sub-para.(4)) refer to the substantive conditions of entitlement; they do not require a claim for JSA (or income support) to have been made. The Commissioner also holds that in para.13(1)(a)(ii)(bb) of Sch.2 the reference to "sub-paragraphs (5), (6) and (7)" has to be read as meaning "sub-paragraphs (5) and (6) or (7)" in order to make sense (see sub-para.(1)(a)(ii)(bb) above which does use the disjunctive, not the conjunctive).

Although sub-para.(4) states that these rules apply where a person is not entitled to income support only because his income and/or capital is too high, sub-para.(5B) also provides that for lone parents and carers covered by sub-para.(5A) the deemed entitlement does not apply if during the relevant period the person would not be entitled to income support because s/he (or any partner) is in remunerative work or s/he is a full-time student (other than one who is eligible for income support) or temporarily absent from Great Britain. Is the effect of this, for example, that if a lone parent finds work after sub-para.(5A) has applied to her for, say, 20 weeks, the deemed entitlement under that sub-paragraph does not apply at all? Although the wording of sub-para.(5B) is not entirely clear, the fact that where the period of work is 12 (or from October 5, 1998, 52 and from October 9, 2006, 104 in the case of a "welfare to work beneficiary" (sub-para.(10)) weeks or less, the linking rule in sub-para.(1)(a)(ii)(bb) will apply so that the period of work can count under sub-para.(5)(c) indicates that this is not the case and that sub-para.(5B) only applies to the periods when the lone parent or carer is in remunerative work, etc. (Note that because sub-para.(3A) now treats deemed receipt of income support as deemed entitlement for the purposes of sub-paras (1), (3) and (3ZA), such a period of 12 (or 104) weeks or less can in fact count directly under sub-para.(1)(a)(ii)(bb) without having to go via the sub-para.(5)(c) route. This is relevant for JSA. Paragraph 13(6) of Sch.2 to the JSA Regulations 1996 contains no equivalent of sub-para.(5)(c), but since such a provision is no longer needed in these circumstances the effect of these rules will be the same for both income support and JSA.) The amendments to sub-para.(1)(a)(ii) introduced on October 7, 1996 have addressed the problem raised in the 1996 edition of J. Mesher and P. Wood, *Income-related Benefits: the Legislation* that the linking rule in that sub-paragraph might not have applied because under its pre-October 1996 form the period of deemed receipt had to fall between periods of *receipt* (or deemed receipt) of income support whereas sub-paras (5) and (5A) treat a person as *entitled* to income support. (There was the same potential problem before October 7, 1996 for people who fell within sub-para.(5) and who, for example, worked for a period of 12 weeks or less between two periods of unemployment.)

Note that if the only reason for non-entitlement to income support is too much income, and the person's income includes payments under a policy taken out to insure against the risk of not being able to meet eligible housing costs, s/he will be **2.837** treated as entitled to income support for the period that the insurance payments are made (sub-para.(6)).

2.838 *Sub-paragraphs (8) and (9)*: If a claim for income support is made by, or in respect of, a person whose payments under a policy to insure against a loss of employment have stopped and who had been getting income support (and/or income-based JSA: reg.32 of the Income Support (General) (Jobseeker's Allowance Consequential Amendments) Regulations 1996, see p.807, and/or, from October 6, 2003, whose former partner had been getting state pension credit: sub-para.(14), and/or, from October 27, 2008, who, or whose partner, or former partner, had been getting income-related ESA) including housing costs within the last 26 weeks, the weeks in between the claims are ignored for the purpose of deciding whether the claimant has been entitled to income support for either the 26- or 39-week qualifying period. Note that sub-para.(9)(a) was omitted with effect from April 1, 2016 following the revocation of para.6 (which contained the 26 week qualifying period), subject to a saving provision—see under "*Waiting period for new claims made on or after April 1, 2016*" above).

2.839 *Sub-paragraph (10)*: The linking period in the case of a "welfare to work beneficiary" was 52 weeks and is 104 weeks from October 9, 2006. See the notes to reg.2(1) in the 2015/16 edition of this volume for when a person counts as a welfare to work beneficiary. The aim of the extended linking period is that the person should not be worse off if he has to reclaim benefit within a year (now two years) because he (or his partner) has again become incapable of work. For JSA there is a similar extension of the linking period where the claimant's partner is a welfare to work beneficiary (see para.13(12) of Sch.2 to the JSA Regulations 1996).

2.840 *Sub-paragraphs (11)–(13)*: To encourage claimants who have already qualified for housing costs back into work, a 52-week linking period also applies if the following conditions are met. A person must stop getting income support on or after April 9, 2001 because he or his partner has started work or increased his hours of work, is taking steps to get work as an employee or in self-employment under certain Training for Work schemes, or is on a New Deal option, an employment zone programme (these programmes have ceased to operate) or the self-employment route, and as a result he or his partner counts as in full-time work or has an income that is too high to be eligible for income support. However, the longer linking period will only apply if immediately before entitlement to income support ceased the person's housing costs were being met (or would have been but for any non-dependant deduction) because he had already served the 8-, 26- or 39-week waiting period. From April 1, 2016, following the revocation of para.6 (subject to a saving provision—see under "*Waiting period for new claims made on or after April 1, 2016*" above), the claimant will have to have served the 39 week waiting period under para.8(1)(a) for the longer linking period to apply; otherwise the linking period will remain 12 weeks. For the equivalent JSA provisions see the amendments to para.13(1) and the new sub-paras (13)–(15) of para.13 of Sch.2 to the JSA Regulations 1996 inserted with effect from April 9, 2001.

Note also the "mortgage interest run-on", introduced on April 9, 2001, to allow housing costs to be met for the first four weeks of employment. This was extended on December 17, 2007 so that it now applies to all housing costs that can be met by income support. See the notes to reg.6.

2.841 *Sub-paragraphs (14) and (15)*: These provide, as referred to above, that for the purposes of the linking rules in this paragraph, if a claimant's former partner was entitled to state pension credit, any reference to income support in this Schedule also includes a reference to state pension credit, and if a claimant, his partner or his former partner was entitled to income-related ESA, any reference to income support in this Schedule also includes a reference to income-related ESA.

Paragraph 15—loans on residential property

The question is whether the loan qualifies (not whether the interest is eligible as it was under the previous form of Sch.3). 2.842

Thus the situation dealt with in *R(IS) 11/95* in which the question was whether interest on a replacement loan was eligible where the original loan had been interest free—see p.264 of J. Mesher and P. Wood, *Income-related Benefits: the Legislation* (1995)—will no longer be an issue. However, even though the question is whether the loan qualifies, not whether the interest is eligible, capital repayments on an interest-free loan do not qualify because reg.17(1)(e) limits the scope of housing costs to "mortgage interest payments or such other housing costs as are prescribed in [Schedule 3]" (*RV v SSWP (IS)* [2013] UKUT 273 (AAC)).

This paragraph (and para.16) deal with whether a loan is for a qualifying purpose. Note the restrictions on loans that will be met in paras 4(2)–(12), 11(4)–(11) and 13.

Clearly there has to be a loan for para.15 to apply. *CIS 14483/1996* concerned a scheme for Muslims operated by the Albaraka International Bank because the Koran prohibits the payment or charging of interest on money loaned. Under the scheme the claimant and the bank jointly purchased the property; the legal estate vested in the claimant who held it on trust for himself and the bank and the beneficial interest was divided into investment shares. The claimant agreed to purchase a number of shares from the bank each month and to pay the bank an amount of "mesne profit" each month to reflect his use of the bank's share in the property. The Commissioner holds that the mesne profit did not constitute "eligible interest" which could be met under para.7(3) of the former Sch.3 because there was no loan. The agreement was not in the nature of a mortgage but was a form of co-partnership, designed specifically to prevent the payment of interest. 2.843

SSWP v UP (JSA) [2010] UKUT 262 (AAC); [2011] AACR 12 also concerned a home financing scheme designed to be compliant with Shari'a principles (i.e. not involving the payment of any interest). Under the HSBC Ijarah method of finance HSBC purchased the property and granted the claimant a 25-year tenancy, under which he was obliged to pay rent and "payments on account". Once the "on account" payments equalled the purchase price the bank would transfer the property into the claimant's name. The tribunal held that the claimant was paying rent relating to a long tenancy which qualified as a housing cost under para.16(1)(a) of Sch.2 to the JSA Regulations 1996 (the equivalent of para.17(1)(a)). Under reg.1(3) of the JSA Regulations 1996 a "long tenancy" is defined as "a tenancy granted for a term of years certain exceeding 21 years" (the same definition applies for the purposes of income support (see reg.2(1)). However, as *R(H)3/07* had pointed out, a lease of more than seven years of registered land "does not operate at law until the relevant registration requirements are met" (see s.27 of the Land Registration Act 2002). Thus until the tenancy had been registered at the Land Registry (which did not happen until after the date of the decision under appeal) a long tenancy did not exist and so no payments of rent made by the claimant could be payments relating to a long tenancy. He was therefore not entitled to housing costs as part of his JSA until the registration had taken place.

In *Secretary of State for Work and Pensions v Mohammad* [2011] EWCA Civ 1358; [2012] AACR 29 following the claimant's divorce in 2007 the former matrimonial home (which had been in her ex-husband's sole name) was transferred into her name. The bank refused to transfer the mortgage into her name but under the ancillary relief proceedings order she undertook to make the mortgage payments. The Secretary of State accepted that the claimant was liable to meet the mortgage payments under para.2 but it was common ground that the mortgage taken out by the husband had not been taken out to acquire an interest in the home. It was argued, however, that the claimant's assumption of liability for the mortgage payments amounted to "taking out" a loan to acquire an interest in the home and therefore fell within sub-para.(1). It was further contended that the loan was "incurred" when the husband took it out in 2002, i.e. before the claimant became entitled to income support in 2003, and therefore the loan did not fall foul of para.4(2). But these arguments were rejected by the Court of Appeal. The claimant has not "taken out" (or even "taken over") a loan when she assumed responsibility for the mortgage payments; the loan remained her husband's loan throughout. The Court also did not accept that a loan could be "taken out" for the purposes of sub-para.(1) at a different time from when it was "incurred" for the purposes of para.4(2). The consequence was that, even if the claimant had succeeded on her first argument, the loan would have been incurred while she was entitled to income support and so she would have been disqualified from receiving housing costs on that loan under para.4(2).

CL v SSWP (IS) [2015] UKUT 259 (AAC) also concerned a claimant who had taken out a loan while on income support. She and her former husband (Mr L) had purchased their then matrimonial home in 1990 but separated in 1992. Divorce proceedings ensued, in the course of which an Order was made under which Mr L was entitled to 33 per cent equity in the property, which was to be sold when the claimant's son (J) was 18. The claimant started to receive income support in December 2007, which included mortgage interest on the original mortgage of £34,000. J reached 18 years of age in February 2008 but became seriously ill around that time and did not recover sufficiently to commence work until August 2011 (although that led to further cardiac problems). After his discharge from hospital in January 2009 he had continued to receive medical supervision and remained in bed for six months; he slept in a ground floor room at the property.

In February 2010 the claimant obtained a loan by way of remortgage: £55,000 of the loan was used to buy out Mr L's interest; £7,000 was spent on repairs; and the remainder was used to redeem the existing mortgage. Mortgage interest on the part of the 2010 loan that had been used to pay off Mr L was refused.

There were two issues: (i) does "loan" in para.15 include deferred sale agreements imposed by court order in the course of divorce proceedings; and (ii) if not, did that amount to unlawful discrimination contrary to art.14, read with art.1 Prot.1 of the ECHR?

The claimant contended that the deferred order for sale was a loan to acquire an interest in a dwelling in that it prevented a forced sale from occurring for the period of J's minority. However, this was rejected by Judge Ward, who accepted the Secretary of State's submissions that (a) "loan" in para.15 means an advance of a sum of money procured at the recipient's request and that the words "taken out" would be otiose if other arrangements, including those imposed by court order, were covered; (b) in *Mohammad* (see above) it had been held that "taken out" could not be extended so as to include "taken over", thus rejecting a wider reading of para.15; (c) the fact that para.15(2) specifically refers to hire purchase agreements indicates that the term "loan" does not capture such agreements and court-imposed orders were yet further away from loans, as ordinarily understood; and (d) para.15 was only engaged by loans taken out to defray "monies" advanced for a specific purpose (rather than financial obligations or obligations capable of financial expression generally).

Turning to the question of discrimination under art.14, a loan taken out to acquire *alternative* accommodation that was more suited to the needs of a disabled person would have escaped the prohibition on mortgage interest on loans taken out while a claimant was entitled to income support (see para.4(9)). However, the 2010 loan secured the right to remain in the *existing* accommodation. Thus the comparison in Judge Ward's view was between someone who does not need to move to another property in order to secure more suited accommodation for a disabled person and cannot in any event do so (it was suggested that J was too ill to move), and someone who can, and does, move to more suitable accommodation for that purpose. However, Judge Ward concluded that any differential treatment there may be in these circumstances was not on the grounds of status. He was, however, just about persuaded that if the disability of a member of the household was such that the household was unable to move following the expiry of a court order, this was capable of amounting to a "status". But if there was discrimination on the grounds of status by that route, it was justified for two substantial reasons. The first was considerations of equity—it could give income support recipients an unjustifiable advantage over people in low paid work who could not get a loan—and the second was the possibility of varying the court order.

Furthermore, if he was wrong that there was no discrimination on the ground of status in failing to allow mortgage interest on a loan taken out to remain in an existing home suitable for the needs of a disabled person when it would have been available had the decision been to move to a different property, that too would be justified because the Secretary of State had "provided for the allocation of resources to [certain categories of] people with disabilities when resources were finite and the potential exposure of public funds, were [mortgage interest] not subject to limitations, very large".

See also *PC v SSWP* [2010] UKUT 112 (AAC) discussed below under *"Interest" includes a "further interest"*.

Sub-paragraph (1): The loan (or any increase in the loan, *CIS 141/1993*) must either be *for the purpose of acquiring an interest in the home, or paying off another loan which was for an approved purpose.* In the second situation the loan will only qualify to the extent that the old loan would have qualified, on which see *CIS 5110/1999*. In *CIS 5110/1999* the claimant's original loan to purchase his home was for £49,000. He then discharged that loan with a loan from a home loans company. That loan was for £50,470 because it included an acceptance fee of £1,470. Subsequently that loan was replaced by a loan from a building society for £50,450. The Commissioner holds that the whole of the third loan, including the sum representing the home loan company's acceptance fee, fell within sub-para.(1)(b). The claimant had had to pay the fee of £1,470 in order to obtain the £49,000 that he needed to discharge his original loan. The £1,470 therefore qualified as money that had been applied for the purpose of paying off a loan within sub-para.(1)(a). Similarly, a repayment administration fee and an early repayment charge fell within para.(1)(b), subject to the qualification that if only part of the loan qualified, any part of those sums attributable to the non-qualifying part was not allowable (*DC v SSWP (JSA)* [2010] UKUT 459 (AAC)). 2.844

The cost of acquiring an interest in the home includes besides the purchase price expenses necessary for the purchase, e.g. stamp duty, legal fees (see *Decision Makers Guide*, para.23576). Loans include hire purchase agreements (sub-para. (2)). An overdraft facility is a loan for this purpose (see *CIS 6010/1995* in the notes to para.16), as is a debt owing on a credit card (see *CCS 4722/1998* decided under the similar child support provision).

Sub-paragraphs (1)(a) and (b) are not mutually exclusive, so eligible interest can be allowed under both heads (see *R(IS) 6/94* below).

CIS 563/1991 considered when money is being *applied* for an approved purpose. Clearly this is the case if it is spent directly on the purchase price and the legal and other expenses of the purchase. The Commissioner considers that it could also include money used for the purchase of goods or some other interest in property that then formed part of the consideration for the transfer of the interest in the home. However, it does not extend to money that has to be spent on some other purpose as a result of a precondition imposed by some other person, e.g. the mortgagee (see *Guest v Chief Adjudication Officer*, unreported, April 2, 1998, CA, below).

"Interest" includes a "further interest"

In *R(IS) 7/93* the claimant had been living in leasehold property for some time and receiving housing costs for the interest on the loan to acquire that interest. He received a further advance to enable him to buy the freehold reversion. It is held that the loan to acquire a further interest was for a qualifying purpose, and it did not matter that he already had one interest. "An interest" in the home should include both legal and equitable interests. In *CIS 465/1994* the Commissioner holds that "acquiring an interest" covers the situation where the owner does not have a 2.845

present right of possession and takes out a mortgage to buy out sitting tenants so that she can move into the property. The tenants were statutory tenants under the Rent Act 1977. The Commissioner states that the primary purpose of Sch.3 was to help with the costs of acquiring or keeping a roof over one's head. Interest in sub-para.(1)(a) was not restricted to "an interest in land" in the Law of Property Act sense, although it did contemplate "an interest of a proprietary nature or some closely analogous right of tenure or occupancy similar to that of a true tenant". Moreover, acquiring an interest could include purchasing an interest only for the purpose of extinguishing it (see *R(IS) 6/95* in the notes to para.3 of Sch.10 which regards a similar transaction as a sale from the tenant's point of view). The Commissioner distinguished *R (IS) 4/95* (see below) on the ground partly that the right of occupation at issue in that case was not a right of exclusive occupation.

In *CIS 679/1992* a loan taken out to purchase a strip of land to extend the claimant's garden was for the purpose of acquiring an interest in what was, at the date of the claim, the dwelling occupied as the home.

In *R(IS) 6/94* the claimant and his wife had bought their home in joint names with the help of a mortgage. They were equitable joint tenants. The claimant was made bankrupt and a trustee in bankruptcy appointed. The trustee in bankruptcy sold the claimant's former interest in the home to the claimant's wife. She obtained a mortgage to pay for this and to discharge the original mortgage (among other things). When the claim for income support was made, interest was only allowed on an amount equal to the original loan under sub-para.(1)(b). The Commissioner points out that on the appointment of the trustee in bankruptcy the claimant's estate vested in him and the equitable joint tenancy was severed (*Re Dennis (a Bankrupt)* [1992] 3 W.L.R. 204). It was replaced by an equitable tenancy in common, under which the trustee and the claimant's wife held equal shares. Therefore, when buying the claimant's former interest in the home, his wife was acquiring a further interest in it and the interest on the part of the mortgage advanced for that purpose was payable under sub-para.(1)(a).

2.846 When a claimant buys a former partner's interest in the home this will constitute acquiring a further interest in a home (but note para.4(2)–(12)). In *CIS 762/1994* the former matrimonial home was transferred to the claimant on the basis that she paid her ex-husband £5,000 and released him from all liability under the mortgage. The original mortgage had been for £43,200 but had increased to just over £52,300 because of arrears. The bank would not agree to the transfer of the house into the claimant's name unless the arrears were discharged. She therefore took out a second loan for £52,300 to discharge the original loan and the arrears. Housing costs on £43,200 only were awarded. But the Commissioner holds that the claimant was entitled to housing costs on the full amount of the second loan. That loan had been applied in part to acquire the husband's interest in the home, the consideration for which included releasing him from all liability under the mortgage, and in part to pay off the original loan of £43,200, and so the whole of it was eligible.

CIS/762/1994 is, however, distinguished on its facts in *PC v SSWP* [2010] UKUT 112 (AAC). When the claimant's wife (Mrs C) was divorced from her previous husband (Mr R) in 1995, Mr R's interest in the former matrimonial home had been transferred to her, subject to Mr R's entitlement to one third of the net proceeds of sale on her remarriage or their daughter attaining 18 years of age. Following the claimant's marriage to Mrs C, Mrs C transferred the property into the joint names of the claimant and herself and a new mortgage was taken out. This was used to discharge the original mortgage, pay the Legal Services Commission's charge and pay Mr R his entitlement. The tribunal found that only the amount used to discharge the original mortgage was eligible as housing costs. Judge Jacobs agreed. Mrs C had acquired absolute title to the property in 1995 and Mr R's right was to a sum of money. Mr R had a charge on the property but that was not the same thing as having an interest in it. The payment to Mr R of his entitlement meant that his charge on the property ceased but that did not give Mrs C any additional interest in the property. See also *R(IS) 4/95*, *R(IS) 18/93* and *CIS/336/1993* below. See also *CL v SSWP (IS)* [2015] UKUT 259 (AAC) discussed above as to whether "loan" in para.15(1)(a) includes deferred sale agreements imposed by court order in the course of divorce proceedings.

However, if the claimant and partner still count as a couple, the acquisition by one of them of the other's interest in the home does not come within sub-para.(1)(a). They are one entity for the purposes of income support, and any transaction between them, when together they previously owned the entire interest, does not give rise to housing costs (*R(IS) 1/95*).

R(IS) 4/95 decides that a Class F land charge (registered by a spouse to protect his or her rights under the Matrimonial Homes Act 1983) is not "an interest in the dwelling occupied as the home", but a mere right of occupation (see *Wroth v Tyler* [1974] Ch. 30). **2.847**

In *R(IS) 18/93* the land certificate of the claimant's home had been deposited with a bank as security for a company loan. When the bank threatened to call in the loan when the company was in trouble, the claimant obtained a mortgage to discharge the debt to the bank. This loan was not for a qualifying purpose. The deposit of the land certificate may have been evidence of the creation of an incumbrance on the claimant's title to the home, but the bank did not acquire an interest in the home. Therefore the mortgage loan was not to acquire the bank's interest. *CIS 336/1993* reaches a similar conclusion. It made no difference that the bank's charge had been created by way of a legal mortgage rather than deposit of the land certificate. By effecting the charge the claimant had not parted with an interest in his home. When he obtained release of the charge he did not acquire any interest.

"Duelling occupied as the home"

R(IS) 11/94 holds that "dwelling occupied as the home" in sub-para.(1)(a) includes any dwelling intended to be occupied as the home, since most properties are acquired before they become a home. If a person acquires a site and then builds a home on it, all the costs connected with the acquisition of the site and the subsequent building work constitute "monies applied" for the purpose of "acquiring an interest" in the home. Such building costs include the value of the claimant's own labour (put in this case at £9,000) and all bank charges (including overdraft interest) necessary to enable the home to be built up to the first day of occupation. However, any interest accruing after the claimant moves into the home is not eligible. **2.848**

CIS 297/1994 holds that the intention to make the property the home has to be formed at the date of acquisition and implemented as soon as practicable. But it would seem at least arguable that the wording of para.15(1)(a) does not actually require this, and that if the dwelling is now occupied as the home, even if this was not the case, or the intention, at the time the interest was acquired, sub-para.(1)(a) can apply. This has now been confirmed by *CIS 401/1999* which disagrees with *CIS 297/1994*. The Commissioner in *CIS 401/1999* points out that sub-para.(1)(a) is worded in general terms in order to cover a range of circumstances but it plainly covers the typical case in which the dwelling does not become the claimant's home until after the purchase has been completed and the claimant moves in. This showed that sub-para.(1)(a) was concerned with the use of the property at the time entitlement to income support was determined rather than at the time of acquisition. The claimant was therefore entitled to housing costs even though the property she was now living in was not originally acquired as a home.

In *Guest v Chief Adjudication Officer*, unreported, April 2, 1998, CA it was a condition of the claimant's loan of £85,000 to purchase his home that there would be a further charge of £30,000 on the property in order that the building society could recoup some of its loss in relation to his previous mortgage. The Commissioner held that this "further advance" of £30,000 was simply a transfer of part of the claimant's liability under the earlier mortgage to his new property and that this did not represent the taking out of a loan for the purposes of para.7(3) of Sch.3 (as in force before October 2, 1995). In addition, it did not fall within para.7(3)(a) (now sub-para.(1)(a)), as this did not extend to money which had to be spent on some other purpose as a result of a precondition imposed by some other person (e.g.

the mortgagee). Paragraph 7(3)(b) (now sub-para.(1)(b)) also did not apply as the provision of alternative security for part of the claimant's pre-existing liability did not amount to "paying off another loan". Moreover, that liability had not been incurred for the purpose of purchasing any interest in his *present* home. The Court of Appeal dismissed the claimant's appeal, holding that no loan as such had been taken out and that the Commissioner's conclusions as to the ambit of para.7(3) were correct. Head (b) had to be read in the light of the essential purpose of Sch.3, which was to provide housing costs in respect of the dwelling occupied as the claimant's home (i.e. his present home). Although there are differences between the former para.7(3) and sub-para.(1), the reasoning in this decision will apply equally to sub-para.(1), as confirmed by *CJSA 4807/2000*. The loans secured on the claimant's home included a loan taken out to purchase a house in which the claimant was living at the time of the loan but which had since been sold. The Commissioner holds that para.14(1)(a) of Sch.2 to the JSA Regulations 1996 (the equivalent of para.15(1)(a)) did not apply to a loan that was used to purchase a dwelling which has since ceased to be occupied as the home, even though it was so occupied at the date of the loan.

See also *R(IS) 14/01*. Under the terms of the claimant's mortgage she paid reduced interest payments during the first three years. The deferred interest was capitalised in another account and at the end of the three years interest was also charged on that sum. The Department refused to include the interest payable on the capitalised interest as part of the claimant's housing costs. The Commissioner accepted that the tribunal had been right to regard the capitalised sum in the second account as a loan as it was in effect a form of secondary financing. However, the sum "lent" to the claimant was not for the purpose of paying interest on the main loan because the interest due on that loan had been reduced. It was lent to allow the claimant to spend money on other things during the first three years. Although this may have had the effect of enabling the claimant to buy the house, this was not sufficient for the loan to qualify under sub-para.(1) (*CIS 3774/1997* not followed). See also *CJSA 888/1999* and *CIS 141/1993* in the note to para.8(1), (1A) and (1B). *CPC/3322/2007* applies those decisions and *R(IS) 14/01* in a case concerning para.11(1) of Sch.II to the State Pension Credit Regulations (the equivalent of para.15(1)).

2.849 *Sub-paragraph (3)*: The proportion of a loan for an eligible purpose defines the proportion of the loan that qualifies under para.15 (subject to the limit in para.11(8)).

Paragraph 16—Loans for repairs and improvements

2.850 *Sub-paragraph (1)*: Loans for the purpose of repairs or improvements to the home, or for service charges to pay for repairs or improvements, or loans to pay off such loans, are eligible (although these are considerably restricted compared with the previous form of Sch.3: see sub-para.(2)).

Placing limitations on the meeting of such costs does not breach art.8 ECHR (respect for private and family life) (*CIS 2056/2002*)).

"Repairs and improvements" are defined in sub-para.(2). Repairs or improvements to any part of the building containing the claimant's home, e.g. the common parts of a block of flats are covered. *R(IS) 5/96* holds that the loan has to be for repairs or improvements to the home that is currently occupied. Thus the claimant was not entitled to interest on a bank loan for central heating after he moved from that home.

2.851 To qualify under sub-para.(1), a loan must be taken out, *and* used for, the purpose set out in heads (a), (b) or (c). *R(IS) 5/06* holds that heads (a), (b) and (c) are to be regarded as a single purpose. Thus, provided that both the initial purpose of the loan and the purpose for which it is used fall within sub-para.(1) as a whole, it is irrelevant that they are not the same purpose. Furthermore, the purpose for which the loan was taken out has to be decided on all the evidence and not just on the understanding of the lender. In that case the claimant had originally taken out the loan to make certain improvements and consolidate loans but had then used a large part of it to adapt her home for the needs of a disabled person when her husband's illness was diagnosed.

The loan has to be used for the repairs, etc. within six months or some further period. If the loan is not so used, the claimant is not entitled to interest on it even during the six months or any extended period (*CIS 257/1994*). The capital amount of the loan is disregarded under para.8(b) of Sch.10.

CIS 6010/1995 decides that the use of an overdraft facility to finance building works could constitute a taking out of a loan for repairs and improvements. The claimant's builders required immediate payment, so she arranged an overdraft in order to pay them before her improvement grant came through. The Department refused payment of the interest on the overdraft on the ground that an overdraft facility was not a loan. The Commissioner holds that the wide ordinary meaning of "loan" as "money borrowed at interest" applied in this context and this covered the drawing of money on overdraft. There was clear evidence that the bank had agreed to grant the overdraft facility for the specific purpose of financing the building works. The Commissioner leaves open the questions whether a loan would be "taken out" where there was no advance arrangement and whether the required purpose could easily be shown in such circumstances.

The overall limit on loans applies (see para.11(5) but note the exception in para.11(9)) as well as the general limits in para.13. Note the increase in the limit for loans that has been introduced for certain claimants by the Social Security (Housing Costs Special Arrangements) (Amendment and Modification) Regulations 2008 (SI 2008/3195), as amended by the Social Security (Housing Costs Special Arrangements) (Amendment) Regulations 2009 (SI 2009/3257) (see the note on these Regulations under "*Modifications to the waiting periods and the cap on loans for certain claimants from January 5, 2009*" and "*Further Modifications from January 5, 2010*" above). But the restriction in para.4(2)–(12) (loans incurred while entitled to income support, income-related ESA or income-based JSA: reg.32 of the Income Support (General) (Jobseeker's Allowance Consequential Amendments) Regulations 1996, see p.807) does not apply to loans for repairs and improvements.

Sub-paragraph (2): To qualify, both repairs and improvements must be undertaken with a view to "maintaining the fitness of the dwelling for human habitation . . .", *and* be one of the listed measures. This is narrower than para.8(3) of the former Sch.3 under which any major repairs were covered if they were "necessary to maintain the fabric" of the home. Now for repairs to be eligible they must not only maintain the home's fitness for human habitation but also come within heads (a)–(l). The test in the former para.8(3) (that applied to improvements only) was that of "improving . . . fitness for occupation" (see *CIS 643/1993* which held that if the claimant considered that the work would improve the property this should be accepted, save in the most exceptional cases). The notion of "maintaining" is narrower than "improving" fitness. Moreover, the new criterion of human habitation seems to be an attempt to move away from the particular needs of the claimant in favour of a more "objective" standard (but see the new head (k) which necessarily will involve consideration of the needs of the disabled person concerned). 2.852

This point is taken up by Judge Mark in *FJ v SSWP* [2009] UKUT 207 (AAC), where he states:

> "It is plain that a dwelling is fit for human habitation as a matter of ordinary English if able bodied persons can live there without a problem, even if it is not adapted for the special needs of a disabled person. It is also plain that it is fit for human habitation in that sense even if it does not provide separate sleeping accommodation for children of different sexes who are part of the claimant's family. It is clear therefore that in the context of this provision, and to make sense of paragraph 16(2)(k) and (l), maintaining the fitness of the home for human habitation means so maintaining it for human habitation by the claimant and her family living there. Further, if the expression has that meaning in relation to (k)

and (l), it must also have the same meaning in relation to the remainder of paragraph 16(2), including sub-paragraph (2)(a)."

The same Judge emphasises in *JT v SSWP (JSA)* [2013] UKUT 184 (AAC) that the test is *maintaining* fitness for habitation, not making fit for habitation. He refers to the Department for Communities and Local Government's publication "*A Decent Home: Definition and guidance for implementation*" (June 2006). While the test of what is a decent home is not the same as whether a home is fit for human habitation, he considered that he could have some regard to the definition as an indication of what a person can reasonably expect in respect of a home.

2.853 *SSWP v AR (IS)* [2010] UKUT 308 (AAC) decides that the test for deciding whether repairs and improvements have been undertaken "with a view to maintaining the fitness of the dwelling for human habitation" was whether they would have been carried out by a sensible and prudent householder properly advised as to the reasonable necessity of the repairs/improvements and the likely consequences if they were not undertaken (as opposed to measures that are undertaken principally out of choice or preference).

The most notable omission from the listed measures was the former head (k), "other improvements which are reasonable in the circumstances" (see the notes to para.8(3) of the former Sch.3 in the 1995 edition of J. Mesher and P. Wood, *Income-related Benefits: the Legislation* as to the ambit of this provision). But the scope of several others was also narrowed. For example, provision of heating is no longer covered, only repairs to an existing heating system under head (b) (the use of the word "system" indicates that a replacement boiler, for example, should be covered as *part* of a heating system and see *CIS 15036/1996* below); head (j) seems considerably more limited than the former head (f) which referred to improvement in the structural condition of the home; and loans for facilities for storing food are no longer included (head (f)). Cupboards and a refrigerator are such facilities (*R(IS) 16/98*); the Commissioner also holds that a loan for a refrigerator would not in any event be covered by para.16 unless it is a fixture within the home (see *CIS 363/1993*). "Provision of" replaced "provision or improvement of" in a number of places (reflecting the change in the overall test from "improving" to "maintaning" the fitness of the home).

"Provision of" would not seem to be limited to initial installation, but could cover repairs to, or replacement of, an existing facility (see *R. v Social Fund Inspector Ex p. Tuckwood* (High Court, April 27, 1995). *CJSA 5439/1999* confirmed that provision includes replacement in this context and note *DC v SSWP (JSA)* [2010] UKUT 459 (AAC) below. See also *R(IS) 2/07* in which the Commissioner states that in the context of sub-para.(2) (and para.17(2)(c)) "provision" means providing something not already in existence or the replacement of something which no longer functions. However, as *JT v SSWP (JSA)* [2013] UKUT 184 (AAC) points out, *R(IS) 2/07* must be read in the light of para.32 of *SSWP v AR (IS)* [2010] UKUT 308 (AAC) which stated that "the reference to 'maintaining' the fitness of the dwelling implies that it is not necessary that the property has fallen in some respect below the standard of fitness before the costs can be allowed".

2.854 Heads (k) and (l) were new and make provision for these two specific situations. Note that a loan to which the new head (k) applies is ignored for the purposes of the ceiling on loans (para.11(9)).

On the meaning of "adapt a dwelling" in head (k), see *R (on the application of Mahmoudi) v London Borough of Lewisham* [2014] EWCA Civ 284; [2014] AACR 14, discussed in the note to para.3(7)(c)(i) above. The question to be asked is whether the process which the dwelling has undergone is a change that makes it more suitable for the needs of the disabled person.

Separate sleeping accommodation

2.855 On head (1) see *CIS 14657/1996*. The Commissioner points out that the loan has to be taken out "for the purpose" of the relevant improvements. The claimant's loan could therefore fall within head (1) where his daughter was aged 10 but her brother would not reach that age for another year or so because the money was being used for something that was bound to happen in the near future. The Commissioner also decides that the cost of a survey could come within head (j) as reasonably incidental to the carrying out of the work covered by that head. *CIS 1678/1999* goes further than *CIS 14657/1996* in holding that it was not necessary for the provision of separate sleeping accommodation to have been the sole or even the main purpose in taking out the loan. It was enough if it was one of two or more purposes (the claimant had wanted her children to have separate bedrooms from the beginning so as not to disturb each other's sleep). Furthermore, it did not matter how long a time had elapsed between the taking out of the loan and the children's attainment of the age of 10 (the loan in question had been incurred while the claimant was expecting her second child). This was because if there were children of different sexes their need for separate sleeping accommodation was a foreseeable and inevitable future need that was likely to have been in the mind of a claimant extending her house. The Commissioner in *CIS 1678/1999* expressly does not follow *CIS 16936/1996* which had decided that the relevant children must all have been at least 10 years old at the date on which the loan was taken out. However, in *CIS 5119/2001* the Commissioner declines to follow *CIS 1678/1999*. In his view it conflicted with *CIS 14657/1998*. But in any event it conflicted with *CIS 2711/1999* (decided by the same Commissioner as *CIS 14657/1998*). In *CIS 2711/1999* the Commissioner had stated that in deciding whether the conditions in head (l) were met it was the circumstances as they stood at the time the loan was taken out and the money was used in carrying out the repairs and improvements that had to be considered, not any later date when a claim for income support was made, or some still later date when during the continuation of a claim a child reached 10. The Commissioner in *CIS 5119/2001* was in complete agreement that the focus had to be on the nature and purpose of the loan at the time when it was taken out rather than any later date. There is therefore a conflict between these various decisions, although the weight of authority would seem to be that the relevant children must be approaching 10 or within a year or two of doing so when the loan is taken out. This conflict was considered in *HMRC v CA* [2009] UKUT 13 (AAC) which concludes that a loan taken out in advance of a child reaching 10 can come within head (l) but how far in advance will depend on the circumstances of the case (preferring *CIS/14657/1996* and *CIS/5119/2001* to *CIS/1678/1999*).

Note the change in the wording of head (l) from November 17, 2008. It now applies if the loan is to provide separate sleeping accommodation for people of different sexes aged 10 or over but under 20 who live with the claimant and for whom the claimant or the claimant's partner is responsible (for the meaning of "responsible"—see reg.15). The previous form of head (l) only applied to the provision of separate sleeping accommodation for male and female *children* aged 10 or over who were members of the claimant's family. As a child is a person under 16 (see s.137 SSCBA), this was ambiguous because a family could include a "qualifying young person" (i.e. a person up to the age of 20) and consequently it has been amended.

Provision of hot water not connected to a central heating system

In *KW v SSWP (IS)* [2012] UKUT 180 (AAC) the claimant was refused housing costs in respect of interest on a loan that he had taken out in order to install solar panels. The claimant had an existing gas central heating system with a boiler, storage tank and hot water cylinder, which provided both heating and hot water. The solar panels were installed to provide hot water only via the cylinder; the gas system would still "kick-in" to heat the water, should the solar panels not provide sufficient energy. The tribunal therefore concluded that the solar panels were providing hot water as part of the whole central heating system and that the loan for the solar panels did not fall within head (a). **2.856**

Judge Ward upheld the tribunal's decision. The words "not connected to a central heating system" must have some purpose and were intended to have an exclusionary effect in relation to the provision of hot water that *is* connected to a central heating system. Judge Ward also held that "necessary associated plumbing" referred to plumbing associated with one of the listed five items, such as connecting the appliance to a water supply or a drain; it did not cover such plumbing when one of the five items was not being provided.

Heating systems

2.857 On the meaning of "repairs to existing heating systems" in head (b), see *CIS 781/2002*. The claimant had two storage radiators in her home. She replaced these with a boiler and ten radiators. The Commissioner considered that repairing an existing system meant changing a part of the system that did not work or putting it back into working order. A repair could have as an incidental effect an improvement in the system. But in the circumstances of this case there had clearly been a replacement of the system, not a repair of the existing system.

Note also *CIS 15036/1996* which concerned whether replacement of a central heating boiler came within para.8(3)(h) of the former Sch.3 ("provision of heating, including central heating"). The Commissioner decides that the installation of the new boiler was an improvement which had been undertaken with a view to "improving fitness for occupation" and so came within para.8(3) (it was not contended that it constituted a major repair necessary to maintain the fabric of the home). The fact that the boiler had merely been replaced by its modern equivalent did not matter. The Commissioner refers to *Morcom v Campbell-Johnson* [1956] 1 Q.B. 106 in which Denning LJ had drawn a distinction between the provision of something new which would constitute an improvement and the replacement of something worn out, albeit with a modern equivalent, which would come within the category of repairs, not improvement. Presumably on the basis of this dictum the replacement of a boiler would also fall within head (b) as it would seem to fulfil the test of maintaining fitness for human habitation. The consequence for the claimant in *CIS 15036/1996* was that the element of her service charge attributable to the new boiler had to be deducted under the former para.9(2)(c) (now para.17(2)(c)).

Damp proofing; insulation

2.858 In *CIS 2132/1998* the claimant had been billed for the cost of renewing a roof over one of the other flats in her block. The Commissioner decides that this did not come within any of the relevant heads in sub-para.(2). Head (g) did not apply as the roof was not part of the dwelling occupied by the claimant as her home. Head (j) was also not applicable, as there was no evidence that the roof had been renewed because of an unsafe structural defect. In addition, although a repair to a roof could, depending on its nature, be a damp-proofing measure, the renewal of a roof did not fall within head (c). In *R(IS)* 2/07 the Commissioner stated that in his view "damp proofing" and "insulation" were terms of art in the building trade which have found their way into ordinary language. As used in head (c), he considered that "damp proofing" was limited to measures taken to prevent rising damp or damp from condensation, and "insulation" in head (g) was similarly restricted to such things as the installation of double-glazing, loft insulation and cavity wall insulation.

SSWP v AR (IS) [2010] UKUT 308 (AAC) did not consider that the reference to "rising damp or damp from condensation" in *R(IS) 2/07* was intended to be an exhaustive list of the causes of damp and that work undertaken for the purpose of curing penetrating damp, such as rendering or re-rendering walls, could constitute damp proof measures, as could internal plastering, depending on the circumstances. Equally the replacement of barge boards and fascias, if they were rotten and their replacement was a necessary accompaniment to the replacement of gutters and downpipes, could also be part of damp proofing (although they might also fall within head (e) (provision of drainage facilities)).

JT v SSWP (JSA) [2013] UKUT 184 (AAC) accepts that the replacement of the claimant's windows was needed to provide adequate insulation for her home.

Provision of facilities for preparing and cooking food

In *DC v SSWP (JSA)* [2010] UKUT 459 (AAC) the work undertaken was a kitchen extension and modernisation because the previous kitchen was very small and in a bad state of repair. Judge Turnbull considered that the provision of facilities for preparing and cooking food was not necessarily limited to the provisions of items such as cookers and worktops but could include the construction or adaptation of the part of the building containing them. Thus, if the previous kitchen was too small and poorly located so that some reconstruction was necessary to render the house habitable, that would amount to the provision of facilities for cooking, notwithstanding that there had previously been a kitchen. However, storage facilities (such as kitchen cupboards) and facilities for eating (such as a "breakfast room") would not be included. **2.859**

A similar approach was taken in *JT v SSWP (JSA)* [2013] UKUT 184 (AAC). The cost of the new sink, cooker, hobs, hood and work surfaces (and associated building and electrical work) was allowed as housing costs but not the base units and cupboards, washing machine, drier and fridge freezer.

Sub-paragraph (3): see the note to para.15(3).

Paragraph 17—other housing costs

This provision lists the other miscellaneous housing costs covered by income support (sub-para.(1)(a)–(f)) and contains the conditions for meeting these costs. **2.860**

Service charges

Of these items, the category of "service charges" (sub-para.(1)(b)) is probably of most interest. This phrase is given no special definition. (It does not include an administration fee charged by a lender where mortgage payments are in arrears (*CIS 392/1994*).) *CIS 157/1989* suggested that it means charges in respect of a service rendered to a tenant by the landlord. The Tribunal of Commissioners in *R(IS) 3/91* and *R(IS) 4/91* decides that the category can extend to owner-occupiers as well. The essence is the determination and arranging of what would otherwise be left for the occupier to do for himself, on the basis of an arrangement which the terms of occupation of the property make binding on all those with the same interest in the property. **2.861**

In *R(IS) 4/91* the claimant, an owner-occupier, had to pay £93 a year to have his cess-pit emptied. The appeal had to be returned to the SSAT for further findings of fact, but it was suggested that if the service was carried out by an outside contractor engaged by the claimant, the cost would not be a service charge.

However, things within the housing benefit definition of ineligible service charges are excluded (sub-para.(2)(b)). This list covers charges in respect of day-to-day living expenses, a number of personal services and other services "not connected with the provision of adequate accommodation" (see *CIS 1460/1995* and the other decisions discussed below under "*Sheltered accommodation*"). *CJSA 5493/1999* expresses the view that "adequate" has a looser meaning than fitness for human habitation but is not to be equated with what is desirable; nor is a provision for bad debt connected with the adequacy of accommodation (although see *CH/3548/2006*). But a provision for future repairs could be: see *CIS 667/2002* and *R(IS) 2/07* below.

In *R(IS) 3/91* a leaseholder's share of the cost of roof repairs was a service charge. The obligation was imposed on the claimant by the conditions of her occupation and the service was connected with the provision of adequate accommodation, so that the exclusion in sub-para.(2)(b) did not bite. In the light of *CIS/2132/1998* and *R(IS) 2/07* (see below) it would seem that the exclusion in sub-para.(2)(c) also did not apply. **2.862**

Under sub-para.(2)(c) charges for the cost of repairs and improvements, as defined in para.16(2), are also deducted. The narrowing of the scope of para.16(2) will mean a corresponding reduction in the exclusion of service charges under sub-para.(2)(c). *CIS/488/2008* highlights a very common difficulty with appeals concerning sub-para.(2)(c), namely a dearth of evidence in relation to the nature of the repairs and improvements for which the service charges are being levied. The Commissioner holds that since the claimant could be expected to have some information as to the state of repair of the building and where the SoS had failed to ask the right questions, the tribunal should have directed an oral hearing and had erred in not doing so.

For interest on loans for service charges for repairs and improvement, see para.16.

2.863 Sub-paragraph (2)(a) provides that if a charge includes fuel charges, deductions are also made (except for charges in respect of communal areas: para.4 of Sch.1 to the Housing Benefit Regulations, confirmed in *CIS 1460/1995*). The standard amounts to be deducted under sub-para.(2)(a) are (from April 2015, not increased in April 2016): heating (apart from hot water), £28.80; hot water, £3.35; lighting, £2.30; cooking, £3.35. The standard amounts can be altered on evidence of the actual or estimated charge.

Note that since housing benefit expenditure is excluded generally under para.4(1)(a), this means that no service charge, payment of which by a tenant is a condition for the occupation of the home (and therefore within the definition of rent), can count under Sch.3.

From April 2000 the "transitional housing benefit scheme" (see Sch.1B to the Housing Benefit Regulations) had allowed certain service charges to be met by housing benefit where the claimant was in supported accommodation. However, this came to an end in April 2003 and the responsibility for meeting such costs passed to local authorities under the "Supporting People" programme. Payments made by local authorities under this programme are disregarded (see para.76 of Sch.9 and para.66 of Sch.10).

2.864 *Insurance charges*: In *R(IS) 4/92* it was held that sums required to be paid by a tenant under the terms of the lease to reimburse the landlord for the cost of property insurance were a service charge within the principles set out in *R(IS) 3/91* and *R(IS) 4/91*. The Commissioner also found that the landlord's obligation to use any money paid out under the insurance policy as a result of fire on reinstatement of the property meant that the charge was connected with the provision of adequate accommodation. The Commissioner in *CSIS 4/1990* doubted that building insurance was so connected (referring to the earlier decision in *CIS 17/1988* where there was a suggestion to the contrary). The Court of Session in the *McSherry* case (which is the appeal in *CSIS 4/1990*) does not deal with this point. However, in *R(IS) 19/93* the Commissioner agrees with *R(IS) 4/92* and dissents from the suggestion in *CIS 17/1988*. The weight of authority would therefore seem to favour the interpretation taken in *R(IS) 4/92* in relation to payments by tenants to reimburse landlords for the cost of building insurance. But note the effect of para.4(1)(a). In *R(IS) 4/92* the Commissioner made his award subject to enquiries whether the reimbursement of the landlord's insurance premiums would be included in the claimant's rent for housing benefit purposes.

In *Dunne v Department of Health and Social Security* (September 10, 1993), the Court of Appeal in Northern Ireland decided that the building insurance premium paid by the claimant as an owner occupier was not a service charge. Although the claimant was obliged to take out such insurance under the terms of both his building lease and his mortgage, it did not fulfill the test laid down in *R(IS) 3/91* and *R(IS) 4/91*. Such a premium was to be distinguished from payment required to be made to the landlord for building insurance by occupiers of a block of flats which clearly was a service charge. In *Secretary of State for Social Security v McSherry* (March 17, 1994) the property insurance premium at issue was mandatory under the terms of the claimant's mortgage. The Court of Session agrees with the decision in *Dunne*, holding that the omission of insurance premiums from para.1 of the former Sch.3 (in contrast to the express provision for routine maintenance and insurance in the supplementary benefit scheme) was deliberate. (*R(SB) 1/90* holds that although decisions of the Court of Appeal of Northern Ireland are not binding on Commissioners in Great Britain, identically worded provisions operating in both Northern Ireland and Great Britain are to be interpreted uniformly. Decisions of the Court of Session are binding.)

R(IS) 19/93 had come to a similar conclusion. The Commissioner states that the claimant's obligation to pay the insurance premium to his building society was not an obligation arising from his interest or estate in the property, but from his mortgage. It was a consequence of the claimant's financial arrangements, not his ownership of the property itself, and thus was not a service charge. In essence, the payment was no different from a house insurance premium paid under an ordinary contract between an owner/occupier and his insurance company (which had been held in *CIS 17/1988* not to constitute a service charge).

The result is that whether the obligation to pay insurance charges or to reimburse a landlord for the payment of insurance premiums constitutes a service charge depends upon it coming within the principles set out in *R(IS) 3/91* and *R(IS) 4/91*. It seems clear that payments required to be made to the landlord from occupiers of a block of flats to cover insurance for the building are a service charge, whereas a building insurance premium payable under the terms of a claimant's mortgage is not. An insurance charge of the kind concerned in *R(IS) 4/92* also constitutes a service charge. On the other hand, an obligation on the claimant to effect insurance under the terms of a lease would not qualify.

Reserve funds: *CIS 667/2002* considered payments into a reserve fund. The Commissioner referred to *CCS 5242/1995* (a child support case) which had decided that payments into a reserve fund could be eligible as housing costs, although there might have to be an apportionment for any relevant deductions under sub-para.(2). The only relevant deductions in this context were those that were not connected with the provision of adequate accommodation and any amounts for repairs and improvements as defined in para.16(2). The Commissioner acknowledges that because the works for which the reserve fund will eventually be used are not yet known an element of speculation is required. But this could be informed by the following factors: (i) the terms governing the use of the reserve fund or the scope of the landlord's powers under the service charge; (ii) information on how the reserve fund has been used in the past; and (iii) details of any work that is planned or anticipated. In this case the only evidence available related to (iii). Future works were to cover roof recovering, repair of a lift, external repointing and redecoration and improvements of the common parts. The Commissioner concluded that none of those constituted a repair or improvement under para.16(2) (see *CIS 2132/1998* in the notes to para.16 in relation to roof renewal) and all related to the provision of adequate accommodation. The consequence was that the whole of the current payment into the reserve fund was an eligible service charge (although in future years the available evidence might justify a different conclusion). 2.865

Payments for future maintenance was also one of the issues in *R(IS) 2/07*. The Secretary of State had argued that the cost of replacement windows and roof repairs provided for in the reserve fund were deductible from the service charge under sub-para.(2)(c) as being in respect of the provision of insulation, natural light, damp proofing or the repair of unsafe structural defects. However, this is rejected by the Commissioner who points out that the purpose of a reserve fund is to avoid the need for the repair of unsafe structural defects and that the repeated use of the word "provision" in para.16(2) implies the furnishing of something not already in existence or the replacement of something which no longer functions. He agrees with *CIS/2132/1998* that damp proofing is not the predominant purpose of a roof. However, he goes on to state that in his view "damp proofing" and "insulation" are terms of art in the building trade which have found their way into ordinary language. As used in para.16(2), he considered that the former was limited to measures taken to prevent rising damp or damp from condensation in an existing building, and the latter to such things as the installation of double-glazing, loft insulation and cavity wall insulation to reduce heat loss in an existing building. Furthermore, the contribution to the reserve fund in respect of future window repairs in the claimant's own flat came within the definition of service charge in *R(IS) 4/91*, para.15. The Commissioner also made the more general observation that even if any of the contingencies itemised in a reserve fund do correspond to the para.16(2) list, what is deductible under sub-para.(2)(c) is the current or recent capital cost of works referred to in para.16(2) incurred within the time prescribed by para.16(1), not the claimant's current contributions to a reserve against such capital costs in the future.

2.866 *Sheltered accommodation*: *CIS 1460/1995* concerned a service charge for residents of sheltered accommodation for the elderly. The claimant lived in a self-contained bungalow and had the use of communal areas (pathways and gardens) and a communal lounge; the service charge covered the costs of broadly the maintenance of the common areas and the structure of the buildings, as well as a resident warden. The Commissioner accepts that the terms of the appendix to *R(IS) 3/91* and *R(IS) 4/91* as a whole (as opposed to the headnote) made it clear that a service charge was only to be excluded under sub-para.(2)(b) to the extent it related to matters specified as ineligible in para.1 of Sch.1 to the Housing Benefit Regulations; there was no overriding test of connection with the adequacy of the accommodation (see para.1(g) of Sch.1). Where an element of a service charge was not dealt with in sub-paras (a)–(f) of para.1 of Sch.1 so that sub-para.(g) had to be considered, a common sense view had to be taken. In general, where a claimant had a right to use a communal lounge, gardens, etc. services related to those communal areas should be accepted as related to the provision of adequate accommodation. Paragraph 1 as a whole did contemplate that charges for communal areas could be eligible (see, for example, sub-para.(a)(ii) (laundry facilities), (iii) (children's play area) and (iv) (cleaning of communal areas)). Moreover, if service charges were thought to be excessive, the appropriate control mechanism was para.10 (now see para.13). (See also *CP v Aylesbury Vale DC* [2011] UKUT 22 (AAC) which confirms that charges for maintaining a communal garden are eligible service charges.) On the meaning of para.1(g) itself, although it excluded services which related purely to meeting the personal needs of residents, this did not mean that in considering whether a service was related to the provision of adequate accommodation the question of suitability for the personal needs of the residents was not relevant (see Sedley J in *R. v North Cornwall DC Ex p. Singer* (High Court, November 26, 1993, 11–12 of the transcript). Paragraph 1 of Sch.1 did envisage that the personal needs of the claimant could be considered (see sub-para.(a)(iv) on window-cleaning and sub-para.(c) on emergency alarm systems where the eligibility of a service charge depended on the claimant's personal circumstances). What was connected to the provision of adequate accommodation, including how far the personal needs of residents should be taken into account, was a question of fact in each case (para.17 of the appendix to *R(IS) 3/91* and *R(IS) 4/91*).

The Commissioner also deals with the meaning of "sheltered accommodation" (see the definition of "communal area" in what was then para.7 (now para.8) of Sch.1 to the Housing Benefit Regulations which includes rooms of common use in sheltered, but not non-sheltered, accommodation). He suggests that the characteristics of such accommodation were the grouping together of individual dwellings, which were offered primarily to those with some special housing need, and where some communal facilites, the employment of a warden and an emergency alarm system, were included. But accommodation could still be sheltered accommodation even without some of these features.

The meaning of "sheltered accommodation" is further considered in *JB v Oxford CC and SSWP (HB)* [2011] UKUT 136 (AAC). The claimant had severe learning difficulties; he had his own bedroom and shared a kitchen, bathroom, toilet, sitting rooms etc. with four other tenants, who had similar difficulties. Care, support and supervision was provided on a 24-hour basis. Judge Levenson held that "sheltered accommodation" clearly meant "something more than ordinary accommodation or shelter . . . this can only really mean that it is accommodation provided for people who are in some way (and probably for some defined reason) more vulnerable than most people are, or are vulnerable in a particular kind of way". There was no need, as the LA had argued, for the accommodation to be self-contained and if there were resident staff, there was no reason for the purposes of the definition for there to be a warden or alarm system (he otherwise agreed with the Commissioner's comments in *CIS/1460/1995*). Although some types of accommodation, such as residential care homes, standard student accommodation and accommodation which was not designed for any kind of vulnerable person, were clearly not "sheltered accommodation", it should be given a broad meaning and clearly encompassed the claimant's accommodation.

This decision was upheld by the Court of Appeal in *Oxford CC v Basey* [2012] EWCA Civ 115; [2012] AACR 38. Sullivan LJ concluded: **2.867**

> "Parliament did not choose to define sheltered accommodation and the Court should not impose a prescriptive definition upon an inherently flexible concept which can take many different forms, and which now includes very sheltered or extra care sheltered accommodation."

In *Liverpool City Council v (1) NM, (2) WD (HB)* [2015] UKUT 523 (AAC) M was a licensee of a room in a supported housing scheme for 16-25 year olds. D was an assured tenant in a sheltered housing scheme for those over 55 and for younger people with disabilities. In both cases their service charges for water rates were broken down into communal water charges, which were stated to be "eligible for HB", and charges for personal use of water (in their room/flat), which were stated to be "not eligible for HB". The local authority disallowed housing benefit in respect of the communal water charges, contending that all water charges, whether for personal or communal use, fell to be deducted under reg.12(B)(5) of the Housing Benefit Regulations 2006. It also contended that communal water charges were ineligible service charges in accordance with Sch.1 to the Housing Benefit Regulations 2006 because they were either for "day-to-day living expenses" within the meaning of para.1(a) or charges which were not connected with the provision of adequate accommodation within the meaning of para.1(g).

Judge Knowles firstly rejected the Council's submission that the accommodation occupied by M was not "sheltered accommodation". Applying *Basey*, "sheltered accommodation" was "an inherently flexible concept" and included accommodation, such as in M's case, where the accommodation was provided on the basis that the licensee accepted support services. She then went on to hold that reg.12(B)(5) was only concerned with the deduction of water charges for personal use when the claimant was not separately billed. It had no application to communal water charges. She also rejected the contention that communal water charges were "day-to-day living expenses" and found that they were clearly charges related to the provision of adequate accommodation, applying *CIS/1460/1995*. The result was that the service charges for the supply of water for communal areas were eligible for housing benefit (and thus are not excluded under para.17(2)(b)), except for water used for the provision of laundry which is ineligible under para.1(a)(ii) of Sch.1. But water charges for the cleaning of a communal laundry are eligible (see para.1(a)(iv)(aa) of Sch.1); this would include the cleaning of laundry equipment (see para.1(a)(ii)).

In *R(IS) 2/07* the claimant owned a leasehold property in a sheltered accommodation complex. Under the terms of her lease she had to pay a service charge which covered services in respect of the buildings, gardens and other ground that formed the complex (but not the insides of any dwelling), as well as personal and communal services for herself and the other owners. One of the issues was the proportion of staff salaries and associated administrative costs that were to be attributed to housing related services (and therefore eligible for income support), as opposed to personal care services (which would be met under the "Supporting People" programme). The tribunal had simply accepted the estimate provided by the company that managed the complex. However, the Commissioner set the tribunal's decision aside, stating that it was necessary to make findings on how many hours the staff actually spent providing accommodation-related services (as opposed to personal services). This ratio should then be applied to the other staff-related costs, such as staff advertising. See also *ET v Rossendale BC [2010] UKUT 222 (AAC)* which concerned whether an allowance for management and administrative costs as part of a concierge charge was excessive (it also considered whether a provision for bad debts and voids included in the charge was excessive).

In *R(PC) 1/07*, which concerned para.13(2)(b) of Sch.II to the State Pension Credit Regulations (the equivalent of sub-para.(2)(b)), the Commissioner recognises that the "gold standard" process for assessing what proportion of service charges are eligible or ineligible put forward in *R(IS) 2/07*, para.28, may not always be necessary or possible and concurs with *CPC/968/2005* that a broad approach is needed. In his view, given, e.g. the terms of the lease relating to the services and service charges, a breakdown of the service charges, details of what service charges (if any) are met by the Supporting People programme and a statement from the warden (or scheme manager as he was referred to in this case) as to how his working hours are usually divided up, it should be possible to make a reasoned estimate of how much of the service charges are accommodation-related. However, each case will depend on its own facts and evidential requirements will vary.

2.868 *R(PC) 1/07* had also taken a different approach to that of *R(IS) 2/07* on the attribution of general administrative costs (e.g. management fees, telephones, audit, accountancy charges, etc.). *R(IS) 2/07* had stated that these should be apportioned in the same ratio as the staff costs (see para.28). *R(PC) 1/07*, however, concluded that general administrative costs had to be apportioned on the same basis as the ratio of eligible to ineligible costs for the rest of the overall budget (see para.8) (following *CPC/968/2005*). This inconsistency is dealt with in *SSWP v DL (SPC)* [2013] UKUT 29 (AAC); [2013] AACR 22, which decides that *R(PC) 1/07* is to be preferred on this point. *SSWP v DL* also contains a useful summary of the general propositions arising from the caselaw on the eligibility/non-eligibility of service charges (see paras 24–28).

R(PC) 2/08 discusses the provisions for supersession in a case where the claimant was awarded housing costs based on an estimate of his service charges for the year and then later (a considerable time later in that case) submits the invoice for his actual service charges for the year in question.

Other miscellaneous housing costs

2.869 Sub-paragraph (a) concerns payments of rent or ground rent relating to a long tenancy (for the definition of "long tenancy" see reg.2(1)). See *SSWP v UP (JSA)* [2010] UKUT 262 (AAC); [2011] AACR 12 which refers to the fact, as *R(H) 3/07* had pointed out, that a lease of more than seven years of registered land "does not operate at law until the relevant registration requirements are met" (see s.27 of the Land Registration Act 2002). Thus until the claimant's tenancy (which was part of a home financing scheme designed to be compliant with Shari'a principles, i.e. not involving the payment of any interest), had been registered at the Land Registry a long tenancy did not exist and so no payments of rent made by the claimant could be payments relating to a long tenancy.

On the meaning of "long tenancy" under Scots law see *NR v SSWP (SPC)* [2013] UKUT 647 (AAC); [2014] AACR 22.

On sub-para.(1)(d) (payments under a co-ownership scheme), see *CJSA 5493/1999*.

Paragraph 18—non-dependent deductions

2.870 Non-dependent is defined in reg.3. The standard deductions depend on whether the non-dependent is in remurative work or not, and the level of earnings (sub-paras (1) and (2)). The same deduction is made for a couple as for a single person (sub-paras (3) and (4)). Note that no deduction is made from the benefit of a claimant who (or whose partner) is severely sight impaired or blind or who is in receipt of attendance allowance, the care component of disability living allowance, the daily living component of personal independence payment or armed forces independence payment for himself (sub-para.(6)). Note also the list in sub-para.(7) of non-dependants for whom no deduction is made. Those covered include those getting a training allowance while on youth training (head (b)); students (head (c)); under-25s on income support or income-based JSA (head (d)); those for whom a deduction has already been made from housing benefit (head (e)); people who would not count as non-dependents under reg.3(2B) but for reg.3(2C) (e.g. co-owners who are close relatives or their partners, where the co-ownership arose after April 11, 1988) (head (f)); patients absent from home for more than 52 weeks (note that with effect from April 10, 2006 the definition of "patient" for the purposes of this provision is to be found in para.3(13)(b); this definition is wide enough to include a person who is in hospital as a private patient) or prisoners (head (g)); people in receipt of state pension credit (head (h)); under 25s who are in receipt of income-related ESA at the assessment phase rate (head (i)); and under 25s whose award of universal credit is calculated on the basis that they do not have any earned income (as defined in reg.52 of the Universal Credit Regulations (sub-para.(9); see Vol.V in this series for the Universal Credit Regulations) (head (j)). See also sub-para.(8).

In *CH/48/2006* (a case concerning the calculation of a non-dependent's earnings for the purposes of council tax benefit) the local authority had applied the highest rate of the non-dependent deduction in respect of the claimant's daughter in the absence of any actual evidence as to what she was earning. She had refused to provide this information. The claimant's evidence was that his daughter was 19-years-old and worked for 20 hours a week in a clothes shop. She occasionally worked overtime. The Commissioner recognised that the local authority was entitled to require evidence from claimants and that, in the absence of such evidence, it could make adverse inferences. However, any such adverse inference had to be based on some sense of reality. The claimant's daughter was only 19 and working in a junior role in an occupation that was not known for paying high wages. It was inherently unlikely that she would have been paid much above the minimum wage. The local authority and the tribunal had a duty to assess, on the evidence available and drawing *reasonable* adverse assumptions where no evidence was available, what was the likely level of the daughter's earnings. On this basis the Commissioner concluded on the balance of probabilities, and drawing the most adverse inferences that could sensibly be taken in the circumstances, that the claimant's daughter's pay was £5 per hour and that she did 10 hours paid overtime a week.

SCHEDULE 3A

[Revoked by the Social Security (Miscellaneous Amendments) Regulations 2006 (SI 2006/588), reg.2(4)(e) with effect from April 3, 2006] **2.871**

SCHEDULE 3B

[Revoked by the Social Security (Miscellaneous Amendments) Regulations 2006 (SI 2006/588), reg.2(4)(f) with effect from April 3, 2006] **2.872**

SCHEDULE 3C

[Revoked by the Social Security (Removal of Residential Allowance and Miscellaneous Amendments) Regulations 2003 (SI 2003/1121), reg.2 and Sch.1, para.7 with effect from October 6, 2003.] **2.873**

SCHEDULE 4

[Revoked by Social Security Amendment (Residential Care and Nursing Homes) Regulations 2001 (SI 2001/3767), reg.2 and Sch. Pt I para.16 with effect from April 8, 2002.] **2.874**

2.875 SCHEDULE 7 [35 **Regulations 21 and 21AA]**

APPLICABLE AMOUNTS IN SPECIAL CASES

Column (1)	*Column (2)*
Patients **1.**—[34 . . .]	**1.**—[34 . . .]
[34 39 **Persons serving a sentence of imprisonment detained in hospital** **2A.**—A person serving a sentence of imprisonment detained in hospital.]	**2A.**—[38 Nil.
2B.—[36. . .]	**2B.**—[36. . .]
3.—[31 37. . .]	**3.**—[31 37. . .]
Column (1)	*Column (2)*
4.—[6. . .]	
5.—[6. . .].	
Claimants without accommodation **6.**—A claimant who is without accommodation.	**6.**—The amount applicable to him under regulation 17[3(1)](a) only.
Members of religious orders **7.**—A claimant who is a member of and fully maintained by a religious order.	**7.**—Nil.
Prisoners **8.**—A person— (a) except where sub-paragraph (b) applies, who is a prisoner; (b) who is detained in custody pending trial or sentence following conviction by a court.	**8.**— (a) Nil; (b) only such amount, if any, as may be applicable under regulation 17[3(1)](e).
9.—A claimant who is a member of a couple and who is temporarily separated from his partner [10where— (a) one member of the couple is— [33 (i) not a patient but is residing in a care home, an Abbeyfield Home or an independent hospital, or] (ii) resident in premises used for the rehabilitation of alcoholics or drug addicts, or (iii) resident in accommodation provided under section 3 of and Part II of the Schedule to, the Polish Resettlement Act 1947 (provision of accommodation in camps), or (iv) participating in arrangements for training made under section 2 of the Employment and Training Act 1973 [12 or section 2 of the Enterprise and	**9.**—Either— (a) the amount applicable to him as a member of a couple under regulation 17; or

Column (1)	*Column (2)*
New Towns (Scotland) Act 1990] or attending a course at an employment rehabilitation centre established under that section [12 of the 1973 Act], where the course requires him to live away from the dwelling occupied as the home, or (v) in a probation or bail hostel approved for the purpose by the Secretary of State; and (b) the other member of the couple is— (i) living in the dwelling occupied as the home, or (ii) a patient, or [33 (iii) residing in a care home, an Abbeyfield Home or an independent hospital.]	(b) the aggregate of his applicable amount and that of his partner assessed under the provisions of these Regulations as if each of them were a single claimant, or a lone parent, whichever is the greater.
Polygamous marriages where one or more partners are temporarily separated **10.**—A claimant who is a member of a polygamous marriage and who is temporarily separated from a partner of his, where one of them is living in the home while the other member is— [33 (a) not a patient but is residing in a care home, an Abbeyfield Home or an independent hospital, or] (b) [33. . .] (c) [1. . .] (d) resident in premises used for the rehabilitation of alcoholics or drug addicts; or (e) attending a course of training or instruction provided or approved by the [12Secretary of State for Employment] where the course requires him to live away from home; or (f) in a probation or bail hostel approved for the purpose by the Secretary of State.	**10.**—Either— (a) the amount applicable to the members of the polygamous marriage under regulation 18; or (b) the aggregate of the amount applicable for the members of the polygamous marriage who remain in the home under regulation 18 and the amount applicable in respect of those members not in the home calculated as if each of them were a single claimant, or a lone parent, whichever is the greater.
[24**Single claimants temporarily in local authority accommodation** **10A.**—[30 . . .]	**10A.**—[30 . . .]
Couples and members of polygamous marriages where one member is or all are temporarily in local authority accommodation **10B.**—[30 . . .] **Lone parents who are in residential accommodation temporarily** **10C.**—[30. . .]	**10B.**—[30 . . .] **10C.**—[30 . . .]]
10D.—[15 . . .]	**10D.**—[15 . . .]

Column (1)	*Column (2)*
Couples where one member is abroad **11.**—[11Subject to paragraph 11A] a claimant who is a member of a couple and whose partner is temporarily not present in [3United Kingdom].	**11.**—For the first four weeks of that absence, the amount applicable to them as a couple under regulation 17, [27. . .] [9 or 21] as the case may be and thereafter the amount applicable to the claimant in Great Britain under regulation 17 [27. . .] or [9 or 21] as the case may be as if the claimant were a single claimant or, as the case may be, a lone parent.
[11**Couple or member of couple taking child or young person abroad for treatment** **11A.**—[15—(1)] A claimant who is a member of a couple where either— (a) he or his partner is, or, (b) both he and his partner are absent from the United Kingdom [14in the circumstances specified in paragraph (2). (2) For the purposes of sub-paragraph (1), the specified circumstances are— (a) in respect of a claimant, those in regulation 4(3)(a) to (d); (b) in respect of a claimant's partner as if regulation 4(3)(a) to (d) applies to that partner.]	**11A.**—For the first eight weeks of that absence, the amount applicable to the claimant under regulation 17(1) [27. . .] or 21, as the case may be, and, thereafter, if the claimant is in Great Britain the amount applicable to him under regulation 17(1) [27. . .] or 21, as the case may be, as if the claimant were a single claimant, or, as the case may be, a lone parent.
Polygamous marriages where any member is abroad **12.**—Subject to paragraph 12A, a claimant who is a member of a polygamous marriage where— (a) he or one of his partners is, or (b) he and one or more of his partners are, or (c) two or more of his partners are, temporarily absent from the United Kingdom.	**12.**—For the first four weeks of that absence, the amount applicable to the claimant under regulations 17 to 21, as the case may be, and thereafter, if the claimant is in Great Britain the amount applicable to him under regulations 18 to 21, as the case may be, as if any member of the polygamous marriage not in the United Kingdom were not a member of the marriage.
Polygamous marriage: taking child or young person abroad for treatment **12A.**—[15—(1)] A claimant who is a member of a polygamous marriage where— (a) he or one of his partners is, (b) he and one or more of his partners are, or (c) two or more of his partners are, absent from the United Kingdom [14in the circumstances specified in paragraph (2). (2) For the purposes of sub-paragraph (1), the specified circumstances are— (a) in respect of a claimant, those in regulation 4(3)(a) to (d);	**12A.**—For the first 8 weeks of that absence the amount applicable to the claimant under regulations 18 to 21, as the case may be, as if any member of the polygamous marriage not in the United Kingdom were not a member of the marriage.]

Column (1)	*Column (2)*
(b) in respect of a claimant's partner or partners, as the case may be, as if regulation 4(3)(a) to (d) applied to that partner or those partners.]	
[24**Persons in residential accommodation.** **13.**—(1) [29 . . .] [30 . . .] (2) [29 . . .]	**13.**—(1) [30 . . .] **13A.**—[30 . . .]
Polish Resettlement (2) [29 . . .]	**13A.**—[30 . . .]
[18**Polish resettlement: Persons temporarily absent from accommodation** **13B.**—[30 . . .]	**13B.**—[30 . . . [29 . . .]]]
Polish resettlement **14.**—[9. . .]	**14.**—[9 . . .]
Resettlement units **15.**—[9. . .]	**15.**—[9 . . .]
Persons temporarily absent from a hostel, residential care or nursing home **16.**—[27. . .]	**16.**—[27. . .]
[25**Partner of a person subject to immigration control** **16A.**—(a) A claimant who is the partner of a person subject to immigration control. (b) Where regulation 18 (polygamous marriages) applies and the claimant is a person— (i) who is not subject to immigration control within the meaning of section 115(9) of the Immigration and Asylum Act; or (ii) to whom section 115 of that Act does not apply by virtue of regulation 2 of the Social Security (Immigration and Security (Immigration and Asylum) Consequential Amendments Regulations 2000; and (iii) who is a member of a couple and one or more of his partners is subject to immigration control within the meaning of section 115(9) of that Act and section 115 of that Act applies to her for the purposes of exclusion from entitlement to income support.]	[31 **16A.**—[31. . .](a) The amount applicable in respect of the claimant only under regulation 17(1)(a), any amount which may be applicable to him under regulation 17(1)(d) plus the amount applicable to him under regulation 17(1)(e), (f) and (g) or, as the case may be, regulation 21. (b) The amount determined in accordance with that regulation or regulation 21 in respect of the claimant and any partners of his who are not subject to immigration control within the meaning of section 115(9) of the Immigration and Asylum Act and to whom section 115 of that Act does not apply for the purposes of exclusion from entitlement to income support.]

Column (1)	*Column (2)*
17.—[25**Person from abroad]**	**17.**—[38 nil]
[24**Persons in residential care or nursing homes who become patients]** **18.**—[27. . .]	**18.**—[27. . .]
Claimants entitled to the disability premium for a past period **19.**—A claimant— (a) whose time for claiming ncome support has been extended under regulation 19(2) of the Social Security (Claims and Payments) Regulations 1987 (time for claiming benefit); and (b) whose partner was entitled to income support in respect of the period beginning with the day on which the claimant's claim is treated as made under [19regulation 6(3) of those Regulations] and [19ending with the day before the day] on which the claim is actually made; and (c) who satisfied the condition in [36 paragraph 11(1)(b)] of Schedule 2 and the additional condition referred to in that paragraph and specified in paragraph 12(1)(b) of that Schedule in respect of that period.	**19.**—The amount only of the disability premium applicable by virtue of [36 paragraph 11(1)(b)] of Schedule 2 as specified in paragraph 15(4)(b) of that Schedule.
[26**Persons who have commenced remunerative work** **19A.**—(1) A person to whom regulation 6(5) (persons not treated as in remunerative work) applies.] (i) Schedule 3 (housing costs); [38 . . .]	**[**26**19A.**—(1) Subect to sub-paragraph (2), the lowest of either— (a) the amount determined in accordance with— (i) Schedule 3 (housing costs); [38 . . .] (ii) as the case may be, Schedule 2 to the Jobseeker's Allowance Regulations 1996 (housing costs), [38 or (iii) as the case may be, Schedule 6 to the Employment and Support Allowance Regulations (housing costs),] which was applicable to the claimant or his partner immediately before he or his partner commenced the remunerative work referred to in regulation 6(5)(a); or (b) the amount of income support [38 , income-related employment and support allowance] or, as the case may be, income-based jobseeker's allowance

Column (1)	Column (2)
	which the claimant or his partner was entitled to in the benefit week immediately before the benefit week in which he or his partner commenced the remunerative work referred to in regulation 6(5) (a) or, where he or his partner was in receipt of a training allowance in that benefit week, the amount of income support or income-based jobseeker's allowance which he would have been entitled to in that week had he not been in receipt of a training allowance. (2) Nothing in sub-paragraph (1) shall prevent any adjustment being made to the amount referredto in (a) or, as the case may be, (b) of that sub-paragraph during the period referred to in regulations 6(6), in order to reflect changes during that period to the amounts prescribed in Schedule 2 [28. . .] or 4 or in this Schedule or to reflect changes in circumstances during that period relating to the matters specified to in sub-paragraph (3). (3) The changes in circumstances referred to in sub-paragraph (2) are changes to the amount of housing costs to be met in accordance with Schedule 3 in the claimant's case occasioned by— (a) the claimant becoming entitled to income support for a continuous period of 26 weeks or more; (b) a change to the standard interest rate; or (c) any non-dependant deduction becoming applicable, or ceasing to be applicable. (4) In sub-paragraph (1), a reference to the claimant or his partner being entitled to and in receipt or an income-based jobseeker's allowance or to an amount being applicable to either of them under the Jobseeker's Allowance Regulations 1996 shall include a reference to the claimant and his partner being entitled to, and in receipt of, a joint-claim jobseeker's allowance and to an amount being applicable to that couple under those Regulations.]
Rounding of fractions **20.**—Where any calculation under this Schedule or as a result of income support being awarded for a period less than one complete benefit week results in a fraction of a penny that fraction shall be treated as a penny.	

AMENDMENTS

1. Income Support (General) Amendment Regulations 1988 (SI 1988/663) reg.33 (April 11, 1988).
2. Employment Act 1988 s.24(3) (May 26, 1988).
3. Income Support (General) Amendment No.4 Regulations 1988 (SI 1988/1445) reg.23 (September 12, 1988).
4. Income Support (General) Amendment No.5 Regulations 1988 (SI 1988/2022) reg.21 (December 12, 1988).
5. Income Support (General) Amendment No.4 Regulations 1988 (SI 1988/1445) Sch.1 para.1 (April 10, 1989).
6. Income Support (General) Amendment No.4 Regulations 1988 (SI 1988/1445) Sch.1 para.1 (April 10, 1989).
7. Income Support (General) Amendment No.4 Regulations 1988 (SI 1988/1445) Sch.1 para.15 (April 10, 1989).
8. Income Support (General) Amendment Regulations 1989 (SI 1989/534) reg.9 (April 10, 1989).
9. Income Support (General) Amendment Regulations 1989 (SI 1989/534) Sch.1 para.13 (October 9, 1989).
10. Income Support (General) Amendment No.3 Regulations 1989 (SI 1989/1678) reg.11 (October 9, 1989).
11. Income Support (General) Amendment Regulations 1990 (SI 1990/547) reg.21 (April 9, 1990).
12. Enterprise (Scotland) Consequential Amendments Order 1991 (SI 1991/387) art.2 (April 1, 1991).
13. Income Support (General) Amendment Regulations 1991 (SI 1991/236) reg.2(1) (April 8, 1991).
14. Income Support (General) Amendment Regulations 1991 (SI 1991/236) reg.13 (April 8, 1991).
15. Income Support (General) Amendment No.4 Regulations 1991 (SI 1991/1559) reg.19 (October 7, 1991).
16. Social Security Benefits (Amendments Consequential Upon the Introduction of Community Care) Regulations 1992 (SI 1992/3147) Sch.1 para.6 (April 1, 1993).
17. Income-related Benefits Schemes (Miscellaneous Amendments) (No.4) Regulations 1993 (SI 1993/2119) reg.21 (October 4, 1993).
18. Income-related Benefits Schemes (Miscellaneous Amendments) (No.5) Regulations 1994 (SI 1994/2139) reg.31 (October 3, 1994).
19. Income-related Benefits Schemes (Miscellaneous Amendments) Regulations 1995 (SI 1995/516) reg.26 (April 10, 1995).
20. Child Benefit, Child Support and Social Security (Miscellaneous Amendments) Regulations 1996 (SI 1996/1803) reg.40 (April 7, 1997).
21. Income-related Benefits and Jobseeker's Allowance (Amendment) (No.2) Regulations 1977 (SI 1997/2197) reg.5(7) (October 6, 1997).
22. Social Security (Miscellaneous Amendments) Regulations 1998 (SI 1998/563) reg.8(1) and (2)(c)(ii) (April 6, 1998).
23. Social Security (Miscellaneous Amendments) Regulations 1998 (SI 1998/563) reg.8(3) (April 6, 1998).
24. Social Security Benefits Up-rating Order 2003 (SI 2003/526) art.17(7) and Sch.4 (April 8, 2002).
25. Social Security (Immigration and Asylum) Consequential Amendments Regulations 2000 (SI 2000/636) reg.3 (April 3, 2000).
26. Social Security (Miscellaneous Amendments) Regulations 2001 (SI 2001/488) reg.7 (April 9, 2001).
27. Social Security Amendment (Residential Care and Nursing Homes) Regulations 2001 (SI 2001/3767) reg.2 and Sch. Pt I para.17 (April 8, 2002).
28. Social Security Amendment (Residential Care and Nursing Homes)

Regulations 2001 (SI 2001/3767) reg.2 and Sch. Pt I para.17 (as amended by Social Security Amendment (Residential Care and Nursing Homes) Regulations 2002 (SI 2002/398) reg.4(2)) (April 8, 2002).

29. Social Security (Hospital In-Patients and Miscellaneous Amendments) Regulations 2003 (SI 2003/1195) reg.3 (May 21, 2003).

30. Social Security (Removal of Residential Allowance and Miscellaneous Amendments) Regulations 2003 (SI 2003/1121) reg.2 and Sch.1 para.8 (October 6, 2003).

31. Social Security (Working Tax Credit and Child Tax Credit) (Consequential Amendments) Regulations 2003 (SI 2003/455) reg.2 and Sch.1 para.21 (April 6, 2004, except in "transitional cases"—see further the note to reg.17 of the Income Support Regulations).

32. Mental Health (Care and Treatment) (Scotland) Act 2003 (Modification of Subordinate Legislation) Order 2005 (SSI 2005/445) art.2 and Sch. para.3(4) (Scotland); Mental Health (Care and Treatment) (Scotland) Act 2003 (Consequential Provisions) Order 2005 (SI 2005/2078) art.15 and Sch.2 para.3(5) (England and Wales) (October 5, 2005).

33. Social Security (Care Homes and Independent Hospitals) Regulations 2005 (SI 2005/2687) reg.2 and Sch.1 para.10 (October 24, 2005).

34. Social Security (Hospital In-Patients) Regulations 2005 (SI 2005/3360) reg.4 (April 10, 2006).

35. Social Security (Miscellaneous Amendments) Regulations 2007 (SI 2007/719) reg.2(8)(a) (April 2, 2007).

36. Social Security (Miscellaneous Amendments) Regulations 2007 (SI 2007/719) reg.2(8)(b) (April 9, 2007).

37. Social Security (Miscellaneous Amendments) Regulations 2007 (SI 2007/719) reg.2(8)(c) (April 8, 2007).

38. Employment and Support Allowance (Consequential Provisions) (No.2) Regulations 2008 (SI 2008/1554) reg.2(1) and (12) (October 27, 2008).

39. Social Security (Persons Serving a Sentence of Imprisonment Detained in Hospital) Regulations 2010 (SI 2010/442) reg.3(1) and (3) (March 25, 2010).

Definitions

"Abbeyfield Home"—see reg.2(1).
"care home"—*ibid.*
"child"—see SSCBA s.137(1).
"claimant"—see reg.2(1).
"couple"—*ibid.*
"family"—see SSCBA s.137(1).
"independent hospital"—see reg.2(1).
"lone parent"—see reg.2(1).
"partner"—*ibid.*
"patient"—see reg.21(3).
"partner of a person subject to immigration control"—*ibid.*
"person from abroad"—*ibid.*
"polygamous marriage"—see reg.2(1).
"prisoner"—see reg.21(3).
"relative"—see reg.2(1).
"single claimant"—*ibid.*
"young person"—*ibid.*, reg.14.

General Note

See the notes to regs 21 and 6(5)–(8). **2.876**

SCHEDULE 8 **Regulations 36(2), 38(2) and 44(6)**

SUMS TO BE DISREGARDED IN THE CALCULATION OF EARNINGS

2.877 [27 **1.**—(1) In the case of a claimant who has been engaged in remunerative work as an employed earner or, had the employment been in Great Britain, would have been so engaged—

(a) any earnings, other than items to which sub-paragraph (2) applies, paid or due to be paid from that employment which terminated before the first day of entitlement to income support;

(b) any earnings, other than a payment of the nature described in [29 sub-paragraph (2)(a) or (b)(ii)], paid or due to be paid from that employment which has not been terminated where the claimant is not-

(i) engaged in remunerative work, or

(ii) suspended from his employment.

(2) This sub-paragraph applies to—

[29 (a) any payment of the nature described in—

(i) regulation 35(1)(e), or

(ii) section 28, 64 or 68 of the Employment Rights Act 1996 (guarantee payments, suspension from work on medical or maternity grounds); and]

(b) any award, sum or payment of the nature described in—

(i) regulation 35(1)(g) or (h), or

(ii) section 34 or 70 of the Employment Rights Act 1996 (guarantee payments and suspension from work: complaints to employment tribunals),

including any payment made following the settlement of a complaint to an employment tribunal or of court proceedings.]

[20 **1A.**—If the claimant's partner has been engaged in remunerative work as an employed earner or, had the employment been in Great Britain, would have been so engaged, any earnings paid or due to be paid on termination of that employment by way of retirement but only if the partner has attained the qualifying age for state pension credit on retirement.]

[27 **2.**—(1) In the case of a claimant to whom this paragraph applies, any earnings (other than a payment of the nature described in [29 paragraph 1(2)(a) or (b)(ii)]) which relate to employment which ceased before the first day of entitlement to income support whether or not that employment has terminated.

(2) This paragraph applies to a claimant who has been engaged in part-time employment as an employed earner or, had the employment been in Great Britain, would have been so engaged; but it does not apply to a claimant who has been suspended from his employment.]

3.—In the case of a claimant who has been engaged in remunerative work or part-time employment as a self-employed earner [1or, had the employment been in Great Britain would have been so engaged] and who has ceased to be so employed, from the date of the cessation of his employment any earnings derived from that employment except earnings to which regulation 30(2) (royalties etc.) applies.

[4**4.**—(1) In a case to which this paragraph applies, [16£20]; but notwithstanding regulation 23 (calculation of income and capital of members of claimant's family and of a polygamous marriage), if this paragraph applies to a claimant it shall not apply to his partner except where, and to the extent that, the earnings of the claimant which are to be disregarded under this paragraph are less than [16£20].

(2) This paragraph applies where the claimant's applicable amount includes, or but for his being an in-patient [18 . . .] [25 . . .] would include, an amount by way of a disability premium under Schedule 2 (applicable amounts).

(3) This paragraph applies where—

(a) the claimant is a member of a couple, and—

(i) his applicable amount would include an amount by way of the disability premium under Schedule 2 but for the higher pensioner premium under that Schedule being applicable; or

(ii) had he not been an in-patient [18 . . .] [25 . . .] his applicable amount would include the higher pensioner premium under that Schedule and had that been the case he would also satisfy the condition in (i) above; and

(b) [20 . . .]

(4) This paragraph applies where—

(a) the claimant's applicable amount includes, or but for his being an in-patient [18 . . .] [25 . . .] would include, an amount by way of the higher pensioner premium under Schedule 2; and

[20 (b) the claimant's partner has attained the qualifying age for state pension credit;]

(c) immediately before attaining that age [20 . . .] his partner was engaged in part-time employment and the claimant was entitled by virtue of sub-paragraph (2) [20 . . .] to a disregard of [16£20]; and

(d) he or, as the case may be, he or his partner has continued in part-time employment.

(5) [15. . .].

(6) [15. . .].

[6(7) For the purposes of this paragraph—

(a) except where head (b) or (c) applies, no account shall be taken of any period not exceeding eight consecutive weeks occurring—

[20 (i) on or after the date on which the claimant's partner attained the qualifying age for state pension credit during which the partner was not engaged in part-time employment or the claimant was not entitled to income support [28 or employment and support allowance]; or]

(ii) immediately after the date on which the claimant or his partner ceased to participate in arrangements for training made under section 2 of the Employment and Training Act 1973 [7or section 2 of the Enterprise and New Towns (Scotland) Act 1990] or to attend a course at an employment rehabilitation centre established under that section [7of the 1973 Act];

(b) in a case where the claimant has ceased to be entitled to income support [28 or employment and support allowance] because he, or if he is a member of a couple, he or his partner becomes engaged in remunerative work, no account shall be taken of any period, during which he was not entitled to income support [28 or employment and support allowance], not exceeding the permitted period determined in accordance with regulation 3A (permitted period) occurring on or after the date on which [20 the claimant's partner attains the qualifying age for state pension credit];

(c) no account shall be taken of any period occurring on or after the date on which [20 the claimant's partner, if he is a member of a couple, attained the qualifying age for state pension credit] during which the claimant was not entitled to income support [28 or employment and support allowance] because he or his partner was participating in arrangements for training made under section 2 of the Employment and Training Act 1973 [7or section 2 of the Enterprise and New Towns (Scotland) Act 1990] or attending a course at an employment rehabilitation centre established under that section [7of the 1973 Act].]]

[13**5.**—In a case where the claimant is a lone parent and paragraph 4 does not apply, [16£20].]

[11**6.**—Where the claimant is a member of a couple—

(a) in a case to which none of paragraphs 4, 6A, 6B, 7 and 8 applies, £10; but notwithstanding regulation 23 (calculation of income and capital of members of claimant's family and of a polygamous marriage), if this paragraph applies to a claimant it shall not apply to his partner except where, and to the extent that, the earnings of the claimant which are to be disregarded under this sub-paragraph are less than £10;

(b) in a case to which one or more of paragraphs 4, 6A, 6B, 7 and 8 applies and the total amount disregarded under those paragraphs is less than £10, so much of the claimant's earnings as would not in aggregate with the amount disregarded under those paragraphs exceed £10.]

[9**6A.**—(1) In a case to which none of paragraphs 4 to 6 applies to the claimant, and subject to sub-paragraph (2), where the claimant's applicable amount includes an amount by way of the carer premium under Schedule 2 (applicable amounts), [16£20] of the earnings of the person who is, or at any time in the preceding eight weeks was, in receipt of [19 carer's allowance] or treated in accordance with paragraph 14ZA(2) of that Schedule as being in receipt of [19 carer's allowance].

(2) Where the carer premium is awarded in respect of the claimant and of any partner of his, their earnings shall for the purposes of this paragraph be aggregated, but the amount to be disregarded in accordance with paragraph (1) shall not exceed [16£20] of the aggregated amount.

6B.—Where the carer premium is awarded in respect of a claimant who is a member of a couple and whose earnings are less than [16£20], but is not awarded in respect of the other member of the couple, and that other member is engaged in an employment—

(a) specified in paragraph 7(1), so much of the other member's earnings as would not when aggregated with the amount disregarded under paragraph 6A exceed [16£20];

(b) other than one specified in paragraph 7(1), so much of the other member's earnings from such other employment up to £5 as would not when aggregated with the amount disregarded under paragraph 6A exceed [16£20].]

7.—(1) In a case to which none of paragraphs [94 to 6B] applies to the claimant, [16£20] of earnings derived from one or more employments as—

(a) [32. . .]

[23 (aa) [32 . . .]]
[24 (ab) [32 . . .]]
[32 (a) a part-time fire-fighter employed by a fire and rescue authority under the Fire and Rescue Services Act 2004 or by the Scottish Fire and Rescue Service established under section 1A of the Fire (Scotland) Act 2005;]
(b) an auxiliary coastguard in respect of coast rescue activities;
(c) a person engaged part time in the manning or launching of a life boat;
(d) a member of any [33 . . .] reserve force prescribed in Part I of [26 Schedule 6 to the Social Security (Contributions) Regulations 2001];

but, notwithstanding regulation 23 (calculation of income and capital of members of claimant's family and of a polygamous marriage), if this paragraph applies to a claimant it shall not apply to his partner except to the extent specified in sub-paragraph (2).

(2) If the claimant's partner is engaged in employment—
(a) specified in sub-paragraph (1) so much of his earnings as would not in aggregate with the amount of the claimant's earnings disregarded under this paragraph exceed [16£20];
(b) other than one specified in sub-paragraph (1) so much of his earnings from that employment up to £5 as would not in aggregate with the claimant's earnings disregarded under this paragraph exceed [16£20].

8.—Where the claimant is engaged in one or more employments specified in paragraph 7(1) but his earnings derived from such employments are less than [16£20] in any week and he is also engaged in any other part-time employment so much of his earnings from that other employment up to £5 as would not in aggregate with the amount of his earnings disregarded under paragraph 7 exceed [16£20].

9.—In a case to which none of paragraphs 4 to 8 applies to the claimant, £5.

[11**10.**—Notwithstanding the foregoing provisions of this Schedule, where two or more payments of the same kind and from the same source are to be taken into account in the same benefit week, because it has not been practicable to treat the payments under regulation 31(1)(b) (date on which income treated as paid) as paid on the first day of the benefit week in which they were due to be paid, there shall be disregarded from each payment the sum that would have been disregarded if the payment had been taken into account on the date on which it was due to be paid.]

11.—Any earnings derived from employment which are payable in a country outside the United Kingdom for such period during which there is a prohibition against the transfer to the United Kingdom of those earnings.

12.—Where a payment of earnings is made in a currency other than sterling, any banking charge or commission payable in converting that payment into sterling.

13.—Any earnings which are due to be paid before the date of claim and which would otherwise fall to be taken into account in the same benefit week as a payment of the same kind and from the same source.

14.—Any earnings of a child or young person [21 . . .].

15.—[21 . . .].

[11[30 **15A.**—(1) Where earnings to which sub-paragraph (2) applies (in aggregate with the claimant's other income (if any) calculated in accordance with this Part) exceed the applicable amount (as specified in Part IV and Schedule 2) less 10 pence, the amount of those earnings corresponding to that excess.

(2) This sub-paragraph applies to earnings, in so far as they exceed the amount disregarded under paragraph 7, derived by the claimant from employment as a member of any [33 . . .] reserve force prescribed in Part 1 of Schedule 6 to the Contributions Regulations in respect of a period of annual continuous training for a maximum of 15 days in any calendar year [33 or in respect of training in the claimant's first year of training as a member of a reserve force for a maximum of 43 days in that year.]]]

[14**15B.**—[22 . . .]]

[17**15C.**—In the case of a person to whom paragraph (5) of regulation 6 (persons not treated as in remunerative work) applies, any earnings.]

16.—In this Schedule "part-time employment" means employment in which the person is not to be treated as engaged in remunerative work under regulation 5 or 6 (persons treated, or not treated, as engaged in remunerative work).

AMENDMENTS

1. Income Support (General) Amendment Regulations 1988 (SI 1988/663) reg.34 (April 11, 1988).

2. Income Support (General) Amendment No.4 Regulations 1988 (SI 1988/1445) reg.24 (September 12, 1988).
3. Income Support (General) Amendment No.4 Regulations 1988 (SI 1988/1445) Sch.1 para.8 (April 10, 1989).
4. Income Support (General) Amendment Regulations 1989 (SI 1989/534) reg.10 and Sch.1 (October 9, 1989).
5. Income Support (General) Amendment No.2 Regulations 1989 (SI 1989/1323) reg.18 (October 9, 1989).
6. Income Support (General) Amendment No.3 Regulations 1989 (SI 1989/1678) reg.12 (October 9, 1989).
7. Enterprise (Scotland) Consequential Amendments Order 1991 (SI 1991/ 387) art.2 and 9 (April 1, 1991).
8. Income Support (General) Amendment Regulations 1992 (SI 1992/468) reg.7 (April 6, 1992).
9. Income-related Benefits Schemes (Miscellaneous Amendments) Regulations 1993 (SI 1993/315) reg.8 (April 12, 1993).
10. Income-related Benefits Schemes (Miscellaneous Amendments) (No.4) Regulations 1993 (SI 1993/2119) reg.22 (October 4, 1993).
11. Income-related Benefits Schemes and Social Fund (Miscellaneous Amendments) Regulations 1996 (SI 1996/1944) reg.6(11) (October 7,1996).
12. Child Benefit, Child Support and Social Security (Miscellaneous Amendments) Regulations 1996 (SI 1996/1803) reg.41 (April 7, 1997).
13. Social Security Amendment (Lone Parents) Regulations 1998 (SI 1998/ 766) reg.13 (April 6, 1998).
14. Social Security (Miscellaneous Amendments) (No.2) Regulations 1999 (SI 1999/2556) reg.2(9) (October 4, 1999).
15. Social Security (Miscellaneous Amendments) Regulations 2000 (SI 2000/681) reg.12(a) (April 3, 2000).
16. Social Security Amendment (Capital Limits and Earnings Disregards) Regulations 2000 (SI 2000/2545) reg.3 and Sch. para.2 (April 9, 2001).
17. Social Security (Miscellaneous Amendments) Regulations 2001 (SI 2001/488) reg.8 (April 9, 2001).
18. Social Security Amendment (Residential Care and Nursing Homes) Regulations 2001 (SI 2001/3767) reg.2(1) and Pt I of Sch. para.18 (April 8, 2002).
19. Social Security Amendment (Carer's Allowance) Regulations 2002 (SI 2002/2497) reg.3 and Sch.2 (April 1, 2003).
20. State Pension Credit (Consequential, Transitional and Miscellaneous Provisions) Regulations 2002 (SI 2002/3019) reg.29(7) (October 6, 2003).
21. Social Security (Working Tax Credit and Child Tax Credit)(Consequential Amendments) Regulations 2003 (SI 2003/455) reg.2 and Sch.1 para.22 (April 6, 2004, except in "transitional cases" and see further the note to reg.17 of the Income Support Regulations).
22. Social Security (Back to Work Bonus and Lone Parent Run-on) (Amendment and Revocation) Regulations 2003 (SI 2003/1589) reg.2(d) (October 25, 2004).
23. Fire and Rescue Services Act 2004 (Consequential Amendments) (England) Order 2004 (SI 2004/3168) art.14 (December 30, 2004) (in relation to England); Fire and Rescue Services Act 2004 (Consequential Amendments) (Wales) Order 2005 (SI 2005/2929 (W.214)) art.15 (October 25, 2005) (in relation to Wales). The amendment does not extend to Scotland.
24. Fire (Scotland) Act 2005 (Consequential Provisions and Modifications) Order 2005 (SI 2005/2060 (S.7)) art.3 and Sch. para.5 (August 2, 2005) (in relation to Scotland only; this amendment also revokes head (a) of para.7(1), again in relation to Scotland only).
25. Social Security (Care Homes and Independent Hospitals) Regulations 2005 (SI 2005/2687) reg.2 and Sch.1 para.11 (October 24, 2005).
26. Social Security (Miscellaneous Amendments) (No.4) Regulations 2006 (SI 2006/2378) reg.5(9) (October 2, 2006).

27. Social Security (Miscellaneous Amendments) (No.5) Regulations 2007 (SI 2007/2618) reg.5(11) (October 1, 2007).
28. Employment and Support Allowance (Consequential Provisions) (No.2) Regulations 2008 (SI 2008/1554) reg.2(13) (October 27, 2008).
29. Social Security (Miscellaneous Amendments) (No.4) Regulations 2009 (SI 2009/2655) reg.2(16) (October 26, 2009).
30. Social Security (Miscellaneous Amendments) (No.2) Regulations 2012 (SI 2012/2575) reg.2(4) (November 5, 2012).
31. Police and Fire Reform (Scotland) Act 2012 (Consequential Provisions and Modifications) Order 2013 (SI 2013/602) art.26 and Sch.2 para.69 (April 1, 2013).
32. Social Security (Miscellaneous Amendments) (No.3) Regulations 2013 (SI 2013/2536) reg.4(7) (October 29, 2013).
33. Social Security (Members of the Reserve Forces) (Amendment) Regulations 2015 (SI 2015/389) reg.2(4) (April 6, 2015).

DEFINITIONS

"benefit week"—see reg.2(1).
"child"—see SSCBA s.137(1).
"claimant"—see reg.2(1).
"couple"—*ibid.*
"date of claim"—*ibid.*
"employed earner"—*ibid.*
"family"—see SSCBA s.137(1).
"first year of training"—see reg.2(1).
"partner"—see reg.2(1).
"polygamous marriage"—*ibid.*
"remunerative work"—*ibid.*
"Social Security Act"—*ibid.*
"supplementary benefit"—*ibid.*
"young person"—*ibid.*, reg.14.

GENERAL NOTE

2.878 Before April 6, 2004 the income (but not the capital) of a child or young person who was a member of the claimant's family was aggregated with the claimant's, subject to the modifications in reg.44. Under the form of this Schedule in force at that time paras 1–10 did not apply to children or young persons (see the form of reg.23(2) then in force) and paras 14 and 15 only applied to children and young persons (see the 2003 edition of this volume for the old form of reg.23 and of paras 14 and 15 of this Schedule). However, with effect from April 6, 2004 (except in "transitional cases"—see the note to reg.17), amounts for children and young persons have been removed from the income support scheme; financial assistance to help with the cost of bringing up a child or young person is now to be provided through the child tax credit system, see Vol.IV of this series. As a consequence, the income of a child or young person is no longer aggregated with the claimant's (see the new form of reg.23 and the notes to that regulation) and so the disregards that applied to such income are no longer needed (although note that part of para.14 has been retained). The former disregards do however remain in force for "transitional cases"—see the note to reg.17.

For income support claimants who had an award of child tax credit before April 6, 2004 see reg.7 of the Social Security (Working Tax Credit and Child Tax Credit) (Consequential Amendments) Regulations 2003 (SI 2003/455) (as amended) on p.812 and the notes to that regulation.

Note that from April 9, 2001, the higher earnings disregard in paras 4, 5, 6A, 6B, 7, 8 and 15 (which has been £15 since the commencement of income support) increased to £20.

Paragraph 1

2.879 This disregard is crucial to entitlement following the termination of full-time employment (i.e. 16 hours or more per week in the case of the claimant, 24 hours or more per week for a partner: reg.5(1) and (1A); references to the "claimant" in Pt V of the Income Support Regulations include his partner (if any), unless the context otherwise requires (reg.23(1)).

For the disregard of a partner's earnings paid on the termination of employment due to retirement see para.1A.

The effect of the new form of para.1 introduced on October 1, 2007, is to significantly extend the disregard that applies to payments made on the termination of full-time work. The new rules are as follows.

- Where the full-time employment terminated before the first day of entitlement to income support, all payments (except those referred to below) made on its cessation, including final earnings, payments in lieu of wages, or in lieu of notice, holiday pay and compensation payments (as defined in reg.35(3)) are ignored (sub-para.(1)(a)). (Note that from April 14, 2008 the definition of "compensation" in reg.35(1)(i) and (3) is amended so that it no longer applies to payments made in respect of full-time employment.) This means that entitlement to income support can begin immediately (subject to the other conditions of entitlement being met). Note, however, that holiday pay that is payable more than four weeks after the termination (or interruption) of employment counts as capital (see reg.48(3)), as may redundancy payments or ex gratia payments, depending on their nature. See further the notes to reg.35(1)(i).

- However, any retainer, and the employment protection payments referred to in reg.35(1)(g) or (h), or ss.34 or 70 of the Employment Rights Act 1996 (including any payment made in settlement of an employment tribunal claim or court action), will be taken into account (sub-para.(2)). But note that these payments are not listed in reg.5(5) (which treats a person who receives earnings of the kind listed in reg.5(5) as in full-time work for the period covered by such earnings (see reg.29(3) and (4)). Thus if any of these payments are made they will not lead to complete disentitlement, although they will, subject to the relevant earnings disregard, be taken into account in calculating the amount of income support (if any) that is payable. See reg.31(1) for the date on which the earnings will be treated as paid; note also reg.29(3) and (4).

  R(IS) 9/95 decided that a guarantee payment under s.12 of the Employment Protection (Consolidation) Act 1978 counted as a retainer, and presumably the same applies to guarantee payments under the current provision, s.28 of the Employment Rights Act 1996. This is confirmed by the amendment to para.1(2)(a) on October 26, 2009 which has the effect that payments in the nature of a retainer (i.e. guarantee payments under s.28 of the Employment Rights Act 1996, and the right to remuneration while suspended on medical grounds under s.64 of that Act or while suspended on maternity grounds under s.68), as well as payments by way of a retainer (i.e. those covered by reg.35(1)(e)), are not disregarded.

  Section 34 of the Employment Rights Act 1996 provides for a complaint to an employment tribunal if an employer fails to pay under s.28 of the Act; and s.70 similarly so provides if an employer fails to pay under s.64 or s.68, or under s.67 fails to offer alternative suitable work where this is available before suspending on maternity grounds.

  Regulation 35(1)(g) applies to compensation awards for unfair dismissal and reg.35(1)(h) to arrears of pay under an order for reinstatement or re-engagement; any sum payable under an award for the continuation of a contract of employment; and remuneration under a protective award.

- Where the employment has not terminated but the claimant is working less than 16 hours a week (or none at all), only payment of any retainer, and (from October 26, 2009) awards under ss.34 or 70 of the Employment Rights Act 1996 (including any payment made in settlement of an employment tribunal claim or court action) are taken into account (subpara. (1)(b)). See above for the meaning of "retainer", which from October 26, 2009 includes payments in the nature of, as well as by way of, a retainer. The employment protection payments referred to in reg.35(1)(g) or (h) will not be applicable if the employment has not terminated. Thus from October 26, 2009 the disregard in these circumstances is no longer more extensive than in the case of termination of full-time employment before the first day of entitlement to income support.

However, if the person has been suspended from his employment the disregard does not apply and earnings will be taken into account in the normal way.

Note that payments of sick pay, maternity pay, paternity pay, shared parental pay or adoption leave pay are taken into account. This is because they do not count as earnings (reg.35(2)) but are taken into account as income (reg.40(4)(a); note the disregards in paras 1, 4 and 4A of Sch.9).

Paragraph 1A

2.880 Since the commencement of the state pension credit scheme on October 6, 2003, claimants who have reached the qualifying age for state pension credit (defined in s.137(1) of the Contributions and Benefits Act 1992—the effect of that definition is that the qualifying age was 60 but from April 2010 it will gradually rise in line with the staged increase in pensionable age for women until it reaches 65 in November 2018 (this equalisation of the state pension age for men and women was previously to have been completed by April 5, 2020 but the timetable for this in the Pensions Act 1995 has been accelerated with effect from April 2016 so that women's state pension age will now be 65 by November 2018; in addition, the increase in state pension age to 66 for both men and women has been brought forward—it will start to rise from 65 in December 2018 to reach 66 by October 2020, see s.1 of the Pensions Act 2011; between 2026 and 2028 it will rise to 67 (see s.26 of the Pensions Act 2014)), or whose partner is entitled to state pension credit, are not entitled to income support (SSCBA s.124(1)(aa) and (g)). There is thus no need for a disregard of a claimant's earnings paid on termination of employment due to retirement at pensionable age (before October 6, 2003 such earnings had been totally disregarded for the purposes of income support). However, provision still needs to be made in relation to a partner's earnings paid on termination of employment due to retirement in cases where the claimant has not reached pensionable age and so is still eligible for income support. Under para.1A such earnings will be disregarded in full, provided that the partner has reached the qualifying age for state pension credit.

Paragraph 2

2.881 The disregard where a person's part-time (i.e. less than 16 hours per week (24 hours in the case of a partner): para.16 and reg.5(1) and (1A)) work has stopped before the claim (provided that he has not been suspended) is also extensive (as was the case before October 1, 2007; the new form of para.2 introduced on October 1, 2007 appears to be merely a recasting of the previous form). But note that with effect from October 26, 2009 not only payments by way of a retainer but also payments in the nature of a retainer (i.e. guarantee payments under s.28 of the Employment Rights Act 1996, and the right to remuneration while suspended on medical grounds under s.64 or while suspended on maternity grounds under s.68, together with awards under ss.34 or 70, of that Act; see further the note to para.1), will be taken into account. However, if the person has been suspended from his employment the disregard does not apply and earnings will be taken into account in the normal way.

It is not necessary for the part-time employment to have ended. On this, see *R(JSA)8/03* which concerned a part-time supply teacher who claimed JSA during the school summer holidays. The Commissioner decides that because she did not have a recognisable cycle of work the equivalent disregard in para.2 of Sch.6 to the JSA Regulations applied. However, if a cycle of work has been established, *R(JSA)*

2/03 holds that a person is to be regarded as engaged in employment (whether remunerative or part-time) during the whole of the cycle and so the disregard in para.2 will not apply. See further the notes to para.2 of Sch.6 to the JSA Regulations.

Payments of sick pay, maternity pay, paternity pay, shared parental pay or adoption leave pay are however taken into account. This is because they do not count as earnings (reg.35(2)) but are taken into account as income (reg.40(4)(a); note the disregards in paras 1, 4 and 4A of Sch.9).

If the part-time work ends while the claimant is claiming income support, termination payments are taken into account as earnings in the usual way.

Paragraph 3

When a self-employed person leaves that employment, only royalties or payments for copyright or public lending rights count. **2.882**

Note also the disregard of business assets in para.6 of Sch.10.

Paragraph 4

This provision allows a disregard of £20 between the claimant and any partner, if the claimant meets the basic conditions for a disability premium or if the conditions for the higher pensioner premium are met with the restrictive extra conditions of sub-para.(4). Note that there appears to be a spare "and" at the end of sub-para.(3) as a result of the amendments made on October 6, 2003 consequent upon the introduction of state pension credit. **2.883**

See the saving provision in reg.4 of the Social Security Amendment (Capital Limits and Earnings Disregards) Regulations 2000 (SI 2000/2545) (p.808) to enable claimants who were entitled to the previous £15 disregard under sub-paras (2) and (3) to meet the condition in sub-para.(4)(c). The saving provision also applies to para.5(4)(c) of Sch.6 to the JSA Regulations 1996.

Paragraph 5

If the claimant is a lone parent the first £20 of net earnings are disregarded. Since April 6, 1998 it has not been necessary for the claimant to be receiving the lone parent rate of the family premium under para.3(1)(a) of Sch.2 for this disregard to apply; *all* lone parent now qualify for a disregard under this paragraph, unless they are entitled to a £20 disregard under para.4. **2.884**

Paragraph 6

From October 7, 1996 the previous £15 disregard for long-term unemployed couples aged less than 60 which applied under this paragraph has been replaced by a £10 earnings disregard that applies to all couples. This is the same as the disregard that applies for JSA. **2.885**

Paragraphs 6A and 6B

Where the carer premium is payable, the first £20 of the earnings of the carer are disregarded. If the carer does not use up the disregard, what is spare may be applied to a (non-carer) partner's earnings under para.6B. Only £5 may be disregarded in this way, except for the employment mentioned in para.7(1). **2.886**

Paragraph 7

Earnings from these activities attract a £20 disregard, but a couple cannot have a total disregard of more than £20. **2.887**

The insertion of a new sub-para.(1)(a) (and the omission of the previous form of sub-para.(1)(a) and of sub-para.(1)(aa)–(ab)) on October 29, 2013 are intended to reflect the policy intention that sub-para.(1)(a) applies to part-time fire-fighters who live in Scotland but are employed by a fire and rescue authority in England and Wales (and those who live in England or Wales but are employed by the Scottish Fire and Rescue Service), as well as those who live and are employed as part-time fire-fighters in the same country.

Paragraph 9

2.888 The basic disregard of net earnings from part-time work is £5.

Paragraph 10

2.889 See notes to reg.32(5).

Paragraph 13

2.890 Where earnings are due before the date of claim, overlaps with payments of the same kind are avoided. See notes to reg.32(5).

Paragraph 14

2.891 See the note at the beginning of the Schedule. The old forms of paras 14 and 15 continue in force for "transitional cases"—see the note to reg.17. It is not entirely clear why this disregard is being retained.

Paragraph 15A

2.892 Under para.15A, as amended from April 6, 2015, earnings as a member of a reserve force from training (i) for a maximum of 43 days in the first year of training (see the definition of "first year of training" in reg.2(1)); or (ii) for a maximum of 15 days' annual continuous training in any calendar year, are disregarded to the extent that, together with any other income, they would have the effect of reducing income support entitlement to less than 10p per week. This disregard is in addition to the £20 disregard of earnings as a member of a reserve force in para.7(1)(d).

The purpose of the disregard is to enable entitlement to income support to continue while a claimant (or partner) is attending such training (note that a person is not treated as in remunerative work for the purposes of income support if s/he is engaged in employment as a member of a reserve force: see reg.6(1)(h)). See also reg.29(2C) which provides that earnings from such reservist training will be taken into account, where the training lasts for the number of days listed in column 1 of the table in reg.29(2C)(c), for the number of days listed in column 2 of the table; or in any other case, for the number of days that the training lasts. The period begins on the date that the earnings are treated as paid under reg.31 (see reg.29(2D)).

Paragraph 15C

2.893 From April 9, 2001 a claimant who, or whose partner, starts remunerative work (i.e. 16 hours or more a week in the case of a claimant, 24 hours in the case of the claimant's partner) after either of them has been in receipt of income support or income-based JSA for at least six months has been allowed a four-week "mortgage interest run-on" (see further reg.6(5)–(8) and the notes to those provisions; from December 17, 2007 this was extended so that it applied to all housing costs that can be met by income support). From October 27, 2008 it also applied where the claimant or partner had been in receipt of income-related ESA for at least six months before starting remunerative work. Note that periods when the run-on applies cannot count towards the required six months' continuous entitlement to benefit. Payment of the run-on will be made direct to the claimant, not the lender. The purpose of the run-on is to tackle some of the hurdles (such as the gap between starting work and receiving wages and the wait for in-work benefits) that face people when they begin full-time work. The amount of benefit paid during the run-on period will be the lower of the amount for housing costs that was being met or the income support/income-based JSA/income-related ESA that was in payment before the claimant or his partner started work (see further the new para.19A of Sch.7). Paragraph 15C provides that all of the person's earnings in the run-on period will be disregarded. See also the disregards in para.74 of Sch.9 and para.62 of Sch.10.

SCHEDULE 9 **Regulation 40(2)**

SUMS TO BE DISREGARDED IN THE CALCULATION OF INCOME OTHER THAN EARNINGS

1.—Any amount paid by way of tax on income which is taken into account under regulation 40 (calculation of income other than earnings). **2.894**

[144 **1A.**—Any payment in respect of any travel or other expenses incurred, or to be incurred, by the claimant in respect of that claimant's participation in [149 a scheme prescribed in regulation 3 of the Jobseeker's Allowance (Schemes for Assisting Persons to Obtain Employment) Regulations 2013] or the Mandatory Work Activity Scheme.]

2.—Any payment in respect of any expenses incurred [77, or to be incurred,] by a claimant who is—

(a) engaged by a charitable or [32voluntary organisation]; or

(b) a volunteer,

if he otherwise derives no remuneration or profit from the employment and is not to be treated as possessing any earnings under regulation 42(6) (notional income).

[133 **2A.**—Any payment in respect of expenses arising out of the [159 claimant participating as a service user].]

3.—In the case of employment as an employed earner, any payment in respect of expenses wholly, exclusively and necessarily incurred in the performance of the duties of the employment.

4.—In the case of a payment [122 under Parts 11 to] 12ZB of the Contributions and Benefits Act] or any remuneration paid by or on behalf of an employer to the claimant who for the time being is unable to work due to illness or maternity [86 or who is taking paternity leave [161 , adoption leave or shared parental leave]]—

(a) any amount deducted by way of primary Class 1 contributions under the Social Security Act [SSCBA];

(b) one-half of any sum paid by the claimant by way of a contribution towards an occupational or personal pension scheme.

[1**4A.**—In the case of the payment of statutory sick pay under Part II of the Social Security (Northern Ireland) Order 1982 [86, statutory maternity pay under Part XII of the Social Security Contributions and Benefits (Northern Ireland) Act 1992 or a payment under any enactment having effect in Northern Ireland corresponding to a payment of [148 [168 . . .] statutory paternity pay] [162 , statutory adoption pay or statutory shared parental pay]]—

(a) any amount deducted by way of primary Class 1 contributions under the Social Security (Northern Ireland) Act 1975;

(b) one-half of any sum paid by way of a contribution towards an occupational or personal pension scheme.]

[131 **5.**—Any housing benefit to which the claimant is entitled.]

[88 **5A.**—(1) Any guardian's allowance.]

[94 **5B.**—(1) Any child tax credit.

(2) Any child benefit.]

[140 (3) Any increase in respect of a dependent child or dependent young person under section 80 or 90 of the Contributions and Benefits Act where—

(a) the claimant has a child or young person who is a member of the claimant's family for the purposes of the claimant's claim for income support, and

(b) the claimant, or that claimant's partner, has been awarded a child tax credit.]

[130 **5C.**—(1) £1.20 in relation to each week in which child benefit is payable to the claimant at the enhanced rate in respect of a child or qualifying young person for whom the claimant is treated as responsible.

(2) 65 pence in relation to each week in which child benefit is payable to the claimant other than at the enhanced rate in respect of a child or qualifying young person for whom the claimant is treated as responsible (and if there is more than one, 65 pence in relation to each such child or young person).

(3) This paragraph does not apply to a claimant in relation to whom regulation 2 of, and Schedule 1 to, the Social Security (Working Tax Credit and Child Tax Credit) (Consequential Amendments) Regulations 2003 have effect.

(4) In this paragraph—

"child" and "qualifying young person" have the meanings given in section 142 of the Contributions and Benefits Act;

"treated as responsible" is to be construed in accordance with section 143 of that Act;

"the enhanced rate" has the meaning given in regulation 2(1)(a) of the Child Benefit (Rates) Regulations 2006.]

6.—[131The] mobility component of disability living allowance [153 or the mobility component of personal independence payment].

7.—Any concessionary payment made to compensate for the non-payment of—

(a) any payment specified in [18paragraph 6 [48 or 9]];

[131 (b) income support;

(c) an income-based jobseeker's allowance; [157 . . .]

(d) an income-related employment and support allowance [157; or

(e) universal credit].]

8.—Any mobility supplement or any payment intended to compensate for the non payment of such a supplement.

[25 **9.**—Any attendance allowance [154 , the care component of disability living allowance or the daily living component of personal independence payment] [90 . . .].]

[29**9A.**—. . .]

10.—Any payment to the claimant as holder of the Victoria Cross or George Cross or any analogous payment.

[97 **11.**—(1) Any payment—

(a) by way of an education maintenance allowance made pursuant to—

(i) regulations made under section 518 of the Education Act 1996;

(ii) regulations made under section 49 or 73(f) of the Education (Scotland) Act 1980;

[131 (iii) directions made under section 73ZA of the Education (Scotland) Act 1980 and paid under section 12(2)(c) of the Further and Higher Education (Scotland) Act 1992; [147 . . .]]

(b) corresponding to such an education maintenance allowance, made pursuant to—

(i) section 14 or section 181 of the Education Act 2002; or

(ii) regulations made under section 181 of that Act [147; or

(c) in England, by way of financial assistance made pursuant to section 14 of the Education Act 2002.]

(2) Any payment, other than a payment to which sub-paragraph (1) applies, made pursuant to—

(a) regulations made under section 518 of the Education Act 1996;

(b) regulations made under section 49 of the Education (Scotland) Act 1980; or

[131 (c) directions made under section 73ZA of the Education (Scotland) Act 1980 and paid under section 12(2)(c) of the Further and Higher Education (Scotland) Act 1992,]

in respect of a course of study attended by a child or a young person or a person who is in receipt of an education maintenance allowance [147 or other payment] made pursuant to any provision specified in sub-paragraph (1).]

[83 **11A.**—Any payment made to the claimant by way of a repayment under regulation 11(2) of the Education (Teacher Student Loans) (Repayment etc) Regulations 2002.]

12.—[64 . . .].

[93 **13.**—(1) Any payment made pursuant to section 2 of the Employment and Training Act 1973 (functions of the Secretary of State) or section 2 of the Enterprise and New Towns (Scotland) Act 1990 (functions in relation to training for employment etc.) except a payment—

(a) made as a substitute for income support, a jobseeker's allowance, incapacity benefit [126 , severe disablement allowance or an employment and support allowance];

(b) of an allowance referred to in section 2(3) of the Employment and Training Act 1973 or section 2(5) of the Enterprise and New Towns (Scotland) Act 1990;

(c) intended to meet the cost of living expenses which relate to any one or more of the items specified in sub-paragraph (2) whilst a claimant is participating in an education, training or other scheme to help him enhance his employment prospects unless the payment is a Career Development Loan paid pursuant to section 2 of the Employment and Training Act 1973 and the period of education or training or the scheme, which is supported by that loan, has been completed; or

(d) made in respect of the cost of living away from home to the extent that the payment relates to rent for which housing benefit is payable in respect of accommodation which is not normally occupied by the claimant as his home.

(2) The items specified in this sub-paragraph for the purposes of sub-paragraph (1)(c) are food, ordinary clothing or footwear, household fuel, rent for which housing benefit is payable, or any housing costs to the extent that they are met under regulation 17(1)(e) or 18(1)(f) (housing costs), of the claimant or, where the claimant is a member of a family, any other member of his family, or any council tax or water charges for which that claimant or member is liable.

(3) For the purposes of this paragraph, "ordinary clothing or footwear" means clothing or footwear for normal daily use, but does not include school uniforms, or clothing or footwear used solely for sporting activities.]

14.—[34 . . .]

[10**15.**—[29[113 (1) Subject to sub-paragraph (3) and paragraph 39, any relevant payment made or due to be made at regular intervals.]

(2) [113. . .]

(3) [113 Sub-paragraph (1)] shall not apply—

(a) to a payment which is made by a person for the maintenance of any member of his family or of his former partner or of his children;

(b) in the case of a person to whom section 23 of the Act [SSCBA, s.126] (trade disputes) applies or in respect of whom section 20(3) of the Act [SSCBA, s.124(1)] (conditions of entitlement to income support) has effect as modified by section 23A(b) of the Act [SSCBA, s.127(b)] (effect of return to work).

(4) [113. . .]

(5) [113. . .]]

[84 (5A) In this paragraph, "relevant payment" means—

(a) a charitable payment;

(b) a voluntary payment;

(c) a payment (not falling within sub-paragraph (a) or (b) above) from a trust whose funds are derived from a payment made in consequence of any personal injury to the claimant;

(d) a payment under an annuity purchased—

(i) pursuant to any agreement or court order to make payments to the claimant; or

(ii) from funds derived from a payment made,

in consequence of any personal injury to the claimant; or

(e) a payment (not falling within sub-paragraphs (a) to (d) above) received by virtue of any agreement or court order to make payments to the claimant in consequence of any personal injury to the claimant.]

[29(6) [79. . .].]

[25**15A.**—[114. . .]]

[38 **15B.**—[90 . . .].]

[35**16.**—Subject to paragraphs 36 and 37, £10 of any of the following, namely—

(a) a war disablement pension (except insofar as such a pension falls to be disregarded under paragraph 8 or 9);

(b) a war widow's pension [81 or war widower's pension];

(c) a pension payable to a person as a [107 widow, widower or surviving civil partner] under [131. . .] any power of Her Majesty otherwise than under an enactment to make provision about pensions for or in respect of persons who have been disabled or have died in consequence of service as members of the armed forces of the Crown;

[102(cc) a guaranteed income payment [131 and, if the amount of that payment has been abated to less than £10 by a [134 pension or payment falling within article 31(1)(a) or (b) of the Armed Forces and Reserve Forces (Compensation Scheme) Order 2005], so much of [134 that pension or payment] as would not, in aggregate with the amount of [134 any] guaranteed income payment disregarded, exceed £10];]

(d) a payment made to compensate for the non-payment of such a pension [102 or payment] as is mentioned in any of the preceding sub-paragraphs;

(e) a pension paid by the government of a country outside Great Britain which is analogous to any of the [102 pensions or payments mentioned in sub-paragraphs (a) to (cc) above];

(f) a pension paid to victims of National Socialist persecution under any special provision made by the law of the Federal Republic of Germany, or any part of it, or of the Republic of Austria.]

[70(g) any widowed mother's allowance paid pursuant to section 37 of the Contributions and Benefits Act;

(h) any widowed parent's allowance paid pursuant to section 39A of the Contributions and Benefits Act.]

17.—Where a person receives income under an annuity purchased with a loan which satisfies the following conditions—

(a) that the loan was made as part of a scheme under which not less than 90 per cent. of the proceeds of the loan were applied to the purchase by the person to whom it was made of an annuity ending with his life or with the life of the survivor of two or more persons (in this paragraph referred to as "the annuitants") who include the person to whom the loan was made;

(b) that the interest on the loan is payable by the person to whom it was made or by one of the annuitants;

(c) that at the time the loan was made the person to whom it was made or each of the annuitants had attained the age of 65;

(d) that the loan was secured on a dwelling in Great Britain and the person to whom the loan was made or one of the annuitants owns an estate or interest in that dwelling; and

(e) that the person to whom the loan was made or one of the annuitants occupies the accommodation on which it was secured as his home at the time the interest is paid,

the amount, calculated on a weekly basis equal to—

[[31](i) here, or insofar as, section 369 of the Income and Corporation Taxes Act 1988 (mortgage interest payable under deduction of tax) applies to the payments of interest on the loan, the interest which is payable after deduction of a sum equal to income tax on such payments at the applicable percentage of income tax within the meaning of section 369(1A) of that Act;]

(ii) in any other case the interest which is payable on the loan without deduction of such a sum.

[[32]**18.**—Any payment made to the claimant by a person who normally resides with the claimant, which is a contribution towards that person's living and accommodation costs, except where that person is residing with the claimant in circumstances to which paragraph 19 or 20 refers.]

[[30]**19.**—Where the claimant occupies a dwelling as his home and the dwelling is also occupied by [[32]another person], and there is a contractual liability to make payments to the claimant in respect of the occupation of the dwelling by that person or a member of his family—

[[121] (a) where the aggregate of any payments made in respect of any one week in respect of the occupation of the dwelling by that person or a member of his family, or by that person and a member of his family, is less than £20, the whole of that amount; or

(b) where the aggregate of any such payments is £20 or more per week, £20.]]

[[30]**20.**—Where the claimant occupies a dwelling as his home and he provides in that dwelling board and lodging accommodation, an amount, in respect of each person for whom such accommodation is provided for the whole or any part of a week, equal to—

(a) where the aggregate of any payments made in respect of any one week in respect of such accommodation provided to such person does not exceed £20.00, 100% of such payments; or

(b) where the aggregate of any such payments exceeds £20.00, £20.00 and 50% of the excess over £20.00.]

[[1]**21.**—(1) [[61]Subject to sub-paragraphs (2) and (3)], except where [[61]regulation 40(4)(b) (provision of support under section 95 or 98 of the Immigration and Asylum Act including support provided by virtue of regulations made under Schedule 9 to that Act in the calculation of income other than earnings) or] regulation 42(4)(a)(i) (notional income) applies or in the case of a person to whom section 23 of the Act [SSCBA, s.126] (trade disputes) applies and for so long as it applies, any income in kind;

(2) The exception under sub-paragraph (1) shall not apply where the income in kind is received from the Macfarlane Trust[[8], the Macfarlane (Special Payments) Trust] [[15], the Macfarlane (Special Payments) (No.2) Trust] [[21], the Fund] [[27], the Eileen Trust] [[136], MFET Limited] [[145], the Skipton Fund, the Caxton Foundation] [[2] or [[26] the Independent Living [[128] Fund (2006)]]].]

[[61](3) The first exception under sub-paragraph (1) shall not apply where the claimant is the partner of a person subject to immigration control and whose partner is receiving support provided under section 95 or 98 of the Immigration and Asylum Act including support provided by virtue of regulations made under Schedule 9 to that Act and the income in kind is support provided in respect of essential living needs of the partner of the claimant and his dependants (if any) as is specified in regulations made under paragraph 3 of Schedule 8 to the Immigration and Asylum Act.]

[[104] (4) The reference in sub-paragraph (1) to "income in kind" does not include a payment to a third party made in respect of the claimant which is used by the third party to provide benefits in kind to the claimant.]

22.—(1) Any income derived from capital to which the claimant is or is treated under regulation 52 (capital jointly held) as beneficially entitled but, subject to sub-paragraph (2), not income derived from capital disregarded under paragraph 1, 2, 4, 6 [[3]12 or 25 to 28] of Schedule 10.

(2) Income derived from capital disregarded under paragraph 2 [[3]4 or 25 to 28] of Schedule 10 but [[24]only to the extent of—

(a) any mortgage repayments made in respect of the dwelling or premises in the period during which that income accrued; or

(b) any council tax or water charges which the claimant is liable to pay in respect of the dwelling or premises and which are paid in the period during which that income accrued.

(3) The definition of "water charges" in regulation 2(1) shall apply to sub-paragraph (2) with the omission of the words "in so far as such charges are in respect of the dwelling which a person occupies as his home".]

23.—Any income which is payable in a country outside the United Kingdom for such period during which there is a prohibition against the transfer to the United Kingdom of that income.

24.—Where a payment of income is made in a currency other than sterling, any banking charge or commission payable in converting that payment into sterling.

25.—(1) Any payment made to the claimant in respect of a child or young person who is a member of his family—

[[20](a) [[109] pursuant to regulations under section 2(6)(b), 3 or 4 of the Adoption and Children Act 2002 or in accordance] with a scheme approved by the [[131] Scottish Ministers under section 51A] of the Adoption (Scotland) Act 1978 (schemes for payment of allowances to adopters) [[143] or in accordance with an adoption allowance scheme made under section 71 of the Adoption and Children (Scotland) Act 2007 (adoption allowances schemes)];

[[49](b) [[131] . . .]

[[135](ba) which is a payment made by a local authority in Scotland in pursuance of section 50 of the Children Act 1975 (payments towards maintenance of children);]

(c) which is a payment made by a local authority in pursuance of section 15(1) of, and paragraph 15 of Schedule 1 to, the Children Act 1989 (local authority contribution to a child's maintenance where the child is living with a person as a result of a [[158] child arrangements] order);

(d) which is a payment made by an authority, as defined in Article 2 of the Children Order, in pursuance of Article 15 of, and paragraph 17 of Schedule 1 to, that Order (contribution by an authority to child's maintenance);]]

[[100](e) in accordance with regulations made pursuant to section 14F of the Children Act 1989 (special guardianship support services);]

[[94] . . .].

[[110] (1A) Any payment, other than a payment to which sub-paragraph (1)(a) applies, made to the claimant pursuant to regulations under section 2(6)(b), 3 or 4 of the Adoption and Children Act 2002.]

(2) [[94] . . .].

[[94] **25A.**—In the case of a claimant who has a child or young person—

(a) who is a member of his family, and

(b) who is residing at an educational establishment at which he is receiving relevant education,

any payment made to that educational establishment, in respect of that child or young person's maintenance by or on behalf of a person who is not a member of the family or by a member of the family out of funds contributed for that purpose by a person who is not a member of the family.]

[[141] **26.**—Any payment made to the claimant with whom a person is accommodated by virtue of arrangements made—

(a) by a local authority under—

(i) section 23(2)(a) of the Children Act 1989 (provision of accommodation and maintenance for a child whom they are looking after),

(ii) section 26 of the Children (Scotland) Act 1995 (manner of provision of accommodation to child looked after by local authority), or

(iii) regulations 33 or 51 of the Looked After Children (Scotland) Regulations 2009 (fostering and kinship care allowances and fostering allowances); or

(b) by a voluntary organisation under section 59(1)(a) of the Children Act 1989 (provision of accommodation by voluntary organisations).]

27.—[[46] Any payment made to the claimant or his partner for a person ("the person concerned"), who is not normally a member of the claimant's household but is temporarily in his care, by—

(a) a health authority;
(b) a local authority [103 but excluding payments of housing benefit made in respect of the person concerned];
(c) a voluntary organisation; or
(d) the person concerned pursuant to section 26(3A) of the National Assistance Act 1948] [73 [131 . . .]
[163 (dza) the person concerned where the payment is for the provision of accommodation in respect of the meeting of that person's needs under section 18 or 19 of the Care Act 2014 (duty and power to meet needs for care and support);]
[156 (da) a clinical commissioning group established under section 14D of the National Health Service Act 2006;
(db) the National Health Service Commissioning Board; or]
(e) [156 . . .]]
[131 (f) a Local Health Board established under section 16BA of the National Health Service Act 1977 or established by an order made under section 11 of the Health Service (Wales) Act.]

[123 **28.**—(1) Any payment made by a local authority in accordance with—
(a) section 17, 23B, 23C or 24A of the Children Act 1989,
(b) section 12 of the Social Work (Scotland) Act 1968, or
(c) section [142 22,] 29 or 30 of the Children (Scotland) Act 1995.

(2) Any payment (or part of a payment) made by a local authority in accordance with section 23C of the Children Act 1989 or section [142 22 or] 29 of the Children (Scotland) Act 1995 (local authorities' duty to promote welfare of children and powers to grant financial assistance to persons in, or formerly in, their care) to a person ("A") which A passes on to the claimant.

(3) Sub-paragraphs (1) and (2) are subject to the following provisions.

(4) Neither of those sub-paragraphs applies where the claimant is a person—
(a) to whom section 126 of the Contributions and Benefits Act (trade disputes) applies, or
(b) in respect of whom section 124(1) of the Contributions and Benefits Act (conditions of entitlement to income support) has effect as modified by section 127 of that Act (effect of return to work).

(5) Sub-paragraph (2) applies only where A—
(a) was formerly in the claimant's care, and
(b) is aged 18 or over, and
(c) continues to live with the claimant.]

[33 **29.**—(1) Subject to sub-paragraph (2) any payment received under an insurance policy, taken out to insure against the risk of being unable to maintain repayments on a loan which qualifies under paragraph 15 or 16 of Schedule 3 (housing costs in respect of loans to acquire an interest in a dwelling, or for repairs and improvements to the dwelling, occupied as the home) and used to meet such repayments, to the extent that it does not exceed the aggregate of—
(a) the amount, calculated on a weekly basis, of any interest on that loan which is in excess of the amount met in accordance with Schedule 3 (housing costs);
(b) the amount of any payment, calculated on a weekly basis, due on the loan attributable to the repayment of capital; and
(c) any amount due by way of premiums on—
  (i) that policy, or
  (ii) a policy of insurance taken out to insure against loss or damage to any building or part of a building which is occupied by the claimant as his home.

(2) This paragraph shall not apply to any payment which is treated as possessed by the claimant by virtue of regulation 42(4)(a)(ii) (notional income).

30.—(1) Except where paragraph 29 [50 or 30ZA] applies, and subject to sub-paragraph (2), any payment made to the claimant which is intended to be used and is used as a contribution towards—
(a) any payment due on a loan if secured on the dwelling occupied as the home which does not qualify under Schedule 3 (housing costs);
(b) any interest payment or charge which qualifies in accordance with paragraphs 15 to 17 of Schedule 3 to the extent that the payment or charge is not met;
(c) any payment due on a loan which qualifies under paragraph 15 or 16 of Schedule 3 attributable to the payment of capital;
(d) any amount due by way of premiums on—
  (i) [36 an insurance policy taken out to insure against the risk of being unable to make the payments referred to in (a) to (c) above;] or
  (ii) a policy of insurance taken out to insure against loss or damage to any building or part of a building which is occupied by the claimant as his home.
(e) his rent in respect of the dwelling occupied by him as his home but only to the extent

that it is not met by housing benefit; or his accommodation charge but only to the extent that the actual charge [79 exceeds] the amount payable by a local authority in accordance with Part III of the National Assistance Act 1948 [164 or Part 1 of the Care Act 2014 (care and support).]

(2) This paragraph shall not apply to any payment which is treated as possessed by the claimant by virtue of regulation 42(4)(a)(ii) (notional income).]

[50 **30ZA.**—(1) Subject to sub-paragraph (2), any payment received under an insurance policy, other than an insurance policy referred to in paragraph 29, taken out to insure against the risk of being unable to maintain repayments under a regulated agreement as defined for the purposes of the Consumer Credit Act 1974 or under a hire-purchase agreement or a conditional sale agreement as defined for the purposes of Part III of the Hire-Purchase Act 1964.

(2) A payment referred to in sub-paragraph (1) shall only be disregarded to the extent that the payment received under that policy does not exceed the amounts, calculated on a weekly basis, which are used to—

(a) maintain the repayments referred to in sub-paragraph (1); and

(b) meet any amount due by way of premiums on that policy.]

[29 **30A.**—(1) Subject to sub-paragraphs (2) and (3), in the case of a claimant [106 residing in a care home, an Abbeyfield Home or an independent hospital], any payment, [118 except a charitable or voluntary payment disregarded under paragraph 15], [116. . .] made to the claimant which is intended to be used and is used to meet the cost of maintaining the claimant in that home [106 or hospital].

(2) This paragraph shall not apply to a claimant for whom accommodation in a [106 care home, an Abbeyfield Home or an independent hospital] is provided by

[165 (a) a local authority under section 26 of the National Assistance Act 1948 [79. . .]; or

(b) a person other than a local authority under arrangements made with the person by a local authority in the exercise of the local authority's functions under section 18 or 19 of the Care Act 2014 (duty and power to meet needs for care and support).]

(3) The amount to be disregarded under this paragraph shall not exceed the difference between—

[79 (a) the claimant's applicable amount; and]

(b) the weekly charge for the accommodation.]

[19 **31.**—Any social fund payment made pursuant to [131 Part 8 of the Contributions and Benefits Act].]

[151 **31A.**—Any local welfare provision.]

32.—Any payment of income which under regulation 48 (income treated as capital) is to be treated as capital.

33.—Any payment under [131 Part 10 of the Contributions and Benefits Act] (pensioners' Christmas bonus).

34.—In the case of a person to whom section 23 of the Act [SSCBA, s.126] (trade disputes) applies and for so long as it applies, any payment up to the amount of the relevant sum within the meaning of sub-section (6) of that section made by a trade union; but, notwithstanding regulation 23 (calculation of income and capital of members of claimant's family and of a polygamous marriage) if this paragraph applies to a claimant it shall not apply to his partner except where, and to the extent that, the amount to be disregarded under this paragraph is less than the relevant sum.

35.—Any payment which is due to be paid before the date of claim which would otherwise fall to be taken into account in the same benefit week as a payment of the same kind and from the same source.

36.—The total of a claimant's income or, if he is a member of a family, the family's income and the income of any person which he is treated as possessing under regulation 23(3) (calculation of income and capital of members of claimant's family and of a polygamous marriage) to be disregarded under regulation 63(2)(b) and 64(1)(c) (calculation of covenant income where a contribution assessed)[11, regulation 66A(2) (treatment of student loans)] [67, regulation 66B(3) (treatment of payments from access funds)] and [117 paragraph 16] shall in no case exceed [39 £20] per week.

37.—Notwithstanding paragraph 36 where two or more payments of the same kind and from the same source are to be taken into account in the same benefit week, there shall be disregarded from each payment the sum which would otherwise fall to be disregarded under this Schedule; but this paragraph shall only apply in the case of a payment which it has not been practicable to treat under regulation 31(1)(b) (date on which income treated as paid) as paid on the first day of the benefit week in which it is due to be paid.

[1 **38.**—[112. . .]

[15 **39.**—(1) Any payment made under [137 or by] the Macfarlane Trust, the Macfarlane

(Special Payments) Trust, the Macfarlane (Special Payments) (No.2) Trust ("the Trusts"), [21the Fund][27, the Eileen Trust] [136 , MFET Limited] [145, the Skipton Fund, the Caxton Foundation] or [26the Independent Living [128 Fund (2006)]].

(2) Any payment by or on behalf of a person who is suffering or who suffered from haemophilia [21or who is or was a qualifying person], which derives from a payment made under [137 or by] any of the Trusts to which sub-paragraph (1) refers and which is made to or for the benefit of—

(a) that person's partner or former partner from whom he is not, or where that person has died was not, estranged or divorced [107 or with whom he has formed a civil partnership that has not been dissolved or, where that person has died, had not been dissolved at the time of that person's death];

(b) any child who is a member of that person's family or who was such a member and who is a member of the claimant's family; or

(c) any young person who is a member of that person's family or who was such a member and who is a member of the claimant's family.

(3) Any payment by or on behalf of the partner or former partner of a person who is suffering or who suffered from haemophilia [21or who is or was a qualifying person] provided that the partner or former partner and that person are not, or if either of them has died were not, estranged or divorced [107 or, where the partner or former partner and that person have formed a civil partnership, the civil partnership has not been dissolved or, if either of them has died, had not been dissolved at the time of the death], which derives from a payment made under [137 or by] any of the Trusts to which sub-paragraph (1) refers and which is made to or for the benefit of—

(a) the person who is suffering from haemophilia [21or who is a qualifying person];

(b) any child who is a member of that person's family or who was such a member and who is a member of the claimant's family; or

(c) any young person who is a member of that person's family or who was such a member and who is a member of the claimant's family.

(4) Any payment by a person who is suffering from haemophilia [21or who is a qualifying person], which derives from a payment under [137 or by] any of the Trusts to which sub-paragraph (1) refers, where—

(a) that person has no partner or former partner from whom he is not estranged or divorced [107 or with whom he has formed a civil partnership that has not been dissolved], nor any child or young person who is or had been a member of that person's family; and

(b) the payment is made either—

(i) to that person's parent or step-parent, or

(ii) where that person at the date of the payment is a child, a young person or a [66 full-time student] student who has not completed his full-time education and has no parent or step-parent, to his guardian,

but only for a period from the date of the payment until the end of two years from that person's death.

(5) Any payment out of the estate of a person who suffered from haemophilia [21or who was a qualifying person], which derives from a payment under [137 or by] any of the Trusts to which sub-paragraph (1) refers, where—

(a) that person at the date of his death (the relevant date) had no partner or former partner from whom he was not estranged or divorced [107 or with whom he had formed a civil partnership that had not been dissolved], nor any child or young person who was or had been a member of his family; and

(b) the payment is made either—

(i) to that person's parent or step-parent, or

(ii) where that person at the relevant date was a child, a young person or a [66 full-time student] who had not completed his full-time education and had no parent or step-parent, to his guardian,

but only for a period of two years from the relevant date.

(6) In the case of a person to whom or for whose benefit a payment referred to in this paragraph is made, any income which derives from any payment of income or capital made under or deriving from any of the Trusts.]

[21(7) For the purposes of sub-paragraphs (2) to (6), any reference to the Trusts shall be construed as including a reference to the Fund [99, the Eileen Trust [136, MFET Limited] [108, the Skipton Fund [146, the Caxton Foundation] and the London Bombings Relief Charitable Fund]].]]

[3**40.**—Any payment made by the Secretary of State to compensate for the loss (in whole or in part) of entitlement to housing benefit.]

[4**41.**—[124 . . .]

42.—[124 . . .]

43.—Any payment made to a juror or a witness in respect of attendance at a court other than compensation for loss of earnings or for the loss of a benefit payable under the benefit Acts.

44.—[[23] . . .].]

[[9]**45.**—[[129] . . .]

[[125] **46.**—Any payment in consequence of a reduction of council tax under section 13 [[152], 13A]or 80 of the Local Government Finance Act 1992 (reduction of liability for council tax).]]

47.—[[131]. . .].]

[[12] [[131] **48.**—(1) Any payment or repayment made—

(a) as respects England, under regulation 5, 6 or 12 of the National Health Service (Travel Expenses and Remission of Charges) Regulations 2003 (travelling expenses and health service supplies);

(b) as respects Wales, under regulation 5, 6 or 11 of the National Health Service (Travelling Expenses and Remission of Charges) (Wales) Regulations 2007 (travelling expenses and health service supplies);

(c) as respects Scotland, under regulation 3, 5 or 11 of the National Health Service (Travelling Expenses and Remission of Charges) (Scotland) (No.2) Regulations 2003 (travelling expenses and health service supplies).

(2) Any payment or repayment made by the Secretary of State for Health, the Scottish Ministers or the Welsh Ministers which is analogous to a payment or repayment mentioned in sub-paragraph (1).

49.—Any payment made to such persons entitled to receive benefits as may be determined by or under a scheme made pursuant to section 13 of the Social Security Act 1988 in lieu of vouchers or similar arrangements in connection with the provision of those benefits (including payments made in place of healthy start vouchers, milk tokens or the supply of vitamins).]

50.—Any payment made either by the Secretary of State for [[120] Justice] or by the [[131] Scottish Ministers] under a scheme established to assist relatives and other persons to visit persons in custody.]

[[19]**51.**—Any payment (other than a training allowance) made, whether by the Secretary of State or by any other person, under the Disabled Persons (Employment) Act 1944 [[93]. . .] to assist disabled persons to obtain or retain employment despite their disability.]

[[131] **52.**—[[150]. . .]

53.—(1) If the claimant is in receipt of any benefit under Part 2, 3 or 5 of the Contributions and Benefits Act, any increase in the rate of that benefit arising under Part 4 (increases for dependants) or section 106(a) (unemployability supplement) of that Act, where the dependant in respect of whom the increase is paid is not a member of the claimant's family.

(2) If the claimant is in receipt of any pension or allowance under Part 2 or 3 of the Naval, Military and Air Forces Etc. (Disablement and Death) Service Pensions Order 2006, any increase in the rate of that pension or allowance under that Order, where the dependant in respect of whom the increase is paid is not a member of the claimant's family.

54.—Any supplementary pension under article 23(2) of the Naval, Military and Air Forces Etc. (Disablement and Death) Service Pensions Order 2006 (pensions to surviving spouses and surviving civil partners) and any analogous payment made by the Secretary of State for Defence to any person who is not a person entitled under that Order.]

55.—In the case of a pension awarded at the supplementary rate under article 27(3) of the Personal Injuries (Civilians) Scheme 1983 (pensions to [[107] widows, widowers or surviving civil partners]), the sum specified in paragraph 1(c) of Schedule 4 to that Scheme.

56.—(1) Any payment which is—

(a) made under any of the Dispensing Instruments to a [[107] widow, widower or surviving civil partner] of a person—

(i) whose death was attributable to service in a capacity analogous to service as a member of the armed forces of the Crown; and

(ii) whose service in such capacity terminated before 31st March 1973; and

[[131] (b) equal to the amount specified in article 23(2) of the Naval, Military and Air Forces Etc. (Disablement and Death) Service Pensions Order 2006.]

(2) In this paragraph "the Dispensing Instruments" means the Order in Council of 19th December 1881, the Royal Warrant of 27th October 1884 and the Order by His Majesty of 14th January 1922 (exceptional grants of pay, non-efective pay and allowances).]

[[41]**57.**—[[119] [[131] . . .]]]

[[42]**58.**—Any payment made [[132] . . .] under section 12B of the Social Work (Scotland) Act 1968 [[138] , or under sections 12A to 12D of the National Health Service Act 2006 (direct payments for health care)] [[166] or under sections 31 to 33 of the Care Act 2014 (direct payments),] [[88a] or under regulations made under section 57 of the Health and Social Care Act 2001 (direct payments)].

59.—[93 . . .]
60.—[93 . . .]
61.—(1) Any payment specified in sub-paragraph (2) to a claimant who was formerly a [69student] and who has completed the course in respect of which those payments were made.
(2) The payments specified for the purposes of sub-paragraph (1) are—
(a) any grant income and covenant income as defined for the purposes of Chapter VIII of Part V;
[57(b) any student loan as defined in Chapter VIII of Part V;
(c) any contribution as defined in Chapter VIII of Part V which—
(i) is taken into account in ascertaining the amount of a student loan referred to in head (b); and
(ii) has been paid.]]
[75 **62.**—[93. . .].]
[82 **62A.**—[93. . .].]
[45**63.**—[93. . .].]
[51**64.**—(1) Subject to sub-paragraph (2), in the case of a person who is receiving, or who has received, assistance under [68 "the self-employment route"] , any payment to the person—
(a) to meet expenses wholly and necessarily incurred whilst carrying on the commercial activity;
(b) which is used or intended to be used to maintain repayments on a loan taken out by that person for the purpose of establshing or carrying on the commercial activity, in respect of which such assistance is or was received.
(2) Sub-paragraph (1) shall apply only in respect of payments which are paid to that person from the special account as defined for the purposes of Chapter IVA of Part V.]
[53**65.**—[93. . .].]
[54**66.**—Any payment made with respect to a person on account of the provision of after-care under section 117 of the Mental Health Act 1983 or [105 section 25 of the Mental Health (Care and Treatment) (Scotland) Act 2003] or the provision of accommodation or welfare services to which [63 Part III of the National Assistance Act 1948 refers or to which the Social Work (Scotland) Act 1968 refers], [167 or the provision of care and support under Part 1 of the Care Act 2014 (care and support),] which falls to be treated as notional income under paragraph (4A) of regulation 42 above (payments made in respect of a person [106 living in a care home, an Abbeyfield Home or an independent hospital]).]
67.—*[Omitted]*
68.—*[Omitted]*
[56**69.**—(1) Any payment of a sports award except to the extent that it has been made in respect of any one or more of the items specified in sub-paragraph (2).
(2) The items specified for the purposes of sub-paragraph (1) are food, ordinary clothing or footwear, household fuel, rent for which housing benefit is payable or any housing costs to the extent that they are met under regulation 17(1)(e) or 18(1)(f) (housing costs) [79. . .], of the claimant or, where the claimant is a member of a family, any other member of his family, or any council tax or water charges for which that claimant or member is liable.
(3) For the purposes of sub-paragraph (2)—

"food" does not include vitamins, minerals or other special dietary supplements intended to enhance the performance of the person in the sport in respect of which the award was made;
"ordinary clothing and footwear" means clothing or footwear for normal daily use but does not include school uniforms or clothing or footwear used solely for sporting activities.]

[59**70.**—[101 . . .]]
[65**71.**—Where the amount of a subsistence allowance paid to a person in a benefit week exceeds the amount of income-based jobseeker's allowance that person would have received in that benefit week had it been payable to him, less 50p, that excess amount.
72.—In the case of a claimant participating in an employment zone programme, any discretionary payment made by an employment zone contractor to the claimant, being a fee, grant, loan or otherwise.]
[85 [92[139**73.**—(1) Any payment of child maintenance made or derived from a liable relative where the child or young person in respect of whom the payment is made is a member of the claimant's family, except where the person making the payment is the claimant or the claimant's partner.
(2) In paragraph (1)—
"child maintenance" means any payment towards the maintenance of a child or young person, including any payment made voluntarily and payments made under—
(a) the Child Support Act 1991;
(b) the Child Support (Northern Ireland) Order 1991;

(c) a court order;
(d) a consent order;
(e) a maintenance agreement registered for execution in the Books of Council and Session or the sheriff court books;

"liable relative" means a person listed in regulation 54 (interpretation) other than a person falling within sub-paragraph (d) of that definition.]]]

[[71]**74.**—In the case of a person to whom paragraph (5) of regulation 6 (persons not treated as in remunerative work) applies, the whole of his income.]

[[76] **75.**—Any discretionary housing payment paid pursuant to regulation 2(1) of the Dis cretionary Financial Assistance Regulations 2001.]

[[87] [[89] **76.**—(1) Any payment made by a local authority, or by the [[131]Welsh Ministers], to or on behalf of the claimant or his partner relating to a service which is provided to develop or sustain the capacity of the claimant or his partner to live independently in his accommodation.]

(2) For the purposes of sub-paragraph (1) "local authority" includes, in England, a county council.]

[[155] **76A.**—Armed forces independence payment.]

[[89] **77.**—[[93] . . .].]

[[91] **78.**—[[93] . . .].]

[[160] **79.**—Any payments to a claimant made under section 49 of the Children and Families Act 2014 (personal budgets and direct payments).]

AMENDMENTS

1. Income Support (General) Amendment Regulations 1988 (SI 1988/663) reg.35 (April 11, 1988).
2. Family Credit and Income Support (General) Amendment Regulations 1988 (SI 1988/999) reg.5 (June 9, 1988).
3. Income Support (General) Amendment No.4 Regulations 1988 (SI 1988/1445) reg.25 (September 12, 1988).
4. Income Support (General) Amendment No.5 Regulations 1988 (SI 1988/2022) reg.22 (December 12, 1988).
5. Income Support (General) Amendment No.4 Regulations 1988 (SI 1988/1445) Sch.1 para.9 (April 10, 1989).
6. Family Credit and Income Support (General) Amendment Regulations 1989 (SI 1989/1034) reg.12 (July 10, 1989).
7. Income Support (General) Amendment Regulations 1989 (SI 1989/534) Sch.1 para.15 (October 9, 1989).
8. Income-related Benefits Schemes Amendment Regulations 1990 (SI 1990/127) reg.3 (January 31, 1990).
9. Income Support (General) Amendment Regulations 1990 (SI 1990/547) reg.22(e) (April 1, 1990).
10. Income Support (General) Amendment Regulations 1990 (SI 1990/547) reg.22 (April 1, 1990).
11. Income-related Benefits Amendment Regulations 1990 (SI 1990/1657) reg.5(4) (September 1, 1990).
12. Income Support (General) Amendment No.3 Regulations 1990 (SI 1990/1776) reg.10 (October 1, 1990).
13. Enterprise (Scotland) Consequential Amendments Order 1991 (SI 1991/387) arts 2 and 9 (April 1, 1991).
14. Income Support (General) Amendment Regulations 1991 (SI 1991/236) reg.14 (April 8, 1991).
15. Income-related Benefits Schemes and Social Security (Recoupment) Amendment Regulations 1991 (SI 1991/1175) reg.5 (May 11, 1991).
16. Income Support (General) Amendment No.4 Regulations 1991 (SI 1991/1559) reg.20 (October 7, 1991).
17. Social Security Benefits Up-rating (No.2) Order 1991 (SI 1991/2910) art.13(13) (April 6, 1992).
18. Disability Living Allowance and Disability Working Allowance (Consequential Provisions) Regulations 1991 (SI 1991/2742) reg.11(6) (April 6, 1992).

19. Income Support (General) Amendment Regulations 1992 (SI 1992/468) reg.8 (April 6, 1992).

20. Income Support (General) Amendment Regulations 1992 (SI 1992/468) Sch. para.9 (April 6, 1992).

21. Income-related Benefits Schemes and Social Security (Recoupment) Amendment Regulations 1992 (SI 1992/1101) reg.6 (May 7, 1992).

22. Social Security Benefits (Amendments Consequential Upon the Introduction of Community Care) Regulations 1992 (SI 1992/3147) Sch.1 para.7 (April 1, 1993).

23. Income-related Benefits Schemes (Miscellaneous Amendments) Regulations 1993 (SI 1993/315) Sch. para.5 (April 1, 1993).

24. Income-related Benefits Schemes (Miscellaneous Amendments) Regulations 1993 (SI 1993/315) reg.9 (council tax and council tax benefit: April 1 1993; otherwise April 12, 1993).

25. Social Security Benefits (Miscellaneous Amendments) Regulations 1993 (SI 1993/518) reg.5 (April 1, 1993).

26. Social Security Benefits (Miscellaneous Amendments) (No.2) Regulations 1993 (SI 1993/963) reg.2(3) (April 22, 1993).

27. Income-related Benefits Schemes and Social Security (Recoupment) Amendment Regulations 1993 (SI 1993/1249) reg.4(4) (May 14, 1993).

28. Income Support (General) Amendment No.3 Regulations 1993 (SI 1993/1679) reg.6 (August 2, 1993).

29. Income-related Benefits Schemes (Miscellaneous Amendments) (No.4) Regulations 1993 (SI 1993/2119) reg.23 (October 4, 1993).

30. Income-related Benefits Schemes (Miscellaneous Amendments) Regulations 1994 (SI 1994/527) reg.9 (April 11, 1994).

31. Income-related Benefits Schemes (Miscellaneous Amendments) (No.5) Regulations 1994 (SI 1994/2139) reg.32 (October 3, 1994).

32. Income-related Benefits Schemes (Miscellaneous Amendments) Regulations 1995 (SI 1995/516) reg.27 (April 10, 1995).

33. Social Security (Income Support and Claims and Payments) Amendment Regulation 1995 (SI 1995/1613) reg.4 and Sch.3 (October 2, 1995).

34. Income-related Benefits Schemes and Social Security (Claims and Payments) (Miscellaneous Amendments) Regulations 1995 (SI 1995/2303) reg.6(9) (October 2, 1995).

35. Income-related Benefits Schemes Amendment (No.2) Regulations 1995 (SI 1995/2792) reg.6(3) (October 28, 1995).

36. Social Security (Income Support, Claims and Payments and Adjudication) Amendment Regulations 1995 (SI 1995/2927) reg.6 (December 12, 1995).

37. Income-related Benefits Schemes (Widows, etc. Pensions Disregards) Amendment Regulations 1995 (SI 1995/3282) reg.2 (December 20, 1995).

38. Income Support (General) Amendment Regulations 1996 (SI 1996/606) reg.2 (April 8, 1996).

39. Income-related Benefits Schemes (Miscellaneous Amendments) Regulations 1996 (SI 1996/462) reg.8 (April 8, 1996).

40. Social Security Benefits Up-rating Order 1996 (SI 1996/599) reg.18(13) (April 8, 1996).

41. Income Support and Social Security (Claims and Payments) (Miscellaneous Amendments) Regulations 1996 (SI 1996/2431) reg.5 (October 15, 1996).

42. Income-related Benefits and Jobseeker's Allowance (Miscellaneous Amendments) Regulations 1997 (SI 1997/65) reg.2(3) (April 7, 1997).

43. Income-related Benefits and Jobseeker's Allowance (Amendment) (No.2) Regulations 1997 (SI 1997/2197) reg.7(7) and (8)(e) (October 6, 1997).

44. Social Security Amendment (New Deal) Regulations 1997 (SI 1997/ 2863) reg.17(7) and (8)(e) (January 5, 1998).

45. Social Security Amendment (New Deal) Regulations 1997 (SI 1997/ 2863) reg.17(9) and (10)(e) (January 5, 1998).

46. Social Security (Miscellaneous Amendments) Regulations 1998 (SI 1998/563) reg.7(3) and (4)(e) (April 6, 1998).
47. Social Security (Miscellaneous Amendments) Regulations 1998 (SI 1998/563) reg.13(1)(c) (April 6, 1998).
48. Social Security (Miscellaneous Amendments) Regulations 1998 (SI 1998/563) reg.15(1) (April 6, 1998).
49. Social Security (Miscellaneous Amendments) Regulations 1998 (SI 1998/563) reg.15(2) (April 6, 1998).
50. Social Security (Miscellaneous Amendments) (No.3) Regulations 1998 (SI 1998/1173) reg.4 (June 1, 1998).
51. Social Security (Miscellaneous Amendments) (No.4) Regulations 1998 (SI 1998/1174) reg.6(4) (June 1, 1998).
52. Social Security (Miscellaneous Amendments) (No.4) Regulations 1998 (SI 1998/1174) reg.7(3) and (4)(e) (June 1, 1998).
53. Social Security Amendment (New Deal) (No.2) Regulations 1998 (SI 1998/2117) reg.4(4) (September 24, 1998).
54. Social Security Amendment (New Deal) (No.2) Regulations 1998 (SI 1998/2117) reg.6(2) (September 24, 1998).
55. Social Security Amendment (Educational Maintenance Allowance) Regulations 1999 (SI 1999/1677) reg.2(1) and (2)(e) (August 16, 1999).
56. Social Security Amendment (Sports Awards) Regulations 1999 (SI 1999/2165) reg.6(4) (August 23, 1999).
57. Social Security Amendment (Students) Regulations 1999 (SI 1999/1935) reg.3(8) (August 30, 1999, or if the student's period of study begins between August 1 and 29, 1999, the first day of the period).
58. Income Support (General) Amendment Regulations 1999 (SI 1999/ 2554) reg.2(3) (October 4, 1999).
59. Social Security (Miscellaneous Amendments) (No.2) Regulations 1999 (SI 1999/2556) reg.2(10) (October 4, 1999).
60. Social Security Amendment (Education Maintenance Allowance) Regulations 2000 (SI 2000/55) reg.2(1) and (2)(c) (February 7, 2000).
61. Social Security (Immigration and Asylum) Consequential Amendments Regulations 2000 (SI 2000/636) reg.3(12) (April 3, 2000).
62. Social Security (Immigration and Asylum) Consequential Amendments Regulations 2000 (SI 2000/636) reg.3(13) (April 3, 2000).
63. Social Security (Miscellaneous Amendments) Regulations 2000 (SI 2000/681) reg.7 (April 3, 2000).
64. Social Security (Miscellaneous Amendments) Regulations 2000 (SI 2000/681) reg.12(a) (April 3, 2000).
65. Social Security Amendment (Employment Zones) Regulations 2000 (SI 2000/724) reg.3(3) (April 3, 2000).
66. Social Security Amendment (Students) Regulations 2000 (SI 2000/1981) reg.5(5) and Sch. (July 31, 2000).
67. Social Security Amendment (Students and Income-related Benefits) Regulations 2000 (SI 2000/1922) reg.2(9) (August 28, 2000, or if the student's period of study begins between August 1 and 27, 2000, the first day of the period).
68. Social Security Amendment (Employment Zones) (No.2) Regulations 2000 (SI 2000/2910) reg.4(1) and (2)(c)(i) (November 27, 2000).
69. Income Support (General) Amendment Regulations 2001 (SI 2001/721) reg.2(c) (March 29, 2001).
70. Social Security Amendment (Bereavement Benefits) Regulations 2000 (SI 2000/2239) reg.2(4) (April 9, 2001).
71. Social Security (Miscellaneous Amendments) Regulations 2001 (SI 2001/488) reg.9 (April 9, 2001).
72. Social Security (Miscellaneous Amendments) (No.3) Regulations 2001 (SI 2001/859) reg.3(5) (April 9, 2001).

73. Social Security (Miscellaneous Amendments) (No.3) Regulations 2001 (SI 2001/859) reg.6(3)(c) (April 9, 2001).

74. Social Security Amendment (New Deal) Regulations 2001 (SI 2001/ 1029) reg.15(10) and (11)(c) (April 9, 2001).

75. Social Security Amendment (New Deal) Regulations 2001 (SI 2001/ 1029) reg.15(12) and (13)(c) (April 9, 2001).

76. Social Security Amendment (Discretionary Housing Payments) Regulations 2001 (SI 2001/2333) reg.2(1)(c) (July 2, 2001).

77. Social Security Amendment (Volunteers) Regulations 2001 (SI 2001/ 2296) reg.2(1) and (2)(c) (September 24, 2001).

78. Children (Leaving Care) Act 2000 (Commencement No.2 and Consequential Provisions) Order 2001 (SI 2001/3070) art.3(2) and para.(c) of Sch.1 (October 1, 2001).

79. Social Security Amendment (Residential Care and Nursing Homes) Regulations 2001 (SI 2001/3767) reg.2(1) and Pt I of Sch. para.19 (April 8, 2002).

80. Social Security Benefits Up-rating Order 2002 (SI 2002/668) art.16(9) (April 8, 2002).

81. Social Security (Miscellaneous Amendments) Regulations 2002 (SI 2002/ 841) reg.2(4) (April 8, 2002).

82. Social Security Amendment (Employment Programme) Regulations 2002 (SI 2002/2314) reg.3(3) (October 14, 2002).

83. Social Security (Miscellaneous Amendments) (No.2) Regulations 2002 (SI 2002/2380) reg.2(a) ((October 14, 2002).

84. Social Security Amendment (Personal Injury Payments) Regulations 2002 (SI 2002/2442) reg.3(1)(d) and (2)(c) (October 28, 2002).

85. Social Security (Child Maintenance Premium and Miscellaneous Amendments) Regulations 2000 (SI 2000/3176) reg.2(1)(b) (in force in relation to any particular case on the day on which s.23 CSPSSA 2000 comes into force in relation to that type of case).

86. Social Security (Paternity and Adoption) Amendment Regulations 2002 (SI 2002/2689) reg.2(6) (December 8, 2002).

87. Social Security (Miscellaneous Amendments) Regulations 2003 (SI 2003/ 511) reg.2(2) (April 1, 2003)

88. Social Security (Working Tax Credit and Child Tax Credit) (Consequential Amendments) Regulations 2003 (SI 2003/455) reg.2 and Sch.1 para.23(a) (April 7, 2003).

88a. Community Care, Services for Carers and Children's Services (Direct Payments) (England) Regulations 2003 (SI 2003/762) reg.11(2) and Sch.2 (April 8, 2003).

89. Social Security (Miscellaneous Amendments) (No.2) Regulations 2003 (SI 2003/2279) reg.2(4) (October 1, 2003).

90. Social Security (Removal of Residential Allowance and Miscellaneous Amendments) Regulations 2003 (SI 2003/1121) reg.2 and Sch.1 para.9 (October 6, 2003).

91. Social Security (Incapacity Benefit Work-focused Interviews) Regulations 2003 (SI 2003/2439) reg.13(a) (October 27, 2003).

92. Social Security (Child Maintenance Premium) Amendment Regulations 2004 (SI 2004/98) reg.2 (in force on: (i) February 16, 2004 in relation to any particular case in respect of which s.23 CSPSSA 2000 has come into force before February 16, 2004; (ii) where this does not apply, the day on which s.23 comes into force in relation to that type of case; (iii) February 16, 2004 in relation to a person who is entitled to income support/income-based JSA on that date and who receives her first payment of child maintenance made voluntarily whilst entitled to income support/income-based JSA on that date; (iv) in such a case where the day that the first voluntary payment is received is after February 16, 2004, the day the payment is received; and (v) February 16, 2004 in relation to a person who makes a claim for income support/income-based JSA on or after that date and receives a payment of child maintenance made voluntarily on or after the date of that claim).

93. Social Security (Miscellaneous Amendments) Regulations 2004 (SI 2004/565) reg.2(3) (April 1, 2004).

94. Social Security (Working Tax Credit and Child Tax Credit) (Consequential

Amendments) Regulations 2003 (SI 2003/455) reg.2 and Sch.1 para.23 (except sub-para.(a) (April 6, 2004, except in "transitional cases" and see further the note to reg.17 of the Income Support Regulations).

95. Social Security (Miscellaneous Amendments) (No.2) Regulations 2004 (SI 2004/1141) reg.4(1) and (2)(c) (May 12, 2004).

96. Social Security (Miscellaneous Amendments) (No.2) Regulations 2004 (SI 2004/1141) reg.4(3) and (4)(c) (May 12, 2004).

97. Social Security (Students and Income-related Benefits) Amendment Regulations 2004 (SI 2004/1708) reg.5(2) (September 1, 2004, or if the student's period of study begins between August 1 and August 31, 2004, the first day of the period).

98. Social Security (Miscellaneous Amendments) (No.3) Regulations 2004 (SI 2004/2308) reg.2(1) and (2)(a) (October 4, 2004).

99. Social Security (Miscellaneous Amendments) (No.3) Regulations 2004 (SI 2004/2308) reg.3(3) and (4)(a) (October 4, 2004).

100. Social Security (Miscellaneous Amendments) (No.3) Regulations 2004 (SI 2004/2308) reg.4(3) and (4)(a) (October 4, 2004).

101. Social Security (Back to Work Bonus and Lone Parent Run-on) (Amendment and Revocation) Regulations 2003 (SI 2003/1589) reg.2(d) (October 25, 2004).

102. Social Security (Miscellaneous Amendments) Regulations 2005 (SI 2005/574) reg.2(7) and (8)(a) (April 4, 2005).

103. Social Security (Miscellaneous Amendments) Regulations 2005 (SI 2005/574) reg.3(5) (April 4, 2005).

104. Social Security (Miscellaneous Amendments) (No.2) Regulations 2005 (SI 2005/2465) reg.2(8)(a) (October 3, 2005).

105. Mental Health (Care and Treatment) (Scotland) Act 2003 (Modification of Subordinate Legislation) Order 2005 (SSI 2005/445) art.2 and Sch., para.3(5) (Scotland); Mental Health (Care and Treatment) (Scotland) Act 2003 (Consequential Provisions) Order 2005 (SI 2005/2078) art.15 and Sch.2 para.3(6) (England and Wales) (October 5, 2005).

106. Social Security (Care Homes and Independent Hospitals) Regulations 2005 (SI 2005/2687) reg.2 and Sch.1 para.12 (October 24, 2005).

107. Civil Partnership (Pensions, Social Security and Child Support) (Consequential, etc. Provisions) Order 2005 (SI 2005/2877) art.2(3) and Sch.3 para.13(8) (December 5, 2005).

108. Income-related Benefits (Amendment) (No.2) Regulations 2005 (SI 2005/3391) reg.2(3) (December 12, 2005).

109. Social Security (Miscellaneous Amendments) (No.2) Regulations 2005 (SI 2005/2465) reg.2(8)(b) (December 30, 2005).

110. Social Security (Miscellaneous Amendments) (No.2) Regulations 2005 (SI 2005/2465) reg.2(8)(c) (December 30, 2005).

111. Housing Benefit and Council Tax Benefit (Consequential Provisions) Regulations 2006 (SI 2006/217) reg.5 and Sch.2 para.1(8) (March 6, 2006).

112. Social Security (Hospital In-Patients) Regulations 2005 (SI 2005/3360) reg.4(6) (April 10, 2006).

113. Social Security (Miscellaneous Amendments) (No.4) Regulations 2006 (SI 2006/2378) reg.5(10)(a) (October 2, 2006).

114. Social Security (Miscellaneous Amendments) (No.4) Regulations 2006 (SI 2006/2378) reg.5(10)(b) (October 2, 2006).

115. Social Security (Miscellaneous Amendments) (No.4) Regulations 2006 (SI 2006/2378) reg.5(10)(c) (October 2, 2006).

116. Social Security (Miscellaneous Amendments) (No.4) Regulations 2006 (SI 2006/2378) reg.5(10)(d) (October 2, 2006).

117. Social Security (Miscellaneous Amendments) (No.4) Regulations 2006 (SI 2006/2378) reg.5(10)(e) (October 2, 2006).

118. Social Security (Miscellaneous Amendments) Regulations 2007 (SI 2007/719) reg.2(9) (April 2, 2007).

119. Asylum and Immigration (Treatment of Claimants, etc.) Act 2004 (c.19) s.12(2)(a)(iii) (June 14, 2007).
120. Secretary of State for Justice Order 2007 (SI 2007/2128) Sch. para.13(2) (August 22, 2007).
121. Social Security (Miscellaneous Amendments) (No.5) Regulations 2007 (SI 2007/2618) reg.5(12) (April 7, 2008).
122. Social Security (Miscellaneous Amendments) Regulations 2008 (SI 2008/698) reg.2(14)(a) (April 14, 2008).
123. Social Security (Miscellaneous Amendments) Regulations 2008 (SI 2008/698) reg.2(14)(b) (April 7, 2008).
124. Social Security (Miscellaneous Amendments) Regulations 2008 (SI 2008/698) reg.2(14)(c) (April 14, 2008).
125. Social Security (Miscellaneous Amendments) Regulations 2008 (SI 2008/698) reg.2(14)(d) (April 14, 2008).
126. Employment and Support Allowance (Consequential Provisions) (No.2) Regulations 2008 (SI 2008/1554) reg.2(14) (October 27, 2008).
127. Social Security (Child Maintenance Amendments) Regulations 2008 (SI 2008/2111) reg.2(9) (October 27, 2008).
128. Social Security (Miscellaneous Amendments) (No.6) Regulations 2008 (SI 2008/2767) reg.2(6) (November 17, 2008).
129. Social Security (Miscellaneous Amendments) (No.6) Regulations 2008 (SI 2008/2767) reg.2(12) (November 17, 2008).
130. Social Security (Child Benefit Disregard) Regulations 2008 (SI 2008/3140) reg.2 (January 5, 2009; this regulation ceases to have effect on April 6, 2009).
131. Social Security (Miscellaneous Amendments) (No.7) Regulations 2008 (SI 2008/3157) reg.2(7) (January 5, 2009).
132. Social Security (Miscellaneous Amendments) Regulations 2009 (SI 2009/583) reg.2(13) (April 6, 2009).
133. Social Security (Miscellaneous Amendments) (No.4) Regulations 2009 (SI 2009/2655) reg.2(17)(a) (October 26, 2009).
134. Social Security (Miscellaneous Amendments) (No.4) Regulations 2009 (SI 2009/2655) reg.2(17)(b) (October 26, 2009).
135. Social Security (Miscellaneous Amendments) (No.4) Regulations 2009 (SI 2009/2655) reg.2(17)(c) (October 26, 2009).
136. Social Security (Miscellaneous Amendments) (No.2) Regulations 2010 (SI 2010/641) reg.2(3)(f) (April 6, 2010).
137. Social Security (Miscellaneous Amendments) (No.2) Regulations 2010 (SI 2010/641) reg.2(7)(e) (April 6, 2010).
138. Social Security (Miscellaneous Amendments) (No.2) Regulations 2010 (SI 2010/641) reg.2(10) (April 6, 2010).
139. Social Security (Miscellaneous Amendments) (No.4) Regulations 2009 (SI 2009/2655) reg.2(17)(d) (April 12, 2010).
140. Social Security (Miscellaneous Amendments) (No.5) Regulations 2010 (SI 2010/2429) reg.2(3)(a) (November 1, 2010).
141. Social Security (Miscellaneous Amendments) (No.5) Regulations 2010 (SI 2010/2429) reg.2(3)(b) (November 1, 2010).
142. Social Security (Miscellaneous Amendments) (No. 5) Regulations 2010 (SI 2010/2429) reg.2(3)(c) (November 1, 2010).
143. Adoption and Children (Scotland) Act 2007 (Consequential Modifications) Order 2011 (SI 2011/1740) art.2 and Sch.1 para.9(3) (July 15, 2011).
144. Social Security (Miscellaneous Amendments) (No.2) Regulations 2011 (SI 2011/1707) reg.4(8)(a) and (9) (August 5, 2011).
145. Social Security (Miscellaneous Amendments) (No.3) Regulations 2011 (SI 2011/2425) reg.7(5) (October 31, 2011).
146. Social Security (Miscellaneous Amendments) (No.3) Regulations 2011 (SI 2011/2425) reg.7(6) (October 31, 2011).

147. Social Security (Miscellaneous Amendments) (No.3) Regulations 2011 (SI 2011/2425) reg.7(8) (October 31, 2011).

148. Social Security (Miscellaneous Amendments) Regulations 2012 (SI 2012/757) reg.3(4) (April 1, 2012).

149. Jobseeker's Allowance (Schemes for Assisting Persons to Obtain Employment) Regulations 2013 (SI 2013/276) reg.13(b) (February 12, 2013).

150. Council Tax Benefit Abolition (Consequential Provision) Regulations 2013 (SI 2013/458) reg.3 and Sch.1 (April 1, 2013).

151. Social Security (Miscellaneous Amendments) Regulations 2013 (SI 2013/443) reg.2(5)(a) (April 2, 2013).

152. Social Security (Miscellaneous Amendments) Regulations 2013 (SI 2013/443) reg.2(5)(b) (April 2, 2013).

153. Personal Independence Payment (Supplementary Provisions and Consequential Amendments) Regulations 2013 (SI 2013/388) reg.8 and Sch. Pt 2 para.11(7)(a) (April 8, 2013).

154. Personal Independence Payment (Supplementary Provisions and Consequential Amendments) Regulations 2013 (SI 2013/388) reg.8 and Sch. Pt 2 para.11(7)(b) (April 8, 2013).

155. Armed Forces and Reserve Forces Compensation Scheme (Consequential Provisions: Subordinate Legislation) Order 2013 (SI 2013/591) art.7 and Sch. para.4(7) (April 8, 2013).

156. National Treatment Agency (Abolition) and the Health and Social Care Act 2012 (Consequential, Transitional and Saving Provisions) Order 2013 (SI 2013/235) art.11 and Sch.2 Pt I para.10(3) (April 1, 2013).

157. Universal Credit (Consequential, Supplementary, Incidental and Miscellaneous Provisions) Regulations 2013 (SI 2013/630) reg.28(8) (April 29, 2013).

158. Child Arrangements Order (Consequential Amendments to Subordinate Legislation) Order 2014 (SI 2014/852) art.2 (April 22, 2014).

159. Social Security (Miscellaneous Amendments) Regulations 2014 (SI 2014/591) reg.2(7) (April 28, 2014).

160. Special Educational Needs (Consequential Amendments to Subordinate Legislation) Order 2014 (SI 2014/2103) art.3(2) (September 1, 2014).

161. Shared Parental Leave and Statutory Shared Parental Pay (Consequential Amendments to Subordinate Legislation) Order 2014 (SI 2014/3255) art.5(6)(a) (December 31, 2014).

162. Shared Parental Leave and Statutory Shared Parental Pay (Consequential Amendments to Subordinate Legislation) Order 2014 (SI 2014/3255) art.5(6)(b)(ii) (December 31, 2014).

163. Care Act 2014 (Consequential Amendments) (Secondary Legislation) Order 2015 (SI 2015/643) art.2 and Sch. para.5(3)(a) (April 1, 2015).

164. Care Act 2014 (Consequential Amendments) (Secondary Legislation) Order 2015 (SI 2015/643) art.2 and Sch. para.5(3)(b) (April 1, 2015).

165. Care Act 2014 (Consequential Amendments) (Secondary Legislation) Order 2015 (SI 2015/643) art.2 and Sch. para.5(3)(c) (April 1, 2015).

166. Care Act 2014 (Consequential Amendments) (Secondary Legislation) Order 2015 (SI 2015/643) art.2 and Sch. para.5(3)(d) (April 1, 2015).

167. Care Act 2014 (Consequential Amendments) (Secondary Legislation) Order 2015 (SI 2015/643) art.2 and Sch. para.5(3)(e) (April 1, 2015).

168. Shared Parental Leave and Statutory Shared Parental Pay (Consequential Amendments to Subordinate Legislation) Order 2014 (SI 2014/3255) art.5(6)(b)(i) (April 5, 2015).

DEFINITIONS

"Abbeyfield Home"—see reg.2(1).
"access funds"—see reg.61(1).
"the Act"—see reg.2(1).

"adoption leave"—*ibid.*
"armed forces independence payment"—*ibid.*
"attendance allowance"—*ibid.*
"the benefit Acts"—*ibid.*
"benefit week"—*ibid.*
"care home"—*ibid.*
"child"—see SSCBA s.137(1).
"the Children Order"—see reg.2(1).
"claimant"—*ibid.*
"claimant participating as a service user"—see reg.2(1B).
"contribution"—see reg.61.
"course of study"—see reg.2(1).
"disability living allowance"—*ibid.*
"dwelling occupied as the home"—*ibid.*
"employed earner"—*ibid.*
"employment zone contractor"—*ibid.*
"employment zone programme"—*ibid.*
"family"—see SSCBA s.137(1).
"full-time student"—see reg.61(1).
"a guaranteed income payment"—see reg.2(1).
"Immigration and Asylum Act"—*ibid.*
"independent hospital"—*ibid.*
"Intensive Activity Period for 50 plus"—*ibid.*
"local welfare provision"—*ibid.*
"the London Bombings Relief Charitable Fund"—*ibid.*
"MFET Limited"—*ibid.*
"the Mandatory Work Activity Scheme"—*ibid.*
"maternity leave"—*ibid.*
"mobility allowance"—see reg.2(1).
"mobility supplement"—*ibid.*
"occupational pension"—*ibid.*
"occupational pension scheme"—see Pension Schemes Act 1993 s.1.
"partner of a person subject to immigration control"—see reg.21(3).
"paternity leave"—see reg.2(1).
"payment"—*ibid.*
"personal independence payment"—*ibid.*
"personal pension scheme"—*ibid.*
"qualifying person"—*ibid.*
"remunerative work"—see reg.2(1) and reg.5.
"self-employment route"—see reg.2(1).
"shared parental leave"—*ibid.*
"Social Security Act"—*ibid.*
"special account"—see reg.39A.
"sports award"—see reg.2(1).
"student loan"—see reg.61.
"subsistence allowance"—see reg.2(1).
"the Caxton Foundation"—*ibid.*
"the Eileen Trust"—*ibid.*
"the Fund"—*ibid.*
"the Independent Living Funds"—*ibid.*
"the Macfarlane (Special Payments) Trust"—*ibid.*
"the Macfarlane (Special Payments) (No.2) Trust"—*ibid.*
"the Macfarlane Trust"—*ibid.*
"the Skipton Fund"—*ibid.*
"training allowance"—*ibid.*
"universal credit" —*ibid.*
"voluntary organisation"—*ibid.*

"war disablement pension"—*ibid.*
"young person"—*ibid.*, and reg.14.

General Note

Paragraph 1

There is no provision in Ch.V itself for deducting tax. So if taxable payments are treated as income under reg.40 a disregard is needed. **2.895**

R(IS) 4/05 decides that "any amount paid by way of tax" includes tax that is to be paid. The claimant's income support claim had been rejected because her state retirement pension exceeded her applicable amount. Her retirement pension was paid gross, with any tax due being payable by her in a lump sum following the end of the tax year. The claimant produced a forecast from the Inland Revenue, which estimated her likely tax liability for the current year. She contended that this amount should be deducted from her retirement pension. The Commissioner agreed. He held that the disregard in para.1 is not concerned with the time at which tax is paid. It applies to tax which at the date of the benefit decision either has been, or is to be, paid, the only condition being that it is tax on income which is being taken into account under reg.40. The tax to be disregarded is the tax paid or due on the income attributable to the benefit weeks in question, not the tax payable in respect of earlier tax years. Where the tax payable is an annual sum, reg.32(1) provides a method for calculating the weekly amount.

As a consequence of this decision guidance has been issued to decision-makers (DMG Letter 04/05) which states that if a claimant provides evidence, such as a forecast from the Inland Revenue, which shows the tax due on income other than earnings paid to him for the current year, the amount of the estimated tax should be disregarded and the net amount taken into account.

Paragraph 1A

Any payment of expenses in relation to participation in the Mandatory Work Activity Scheme or a scheme listed in reg.3 of the Jobseeker's Allowance (Schemes for Assisting Persons to Obtain Employment) Regulations 2013 is ignored. **2.896**

Paragraph 2

A payment purely of expenses to a volunteer or someone working for a charity or a voluntary organisation is disregarded unless the person is caught by reg.42(6) on underpaid services. The September 2001 amendment allows an advance payment of expenses to be disregarded. A volunteer is someone who without any legal obligation performs a service for another person without expectation of payment (*R(IS) 12/92*). **2.897**

Paragraph 2A

Payments of expenses in respect of a "claimant participating as a service user" (see reg.2(1B) for those to whom this refers) are ignored. This disregard is needed because if those who come within reg.2(1B) are paid for their involvement as well as receiving expenses the disregard under para.2 does not apply. Payments of expenses in respect of a claimant participating as a service user are excluded from the definition of "earnings" by reg.35(2)(f). But any payment (e.g. for attending meetings) that results from a claimant participating as a service user will count as earnings, subject to the appropriate disregard. Note, however, that the notional income rules do not apply to either expenses *or* earnings as a result of a claimant participating as a service user (see reg.42(2)(ga) and reg.42(8ZA)). **2.898**

Paragraph 3

Such payments are not earnings (reg.35(2)), but are income (reg.40(4)). See the notes to reg.35(1)(f) for "wholly, exclusively and necessarily." *CFC/2/1989* might suggest that payments made by the employee for necessary, etc. expenses out of such income are to be deducted from that income. But that is not consistent with the **2.899** scheme of the legislation and is rejected in *R(FC) 1/90*, *R(IS) 16/93* and *CIS/77/1993*. See the notes to reg.35(2). However, note the effect of the application of the principle in *Parsons v Hogg* to the meaning of "gross earnings" (see the notes to reg.36(3)).

Paragraphs 4 and 4A

2.900 The standard deductions are to be made from contractual or statutory sick, maternity, paternity, shared parental or adoption leave pay, which are not earnings (reg.35(2)), but are income (reg.40(4)).

Paragraph 5

2.901 See also paras 40, 42, 45, 46 and 52.

In *CIS/521/2002* the claimant was one of four partners who ran a hotel providing board and lodging accommodation for the homeless. Under reg.37(2)(a) payments received for providing board and lodging accommodation do not count as earnings from self-employment. They count as income under reg.40(4)(a) and thus any appropriate disregard in Sch.9 may apply. The board and lodging charges were primarily met by housing benefit which was paid direct to the partnership. The Commissioner raises the point that such payments would seem to come within para.5 (although he did not have to reach a conclusion on the issue). However, to apply the disregard to direct payments of housing benefit to landlords would draw a line between such landlords and those receiving rent from tenants who had housing benefit paid to them and there seemed to be no reason for such a distinction. For further discussion of *CIS/521/2002* see the note to para.20 below.

The inclusion of the words "to which the claimant is entitled" are intended to make clear that it is only payments of housing benefit to which the claimant is entitled that are ignored under para.5 and that the disregard does not extend to housing benefit paid direct to the claimant as a landlord. This amendment was made as a result of the Commissioner's decision in *CH/2321/2002* on the ambit of the disregard in para.27(b) (see the note to para.27) but it also deals with the point raised by the Commissioner in *CIS/521/2002*.

Paragraph 5A

2.902 A new disregard of guardian's allowance has been introduced as part of the changes associated with the start of child tax credit in April 2003.

Paragraph 5B

2.903 With effect from April 6, 2004 (except in "transitional cases"—see the note to reg.17), amounts for children and young persons have been removed from the income support scheme; financial assistance to help with the cost of bringing up a child or young person is now provided through the child tax credit system, see Vol. IV of this series. As part of the changes associated with the introduction of child tax credit, child tax credit is ignored, as is child benefit (except in "transitional cases—see the note to reg.17).

For income support claimants who had an award of child tax credit before April 6, 2004 see reg.7 of the Social Security (Working Tax Credit and Child Tax Credit) (Consequential Amendments) Regulations 2003 (SI 2003/455) (as amended) on p.812 and the notes to that regulation.

Note that the £10.50 disregard of child benefit in respect of a child under one in transitional cases (see reg.7(6) and (7) of the 2003 Regulations) has been abolished with effect from April 11, 2011 in line with the abolition of the "baby element" in child tax credit from that date.

The effect of the new sub-para.(3) inserted on November 2010 is that any child dependency increase paid with another benefit, such as incapacity benefit or carer's allowance, is disregarded if the claimant has been awarded child tax credit. The disregard does not apply to those claimants who continue to receive amounts for their children as part of their income support.

Paragraph 5C

This paragraph had a very short shelf-life, as it was only in force from January 5 to April 6, 2009. The reason it was introduced was as follows. 2.904

The 2009 annual up-rating of child benefit was brought forward to January 5, 2009 as part of the Government's strategy to reduce child poverty and in the light of the prevailing economic situation. This was achieved by the Child Benefit (Rates) (Amendment) Regulations 2008 (SI 2008/3246), together with the Rates of Child Benefit (Commencement) Order 2008 (SI 2008/3247). The increase in child benefit was £1.20 per week for an only or eldest child and 65 pence for other children. The purpose of para.5C was to disregard these increases but only until the amount of the income support child personal allowance was up-rated in April 2009 (hence its short shelf-life). It only applied in "transitional cases" (see the notes to reg.17), since child benefit is already fully disregarded for claimants in receipt of child tax credit.

Paragraph 6

The mobility component of disability living allowance and the mobility component of personal independence payment is disregarded. See also paras 7 and 8. 2.905

Paragraph 9

The general rule is that attendance allowance, the care component of disability living allowance and the daily living component of personal independence payment is disregarded. 2.906

However, for most claimants in residential care, these benefits will normally cease to be payable after a claimant has been a resident in a residential care or nursing home for four weeks.

From October 6, 2003 there is no longer any special provision under this paragraph for claimants living in Polish resettlement homes (with the introduction of state pension credit on October 6, 2003, claimants living in Ilford Park Polish Home, the only remaining resettlement home, are unlikely to qualify for income support in any event because of their age). See the 2003 edition of this volume for the form of para.9 in force before October 6, 2003 (and the notes to that paragraph for the other special cases previously dealt with in para.9).

Paragraph 11

Education maintenance allowances (EMAs) (which now only apply in Wales and Scotland) are disregarded in full. 2.907

A national scheme for the payment of EMAs was introduced from the start of the 2004/5 academic year (this replaced the previous pilot project). EMAs are payable for up to three years to 16–19-year-olds who remain in non-advanced education after the age of 16. Under the national scheme they include weekly payments (depending on income), together with periodic bonuses. The allowance is fully disregarded when calculating entitlement to income support, JSA, ESA, working tax credit and child tax credit (as well as housing benefit and, until its abolition on April 1, 2013, council tax benefit). For the capital disregard see para.63 of Sch.10.

The October 31, 2011 amendments to para.11 allow for payments made from the "16–19 Bursary Fund" to be disregarded in the same way as EMAs. The bursary scheme was introduced in September 2011 to help vulnerable 16–19 year olds continue in full-time education and replaces the education maintenance allowance in England.

Paragraph 11A

As part of the Government's strategy to recruit and retain teachers, s.186 of the Education Act 2002 and the Education (Teacher Student Loans) (Repayment, etc.) Regulations 2002 provide for the reduction/extinguishment of the amount owing on student loans for newly qualified teachers in shortage subjects working in England and Wales. The scheme operates differently depending on where the student loan was originally incurred. For those teachers who took out student loans while living in England and Wales the Department for Education and Skills will simply waive 2.908

repayment. However, for those who took out their loans while living in Scotland, Northern Ireland or another EEA country, annual payments will be made to the teacher over a number of years to enable them to repay the Student Loan Company. Under the new para.11A any such payments are disregarded.

Paragraph 13

2.909 The new form of para.13 in force from April 1, 2004 has been introduced in order to provide a single disregard of the various allowances, grants and other payments made under s.2 of the Employment and Training Act 1973 or s.2 of the Enterprise and New Towns (Scotland) Act 1990 to people participating in New Deals and other training and welfare to work schemes. Before April 1, 2004 separate disregards had existed in respect of such payments under a number of the provisions in this Schedule. As a consequence of this change, those provisions have been revoked or amended. The revoked paragraphs are paras 59, 60, 62, 62A, 63, 65, 77 and 78; the two paragraphs that have been amended are paras 51 and 70.

Sub-paragraph (1) provides that payments under s.2 of the 1973 Act or s.2 of the 1990 Act are ignored *unless* they are: (i) paid instead of income support, JSA, incapacity benefit, ESA or severe disablement allowance (sub-para.(1)(a)); (ii) payments of a "bridging allowance" to a young person under s.2(3) of the 1973 Act (s.2(5) of the 1990 Act) (sub-para.(1)(b)); (iii) intended to cover food, ordinary clothing or footwear (defined in sub-para.(3)), fuel, housing costs met by income support or rent for which housing benefit is payable, council tax or water charges while the claimant is on an education, training or other scheme to help "enhance his employment prospects", but not if the payment is a Career Development Loan and the period of education or training in respect of which the loan was paid has ended (sub-paras (1)(c) and (2)); or (iv) paid for living away from home costs which overlap with housing benefit (sub-para.(1)(d)).

A single capital disregard of such payments has also been introduced at the same time. See para.30 of Sch.10. If these payments do count as capital they are only ignored for 52 weeks from the date of receipt.

Paragraph 15

2.910 With effect from October 2, 2006, charitable and voluntary payments and payments from funds derived from a personal injury award to the claimant, made or due to be made at regular intervals, are totally disregarded. Note the payments to which the disregard does not apply in sub-para.(3) and para.39.

This provision assumes that such regular charitable, voluntary or personal injury payments amount to income. Irregular charitable or voluntary payments count as capital (reg.48(9)). See reg.41(7) which treats any periodical payments paid under an agreement or court order to a claimant in consequence of personal injury to him, other than payments deemed to be capital under reg.48(4), as income. Since the amendments to reg.48(4) on October 2, 2006, not only capital disregarded under para.12 (trusts of personal injury compensation) but also capital disregarded under paras 44 and 45 (funds held in court derived from compensation for personal injury or the death of a parent) are excepted from the rule in reg.48(4); thus regular payments from such sources will count as income in the normal way.

In the case of personal injury payments, the disregard is applicable whether the payments are made from a trust fund, or under an annuity, or by virtue of an agreement or court order. This thus ameliorates the problem highlighted by *Beattie v Secretary of State for Social Security*, reported as part of *R(IS) 10/01* (see the note to reg.41(2)).

2.911 A monthly NHS pension payable as a result of an injury the claimant had suffered in the course of his employment did not, however, come within sub-para.(5A)(e) (*Malekout v Secretary of State for Work and Pensions* [2010] EWCA Civ 162; [2010] AACR 28). The claimant argued that the pension fell within the words "received by virtue of any agreement" in head (e) because he had a contract of employment with the NHS; the NHS Pension Scheme and the regulations governing it were to be read into his contract of employment; and so he was entitled to the pension by virtue of that agreement. The Court of Appeal, however, disagreed. The word "agreement" in head (e) had to be read in context. One element of that context was that heads (c) and (d) relate to the situation where a claimant has been injured and the consequential damages are put into a trust or used to purchase an annuity. This suggested that head (e) was there to deal with the situation where a similar payment was made, but not via a trust or an annuity. A second piece of context was that the word "agreement" appeared in the phrase "agreement or court order". This indicated an agreement that was reached instead of a court order after the injury had occurred. Thus the proper construction of head (e) was that it was the agreement or court order that had to be "in consequence of any personal injury" and so had to postdate the personal injury. The result was that the claimant's pension could not be disregarded under head (e).

In *Lloyd v London Borough of Lewisham and Secretary of State for Work and Pensions* [2013] EWCA Civ 923; [2013] AACR 28 the claimant had been assaulted while working as a traffic warden and under the terms of her employment became entitled to an income loss award of £15,000 a year. The Court of Appeal found the reasoning in *Malekout* highly persuasive and concluded that payments made under "pre-injury" agreements (as in Ms Lloyd's case) are not disregarded under para.14(1)(e) of Sch.5 to the Housing Benefit Regulations 2006 (the equivalent provision to head (e)). Paragraph 14(1)(e) only applies to sums paid under agreements (or court orders) which are made *after* the injury occurs.

Note that the payment must derive from an award for personal injury *to the claimant*. Compare the capital disregards of payments for personal injury and of trust funds of personal injury compensation in paras 12 and 12A of Sch.10 which (since October 2, 2006) also apply where the injury was to the claimant's partner (and note the exemptions from the notional capital rules in reg.51(1) and (2) for trusts of personal injury compensation which simply refer to trusts of payments made in consequence of "personal injury"). See *R(IS) 3/03*, discussed in the notes to para.12 of Sch.10 in the 2006 edition of this volume, in which the Commissioner considered that, at least on the facts of that case, the reference to "the claimant" in para.12 before the October 2, 2006 amendment did not, by virtue of reg.23(1), include the claimant's partner. See also *CP v SSWP (IS)* [2011] UKUT 157 (AAC) discussed in the notes to paras 12 and 44 of Sch.10. It is not clear why the wording of the income disregard of personal injury payments has not been amended to include payments in respect of an injury to the claimant's partner in line with the change to the capital disregard.

There is no special definition of "charitable" or "voluntary". The words must **2.912** be applied to whoever makes the payment. In *R. v Doncaster BC ex p. Boulton, The Times*, December 31, 1992, on the equivalent provision in housing benefit, Laws J holds that the word "charitable" appearing in a statute providing for the distribution and calculation of legal rights must refer only to payments under a charitable trust, rather than referring to acts done for some generous motive. He finds the legislative purpose to be to allow charities to make payments to claimants knowing that they will not simply reduce the amount of benefit. That decision must be highly persuasive, but does not preempt the income support position.

Laws J also takes a different view to that expressed in the 1992 edition of J. Mesher, *Income-related Benefits: the Legislation*, on the meaning of "voluntary." He holds that it does not refer to a payment which is not compulsory or not legally enforceable, but to a payment for which the person making the payment gets nothing in return. It does not matter that in voluntarily undertaking the payment the person comes under an obligation. The legislative purpose would then be consistent with that for charitable payments. He then had to apply this principle to payments by the National Coal Board in lieu of concessionary coal to a miner's widow. The concessionary coal scheme and the conditions for the payment of cash in lieu, including to widows, is contained in a collective agreement which is incorporated into miners' contracts of employment. Laws J holds that neither he nor the Housing Benefit Review Board had sufficient evidence of the particular contractual arrangements to be able to conclude that under the principle of *Beswick v Beswick* [1968] A.C. 58 the widow could as administratrix of her husband's estate obtain specific performance of the contract to make payments to his widow. However, he was satisfied that the NCB did receive something in return for payments made under the collective agreement, in the promotion of the efficient running of the coal industry. An element of this purpose was seeing that employees, ex-employees and their spouses were properly looked after. Therefore, he finds that the payments were not voluntary and the disregard did not apply. On this point also, the *Boulton* case cannot be conclusive for income support purposes, but is cogently argued and persuasive. It has been applied to para.15 in *R(IS) 4/94*. In *CIS 702/1991* an annuity had been purchased for the claimant under the terms of her friend's will. It was argued that the payments under the annuity were "voluntary" as in essence there was a gift of them from the friend under the will. It is held that the disregard in para.15 did not apply since the payments under the annuity were contractual in nature. That was consistent with the decision of Laws J in the *Boulton* case. See also *CIS 492/1992.*

However, the irregular payments received by the claimant in *R(H) 5/05* from a friend and his parents following his inability to work after a stroke were "voluntary". The friend had written a letter which indicated that the payments from her were by way of a loan to be repaid at some unspecified date. But in the Commissioner's view the payments were made without any clear thought about their legal nature. The overall circumstances showed that no legally enforceable rights or obligations were created by the payments to the claimant and that she obtained nothing in return for the payments. The Commissioner commented that "if something like the maintenance of a relationship of affection or of familial duty on the part of the payer or the creation of a merely moral obligation on the part of the payee, dependent on undefined future developments, takes a case out of the category of "voluntary payment" nothing significant would be left". Thus, applying *Boulton*, since the friend had obtained nothing in return for the payments she made to the claimant by way of loan, they were voluntary payments within the meaning of reg.40(6) of the Housing Benefit Regulations (the equivalent of reg.48(9); it was accepted that the payments were not regular and therefore fell to be treated as capital. The payments from the claimant's parents, where the presumption of gift applied in the absence of evidence to the contrary, also fell within reg.40(6).

2.913 In *CIS/1813/2007* payments of working tax credit made to the claimant after she had notified the Revenue that she had ceased work and had asked for the payments to stop were "voluntary" payments. This was because once the claimant had made proper disclosure, and even more so where she had asked not to be paid, it was entirely a matter for the Revenue whether to continue payment. For further discussion of *CIS/1813/2007* see the note to reg.23 under "*What constitutes income?*"

See also *CJSA/2336/2005* discussed in the note to reg.48(9) which held that the loans from the claimant's mother to pay her rent pending the outcome of her benefit claims were voluntary payments. *R(H) 8/08* also concerned loans to pay rent while a claim for housing benefit was being determined. The Commissioner concludes that just because there was no immediate obligation to repay the loans it did not automatically follow that they were properly to be considered income. It was necessary to examine all the facts before reaching such a conclusion in relation to all or some of the loans. He does not refer to *CJSA/2336/2005* or go on to deal with the question of whether the loans were voluntary payments.

If regular payments are not charitable or voluntary or made from funds derived from a personal injury award to the claimant, they count as ordinary income with no disregard.

Paragraph 15A

The disregard in this paragraph is no longer needed in view of the October 2, 2006 amendments to para.15. **2.914**

Paragraph 16

The £10 disregard under sub-para.(a) only applies if the payment is not fully disregarded under paras 8 or 9. **2.915**

"War disablement pension" was not originally defined in either these Regulations or any relevant part of the Contributions and Benefits Act 1992 (but now see the definition in reg.2(1)). However, it was defined in s.84(1) of the Social Security Act 1986. When these regulations were first introduced they were made under the 1986 Act. Thus, in the absence of any other definition, the meaning in s.84(1) applies (*CIS 276/1998*; see Interpretation Act 1978 s.11). Section 84(1) defined a war disablement pension as:

> "(a) any retired pay, pension or allowance granted in respect of disablement under powers conferred by or under the Air Force (Constitution) Act 1917, the Personal Injuries (Emergency Provisions) Act 1939, the Pensions (Navy, Army, Air Force and Mercantile Marine) Act 1939, the Polish Resettlement Act 1947 or Part VII or section 151 of the Reserve Forces Act 1980;
> (b) without prejudice to paragraph (a) of this definition, any retired pay or pension to which sub-section (1) of section 365 of the Income and Corporation Taxes Act 1970 applies".

The claimant in *CIS 276/1998* was discharged from the RAF on medical grounds and was awarded a service invaliding pension. This pension was exempt from income tax under s.315 of the Income and Corporation Taxes Act 1988 (formerly s.365 of the 1970 Act). The Department treated the pension as an occupational pension. But the Commissioner holds that the concepts of occupational pension and war disablement pension were not mutually exclusive. The claimant's pension clearly fell within para.(b) of the definition in s.84(1) and so it was also a war disablement pension. He was thus entitled to a £10 disregard under sub-para.(a).

On sub-para.(cc), see the note to the definition of *"the Armed Forces and Reserve Forces Compensation Scheme"* in reg.2(1). **2.916**

Under sub-para.(f), the £10 disregard applies to pensions paid to victims of National Socialist persecution by the German and Austrian Governments. In *MN v Bury Council and SSWP* [2014] UKUT 187 (AAC) (a case which concerned para.15(g) of Sch.5 to the Housing Benefit Regulations 2006, the equivalent of sub-para.(f)) Judge Williams holds that the failure to extend the disregard to people receiving a pension as a victim of such persecution under the Netherlands WUV scheme was discriminatory in breach of art.1 Protocol 1, read with art.14, ECHR, and that such discrimination was manifestly without reasonable justification (see *Humphreys v Her Majesty's Revenue and Customs* [2012] UKSC 18; [2012] AACR 46). By way of remedy Judge Williams referred the matter to the attention of the Secretary of State for him to decide how best to reformulate the provision so as to exclude the discrimination that had been identified (as well as directing that the Council was to reconsider its decision in the light of his provisional decision).

Paragraph 17

If a person takes out one of these schemes for converting the capital value of the home into income, then so much of the annuity as goes to the mortgage interest is disregarded. The conditions are complicated. Only schemes entered by those aged at least 65 count. **2.917**

Paragraph 18

The inter-relationship of this and the following two paragraphs is now much clearer. The new form of this paragraph, together with the amendment to para.19, was **2.918** introduced in April 1995, following the decision in *CIS 82/1993*. The Commissioner held that on the previous wording the dividing line between paras 18 and 19 was not whether a payment for accommodation was made under a contractual obligation, but whether or not the payment was made by a person who normally resided with the claimant. Paragraph 19 only applied where the person did not normally reside with the claimant. (See the 1994 Supplement to J. Mesher and P. Wood, *Income-related Benefits: the Legislation* for a summary of the Commissioner's reasoning.) "Normally resides" in para.18 had no special meaning (cf. reg.3) and could include someone who was liable to make payments to the claimant for his occupation of the claimant's home. On the facts, the two "lodgers" who shared the claimant's flat, and each paid him £70 per week, did reside with him. The result was that para.18, not para.19, applied. "Payment" could include part of a payment (see reg.2(1)), so the proportion of each payment that went to meeting the "lodger's" living and accommodation costs could be disregarded under para.18 (*CIS 422/1992* followed). The evidence was that the benefit of the outgoings on the flat was shared more or less equally between the three occupants, so the Commissioner divided the rent, water rates and fuel costs by three and added to this the cost of the services provided by the claimant (e.g. laundry, routine repairs and replacements). This led to a much larger proportion of each payment (£47) being disregarded, than would have been the case if para.19 applied.

The new form of para.18, and the amendment to para.19, have dealt with most of the difficulties exposed in *CIS 82/1993* regarding the inter-relationship of these two paragraphs. Paragraphs 18, 19 and 20 can now all apply where the person is residing with the claimant, so the problem identified in the 1994 edition of J. Mesher and P. Wood, *Income-related Benefits: the Legislation* no longer exists. If para.18 applies, payments by someone who normally resides with the claimant towards his own living and accommodation costs continue to be wholly disregarded. The new wording confirms, as decided in *CIS 422/1992* and *CIS 82/1993*, that it is only payments towards the "lodger's" living expenses that are disregarded (see above). However, para.18 does not apply in the circumstances covered by paras 19 and 20, so that those provisions must be looked at first. The intention is that payments from sub-tenants and licensees should fall within para.19, not para.18 (see below).

If the person making the payment is a non-dependant (see reg.3), note that standard deductions are made from housing costs for the presence of a non-dependant in the household (see para.18 of Sch.3).

Paragraph 19

2.919 Whenever the person occupying the claimant's home has a contractual liability to make payments (an oral agreement will suffice: *CIS 1501/2002*), this paragraph will now apply. This is certainly wide enough to cover income from subtenants and licensees. People referred to in paras 18 and 20 are no longer excluded, but para.18 does not apply if the circumstances come within para.19 (see above). Although some payments could fall within both para.19 and para.20, it does not matter that there is no provision for choosing between them, for a claimant can simply take advantage of the more generous disregard in para.20 when the conditions of that paragraph are met (*CIS 82/1993*).

In *CIS 82/1993* the Commissioner raised the possibility of whether the disregard in para.30(d) (now para.30(1)(e)) (contribution intended and used towards rent) might apply to payments by a sub-tenant or licensee of a tenant. He accepted the Department's submission that in view of the specific provisions in paras 18, 19 and 20, para.30(d) (now (1)(e)) did not cover such payments, but did consider that legislative clarification of the relationship between para.30 and para.18, 19 and 20 would be useful. It is not clear on the wording of para.30(1)(e) why payments from a sub-tenant or licensee should be excluded, provided that they are intended and used as a contribution towards rent not met by housing benefit. Payments may be disregarded under more than one paragraph of Sch.9, provided this is not specifically prescribed. Paragraph 30(1)(e) does not refer to payments under paras 18, 19 or 20; the only payments that are specifically excluded from para.30 are those covered by para.29. Indeed this was the approach taken by the Commissioner in *CIS 13059/1996*, who declined to follow *CIS 82/1993* on this point. He decides that para.30 can apply at the same time as any of paras 18 to 20 because paras 18 to 20 are not concerned with the same sort of payments as para.30. Paragraph 30 makes provision for disregarding payments designed to help meet certain elements of a claimant's housing expenditure, whereas this is not the specific purpose of paras 18 to 20. See further the notes to para.30.

In April 1994 the wording of para.19 was tightened up so that only one disregard per week applies to payments for each licence or subtenancy. On the pre-April 1994 form a separate disregard could have applied to each payment regardless of the period covered by it (e.g. daily).

A further change was made on April 7, 2008 when the previous two-tier disregard in para.19 (see the 2007 edition of this volume) was replaced by a single disregard of £20 per week per sub-tenancy or licence. If the income is less than £20 per week the whole of it will be ignored.

Paragraph 20

This disregard (and not para.18) applies when a person provides board and lodging accommodation in his home. The post-April 1994 form makes it clear that only one disregard is allowed per week per boarder (see the notes to para.19). **2.920**

Under reg.37(2)(a) payments received for providing board and lodging accommodation do not count as earnings from self-employment. They count as income under reg.40(4)(a) and thus any appropriate disregard in Sch.9 may apply. In *CIS 521/2002* the claimant was a partner in a board and lodging business run in what was formerly a fully-fledged hotel. As the claimant lived in the hotel (and on the basis that she was to be regarded as living in the whole hotel as her home) para.20 applied. The issue was how her income was to be calculated. The Commissioner holds that the full disregard under sub-para.(b) in respect of each boarder was to be applied to her share of the weekly board and lodging payments. As the Commissioner points out, there is no provision in para.20 for cases of partnerships or for taking into account only a proportion of the total number of persons being provided with board and lodging. The consequence was that the claimant had no income to be taken into account for the purposes of income support. For further discussion of *CIS 521/2002* see the note to reg.37(2). See also the note to para.5 above.

Paragraph 21

Income in kind is normally disregarded but note the exceptions. Earnings in kind are not earnings (reg.35(2)), but are income. There is some scope for benefit planning here, but note *R(IS) 2/98* in the notes to reg.42(6) (notional earnings). On the first exception in sub-para.(1) and on sub-para.(3) see the notes to reg.21(3). **2.921**

Sub-paragraph (4), added with effect from October 3, 2005, provides that the disregard of income in kind under para.21 does not apply to payments to a third party which are used by the third party to provide benefits in kind to the claimant. See further the note to reg.42(4).

Paragraph 22

The general rule is that the actual income derived from capital is disregarded as income. It can go to increase the amount of capital under reg.48(4). But income in the categories specified—premises, business assets and trusts of, and funds held in court that derive from, personal injury compensation (see the note to reg.48(4))—is not disregarded. Where this income is from premises whose capital value is disregarded, any mortgage repayments, water charges and council tax can be set off against it. Mortgage repayments in sub-para.(2)(a) include capital and interest, buildings insurance, and if an endowment policy is a condition of the mortgage, premiums on that policy (*CFC 13/1993*). *CIS 563/1991* deals with the situation where both a disregard in the excepted categories and a disregard under some other paragraph of Sch.10 apply. See the notes to reg.48(4). **2.922**

Paragraph 24

2.923 In *CIS 627/1995* the Commissioner puts forward the view that since para.24 disregards the *cost* of converting a payment into sterling, it was the *gross* sterling equivalent of the claimant's Canadian pension that had to be taken into account (i.e. the cost of conversion had to be added back to the net amount paid to the claimant). However, it is respectfully suggested that the purpose of para.24 is not to disregard any banking charge or commission *as a cost*, but simply to ensure that the amount of any banking charge or commission is not included in the income taken into account. Although the wording of para.24 could be clearer, it seems unlikely that the Commissioner's interpretation is the intended one. It is also not the approach taken in the *Decision Makers Guide* (see para.28415).

Paragraph 25

2.924 With effect from April 6, 2004 (except in "transitional cases"—see the note to reg.17) amounts for children and young persons have been removed from the income support scheme; financial assistance to help with the cost of bringing up a child or young person is now to be provided through the child tax credit system, see Vol.IV of this series. As a consequence the disregard in para.25 has been amended with effect from April 6, 2004 (except in "transitional cases"—see the note to reg.17) so that payments made to adopters in respect of a child or young person who is a member of the claimant's family are fully disregarded. The same applies to payments from local authorities towards the maintenance of children by subparas (ba)–(d). Subparagraph (e) covers payments by local authorities to special guardians (s.115 of the Adoption and Children Act 2002 amended the Children Act 1989 to introduce from December 30, 2005 a new special guardianship order, which is intended to provide permanence for children for whom adoption is not appropriate; the special guardian has parental responsibility for the child but the child's legal relationship with his birth parents is not severed). For the capital disregard of such payments see para.68A of Sch.10.

The old form of para.25(1) and (2) (see the 2003 edition of this volume), but as amended on October 4, 2004, remains in force for "transitional cases"—see the note to reg.17.

In addition, any payment, other than one that falls under subpara.(1)(a), that is made in accordance with regulations under ss.2(6)(b), 3 or 4 of the Adoption and Children Act 2002 (see the Adoption Support Services Regulations 2005 (SI 2005/691) and the Adoption Support Services (Local Authorities) (Wales) Regulations 2005 (SI 2005/1512)) that is not in respect of a child or young person who is a member of the claimant's family is ignored in full (sub-para.(1A)). This could apply, for example, to payments made before placing the child with the family. Note that *any* payment made under ss.2(6), 3 or 4 of the Adoption and Children Act 2002 that counts as capital is fully disregarded (see para.68 of Sch.10).

Paragraph 25A

2.925 With effect from April 6, 2004 (except in "transitional cases"—see the note to reg.17) amounts for children and young persons have been removed from the income support scheme; financial assistance to help with the cost of bringing up a child or young person is now to be provided through the child tax credit system, see Vol.IV of this series. Income support has in effect become an "adults only" benefit. Accordingly the income (as well as the capital) of a child or young person who is a member of the claimant's family is not aggregated with the claimant's (see the new form of reg.23(2)) and the income support applicable amount no longer includes any personal allowance for a child or young person, the family premium, the disabled child premium or an enhanced disability premium for a child or young person.

This new disregard is another of the consequential changes that apply from April 6, 2004 (except in "transitional cases"—see the note to reg.17) as a result of the new system. Under this paragraph payments to a boarding school for the maintenance of a child or young person, who is a member of the claimant's family, made by a third party or out of funds provided by a third party are ignored in full (compare the previous form of this provision in reg.44(2) (now revoked, except in "transitional cases"—

see the note to reg.17; see the 2003 edition of this volume for reg.44 and the notes to that regulation) which applied when the income of a child or young person who was a member of the claimant's family was, subject to the modifications in reg.44, aggregated with the claimant's (see the old form of reg.23 in the 2003 edition)).

Paragraph 26

Payments to foster-parents are disregarded completely. Foster-children are not members of the family (reg.16(4)). **2.926**

Paragraph 27

CIS 17020/1996 concerned a local authority scheme for placing disabled people in the carers' own homes. In order to attempt to take advantage of the disregard in para.27 the local authority sent the disabled person a bill for his care and accommodation and then paid the money to the claimant, instead of the disabled person paying the claimant directly. However, the Commissioner decides that para.27 only applied to payments made by a local authority from its own resources. The appropriate disregard was in para.20. He also discusses the meaning of the words "not normally a member of the claimant's household but is temporarily in his care". In his view the word "normally" referred to the period of the membership, not the manner of it. The question of whether the disabled person was temporarily in the claimant's care was one of fact, having regard to the intention of the parties and the length of the stay. **2.927**

In *CH/2321/2002* (which concerned para.25 of Sch.4 to the Housing Benefit Regulations, the equivalent of para.27), the Commissioner decided that the disregard could apply to payments of housing benefit paid direct to the claimant in respect of a person in their care. However this was not the policy intention; in addition it was felt that this interpretation created an anomaly since the full disregard under sub-para.(b) would not apply where the housing benefit was paid to the tenant and he used it to pay for board and lodging; in that case only the more limited disregard in para.20 would apply. Sub-paragraph (b) has therefore been amended with effect from April 4, 2005 to exclude payments of housing benefit from the disregard. See also the amendment to para.5.

Paragraph 28

This disregard does not apply in trade dispute cases (sub-para.(4)). Outside that special situation payments under the legislation (broadly to prevent children going into care, or to support certain care leavers) can be capital or income (*R(SB) 29/85*). Income is disregarded here and capital under para.17 of Sch.10. **2.928**

The disregard under para.28 has been extended with effect from April 7, 2008 so that it also applies where a person who was formerly in the care of the claimant continues to live with the claimant after he reaches 18 and pays the money to the claimant.

Paragraph 29

Since October 1995 the proceeds of mortgage protection policies can be used to cover payments in respect of *any* interest on a loan that qualifies under paras 15 or 16 of Sch.3 that is not met by income support, capital repayments due on a qualifying loan and any premiums due on the policy and any building insurance policy. (Despite the "or" in head (c) the disregard presumably applies to premiums on both types of policy if premiums on both are due). Any excess counts as income (confirmed in *KS v SSWP* [2009] UKUT 202 (AAC)). *KS v SSWP* also confirms that payments under more than one policy can be disregarded under para.29. According to the *Decision Makers Guide* "capital repayments" include not only repayments of capital on a repayment mortgage but also payments into endowment policies, individual savings accounts (ISAs), personal pension plans and other investment plans that have been taken out to repay a mortgage or loan (para.28231). Note reg.7(15) and (16) of the Decisions and Appeals Regulations 1999 which provides that certain changes in the loan interest payable will not lead to an immediate review of the amount disregarded under this paragraph. **2.929**

Sub-paragraph (2) seems merely declaratory as the disregard only applies to payments for housing costs that are not met by income support.

If the loan is not a qualifying loan see para.30. Paragraph 30 will also be relevant rather than this paragraph where the policy is a general income protection policy taken out only partly to meet housing costs (*R(IS) 13/01*).

Paragraph 30

2.930 Payments other than those disregarded under para.29 or, from June 1, 1998, para.30ZA, earmarked for these elements of housing expenditure, are ignored (sub-para.(1)). Note that payments from liable relatives are dealt with in reg.54.

If payments are made for purposes within sub-para.(1)(a) to (e), it should be assumed, in the absence of clear evidence to the contrary, that they are made out of income "intended to be used" for those purposes (*R(IS) 13/01*). See also *CIS 13059/1996* below.

However, *CIS 4255/2002* holds that the disregard under sub-para.(1) does not extend to payments from social security benefits. Benefits such as incapacity benefit, child benefit and invalid care allowance (now carer's allowance) were no more closely connected with or referable to housing costs than to a claimant's expenses generally and thus could not be said to be "intended to be used . . . as a contribution towards" the expenses in sub-para.(1). The necessary connection that had been found to exist in *CIS 13059/1996* (see below) and in *R(IS) 13/01* (because in that case the income protection policy had been taken out a few days after the mortgage from which it could be inferred that there was an intention that income from the policy would be used, if necessary, to pay the mortgage) was not present. A similar approach was taken in *CIS 3911/1998* which held that payments from an occupational pension scheme could not be disregarded under sub-para.(1).

2.931 Since October 1995 the disregard extends to payments on *any* loan secured on the home that is not a qualifying loan under Sch.3 (e.g. a loan for business purposes) (head (a)); any housing cost that is eligible under Sch.3 to the extent that it is not met by income support (head (b)); capital repayments on a qualifying loan (head c)), and premiums on any buildings insurance policy and (since December 1995) any policy taken out to insure against the risk of not being able to make the payments in heads (a)–(c) (head (d)). On the meaning of capital repayments see the note to para.29. Note reg.7(15) and (16) of the Decisions and Appeals Regulations 1999 which provides that certain loan interest changes will not lead to an immediate review of the amount disregarded under heads (a)–(c).

CIS 13059/1996 decides (contrary to the view taken in *CIS 82/1993*, see the note to para.19) that sub-para.(1) can apply to payments made by a tenant (or licensee) of the claimant who lives in her home. The claimant's mortgage interest was met by income support but only to the extent of the interest on £125,000 (there was about £160,000 owing on her mortgage). There were two tenants living in her flat. The AO decided that the rent received from the tenants had to be taken into account in calculating the claimant's income support, subject only to the disregard in para.19. However, the Commissioner concludes that para.30 could apply at the same time as para.19 (or paras 18 or 20) because these paragraphs were not concerned with the same sort of payments. Paragraphs 18 to 20 were not intended to make specific provision for disregarding payments designed to help meet a claimant's housing costs, whereas para.30 was so intended. Moreover, there was no reason why para.30 should not apply to payments made under a contractual liability. The Commissioner also deals with the meaning of the phrase "payment . . . which is intended to be used and is used as a contribution towards" in para.(1). He rejects the argument that it was only necessary to look at the intention of the claimant. But he holds that it was possible to infer from a tenancy agreement that the tenant intended the landlord to use the rent, so far as necessary, to pay the landlord's own liabilities on the property so that the tenant could continue to occupy it. "Intended" in para.(1) was used in the sense of "designed" or "calculated" and it was necessary to look at the general context in which payments were made in order to ascertain the intention of the parties. The

Commissioner also confirms that there was no reason why part of a payment could not be disregarded under para.30 in addition to part being disregarded under any of paras 18–20. (See reg.2(1): "payment" includes part of a payment). Thus in addition to the para.19 disregard, a further amount to cover the claimant's mortgage interest that was not met under paras 7 and 8 of Sch.3 as then in force could be disregarded from the rent payments.

The same Commissioner again considered the operation of the para.30 disregard in *R(IS) 13/01*. The claimant had an income protection policy, not a mortgage protection policy, so para.29 did not apply. The Commissioner holds that the difference between the amount the claimant was "due to pay" his building society (rather than the amount actually debited from his mortgage account—see *CIS 632/1992* upheld by the Court of Appeal in *Brain v Chief Adjudication Officer*, December 2, 1993 in the notes to para.1 of Sch.3) and the amount of mortgage interest met by income support, to the extent that the claimant actually made up that difference, could be deducted from the income he received under the income protection policy under heads (a) and (b) of sub-para.(1). In addition, head (c) covered the premiums on his endowment policy because the premiums were "due on a loan attributable to the payment of capital" (following *CIS 642/1992* rather than the approach he had taken in *CIS 13059/1996*). The claimant's building insurance premiums also fell within head (d)(ii). However, the premiums on the income protection policy itself could not be disregarded under para.30. Head (d)(i) did not apply as the policy had not been *taken out* to insure against the risk of being unable to maintain his mortgage payments.

Again, sub-para.(2) seems merely declaratory as the disregard under para.(1) only applies to elements of housing expenditure that are not met by income support.

Paragraph 30ZA

This provides for a disregard of payments received under so-called "creditor insurance" policies. It will apply to payments received under an insurance policy to cover, for example, hire-purchase payments or loan or similar payments. But any excess above the amount of the payment due, plus any premiums on the policy concerned, counts as income. **2.932**

Paragraph 30A

Where a claimant is in a care home, Abbeyfield Home or independent hospital (for the definitions of these terms see reg.2(1)) and the accommodation has not been arranged by a local authority, payments towards the cost of the home's fees are disregarded. The amount ignored is the difference between the claimant's applicable amount and the weekly charge for the accommodation. However, if the payment is a charitable or voluntary payment (which may well be the case), it is fully disregarded under para.15 (see the notes to para.15 for what counts as a charitable or voluntary payment). **2.933**

Paragraph 31A

For the definition of "local welfare provision" see reg.2(1). It is financial or other assistance under local schemes set up by the local authority (at the local authority's discretion) (in England) or by the devolved administrations (in Wales and Scotland) and intended to replace social fund community care grants and crisis loans which were abolished in April 2013. **2.934**

Paragraph 34

This is the compensation for the automatic counting of the "relevant sum" as part of the family's income under s.126(5)(b) of the Contributions and Benefits Act. From April 2015 (not up-rated in April 2016) the relevant sum is £40.50. **2.935**

Paragraph 35

See notes to reg.32(5). **2.936**

Paragraph 37

See notes to reg.32(5). **2.937**

Paragraph 39

2.938 The disregard now extends to payments to haemophiliacs from the three trusts, and to non-haemophiliacs from the Fund, the Eileen Trust, MFET Limited, the Skipton Fund and the Caxton Foundation, and to distributions of income payments to the close family, or to a slightly wider class for the two years following such a person's death. Such distribution of income payments are also ignored if they derive from a payment from the London Bombings Relief Charitable Fund (it is understood that no disregard under sub-para.(1) is considered necessary because these funds only provide lump sum payments). Any payments from the Independent Living Fund (2006) are ignored.

Sub-paragraphs (4)(b)(i) and (ii) and (5)(b)(i) and (ii) include references to step-parents. Note that from December 5, 2005, references to "step" relationships and "in laws" are to be read as including relationships arising through civil partnership in any provision to which s.246 of the Civil Partnership Act 2004 applies. Section 246 is applied to sub-paras (4)(b)(i) and (ii) and (5)(b)(i) and (ii) by art.3 of and para.22 of the Schedule to the Civil Partnership Act 2004 (Relationships Arising Through Civil Partnership) Order 2005 (SI 2005/3137).

Paragraph 46

2.939 The reference to s.13A of the Local Government Act 1992 (inserted on April 2, 2013) should cover any payment under local council tax reduction schemes which have replaced council tax benefit from April 2013.

Paragraph 51

2.940 Payments to a disabled person to assist him to obtain or retain employment under the Disabled Persons (Employment) Act 1994 are ignored. The previous form of this paragraph also referred to payments for this purpose under s.2 of the Employment and Training Act 1973. However from April 1, 2004 a single disregard has been introduced in relation to payments under all s.2 schemes. See para.13.

Paragraph 53

2.941 Increases for dependants who are not residing with the claimant paid with certain benefits (e.g. retirement pension) or war pensions are disregarded. Such increases are only paid if the claimant is contributing at least that amount to the maintenance of the dependant.

Paragraphs 54–56

2.942 See para.47. These new disregards arose from the transfer of responsibility for the payment of most pre-1973 war widows' (and widowers') pensions from the Ministry of Defence to the DSS from October 1994. From December 5, 2005 these paragraphs also apply to pensions payable under the relevant provisions to surviving civil partners.

Paragraph 57

2.943 Pararaph 57 provided for a disregard of any income support to which a person was entitled under reg.21ZB (reg.21ZB allowed asylum seekers to claim income support retrospectively if their refugee status was subsequently recognised by the IND). It was revoked on June 14, 2007 (as was reg.21ZB). However under art.2(3) of the Asylum and Immigration (Treatment of Claimants, etc.) Act 2004 (Commencement No.7 and Transitional Provisions) Order 2007 the revocation of para.57 did not apply in the case of a person who is recorded as a refugee on or before June 14, 2007. For these purposes a person is recorded as a refugee on the day that the Secretary of State notifies him that he has been recognised as a refugee (art.2(4) of the Order). See further the note to para.18A of Sch.1B. Paragraph 57 was finally fully revoked on January 5, 2009.

Paragraph 58

Payments by local authorities in lieu of community care services are to be ignored. 2.944

In *CIS/1068/2006* the claimant's wife paid the community care payments that she received to her husband in consideration of the care services he provided to her. The Commissioner held that these payments counted as "earnings" because the claimant had been engaged by his wife to provide care services for reward. They therefore fell to be taken into account in calculating his income support. The Commissioner rejected the claimant's argument that the payments should be disregarded under para.58. In his view the policy that underlaid the exemption for direct payments in para.58 was that the direct payments were intended to be spent in purchasing from a third party care services which would otherwise have had to be provided by the local authority. Thus the payments *to the claimant's wife* were disregarded under para.58 but not to take her payments *to the claimant* into account would have been to put them in a more advantageous position than they would have been had she paid a third party for care services.

The claimant appealed to the Court of Appeal against this decision but his appeal was dismissed (*Casewell v Secretary of State for Work and Pensions* [2008] EWCA Civ 10, reported as *R(IS) 7/08*). The claimant contended that s.136 of the Contributions and Benefits Act requires that payments made to a member of the family are counted when they come into the family, and if at that point they are disregarded, they cannot be counted again if they are transferred from one member of the family to another. However the Court agreed with the Commissioner that the payments to the claimant by his wife were earnings in respect of the care he provided and in the claimant's hands they became his income under s.136(1). It should be noted that the payments to the claimant's wife in this case were made on the basis that she was instructed to pay the claimant the appropriate sum each week against a payslip. There was therefore a specific obligation for the claimant's wife to deal with the payments in a particular way, which had the result that the money paid to her husband was treated as earnings. Thus this was a somewhat different situation from the more usual informal transfer of resources between family members.

Modification of paragraph 58

With effect from April 1, 2014, the disregard in para.58 is modified by art.2 of, and para.1 of the Schedule to, the Social Care (Self-directed Support) (Scotland) Act 2013 (Consequential Modifications and Savings) Order 2014 (SI 2014/513) so that the words "as a direct payment as defined in section 4(2) of the Social Care (Self-directed Support) (Scotland) Act 2013" are substituted for the words "under section 12B of the Social Work (Scotland) 1968". However, under art.3 of the Order, this modification does not apply if a payment is made under s.12B of the 1968 Act on or after April 1, 2014. 2.945

Paragraphs 59–60

For the previous form of these paragraphs, which concerned Career Development Loans, see the 2003 edition of this volume. However they have been omitted with effect from April 1, 2004 because from that date para.13 contains a single disregard in relation to payments made under s.2 of the Employment and Training Act 1973 or s.2 of the Enterprise and New Towns (Scotland) Act 1990 to people participating in New Deals and other training and welfare to work schemes. See the note to para.13. 2.946

Paragraph 61

Any grant or covenant income, student loan or contribution (for definitions see reg.61) left over at the end of a person's course is ignored. See regs 29(2B), 32(6A) and 40(3B) for the position where part or all of a student's grant is repayable because he has left or is dismissed from his course before it finishes. 2.947

Paragraphs 62, 62A and 63

2.948 For the previous form of these paragraphs see the 2003 edition of this volume. However, they have been omitted with effect from April 1, 2004 because from that date para.13 contains a single disregard in relation to payments made under s.2 of the Employment and Training Act 1973 or s.2 of the Enterprise and New Towns (Scotland) Act 1990 to people participating in New Deals and other training and welfare to work schemes. See the note to para.13.

Paragraph 64

2.949 (*Note*: this is a new para.64; the previous para.64 is now para.66).

This disregards any payment to a person, who is on, or has left, the "self-employment route" (defined in reg.2(1)), from his "special account" (defined in reg.39A) if it is: (i) to meet expenses wholly and necessarily incurred in his business while on the self-employment route; or (ii) used, or intended to be used, to make repayments on a loan taken out for the purposes of that business. For the treatment of a person's income from "test-trading" while on the self-employment route, see regs 39A to 39D and the note to reg.102C of the JSA Regulations.

See also the disregard in para.13.

Paragraph 65

2.950 See the note to paras 62, 62A and 63 above.

Paragraph 66

2.951 This is the renumbered para.64. See the note to reg.42(4A).

Paragraph 69

2.952 A "sports award" (defined in reg.2(1)) is ignored, except to the extent that it has been made for any of the items listed in sub-para.(2) (note the definitions in sub-para.(3)). For the disregard where the sports award counts as capital see para.56 of Sch.10 but note that under para.56 the disregard only applies for 26 weeks from the date of receipt. See also reg.6(1)(m) under which a person will be deemed not to be in remunerative work while engaged in activity for which the only payment he is, or will be, receiving is a sports award and reg.37(2)(c) which ensures that the award is not treated as self-employed earnings.

Paragraphs 71 and 72

2.953 See the note to reg.42(5A).

Paragraph 73

2.954 The disregard under this paragraph was originally introduced as part of the child support reforms under the Child Support, Pensions and Social Security Act 2000. It replaced the child maintenance bonus scheme under s.10 of the Child Support Act 1995 which allowed income support and income-based JSA claimants receiving child maintenance to build up a "child maintenance bonus" (see the 2008/2009 edition of this volume for s.10 and the Social Security (Child Maintenance Bonus) Regulations 1996 (SI 1996/3195)). Section 23 of the Child Support, Pensions and Social Security Act 2000 which repealed s.10 was brought fully into force by the Child Support, Pensions and Social Security Act 2000 (Commencement No.14) Order 2008 (SI 2008/2545) (c.109) art.4, with effect from October 27, 2008. The result was that from October 27, 2008 it was no longer possible for any person to accrue a child maintenance bonus.

The disregard was initially a partial disregard but from April 12, 2010 any payment of child maintenance is fully disregarded as income. For the definition of "child maintenance" see sub-para.(2) and note also the definition of "liable relative" for the purposes of para.73. The special rules for the treatment of child maintenance in Ch.VII of these Regulations have also been omitted from April 12, 2010. It would seem that a lump sum payment of child maintenance will count as capital.

Paragraph 74

This provides for the whole of a claimant's income to be disregarded during any "mortgage run-on" period. See the notes to reg.6(5)–(8) as to when this applies (note that from December 17, 2007 it has been extended so that it now applies to all housing costs that can be met by income support). See also the disregards in para.15C of Sch.8 and para.62 of Sch.10 and the note to para.15C. **2.955**

Paragraph 75

Discretionary housing payments can be made by a local authority to claimants who need extra help with the cost of their housing liability. They replaced the previous system of exceptional circumstances payments and exceptional hardship payments with effect from July 2, 2001. Any such payments are ignored as income; for the capital disregard see para.7 of Sch.10. **2.956**

Paragraph 76

From April 1, 2003 the responsibility for meeting the cost of housing-related services for people in supported accommodation passed to local authorities under the "Supporting People" programme (between April 2000 and April 2003 under the "Transitional Housing Benefit Scheme" certain service charges for claimants in supported accommodation had been met by housing benefit (see Sch.1B to the Housing Benefit Regulations which ceased to have effect on April 7, 2003)). **2.957**

This paragraph provides for payments under this programme to be ignored. The previous form of the disregard (see the 2003 edition of this volume) referred to payments from a local authority in respect of "welfare services" within the meaning of s.93(1) or (2) of the Local Government Act 2000 (in Scotland "housing support services" under s.91(1) of the Housing (Scotland) Act 2001). However the form in force from October 1, 2003 has been reworded to remove those legislative references in order to ensure that the disregard covers all payments made under the Supporting People programme.

For the indefinite capital disregard of such payments see para.66 of Sch.10.

Paragraphs 77 and 78

For the previous form of these paragraphs, which concerned the Employment, Retention and Advancement (ERA) scheme and the Return to Work Credit scheme respectively, see the 2003/2004 Supplement to this volume. However these paragraphs have been omitted with effect from April 1, 2004 because from that date para.13 contains a single disregard in relation to payments made under s.2 of the Employment and Training Act 1973 or s.2 of the Enterprise and New Towns (Scotland) Act 1990 to people participating in New Deals and other training and welfare to work schemes. See the note to para.13. **2.958**

Paragraph 79

This provides for an income disregard of payments under s.49 of the Children and Families Act 2014. Under s.49, parents of a child/young person with an education, health and care plan ("an EHC plan") will have the option of a personal budget, through which they will have control over how some of the provision in the EHC plan will be delivered. EHC plans will gradually replace special educational needs statements and learning disability assessments in England. For the capital disregard of payments under s.49, see para.71 of Sch.10. **2.959**

SCHEDULE 10

Regulation 46(2)

CAPITAL TO BE DISREGARDED

1.—The dwelling occupied as the home but, notwithstanding regulation 23 (calculation of income and capital of members of claimant's family and of a polygamous marriage), only one dwelling shall be disregarded under this paragraph. **2.960**

[96 **1A.**—Any payment in respect of any travel or other expenses incurred, or to be incurred, by the claimant in respect of that claimant's participation in [100 a scheme prescribed in regulation 3 of the Jobseeker's Allowance (Schemes for Assisting Persons to Obtain Employment) Regulations 2013] or the Mandatory Work Activity Scheme, but only for 52 weeks beginning with the date of receipt of the payment.]

2.—Any premises acquired for occupation by the claimant which he intends to occupy [4as his home] within 26 weeks of the date of acquisition or such longer period as is reasonable in the circumstances to enable the claimant to obtain possession and commence occupation of the premises.

3.—Any sum directly attributable to the proceeds of sale of any premises formerly occupied by the claimant as his home which is to be used for the purchase of other premises intended for such occupation within 26 weeks of the date of sale or such longer period as is reasonable in the circumstances to enable the claimant to complete the purchase.

4.—Any premises occupied in whole or in part by—

(a) a partner or relative of [12a single claimant or any member of] the family [4as his home] where that person [92 has attained the qualifying age for state pension credit] or is incapacitated;

(b) the former partner of a claimant [2 . . .] as his home; but this provision shall not apply where the former partner is a person from whom the claimant is estranged or divorced [71 or with whom he formed a civil partnership that has been dissolved].

[26**5.**—Any future interest in property of any kind, other than land or premises in respect of which the claimant has granted a subsisting lease or tenancy, including sub-leases or sub-tenancies.]

6.—[12(1)] The assets of any business owned in whole or in part by the claimant and for the purposes of which he is engaged as a self-employed earner or, if he has ceased to be so engaged, for such period as may be reasonable in the circumstances to allow for disposal of any such asset.

[12(2) The assets of any business owned in whole or in part by the claimant where—

(a) he is not engaged as a self-employed earner in that business by reason of some disease or bodily or mental disablement; but

(b) he intends to become engaged (or, as the case may be, re-engaged) as a self-employed earner in that business as soon as he recovers or is able to become engaged, or re-engaged, in that business;

for a period of 26 weeks from the date on which the claim for income support is made, or is treated as made, or, if it is unreasonable to expect him to become engaged or re-engaged in that business within that period for such longer period as is reasonable in the circumstances to enable him to become so engaged or re-engaged.]

[33(3) In the case of a person who is receiving assistance under [44 the self-employment route], the assets acquired by that person for the purpose of establishing or carrying on the commercial activity in respect of which such assistance is being received.

(4) In the case of a person who has ceased carrying on the commercial activity in respect of which assistance was received as specified in sub-paragraph (3), the assets relating to that activity for such period as may be reasonable in the circumstances to allow for disposal of any such asset.]

7.—[55—(1) Subject to sub-paragraph (2),] any arrears of, or any concessionary payment made to compensate for arrears due to the non-payment of—

(a) any payment specified in paragraph 6, [168[55 or 9]] of Schedule 9 (other income to be disregarded);

[82 (b) an income-related benefit [87 , an income-related employment and support allowance] or an income-based jobseeker's allowance, child tax credit or working tax credit under Part 1 of the Tax Credits Act 2002;]

[29(c) [68 . . .]]

[50(d) any discretionary housing payment paid pursuant to regulation 2(1) of the Discretionary Financial Assistance Regulations 2001] [103 ; or

(e) universal credit]

but only for a period of 52 weeks from the date of the receipt of the arrears or of the concessionary payment.

[55 (2) In a case where the total of any arrears and, if appropriate, any concessionary payment referred to in sub-paragraph (1) relating to any one of the specified payments, benefits or allowances amounts to £5,000 or more (referred to in this sub-paragraph and in sub-paragraph (3) as the "relevant sum") and is—

(a) paid in order to rectify, or to compensate for, an official error as defined in regulation

1(3) of the Social Security and Child Support (Decisions and Appeals) Regulations 1999, and

(b) received by the claimant in full on or after 14th October 2001,

sub-paragraph (1) shall have effect in relation to such arrears or concessionary payment either for a period of 52 weeks from the date of receipt, or, if the relevant sum is received in its entirety during the award of income support, for the remainder of that award if that is a longer period.

(3) For the purposes of sub-paragraph (2), "the award of income support" means—

(a) the award [103 of any of] income support [87 , an income-related employment and support allowance] [103 , an income-based jobseeker's allowance or universal credit] in which the relevant sum (or first part thereof where it is paid in more than one instalment) is received, and

(b) where that award is followed by one or more further awards which in each case may be [103 any] of income support [87 , an income-related employment and support allowance] [103 , an income-based jobseeker's allowance or universal credit] and which, or each of which, begins immediately after the end of the previous award, such further awards until the end of the last such award, provided that for any such further awards the claimant—

(i) is the person who received the relevant sum, or

(ii) is the partner of the person who received the relevant sum, or was that person's partner at the date of his death, or

(iii) in the case of a joint-claim jobseeker's allowance, is a joint-claim couple either member or both members of which received the relevant sum] [103 , or

(iv) in a case where universal credit is awarded to the claimant and another person as joint claimants, either the claimant or the other person, or both of them, received the relevant sum].

8.—Any sum—

(a) paid to the claimant in consequence of damage to, or loss of the home or any personal possession and intended for its repair or replacement; or

(b) acquired by the claimant (whether as a loan or otherwise) on the express condition that it is to be used for effecting essential repairs or improvements to the home,

and which is to be used for the intended purpose, for a period of 26 weeks from the date on which it was so paid or acquired or such longer period as is reasonable in the circumstances to enable the claimant to effect the repairs, replacement or improvements.

9.—Any sum—

(a) deposited with a housing association as defined in section 189(1) of the Housing Act 1985 or section 338(1) of the Housing (Scotland) Act 1987 as a condition of occupying the home;

(b) which was so deposited and which is to be used for the purchase of another home, for the period of 26 weeks of such longer period as is reasonable in the circumstances to complete the purchase.

10.—Any personal possessions except those which had or have been acquired by the claimant with the intention of reducing his capital in order to secure entitlement to [83 . . .] income support or to increase the amount of that benefit.

11.—The value of the right to receive any income under an annuity and the surrender value (if any) of such an annuity.

[12**12.**—Where the funds of a trust are derived from a payment made in consequence of any personal injury to the claimant [76 or the claimant's partner], the value of the trust fund and the value of the right to receive any payment under that trust.]

[77**12A.**— (1) Any payment made to the claimant or the claimant's partner in consequence of any personal injury to the claimant or, as the case may be, the claimant's partner.

(2) But sub-paragraph (1)—

(a) applies only for the period of 52 weeks beginning with the day on which the claimant first receives any payment in consequence of that personal injury;

(b) does not apply to any subsequent payment made to him in consequence of that injury (whether it is made by the same person or another);

(c) ceases to apply to the payment or any part of the payment from the day on which the claimant no longer possesses it;

(d) does not apply to any payment from a trust where the funds of the trust are derived from a payment made in consequence of any personal injury to the claimant.

(3) For the purposes of sub-paragraph (2)(c), the circumstances in which a claimant no longer possesses a payment or a part of it include where the claimant has used a payment or part of it to purchase an asset.

(4) References in sub-paragraphs (2) and (3) to the claimant are to be construed as including references to his partner (where applicable).]

13.—The value of the right to receive any income under a life interest or from a liferent.

14.—The value of the right to receive any income which is disregarded under paragraph 11 of Schedule 8 or paragraph 23 of Schedule 9 (earnings or other income to be disregarded).

15.—The surrender value of any policy of life insurance.

16.—Where any payment of capital falls to be made by instalments, the value of the right to receive any outstanding instalments.

[84 **17.**—(1) Any payment made by a local authority in accordance with—

(a) section 17, 23B, 23C or 24A of the Children Act 1989,

(b) section 12 of the Social Work (Scotland) Act 1968, or

(c) section 29 or 30 of the Children (Scotland) Act 1995.

(2) Any payment (or part of a payment) made by a local authority in accordance with section 23C of the Children Act 1989 or section 29 of the Children (Scotland) Act 1995 (local authorities' duty to promote welfare of children and powers to grant financial assistance to persons in, or formerly in, their care) to a person ("A") which A passes on to the claimant.

(3) Sub-paragraphs (1) and (2) are subject to the following provisions.

(4) Neither of those sub-paragraphs applies where the claimant is a person—

(a) to whom section 126 of the Contributions and Benefits Act (trade disputes) applies, or

(b) in respect of whom section 124(1) of the Contributions and Benefits Act (conditions of entitlement to income support) has effect as modified by section 127 of that Act (effect of return to work).

(5) Sub-paragraph (2) applies only where A—

(a) was formerly in the claimant's care, and

(b) is aged 18 or over, and

(c) continues to live with the claimant.]

[17**18.**—Any social fund payment made pursuant to [90 Part 8 of the Contributions and Benefits Act].]

[101 **18A.**—Any local welfare provision.]

19.—Any refund of tax which fell to be deducted under [90 section 369 of the Income and Corporation Taxes Act 1988 (mortgage interest payable under deduction of tax)] on a payment of relevant loan interest for the purpose of acquiring an interest in the home or carrying out repairs or improvements in the home.

20.—Any capital which under [11regulation 41 [61 . . .] or 66A (capital treated as income [61 . . .] or treatment of student loans)] is to be treated as income.

21.—Where a payment of capital is made in a currency other than sterling, any banking charge or commission payable in converting that payment into sterling.

[1**22.**—[14(1) Any payment made under [94 or by] the Macfarlane Trust, the Macfarlane (Special Payments) Trust, the Macfarlane (Special Payments) (No.2) Trust ("the Trusts"), [19the Fund] [23, the Eileen Trust] [93, MFET Limited] [63, the Independent Living [88 Fund (2006)] [72, the Skipton Fund [98, the Caxton Foundation] or the London Bombings Relief Charitable Fund]].

(2) Any payment by or on behalf of a person who is suffering or who suffered from haemophilia [19or who is or was a qualifying person], which derives from a payment made under [94 or by] any of the Trusts to which sub-paragraph (1) refers and which is made to or for the benefit of—

(a) that person's partner or former partner from whom he is not, or where that person has died was not, estranged or divorced [71 or with whom he has formed a civil partnership that has not been dissolved or, where that person has died, had not been dissolved at the time of that person's death];

(b) any child who is a member of that person's family or who was such a member and who is a member of the claimant's family; or

(c) any young person who is a member of that person's family or who was such a member and who is a member of the claimant's family.

(3) Any payment by or on behalf of the partner or former partner of a person who is suffering or who suffered from haemophilia [19or who is or was a qualifying person] provided that the partner or former partner and that person are not, or if either of them has died were not, estranged or divorced [71 or, where the partner or former partner and that person have formed a civil partnership, the civil partnership has not been dissolved or, if either of them has died, had not been dissolved at the time of the death], which derives from a payment made under [94 or by] any of the Trusts to which sub-paragraph (1) refers and which is made to or for the benefit of—

(a) the person who is suffering from haemophilia [19or who is a qualifying person];

(b) any child who is a member of that person's family or who was such a member and who is a member of the claimant's family; or
(c) any young person who is a member of that person's family or who was such a member and who is a member of the claimant's family.

(4) Any payment by a person who is suffering from haemophilia [[19]or who is a qualifying person], which derives from a payment under [[94] or by] any of the Trusts to which sub-paragraph (1) refers, where—
(a) that person has no partner or former partner from whom he is not estranged or divorced [[71]or with whom he has formed a civil partnership that has not been dissolved], nor any child or young person who is or had been a member of that person's family; and
(b) the payment is made either—
(i) to that person's parent or step-parent, or
(ii) where that person at the relevant date was a child, a young person or a [[43] full-time student] who had not completed his full-time education and had no parent or step-parent, to his guardian,

but only for a period of two years from the date of the payment until the end of two years from that person's death.

(5) Any payment out of the estate of a person who suffered from haemophilia [[19]or who was a qualifying person], which derives from a payment under [[94] or by] any of the Trusts to which sub-paragraph (1) refers, where—
(a) that person at the date of his death (the relevant date) had no partner or former partner from whom he was not estranged or divorced [[71] or with whom he had formed a civil partnership that had not been dissolved], nor any child or young person who was or had been a member of his family; and
(b) the payment is made either—
(i) to that person's parent or step-parent, or
(ii) where that person at the relevant date was a child, a young person or a [[43] full-time student] who had not completed his full-time education and had no parent or step-parent, to his guardian,

but only for a period of two years from the relevant date.

(6) In the case of a person to whom or for whose benefit a payment referred to in this paragraph is made, any capital resource which derives from any payment of income or capital made under or deriving from any of the Trusts.]

[[19](7) For the purposes of sub-paragraphs (2) to (6), any reference to the Trusts shall be construed as including a reference to the Fund [[64], the Eileen Trust [[93] , MFET Limited] [[72], the Skipton Fund [[98], the Caxton Foundation] and the London Bombings Relief Charitable Fund]].]

[[69] **22A.**—[[72] . . .]]

23.—The value of the right to receive an occupational [[15]or personal] pension.

[[26]**23A.**—The value of any funds held under a personal pension scheme [[79] . . .].]

24.—The value of the right to receive any rent [[26]except where the claimant has a reversionary interest in the property in respect of which rent is due.]]

[[2]**25.**—Where a claimant has ceased to occupy what was formerly the dwelling occupied as the home following his estrangement or divorce from [[71], or dissolution of his civil partnership with,] his former partner, that dwelling for a period of 26 weeks from the date on which he ceased to occupy that dwelling [[56] or, where that dwelling is occupied as the home by the former partner who is a lone parent, for as long as it is so occupied].

26.—Any premises where the claimant is taking reasonable steps to dispose of those premises, for a period of 26 weeks from the date on which he first took such steps, or such longer period as is reasonable in the circumstances to enable him to dispose of those premises.

[[5]**27.**—Any premises which the claimant intends to occupy as his home, and in respect of which he is taking steps to obtain possession and has sought legal advice or has commenced legal proceedings, with a view to obtaining possession, for a period of 26 weeks from the date on which he first sought such advice or first commenced such proceedings whichever is earlier, or such longer period as is reasonable in the circumstances to enable him to obtain possession and commence occupation of those premises.]

28.—Any premises which the claimant intends to occupy as his home to which essential repairs or alterations are required in order to render them fit for such occupation, for a period of 26 weeks from the date on which the claimant first takes steps to effect those repairs or alterations, or such longer period as is reasonable in the circumstances to enable those repairs or alterations to be carried out and the claimant to commence occupation of the premises.]

[[4]**29.**—Any payment in kind made by a charity [[8]or under [[94] or by] the Macfarlane (Special Payments) Trust][[19], the Macfarlane (Special Payments) (No.2) Trust][[22], [[81] the

Fund [89. . .] [96, MFET Limited] [97, the Skipton Fund, the Caxton Foundation] or the Independent Living Fund (2006)]].

[60**30.**—Any payment made pursuant to section 2 of the Employment and Training Act 1973 or section 2 of the Enterprise and New Towns (Scotland) Act 1990, but only for the period of 52 weeks beginning on the date of receipt of the payment.]

31.—Any payment made by the Secretary of State to compensate for the loss (in whole or in part) of entitlement of housing benefit.]

[5**32.**—[85 . . .]

33.—[85 . . .]

34.—Any payment made to a juror or a witness in respect of attendance at a court other than compensation for loss of earnings or for the loss of a benefit payable under the benefit Acts.

35.—[20 . . .].]

[9**36.**—Any payment in consequence of a reduction of [20 [86 . . .] council tax under section 13 [102, 13A] or, as the case may be, section 80 of the Local Government Finance Act 1992 (reduction of liability for council tax)] but only for a period of 52 weeks from the date of the receipt of the payment.]

[10**37.**—Any grant made to the claimant in accordance with a scheme made under section 129 of the Housing Act 1988 or section 66 of the Housing (Scotland) Act 1988 (schemes for payments to assist local housing authority and local authority tenants to obtain other accommodation) which is to be used—

(a) to purchase premises intended for occupation as his home; or

(b) to carry out repairs or alterations which are required to render premises fit for occupation as his home

for a period of 26 weeks from the date on which he received such a grant or such longer period as is reasonable in the circumstances to enable the purchase, repairs or alterations to be completed and the claimant to commence occupation of those premises as his home.]

[12 [90 **38.**—(1) Any payment or repayment made—

(a) as respects England, under regulation 5, 6 or 12 of the National Health Service (Travel Expenses and Remission of Charges) Regulations 2003 (travelling expenses and health service supplies);

(b) as respects Wales, under regulation 5, 6 or 11 of the National Health Service (Travelling Expenses and Remission of Charges) (Wales) Regulations 2007 (travelling expenses and health service supplies);

(c) as respects Scotland, under regulation 3, 5 or 11 of the National Health Service (Travelling Expenses and Remission of Charges) (Scotland) (No.2) Regulations 2003 (travelling expenses and health service supplies),

but only for a period of 52 weeks from the date of receipt of the payment or repayment.

(2) Any payment or repayment made by the Secretary of State for Health, the Scottish Ministers or the Welsh Ministers which is analogous to a payment or repayment mentioned in sub-paragraph (1), but only for a period of 52 weeks from the date of receipt of the payment or repayment.

39.—Any payment made to such persons entitled to receive benefits as may be determined by or under a scheme made pursuant to section 13 of the Social Security Act 1988 in lieu of vouchers or similar arrangements in connection with the provision of those benefits (including payments made in place of healthy start vouchers, milk tokens or the supply of vitamins), but only for a period of 52 weeks from the date of receipt of the payment.]

[91 **39A.**—Any payment made under Part 8A of the Contributions and Benefits Act (entitlement to health in pregnancy grant).]

40.—Any payment made either by the Secretary of State for [80 Justice] or by the [90 Scottish Ministers] under a scheme established to assist relatives and other persons to visit persons in custody, but only for a period of 52 weeks from the date of receipt of the payment.

[90 **41.**—Any arrears of supplementary pension which is disregarded under paragraph 54 of Schedule 9 (sums to be disregarded in the calculation of income other than earnings) or of any amount which is disregarded under paragraph 55 or 56 of that Schedule, but only for a period of 52 weeks from the date of receipt of the arrears.]]

[17**42.**—Any payment (other than a training allowance[60 . . .]) made, whether by the Secretary of State or by any other person, under the Disabled Persons (Employment) Act 1944 [60 . . .] to assist disabled persons to obtain or retain employment despite their disability.

43.—Any payment made by a local authority under section 3 of the Disabled Persons (Employment) Act 1958 to homeworkers under the Blind Homeworkers' Scheme.]

[25[78**44.**—(1) Any sum of capital to which sub-paragraph (2) applies and—

(a) which is administered on behalf of a person by the High Court or the County Court under Rule 21.11(1) of the Civil Procedure Rules 1998 or by the Court of Protection;

(b) which can only be disposed of by order or direction of any such court; or
(c) where the person concerned is under the age of 18, which can only be disposed of by order or direction prior to that person attaining age 18.

(2) This sub-paragraph applies to a sum of capital which is derived from—
(a) an award of damages for a personal injury to that person; or
(b) compensation for the death of one or both parents where the person concerned is under the age of 18.]]

45.—Any sum of capital administered on behalf of a person [[31]. . .] in accordance with an order made under [[58] section 13 of the Children (Scotland) Act 1995], or under Rule 36.14 of the Ordinary Cause Rules 1993 or under Rule 128 of the Ordinary Cause Rules, where such sum derives from—
(a) an award of damages for a personal injury to that person; or
(b) compensation for the death of one or both parents [[31] where the person concerned is under the age of 18].]

[[27]**46.**—Any payment to the claimant as holder of the Victoria Cross or George Cross.]

[[30]**47.**—[[90] . . .]

48.—[[90]. . .]

49.—[[90] . . .]]

[[48] **50.**—[[60]. . .].]

[[54] **50A.**—[[60]. . .].]

[[32] **51.**—[[60]. . .].]

[[35] **52.**—In the case of a person who is receiving, or who has received, assistance under [[44] the self-employment route], any sum of capital which is acquired by that person for the purpose of establishing or carrying on the commercial activity in respect of which such assistance is or was received but only for a period of 52 weeks from the date on which that sum was acquired.]

[[36]**53.**—[[60]. . .].]

54.—*[Omitted.]*

55.—*[Omitted.]*

[[37]**56.**—(1) Any payment of a sports award for a period of 26 weeks from the date of receipt of that payment except to the extent that it has been made in respect of any one or more of the items specified in sub-paragraph (2).

(2) The items specified for the purposes of sub-paragraph (1) are food, ordinary clothing or footwear, household fuel, rent for which housing benefit is payable or any housing costs to the extent that they are met under regulation 17(1)(e) or 18(1)(f) (housing costs) [[53]. . .], of the claimant or, where the claimant is a member of a family, any other member of his family, or any council tax or water charges for which that claimant or member is liable.

(3) For the purposes of sub-paragraph (2)—

"food" does not include vitamins, minerals or other special dietary supplements intended to enhance the performance of the person in the sport in respect of which the award was made;

"ordinary clothing and footwear" means clothing or footwear for normal daily use but does not include school uniforms or clothing or footwear used solely for sporting activities.]

[[38]**57.**—[[67]. . .]]

[[42]**58.**—In the case of a claimant participating in an employment zone programme, any discretionary payment made by an employment zone contractor to the claimant, being a fee, grant, loan or otherwise, but only for the period of 52 weeks from the date of receipt of the payment.

59.—Any arrears of subsistence allowance paid as a lump sum but only for the period of 52 weeks from the date of receipt of the payment.]

60.—*[Omitted.]*

[[45] **61.**—Where an ex-gratia payment of £10,000 has been made by the Secretary of State on or after 1st February 2001 in consequence of the imprisonment or internment of—
(a) the claimant;
(b) the claimant's partner;
(c) the claimant's deceased spouse [[71] or deceased civil partner]; or
(d) the claimant's partner's deceased spouse [[71] or deceased civil partner],

by the Japanese during the Second World War, £10,000.]

[[46]**62.**—In the case of a person to whom paragraph (5) of regulation 6 (persons not treated as in remunerative work) applies, the whole of his capital.]

[[65] **63.**—(1) Any payment—
(a) by way of an education maintenance allowance made pursuant to—
(i) regulations made under section 518 of the Education Act 1996;

(ii) regulations made under section 49 or 73(f) of the Education (Scotland) Act 1980;

[90 (iii) directions made under section 73ZA of the Education (Scotland) Act 1980 and paid under section 12(2)(c) of the Further and Higher Education (Scotland) Act 1992; [99 . . .]]

(b) corresponding to such an education maintenance allowance, made pursuant to—

(i) section 14 or section 181 of the Education Act 2002; or

(ii) regulations made under section 181 of that Act [99; or

(c) in England, by way of financial assistance made pursuant to section 14 of the Education Act 2002.]

(2) Any payment, other than a payment to which sub-paragraph (1) applies, made pursuant to—

(a) regulations made under section 518 of the Education Act 1996;

(b) regulations made under section 49 of the Education (Scotland) Act 1980; or

[90 (c) directions made under section 73ZA of the Education (Scotland) Act 1980 and paid under section 12(2)(c) of the Further and Higher Education (Scotland) Act 1992,]

in respect of a course of study attended by a child or a young person or a person who is in receipt of an education maintenance allowance [99 or other payment] made pursuant to any provision specified in sub-paragraph (1)].

[49**64.**—(1) Subject to sub-paragraph (2), the amount of any trust payment made to a claimant or a member of a claimant's family who is—

(a) a diagnosed person;

(b) the diagnosed person's partner or the person who was the diagnosed person's partner at the date of the diagnosed person's death;

(c) a parent of a diagnosed person, a person acting in the place of the diagnosed person's parents or a person who was so acting at the date of the diagnosed person's death; or

(d) a member of the diagnosed person's family (other than his partner) or a person who was a member of the diagnosed person's family (other than his partner) at the date of the diagnosed person's death.

(2) Where a trust payment is made to—

(a) a person referred to in sub-paragraph (1)(a) or (b), that sub-paragraph shall apply for the period beginning on the date on which the trust payment is made and ending on the date on which that person dies;

(b) a person referred to in sub-paragraph (1)(c), that sub-paragraph shall apply for the period beginning on the date on which the trust payment is made and ending two years after that date;

(c) a person referred to in sub-paragraph (1)(d), that sub-paragraph shall apply for the period beginning on the date on which the trust payment is made and ending—

(i) two years after that date; or

(ii) on the day before the day on which that person—

(aa) ceases receiving full-time education; or

(bb) attains the age of [75 20],

whichever is the latest.

(3) Subject to sub-paragraph (4), the amount of any payment by a person to whom a trust payment has been made, or of any payment out of the estate of a person to whom a trust payment has been made, which is made to a claimant or a member of a claimant's family who is—

(a) the diagnosed person's partner or the person who was the diagnosed person's partner at the date of the diagnosed person's death;

(b) a parent of a diagnosed person, a person acting in the place of the diagnosed person's parents or a person who was so acting at the date of the diagnosed person's death; or

(c) a member of the diagnosed person's family (other than his partner) or a person who was a member of the diagnosed person's family (other than his partner) at the date of the diagnosed person's death,

but only to the extent that such payments do not exceed the total amount of any trust payments made to that person.

(4) Where a payment as referred to in sub-paragraph (3) is made to—

(a) a person referred to in sub-paragraph (3)(a), that sub-paragraph shall apply for the period beginning on the date on which that payment is made and ending on the date on which that person dies;

(b) a person referred to in sub-paragraph (3)(b), that sub-paragraph shall apply for the period beginning on the date on which that payment is made and ending two years after that date;

(c) a person referred to in sub-paragraph (3)(c), that sub-paragraph shall apply for the period beginning on the date on which that payment is made and ending—

(i) two years after that date; or

(ii) on the day before the day on which that person—

(aa) ceases receiving full-time education; or

(bb) attains the age of [75 20],

whichever is the latest.

(5) In this paragraph, a reference to a person—

(a) being the diagnosed person's partner;

(b) being a member of the diagnosed person's family; or

(c) acting in the place of the diagnosed person's parents,

at the date of the diagnosed person's death shall include a person who would have been such a person or a person who would have been so acting, but for the diagnosed person [70 residing in a care home, an Abbeyfield Home or an independent hospital] on that date.

(6) In this paragraph—

"diagnosed person" means a person who has been diagnosed as suffering from, or who, after his death, has been diagnosed as having suffered from, variant Creutzfeldt-Jakob disease;

"relevant trust" means a trust established out of funds provided by the Secretary of State in respect of persons who suffered, or who are suffering, from variant Creutzfeldt-Jakob disease for the benefit of persons eligible for payments in accordance with its provisions;

"trust payment" means a payment under a relevant trust.]

[52**65.**—The amount of a payment, other than a war pension [90. . .], to compensate for the fact that the claimant, the claimant's partner, the claimant's deceased spouse [71 or deceased civil partner] or the claimant's partner's deceased spouse [71 or deceased civil partner]—

(a) was a slave labourer or a forced labourer;

(b) had suffered property loss or had suffered personal injury; or

(c) was a parent of a child who had died,

during the Second World War.]

[56[58 **66.**—(1) Any payment made by a local authority, or by the [90 Welsh Ministers], to or on behalf of the claimant or his partner relating to a service which is provided to develop or sustain the capacity of the claimant or his partner to live independently in his accommodation.]

(2) For the purposes of sub-paragraph (1) "local authority" includes, in England, a county council.]

[58 **67.**—Any payment made under [91. . .] [105 sections 31 to 33 of the Care Act 2014 (direct payments) or under] regulations made under section 57 of the Health and Social Care Act 2001 or under section 12B of the Social Work (Scotland) Act 1968 [95 , or under sections 12A to 12D of the National Health Service Act 2006 (direct payments for health care)].

[73 **68.**—Any payment made to the claimant pursuant to regulations under section 2(6)(b), 3 or 4 of the Adoption and Children Act 2002.]

[66 **68A.**—Any payment made to the claimant in accordance with regulations made pursuant to section 14F of the Children Act 1989 (special guardianship support services).]

69.—[60. . .].]

[59 **70.**—[60. . .].]

[104 **71.**—Any payments to a claimant made under section 49 of the Children and Families Act 2014 (personal budgets and direct payments).]

AMENDMENTS

1. Income Support (General) Amendment Regulations 1988 (SI 1988/663) reg.36 (April 11, 1988).

2. Income Support (General) Amendment No.2 Regulations 1988 (SI 1988/910) reg.3 (May 30, 1988).

3. Family Credit and Income Support (General) Amendment Regulations 1988 (SI 1988/999) reg.5 (June 9, 1988).

4. Income Support (General) Amendment No.4 Regulations 1988 (SI 1988/1445) reg.26 (September 12, 1988).

5. Income Support (General) Amendment No.5 Regulations 1988 (SI 1988/2022) reg.23 (December 12, 1988).

6. Family Credit and Income Support (General) Amendment Regulations 1989 (SI 1989/1034) reg.12 (July 10, 1989).
7. Income Support (General) Amendment Regulations 1989 (SI 1989/534) Sch.1 para.18 (October 9, 1989).
8. Income-related Benefits Schemes Amendment Regulations 1990 (SI 1990/127) reg.3 (January 31, 1990).
9. Income Support (General) Amendment Regulations 1990 (SI 1990/547) reg.23(*a*) (April 1, 1990).
10. Income Support (General) Amendment Regulations 1990 (SI 1990/547) reg.23(*b*) (April 9, 1990).
11. Social Security Benefits (Student Loans and Miscellaneous Amendments) Regulations 1990 (SI 1990/1549) reg.5(9) (September 1, 1990).
12. Income Support (General) Amendment No.3 Regulations 1990 (SI 1990/1776) reg.11 (October 1, 1990).
13. Enterprise (Scotland) Consequential Amendments Order 1991 (SI 1991/387) arts 2 and 9 (April 1, 1991).
14. Income-related Benefits Schemes and Social Security (Recoupment) Amendment Regulations 1991 (SI 1991/1175) reg.5 (May 11, 1991).
15. Income Support (General) Amendment No.4 Regulations 1991 (SI 1991/1559) reg.21 (October 7, 1991).
16. Disability Living Allowance and Disability Working Allowance (Consequential Provisions) Regulations 1991 (SI 1991/2742) reg.11(7) (April 6, 1992).
17. Income Support (General) Amendment Regulations 1992 (SI 1992/468) reg.9 (April 6, 1992).
18. Income Support (General) Amendment Regulations 1992 (SI 1992/468) Sch. para.10 (April 6, 1992).
19. Income-related Benefits Schemes and Social Security (Recoupment) Amendment Regulations 1992 (SI 1992/1101) reg.6(8) (May 7, 1992).
20. Income-related Benefits Schemes (Miscellaneous Amendments) Regulations 1993 (SI 1993/315) Sch. para.6 (April 1, 1993).
21. Social Security Benefits (Miscellaneous Amendments) (No.2) Regulations 1993 (SI 1993/963) reg.2(3) (April 22, 1993).
22. Social Security Benefits (Miscellaneous Amendments) (No.2) Regulations 1993 (SI 1993/963) reg.2(5) (April 22, 1993).
23. Income-related Benefits Schemes and Social Security (Recoupment) Amendment Regulations 1993 (SI 1993/1249) reg.4(5) (May 14, 1993).
24. Income-related Benefits Schemes (Miscellaneous Amendments) (No.4) Regulations 1993 (SI 1993/2119) reg.24 (October 4, 1993).
25. Income-related Benefits Schemes (Miscellaneous Amendments) (No.5) Regulations 1994 (SI 1994/2139) reg.33 (October 3, 1994).
26. Income-related Benefits Schemes and Social Security (Claims and Payments) (Miscellaneous Amendments) Regulations 1995 (SI 1995/2303) reg.6(10) (October 2, 1995).
27. Income-related Benefits Schemes (Miscellaneous Amendments) Regulations 1996 (SI 1996/462) reg.11(1) (April 8, 1996).
28. Income Support (General) (Jobseeker's Allowance Consequential Amendments) Regulations 1996 (SI 1996/206) reg.26 (October 7, 1996).
29. Income-related Benefits Schemes and Social Fund (Miscellaneous Amendments) Regulations 1996 (SI 1944) reg.13 and Sch. para.7 (October 7, 1996).
30. Income Support and Social Security (Claims and Payments) (Miscellaneous Amendments) Regulations 1996 (SI 1996/2431) reg.6 (October 15, 1996).
31. Income-related Benefits and Jobseeker's Allowance (Amendment) (No.2) Regulations 1997 (SI 1997/2197) reg.7(9) and (10)(e) (October 6, 1997).
32. Social Security Amendment (New Deal) Regulations 1997 (SI 1997/ 2863) reg.17(11) and (12)(e) (January 5, 1998).
33. Social Security (Miscellaneous Amendments) (No.4) Regulations 1998 (SI 1998/1174) reg.7(7) and (8)(e) (June 1, 1998).

34. Social Security (Miscellaneous Amendments) (No.4) Regulations 1998 (SI 1998/1174) reg.7(9) and (10)(e) (June 1, 1998).
35. Social Security (Miscellaneous Amendments) (No.4) Regulations 1998 (SI 1998/1174) reg.7(11) and (12)(e) (June 1, 1998).
36. Social Security Amendment (New Deal) (No.2) Regulations 1998 (SI 1998/2117) reg.5(2) and (3)(c) (September 24, 1998).
37. Social Security Amendment (Sports Awards) Regulations 1999 (SI 1999/2165) reg.6(5) (August 23, 1999).
38. Social Security (Miscellaneous Amendments) (No.2) Regulations 1999 SI 1999/2556) reg.2(11) (October 4, 1999).
39. Social Security Amendment (Education Maintenance Allowance) Regulations 2000 (SI 2000/55) reg.2(3) and (4)(c) (February 7, 2000).
40. Social Security (Miscellaneous Amendments) Regulations 2000 (SI 2000/681) reg.9 (April 3, 2000).
41. Social Security (Immigration and Asylum) Consequential Amendments Regulations 2000 (SI 2000/636) reg.3(13) (April 3, 2000).
42. Social Security Amendment (Employment Zones) Regulations 2000 (SI 2000/724) reg.3(4) (April 3, 2000).
43. Social Security Amendment (Students) Regulations 2000 (SI 2000/1981) reg.5(5) and Sch. (July 31, 2000).
44. Social Security Amendment (Employment Zones) (No.2) Regulations 2000 (SI 2000/2910) reg.4(1) and (2)(c)(ii) (November 27, 2000)
45. Social Security Amendment (Capital Disregards) Regulations 2001 (SI 2001/22) reg.2(a) (February 1, 2001).
46. Social Security (Miscellaneous Amendments) Regulations 2001 (SI 2001/488) reg.10 (April 9, 2001).
47. Social Security (Miscellaneous Amendments) (No.3) Regulations 2001 (SI 2001/859) reg.3(6) (April 9, 2001).
48. Social Security Amendment (New Deal) Regulations 2001 (SI 2001/1029) reg.15(14) and (15)(c) (April 9, 2001).
49. Social Security Amendment (Capital Disregards and Recovery of Benefits) Regulations 2001 (SI 2001/1118) reg.2(1) (April 12, 2001).
50. Social Security Amendment (Discretionary Housing Payments) Regulations 2001 (SI 2001/2333) reg.2(2)(c) (July 2, 2001).
51. Children (Leaving Care) Act 2000 (Commencement No.2 and Consequential Provisions) Order 2001 (SI 2001/3070) art.3(2) and para.(c) of Sch.1 (October 1, 2001).
52. Social Security Amendment (Capital Disregards) (No.2) Regulations 2001 (SI 2001/3481) reg.2 (November 19, 2001).
53. Social Security Amendment (Residential Care and Nursing Homes) Regulations 2001 (SI 2001/3767) reg.2(1) and Pt I of Sch. para.20 (April 8, 2002).
54. Social Security Amendment (Employment Programme) Regulations 2002 (SI 2002/2314) reg.3(4) (October 14, 2002).
55. Social Security (Miscellaneous Amendments) (No.2) Regulations 2002 (SI 2002/2380) reg.2(b) (October 14, 2002).
56. Social Security (Miscellaneous Amendments) Regulations 2003 (SI 2003/511) reg.2(3) (April 1, 2003).
57. Social Security (Working Tax Credit and Child Tax Credit) (Consequential Amendments) Regulations 2003 (SI 2003/455) reg.2 and Sch.1 para.24(a) (April 7, 2003).
58. Social Security (Miscellaneous Amendments) (No.2) Regulations 2003 (SI 2003/2279) reg.2(5) (October 1, 2003).
59. Social Security (Incapacity Benefit Work-focused Interviews) Regulations 2003 (SI 2003/2439) reg.13(b) (October 27, 2003).
60. Social Security (Miscellaneous Amendments) Regulations 2004 (SI 2004/565) reg.2(4) (April 1, 2004).
61. Social Security (Working Tax Credit and Child Tax Credit) (Consequential Amendments) Regulations 2003 (SI 2003/455) reg.2 and Sch.1 para.24(b) (April 6,

2004, except in "transitional cases" and see further the note to reg.17 of the Income Support Regulations).

62. Social Security (Miscellaneous Amendments) (No.2) Regulations 2004 (SI 2004/1141) reg.3(1) and (2)(c) (May 12, 2004).

63. Social Security (Miscellaneous Amendments) (No.2) Regulations 2004 (SI 2004/1141) reg.3(3) and (4)(c) (May 12, 2004).

64. Social Security (Miscellaneous Amendments) (No.2) Regulations 2004 (SI 2004/1141) reg.3(5) and (6)(c) (May 12, 2004).

65. Social Security (Students and Income-related Benefits) Amendment Regulations 2004 (SI 2004/1708) reg.5(3) (September 1, 2004, or if the student's period of study begins between August 1 and August 31, 2004, the first day of the period).

66. Social Security (Miscellaneous Amendments) (No.3) Regulations 2004 (SI 2004/2308) reg.4(5) (October 4, 2004).

67. Social Security (Back to Work Bonus and Lone Parent Run-on) (Amendment and Revocation) Regulations 2003 (SI 2003/1589) reg.2(d) (October 25, 2004).

68. Social Security (Miscellaneous Amendments) Regulations 2005 (SI 2005/574) reg.3(6) (April 4, 2005).

69. Income-related Benefits (Amendment) Regulations 2005 (SI 2005/2183) reg.2 (August 5, 2005).

70. Social Security (Care Homes and Independent Hospitals) Regulations 2005 (SI 2005/2687) reg.2 and Sch.1 para.13 (October 24, 2005).

71. Civil Partnership (Pensions, Social Security and Child Support) (Consequential, etc. Provisions) Order 2005 (SI 2005/2877) art.2(3) and Sch.3 para.13(9) (December 5, 2005).

72. Income-related Benefits (Amendment) (No.2) Regulations 2005 (SI 2005/3391) reg.2(5) (December 12, 2005).

73. Social Security (Miscellaneous Amendments) (No.2) Regulations 2005 (SI 2005/2465) reg.2(9) (December 30, 2005).

74. Housing Benefit and Council Tax Benefit (Consequential Provisions) Regu lations 2006 (SI 2006/217) reg.5 and Sch.2 para.1(9) (March 6, 2006).

75. Social Security (Young Persons) Amendment Regulations 2006 (SI 2006/718) reg.2(9) (April 10, 2006).

76. Social Security (Miscellaneous Amendments) (No.4) Regulations 2006 (SI 2006/2378) reg.5(11)(a) (October 2, 2006).

77. Social Security (Miscellaneous Amendments) (No.4) Regulations 2006 (SI 2006/2378) reg.5(11)(b) (October 2, 2006).

78. Social Security (Miscellaneous Amendments) (No.4) Regulations 2006 (SI 2006/2378) reg.5(11)(c) (October 2, 2006).

79. Social Security (Miscellaneous Amendments) (No.3) Regulations 2007 (SI 2007/1749) reg.2(8) (July 16, 2007).

80. Secretary of State for Justice Order 2007 (SI 2007/2128) Sch. para.13(3) (August 22, 2007).

81. Independent Living Fund (2006) Order 2007 (SI 2007/2538) reg.2(3) (October 1, 2007).

82. Social Security (Miscellaneous Amendments) Regulations 2008 (SI 2008/698) reg.2(15)(a) (April 14, 2008).

83. Social Security (Miscellaneous Amendments) Regulations 2008 (SI 2008/698) reg.2(15)(b) (April 14, 2008).

84. Social Security (Miscellaneous Amendments) Regulations 2008 (SI 2008/698) reg.2(15)(c) (April 7, 2008).

85. Social Security (Miscellaneous Amendments) Regulations 2008 (SI 2008/698) reg.2(15)(d) (April 14, 2008).

86. Social Security (Miscellaneous Amendments) Regulations 2008 (SI 2008/698) reg.2(15)(e) (April 14, 2008).

87. Employment and Support Allowance (Consequential Provisions) (No.2) Regulations 2008 (SI 2008/1554) reg.2(15) (October 27, 2008).

88. Social Security (Miscellaneous Amendments) (No.6) Regulations 2008 (SI 2008/2767) reg.2(6) (November 17, 2008).

89. Social Security (Miscellaneous Amendments) (No.6) Regulations 2008 (SI 2008/2767) reg.2(13) (November 17, 2008).

90. Social Security (Miscellaneous Amendments) (No.7) Regulations 2008 (SI 2008/3157) reg.2(8) (January 5, 2009).

91. Social Security (Miscellaneous Amendments) Regulations 2009 (SI 2009/583) reg.2(14) (April 6, 2009).

92. Social Security (Equalisation of State Pension Age) Regulations 2009 (SI 2009/1488) reg.4 (April 6, 2010).

93. Social Security (Miscellaneous Amendments) (No.2) Regulations 2010 (SI 2010/641 reg.2(3)(g) (April 6, 2010).

94. Social Security (Miscellaneous Amendments) (No.2) Regulations 2010 (SI 2010/641 reg.2(7)(f) (April 6, 2010).

95. Social Security (Miscellaneous Amendments) (No.2) Regulations 2010 (SI 2010/641 reg.2(10) (April 6, 2010).

96. Social Security (Miscellaneous Amendments) (No.2) Regulations 2011 (SI 2011/1707) reg.4(10)(a) and (11) (August 5, 2011).

97. Social Security (Miscellaneous Amendments) (No.3) Regulations 2011 (SI 2011/2425) reg.7(5) (October 31, 2011).

98. Social Security (Miscellaneous Amendments) (No.3) Regulations 2011 (SI 2011/2425) reg.7(6) (October 31, 2011).

99. Social Security (Miscellaneous Amendments) (No.3) Regulations 2011 (SI 2011/2425) reg.7(8) (October 31, 2011).

100. Jobseeker's Allowance (Schemes for Assisting Persons to Obtain Employment) Regulations 2013 (SI 2013/276) reg.13(b) (February 12, 2013).

101. Social Security (Miscellaneous Amendments) Regulations 2013 (SI 2013/443) reg.2(6)(a) (April 2, 2013).

102. Social Security (Miscellaneous Amendments) Regulations 2013 (SI 2013/443) reg.2(6)(b) (April 2, 2013).

103. Universal Credit (Consequential, Supplementary, Incidental and Miscellaneous Provisions) Regulations 2013 (SI 2013/630) reg.28(9) (April 29, 2013).

104. Special Educational Needs (Consequential Amendments to Subordinate Legislation) Order 2014 (SI 2014/2103) art.3(3) (September 1, 2014).

105. Care Act 2014 (Consequential Amendments) (Secondary Legislation) Order 2015 (SI 2015/643) art.2 and Sch. para.5(4) (April 1, 2015).

Definitions

"Abbeyfield Home"—see reg.2(1).
"the Act"—*ibid.*
"the benefit Acts"—*ibid.*
"care home"—*ibid.*
"child"—see SSCBA s.137(1).
"claimant"—see reg.2(1).
"dwelling occupied as the home"—*ibid.*
"employment zone contractor"—*ibid.*
"employment zone programme"—*ibid.*
"family"—see SSCBA s.137(1).
"full-time student"—see reg.61(1).
"independent hospital"—see reg.2(1).
"Intensive Activity Period for 50 plus"—*ibid.*
"local welfare provision" —*ibid.*
"the London Bombings Relief Charitable Fund"—*ibid.*
"lone parent"—*ibid.*
"the Mandatory Work Activity Scheme"—*ibid.*
"MFET Limited"—*ibid.*

"occupational pension"—*ibid.*
"partner"—*ibid.*
"payment"—*ibid.*
"personal pension scheme"—*ibid.*
"policy of life insurance"—*ibid.*
"qualifying age for state pension credit"—see SSCBA s.137(1).
"qualifying person"—see reg.2(1).
"relative"—*ibid.*
"remunerative work"—*ibid.*
"self-employed earner"—*ibid.*
"self-employment route"—*ibid.*
"sports award"—*ibid.*
"subsistence allowance"—*ibid.*
"supplementary benefit"—*ibid.*
"the Caxton Foundation"—*ibid.*
"the Eileen Trust"—*ibid.*
"the Independent Living Funds"—*ibid.*
"the Macfarlane (Special Payments) Trust"—*ibid.*
"the Macfarlane (Special Payments) (No.2) Trust"—*ibid.*
"the Macfarlane Trust"—*ibid.*
"the Skipton Fund"—*ibid.*
"training allowance"—*ibid.*
"universal cerdit"—*ibid.*
"young person"—*ibid.*, reg.14.

General Note

2.961 Capital may be disregarded under more than one paragraph of Sch.10 at the same time, or in succession. There is no provision in reg.46(2) or Sch.10 for establishing any order of priority if different paragraphs of Sch.10 are applicable, so the claimant will be entitled to the benefit of the most favourable disregard (this is also the case for Sch.9). The disregards in Sch.10 apply to notional capital (*CIS 25/1990*, *CIS 81/1991*, *CIS 562/1992* and *CIS 30/1993*), provided that their conditions are met (*CIS 30/1993*). See the note to para.26 and to reg.51(6).

In *R(IS) 15/96* the Commissioner expresses the view that claimants should be advised by the Benefits Agency of the existence of relevant disregards so that they can take advantage of them. In that case the claimant had received a criminal injuries compensation award so he could have taken steps to utilise the disregard in para.12.

A number of the provisions in Sch.10 allow for a disregard to apply for a set period "or such longer period as is reasonable in the circumstances". In *Guildford BC v MW (HB)* [2014] UKUT 49 (AAC) (a case on Sch.6 to the Housing Benefit Regulations 2006, the equivalent to Sch.10), Judge Wright confirms that whether a capital disregard is to be extended is a matter for a tribunal on appeal to determine entirely afresh and by assessing reasonableness for itself.

Paragraph 1

2.962 The value of the home is disregarded. Paragraph 3 of Sch.3 contains rules about when a person is or is not to be treated as occupying a dwelling as his home. The fact that Sch.10 did not originally contain paras 25–28 gave rise to a number of problems (for which see p.178 of J. Mesher, *Income Support, the Social Fund and Family Credit: the Legislation* (1988)). The introduction of, in particular, a disregard of the value of premises which are for sale will solve, or at least postpone, many of the problems. See reg.17(f) and (2)–(7) for transitional protection for those excluded from income support from April 11, 1988 to May 29, 1988, and the now revoked Sch.9 para.41 and Sch.10 para.32.

On the meaning of "dwelling occupied as the home", see notes to reg.2(1).

Paragraph 1 can apply to notional capital (*CIS 81/1991* (although it was not necessary to the decision) and *CIS 30/1993*).

Paragraph 1A

Any payment of expenses in relation to participation in the Mandatory Work Activity Scheme or a scheme listed in reg.3 of the Jobseeker's Allowance (Schemes for Assisting Persons to Obtain Employment) Regulations 2013 is ignored but if it counts as capital, only for 52 weeks from the date of receipt. **2.963**

Paragraph 2

In *JH v SSWP* [2009] UKUT 1 (AAC) Judge Mesher points out that the form of para.2 of Sch.8 to the JSA Regulations 1996 (which is the same as this paragraph) is different from that of the disregard of the value of premises in some of the other paragraphs in Sch.8 (and in this Schedule). It does not provide that it applies for a period of 26 weeks or such longer period as is reasonable. Instead, it makes it a condition of its application week by week that the claimant intends to occupy the premises as his home within 26 weeks of its acquisition or such longer period as is reasonable. Thus the commentary to this paragraph in the 2008/09 edition (and previous editions) of this volume was wrong in saying that the value of the premises must be disregarded for the first 26 weeks after the acquisition (and had been wrong since he originally wrote that in 1988!). There is no such automatic disregard. **2.964**

All the circumstances must be looked at in deciding whether a longer period is reasonable. There must be some realistic prospect of occupation starting.

It might be thought that the requirement that the premises have been "acquired for occupation by the claimant" would exclude some forms of acquisition (e.g. inheritance). But according to para.29553 of the *Decision Makers Guide*, a person may acquire premises if he buys, is given or inherits them.

"Premises" is to be given a reasonably wide meaning; thus acquiring land on which a person intends to build his home is covered by the disregard (see *CIS 8475/1995* in the note to para.3). But the disregard under para.2 does not extend to money in the claimant's bank account, even though it is intended for use for the purchase of premises (*GS v Department for Social Development (IS)* [2012] NI Com 284, a decision of a Northern Ireland Commissioner). **2.965**

The income from premises whose value is disregarded under this provision counts as income (Sch.9 para.22), but mortgage repayments, water charges and council tax can be set off against it.

Paragraph 3

The sum must be directly attributable to the actual (*R(IS) 4/96*) proceeds of sale of a home, and must be intended for the purchase of another home (not repairs or refurbishment: *R(SB) 14/85; CIS 368/1993*). Money paid out on the surrender of endowment policies that had not been used to repay the claimant's mortgage on his former home was not "directly attributable to the proceeds of sale" of that home (*CFC 2493/1997*). *R(IS)6/95* decides that para.3 is not restricted to circumstances where a claimant is free to sell to a third party but can apply where a statutory tenancy of a home has been surrendered to the landlord. The claimant had sold his home, albeit technically by a surrender rather than a sale, and it was irrelevant to whom he had sold it. **2.966**

As well as the purchase of a home that is already erected, the disregard also covers buying land and building a house on it (*CIS 8475/1995*). In *CIS 8475/1995* the claimant decided to use the proceeds of sale of his former home to buy a plot of land and build a bungalow on it. When he made his claim for income support the sale proceeds were held on deposit. By the date of the tribunal hearing the claimant had used the majority of the proceeds to purchase and clear the land. He had about £10,000 left for materials and labour to build the bungalow. The Commissioner decides that the claimant's intended use of the proceeds of sale fell within para.3. The words "purchase of other premises" in para.3 were to be given a reasonably wide meaning and included the outlay of money in stages to acquire land and build a house on it. This approach was consistent with that adopted in *R(IS) 11/94* in relation to housing costs met by income support (see the notes to para.15 of Sch.3); the Commissioner also agrees with *R(IS) 3/96* that the word "premises" in the first four paragraphs of this Schedule has a similar meaning (see the note to para.4). But the disregard in para.3 only applied to sums of money. Once the claimant had acquired the plot of land, the land and the partly-built bungalow as the work progressed, fell to be disregarded under para.2. On the facts of this case it was reasonable for the period of the disregard under paras 2 and 3 to be extended to 18 months from the date of the claim for income support. The Commissioner comments that in self-build cases a disregard of 12 months rather than six will normally be reasonable.

In *CIS 8475/1995* the Commissioner also makes the point that there is a difference between the wording "is to be used" in para.3 and the tests of intended occupation in, for example, paras 2, 27 and 28. In his view, para.3 required an element of practical certainty as well as subjective intent. This could be shown, for example, by a binding contract for purchase which had not yet been completed, or an agreement "subject to contract" in circumstances where it seemed likely that the money would not be diverted to other purposes. On the facts of that case the Commissioner found obtaining planning permission, placing the purchase in the hands of solicitors and accepting a builder's quote to be sufficient. *CIS 685/1992*, however, decides that it is not necessary, in order for there to be an extension of the primary 26-week period, that an intention to occupy specific premises should have been formed before the end of that period. If the proceeds of sale had not been used at the end of the 26 weeks there was a general discretion for the Department (or tribunal) to allow a longer period for the finding of another home and the completion of its purchase. However, a mere hope that the proceeds might be used at some future date for another home was not sufficient. In *R(IS) 7/01* the Commissioner considers that these two decisions are not irreconcilable and, adopting the approach of *CIS 15984/1996* to the words "to be used", concludes that the test under para.3 is that there must not only be an intention to use the capital to buy another home but also reasonable certainty that it will be used within 26 weeks or such further period as may be reasonable. In *CIS/4757/2003*, the same Commissioner confirms that personal circumstances (such as illness, as in that case, or awaiting the outcome of job applications that might determine the location of the new home as in *CIS/15984/1996*) can justify an extension beyond the 26 weeks. If the claimant can still demonstrate an intention to use the proceeds of sale to purchase another home, and it is reasonably certain that a property will be purchased within a further identifiable period, an extension of time will generally be appropriate.

2.967 Note also *CIS/4269/2003* which confirms that there is nothing in para.3 which says that the proceeds of sale must be of the property that was occupied immediately before the property which is to be purchased. The disregard in para.3 can still apply if a claimant who has a sum directly attributable to the proceeds of sale of home A is currently living in home B, providing that the condition that the sum is to be used to purchase home C within 26 weeks (or reasonable longer period) of the sale of home A is met. But the disregard in para.3 does not apply if the claimant has already purchased his new home prior to the sale of his former home and at the time of the purchase it was not intended that the former home would be sold (*WT v Department for Social Development (IS)* [2011] NI Com 203, a decision of the Northern Ireland Chief Commissioner).

In *CIS 222/1992* the claimant intended to use her share of the proceeds of sale of her deceased mother's house to purchase her own council house. The claimant had lived in her mother's house for a short time some 10 years before. The Commissioner rejects the argument that the claimant was entitled to the benefit of the disregard in para.3 because she formerly occupied her mother's home as her home. He finds that the conditions for a purposive construction of para.3 were satisfied (see Lord Diplock at 105 in *Jones v Wrotham Park Settled Estates Ltd* [1980]

A.C. 74), and holds that para.3 only applied where the claimant had owned the property when she had lived there.

Paragraph 4

In *R(IS) 3/96* the Commissioner rejects a submission from the Secretary of State (said to reflect the policy intention) that para.4 applied to disregard premises of any kind and extent. He decides that "premises" in para.4 was to be interpreted in accordance with the definition of "dwelling occupied as the home" in reg.2(1). The first four paragraphs of Sch.10 were all concerned with disregarding the claimant's home or what would be the home if the claimant was in actual occupation, and thus it was entirely consistent for "premises" in paras 2, 3 and 4 to be given a similar interpretation. Thus when the claimant went to live in a residential care home the farmhouse she jointly owned with her husband could be ignored under para.4(b), but not the farmland which had its own access and could have been sold separately. **2.968**

"Relative" is defined in reg.2(1). "Incapacitated" is not. Paragraph 29437 of the *Decision Makers Guide* suggests that receipt of incapacity benefit, statutory sick pay, or the disability element of working tax credit (as well as more rigorous benefits like severe disablement allowance, attendance allowance and disability living allowance) or an equivalent degree of incapacity will do. Presumably from October 27, 2008 receipt of ESA, and from April 8, 2013 personal independence payment, or armed forces independence payment, will also do. Under supplementary benefit, occupation was held to connote occupation as a residence, not merely as a holiday home *(R(SB) 1/85)*. Under sub-para.(b) it does not now matter that the claimant also occupies the home.

Occupation by a former partner does not count if there has been estrangement or divorce or dissolution of a civil partnership, but see the disregard in para.25 in these circumstances.

Estrangement is not the same as separation *(CIS/4843/2002, R(IS) 5/07)*. **2.969**
R(IS) 5/05 agrees with *R(SB) 2/87* that estrangement has a "connotation of emotional disharmony", whereas separation does not necessarily imply estrangement. However, when a woman talks of being "separated" from her husband, she is not usually referring to physical separation but to a separation prompted by emotional disharmony (presumably the Commissioner would also consider that the same applied if a husband referred to being "separated"!). The essential question was whether the parties had ceased to consider themselves as a couple and not whether, despite that, they continued to maintain friendly relations. In *CH/117/2005*, which concerned the equivalent provision in para.4(b) of Sch.5 to the Housing Benefit Regulations, the Commissioner did not agree with *R(IS) 5/05* that emotional disharmony must necessarily be a feature of estrangement. In his view a couple who have decided that their relationship is at an end could remain the best of friends but would be estranged for the purposes of housing benefit or income support. But the Commissioner does agree with *R(IS) 5/05* that the central question is whether the couple have ceased to consider themselves as a couple. Thus a couple will not be estranged if they have retained all the indicia of partners apart from physical presence in the same household.

However, with respect to the Commissioner in *CH/117/2005*, in order to distinguish estrangement from the position of a couple who still regard themselves as such but who are classed as former partners because they have ceased to have a common household, the question must surely be whether the relationship between the former partners as partners has ended, which will normally involve at least some element of "emotional disharmony". Indeed the Commissioner himself appears to recognise this in *CPC/683/2007* (a case on the equivalent provision in para.4(b) of Sch.V to the State Pension Credit Regulations) when he says that on the facts of that case there was no emotional disharmony between the claimant and his wife as adults but there was emotional disharmony between them as partners and that this was a key distinction. In *CPC/683/2007* the claimant's evidence was that he continued to feel responsible for his wife and did odd jobs to assist her but he accepted that his wife would never resume living together with him because of his affair. The Commissioner in *CPC/683/2007* comments that he did not consider that there was any inconsistency between his decision in *CH/117/2005* and *R(IS) 5/05*. Any difference was accounted for by the facts of the cases and the different emphasis given in explaining the decisions. To the extent that there is any inconsistency, however, *R(IS) 5/05* as a reported decision is to be preferred.

See also *CIS/4096/2005* in which the Commissioner reviewed the authorities on estrangement, in the context of reg.13(1)(d). She concluded that estrangement does not require mutuality of feeling, as had been suggested in *CIS/4498/2001*. Disharmony can arise from one person's attitude to another even though the other party may not wish the situation to be as it is. Further, as the Commissioner in *CIS/2660/1998* (which concerned estrangement in the context of a social fund funeral payment) had stated, the position was to be considered from the point of view of the claimant. The legislative test (in reg.13, paras 4(b), 25 and 26 of this Schedule and para.4(b) of Sch.5 to the Housing Benefit Regulations 1987 (now para.4(b) of Sch.6 to the Housing Benefit Regulations 2006) was whether the *claimant* was estranged *from* [the appropriate party according to the benefit involved]. None of the legislative provisions concerning estrangement referred to the "estrangement of, (or between), the parties". (The test is also the same in para.4(b) of Sch.V to the State Pension Credit Regulations; in reg.8(1)(c) of the Social Fund Maternity and Funeral Expenses Regulations the wording is: "any of the immediate family members . . . was not estranged from the deceased".) In the context of para.4(b) this means that the position has to be judged from the point of view of the claimant and not his former partner. However, in *CPC/683/2007* the Commissioner did not consider that *CIS/2660/2008* was authority for the proposition that the position had to be looked at from the claimant's viewpoint, but even if it was, he considered that the tribunal had been correct to conclude that the claimant and his wife were estranged as partners.

2.970 In a further decision on this subject (*CH/3777/2007*), the Commissioner states that "estranged" in this context simply implies that the relationship between the couple has broken down; there is no requirement that the dealings and communications between them should be acrimonious. He also did not agree that "estranged" required an element of disharmony because otherwise it added nothing to the reference to a "former partner". This view thus accords with that in *CH/117/2005*. Whether emotional disharmony is a necessary feature may therefore depend on the context.

Renewed contact does not necessarily end estrangement; it is question of fact in each case (*R 1/02(SF)*, *AC v SSWP (IS)* [2015] UKUT 49 (AAC)).

In *CIS 231/1991* the claimant had transferred his former home to his parents who were both over 60 (which was the age limit in para.4(a) at that time). When he claimed income support they were living in the home. The Commissioner decides that para.4(a) applied to the former home; the disregard applied to notional, as well as actual, capital.

Note that from April 6, 2010, as a result of the start of the equalisation of state pension age, the age limit in para.4(a) is "the qualifying age for state pension credit" (defined in s.137(1) of the Contributions and Benefits Act 1992—the effect of that definition is that the qualifying age was 60 but from April 2010 it will gradually rise in line with the staged increase in pensionable age for women until it reaches 65 in November 2018 (this equalisation of the state pension age for men and women was previously to have been completed by April 5, 2020 but the timetable for this in the Pensions Act 1995 has been accelerated with effect from April 2016 so that women's state pension age will now be 65 by November 2018; in addition, the increase in state pension age to 66 for both men and women has been brought forward—it will start to rise from 65 in December 2018 to reach 66 by October 2020, see s.1 of the Pensions Act 2011, and between 2026 and 2028 it will rise to 67 (see s.26 of the Pensions Act 2014)).

Paragraph 5

Before October 2, 1995 the disregard in para.5 applied to "any reversionary interest". The new form is in response to the Court of Appeal's decision in *Chief Adjudication Officer v Palfrey,* reported as part of *R(IS) 26/95,* which upheld the Tribunal of Commissioners' decision in *CIS 85/1992* that property subject to a tenancy was a reversionary interest and so was to be disregarded. The Commissioners had held that *R(SB) 3/86* (which decided that a reversionary interest was "something which does not afford any present enjoyment but carries a vested or contingent right to enjoyment in the future" and that a landlord's interest in a freehold property was not merely such an interest) was not to be followed. In *CIS 85/1992* the rented property was freehold, but *CIS 563/1991* and *CIS 615/1993* confirmed that the disregard under the previous form of para.5 applied to leasehold property as well. 2.971

It was considered that the effect of these decisions was to create an easy loophole which could enable a claimant to have the capital value of property disregarded simply by letting it, and so the new form of para.5 was introduced. Under the new form, the disregard applies to future interests in property but not land or premises which have been let by the claimant. A future interest in property is one that does not take effect immediately. An example would be where the claimant's entitlement only arises on the death of a person who has a life interest in the particular fund or property. Note that for the exception to operate, the lease, etc. has to be granted by the claimant. So, if the tenancy was granted by someone else (e.g. before the claimant owned the property) the disregard should still apply.

CIS 635/1994 suggests that the disregard could also apply if the property was subject to an irrevocable licence (rather than a lease or tenancy). The Commissioner expressed doubts as to whether a freehold or leasehold interest in a property subject to a tenancy could be said to be a future interest, but considered that the way the exception was put appeared to assume that it was. This meant that the new disregard might not be limited (as at first sight it seemed to be) to future interests in the sense of interests where there was no right at all until the future event happened. If the consequence is that the new form of para.5 covers situations where the claimant's interest affords no present enjoyment (and is a future interest in that sense) then, leaving aside the exception, the disregard itself may not be significantly different. Indeed it could be argued that a future interest is wider than a reversionary interest as it could include not only an interest that will revert to the claimant but also one that will only take effect in the future. (Note that in *Palfrey* both the Court of Appeal and the Commissioners considered that the capital value of the element of possession involved in a tenanted property fell to be disregarded under para.24 (in its previous form); it was the right to regain possession of the property at the end of the term which was a purely reversionary right that was covered by the old form of para.5.)

See also *R(IS) 1/97.* The claimant on separating from his wife had agreed that she could remain in the former matrimonial home (which was in his sole name) for her lifetime. There was no written agreement. The Commissioner decides that in the circumstances an irrevocable licence had been granted or could be inferred which gave rise to a constructive trust which in turn made the wife a tenant for life for the purposes of the Settled Land Act 1925. The Commissioner decides that the test laid down in *Ashburn Anstalt v Arnold* [1989] Ch. 1 for imposing a constructive trust, that is, that the owner of the property had so conducted himself that it would be inequitable to allow him to deny the beneficiary an interest in the property, was satisfied. The result was that the claimant's interest in the former matrimonial home was a reversionary one as it did not afford any present enjoyment. If the claimant's interest can similarly be ignored under the new form of para.5 (see above), this decision may have potentially wide implications for separating couples. See *R(IS) 5/07* in which the Commissioner stated that further information about the terms on which the claimant's husband continued to live in the former matrimonial home was needed but clearly considered that the disregard in para.5 might be applicable. 2.972

Note also *R(IS) 4/96* which decides that a charge on a former matrimonial home which was not to be enforced until the claimant's ex-wife died, remarried or cohabited for longer than six months was not a reversionary interest but gave the claimant a secured debt payable at a future date (see *Re Fisher* [1943] Ch. 377).

See also the amendment to para.24.

Rent from tenanted property, as and when it is received, will generally count as capital, not income (Sch.9 para.22), under reg.48(4). But note the excepted cases, e.g. if the property is up for sale (and so disregarded under para.26). See the notes to reg.48(4) and para.22 of Sch.9 and note *CIS 563/1991* discussed in the note to reg.48(4).

Paragraph 6

2.973 The business assets of a self-employed person are primarily disregarded under sub-para.(1) if he is engaged in the business. Paragraph 29371 of the *Decision Makers Guide* states that a person should be treated as engaged in a business for as long as he performs some work in it in a practical sense.

Business assets have to be distinguished from personal assets by asking if they are "part of the fund employed and risked in the business" (*R(SB) 4/85*). The income tax and accounting position are factors to be taken into account, but are not conclusive (*CFC 10/1989*), although see *CIS 5481/1997* which emphasises the relevance of accounting practice.

See also *R(H) 7/08* which concluded that "personal" distinguished between things held for personal and for business use and that there was no room for any third category of physical assets other than land. In *JJ v SSWP (IS)* [2012] UKUT 253 (AAC) the Aston Martin which the claimant had purchased with the intention of starting a classic car rental business was a business asset and not a personal possession, even though the claimant did not proceed with his project. The new tribunal would need to decide whether the claimant could be regarded as engaged in the business so that the disregard in sub-para.(1) applied, and if so, for what period.

2.974 *CIS/2467/2003* concerned a self-employed author who received advances on contracting to write a book and subsequent royalties on sales. The Commissioner rejected his argument that money paid by way of advances was not legally owned by him because the advances were repayable if he did not fulfill the contract. In his view the advances fully belonged to the claimant as soon as they were received. He further concluded that the receipts from the claimant's business were capital (see further the note to reg.30) and that they could not be disregarded under para.6. This was because, applying the test in *R(SB) 4/85*, the money was not employed in and risked in the business. The Commissioner rejected the claimant's argument that the ISA into which advances had been paid constituted a long-term reserve fund that underwrote and underpinned his business. It was a Maxi ISA; these are designed for personal savings by investment on a medium and long-term basis. The money in it was thus not employed in the business but in the personal sphere as the proceeds of the business. As the claimant was the business, if things went wrong he might need to draw on the value of the investment but this would represent a putting back into the business of resources from the claimant's personal sphere. The claimant also had a joint account with his wife into which some business receipts were paid and which was used for domestic purposes. The Commissioner emphasised that if a claimant wished to benefit from the disregard in para.6 in relation to money which is not in a separate business account, he must show that there is some positive demarcation between the assets of the business and personal assets. The claimant had failed to do this and the consequence was that none of the capital in his accounts fell to be disregarded under para.6.

R(FC) 2/92 holds that the ownership by an individual of a tenanted house is not a business, although there may come a point, depending on the circumstances, at which the amount of administration and/or activity involved even in the letting out of a single property could amount to self-employment (*CCS 2128/2001*; *CIB 1595/2000* and *CIB 2114/2000*). See also *CFC 4238/1997*. In *CH/4258/2004*, which concerned para.7(1) of Sch.5 to the Housing Benefit Regulations (the equivalent of para.6(1)), the claimant ran a retail business from the ground floor and basement of a building which also included three flats on the upper floors. She purchased the freehold of the whole building (as the owner was not prepared to sell the retail part separately). The Comissioner concludes that the flats (which were let to tenants) were not used for the retail business (the fact that one business loan had been used to purchase the whole building did not affect this). Nor, applying *R(FC) 2/92*, were they assets of another business. As a consequence their value counted as the claimant's capital. Note that since October 2, 1995 a property that the claimant has let to tenants is not ignored as a reversionary interest (see the notes to para.5).

In *R(IS) 14/98* although the claimant was only a sleeping partner, the Commissioner decides that she continued to be gainfully employed and so a self-employed earner (s.2(1)(b) of the Contributions and Benefits Act 1992) in the farm business she owned with her son. The claimant had ceased to take an active role, having gone to live permanently in a residential care home, but she remained entitled to a share of the profits and capital and jointly and severally liable for the partnership's losses. Thus her share of the partnership assets, including the farm, fell to be disregarded under para.6. See also *CG 19/1994* where the claimant who had become a partner in her husband's business solely for tax purposes was held to be gainfully employed in the business. But the decision in *R(IS) 14/98* was appealed to the Court of Appeal, which allowed the appeal (*Chief Adjudication Officer v Knight*, reported as part of *R(IS) 14/98*). The Court held that for the disregard in para.6 to apply, a financial commitment to a business on its own was insufficient. The claimant had to be involved or engaged in the business in some practical sense as an earner. Thus a sleeping partner in a business managed and worked exclusively by others could not benefit from para.6.

If the claimant ceases to be engaged in the business, the value of the assets is disregarded for a period which is reasonable to allow them to be disposed of. In *CIS 5481/1997* the partnership that the claimant had been involved in had ceased trading. The Commissioner points out that a partnership did not cease to exist when it stopped trading. It ceased to exist when it was dissolved (which might or might not be the same time as it stopped trading). The assets remained business assets until the partnership was dissolved. However, the disregard in para.6 operated while a person was engaged as a self-employed earner for the purposes of the business and for such further time as was reasonable to allow for the disposal of the business's assets. The point when a person ceased to be engaged as a self-employed earner might be at the same time as a partnership ceased trading, or when it was dissolved, or at some other time (e.g. see *Knight* above). Thus in considering what was a reasonable time for disposal of assets under para.6 account had to be taken of the obligation on partners to sort out the partnership debts before distributing the assets. This would depend on the terms of any partnership deed or agreement or the Partnership Act 1890, and what was a reasonable period of time might alter if the circumstances changed. It may be useful for a tribunal dealing with a case of this kind to include a financially qualified member in view of the nature of the issues involved. **2.975**

Where the self-employed person is temporarily not engaged in the business because of illness, there is a disregard under sub-para.(2). The reference to engagement or re-engagement clearly contemplates that the person may not previously have been engaged in the business (*JJ v SSWP (IS)* [2012] UKUT 253 (AAC)).

Sub-paragraphs (3) and (4) disregard any assets of a business carried on while a person is participating in the "self-employment route" (defined in reg.2(1)), and, if the person later ceases to be engaged in that business, for a period which is reasonable to allow them to be disposed of. See also para.52 under which any capital acquired for the purposes of such a business is ignored for 52 weeks from the date of receipt.

Note in addition the general disregard of payments made under s.2 of the Employment and Training Act 1973 or s.2 of the Enterprise and New Towns (Scotland) Act 1990 for 52 weeks from the date of receipt in para.30. **2.976**

Income from capital disregarded under para.6 is not disregarded (Sch.9 para.22).

Paragraph 7

2.977 Arrears of benefit which would be income when paid on the proper date retain their character as income (*R(SB) 4/89*). However, if any money is left after the end of the period to which the benefit is attributed as income then this will be capital (see notes to regs 23 and 40(1)).

Paragraph 7 applies, under sub-para.(1)(a), to mobility allowance or supplement, attendance allowance, any care or mobility component of disability living allowance and the daily living component or mobility component of personal independence payment; and under sub-para.(1)(b), to income support, income-based JSA, income-related ESA, child tax credit, working tax credit, housing benefit and council tax benefit (note that council tax benefit was abolished on April 1, 2013). (Sub-paragraph (1)(c) which applied to earnings top-up, a pilot scheme for people in low-paid work who did not have children which came to an end in October 1999, was revoked on April 4, 2005.) From July 2, 2001 it also applies under sub-para.(1)(d) to discretionary housing payments. These are payments that can be made by a local authority to claimants who need extra help with their housing liability. They replaced the previous system of exceptional circumstances payments and exceptional hardship payments with effect from July 2, 2001. Under sub-para.(e), added with effect from April 29, 2013, it applies to universal credit.

For these benefits there is a disregard for 52 weeks from the date of receipt under sub-para.(1), unless the more extensive disregard in sub-para.(2) applies.

2.978 The effect of sub-para.(2) is that if, on or after October 14, 2001, as a consequence of an official error (as defined in reg.1(3) of the Decisions and Appeals Regulations 1999, see Vol.III of this series), a claimant receives arrears and/or concessionary payment(s) totalling £5,000 or more in relation to any one of the benefits listed in sub-para.(1) ("the relevant sum"), this will be ignored indefinitely while the award during which the payment(s) are made continues, or for 52 weeks from the date of receipt, whichever is the longer. Award for this purpose means the award of income support, income-related ESA, income-based JSA or universal credit during which the arrears/concessionary payment (or first instalment thereof) was received and includes subsequent awards of income support, income-related ESA, income-based JSA or universal credit, provided that such awards are continuous and that the claimant is either the person who received the relevant sum or the partner of that person, or was his partner at the date of his death, or in the case of joint-claim JSA is a joint-claim couple, either or both of whom received the relevant sum (sub-para.(3)). Thus the sub-para.(2) disregard will not apply and a claimant will be restricted to the 52-week disregard under sub-para.(1) if the relevant sum (or part thereof) was paid before income support/income-based JSA/income-related ESA/universal credit was claimed. It also seems that £5,000 or more must have been paid in respect of one of the listed benefits for the indefinite disregard to apply; payments in relation to more than one of these benefits cannot be aggregated for this purpose. Further, the requirement that a subsequent award should begin immediately after the end of the previous award for the indefinite disregard to continue to apply may cause difficulties, since there can often be a gap between claims when a claimant moves between benefits and the limited circumstances in which claims can be backdated may not apply.

MK v SSWP (IS) [2013] UKUT 629 (AAC) confirms that the disregard in para.7 only applies to the arrears of benefit that are paid and not to a sum equivalent to the arrears.

CIS/2448/2006, followed in *R(IS)5/08*, decides that a refund of charges by a local authority to a claimant because the claimant had been wrongly charged for after-care services under s.117 of the Mental Health Act 1983 (see *R. v Manchester City Council Ex p. Stennett* [2002] UKHL 34 in which the House of Lords held that a local authority was not entitled to charge for such after-care) was not "arrears of income support" and therefore could not be disregarded under para.7. The fact that the charges had been paid out of the claimant's income support did not turn the repayment of charges wrongly made into a payment of arrears of income support.

Note also the disregards in paras 38–41.

Paragraph 8

This meets the problems in *R(SB) 14/81* and para.8(2) of *R(SB) 14/85*. Such sums may not be part of the claimant's capital anyway (see *CSB 975/1985* and the notes to reg.46). **2.979**

R(IS) 6/95 decides that sub-para.(a) only applies where the claimant has suffered damage to, or the loss of, his property against his will, not where he has deliberately brought this about. Thus it did not cover payment received for the surrender of a statutory tenancy of the claimant's home. *JM v SSWP* [2009] UKUT 87 (AAC) holds that the caselaw on the meaning of "to be used" in para.3 is equally applicable to para.8 (see the note to para.3 for this caselaw). In *JM* the claimant had received compensation some five years earlier for the destruction of his home in a gas explosion. He had not yet bought another property as he was caring for his disabled cousin but he intended to do so once his caring role ended (the date of which was uncertain). In these circumstances his intention to use the money to purchase a replacement home was no more than an aspiration and the disregard in sub-para.(a) did not apply from the outset. The claimant had also received a further sum for the sale of the land on which his house had stood. In the Upper Tribunal Judge's view this did not fall within sub-para.(a) which relates to sums paid for damage to, or loss of, the *home*; it could fall within para.3 but again the disregard in that paragraph did not apply because the claimant did not have a sufficient intention to use the money for the purpose envisaged by para.3.

CIS/368/1993 rejects the argument that money (in that case proceeds of sale of a previous home) ear-marked for the renovation of the claimant's home came within sub-para.(b). The Commissioner decides that the money had not been "acquired on the express condition" that it was to be used for the renovation, but as a consequence of the sale.

Paragraph 9

Sub-paragraph (b) gets round the problem in *R(SB) 4/87*. **2.980**

Paragraph 10

Only possessions bought with the intention of reducing capital so as to gain income support count. See the notes to reg.51(1) for "purpose". Note that the corresponding paragraph under JSA (para.15 of Sch.8 to the JSA Regulations 1996) applies if a person has bought possessions with the intention of reducing capital in order to secure entitlement to or increase the amount of JSA *or income support*. That avoids the question that might otherwise have arisen on a claimant transferring from income support to JSA as to whether possessions that had been bought only for the purpose of income support could be caught by para.15 of Sch.8. Similarly para.14 of Sch.9 to the ESA Regulations 2008 (see Vol.1 in this series) applies if a person has bought possessions with the intention of reducing capital in order to secure entitlement to or increase the amount of ESA *or income support or JSA*. However, para.10 has not been amended along those lines. **2.981**

If the value of personal possessions does count, it is their current market value, i.e. their second hand value, not what was paid for them (*CIS/494/1990, CIS/2208/2003*), which must be included, less 10 per cent if there would be expenses in selling. For the possible problems of double counting and the interaction of this paragraph if personal possessions are not ignored and reg.51(1), see *CIS 494/1990* and *R(IS)8/04,* discussed under "*Deprivation*" in the notes to reg.51(1).

Presumably anything which is not real property is a personal possession. Providing that it is an object and not a right to sue for something, like a debt. But hard lines might have to be drawn between coins and bank-notes (obviously capital) and investments like paintings, stamps, furniture (apparently disregarded). What about gold bars?

In *R(H) 7/08* the Commissioner concludes that "personal possessions" means any physical assets other than land and assets used for business purposes. Thus the claimant's caravan was a personal possession and fell to be disregarded under this paragraph. In *JH v SSWP* [2009] UKUT 1 (AAC) a beach hut was a personal possession to which the disregard in para.15 of Sch.8 to the JSA Regulations 1996 (the equivalent of this paragraph) applied. But the right under a contractual licence to put the hut on the site was not a personal possession, did count as capital and had a market value.

Paragraph 12

2.982 There is an unlimited disregard of the value of a trust fund deriving from payment made in consequence of personal injury to the claimant or (from October 2, 2006) the claimant's partner. This seems particularly generous compared to the treatment of other forms of capital.

Note that "personal injury" includes a disease and any injuries suffered as a result of a disease (e.g. amputation of both legs following meningitis and septicaemia), as well as any accidental or criminal injury (*R(SB) 2/89*).

Compensation for personal injury includes all heads of an award for personal injury (*Peters v East Midland Strategic Heath Authority* [2009] EWCA Civ 145, [2009] 3 WLR 737, a decision of the meaning of "an award of damages for a personal injury" in para.44(2)(a) but the same reasoning will apply). In particular, it is not restricted to general damages for pain, suffering and loss of amenity, but can include other heads of loss, such as loss of earnings and any sum awarded by a court in respect of the cost of providing accommodation and care. See also *R(IS) 15/96* (para.18).

2.983 *KQ v SSWP (IS)* [2011] UKUT 102 (AAC); [2011] AACR 43 holds that a compensation payment received from negligent solicitors, which purely related to what would have been claimed from the negligent surgeon, was in consequence of the personal injury to the claimant. Judge Levenson accepts that the chain of causation does not go on for ever and so damages for the stress caused by the negligent solicitors or an element of punitive damages might not come within the disregard in para.12 (or para.12A). But there was no such element in the compensation in this case.

From October 2, 2006 the disregard applies where the injury was to the claimant *or* the claimant's partner. Before that date para.12 had simply referred to a trust derived from a payment made in compensation of any personal injury to the claimant. See *R(IS) 3/03* (discussed in the notes to para.12 of the 2006 edition of this volume) in which the Commissioner considered, at least on the facts of that case, that the reference to "the claimant" in para.12 did not include, by virtue of reg.23(1), a reference to the claimant's partner.

The disregard does not apply where the compensation was an award under the Fatal Accidents Act 1976 (*CP v SSWP (IS)* [2011] UKUT 157 (AAC)). In *CP v SSWP* the claimant, who had Down's syndrome, received substantial compensation under the 1976 Act after her mother (and primary carer) was killed in a road traffic accident. Paragraph 12 did not bite on such an award where the personal injury (or rather the fatality) was suffered by the claimant's mother, not the claimant.

2.984 Before October 2, 2006, if there was no trust, the compensation counted as capital. But now see para.12A, inserted with effect from October 2, 2006, which provides a general capital disregard of payments made in consequence of personal injury either to the claimant or the claimant's partner for 52 weeks from the date that the claimant first receives any payment in respect of the injury. Paragraph 12A thus introduces a "grace period" during which a trust fund can be set up, or an annuity purchased (see the disregard in para.11), or the money spent. See further the notes to para.12A.

If para.12A does not, or has ceased to, apply, and there is no trust, etc. the compensation counts as capital, even though it is in a solicitor's hands (*Thomas v Chief Adjudication Officer*, reported as (*R(SB) 17/87*; see also *R(IS) 15/96* in the notes to reg.46. But note *CIS 984/2002* which holds that money held by the claimant's solicitor pending quantification of the statutory charge to the Legal Services Commission under s.10(7) of the Access to Justice Act 1999 was not part of the claimant's capital: see further the note to reg.46).

If the claimant then transfers the compensation to trustees, the exception in reg.51(1)(a) operates so that he will not be treated as having deprived himself of the capital placed on trust. Although putting money into a trust would normally count as deprivation, to do so in the case of trusts of personal injury compensation would defeat the purpose of para.12. It is not necessary for the trust to be set up before the compensation is received. Furthermore, since para.12 refers to funds "derived" from personal injury compensation, it is certainly arguable that the disregard should also apply even if the compensation was initially used for other purposes before being placed on trust. An example could be if the compensation was used to buy a home but this was later sold and the proceeds of sale put on trust. If the money placed on trust derived (in the sense of "originated") from personal injury compensation, there would seem to be no policy reason why the disregard in para.12 should not apply. The purpose of the disregard is presumably to allow such compensation payments to be used for the person's disablement needs that have arisen as a result of the injury. The fact that the funds have been employed elsewhere for an intermediate period would not seem to affect this policy intention.

CIS 368/1994 decides that the disregard in para.12 applied where the compensation was held and administered by a combination of the Public Trustee and the Court of Protection. In the Commissioner's view, the word "trust" was used to cover the situation where the legal estate was in one person and the beneficial interest in another. It did not matter for the purposes of para.12 whether a particular trust had been set up or whether there was in operation a statutory scheme involving, for example, the Court of Protection. The effect of this decision would seem to be that the disregard in para.12 can apply whether the money is administered by the Court of Protection itself or held in the name of the receiver or the Public Trustee. For further discussion of the position of funds held by the Court of Protection, see *R(IS) 9/04* in the note to reg.46. **2.985**

Now see paras 44 and 45 which have introduced a specific disregard for funds held in court that derive from damages for personal injury or compensation for the death of a parent. See the notes to paras 44 and 45.

Any payment from the trust will be income or capital depending on the nature of the payment (income from trusts disregarded under this paragraph is one of the excepted cases from the general rule in reg.48(4) that income from capital counts as capital). But note that from October 2, 2006, income payments, made or due to be made at regular intervals, from a trust fund derived from a payment made in consequence of any personal injury to the claimant is fully disregarded under para.15 of Sch.9. For reasons that are not entirely clear this income disregard has not been amended to include payments in respect of an injury to the claimant's partner in line with the disregard under this paragraph and para.12A. See further the notes to para.15 of Sch.9. Note also the rules for payments to third parties in regs 42(4) and 51(3). The notional income rule in reg.42(2) (income available on application) and the notional capital rules in reg.51(1) (deprivation of capital) and reg.51(2) (capital available on application) do not apply to trusts of personal injury compensation.

Paragraph 12A

Paragraph 12A provides for a general capital disregard of payments for personal injury (for the disregard where the personal injury payment has been placed on trust, see para.12 or where it is being administered by a court, see paras 44 and 45). The disregard applies to a payment made in consequence of a personal injury to *either* the claimant *or* the claimant's partner. It does not apply to payments from a trust fund. But note that the disregard only applies for 52 weeks from the date that the claimant *first* receives any payment in respect of the injury; it does not apply to any subsequent payment (even if made by another person). This is because the **2.986** purpose of the disregard is to introduce a "grace period" during which a trust fund can be set up (the disregard in para.12 will then apply), or an annuity purchased (see the disregard in para.11), or the money spent.

The disregard under para.12A will cease to apply to the payment or any part of it when the claimant no longer possesses it. See sub-para.(3) which specifically provides that this includes the situation where the claimant has used the payment or part of it to purchase an asset. Unless any of the other disregards in Sch.10 apply (e.g. para.10), it will then be taken into account as capital.

Note also that from October 2, 2006, regular income payments from funds derived from a personal injury award to the claimant are fully disregarded (see para.15 of Sch.9 and the notes to that paragraph). For reasons that are not entirely clear this income disregard has not been amended to include payments in respect of an injury to the claimant's partner in line with the disregard under para.12 and this paragraph.

Paragraph 13

2.987 This reverses the result of *R(SB) 43/84*.

Paragraph 14

2.988 The provisions mentioned deal with situations where foreign income or earnings cannot be transmitted to the United Kingdom.

Paragraph 15

2.989 The surrender value of all life insurance policies is disregarded. In supplementary benefit there was a limit of £1,500.

In *R(IS) 7/98* the claimant had placed her capital in an "investment bond". This provided for a low guaranteed minimum death benefit if the investment had not been fully cashed in before death. But it also included, among other surrender options, a "monthly withdrawal plan", under which the claimant received a sum of £75.20 a month by way of partial encashment until the value of the investment was exhausted. The Commissioner decides that the bond fell within the definition of "policy of life insurance" in reg.2(1). For this definition to apply, it was not necessary for death of the investor to be the only contingency under which money was payable (see *CIS 122/1991*), nor was the relative size of the death benefits on one hand, and the investments benefits on the other, relevant (see *Gould v Curtis* [1913] 3 K.B. 84). The value of the bond therefore fell to be disregarded under para.15 (even though its full investment value was obtainable on demand and so would have come within reg.51(2) (capital available on demand), except for para.15). However, in relation to the original decision to purchase the bond, the deprivation rule in reg.51(1) would have to be considered (see *CIS 112/1994* (and *CIS 109/1994*) in the notes to reg.51). Moreover, since the £75.20 monthly payments represented payments of capital by instalments, for as long as the total outstanding under the policy together with any other capital belonging to the claimant exceeded £8,000 (the then capital limit), such payments would count as income for the period they were paid under reg.41. (See para.16 as regards the right to receive these payments.)

Paragraph 16

2.990 See reg.41(1) and *R(IS) 7/98* in the note to para.15.

Paragraph 17

2.991 See the notes to para.28 of Sch.9.

Paragraph 18A

2.992 See the note to para.31A of Sch.9.

Paragraph 20

2.993 This is to avoid double counting. Note that the amendments made to this provision on April 6, 2004 do not apply in "transitional cases"—see the note to reg.17. The amendments were made because with effect from April 6, 2004 (except in "transitional cases"—see the note to reg.17) amounts for children and young persons were removed from the income support scheme (financial support for children and young persons is now to be provided through the child tax credit system, see Vol.IV in this series) and income support became in effect an "adults only" benefit. See the 2003 edition of this volume for the old form of para.20.

Paragraph 22

The disregard now extends to payments to haemophiliacs from the three trusts and to non-haemophiliacs from the Fund, the Eileen Trust, MFET Limited, the Skipton Fund, the Caxton Foundation and the London Bombings Relief Charitable Fund, and to distributions of capital payments to the close family, or a slightly wider class for the two years following such a person's death. Any payments from the Independent Living Fund are ignored. **2.994**

A disregard of an amount equal to any interim assistance grant paid by the London Bombings Relief Charitable Fund had been introduced on August 5, 2005 (see para.22A in the Supplement to the 2005 edition of this volume) but on December 12, 2005 para.22A was revoked and replaced by the disregard under this paragraph.

Sub-paragraphs (4)(b)(i) and (ii) and (5)(b)(i) and (ii) include references to step-parents. Note that from December 5, 2005, references to "step" relationships and "in laws" are to be read as including relationships arising through civil partnership in any provision to which s.246 of the Civil Partnership Act 2004 applies. Section 246 is applied to sub-paras (4)(b)(i) and (ii) and (5)(b)(i) and (ii) by art.3 of and para.23 of the Schedule to the Civil Partnership Act 2004 (Relationships Arising Through Civil Partnership) Order 2005 (SI 2005/3137).

Paragraph 23

Accrued rights to receive an occupational or personal pension in the future are often amongst a person's most valuable assets, but they are not capable of being bought or sold, and so have no market value anyway. **2.995**

Paragraph 23A

See the notes to reg.42(2)(g) and (2ZA) to (2CA). **2.996**

Paragraph 24

This paragraph was amended on October 2, 1995 at the same time as the new form of para.5 was introduced. See the notes to para.5. Since the annual amount of the rent due can be used to calculate the value of a tenanted property the amendment will prevent the annual rent (and thus the capital value of the property) from being reduced to nil because of the disregard. **2.997**

Paragraph 25

This paragraph applies where a claimant has ceased to be part of a couple because of estrangement or divorce, or dissolution of a civil partnership, and has left what was formerly the home. In these circumstances the claimant may well have an actual or deemed (see reg.52) interest in the dwelling, but no longer be able to get within para.1. But see the notes to reg.52 under "*Former matrimonial assets*" and "*Valuation under regulation 52*" and *R(IS) 1/97* in the notes to para.5. **2.998**

Divorce is an easily proved event, but estrangement is a less hard-edged concept. See the note to para.4 for a discussion of the meaning of "estrangement".

The disregard used to be limited to 26 weeks from the date on which the claimant left the dwelling, with no extension. However, with effect from April 1, 2003 it applies without limit if the former partner who occupies the home is a lone parent. This brings the disregard into line with that which applies for the purpose of housing benefit and, until its abolition on April 1, 2013, applied for council tax benefit.

Paragraph 26

2.999 This provision restores some of the effect of the similar supplementary benefit disregard. It will ease some of the problems noted on p.178 of J. Mesher, *Income Support, the Social Fund and Family Credit: the Legislation* (1988), but not all of them. It applies if reasonable steps are being taken to dispose of premises. "Premises" in para.26 is to be construed widely and includes land without buildings (*R(IS) 4/97*, preferring *CSB 222/1986* to *CIS 673/1993*). See also *R(IS) 3/96* and *CIS 8475/1995* in the notes to paras 3 and 4. What are reasonable steps must be a question of fact. The Commissioner in *R(IS) 4/97* considers that the test is an objective one. So, if the sale price was totally unrealistic, that attempt at sale should be disregarded and the period of the disregard would not start to run until reasonable steps to dispose of the premises were *first* taken. In his view the period of the disregard must be continuous. *CIS 6908/1995* also confirms that the disregard starts when the claimant first takes steps to dispose of the premises, which may well be before a property is put on the open market. Making a genuine approach to the other tenant in common to agree to a sale, or reaching agreement on an auctioneer and a conveyancer, could constitute taking reasonable steps (*JH v SSWP* [2009] UKUT 1 (AAC)). In *JT v Leicester CC (CTB)* [2012] UKUT 445 (AAC) obtaining a solicitor's quotation for charges associated with a sale and a written valuation from an estate agent were undoubtedly "steps". They were also reasonable steps up to the point when the claimant stopped taking steps to dispose of the property, at which point the disregard in para.26 ceased to apply.

In *R(IS) 5/05* the Commissioner points out that the bringing of ancillary relief proceedings within a divorce suit may have been a necessary preliminary step before a former matriomonial home was put on the market; there also seemed no reason why the para.26 disregard should not apply while arrangements were being made for a former partner to buy the interest of the claimant, which avoided putting the home on the market at all. He added that if the claimant was proposing to buy out the former partner and move back into the matrimonial home herself, the disregard in para.27 might be applicable instead.

CIS/1915/2007 confirms that bringing divorce proceedings could constitute reasonable steps. But the Commissioner also emphasises that a flexible approach had to be taken to the question of reasonableness. If there was a temporary suspension of the divorce proceedings and the resulting disposal of the property, because of family pressures, or threats of violence, or to see if a reconciliation could be achieved, all the circumstances had to be considered to determine whether the claimant was still taking reasonable steps. By putting her divorce proceedings on hold until she had moved to other accommodation and so was in a position where she could safely proceed the claimant was continuing to take such steps. See also *JC-W v Wirral MBC (HB)* [2011] UKUT 501 (AAC) (paras 26–27) decided by the same Commissioner (now Judge).

2.1000 The initial disregard is for 26 weeks, but can be extended where reasonable to enable the disposal to be carried out.

In *CIS 562/1992* it is held that the 26 weeks does not run from the beginning of each fresh claim for income support, but from the day on which the claimant first took steps to dispose of the property. On its particular facts (it was several years since the property was first put on the market and the claimant had transferred ownership of it to his son for some time but then taken it back) this decision seems right. However, if a property is up for sale, then is genuinely taken off the market and put up for sale again later, it must be arguable that the time under para.26 starts running afresh from the second occasion of taking steps to dispose of the property. This approach is supported by *CIS/2668/1998* and *CJSA/2379/1998* (see in particular para.9). As the Commissioner in those cases confirms, it will depend on the circumstances of each case. See also *SP v SSWP* [2009] UKUT 255 (AAC) which states that para.29585 of the *Decision Makers Guide*, in taking the view that the disregard always runs from the date the person first took steps, does not properly reflect the law on this point. (Note that the current version of para.29585 does acknowledge that there may be exceptional circumstances where the first date may change due to a break in attempts to market the property.)

A further question is how for long the disregard should apply. This again is pre-eminently a question of fact (*SP v SSWP*; *CIS/6908/1995*). In *CIS/6908/1995* the Commissioner suggests some of the factors that might be relevant in deciding whether the 26 weeks should be extended. Besides the efforts made by the claimant to dispose of the property, other factors might be the state of the housing market, the claimant's intentions as regards the proceeds of sale, the value of his interest in the property and his ability to borrow money on the strength of that interest. *SP v SSWP* suggests that a person's state of health may also be a relevant consideration (see *CIS/4757/2003* decided in the context of the disregard under para.3 of this Schedule).

CIS/6908/1995 accepts that the 26 weeks could run while the property was being 2.1001
disregarded under some other paragraph of Sch.10. But it would often be right to extend the period to a date (at least) 26 weeks after the property had ceased to be disregarded under that other paragraph (because otherwise the effect could be to deprive a claimant of the benefit of para.26).

CIS 30/1993 decides that this disregard cannot apply to notional capital if the claimant has already disposed of the same capital so as to trigger reg.51(1). This is because para.26 is only applicable where the *claimant* is taking steps to dispose of premises. The Commissioner in *CIS 30/1993* acknowledges that this view is different from that taken in some other decisions, but having reviewed these (*R(SB) 9/91*, *CIS 25/1990*, *CIS 81/1991* and *CIS 562/1992*) concludes that the only one in which this question had been central to the appeal was *CIS 25/1990* and in that case the point had not been argued in any detail. He was therefore not bound by it (*R1/92 (IS)*, a decision of the Chief Commissioner in Northern Ireland, had come to the same conclusion as he had done). It had been argued on behalf of the claimant that if the property was put up for sale by the actual possessor of it, para.26 should apply. The Secretary of State had submitted, first, that the wording of para.26 made it clear that the disregard only applied if the claimant was taking steps to dispose of the premises; second, that the purpose of the disregard in para.26 was to allow the claimant a reasonable time to liquidate assets to provide money to live on. There could be no guarantee that the third party would allow the proceeds of sale to be used to support the claimant and thus there was no reason to delay counting the notional capital. The Commissioner holds that the words of para.26 were plain and unambiguous and could not apply because the claimant could not be taking steps to dispose of what she had already disposed of. This seems unfair in that a claimant deemed to have notional capital may suffer an additional penalty through not being able to benefit from the disregard in para.26. But the Commissioner's conclusion is cogently argued.

Paragraph 27

In these circumstances the claimant will have an interest in the premises, but it 2.1002
would be unfair to count the value of the interest. The initial disregard is for 26 weeks, with an extension as reasonable.

In *CIS 240/1992* the legal advice given to the claimant was that he could not obtain possession of the premises until the end of the current tenancy. The Commissioner states that for para.27 to apply the claimant must be taking steps to obtain possession and rejects a submission that a failure to take steps that were bound to be unsuccessful did not preclude the application of para.27. But in seeking legal advice was not the claimant taking such steps? Paragraph 27 does not require the claimant to have commenced legal proceedings for the disregard to apply; it is sufficient if he has sought legal advice with a view to obtaining possession. Provided that a claimant is willing to commence proceedings immediately the tenancy ends (which did not appear to be the case in *CIS 240/1992*) it is difficult to see what other steps he could take in such circumstances.

Paragraph 28

2.1003 Since the value of the home is disregarded, this is a limited extension. Then the disregard is for 26 weeks, with an extension as reasonable.

The scope of the similar disregard in para.27 of Sch.5 to the Housing Benefit Regulations was considered in *R. v Tower Hamlets LBC Housing Benefit Review Board Ex p. Kapur, The Times*, June 28, 2000, HC. The claimant, who was in receipt of housing and council tax benefit, owned a house valued at £240,000 which was vacant and unfit for human habitation. He wanted to move into the property and made several unsuccessful attempts to obtain finance to effect repairs to it. The local authority decided that the value of the property could not be disregarded because the steps taken by the applicant to raise finance were merely preparatory and were not steps taken to effect repairs. Scott Baker J held that this was the wrong approach. He referred to the *Adjudication Officer's Guide* which stated, in relation to the income support disregard in para.28, that steps could include getting a grant or loan to pay for repairs or alterations, employing an architect, getting planning permission or finding someone to do the work, and the date that a person first took such steps could be the date he first started making these inquiries. It was a question of fact as to when the first steps were taken but the Board's approach had been too narrow. Now see paras 29572–6 of the *Decision Makers Guide*.

Paragraph 29

2.1004 Payments of earnings or other income in kind are disregarded (see regs 35(2) and 40(4) and Sch.9 para.21). Most payments of capital in kind would be personal possessions (see para.10).

Paragraph 30

2.1005 The new form of this paragraph in force from April 1, 2004 provides a blanket capital disregard of the various allowances, grants and other payments made under s.2 of the Employment and Training Act 1973 or s.2 of the Enterprise and New Towns (Scotland) Act 1990 to people participating in New Deals and other training and welfare to work schemes. However if these payments do count as capital they are only ignored for 52 weeks from the date of receipt.

Before April 1, 2004 separate disregards had existed in respect of such payments under a number of the provisions in this Schedule. As a consequence of this change, those provisions have been revoked or amended. The revoked paragraphs are paras 50, 50A, 51, 53, 69 and 70; the amended paragraph is para.42.

For the income disregard of payments under s.2 of the 1973 Act and s.2 of the 1990 Act see para.13 of Sch.9.

Paragraph 36

2.1006 See the note to para.46 of Sch.9 but if any such payment does count as capital the disregard only applies for 52 weeks from the date of receipt of the payment.

Paragraph 42

2.1007 These are capital payments from special Department of Employment schemes to assist disabled people, such as the "business on own account' scheme and the "personal reader service."

Paragraph 43

2.1008 Start-up capital payments under the Blind Homeworkers' Scheme are disregarded, but payments of income are taken into account.

Paragraphs 44–45

2.1009 These paragraphs were amended in October 1997 so that the disregard of funds held in court that derive from damages for personal injury is no longer restricted to under 18-year-olds but now applies without age limit. However, where the compensation was awarded for the death of a parent (or parents), the person concerned must be under 18 for the disregard to apply. Death benefits under a pension or insurance policy are not compensation, since this implies the replacement of something lost, whereas such benefits are paid on the basis of a contract made by the deceased (*McAuley v Department for Social Development*, Court of Appeal of Northern Ireland, reported as *R 3/01(IS)*).

See para.12 for the disregard of compensation payments for personal injury placed on trust. *CIS 368/1994* decided that the disregard in para.12 applied to compensation for personal injury that was held and administered by the Court of Protection, since in the circumstances such an arrangement amounted to a "trust". (For further discussion of the position of funds held by the Court of Protection, see *R(IS) 9/04* in the note to reg.46.) The disregard in para.44(2)(a) will now apply to damages for personal injury held by the Court of Protection (and also the High Court and the County Court, and, under para.45(a), the equivalent Scottish courts).

The term "Court of Protection" in para.44 is apt to refer to the current Court of Protection (established under the Mental Capacity Act 2005 with effect from October 1, 2007) which replaced the former Court of Protection (which was an office of the Supreme Court constituted under the Mental Health Act 1983) (*R(ZYN) v Walsall MBC* [2014] EWHC 1918 (Admin)).

Note that the award must be for injury "to that person". The disregard under para.44(2)(a) does not apply where the award was under the Fatal Accidents Act 1976 (*CP v SSWP (IS)* [2011] UKUT 157 (AAC)). In *CP v SSWP* the claimant, who had Down's syndrome, received substantial compensation under the 1976 Act after her mother (and primary carer) was killed in a road traffic accident. Paragraph 44(2)(a) did not apply because the personal injury (or rather the fatality) was suffered by the claimant's mother, not the claimant. Furthermore, the fact that it did not apply was not contrary to ECHR. **2.1010**

CP v SSWP also decides that the disregard in para.44(2)(b) only applies while the person concerned is under 18. As the claimant was 22 when she first claimed income support, para.44(2)(b) did not apply.

A new form of para.44 was substituted with effect from October 2, 2006, so that it applies not only to capital administered by a court but also to capital "which can only be disposed of by order or direction of [a] court" (see sub-para.(1)(b) and (c)). This amendment is apparently to allow for the contracting-out of the administering of court funds to the private sector, which the DCA, now the Ministry of Justice, is apparently contemplating.

"Personal injury" includes a disease and any injuries suffered as a result of a disease (e.g. amputation of both legs following meningitis and septicaemia), as well as any accidental or criminal injury (*R(SB) 2/89*). **2.1011**

"An award of damages for a personal injury" covers all heads of an award of damages for personal injury (*Peters v East Midland Strategic Heath Authority* [2009] EWCA Civ 145, [2009] 3 W.L.R. 737). In particular, it is not restricted to general damages for pain, suffering and loss of amenity, but can include other heads of loss, such as loss of earnings and any sum awarded by a court in respect of the cost of providing accommodation and care. See also *R(IS) 15/96* (para.18).

Note that with effect from October 2, 2006, paras 44 and 45 have been added to the list of exceptions from the general rule in reg.48(4) that income from capital counts as capital. Payments to a claimant from funds disregarded under para.44 or 45 will therefore count as income or capital depending on the nature of the payments. The intention is to align the treatment of payments from funds held in court that derive from personal injury with that of payments from trusts of personal injury compensation, and that the disregard in para.15 of Sch.9, which from October 2, 2006 is a total disregard, should equally apply to regular payments from personal injury funds held in court. Presumably it is considered that, applying *CIS/368/1994*, payments from such court funds are covered by para.15(5A)(c) (payments from a trust fund derived from a payment made in consequence of any personal injury to the claimant). In addition, they may fall within para.15(5A)(e) (payments "received by virtue of any agreement or court order to make payments to the claimant in consequence of any personal injury to the claimant"). Note that the income disregard in para.15 of Sch.9 only applies to payments made as a consequence of personal injury to the claimant (see further the notes to para.15 of Sch.9). The disregard in para.15 would not normally seem to apply where the funds held in court are derived from compensation for the death of one or both parents.

Note also that funds disregarded under para.44(2)(a) and para.45(a) are excluded from the notional income rule in reg.42(2) (income available on application) and the notional capital rules in reg.51(1)(c) and (2)(e) (deprivation of capital and capital available on application).

Paragraphs 50, 50A and 51

2.1012 For the previous form of these paragraphs see the 2003 edition of this volume. However they have been omitted with effect from April 1, 2004 because from that date para.30 contains a blanket disregard in relation to payments made under s.2 of the Employment and Training Act 1973 or s.2 of the Enterprise and New Towns (Scotland) Act 1990 to people participating in New Deals and other training and welfare to work schemes. But note that if such payments do count as capital they are only ignored for 52 weeks from the date of receipt. See further the note to para.30.

Paragraph 52

2.1013 Any capital acquired for the purposes of a business carried on while a person is participating in the "self-employment route" (defined in reg.2(1)) is ignored for 52 weeks from the date of receipt.

See also the disregard of business assets for people participating in the self-employment route in para.6(3) and (4) and the general disregard of payments made under s.2 of the Employment and Training Act 1973 or s.2 of the Enterprise and New Towns (Scotland) Act 1990 in para.30.

Paragraph 53

2.1014 See the note to paras 50, 50A and 51 above.

Paragraph 56

2.1015 See the note to para.69 of Sch.9. Note that if a sports award (or part of it) counts as capital, the payment will only be disregarded for 26 weeks from the date of receipt.

Paragraphs 58 and 59

2.1016 See the note to reg.42(5A).

Paragraph 60

2.1017 This paragraph has not been reproduced as it only related to a pilot scheme to reduce under-occupation operating in three London boroughs (Croydon, Haringey and Newham) from April 3, 2000. It was added by reg.12 of the Social Security (Payments to Reduce Under-occupation) Regulations 2000 (SI 2000/637) on April 3, 2000 and provided that a payment made under the scheme would be ignored for 52 weeks from the date of payment. The pilot scheme lasted for three years and the Payments to Reduce Under-occupation Regulations ceased to have effect on March 31, 2003.

Paragraph 61

2.1018 This allows ex-gratia payments of £10,000, made to former Japanese prisoners of war or to their surviving spouse or civil partner, on or after February 1, 2001, to be disregarded indefinitely.

Paragraph 62

2.1019 This provides for the whole of a claimant's capital to be disregarded during any "mortgage run-on" period. See the notes to reg.6(5)–(8) as to when this applies (note that from December 17, 2007 it has been extended so that it now applies to all housing costs that can be met by income support). See also the disregards in para.15C of Sch.8 and para.74 of Sch.9 and the note to para.15C.

Paragraph 63

See the note to para.11 of Sch.9. Note that the new form of para.63 in force from the start of the national scheme of education maintenance allowances (EMAs) provides for an indefinite disregard of any part of the EMA that counts as capital. **2.1020**

The October 31, 2011 amendments to para.63 allow for payments made from the "16–19 Bursary Fund" to be disregarded in the same way as EMAs. The bursary scheme was introduced in September 2011 to help vulnerable 16–19 year olds continue in full-time education and replaces the education maintenance allowance in England.

Paragraph 64

This refers to payments from, or derived from, the government-funded trust funds set up to help those who have contracted variant Creutsfeldt-Jakob disease. The disregard extends to distribution of capital to the partner of the "diagnosed person" (defined in sub-para.(6)), to any child for two years from the date of the payment, or until he leaves full-time education or becomes 20, if this is later, or to any parent for two years from the date of the payment. **2.1021**

Paragraph 65

This provides for an indefinite disregard of compensation paid because the claimant, his partner, his deceased spouse or deceased civil partner or his partner's deceased spouse or deceased civil partner was forced to work, lost property or suffered personal injury, or was the parent of a child who died, during the Second World War. **2.1022**

Paragraph 66

See the note to para.76 of Sch.9. **2.1023**

Paragraph 67

This disregard has been introduced to ensure that if payments for community care services which a local authority makes direct to the person concerned do count as capital they are not taken into account. For the income disregard see para.58 of Sch.9. **2.1024**

Modification of para.67

With effect from April 1, 2014, the disregard in para.67 is modified by art.2 of, and para.1 of the Schedule to, the Social Care (Self-directed Support) (Scotland) Act 2013 (Consequential Modifications and Savings) Order 2014 (SI 2014/513) so that the words "as a direct payment as defined in section 4(2) of the Social Care (Self-directed Support) (Scotland) Act 2013" are substituted for the words "under section 12B of the Social Work (Scotland) 1968". However, under art.3 of the Order, this modification does not apply if a payment is made under s.12B of the 1968 Act on or after April 1, 2014. **2.1025**

Paragraph 68

For the regulations under ss.2(6)(b), 3 or 4 of the Adoption and Children Act 2002 see the Adoption Support Services Regulations 2005 (SI 2005/691) and the Adoption Support Services (Local Authorities) (Wales) Regulations 2005 (SI 2005/1512). Any payments to adopters or potential adopters made under these provisions are fully disregarded. **2.1026**

Paragraph 68A

Section 115 of the Adoption and Children Act 2002 amended the Children Act 1989 to introduce a new special guardianship order, which is intended to provide permanence for children for whom adoption is not appropriate; the special guardian has parental responsibility for the child but the child's legal relationship with his birth parents is not severed. The special guardianship provisions came into force on December 30, 2005. Payments made by local authorities to special guardians are ignored. For the income disregard see para.25(1)(e) of Sch.9. **2.1027**

Paragraphs 69 and 70

2.1028 For the previous form of these paragraphs, which concerned the Employment, Retention and Advancement ("ERA") scheme and the Return to Work Credit scheme respectively, see the 2003/2004 Supplement to this volume. However these paragraphs have been omitted with effect from April 1, 2004 because from that date para.30 contains a blanket disregard in relation to payments made under s.2 of the Employment and Training Act 1973 or s.2 of the Enterprise and New Towns (Scotland) Act 1990 to people participating in New Deals and other training and welfare to work schemes. But note that if such payments do count as capital they are only ignored for 52 weeks from the date of receipt. See further the note to para.30.

Paragraph 71

2.1029 This provides for a capital disregard of payments under s.49 of the Children and Families Act 2014. See further the annotation to para.79 of Sch.9, under which payments under s.49 are disregarded as income.

The Income Support (Liable Relatives) Regulations 1990

(SI 1990/1777) (AS AMENDED)

Made by the Secretary of State under s.166(1) to (3A) of the Social Security Act 1975 and ss.24A(1), 24B(5) and 84(1) of the Social Security Act 1986

Citation, commencement and interpretation

2.1030 **1.**—(1) These Regulations may be cited as the Income Support (Liable Relatives) Regulations 1990 and shall come into force on 15th October 1990.

(2) In these Regulations—

"the Act" means the Social Security Act 1986; and

"the Income Support Regulations" means the Income Support (General) Regulations 1987.

Prescribed amounts for the purposes of section 24A of the Act [SSAA, s.107]

2.1031 **2.**—(1) For the purposes of section 24A of the Act [SSAA, s.107] (recovery of expenditure on income support: additional amounts and transfer of orders) the amount which may be included in the sum which the court may order the other parent to pay under section 24(4) of the Act [SSAA, s.106(2)] shall be the whole of the following amounts which are payable to or for the claimant—

(a) any personal allowance under paragraph 2 of Part I of Schedule 2 to the Income Support Regulations for each of the children whom the other parent is liable to maintain;

(b) any family premium under paragraph 3 of Part II of that Schedule;

(c) any lone parent premium under paragraph 8 of Part III of that Schedule;

(d) any disabled child premium under paragraph 14 of Part III of that Schedule in respect of a child whom the other parent is liable to maintain; and

(e) any carer premium under paragraph 14ZA of Part III of that Schedule if, but only if, that premium is payable because the claimant is in receipt, or is treated as being in receipt, of [1 a carer's allowance] by reason of the fact that he is caring for a severely disabled child or young person whom the other parent is liable to maintain.

(2) If the court is satisfied that in addition to the amounts specified in paragraph (1) above the liable parent has the means to pay, the sum which the court may order him to pay under section 24 of the Act [SSAA, s.106] may also include all or some of the amount of any personal allowance payable to or for the claimant under paragraph 1 of Part I of Schedule 2 to the Income Support Regulations.

AMENDMENT

1. Social Security Amendment (Carer's Allowance) Regulations 2002 (SI 2002/2497) reg.3 and Sch.2 (April 1, 2003).

Notice to the Secretary of State of applications to alter etc. maintenance orders

3.—(1) For the purposes of section 24B(5) of the Act [SSAA, s.108(5)] **2.1032**
(prescribed person in prescribed circumstances to notify the Secretary of State of application to alter etc. a maintenance order) the prescribed person is, and in paragraph (2) below that expression means,—

(a) in England and Wales—
   (i) in relation to the High Court, where the case is proceeding in the deputy principal registry the senior registrar of that registry, and where the case is proceeding in a district registry the district registrar;
   (ii) in relation to a county court, the proper officer of that court within the meaning of Order 1, Rule 3 of the County Court Rules 1981; and
   (iii) in relation to a magistrates' court, the clerk to the justices of that court; and
(b) in Scotland—
   (i) in relation to the Court of Session, the deputy principal clerk of session; and
   (ii) in relation to a sheriff court, the sheriff clerk.

(2) For the purposes of that subsection the prescribed circumstances are that before the final determination of the application the Secretary of State has made a written request to the prescribed person that he be notified of any such application, and has not made a written withdrawal of that request.

GENERAL NOTE

See the notes to ss.107 and 108 of the Administration Act in Vol.III of **2.1033**
this series.

The Income Support (Transitional) Regulations 1987

(SI 1987/1969)

2.1034 *These regulations have been omitted in order to save space and because they are now only likely to be relevant to a very few cases. For the full text of these Regulations, see Vol.II of Social Security Legislation 2000*

The Income Support (General) Amendment No.6 Regulations 1991

(SI 1991/2334) (AS AMENDED)

Made by the Secretary of State under ss.22(1) and 84(1) of the Social Security Act 1986 and s.166(1) to (3A) of the Social Security Act 1975

[IN FORCE NOVEMBER 11, 1991]

Saving Provision in relation to Severe Disability Premium

2.1035 4.—(1) The provisions of this regulation are subject to regulation 5.

(2) Where paragraph (3), (4), (5) or (6) applies to a claimant, sub-paragraph (2)(a)(ii), or, as the case may be, sub-paragraph (2)(b)(iii) of paragraph 13 of Schedule 2 to the General Regulations shall have effect as if the relevant amendment had not been made.

(3) This paragraph applies to a claimant who satisfied both the qualifying conditions in the week immediately preceding 21st October 1991.

(4) This paragraph applies to a claimant—

(a) who satisfied both the qualifying conditions in at least one of the eight weeks immediately preceding 21st October 1991, but did not satisfy either or both of those conditions in the week immediately preceding that date; and

(b) who in a week commencing not more than eight weeks after the date on which he last satisfied both the qualifying conditions, would again have satisfied both those conditions if the relevant amendment had not been made.

(5) This paragraph applies to a claimant—

(a) who ceased to be entitled to income support because he became engaged in remunerative work for a period not exceeding the permitted period determined in accordance with regulation 6 and that period had commenced but had not ended before 21st October 1991; and

(b) who satisfied both the qualifying conditions in the week ending on the day before the first day of that period commenced; and

(c) who in the week which commences on the day immediately following the day on which that period ends, would again have satisfied both the qualifying conditions if the relevent amendment had not been made.

(6) This paragraph applies to a claimant—

(a) who satisfied both the qualifying conditions immediately before he—

(i) participated in arrangements for training made under section 2 of the Employment and Training Act 1973 or section 2 of the Enterprise and New Towns (Scotland) Act 1990; or

(ii) attended a course at an employment rehabilitation centre established under section 2 of the Employment and Training Act 1973,

and he had begun the training or joined the course before 21st October 1991 and was still continuing with the training or course at that date; and

(b) who in the week which commences on the day immediately following the last day he attended the training or course, would again have satisfied both the qualifying conditions if the relevant amendment had not been made.

(7) The "qualifying conditions" means the two qualifying conditions set out in paragraph (8)(a) and (b) below.

(8) For the purposes of paragraph (7)—

(a) the first qualifying condition is that the claimant—

(i) has made a claim for income support which has not been determined, but had it been determined and an award made, his applicable amount would have included severe disability premium; or

(ii) has a current award of income support and the applicable amount appropriate to that award includes severe disability premium; or

(iii) has a current award of income support and has before 21st October 1991 made an application in writing in accordance with section 104(2) of the Social Security Act requesting a review of that award, where the ground, or one of the grounds for review, is that—

(aa) he has become a co-owner with a close relative of the dwelling which he and that close relative jointly occupy as their home; or

(bb) he has become jointly liable with a close relative to make payments to a landlord in respect of the dwelling which he and that close relative jointly occupy as their home,

whether or not there are other co-owners or other persons jointly liable to make such payments and, if revised, the applicable amount appropriate to the award includes severe disability premium in respect of a period prior to that date;

(b) the second qualifying condition is that the person is—

(i) a co-owner, with a close relative, of the dwelling he and that close relative jointly occupy as their home, whether or not there are other co-owners; or

(ii) jointly liable, with a close relative, to make payments to a landlord in respect of the dwelling he and that close relative jointly occupy as their home, whether or not there are other persons jointly liable to make such payments.

[[1](9) For the purposes of paragraph (8)(b) and regulation 5(2)(b), where a person has satisfied the second qualifying condition, but his circumstances change so that he no longer satisfies it, he shall nonetheless be treated as satisfying it for so long as he is a person to whom paragraph (10) applies.

(10) This paragraph applies to a person—

(a) who was, together with a close relative of his, either a co-owner of, or jointly liable to make payments to a landlord in respect of, the dwelling which he and that close relative jointly occupied as their home; and

(b) who has since become, with that close relative or any other close relative, either—

(i) jointly liable to make payments to a landlord in respect of that dwelling or any other dwelling; or

(ii) a co-owner of that dwelling or any other dwelling,

which he and the close relative jointly occupy as their home (whether or not there are other co-owners, or other persons jointly liable to make such payments).]

AMENDMENT

1. Income-related Benefits Schemes (Miscellaneous Provisions) Amendment Regulations 1991 (SI 1991/2695) reg.5 (December 27, 1991).

DEFINITIONS

"claimant"—see Income Support Regulations reg.2(1).
"close relative"—*ibid.*
"dwelling occupies as the home"—*ibid.*
"partner"—*ibid.*
"permitted period"—see reg.6.
"relevant amendment"—see General Note.
"remunerative work"—see Income Support Regulations reg.2(1).
"Social Security Act"—*ibid.*

GENERAL NOTE

2.1036 The "relevant amendment" is the amendment to the definition of non-dependant in reg.3 of the Income Support Regulations with effect from November 11, 1991, by reg.2 of these Regulations (reg.1(3)). These Regulations were made on October 21, 1991, which is why that is the date used in reg.4 to fix the transitional protection. Regulation 4 allows existing claimants to continue to receive the benefit of the severe disability premium where they previously met the new conditions for joint occupiers of the home, except that the joint occupation was with a close relative.

Regulation 5 defines when the protection of reg.4 ceases to apply.

Circumstances in which regulation 4 ceases to apply

2.1037 **5.**—(1) Regulation 4 shall cease to apply to a claimant, or his partner, on the relevant day and shall not apply on any day thereafter.

(2) The relevant day is the first day after a period of eight consecutive weeks throughout which—

(a) subject to paragraph (3), he is not entitled to income support; or

(b) he is unable to satisfy, or be treated as satisfying, the second qualifying condition.

(3) For the purpose of calculating a period in excess of eight weeks in paragraph (2)(a) above the following periods shall be disregarded—

(a) where the claimant, or his partner, becomes engaged in remunerative work, any period during which he, or his partner, was not entitled to income support, not exceeding the permitted period determined in accordance with regulation 6;

(b) any period during which the claimant, or his partner, was participating in arrangements for training made under section 2 of the Employment and Training Act 1973 or section 2 of the Enterprise and New Towns (Scotland) Act 1990 or attending a course at an employment rehabilitation centre established under section 2 of the Employment and Training Act 1973.

DEFINITIONS

"claimant"—see Income Support Regulations reg.2(1).
"partner"—*ibid.*
"permitted period"—see reg.6.
"qualifying condition"—see reg.4(7).

Definition of "permitted period" for the purposes of regulations 4 and 5

6.—(1) For the purposes of regulations 4(5) and 5(3)(a), where a claimant has ceased to be entitled to income support because he or his partner became engaged in remunerative work, [1. . .] the permitted period shall be a period of 12 consecutive weeks. **2.1038**

(2) [1 . . .]
(3) [1 . . .]

AMENDMENT

1. Income Support (General) (Jobseeker's Allowance Consequential Amendments) Regulations 1996 (SI 1996/206) reg.31 (October 7, 1996).

DEFINITIONS

"claimant"—see Income Support Regulations reg.2(1).
"partner"—*ibid.*
"relevant education"—see Income Support Regulations reg.12.
"remunerative work"—see Income Support Regulations reg.2(1).
"student"—*ibid.*

The Income Support (General) Amendment No.3 Regulations 1993

(SI 1993/1679)

Made by the Secretary of State under ss.135(1), 136(5)(b), 137(1) and 175(1) to (4) of the Social Security Contributions and Benefits Act 1992

[In force August 2, 1993]

2.—(4) In the case of a claimant who was entitled to income support by virtue of regulation 70 of the Income Support Regulations for the benefit week which includes 2nd August 1993, then in respect of each day after that date on which the claimant's entitlement to income support continues, regulation 70 shall continue to apply in his case as if the preceding provisions of this regulation had not been made. **2.1039**

General Note

2.1040 See the notes to reg.70(3) in the 1995 edition of J. Mesher and R. Wood, *Income-related Benefits: the Legislation*. Regulation 70(3) was amended by reg.2(1)–(3) of these Regulations on August 2, 1993.

Saving

2.1041 **4.**—(1) In the case of a claimant who was entitled to income support for the benefit week which included 2nd August 1993 then, but subject to paragraph (3), in respect of each day after that date on which the claimant's entitlement to income support continues, Schedule 3 to the Income Support Regulations shall continue to apply in his case as if regulation 3 of these Regulations had not been made.

(2) Heads (c) to (f) of sub-paragraph (9) of paragraph 7 of Schedule 3 to the Income Support Regulations shall apply to paragraph (1) above as they apply to sub-paragraph (1) of paragraph 7, but with the modification that for the words "in receipt of income support", wherever they occur, there were substituted the words "entitled to income support" and that the words "Subject to sub-paragraphs (10) and (11)" were omitted.

(3) In its application to any loan taken out or increased after 2nd August 1993 Schedule 3 to the Income Support Regulations shall have effect as amended by regulation 3 of these Regulations.

(4) Paragraphs (1) and (3) above shall apply as from 11th April 1994 as if for the references to "2nd August 1993" wherever they occur there were substituted references to "11th April 1994".

General Note

2.1042 See the notes to para.7(6B)–(6F) of the former Sch.3 to the Income Support Regulations in the 1995 edition of J. Mesher and P. Wood, *Income-related Benefits: the Legislation*. Paragraph 7 of the former Sch.3 was amended by reg.3 of these regulations on August 2, 1993. See also notes to para.11(4)–(11) of the new Sch.3.

The Income-related Benefits Schemes (Miscellaneous Amendments) (No.3) Regulations 1994

(SI 1994/1807)

Made by the Secretary of State under ss.131(3)(b), 135(1), 137(1) and (2)(i) and 175(1), (3) and (4) of the Social Security Contributions and Benefits Act 1992

[In force August 1, 1994]

General Note

2.1043 See the amendment to reg.21(3) of the Income Support Regulations inserted by reg.4(1) of these Regulations.

These regulations were revoked by reg.11(1)(a) of the Social Security (Persons From Abroad) Amendment Regulations 2006 (SI 2006/1026) with effect from April 30, 2006.

The Disability Working Allowance and Income Support (General) Amendment Regulations 1995

(SI 1995/482) (AS AMENDED)

Made by the Secretary of State under ss.124(1)(d)(i) and (3), 129(2B)(b) and (c) and (8), 135(1), 137(1) and 175(1), (3) and (4) of the Social Security Contributions and Benefits Act 1992 and s.12(1) of the Social Security (Incapacity for Work) Act 1994

[In force April 13, 1995]

Transitional provisions with respect to the Income Support Regulations

19.—(1) Sickness benefit shall be a qualifying benefit for the purposes of regulation 9(2)(a)(i) of the Income Support Regulations, and for this purpose "sickness benefit" means sickness benefit under section 31 of the Social Security Contributions and Benefits Act 1992 as in force on 12th April 1995. 2.1044

(2) Where the disability premium was applicable to a claimant on 12th April 1995 by virtue of paragraph 12(1)(b) of Schedule 2 to the Income Support Regulations as in force on that date, the disability premium shall continue to be applicable to that claimant for so long as paragraph 12(1)(b)(i) of that Schedule applies to him.

(3) Paragraph (2) shall not apply to a claimant to whom paragraph 12(1)(b)(i) of Schedule 2 to the Income Support Regulations has ceased to apply for a period of more than 56 continuous days.

(4) Where on 12th April 1995 paragraph 5 of Schedule 1 to the Income Support Regulations (persons incapable of work) as in force on that date applied to a claimant, but the disability premium was not applicable to him, that claimant shall be treated for the purposes of paragraph 12(1) of Schedule 2 to the Income Support Regulations as if, throughout the period that paragraph 5 of Schedule 1 had applied to him, paragraph 12(1)(b)(i) of Schedule 2 applied to him.

(5) [[2] Where it is determined on or after 13th April, 1995] that a claimant fails to satisfy the incapacity for work test, in accordance with regulations made under section 171C of the Contributions and Benefits Act (the all work test), on its first application to the claimant concerned, and the claimant, immediately prior to [[1]13th April 1995], was either—

(a) incapable of work and had been so for a continuous period of 28 weeks in circumstances to which paragraph 5 of Schedule 1 of the Income Support Regulations refers (persons incapable of work not required to be available for employment); or

(b) in receipt of invalidity benefit or severe disablement allowance,

then, in a case in which either regulations 8(2A) or 11(2A) of the Income Support Regulations applies (persons not required to be available for employment and registration for employment), notwithstanding regulation 22(1A) and (5A) of the Income Support Regulations (reductions in applicable amounts), the amount of any income support to which the claimant is entitled shall be calculated in accordance with regulation 17 of those Regulations.

[1(6) Where—

(a) a determination of the amount of a person's benefit has been made in a case to which paragraph (5) of this regulation, as originally made, had effect; and

(b) an appeal to which regulation 8(2A) or 11(2A) of the Income Support Regulations (persons not required to be available or registered for employment) refers, remains outstanding on 2nd October 1995;

the amount of any benefit to which he is entitled shall continue to be determined under paragraph (5), as originally made, until the determination of the appeal.]

AMENDMENTS

1. Income-related Benefits Schemes and Social Security (Claims and Payments) (Miscellaneous Amendments) Regulations 1995 (SI 1995/2303) reg.8(2) (October 2, 1995).

2. Social Security Act 1998 (Commencement No.9 and Savings and Consequential and Transitional Provisions) Order 1999 (SI 1999/2422 (C.61)) art.3(12) and Sch.11 (September 6, 1999).

Savings with respect to the Income Support Regulations

2.1045 **20.**—(1) Where a person was not required to be available for employment on 12th April 1995 by virtue of regulation 8(2) of the Income Support Regulations as in force on that date, that regulation shall continue to apply in that person's case as if regulation 6 of these Regulations had not been made.

(2) Where a claimant was not required to register for employment on 12th April 1995 by virtue of regulation 11(2) of the Income Support Regulations as in force on that date, that regulation shall continue to apply in that claimant's case as if regulation 8 of these Regulations had not been made.

(3) Where a claimant appeals against a decision of an adjudication officer that he is not incapable of work, and that decision was made on or before 12th April 1995, regulations 8 and 11 of the Income Support Regulations shall apply in that claimant's case as if these Regulations had not been made.

(4) Where the higher pensioner premium was applicable to a claimant on, or at any time during the 8 weeks immediately preceding, 12th April 1995 by virtue of paragraph 12(1)(c)(i) of Schedule 2 to the Income Support Regulations as in force on that date, paragraph 12 of that Schedule shall continue to apply in that claimant's case as if regulation 16 of these Regulations had not been made.

GENERAL NOTE

2.1046 These transitional and saving provisions relate to some of the amendments made to the Income Support Regulations as a consequence of the introduction of incapacity benefit and the new tests for deciding incapacity for work from April 13, 1995. See the notes to reg.22A of, and paras 24–25 of Sch.1B to, the Income Support Regulations.

Regulation 19(5) was amended on October 2, 1995 to make it clear that it only applied to people who had been incapable of work for 28 weeks or in receipt of invalidity benefit or severe disablement allowance immediately before April 13, 1995 (and not to people who were so incapable, etc. by the date of the adjudication officer's decision). Regulation 19(6) allows payment of full income support under the previous form of reg.19(5) to those whose appeals are outstanding on October 2, 1995 until the appeal has been determined. This should mean the final determination of the appeal, e.g. if it is taken to the Social Security Commissioner (now Upper Tribunal).

See the further transitional protection in reg.27(3) of the Income Support (General) (Jobseeker's Allowance Consequential Amendments) Regulations 1996 (p.806).

The Income-related Benefits Schemes (Miscellaneous Amendments) Regulations 1995

(SI 1995/516)

Made by the Secretary of State under ss.123(1)(a) to (c), 128(5), 129(4) and (8), 135(1), 136(3), (5)(a) and (b), 137(1), (2)(c) and (d)(i) and 175(1), (3) and (4) of the Social Security Contributions and Benefits Act 1992

[In force April 10, 1995]

Saving

28.—(1) In the case of a claimant who was entitled to income support for the benefit week which included 9th April 1995 then, but subject to paragraph (3), in respect of each day after that date on which the claimant's entitlement to income support continues, Schedule 3 to the Income Support Regulations shall continue to have effect as though regulation 25(c) of these Regulations had not been made. **2.1047**

(2) Heads (c) to (f) of sub-paragraph (9) of paragraph 7 of Schedule 3 to the Income Support Regulations shall apply to paragraph (1) above as they apply to sub-paragraph (1) of paragraph 7, but with the modification that for the words "in receipt of income support", wherever they appear, there were substituted the words "entitled to income support" and that the words "Subject to sub-paragraphs (10) and (11)" were omitted.

(3) In its application to any loan taken out or increased after 9th April 1995, Schedule 3 to the Income Support Regulations shall have effect as amended by regulation 25(c) of these Regulations.

Definition

"claimant"—see Income Support Regulations reg.2(1).

General Note

See the notes to para.7(6B)–(6F) of the former Sch.3 to the Income Support Regulations in the 1995 edition of J. Mesher and P. Wood, *Income-related Benefits: the Legislation*. Paragraph 7(6C) of the former Sch.3 was amended by reg.25(c) of these Regulations on April 10, 1995. See also the notes to para.11(4)–(11) of the new Sch.3. **2.1048**

The Social Security (Income Support and Claims and Payments) Amendment Regulations 1995

(SI 1995/1613)

Made by the Secretary of State under ss.135(1), 136(5)(b), 137(1) and 175(1) and (3)–(5) of the Social Security Contributions and Benefits Act 1992 and ss.5(1)(p). 15A(2), 189(1) and (4) and 191 of the Social Security Administration Act 1992

[In force October 2, 1995]

Revocations and savings

2.1049 **5.**—(2) The revocation by paragraph (1) above and Schedule 4 to these Regulations of any provision previously amended or substituted but subject to a saving for existing beneficiaries does not affect the continued operation of those savings.

General Note

2.1050 See the notes to para.11(4)–(11) of Sch.3 to the Income Support Regulations.

The Income Support (General) Amendment and Transitional Regulations 1995

(SI 1995/2287)

Made by the Secretary of State under ss.135(1), 137(1) and 175(1) and (3) to (5) of the Social Security Contributions and Benefits Act 1992

[In force October 2, 1995]

Transitional protection

2.1051 **3.**—(1) Where a claimant for income support whose applicable amount, in the benefit week which included 1st October 1995, included an amount in respect of the interest on a loan or part of a loan by virtue of paragraph 7(6), 7(7) or 8(1)(a) of Schedule 3 to the Income Support Regulations (housing costs) ("the former paragraphs") as then in force and that loan or part of a loan is not a qualifying loan for the purposes of paragraphs 15 and 16 of Schedule 3 to the Income Support Regulations, paragraphs (2) and (3) shall have effect in his case.

(2) A loan or part of a loan to which paragraph (1) applies shall qualify as a loan to which paragraph 15 or 16, as the case may be, of Schedule 3 to the Income Support Regulations applies, for as long as any of the former paragraphs would have continued to be satisfied had it remained in force and the claimant remains in receipt of income support or is treated as being in receipt of income support.

(3) Heads (a), (c) and (e) of sub-paragraph (1) of paragraph 14 of Schedule 3 to the Income Support Regulations shall apply to paragraph (2) above as they apply to Schedule 3, but as if the words "Subject to sub-paragraph (2)" at the beginning were omitted.

DEFINITION

"claimant"—see Income Support Regulations reg.2(1).

GENERAL NOTE

See the note to para.7 of Sch.3 to the Income Support Regulations. 2.1052

The Income-related Benefits Schemes and Social Security (Claims and Payments) (Miscellaneous Amendments) Regulations 1995

(SI 1995/2303)

Made by the Secretary of State under ss.123(1), 124(1)(d), 129(3), 130(2) and (4), 135(1), 136(1) and (3)–(5), 137(1) and (2)(b), (d), (h), (i) and (l) and 175(1) and (3)–(6) of the Social Security Contributions and Benefits Act 1992 and ss.5(1)(h), (i) and (o), 6(1)(h) and (i) and 189 of the Social Security Administration Act

[In force October 2, 1995]

Transitional provision with respect to the Income Support Regulations

8.—(1) In determining whether a claimant is entitled to income support on or after 2nd October 1995 and whether he satisfies the provisions of either— 2.1053

(a) regulation 4(2)(c)(v) of the Income Support Regulations(temporary absence from Great Britain); or

(b) paragraph 7 of Schedule 1 to those Regulations (disabled students not required to be available for work);

in a case where the claimant, for a period up to and including 12th April 1995, was continuously incapable of work for the purposes of paragraph 5 of Schedule 1 to the Income Support Regulations, as it was then in force, that period of incapacity shall be treated as forming part of a subsequent period of incapacity beginning not later than 7th June 1995 to which the provisions referred to in paragraphs (a) or (b) above refer and which is continuous to the date of the determination in question.

DEFINITION

"claimant"—see Income Support Regulations reg.2(1).

GENERAL NOTE

See the notes to reg.4(2)(c)(v) of the Income Support Regulations. For para.7 of Sch.1 see the 1996 edition of J. Mesher and P. Wood, *Income-related Benefits: the Legislation*. 2.1054

The Income Support (General) (Jobseeker's Allowance Consequential Amendments) Regulations 1996

(SI 1996/206) (AS AMENDED)

Made by the Secretary of State under s.40 of the Jobseekers Act 1995 and ss.124(1)(e), 137(1) and 175(1) to (4) of the Social Security Contributions and Benefits Act 1992

[In force October 7, 1996]

Transitional provisions

2.1055 **27.**—(1) Where on 6th October 1996 or at any time during the eight weeks immediately preceding that date paragraph 4(1) of Schedule 1 to the principal Regulations (persons caring for another person) as in force on that date applied to a claimant, or would have applied to him if he had made a claim for income support the claimant shall be treated for the purposes of paragraphs 5 and 6 of Schedule 1B to the principal Regulations as if, throughout the period that paragraph 4(1) of Schedule 1 applied or would have applied to him, paragraph 4 of Schedule 1B had applied or would have applied to him.

(2) Where on 6th October 1996 paragraph 5 of Schedule 1 to the principal Regulations (persons incapable of work) as in force on that date applied to a claimant, the claimant shall be treated for the purposes of regulation 4(2)(c)(v) of and paragraph 10 of Schedule 1B to the principal Regulations as if, throughout the period that paragraph 5 of Schedule 1 applied to him, paragraph 7 of Schedule 1B had applied to him.

(3) Where—

(a) a determination of the amount of a person's benefit has been made in a case to which regulation 19(5) of The Disability Working Allowance and Income Support (General) Amendment Regulations 1995 as originally made had effect (amendments consequential on the coming into force of the Social Security (Incapacity for Work) Act 1994: transitional provisions); and

(b) an appeal to which regulations 8(2A) or 11(2A) of the principal Regulations as in force on 2nd October 1995 referred (persons not required to be available or registered for employment), has still to be determined,

regulation 22A(1) of the principal Regulations (reduction in applicable amount where the claimant is appealing against a decision that he is not incapable of work) shall not apply to that person.

DEFINITION

"claimant"—see Income Support Regulations reg.2(1).

GENERAL NOTE

2.1056 These transitional provisions relate to the some of the changes made to the income support scheme as a result of the introduction of JSA on October 7, 1996. On para.(3) see the notes to regs 19 and 20 of the Disability Working Allowance and Income Support (General) Amendment Regulations 1995 on p.802 and reg.22A of the Income Support Regulations.

Continuity with jobseeker's allowance

32.—In determining whether a person is entitled to income support [1or is to be treated as being in receipt of income support or whether any amount is applicable or payable— 2.1057

(a) entitlement to an income-based jobseeker's allowance shall be treated as entitlement to income support for the purposes of any requirement that a person is or has been entitled to income support for any period of time; and

(b) a person who is treated as being in receipt of income-based jobseeker's allowance shall be treated as being in receipt of income support for the purposes of any requirement that he is or has been treated as being in receipt of income support for any period of time.]

AMENDMENT

1. Income-related Benefits Schemes and Social Fund (Miscellaneous Amendments) Regulations 1996 (SI 1996/1944) reg.12 (October 7, 1996).

GENERAL NOTE

Paragraph (a) of this important provision allows entitlement to income-based JSA to count as entitlement to income support for the purposes of satisfying any requirement that the person is or has been entitled to income support for any period of time. Paragraph (b) has the same effect where the requirement is that the person is or has been treated as being in receipt of income support. This could be relevant, for example, in relation to waiting periods or the linking rules for payment of housing costs. For the JSA provision see para.18(1)(c) of Sch.2 to the JSA Regulations 1996; for the ESA provision see para.20(1)(c) of Sch.6 to the ESA Regulations 2008 in Vol.I of this series. 2.1058

The Income-related Benefits and Jobseeker's Allowance (Personal Allowances for Children and Young Persons) (Amendment) Regulations 1996

(SI 1996/2545)

Made by the Secretary of State under ss.128(1)(a)(i) and (5), 129(1)(c)(i) and (8), 135(1), 136(3) and (4), 137(1) and 175(1), (3) and (4) of the Social Security Contributions and Benefits Act 1992 and ss.4(5), 35(1) and 36(1), (2) and (4) of the Jobseekers Act 1995

[In force April 7, 1997].

Transitional provisions

10.—(1) Where, in relation to a claim for income support, jobseeker's allowance, housing benefit or council tax benefit, a claimant's weekly applicable amount includes a personal allowance in respect of one or more children or young persons who are, as at the day before the appropriate date these Regulations come into force for the purpose of those benefits in accordance with regulation 1 of these Regulations (referred to in this regulation as "the appropriate date"), aged 11, 16 or 18, the provisions specified in regulation 2(7) of these Regulations shall have effect, for the period specified in paragraph (2) below, as if regulation 2 of these Regulations had not been made. 2.1059

(2) The period specified for the purposes of paragraph (1) above shall be, in relation to each particular child or young person referred to in that paragraph, the period beginning on the appropriate date and ending—

(a) where that child or young person is aged 11 or 16 as at the day before the appropriate date, on 31st August 1997;

(b) where that young person is aged 18 as at the day before the appropriate date, on the day preceding the day that young person ceases to be a person of a prescribed description for the purposes of regulation 14 of the Income Support Regulations, regulation 76 of the Jobseeker's Allowance Regulations, regulation 13 of the Housing Benefit Regulations or regulation 5 of the Council Tax Benefit Regulations.

DEFINITIONS

"child"—see SSCBA s.137(1).
"claimant"—see Income Support Regulations reg.2(1).
"young person"—see Income Support Regulations regs 2(1) and 14.

GENERAL NOTE

2.1060 See the notes to para.2 of Sch.2 to the Income Support Regulations. Paragraph 2 of Sch.2 and para.2 of Sch.1 to the JSA Regulations 1996 were amended by reg.2 of these Regulations on April 7, 1997.

The weekly amount for a person aged not less than 18 in sub-para.(d) of the previous form of para.2 of Sch.2 and para.2 of Sch.1 to the JSA Regulations was increased to £38.90 from April 7, 1997 (Social Security Benefits Up-rating Order 1997 (SI 1997/543) art.18(4) and 24(4)). The weekly amounts in sub-paras (a), (b) and (c) were also increased and were the same as the amounts in sub-paras (a), (b) and (c) of the 1997 form of the respective paras.

The Social Security Amendment (Capital Limits and Earnings Disregards) Regulations 2000

(SI 2000/2545) (AS AMENDED)

Made by the Secretary of State under ss.123(1)(a), (d) and (e), 134(1), 136(2) and (5)(b) and (d), 137(1) and 175(1), (3) and (4) of the Social Security Contributions and Benefits Act 1992 and ss.12(4)(b) and (d), 13(1) and (3), 35(1) and 36(1), (2) and (4) of the Jobseekers Act 1995

[In force April 9, 2001]

Saving

2.1061 **4.**—[1 . . .], paragraph 4(4)(c) of Schedule 8 to the Income Support Regulations and paragraph 5(4)(c) of Schedule 6 to the Jobseeker's Allowance Regulations shall have effect as if regulation 3 above had not been made in a case where the claimant was entitled, by virtue of sub-paragraph (2) or (3) of those paragraphs as in force immediately before the coming into force of these Regulations, to a disregard of £15.

AMENDMENT

1. Housing Benefit and Council Tax Benefit (Consequential Provisions) Regulations 2006 (SI 2006/217) reg.3 and Sch.1 (March 6, 2006).

GENERAL NOTE

See the note to para.4 of Sch.8 to the Income Support Regulations. Paragraph 4 of Sch.8 and para.5 of Sch.6 to the JSA Regulations 1996 were amended by reg.3 of, and the Sch. to, these Regulations on April 9, 2001. **2.1062**

The Child Support (Consequential Amendments and Transitional Provisions) Regulations 2001

(SI 2001/158) (AS AMENDED)

Made by the Secretary of State under s.29(2) of the Child Support, Pensions and Social Security Act 2000

[In force in relation to a particular case on the date on which s.1 of the 2000 Act comes into force in relation to that type of case]

PART III

SAVINGS

Savings for particular cases

10.—[1 (Z1) This regulation is subject to the Child Support (Transitional Provisions) Regulations 2000.] **2.1063**

(1) Where, in respect of a particular case there is a maintenance assessment the effective date of which is before the date that these Regulations come into force with respect to that type of case ("the commencement date"), these Regulations shall not apply for the purposes of—

(a) *[omitted]*;
(b) the Income Support Regulations, in relation to a person who is entitled to income support for a period beginning on or before the day before the commencement date;
(c) the Jobseeker's Allowance Regulations, in relation to a person who is entitled to a jobseeker's allowance for a period beginning on or before the day before the commencement date; and
(d) *[omitted]*.

(2) These Regulations shall not apply with respect to the Income Support Regulations and the Jobseeker's Allowance Regulations in relation to a person who is entitled to income support or a jobseeker's allowance, as the case may be, for a period beginning on or before the day before the commencement date.

AMENDMENT

1. Child Support (Transitional Provision) (Miscellaneous Amendments) Regulations 2003 (SI 2003/347) reg.2(3) and (4)(b) (March 3, 2003).

GENERAL NOTE

2.1064 These regulations made amendments to regs 60A and 60C(6)(a) of, and para.14(2) of Sch.3 to, the Income Support Regulations and to regs 125 and 128(6)(a) of, and para.13(2) of Sch.2 to, the JSA Regulations 1996. See the note to reg.60A of the Income Support Regulations in the 2008/09 edition of this volume.

The Social Security (Working Tax Credit and Child Tax Credit) (Consequential Amendments) Regulations 2003

(SI 2003/455) (AS AMENDED)

Made by the Secretary of State under ss.1(1C) and 189(1) of the Social Security Administration Act 1992, ss.22(5), 122(1), 123(1)(a), (d) and (e), 124(1)(e), 135(1), 136(1), (3), (4) and (5), 137(1), 138(1)(a), (2) and (4), and 175(1) and (3) to (5) of the Social Security Contributions and Benefits Act 1992, ss.4(5), 12, 13(2), 35(1), 36(2) and (4) of the Jobseekers Act 1995

Citation, commencement and interpretation

2.1065 **1.**—(1) These Regulations may be cited as the Social Security (Working Tax Credit and Child Tax Credit) (Consequential Amendments) Regulations 2003 and this regulation shall come into force on 1 April 2003.

(2) Subject to paragraph (5), in a case where a claimant for income support—

(a) has a child or young person who is a member of his family for the purposes of his claim for income support, and

(b) is awarded, or his partner is awarded, a child tax credit for a period beginning before 6 April 2004,

regulation 7 shall have effect from the first day of the first benefit week to commence for that claimant on or after the day from which that award of child tax credit begins and regulation 2 and Schedule 1 shall have effect from the first day of the first benefit week to commence for that claimant on or after 6 April 2004.

(3) Subject to [1 paragraphs (4A) to (5)], in a case where a claimant for income support—

(a) has a child or young person who is a member of his family for the purposes of his claim for income support, and

(b) has not been awarded, or his partner has not been awarded, a child tax credit for a period beginning before 6 April 2004,

regulations 2 and 7 and Schedule 1 shall have effect from the first day of the first benefit week to commence for that claimant on or after the day on which his, or his partner's, award of child tax credit begins.

(4) Subject to [1 paragraphs (4A) to (5)], in a case where paragraph (2)(a) or (3)(a) does not apply to a claimant for income support, regulation 2 and Schedule 1 shall have effect from the first day of the first benefit week to commence for that claimant on or after 6 April 2004.

[1 (4A) the case of a person who makes a claim for income support on or after 8th September 2005, regulation 2 and Schedule 1 shall have effect from the date that claim is made.

(4B) Subject to paragraph (4C), in the case of a claimant for income support who applies on or after 8th September 2005 for an amount to be included in his applicable amount in respect of a child or young person, regulation 2 and Schedule 1 shall have effect from the date of that application.

(4C) Paragraph (4B) shall not apply to a claimant for income support who already has an amount included in his applicable amount in respect of a child or young person on the date he makes the application referred to in that paragraph.]

(5) *[Omitted.]*

(6) Subject to [1 paragraphs (8A) to (9)], in a case where a claimant for a jobseeker's allowance—

(a) has a child or young person who is a member of his family for the purposes of his claim for jobseeker's allowance, and

(b) is awarded, or his partner is awarded, a child tax credit for a period beginning before 6 April 2004, regulation 8 shall have effect from the first day of the first benefit week to commence for that claimant on or after the day from which that award of child tax credit begins and regulation 3 and Schedule 2 shall have effect from the first day of the first benefit week to commence for that claimant on or after 6th April 2004.

(7) Subject to [1 paragraphs (8A) to (9)], in a case where a claimant for a jobseeker's allowance—

(a) has a child or young person who is a member of his family for the purposes of his claim for jobseeker's allowance, and

(b) has not been awarded, or his partner has not been awarded, a child tax credit for a period beginning before 6th April, 2004.

regulations 3 and 8 and Schedule 2 shall have effect from the first day of the first benefit week to commence for that claimant on or after the day on which his, or his partner's, award of child tax credit begins.

(8) Subject to [1 paragraphs (8A) to (9)], in a case where paragraph (6)(a) or (7)(a) does not apply to a claimant for jobseeker's allowance, regulation 3 and Schedule 2 shall have effect from the first day of the first benefit week to commence for that claimant on or after 6 April 2004.

[1 (8A) In the case of a person who makes a claim for a jobseeker's allowance on or after 8th September 2005, regulation 3 and Schedule 2 shall have effect from the date that claim is made.

(8B) Subject to paragraph (8C), in the case of a claimant for a jobseeker's allowance who applies on or after 8th September 2005 for an amount to be included in his applicable amount in respect of a child or young person, regulation 3 and Schedule 2 shall have effect from the date of that application.

(8C) Paragraph (8B) shall not apply to a claimant for a jobseeker's allowance who already has an amount included in his applicable amount in respect of a child or young person on the date he makes the application referred to in that paragraph.]

(9)–(10) *[Omitted.]*

(11) In paragraphs (2) to (5) and regulation 7, the expressions "benefit week", "claimant" and "partner" have the same meaning as in regulation 2(1) of the Income Support Regulations and in paragraphs (6) to (9) and regulation 8, the expressions "benefit week" and "partner" have the same meaning as in regulation 1(3) of the Jobseeker's Allowance Regulations.

(12) In these Regulations—
[Omitted].
"the Income Support Regulations" means the Income Support (General) Regulations 1987; and
"the Jobseeker's Allowance Regulations" means the Jobseeker's Allowance Regulations 1996.

2.1066 **2.–6.** *[Omitted.]*

AMENDMENT

1. Social Security (Tax Credit) Regulations 2005 (SI 2005/2294) reg.2(2) (September 8, 2005).

Income Support—transitional arrangements

2.1067 7.—(1) [1 Subject to paragraph (2) and regulation 31(3) of the Income Support Regulations,] in the case of a claimant for income support who makes a claim, or whose partner makes a claim, for a child tax credit, the Secretary of State shall treat that claimant's income as including an amount equivalent to the amount of child tax credit to which he, or his partner, is entitled for the period specified in pargraph (3).

(2) In a case where a claimant for income support—

(a) has a child or young person who is a member of his family for the purposes of his claim for income support; and

(b) is, or has a partner who is, aged not less than 60.

the Secretary of State shall, [1 in the benefit week which begins on or includes 5 October 2003, disregard from his income an amount equivalent to the amount of child tax credit to which he is entitled.]

(3) For the purposes of [1 paragraph (1)], the specified period begins on the first day of the first benefit week to commence for that claimant on or after 7 April 2003, or the date the award of child tax credit begins if later, and ends on the day before the first day of the first benefit week to commence for that claimant on or after 6 April 2004.

(4) In the case of a claimant for income support who applies for an applicable amount under regulation 17 or 18 of the Income Support Regulations on or after 7 April 2003 in respect of a child or young person who is a member of his family, the Secretary of State shall treat that claimant's income as including an amount equivalent to the amount of child benefit to which he, or his partner, is entitled in respect of that child or young person for the period specified in paragraph (5).

(5) For the purposes of paragraph (4), the specified period begins on the first day of the first benefit week to commence for that claimant on or after the date from which his claim includes that applicable amount and ends on—

(a) in a case where the claimant, or his partner, is awarded child tax credit for a period beginning before 6th April 2004, the first day of the first benefit week to commence for that claimant on or after 6 April 2004;

(b) in the case where the claimant, or his partner, is awarded child tax credit for a period beginning on or after 6th April 2004 the first day of the first benefit week to commence for that claimant on or after the day that award of child tax credit begins; or

(c) the first day of the first benefit week in which his applicable amount in respect of that child or young person ends, if earlier.

(6) [3. . .]

(7) [3. . .]

AMENDMENTS

1. Social Security (Working Tax Credit and Child Tax Credit) (Consequential Amendments) (No.3) Regulations 2003 (SI 2003/1731) reg.6 (August 8, 2003).

2. Social Security (Miscellaneous Amendments) Regulations 2004 (SI 2004/565) reg.11 (April 12, 2004).

3. Social Security (Miscellaneous Amendments) Regulations 2011 (SI 2011/674) reg.11(a) (April 11, 2011).

Jobseeker's allowance—transitional arrangements

8.—(1) [1 Subject to regulation 96(3) of the Jobseeker's Allowance Regulations,] in the case of a claimant for jobseeker's allowance who makes a claim, or whose partner makes a claim, for a child tax credit, the Secretary of State shall treat that claimant's income as including an amount equivalent to the amount of child tax credit to which he, or his partner, is entitled for the period specified in pararaph (2). **2.1068**

(2) For the purposes of paragraph (1) the specified period begins on the first day of the first benefit week to commence for that claimant on or after 7 April 2003, or the date that award of child tax credit begins if later, and ends on the day before the first day of the first benefit week to commence for that claimant on or after 6 April 2004.

(3) In the case of a claimant for jobseeker's allowance who applies for an applicable amount under regulation 83 or 84 of the Jobseeker's Allowance Regulations on or after 7 April 2003 in respect of a child or young person who is a member of his family, the Secretary of State shall treat the claimant's income as including an amount equivalent to the amount of child benefit to which he, or his partner, is entitled in respect of that child or young person for the period specified in paragraph (4).

(4) For the purposes of paragraph (3), the specified period begins on the first day of the first benefit week to commence for that claimant on or after the date from which his claim includes that applicable amount and ends on—

(a) in a case where the claimant, or his partner, is awarded child tax credit for a period beginning before 6 April 2004, the first day of the first benefit week to commence for that claimant on or after 6 April 2004;

(b) in a case where the claimant, or his partner, is awarded child tax credit for a period beginning on or after 6 April 2004, the first day of the first benefit week to commence for that claimant on or after the day on which that award of child tax credit begins; or

(c) the first day of the first benefit week in which his applicable amount in respect of that child or young person ends, if earlier.

(5) [3. . .]

(6) [3. . .]

AMENDMENTS

1. Social Security (Working Tax Credit and Child Tax Credit) (Consequential Amendments) (No.3) Regulations 2003 (SI 2003/1731) reg.6(1) and (3) (August 8, 2003).

2. Social Security (Miscellaneous Amendments) Regulations 2004 (SI 2004/565) reg.11 (April 12, 2004).

3. Social Security (Miscellaneous Amendments) Regulations 2011 (SI 2011/674) reg.11(b) (April 11, 2011).

GENERAL NOTE

2.1069 These regulations make transitional provisions for IS and JSA claimants who are responsible for a child or young person and who are also awarded child tax credit (see Vol.IV) which was introduced on April 7, 2003.

It is intended that starting from April 6, 2004, IS and JSA will become "adults only" benefits with all means-tested state financial help towards the cost of bringing up a child being met through child tax credit. To this end, reg.2 and Sch.1 and reg.3 and Sch.2 (which are referred to above) amend, respectively, the IS Regulations and the JSA Regulations 1996 from that date (except in "transitional cases"—see the note to reg.17 of the Income Support Regulations) so as to abolish the family premium and personal allowances for children and young persons and child-related premiums.

Regulations 7(1)–(3) and 8(1)–(2) deal with the period between April 7, 2003 and April 6, 2004. The general rule is that child tax credit counts as income for income support and JSA so that the claimant does not receive a double benefit.

2.1070 Note that regs 7(6)–(7) and 8(5)–(6) provided for a £10.50 disregard of child benefit in respect of a child under one in transitional cases to mirror the "baby element" in child tax credit. However these paragraphs were revoked with effect from April 11, 2011 in line with the abolition of the child tax credit baby element from April 6, 2011.

Regulation 1(5), (9) and (10) which are not reproduced here amend other regulations with effect from April 7, 2003. Their effect is noted in the text of those regulations where appropriate.

In *R(IS) 3/05* the Commissioner acknowledges that there were several problems in working out the meaning of reg.7(1) but on the facts of that case he saw no difficulty in interpreting reg.7(1) as deeming the claimant's income to include the amount equivalent to that contained in the operative award of child tax credit. The main issue was whether the claimant had made a valid claim for child tax credit (the claimant having discovered that he would be better off not claiming child tax credit); the Commissioner decided that an effective claim had been made.

However, the Commissioner did have to grapple with the meaning of reg.7(1) in *CIS/1064/2004*. The claimant, who had two young children, had been awarded working tax credit and child tax credit for the period April 6, 2003 to April 5, 2004. However she had stopped working, it seems in early August 2003 (it was not exactly clear when). This resulted in a change in the tax credit decisions. The award of working tax credit was stopped and the overpayment of working tax credit that was said to have arisen was set off against the child tax credit that remained payable, leaving very little in payment. But, when calculating her income support the maximum amount of child tax credit was taken into account. The claimant appealed. The tribunal reluctantly dismissed her appeal, deciding that as reg.7(1) used the word "entitled", rather than "paid", and as a person who is in receipt of income support is entitled to the maximum award of child tax credit (see ss.7(2) and 13(1) of the Tax Credits Act 2002 and reg.4 of the Tax Credits (Income Thresholds and Determination of Rates) Regulations 2002 (SI 2002/2008) in Vol. IV of this series), it was the amount of that entitlement that had to be taken into account.

2.1071 In a very detailed analysis the Commissioner firstly rejects the claimant's contention that reg.7(1) did not apply where a person who already had an award of child tax credit made a claim for income support during the tax year 2003/2004 but only applied where a person who was already in receipt of income support applied for child tax credit. He decided that the order in which the claims were made did not matter. He then went on to consider the application of reg.7(1) in the claimant's case. Identifying the effect of reg.7(1) was, in his view, "a matter of considerable difficulty and complexity". However, he concludes that the most natural reading of reg.7(1) was that it required identification of the amount of child tax credit to which the particular claimant was actually "entitled" week by week during the period that was in question for income support purposes. It did not simply deem the claimant to be receiving the maximum amount of child tax credit for the children for whom she was responsible. However, the question remained of what was meant by "is entitled". The Commissioner concluded that it referred to the amount of child tax credit attributable, in accordance with the most recent award or amended award made by the Board, to the period from the effective date of the award or amended award to the end of the tax year. This result was consistent with the overall scheme of decision-making under the Tax Credits Act 2002. It also had the merit of being consistent with the general principle that the income support scheme was designed to meet financial needs when they arose through a shortfall in resources available at the time in question.

Applying this to the facts of the claimant's case, the Commissioner finds that the Board must have made a decision under s.28(5) of the 2002 Act (because the child tax credit had been reduced to recoup the overpayment of working tax credit), although he thought that there must also have been a use of the duty under reg.12(3) of the Tax Credits (Payments by the Board) Regulations 2002 (SI 2002/2173) (see Vol.IV in this series) to adjust the amount of the child tax credit payment in consequence of the amendment of the child tax credit award. Therefore, as there had been an amended award, the effect of reg.7(1) and (3) was that the clamant had to be treated as receiving an amount of income equivalent to the amount of child tax credit to which she was entitled under that amended award. The result was that it was the amount of child tax credit that she was actually receiving that was to be taken into account in calculating her income support. Note that the Commissioner left open how reg.7(1) and (3) applied in a case where the award of child tax credit had not been amended but by some administrative action there had simply been an adjustment of the amount paid without an amendment of the award.

The final question was how much of the amount under the amended child tax credit award was to be taken into account for the period specified in reg.7(1) and (3). The answer to this was to be found in reg.31(3) of the Income Support Regulations, although this did not supply a complete rule for the taking into account of income arising from awards of child tax credit and working tax credit. This was because it does not say how a weekly amount of income is to be derived from the amount of a tax credit award. The Commissioner therefore considered that reg.32 of the Income Support Regulations, substituting for the word "payment" in that regulation the amount of the tax credit award or amended award, should be applied (either directly or by a process of analogy to flesh out reg.31(3)). The period of the most recent child tax credit or working tax credit award had to be considered. Thus, where there had been an amended award, the period over which the amount of the amended award would be taken into account would be only the period after the effective date of the amendment. The weekly amount so calculated had then to be taken into account, but only from the first day of the benefit week identified under reg.31(3). The weekly amount had to be attributed to all the benefit weeks in the period after the effective date of the amendment to the end of the tax year, regardless of the way in which payments of tax credit were actually being made. If a tax credit award was terminated or amended later in the year there would either no longer be any amount to be taken into account or there would have to be a fresh application of reg.31(3)(b) or (c).

Note also *CSTC/326/2005* which holds that a claimant who was in receipt of income support and transferring to child tax credit could only be awarded child tax credit from the date of his claim – it could not be backdated for three months. For further discussion of this case see Vol.IV in this series.

The Social Security (Housing Costs Special Arrangements) (Amendment and Modification) Regulations 2008

(SI 2008/3195) (AS AMENDED)

Made by the Secretary of State for Work and Pensions under ss.123(1)(a), 135(1), 137(1) and 175(1) and (3) and (4) of the Social Security Contributions and Benefits Act 1992, ss.4(5), 35(1) and 36(2) and (4) of the Jobseekers Act 1995, ss.2(3)(b), 17(1) and 19(1) of the State Pension Credit Act 2002, and ss.4(2)(a) and (3), 24(1) and 25(2), (3) and (5) of the Welfare Reform Act 2007.

REGULATIONS REPRODUCED

GENERAL NOTE

2.1073 The modifications to the rules for housing costs for income support, income-based JSA, income-related ESA and state pension credit made by these Regulations only apply to certain claimants, even after the January 2010 amendments. See the note to Sch.3 to the Income Support Regulations under "*Modifications to the waiting periods and the cap on loans for certain claimants from January 5, 2009*" and "*Further Modifications from January 5, 2010*".

The modifications relating to waiting periods made by these Regulations were revoked on April 1, 2016 (subject to a saving provision: see p.824) but the modifications which concern the capital limit for eligible loans (together with the time limit for receipt of housing costs in the case of JSA) continue in effect.

Citation, commencement and interpretation

1.—(1) These Regulations may be cited as the Social Security (Housing Costs Special Arrangements) (Amendment and Modification) Regulations 2008. 2.1074

(2) Regulations 4 to 6, in so far as they relate to a particular person, come into force on the first day of the first benefit week to commence for that person on or after 5th January 2009.

(3) The remaining provisions of these Regulations come into force on 5th January 2009.

(4) In these Regulations—

"benefit week" has the same meaning as in—

[(a) omitted as not relating to income support, income-based JSA or state pension credit]

(b) regulation 2(1) of the Income Support Regulations, where the relevant benefit is income support;

(c) regulation 1(2) of the Jobseeker's Allowance Regulations, where the relevant benefit is a jobseeker's allowance;

"housing costs" has the same meaning as in paragraph 1(1) (housing costs) of—

[(a) omitted as not relating to income support, income-based JSA or state pension credit]

(b) Schedule 3 to the Income Support Regulations, where the relevant benefit is income support;

(c) Schedule 2 to the Jobseeker's Allowance Regulations, where the relevant benefit is a jobseeker's allowance;

"relevant benefit" means—

(a) an employment and support allowance;

(b) income support;

(c) a jobseeker's allowance;

[Definition omitted as not relating to income support, income-based JSA or state pension credit]

"the Income Support Regulations" means the Income Support (General) Regulations 1987;

"the Jobseeker's Allowance Regulations" means the Jobseeker's Allowance Regulations 1996;

"the State Pension Credit Regulations" means the State Pension Credit Regulations 2002.

PART 2

MODIFICATIONS RELATING TO CERTAIN CLAIMANTS WHO ARE ENTITLED TO A RELEVANT BENEFIT ON 4TH JANUARY 2009

Application

3.—(1) This Part applies in relation to a person who— 2.1075

(a) is entitled to a relevant benefit on 4th January 2009; and
(b) on or after that date falls within paragraph (3) or (4).

(2) This Part ceases to apply in relation to a person who makes a further claim to the same, or claims another, relevant benefit after 4th January 2009.

(3) A person falls within this paragraph if, apart from these Regulations, the housing costs to be met in the benefit week that includes 4th January 2009 would be nil in that person's case because [1 that person] has not been entitled to the relevant benefit concerned for the period mentioned in sub-paragraph (1)(a) in any of the following provisions—

[(a) omitted as not relating to income support or income-based JSA]
(b) paragraph 6 (existing housing costs) or paragraph 8 (new housing costs) of Schedule 3 to the Income Support Regulations;
(c) paragraph 6 (existing housing costs) or paragraph 7 (new housing costs) of Schedule 2 to the Jobseeker's Allowance Regulations.

(4) A person falls within this paragraph if [1 that person] has been entitled to a relevant benefit for a continuous period, which includes 4th January 2009, for at least 8 weeks but less than 26 weeks under any of the provisions mentioned in paragraph (5) as in force apart from these Regulations.

(5) The provisions are—

[(a) omitted as not relating to income support or income-based JSA]
(b) paragraph 6(1)(b) (existing housing costs) or paragraph 8(4) (new housing costs) of Schedule 3 to the Income Support Regulations;
(c) paragraph 6(1)(b) (existing housing costs) or paragraph 7(6) (new housing costs) of Schedule 2 to the Jobseeker's Allowance Regulations.

AMENDMENT

1. Social Security (Housing Costs Special Arrangements) (Amendment) Regulations 2009 (SI 2009/3257) reg.2 (January 5, 2010).

Modification of the Income Support Regulations

2.1076 **5.**—Schedule 3 (housing costs) to the Income Support Regulations applies in relation to a person to whom this Part applies as if—

(a) [1 . . .]
(b) [1 . . .]
(c) in paragraph 11(5) (general provisions applying to new and existing housing costs) the reference to "£100,000" were to "£200,000";
(d) [1 . . .]

AMENDMENT

1. Social Security (Housing Costs Amendments) Regulations 2015 (SI 2015/1647) reg.7(1) (April 1, 2016). Note that the revocation of these paragraphs is subject to the saving provision in reg.8 of SI 2015/1647. See p.824 for this saving provision.

Modification of the Jobseeker's Allowance Regulations

2.1077 **6.**—Schedule 2 (housing costs) to the Jobseeker's Allowance Regulations applies in relation to a person to whom this Part applies as if—

(a) after paragraph 4 (housing costs not met) there were inserted—

"Housing costs: limitation applicable to qualifying loans

2.1078 **4A.**—(1) Subject to sub-paragraphs (2) and (3), no amount may be met in respect of housing costs under paragraph 14 or 15 where the claimant has been in receipt of housing costs under either or both of those paragraphs for a total of 104 weeks.

(2) No week in which the appropriate amount specified in paragraph 10(4) is £100,000 in relation to that claimant is to count towards the 104 week total.

(3) Sub-paragraph (1) does not apply where—

(a) the claimant or his [1 . . .] partner or, if the claimant is a member of a joint-claim couple, the other member of the couple, was previously entitled to income support or employment and support allowance; and

(b) 12 weeks or less has elapsed since the last day of that entitlement and the first day of entitlement to a jobseeker's allowance.

[2(4) In determining whether the exemption provided for in sub-paragraph (3) applies, where the claimant or his partner or, if the claimant is a member of a joint-claim couple, the other member of the couple was in receipt of a jobseeker's allowance immediately before becoming entitled to income support by virtue of regulation 6(6) of the Income Support Regulations, no account shall be taken of entitlement arising by virtue of that regulation.]"

(b) [3 . . .]

(c) [3 . . .]

(d) in paragraph 10(4) (general provisions applying to new and existing housing costs) the reference to "£100,000" were to "£200,000";

(e) [3 . . .]

AMENDMENTS

1. Social Security (Housing Costs Special Arrangements) (Amendment) Regulations 2009 (SI 2009/3257) reg.3 (January 5, 2010).

2. Social Security (Miscellaneous Amendments) (No.3) Regulations 2011 (SI 2011/2425) reg.26(2) (October 31, 2011).

3. Social Security (Housing Costs Amendments) Regulations 2015 (SI 2015/1647) reg.7(1) (April 1, 2016). Note that the revocation of these paragraphs is subject to the saving provision in reg.8 of SI 2015/1647. See p.824 for this saving provision.

Saving

7.—[1 . . .] 2.1079

AMENDMENT

1. Social Security (Housing Costs Amendments) Regulations 2015 (SI 2015/1647) reg.7(1) (April 1, 2016). Note that the revocation of this regulation is subject to the saving provision in reg.8 of SI 2015/1647. See p.824 for this saving provision.

PART 3

MODIFICATIONS RELTING TO CERTAIN PERSONS WHO CLAIM A RELEVANT BENEFIT AFTER 4TH JANUARY 2009

Application and interpretation

[1**8.**—(1) This Part applies on and after 5th January 2010 to a person ("C") who— 2.1080

(a) claims a relevant benefit after 4th January 2009; and
(b) satisfies any of the following conditions.

(2) The first condition is that Part 2 applied to C at any time.

(3) The second condition is that this Part (as it has effect on and after 5th January 2010) applied to C in relation to a previous award.

(4) The third condition is that—

(a) neither C nor C's partner has been awarded a relevant benefit as the result of an earlier claim (whether the award was made before or on or after 5th January 2009);
(b) neither C nor C's partner is in receipt of state pension credit before the date on which C's claim is made or treated as made; and
(c) C does not fall to be treated under a linking rule as being in continuous receipt of the benefit to which C's claim relates in respect of a period which begins on or before 4th January 2009 and which ends immediately before the date on which C's claim is made or is treated as made.

(5) The fourth condition is that—

(a) C is not in receipt of a relevant benefit immediately before the date on which a claim made by C after 4th January 2009 is made or treated as made;
(b) neither C nor C's partner is in receipt of state pension credit before that claim is made or treated as made;
(c) C or C's partner was awarded a relevant benefit as the result of a claim made or treated as made before that claim; and
(d) C does not fall to be treated under a linking rule as being in continuous receipt of a relevant benefit during the period which falls immediately between the date on which a claim to which this provision relates is made or treated as made and the last period to occur before that date in respect of which C was in receipt of a relevant benefit (whether as a single person or as a member of a couple or polygamous marriage).

(6) The fifth condition is that—

(a) C or C's partner is in receipt of state pension credit before the date on which any claim for a relevant benefit made by C or C's partner after 4th January 2009 is made or treated as made; and
(b) none of the following provisions apply in relation to any such claim—
   (i) paragraph 3(2) (previous entitlement to other income-related benefits) of Schedule 6 (housing costs) to the Employment and Support Allowance Regulations;
   (ii) paragraph 1A(1A) (previous entitlement to income-based jobseeker's allowance, income-related employment and support allowance or state pension credit) of Schedule 3 (housing costs) to the Income Support Regulations;
   (iii) paragraph 1A(1ZA) or (1B) (previous entitlement to income support, income-related employment and support allowance or state pension credit) of Schedule 2 (housing costs) to the Jobseeker's Allowance Regulations.

(7) In this regulation—

a "linking rule" means a provision of—

(a) paragraph 15 (linking rule) of Schedule 6 (housing costs) to the Employment and Support Allowance Regulations,

(b) paragraph 14 (linking rule) of Schedule 3 (housing costs) to the Income Support Regulations, or (as the case may be)
(c) paragraph 13 (linking rule) of Schedule 2 (housing costs) to the Jobseeker's Allowance Regulations;

"partner" has the same meaning as in regulation 1(3) (citation, commencement and interpretation) of the Jobseeker's Allowance Regulations.]

AMENDMENT

1. Social Security (Housing Costs Special Arrangements) (Amendment) Regulations 2009 (SI 2009/3257) reg.4 (January 5, 2010).

Modification of the Income Support Regulations

10.—Schedule 3 (housing costs) to the Income Support Regulations applies in relation to a person to whom this Part applies as if— 2.1081

(a) [1 . . .]
(b) [1 . . .]
(c) [1 . . .]
(d) [1 . . .]
(e) [1 . . .]
(f) in paragraph 11 (general provisions applying to new and existing housing costs)—
  (i) [1 . . .]
  (ii) [1 . . .]
  (iii) in sub-paragraph (5), the reference to "£100,000" were to "£200,000";
(g) [1 . . .]
(h) [1 . . .]

AMENDMENT

1. Social Security (Housing Costs Amendments) Regulations 2015 (SI 2015/1647) reg.7(1) (April 1, 2016). Note that the revocation of most of this regulation (with the exception of para.(f)(iii)) is subject to the saving provision in reg.8 of SI 2015/1647. See p.824 for this saving provision.

Modification of the Jobseeker's Allowance Regulations

11.—Schedule 2 (housing costs) to the Jobseeker's Allowance Regulations applies in relation to a person to whom this Part applies as if— 2.1082

(a) [3 . . .]
[1(b) after paragraph 4 (housing costs not met) there were inserted—

"Housing costs: limitation applicable to qualifying loans

4A.—(1) Except as mentioned below, no amount may be met in respect of housing costs under paragraph 14 or 15 after the claimant has been in receipt of housing costs under either or both of those paragraphs ("relevant housing costs") for a cumulative total of 104 weeks, beginning on or after 5th January 2009. 2.1083

(2) Sub-paragraphs (3) to [2(7)] apply for the purposes of sub-paragraph (1).

(3) No week in which the appropriate amount specified in paragraph 10(4) is £100,000 in relation to the claimant is to count towards the 104 week total.

(4) Where sub-paragraph (5) applies to the claimant, relevant housing costs awarded to him in respect of a previous award of a jobseeker's allowance are to be disregarded.

(5) This sub-paragraph applies to the claimant where he does not fall to be treated under paragraph 13 (linking rule) as being in receipt of a jobseeker's allowance for a continuous period beginning with the first day of the last period in respect of which he was not in receipt of a jobseeker's allowance and ending immediately before his most recent claim is made or is treated as made.

(6) Sub-paragraph (1) does not apply where—

(a) the claimant or his partner or, if the claimant is a member of a joint-claim couple, the other member of the couple, was entitled to an employment and support allowance or income support before one of them becomes entitled to a jobseeker's allowance; and

(b) 12 weeks or less has elapsed since the last day of that entitlement and the first day of entitlement to a jobseeker's allowance.]

[2 (7) In determining whether the exemption provided for in sub-paragraph (6) applies, where the claimant or his partner or, if the claimant is a member of a joint-claim couple, the other member of the couple was in receipt of a jobseeker's allowance immediately before becoming entitled to income support by virtue of regulation 6(6) of the Income Support Regulations, no account shall be taken of entitlement arising by virtue of that regulation.]"

(c) [3 . . .]
(d) [3 . . .]
(e) [3 . . .]
(f) [3 . . .]
(g) in paragraph 10 (general provisions applying to new and existing housing costs)—
(i) [3 . . .]
(ii) [3 . . .]
(iii) in sub-paragraph (4), the reference to "£100,000" were to "£200,000";
(h) [3 . . .]
(i) [3 . . .]
(j) [3 . . .]

AMENDMENTS

1. Social Security (Housing Costs Special Arrangements) (Amendment) Regulations 2009 (SI 2009/3257) reg.5 (January 5, 2010).

2. Social Security (Miscellaneous Amendments) (No.3) Regulations 2011 (SI 2011/2425) reg.26(3) (October 31, 2011).

3. Social Security (Housing Costs Amendments) Regulations 2015 (SI 2015/1647) reg.7(1) (April 1, 2016). Note that the revocation of most of this regulation (with the exception of paras (b) and (g)(iii)) is subject to the saving provision in reg.8 of SI 2015/1647. See p.824 for this saving provision.

PART 4

Modifications relating to certain persons who claim State Pension Credit

Modifications relating to certain persons who claim State Pension Credit

12.—(1) This Part applies where— 2.1084

(a) a person becomes entitled to state pension credit;

(b) that person or that person's partner ceases to be entitled to a relevant benefit;

(c) that person or [1 that person's] partner is a person to whom [1 —

(i) Part 2 applies, or

(ii) Part 3 (as it has effect, in relation to the person or that person's partner, on and after 5th January 2010) applies or would have applied had the person claiming state pension credit remained entitled to a relevant benefit.]

(d) the last day on which the person or [1 that person's] partner was entitled to a relevant benefit was no more than 12 weeks before—

(i) except where head (ii) applies, the first day of entitlement to state pension credit; or

(ii) where the claim for state pension credit was treated as made on a day earlier than the day on which it was actually made ("the actual date"), the day which would have been the first day of entitlement to state pension credit had the claim been treated as made on the actual date; and

(e) in the period immediately before the date on which the person's entitlement to the relevant benefit ended, [1 that person's] applicable amount included an amount in respect of housing costs under any of the provisions mentioned below.

(2) The provisions are—

(a) paragraph 16 (loans on residential property) or 17 (loans for repairs and improvements to the dwelling occupied as the home) of Schedule 6 to the Employment and Support Allowance Regulations;

(b) paragraph 15 (loans on residential property) or 16 (loans for repairs and improvements to the dwelling occupied as the home) of Schedule 3 to the Income Support Regulations;

(c) paragraph 14 (loans on residential property) or 15 (loans for repairs and improvements to the dwelling occupied as the home) of Schedule 2 to the Jobseeker's Allowance Regulations.

(3) Paragraph 8(2) (general provisions applying to housing costs) of Schedule 2 to the State Pension Credit Regulations is to apply in relation to a person to whom this Part applies as if the reference to "£100,000" were to "£200,000".

AMENDMENT

1. Social Security (Housing Costs Special Arrangements) (Amendment) Regulations 2009 (SI 2009/3257) reg.6 (January 5, 2010).

The Social Security (Housing Costs Amendments) Regulations 2015

(SI 2015/1647)

Made by the Secretary of State for Work and Pensions under ss.123(1)(a), 135(1), 137(1) and 175(1), (3) and (4) of the Social Security Contributions and Benefits Act 1992, ss.4(5), 35(1) and 36(2) and (4) of the Jobseekers Act 1995, ss.4(2)(a), 24(1) and 25(2), (3) and (5) of the Welfare Reform Act 2007 and ss.11(4) and (5)(b), 40, 42(1), (2) and (3) of, and para.1 of Sch.6 to, the Welfare Reform Act 2012.

[In force April 1, 2016]

GENERAL NOTE

2.1085 See the notes to the Social Security (Housing Costs Special Arrangements) (Amendment and Modification) Regulations 2008 above and to Sch.3 to the Income Support Regulations.

Saving provision

2.1086 **8.**—(1) This regulation applies to a person ("P") where, for the purpose of determining whether P's entitlement to a relevant benefit includes an amount for housing costs, the Secretary of State determines that P is entitled or required to be treated as entitled to one or more relevant benefits for a continuous period which includes 31st March 2016.

(2) Where this regulation applies to P, the provisions of—

(a) Schedule 6 to the Employment and Support Allowance Regulations 2008;

(b) Schedule 3 to the Income Support (General) Regulations 1987; and

(c) Schedule 2 to the Jobseeker's Allowance Regulations 1996,

as modified by the Social Security (Housing Costs Special Arrangements) (Amendment and Modification) Regulations 2008 are to have effect in relation to P as if the amendments made by regulations 2 to 4 of these Regulations and the revocation made by regulation 7(1) had not been made.

(3) Where this regulation applies to P, the provisions of Schedule 5 to the Universal Credit Regulations 2013 are to have effect in relation to P as if the amendments made by regulations 5 and 6 of these Regulations had not been made.

(4) In this regulation, "relevant benefit" means—

(a) an employment and support allowance under Part 1 of the Welfare Reform Act 2007;

(b) income support under the Income Support (General) Regulations 1987;

(c) a jobseeker's allowance under the Jobseeker's Allowance Regulations 1996; and

(d) universal credit under Part 1 of the Welfare Reform Act 2012.

The Income Support (Prescribed Categories of Person) Regulations 2009

(SI 2009/3152)

With effect from December 30, 2009, reg.2 of these Regulations revoked reg.13(2)(b) and (bb) of, and paras 7(a) and (b), 10, 12 and 13 of Sch.1B to, the Income Support Regulations, subject to a saving provision for certain claimants. See the 2015/16 edition of this book for these Regulations and the notes to them. 2.1087

The Social Security (Miscellaneous Amendments) (No.5) Regulations 2009

(SI 2009/3228)

Made by the Secretary of State under ss.123(1)(a), 124(1)(e), 135(1), 136(3), (4) and (5)(a), (b) and (c), 137(1) and (2)(d), and 175(1), (3) and (4) of the Social Security Contributions and Benefits Act 1992, ss.4(5), 12(1), (2) and (4)(a), (b) and (c), 13, 35(1) and 36(1), (2) and (4) of, and paras 1(2)(b) and 8A of Sch.1 to, the Jobseekers Act 1995, s.115(3), (4) and (7), 166(3) and 167(1) of the Immigration and Asylum Act 1999, and ss.17(1), (2) and (3)(a), (b) and (c), 24(1), 25(1), (2), (3) and (5) of, and para.6(3)(b) of Sch.1 to, the Welfare Reform Act 2007.

[In force January 25, 2010]

Citation, commencement and interpretation

1.—(1) These Regulations may be cited as the Social Security (Miscellaneous Amendments) (No.5) Regulations 2009. 2.1088

(2)–(3) . . .

(4) In this regulation—

. . .

"the Employment and Support Allowance Regulations" means the Employment and Support Allowance Regulations 2008;

"the Immigration and Asylum Regulations" means the Social Security (Immigration and Asylum) Consequential Amendments Regulations 2000;

"the Income Support Regulations" means the Income Support (General) Regulations 1987; and

"the Jobseeker's Allowance Regulations" means the Jobseeker's Allowance Regulations 1996.

Abolition (subject to savings) of urgent case payments

2.—(1) Subject to paragraphs (2) to (4), the following provisions are revoked— 2.1089

(a) Part 6 of the Income Support Regulations (urgent cases);
(b) Part 10 of the Jobseeker's Allowance Regulations (urgent cases);
(c) regulation 12(3) of the Immigration and Asylum Regulations (transitional arrangements and savings);

(d) Part 13 of the Employment and Support Allowance Regulations (urgent cases).

(2) The provisions referred to in paragraph (1) ("the relevant provisions") continue to have effect in relation to a person who, on the day before the day on which these Regulations come into force, is a person ("P") to whom regulation 70(2)(b) of the Income Support Regulations, regulation 147(2)(b) of the Jobseeker's Allowance Regulations or (as the case may be) regulation 162(2) of the Employment and Support Allowance Regulations applies.

(3) Where on the day before the day on which these Regulations come into force P falls within paragraph 1 of Part 1 of the Schedule to the Immigration and Asylum Regulations, the relevant provisions continue to have effect in relation to P until—

(a) the expiry of the period, or the aggregate of any periods, of 42 days during any one period of leave to which paragraph 1 of Part 1 of that Schedule applies, or

(b) the day on which P no longer falls within paragraph 1 of Part 1 of that Schedule,

whichever shall first occur.

(4) In any other case, the relevant provisions continue to have effect in relation to P until the day on which regulation 70(2)(b) of the Income Support Regulations, regulation 147(2)(b) of the Jobseeker's Allowance Regulations or (as the case may be) regulation 162(2) of the Employment and Support Allowance Regulations ceases to apply to P.

GENERAL NOTE

2.1090 See the commentary to Pt 6 (regs 70–72) of the Income Support Regulations.

Abolition of urgent case payments: supplementary provisions

2.1091 **3.**—. . .

Revocation (subject to savings) of provisions specifying that certain persons are to be treated as not engaged in remunerative work

2.1092 **4.**—(1) Subject to paragraphs (3) to (7), the following provisions are revoked—

(a) in the Income Support Regulations—

(i) regulation 6(4)(a) and (d) (persons not treated as engaged in remunerative work), and

(ii) paragraphs 8 and 9 of Schedule 1B (prescribed categories of persons);

(b) in the Jobseeker's Allowance Regulations—

(i) regulation 53(c) and (h) (persons treated as not engaged in remunerative work), and

(ii) paragraphs 7 and 8 of Schedule A1 (categories of members of a joint-claim couple who are not required to satisfy the conditions in section 1(2B)(b));

(c) regulation 43(2)(a) and (d) of the Employment and Support Allowance Regulations (circumstances under which partners of claimants entitled to an income-related allowance are not to be treated as engaged in remunerative work).

(2) . . .

(3) Paragraphs (4) to (6) apply to a person ("P") who in respect of a period which includes the day before the date on which these Regulations come into force—

(a) is entitled to a specified benefit (irrespective of whether P claims the benefit before, on or after that day), and

(b) falls within one of the provisions referred to in paragraph (1).

(4) Where the specified benefit is income support, regulation 6(4)(a) and (d) of, and paragraphs 8 and 9 of Schedule 1B to, the Income Support Regulations continue to have effect in relation to P's entitlement to that benefit.

(5) Where the specified benefit is a jobseeker's allowance, regulation 53(c) and (h) of, and paragraphs 7 and 8 of Schedule A1 to, the Jobseeker's Allowance Regulations continue to have effect in relation to P's entitlement to that benefit.

(6) Where the specified benefit is an employment and support allowance, regulation 43(2)(a) and (d) of the Employment and Support Allowance Regulations continue to have effect in relation to P's entitlement to that benefit.

(7) The provisions saved by paragraphs (4), (5) and (6) continue to have effect in relation to P's entitlement to the specified benefit until the day on which—

(a) P first ceases to fall within a provision referred to in paragraph (1), or,

(b) P first ceases to be entitled to that benefit,

whichever shall first occur.

(8) In this regulation "specified benefit" means income support, a jobseeker's allowance or an employment and support allowance.

General Note

See the commentary to reg.6 of the Income Support Regulations. **2.1093**

The Social Security (Lone Parents and Miscellaneous Amendments) Regulations 2012

(SI 2012/874)

Made by the Secretary of State for Work and Pensions under ss. 2(A)(1), 189(1), (4) and (5) and 191 of the Social Security Administration Act 1992, ss. 123(1), 124(1)(c), 137(1) and 175(1) and (3) to (5) of the Social Security Contributions and Benefits Act 1992, ss. 6(4), 7(4), 35(1) and 36(2) of the Jobseekers Act 1995 and ss. 2(4)(a), 4(6)(a) and 24(1) of the Welfare Reform Act 2007.

[In force May 21, 2012]

Savings and transitional provisions applicable to certain lone parents following a full-time course

7.—(1) This regulation applies to a lone parent if the following conditions are met. **2.1094**

(2) The first condition is that—

(a) immediately before the specified day the lone parent was entitled to income support and fell within paragraph 1 (lone parents) of Schedule 1B (prescribed categories of person) to the Income Support Regulations;

(b) no other paragraph of Schedule 1B applies to the lone parent; and

(c) on and after the specified day, the lone parent is responsible for and a member of the same household as—

(i) a single child aged 5 or over, or

(ii) more than one child where the youngest child is aged 5 or over.

(3) The second condition is that immediately before the specified day, and on and after that day, the lone parent is also—

(a) a full-time student attending or undertaking a full-time course of advanced education, a full-time course of study or a sandwich course, or

(b) following a full-time course of training or instruction provided pursuant to arrangements made by the Secretary of State or pursuant to a scheme which has been approved by the Secretary of State as supporting the objectives set out in section 2 of the Employment and Training Act 1973.

(4) This regulation does not apply, or (as the case may be) it ceases to apply, to a lone parent if the lone parent makes a further claim for income support on or after the specified day.

(5) Where this regulation applies to a lone parent—

(a) paragraph 1 of Schedule 1B to the Income Support Regulations as in force in relation to the lone parent at the beginning of the period of study referred to in paragraph (3)(a) shall continue to have effect in relation to the lone parent for so long as the lone parent remains a full-time student;

(b) paragraph 1 of Schedule 1B to the Income Support Regulations as in force at the beginning of the particular course of training or instruction referred to in paragraph (3)(b) shall continue to have effect in relation to the lone parent for so long as the lone parent is following that full-time course; and

(c) any requirement to take part in a work-focused interview every 13 weeks in accordance with regulation 2ZA of the Lone Parents Regulations or regulation 4A of the Jobcentre Plus Regulations shall continue to apply in relation to the lone parent at a time when, apart from this paragraph, the requirement would cease to apply because the lone parent's child's or youngest child's, age exceeds the age specified in those regulations.

(6) For the purposes of this regulation—

"full-time course of advanced education", "full-time course of study" and "sandwich course" have the same meaning as in regulation 61 of the Income Support Regulations;

"full-time student" and "period of study" have the same meaning as in regulation 2(1) of the Income Support Regulations;

"specified day" means 21st May 2012.

General Note

2.1095 See the note to para.1 of Sch.1B to the Income Support Regulations.

The Income Support (Work-Related Activity) and Miscellaneous Amendments Regulations 2014

(SI 2014/1097)

Made by the Secretary of State for Work and Pensions under ss.2A(1), (3), (6) and (8), 2D(1), (4)(a), (b), (d), (f) and (h) and (5) to (9)(c), 2E(3)(a) and (b), (4) and (5)(a) and (d), 2G(2)(a) and (4), 2H, 189(1) and (4) to (6) and 191 of the Social Security Administration Act 1992, ss. 9(1), 10(3) and (6) and 84 of the Social Security Act 1998, ss.11E(1)(a), 13(2)(a), 24(1) and 25(2) and (3) of the Welfare Reform Act 2007 and ss.20(1)(a), 21(1)(b) and (5), 40 and 42(2) and (3) of the Welfare Reform Act 2012. **2.1096**

[*In force April 28, 2014]*

REGULATIONS REPRODUCED

PART 1

GENERAL

PART 2

WORK-RELATED ACTIVITY

GENERAL NOTE

See the note to para.1 of Sch. IB to the Income Support Regulations. **2.1097**

PART 1

GENERAL

Citation, commencement and interpretation

1.—(1) These Regulations may be cited as the Income Support (Work-Related Activity) and Miscellaneous Amendments Regulations 2014 and come into force on the day after the day on which they are made. **2.1098**

(2) In these Regulations—

"action plan" means an action plan given in accordance with regulation 3;
"working day" means any day other than a Saturday, a Sunday, Christmas Day, Good Friday or a day which is a bank holiday under the Banking and Financial Dealings Act 1971.

PART 2

WORK-RELATED ACTIVITY

Requirement to undertake work-related activity

2.1099 **2.**—(1) The Secretary of State may require a person who satisfies the conditions in paragraph (2) to undertake work-related activity as a condition of continuing to be entitled to the full amount of income support payable apart from these Regulations.

(2) The conditions referred to in paragraph (1) are that the person—

(a) is entitled to income support;

(b) is subject to a requirement imposed under section 2A of the Social Security Administration Act 1992;

(c) is not a lone parent of a child under the age of 3; and

(d) falls within paragraph 1(1) of Schedule 1B to the Income Support (General) Regulations 1987 and no other paragraph within that Schedule.

(3) A requirement imposed under paragraph (1)—

(a) must be reasonable in the view of the Secretary of State, having regard to the person's circumstances; and

(b) may not require the person to apply for a job or undertake work, whether as an employee or otherwise.

Notification of work-related activity

2.1100 **3.**—(1) The Secretary of State must notify a person of a requirement to undertake work-related activity by including the requirement in a written action plan which is given to the person.

(2) The action plan must contain—

(a) particulars of the work-related activity which the person is to undertake; and

(b) any other information that the Secretary of State considers appropriate.

Requirement to undertake work-related activity at a certain time not to apply

2.1101 **4.**—The Secretary of State may determine that a requirement as to the time at, or by, which work-related activity is to be undertaken is not to apply, or is to be treated as not having applied, if in the view of the Secretary of State it would be, or would have been, unreasonable to require the person to undertake the activity at or by that time.

Reconsideration of action plans

5.—(1) A person may request the reconsideration of an action plan. **2.1102**

(2) On receipt of a request the Secretary of State must reconsider the action plan.

(3) A decision of the Secretary of State following a request must be in writing and given to the person.

Failure to undertake work-related activity

6.—(1) A person who is required to undertake work-related activity but fails to do so must show good cause for the failure before the end of five working days beginning with the date on which the Secretary of State gives notice to the person of the failure. **2.1103**

(2) The Secretary of State must determine whether a person who is required to undertake work-related activity has failed to do so and, if so, whether the person has shown good cause for the failure.

(3) In a case where within one month of the date on which the Secretary of State gave notice to a person of their failure to undertake work-related activity—

(a) the person brings new facts to the attention of the Secretary of State which could not reasonably have been brought to the attention of the Secretary of State within the period specified in paragraph (1); and

(b) those facts show that the person had good cause for failing to undertake work-related activity,

paragraph (1) applies with the modification that for the words "five working days" there is substituted "one month".

(4) Where a notice under paragraph (1) is sent by post it is taken to have been received on the second working day after it is sent.

Good cause

7.—Matters to be taken into account by the Secretary of State in determining whether a person has shown good cause for failing to undertake work-related activity for the purposes of regulation 6(2) include that— **2.1104**

(a) the person misunderstood the requirement to undertake work-related activity due to any learning, language or literacy difficulties of the person or any misleading information given to the person by the Secretary of State;

(b) the person was attending a medical or dental appointment, or accompanying someone for whom they have caring responsibilities to such an appointment, and that it would have been unreasonable, in the circumstances, for the person to undertake work-related activity;

(c) the person had difficulties with their normal mode of transport and that no reasonable alternative was available;

(d) the established customs and practices of the religion to which the person belongs prevented the person undertaking work-related activity on that day or at that time;

(e) the person was attending an interview with an employer with a view to obtaining employment;

(f) the person was pursuing employment opportunities as a self-employed earner;
(g) the person, a dependant of the person or someone for whom the person provides care suffered an accident, sudden illness or relapse of a physical or mental health condition;
(h) the person was attending the funeral of a close friend or relative on the day fixed for the work-related activity;
(i) a disability from which the person suffers made it impracticable to attend at the time fixed for the work-related activity;
(j) the availability of childcare.

Reduction of income support

2.1105 **8.**—(1) Subject to paragraph (4), where the Secretary of State has determined that a person who was required to undertake work-related activity has failed to do so and has not shown good cause for that failure in accordance with regulation 6 (failure to undertake work-related activity), the amount of income support payable to the person is to be reduced in accordance with paragraph (2).

(2) Subject to paragraphs (3) and (4), the amount of the reduction of income support in relation to each failure is 20 per cent. of the amount applicable in respect of a single claimant for income support aged not less than 25 as prescribed in paragraph 1(1)(e) of Schedule 2 to the Income Support (General) Regulations 1987.

(3) In any benefit week, the amount of income support payable to a person is not, by virtue of paragraph (1), to be reduced below 10 pence.

(4) The amount of income support payable to a person is not to be reduced in accordance with paragraph (1) if that amount—

(a) is, at the time a determination falls to be made in respect of the current failure, being paid at a reduced rate in accordance with paragraphs (1) and (2), regulations 7(3) and 8 of the Social Security (Work-focused Interviews for Lone Parents) and Miscellaneous Amendments Regulations 2000 or regulation 12(2)(c) of the Social Security (Jobcentre Plus Interviews) Regulations 2002; and
(b) was last reduced not more than two weeks before the date of the current failure.

(5) In this regulation—

"benefit week" means any period of seven days corresponding to the week in respect of which income support is due to be paid;

"current failure" means a failure which, in relation to a person, may lead to a reduction in income support under paragraph (1) in relation to which the Secretary of State has not yet determined whether the amount of income support payable to the person is to be reduced in accordance with those paragraphs.

Circumstances where reduction under regulation 8(1) and (2) ceases to have effect

2.1106 **9.**—(1) The reduction in income support set out in regulation 8(1) in respect of a failure to undertake work-related activity ceases to have effect in respect of a person from whichever is the earlier of—

(a) the date on which the person is no longer required to take part in a work-related activity as a condition of continuing to be entitled to the full amount of benefit which is payable apart from these Regulations; or

(b) the first day of the benefit week in which the person satisfies a compliance condition.

(2) In paragraph (1)(b), "compliance condition" means a requirement to—

(a) undertake work-related activity; or

(b) take part in a work-focused interview.

Restrictions on availability

10.—(1) Subject to paragraph (2), a person to whom regulation 2 applies may restrict the times at which they are required to undertake work-related activity. **2.1107**

(2) A person may not restrict the times at which they are required to undertake work-related activity by virtue of paragraph (1) to exclude—

(a) their child's normal school hours; or

(b) any period during which the person entrusts temporary supervision of their child to a person over the age of 18, not including any form of health care for the child.

Contracting out

11.—(1) Any function of the Secretary of State under this Part specified in paragraph (2) may be exercised by, or by employees of, such person (if any) as the Secretary of State may authorise for that purpose. **2.1108**

(2) The functions are any function under—

(a) regulation 2 (requirement to undertake work-related activity);

(b) regulation 3 (notification of work-related activity);

(c) regulation 4 (requirement to undertake work-related activity at a certain time not to apply);

(d) regulation 5 (reconsideration of action plans).

The Shared Parental Leave and Statutory Shared Parental Pay (Consequential Amendments to Subordinate Legislation) Order 2014

(2014/3255)

Made by the Secretary of State under section 135(3) and 136(1) and (2) of the Children and Families Act 2014.

[In force December 31, 2014 and 5 April, 2015]

GENERAL NOTE

This Order makes consequential amendments to secondary legislation following the introduction of shared parental leave and statutory shared parental pay in place of additional paternity leave and additional statutory paternity pay by Part 7 of the Children and Families Act 2014. Those amendments that come into force on April 5, 2015 are subject to the transitional provisions in art.35. **2.1109**

Citation and commencement

2.1110 **1.**—(1) This Order may be cited as the Shared Parental Leave and Statutory Shared Parental Pay (Consequential Amendments to Subordinate Legislation) Order 2014.

(2) The provisions of this Order specified in article 37 come into force on 31st December 2014.

(3) The remaining provisions of this Order come into force on 5th April 2015.

2.–34. *[Omitted.]*

Transitional provisions

2.1111 **35.**—(1) The amendments made by this Order in those articles which come into force on 5th April 2015 in accordance with 1(3) (amendments relating to references to ordinary and additional paternity leave and to ordinary and additional statutory paternity pay) do not have effect in relation to—

(a) ordinary statutory paternity pay which is paid;
(b) additional statutory paternity pay which is paid;
(c) a period in respect of which additional statutory paternity pay is payable which begins, or continues;
(d) ordinary paternity leave which is taken; or
(e) additional paternity leave which is taken;

on or after 5th April 2015.

(2) In this article—

"additional paternity leave" means leave under section 80AA or 80BB of the Employment Rights Act 1996;

"additional statutory paternity pay" means pay under section 171ZEA or 171ZEB of the Social Security Contributions and Benefits Act 1992;

"ordinary paternity leave" means leave under section 80A or 80B of the Employment Rights Act 1996;

"ordinary statutory paternity pay" means pay under section 171ZA or 171ZB of the Social Security Contributions and Benefits Act 1992.

36.–37. *[Omitted.]*

The Social Security (Persons from Abroad) Miscellaneous Amendments Regulations 1996

(SI 1996/30) (AS AMENDED)

Made by the Secretary of State under ss.64(1), 68(4)(c)(i), 70(4), 71(6), 123(1), 124(1), 128(1), 129(1), 130(1) and (2), 131(1) and (3), 135, 137(1) and (2)(a) and (i) and 175(1) and (3)–(5) of the Social Security Contributions and Benefits Act 1992 and s.5(1)(r) of the Social Security Administration Act 1992

[In force February 5, 1996]

Saving

12.—(1) Where, before the coming into force of these Regulations, a person who becomes an asylum seeker under regulation 4A(5)(a)(i) of the Council Tax Benefit Regulations, regulation 7A(5)(a)(i) of the Housing Benefit Regulations or regulation 70(3A)(a) of the Income Support Regulations, as the case may be, is entitled to benefit under any of those Regulations, those provisions of those Regulations as then in force shall continue to have effect [1 . . .] [2 (both as regards him and as regards persons who are members of his family at the coming into force of these Regulations)] as if regulations 3(a) and (b), 7(a) and (b) or 8(2) and (3)(c), as the case may be, of these Regulations had not been made. 2.1112

(2) Where, before the coming into force of these Regulations, a person in respect of whom an undertaking was given by another person or persons to be responsible for his maintenance and accommodation, claimed benefit to which he is entitled, or is receiving benefit, under the Council Tax Benefit Regulations, the Housing Benefit Regulations or the Income Support Regulations, as the case may be, those Regulations as then in force shall have effect as if regulations 3, 7 or 8, as the case may be, of these Regulations had not been made.

AMENDMENTS

1. Added by the Asylum and Immigration Act 1996 Sch.1 para 5 (July 24, 1996) and repealed by Immigration and Asylum Act 1999 Sch.14 para.113 (April 3, 2000).

2. Social Security (Immigration and Asylum) Consequential Amendments Regulations 2000 (SI 2000/636) reg.12(11)(a) (April 3, 2000).

GENERAL NOTE

See the notes to "persons subject to immigration control" in SI 2000/636 and to reg.70 of the Income Support Regulations. 2.1113

The transitional protection established by reg.12 is unaffected by anything in the Social Security (Persons from Abroad) Amendment Regulations 2006 (SI 2006/1026)—see reg.11(2)(a) of SI 2006/1026.

The Social Security (Immigration and Asylum) Consequential Amendments Regulations 2000

(SI 2000/636) (AS AMENDED)

Made by the Secretary of State under ss.115(3), (4) and (7), 1235) and (6), 166(3) and 167 of the Immigration and Asylum Act 1999, ss.64(1), 68(4), 70(4), 71(6), 123(1)(a), (d) and (e), 135(1), 136(3) and (4), 137(1) and (2)(i) and 175(1), (3) and (4) of the Social Security Contributions and Benefits Act 1992, ss.5(1)(a) and (b), 189(1) and (4) and 191 of the Social Security Administration Act 1992, ss.12(1) and (2), 35(1) and 36(2) and (4) of the Jobseekers Act 1995

[In force April 3, 2000]

GENERAL NOTE

2.1114 These regulations are made under s.115 of the Immigration and Asylum Act 1999 which excludes "persons subject to immigration control" from certain benefits. Regulation 2 and the Schedule provide for exceptions to that exclusion. The combined effect of those provisions is as follows.

"Person subject to immigration control" is defined by s.115(9). Note first of all that a British citizen can never be a person subject to immigration control for social security purposes—*R(PC)2/07*. Neither can a person who is a national of a European Economic Area ("EEA") state (i.e. of the 28 EU countries—Austria, Belgium, Bulgaria, Croatia, Cyprus, the Czech Republic, Denmark, Estonia, Finland, France, Germany, Greece, Hungary, Ireland, Italy, Latvia, Lithuania, Luxembourg, Malta, the Netherlands, Poland, Portugal, Romania, Slovakia, Slovenia, Spain, Sweden and the UK—or of Iceland, Liechtenstein or Norway).

Nationals of other countries are subject to immigration control if they are within one of the following four categories:

(a) A person who requires leave to enter or remain in the UK but does not have it

2.1115 This category (s.115(9)(a)) covers illegal entrants, overstayers, people who are subject to a deportation order, those allowed temporary admission to the UK and, subject to *R(SB) 11/88* (below), anyone whose immigration status has yet to be determined.

The practice of the UK Border Agency of the Home Office ("UKBA") is to grant temporary admission to asylum seekers (except those who are detained) pending investigation of their claims (see *CIS 3108/97*). Section 115 therefore has the effect of excluding all asylum seekers from benefit with effect from April 3, 2000. The intention is that asylum seekers who are destitute will instead receive support from a Home Office agency, the National Asylum Support Service, under ss.95–100 of the Immigration and Asylum Act. Note, however, that reg.70(2A) of the IS Regulations reg.147(2A) of the JSA Regulations reg.12(1) of the Social Security (Persons From Abroad) Miscellaneous Amendments Regulations 1996 (SI 1996/30) and regs 2(4)(a) and (5) and 12(3) of SI 2000/636 contain important transitional protection for claimants who became asylum seekers on or before April 2, 2000.

For social security purposes, whether or not a person requires leave to enter or remain in the UK is a matter for the decision-maker (or, on appeal, for the appeal tribunal or Commissioner) to determine and any decision by the UKBA is not binding (*R(SB) 11/88* but see *R(SB) 2/85* and *R(SB) 25/85* as to the terms on which leave is granted).

Nationals of the Isle of Man and the Channel Islands have freedom of travel within the UK and do not require leave to enter or remain (Immigration Act 1971 s.1(3)). Certain commonwealth citizens cannot be deported (Immigration Act 1971 s.7(1)).

Finally, note the Displaced Persons (Temporary Protection) Regulations 2005 (SI 2005/1379) (below), which, for benefit purposes, treat some displaced persons as if they have been granted exceptional leave to remain (i.e. with the result that those persons are not persons subject to immigration control under s.115(9)(a)).

(b) A person who has leave to enter or remain but subject to a condition that he does not have recourse to public funds

2.1116 Limited leave to enter or remain subject to there being no recourse to public funds is given under s.33(1) of the Immigration Act 1971. From April 6, 2016, "public funds" are defined by rule 6 of the Immigration Rules as attendance allowance, severe disablement allowance, carer's allowance, disability living allowance, income support, (the former) council tax benefit and housing benefit, a social fund payment, child benefit, income-based JSA, income-related ESA, state pension credit, child tax credit, working tax credit, universal credit, personal independence payment, council tax reduction, certain publicly funded housing, and payments from local welfare funds under s.1 of the Localism Act 2011, the Welfare Funds (Scotland) Act 2015, or regulations made under art.135 of the Welfare Reform (Northern Ireland) Order 2015. Note however the clarifications of that definition in rules 6A–6C, as follows:

> "6A. For the purpose of these Rules, a person (P) is not to be regarded as having (or potentially having) recourse to public funds merely because P is (or will be) reliant in whole or in part on public funds provided to P's sponsor unless, as a result of P's presence in the United Kingdom, the sponsor is (or would be) entitled to increased or additional public funds (save where such entitlement to increased or additional public funds is by virtue of P and the sponsor's joint entitlement to benefits under the regulations referred to in paragraph 6B).
>
> 6B. Subject to paragraph 6C, a person (P) shall not be regarded as having recourse to public funds if P is entitled to benefits specified under section 115 of the Immigration and Asylum Act 1999 by virtue of regulations made under subsections (3) and (4) of that section or section 42 of the Tax Credits Act 2002. For an example of this principle, see *OD v SSWP (JSA)* [2015] UKUT 0438 (AAC).
>
> 6C. A person (P) making an application from outside the United Kingdom will be regarded as having recourse to public funds where P relies upon the future entitlement to any public funds that would be payable to P or to P's sponsor as a result of P's presence in the United Kingdom, (including those benefits to which P or the sponsor would be entitled as a result of P's presence in the United Kingdom under the regulations referred to in to paragraph 6B)."

Such a condition is typically applied to those seeking to join relatives who are settled in the UK, to people coming to the UK to study, to work or just for a visit.

For this category (s.115(9)(b)) and the following two (s.115(9)(c) and (d)) to apply, it is necessary that the person should actually require leave to enter or remain in the UK. So, for example, if the UKBA mistakenly grants conditional leave to a person who is in fact a British citizen and does not require leave at all, the mistake does not cause that person to become subject to immigration control for social security purposes (see *R(SB) 11/88*). However, where it is clear that leave is required, the decision of the UKBA as to the terms on which leave is granted is conclusive (see *R(SB) 2/85* and *R(SB) 25/85*). A proper statement of the terms of leave should be obtained from the Home Office (*CSSB 137/82*).

Until October 28, 2013 there was one exception to the exclusion from benefit in s.115(9)(b). That exception was established by reg.2(1) and para.1 of Pt I of the Schedule and applied to those who had previously supported themselves without recourse to public funds but found themselves temporarily without money because remittances from abroad had been disrupted. In such circumstances, income support, income-based JSA, income-related ESA and social fund payments could be paid as long as there was a reasonable expectation that the supply of funds would be resumed. However, that exception was abolished with effect from October 29, 2013, by reg.9(1) and (3) of the Social Security (Miscellaneous Amendments) (No.3) Regulations 2013 (SI 2013/2536). For details of the law as it stood before that date, see pp.375, 800–801 and 809–810 of Vol.II of the 2013/14 edition.

(c) A person who has leave to enter or remain which was given as a result of a maintenance undertaking

"Maintenance undertaking" is defined by s.115(10) as "a written undertaking given by another person in pursuance of the immigration rules to be responsible for [the claimant's] maintenance and accommodation". Under r.35 of the Immigration Rules such undertakings may be demanded from "a sponsor of a person seeking leave to enter or variation of leave to enter or remain in the United **2.1117**

Kingdom" but are normally only required from the sponsors of elderly or other dependent relatives. The purpose of the undertaking is to reinforce a condition that the person seeking leave to enter or remain should not have recourse to public funds by

- demonstrating that the sponsor has sufficient resources to maintain and accommodate the relative without the latter claiming public funds; and
- making the sponsor legally "liable to maintain" the relative. This has the effect that, if the Secretary of State does for any reason have to pay income support to the relative (and, in most cases, the mere existence of an undertaking will mean that the relative has no such entitlement), the sponsor may, in certain circumstances, be subject to a criminal penalty and the Secretary of State may recoup the benefit paid by making a complaint in a magistrates' court (see, respectively ss.105 and 106 of the SSAA 1992 in Vol.III).

The requirement in the definition that the undertaking has been given "in pursuance of the immigration rules" cannot mean "in pursuance of a requirement in the immigration rules" because the decision whether to ask for an undertaking is a discretionary one. Rather, it means "under" or "further to" the immigration rules, see *CIS/1697/2004*, paras 41 and 42. In that case, the Deputy Commissioner held that it was sufficient that the sponsor was making a promise in furtherance of the claimant's application for indefinite leave to remain.

It is not necessary that the undertaking should be given on one of the official Home Office forms (either Form RON 112 or the Form SET(F) that replaced it)—see *R. (Begum) v Social Security Commissioner* [2003] EWHC 3380 (Admin), QBD (Sir Christopher Bellamy), November 6, 2003 confirming *CIS/2474/1999*, *CIS/2816/2002* and, on this point, *CIS/47/2002*. Those forms "are expressly in the language of undertaking and emphasise the significance of such undertakings" (see Rix LJ at [36] of *Ahmed v Secretary of State for Work & Pensions* [2005] EWCA Civ 535, CA (May, Rix and Jacob LJJ), April 19, 2005 (reported as *R(IS) 8/05*). But if an official form is not used, consideration may need to be given to whether the document signed by the sponsor amounts to an "undertaking" at all. In *Ahmed* the Court of Appeal held (upholding the Commissioner in *CIS/426/2003* and disagreeing, on this point, with the Commissioner in *CIS/47/2002* in which the disputed document was in similar terms) that the issue is one of substance rather than form and that the legal test is whether or not the document contains a promise or agreement about what the sponsor will do in the future rather than a statement about his or her present abilities and intentions:

> "**47.** . . . It seems to me that an undertaking has to be something in the nature of a promise or agreement and the language that 'I am able and willing to maintain and accommodate' is language which has reference, essentially, to current ability and intention and does not amount to a promise for the future. The essence of an undertaking is a promise as to the future, as typically found in the language 'I will.'
>
> **48.** I accept that the use of any particular language is not a condition precedent. The absence of an express reference to 'I undertake', such as is found in the Home Office's forms, or to 'I promise' or 'I agree', will not necessarily be critical if it is still clear that the substance of what is said is a promise for the future." (per Rix LJ)

2.1118 So, the declaration in the *Ahmed* case that the sponsor was "able and willing to maintain and accommodate the applicant without recourse to public funds and in suitable accommodation" was not an undertaking because it only related to present facts and intentions. For a further example (in which the opposite conclusion was reached on the facts) see *CIS/1697/2004*. That decision also holds that neither a commissioner, nor (by necessary implication) a tribunal, has any power to grant rectification of a defective maintenance undertaking .

In *CIS 3508/2001* it was held that leave to enter or remain was given "as a result of" a maintenance undertaking if the existence of that undertaking was a factor in the decision to grant leave. It does not have to be the only, or even a major, factor. It is sufficient that it was of some relevance. It seems that that will almost always be the case if the immigration decision-maker acts within the Immigration Rules. In *Shah v Secretary of State for Work and Pensions* [2002] EWCA Civ 285 (reported as *R(IS) 2/02)*, the Court of Appeal held that a maintenance undertaking should be regarded as a continuing obligation and therefore applied even if the claimant had left the UK (thereby causing his or her indefinite leave to remain to lapse) and had been made a fresh grant of indefinite leave to remain as a returning residence on his or her return. *Shah* was decided under the pre-April 2000 law, but it is suggested that the same principles also apply to s.115(9)(c).

Under the principles set out by the House of Lords in *Kerr v Department for Social Development* [2004] UKHL 23; *R1/04 (SF)*, it is for the Secretary of State to show that the maintenance undertaking was a factor in the decision to grant leave: see *R(PC) 1/09*. In that case, where the decision to grant leave was made outside the Immigration Rules, the causal connection could not be inferred and had not been established: see also *SSWP v SS (SPC)* [2010] UKUT 0483 (AAC) and *SJ v SSWP* [2015] UKUT 0505 (AAC).

People who are granted leave to enter or remain as a result of a maintenance undertaking are not entitled to income support income-based JSA until they have been resident in the UK for a period of at least five years from the date of entry or the date on which the undertaking was given, whichever is later. The only exceptions are where the sponsored immigrant becomes a British citizen during the five-year period (see *R(PC) 2/07*) and where the person (or all the people if there was more than one) who gave the maintenance undertaking has died before the end of the five-year period. See para.3 of Pt I of the Schedule. The five years' residence need not be continuous: it can be made up of shorter periods (see paras 74–75 of the Commissioner's decision in *R(IS) 2/02*). In *CPC/1035/2005* the Commissioner considered the position of a Pakistani national who had been given leave to enter the UK under a maintenance undertaking. Since entering the UK in October 1996, she had returned to Pakistan for periods of 17 months, nearly 14 months and 21 months in order to look after her parents. In July 2004, over $7^{1/2}$ years after she first entered, she claimed—and, in August 2004, was refused—SPC. The Commissioner upheld that refusal. Although it was not necessary for the claimant to be physically present in the UK in order to be resident here, "whether a person is or is not resident in a particular place during a period of physical absence depends on a calculus consisting of the duration and circumstances of the absence". Some absences affect residence simply on account of their length. Each period of absence had to be considered individually but none of the periods listed above, not even the shortest, was compatible with the claimant remaining resident in the UK. It followed that as the claimant had not been resident in the UK for nearly 58 months (4 years and 10 months) of the period between October 1996 and August 2004, she had not been resident for a total of five years since the date of her entry and was therefore still excluded from benefit. 2.1119

Sponsored immigrants are not excluded from social fund payments (see para.4 of Pt II of the Schedule) but in practice are unlikely to be eligible for anything other than a crisis loan or a winter fuel payment. This is because, as persons subject to immigration control, they are excluded from the qualifying benefits for maternity and funeral expenses payments, community care grants, budgeting loans and cold weather payments. Sponsored immigrants are also not excluded from entitlement to attendance allowance, severe disablement allowance, health in pregnancy grants, carer's allowance or disability living allowance.

(d) A person who has leave to enter or remain only because he is appealing against certain immigration decisions

Under s.82 of the Nationality, Immigration and Asylum Act 2002 (the successor to s.61 of the 1999 Act referred to in to para.17 of Sch.4 to that Act), a person with limited 2.1120 leave to enter or remain in the UK has a right of appeal against a decision to vary, or to refuse to vary, his leave. Section 3C of the Immigration Act 1971 (the successor to para.17 of Sch.4 to the 1999 Act) provides that while such an appeal is pending, the leave to which the appeal relates and any conditions subject to which it was granted continue to have effect. Section 115(9)(d) provides that those whose leave has automatically been extended by para.17 are persons subject to immigration control.

The ECSMA Agreement and the European Social Charter

2.1121 Nationals of those countries which are not members of the EEA but which have ratified the European Convention on Social and Medical Assistance ("the ECSMA Agreement") or the European Social Charter (both of which are treaties concluded under the auspices of the Council of Europe (ETS Nos 14 and 35 respectively) are not excluded from income support, income-based jobseeker's allowance, income-related ESA, universal credit, housing benefit, social fund payments or (before April 1, 2013) council tax benefit: see *OD v SSWP (JSA)* [2015] UKUT 0438 (AAC). This affects nationals of Turkey (ECSMA Agreement and Social Charter), Switzerland (Social Charter) and the Former Yugoslav Republic of Macedonia (Social Charter). Turkey ratified the Social Charter on November 24, 1999 and the ECSMA Agreement on December 2, 1996. Switzerland ratified the Social Charter on May 6, 1976 and Macedonia ratified it on March 31, 2005. Records of which States have ratified a Council of Europe treaty are maintained by the Council's Treaty Office and are available from its website at *http://www.conventions.coe.int/*. Note, finally, that there are two European Social Charters. For the purposes of these regulations it is the original Charter (which was opened for signature in Turin on October 18, 1961) that is relevant, not the Revised Social Charter (ETS 163) (which was opened for signature in Strasbourg on May 3, 1996).

The meaning of "lawfully present" was considered by the House of Lords in *Szoma v Secretary of State for Work and Pensions* [2005] UKHL 64 (reported as *R(IS) 2/06*). That appeal was a challenge to the decision of the Court of Appeal in *Kaya v Haringey LBC* [2001] EWCA Civ 677, in which it had been held, following the decision of the House of Lords in *In re Muisi* (reported *sub nom. R. v Home Secretary Ex p. Bugdaycay* [1987] A.C. 514), that a person granted temporary admission to the UK could not be "lawfully present" because he or she was deemed by s.11 of the Immigration Act 1971 not to be present in the UK at all. In *Szoma*, their Lordships overruled *Kaya* and held that lawful presence did not require

> "More by way of positive legal authorisation for someone's presence in the UK than that they are at large here pursuant to the express written authority of an immigration officer provided for by statute."

Note that an ECSMA national who is not excluded from benefit by virtue of para.4 of Pt I of the Schedule, may nevertheless be excluded by virtue of the habitual residence and right to reside tests—see *Yesilov v London Borough of Camden and SSWP* [2009] EWCA Civ 415 *(R(H) 7/09)*.

Spouses and family members of EEA nationals

2.1122 A person who is not an EEA national but who is a family member of such a national is not excluded from social fund payments (and certain non-contributory, non-means-tested benefits covered by Vol.I) (para.1 of Pt II of the Schedule. In *CDLA/708/2007*, the Deputy Commissioner held that para.1 only applied where the EEA national is "exercising his or her rights or freedoms under the EEA Agreement (whether or not he or she also has equivalent rights under EC law) and where the family member is a person who has rights under the EEA Agreement as a family member. However, in *JFP v DSD (DLA)* [2012] NI Com 267, the Chief Commissioner of Northern Ireland declined to follow *CDLA/708/2007*. In his view, there was no reason not to give para.1 of Pt II of the Schedule its natural meaning so that s.115 does not exclude any family member of any EEA national from entitlement to attendance allowance, disability living allowance, carer's allowance, child benefit, a social fund payment or any of the other benefits set out in the heading to that Part of the Schedule. In *MS v SSWP (DLA)* [2016] UKUT 0042 (AAC) a judge of the Upper Tribunal in Great Britain considered the reasoning in both decisions and preferred that in *CDLA/708/2007*. The judge's views on this point were obiter because he had already decided that the claimant did not satisfy the conditions of entitlement to DLA. However, the practical effect of *MS v SSWP* is to create a conflict of precedent between Great Britain and Northern Ireland. The strict position has always been that the FTT in Great Britain was bound to follow *CDLA/708/2007* and appeal tribunals in Northern Ireland were bound by the decision of the Chief Commissioner. However, most tribunals in Great Britain would in practice have regarded themselves as free to follow *JFP v DSD* because, although it was given in another jurisdiction, it was of considerable persuasive authority, had considered *CDLA/708/2007* in detail, and disapproved it. That line of argument is no longer open following *MS v SSWP*.

As regards entitlement to social fund payments, see the note on sponsored immigrants (above) as to the practical restrictions on eligibility.

EEA reciprocal agreements

Under art.310 (formerly art.238) of the Treaty establishing the European Community (as amended by the Treaty of Amsterdam), the EC "may conclude with one or more States or international organisations agreements establishing an association involving reciprocal rights and obligations, common action and special procedure". Paragraphs 2 and 3 of Pt II of the Schedule apply when such a reciprocal agreement provides for equal treatment in the field of social security of workers who are nationals of the signatory State and their families. In those circumstances, nationals of the non-EC State who are lawfully working in the UK and members of their families who are living with them are not excluded by s.115 from entitlement to social fund payments, attendance allowance, SDA, health in pregnancy grants, carer's allowance, DLA and child benefit. For an example of how an association agreement affected entitlement to family credit under the pre-April 3, 2000 law see *R(FC) 1/01* which also decides that where such an Agreement does not provide for equal treatment in the field of social security but a Decision of an Association Council constituted under the Agreement and required by the Agreement to adopt social security measures does so provide, the Decision of the Association Council must be regarded as made under the Agreement so that (in terms of the current law) paras 2 and 3 of Pt II of the Schedule would apply. **2.1123**

From time to time, tribunals can be called on to decide legal issues arising under the terms of the individual Association Agreements and the Decisions of the Association Councils established by those Agreements. Useful guidance for those who need to apply the Agreement between the EC and Turkey may be found in two decisions of Commissioner Mesher, *CJSA/4705/1999* and *CIS/5707/1999*. In the latter appeal, the Commissioner holds that income support is not within the material scope of Decision 3/80 of the Association Council under that Agreement (and therefore that IS claimants may not benefit from its terms). In the former appeal, it was held that JSA was within the material scope of the Decision but, following the decision of the ECJ in *Sürül v Bundesanstalt für Arbeit* (C–262/96) [1999] E.C.R. I-2685, a person may only rely on the Decision if authorised to reside in the Member State concerned and lawfully resident there. In *CJSA/4705/1999*, the claimant was an overstayer and therefore not authorised to reside in the United Kingdom. He could not therefore benefit from Decision 3/80.

The habitual residence test and the right to reside

Note that, even if claimants are not excluded from benefit as a person subject to immigration control, entitlement to IS, JSA and SPC is also dependent upon their being (or treated as being) habitually resident. For EEA and Swiss nationals, this includes a requirement that they should have a "right to reside" in the Common Travel Area. See generally the notes to the definition of "person from abroad" in reg.21AA of the IS Regulations. **2.1124**

Citation, commencement and interpretation

2.1125 **1.**—(1) These Regulations may be cited as the Social Security (Immigration and Asylum) Consequential Amendments Regulations 2000.

(2) These Regulations shall come into force on 3rd April 2000.

(3) In these Regulations—

"the Act" means the Immigration and Asylum Act 1999;

"the Attendance Allowance Regulations" means the Social Security (Attendance Allowance) Regulations 1991;

"the Claims and Payments Regulations" means the Social Security (Claims and Payments) Regulations 1987;

"the Contributions and Benefits Act" means the Social Security Contributions and Benefits Act 1992;

[1 . . .];

"the Disability Living Allowance Regulations" means the Social Security (Disability Living Allowance) Regulations 1991;

[2 "the Employment and Support Allowance Regulations" means the Employment and Support Allowance Regulations 2008;]

[1 . . .];

"the Income Support Regulations" means the Income Support (General) Regulations 1987;

"the Invalid Care Allowance Regulations" means the Social Security (Invalid Care Allowance) Regulations 1976;

"the Jobseeker's Allowance Regulations" means the Jobseeker's Allowance Regulations 1996;

[3 "personal independence payment" means personal independence payment under Part 4 of the Welfare Reform Act 2012;]

"the Persons from Abroad Regulations" means the Social Security (Persons from Abroad) Miscellaneous Amendments Regulations 1996;

"the Severe Disablement Allowance Regulations" means the Social Security (Severe Disablement Allowance) Regulations 1984.

[2 "income-related employment and support allowance" means an income-related allowance under Part 1 of the Welfare Reform Act 2007 (employment and support allowance) [4 ;

"universal credit" means universal credit under Part 1 of the Welfare Reform Act 2012].]

(4) In these Regulations, unless the context otherwise requires, a reference—

(a) to a numbered regulation or Schedule is to the regulation in, or the Schedule to, these Regulations bearing that number;

(b) in a regulation or Schedule to a numbered paragraph is to the paragraph in that regulation or Schedule bearing that number.

AMENDMENTS

1. Housing Benefit and Council Tax Benefit (Consequential Provisions) Regulations 2006 (SI 2006/217) reg.3 and Sch.1 (March 6, 2006).

2. Employment and Support Allowance (Consequential Provisions) (No.2) Regulations 2008 (SI 2008/1554) reg.69(1) and (2) (October 27, 2008).

3. Personal Independence Payment (Supplementary Provisions and Consequential Amendments) Regulations 2013 (SI 2013/388) reg.8 and Sch. para.23(1) and (2) (April 8, 2013).

4. Universal Credit (Consequential, Supplementary, Incidental and Miscellaneous Provisions) Regulations 2013 (SI 2013/630) reg.31(1) and (2) (April 29, 2013).

GENERAL NOTE

With effect from April 7, 2003 the definition of "the Claims and Payments Regulations" was revoked in so far as it related to child benefit and guardian's allowance (reg.43 of and Pt I of Sch.3 to the Child Benefit and Guardian's Allowance (Administration) Regulations 2003). The definition remains in force for the purposes of other benefits. **2.1126**

Persons not excluded from specified benefits under section 115 of the Immigration and Asylum Act 1999

2.—(1) For the purposes of entitlement to income-based jobseeker's allowance, income support, a social fund payment, housing benefit [6 . . .] under the Contributions and Benefits Act, [3 income-related employment and support allowance,] [2 or state pension credit under the State Pension Credit Act 2002,] as the case may be, a person falling within a category or description of persons specified in Part I of the Schedule is a person to whom section 115 of the Act does not apply. **2.1127**

[8 (1A) For the purposes of entitlement to universal credit, a person falling within a category or description of persons specified in paragraphs 2, 3 and 4 of Part I of the Schedule is a person to whom section 115 of the Act does not apply.]

(2) For the purposes of entitlement to attendance allowance, severe disablement allowance, [1 carer's allowance], disability living allowance, a social fund payment [4 , health in pregnancy grant] or child benefit under the Contributions and Benefits Act [7 or personal independence payment], as the case may be, a person falling within a category or description of persons specified in Part II of the Schedule is a person to whom section 115 of the Act does not apply.

(3) For the purposes of entitlement to child benefit, attendance allowance or disability living allowance under the Contributions and Benefits Act [7 or personal independence payment], as the case may be, a person in respect of whom there is an Order in Council made under section 179 of the Social Security Administration Act 1992 giving effect to a reciprocal agreement in respect of one of those benefits, as the case may be, is a person to whom section 115 of the Act does not apply.

(4) For the purposes of entitlement to—

(a) income support, a social fund payment, housing benefit [6 . . .] under the Contributions and Benefits Act, [3 or income-related employment and support allowance,] as the case may be, a person who is entitled to or is receiving benefit by virtue of paragraph (1) or (2) of regulation 12 of the Persons from Abroad Regulations is a person to whom section 115 of the Act does not apply;

(b) attendance allowance, disability living allowance, [1carer's allowance, severe disablement allowance, a social fund payment or child benefit under the Contributions and Benefits Act, as the case may be, a person who is entitled to or is receiving benefit byvirtue of paragraph (10) of regulation 12 is a person to whom section 115 of the Act does not apply.

[2(c) state pension credit under the State Pension Credit Act 2002, a person to whom sub-paragraph (a) would have applied but for the fact that they have attained the qualifying age for the purposes of state pension credit, is a person to whom section 115 of the Act does not apply.]

[5 (5) For the purposes of entitlement to [8 universal credit,] income support, [8 an income-based jobseeker's allowance under the Jobseekers Act 1995], an [8 income-related] employment and support allowance or a social fund payment under the Contributions and Benefits Act, as the case may be, a person who is an asylum seeker within the meaning of paragraph (4) of regulation 12 who has not ceased to be an asylum seeker by virtue of paragraph (5) of that regulation is a person to whom section 115 of the Act does not apply.]

(6) For the purposes of entitlement to housing benefit [6 . . .] or a social fund payment under the Contributions and Benefits Act, as the case may be, a person to whom regulation 12(6) applies is a person to whom section 115 of the Act does not apply.

[2 (7) For the purposes of entitlement to state pension credit under the State Pension Credit Act 2002, a person to whom paragraph (5) would have applied but for the fact that they have attained the qualifying age for the purposes of state pension credit, is a person to whom section 115 of the Act does not apply.

(8) [9 . . .]]

AMENDMENTS

1. Social Security Amendment (Carer's Allowance) Regulations 2002 (SI 2002/2497) reg.3 and Sch.2 (April 1, 2003).

2. State Pension Credit (Transitional and Miscellaneous Provisions) Amendment Regulations 2003 (SI 2003/2274) reg.6 (October 6, 2003).

3. Employment and Support Allowance (Consequential Provisions) (No.2) Regulations 2008 (SI 2008/1554) reg.69(1) and (3) (October 27, 2008).

4. Health in Pregnancy Grant (Entitlement and Amount) Regulations 2008 (SI 2008/3108) reg.8(2) (January 1, 2009).

5. Social Security (Miscellaneous Amendments) (No.5) Regulations 2009 (SI 2009/3228) reg.3(5) (January 25, 2010).

6. Council Tax Benefit Abolition (Consequential Provision) Regulations 2013 (SI 2013/458) reg.3 and Sch.1 (April 1, 2013).

7. Personal Independence Payment (Supplementary Provisions and Consequential Amendments) Regulations 2013 (SI 2013/388) reg.8 and Sch. para.23(1) and (3) (April 8, 2013).

8. Universal Credit (Consequential, Supplementary, Incidental and Miscellaneous Provisions) Regulations 2013 (SI 2013/630) reg.31(1) and (3) (April 29, 2013).

9. Social Security (Miscellaneous Amendments) (No.3) Regulations 2013 (SI 2013/2536) reg.9(2) (October 29, 2013).

Transitional arrangements and savings

2.1128 **12.**—(1) and (2) [2 . . .]

(3) [3 . . .]

(4) An asylum seeker within the meaning of this paragraph is a person who—

(a) submits on his arrival (other than on his re-entry) in the United Kingdom from a country outside the Common Travel Area a claim for asylum on or before 2nd April 2000 to the Secretary of State that it would be contrary to the United Kingdom's obligations under the Convent for him to be removed or required to leave, the United Kingdom and that claim is recorded by the Secretary of State as having been made before that date; or

(b) on or before 2nd April 2000 becomes, while present in Great Britain, an asylum seeker when—
   (i) the Secretary of State makes a declaration to the effect that the country of which he is a national is subject to such a fundamental change of circumstances that he would not normally order the return of a person to that country; and
   (ii) he submits, within a period of three months from the date that declaration was made, a claim for asylum to the Secretary of State under the Convention relating to the Status of Refugees, and
   (iii) his claim for asylum under that Convention is recorded by the Secretary of State has having been made; and

(c) in the case of a claim for jobseeker's allowance, holds a work permit or has written authorisation from the Secretary of state permitting him to work in the United Kingdom.

(5) A person ceases to be an asylum seeker for the purposes of this paragraph when his claim for asylum is recorded by the Secretary of State as having been decided (other than on appeal) or abandoned

(6)–(8) [*Omitted as applying only to housing benefit and council tax benefit.*]

(9) In paragraphs (4) and (7) "the Common Travel Area" means the United Kingdom, the Channel Islands, the Isle of Man and the Republic of Ireland collectively and "the Convention" means the Convention relating to the Status of Refugees done at Geneva on 28th July 1951 as extended by Article 2(1) of the Protocol relating to the Status of Refugees done at New York on 31st January 1967.

(10) Where, before the coming into force of these Regulations, a person has claimed benefit to which he is entitled or is receiving benefit by virtue of regulation 12(3) of the Persons from Abroad Regulations or regulation 14B(g) of the Child Benefit (General) Regulations 1976, as the case may be, those provisions shall continue to have effect, for the purposes of entitlement to attendance allowance, disability living allowance, [1 carer's allowance], severe disablement allowance or child benefit, as the case may be, until such time as—

(a) his claim for asylum (if any) is recorded by the Secretary of State as having been decided or abandoned; or
(b) his entitlement to that benefit is revised or superseded under section 9 or 10 of the Social Security Act 1998, if earlier,

as if regulations 8, 9, 10 and 11 and paragraph (2) or paragraph (3), as the case may be, of regulation 13, had not been made.

(11) In the Persons from Abroad Regulations—

(a) in paragraph (1) of regulation 12, after the words "shall continue to have effect" there shall be inserted the words "both as regards him as regards persons who are members of his family at the coming into force of these Regulations)"; and
(b) notwithstanding the amendments and revocations in regulations 3, 6 and 7, regulations 12(1) and (2) of the Persons from Abroad Regulations shall continue to have effect as they had effect before those amendments and revocations came into force.

AMENDMENTS

1. Social Security Amendment (Carer's Allowance) Regulations 2002 (SI 2002/2497) reg.3 and Sch.2 (April 1, 2003).

2. Asylum and Immigration (Treatment of Claimants, etc.) Act 2004 (c.19) s.12(3) (June 14, 2007).

3. Social Security (Miscellaneous Amendments) (No.5) Regulations 2009 (SI 2009/3228) reg.2(1)(c) (January 25, 2010).

GENERAL NOTE

2.1129 Paragraphs (1) and (2) made transitional provision for asylum seekers who claimed asylum before April 3, 2000, by preserving the effect of s.11(2) of the Asylum and Immigration Act 1996 (which was repealed by the Immigration and Asylum Act 1999 with effect from that date). They were revoked on June 14, 2007. However, by art.2(3) of the Asylum and Immigration (Treatment of Claimants, etc.) Act 2004 (Commencement No.7 and Transitional Provisions) Order 2007 (SI 2007/1602), the revocation of reg.21ZB "shall not apply to a person who is recorded as a refugee on or before June 14, 2007". For those purposes a person is recorded as a refugee on the day on which the Home Secretary notifies him that he has been recognised as a refugee and granted asylum in the UK (see art.2(4)). For cases in which the claim for asylum was made before April 3, 2000 and the decision granting refugee status was notified on or before June 14, 2007, see pp.698–699 of the 2007 edition.

Until January 25, 2010, para.(3) allowed pre-April 3, 2000 asylum seekers to claim income support (and, from October 27, 2008, employment and support allowance: see reg.69(1) and (4) of SI 2008/1554) at the reduced "urgent cases" rate. Paragraph (3) was revoked on January 25, 2010. From that date, if there are still any pre-April 3, 2000 asylum seekers (as defined in para.(4)) who have not ceased to be an asylum seekers under para.(5), they can claim income support, jobseeker's allowance, employment and support allowance and social fund payments at the full rate under reg.2(5). For income support, such claimants will fall within the amended prescribed category "Persons from abroad" in para.21 of Sch.1B to the Income Support Regulations.

SCHEDULE **Regulation 2**

PERSONS NOT EXCLUDED FROM CERTAIN BENEFITS UNDER SECTION 115 OF THE IMMIGRATION AND ASYLUM ACT 1999

PART I

2.1130 *Persons not excluded under section 115 of the Immigration and Asylum Act from entitlement to [5 universal credit,] income-based jobseeker's allowance, income support, [3 income-related employment and support allowance,] a social fund payment, housing benefit or council tax benefit.*

1.[7 . . .]

2. A person who has been given leave to enter or remain in, the United Kingdom by the Secretary of State upon an undertaking by another person or persons pursuant to the immigration rules within the meaning of the Immigration Act 1971, to be responsible for his maintenance and accommodation and who has not been resident in the United Kingdom for a period of at least five years beginning on the date of entry or the date on which the undertaking was given in respect of him, whichever date is the later and the person or persons who gave the undertaking to provide for his maintenance and accommodation has, or as the case may be, have died

3. A person who—

(a) has been given leave to enter or remain in, the United Kingdom by the Secretary of State upon an undertaking by another person or persons pursuant to the immigration rules within the meaning of the Immigration Act 1971, to be responsible for his maintenance and accommodation; and
(b) has been resident in the United Kingdom for a period of at least five years beginning on the date of entry or the date on which the undertaking was given in respect of him, whichever date is the later.

4. A person who is a national of a state which has ratified the European Convention on Social and Medical Assistance (done in Paris on 11th December 1953) or a state which has ratified the Council of Europe Social Charter (signed in Turin on 18th October 1961) and who is lawfully present in the United Kingdom.

PART II

Persons not excluded under section 115 of the Immigration and Asylum Act from entitlement to attendance allowance, severe disablement allowance, [1carer's allowance], disability living allowance, [4 personal independence payment,] a social fund payment [2 , Health in Pregnancy Grant] or child benefit. **2.1131**

1. A member of a family of a national of a State contracting party to the Agreement on the European Economic Area signed at Oporto on 2nd May 1992 as adjusted by the Protocol signed at Brussels on 17th March 1993 [6 as modified or supplemented from time to time].

2. A person who is lawfully working in Great Britain and is a national of a State with which the Community has concluded an agreement under Article 310 of the Treaty of Amsterdam amending the Treaty on European Union, the Treaties establishing the European Communities and certain related Acts providing, in the field of social security, for the equal treatment of workers who are nationals of the signatory State and their families.

3. A person who is a member of a family of, and living with, a person specified in paragraph 2.

4. A person who has been given leave to enter, or remain in, the United Kingdom by the Secretary of State upon an undertaking by another person or persons pursuant to the immigration rules within the meaning of the Immigration Act 1971, to be responsible for his maintenance and accommodation.

AMENDMENTS

1. Social Security Amendment (Carer's Allowance) Regulations 2002 (SI 2002/2497) reg.3 and Sch.2 (April 1, 2003).
2. Health in Pregnancy Grant (Entitlement and Amount) Regulations 2008 (SI 2008/3108) reg.8(3) (January 1, 2009).
3. Employment and Support Allowance (Consequential Provisions) (No.2) Regulations 2008 (SI 2008/1554) reg.69(1) and (5) (October 27, 2008).
4. Personal Independence Payment (Supplementary Provisions and Consequential Amendments) Regulations 2013 (SI 2013/388) reg.8 and Sch. para.23(1) and (4) (April 8, 2013).
5. Universal Credit (Consequential, Supplementary, Incidental and Miscellaneous Provisions) Regulations 2013 (SI 2013/630) reg.31(1) and (4) (April 29, 2013).
6. Social Security (Croatia) Amendment Regulations 2013 (SI 2013/1474) reg.8 (July 1, 2013).
7. Social Security (Miscellaneous Amendments) (No.3) Regulations 2013 (SI 2013/2536) reg.9(3) (October 29,2013).

The Social Security (Habitual Residence) Amendment Regulations 2004

(SI 2004/1232)

Made by the Secretary of State under ss.123(1)(a), (d) and (e), 131(3)(b), 135(1) and (2), 137(1) and (2)(i) and 175(1), (3) and (4) of the Social Security Contributions and Benefits Act 1992, ss.4(5), 35(1) and 36(2) and

(4) of the Jobseekers Act 1995 and ss.1(5)(a) and 17(1) of the State Pension Credit Act 2002

[In force May 1, 2004]

General Note

2.1132 See the commentary to reg.21AA of the Income Support Regulations.

These regulations were completely revoked by reg.11(1)(d) of SI 2006/1026 with effect from April 30, 2006 but with a saving (in reg.11(2)(b)) for the transitional protection in reg.6 below.

Transitional arrangements and savings

2.1133 **6.**—(1) Paragraph (2) shall apply where a person—

(a) is entitled to a specified benefit in respect of a period which includes 30th April 2004;

(b) claims a specified benefit on or after 1 May 2004 and it is subsequently determined that he is entitled to that benefit in respect of a period which includes 30 April 2004;

(c) claims a specified benefit on or after 1 May 2004 and it is subsequently determined that he is entitled to such a benefit in respect of a period which is continuous with a period of entitlement to the same or another specified benefit which includes 30 April 2004;

[1 (ca) to whom sub-paragraph (c) applied, claims an employment and support allowance and it is subsequently determined that he is entitled to that benefit, and this entitlement is linked to a previous period of entitlement by virtue of regulation 145(1) of the Employment and Support Allowance Regulations (linking rules);]

(d) claims jobseeker's allowance on or after 1 May 2004 and it is subsequently determined that he is entitled to jobseeker's allowance in respect of a period of entitlement to that benefit which is linked to a previous period of entitlement which includes 30 April 2004 by virtue of regulations made under paragraph 3 of Schedule 1 to the Jobseekers Act 1995.

(2) Where this paragraph applies—

(a) *[Omitted]*;

(b) regulation 21 of the Income Support Regulations shall continue to have effect as if regulation 3 had not been made;

(c) regulation 85 of the Jobseeker's Allowance Regulations shall continue to have effect as if regulation 4 had not been made; [1 . . .]

(d) regulation 2 of the State Pension Credit Regulations shall continue to have effect as if regulation 5 had not been made. [1 ; and

(e) regulation 70(2) to (4) of the Employment and Support Allowance Regulations (special cases: supplemental – persons from abroad) does not apply.]

(3) The provisions saved by paragraph (2) shall continue to have effect until the date on which entitlement to a specified benefit for the purposes of paragraph (1) ceases, and if there is more than one such specified benefit, until the last date on which such entitlement ceases.

[1 (4) In this regulation—

(a) "the Employment and Support Allowance Regulations" means the Employment and Support Allowance Regulations 2008; and

(b) "specified benefit" means income support, housing benefit, council tax benefit, jobseeker's allowance, state pension credit and employment and support allowance.]

AMENDMENT

1. Social Security (Miscellaneous Amendments) (No.3) Regulations 2011 (SI 2011/2425) reg.17 (October 31, 2011).

MODIFICATION

Regulation 6 is modified by Sch.2 para.27 of the Employment and Support Allowance (Transitional Provisions, Housing Benefit and Council Tax Benefit) (Existing Awards) (No.2) Regulations 2010 (SI 2010/1907) (as amended) for the purposes specified in reg.16(1). For details of the modification, see the text of those Regulations in Vol.I.

The Accession (Immigration and Worker Registration) Regulations 2004

(SI 2004/1219) (AS AMENDED)

Made by the Home Secretary, under section 2(2) of the European Communities Act 1972 and section 2 of the European Union (Accessions) Act 2003

[In force May 1, 2004]

GENERAL NOTE

See the commentary to reg.21AA of the Income Support Regulations. 2.1134

With two exceptions, these Regulations were revoked by reg.2 of the Accession (Immigration and Worker Registration) (Revocation, Savings and Consequential Provisions) Regulations 2011 (SI 2011/544) with effect from May 1, 2011. For the text of the Regulations prior to revocation, see pp.792–798 of Vol.II of the 2011/12 edition.

The exceptions are that:

- reg.8 remains in force (as amended) until April 30, 2012 (see reg.3(1)–(3) of SI 2011/544); and
- the whole of the regulations continue to have effect to the extent necessary for the purposes of reg.7A of the Immigration (European Economic Area) Regulations 2006 which is introduced by reg.5 of and Sch.2 to SI 2011/544.

Registration card and registration certificate

8.—(1) An application for a registration certificate authorising an accession State worker requiring registration to work for an employer may only be made by an applicant who is working for that employer at the date of the application. 2.1135

(2) The application shall be in writing and shall be made to the Secretary of State.

(3) The application shall state—

(a) the name, address, and date of birth of the applicant;

(b) the name and address of the head or main office of the employer;
(c) the date on which the applicant began working for that employer;
(d) where the applicant has been issued with a registration card, the reference number of that card.

(4) Unless the applicant has been issued with a registration card under paragraph (5), the application shall be accompanied by—
(a) a registration fee of [[1] [[2] £90]];
(b) two passport size photographs of the applicant;
(c) the applicant's national identity card or passport issued by the applicant's State;
(d) a letter from the employer concerned confirming that the applicant began working for the employer on the date specified in the application.

(5) In the case of an application by an applicant who has not been issued with a registration card under this paragraph, the Secretary of State shall, where he is satisfied that the application is made in accordance with this regulation and that the applicant—
[[3] (a) was an accession State worker requiring registration at the date on which the applicant began working for that employer; and]
(b) began working for the employer on the date specified in the application,

send the applicant a registration card and a registration certificate authorising the worker to work for the employer specified in the application, and shall return the applicant's national identity card or passport.

(6) In the case of any other application, the Secretary of State shall, if he is satisfied as mentioned in paragraph (5), send the applicant a registration certificate authorising the worker to work for the employer specified in the application.

(7) A registration card issued under paragraph (5) shall contain—
(a) the name, nationality and date of birth of the applicant;
(b) a photograph of the applicant;
(c) a reference number.

(8) A registration certificate issued under paragraph (5) or (6) shall contain—
(a) the name of the applicant;
(b) the reference number of the applicant's registration card;
(c) the name and address of the head or main office of the employer, as specified in the application;
(d) the date on which the applicant began working for the employer, as specified in the application; and
(e) the date on which the certificate is issued.

(9) Where the Secretary of State receives an application made in accordance with this regulation and he is not satisfied as mentioned in paragraph (5), he shall—
(a) send the applicant a notice of refusal; and
(b) return any documents and fee that accompanied the application to the applicant.

(10) Where the Secretary of State sends a registration certificate or notice of refusal to an applicant under this regulation he shall, at the same time, send a copy of the certificate or notice to the employer concerned at the address specified in the application for that employer.

(11) Certificates and notices, and copies of these documents, sent under this regulation shall be sent by post.

AMENDMENTS

1. Accession (Immigration and Worker Registration) (Amendment) Regulations 2005 (SI 2005/2400) reg.2 (October 1, 2005).
2. Accession (Immigration and Worker Registration) (Amendment) Regulations 2007 (SI 2007/928) regs 2 and 3 (April 2, 2007).
3. Accession (Immigration and Worker Registration) (Revocation, Savings and Consequential Provisions) Regulations 2011 (SI 2011/1544) reg.3 (May 1, 2011).

The Displaced Persons (Temporary Protection) Regulations 2005

(SI 2005/1379)

Made by the Secretary of State under s.2(2) of the European Communities Act 1972

[In force June 15, 2005]

GENERAL NOTE

These Regulations form part of the implementation of Council Directive 2001/55 on minimum standards for giving temporary protection in the event of a mass influx of displaced persons. Essentially, those granted temporary protection as displaced persons are treated for benefit purposes as if they had been granted exceptional leave to remain. They are therefore not "persons subject to immigration control" within s.115 of the Immigration and Asylum Act 1999. In addition, they do not have to satisfy the right to reside test for income support, income-based JSA, income-related ESA, SPC and universal credit (see reg.21AA(4)(h)(iii) of the Income Support Regulations, reg.85A(4)(h)(iii) of the Jobseeker's Allowance Regulations, reg.70(4)(h)(iii) of the Employment and Support Allowance Regulations, reg.2(4)(h)(iii) of the State Pension Credit Regulations, and reg.9(4)(e)(iii) of the Universal Credit Regulations). **2.1136**

Interpretation

2.—(1) In these Regulations— **2.1137**
(a)–(g) *[Omitted]*
(h) "temporary protection" means limited leave to enter or remain granted pursuant to Part 11A of the Immigration Rules; and
(i) "Temporary Protection Directive" means Council Directive 2001/55/ EC of 20 July 2001 on minimum standards for giving temporary protection in the event of a mass influx of displaced persons and on measures promoting a balance of efforts between member States in receiving such persons and bearing the consequences thereof.

Means of subsistence

3.—(1) Any person granted temporary protection as a result of a decision of the Council of the European Union made pursuant to Article 5 of the Temporary Protection Directive shall be deemed for the purposes of the provision of means of subsistence to have been granted leave to enter or remain in the United Kingdom exceptionally, outside the Immigration Rules. **2.1138**

(2) Subject to paragraph (3), paragraph (1) shall cease to apply on the date when the period of mass influx of displaced persons to which the grant of temporary protection relates ends in accordance with Chapter II of the Temporary Protection Directive.

(3) Paragraph (1) shall continue to apply for a period not exceeding 28 days from the date referred to in paragraph (2) for as long as the conditions in paragraph (4) are satisfied and the person is in the United Kingdom.

(4) Those conditions are—

(a) the person's grant of temporary protection has expired; and

(b) the person is taking all reasonable steps to leave the United Kingdom or place himself in a position in which he is able to leave the United Kingdom, which may include co-operating with a voluntary return programme.

4.—"Means of subsistence" in regulation 3 means any means of subsistence governed by—

(a) Part VII of the Social Security Contributions and Benefits Act 1992;

(b) Part VII of the Social Security Contributions and Benefits (Northern Ireland) Act 1992;

(c) sections 1 and 3 of Part I of the Jobseekers Act 1995;

(d) articles 3 and 5 of Part II of the Jobseekers (Northern Ireland) Order 1995;

(e) the State Pension Credit Act 2002; or

(f) the State Pension Credit Act (Northern Ireland) 2002.

The Immigration (European Economic Area) Regulations 2006

(SI 2006/1003)

REGULATIONS REPRODUCED

PART 1

INTERPRETATION ETC

PART 2

EEA RIGHTS

PART 3

RESIDENCE DOCUMENTATION

PART 4

REFUSAL OF ADMISSION AND REMOVAL ETC

PART 5

PROCEDURE IN RELATION TO EEA DECISIONS

PART 6

APPEALS UNDER THESE REGULATIONS

The Secretary of State, being a Minister designated for the purposes of section 2(2) of the European Communities Act 1972 in relation to measures relating to rights of entry into, and residence in, the United Kingdom, in exercise of the powers conferred upon him by that section, and of the powers conferred on him by section 109 of the Nationality, Immigration and Asylum Act 2002, makes the following Regulations:
[In Force April 30, 2006]

GENERAL NOTE

2.1140 See the commentary to reg.21AA of the Income Support Regulations.

PART 1

INTERPRETATION ETC

Citation and commencement

2.1141 **1.**—These Regulations may be cited as the Immigration (European Economic Area) Regulations 2006 and shall come into force on 30th April 2006.

General interpretation

2.1142 **2.—**(1) In these Regulations—
"the 1971 Act" means the Immigration Act 1971;
"the 1999 Act" means the Immigration and Asylum Act 1999;
"the 2002 Act" means the Nationality, Immigration and Asylum Act 2002;
[8 "the 2014 Act" means the Immigration Act 2014;]
[2 "the Accession Regulations" means the Accession (Immigration and Worker Registration) Regulations 2004;]
[3 "civil partner" does not include—
(a) a party to a civil partnership of convenience; or
(b) the civil partner ("C") of a person ("P") where a spouse, civil partner or durable partner of C or P is already present in the United Kingdom;]

"decision maker" means the Secretary of State, an immigration officer or an entry clearance officer (as the case may be);

[1 "deportation order" means an order made pursuant to regulation 24(3);]

[3 "derivative residence card" means a card issued to a person, in accordance with regulation 18A, as proof of the holder's derivative right to reside in the United Kingdom as at the date of issue;]

"document certifying permanent residence" means a document issued to an EEA national, in accordance with regulation 18, as proof of the holder's permanent right of residence under regulation 15 as at the date of issue;

[3 "durable partner" does not include the durable partner ("D") of a person ("P") where a spouse, civil partner or durable partner of D or P is already present in the United Kingdom and where that marriage, civil partnership or durable partnership is subsisting;]

[3 "EEA decision" means a decision under these Regulations that concerns—

(a) a person's entitlement to be admitted to the United Kingdom;

(b) a person's entitlement to be issued with or have renewed, or not to have revoked, a registration certificate, residence card, derivative residence card, document certifying permanent residence or permanent residence card;

(c) a person's removal from the United Kingdom; or

(d) the cancellation, pursuant to regulation 20A, of a person's right to reside in the United Kingdom [7 ;

but does not include decisions under regulations 24AA (human rights considerations and interim orders to suspend removal) or 29AA (temporary admission in order to submit case in person)];

"EEA family permit" means a document issued to a person, in accordance with regulation 12, in connection with his admission to the United Kingdom;

"EEA national" means a national of an EEA State [4 who is not also a [5 British citizen]];

"EEA State" means—

(a) a member State, other than the United Kingdom;

(b) Norway, Iceland or Liechtenstein; or

(c) Switzerland;

"entry clearance" has the meaning given in section 33(1) of the 1971 Act;

"entry clearance officer" means a person responsible for the grant or refusal of entry clearance;

[1 "exclusion order" means an order made under regulation 19(1B)]

"immigration rules" has the meaning given in section 33(1) of the 1971 Act;

"military service" means service in the armed forces of an EEA State;

"permanent residence card" means a card issued to a person who is not an EEA national, in accordance with regulation 18, as proof of the holder's permanent right of residence under regulation 15 as at the date of issue;

[6 "[7 . . .] qualifying EEA State residence card" means—

(a) [8 a valid document] called a "Residence card of a family member of a Union Citizen" issued under Article 10 of Council Directive

2004/38/EC (as applied, where relevant, by the EEA Agreement) by an EEA State listed in sub-paragraph (b) to a non-EEA family member of an EEA national as proof of the holder's right of residence in that State;

(b) [8 any EEA State, except Switzerland];]

"registration certificate" means a certificate issued to an EEA national, in accordance with regulation 16, as proof of the holder's right of residence in the United Kingdom as at the date of issue;

"relevant EEA national" in relation to an extended family member has the meaning given in regulation 8(6);

"residence card" means a card issued to a person who is not an EEA national, in accordance with regulation 17, as proof of the holder's right of residence in the United Kingdom as at the date of issue;

[3 spouse" does not include—

(a) a party to a marriage of convenience; or

(b) the spouse ("S") of a person ("P") where a spouse, civil partner or durable partner of S or P is already present in the United Kingdom;]

[5 . . .]

(2) Paragraph (1) is subject to paragraph 1(a) of Schedule 4 (transitional provisions).

[1 (3) Section 11 of the 1971 Act (construction of references to entry) shall apply for the purpose of determining whether a person has entered the United Kingdom for the purpose of these Regulations as it applies for the purpose of determining whether a person has entered the United Kingdom for the purpose of that Act.]

AMENDMENTS

1. Immigration (European Economic Area) (Amendment) Regulations 2009 (SI 2009/1117) reg.2 and Sch.1 para.1 (1 June 2009).

2. Accession (Immigration and Worker Registration) (Revocation, Savings and Consequential Provisions) Regulations 2011 (SI 2011/544) reg.5 and Sch.2 para.1 (May 1, 2011).

3. Immigration (European Economic Area) (Amendment) Regulations 2012 (SI 2012/1547) reg.2 and Sch.1 para.1 (July 16, 2012).

4. Immigration (European Economic Area) (Amendment) Regulations 2012 (SI 2012/1547) reg.2 and Sch.1 para.1(d) (October 16, 2012).

5. Immigration (European Economic Area) (Amendment) (No.2) Regulations 2012 (SI 2012/2560) reg.2 and Sch. para.7 (November 8, 2012).

6. Immigration (European Economic Area) (Amendment) (No.2) Regulations 2013 (SI 2013/3032) reg.4 and Sch.1 para.1 (January 1, 2014).

7. Immigration (European Economic Area) (Amendment) (No.2) Regulations 2014 (SI 2014/1976) reg.3 and Sch. para.1 (July 28, 2014).

8. Immigration (European Economic Area) (Amendment) Regulations 2015 (SI 2015/694) reg.4 and Sch.1 para.1 (April 6, 2015).

GENERAL NOTE

2.1143 The change to the definition of "EEA National" made by para.1(d) of SI 2012/1547 with effect from October 16, 2012 was subject to the transitional provisions in Sch.3 to SI 2012/1547, which is given effect by reg.4 of that instrument and which is in the following terms:

"SCHEDULE 3

TRANSITIONAL PROVISIONS

Interpretation

1.—In this Schedule— 2.1144

(a) the "2006 Regulations" means the Immigration (European Economic Area) Regulations 2006; and

(b) the terms "EEA family permit", "EEA State", "family member", "registration certificate" and "residence card" have the meanings given in regulation 2(1) of the 2006 Regulations.

Amendments to the definition of EEA national

2.—(1) Where the right of a family member ("F") to be admitted to, or reside in, the United Kingdom pursuant to the 2006 Regulations depends on the fact that a person ("P") is an EEA national, P will, notwithstanding the effect of paragraph 1(d) of Schedule 1 to these Regulations, continue to be regarded as an EEA national for the purpose of the 2006 Regulations where the criteria in subparagraphs (2), (3) or (4) are met and for as long as they remain satisfied in accordance with subparagraph (5). 2.1145

(2) The criterion in this subparagraph is met where F was on 16th July 2012 a person with a permanent right to reside in the United Kingdom under the 2006 Regulations.

(3) The criteria in this subparagraph are met where F—

(a) was on the 16th July 2012 a person with a right to reside in the United Kingdom under the 2006 Regulations; and

(b) on the 16th October 2012—

(i) held a valid registration certificate or residence card issued under the 2006 Regulations;

(ii) had made an application under the 2006 Regulations for a registration certificate or residence card which had not been determined; or

(iii) had made an application under the 2006 Regulations for a registration certificate or residence card which had been refused and in respect of which an appeal under regulation 26 could be brought while the appellant is in the United Kingdom (excluding the possibility of an appeal out of time with permission) or was pending (within the meaning of section 104 of the Nationality, Immigration and Asylum Act 2002).

(4) The criteria in this subparagraph are met where F—

(a) had, prior to the 16th July 2012, applied for an EEA family permit pursuant to regulation 12 of the 2006 Regulations; or

(b) has applied for and been refused an EEA family permit and where, on the 16th July 2012, an appeal under regulation 26 against that decision could be brought (excluding the possibility of an appeal out of time with permission) or was pending (within the meaning of section 104 of the 2002 Act).

(5) Where met, the criteria in subparagraph (2), (3) and (4) remain satisfied until the occurrence of the earliest of the following events—

(a) the date six months after an EEA family permit has been issued if F has not within that period been admitted to the United Kingdom;

(b) the date on which an appeal against a decision referred to in subparagraph (3)(b)(iii) or (4)(b) can no longer be brought (ignoring the possibility of an appeal out of time with permission) where no such appeal has been brought;

(c) the date on which any appeal against a decision referred to in subparagraph (3)(b)(iii) or (4)(b) is finally determined, is withdrawn or is abandoned (within the meaning of section 104 of the 2002 Act) (save where the outcome of the appeal process is that the document in question falls to be granted);

(d) the date on which F ceases to be the family member of an EEA national; or

(e) the date on which a right of permanent residence under regulation 15 of the 2006 Regulations is lost in accordance with regulation 15(2) of those Regulations.

(6) P will only continue to be regarded as an EEA national for the purpose of considering the position of F under the 2006 Regulations."

Continuity of residence

3.—(1) This regulation applies for the purpose of calculating periods of continuous residence in the United Kingdom under regulation 5(1) and regulation 15. 2.1146

(2) Continuity of residence is not affected by—

(a) periods of absence from the United Kingdom which do not exceed six months in total in any year;

(b) periods of absence from the United Kingdom on military service; or

(c) any one absence from the United Kingdom not exceeding twelve months for an important reason such as pregnancy and childbirth, serious illness, study or vocational training or an overseas posting.

(3) But continuity of residence is broken if a person is removed from the United Kingdom under [1 these Regulations].

AMENDMENT

1. Immigration (European Economic Area) (Amendment) Regulations 2009 (SI 2009/1117) reg.2 and Sch.1 para.2 (June 1, 2009).

DEFINITION

"military service"—see reg.2(1).

"Worker", "self-employed person", "self-sufficient person" and "student"

2.1147 **4.**—(1) In these Regulations—

(a) "worker" means a worker within the meaning of [4 Article 45 of the Treaty on the Functioning of the European Union];

(b) "self-employed person" means a person who establishes himself in order to pursue activity as a self-employed person in accordance with [4 Article 49 of the Treaty on the Functioning of the European Union];

(c) "self-sufficient person" means a person who has—

(i) sufficient resources not to become a burden on the social assistance system of the United Kingdom during his period of residence; and

(ii) comprehensive sickness insurance cover in the United Kingdom;

(d) "student" means a person who—

[3 (i) is enrolled, for the principal purpose of following a course of study (including vocational training), at a public or private establishment which is—

(aa) financed from public funds; or

(bb) otherwise recognised by the Secretary of State as an establishment which has been accredited for the purpose of providing such courses or training within the law or administrative practice of the part of the United Kingdom in which the establishment is located;]

(ii) has comprehensive sickness insurance cover in the United Kingdom; and

(iii) assures the Secretary of State, by means of a declaration, or by such equivalent means as the person may choose, that he has sufficient resources not to become a burden on the social assistance system of the United Kingdom during his period of residence.

(2) For the purposes of paragraph 1(c) [6 or (d)], where family members

of the person concerned reside in the United Kingdom and their right to reside is dependent upon their being family members of that person—

(a) the requirement for that person to have sufficient resources not to become a burden on the social assistance system of the United Kingdom during his period of residence shall only be satisfied if his resources and those of the family members are sufficient to avoid him and the family members becoming such a burden;

(b) the requirement for that person to have comprehensive sickness insurance cover in the United Kingdom shall only be satisfied if he and his family members have such cover.

(3) [6 . . .]

[2 (4) For the purposes of paragraphs (1)(c) and (d) and [6 paragraph (2)], the resources of the person concerned and, where applicable, any family members, are to be regarded as sufficient if—

(a) they exceed the maximum level of resources which a [5 British citizen] and his family members may possess if he is to become eligible for social assistance under the United Kingdom benefit system; or

(b) paragraph (a) does not apply but, taking into account the personal situation of the person concerned and, where applicable, any family members, it appears to the decision maker that the resources of the person or persons concerned should be regarded as sufficient.]

[3(5) For the purpose of regulation 15A(2) references in this regulation to "family members" includes a "primary carer" as defined in regulation 15A(7).]

AMENDMENTS

1. Secretaries of State for Children, Schools and Families, for Innovation, Universities and Skills and for Business, Enterprise and Regulatory Reform Order 2007 (SI 2007/3224) art.15 and Sch. para.60 (December 12, 2007).

2. Immigration (European Economic Area) (Amendment) Regulations 2011 (SI 2011/1247) reg.2(1) and (2) (2 June 2011).

3. Immigration (European Economic Area) (Amendment) Regulations 2012 (SI 2012/1547) reg.2 and Sch.1 para.2 (July 16, 2012).

4. The Treaty of Lisbon (Changes in Terminology or Numbering) Order 2012 (SI 2012/1809) art.3(1) and Sch. Pt.2 (August 1, 2012).

5. Immigration (European Economic Area) (Amendment) (No.2) Regulations 2012 (SI 2012/2560) reg.2 and Sch. para.7 (November 8, 2012).

6. Immigration (European Economic Area) (Amendment) Regulations 2015 (SI 2015/694) reg.4 and Sch.1 para.2 (April 6, 2015).

"Worker or self-employed person who has ceased activity"

5.—(1) In these Regulations, "worker or self-employed person who has ceased activity" means an EEA national who satisfies the conditions in paragraph (2), (3), (4) or (5). **2.1148**

(2) A person satisfies the conditions in this paragraph if he—

(a) terminates his activity as a worker or self-employed person and—

(i) has reached the age at which he is entitled to a state pension on the date on which he terminates his activity; or

(ii) in the case of a worker, ceases working to take early retirement;

(b) pursued his activity as a worker or self-employed person in the United Kingdom for at least twelve months prior to the termination; and

(c) resided in the United Kingdom continuously for more than three years prior to the termination.

(3) A person satisfies the conditions in this paragraph if—

(a) he terminates his activity in the United Kingdom as a worker or self-employed person as a result of a permanent incapacity to work; and

(b) either—

(i) he resided in the United Kingdom continuously for more than two years prior to the termination; or

(ii) the incapacity is the result of an accident at work or an occupational disease that entitles him to a pension payable in full or in part by an institution in the United Kingdom.

(4) A person satisfies the conditions in this paragraph if—

(a) he is active as a worker or self-employed person in an EEA State but retains his place of residence in the United Kingdom, to which he returns as a rule at least once a week; and

(b) prior to becoming so active in that EEA State, he had been continuously resident and continuously active as a worker or self-employed person in the United Kingdom for at least three years.

(5) A person who satisfies the condition in paragraph (4)(a) but not the condition in paragraph (4)(b) shall, for the purposes of paragraphs (2) and (3), be treated as being active and resident in the United Kingdom during any period in which he is working or self-employed in the EEA State.

(6) The conditions in paragraphs (2) and (3) as to length of residence and activity as a worker or self-employed person shall not apply in relation to a person whose spouse or civil partner is a [2 British citizen].

(7) [1 Subject to [3 "regulations 6(2), 7A(3) or 7B(3)], for the purposes of this regulation—]

(a) periods of inactivity for reasons not of the person's own making;

(b) periods of inactivity due to illness or accident; and

(c) in the case of a worker, periods of involuntary unemployment duly recorded by the relevant employment office,

shall be treated as periods of activity as a worker or self-employed person, as the case may be.

AMENDMENTS

1. Accession (Immigration and Worker Registration) (Revocation, Savings and Consequential Provisions) Regulations 2011 (SI 2011/544) reg.5 and Sch.2 para.2 (May 1, 2011).

2. Immigration (European Economic Area) (Amendment) (No.2) Regulations 2012 (SI 2012/2560) reg.2 and Sch. para.7 (November 8, 2012).

3. Immigration (European Economic Area) (Amendment) (No.2) Regulations 2013 (SI 2013/3032) reg.4 and Sch.1 para.2 (January 1, 2014).

DEFINITIONS

"civil partner"—see reg.2(1).
"EEA national"—*ibid.*
"EEA State"—*ibid.*
"self-employed person"—see reg.4(1).
"spouse"—see reg.2(1).
"worker"—see reg.4(1).

GENERAL NOTE

2.1149 For the rules on continuity of residence see reg.3.

"Qualified person"

6.—(1) In these Regulations, "qualified person" means a person who is an EEA national and in the United Kingdom as— 2.1150

(a) a jobseeker;
(b) a worker;
(c) a self-employed person;
(d) a self-sufficient person; or
(e) a student.

(2) [[1] Subject to [[2] regulations 7A(4) and 7B(4)], a person who is no longer working shall not cease to be treated as a worker for the purpose of paragraph (1)(b) if—]

(a) he is temporarily unable to work as the result of an illness or accident;

[[2] (b) he is in duly recorded involuntary unemployment after having been employed in the United Kingdom for at least one year, provided that he—

(i) has registered as a jobseeker with the relevant employment office; and
(ii) satisfies conditions A and B;

(ba) he is in duly recorded involuntary unemployment after having been employed in the United Kingdom for less than one year, provided that he—

(i) has registered as a jobseeker with the relevant employment office; and
(ii) satisfies conditions A and B;]

(c) he is involuntarily unemployed and has embarked on vocational training; or

(d) he has voluntarily ceased working and embarked on vocational training that is related to his previous employment.

[[2] (2A) A person to whom paragraph (2)(ba) applies may only retain worker status for a maximum of six months.]

(3) A person who is no longer in self-employment shall not cease to be treated as a self-employed person for the purpose of paragraph (1)(c) if he is temporarily unable to pursue his activity as a self-employed person as the result of an illness or accident.

[[2] (4) For the purpose of paragraph (1)(a), a "jobseeker" is a person who satisfies conditions [[3] A, B and, where relevant, C].

(5) Condition A is that the person—

(a) entered the United Kingdom in order to seek employment; or
(b) is present in the United Kingdom seeking employment, immediately after enjoying a right to reside pursuant to paragraph (1)(b) to (e) (disregarding any period during which worker status was retained pursuant to paragraph (2)(b) or (ba)).

(6) Condition B is that the person can provide evidence that he is seeking employment and has a genuine chance of being engaged.

(7) A person may not retain the status of a worker pursuant to paragraph (2)(b), or jobseeker pursuant to paragraph (1)(a), for longer than [[3] the relevant period] unless he can provide compelling evidence that he is continuing to seek employment and has a genuine chance of being engaged.]

[[3] (8) In paragraph (7), "the relevant period" means—

(a) in the case of a person retaining worker status pursuant to paragraph (2)(b), a continuous period of six months;

(b) in the case of a jobseeker, [4 91] days, minus the cumulative total of any days during which the person concerned previously enjoyed a right to reside as a jobseeker, not including any days prior to a continuous absence from the United Kingdom of at least 12 months.

(9) Condition C applies where the person concerned has, previously, enjoyed a right to reside under this regulation as a result of satisfying conditions A and B—

(a) in the case of a person to whom paragraph (2)(b) or (ba) applied, for at least six months; or

(b) in the case of a jobseeker, for at least [4 91] days in total,

unless the person concerned has, since enjoying the above right to reside, been continuously absent from the United Kingdom for at least 12 months.

(10) Condition C is that the person has had a period of absence from the United Kingdom.

(11) Where condition C applies—

(a) paragraph (7) does not apply; and

(b) condition B has effect as if "compelling" were inserted before "evidence".]

AMENDMENTS

1. Accession (Immigration and Worker Registration) (Revocation, Savings and Consequential Provisions) Regulations 2011 (SI 2011/544) reg.5 and Sch.2 para.3 (May 1, 2011).

2. Immigration (European Economic Area) (Amendment) (No.2) Regulations 2013 (SI 2013/3032) reg.4 and Sch.1 para.3 (January 1, 2014).

3. Immigration (European Economic Area) Regulations 2006 (SI 2014/1451) reg.3 (July 1, 2014).

4. Immigration (European Economic Area) (Amendment) (No.3) Regulations 2014 (SI 2014/2761) reg.3 (November 10, 2014).

DEFINITIONS

"EEA national"—see reg.2(1).
"self-employed person"—see reg.4(1).
"self-sufficient person"—*ibid.*
"student"—*ibid.*
"worker"—*ibid.*

MODIFICATIONS

From May 1, 2004 to April 30, 2011, this regulation was modified as it affects nationals of A8 States (the Czech Republic, Estonia, Hungary, Latvia, Lithuania, Poland, Slovakia and Slovenia) by reg.5 of the Accession (Immigration and Worker Registration) Regulations 2004 (SI 2004/1219) as amended. For the text of the A8 Regulations as it stood immediately prior to their revocation, see pp.792–798 of Vol.II of the 2011/12 edition.

From July 1, 2013, this regulation is modified as it affects nationals of Croatia by regs 5 and 7 of the Accession of Croatia (Immigration and Worker Authorisation) Regulations 2013 (SI 2013/1460).

The modifications made by reg.5 are that:

- an accession state national subject to worker authorisation who is seeking employment in the United Kingdom shall not be treated as a jobseeker for the purposes of the definition of "qualified person" in reg.6(1) of the EEA

Regulations, and such a person shall be treated as a worker for the purposes of that definition only during a period in which he holds an accession worker authorisation document and is working in accordance with the conditions set out in that document; and that

- reg.6(2) shall not apply to an accession state national subject to worker authorisation who ceases to work.

The modifications made by reg.7 are that during the accession period, para.(1) has effect as if:

- after "EEA national", there were inserted ", except an accession state national subject to worker authorisation within the meaning of regulation 2 of the Croatian Regulations," and
- and after para.(1), there were inserted—

"(1A) In these Regulations, a "qualified person" also means a person who is an accession State national subject to worker authorisation within the meaning of regulation 2 of the Croatian Regulations and in the United Kingdom as—

(a) a self-employed person;
(b) a self-sufficient person;
(c) a student; or
(d) a highly skilled person who is seeking employment or is employed in the United Kingdom.

(1B) In regulation 16(5), a "qualified person" includes an accession State national subject to worker authorisation within the meaning of regulation 2 of the Croatian Regulations.

(1C) In these Regulations—

(a) "the Croatian Regulations" means the Accession of Croatia (Immigration and Worker Authorisation) Regulations 2013; and
(b) "highly skilled worker" has the meaning given in regulation 1 of the Croatian Regulations."

GENERAL NOTE

The amendments made to reg.6(2)(b), and subsequent paragraphs and sub-paragraphs of that regulation, by para.3(b) to (e) of Sch.1 to SI 2013/3032 were subject to the following transitional provision: **2.1151**

"(a) any period of employment in the United Kingdom before the coming into force of [SI 2013/3032] is to be treated as a period of employment under regulation 6 of the 2006 Regulations as amended by these Regulations; and

(b) any period—

(i) of duly recorded involuntary unemployment; or
(ii) during which a person was a jobseeker for the purposes of regulation 6(1)(a) of the 2006 Regulations, before the coming into force of these Regulations is to be disregarded."

See Sch.3 para.1 to SI 2013/3032.

The amendments made to reg.6(4) and (7) and the coming into effect of paras (8)–(11) were subject to the following transitional provision:

"Any period after 31st December 2013 during which a person was a jobseeker for the purposes of regulation 6(1)(a) of the [the Immigration (European Economic Area) Regulations 2006] is, where relevant, to be taken into consideration when determining—

(a) the length of the relevant period; and

(b) whether condition C applies,

for the purposes of regulation 6 of the 2006 Regulations as amended by these Regulations."

See regs 4 and 2 of SI 2014/1451.

Family member

2.1152 7.—(1) Subject to paragraph (2), for the purposes of these Regulations the following persons shall be treated as the family members of another person—

(a) his spouse or his civil partner;

(b) direct descendants of his, his spouse or his civil partner who are—

(i) under 21; or

(ii) dependants of his, his spouse or his civil partner;

(c) dependent direct relatives in his ascending line or that of his spouse or his civil partner;

(d) a person who is to be treated as the family member of that other person under paragraph (3).

(2) A person shall not be treated under paragraph (1)(b) or (c) as the family member of a student residing in the United Kingdom after the period of three months beginning on the date on which the student is admitted to the United Kingdom unless—

(a) in the case of paragraph (b), the person is the dependent child of the student or of his spouse or civil partner; or

(b) the student also falls within one of the other categories of qualified persons mentioned in regulation 6(1).

(3) Subject to paragraph (4), a person who is an extended family member and has been issued with an EEA family permit, a registration certificate or a residence card shall be treated as the family member of the relevant EEA national for as long as he continues to satisfy the conditions in regulation 8(2), (3), (4) or (5) in relation to that EEA national and the permit, certificate or card has not ceased to be valid or been revoked.

(4) Where the relevant EEA national is a student, the extended family member shall only be treated as the family member of that national under paragraph (3) if either the EEA family permit was issued under regulation 12(2), the registration certificate was issued under regulation 16(5) or the residence card was issued under regulation 17(4).

DEFINITIONS

"civil partner"—see reg.2(1).
"EEA family permit"—*ibid.*
"EEA national"—*ibid.*
"qualified person"—see reg.6(1).
"registration certificate"— see reg.2(1).
"relevant EEA national"—*ibid.*, and reg.8(6).
"residence card"—*ibid.*
"spouse"—*ibid.*
"student"—see reg.4(1).

[1 Application of the Accession Regulations

2.1153 **7A.**—(1) This regulation applies to an EEA national who was an accession State worker requiring registration on 30th April 2011 ("an accession worker").

(2) In this regulation—

"accession State worker requiring registration" has the same meaning as in regulation 1(2)(d) of the Accession Regulations;

"legally working" has the same meaning as in regulation 2(7) of the Accession Regulations.

(3) In regulation 5(7)(c), where the worker is an accession worker, periods of involuntary unemployment duly recorded by the relevant employment office shall be treated only as periods of activity as a worker—

(a) during any period in which regulation 5(4) of the Accession Regulations applied to that person; or

(b) when the unemployment began on or after 1st May 2011.

(4) Regulation 6(2) applies to an accession worker where he—

(a) was a person to whom regulation 5(4) of the Accession Regulations applied on 30th April 2011; or

(b) became unable to work, became unemployed or ceased to work, as the case maybe, on or after 1st May 2011.

(5) For the purposes of regulation 15, an accession worker shall be treated as having resided in accordance with these Regulations during any period before 1st May 2011 in which the accession worker—

(a) was legally working in the United Kingdom; or

(b) was a person to whom regulation 5(4) of the Accession Regulations applied.

(6) Subject to paragraph (7), a registration certificate issued to an accession worker under regulation 8 of the Accession Regulations shall, from 1st May 2011, be treated as if it was a registration certificate issued under these Regulations where the accession worker was legally working in the United Kingdom for the employer specified in that certificate on—

(a) 30th April 2011; or

(b) the date on which the certificate is issued where it is issued after 30th April 2011.

(7) Paragraph (6) does not apply—

(a) if the Secretary of State issues a registration certificate in accordance with regulation 16 to an accession worker on or after 1st May 2011; and

(b) from the date of registration stated on that certificate.]

AMENDMENT

1. Accession (Immigration and Worker Registration) (Revocation, Savings and Consequential Provisions) Regulations 2011 (SI 2011/544) reg.5 and Sch.2 para.4 (May 1, 2011).

DEFINITIONS

"EEA national"—see reg.2(1).
"registration certificate"—*ibid.*

GENERAL NOTE

The Accession (Immigration and Worker Registration) Regulations 2004 ("the A8 Regulations") were revoked with effect from May 1, 2011 by reg.2 of the Accession (Immigration and Worker Registration) (Revocation, Savings and Consequential Provisions) Regulations 2011. However, that revocation was subject to the savings in reg.3, which: **2.1154**

- provide that reg.8 of the A8 Regulations shall continue to have effect until April 30, 2012;
- amend reg.8(5)(a) of the A8 Regulations to read:

  "(a) was an accession State worker requiring registration at the date on which the applicant began working for that employer; and"
- provide that the A8 Regulations as a whole "shall continue to have effect to the extent necessary for the purposes of regulation 7A" above.

For the text of the A8 Regulations as it stood immediately prior to their revocation, see pp.792–798 of Vol.II of the 2011/12 edition.

[1 Application of the EU2 Regulations

2.1155 **7B.**—(1) This regulation applies to an EEA national who was an accession State national subject to worker authorisation before 1st January 2014.

(2) In this regulation—

"accession State national subject to worker authorisation" has the same meaning as in regulation 2 of the EU2 Regulations;

"the EU2 Regulations" means the Accession (Immigration and Worker Authorisation) Regulations 2006.

(3) Regulation 2(12) of the EU2 Regulations (accession State national subject to worker authorisation: legally working) has effect for the purposes of this regulation as it does for regulation 2(3) and (4) of the EU2 Regulations.

(4) In regulation 5(7)(c), where the worker is an accession State national subject to worker authorisation, periods of involuntary unemployment duly recorded by the relevant employment office must only be treated as periods of activity as a worker when the unemployment began on or after 1st January 2014.

(5) Regulation 6(2) applies to an accession State national subject to worker authorisation where the accession State national subject to worker authorisation became unable to work, became unemployed or ceased to work, as the case may be, on or after 1st January 2014.

(6) For the purposes of regulation 15, an accession State national subject to worker authorisation must be treated as having resided in accordance with these Regulations during any period before 1st January 2014 in which the accession State national subject to worker authorisation was legally working in the United Kingdom.

(7) An accession worker card issued to an accession State national subject to worker authorisation under regulation 11 of the EU2 Regulations before 1st January 2014 must be treated as if it were a registration certificate issued under these Regulations so long as it has not expired.]

AMENDMENT

1. Immigration (European Economic Area) (Amendment) (No.2) Regulations 2013 (SI 2013/3032) reg.4 and Sch.1 para.4 (January 1, 2014).

"Extended family member"

2.1156 **8.**—(1) In these Regulations "extended family member" means a person who is not a family member of an EEA national under regulation 7(1)(a), (b) or (c) and who satisfies the conditions in paragraph (2), (3), (4) or (5).

(2) A person satisfies the condition in this paragraph if the person is a relative of an EEA national, his spouse or his civil partner and—

(a) the person is residing in [1 a country other than the United Kingdom] [2 . . .] and is dependent upon the EEA national or is a member of his household;

(b) the person satisfied the condition in paragraph (a) and is accompanying the EEA national to the United Kingdom or wishes to join him there; or

(c) the person satisfied the condition in paragraph (a), has joined the EEA national in the United Kingdom and continues to be dependent upon him or to be a member of his household.

(3) A person satisfies the condition in this paragraph if the person is a relative of an EEA national or his spouse or his civil partner and, on serious health grounds, strictly requires the personal care of the EEA national his spouse or his civil partner.

(4) A person satisfies the condition in this paragraph if the person is a relative of an EEA national and would meet the requirements in the immigration rules (other than those relating to entry clearance) for indefinite leave to enter or remain in the United Kingdom as a dependent relative of the EEA national were the EEA national a person present and settled in the United Kingdom.

(5) A person satisfies the condition in this paragraph if the person is the partner of an EEA national (other than a civil partner) and can prove to the decision maker that he is in a durable relationship with the EEA national.

(6) In these Regulations "relevant EEA national" means, in relation to an extended family member, the EEA national who is or whose spouse or civil partner is the relative of the extended family member for the purpose of paragraph (2), (3) or (4) or the EEA national who is the partner of the extended family member for the purpose of paragraph (5).

AMENDMENTS

1. Immigration (European Economic Area) (Amendment) Regulations 2011 (SI 2011/1247) reg.2(1) and (3) (June 2, 2011).

2. Immigration (European Economic Area) (Amendment) (No.2) Regulations 2012 (SI 2012/2560) reg.2 and Sch. para.1 (November 8, 2012).

DEFINITIONS

"civil partner"—see reg.2(1).
"decision maker"—*ibid.*
"EEA national"—*ibid.*
"EEA State"—*ibid.*
"family member"—see reg.7.
"entry clearance"— see reg.2(1).
"immigration rules"—*ibid.*
"registration certificate"—*ibid.*
"spouse"—*ibid.*

[1 Family members of British citizens

9.—(1) If the conditions in paragraph (2) are satisfied, these Regulations apply to a person who is the family member of a British citizen as if the British citizen ("P") were an EEA national. **2.1157**

(2) The conditions are that—

(a) P is residing in an EEA State as a worker or self-employed person or was so residing before returning to the United Kingdom;
(b) if the family member of P is P's spouse or civil partner, the parties are living together in the EEA State or had entered into the marriage or civil partnership and were living together in the EEA State before the British citizen returned to the United Kingdom; and
(c) the centre of P's life has transferred to the EEA State where P resided as a worker or self-employed person.

(3) Factors relevant to whether the centre of P's life has transferred to another EEA State include—
(a) the period of residence in the EEA State as a worker or self-employed person;
(b) the location of P's principal residence;
(c) the degree of integration of P in the EEA State.

(4) Where these Regulations apply to the family member of P, P is to be treated as holding a valid passport issued by an EEA State for the purpose of the application of regulation 13 to that family member.]

Amendments

1. Immigration (European Economic Area) (Amendment) (No.2) Regulations 2012 (SI 2012/2560) reg.2 and Sch. para.7 (November 8, 2012).
2. Immigration (European Economic Area) (Amendment) (No.2) Regulations 2013 (SI 2013/3032) reg.4 and Sch.1 para.5 (January 1, 2014).

Definitions

"civil partner"—see reg.2(1).
"EEA national"—*ibid.*
"EEA State"—*ibid.*
"family member"—see reg.7.
"self-employed person"—see reg.4(1).
"spouse"— see reg.2(1).
"worker"—see reg.4(1).

General Note

2.1158 The substitution of reg.9 by SI 2013/3032 Sch.1 para.5 with effect from January 1, 2014 was subject to the following transitional provision:

"(1) [The substitution] has no effect in relation to the family member ("F") of a British citizen where the criteria in subparagraphs (2) or (3) are met.

(2) The criterion in this subparagraph is met where, upon the coming into force of these Regulations, F was a person with a permanent right to reside in the United Kingdom under the 2006 Regulations.

(3) The criteria in this subparagraph are met where, upon the coming into force of these Regulations, F was a person with a right to reside under the 2006 Regulations; and
(a) held a valid registration certificate, residence card or EEA family permit issued under the 2006 Regulations;
(b) had made an application under the 2006 Regulations for a registration certificate, residence card or EEA family permit which had not been determined; or
(c) had made an application under the 2006 Regulations for a registration certificate or residence card which had been refused and in respect of which an appeal under regulation 26 of the 2006 Regulations could be brought while the appellant is in the United Kingdom (excluding the possibility of an

appeal out of time with permission) or was pending (within the meaning of regulation 25(2) of the 2006 Regulations).

(4) Where met, the criteria in subparagraphs (2) and (3) remain satisfied until the occurrence of the earliest of the following events—

(a) the date six months after an EEA family permit has been issued if F has not within that period been admitted to the United Kingdom;

(b) the date on which an appeal against a decision referred to in subparagraph (3)(c) can no longer be brought (ignoring the possibility of an appeal out of time with permission) where no such appeal has been brought;

(c) the date on which any appeal against a decision referred to in subparagraph 3(c) is finally determined, is withdrawn or is abandoned (within the meaning of regulation 25(2) of the 2006 Regulations), save where the outcome of the appeal process is that the document in question falls to be granted;

(d) the date on which F ceases to be the family member of an EEA national or a family member who has retained the right of residence, within the meaning of regulation 10 of the 2006 Regulations; or

(e) the date on which F's right of residence under regulation 15 of the 2006 Regulations (permanent right of residence) is lost in accordance with paragraph (2) of that regulation (right of permanent residence lost through more than two years' consecutive absence)."

See Sch.3 para.2 to SI 2013/3032.

"Family member who has retained the right of residence"

10.—(1) In these Regulations, "family member who has retained the right of residence" means, subject to paragraph (8), a person who satisfies the conditions in paragraph (2), (3), (4) or (5). **2.1159**

(2) A person satisfies the conditions in this paragraph if—

[1 (a) he was a family member of a qualified person or of an EEA national with a permanent right residence when that person died;]

(b) he resided in the United Kingdom in accordance with these Regulations for at least the year immediately before the death of [1 the qualified person or the EEA national with a permanent right of residence]; and

(c) he satisfies the condition in paragraph (6).

(3) A person satisfies the conditions in this paragraph if—

(a) he is the direct descendant of—

(i) [1 a qualified person or an EEA national with a permanent right of residence] who has died;

(ii) a person who ceased to be the qualified person on ceasing to reside in the United Kingdom; or

(iii) the person who was the spouse or civil partner of [1 the qualified person or the EEA national with a permanent right of residence] mentioned in sub-paragraph (i) when he died or is the spouse or civil partner of the person mentioned in sub-paragraph (ii); and

(b) he was attending an educational course in the United Kingdom immediately before [1 the qualified person or the EEA national with a permanent right of residence] died or ceased to be a qualified person and continues to attend such

(4) A person satisfies the conditions in this paragraph if the person is the parent with actual custody of a child who satisfies the condition in paragraph (3).

(5) A person satisfies the conditions in this paragraph if—

[1 (a) he ceased to be a family member of a qualified person or of an EEA national with a permanent right of residence on the termination of the marriage or civil partnership of that person;]

(b) he was residing in the United Kingdom in accordance with these Regulations at the date of the termination;

(c) he satisfies the condition in paragraph (6); and

(d) either—

(i) prior to the initiation of the proceedings for the termination of the marriage or the civil partnership the marriage or civil partnership had lasted for at least three years and the parties to the marriage or civil partnership had resided in the United Kingdom for at least one year during its duration;

(ii) the former spouse or civil partner of the qualified person has custody of a child of [[1] the qualified person or the EEA national with a permanent right of residence];

[[1] (iii) the former spouse or civil partner of the qualified person or the EEA national with a permanent right of residence has the right of access to a child of the qualified person or the EEA national with a permanent right of residence, where the child is under the age of 18 and where a court has ordered that such access must take place in the United Kingdom; or]

(iv) the continued right of residence in the United Kingdom of the person is warranted by particularly difficult circumstances, such as he or another family member having been a victim of domestic violence while the marriage or civil partnership was subsisting.

(6) The condition in this paragraph is that the person—

(a) is not an EEA national but would, if he were an EEA national, be a worker, a self-employed person or a self-sufficient person under regulation 6; or

(b) is the family member of a person who falls within paragraph (a).

(7) In this regulation, "educational course" means a course within the scope of Article 12 of Council Regulation (EEC) No. 1612/68 on freedom of movement for workers.

(8) A person with a permanent right of residence under regulation 15 shall not become a family member who has retained the right of residence on the death or departure from the United Kingdom of [[1] the qualified person or the EEA national with a permanent right of residence] or the termination of the marriage or civil partnership, as the case may be, and a family member who has retained the right of residence shall cease to have that status on acquiring a permanent right of residence under regulation 15.

AMENDMENT

1. Immigration (European Economic Area) (Amendment) Regulations 2012 (SI 2012/1547) reg.2 and Sch.1 para.3 (July 16, 2012).

DEFINITIONS

"civil partner"—see reg.2(1).
"EEA national"—*ibid.*
"family member"—see reg.7.
"qualified person"—see reg.6(1).
"self-employed person"—see reg.4(1).
"self-sufficient person"—*ibid.*

"spouse"—see reg.2(1).
"worker"—see reg.4(1).

PART 2

EEA RIGHTS

Right of admission to the United Kingdom

11.—(1) An EEA national must be admitted to the United Kingdom if he produces on arrival a valid national identity card or passport issued by an EEA State. 2.1160

[3 (2) A person who is not an EEA national must be admitted to the United Kingdom if he is—

(a) a family member of an EEA national and produces on arrival a valid passport and a qualifying EEA State residence card, provided the conditions in regulation 19(2)(a) (non-EEA family member to be accompanying or joining EEA national in the United Kingdom) and (b) (EEA national must have a right to reside in the United Kingdom under these Regulations) are met; or

(b) a family member of an EEA national, a family member who has retained the right of residence, a person who meets the criteria in paragraph (5) or a person with a permanent right of residence under regulation 15 and produces on arrival—

(i) a valid passport; and

(ii) an EEA family permit, a residence card, a derivative residence card or a permanent residence card.]

[3 (3) An immigration officer must not place a stamp in the passport of a person admitted to the United Kingdom under this regulation who is not an EEA national if the person produces a residence card, a derivative residence card, a permanent residence card or a qualifying EEA State residence card.]

(4) Before an immigration officer refuses admission to the United Kingdom to a person under this regulation because the person does not produce on arrival a document mentioned in paragraph (1) or (2), the immigration officer must give the person every reasonable opportunity to obtain the document or have it brought to him within a reasonable period of time or to prove by other means that he is—

(a) an EEA national;

(b) a family member of an EEA national with a right to accompany that national or join him in the United Kingdom; [4 . . .

(ba) a person who meets the criteria in paragraph (5); or]

(c) a family member who has retained the right of residence or a person with a permanent right of residence under regulation 15.

[1 (5) A person ("P") meets the criteria in this paragraph where—

(a) P previously resided in the United Kingdom pursuant to regulation 15A(3) and would be entitled to reside in the United Kingdom pursuant to that regulation were P in the country;

(b) P is accompanying an EEA national to, or joining an EEA national in, the United Kingdom and P would be entitled to reside in the

United Kingdom pursuant to regulation 15A(2) were P and the EEA national both in the United Kingdom;

(c) P is accompanying a person ("the relevant person") to, or joining the relevant person in, the United Kingdom and—

(i) the relevant person is residing, or has resided, in the United Kingdom pursuant to regulation 15A(3); and

(ii) P would be entitled to reside in the United Kingdom pursuant to regulation 15A(4) were P and the relevant person both in the [2 United Kingdom.]

(d) P is accompanying a person who meets the criteria in (b) or (c) ("the relevant person") to the United Kingdom and—

(i) P and the relevant person are both—

(aa) seeking admission to the United Kingdom in reliance on this paragraph for the first time; or

(bb) returning to the United Kingdom having previously resided there pursuant to the same provisions of regulation 15A in reliance on which they now base their claim to admission; and

(ii) P would be entitled to reside in the United Kingdom pursuant to regulation 15A(5) were P and the relevant [2 person there; or

(e) P is accompanying a British citizen to, or joining a British citizen in, the United Kingdom and P would be entitled to reside in the United Kingdom pursuant to regulation 15A(4A) were P and the British citizen both in the United Kingdom.]

(6) Paragraph (7) applies where—

(a) a person ("P") seeks admission to the United Kingdom in reliance on [2 paragraph 5(b), (c) or (e)]; and

(b) if P were in the United Kingdom, P would have a derived right of residence by virtue of regulation 15A(7)(b)(ii).

(7) Where this paragraph applies a person ("P") will only be regarded as meeting the criteria in [2 paragraph 5(b), (c) or (e)] where P—

(a) is accompanying the person with whom P would on admission to the United Kingdom jointly share care responsibility for the purpose of regulation 15A(7)(b)(ii); or

(b) has previously resided in the United Kingdom pursuant to regulation [2 15A(2), (4) or (4A)] as a joint primary carer and seeks admission to the United Kingdom in order to reside there again on the same basis.]

[1 8] But this regulation is subject to regulations 19(1) [4, (1A)] [3, (1AB) and (2)] [5 and 23A].

AMENDMENTS

1. Immigration (European Economic Area) (Amendment) Regulations 2012 (SI 2012/1547) reg.2 and Sch.1 para.4 (July 16, 2012).

2. Immigration (European Economic Area) (Amendment) (No.2) Regulations 2012 (SI 2012/2560) reg.2 and Sch. para.2 (November 8, 2012).

3. Immigration (European Economic Area) (Amendment) (No.2) Regulations 2013 (SI 2013/3032) reg.4 and Sch.1 para.6 (January 1, 2014).

4. Immigration (European Economic Area) (Amendment) (No.2) Regulations 2014 (SI 2014/1976) reg.3 and Sch. para.2 (July 28, 2014).

5. Immigration (European Economic Area) (Amendment) Regulations 2015 (SI 2015/694) reg.4 and Sch.1 para.3 (April 6, 2015).

DEFINITION

"derivative residence card"—see reg.2(1).

MODIFICATION

Regulation 11 is modified in its application to the Channel Tunnel by art.7 of, and para.5 of Sch.4 to, the Channel Tunnel (International Arrangements) Order 1993 (SI 1993/1815) as amended.

DEFINITIONS

"EEA family permit"—see reg.2(1).
"EEA national"—*ibid.*
"EEA State"—*ibid.*
"family member"—see reg.7.
"family member who has retained the right of residence"—see reg.10(1).
"permanent residence card"—see reg.2(1).
"relevant"—*ibid.*, and reg.8(6).
"residence card"—see reg.2(1).

Issue of EEA family permit

12.—(1) An entry clearance officer must issue an EEA family permit to a person who applies for one if the person is a family member of an EEA national and— **2.1161**

(a) the EEA national—

(i) is residing in the UK in accordance with these Regulations; or

(ii) will be travelling to the United Kingdom within six months of the date of the application and will be an EEA national residing in the United Kingdom in accordance with these Regulations on arrival in the United Kingdom; and

[2 (b) the family member will be accompanying the EEA national to the United Kingdom or joining the EEA national there.]

[3 (1A) An entry clearance officer must issue an EEA family permit to a person who applies and provides proof that, at the time at which he first intends to use the EEA family permit, he—

(a) would be entitled to be admitted to the United Kingdom by virtue of regulation 11(5); and

(b) will (save in the case of a person who would be entitled to be admitted to the United Kingdom by virtue of regulation 11(5)(a)) be accompanying to, or joining in, the United Kingdom any person from whom his right to be admitted to the United Kingdom under regulation 11(5) will be derived.

(1B) An entry clearance officer must issue an EEA family permit to a family member who has retained the right of residence.]

(2) An entry clearance officer may issue an EEA family permit to an extended family member of an EEA national who applies for one if—

(a) the relevant EEA national satisfies the condition in paragraph (1)(a);

(b) the extended family member wishes to accompany the relevant EEA national to the United Kingdom or to join him there; and

(c) in all the circumstances, it appears to the entry clearance officer appropriate to issue the EEA family permit.

(3) Where an entry clearance officer receives an application under paragraph (2) he shall undertake an extensive examination of the personal

circumstances of the applicant and if he refuses the application shall give reasons justifying the refusal unless this is contrary to the interests of national security.

(4) An EEA family permit issued under this regulation shall be issued free of charge and as soon as possible.

(5) But an EEA family permit shall not be issued under this regulation if the applicant or the EEA national concerned [1 3 . . .][3 is not entitled to be admitted to the United Kingdom as a result of regulation 19(1A) or [4 (1AB) or] falls to be excluded in accordance with regulation 19(1B)].

[3 (6) An EEA family permit will not be issued under this regulation to a person ("A") who is the spouse, civil partner or durable partner of a person ("B") where a spouse, civil partner or durable partner of A or B holds a valid EEA family permit.]

AMENDMENTS

1. Immigration (European Economic Area) (Amendment) Regulations 2009 (SI 2009/1117) reg.2 and Sch.1 para.3 (June 1, 2009).
2. Immigration (European Economic Area) (Amendment) Regulations 2011 (SI 2011/1247) reg.2(1) and (4) (June 2, 2011).
3. Immigration (European Economic Area) (Amendment) Regulations 2012 (SI 2012/1547) reg.2 and Sch.1 para.5 (July 16, 2012).
4. Immigration (European Economic Area) (Amendment) (No.2) Regulations 2013 (SI 2013/3032) reg.4 and Sch.1 para.7 (January 1, 2014).

DEFINITIONS

"civil partner"—see reg.2(1).
"deportation order"—*ibid.*
"durable partner"—*ibid.*
"EEA family permit"—*ibid.*
"EEA national"—*ibid.*
"EEA State"—*ibid.*
"exclusion order"—*ibid.*
"extended family member"—see reg.8(1).
"family member"—see reg.7.
"entry clearance"—see reg.2(1).
"entry clearance officer"—*ibid.*
"immigration rules"—*ibid.*
"relevant EEA national"—*ibid.*, and reg.8(6).
"spouse"—*ibid.*

Initial right of residence

2.1162 **13.**—(1) An EEA national is entitled to reside in the United Kingdom for a period not exceeding three months beginning on the date on which he is admitted to the United Kingdom provided that he holds a valid national identity card or passport issued by an EEA State.

(2) A family member of an EEA national [1 or a family member who has retained the right of residence who is] residing in the United Kingdom under paragraph (1) who is not himself an EEA national is entitled to reside in the United Kingdom provided that he holds a valid passport.

[1 (3) An EEA national or his family member who becomes an unreasonable burden on the social assistance system of the United Kingdom will cease to have a right to reside under this regulation.

(4) A person who otherwise satisfies the criteria in this regulation will not be entitled to reside in the United Kingdom under this regulation where the Secretary of State [3 or an immigration officer] has made a decision under [2 —

(a) regulation 19(3)(b), 20(1) [3, 20A(1) or 23A]; or
(b) regulation 21B(2), where that decision was taken in the preceding twelve months.]]

AMENDMENTS

1. Immigration (European Economic Area) (Amendment) Regulations 2012 (SI 2012/1547) reg.2 and Sch.1 para.6 (July 16, 2012).
2. Immigration (European Economic Area) (Amendment) (No.2) Regulations 2013 (SI 2013/3032) reg.4 and Sch.1 para.8 (January 1, 2014).
3. Immigration (European Economic Area) (Amendment) Regulations 2015 (SI 2015/694) reg.4 and Sch.1 para.4 (April 6, 2015).

DEFINITIONS

"EEA national"—see reg.2(1).
"EEA State"—*ibid.*
"family member"—see reg.7.

Extended right of residence

14.—(1) A qualified person is entitled to reside in the United Kingdom for so long as he remains a qualified person. **2.1163**

(2) A family member of a qualified person residing in the United Kingdom under paragraph (1) or of an EEA national with a permanent right of residence under regulation 15 is entitled to reside in the United Kingdom for so long as he remains the family member of the qualified person or EEA national.

(3) A family member who has retained the right of residence is entitled to reside in the United Kingdom for so long as he remains a family member who has retained the right of residence.

(4) A right to reside under this regulation is in addition to any right a person may have to reside in the United Kingdom under regulation 13 or 15.

[1 (5) A person who otherwise satisfies the criteria in this regulation will not be entitled to a right to reside in the United Kingdom under this regulation where the Secretary of State [3 or an immigration officer] has made a decision under [2 —

(a) regulation 19(3)(b), 20(1) [3, 20A(1) or 23A]; or
(b) regulation 21B(2) (not including such a decision taken on the basis of regulation 21B(1)(a) or (b)), where that decision was taken in the preceding twelve months.]]

AMENDMENTS

1. Immigration (European Economic Area) (Amendment) Regulations 2012 (SI 2012/1547) reg.2 and Sch.1 para.7 (July 16, 2012).
2. Immigration (European Economic Area) (Amendment) (No.2) Regulations 2013 (SI 2013/3032) reg.4 and Sch.1 para.9 (January 1, 2014).
3. Immigration (European Economic Area) (Amendment) Regulations 2015 (SI 2015/694) reg.4 and Sch.1 para.5 (April 6, 2015).

Definitions

"EEA national"—see reg.2(1).
"family member"—see reg.7.
"family member who has retained the right of residence"—see reg.10(1).
"qualified person"—see reg.6(1).

Permanent right of residence

2.1164 **15.**—(1) The following persons shall acquire the right to reside in the United Kingdom permanently—

(a) an EEA national who has resided in the United Kingdom in accordance with these Regulations for a continuous period of five years;

(b) a family member of an EEA national who is not himself an EEA national but who has resided in the United Kingdom with the EEA national in accordance with these Regulations for a continuous period of five years;

(c) a worker or self-employed person who has ceased activity;

(d) the family member of a worker or self-employed person who has ceased activity;

(e) a person who was the family member of a worker or self-employed person where—

  (i) the worker or self-employed person has died;

  (ii) the family member resided with him immediately before his death; and

  (iii) the worker or self-employed person had resided continuously in the United Kingdom for at least the two years immediately before his death or the death was the result of an accident at work or an occupational disease;

(f) a person who—

  (i) has resided in the United Kingdom in accordance with these Regulations for a continuous period of five years; and

  (ii) was, at the end of that period, a family member who has retained the right of residence.

[[1] (1A) Residence in the United Kingdom as a result of a derivative right of residence does not constitute residence for the purpose of this regulation.]

(2) [[1] . . . The] right of permanent residence under this regulation shall be lost only through absence from the United Kingdom for a period exceeding two consecutive years.

[[1] (3) A person who satisfies the criteria in this regulation will not be entitled to a permanent right to reside in the United Kingdom where the Secretary of State [[3] or an immigration officer] has made a decision under [[2] —

(a) regulation 19(3)(b), 20(1) [[3], 20A(1) or 23A]; or

(b) regulation 21B(2) (not including such a decision taken on the basis of regulation 21B(1)(a) or (b)), where that decision was taken in the preceding twelve months.]]

Amendments

1. Immigration (European Economic Area) (Amendment) Regulations 2012 (SI 2012/1547) reg.2 and Sch.1 para.8 (July 16, 2012).

2. Immigration (European Economic Area) (Amendment) (No.2) Regulations 2013 (SI 2013/3032) reg.4 and Sch.1 para.10 (January 1, 2014).

3. Immigration (European Economic Area) (Amendment) Regulations 2015 (SI 2015/694) reg.4 and Sch.1 para.6 (April 6, 2015).

DEFINITIONS

"EEA national"—see reg.2(1).
"family member"—see reg.7.
"family member who has retained the right of residence"—see reg.10(1).
"self-employed person"—see reg.4(1).
"worker"—*ibid.*
"Worker or self-employed person who has ceased activity"—see reg.5(1).

GENERAL NOTE

For the rules on continuity of residence see reg.3. 2.1165
For the treatment of residence before April 30, 2006, see Sch.4 para.6.

[1 Derivative right of residence

15A.—(1) A person ("P") who is not [2 an exempt person] and who satisfies the criteria in paragraph (2), (3), (4) [2, (4A)] or (5) of this regulation is entitled to a derivative right to reside in the United Kingdom for as long as P satisfies the relevant criteria. 2.1166

(2) P satisfies the criteria in this paragraph if—
(a) P is the primary carer of an EEA national ("the relevant EEA national"); and
(b) the relevant EEA national—
(i) is under the age of 18;
(ii) is residing in the United Kingdom as a self-sufficient person; and
(iii) would be unable to remain in the United Kingdom if P were required to leave.

(3) P satisfies the criteria in this paragraph if—
(a) P is the child of an EEA national ("the EEA national parent");
(b) P resided in the United Kingdom at a time when the EEA national parent was residing in the United Kingdom as a worker; and
(c) P is in education in the United Kingdom and was in education there at a time when the EEA national parent was in the United Kingdom.

(4) P satisfies the criteria in this paragraph if—
(a) P is the primary carer of a person meeting the criteria in paragraph (3) ("the relevant person"); and
(b) the relevant person would be unable to continue to be educated in the United Kingdom if P were required to leave.

[2 (4A) P satisfies the criteria in this paragraph if—
(a) P is the primary carer of a British citizen ("the relevant British citizen");
(b) the relevant British citizen is residing in the United Kingdom; and
(c) the relevant British citizen would be unable to reside in the UK or in another EEA State if P were required to leave.]

(5) P satisfies the criteria in this paragraph if—
(a) P is under the age of 18;
(b) P's primary carer is entitled to a derivative right to reside in the United Kingdom by virtue of paragraph (2) or (4);
(c) P does not have leave to enter, or remain in, the United Kingdom; and

(d) requiring P to leave the United Kingdom would prevent P's primary carer from residing in the United Kingdom.

(6) For the purpose of this regulation—

(a) "education" excludes nursery education; [2 . . .]

(b) "worker" does not include a jobseeker or a person who falls to be regarded as a worker by virtue of [2 regulation 6(2); and

(c) "an exempt person" is a person—

(i) who has a right to reside in the United Kingdom as a result of any other provision of these Regulations;

(ii) who has a right of abode in the United Kingdom by virtue of section 2 of the 1971 Act;

(iii) to whom section 8 of the 1971 Act, or any order made under subsection (2) of that provision, applies; or

(iv) who has indefinite leave to enter or remain in the United Kingdom.]

(7) P is to be regarded as a "primary carer" of another person if

(a) P is a direct relative or a legal guardian of that person; and

(b) P—

(i) is the person who has primary responsibility for that person's care; or

[2 (ii) shares equally the responsibility for that person's care with one other person who is not an exempt person.]

[2 (7A) Where P is to be regarded as a primary carer of another person by virtue of paragraph (7)(b)(ii) the criteria in paragraphs (2)(b)(iii), (4)(b) and (4A)(c) shall be considered on the basis that both P and the person with whom care responsibility is shared would be required to leave the United Kingdom.

(7B) Paragraph (7A) does not apply if the person with whom care responsibility is shared acquired a derivative right to reside in the United Kingdom as a result of this regulation prior to P assuming equal care responsibility.]

(8) P will not be regarded as having responsibility for a person's care for the purpose of paragraph (7) on the sole basis of a financial contribution towards that person's care.

(9) A person who otherwise satisfies the criteria in paragraph (2), (3), (4) [2, (4A)] or (5) will not be entitled to a derivative right to reside in the United Kingdom where the Secretary of State [4 or an immigration officer] has made a decision under [3 —

(a) regulation 19(3)(b), 20(1) [4, 20A(1) or 23A]; or

(b) regulation 21B(2), where that decision was taken in the preceding twelve months.]]

AMENDMENTS

1. Immigration (European Economic Area) (Amendment) Regulations 2012 (SI 2012/1547) reg.2 and Sch.1 para.9 (July 16, 2012).

2. Immigration (European Economic Area) (Amendment) (No.2) Regulations 2012 (SI 2012/2560) reg.2 and Sch. para.3 (November 8, 2012).

3. Immigration (European Economic Area) (Amendment) (No.2) Regulations 2013 (SI 2013/3032) reg.4 and Sch.1 para.11 (January 1, 2014).

4. Immigration (European Economic Area) (Amendment) Regulations 2015 (SI 2015/694) reg.4 and Sch.1 para.7 (April 6, 2015).

DEFINITIONS

"EEA national"—see reg.2(1).
"exempt person"—see para.(6)(c).
"primary carer"—see paras (7)–(7B).
"worker"—see reg.4(1) but see also para.(6)(b).

[1 Continuation of a right of residence

15B.—(1) This regulation applies during any period in which, but for the effect of regulation 13(4), 14(5), 15(3) or 15A(9), a person ("P") who is in the United Kingdom would be entitled to reside here pursuant to these Regulations. 2.1167

(2) Where this regulation applies, any right of residence will (notwithstanding the effect of regulation 13(4), 14(5), 15(3) or 15A(9)) be deemed to continue during any period in which—

(a) an appeal under regulation 26 could be brought, while P is in the United Kingdom, against a relevant decision (ignoring any possibility of an appeal out of time with permission); or
(b) an appeal under regulation 26 against a relevant decision, brought while P is in the United Kingdom, is pending [3 . . .].

(3) Periods during which residence pursuant to regulation 14 is deemed to continue as a result of paragraph (2) will not constitute residence for the purpose of regulation 15 unless and until—

(a) a relevant decision is withdrawn by the Secretary of State; or
(b) an appeal against a relevant decision is allowed and that appeal is finally determined [3 . . .].

(4) Periods during which residence is deemed to continue as a result of paragraph (2) will not constitute residence for the purpose of regulation 21(4)(a) unless and until—

(a) a relevant decision is withdrawn by the Secretary of State; or
(b) an appeal against a relevant decision is allowed and that appeal is finally determined [3 . . .].

(5) A "relevant decision" for the purpose of this regulation means a decision pursuant to regulation [2 19(3)(b) or (c)], 20(1) or 20A(1) which would, but for the effect of paragraph (2), prevent P from residing in the United Kingdom pursuant to these Regulations.]

[3 (6) This regulation does not affect the ability of the Secretary of State to give directions for P's removal while an appeal is pending or before it is finally determined.

(7) In this regulation, "pending" and "finally determined" have the meanings given in section 104 of the 2002 Act.]

AMENDMENTS

1. Immigration (European Economic Area) (Amendment) Regulations 2012 (SI 2012/1547) reg.2 and Sch.1 para.10 (July 16, 2012).

2. Immigration (European Economic Area) (Amendment) (No.2) Regulations 2013 (SI 2013/3032) reg.4 and Sch.1 para.12 (January 1, 2014).

3. Immigration (European Economic Area) (Amendment) (No.2) Regulations 2014 (SI 2014/1976) reg.3 and Sch. para.3 (July 28, 2014).

PART 3

RESIDENCE DOCUMENTATION

Issue of registration certificate

2.1168 **16.**—(1) The Secretary of State must issue a registration certificate to a qualified person immediately on application and production of—

(a) a valid identity card or passport issued by an EEA State;

(b) proof that he is a qualified person.

(2) In the case of a worker, confirmation of the worker's engagement from his employer or a certificate of employment is sufficient proof for the purposes of paragraph (1)(b).

(3) The Secretary of State must issue a registration certificate to an EEA national who is the family member of a qualified person or of an EEA national with a permanent right of residence under regulation 15 immediately on application and production of—

(a) a valid identity card or passport issued by an EEA State; and

(b) proof that the applicant is such a family member.

(4) The Secretary of State must issue a registration certificate to an EEA national who is a family member who has retained the right of residence on application and production of—

(a) a valid identity card or passport; and

(b) proof that the applicant is a family member who has retained the right of residence.

(5) The Secretary of State may issue a registration certificate to an extended family member not falling within regulation 7(3) who is an EEA national on application if—

(a) the relevant in relation to the extended family member is a qualified person or an EEA national with a permanent right of residence under regulation 15; and

(b) in all the circumstances it appears to the Secretary of State appropriate to issue the registration certificate.

(6) Where the Secretary of State receives an application under paragraph (5) he shall undertake an extensive examination of the personal circumstances of the applicant and if he refuses the application shall give reasons justifying the refusal unless this is contrary to the interests of national security.

(7) A registration certificate issued under this regulation shall state the name and address of the person registering and the date of registration [[2] . . .].

(8) [[1] But this regulation is subject to regulations 7A(6) and 20(1).]

AMENDMENTS

1. Accession (Immigration and Worker Registration) (Revocation, Savings and Consequential Provisions) Regulations 2011 (SI 2011/544) reg.5 and Sch.2 para.5 (May 1, 2011).

2. Immigration (European Economic Area) (Amendment) Regulations 2013 (SI 2013/1391) reg.2(a) (July 1, 2013).

DEFINITIONS

"EEA national"—see reg.2(1).
"EEA State"—*ibid.*
"extended family member"—see reg.8(1).
"family member"—see reg.7.
"family member who has retained the right of residence"—see reg.10(1).
"qualified person"—see reg.6(1).
"registration certificate"—see reg.2(1).
"relevant EEA national"—*ibid.*, and reg.8(6).
"worker"—see reg.4(1).

Issue of residence card

17.—(1) The Secretary of State must issue a residence card to a person who is not an EEA national and is the family member of a qualified person or of an EEA national with a permanent right of residence under regulation 15 on application and production of— **2.1169**

(a) a valid passport; and
(b) proof that the applicant is such a family member.

(2) The Secretary of State must issue a residence card to a person who is not an EEA national but who is a family member who has retained the right of residence on application and production of—

(a) a valid passport; and
(b) proof that the applicant is a family member who has retained the right of residence.

(3) On receipt of an application under paragraph (1) or (2) and the documents that are required to accompany the application the Secretary of State shall immediately issue the applicant with a certificate of application for the residence card and the residence card shall be issued no later than six months after the date on which the application and documents are received.

(4) The Secretary of State may issue a residence card to an extended family member not falling within regulation 7(3) who is not an EEA national on application if—

(a) the relevant EEA national in relation to the extended family member is a qualified person or an EEA national with a permanent right of residence under regulation 15; and
(b) in all the circumstances it appears to the Secretary of State appropriate to issue the residence card.

(5) Where the Secretary of State receives an application under paragraph (4) he shall undertake an extensive examination of the personal circumstances of the applicant and if he refuses the application shall give reasons justifying the refusal unless this is contrary to the interests of national security.

(6) A residence card issued under this regulation may take the form of a stamp in the applicant's passport and shall be [1 . . .] be valid for—

(a) five years from the date of issue; or
(b) in the case of a residence card issued to the family member or extended family member of a qualified person, the envisaged period of residence in the United Kingdom of the qualified person,

whichever is the shorter.

[1 (6A) A residence card issued under this regulation shall be entitled "Residence card of a family member of an EEA national" or "Residence card of a family member who has retained the right of residence", as the case may be.]

(7) [2 . . .]

(8) But this regulation is subject to [1 regulations 20(1) and (1A)].

AMENDMENTS

1. Immigration (European Economic Area) (Amendment) Regulations 2009 (SI 2009/1117) reg.2 and Sch.1 para.4 (June 1, 2009).

2. Immigration (European Economic Area) (Amendment) Regulations 2013 (SI 2013/1391) reg.2(b) (July 1, 2013).

DEFINITIONS

"EEA national"—see reg.2(1).
"extended family member"—see reg.8(1).
"family member"—see reg.7.
"family member who has retained the right of residence"—see reg.10(1).
"qualified person"—see reg.6(1).
"relevant EEA national"—see reg.2(1) and reg.8(6).
"residence card"—see reg.2(1).

Issue of a document certifying permanent residence and a permanent residence card

2.1170 **18.**—(1) The Secretary of State must issue an EEA national with a permanent right of residence under regulation 15 with a document certifying permanent residence as soon as possible after an application for such a document and proof that the EEA national has such a right is submitted to the Secretary of State.

(2) The Secretary of State must issue a person who is not an EEA national who has a permanent right of residence under regulation 15 with a permanent residence card no later than six months after the date on which an application for a permanent residence card and proof that the person has such a right is submitted to the Secretary of State.

(3) Subject to paragraph (5) [1 . . .], a permanent residence card shall be valid for ten years from the date of issue and must be renewed on application.

(4) [2 . . .]

(5) A document certifying permanent residence and a permanent residence card shall cease to be valid if the holder ceases to have a right of permanent residence under regulation 15.

[1 (6) But this regulation is subject to regulation 20.]

AMENDMENTS

1. Immigration (European Economic Area) (Amendment) Regulations 2009 (SI 2009/1117) reg.2 and Sch.1 para.5 (June 1, 2009).

2. Immigration (European Economic Area) (Amendment) Regulations 2013 (SI 2013/1391) reg.2(c) (July 1, 2013).

DEFINITIONS

"document certifying permanent residence"—see reg.2(1).
"EEA national"—*ibid.*
"permanent residence card"—*ibid.*

[1 Issue of a derivative residence card

18A.—(1) The Secretary of State must issue a person with a derivative residence card on application and on production of— 2.1171

(a) a valid identity card issued by an EEA State or a valid passport; and
(b) proof that the applicant has a derivative right of residence under regulation 15A.

(2) On receipt of an application under paragraph (1) the Secretary of State must issue the applicant with a certificate of application as soon as possible.

(3) A derivative residence card issued under paragraph (1) may take the form of a stamp in the applicant's passport and will be valid until—

(a) a date five years from the date of issue; or
(b) any other date specified by the Secretary of State when issuing the derivative residence card.

(4) A derivative residence card issued under paragraph (1) must be issued [2 . . .] as soon as practicable.

(5) But this regulation is subject to regulations 20(1) and 20(1A).]

AMENDMENTS

1. Immigration (European Economic Area) (Amendment) Regulations 2012 (SI 2012/1547) reg.2 and Sch.1 para.11 (July 16, 2012).

2. Immigration (European Economic Area) (Amendment) Regulations 2013 (SI 2013/1391) reg.2(d) (July 1, 2013).

DEFINITION

"derivative residence card"—see reg.2(1).

PART 4

REFUSAL OF ADMISSION AND REMOVAL ETC 2.1172

PART 5

PROCEDURE IN RELATION TO EEA DECISIONS 2.1173

PART 6

APPEALS UNDER THESE REGULATIONS 2.1174

PART 7

GENERAL

[1 Alternative evidence of identity and nationality

29A.—(1) Subject to paragraph (2), where a provision of these Regulations requires a person to hold or produce a valid identity card issued by an EEA 2.1175

State or a valid passport the Secretary of State may accept alternative evidence of identity and nationality where the person is unable to obtain or produce the required document due to circumstances beyond his or her control.

(2) This regulation does not apply to regulation 11.]

AMENDMENT

1. Immigration (European Economic Area) (Amendment) (No.2) Regulations 2012 (SI 2012/2560) reg.2 and Sch. para.6 (November 8, 2012).

DEFINITION

"EEA State"—see reg.2(1).

Effect on other legislation

2.1176 **30.**—Schedule 2 (effect on other legislation) shall have effect.

Revocations, transitional provisions and consequential amendments

2.1177 **31.**—(1) *[Omitted.]*

(2) Schedule 4 (transitional provisions) and Schedule 5 (consequential amendments) shall have effect.

SCHEDULE 1

APPEALS TO [1 FIRST-TIER TRIBUNAL] THE TRIBUNAL

[Omitted.]

Regulation 30

SCHEDULE 2

EFFECT ON OTHER LEGISLATION

Leave under the 1971 Act

2.1178 **1.**—(1) In accordance with section 7 of the Immigration Act 1988, a person who is admitted to or acquires a right to reside in the United Kingdom under these Regulations shall not require leave to remain in the United Kingdom under the 1971 Act during any period in which he has a right to reside under these Regulations but such a person shall require leave to remain under the 1971 Act during any period in which he does not have such a right.

(2) [1 Subject to sub-paragraph (3),] where a person has leave to enter or remain under the 1971 Act which is subject to conditions and that person also has a right to reside under these Regulations, those conditions shall not have effect for as long as the person has that right to reside.

[1 (3) Where the person mentioned in sub-paragraph (2) is an accession State national subject to worker authorisation working in the United Kingdom during the accession period and the document endorsed to show that the person has leave is an accession worker authorisation document, any conditions to which that leave is subject restricting his employment shall continue to apply.

(4) In sub-paragraph (3)—

(a) "accession period" has the meaning [3 given in—

(i) regulation 1(2)(c) of the Accession (Immigration and Worker Authorisation) Regulations 2006, in relation to a person who is an accession State national subject to worker authorisation within the meaning of regulation 2 of those Regulations; and

(ii) regulation 1(2) of the Accession of Croatia (Immigration and Worker Authorisation) Regulations 2013, in relation to a person who is an accession State national subject to worker authorisation within the meaning of regulation 2 of those Regulations;]

(b) "accession State national subject to worker authorisation" has the meaning [3 given in—
(i) regulation 2 of the Accession (Immigration and Worker Authorisation) Regulations 2006; and
(ii) regulation 2 of the Accession of Croatia (Immigration and Worker Authorisation) Regulations 2013; and]
(c) "accession worker authorisation document" has the meaning [3 given in—
(i) regulation 9(2) of the Accession (Immigration and Worker Authorisation) Regulations 2006, in relation to a person who is an accession State national subject to worker authorisation within the meaning of regulation 2 of those Regulations; and
(ii) regulation 1(2) of the Accession of Croatia (Immigration and Worker Authorisation) Regulations 2013, in relation to a person who is an accession State national subject to worker authorisation within the meaning of regulation 2 of those Regulations.]]

Persons not subject to restriction on the period for which they may remain

2.—(1) For the purposes of the 1971 Act and the British Nationality Act 1981, a person who has a permanent right of residence under regulation 15 shall be regarded as a person who is in the United Kingdom without being subject under the immigration laws to any restriction on the period for which he may remain. **2.1179**

(2) But a qualified person, the family member of a qualified person [2, a person with a derivative right of residence] and a family member who has retained the right of residence shall not, by virtue of that status, be so regarded for those purposes.

Carriers' liability under the 1999 Act

3. [Omitted.] **2.1180**

Appeals under the 2002 Act and previous immigration Acts

4. [Omitted.] **2.1181**

Amendments

1. Accession (Immigration and Worker Authorisation) Regulations 2006 (SI 2006/3317) reg.1(3) and Sch.2 para.2(2) (January 1, 2007).
2. Immigration (European Economic Area) (Amendment) Regulations 2012 (SI 2012/1547) reg.2 and Sch.1 para.22 (July 16, 2012).
3. Accession of Croatia (Immigration and Worker Authorisation) Regulations 2013 (SI 2013/1460) reg.1(3) and Sch.2 (July 1, 2013).

Definitions

"the 1971 Act"—see reg.2(1).
"the 1999 Act"—*ibid.*
"the 2002 Act—*ibid.*
"family member"—see reg.7.
"family member who has retained the right of residence"—see reg.10(1).
"qualified person"—see reg.6(1).
"worker"—see reg.4(1).

SCHEDULE 3

REVOCATIONS AND SAVINGS

2.1182 *[Omitted.]*

Regulation 31(2)

SCHEDULE 4

TRANSITIONAL PROVISIONS

Interpretation

2.1183 **1.**—In this Schedule—

(a) the "2000 Regulations" means the Immigration (European Economic Area) Regulations 2000 and expressions used in relation to documents issued or applied for under those Regulations shall have the meaning given in regulation 2 of those Regulations;

(b) the "Accession Regulations" means the Accession (Immigration and Worker Registration) Regulations 2004.

Existing documents

2.1184 **2.**—(1) An EEA family permit issued under the 2000 Regulations shall, after 29th April 2006, be treated as if it were an EEA family permit issued under these Regulations.

(2) Subject to paragraph (4), a residence permit issued under the 2000 Regulations shall, after 29th April 2006, be treated as if it were a registration certificate issued under these Regulations.

(3) Subject to paragraph (5), a residence document issued under the 2000 Regulations shall, after 29th April 2006, be treated as if it were a residence card issued under these Regulations.

(4) Where a residence permit issued under the 2000 Regulations has been endorsed under the immigration rules to show permission to remain in the United Kingdom indefinitely it shall, after 29th April 2006, be treated as if it were a document certifying permanent residence issued under these Regulations and the holder of the permit shall be treated as a person with a permanent right of residence under regulation 15.

(5) Where a residence document issued under the 2000 Regulations has been endorsed under the immigration rules to show permission to remain in the United Kingdom indefinitely it shall, after 29th April 2006, be treated as if it were a permanent residence card issued under these Regulations and the holder of the permit shall be treated as a person with a permanent right of residence un(6) Paragraphs (4) and (5) shall also apply to a residence permit or residence document which is endorsed under the immigration rules on or after 30th April 2006 to show permission to remain in the United Kingdom indefinitely pursuant to an application for such an endorsement made before that date.

Outstanding applications

2.1185 **3.**—(1) An application for an EEA family permit, a residence permit or a residence document made but not determined under the 2000 Regulations before 30 April 2006 shall be treated as an application under these Regulations for an EEA family permit, a registration certificate or a residence card, respectively.

(2) But the following provisions of these Regulations shall not apply to the determination of an application mentioned in sub-paragraph (1)—

(a) the requirement to issue a registration certificate immediately under regulation 16(1); and

(b) the requirement to issue a certificate of application for a residence card under regulation 17(3).

Decisions to remove under the 2000 Regulations

2.1186 *4. [Omitted.]*

Appeals

2.1187 *5. [Omitted.]*

[1 Periods of residence prior to the entry into force of these Regulations

6.—(1) Any period during which a person ("P"), who is an EEA national, carried out an activity or was resident in the United Kingdom in accordance with the conditions in subparagraph (2) or (3) is to be treated as a period during which the person carried out that activity or was resident in the United Kingdom in accordance with these Regulations for the purpose of calculating periods of activity and residence there under. **2.1188**

(2) P carried out an activity, or was resident, in the United Kingdom in accordance with this subparagraph where such activity or residence was at that time in accordance with—

(a) the 2000 Regulations;
(b) the Immigration (European Economic Area) Order 1994 ("the 1994 Order"); or
(c) where such activity or residence preceded the entry into force of the 1994 Order, any of the following Directives which was at the relevant time in force in respect of the United Kingdom—
  (i) Council Directive 64/221/EEC;
  (ii) Council Directive 68/360/EEC;
  (iii) Council Directive 72/194/EEC;
  (iv) Council Directive 73/148/EEC;
  (v) Council Directive 75/34/EEC;
  (vi) Council Directive 75/35/EEC;
  (vii) Council Directive 90/364/EEC;
  (viii) Council Directive 90/365/EEC; and
  (ix) Council Directive 93/96/EEC.

(3) P carried out an activity or was resident in the United Kingdom in accordance with this subparagraph where P—

(a) had leave to enter or remain in the United Kingdom; and
(b) would have been carrying out that activity or residing in the United Kingdom in accordance with these Regulations had the relevant state been an EEA State at that time and had these Regulations at that time been in force.

(4) Any period during which P carried out an activity or was resident in the United Kingdom in accordance with subparagraph (2) or (3) will not be regarded as a period during which P carried out that activity or was resident in the United Kingdom in accordance with these Regulations where it was followed by a period—

(a) which exceeded two consecutive years and for the duration of which P was absent from the United Kingdom; or
(b) which exceeded two consecutive years and for the duration of which P's residence in the United Kingdom—
  (i) was not in accordance with subparagraph (2) or (3); or
  (ii) was not otherwise in accordance with these Regulations.

(5) The relevant state for the purpose of subparagraph (3) is the state of which P is, and was at the relevant time, a national.]

AMENDMENT

1. Immigration (European Economic Area) (Amendment) Regulations 2012 (SI 2012/1547) reg.2 and Sch.1 para.25 (July 16, 2012).

DEFINITIONS

"document certifying permanent residence"—*ibid.*
"EEA family permit"—*ibid.*
"immigration rules"—*ibid.*
"permanent residence card"—*ibid.*
"registration certificate"—*ibid.*
"residence card"—*ibid.*

SCHEDULE 5

CONSEQUENTIAL AMENDMENTS

[Omitted.] **2.1189**

The Social Security (Persons from Abroad) Amendment Regulations 2006

(2006/1026)

Made by the Secretary of State under sections 123(1)(a), (d) and (e), 131(3)(b), 135(1) and (2), 137(1) and (2), 138(1)(a) and (4) and 175(1), (3) and (4) of the Social Security Contributions and Benefits Act 1992, sections 4(5) and (12), 35(1) and 36(2) and (4) of, and paragraph 11 of Schedule 1 to, the Jobseekers Act 1995 and sections 1(5)(a) and 17(1) of the State Pension Credit Act 2002, after agreement by the Social Security Advisory Committee that proposals to make these Regulations should not be referred to it;

ARRANGEMENT OF REGULATIONS

[30th April 2006]

Citation and commencement

2.1191 **1.**—These Regulations shall be cited as the Social Security (Persons from Abroad) Amendment Regulations 2006 and shall come into force on 30th April 2006.

[Regulations 2–5 omitted as relating solely to housing benefit and council tax benefit]

[Regulations 6–9 noted at the appropriate places in the text of the amended regulations]

Nationals of Norway, Iceland, Liechtenstein and Switzerland

2.1192 **10.**—The following provisions shall apply in relation to a national of Norway, Iceland, Liechtenstein or Switzerland or a member of his family (within the meaning of Article 2 of Council Directive No. 2004/38/EC) as if such a national were a national of a member State—

(a)–(d) *[Omitted as relating solely to housing benefit and council tax benefit]*

(e) regulation 21AA(4)(a) to (e) of the Income Support (General) Regulations 1987;

(f) regulation 85A(4)(a) to (e) of the Jobseeker's Allowance Regulations 1996;

(g) regulation 7(10) of the Social Fund Maternity and Funeral Expenses (General) Regulations 2005; and

(h) regulation 2(4)(a) to (e) of the State Pension Credit Regulations 2002.

Revocations and savings

2.1193 **11.**—(1) The following Regulations are revoked—

(a)–(d) *[Noted at the appropriate places in the text of the revoked regulations]*

(2) Nothing in these Regulations shall affect the continued operation of the transitional arrangements and savings provided for in—

(a) regulation 12 of the Social Security (Persons From Abroad) Miscellaneous Amendments Regulations 1996;

(b) regulation 6 of the Social Security (Habitual Residence) Amendment Regulations 2004; or

(c) *[Omitted as applying solely to housing benefit and council tax benefit]*

The Accession (Immigration and Worker Authorisation) Regulations 2006

(SI 2006/3317) (AS AMENDED)

Made by the Home Secretary under section 2 of the European Communities Act 1972 and section 2 of the European Union (Accessions) Act 2006

[January 1, 2007]

GENERAL NOTE

See the commentary to reg.21AA of the Income Support Regulations. 2.1194

The accession period, during which these Regulations restricted the rights of A2 nationals (i.e. nationals of Bulgaria and Romania) to reside in the UK as workers and jobseekers, ended on December 31, 2013 (see reg.1(2)(c)). From January 1, 2014, A2 nationals have the same rights as any other EU citizen (except for Croatian nationals, see below). However, the Regulations remain relevant in appeals where an A2 national seeks to establish that he or she has a permanent right of residence based on lawful residence in the UK between January 1, 2007 and December 31, 2013.

PART 1

GENERAL

CITATION, COMMENCEMENT, INTERPRETATION AND CONSEQUENTIAL AMENDMENTS

1.—(1) These Regulations may be cited as the Accession (Immigration and Worker Authorisation) Regulations 2006 and shall come into force on 1st January 2007. 2.1195

(2) In these Regulations—

(a) "the 1971 Act" means the Immigration Act 1971;

(b) "the 2006 Regulations" means the Immigration (European Economic Area) Regulations 2006;

(c) "accession period" means the period beginning on 1st January 2007 and ending on [1 31st December 2013];

(d) "accession State national subject to worker authorisation" has the meaning given in regulation 2;

(e) "accession worker authorisation document" shall be interpreted in accordance with regulation 9(2);

(f) "authorised category of employment" means a category of employment listed in the first column of the table in Schedule 1;

(g) "authorised family member" has the meaning given in regulation 3;
(h) "civil partner" does not include a party to a civil partnership of convenience;
(i) "EEA State" means—
  (i) a member State, other than the United Kingdom;
  (ii) Norway, Iceland or Liechtenstein;
  (iii) Switzerland;
(j) "employer" means, in relation to a worker, the person who directly pays the wage or salary of that worker;
(k) "family member" shall be interpreted in accordance with regulation 7 of the 2006 Regulations;
(l) "highly skilled person" has the meaning given in regulation 4;
(m) "immigration rules" means the rules laid down as mentioned in section 3(2) of the 1971 Act applying on 1st January 2007;
(n) "letter of approval under the work permit arrangements" has the meaning given in paragraph 1(b) of Schedule 1;
(o) "registration certificate" means a certificate issued in accordance with regulation 16 of the 2006 Regulations;
(p) "relevant requirements" means, in relation to an authorised category of employment, the requirements set out in the second column of the table in Schedule 1 for that category;
(q) "Sectors Based Scheme" has the meaning given in paragraph 1(f) of Schedule 1;
(r) "spouse" does not include a party to a marriage of convenience;
(s) "student" has the meaning given in regulation 4(1)(d) of the 2006 Regulations;
(t) "worker" means a worker within the meaning of Article 39 of the Treaty establishing the European Community, and "work" and "working" shall be construed accordingly.

(3) *[Omitted as relating to consequential amendments only.]*

AMENDMENT

1. Accesssion (Immigration and Worker Authorisation) (Amendment) Regulations 2011 (SI 2011/2816) reg.2 (December 30, 2011).

"Accession State national subject to worker authorisation"

2.1196 **2.**—(1) Subject to the following paragraphs of this regulation, in these Regulations "accession State national subject to worker authorisation" means a national of Bulgaria or Romania.

[[1] (2) A national of Bulgaria or Romania is not an accession State national subject to worker authorisation if on 31st December 2006 he had leave to enter or remain in the United Kingdom under the 1971 Act that was not subject to any condition restricting his employment or he is given such leave after that date.]

(3) A national of Bulgaria or Romania is not an accession State national subject to worker authorisation if he was legally working in the United Kingdom on 31st December 2006 and had been legally working in the United Kingdom without interruption throughout the period of 12 months ending on that date.

(4) A national of Bulgaria or Romania who legally works in the United Kingdom without interruption for a period of 12 months falling partly or wholly after 31st December 2006 shall cease to be an accession State national subject to worker authorisation at the end of that period of 12 months.

(5) A national of Bulgaria or Romania is not an accession State national subject to worker authorisation during any period in which he is also a national of—

(a) the United Kingdom; or

(b) an EEA State, other than Bulgaria or Romania.

[[3] (5A) A national of Bulgaria or Romania is not an accession State national subject to worker authorisation during any period in which that national is the spouse, civil partner or child under 18 of a person who has leave to enter or remain in the United Kingdom under the 1971 Act that allows that person to work in the United Kingdom.]

(6) A national of Bulgaria or Romania is not an accession State national subject to worker authorisation during any period in which he is the spouse or civil partner of a national of the United Kingdom or of a person settled in the United Kingdom.

[[2] (6A) A national of Bulgaria or Romania is not an accession State national subject to worker authorisation during any period in which he is a member of a mission or other person mentioned in section 8(3) of the 1971 Act (member of a diplomatic mission, the family member of such a person, or a person otherwise entitled to diplomatic immunity), other than a person who, under section 8(3A) of that Act, does not count as a member of a mission for the purposes of section 8(3).]

(7) A national of Bulgaria or Romania is not an accession State national subject to worker authorisation during any period in which he has a permanent right of residence under regulation 15 of the 2006 Regulations.

[[2] (8) A national of Bulgaria or Romania is not an accession State national subject to worker authorisation during any period in which he is a family member of—

(a) an EEA national who has a right to reside in the United Kingdom under the 2006 Regulations, other than—

(i) an accession State national subject to worker authorisation; or

(ii) a person who is not an accession State national subject to worker authorisation solely by virtue of being the family member of a person mentioned in sub-paragraph (b) [[3] or a worker mentioned in paragraph (8A)]; or

(b) an accession State national subject to worker authorisation who has a right to reside under regulation 14(1) of the 2006 Regulations by virtue of being a self-employed person, a self-sufficient person or a student falling within sub-paragraph (c), (d) or (e) of regulation 6(1) of those Regulations ("qualified person").]

[[3] (8A) A national of Bulgaria or Romania is not an accession State national subject to worker authorisation during any period in which that national is the spouse, civil partner or descendant of an accession State national subject to worker authorisation who has a right to reside under regulation 14(1) of the 2006 Regulations by virtue of being a worker falling within sub-paragraph (b) of regulation 6(1) of those Regulations ("qualified person") provided that, in the case of a descendant, the descendant is under 21 or dependent on the accession State national subject to worker authorisation.]

(9) A national of Bulgaria or Romania is not an accession State national subject to worker authorisation during any period in which he is a highly skilled person and holds a registration certificate that includes a statement that he has unconditional access to the United Kingdom labour market.

[[1](10) A national of Bulgaria or Romania is not an accession State national subject to worker authorisation during any period in which he is in the United Kingdom as a student and—

(a) holds a registration certificate that includes a statement that he is a student who may work in the United Kingdom whilst a student in accordance with the condition set out in paragraph (10A); and

(b) complies with that condition.

(10A) The condition referred to in paragraph (10) is that the student shall not work for more than 20 hours a week unless—

(a) he is following a course of vocational training and is working as part of that training; or

(b) he is working during his vacation.

(10B) A national of Bulgaria or Romania who ceases to be a student at the end of his course of study is not an accession State national subject to worker authorisation during the period of four months beginning with the date on which his course ends provided he holds a registration certificate that was issued to him before the end of the course that includes a statement that he may work during that period.]

(11) A national of Bulgaria or Romania is not an accession State national subject to worker authorisation during any period in which he is a posted worker.

(12) For the purposes of paragraphs (3) and (4) of this regulation—

(a) a person working in the United Kingdom during a period falling before 1st January 2007 was working legally in the United Kingdom during that period if—

(i) he had leave to enter or remain in the United Kingdom under the 1971 Act for that period, that leave allowed him to work in the United Kingdom, and he was working in accordance with any condition on that leave restricting his employment; or

[[2] (ia) he was exempt from the provisions of the 1971 Act by virtue of section 8(3) of that Act; or]

(ii) he was entitled to reside in the United Kingdom for that period under the Immigration (European Economic Area) Regulations 2000 or the 2006 Regulations without the requirement for such leave;

(b) a person working in the United Kingdom on or after 1st January 2007 is legally working during any period in which he—

(i) falls within paragraphs (5) to [[1] (10B)]; or

(ii) holds an accession worker authorisation document and is working in accordance with the conditions set out in that document;

(c) a person shall be treated as having worked in the United Kingdom without interruption for a period of 12 months if he was legally working in the United Kingdom at the beginning and end of that period and any intervening periods in which he was not legally working in the United Kingdom do not, in total, exceed 30 days.

(13) In this regulation—

(a) "posted worker" means a worker who is posted to the United Kingdom, within the meaning of Article 1(3) of Directive 96/71/EC concerning the posting of workers , by an undertaking established in an EEA State;

(b) the reference to a person settled in the United Kingdom shall be interpreted in accordance with section 33(2A) of the 1971 Act.

AMENDMENTS

1. Accession (Immigration and Worker Authorisation) (Amendment) Regulations 2007 (SI 2007/475) reg.2(2) (March 16, 2007).
2. Accession (Worker Authorisation and Worker Registration) (Amendment) Regulations 2007 (SI 2007/3012) reg.2(2) (November 19, 2007).
3. Accession (Worker Authorisation and Worker Registration) (Amendment) Regulations 2009 (SI 2009/2426) reg.2(1) and (2) (October 2. 2009).

GENERAL NOTE

Paragraphs (10)–(10B). Regulation 4 of SI 2007/475 contains transitional protection for students who had access to the UK labour market for 20 hours a week to whom a registration certificate had been issued before March 16, 2007. **2.1197**

Authorised family member

[1 **3.**—A person is an authorised family member for the purpose of these Regulations if that person is the family member of an accession State national subject to worker authorisation who has a right to reside in the United Kingdom under regulation 14(1) of the 2006 Regulations as a worker, unless— **2.1198**

(a) the worker is only authorised to work under these Regulations by virtue of holding an accession worker card issued in accordance with regulation 11 pursuant to an application as an authorised family member; or

(b) the family member is the spouse or civil partner of the worker or a descendant of the worker who is under 21 or dependent on the worker.]

AMENDMENT

1. Accession (Worker Authorisation and Worker Registration) (Amendment) Regulations 2009 (SI 2009/2426) reg.2(1) and 3) (October 2, 2009).

GENERAL NOTE

For the amendments to the previous version of this regulation (and the transitional provision made by the amending regulations) see p.714 of Vol.II of the 2007 edition and p.757 of Vol.II of the 2009/10 edition. **2.1199**

"Highly skilled person"

4.—(1) In these Regulations "highly skilled person" means a person who— **2.1200**

(a) meets the criteria specified by the Secretary of State for the purpose of paragraph 135A(i) of the immigration rules (entry to the United Kingdom under the Highly Skilled Migrant Programme) and applying on 1st January 2007, other than the criterion requiring a proficiency in the English language; or

(b) has been awarded one of the following qualifications and applies for a registration certificate or submits a registration certificate to the Secretary of State under regulation 7(4) within 12 months of being awarded the qualification—

[[1] (i) a Higher National Diploma awarded by a relevant institution in Scotland; or

(ii) a degree, postgraduate certificate or postgraduate diploma awarded by a relevant institution in the United Kingdom.]

(2) In paragraph (1)(b), "relevant institution" means an institution that is financed from public funds or included on the Department for Education and Skills' Register of Education and Training Providers on 1st January 2007.

AMENDMENT

1. Accession (Worker Authorisation and Worker Registration) (Amendment) Regulations 2007 (SI 2007/3012) reg.2(4) (November 19, 2007).

Derogation from provisions of Community law relating to workers

2.1201 **5.**—Regulations 6, 7 and 9 derogate during the accession period from Article 39 of the Treaty establishing the European Communities, Articles 1 to 6 of Regulation (EEC) No. 1612/68 on freedom of movement for workers within the Community and Council Directive 2004/38/EC on the right of citizens of the Union and their family members to move and reside freely within the territory of the Member States.

PART 2

IMMIGRATION

Right of residence of an accession State national subject to worker authorisation

2.1202 **6.**—(1) An accession State national subject to worker authorisation shall, during the accession period, only be entitled to reside in the United Kingdom in accordance with the 2006 Regulations, as modified by this regulation.

(2) An accession State national subject to worker authorisation who is seeking employment in the United Kingdom shall not be treated as a job-seeker for the purpose of the definition of "qualified person" in regulation 6(1) of the 2006 Regulations and such a person shall be treated as a worker for the purpose of that definition only during a period in which he holds an accession worker authorisation document and is working in accordance with the conditions set out in that document.

(3) Regulation 6(2) of the 2006 Regulations shall not apply to an accession State national subject to worker authorisation who ceases to work.

Issuing registration certificates and residence cards to nationals of Bulgaria and Romania and their family members during the accession period

7.—(1) Subject to paragraph (2), an accession State national subject to worker authorisation shall not be treated as a qualified person for the purposes of regulations 16 and 17 of the 2006 Regulations (issue of registration certificates and residence cards) during the accession period unless he falls within sub-paragraphs (c), (d) or (e) of regulation 6(1) of the 2006 Regulations. **2.1203**

(2) [[2] During the accession period, the Secretary] of State shall issue a registration certificate to an accession State national subject to worker authorisation on application if he is satisfied that the applicant—

(a) is seeking employment in the United Kingdom; and

(b) is a highly skilled person.

(3) Where the Secretary of State issues a registration certificate during the accession period to a Bulgarian or Romanian national under paragraph (2) or in any case where he is satisfied that the Bulgarian or Romanian national is not an accession State national subject to worker authorisation [[1] (other than solely by virtue of falling within paragraph (10) or (10B) of regulation 2)], the registration certificate shall include a statement that the holder of the certificate has unconditional access to the United Kingdom labour market.

(4) A Bulgarian or Romanian national who holds a registration certificate that does not include a statement that he has unconditional access to the United Kingdom labour market may, during the accession period, submit the certificate to the Secretary of State for the inclusion of such a statement.

(5) The Secretary of State shall re-issue a certificate submitted to him under paragraph (4) with the inclusion of a statement that the holder has unconditional access to the United Kingdom labour market if he is satisfied that the holder—

(a) is a highly skilled person; or

(b) has ceased to be an accession State national subject to worker authorisation other than solely by virtue of falling within [[1] paragraph (10) or (10B) of regulation 2].

(6) A registration certificate issued to a Bulgarian or Romanian student during the accession period shall include a statement that the holder of the certificate is a student who [[1] may work in the United Kingdom whilst a student in accordance with the condition set out in regulation 2 (10A) and who, on ceasing to be a student, may work during the period referred to in regulation 2(10B)], unless it includes a statement under paragraph (3) or (5) that the holder has unconditional access to the United Kingdom labour market.

(7) But this regulation is subject to regulation 20 of the 2006 Regulations (power to refuse to issue and to revoke registration certificates).

AMENDMENTS

1. Accession (Immigration and Worker Authorisation) (Amendment) Regulations 2007 (SI 2007/475) reg.2(4) (March 16, 2007).

2. Immigration (European Economic Area) (Amendment) (No.2) Regulations 2013 (SI 2013/3032) reg.5 and Sch.2 para.3(1) and (2) (January 1, 2014).

Transitional provisions to take account of the application of the 2006 Regulations to nationals of Bulgaria and Romania and their family members on 1st January 2007

2.1204 **8.**—(1) Where before 1st January 2007 directions have been given for the removal of a Bulgarian or Romanian national or the family member of such a national under paragraphs 8 to 10A of Schedule 2 to the 1971 Act or section 10 of the 1999 Act, those directions shall cease to have effect on and after that date.

(2) Where before 1st January 2007 the Secretary of State has made a decision to make a deportation order against a Bulgarian or Romanian national or the family member of such a national under section 5(1) of the 1971 Act—

(a) that decision shall, on and after 1st January 2007, be treated as if it were a decision under regulation 19(3)(b) of the 2006 Regulations; and

(b) any appeal against that decision, or against the refusal of the Secretary of State to revoke the deportation order, made under section 63 of the 1999 Act or section 82(2)(j) or (k) of the 2002 Act before 1st January 2007, shall, on or after that date, be treated as if it had been made under regulation 26 of the 2006 Regulations.

(3) In this regulation—

(a) "the 1999 Act" means the Immigration and Asylum Act 1999;

(b) "the 2002 Act" means the Nationality, Immigration and Asylum Act 2002;

(c) any reference to the family member of a Bulgarian or Romanian national is a reference to a person who on 1st January 2007 acquires a right to reside in the United Kingdom under the 2006 Regulations as the family member of a Bulgarian or Romanian national.

Part 3

Accession State worker authorisation

Requirement for an accession State national subject to worker authorisation to be authorised to work

2.1205 **9.**—(1) An accession State national subject to worker authorisation shall only be authorised to work in the United Kingdom during the accession period if he holds an accession worker authorisation document and is working in accordance with the conditions set out in that document.

(2) For the purpose of these Regulations, an accession worker authorisation document is—

(a) a passport or other travel document endorsed before 1st January 2007 to show that the holder has leave to enter or remain in the United Kingdom under the 1971 Act, subject to a condition restricting his employment in the United Kingdom to a particular employer or category of employment;

(b) a seasonal agricultural work card, except where the holder of the card has a document mentioned in sub-paragraph (a) giving him leave to enter the United Kingdom as a seasonal agricultural worker; or

(c) an accession worker card issued in accordance with regulation 11.

(3) But a document shall cease to be treated as an accession worker authorisation document under paragraph (2)—

(a) in the case of a document mentioned in paragraph (2)(a), at the end of the period for which leave to enter or remain is given;

(b) in the case of a seasonal agricultural work card, at the end of the period of six months beginning with the date on which the holder of the card begins working for the agricultural employer specified in the card;

(c) in the case of an accession worker card, on the expiry of the card under regulation 11(7).

(4) For the purpose of this regulation—

(a) "seasonal agricultural work card" means a Home Office work card issued by the operator of a seasonal agricultural workers scheme approved by the Secretary of State for the purpose of paragraph 104(ii) of the immigration rules;

(b) the reference to a travel document other than a passport is a reference to a document which relates to a national of Bulgaria or Romania and which is designed to serve the same purpose as a passport.

Application for an accession worker card

10.—(1) An application for an accession worker card may be made by an accession State national subject to worker authorisation who wishes to work for an employer in the United Kingdom if— **2.1206**

(a) the employment concerned falls within an authorised category of employment; or

(b) the applicant is an authorised family member.

(2) The application shall be in writing and shall be made to the Secretary of State.

(3) The application shall state—

(a) the name, address, and date of birth of the applicant;

(b) the name and address of the employer for whom the applicant wishes to work; and

(c) unless the applicant is an authorised family member, the authorised category of employment covered by the application.

(4) The application shall be accompanied by—

(a) the applicant's national identity card or passport; and

(b) two passport size photographs of the applicant.

(5) Where the applicant is not an authorised family member, the application shall, in addition to the documents required by paragraph (4), be accompanied by—

(a) where the relevant requirements for the authorised category of employment specified in the application require the applicant to hold a letter of approval under the work permit arrangements, that letter;

(b) where sub-paragraph (a) does not apply, a letter from the employer specified in the application confirming that the applicant has an offer of employment with the employer; and

(c) any other proof that the applicant wishes to provide to establish that he meets the relevant requirements.

(6) where the applicant is an authorised family member, the application shall, in addition to the documents required by paragraph (4), be accompanied by—

(a) a letter from the employer specified in the application confirming that the applicant has an offer of employment with the employer; and
(b) proof that the applicant is an authorised family member.

(7) In this regulation "address" means, in relation to an employer which is a body corporate or partnership, the head or main office of that employer.

Issuing an accession worker card etc

2.1207 **11.**—(1) [[1] During the accession period, subject] to paragraph (2), the Secretary of State shall issue an accession worker card pursuant to an application made in accordance with regulation 10 if he is satisfied that the applicant is an accession State national subject to worker authorisation who—
(a) is an authorised family member; or
(b) meets the relevant requirements for the authorised category of employment covered by the application.

(2) The Secretary of State shall not issue an accession worker card if he has decided to remove the applicant from the United Kingdom under regulation 19(3)(b) of the 2006 Regulations (removal on grounds of public policy, public security or public health).

(3) An accession worker card issued under this regulation to an authorised family member shall include a condition restricting the applicant's employment to the employer specified in the application.

(4) An accession worker card issued under this regulation pursuant to an application that was accompanied by a letter of approval under the work permit arrangements shall include the following conditions—
(a) a condition restricting the applicant's employment to the employer specified in the application and any secondary employer; and
(b) a condition restricting him to the type of employment specified in the letter of approval under the work permit arrangements.

(5) In any other case, an accession worker card issued under this regulation shall include the following conditions—
(a) a condition restricting the applicant's employment to the employer specified in the application; and
(b) a condition restricting him to the authorised category of employment specified in the application.

(6) An accession worker card issued under this regulation shall include a photograph of the applicant and shall set out—
(a) the name, nationality and date of birth of the applicant;
(b) the name and address of the employer specified in the application;
(c) the conditions required by paragraph (3), (4) or (5), as the case may be; and
(d) the date on which the card was issued.

(7) An accession worker card shall expire if the holder of the card ceases working for the employer specified in the application.

(8) Where the Secretary of State is not satisfied as mentioned in paragraph (1) or where paragraph (2) applies, he shall refuse the application and issue a notice of refusal setting out the reasons for the refusal.

(9) An accession worker card or notice of refusal issued under this regulation shall be sent to the applicant by post together with the identity card or passport that accompanied the application.

(10) In this regulation, "secondary employer" means, in relation to an applicant, an employer who is not specified in his application and who

employs the applicant for no more than 20 hours a week when the applicant is not working for the employer who is specified in the application.

AMENDMENT

1. Immigration (European Economic Area) (Amendment) (No.2) Regulations 2013 (SI 2013/3032) reg.5 and Sch.2 para.3(1) and (3) (January 1, 2014).

*[***12.–15.** *Omitted.]* 2.1208

SCHEDULE 1 **Regulation 1(2)**

Authorised categories of employment and relevant requirements

2.1209

Column (1)	*Column (2)*
Authorised category of employment	*Relevant requirements in relation to authorised category of employment*
Authorised categories of employment requiring a letter of approval under the work permit arrangements	
Employment under the Sectors Based Scheme	The applicant— (1) holds a letter of approval under the work permit arrangements issued under the Sectors-Based Scheme; and (2) is capable of undertaking the employment specified in that letter.
Training or work experience	The applicant— (1) holds a letter of approval under the work permit arrangements issued under the Training and Work Experience Scheme; and (2) is capable of undertaking the training or work experience as specified in that letter.

Column (1)	*Column (2)*
Work permit employment	The applicant— (1) holds a letter of approval under the work permit arrangements issued in relation to work permit employment; and (2) is capable of undertaking the employment specified in that letter.
Other authorised categories of employment	
Airport based operational ground an overseas air line	The applicant has been transferred staff of to the United Kingdom by an overseas-owned airline operating services to and from the United Kingdom to take up duty at an international airport as station manager, securitymanager or technical manager.
Au pair placement	The applicant – (1) has and intends to take up an offer of an au pair placement; (2) is aged between 17 to 27 inclusive; (3) is unmarried and is not in a civil partnership; and (4) is without dependants.

Column (1)	*Column (2)*
Domestic worker in a private household	The applicant— (1) is over 18; (2) has been employed for at least a year outside the United Kingdom as a domestic worker under the same roof as his employer or in a household that the employer uses for himself on a regular basis; and (3) intends to be so employed by that employer in the United Kingdom.
Minister of religion, missionary or member of a religious order	The applicant— (1) if a minister of religion— (a) has either been working for at least one year as a minister of religion in any of the five years immediately prior to the date on which the application for the worker accession card is made or, where ordination is prescribed by a religious faith as the sole means of entering the ministry, has been ordained as a minister of religion following at least one year's full time or two years' part.time training for the ministry; and (b) holds an International English Language Testing System Certificate issued to him to certify that he has achieved level 4 competence in spoken English, and the Certificate is dated not more than two years prior to the date on which the application for an accession worker card is made; (2) if a missionary, has been trained as a missionary or has worked as a missionary and is being sent or has been sent to the United Kingdom by an overseas organisation; (3) if a member of a religious order, is living or coming to live in a community maintained by the religious order of which he is a member and, if intending to teach, does not intend to do so save at an establishment maintained by his order; and (4) intends to work in the United Kingdom as a minister of religion, missionary or for the religious order of which he is a member.
Overseas government employment	The applicant intends to work in the United Kingdom for an overseas government or the United Nations or other international organisation of which the United Kingdom is a member.
Postgraduate doctors, dentists and trainee general practitioners	The applicant— (1) is a graduate from a medical or dental school who is eligible for provisional or limited registration with the General Medical Council or General Dental Council and intends to work in the United Kingdom as a doctor or dentist as part.of his training; or

Column (1)	*Column (2)*
	(2) is a doctor, dentist or trainee general practitioner eligible for full or limited registration with the General Medical Council or the General Dental Council and intends to work in the United Kingdom as part of his postgraduate training or general practitioner training in a hospital or the Community Health Services.
Private servant in a diplomatic household	The applicant— (1) is over 18; and (2) intends to work in the United Kingdom as a private servant in the household of a member of staff of a diplomatic or consular mission who enjoys diplomatic privileges and immunity within the meaning of the Vienna Convention on Diplomatic Relations.
Representative of an overseas newspaper, news agency or broadcasting organisation	The applicant has been engaged by an overseas newspaper, news agency or broadcasting organisation outside the United Kingdom and is being posted to the United Kingdom by that newspaper, agency or organisation to act as its representative.
Sole representative	The applicant— (1) has been employed outside the United Kingdom as a representative of a firm that has its headquarters and principal place of business outside the United Kingdom and has no branch, subsidiary or other representative in the United Kingdom; (2) intends to work as a senior employee with full authority to take operational decisions on behalf of the overseas firm for the purpose of representing it in the United Kingdom by establishing and operating a registered branch or wholly owned subsidiary of that overseas firm; and (3) is not a majority shareholder in that overseas firm.
Teacher or language assistant	The applicant intends to work at an educational establishment in the United Kingdom under an exchange scheme approved by the Department for Education and Skills, the Scottish or Welsh Office of Education or the Department of Education, Northern Ireland, or administered by the British Council's Education and Training Group.
Overseas qualified nurses	The applicant— (1) has obtained confirmation from the Nursing and Midwifery Council that he is eligible for admission to the Overseas Nurses Programme; and (2) has been offered and intends to take up a supervised practice placement through an education provider that is recognised by the Nursing and Midwifery Council or a midwifery or a midwifery adaptation programme placement in a setting approved by that Council.

2.1210 **1.**—In this Schedule—

(a) "au pair placement" means an arrangement whereby a young person—
  (i) comes to the United Kingdom for the purpose of learning English;
  (ii) lives for a time as a member of an English speaking family with appropriate opportunities for study; and
  (iii) helps in the home for a maximum of 5 hours per day in return for an allowance and with two free days per week;

(b) "letter of approval under the work permit arrangements" means a letter issued by the Secretary of State under the work permit arrangements stating that employment by the employer specified in the letter of the person so specified for the type of employment so specified satisfies the labour market criteria set out in those arrangements;

(c) "member of a religious order" means a person who lives in a community run by that order;

(d) "minister of religion" means a religious functionary whose main regular duties comprise the leading of a congregation in performing the rites and rituals of the faith and in preaching the essentials of the creed;

(e) "missionary" means a person who is directly engaged in spreading a religious doctrine and whose work is not in essence administrative or clerical;

(f) "Sectors Based Scheme" means the scheme established by the Secretary of State for the purpose of paragraph 135I(i) of the immigration rules (requirements for leave to enter the United Kingdom for the purpose of employment under the Sectors Based Scheme);

(g) "Training and Work Experience Scheme" means the scheme established by the Secretary of State for the purpose of paragraph 116(i) of the immigration rules (requirement for leave to enter the United Kingdom for approved training or work experience);

(h) "work permit arrangements" means the arrangements published by the Secretary of State setting out the labour market criteria to be applied for the purpose of issuing the work permits referred to in paragraphs 116(i) (Training and Work Experience Scheme) and 128(i) of the immigration rules and the immigration employment document referred to in paragraph 135I(i) (Sectors Based Scheme) of the immigration rules;

(i) "work permit employment" means a category of employment covered by the work permit arrangements, other than employment covered by the Sectors Based Scheme and the Training and Work Experience Scheme.

[Schedule 2 Omitted.]

The Accession of Croatia (Immigration and Worker Authorisation) Regulations 2013

(SI 2013/1460)

IN FORCE JULY 1, 2013

ARRANGEMENT OF REGULATIONS

PART 1

INTERPRETATION ETC.

PART 2

APPLICATION OF THE EEA REGULATIONS AND OTHER INSTRUMENTS

PART 3

ACCESSION STATE WORKER AUTHORISATION AND ASSOCIATED DOCUMENTATION

PART 4

PENALTIES AND OFFENCES

SCHEDULE

CONSEQUENTIAL AMENDMENTS

GENERAL NOTE

Croatia acceded to the EU on July 1, 2013 under the Treaty concerning the accession of the Republic of Croatia to the European Union, signed at Brussels on December 9, 2011, to which effect is given in UK domestic law by ss.1 and 3 of the European Union (Croatian Accession and Irish Protocol) Act 2013. Section 4 of that Act empowers the Secretary of State to make provision for "the entitlement of a Croatian national to enter or reside in the United Kingdom as a worker, and . . . any matter ancillary to that entitlement". That power has been exercised to make these Regulations, which provide that during a transitional period of five years, a Croatian national who is an "accession State national subject to worker authorisation" (i.e. any **2.1212**

Croatian national who does not fall within the exceptions listed in reg.2(2)–(20)) does not have a right of residence of the UK as a "jobseeker" and only has a right to reside as a worker during a period in which s/he "holds an accession worker authorisation document and is working in accordance with the conditions set out in that document".

The structure of the scheme is similar to that which applied to nationals of Bulgaria and Romania before January 1, 2014 under the Accession (Immigration and Worker Authorisation) Regulations 2006 (see above). It requires that the employment of accession state national subject to worker authorisation should be authorised in advance in order to be lawful. It therefore differs from the scheme of registration that applied to nationals of the A8 states between May 1, 2004 and April 30, 2011.

See further the commentary to reg.21AA of the Income Support Regulations.

The Secretary of State makes the following Regulations in exercise of the powers conferred by section 4 of the European Union (Croatian Accession and Irish Protocol) Act 2013.

In accordance with section 5(1) of that Act, a draft of this instrument was laid before Parliament and approved by resolution of each House of Parliament.

PART 1

Interpretation Etc

Citation, commencement, interpretation and consequential amendments

2.1213 **1.**—(1) These Regulations may be cited as the Accession of Croatia (Immigration and Worker Authorisation) Regulations 2013 and come into force on 1st July 2013.

(2) In these Regulations—

"the 1971 Act" means the Immigration Act 1971;

"the 2006 Act" means the Immigration, Asylum and Nationality Act 2006;

"accession period" means the period beginning with 1st July 2013 and ending with 30th June 2018;

"accession State national subject to worker authorisation" has the meaning given in regulation 2;

"accession worker authorisation document" has the meaning given in regulation 8(2);

"authorised category of employment" means—

(a) employment for which the applicant has been issued by a sponsor with a valid certificate of sponsorship under Tier 2 or Tier 5 of the Points-Based System; or

(b) employment as—

(i) a representative of an overseas business;

(ii) a postgraduate doctor or dentist; or

(iii) a domestic worker in a private household;

"certificate of sponsorship" has the meaning given in paragraph 6 of the immigration rules, except that the reference to an application or potential application for entry clearance or leave to enter or remain as a Tier 2 migrant or a Tier 5 migrant is to be read as including a reference to an application or potential application for a worker authorisation registration certificate;

"certificate of sponsorship checking service" has the meaning given in paragraph 6 of the immigration rules, except that the reference to an application or potential application for entry clearance or leave to enter or remain as a Tier 2 migrant or a Tier 5 migrant is to be read as including a reference to an application or potential application for a worker authorisation registration certificate;

"civil partner" does not include a party to a civil partnership of convenience;

"EEA registration certificate" means a certificate issued in accordance with regulation 16 of the EEA Regulations;

"the EEA Regulations" means the Immigration (European Economic Area) Regulations 2006;

"EEA State" excludes the United Kingdom and includes Switzerland;

"employer" means, in relation to a worker, the person who directly pays the wage or salary of that worker, and "employ", "employment" and "employs" shall be construed accordingly;

"the EU2 Regulations" means the Accession (Immigration and Worker Authorisation) Regulations 2006;

"extended family member" has the meaning given in regulation 8 of the EEA Regulations;

"family member" has the meaning given in regulation 7 of the EEA Regulations;

"highly skilled person" has the meaning given in regulation 3;

"immigration rules" means the rules laid down as mentioned in section 3(2) of the 1971 Act applying (except for in the definition of "relevant requirements") [2 —

(a) for the purposes of regulation 3(1)(a) (highly skilled person: Tier 1 (Exceptional Talent) migrant), on 6th November 2014; and

(b) for all other purposes, on 1st July 2013];

"Points-Based System" means the system established under Part 6A of the immigration rules;

"relevant requirements" means, in relation to an authorised category of employment, the requirements which, subject to any necessary modifications, a person in that category of employment was obliged to meet under the immigration rules in force on 9th December 2011 in order to obtain entry clearance or leave to enter or remain in the United Kingdom and which are set out in the relevant statement;

[1 "relevant statement" means the statement entitled "the Statement of relevant requirements" dated [2 March 2015] and published by the Secretary of State;]

"right to reside" shall be interpreted in accordance with the EEA Regulations and "entitled to reside" and "right of residence" shall be construed accordingly;

"sponsor" means the holder of a sponsor licence;

"sponsor licence" has the meaning given in paragraph 6 of the immigration rules;

"spouse" does not include a party to a marriage of convenience;

"student" has the meaning given in regulation 4(1)(d) of the EEA Regulations;

[2 "Student Union Sabbatical Officer" and "national National Union of Students (NUS) position" have the same meaning as in paragraph 245ZW of the immigration rules;]

"Tier 2" and "Tier 5" shall be construed in accordance in paragraph 6 of the immigration rules, except that the reference to the grant of leave is to be read as including a reference to the issuing of a worker authorisation registration certificate;

"unmarried or same sex partner" means a person who is in a durable relationship with another person;

"work" and "working" shall be construed in accordance with the meaning of "worker"; and

"worker authorisation registration certificate" means a certificate issued in accordance with regulation 10 of these Regulations.

(3) The Schedule (consequential amendments) shall have effect.

AMENDMENTS

1. Accession of Croatia (Immigration and Worker Authorisation) (Amendment) Regulations 2014 (SI 530/2014) reg.2(1) and (2) (April 6, 2014).

2. Immigration (European Economic Area) (Amendment) Regulations 2015 (SI 2015/694) reg.5 and Sch.2 para.1 (April 6, 2015).

"Accession State national subject to worker authorisation"

2.1214 **2.**—(1) Subject to the following paragraphs of this regulation, other than where these Regulations expressly refer to an accession State national subject to worker authorisation within the meaning of regulation 2 of the EU2 Regulations, in these Regulations "accession State national subject to worker authorisation" means a Croatian national.

(2) A Croatian national is not an accession State national subject to worker authorisation if, on 30th June 2013, he had leave to enter or remain in the United Kingdom under the 1971 Act that was not subject to any condition restricting his employment [1 (other than a condition restricting his employment as a doctor in training or as a dentist in training or as a professional sportsperson (including as a sports coach))], or he is given such leave after that date.

(3) A Croatian national is not an accession State national subject to worker authorisation if he was legally working in the United Kingdom on 30th June 2013 and had been legally working in the United Kingdom without interruption throughout the preceding period of 12 months ending on that date.

(4) A Croatian national who legally works in the United Kingdom without interruption for a period of 12 months falling partly or wholly after 30th June 2013 ceases to be an accession State national subject to worker authorisation at the end of that period of 12 months.

(5) For the purposes of paragraphs (3) and (4) of this regulation—

(a) a person working in the United Kingdom during a period falling before 1st July 2013 was legally working in the United Kingdom during that period if—

(i) he had leave to enter or remain in the United Kingdom under the 1971 Act for that period, that leave allowed him to work in the United Kingdom, and he was working in accordance with any condition of that leave restricting his employment;

(ii) he was exempt from the provisions of the 1971 Act by virtue of section 8(2) or (3) of that Act (persons exempted by order or membership of diplomatic mission); or

(iii) he was entitled to reside in the United Kingdom for that period under the EEA Regulations without the requirement for such leave;

(b) a person working in the United Kingdom on or after 1st July 2013 is legally working in the United Kingdom during any period in which he—

(i) falls within any of paragraphs (6) to (16) or (18); or

(ii) holds an accession worker authorisation document and is working in accordance with the conditions set out in that document; and

(c) a person shall be treated as having worked in the United Kingdom without interruption for a period of 12 months if—

(i) he was legally working in the United Kingdom at the beginning and end of that period; and

(ii) during that period of 12 months, if his work in the United Kingdom was interrupted, any intervening periods of interruption did not exceed 30 days in total.

(6) Other than during any period in which he is also an accession State national subject to worker authorisation within the meaning of regulation 2 of the EU2 Regulations, a Croatian national is not an accession State national subject to worker authorisation during any period in which he is also a national of—

(a) the United Kingdom; or

(b) an EEA State, other than Croatia.

(7) A Croatian national is not an accession State national subject to worker authorisation during any period in which he is also an accession State national subject to worker authorisation within the meaning of regulation 2 of the EU2 Regulations and is working in accordance with those Regulations.

(8) A Croatian national is not an accession State national subject to worker authorisation during any period in which he is the spouse, civil partner, unmarried or same sex partner, or child under 18 of a person who has leave to enter or remain in the United Kingdom under the 1971 Act and that leave allows him to work in the United Kingdom.

(9) A Croatian national is not an accession State national subject to worker authorisation during any period in which he is the spouse, civil partner, unmarried or same sex partner of—

(a) a national of the United Kingdom; or

(b) a person that is settled in the United Kingdom in accordance with the meaning given in section 33(2A) (interpretation – meaning of "settled") of the 1971 Act.

(10) A Croatian national is not an accession State national subject to worker authorisation during any period in which he is a member of a mission or other person mentioned in section 8(3) (member of a diplomatic mission, the family member of such a person, or a person otherwise entitled to diplomatic immunity) of the 1971 Act, other than a person who, under section 8(3A) (conditions of membership of a mission) of that Act, does not count as a member of a mission for the purposes of section 8(3).

(11) A Croatian national is not an accession State national subject to worker authorisation during any period in which he is a person who is exempt from all or any of the provisions of the 1971 Act by virtue of an order made under section 8(2) (exemption for persons specified by order) of that Act.

(12) A Croatian national is not an accession State national subject to worker authorisation during any period in which he has a permanent right of residence under regulation 15 of the EEA Regulations.

(13) Subject to paragraph (14), a Croatian national is not an accession

State national subject to worker authorisation during any period in which he is a family member (X) of an EEA national (Y) who has a right to reside in the United Kingdom.

(14) Where Y is an accession State national subject to worker authorisation under these Regulations or an accession State national subject to worker authorisation within the meaning of regulation 2 of the EU2 Regulations, paragraph (13) only applies where X is the—

(a) spouse or civil partner of Y;

(b) unmarried or same sex partner of Y; or

(c) a direct descendant of Y, Y's spouse or Y's civil partner who is—

(i) under 21; or

(ii) dependant of Y, Y's spouse or Y's civil partner.

(15) A Croatian national is not an accession State national subject to worker authorisation during any period in which he is a highly skilled person and holds an EEA registration certificate issued in accordance with regulation 7 that includes a statement that he has unconditional access to the United Kingdom labour market.

(16) A Croatian national is not an accession State national subject to worker authorisation during any period in which he is in the United Kingdom as a student and either—

(a) holds an EEA registration certificate that includes a statement that he is a student who may work in the United Kingdom whilst a student in accordance with the condition set out in paragraph (17) and complies with that condition; or

(b) has leave to enter or remain under the 1971 Act as a student and is working in accordance with any conditions attached to that leav

(17) The condition referred to in paragraph (16)(a) is that the student shall not work for more than 20 hours a week unless—

(a) he is following a course of vocational training and is working as part of that training; [2 . . .]

(b) he is working during his vacation [; or

(c) he works for no more than 2 years as a Student Union Sabbatical Officer, provided the appointment to the post is by election and the post is—

(i) either at the institution at which the Croatian national is enrolled as a student; or

(ii) a national National Union of Students (NUS) position].

(18) A Croatian national who ceases to be a student at the end of his course of study is not an accession State national subject to worker authorisation during the period of four months beginning with the date on which his course ends provided he holds an EEA registration certificate that was issued to him before the end of the course that includes a statement that he may work during that period.

(19) A Croatian national is not an accession State national subject to worker authorisation during any period in which he is a posted worker.

(20) In paragraph (19), "posted worker" means a worker who is posted to the United Kingdom, within the meaning of Article 1(3) of the Council Directive 96/71/EC of the European Parliament and of the Council of 16 December 1996 concerning the posting of workers in the framework of the provision of services, by an undertaking established in an EEA State.

AMENDMENTS

1. Accession of Croatia (Immigration and Worker Authorisation) (Amendment) Regulations 2014 (SI 530/2014) reg.2(1) and (3) (April 6, 2014).

2. Immigration (European Economic Area) (Amendment) Regulations 2015 (SI 2015/694) reg.5 and Sch.2 para.2 (April 6, 2015).

"Highly skilled person"

3.—(1) In these Regulations "highly skilled person" means a person who— 2.1215

(a) meets the requirements specified by the Secretary of State for the purpose of paragraph 245BB(c) (requirements for entry clearance as a Tier 1 (Exceptional Talent) migrant) of the immigration rules; or

(b) has been awarded one of the following qualifications and applies for an EEA registration certificate within 12 months of being awarded the qualification—

  (i) a recognised bachelor, masters or doctoral degree;

  (ii) a postgraduate certificate in education or professional graduate diploma of education; or

  (iii) a higher national diploma awarded by a Scottish higher education institution.

(2) For the purposes of paragraph (1)(b), the qualification must have been awarded by a higher education institution which, on the date of the award, is a UK recognised body or an institution that is not a UK recognised body but which provides full courses that lead to the award of a degree by a UK recognised body.

(3) For the purposes of paragraph (1)(b)(iii), to qualify as a higher national diploma from a Scottish institution, a qualification must be at level 8 on the Scottish credit and qualifications framework.

(4) In this regulation, a "UK recognised body" means an institution that has been granted degree awarding powers by a Royal Charter, an Act of Parliament or the Privy Council.

PART 2

APPLICATION OF THE EEA REGULATIONS AND OTHER INSTRUMENTS

Derogation from provisions of European Union law relating to workers

4.—Pursuant to Annex V of the treaty concerning the accession of the Republic of Croatia to the European Union, signed at Brussels on 9 December 2011, Regulations 5 and 7 to 10 derogate during the accession period from Article 45 of the Treaty on the Functioning of the European Union, Articles 1 to 6 of Regulation (EEC) No. 1612/68 of the Council of 15 October 1968 on freedom of movement for workers within the Community and Directive 2004/38/EC of the European Parliament and of the Council of 29 April 2004 on the right of citizens of the Union and their family members to move and reside freely within the territory of the member States, amending Regulation (EEC) No. 1612/68, and repealing Directives 64/221/EEC, 68/360/EEC, 72/194/EEC, 73/148/EEC, 75/34/EEC, 75/35/EEC, 90/364/EEC, 90/365/EEC and 93/96/EEC. 2.1216

Right of residence of an accession State national subject to worker authorisation

2.1217 [1 **5.**—During the accession period, an accession State national subject to worker authorisation who is seeking employment in the United Kingdom shall not be treated as a jobseeker and shall be treated as a worker only in so far as it gives him a right to reside and only during a period in which he holds an accession worker authorisation document and is working in accordance with the conditions set out in that document.]

AMENDMENT

1. Accession of Croatia (Immigration and Worker Authorisation) (Amendment) Regulations 2014 (SI 530/2014) reg.2(1) and (4) (April 6, 2014).

Transitional provisions to take account of the application of the EEA Regulations to Croatian nationals and their family members on 1st July 2013

2.1218 **6.**—(1) Where, before 1st July 2013, any direction has been given for the removal of a Croatian national or the family member of such a national under paragraphs 8 to 10A of Schedule 2 (removal of persons refused leave to enter and illegal entrants) to the 1971 Act, section 10 (removal of certain persons unlawfully in the United Kingdom) of the 1999 Act or section 47 (removal: persons with statutorily extended leave) of the 2006 Act, that direction shall cease to have effect on that date.

(2) Where before 1st July 2013 the Secretary of State has made a deportation order against a Croatian national or the family member of such a national under section 5(1) (deportation orders) of the 1971 Act—

(a) that order shall, on and after 1st July 2013, be treated as if it were a decision under regulation 19(3)(b) of the EEA Regulations; and

(b) any appeal against that order, or against the refusal of the Secretary of State to revoke the deportation order, made before 1st July 2013 under section 63 (deportation orders) of the 1999 Act, or under section 82(2)(j) or (k) (right of appeal: general) of the 2002 Act shall, on or after that date, be treated as if it had been made under regulation 26 of the EEA Regulations.

(3) In this regulation—

(a) "the 1999 Act" means the Immigration and Asylum Act 1999;

(b) "the 2002 Act" means the Nationality, Immigration and Asylum Act 2002; and

(c) any reference to the family member of a Croatian national is, in addition to the definition set out in regulation 1(2), a reference to a person who on 1st July 2013 acquires a right to reside in the United Kingdom under the EEA Regulations as the family member of a Croatian national.

Issuing EEA registration certificates and residence cards

2.1219 **7.**—(1) During the accession period, regulation 6 of the EEA Regulations has effect as if, in paragraph (1), after "EEA national", there were inserted

", except an accession State national subject to worker authorisation within the meaning of regulation 2 of the Croatian Regulations," and after paragraph (1), there were inserted—

"(1A) In these Regulations, a "qualified person" also means a person who is an accession State national subject to worker authorisation within the meaning of regulation 2 of the Croatian Regulations and in the United Kingdom as—

(a) a self-employed person;
(b) a self-sufficient person;
(c) a student; or
(d) a highly skilled person who is seeking employment or is employed in the United Kingdom.

[1 (1B) In regulation 14(2), regulation 16(3) and (5) and regulation 17(1) and (4) a "qualified person" includes an accession State national subject to worker authorisation within the meaning of regulation 2 of the Croatian Regulations where that accession State national subject to worker authorisation has a right to reside.]

(1C) In these Regulations—

(a) "the Croatian Regulations" means the Accession of Croatia (Immigration and Worker Authorisation) Regulations 2013; and
(b) "highly skilled worker" has the meaning given in regulation 1 of the Croatian Regulations."

(2) Subject to paragraph (6), an EEA registration certificate issued to a Croatian national during the accession period shall include a statement that the holder of the certificate has unconditional access to the United Kingdom labour market, unless that person is not an accession State national subject to worker authorisation solely by virtue of falling within paragraph (16) or (18) of regulation 2.

(3) A Croatian national who holds an EEA registration certificate that does not include a statement that he has unconditional access to the United ingdom labour market may, during the accession period, submit the certificate to the Secretary of State for the inclusion of such a statement.

(4) The Secretary of State must re-issue a EEA certificate submitted to her under paragraph (3) with the inclusion of a statement that the holder has unconditional access to the United Kingdom labour market if she is satisfied that the holder—

(a) is a qualified person within the meaning of paragraph (1A) of regulation 6 of the EEA Regulations as applied by paragraph (1); or
(b) has ceased to be an accession State national subject to worker authorisation other than solely by virtue of falling within paragraph (16) or (18) of regulation 2.

(5) An EEA registration certificate issued to a Croatian national who is a student during the accession period shall include a statement that the holder of the certificate is a student who may work in the United Kingdom whilst a student in accordance with the condition set out in paragraph (17) of regulation 2 and who, on ceasing to be a student, may work during the period referred to in paragraph (18) of regulation 2, unless it includes a statement under paragraph (2) or (4) that the holder has unconditional access to the United Kingdom labour market.

(6) Where under paragraph (5) of regulation 16 of the EEA Regulations an EEA registration certificate is issued to a Croatian national extended family member [1 , with the exception of an extended family member who is an unmarried partner (including a same sex partner),] of an accession

State national subject to worker authorisation, the certificate must include a statement that the certificate does not confer a permission to work.

[1 (7) Where under paragraph (1) or (4) of regulation 17 of the EEA Regulations a residence card is issued to a family member or an extended family member of an accession State national subject to worker authorisation—

(a) paragraph (6) of regulation 17 of the EEA Regulations shall not apply;

(b) the duration of that card shall be twelve months from the date of issue; and

(c) that card shall be entitled "Accession Residence Card".]

AMENDMENT

1. Accession of Croatia (Immigration and Worker Authorisation) (Amendment) Regulations 2014 (SI 530/2014) reg.2(1) and (5) (April 6, 2014).

PART 3

ACCESSION STATE WORKER AUTHORISATION AND ASSOCIATED DOCUMENTATION

Requirement for an accession State national subject to worker authorisation to be authorised to work

2.1220 **8.**—(1) An accession State national subject to worker authorisation shall only be authorised to work in the United Kingdom during the accession period if he holds an accession worker authorisation document and is working in accordance with the conditions set out in that document.

(2) For the purpose of these Regulations, an accession worker authorisation document means—

(a) a passport or other travel document endorsed before 1st July 2013 to show that the holder has leave to enter or remain in the United Kingdom under the 1971 Act, subject to a condition restricting his employment in the United Kingdom to a particular employer or category of employment; or

(b) a worker authorisation registration certificate endorsed with a condition restricting the holder's employment to a particular employer and authorised category of employment.

(3) In the case of a document mentioned in paragraph (2)(a), the document ceases to be a valid accession worker authorisation document at the point at which—

(a) the period of leave to enter or remain expires; or

(b) the document holder ceases working for the employer, or in the employment, specified in the document for a period of time that exceeds 30 days in total.

(4) In the case of a document mentioned in paragraph (2)(b), the document ceases to be a valid accession worker authorisation document at the point at which—

(a) the document expires;

(b) the document holder ceases working for the employer, or in the authorised category of employment, specified in the document for a period of time that exceeds 30 days in total; or

(c) the document is revoked.

(5) For the purposes of this regulation, and regulations 9 and 11, the reference to a travel document other than a passport is a reference to a document which relates to a Croatian national and which can serve the same purpose as a passport.

Application for a worker authorisation registration certificate as an accession worker authorisation document

9.—(1) An application for a worker authorisation registration certificate may be made by an accession State national subject to worker authorisation who wishes to work for an employer in the United Kingdom if the employment concerned falls within an authorised category of employment. 2.1221

(2) The application shall be in writing and shall be made to the Secretary of State.

(3) The application shall state—

(a) the name, address in the United Kingdom or in Croatia, and date of birth, of the applicant;

(b) the name and address of the employer for whom the applicant wishes to work; and

(c) the authorised category of employment covered by the application.

(4) The application shall be accompanied by—

(a) proof of the applicant's identity in the form of—

(i) a national identity card;

(ii) a passport; or

(iii) other travel document as defined by regulation 8(5);

(b) two passport size photographs of the applicant;

(c) where the relevant requirements require the applicant to hold a certificate of sponsorship, the certificate of sponsorship reference number;

(d) where sub-paragraph (c) does not apply, a letter from the employer specified in the application confirming that the applicant has an offer of employment with the employer; and

(e) a fee of £55.

(5) In this regulation "address" means, in relation to an employer which is a body corporate or partnership, the head or main office of that employer.

Issuing and revoking a worker authorisation registration certificate

10.—(1) Subject to paragraph (3), the Secretary of State shall issue a worker authorisation registration certificate pursuant to an application made in accordance with the provisions of regulation 9 if the Secretary of State is satisfied that the applicant is an accession State national subject to worker authorisation who meets the relevant requirements. 2.1222

(2) A worker authorisation registration certificate shall include—

(a) a condition restricting the employment of the document holder to the employer and the authorised category of employment specified in the application;

(b) a statement that the document holder has a right of residence in the United Kingdom as a worker whilst working in accordance with any conditions specified in the certificate;

(c) where the authorised category of employment specified in the application is one for which a certificate of sponsorship is required, a statement that the holder of the document has a right to engage in supplementary employment; and

(d) where the period of authorised employment is less than 12 months, a statement specifying the date on which the worker authorisation registration certificate expires.

(3) The Secretary of State may—

(a) refuse to issue, revoke or refuse to renew a worker authorisation registration certificate if the refusal or revocation is justified on grounds of public policy, public security or public health,

(b) refuse the application where the Secretary of State is not satisfied that regulation 9 or this regulation has been complied with or satisfied, or

(c) revoke a worker authorisation registration certificate where—

(i) the document holder ceases working for the employer, or in the employment, specified in the document for a period of time that exceeds 30 days in total,

(ii) deception was used in order to obtain the document, or

(iii) the document was obtained on the basis of sponsorship by a sponsor whose licence has been withdrawn,

and where the Secretary of State has refused to issue, revoked or refused to renew a worker authorisation registration certificate, she shall issue a notice setting out the reasons.

(4) A worker authorisation registration certificate or notice of refusal or revocation issued under this regulation shall be sent to the applicant by post together with the identity card or passport that accompanied the application.

(5) Subject to paragraph (6), in this regulation, "supplementary employment" means—

(a) employment in a job which appears on the shortage occupation list in Appendix K of the immigration rules; or

(b) employment in the same profession and at the same professional level as the employment for which the applicant has been issued with a certificate of sponsorship.

(6) "Supplementary employment" is subject to the condition that—

(i) the applicant remains working for the sponsor in the employment that the certificate of sponsorship checking service records that the applicant has been sponsored to do; and

(ii) the supplementary employment does not exceed 20 hours per week and takes place outside of the hours when the applicant is contracted to work for the sponsor in the employment the applicant is being sponsored to do.

(7) The Secretary of State shall ensure that the relevant statement is available to the public through her website and the library of the Home Office.

PART 4

PENALTIES AND OFFENCES

Unauthorised employment of accession State national - penalty for employer

11.—(1) It is contrary to this regulation to employ an accession State national subject to worker authorisation during the accession period if that person is not the holder of a valid accession worker authorisation document or, where that person holds such a document, the person would be in breach of a condition of that document in undertaking the employment. **2.1223**

(2) The Secretary of State may give an employer who acts contrary to this regulation a notice requiring him to pay a penalty of a specified amount not exceeding £5,000.

(3) The Secretary of State may give a penalty notice without having established whether the employer is excused under paragraph (5).

(4) A penalty notice must—

(a) state why the Secretary of State thinks the employer is liable to the penalty;

(b) state the amount of the penalty;

(c) specify a date, at least 28 days after the date specified in the notice as the date on which it is given, before which the penalty must be paid;

(d) specify how the penalty must be paid;

(e) provide a reference number;

(f) explain how the employer may object to the penalty; and

(g) explain how the Secretary of State may enforce the penalty.

(5) Subject to paragraph (7), an employer is excused from paying a penalty under this regulation if—

(a) before the commencement of the employment, the employee or prospective employee produces to the employer any of the following documents—

(i) an accession worker authorisation document that authorises the employee or prospective employee to take the employment in question;

(ii) an EEA registration certificate which includes a statement that the holder has unconditional access to the United Kingdom labour market; or

(iii) one of the following documents confirming that the document holder is not an accession State national subject to worker authorisation by virtue of regulation 2(6)—

(aa) a passport;

(bb) a national identity card; or

(cc) other travel document as defined by regulation 8(5); and

(b) the employer complies with the requirements set out in paragraph (6) of this regulation.

(6) The requirements are that—

(a) the employer takes all reasonable steps to check the validity of the document;

(b) the employer has satisfied himself that the photograph on the document is of the employee or prospective employee;

(c) the employer has satisfied himself that the date of birth on the document is consistent with the appearance of the employee or prospective employee;

(d) the employer takes all other reasonable steps to check that the employee or prospective employee is the rightful holder of the document; and

(e) the employer securely retains a dated copy of the whole of the document in a format which cannot be subsequently altered for a period of not less than two years after the employment has come to an end.

(7) An employer is not excused from paying a penalty if the employer knew, at any time during the period of the employment, that the employment was contrary to this regulation.

(8) Nothing in these regulations permits an employer to retain documents produced by an employee or prospective employee for the purposes of paragraph (5) for any period longer than is necessary for the purposes of ensuring compliance with paragraph (6).

(9) The Secretary of State may issue a code of practice specifying factors to be considered by her in determining the amount of a penalty imposed under paragraph (2) of this regulation.

(10) The Secretary of State shall lay a code issued under paragraph (9) before Parliament and publish it.

(11) The Secretary of State may from time to time review the code and may revoke, or revise and re-issue it, following a review; and a reference in this section to the code includes a reference to the code as revised.

Unauthorised employment of accession State national – penalty for employer – objection

2.1224 **12.** *[Omitted.]*

Unauthorised employment of accession State national – penalty for employer – appeal

2.1225 **13.** *[Omitted.]*

Unauthorised employment of accession State national – penalty for employer – enforcement

2.1226 **14.** *[Omitted.]*

Unauthorised employment of accession State national – employer offence

2.1227 **15.**—(1) A person commits an offence if he employs another ("the employee") knowing that the employee is an accession State national subject to worker authorisation and that—

(a) the employee is not the holder of a valid accession worker authorisation document; or

(b) the employee is prohibited from undertaking the employment because of a condition in his accession worker authorisation document.

(2) A person guilty of an offence under this section shall be liable on summary conviction—

(a) to imprisonment for a term not exceeding 51 weeks in England and Wales or 6 months in Scotland or Northern Ireland;
(b) to a fine not exceeding level 5 on the standard scale; or
(c) to both.

(3) An offence under this regulation shall be treated as—
(a) a relevant offence for the purpose of sections 28B (search and arrest by warrant) and 28D (entry and search of premises) of the 1971 Act; and
(b) an offence under Part 3 of that Act (criminal proceedings) for the purposes of sections 28E (entry and search of premises following arrest), 28G (searching arrested persons) and 28H (searching persons in police custody).

(4) In relation to an offence committed before the commencement of section 281(5) (alteration of penalties for other summary offences) of the Criminal Justice Act 2003, the reference to 51 weeks in paragraph (2)(a) shall be read as a reference to 6 months.

(5) For the purposes of paragraph (1), a body (whether corporate or not) shall be treated as knowing a fact about an employee if a person who has responsibility within the body for an aspect of the employment knows the fact.

Unauthorised working by accession State national - employee offence and penalty

16.—(1) Subject to paragraph (2), an accession State national subject to worker authorisation who works in the United Kingdom during the accession period shall be guilty of an offence if he does not hold a valid accession worker authorisation document. 2.1228

(2) A person guilty of an offence under this regulation shall be liable on summary conviction—
(a) to imprisonment for a term not exceeding more than three months;
(b) to a fine not exceeding level 5 on the standard scale; or
(c) to both.

(3) A constable or immigration officer who has reason to believe that a person has committed an offence under this regulation may give that person a notice offering him the opportunity of discharging any liability to conviction for that offence by payment of a penalty of £1000 in accordance with the notice.

(4) Where a person is given a notice under paragraph (3) in respect of an offence under this regulation—
(a) no proceedings may be instituted for that offence before the expiration of the period of 21 days beginning with the day after the date of the notice; and
(b) he may not be convicted of that offence if, before the expiration of that period, he pays the penalty in accordance with the notice.

(5) A notice under paragraph (3) must give such particulars of the circumstances alleged to constitute the offence as are necessary for giving reasonable information of the offence.

(6) A notice under paragraph (3) must also state—
(a) the period during which, by virtue of paragraph (4), proceedings will not be instituted for the offence;
(b) the amount of the penalty; and

(c) that the penalty is payable to the Secretary of State at the address specified in the notice.

(7) Without prejudice to payment by any other method, payment of a penalty in pursuance of a notice under paragraph (3) may be made by pre-paying and posting a letter by registered post or the recorded delivery service containing the amount of the penalty (in cash or otherwise) to the Secretary of State at the address specified in the notice.

(8) Where a letter is sent in accordance with paragraph (7) payment is to be regarded as having been made at the time at which that letter would be delivered in the ordinary course of registered post or the recorded delivery service.

(9) A constable or immigration officer may withdraw a penalty notice given under paragraph (3) if the constable or immigration officer decides that—

(a) the notice was issued in error;
(b) the notice contains material errors; or
(c) he has reasonable grounds to believe that the employee has committed an offence under regulation 17.

(10) A penalty notice may be withdrawn—

(a) whether or not the period specified in paragraph (4)(a) has expired;
(b) under paragraph (9)(a) and (b), whether or not the penalty has been paid; and
(c) under paragraph (9)(c), only where the penalty has not yet been paid.

(11) Where a penalty notice has been withdrawn under paragraph (9)—

(a) notice of the withdrawal must be given to the recipient; and
(b) any amount paid by way of penalty in pursuance of that notice must be repaid to the person who paid it.

(12) Subject to paragraph (13), proceedings shall not be continued or instituted against an employee for an offence under paragraph (1) in connection with which a withdrawal notice was issued.

(13) Proceedings may be continued or instituted for an offence in connection with which a withdrawal notice was issued if—

(a) where the withdrawal notice was withdrawn pursuant to paragraph (9)(b)—
  (i) a further penalty notice in respect of the offence was issued at the same time as the penalty notice was withdrawn; and
  (ii) the penalty has not been paid pursuant to that further penalty notice in accordance with paragraph (4)(a); or
(b) the withdrawal notice was withdrawn pursuant to paragraph (9)(c).

Deception—employee offence

2.1229 17. *[Omitted.]*

Offences under regulations 16 and 17—search, entry and arrest

2.1230 **18.** *[Omitted.]*

SCHEDULE

CONSEQUENTIAL AMENDMENTS

[Omitted.]

The Community Charges (Deductions from Income Support) (No.2) Regulations 1990

(SI 1990/545) (AS AMENDED)

Made by the Secretary of State under ss.22(3) and 146(6) and Sch.4 para.6 of the Local Government Finance Act 1988

GENERAL NOTE

The first version of these Regulations (SI 1990/107) was defective and was replaced. 2.1231

The Community Charges (Deductions from Income Support) (Scotland) Regulations 1989 (SI 1989/507) made provision for Scotland from April 10, 1989. They have been amended by SI 1990/113 to bring them into line with these Regulations, but are not reproduced.

Citation, commencement and interpretation

1.—(1) These Regulations may be cited as the Community Charges (Deductions from Income Support) (No.2) Regulations 1990 and shall come into force on 1 April 1990. 2.1232

(2) In these Regulations, unless the context otherwise requires—

[3. . .];

"the 1986 Act" means the Social Security Act 1986;

[3. . .];

[4"the 1998 Act" means the Social Security Act 1998;]

"appropriate social security office" means an office of the Department of Social Security which is normally open to the public for the receipt of claims for income support and includes an office of the [1Department for Education and Employment] which is normally open to the public for the receipt of claims for [1jobseeker's allowance and income support];

[8 "assessment period" means the period prescribed by regulation 21 of the UC Regulations;]

[5"Commissioner" has the meaning it bears in section 39(1) of the 1998 Act;]

[2"contribution-based jobseeker's allowance", except in a case to which paragraph (b) of the definition of income-based jobseeker's allowance applies, means a contribution-based jobseeker's allowance under Part I of the Jobseekers Act 1995, but does not include any back to work bonus under section 26 of the Jobseekers Act which is paid as jobseeker's allowance;]

"couple" means a married or unmarried couple;

"debtor" means a person against whom a liability order has been obtained;

"5 per cent. of the personal allowance for a single claimant aged not less than 25" and

"5 per cent. of the personal allowance for a couple where both members are aged not less than 18" means, in each case, where the percentage is not a multiple of 5 pence, the sum obtained by rounding that 5 per cent. to the next higher such multiple;

"income support" means income support within the meaning of the 1986 Act [[1]but does not include any back to work bonus under section 26 of the Jobseekers Act which is paid as income support;]

[[2]"income-based jobseeker's allowance" means—

(a) an income-based jobseeker's allowance under Part I of the Jobseekers Act 1995; and

(b) in a case where, if there was no entitlement to contribution-based jobseeker's allowance, there would be entitlement to income-based jobseeker's allowance at the same rate, contribution-based jobseeker's allowance;]

but does not include any back to work bonus under section 26 of the Jobseekers Act which is paid as jobseeker's allowance;]

[[1]"Jobseekers Act" means the Jobseekers Act 1995;

"jobseeker's allowance" means an allowance under Part I of the Jobseekers Act but does not include any back to work bonus under section 26 of that Act which is paid as jobseeker's allowance;]

"liability order" means an order under regulation 29 of the Community Charges (Administration and Enforcement) Regulations 1989;

"married couple" has the meaning ascribed to it in section 20(11) of the 1986 Act [SSCBA, s.137(1)];

"payments to third parties" means direct payments to third parties in accordance with Schedule 9 to the Social Security (Claims and Payments) Regulations 1987 [[8] or Schedule 6 to the UC etc. Claims and Payments Regulations,];

"polygamous marriage" means a marriage to which section 22B of the Social Security Act 1986 [SSCBA, s.133] refers;

"single debtor" means a debtor who is not a member of a couple;

[[7] "state pension credit" means the benefit of that name payable under the State Pension Credit Act 2002;]

[[6]"tribunal" means an appeal tribunal constituted under Chapter I of Part I of the 1998 Act;]

[[8] "the UC Regulations" means the Universal Credit Regulations 2013; and

"the UC etc. Claims and Payments Regulations" means the Universal Credit, Personal Independence Payment, Jobseeker's Allowance and Employment and Support Allowance (Claims and Payments) Regulations 2013;

"universal credit" means universal credit under Part 1 of the Welfare Reform Act 2012;]

"unmarried couple" has the meaning ascribed to it in section 20(11) of the 1986 Act [SSCBA, s.137(1)].

(3) Unless the context otherwise requires, any reference in these Regulations to a numbered regulation or Schedule is a reference to the regulation and Schedule bearing that number in the Regulations and any reference in a regulation or Schedule to a numbered paragraph is a reference to the paragraph of that regulation or Schedule having that number.

AMENDMENTS

1. Social Security (Jobseeker's Allowance Consequential Amendments) (Deductions) Regulations 1996 (SI 1996/2344) reg.6 (October 7, 1996).
2. Social Security (Miscellaneous Amendments) Regulations 1998 (SI 1998/563) regs 3(1) and (2)(a) (April 1, 1998). (Note that the commencement date for this provision was amended by Social Security (Miscellaneous Amendments) (No.2) Regulations 1998 (SI 1998/865) reg.2 (March 20, 1998).)
3. Social Security Act 1998 (Commencement No.12, and Consequential and Transitional Provisions) Order 1999 (SI 1999/3178 (C.81)) art.3(11) and Sch.11 para.1(a).
4. Social Security Act 1998 (Commencement No.12, and Consequential and Transitional Provisions) Order 1999 (SI 1999/3178 (C.81)) art.3(11) and Sch.11 para.1(b) (November 29, 1999).
5. Social Security Act 1998 (Commencement No.12, and Consequential and Transitional Provisions) Order 1999 (SI 1999/3178 (C.81)) art.3(11) and Sch.11 para.1(c) (November 29, 1999).
6. Social Security Act 1998 (Commencement No.12, and Consequential and Transitional Provisions) Order 1999 (SI 1999/3178 (C.81)) art.3(11) and Sch.11 para.1(d) (November 29, 1999).
7. State Pension Credit (Consequential, Transitional and Miscellaneous Provisions) Regulations 2002 (SI 2002/3019) reg.35 (October 6, 2003).
8. Fines, Council Tax and Community Charges (Deductions from Universal Credit and Other Benefits) Regulations 2013 (SI 2013/612) regs 13 and 14 (April 29, 2013). (The extraneous comma at the end of the amended definition of "payments to third parties" is required by reg.14(3) and is not an editorial error.)

MODIFICATION

Regulation 1 is modified by Sch.2 para.23 of the Employment and Support Allowance (Transitional Provisions, Housing Benefit and Council Tax Benefit) (Existing Awards) (No.2) Regulations 2010 (SI 2010/1907) (as amended) for the purposes specified in reg.16(1). For details of the modification, see the text of those Regulations in Vol.I.

[3[4Application for deductions] from income support, [8 universal credit,] [6, state pension credit] [7, jobseeker's allowance or employment and support allowance]]

2.—(1) Where a debtor is entitled to income support [6, state pension credit] [3or jobseeker's allowance], an authority may apply to the Secretary of State by sending an application in respect of the debtor or, where a liability order is made against a couple in respect of both of the couple, to an appropriate social security office asking the Secretary of State to deduct sums from any amount payable to the debtor, or as the case may be either of the couple by way of income support [3[7, jobseeker's allowance or employment and support allowance]]. 2.1233

[8 (1A) Subject to paragraphs (1B), (1C) and (4A) and regulation 4, where the Secretary of State receives an application from an authority in respect of a debtor who is entitled to universal credit, the Secretary of State may deduct an amount from the universal credit payable to the debtor which is equal to 5 per cent. of the appropriate universal credit standard allowance and pay that sum to the authority towards satisfaction of any outstanding sum which is, or forms part of, the amount in respect of which the liability order was made.

(1B) No amount may be deducted under paragraph (1A) where it would reduce the amount of universal credit payable to the debtor to less than 1 penny.

(1C) For the purpose of paragraph (1A), where 5 per cent. of the appropriate universal credit standard allowance results in a fraction of a penny, that fraction is to be disregarded if it is less than half a penny and otherwise it is to be treated as a penny.

(1D) In paragraphs (1A) and (1C), "appropriate universal credit standard allowance" means the appropriate universal credit standard allowance for the debtor for the assessment period in question under regulation 36 of the UC Regulations.]

(2) An application from an authority shall be in writing and shall contain the following particulars—

(a) the name and address of the debtor or where the liability order is made against a couple, the names and address of both of them;

(b) the name and place of the court which made the liability order;

(c) the date when the liability order was made;

(d) the total amount of the arrears specified in the liability order;

(e) the total amount which the authority wishes to have deducted from income support [6, state pension credit] [3[7, jobseeker's allowance or employment and support allowance]].

(3) Where it appears to the Secretary of State that an application from an authority gives insufficient particulars to enable the debtor to be identified he may require the authority to furnish such further particulars as may reasonably be required.

(4) [5. . .].

[8(4A) Before making a deduction under paragraph (1A), the Secretary of State must make any deduction which falls to be made in respect of a liability mentioned in paragraph 5(2)(a) to (c) of Schedule 6 to the UC etc. Claims and Payments Regulations.]

(5) [5. . .].

(6) [5. . .].

AMENDMENTS

1. Social Security (Claims and Payments) Amendment Regulation 1992 (SI 1992/1026) reg.7 (May 25, 1992).

2. Social Security (Claims and Payments) Amendment (No.3) Regulations 1993 (SI 1993/2113) reg.5 (September 27, 1993).

3. Social Security (Jobseeker's Allowance Consequential Amendments) (Deductions) Regulations 1996 (SI 1996/2344) reg.7 (October 7, 1996).

4. Social Security Act 1998 (Commencement No.12, and Consequential and Transitional Provisions) Order 1999 (SI 1999/3178 (C.81)) art.3(11) and Sch.11 para.2(1) (November 29, 1999).

5. Social Security Act 1998 (Commencement No.12, and Consequential and Transitional Provisions) Order 1999 (SI 1999/3178 (C.81)) art.3(11) and Sch.11 para.2(2) (November 29, 1999).

6. State Pension Credit (Consequential, Transitional and Miscellaneous Provisions) Regulations 2002 (SI 2002/3019) reg.35 (October 6, 2003).

7. Employment and Support Allowance (Consequential Provisions) (No.2) Regulations 2008 (SI 2008/1554) reg.53(1) and (2) (October 27, 2008).

8. Fines, Council Tax and Community Charges (Deductions from Universal Credit and Other Benefits) Regulations 2013 (SI 2013/612) regs 13 and 15 (April 29, 2013).

DEFINITIONS

"adjudication officer"—see reg.1(2).
"authority"—see Local Government Finance Act 1988 s.144.
"appropriate social security officer"—see reg.1(2).
"couple"—*ibid.*
"debtor"—*ibid.*
"5 per cent. of the personal allowance for a single claimant aged not less than 25"—*ibid.*
"5 per cent. of the personal allowance for a couple where both members are aged not less than 18"—*ibid.*
"income support"—*ibid.*
"Jobseekers Act"—*ibid.*
"jobseeker's allowance"—*ibid.*
"liability order"—*ibid.*
"payments to third parties"—*ibid.*
"polygamous marriage"—*ibid.*

GENERAL NOTE

R(IS) 3/92 held that if the Secretary of State accepted the validity (i.e. the form and content) of an application under para.(2), the AO or SSAT also had to accept it. But where there is an issue as to whether the claimant is a "debtor" (defined in reg.1(2)) at all, the tribunal must satisfy itself that the basic conditions for the operation of the procedure exist: namely that there *is* a subsisting liability order, properly obtained, under which there *is* outstanding a sum due of the amount sought to be deducted from income support (*R(IS) 1/98*). In that case neither the alleged liability order nor any evidence from the local authority confirming that an amount was still due from the claimant had been produced, whereas the claimant had produced evidence which appeared to substantiate that she was in fact in credit on her community charge account. The Commissioner therefore decided that there was no jurisdiction to make any deduction from the claimant's income support in respect of the community charge. 2.1234

[1 Deductions from debtor's income support [2, [4 universal credit,] state pension credit] or [3, jobseeker's allowance or employment and support allowance]

3.—(1) Subject to paragraph (4) and regulation 4, where the Secretary of State receives an application from an authority in respect of a debtor who is entitled to income support [2, state pension credit] [3, income-based jobseeker's allowance or income-related employment and support allowance] and the amount payable by way of that benefit, after any deduction under this paragraph, is 10 pence or more, the Secretary of State may deduct a sum from that benefit which is equal to 5 per cent. of the personal allowance— 2.1235

(a) set out in paragraph 1(1)(e) of Schedule 2 to the Income Support (General) Regulations 1987 or, as the case may be, of Schedule 1 to the Jobseeker's Allowance Regulations 1996 for a couple where—
  (i) a liability order is made; and
  (ii) that benefit is payable, in respect of both members of a couple both of whom are aged not less than 18; and
(b) in any other case, for a single claimant aged not less than 25 set out in paragraph 1(3)(c) of Schedule 2 to the Income Support (General) Regulations 1987 or, as the case may be, paragraph 1(3)(e) of Schedule 1 to the Jobseeker's Allowance Regulations 1996,

and pay that sum to the authority towards satisfaction of any outstanding sum which is or forms part of the amount in respect of which the liability order was made.

[4 (1A) Subject to paragraphs (1B), (1C) and (4A) and regulation 4, where the Secretary of State receives an application from an authority in respect of a debtor who is entitled to universal credit, the Secretary of State may deduct an amount from the universal credit payable to the debtor which is equal to 5 per cent. of the appropriate universal credit standard allowance and pay that sum to the authority towards satisfaction of any outstanding sum which is, or forms part of, the amount in respect of which the liability order was made.

(1B) No amount may be deducted under paragraph (1A) where it would reduce the amount of universal credit payable to the debtor to less than 1 penny.

(1C) For the purpose of paragraph (1A), where 5 per cent. of the appropriate universal credit standard allowance results in a fraction of a penny, that fraction is to be disregarded if it is less than half a penny and otherwise it is to be treated as a penny.

(1D) In paragraphs (1A) and (1C), "appropriate universal credit standard allowance" means the appropriate universal credit standard allowance for the debtor for the assessment period in question under regulation 36 of the UC Regulations.]

(2) Subject to paragraph (3) and regulation 4, where—

(a) the Secretary of State receives an application from an authority in respect of a debtor who is entitled to contribution-based job-seeker's allowance; and

(b) the amount of contribution-based jobseeker's allowance payable before any deduction under this paragraph is equal to or more than one-third of the age-related amount applicable to the debtor under section 4(1)(a) of the Jobseekers Act,

the Secretary of State may deduct a sum from that benefit which is equal to one-third of the age-related amount applicable to the debtor under section 4(1)(a) of the Jobseekers Act and pay that sum to the authority towards satisfaction of any outstanding sum which is or forms part of the amount in respect of which the liability order was made.

(3) Where the sum that would otherwise fall to be deducted under paragraph (2) includes a fraction of a penny, the sum to be deducted shall be rounded down to the next whole penny.

(4) Before making a deduction under paragraph (1) the Secretary of State shall make any deduction which falls to be made in respect of a liability mentioned in any of the following provisions of the Social Security (Claims and Payments) Regulations 1987—

(a) regulation 34A (mortgage interest);

(b) paragraph 3 (housing costs) of Schedule 9;

(c) paragraph 5 (rent and certain service charges for fuel) of Schedule 9;

(d) paragraph 6 (fuel costs) of Schedule 9; and

(e) paragraph 7 (water charges) of Schedule 9.

[4 (4A) Before making a deduction under paragraph (1A), the Secretary of State must make any deduction which falls to be made in respect of a liability mentioned in paragraph 5(2)(a) to (c) of Schedule 6 to the UC etc. Claims and Payments Regulations.]

(5) Subject to regulations 5 and 6, a decision of the Secretary of State under this regulation shall be final.

(6) The Secretary of State shall notify the debtor in writing of a decision to make a deduction under this regulation as soon as is practicable and at the same time shall notify the debtor of his right of appeal.]

AMENDMENTS

1. Social Security Act 1998 (Commencement No.12, and Consequential and Transitional Provisions) Order 1999 (SI 1999/3178 (C.81)) art.3(11) and Sch.11 para.3 (November 29, 1999).
2. State Pension Credit (Consequential, Transitional and Miscellaneous Provisions) Regulations 2002 (SI 2002/3019) reg.35 (October 6, 2003).
3. Employment and Support Allowance (Consequential Provisions) (No.2) Regulations 2008 (SI 2008/1554) reg.53(1) and (3) (October 27, 2008).
4. Fines, Council Tax and Community Charges (Deductions from Universal Credit and Other Benefits) Regulations 2013 (SI 2013/612) regs 13 and 16 (April 29, 2013).

Circumstances, time of making and termination of deductions

4.—[2(1) The Secretary of State— 2.1236
(a) shall make deductions under [5 regulation 3(1) or (2)] only where the debtor is entitled to income support [3 , state pension credit] [4, jobseeker's allowance or employment and support allowance] throughout any benefit week; and
(b) shall not determine any application under regulation 2 which relates to a debtor in respect of whom—
 (i) he is making deductions; or
 (ii) deductions fall to be made,

pursuant to an earlier application under regulation 3 until no deductions pursuant to that earlier application fall to be made.]

[5 (1A) The Secretary of State may make deductions from universal credit under regulation 3(1A) only if—
(a) the debtor is entitled to universal credit throughout any assessment period; and
(b) no deductions are being made in respect of the debtor under any other application.]

(2) The Secretary of State shall make deductions from income support [3, [5 universal credit,] state pension credit] [1[4, jobseeker's allowance or employment and support allowance] at a time which corresponds to the payment of income support [3, [5 universal credit,] state pension credit] [1[4, jobseeker's allowance or employment and support allowance]] to the debtor and he shall cease making deductions when—
(a) a payment to a third party has priority;
(b) there is insufficient entitlement to income support [3, [5 universal credit,] state pension credit] [1[4, jobseeker's allowance or employment and support allowance]] to enable him to make the deduction;
(c) entitlement to income support [3, [5 universal credit,] state pension credit] [1[4, jobseeker's allowance or employment and support allowance]] ceases;
(d) an authority withdraws its application for deductions to be made; or
(e) the debt in respect of which he was making the deductions is discharged.

(3) Payments shall be made to the authority at such intervals as the Secretary of State may decide.

AMENDMENTS

1. Social Security (Jobseeker's Allowance Consequential Amendments) (Deductions) Regulations 1996 (SI 1996/2344) reg.9 (October 7, 1996).
2. Social Security Act 1998 (Commencement No.12, and Consequential and Transitional Provisions) Order 1999 (SI 1999/3178 (C.81)) art.3(11) and Sch.11 para.4 (November 29, 1999).
3. State Pension Credit (Consequential, Transitional and Miscellaneous Provisions) Regulations 2002 (SI 2002/3019) reg.35 (October 6, 2003).
4. Employment and Support Allowance (Consequential Provisions) (No.2) Regulations 2008 (SI 2008/1554) reg.53(1) and (4) (October 27, 2008).
5. Fines, Council Tax and Community Charges (Deductions from Universal Credit and Other Benefits) Regulations 2013 (SI 2013/612) regs 13 and 17 (April 29, 2013).

DEFINITIONS

"adjudication officer"—see reg.1(2).
"authority"—see Local Government Finance Act 1988 s.144.
"debtor"—see reg.1(2).
"income support"—*ibid.*
"jobseeker's allowance"—*ibid.*

[1Revision and supersession

2.1237 **5.**—Any decision of the Secretary of State under regulation 3 may be revised under section 9 of the 1998 Act or superseded under section 10 of that Act as though the decision were made under section 8(1)(c) of that Act.]

AMENDMENT

1. Social Security Act 1998 (Commencement No.12, and Consequential and Transitional Provisions) Order 1999 (SI 1999/3178 (C.81)) art.3(11) and Sch.11 para.5 (November 29, 1999).

[1 Appeal

2.1238 **6.**—Any decision of the Secretary of State under regulation 3 (whether as originally made or as revised under regulation 5) may be appealed to a tribunal as though the decision were made on an award of a relevant benefit (within the meaning of section 8(3) of the 1998 Act) under section 8(1)(c) of the 1998 Act.]

AMENDMENT

1. Social Security Act 1998 (Commencement No.12, and Consequential and Transitional Provisions) Order 1999 (SI 1999/3178 (C.81)) art.3(11) and Sch.11 para.5 (November 29, 1999).

Correction of accidental errors

2.1239 **7.**—[1 . . .]

AMENDMENT

1. Social Security Act 1998 (Commencement No.12, and Consequential and Transitional Provisions Order 1999 (SI 1999/3178 (C.81)) art.3(11) and Sch.11 para.6 (November 29, 1999).

Setting aside decisions on certain grounds

8.—[1 . . .] 2.1240

AMENDMENT

1. Social Security Act 1998 (Commencement No.12, and Consequential and Transitional Provisions Order 1999 (SI 1999/3178 (C.81)) art.3(11) and Sch.11 para.6 (November 29, 1999).

Provisions common to regulations 7 and 8

9.—[1 . . .] 2.1241

AMENDMENT

1. Social Security Act 1998 (Commencement No.12, and Consequential and Transitional Provisions) Order 1999 (SI 1999/3178 (C.81)) art.3(11) and Sch.11 para.6 (November 29, 1999).

The Fines (Deductions from Income Support) Regulations 1992

(SI 1992/2182) (AS AMENDED)

Made by the Secretary of State under ss.24 and 30 of the Criminal Justice Act 1991

Citation, commencement and interpretation

1.—(1) These Regulations may be cited as the Fines (Deductions from Income Support) Regulations 1992 and shall come into force on 1 October 1992. 2.1242

(2) In these Regulations, unless the context otherwise requires—

"the 1971 Act" means the Vehicles (Excise) Act 1971;

"the 1973 Act" means the Powers of the Criminal Courts Act 1973;

[4 "the 1998 Act" means the Social Security Act 1998;]

[9 "the 2012 Act" means the Welfare Reform Act 2012;]

[4 . . .];

"application" means an application made under regulation 2 [6 . . .] containing the information specified in regulation 3(1);

[4. . .];

[9 "assessment period" means the period prescribed by regulation 21 of the UC Regulations;]

"benefit week" has the meaning prescribed in regulation 2(1) of the Income Support Regulations [2or, as the case may be, [7 regulation 1(2) of the State Pension Credit Regulations 2002 or] regulation 1(3) of the Jobseeker's Allowance Regulations 1996 [8 or regulation 2(1) of the Employment and Support Allowance Regulations];]

"the Claims and Payments Regulations" means the Social Security (Claims and Payments) Regulations 1987;

[4 "Commissioner" has the meaning it bears in section 39(1) of the 1998 Act;]

[3 "contribution-based jobseeker's allowance", except in a case to which paragraph (b) of the definition of income-based jobseeker's allowance applies, means a contribution-based jobseeker's allowance under Part I of the Jobseekers Act 1995 [9 as amended by the provisions of Part 1 of Schedule 14 to the 2012 Act that remove references to an income-based allowance or under Part 1 of the Jobseekers Act 1995 as it has effect apart from those amendments], but does not include any back to work bonus under section 26 of the Jobseekers Act which is paid as jobseeker's allowance;]

[8 "contributory employment and support allowance" means a contributory allowance under Part 1 of the Welfare Reform Act [9 as amended by the provisions of Schedule 3, and Part 1 of Schedule 14, to the 2012 Act that remove references to an income-related allowance or under Part 1 of the Welfare Reform Act as it has effect apart from those amendments];]

"court" means in England and Wales a magistrates' court and in Scotland a court;

[8 "the Employment and Support Allowance Regulations" means the Employment and Support Allowance Regulations 2008;]

"5 per cent. of the personal allowance for a single claimant aged not less than 25" means, where the percentage is not a multiple of 5 pence, the sum obtained by rounding that 5 per cent. to the next higher such multiple;

[2 "income support" means income support under Part VII of the Social Security Contributions and Benefits Act 1992, but does not include any back to work bonus under section 26 of the Jobseekers Act which is paid as income support;]

"Income Support Regulations" means the Income Support (General) Regulations 1987;

[3 "income-based jobseeker's allowance" means—

(a) an income-based jobseeker's allowance under Part I of the Job-seekers Act 1995; and

(b) in a case where, if there was no entitlement to contribution-based jobseeker's allowance, there would be entitlement to income-based jobseeker's allowance at the same rate, contribution-based jobseeker's allowance,

but does include any back to work bonus under section 26 of the Jobseekers Act which is paid as jobseeker's allowance;]

[8 "income-related employment and support allowance" means—

(a) an income-related allowance under Part 1 of the Welfare Reform Act; and

(b) in a case where, if there was no entitlement to contributory employment and support allowance, there would be entitlement to income-related employment and support allowance at the same rate, contributory employment and support allowance;]

[2 "Jobseekers Act" means the Jobseekers Act 1995;

"jobseeker's allowance" means an allowance under Part I of the Jobseekers Act but does not include any back to work bonus under section 26 of that Act which is paid as jobseeker's allowance;]

"payments to third parties" means direct payments to third parties in accordance with Schedules 9 and 9A to the Claims and Payments

Regulations [9 Schedule 6 to the Universal Credit, Personal Independence Payment, Jobseeker's Allowance and Employment and Support Allowance (Claims and Payments) Regulations 2013,], regulation 2(4) of the Community Charges (Deductions from Income Support) (No.2) Regulations 1990 and regulation 2(4) of the Community Charges (Deductions from Income Support) (Scotland) Regulations 1989 [1and regulation 2 of the Council Tax (Deductions from Income Support) Regulations 1993];

[7 "personal allowance for a single claimant aged not less than 25" means—

(a) in the case of a person who is entitled to either income support or state pension credit, the amount for the time being specified in paragraph 1(1)(e) of column (2) of Schedule 2 to the Income Support Regulations; or

(b) in the case of a person who is entitled to an income-based jobseeker's allowance, the amount for the time being specified in paragraph 1(1)(e) of column (2) of Schedule 1 to the Jobseeker's Allowance Regulations 1996;]

[8 (c) in the case of a person who is entitled to an income-related employment and support allowance, the amount specified for the time being in paragraph 1(1)(b) of column 2 of Schedule 4 to the Employment and Support Allowance Regulations;]

"social security office" means an office of the [5 Department for Work and Pensions which is open to the public for the receipt of claims for income support or a [8 , jobseeker's allowance or an employment and support allowance]].

[7 "state pension credit" means the benefit of that name payable under the State Pension Credit Act 2002]

[4 "tribunal" means an appeal tribunal constituted under Chapter 1 of Part I of the 1998 Act.]

[9 "the UC Regulations" means the Universal Credit Regulations 2013;

"universal credit" means universal credit under Part 1 of the 2012 Act;]

[8 "the Welfare Reform Act" means the Welfare Reform Act 2007;]

(3) Unless the context otherwise requires, any reference in these Regulations to a numbered regulation, Part or Schedule bearing that number in these Regulations and any reference in a regulation or Schedule to a numbered paragraph is a reference to the paragraph of that regulation or Schedule having that number.

AMENDMENTS

1. Deductions from Income Support (Miscellaneous Amendment) Regulations 1993 (SI 1993/495) reg.3 (April 1, 1993).

2. Social Security (Jobseeker's Allowance Consequential Amendments) (Deductions) Regulations 1996 (SI 1996/2344) reg.10 (October 7, 1996).

3. Social Security (Miscellaneous Amendments) Regulations 1998 (SI 1998/563) reg.3(1) and (2)(d) (April 1, 1998). (Note that the commencement date for this provision was amended by Social Security (Miscellaneous Amendments) (No.2) Regulations 1998 (SI 1998/865) reg.2 (March 20, 1998).)

4. Social Security Act 1998 (Commencement No.12, and Consequential and Transitional Provisions) Order 1999 (SI 1999/3178 (C.81)) art.3(12) and Sch.12 para.1 (November 29, 1999).

5. Secretaries of State for Education and Skills and for Work and Pensions Order 2002 (SI 2002/1397) art.12 and Sch. para.22 (June 27, 2002).

6. Fines (Deductions from Income Support) (Amendment) Regulations 2003 (SI 2003/1360) reg.2(a) (June 20, 2003).

7. State Pension Credit (Consequential, Transitional and Miscellaneous Provisions) Regulations 2002 (SI 2002/3019) reg.32 (October 6, 2003).

8. Employment and Support Allowance (Consequential Provisions) (No.2) Regulations 2008 (SI 2008/1554) reg.54(1) and (2) (October 27, 2008).

9. Fines, Council Tax and Community Charges (Deductions from Universal Credit and Other Benefits) Regulations 2013 (SI 2013/612) regs 2 and 3 (April 29, 2013). (The double comma in the definition of "payments to third parties" is required by reg.3(6) and is not an editorial error.)

MODIFICATION

Regulation 1 is modified by Sch.2 para.24 of the Employment and Support Allowance (Transitional Provisions, Housing Benefit and Council Tax Benefit) (Existing Awards) (No.2) Regulations 2010 (SI 2010/1907) (as amended) for the purposes specified in reg.16(1). For details of the modification, see the text of those Regulations in Vol.I.

[1Application for deductions from support [2, [4 universal credit,] state state pension credit] or [3, jobseeker's allowance or employment and support allowance]]

2.1243 **2.**—(1) Where a fine has been imposed on an offender by a court or a sum is required to be paid by a compensation order which has been made against an offender by a court and (in either case) the offender is entitled to income support [2, [4 universal credit,] state pension credit] [1[3, jobseeker's allowance or employment and support allowance]], the court may, subject to paragraph (2), apply to the Secretary of State asking him to deduct sums from any amounts payable to the offender by way of income support [2, [4 universal credit,] state pension credit] [1[3, jobseeker's allowance or employment and support allowance]], in order to secure the payment of any sum which is or forms part of the fine or compensation.

(2) Before making an application the court shall make an enquiry as to the offender's means.

AMENDMENTS

1. Social Security (Jobseeker's Allowance Consequential Amendments) (Deductions) Regulations 1996 (SI 1996/2344) reg.11 (October 7, 1996).

2. State Pension Credit (Consequential, Transitional and Miscellaneous Provisions) Regulations 2002 (SI 2002/3019) reg.32 (October 6, 2003).

3. Employment and Support Allowance (Consequential Provisions) (No.2) Regulations 2008 (SI 2008/1554) reg.54(1) and (3) (October 27, 2008).

4. Fines, Council Tax and Community Charges (Deductions from Universal Credit and Other Benefits) Regulations 2013 (SI 2013/612) regs 2 and 4 (April 29, 2013).

DEFINITIONS

"court"—see reg.1(2).
"income support"—*ibid.*
"jobseeker's allowance"—*ibid.*

[1 Information that the court may require

2A.—(1) Where an application is made the court may require the offender to provide his full name, full address, date of birth, national insurance number and the name of any benefits to which he is entitled. 2.1244

(2) For the purposes of this regulation "benefits" means income support, state pension credit [2 , a jobseeker's allowance or an employment and support allowance].]

AMENDMENTS

1. Fines (Deductions from Income Support)(Amendment) Regulations 2004 reg.2(a) (December 18, 2004).
2. Employment and Support Allowance (Consequential Provisions) (No.2) Regulations 2008 (SI 2008/1554) reg.54(1) and (4) (October 27, 2008).

Contents of application

3.—(1) An application [1. . .] shall contain the following information — 2.1245

(a) the name and address of the offender, and, if it is known, his date of birth;
(b) the date when the fine was imposed or the compensation order made;
(c) the name and address of the court imposing the fine or making the compensation order;
(d) the amount of the fine or the amount payable by the compensation order as the case may be;
(e) the date on which the application is made;
(f) the date on which the court enquired into the offender's means;
(g) whether the offender has defaulted in paying the fine, compensation order or any instalment of either.

(2) A court making an application shall serve it on the Secretary of State by sending or delivering it to a social security office.

(3) Where it appears to the Secretary of State that an application from a court gives insufficient information to enable the offender to be identified, he may require the court to furnish such further information as he may reasonably require for that purpose.

AMENDMENT

1. Fines (Deductions from Income Support) (Amendment) Regulations 2003 (SI 2003/1360) reg.2(b) (June 20, 2003).

DEFINITIONS

"application"—see reg.1(2).
"court"—*ibid.*
"social security office"—*ibid.*

[1Deductions from offender's income support [2, [5 universal credit,] state pension credit] or jobseeker's allowance

4.—(1) Subject to regulation 7, where— 2.1246

(a) the Secretary of State receives an application from a court in respect of an offender who is entitled to income support [2 , state pension credit] [4, income-based jobseeker's allowance or income-related employment and support allowance];

(b) the amount payable by way of that benefit, after any deduction under this paragraph, is 10 pence or more; and

(c) the aggregate amount payable under one or more of the following provisions, namely, paragraphs 3(2)(a), 5(6), 6(2)(a) and 7(3)(a) and (5)(a) of Schedule 9 to the Claims and Payments Regulations, and regulation 2 of the Council Tax (Deductions from Income Support) Regulations 1993, together with the amount to be deducted under this paragraph does not exceed an amount equal to 3 times 5 per cent. of the personal allowance for a single claimant aged not less than 25 years,

the Secretary of State may deduct a sum from that benefit which is equal to 5 per cent. of the personal allowance for a single claimant aged not less than 25 [3 or £5, whichever is the greater amount allowed by sub-paragraphs (b) and (c)] and pay that sum to the court towards satisfaction of the fine or the sum required to be paid by compensation order.

[5 (1A) Subject to paragraphs (1C) and (1D) and regulation 7, where the Secretary of State receives an application from a court in respect of an offender who is entitled to universal credit, the Secretary of State may deduct from the universal credit payable to the offender an amount permitted by paragraph (1B) and pay that amount to the court towards satisfaction of the fine or the sum required to be paid by compensation order.

(1B) The amount that may be deducted under paragraph (1A) is any sum which is no less than 5 per cent. of the appropriate universal credit standard allowance for the offender for the assessment period in question under regulation 36 of the UC Regulations but no greater than £108.35.

(1C) No amount may be deducted under paragraph (1A) where it would reduce the amount of universal credit payable to the offender to less than 1 penny.

(1D) For the purpose of paragraph (1B), where 5 per cent. of the appropriate universal credit standard allowance results in a fraction of a penny, that fraction is to be disregarded if it is less than half a penny and otherwise it is to be treated as a penny.]

[5(2) Subject to paragraph (3) and regulation 7, where—

(a) the Secretary of State receives an application from a court in respect of an offender who is entitled to contribution-based jobseeker's allowance or contributory employment and support allowance; and

(b) the amount of that allowance payable, before any deduction under this paragraph, is 10 pence or more,

the Secretary of State may deduct a sum from that allowance, up to the appropriate maximum specified in paragraph (2A), and pay that sum to the court towards satisfaction of the fine or the sum required to be paid by compensation order.

(2A) The appropriate maximum is 40 per cent. of the appropriate age-related amount for the offender specified—

(a) where the offender is entitled to contribution-based jobseeker's allowance, in regulation 79 of the Jobseeker's Allowance Regulations 1996 or, as the case may be, regulation 49 of the Jobseeker's Allowance Regulations 2013;

(b) where the offender is entitled to contributory employment and support allowance, in paragraph 1(1) of Schedule 4 to the Employment and Support Allowance Regulations or, as the case may be, regulation 62(1)(b) of the Employment and Support Allowance Regulations 2013.]

(3) No deduction shall be made under paragraph (2) where a deduction is being made from the offender's contribution-based jobseeker's allowance under the Community Charges (Deductions from Income Support) (No.2) Regulations 1990, the Community Charges (Deductions from Income Support) (Scotland) Regulations 1989 or the Council Tax (Deductions from Income Support) Regulations 1993.

[5 . . .]

(5) The Secretary of State shall notify the offender and the court in writing of a decision to make a deduction under this regulation so far as is practicable within 14 days from the date on which he made the decision and at the same time shall notify the offender of his right of appeal.]

Amendments

1. Social Security Act 1998 (Commencement No.12, and Consequential and Transitional Provisions) Order 1999 (SI 1999/3178 (C.81)) art.3(12) and Sch.12 para.2 (November 29, 1999).

2. State Pension Credit (Consequential, Transitional and Miscellaneous Provisions) Regulations 2002 (SI 2002/3019) reg.32 (October 6, 2003).

3. Fines (Deductions from Income Support) (Amendment) Regulations 2004 reg.2(b) (December 18, 2004).

4. Employment and Support Allowance (Consequential Provisions) (No.2) Regulations 2008 (SI 2008/1554) reg.54(1) and (5) (October 27, 2008).

5. Fines, Council Tax and Community Charges (Deductions from Universal Credit and Other Benefits) Regulations 2013 (SI 2013/612) regs 2 and 5 (April 29, 2013).

General Note

The replacement of para.(2) with paras (2) and (2A) by regs 2 and 5(4) of SI 2013/612 does not have effect in respect of an application received by the Secretary of State from the court in respect of an offender before April 29, 2013: see reg.5(6) of SI 2013/612. 2.1247

Notification of decision

5.—[1 . . .] 2.1248

Amendment

1. Social Security Act 1998 (Commencement No.12, and Consequential and Transitional Provisions) Order 1999 (SI 1999/3178 (C.81)) art.3(12) and Sch.12 para.2 (November 29, 1999).

[1Deductions from offender's income support or income-based jobseeker's allowance]

6.—[2 . . .] 2.1249

AMENDMENTS

1. Social Security (Jobseeker's Allowance Consequential Amendments) (Deductions) Regulations 1996 (SI 1996/2344) reg.13 (October 7, 1996).
2. Social Security Act 1998 (Commencement No.12, and Consequential and Transitional Provisions) Order 1999 (SI 1999/3178 (C.81)) art.3(12) and Sch.12 para.2 (November 29, 1999).

DEFINITIONS

"adjudication officer"—see reg.1(2).
"court"—*ibid.*
"5 per cent. of the personal allowance for a single claimant aged not less than 25"—*ibid.*

[1Deductions from offender's contribution-based jobseeker's allowance

2.1250 **6A.**—[2 . . .]

AMENDMENTS

1. Social Security (Jobseeker's Allowance Consequential Amendments) (Deductions) Regulations 1996 (SI 1996/2344) reg.14 (October 7, 1996).
2. Social Security Act 1998 (Commencement No.12, and Consequential and Transitional Provisions) Order 1999 (SI 1999/3178 (C.81)) art.3(12) and Sch.12 para.2 (November 29, 1999).

Circumstances, time of making and termination of deductions

2.1251 **7.**—(1) The Secretary of State may make deductions from income support [4, state pension credit] [1[5, jobseeker's allowance or employment and support allowance]] under [2 under [6 regulation 4(1) or (2)]] only if—
(a) the offender is entitled to income support [4, state pension credit] [1[5, jobseeker's allowance or employment and support allowance]] throughout any benefit week; and
(b) no deductions are being made in respect of the offender under any other application.

[6 (1A) The Secretary of State may make deductions from universal credit under regulation 4(1A) only if—
(a) the offender is entitled to universal credit throughout any assessment period; and
(b) no deductions are being made in respect of the offender under any other application.]

(2) The Secretary of State shall not make a deduction unless—
(a) the offender at the date of application by the court is aged not less than 18;
(b) the offender is entitled to income support [4, [6 universal credit,] state pension credit] [1[5, jobseeker's allowance or employment and support allowance]]; and
(c) the offender has defaulted in paying the fine, compensation order or any instalment of either.

(3) The Secretary of State shall make deductions from income support [4, [6 universal credit,] state pension credit] [1[5, jobseeker's allowance or employment and support allowance]] by reference to the times at which

payment of income support [4 , state pension credit] [1 [5, jobseeker's allowance or employment and support allowance]] is made to the offender.

(4) The Secretary of State shall cease making deductions from income support [4, [6 universal credit,] state pension credit] [1 [5, jobseeker's allowance or employment and support allowance]] if—

(a) there is no longer sufficient entitlement to income support [4, state pension credit] [1 [5, jobseeker's allowance or employment and support allowance]] to enable him to make the deduction;

(b) entitlement to income support [4, [6 universal credit,] state pension credit] [1 [5, jobseeker's allowance or employment and support allowance]] ceases;

(c) a court withdraws its application for deductions to be made; or

(d) the liability to make payment of the fine or under the compensation order as the case may be has ceased.

[3 (5) The Secretary of State shall not determine any application under regulation 2 which relates to an offender in respect of whom—

(a) he is making deductions; or

(b) deductions fall to be made,

pursuant to an earlier application under that regulation until no deductions pursuant to that earlier application fall to be made.]

(6) Payments of sums deducted from income support [4, [6 universal credit,] state pension credit] [1 [5 , jobseeker's allowance or employment and support allowance]] by the Secretary of State under these Regulations shall be made to the court at intervals of 13 weeks.

(7) Where the whole of the amount to which the application relates has been paid, the court shall so far as is practicable give notice of that fact within 21 days to the Secretary of State.

(8) The Secretary of State shall notify the offender in writing of the total of the sums deducted by him under any application—

(a) on receipt of a written request for such information from the offender; or

(b) on the termination of deductions made under any such application.

AMENDMENTS

1. Social Security (Jobseeker's Allowance Consequential Amendments) (Deductions) Regulations 1996 (SI 1996/2344) reg.15 (October 7, 1996).

2. Social Security Act 1998 (Commencement No.12, and Consequential and Transitional Provisions) Order 1999 (SI 1999/3178 (C.81)) art.3(12) and Sch.12 para.3(a) (November 29, 1999).

3. Social Security Act 1998 (Commencement No.12, and Consequential and Transitional Provisions) Order 1999 (SI 1999/3178 (C.81)) art.3(12) and Sch.12 para.3(b) (November 29, 1999).

4. State Pension Credit (Consequential, Transitional and Miscellaneous Provisions) Regulations 2002 (SI 2002/3019) reg.32 (October 6, 2003).

5. Employment and Support Allowance (Consequential Provisions) (No.2) Regulations 2008 (SI 2008/1554) reg.54(1) and (6) (October 27, 2008).

6. Fines, Council Tax and Community Charges (Deductions from Universal Credit and Other Benefits) Regulations 2013 (SI 2013/612) regs 2 and 6 (April 29, 2013).

DEFINITIONS

"adjudication officer"—see reg.1(2).
"authority"—*ibid.*

"benefit week"—*ibid.*
"court"—*ibid.*
"income support"—*ibid.*
"jobseeker's allowance"—*ibid.*

Withdrawal of application

2.1252 **8.**—A court may withdraw an application at any time by giving notice in writing to the social security office to which the application was sent or delivered.

DEFINITIONS

"application"—see reg.1(2).
"court"—*ibid.*
"social security office"—*ibid.*

[[1]Revision and supersession

2.1253 **9.**—Any decision of the Secretary of State under regulation 4 may be revised under section 9 of the 1998 Act or superseded under section 10 of that Act as though the decision were made under section 8(1)(c) of that Act.]

AMENDMENT

1. Social Security Act 1998 (Commencement No.12, and Consequential and Transitional Provisions) Order 1999 (SI 1999/3178 (C.81)) art.3(12) and Sch.12 para.4 (November 29, 1999).

[[1]Appeal

2.1254 **10.**—Any decision of the Secretary of State under regulation 4 (whether as originally made or as revised under regulation 9) may be appealed to a tribunal as though the decision were made on an award of a relevant benefit (within the meaning of section 8(3) of the 1998 Act) under section 8(1)(c) of the 1998 Act.]

AMENDMENT

1. Social Security Act 1998 (Commencement No.12, and Consequential and Transitional Provisions) Order 1999 (SI 1999/3178 (C.81)) art.3(12) and Sch.12 para.4 (November 29, 1999).

Correction of accidental errors

2.1255 **11.**—[[1] . . .]

AMENDMENT

1. Social Security Act 1998 (Commencement No.12, and Consequential and Transitional Provisions) Order 1999 (SI 1999/3178 (C.81)) art.3(12) and Sch.12 para.5 (November 29, 1999).

Setting aside decisions on certain grounds

2.1256 **12.**—[[2] . . .]

AMENDMENTS

1. Deductions from Income Support (Miscellaneous Amendment) Regulations 1993 (SI 1993/495) reg.3 (April 1, 1993).
2. Social Security Act 1998 (Commencement No.12, and Consequential and Transitional Provisions) Order 1999 (SI 1999/3178 (C.81)) art.3(12) and Sch.12 para.5 (November 29, 1999).

Provisions common to regulations 11 and 12

13.—[1 . . .] 2.1257

AMENDMENT

1. Social Security Act 1998 (Commencement No.12, and Consequential and Transitional Provisions) Order 1999 (SI 1999/3178 (C.81)) art.3(12) and Sch.12 para.5 (November 29, 1999).

Manner of making applications or appeals and time limits

14.—[1 . . .] 2.1258

AMENDMENT

1. Social Security Act 1998 (Commencement No.12, and Consequential and Transitional Provisions) Order 1999 (SI 1999/3178 (C.81)) art.3(12) and Sch.12 para.5 (November 29, 1999).

Manner and time for the service of notices etc.

15.—[2 . . .] 2.1259

AMENDMENTS

1. Deductions from Income Support (Miscellaneous Amendment) Regulations 1993 (SI 1993/495) reg.3 (April 1, 1993).
2. Social Security Act 1998 (Commencement No.12, and Consequential and Transitional Provisions) Order 1999 (SI 1999/3178 (C.81)) art.3(12) and Sch.12 para.5 (November 29, 1999).

SCHEDULE 1

TIME LIMITS FOR MAKING APPLICATIONS OR APPEALS

[1 . . .] 2.1260

AMENDMENT

1. Social Security Act 1998 (Commencement No.12, and Consequential and Transitional Provisions) Order 1999 (SI 1999/3178 (C.81)) art.3(12) and Sch.12 para.5 (November 29, 1999).

SCHEDULE 2

CONDUCT AND PROCEDURE IN RELATION TO APPEALS AND APPLICATIONS

[1 . . .] 2.1261

AMENDMENT

1. Social Security Act 1998 (Commencement No.12, and Consequential and Transitional Provisions) Order 1999 (SI 1999/3178 (C.81)) art.3(12) and Sch.12 para.5 (November 29, 1999).

SCHEDULE 3

FORM

APPLICATION TO SECRETARY OF STATE UNDER THE FINES (DEDUCTIONS FROM INCOME SUPPORT) REGULATIONS 1992

2.1262 [1 . . .]

AMENDMENT

1. Fines (Deductions from Income Support) (Amendment) Regulations 2003 (SI 2003/1360) reg.2(c) (June 20, 2003).

The Council Tax (Deductions from Income Support) Regulations 1993

(SI 1993/494) (AS AMENDED)

Made by the Secretary of State under ss.14(3), 97(5), 113 and 116(1) of and Schs 4, paras 1 and 6, and 8, para.6, to the Local Government Finance Act 1992

Citation, commencement and interpretation

2.1263 **1.**—(1) These Regulations may be cited as the Council Tax (Deductions from Income Support) Regulations 1993 and shall come into force on 1st April 1993.

(2) In these Regulations, unless the context otherwise requires—

[3 "the 1998 Act" means the Social Security Act 1998;]

[7 "the 2012 Act" means the Welfare Reform Act 2012;]

[3 . . .]

"application means an application made under regulation 2 or regulation 3 containing the information specified in regulation 4;

[3 . . .]

[7 "assessment period" means the period prescribed by regulation 21 of the UC Regulations;]

"authority" means—

(a) in relation to England and Wales, a billing authority, and

(b) in relation to Scotland, a levying authority;

"benefit week" has the meaning prescribed in regulation 2(1) of the Income Support (General) Regulations 1987 [1or, as the case may be, [5 regulation 1(2) of the State Pension Credit Regulations 2002 [6 , regulation 2(1) of the Employment and Support Allowance Regulations 2008] or] regulation 1(3) of the Jobseeker's Allowance Regulations 1996;]

"Claims and Payments Regulations" means the Social Security (Claims and Payments) Regulations 1987;

[3 "Commissioner" has the meaning it bears in section 39(1) of the 1998 Act;]

[2 "contribution-based jobseeker's allowance", except in a case to which paragraph (b) of the definition of income-based jobseeker's allowance applies, means a contribution-based jobseeker's allowance under Part I of the Jobseekers Act 1995 [7 as amended by the provisions of Part 1 of Schedule 14 to the 2012 Act that remove references to an income-based allowance or under Part 1 of the Jobseekers Act 1995 as it has effect apart from those amendments], but does not include any back to work bonus under section 26 of the Jobseekers Act which is paid as jobseeker's allowance;]

[6 "contributory employment and support allowance" means a contributory allowance under Part 1 of the Welfare Reform Act (employment and support allowance) [7 as amended by the provisions of Schedule 3, and Part 1 of Schedule 14, to the 2012 Act that remove references to an income-related allowance or under Part 1 of the Welfare Reform Act as it has effect apart from those amendments];]

"debtor"—

(a) in relation to England and Wales, has the same meaning as in paragraph 6 of Schedule 4 to the Local Government Finance Act, and

(b) in relation to Scotland, has the same meaning as in paragraph 6 of Schedule 8 to that Act;

"5 per cent. of the personal allowance for a single claimant aged not less than 25" means, where the percentage is not a multiple of 5 pence, the sum obtained by rounding that 5 per cent. to the next higher such multiple;

"income support" means income support within the meaning of the Social Security Contributions and Benefits Act 1992 [1but does not include any back to work bonus under section 26 of the Jobseekers Act which is paid as income support;]

[2 "income-based jobseeker's allowance" means—

(a) an income-based jobseeker's allowance under Part I of the Jobseekers Act 1995; and

(b) in a case where, if there was no entitlement to contribution-based jobseeker's allowance, there would be entitlement to income-based jobseeker's allowance at the same rate, contribution-based jobseeker's allowance,

but does not include any back to work bonus under section 26 of the Jobseekers Act which is paid as jobseeker's allowance;]

[6 "income-related employment and support allowance" means—

(a) an income-related allowance under Part 1 of the Welfare Reform Act; and

(b) in a case where, if there was no entitlement to contributory employment and support allowance, there would be entitlement to income-related employment and support allowance at the same rate, contributory employment and support allowance;]

[1 "Jobseekers Act" means the Jobseekers Act 1995;

"jobseeker's allowance" means an allowance under Part I of the Jobseekers Act but does not include any back to work bonus under section 26 of that Act which is paid as jobseeker's allowance;]

"the Local Government Finance Act" means the Local Government Finance Act 1992;

[5 "personal allowance for a single claimant aged not less than 25" means—

(a) in the case of a person who is entitled to either income support or state pension credit, the amount for the time being specified in paragraph 1(1)(e) of column (2) of Schedule 2 to the Income Support Regulations; [6 . . .]

(b) in the case of a person who is entitled to an income-based jobseeker's allowance, the amount for the time being specified in paragraph 1(1)(e) of column (2) of Schedule 1 to the Jobseeker's Allowance Regulations 1996;] [6 or

(c) in the case of a person who is entitled to income-related employment and support allowance, the amount specified for the time being in paragraph 1 of column 2 of Schedule 4 to the Employment and Support Allowance Regulations 2008;]

"social security office" means an office of the [4 Department for Work and Pensions which is open to the public for the receipt of claims for income support [6 , a jobseeker's allowance or an employment and support allowance].]

[5 "state pension credit" means the benefit of that name payable under the State Pension Credit Act 2002;]

[3 "tribunal" means an appeal tribunal constituted under Chapter 1 of Part I of the 1998 Act.]

[7 "the UC Regulations" means the Universal Credit Regulations 2013;

"universal credit" means universal credit under Part 1 of the 2012 Act;]

[6 "the Welfare Reform Act" means the Welfare Reform Act 2007.]

(3) Unless the context otherwise requires, any reference in these Regulations to a numbered regulation or Schedule is a reference to the regulation or Schedule bearing that number in these Regulations and any reference in a regulation or Schedule to a numbered paragraph is a reference to the paragraph of that regulation or Schedule having that number.

AMENDMENTS

1. Social Security (Jobseeker's Allowance Consequential Amendments) (Deductions) Regulations 1996 (SI 1996/2344) reg.17 (October 7, 1996).

2. Social Security (Miscellaneous Amendments) Regulations 1998 (SI 1998/563) reg.3(1) and (2)(c) (April 1, 1998). (Note that the commencement date for this provision was amended by Social Security (Miscellaneous Amendments) (No.2) Regulations 1998 (SI 1998/865) reg.2 (March 20, 1998).)

3. Social Security Act 1998 (Commencement No.12, and Consequential and Transitional Provisions) Order 1999 (SI 1999/3178) art.3(13) and Sch.13 para.1 (November 29, 1999).

4. Secretaries of State for Education and Skills and for Work and Pensions Order 2002 (SI 2002/1397) art.12 and Sch. para.23 (June 27, 2002).

5. State Pension Credit (Consequential, Transitional and Miscellaneous Provisions) Regulations 2002 (SI 2002/3019) reg.33 (October 6, 2003).

6. Employment and Support Allowance (Consequential Provisions) (No.2) Regulations 2008 (SI 2008/1554) reg.55(1) and (2) (October 27, 2008).

7. Fines, Council Tax and Community Charges (Deductions from Universal Credit and Other Benefits) Regulations 2013 (SI 2013/612) regs 7 and 8 (April 29, 2013).

MODIFICATION

Regulation 1 is modified by Sch.2 para.25 of the Employment and Support Allowance (Transitional Provisions, Housing Benefit and Council Tax Benefit) (Existing Awards) (No.2) Regulations 2010 (SI 2010/1907) (as amended) for the purposes specified in reg.16(1). For details of the modification, see the text of those Regulations in Vol.I.

[1Application for deductions from income support [2, [4 universal credit,] state pension credit] or [3 , jobseeker's allowance or employment and support allowance]: England and Wales]

2.—Where a liability order has been made against a debtor by a magistrates' court and the debtor is entitled to income support [2, [4 universal credit,] state pension credit] [1 [3, a jobseeker's allowance or an employment and support allowance]] the billing authority concerned may apply to the Secretary of State asking him to deduct sums from any amounts payable to the debtor by way of to income support [2, [4 universal credit,] state pension credit] [1 [3, a pension credit] [1 [3 , a jobseeker's allowance or an employment and support allowance]] in order to secure the payment of any outstanding sum which is or forms part of the amount in respect of which the liability order was made. 2.1264

AMENDMENTS

1. Social Security (Jobseeker's Allowance Consequential Amendments) (Deductions) Regulations 1996 (SI 1996/2344) reg.18 (October 7, 1996).
2. State Pension Credit (Consequential, Transitional and Miscellaneous Provisions) Regulations 2002 (SI 2002/3019) reg.33 (October 6, 2003).
3. Employment and Support Allowance (Consequential Provisions) (No.2) Regulations 2008 (SI 2008/1554) reg.55(1) and (3) (October 27, 2008).
4. Fines, Council Tax and Community Charges (Deductions from Universal Credit and Other Benefits) Regulations 2013 (SI 2013/612) regs 7 and 9 (April 29, 2013).

DEFINITIONS

"debtor"—see reg.1(2).
"income support"—*ibid.*
'jobseeker's allowance"—*ibid.*

[2Application for deductions from income support [2, [5 universal credit,] state pension credit] [4 , jobseeker's allowance or employment and support allowance]: Scotland]

3.—(1) Where a levying authority has obtained a summary warrant or a decree against a debtor in respect of arrears of sums payable under paragraph 1(1) of Schedule 8 to the [1Local Government Finance Act] and the debtor is entitled to income support [2, [5 universal credit,] state pension credit] [2 [4 , a jobseeker's allowance or an employment and support allowance]] the levying authority may, without prejudice to its right to pursue any other means of recovering such arrears, apply to the Secretary of State asking him to deduct sums from any amounts payable to the debtor by way of income support [2, [5 universal credit,] state pension credit] [2 [4 , a jobseeker's allowance or an employment and support allowance]] in order 2.1265 to secure the payment of any outstanding sum which is or forms part of the amount in respect of which the summary warrant or decree was granted.

AMENDMENTS

1. Social Security (Claims and Payments) Amendment (No.3) Regulations 1993 (SI 1993/2113) reg.6 (September 27, 1993).
2. Social Security (Jobseeker's Allowance Consequential Amendments) (Deductions) Regulations 1996 (SI 1996/2344) reg.19 (October 7, 1996).
3. State Pension Credit (Consequential, Transitional and Miscellaneous Provisions) Regulations 2002 (SI 2002/3019) reg.33 (October 6, 2003).
4. Employment and Support Allowance (Consequential Provisions) (No.2) Regulations 2008 (SI 2008/1554) reg.55(1) and (4) (October 27, 2008).
5. Fines, Council Tax and Community Charges (Deductions from Universal Credit and Other Benefits) Regulations 2013 (SI 2013/612) regs 7 and 10 (April 29, 2013).

DEFINITIONS

"debtor"—see reg.1(2).
"income support"—*ibid.*
"jobseeker's allowance"—*ibid.*
"Local Government Finance Act"—*ibid.*

Contents of application

2.1266 **4.**—(1) An application shall contain the following particulars—
(a) the name and address of the debtor;
(b) the name and address of the authority making the application;
(c) the name and place of the court which made the liability order or granted the summary warrant, or decree as the case may be;
(d the date on which the liability order was made or the summary warrant or decree granted as the case may be;
(e) the amount specified in the liability order, summary warrant or decree as the case may be;
(f) the total sum which the authority wishes to have deducted from income support [2 , state pension credit] [1 [3 , a jobseeker's allowance or an employment and support allowance]].

(2) An authority making application shall serve it on the Secretary of State by sending or delivering it to a social security office.

(3) Where it appears to the Secretary of State that an application from an authority gives insufficient particulars to enable the debtor to be identified he may require the authority to furnish such further particulars as may reasonably be required for that purpose.

AMENDMENTS

1. Social Security (Jobseeker's Allowance Consequential Amendments) (Deductions) Regulations 1996 (SI 1996/2344) reg.20 (October 7, 1996).
2. State Pension Credit (Consequential, Transitional and Miscellaneous Provisions) Regulations 2002 (SI 2002/3019) reg.33 (October 6, 2003).
3. Employment and Support Allowance (Consequential Provisions) (No.2) Regulations 2008 (SI 2008/1554) reg.55(1) and (5) (October 27, 2008).

DEFINITIONS

"application"—see reg.1(2).
"authority"—*ibid.*

"debtor"—*ibid.*
"jobseeker's allowance"—*ibid.*
"social security office"—*ibid.*

GENERAL NOTE

On regs 2, 3 and 4 see *R(IS) 3/92* and *R(IS) 1/98* in the notes to reg.2 of the Community Charges (Deductions from Income Support) (No.2) Regulations 1990. *CIS 1725/1997* confirms that *R(IS) 1/98* applies to deductions for council tax arrears as well as those for arrears of the community charge. **2.1267**

[1Deductions from debtor's income support [2, [4 universal credit,] state pension credit] [3 , jobseeker's allowance or employment and support allowance]

5.—(1) Subject to regulation 8, where— **2.1268**

(a) the Secretary of State receives an application from an authority in respect of a debtor who is entitled to income support [2 , state pension credit] [3 , a jobseeker's allowance or an employment and support allowance];

(b) the amount payable by way of that benefit, after any deduction under this paragraph, is 10 pence or more; and

(c) the aggregate amount payable under one or more of the following provisions, namely, paragraphs 3(2)(a), 5(6), 6(2)(a) and 7(3)(a) and (5)(a) of Schedule 9 to the Claims and Payments Regulations together with the amount to be deducted under this paragraph does not exceed an amount equal to 3 times 5 per cent. of the personal allowance for a single claimant aged not less than 25 years,

the Secretary of State may deduct a sum from that benefit which is equal to 5 per cent. of the personal allowance for a single claimant aged not less than 25 and pay that sum to the authority towards satisfaction of any outstanding sum which is or forms part of the amount in respect of which the liability order was made or the summary warrant or the decree was granted.

[4 (1A) Subject to paragraphs (1B) and (1C) and regulation 8, where the Secretary of State receives an application from an authority in respect of a debtor who is entitled to universal credit, the Secretary of State may deduct from the universal credit payable to the debtor an amount equal to 5 per cent. of the appropriate universal credit standard allowance and pay that sum to the authority towards satisfaction of any outstanding sum which is, or forms part of, the amount in respect of which the liability order was made or the summary warrant or decree was granted.

(1B) No amount may be deducted under paragraph (1A) where it would reduce the amount of universal credit payable to the debtor to less than 1 penny.

(1C) For the purpose of paragraph (1A), where 5 per cent. of the appropriate universal credit standard allowance results in a fraction of a penny, that fraction is to be disregarded if it is less than half a penny and otherwise it is to be treated as a penny.

(1D) In paragraphs (1A) and (1C), "appropriate universal credit standard allowance" means the appropriate universal credit standard allowance for the debtor for the assessment period in question under regulation 36 of the UC Regulations.]

[4 (2) Subject to regulation 8, where—

(a) the Secretary of State receives an application from an authority in respect of a debtor who is entitled to contribution-based jobseeker's allowance or contributory employment and support allowance; and

(b) the amount of that allowance payable, before any deduction under this paragraph, is 10 pence or more,

the Secretary of State may deduct a sum from that allowance, up to the appropriate maximum specified in paragraph (2A), and pay that sum to the authority towards satisfaction of any outstanding sum which is, or forms part of, the amount in respect of which the liability order was made or the summary warrant or decree was granted.

(2A) The appropriate maximum is 40 per cent. of the appropriate age-related amount for the debtor specified—

(a) where the debtor is entitled to contribution-based jobseeker's allowance, in regulation 79 of the Jobseeker's Allowance Regulations 1996 or, as the case may be, regulation 49 of the Jobseeker's Allowance Regulations 2013;

(b) where the debtor is entitled to contributory employment and support allowance, in paragraph 1(1) of Schedule 4 to the Employment and Support Allowance Regulations 2008 or, as the case may be, regulation 62(1)(b) of the Employment and Support Allowance Regulations 2013.]

[4 . . .]

(4) The Secretary of State shall notify the debtor and the authority concerned in writing of a decision to make a deduction under this regulation so far as is practicable within 14 days from the date on which he made the decision and at the same time shall notify the debtor of his right of appeal.]

AMENDMENTS

1. Social Security Act 1998 (Commencement No.12, and Consequential and Transitional Provisions) Order 1999 (SI 1999/3178 (C.81)) art.3(13) and Sch.13, para.2 (November 29, 1999).

2. State Pension Credit (Consequential, Transitional and Miscellaneous Provisions) Regulations 2002 (SI 2002/3019) reg.33 (October 6, 2003).

3. Employment and Support Allowance (Consequential Provisions) (No.2) Regulations 2008 (SI 2008/1554) reg.55(1) and (6) (October 27, 2008).

4. Fines, Council Tax and Community Charges (Deductions from Universal Credit and Other Benefits) Regulations 2013 (SI 2013/612) regs 7 and 11 (April 29, 2013).

GENERAL NOTE

2.1269 The replacement of para.(2) with paras (2) and (2A) by regs 2 and 11(4) of SI 2013/612 does not have effect in respect of an application received by the Secretary of State from the court in respect of an offender before April 29, 2013: see reg.11(6) of SI 2013/612.

Notification of decision

2.1270 **6.**—[1 . . .]

AMENDMENT

1. Social Security Act 1998 (Commencement No.12, and Consequential and Transitional Provisions) Order 1999 (SI 1999/3178 (C.81)) art.3(13) and Sch.13 para.2 (November 29, 1999).

[1Deductions from debtor's income support or income-based jobseeker's allowance]

7.—[2 . . .] 2.1271

AMENDMENTS

1. Social Security (Jobseeker's Allowance Consequential Amendments) (Deductions) Regulations 1996 (SI 1996/2344) reg.22 (October 7, 1996).
2. Social Security Act 1998 (Commencement No.12, and Consequential and Transitional Provisions) Order 1999 (SI 1999/3178 (C.81)) art.3(13) and Sch.13 para.2 (November 29, 1999).

[1Deductions from debtor's contribution-based jobseeker's allowance]

7A.—[2 . . .] 2.1272

AMENDMENTS

1. Social Security (Jobseeker's Allowance Consequential Amendments) (Deductions) Regulations 1996 (SI 1996/2344) reg.23 (October 7, 1996).
2. Social Security Act 1998 (Commencment No.12 and Consequential and Transitional Provisions) Order 1999 (SI 1999/3178 (C.81)) art.3(13) and Sch.13 para.2 (November 29, 1999).

Circumstances, time of making and termination of deductions

8.—(1) The Secretary of State may make deductions from [1income support [3, state pension credit] [4, jobseeker's allowance or employment and support allowance] under [4 [5 regulation 5(1) or (2)]] only if— 2.1273

(a) the debtor is entitled to income support [3, state pension credit] [1 [4, jobseeker's allowance or employment and support allowance]] throughout any benefit week;
(b) no deductions are being made in respect of the debtor under any other application; and
(c) no payments are being made under regulation 2 of the Community Charge (Deductions from Income Support) (Scotland) Regulations 1989 or regulation 2 of the Community Charge (Deductions from Income Support) (No.2) Regulations 1990.

[5 (1A) The Secretary of State may make deductions from universal credit under regulation 5(1A) only if—

(a) the debtor is entitled to universal credit throughout any assessment period;
(b) no deductions are being made in respect of the debtor under any other application; and
(c) no payments are being made under regulation 2 of the Community Charge (Deductions from Income Support)(Scotland) Regulations 1989(12) or regulation 2 of the Community Charge (Deductions from Income Support)(No.2) Regulations 1990.]

(2) The Secretary of State shall make deductions from income support [3, [5 universal credit,] state pension credit] [1 [4, jobseeker's allowance or employment and support allowance]] by reference to the times at which payment of income support [3, [5 universal credit,] state pension credit] [1 [4, jobseeker's allowance or employment and support allowance]] is made to the debtor.

(3) The Secretary of State shall cease making deductions from income support [3, [5 universal credit,] state pension credit] [1[4, jobseeker's allowance or employment and support allowance]] if—

(a) there is no longer sufficient entitlement to income support [3, [5 universal credit,] state pension credit] [1 [4, jobseeker's allowance or employment and support allowance]] to enable him to make the deduction;

(b) an authority withdraws its application for deductions to be made; or

(c) the debt in respect of which he was making deductions is discharged.

[2(4) The Secretary of State shall not determine any application under regulation 2 or 3 which relates to a debtor in respect of whom—

(a) he is making deductions; or

(b) deductions fall to be made,

pursuant to an earlier application under either of those regulations until no deductions pursuant to that earlier application fall to be made.]

(5) Payments of sums deducted from income support [3, [5 universal credit,] state pension credit] [1 [4, jobseeker's allowance or employment and support allowance]] by the Secretary of State under these Regulations shall be made to the authority concerned, as far as is practicable, at intervals not exceeding 13 weeks.

(6) Where the whole of the amount to which the application relates has been paid, the authority concerned shall, so far as is practicable, give notice of that fact within 21 days to the Secretary of State.

(7) The Secretary of State shall notify the debtor in writing of the total of the sums deducted by him under any application—

(a) on receipt of a written request for such information from the debtor; or

(b) on the termination of deductions made under any such application.

AMENDMENTS

1. Social Security (Jobseeker's Allowance Consequential Amendments) (Deductions) Regulations 1996 (SI 1996/2344) reg.24 (October 7, 1996).

2. Social Security Act 1998 (Commencement No.12, and Consequential and Transitional Provisions) Order 1999 (SI 1999/3178 (C.81)) art.3(13) and Sch.13 para.3 (November 29, 1999).

3. State Pension Credit (Consequential, Transitional and Miscellaneous Provisions) Regulations 2002 (SI 2002/3019) reg.33 (October 6, 2003).

4. Employment and Support Allowance (Consequential Provisions) (No.2) Regulations 2008 (SI 2008/1554) reg.55(1) and (7) (October 27, 2008).

5. Fines, Council Tax and Community Charges (Deductions from Universal Credit and Other Benefits) Regulations 2013 (SI 2013/612) regs 7 and 12 (April 29, 2013).

Withdrawal of application

2.1274 **9.**—An authority may withdraw an application at any time by giving notice in writing to the social security office to which the application was sent or delivered.

[1Revision and supersession

2.1275 **10.**—Any decision of the Secretary of State under regulation 5 may be revised under section 9 of the 1998 Act or superseded under section 10 of that Act as though the decision were made under section 8(1)(c) of that Act.]

AMENDMENT

1. Social Security Act 1998 (Commencement No.12, and Consequential and Transitional Provisions) Order 1999 (SI 1999/3178 (C.81)) art.3(13) and Sch.13 para.4 (November 29, 1999).

[[1]Appeal

11.—Any decision of the Secretary of State under regulation 5 (whether as originally made or as revised under regulation 10) may be appealed to a tribunal as though the decision were made on an award of a relevant benefit (within the meaning of section 8(3) of the 1998 Act) under section 8(1)(c) of the 1998 Act.] **2.1276**

AMENDMENT

1. Social Security Act 1998 (Commencement No.12, and Consequential and Transitional Provisions) Order 1999 (SI 1999/3178 (C.81)) art.3(13) and Sch.13 para.4 (November 29, 1999).

Correction of accidental errors

12.—[[1] . . .] **2.1277**

AMENDMENT

1. Social Security Act 1998 (Commencement No.12, and Consequential and Transitional Provisions) Order 1999 (SI 1999/3178 (C.81)) art.3(13) and Sch.13 para.5 (November 29, 1999).

Setting aside decisions on certain grounds

13.—[[1] . . .] **2.1278**

AMENDMENT

1. Social Security Act 1998 (Commencement No.12, and Consequential and Transitional Provisions) Order 1999 (SI 1999/3178 (C.81)) art.3(13) and Sch.13 para.5 (November 29, 1999).

Provisions common to regulations 12 and 13

14.—[[1] . . .] **2.1279**

AMENDMENT

1. Social Security Act 1998 (Commencement No.12, and Consequential and Transitional Provisions) Order 1999 (SI 1999/3178 (C.81)) art.3(13) and Sch.13 para.5 (November 29, 1999).

Manner of making applications or appeals and time limits

15.—[[1] . . .] **2.1280**

AMENDMENT

1. Social Security Act 1998 (Commencement No.12, and Consequential and Transitional Provisions) Order 1999 (SI 1999/3178 (C.81)) art.3(13) and Sch.13 para.5 (November 29, 1999).

Manner and time for the service of notices etc.

2.1281 **16.**—[1 . . .]

AMENDMENT

1. Social Security Act 1998 (Commencement No.12, and Consequential and Transitional Provisions) Order 1999 (SI 1999/3178 (C.81)) art.3(13) and Sch.13 para.5 (November 29, 1999).

SCHEDULE 1

TIME LIMITS FOR MAKING APPLICATIONS OR APPEALS

2.1282 [1 . . .]

AMENDMENT

1. Social Security Act 1998 (Commencement No.12, and Consequential and Transitional Provisions) Order 1999 (SI 1999/3178 (C.81)) art.3(13) and Sch.13 para.5 (November 29, 1999).

SCHEDULE 2

CONDUCT AND PROCEDURE IN RELATION TO APPEALS AND APPLICATIONS

2.1283 [1 . . .]

AMENDMENT

1. Social Security Act 1998 (Commencement No.12, and Consequential and Transitional Provisions) Order 1999 (SI 1999/3178 (C.81)) art.3(13) and Sch.13 para.5 (November 29, 1999).

The Social Security Benefits (Maintenance Payments and Consequential Amendments) Regulations 1996

(SI 1996/940) (AS AMENDED)

Made by the Secretary of State under ss.74A(5) and (6), 189(1) and (3)–(5) and 191 of the Social Security Administration Act 1992 and ss.136(5)(b), 137(1) and 175(1)–(4) of the Social Security Contributions and Benefits Act 1992

[In force April 19, 1996]

Interpretation for the purposes of section 74A of the Act

2.—In section 74A of the Act (payment of benefit where maintenance payments collected by Secretary of State)— 2.1284

(a) "child maintenance" means any payment towards the maintenance of a child or young person, including payments made—
   (i) under a court order;
   (ii) under a maintenance [1 calculation] made under the Child Support Act 1991;
   (iii) under an agreement for maintenance; or
   (iv) voluntarily,

   and for this purpose a "young person" is a person referred to in regulation 3 of these Regulations (persons of a prescribed description);

(b) "spousal maintenance" means any payment made by a person towards the maintenance of that person's spouse [2 or civil partner], including payments made—
   (i) under a court order;
   (ii) under an agreement for maintenance; or
   (iii) voluntarily;

(c) "relevant income" means—
   (i) any income which is taken into account under Part V of the Income Support Regulations for the purposes of calculating the amount of income support to which the claimant is entitled; or
   (ii) any income which is taken into account under Part VIII of the Jobseeker's Allowance Regulations for the purposes of calculating the amount of jobseeker's allowance to which the claimant is entitled [3 or
   (iii) any income which is taken into account under Part 10 of the Employment and Support Allowance Regulations for the purposes of calculating the amount of employment and support allowance to which the claimant is entitled.]

AMENDMENTS

1. Child Support (Consequential Amendments and Transitional Provisions) Regulations 2001 (SI 2001/158) reg.8 (in force in relation to a particular case from the date on which CSPSSA 2000 s.1 comes into force in relation to that type of case).

2. Civil Partnership (Pensions, Social Security and Child Support) (Consequential, etc. Provisions) Order 2005 (SI 2005/2877) art.2(3) and Sch.3 para.27 (December 5, 2005).

3. Employment and Support Allowance (Consequential Provisions) (No.2) Regulations 2008 (SI 2008/1554) reg.59(3) (October 27, 2008).

Persons of a prescribed description

3.—For the purposes of the definition of "family" in section 74A(5) of the Act, a person of a prescribed description is any person who— 2.1285

(a) is referred to as a "young person" in the Income Support Regulations by virtue of regulation 14 of those Regulations; or
(b) is referred to as a "young person" in the Jobseeker's Allowance Regulations by virtue of regulation 76 of those Regulations [1 or
(c) is referred to as a "young person" in the Employment and Support Allowance Regulations by virtue of regulation 2(1) of those Regulations.]

AMENDMENT

1. Employment and Support Allowance (Consequential Provisions) (No.2) Regulations 2008 (SI 2008/1554) reg.59(4) (October 27, 2008).

Circumstances in which a person is to be treated as responsible for another

2.1286 **4.**—A person shall be treated as responsible for another for the purposes of section 74A of the Act if he is treated as responsible for that other person under either regulation 15 of the Income Support Regulations or regulation 77 of the Jobseeker's Allowance Regulations.

Circumstances in which persons are to be treated as being members of the same household

2.1287 **5.**—Persons shall be treated as members of the same household for the purposes of section 74A of the Act if they are treated as members of the same household under [1. . .] regulation 16 of the Income Support Regulations or regulation 78 of the Jobseeker's Allowance Regulations [1 or regulation 156 of the Employment and Support Allowance Regulations].

AMENDMENT

1. Employment and Support Allowance (Consequential Provisions) (No.2) Regulations 2008 (SI 2008/1554) reg.59(5) (October 27, 2008).

GENERAL NOTE

2.1288 For s.74A of the Social Security Administration Act, see Vol.III of this series. See the note to para.73 of Sch.9 to the Income Support Regulations.

The Care Planning, Placement and Case Review (England) Regulations 2010

(SI 2010/959)

Made by the Secretary of State for Children, Schools and Families under ss.22C(11), 23ZA(3) and (4), 23ZB(1)(a), 23D(2), 23E(1) and (2), 25A(4), 25B(1)(b) and (2)(a), 26(1) and (2), 31A(3), 34(8) and 104(4) of, and paras 12A–12E, 12F(1)(a), 12G and 19B(2)(b), (3), (7) and (8) of Sch.2 to, the Children Act 1989

[In force April 1, 2011]

REGULATIONS REPRODUCED

2.1289 40. Eligible children
48. Application of these Regulations with modifications to short breaks

General note

See the notes to reg.2 of the Children (Leaving Care) Social Security Benefits Regulations 2001. 2.1290

Eligible children

Meaning of eligible child

40.—(1) For the purposes of paragraph 19B(2)(b) of Schedule 2 to the 1989 Act (meaning of eligible child), the prescribed period is 13 weeks and the prescribed age is 14. 2.1291

(2) For the purposes of paragraph 19B(3)(b) of that Schedule, if C is a child to whom regulation 48 applies, C is not an eligible child despite falling within paragraph 19B(2) of that Schedule.

Application of these Regulations with modifications to short breaks

48.—(1) In the circumstances set out in paragraph (2) these Regulations apply with the modifications set out in paragraph (3). 2.1292

(2) The circumstances are that—

(a) C is not in the care of the responsible authority,

(b) the responsible authority have arranged to place C in a series of short-term placements with the same person or in the same accommodation ("short breaks"), and

(c) the arrangement is such that—

(i) no single placement is intended to last for longer than 17 days,

(ii) at the end of each such placement, C returns to the care of C's parent or a person who is not C's parent but who has parental responsibility for C, and

(iii) the short breaks do not exceed 75 days in total in any period of 12 months.

(3) *[Omitted]*.

The Care Leavers (England) Regulations 2010

(SI 2010/2571)

Made by the Secretary of State for Education under ss.23A(3), 23B(8)(c) and (10), 23D(2), 23E(1), (1B), (1C) and (2), 24B(6) and 104(4) of, and para.19B(2), (3), (7) and (8) of Sch.2 to, the Children Act 1989

[In force April 1, 2011]

General note

See the note to reg.2 of the Children (Leaving Care) Social Security Benefits Regulations 2001. 2.1293

Relevant children

3.—(1) For the purposes of section 23A(3), children falling within paragraph (2) are an additional category of relevant children. 2.1294

(2) Subject to paragraph (3), a child falls within this paragraph if—

(a) the child is aged 16 or 17,

(b) the child is not subject to a care order, and

(c) on attaining the age of 16 the child was detained, or in hospital, and immediately before being detained or admitted to hospital had been looked after by a local authority for a period or periods amounting in total to at least 13 weeks, which began after the child attained the age of 14.

(3) In calculating the period of 13 weeks referred to in paragraph (2)(b), no account is to be taken of any period in which the child was looked after by a local authority in the course of a pre-planned series of short-term placements, none of which individually exceeded four weeks, where at the end of each such placement the child returned to the care of their parent, or a person who is not a parent but who has parental responsibility for them.

(4) For the purposes of this regulation—

(a) "detained" means detained in a remand centre, a young offender institution or a secure training centre, or any other institution pursuant to an order of a court [1, but excludes remand to youth detention accommodation], and

(b) "hospital" has the meaning given in section 275(1) of the National Health Service Act 2006

[1 (c) "remand to youth detention accommodation" has the meaning given in section 102(1) of the Legal Aid, Sentencing and Punishment of Offenders Act 2012.]

(5) Subject to paragraph (6), a child who has lived for a continuous period of six months or more (whether that period commenced before or after they ceased to be looked after) with—

(a) their parent,

(b) someone who is not their parent but who has parental responsibility for them, or

(c) where they were in care and there was a [2 child arrangements] order in force immediately before the care order was made, a person [2 named in the child arrangements order as a person with whom they were to live],

is not a relevant child despite falling within section 23A(2).

[2 (5A) For the purposes of paragraph (5), a child arrangements order is one that consists of, or includes, arrangements relating to either or both of the following—

(i) with whom the child is to live, and

(ii) when the child is to live with any person.]

(6) Where living arrangements described in paragraph (5) break down and the child ceases to live with the person concerned, the child is a relevant child.

AMENDMENTS

1. Care Planning, Placement and Case Review (England) (Miscellaneous Amendments) Regulations 2013 (SI 2013/706) reg.12 (April 19, 2013).

2. Child Arrangements Order (Consequential Amendments to Subordinate Legislation) Order 2014 (SI 2014/852) art.19 (April 22, 2014).

The Care Planning, Placement and Case Review (Wales) Regulations 2015

(SI 2015/1818)

Made by the Welsh Ministers under ss. 81(6)(d), 83(5), 84, 87, 97(4)(a), 97(5), 98(1)(a), 100(1)(b), 100(2)(a), 102(1), 102(2), 104(2)(c), 104(6), 106(4), 107(7)(c), 107(8), 107(9), 108(6) and 196(2) of the Social Services and Well-being (Wales) Act 2014 and ss. 31A and 34(8) of the Children Act 1989

[In force April 6, 2016]

REGULATIONS REPRODUCED

Title, commencement and application

1.—(1) The title of these Regulations is the Care Planning, Placement and Case Review (Wales) Regulations 2015 and they come into force on 6 April 2016. **2.1296**

(2) These Regulations apply in relation to Wales.

Meaning of category 1 young person

47.—(1) For the purposes of section 104(2) of the 2014 Act the prescribed period is 13 weeks and the prescribed age is 14. **2.1297**

(2) For the purposes of section 104(6)(b) of the 2014 Act, if C is a child to whom regulation 62 applies, C is not a category 1 young person despite falling within section 104(2) of that Act.

Application of these Regulations with modifications to short breaks

62.—(1) In the circumstances set out in paragraph (2), these Regulations apply with the modifications set out in paragraph (3). **2.1298**

(2) The circumstances are that—

(a) C is not in the care of the responsible authority,

(b) the responsible authority has arranged to place C in a series of short-term placements with the same person or in the same accommodation ("short breaks"), and

(c) the arrangement is such that—

(i) no single placement is intended to last for more than 4 weeks,

(ii) at the end of each such placement C returns to the care of C's parent or a person who is not C's parent but who has parental responsibility for C, and

(iii) the short breaks do not exceed 120 days in total in any period of 12 months.

(3) *[Omitted]*

The Care Leavers (Wales) Regulations 2015

(SI 2015/1820)

Made by the Welsh Ministers under ss. 104(2) and (6), 106(4), 107(7)(c) and (8), 108(6), 109(1) and (3), 116(2) and 196(2) of the Social Services and Well-being (Wales) Act 2014

[In force April 6, 2016]

REGULATIONS REPRODUCED

Title, commencement and application

2.1300 **1.**—(1) The title of these Regulations is the Care Leavers (Wales) Regulations 2015 and they come into force on 6 April 2016.

(2) These Regulations apply in relation to Wales.

Category 2 young persons

2.1301 **3.**—(1) For the purposes of section 104(6)(a) of the Act, children falling within paragraph (2) are an additional category of category 2 young person.

(2) Subject to paragraph (3), a child falls within this paragraph if—

(a) the child is aged 16 or 17,

(b) the child is not subject to a care order, and

(c) on attaining the age of 16 the child was detained, or in hospital, and immediately before being detained or admitted to hospital had been looked after by a local authority for a period or periods amounting in total to at least 13 weeks, which began after the child attained the age of 14.

(3) In calculating the period of 13 weeks referred to in paragraph (2)(c), no account is to be taken of any period in which the child was looked after by a local authority or a local authority in England in the course of a pre-planned series of short-term placements, none of which individually exceeded four weeks, where at the end of the each such placement the child returned to the care of their parent or a person who is not a parent but who has parental responsibility for them.

(4) Subject to paragraph (5), a child who has lived for a continuous period of six months or more (whether that period commenced before or after they ceased to be looked after) with—

(a) their parent,

(b) someone who is not their parent but who has parental responsibility for them, or

(c) where they were in care and there was a child arrangements order in force immediately before the care order was made, a person named in the child arrangements order as the person with whom they were to live, is not to be treated as a category 2 young person despite falling within the definition set out in section 104(2) of the Act.

(5) Where living arrangements described in paragraph (4) break down and the child ceases to live with the person concerned, the child is to be treated as a category 2 young person.

(6) For the purposes of paragraph (4), a child arrangements order is one that consists of, or includes, arrangements relating to either or both of the following—

(a) with whom the child is to live, and

(b) when the child is to live with any person.

(7) For the purposes of this regulation—

"child arrangements order" has the meaning given in section 8(1) of the Children Act 1989; and

"hospital" has the same meaning as in the Mental Health Act 1983.

The Children (Leaving Care) Social Security Benefits Regulations 2001

(SI 2001/3074) (AS AMENDED)

Made by the Secretary of State for Work and Pensions under s.6(3), (5), (6) and (7) of the Children (Leaving Care) Act 2000

[In force October 1, 2001]

REGULATIONS REPRODUCED

Entitlement to Benefits

2.—(1) Section 6 (exclusion from benefits) shall not apply for the purposes of entitlement to income support [2 , income-based jobseeker's allowance or income-related employment and support allowance] where a person— 2.1303

(a) falls within subsection (2)(a) or (b) of that section; and

(b) falls within a category of person prescribed in—

(i) provided the person is a lone parent, regulation 13(2)(a) (circumstances in which persons in relevant education may be entitled to income support) of; [3 or]

(ii) [3 . . .]

(iii) paragraph 1, 2, 7, 8, [3 . . .] 11, [3 . . .] [3 . . .] 24 or 25 of Schedule 1B (prescribed categories of person) to,

the Income Support (General) Regulations 1987 ("the Income Support Regulations").

(2) Section 6 shall not apply to a person who falls within subsection (2) (a) or (b) of that section who has not been looked after by a local authority for the purposes of paragraph 19B of Schedule 2 to the Children Act 1989 on or after 1st October 2001.

(3) Where a person who falls within subsection (2)(a) or (b) of section 6

is residing in Scotland but is not supported by a local authority in England or Wales then, notwithstanding that he has been looked after by such a local authority for the purposes of paragraph 19B of Schedule 2 to the 1989 Act on or after 1st October 2001, section 6 shall not apply to that person [1 provided that he ceased to be so looked after before 1st April 2004].

(4) In paragraph (1)(b)(i) above, "lone parent" has the meaning it bears in regulation 2(1) of the Income Support Regulations.

AMENDMENTS

1. Social Security (Miscellaneous Amendments) Regulations 2004 (SI 2004/565) reg.12 (April 1, 2004).

2. Employment and Support Allowance (Consequential Provisions) (No.2) Regulations 2008 (SI 2008/1554) reg.70 (October 27, 2008).

3. Income Support (Prescribed Categories of Person) Regulations 2009 (SI 2009/3152) reg.3(3) and 3(7) (December, 30, 2009). Regulation 3(3) amended reg.2(1)(b) with effect from December 30, 2009 but reg.3(7) provided that this did not apply in the case of a person who was subject to the saving provisions in reg.2(2) of those Regulations. See the 2015/16 edition of this volume for these Regulations and the notes to them.

GENERAL NOTE

2.1304 This regulation deals with the exceptions to the exclusion from benefit in s.6(2)(a) and (b) of the Children (Leaving Care) Act 2000 (see the note to the Children (Leaving Care) Act 2000). See the Children (Leaving Care) Social Security Benefits (Scotland) Regulations 2004 (SI 2004/747) below which provide for similar exceptions to the exclusion under s.6(2)(c) of the 2000 Act (as well as defining the scope of the exclusion under that provision).

Note that s.6 of the 2000 Act has not been amended following the introduction of ESA on October 27, 2008 so as to also exclude entitlement to income-related ESA. This would appear to be an oversight as a purported amendment to reg.2(1) has been made to include a reference to income-related ESA. However, in view of the fact that s.6 has not been amended to exclude an "eligible child" or a "relevant child" from entitlement to ESA, such an amendment is not necessary (and is ultra vires).

Note also that this regulation has not been amended to include a person who falls within subs.(2)(ba) or (bb) of s.6 of the Children (Leaving Care) Act 2000. Subsection (2)(ba) and (bb) came into force on April 6, 2016 and refer to a "category 1 young person" and a "category 2 young person" respectively within the meaning of s.104(2) of the Social Services and Well-being (Wales) Act 2014 (see p.195–196). A "category 1 young person" is the equivalent in Wales of an "eligible child" and a "category 2 young person" is the equivalent in Wales of a "relevant child". It is not known why this regulation has not been amended to include a person who falls within subs.(2)(ba) or (bb). However, the result, at least for the time being, is that category 1 and category 2 young people would not seem to be covered by the exceptions in this regulation to the exclusion from benefit in s.6(2) of the 2000 Act.

Eligible and relevant children

2.1305 Under s.6, an "eligible child" (defined in para.19B of Sch.2 to the Children Act 1989) or a "relevant child" (defined in s.23A of the 1989 Act) is not entitled to income-based JSA, income support or housing benefit (subss.(1), (2)(a) and (2)(b)). (Nor is a category 1 or category 2 young person.) See also the consequential amendments to reg.4ZA of the Income Support Regulations and reg.57 of the JSA Regulations 1996 made by the Children (Leaving Care) Act 2000 (Commencement No.2 and Consequential Provisions) Order 2001 (SI 2001/ 3070) with effect from October 1, 2001.

Paragraph 19B of Sch.2 to, and s.23A of, the Children Act 1989 were inserted by ss.1 and 2 respectively of the Children (Leaving Care) Act 2000 (p.194). 2.1306

Under para.19B, together with regs 40 and 48 of the Care Planning, Placement and Case Review (England) Regulations 2010 (SI 2010/959) ("the English Regulations (eligible children)"), an "eligible child" is a 16-or 17-year-old who is being looked after by a local authority and who has, since the age of 14, been looked after by a local authority for a period of at least 13 weeks, or periods totalling at least 13 weeks, which ended after he became 16. However, periods of respite care are excluded. Thus the child will not be an eligible child if he is not in the care of the responsible authority and has been/is placed by the responsible authority in a series of short-term placements with the same person or in the same accommodation, none of which are intended to exceed 17 days and which do not total more than 75 days in any 12-month period and the child returns to the care of his parent or the person who has parental responsibility for him at the end of each placement (see reg.48 of the English Regulations).

A "relevant child" is a 16- or 17-year-old who was an eligible child but who is no longer being looked after by a local authority (s.23A(2) of the 1989 Act). It also includes a 16- or 17-year-old (not subject to a care order) who at the age of 16 was in hospital or detained in a remand centre, a young offenders institution, a secure training centre, or any other institution pursuant to an order of a court (other than remand to youth detention accommodation), and who immediately before he was in hospital or detained, had, since the age of 14, been looked after by a local authority for a period or periods totalling at least 13 weeks (reg.3(2) of the Care Leavers (England) Regulations 2010 (SI 2010/2571) ("the English Regulations (relevant children)"). In calculating the 13 weeks any pre-planned short-term placement which does not exceed four weeks and at the end of which the child returns to the care of his parent or the person who has parental responsibility for him is ignored (reg.3(3) of the English Regulations (relevant children)). However, a child who has lived with his parent, the person who has parental responsibility for him or, in the case of a child subject to a care order, the person in whose favour a child arrangements order had been made before the care order was made for at least six months, whether or not the six months started before or after the child stopped being looked after by a local authority, does not count as a relevant child (reg.3(5) of the English Regulations (relevant children)) but will do so if the living arrangements break down and the child ceases to live with the person concerned (reg.3(6) of the English Regulations (relevant children)).

Once an eligible or relevant child becomes 18 he ceases to count as such and the exclusion from benefit in s.6 will not apply. 2.1307

If there is a dispute over whether the s.6 exclusion applies, it may be necessary for decision-makers (and appeal tribunals) to decide whether a child falls within either definition. For this reason the text of the relevant parts of both the English and the Welsh Regulations has been included (see pp.950–955, but note what is said above about the fact that this regulation has not been amended to include a person who falls within subs.(2)(ba) or (bb) of s.6 of the Children (Leaving Care) Act 2000). Clearly information from the relevant social services department will be useful in determining these issues. But if, for example, a local authority has decided that living arrangements have broken down with the result that the person concerned is again treated as a relevant child, is a tribunal bound by the local authority decision or can it reach a different conclusion? As this will be largely a question of fact, there seems to be no reason why the tribunal cannot consider this issue in deciding whether the s.6 exclusion applies.

See also the amendments to reg.14 of the Income Support Regulations and reg.76(2) of the JSA Regulations 1996 made by the Children (Leaving Care) Act 2000 (Commencement No.2 and Consequential Provisions) Order 2001 (SI 2001/3070) with effect from October 1, 2001. The result of these amendments is that a person to whom the s.6 exclusion applies cannot form part of a claimant's family for the purposes of income support and income-based JSA.

Category 1 and Category 2 young persons

2.1308 The definition of a category 1 young person in s.104(2) of the Social Services and Well-being (Wales) Act 2014 is to all intents and purposes the same as the definition of "eligible child" in para.19B of Sch.2 to the Children Act 1989. Similarly, the definition of a category 2 young person in s.104(2) replicates the definition of "relevant child" in s.23A(2) of the 1989 Act.

In addition, the provisions of regs 47 and 62 of the Care Planning, Placement and Case Review (Wales) Regulations 2015 (SI 2015/1818), which relate to category 1 young persons, are the same as those in regs 40 and 48 of the Care Planning, Placement and Care Review (England) Regulations 2010, which relate to eligible children, except that in Wales the limit for the intended length of a short-term placement is four weeks (as opposed to 17 days) and the overall limit on the length of time the child can spend in such short breaks is 120 (as opposed to 75) days. As regards category 2 young persons, reg.3 of the Care Leavers (Wales) Regulations 2015 (SI 2015/1820) is the same as reg.3 of the Care Leavers (England) Regulations 2010, which concerns relevant children.

The s.6 exclusion

2.1309 The circumstances in which the s.6 exclusion will not apply are set out in reg.2.

Note firstly that the exclusion only applied to an eligible or relevant child who had been looked after by a local authority on or after October 1, 2001 (para.(2)) (i.e. it did not apply to a 16- or 17-year-old who left local authority care before that date). It also did not originally apply if an eligible or relevant child who would otherwise be caught by s.6 was living in Scotland, provided that he was not being supported by an English or Welsh local authority (para.(3)). However, this now only applies if the person ceased to be so looked after before April 1, 2004. This is because, with the exception of s.6, the Children (Leaving Care) Act 2000 did not apply to Scotland and so 16- or 17-year-olds who left Scottish local authority care remained potentially entitled to income support, income-based JSA and housing benefit, whether they were in Scotland, England or Wales. However, with effect from April 1, 2004 equivalent legislation came into force in Scotland and so 16- or 17-year-olds leaving Scottish local authority care then came within s.6. See the Support and Assistance of Young People Leaving Care (Scotland) Regulations 2003 (SSI SI 2003/608).

In addition to these general exceptions, para.(1) provides that an eligible child or a relevant child can still qualify for income support or income-based JSA if he is: (i) in relevant education and a lone parent (as defined in reg.2(1) of the Income Support Regulations (para.(4)); or (ii) a lone parent, a single foster parent, incapable of work or appealing against a decision that he is capable of work, or a disabled worker within the meaning of para.8 of Sch.1B to the Income Support Regulations (but note that para.8 was revoked on January 25, 2010, although there is some transitional protection: see the note to para.8). (Paragraph 11 of Sch.1B is also listed in para.(1)(b)(iii) but is no longer of any application). But note that there is no exception under para.(1) to the exclusion from housing benefit even if the person does fall within any of these categories.

Note the amendments made to para.(1)(b) by the Income Support (Prescribed Categories of Person) Regulations 2009 (SI 2009/3152) with effect from December 30, 2009. However, the amendments did not apply to claimants to whom the savings provisions in reg.2(2) of the 2009 Regulations applied. See the 2015/16 edition of this volume for the 2009 Regulations and the notes to those Regulations. It is not known why sub-paras (a) and (b) of para.7 of Sch.1B (incapacity for work) have not also been omitted.

As pointed out at the beginning of this note, however, an eligible child, relevant child, category 1 young person or category 2 young person can claim ESA as the s.6 exclusion does not include ESA. But note, as has also already been pointed out, reg.2 has not been amended to take account of the changes in Wales made by the Social Services and Well-being (Wales) Act 2014. Thus, as things stand at the moment, the exceptions to the s.6 exclusion do not apply in Wales with effect from April 6, 2016.

The Children (Leaving Care) Social Security Benefits (Scotland) Regulations 2004

(SI 2004/747)

Made by the Secretary of State for Work and Pensions under ss.6(4), (6) and (7) of the Children (Leaving Care) Act 2000

[In force April 1, 2004]

REGULATIONS REPRODUCED

Entitlement to Benefits (Scotland)

2.—(1) For the purposes of section 6(2)(c) of the Children (Leaving Care) Act 2000 (exclusion from benefits of persons of a prescribed description)— **2.1311**

(a) a person of the description set out in paragraph (2) is hereby prescribed unless he is a person to whom paragraph (3)(b) applies; and

(b) a person of the description set out in paragraph (3) is hereby prescribed in relation only to entitlement to housing benefit.

(2) The description of person mentioned in paragraph (1)(a) is a person—

(a) who is less than 18 years of age,

(b) to whom a local authority in Scotland is obliged to provide advice, guidance and assistance in terms of section 29(1) of the Children (Scotland) Act 1995 (duty of local authorities to provide after-care to persons who at the time when they cease to be of school age or at any subsequent time were, but are no longer, looked after by a local authority),

(c) who ceased to be looked after on or after 1st April 2004 and since the age of 14 has been looked after and accommodated for a period of, or periods totaling, 13 weeks or more, and

(d) who either—

(i) is not living with his family, or

(ii) is living with his family and is provided with regular financial assistance in terms of that section.

(3) The description of person mentioned in paragraph (1)(b) is a person—

(a) who falls within the description set out in paragraph (2)(a) to (d), and

(b) who also falls within a category of person prescribed in—

(i) provided the person is a lone parent, regulation 13(2)(a) (circumstances in which persons in relevant education may be entitled to income support) of; [1 or]

(ii) [1 . . .]

(iii) paragraph 1, 2, 7, 8, [1 . . .] 11, [1 . . .] [1 . . .] 24 or 25 of Schedule 1B (prescribed categories of person) to,

the Income Support (General) Regulations 1987 ("the Income Support Regulations").

(4) In this regulation—

(a) in calculating the period of, or periods, totaling 13 weeks referred to in paragraph (2)(c) no account shall be taken of any pre-planned series of short-term placements, of 4 weeks or less where the person returns to his family at the end of each such placement,

(b) "accommodated" means provided with accommodation by a local authority pursuant to its duties under section 25 of the Children (Scotland) Act 1995 or [2 by giving effect to a compulsory supervision order and a requirement within that order of the type mentioned in section 83(2)(a) of the Children's Hearings (Scotland) Act 2011,] but does not include circumstances where a person has been placed with his family either under arrangements made under section 26(1)(c) of [2 the Children (Scotland) Act 1995 or by giving effect to a requirement within a compulsory supervision order under the Children's Hearings (Scotland) Act 2011,]

(c) "family" includes any person who has parental responsibility for another person who is less than 18 years of age and any person with whom that other person was living prior to being looked after by a local authority, but does not include a local authority,

(d) "lone parent" has the meaning assigned to it in regulation 2(1) of the Income Support Regulations,

(e) "looked after" has the meaning assigned to it in section 17(6) of the Children (Scotland) Act 1995.

AMENDMENTS

1. Income Support (Prescribed Categories of Person) Regulations 2009 (SI 2009/3152) reg.3(5) and 3(7) (December, 30, 2009). Regulation 3(5) amended reg.2(3)(b) with effect from December 30, 2009 but reg.3(7) provided that this did not apply in the case of a person who was subject to the saving provisions in reg.2(2) of those Regulations. See the 2015/16 edition of this volume for these Regulations and the notes to them.

2. Children's Hearings (Scotland) Act 2011 (Consequential and Transitional Provisions and Savings) Order 2013 (SI 2013/1465) art.17(1) and Sch.1 Pt 2 para.20 (June 24, 2013).

GENERAL NOTE

2.1312 See the note to the Children (Leaving Care) Act 2000 and the Children (Leaving Care) Social Security Benefits Regulations 2001. The effect of these regulations and s.6 of the 2000 Act is to remove entitlement to income support, income-based JSA and housing benefit for most 16- or 17-year-old Scottish care-leavers with effect from April 1, 2004, thus bringing the rules in Scotland broadly into line with those that already existed in England and Wales. Note that the rules only apply to 16- or 17-year-olds who stop being looked after by a Scottish local authority on or after April 1, 2004 (i.e. they do not apply to a 16- or 17-year-old who left Scottish local authority care before that date). Note also that in Scotland the s.6 exclusion does not apply if the care leaver is living with his family (unless he is receiving regular financial assistance from the local authority under s.29(1) of the Children (Scotland) Act 1995). The exceptions to the s.6 exclusion in para.(3)(b) are the same as in reg. 2(1)(b) of the Children (Leaving Care) Social Security Benefits Regulations 2001 (again there is no exception to the exclusion from housing benefit).

Note the amendments made to para.(3)(b) by the Income Support (Prescribed Categories of Person) Regulations 2009 (SI 2009/3152) with effect from December 30, 2009. However, the amendments did not apply to claimants to whom the savings provisions in reg.2(2) of the 2009 Regulations applied. See the 2015/16 edition of this volume for the 2009 Regulations and the notes to those Regulations.

It is not known why para.7 (or at least sub-paras (a) and (b) of para.7) of Sch.1B (incapacity for work) has not also been omitted.

As pointed out at the beginning of the note to the Children (Leaving Care) Social Security Benefits Regulations 2001, however, an eligible child, relevant child, category 1 young person or category 2 young person can claim ESA as the s.6 exclusion does not include ESA.

The Child Support (Maintenance Calculations and Special Cases) Regulations 2000

(SI 2001/155) (AS AMENDED)

Made by the Secretary of State under various provisions of the Child Support Act 1991

REGULATIONS REPRODUCED

PART II

CALCULATION OF CHILD SUPPORT MAINTENANCE

4. Flat rate. 2.1313

GENERAL NOTE

See the note to s.43 of the Child Support Act 1991. 2.1314

Flat rate

4.—(1) The following benefits, pensions and allowances are prescribed for the purposes of paragraph 4(1)(b) of Schedule 1 to the Act— 2.1315

(a) under the Contributions and Benefits Act—
 (i) bereavement allowance under section 39B;
 (ii) category A retirement pension under section 44;
 (iii) category B retirement pension under section 48C;
 (iv) category C and category D retirement pensions under section 78;
 (v) incapacity benefit under section 30A;
 (vi) [1 carer's allowance] under section 70;
 (vii) maternity allowance under section 35 [8 or 35B];
 (viii) severe disablement allowance under section 68;
 (ix) industrial injuries benefit under section 94;
 (x) widowed mother's allowance under section 37;
 (xi) widowed parent's allowance under section 39A; and
 (xii) widow's pension under section 38;
(b) contribution-based jobseeker's allowance under section 1 of the Jobseekers Act;
(c) a social security benefit paid by a country other than the United Kingdom;
(d) a training allowance (other than work-based training for young people or, in Scotland, Skillseekers training); [4 . . .]
(e) a war disablement pension [3 . . .] within the meaning of section 150(2) of the Contributions and Benefits Act or a pension which is analogous to such a pension paid by the government of a country outside Great Britain [3 [4 . . .]

[5 (f) a war widow's pension, war widower's pension or surviving civil partner's war pension;]] [4 [6 . . .]

(g) a payment under a scheme mentioned in section 1(2) of the Armed Forces (Pensions and Compensation) Act 2004 (compensation schemes for armed and reserve forces);] [6 [9 . . .]

(h) contributory employment and support allowance under section 2 of the Welfare Reform Act] [9 ; and

(i) a state pension under Part 1 of the Pensions Act 2014.]

(2) The benefits prescribed for the purposes of paragraph 4(1)(c) of Schedule 1 to the Act are—

(a) income support under section 124 of the Contributions and Benefits Act; and

(b) income-based jobseeker's allowance under section 1 of the Jobseekers Act [2 and

(c) state pension credit] [6[7 . . .]

(d) income-related employment and support allowance under section 4 of the Welfare Reform Act] [7 ; and

(e) universal credit under Part 1 of the Welfare Reform Act 2012, where the award of universal credit is calculated on the basis that the non-resident parent does not have any earned income].

(3) Where the non-resident parent is liable to a pay a flat rate by virtue of paragraph 4(2) of Schedule 1 to the Act—

(a) if he has one partner, then the amount payable by the non-resident parent shall be half the flat rate; and

(b) if he has more than one partner, then the amount payable by the non-resident parent shall be the result of apportioning the flat rate equally among him and his partners.

[7 (4) For the purposes of paragraph (2)(e) and regulation 5(d), "earned income" has the meaning given in regulation 52 of the Universal Credit Regulations 2013 (earned income).]

AMENDMENTS

1. Social Security Amendment (Carer's Allowance) Regulations 2002 (SI 2002/2497) reg.3 and Sch.2 (April 1, 2003).

2. State Pension Credit (Consequential, Transitional and Miscellaneous Provisions) Regulations 2002 (SI 2002/3019) reg.27(3) (October 6, 2003).

3. Child Support (Miscellaneous Amendments) (No.2) Regulations 2003 (SI 2003/2779) reg.6(3) (November 5, 2003).

4. Child Support (Miscellaneous Amendments) Regulations 2005 (SI 2005/785) reg.6(2) (March 16, 2005).

5. Civil Partnership (Pensions, Social Security and Child Support) (Consequential, etc. Provisions) Order 2005 (SI 2005/2877) art.2(4) and Sch.4 para.7(3) (December 5, 2005).

6. Employment and Support Allowance (Consequential Provisions) (No.2) Regulations 2008 (SI 2008/1554) reg.61(3) (October 27, 2008).

7. Universal Credit (Consequential, Supplementary, Incidental and Miscellaneous Provisions) Regulations 2013 (SI 2013/630) reg.43(3) (April 29, 2013).

8. Social Security (Maternity Allowance) (Miscellaneous Amendments) Regulations 2014 (SI 2014/884) reg.3(2) (May 18, 2014).

9. Pensions Act 2014 (Consequential, Supplementary and Incidental Amendments) Order 2015 (SI 2015/1985) art.19 (April 6, 2016).

The Child Support Maintenance Calculation Regulations 2012

(SI 2012/2677) (AS AMENDED)

Made by the Secretary of State under various provisions of the Child Support Act 1991

REGULATIONS REPRODUCED

PART 4

THE MAINTENANCE CALCULATION RULES

GENERAL NOTE

See the note to s.43 of the Child Support Act 1991. 2.1317

Flat rate

44.—(1) The following benefits, pensions or allowances are prescribed for the purposes of paragraph 4(1)(b) of Schedule 1 to the 1991 Act (that is the benefits, pensions or allowances that qualify the non-resident parent for the flat rate)— 2.1318

(a) under the Social Security Contributions and Benefits Act 1992—
  (i) bereavement allowance under section 39B,
  (ii) category A retirement pension under section 44,
  (iii) category B retirement pension under section 48C,
  (iv) category C and category D retirement pension under section 78,
  (v) incapacity benefit under section 30A,
  (vi) carer's allowance under section 70,
  (vii) maternity allowance under section 35 [2 or 35B],
  (viii) severe disablement allowance under section 68,
  (ix) industrial injuries benefit under section 94,
  (x) widowed mother's allowance under section 37,
  (xi) widowed parent's allowance under section 39A, and
  (xii) widow's pension under section 38;
(b) contribution-based jobseeker's allowance under the Jobseekers Act 1995;
(c) a social security benefit paid by a country other than the United Kingdom;
(d) a training allowance (other than work-based training for young people or, in Scotland, Skillseekers training);
(e) a war disablement pension within the meaning of section 150(2) of the Social Security Contributions and Benefits Act 1992 or a pension which is analogous to such a pension paid by the government of a country outside Great Britain;

(f) a war widow's pension, war widower's pension or surviving civil partner's war pension within the meaning of that section;
(g) a payment under a scheme mentioned in section 1(2) of the Armed Forces (Pensions and Compensation) Act 2004 (compensation schemes for armed and reserve forces); [3 . . .]
(h) contributory employment and support allowance [; and
(i) a state pension under Part 1 of the Pensions Act 2014.]

(2) The following benefits are prescribed for the purposes of paragraph 4(1)(c) of Schedule 1 to the 1991 Act (that is the benefits that qualify the non-resident parent for the flat rate if received by the non-resident parent or their partner)—
(a) income support;
(b) income-based jobseeker's allowance;
(c) income-related employment and support allowance; [1. . .]
(d) state pension credit [1 and
(e) universal credit under Part 1 of the Welfare Reform Act 2012, where the award of universal credit is calculated on the basis that the non-resident parent does not have any earned income].

(3) Where the conditions referred to in paragraph 4(2) of Schedule 1 to the 1991 Act are satisfied (that is where an income-related benefit is payable to the non-resident parent or their partner and a maintenance calculation is in force in respect of each of them) the flat rate of maintenance payable is half the flat rate that would otherwise apply.

(4) In paragraph (1)(d) "training allowance" means a payment under section 2 of the Employment and Training Act 1973 or section 2 of the Enterprise and New Towns (Scotland) Act 1990 which is paid to a person for their maintenance while they are undergoing training.

[1 (5) For the purposes of paragraph (2)(e) and regulation 45(1)(c), "earned income" has the meaning given in regulation 52 of the Universal Credit Regulations 2013.]

AMENDMENTS

1. Universal Credit (Consequential, Supplementary, Incidental and Miscellaneous Provisions) Regulations 2013 (SI 2013/630) reg. 44(3) (April 29, 2013).

2. Social Security (Maternity Allowance) (Miscellaneous Amendments) Regulations 2014 (SI 2014/884) reg.3(3) (May 18, 2014).

3. Pensions Act 2014 (Consequential, Supplementary and Incidental Amendments) Order 2015 (SI 2015/1985) art.38 (April 6, 2016).

PART III

OLD STYLE JOBSEEKER'S ALLOWANCE

The Jobseeker's Allowance Regulations 1996

(SI 1996/207) (AS AMENDED)

Made by the Secretary of State for Education and Employment and the Secretary of State for Social Security under various powers in the Jobseekers Act 1995, the Social Security Administration Act 1992 and the Social Security Contributions and Benefits Act 1992

ARRANGEMENT OF REGULATIONS

PART I

GENERAL

PART IA

JOINT-CLAIM COUPLES

PART II

JOBSEEKING

Chapter I

Interpretation

Chapter II

Availability for employment

Chapter III

Actively seeking employment

Chapter IV

Attendance, information and evidence

Chapter V

Jobseeker's agreement

Part III

Other Conditions of Entitlement

Part IV

Young Persons

PART V

SANCTIONS

PART VI

MEMBERSHIP OF THE FAMILY

PART VII

AMOUNTS

Part VIII

Income and Capital

Chapter I

General

Chapter II

Income

Chapter III

Employed earners

Chapter IV

Self-employed earners

Chapter IVA

Participants in the self-employment route

Chapter V

Other income

Chapter VI

Capital

Chapter VII

Liable relative payments

Chapter VIII

Child support

Chapter IX

Students

PART IX

HARDSHIP

PART IXA

HARDSHIP FOR JOINT-CLAIM COUPLES

SCHEDULES

GENERAL NOTE

These regulations are those that continue to apply in relation to old style JSA and the old style Jobseekers Act 1995, i.e. in cases where universal credit has not come into operation and in which the new style Jobseekers Act 1995 and the JSA Regulations 2013 (set out in Pt VI of this volume) have not come into effect. See the introductory note to the JSA Regulations 2013 for a brief summary of the process by which universal credit is gradually being brought into force. 3.2

PART I

GENERAL

[81 Citation, commencement, interpretation and application]

1.—(1) These Regulations may be cited as the Jobseeker's Allowance Regulations 1996. 3.3

(2) These Regulations shall come into force on 7th October 1996.

[81 (2A) These Regulations do not apply to a particular case on any day on which section 33(1)(a) of the 2012 Act (abolition of income-based jobseeker's allowance) is in force and applies in relation to that case.]

(3) In these Regulations—

[79 "the 2012 Act" means the Welfare Reform Act 2012;]

[40 "Abbeyfield Home" means an establishment run by the Abbeyfield Society including all bodies corporate or incorporate which are affiliated to that Society;]

"the Act" means the Jobseekers Act 1995;

[31 "adoption leave" means a period of absence from work on ordinary or additional adoption leave by virtue of section 75A or 75B of the Employment Rights Act 1996;]

[38 "the Armed Forces and Reserve Forces Compensation Scheme" means the scheme established under section 1 (2) of the Armed Forces (Pensions and Compensation) Act 2004;]

[80 "armed forces independence payment" means armed forces independence payment under the Armed Forces and Reserve Forces (Compensation Scheme) Order 2011;]

"attendance allowance" means—
(a) an attendance allowance under section 64 of the Benefits Act;
(b) an increase of disablement pension under section 104 or 105 of the Benefits Act (increases where constant attendance needed and for exceptionally severe disablement);
(c) a payment under regulations made in accordance with section 111 of, and paragraph 7(2) of Schedule 8 to, the Benefits Act (payments for constant attendance in workmen's compensation cases);
(d) an increase in allowance which is payable in respect of constant attendance under section 111 of, and paragraph 4 of Schedule 8 to, the Benefits Act (industrial diseases benefit schemes);
(e) a payment by virtue of article 14, 15, 16, 43 or 44 of the Personal Injuries (Civilians) Scheme 1983 or any analogous payment;
(f) any payment based on the need for attendance which is paid as an addition to a war disablement pension;

[[56] "Back to Work Session" means a seminar or appointment referred to as "a Back to Work Session" arranged by or on behalf of the Secretary of State, the purpose of which is to provide a person who attends with information, support and advice with a view to assisting him to find employment or to improve his chances of finding employment;]

[[57] "basic rate", where it relates to the rate of tax, has the same meaning as in the Income Tax Act 2007 (see section 989 of that Act).]

[[55] "the Benefit Acts" means the Act, the Benefits Act [[79] , Part 1 of the Welfare Reform Act 2007 [[93], Part 4 of the 2012 Act and the Pensions Act 2014]];]

[[59] "benefit week" means—
(a) a period of 7 days ending with a day determined in accordance with paragraph (b) unless, in any particular case or class of case, the Secretary of State arranges otherwise;
(b) the day specified for the purposes of paragraph (a) is the day in column (2) which corresponds to the series of numbers in column (1) which includes the last 2 digits of the person's national insurance number—

(1)	*(2)*
00 to 19	Monday
20 to 39	Tuesday
40 to 59	Wednesday
60 to 79	Thursday
80 to 99	Friday;]

"board and lodging accommodation" means—
(a) accommodation provided to a person or, if he is a member of a family, to him or any other member of his family, for a charge which is inclusive of the provision of that accommodation and at least some cooked or prepared meals which both are cooked or prepared (by a person other than the person to whom the accommodation is provided or a member of his family) and are consumed in that accommodation or associated premises; or

(b) accommodation provided to a person in a hotel, guest house, lodging house or some similar establishment,

except accommodation provided by a close relative of his or of any other member of his family, or other than on a commercial basis;

[[40]"care home" in England and Wales has the meaning assigned to it by section 3 of the Care Standards Act 2000, and in Scotland means a care home service within the meaning assigned to it by [[20] paragraph 2 of schedule 12 to the Public Services Reform (Scotland) Act 2010];]

[[71] "the Caxton Foundation" means the charitable trust of that name established on 28th March 2011 out of funds provided by the Secretary of State for the benefit of certain persons suffering from hepatitis C and other persons eligible for payment in accordance with its provisions;]

[[32] "child tax credit" means a child tax credit under section 8 of the Tax Credits Act 2002;]

[[7]"the Children Order" means the Children (Northern Ireland) Order 1995;]

"Claims and Payments Regulations" means the Social Security (Claims and Payments) Regulations 1987;

"close relative" means, except in Parts II [[4] . . .] and V, a parent, parent-in-law, son, son-in-law, daughter, daughter-in-law, step parent, step-son, step-daughter, brother, sister, [[41]or, if any of the preceding persons is one member of a couple, the other member of that couple];

"college of further education" means a college of further education within the meaning of Part I of the Further and Higher Education (Scotland) Act 1992;

"concessionary payment" means a payment made under arrangements made by the Secretary of State with the consent of the Treasury which is charged either to the National Insurance Fund or to a Departmental Expenditure Vote to which payments of benefit [[55] or tax credits under the benefit Acts or the Tax Credits Act 2002] are charged;

[[75] "the Contributions Regulations" means the Social Security (Contributions) Regulations 2001;]

[[81] "contributory employment and support allowance" means an allowance under Part 1 of the Welfare Reform Act as amended by the provisions of Schedule 3, and Part 1 of Schedule 14, to the 2012 Act that remove references to an income-related allowance, and a contributory allowance under Part 1 of the Welfare Reform Act as that Part has effect apart from those provisions;]

"co-ownership scheme" means a scheme under which a dwelling is let by a housing association and the tenant, or his personal representative, will, under the terms of the tenancy agreement or of the agreement under which he became a member of the association, be entitled, on his ceasing to be a member and subject of any condition stated in either agreement, to a sum calculated by reference directly or indirectly to the value of the dwelling;

[[41] [[83 85] "couple" means—

(a) two people who are married to, or civil partners of, each other and are members of the same household; or

(b) two people who are not married to, or civil partners of, each other but are living together as a married couple;]]

"course of advanced education" means—

(a) a course leading to a postgraduate degree or comparable qualification, a first degree or comparable qualification, a diploma of higher education or a higher national diploma; or

(b) any other course which is of a standard above advanced GNVQ or equivalent, including a course which is of a standard above a general certificate of education (advanced level), [[36] a Scottish national qualification (higher or advanced higher)]

[[16] "course of study" means any course of study, whether or not it is a sandwich course and whether or not a grant is made for attending or undertaking it;]

[[89] "Crown servant" means a person holding an office or employment under the Crown;]

"Crown tenant" means a person who occupies a dwelling under a tenancy or licence where the interest of the landlord belongs to Her Majesty in right of the Crown or to a government department or is held in trust for Her Majesty for the purposes of a government department, except (in the case of an interest belonging to Her Majesty in right of the Crown) where the interest is under the management of the Crown Estate Commissioners;

"date of claim" means the date on which the claimant makes, or is treated as making, a claim for a jobseeker's allowance for the purposes of regulation 6 of the Claims and Payments Regulations;

"disability living allowance" means a disability living allowance under section 71 of the Benefits Act;

[[32] . . .]

"dwelling occupied as the home" means the dwelling together with any garage, garden and outbuildings, normally occupied by the claimant as his home including any premises not so occupied which it is impracticable or unreasonable to sell separately, in particular, in Scotland, any croft land on which the dwelling is situated;

"earnings" has the meaning specified, in the case of an employed earner, in regulation 98, or in the case of a self-employed earner, in regulation 100;

[[39] . . .]

"the Eileen Trust" means the charitable trust of that name established on 29th March 1993 out of funds provided by the Secretary of State for the benefit of persons eligible for payment in accordance with its provisions;

[[53] "the Employment and Support Allowance Regulations" means the Employment and Support Allowance Regulations 2008;]

"employment-related course" means a course the purpose of which is to assist persons to acquire or enhance skills required for employment, for seeking employment or for a particular occupation;

[[69] "the Employment, Skills and Enterprise Scheme" means a scheme under section 17A (schemes for assisting persons to obtain employment: "work for your benefit" schemes etc.) of the Jobseekers Act 1995 known by that name and provided pursuant to arrangements made by the Secretary of State that is designed to assist claimants to obtain employment, including self-employment, and which may include for any individual work-related activity (including work experience or job search);]

[[12] "employment zone" means an area within Great Britain designated for the purposes of section 60 of the Welfare Reform and Pensions Act 1999 and an "employment zone programme" means a programme established for such an area or areas designed to assist claimants for a jobseeker's allowance to obtain sustainable employment;

"employment zone contractor" means a person who is undertaking the provision of facilities in respect of an employment zone programme on behalf of the Secretary of State [52 . . .];]

[61 "enactment" includes an enactment comprised in, or in an instrument made under, an Act of the Scottish Parliament [82 or the National Assembly for Wales];]

[35 . . .]

[24 . . .]

[91 "first year of training" means a period of one year beginning with a person's first day of training.]

[60 "the Flexible New Deal" means the employment programme specified in regulation 75(1)(a)(v);]

"full-time course of advanced education" means a course of advanced education which is [16. . .]—

(a) [16. . .] a full-time course of study which is not funded in whole or in part by [24 the [65 [74 Secretary of State under section 14 of the Education Act 2002] [92 or under section 100 of the Apprenticeships, Skills, Children and Learning Act 2009]] or by the [45 55 Welsh Ministers]] or a full-time course of study [1 . . .] which is not funded in whole or in part by the Secretary of State for Scotland at a college of further education [1 or a full-time course of study which is a course of higher education and is funded in whole or in part by the Secretary of State for Scotland;]

[24(b) a course of study which is funded in whole or in part by the [65 [74 Secretary of State under section 14 of the Education Act 2002] [92 or under section 100 of the Apprenticeships, Skills, Children and Learning Act 2009]] or by the [45 55 Welsh Ministers] if it involves more than 16 guided hours per week for the student in question, according to the number of guided learning hours per week for that student set out—

[65 (i) in the case of a course funded by the [74 Secretary of State [92 . . .]] [92 . . .], in the student's learning agreement signed on behalf of the establishment which is funded by [92 the Secretary of State] for the delivery of that course; or]

(ii) in the case of a course funded by the [45 55 Welsh Ministers], in a document signed on behalf of the establishment which is funded by the National Council for Education and Training for Wales for the delivery of that course; or,]

(c) [16. . .] a course of study (not being higher education) which is funded in whole or in part by the Secretary of State for Scotland at a college of further education if it involves—

(i) more than 16 hours per week of classroom-based or workshop-based programmed learning under the direct guidance of teaching staff according to the number of hours set out in a document signed on behalf of the college; or

(ii) 16 hours or less per week of classroom-based or workshop-based programmed learning under the direct guidance of teaching staff and it involves additional hours using structured learning packages supported by the teaching staff where the combined total of hours exceeds 21 per week, according to the number of hours set out in a document signed on behalf of the college;

"full-time student" means a person, other than a person in receipt of a training allowance [44 or a person who is a qualifying young person or child within the meaning of section 142 of the Benefits Act (child and qualifying young person)], who is—

(a) aged less than 19 and [63 attending or undertaking] a full-time course of advanced education or

(b) aged 19 or over but under pensionable age and—

(i) attending [63 or undertaking] a full-time course of study which is not funded in whole or in part by [24 the [65 [74 Secretary of State under section 14 of the Education Act 2002] [92 or under section 100 of the Apprenticeships, Skills, Children and Learning Act 2009]] or by the [45 55 Welsh Ministers]] or a full-time course of study [1 . . .] which is not funded in whole or in part by the Secretary of State for Scotland at a college of further education [1 or a full-time course of study which is a course of higher education and is funded in whole or in part by the Secretary of State for Scotland;]

[24(ii) [63 attending or undertaking] a course of study which is funded in whole or in part by the [65 [74 Secretary of State under section 14 of the Education Act 2002] [92 or under section 100 of the Apprenticeships, Skills, Children and Learning Act 2009]] or by the [45 55 Welsh Ministers] if it involves more than 16 guided hours per week for the student in question, according to the number of guided learning hours per week for that student set out—

[65 (aa) in the case of a course funded by the [74 Secretary of State [92 . . .]] [92 . . .], in the student's learning agreement signed on behalf of the establishment which is funded by [92 the Secretary of State] for the delivery of that course; or,]

(bb) in the case of a course funded by the National Council for Education and Training for Wales, in a document signed on behalf of the establishment which is funded by the [45 55 Welsh Ministers] for the delivery of that course; or]

(iii) [63 attending or undertaking] a course of study (not being higher education) which is funded in whole or in part by the Secretary of State for Scotland at a college of further education if it involves—

(aa) more than 16 hours per week of classroom-based or workshop-based programmed learning under the direct guidance of teaching staff according to the number of hours set out in a document signed on behalf of the college; or

(bb) 16 hours or less per week of classroom or workshop based programmed learning under the direct guidance of teaching staff and it involves additional hours using structured learning packages supported by the teaching staff where the combined total of hours exceeds 21 per week, according to the number of hours set out in a document signed on behalf of the college;

"the Fund" means moneys made available from time to time by the Secretary of State for the benefit of persons eligible for payment in accordance with the provisions of a scheme established by him on 24th April 1992 or, in Scotland, on 10th April 1992;

[38 "a guaranteed income payment" means a payment made under article 14(1)(b) or article 21(1)(a) of the Armed Forces and Reserve Forces (Compensation Scheme) Order 2005;]

[89 "Her Majesty's forces" has the meaning in the Armed Forces Act 2006;]

[54 "Health Service Act" means the National Health Service Act 2006;

"Health Service (Wales) Act" means the National Health Service (Wales) Act 2006;]

"higher education" means higher education within the meaning of Part II of the Further and Higher Education (Scotland) Act 1992;

"housing association" has the meaning assigned to it by section 1(1) of the Housing Associations Act 1985;

[5"housing benefit expenditure" means expenditure in respect of which housing benefit is payable as specified in [43 regulation 12(1) of the Housing Benefit Regulations 2006] but does not include any such expenditure in respect of which an amount is applicable under regulation 83(f) or 84(1)(g) (housing costs);]

[14 "Immigration and Asylum Act" means the Immigration and Asylum Act 1999;]

"Income Support Regulations" means the Income Support (General) Regulations 1987;

[40 [66 "independent hospital"—

(a) in England, means a hospital as defined by section 275 of the National Health Service Act 2006 that is not a health service hospital as defined by that section;

(b) in Wales, has the meaning assigned to it by section 2 of the Care Standards Act 2000; and

[72 (c) in Scotland, means an independent health care service as defined in section 10F(1)(a) and (b) of the National Health Service (Scotland) Act 1978;]

[54 . . .]

[49 "the Independent Living Fund (2006)" means the Trust of that name established by a deed dated 10th April 2006 and made between the Secretary of State for Work and Pensions of the one part and Margaret Rosemary Cooper, Michael Beresford Boyall and Marie Theresa Martin of the other part;]

[54 . . .]

[23 52 . . .]

"invalid carriage or other vehicle" means a vehicle propelled by a petrol engine or by electric power supplied for use on the road and to be controlled by the occupant;

"jobseeking period" means the period described in regulation 47 [8except where otherwise provided];

"last day of the course" has the meaning prescribed in regulation 130 for the purposes of the definition of "period of study" in this paragraph;

"liable relative" has the meaning prescribed in regulation 117;

[78 "local welfare provision" means occasional financial or other assistance given by a local authority, the Scottish Ministers or the Welsh Ministers, or a person authorised to exercise any function of, or provide a service to, them, to or in respect of individuals for the purpose of—

(a) meeting, or helping to meet, an immediate short term need—

(i) arising out of an exceptional event, or exceptional circumstances; and

(ii) that requires to be met in order to avoid a risk to the well-being of an individual; or

(b) enabling individuals to establish or maintain a settled home, where those individuals have been or, without the assistance, might otherwise be—

(i) in prison, hospital, a residential care establishment or other institution; or

(ii) homeless or otherwise living an unsettled way of life;]

[42"the London Bombings Relief Charitable Fund" means the company limited by guarantee (number 5505072) and registered charity of that name established on 11th July 2005 for the purpose of (amongst other things) relieving sickness, disability or financial need of victims (including families or dependants of victims) of the terrorist attacks carried out in London on 7th July 2005;]

"lone parent" means a person who has no partner and who is responsible for, and a member of the same household as, a child or young person;

"long tenancy" means a tenancy granted for a term of years certain exceeding twenty one years, whether or not the tenancy is, or may become, terminable before the end of that term by notice given by or to the tenant or by re-entry, forfeiture (or, in Scotland, irritancy) or otherwise and includes a lease for a term fixed by law under a grant with a covenant or obligation for perpetual renewal unless it is a lease by subdemise from one which is not a long tenancy;

[47 "long-term patient" means a person who—

(a) is a patient within the meaning of regulation 85(4); and

(b) has been such a patient for a continuous period of more than 52 weeks;]

[51 . . .]

"the Macfarlane (Special Payments) Trust" means the trust of that name, established on 29th January 1990 partly out of funds provided by the Secretary of State for the benefit of certain persons suffering from haemophilia;

"the Macfarlane (Special Payments) (No.2) Trust" means the trust of that name, established on 2nd May 1991 partly out of funds provided by the Secretary of State, for the benefit of certain persons suffering from haemophilia and other beneficiaries;

"the Macfarlane Trust" means the charitable trust, established partly out of funds provided by the Secretary of State to the Haemophilia Society, for the relief of poverty or distress among those suffering from haemophilia;

"making a claim" includes treated as making a claim;

[68 "the Mandatory Work Activity Scheme" means a scheme within section 17A (schemes for assisting persons to obtain employment:

"work for your benefit" schemes etc.) of the Jobseekers Act 1995 known by that name and provided pursuant to arrangements made by the Secretary of State that is designed to provide work or work-related activity for up to 30 hours per week over a period of four consecutive weeks with a view to assisting claimants to improve their prospects of obtaining employment;]

"maternity leave" means a period during which a woman is absent from work because she is pregnant or has given birth to a child, and at the end of which she has a right to return to work either under the terms of her contract of employment or under [50 Part VIII of the Employment Rights Act 1996];

[63 MFET Limited" means the company limited by guarantee (number 7121661) of that name, established for the purpose in particular of making payments in accordance with arrangements made with the Secretary of State to persons who have acquired HIV as a result of treatment by the NHS with blood or blood products;]

"mobility supplement" means any supplement under [55 article 20 of the Naval, Military and Air Forces Etc. (Disablement and Death) Service Pensions Order 2006] including such a supplement by virtue of any other scheme or order or under article 25A of the Personal Injuries (Civilians) Scheme 1983;

"net earnings" means such earnings as are calculated in accordance with regulation 99;

"net profit" means such profit as is calculated in accordance with regulation 101;

[15 "the New Deal options" means the employment programmes specified in regulation 75(1)(a)(ii) and the training scheme specified in regulation 75(1)(b)(ii);]

"non-dependant" has the meaning prescribed in regulation 2;

"non-dependant deduction" means a deduction that is to be made under regulation 83(f) and paragraph 17 of Schedule 2;

[40 . . .]

"occupational pension" means any pension or other periodical payment under an occupational pension scheme but does not include any discretionary payment out of a fund established for relieving hardship in particular cases;

"partner" means where a claimant—

(a) is a member of [41 a couple], the other member of that couple;

(b) is married polygamously to two or more members of his household, any such member;

[19but in so far as this definition applies to a member of a joint-claim couple, it shall only apply to such a member specified in regulation 3E(2)].

"part-time student" means a person who is attending or undertaking a course of study and who is not a full-time student;

[31 73 "paternity leave" means a period of absence from work on [87 . . .] paternity leave by virtue of section 80A or 80B of the Employment Rights Act 1996 [87 . . .];]

"payment" includes a part of a payment;

"pay period" means the period in respect of which a claimant is, or expects to be, normally paid by his employer, being a week, a fortnight, four weeks, a month or other longer or shorter period as the case may be;

"period of study" except in Parts II, IV and V means—

(a) in the case of a course of study for one year or less, the period beginning with the start of the course and ending with the last day of the course;

(b) in the case of a course of study for more than one year, in the first or, as the case may be, any subsequent year of the course, other than the final year of the course, the period beginning with the start of the course or, as the case may be, that year's start and ending with either —

[[17](i) the day before the start of the next year of the course in a case where the student's grant or loan is assessed at a rate appropriate to his studying throughout the year, or, if he does not have a grant or loan, where a loan would have been assessed at such a rate had he had one; or]

(ii) in any other case the day before the start of the normal summer vacation appropriate to his course;

(c) in the final year of a course of study of more than one year, the period beginning with that year's start and ending with the last day of the course;

[[79] "personal independence payment" means personal independence payment under Part 4 of the 2012 Act;]

"policy of life insurance" means any instrument by which the payment of money is assured on death (except death by accident only) or the happening of any contingency dependent on human life, or any instrument evidencing a contract which is subject to payment of premiums for a term dependent on human life;

"polygamous marriage" means any marriage during the subsistence of which a party to it is married to more than one person and the ceremony of marriage took place under the law of a country which permits polygamy;

[[25] . . .]

[[62] "qualifying age for state pension credit" means—

(a) in the case of a woman, pensionable age; or

(b) in the case of a man, the age which is pensionable age in the case of a woman born on the same day as the man;]

[[61] "public authority" includes any person certain of whose functions are functions of a public nature;]

"qualifying person" means a person in respect of whom payment has been made from the Fund [[37], the Eileen Trust [[63] , MFET Limited] [[42], the Skipton Fund [[71], the Caxton Foundation] or the London Bombings Relief Charitable Fund]];

"relative" means close relative, grand-parent, grand-child, uncle, aunt, nephew or niece;

"relevant enactment" has the meaning prescribed in [[2] regulation 78(9)(a)];

"remunerative work" has the meaning prescribed in regulation 51(1);

[[40] . . .]

[[33] . . .]

[[40] . . .]

[[17] [54] "sandwich course" has the meaning prescribed in regulation 2(9) of the Education (Student Support) Regulations 2008, regulation 4(2) of the Education (Student Loans) (Scotland) Regulations 2007, regulation 2(8) of the Education (Student Support) Regulations (Northern Ireland) 2007;]

[94 "Scottish basic rate" means the rate of income tax of that name calculated in accordance with section 6A of the Income Tax Act 2007;

"Scottish taxpayer" has the same meaning as in Chapter 2 of Part 4A of the Scotland Act 1998;]

"self-employed earner" has the meaning it has in Part I of the Benefits Act by virtue of section 2(1)(b) of that Act;

[18 30 36 "self-employment route" means assistance in pursuing self-employed earner's employment whilst participating in—

(a) an employment zone programme; [69 . . .]

(b) a programme provided or other arrangements made pursuant to section 2 of the Employment and Training Act 1973 (functions of the Secretary of State) or section 2 of the Enterprise and New Towns (Scotland) Act 1990 (functions in relation to training for employment etc.)] [69 76 ; or

(c) a scheme prescribed in regulation 3 of the Jobseeker's Allowance (Schemes for Assisting Persons to Obtain Employment) Regulations 2013;]

[61 [84 . . .]

[86 "shared parental leave" means leave under section 75E to 75G of the Employment Rights Act 1996;]

"single claimant" means a claimant who neither has a partner nor is a lone parent;

[37 "the Skipton Fund" means the ex-gratia payment scheme administered by the Skipton Fund Limited, incorporated on 25th March 2004, for the benefit of certain persons suffering from hepatitis C and other persons eligible for payment in accordance with the scheme's provisions;]

[11 "sports award" means an award made by one of the Sports Councils named in section 23(2) of the National Lottery etc. Act 1993 out of sums allocated to it for distribution under that section;]

[50 57 . . .]

[13 "subsistence allowance" means an allowance which an employment zone contractor has agreed to pay to a person who is participating in an employment zone programme;]

"terminal date" in respect of a claimant means the terminal date in his case for the purposes of regulation 7 of the Child Benefit (General) Regulations 1976;

"training allowance" means an allowance (whether by way of periodical grants or otherwise) payable—

(a) out of public funds by a Government department or by or on behalf of the Secretary of State [52 . . .], [58 Skills Development Scotland,] Scottish Enterprise or Highlands and Islands Enterprise [21 , [74 . . . [65 . . .] [92 . . .] or the [55 Welsh Ministers]]; and

(b) to a person for his maintenance or in respect of a member of his family; and

(c) for the period, or part of the period, during which he is following a course of training or instruction provided by, or in pursuance of arrangements made with, that department or approved by that department in relation to him or so provided or approved by or on behalf of the Secretary of State [52 . . .], [58 Skills Development Scotland,] Scottish Enterprise or Highlands and Islands Enterprise [22 or the [55 Welsh Ministers]],

but it does not include an allowance paid by any Government department to or in respect of a person by reason of the fact that he is following a course of full-time education, other than under arrangements made under section 2 of the Employment and Training Act 1973 [3 or section 2 of the Enterprise and New Towns (Scotland) Act 1990,] or is training as a teacher;

[90 "traineeship" means a course which—

(a) is funded (in whole or in part) by, or under arrangements made by, the—

(i) Secretary of State under section 14 of the Education Act 2002, or

(ii) [92 . . .]

(b) lasts no more than 6 months;

(c) includes training to help prepare the participant for work and a work experience placement; and

(d) is open to persons who on the first day of the course have attained the age of 16 but not 25;]

[81 "universal credit" means universal credit under Part 1 of the 2012 Act;]

[79 "the Universal Credit etc. Claims and Payments Regulations" means the Universal Credit, Personal Independence Payment, Jobseeker's Allowance and Employment and Support Allowance (Claims and Payments) Regulations 2013;]

"voluntary organisation" means a body, other than a public or local authority, the activities of which are carried on otherwise than for profit;

[55 "war disablement pension" means any retired pay or pension or allowance payable in respect of disablement under an instrument specified in section 639(2) of the Income Tax (Earnings and Pensions) Act 2003;

"war pension" means a war disablement pension, a war widow's pension or a war widower's pension;

"war widow's pension" means any pension or allowance payable to a woman as a widow under an instrument specified in section 639(2) of the Income Tax (Earnings and Pensions) Act 2003 in respect of the death or disablement of any person;

"war widower's pension" means any pension or allowance payable to a man as a widower or to a surviving civil partner under an instrument specified in section 639(2) of the Income Tax (Earnings and Pensions) Act 2003 in respect of the death or disablement of any person;]

"water charges" means—

(a) as respects England and Wales, any water and sewerage charges under Chapter 1 of Part V of the Water Industry Act 1991;

(b) as respects Scotland, any water and sewerage charges under Schedule 11 to the Local Government Finance Act 1992;

in so far as such charges are in respect of the dwelling which a person occupies as his home;

"week" in [6 the definitions of "full-time course of advanced education" and of "full-time student" and] [3 Parts III, VI, VII, VIII, IX, X, XI, XII and XIII] means a period of 7 days;

[53 "the Welfare Reform Act" means the Welfare Reform Act 2007;]

[9"welfare to work beneficiary" means a person—

(a) to whom regulation 13A(1) of the Social Security (Incapacity for Work) (General) Regulations 1995 applies; and

(b) who again becomes incapable of work for the purposes of Part XIIA of the Contributions and Benefits Act 1992;]

[67 "Work Experience" means the employment programme specified in regulation 75(1)(a)(vi);]

[32 "working tax credit" means a working tax credit under section 10 of the Tax Credits Act 2002;]

[32 . . .]

"year of assessment" has the meaning prescribed in section 832(1) of the Income and Corporation Taxes Act 1988;

"young person" except in Part IV has the meaning prescribed in regulation 76.

[16 (3A) For the purposes of the definition of "full-time student" in paragraph (3) but subject to paragraph (3D), a person shall be regarded as attending or, as the case may be, undertaking a course of study or as being on a sandwich course—

(a) subject to paragraph (3B), in the case of a person attending or undertaking a part of a modular course which would be a full-time course of study, for a period beginning on the day on which that part of the course starts and ending—

(i) on the last day on which he is registered with the educational establishment as attending or undertaking that part as a full-time course of study; or

(ii) on such earlier date (if any) as he finally abandons the course or is dismissed from it;

(b) in any other case, throughout the period beginning on the date on which he starts attending or undertaking the course and ending on the last day of the course or on such earlier date (if any) as he finally abandons it or is dismissed from it.

(3B) For the purpose of sub-paragraph (a) of paragraph (3A), the period referred to in that sub-paragraph shall include—

(a) where a person has failed examinations or has failed to successfully complete a module relating to a period when he was attending or undertaking a part of the course as a full-time course of study, any period in respect of which he attends or undertakes the course for the purpose of retaking those examinations or that module;

(b) any period of vacation within the period specified in that paragraph or immediately following that period except where the person has registered with the educational establishment to attend or undertake the final module in the course and the vacation immediately follows the last day on which he is required to attend or undertake the course.

(3C) In paragraph (3A), "modular course" means a course of study which consists of two or more modules, the successful completion of a specified number of which is required before a person is considered by the educational establishment to have completed the course.

(3D) A full-time student shall not be regarded as undertaking a full-time course of advanced education or a full-time course of study for the period specified in paragraph (3E) if—

(a) at any time during an academic year, with the consent of the relevant educational establishment, he ceases to attend or undertake a course because he is—

(i) engaged in caring for another person; or

(ii) ill;

(b) he has subsequently ceased to be engaged in caring for that person or, as the case may be, he has subsequently recovered from that illness; and

(c) he is not eligible for a grant or a student loan (as defined in regulation 130) in respect of the period specified in paragraph (3E).

(3E) The period specified for the purposes of paragraph (3D) is the period, [[29], not exceeding one year,] beginning on the day on which he ceased to be engaged in caring for that other person or, as the case may be, the day on which he recovered from that illness and ending on the day before—

(a) the day on which he resumes attending or undertaking the course; or

[[29](b) the day from which the relevant educational establishment has agreed that he may resume attending or undertaking the course,

whichever shall first occur.]

[[25] (3F) For the purposes of these Regulations, where a person's principal place of residence is a [[40]care home, an Abbeyfield Home or an independent hospital and he is temporarily absent from that home or hospital, he shall be regarded as continuing to reside in that home or hospital]—

(a) where he is absent because he is a patient, for the first [[34] 52] weeks of any such period of absence and for this purpose—

(i) "patient" has the meaning it has in Schedule 5 by virtue of regulation 85; and

(ii) periods of absence separated by not more than 28 days shall be treated as a single period of absence equal in duration to all those periods; and

(b) for the first three weeks of any other period of absence.]

[[84] (3G) References in these Regulations to a claimant participating as a service user are to—

(a) a person who is being consulted by or on behalf of—

(i) a body which has a statutory duty to provide services in the field of health, social care or social housing; or

(ii) a body which conducts research or undertakes monitoring for the purpose of planning or improving such services, in their capacity as a user, potential user, carer of a user or person otherwise affected by the provision of those services;

[[88] (ab) a person who is being consulted by or on behalf of—

(i) the Secretary of State in relation to any of the Secretary of State's functions in the field of social security or child support or under section 2 of the Employment and Training Act 1973; or

(ii) a body which conducts research or undertakes monitoring for the purpose of planning or improving such functions,

in their capacity as a person affected or potentially affected by the exercise of those functions or the carer of such a person;] or

(b) the carer of a person consulted under [[88] sub-paragraphs (a) or (ab)].]

(4) In these Regulations, unless the context otherwise requires, a reference—

(a) to a numbered section is to the section of the Act bearing that number;

(b) to a numbered Part is to the Part of these Regulations bearing that number;

(c) to a numbered regulation or Schedule is to the regulation in or Schedule to these Regulations bearing that number;

(d) in a regulation or Schedule to a numbered paragraph is to the paragraph in that regulation or Schedule bearing that number;

(e) in a paragraph to a lettered or numbered sub-paragraph is to the sub-paragraph in that paragraph bearing that letter or number.

(5) Unless the context requires otherwise, any reference to the claimant's family or, as the case may be, to a member of his family, shall be construed for the purposes of these Regulations as if it included in relation to a polygamous marriage a reference to any partner and to any child or young person who is treated as the responsibility of the claimant or his partner, where that child or young person is a member of the claimant's household.

[[70] (6) In such cases and subject to such conditions or requirements as the Secretary of State may specify by means of a direction, any requirement imposed by or under these Regulations for a signature may be satisfied by means of an electronic signature (within the meaning given in section 7(2) of the Electronic Communications Act 2000.)]

AMENDMENTS

1. Jobseeker's Allowance (Amendment) Regulations 1996 (SI 1996/1516) reg.2 (October 7, 1996).

2. Jobseeker's Allowance (Amendment) Regulations 1996 (SI 1996/1516) reg.20 and Sch. (October 7, 1996).

3. Jobseeker's Allowance and Income Support (General) (Amendment) Regulations 1996 (SI 1996/1517) reg.2 (October 7, 1996).

4. Social Security and Child Support (Jobseeker's Allowance) (Miscellaneous Amendments) Regulations 1996 (SI 1996/2538) reg.2(2) (October 28, 1996).

5. Income-related Benefits and Jobseeker's Allowance (Miscellaneous Amendments) Regulations 1997 (SI 1997/65) reg.4(2) (April 7, 1997).

6. Social Security (Miscellaneous Amendments) Regulations 1997 (SI 1997/454) reg.2(2) (April 7, 1997).

7. Social Security (Miscellaneous Amendments) Regulations 1998 (SI 1998/563) reg.5(1) and (2)(f) (April 6, 1998).

8. Social Security Amendment (New Deal) Regulations 1998 (SI 1998/1274) reg.2 (June 1, 1998).

9. Social Security (Welfare to Work) Regulations 1998 (SI 1998/2231) reg.14(2) (October 5, 1998).

10. Social Security and Child Support (Tax Credits) Consequential Amendments Regulations 1999 (SI 1999/2566) reg.2(3) and Sch.2 Pt III (October 5, 1999).

11. Social Security Amendment (Sports Award) Regulations 1999 (SI 1999/2165) reg.2(1) and (2)(e) (August 23, 1999).

12. Social Security Amendment (Employment Zones) Regulations 2000 (SI 2000/724) reg.2(1) (April 3, 2000).

13. Social Security Amendment (Employment Zones) Regulations 2000 (SI 2000/724) reg.2(1) (April 3, 2000).

14. Social Security (Immigration and Asylum) Consequential Amendments Regulations 2000 (SI 2000/636) reg.4(2) (April 3, 2000).

15. Jobseeker's Allowance (Amendment) Regulations 2000 reg.2(2) (March 6, 2000).

16. Social Security Amendment (Students) Regulations 2000 (SI 2000/1981) reg.6(2) (July 31, 2000).

17. Social Security Amendment (Students and Income-related Benefits) Regulations 2000 (SI 2000/1922) reg.3(2) (August 28, 2000, or if the student's period of study begins between August 1 and 27, 2000, the first day of the period).

18. Social Security Amendment (Employment Zones) (No.2) Regulations 2000 (SI 2000/2910) reg.2(3) (November 27, 2000).

19. Jobseeker's Allowance (Joint Claims) Regulations 2000 (SI 2000/1978) reg.2(5) and Sch.2 para.(1) (March 19, 2001).

20. Social Security (Miscellaneous Amendments) (No.2) Regulations 2001 (SI 2001/652) reg.2(a) (March 26, 2001).

21. Social Security (Miscellaneous Amendments) (No.2) Regulations 2001 (SI 2001/652) reg.2(b)(i) (March 26, 2001).

22. Social Security (Miscellaneous Amendments) (No.2) Regulations 2001 (SI 2001/652) reg.2(b)(ii) (March 26, 2001).

23. Social Security Amendment (New Deal) Regulations 2001 (SI 2001/1029) reg.2 (April 9, 2001).

24. Jobseeker's Allowance (Amendment) Regulations 2001 (SI 2001/1434) reg.2(2)(a) (April 1, 2001).

25. Social Security Amendment (Residential Care and Nursing Homes) Regulations 2001 (SI 2001/3767) reg.2 and Sch. Pt II para.1 (April 8, 2002).

26. Social Security (Miscellaneous Amendments) Regulations 2002 (SI 2002/841) reg.3 (April 8, 2002).

27. Income Support (General) and Jobseeker's Allowance Amendment Regulations 2002 (SI 2002/1411) reg.2 (June 17, 2002).

28. Social Security Amendment (Students and Income-related Benefits) Regulations 2002 (SI 2002/1589) reg.2(3) (August 1, 2002).

29. Social Security Amendment (Intercalating Students) Regulations 2002 (SI 2002/1763) reg.2 (August 1, 2002).

30. Social Security Amendment (Employment Programme) Regulations 2002 (SI 2002/2314) reg.2(2) (October 14, 2002).

31. Social Security (Paternity and Adoption) Amendment Regulations 2002 (SI 2002/2689) reg.3 (December 8, 2002).

32. Income-related Benefits and Jobseeker's Allowance (Working Tax Credit and Child Tax Credit) (Amendment) Regulations 2002 (SI 2002/2402) reg.3 and Sch.2 para.1 (April 6, 2003).

33. Social Security (Removal of Residential Allowance and Miscellaneous Amendments) Regulations 2003 (SI 2003/1121) reg.4 and Sch.2 para.1 (October 6, 2003).

34. Social Security (Hospital In-Patients and Miscellaneous Amendments) Regulations 2003 (SI 2003/1195) reg.6 (May 21, 2003).

35. Social Security (Miscellaneous Amendments) Regulations 2004 (SI 2004/565) reg.5(2) (April 1, 2004).

36. Social Security (Income-Related Benefits Self-Employment Route Amendment) Regulations 2004 (SI 2004/963) reg.2 (May 4, 2004).

37. Social Security (Miscellaneous Amendments) (No.2) Regulations 2004 (SI 2004/1141) reg.2(a) (May 12, 2004).

38. Social Security (Miscellaneous Amendments) Regulations 2005 (SI 2005/574) reg.2 (April 4, 2005).

39. Social Security (Miscellaneous Amendments) Regulations 2005 (SI 2005/574) reg.6 (April 4, 2005).

40. Social Security (Care Homes and Independent Hospitals) Regulations 2005 (SI 2005/2687) reg.3 and Sch.2 para.2 (October 24, 2005).

41. Civil Partnership (Pensions, Social Security and Child Support) (Consequential, etc. Provisions) Order 2005 (SI 2005/2877) art.2(3) and Sch.3 para.26(2) (December 5, 2005).

42. Income-related Benefits (Amendment) (No.2) Regulations 2005 reg.5 (December 12, 2005).

43. Housing Benefit and Council Tax Benefit (Consequential Provisions) Regulations 2006 (SI 2006/217) reg.5 and Sch.3 para.8 (March 6, 2006).

44. Social Security (Young Persons) Amendment Regulations 2006 (SI 2006/718) reg.3(2) (April 10, 2006).

45. National Council for Education and Training for Wales (Transfer of Functions to the National Assembly for Wales and Abolition) Order 2005 art.9(2) and Sch.2 para.8 (April 1, 2006).

46. Social Security (Miscellaneous Amendments) (No.4) Regulations 2006 (SI 2006/2378) reg.13(2) (October 2, 2006).

47. Social Security (Miscellaneous Amendments) Regulations 2007 (SI 2007/719) reg.3(2) (April 9, 2007).

48. Social Security (Miscellaneous Amendments) (No.3) Regulations 2007 (SI 2007/1749) reg.3(2) (July 17, 2007).

49. Independent Living Fund (2006) Order 2007 (SI 2007/2538) reg.4 (October 1, 2007).

50. Social Security (Miscellaneous Amendments) (No.5) Regulations 2007 (SI 2007/2618) reg.8(2) (October 1, 2007).

51. Social Security (Miscellaneous Amendments) (No.5) Regulations 2007 (SI 2007/2618) reg.2 and Sch.1 (October 1, 2007).

52. Social Security (Miscellaneous Amendments) Regulations 2008 (SI 2008/698) reg.4(2) (April 14, 2008).

53. Employment and Support Allowance (Consequential Provisions) (No.2) Regulations 2008 (SI 2008/1554) reg.3(1) and (2) (October 27, 2008).

54. Social Security (Miscellaneous Amendments) (No.6) Regulations 2008 (SI 2008/2767) reg.4(1) and (2) (November 17, 2008).

55. Social Security (Miscellaneous Amendments) (No.7) Regulations 2008 (SI 2008/3157) reg.3(1) and (2) (January 5, 2009).

56. Social Security (Flexible New Deal) Regulations 2009 (SI 2009/480) reg.2(2)(a) (April 6, 2009).

57. Social Security (Miscellaneous Amendments) Regulations 2009 (SI 2009/583) reg.4(1) and (2) (April 6, 2009).

58. Social Security (Miscellaneous Amendments) Regulations 2009 (SI 2009/583) reg.4(1) and (3) (April 6, 2009).

59. Social Security (Claims and Payments) Amendment Regulations 2009 (SI 2009/604) reg.3 (April 6, 2009).

60. Social Security (Flexible New Deal) Regulations 2009 (SI 2009/480) reg.2(2)(b) (October 5, 2009).

61. Social Security (Miscellaneous Amendments) (No.4) Regulations 2009 (SI 2009/2655) reg.4(1) and (2) (October 26, 2009).

62. Social Security (Equalisation of State Pension Age) Regulations 2009 (SI 2009/1488) reg.10 (April 6, 2010). That the definition is not in alphabetical order is required by the amending legislation and is not a publishing error.

63. Social Security (Miscellaneous Amendments) (No.2) Regulations 2010 (SI 2010/641) reg.4 (April 6, 2010).

64. Housing and Regeneration Act 2008 (Consequential Provisions) (No.2) Order 2010 art.4 and Sch.1 para.15 (April 1, 2010).

65. Apprenticeships, Skills, Children and Learning Act 2009 (Consequential Amendments to Subordinate Legislation) (England) Order 2010 (SI 2010/1941) reg.5(1) and (2) (September 1, 2010).

66. Health and Social Care Act 2008 (Miscellaneous Consequential Amendments) Order 2010 (SI 2010/1881) regs 2 and 8 (October 1, 2010).

67. Jobseeker's Allowance (Work Experience) (Amendment) Regulations 2011 (SI 2011/798) reg.2(2) (April 5, 2011).

68. Jobseeker's Allowance (Mandatory Work Activity Scheme) Regulations 2011 (SI 2011/688) reg.11 (April 25, 2011).

69. Jobseeker's Allowance (Employment, Skills and Enterprise Scheme) Regulations 2011 (SI 2011/917) reg.11 (May 20, 2011).

70. Social Security (Electronic Communications) Order 2011 (SI 2011/1498) art.3(2) (June 20, 2011)

71. Social Security (Miscellaneous Amendments) (No. 3) Regulations 2011 (SI 2011/2425) reg.10(1) and (2) (October 31, 2011).

72. Public Services Reform (Scotland) Act 2010 (Consequential Modifications of Enactments) Order 2011 (SI 2011/2581) art.2 and Sch.2 para.20 (October 28, 2011).

73. Social Security (Miscellaneous Amendments) Regulations 2012 (SI 2012/757) reg.4(1) and (2) (April 1, 2012).

74. Young People's Learning Agency Abolition (Consequential Amendments to Subordinate Legislation) (England) Order 2012 (SI 2012/956) reg.5(2) (May 1, 2012).

75. Jobseeker's Allowance (Members of the Reserve Forces) Regulations 2012 (2012/1616) reg.2(1) and (2) (July 30, 2012).

76. Jobseeker's Allowance (Schemes for Assisting Persons to Obtain Employment) Regulations 2013 (SI 2013/276) reg.8(1)(c) and (2) (February 12, 2013). (The former para.(c) in the definition of "self-employment route"—see p.882 of Vol II of the 2012/13 edition—was inserted by SI 2011/917 (see point 69 above). Section 1(14) of the Jobseekers (Back to Work Schemes) Act 2013 provides that SI 2011/917 (which was held to be ultra vires by the Court of Appeal in *R. (Reilly and Wilson) v Secretary of State for Work and Pensions* [2013] EWCA Civ 66) is to be treated as having been revoked by SI 2013/276 upon the coming into force of the latter instrument).

77. National Treatment Agency (Abolition) and the Health and Social Care Act 2012 (Consequential, Transitional and Saving Provisions) Order 2013 (SI 2013/235) art.9 and Sch.1 para.27(1) and (2) (April 1, 2013).

78. Social Security (Miscellaneous Amendments) Regulations 2013 (SI 2013/443) reg.4(1) and (2) (April 2, 2013).

79. Personal Independence Payment (Supplementary Provisions and Consequential Amendments) Regulations 2013 (SI 2013/388) reg.8 and Sch. para.16(1) and (2) (April 8, 2013).

80. Armed Forces and Reserve Forces Compensation Scheme (Consequential Provisions: Subordinate Legislation) Order 2013 (SI 2013/591) art.7 and Sch. para.10(1) and (2) (April 8, 2013).

81. Universal Credit (Consequential, Supplementary, Incidental and Miscellaneous Provisions) Regulations 2013 (SI 2013/630) reg.30(1) and (2) (April 29, 2013).

82. Social Security (Miscellaneous Amendments) (No.3) Regulations 2013 (SI 2013/2536) reg.6(1) and (2) (October 29, 2013).

83. Marriage (Same Sex Couples) Act 2013 (Consequential Provisions) Order 2014 (SI 2014/107) reg.2 and Sch.1 para.16 (March 13, 2014). The amendment extends to England and Wales only (see SI 2014/107 art.1(4)).

84. Social Security (Miscellaneous Amendments) Regulations 2014, (SI 2014/591) reg.4(1) and (2) (April 28, 2014).

85. Marriage and Civil Partnership (Scotland) Act 2014 and Civil Partnership Act 2004 (Consequential Provisions and Modifications) Order 2014 (SI 2014/3229) art.29 and Sch.6 para.11 (December 16, 2014). The amendment relates only to Scotland (see SI 2014/3229 art.3(4)) but is in the same terms as the amendments made in relation to England and Wales by SI 2014/107 (see point 83 above).

86. Shared Parental Leave and Statutory Shared Parental Pay (Consequential Amendments to Subordinate Legislation) Order 2014 (SI 2014/3255) art.7(1) and (2)(c) (December 31, 2014).

87. Shared Parental Leave and Statutory Shared Parental Pay (Consequential Amendments to Subordinate Legislation) Order 2014 (SI 2014/3255) art.7(1) and (2)(a) and (b) (April 5, 2015). The amendment is subject to the transitional provision in art.35 of SI 2014/3255, which is reproduced below.

88. Social Security (Miscellaneous Amendments) Regulations 2015 (SI 2015/67) reg.2(1)(b) and (2) (February 23, 2015).

89. Jobseeker's Allowance (Habitual Residence) Amendment Regulations 2014 (SI 2014/2735) reg.2 (November 9, 2014).

90. Social Security (Traineeships and Qualifying Young Persons) Amendment Regulations 2015 (SI 2015/336) reg.2(1) and (2) (March 27, 2015).

91. Social Security (Members of the Reserve Forces) (Amendment) Regulations 2015 (SI 2015/389) reg.3(1) and (2) (April 6, 2015).

92. Deregulation Act 2015 (Consequential Amendments) Order 2015 (SI 2015/971) art.2 and Sch.3 para.4(1) and (2) (May 26, 2015).

93. Pensions Act 2014 (Consequential, Supplementary and Incidental Amendments) Order 2015 (SI 2015/1985) art.16(1) and (2) (April 6, 2016).

94. Social Security (Scottish Rate of Income Tax etc.) (Amendment) Regulations 2016 (SI 2016/233) reg.3(1) and (2) (April 6, 2016).

DEFINITIONS

"Benefits Act"—see Jobseekers Act 1995 s.35(1).
"child"—*ibid.*
"claimant"—*ibid.*
"family"—*ibid.*
"occupational pension scheme"—*ibid.*

GENERAL NOTE

See the notes to reg.2(1) of the Income Support Regulations for points on some of these definitions, namely, "board and lodging accommodation", "close relative", "couple", "dwelling occupied as the home", "occupational pension", "self-employed earner", "self-employment route", "the Skipton fund", "training allowance" and "welfare to work beneficiary". Otherwise, the significance of particular definitions is dealt with in the notes to the regulations in which they occur. 3.4

Note also the additional definitions in reg.3 and the definitions in reg.4 for the purposes of Pt II (jobseeking), Pt IV (young persons), Pt V (sanctions) and various sections of the Jobseekers Act.

On the definitions relating to students and on paras (3A)–(3E), see the note to reg.130.

Definition of non-dependant

2.—(1) In these Regulations, "non-dependant" means any person, except a person to whom paragraph (2), (3) or (4) applies, who normally resides with the claimant or with whom the claimant normally resides. 3.5

(2) This paragraph applies to—

(a) any member of the claimant's family;

(b) a child or young person who is living with the claimant but who is not a member of his household by virtue of regulation 78 (circumstances in which a person is to be treated as being or not being a member of the household);

(c) a person who lives with the claimant in order to care for him or for the claimant's partner and who is engaged for that purpose by a charitable or voluntary organisation (other than a public or local authority) which makes a charge to the claimant or the claimant's partner for the care provided by that person;

(d) the partner of a person to whom sub-paragraph (c) applies.

(3) This paragraph applies to a person, other than a close relative of the claimant or the claimant's partner,—

(a) who is liable to make payments on a commercial basis to the claimant or the claimant's partner in respect of his occupation of the claimant's dwelling;

(b) to whom the claimant or the claimant's partner is liable to make payments on a commercial basis in respect of his occupation of that person's dwelling;

(c) who is a member of the household of a person to whom subparagraph (a) or (b) applies.

(4) Subject to paragraph (5), this paragraph applies to—

(a) a person who jointly occupies the claimant's dwelling and who is either—

(i) a co-owner of that dwelling with the claimant or the claimant's partner (whether or not there are other co-owners); or

(ii) jointly liable with the claimant or the claimant's partner to make payments to a landlord in respect of his occupation of that dwelling; or

(b) a partner of a person to whom sub-paragraph (a) applies.

(5) Where a person is a close relative of the claimant or the claimant's partner, paragraph (4) shall apply to him only if the claimant's, or the claimant's partner's, co-ownership, or joint liability to make payments to a landlord in respect of his occupation, of the dwelling arose either before 11th April 1988, or, if later, on or before the date upon which the claimant or the claimant's partner first occupied the dwelling in question.

(6) For the purposes of this regulation a person resides with another only if they share any accommodation except a bathroom, a lavatory or a communal area but not if each person is separately liable to make payments in respect of his occupation of the dwelling to the landlord.

(7) In this regulation "communal area" means any area (other than rooms) of common access (including halls and passageways) and rooms of common use in sheltered accommodation.

DEFINITIONS

"child"—see Jobseekers Act 1995 s.35(1).
"claimant"—*ibid.*
"close relative"—see reg.1(3).
"family"—see s.35(1).
"partner"—see reg.1(3).
"voluntary organisation"—*ibid.*

GENERAL NOTE

3.6 See the notes to reg.3 of the Income Support Regulations.

[1Disapplication of section 1(1A) of the Administration Act

3.7 **2A.**—Section 1(1A) of the Administration Act (requirement to state national insurance number) shall not apply—

(a) [2 . . .]

(b) to any claim for jobseeker's allowance made or treated as made before 5th October 1998].

[3 (c) to a person who—

(i) is a person in respect of whom a claim for jobseeker's allowance is made;

(ii) is subject to immigration control within the meaning of section 115(9)(a) of the Immigration and Asylum Act;

(iii) is not entitled to any jobseeker's allowance for the purposes of section 1 of the Act; and
(iv) has not previously been allocated a national insurance number.]

AMENDMENTS

1. Social Security (National Insurance Number Information: Exemption) Regulations 1997 (SI 1997/2676) reg.12 (December 1, 1997).
2. Social Security (Working Tax Credit and Child Tax Credit) (Consequential Amendments) Regulations 2003 (SI 2003/455) reg.3 and Sch.2 para.1 (April 6, 2004, except in "transitional cases" and see further the note to reg.83 and to reg.17 of the Income Support Regulations).
3. Social Security (National Insurance Number Information: Exemption) Regulations 2009 (SI 2009/471) reg.7 (April 6, 2009).

DEFINITIONS

"child"—see Jobseekers Act 1995 s.35(1).
"young person"—see reg.76.

GENERAL NOTE

See the notes to s.1(1A)–(1C) of the Administration Act and reg.2A of the Income Support Regulations. Note that in the case of jobseeker's allowance, unlike income support, the requirement to have, or apply for, a national insurance number as a condition of entitlement to benefit does not apply to any claim made or treated as made before October 5, 1998 (para.(b)). 3.8

Meanings of certain expressions used in the Jobseekers Act 1995

3.—For the purposes of the Act and of these Regulations— 3.9
"employed earner" has the meaning it has in Part I of the Benefits Act by virtue of section 2(1)(a) of that Act;
[[1]"employment", except as provided in regulations 4 and 75, includes any trade, business, profession, office or vocation;]
"pensionable age" has the meaning it has in Parts I to VI of the Benefits Act by virtue of section 122(1) of that Act.

AMENDMENT

1. Social Security Amendment (New Deal) Regulations 1997 (SI 1997/2863) reg.2 (January 5, 1998).

DEFINITION

"the Benefits Act"—see Jobseekers Act 1995 s.35(1).

GENERAL NOTE

"*Employed earner*". See the note to reg.2(1) of the Income Support Regulations. 3.10
"*Employment*". The 1998 amendments to this definition and to the definition of "employment" in reg.4 were made as a consequence of the introduction of the "New Deal" for 18–24- year olds. The amendments removed Pt V of these Regulations and s.19 of the Jobseekers Act 1995 from the list of provisions in reg.4 in which employment only refers to work as an employee and does not include self-employment (unless otherwise stated); employment for the purposes of Pt V and s.19 was then defined in reg.75. The intention behind the amendments was that the fixed term sanctions of two or four weeks would apply to all people taking part in the New Deal, regardless of whether they were employed or in receipt of an allowance. The New Deal programmes no longer exist.

The definition of "employment" in reg.75 was further amended (and other amendments were made to reg.75) as a result of the new JSA sanctions regime that came into force in October 2012.

Note also the definition of employment in s.7(8) of the Act for the purposes of regs 18–22.

"*Pensionable age*". Pensionable age is currently 65 for men and 60 for women born before April 6, 1950. Women born between April 6, 1950 and November 6, 1953 will reach pensionable age at a date between their sixtieth and sixty-fifth birthday (the exact days are set out in Pt I of Sch.4 to the Pensions Act 1995). In addition, the increase in state pension age for both men and women will start to rise from 65 in December 2018 to reach 66 by October 2020; it will rise to 67 between 2026 and 2028.

[1 PART IA

JOINT-CLAIM COUPLES

Prescribed description of a joint-claim couple for the purposes of section 1(4)

3.11 **3A.**—(1) For the purposes of section 1(4), a joint-claim couple shall include any joint-claim couple within the meaning given in section 1(4) of the Act where at least one member [2 is aged 18 or over and] was born after [3 28th October [41947]], unless a member of the couple is treated as responsible for a child or young person under regulation 77(3), or the couple has care of a child or young person in one or more of the circumstances mentioned in regulation 78(4), or a child or young person is living with either member of the couple in the circumstances mentioned in regulation 78(8).

(2) In a case where a person would (but for these Regulations) be a member of more than one joint-claim couple, a joint-claim couple means the couple of which he is a member which that person nominates (or in default of such nomination, which the Secretary of State nominates), to the exclusion of any other couple of which he is a member.]

AMENDMENTS

1. Jobseeker's Allowance (Joint Claims) Regulations 2000 (SI 2000/1978) reg.2(2) (March 19, 2001).

2. Social Security Amendment (Joint Claims) Regulations 2001 (SI 2001/518) reg.2(2) (March 19, 2001).

3. Jobseeker's Allowance (Joint Claims) Amendment Regulations 2002 (SI 2002/1701) reg.2(a) (October 28, 2002).

4. Jobseeker's Allowance (Joint Claims) Amendment Regulations 2008 (SI 2008/13) reg.2(2) (February 25, 2008).

GENERAL NOTE

3.12 The standard JSA picture had been one of a claimant claiming in his own right a contribution-based jobseeker's allowance and of a claimant claiming income-based jobseeker's allowance for himself, and any partner and/or children, with consequent aggregation of needs and resources. From March 19, 2001, a new dimension was added: the requirement that a "joint-claim couple" make a joint claim for jobseeker's allowance (what in reality is a joint-claim income-based jobseeker's allowance) (s.1(2B)–(2D)). This aspect of the scheme goes beyond the familiar notion of aggregation of needs and resources (although "joint-claim jobseeker's allowance" embodies that too (see ss.3A and 4)) since that traditional model embodies the notion of one partner in a couple being dependent on the other, the latter being the claimant having to fulfil the conditions of entitlement. The "joint-claim couple" aspect goes further than this in that each partner is party to the claim and each must satisfy the conditions of entitlement in s.1(2)(a)–(c) and (e)–(i). In other words, each partner of a joint-claim couple must: (i) be available for employment; (ii) have entered into a jobseeker's agreement; (iii) be actively seeking employment; (iv) not be engaged in remunerative work; (v) be capable of work; (vi) not be receiving relevant education; (vii) be under pensionable age; and (viii) be in Great Britain.

The "joint-claim" scheme has, legislatively speaking, required the adaptation of rules designed for a single claimant to deal instead with two people. Of particular note are the provisions for entitlement notwithstanding that one member of the couple does not meet the "labour market conditions" (see JSA Regulations reg.3D) and the provisions enabling one member of the couple to receive a reduced rate jobseeker's allowance where the other is caught by a sanction.

Jobseekers Act 1995 s.1(4) defines "joint-claim couple" as a couple, of a prescribed description, who are not members of any family that includes someone for whom one of the members of the couple is entitled to child benefit. JSA Regulations reg.3A, as amended from February 25, 2008, gives the prescribed description: where one of the members of the couple is aged 18 or over and was born after October 28, 1947. Such a couple, however, will not be of a prescribed description if:

(a) under reg.77(3), one of its members is treated as responsible for a child or young person;

(b) the couple has care of a child or young person in one or more of the circumstances mentioned in JSA Regulations reg.78(4) (where they are fosterers or the child has been placed with them for adoption); or

(c) a child or young person is living with the couple in the circumstances mentioned in JSA Regulations reg.78(8) (a child living with the couple when he is away from home while at school).

[1Entitlement of a former joint-claim couple to a jobseeker's allowance

3B.—(1) Where a joint-claim couple cease to be a joint-claim couple because they become, or are treated as, responsible for one or more children— 3.13

(a) any claim made by both members of that couple for a jobseeker's allowance may be treated as a claim for a jobseeker's allowance made by either member of that couple;

(b) any award of a joint-claim jobseeker's allowance in respect of that couple may be terminated and may be replaced by a replacement award,

where the conditions specified in paragraph (2) have been complied with.

(2) The conditions specified in this paragraph are that a member of the couple—

(a) provides such evidence as the Secretary of State may require confirming that the couple are responsible for one or more children; and

(b) advises the Secretary of State as to which member of the couple is to be the claimant.

(3) The claim by a member of the couple for a jobseeker's allowance referred to in paragraph (1)(a) shall be treated as made on the date on which he and his partner were treated as having claimed a jobseeker's allowance as a joint-claim couple as determined in accordance with regulation 6 of the Claims and Payments Regulations.

(4) In this regulation, "replacement award" shall have the meaning ascribed to it by paragraph 9A of Schedule 1 to the Act.]

AMENDMENT

1. Jobseeker's Allowance (Joint Claims) Regulations 2000 (SI 2000/1978) reg.2(2) (March 19, 2001).

GENERAL NOTE

3.14 This regulation sets out what happens if a joint-claim couple become responsible for a child (and therefore cease to be a joint-claim couple—see the definition in reg.3A(1)). The existing joint claim can be treated as a claim by either member of the couple and the joint award of benefit is terminated and replaced by a "replacement award". If the couple wish this to happen, they must provide the Secretary of State with evidence that they have become responsible for a child and notify him as to which member of the couple is to be the claimant.

[[1]Entitlement of a new joint-claim couple to a jobseeker's allowance

3.15 **3C.**—(1) Paragraph (2) shall apply where a couple become a joint-claim couple because the child, or all the children, for which they were responsible have—

(a) died;

(b) ceased to be a child or children for whom they are responsible; or

(c) reached the age of 16 and are [[2] not qualifying young persons within the meaning of section 142 of the Benefits Act (child and qualifying young person)].

(2) In a case to which this paragraph applies—

(a) any claim made by either member of that couple for a jobseeker's allowance may be treated as a claim made by both members of the couple;

(b) any award of an income-based jobseeker's allowance, or a replacement award, in respect of either member of that couple may be terminated and may be replaced by a new award in respect of the couple,

where the conditions specified in paragraph (3) have been complied with.

(3) The conditions specified in this paragraph are that the Secretary of State—

(a) has sufficient evidence to decide whether a new award should be made; and

(b) is informed as to which member of the couple is to be the nominated member for the purposes of section 3B.

(4) The claim by both members of the joint-claim couple for a jobseeker's allowance referred to in paragraph (2)(a) shall be treated as made on the date on which the claim by a member of that couple was treated as made in accordance with regulation 6 of the Claims and Payments Regulations.

(5) For the purposes of paragraphs 6 and 7 of Schedule 2 (housing costs), any award of an income-based jobseeker's allowance which related to the day before the day on which the relevant event specified in paragraph (1) occurred and any new award referred to in paragraph (2)(b) shall be treated as a continuous award of an income-based jobseeker's allowance.

(6) In this regulation, "new award" shall have the meaning ascribed to it by paragraph 9C of Schedule 1 to the Act.]

AMENDMENTS

1. Jobseeker's Allowance (Joint Claims) Regulations 2000 (SI 2000/1978) reg.2(2) (March 19, 2001).

2. Social Security (Young Persons) Amendment Regulations 2006 (SI 2006/718) reg.3(3) (April 10, 2006).

GENERAL NOTE

Regulation 3C is the mirror image of reg.3B. The latter regulation sets out what happens when a couple become responsible for a child and therefore cease to be a joint-claim couple whereas reg.3C sets out what happens when a couple becomes a joint-claim couple because they are no longer responsible for a child. In the circumstances listed in para.(1), any claim by either member of the couple may be treated as a joint claim and any award in favour of either may be terminated and replaced with a joint award. 3.16

[1Further circumstances in which a joint-claim couple may be entitled to a joint-claim jobseeker's allowance

3D.—(1) Subject to paragraph (2), a joint-claim couple are entitled to a joint-claim jobseeker's allowance where— 3.17

(a) the members of that couple claim a jobseeker's allowance jointly;
(b) one member satisfies the conditions set out in section 1(2)(a) to (c) and (e) to (i); and
[2 (c) the other member satisfies the condition in section 1(2)(e) and (h) but is not required to satisfy the other conditions in section 1(2B)(b) because, subject to paragraph (3), he is a person to whom any paragraph in Schedule A1 applies; and]
(d) the conditions set out in section 3A are satisfied in relation to the couple.

(2) A member of a joint-claim couple who falls within any paragraph in Schedule A1 for the purposes of this regulation for any day in a benefit week shall fall within that category for the whole of that week.

(3) Subject to paragraph (4), paragraph 2 of Schedule A1 (students) may only apply to a member of a joint-claim couple in respect of one claim for a jobseeker's allowance made jointly by that couple in respect of a jobseeking period applying to the other member of that couple.

(4) Notwithstanding paragraph (3), paragraph 2 of Schedule A1 may apply to a member of a joint-claim couple in respect of a further claim for a jobseeker's allowance made jointly by the couple where the couple's previous entitlement to a joint-claim jobseeker's allowance ceased because one member of the couple—

(a) was engaged in remunerative work;
(b) had been summoned to jury service; or
(c) was within a linked period as prescribed in regulation 48(2).]

AMENDMENTS

1. Jobseeker's Allowance (Joint Claims) Regulations 2000 (SI 2000/1978) reg.2(2) (March 19, 2001).

2. Social Security Amendment (Joint Claims) Regulations 2001 (SI 2001/518) reg.2(3) (March 19, 2001).

GENERAL NOTE

3.18 In the circumstances set out in reg.3D, a joint-claim couple can be entitled to JSA even though only one of them satisfies the labour market conditions. This applies if one member is in Great Britain, under pensionable age, capable of, available for and actively seeking work, has a jobseeker's agreement, and is neither in remunerative work nor receiving relevant education. The other member must be under pensionable age and not in remunerative work and must fall into one of the prescribed categories listed in Sch.A1.

Note that this regulation only dispenses the "failing" member from compliance with the labour market conditions. It is still necessary for the couple to make a joint claim and to meet the requirements of s.3A of the Jobseekers Act 1995.

[1Entitlement of a member of a joint-claim couple to a jobseeker's allowance without a claim being made jointly by the couple

3.19 **3E.**—(1) A member of a joint-claim couple is entitled to a jobseeker's allowance if, without making a claim jointly for that allowance with the other member of the couple—

(a) he satisfies the conditions set out in section 1(2) (a) to (c) and (e) to (i);

(b) he satisfies the conditions set out in section 3; and

(c) the other member of that couple fails to meet the conditions of entitlement set out in section 1(2B)(b) and is a person to whom paragraph (2) applies.

(2) This paragraph applies to a member of a joint-claim couple—

(a) who has failed to attend at the time and place specified by the employment officer for the purposes of regulation 6 of the Claims and Payments Regulations;

(b) in respect of whom it has been determined by the Secretary of State that the conditions in section 1(2)(a) to (c) have not been satisfied but only for so long as it has been so determined in respect of that member;

(c) who is temporarily absent from Great Britain;

(d) who is a person from abroad as defined for the purposes of regulation [485A] and Schedule 5;

(e) who is subject to immigration control within the meaning of section 115(9) of the Immigration and Asylum Act;

(f) who is over pensionable age;

(g) who is engaged, or has agreed to be engaged, in remunerative work for [2 16 hours or more] per week but less than 24 hours per week;

(h) who has claimed a maternity allowance payable in accordance with section 35 [7 or 35B] of the Benefits Act or who has claimed statutory maternity pay payable in accordance with Part XII of that Act;

(i) who is or has been pregnant and to whom sub-paragraph (h) does not apply but only for the period commencing 11 weeks before the expected week of confinement and ending [6twenty eight weeks after the date on which the pregnancy ends];

(j) in respect of whom there is an Order in Council under section 179 of the Administration Act giving effect to a reciprocal agreement which, for the purposes of jobseeker's allowance, has effect as if a payment made by another country is to be treated as a payment of a jobseeker's allowance; [3 . . .]

(k) who is in receipt of statutory sick pay and who, immediately before he became incapable of work, was engaged in remunerative work for 16 hours or more per week; [3 or

(l) where the other member was entitled to an income-based jobseeker's allowance on [5 24th February 2008], save that this sub-paragraph shall apply only until the day on which he is required to attend at a place specified by an employment officer in a notification given or sent to him.]]

AMENDMENTS

1. Jobseeker's Allowance (Joint Claims) Regulations 2000 (SI 2000/1978) reg.2(2) (March 19, 2001).
2. Social Security Amendment (Joint Claims) Regulations 2001 (SI 2001/518) reg.2(4) (March 19, 2001).
3. Jobseeker's Allowance (Joint Claims) Amendment Regulations 2002 (SI 2002/1701) reg.2(b) (October 28, 2002).
4. Social Security (Miscellaneous Amendments) Regulations 2007 (SI 2007/719) reg.3(3) (April 2, 2007).
5. Jobseeker's Allowance (Joint Claims) Amendment Regulations 2008 (SI 2008/13) reg.2(3) (February 25, 2008).
6. Social Security (Miscellaneous Amendments) (No.2) Regulations 2010 (SI 2010/641) reg.4(4) (April 6, 2010).
7. Social Security (Maternity Allowance) (Miscellaneous Amendments) Regulations 2014 (SI 2014/884) reg. 4(2) (May 18, 2014).

GENERAL NOTE

In the circumstances set out in reg.3E, one member of a joint-claim couple can make a standard claim for JSA (i.e. not jointly with the other member) as long as s/he meets the labour market conditions and the conditions in s.3 of the Jobseekers Act 1995. The circumstances in which this is possible are listed in para.(2) and are self-explanatory. 3.20

[1Transitional case couples: prescribed circumstances and period for the purposes of paragraph 8A(2) of Schedule 1

3F.—[2 . . .]] 3.21

AMENDMENTS

1. Jobseeker's Allowance (Joint Claims) Regulations 2000 (SI 2000/1978) reg.2(2) (March 19, 2001).
2. Jobseeker's Allowance (Joint Claims) Amendment Regulations 2008 (SI 2008/13) reg.2(4) (February 25, 2008).

[1 Supply of information

3G.—Where a claim for a jobseeker's allowance has been made jointly by a joint-claim couple, information relating to that claim may be supplied by the Secretary of State to either or both members of that couple for any purpose connected with that claim.] 3.22

AMENDMENT

1. Jobseeker's Allowance (Joint Claims) Regulations 2000 (SI 2000/1978) reg.2(2) (March 19, 2001).

GENERAL NOTE

3.23 This regulation is self-explanatory. Normally information provided in connection with a claim is confidential to the claimant. With a joint claim, the Secretary of State may discuss the claim with either or both claimants.

PART II

JOBSEEKING

Chapter I

Interpretation

Interpretation of Parts II, IV and V

3.24 **4.**—In Parts II, IV and V and, as provided below, the Act—

"appropriate office" means the office of the Department for [6 Work and Pensions] which the claimant is required to attend in accordance with a notice under regulation 23, or any other place which he is so required to attend;

"caring responsibilities" means responsibility for caring for a child or for an elderly person or for a person whose physical or mental condition requires him to be cared for, who is either in the same household or a close relative;

"casual employment" means employment from which the employee can be released without his giving any notice [3except where otherwise provided];

"close relative" means [1, except in Part IV] [5a member of a couple], parent, step-parent, grandparent, parent-in-law, son, step-son, son-in-law, daughter, step-daughter, daughter-in-law, brother, sister, grandchild, [5or if any of the preceding persons is one member of a couple, the other member of that couple];

"elderly person" means a person of over pensionable age;

"employment" in sections 1, 3, 6, 8, 14 [2 . . .] and 20 and paragraph 8 of Schedule 1 to the Act and in [2Parts II and IV] means employed earner's employment except where otherwise provided;

[8 . . . ;]

[3"examination" in relation to a qualifying course means an examination which is specified as an examination related to the qualifying course in a document signed on behalf of the establishment at which the qualifying course is being undertaken;

"made a claim for a jobseeker's allowance" includes treated as having made a claim for the allowance and treated as having an award of the allowance in accordance with regulation 5, 6 or 7 of the Jobseeker's Allowance (Transitional Provisions) Regulations 1996;]

"Outward Bound course" means any course or programme for personal development which is made available to persons who are not in employment by the charitable trust known as the Outward Bound Trust Limited;

"part-time member of a fire brigade" means a person who is a part-time member of a fire brigade maintained in pursuance of the Fire Services Acts 1947–1959;

"pattern of availability" has the meaning given in regulation 7;

[4 "period of study" means—

(a) the period during which the student is regarded as attending or undertaking the course of study; and

(b) any period of attendance by the student at his educational establishment or any period of study undertaken by the student, in connection with the course, which occurs before or after the period during which he is to be regarded as undertaking the course of study;]

"a person who is kept on short-time" means a person whose hours of employment have been reduced owing to temporary adverse industrial conditions;

"a person who is laid off" means a person whose employment has been suspended owing to temporary adverse industrial conditions;

[3"qualifying course" has the meaning given in regulation 17A;

"term-time" in relation to a qualifying course means the period specified as term-time in relation to a person to whom regulation 17A(2) applies in a document signed on behalf of the establishment at which the qualifying course is being undertaken;

"vacation" in relation to a qualifying course means any period falling within the period of study, which is not term-time;]

"voluntary work" means work for an organisation the activities of which are carried on otherwise than for profit, or work other than for a member of the claimant's family, where no payment is received by the claimant or the only payment due to be made to him by virtue of being so engaged is a payment in respect of any expenses reasonably incurred by him in the course of being so engaged;

"week" in sections 6 and 7 and in Parts II and IV means benefit week except where provided otherwise in Parts II and IV;

"work camp" means any place in Great Britain where people come together under the auspices of a charity, a local authority or a voluntary organisation to provide a service of benefit to the community or the environment.

AMENDMENTS

1. Social Security and Child Support (Jobseeker's Allowance) (Miscellaneous Amendments) Regulations 1996 (SI 1996/2538) reg.2(3) (October 28, 1996).

2. Social Security Amendment (New Deal) Regulations 1997 (SI 1997/2863) reg.3 (January 5, 1998).

3. Social Security Amendment (New Deal) Regulations 1998 (SI 1998/1274) reg.3 (June 1, 1998).

4. Social Security Amendment (Students) Regulations 2000 (SI 2000/1981) reg.6(3) (July 31, 2000).

5. Civil Partnership (Pensions, Social Security and Child Support) (Consequential, etc. Provisions) Order 2005 (SI 2005/2877) art.2(3) and Sch.3 para.26 (December 5, 2005).

6. Social Security (Miscellaneous Amendments) Regulations 2008 (SI 2008/698) reg.4(3) (April 14, 2008).

7. Jobseeker's Allowance (Sanctions for Failure to Attend) Regulations 2010 (SI 2010/509) reg.2(2) (April 6, 2010).

8. Jobseeker's Allowance (Sanctions) (Amendment) Regulations 2012 (SI 2012/2568) reg.5(2) (October 22, 2012).

DEFINITIONS

"benefit week"—see reg.1(3).
"child"—see Jobseekers Act 1995 s.35(1).
"couple"—*ibid.*
"course of study"—*ibid.*
"payment"—*ibid.*
"pensionable age"—see reg.3.
"voluntary organisation"—see reg.1(3).

GENERAL NOTE

3.25 "*Close relative*". See the note to reg.2(1) of the Income Support Regulations.

"*Employment*". See the note to the definition of "employment" in reg.3.

"Part-time member of a fire brigade": as regards Wales, with effect from October 25, 2005, the definition was modified by the Fire and Rescue Services Act 2004 (Consequential Amendments) (Wales) Order 2005 (SI 2005/2929) art.36(2) to read as follows:

> "'*Part-time member of a fire brigade*' means a person who is a part-time member of a fire brigade maintained in pursuance of the Fire Services Acts 1947–1959 [or, in England or Wales, a part-time fire-fighter employed by a fire and rescue authority]."

As regards Scotland, the definition was modified with effect from August 5, 2005 by the Fire (Scotland) Act 2005 (Consequential Provisions and Modifications) Order 2005 (SI 2005/2060 (S7)) art.3 and Sch. para.10(2) to read as follows:

> "'*Part-time member of a fire brigade*' means a person who is a part-time [fire-fighter employed by a fire and rescue authority (as defined in section 1 of the Fire (Scotland) Act 2005 (asp 5)) or a joint fire and rescue board constituted by an amalgamation scheme made under section 2(1) of that Act]."

"*Period of study*". See *R(JSA) 2/02*.

Chapter II

Availability for employment

Exceptions to requirement to be available immediately: carers, voluntary workers, persons providing a service and persons under an obligation to provide notice

3.26 **5.**—[1(1) [4 Subject to paragraph (1A),] in order to be regarded as available for employment—

(a) [2. . .];
(b) a person who is engaged in voluntary work [2or who has caring responsibilities] is not required to be able to take up employment immediately, providing he is willing and able—

(i) to take up employment on being given one week's notice; and

(ii) to attend for interview in connection with the opportunity of any such employment on being given 48 hours' notice.]

[4 (1A) In order to be regarded as available for employment, a person who has caring responsibilities in relation to a child is not required to take up employment or attend for interview within the periods referred to in paragraph (1) if those responsibilities make it unreasonable for him to do so, providing he is willing and able—

(a) to take up employment on being given 28 days notice; and

(b) to attend for interview in connection with the opportunity of any such employment on being given 7 days notice.

(1B) For the purposes of paragraph (1A), it is for the claimant to show that it is unreasonable for him to take up employment or attend for interview within the periods referred to in paragraph (1).]

(2) In order to be regarded as available for employment, a person who is engaged, whether by contract or otherwise, in providing a service with or without remuneration, other than a person who has caring responsibilities or who is engaged in voluntary work, is not required to be able to take up employment immediately, providing he is willing and able to take up employment on being given 24 hours' notice.

(3) In order to be regarded as available for employment, a person who is in employed earner's employment and is not engaged in remunerative work and who is required by [3section 86 of the Employment Rights Act 1996] to give notice to terminate his contract is not required to be able to take up employment immediately, providing he is willing and able to take up employment immediately he is able to do so in accordance with his statutory obligations.

(4) Where in accordance with regulation 7, 13[5, 13A] or 17 a person is only available for employment at certain times, he is not required to be able to take up employment at a time at which he is not available, but he must be willing and able to take up employment immediately he is available.

(5) Where in accordance with paragraph [4(1), (1A) or (2)] a person is not required to be able to take up employment immediately, the [4 . . .] periods referred to in those paragraphs include periods when in accordance with regulation 7[5, 13 or 13A] he is not available.

[1(6) In this regulation "week" means any period of seven consecutive days.]

AMENDMENTS

1. Jobseeker's Allowance (Amendment) Regulations 2002 (SI 2002/3072) reg.3 (January 1, 2003).

2. Social Security (Income Support and Jobseeker's Allowance) Amendment Regulations 2006 (SI 2006/1402) reg.2(2) (May 30, 2006).

3. Social Security (Miscellaneous Amendments) (No.5) Regulations 2007 (SI 2007/2618) reg.8(3) (October 1, 2007).

4. Social Security (Lone Parents and Miscellaneous Amendments) Regulations 2008 (SI 2008/3051) reg.11(2) (November 4, 2008).

5. Jobseeker's Allowance (Lone Parents) (Availability for Work) Regulations 2010 (SI 2010/837) reg.2(2) (April 26, 2010).

DEFINITIONS

"caring responsibilities"—see reg.4.
"child"—see Jobseekers Act 1995 s.35(1).
"claimant"—*ibid.*
"employed eamer's employment"—see Jobseekers Act 1995 s.6(9); SSCBA 1992 s.2(1)(a).
"employment"—see reg.4.
"remunerative work"—see regs 1(3) and 51(1).
"voluntary work"—see reg.4.

GENERAL NOTE

3.27 The general rule on availability set out in s.6(1) of the old style Jobseekers Act 1995 requires that a claimant be willing and able to take up *immediately* any employed earner's employment (on which see s.6(9) of that Act and SSCBA 1992 ss.2(1)(a) and 122(1)). This regulation provides qualifications of and exceptions to that general rule.

Paragraph (4) qualifies the "immediately" condition by requiring that it be related to the claimant's "pattern of availability" (the times at which he is available to take up employment) permitted by regs 7 (enabling restriction of hours to 40 or more), 13 (enabling carers to restrict hours of availability to between 16 and 40 hours to suit caring responsibilities, and the sick/disabled to restrict times and/or hours of availability so far as reasonable in light of physical or mental condition), 13A (certain lone parents) and 17 (treating as available persons laid off from employment or put on short-time). Paragraph (4) stipulates that a claimant, available only at certain times in accordance with any of those provisions, is not required to be able to take up employment during one of his permitted periods of non-availability, but must be willing and able to take up employment immediately in one of his spells of availability. In addition, paras (1)–(3) give varying periods of grace within which one must be willing and able to take up employment, to carers, voluntary workers, to other service-providers, and to persons employed for less than 16 hours per week and under a specific statutory obligation to provide notice. These provisions are discussed further below.

Carers (paras (1), (1A), (1B) and (5))

3.28 A carer (someone "who has caring responsibilities", defined as discussed below) has from May 30, 2006 the benefit of an enhanced relaxation of the rules on immediate availability. Such persons are from that date exempt from the requirement to be immediately available provided that they are willing and able to take up employed earner's employment on being given one weeks' notice (rather than the 48 hours concession prior to May 30, 2006) so long as they are also willing and able to attend for interview in connection with the opportunity of any such employment on being given 48 hours' notice. In *CIS 142/1993* the Commissioner decided that the same phrase (except that the required notice was only 24 hours) in reg.12(1) of the Unemployment, Sickness and Invalidity Benefit Regulations 1983 meant that the notice should only start to run when the claimant would receive notification of the job (in that case by a telephone call from his parents in the evening as he was doing voluntary work during the day). See also para.21236 of the *DMG*. From November 24, 2008, carers for children were given a further concession: if they can establish that complying with the one week or 48 hours requirement in para.(1) is unreasonable because of their caring responsibilities, they will not be required to comply with those limits so long as they are willing and able to take up employment on being given 28 days' notice or to attend for interview for such employment on being given seven days' notice (see paras (1A) and (1B)). Paragraph (5) makes clear that the one week or 48-hour notice periods includes periods of non-availability in accordance with regs 7, 13 or 13A. Regulation 7 enables restriction of hours to 40 or more in an pattern of employment recorded in the current jobseeker's agreement. Under reg.13, so long as he has reasonable prospects of employment despite the restriction, a carer can restrict availability to such hours between 16 and 40 hours per week as his caring responsibilities allow, and for the specific hours those responsibilities allow (reg.13(4), (5), and 8). Reg.13 also permits anyone to restrict his times and/or hours of availability so far as reasonable in light of his physical or mental condition (reg.13(3)). Regulation 13A allows a lone parent, who is both responsible for and a member of the same household as a child under 13, to restrict their availability to the child's normal school hours.

A carer (a person "who has caring responsibilities") is someone who has responsibility for caring for a child or for an elderly person or for a person whose physical or mental condition requires them to be cared for. But the child, the elderly person and the person whose condition requires being cared for must either be a close relative or in the same household (reg.4). "Close relative" means a spouse or other member of an unmarried couple, parent, step-parent, grandparent, parent-in-law, son, step-son, son-in-law, daughter, step-daughter, daughter-in-law, brother, sister, grandchild or the spouse of any of these persons or, if that person is one of an unmarried couple, the other member of that couple (*ibid.*). On "unmarried couple" see old style Jobseekers Act 1995 s.35(1) and the note thereto.

Voluntary workers (paras (1) and (5))

A voluntary worker ("a person who is engaged . . . in voluntary work", discussed below) is exempt from the requirement to be immediately available, subject to being willing and able to take up employed earner's employment on being given one week's notice, and to attend for interview in connection with the opportunity of any such employment on being given 48 hours' notice. The "one week" and 48-hour periods include periods when in accordance with regs.7, 13 or 13A the claimant is not available (para.(5)). **3.29**

"Voluntary work" covers work for an organisation, the activities of which are carried on otherwise than for profit, or work other than for a member of the claimant's family, where no payment is received by the claimant or the only payment due to be made to him by virtue of being so engaged is one in respect of any expenses reasonably incurred by him in the course of being engaged in the work (reg.4). On "family", see old style Jobseekers Act 1995 s.35(1) and regs 76–78.

See also reg.12 on cases where claimants have restricted the number of hours for which they are available. Time engaged in voluntary work and the extent to which it may have improved prospects of employment is to be taken into account in determining whether in any week the claimant has taken all the steps that are reasonable for the purposes of the actively seeking employment test (reg.18(2)(g)).

Others providing a service (paras (2) and (5))

These paragraphs cover those engaged in providing a service, other than carers or voluntary workers, who are, in any event, more generously treated under para.(1), examined above. It is irrelevant whether the service is provided by contract or not. Nor is it material whether the service is or is not remunerated. Those engaged in providing a service do not have to be available immediately. It suffices that they are available on being given 24 hours' notice. That 24-hour period includes periods when, in accordance with regs 7, 13 or 13A, the service-provider is not available (para.(5)). **3.30**

The provision is similar to, but wider than, its predecessor (USI Regulations reg.12(1)), which was interpreted in *CU/96/1994*. There Commissioner Skinner considered the phrase "providing a service with or without remuneration" found both in USI Regulations reg.12(1) and in the old style JSA provision now under consideration. The claimant in *CU/96/1994* had been found not to be available for work because he was not in a position to accept a job offer at once, but would require 24 hours' notice in order to make arrangements for his wife and two teenage children to be able to make their way to college and school and return from there to home. In setting aside the tribunal decision as erroneous in law, Commissioner Skinner opined that the phrase was "a wide one", capable of embracing the necessary help given to members of one's own family: "The service provided does not have to be for the public, it does not have to arise under a contract of employment" (para.5). The contrast between the wording of paras (1) and (1A) (service as a volunteer) (the same contrast as between paras (1) and (2) of this regulation) reinforced his view, as did the *Shorter Oxford English Dictionary* definition of "service" as "the action of serving, helping or benefiting: conduct tending to the welfare or advantage of another: an act of helping or benefiting". That was the sense in which the word was used in para.(1) of the regulation:

> "So consequently if the claimant does an act which helps or benefits a member of his family or does something which tends to their welfare or advantage, he can be said to be rendering a service. However it must be necessary service not some fanciful help. No doubt many unemployed people may be able to satisfy that criteria". (para.5)

But the claimant taking his children to school could not be a "service" in the sense of the regulation; it was merely an exercise of parental responsibility, fulfilling a parental duty rather than rendering a service to his children. Transporting his wife to and from her nursing course, however, was in law capable of amounting to a "service":

> "It was something done for the wife's benefit and it does not seem that the claimant had any duty or responsibility so to transport her. No doubt it was a worthwhile and kindly thing to do, but he did not have to do it, and I accept that he could in law provide a service". (para.7)

Commissioner Skinner thought the real restriction on the operation of USI Regulations reg.12(1) to be the requirement therein that the circumstances be such that it would not be reasonable to expect the claimant to be ready for suitable employment on less than 24 hours' notice. That restriction is not embodied in the old style JSA provision now under consideration.

Those working less than 16 hours per week and under an obligation to provide notice (para.(3))

3.31 This provision covers claimants, employed in employed earner's employment, who are not "engaged in remunerative work" and so not precluded from JSA. In short, it embraces those working but for less than 16 hours a week, who are statutorily obliged to give notice (i.e. those continuously employed for one month or more) (s.86 of the Employment Rights Act 1996 requires a minimum of one week's notice). Such persons are not required to be available to take up employment immediately, provided they are willing to and can do so immediately their statutory obligations permit. Should that occur during a permitted spell of non-availability under regs.7, 13 or 13A, they will not be ruled out by the "immediately" requirement, so long as they are willing and able to take up employment immediately that spell of non-availability ends (para.(4)).

The effect of para.(5)

3.32 In calculating the expiry of the 48-hour period allowed to carers and voluntary workers and also the 24-hour period allowed to other service providers (the groups embraced by paras (1) and (2)), there must be included any period of permitted non-availability under regs 7, 13 or 13A. See further the notes on those groups.

Employment of at least 40 hours per week

3.33 **6.**—(1) In order to be regarded as available for employment, a person must be willing and able to take up employment of at least 40 hours per week, unless he has restricted his availability in accordance with paragraph

[1 (3), (3A) or (4)] of regulation [2 13, regulation 13A or] paragraph (2) of regulation 17 or two or more of those provisions.

(2) In order to be regarded as available for employment, a person must be willing and able to take up employment of less than 40 hours per week but not for a greater number of hours per week than the number for which he is available in accordance with paragraph [1 (3), (3A) or (4)] of regulation [2 13, regulation 13A] or paragraph (2) of regulation 17 or two or more of those provisions.

AMENDMENTS

1. Social Security (Lone Parents and Miscellaneous Amendments) Regulations 2008 (SI 2008/3051) reg.11(3) (November 4, 2008).

2. Jobseeker's Allowance (Lone Parents) (Availability for Work) Regulations 2010 (SI 2010/837) reg.2(3) (April 26, 2010).

DEFINITIONS

"employment"—see reg.4.
"week"—*ibid.*

GENERAL NOTE

Under the previous regime of benefits for the unemployed, being available for part-time work only did not of itself necessarily preclude availability (*CU109/48(KL); CU22/91*, paras 9 and 10). Under the old style Jobseekers Act 1995, the general rule is different. Section 6(1) states simply that someone is available for employment if willing and able to take up immediately *any* employed earner's employment. But that is subject to qualification and modification by regulations. This regulation stipulates that, normally, in order to be regarded as available for employment, a person must be willing and able to take up employment for a minimum of 40 hours per week, but also be willing to take up employment of less than 40 hours per week. In other words, being available merely for part-time employment (less than 40 hours per week) does not suffice, but to be available one must not only be available for full-time employment (40 or more hours per week) but be willing and able to accept part-time employment (less than 40 hours per week), if offered. 3.34

The general rule stated in this regulation is itself subject to exceptions for those in certain protected groups—those covered by reg.13(3), (3A) or (4), reg.13A or reg.17(2)—who are permitted to reduce their hours of availability to a level below 40 per week (e.g. to 26 because of caring responsibilities) and cannot be required to take up work for a number of hours below 40 but above that permitted level. The first protected group is the sick/disabled, who can impose *any* restrictions on availability which are reasonable in light of physical or mental condition (reg.13(3)). Carers (the second protected group) can restrict their hours to between 16 and 40 per week, so long as they are available for as many hours as their caring responsibilities allow and for the specific hours those responsibilities permit so long as there are reasonable prospects of employment despite the restriction (reg.13(4)). A lone parent, who is both responsible for and a member of the same household as a child under 13, can restrict their availability to the child's normal school hours (reg.13A). Those in employment but currently kept on short time (defined in reg.4) (the fourth group) are treated as available for up to 13 weeks so long as they are willing and able to resume that employment (it is obviously beneficial for all concerned to aid their ultimate return to full-time working in that job) and are available for casual employment so that the total number of hours for which they work and are available for casual employment is at least 40 per week (reg.17).

For availability purposes, "week" means "benefit week": generally the period of seven days ending with the day corresponding to the claimant's "signing"/attendance day (regs 4 and 1(3)).

In *CJSA/1434/00*, Commissioner Bano held that reg.6 was not contrary to EC Council Directive 79/7 as indirectly discriminatory on grounds of sex. He stated:

> "Because regulation 13(4) of the Jobseeker's Allowance Regulations exempts claimants with caring responsibilities from the requirement in regulation 6 to be willing and able to take up employment for 40 hours per week and regulation 13(3) enables claimants with physical and mental disabilities to restrict their availability in any way, provided that the restrictions are reasonable, it has not been possible to identify any category of claimant unable to comply with the 40 hour availability requirement. In the absence of evidence of the existence of any such category, I agree with Ms. Bergmann that compliance with regulation 6 must be regarded as a matter of choice for each individual claimant. The regulation therefore does not create a condition with which a claimant either can or cannot comply, and no statistical comparison of men and women on that basis is therefore possible. The elements necessary to establish a claim of indirect discrimination on a statistical, or demographic, basis in accordance with the approach of the European Court of Justice in *Seymour-Smith* and of the Court of Appeal in *Jones* are therefore lacking in this case, and I therefore consider that the claimant's claim of indirect discrimination on that basis must fail. Having reached that conclusion, I do not consider it necessary to deal with Ms Bergmann's alternative submission that the 40 hour availability rule is objectively justified". (para.14)

Restriction of hours for which a person is available to 40 hours per week

3.35 **7.**—(1) Except as provided in [1 regulations 13, 13A and 17(2)], a person may not restrict the total number of hours for which he is available for employment to less than 40 hours in any week.

(2) A person may restrict the total number of hours for which he is available for employment in any week to 40 hours or more providing—

(a) the times at which he is available to take up employment (his"pattern of availability") are such as to afford him reasonable prospects of securing employment;

(b) his pattern of availability is recorded in his jobseeker's agreement and any variations in that pattern are recorded in a varied agreement and

(c) his prospects of securing employment are not reduced considerably by the restriction imposed by his pattern of availability.

(3) A person who has restricted the total number of hours for which he is available in accordance with paragraph (2) and who is not available for employment, and is not to be treated as available for employment in accordance with regulation 14, for one day or more in a week in accordance with his pattern of availability shall not be regarded as available for employment even if he was available for employment for a total of 40 hours or more during that week.

AMENDMENT

1. Jobseeker's Allowance (Lone Parents) (Availability for Work) Regulations 2010 (SI 2010/837) reg.2(4) (April 26, 2010).

DEFINITIONS

"employment"—see reg.4.
"week"—*ibid.*

GENERAL NOTE

For availability purposes, "week" means "benefit week": generally the period of seven days ending with the day corresponding to the claimant's "signing"/ attendance day (regs 4 and 1(3)). 3.36

Paragraph (1)

This paragraph reinforces the general rule, stated in reg.6(1), that, save for those in the groups protected by regs.13 (the sick/disabled, carers), 13A (lone parents responsible for a child under 13 in the same household) and 17(2) (those working short time), in order to be available for employment, one must be willing and able to take up employment of at least 40 hours per week: this paragraph stipulates that a person not in a protected group may not restrict the total number of hours for which he is available to less than 40 hours in any week. 3.37

Paragraph (2)

Section 6(1) of the old style Jobseekers Act 1995 stipulates that a person is available for employment if willing and able to take up immediately *any employed earner's employment*. This paragraph qualifies the rigour of that by enabling any claimant to set a ceiling at or above 40 hours on the total number of hours, and on what days, for which he is available in any week. This involves the claimant and an employment officer agreeing a "pattern of availability"—the times at which he is available to take up employment (sub-para.(a))—which must be recorded in his job-seeker's agreement (sub-para.(b)). On the jobseeker's agreement, see old style Jobseekers Act 1995 s.9. Any variation in that pattern must be agreed with an employment officer and recorded in a varied agreement (on variation see old style Jobseekers Act 1995 s.10). A ceiling on total hours of availability can only be set in this way if the pattern of availability is such as to afford the claimant reasonable prospects of securing employment and those prospects are not reduced considerably by the restriction imposed by the pattern of availability (sub-paras (a) and (c)). The burden of establishing reasonable prospects of employment rests on the claimant (reg.10(2)). In deciding that issue, regard must be had in particular to: the claimant's skills, qualifications and experience; the type and number of vacancies within daily travelling distance of his home; how long he has been unemployed; what job applications he has made and their outcome (reg.10(1)(a)–(d)). If he also wishes to place restrictions on the nature of the employment he is prepared to accept (under reg.8 or 13(2)), regard must also be had to whether he is willing to move home to take up employment (reg.10(1)(e)). 3.38

To make proper sense, para.(2) needs to be read by looking at the whole of the regulation (*R(JSA) 2/07*, para.12). "[R]egulation 7 covers cases of restrictions not just on the total hours to be worked in a week or on the start and finish times on a day, but also restrictions on the days of the week on which a claimant is available. The phrase "the times at which he is available" in regulation 7(2)(a) has a broad enough meaning to cover such cases. There is then also a neat fit with regulation 8, which deals with restrictions on the nature, terms and conditions or locality of employment" (para.13). Paragraph (2)(b) accordingly requires that to be available the claimant must adhere in practice to the pattern of availability (either strictly or by following an even less restrictive pattern) embodied in the jobseeker's agreement unless and until that agreement is varied pursuant to old style Jobseekers Act 1995 s.10 (*ibid.*, para.14). So, in *R(JSA) 2/07*, the claimant who had agreed to Saturday working in his jobseeker's agreement, but adopted an actual pattern which excluded Saturday, was not protected by reg.7(2) and so was not available. If the claimant is unhappy about the pattern proposed for the agreement, he has a number of choices. First, he can refuse to sign and ask for the agreement to be referred to the Secretary of State, hoping that the Secretary of State will agree with him about its terms and will also backdate the agreement so that the claimant, without benefit until the matter is decided, will not have lost but merely postponed benefit. Alternatively, he can sign under protest and immediately seek a variation of the agreement. But if he does so, he must, if he is to retain benefit pending the variation adhere to the "agreed" pattern set out in the agreement.

In *CJSA 1279/98* and *R(JSA) 3/01* (considered in the notes to para.(3), below), Commissioner Levenson, taking a "whole week" approach to this regulation, seems to take the view that if the claimant has not expressly restricted his hours to less than 40 hours per week he must be taken to have restricted them to 40 hours or more so that this paragraph and para.(3) interact, unless some other exception applies, so that non-availability even for one day in a week will preclude availability throughout the benefit week. It may even apply where others effect the restriction (e.g. the police taking the claimant into custody). In *R(JSA) 3/01*, however, the Commissioner held that the claimant was saved by reg.13(3): the restriction was reasonable in view of his physical condition (incarceration). That "saving" was rejected as erroneous in law by the Court of Appeal in *CAO v David* (reported in *R(JSA) 3/01*) (see notes to para.(3), below). *David* was applied in *CJSA/5944/99*, another case of someone detained in police custody. See further commentary to reg.14.

Paragraph (3)

3.39 This at first sight baffling provision stresses that a claimant must ensure availability each week in accordance with his agreed pattern of availability; failure to be available on one or more days in a week in accordance with the agreed pattern will preclude entitlement even though the claimant was available for a total of 40 hours or more in that week unless, with respect to the day(s) of nonavailability the claimant is protected by a "deemed availability" rule in reg.14. So, if a claimant with an agreed pattern of availability under para.(2) goes away on a holiday which includes one of his agreed days of availability without informing an employment officer and agreeing a revised pattern in accordance with para.(2), this paragraph precludes availability for the whole of that benefit week, despite the claimant's being available for 40 or more hours spread over the other days of that week (see also AOG, para.26231, now DMG 21231); similarly (until May 30, 2006) if the day of non-availability arose because the claimant was in custody. From that date, a degree of deemed availability is afforded those in police custody (reg.14(1)(s)).

But what of persons not available on a particular day(s) for similar reasons, but who do not have a para.(2) pattern of availability (e.g. because they are willing to do any job, whatever hours at any time)? AOG, para.26233 (now DMG 21233) advises decision-makers to treat them as not available throughout that week, despite their being available in the rest of the week for 40 hours or more (if action took them below 40 hours availability reg.6(1) would, of course, rule them non-available). That preclusion throughout the week clearly cannot be founded on para.(3) which only applies where a claimant "has *restricted* the total number of hours for which he is available *in accordance with paragraph (2)*" (emphasis supplied). The person away on holiday may have de facto "restricted" his hours but, not having sought or obtained a revision of his jobseeker's agreement, has not done so "in accordance with paragraph (2)"; nor has the person in custody who might in any event not properly be regarded as having restricted his hours as opposed to having them restricted for him by the action of others which may or may not have been warranted. Clearly such claimants are not available on the particular days of non-availability (unless the day(s) can be brought within one of the situations of deemed availability in reg.14). But does this not mean that, if satisfying the "40 or more hours rule" in reg.6 they should be regarded as available on the other days of the week and entitled to a proportionate rate of benefit? The Departmental view on this is apparently that one must read old style Jobseekers Act 1995 s.6(1) with s.1 of that Act. Taking that "total" availability rule ("a person is available for employment if he is willing and able to take up immediately any employed earner's employment") with the weekly basis of JSA ("a jobseeker's allowance is payable in respect of a week": s.1(3)), the requirement is that one be available throughout the week in the absolute terms set by s.6(1), unless specifically relieved from that requirement by means of the concessions set out in the JSA Regulations 1996 dealing with availability: so that a single unprotected day of non-availability precludes entitlement for that benefit week. The difficulties with that approach are that neither s.6 nor s.1 are explicit on that point and that the preclusion for a full week because of a single day of non-availability for those with a pattern of availability (the para.(2) situation) is specifically sanctioned by para.(3). That is something which is arguably suggestive of a view that such a result does not necessarily flow from the asserted general principles of the Act itself. If this paragraph is thought necessary to deal with those departing from an agreed pattern of availability (something less than 7 days × 24 hours) whilst complying with the "40 hours rule" in reg.6, surely a similar specific rule is needed to preclude for the whole week those without such a pattern? Or is para.(3) there out of an excess of caution to emphasise that the "concession" afforded by para.(2) is a limited one? In short, while the policy intention may be clear, if harsh, it is by no means clear that it has successfully been translated into law.

Commissioner Levenson has considered the approach to reg.7 in two decisions. He supports a "whole week" approach. In *R(JSA) 3/01* he thought it clear that—

> "there is no provision (other than for exceptions that do not apply in this case) to award jobseeker's allowance for parts of the week or to find that a claimant was available for employment during part of a week but not during the rest of the week. The claimant is either available for employment during a particular week or he is not so available". (para.4)

In consequence, as regards holidays, Commissioner Levenson has supported the Department's approach. In *CJSA 1279/98*, the claimant's signing-on day was Tuesday, so that his benefit week ran from Wednesday to Tuesday. He went on holiday, having informed the Jobcentre, from Saturday to Saturday for one week, stating that in that period he would not be available for work. Commissioner Levenson upheld the finding that pursuant to paras (2) and (3) of this regulation, his non-availability even for one day in each of the benefit weeks meant he was not entitled to benefit in either of those weeks. The Commissioner took the view that since he had not restricted his hours of availability to less than 40 hours per week, he must be taken to have restricted them to 40 hours or more under para.(2), so that the preclusive effect of para.(3) came into operation. It is submitted that it could equally be argued that the claimant had not in fact invoked para.(2): the real question should have been whether in each of the weeks in question he was, in the days prior to and after his holiday, available for at least 40 hours (see CPAG, *Welfare Rights Bulletin* 153, p.19). **3.40**

In *R(JSA) 3/01* the Commissioner dealt with someone in police custody for two days of his benefit week. He held here that, even though someone else imposed the restrictions, that is the police, reg.13(3) protected the claimant from the preclusive effect of reg.7: the restriction (two days in police custody) was reasonable (indeed inevitable) in light of his physical condition which was such that he was not free, legally or practically to leave (para.6). On appeal, however, the Court of Appeal held that Commisioner Levenson had erred in law (*CAO v David*, reported in *R(JSA) 3/01*: see the notes to reg.13(3) below). Simon Brown LJ expressed some concerns about the justice of the result, saying in paras 25 and 26:

> "The first of these relates to the jobseeker's agreement itself. Section 6 of the Act, as noted, requires the claimant to be willing and able to take up employment 'immediately'. That 'immediately' means within a very short space of time indeed is clear not only from the word itself but also from regulation 5 which provides for exceptions to this requirement in the case of those with caring responsibilities or engaged in voluntary work (who need only be willing and able to take up employment on 48 hours' notice) and certain others engaged in providing a service (who get 24 hours' notice). No doubt the requirement for immediate availability allows

the claimant time to wash, dress and have his breakfast, but strictly it would seem inconsistent with, say, a claimant's stay overnight with a friend or relative, or attendance at a weekend cricket match, or even an evening at the cinema (unless perhaps he had left a contact number and had not travelled far).

In these circumstances, claimants ought clearly to be wary of entering into an agreement which offers unrestricted availability throughout the entire week, day and night, weekdays and weekends."

The judge was also concerned, particularly in view of the presumption of innocence, that mere detention by the police for some part of one day should lead to loss of entitlement to JSA for a whole benefit week and suggested that some amendment should be considered. Regulation 14(1)(s) now contains a deeming of availability in circumstances like those of *David*, limited to 96 hours.

Other restrictions on availability

3.41 **8.**—Subject to regulations 6, 7 and 9, any person may restrict his availability for employment by placing restrictions on the nature of the employment for which he is available, the terms or conditions of employment for which he is available (including the rate of remuneration) and the locality or localities within which he is available, providing he can show that he has reasonable prospects of securing employment notwithstanding those restrictions and any restrictions on his availability in accordance with regulations 7(2), [113(2), (3), (3A) or (4)][2, 13A] or 17(2).

AMENDMENTS

1. Social Security (Lone Parents and Miscellaneous Amendments) Regulations 2008 (SI 2008/3051) reg.11(4) (November 4, 2008).

2. Jobseeker's Allowance (Lone Parents) (Availability for Work) Regulations 2010 (SI 2010/837) reg.2(5) (April 26, 2010).

DEFINITION

"employment"—see reg.4.

GENERAL NOTE

3.42 Section 6(1) of the old style Jobseekers Act 1995 states that a claimant is available for employment if he is willing and able to take up immediately *any employed earner's employment*. This regulation mitigates the rigour of that by enabling a claimant to restrict his availability by placing restrictions on the nature of the employment for which he is available, on its terms and conditions (including rate of remuneration) and on the locality or localities within which he is available. The regulation is subject to regs 6, 7 and 9, so the apparent width of this regulation cannot be used to circumvent the limitations imposed by those regulations. This means that a claimant cannot under this regulation restrict hours of work to below 40 (reg.6), the pattern of availability (the times at which he is available to take up employment) must conform to the criteria in reg.7, and no remuneration restrictions are permissible after six months from the date of claim (reg.9). Moreover, restrictions are only allowable under this regulation if the claimant can establish that he has reasonable prospects of securing employment despite these restrictions and any other restrictions imposed under other availability regulations (namely, regs 7(2), 13(2), (3) or (4), 13A and 17(2)). Regulation 10(2) emphasises that the burden of establishing this lies on the claimant. In determining whether he has reasonable prospects of employment, regard must be had in particular to: his skills, qualifications and experience; the type and number of vacancies within daily travelling distance of his home; how long he has been unemployed; what job applications he has made and their outcome (reg.10(1)(a)–(d)). If the restrictions include ones on the nature of the employment the claimant is prepared to accept (both regs 8 and 13(2) enable such restrictions), regard must also be had to whether he is willing to move home to take up employment (reg.10(1)(e)). Note that the standard is "reasonable prospects" of employment, not the higher standard of "good prospects" (see Commissioner Levenson in *CJSA/4435/1998*).

Note that claimants who are allowed by some of the provisions of reg.13 to impose restrictions on the nature of the employment for which they are available (in particular where the restrictions are reasonable in the light of the claimant's physical or mental condition: reg.13(3); and where a person with caring responsibilities for a child is subject to a parenting order or a parenting contract: reg.13(3A)) do not have to meet the condition of having reasonable prospects of employment subject to those restrictions to take the benefit of reg.13. Nor does a lone parent responsible for a child under the age of 13 who is allowed by reg.13A to restrict availability to that child's normal school hours. The reasonable prospects condition is built in to reg.13(2) (religious belief or conscientious objection) and (4) (caring responsibilities and available for less than 40 hours but at least 16 per week). Note also the categories of deemed availability in regs 14 and 14A and 16–17B and the special rules about what availability means in reg.5.

No restrictions on pay after six months

9.—After the expiry of the six month period beginning with the date of claim, a person may not restrict his availability for employment by placing restrictions on the level of remuneration in employment for which he is available. 3.43

DEFINITIONS

"date of claim"—see reg.1(3).
"employment"—see reg.4.

GENERAL NOTE

Regulation 8 (and possibly reg.13(3)) allow restrictions as to remuneration in the employment for which a claimant is available. This regulation stipulates that restrictions on the level of remuneration in the employment for which a claimant is available are allowable, if at all, only for maximum of six months beginning with the date of claim. The "date of claim" means the date on which the claimant makes, or is treated as making, a claim for a jobseeker's allowance for the purposes of reg.6 of the Social Security (Claims and Payments) Regulations 1987 (see reg.1(3)). 3.44

Reasonable prospects of employment

10.—(1) For the purposes of regulations 7 and 8 and paragraphs (2) and (4) of regulation 13, in deciding whether a person has reasonable prospects of securing employment, regard shall be had, in particular, to the following matters— 3.45

- (a) his skills, qualifications and experience;
- (b) the type and number of vacancies within daily travelling distance from his home;
- (c) the length of time for which he has been unemployed;
- (d) the job applications which he has made and their outcome;
- (e) if he wishes to place restrictions on the nature of the employment for which he is available, whether he is willing to move home to take up employment.

(2) It shall be for the claimant to show that he has reasonable prospects of securing employment if he wishes to restrict his availability in accordance with regulation 7 or 8 or paragraph (2) or (4) of regulation 13.

DEFINITION

"employment"—see reg.4.

GENERAL NOTE

3.46 A number of regulations enabling the claimant to restrict his availability make the permissibility of restrictions depend on whether, despite all the restrictions he imposes, he has reasonable prospects of securing employment (see regs 7, 8, 13(2), (4)). Paragraph (2) of this regulation places on the claimant the burden of showing that such is the case. Paragraph (1) of this regulation requires that in deciding the matter of "reasonable prospects", regard must be had *in particular* (the list is thus not exhaustive) to: the claimant's skills, qualifications and experience; the type and number of vacancies within daily travelling distance of his home; how long he has been unemployed; what job applications he has made and their outcome (sub-paras (a)–(d)). If the restrictions include ones on the nature of the employment he is prepared to accept (both regs 8 and 13(2) enable such restrictions), regard must also be had to whether he is willing to move home to take up employment (sub-para.(e)). Note that the standard is "reasonable prospects" of employment, not the higher standard of "good prospects" (see Commissioner Levenson in *CJSA/4435/1998*).

Part-time students

3.47 **11.**—(1) If in any week a person is a part-time student and—

(a) he falls within paragraph (2)

(b) he has restricted the total number of hours for which he is available in accordance with regulation 7(2), [1 [5 13(3), (3A) or (4)]] [6 , 13A] or 17(2); and

(c) the hours of his course of study fall in whole or in part within his pattern of availability,

in determining whether he is available for employment no matter relating to his course of study shall be relevant providing he is willing and able to re-arrange the hours of his course in order to take up employment at times falling within his pattern of availability, to take up such employment immediately or, if he falls within paragraph [5 (1), (1A), (2) or (3)] of regulation 5, at the time specified in that paragraph and providing he complies with the requirements of regulation 6.

(2) A person falls within this paragraph if—

(a) for a continuous period of not less than 3 months falling immediately before the date on which he first attended the course of study he was in receipt of jobseeker's allowance[4, incapacity benefit or employment and support allowance] or was on a course of training or he was in receipt of income support and he fell within paragraph 7 of Schedule 1B to the Income Support Regulations or

(b) during the period of 6 months falling immediately before the date on which he first attended the course of study he was—

(i) for a period, or periods in the aggregate, of not less than 3 months in receipt of jobseeker's allowance[4, incapacity benefit or employment and support allowance] or on a course of training or he was in receipt of income support and he fell within paragraph 7 of Schedule 1B to the Income Support Regulations and

(ii) after the period referred to in (i), or in the case of periods in the aggregate, after the first such period and throughout the remainder of the 6 months for which that sub-paragraph did not apply to him, engaged in remunerative work or other work the emoluments of which are such as to disentitle him from receipt of jobseeker's allowance[4, incapacity benefit or employment and support allowance] or from receipt of income support which would have been payable because he fell within paragraph 7 of Schedule 1B to the Income Support Regulations

and the period of 3 months referred to in sub-paragraph (i) or, as the case may be, the period of 6 months referred to in sub-paragraph (ii), fell wholly after the terminal date.

(3) In this regulation, "training" means training for which persons aged under 18 are eligible and for which persons aged 18 to 24 may be eligible [3 secured in England and Wales by the Learning and Skills Council for England or by the National Council for Education and Training for Wales, and in Scotland, provided] directly or indirectly by a Local Enterprise Company pursuant to its arrangement with, as the case may be, Scottish Enterprise or Highlands and Islands Enterprise (whether that arrangement is known as an Operating Contract or by any other name).

AMENDMENTS

1. Jobseeker's Allowance and Income Support (General) (Amendment) Regulations 1996 (SI 1996/1517) reg.3 (October 7, 1996).

2. Jobseeker's Allowance (Amendment) (No.2) Regulations 1999 (SI 1999/3087) reg.2 (November 30, 1999).

3. Jobseeker's Allowance (Amendment) Regulations 2001 (SI 2001/1434) reg.2(3) (March 26, 2001).

4. Employment and Support Allowance (Consequential Provisions) (No.2) Regulations 2008 (SI 2008/1554) reg.3(3) (October 27, 2008).

5. Social Security (Lone Parents and Miscellaneous Amendments) Regulations 2008 (SI 2008/3051) reg.11(5) (November 24, 2008).

6. Jobseeker's Allowance (Lone Parents) (Availability for Work) Regulations 2010 (SI 2010/837) reg.2(6) (April 26, 2010).

DEFINITIONS

"course of study"—see reg.1(3).
"employment"—see reg.4.
"part-time student"—see reg.1(3).
"pattern of availability"—see regs 4 and 7(2)(a).
"terminal date"—see reg.1(3).
"week"—see reg.4.

GENERAL NOTE

The effect of this provision, broadly, is to disregard a part-time student's course of study when deciding whether he is available for employment, as long as he is prepared and able to re-arrange the hours of the course in order to take up employment, to start work immediately, or on notice if reg.5(1), (1A), (2) or (3) applies, and he complies with reg.6. However, it only applies to part-time students who satisfy the conditions in para.(2) and who have restricted the hours for which they are available under regs 7(2), 13(3), (3A) or (4), 13A or 17(2). Note that if a part- **3.48** time student's hours of study fall completely outside the times he has agreed to be available for work he will not need to rely on this provision as his availability will not be affected.

A part-time student is a person who is undertaking a course of study who is not a full-time student (reg.1(3)). See reg.1(3) for the definitions of "full-time student" and "course of study" and the notes to reg.130.

This regulation does not apply to a person in relevant education (defined in reg.54(1) and (2); see the notes to reg.54) because such a person is excluded from JSA (s.1(2)(g) of the old style Jobseekers Act 1995). But note that under reg.54(3) a young person (i.e. under 19: reg.76) who is a part-time student on a course other than one of advanced education or of a kind within para.(b) of the definition of full-time student in reg.1(3) and who satisfies para.(2) of this regulation does not count as in relevant education (and will not do so after he finishes or leaves his part-time course (reg.54(4))). Thus para.(1) may apply to such a young person.

A part-time student (except a person whose course does not conflict with his permitted pattern of availability) who does not satisfy the conditions in this regulation will probably not be treated as available unless prepared to abandon the course in order to take up employment. But note reg.17A, in force from June 1, 1998, under which a claimant aged 25 or over may be able to attend a full-time employment-related course while continuing to receive old style JSA, and the more limited deeming of availability in reg.14(1)(a), (aa) and (f).

Paragraph (2)

3.49 The main condition (sub-para.(a)) is that for the whole three months immediately before the course the claimant was either in receipt of JSA, incapacity benefit, ESA or income support while sick or on Work Based Training for Young People (see the definition of training in para.(3)). Receipt of benefit means entitlement to benefit, whether benefit is actually in payment or not (*R(SB) 12/87*). The intention is that the claimant should be primarily unemployed and not simply wishing to continue to study on benefit. A person who leaves school in the summer will not be entitled to old style JSA until the first Monday in September (see reg.54(2)) and thus will not have had three months on benefit in time to start a course before January.

The three months (or the six months in sub-para.(b), see below) cannot begin until after the "terminal date", that is, after the person has ceased to be treated as in relevant education. If the claimant starts (say in September) a course whose contact hours are below 12, so as to be outside the definition of relevant education (see the notes to reg.54), and after three months on benefit increases the hours, it may be difficult to decide when the claimant first attended "the" course. The official view in the previous edition of the *Adjudication Officer's Guide* (para.25529) (in relation to the 21-hour rule in the former reg.9 of the Income Support Regulations, see J. Mesher and P. Wood, *Income-Related Benefits: The Legislation* (1996)) was that a mere change in hours did not mean that a new course was starting, so that the three months' benefit would have been at the wrong time, but that if the subjects taken had changed there would have been a new course.

Under sub-para.(b) a claimant can mix receipt of a relevant benefit, Work Based Training and work over the six months, provided that the relevant benefit and the Work Based Training add up to at least three months.

3.50 *The transition from new style JSA*

In para.(2)(a) the reference to jobseeker's allowance is, where art.13(1) and (2) of the Welfare Reform Act 2012 (Commencement No.9 and Transitional and Transitory Provisions and Commencement No.8 and Savings and Transitional Provisions (Amendment)) Order 2013 (as amended and set out in the 2014/15

Supplement) applies, to be read as if it included a reference to new style JSA (art.13(3)(za) of that Order, in force from June 16, 2014).

Volunteers

[1 **12.**—(1) Paragraph (2) applies if in any week a person is engaged in voluntary work and— 3.51

(a) he has restricted the total number of hours for which he is available in accordance with regulation 7(2),[2 13(3), (3A) or (4)] [3, 13A] or 17(2); and

(b) the hours in which he is engaged in voluntary work fall in whole or in part within his pattern of availability.

(2) In determining whether a person to whom this paragraph applies is available for employment no matter relating to his voluntary work shall be relevant providing—

(a) on being given one week's notice, he is willing and able to re-arrange the hours in which he is engaged in voluntary work in order to take up employment at times falling within his pattern of availability; and

(b) on being given 48 hours' notice, he is willing and able to re-arrange the hours in which he is engaged in voluntary work in order to attend for interview at times falling within his pattern of availability in connection with the opportunity of any such employment; and

(c) he complies with the requirements of regulation 6.

(3) In paragraph (2) "week" means any period of seven consecutive days.]

AMENDMENTS

1. Jobseeker's Allowance (Amendment) Regulations 2002 (SI 2002/3072) reg.4 (January 1, 2003).
2. Social Security (Lone Parents and Miscellaneous Amendments) Regulations 2008 (SI 2008/3051) reg.11(6) (November 4, 2008).
3. Jobseeker's Allowance (Lone Parents) (Availability for Work) Regulations 2010 (SI 2010/837) reg.2(7) (April 26, 2010).

DEFINITIONS

"employment"—see reg.4.
"pattern of availability"—*ibid.*, and reg.7(2)(a).
"voluntary work"—see reg.4.

GENERAL NOTE

Section 6(1) of the old style Jobseekers Act 1995 stipulates that a claimant is available for employment if willing and able to take up immediately *any employed earner's employment*. This regulation mitigates the rigour of that section as regards determining the availability of a claimant engaged in voluntary work (defined below). 3.52

If a person has restricted his hours of availability under regs.7(2), 13(3) or (4), 13A or 17(2), any voluntary work (defined in reg.4) that he does which coincides with the times he has agreed to be available for work will be disregarded when deciding whether he is available for work, as long as he is prepared and able, on one week's notice, to re-arrange the hours in which he is engaged in voluntary work in order to take up employment at times falling within his pattern of availability, and, on 48 hours' notice, to re-arrange the hours in which he is engaged in voluntary work in order to attend for interview at times falling within his pattern of availability in connection with the opportunity of any such employment. He must, however, comply with reg.6. If a person's voluntary work falls outside the hours of agreed availability this regulation does not apply as availability will not be affected.

See also reg.5(1)(b) under which a person doing voluntary work only has to be available to take up employment on one week's notice and to attend for interview for such employment on 48 hours' notice.

A claimant is engaged in voluntary work when working for an organisation the activities of which are carried on otherwise than for profit, or for someone other than a member of his family, where he receives no payment by virtue of such engagement or the only payment due for it is one in respect of his reasonable expenses of such engagement (reg.4). For availability purposes, "week" means "benefit week": generally the period of seven days ending with the day corresponding to the claimant's "signing"/attendance day (regs 4 and 1(3)).

Note also that reg.18(3)(g) requires time engaged in voluntary work and the extent to which it may have improved prospects of employment to be taken into account in determining for the purposes of the actively seeking employment test whether a claimant has taken all reasonably expected steps to have the best prospects of securing employment.

Additional restrictions on availability for certain groups

3.53 **13.**—(1) In any week a person may restrict his availability for employment in the following ways, if the circumstances set out apply.

(2) Subject to regulations 6, 7 and 9, a person may impose restrictions on the nature of the employment for which he is available by reason of a sincerely held religious belief, or a sincerely held conscientious objection providing he can show that he has reasonable prospects of employment notwithstanding those restrictions and any restrictions on his availability in accordance with regulation 7(2), 8, paragraph [[1](3), (3A) or (4)] of this regulation[[2], regulation 13A or] or regulation 17(1) or (2).

(3) A person may restrict his availability in any way providing the restrictions are reasonable in the light of his physical or mental condition.

[[1] (3A) A person who has caring responsibilities in relation to a child and who—

(a) is the subject of a parenting order concerning that child under section 8 of the Crime and Disorder Act 1998, section 20 of the Anti-social Behaviour Act 2003("the 2003 Act"), or in relation to Scotland, under section 102 of the Antisocial Behaviour etc. (Scotland) Act 2004, or

(b) has entered into a parenting contract concerning that child under section 19 of the 2003 Act,

may restrict his availability in any way providing the restrictions are reasonable in the light of the terms of the order or contract.]

(4) A person with caring responsibilities may restrict the total number of hours for which he is available for employment to less than 40 hours in any week providing—

(a) in that week he is available for employment for as many hours as his caring responsibilities allow and for the specific hours that those responsibilities allow and

(b) he has reasonable prospects of securing employment notwithstanding that restriction and

(c) he is available for employment of at least 16 hours in that week.

(5) In deciding whether a person satisfies the conditions in paragraph (4)(a), regard shall be had, in particular, to the following matters—

(a) the particular hours and days spent in caring;

(b) whether the caring responsibilities are shared with another person;

(c) the age and physical and mental condition of the person being cared for.

[[1](6) This paragraph applies to a person who has caring responsibilities in relation to a child if an employment officer determines that, due to the type and number of employment vacancies within daily travelling distance of the person's home, he would not satisfy the condition in paragraph (4)(b).

(7) Paragraph (4) has effect in relation to a person to whom paragraph (6) applies as if sub-paragraph (b) were omitted.]

AMENDMENTS

1. Social Security (Lone Parents and Miscellaneous Amendments) Regulations 2008 (SI 2008/3051) reg.11(7) (November 4, 2008).

2. Jobseeker's Allowance (Lone Parents) (Availability for Work) Regulations 2010 (SI 2010/837) reg.2(8) (April 26, 2010).

DEFINITIONS

"caring responsibilities"—see reg.4.
"child"—see Jobseekers Act 1995 s.35(1).
"employment"—see reg.4.
"employment officer"—see Jobseekers Act 1995 s.35(1).
"week"—see reg.4.

GENERAL NOTE

Section 6(1) of the old style Jobseekers Act 1995 stipulates that a claimant is available for employment if he is willing and able to take up immediately *any employed earner's employment*. This regulation mitigates the rigour of that by enabling certain claimants to impose restrictions on availability without thereby precluding entitlement to JSA. For availability purposes, "week" means "benefit week": generally the period of seven days ending with the day corresponding to the claimant's "signing"/attendance day (regs 4 and 1(3)). 3.54

Paragraph (1)

This makes clear that in any week a claimant may be able to impose restrictions under more than one of the other paragraphs in this regulation; this paragraph reads "may restrict his availability for employment in the following *ways*" (emphasis added by annotator). 3.55

Paragraph (2)

A claimant complying with the dictates of regs 6, 7 and 9 can impose restrictions on the nature of the employment for which he is available because of a sincerely held religious belief or conscientious objection, so long as he can show that he has reasonable prospects of employment despite those and any other restrictions imposed under other availability regulations (namely, regs 7(2); 8, paras (3) and (4) of this regulation, reg.13A and regs 17(1) and (2)). Regulation 10(2) provides that the burden of establishing this lies on the claimant. In determining whether he has reasonable prospects of employment, regard must be had in particular to: his skills, qualifications and experience; the type and number of vacancies within daily 3.56

travelling distance of his home; how long he has been unemployed; what job applications he has made and their outcome (reg.10(1)(a)–(d)). Since his restrictions include ones on the nature of the employment he is prepared to accept, regard must also be had to whether he is willing to move home to take up employment (reg.10(1)(e)).

Paragraph (3)

3.57 This provides protection for the sick/disabled: those who are in some way physically or mentally incapacitated and who are unable or unwilling (especially in the light of regs 55, 55ZA and 55A allowing an old style JSA claimant to be treated as capable of work or as not having limited capability for work during short and shortish periods of actual inability to work) to claim an incapacity benefit or ESA. Where and for so long as any of regs 55, 55ZA or 55A apply a claimant is deemed by reg.14(1)(l) to be available for employment and by reg.19(1)(l), (lzl) or (ll), as the case may be, to be actively seeking employment. Thus for those periods what restrictions are permissible under reg.13(3) is less important, although it appears that any restrictions should still be recorded in the claimant's jobseeker's agreement (reg.31(c)) as well as the general pattern of availability. Regulation 13(3) becomes more important where the deeming mentioned above does not apply and provides a general protection to take reasonable account of the particular nature of the claimant's physical or mental condition. Regard must also be had to a claimant's physical or mental limitations when determining under the actively seeking employment condition whether all reasonably expected steps have been taken to secure employment (reg.18(3)(b)).

Under this paragraph, claimants can restrict their availability *in any way*. This can therefore include restrictions on the rate of pay acceptable as well as on the nature or location of employment, terms and conditions, hours and days of availability etc. The essential test is that such restrictions are reasonable in light of their physical or mental condition. If all the restrictions imposed can be so justified, no issue of "reasonable prospects of employment" arises. If, however, restrictions are imposed which require justification under certain other provisions (regs 7, 8 or para.(2) of this regulation), then the claimant has to show that he has reasonable prospects of employment despite the totality of restrictions imposed (including those justified under this paragraph). In such a case, reg.10(2) requires that the burden of establishing this lies on the claimant. In determining whether he has reasonable prospects of employment, regard must be had in particular to: his skills, qualifications and experience; the type and number of vacancies within daily travelling distance of his home; how long he has been unemployed; what job applications he has made and their outcome (reg.10(1)(a)–(d)). If the restrictions include ones on the nature of the employment he is prepared to accept (this and regs 8 and 13(2) enable such restrictions), regard must also be had to whether he is willing to move home to take up employment (reg.10(1)(e)). If, however, the only other restrictions imposed are those as a carer on hours and pattern of availability justifiable under para.(4), the reasonable prospects issue focuses only on the restrictions imposed under that paragraph. Note that, in contrast to para.(4), this paragraph sets no minimum on hours of availability; the touchstone is reasonableness in light of physical or mental condition.

This provision is potentially quite wide. It permits *any* restrictions on availability that are reasonable because of the claimant's physical or mental condition. Indeed, in *R(JSA) 3/01*, Commissioner Levenson held that, even though someone else imposed the restrictions, that is the police, reg.13(3) protected the claimant from the preclusive effect of reg.7: the restriction (two days in police custody) was reasonable (indeed inevitable) in light of his physical condition which was such that he was not free, legally or practically, to leave (para.6). On appeal, however, the Court of Appeal held that Commisioner Levenson had erred in law (*CAO v David*, reported in *R(JSA) 3/01*). Simon Brown LJ said:

> "In short, the Commissioner took the view, first that the expression in regulation 13(3) 'physical or mental condition' is apt to refer not only to some dis-

ability on the claimant's part but also to any extraneous physical constraints that may be placed upon him; and second that it is unnecessary under this regulation for the claimant himself to have invoked his 'condition' so as to justify restricting his availability in advance of the week in question; rather the claimant's non-availability can retrospectively be overlooked under this provision.

I have to say that to my mind both limbs of this construction are impossible. The reference to the claimant's 'physical or mental condition' seems to me clearly confined to some personal disability. And it seems to me no less clear that the provision applies prospectively only and specifically with regard to the completion of the jobseeker's agreement. That this is so is surely demonstrated also by regulation 55 which deals with short periods of sickness ... .

On the Commissioner's approach there would be no need for regulation 55: such a person could instead invoke regulation 13(3) and, notwithstanding his jobseeker's agreement, assert that his availability was restricted by his temporary physical incapacity.

It follows that in my judgment the Commissioner was wrong in his decision and that, so far from resolving the appeal in favour of the claimant (who had not appealed), he should have decided it in favour of the adjudication officer (who had)". (paras 19–22 of the judgment)

Note that para.(3) is not made subject to any other provisions. Thus, for example, although restrictions on the rate of pay may only be imposed for six months under reg.9, it is apparently accepted that restrictions under para.(3) can include limits on the rate of pay the claimant will accept *after* six months, as long as the restriction is reasonable in the light of his condition, e.g. because of additional transport costs (see *Welfare Rights Bulletin* 138, p.4).

Paragraph (3A)

Since November 24, 2008, carers with responsibilities for caring for a child, who are subject in respect of that child to parenting orders under the anti-social behaviour legislation, or who have entered in respect of that child into a parenting contract under that legislation, can restrict availability in any way so long as the restrictions are reasonable in the light of the terms of that order or contract. **3.58**

Paragraphs (4) and (5)

These paragraphs provide assistance to a claimant who is a carer ("a person with caring responsibilities", discussed below), enabling him to restrict his total hours of availability in any week to below 40 hours but not less than 16 hours per week, provided that in that week he is available for employment for as many hours as his caring responsibilities permit and for the specific hours they allow, and provided that he has reasonable prospects of employment notwithstanding that restriction (para. (4)). In determining whether in any week he is available for as many hours as his caring responsibilities allow and for the specific hours they allow ("the conditions in paragraph (4)(a)"), regard must be had, in particular (the list is not exhaustive), to: the particular hours and days spent in caring; whether the caring responsibilities are shared with someone else; the age, physical and mental condition of the person being cared for by the claimant (para.(5)). In determining whether he has reasonable prospects of employment (and the burden of establishing this lies on the claimant: reg.10(2)), regard must be had in particular to: his skills, qualifications and experience; the type and number of vacancies within daily travelling distance of his home; how long he has been unemployed; what job applications he has made and their outcome (reg.10(1)(a)–(d)). If the claimant has placed other restrictions on his availability under regs 7, 8 or para.(2) of this regulation, the matter of "reasonable prospects" must be looked at in the context of the totality of restrictions imposed, although that flows from those other provisions rather than this. If those restrictions include ones on the nature of the employment he is prepared to accept **3.59** (reg.8 and para.(2) of this regulation enable such restrictions), regard must also be had to whether he is willing to move home to take up employment (reg.10(1)(e)). If, however, the only restrictions imposed apart from those under para.(4) are ones justified under para.(3) of this regulation (reasonable in light of physical or mental condition), the "reasonable prospects" issue would fall to be decided only with regard to the total hours and pattern of availability restrictions imposed under para.(4).

A carer (a person "who has caring responsibilities") is someone who has responsibility for caring for a child or for an elderly person or for a person whose physical or mental condition requires him to be cared for. But the child, the elderly person and the person whose conditions requires him to be cared for must either be a close relative or in the same household (reg.4). "Close relative" means a spouse or other member of an unmarried couple, parent, step-parent, grandparent, parent-in-law, son, step-son, son-in-law, daughter, step-daughter, daughter-in-law, brother, sister, grandchild or the spouse of any of these persons or, if that person is one of an unmarried couple, the other member of that couple (*ibid.*). On "unmarried couple" see old style Jobseekers Act 1995 s.35(1) and note thereto.

[1 Additional restrictions on availability for lone parents

3.60 **13A.**—A lone parent who in any week is responsible for, and a member of the same household as, a child under the age of 13 may restrict his availability for employment to the child's normal school hours.]

AMENDMENT

1. Jobseeker's Allowance (Lone Parents) (Availability for Work) Regulations 2010 (SI 2010/837) reg.2(9) (April 26, 2010).

DEFINITIONS

"lone parent"—see reg.1(3).
"week"—see reg.4.

GENERAL NOTE

3.61 From April 26, 2010, this allows a lone parent, who in any week is both responsible for (see regs 77 and 78) and a member of the same household as a child under 13, to restrict their hours of availability to that child's normal school hours.

Circumstances in which a person is to be treated as available

3.62 **14.**—(1) A person [16. . .] shall be treated as available for employment in the following circumstances for as long as those circumstances apply, subject to any maximum period specified in this paragraph—

(a) notwithstanding regulation [815(1)(a)], if he is participating as a full-time student in an employment-related course where participation by him has been approved before the course started by an employment officer, for a maximum of 2 weeks and one such course in any period of 12 months;

[16(aa) notwithstanding regulation 15(1)(a), if he is participating in a traineeship;]

(b) if he is attending a residential work camp, for a maximum of 2 weeks and one such occasion in any period of 12 months;

(c) if he is temporarily absent from Great Britain because he is taking a member of his family who is a child or young person abroad for treatment, for a maximum of 8 weeks;

(d) if he is engaged in the manning or launching of a lifeboat or in the performance of duty as a part-time member of a fire brigade or engaged during an emergency in duties for the benefit of others;

(e) if he is a member of a couple and is looking after a member of his family who is a child while the other member is temporarily absent from the United Kingdom, for a maximum of 8 weeks;

(f) if he is following an Open University course and is attending, as a requirement of that course, a residential course, for a maximum of one week per course;

(g) if he is temporarily looking after a child full-time because the person who normally looks after the child is ill or temporarily absent from home or the person is looking after a member of the family who is ill, for a maximum of 8 weeks;

(h) if he has been discharged from detention in a prison, remand centre or youth custody institution [12and he is not given notice to participate in [13a scheme prescribed in regulation 3 of the Jobseeker's Allowance (Schemes for Assisting Persons to Obtain Employment) Regulations 2013]], for one week commencing with the date of his discharge;

[2(i) if the period beginning on the date of claim and ending on the day before the beginning of the first week after the date of claim is less than 7 days and the circumstances in paragraph (2A) apply, for any part of that period when he is not treated as available for employment under any other provision of this regulation;]

[1(j) if the award is terminated other than on the last day of a week, for the period beginning with the beginning of the week in which the award is terminated and ending on the day on which the award is terminated;]

(k) notwithstanding regulation [815(1)(a)], if he is participating in a programme provided by the Venture Trust in pursuance of an arrangement made by [7 the Scottish Ministers], for a maximum of 4 weeks and one such programme in any period of 12 months;

(l) if he is treated as capable of work [10or as not having limited capability for work] in accordance with regulation 55, [1755ZA or 55A], for the period determined in accordance with that regulation;

[5(ll) [17...]

(m) if he is temporarily absent from Great Britain to attend an interview for employment and has given notice to an employment officer, in writing if so required by the employment officer, that he will be so absent for a maximum of one week;

(n) if he is a member of a couple [4 other than a joint-claim couple] and he and his partner are both absent from Great Britain and a premium referred to in paragraph 10, 11, 12, 13 or 15 of Schedule 1 (applicable amounts) is applicable in respect of his partner, for a maximum of 4 weeks.

[4(nn) if he is a member of a joint-claim couple and he and his partner are both absent from Great Britain and a premium referred to in paragraph 20E, 20F, 20G or 20I of Schedule 1 (applicable amounts) is applicable in respect of his partner, for a maximum of 4 weeks;]

[3(o) if—

(i) he is available for employment, or is treated as such, on the day he makes his claim for a jobseeker's allowance; and

(ii) the Secretary of State has directed that the prescribed time for claiming a jobseeker's allowance be extended under regulation 19(6) of the Claims and Payments Regulations where the circumstances specified in regulation 19(7)(d) of those Regulations applied in relation to an entitlement to incapacity benefit[[10], employment and support allowance] or an entitlement to income support by virtue of paragraph 7 of Schedule 1B to the Income Support Regulations,

for the period of that extension.]

[[4](p) if he is temporarily absent from Great Britain in the circumstances prescribed in regulation 50(6B)(a) or (c) for the period of any such temporary absence.]

[[5](q) if he is temporarily absent from Great Britain in the circumstances prescribed in regulation 50(6AA) or, as the case may be, (6C).]

[[6](r) if he is required to attend a court or tribunal as a justice of the peace, a party to any proceedings, a witness or a juror;

(s) if, for a maximum of 96 hours before being released, he is in—

(i) police detention within the meaning in section 118(2) of the Police and Criminal Evidence Act 1984 (general interpretation), or

(ii) legal custody within the meaning in section 295 of the Criminal Procedure (Scotland) Act 1995 (legal custody in Scotland) but is not a prisoner as defined by regulation 85(4) (special cases).]

[[9](t) he is looking after a child for whom he has caring responsibilities during the child's school holidays or another similar vacation period and it would be unreasonable for him to make other arrangements for the care of that child;

(u) he is looking after a child for whom he has caring responsibilities at a time when the child—

(i) is excluded from school or another educational establishment, and

(ii) is not receiving education pursuant to arrangements made by a local education authority or (in Scotland) an education authority, and

there are no other arrangements for the care of that child it would be reasonable for him to make.]

[[18](v) if he is a member of a reserve force prescribed in Part I of Schedule 6 to the Contributions Regulations, either—

(i) if he is engaged in his first year of training, for a maximum of 43 days in that year; or

(ii) if he is engaged in annual continuous training, for a maximum of 15 days in any calendar year.]

(2) [[9]Subject to [[14]paragraphs (2ZB), (2ZC) and (2ZD)] a person [[16]. . .] shall be treated as available for employment in the following circumstances—

(a) if there is a death or serious illness of a close relative or close friend of his;

(b) if there is a domestic emergency affecting him or a close relative or close friend of his;

(c) if there is a funeral of a close relative or close friend of his;

(d) if he has caring responsibilities and the person being cared for has died;

for the time required to deal with the emergency or other circumstance and for a maximum of one week on the occurrence of any of the circumstances set out in sub-paragraphs (a) to (d), or any combination of those circumstances, and on no more than 4 such periods in any period of 12 months.

[[9](2ZA) A person who has caring responsibilities in relation to a child may be treated as available for employment for more than one week, but for no more than 8 weeks, on the occurrence of any of the circumstances set out in paragraph (2)(a) or (b), or any combination of those circumstances, but on no more than one occasion in any period of 12 months.

(2ZB) Where a claimant has been treated as available for employment under paragraph (2ZA) in any period of 12 months, the first week in which he is so treated shall count towards the 4 periods allowable under paragraph (2).]

[[15](2ZC) A person who has recently become homeless shall be treated as available for employment under paragraph (2)(b) only where he takes such steps as are reasonable for him to take to find living accommodation.

(2ZD) A person to whom paragraph (2ZC) applies may be treated as available for employment under paragraph (2)(b) for periods of longer than one week and on more than 4 occasions in any 12 months.]

[[2](2A) A person shall be treated as available for employment under paragraph (1)(i) only if—

- (a) where a pattern of availability is recorded in his jobseeker's agreement, or where he has restricted the hours for which he is available in accordance with regulations [[9] 13(3), (3A) or (4)] [[11], 13A] or 17(2) and that restriction has been agreed with an employment officer, he is available for employment during such of the period referred to in paragraph (1)(i) as he is not treated as available for employment under any other provision of this regulation, in accordance with—
  - (i) his pattern of availability or, as the case may be, the hours to which he has restricted his availability in accordance with regulations [[9]13(3), (3A) or (4)][[11], 13A] or 17(2), and
  - (ii) any other restrictions he has placed on his availability for employment which will apply in the first week after the date of claim, provided those restrictions have been agreed with an employment officer, and
  - (iii) if he falls within regulation 5, that regulation;
- (b) where no pattern of availability is recorded in his jobseeker's agreement, he is available for employment during such of the period referred to in paragraph (1)(i) as he is not treated as available for employment under any other provision of this regulation—
  - (i) in accordance with any restrictions he has placed on his availability for employment which will apply in the first week after the date of claim, provided those restrictions have been agreed with an employment officer, and
  - (ii) for 8 hours on each day falling within that period on which he is not treated as available for employment to any extent under any other provision of this regulation, and
  - (iii) if he falls within regulation 5, in accordance with that regulation.]

[[6] (2B) A person shall not be treated as available for employment under paragraph (1)(r)—

(a) for more than eight weeks,
(b) where he does not, before the period during which he is required to attend the court or tribunal, give an employment officer notice, in writing where requested by the employment officer, that he is so required, or
(c) where he is a prisoner as defined by regulation 85(4) (special cases).]

(3) If any of the circumstances set out in paragraph (1), except those in sub-paragraphs (i) and (j), or any of those set out in paragraph (2) apply to a person for part of a week, he shall for the purposes of regulation 7(1) be treated as available for 8 hours on any day on which those circumstances applied subject to the maximum specified in paragraph (1) or (2), unless he has restricted the total number of hours for which he is available in a week in accordance with regulation 7(2), [1 13(4)] or 17(2). If he has so restricted the total number of hours for which he is available, he shall, for the purposes of regulation [1 7(1), 13(4) or 17(2)], be treated as available for the number of hours for which he would be available on that day in accordance with his pattern of availability recorded in his jobseeker's agreement, if any of the circumstances set out in paragraph (1) except those in sub-paragraphs (i) and (j) or any of those set out in paragraph (2) applied on that day, subject to the maximum specified in paragraph (1) or (2).

(4) In paragraph (1)(c), "treatment" means treatment for a disease or bodily or mental disablement by or under the supervision of a person qualified to provide medical treatment, physiotherapy or a form of treatment which is similar to, or related to, either of those forms of treatment.

(5) For the purposes of paragraph (1)(d),
(a) a person is engaged in duties for the benefit of others while—
  (i) providing assistance to any person whose life may be endangered or who may be exposed to the risk of serious bodily injury or whose health may be seriously impaired,
  (ii) protecting property of substantial value from imminent risk of serious damage or destruction, or
  (iii) assisting in measures being taken to prevent a serious threat to the health of the people,

as a member of a group of persons organised wholly or partly for the purpose of providing such assistance or, as the case may be, protection;
(b) events which may give rise to an emergency include—
  (i) a fire, a flood or an explosion,
  (ii) a natural catastrophe,
  (iii) a railway or other transport accident,
  (iv) a cave or mountain accident,
  (v) an accident at sea,
  (vi) a person being reported missing and the organisation of a search for that person.

(6) In paragraph (1), except in sub-paragraphs (i) and (j), and in paragraph (2), "week" means any period of 7 consecutive days.

[6 (7) In this regulation, "tribunal" means any tribunal listed in Schedule 1 to the Tribunals and Inquiries Act 1992.]

AMENDMENTS

1. Jobseeker's Allowance and Income Support (General) (Amendment) Regulations 1996 (SI 1996/1517) reg.5 (October 7, 1996).

2. Social Security (Jobseeker's Allowance and Mariners' Benefits) (Miscellaneous Amendments) Regulations 1997 (SI 1997/563) reg.2 (March 11, 1997).
3. Jobseeker's Allowance (Amendment) (No.2) Regulations 1999 (SI 1999/3807) reg.3 (November 30, 1999).
4. Jobseeker's Allowance (Joint Claims: Consequential Amendments) Regulations 2000 (SI 2000/3336) reg.2 (March 19, 2001).
5. Social Security (Income Support and Jobseeker's Allowance) Amendment Regulations 2004 (SI 2004/1869) reg.3(2) (October 4, 2004).
6. Social Security (Income Support and Jobseeker's Allowance) Amendment Regulations 2006 (SI 2006/1402) reg.2(3) (May 30, 2006).
7. Social Security (Miscellaneous Amendments) Regulations 2008 (SI 2008/698) reg.4(4) (April 14, 2008).
8. Social Security (Students Responsible for Children or Young Persons) Amendment Regulations 2008 (SI 2008/1826) reg.3(5) (July 9, 2008).
9. Social Security (Lone Parents and Miscellaneous Amendments) Regulations 2008 (SI 2008/3051) reg.11(8) (November 4, 2008).
10. Employment and Support Allowance (Consequential Provisions) (No.2) Regulations 2008 (SI 2008/1554) reg.4(4) (October 27, 2008).
11. Jobseeker's Allowance (Lone Parents) (Availability for Work) Regulations 2010 (SI 2010/837) reg.2(10) (April 26, 2010).
12. Jobseeker's Allowance (Jobseeking and Work for Your Benefit) (Amendment and Revocation) Regulations 2012 (SI 2012/397) reg.2 (March 1, 2012).
13. Jobseeker's Allowance (Schemes for Assisting Persons to Obtain Employment) Regulations 2013 (SI 2013/276) reg.14 (February 12, 2013 at 6.45 pm).
14. Jobseeker's Allowance (Homeless Claimants) Amendment Regulations 2014 (SI 2014/1623) reg.2(2) (July 21, 2014).
15. Jobseeker's Allowance (Homeless Claimants) Amendment Regulations 2014 (SI 2014/1623) reg.2(3) (July 21, 2014).
16. Social Security (Traineeships and Qualifying Young Persons) Amendment Regulations 2015 (SI 2015/336) reg.2(3) (March 27, 2015).
17. Jobseeker's Allowance (Extended Period of Sickness) Amendment Regulations 2015 (SI 2015/339) reg.2(2) (March 30, 2015).
18. Social Security (Members of the Reserve Forces) (Amendment) Regulations 2015 (SI 2015/389) reg.3(3) (April 6, 2015).

DEFINITIONS

"a joint-claim couple"—see Jobseekers Act 1995 s.1(4).
"capable of work"—see Jobseekers Act 1995 s.35(2) and Sch.1 para.2; reg.55.
"caring responsibilities"—see reg.4.
"child"—see Jobseekers Act 1995 s.35(1).
"close relative"—see reg.4.
"Contributions Regulations"—see reg.1(3).
"couple"—*ibid.*
"date of claim"—*ibid.*
"employment"—see reg.4.
"employment officer"—see Jobseekers Act 1995 s.35(1).
"employment-related course"—see reg.1(3).
"family"—see Jobseekers Act 1995 s.35(1).
"first year of training"—see reg.1(3).
"full-time student"—*ibid.*
"Great Britain"—see Jobseekers Act 1995 s.35(1).
"partner"—see reg.1(3).
"part-time member of a fire brigade"—see reg.4.
"traineeship"—see reg.1(3).
"week" (except in paras (1)(i) and (j) and (2))—see para.(6).
"week" (in paras (1)(i) and (j) and (2))—see reg.4.

"work camp"—see reg.4.
"young person"—see regs 1(3) and 76.

GENERAL NOTE

3.63 This regulation sets out in paras (1) and (2) a diverse range of specific situations in which, for the periods specified, someone is to be treated as available for employment even though the person might otherwise fail to satisfy the test of availability for work in s.6(1) of the old style Jobseekers Act 1995 as modified by these Regulations. The express exception at the beginning of para.(1) where reg.15(1)(a), (b), (bc) or (c) applies has now been removed (with effect from March 30, 2015). The specific provision in para.(1)(a), (aa) and (k) for those sub-paras to apply notwithstanding reg.15(1)(a) would suggest the intention that, apart from those circumstances, a person deemed under reg.15(1) not to be available cannot take advantage of reg.14. However, that result is expressly achieved by the new reg.15(5). See the notes to reg.15 for the treatment of full-time students, to which para.(1)(a) and (k) is relevant.

The categories set out in para.(1) need to be examined carefully. They cannot apply for longer than the circumstances prescribed last. However, some categories contain more stringent limits. Sub-paragraph (l) is an important element of the protection given to those who are treated as capable of work or as not having limited capability for work under regs 55, 55ZA or 55A, by deeming such persons to be available for employment (and see reg.19(1)(l), (lzl) and (ll) on deemed actively seeking employment). However, claimants who fall outside those regulations but who restrict their availability as reasonable in the light of their physical or mental condition (reg.13(3)) still have to meet the s.6(1) test in relation to whatever is left after applying those restrictions.

The remainder of the categories specified in para.(1) fall into four main groups (sometimes overlapping): those taking part in certain educational or training activities (sub-paras (a), (aa), (b), (f), (k) and (v)); those involving temporary absence from Great Britain (sub-paras (c), (e), (m), (n), (nn), (p) and (q)); those involving caring for others (sub-paras (e), (g), (t) and (u)); and those involving some public service (sub-paras (d), with para.(5), (r) and (v)). The remaining miscellaneous categories, often to do with the beginning or end of a period of entitlement, are in sub-paras (h), (i), (j), (o) and (s).

Paragraph (2), unless any of the contrary rules in reg.15(1) apply (see reg.15(5)), requires claimants to be treated as available for employment when affected by various adverse personal circumstances, such as the death or serious illness of a close relative (defined) or close friend (not defined) (sub-para.(a)) or the funeral of such a person (sub-para.(c)). However, the deeming lasts only for the time required to deal with the circumstance up to a maximum of one week for each occurrence, subject to the potential extensions mentioned below. There can ordinarily only be four periods of such deeming within any 12-month period. There is a more general category of deeming under para.(2)(b) covering a domestic emergency (not defined) affecting the claimant or a close relative or close friend. Since July 21, 2014 there has, under para.(2ZC), been a limitation on the application of para.(2)(b) if the claimant has recently become homeless (not defined), when the claimant must take such steps as are reasonable to find living accommodation (not defined) to benefit from the deeming. However, if that condition is met, both the one-week limit and the four occasions rule do not apply (para.(2ZD)). Paragraph (2)(d) applies to a person with caring responsibilities (defined in reg.4 to require the person cared for to be a close relative or a member of the same household) when the person cared for has died, subject to the ordinary limits. Paragraph (2ZA) allows the one-week limit in relation to para.(2)(a) or (b) to be extended to eight weeks where the claimant has caring responsibilities for a child (and see para.(1)(t) and (u)). The mere death of a child for whom the claimant has caring responsibilities but who is not a close relative (see para.(2)(a)) cannot trigger the extension in para.(2ZA) except on the rather artificial basis either that the child was a "close friend" or that there is a domestic emergency.

In *CAO v David* (reported as *R(JSA)3/01* alongside the decision of Commissioner Levenson, whose reasoning the Court rejected)(see further the commentary to reg.7(3)), the Court of Appeal thought that the scheme of deemed availability should be extended to cover those, like Mr David, unavailable through circumstances beyond their control (detention in police custody). This was effected by para.(1)(s) from May 30, 2006. *David* was applied in *CJSA/5944/99*, another case of someone detained in police custody. Commissioner Angus held that reg.14(1)(h) did not aid the claimant: **3.64**

> "I have come to the conclusion that the submission by the adjudication officer is correct and the wording of sub-paragraph (h) is not apt to describe a class of detention establishments which would include the cells in a police station. My reasoning is slightly different from what I understand to be the adjudication officer's and the Secretary of State's representative's reasoning.
>
> 11. It seems to me that the three establishments specified in sub-paragraph (h) are all establishments to which a person can be committed by the Court to await further court procedures or to serve a custodial sentence. Detention in one of those establishments, whether on sentence or on remand, can be prolonged. Detention in a police cell, however, is normally temporary pending charge and the first appearance in court and is normally for not more than 48 hours. Therefore to my mind the police cell is not an establishment in the same genus as the establishments specified in sub-paragraph (h) and regulation 14(1) does not assist the claimant."

Paragraph.(3) concerns the situation in which para.(1) protections (other than those in sub-paras (i) and (j)) and para.(2) protections apply only in respect of part of a benefit week (generally the period of seven days ending with the day corresponding to the claimant's "signing"/attendance day; see regs 4 and 1(3)). The protection offered by para.(1)(i) only extends to claimants meeting the conditions in para.(2A). The protection offered by para.(1)(r) only extends to claimants meeting the conditions in para.(2B).The remainder of the regulation contains relevant definitions.

In applying this regulation, careful note should be taken of the specific definition of certain terms (listed under "Definitions", above), in particular the different meanings of "week". One must also remember and maintain the distinction between Great Britain (England, Scotland and Wales) on the one hand, and the United Kingdom (of Great Britain and Northern Ireland) on the other.

Note that where it has been decided that a person is to be treated as available for employment in any benefit week, a subsequent revision or supersession of that decision can embrace also the question whether in that week the person was actually available for employment (old style Jobseekers Act 1995 s.6(6)). Note further that unlike the position with UB, where full benefit remained in payment pending resolution of the issue (see USI Regs reg.12A), under old style JSA if there remains an unresolved issue as to the claimant's availability for work there will be no entitlement to benefit, although the person excluded may be eligible for a hardship payment (see regs 140–146 ("standard" cases) and regs 146A–146H ("joint-claim" couples, below).

[1 14A.—(1) Paragraph (2) applies where a person (V) notifies the Secretary of State, in such manner as the Secretary of State specifies, that— **3.65**

(a) domestic violence has been inflicted on or threatened against V by V's partner or former partner or a family member, during the period of 26 weeks ending on the date of the notification; and
(b) at the time of the notification, V is not living at the same address as the person who inflicted domestic violence on or threatened it against V.

(2) Where this paragraph applies V is to be treated as being available for employment for a period of 4 weeks ("the 4 week exemption period") beginning on the date of V's notification to the Secretary of State under paragraph (1).

(3) V is to be treated as available for employment under paragraph (2)—

(a) whether or not V is entitled to a jobseeker's allowance for the whole or part of the 4 week exemption period; and

(b) on only one occasion in any 12 month period.

(4) Paragraph (6) applies where domestic violence has been inflicted on or threatened against V by V's partner or former partner or a family member.

(5) Domestic violence is only to be regarded as having been inflicted on or threatened against V for the purpose of paragraph (4) if V provides relevant evidence to the Secretary of State during the 4 week exemption period.

(6) Where this paragraph applies, V is to be treated as being available for employment for a period of 13 weeks ("the 13 week exemption period") beginning on the date of V's notification to the Secretary of State under paragraph (1).

(7) Subject to paragraphs (8) and (9), the 13 week exemption period shall apply for 13 consecutive weeks, whether or not V is entitled to a jobseeker's allowance for the whole or part of that period.

(8) After the first 4 weeks of the 13 week exemption period, V may notify the Secretary of State that V no longer wishes to be treated as available for employment by virtue of paragraph (6).

(9) Where V gives such a notification to the Secretary of State, the 13 week exemption period—

(a) shall be suspended from the date of the notification until the date on which V gives a further notification to the Secretary of State that V wishes again to be treated as available for employment by virtue of paragraph (6); and

(b) shall not apply at any time after the expiry of 12 months from the date of the notification referred to in paragraph (1).

(10) For the purpose of this regulation—

[[3] "coercive behaviour" means an act of assault, humiliation or intimidation or other abuse that is used to harm, punish or frighten V;

"controlling behaviour" means an act designed to make V subordinate or dependent by isolating them from sources of support, exploiting their resources and capacities for personal gain, depriving them of the means needed for independence, resistance or escape or regulating their everyday behaviour;

"domestic violence" means any incident or pattern of incidents of controlling behaviour, coercive behaviour, violence or abuse including but not limited to—

(a) psychological abuse;
(b) physical abuse;
(c) sexual abuse;
(d) financial abuse; and
(e) emotional abuse;

regardless of the gender or sexuality of V;]

"family member" means the following members of the family of V, V's partner or V's former partner – grandparent, grandchild, parent, parent-in-law, son, son-in-law, daughter, daughter-in-law, step-parent, step-son, step-daughter, brother, brother-in-law, sister, sister-in-law, or, if any of the preceding persons is a member of a couple, the other member of that couple,

"health care professional" means a person who is a member of a profession regulated by a body mentioned in section 25(3) of the National Health Service Reform and Health Care Professions Act 2002,

"person acting in an official capacity" means a health care professional, a police officer, a registered social worker, V's employer or a representative of V's trade union and any public, voluntary or charitable body which has had direct contact with V in connection with domestic violence,

"registered social worker" means a person registered as a social worker in a register maintained by—

[2(a) the Health and Care Professions Council,]

(b) the Care Council for Wales,

(c) the Scottish Social Services Council, or

(d) the Northern Ireland Social Care Council,

"relevant evidence" means written evidence from a person acting in an official capacity showing that—

(a) V's circumstances are consistent with those of a person who has had domestic violence inflicted on or threatened against them during the period of 26 weeks ending on the date of the notification referred to in paragraph (1); or

(b) V has made contact with the person acting in an official capacity in relation to such an incident, which occurred during that period.]

AMENDMENTS

1. Jobseeker's Allowance (Domestic Violence) (Amendment) Regulations 2012 (SI 2012/853) reg.2(2) (April 23, 2012).

2. Health and Social Care Act 2012 (Consequential Provisions—Social Workers) Order 2012 (SI 2012/1479) Sch. para.70 (August 1, 2012).

3. Jobseeker's Allowance (Domestic Violence) (Amendment) Regulations 2013 (SI 2013/2722) reg.2 (October 29, 2013).

DEFINITIONS

"couple"—see reg.1(3).
"employment"—see reg.4.
"partner"—see reg.1(3).
"week"—see reg.4.

GENERAL NOTE

This regulation operates in combination with reg.19(1)(x) and reg.34(g). In combination they provide that an old style JSA claimant (V) who has been a victim of domestic violence can, if the conditions of this regulation are met, be treated both as available for employment (this reg.) and actively seeking work (reg.19(1)(x)), and also as having a jobseeker's agreement if they do not already have one (reg.34(g)). V can be so treated for a set 13-week "exemption period" commencing with V's notification to the Secretary of State if s/he provides relevant evidence during the initial four weeks of the period. **3.66**

Victims remain entitled to JSA provided they meet the other conditions of entitlement. The 13 weeks run consecutively—unless suspended in accordance with paras (8) and (9)—and whether or not V is entitled to JSA for all or only part of that period (para.(7))

Initially, the definition of "domestic violence" in para.(10) was in terms of abuse as specified on a particular page of the December 2005 Department of Health document *Responding to domestic abuse: a handbook for health professionals*. It was not very satisfactory for an important definition not only not to be set out in the Regulations, but to be in a publication that was difficult to find (the text was reproduced in the note to reg.98 of the Universal Credit Regulations in Vol.V, *Universal Credit*, 2013/14 ed), and its terms were perhaps not well-suited to the particular benefits context. The new definition in para.(10), expanded into various forms of abuse and into further definitions of coercive and controlling behaviour, is still very wide. It uses the terms of the government's official approach to the meaning of domestic violence across departments, which had not previously been used as a statutory definition. Note that the new criminal offence of controlling or coercive behaviour in intimate or familial relationships under s.76 of the Serious Crime Act 2015, while using the terms of controlling and coercive behaviour (the meaning of which is discussed in Home Office Statutory Guidance of December 2015) contains conditions that are different from those in reg.14A. While the definition here expressly includes coercive behaviour and controlling behaviour (both given their own definitions in para.(10)), any other incident of abuse of any kind can come within the ambit of domestic violence. Thus, although the specific definition of "coercive behaviour" requires the act or abuse to be used to harm, punish or frighten the victim and the specific definition of "controlling behaviour" is restricted to acts designed to make the victim subordinate or dependant by particular means (as taken to extremes by the vile Rob Titchener in *The Archers*), abuse of similar kinds where that specific form of intention or purpose is not present or is difficult to prove can nonetheless be domestic violence. The width of that approach makes the specification in para.(1) of the circumstances in which reg.14A applies more important. Victims can be of any gender and their sexuality is immaterial. The person perpetrating or threatening the domestic violence must be V's partner, former partner or a family member (defined in para.(10) to cover a wide range of members of the family of V, V's partner or V's former partner).

3.67 The regulation applies only if V notifies the Secretary of State in the specified manner and at that time V is not living at the same address as the perpetrator of the domestic violence or the person threatening it (para.(1)). It covers domestic violence perpetrated or threatened in the 26 weeks prior to the notification (*ibid.*). The four week period is designed to enable V to gather "relevant evidence" (see para.(10)) of the domestic violence. It also allows V time to deal with pressing issues resulting from leaving an abusive relationship such as getting new accommodation, legal advice or children settled in new schools. "Relevant evidence" is written evidence from someone in an official capacity (as quite widely defined in para.(10)) showing either: (i) that V has contacted that person in relation to an incident of domestic violence during the 26-week period prior to V's notification to the Secretary of State, or (ii) that V's circumstances are consistent with those of someone who has in that period had domestic violence threatened against them or inflicted on them. The evidence must be furnished to the Secretary of State within four weeks of V's initial notification (para.(5)).

Note that there can only be one four-week evidence-gathering period and 13-week "exemption period" (of which the four-week period forms part) in any 12-month period (para.(3)). After four weeks of being treated as available, V can by notifying the Secretary of State suspend the remainder of the 13-week period of deemed availability and actively seeking work and resurrect it within a year from the initial notification setting the exemption period regulation in motion (paras (8), (9)).

The transition from new style JSA

3.68 Paragraph (3)(b) is, where art.13(1) and (2) of the Welfare Reform Act 2012 (Commencement No.9 and Transitional and Transitory Provisions and Commencement No. 8 and Savings and Transitional Provisions (Amendment))

Order 2013 (as amended and set out in the 2014/15 Supplement) applies, to be read as if para.(2) had applied where the person had been treated as available for employment under reg.15 of the JSA Regulations 2013 (art.13(3)(a) of that Order).

Circumstances in which a person is not to be regarded as available

15.—[4 (1)] A person shall not be regarded as available for employment in the following circumstances— 3.69

[4 (a) [7. . .] if he is full-time student during the period of study];

(b) if he is a prisoner on temporary release in accordance with the provisions of the Prison Act 1952 or rules made under section 39(6) of the Prisons (Scotland) Act 1989;

[1(bb) if the period beginning on the date of claim and ending on the day before the beginning of the first week after the date of claim is less than 7 days, for that period, unless he is treated as available for employment for that period in accordance with regulation 14;]

[2(bc) if he is on paternity leave[6, shared paternity leave] or ordinary [3 or additional] adoption leave by virtue of section 75A [3 or 75B] of the Employment Rights Act 1996;]

[5(c) if she is in receipt of a maternity allowance under section 35 or 35B of the Benefits Act or maternity pay in accordance with sections 164–171 of that Act.]

[4 (2) [7 Paragraph (1)(a) shall not apply to a full-time student] during the period of the summer vacation appropriate to his course, but only if the first and second conditions are satisfied.

(3) The first condition is satisfied if—

(a) in the case of a student with a partner, the partner is also a full-time student and either of them is treated as responsible for a child or a young person; or

(b) in any other case, the student is treated as responsible for a child or young person.

(4) The second condition is satisfied if the student is—

(a) available for employment in accordance with this Chapter; or

(b) treated as available for employment in accordance with regulation 14(1)(a) or (k).]

[7(5) Any provision of these Regulations under which a person is treated as available for employment is subject to paragraph (1) except to the extent that these Regulations expressly provide otherwise.]

AMENDMENTS

1. Social Security (Jobseeker's Allowance and Mariners' Benefits) (Miscellaneous Amendments) Regulations 1997 (SI 1997/563) reg.3 (March 11, 1997).

2. Jobseeker's Allowance (Amendment) Regulations 2002 (SI 2002/3072) reg.5 (December 13, 2002).

3. Social Security (Miscellaneous Amendments) Regulations 2008 (SI 2008/698) reg.4(5) (April 14, 2008).

4. Social Security (Students Responsible for Children or Young Persons) Amendment Regulations 2008 (SI 2008/1826) reg.3(2)–(4) (July 9, 2008).

5. Social Security (Maternity Allowance) (Miscellaneous Amendments) Regulations 2014 (SI 2914/884) reg.4(3) (May 18, 2014).

6. Shared Parental Leave and Statutory Shared Parental Pay (Consequential

Amendments and Subordinate Legislation) Order 2014 (SI 2914/3255) art.7(3) (December 31, 2014).

7. Social Security (Traineeships and Qualifying Young Persons) Amendment Regulations 2015 (SI 2015/336) reg.2(4) (March 27, 2015).

DEFINITIONS

"child"—see Jobseekers Act 1995 s.35(1).
"data of claim"—see reg.1(3).
"employment"—see reg.4.
"full-time student"—reg.1(3).
"partner"—*ibid.*
"period of study"—see reg.4.
"week"—*ibid.*
"young person"—see regs 1(3) and 76.

GENERAL NOTE

3.70 This regulation excludes certain groups from entitlement to old style JSA by treating them (whatever would be the reality of the situation applying the standard availability test) as not available for employment. Paragraph (5) now confirms that the exclusionary effect of para.(1) trumps any other provision in these Regulations unless it contains something expressly to the contrary, as some of the entries in regs 14 and 17A do. The excluded groups (and the circumstances of their exclusion) are set out below.

(1) Full-time students (paras (1)(a), (2), (3) and (4)).

With two exceptions, any claimant who is a full-time student (defined in reg.1(3)) is treated as not available for employment throughout the "period of study": the period beginning with the start of the claimant's course of study and ending on its last day or on such earlier date as he abandons it or is dismissed from it (reg.4). Note that the "period of study" includes any period of his attendance at his educational establishment, or any period of study undertaken by him, in connection with his course whether occurring before or after the period of the course (*ibid.*, and see further *CJSA/1457/1999*). The fact that this includes a student who is not attending college for a year while he resits exams externally is not contrary to art.14, read with art.1 Prot.1 of the ECHR (*MS v SSWP* [2009] UKUT 9 (AAC)).

The first exception covers claimants falling within reg.17A (employment-related courses for certain over-25s). The second exception covers the situation where both claimant and partner are full-time students and one is treated for child benefit purposes as responsible for a child or young person. Following the decision in *CJSA/2663/2006*, from July 9, 2008 it also covers the situation where a single student is treated as responsible for a child or young person. In either case, the exception only applies, however, during the summer vacation of the claimant's course, and only then if he is actually available for work in accordance with the usual rules on availability or is treated as available under reg.14(1)(a) (when participating in an approved employment-related course) or reg.14(1)(k) (when participating in a Venture Trust programme). See also *MB v SSWP (JSA)* [2013] UKUT 535 (AAC), in which Judge Wikeley discusses the case of a lone parent mature student.

(2) Prisoners on temporary release (para.(1)(b)).

(3) Women receiving maternity allowance (see SSCBA 1992 ss.35 or 35B) or statutory maternity pay (see SSCBA 1992 ss.164–171) (para.(1)(c)).

(4) Claimants in respect of part weeks at the beginning of a claim (para.(1)(bb))

This provides that a claimant is not to be regarded as available for employment (and is therefore excluded from JSA) for a part-week at the beginning of a claim unless he is treated as available for that period by one of the provisions in reg.14, above.

(5) Persons on paternity leave or shared parental leave or ordinary or additional adoption leave (para.(1)(bc)).

Further circumstances in which a person is to be treated as available: permitted period

16.—(1) A person who is available for employment— 3.71

(a) only in his usual occupation;

(b) only at a level of remuneration not lower than that which he is accustomed to receive, or

(c) only in his usual occupation and at a level of remuneration not lower than that which he is accustomed to receive

may be treated for a permitted period as available for employment in that period.

(2) Whether a person should be treated as available for a permitted period and if so, the length of that permitted period shall be determined having regard to the following factors—

(a) the person's usual occupation and any relevant skills or qualifications which he has;

(b) the length of any period during which he has undergone training relevant to that occupation;

(c) the length of the period during which he has been employed in that occupation and the period since he was so employed;

(d) the availability and location of employment in that occupation.

(3) A permitted period shall be for a minimum of one week and a maximum of 13 weeks and shall start on the date of claim and in this paragraph "week" means any period of 7 consecutive days.

DEFINITIONS

"date of claim"—see reg.1(3).
"employment"—see reg.4.

GENERAL NOTE

Section 6(1) of the old style Jobseekers Act 1995 stipulates that a claimant is available for employment if willing and able to take up immediately *any employed earner's employment*. This regulation mitigates the rigour of that by enabling a claimant who has a usual occupation to be treated, for a permitted period of between one and 13 weeks, as available for employment even though only available for employment in his usual occupation and/or at his accustomed level of remuneration (paras (1), (3)). Here "week" in para.(3) means any period of seven days, not a benefit week, and the permitted period begins on the date of claim (para.(3)). Whether a claimant should be so treated and for how long is to be determined having regard to: his usual occupation and any of his relevant skills and qualifications; the length of any period of training, relevant to that occupation, which he has undergone; how long he was employed in that occupation and the length of time elapsed since he was last employed in it; the location and availability of employment in that occupation. Note also that under reg.20(1), such a claimant can be treated as actively seeking employment for a corresponding period. Furthermore, under reg.20(2), someone who has at any time in the 12 months prior to his date of claim for old style JSA been engaged in self-employment in his usual occupation, can be treated as actively seeking employment during the "permitted period" even though he confines his jobsearch to employment, self-employment, or both, only in his usual occupation, 3.72

or only at his accustomed rate of remuneration, or only in his usual occupation and at his accustomed rate. But under the terms of this regulation, he must still be available for *employment* as opposed to *self-employment*. Whether a claimant has a usual occupation will be a question of fact looking to his employment history and the time for which he has followed a particular occupation.

For limitations on the application of this regulation in the case of a claimant laid-off from employment or working short-time, see reg.17(4).

Laid off and short-time workers

3.73 **17.**—(1) A person who is laid off shall be treated as available for employment providing he is willing and able to resume immediately the employment from which he has been laid off and to take up immediately any casual employment which is within daily travelling distance of his home or, if he falls within paragraph [[2](1), (1A) or (2)] of regulation 5, at the time specified in that regulation.

(2) [[1](a)] A person who is kept on short-time shall be treated as available for employment, providing he is willing and able to resume immediately the employment in which he is being kept on short-time and to take up immediately any casual employment which is within daily travelling distance of his home or, if he falls within paragraph (1) or (2) of regulation 5, at the time specified in that regulation in the hours in which he is not working short-time but the total number of hours for which he works and is available for casual employment must be at least 40 in any week [[1]unless paragraph (b) or (c) applies.

(b) The total number of hours for which a person kept on short-time works and is available for casual employment may be less than 40 in any week if that person has imposed restrictions on his availability which are reasonable in the light of his physical or mental condition;

(c) The total number of hours for which a person kept on short-time works and is available for casual employment may be less than 40 in any week if he has caring responsibilities providing the total number of hours for which he works and is available for casual employment is as many as his caring responsibilities allow and for the specific hours those responsibilities allow and is at least 16 in any week;]

(3) A person shall not be treated as available for employment in accordance with this regulation for more than 13 weeks, starting with the day after the day he was laid off or first kept on short-time.

(4) A person who is laid off or kept on short-time may not be treated as available for employment for a permitted period in accordance with regulation 16, unless he ceases to be laid off or kept on short-time within 13 weeks of the day on which he was laid off or first kept on short time, in which case he may be treated as available for employment for a permitted period ending a maximum of 13 weeks after the date of claim.

(5) In paragraphs (3) and (4), "week" means any period of 7 consecutive days.

AMENDMENTS

1. Jobseeker's Allowance and Income Support (General) (Amendment) Regulations 1996 (SI 1996/1517) reg.6 (October 7, 1996).

2. Social Security (Lone Parents and Miscellaneous Amendments) Regulations 2008 (SI 2008/3051) reg.11(9) (November 4, 2008).

DEFINITIONS

"casual employment"—see reg.4.
"employment"—*ibid.*
"permitted period"—see reg.16(3).
"a person who is kept on short-time"—see reg.4.
"a person who is laid off "—*ibid.*
"week" (in paras (3), (4))—see para.(5).
"week" (in para.(2))—see reg.4.

GENERAL NOTE

For up to 13 weeks from the day after he was laid off or put on short time, as the case may be, this regulation enables a claimant who is laid off or kept on short time to be treated as available for employment (paras (1)–(3)). It also sets limitations on treating such a claimant as available for employment during the permitted period under reg.16 (para.(4)). Its aim is to assist for a short period a claimant whose employment has been affected by temporary adverse industrial conditions in the hope that before the end of that period a recovery will mean that he can return to working or to usual hours of working in that employment and thus cease to need old style JSA. 3.74

A claimant who is laid off (para.(1))

A person is laid off when his employment has been suspended owing to temporary adverse industrial conditions (reg.4). A claimant who is laid off must be treated as available for employment provided (1) that he is willing and able to resume immediately the employment from which he has been laid off, and (2) that he is willing and able to take up, immediately or, if a carer, voluntary worker or person providing a service, within the period of grace afforded by reg.5(1), (1A) or (2), any casual employment within daily travelling distance of his home (para.(1)). "Casual employment" means employment from which the employee can be released without giving notice (reg.4). 3.75

A claimant who is kept on short-time (para.(2))

A person is kept on short time when his hours of employment have been reduced owing to temporary adverse industrial conditions (reg.4). Given that the remunerative work exclusion precludes claims by those working 16 or more hours per week (old style Jobseekers Act 1995 s.1(2)(e); regs 51–53), the reduction must take the claimant below that threshold. Nor must his earnings exceed the prescribed amount (old style Jobseekers Act 1995 s.2(1)(c); JSA Regulations 1996 reg.56), since that also precludes entitlement. A claimant who is kept on short time in an employment must be treated as available for employment, provided he is willing and able to resume immediately that employment and to take up, generally immediately, any casual employment within daily travelling distance of his home in the hours he is not working short time. Usually, however, the total number of hours for which he works and is available for casual employment must be at least 40 in any [benefit] week (para.(2)(a), regs 4 and 1(3)). "Casual employment" is employment from which the employee can be released without giving notice (reg.4). As regards willingness and ability to take up casual employment, the general requirement "immediately" does not apply to carers, voluntary workers, and those providing a service, who are afforded the appropriate period of grace in reg.5(1) and (2): 48 hours for carers and voluntary workers; 24 hours for those providing a service (para.(2)(a)). The total hours rule (at least 40) does not apply to a claimant who has imposed restrictions on his availability which are reasonable in the light of his physical or mental condition (para.(2)(b)). Nor does it apply to a claimant who is a carer (a person with caring responsibilities as defined in reg.4): in any week in such a case the total of hours worked and those of availability for casual employment can be as many hours between 16 and 40 as his caring responsibilities allow (para.(2)(c)). 3.76

Paragraph (3)

3.77 Some claimants will only experience lay off, others only being kept on short time. For others, short time may be followed by lay-off. This paragraph stipulates that, whichever of these situations is the case, a claimant can only be treated as available under this regulation for up to 13 weeks from the day after the day he was laid off or first kept on short time.

Paragraph (4)

3.78 The effect of this is that a claimant who is laid off or kept on short time for 13 weeks cannot then take advantage of the one to 13 weeks permitted period afforded by reg.16 during which, for example, a claimant can confine his availability to employment in his usual occupation. A claimant, laid off or kept on short time, can only be eligible for protection under reg.16 if he ceases to be laid off or kept on short time within the 13-week period afforded by this regulation. If he does so, in reality by becoming wholly unemployed, he can be treated as available under reg.16 for a permitted period ending no more than 13 weeks from the date of claim. The date of claim is the date the claimant makes, or is treated as making, a claim for old style JSA for the purposes of reg.6 of the Claims and Payments Regulations (reg.1(3)). In many (but not necessarily all) cases that will be immediately after the day he was first laid off or put on short time, so that in such a case, for example, a claimant who has had 10 weeks' protection under this regulation, could get no more than three weeks' protection under reg.16.

[1Further circumstances in which a person is to be treated as available: full-time students participating in a qualifying course

3.79 **17A.**—(1) A person to whom paragraph (2) applies shall, notwithstanding regulation [515(1)(a)], be treated as available for employment in accordance with paragraph (3).

(2) This paragraph applies to a person—

(a) who is aged 25 years or over; and

(b) [2subject to paragraph (2A),] who has made a claim for a jobseeker's allowance and has been receiving benefit within a jobseeking period for not less than 2 years as at the date he started, or is due to start, the qualifying course and for the purposes of this paragraph the linking provision set out in regulation 48 shall apply.

[2(2A) A person who has been receiving benefit in accordance with paragraph (b) of the definition of "receiving benefit" in paragraph (7) shall, for the purposes of paragraph (2)(b), be treated as having received benefit within a jobseeking period.]

(3) Subject to paragraph (4), where an employment officer has determined, having regard to the factors specified in paragraph (5), that a person to whom paragraph (2) applies may undertake a qualifying course, that person shall be treated as available for employment in any week in which he is undertaking the qualifying course as a full-time student and—

(a) which falls wholly or partly in term-time, providing he—

(i) provides evidence, as often as may be required by an employment officer, within 5 days of being so required by the employment officer, consisting of a document signed by him and on behalf of the establishment at which he is undertaking the qualifying course, confirming that he is attending the establishment when required to attend, in such form as may be required by the employment officer; and

(ii) provides evidence, as often as may be required by an employment officer, within 5 days of being so required by the employment officer, consisting of a document signed by him and on behalf of the establishment at which he is undertaking the qualifying course, confirming that he is making satisfactory progress on the course, in such form as may be required by the employment officer;

(b) in which he is taking examinations relating to the qualifying course; or

(c) which falls wholly in a vacation from the qualifying course, if he is willing and able to take up immediately any casual employment.

(4) In a case where the combined duration of—

(a) any qualifying course, other than one falling within paragraph (6), which a person to whom paragraph (2) applies has previously undertaken in respect of which he was, for any part of such qualifying course, treated as available for employment in accordance with paragraph (3); and

(b) the qualifying course which he is currently undertaking

is more than 1 year, the person shall only be treated as available for employment in accordance with paragraph (3) if he has been receiving benefit within a jobseeking period for not less than 2 years since the last day of the most recent such qualifying course in respect of which he was, for any part, treated as available in accordance with paragraph (3), and for the purposes of this paragraph the linking provision set out in regulation 48 shall apply.

(5) The factors which an employment officer must take into account when determining whether a person may undertake a qualifying course are—

(a) the skills, qualifications and abilities of that person;

(b) whether the course would assist him to acquire new skills and qualifications;

(c) whether he would have to give up a course of study in order to undertake this course;

(d) any needs arising from his physical or mental condition;

(e) the time which has elapsed since he was last engaged in employment as an employed earner or as a self-employed earner;

(f) his work experience;

(g) the number of jobs in the labour market and, if relevant, the local labour market, which require the skills and qualifications which he would acquire on the course; and

(h) any evidence about whether this course or this type of course has facilitated the obtaining by persons of work.

(6) A qualifying course falls within this paragraph if the person had [6 a good reason] for any act or omission for the purposes of section [6 19A(2)(d), (e) or (f)] in relation to that course.

(7) In this regulation—

[3 "benefit" means—

(a) income support, unemployment benefit, a jobseeker's allowance or any earnings credited to a person in accordance with regulation 8A or 9A of the Social Security (Credits) Regulations 1975 or which would be credited to a person in accordance with paragraph (1) of that regulation 9A but are not so credited by reason only of the fact that no further earnings are in his case required for the purpose mentioned in that paragraph; or

(b) any earnings credited to a person for unemployment in accordance with regulation 9 of the Social Security (Credits) Regulations 1975 as it applied before 7th October 1996 and]

"receiving benefit" means [[2]receiving—

(a) benefit which that person has claimed and received as an unemployed person or in accordance with Part I of the Act [[4] or in accordance with regulation 9A of the Social Security (Credits) Regulations 1975] or

(b) income support which that person has claimed and received as an asylum seeker pursuant to regulation 70(3A) of the Income Support Regulations but only to the extent that—

(i) any periods in respect of which he was in receipt of income support as an asylum seeker pursuant to regulation 70(3A) of the Income Support Regulations link with the jobseeking period which includes the date on which he started, or is due to start, the qualifying course and for this purpose, such periods shall link where they are separated by a period of 12 weeks or less in respect of which he was not in receipt of income support; and

(ii) he is, at the date he started, or is due to start, the qualifying course, a person to whom paragraph (7A) applies;]

"casual employment" means employment from which the employee can be released without his giving any notice or, if he is required to give notice, employment from which he can be released before the end of the vacation;

"duration" in relation to a qualifying course means the period beginning with the start of the course and ending with the last day of the course;

"jobseeking period" means the period described in regulation 47 and any period treated as a jobseeking period pursuant to regulation 47A;

"last day" in relation to a qualifying course means the date on which the last day of the course falls, or the date on which the final examination relating to that course is completed, whichever is the later;

"qualifying course" means a course which—

(a) is an employment-related course;

(b) lasts no more than 12 consecutive months; and

(c) except where it falls within paragraph (8), is either—

(i) a course of a description falling within Schedule 2 to the Further and Higher Education Act 1992; or

(ii) a programme of learning falling within section 6 of the Further and Higher Education (Scotland) Act 1992.

[[2](7A) Subject to paragraph (7B), this paragraph shall apply in the case of a person—

(a) who—

(i) is a refugee within the definition of Article 1 of the Convention relating to the Status of Refugees done at Geneva on 28th July 1951, as extended by Article 1(2) of the Protocol relating to the Status of Refugees done at New York on 31st January 1967; or

(ii) has been granted exceptional leave—

(aa) to enter the United Kingdom by an immigration officer appointed for the purposes of the Immigration Act 1971; or

(bb) to remain in the United Kingdom by the Secretary of State; and

(b) who was in receipt of income support as an asylum seeker pursuant to regulation 70(3A) of the Income Support Regulations at any time during the period of 12 weeks immediately preceding the beginning of the jobseeking period which includes the date on which he started, or is due to start, the qualifying course.

(7B) Paragraph (7A) shall include a person who has been recorded as a refugee by the Secretary of State within the definition in sub-paragraph (a) of that paragraph and whose claim for income support was determined in accordance with regulation 21ZA(2) or (3) of the Income Support Regulations (treatment of refugees).]

(8) A course or a programme of learning which is of a standard above that of a course or programme of learning falling within paragraph (c) of the definition of "qualifying course" falls within this paragraph if an employment officer so determines in a particular case.]

AMENDMENTS

1. Social Security Amendment (New Deal) Regulations 1998 (SI 1998/1274) reg.4 (June 1, 1998).
2. Jobseeker's Allowance Amendment (New Deal) Regulations 1998 (SI 1998/2874) reg.2 (November 24, 1998).
3. Jobseeker's Allowance Amendment (New Deal) Regulations 1999 (SI 1999/3083) reg.2(2) (November 30, 1999).
4. Jobseeker's Allowance Amendment (New Deal) Regulations 1999 (SI 1999/3083) reg.2(3) (November 30, 1999).
5. Social Security (Students Responsible for Children or Young Persons) Amendment Regulations 2008 (SI 2008/1826) reg.3(5) (July 9, 2008).
6. Jobseeker's Allowance (Sanctions) (Amendment) Regulations 2012 (SI 2012/2568) reg.7(3) (October 22, 2012).

DEFINITIONS

"course of study"—see reg.1(3).
"employed earner"—see reg.3 and SSCBA 1992 s.2(1)(a).
"employment"—see reg.4.
"employment officer"—see Jobseekers Act 1995 s.35(1).
"employment-related course"—see reg.1(3).
"examination"—see reg.4.
"full-time student"—see reg.1(3).
"made a claim for jobseeker's allowance"—see reg.4.
"self-employed earner"—see reg.1(3) and SSCBA 1992 s.2(1)(b).
"term-time"—see reg.4.
"vacation"—*ibid.*
"week"—*ibid.*

GENERAL NOTE

One element of equipping people for work is that of encouraging education in terms of following an employment-related course to acquire new or better skills. **3.80**

This regulation allows a claimant doing so, in certain limited circumstances, to be treated as available for employment (and see reg.21A for actively seeking employment). The claimant must be 25 or over, have made a claim for old style JSA and been "receiving benefit" (see below) for at least two years within a jobseeking period (the linking provision in reg.48 applies) as at the start date for the course, and must be undertaking a qualifying course with the agreement of an employment officer. A qualifying course is one meeting the criteria set out in para.(7) read with para.(8): in essence a course of further or higher education (or one at a level superior to that if an employment officer so determines in a particular case) which is employment related and lasts no more than 12 months. In determining whether to agree that a claimant can undertake such a course, an employment officer must take into account the factors listed in para.(5). Basically, such a claimant must be treated as available for employment in any week in which he is undertaking such a course which falls: (i) wholly or partly within term-time (note the evidence requirements in para.(3)(a) including one with respect to "satisfactory progress"), (ii) which is one in which he is taking examinations relating to the course, or (iii) which falls wholly in a vacation from the course provided in this third case that he is willing and able to take up immediately any casual employment (defined for these purposes in para.(7) rather than according to the general definition in reg.4 (para.(3)). Note, however, that para.(3) is expressed to be "subject to paragraph (4)". Paragraph (4) deals with the situation where the claimant has already been treated as available with respect to one qualifying course and is now undertaking another. If the combined duration of the two courses is more than a year, then the claimant cannot be treated as available under this regulation unless he has been receiving benefit within a jobseeking period for at least two years (the linking provision in reg.48 applies) since the last day of the most recent qualifying course in respect of which he was for any part of that course treated as available by para.(3) of this regulation. In short, a claimant can only be treated as available under this regulation for up to one year without having to serve a two-year requalification period in receipt of benefit. Note, however, when looking to the combined duration of qualifying courses that one ignores any course where the claimant had a good reason for the purposes of s.19A(2)(d), (e) or (f) (neglect to avail himself of a place on a course, refusing to apply for a vacant place or accept it when offered, giving up such a place or failing to attend the course) with respect to any act or omission in relation to that course (para.(6)).

These rules became effective on June 1, 1998. "Receiving benefit" is not just confined to receiving benefit (income support, UB or JSA) as an unemployed person or in accordance with Pt I of the old style Jobseekers Act 1995 (para.7). However, note in relation to paras (7A) and (7B) that both reg.70 and reg.21ZA of the Income Support Regulations have been revoked, the former with effect from January 25, 2000 and the latter with effect from April 3, 2000. The revocations were subject to savings, which now seem very unlikely to have any scope for operation. With effect from November 30, 1999, "benefit" and "receiving benefit" also includes receipt of earnings credited for contributions purposes in respect of unemployment and of men born before October 6, 1954 but who have not yet attained 65.

Note, finally, that during any week in which a person is treated as available under this regulation he will be treated also as actively seeking work. Where the week is during a vacation from the course, he must however show that during that week he has taken such steps as he can reasonably be expected to have to take to have the best prospects of securing the casual employment for which reg.17A requires him to be available (see reg.21A below).

The transition from new style JSA

3.81 In para.(a) of the definition of "benefit" in para.(7), the reference to jobseeker's allowance is, where art.13(1) and (2) of the Welfare Reform Act 2012 (Commencement No.9 and Transitional and Transitory Provisions and Commencement No.8 and Savings and Transitional Provisions (Amendment)) Order 2013 (as amended and set out in the 2014/15 Supplement) applies, to be read as if it included a reference to new style JSA (art.13(3)(aa) of that Order, in force from June 16, 2014).

[[1]Further circumstances in which a person is to be treated as available: lone parents with children aged 5 not in full-time education

17B.—A lone parent shall be treated as available for employment in any week where— 3.82

(a) the lone parent is responsible for, and a member of the same household as, a child who is aged 5;

(b) the child—

(i) is not receiving full-time education by regular attendance at school or otherwise; and

(ii) is not required by law to receive full-time education; and

(c) it would be unreasonable for the lone parent to make other arrangements for the care of that child.]

AMENDMENT

1. Social Security (Lone Parents and Miscellaneous Amendments) Regulations 2012 (SI 2012/874) reg.3(2) (May 21, 2012, subject to special commencement provisions in the Sch. to this amending instrument).

DEFINITIONS

"child"—see Jobseekers Act 1995 s.35(1).
"lone parent"—see reg.1(3).
"week"—see reg.4.

Chapter III

Actively seeking employment

Steps to be taken by persons actively seeking employment

18.—[[1](1) For the purposes of section 7(1) (actively seeking employment) a person shall be expected to have to take more than two steps in any week unless taking one or two steps is all that is reasonable for that person to do in that week.] 3.83

(2) Steps which it is reasonable for a person to be expected to have to take in any week include—

(a) oral or written applications (or both) for employment made to persons—

(i) who have advertised the availability of employment; or

(ii) who appear to be in a position to offer employment;

(b) seeking information on the availability of employment from—

(i) advertisements;

(ii) persons who have placed advertisements which indicate the availability of employment;

(iii) employment agencies and employment businesses;

(iv) employers;

(c) registration with an employment agency or employment business;

(d) appointment of a third party to assist the person in question in finding employment;

(e) seeking specialist advice, following referral by an employment officer, on how to improve the prospects of securing employment having regard to that person's needs and in particular in relation to any mental or physical limitations of that person;

(f) drawing up a curriculum vitae;
(g) seeking a reference or testimonial from a previous employer;
(h) drawing up a list of employers who may be able to offer employment to him with a view to seeking information from them on the availability of employment;
(i) seeking information about employers who may be able to offer employment to him;
(j) seeking information on an occupation with a view to securing employment in that occupation.

(3) In determining whether, in relation to any steps taken by a person, the requirements of section 7(1) are satisfied in any week, regard shall be had to all the circumstances of the case, including—

(a) his skills, qualifications and abilities;
(b) his physical or mental limitations;
(c) the time which has elapsed since he was last in employment and his work experience;
(d) the steps which he has taken in previous weeks and the effectiveness of those steps in improving his prospects of securing employment;
(e) the availability and location of vacancies in employment;
(f) any time during which he was—
 (i) engaged in the manning or launching of a lifeboat or in the performance of duty as a part-time member of a fire brigade or engaged during an emergency in duties for the benefit of others.
 (ii) attending an Outward Bound course,
 (iii) in the case of a blind person, participating in a course of training in the use of guide dogs,
 (iv) participating in training in the use of aids to overcome any physical or mental limitations of his in order to improve his prospects of securing employment,
 [2(v) engaged in duties as a member of any territorial or reserve force prescribed in Part I of [Schedule 6 to the Social Security (Contributions) Regulations 2001,]
 (vi) participating as a part-time student in an employment-related course,
 (vii) participating for less than 3 days in an employment or training programme for which a training allowance is not payable;
(g) any time during which he was engaged in voluntary work and the extent to which it may have improved his prospects of securing employment;
(h) whether he is treated as available for employment under regulation 14;
(i) whether he has applied for, or accepted, a place on, or participated in, a course or programme the cost of which is met in whole or in part out of central funds or by the European Community and the purpose of which is to assist persons to select, train for, obtain or retain employed earner's employment or self-employed earner's employment; and
(j) where he had no living accommodation in that week the fact that he had no such accommodation and the steps which he needed to take and has in fact taken to seek such accommodation.

(4) Any act of a person which would otherwise be relevant for purposes of section 7 shall be disregarded in the following circumstances—

(a) where, in taking the act, he acted in a violent or abusive manner,
(b) where the act comprised the completion of an application for employment and he spoiled the application,
(c) where by his behaviour or appearance he otherwise undermined his prospects of securing the employment in question,

unless those circumstances were due to reasons beyond his control.

(5) In this regulation—

"employment agency" and "employment business" mean an employment agency or (as the case may be) employment business within the meaning of the Employment Agencies Act 1973;

"employment or training programme" means a course or programme the person's participation in which is attributable to arrangements made by the Secretary of State under section 2 of the Employment and Training Act 1973 for the purpose of assisting persons to select, train for, obtain or retain employed earner's employment.

AMENDMENTS

1. Jobseeker's Allowance (Amendment) Regulations 2004 (SI 2004/1008) reg.2(2) (April 19, 2004 [new claimants]; October 18, 2004 [existing claimants and existing recipients of jobseeking credits]).

2. Social Security (Miscellaneous Amendments) (No.4) Regulations 2006 (SI 2006/2378) reg.13(3)(a) (October 2, 2006).

DEFINITIONS

"employment"—see Jobseekers Act 1995 s.7(8).
"employment officer"—see Jobseekers Act 1995 s.35(1).
"employment-related course"—see reg.1(3).
"engaged during an emergency in duties for the benefit of others"—see reg.22.
"Outward Bound course"—see reg.4.
"part-time member of a fire brigade"—*ibid.*
"part-time student"—see reg.1(3).
"training allowance"—*ibid.*
"voluntary work"—see reg.4.
"week"—*ibid.*

GENERAL NOTE

For the purposes of the old style Jobseekers Act 1995, in any week a person is actively seeking employment if during that week he takes such steps as he can reasonably be expected to have to take in order to have the best prospects of securing employment (s.7(1)). See regs 19–21B below for circumctances in which a claimant is deemed to be actively seeking employment. In its original form, para.(1) of this regulation amplified that "touchstone test" by stipulating that a person will be expected to take more than one step on one occasion in any week unless taking one step on a single occasion in the week is all that it is reasonable for that person to do in that week. (see *CJSA/2162/2001*, noted in the commentary to old style Jobseekers Act 1995 ss.7 and 9). A new version was substituted with effect from April 19, 2004 for new claimants and from October 18, 2004 for those who were existing claimants at April 19 or then in receipt of jobseeking credits. The substitution increased the minimum number of steps that a jobseeker must take to be actively seeking employment from at least two to at least three in a week, unless taking one or two steps is all that it is reasonable to do in that week. The qualification is an important one. A claimant's responsibility has, in the past at least, been misstated in jobseekers' agreements in terms of a declaration that "I know that I must take at least three steps each week". 3.84

Concerns were expressed by the SSAC (see Cmd.6145) about the lack of need for and the effect of the change at a time of national low unemployment, and against a background of manpower cuts at Jobcentres. Despite this, the change was made. The Secretary of State was of the view that tailored support was an important way to help people return to work but that, in addition to special provision, it was reasonable in a buoyant labour market to increase expectations of the claimant unemployed through measures designed to be adapted to the individual to increase prospects of getting a job more quickly. There was no change to reduce the minimum number of steps in the more recent periods of high unemployment.

In deciding whether the "touchstone" test is met, the focus should be on what the claimant did in the week in question rather than on whether each of the steps set out in the jobseeker's agreement were performed (*CJSA/1814/2007*, noted in more detail in the commentary to old style Jobseekers Act 1995 s.7, above).

3.85 In past editions it has been suggested, relying in part on Commissioner's decision *CJSA/2162/2001* (see above), that there might be circumstances in which the application of the "touchstone test" would result in a conclusion that there were no steps that it was reasonable for the claimant to take in a particular week, so that the test in s.7(1) could be satisfied by taking no steps. It is now submitted that that is wrong. Despite the view expressed there by Commissioner Williams that reg.18 read as a whole did not preclude such a conclusion, it is hard to read reg.18(1) as requiring anything less than an absolute minimum of one step in any week to satisfy s.7(1). It must also be remembered that reg.19 sets out a wide variety of deserving circumstances in which a claimant is to be treated as actively seeking employment, whether or not s.7(1) would otherwise be satisfied, and that regs 20–21B cover some more specific circumstances.

In determining the number of steps taken in any week it is now accepted that doing the same type of act (e.g. looking in a local newspaper for job advertisements) on three different occasions during a week counts as three steps. That was decided in Commissioner's decision *CJSA/3146/2009*, as followed in *CSJSA/548/2014*. By the same token, applying for three vacancies or making enquiries to three employers on the same day would count as three steps. However, those decisions rightly stress that that would only get a claimant over the normal minimum limit in reg.18(1) and it still has to be asked, however many steps over the minimum have been taken, whether the claimant has taken such steps as can reasonably be expected.

CJSA/3146/2009 also contains some helpful guidance about the significance of the contents of a jobseeker's agreement to the actively seeking employment test. The plain (although not uncommonly forgotten) basis is that the test is not that the claimant must carry out all the activities as specified in the jobseeker's agreement. The test is the "touchstone test" of reasonableness in all the circumstances, as modified by reg.18. However, the jobseeker's agreement can set the context for a claimant's job search activities in forming a starting point in identifying the sorts of things that the claimant might reasonably be expected to do (see para.33 of the decision).

3.86 The remainder of the regulation supplies further detail to flesh out that "touchstone test" in terms of providing a partial definition of "steps" (para.(2)), stipulating circumstances to be taken into account in determining whether the test is met in any week (para.(3)) and, most controversially, setting out the circumstances in which otherwise relevant acts are to be disregarded (para.(4)). Paragraph (5) provides definitions of certain terms used in this regulation: "employment agency", "employment business" and "employment or training programme". "Week" means "benefit week" (reg.4); that is, generally, the period of seven days ending with the claimant's "signing"/attendance day (reg.1(3)).

Paragraph.(2) provides a partial definition of "steps" and thus gives a general indication of the type of action claimants must take in order not to fall foul of the actively seeking work test. The list, albeit much longer than its predecessor (USI Regulations reg.12B) is not exhaustive: the provision reads "steps which it is reasonable to expect a person to have to take in any week *include*" (emphasis supplied by annotator). Regard must still be had to all the steps taken by the claimant to try to get employment: the "touchstone test" remains that in the statute: "such steps as he can reasonably be expected to have to take in order to have the best prospects of securing employment". To determine whether in a particular week any steps taken by a particular claimant satisfy that test, para.(3) requires that regard must be had to all the circumstances of the case, including those specifically there listed. In para.(2) the specifically listed "steps" are:

(a) written and/or oral applications for employment to those who have advertised its availability or who appear to be in a position to offer it;
(b) seeking information on the availability of employment from advertisements, advertisers and employers, or from employment agencies and employment businesses within the meaning of the Employment Agencies Act 1973;
(c) registration with an employment agency or employment business within the meaning of the Employment Agencies Act 1973;
(d) the appointment of a third party to assist the claimant in finding employment (an actor appointing an agent might be an example);
(e) seeking specialist advice, after referral by an employment officer, on how to improve prospects of securing employment having regard to the claimant's needs and in particular any of his physical or mental limitations;
(f) drawing up a curriculum vitae (CV);
(g) seeking a testimonial or reference from a former employer;
(h) drawing up a list of possible employers with a view to seeking information from them on the availability of employment;
(i) seeking information about possible employers; and
(j) seeking information on an occupation with a view to securing employment in it.

The statutory touchstone test of actively seeking employment requires the claimant to take in any week "such steps as he can reasonably be expected to have to take in order to have the best prospects of securing employment". To determine whether in a particular week any steps taken by a particular claimant (whether listed in para.(2) or not—that list not being exhaustive) satisfy that test, para.(3) requires that regard must be had to all the circumstances of the claimant's case, including those specifically listed. The listed circumstances are:

(a) his skills, qualifications and abilities;
(b) his physical or mental limitations (something important to those once on ESA who have been found capable of work and therefore have to look to JSA);
(c) his work experience and how long he has been unemployed;
(d) what he has done in previous weeks to find employment and the effectiveness of that in improving his prospects of finding it;
(e) what jobs are available and where they are;
(f) time spent in certain worthwhile activities; lifeboatman or part-time fireman; as someone undertaking duties in an emergency (on which see reg.22); attendance at an Outward Bound course; or, if blind, taking part in a course of training in the use of guide dogs; or participating in training in the use of aids to overcome any physical or mental limitations in order to improve prospects of securing employment; engagement in a prescribed territorial or reserve force; participation as a part-time student in an employment-related course (one whose purpose is to assist persons to acquire or enhance skills required for seeking employment, for a particular occupation or for employment—see reg.1(3)); participating for less than three days in an employment or training programme (as defined in para.(5)) for which a training allowance is not payable;
(g) engagement in voluntary work and the extent to which it may have improved his prospects of securing employment;
(h) whether he is treated as available for work under reg.14 (para.(1)(d) of which is in identical terms to para.(f)(i) of this regulation—lifeboatman, part-time fireman, someone undertaking duties in an emergency);

(i) whether he has applied for, or accepted a place on, or participated in, a wholly or partially centrally or European Community-funded course or programme designed to help people select, train for, obtain and retain employment or self-employment; and

(j) the fact that he is homeless, the steps taken and those that he needed to take to find somewhere to live.

3.87 It must, however, be stressed that this list of particular factors is not exhaustive; regard must be had to all the circumstances of the claimant's case to decide whether he meets the touchstone test, the hallmark of which is flexibility and adaptability to different claimants and different labour markets by setting a general target and allowing flexibility of interpretation and application to the individual case, to decide what should be the appropriate extent of job search for a particular individual at a particular time and place. For instance, since it is possible for a claimant to satisfy the condition in s.1(2)(e) of the old style Jobseekers Act 1995 of not being in remunerative work while working for less than 16 hours a week on average or while, say, being on a zero hours contract currently producing few or no hours but likely to produce more in the future, it is arguable that it would be relevant to consider how reasonable it is to expect the claimant to take steps to seek alternative employment.

The aim of the controversial provision in para.(4) was to "enable a person's job-seeking activity to be disregarded if he behaves or presents himself in such a way as deliberately to reduce or extinguish his chance of receiving offers of employment" (DSS, *Notes on Clauses* [with respect to the Jobseekers Bill]). It provides that an otherwise relevant act of a person is to be disregarded in a number of circumstances unless the circumstances were due to reasons beyond his control: (i) where in taking the act he acted in a violent or abusive manner; (ii) where the act comprised the completion of an application for employment and he spoiled the application; and (iii) where, by his behaviour or appearance, he otherwise undermined his prospects of securing the employment in question.

The paragraph, particularly in head (iii) thus involves a more explicit "policing" of behaviour, appearance and, possibly, form-filling competence by Jobcentre Plus personnel, decision-makers and tribunals. The concept of "spoiled the application" in head (ii) is by no means crystal clear. The saving for circumstances beyond one's control will presumably protect the dyslexic and the illiterate, but what about the semi-literate? Electoral law, of course, has the concept of the "spoilt ballot paper", which covers the situation in which the voter has, in that context inadvertently, dealt with his ballot paper in such a manner that it cannot conveniently be used as a ballot paper, but whether that in any way provides a valid analogy for "spoiled" in this regulation remains to be seen. On "spoiled", see the remarks of Commissioner Howell in *CJSA/4665/01*, noted in the commentary to old style Jobseekers Act 1995 s.19(2)(c). Given the aim of the provision, it might have been better for the sake of clarity to have worded it "deliberately spoiled". A further sanction for some such behaviour lies in the preclusion of payment of benefit under s.19(2)(c) in respect of the person having, without a good reason, neglected to avail himself of a reasonable opportunity of employment; the equivalent provision in the unemployment benefit regime enabled disqualification of a claimant who had attended an interview for a job as a parcel porter in a "dirty and unshaven state" (*R(U)28/55*). Care will have to be taken to avoid applying the provision in a manner discriminatory on grounds of sex or race (e.g. to penalise men with long hair or Rastafarians with dreadlocks).

For an interesting consideration of para.(4) and old style Jobseekers Act 1995 s.7(3), see N. Wikeley, "What the Unemployed Need is a Good Haircut . . ." in [1996] 25 I.L.J. 71.

[1Actively seeking employment in the period at the beginning of a claim

3.88 **18A.**—(1) Paragraph (2) applies in any case [2other than a case which falls within regulation 19(1)(i) or (s),] where the period beginning on the date of claim and ending on the day before the beginning of the first week after the date of claim is less than 7 days.

(2) Where this paragraph applies, a person is actively seeking employment in the period referred to in paragraph (1) if he takes in that period such steps as he can reasonably be expected to have to take in order to have the best prospects of securing employment and in determining whether a person has taken such steps—

(a) the steps which it is reasonable for him to be expected to have to take include those referred to in regulation 18(2); and

(b) regard shall be had to all the circumstances of the case, including those matters referred to in regulation 18(3).]

AMENDMENTS

1. Social Security (Jobseeker's Allowance and Mariners' Benefits) (Miscellaneous Amendments) Regulations 1997 (SI 1997/563) reg.4 (March 11, 1997).

2. Jobseeker's Allowance (Amendment) (No.2) Regulations 1999 (SI 1999/3087) reg.4 (November 30, 1999).

DEFINITIONS

"data of claim"—see reg.1(3).
"employment"—see Jobseekers Act 1995 s.7(8).
"week"—see reg.4.

GENERAL NOTE

The actively seeking employment test in old style Jobseekers Act 1995 s.7 is expressed in terms of each week. This regulation, inserted with effect from March 11, 1997, adapts that test to cover a part-week at the beginning of a claim, so that a claimant will satisfy the test if in that part-week period he takes such steps as he can reasonably be expected to have to take in order to have the best prospects of securing employment, having regard to all the circumstances of the case including the matters set out in reg.18(3), above. "Steps" include those referred to in reg.18(2), above. **3.89**

The practical application of reg.18A will be limited by the extension to seven from October 27, 2014 of the number of "waiting days" under para.4 of Sch.1 to the old style Jobseekers Act 1995, but there may not necessarily be waiting days to serve at the beginning of each claim (see reg.46 and the meaning of "jobseeking period").

Circumstances in which a person is to be treated as actively seeking employment

19.—(1) A person shall be treated as actively seeking employment in the following circumstances, subject to [[7]paragraphs (2) and (2A)] and to any maximum period specified in this paragraph— **3.90**

(a) in any week during which he is participating for not less than 3 days as a full-time student in an employment-related course where participation by him has been approved before the course started by an employment officer, for a maximum of 2 weeks and one such course in any period of 12 months;

[[15](aa) for any period for which he is treated as available for employment under regulation 14(1)(aa) (traineeships);]

(b) in any week during which he is attending for not less than 3 days a residential work camp, for a maximum of 2 weeks and one such occasion in any period of 12 months;

(c) in any week during which he is temporarily absent from Great Britain for not less than 3 days because he is taking a member of his family who is a child or young person abroad for treatment, for a maximum of 8 weeks;

(d) in any week during which he is engaged for not less than 3 days in the manning or launching of a lifeboat or in the performance of duty as a part-time member of a fire brigade or engaged during an emergency in duties for the benefit of others;

(e) if he is a member of a couple, in any week during which he is for not less than 3 days looking after a member of his family who is a child while the other member is temporarily absent from the United Kingdom, for a maximum of 8 weeks;

(f) if he is following an Open University course, in any week during which he is attending for not less than 3 days, as a requirement of that course, a residential course, for a maximum of one week per course;

(g) in any week during which he is for not less than 3 days temporarily looking after a child full-time because the person who normally looks after the child is ill or temporarily absent from home or the person is looking after a member of the family who is ill, for a maximum of 8 weeks;

(h) in the first week after the date of claim if he is treated as available for employment to any extent in that week under regulation 14(1)(h);

[[3](i) for any period if he is treated as available for employment to any extent in that period under regulation 14(1)(h);]

[[1](j) if the award is terminated other than on the last day of a week, for the period beginning with the beginning of the week in which the award is terminated and ending on the day on which the award is terminated;]

(k) in any week during which he is participating for not less than 3 days in a programme provided by the Venture Trust in pursuance of an arrangement made by [[8] the Scottish Ministers], for a maximum of 4 weeks and one such programme in any period of 12 months;

(l) in any week during which he is for not less than 3 days treated as capable of work [[12]or as not having limited capability for work] in accordance with regulation 55;

[[16](lzl) in any week during which he is treated as capable of work or as not having limited capability for work under regulation 55ZA unless it would be reasonable for him to take steps in that week to seek employment and he has not taken such steps.]

[[6](ll) in any week during which he is for not less than 3 days treated as capable of work [[12]or as not having limited capability for work] in accordance with regulation 55A;]

(m) in any week during which he is temporarily absent from Great Britain for not less than 3 days in order to attend an interview for employment and has given notice to an employment officer, in writing if so required by the employment officer, that he will be so absent, for a maximum of 1 week;

(n) if he is a member of a couple [[5] other than a joint-claim couple], in any week during which he and his partner are both absent from Great Britain for not less than 3 days and in which a premium referred to in paragraph 10, 11, 12, 13 or 15 of Schedule 1 (applicable amounts) is applicable in respect of his partner for a maximum of 4 weeks;

[5(nn) if he is a member of a joint-claim couple, in any week during which he and his partner are both absent from Great Britain for not less than 3 days and in which a premium referred to in paragraph 20E, 20F, 20G or 20I of Schedule 1 (applicable amounts) is applicable in respect of his partner, for a maximum of 4 weeks;]

(o) in any week during which he is treated as available for employment on not less than 3 days under regulation [9 14(2)or (2ZA)];

(p) in any week in respect of which he has given notice to an employment officer, in writing if so required by the employment officer, that—
  (i) he does not intend to be actively seeking employment, but
  (ii) he does intend to reside at a place other than his usual place of residence for at least one day;

(q) in any week during which he is participating for not less than 3 days in an employment or training programme [13(other than Work Experience)] for which a training allowance is not payable;

[2(r) in any week, being part of a single period not exceeding 8 weeks falling within a period of continuous entitlement to a jobseeker's allowance, during which he is taking active steps to establish himself in self-employed earner's employment under any scheme for assisting persons to become so employed—
  (i) where, in Wales, his participation under the scheme is attributable to arrangements made by the Secretary of State under section 2 of the Employment and Training Act 1973,
  (ii) where, in Scotland, the scheme—
    (aa) is established by virtue of arrangements made by [10 Skills Development Scotland,] Scottish Enterprise or Highlands and Islands Enterprise under section 2(3) of the Enterprise and New Towns (Scotland) Act 1990 or
    (bb) is directly or indirectly provided by, or with financial assistance from, the Secretary of State,
  (iii) where, in England, the scheme is directly or indirectly provided by, or with financial assistance from, the Secretary of State, the [11 Homes and Communities Agency] an urban development corporation or a housing action trust,

and the single period referred to above shall begin with the week in which he is accepted on a place under the scheme.]

[4(s) for any period if he is treated as available for employment to any extent in that period under regulation 14(1)(o).]

[5(t) if he is temporarily absent from Great Britain in the circumstances prescribed in regulation 50(6B)(a) or (c), for the period of any such temporary absence.]

[6(u) if he is temporarily absent from Great Britain in the circumstances prescribed in regulation 50(6AA) or, as the case may be (6C).]

[7(v) in any week during which he is, for not less than three days, required to attend a court or tribunal as a justice of the peace, a party to any proceedings, a witness or a juror;

(w) if, for a maximum of 96 hours before being released, he is in—
  (i) police detention within the meaning in section 118(2) of the Police and Criminal Evidence Act 1984 (general interpretation), or
  (ii) legal custody within the meaning in section 295 of the Criminal Procedure (Scotland) Act 1995 (legal custody in Scotland) but is not a prisoner as defined by regulation 85(4) (special cases).]

[14(x) in any week during which he is treated as available for employment under regulation 14A;]

[17(y) in any week during which he is engaged for not less than 3 days in training as a member of a reserve force prescribed in Part I of Schedule 6 to the Contributions Regulations, either—

(i) if he is engaged in his first year of training, for a maximum of 43 days in that year; or

(ii) if he is engaged in annual continuous training, for a maximum of 15 days in any calendar year.]

(2) In any period of 12 months a person shall be treated as actively seeking employment under paragraph (1)(p) only for the number of weeks specified in one of the following subparagraphs—

(a) a maximum of 2 weeks; or

(b) a maximum of 3 weeks during which he is attending for at least 3 days in each such week an Outward Bound course; or

(c) if he is a blind person, a maximum of 6 weeks during which, apart from a period of no more than 2 weeks, he participates for a maximum period of 4 weeks in a course of training in the use of guide dogs of which at least 3 days in each such week is spent in that training.

[7(2A) A person shall not be treated as actively seeking employment under paragraph (1)(v)—

(a) for more than eight weeks,

(b) where he does not, before the period during which he is required to attend the court or tribunal, give an employment officer notice, in writing where requested by the employment officer, that he is so required, or

(c) where he is a prisoner as defined by regulation 85(4) (special cases).]

(3) In this regulation—

"employment or training programme" means a course or programme the person's participation in which is attributable to arrangements made by the Secretary of State under section 2 of the Employment and Training Act 1973 for the purpose of assisting persons to select, train for, obtain or retain employment;

"housing action trust" means a corporation established by an order of the Secretary of State pursuant to section 62(1) of the Housing Act 1988;

"treatment" means treatment for a disease or bodily or mental disablement by or under the supervision of a person qualified to provide medical treatment, physiotherapy or a form of treatment which is similar to, or related to, either of those forms of treatment;

[7"tribunal" means any tribunal listed in Schedule 1 to the Tribunals and Inquiries Act 1992;]

"urban development corporation" means a corporation established by an order of the Secretary of State pursuant to section 135(1) of the Local Government, Planning and Land Act 1980;

[11 . . .]

AMENDMENTS

1. Jobseeker's Allowance and Income Support (General) (Amendment) Regulations 1996 (SI 1996/1517) reg.7 (October 7, 1996).

2. Social Security Amendment (New Deal) Regulations 1998 (SI 1998/1274) reg.5 (June 1, 1998).

3. Jobseeker's Allowance (Amendment) (No.2) Regulations 1999 (SI 1999/3087) reg.5(2) (November 30, 1999).
4. Jobseeker's Allowance (Amendment) (No.2) Regulations 1999 (SI 1999/3087) reg.5(3) (November 30, 1999).
5. Jobseeker's Allowance (Joint Claims: Consequential Amendments) Regulations 2000 (SI 2000/3336) reg.2 (March 19, 2001).
6. Social Security (Income Support and Jobseeker's Allowance) Amendment Regulations 2004 (SI 2004/1869) reg.3(3) (October 4, 2004).
7. Social Security (Income Support and Jobseeker's Allowance) Amendment Regulations 2006 (SI 2006/1402) reg.2(4) (May 30, 2006).
8. Social Security (Miscellaneous Amendments) Regulations 2008 (SI 2008/698) reg.4(6) (April 14, 2008).
9. Social Security (Lone Parents and Miscellaneous Amendments) Regulations 2008 (SI 2008/3051) reg.11(10) (November 4, 2008).
10. Social Security (Miscellaneous Amendments) Regulations 2009 (SI 2009/583) reg.4(3) (April 6, 2009).
11. The Housing and Regeneration Act 2008 (Consequential Provisions) (No.2) Order 2008 (SI 2008/2831) Sch.1 para.7 (December 1, 2008).
12. Employment and Support Allowance (Consequential Provisions) (No.2) Regulations 2008 (SI 2008/1554) reg.3(5) (October 27, 2008).
13. Jobseeker's Allowance (Work Experience) (Amendment) Regulations 2011 (SI 2011/789) reg.2(3) (April 5, 2011).
14. Jobseeker's Allowance (Domestic Violence) (Amendment) Regulations 2012 (SI 2012/853) reg.2(3) (April 23, 2012).
15. Social Security (Traineeships and Qualifying Young Persons) Amendment Regulations 2015 (SI 2015/336) reg.2(5) (March 27, 2015).
16. Jobseeker's Allowance (Extended Period of Sickness) Amendment Regulations 2015 (SI 2015/339) reg.2(3) (March 30, 2015).
17. Social Security (Members of the Reserve Forces) (Amendment) Regulations 2015 (SI 2015/389) reg.3(4) (April 6, 2015).

DEFINITIONS

"a joint-claim couple"—see Jobseekers Act 1995 s.1(4).
"capable of work"—see Jobseekers Act 1995 s.35(2) and Sch.1 para.2; reg.55.
"child"— see Jobseekers Act 1995 s.35(1).
"the Contributions Regulations"—see reg.1(3).
"couple"—*ibid.*
"date of claim"—*ibid.*
"employed earner's employment"—see Jobseekers Act 1995 s.7(8); SSCBA 1992 s.2(1)(a).
"employment"—see Jobseekers Act 1995 s.7(8).
"employment officer"—see Jobseekers Act 1995 s.35(1).
"employment-related course"—see reg.1(3).
"engaged during an emergency in duties for the benefit of others"—see reg.22.
"family"—see Jobseekers Act 1995 s.35(1).
"first year of training"—see reg.1(3).
"full-time student"—*ibid.*
"Great Britain"—see Jobseekers Act 1995 s.35(1).
"partner"—see reg.1(3).
"part-time member of a fire brigade"—see reg.4.
"self-employed earner's employment"—see Jobseekers Act 1995 s.7(8); SSCBA 1992 s.2(1)(b).
"training allowance"—see reg.1(3).
"week"—see reg.4.
"work camp"—*ibid.*
"young person"—see regs 1(3) and 76.

General Note

3.91 Like its predecessor under the unemployment benefit regime (USI Regulations reg.12D), this regulation sets out in para.(1) a range of situations in which, for the periods specified therein or in para.(2), someone is to be treated as actively seeking employment, even though, were it applied to him, he might fail to satisfy the touchstone test of actually actively seeking work set out in old style Jobseekers Act 1995 s.7(1) as amplified by reg.18. Note, however, that where it has been decided that a person is to be treated as actively seeking employment in any week, a subsequent revision and supersession of that decision can embrace also the question whether in that week the person was actually actively seeking employment (old style Jobseekers Act 1995 s.7(7)). In applying the regulation, careful note should be taken of the specific definition of certain terms (listed in "Definitions", above and in para.(3)). One must also remember the distinction between *Great Britain* (England, Scotland and Wales) and the *United Kingdom* (of Great Britain and Northern Ireland).

The categories set out on para.(1) need to be examined carefully. They cannot apply for longer than the circumstances prescribed last. However, some categories contain more stringent limits. Sub-paragraphs (l), (lza) and (ll) are an important element of the protection given to those who are treated as capable of work or as not having limited capability for work under regs 55, 55ZA or 55A, by deeming such persons to be actively seeking employment (and see reg.14(1)(l) on deemed availability). Another particularly interesting category, in the light of the state of the rules on potential availability for employment while claimants are on holiday (see the notes to s.6 of the old style Jobseekers Act 1995), is sub-para.(p), covering weeks in respect of which a claimant has given (advance) notice to an employment officer of the absence of an intention to be actively seeking employment and an intention to reside for at least a day in that week at a place other than the claimant's usual place of residence. Under para.(2) advantage can generally only be taken of sub-para.(p) for two weeks in any 12 months, although there are specific extensions for Outward Bound courses and guide dog training for the blind.

The remainder of the categories specified in para.(1) fall into four main groups (sometimes overlapping): those taking part in certain educational or training activities (sub-paras (a), (aa), (b), (f), (k), (q) and (y)); those involving temporary absence from Great Britain (sub-paras (c), (e), (m), (n), (nn), (t) and (u)); those involving caring for others (sub-paras (e), (g), (t) and (u)); and those involving some public service (sub-paras (d), (v) and (y)). The remaining miscellaneous categories, often to do with the beginning or end of a period of entitlement, are in sub-paras (h), (i), (j), (o), (r), (s), (w) and (x).

The transition from new style JSA

3.92 In para.(1)(r) the reference to jobseeker's allowance is, where art.13(1) and (2) of the Welfare Reform Act 2012 (Commencement No.9 and Transitional and Transitory Provisions and Commencement No.8 and Savings and Transitional Provisions (Amendment)) Order 2013 (as amended and set out in the 2014/15 Supplement) applies, to be read as if it included a reference to new style JSA (art.13(3)(ab) of that Order, in force from June 16, 2014).

Further circumstances in which a person is to be treated as actively seeking employment: permitted period

3.93 **20.**—(1) A person to whom paragraph (2) does not apply shall be treated as actively seeking employment in any week during any permitted period determined in his case in accordance with regulation 16, if he is actively seeking employment in that week—

(a) only in his usual occupation,

(b) only at a level of remuneration not lower than that which he is accustomed to receive, or
(c) only in his usual occupation and at a level of remuneration not lower than that which he is accustomed to receive.

(2) A person to whom this paragraph applies shall be treated as actively seeking employment in any week during any permitted period determined in his case in accordance with regulation 16, if he is actively seeking employment, self-employed earner's employment, or employment and self-employed earner's employment in that week—
(a) only in his usual occupation,
(b) only at a level of remuneration not lower than that which he is accustomed to receive, or
(c) only in his usual occupation and at a level of remuneration not lower than that which he is accustomed to receive.

(3) Paragraph (2) applies to a person who has, at any time during the period of 12 months immediately preceding the date of claim, been engaged in his usual occupation in self-employed earner's employment.

DEFINITIONS

"employment"—see Jobseekers Act 1995 s.7(8).
"employed earner's employment"—see Jobseekers Act 1995 s.7(8); SSCBA 1992 s.2(1)(a).
"self-employed earner's employment"—see Jobseekers Act 1995 s.7(8); SSCBA 1992 s.2(1)(b).
"week"—see reg.4.

GENERAL NOTE

Under the old style Act, all claimants must be available for employment (as opposed to self-employment). For a "permitted period" of up to 13 weeks, a claimant can be treated as available even though only available for employment in his usual occupation and/or at his accustomed level of remuneration (reg.16). Paragraph (1) of this regulation enables such a person to be treated as actively seeking employment for that period. Under para.(2), someone who has at any time in the 12 months prior to his date of claim for old style JSA been engaged in self-employment in his usual occupation can be treated as actively seeking employment during the "permitted period", even though he confines his jobsearch to employment, self-employment or both, only in his usual occupation, or only at his accustomed rate of remuneration, or only in his usual occupation and at his accustomed rate. But he must, of course, still be available for employment as an employed earner. On determining whether a particular claimant can have such a "permitted period" and, if so, its length, see reg.16(2). For limitations on the application of the period in the case of a claimant laid of from, or kept on short time in, his employment, see reg.17(4). 3.94

Further circumstances in which a person is to be treated as actively seeking employment: laid off and short time workers

21.—A person who has restricted his availability for employment in accordance with regulation 17(1) or, as the case may be, regulation 17(2), shall in any week in which he has so restricted his availability for not less than 3 days be treated as actively seeking employment in that week if he takes such steps as he can reasonably be expected to have to take in order to have the best prospects of securing employment for which he is available under regulation 17. 3.95

DEFINITIONS

"employment"—see reg.4.
"week"—*ibid.*

GENERAL NOTE

3.96 Under reg.17, a claimant laid off from employment or put on short time owing to temporary adverse industrial conditions can, for up to 13 weeks, be treated as available for employment, provided he is willing and able to resume immediately the employment from which, as the case may be, he is laid off or kept on short time, and to take up immediately any casual employment within daily travelling distance of his home. The requirement of immediacy is modified for carers and volunteers (48 hours' notice) and those providing a service (24 hours' notice), protected by reg.5(1) and (2).

This regulation stipulates that a claimant who has restricted his availability in that way for not less than three days in a particular week is to be treated as actively seeking employment in that week, provided he takes such steps as he can reasonably be expected to have to take in order to have the best prospects of securing the employment for which, under reg.17, he is available. In short, for up to 13 weeks of short time or lay off, he can confine his jobsearch to the job with respect to which he has been laid off or kept on short time and casual employment within daily travelling distance of his home.

[1Further circumstances in which a qualifying person is to be treated as actively seeking employment: full-time students participating in a qualifying course

3.97 **21A.**—A person who is treated as available for employment in accordance with regulation 17A(3) shall be treated as actively seeking employment in any week—

(a) which, in relation to the qualifying course, falls wholly or partly in term-time;
(b) in which he is taking examinations relating to the qualifying course; or
(c) which falls wholly in a vacation from the qualifying course, if in that week he takes such steps as he can reasonably be expected to have to take in order to have the best prospects of securing employment for which he is available under regulation 17A(3)(c).]

AMENDMENT

1. Social Security Amendment (New Deal) Regulations 1998 (SI 1998/1274) reg.6 (June 1, 1998).

DEFINITIONS

"employment"—see Jobseekers Act 1995 s.7(8).
"employed earner's employment"—see Jobseekers Act 1995 s.7(8); SSCBA 1992 s.2(1)(a).
"examination"—see reg.4.
"qualifying course"—*ibid.*, reg.17A(7).
"term-time"—see reg.4.
"vacation"—*ibid.*
"week"—*ibid.*

General Note

Complementing reg.17A, reg.21A provides that during any week in which a person is treated as available under reg.17A, he will be treated also as actively seeking work. Where the week is during a vacation from the course, he must however show that during that week he has taken such steps as he can reasonably be expected to have to take to have the best prospects of securing the casual employment for which reg.17A requires him to be available. 3.98

[1Further circumstances in which a person is to be treated as actively seeking employment: lone parents with children aged 5 not in full-time education

21B.—A lone parent who is treated for any period as being available for employment under regulation 17B shall be treated as actively seeking employment for the same period.] 3.99

Amendment

1. Social Security (Lone Parents and Miscellaneous Amendments) Regulations 2012 (SI 2012/874) reg.3(2) (May 21, 2012, subject to special commencement provisions in the Sch. to this amending instrument).

Interpretation of certain expressions for the purposes of regulations 18(3)(f)(i) and 19(1)(d)

22.—For the purposes of regulations 18(3)(f)(i) and 19(1)(d)— 3.100
(a) a person is engaged in duties for the benefit of others while—
(i) providing assistance to any person whose life may be endangered or who may be exposed to the risk of serious bodily injury or whose health may be seriously impaired,
(ii) protecting property of substantial value from imminent risk of serious damage or destruction, or
(iii) assisting in measures being taken to prevent a serious threat to the health of the people,
as a member of a group of persons organised wholly or partly for the purpose of providing such assistance or, as the case may be, protection;
(b) events which may give rise to an emergency include—
(i) a fire, a flood or an explosion,
(ii) a natural catastrophe,
(iii) a railway or other transport accident,
(iv) a cave or mountain accident,
(v) an accident at sea,
(vi) a person being reported missing and the organisation of a search for that person.

General Note

Regulation 18(3)(f)(i) provides that in applying the touchstone test of actively seeking employment to a claimant's jobseeking activity in a week, the fact that a claimant was engaged during an emergency in duties for the benefit of others is one of the circumstances to be taken into account. Under reg.19(1)(d) a claimant so engaged for at least three days in a week is treated as actively seeking work in that week. For the purposes of those provisions, this regulation provides in para.(1) a complete definition of when "a person is engaged in duties for the benefit of others" 3.101

and in para.(b) an indication of what events can give rise to an "emergency". Paragraph (b) is not, however, exhaustive; it reads "events which may give rise to an emergency *include*" (emphasis supplied by annotator). See further reg.14, where the same definitions are deployed, and the annotations to that provision.

Chapter IV

Attendance, information and evidence

Attendance

3.102 **23.**—[[1]A claimant shall [[2] participate in an interview in such manner, time and place] as an employment officer may specify by a notification which is given or sent to the claimant and which may be in writing, by telephone or by electronic means.]

AMENDMENTS

1. Jobseeker's Allowance (Amendment) (No.3) Regulations 2000 (SI 2000/2194) reg.2(2) (September 11, 2000).
2. Jobseeker's Allowance (Sanctions) (Amendment) Regulations 2012 (SI 2012/2568) reg.5(4) (October 22, 2012).

DEFINITIONS

"claimant"—see Jobseekers Act 1995 s.35(1).
"employment officer"—*ibid.*
"writing"—see Interpretation Act 1978 Sch.1.

GENERAL NOTE

3.103 *"Sent"*: In *R(JSA) 1/04*, the claimant had been sent a notice, dated October 8, 2001 calling him for interview on October 25, 2001, but, Commissioner Turnbull accepted, had probably not received it. The Commissioner held that the proper interpretation of "sent" in reg.23 in accordance with s.7 of the Interpretation Act 1978, as applied by s.23 of that Act to subordinate legislation, meant that the claimant was entitled to prove non-receipt in order to say it had not been "sent" with the consequence that his entitlement to JSA could not be terminated since he had not "failed to attend" the interview. No particular period of notification is required, but in the case of unreasonably short notice, the claimant's remedy appears to lie in contacting the employment officer within five days after the notified date and thus avoiding the ending of entitlement (reg.25(1)(a) and (b)). Unreasonable notice would also be relevant to a good reason for failing to comply with reg.23 and to the possibility of a sanction under s.19A(2)(a) of the Act (see the notes to reg.25 below).

The Interpretation Act presumption only applies where the letter containing the notice was properly addressed. The decisions in *CJSA/4720/2014* (not at present on the AAC website) and *DD v SSWP (JSA)* [2015] UKUT 318 (AAC) arose under the SAPOE Regulations (below), where reg.2(2) provides that where a notice is sent by post it is to be taken to have been received on the second working day after posting. The judges in both cases held that that provision only applied if the letter was correctly addressed, and that outside any presumption the question was whether the Secretary of State had shown on the balance of probabilities that the notice had been received. The cases concerned the same claimant and the same mistake in the address, but different letters and notices to participate in schemes and it is evident that neither Upper Tribunal judge knew of the existence of the other appeal. The first line and the postcode was correct, but the address included the name of an estate some miles away from the estate on which the claimant lived. The claimant denied receiving the letters in question. In *CJSA/4720/2014*, the First-tier Tribunal decided that, in the light of the claimant's history of non-attendance at Work Programme appointments and of sending back letters from the provider unopened, she did in fact receive the letter in question so that the sanction (presumably under s.19A(2)(b) of the old style Jobseekers Act 1995, as only Mandatory Work Activity is prescribed for the purposes of s.19(2)(e)) was upheld. Judge West set that decision aside on the basis (perhaps only doubtfully made out on the extracts cited) that the tribunal had regarded it as crucial that the correct postcode had been used and that, as asserted on behalf of the Secretary of State, that would have enabled delivery to the correct address before the appointment. However, there was a reference to a new tribunal to give the Secretary of State the opportunity to produce evidence from the Royal Mail in support of the assertion that use of the correct postcode would enable the correct delivery of a letter when other parts of the address are incorrect. By contrast, in *DD* Judge Mark, on the material before him, while accepting that the Royal Mail would have had little difficulty in identifying the correct address, considered that the doubt about how long that process would take meant that on the balance of probabilities it had not been shown that a letter said to have been posted on January 9, 2014 (a Thursday) had been received by Wednesday January 15, 2014 in time for the claimant to know that she was required to attend on that day. He substituted a decision setting aside the sanction imposed on the claimant. The judge also queried whether evidence that a letter had been issued on a particular date was necessarily evidence of posting on that day, given common office practice of post put in an out-tray after mid-afternoon not in fact being posted until the following working day.

There is some doubt, as was raised in *CS v SSWP (JSA)* [2015] UKUT 61 (AAC), whether the provision that the notification of the manner, time and place of the interview "may" be in writing, by telephone or by electronic means is exhaustive or merely illustrative. The issue potentially raised in that case was whether an oral notification given in the course of face to face contact between the claimant and the employment officer qualified. In the event, Judge Wikeley did not have to decide that point of interpretation, because the Secretary of State conceded that, in the absence of any entry in the claimant's Action Plan for the date on which it was said that the employment officer had told him orally that he was to sign on in seven days' time rather than on the previous fortnightly basis, the First-tier Tribunal erred in law by accepting the DWP's assertion that notification had been given in preference to the claimant's evidence that he had not been told that he had to attend on any particular date and time different from his previous pattern. Judge Wikeley accepted that concession, suggesting that, just as in sanctions cases (see *DL v SSWP (JSA)* [2013] UKUT 295 (AAC)), the legislation should be construed strictly, giving the claimant the benefit of any doubt that might reasonably arise. The Secretary of State's submission in *CS* had been that the provision is purely illustrative, so that a properly proved oral notification comes within reg.23. The contrary argument is that there would appear to be little point in specifying the particular means of communication if the intention was to be purely illustrative and that "may be" can often properly be construed as setting out the permissible means of doing something. It is of course to be implied that the notification is in a form that the particular claimant is reasonably to be known to be capable of comprehending.

It was accepted in *CS* that a proper notification would have to specify the time (including date) and place of the interview. It remains unclear just what has to be specified about the manner in which the claimant is to participate in the interview. Regulation 25 makes it a condition for terminating entitlement on a failure to comply with regs 23, 23A or 24(6) and (10) that the claimant has failed to make contact with an employment officer "in the manner set out in [a reg.23 or 23A] notification" before the end of the period of five working days from the failure to comply. Thus, the notification should tell the claimant by what means contact can be made with an employment officer if the day or time of the interview is missed **3.104** and/or if a signed declaration was not provided on the notified day. It may be arguable, applying the strict interpretation principle suggested in *CS*, that if the notification fails to provide that information, reg.25 cannot be applied.

In *CJSA/1080/2002*, Commissioner Rowland held that the requirement to attend as a condition of entitlement to JSA lapses once the claimant has been informed that his claim for JSA has been rejected. In that case, the letter so informing the claimant may have been meant to refer only to IBJSA but was so worded that a reasonable claimant would understand it to reject her claim for both IBJSA and CBJSA. Accordingly, the tribunal had erred in not considering title to CBJSA: the requirement to attend having lapsed, regs 25 and 26 were inapplicable, so that there was no limit to the period for which the tribunal could have awarded CBJSA on the appeal.

Judge Rowland followed *CJSA/1080/2002*, with the apparent agreement of the Secretary of State, in *GM v SSWP (JSA)* [2014] UKUT 57 (AAC). The principle therefore seems to be accepted, although the technical mechanism to implement it is not entirely clear. Perhaps the requirement under reg.23 (or 23A) is simply to be regarded as of no effect in such circumstances.

3.105 Note that the test has now become, in line with universal credit and new style JSA, not merely attendance at an interview at the notified date and time, but participation in the interview. This would appear to mean that a claimant can be required to participate in an interview over the telephone, providing that notification has been given of that manner of conducting it. However, in an ambiguous Parliamentary answer on November 24, 2015 (UIN 17005), the Minister of State, Priti Patel, said:

> "Under JSA, claimants are not sanctioned for failing to answer their telephone. In Universal Credit, claimants who have a prearranged telephone interview with their Work Coach, and who fail to participate without good reason, can be referred for a sanction decision."

There is no further provision about what participation means. It must at least entail turning up at the place and time specified, although the decision of Judge Knowles in *SA v SSWP (JSA)* [2015] UKUT 454 (AAC) (see the notes to s.19A(2)(c) of the old style Jobseekers Act 1995 for full discussion) would indicate that tribunals should consider, in cases where the claimant arrives not very late, whether it is proportionate to the nature of all the circumstances to regard that as a failure to participate in an interview. There were all sorts of mitigating circumstances in *SA*, that may well not be present in other cases. Also, there is specific provision in reg.25(1)(b) for cases where a claimant makes contact with an employment officer on the right day, but does not participate in an interview at the right time, which may provide a significantly different context. As discussed further below, it is relatively easy for claimants to avoid a ceasing of entitlement under reg.25, but they may still be subject to a sanction under s.19A(2)(a). The approach in *SA* might be more relevant in that context.

Participation must also extend to making some meaningful contribution to the interview, but the limits will probably not be established until some more appeals have reached the Upper Tribunal. Behaviour that leads to the premature termination of the interview may well amount to a failure to participate (see the facts of *DM v SSWP (JSA)* [2015] UKUT 67 (AAC) in the notes to s.19A(2)(c)). There may, though, in cases of uncooperative claimants or heavy-handed officials or a combination, be difficult questions about when an interview has ceased to exist, so that subsequent behaviour cannot be relevant to whether there has been a failure to participate (see *PH v SSWP (ESA)* [2016] UKUT 119 (AAC) on failing to submit to a medical examination).

A failure to comply with a requirement under s.8(1) can lead to the ceasing of entitlement under paras 25–27 below, as authorised by s.8(2), and also to a sanction under s.19A(2)(a) of the old style Jobseekers Act 1995. Regulation 25(1) specifies in sub-paras (a) and (b) that a failure to participate in a notified interview and to contact the employment officer within five working days after the notified date leads to the ceasing of entitlement. Sub-paragraph.(c) specifies that result where a claimant fails to provide a signed declaration on the day required under reg.24(10). See the notes to reg.25 for the details.

In relation to reg.25(1)(a) and (b), on failing to comply with a requirement under regs 23 or 23A, the cessation of entitlement cannot be applied where the claimant has made contact with an employment officer within the appropriate five-day period, however feeble the reason for not participating in the interview on the right day or at the right time. In those circumstances, the claimant will still have failed to comply with a requirement under either reg.23 or 23A, by failing to participate in an interview on the right date or at the right time. That is a sanctionable failure under s.19A(2)(a) of the old style Jobseekers Act 1995 if the claimant does not have a good reason for the failure to comply, which reg.70A(2)(b), (3) and (4) allows to lead to a reduction in benefit for the appropriate fixed period under reg.69A. If the claimant has not made contact within the five-day period, the cessation of entitlement under reg.25(1)(a) or (b) must follow. However, in those circumstances there can be no reduction in benefit following the sanctionable failure. Regulation 70A(2)(b), (3)(b) and (4)(d) requires that result in regs 23 or 23A cases, except where the claimant has made contact with an employment officer within the prescribed period. The sanctionable failure then does not count as a previous failure for the purpose of calculating the period of reduction of benefit on any subsequent "offence" (reg.69A(2)(a)).

[1Attendance by members of a joint-claim couple

23A.—Each member of a joint-claim couple shall [2participate in an interview in such manner, time and place] as the employment officer may specify by a notification which is given or sent to that member and which may be in writing, by telephone or by electronic means.] 3.106

AMENDMENTS

1. Jobseeker's Allowance (Joint Claims) Regulations 2000 (SI 2000/1978) Sch.2 para.2 (March 19, 2001).

2. Jobseeker's Allowance (Sanctions) (Amendment) Regulations 2012 (SI 2012/2568) reg.5(4) (October 22, 2012).

DEFINITIONS

"employment officer"—see Jobseekers Act 1995 s.35(1).
"joint claim couple"—see Jobseekers Act 1995 ss.35(1) and 1(4).

GENERAL NOTE

This makes the same provision as in reg.23 for both members of a joint-claim couple. See the notes to reg.23. 3.107

Provision of information and evidence

24.—(1) A claimant shall provide such information as to his circumstances, his availability for employment and the extent to which he is actively seeking employment as may be required by the Secretary of State in order to determine the entitlement of the claimant to a jobseeker's allowance, whether that allowance is payable to him and, if so, in what amount. 3.108

[1(1A) A member of a joint-claim couple shall provide such information as to the circumstances of each or either member of a couple, the availability for employment of each or either member of the couple and the extent to which each or either member of the couple is actively seeking employment as may be required by the Secretary of State in order to determine the entitlement of the couple to a jobseeker's allowance, whether that allowance is payable to the couple and, if so, in what amount.]

(2) A claimant shall furnish such other information in connection with the claim, or any question arising out of it, as may be required by the Secretary of State.

(3) Where—

(a) a jobseeker's allowance may be claimed by either member of a couple, or

(b) entitlement to a jobseeker's allowance or whether that allowance is payable and, if so, in what amount, is or may be affected by the circumstances of either member of a couple or any member of a polygamous marriage,

the Secretary of State may require the member of the couple other than the claimant to certify in writing whether he agrees to the claimant's making the claim, or that he, or any member of a polygamous marriage, confirms the information given about his circumstances [[1], and in this paragraph "couple" does not include a joint-claim couple.

(3A) Where entitlement to a joint-claim jobseeker's allowance or whether that allowance is payable and, if so, in what amount, is or may be affected by the circumstances of any member of a polygamous marriage, the Secretary of State may require either member of the joint-claim couple to certify in writing that any member of the polygamous marriage confirms the information given about that member's circumstances.]

(4) A claimant shall furnish such certificates, documents and other evidence as may be required by the Secretary of State for the determination of the claim.

(5) A claimant shall furnish such certificates, documents and other evidence affecting his continuing entitlement to a jobseeker's allowance, whether that allowance is payable to him and, if so, in what amount as the Secretary of State may require.

[[1](5A) A member of a joint-claim couple shall furnish such certificates, documents and other evidence affecting the continuing entitlement of the couple to a jobseeker's allowance, whether that allowance is payable to the couple and, if so, in what amount as the Secretary of State may require.]

(6) A claimant shall, if the Secretary of State requires him to do so, provide a signed declaration to the effect that—

(a) since making a claim for a jobseeker's allowance or since he last provided a declaration in accordance with this paragraph he has either been available for employment or satisfied the circumstances to be treated as available for employment, save as he has otherwise notified the Secretary of State.

(b) since making a claim for a jobseeker's allowance or since he last provided a declaration in accordance with this paragraph he has either been actively seeking employment to the extent necessary to give him his best prospects of securing employment or he has satisfied the circumstances to be treated as actively seeking employment, save as he has otherwise notified the Secretary of State, and

(c) since making a claim for a jobseeker's allowance or since he last provided a declaration in accordance with this paragraph there has been no change to his circumstances which might affect his entitlement to a jobseeker's allowance or the amount of such an allowance, save as he has notified the Secretary of State.

(7) A claimant shall notify the Secretary of State—

(a) of any change of circumstances which has occurred which he might reasonably be expected to know might affect his entitlement to a jobseeker's allowance [[1]or, in the case of a joint-claim couple, the entitlement of the couple to a joint-claim jobseeker's allowance] or the payability or amount of such an allowance; and

(b) of any such change of circumstances which he is aware is likely so to occur,

and shall do so as soon as reasonably practicable after its occurrence or, as the case may be, after he becomes so aware, by giving notice [[3]of the change to an office of the Department for Work and Pensions specified by the Secretary of State—

(i) in writing or by telephone (unless the Secretary of State determines in any particular case that notice must be in writing or may be given otherwise than in writing or by telephone); or

(ii) in writing if in any class of case he requires written notice (unless he determines in any particular case to accept notice given otherwise than in writing).]

(8) Where, pursuant to paragraph (1) [[1](1A)] or (2), a claimant is required to provide information he shall do so [[5]at the time he is required to participate in an interview] in accordance with a [[2]notification] under regulation 23 [[1]or 23A], if so required by the Secretary of State, or within such period as the Secretary of State may require.

(9) Where, pursuant to paragraph (4) [[4] . . .], a claimant is required to provide certificates, documents or other evidence he shall do so within seven days of being so required or such longer period as the Secretary of State may consider reasonable.

[[4](9A) Where, pursuant to paragraph (5) or (5A), a claimant is required to provide certificates, documents or other evidence, he shall do so within the period applicable under regulation 17(4) of the Social Security and Child Support (Decisions and Appeals) Regulations 1999.]

(10) Where, pursuant to paragraph (6), a claimant is required to provide a signed declaration he shall provide it [[5]on the day on which he is required to participate in an interview] in accordance with a [[2]notification] under regulation 23 [[1]or 23A] or on such other day as the Secretary of State may require.

AMENDMENTS

1. Jobseeker's Allowance (Joint Claims) Regulations 2000 (SI 2000/1978) Sch.2 para.3 (March 19, 2001).

2. Jobseeker's Allowance (Amendment) (No.3) Regulations 2000 (SI 2000/2194) reg.2(3) (September, 11, 2000).

3. Social Security (Miscellaneous Amendments) (No.2) Regulations 2006 (SI 2006/832) reg.4 (April 10, 2006).

4. Social Security (Suspension of Payment of Benefits and Miscellaneous Amendments) Regulations 2012 (SI 2012/824) reg.3 (April 17, 2012).

5. Jobseeker's Allowance (Sanctions) (Amendment) Regulations 2012 (SI 2012/2568) reg.5(5) (October 22, 2012).

DEFINITIONS

"claimant"—see Jobseekers Act 1995 s.35(1).
"couple"—*ibid.*
"employment"—see reg.4.
"a joint-claim couple"—see Jobseekers Act 1995 ss.35(1) and 1(4).

"polygamous marriage"—see reg.1(3).
"writing"—see Interpretation Act 1978 Sch.1.

General Note

3.109 A failure to provide a signed declaration in accordance with reg.24(6) and (10) means loss of entitlement to old style JSA (see reg.25(1)(c), subject to reg.27). The mere non-furnishing of the evidence contemplated by the other provisions in reg.24 has no such automatic preclusive effect, but could lead to a sanction under s.19A(2)(a) of the old style Jobseekers Act 1995 if there was no good reason for the failure to comply, if it were not for the prohibition in reg.70A(2)(a) on any reduction in benefit under s.19A for any failure to comply with reg.24. It, may also, of course, cause a decision-maker or tribunal to doubt assertions about actively seeking work (see Commissioner Brown in the Northern Ireland decisions *C1/00–01 (JSA)* and *C2/00–01 (JSA)*, [35]).

[[1]Alternative means of notifying changes of circumstances

3.110 **24A.**—(1) In such cases and subject to such conditions as the Secretary of State may specify, the duty in regulation 24(7) to notify a change of circumstances may be discharged by notifying the Secretary of State as soon as reasonably practicable—

(a) where the change of circumstances is a birth or death, through a relevant authority, or a county council in England, by personal attendance at an office specified by that authority or county council, provided the Secretary of State has agreed with that authority or county council for it to facilitate such notification; or
(b) where the change of circumstances is a death, by telephone to a telephone number specified for that purpose by the Secretary of State.

(2) In this regulation "relevant authority" has the same meaning as in the Housing Benefit Regulations 2006 [[2]. . .].]

Amendments

1. Inserted by the Social Security (Notification of Change of Circumstances) Regulations 2010 (SI 2010/444) reg.3 (April 5, 2010).
2. Council Tax Benefit Abolition (Consequential Provision) Regulations 2013 (SI 2013/458) reg.3 and Sch.1 (April 1, 2013).

General Note

3.111 This allows the Secretary of State to enable a broadening of the routes by which the duty to notify changes of circumstances imposed by reg.24(7) may be discharged. "Relevant authority" is defined in reg.2(1) of the Housing Benefit Regulations 2006 as an authority administering housing benefit.

[[1]Information given electronically

3.112 **24B.**—(1) A person may give any certificate, notice, information or evidence required to be given and in particular may give notice of a change of circumstances required to be notified under regulation 24 by means of an electronic communication, in accordance with the provisions set out in Schedule 9ZC to the Claims and Payments Regulations.

(2) In this regulation, "electronic communication" has the meaning given in section 15(1) of the Electronic Communications Act 2000.]

AMENDMENT

1. Social Security (Electronic Communications) Order 2011 (SI 2011/1498) art.3(3) (June 20, 2011).

DEFINITION

"Claims and Payments Regulations"—see reg.1(3).

Entitlement ceasing on a failure to comply

25.—(1) [4Entitlement] to a jobseeker's allowance shall cease in the following circumstances— 3.113

[4(a) if a claimant fails to [8 participate in an interview] on the day specified in a relevant notification, and fails to make contact with an employment officer in the manner set out in that notification before the end of the period of five working days beginning with the first working day after the day on which the claimant failed to [8participate in an interview;]2

(b) if—

[1(i) [8that claimant makes contact with an employment officer on the day specified in the relevant notification but fails to participate in an interview at the time specified in that notification, and the Secretary of State has informed that claimant in writing that a failure to participate in an interview, on the next occasion on which he is required to participate in an interview], at the time specified in such a [2notification] may result in his entitlement to a jobseeker's allowance ceasing [4or the benefit not being payable for a period], and

(ii) he fails to [8 participate in an interview] at the time specified in such a [2notification] on the next occasion; [4and

(iii) that claimant fails to make contact with an employment officer in the manner set out in such a notification before the end of the period of five working days beginning with the first working day after the day on which that claimant failed to [8 participate in an interview] at the time specified;]

(c) [4subject to regulation 27,] if [3that claimant] was required to provide a signed declaration as referred to in regulation 24(6) and he fails to provide it on the day on which he ought to do so in accordance with regulation 24(10).]

[4(1A) In this regulation and in regulations 27A, 28 and 30—

"relevant notification" means a notification under regulation 23 or 23A, other than a notification requiring attendance under an employment programme or a training scheme[7, under a scheme prescribed in regulation 3 of the Jobseeker's Allowance (Schemes for Assisting Persons to Obtain Employment) Regulations 2013][9, under a scheme prescribed in regulation 3 of the Jobseeker's Allowance (18–21 Work Skills Pilot Scheme) Regulations 2014][6, under the Employment, Skills and Enterprise Scheme] [5or under the Mandatory Work Activity Scheme];

"working day" means any day on which the appropriate office is not closed.]

(2) In this regulation, "an employment programme" and "a training scheme" have the meaning given in regulation 75.

AMENDMENTS

1. Jobseeker's Allowance (Amendment Regulations) 1999 (SI 1999/530) reg.2 (March 25, 1999).

2. Jobseeker's Allowance (Amendment) (No.3) Regulations 2000 (SI 2000/2194) reg.2(4) (September 11, 2000).

3. Jobseeker's Allowance (Joint Claims) Regulations 2000 (SI 2000/1978) Sch.2 para.4 (March 19, 2001).

4. Jobseeker's Allowance (Sanctions for Failure to Attend) Regulations 2010 (SI 2010/509) reg.2 (April 6, 2010).

5. Jobseeker's Allowance (Mandatory Work Activity Scheme) Regulations 2011 (SI 2011/688) reg.16(a) (April 25, 2011).

6. Jobseeker's Allowance (Employment, Skills and Enterprise Scheme) Regulations 2011 (SI 2011/917) reg.16(a) (May 20, 2011).

7. Jobseeker's Allowance (Schemes for Assisting Persons to Obtain Employment) Regulations 2013 (SI 2013/276) reg.14(b) (February 12, 2013 at 6.45 pm).

8. Social Security (Miscellaneous Amendments) Regulations 2013 (SI 2013/443) reg.4(3) (April 2, 2013).

9. Jobseeker's Allowance (18–21 Work Skills Pilot Scheme) Regulations 2014 (SI 2014/3117) reg.19 (November 25, 2014).

DEFINITIONS

"claimant"—see Jobseekers Act 1995 s.35(1).
"employment officer"—*ibid.*
"an employment programme"—see reg.75(1).
"a training scheme"—see reg.75(1).

GENERAL NOTE

3.114 Sub-paragraphs (a) and (b) of para.(1) specify that a failure to participate in a notified interview and to contact the employment officer within five working days after the notified date leads to the ceasing of entitlement, on the day specified in reg.26. Sub-para.(c) specifies that result where a claimant fails to provide a signed declaration on the day required under reg.24(10), but not where there is a failure to comply with any other requirement under reg.24. Under all of sub-paras (a), (b) and (c) it is irrelevant, if the claimant has not made contact with an employment officer within the relevant five-day period, how good the reasons might have been for not participating in the interview or for not providing the signed declaration. The claimant's basic remedy is to make a new claim and possibly apply for the back-dating of the claim (available only in restricted circumstances under reg.19 of the Claims and Payments Regulations). See further the notes to reg.26 below.

If the claimant has made contact within the five-day period there cannot be a termination of entitlement. Although sub-para.(c) is subject to reg.27, which purports to make it an extra condition in such cases that the claimant shows, within that period, a good reason for failing to comply, the reasoning of Commissioner Stockman in the Northern Ireland decision in *LDG v DSD (JSA)* [2015] NICom 16 indicates that that condition is not valid, having been imposed outside the power given by s.8(2) of the old style Jobseekers Act 1995. Section 8(2) only allows regulations to provide for entitlement to cease if the claimant does not make the prescribed contact within a prescribed period. It does not allow the addition of the extra condition that, as well as making contact in the way prescribed, the claimant must also do something different in showing a good reason. In *KH v SSWP (JSA)* [2015] UKUT 497 (AAC) Judge Hemingway applied the exception to reg.25(1)(c) in reg.27 without consideration of the convincing reasoning of Commissioner Stockman in *LDG*. As the judge had not been referred to *LDG*, the decision in *KH* cannot be taken as undermining the force of the reasoning in *LDG* in any way. See the notes to reg.27 for further details. If the extra condition were valid, it appears that the good reason has to be shown within the five-day period (see the reasoning in paras 255–268 of *SSWP v TJ (JSA)* [2015] UKUT 56 (AAC)). See the notes to reg.23 for what must be specified in a regs 23 or 23A notification.

Sub-paragraph (a) is relatively straightforward in its terms. It appears to apply where the claimant does not turn up at all on the day, or at least makes no contact with an employment officer on that day, specified in a notification under regs 23 or 23A. See the notes to reg.23 for what a failure to participate in an interview might entail. Sub-paragraph (b) is much more convoluted and there is some difficulty, stemming partly from the conventional use of the present tense in legislation, in working out the order in which things have to happen and at what point the duty to bring an end to entitlement is triggered. It appears to work in the following way. First, a claimant who has been notified to participate in an interview on a particular day turns up on the right day but at the wrong time and sees an employment officer, who gives a written warning that a failure to participate in an interview on the next day on which he is notified to participate may result in the ceasing of entitlement or a sanction (sub-para.(b)(i)). Those circumstances do not fall within sub-para.(a) because, although the claimant has failed to participate in an interview on the notified day, there has been contact with an employment officer. Then, if heads (ii) and (iii) of sub-para.(b) are both satisfied, requiring the expiry of five working days without contact with an employment officer in the manner set out in the latest notification and a failure to participate in an interview at the right time on the next notified day, the duty to bring an end to entitlement is triggered. Under reg.26(b), the day on which the claimant was required to participate in an interview must presumably refer, in the case of sub-para.(b) of reg.25(1), to that final day on which the operation of the provision was triggered. See further the notes to reg.26.

In relation to sub-paras (a) and (b), the cessation of entitlement cannot be applied where the claimant has made contact with an employment officer within the appropriate five-day period in the manner set out in the relevant notification, however feeble the reason for not participating in the interview on right day or at the right time. In those circumstances, the claimant will still have failed to comply with a requirement under regs 23 or 23A, by failing to participate in an interview on the right date or at the right time. That is a sanctionable failure under s.19A(2)(a) of the old style Jobseekers Act 1995 if the claimant does not have a good reason for the failure to comply, which reg.70A(2)(b), (3) and (4) allows to lead to a reduction in benefit for the appropriate fixed period under reg.69A. If the claimant has not made contact within the five-day period, the cessation of entitlement under reg.25(1)(a) or (b) must follow. However, in those circumstances there can be no reduction in benefit following the sanctionable failure. Regulation 70A(2)(b), (3)(b) and (4)(d) requires that result in regs 23 or 23A cases except where the claimant has made contact with an employment officer within the prescribed period. The sanctionable failure then does not count as a previous failure for the purpose of calculating the period of reduction of benefit on any subsequent "offence" (reg.69A(2)(a)).

In relation to sub-para.(c), reg.27 provides that entitlement is not to cease if the claimant not only contacts an employment officer within five working days in the manner set out in the notification to participate in an interview on the day on which the declaration was to be signed but also shows a good reason for the failure to provide the signed declaration. On the basis, discussed above, that that extra condition is not valid, where the claimant makes contact within the relevant period, there would still have been a sanctionable failure under s.19A(2)(a) of the old style Jobseekers Act 1995, unless there was a good reason for the failure. However, reg.70A(2)(a) prevents there being any reduction in benefit as a result and reg.69A(2)(a) applies as above. If entitlement ceases under sub-para.(c), there may be such a sanctionable failure. However, there can, for the same reason, be no reduction of benefit as a result (which in any case could only bite on entitlement under a new claim). See the notes to reg.26 for the date from which entitlement ceases. 3.115

In *CJSA/3139/2001*, Commissioner Rowland held that someone who attended on the right day but failed to sign the required declaration, could not lose entitlement because of reg.25(1)(a) or (b) but was instead caught by reg.25(1)(c). Here the claimant knew he had to sign on, but left the Jobcentre rather than waiting for a member of staff to return to the enquiries desk. Accordingly, he did not have good cause for the failure to sign.

Time at which entitlement is to cease

3.116 **26.**—Entitlement to a jobseeker's allowance shall cease in accordance with regulation 25 on whichever is the earlier of—

(a) the day after the last day in respect of which [4 that claimant] has provided information or evidence which [2 shows that he continues to be entitled] to a jobseeker's allowance,

(b) if [1 regulation 25(1)(a) or (b)] applies, the day on which he was required to [5 participate in an interview], and

(c) if [1 regulation 25(1)(c)] applies, the day on which he ought to have provided the signed declaration,

provided that it shall not cease earlier than the day after he last [5 participated in an interview] in compliance with a [3notification] under regulation 23 [4or 23A].

Amendments

1. Jobseeker's Allowance (Amendment) Regulations 1996 (SI 1996/1516) reg.8 and Sch. (October 7, 1996).
2. Jobseeker's Allowance and Income Support (General) (Amendment) Regulations 1996 (SI 1996/1517) reg.9 (October 7, 1996).
3. Jobseeker's Allowance (Amendment) (No.3) Regulations 2000 (SI 2000/2194) reg.2(5) (September 11, 2000).
4. Jobseeker's Allowance (Joint Claims) Regulations 2000 (SI 2000/1978) Sch.2 para.5 (March 19, 2001).
5. Social Security (Miscellaneous Amendments) Regulations 2013 (SI 2013/443) reg.4(4) (April 2, 2013).

General Note

3.117 In *CJSA/2652/2001*, Commissioner Williams approved the approach in *CJSA/3139/2001*, noted in the commentary to reg.25, above. It did not, however, apply to his case. He attempted in the case to elucidate regs 23–26 and, in particular, to make some sense of reg.26. His approach was, however, overturned on appeal by the Court of Appeal in *Ferguson v Secretary of State for Work and Pensions* [2003] EWCA Civ 56, reported as *R(JSA)6/03*. Arden LJ, giving the judgment of the Court, stated:

> "**38.** I turn to the first of the substantial issues, which I would call the devoid issue. I accept, for the reasons I have already given, the submission of the Secretary of State that there is a clear distinction between regulations 25 and 26. They reflect the enabling power and deal separately with cessation events and the effective date for cessation of a benefit. When we examine regulation 26(a) it is clear that that is directed to ensuring that the claimant only receives benefit for the period in respect of which he fulfils all the conditions of entitlement, otherwise there would be no point in having paragraph 26(a). It is necessary, of course, to fix a date other than that of the cessation event, and regulation 26 has that object because it refers, as I have said, to the earlier of certain events. The purpose of regulation 26(a), in contrast to 26(b) and (c), seems to me clearly to be to fix the date so that the claimant only receives benefit for the period in which he fulfils all the conditions of entitlement and has demonstrated that. As I have said, the proviso confirms that. It is also important

to note that, contrary to the conclusion of the Commissioner, regulation 26(a) is dealing with a factual situation; namely, it is establishing the date as the day after the last day in respect of which the claimant provided information or evidence of the requisite kind. It is not dealing in terms with a failure to provide information or evidence; it is directed simply to a factual situation. Had it been intended to deal with a failure to comply with a requirement to produce information or evidence, as it seems to me, it would necessarily have been differently worded.

39. As I see it, the answer to the devoid issue must be that 26(a) does not render 26(b) and (c) devoid of meaning. Circumstances can arise in which no declaration is required, in which case 26(b) and (c) will become operative. Circumstances can also arise where there is a failure to attend and reasonable cause for non-attendance is not shown but the claimant does produce satisfactory evidence of compliance with the conditions. On this point I would turn to the evidence of Mr Anthony Booth, an administrator in the Department for Work and Pensions responsible for certain policy aspects of the JSA. His witness statement is dated 13th November 2002. He says this:

> '3. JSA claimants are normally required to attend the Jobcentre each fortnight. They lose entitlement if they fail to do so, unless they can show good cause for the failure within the next five working days. In the second quarter of 2002, about 180,000 JSA claims were terminated in these circumstances.
>
> 4. Most of those failing to attend make no contact with the Jobcentre during the five days. Consequently in terminating their entitlement, the Jobcentre has no information as to whether the JSA conditions were satisfied during the preceding fortnight. Entitlement is therefore terminated indefinitely with effect from the day after their last correct attendance.
>
> 5. Of those whose entitlement is terminated on a failure to attend, a minority make contact during the next five days but are found not to have good cause for their failure. They can, however, usually show that they satisfied the JSA conditions during the previous fortnight. Their entitlement is therefore terminated with effect from the date of failure only. They are also in a position to make an immediate new claim, so that their period of disentitlement lasts only from the date of failure to the date of renewal. About 30,000 people fell into this category in the second quarter of 2002.'

40. Pausing there, as Keene L.J. pointed out, the date of failure to which Mr Booth referred is the date of failure to attend. So circumstances can arise in which a person fails to attend but produces subsequently, and is accepted as producing, evidence of entitlement, so that paragraph (a) of regulation 26 would not apply.

41. Before I leave Mr Booth's statement on this point, I note that in the next paragraph he draws the conclusion that, although it cannot be substantiated, it is probable that a significant proportion of the people who fail to attend and make no contact with the Jobcentre have in fact ceased to satisfy the JSA entitlement conditions at some point between their last attendance and the date of failure. He adds:

> 'Paying JSA to them for that period therefore risks making an overpayment.'

42. Therefore, this evidence illustrates that section 26(a) does not render the subsequent paragraphs of that regulation inoperative or ineffective. Regulation 26(a) does not, moreover, provide that the necessary information can only be provided on the specified date for interview or in the window of opportunity permitted by regulation 27.

> **43.** I therefore turn to the next substantial issue of construction, which I will call the analogue issue. That is the question which much concerned the Commissioner. It is as to whether there was a sanction for failure to comply with a requirement under regulation 24(5) to produce information or evidence. As I see it, the answer to this issue has been provided by the Secretary of State's reference to the Social Security and Child Support (Decisions and Appeals) Regulations 1999, from which I have read extracts. Accordingly, there is separate statutory machinery which comes into operation if there is a failure to provide information or evidence and therefore it is not significant, in my judgment, that the failure to provide information or evidence is not a cessation event for the purpose of regulation 25."

Although, since this decision, the regulation was amended from April 2, 2013 substituting "failure to participate in an interview" for "failure to attend", this does not affect the interpretation given in the judgment with regard to the consequences of the relevant "failure"; one simply reads its references to "failure to attend" as "failure to participate in an interview".

The Court also held that the term "evidence" in para.(a) includes the declaration required by regs 24(6) and 25(1)(c) (para.44). Regulation 26(c) is not limited to "postal signers" (para.48). Arden LJ considered the conclusion the court had reached to be a "logical one" (para.50). Commissioner Williams had erred in failing

> "to give appropriate weight in his conclusion to two important textual points from these Regulations. The first point is that regulations 25 and 26 cover different subject matters. They have a different scope. Regulation 25 deals with cessation events; regulation 26 deals with the effective date of cessation of benefit. In addition, the Commissioner failed, in my judgment, to give appropriate weight to the 'earlier' point. As I see it, regulation 26 compels reference to the earlier of two dates. The court must give effect to those words and apply the regulation so that benefit terminates on whichever of those dates first occurs. It seems to me that the regulation was probably correct to say 'earlier' rather than 'earliest', since only one of the cessation events in paragraphs (b) and (c) of regulation 26 will occur. Once it occurs, the benefit terminates and any subsequent event is irrelevant. Contrary to Mr Ferguson's submission, I cannot treat as subsumed within a failure to attend a failure to provide information or to sign a declaration with which a requirement to attend was coupled. It seems to me that those two matters must be decoupled in order to apply the regulation properly in accordance with its wording.
>
> **50.** The conclusion which I reach is, in my judgment, a logical one. Entitlement to JSA depends on eligibility. Eligibility depends for one of its requirements on showing entitlement at the end of the 14-day period. On the interpretation which I prefer, benefit will cease as at the date immediately following the last date for which the necessary proof was given if there is a failure to attend in accordance with regulation 25(a) or (b) or a failure to sign a declaration. As Mr Forsdick put it, the Commissioner's construction gives the claimant who is in default an additional two-week period of grace for which he cannot in fact prove eligibility. That seems to me to be contrary to the scheme of the Regulations. In addition, it seems to me to undermine regulations 27 and 28, which give a window of opportunity for five days only provided that the claimant can establish a reasonable cause for nonattendance. As I see it, the Commissioner's construction, with respect to him, was inconsistent with and undermined those regulations. Accordingly, on the main issue of construction I would allow the appeal". (paras 49 and 50)

3.118 In *R(JSA)2/04*, Commissioner Rowland considered *Ferguson* and noted that, as the Secretary of State submitted in *Ferguson* at para.18:

"regulation 26(a) is intended to avoid overpayments by allowing the Secretary of State to terminate promptly an award of jobseeker's allowance in a case where a claimant has failed to 'sign on' and has not shown continued entitlement during the previous fortnight. However, I am satisfied that the language used does not prevent the Secretary of State's decision from being adjusted on revision or appeal if the claimant takes appropriate action within the time allowed under the Social Security and Child Support (Decisions and Appeals) Regulations 1999 and provides the information or evidence before a further decision is made".

The Commissioner had accepted that if a claimant fails to make contact with an employment officer within the relevant five working days it is proper for a decision-maker to make a decision that entitlement ceased from the date identified in reg.26(a). Since JSA is paid fortnightly in arrears and most claimants are required to attend fortnightly and sign a declaration as to their availability and actively seeking employment in the days since their previous signing day, the earliest day for cessation of entitlement will usually be the day after that previous signing day when the last declaration under reg.24(10) had been provided (reg.26(a)). However, he went on to hold that, if the claimant later (for instance on turning up at the next fortnightly signing day having missed the previous one) came forward with evidence and information to show that they had satisfied the conditions of entitlement to JSA throughout the previous four weeks, that would indicate that the original reg.26(a) date was now wrong, so that the date in either (b) or (c) as appropriate was to be taken as the date of cessation of entitlement. Thus the Secretary of State should revise the original decision. If the claimant had made a new claim for JSA and asked for backdating to the day after the last day of entitlement under the previous award which was refused, any appeal would encompass an appeal against the decision terminating entitlement, on which the approach above could be taken into account. Although that result was apparently supported by the Secretary of State in *R(JSA) 2/04*, there remains some doubt about the reasoning. If reg.26(a) cannot be interpreted as referring to anything other than the last day that the claimant provided information or evidence showing entitlement before the day on which the failure to comply occurred, then the chain appears to be broken. A subsequent provision of such information or evidence could then not alter the reg.26(a) date.

[1Where entitlement is not to cease under regulation 25(1)(c)

27.—Entitlement to a jobseeker's allowance is not to cease by virtue of regulation 25(1)(c) if, before the end of the period of five working days beginning with the first working day after the day on which a claimant ("C") failed to provide a signed declaration in accordance with regulation 24(10), C makes contact with an employment officer in the manner set out in a notification under regulation 23 or 23A and shows that C had [2a good reason] for the failure.] 3.119

AMENDMENTS

1. Jobseeker's Allowance (Sanctions for Failure to Attend) Regulations 2010 (SI 2010/509) reg.2(4) (April 6, 2010).

2. Jobseeker's Allowance (Sanctions) (Amendment) Regulations 2012 (SI 2012/2568) reg.5(6) (October 22, 2012).

GENERAL NOTE

See the annotations to reg.25. 3.120

Note in particular that the decision of Commissioner Stockman in the Northern Ireland decision in *LDG v DSD (JSA)* [2015] NICom 16 indicates that the condition that the claimant is to show a good reason for failing to provide a signed declaration under reg.24(10) within the five working days after the failure is not valid, having been imposed outside the power given by s.8(2) of the old style Jobseekers Act 1995. Section 8(2) only allows regulations to provide for entitlement to cease if the claimant does not make the prescribed contact within a prescribed period. It does not allow the addition of the extra condition that to escape the cessation of employment the claimant, as well as making contact in the way prescribed in reg.27 (by making contact with an employment officer in the manner set out in the regs 23 or 23A notification), must also do something different in showing a good reason.

In *KH v SSWP (JSA)* [2015] UKUT 497 (AAC) Judge Hemingway set aside a decision of a First-tier Tribunal for failing to give proper consideration to whether a letter received from the claimant within five days of failing to provide a signed declaration under reg.24(6) and (10) might have contained information relevant to whether she had a good reason for the failure, so as, according to the terms of reg.27, to prevent the termination of entitlement under reg.25(1)(c). However, he had not been referred to and did not take into account the convincing reasoning in *LDG* that the requirement in reg.27 for a claimant to show a good reason for the failure to provide the signed declaration, in addition to making contact with an employment officer within the five days, is not valid. The judge was inclined to say that the claimant's letter (which was not in the papers before him) was, in the absence of any submission to the contrary from the Secretary of State, a making of contact in the manner set out in the relevant notification under reg.23. Thus, if the reasoning in *LDG* had been adopted, he might well have been able to substitute a decision in the claimant's favour, rather than remit the case to a new tribunal for rehearing. In view of the complete lack of any reference to *LDG*, the decision in *KH* should not be taken as in any way undermining the force and authority of the reasoning in *LDG*.

Judge Hemingway rightly criticised the apparent lack of care in the decision-making process and in the presentation of the case to the First-tier Tribunal, in failing to provide copies of potentially relevant documents or of a decision under appeal. He stressed that "decisions which result in a claimant ceasing to have income can have potentially very serious consequences such that considerable care ought to be taken at all stages in the decision-making process and the explanation of that process once an appeal is lodged."

DEFINITIONS

"claimant"—see Jobseekers Act 1995 s.35(1).
"employment officer"—*ibid.*

Regs 27A – 30 revoked by Jobseeker's Allowance (Sanctions) (Amendment) Regulations 2012 (SI 2012/2568) reg.5(7) (October 22, 2012).

Chapter V

Jobseeker's Agreement

GENERAL NOTE

3.121 The terms and effects of the regulations in this Chapter (regs 31–40) are noted in the annotations to ss.9 and 10 of the Jobseekers Act 1995 as follows:

Section 9 (the jobseeker's agreement): regs 31–36.
Section 10 (variation of jobseeker's agreement): regs 37–40.

Contents of Jobseeker's Agreement

3.122 **31.**—The prescribed requirements for a jobseeker's agreement are that it shall contain the following information—

(a) the claimant's name;
(b) where the hours for which the claimant is available for employment are restricted in accordance with regulation 7, the total number of hours for which he is available and any pattern of availability;
(c) any restrictions on the claimant's availability for employment, including restrictions on the location or type of employment, in accordance with regulations 5, 8, 13[5, or 13A] and 17;
(d) a description of the type of employment which the claimant is seeking;
(e) the action which the claimant will take—
  (i) to seek employment; and
  (ii) to improve his prospects of finding employment;
(f) the dates of the start and of the finish of any permitted period in his case for the purposes of sections 6(5) and 7(5);
(g) a statement of the claimant's right—
  (i) to have a proposed jobseeker's agreement referred to [1the Secretary of State];
  (ii) to seek a [2 revision or supersession] of any determination of, or direction given by, [1 the Secretary of State]; and
  (iii) to appeal to [3an appeal tribunal] against any determination of, or direction given by [1the Secretary of State] [4 following a revision or supersession];
(h) the date of the agreement.

AMENDMENTS

1. Social Security Act 1998 (Commencement No.11, and Savings and Consequential and Transitional Provisions) Order 1999 Sch.12 para.2 (SI 1999/2860) (C.75)) (October 18, 1999).
2. Social Security Act 1998 (Commencement No.11, and Savings and Consequential and Transitional Provisions) Order 1999 Sch.12 para.1(a) (SI 1999/2860) (C.75)) (October 18, 1999).
3. Social Security Act 1998 (Commencement No.11, and Savings and Consequential and Transitional Provisions) Order 1999 Sch.12 para.1(b)(i) (SI 1999/2860) (C.75)) (October 18, 1999).
4. Social Security Act 1998 (Commencement No.11, and Savings and Consequential and Transitional Provisions) Order 1999 Sch.12 para.1(b)(ii) (SI 1999/2860) (C.75)) (October 18, 1999).
5. Jobseeker's Allowance (Lone Parents) (Availability for Work) Regulations 2010 (SI 2010/837) reg.2(11) (April 26, 2010).

DEFINITIONS

"claimant"—see Jobseekers Act 1995 s.35(1).
"employment"—see reg.4.
"pattern of availability"—see regs 4 and 7(2)(a).

Back-dating of a Jobseeker's Agreement [1 . . .]

32.—In giving a direction under section 9(7)(c), the [2 Secretary of State] shall take into account all relevant matters including— **3.123**
(a) where the claimant refused to accept the agreement proposed by the employment officer, whether he was reasonable in so refusing;
(b) where the claimant has signified to the employment officer or to the [2 Secretary of State] that the claimant is prepared to accept an agree-

ment which differs from the agreement proposed by the employment officer, whether the terms of the agreement which he is prepared to accept are reasonable;

(c) where the claimant has signified to the employment officer or to the [2 Secretary of State] that the claimant is prepared to accept the agreement proposed by the employment officer, that fact;

(d) the date on which, in all the circumstances, he considers that the claimant was first prepared to enter into an agreement which the [2 Secretary of State] considers reasonable; and

(e) where the date on which the claimant first had an opportunity to sign a jobseeker's agreement was later than the date on which he made a claim, that fact.

AMENDMENTS

1. Social Security Act 1998 (Commencement No.11, and Savings and Consequential and Transitional Provisions) Order 1999 Sch.12 para.3 (SI 1999/2860) (C.75)) (October 18, 1999).

2. Social Security Act 1998 (Commencement No.11, and Savings and Consequential and Transitional Provisions) Order 1999 Sch.12 para.2 (SI 1999/2860) (C.75)) (October 18, 1999).

DEFINITIONS

"claimant"—see Jobseekers Act 1995 s.35(1).
"employment officer"—*ibid.*

Notification of Determinations and Directions under Section 9

3.124 **33.**—The claimant shall be notified of—

(a) any determination of the [1 Secretary of State] under section 9;

(b) any direction given by the [1 Secretary of State] under section 9;

AMENDMENT

1. Social Security Act 1998 (Commencement No.11, and Savings and Consequential and Transitional Provisions) Order 1999 Sch.12 para.2 (SI 1999/2860) (C.75)) (October 18, 1999).

DEFINITION

"claimant"—see Jobseekers Act 1995 s.35(1).

Jobseeker's Agreement treated as having been made

3.125 **34.**—A claimant is to be treated as having satisfied the condition mentioned in section 1(2)(b)—

(a) where he is permitted to make a claim for a jobseeker's allowance without attending at an office of the [3Department for Work and Pensions], for the period beginning with the date of claim and ending on the date on which he has an interview with an employment officer for the purpose of drawing up a jobseeker's agreement;

(b) where, after the date of claim, the claim is terminated before he has an interview with an employment officer for the purpose of drawing up a jobseeker's agreement;

(c) as long as he is treated as available for employment in accordance with regulation 14 where the circumstances set out in that regulation arise after the date of claim and before he has an interview with an employment officer for the purpose of drawing up a job-seeker's agreement;

(d) as long as there are circumstances not peculiar to the claimant which make impracticable or unduly difficult the normal operation of the provisions governing, or the practice relating to, the claiming, awarding or payment of jobseeker's allowance;

[[1](e) where the claimant was in receipt of a training allowance and was, in accordance with regulation 170, entitled to an income-based jobseeker's allowance without being available for employment, having entered into a jobseeker's agreement or actively seeking employment, for the period beginning with the date on which regulation 170 ceased to apply to him and ending on the date on which he has an interview with an employment officer for the purpose of drawing up a jobseeker's agreement.]

[[2] (f) if he is temporarily absent from Great Britain in the circumstances prescribed in regulation 50(6B)(a) or (c), for the period of any such temporary absence.]

[[4](g) in any period during which he is treated as available for employment under regulation 14A if the claimant has not entered into a jobseeker's agreement before that period begins.]

AMENDMENTS

1. Jobseeker's Allowance (Amendment) Regulations 1996 (SI 1996/1516) reg.3 (October 7, 1996).

2. Jobseeker's Allowance (Joint Claims) Regulations 2000 (SI 2000/1978) Sch.2 para.9 (March 19, 2001).

3. Secretaries of State for Education and Skills and for Work and Pensions Order 2002 (SI 2002/1397) art.12 and Sch. para.26 (June 27, 2002).

4. Jobseeker's Allowance (Domestic Violence) (Amendment) Regulations 2012 (SI 2012/853) reg.2(4) (April 23, 2012).

DEFINITIONS

"date of claim"—see reg.1(3).
"employment"—see reg.4.
"employment officer"—see Jobseekers Act 1995 s.35(1).
"training allowance"—see reg.1(3).

Automatic Back-dating of Jobseeker's Agreement

35.—Where a jobseeker's agreement is signed on a date later than the date of claim and there is no reference of that agreement to [[1]the Secretary of State] under section 9(6), the agreement shall be treated as having effect on the date of claim. **3.126**

AMENDMENT

1. Social Security Act 1998 (Commencement No.11, and Savings and Consequential and Transitional Provisions) Order 1999 Sch.12 para.2 (SI 1999/2860) (C.75)) (October 18, 1999).

DEFINITION

"date of claim"—see reg.1(3).

Jobseeker's Agreement to remain in effect

3.127 **36.**—A jobseeker's agreement entered into by a claimant shall not cease to have effect on the coming to an end of an award of a jobseeker's allowance made to him—

(a) where a further claim for a jobseeker's allowance is made within a period not exceeding 14 days; or

(b) in respect of any part of a period of suspension, where—

 (i) the Secretary of State has directed under regulation 37(1A) of the Claims and Payments Regulations that payment under an award be suspended for a definite or indefinite period on the ground that a question arises whether the conditions for entitlement to that allowance are or were fulfilled or the award ought to be revised,

 (ii) subsequently that suspension expires or is cancelled in respect of a part only of the period for which it has been in force, and

 (iii) it is then determined that the award should be revised to the effect that there was no entitlement to the allowance in respect of all or any part of the period between the start of the period over which the award has been suspended and the date when the suspension expires or is cancelled; or

(c) for as long as the claimant satisfies the conditions of entitlement to national insurance credits, other than any condition relating to the existence of a jobseeker's agreement, in accordance with the Social Security (Credits) Regulations 1975.

DEFINITIONS

"claimant"—see Jobseekers Act 1995 s.35(1).
"Claims and Payments Regulations"—see reg.1(3).

Variation of Jobseeker's Agreement

3.128 **37.**—The prescribed manner for varying a jobseeker's agreement shall be in writing and signed by both parties in accordance with section 10(2) on the proposal of the claimant or the employment officer.

DEFINITIONS

"claimant"—see Jobseekers Act 1995 s.35(1).
"employment officer"—*ibid.*

Direction to vary Agreement: time for compliance

3.129 **38.**—The prescribed period for the purposes of section 10(6)(c) shall be the period of 21 days beginning with the date on which the direction was issued.

Variation of Agreement: matters to be taken into account

3.130 **39.**—In giving a direction under section 10(6)(b) or (d) [[1]the Secretary of State] shall take into account the preference of the claimant if he considers that both the claimant's proposals and those of employment officer satisfy the requirements of section 10(5).

AMENDMENT

1. Social Security Act 1998 (Commencement No.11, and Savings and Consequential and Transitional Provisions) Order 1999 Sch.12 para.2 (SI 1999/2860) (C.75)) (October 18, 1999).

DEFINITIONS

"claimant"—see Jobseekers Act 1995 s.35(1).
"employment officer"—*ibid.*

Notification of Determinations and Directions under Section 10

40.—The claimant shall be notified of— 3.131

(a) any determination of [1 the Secretary of State] under section 10;
(b) any direction of [1 the Secretary of State] under section 10.

AMENDMENT

1. Social Security Act 1998 (Commencement No.11, and Savings and Consequential and Transitional Provisions) Order 1999 Sch.12 para.2 (SI 1999/2860) (C.75)) (October 18, 1999).

DEFINITION

"claimant" —see Jobseekers Act 1995 s.35(1).

[Regulations 41–45 were revoked by Social Security Act 1998 (Commencement No.11, and Savings and Consequential and Transitional Provisions) Order 1999 Sch.12 para.4 (SI 1999/2860) (October 18, 1999).]

PART III

OTHER CONDITIONS OF ENTITLEMENT

[1The contribution-based conditions and relevant earnings

45A.—(1) A claimant's relevant earnings for the purposes of section 2(2) 3.132
(b) of the Act are the total amount of the claimant's earnings at the lower earnings limit for the base year.

(2) For the purposes of paragraph (1), earnings which exceed the lower earnings limit are to be disregarded.]

AMENDMENT

1. Social Security (Contribution Conditions for Jobseeker's Allowance and Employment and Support Allowance) Regulations 2010 (SI 2010/2446) reg.2 (November 1, 2010).

DEFINITIONS

"claimant"—see Jobseekers Act 1995 s.35(1).
"earnings"—see reg.1(3).

"lower earnings limit"—see Jobseekers Act 1995 s.2(4)(c) and SSCBA 1992 s.5(1)(a).

GENERAL NOTE

3.133 The changes effected by s.12 of the Welfare Reform Act 2009 and this regulation made in consequence significantly tighten the contribution conditions for CBJSA. Together they mean that the requisite level of "relevant earnings" in the tax year relied on for the first contribution condition is now 26 times that year's lower earnings limit, rather than 25. This new regulation defines "relevant earnings" to cover only earnings at that lower earnings limit, so that new claimants will have to have worked for at least 26 weeks in one of the last two tax years (April 6 to April 5) complete before the start of the benefit year (beginning in early January) which includes the first day of claim in the relevant jobseeking period.

[1Relaxation of the first set of conditions

3.134 **45B.**—(1) A claimant who [2. . .] satisfies the condition in paragraph (2) is to be taken to satisfy the first set of conditions if the claimant has—

(a) paid Class 1 contributions before the relevant benefit week in respect of any one tax year; and
(b) earnings at the lower earnings limit in that tax year on which primary Class 1 contributions have been paid or treated as paid which in total, and disregarding any earnings which exceed the lower earnings limit for that year, are not less than that limit multiplied by 26.

(2) The condition referred to in paragraph (1) is that the claimant, in respect of any week during the last complete tax year preceding the relevant benefit year, is entitled to be credited with earnings in accordance with regulation 9E of the Social Security (Credits) Regulations 1975 (credits for certain spouses and civil partners of members of Her Majesty's forces).]

AMENDMENTS

1. Social Security (Contribution Conditions for Jobseeker's Allowance and Employment and Support Allowance) Regulations 2011 (SI 2011/2862) reg.2 (January 1, 2012).

2. Social Security (Miscellaneous Amendments) (No.3) Regulations 2013 (SI 2013/2536) reg.6(4) (October 29, 2013).

DEFINITIONS

"claimant"—see Jobseekers Act 1995 s.35(1).
"earnings"—see reg.1(3).
"the first set of conditions"—see Jobseekers Act 1995 s.2(3C).
"lower earnings limit"—see Jobseekers Act 1995 s.2(4)(c) and SSCBA 1992 s.5(1)(a).
"primary Class 1 contributions"—see Jobseekers Act 1995 s.2(4)(c) and SSCBA 1992 ss.6 and 8.

GENERAL NOTE

3.135 From January 1, 2012, some spouses and civil partners, accompanying a member of Her Majesty's forces on a posting abroad after April 2010, will on return from that posting be able to benefit from the relaxation of the first National Insurance (NI) contribution condition effected by this regulation when they make a claim for CESA or CBJSA where they would not have otherwise met the first NI contribution condition.

The regulation covers such spouses and civil partners in respect of any week during the last complete tax year preceding the start of the benefit year in which the claim for benefit was made, provided they have been awarded a NI credit under regulation 9E of the Social Security (Credits) Regulations 1975 in respect of at least one week during the last complete tax year prior to their claim to benefit from the change effected by this regulation. The relaxation allows them to be taken to have satisfied the first contribution condition in s.2(1)(a) and (2) of the old style Jobseekers Act 1995. where they had paid sufficient NI contributions in any previous complete tax year before the beginning of the relevant benefit year. Under the current rules sufficient NI contributions must have been paid in one of the last two complete tax years before the beginning of the relevant benefit year.

Waiting days

46.—(1) Paragraph 4 of Schedule 1 to the Act shall not apply in a case where— **3.136**

(a) a person's entitlement to a jobseeker's allowance commences within 12 weeks of an entitlement of his to income support, incapacity benefit[[3], employment and support allowance] or [[2]carer's allowance] coming to an end; or

(b) a claim for a jobseeker's allowance falls to be determined by reference to section 3(1)(f)(ii) (persons under the age of 18);[[1]or

(c) a joint-claim couple are entitled to a joint-claim jobseeker's allowance in respect of themselves and that paragraph of that Schedule has already applied to one member of that couple in respect of a jobseeking period which is linked to a jobseeking period relating to that member which has commenced by virtue of his having claimed a jobseeker's allowance as a member of that couple;

(d) a joint-claim couple have claimed a jobseeker's allowance jointly within 12 weeks of either member of that couple being entitled to a jobseeker's allowance, income support, incapacity benefit [[3], employment and support allowance] or [[2] carer's allowance];

(e) a member of a joint-claim couple is both in receipt of a training allowance and the nominated member for the purposes of section 3B.]

(2) In the case of a person to whom paragraph 4 of Schedule 1 to the Act applies, the number of days is [[4]7].

AMENDMENTS

1. Jobseeker's Allowance (Joint Claims) Regulations 2000 (SI 2000/1978) Sch.2 para.10 (March 19, 2001).

2. Social Security (Miscellaneous Amendments) Regulations 2003 (SI 2003/511) reg.3(5) (April 1, 2003).

3. Employment and Support Allowance (Consequential Provisions) (No.2) Regulations 2008 (SI 2008/1554) reg.3(6) (October 27, 2008).

4. Social Security (Jobseeker's Allowance and Employment and Support Allowance) (Waiting Days) Amendment Regulations 2014 (SI 2014/2309) reg.2(1) (October 27, 2014).

DEFINITION

"the Act"—see reg.1(3).
"couple"—see Jobseekers Act 1995 s.35(1).
"jobseeking period"—see reg.1(3).
"a joint-claim couple"—see Jobseekers Act 1995 ss.35(1) and 1(4).
"a joint-claim jobseeker's allowance"—*ibid.*
"training allowance"—see reg.1(3).

General Note

3.137 Unemployment benefit was a daily benefit payable in respect of a six-day week. JSA is a weekly benefit. Nonetheless, through para.4 of Sch.1 to the old style Jobseekers Act 1995, as amplified by this regulation, it deploys the traditional concept of "waiting days".

There is no entitlement to old style JSA for a number of days (initially three, but extended to seven with effect from October 27, 2014 (see para.(2)) at the start of a jobseeking period. The amendment to increase the number of waiting days to seven does not apply where the relevant jobseeking period began before October 27, 2014 (reg.4(1) of the amending regulations). Seven days' worth of benefit is a substantial amount, so that the provision in the Social Security (Payments on Account of Benefit) Regulations 2013 (Vol.III) for the making of payments on account of benefit, in certain cases of financial need (restrictively defined), has become more important. However, the claimant has to repay the "advance" out of future payments of JSA. On "jobseeking period" and the effect of "linking", see notes to regs 47 and 48 below.

Note further that the "waiting days" rule does not apply where the claimant's entitlement to JSA begins within 12 weeks of the ending of entitlement to income support, incapacity benefit or carer's allowance, nor where the claim for income-based JSA has to be determined by reference to s.3(1)(f)(ii) (i.e. the person is 16 or 17, registered for training but is not being provided with any, severe hardship will result to him if JSA is not paid, and the (Secretary of State directs that s.16 is to apply to him) (para.(1)(a), (b)).

3.138 As regards a "joint-claim couple", the waiting days will not have to be served again where the jobseeking period commenced because of a claim as a "joint claim couple" links to a jobseeking period in which one of the members had already served the waiting days (para.(1)(c)). Nor will they need to be served where the joint-claim is within 12 weeks of either member's entitlement to JSA, income support, incapacity benefit or invalid care allowance (para.(1)(d)). Nor do the waiting days have to be served if the nominated member (see Jobseekers Act 1995 s.3B) of the couple is receiving a training allowance (para.(1)(e)).

A sanction imposed under ss.19 or 19A of the Act (see Pt V of these Regulations) will not begin until after any waiting days have been served. But a claimant who is entitled to IBJSA will qualify for maximum housing benefit during any waiting days (see reg.2(3)(b) of the Housing Benefit Regulations 2006).

The transition from new style JSA

3.139 In para.(1)(a) and (d) the references (second reference in sub-para.(d)) to jobseeker's allowance are, where art.13(1)(a) and (2)(b) of the Welfare Reform Act 2012 (Commencement No.9 and Transitional and Transitory Provisions and Commencement No.8 and Savings and Transitional Provisions (Amendment)) Order 2013 (as amended and set out in the 2014/15 Supplement) applies and the claimant was entitled to new style JSA under reg.36(1) of the JSA Regulations 2013 during what would otherwise have been waiting days when that award continued as an award of old style JSA, to be read as if it included a reference to the new style JSA award (art.13(3)(b) of that Order).

Jobseeking period

3.140 **47.**—(1) For the purposes of the Act, but subject to paragraphs (2) and (3), the "jobseeking period" means any period throughout which the claimant satisfies or is treated as satisfying the conditions specified in paragraphs (a) to (c) and (e) to (i) of subsection (2) of section 1 (conditions of entitlement to a jobseeker's allowance).

(2) Any period in which—

(a) a claimant does not satisfy any of the requirements in section 1(2)(a) to (c), and

(b) a jobseeker's allowance is payable to him in accordance with Part IX (Hardship), [3or, where the claimant is a member of a joint-claim couple, a jobseeker's allowance is payable in accordance with Part IXA (hardship)]

shall, for the purposes of paragraph (1), be treated as a period in which the claimant satisfies the conditions specified in paragraphs (a) to (c) of subsection (2) of section 1.

[1(2A) Any period in which a claimant is entitled to a jobseeker's allowance in accordance with regulation 11(3) of the Jobseeker's Allowance (Transitional Provisions) Regulations 1995 shall, for the purposes of paragraph (1), be treated as a period in which he satisfies the conditions specified in paragraphs (a) to (c) and (e) to (i) of subsection (2) of section 1.]

(3) The following periods shall not be, or be part of, a jobseeking period—

(a) any period in respect of which no claim for a jobseeker's allowance has been made or treated as made;

(b) such period as falls before the day on which a claim for a jobseeker's allowance is made or treated as made [2. . .];

(c) where a claim for a jobseeker's allowance has been made or treated as made but no entitlement to benefit arises in respect of a period before the date of claim by virtue of section 1(2) of the Administration Act (limits for backdating entitlement), that period;

(d) where—

(i) a claimant satisfies the conditions specified in paragraphs (a) to (c) and (e) to (i) of subsection (2) of section 1; and

(ii) entitlement to a jobseeker's allowance ceases in accordance with regulation 25 (entitlement ceasing on a failure to comply),

the period beginning with the date in respect of which, in accordance with regulation 26, entitlement ceases and ending with the day before the date in respect of which the claimant again becomes entitled to a jobseeker's allowance; or

(e) any week in which a claimant is not entitled to a jobseeker's allowance in accordance with section 14 (trade disputes).

[2(f) subject to regulation 2A, any period in respect of which the claimant is not entitled to a jobseeker's allowance because section 1(1A) of the Administration Act (requirement to state national insurance number) applies.]

(4) For the purposes of section 5 (duration of a contribution-based jobseeker's allowance) any day—

(a) which falls within a jobseeking period; [0and either

(b) (i) on which the claimant satisfies the conditions specified in section 2 (the contribution-based conditions) other than the conditions specified in subsection (1)(c) and (d) of that section; and

(ii) on which a contribution–based jobseeker's allowance is not payable to the claimant by virtue of [10section 19 or 19A or regulation 69B] [4or on which the claimant is a member of a joint-claim couple and a joint-claim jobseeker's allowance is not payable or is reduced because he is subject to sanctions by virtue of [10section 19 or 19A or regulation 69B]] [5or by virtue of a restriction imposed pursuant [7 . . .] [6to section [96B], 7, 8 or 9 of the Social Security Fraud Act 2001 (loss of benefit provisions)]];

shall be treated as if it was a day in respect of which he was entitled to a contribution-based jobseeker's allowance.

AMENDMENTS

0. Jobseeker's Allowance and Income Support (General) (Amendment) Regulations 1996 (SI 1996/1517) reg.14(3) (October 7, 1996).

1. Social Security and Child Support (Jobseeker's Allowance) (Miscellaneous Amendments) Regulations 1996 (SI 1996/2538) reg.2(4) (October 28, 1996).

2. Social Security (Incapacity Benefit and Jobseeker's Allowance) Amendment Regulations 1999 (SI 1999/2226) reg.3 (September 6, 1999).

3. Jobseeker's Allowance (Joint Claims) Regulations 2000 (SI 2000/1978) Sch.2 para.11 (March 19, 2001).

4. Social Security Amendment (Joint Claims) Regulations 2001 (SI 2001/ 518) reg.2(5) (March 19, 2001).

5. Social Security (Breach of Community Order) (Consequential Amendments) Regulations 2001 (SI 2001/1711) reg.2(4) (October 15, 2001).

6. Social Security (Loss of Benefit) (Consequential Amendments) Regulations 2002 (SI 2002/490) reg.7 (April 1, 2002).

7. Welfare Reform Act 2009 (Section 26) (Consequential Amendments) Regulations 2010 (SI 2010/424) reg.3(2) (March 22, 2010, but where someone is subject to a restriction under ss.62 or 63 of the Child Support, Pensions and Social Security Act 2000 immediately before that date, on the first day of the first benefit week to commence for that person on or after March 22, 2010).

8. Jobseekers Allowance (Sanctions for Failure to Attend) Regulations 2010 (SI 2010/509) reg.2(7) (April 6, 2010).

9. Social Security (Loss of Benefit) (Amendment) Regulations 2010 (SI 2010/1160) reg.11(2) (April 1, 2010).

10. Jobseeker's Allowance (Sanctions) (Amendment) Regulations 2012 (SI 2012/2568) reg.5(8) (October 22, 2012).

DEFINITIONS

"the Administration Act"—see Jobseekers Act 1995 s.35(1).
"the Act"—see reg.1(3).
"claimant"—see Jobseekers Act 1995 s.35(1).
"contribution-based jobseeker's allowance"—see ss.35(1) and 1(4).
"jobseeking period"—see para.(1).

GENERAL NOTE

Paragraphs (1)–(3)

3.141 This regulation, read with regs 48 and 49 below and para.3 of Sch.1 to the old style Jobseekers Act 1995, provides some relief to those whose unemployment is intermittent, interspersed with, say, periods of employment, of incapacity for work, of training for work or periods when pregnant. It uses, somewhat after the fashion of unemployment benefit and its notion of "period of interruption of employment" ("PIE"), for the concept of "linking" and "linked periods" where what would otherwise be separate jobseeking periods are fused into one and certain periods ("linked periods") do not "break" a jobseeking period.

There are three particular purposes for which the concept of the jobseeking period is relevant: (a) in the identification of the tax years in which the two contribution conditions in s.2(1)(a) and (b) of the Act must be satisfied; (b) in the application of the waiting days rule in para.4 of Sch.1 to the Act only once in each jobseeking period; and (c) in the possibly redundant provisions in para.(3) about days which count towards the 182-day limit on a period of entitlement under s.5 of the Act.

Regulation 47 provides the general definition of "jobseeking period" and some important exceptions. Regulation 47A deals with cases going back into the unemployment benefit regime. Regulations 48 and 49 deal with linking.

A "jobseeking period" is under para.(1) any period throughout which the claimant satisfies (or is treated as satisfying) the conditions of entitlement to JSA set out in the old style Jobseekers Act 1995 s.1(2)(a)–(c) and (e)–(i): available for employment; a current jobseeker's agreement; actively seeking employment; not in remunerative work; not receiving relevant education; under pensionable age; and in Great Britain (para.(1)) (note that reg.49, below, treats certain days as ones meeting those conditions in respect of men over 60 but under pensionable age). Where a hardship payment under Pts IX or IXA (joint-claim couple) of these Regulations is paid to a claimant who does not satisfy a labour market condition (any of the conditions in the old style Jobseekers Act 1995 s.1(2)(a)–(c): availability; actively seeking; jobseeker's agreement), he is to be treated as satisfying them for purposes of applying the above definition of jobseeking period (para.(2)). Note that Transitional Reg.11(3) in para.(2A) is now reg.13(3) of the JSA (Transitional) Regs 1996. 3.142

Certain periods listed in para.(3) cannot constitute, or be part of, a jobseeking period: (i) any period in which no claim for JSA has been made or treated as made; (ii) any period before the day on which a claim is made; (iii) a period caught by the 12-month limit on backdating entitlement under s.1(2) of the AA 1992; (iv) a period of disentitlement under regs 25 and 26; (v) any week of disentitlement because the claimant is caught by the trade dispute rule in Jobseekers Act 1995 s.14; and (vi) any period that the claimant is not entitled to JSA because he has not provided the required information or evidence about his national insurance number or that of any adult dependant included in his claim (para.(3)). Paragraph (3)(f) will apply to days falling on or after September 6, 1999 but not to any period before that date. The amendment is considered necessary to avoid a possible advantage being gained by a person who makes a further claim to JSA that links to the earlier disallowed claim. Without this provision the jobseeking period formed by the earlier claim would determine what tax years were used to decide entitlement to CBJSA and the claimant would not need to serve the three waiting days on the second claim.

Under para.(4), for the purpose only of the rules in s.5 of the Act limiting the duration of entitlement to 182 days, a day which would otherwise fall within a jobseeking period, but on which someone satisfying the two contribution conditions in s.2 is subject to a JSA sanction or a fraud sanction so that JSA is not payable, is nonetheless to be treated as a day of entitlement to JSA, so that it will count as one of the 182 days. This provision is arguably unnecessary because sanctions under ss.19 and 19A of the Act and restrictions under the Social Security Fraud Act 2001 only affect the payability of benefit or the amount payable, not entitlement.

The transition from new style JSA

Regulation 47 as a whole is, where art.13(1) and (2) of the Welfare Reform Act 2012 (Commencement No.9 and Transitional and Transitory Provisions and Commencement No.8 and Savings and Transitional Provisions (Amendment)) Order 2013 (as amended and set out in the 2014/15 Supplement) applies, to be read as if a jobseeking period includes any period that formed part of a jobseeking period under reg.37 of the JSA Regulations 2013 and in para.(4) as if the reference to a day treated as a day on which the claimant was entitled to contribution-based JSA included a reference to a day treated under reg.37(3) of the JSA Regulations 2013 as a day of entitlement to new style JSA (art.13(3)(c) of that Order). 3.143

[1 Jobseeking periods: periods of interruption of employment

3.144 [3 **47A.**—(1)] For the purposes of section 2(4)(b)(i) and for determining any waiting days—

[2(za) where a linked period commenced before 7th October 1996 [3. . .], any days of unemployment which form part of a period of interruption of employment where the last day of unemployment in that period of interruption of employment was no more than 8 weeks before the date upon which that linked period commenced;]

(a) where a jobseeking period or a linked period commences on 7th October 1996, any period of interruption of employment ending within the 8 weeks preceding that date; or

(b) where a jobseeking period or a linked period commences after 7th October 1996, any period of interruption of employment ending within the 12 weeks preceding the day the jobseeking period or linked period commenced,

shall be treated as a jobseeking period [2and, for the purposes of paragraph (za), a day shall be treated as being, or not being, a day of unemployment in accordance with section 25A of the Social Security Contributions and Benefits Act 1992 and with any regulations made under that section, as in force on 6th October 1996].]

[3(2) In paragraph (1) "period of interruption of employment" in relation to a period prior to 7th October 1996 has the same meaning as it had in the Benefits Act by virtue of section 25A of that Act (determination of days for which unemployment benefit is payable) as in force on 6th October 1996.]

AMENDMENTS

1. Social Security and Child Support (Jobseeker's Allowance) (Miscellaneous Amendments) Regulations 1996 (SI 1996/2538) reg.2(5) (October 28, 1996).
2. Jobseeker's Allowance (Amendment) (No.2) Regulations 1997 (SI 1997/2677) reg.2 (December 1, 1997).
3. Social Security (Miscellaneous Amendments) Regulations 1998 (SI 1998/563) reg.16 (April 1, 1998).

DEFINITIONS

"the Benefits Act"—see Jobseekers Act 1995 s.35(1).
"jobseeking period"—see reg.47(1).
"linked period"—see reg.48(2).

GENERAL NOTE

3.145 Some spells of unemployment are continuous, others intermittent. A jobseeking period can consist of a long chain of such spells, interspersed with spells of work or entitlement to certain other benefits. This regulation enables such a chain to go back to the benefits regime before October 7, 1996, when JSA was introduced, for the purposes of the contribution conditions and the waiting days rule. Then the relevant concept was "period of interruption of employment" (PIE) and the regime worked on an eight-week linking rule where two or more ostensibly separate PIEs were fused into a single one where they were not more than eight weeks apart. Old style JSA works on a 12-week linking period (see reg.48(1) and (3)), as does new style JSA.

Linking periods

48.—(1) For the purposes of the Act, two or more jobseeking periods shall be treated as one jobseeking period where they are separated by a period comprising only— 3.146

(a) any period of not more than 12 weeks;
(b) a linked period;
(c) any period of not more than 12 weeks falling between—
(i) any two linked periods; or
(ii) a jobseeking period and a linked period;
[1(d) a period in respect of which the claimant is summoned for jury service and is required to attend court.]

(2) Linked periods for the purposes of the Act are any of the following periods—

(a) to the extent specified in paragraph (3), any period throughout which the claimant is entitled to [8 a carer's allowance] under section 70 of the Benefits Act;
(b) any period throughout which the claimant is incapable of work, or is treated as incapable of work, in accordance with Part XIIA of the Benefits Act;
[10(bb) any period throughout which the claimant has, or is treated as having, limited capability for work for the purposes of Part 1 of the Welfare Reform Act;]
(c) any period throughout which the claimant was entitled to a maternity allowance under section 35[11or 35B] of the Benefits Act;
(d) any period throughout which the claimant was engaged in training for which a training allowance is payable.
[2(e) a period which includes 6th October [31996] during which the claimant attends court in response to a summons for jury service and which was immediately preceded by a period of entitlement to unemployment benefit.]
[4(f) any period throughout which the claimant was participating—
(i) in the [7 Self-Employed] Employment Option of the New Deal as specified in regulation 75(1)(a)(ii)(aa);
[6(ii) in the Voluntary Sector Option of the New Deal specified in regulation 75(1)(a)(ii)(bb), in the Environment Task Force Option of the New Deal specified in regulation 75(1)(a)(ii)(cc), [9 or in the Intensive Activity Period specified in regulation 75(1)(a)(iv)] and was not entitled to a jobseeker's allowance because, as a consequence of his participation, the claimant was engaged in remunerative work or failed to satisfy the condition specified either in section 2(1)(c) or in section 3(1)(a).]
[5(g) any period throughout which the claimant was participating in an employment zone programme and was not entitled to a job-seeker's allowance because, as a consequence of his participation in that programme, he was engaged in remunerative work or failed to satisfy the condition specified in section 2(1)(c) or in section 3(1)(a).]

[2(2A) A period is a linked period for the purposes of section 2(4)(b)(ii) of the Act only where it ends within 12 weeks or less of the commencement of a jobseeking period or of some other linked period.]

(3) A period of entitlement to invalid care allowance shall be a linked period only where it enables the claimant to satisfy contributions for entitle-

ment to a contribution-based jobseeker's allowance which he would otherwise be unable to satisfy.

AMENDMENTS

1. Jobseeker's Allowance and Income Support (General) (Amendment) Regulations 1996 (SI 1996/1517) reg.15 (October 7, 1996).
2. Social Security and Child Support (Jobseeker's Allowance) (Miscellaneous Amendments) Regulations 1996 (SI 1996/2538) reg.2(6) (October 28, 1996).
3. Social Security (Miscellaneous Amendments) Regulations 1997 (SI 1997/454) reg.2(4) (April 7, 1997).
4. Social Security Amendment (New Deal) Regulations 1997 (SI 1997/2863) reg.4 (January 5, 1998).
5. Social Security Amendment (Employment Zones) Regulations 2000 (SI 2000/724) reg.4(4)(a) (April 3, 2000).
6. Social Security Amendment (New Deal) Regulations 2001 (SI 2001/1029) reg.3 (April 9, 2001).
7. Social Security Amendment (Employment Programme) Regulations 2002 (SI 2002/2314) reg.2(3) (October 14, 2002).
8. Social Security (Miscellaneous Amendments) Regulations 2003 (SI 2003/511) reg.3(5) (April 1, 2003).
9. Social Security (Miscellaneous Amendments) Regulations 2008 (SI 2008/698) reg.4(7) (April 14, 2008).
10. Employment and Support Allowance (Consequential Provisions) (No.2) Regulations 2008 (SI 2008/1554) reg.3(7) (October 27, 2008).
11. Social Security (Maternity Allowance) (Miscellaneous Amendments) Regulations 2014 (SI 2914/884) reg.4(4) (May 18, 2014).

DEFINITIONS

"the Act"—see s.35(1).
"the Benefits Act"—*ibid.*
"claimant"—*ibid.*
"employment zone programme"—see reg.1(3).
"jobseeking period"—see reg.47(1)–(3).
"linked period"—see paras (2) and (3).
"training allowance"—see reg.1(3).
"week"—see reg.1(3).

GENERAL NOTE

3.147 Under para.(1), two or more jobseeking periods as defined in reg.47 must be fused into a single jobseeking period where separated by no more than 12 weeks, by a linked period (defined in para.(2)), by any period of not more than 12 weeks falling between any two linked periods or a jobseeking period and a linked period, or by a period in respect of which the claimant is summoned for jury service and is required to attend court. Thus, through the list of categories in para.(2), are the intermittently unemployed protected, while oscillating between unemployment and work or training, or unemployment and sickness/disability related inability to work, or unemployment and maternity or performing jury service, or caring, or any combination of these. Not all linked periods count as such for all purposes. Thus, a period of entitlement to a carer's allowance (para.(2)(a)) counts only to enable the JSA claimant to satisfy the JSA contribution conditions (old style Jobseekers Act 1995 s.2(1)(a) and (b)) that otherwise would not be satisfied (para.(3)). Similarly, to rank for the purposes of s.2(4)(b)(ii) (identifying the "relevant benefit year" for contributions conditions purposes as earlier than the start of the benefit year in which the JSA claim is made) a linked period counts only if it ended within 12 weeks of the start of a jobseeking period or another linked period (para.(2A)). It is hard to see why this result is not already achieved by para.(1)(a) and (c).

Note that linked periods or intervening periods of 12 weeks or less cannot themselves form part of a jobseeking period.

Note also s.47A with respect to linking back to a period of interruption of employment before JSA came into operation for purposes of identifying the relevant benefit year for contributions conditions purposes for CBJSA and for determining any waiting days.

Persons approaching retirement and the jobseeking period

49.—(1) [2 Subject to paragraph (5),] the provisions of this regulation apply only to days which fall— 3.148

(a) after 6th October 1996; and

(b) within a tax year in which the claimant has attained [4 the qualifying age for state pension credit] but is under pensionable age;

and in respect of which a jobseeker's allowance is not payable because the decision of the determining authority is that the claimant—

(i) has exhausted his entitlement to a contribution-based jobseeker's allowance; or

(ii) fails to satisfy one or both the contribution conditions specified in section 2(1)(a) and (b); or

(iii) is entitled to a contribution-based jobseeker's allowance but the amount payable is reduced to Nil by virtue of deductions made in accordance with regulation 81 for pension payments.

[1(2) For the purposes of paragraph (1) of regulation 47 (jobseeking period) but subject to paragraphs [33, 4 and 4A], any days to which paragraph (1) applies and in respect of which the person does not satisfy or is not treated in accordance with regulation 14, 16, 17, 19, 20, 21 or 34 as satisfying the conditions specified in paragraphs (a) to (c) of subsection (2) of section (1) (conditions of entitlement to a jobseeker's allowance), shall be days on which the person is treated as satisfying the condition in paragraphs (a) to (c) and (e) to (i) of subsection (2) of section (1).]

(3) Where a person—

(a) [1. . .]

(b) is employed as an employed earner or a self-employed earner for a period of more than 12 weeks,

then no day which falls within or follows that period shall be days on which the person is treated as satisfying those conditions so however that this paragraph shall not prevent paragraph (2) from again applying to a person who makes a claim for a jobseeker's allowance after that period.

(4) Any day which is, for the purposes of section 30C of the Benefits Act, a day of incapacity for work falling within a period of incapacity for work shall not be a day on which the person is treated as satisfying the conditions referred to in paragraph (2).

[3(4A) Any day which, for the purposes of Part 1 of the Welfare Reform Act, is a day where the person has limited capability for work falling within a period of limited capability for work shall not be a day on which the person is treated as satisfying the conditions referred to in paragraph (2).]

[2(5) This regulation shall not apply in respect of any days in respect of which a joint-claim jobseeker's allowance has been claimed.]

AMENDMENTS

1. Jobseeker's Allowance and Income Support (General) (Amendment) Regulations 1996 (SI 1996/1517) reg.16 (October 7, 1996).

2. Jobseeker's Allowance (Joint Claims) Regulations 2000 (SI 2000/1978) Sch.2 para.12 (March 19, 2001).

3. Employment and Support Allowance (Consequential Provisions) (No.2) Regulations 2008 (SI 2008/1554) reg.3(8) (October 27, 2008).

4. Social Security (Equalisation of State Pension Age) Regulations 2009 (SI 2009/1488) reg.11 (April 6, 2010).

DEFINITIONS

"the Benefits Act"—see Jobseekers Act 1995 s.35(1).
"claimant"—*ibid.*
"a contribution-based jobseeker's allowance"—see Jobseekers Act 1995 ss.35(1) and 1(4).
"employed earner"—see reg.3.
"a joint-claim jobseeker's allowance"—see Jobseekers Act 1995 ss.35(1) and 1(4).
"pensionable age"—see reg.3.
"qualifying age for state pension credit"—see reg.1(3).
"self-employed earner"—*ibid.*
"tax year"—see Jobseekers Act 1995 s.35(1).
"the Welfare Rights Act"—see reg.1(3).

GENERAL NOTE

3.149 This provision benefits persons (in practice only men: para.(1)(b)) for some days falling after October 6, 1996 during the tax year in which they reach the qualifying age for SPC. The days are ones in that tax year prior to actual attainment of pensionable age on which JSA is not payable because of exhaustion of entitlement, failure to satisfy one or both contribution conditions (old style Jobseekers Act 1995 s.2(1)(a) and (b)), or because the JSA amount has been reduced to nil under reg.81 because of pension payments. Any such days (other than those excluded by any of paras (3)–(5)) are to be days in a jobseeking period notwithstanding that the claimant is not available for and actively seeking work and has not entered into a jobseeker's agreement.

Days which were ones of incapacity for work within a period of incapacity for work cannot form part of a jobseeking period in this way (para.(4)). Nor can days of limited capability for work forming part of a period of limited capability for work (para.(4A)). But both such situations rank as linked periods under reg.48(2)(b). Further, where someone works in employment or self-employment for more than 12 weeks, no day within or after that period can be treated as part of a jobseeking period in this way, but the protection afforded by paras (1) and (2) of the regulation can apply again after such a period when the person makes a claim for JSA (para. (3)).

Note that this regulation cannot apply to days which are the subject of a claim for joint-claim JSA (para.(5)).

Persons temporarily absent from Great Britain

3.150 **50.**—(1) For the purposes of the Act, a claimant shall be treated as being in Great Britain during any period of temporary absence from Great Britain—

(a) not exceeding 4 weeks in the circumstances specified in paragraphs (2), (3) and (4);
(b) not exceeding 8 weeks in the circumstances specified in paragraph (5).

(2) The circumstances specified in this paragraph are that—
(a) the claimant is in Northern Ireland and satisfies the conditions of entitlement to a jobseeker's allowance; and
(b) immediately preceding the period of absence from Great Britain the claimant was entitled to a jobseeker's allowance; and
(c) the period of absence is unlikely to exceed 52 weeks.
(3) The circumstances specified in this paragraph are that—
(a) immediately preceding the period of absence from Great Britain the claimant was entitled to a jobseeker's allowance; and
(b) the period of absence is unlikely to exceed 52 weeks; and
(c) while absent from Great Britain, the claimant continues to satisfy, or be treated as satisfying, the other conditions of entitlement to a jobseeker's allowance; and
(d) is one of a couple, both of whom are absent from Great Britain, where a premium referred to in paragraphs 10, 11, 12, 13 or 15 of Schedule 1 (applicable amounts) is applicable in respect of the claimant's partner.
(4) The circumstances of this paragraph are that—
(a) while absent from Great Britain the person is in receipt of a training allowance; and
(b) regulation 170 (person in receipt of training allowance) applies in his case; and
(c) immediately preceding his absence from Great Britain, he was entitled to a jobseeker's allowance.
(5) The circumstances specified in this paragraph are that—
(a) immediately preceding the period of absence from Great Britain, the claimant was entitled to a jobseeker's allowance; and
(b) the period of absence is unlikely to exceed 52 weeks; and
(c) the claimant continues to satisfy or be treated as satisfying the other conditions of entitlement to a jobseeker's allowance; and
(d) the claimant is, or the claimant and any other member of his family are, accompanying a member of the claimant's family who is a child or young person solely in connection with arrangements made for the treatment of that child or young person for a disease or bodily or mental disablement; and
(e) those arrangements related to treatment—
  (i) outside Great Britain;
  (ii) during the period whilst the claimant is, or the claimant and any member of his family are, temporarily absent from Great Britain; and
  (iii) by, or under the supervision of, a person appropriately qualified to carry out that treatment.

(6) A person shall also be treated, for the purposes of the Act, as being in Great Britain during any period of temporary absence from Great Britain where—
(a) the absence is for the purpose of attending an interview for employment; and
(b) the absence is for 7 consecutive days or less; and
(c) notice of the proposed absence is given to the employment officer before departure, and is given in writing if so required by the officer; and
(d) on his return to Great Britain the person satisfies the employment

officer that he attended for the interview in accordance with his notice.

[[1](6A) A member of a joint-claim couple shall be treated, for the purposes of the Act, as being in Great Britain where he is a member of a transitional case couple as defined for the purposes of paragraph 8A(2) of Schedule 1 to the Act and, as at the date on which Schedule 7 to the Welfare Reform and Pensions Act 1999 comes into force—

(a) he is temporarily absent from Great Britain; or

(b) he has made definite arrangements to be temporarily absent from Great Britain from some future date,

and that member shall be so treated during any such period of temporary absence from Great Britain.

[[2](6AA) For the purposes of the Act a claimant shall be treated as being in Great Britain during any period of temporary absence from Great Britain if—

(a) he was entitled to a jobseeker's allowance immediately before the beginning of that period of temporary absence; and

(b) that period of temporary absence is for the purpose of the claimant receiving treatment at a hospital or other institution outside Great Britain where that treatment is being provided—

(i) under section 3 of the National Health Service Act 1977 (services generally);

(ii) pursuant to arrangements made under section 23 of that Act (voluntary organisations and other bodies); or

(iii) pursuant to arrangements made under paragraph 13 of Schedule 2 to the National Health Service and Community Care Act 1990 (National Health Service Trusts—specific powers).]

(6B) A member of a joint-claim couple shall be treated, for the purposes of the Act, as being in Great Britain during any period of temporary absence from Great Britain—

(a) not exceeding 4 weeks where he is in Northern Ireland and the period of absence is unlikely to exceed 52 weeks;

(b) not exceeding 4 weeks where he is in receipt of a training allowance during the period of absence and regulation 170 applies in his case; or

(c) not exceeding 7 days where the absence is for the purpose of attending an interview for employment,

where that member is so temporarily absent as at the date of claim by the other member of that couple.]

[[2](6C) For the purposes of the Act a member of a joint-claim couple ("the first member") shall be treated as being in Great Britain during any period of temporary absence if—

(a) he and the other member of that couple were entitled to a joint-claim jobseeker's allowance immediately before the beginning of that period of temporary absence; and

(b) that period of temporary absence is for the purpose of the first member receiving treatment at a hospital or other institution outside Great Britain where that treatment is being provided—

(i) under section 3 of the National Health Service Act 1977;

(ii) pursuant to arrangements made under section 23 of that Act; or

(iii) pursuant to arrangements made under paragraph 13 of Schedule 2 to the National Health Service and Community Care Act 1990.]

[3(6D) For the purposes of the Act, a person ("P") shall be treated as being in Great Britain during any period of temporary absence from Great Britain not exceeding 15 days where—

(a) P's absence is for the purpose of taking part in annual continuous training as a member of any territorial or reserve force prescribed in Part 1 of Schedule 6 to the Contributions Regulations; and

(b) P or P's partner was entitled to a jobseeker's allowance immediately before the period of absence began.]

(7) In this regulation—

"appropriately qualified" means qualified to provide medical treatment, physiotherapy or a form of treatment which is similar to, or related to, either of those forms of treatment;

"employment officer" means a person who is an employment officer for the purposes of sections 9 and 10.

AMENDMENTS

1. Jobseeker's Allowance (Joint Claims) Regulations 2000 (SI 2000/1978) Sch.2 para.13 (March 19, 2001).

2. Social Security (Income Support and Jobseeker's Allowance) Amendment Regulations 2004 (SI 2004/1869) reg.3(4) (October 4, 2004).

3. Social Security (Miscellaneous Amendments) (No 2) Regulation 2012 (SI 2012/2575) reg.3 (November 5, 2012).

DEFINITIONS

"the Act"—see reg.1(3).
"child"—see Jobseekers Act 1995 s.35(1).
"claimant"—*ibid.*
"employment"—see reg.3.
"employment officer"—see para.(7); Jobseekers Act 1995 s.9(13).
"entitled"—see Jobseekers Act 1995 s.35(1).
"family"—*ibid.*
"joint-claim couple"—see Jobseekers Act 1995 s.1(4).
"Great Britain"—see Jobseekers Act 1995 s.35(1).
"training allowance"—see reg.1(3).
"week"—*ibid.*
"young person"—see regs 1(3) and 76.

GENERAL NOTE

Paragraph (1)

Entitlement to JSA is dependent on the claimant being in Great Britain (old style Jobseekers Act 1995 s.1(2)(i)). This regulation treats a claimant as being in Great Britain during a range of periods of temporary absence from Great Britain, thus rendering him eligible for JSA. On "temporary absence", see notes on Persons Abroad Regulations 1975 reg.2 in D. Bonner, I. Hooker and R. White, *Social Security Legislation 2002: Vol.I. Non-Means Tested Benefits*. Note, however, that in contrast to that regulation, some of the paragraphs defining the circumstances in which someone is to be treated as if in Great Britain themselves set a requirement that the absence must be unlikely to exceed a specified number of weeks. **3.151**

Paragraph (2) read with para.(1)(a)

A claimant entitled to old style JSA immediately prior to the absence can be treated as being in Great Britain for up to four weeks of temporary absence from Great Britain where the period of absence is unlikely to exceed 52 weeks, he is in Northern Ireland, and satisfies the conditions of entitlement to JSA. **3.152**

Paragraph (3) read with para.(1)(a)

3.153 A claimant entitled to old style SA immediately prior to the absence can be treated as being in Great Britain for up to four weeks of temporary absence from Great Britain where the period of absence is unlikely to exceed 52 weeks, and during the absence he continues to satisfy or be treated as satisfying the other conditions of entitlement to JSA, provided that the claimant is one of a couple and a premium is applicable to his partner under any of paras 10–13 or 15 of Sch.1. The relevant premiums are: pensioner premium for persons over 60; pensioner premium for a partner 75 or over; higher pensioner premium; disability premium; and severe disability premium.

Paragraph (4) read with para.(1)(a)

3.154 A claimant entitled to old style JSA immediately prior to the absence can be treated as being in Great Britain for up to four weeks of temporary absence from Great Britain provided that while absent he is entitled to a training allowance but training is not being provided so that reg.170 applies to him. This would appear to limit this provision to claimants under 25.

Paragraph (5) read with para.(1)(b)

3.155 A claimant entitled to old style JSA immediately prior to the absence can be treated as being in Great Britain for up to eight weeks of temporary absence from Great Britain where the period of absence is unlikely to exceed 52 weeks, and during the absence he continues to satisfy or be treated as satisfying the other conditions of entitlement to JSA, provided that the claimant (or the claimant and another family member) is (are) accompanying a child or young person of the claimant's family solely in connection with arrangements made for the treatment of that child or young person for a disease or bodily or mental disablement outside Great Britain and during the period of absence, by or under the supervision of someone appropriately qualified to carry out that treatment. "Appropriately qualified" means qualified to provide medical treatment, physiotherapy or a similar or related form of treatment (para.(7)).

Paragraph (6)

3.156 A person must also be treated as being in Great Britain during a period of temporary absence of up to seven days where the absence is for the purpose of attending an interview for employment, notice (in writing if required) of the absence was given to an employment officer before his departure, and on return he satisfies an employment officer that he attended for the interview in accordance with the notice. An "employment officer" is an officer of the Secretary of State or any other person designated as employment officer by the Secretary of State (para.(7), Jobseekers Act 1995 s.9(13)); in reality, an officer in the Employment Service.

Paragraphs (6A)–(6C)

3.157 These apply only to members of a joint-claim couple.

Paragraph (6D)

This establishes a special rule for partners of members of the territorial or reserve forces temporarily absent from Great Britain for training of the specified kind.

The transition from new style JSA

3.158 In paras (2)(b), (3)(a) and (c), (5)(a) and (c), (6AA)(a) and (6D)(b) the references to entitlement to jobseeker's allowance are, where art.13(1)(b) of the Welfare Reform Act 2012 (Commencement No.9 and Transitional and Transitory Provisions and Commencement No.8 and Savings and Transitional Provisions (Amendment)) Order 2013 (as amended and set out in the 2014/15 Supplement) applies, to be read as if they included a reference to entitlement under a new style JSA award (art.13(3)(d) of that Order).

Remuneratives work

51.—(1) For the purposes of the Act "remunerative work" means— 3.159

(a) in the case of [5 a claimant], work in which he is engaged or, where his hours of work fluctuate, is engaged on average, for not less than 16 hours per week; and

(b) in the case of any partner of the claimant, work in which he is engaged or, where his hours of work fluctuate, is engaged on average, for not less than 24 hours per week; [1 and

(c) in the case of a non-dependant, or of a child or young person to whom paragraph 18 of Schedule 6 refers, work in which he is engaged or, where his hours of work fluctuate, is engaged on average, for not less than 16 hours per week,]

and for those purposes, [3 "work" is work] for which payment is made or which is done in expectation of payment.

(2) For the purposes of paragraph (1), the number of hours in which [5 a claimant] or his partner is engaged in work shall be determined—

(a) where no recognisable cycle has been established in respect of a person's work, by reference to the number of hours or, where those hours are likely to fluctuate, the average of the hours, which he is expected to work in a week;

(b) where the number of hours for which he is engaged fluctuate, by reference to the average of hours worked over—

(i) if there is a recognisable cycle of work, and sub-paragraph (c) does not apply, the period of one complete cycle (including, where the cycle involves periods in which the person does not work, those periods but disregarding any other absences);

(ii) in any other case, the period of five weeks immediately before the date of claim or the date of [4 supersession], or such other length of time as may, in the particular case, enable the person's average hours of work to be determined more accurately;

(c) [7 . . .]

(3) In determining in accordance with this regulation the number of hours for which a person is engaged in remunerative work—

(a) that number shall include any time allowed to that person by his employer for a meal or for refreshments, but only where the person is, or expects to be, paid earnings in respect of that time;

(b) no account shall be taken of any hours in which the person is engaged in an employment or scheme to which any one of paragraphs (a) to (h) of regulation 53 (person treated as not engaged in remunerative work) applies;

(c) no account shall be taken of any hours in which the person is engaged otherwise than in an employment as an earner in caring for—

(i) a person who is in receipt of attendance allowance [1 . . .] [9 , the care component of disability living allowance at the highest or middle rate [10 , armed forces independence payment] or the daily living component of personal independence payment at the standard or enhanced rate]; or

(ii) a person who has claimed an attendance allowance [1 . . .] [9, disability living allowance [10 , armed forces independence payment] or personal independence payment], but only for the period beginning with the date of claim and ending on the date the claim is determined or, if earlier, on the expiration of the period of 26 weeks from the date of claim; or

(iii) another person [2 and] is in receipt of [6 carer's allowance] under Section 70 of the [1Benefits Act; or

(iv) a person who has claimed either attendance allowance or disability living allowance and has an award of attendance allowance or the care component of disability living allowance at one of the two higher rates prescribed under section 72(4) of the Benefits Act for a period commencing after the date on which that claim was made] [9 ; or

(v) a person who has claimed personal independence payment and has an award of the daily living component at the standard or enhanced rate under section 78 of the 2012 Act for a period commencing after the date on which that claim was made] [10 ; or

(vi) a person who has claimed and has an award of armed forces independence payment for a period commencing after the date on which that claim was made.]

[8 ...]

AMENDMENTS

1. Jobseekers's Allowance (Amendment) Regulations 1996 (SI 1996/15160) reg.9 (October 7, 1996).

2. Jobseekers's Allowance (Amendment) Regulations 1996 (SI 1996/1516) reg.20 and Sch. (October 7, 1996).

3. Social Security (Miscellaneous Amendments) Regulations 1997 (SI 1997/454) reg.2(5) (April 7, 1997).

4. Social Security Act 1998 (Commencement No.11, and Savings and Consequential and Transitional Provisions) Order 1999 (SI 1999/2860 (C.75)) art.3(1) and (12) and Sch.12 para.5 (October 18, 1999)

5. Jobseeker's Allowance (Joint Claims) Regulations 2000 (SI 2000/1978) reg.2(5) and Sch.2 para.14 (March 19, 2001).

6. Social Security (Miscellaneous Amendments) Regulations 2003 (SI 2003/511) reg.3(4) and (5) (April 1, 2003).

7. Social Security (Miscellaneous Amendments) Regulations 2009 (SI 2009/583) reg.4(1) and (4) (April 6, 2009).

8. Social Security (Miscellaneous Amendments) (No.3) Regulations 2011 (SI 2011/2425) reg.10(1) and (3) (October 31, 2011).

9. Personal Independence Payment (Supplementary Provisions and Consequential Amendments) Regulations 2013 (SI 2013/388) reg.8 and Sch. para.16(1) and (3) (April 8, 2013).

10. Armed Forces and Reserve Forces Compensation Scheme (Consequential Provisions: Subordinate Legislation) Order 2013 (SI 2013/591) art.7 and Sch. para.10(1) and (3) (April 8, 2013).

DEFINITIONS

"the Act"—see reg.1(3).
"attendance allowance"—*ibid.*
"the Benefits Act"—see Jobseekers Act s.35(1).
"child"—*ibid.*
"claimant"—*ibid.*
"date of claim"—see reg.1(3).
"disability living allowance"—*ibid.*
"earnings"—*ibid.*

"employment"—see reg.3.
"partner"—see reg.1(3).
"payment"—*ibid.*
"week"—*ibid.*
"young person"—*ibid.*, reg.76.

General Note

A person who is in remunerative work is not entitled to JSA (s.1(2)(e) of the Jobseekers Act). This applies to both contribution-based and income-based JSA. For income-based JSA there is also no entitlement if a person is a member of a couple whose partner is engaged in remunerative work (s.3(1)(e) of the Jobseekers Act). 3.160

Paragraph (1) contains the basic rule. Remunerative work is work for 16 hours or more on average a week in the case of the claimant (sub-para.(a)), or a non-dependent (see reg.2) or (in "transitional cases"—see notes to reg.83 and reg.17 of the Income Support Regulations) a child or young person who has left school and is treated as in relevant education until the next terminal date (sub-para.(c)). (Whether a non-dependent or such a child or young person is in remunerative work is relevant to income-based JSA: see para.17 of Sch.2 (non-dependent deductions from housing costs) and para.18 of Sch.6 (earnings of a child or young person not disregarded)). But in the case of a partner remunerative work is 24 hours or more a week (sub-para.(b)). Work is remunerative if payment is made for it, or it is done in the expectation of payment. See further the notes to reg.5 of the Income Support Regulations.

Paragraph (2) is similar to reg.5(2) and (3B) and para.(3)(a) and (b) to reg.5(7) and (6) respectively of the Income Support Regulations. On para.(3)(c) see the note to reg.53 below. Like reg.5(2) of the Income Support Regulations, the opening words of para.(2) suggest a mechanism for determining the hours worked in all cases but sub-paras (a), (b) and (c) do not cover all situations. In particular, a person who works for a regular number of contracted hours seems to fall outside para.(2) and inside para.(1).

The notes to reg.5 of the IS Regulations must, however, be read subject to the decision of the Tribunal of Commissioners in *R(JSA) 4/03*, which held that reg.51(2)(c) of the JSA Regulations (which is in similar terms to reg.5(3B) of the Income Support Regulations) discriminated indirectly against women and could not be objectively justified by reference to factors other than sex and therefore was inconsistent with EC Directive 79/7 (see Vol.III). In consequence reg.51(2)(c) was to be regarded as being of no effect. It has now been revoked with effect from April 6, 2009. 3.161

For an example of the application of the principles in *R(JSA) 5/03* (and, in particular, the treatment of paid public or extra-statutory holidays falling outside term-time) see the decision of Commissioner Mesher in *CJSA 1638/2003*.

It is important to note that the above decisions were all concerned with JSA, *not* IS. The Government conceded that, as had been held by the Court of Appeal in *Hockenjos v Secretary of State for Social Security* [2001] EWCA Civ 624 (CA), JSA was within the material scope of Directive 79/7. By contrast the ECJ held in *Jackson and Cresswell v Chief Adjudication Officer* (C-63/91 and C-64/91) [1992] E.C.R. I-4737 (also reported as an appendix to *R(IS) 10/91*) that IS was *not* within the material scope of the Directive because it provided protection against poverty rather than against any of the risks listed in art.3 of the Directive. Therefore reg.5(3B) of the Income Support Regulations (as interpreted by the HL in *Stafford and Banks*) remains good law even though the equivalent JSA Regulation is of no effect.

Note also that all those who stand to benefit from the disapplication of reg.51(2)(c) will ex hypothesi be workers and will therefore inevitably come within the personal scope of the Directive as defined by art.2.

Paragraphs (4) and (5)

3.162 Regulations 22–24 of the Income Support (General) Amendment No.4 Regulations 1991 (SI 1991/1559) provided transitional protection for existing income support claimants when the limit for remunerative work for income support was reduced from 24 to 16 hours per week in April 1992. The effect of paras (4) and (5) was to continue that protection for claimants on the transfer to jobseeker's allowance. They were revoked by SI 2011/2425 with effect from October 31, 2011.

Persons treated as engaged in remunerative work

3.163 **52.**—(1) Except in the case of a person on maternity leave [6, paternity leave, adoption leave] [10 , shared parental leave] or absent from work through illness, a person shall be treated as engaged in remunerative work during any period for which he is absent from work referred to in regulation 51(1) (remunerative work) where the absence is either without [9 a good reason] or by reason of a recognised, customary or other holiday.

(2) For the purposes of an income-based jobseeker's allowance, [3 but not a joint-claim jobseeker's allowance] the partner of a claimant shall be treated as engaged in remunerative work where—

(a) the partner is or was involved in a trade dispute; and
(b) had the partner claimed a jobseeker's allowance, section 14 (trade disputes) would have applied in his case; and
(c) the claimant was not entitled to an income-based jobseeker's allowance when the partner became involved in the trade dispute;

and shall be so treated for a period of 7 days beginning on the date the stoppage of work at the partner's place of employment commenced, or if there was no stoppage of work, the date on which the partner first withdrew his labour in furtherance of the trade dispute.

[4(2A) For the purposes of a joint-claim jobseeker's allowance, a member of a joint-claim couple shall be treated as engaged in remunerative work where—

(a) he is or was involved in a trade dispute;
(b) had the joint-claim couple of which he is a member claimed a jobseeker's allowance jointly, section 14 (trade disputes) would have applied in the case of one or both members of that couple; and
(c) the joint-claim couple were not entitled to a joint-claim jobseeker's allowance when that member of the joint-claim couple became involved in the trade dispute,

and shall be so treated for a period of 7 days beginning on the date the stoppage of work commenced at that member's place of employment or, if there was no stoppage of work, the date on which that member first withdrew his labour in furtherance of the trade dispute.]

(3) [7 Subject to paragraph (3A), a person] who was, or was treated as being, engaged in remunerative work and in respect of that work earnings to which [1 8 regulation 98(1)(c)] (earnings of employed earners) applies are paid, shall be treated as engaged in remunerative work for the period for which those earnings are taken into account in accordance with Part VIII.

[7 (3A) Paragraph (3) shall not apply to earnings disregarded under paragraph 1 of Schedule 6 to these regulations.]

[5(4)–(6) . . .]

AMENDMENTS

1. Jobseekers's Allowance (Amendment) Regulations 1996 (SI 1996/1516) reg.20 and Sch. (October 7, 1996).
2. Social Security (Miscellaneous Amendments) (No.2) Regulations 1999 (SI 1999/2556) reg.3 (October 4, 1999).
3. Jobseeker's Allowance (Joint Claims) Regulations 2000 (SI 2000/1978) reg.2(5) and Sch.2 para.15(a) (March 19, 2001).
4. Jobseeker's Allowance (Joint Claims) Regulations 2000 (SI 2000/1978) reg.2(5) and Sch.2 para.15(b) (March 19, 2001).
5. Social Security (Miscellaneous Amendments) Regulations 2001 (SI 2001/488) reg.12(a) (April 9, 2001).
6. Social Security (Paternity and Adoption) Amendment Regulations 2002 (SI 2002/2689) reg.3 (December 8, 2002).
7. Social Security (Miscellaneous Amendments) (No.5) Regulations 2007 (SI 2007/2618) reg.8(4) (October 1, 2007).
8. Social Security (Miscellaneous Amendments) Regulations 2008 (SI 2008/698) reg.4(8) (April 14, 2008).
9. Jobseeker's Allowance (Sanctions) (Amendment) Regulations 2012 (SI 2012/2568) reg.5(9) (October 22, 2012).
10. Shared Parental Leave and Statutory Shared Parental Pay (Consequential Amendments to Subordinate Legislation) Order 2014 (SI 2014/3255) art.7(1) and (4) (December 31, 2014).

DEFINITIONS

"maternity leave"—see reg.1(3).
"partner"—*ibid.*
"remunerative work"—see reg.51(1).
"trade dispute"—see Jobseekers Act s.35(1).

GENERAL NOTE

This provision deems people to be in remunerative work in certain circumstances. **3.164**

Paragraph (1)

See reg.5(3) and (3A) of the Income Support Regulations and the notes to those paragraphs. See also the discussion under the heading "Term-time only workers" in the notes to reg.5. **3.165**

Paragraph (2)

See the notes to s.15 of the Jobseekers Act. **3.166**

Paragraph (3)

Where (within four weeks) holiday pay is paid, the person is treated as in remunerative work for the period covered. See regs 94 and 96. Following the increased disregard of payments made on the termination of full-time employment that was introduced on October 1, 2007 (see para.1 of Sch.6 and the notes to that paragraph) this provision will only apply where a person's employment has been suspended. **3.167**

Persons treated as not engaged in remunerative work

53.—A person shall be treated as not engaged in remunerative work in so far as— **3.168**

(a) he is engaged by a charity or a voluntary organisation or is a volunteer where the only payment received by him or due to be paid to him is a payment which is to be disregarded under regulation 103(2) and paragraph 2 of Schedule 7 (sums to be disregarded in the calculation of income other than earnings) [[12] and in this paragraph "volunteer" means a person who is engaged in voluntary work, otherwise than for a relative, where the only payment received, or due to be paid to the person by virtue of being so engaged, is in respect of any expenses reasonably incurred by the person in connection with that work];

(b) he is engaged on a scheme for which a training allowance is being paid;

[[3](bb) he is receiving assistance [[7]under the self-employment route]

[[59](c) [[11] . . .]]

(d) he is engaged in employment as—

[[8 18] . . .]

[[18] (i) a part-time fire-fighter employed by a fire and rescue authority under the Fire and Rescue Services Act 2004 or by the Scottish Fire and Rescue Service established under section 1A of the Fire (Scotland) Act 2005;]

[[6](ia) [[18] . . .]]

[[8](ib) [[18] [[17]]. . .]]

(ii) an auxiliary coastguard in respect of coastal rescue activities;

(iii) a person engaged part-time in the manning or launching of a lifeboat;

(iv) a member of any [[19] . . .] reserve force prescribed in Part I of [[10] Schedule 6 to the Social Security (Contributions) Regulations 2001];

(e) he is performing his duties as a councillor, and for this purpose "councillor" has the same meaning as in section 171F(2) of the Benefits Act;

(f) he is engaged in caring for a person who is accommodated with him by virtue of arrangements made under any of the provisions referred to in paragraph 27 or 28 of Schedule 7 (sums to be disregarded in the calculation of income other than earnings), and is in receipt of any payment specified in that paragraph;

(g) he is—

(i) the partner of the claimant; and

(ii) involved in a trade dispute; and

(iii) not a person to whom regulation 52(2) applies,

and had he claimed a jobseeker's allowance, section 14 (trade disputes) would have applied in his case;

[[4](gg) he is—

(i) a member of a joint-claim couple; and

(ii) involved in a trade dispute; and

(iii) not a person to whom regulation 52(2A) applies,

and had the joint-claim couple of which he is a member claimed a jobseeker's allowance jointly, section 14 (trade disputes) would have applied in the case of one or both members of that couple;]

(h) [[11] . . .]

[[2](i) he is engaged in an activity in respect of which—

(i) a sports award has been made, or is to be made, to him; and

(ii) no other payment is made or is expected to be made to him].

(j) [*Omitted.*]

[[13] (k) he is engaged in the programme known as Work Experience.]

[14 (l) he is participating in the Mandatory Work Activity Scheme.]
[15 16 (m) he is participating in a scheme prescribed in regulation 3 of the Jobseeker's Allowance (Schemes for Assisting Persons to Obtain Employment) Regulations 2013.]

AMENDMENTS

1. Jobseekers's Allowance (Amendment) Regulations 1996 (SI 1996/1516) reg.20 and Sch. (October 7, 1996).
2. Social Security Amendment (Sports Awards) Regulations 1999 (SI 1999/2165) reg.7(2) (August 23, 1999).
3. Social Security Amendment (Employment Zones) (No.2) Regulations 2000 (SI 2000/2910) reg.3 (November 27, 2000).
4. Jobseeker's Allowance (Joint Claims) Regulations 2000 (SI 2000/1978) reg.2(5) and Sch.2 para.16 (March 19, 2001).
5. Social Security Amendment (Residential Care and Nursing Homes) Regulations 2001 (SI 2001/3767) reg.2 and Sch. Pt II para.2 (April 8, 2002).
6. Fire and Rescue Services Act 2004 (Consequential Amendments) (England) Order 2004 (SI 2004/3168) reg.36(3) (December 30, 2004) (in relation to England); Fire and Rescue Services Act 2004 (Consequential Amendments) (Wales) Order 2005 (WSI 2005/2929 (W.214)) reg.33(6) (October 25, 2005) (in relation to Wales). The amendment does not extend to Scotland.
7. Social Security (Income-Related Benefits Self-Employment Route Amendment) Regulations 2004 (SI 2004/963) reg.4 (May 4, 2004).
8. Fire (Scotland) Act 2005 (Consequential Provisions and Modifications) Order 2005 (SI 2005/2060) art.3 and Sch. para.10(3) (August 2, 2005).
9. Social Security (Care Homes and Independent Hospitals) Regulations 2005 (SI 2005/2687) reg.3 and Sch.2 para.2 (October 24, 2005).
10. Social Security (Miscellaneous Amendments) (No.4) Regulations 2006 (SI 2006/2378) reg.13(3) (October 2, 2006).
11. Social Security (Miscellaneous Amendments) (No.5) Regulations 2009 (SI 2009/3228) reg.4(b)(i) (January 25, 2010).
12. Social Security (Miscellaneous Amendments) (No.2) Regulations 2010 (SI 2010/641) reg.4(1) and (5) (April 6, 2010).
13. Jobseeker's Allowance (Work Experience) (Amendment) Regulations 2011(SI 2011/798) reg.2(4) (April 5, 2011).
14. Jobseeker's Allowance (Mandatory Work Activity Scheme) Regulations 2011 (SI 2011/688) reg.16(c) (April 25, 2011).
15. Jobseeker's Allowance (Employment, Skills and Enterprise Scheme) Regulations 2011 (SI 2011/917) reg.16(b) (May 20, 2011).
16. Jobseeker's Allowance (Schemes for Assisting Persons to Obtain Employment) Regulations 2013 (SI 2013/276) reg.14(c) (February 12, 2013).
17. Police and Fire Reform (Scotland) Act 2012 (Consequential Provisions and Modifications) Order 2013 (SI 2013/602) art.26 and Sch.2 para.74(1) and (3) (April 1, 2013).
18 Social Security (Miscellaneous Amendments) (No.3) Regulations 2013 (SI 2013/2536) reg.6(1) and (5) (October 29,2013).
19. Social Security (Members of the Reserve Forces) (Amendment) Regulations 2015 (SI 2015/389) reg.3(1) and (7)(c) (April 6, 2015).

DEFINITIONS

"Abbeyfield Home"—see reg.1(3).
"the Benefits Act"—see Jobseekers Act s.35(1).
"care home"—see reg.1(3).
"earnings"—*ibid.*
"employment"—see reg.3.

"independent hospital"—see reg.1(3).
"partner"—*ibid.*
"remunerative work"—see reg.51(1).
"trade dispute"—see Jobseekers Act s.35(1).
"training allowance"—see reg.1(3).
"voluntary organisation"—*ibid.*

GENERAL NOTE

3.169 See the notes to reg.6 of the Income Support Regulations. The categories are similar to those in paras (1) and (4) of reg.6 but there are slight differences. On para. (g), see the notes to s.15 of the Jobseekers Act.

Unlike income support (see reg.6(4)(c)), carers are not covered by reg.53. Instead, unless they are "employed as an earner", no account is taken of the hours they spend in caring in deciding whether they are engaged in remunerative work (see reg.52(3)(c)).

There is no equivalent to reg.6(b). So a childminder working 16 or more hours a week (or 24 if she is the partner of a claimant) may count as in remunerative work.

The revocations of paras (c) and (h) with effect from January 25, 2010 are subject to savings provisions in reg.4 of SI 2009/3228 (above). Those provisions apply where a claimant is entitled to jobseeker's allowance for a period including January 24, 2010 (irrespective of when jobseeker's allowance was claimed) and falls within paras (c) or (h) on that date. In those circumstances, para.(c) or (h)—and also para.7 or 8 of Sch.A1 (which were revoked on the same date)—continue to apply to the claimant until either they cease to fall within para.(c) or (h) or they cease to be entitled to jobseeker's allowance, whichever is earlier: see reg.4(3), (5), (7) and (8) of SI 2009/3228.

Relevant education

3.170 **54.**—(1) Only full-time education which is undertaken by a child or young person and which is not a course of advanced education shall be treated as relevant education for the purposes of the Act.

[2 (2) A child or young person shall be treated as receiving full-time education where he is a qualifying young person or child within the meaning of section 142 of the Benefits Act (child and qualifying young person).]

(3) A young person who—

(a) is a part-time student; and
(b) before he became a part-time student fulfilled the requirements specified for a person falling within paragraph (2) of regulation 11 (part-time students); and
(c) is undertaking a course of study, other than a course of advanced education or a course of study of a kind specified in head (i), (ii) or (iii) of the definition of "full-time student" in regulation 1(3),

shall not be treated as receiving relevant education.

(4) A young person to whom paragraph (3) applied and who has completed or terminated his course of part-time study shall not be treated as receiving relevant education.

[3 (4A) A young person who is participating in a traineeship shall not be treated as receiving relevant education.]

[1(5) [4 . . .]]

AMENDMENTS

1. Social Security Amendment (New Deal) Regulations 1997 (SI 1997/2863) reg.5 (January 5, 1998).
2. Social Security (Young Persons) Amendment Regulations 2006 (SI 2006/718) reg.3(4) (April 10, 2006).
3. Social Security (Traineeships and Qualifying Young Persons) Amendment Regulations 2015 (SI 2015/336) reg.2(6)(a) (March 27, 2015).
4. Social Security (Traineeships and Qualifying Young Persons) Amendment Regulations 2015 (SI 2015/336) reg.2(6)(b) (March 27, 2015).

DEFINITIONS

"the Benefits Act"—see Jobseekers Act s.35(1).
"child"—*ibid.*
"course of advanced education"—see reg.1(3).
"course of study"—*ibid.*
"part-time student"—*ibid.*
"traineeship" – *ibid.*
"young person"—*ibid.*, reg.76.

GENERAL NOTE

Paragraphs (1) and (2)

Under s.1(2)(g) of the Jobseekers Act a person is excluded from JSA if he is in relevant education. 3.171

Paragraphs (1) and (2) provide an exhaustive test of when a person is to be treated as receiving relevant education. On para.(2), see the note to reg.12 of the Income Support Regulations.

Note that some claimants may be able to receive income support though in relevant education (see reg.13 of, and paras 15 and 15A of Sch.IB to, the Income Support Regulations), in which case some may also be eligible for JSA (see regs 57(1) (meaning of "young person"), 57(2) and (4)(a) and 61(1)(c)). It will normally be better for most young people to claim income support in these circumstances, so as to avoid the risk of being sanctioned for not complying with the JSA labour market conditions.

Paragraphs (3) and (4)

Under para.(3) a young person (as defined in reg.76) who is a part-time student (see the definitions of full-time and part-time student in reg.1(3); note also reg.1(3A)–(3E)) undertaking a course other than one of advanced education or of a kind within para.(b) of the definition of "full-time student" in reg.1(3) who satisfies the conditions in sub-para. (b) does not count as in relevant education (and will not so count after he finishes or leaves his part-time course (para.(4)). The conditions in para.(3)(b) are that for the three months before he started his course he was in receipt of JSA, ESA, incapacity benefit or income support while sick or on a course of "training" (see reg.11(3)) or in the six months before the course was in receipt of any of these benefits or on a course of "training" for a total of three months and for the remainder of the time was in remunerative work (see reg.51) or earning too much to be entitled to benefit (in both cases the three and the six months must be after the young person has ceased to be in relevant education). 3.172

See reg.11 which may enable such a part-time student to be accepted as available for work even though his hours of study coincide with the times he is required to be available for employment.

Paragraph (4A)

3.173 This provision ensures that a young person who is on a "traineeship" is not treated as in relevant education. A "traineeship" is a course of up to six months which helps 16–24 year olds to prepare for work and is funded by, or under arrangements made by, the Secretary of State under s.14 of the Education Act 2002 (see the definition in reg.1(3)). A person who is on a traineeship is treated as available for, and actively seeking, work (see regs 14(1)(aa) and 19(1)(aa)) and so may be eligible for JSA.

Short periods of sickness

3.174 55.—(1) Subject to the following provisions of this regulation, a person who—

(a) [1 has been awarded a jobseeker's allowance] [10 . . .]; and
(b) proves to the satisfaction of [2 the Secretary of State] that he is unable to work on account of some specific disease or disablement; and
(c) [12 during the period of his disease or disablement, satisfies] the requirements for entitlement to a jobseeker's allowance other than those specified in section 1(2)(a), (c) and (f) (available for and actively seeking employment, and capable of work [5 or not having limited capability for work]),

shall be treated for a period of not more than 2 weeks as capable of work [5 or as not having limited capability for work], except where the claimant states in writing that for the period of his disease or disablement he proposes to claim or has claimed incapacity benefit, [5 employment and support allowance,] [12 universal credit,] severe disablement allowance or income support.

(2) The evidence which is required for the purposes of paragraph (1)(b) is a declaration made by the claimant in writing, in a form approved for the purposes by the Secretary of State, that he has been unfit for work from a date or for a period specified in the declaration.

(3) [12 Paragraph (1) does] not apply to a claimant on more than two occasions in any one jobseeking period or where a jobseeking period exceeds 12 months, in each successive 12 months within that period and for the purposes of calculating any period of 12 months, the first 12 months in the jobseeking period commences on the first day of the jobseeking period.

[11(4) [12 Paragraph (1) does] not apply to any person where the first day in respect of which they are unable to work falls within eight weeks beginning with the day the person ceased to be entitled to statutory sick pay.]

[4(5) [12 Paragraph (1) does] not apply to a claimant who is temporarily absent from Great Britain in the circumstances prescribed by regulation 50(6AA) or, as the case may be, (6C).]

[12 (6) Paragraph (1) does not apply to any person—

(a) during any period where the person is treated as capable of work or as not having limited capability for work under regulation 55ZA (extended period of sickness); or
(b) where the first day in respect of which that person would, apart from this sub-paragraph, have been treated as capable of work or as not having limited capability for work under this regulation falls immediately after the last day on which the person is so treated under regulation 55ZA.]

AMENDMENTS

1. Jobseeker's Allowance and Income Support (General) (Amendment) Regulations 1996 (SI 1996/1517) reg.17 (October 7, 1996).
2. Social Security Act 1998 (Commencement No.11, and Savings and Consequential and Transitional Provisions) Order 1999 (SI 1999/2860) art.3(12) and Sch.12 para.2 (October 18, 1999).
3. Jobseeker's Allowance (Joint Claims) Regulations 2000 (SI 2000/1978) reg.2(5) and Sch.2 para.17 (March 19, 2001).
4. Social Security (Income Support and Jobseeker's Allowance) Amendment Regulations 2004 (SI 2004/1869) reg.3(5) (October 4, 2004).
5. Employment and Support Allowance (Consequential Provisions) (No.2) Regulations 2008 (SI 2008/1554) reg.3(9) (October 27, 2008).
6. Jobseeker's Allowance (Sanctions for Failure to Attend) Regulations 2010 (SI 2010/509) reg.2(8) (April 6, 2010).
7. Employment and Support Allowance (Transitional Provisions, Housing Benefit and Council Tax Benefit) (Existing Awards) (No.2) Regulations 2010 (SI 2010/1907) as amended by the Employment and Support Allowance (Transitional Provisions, Housing Benefit and Council Tax Benefit) (Existing Awards) (No. 2) (Amendment) Regulations 2010 (SI 2010/2430) reg.26 and Sch.4 para.1A(1) (January 31, 2011).
8. Social Security (Miscellaneous Amendments) Regulations 2011 (SI 2011/674) reg.7(2) (April 11, 2011).
9. Jobseeker's Allowance (Mandatory Work Activity Scheme) Regulations 2011 (SI 2011/688) reg.16(d) (April 25, 2011).
10. Jobseeker's Allowance (Sanctions) (Amendment) Regulations 2012 (SI 2012/2568) reg.5(10) (October 22, 2012).
11. Social Security (Miscellaneous Amendments) (No.3) Regulations 2013 (SI 2013/2536) reg.6(6) (October 29, 2013).
12. Jobseeker's Allowance (Extended Period of Sickness) Amendment Regulations 2015 (SI 2015/339) reg. 2(4) (March 30, 2015).

DEFINITIONS

"claimant"—see Jobseekers Act s.35(1).
"jobseeking period"—see regs 1(3) and 47(1)–(3).
"limited capability for work"—see Jobseekers Act s.35(2) and Sch.1 para.2.

GENERAL NOTE

Paragraph (1) (along with regs 14(1)(l) and 19(1)(l)—see below) allows a JSA award to continue for up to two weeks while a claimant is unable to work due to illness or disablement by treating him as capable of work, or as not having limited capability for work, for that period. However, this does not apply if the claimant has stated in writing that he proposes to claim, or has claimed, ESA or universal credit (it is no longer possible to make a claim for severe disablement allowance, incapacity benefit or income support on the grounds of incapacity for work). Presumably the intention is to avoid a claimant having to chop and change between benefits where his period of unfitness is only likely to be short. 3.175

This provision is subject to a limit of two such periods in one jobseeking period or, if the jobseeking period lasts longer than 12 months, in each successive 12-month period—see para.(3).

Note that under para.(1)(b) the claimant only has to show that he is unable to work on account of some specific disease or disablement (not further defined). This is achieved by the claimant providing a written declaration in a form approved by the Secretary of State that he has been unfit for work from a certain date or for a specified period (para.(2)).

3.176 Regulation 55 does not apply if the first day that the claimant is unable to work falls within eight weeks of the day on which he ceased to be entitled to statutory sick pay (para.(4)) or if he is temporarily absent from Great Britain for the purpose of receiving NHS treatment abroad (para.(5)). On para.(5), see the note to reg.55A.

Under para.(6), inserted with effect from March 30, 2015, this provision does not apply during any period when reg.55ZA applies (sub-para.(a)); or if the two-week period would follow *immediately* after the last day of a period to which reg.55ZA applied (sub-para.(b)).

While a person is treated as not having limited capability for work under this regulation, he is treated as available for work (see reg.14(1)(l)); he is also treated as actively seeking work in any week in which he is covered by this regulation for at least three days in that week (see reg.19(1)(l)).

3.177 However, a person can still choose to claim benefit on the ground of limited capability for work in the circumstances to which this regulation applies if he wishes to do so.

See further reg.55ZA and the notes to that regulation.

In *CIS 2107/1998* the claimant who had been in receipt of income-based JSA was advised to claim incapacity benefit when he became unfit for work. This was refused but income support was awarded from a later date. The claimant appealed against the refusal to backdate his income support. The Commissioner states that when a claimant appeals against a gap in benefit, that should be taken as an appeal against *all* the decisions that gave rise to that gap (in this case potentially JSA, incapacity benefit and income support). He also held that the proviso at the end of para.(1) should be construed narrowly in order not to defeat the primacy of the rule in reg.55. In his view the proviso meant that there had to be some written statement by the claimant, other than the claim form for incapacity benefit; moreover, the statement had to make it clear that it applied to the whole period of sickness. The result was that the proviso did not operate in this case and the claimant was entitled to JSA for the two week period after he became ill (which period coincided with the gap in his claim).

[1 Extended period of sickness

3.178 **55ZA.**—(1) This regulation applies to a person who—

(a) has been awarded a jobseeker's allowance;

(b) proves to the satisfaction of the Secretary of State that he is unable to work on account of some specific disease or disablement;

(c) either—

(i) declares that he has been unable to work, or expect to be unable to work, on account of that disease or disablement for more than 2 weeks but he does not expect to be unable to work on account of that disease or disablement for more than 13 weeks; or

(ii) is not a person to whom regulation 55(1) (short periods of sickness) applies by virtue of paragraph (3) of that regulation;

(d) during the period of his disease or disablement, satisfies the requirements for entitlement to a jobseeker's allowance other than those specified in section 1(2)(a), (c) and (f) (availability for and actively seeking employment and capable of work or not having limited capability for work); and

(e) has not stated in writing that for the period of his disease or disablement he proposes to claim or has claimed an employment and support allowance or universal credit.

(2) The evidence which is required for the purposes of paragraph (1)(b) in a case where paragraph (1)(c)(i) applies is—

(a) evidence of incapacity for work or limited capability for work in accordance with the Social Security (Medical Evidence) Regulations 1976 (which prescribe the form of a doctor's statement or other evidence required in each case); and

(b) any such additional information as the Secretary of State may request.

(3) The evidence which is required for the purposes of paragraph (1)(b) in a case where paragraph (1)(c)(ii) applies is a declaration made by the person in writing, in a form approved for the purposes by the Secretary of State, that the person has been unfit for work from a date or for a period specified in the declaration.

(4) Subject to the following paragraphs, a person to whom this regulation applies is to be treated as capable of work or as not having limited capability for work for the continuous period beginning on the first day on which he is unable to work on account of the disease or disablement ("the first day") and ending on—

(a) the last such day; or

(b) if that period would otherwise exceed 13 weeks, the day which is 13 weeks after the first day.

(5) This regulation does not apply to a person on more than one occasion in any one period of 12 months starting on the first day applying for the purpose of paragraph (4).

(6) Paragraphs (4) and (5) of regulation 55 apply for the purposes of this regulation as they apply for the purposes of paragraph (1) of regulation 55.]

AMENDMENT

1. Jobseeker's Allowance (Extended Period of Sickness) Amendment Regulations 2015 (SI 2015/339) reg.2(5) (March 30, 2015).

DEFINITION

"limited capability for work"—see Jobseekers Act s.35(2) and Sch.1 para.2.

GENERAL NOTE

This provision allows a JSA claimant to remain on JSA despite being unable to work due to illness or disablement for up to 13 weeks (referred to by the DWP as an extended period of sickness ("EPS")). The intention is apparently to keep claimants more engaged with the labour market and to support a return to work more quickly, as well as reducing the administrative burden of requiring claimants to switch from JSA to ESA for a short period of time. **3.179**

This regulation applies in addition to the two periods of two weeks' sickness that is allowed under reg.55. If therefore a claimant has already had two periods of two weeks' sickness in his jobseeking period (or, if the jobseeking period lasts longer than 12 months, in each successive 12 month period—see reg.55(3)), this regulation may apply in the case of a third period of sickness. It may also apply if a claimant's sickness turns out to last more than two weeks (although it seems that any days covered by reg.55 will count towards the 13-week limit under this regulation—see para.(4) which states that the 13-week period starts on the first day on which the claimant is unable to work due to the illness or disablement). However, in such a case it seems that reg.55 could still apply for two periods of two weeks in the jobseeking period/successive 12-month period—see reg.55(6)(a) which provides that reg.55 does not apply during any period when a person is covered by reg.55ZA. Note also that a claimant cannot start a two-week period under reg.55 *immediately* after the last day of a period in which he was treated as not having limited capability for work under this regulation (see reg.55(6)(b)).

Regulation 55ZA can only apply on one occasion in any period of 12 months (para.(5)); the 12-month period starts on the first day that the person is unable to work due to illness or disablement (see the definition of "the first day" in para.(4))—presumably this means the first day on which the claimant's inability to work is accepted by the Secretary of State. Note that this 12-month period is therefore not the same 12-month period as that which applies under reg.55(3); the 12-month period under reg.55(3) starts from the beginning of the claimant's jobseeking period (or, if the jobseeking period lasts longer than 12 months, from the start of each successive 12-month period).

3.180 Note that for reg.55ZA to apply, the person only has to show that he is unable to work on account of some specific disease or disablement (not further defined). In addition, the claimant must either declare that due to that illness or disablement he has been unable to work or expects to be unable to work, for more than two weeks but does not expect this to be the case for more than 13 weeks; *or* be a person who has already had two periods of up to two weeks' sickness within his jobseeking period (or, if the jobseeking period lasts longer than 12 months, within each successive 12-month period—see reg.55(3)); *and* satisfy the conditions for an award of JSA (other than the requirements of being available for, and of actively seeking, work and of not having limited capability for work); *and* not have stated in writing that he proposes to claim ESA or universal credit (para.(1)).

Regulation 55ZA does not apply if the first day that the claimant is unable to work falls within eight weeks of the day on which he ceased to be entitled to statutory sick pay or if he is temporarily absent from Great Britain for the purpose of receiving NHS treatment abroad (para.(6)).

If the claimant declares that he is unable to work for more than two but not more than 13 weeks, he has to provide a doctor's statement or other evidence in accordance with the Social Security (Medical Evidence) Regulations 1976 (see Vol.III in this series), together with any other information the Secretary of State may require (para.(2)). If he is a person who has already had two periods of up to two weeks sickness (i.e. this is in effect a third period of short sickness), he has to provide a written declaration in a form approved by the Secretary of State that he has been unfit for work from a certain date or for a specified period (para.(3)).

3.181 If the conditions in reg.55ZA are met, the claimant is treated as capable of work or as not having limited capability for work, for a continuous period from the first day on which he is unable to work due to the illness or disablement to the last such day, or for 13 weeks after the first day, if the period is longer than 13 weeks (para.(4)).

It remains possible for a claimant to still claim benefit on the ground of limited capability for work in the circumstances to which reg.55ZA applies if he wishes to do so.

While a claimant is treated as not having limited capability for work under reg.55ZA, he is treated as available for work (see reg.14(1)(l)). He is also treated as actively seeking work in any week to which reg.55ZA applies, provided that there are no steps that it would be reasonable for him to take to seek employment in that week (see reg.19(1)(lzl)).

[1Periods of sickness and persons receiving treatment outside Great Britain

3.182 **55A.**—(1) A person—

(a) who has been awarded a jobseeker's allowance, a joint-claim jobseeker's allowance [6. . .]; and
(b) who is temporarily absent from Great Britain in the circumstances prescribed by regulation 50(6AA) or, as the case may be, (6C); and
(c) who proves to the satisfaction of the Secretary of State that he is

unable to work on account of some specific disease or disablement; and

(d) but for his disease or disablement, would satisfy the requirements for entitlement to a jobseeker's allowance other than those specified in section 1(2)(a), (c) and (f) (available for and actively seeking employment and capable of work [2 or not having limited capability for work]),

shall be treated during that period of temporary absence abroad as capable of work [2or as not having limited capability for work], except where that person has stated in writing before that period of temporary absence abroad begins that immediately before the beginning of the period of that temporary absence abroad he has claimed [4 . . .] [2 employment and support allowance] [4 . . .].

(2) The evidence which is required for the purposes of paragraph (1)(c) is a declaration made by that person in writing, in a form approved for the purposes by the Secretary of State, that he will be unfit for work from a date or for a period specified in the declaration.]

AMENDMENTS

1. Social Security (Income Support and Jobseeker's Allowance) Amendment Regulations 2004 (SI 2004/1869) reg.3(6) (October 4, 2004).

2. Employment and Support Allowance (Consequential Provisions) (No.2) Regulations 2008 (SI 2008/1554) reg.3(10) (October 27, 2008).

3. Jobseeker's Allowance (Sanctions for Failure to Attend) Regulations 2010 (SI 2010/509) reg.2(9) (April 6, 2010).

4. Employment and Support Allowance (Transitional Provisions, Housing Benefit and Council Tax Benefit) (Existing Awards) (No.2) Regulations 2010 (SI 2010/1907) as amended by the Employment and Support Allowance (Transitional Provisions, Housing Benefit and Council Tax Benefit) (Existing Awards) (No. 2) (Amendment) Regulations 2010 (SI 2010/2430) reg.26 and Sch.4 para.1A(2) (January 31, 2011).

5. Jobseeker's Allowance (Mandatory Work Activity Scheme) Regulations 2011 (SI 2011/688) reg.16(e) (April 25, 2011).

6. Jobseeker's Allowance (Sanctions) (Amendment) Regulations 2012 (SI 2012/2568) reg.5(11) (October 22, 2012).

DEFINITIONS

"joint-claim jobseeker's allowance"—see Jobseekers Act 1995 s.35(1) and s.1(4).

"limited capability for work"—see Jobseekers Act s.35(2) and Sch.1 para.2.

GENERAL NOTE

The purpose of this provision, together with the amendments that have been made to regs 14, 19, 50 and 55, is to enable entitlement to JSA to continue during any period that the claimant (including a member of a joint-claim couple) goes abroad temporarily for the purpose of receiving treatment funded by the NHS. Regulation.55A treats such a person as capable of work, or as not having limited capability for work, provided that he supplies a written declaration on an approved form that he is unfit for work from a stated date or for a specified period and satisfies the conditions for an award of JSA (other than the requirements of being available for, and of actively seeking, work and of not having limited capability for work). However, he will not be treated as capable of work, or as not having limited capability for work, if he has stated in writing before the absence abroad begins that he has claimed ESA. Thus a person in these circumstances can choose to remain in receipt of JSA or to claim benefit on the ground of limited capability for work if he wishes to do so. **3.183**

Prescribed amount of earnings

3.184 **56.**—(1) The prescribed amount of earnings for the purposes of section 2(1)(c) (the contribution-based conditions) shall be calculated by applying the formula—

$$(A + D) - £0.01$$

where—

A is the age-related amount applicable to the claimant in accordance with section 4(2); and

D is any amount disregarded from the claimant's earnings in accordance with regulation 99(2) (calculation of net earnings of employed earners) or regulation 101(2) (calculation of net profit of self-employed earners) and Schedule 6.

(2) For the avoidance of doubt in calculating the amount of earnings in accordance with paragraph (1), only the claimant's earnings shall be taken into account.

General Note

3.185 Under old style Jobseekers Act 1995 s.2(1)(c), to be entitled to contribution-based JSA, a claimant "must not have earnings in excess of the prescribed amount". This regulation gives the set formula for determining that prescribed amount, which amount is not the same for everyone. The prescribed amount is a level equal to the claimant's personal age-related rate of CBJSA (determined in accordance with old style Jobseekers Act 1995 s.4 and reg.79) (A in the formula) plus the appropriate disregards from his earnings (D in the formula), minus one penny.

Part IV

Young Persons

Interpretation of Part IV

3.186 **57.**—(1) In this Part—

[14 ...]

[7 "child benefit extension period" means the extension period within the meaning of regulation 5(3) of the Child Benefit (General) Regulations 2006 (extension period: 16 and 17 year olds).]

"chronically sick or mentally or physically disabled" has the same meaning as in regulation 13(3)(b) of the Income Support Regulations (circumstances in which persons in relevant education may be entitled to income support);

[4 [12 [14 ...]]]

"full-time education" has the same meaning as in regulation 1 of the Child Benefit (General) Regulations 1976;

"suitable training" means training which is suitable for that young person in vocationally relevant respects, namely his personal capacity, aptitude, his preference, the preference of the training provider, the level of approved qualification aimed at, duration of the training, proximity and prompt availability of the training;

"training" in sections 3, 16 and 17 and in this Part except in regulation 65 read with section 7 and except in the phrase "suitable training", means training for which persons aged under 18 are eligible and for which persons aged 18 to 24 may be eligible [5 secured by the [13 [15 Secretary of State] [16 . . .]] or by the [8 9 Welsh Ministers] and, in Scotland, provided] directly or indirectly by a Local Enterprise Company pursuant to its arrangement with, as the case may be, [10 Skills Development, Scotland] Scottish Enterprise or Highlands and Islands Enterprise (whether that arrangement is known as an Operating Contract or by any other name);

"treatment" means treatment for a disease or bodily or mental disablement by or under the supervision of a person qualified to provide medical treatment, physiotherapy or a form of treatment which is similar to, or related to, either of those forms of treatment;

[1 "young person" means a person—

(a) who has reached the age of 16 but not the age of 18;

(b) who does not satisfy the conditions in section 2 or whose entitlement to a contribution-based jobseeker's allowance has ceased as a result of section 5(1); and

(c) who is not a person to whom section 6 of the Children (Leaving Care) Act 2000 (exclusion from benefits) applies.]

(2) A young person falls within this paragraph if he is—

(a) a member of a married couple [6 or of a civil partnership] where the other member of that couple [6 or civil partnership]—

(i) has reached the age of 18 or

(ii) is a young person who has registered for employment and training in accordance with regulation 62 or

(iii) is a young person to whom paragraph (4) applies;

(b) a person who has no parent nor any person acting in the place of his parents;

(c) a person who—

(i) is not living with his parents nor any person acting in the place of his parents; and

(ii) immediately before he attained the age of 16 was—

(aa) [2 in England and Wales] being looked after by a local authority pursuant to a relevant enactment which placed him with some person other than a close relative of his [2 . . .]

(bb) in custody in any institution to which the Prison Act 1952 applies or under [2 the Prisons (Scotland) Act 1989; or]

[2(cc) in Scotland, in the care of a local authority under a relevant enactment and whilst in that care was not living with his parents or any close relative.]

(d) a person who is in accommodation which is other than his parental home and which is other than the home of a person acting in the place of his parents, who entered that accommodation—

(i) as part of a programme of rehabilitation or resettlement, that programme being under the supervision of the probation service or a local authority; or

(ii) in order to avoid physical or sexual abuse; or

(iii) because of a mental or physical handicap or illness and he needs such accommodation because of his handicap or illness;

(e) a person who is living away from his parents and any person who is

acting in the place of his parents in a case where his parents are or, as the case may be, that person is, unable financially to support him and his parents are, or that person is—
(i) chronically sick or mentally or physically disabled; or
(ii) detained in custody pending trial or sentence upon conviction or under a sentence imposed by a court; or
(iii) prohibited from entering or re-entering Great Britain;
(f) a person who of necessity has to live away from his parents and any person acting in the place of his parents because—
(i) he is estranged from his parents and that person; or
(ii) he is in physical or moral danger; or
(iii) there is a serious risk to his physical or mental health.

[2(3)(a) In England and Wales, any reference in this regulation to a person acting in place of a person's parents includes a reference to—
(i) where the person is being looked after by a local authority or voluntary organisation which places him with a family, a relative of his, or some other suitable person, the person with whom the person is placed, whether or not any payment is made to him in connection with the placement; or
(ii) in any other case, any person with parental responsibility for the child, and for this purpose "parental responsibility" has the meaning it has in the Children Act 1989 by virtue of section 3 of that Act; and
(b) in Scotland, any reference in this regulation to a person acting in place of a person's parents includes a reference to a local authority or voluntary organisation where the person is in its care under a relevant enactment, or to a person with whom the person is boarded out by a local authority or voluntary organisation whether or not any payment is made by it.]

(4) This paragraph applies to—
(a) a person who falls under any of the following paragraphs of Schedule 1B to the Income Support Regulations—

Paragraph 1	(lone parents)
Paragraph 2	(single person looking after foster children)
Paragraph 3	(persons temporarily looking after another person)
Paragraph 4	(persons caring for another person)
[11 . . .]	
Paragraph 11	
[11 . . .]	
[11 . . .]	
Paragraph 14	(pregnancy)
Paragraph 15	(persons in education)
Paragraph 18	(refugees)
Paragraph 21	(persons from abroad)
Paragraph 23	(member of couple looking after children while other member temporarily abroad)
Paragraph 28	(persons in receipt of a training allowance);

(b) a person who is a member of a couple and is treated as responsible for a child who is a member of his household;
(c) a person who is laid off or kept on short-time, who is available for employment in accordance with section 6 and Chapter II of Part

II read with regulation 64 and who has not been laid off or kept on short-time for more than 13 weeks;

(d) a person who is temporarily absent from Great Britain because he is taking a member of his family who is a child or young person abroad for treatment, and who is treated as being in Great Britain in accordance with regulation 50(1)(b) or whose entitlement to income support is to continue in accordance with regulation 4(3) of the Income Support Regulations and who is not claiming a jobseeker's allowance or income support;

(e) a person who is incapable of work and training by reason of some disease or bodily or mental disablement if, in the opinion of a medical practitioner, that incapacity is unlikely to end within 12 months because of the severity of that disease or disablement.

AMENDMENTS

1. Children (Leaving Care) Act 2000 (Commencement No. 2 and Consequential Provisions) Order 2001 (SI 2001/3070) art.3(5) and Sch.4.

2. Jobseeker's Allowance and Income Support (General) (Amendment) Regulations 1996 (SI 1996/1517) reg.11 (October 7, 1996).

3. Jobseeker's Allowance (Amendment) (No. 2) Regulations 1998 (SI 1998/1698) reg.2 (August 4, 1998).

4. Social Security (Miscellaneous Amendments) (No. 2) Regulations 2001 (SI 2001/652) reg.5(a) (April 1, 2001).

5. Social Security (Miscellaneous Amendments) (No. 2) Regulations 2001 (SI 2001/652) reg.5(c) (March 26, 2001).

6. Civil Partnership (Pensions, Social Security and Child Support) (Consequential, etc. Provisions) Order 2005 (SI 2005/2877) art.2(3) and Sch.3 para.26(4) (December 5, 2005).

7. Social Security (Young Persons) Amendment Regulations 2006 (SI 2006/718) reg.3(5) (April 10, 2006).

8. National Council for Education and Training for Wales (Transfer of Functions to the National Assembly for Wales and Abolition) Order 2005 (SI 2005/3238) art.9(2) and Sch.2 para.8 (April 1, 2006).

9. Social Security (Miscellaneous Amendments) (No.7) Regulations 2008 (SI 2008/3157) reg.3(1) and (4) (January 5, 2009).

10. Social Security (Miscellaneous Amendments) Regulations 2009 (SI 2009/583) reg.4(1) and (3) (April 6, 2009).

11. Social Security (Miscellaneous Amendments) (No.2) Regulations 2010 (SI 2010/641) reg.4(1) and (6) (April 6, 2010).

12. Education and Inspections Act 2006 and Education and Skills Act 2008 (Consequential Amendments to Subordinate Legislation) (England) Regulations 2010 (SI 2010/1939) reg.2 (September 1, 2010).

13. Apprenticeships, Skills, Children and Learning Act 2009 (Consequential Amendments to Subordinate Legislation) (England) Order 2010 (SI 2010/1941) reg.5(1) and (4) (September 1, 2010).

14. Social Security (Miscellaneous Amendments) (No. 3) Regulations 2011 (SI 2011/2425) reg.10(1) and (4) (October 31, 2011).

15. Young People's Learning Agency Abolition (Consequential Amendments to Subordinate Legislation) (England) Order 2012 (SI 2012/956) reg.5(4) (May 1, 2012).

16. Deregulation Act 2015 (Consequential Amendments) Order 2015 (SI 2015/971) art.2 and Sch.3 para.4(1) and (4) (May 26, 2015).

DEFINITIONS

"the Benefits Act"—see Jobseekers Act s.35(1).

"child"—*ibid.*
"close relative"—see reg.4.
"couple"—see reg.1(3).
"employment"—see reg.4.
"married couple"—see Jobseekers Act s.35(1).
"a person who is kept on short-time"—see reg.4.
"a person who is laid off "—*ibid.*
"relative"—see reg.1(3).
"voluntary organisation"—*ibid.*

GENERAL NOTE

Paragraph (1)

3.187 "*Young person*". To be entitled to income-based JSA, a person must in general be 18 (s.3(1)(f)(i) of the Jobseekers Act). This Part of the Regulations deals with the exceptions to this general exclusion (see s.3(1)(f)(ii) and (iii) of the Jobseekers Act). The lower age limit does not apply to contribution-based JSA, although in practice people below 18 will be unlikely to satisfy the contribution conditions (see s.2(1) of the Jobseekers Act). If a 16- or 17-year-old does qualify for contribution-based JSA, he does not count as a young person for the purposes of this Part.

The categories of 16- and 17-year-olds who under regs 58–61 are entitled to income-based JSA are similar (but not identical) to those who qualified for income support before October 7, 1996. (16- and 17-year-olds who are entitled to benefit while in relevant education can still claim income support under reg.13 of the Income Support Regulations, see para.15 of Sch.1B to those Regulations.) In *some* cases (see reg.61), a 16- or 17-year-old who is eligible for income-based JSA will also be eligible for income support. Because of the stricter benefit regime associated with JSA, it will usually be better for such a young person to claim income support. If the claimant does not come within one of the prescribed circumstances for JSA there is still the possibility of a severe hardship direction being made by the Secretary of State under s.16 of the Jobseekers Act, which then exempts the young person from the lower age limit (see s.3(1)(f)(ii)).

It is important to remember that satisfying an exception only gets the young person past the age condition for income-based JSA. All the other conditions of entitlement (see ss.1 and 3 of the Jobseekers Act) must be met. In order to meet the labour market conditions the young person will have to: (i) register for work and training (reg.62); (ii) be available for work, although if he has not been "sanctioned" for a training-related "offence" or refusing a job opportunity or voluntary unemployment or losing a job through misconduct, laid off or put on short-time or accepted an offer to enlist in the armed forces within the next eight weeks, he can restrict his availability to employment where the employer provides "suitable training" (defined in reg.57(1)) (reg.64); (iii) actively seek work and training (reg.65); and (iv) enter into a jobseeker's agreement (reg.66).

Paragraphs (2)–(4)

3.188 See the notes to regs 58–61.

The amendments made to para.(4) by SI 2010/641 (which consisted in the deletion of the references to paras 10 (disabled students), 12 (which relates to deaf students) and 13 (blind persons) of Sch.1B to the Income Support Regulations) do not apply to young people who fall within reg.2(2) of the Income Support (Prescribed Categories of Person) Regulations (SI 2009/3152) (see the *Transitional, Savings and Modifications* section, above).

[[1]Young persons to whom section 3(1)(f)(iii) or 3A(1)(e)(ii) applies

3.189 **58.**—For the period specified in relation to him, a young person to whom regulation 59, 60 or 61 applies shall be regarded as a person within prescribed circumstances for the purposes of section 3(1)(f)(iii) or section 3A(1)(e)(ii) (conditions of entitlement for certain persons under the age of 18).]

AMENDMENT

1. Jobseeker's Allowance (Joint Claims) Regulations 2000 (SI 2000/1978) reg.2(5) and Sch.2 para.18 (March 19, 2001).

DEFINITION

"young person"—see reg.57(1).

GENERAL NOTE

This regulation, together with regs 59, 60 and 61, prescribes the circumstances in which, and the periods for which, 16- and 17-year-olds can be exempted from the lower age limit of 18 imposed by s.3(1)(f)(i) of the Jobseekers Act. See the notes to regs 59, 60 and 61. 3.190

Young persons in the child benefit extension period

59.—(1) For the period specified in paragraph (2), this regulation applies to a young person who falls within paragraph (2) of regulation 57. 3.191

(2) The period in the case of any person falling within paragraph (1) is the child benefit extension period, except where regulation 61(1)(d) or (e) applies.

DEFINITIONS

"child benefit extension period"—see reg.57(1).
"young person"—*ibid.*

GENERAL NOTE

A 16- or 17-year-old who comes within any of the categories in reg.57(2) is exempt from the ordinary lower age limit for income-based JSA imposed by s.3(1)(f)(i) of the Jobseekers Act until the end of the child benefit extension period, unless reg.61(1)(d) or (e) applies (see below). See reg.57(1) for the definition of the "child benefit extension period" and the notes to reg.54. Note that reg.59 only gets the young person past the age condition for income-based JSA. All the other conditions of entitlement must be met (see the note to the definition of "young person" in reg.57(1)). 3.192

The categories in reg.57(2) are broadly the same as those in the former Pt II of Sch.1A to the Income Support Regulations (revoked on October 7, 1996) (16- or 17-year-olds exempt from the age test for income support during the child benefit extension period). Note, however, the slightly different conditions in reg.57(2)(a)(ii) (the young person must have registered for employment *and* training), and in reg.57(4)(c) and (d).

If, in the circumstances set out in reg.62, the young person registers for employment and training with Jobcentre Plus, rather than the person specified by the Secretary of State under that regulation, then reg.61(1)(d) or (e) will apply to him. In that case, he will be exempt from the lower age limit for JSA for the (normally shorter) periods specified in, respectively, reg.61(2)(c) or (d) (see below) rather than for the whole of the child benefit extension period. He must therefore register with the specified person before the expiry of those time limits if he is to continue to receive JSA.

See also regs 60 and 61.

Young persons at the end of the child benefit extension period

3.193 **60.**—(1) For the period specified in relation to him in paragraph (2), this regulation applies to a young person who is—

(a) a person who has ceased to live in accommodation provided for him by a local authority under Part III of the Children Act 1989 (local authority support for children and families) and is of necessity living away from his parents and any person acting in place of his parents;

(b) a person who has been discharged from any institution to which the Prison Act 1952 applies or from custody under the Criminal Procedure (Scotland) Act 1975 after the child benefit extension period and who is a person falling within paragraph (2) of regulation 57.

(2)(a) Except where regulation 61(1)(d) or (e) applies, the period in the case of a person falling within paragraph 1(a) is the period which begins on the day on which that paragraph first applies to that person and ends on the day before the day on which that person attains the age of 18 or the day at the end of a period of 8 weeks immediately following the day on which paragraph 1(a) first had effect in relation to him, whichever is the earlier; and this period may include any week in which regulation 7 of the Child Benefit (General) Regulations 1976 (circumstances in which a person who has ceased to receive full-time education is to continue to be treated as a child) also applies to that person;

(b) except where regulation 61(1)(d) or (e) applies, the period in the case of any person falling within paragraph 1(b) is the period beginning on the day [[1] . . .] he was discharged, and ends on the last day of the period of 8 weeks beginning with the date on which the period began or on the day before the date on which that person attains the age of 18, whichever first occurs.

(3) In this regulation, "week" means any period of 7 consecutive days.

AMENDMENT

1. Social Security (Miscellaneous Amendments) (No.4) Regulations 2009 (SI 2009/2655) regs 4(1) and (3) (October 29, 2009).

DEFINITIONS

"child benefit extension period"—see reg.57(1).
"young person"—*ibid.*

GENERAL NOTE

3.194 This provision is similar to the former reg.13A(4)(c) and (d) of the Income Support Regulations (now revoked). The effect, with reg.58, is to exempt 16- and 17-year-olds from the ordinary lower age limit for income-based JSA (see s.3(1)(f)(i) of the Jobseekers Act) if they leave local authority care and have to live away from their parents and any substitute (para.(1)(a)), or if they have been discharged from custody after the end of the child benefit extension period and one of the conditions in reg.57(2) applies (para.(1)(b)). Except where reg.61(1)(d) or (e) applies (see the note to reg.59 above as to when these apply), the exemption lasts for eight weeks, or until the person reaches 18, if sooner (para.(2)). If the exemption is under para.(1)(a), any week in the child benefit extension period can count in the eight weeks (it is understood that this is the intended meaning, although para.(2)(a) refers to reg.7, not reg.7D, of the Child Benefit Regulations).

Note that there is no equivalent to the former reg.13A(4)(a) (incapacity for work and training which is likely to end within 12 months). Such a young person could claim income support: see para.7 of Sch.1B to the Income Support Regulations.

It is important to remember that reg.60 only gets the young person past the age condition for income-based JSA. All the other conditions of entitlement must be met (see the note to the definition of "young person" in reg.57(1)).

See also reg.61.

Other young persons in prescribed circumstances

61.—(1) For the period specified in relation to him in paragraph (2), this regulation applies to a young person— 3.195

(a) who is a person who is laid off or kept on short-time and is available for employment in accordance with section 6 and Chapter II of Part II read with regulation 64;

(b) who is a member of a couple and is treated as responsible for a child who is a member of his household;

(c) who falls within a prescribed category of persons for the purposes of section 124(1)(e) of the Benefits Act and who is not claiming income support;

[[6] (d) to whom section 3(1)(f)(ii) or section 3A(1)(e)(i) does not apply, who is a person falling within paragraph (2) of regulation 57, sub-paragraph (a) or (b) of paragraph (1) of regulation 60, or sub-paragraph (b) or (c) of this paragraph, and who registers with Jobcentre Plus in accordance with regulation 62(2)(a); and

(e) to whom section 3(1)(f)(ii) or section 3A(1)(e)(i) does not apply, who is a person falling within paragraph (2) of regulation 57, sub-paragraph (a) or (b) of paragraph (1) of regulation 60, or sub-paragraph (b) or (c) of this paragraph, and who registers with Jobcentre Plus in accordance with regulation 62(2)(b).]

(f) who has accepted a firm offer of enlistment by one of the armed forces with a starting date not more than 8 weeks after the offer was made who was not in employment or training at the time of that offer and whose jobseeker's allowance has never been reduced in accordance with regulation 63 or [[7] section 19(2)(c) or (d) or section 19A(2)(d), (e), (f) or (g)] read with regulation 68 or [[7] reduced in accordance with section 19(2)(a) or (b)] read with Part V.

[[5] (g) who has limited capability for work for the purposes of Part 1 of the Welfare Reform Act.]

(2)(a) The period in the case of any person falling within paragraph (1)(a) is the period starting with the date on which he was laid off or first kept on short-time and ending on the date on which he ceases to be laid off or kept on short-time or the day before the day he attains the age of 18 or at the expiry of the 13 week period starting with the date of the lay off, or date he was first kept on short-time, whichever first occurs;

(b) except where paragraph (1)(d) or (e) applies, the period in the case of any person falling within paragraph [[5] 1(b), (c) or (g)] is the period until the day before that person attains the age of 18 or until paragraph [[5] 1(b), (c) or (g)] ceases to apply, whichever first occurs;

(c) the period in the case of any person falling within paragraph (1)(d) is the period starting with the date of registration with [6 Jobcentre Plus] and ending on the day on which the person is next due to attend in accordance with regulation 23 [3 or regulation 23A] or on the date on which the period calculated in accordance with regulation 59(2) or 60(2) or sub-paragraph (b) would have expired, whichever first occurs;

(d) the period in the case of any person falling within paragraph 1(e) is the period starting on the date of registration with [6 Jobcentre Plus] and ending five days after that date or on the day after the day on which he registered with [6 a person other than Jobcentre Plus specified by the Secretary of State for the purposes of regulation 62(1)], or on the date on which the period calculated in accordance with regulation 59(2) or 60(2) or sub-paragraph (b) would have expired, whichever first occurs;

(e) the period in the case of any person falling within paragraph 1(f) is the period starting with the date of claim and ending with the day before the day on which he is due to enlist or the day before he attains the age of 18, whichever first occurs.

(3) In this regulation "week" means a period of 7 consecutive days.

AMENDMENTS

1. Jobseeker's Allowance (Joint Claims) Regulations 2000 (SI 2000/1978) reg.2(5) and Sch.2 para.19(a) (March 19, 2001).
2. Jobseeker's Allowance (Joint Claims) Regulations 2000 (SI 2000/1978) reg.2(5) and Sch.2 para.19(b) (March 19, 2001).
3. Jobseeker's Allowance (Joint Claims) Regulations 2000 (SI 2000/1978) reg.2(5) and Sch.2 para.19(c) (March 19, 2001).
4. Social Security (Miscellaneous Amendments) (No.2) Regulations 2001 (SI 2001/652) reg.5(b) (April 1, 2001).
5. Employment and Support Allowance (Consequential Provisions) (No.2) Regulations 2008 (SI 2008/1554) reg.3(1) and (11) (October 27, 2008).
6. Social Security (Miscellaneous Amendments) (No.3) Regulations 2011 (SI 2011/2425) reg.10(1) and (5) (October 31, 2011).
7. Jobseeker's Allowance (Sanctions) (Amendment) Regulations 2012 (SI 2012/2568) reg.5(12) (October 22, 2012).

DEFINITIONS

"the Benefits Act"—see Jobseekers Act s.35(1).
"child"—see Jobseekers Act s.35(1).
"couple"—see reg.1(3).
"a person who is kept on short-time"—see reg.4.
"a person who is laid off"—*ibid.*

GENERAL NOTE

3.196 This sets out additional circumstances in which a 16- or 17-year-old will be exempt from the lower age limit imposed by s.3(1)(f)(i) of the Jobseekers Act. Paragraph.(1) defines the categories covered and para.(2) the length of the exemption.

Paragraph (1)(a). A person who is laid off or on short-time working and who is available for work (see reg.64) will be exempt for up to 13 weeks (para.(2)(a)).

Paragraph (1)(b). A person who is a member of a couple and responsible for a child (see regs 77 and 78) is exempt until 18 (except where para.(1)(d) or (1)(e) applies, see below) (para.(2)(b)).

Paragraph (1)(c). A person who falls within para.4ZA of, and Sch.1B to, the Income Support Regulations (which prescribe the categories of people entitled to income support under s.124(1)(e) of the SSCBA), and who is not claiming income support, is exempt until 18 (except where para.(1)(d) or (e) applies, see below) (para.(2)(b)). As the age limit for income support is now 16 (see s.124(1)(a) of the SSCBA, amended with effect from October 7, 1996), it will be better for most young people who come within Sch.1B to claim income support so as to avoid the risk of being sanctioned for not complying with the JSA labour market conditions.

Paragraph (1)(d) and (e). These sub-paras do not apply if a severe hardship direction has been made. Except for a young person who is laid off or on short-time (sub-para.(a)) or has accepted an offer to enlist in the armed forces in the next eight weeks (sub-para.(f)), a 16-or 17-year-old who is eligible for income-based JSA must register for employment and training with "such person as the Secretary of State may specify". However, if s/he is unable to do so because of "an emergency affecting that person such as a strike or fire" (reg.62(2))(a)) or because s/he "would suffer hardship because of the extra time it would take to register with that person" (reg.62(2)(b)), the young person must register with Jobcentre Plus instead. If he does so, the young person will be exempt from the lower age limit for JSA for the period until his next signing on day (normally two weeks) if reg.61(1)(d) applies (see reg.61(2)(c)), or five days if reg.61(1)(e) applies (see reg.61(2)(d)) (or until he ceases to be eligible for JSA under regs. 59 or 60 or reaches 18, if that is earlier).

Paragraph (1)(f). This applies to a person who has accepted an offer (made when he was not employed or in training) to enlist in the armed forces within the next eight weeks and who has never been sanctioned for a training-related "offence" or refusing a job opportunity or voluntary unemployment or losing a job through misconduct. The exemption lasts until he enlists (para.(2)(e)).

Note that reg.61 only gets the young person past the age condition for income-based JSA. All the other conditions of entitlement must be met (see the note to the definition of "young person" in reg.57(1)).

Registration

62.—(1) Except in the circumstances set out in paragraphs (2) and (3) a young person to whom section 3(1)(f)(ii) or (iii) [1 or section 3A(1)(e)(i) or (ii)] applies other than one falling within regulation 61(1)(a) or (f), must register with [3 such person as the Secretary of State may specify [2 ...]] for both employment and training. **3.197**

[3 (2) A young person must register with Jobcentre Plus for both employment and training where the Secretary of State has specified a person other than Jobcentre Plus for the purposes of paragraph (1) and—

(a) the young person is unable to register with that person because of an emergency affecting that person such as a strike or fire, or

(b) the young person would suffer hardship because of the extra time it would take to register with that person.]

AMENDMENTS

1. Jobseeker's Allowance (Joint Claims) Regulations 2000 (SI 2000/1978), reg.2(5) and Sch.2 para.20 (March 19, 2001).
2. Social Security (Miscellaneous Amendments) (No.2) Regulations 2001 (SI 2001/652) reg.5(b) (April 1, 2001).
3. Social Security (Miscellaneous Amendments) (No.3) Regulations 2011 (SI 2011/2425) reg.10(1) and (6) (October 31, 2011).

DEFINITIONS

"employment"—see reg.4.
"training"—see reg.57(1).
"young person"—*ibid.*

GENERAL NOTE

3.198 Except for a young person who is laid off or on short-time, or who has never been sanctioned for a training-related "offence" or refusing a job opportunity or voluntary unemployment or losing a job through misconduct and has accepted an offer to enlist in the armed forces within the next eight weeks, a 16- or 17-year-old who is exempt from the lower age limit for income-based JSA has to register with "such person as the Secretary of State may specify" (para.(1)). For para.(2) see the commentary to reg.61(1)(d) and (e) above.

While paras (2) or (3) apply, he will be deemed to have entered into a jobseeker's agreement (reg.66(2)).

See also regs 64–66.

Reduced payments under section 17

3.199 **63.**—(1) Except as provided in paragraph (3), the amount of an income-based jobseeker's allowance which would otherwise be payable to a young person shall be reduced by[1, if he is a single person or a lone parent,] a sum equal to 40 per cent of the amount applicable in his case by way of a personal allowance determined [1 in accordance with paragraph 1(1) or 1(2) of Schedule 1 (as the case may be) or, if he is a member of a couple, a sum equal to 40 per cent of the amount which would have been applicable in his case if he had been a single person determined in accordance with paragraph 1(1) of Schedule 1] for the period set out in paragraph (2) if—

(a) he was previously entitled to an income-based jobseeker's allowance and that entitlement ceased by virtue of the revocation of a direction under section 16 because he had failed to pursue an opportunity of obtaining training or rejected an offer of training;

(b) his allowance has at any time in the past been reduced in accordance with this regulation or in accordance with regulation 68 because he has done an act or omission falling within [7 section 19(2)(a) or (b) or section 19A(2)(c) to (g)] and he has—

(i) failed to pursue an opportunity of obtaining training without showing [7 a good reason] for doing so,

(ii) rejected an offer of training without showing [7 a good reason] for doing so or

(iii) failed to complete a course of training and no certificate has been issued to him under subsection (4) of section 17 with respect to that failure;

(c) he has—

(i) done an act or omission falling within section 16(3)(b)(i) or (ii) and has not shown [7 a good reason] for doing so or done an act or omission falling within [7 section 19A(2)(d) or (e) or failed to attend a training scheme or employment programme] [4 7 . . .] without [7 a good reason] or done an act or omission falling within [7 section 19A(2)(d) or (e) or failed to attend a training scheme or employment programme] [4 7 . . .] for which he was regarded as having [7 a good reason] in accordance with regulation 67(1) and

(ii) after that act or omission failed to complete a course of training and no certificate has been issued to him under subsection (4) of section 17 with respect to that failure and at the time he did the act or omission falling within subparagraph (i) he was a new jobseeker;

(d) he has—

(i) failed to complete a course of training and no certificate has been issued to him under subsection (4) of section 17 with respect to that failure or [7 given up a place on a training scheme or employment programme] [5 7 . . .] without [7 a good reason] or [7 given up a place on a training scheme or employment programme] [5 7 . . .] for which he was regarded as having [7 a good reason] in accordance with regulation 67(1) and

(ii) after that failure he has failed to complete a course of training and no certificate has been issued to him under subsection (4) of section 17 with respect to that failure and on the day before the day he first attended the course referred to in sub-paragraph (i) he was a new jobseeker; or

(e) he has failed to complete a course of training and no certificate has been issued to him under subsection (4) of section 17 with respect to that failure and on the day before he first attended the course he was not a new jobseeker; or

(f) he has failed to complete a course of training and no certificate has been issued to him under subsection (4) of section 17 with respect to that failure and he lost his place on the course through his misconduct.

(2) The period shall start with the date on which the first severe hardship direction is made under section 16 after the act or acts referred to in paragraph (a), (b), (c), (d), (e) or (f) of paragraph (1) have taken place and shall end fourteen days later.

(3) In the case of a young person who is pregnant or seriously ill who does an act falling within sub-paragraphs (a)–(f) of paragraph (1), the reduction shall be [1 if he is a single person or a lone parent] of 20 per cent of the amount applicable in his case by way of a personal allowance [1 determined in accordance with paragraph 1(1) or 1(2) of Schedule 1 (as the case may be) or, if he is a member of a couple, of 20 per cent of the amount which would have been applicable in his case if he had been a single person determined in accordance with paragraph 1(1) of Schedule 1].

(4) For the purposes of this regulation, "new jobseeker" means a young person who has not since first leaving full-time education been employed or self-employed for 16 or more hours per week or completed a course of

train in or failed to complete a course of training and no certificate has been issued to him to show [7 a good reason] for that failure under subsection (4) of section 17 or [7 given up a place on a training scheme or employment programme [6 7 . . .] without [7 a good reason] or done an act or omission falling within [7 section 19A(2)(g)] [6 7 . . .]].

(5) A reduction under paragraph (1) or (3) shall, if it is not a multiple of 5p, be rounded to the nearest such multiple or, if it is a multiple of 2.5p but not of 5p, to the next lower multiple of 5p.

AMENDMENTS

1. Social Security and Child Support (Miscellaneous Amendments) Regulations 1997 (SI 1997/827) reg.2 (April 7, 1997).
2. Jobseeker's Allowance (Joint Claims) Regulations 2000 (SI 2000/1978) reg.2(5) and Sch.2 para.21(a)(i)(aa) (March 19, 2001).
3. Jobseeker's Allowance (Joint Claims) Regulations 2000 (SI 2000/1978) reg.2(5) and Sch.2 para.21(a)(i)(bb) (March 19, 2001).
4. Jobseeker's Allowance (Joint Claims) Regulations 2000 (SI 2000/1978) reg.2(5) and Sch.2 para.21(a)(ii) (March 19, 2001).
5. Jobseeker's Allowance (Joint Claims) Regulations 2000 (SI 2000/1978) reg.2(5) and Sch.2 para.21(a)(iii) (March 19, 2001).
6. Jobseeker's Allowance (Joint Claims) Regulations 2000 (SI 2000/1978) reg.2(5) and Sch.2 para.21(b) (March 19, 2001).
7. Jobseeker's Allowance (Sanctions) (Amendment) Regulations 2012 (SI 2012/2568) reg.5(13) (October 22, 2012).

DEFINITIONS

"full-time education"—see reg.57(1).
"income-based jobseeker's allowance"—see Jobseekers Act s.1(4).
"training"—see reg.57(1).
"young person"—*ibid.*

GENERAL NOTE

Paragraph (1)

3.200 Section 20(2) of the Act provides that where a severe hardship direction is in force and the young person has without a good reason failed to pursue an opportunity, or rejected an offer, of training or failed to complete a training course, a s.19A sanction will not be applied. Instead, the circumstances in which income-based JSA payable under a severe hardship direction will be paid at a reduced rate are set out in this regulation. The reduction is 40 per cent of the appropriate single person or lone parent personal allowance under para.1 of Sch.1, or 20 per cent if the young person is pregnant or seriously ill (not defined) (para.(3)), and lasts for two weeks (para.(2)). If the person is a member of a couple, the same reduction is applied as if he was a single claimant.

The effect of para.(1) is that in some cases, e.g. where the person was previously a "new jobseeker," the reduction will only be applied where it is a "second offence". The detailed rules provide for the reduction to be imposed if:

(i) a previous severe hardship direction was revoked because the person failed to pursue an opportunity, or rejected an offer, of training without a good reason (sub-para.(a));
(ii) at any time in the past the person's JSA has been subject to a reduction under this regulation, or reg.68 for a training-related "offence" or stopped because of voluntary unemployment or losing a job through misconduct, and then without a good reason he fails to pursue an opportunity, or rejects an offer, or fails to complete a course, of training (sub-para.(b));

(iii) while he was a new jobseeker (defined in para.(4)) he failed to pursue an opportunity, or rejected an offer, of training without a good reason while a severe hardship direction was in force, or did not avail himself of, or failed to apply for or accept after having been notified of, or failed to attend, a place on a training scheme or employment programme either without a good reason, or only with a deemed good reason under reg.67(1), and then fails without a good reason to complete a course of training (sub-para.(c));

(iv) he has failed to complete a course of training without a good reason while a severe hardship direction was in force, or given up a training scheme or employment programme place either without a good reason or only with a deemed good reason under reg.67(1), and was a new jobseeker (defined in para.(4)) on the day before he started the course, and then fails to complete a course of training without a good reason (sub-para.(d));

(v) he has failed to complete a course of training without a good reason and was not a new jobseeker on the day before he started the course (sub-para.(e)); or

(vi) he has lost his training place through misconduct before finishing the course (sub-para.(f)).

The above is a summary of the very detailed rules in para.(1) but the reader is advised to check the text of the regulation where there is any doubt as to whether a particular sub-paragraph applies.

Paragraph (4)

A new jobseeker is a 16- or 17-year-old who since leaving full-time education (see reg.57(1)) has not been employed or self-employed for 16 hours or more a week, or finished a training course, or failed to finish a training course without a good reason or given up without a good reason or lost through misconduct a training scheme or employment programme place. **3.201**

Availability for employment

64.—(1) A young person is required to be available for employment in accordance with section 6 and Chapter II of Part II except as provided in paragraphs (2) and (3). **3.202**

(2) A young person whose jobseeker's allowance has not been reduced in accordance with regulation 63 or in accordance with regulation 68 because he has done an act or omission falling within [2 section 19A(2)(d), (e), (f) or (g) or section 19(2)(c) or (d) or in accordance with section 19(2)(a) or (b)] read with Part V and who does not fall within regulation 61(1)(a) or (f) may restrict his availability for employment to employment where suitable training is provided by the employer.

(3) A young person who places restrictions on the nature of employment for which he is available as permitted by paragraph (2) does not have to show that he has reasonable prospects of securing employment notwithstanding those restrictions.

Amendments

1. Jobseeker's Allowance (Joint Claims: Consequential Amendments) Regulations 2000 (SI 2000/3336) reg.2(8) (March 19, 2001).

2. Jobseeker's Allowance (Sanctions) (Amendment) Regulations 2012 (SI 2012/2568) reg.5(14) (October 22, 2012).

Definitions

"employment"—see reg.4.

"suitable training"—see reg.57(1).

General Note

3.203 In order to be entitled to JSA, a young person has to be available for work under the normal rules (see s.6 of the Jobseekers Act and regs 5–17) (para.(1)). However, provided that he is not subject to a sanction under reg.63 or under reg.68 for a training-related "offence" or refusing a job opportunity or voluntary unemployment or losing a job through misconduct, a 16- or 17-year-old can restrict his availability to employment where the employer provides "suitable training" (para.(2)). See reg.57(1) for the definition of suitable training. This does not apply to a young person who has been laid off or is on short-time working, or who has never been sanctioned for a training-related "offence" or refusing a job opportunity or voluntary unemployment or losing a job through misconduct and has accepted an offer to join the armed forces in the next eight weeks. Presumably this is because such a young person is only expected to be unemployed for a short time and so it would not be reasonable to require an employer to provide him with training. The young person does not have to show that he still has reasonable prospects of obtaining work (para.(3)). Note also reg.67(2).

In addition, see regs 62 and 65–66.

Active seeking

3.204 **65.**—(1) Subject to the following paragraphs, Section 7 and Chapter III of Part II shall have effect in relation to a young person as if "employment" included "training".

(2) Subject to paragraphs (4) and (5), in order to have the best prospects of securing employment or training a young person can be expected to have to take more than one step on one occasion in any week unless taking one step on one occasion is all that it is reasonable for that person to do in that week, and unless it is reasonable for him to take only one step on one occasion, he can be expected to have to take at least one step to seek training and one step to seek employment in that week.

(3) Subject to paragraph (4), steps which it is reasonable for a young person to be expected to have to take include, in addition to those set out in regulation 18(2)—

(a) seeking training and

(b) seeking full-time education.

(4) Paragraphs (1), (2) and (3) do not apply to a young person falling within regulation 61(1)(a) or (f).

(5) Paragraphs (1) and (2) do not apply to a young person [2 [3 . . .]] who has had his jobseeker's allowance reduced in accordance with regulation 63 or regulation 68 because he has done an act or omission falling within [3 section 19A(2)(a), (d), (e), (f) or (g) or section 19(2)(c) or (d) or in accordance with section 19(2)(a) or (b)] read with Part V but paragraph (3) does apply to such a young person.

(6) "Training" in section 7 and in this regulation means suitable training.

Amendments

1. Jobseeker's Allowance (Joint Claims: Consequential Amendments) Regulations 2000 (SI 2000/3336) reg.2(9) (March 19, 2001).

2. Jobseeker's Allowance (Sanctions for Failure to Attend) Regulations 2010 (SI 2010/509) reg.2(10) (April 6, 2010).

3. Jobseeker's Allowance (Sanctions) (Amendment) Regulations 2012 (SI 2012/2568) reg.5(15) (October 22, 2012).

DEFINITIONS

"employment"—see reg.4.
"full-time education"—see reg.57(1).
"suitable training"—*ibid.*
"young person"—*ibid.*

GENERAL NOTE

The normal rules in relation to actively seeking work apply to young people (see s.7 of the Jobseekers Act and regs 18–22) but they must seek training (which means suitable training (para.(6)) as well as work (para.(1)). See reg.57(1) for the definition of "suitable training". They are expected to take more than one step (see reg.18(2)) each week, including at least one step to find work and one to find training, unless it is reasonable to take only one step that week (para.(2)). In the case of a young person, "steps" include, as well as those referred to in reg.18(2), seeking training and seeking full-time education (para.(3)). 3.205

These special rules do not apply to a young person who is laid off or on short-time working or who has never been sanctioned for a training-related "offence" or refusing a job opportunity or voluntary unemployment or losing a job through misconduct and has accepted an offer to join the armed forces within the next eight weeks (para.(4)). Presumably this is because they are only expected to be unemployed for a short time and so it would not be reasonable to require them to seek training or education in that time, only work.

Paragraph (5) appears to provide that a young person whose JSA is subject to a sanction under reg.63 or under reg.68 for a training-related "offence" or refusing a job opportunity or voluntary unemployment or losing a job through misconduct is not required to seek training as well as work, since it states that paras (1) and (2) do not apply to such a person. But this is followed by the somewhat contradictory statement that para.(3) does apply; that is, such a young person *is* required to seek training and full-time education. The policy intention apparently is that a 16- or 17-year-old who has been sanctioned should only be seeking training (and education) with a view to finding work and not as an end in itself.

See also regs 62, 64, 65A and 66.

[1Attendance, information and evidence

65A.—A young person who does not fall within regulation 61(1)(a) or (f) shall, if the Secretary of State requires him to do so, provide, in addition to the declaration specified in regulation 24(6), a declaration to the effect that since making a claim for a jobseeker's allowance or since he last provided a declaration in accordance with this regulation he has been actively seeking suitable training to the extent necessary to give him his best prospects of securing suitable training save as he has otherwise notified the Secretary of State.] 3.206

AMENDMENT

1. Jobseeker's Allowance and Income Support (General) (Amendment) Regulations 1996 (SI 1996/1517) reg.12 (October 7, 1996).

DEFINITIONS

"suitable training"—see reg.57(1).
"young person"—*ibid.*

GENERAL NOTE

3.207 This regulation provides that a 16- or 17-year-old may be required to declare that he has been actively seeking suitable training as well as work when he signs on. There is the usual exception from this rule for a young person who has been laid off or is on short-time working, or who has never been sanctioned for a training-related "offence" or refusing a job opportunity or voluntary unemployment or losing a job through misconduct and has accepted an offer to join the armed forces within the next eight weeks.

See also regs 62, 64, 65 and 66.

The jobseeker's agreement

3.208 **66.**—(1) In a jobseeker's agreement with a young person, other than one falling within regulation 61(1)(a) or (f), the following information is required in addition to that prescribed in Chapter V of Part II: a broad description of the circumstances in which the amount of the person's benefit may be reduced in accordance with section 17 and regulation 63, or [4 section 19(2)(a), (b), (c) or (d) or section 19A(2)(a), (c), (d), (e), (f) or (g)] and regulation 68.

(2) A young person is to be treated as having entered into a jobseeker's agreement and as having satisfied the condition mentioned in section 1(2)(b) as long as the circumstances set out in [1regulation 62(2) or 62(3) apply.]

AMENDMENTS

1. Jobseekers's Allowance (Amendment) Regulations 1996 (SI 1996/1516) reg.8 and Sch. (October 7, 1996).
2. Jobseeker's Allowance (Joint Claims) Regulations 2000 (SI 2000/1978) reg.2(5) and Sch.2 para.22 (March 19, 2001).
3. Jobseeker's Allowance (Sanctions for Failure to Attend) Regulations 2010 (SI 2010/509) reg.2(11) (April 6, 2010).
4. Jobseeker's Allowance (Sanctions) (Amendment) Regulations 2012 (SI 2012/2568) reg.5(16) (October 22, 2012).

DEFINITIONS

"jobseeker's agreement"—see Jobseekers Act s.9(1).
"young person"—see reg.57(1).

GENERAL NOTE

3.209 See the notes to ss.9–11 of the Jobseekers Act and regs 31–45 for the rules relating to jobseeker's agreements.

Paragraph (1)

3.210 A 16- or 17-year-old has to enter into a jobseeker's agreement as a condition of receiving JSA in the normal way. But the agreement must contain additional information as to the sanctions that can be applied. There is the usual exception from this rule for a young person who has been laid off or is on short-time working, or who has never been sanctioned for a training-related "offence" or refusing a job opportunity or voluntary unemployment or losing a job through misconduct and has accepted an offer to join the armed forces within the next eight weeks.

Paragraph (2)

3.211 A young person will be deemed to have entered into a jobseeker's agreement while he has to register with Jobcentre Plus for work and training instead of the person specified by the Secretary of State under reg.62(1) due to an emergency or because the extra time involved in registering with the Careers Service would cause him hardship.

Regulation 62(3) was revoked by reg.10(6)(b) of SI 2011/2425 with effect from October 31, 2011. However, the reference to it in para.(2) has not been revoked.

Sanctions

67.—(1) Without prejudice to any other circumstances in which a person may be regarded as having [9 a good reason] for any act or omission for the purposes of [9 section 19A(2)(d), (e) or (f)] and in addition to the circumstances listed in regulation 73, a young person is to be regarded as having [9 a good reason] for any act or omission for the purposes of [9 section 19A(2)(d), (e) or (f)] where— 3.212

(a) this is the first occasion on which he has done an act or omission falling within [9 section 19A(2)(d), (e) or (f)] and he has not while claiming a jobseeker's allowance failed to pursue an opportunity of obtaining training without [9 a good reason] or rejected an offer of training without [9 a good reason] or failed to complete a course of training and no certificate has been issued to him under subsection (4) of section 17 with respect to that training; and

(b) at the time he did the act or omission falling within [9 section 19A(2)(d) or (e) or failed to attend a training scheme or employment programme] he was [1. . .] a new jobseeker or, [9 in the case where he has given up a place on a training scheme or employment programme] at the time he first attended the scheme or programme he was [1. . .] a new jobseeker.

(2) Without prejudice to any other circumstances in which a person may be regarded as having [9 a good reason] for any act or omission for the purposes of [9 [10 section 19(2)(c) or (d]] a young person is to be regarded as having [9 a good reason] for any act or omission for the purposes of [9 [10 section 19(2)(c) or (d]] where the employer did not offer suitable training unless he falls within regulation 61(1)(a) or (f) or his jobseeker's allowance has been reduced in accordance with regulation 63 or in accordance with regulation 68 because he has done an act or omission falling within [9 section 19A(2)(d), (e), (f) or (g)] or [9 section 19A(2)(c) or (d)] [9] [10 section 19(2)(a), (b), (c) or (d) read with Part V].

(3) For the purposes of this regulation, "new jobseeker" means a young person who has not since first leaving full-time education been employed or self-employed for 16 or more hours per week or completed a course of training or failed to complete a course of training and no certificate has been issued to him to show [9 a good reason] for that failure under subsection (4) of section 17 or [9 given up a place on a training scheme or employment programme] without [9 a good reason] or done an act or omission falling within [9 section 19A(2)(g)].

AMENDMENTS

1. Jobseeker's Allowance and Income Support (General) (Amendment) Regulations 1996 (SI 1996/1517) reg.13 (October 7, 1996).

2. Jobseeker's Allowance (Joint Claims) Regulations 2000 (SI 2000/1978) reg.2(5) and Sch.2 para.23(a)(i) (March 19, 2001).

3. Jobseeker's Allowance (Joint Claims) Regulations 2000 (SI 2000/1978) reg.2(5) and Sch.2 para.23(a)(ii) (March 19, 2001).

4. Jobseeker's Allowance (Joint Claims) Regulations 2000 (SI 2000/1978) reg.2(5) and Sch.2 para.23(b)(i) (March 19, 2001).

5. Jobseeker's Allowance (Joint Claims) Regulations 2000 (SI 2000/1978) reg.2(5) and Sch.2 para.23(b)(ii) (March 19, 2001).
6. Jobseeker's Allowance (Joint Claims) Regulations 2000 (SI 2000/1978) reg.2(5) and Sch.2 para.23(b)(iii) (March 19, 2001).
7. Jobseeker's Allowance (Joint Claims) Regulations 2000 (SI 2000/1978) reg.2(5) and Sch.2 para.23(c)(i) (March 19, 2001).
8. Jobseeker's Allowance (Joint Claims) Regulations 2000 (SI 2000/1978) reg.2(5) and Sch.2 para.23(c)(ii) (March 19, 2001).
9. Jobseeker's Allowance (Sanctions) (Amendment) Regulations 2012 (SI 2012/2568) reg.5(17) (October 22, 2012).
10. Social Security (Miscellaneous Amendments) Regulations 2013 (SI 2013/443) reg.4(1) and (5) (April 2, 2013).

DEFINITIONS

"full-time education"—see reg.57(1).
"suitable training"—*ibid.*
"training"—*ibid.*
"young person"—*ibid.*

GENERAL NOTE

3.213 See the notes to ss.19–19B of the Jobseekers Act and Pt V of the JSA Regulations for the circumstances in which sanctions may be applied.

Paragraph (1)

3.214 The broad effect of paragraph (1) is to give a "new jobseeker" (see para.(3)) a second chance in certain circumstances where a sanction might otherwise be imposed. He will be deemed to have a good reason for the purposes of s.19A(2)(d), (e) or (f) if this is the first time he has refused or given up, etc. a training scheme or employment programme opportunity.

Paragraph (2)

3.215 This provides that unless a young person has been sanctioned under reg.63 or under reg.68 for a training-related "offence" or refusing a job opportunity or voluntary unemployment or losing a job through misconduct, he will have a good reason for failing to apply for or accept a notified job, or for not taking advantage of a reasonable opportunity of employment if the employer does not offer suitable training (defined in reg.57(1)). There is the usual exception from this rule for a young person who has been laid off or is on short-time working, or who has never been sanctioned for a training-related "offence" or refusing a job opportunity or voluntary unemployment or losing a job through misconduct and has accepted an offer to join the armed forces within the next eight weeks. See also s.64 which provides that a 16- or 17-year-old may limit his availability to employment where the employer provides suitable training.

Paragraph (3)

3.216 See the note to reg.63(4).

Reduced amount of allowance

3.217 **68.**—(1) Subject to paragraphs (2) and (4), the amount of an income-based jobseeker's allowance which would otherwise be payable to a young person shall be reduced by [1, if he is a single person or a lone parent,] a sum equal to 40 per cent of the amount applicable in his case by way of a peronal allowance determined [1in accordance with paragraph 1(1) or 1(2) of Schedule 1 (as the case may be) or, if he is a member of a couple [3(including a joint-claim couple)], sum equal to 40 per cent of the amount which would have been applicable in his case if he had been a single person determined in accordance with paragraph 1(1) of Schedule 1] for a period of two weeks from the beginning of the first week after [2the Secretary of State]'s decision where the young person [4 5 . . .] has done any act or omission falling within [5 section 19(2)(c) or (d) or section 19A(2)(a), (c), (d), (e), (f) or (g)] unless the young person reaches the age of 18 before that two week period expires, in which case the allowance shall be payable at the full rate applicable in his case from the date he reaches the age of 18.

(2) Subject to paragraph (4), in a case where the young person or any member of his family is pregnant or seriously ill the amount of an income-based job-seeker's allowance which would otherwise be payable to the young person shall be reduced by [1, if he is a single person or a lone parent,] a sum equal to 20 per cent of the amount applicable in his case by way of a personal allowance determined [1 in accordance with paragraph 1(1) or 1(2) of Schedule 1 (as the case may be) or, if he is a member of a couple, a sum equal to 20 per cent of the amount which would have been applicable in his case if he had been a single person determined in accordance with paragraph 1(1) of Schedule 1] for a period of two weeks from the beginning of the first week after [2 the Secretary of State]'s decision where the young person [4 5 . . .] has done any act or omission falling within [5 section 19(2)(c) or (d) or section 19A(2)(a), (c), (d), (e), (f) or (g)] unless the young person reaches the age of 18 before that two week period expires, in which case the allowance shall be payable at the full rate applicable in his case from the date he reaches the age of 18.

(3) A reduction under paragraph (1) or (2) shall, if it is not a multiple of 5p, be rounded to the nearest such multiple or if it is a multiple of 2.5p but not of 5p, to the next lower multiple of 5p.

(4) If a young person's claim for an income-based jobseeker's allowance is terminated before the expiry of the period determined in accordance with paragraphs (1) and (2), and he makes a fresh claim for the allowance, it shall be payable to him at the reduced rate determined in accordance with paragraph (1) or (2) for the balance of the time remaining of that two weeks, unless the young person reaches the age of 18 before that two week period expires, in which case the allowance shall be payable at the full rate applicable in his case from the date he reaches the age of 18.

(5) An income-based jobseeker's allowance shall be payable to a young person at the full rate applicable in his case after the expiry of the two week period referred to in paragraphs (1) and (2).

AMENDMENTS

1. Social Security and Child Support (Miscellaneous Amendments) Regulations 1997 (SI 1997/827) reg.3 (April 7, 1997).

2. Social Security Act 1998 (Commencement No.11, and Savings and Consequential and Transitional Provisions) Order 1999 (SI 1999/2860 (C.75)) art.3(1) and (12) and Sch.12 para.2 (October 18 1999).

3. Jobseeker's Allowance (Joint Claims) Regulations 2000 (SI 2000/1978) reg.2(5) and Sch.2 para.24 (March 19, 2001).

4. Jobseeker's Allowance (Sanctions for Failure to Attend) Regulations 2010 (SI 2010/509) reg.2(12) (April 6, 2010).

5. Jobseeker's Allowance (Sanctions) (Amendment) Regulations 2012 (SI 2012/2568) reg.5(18) (October 22, 2012).

DEFINITIONS

"income-based jobseeker's allowance"—see Jobseekers Act s.1(4).
"young person"—see reg.57(1).

GENERAL NOTE

3.218 See the notes to ss.19–19B of the Jobseekers Act and Pt V of the JSA Regulations as to the circumstances in which sanctions may be applied.

The rules as to the amount and duration of a benefit sanction are different from those for adults. A person aged 18 or over who is sanctioned will only be paid JSA (at a reduced rate) if he is in hardship; see regs 140–146. If a young person is "sanctioned" under s.19(2)(c) or (d) or s.19A(2)(a), (c), (d),(e), (f) or (g), his income-based JSA will continue to be paid but at a reduced rate. (Note that this does not apply if the sanction is imposed under s.19(2)(a) or (b), or s.19A(2)(b), in such a case the young person will only qualify for JSA if he can show hardship.) The reduction is 40 per cent of the appropriate single person or lone parent personal allowance under para.1 of Sch.1 or 20 per cent if the young person or any member of the family is pregnant or seriously ill. If the person is a member of a couple the same reduction is applied as if he was a single claimant. It lasts for two weeks but will cease if the young person becomes 18 within that time. If the young person stops receiving JSA before the end of the two weeks but then claims JSA again, the reduction will be applied for the unexpired balance of the two-week period or until the person reaches 18.

PART V

SANCTIONS

[[1]The period of a reduction under section 19: higher-level sanctions

3.219 **69.**—(1) Subject to paragraphs (3) and (4), a reduction under section 19 (higher level sanctions) is to have effect for—

(a) 13 weeks, where there has been no previous sanctionable failure by the claimant that falls within paragraph (2);
(b) 26 weeks, where there has been only one previous sanctionable failure by the claimant that falls within paragraph (2);
(c) 156 weeks, where there have been two or more previous sanctionable failures by the claimant that fall within paragraph (2)(a) and, if applicable, (b) and the most recent of those failures—
    (i) falls within paragraph (2)(c), and
    (ii) resulted in a reduction that has effect for 26 weeks under sub-paragraph (b) or 156 weeks under this sub-paragraph, or would have done but for paragraph (4).

(2) A previous sanctionable failure referred to in paragraph (1) falls within this paragraph if—

(a) the failure resulted in a decision to reduce the claimant's award in accordance with section 19;

(b) in the case of a joint-claim couple, the failure was by the same claimant; and
(c) the date of the failure is within 52 weeks but not within 2 weeks of the date of the claimant's current sanctionable failure.

(3) Where a claimant's award has been reduced in relation to a sanctionable failure which is specified in section 19(2)(a), (b) or (d) and which occurred before the date of claim for a jobseeker's allowance, any such failure must not be counted for the purpose of determining the period of a reduction for a subsequent sanctionable failure under section 19.

(4) Where a sanctionable failure which is specified in section 19(2)(a), (b) or (d) occurs on or before the date on which a claim for a jobseeker's allowance is made—

(a) except where sub-paragraph (b) applies, the reduction relating to that failure is to have effect for the period set out in paragraph (1) that applies in the claimant's case (the "applicable sanction period") minus the period beginning with the day after the date of the sanctionable failure and ending with the day before the date of claim;
(b) if—
  (i) the failure was in relation to employment which was due to last for a limited period,
  (ii) the limited period ends on or before the end of the applicable sanction period, and
  (iii) the date of claim is on or before the last day of the limited period,

the reduction relating to that failure is to have effect for the period beginning with the day after the date of the sanctionable failure and ending with the last day of the limited period minus the period beginning with the day after the date of the sanctionable failure and ending with the day before the date of claim.

(5) In paragraph (4)(b), "limited period" means a specific term which is fixed, or which can be ascertained, before it begins, by reference to some relevant circumstance.

(6) The period of a reduction under section 19 begins—

(a) on the first day of the benefit week in which the sanctionable failure occurred where, on the date of the determination to reduce the award, the claimant has not been paid a jobseeker's allowance since the sanctionable failure occurred; or
(b) in any other case, on the first day of the benefit week after the end of the benefit week in respect of which the claimant was last paid a jobseeker's allowance.]

AMENDMENT

1. Jobseeker's Allowance (Sanctions) (Amendment) Regulations 2012 (SI 2012/2568) reg.2(2) (October 22, 2012).

DEFINITIONS

"current sanctionable failure"—see reg.75(5).
"sanctionable failure"—*ibid*.

GENERAL NOTE

3.220 Higher-level sanctions are applicable to failures under s.19 of the old style Jobseekers Act 1995. No failures under s.19A can come within the present regulation. If the circumstances fall within both sections only the s.19 sanction can apply (s.19A(3)). There is a distinction between certain sanctionable failures that occurred on or before the date of claim and other failures within s.19. The pre-claim failures identified in para.(4) are losing employment through misconduct, without a good reason voluntarily leaving employment and without a good reason neglecting to avail oneself of a reasonable opportunity of employment.

The general rule in para.(1)(a) for all cases is that the reduction period is 13 weeks if there have been no other higher-level sanctionable failures in the previous 52 weeks, 26 weeks if there has been one other such failure in that period and 156 weeks (three years) if there have been two or more such failures in that previous 52 weeks. The failure must be by the same person concerned, even in the case of a joint-claim couple (para.(2)(b)). The general rule is subject first to the rule in para.(2)(a) that only a sanctionable failure that resulted in a reduction in benefit counts for this purpose as a previous failure. Secondly, under para.(2)(c) any sanctionable failure occurring within two weeks of the date of claim is disregarded. The pre-claim failures identified in para.(4) are also disregarded for this purpose (para.(3)).

For pre-claim sanctionable failures under para.(4)(a) the number of days between the date of the failure and the date of the relevant claim is deducted from the number of days in the reduction period calculated as under para.(1). That is subject to the further rule that if the sanctionable failure relates to paid work that was due to last only for a limited period, the period down to the date when the work was due to end is substituted for the para.(4)(a) period in the calculation. Presumably that is to give an incentive to people to take such work. See also reg.70A(1) (removing the possibility of a reduction of benefit if the JSA claim is made outside the period of reduction that would otherwise have applied to such a pre-claim failure).

Paragraph (6) stipulates when the period of reduction under a s.19 sanction starts. The amount of the reduction is set by reg.70.

The form of paras (1) and (2) is to be amended with effect from July 25, 2016 by SI 2016/678 to clarify their operation and close some unintended gaps.

[1The period of a reduction under section 19A: Other sanctions

3.221 **69A.**—(1) A reduction under section 19A (other sanctions) is to have effect for—

(a) 4 weeks, where there has been no previous sanctionable failure by the claimant that falls within paragraph (2); or

(b) 13 weeks, where there has been—

(i) only one previous sanctionable failure by the claimant that falls within paragraph (2), or

(ii) more than one previous sanctionable failure and the most recent of those failures falls within paragraph (2).

(2) A previous sanctionable failure falls within this paragraph if—

(a) the failure resulted in a decision to reduce the claimant's award in accordance with section 19A;

(b) in the case of a joint-claim couple, the failure was by the same claimant; and

(c) the date of the failure is within 52 weeks but not within 2 weeks of the date of the claimant's current sanctionable failure.

(3) The period of a reduction under section 19A begins—

(a) on the first day of the benefit week in which the sanctionable failure occurred where, on the date of the determination to reduce the award, the claimant has not been paid a jobseeker's allowance since the sanctionable failure occurred; or

(b) in any other case, on the first day of the benefit week after the end of the benefit week in respect of which the claimant was last paid a jobseeker's allowance.]

AMENDMENT

1. Jobseeker's Allowance (Sanctions) (Amendment) Regulations 2012 (SI 2012/2568) reg.2(2) (October 22, 2012).

DEFINITIONS

"benefit week"—see reg.1(3).
"claimant"—see Jobseekers Act 1995 s.35(1).
"current sanctionable failure"—see reg.75(5).
"a joint-claim couple"—see Jobseekers Act 1995 ss.35(1) and 1(4).
"sanctionable failure"—see reg.75(5).
"week"—see reg.75(3).

GENERAL NOTE

Made under s.19A, which sets out other conduct ranking as a sanctionable failure in respect of which an award of old style JSA is to be reduced, this provision sets the period for which the reduction is to apply. Basically, looking at things over a 52-week period and looking at the same person (whether single or the defaulting member in a joint couple), the period is four weeks for a first "offence" and 13 weeks for a subsequent offence (paras (1) and (2)). At least two weeks must have elapsed between "offences" (para.(2)(c)). Paragraph (3) stipulates when the period of reduction under s.19A begins. The amount of reduction is set by reg.70. 3.222

Note that reg.70A(2)–(5) prevents a reduction in benefit following from certain s.19A sanctionable failures.

The form of paras (1) and (2) is to be amended with effect from July 25, 2016 by SI 2016/678 to clarify their operation and close some unintended gaps.

[[1]The period of a reduction under section 19B: Claimants ceasing to be available for employment etc.

69B.—(1) Subject to paragraph (5), the amount of an award of a jobseeker's allowance, other than a joint-claim jobseeker's allowance, is to be reduced in accordance with this regulation and regulation 70 (amount of a reduction) if the claimant— 3.223

(a) was previously entitled to a jobseeker's allowance, or was a member of a couple entitled to a joint-claim jobseeker's allowance; and
(b) ceased to be so entitled by failing to comply with the condition in section 1(2)(a) or (c) (availability for employment and actively seeking employment).

(2) Subject to paragraph (5), the amount of an award of a joint-claim jobseeker's allowance is to be reduced in accordance with this regulation and regulation 70 (amount of a reduction) if the case falls within either paragraph (3) or (4).

(3) A case falls within this paragraph if—

(a) one of the claimants was previously entitled to a jobseeker's allowance, other than a joint-claim jobseeker's allowance; and
(b) ceased to be so entitled by failing to comply with the condition in section 1(2)(a) [[2]or (c)] .

(4) A case falls within this paragraph if—

(a) the couple were previously entitled to a joint-claim jobseeker's allowance but ceased to be so entitled by either or both of them failing to comply with the condition in section 1(2)(a) or (c); or

(b) either member of the couple was a member of another couple previously entitled to such an allowance and that couple ceased to be so entitled by that person failing to comply with the condition in section 1(2)(a) or (c).

(5) This regulation does not apply where—

(a) the claimant had been treated as available for work under regulation 14 (circumstances in which a person is to be treated as available), or as actively seeking employment under regulation 19 (circumstances in which a person is to be treated as actively seeking employment);

(b) the claimant ceased to be so treated due to no longer falling within regulation 14 or 19;

(c) as a result of (b), the claimant's award was terminated for failing to comply with the conditions in section 1(2)(a) or (c) (availability for employment and actively seeking employment); and

(d) the Secretary of State considers that a reduction is not appropriate in the claimant's circumstances.

(6) Subject to paragraph (7), a reduction under this regulation is to have effect for a period of—

(a) 4 weeks, where there has been only one occasion on which the claimant's previous entitlement ceased; or

(b) 13 weeks, where there have been two or more occasions on which the claimant's previous entitlement ceased and the date of the most recent occasion was within 52 weeks but not within 2 weeks of the last previous occasion.

(7) The period specified in paragraph (6) is to be reduced by the period beginning with the first day of the benefit week following the benefit week in which the claimant was last paid an award of jobseeker's allowance and ending with the day before the date of claim [2 or where regulation 3(g) of the Claims and Payments Regulations applies, the day before the suspension ends].

(8) The period of a reduction under this regulation begins on the date of claim] [2 or where regulation 3(g) of the Claims and Payments Regulations applies, the date on which the suspension ends.]

AMENDMENTS

1. Jobseeker's Allowance (Sanctions) (Amendment) Regulations 2012 (SI 2012/2568) reg.2(2) (October 22, 2012).

2. Social Security (Miscellaneous Amendments) Regulations 2013 (SI 2013/443) reg.4(8) (April 2, 2013).

DEFINITIONS

"Claims and Payments Regulations"—see reg.1(3).
"couple"—*ibid.*
"a joint-claim jobseeker's allowance"—see Jobseekers Act 1995 ss.35(1) and 1(4).
"week"—see reg.75(3).

GENERAL NOTE

3.224 Section 19B of the old style Jobseekers Act 1995 enables regulations to provide for an award of old style JSA to be reduced in respect of a claim for a period not exceeding 13 weeks where a previous JSA entitlement had ended because of failing to be available for or actively seeking employment. When a reduction is to apply is set out in paras (1)–(5) of this regulation. Paragraph (1) deals with JSA claims other than joint claims. Paragraphs (2)–(4) deal with joint claims, differentiating situations: (i) where one of the joint-claim couple had previously been entitled to non-joint-claim JSA terminated because of non-availability (para.(3)); and (ii) where a previous joint-claim award of JSA ended because one or both had not complied with availability and/or actively seeking employment requirements (para.(4)). The regulation does not apply in cases covered by para.(5). This deals with the situation where the claimant's award of JSA had been terminated because of no longer being being treated as available or actively seeking employment under regs 14 or 19 (paras (5)(a)–(c)). In such a case this regulation will not apply where the Secretary of State considers that a reduction is not appropriate to the claimant's circumstances (para. (5)(d)).

The period of reduction is set by paras (6) and (7) (broadly speaking four weeks for a first offence and 13 weeks for a subsequent one). There must be at least two weeks between "offences". The start of the period of reduction is stipulated as the date of claim (reg.69(8)). The amount of reduction is set by reg.70.

Regulation 70A does not apply to reductions under s.19B.

The form of paras (1) and (2) is to be amended with effect from July 25, 2016 by SI 2016/678 to clarify their operation and close some unintended gaps.

[1The amount of a reduction under section 19 and 19A and regulation 69B

70.—(1) Subject to paragraph (2), the amount of a reduction under section 19 or 19A or regulation 69B is— 3.225

(a) 100% of the allowance payable to the claimant; or

(b) in the case of a joint-claim couple—

(i) 100% of the allowance payable to the couple, where the reduction relates to a sanctionable failure by each member of the couple, or

(ii) an amount calculated in accordance with paragraph (3), where the reduction relates to a sanctionable failure by only one member of the couple.

(2) In a case where the following circumstances apply —

(a) a claimant's award is already reduced in accordance with section 19 or 19A or regulation 69B; or

(b) in the case of a joint-claim couple, an award of a joint-claim jobseeker's allowance is already reduced in accordance with section 19 or 19A or regulation 69B as a result of a sanctionable failure by one or each member of the couple and the current sanctionable failure is by the same claimant,

no reduction is to be made for any days when those circumstances apply.

(3) The amount referred to in paragraph (1)(b)(ii) is such amount which, after its deduction from the full amount of the award of a joint-claim jobseeker's allowance, leaves the following amount—

(a) in any case in which the member of the couple, who is not the member whose sanctionable failure led to the reduction, satisfies the conditions set out in section 2 of the Act (contribution based conditions), a rate equal to the amount calculated in accordance with section 4(1) (amount payable by way of a jobseeker's allowance);

(b) in any case where the couple are a couple in hardship for the purposes of Part IXA, a rate equal to the amount calculated in accordance with regulation 146G (applicable amount in hardship cases for joint-claim couples);

(c) in any other case, a rate calculated in accordance with section 4(3A)(5) (amount payable by way of a joint-claim jobseeker's allowance) save that the applicable amount shall be the amount determined by reference to paragraph 1(1) of Schedule 1 which would have been the applicable amount had the member of the couple who is not subject to sanctions been a single claimant.

AMENDMENT

1. Jobseeker's Allowance (Sanctions) (Amendment) Regulations 2012 (SI 2012/2568) reg.2(3) (4) (October 22, 2012).

DEFINITIONS

"the Act"—see reg.1(3).
"claimant"—see Jobseekers Act 1995 s.35(1).
"current sanctionable failure"—see reg.75(5).
"a joint-claim couple"—see Jobseekers Act 1995 ss.35(1) and 1(4).
"a joint-claim jobseeker's allowance"—*ibid.*
"sanctionable failure"—see reg.75(5).

GENERAL NOTE

3.226 This sets the amount of the reduction under ss.19 or 19A of the Act and under reg.69B. Basically, this means a reduction of 100 per cent for a single claimant and where each member of a joint-claim couple commits a sanctionable failure (para. (1)(a) and (b)(i)), with a lesser reduction where the sanctionable failure is only by one member of such a couple (paras (1)(b)(ii), (3)). No reduction is, however, to be made for any days when the circumstances in para.(2) apply.

[1Cases in which no reduction is to be made under section 19 or 19A

3.227 **70A.**—(1) No reduction is to be made under section 19 (higher-level sanctions) where—

(a) the sanctionable failure is listed in section 19(2)(a), (b), or (d);

(b) the sanctionable failure occurs before a claim to a jobseeker's allowance is made; and

(c) the period of the reduction as calculated under sub-paragraph (a) or (b) of regulation 69(4) is the same as, or shorter than, the period between the date of the sanctionable failure and the date of claim.

(2) No reduction is to be made under section 19A (other sanctions) where the sanctionable failure is specified in section 19A(2)(a) (failure to comply with regulations under section 8(1) or (1A)) and—

(a) is a failure to comply with regulation 24 (provision of information and evidence); or

(b) unless paragraph (3) or (4) applies, is a failure to comply with regulation 23 (attendance) or 23A (attendance by members of a joint-claim couple)(6).

(3) This paragraph applies where the claimant—

(a) fails to [2participate] on the day specified in a relevant notification;

(b) makes contact with an employment officer in the manner set out in a relevant notification before the end of the period of five working days beginning with the first working day after the day on which the claimant failed to [2participate] on the day specified; and

(c) fails to show a good reason for that failure to [²participate].

(4) This paragraph applies where—

[²(a) the claimant fails to participate in an interview at the time specified in a relevant notification, but makes contact with an employment officer in the manner set out in the notification on the day specified in the notification;]

[²(b) the Secretary of State has informed the claimant in writing that a failure to participate in an interview at the time specified in a relevant notification, on the next occasion on which a claimant is required to participate in an interview] may result in the claimant's entitlement to a jobseeker's allowance or a joint-claim jobseeker's allowance ceasing or the award being subject to a reduction;

(c) the claimant fails to [²participate in an interview at the time specified] in a relevant notification on the next occasion;

(d) the claimant makes contact with an employment officer in the manner set out in a relevant notification before the end of the period of five working days after the day on which the claimant failed to [²participate in an interview at the time specified]; and

(e) the claimant fails to show a good reason for that failure to [²participate in an interview at the time specified].

(5) In this regulation, "relevant notification" has the meaning given in regulation 25.]

AMENDMENTS

1. Jobseeker's Allowance (Sanctions) (Amendment) Regulations 2012 (SI 2012/2568) reg.2(3) and (4) (October 22, 2012).

2. Social Security (Miscellaneous Amendments) Regulations 2013 (SI 2013/443) reg.4(7) (April 2, 2013).

DEFINITIONS

"claimant"—see Jobseekers Act 1995 s.35(1).
"date of claim"—see reg.1(3).
"employment officer"—see Jobseekers Act 1995 s.35(1).
"a joint-claim jobseeker's allowance"—see Jobseekers Act 1995 ss.35(1) and 1(4).
"relevant notification"—see para.(5); reg.25.
"sanctionable failure"—see reg.75(5).

GENERAL NOTE

Paragraph (1)

This sets out the situations in which no reduction is to be made in respect of certain sanctionable failures in s.19 (higher-level sanctions). The potentially relevant failures are those under s.19(2)(a) (misconduct), (b) (voluntarily leaving or (d) (neglect to avail) which occurred before the JSA claim was made. In such a case, no reduction of JSA is to be made where the otherwise applicable period of the reduction under reg.69 is the same as or shorter than the period of no-claim after the date of the sanctionable failure. **3.228**

Paragraphs (2)–(4)

This stipulates that no reduction is to be made in respect of sanctionable failures under s.19A(2)(a) (failure to comply with regulations made under s.8(1) or (1A) of the Act) where the failure is failure to comply with reg.24 (provision of information or evidence). Nor is one to be made in respect of failure to comply with regs 23 or 23A (attendance, i.e. participation in an interview, by single claimant or joint-claim **3.229** couple), unless either para.(3) or (4) applies. See the annotations to regs 23 and 24 for the interactions.

[1Sanctionable failures under section 19: schemes under section 17A(1)

3.230 **70B.**—(1) Mandatory Work Activity is a prescribed scheme for the purposes of section 19(2)(e) (higher level sanctions).

(2) In paragraph (1) "Mandatory Work Activity" means a scheme under section 17A(1) (schemes for assisting persons to obtain employment; "work for your benefit" schemes etc) designed to provide work or work-related activity for up to 30 hours per week over a period of four consecutive weeks with a view to assisting claimants to improve their prospects of obtaining employment.]

Amendment

1. Jobseeker's Allowance (Sanctions) (Amendment) Regulations 2012 (SI 2012/2568) reg.2(3) and (4) (October 22, 2012).

General Note

3.231 This makes Mandatory Work Activity (as defined in para.(2)) a prescribed scheme for the purposes of the sanctionable failure set out in s.19(2)(e), applying a higher level sanction in respect of failure to participate in a scheme within s.17A designed to assist in obtaining employment, which is prescribed for purposes of s.19.

Mandatory Work Activity is a scheme under s.17A(1) by virtue of the Jobseeker's Allowance (Mandatory Work Activity Scheme) Regulations 2011, which have been found to be validly made by the Court of Appeal in *Smith v Secretary of State for Work and Pensions* ([2015] EWCA Civ 229, affirming the decision of Hickinbottom J ([2014] EWHC 843 (Admin)) on essentially the same reasoning. See further the annotations to s.17A and to the MWAS Regulations.

[1Application of a reduction to a new award

3.232 **70C.**—(1) Subject to paragraph (4), this regulation applies where—

(a) the amount of an award is reduced in accordance with section 19 or 19A or regulation 69B;

(b) that award ("the previous award") is terminated;

(c) the reduction period had either not yet begun or not ended when the previous award was terminated;

(d) a new award is made to the claimant who had been entitled to the previous award; and

(e) in the case of an award of a joint-claim jobseeker's allowance, the reduction to the previous award was made in relation to a sanctionable failure by the claimant who is entitled to the new award.

(2) Where this regulation applies, the reduction period that would have applied to the previous award but for the award having terminated applies to the new award from the first day of the benefit week in which the claim for the new award is made for the outstanding period.

(3) In this regulation—

"outstanding period" means the period determined under regulation 69, 69A or 69B in relation to the previous award minus—

(a) the benefit weeks in respect of which the previous award was reduced; and

(b) the period beginning with the first day of the benefit week after the benefit week in which the previous award was terminated and ending with the first day of the benefit week in which entitlement to the new award begins;

"reduction period" means the period determined under regulation 69, 69A or 69B in relation to the previous award.

(4) This regulation does not apply where the Secretary of State is satisfied that, since the date of the most recent sanctionable failure, the claimant has been in employment for a period of, or more than one period where the total of those periods amounts to, at least 26 weeks.]

AMENDMENT

1. Jobseeker's Allowance (Sanctions) (Amendment) Regulations 2012 (SI 2012/2568) reg.2(3) and (4) (October 22, 2012).

DEFINITIONS

"benefit week"—see reg.1(3).
"claimant"—see Jobseekers Act 1995 s.35(1).
"a joint-claim jobseeker's allowance"—see Jobseekers Act 1995 ss.35(1) and 1(4).
"sanctionable failure"—see reg.75(5).
"week"—see reg.75(3).

GENERAL NOTE

This deals with the situation where a reduction of old style JSA has been made under ss.19 or 19A or reg.69B, but the award was terminated before the reduction period began or before it had ended. In such a case, the unexpired part of the reduction period (eroded by the intervening weeks before the beginning of the new award: head (b) of definition of "outstanding period" in para.(3)) is carried over into a new award of JSA to the person entitled to the previous award subject to the sanction. Note that under para.(4) this does not apply where the Secretary of State is satisfied that since the date of the most recent sanctionable failure the claimant has been in work for a period of 26 weeks or combined periods totalling 26 weeks. 3.233

Voluntary redundancy

71.—(1) A claimant is to be treated as not having left his employment voluntarily— 3.234

(a) where he has been dismissed by his employer by reason of redundancy after volunteering or agreeing to be so dismissed, [1 . . .]
(b) where he has left his employment on a date agreed with his employer without being dismissed, in pursuance of an agreement relating to voluntary redundancy, [1 or
(c) where he has been laid-off or kept on short-time to the extent specified in [2 section 148 of the Employment Rights Act 1996], and has complied with the requirements of that section.]

(2) In paragraph (1) "redundancy" means one of the facts set out in paragraphs (a) and (b) of section [2 139(1) of the Employment Rights Act 1996].

AMENDMENTS

1. Jobseeker's Allowance (Amendment) Regulations 1996 (SI 1996/1516) reg.5 (October 7, 1996).
2. Social Security (Miscellaneous Amendments) (No.5) Regulations 2007 (SI 2007/2618) reg.8(5) (October 1, 2007).

DEFINITIONS

"claimant"—see Jobseekers Act s.35(1).
"employment"—see reg.75(4).

GENERAL NOTE

3.235 Section 19(7) of the old style Jobseekers Act 1995 enables the making of regulations setting out circumstances in which a person who might otherwise be regarded, under the normal rules discussed in the notes to s.19(6), as having left employment voluntarily, is to be treated as not having left voluntarily. This regulation is the result, covering a number of instances of voluntary redundancy.

Regulation 71 provides that a claimant is not to be treated as having left voluntarily in three situations. First, it protects the claimant who has been dismissed by his employer by reason of redundancy after volunteering or agreeing to be so dismissed. The reference to "dismissal" might be thought unfortunate if it were to perpetuate or risk reopening old controversies on its precise meaning. Were it the sole protective limb, *R(U)3/91* ought probably to be followed to give it a wide meaning. But in any event the narrower meaning cannot, given the wording and structure of the new provision, have the same detrimental consequences, since the second limb of reg.71(1) now protects a claimant who has left his employment on a date agreed with his employer *without being dismissed*, in pursuance of an agreement relating to voluntary redundancy. "Redundancy", rather than dismissal, is thus the key limiting factor in these protective limbs. It means one of the facts set out in s.139(1) of the Employment Rights Act 1996 (reg.71(2)). That subsection provides two facts: (a) the fact that the employer has ceased, or intends to cease, to carry on the business in the place where the employee [the JSA claimant] was employed; and (b) the fact that the requirements of that business for employees to carry out work of a particular kind, or for employees to carry out work of a particular kind in the place where [the claimant] was employed, have ceased or diminished or are expected to cease do diminish.

The third situation of protection afforded by reg.71 embraces the claimant who has been laid off or kept on short-time to the extent specified in s.148 of the Employment Rights Act 1996 and has complied with the requirements of that section, thus protecting claimants like the one in *CU/71/94* and thereby going wider than the range of protections previously afforded by SSCBA 1992 s.28(4), even when that section was interpreted broadly. Section 148 of the 1996 Act enables a person laid off or kept on short time to claim a redundancy payment if he serves on his employer written notice of his intention to do so. He must have been laid off or kept on short time either for four or more consecutive weeks or for a series of six or more weeks within a period of 13 weeks prior to service of the notice. To get the s.148 payment, the employee must terminate the contract of employment and not be dismissed by the employer.

[1Good reason for the purpose of section 19(2)(c) and (d) and 19A(2)(c)

3.236 **72.**—A person is not to be regarded as having a good reason for any act or omission for the purposes of section 19(2)(c) and (d) and section 19A(2)(c) if, and to the extent that, the reason for that act or omission relates to the time it took, or would normally take, for the person to travel from his home to the place of the employment, or a place mentioned in the jobseeker's direction, and back to his home where that time was or is normally less than [2one hour and thirty minutes either way,] by a route and means appropriate to his circumstances and to the employment, or to the carrying out of the jobseeker's direction, unless, in view of the health of the person or any caring responsibilities of his, that time was or is unreasonable.]

AMENDMENTS

1. Jobseeker's Allowance (Sanctions) (Amendment) Regulations 2012 (SI 2012/2568) reg.2(5) (October 22, 2012)

2. Social Security (Miscellaneous Amendments) (No.2) Regulations 2012 (SI 2012/2575) reg.3(3) (November 5, 2012).

Regulations 73 and 73A revoked by Jobseeker's Allowance (Sanctions) (Amendment) Regulations 2012 (SI 2012/2568) reg.2(6) from October 22, 2012.

Person of prescribed description for the purpose of section 20(3)

74.—(1) Subject to paragraph (2), a person shall be of a prescribed description for the purposes of section 20(3) [1. . .] (exemption from non-payment of jobseeker's allowance) and shall not fall within [1section 19(2)(b) or (d)] [1. . .] if he has neither worked in employed earner's employment, nor has been a self-employed earner, nor been a full-time student nor been in relevant education, during the period of 13 weeks preceding the day of the commencement of the employment. 3.237

(2) For the purposes of paragraph (1), a person shall not be regarded as having—

(a) worked in employed earner's employment; or

(b) been a self-employed earner; or

(c) been a full-time student or been in relevant education;

by reason only of any engagement in an activity referred to in paragraph (3) or by his attendance for a period of up to 14 days at a work camp.

(3) The activities referred to in this paragraph are—

(a) the manning or launching of a lifeboat; or

(b) the performance of duty as a part-time member of a fire brigade.

(4) A trial period in section 20(3) [1. . .] means a period of 8 weeks beginning with the commencement of the fifth week of the employment in question and ending at the end of the twelfth week of that employment and for the purposes of this definition in determining the time at which the fifth week of the employment in question commences or at which the twelfth week of that employment ends, any week in which a person has not worked in the employment for at least 16 hours shall be disregarded.

AMENDMENT

1. Jobseeker's Allowance (Sanctions) (Amendment) Regulations 2012 (SI 2012/2568) reg.2(7) (October 22, 2012).

DEFINITIONS

"employed earner"—see regs 3 and 75(4); SSCBA 1992 s.2(1)(a).
"employment"—see reg.75(4).
"full-time student"—see reg.1(3).
"part-time member of a fire brigade"—see reg.4.
"relevant education"—see Jobseekers Act 1995 s.35(2) and Sch.1 para.14 and reg.54.
"self-employed earner"—see reg.1(3); SSCBA 1992 s.2(1)(b).
"week"—see reg.75(3).
"work camp"—see reg.4.

GENERAL NOTE

3.238 Taken together, s.20(3) of the old style Jobseekers Act 1995 and this regulation protect from preclusion from JSA under the voluntarily leaving employment without good reason head of s.19(2)(b) or under s.19(2)(d) (neglect without a good reason to avail oneself of a reasonable opportunity of employment) certain persons who leave employment voluntarily without a good reason at any time during a trial period.

These provisions are designed to encourage people to enter or re-enter employment who may be apprehensive about taking up work, fearful that they might not be able to handle it or that it might prove unsuitable and they might have to leave it. The encouragement is afforded by reducing the fear of preclusion from benefit should their fears be realised and they have to give up the job. An example of such people might be carers who have been out of the job market caring for sick or elderly relatives, but the provisions are by no means so limited. Specifically, the persons protected by the provisions are those who have neither worked in employed earner's employment nor been a self-employed earner, nor a full-time student or in relevant education during the 13-week period preceding the day of commencement of the employment. It is specifically stated that engagement in certain activities does not constitute working in employed earner's employment, being a self-employed earner or having been a full-time student or in relevant education: the manning or launching of a lifeboat; the performance of duty as a part-time member of a fire brigade; or attendance for a period of up to 14 days at a work camp (paras (2) and (3)).

"Trial period" is a period of eight weeks beginning with the commencement of the fifth week of the employment in question and ending at the end of the 12th week of that employment. In determining when the fifth week commences or when the 12th week ends, one disregards any week in which the claimant worked in the employment for less than 16 hours.

3.239 Note that there appears to be no requirement that the claimant has taken up the employment on a "trial basis". Note also that protection is afforded those persons "who leave that employment voluntarily *and without good reason*" (subs.(3), emphasis supplied by annotator). In some circumstances those who leave employment taken on a trial basis because it proves unsuitable may well have good reason for voluntarily leaving, thus obviating the need to rely on this subsection, being protected from preclusion under s.19(2)(b) by the terms of that provision, if interpreted in the light of case law on "just cause" from the comparable UB context. Since establishing "just cause" may well be more difficult to establish than "good reason" (see further the notes to s.19(2)(b)), such persons would surely also have "good reason" so as to protect them from the "neglect to avail" preclusion in s.19(2)(d).

"Week" is defined for the purposes of this regulation as any period of seven consecutive days (reg.75(3)). That differs from the predecessor "trial period" provisions where week then meant a period of seven days beginning with a Sunday. But even had the new definition then been applicable, it would not have assisted the unfortunate claimant in *R(U)1/92*, since he had only completed the requisite number of "working" as opposed to "seven day" weeks.

3.240 *Regulation 74A revoked by Social Security (Miscellaneous Amendments) (No.2) Regulations 2012 (SI 2012/2575) reg.3 from November 5, 2012.*

3.241 *Regulation 74B revoked by Jobseeker's Allowance (Sanctions) (Amendment) Regulations 2012 (SI 2012/2568) reg.2(8) from October 22, 2012.*

Interpretation

3.242 **75.**—(1) For the purposes of [2 section 19A] and of this Part:

[2 (a) "an employment programme" means a programme or scheme which is designed to assist a claimant to prepare for or move into work;
(b) "a training scheme" means a scheme or course which is designed to assist a claimant to gain the skills, knowledge or experience that will make it more likely, in the opinion of the Secretary of State, that the claimant will obtain work or be able to do so;
(2) [2 . . .]

[2(3) In section 19A and in this Part, "week" means any period of 7 consecutive days.]

[3(4) In section 19 and 19A][3 and in this Part, "employment" means employed earner's employment other than such employment in which a person is employed whilst participating in an employment programme falling within paragraph (1)(a) and "employed earner" shall be construed accordingly; and for the purposes of paragraph (4) of regulation 70C includes self-employment where the claimant's income as calculated under Part VIII exceeds his applicable amount as calculated under sections 4(1), 12 and 13 of the Act.]

(5) [2 In this Part,

"current sanctionable failure" means a failure which is sanctionable under section 19 (higher-level sanctions), 19A (other sanctions) or 19B (claimants ceasing to be available for employment etc) in relation to which the Secretary of State has not yet determined whether the amount of an award is to be reduced in accordance with section 19 or 19A or regulation 69B;]

[3 . . .];

[2"sanctionable failure" means a failure which is sanctionable under section 19 (higher-level sanctions), 19A (other sanctions) or 19B (claimants ceasing to be available for employment etc).]

AMENDMENTS

1. Social Security (Miscellaneous Amendments) Regulations 2008 (SI 2008/698) reg.4(9) (April 14, 2008).
2. Jobseeker's Allowance (Sanctions) (Amendment) Regulations 2012 (SI 2012/2568) reg.2(9) (October 22, 2012).
3. Social Security (Miscellaneous Amendments) Regulations 2013 (SI 2013/443) reg.4(6) (April 2, 2013).

DEFINITIONS

"the Act"—see reg.1(3).
"claimant"—see Jobseekers Act 1995 s.35(1).
"employed earner"—see reg.3.

PART VI

MEMBERSHIP OF THE FAMILY

Persons of a prescribed description

76.—(1) Subject to paragraph (2), a person of a prescribed description for the purposes of the definition of "family" in section 35(1) of the Act is a **3.243**

person [3 who falls within the definition of qualifying young person in section 142 of the Benefits Act (child and qualifying young person)], and in these Regulations, except in Part IV, such a person is referred to as a "young person".

(2) Paragraph (1) shall not apply to a person who is—

(a) [3 . . .]

(b) entitled to a jobseeker's allowance or would, but for section 3(1)(d) of the Act (provision against dual entitlement) be so entitled; or

(c) entitled to income support or would, but for section 134(2) of the Benefits Act (exclusion from benefit) be [2 so entitled; or

(d) a person to whom section 6 of the Children (Leaving Care) Act 2000 (exclusion from benefits) applies.] [4 or

(e) entitled to an income-related employment and support allowance or would, but for paragraph 6(1)(d) of Schedule 1 to the Welfare Reform Act (conditions of entitlement to income-related employment and support allowance), be entitled [5 ; or

(f) entitled to universal credit].]

[1(3) A person of a prescribed description for the purposes of the definition of "family" in section 35(1) of the Act includes a child or young person in respect of whom section 145A of the Benefits Act applies for the purposes of entitlement to child benefit but only for the period prescribed under section 145A(1) of that Act.]

Definitions

"the Act"—see reg.1(3).
"course of advanced education"—*ibid.*

Amendments

1. Income-related Benefits and Jobseeker's Allowance (Working Tax Credit and Child Credit) (Amendment) Regulations 2002 (SI 2002/2402) reg.3 and Sch.2 para.2 (April 6, 2003).

2. Children (Leaving Care) Act 2000 (Commencement No.2 and Consequential Provisions) Order 2001 (SI 2001/3070) art.3(5) and Sch.4.

3. Social Security (Young Persons) Amendment Regulations 2006 (SI 2006/718) reg.3(6) (April 10, 2006).

4. Employment and Support Allowance (Consequential Provisions) (No.2) Regulations 2008 (SI 2008/1554) reg.3(1) and (12) (October 27, 2008).

5. Universal Credit (Consequential, Supplementary, Incidental and Miscellaneous Provisions) Regulations 2013 (SI 2013/630) reg.30(1) and (3) (April 29, 2013).

General Note

3.244 This regulation is very similar to reg.14 of the Income Support Regulations, except that para.(2) contains an additional exception that the person must not be entitled to income support in their own right (sub-para.(c)). Note that para.(1) expressly provides that this definition of "young person" does not apply for the purposes of Pt IV (entitlement of 16- and 17-year-olds to JSA).

See the note to reg.14 of the Income Support Regulations.

Circumstances in which a person is to be treated as responsible or not responsible for another

3.245 **77.**—(1) Subject to the following provisions of this regulation, a person is to be treated for the purposes of the Act as responsible for a child or young person for whom he is receiving child benefit [1and this includes a child or young person to whom paragraph (3) of regulation 76 applies.]

(2) In a case where a child ("the first child") is in receipt of child benefit in respect of another child ("the second child"), the person treated as responsible for the first child in accordance with the provisions of this regulation shall also be treated as responsible for the second child.

(3) In the case of a child or young person in respect of whom no person is receiving child benefit, the person who shall be treated as responsible for that child or young person shall be—

(a) except where sub-paragraph (b) applies, the person with whom the child or young person usually lives; or

(b) where only one claim for child benefit has been made in respect of the child or young person, the person who made that claim.

(4) Where regulation 78(7) (circumstances in which a person is to be treated as being or not being a member of the household) applies in respect of a child or young person, that child or young person shall be treated as the responsibility of the claimant for that part of the week for which he is under that regulation treated as being a member of the claimant's household.

(5) Except where paragraph (4) applies, a child or young person shall be treated as the responsibility of only one person in any benefit week and any person other than the one treated as responsible for the child or young person under this regulation shall be treated as not so responsible.

AMENDMENT

1. Income-related Benefits and Jobseeker's Allowance (Working Tax Credit and Child Tax Credit) (Amendment) Regulations 2002 (SI 2002/2402) reg. and Sch.2 para.3 (April 6, 2003).

DEFINITIONS

"the Act"—see reg.1(3).
"benefit week"—*ibid.*
"child"—see Jobseekers Act s.35(1).
"claimant"—*ibid.*
"week"—*ibid.*
"young person"—see reg.76.

GENERAL NOTE

The definition of family in s.35(1) of the Jobseekers Act refers to a person being responsible for a child or young person (on which see reg.76). This provision mirrors that in reg.15 of the Income Support Regulations and makes the test of responsibility for a child or young person receipt of child benefit. See the notes to reg.15. **3.246**

Note however, the decision of the Court of Appeal in *Hockenjos v Secretary of State for Social Security* [2004] EWCA Civ 1749 (on appeal from *CJSA 4890/1998*) that paras (1)–(3) and (5) of this regulation discriminated against men contrary to art.4 of Directive 79/7 (see Vol.III) and that such discrimination was not objectively justifiable. Those provisions therefore could not be applied to Mr Hockenjos or, by implication, any man within the personal scope of that Directive. In such a case, whether or not a child or young person was a member of the claimant's "family" was to be decided by applying the definition in s.35 of the Jobseekers Act as if reg.77 did not exist, i.e. by asking whether that child or young person was a member of the same household for whom the claimant or any partner was responsible. Applying that test to Mr Hockenjos (who had shared parental responsibility and whose daughters lived with him for substantial parts, though not the majority, of each week under a joint residence order made by a court) there was no doubt that it was satisfied. The effect was that Mr Hockenjos was entitled to JSA for his children on the same basis as if they lived with him full time and, as the "one claimant per child" rule in reg.77(5) was indirectly discriminatory, the fact the Secretary of State might also have to pay income support or JSA for the children to their mother on the same basis did not affect that conclusion. The Secretary of State petitioned the House of Lords for leave to appeal, but leave was refused.

CJSA/2507/2002 decides that a woman who is the substantial minority carer of her children cannot rely on *Hockenjos* because she cannot establish direct or indirect discrimination against her *as a woman*. The decision also holds that reg.77 does not infringe such a woman's Convention Rights.

3.247 For an example where, on somewhat unusual facts, a man could not claim the benefit of *Hockenjos* see *CJSA/2811/2006*. That decision leaves open the possibility that the rules might discriminate unlawfully against a man who, following a period of joint care, becomes a child's sole carer in comparison with a woman in the same position (see para.12).

For the reasons given in the note to reg.15 of the IS Regulations, the *Hockenjos* decision does not apply to income support.

Circumstances in which a person is to be treated as being or not being a member of the household

3.248 **78.**—(1) Subject to paragraphs (2) to (5), the claimant and any partner and, where the claimant or his partner is treated as responsible under regulation 77 (circumstances in which a person is to be treated as responsible or not responsible for another) for a child or young person, that child or young person and any child of that child or young person shall be treated for the purposes of the Act as members of the same household notwithstanding that any of them is temporarily living away from the other members of his family.

[3(1A) Subject to paragraphs (2) and (3), the members of a joint-claim couple shall be treated for the purposes of the Act as members of the same household notwithstanding that they are temporarily living away from each other.]

(2) [4Paragraphs (1) and (1A)] shall not apply to a person who is living away from the other members of his family where—

(a) that person does not intend to resume living with the other members of his family; or

(b) his absence from the other members of his family is likely to exceed 52 weeks, unless there are exceptional circumstances (for example the person is in hospital or otherwise has no control over the length of his absence), and the absence is unlikely to be substantially more than 52 weeks.

(3) [5 Paragraphs (1) and (1A)] shall not apply in respect of any member of a couple or of a polygamous marriage where—

(a) one, both or all of them are patients detained in a hospital provided under section 4 of the National Health Service Act 1977 ([9 high security psychiatric services]) or [8 section 102 of the National Health Service (Scotland) Act 1978[24] (state hospitals)]; or

[2(b) one, both or all of them are—

(i) detained in custody pending trial or sentence upon conviction or under a sentence imposed by a court; or

(ii) on temporary release in accordance with the provisions of the Prison Act 1952 or rules made under section 39(6) of the Prisons (Scotland) Act 1989]

(c) [6 a claimant] is abroad and does not satisfy the conditions of regulation 50 (persons absent from Great Britain); or

(d) one of them is permanently [7 residing in a care home, an Abbeyfield Home or an independent hospital].

(4) A child or young person shall not be treated as a member of the claimant's household where he is—

(a) placed with the claimant or his partner by a local authority under section 23(2)(a) of the Children Act 1989 or by a voluntary organisation under section 59(1)(a) of that Act; or

(b) placed with the claimant or his partner prior to adoption; or

(c) in accordance with a relevant Scottish enactment, boarded out with the claimant or his partner, whether or not with a view to adoption; or

(d) placed for adoption with the claimant or his partner pursuant to a decision under the Adoption Agencies Regulations 1983 or the Adoption Agencies (Scotland) Regulations 1984.

(5) Subject to paragraphs (6) and (7), paragraph (1) shall not apply to a child or young person who is not living with the claimant and who—

(a) in a case which does not fall within sub-paragraph (b), has been continuously absent from Great Britain for a period of more than four weeks commencing—

(i) where he went abroad before the date of the claim for a jobseeker's allowance, with that date;

(ii) in any other case, on the day which immediately follows the day on which he went abroad; or

(b) where [1regulation 50(5)] or paragraph 11 or 13 of Schedule 5 (temporary absence abroad for the treatment of a child or young person) applies, has been continuously absent from Great Britain for a period of more than 8 weeks, that period of 8 weeks commencing—

(i) where he went abroad before the date of the claim for a jobseeker's allowance, on the date of that claim;

(ii) in any other case, on the day which immediately follows the day on which he went abroad; or

(c) has been an in-patient or in accommodation [7 . . .] for a continuous period of more than 12 weeks commencing—

(i) where he became an in-patient or, as the case may be, entered that accommodation before the date of the claim for a jobseeker's allowance, with that date; or

(ii) in any other case, with the date on which he became an in-patient or entered that accommodation,

and, in either case, has not been in regular contact with either the claimant or any member of the claimant's household; or

(d) is being looked after by a local authority under a relevant enactment; or

(e) has been placed with a person other than the claimant prior to adoption, or

(f) is in the care of a local authority under a relevant Scottish enactment; or

(g) has been boarded out under a relevant Scottish enactment with a person other than the claimant prior to adoption; or

(h) has been placed for adoption pursuant to a decision under the

Adoption Agencies Regulations 1983 or the Adoption Agencies (Scotland) Regulations 1984; or

(i) is detained in custody pending trial or sentence upon conviction or under a sentence imposed by a court.

(6) In the case of a person who was entitled to income support [[10] or an income-related employment and support allowance] immediately before his entitlement to a jobseeker's allowance commenced, sub-paragraphs (a), (b) and (c) of paragraph (5) [[1]shall] each have effect as if head (i) was omitted.

(7) A child or young person to whom any of the circumstances mentioned in [[1]sub-paragraphs (d), (f) or (i)] of paragraph (5) applies shall be treated as being a member of the claimant's household only for that part of any benefit week where that child or young person lives with the claimant.

(8) Where a child or young person for the purposes of attending the educational establishment at which he is receiving relevant education is living with the claimant or his partner and neither one is treated as responsible for that child or young person that child or young person shall be treated as being a member of the household of the person treated as responsible for him and shall not be treated as a member of the claimant's household.

(9) In this regulation—

[[7] (za) "accommodation" means accommodation provided by a local authority in a home owned or managed by that local authority—

(i) under sections 21 to 24 of the National Assistance Act 1948 (provision of accommodation),

[[11] (ia) under section 18 or 19 of the Care Act 2014 (duty and power to meet needs for care and support); or]

(ii) in Scotland, under section 13B or 59 of the Social Work (Scotland) Act 1968 (provision of residential or other establishment), or

(iii) under section 25 of the Mental Health (Care and Treatment) (Scotland) Act 2003 (care and support services etc.),

where the accommodation is provided for a person whose stay in that accommodation has become other than temporary;]

(a) "relevant enactment" means the Army Act 1955, the Social Work (Scotland) Act 1968, the Matrimonial Causes Act 1973, the Adoption (Scotland) Act 1978, the Family Law Act 1986 and the Children Act 1989;

(b) "relevant Scottish enactment" means the Army Act 1955, the Air Force Act 1955, the Naval Discipline Act 1957, the Adoption Act 1958, the Matrimonial Proceedings Children Act 1958, the Children Act 1958, the Social Work (Scotland) Act 1968, the Family Law Reform Act 1969, the Children and Young Persons Act 1969, the Matrimonial Causes Act 1973, the Guardianship Act 1973, the Children Act 1975, the Domestic Proceedings and Magistrates' Courts Act 1978, the Adoption (Scotland) Act 1978, the Child Care Act 1980, and the Foster Children Act 1980;

(c) "voluntary organisation" has the meaning assigned to it in the Children Act 1989 or, in Scotland, the Social Work (Scotland) Act 1968.

AMENDMENTS

1. Jobseeker's Allowance (Amendment) Regulations 1996 (SI 1996/1516) reg.20 and Sch. (October 7, 1996).

2. Jobseeker's Allowance and Income Support (General) (Amendment) Regulations 1996 (SI 1996/1517) reg.18 (October 7, 1996).
3. Jobseeker's Allowance (Joint Claims) Regulations 2000 (SI 2000/1978) reg.2(5) and Sch.2 para.33(a) (March 19, 2001).
4. Jobseeker's Allowance (Joint Claims) Regulations 2000 (SI 2000/1978) reg.2(5) and Sch.2 para.33(b) (March 19, 2001).
5. Jobseeker's Allowance (Joint Claims) Regulations 2000 (SI 2000/1978) reg.2(5) and Sch.2 para.33(c)(i) (March 19, 2001).
6. Jobseeker's Allowance (Joint Claims) Regulations 2000 (SI 2000/1978) reg.2(5) and Sch.2 para.33(c)(ii) (March 19, 2001).
7. Social Security (Care Homes and Independent Hospitals) Regulations 2005 (SI 2005/2687) reg.3 and Sch.2 para.3 (October 24, 2005).
8. Social Security (Miscellaneous Amendments) Regulations 2006 (SI 2006/588) reg.3 (April 1, 2006).
9. Social Security (Miscellaneous Amendments) (No.4) Regulations 2006 (SI 2006/2378) reg.13(4) (October 2, 2006).
10. Employment and Support Allowance (Consequential Provisions) (No.2) Regulations 2008 (SI 2008/1554) reg.3(1) and (13) (October 27, 2008).
11. Care Act 2014 (Consequential Amendments) (Secondary Legislation) Order 2015 (SI 2015/643) art.2 and Sch. para.9(2) (April 1, 2015).

Definitions

"Abbeyfield Home"—see reg.1(3).
"the Act"—*ibid.*
"care home"—*ibid.*
"claimant"—see Jobseekers Act s.35(1).
"child"—*ibid.*
"couple"—see reg.1(3).
"date of claim"—*ibid.*
"family"—see Jobseekers Act s.35(1).
"independent hospital"—see reg.1(3).
"partner"—*ibid.*
"polygamous marriage"—*ibid.*
"young person"—see reg.76.

General Note

This regulation is very similar to reg.16 of the Income Support Regulations. **3.249**
Unlike the Income Support Regulations, the JSA Regulations make separate reference to the Scottish legislation in the case of provisions that were amended in the Income Support Regulations as a consequence of the Children Act 1989 (see para. (4)(c), para.(5)(f) and (g) and (9)(b)).

See the notes to reg.16 of the Income Support Regulations.

Part VII

Amounts

Weekly amounts of contribution-based jobseeker's allowance

79.—(1) In the case of a contribution-based jobseeker's allowance, the age-related amount applicable to a claimant for the purposes of section 4(1)(a) shall be— **3.250**

[1(a) in the case of a person who has not attained the age of 25, [2£57.90] per week;]

[1. . .]

(c) in the case of a person who has attained the age of 25, [2£73.10] per week.

(2) Where the amount of any contribution-based jobseeker's allowance would, but for this paragraph, include a fraction of one penny, that fraction shall be treated as one penny.

AMENDMENTS

1. Social Security (Miscellaneous Amendments) (No.3) Regulations 2013 (SI 2013/2536) reg.6(6) (October 29, 2013).

2. Welfare Benefits Up-rating Order 2015 (SI 2015/30) art.8 (April 6, 2015).

DEFINITIONS

"contribution-based jobseeker's allowance"—see Jobseekers Act 1995 ss.35(1) and 1(4).

"week"—see reg.1(3).

GENERAL NOTE

3.251 If a claimant is entitled to a contribution-based JSA, the first step in calculating the amount payable under the old style Jobseekers Act 1995 s.4(1) is to determine the age-related amount payable (s.4(1)(a)). Paragraph (1) of this regulation sets out those amounts. There are now only two rates: a lower rate for under 25s (sub-para. (a)) and a higher rate for those aged 25 and over (sub-para.(c)).

Given the contribution conditions it is difficult to see how anyone under 18 could qualify save in highly unusual circumstances, unless there is an alteration to the rules on when contribution credits can be awarded (see annotations to old style Jobseekers Act 1995 s.2(1)(a) and (b) and (2)–(4)). Differential rates for the basic part of benefit seem hard to justify, given that the ability to receive JSA regardless of means (the Government's description: see White Paper para.4.21) rests on the same level of contributions for all, regardless of age (see annotations to s.2). The stated justification—that some 75 per cent of under-25s do not live independently and have fewer financial commitments—per Mr R. Evans, Parliamentary Under-Secretary of State, *House of Commons Standing Committee B Debates on the Jobseekers Bill*, col.247—may well be accurate, but the resultant rule paints with too broad a brush, relegates social security contributions very much to the realm of earmarked taxation rather than insurance for the future, and seems more appropriate to a means-tested than a contributory benefit payable in consequence of the insured risk materialising. Nevertheless, in *R (on the application of Carson and Reynolds) v Secretary of State for Work and Pensions* [2005] UKHL 37, [2006] 1 A.C. 173, the House of Lords unanimously dismissed an appeal from the Court of Appeal in *Reynolds* in holding that the differential treatment of those under 25 was not discriminatory contrary to the Human Rights Act 1998 and art.14 of the European Convention on Human Rights. Lord Hoffmann considered that the circumstances of JSA and income support claimants aged up to and over 25 were relevantly different. Those under 25 were likely to have lower living expenses, e.g. from living with parents or otherwise not in an independent household, and to have lower earnings expectations. Also, a line had to be drawn somewhere, so that there would have been justification if similar circumstances had been treated differently. The companion case of *Carson* (to do with payment of increases in retirement pensions to pensioners living in some overseas countries and not others) was taken to the European Court of Human Rights, where the Grand Chamber ruled that there was no breach of art.14 (*Carson v United Kingdom* [2010] ECHR 338). *Reynolds* was not taken to the ECHR. See further the annotations to Sch.1 to the Human Rights Act in Vol.III.

Paragraph (2) provides with respect to contribution-based JSA that fractions of a penny shall be treated as one penny.

Deductions in respect of earnings

80.—(1) The deduction in respect of earnings which falls to be made in accordance with section 4(1)(b) from the amount which, apart from this regulation, would be payable by way of a contribution-based jobseeker's allowance for any benefit week is an amount equal to the weekly amount of the claimant's earnings calculated in accordance with Part VIII (income and capital). 3.252

(2) For the avoidance of doubt, in calculating the amount of earnings for the purposes of this regulation, only the claimant's earnings shall be taken into account.

DEFINITIONS

"claimant"—see Jobseekers Act 1995 s.35(1).
"contribution-based jobseeker's allowance"—see Jobseekers Act 1995 ss.35(1) and 1(4).
"earnings"—see regs 98 (employed earner) and 100 (self-employed earner).
"week"—see reg.1(3).

GENERAL NOTE

Section 4(1) of the old style Jobseekers Act 1995 provides that one calculates the amount of contribution-based JSA payable to a claimant by first determining the age-related amount applicable (see reg.79) and then making prescribed deductions from that in respect of: (a) earnings (the subject-matter of this regulation), and (b) pension payments (the subject-matter of reg.81). The provisions, subjecting CBJSA to a form of means-testing not applicable to UB, represent one of the ways in which the scheme deals with the problem of partial unemployment, where a claimant is working below the 16-hour threshold set for the remunerative work exclusion, whether in employment or self-employment. "Earnings" means those of employed earners (reg.98) and self-employed earners (reg.100). Only the claimant's own earnings count for purposes of CBJSA (para.(2); cf. reg.88). Under para.(1), the deduction to be made from the appropriate age-related amount in respect of earnings is an amount equal to the weekly amount of earnings as calculated in accordance with Pt VIII of these Regulations. Essentially, in the case of an employed earner, one takes account of net earnings less appropriate disregards and, in the case of a self-employed earner, net profit, less appropriate disregards. Note, in this regard, that the range of disregards for purposes of this regulation is narrower than those applicable when calculating earnings for purposes of IBJSA (does income exceed the applicable amount?) or for purposes of ascertaining whether the claimant's weekly earnings exceed the "prescribed amount" for the purposes of reg.56 and the preclusion from entitlement to CBJSA set by the old style Jobseekers Act 1995 s.2(1)(c) (see regs 99(3) and 101(3), contrasting them with regs 99(2) and 101(2)). 3.253

Payments by way of pensions

81.—(1) The deduction in respect of pension payments [3, PPF payments or FAS payments] from the amount which apart from this regulation would be payable to a claimant by way of a contribution-based jobseeker's allowance for any [1benefit week] shall be a sum equal to the amount by which that payment exceeds or, as the case may be, the aggregate of those payments exceed £50 per benefit week. 3.254

[1(1A) Where pension payments[3, PPF payments or FAS payments] first begin to be made to a person for a period starting other than on the first day of a benefit week, the deduction referred to in paragraph (1) shall have effect from the beginning of that benefit week.

(1B) Where pension payments[3, PPF payments or FAS payments] are already in payment to a person and a change in the rate of payment takes effect in a week other than at the beginning of the benefit week, the deduction referred to in paragraph (1) shall have effect from the first day of that benefit week.]

(2) In determining the amount of any pension payments[3, PPF payments or FAS payments] for the purposes of paragraph (1), there shall be disregarded—

(a) [1. . .]

(b) [1. . .]

[2(c) any payments from a personal pension scheme, an occupational pension scheme or a public service pension scheme which are payable to him and which arose in accordance with the terms of such a scheme on the death of a person who was a member of the scheme in question.] [3; and

(d) any PPF payments or FAS payments which are payable to him and which arose on the death of a person who had an entitlement to such payments.]

(3) Subject to the provisions of paragraph (2), where a pension payment[3, PPF payment or FAS payment], or an aggregate of such payments, as the case may be, is paid to a person for a period other than a week, such payments shall be treated as being made to that person by way of weekly pension payments[3, weekly PPF payments or weekly FAS payments] and the weekly amount shall be determined—

(a) where payment is made for a year, by dividing the total by 52;

(b) where payment is made for three months, by dividing the total by 13;

(c) where payment is made for a month, by multiplying the total by 12 and dividing the result by 52;

(d) where payment is made for two or more months, otherwise than for a year or for three months, by dividing the total by the number of months, multiplying the result by 12 and dividing the result of that multiplication by 52; or

(e) in any other case, by dividing the amount of the payment by the number of days in the period for which it is made and multiplying the result by 7.

AMENDMENTS

1. Jobseeker's Allowance and Income Support (General) (Amendment) Regulations 1996 (SI 1996/1517) reg.19 (October 7, 1996).

2. Social Security (Miscellaneous Amendments) Regulations 1997 (SI 1997/454) reg.2(9) (April 7, 1997).

3. Social Security (PPF Payments and FAS Payments) (Consequential Amendments) Regulations 2006 (SI 2006/1069) reg.5 (May 5, 2006).

DEFINITIONS

"FAS payments"—see Jobseekers Act 1995 s.35(1).
"pension payments"—*ibid.*
"PPF payments"—*ibid.*

GENERAL NOTE

Section 4(1) of the old style Jobseekers Act 1995 provides that one calculates the amount of contribution-based JSA payable to a claimant by first determining the age-related amount applicable (see reg.79) and then making prescribed deductions from that in respect of: (a) earnings (the subject-matter of reg.80), and (b) pension payments, FAS payments and PPF payments (the subject-matter of this regulation). There is thus brought into CBJSA generally the concept of abatement of benefit in respect of payments by way of occupational or personal pension previously applied in unemployment benefit only to claimants 55 or over pursuant to the now-repealed SSCBA 1992 s.30. **3.255**

"Pension payments" and the other payments are defined in Jobseekers Act 1995 s.35(1). The rules on taking them into account (paras (1), (1A) and (1B)), determining a weekly equivalent (para.(3)) and on which payments can be disregarded (para.(2)(c)) are set out in this regulation. The definition of the pension payments covered is not the same as "payments by way of occupational or personal pension" applicable to unemployment benefit under SSCBA 1992 s.122(1). Nor are the rules in this regulation exactly the same as those which applied to UB. Unless falling within the disregarded class (para.(2)(c)), a pension payment must be taken into account once its weekly equivalent (or if several, their aggregate weekly equivalent), determined in accordance with para.(3), exceeds £50, regardless of the age of the claimant. It is notable that the £50 figure has not changed for over 15 years.

"Pension payments" are periodical payments made in relation to a person, under a personal pension scheme or, in connection with the coming to an end of an employment of his, under an occupational pension scheme or a public service pension scheme, and also such other payments as may be prescribed in regulations (Jobseekers Act 1995 s.35(1)). A "personal pension scheme" embraces a contract or trust scheme approved under Ch.III of Pt XIV of the Income and Corporation Taxes Act 1988; a personal pension scheme approved under Ch.IV of that Part of that Act; and a personal pension scheme as defined in s.1 of the Pension Schemes Act 1993 ("any scheme or arrangement which is comprised in one or more instruments or agreements and which has, or is capable of having, effect so as to provide benefits, in the form of pensions or otherwise, payable on death or retirement to or in respect of employed earners who have made arrangements with the trustees or managers of the scheme for them to become members of it") (s.35(1)). An "occupational pension scheme" is—

> "any scheme or arrangement which is comprised in one or more instruments or agreements and which has, or is capable of having, effect in relation to one or more descriptions or categories of employments so as to provide benefits, in the form of pensions or otherwise, payable on termination of service, or on death or retirement, to or in respect of earners with qualifying service in an employment of any such description or category." (Pension Schemes Act 1993 s.1, applied here by virtue of Jobseekers Act 1995 s.35(1).)

A "public service pension scheme" is— **3.256**

> "an occupational pension scheme [as just defined] established by or under an enactment or the Royal prerogative or a Royal charter, being a scheme (a) all the particulars of which are set out in, or in a legislative instrument made under, an enactment, Royal warrant or charter, or (b) which cannot come into force, or be amended, without the scheme or amendment being approved by a Minister of the Crown or government department."

The term includes—

> "any occupational pension scheme established, with the concurrence of the Treasury, by or with the approval of any Minister of the Crown and any occu-

pational pension scheme prescribed by regulations made by the Secretary of State and the Treasury jointly as being a scheme which ought in their opinion to be treated as a public service pension scheme for the purposes of this Act". (Pension Schemes Act 1993 s.1, applied here by virtue of Jobseekers Act 1995, s.35(1).)

The May 2006 amendments provide for PPF (Pensions Protection Fund) payments and Financial Assistance Scheme (FAS) payments to be treated in the same way as occupational pension income in respect of CBJSA. The terms are defined s.35(1).The PPF is a statutory fund run by the Board of the PPF. It became operational on April 6, 2005. The PPF aims to provide compensation for members of defined benefit occupational pension schemes and the defined benefit element of hybrid pension schemes should the employer become insolvent and the pension scheme is underfunded at a certain level. The FAS offers help to some people who have lost out on their defined benefit occupational pension because their scheme was underfunded when it wound up and the employer is insolvent or no longer exists. In addition, it also provides assistance for certain surviving spouses and civil partners. The FAS is aimed at pension schemes that began to wind up between January 1, 1997 and April 5, 2005. Schemes that begun winding up after this period may be eligible for help from the PPF.

3.257 In determining the amount of any pension or other payments for abatement purposes, there must be disregarded any payable to the claimant which arose in accordance with the terms of a personal pension scheme, occupational pension scheme or a public service pension scheme on the death of someone who was a member of that scheme (para.(2)(c) and (d)).

In *R(JSA)1/01* Commissioner Howell considered the case of a claimant for CBJSA. The claimant was a former civil servant with the Property Services Agency who received annual compensation payments for his redundancy which came about when the agency was sold off to the private sector. These annual payments were not part of his retirement benefits but were "contractual payments made by his private employer, not under any separate funded scheme but out of its own operational assets, in satisfaction of the redundancy terms negotiated with him as part of his contract of employment on transfer of employment to them" (para.6). Clearly these payments were not earnings under reg.98 since para.(2)(b) thereof excludes from the definition of earnings "any periodic sum paid to a claimant on account of the termination of his employment by reasons of redundancy". Following the Court of Appeal in *Westminster CC v Haywood* [1998] Ch. 377 and Hart J in *City and Council of Swansea v Johnson* [1999] Ch. 189, Commissioner Howell held that the annual payments were ones of occupational pension and subject to the abatement of JSA rules in reg.81. He commented:

> "I do not for my part consider there to be any absurdity or inconsistency in this result. Periodical payments under an employer's scheme or arrangement of this type after employment terminates appear to me to have the same essential characteristic of deferred or contingent 'pay' for this purpose, whether the reason is permitted early retirement or premature termination on redundancy. It seems to me consistent to treat both in the same way as 'pension payments' under regulation 81 whether or not they come from the same source. Nor do I find any absurdity or inconsistency in their both being taken into account as pension payments though excluded from counting as 'earnings'. The point of excluding both from the definition of 'earnings' in regulation 98 is not to remove them from the reckoning altogether, but to allow the first £50 a week of these types of payment to be left out of account while continued current earnings left within regulation 80 would be fully deductible". (See para.28.)

To apply this regulation it is vital to identify the source of the payment. Failure so to do is an error of law (*R(JSA)2/01; CJSA/4316/1998*). It would be helpful if the correspondence from employer to claimant indicated the source of the payment

(*R(JSA)2/01*). In *R(JSA)2/01* and *CJSA/4316/1998*, the source of the annual compensation payment was the Civil Service Pension Scheme. Following *R(JSA)1/01* and the statements of Millett LJ in *Westminster CC v Haywood* [1998] Ch. 377, at 404–405, this was held, both in *R(JSA)2/01* and *CJSA/4316/1998*, to fall within the JSA definitions of pension payment, notwithstanding that in *R(JSA)2/01* the claimant got that compensation payment because he did not get what the civil service scheme called a pension (*R(JSA)2/01*, at para.7).

In *R(JSA)6/02, R(JSA)1/01* was followed to hold that "three months' redundancy payment" on termination of employment with London and Manchester (Management Services) Limited constituted periodical pension payments abating CBJSA. **3.258**

In *CJSA 1542/2000*, Commissioner Rowland followed *R(JSA)6/02* to hold that a lump sum payment amounting to three months' redundancy payment was a pension payment for the purposes of this regulation.

[1 Income-based jobseeker's allowance

82.—(1) Regulations 83 to [2 85] and 87 apply in the case of an income-based jobseeker's allowance but not a joint-claim jobseeker's allowance. **3.259**

(2) Regulations 86A to [2 86C] only apply in the case of a joint-claim jobseeker's allowance.]

AMENDMENTS

1. Jobseeker's Allowance (Joint Claims) Regulations 2000 (SI 2000/1978) reg.2(5) and Sch.2 para.34 (March 19, 2001).

2. Social Security Amendment (Residential Care and Nursing Homes) Regulations 2001 (SI 2001/3767) reg.2 and Sch. Pt II para.3 (April 8, 2002).

Applicable amounts

83.—Except in the case of a claimant to whom regulation 84, 85, [1. . .] [4 . . .] (applicable amounts in other cases [4 . . .]) applies, a claimant's weekly applicable amount shall be the aggregate of such of the following amounts as may apply in this case— **3.260**

(a) an amount in respect of himself or if he is a member of a couple, an amount in respect of both of them, determined in accordance with sub-paragraph (1), (2) or (3), as the case may be, of paragraph 1 of Schedule 1;
(b) [3 . . .]
(c) [2 . . .]
(d) [3 . . .]
(e) the amount of any premiums which may be applicable to him, determined in accordance with Parts III and IV of Schedule 1 (premiums); and
(f) any amounts determined in accordance with Schedule 2 (housing costs) which may be applicable to him in respect of mortgage interest payments or such other housing costs as are prescribed in that Schedule.

AMENDMENTS

1. Social Security Amendment (Residential Care and Nursing Homes) Regulations 2001 (SI 2001/3767) reg.2 and Sch. Pt II para.4 (April 8, 2002).

2. Social Security (Removal of Residential Allowance and Miscellaneous Amendments) Regulations 2003 (SI 2003/1121) reg.4 and Sch.2 para.2 (October 6, 2003).

3. Social Security (Working Tax Credit and Child Tax Credit) (Consequential Amendments) Regulations 2003 (SI 2003/455) reg.3 and Sch.2 para.2 (April 6, 2004, except in "transitional cases" and see further the note to this regulation and to reg.17 of the Income Support Regulations).

4. Social Security (Miscellaneous Amendments) (No.5) Regulations 2009 (SI 2009/3228) reg.3(3)(a) (January 25, 2010).

DEFINITIONS

"child"—see Jobseekers Act s.35(1).
"claimant"—*ibid.*
"couple"—see reg.1(3).
"family"—see Jobseekers Act s.35(1).
"young person"—see reg.76.

GENERAL NOTE

3.261 This provision only applies to income-based JSA (reg.82).

Income-based JSA uses the same formula as income support for calculating the amount of a claimant's benefit, that is, by setting his "applicable amount" against his income. Regulation 83 sets out the categories which go towards the total applicable amount which are the same as those in reg.17 of the Income Support Regulations. See the notes to reg.17. There is no equivalent to reg.17(1)(f) and (g) and (2) to (7) which contain various transitional protection provisions. But note the rules for "transitional supplement" to income-based JSA in reg.87 which preserve the effect of these and other income support transitional protection provisions for JSA claimants who would have been covered by them had they been entitled to claim income support after October 6, 1996 (for claimants entitled to a special transitional addition or transitional addition under the Income Support (Transitional) Regulations before October 7, 1996, see para.(1) of reg.87).

As with income support there are special rules for particular categories, see regs 84–86D.

Subject to exceptions in "transitional cases", JSA became an "adults only" benefit on April 6, 2004 with all support for the costs of bringing up children and young persons transferred to child tax credit and regs 83(b) and 84(c) (personal allowances for children and young persons), regs 383(d) and 84(e) (family premium) and para.16 of Sch.1 (disabled child premium) were revoked from that date. At the same time para.15A(1)(b) of Sch.1 was amended to remove the possibility of claiming the enhanced disability premium for a child. For JSA the rules which create "transitional cases" are contained in reg.1(6)–(8) of SI 2003/455 (p.811) and are the same as the rules for income support in reg.1(2)–(4). For a detailed discussion, see the note to reg.17 of the Income Support Regulations.

Polygamous marriages

3.262 **84.**—(1) Except in the case of a claimant to whom regulation 83, [2or 85] (applicable amounts in special cases) [2. . .] [5. . .] or paragraph (2) applies, where a claimant is a member of a polygamous marriage his weekly applicable amount shall be the aggregate of such of the following amounts as may apply in his case—

(a) the highest amount applicable to him and one of his partners determined in accordance with sub-paragraph (3) of paragraph 1 of Schedule 1 as if he and that partner were a couple;

(b) an amount equal to the difference between the amounts specified in [1sub-paragraph (3)(e)] and (1)(e) of paragraph 1 of Schedule 1 in respect of each of his other partners;

(c) [4. . .]
(d) [3. . .]
(e) [4. . .]
(f) the amount of any premiums which may be applicable to him determined in accordance with Parts III and IV of Schedule 1 (premiums); and
(g) any amounts determined in accordance with Schedule 2 (housing costs) which may be applicable to him in respect of mortgage interest payments or such other housing costs as are prescribed in that Schedule.

(2) In the case of a partner who is aged less than 18 the amount which applies in respect of that partner shall be Nil unless that partner—
(a) is treated as responsible for a child; or
(b) is a person who, had he not been a member of a polygamous marriage, would have qualified for a jobseeker's allowance by virtue of section 3(1)(f)(ii) or section 3(1)(f)(iii) and the regulations made thereunder (jobseeker's allowance for persons aged 16 or 17).

AMENDMENTS

1. Jobseeker's Allowance (Amendment) Regulations 1996 (SI 1996/1516) reg.20 and Sch. (October 7, 1996).
2. Social Security Amendment (Residential Care and Nursing Homes) Regulations 2001 (SI 2001/3767) reg.2 and Sch. Pt II para.5 (April 8, 2002).
3. Social Security (Removal of Residential Allowance and Miscellaneous Amendments) Regulations 2003 (SI 2003/1121) reg.4 of and Sch.2 para.3 (October 6, 2003).
4. Social Security (Working Tax Credit and Child Tax Credit) (Consequential Amendments) Regulations 2003 (SI 2003/455) reg.3 and Sch.2 para.3 (April 6, 2004, except in "transitional cases" and see further the note to regs 83 and to 17 of the Income Support Regulations).
5. Social Security (Miscellaneous Amendments) (No.5) Regulations 2009 (SI 2009/3228) reg.3(3)(b) (January 25, 2010).

DEFINITIONS

"child"—see Jobseekers Act s.35(1).
"claimant"—*ibid.*
"couple"—see reg.1(3).
"family"—see Jobseekers Act s.35(1).
"young person"—see reg.76.

GENERAL NOTE

Regulation 84 contains the special rules for polygamous marriages but not for other kinds of relationships. There the ordinary living together as husband and wife rule in s.35(1) of the Jobseekers Act applies. **3.263**

This provision only applies to income-based JSA (reg.82).

Special cases

85.—(1) [9 [18. . .]] in the case of a person to whom any paragraph in column (1) of Schedule 5 applies (applicable amounts in special cases) the amount included in the claimant's weekly applicable amount in respect of him shall be the amount prescribed in the corresponding paragraph in column (2) of that Schedule [11. . .]. **3.264**

(2) [19. . .]

[9(2A) [10. . .]]
(3) [16 . . .]
(4) [3 [12 17 In this regulation] and Schedule 5—
[7 . . .]
[7 "partner of a person subject to immigration control" means a person—
(i) who is not subject to immigration control within the meaning of section 115(9) of the Immigration and Asylum Act; or
(ii) to whom section 115 of that Act does not apply by virtue of regulation 2 of the Social Security (Immigration and Asylum) Consequential Amendments Regulations 2000; and
(iii) who is a member of a couple and [15 the member's] partner is subject to immigration control within the meaning of section 115(9) of that Act and section 115 of that Act applies to [15 the partner] for the purposes of exclusion from entitlement to jobseeker's allowance;]
[17 "person from abroad" has the meaning given in regulation 85A]
"patient" means a person (other than a prisoner) who is regarded as receiving free in-patient treatment within the meaning of [16 regulation 2(4) and (5) of the Social Security (Hospital In-Patients) Regulations 2005];
"prisoner" means a person who—
(a) is detained in custody pending trial or sentence upon conviction or under a sentence imposed by a court; or
(b) is on temporary release in accordance with the provisions of the Prison Act 1952 or the Prisons (Scotland) Act 1989,

other than a person [5who is detained in hospital under the provisions of the Mental Health Act 1983, or, in Scotland, under the provisions of the [13 Mental Health (Care and Treatment) (Scotland) Act 2003] or the Criminal Procedure (Scotland) Act 1995;]

[14 . . .]
(4A) [3 17 . . .]
(4B) [12 17 . . .]
(5) [14 . . .]
(6) [14 . . .]

AMENDMENTS

1. Jobseeker's Allowance (Amendment) Regulations 1996 (SI 1996/1516) reg.10(1) (October 7, 1996).
2. Jobseeker's Allowance (Amendment) Regulations 1996 (SI 1996/1516) reg.20 and Sch. (October 7, 1996).
3. Social Security and Child Support (Jobseeker's Allowance) (Miscellaneous Amendments) Regulations 1996 (SI 1996/2538) reg.2(7) (October 28, 1996).
4. Social Security (Miscellaneous Amendments) Regulations 1997 (SI 1997/454) reg.2(10) (April 7, 1997).
5. Social Security (Miscellaneous Amendments) Regulations 1998 (SI 1998/563) reg.8(1) and (2)(d) (April 6, 1998).
6. Social Security (Miscellaneous Amendments) Regulations 1998 (SI 1998/563) reg.18(3) and (4)(d) (April 6, 1998).
7. Social Security (Immigration and Asylum) Consequential Amendments Regulations 2000 (SI 2000/636) reg.4(3)(a) (April 3, 2000).
8. Income-related Benefits and Jobseeker's Allowance (Amendment) Regulations 2000 (SI 2000/979) reg.3 (May 2, 2000).
9. Social Security Amendment (Residential Care and Nursing Homes) Regulations 2001 (SI 2001/3767) reg.2 and Sch. Pt II para.6 (April 8, 2002).

10. Social Security (Removal of Residential Allowance and Miscellaneous Amendments) Regulations 2003 (SI 2003/1121) reg.4 and Sch.2 para.4 (October 6, 2003).

11. Social Security (Working Tax Credit and Child Tax Credit) (Consequential Amendments) Regulations 2003 (SI 2003/455) reg.3 and Sch.4 para.1 (April 6, 2004, except in "transitional cases" and see further the note to regs 83 and to 17 of the Income Support Regulations).

12. Social Security (Habitual Residence) Amendment Regulations 2004 (SI 2004/1232) reg.4 (May 1, 2004).

13. Mental Health (Care and Treatment) (Scotland) Act 2003 (Modification of Subordinate Legislation) Order 2005 (SSI 2005/445) art.2 and Sch. para.23(2) (Scotland); Mental Health (Care and Treatment) (Scotland) Act 2003 (Consequential Provisions) Order 2005 (SI 2005/2078) art.15 and Sch.2 para.17(3) (England and Wales) (October 5, 2005).

14. Social Security (Care Homes and Independent Hospitals) Regulations 2005 (SI 2005/2687) reg.3 and Sch.2 para.4 (October 24, 2005).

15. Civil Partnership (Pensions, Social Security and Child Support) (Consequential, etc. Provisions) Order 2005 (SI 2005/2877) art.2(3) and Sch.3 para.26(5) (December 5, 2005).

16. Social Security (Hospital In-Patients) Regulations 2005 (SI 2005/3360) reg.6 (April 10, 2006).

17. Social Security (Persons from Abroad) Amendment Regulations 2006 (SI 1026/2006) reg.7(2) (April 30, 2006).

18. Social Security (Miscellaneous Amendments) (No.5) Regulations 2007 (SI 2007/2618) reg.8(6) (October 1, 2007).

19. Social Security (Miscellaneous Amendments) Regulations 2009 (SI 2009/583) reg.4(1) and (5) (April 6, 2009).

DEFINITIONS

"child"—see Jobseekers Act s.35(1).
"claimant"—*ibid.*
"Income Support Regulations"—see reg.1(3).
"young person"—see reg.76.

GENERAL NOTE

This regulation only applies to income-based JSA (reg.82). **3.265**

Applicable amounts in special cases are to be as prescribed in Sch.5.

This provision is similar to reg.21 of the Income Support Regulations. See the notes to that regulation.

[1 Special cases: supplemental – persons from abroad

85A.—(1) "Person from abroad" means, subject to the following provisions of this regulation, a claimant who is not habitually resident in the United Kingdom, the Channel Islands, the Isle of Man or the Republic of Ireland. **3.266**

[10 (2) No claimant shall be treated as habitually resident in the United Kingdom, the Channel Islands, the Isle of Man or the Republic of Ireland unless—

(a) [12 subject to the exceptions in paragraph (2A),] the claimant has been living in any of those places for the past three months; and
(b) the claimant has a right to reside in any of those places, other than a right to reside which falls within paragraph (3).]

[12 (2A) The exceptions are where the claimant has at any time during the period referred to in paragraph (2)(a)—

(a) paid either Class 1 or Class 2 contributions by virtue of regulation 114, 118, 146 or 147 of the Social Security (Contributions) Regulations 2001 or by virtue of an Order in Council having effect under section 179 of the Social Security Administration Act 1992; or

(b) been a Crown servant posted to perform overseas the duties of a Crown servant; or

(c) been a member of Her Majesty's forces posted to perform overseas the duties of a member of Her Majesty's forces.]

(3) A right to reside falls within this paragraph if it is one which exists by virtue of, or in accordance with, one or more of the following—

(a) regulation 13 of the Immigration (European Economic Area) Regulations 2006; or

[7 (aa) regulation 15A(1) of those Regulations, but only in a case where the right exists under that regulation because the claimant satisfies the criteria in regulation 15A(4A) of those Regulations;]

(b) Article 6 of Council Directive No.2004/38/EC [7 ; or

(c) Article 20 of the Treaty on the Functioning of the European Union (in a case where the right to reside arises because a British citizen would otherwise be deprived of the genuine enjoyment of the substance of their rights as a European Union citizen).]

(4) A claimant is not a person from abroad if he is—

[11 (za) a qualified person for the purposes of regulation 6 of the Immigration (European Economic Area) Regulations 2006 as a worker or a self-employed person;

(zb) a family member of a person referred to in sub-paragraph (za) within the meaning of regulation 7(1)(a), (b) or (c) of those Regulations;

(zc) a person who has a right to reside permanently in the United Kingdom by virtue of regulation 15(1)(c), (d) or (e) of those Regulations;]

(g) a refugee within the definition in Article 1 of the Convention relating to the Status of Refugees done at Geneva on 28th July 1951, as extended by Article 1(2) of the Protocol relating to the Status of Refugees done at New York on 31st January 1967;

[3 [9 (h) a person who has been granted leave or who is deemed to have been granted leave outside the rules made under section 3(2) of the Immigration Act 1971 where that leave is—

(i) discretionary leave to enter or remain in the United Kingdom;

(ii) leave to remain under the Destitution Domestic Violence concession; or

(iii) leave deemed to have been granted by virtue of regulation 3 of the Displaced Persons (Temporary Protection) Regulations 2005(19);]]

(hh) a person who has humanitarian protection granted under those rules;] [9 or]

(i) a person who is not a person subject to immigration control within the meaning of section 115(9) of the Immigration and Asylum Act and who is in the United Kingdom as a result of his deportation, expulsion or other removal by compulsion of law from another country to the United Kingdom; [5 . . .]

[9 . . .]

AMENDMENTS

1. Social Security (Persons from Abroad) Amendment Regulations 2006 (SI 1026/2006) reg.7(3) (April 30, 2006).
2. Social Security (Lebanon) Amendment Regulations 2006 (SI 2006/1981) reg.3 (July 25, 2006). The amendment ceased to have effect from January 31, 2007.
3. Social Security (Persons from Abroad) Amendment (No.2) Regulations 2006 (SI 2006/2528) reg.3 (October 9, 2006).
4. Social Security (Bulgaria and Romania) Amendment Regulations 2006 (SI 2006/3341) reg.3 (January 1, 2007).
5. Social Security (Habitual Residence) (Amendment) Regulations 2009 (SI 2009/362) reg.3 (March 18, 2009).
6. Social Security (Miscellaneous Amendments) (No.3) Regulations 2011 (SI 2011/2425) reg.10(1) and (7) (October 31, 2011).
7. Social Security (Habitual Residence) (Amendment) Regulations 2012 (SI 2012/2587) reg.3 (November 8, 2012).
8. Social Security (Croatia) Amendment Regulations 2013 (SI 2013/1474) reg.3 (July 1, 2013).
9. Social Security (Miscellaneous Amendments) (No.3) Regulations 2013 (SI 2013/2536) reg.6(1) and (8) (October 29,2013).
10. Jobseeker's Allowance (Habitual Residence) Amendment Regulations 2013 (SI 3196/2013) reg.2 (January 1, 2014).
11. Social Security (Habitual Residence) (Amendment) Regulations 2014 (SI 2014/902) reg.3 (May 31, 2014).
12. Jobseeker's Allowance (Habitual Residence) Amendment Regulations 2014 (SI 2014/2735) reg.3 (November 9, 2014).

GENERAL NOTE

See the commentary to reg.21AA of the IS Regulations. Note, in particular, the difference in wording between reg.21AA(3) and reg.85A(3), the effect of which is that, from April 30, 2006, any claimant seeking to establish a right to reside as a workseeker for social security purposes must claim JSA rather than IS if his or her claim is not to be defeated by reg.21AA. 3.267

From April 30, 2006, subparas (a)–(e) of para.(4) apply to nationals of Switzerland as well as to nationals of Iceland, Liechtenstein and Norway—and to members of their families as defined by art.2 of the Rights of Residence Directive—as if those nationals were EU nationals (see reg.10(f) of SI 1026/2006). Paragraph 4 has been amended many times, so that sub-paras (a)–(e) are now sub-paras (za)–(f)—without reg.10 of SI 2006/1026 being changed to refer to the amended law. However, ss.17(2) and 23 of the Interpretation Act 1978 have the effect that reg.10 must be interpreted as referring to para.(4) in its current form.

Applicable amounts for persons in residential care and nursing homes

86.—[1. . .] 3.268

AMENDMENT

1. Social Security Amendment (Residential Care and Nursing Homes) Regulations 2001 (SI 2001/3767) reg.2 and Sch. Pt II para.7 (April 8, 2002).

[1Applicable amounts for joint-claim couples

86A.—Except in the case of a joint-claim couple where regulation 86B (polygamous marriages), [2or 86C] (special cases) [2. . .] [5. . .] applies, 3.269

the applicable amount of a joint-claim couple who are jointly claiming a jobseeker's allowance shall be the aggregate of such of the following amounts as may apply in their case—

(a) an amount in respect of the joint-claim couple determined in accordance with sub-paragraph (3) of paragraph 1 of Schedule 1;
(b) [[3]. . .]
(c) the amount of any premiums which may be applicable to either or both members of the joint-claim couple, determined in accordance with Parts IVA and IVB of Schedule 1 (premiums); and
(d) any amounts determined in accordance with Schedule 2 (housing costs) which may be applicable to the joint-claim couple in respect of mortgage interest payments or such other housing costs as are prescribed in that Schedule.]

AMENDMENTS

1. Jobseeker's Allowance (Joint Claims) Regulations 2000 (SI 2000/1978) reg.2(5) and Sch.2 para.35 (March 19, 2001).

2. Social Security Amendment (Residential Care and Nursing Homes) Regulations 2001 (SI 2001/3767) reg.2 and Sch. Pt II para.8 (April 8, 2002).

3. Social Security (Removal of Residential Allowance and Miscellaneous Amendments) Regulations 2003 (SI 2003/1121) reg.4 and Sch.2 para.5 (October 6, 2003).

4. Social Security (Hospital In-Patients) Regulations 2005 (SI 2005/3360) reg.6 (April 10, 2006).

5. Social Security (Miscellaneous Amendments) (No.5) Regulations 2009 (SI 2009/3228) reg.3(3)(c) (January 25, 2010).

GENERAL NOTE

3.270 This regulation applies to income-based JSA only (see reg.82). It makes provision corresponding to reg.83 for joint-claim couples.

[[1]Applicable amounts for joint-claim couples: polygamous marriages

3.271 **86B.**—Except in the case of a joint-claim couple where regulation 86A, [[2]or 86C] (special cases) [[2]. . .] [[4]. . .] applies, the applicable amount of a joint-claim couple who are jointly claiming a jobseeker's allowance where either or both members of that couple are members of a polygamous marriage, shall be the aggregate of such of the following amounts as may apply in their case—

(a) the highest amount applicable to a member of the joint-claim couple and one other member of that marriage determined in accordance with sub-paragraph (3) of paragraph 1 of Schedule 1 as if those members were a couple;
(b) an amount equal to the difference between the amounts specified in sub-paragraphs (3)(e) and (1)(e) of paragraph 1 of Schedule 1 in respect of each of the other members of the polygamous marriage who are members of that household;
(c) [[3] . . .]
(d) the amount of any premiums which may be applicable to a member of the joint-claim couple determined in accordance with Parts IVA and IVB of Schedule 1 (premiums); and
(e) any amounts determined in accordance with Schedule 2 (housing costs) which may be applicable to the joint-claim couple in respect

of mortgage interest payments or such other housing costs as are prescribed in that Schedule.]

AMENDMENTS

1. Jobseeker's Allowance (Joint Claims) Regulations 2000 (SI 2000/1978) reg.2(5) and Sch.2 para.35 (March 19, 2001).
2. Social Security Amendment (Residential Care and Nursing Homes) Regulations 2001 (SI 2001/3767) reg.2 and Sch. Pt II para.8 (April 8, 2002).
3. Social Security (Removal of Residential Allowance and Miscellaneous Amendments) Regulations 2003 (SI 2003/1121) reg.4 and Sch.2 para.6 (October 6, 2003).
4. Social Security (Miscellaneous Amendments) (No.5) Regulations 2009 (SI 2009/3228) reg.3(3)(d) (January 25, 2010).

GENERAL NOTE

This regulation applies to income-based JSA only (see reg.82). It makes provision corresponding to reg.84 for joint-claim couples. 3.272

[1Joint-claim couples: special cases

86C.—(1) [2[3Where]] a member of a joint-claim couple is a person to whom any paragraph in column (1) of Schedule 5A applies (applicable amounts in special cases for joint-claim couples), the amount included in the joint-claim couple's weekly applicable amount shall be the amount prescribed in the corresponding paragraph in column (2) of that Schedule. 3.273

(2) Except where the amount prescribed in Schedule 5A in respect of a joint-claim couple includes an amount applicable under regulation 86A(c) or 86B(d), a person to whom paragraph (1) applies shall be treated as not falling within the conditions specified in paragraph 20I of Schedule 1 (severe disability premium).

[2(2A) [3. . .]

(3) [4 . . .]

(4) Expressions used in this regulation and in Schedule 5A shall have the same meaning as those expressions have for the purposes of regulation 85 and Schedule 5 save that for the purposes of this regulation and of Schedule 5A, the definition of "person from abroad" in regulation 85(4) shall have effect as if after the words "a claimant" there were inserted the words ",other than a member of a joint-claim couple who is not the nominated member for the purposes of section 3B,".]

AMENDMENTS

1. Jobseeker's Allowance (Joint Claims) Regulations 2000 (SI 2000/1978) reg.2(5) and Sch.2 para.35 (March 19, 2001).
2. Social Security Amendment (Residential Care and Nursing Homes) Regulations 2001 (SI 2001/3767) reg.2 and Sch. Pt II para.9 (April 8, 2002).
3. Social Security (Miscellaneous Amendments) Regulations 2004 (SI 2004/565) reg.6 (April 1, 2004).
4. Social Security (Hospital In-Patients) Regulations 2005 (SI 2005/3360) reg.6 (April 10, 2006).

GENERAL NOTE

This regulation applies to income-based JSA only (see reg.82). It makes provision corresponding to reg.85 for joint-claim couples. 3.274

[1Applicable amount for a joint-claim couple where a member is in residential care or a nursing home

3.275 **86D.**—[2. . .]]

Amendments

1. Jobseeker's Allowance (Joint Claims) Regulations 2000 (SI 2000/1978) reg.2(5) and Sch.2 para.35 (March 19, 2001).

2. Social Security Amendment (Residential Care and Nursing Homes) Regulations 2001 (SI 2001/3767) reg.2 and Sch. Pt II para.10 (April 8, 2002).

General Note

3.276 This regulation applied to income-based JSA only (see reg.82). It made provision corresponding to reg.86 for joint-claim couples.

Transitional supplement to income-based jobseeker's allowance

3.277 87.—(1) In the case of a person who, before 7th October 1996 was entitled to a special transitional addition or transitional addition in accordance with the Income Support (Transitional) Regulations 1987, the amount of any income-based jobseeker's allowance payable to him shall be increased by an amount equal to those additions, but the increase shall continue to be payable only for so long as the claimant continues to satisfy the requirements imposed in those Regulations for payment of the addition.

(2) A claimant's weekly applicable amount shall include an amount (the "protected sum") equal to any protected sum which would have been applicable in his case under regulation 17(1)(g) or 18(1)(h) of, and Schedules 3A and 3B to, the Income Support Regulations had he been entitled to income support and not a jobseeker's allowance.

(3) In the case of any person who had he been entitled to income support and not a jobseeker's allowance, would in any week have had a higher applicable amount, in accordance with regulation 17(2) to (6A) of the Income Support Regulations, than the amount applicable to him in accordance with regulation 82 or, as the case may be, 83 then that amount shall be substituted for the applicable amount determined under that regulation.

(4) Paragraph (5) applies to a person who, had he been entitled to income support and not a jobseeker's allowance, would have been a person to whom any of the following transitional or savings provisions would have applied—

(a) the Income Support (General) Amendment No.3 Regulations 1993 ("the 1993 Regulations"), regulation 4;
(b) the Income-related Benefits Schemes (Miscellaneous Amendments) Regulations 1995 ("the 1995 Regulations"), regulation 28.

(5) Where this paragraph applies, the amount of housing costs applicable in the particular case shall be determined as if, in Schedule 2—

(a) in a case to which regulation 4(1) of the 1993 Regulations would have applied, paragraph 10(4) to (9) was omitted;
(b) in a case to which regulation 4(4) of the 1993 Regulations would have applied, in [1paragraph 10(4)] for the reference to £100,000 there was substituted a reference to £150,000; and

(c) in a case to which the 1995 Regulations apply, in [1paragraph 10(4)] for the reference to £100,000 there was substituted a reference to £125,000.

(6) In determining for the purposes of this regulation whether, if the claimant were entitled to income support—

(a) an amount would be applicable;
(b) an amount would be payable; or
(c) if an amount was payable, the rate at which it would be payable,

any requirement that the person be entitled to income support, or to income support for any period of time, shall be treated as if the reference to income support included also a reference to an income-based jobseeker's allowance.

(7) [2For the purposes of applying paragraph (1), regulation 2A of the Income Support (Transitional) Regulations, and for the purposes of paragraph (6), regulation 3A of the Income Support Regulations shall have effect in accordance with the following sub-paragraphs]—

(a) as if in paragraph (1)(a), after the words "permitted period", there was included the words "subject to paragraph 2A"; and
(b) with the addition after paragraph (1) of the following paragraphs—

"(2A) Subject to paragraph (2B) where the claimant or his partner has ceased to be engaged in remunerative work, the permitted period shall be 8 weeks if—

(a) a jobseeker's allowance [2is not payable] to the claimant in the circumstances mentioned in [3 section 19(2)(a) or (b)] of the Jobseekers Act 1995 (employment left voluntarily or lost through misconduct); or
(b) the claimant or his partner has ceased to be engaged in that work within 4 weeks of beginning it; or
(c) at any time during the period of 13 weeks immediately preceding the beginning of that work, the person who has ceased to be engaged in it—
  (i) was engaged in remunerative work; or
  (ii) was in relevant education; or
  (iii) was a student.

(2B) [1Paragraph (2A)(b) or (2A)(c)] shall not apply in the case of a person who, by virtue of regulation 74 of the Jobseeker's Allowance Regulations 1996, is a person to whom [3 section 19(2)(b)] of the Jobseekers Act 1995 does not apply.

(2C) In this regulation, 'remunerative work' means remunerative work for the purposes of the Jobseekers Act 1995."

AMENDMENTS

1. Jobseeker's Allowance (Amendment) Regulations 1996 (SI 1996/1516) reg.20 and Sch. (October 7, 1996).

2. Jobseeker's Allowance and Income Support (General) (Amendment) Regulations 1996 (SI 1996/1517) reg.20 (October 7, 1996).

3. Jobseeker's Allowance (Sanctions) (Amendment) Regulations 2012 (SI 2012/2568) reg.5(19) (October 22, 2012).

DEFINITIONS

"claimant"—see Jobseekers Act s.35(1).
"Income Support Regulations"—*ibid.*
"remunerative work"—see reg.51(1).

General Note

3.278 This provision only applies to income-based JSA (reg.82).

Paragraphs (2)–(5) preserve the effect of various income support transitional protection provisions for JSA claimants who would have been covered by them had they been entitled to claim income support after October 6, 1996. Paragraph (1) concerns those who were entitled to a special transitional addition or transitional addition under the Income Support (Transitional) Regulations before October 7, 1996. For the regulations referred to in para.(4) see pp.800 and 803. The effect of those Regulations is explained in the notes to para.11((4)–(11) of Sch.3 to the Income Support Regulations.

[1Minimum amount of a jobseeker's allowance

3.279 **87A.**—Where the amount of a jobseeker's allowance is less than 10 pence a week that allowance shall not be payable.]

Amendment

1. Jobseeker's Allowance and Income Support (General) (Amendment) Regulations 1996 (SI 1996/1517) reg.21 (October 7, 1996).

Part VIII

Income and Capital

Chapter I

General

Calculation of income and capital of members of claimant's family and of a polygamous marriage

3.280 **88.**—(1) Subject to [3 paragraph] (3) [2and [3regulation] 88ZA (calculation of income and capital of a joint-claim couple)] [3 . . .], the income and capital of a claimant's partner [3. . .] which by virtue of section 13(2) is to be treated as the income and capital of the claimant, shall be calculated in accordance with the following provisions of this Part in like manner as for the claimant; and any reference to the "claimant" shall, except where the context otherwise requires, be construed, for the purposes of this Part, as if it were a reference to his partner [3. . .].

[3(2) Subject to the following provisions of this Part, the income paid to, or in respect of, and capital of, a child or young person who is a member of the claimant's family shall not be treated as the income or capital of the claimant.]

(3) Where at least one member of a couple is aged less than 18 and the applicable amount of the couple falls to be determined under [1paragraph 1(3)(b), (c), (g) or (h)] of Schedule 1 (applicable amounts), the income of the claimant's partner shall not be treated as the income of the claimant to the extent that—

(a) in the case of a couple where both members are aged less than 18, the amount specified in paragraph 1(3)(a) of that Schedule exceeds the amount specified in paragraph 1(3)(c) of that Schedule; and

(b) in the case of a couple where only one member is aged less than 18, the amount specified in paragraph 1(3)(e) of that Schedule exceeds the amount which applies in that case which is specified in [1paragraph 1(3)(g) or (h)] of that Schedule.

(4) Subject to paragraph (5), where a claimant is married polygamously to two or more members of his household—

(a) the claimant shall be treated as possessing capital and income belonging to each such member [3 . . .]; and

(b) the income and capital of that member [3 . . .] shall be calculated in accordance with the following provisions of this Part in like manner as for the claimant [3 . . .].

(5) Where a member of a polygamous marriage is a partner aged less than 18 and the amount which applies in respect of him under regulation 84(2) (polygamous marriages) is nil, the claimant shall not be treated as possessing the income of that partner to the extent that an amount in respect of him would have been included in the applicable amount if he had fallen within the circumstances set out in regulation 84(2)(a) or (b).

AMENDMENTS

1. Jobseeker's Allowance (Amendment) Regulations 1996 (SI 1996/1516) reg.20 and Sch. (October 7, 1996).

2. Jobseeker's Allowance (Joint Claims) Regulations 2000 (SI 2000/1978) reg.2(5) and Sch.2 para.36 (March 19, 2001).

3. Social Security (Working Tax Credit and Child Tax Credit) (Consequential Amendments) Regulations 2003 (SI 2003/455) reg.3 and Sch.2 para.6 (April 6, 2004, except in "transitional cases" and see further the note to reg.83 and to reg.17 of the Income Support Regulations).

DEFINITIONS

"child"—see Jobseekers Act s.35(1).
"claimant"—*ibid.*
"family"—*ibid.*
"joint-claim couple"—see JSA s.1(4).
"partner"—see reg.1(3).
"polygamous marriage"—*ibid.*
"young person"—see reg.76.

GENERAL NOTE

This regulation contains the basic rule on aggregation of resources which is the same as that in reg.23 of the Income Support Regulations. With effect from April 6, 2004 (except in "transitional cases"—see the note to reg. 83 and to reg.17 of the Income Support Regulations), only the income and capital of the claimant's partner is treated as the claimant's. 3.281

Under the form of reg.88 in force before April 6, 2004 (the old form continues to apply for "transitional cases"—see the note to reg.83 and to reg.17 of the Income Support Regulations) the income (but not the capital) of a child or young person who was a member of the claimant's family was aggregated with the claimant's (see the 2003 edition of this volume for the old form of reg.88 and the notes to that regulation for further details of the former rules relating to treatment of a child or young person's income and capital). However, with effect from April 6, 2004 (except in "transitional cases") amounts for children and young persons have been removed from income-based JSA; financial assistance to help with the cost of bringing up a child or young person is now to be provided through the child tax credit system, see Vol.IV of this series. As a consequence the new form of para.(2) provides that income paid to, or in respect of, and the capital of, a child or young person does not count as that of the claimant. Note the new disregards of child benefit and child tax credit (see para.6B of Sch.7) (for income-based JSA claimants who had an award of child tax credit before April 6, 2004 see reg.8 of the Social Security (Working Tax Credit and Child Tax Credit) (Consequential Amendments) Regulations 2003 (SI 2003/455) (as amended) on p.813 and the notes to that regulation).

See further the notes to reg.23.

The aggregation rule is primarily relevant to income-based JSA (although reg.88 applies to both contribution and income-based JSA), since for contribution-based JSA only the *claimant's* earnings and pension payments are taken into account (see s.2(1)(c) and 4(1) of the Jobseekers Act and regs 56(2), 80(2) and 81).

[1 Calculation of income and capital of a joint-claim couple

3.282 **88ZA.**—(1) Subject to paragraphs (2) and (4), the income and capital of a joint-claim couple shall be calculated by—

(a) determining the income and capital of each member of that couple in accordance with this Part; and

(b) aggregating the amount determined in respect of each member in accordance with sub-paragraph (a) above.

(2) Where—

(a) a member of a joint-claim couple is aged less than 18;

(b) the other member is aged over 18; and

(c) the applicable amount of the couple falls to be determined under paragraph 1(3)(g) or (h) of Schedule 1 (applicable amounts),

the income of the joint-claim couple shall not be aggregated to the extent that the amount specified in paragraph 1(3)(e) of that Schedule exceeds the amount which applies in that case which is specified in paragraph 1(3)(g) or (h) of that Schedule.

(3) Where a member of a joint-claim couple is married polygamously to two or more members of his household, the joint-claim couple shall be treated as possessing income and capital belonging to each such member and the income and capital of that member shall be calculated in accordance with the following provisions of this Part in like manner as for each member of the joint-claim couple.

(4) Regulations 99(2) and 101(2) in so far as they relate to paragraphs 5,7, 8 and 11 of Schedule 6 (earnings to be disregarded) shall not apply to a member of a joint-claim couple but there shall instead be disregarded from the net earnings of a member of a joint-claim couple any sum, where applicable, specified in—

(a) paragraphs 1 to 4 and 13 to 16 of Schedule 6; and

(b) paragraphs 1 to 6 of Schedule 6A.]

AMENDMENT

1. Jobseeker's Allowance (Joint Claims) Regulations 2000 (SI 2000/1978) reg.2(5) and Sch.2, para.37 (March 19, 2001).

DEFINITIONS

"joint-claim couple"—see JSA s.1(4).
"polygamous marriage"—see reg.1(3).

[1 Income of participants in the self-employment route [2. . .]

88A.—Chapters II, III, IV, V, VII and VIII of this Part and regulations 131 to 136, 138 and 139 shall not apply to any income which is to be calculated in accordance with Chapter IVA of this Part (participants in the self-employment route [2. . .]).] 3.283

AMENDMENTS

1. Social Security (Miscellaneous Amendments) (No.4) Regulations 1998 (SI 1998/1174) reg.3(3) (June 1, 1998).
2. Social Security Amendment (Employment Zones) (No.2) Regulations 2000 (SI 2000/2910) reg.5(2)(a) (November 27, 2000).

DEFINITION

"self-employment route"—see reg.1(3).

GENERAL NOTE

Regulation 88A takes any gross receipts from trading while on the self-employment route (defined in reg.1(3)) out of the categories of earnings, self-employed earnings and income other than earnings. The rules for liable relative payments and student income (except reg.137) also do not apply. Any such receipts may only be taken into account in accordance with regs 102A–102D. 3.284

[2[4. . .]] liable relative payments

89.—Regulations 94 to [1 105], 108 to 115 and Chapter IX of this Part shall not apply to any payment which is to be calculated in accordance with Chapter VII thereof ([3 [5 . . .] liable relative payments]). 3.285

AMENDMENTS

1. Social Security (Working Tax Credit and Child Tax Credit) (Consequential Amendments) Regulations 2003 (SI 2003/455) reg.3 and Sch.2 para.7 (April 6, 2004, except in "transitional cases" and see further the note to reg.83 and to reg.17 of the Income Support Regulations).
2. Social Security (Child Maintenance Amendments) Regulations 2008 (SI 2008/2111) reg.3(2) (October 27, 2008).
3. Social Security (Child Maintenance Amendments) Regulations 2008 (SI 2008/2111) reg.3(3) (October 27, 2008).
4. Social Security (Miscellaneous Amendments) (No.4) Regulations 2009 (SI 2009/2655) reg.4(4) (April 12, 2010).
5. Social Security (Miscellaneous Amendments) (No.4) Regulations 2009 (SI 2009/2655) reg.4(5) (April 12, 2010).

GENERAL NOTE

See reg.25 of the Income Support Regulations. 3.286

Child support

90.—[1 . . .] 3.287

AMENDMENT

1. Social Security (Child Maintenance Amendments) Regulations 2008 (SI 2008/2111) reg.3(4)(a) (October 27, 2008).

Calculation of income and capital of full-time students

3.288 **91.**—The provisions of Chapters II to VI of this Part (income and capital) shall have effect in relation to full-time students and their partners subject to the modifications set out in Chapter IX thereof (full-time students).

DEFINITIONS

"full-time student"—see reg.1(3).
"partner"—*ibid.*

GENERAL NOTE

3.289 See reg.26 of the Income Support Regulations.

Rounding of fractions

3.290 **92.**—Where any calculation under this Part results in a fraction of a penny that fraction shall, if it would be to the claimant's advantage, be treated as a penny, otherwise it shall be disregarded.

CHAPTER II

INCOME

Calculation of income

3.291 **93.**—(1) For the purposes of [1 sections 3(1) (the income-based conditions) and 3A(1) (the conditions for claims by joint-claim couples)] (the income-based conditions) the income of a claimant shall be calculated on a weekly basis—

(a) by determining in accordance with this Part, other than Chapter VI, the weekly amount of his income; and
(b) by adding to that amount the weekly income calculated under regulation 116 (calculation of tariff income from capital).

(2) For the purposes of paragraph (1) "income" includes capital treated as income under regulation 104 and income which a claimant is treated as possessing under regulation 105 (notional income).

AMENDMENT

1. Jobseeker's Allowance (Joint Claims) Regulations 2000 (SI 2000/1978) reg.2(5) and Sch.2 para.38 (March 19, 2001).

DEFINITIONS

"claimant"—see JSA s.35(1).
"joint-claim couple"—see JSA s.1(4).

General Note

This confirms that for the purposes of income-based JSA all resources which come under the description of income, including resources specifically treated as earnings or income, are to be taken into account in the income calculation. 3.292

Calculation of earnings derived from employed earner's employment and income other than earnings

94.—(1) Earnings derived from employment as an employed earner and income which does not consist of earnings shall be taken into account over a period determined in accordance with the following paragraphs and at a weekly amount determined in accordance with regulation 97 (calculation of weekly amount of income). 3.293

(2) Subject to the following provisions of this regulation, the period over which a payment is to be taken into account shall be—

[6 (a) where the payment is monthly, a period equal to the number of weeks from the date on which the payment is treated as paid to the date immediately before the date on which the next monthly payment would have been so treated as paid whether or not the next monthly payment is actually paid;

(aa) where the payment is in respect of a period which is not monthly, a period equal to the length of the period for which payment is made;]

[9 (b) in any other case, a period equal to such number of weeks as is equal to the number obtained by applying the formula—

$$\frac{E}{J+D}$$

where—

E is the amount of net earnings, or in the case of income which does not consist of earnings, the amount of that income less any amount paid by way of tax on that income which is disregarded under paragraph 1 of Schedule 7 (sums to be disregarded in the calculation of income other than earnings);

J is the amount of jobseeker's allowance which would be payable had the payment not been made;

D is an amount equal to the total of the sums which would fall to be disregarded from that payment under Schedule 6 and Schedule 6A (sums to be disregarded in the calculation of earnings) or, as the case may be, any paragraph of Schedule 7 other than paragraph 1 of that Schedule, as is appropriate in the claimant's case,]

and that period shall begin on the date on which the payment is treated as paid under regulation 96.

[1(2A) The period over which a Career Development Loan, which is paid pursuant to section 2 of the Employment and Training Act 1973, shall be taken into account shall be the period of education and training intended to be supported by that loan.

(2B) Where grant income as defined in Chapter IX of this Part has been paid to a person who ceases to be a full-time student before the end of the period in respect of which that income is payable and, as a consequence, the whole or part of that income falls to be repaid by that person, that income shall be taken into account over the period beginning on the date on which that income is treated as paid under regulation 96 and ending—

(a) on the date on which repayment is made in full; or

[[2](aa) where the grant is paid in instalments, on the day before the next instalment would have been paid had the claimant remained a student; or]

(b) on the last date of the academic term or vacation during which that person ceased to be a full-time student

whichever shall first occur.]

[[7] [[10] (2C)(a) This paragraph applies where earnings are derived by a claimant as a member of a reserve force prescribed in Part 1 of Schedule 6 to the Contributions Regulations—

(i) in respect of a period of annual continuous training for a maximum of 15 days in any calendar year; or

(ii) in respect of training in the claimant's first year of training as a member of a reserve force for a maximum of 43 days in that year.

(b) Earnings, whether paid to the claimant alone or together with other earnings derived from the same source, are to be taken into account—

(i) in the case of a period of training which lasts for the number of days listed in column 1 of the table in sub-paragraph (c), over a period of time which is equal to the number of days set out in the corresponding row in column 2 of that table; or

(ii) in any other case, over a period of time which is equal to the number of days of the training period.

(c) This is the table referred to in sub-paragraph (b)(i)—

Column 1 *Period of training in days*	*Column 2* *Period of time over which earnings are to be taken into account in days*
8 to 10	7
15 to 17	14
22 to 24	21
29 to 31	28
36 to 38	35
43	42]

(2D) The period referred to in paragraph (2C) over which earnings are to be taken into account shall begin on the date on which they are treated as paid under regulation 96.]

(3) Where earnings not of the same kind are derived from the same source and the periods in respect of which those earnings would, but for this paragraph, fall to be taken into account—

(a) overlap, wholly or partly, those earnings shall be taken into account over a period equal to the aggregate length of those periods;

(b) and that period shall begin with the earliest date on which any part of those earnings would otherwise be treated as paid under regulation 96 (date on which income is treated as paid).

(4) In a case to which paragraph (3) applies, earnings under regulation 98 (earnings of employed earners) shall be taken into account in the following order of priority—

(a) earnings normally derived from the employment;
(b) any compensation payment;
(c) any holiday pay.

(5) Where earnings to which regulation 98(1)(b) or (c) (earnings of employed earners) applies are paid in respect of part of a day, those earnings shall be taken into account over a period equal to a day.

(6) Subject to paragraph (7), the period over which a compensation payment is to be taken into account shall be the period beginning on the date on which the payment is treated as paid under regulation 96 (date on which income is treated as paid) and ending—

(a) subject to sub-paragraph (b), where the person who made the payment represents that it, or part of it, was paid in lieu of notice of termination of employment or on account of the early termination of a contract of employment for a term certain, on the expiry date;
(b) in a case where the person who made the payment represents that it, or part of it, was paid in lieu of consultation under section 188 of the Trade Union and Labour Relations (Consolidation) Act 1992, on the later of—
   (i) the date on which the consultation period under that section would have ended;
   (ii) in a case where sub-paragraph (a) also applies, the expiry date; or
   (iii) the standard date;
(c) in any other case, on the standard date.

(7) The maximum length of time over which a compensation payment may be taken into account under paragraph (6) is 52 weeks from the date on which the payment is treated as paid under regulation 96.

(8) In this regulation—

(a) "compensation payment" means any payment to which paragraph (3) of regulation 98 (earnings of employed earners) applies;
(b) "the expiry date" means in relation to the termination of a person's employment—
   (i) the date on which the period of notice applicable to the person was due to expire, or would have expired had it not been waived; and for this purpose "period of notice" means the period of notice of termination of employment to which a person is entitled by statute or by contract, whichever is the longer, or, if he is not entitled to such notice, the period of notice which is customary in the employment in question; or
   (ii) subject to paragraph (9), where the person who made the payment represents that the period in respect of which that payment is made is longer than the period of notice referred to in head (i) above, the date on which that longer period is due to expire; or
   (iii) where the person had a contract of employment for a term certain, the date on which it was due to expire;
(c) "the standard date" means the earlier of—
   (i) the expiry date; and
   (ii) the last day of the period determined by dividing the amount of the compensation payment by the maximum weekly amount which, on the date on which the payment is treated as paid under regulation 96, is specified in [5 section 227(1) of the

Employment Rights Act 1996], and treating the result (less any fraction of a whole number) as a number of weeks.

(9) For the purposes of paragraph (8), if it appears to [3the Secretary of State] in a case to which sub-paragraph (b)(ii) of that paragraph applies that, having regard to the amount of the compensation payment and the level of remuneration normally received by the claimant when he was engaged in the employment in respect of which the compensation payment was made, it is unreasonable to take the payment into account until the date specified in that sub-paragraph, the expiry date shall be the date specified in paragraph (8)(b)(i).

(10) For the purposes of this regulation the claimant's earnings and income which does not consist of earnings shall be calculated in accordance with Chapters III and V respectively of this Part.

[9 (11) For the purposes of the number obtained as referred to in paragraph (2)(b), any fraction is to be treated as a corresponding fraction of a week.]

AMENDMENTS

1. Income-related Benefits and Jobseeker's Allowance (Miscellaneous Amendments) Regulations 1997 (SI 1997/65) reg.5(2) (April 7, 1997).
2. Social Security (Miscellaneous Amendments) Regulations 1998 (SI 1998/563) reg.12 (April 6, 1998).
3. Social Security Act 1998 (Commencement No.11, and Savings and Consequential and Transitional Provisions) Order 1999 (SI 1999/2860 (C.75)) art.3(12) and Sch.12 para.2 (October 18, 1999).
4. Jobseeker's Allowance (Joint Claims) Regulations 2000 (SI 2000/1978) reg.2(5) and Sch.2 para.39 (March 19, 2001).
5. Social Security (Miscellaneous Amendments) (No.5) Regulations 2007 (SI 2007/2618) reg.8(7) (October 1, 2007).
6. Social Security (Miscellaneous Amendments) Regulations 2008 (SI 2008/698) reg.4(10) (April 14, 2008).
7. Jobseeker's Allowance (Members of the Reserve Forces) Regulations 2012 (SI 2012/1616) reg.2(6) (July 30, 2012).
8. Social Security (Miscellaneous Amendments) (No.2) Regulations 2012 (SI 2012/2575) reg.3(5) (November 5, 2012).
9. Social Security (Miscellaneous Amendments) (No.3) Regulations 2013 (SI 2013/2536) reg.6(9) (October 29, 2013).
10. Social Security (Members of the Reserve Forces) (Amendment) Regulations 2015 (SI 2015/389) reg.3(5) (April 6, 2015).

DEFINITIONS

"claimant"—*ibid.*, reg.88(1)
"earnings"—see reg.1(3).
"employed earner"—see reg.3 and SSCBA s.2(1)(a).
"first year of training"—see reg.1(3).
"full-time student"—see reg.1(3).
"grant income"—see reg.130.

GENERAL NOTE

3.294 On paras (1)–(5) see the notes to reg.29(1)–(4A) of the Income Support Regulations. In relation to paras (2C) and (2D) note the disregard in para.19 of Sch.6. A claimant is treated as available for work while engaged in such reservist training (see reg.14(1)(v)) and as actively seeking work in any week in which he is taking part in such training for three or more days a week (see reg.19(1)(y)).

Paragraphs (3) and (4) will be of less relevance following the increased disregard of payments made on the termination of full-time employment introduced on October 1, 2007 (see para.1 of Sch.6 and the notes to that paragraph). However they will still apply where part-time work ends while the claimant is claiming JSA, or where full-time employment has been suspended.

Note that para.(2)(b) was rewritten and a new para.(11) was added on October 29, 2013 so as to match the equivalent provisions for new style JSA (see reg.54(2)(c) and (13) of the Jobseeker's Allowance Regulations 2013 (SI 2013/378) in Pt VI of this Volume) but the substance remains the same.

Paragraphs (6)–(9)

These provisions define the length of the period for which a "compensation payment" (defined in reg.98(3)) is to be taken into account. Note that from October 1, 2007 such compensation payments are ignored except in the case of part-time work which ends while the person is claiming JSA. There is no equivalent to reg.29(4C) of the Income Support Regulations so it seems that a compensation payment made on the termination of such part-time employment will be taken into account as earnings for the period covered by the payment. The "maximum weekly amount" referred to in para.(8)(c)(ii) is the amount specified at the relevant time as the amount to be used in calculating the basic award for unfair dismissal and redundancy payments. The figure in effect from April 6, 2016 is £479. 3.295

Note *CJSA 5529/1997* in which the effect of para.(6) was that the period to which the claimant's compensation payment was to be attributed ended before it started. On October 1, 1996 the claimant agreed with her employer that her employment would end on December 31, 1996 by way of voluntary redundancy. She was to receive a payment of £41,500 on January 4, 1997, which would not include any sum in lieu of notice. She claimed JSA with effect from January 1, 1997. The Commissioner states that the period for which the compensation period was to be taken into account under para.(6) ended on the "standard date". Under para.(8)(c) the standard date was the earlier of the "expiry date" and what might be termed the "apportionment date". The expiry date in this case was no later than December 31, 1996 because the claimant was entitled to 12 weeks' (or three months') notice and the agreement for redundancy had been made on October 1, 1996 (see para.(8)(b)(i)). The result was that there was no period in respect of which the compensation payment was to be taken into account and thus no period during which she was to be treated as in remunerative work after December 31, 1996.

Calculation of earnings of self-employed earners

95.—(1) Except where paragraph (2) applies, where a claimant's income consists of earnings from employment as a self-employed earner the weekly amount of his earnings shall be determined by reference to his average weekly earnings from that employment— 3.296

(a) over a period of one year; or

(b) where the claimant has recently become engaged in that employment or there has been a change which is likely to affect the normal pattern of business, over such other period as may, in any particular case, enable the weekly amount of his earnings to be determined more accurately.

(2) Where the claimant's earnings consist of [2 any items to which paragraph (2A) applies] those earnings shall be taken into account over a period equal to such number of weeks as is equal to the number obtained (and any fraction shall be treated as a corresponding fraction of a week) by dividing the earnings by the amount of jobseeker's allowance which would be payable had the payment not been made plus an amount equal to the total

of the sums which would fall to be disregarded from the payment under Schedule 6 [1 and Schedule 6A] (earnings to be disregarded) as is appropriate in the claimant's case.

[2 [3 (2A) This paragraph applies to—

(a) royalties or other sums paid as a consideration for the use of, or the right to use, any copyright, design, patent or trade mark; or

(b) any payment in respect of any—

(i) book registered under the Public Lending Right Scheme 1982; or

(ii) work made under any international public lending right scheme that is analogous to the Public Lending Right Scheme 1982,

where the claimant is the first owner of the copyright, design, patent or trade mark, or an original contributor to the book or work concerned.]]

(3) For the purposes of this regulation the claimant's earnings shall be calculated in accordance with Chapter IV of this Part.

AMENDMENTS

1. Jobseeker's Allowance (Joint Claims) Regulations 2000 (SI 2000/1978) reg.2(5) and Sch.2 para.40 (March 19, 2001).

2. Social Security (Miscellaneous Amendments) Regulations 2008 (SI 2008/698) reg,.4(11) (April 7, 2008).

3. Social Security (Miscellaneous Amendments) Regulations 2009 (SI 2009/583) reg.4(6) (April 6, 2009).

DEFINITIONS

"claimant"—see Jobseekers Act s.35(1) and reg.88(1).

"earnings"—see reg.1(3).

"self-employed earner"—*ibid.*, SSCBA s.2(1)(b).

GENERAL NOTE

3.297 See the notes to reg.30 of the Income Support Regulations.

Note the more general exception to the rule in para.(1)(a) that is hidden in reg.101(11) which allows the amount of any item of income or expenditure to be calculated over a different period if that will produce a more accurate figure.

Date on which income is treated as paid

3.298 **96.**—(1) Except where paragraph [5 [(2) [6 applies]], a payment of income to which regulation 94 (calculation of earnings derived from employed earner's employment and income other than earnings) applies shall be treated as paid—

(a) in the case of a payment which is due to be paid before the first benefit week pursuant to the claim, on the date on which it is due to be paid;

(b) in any other case, on the first day of the benefit week in which it is due to be paid or the first succeeding benefit week in which it is practicable to take it into account.

(2) Income support, maternity allowance, short-term or long-term incapacity benefit, severe disablement allowance [4 , jobseeker's allowance [7, employment and support allowance or universal credit]] shall be treated as paid [7 on any day] in respect of which it is payable.

[3 (3) [6 . . .]]
[5 (4) [6 . . .]]

AMENDMENTS

1. Social Security (Miscellaneous Amendments) Regulations 2000 (SI 2000/681) reg.3(2) (April 3, 2000).
2. Income-related Benefits and Jobseeker's Allowance (Working Tax Credit and Child Tax Credit) (Amendment) Regulations 2002 (SI 2002/2402) reg.3 and Sch.2 para.4 (April 6, 2003).
3. Social Security (Working Tax Credit and Child Tax Credit) (Consequential Amendments) (No.3) Regulations 2003 (SI 2003/1731) reg.4 (August 8, 2003).
4. Employment and Support Allowance (Consequential Provisions) (No.2) Regulations 2008 (SI 2008/1554) reg.3(14) (October 27, 2008).
5. Social Security (Miscellaneous Amendments) (No.6) Regulations 2008 (SI 2008/2767) reg.4(4) (November 17, 2008).
6. Social Security (Miscellaneous Amendments) Regulations 2011 (SI 2011/674) reg.7(3) (April 11, 2011).
7. Universal Credit (Consequential, Supplementary, Incidental and Miscellaneous Provisions) Regulations 2013 (SI 2013/630) reg.30(4) (April 29, 2013).

DEFINITIONS

"benefit week"—see reg.1(3).
"child tax credit"—*ibid.*
"universal credit"—*ibid.*
"working tax credit"—*ibid.*

GENERAL NOTE

See the notes to reg.31 of the Income Support Regulations. **3.299**

Calculation of weekly amount of income

97.—(1) For the purposes of regulation 94 (calculation of earnings derived from employed earner's employment and income other than earnings) [4[5 . . .]], subject to paragraphs (2) to [2(7)], where the period in respect of which a payment [4 of income or tax credit] is made— **3.300**

(a) does not exceed a week, the weekly amount shall be the amount of that payment;
(b) exceeds a week, the weekly amount shall be determined—
  (i) in a case where that period is a month, by multiplying the amount of the payment by 12 and dividing the product by 52;
  (ii) in a case where that period is three months, by multiplying the amount of the payment by 4 and dividing the product by 52;
  [4 (iii) in a case where that period is a year and the payment is an award of working tax credit, by dividing the payment by the number of days in the year and multiplying the result by 7;
  (iiia) in a case where that period is a year and the payment is income other than an award of working tax credit, by dividing the amount of the payment by 52;]
  (iv) in any other case by multiplying the amount of the payment by 7 and dividing the product by the number equal to the number of days in the period in respect of which it is made.

(2) Where a payment for a period not exceeding a week is treated under regulation 96(1)(a) (date on which income is treated as paid) as paid before the first benefit week and a part is to be taken into account for some days only in that week ("the relevant days"), the amount to be taken into account for the relevant days shall be calculated by multiplying the amount of the payment by the number equal to the number of relevant days and dividing the product by the number of days in the period in respect of which it is made.

(3) Where a payment is in respect of a period equal to or in excess of a week and a part thereof is to be taken into account for some days only in a benefit week ("the relevant days"), the amount to be taken into account for the relevant days shall, except where paragraph (4) applies, be calculated by multiplying the amount of the payment by the number equal to the number of relevant days and dividing the product by the number of days in the period in respect of which it is made.

(4) In the case of a payment of—

(a) maternity allowance, short-term or long-term incapacity benefit or severe disablement allowance, the amount to be taken into account for the relevant days shall be the amount of benefit payable in respect of those days;

(b) jobseeker's allowance [[3], income support or employment and support allowance], the amount to be taken into account for the relevant days shall be calculated by multiplying the weekly amount of the benefit by the number of relevant days and dividing the product by seven.

(5) Except in the case of a payment which it has not been practicable to treat under regulation 96(1)(b) as paid on the first day of the benefit week in which it is due to be paid, where a payment of income from a particular source is or has been paid regularly and that payment falls to be taken into account in the same benefit week as a payment of the same kind and from the same source, the amount of that income to be taken into account in any one benefit week shall not exceed the weekly amount determined under paragraph (1)(a) or (b), as the case may be, of the payment which under regulation 96(1)(b) (date on which income is treated as paid) is treated as paid first.

(6) Where the amount of the claimant's income fluctuates and has changed more than once, or a claimant's regular pattern of work is such that he does not work every week, the foregoing paragraphs may be modified so that the weekly amount of his income is determined by reference to his average weekly income—

(a) if there is a recognisable cycle of work, over a period of one complete cycle (including, where the cycle involves periods in which the claimant does no work, those periods but disregarding any other absences);

(b) in any other case, over a period of five weeks or such other period as may, in the particular case, enable the claimant's average weekly income to be determined more accurately.

[[1](7) Where income is taken into account under paragraph (2B) of regulation 94 over the period specified in that paragraph, the amount of that income to be taken into account in respect of any week in that period shall be an amount equal to the amount of that income which would have been taken into account under regulation 131 had the person to whom that income was paid not ceased to be a full-time student.]

AMENDMENTS

1. Income-related Benefits and Jobseeker's Allowance (Miscellaneous Amendments) Regulations 1997 (SI 1997/65) reg.6(2) (April 7, 1997).
2. Social Security (Miscellaneous Amendments) Regulations 1997 (SI 1997/454) reg.2(11) (April 7, 1997).
3. Employment and Support Allowance (Consequential Provisions) (No.2) Regulations 2008 (SI 2008/1554) reg.3(15) (October 27, 2008).
4. Social Security (Miscellaneous Amendments) (No.6) Regulations 2008 (SI 2008/2767) reg.4(5) (November 17, 2008).
5. Social Security (Miscellaneous Amendments) Regulations 2011 (SI 2011/674) reg.7(4) (April 11, 2011).

DEFINITIONS

"benefit week"—see reg.1(3).
"claimant"—see Jobseekers Act s.35(1) and reg.88(1).
"full-time student"—see reg.1(3).

GENERAL NOTE

See the notes to reg.32 of the Income Support Regulations. In relation to para. (5), the JSA disregards corresponding to the income support disregards referred to in those notes are in Sch.6 para.13, Sch.7 para.39, Sch.6 para.16 and Sch.7 para.37. 3.301

Note that there is no equivalent of reg.32(7) as the JSA rules for the treatment of compensation payments made on the termination of part-time employment are different from those under the income support scheme (see reg.98(1)(b) and (3) and the note to reg.94(6)–(9)).

On calculation of entitlement to income-based JSA for part-weeks, see reg.150.

Chapter III

Employed Earners

Earnings of employed earners

98.—(1) Subject to paragraphs (2) and (3), "earnings" means in the case of employment as an employed earner, any remuneration or profit derived from that employment and includes— 3.302

(a) any bonus or commission;
(b) any compensation payment;
(c) any holiday pay except any payable more than four weeks after the termination or interruption of employment but this exception shall not apply to a person who is, or would be, prevented from being entitled to a jobseeker's allowance by section 14 (trade disputes);
(d) any payment by way of a retainer;
(e) any payment made by the claimant's employer in respect of expenses not wholly, exclusively and necessarily incurred in the performance of the duties of the employment, including any payment made by the claimant's employer in respect of—
    (i) travelling expenses incurred by the claimant between his home and place of employment;

(ii) expenses incurred by the claimant under arrangements made for the care of a member of his family owing to the claimant's absence from home;

[1(f) any payment or award of compensation made under section [6 112(4), 113, 117(3)(a), 128, [8131 or 132] of the Employment Rights Act 1996 (the remedies: orders and compensation, the orders, enforcement of order and compensation, interim relief)];

(ff) any payment or remuneration made under section [6 28, 34, 64, 68 or 70 of the Employment Rights Act 1996 (right to guarantee payments, remuneration on suspension on medical or maternity grounds, complaints to employment tribunals)]:]

(g) any award of compensation made under section 156, [6 . . .] 161 to 166, 189 or 192 of the Trade Union and Labour Relations (Consolidation) Act 1992 (compensation for unfair dismissal or redundancy on grounds of involvement in trade union activities, and protective awards).

[3(h) the amount of any payment by way of a non-cash voucher which has been taken into account in the computation of a person's earnings in accordance with [5 Part 5 of Schedule 3 to the Social Security (Contributions) Regulations 2001].]

(2) "Earnings" shall not include—

(a) [3 Subject to paragraph (2A),] any payment in kind;

(b) any periodic sum paid to a claimant on account of the termination of his employment by reason of redundancy;

(c) any remuneration paid by or on behalf of an employer to the claimant in respect of a period throughout which the claimant is on maternity leave [4, paternity leave, adoption leave] [10, shared parental leave] or is absent from work because he is ill;

(d) any payment in respect of expenses wholly, exclusively and necessarily incurred in the performance of the duties of the employment;

(e) any occupational pension;

(f) any redundancy payment within the meaning of [6 section 135(1) of the Employment Rights Act 1996];

[2(g) any lump sum payment made under the Iron and Steel Re-adaptation Benefits Scheme].

[7 (h) any payment in respect of expenses arising out of the [9 claimant participating as a service user].]

[3(2A) Paragraph (2)(a) shall not apply in respect of any non-cash voucher referred to in paragraph (1)(h).]

(3) In this regulation "compensation payment" means any payment made in respect of the termination of employment other than—

(a) any remuneration or emolument (whether in money or in kind) which accrued in the period before the termination;

(b) any holiday pay;

(c) any payment specified in paragraphs (1)(f)[,1(ff),] or (g) or (2);

(d) any refund of contributions to which that person was entitled under an occupational pension scheme.

AMENDMENTS

1. Jobseeker's Allowance and Income Support (General) (Amendment) Regulations 1996 (SI 1996/1517) reg.22 (October 7, 1996).

2. Social Security (Miscellaneous Amendments) Regulations 1997 (SI 1997/454) reg.2(12) (April 7, 1997).
3. Social Security Amendment (Non-Cash Vouchers) Regulations 1999 (SI 1999/1509) reg.2(6) (July 1, 1999).
4. Social Security (Paternity and Adoption) Amendment Regulations 2002 (SI 2002/2689) reg.3(5) (December 8, 2002).
5. Social Security (Miscellaneous Amendments) (No.4) Regulations 2006 (SI 2006/2378) reg.13(5) (October 2, 2006).
6. Social Security (Miscellaneous Amendments) (No.5) Regulations 2007 (SI 2007/2618) reg.8(8) (October 1, 2007).
7. Social Security (Miscellaneous Amendments) (No.4) Regulations 2009 (SI 2009/2655) reg.4(6) (October 26, 2009).
8. Social Security (Miscellaneous Amendments) (No.3) Regulations 2013 (SI 2013/2536) reg.6(10) (October 29, 2013).
9. Social Security (Miscellaneous Amendments) Regulations 2014 (SI 2014/591) reg.4(3) (April 28, 2014).
10. Shared Parental Leave and Statutory Shared Parental Pay (Consequential Amendments to Subordinate Legislation) Order 2014 (SI 2014/3255) art.7(5) (December 31, 2014).

DEFINITIONS

"adoption leave"—see reg.1(3).
"claimant"—see Jobseekers Act s.35(1) and reg.88(1).
"claimant participating as a service user"—see reg.1(3G).
"employed earner"—see reg.3 and SSCBA s.2(1)(a).
"family"—see Jobseekers Act, s.35(1).
"maternity leave"—see reg.1(3).
"occupational pension"—*ibid.*
"paternity leave"—*ibid.*
"shared parental leave"—*ibid.*

GENERAL NOTE

3.303 Regulation 98 applies to earnings from employment as an employed earner. It is similar to reg.35 of the Income Support Regulations but there are some differences which are referred to below. Otherwise see the notes to reg.35.

Like reg.35(1), para.(1) first provides a general definition of earnings from employment as an employee—any remuneration or profit derived from that employment—and then deems certain payments to be earnings. Paragraph (2) provides a number of exceptions and Sch.6 lists items which would otherwise count as earnings which are to be disregarded.

See in particular paras 1–3 of Sch.6 which concern the earnings that are ignored on the termination of employment or where hours of work are reduced (possibly to nil). The disregard that applies to payments made on the termination of full-time employment (i.e. 16 hours or more per week in the case of the claimant, 24 hours or more per week for a partner) was significantly extended with effect from October 1, 2007. See the new form of para.1 of Sch.6 and the notes to that paragraph.

Paragraph (1)

3.304 Note that the particular categories that are deemed to be earnings are the same as for income support, except that there is no equivalent of reg.35(1)(b), (c) and (i); instead sub-para.(b) refers to "any compensation payment" (defined in para.(3)). In addition, sub-paras (f), (ff) and (g) slightly expand on the list of awards of compensation or pay made by an employment tribunal and other payments under the employment protection legislation that are specifically deemed to count as earnings (compare reg.35(1)(g), (gg) and (h)). Holiday pay outside the period in sub-para.(c) is capital (reg.110(3)).

See the notes to reg.35(1) for further discussion.

Paragraph (2)

3.305 Sub-paragraphs (b) and (f) contain two additions to the list of payments that do not count as earnings, which otherwise are the same as for income support. Sub-para.(b) in fact contains the same provision that in the Income Support Regulations is expressed as an exception to reg.35(1)(b). But by placing it in the para.(2) list the JSA rules make it clear that such periodic redundancy payments although not earnings will count as income (see below). Sub-paragraph (f) expressly states that redundancy payments "within the meaning of s.135(1) of the Employment Rights Act 1996" are not earnings, nor are lump sum payments under the Iron and Steel Re-adaptation Benefits Scheme (sub-para.(g)). On the meaning of redundancy payment under sub-para.(f) see *CJSA 82/1998* in the notes to reg.35(1) of the Income Support Regulations.

Note that although the payments listed in para.(2)(a)–(e) are deemed not to be earnings they do count as other income (reg.103(6)). However, income in kind is disregarded (Sch.7 para.22) and so are payments of necessary expenses (Sch.7 para.3). Payment of expenses that result from a "claimant participating as a service user" (sub-para.(h)—see reg.1(3G) for those to whom this refers) are also ignored (para.2A of Sch.7). Under sub-paras (f) and (g) redundancy payments and lump sum payments under the Iron and Steel Re-adaptation Benefits Scheme will count as capital.

See the notes to reg.35(2) for further discussion.

Paragraph (3)

3.306 This provision is different from reg.35(1)(i) and (3) of the Income Support Regulations but is based on the previous unemployment benefit rule. It provides a broad definition of a "compensation payment" as "any payment made in respect of the termination of employment" but then lists those payments which are not to count as compensation payments.

If a payment is a compensation payment it counts as earnings under para.(1)(b). However from October 1, 2007 such earnings are disregarded (except in the case of part-time work which ends while the person is claiming JSA: see paras 1–2 of Sch.6 and the notes to those paragraphs). The consequence of the different definition of compensation payment for JSA is that contractual redundancy payments, ex gratia payments and other kinds of compensation (other than employment tribunal awards and "out of court" settlements) are ignored (for income support they count as capital).

Calculation of net earnings of employed earners

3.307 **99.**—(1) For the purposes of regulation 94 (calculation of earnings of employed earners) the earnings of a claimant derived from employment as an employed earner to be taken into account shall, subject to paragraph (2), be his net earnings.

(2) Subject to paragraph (3), there shall be disregarded from a claimant's net earnings, any sum, where applicable, specified in paragraphs 1 to 16 and 19 of Schedule 6.

(3) [*Omitted as not relating to income-based jobseeker's allowance.*]

(4) For the purposes of paragraph (1) net earnings shall be calculated by taking into account the gross earnings of the claimant from that employment less—

(a) any amount deducted from those earnings by way of—
  (i) income tax;
  (ii) primary Class 1 contributions payable under the Benefits Act; and

(b) one-half of any sum paid by the claimant in respect of a pay period by way of a contribution towards an occupational or personal pension scheme.

Definitions

"the Benefits Act"—see Jobseekers Act s.35(1).
"claimant"—*ibid.*, reg.88(1).
"employed earner"—see reg.3 and SSCBA s.2(1)(a).
"occupational pension scheme"—see Jobseekers Act s.35(1).
"pay period"—see reg.1(3).
"personal pension scheme"—see Jobseekers Act s.35(1).

General Note

See the notes to reg.36 of the Income Support Regulations. **3.308**

One of the issues discussed in those notes is the decision of the ECJ in *Cresswell v Chief Adjudication Officer, Jackson v Chief Adjudication Officer* [1992] E.C.R. I-4737, also reported as *R(IS)10/91*, which held that income support did not come within Directive 79/7 or Directive 76/207. The position of income-based JSA however seemed to be different. Income-based JSA is clearly directly concerned with one of the risks in art.3(1) of Directive 79/7, namely unemployment. Furthermore, Directive 76/207 may also be applicable. Further challenges against discriminatory aspects of income-based JSA, such as the lack of a child care costs disregard for part-time earnings, may therefore be possible (although note the final result of the *Meyers* case also referred to in the note to s.36). And now see *Hockenjos v Secretary of State* [2001] EWCA Civ 624; [2001] 2 C.M.L.R. 51; [2001] I.C.R. 966, also reported as *R(JSA) 1/05*, in which the Court of Appeal has held that JSA is a unitary statutory scheme to provide against the risk of unemployment. The result is that both contribution-based and income-based JSA are within the scope of Directive 79/7.

Chapter IV

Self-Employed Earners

Earnings of self-employed earners

100.—(1) Subject to paragraph (2), "earnings", in the case of employment as a self-employed earner, means the gross receipts of the employment and shall include any allowance paid under any scheme referred to in regulation 19(1)(r) (circumstances in which a person is to be treated as actively seeking employment: schemes for assisting persons to become self-employed earners) to the claimant for the purpose of assisting him in carrying on his business. **3.309**

(2) "Earnings" shall not include—

(a) where a claimant is involved in providing board and lodging accommodation for which a charge is payable, any payment by way of such a charge;

(b) any payment to which paragraph 27 or 28 of Schedule 7 refers (payments in respect of a person accommodated with the claimant under an arrangement made by a local authority or voluntary organisation, and payments made to the claimant by a health authority, local authority or voluntary organisation in respect of persons temporarily in the claimant's care).

[[1](c) any sports award.]

AMENDMENT

1. Social Security Amendment (Sports Awards) Regulations 1999 (SI 1999/2165) reg.7(3) (August 23, 1999).

DEFINITIONS

"board and lodging accommodation"—see reg.1(3).
"claimant"—see Jobseekers Act s.35(1) and reg.88(1).
"employment"—see reg.3.
"self-employed earner"—see reg.1(3), SSCBA s.2(1)(b).
"sports award"—see reg.1(3).
"voluntary organisation"—*ibid.*

GENERAL NOTE

3.310 See the notes to reg.37 of the Income Support Regulations.

The payments in para.(2)(a) count as income under reg.103(6) but subject to disregards. Paragraph (2)(b) applies to payments to foster-parents and to people for providing temporary care in their home. These payments are disregarded as income other than earnings under paras 27 and 28 of Sch.7. Paragraph (2)(b) ensures that they are not treated as earnings. See also reg.53(f). In relation to para.(2)(c), see the disregard in para 67 of Sch.7 and para.51 of Sch.8. See also reg.53(i).

Calculation of net profit of self-employed earners

3.311 **101.**—(1) For the purposes of regulation 95 (calculation of earnings of self-employed earners), the earnings of a claimant to be taken into account shall be—

(a) in the case of a self-employed earner who is engaged in employment on his own account, the net profit derived from that employment;

(b) in the case of a self-employed earner whose employment is carried on in partnership, or is that of a share fisherman within the meaning of regulation 156, his share of the net profit derived from that employment less—

(i) an amount in respect of income tax and of [2national insurance contributions] payable under the Benefits Act calculated in accordance with regulation 102 (deduction of tax and contributions for self-employed earners); and

(ii) one half of any premium paid in the period that is relevant under regulation 95 in respect of a personal pension scheme.

(2) Subject to paragraph (3), there shall be disregarded from a claimant's net profit any sum, where applicable, specified in paragraphs 1 to 16 of Schedule 6.

(3) For the purposes of calculating the amount to be deducted in respect of earnings under regulation 80 (contribution-based jobseeker's allowance: deductions in respect of earnings) the disregards in paragraphs 5 to 8 and 11 of Schedule 6 shall not apply.

(4) For the purposes of paragraph (1)(a) the net profit of the employment shall, except where paragraph (10) applies, be calculated by taking into account the earnings of the employment over the period determined under regulation 95 (calculation of earnings of self-employed earners) less—

(a) subject to paragraphs (6) to (8), any expenses wholly and exclusively defrayed in that period for the purposes of that employment;

(b) an amount in respect of—

(i) income tax; and
(ii) [[2]national insurance contributions] payable under the Benefits Act, calculated in accordance with regulation 102 (deductions of tax and contributions for self-employed earners); and
(c) one-half of any premium paid in the period that is relevant under regulation 95 in respect of a personal pension scheme.

(5) For the purposes of paragraph (1)(b), the net profit of the employment shall be calculated by taking into account the earnings of the employment over the period determined under regulation 95 less, subject to paragraphs (6) to (8), any expenses wholly and exclusively defrayed in that period for the purposes of that employment.

(6) Subject to paragraph (7), no deduction shall be made under paragraph (4)(a) or (5) in respect of—
(a) any capital expenditure;
(b) the depreciation of any capital asset;
(c) any sum employed or intended to be employed in the setting up or expansion of the employment;
(d) any loss incurred before the beginning of the period determined under regulation 95;
(e) the repayment of capital on any loan taken out for the purposes of the employment;
(f) any expenses incurred in providing business entertainment.

(7) A deduction shall be made under paragraph (4)(a) or (5) in respect of the repayment of capital on any loan used for—
(a) the replacement in the course of business of equipment or machinery; and
(b) the repair of an existing business asset except to the extent that any sum is payable under an insurance policy for its repair.

(8) [[1]The Secretary of State] shall refuse to make a deduction under paragraph (4)(a) or (5) in respect of any expenses where he is not satisfied that the expense has been defrayed or, having regard to the nature of the expense and its amount, that it has been reasonably incurred.

(9) For the avoidance of doubt—
(a) a deduction shall not be made under paragraph (4)(a) or (5) in respect of any sum unless it has been expended for the purposes of the business;
(b) a deduction shall be made there under in respect of—
(i) the excess of any VAT paid over VAT received in the period determined under regulation 95;
(ii) any income expended in the repair of an existing asset except to the extent that any sum is payable under an insurance policy for its repair;
(iii) any payment of interest on a loan taken out for the purposes of the employment.

(10) Where a claimant is engaged in employment as a child-minder the net profit of the employment shall be one-third of the earnings of that employment, less—
(a) an amount in respect of—
(i) income tax; and
(ii) [[2] national insurance contributions] payable under the Benefits Act, calculated in accordance with regulation 102 (deductions of tax and contributions for self-employed earners); and

(b) one half of any premium paid in the period that is relevant under regulation 95 in respect of a personal pension scheme.

(11) Notwithstanding regulation 95 and the foregoing paragraphs, [1the Secretary of State] may assess any item of a claimant's income or expenditure over a period other than that determined under regulation 95 such as may, in the particular case, enable the weekly amount of that item of income or expenditure to be determined more accurately.

(12) For the avoidance of doubt where a claimant is engaged in employment as a self-employed earner and he is engaged in one or more other employments as a self-employed or employed earner, any loss incurred in any one of his employments shall not be offset against his earnings in any other of his employments.

AMENDMENTS

1. Social Security Act 1998 (Commencement No.11, and Savings and Consequential and Transitional Provisions) Order 1999 (SI 1999/2860 (c.75)) art.3(12) and Sch.12 para.2 (October 18, 1999).

2. Social Security (Miscellaneous Amendments) (No.3) Regulations 2013 (SI 2013/2536) reg.6(11) (October 29, 2013).

DEFINITIONS

"the Benefits Act"—see Jobseekers Act s.35(1).
"claimant"—*ibid.*, and reg.88(1).
"earnings"—see reg.1(3) and reg.100.
"employment"—see reg.3.
"personal pension scheme"—see Jobseekers Act s.35(1).
"self-employed earner"—see reg.1(3) and SSCBA s.2(1)(b).

GENERAL NOTE

3.312 See the notes to reg.38 of the Income Support Regulations.

[1 Deduction of tax and contributions for self-employed earners

3.313 **102.**—(1) Subject to paragraph (2), the amount to be deducted in respect of income tax under regulation 101(1)(b)(i), (4)(b)(i) or (10)(a)(i) (calculation of net profit of self-employed earners) is to be calculated—

(a) on the basis of the amount of chargeable income; and

[3 (b) as if that income was assessable to income tax at the basic rate, or in the case of a Scottish taxpayer, the Scottish basic rate, of tax less only the personal reliefs to which the claimant is entitled under Chapters 2, 3 and 3A of Part 3 of the Income Tax Act 2007 as are appropriate to their circumstances.]

(2) If the period determined under regulation 95 is less than a year, the earnings to which the basic rate [3 , or the Scottish basic rate,] of tax is to be applied and the amount of the [3 personal reliefs deductible under paragraph (1) are] to be calculated on a pro rata basis.

(3) Subject to paragraph (4), the amount to be deducted in respect of national insurance contributions under regulation 101(1)(b)(i), (4)(b)(ii) or (10)(a)(ii) is to be the total of—

(a) the amount of Class 2 contributions payable under section [2 11(2)] or, as the case may be, [2 11(8)] of the Benefits Act at the rate applicable at the date of claim except where the claimant's chargeable income is less than the amount specified in section 11(4) of that Act ([2 small profits threshold]) for the tax year in which the date of claim falls; and

(b) the amount of Class 4 contributions (if any) which would be payable under section 15 of that Act (Class 4 contributions recoverable under the Income Tax Acts) at the percentage rate applicable at the date of claim on so much of the chargeable income as exceeds the lower limit but does not exceed the upper limit of profits and gains applicable for the tax year in which the date of claim falls.

(4) If the period determined under regulation 95 is less than a year—

(a) the amount specified for the tax year referred to in paragraph (3)(a) is to be reduced pro rata; and

(b) the limits referred to in paragraph (3)(b) are to be reduced pro rata.

(5) In this regulation "chargeable income" means—

(a) except where sub-paragraph (b) applies, the earnings derived from the employment less any expenses deducted under regulation 101(4)(a) or, as the case may be, (5); and

(b) in the case of employment as a child minder, one-third of the earnings of that employment.]

AMENDMENTS

1. Social Security (Miscellaneous Amendments) (No.3) Regulations 2013 (SI 2013/2536) reg.6(12) (October 29, 2013).

2. Social Security (Miscellaneous Amendments No.2) Regulations 2015 (SI 2015/478) reg.29 (April 6, 2015).

3. Social Security (Scottish Rate of Income Tax etc.) (Amendment) Regulations 2016 (SI 2016/233) reg.3(3) (April 6, 2016).

DEFINITIONS

"the Benefits Act"—see Jobseekers Act s.35(1).
"claimant"—*ibid.*, reg.88(1).
"date of claim"—see reg.1(3).
"earnings"—*ibid.*, reg.100.
"Scottish basic rate"—see reg.1(3).
"Scottish taxpayer"—*ibid.*

GENERAL NOTE

See the notes to reg.39 of the Income Support Regulations. **3.314**

Regulation 102 was rewritten on October 29, 2013 so as to match the equivalent provision for new style JSA (see reg.62 of the Jobseeker's Allowance Regulations 2013 (SI 2013/378) in Pt VI of this Volume) but the substance remains the same.

[1Chapter IVA

Participants in the self-employment route [3 . . .]

Interpretation

3.315 **102A.**—In this Chapter—

[2 . . .]

"special account" means, where a person was carrying on a commercial activity in respect of which assistance was received under the self-employment route, the account into which the gross receipts from that activity were payable during the period in respect of which such assistance was received.]

AMENDMENTS

1. Social Security (Miscellaneous Amendments) (No.4) Regulations 1998 (SI 1998/1174) reg.3(4) (June 1, 1998).
2. Social Security Amendment (Employment Zones) (No.2) Regulations 2000 (SI 2000/2910) reg.5(2)(b) (November 27, 2000).
3. Social Security Amendment (Employment Zones) (No.2) Regulations 2000 (SI 2000/2910) reg.5(2)(c) (November 27, 2000).

DEFINITION

"self-employment route"—see reg.1(3).

GENERAL NOTE

3.316 For the definition of the "self-employment route" see reg.1(3).
See the note to reg.102C.

[1 Treatment of gross receipts of participants in the self-employment route [2 . . .]

3.317 **102B.**—The gross receipts of a commercial activity carried on by a person in respect of which assistance is received under the self-employment route, shall be taken into account in accordance with the following provisions of this Chapter.]

AMENDMENTS

1. Social Security (Miscellaneous Amendments) (No.4) Regulations 1998 (SI 1998/1174) reg.3(4) (June 1, 1998).
2. Social Security Amendment (Employment Zones) (No.2) Regulations 2000 (SI 2000/2910) reg.5(2)(c) (November 27, 2000).

DEFINITION

"self-employment route"—see reg.1(3).

[1 Calculation of income of participants in the self-employment route [2 . . .]

3.318 **102C.**—(1) The income of a person who has received assistance under the self-employment route shall be calculated by taking into account the whole of the monies in the special account at the end of the last day upon which such assistance was received and deducting from those monies—

(a) an amount in respect of income tax calculated in accordance with regulation 102D (deduction in respect of tax for participants in the self-employment route [2 . . .]).

(b) any sum to which paragraph (4) refers.

(2) Income calculated pursuant to paragraph (1) shall be apportioned equally over a period which starts on the date the income is treated as paid under paragraph (3) and is equal in length to the period beginning with the day upon which assistance was first received under the self-employment route and ending on the last day upon which such assistance was received.

(3) Income calculated pursuant to paragraph (1) shall be treated as paid—

(a) in the case where it is due to be paid before the first benefit week in respect of which the participant or his partner [3 or, in the case of a joint-claim couple, the participant and the other member of the couple of which the participant is a member,] first claims a jobseeker's allowance following the last day upon which assistance was received under the self-employment route, on the day in the week in which it is due to be paid which corresponds to the first day of the benefit week;

(b) in any other case, on the first day of the benefit week in which it is due to be paid.

(4) This paragraph refers, where applicable in each benefit week in respect of which income calculated pursuant to paragraph (1) is taken into account pursuant to paragraphs (2) and (3), to the sums which would have been disregarded under paragraphs 5 to 8, 11 and 12 of Schedule 6 [3 or paragraphs 1, 2, 5 and 6 of Schedule 6A] had the income been earnings.]

AMENDMENTS

1. Social Security (Miscellaneous Amendments) (No.4) Regulations 1998 (SI 1998/1174) reg.3(4) (June 1, 1998).

2. Social Security Amendment (Employment Zones) (No.2) Regulations 2000 (SI 2000/2910) reg.5(2)(c) (November 27, 2000).

3. Jobseeker's Allowance (Joint Claims) Regulations 2000 (SI 2000/1978) reg.2(5) and Sch.2 para.41 (March 19, 2001).

DEFINITIONS

"benefit week"—see reg.1(3).
"joint-claim couple"—see JSA s.1(4).
"self-employment route"—see reg.1(3).
"special account"—*ibid.*
"week"—see reg.1(3).

GENERAL NOTE

This regulation, together with reg.102D, applies to the income from "test-trading" of people who have taken part in the "self-employment route" (defined in reg.1(3)). See also reg.88A which takes any gross receipts from trading while on the self-employment route out of the categories of earnings, self-employed earnings and income other than earnings. The rules for liable relative payments and student income (except reg.137) also do not apply. Any such receipts may only be taken into account in accordance with regs 102A–102D. For an example of a case in which regs 102A–102D applied, see *JL v SSWP (JSA)* [2012] UKUT 72 (AAC). 3.319

There are several issues raised by reg.102C that need clarifying. The intention seems to be that, after deducting an amount for income tax in accordance with reg.102D and applying the relevant earnings disregard under paras 5–8, 11 or 12 of Sch.6 in each benefit week that would have been applicable if the income had been earnings, the balance of the money in the person's "special account" (defined in reg.102A) at the end of the day on which he ceases to receive "assistance" (not defined) under the self-employment route is to be spread over a period equal in length to the period that the person received such assistance. The period starts on the date that the income is treated as paid under para.(3). Under para.(3)(a), if the income is due to be paid before the first benefit week pursuant to the claimant's (or his partner's) first JSA claim after assistance under the self-employment route finishes, it is treated as paid on the day that corresponds to the first day of the benefit week. In any other case it is treated as paid on the first day of the benefit week in which it is due (para.(3)(b)).

But when is this income due to be paid and what or who determines this? According to the guidance (see AM(AOG)82), it is due to be paid on the day after: (i) the person leaves the self-employment route if he is not entitled to JSA or income support immediately after leaving the self-employment route; (ii) his entitlement to JSA or income support ends if that entitlement stops within 13 weeks of the day after he left the self-employment route; or (iii) the expiry of 13 weeks starting on the day after he left the self-employment route if he is entitled to JSA or income support throughout that period. These rules are presumably part of the terms of the New Deal, since such provisions do not appear in the JSA (or Income Support) Regulations themselves. The 13-week "period of grace" in (iii) may perhaps be related to the fact that according to Employment Service guidance a person can continue to receive assistance in connection with trying to establish himself in self-employment for a further 13 weeks after his participation in the self-employment route ends. Presumably the intention is that any profit from his "test-trading" should not affect his benefit entitlement until after that period.

3.320 Note also that para.(1) refers to "the whole of the monies" in the person's special account but reg.102B refers to the "gross receipts" of the activity carried on while on the self-employment route. The normal rules for the calculation of earnings of self-employed earners (see regs 100–102) do not apply (see reg.88A), although presumably the case law on the meaning of "gross receipts" for self-employed earners will be relevant (see the notes to reg.37 of the Income Support Regulations). However, certain sums are ignored in calculating the person's income in his "special account". Thus any payment to him from this account (whether before or after he leaves the self-employment route) will disregarded if it is: (i) to meet expenses wholly and necessarily incurred in his business while on the self-employment route; or (ii) used, or intended to be used, to make repayments on a loan taken out for the purposes of that business (see para.62 of Sch.7). See also para.11(3) and (4) of Sch.8, which disregard any assets of the business while the person is participating in the self-employment route and, if the person later ceases to be engaged in that business, for a period which is reasonable to allow them to be disposed of. In addition, any capital acquired for the purposes of the business is ignored for 52 weeks from the date of receipt (para.47 of Sch.8).

See also regs 23A and 39A–39D of, and para.64 of Sch.9 and paras 6(3) and (4) and 52 of Sch.10 to, the Income Support Regulations which introduce similar provisions for the treatment of income from "test-trading" while on the self-employment route when the person or his partner claims income support.

[1 Deduction in respect of tax for participants in the self-employment route [2 . . .]

3.321 **102D.**—(1) The amount to be deducted in respect of income tax under regulation 102C(1)(a) (calculation of income of participants in the self-employment route [2 . . .]) in respect of the period determined under regulation 102C(2) shall be calculated as if—

(a) the chargeable income is the only income chargeable to tax;

[6 (b) the personal reliefs applicable to the person receiving assistance under the self-employment route under Chapters 2, 3 and 3A of Part 3 of the Income Tax Act 2007 are allowable against that income; and

(c) the rate at which the chargeable income less the personal reliefs is assessable to income tax is the basic rate, or in the case of a Scottish taxpayer, the Scottish basic rate, of tax.]

(2) For the purpose of paragraph (1), the [4 [5 basic] rate] [6 , or the Scottish basic rate,] of tax to be applied and the amount of the [3 [6 personal reliefs]] deductible shall, where the period determined under regulation 102C(2) is less than a year, be calculated on a pro rata basis.

(3) In this regulation, "chargeable income" means the monies in the special account at the end of the last day upon which assistance was received under the self-employment route.]

AMENDMENTS

1. Social Security (Miscellaneous Amendments) (No.4) Regulations 1998 (SI 1998/1174) reg.3(4) (June 1, 1998).

2. Social Security Amendment (Employment Zones) (No.2) Regulations 2000 (SI 2000/2910) reg.5(2)(c) (November 27, 2000).

3. Social Security (Miscellaneous Amendments) (No.3) Regulations 2007 (SI 2007/1749) reg.3(3) (July 16, 2007).

4. Social Security (Miscellaneous Amendments) (No.5) Regulations 2007 (SI 2007/2618) reg.8(10) (October 1, 2007).

5. Social Security (Miscellaneous Amendments) Regulations 2009 (SI 2009/583) reg.4(8) (April 6, 2009).

6. Social Security (Scottish Rate of Income Tax etc.) (Amendment) Regulations 2016 (SI 2016/233) reg.3(4) (April 6, 2016).

DEFINITIONS

"Scottish basic rate"—see reg.1(3).
"Scottish taxpayer"—*ibid.*
"self-employment route"—*ibid.*
"special account"—*ibid.*

GENERAL NOTE

See the note to reg.102C above. 3.322

Chapter V

Other Income

Calculation of income other than earnings

103.—(1) For the purposes of regulation 94 (calculation of income other than earnings) [10 [11 . . .]] the income of a claimant which does not consist of earnings to be taken into account shall, subject to the following 3.323

provisions of this regulation, be his gross income and any capital treated as income under [6 regulation 104 (capital treated as income)].

(2) There shall be disregarded from the calculation of a claimant's gross income under paragraph (1) any sum, where applicable, specified in Schedule 7.

(3) Where the payment of any benefit under the Act or under the Benefits Act is subject to any deduction by way of recovery, the amount to be taken into account under paragraph (1) shall be the gross amount to which the beneficiary is entitled.

(4) [7 . . .]

[5 (5) [8 Paragraphs (5ZA) and (5AZA) apply] where—

(a) a relevant payment has been made to a person in an academic year; and

(b) that person abandons, or is dismissed from, his course of study before the payment to him of the final instalment of the relevant payment.

(5ZA) [8 Where a relevant payment is made quarterly, the] amount of a relevant payment to be taken into account for the assessment period for the purposes of paragraph (1) in respect of a person to whom paragraph (5) applies, shall be calculated by applying the formula—

$$\frac{A - (B \times C)}{D}$$

where—

A = the total amount of the relevant payment which that person would have received had he remained a student until the last day of the academic term in which he abandoned, or was dismissed from, his course, less any deduction under regulation 136(5);

B = the number of benefit weeks from the benefit week immediately following that which includes the first day of that academic year to the benefit week immediately before that which includes the day on which the person abandoned, or was dismissed from, his course;

C = the weekly amount of the relevant payment, before the application of the £10 disregard, which would have been taken into account as income under regulation 136(2) had the person not abandoned or been dismissed from, his course and, in the case of a person who was not entitled to a jobseeker's allowance immediately before he abandoned or was dismissed from his course, had that person, at that time, been entitled to a jobseeker's allowance;

D = the number of benefit weeks in the assessment period.

[8 (5AZA) Where a relevant payment is made by two or more instalments in a quarter, the amount of a relevant payment to be taken into account for the assessment period for the purposes of paragraph (1) in respect of a person to whom paragraph (5) applies, shall be calculated by applying the formula in paragraph (5ZA) but as if—

A = the total amount of relevant payments which that person received, or would have received, from the first day of the academic year to the day the person abandoned the course, or was dismissed from it, less any deduction under regulation 136(5).]

(5ZB) [8 In this regulation]—

"academic year" and "student loan" shall have the same meanings as for the purposes of Chapter IX of this Part;

[8 "assessment period" means—

(a) in a case where a relevant payment is made quarterly, the period beginning with the benefit week which includes the day on which the person abandoned, or was dismissed from, his course and ending with the benefit week which includes the last day of the last quarter for which an instalment of the relevant payment was payable to that person;

(b) in a case where the relevant payment is made by two or more instalments in a quarter, the period beginning with the benefit week which includes the day on which the person abandoned, or was dismissed from, his course and ending with the benefit week which includes—

(i) the day immediately before the day on which the next instalment of the relevant payment would have been due had the payments continued; or

(ii) the last day of the last quarter for which an instalment of the relevant payment was payable to that person ,

whichever of those dates is earlier;]

[8 "quarter" in relation to an assessment period means a period in that year beginning on—

(a) 1st January and ending on 31st March;

(b) 1st April and ending on 30th June;

(c) 1st July and ending on 31st August; or

(d) 1st September and ending on 31st December;]

"relevant period" means either a student loan or an amount intended for the maintenance of dependants referred to in regulation 131(5A) or both.]

[2(5A) In the case of income to which regulation 94(2B) applies (calculation of income of former full-time students), the amount of income to be taken into account for the purposes of paragraph (1) shall be the amount of that income calculated in accordance with regulation 97(7) and on the basis that none of that income has been repaid.]

[9 (5B) Where the claimant—

(a) is a member of a couple;

(b) his partner is receiving a contributory employment and support allowance; and

(c) that benefit has been reduced under regulation 63 of the Employment and Support Allowance Regulations [12 or section 11J of the Welfare Reform Act as the case may be],

the amount of that benefit to be taken into account is the amount as if it had not been reduced.]

(6) For the avoidance of doubt there shall be included as income to be taken into account under paragraph (1)—

[4(a) any payment to which regulation 98(2)(a) to (e) or 100(2) (payments not earnings) applies; or

(b) in the case of a claimant who is receiving support under section 95 or 98 of the Immigration and Asylum Act including support provided by virtue of regulations made under Schedule 9 to that Act, the amount of such support provided in respect of essential living needs of the claimant and his [6 parter] (if any) as is specified in regulations made under paragraph 3 of Schedule 8 to the Immigration and Asylum Act.]

AMENDMENTS

1. Jobseeker's Allowance and Income Support (General) (Amendment) Regulations 1996 (SI 1996/1517) reg.23 (October 7, 1996).

2. Income-related Benefits and Jobseeker's Allowance (Miscellaneous Amendments) Regulations 1997 (SI 1997/65) reg.7(2) (April 7, 1997).

3. Social Security (Miscellaneous Amendments) Regulations 1997 (SI 1997/454), reg.2(13) April 7, 1997).

4. Social Security (Immigration and Asylum) Consequential Amendments Regulations 2000 (SI 2000/636) reg.4(4) (April 3, 2000).

5. Social Security Amendment (Students and Income-related Benefits) Regulations 2001 (SI 2001/2319) reg.5(2) (August 1, 2001).

6. Social Security (Working Tax Credit and Child Tax Credit) (Consequential Amendments) Regulations 2003 (SI 2003/455) reg.3 and Sch.2 para.8 (April 6, 2004, except in "transitional cases" and see further the note to reg.83 and to reg.17 of the Income Support Regulations).

7. Social Security (Miscellaneous Amendments) Regulations 2005 (SI 2005/574) reg.6(3) (April 4, 2005).

8. Social Security (Students and Miscellaneous Amendments) Regulations 2008 (SI 2008/1599) reg.4(2) (September 1, 2008, or if the student's period of study begins between August 1 and 31, 2008, the first day of the period).

9. Employment and Support Allowance (Consequential Provisions) (No.2) Regulations 2008 (SI 2008/1554) reg.3(16) (October 27, 2008).

10. Social Security (Miscellaneous Amendments) (No.4) Regulations 2009 (SI 2009/2655) reg.4(7) (October 26, 2009).

11. Social Security (Miscellaneous Amendments) Regulations 2011 (SI 2011/674) reg.7(5) (April 11, 2011).

12. Universal Credit (Consequential, Supplementary, Incidental and Miscellaneous Provisions) Regulations 2013 (SI 2013/630) reg.30(5) (April 29, 2013).

DEFINITIONS

"academic year"—see reg.130.
"the Act"—see reg.1(3).
"the Benefits Act"—see Jobseekers Act s.35(1).
"benefit week"—see reg.1(3).
"claimant"—see Jobseekers Act s.35(1) and reg.88(1).
"earnings"—see reg.1(3).
"full-time student"—*ibid.*
"Immigration and Asylum Act"—*ibid.*
"student loan"—see reg.130.
"Welfare Reform Act"—see reg.1(3).

GENERAL NOTE

3.324 On paras (1)–(3) and (5)–(6), see the notes to reg.40 of the Income Support Regulations but in relation to para.(6)(b) note that there is no equivalent to reg.40(5).

Capital treated as income

3.325 **104.**—(1) Any capital payable by instalments which are outstanding on the first day in respect of which an income-based jobseeker's allowance is payable, or, in the case of a [3supersession], the date of that [3supersession], shall, if the aggregate of the instalments outstanding and the amount of the claimant's capital otherwise calculated in accordance with Chapter VI of this Part exceeds [8 . . .] [£16,000], be treated as income.

(2) Any payment received under an annuity shall be treated as income.

(3) [7 . . .]

(4) Any earnings to the extent that they are not a payment of income shall be treated as income.

[2(5) Any Career Development Loan paid pursuant to section 2 of the Employment and Training Act 1973 shall be treated as income.]

[6 (6) Where an agreement or court order provides that payments shall be made to the claimant in consequence of any personal injury to the claimant and that such payments are to be made, wholly or partly, by way of periodical payments, any such periodical payments received by the claimant (but not a payment which is treated as capital by virtue of this Part), shall be treated as income.]

AMENDMENTS

1. Income-related Benefits and Jobseeker's Allowance (Miscellaneous Amendments) Regulations 1997 (SI 1997/65) reg.3(2) (April 7, 1997).

2. Income-related Benefits and Jobseeker's Allowance (Miscellaneous Amendments) Regulations 1997 (SI 1997/65) reg.3(3) (April 7, 1997).

3. Social Security Act 1998 (Commencement No.11, and Savings and Consequential and Transitional Provisions) Order 1999 (SI 1999/2860 c.75)) art.3(12) and Sch.12 para.5 (October 18, 1999).

4. Social Security Amendment (Capital Limits and Earnings Disregards) Regulations 2000 (SI 2000/2545) reg.2(2)(a) (April 9, 2001).

5. Children (Leaving Care) Act 2000 (Commencement No.2 and Consequential Provisions) Order 2001 (SI 2001/3070) art.3(5) and Sch.4 para.(c) (October 1, 2001).

6. Social Security Amendment (Personal Injury Payments) Regulations 2002 (SI 2002/2442) reg.2 (October 28, 2002).

7. Social Security (Working Tax Credit and Child Tax Credit) (Consequential Amendments) Regulations 2003 (SI 2003/455) reg.3 and Sch.2 para.9 (April 6, 2004, except in "transitional cases" and see further the note to reg.83 and to reg.17 of the Income Support Regulations).

8. Social Security (Miscellaneous Amendments) (No.2) Regulations 2005 (SI 2005/2465) reg.3(2) (April 10, 2006).

DEFINITIONS

"claimant"—see Jobseekers Act s.35(1) and reg.88(1).
"payment"—see reg.1(3).

GENERAL NOTE

See the notes to reg.41 of the Income Support Regulations. 3.326

Paragraph (3) was omitted with effect from April 6, 2004 by reg.3 of and para.9 of Sch.2 to the Social Security (Working Tax Credit and Child Tax Credit) (Consequential Amendments) Regulations 2003 (SI 2003/455), except in "transitional cases" (i.e. those cases in which the claimant is still receiving amounts for his children in his income-based JSA—see further the notes to reg.83 and reg.17 of the Income Support Regulations). For "transitional cases" para.(3) continues in force (see the 2003 edition of this volume for this provision). With effect from May 12, 2004, reg.5 of the Social Security (Miscellaneous Amendments) (No.2) Regulations 2004 (SI 2004/1141) substituted the words "section 12 of the Social Work (Scotland) Act 1968 or sections 29 or 30 of the Children (Scotland) Act 1995" for the words "section 12, 24 or 26 of the Social Work (Scotland) Act 1968" in para.(3). The effect of this amendment is simply to update the references to the Scottish legislation referred to in para.(3).

Notional income

3.327 **105.**—[47(1) A claimant is to be treated as possessing income of which the claimant has deprived themselves for the purpose of securing entitlement to a jobseeker's allowance or increasing the amount of that allowance, or for the purpose of securing entitlement to, or increasing the amount of income support or an employment and support allowance.]

(2) Except in the case of—

(a) a discretionary trust;

(b) a trust derived from a payment made in consequence of a personal injury;

[1(c) [19 . . .]]

(d) [18 working tax credit or child tax credit];

(e) a jobseeker's allowance;

(f) [21 . . .]

(g) a personal pension scheme [24 [29, occupational pension scheme or a payment made by the Board of the Pension Protection Fund]] where the claimant [43 has not attained the qualifying age for state pension credit]; [2 or

[41 (ga) any sum to which paragraph (15A) applies;]

[30 (h) any sum to which paragraph 42(2)(a) of Schedule 8 (capital to be disregarded) applies which is administered in the way referred to in paragraph 42(1)(a);

(ha) any sum to which paragraph 43(a) of Schedule 8 refers; or]]

[5 (i) rehabilitation allowance made under section 2 of the Employment and Training Act 1973],

income which would become available to the claimant upon application being made but which has not been acquired by him shall be treated as possessed by him but only from the date on which it could be expected to be acquired were an application made.

[1 (2A) [19 . . .]]

[25 (2B) A claimant who has attained the [43 qualifying age for state pension credit] shall be treated as possessing—

(a) the amount of any income from an occupational pension scheme [29 a personal pension scheme or the Board of the Pension Protection Fund]—

(i) for which no claim has been made, and

(ii) to which he might expect to be entitled if a claim for it were made;

(b) income from an occupational pension scheme which the claimant elected to defer,

but only from the date on which it could be expected to be acquired were an application for it to be made.]

[32 (3) This paragraph applies where a person [43 who has attained the qualifying age for state pension credit]—

(a) is entitled to money purchase benefits under an occupational pension scheme or a personal pension scheme;

(b) fails to purchase an annuity with the funds available in that scheme; and

(c) either—

(i) defers in whole or in part the payment of any income which would have been payable to him by his pension fund holder, or

(ii) fails to take any necessary action to secure that the whole of any income which would be payable to him by his pension fund holder upon his applying for it, is so paid, or

(iii) income withdrawal is not available to him under that scheme.

(3A) Where paragraph (3) applies, the amount of any income foregone shall be treated as possessed by that person, but only from the date on which it could be expected to be acquired were an application for it to be made.]

(4) The amount of any income foregone in a case [32 where paragraph (3)(c)(i) or (ii)] applies shall be the maximum amount of income which may be withdrawn from the fund and shall be determined by [9 the Secretary of State] who shall take account of information provided by the pension fund holder in accordance with regulation 7(5) of the Social Security (Claims and Payments) Regulations 1987.

(5) The amount of any income foregone in a case [32 where paragraph (3)(c)(iii)] applies shall be the income that the claimant could have received without purchasing an annuity had the fund held under the relevant [27 occupational or personal pension scheme been held under a scheme] where income withdrawal was available and shall be determined in the manner specified in paragraph (4).

[28 (5A) In paragraph (3), "money purchase benefits" has the meaning it has in the Pension Schemes Act 1993.]

(6) Subject to paragraph (7), any income which is due to be paid to the claimant but has not been paid to him, shall be treated as possessed by the claimant.

(7) Paragraph (6) shall not apply to—

(a) any amount to which paragraph (8) or (9) applies;

(b) a payment to which section 74(2) or (3) of the Administration Act applies (abatement of prescribed payments from public funds which are not made before the prescribed date, and abatement from prescribed benefits where maintenance not paid); and

(c) a payment from a discretionary trust, or a trust derived from a payment made in consequence of a personal injury.

[12(d) any earnings which are due to an employed earner on the termination of his employment by reason of redundancy but which have not been paid to him.]

(8) This paragraph applies to an amount which is due to be paid to the claimant under an occupational pension scheme but which is not paid because the trustees or managers of the scheme have suspended or ceased payment due to an insufficiency of resources.

(9) This paragraph applies to any amount by which a payment made to the claimant from an occupational pension scheme falls short of the payment to which he was due under the scheme where the shortfall arises because the trustees or managers of the scheme have insufficient resources available to them to meet in full the scheme's liabilities.

(10) [6Any payment of income, other than a payment of income specified in paragraph (10A)], made—

(a) to a third party in respect of a single claimant or in respect of a single claimant or [19 his partner] shall be treated—

(i) in a case where that payment is derived from a payment of any benefit under the [38 benefit Acts, a payment from the Armed Forces and Reserve Forces Compensation Scheme, a war disablement pension, war widow's pension or war widower's pension or a pension payable to a person as a widow, widower or surviving civil partner under any power of Her Majesty otherwise than under an enactment to make provision about pensions for or in respect of persons who have been disabled or have died in consequence of service as members of the armed forces of the Crown] as possessed by that single claimant, if it would normally be paid to him, or as possessed [19 by his partner, if it would normally be paid to his partner];

[10 (ia) in a case where that payment is a payment of an occupational pension [29, a pension or other periodical payment made under a personal pension scheme or a payment made by the Board of the Pension Protection Fund], as possessed by that single claimant or, as the case may be, by [19 the claimant's partner];]

(ii) in any other case, as possessed by that single claimant [19 or his partner] to the extent that it is used for the food, ordinary clothing or footwear, household fuel, rent for which housing benefit is payable, or any housing costs to the extent that they are met under regulation 83(f) [15, 84(1)(g), 86A(d) or 86B(e)], of that single claimant or, as the case may be, [19 of his partner], or is used for any council tax or water charges for which that claimant or [19 partner is liable];

[19 (b) to a single claimant or his partner in respect of a third party (but not in respect of another member of his family) shall be treated as possessed by that single claimant or, as the case may be, his partner, to the extent that it is kept or used by him or used by or on behalf of his partner;]

but, except where sub-paragraph (a)(i) applies and in the case of a person who is, or would be, prevented from being entitled to a jobseeker's allowance by section 14 (trade disputes), this paragraph shall not apply to any payment in kind [22 to the third party].

[6(10A) Paragraph (10) shall not apply in respect of a payment of income made—

(a) under [44 or by] the Macfarlane Trust, the Macfarlane (Special Payments) Trust, the Macfarlane (Special Payments) (No.2) Trust, the Fund, the Eileen Trust [42 , MFET Limited] [48, the Skipton Fund, the Caxton Foundation] or the Independent Living [37 Fund (2006)];

(b) pursuant to section 19(1)(a) of the Coal Industry Act 1994 (concessionary coal); or

(c) pursuant to section 2 of the Employment and Training Act 1973 in respect of a person's participation—

(i) in an employment programme specified in regulation 75(1)(a)(ii);

(ii) in a training scheme specified in regulation 75(1)(b)(ii); or

[16 (iia) [36 . . .] in the Intensive Activity Period specified in regulation 75(1)(a)(iv); or]

(iii) in a qualifying course within the meaning specified in regulation 17A(7)] [40 ; or

(iv) in the Flexible New Deal.]

(ca) [*Omitted*]

[45 (cb) in respect of a person's participation in the Mandatory Work Activity Scheme;]

[46 (cc) [50 . . .]]

[49 (cc) in respect of a claimant's participation in a scheme prescribed in regulation 3 of the Jobseeker's Allowance (Schemes for Assisting Persons to Obtain Employment) Regulations 2013;]

(cd) *[Omitted]*

(ce) *[Omitted]*

[11(d) under an occupational pension scheme [29, in respect of a pension or other periodical payment made under a personal pension scheme or a payment made by the Board of the Pension Protection Fund] where—

(i) a bankruptcy order has been made in respect of the person in respect of whom the payment has been made or, in Scotland, the estate of that person is subject to sequestration or a judicial factor has been appointed on that person's estate under section 41 of the Solicitors (Scotland) Act 1980;

(ii) the payment is made to the trustee in bankruptcy or any other person acting on behalf of the creditors; and

(iii) the person referred to in (i) and [19 his partner (if any)] does not possess, or is not treated as possessing, any other income apart from that payment.]

(11) Where the claimant [23 resides in a care home, an Abbeyfield Home or an independent hospital, or is temporarily absent from such a home or hospital], any payment made by a person other than the claimant or a member of his family in respect of some or all of the cost of maintaining the claimant [19 or his partner in that home [37 or hospital] shall be treated as possessed by the claimant or his partner].

[14(11A) Where the amount of a subsistence allowance paid to a claimant in a benefit week is less than the amount of income-based jobseeker's allowance that person would have received in that benefit week had it been payable to him, less 50p, he shall be treated as possessing the amount which is equal to the amount of income-based jobseeker's allowance which he would have received in that week, less 50p.]

(12) Where a claimant's earnings are not ascertainable at the time of the determination of the claim or of any [9 review or supersession] [9the Secretary of State] shall treat the claimant as possessing such earnings as is reasonable in the circumstances of the case having regard to the number of hours worked and the earnings paid for comparable employment in the area.

(13) [13 Subject to paragraph (13A),] where—

(a) a claimant performs a service for another person; and

(b) that person makes no payment of earnings or pays less than that paid for a comparable employment in the area,

[9 the Secretary of State] shall treat the claimant as possessing such earnings (if any) as is reasonable for that employment unless the claimant satisfies him that the means of that person are insufficient for him to pay or to pay more for the service [13 . . .].

[13(13A) Paragraph (13) shall not apply—

(a) to a claimant who is engaged by a charitable or voluntary organisation or who is a volunteer if the Secretary of State is satisfied in any of those cases that it is reasonable for him to provide those services free of charge;

(b) in a case where the service is performed in connection with—

(i) the claimant's participation in an employment or training programme in accordance with regulation 19(1)(q) [16, other than where the service is performed in connection with the claimant's participation [36 . . .] in the Intensive Activity Period specified in regulation 75(1)(a)(iv)]; or

(ii) the claimant's or the claimant's partner's participation in an employment or training programme as defined in regulation 19(3) for which a training allowance is not payable or, where such an allowance is payable, it is payable for the sole purpose of reimbursement of travelling or meal expenses to the person participating in that programme] [33; or

(c) to a claimant who is participating in a work placement approved by the Secretary of State (or a person providing services to the Secretary of State) before the placement starts.]

(14) Where a claimant is treated as possessing any income under any of paragraphs (1) to (11) the foregoing provisions of this Part shall apply for the purposes of calculating the amount of that income as if a payment had actually been made and as if it were actual income which he does possess.

(15) Where a claimant is treated as possessing any earnings under paragraphs (12) or (13) the foregoing provisions of this Part shall apply for the purposes of calculating the amount of those earnings as if a payment had actually been made and as if they were actual earnings which he does possess, except that paragraph (4) of regulation 99 (calculation of net earnings of employed earners) shall not apply and his net earnings shall be calculated by taking into account the earnings which he is treated as possessing, less—

(a) an amount in respect of income tax equivalent to an amount calculated by applying to those earnings [39 . . .] the basic rate [52, or in the case of a Scottish taxpayer, the Scottish basic rate,] of tax in the year of assessment less only the [52 personal reliefs to which the claimant is entitled under Chapters 2, 3 and 3A of Part 3 of the Income Tax Act 2007 as are] appropriate to his circumstances; but, if the period over which those earnings are to be taken into account is less than a year, the earnings to which the [34 [39 basic] rate] [52, or the Scottish basic rate,] of tax is to be applied and the amount of the [52 personal reliefs] deductible under this paragraph shall be calculated on a pro rata basis;

(b) where the weekly amount of those earnings equals or exceeds the lower earnings limit, an amount representing primary Class 1 contributions under the Benefits Act, calculated by applying to those earnings the initial and main primary percentages in accordance with section 8(1)(a) and (b) of that Act; and

(c) one-half of any sum payable by the claimant in respect of a pay period by way of a contribution towards an occupational or personal pension scheme.

[41 (15A) Paragraphs (1), (2), (6), (10), (12) and (13) shall not apply in respect of any amount of income other than earnings, or earnings derived from employment as an employed earner, arising out of the [51 claimant participating as a service user].]

(16) In this regulation—

"ordinary clothing or footwear" means clothing or footwear for normal daily use, but does not include school uniforms, or clothing or footwear used solely for sporting activities;

"pension fund holder" means with respect to a personal pension scheme [32 or an occupational pension scheme] the trustees, managers or scheme administrators, as the case may be, of the scheme concerned;

"resources" has the same meaning as in section 181 of the Pension Schemes Act 1993;

[35 "work placement" means practical work experience which is not undertaken in expectation of payment.]

AMENDMENTS

1. Child Benefit, Child Support and Social Security (Miscellaneous Amendments) (Regulation 1996 (SI 1996/1803) reg.42 (April 7, 1997).

2. Income-related Benefits and Jobseeker's Allowance (Amendment) (No.2) Regulations 1997 (SI 1997/2197) reg.6 (October 6, 1997).

3. Income-related Benefits and Jobseeker's Allowance (Amendment) (No.2) Regulations 1997 (SI 1997/2197) reg.7(3) and (4)(f) (October 6, 1997).

4. Social Security Amendment (New Deal) Regulations 1997 (SI 1997/2863) reg.9 (January 5, 1998).

5. Social Security (Miscellaneous Amendments) Regulations 1998 (SI 1998/563) reg.6(1) and (2)(f) (April 6, 1998).

6. Social Security Amendment (New Deal) (No.2) Regulations 1998 (SI 1998/2117) reg.2(1) (September 24, 1998).

7. Social Security and Child Support (Tax Credits) Consequential Amendments Regulations 1999 (SI 1999/2566) reg.2(1) and Sch.2 Pt I (October 5, 1999).

8. Social Security and Child Support (Tax Credits) Consequential Amendments Regulations 1999 (SI 1999/2566) reg.2(2) and Sch.2 Pt II (October 5, 1999).

9. Social Security Act 1998 (Commencement No.11, and Savings and Consequential and Transitional Provisions) Order 1999 (SI 1999/2860 (C.75)) art.3(12) and Sch.12 (October 18, 1999).

10. Social Security Amendment (Notional Income and Capital) Regulations 1999 (SI 1999/2640) reg.2(1)(b) (November 15, 1999).

11. Social Security Amendment (Notional Income and Capital) Regulations 1999 (SI 1999/2640) reg.2(3)(d) (November 15, 1999).

12. Income Support (General) and Jobseeker's Allowance Amendment (No.2) Regulations 1999 (SI 1999/3324) reg.2 (January 7, 2000).

13. Social Security (Approved Work) Regulations 2000 (SI 2000/678) reg.2(1) (April 3, 2000).

14. Social Security Amendment (Employment Zones) Regulations 2000 (SI 2000/724) reg.3(1) (April 3, 2000).

15. Jobseeker's Allowance (Joint Claims) Regulations 2000 (SI 2000/1978) reg.2(5) and Sch.2 para.42 (March 19, 2001).

16. Social Security Amendment (New Deal) Regulations 2001 (SI 2001/1029) reg.7 (April 9, 2001).

17. Social Security (Miscellaneous Amendments) Regulations 2002 (SI 2002/841) reg.3(2) (April 8, 2002).

18. Social Security (Working Tax Credit and Child Tax Credit) (Consequential Amendments) Regulations 2003 (SI 2003/455) reg.3 and Sch.2 para.10(b) (April 7, 2003).

19. Social Security (Working Tax Credit and Child Tax Credit) (Consequential Amendments) Regulations 2003 (SI 2003/455) reg.3 and Sch.2 para.10 (except sub-para.(b)) (April 6, 2004, except in "transitional cases" and see further the note to reg.83 and to reg.17 of the Income Support Regulations).

20. Social Security (Miscellaneous Amendments) Regulations 2005 (SI 2005/574) reg.2(6) (April 4, 2005).

21. Social Security (Miscellaneous Amendments) Regulations 2005 (SI 2005/574) reg.6(4) (April 4, 2005).

22. Social Security (Miscellaneous Amendments) (No.2) Regulations 2005 (SI 2005/2465) reg.3(3)(f) (October 3, 2005).

23. Social Security (Care Homes and Independent Hospitals) Regulations 2005 (SI 2005/2687) reg.3 and Sch.2 para.5 (October 24, 2005).

24. Social Security (Miscellaneous Amendments) (No.2) Regulations 2005 (SI 2005/2465) reg.3(3)(a) (April 6, 2006).

25. Social Security (Miscellaneous Amendments) (No.2) Regulations 2005 (SI 2005/2465) reg.3(3)(b) (April 6, 2006).

26. Social Security (Miscellaneous Amendments) (No.2) Regulations 2005 (SI 2005/2465) reg.3(3)(c) (April 6, 2006).

27. Social Security (Miscellaneous Amendments) (No.2) Regulations 2005 (SI 2005/2465) reg.3(3)(d) (April 6, 2006).

28. Social Security (Miscellaneous Amendments) (No.2) Regulations 2005 (SI 2005/2465) reg.3(3)(e) (April 6, 2006).

29. Social Security (Miscellaneous Amendments) Regulations 2006 (SI 2006/588) reg.3(3) (April 6, 2006).

30. Social Security (Miscellaneous Amendments) Regulations 2007 (SI 2007/719) reg.3(4) (April 2, 2007).

31. Social Security (Miscellaneous Amendments) (No.3) Regulations 2007 (SI 2007/1749) reg.3(3) (July 16, 2007).

32. Social Security (Miscellaneous Amendments) (No.3) Regulations 2007 (SI 2007/1749) reg.3(4) (July 16, 2007).

33. Social Security (Miscellaneous Amendments) (No.5) Regulations 2007 (SI 2007/2618) reg.8(11)(a) (October 1, 2007).

34. Social Security (Miscellaneous Amendments) (No.5) Regulations 2007 (SI 2007/2618) reg.8(11)(b) (October 1, 2007).

35. Social Security (Miscellaneous Amendments) (No.5) Regulations 2007 (SI 2007/2618) reg.8(11)(c) (October 1, 2007).

36. Social Security (Miscellaneous Amendments) Regulations 2008 (SI 2008/698) reg.4(12)(a) (April 14, 2008).

37. Social Security (Miscellaneous Amendments) (No.6) Regulations 2008 (SI 2008/2767) reg.4(6) (November 17, 2008).

38. Social Security (Miscellaneous Amendments) (No.7) Regulations 2008 (SI 2008/3157) reg.3(6) (January 5, 2009).

39. Social Security (Miscellaneous Amendments) Regulations 2009 (SI 2009/583) reg.4(7) (April 6, 2009).

40. Social Security (Flexible New Deal) Regulations 2009 (SI 2009/480) reg.2(6) (October 5, 2009).

41. Social Security (Miscellaneous Amendments) (No.4) Regulations 2009 (SI 2009/2655) reg.4(8) (October 26, 2009).

42. Social Security (Miscellaneous Amendments) (No.2) Regulations 2010 (SI 2010/641) reg.4(3)(b) (April 6, 2010).

43. Social Security (Miscellaneous Amendments) (No.2) Regulations 2010 (SI 2010/641) reg.4(7) (April 6, 2010).

44. Social Security (Miscellaneous Amendments) (No.2) Regulations 2010 (SI 2010/641) reg.4(8)(a) (April 6, 2010).

45. Jobseeker's Allowance (Mandatory Work Activity Scheme) Regulations 2011 (SI 2011/688) reg.12(1)(d) and (2) (April 25, 2011).

46. Jobseeker's Allowance (Employment, Skills and Enterprise Scheme) Regulations 2011 (SI 2011/917) reg.12(1)(d) and (2) (May 20, 2011).

47. Social Security (Miscellaneous Amendments) (No.3) Regulations 2011 (SI 2011/2425) reg.10(8) (October 31, 2011).

48. Social Security (Miscellaneous Amendments) (No.3) Regulations 2011 (SI 2011/2425) reg.10(9) (October 31, 2011).

49. Jobseeker's Allowance (Schemes for Assisting Persons to Obtain Employment) Regulations 2013 (SI 2013/276) reg.9(1)(d) and (2) (February 12, 2013).

50. Jobseekers (Back to Work Schemes) Act 2013 s.1(14) (March 26, 2013).

51. Social Security (Miscellaneous Amendments) Regulations 2014 (SI 2014/591) reg.4(4) (April 28, 2014).
52. Social Security (Scottish Rate of Income Tax etc.) (Amendment) Regulations 2016 (SI 2016/233) reg.3(5) (April 6, 2016).

DEFINITIONS

"Abbeyfield Home"—see reg.1(3).
"the Act"—*ibid.*
"the Armed Forces and Reserve Forces Compensation Scheme"—*ibid.*
"the Benefits Act"—see Jobseekers Act s.35(1).
"care home"—see reg.1(3).
"the Caxton Foundation"—*ibid.*
"child tax credit"—*ibid.*
"claimant"— *ibid.*, and reg.88(1).
"claimant participating as a service user"—see reg.1(3G).
"earnings"—see reg.1(3).
"the Employment, Skills and Enterprise Scheme"—*ibid.*
"family"—Jobseekers Act s.35(1).
"independent hospital"—see reg.1(3).
"Intensive Activity Period for 50 plus"—*ibid.*
"the Mandatory Work Activity Scheme"—*ibid.*
"MFET Limited"—*ibid.*
"occupational pension"—*ibid.*
"occupational pension scheme"—see Jobseekers Act s.35(1).
"partner"—see reg.1(3).
"pay period"—*ibid.*
"payment"—*ibid.*
"personal pension scheme"—see Jobseekers Act s.35(1).
"qualifying age for state pension credit"—see reg.1(3).
"Scottish basic rate"—*ibid.*
"Scottish taxpayer" —*ibid.*
"single claimant"—*ibid.*
"the Skipton Fund"—*ibid.*
"subsistence allowance"—*ibid.*
"the Eileen Trust"—*ibid.*
"the Fund"—*ibid.*
"the Independent Living Funds"—*ibid.*
"the Macfarlane (Special Payments) Trust"—*ibid.*
"the Macfarlane (Special Payments) (No.2) Trust"—*ibid.*
"the Macfarlane Trust"—*ibid.*
"training allowance"—*ibid.*
"voluntary organisation"—*ibid.*
"war disablement pension"—*ibid.*
"war widow's pension"—*ibid.*
"war widower's pension"—*ibid.*
"water charges"—*ibid.*
"working tax credit"—*ibid.*
"year of assessment"—*ibid.*

GENERAL NOTE

See the notes to reg.42 of the Income Support Regulations. There are some differences which are mainly related to the different nature of the two benefits (for example, there is no equivalent in reg.105 to reg.42(6A)(c) as this relates to lone parents). **3.328**

See also the new head (iv) inserted in para.(10A)(c) on October 5, 2009 which has not been reproduced in reg.42(4ZA)(c) of the Income Support Regulations.

Note that a new para.(10A)(cc) has been inserted with effect from February 12, 2013 and the original para.(10A)(cc) (which related to a claimant's participation in the Employment, Skills and Enterprise Scheme) has been treated as revoked from that date as a result of s.1(14) of the Jobseekers (Back to Work Schemes) Act 2013. The Jobseeker's Allowance (Employment, Skills and Enterprise Scheme) Regulations 2011 (SI 2011/917) were held to be ultra vires by the Court of Appeal in *R (Reilly and Wilson) v Secretary of State for Work and Pensions* [2013] EWCA Civ 66. The appeal against this decision was allowed by the Supreme Court on October 30, 2013 (*R (on the application of Reilly) v Secretary of State for Work and Pensions* [2013] UKSC 68) but "on the basis only that the Jobseekers (Back to Work Schemes) Act 2013 has come into force" (the 2013 Act came into force on March 26, 2013).

3.329 Sub-paras (ca), (cd) and (ce) of para.(10A) have not been included. This is because they only apply to pilot schemes in certain areas of the country.

Paragraph (ca) was inserted by reg.14(1)(d) and (2) of the Jobseeker's Allowance (Work for Your Benefit Pilot Scheme) Regulations 2010 (SI 2010/1222) to ensure that a person who was participating in the Work for Your Benefit Pilot Scheme was not treated as possessing notional income as a result of expenses paid in respect of that participation. These Regulations came into force on November 22, 2010 and were to cease to have effect on November 21, 2013 but in fact were revoked on March 1, 2012.

Paragraph (cd) was inserted by reg.11(1)(c) and (2) of the Jobseeker's Allowance (Supervised Jobsearch Pilot Scheme) Regulations 2014 (SI 2014/1913); its effect was that a person who was participating in the Supervised Jobsearch Pilot Scheme would not be treated as possessing notional income as a result of expenses paid in respect of that participation. These Regulations came into force on July 18, 2014 and ceased to have effect on April 30, 2015.

Paragraph (ce) was inserted by reg.15(1)(c) and (2) of the Jobseeker's Allowance (18–21 Work Skills Pilot Scheme) Regulations 2014 (SI 2014/3117) and makes the same provision as regards notional income in respect of a person's participation in the 18–21 Work Skills Pilot Scheme. These Regulations came into force on November 25, 2014 and will cease to have effect two years after they came into force.

Paragraph (1)

3.330 Until October 31, 2011 para.(1) applied if the deprivation had been for the purpose of securing entitlement to, or increasing the amount of, JSA *or income support*. This avoided the question that might otherwise have arisen on a claimant transferring from income support to JSA whether a deprivation which had only been for the purposes of income support was caught by para.(1). But para.(1) was not amended on the introduction of ESA to include a reference to a deprivation for the purposes of ESA. The question could therefore have arisen on a claimant transferring from ESA to JSA as to whether a deprivation which had only been for the purposes of ESA was caught by para.(1).

Paragraph (1) has, however, been amended with effect from October 31, 2011 so that it now applies if the person has deprived himself of income in order to secure entitlement to, or increase the amount of, JSA, income support or ESA. A similar amendment has been made to reg.42(1) of the Income Support Regulations, so that it now also applies if the deprivation was for the purpose of securing entitlement to, or increasing the amount of, income support, JSA or ESA. The Explanatory Memorandum which accompanied the SI that made these amendments describes this as a "minor" change, the need for which was apparently overlooked when ESA was introduced. However, the change to para.(1) could have a significant effect in certain cases because a deprivation of income now counts for the purposes of all three benefits. It is suggested that para.(1) would not previously have bitten if the deprivation had been for the purpose of securing, or increasing, entitlement to ESA.

Note that the JSA deprivation of capital rule (reg.113(1)) has not been amended;

it continues to apply only where the deprivation was for the purposes of securing entitlement to, or increasing the amount of, JSA or income support.

Modifications in respect of children and young persons

106.—[1. . .] 3.331

AMENDMENT

1. Social Security (Working Tax Credit and Child Tax Credit) (Consequential Amendments) Regulations 2003 (SI 2003/455) reg.3 and Sch.2 para.11 (April 6, 2004, except in "transitional cases" and see further the note to reg.83 and to reg.17 of the Income Support Regulations).

GENERAL NOTE

See the notes to reg.44 of the Income Support Regulations. 3.332

Chapter VI

Capital

[1Capital limit

107.—For the purposes of section 13(1) and (2A) (no entitlement to an income-based jobseeker's allowance if capital exceeds a prescribed amount), the prescribed amount is £16,000.] 3.333

AMENDMENT

1. Social Security (Miscellaneous Amendments) (No.2) Regulations 2005 (SI 2005/2465) reg.3(4) (April 10, 2006).

DEFINITION

"claimant"—see Jobseekers Act s.35(1) and reg.88(1).

GENERAL NOTE

Under s.13(1) of the Jobseekers Act there is no entitlement to income-based JSA if the claimant's capital exceeds the prescribed amount. The limit is the same as it is for income support, that is from April 10, 2006 it is £16,000 for all claimants, thus bringing income-based JSA and income support into line with housing benefit and, until its abolition on April 1, 2013, council tax benefit. In addition, the amount above which the tariff income rule applies has been increased to £6,000, except in the case of residents in a care home, Abbeyfield Home or independent hospital, for whom the tariff income rule will continue to apply only to capital above £10,000 (see reg.116). 3.334

The capital of a claimant's partner is aggregated with the claimant's (reg.88(1)), but not that of children and young persons (reg.88(2)).

See the notes to reg.45 of the Income Support Regulations.

Calculation of capital

108.—(1) Subject to paragraph (2), the capital of a claimant to be taken into account shall be the whole of his capital calculated in accordance with this Part and any income treated as capital under regulation 110. 3.335

(2) There shall be disregarded from the calculation of a claimant's capital under paragraph (1) any capital, where applicable, specified in Schedule 8.

DEFINITION

"claimant"—see Jobseekers Act s.35(1) and reg.88(1).

GENERAL NOTE

3.336 See the notes to reg.46 of the Income Support Regulations.

Disregard of capital of child or young person

3.337 **109.**—[1. . .]

AMENDMENT

1. Social Security (Working Tax Credit and Child Tax Credit) (Consequential Amendments) Regulations 2003 (SI 2003/455) reg.3 and Sch.2 para.11 (April 6, 2004, except in "transitional cases" and see further the note to reg.83 and to reg.17 of the Income Support Regulations).

GENERAL NOTE

3.338 See the notes to reg.47 of the Income Support Regulations.

Income treated as capital

3.339 **110.**—(1) Any bounty derived from employment to which paragraph 9 of Schedule 6 applies and paid at intervals of at least one year shall be treated as capital.

(2) Except in the case of an amount to which section 15(2)(c)(i) (refund of tax in trade dispute cases) applies, any amount by way of a refund of income tax deducted from profits or emoluments chargeable to income tax under Schedule D or E shall be treated as capital.

(3) Any holiday pay which is not earnings under regulation 98(1)(c) (earnings of employed earners) shall be treated as capital.

(4) Except any income derived from capital disregarded under paragraphs 1, 2, 4 to 8, 11 [4, 17, 42 or 43] of Schedule 8, any income derived from capital shall be treated as capital but only from the date it is normally due to be credited to the claimant's account.

(5) Subject to paragraph (6), in the case of employment as an employed earner, any advance of earnings or any loan made by the claimant's employer shall be treated as capital.

(6) Paragraph (5) shall not apply to a person who is, or would be, prevented from being entitled to a jobseeker's allowance by section 14 (trade disputes).

(7) Any payment under section 30 of the Prison Act 1952 (payments for discharged prisoners) or allowance under section 17 of the Prisons (Scotland) Act 1989 (allowances to prisoners on discharge) shall be treated as capital.

(8) [3. . .]

(9) Any charitable or voluntary payment which is not made or not due to be made at regular intervals, other than one to which paragraph (10) applies, shall be treated as capital.

(10) This paragraph applies to a payment—

(a) which is made to a person who is, or would be, prevented from being entitled to a jobseeker's allowance by section 14 (trade disputes);

(b) [3 . . .]

(c) which is made under [7 or by] the Macfarlane Trust, the Macfarlane (Special Payments) Trust, the Macfarlane (Special Payments) (No.2) Trust, the Fund, the Eileen Trust [6 , MFET Limited] [8 , the Skipton Fund, the Caxton Foundation] or the Independent Living [5 Fund (2006)].

[2(11) Any arrears of subsistence allowance which are paid to a claimant as a lump sum shall be treated as capital.]

AMENDMENTS

1. Social Security (Miscellaneous Amendments) Regulations 1998 (SI 1998/563) reg.14(2) (April 6, 1998).

2. Social Security Amendment (Employment Zones) Regulations 2000 (SI 2000/724) reg.3(2) (April 3, 2000).

3. Social Security (Working Tax Credit and Child Tax Credit) (Consequential Amendments) Regulations 2003 (SI 2003/455) reg.3 and Sch.2 para.12 (April 6, 2004, except in "transitional cases" and see further the note to reg.83 and to reg.17 of the Income Support Regulations).

4. Social Security (Miscellaneous Amendments) (No.4) Regulations 2006 (SI 2006/2378) reg.13(6) (October 2, 2006).

5. Social Security (Miscellaneous Amendments) (No.6) Regulations 2008 (SI 2008/2767) reg.4(7) (November 17, 2008).

6. Social Security (Miscellaneous Amendments) (No.2) Regulations 2010 (SI 2010/641) reg.4(3)(c) (April 6, 2010).

7. Social Security (Miscellaneous Amendments) (No.2) Regulations 2010 (SI 2010/641) reg.4(8)(b) (April 6, 2010).

8. Social Security (Miscellaneous Amendments) (No.3) Regulations 2011 (SI 2011/2425) reg.10(9) (October 31, 2011).

DEFINITIONS

"child"—see Jobseekers Act s.35(1).
"the Caxton Foundation"—see reg.1(3).
"the Children Order"— *ibid.*
"claimant"—Jobseekers Act, s.35(1) and reg.88(1).
"earnings"—see reg.1(3).
"employed earner"—see reg.3 and SSCBA s.2(1)(a).
"family"—see Jobseekers Act s.35(1).
"the Eileen Trust"—see reg.1(3).
"the Fund"—*ibid.*
"the Independent Living Funds"—*ibid.*
"the Macfarlane (Special Payments) Trust"—*ibid.*
"the MacFarlane (Special Payments) (No.2) Trust"—*ibid.*
"the Macfarlane Trust"—*ibid.*
"MFET Limited"—*ibid.*
"the Skipton Fund"—*ibid.*
"subsistence allowance"—*ibid.*

GENERAL NOTE

See the notes to reg.48 of the Income Support Regulations. Most of the categories **3.340** deemed to be capital are self-explanatory. They are then disregarded as income (Sch.7 para.34).

[1 Calculation of capital in the United Kingdom

3.341 **111.**—Capital which a claimant possesses in the United Kingdom shall be calculated at its current market or surrender value less—

(a) where there would be expenses attributable to sale, 10 per cent ; and

(b) the amount of any incumbrance secured on it.]

AMENDMENT

1. Social Security (Miscellaneous Amendments) (No.5) Regulations 2007 (SI 2007/2618) reg.8(12) (October 1, 2007).

DEFINITION

"claimant"—see Jobseekers Act s.35(1) and reg.88(1).

GENERAL NOTE

3.342 See the notes to reg.49 of the Income Support Regulations.

Calculation of capital outside the United Kingdom

3.343 **112.**—Capital which a claimant possesses in a country outside the United Kingdom shall be calculated—

(a) in a case in which there is no prohibition in that country against the transfer to the United Kingdom of an amount equal to its current market or surrender value in that country, at that value;

(b) in a case where there is such a prohibition, at the price which it would realise if sold in the United Kingdom to a willing buyer,

less, where there would be expenses attributable to sale, 10 per cent, and the amount of any incumbrance secured on it.

DEFINITION

"claimant"—see Jobseekers Act s.35(1) and reg.88(1).

GENERAL NOTE

3.344 See the note to reg.50 of the Income Support Regulations.

Notional capital

3.345 **113.**—(1) A claimant shall be treated as possessing capital of which he has deprived himself for the purpose of securing entitlement to a jobseeker's allowance or increasing the amount of that allowance, or for the purpose of securing entitlement to or increasing the amount of income support, except—

(a) where that capital is derived from a payment made in consequence of a personal injury and is placed on trust for the benefit of the claimant; or

(b) to the extent that the capital he is treated as possessing is reduced in accordance with regulation 114 (diminishing notional capital rule); [1or

[16 (c) any sum to which paragraph 42(2)(a) of Schedule 8 (capital to be disregarded) applies which is administered in the way referred to in paragraph 42(1)(a); or

(d) any sum to which paragraph 43(a) of Schedule 8 refers.]]

(2) Except in the case of—

(a) a discretionary trust;

(b) a trust derived from a payment made in consequence of a personal injury;

(c) any loan which would be obtainable only if secured against capital disregarded under Schedule 8; or

(d) a personal pension scheme; [1or

[14 (da) an occupational pension scheme [15 or a payment made by the Board of the Pension Protection Fund] where the claimant [24 has not attained the qualifying age for state pension credit]; or]

[17 (e) any sum to which paragraph 42(2)(a) of Schedule 8 (capital to be disregarded) applies which is administered in the way referred to in paragraph 42(1)(a); or

(f) any sum to which paragraph 43(a) of Schedule 8 refers,]]

any capital which would become available to the claimant upon application being made but which has not been acquired by him shall be treated as possessed by him but only from the date on which it could be expected to be acquired were an application made.

(3) [3Any payment of capital, other than a payment of capital specified in paragraph (3A)], made—

(a) to a third party in respect of a single claimant or [10 his partner] shall be treated—

(i) in a case where that payment is derived from a payment of any benefit under the [20 benefit Acts, a payment from the Armed Forces and Reserve Forces Compensation Scheme, a war disablement pension, war widow's pension or war widower's pension or a pension payable to a person as a widow, widower or surviving civil partner under any power of Her Majesty otherwise than under an enactment to make provision about pensions for or in respect of persons who have been disabled or have died in consequence of service as members of the armed forces of the Crown], as possessed by that single claimant, if it would normally be paid to him, or as possessed [10 by his partner, if it would normally be paid to his partner];

[4(ia) in a case where that payment is a payment of an occupational pension [15, a pension or other periodical payment made under a personal pension scheme or a payment made by the Board of the Pension Protection Fund], as possessed by that single claimant or, as the case may be, by [10 the claimant's partner];]

(ii) in any other case, as possessed by that single claimant [10 or his partner] to the extent that it is used for the food, ordinary clothing or footwear, household fuel, rent for which housing benefit [8 is payable] or any housing costs to the extent that they are met under regulation 83(f) [684(1)(g), 86A(d) or 86B(e)] [8 . . .], of that single claimant or, as the case may be, [10 of his partner], or is used for any council tax or water charges for which that claimant or [10 partner is liable];

[10 (b) to a single claimant or his partner in respect of a third party (but not in respect of another member of his family) shall be treated as possessed by that single claimant or, as the case may be, his partner, to the extent that it is kept or used by him or used by or on behalf of his partner.]

[3(3A) Paragraph (3) shall not apply in respect of a payment of capital made—

(a) under [23 or by] the Macfarlane Trust, the Macfarlane (Special Payments) Trust, the Macfarlane (Special Payments) (No.2) Trust, the Fund, the Eileen Trust [22 , MFET Limited] [11, the Independent Living [19 Fund (2006)] [13, the Skipton Fund [27, the Caxton Foundation] or the London Bombings Relief Charitable Fund]]; or

(b) pursuant to section 2 of the Employment and Training Act 1973 in respect of a person's participation—

(i) in an employment programme specified in regulation 75(1)(a)(ii);

(ii) in a training scheme specified in regulation 75(1)(b)(ii); or

[7 (iia) [18 . . .] in the Intensive Activity Period specified in regulation 75(1)(a)(iv); or]

(iii) in a qualifying course within the meaning specified in regulation 17A(7)] [21; or

(iv) in the Flexible New Deal.]

(ba) [*Omitted*]

[25(bb) in respect of a person's participation in the Mandatory Work Activity Scheme;]

[26 (bc) [29 . . .]]

[28 (bc) in respect of a claimant's participation in a scheme prescribed in regulation 3 of the Jobseeker's Allowance (Schemes for Assisting Persons to Obtain Employment) Regulations 2013;]

(bd) *[Omitted]*

(be) *[Omitted]*

[5(c) under an occupational pension scheme [15, in respect of a pension or other periodical payment made under a personal pension scheme or a payment made by the Board of the Pension Protection Fund] where—

(i) a bankruptcy order has been made in respect of the person in respect of whom the payment has been made or, in Scotland, the estate of that person is subject to sequestration or a judicial factor has been appointed on that person's estate under section 41 of the Solicitors (Scotland) Act 1980;

(ii) the payment is made to the trustee in bankruptcy or any other person acting on behalf of the creditors; and

(iii) the person referred to in (i) and [10 his partner (if any)]does not possess, or is not treated as possessing, any other income apart from that payment.]

(4) Where a claimant stands in relation to a company in a position analogous to that of a sole owner or a partner in the business of that company, he shall be treated as if he were such sole owner or partner and in such a case—

(a) the value of his holding in that company shall, notwithstanding regulation 108 (calculation of capital), be disregarded; and

(b) he shall, subject to paragraph (5), be treated as possessing an amount of capital equal to the value or, as the case may be, his share of the value of the capital of that company and the foregoing provisions of this Chapter shall apply for the purposes of calculating that amount as if it were actual capital which he does possess.

(5) For so long as the claimant undertakes activities in the course of the business of the company, the amount which he is treated as possessing under paragraph (4) shall be disregarded.

(6) Where a claimant is treated as possessing any capital under any of paragraphs (1) to (4) the foregoing provisions of this Chapter shall apply for the purposes of calculating the amount of that capital as if it were actual capital which he does possess.

(7) For the avoidance of doubt a claimant is to be treated as possessing capital under paragraph (1) only if the capital of which he has deprived himself is actual capital.

(8) In paragraph (3) the expression "ordinary clothing or footwear" means clothing or footwear for normal daily use, but does not include school uniforms, or clothing or footwear used solely for sporting activities.

AMENDMENTS

1. Income-related Benefits and Jobseeker's Allowance (Amendment) (No.2) Regulations 1997 (SI 1997/2197) reg.6 (October 6, 1997).

2. Social Security Amendment (New Deal) Regulations 1997 (SI 1997/2863) reg.10 (January 5, 1998).

3. Social Security Amendment (New Deal) (No.2) Regulations 1998 (SI 1998/2117) reg.3(1) (September 24, 1998).

4. Social Security Amendment (Notional Income and Capital) Regulations 1999 (SI 1999/2640) reg.2(1)(b) (November 15, 1999).

5. Social Security Amendment (Notional Income and Capital) Regulations 1999 (SI 1999/2640) reg.2(3)(d) (November 15, 1999).

6. Jobseeker's Allowance (Joint Claims) Regulations 2000 (SI 2000/1978) reg.2(5) and Sch.2 para.44 (March 19, 2001).

7. Social Security Amendment (New Deal) Regulations 2001 (SI 2001/1029) reg.8 (April 9, 2001).

8. Social Security Amendment (Residential Care and Nursing Homes) Regulations 2001 (SI 2001/3767) reg.2(2) and Pt II of Sch. para.11 (April 8, 2002).

9. Social Security (Miscellaneous Amendments) Regulations 2002 (SI 2002/841) reg.3(3) (April 8, 2002).

10. Social Security (Working Tax Credit and Child Tax Credit) (Consequential Amendments) Regulations 2003 (SI 2003/455) reg.3 and Sch.2 para.13 (April 6, 2004, except in "transitional cases" and see further the note to regs 83 and 17 of the Income Support Regulations).

11. Social Security (Miscellaneous Amendments) (No.3) Regulations 2004 (SI 2004/2308) reg.3(1) and (2)(d) (October 4, 2004).

12. Social Security (Miscellaneous Amendments) Regulations 2005 (SI 2005/574) reg.2(6) (April 4, 2005).

13. Income-related Benefits (Amendment) (No.2) Regulations 2005 (SI 2005/3391) reg.5(3) (December 12, 2005).

14. Social Security (Miscellaneous Amendments) (No.2) Regulations 2005 (SI 2005/2465) reg.3(5) (April 6, 2006).

15. Social Security (Miscellaneous Amendments) Regulations 2006 (SI 2006/588) reg.3(4) (April 6, 2006).

16. Social Security (Miscellaneous Amendments) Regulations 2007 (SI 2007/719) reg.3(5)(a) (April 2, 2007).

17. Social Security (Miscellaneous Amendments) Regulations 2007 (SI 2007/719) reg.3(5)(b) (April 2, 2007).

18. Social Security (Miscellaneous Amendments) Regulations 2008 (SI 2008/698) reg.4(12)(b) (April 14, 2008).

19. Social Security (Miscellaneous Amendments) (No.6) Regulations 2008 (SI 2008/2767) reg.4(7) (November 17, 2008).

20. Social Security (Miscellaneous Amendments) (No.7) Regulations 2008 (SI 2008/3157) reg.3(6) (January 5, 2009).

21. Social Security (Flexible New Deal) Regulations 2009 (SI 2009/480) reg.2(7) (October 5, 2009).

22. Social Security (Miscellaneous Amendments) (No.2) Regulations 2010 (SI 2010/641) reg.4(3)(d) (April 6, 2010).

23. Social Security (Miscellaneous Amendments) (No.2) Regulations 2010 (SI 2010/641) reg.4(8)(c) (April 6, 2010).

24. Social Security (Miscellaneous Amendments) (No.2) Regulations 2010 (SI 2010/641) reg.4(9) (April 6, 2010).

25. Jobseeker's Allowance (Mandatory Work Activity Scheme) Regulations 2011 (SI 2011/688) reg.13(1)(d) and (2) (April 25, 2011).

26. Jobseeker's Allowance (Employment, Skills and Enterprise Scheme) Regulations 2011 (SI 2011/917) reg.13(1)(d) and (2) (May 20, 2011).

27. Social Security (Miscellaneous Amendments) (No.3) Regulations 2011 (SI 2011/2425) reg.10(10) (October 31, 2011).

28. Jobseeker's Allowance (Schemes for Assisting Persons to Obtain Employment) Regulations 2013 (SI 2013/276) reg.10(1)(d) and (2) (February 12, 2013).

29. Jobseekers (Back to Work Schemes) Act 2013 s.1(14) (March 26, 2013).

DEFINITIONS

"the Act"—see reg.1(3).
"the Armed Forces and Reserve Forces Compensation Scheme"—*ibid.*
"the Benefits Act"—see Jobseekers Act s.35(1).
"the Caxton Foundation"—see reg.1(3).
"claimant"—see Jobseekers Act s.35(1) and reg.88(1).
"the Employment, Skills and Enterprise Scheme"—see reg.1(3).
"family"—see Jobseekers Act s.35(1).
"occupational pension"—see reg.1(3).
"payment"—*ibid.*
"personal pension scheme"—see Jobseekers Act s.35(1).
"the Eileen Trust"—see reg.1(3).
"the Fund"—*ibid.*
"the Independent Living Funds"—*ibid.*
"the London Bombings Relief Charitable Fund"—*ibid.*
"the Macfarlane (Special Payments) Trust"—*ibid.*
"the Macfarlane (Special Payments) (No.2) Trust"—*ibid.*
"the Macfarlane Trust"—*ibid.*
"the Mandatory Work Activity Scheme"—*ibid.*
"MFET Limited"—*ibid.*
"qualifying age for state pension credit"—*ibid.*
"the Skipton Fund"—*ibid.*
"single claimant"—*ibid.*
"war disablement pension"—*ibid.*
"war widow's pension"—*ibid.*
"war widower's pension"—*ibid.*
"water charges"—*ibid.*

GENERAL NOTE

3.346 See the notes to reg.51 of the Income Support Regulations. Note that para.(3A)(b)(iv), (bb) and (bc) have not been reproduced in reg.51.

In relation to para.(3A)(bc), note that a further para.(3A)(bc) was inserted on February 12, 2013, and the original para.(3A)(bc) has been treated as revoked from that date as a result of s.1(14) of the Jobseekers (Back to Work Schemes) Act 2013. The original para.(3A)(bc) related to a claimant's participation in the Employment,

Skills and Enterprise Scheme. The Jobseeker's Allowance (Employment, Skills and Enterprise Scheme) Regulations 2011 (SI 2011/917) were held to be ultra vires by the Court of Appeal in *R (Reilly and Wilson) v Secretary of State for Work and Pensions* [2013] EWCA Civ 66. The appeal against this decision was allowed by the Supreme Court on October 30, 2013 (*R (on the application of Reilly) v Secretary of State for Work and Pensions* [2013] UKSC 68) but "on the basis only that the Jobseekers (Back to Work Schemes) Act 2013 has come into force" (the 2013 Act came into force on March 26, 2013).

Sub-paragraphs (ba), (bd) and (be) of para.(3A) have not been included. This is because they only apply to pilot schemes in certain areas of the country.

Paragraph (ba) was inserted by reg.15(1)(d) and (2) of the Jobseeker's Allowance (Work for Your Benefit Pilot Scheme) Regulations 2010 (SI 2010/1222) to ensure that a person who was participating in the Work for Your Benefit Pilot Scheme was not treated as possessing notional capital as a result of expenses paid in respect of that participation. These Regulations came into force on November 22, 2010 and were to cease to have effect on November 21, 2013 but in fact were revoked on March 1, 2012. 3.347

Paragraph (bd) was inserted by reg.12(1)(c) and (2) of the Jobseeker's Allowance (Supervised Jobsearch Pilot Scheme) Regulations 2014 (SI 2014/1913); its effect was that a person who was participating in the Supervised Jobsearch Pilot Scheme would not be treated as possessing notional capital as a result of expenses paid in respect of that participation. These Regulations came into force on July 18, 2014 and ceased to have effect on April 30, 2015.

Paragraph (be) was inserted by reg.16(1)(c) and (2) of the Jobseeker's Allowance (18–21 Work Skills Pilot Scheme) Regulations 2014 (SI 2014/3117) and makes the same provision as regards notional capital in respect of a person's participation in the 18–21 Work Skills Pilot Scheme. These Regulations came into force on November 25, 2014 and will cease to have effect two years after they came into force.

Paragraph (1)

Under para.(1) if a person has deprived himself of capital he will be caught by this rule if the purpose of the deprivation was to secure entitlement to or increase the amount of jobseeker's allowance *or income support*. This avoids the question that might otherwise have arisen on a claimant transfering from income support to jobseeker's allowance whether a deprivation which had only been for the purposes of income support could be caught by para.(1). But note that para.(1) has not been amended to include a reference to a deprivation for the purposes of ESA. Such an amendment, however, was made to para.(1) of reg.105 on October 31, 2011. 3.348

Diminishing notional capital rule

114.—(1) Where a claimant is treated as possessing capital under regulation 113(1) (notional capital), the amount which he is treated as possessing— 3.349

(a) in the case of a week that is subsequent to—
  (i) the relevant week in respect of which the conditions set out in paragraph (2) are satisfied, or
  (ii) a week which follows that relevant week and which satisfies those conditions,

  shall be reduced by an amount determined under paragraph (2);

(b) in the case of a week in respect of which paragraph (1)(a) does not apply but where—
  (i) that week is a week subsequent to the relevant week, and
  (ii) that relevant week is a week in which the condition in paragraph (3) is satisfied,

  shall be reduced by an amount determined under paragraph (3).

(2) This paragraph applies to a benefit week or part week where the claimant satisfies the conditions that—

(a) he is in receipt of a jobseeker's allowance; and

(b) but for regulation 113(1), he would have received an additional amount of jobseeker's allowance in that benefit week or, as the case may be, that part week;

and in such a case, the amount of the reduction for the purposes of paragraph (1)(a) shall be equal to that additional amount.

(3) Subject to paragraph (4), for the purposes of paragraph (1)(b) the condition is that the claimant would have been entitled to an income-based jobseeker's allowance in the relevant week but for regulation 113(1), and in such a case the amount of the reduction shall be equal to the aggregate of—

(a) the amount of jobseeker's allowance to which the claimant would have been entitled in the relevant week but for regulation 113(1); and for the purposes of this sub-paragraph if the relevant week is a part-week that amount shall be determined by dividing the amount of jobseeker's allowance to which he would have been entitled by the number equal to the number of days in the part-week and multiplying the quotient by 7;

(b) the amount of housing benefit (if any) equal to the difference between his maximum housing benefit and the amount (if any) of housing benefit which he is awarded in respect of the benefit week which includes the last day of the relevant week, and for this purpose "benefit week" has the same meaning as in regulation 2(1) of [[1] the Housing Benefit Regulations 2006] (interpretation);

(c) the amount of council tax benefit (if any) equal to the difference between his maximum council tax benefit and the amount (if any) of council tax benefit which he is awarded in respect of the benefit week which includes the last day of the relevant week, and for this purpose "benefit week" [[2] means a period of 7 consecutive days beginning on a Monday and ending on a Sunday].

(4) The amount determined under paragraph (3) shall be re-determined under that paragraph if the claimant makes a further claim for a jobseeker's allowance and the conditions in paragraph (5) are satisfied, and in such a case—

(a) sub-paragraphs (a), (b) and (c) of paragraph (3) shall apply as if for the words "relevant week" there were substituted the words "relevant subsequent week"; and

(b) subject to paragraph (6), the amount as re-determined shall have effect from the first week following the relevant subsequent week in question.

(5) The conditions referred to in paragraph (4) are that—

(a) a further claim is made 26 or more weeks after—

(i) the date on which the claimant made a claim for a jobseeker's allowance in respect of which he was first treated as possessing the capital in question under regulation 113(1); or

(ii) in a case where there has been at least one re-determination in accordance with paragraph (4), the date on which he last made a claim for a jobseeker's allowance which resulted in the weekly amount being re-determined; or

(iii) the date on which he last ceased to be in receipt of a jobseeker's allowance;

whichever last occurred; and

(b) the claimant would have been entitled to a jobseeker's allowance but for regulation 113(1).

(6) The amount as re-determined pursuant to paragraph (4) shall not have effect if it is less than the amount which applied in that case immediately before the re-determination and in such a case the higher amount shall continue to have effect.

(7) For the purposes of this regulation—

(a) "part-week" has the same meaning as in regulation 150(3);

(b) "relevant week" means the benefit week or part-week in which the capital in question of which the claimant has deprived himself within the meaning of regulation 113(1)—

(i) was first taken into account for the purposes of determining his entitlement to a jobseeker's allowance or income support; or

(ii) was taken into account on a subsequent occasion for the purposes of determining or re-determining his entitlement to a jobseeker's allowance or income support on that subsequent occasion and that determination or re-determination resulted in his beginning to receive, or ceasing to receive, a jobseeker's allowance or income support;

and where more than one benefit week or part-week is identified by reference to heads (i) and (ii) of this sub-paragraph, the later or latest such benefit week or part-week;

(c) "relevant subsequent week" means the benefit week or part-week which includes the day on which the further claim or, if more than one further claim has been made, the last such claim was made.

AMENDMENTS

1. Housing Benefit and Council Tax Benefit (Consequential Provisions) Regulations 2006 (SI 2006/217) reg.5 and Sch.2 para.8(3) (March 6, 2006).

2. Council Tax Benefit Abolition (Consequential Provision) Regulations 2013 (SI 2013/458) reg.4 and Sch.2 para.3 (April 1, 2013).

DEFINITIONS

"benefit week"—see reg.1(3).
"claimant"—see Jobseekers Act s.35(1) and reg.88(1).
"week"—see Jobseekers Act s.35(1).

GENERAL NOTE

See the notes to reg.51A of the Income Support Regulations. 3.350

Capital jointly held

115.—Except where a claimant possesses capital which is disregarded under regulation 113(4) (notional capital), where a claimant and one or more persons are beneficially entitled in possession to any capital asset, they shall be treated as if each of them were entitled in possession [[1]to the whole beneficial interest therein in an equal share and the foregoing provisions of this Chapter shall apply for the purposes of calculating the amount of capital which the claimant is treated as possessing as if it were actual capital which the claimant does possess.] 3.351

AMENDMENT

1. Social Security Amendment (Capital) Regulations 1998 (SI 1998/2250) reg.2 (October 12, 1998).

DEFINITION

"claimant"—see Jobseekers Act s.35(1) and reg.88(1).

GENERAL NOTE

3.352 See the notes to reg.52 of the Income Support Regulations.

Calculation of tariff income from capital

3.353 **116.**—(1) [1Except in a case to which paragraph [7 . . .] (1B) applies,] where the claimant's capital calculated in accordance with this Part exceeds [7£6,000] it shall be treated as equivalent to a weekly income of £1 for each complete £250 in excess of [7£6,000] but not exceeding [7£16,000].

[4 (1ZA) [7 . . .]]

[1(1A) In the case of a claimant to whom paragraph (1B) applies and whose capital calculated in accordance with Chapter VI of Part VIII exceeds £10,000, it shall be treated as equivalent to a weekly income of £1 for each complete £250 in excess of £10,000 but not exceeding £16,000.

(1B) This paragraph applies where the claimant lives permanently in—

[6 (a) a care home or an independent hospital;

(b) an Abbeyfield Home;]

(c) accommodation provided under section 3 of, and Part II of the Schedule to, the Polish Resettlement Act 1947 (provision of accommodation in camps) where the claimant requires personal care [3by reason of old age, disablement, past or present dependence on alcohol or drugs, past or present mental disorder or a terminal illness and the care is provided in the home];

[2(d) [6 . . .].]

(1C) For the purpose of paragraph (1B), a claimant shall be treated as living permanently in such home [6, hospital] or accommodation where he is absent—

[5(a) from a home [6, hospital] or accommodation referred to in sub-paragraph (a) [6 or (b)] of paragraph (1B) for a period not exceeding 13 weeks;]

(b) from accommodation referred to in sub-paragraph (c) of paragraph (1B), but intends, with the agreement of the manager of the accommodation, to return to the accommodation in due course.]

(2) Notwithstanding [1paragraphs (1) [7 . . .] and (1A)], where any part of the excess is not a complete £250 that part shall be treated as equivalent to a weekly income of £1.

(3) For the purposes of [1paragraphs (1) [7 . . .] and (1A)], capital includes any income treated as capital under regulations 110 and 124 (income treated as capital and liable relative payments treated as capital).

[1(4) [6 . . .].]

AMENDMENTS

1. Jobseeker's Allowance (Amendment) Regulations 1996 (SI 1996/1516) reg.12 (October 7, 1996).

2. Income-related Benefits and Jobseeker's Allowance (Miscellaneous Amendments) Regulations 1997 (SI 1997/65) reg.8 (April 7, 1997).
3. Income-related Benefits and Jobseeker's Allowance (Amendment) (No.2) Regulations 1997 (SI 1997/2197) reg.7(5) and (6)(b) (October 6, 1997).
4. Social Security Amendment (Capital Limits and Earnings Disregards) Regulations 2000 (SI 2000/2545) reg.2(2)(c) (April 9, 2001).
5. Social Security Amendment (Residential Care and Nursing Homes) Regulations 2001 (SI 2001/3767) reg.2(2) and Pt II of Sch. para.12 (April 8, 2002).
6. Social Security (Care Homes and Independent Hospitals) Regulations 2005 (SI 2005/2687) reg.3 and Sch.2 para.6 (October 24, 2005).
7. Social Security (Miscellaneous Amendments) (No.2) Regulations 2005 (SI 2005/2465) reg.3(6) (April 10, 2006).

DEFINITIONS

"Abbeyfield Home"—see reg.1(3).
"care home"—*ibid.*
"claimant"—see Jobseekers Act s.35(1) and reg.88(1).
"independent hospital"—see reg.1(3).

GENERAL NOTE

See the notes to reg.53 of the Income Support Regulations. 3.354

Chapter VII

[4[6 . . .] Liable Relative Payments]

Interpretation

117.—In this Chapter, unless the context otherwise requires— 3.355
[5 [7. . .]]
"claimant" includes a young claimant;
[5 "claimant's family" shall be construed in accordance with section 35(1) of the Jobseekers Act 1995 (interpretation);]
[5 "housing costs" means those costs which may be met under regulation 83(f) or 84(1)(g) (housing costs);]
"liable relative" means—
(a) a spouse [2, former spouse, civil partner or former civil partner] of a claimant or of a member of the claimant's family;
(b) a parent of a young claimant or of a child or young person who is a member of a claimant's family;
(c) a person who has not been adjudged to be the father of a young claimant or of a child or young person who is a member of a claimant's family, where that person is contributing to the maintenance of that young claimant, child or young person and by reason of that contribution he may reasonably be treated as the father of that young claimant, child or young person;
(d) a person liable to maintain another person by virtue of section 78(6)(c) of the Administration Act where the latter is the claimant or a member of the claimant's family,

and, in this definition, a reference to a child's, young person's or young claimant's parent includes any person in relation to whom the child, young person or young claimant was treated as a child or a member of the family;

[5 "ordinary clothing and footwear" means clothing and footwear for normal daily use but does not include school uniforms;]

"payment" means a periodical payment or any other payment made by or derived from a liable relative [5 . . .]; but it does not include any payment—

(a) arising as a consequence of a disposition of property made in contemplation of, or as a consequence of—
  (i) an agreement to separate; or
  (ii) any proceedings for judicial separation, divorce or nullity of marriage; [2 or
  (iii) any proceedings for separation, dissolution or nullity in relation to a civil partnership;]

(b) made after the death of the liable relative;

(c) made by way of a gift but not in aggregate or otherwise exceeding £250 in the period of 52 weeks beginning with the date on which the payment, or if there is more than one such payment the first payment, is made; and in the case of a claimant who continues to be in receipt of an income-based jobseeker's allowance at the end of the period of 52 weeks, this provision shall continue to apply thereafter with the modification than any subsequent period of 52 weeks shall begin with the first day of the benefit week in which the first payment is made after the end of the previous period of 52 weeks;

(d) [1 . . .]

[5 (e) made to a third party, or in respect of a third party, unless the payment is—
  (i) in relation to the claimant or the claimant's [7 partner or is made or derived from a person falling within sub-paragraph (d) of the definition of liable relative]; and
  (ii) [8 . . .] in respect of food, ordinary clothing or footwear, fuel, [8 rent for which housing benefit is payable, housing costs to the extent that they are met under regulations 83(f) or 84(1)(g) (housing costs),] council tax or water charges;]

(f) in kind;

(g) to or in respect of a child or young person who is to be treated as not being a member of the claimant's household under regulation 78;

(h) which is not a periodical payment, to the extent that any amount of that payment—
  (i) has already been taken into account under this Part by virtue of a previous claim or determination; or
  (ii) has been recovered under section 74(1) of the Administration Act (prevention of duplication of payments) or is currently being recovered; or
  (iii) at the time the determination is made, has been used by the claimant except where he has deprived himself of that amount for the purpose of securing entitlement to a job-seeker's allowance or increasing the amount of that allowance;

[7 (i) to which paragraph 70 of Schedule 7 (sums to be disregarded in the calculation of income other than earnings) applies;]

"periodical payment" means—

(a) a payment which is made or is due to be made at regular intervals [5 . . .];

(b) in a case where the liable relative has established a pattern of making payments at regular intervals, any such payment;
(c) any payment [5 [7 . . .] that does not exceed] the amount of jobseeker's allowance payable had that payment not been made;
(d) any payment representing a commutation of payments to which subparagraph (a) or (b) of this definition applies whether made in arrears or in advance,

but does not include a payment due to be made before the benefit week in which the claimant first became entitled to an income-based jobseeker's allowance, which was not so made;

"young claimant" means a person aged 16 or over but under [3 20] who makes a claim for a jobseeker's allowance.

AMENDMENTS

1. Social Security (Working Tax Credit and Child Tax Credit) (Consequential Amendments) Regulations 2003 (SI 2003/455) reg.3 and Sch.2 para.14 (April 6, 2004, except in "transitional cases" and see further the note to reg.83 and to reg.17 of the Income Support Regulations).

2. Civil Partnership (Pensions, Social Security and Child Support) (Consequential, etc. Provisions) Order 2005 (SI 2005/2877) art.2(3) and Sch.3 para.26(6) (December 5, 2005).

3. Social Security (Young Persons) Amendment Regulations 2006 (SI 2006/718) reg.3(7) (April 10, 2006).

4. Social Security (Child Maintenance Amendments) Regulations 2008 (SI 2008/2111) reg.3(5) (October 27, 2008).

5. Social Security (Child Maintenance Amendments) Regulations 2008 (SI 2008/2111) reg.3(6) (October 27, 2008).

6. Social Security (Miscellaneous Amendments) (No.4) Regulations 2009 (SI 2009/2655) reg.4(5) (April 12, 2010).

7. Social Security (Miscellaneous Amendments) (No.4) Regulations 2009 (SI 2009/2655) reg.4(9) (April 12, 2010).

8. Social Security (Miscellaneous Amendments) Regulations 2013 (SI 2013/443) reg.4(9) (April 2, 2013).

DEFINITIONS

"benefit week"—see reg.1(3).
"child"—see Jobseekers Act s.35(1).
"claimant"—*ibid.*, and reg.88(1).
"family"—see Jobseekers Act s.35(1).
"young person"—see reg.76.

GENERAL NOTE

See the notes to reg.54 of the Income Support Regulations. 3.356

Treatment of [1 [3 . . .]] liable relative payments

118.—Subject to regulation 119 [4 . . .[2 . . .]] a payment shall— 3.357
(a) to the extent that it is not a payment of income, be treated as income;
(b) be taken into account in accordance with the following provisions of this Chapter.

AMENDMENTS

1. Social Security (Child Maintenance Amendments) Regulations 2008 (SI 2008/2111) reg.3(2)(b) (October 27, 2008).
2. Social Security (Child Maintenance Amendments) Regulations 2008 (SI 2008/2111) reg.3(7) (October 27, 2008).
3. Social Security (Miscellaneous Amendments) (No.4) Regulations 2009 (SI 2009/2655) reg.4(4) (April 12, 2010).
4. Social Security (Miscellaneous Amendments) (No.4) Regulations 2009 (SI 2009/2655) reg.4(10) (April 12, 2010).

DEFINITION

"payment"—*ibid.*

GENERAL NOTE

3.358 See the note to reg.55 of the Income Support Regulations.

Disregard of payments treated as not relevant income

3.359 **119.**—Where the Secretary of State treats any payment as not being relevant income for the purposes of section 74A of the Administration Act (payment of benefit where maintenance payments collected by Secretary of State), that payment shall be disregarded in calculating a claimant's income.

DEFINITIONS

"payment"—see reg.117.
"relevant income"—see reg.2(c), Social Security Benefits (Maintenance Payments and Consequential Amendments) Regulations 1996 (SI 1996/940) (p.949).

GENERAL NOTE

3.360 See reg.55A of the Income Support Regulations and the note to s.74A of the Administration Act in Vol.III of this series.

Period over which periodical payments are to be taken into account

3.361 **120.**—(1) The period over which a periodical payment is to be taken into account shall be—

(a) in a case where the payment is made at regular intervals, a period equal to the length of that interval;
(b) in a case where the payment is due to be made at regular intervals but is not so made, such number of weeks as is equal to the number obtained (and any fraction shall be treated as a corresponding fraction of a week) by dividing the amount of that payment by the weekly amount of that periodical payment as calculated in accordance with regulation 122(4);
(c) in any other case, a period equal to a week.

(2) The period under paragraph (1) shall begin on the date on which the payment is treated as paid under regulation 123.

DEFINITION

"periodical payment"—see reg.117.

General Note

See the note to reg.56 of the Income Support Regulations. 3.362

[1 Period over which payments other than periodical payments are to be taken into account

121.—(1) The period over which a payment other than a periodical payment (a "non-periodical payment") is to be taken account shall be determined as follows. 3.363

(2) Except in a case where paragraph (4) applies, the number of weeks over which a non-periodical payment is to be taken into account shall be equal to the number obtained by dividing that payment by the amount referred to in paragraph (3).

(3) The amount is the aggregate of £2 and—

(a) the amount of jobseeker's allowance that would be payable had no payment been made [2 . . .]

(b) [2 . . .].

(4) This paragraph applies in a case where a liable relative makes a periodical payment and a non-periodical payment concurrently and the weekly amount of the periodical payment (as calculated in accordance with regulation 122) is less than B.

(5) In a case where paragraph (4) applies, the non-periodical payment shall, subject to paragraphs (6) and (7), be taken into account over a period of the number of weeks equal to the number obtained by applying the formula—

$$\frac{A}{B - C}$$

(6) If the liable relative ceases to make periodical payments, the balance (if any) of the non-periodical payment shall be taken into account over the number of weeks equal to the number obtained by dividing that balance by the amount referred to in paragraph (3).

(7) If the amount of any subsequent periodical payment varies, the balance (if any) of the non-periodical payment shall be taken into account over a period of the number of weeks equal to the number obtained by applying the formula—

$$\frac{D}{B - E}$$

(8) The period under paragraph (2) or (4) shall begin on the date on which the payment is treated as paid under regulation 123 (date on which a liable relative payment is treated as paid) and the period under paragraph (6) and (7) shall begin on the first day of the benefit week in which the cessation or variation of the periodical payment occurred.

(9) Any fraction which arises by applying a calculation or formula referred to in this regulation shall be treated as a corresponding fraction of a week.

(10) In paragraphs (4) to (7)—

A = the amount of the non-periodical payment;

B = the aggregate of £2 and the amount of jobseeker's allowance that would be payable had the periodical payment not been made [2 . . .];

C = the weekly amount of the periodical payment;

D = the balance (if any) of the non-periodical payment;
E = the weekly amount of any subsequent periodical payment.]

Amendments

1. Social Security (Child Maintenance Amendments) Regulations 2008 (SI 2008/2111) reg.3(8) (October 27, 2008).
2. Social Security (Miscellaneous Amendments) (No.4) Regulations 2009 (SI 2009/2655) reg.4(11) (April 12, 2010).

Definitions

"benefit week"—see reg.1(3).
"liable relative"—see reg.117.
"payment"—*ibid.*
"periodical payment"—*ibid.*

General Note

3.364 See the note to reg.57 of the Income Support Regulations.

Calculation of the weekly amount of a [1[2 . . .]] liable relative payment

3.365 **122.**—(1) Where a periodical payment is made or is due to be made at intervals of one week, the weekly amount shall be the amount of that payment.

(2) Where a periodical payment is made or is due to be made at intervals greater than one week and those intervals are monthly, the weekly amount shall be determined by multiplying the amount of the payment by 12 and dividing the product by 52.

(3) Where a periodical payment is made or is due to be made at intervals and those intervals are neither weekly or monthly, the weekly amount shall be determined by dividing that payment by the number equal to the number of weeks (including any part of a week) in that interval.

(4) Where a payment is made and that payment represents a commutation of periodical payments whether in arrears or in advance, the weekly amount shall be the weekly amount of the individual periodical payments so commuted as calculated under paragraphs (1) to (3) as appropriate.

(5) The weekly amount of a payment to which regulation 121 applies (period over which payments other than periodical payments are to be taken into account) shall be equal to the amount of the divisor used in calculating the period over which the payment or, as the case may be, the balance is to be taken into account.

Amendments

1. Social Security (Child Maintenance Amendments) Regulations 2008 (SI 2008/2111) reg.3(2)(c) (October 27, 2008).
2. Social Security (Miscellaneous Amendments) (No.4) Regulations 2009 (SI 2009/2655) reg.4(4) (April 12, 2010).

Definitions

"payment"—*ibid.*
"periodical payment"—*ibid.*

General Note

See the note to reg.58 of the Income Support Regulations. 3.366

Date on which a [1[2 . . .]] liable relative payment is to be treated as paid

123.—(1) A periodical payment is to be treated as paid— 3.367

(a) in the case of a payment which is due to be made before the benefit week in which the claimant first became entitled to an income-based jobseeker's allowance, on the day in the week in which it is due to be paid which corresponds to the first day of the benefit week;

(b) in any other case, on the first day of the benefit week in which it is due to be paid unless, having regard to the manner in which jobseeker's allowance is due to be paid in the particular case, it would be more practicable to treat it as paid on the first day of a subsequent benefit week.

(2) Subject to paragraph (3), any other payment shall be treated as paid—

(a) in the case of a payment which is made before the benefit week in which the claimant first became entitled to an income-based jobseeker's allowance, on the day in the week in which it is paid which corresponds to the first day of the benefit week;

(b) in any other case, on the first day of the benefit week in which it is paid unless, having regard to the manner in which jobseeker's allowance is due to be paid in the particular case, it would be more practicable to treat it as paid on the first day of a subsequent benefit week.

(3) Any other payment paid on a date which falls within the period in respect of which a previous payment is taken into account, not being a periodical payment, is to be treated as paid on the first day following the end of that period.

Amendments

1. Social Security (Child Maintenance Amendments) Regulations 2008 (SI 2008/2111) reg.3(2)(d) (October 27, 2008).

2. Social Security (Miscellaneous Amendments) (No.4) Regulations 2009 (SI 2009/2655) reg.4(4) (April 12, 2010).

Definitions

"benefit week"—see reg.1(3).
"payment"—*ibid.*
"periodical payment"—*ibid.*

General Note

See the notes to reg.59 of the Income Support Regulations. 3.368

Liable relative payments to be treated as capital

124.—[1 . . .] 3.369

AMENDMENT

1. Social Security (Child Maintenance Amendments) Regulations 2008 (SI 2008/2111) reg.3(4)(b) (October 27, 2008).

Chapter VIII

Child Support

Interpretation

3.370 **125.**—[1 . . .]

AMENDMENT

1. Social Security (Child Maintenance Amendments) Regulations 2008 (SI 2008/2111) reg.3(4)(c) (October 27, 2008).

Treatment of child support maintenance

3.371 **126.**—[1 . . .]

AMENDMENT

1. Social Security (Child Maintenance Amendments) Regulations 2008 (SI 2008/2111) reg.3(4)(c) (October 27, 2008).

Disregard of payments treated as not relevant income

3.372 **127.**—[1 . . .]

AMENDMENT

1. Social Security (Child Maintenance Amendments) Regulations 2008 (SI 2008/2111) reg.3(4)(c) (October 27, 2008).

Calculation of the weekly amount of child support maintenance

3.373 **128.**—[1 . . .]

AMENDMENT

1. Social Security (Child Maintenance Amendments) Regulations 2008 (SI 2008/2111) reg.3(4)(c) (October 27, 2008).

Date on which child support maintenance is to be treated as paid

3.374 **129.**—[1 . . .]

AMENDMENT

1. Social Security (Child Maintenance Amendments) Regulations 2008 (SI 2008/2111) reg.3(4)(c) (October 27, 2008).

Chapter IX

[4 Students]

Interpretation

130.—In this Chapter, unless the context otherwise requires— 3.375

[7 "academic year" means the period of twelve months beginning on 1st January, 1st April, 1st July or 1st September according to whether the course in question begins in the winter, the spring, the summer or the autumn respectively but if students are required to begin attending the course during August or September and to continue attending through the autumn, the academic year of the course shall be considered to begin in the autumn rather than the summer;]

[5 "access funds" means—

(a) grants made under section [14 68] of the Further and Higher Education Act 1992 [14 . . .] [7 for the purpose of providing funds on a discretionary basis to be paid to students];

(b) grants made under sections 73(a) and (c) and 74(1) of the Education (Scotland) Act 1980; [7 . . .]

(c) grants made under Article 30 of the Education and Libraries (Northern Ireland) Order 1993, or grants, loans or other payments made under Article 5 of the Further Education (Northern Ireland) Order 1997 in each case being grants, or grants, loans or other payments as the case may be, made for the purpose of assisting students in financial difficulties;] [7 [8 . . .]

(d) discretionary payments, known as "learner support funds", which are made available to students in further education by institutions out of funds provided by the [17 [18 Secretary of State under section 14 of the Education Act 2002] or [19 . . .] under sections 100 and 101 of [18 the Apprenticeships, Skills, Children and Learning Act 2009]];] [8 or

(e) Financial Contingency Funds made available by the [12 Welsh Ministers];]

[13 "contribution" means—

(a) any contribution in respect of the income of a student or any person which the Secretary of State, the Scottish Ministers or an education authority takes into account in ascertaining the amount of a student's grant or student loan; or

(b) any sums, which in determining the amount of a student's allowance or bursary in Scotland under the Education (Scotland) Act 1980, the Scottish Ministers or education authority takes into account being sums which the Scottish Ministers or education authority consider that it is reasonable for the following persons to contribute towards the holder's expenses—

(i) the holder of the allowance or bursary;

(ii) the holder's parents;

(iii) the holder's parent's spouse, civil partner or person ordinarily living with the holder's parent as if he or she were the spouse or civil partner of that parent; or

(iv) the holder's spouse or civil partner;]

"covenant income" means the income payable to a student under a deed of covenant by a person whose income is, or is likely to be, taken into account in assessing the student's grant or award;

"education authority" means a government department, [16 a local authority as defined in section 579 of the Education Act 1996], a local education authority as defined in section 123 of the Local Government (Scotland) Act 1973, an education and library board established under article 3 of the Education and Libraries (Northern Ireland) Order 1986, any body which is a research council for the purposes of the Science and Technology Act 1965 or any analogous government department, authority, board or body, of the Channel Islands, Isle of Man or any other country outside Great Britain;

[5 "grant" (except in the definition of "access funds") means any kind of educational grant or award and includes any scholarship, studentship, exhibition, allowance or bursary but does not include a payment from access funds [9 or any payment to which paragraph 12 of Schedule 7 or paragraph 52 of Schedule 8 applies];]

"grant income" means—

(a) any income by way of a grant;

(b) in the case of a student other than one to whom sub-paragraph (c) refers, any contribution that has been taken into account whether or not it has been paid;

(c) in the case of a student who satisfies the additional conditions for a disability premium in paragraph 14 of Schedule 1 (applicable amounts), any contribution which has been taken into account and which has been paid,

and any such contribution which is paid by way of a covenant shall be treated as part of the student's grant income;

[3 . . .]

[15 "last day of the course" means the date on which the last day of the final academic term falls in respect of the course in which the student is enrolled;]

[8 "periods of experience" means periods of work experience which form part of a sandwich course;]

"standard maintenance grant" means—

(a) except where paragraph (b) or (c) applies, in the case of a student attending [3 or undertaking] a course of study at the University of London or an establishment within the area comprising the City of London and the Metropolitan Police District, the amount specified for the time being in paragraph 2(2)(a) of Schedule 2 to the Education (Mandatory Awards) Regulations 1995 ("the 1995 regulations") for such a student;

(b) except where paragraph (c) applies, in the case of a student residing at his parents' home, the amount specified in paragraph 3(2) thereof;

[7 (c) in the case of a student receiving an allowance or bursary under the Education (Scotland) Act 1980, the amount of money specified as the "standard maintenance allowance" for the relevant year appropriate for the student set out in the Student Support in Scotland Guide issued by the Student Awards Agency for Scotland, or its nearest equivalent in the case of a bursary provided by a college of further education or a local education authority [11 . . .];]

(d) in any other case, the amount specified in paragraph 2(2) of the 1995 regulations other than in sub-paragraph (a) or (b) thereof;

[6 . . .]

[2 "student loan" means a loan towards a student's maintenance pursuant to any regulations made under section 22 of the Teaching and Higher Education Act 1998, section 73 of the Education (Scotland) Act 1980 or Article 3 of the Education (Student Support) (Northern Ireland) Order 1998 [7 and shall include, in Scotland, a young student's bursary paid under regulation 4(1)(c) of the Students' Allowances (Scotland) Regulations 1999];

[7 . . .]

AMENDMENTS

1. Social Security (Miscellaneous Amendments) Regulations 1998 (SI 1998/563) reg.4(1) and (2)(f) (April 6, 1998).

2. Social Security Amendment (Students) Regulations 1999 (SI 1999/1935) reg.2(2) (August 30, 1999, or if the student's period of study begins between August 1 and 29, 1999, the first day of the period).

3. Social Security Amendment (Students) Regulations 2000 (SI 2000/1981) reg.6(4) (July 31, 2000).

4. Social Security Amendment (Students and Income-related Benefits) Regulations 2000 (SI 2000/1922) reg.3(3) (August 28, 2000, or if the student's period of study begins between August 1 and 27, 2000, the first day of the period).

5. Social Security Amendment (Students and Income-related Benefits) Regulations 2000 (SI 2000/1922) reg.3(4) (August 28, 2000, or if the student's period of study begins between August 1 and 27, 2000, the first day of the period).

6. Social Security Amendment (Students and Income-related Benefits) Regulations 2000 (SI 2000/1922) reg.3(5) (August 28, 2000, or if the student's period of study begins between August 1 and 27, 2000, the first day of the period).

7. Social Security Amendment (Students and Income-related Benefits) Regulations 2001 (SI 2001/2319) reg.2(1)(a) and (2)(d) (August 1, 2001).

8. Social Security Amendment (Students and Income-related Benefits) Regulations 2002 (SI 2002/1589) reg.2(3)(b) (August 1, 2002).

9. Social Security (Students and Income-related Benefits) Amendment Regulations 2004 (SI 2004/1708) reg.6(2) (September 1, 2004, or if the student's period of study begins between August 1 and August 31, 2004, the first day of the period).

10. Civil Partnership (Pensions, Social Security and Child Support) (Consequential, etc. Provisions) Order 2005 (SI 2005/2877) art.2(3) and Sch.3 para.26(7) (December 5, 2005).

11. Social Security (Miscellaneous Amendments) (No.6) Regulations 2008 (SI 2008/2767) reg.4(8) (November 17, 2008).

12. Social Security (Miscellaneous Amendments) (No.7) Regulations 2008 (SI 2008/3157) reg.3(7) (January 5, 2009).

13. Social Security (Miscellaneous Amendments) Regulations 2009 (SI 2009/583) reg.4(9) (April 6, 2009).

14. Social Security (Miscellaneous Amendments) (No.4) Regulations 2009 (SI 2009/2655) reg.4(12) (October 26, 2009).

15. Social Security (Miscellaneous Amendments) (No.2) Regulations 2010 (SI 2010/641) reg.4(10) (April 6, 2010).

16. Local Education Authorities and Children's Services Authorities (Integration of Functions) (Local and Subordinate Legislation) Order 2010 (SI 2010/1172) art.5 and Sch.3 para.27(3) (May 5, 2010).

17. Apprenticeships, Skills, Children and Learning Act 2009 (Consequential Amendments to Subordinate Legislation) (England) Order 2010 (SI 2010/1941) art.5(6) (September 1, 2010).

18. Young People's Learning Agency Abolition (Consequential Amendments to

Subordinate Legislation) (England) Order 2012 (SI 2012/956) art.5(6) (May 1, 2012).

19. Deregulation Act 2015 (Consequential Amendments) Order 2015 (SI 2015/971) art.2 and Sch.3 para.4(5) (May 26, 2015).

DEFINITIONS

"full-time student"—see reg.1(3).
"sandwich course"—*ibid.*

GENERAL NOTE

3.376 See the notes to reg.61 of the Income Support Regulations.

Under JSA the definitions applying to full-time students are in a slightly different form. The main definitions for the purpose of defining full-time student status are in reg.1(3) (namely "course of advanced education", "course of study", "full-time course of advanced education", "full-time student" and "part-time student"); see also paras (3A)–(3E) of reg.1 which apply for the purposes of the definition of "full-time student". Since the amendments made to both the Income Support Regulations and the JSA Regulations on July 31, 2000 by SI 2000/1981 the differences from income support are less marked.

On the pre-July 31, 2000 form, see *CJSA 836/1996*, discussed in the notes to reg.61 of the Income Support Regulations under "*Difference between income support and JSA definition*". The Commissioner in that case took the view that the differences between the then form of the JSA and income support definitions were material. In his view the result was that for the purposes of JSA the question whether a person was attending or undertaking a full- or part-time course had to be determined by looking at the situation at the time in question (rather than at the commencement of the course, as was the case for income support). (Note that *CJSA 836/1996* was not followed in *C5/98(JSA)* (a Northern Ireland decision)). However, since the insertion of paras (3A)–(3C) into reg.1 (which provisions parallel reg.61(2)–(4) of the Income Support Regulations) with effect from July 31, 2000, the Commissioner's reasoning in *CJSA 836/1998* no longer applies. This is because the deeming of full-time student status for the entire length of a course (subject to earlier final abandonment or dismissal) is now contained in reg.1(3A)(b), rather than the definition of "course of study" in reg.1(3).

3.377 Note paras (3D) and (3E) inserted into reg.1 at the same time. (There is no equivalent to these provisions in the Income Support Regulations.) The effect of these provisions is to allow a full-time student who has taken time out of his course with the consent of his university or college because of illness or caring responsibilities (not defined), and who has now recovered or whose caring responsibilities have ended, to claim JSA until the earlier of the day before he rejoins his course or the date the relevant educational establishment has agreed that he can rejoin (subject to a maximum of one year). This does not apply if the person is eligible for a grant or student loan during this period.

In *CJSA 1920/1999* the claimant was a full-time student who had applied for a fixed term leave of absence from her course because she was pregnant. Her claim for JSA was refused because she was deemed to be a full-time student. The Commissioner decided (disagreeing with *CJSA 4890/1998*) that JSA was a single benefit and was within the scope of EC Directive 79/7 (on equal treatment in social security). He also concluded that discrimination against a pregnant student was direct discrimination against women in breach of art.4 of Directive 79/7, that there was such discrimination under the JSA Regulations and that no justification for that discrimination had been established.

The Commissioner in *CJSA 1920/1999* granted the Secretary of State leave to appeal to the Court of Appeal. But in the meantime on May 2, 2001 the Court of Appeal allowed the claimant's appeal against the decision in *CJSA 4890/1998* (*Hockenjos v Secretary of State,* [2001] EWCA Civ 624; [2001] 2 C.M.L.R. 51;

[2001] I.C.R. 966, also reported as *R(JSA) 1/05*). The Court of Appeal held that the Jobseekers Act 1995 had set up a unitary statutory scheme to provide against the risk of unemployment which was covered by art.3(1)(a) of the Directive. Thus both contribution-based and income-based JSA were within the scope of Directive 79/7.

However, the Court of Appeal allowed the Secretary of State's appeal against the decision in *CJSA 1920/1999* (*Secretary of State for Social Security v Walter* [2001] EWCA Civ 1913; reported as *R(JSA) 3/02*). The Court disagreed with the Commissioner's conclusion that the JSA Regulations directly discriminate against pregnant women, although the question of whether they may indirectly discriminate was left open. **3.378**

The argument that refusal of JSA to a pregnant student constituted indirect discrimination contrary to Directive 79/7 was raised in *CJSA/825/2004* but the Commissioner considered that evidence that women were disproportionately affected was needed.

In *CM v SSWP* [2009] UKUT 43 (AAC), reported as *R(IS) 7/09*, the Upper Tribunal Judge accepted statistical evidence was not necessary to establish indirect discrimination in this situation since only women could become pregnant and this was the only difference between female and male intercalating students that was being argued before him. The Secretary of State conceded that pregnancy was an "other status" for the purposes of art.14 ECHR. However, the discrimination against pregnant students who are intercalating was justified because the Government's policy was that students who intercalate for essentially transient reasons should not be supported by benefits. Students in the later stages of pregnancy were thus being treated in a similar way to those who were ill or had caring responsibilities and the inclusion of pregnant students within that policy was objectively justifiable. There was therefore no breach of art.14, read with art.1 Prot.1 of the ECHR. It had also been argued that the denial of income support meant that pregnant students were more likely to be forced to abandon their course so as to have a means of subsistence. However, the Upper Tribunal Judge held that this did not bring this case within art.2 Prot.1 (right to education) because the claimant had not in fact abandoned her course but had chosen to intercalate.

Note also *MS v SSWP* [2009] UKUT 9 (AAC) which holds that the denial of JSA to a student who is not attending college for a year while he resits exams externally is not contrary to art.14, read with art.1 Prot.1 of the ECHR.

Calculation of grant income

131.—(1) The amount of a student's grant income to be taken into account shall, subject to paragraphs [4(2) and (3)], be the whole of his grant income. **3.379**

(2) There shall be disregarded from the amount of a student's grant income any payment—

(a) intended to meet tuition fees or examination fees;

(b) intended to meet additional expenditure incurred by a disabled student in respect of his attendance on a course;

(c) intended to meet additional expenditure connected with term time residential study away from the student's educational establishment;

(d) on account of the student maintaining a home at a place other than that at which he resides while attending his course but only to the extent that his rent is not met by housing benefit;

(e) on account of any other person but only if that person is residing outside the United Kingdom and there is no applicable amount in respect of him;

(f) intended to meet the cost of books and equipment [1 . . .] [3 . . .];

(g) intended to meet travel expenses incurred as a result of his attendance on the course.

[[12](h) intended for the maintenance [[13]. . .] of a child dependent].

[[13](i) intended for the child care costs of a child dependant.]

[[18] (j) of higher education bursary for care leavers made under Part III of the Children Act 1989.]

[[3](3) Where a student does not have a student loan and is not treated as possessing such a loan, there shall be excluded from the student's grant income—

(a) the sum of [[16][[19]£303] per academic year] in respect of travel costs; and

[[6](b) the sum of [[17][[20]£390] per academic year] towards the costs of books and equipment,]

whether or not any such costs are incurred.]

[[7][[12] (3A) [[14][[15]. . .]]]]

(4) [[4] Subject to paragraph (5A), a student's grant income except for any amount intended for the maintenance of [[12] adult] dependants under Part III of Schedule 2 to the Education (Mandatory Awards) Regulations 1999 [[12] . . .]] shall be apportioned—

(a) subject to paragraph (6), in a case where it is attributable to the period of study, equally between the weeks [[10] in the period beginning with the benefit week, the first day of which coincides with, or immediately follows, the first day of the period of study and ending with the benefit week, the last day of which coincides with, or immediately precedes, the last day of the period of study];

(b) in any other case, equally between the weeks in the period [[10]beginning with the benefit week, the first day of which coincides with, or immediately follows, the first day of the period for which it is payable and ending with the benefit week, the last day of which coincides with, or immediately precedes, the last day of the period for which it is payable].

(5) [[8]Any grant paid under section 63(6) of the Health Services and Public Health Act 1968 (grants in respect of the provision of instruction to officers of hospital authorities) and] any amount intended for the maintenance of [[12] an adult dependant] under the provisions referred to in paragraph (4) shall be apportioned equally over a period of 52 weeks, or if there are 53 weeks (including part-weeks) in the year, 53.

[[4](5A) [[10] In a case where a student is in receipt of a student loan or where he could have acquired a student loan by taking reasonable steps but had not done so,] any amount intended for the maintenance of [[12]an adult dependant] under provisions other than those referred to in paragraphs (4) and (5), shall be apportioned over the same period as the student's loan is apportioned or [[10], as the case may be, would have been apportioned]].

(6) In the case of a student on a sandwich course, any periods of experience within the period of study shall be excluded and the student's grant income shall be apportioned equally between [[10]the weeks in the period beginning with the benefit week, the first day of which immediately follows the last day of the period of experience and ending with the benefit week, the last day of which coincides with, or immediately precedes, the last day of the period of study].

AMENDMENTS

1. Jobseeker's Allowance (Amendment) Regulations 1996 (SI 1996/1516) reg.20 and Sch. (October 7, 1996).

2. Social Security (Student Amounts Amendment) Regulations 1998 (SI 1998/1379) reg.2 (August 31, 1998, or if the student's period of study begins between August 1, and 30, 1998, the first day of the period).

3. Social Security Amendment (Students) Regulations 1999 (SI 1999/1935) reg.2(3) (August 30, 1999, or if the student's period of study begins between August 1 and 29, 1999, the first day of the period).

4. Social Security Amendment (Students and Income-related Benefits) Regulations 2000 (SI 2000/1922) reg.3(6) (August 28, 2000, or if the student's period of study begins between August 1 and 27, 2000, the first day of the period).

5. Social Security Amendment (Students and Income-related Benefits) Regulations 2001 (SI 2001/2319) reg.3(1) and (3)(d) (August 27, 2001, or if the student's period of study begins between August 1 and 26, 2001, the first day of the period).

6. Social Security Amendment (Students and Income-related Benefits) Regulations 2001 (SI 2001/2319) reg.3(2) and (3)(d) (August 27, 2001, or if the student's period of study begins between August 1 and 26, 2001, the first day of the period).

7. Social Security Amendment (Students and Income-related Benefits) Regulations 2001 (SI 2001/2319) reg.3(4) (August 27, 2001, or if the student's period of study begins between August 1 and 26, 2001, the first day of the period).

8. Social Security Amendment (Students and Income-related Benefits) Regulations 2001 (SI 2001/2319) reg.6 (August 27, 2001, or if the student's period of study begins between August 1 and 26, 2001, the first day of the period).

9. Social Security Amendment (Students and Income-related Benefits) Regulations 2002 (SI 2002/1589) reg.3 (August 26, 2002, or if the student's period of study begins between August 1 and 25, 2002, the first day of the period).

10. Social Security Amendment (Students and Income-related Benefits) Regulations 2002 (SI 2002/1589) reg.4 (August 26, 2002, or if the student's period of study begins between August 1 and 25, 2002, the first day of the period).

11. Social Security Amendment (Students and Income-related Benefits) (No.2) Regulations 2002 (SI 2002/2207) reg.2 (September 2, 2002).

12. Social Security (Working Tax Credit and Child Tax Credit) (Consequential Amendments) Regulations 2003 (SI 2003/455) reg.3 and Sch.2 para.16 (April 6, 2004, except in "transitional cases" and see further the note to regs 83 and 17 of the Income Support Regulations), as amended by Social Security (Working Tax Credit and Child Tax Credit) (Consequential Amendments) (No.3) Regulations 2003 (SI 2003/1731), reg.6(5)(a) (August 8, 2003).

13. Social Security (Students and Income-related Benefits) Amendment Regulations 2004 (SI 2004/1708) reg.3(4) (September 1, 2004, or if the student's period of study begins between August 1 and August 31, 2004, the first day of the period).

14. Social Security (Students and Income-related Benefits) Amendment Regulations 2005 (SI 2005/1807) reg.2(7) (September 1, 2005, or if the student's period of study begins between August 1 and August 31, 2005, the first day of the period).

15. Social Security (Students and Income-related Benefits) Amendment Regulations 2006 (SI 2006/1752) regs 5(3) and 6 (September 1, 2006, or if the student's period of study begins between August 1 and August 31, 2006, the first day of the period).

16. Social Security (Students and Income-related Benefits) Amendment Regulations 2007 (SI 2007/1632) reg.3(2)(a) (September 1, 2007, or if the student's period of study begins between August 1 and 31, 2007, the first day of the period).

17. Social Security (Students and Income-related Benefits) Amendment

Regulations 2007 (SI 2007/1632) reg.3(2)(b) (September 1, 2007, or if the student's period of study begins between August 1 and 31, 2007, the first day of the period).

18. Social Security (Miscellaneous Amendments) Regulations 2009 (SI 2009/583) reg.4(10) (April 6, 2009).

19. Social Security (Students and Miscellaneous Amendments) Regulations 2009 (SI 2009/1575) reg.2(2) and (4)(b) (September 1, 2009, or if the student's period of study begins between August 1 and 31, 2009, the first day of the period).

20. Social Security (Students and Miscellaneous Amendments) Regulations 2009 (SI 2009/1575) reg.2(3) and (4)(b) (September 1, 2009, or if the student's period of study begins between August 1 and 31, 2009, the first day of the period).

DEFINITIONS

"grant"—see reg.130.
"grant income"—*ibid.*
"period of study"—see reg.1(3).
"periods of experience"—see reg.130.
"sandwich course"—see reg.1(3).
"student loan"—see reg.130.

GENERAL NOTE

3.380 See the notes to reg.62 of the Income Support Regulations.

The disregard in para.(2)(h) is a general disregard of any payment intended for the maintenance of a child and that in para.(2)(i) is a general disregard of any payment intended for child care costs. They replaced the various disregards for students with child care responsibilities previously contained in para.(3A). Paragraph (3A) had gone through a number of forms and parts of the penultimate form of it remained in force in "transitional cases" (i.e. those cases in which the claimant is still receiving amounts for his children in his income-based JSA—see the note to reg.83 and to reg.17 of the Income Support Regulations) but the one remaining sub-para. that was still in force for transitional cases (sub-para.(e)) was omitted on September 1, 2006 (or if the student's period of study begins between August 1 and 31, 2006, on the first day of the period) by reg.5(3) of the Social Security (Students and Income-related Benefits) Amendment Regulations 2006 (SI 2006/1752) (see further the notes to this regulation in the 2006 edition of this volume and in the 2006/2007 Supplement to this series).

Calculation of covenant income where a contribution is assessed

3.381 **132.**—(1) Where a student is in receipt of income by way of a grant during a period of study and a contribution has been assessed, the amount of his covenant income to be taken into account for that period and any summer vacation immediately following shall be the whole amount of his covenant income less, subject to paragraph (3), the amount of the contribution.

(2) The weekly amount of the student's covenant income shall be determined—

(a) by dividing the amount of income which falls to be taken into account under paragraph (1) by 52 or, if there are 53 benefit weeks (including part-weeks) in the year, 53; and

(b) by disregarding £5 from the resulting amount.

(3) For the purposes of paragraph (1), the contribution shall be treated as increased by the amount, if any, by which the amount excluded under regulation 131(2)(g) falls short of the amount for the time being specified in paragraph 7(4)(i) of Schedule 2 to the Education (Mandatory Awards) Regulations 1995 (travel expenditure).

DEFINITIONS

"benefit week"—see reg.1(3).
"contribution"—see reg.130.
"covenant income"—*ibid.*
"grant"—*ibid.*
"period of study"—see reg.1(3).

GENERAL NOTE

See the note to reg.63 of the Income Support Regulations. 3.382

Covenant income where no grant income or no contribution is assessed

133.—(1) Where a student is not in receipt of income by way of a grant the amount of his covenant income shall be calculated as follows— 3.383

(a) any sums intended for any expenditure specified in regulation 131(2)(a) to (e), necessary as a result of his attendance on the course, shall be disregarded;
(b) any covenant income, up to the amount of the standard maintenance grant, which is not so disregarded, shall be apportioned equally between the weeks of the period of study and there shall be disregarded from the covenant income to be so apportioned the amount which would have been disregarded under regulation 131(2)(f) and (g) and (3) had the student been in receipt of the standard maintenance grant;
(c) the balance, if any, shall be divided by 52 or, if there are 53 benefit weeks (including part-weeks) in the year, 53 and treated as weekly income of which £5 shall be disregarded.

(2) Where a student is in receipt of income by way of a grant and no contribution has been assessed, the amount of his covenant income shall be calculated in accordance with paragraph (1), except that—

(a) the value of the standard maintenance grant shall be abated by the amount of his grant income less an amount equal to the amount of any sums disregarded under regulation 131(2)(a) to (e); and
(b) the amount to be disregarded under paragraph (1)(b) shall be abated by an amount equal to the amount of any sums disregarded under regulation 131(2)(f) and (g) and (3).

DEFINITIONS

"benefit week"—see reg.1(3).
"contribution"—see reg.130.
"covenant income"—*ibid.*
"grant income"—*ibid.*

GENERAL NOTE

See the note to reg.64 of the Income Support Regulations. 3.384

Relationship with amounts to be disregarded under Schedule 7

134.—No part of a student's covenant income or grant income shall be disregarded under paragraph 15 of Schedule 7 (charitable and voluntary payments) [1. . .]. 3.385

AMENDMENT

1. Social Security (Miscellaneous Amendments) (No.4) Regulations 2006 (SI 2006/2378) reg.13(7) (October 2, 2006).

DEFINITIONS

"covenant income"—see reg.130.
"grant income"—*ibid.*

GENERAL NOTE

3.386 See reg.65 of the Income Support Regulations.

Other amounts to be disregarded

3.387 **135.**—(1) For the purposes of ascertaining income other than grant income, covenant income, and loans treated as income in accordance with regulation 136, any amounts intended for any expenditure specified in regulation 131(2) (calculation of grant income) necessary as a result of the student's attendance on the course shall be disregarded but only if, and to the extent that, the necessary expenditure exceeds or is likely to exceed the amount of the sums disregarded under regulation 131(2) and (3), 132(3) [1, 133(1)(a) or (b) and 136(5) (calculation of grant income, covenant income and treatment of student loans)] on like expenditure.

(2) Where a claim is made in respect of any period in the normal summer vacation and any income is payable under a deed of covenant which commences or takes effect after the first day of that vacation, that income shall be disregarded.

AMENDMENT

1. Social Security Amendment (Students) Regulations 1999 (SI 1999/1935) reg.2(4) (August 30, 1999, or if the student's period of study begins between August 1 and 29, 1999, the first day of the period).

DEFINITIONS

"covenant income"—see reg.130.
"grant income"—*ibid.*
"student loan"—*ibid.*

GENERAL NOTE

3.388 See the note to reg.66 of the Income Support Regulations.

Treatment of student loans

3.389 **136.**—[2(1) A student loan shall be treated as income [10 . . .].

(1A) [10 . . .]

(2) In calculating the weekly amount of the loan to be taken into account as income—

[7(a) in respect of a course that is of a single academic year's duration or less, a loan which is payable in respect of that period shall be apportioned equally between the weeks in the period beginning with—

(i) except in a case where (ii) below applies, the benefit week, the first day of which coincides with, or immediately follows, the first day of the single academic year;

(ii) where the student is required to start attending the course in August or where the course is of less than an academic year's duration, the benefit week, the first day of which coincides with, or immediately follows, the first day of the course,

and ending with the benefit week, the last day of which coincides with, or immediately precedes, the last day of the course;]

[5(aa) in respect of an academic year of a course which starts other than on 1st September, a loan which is payable in respect of that academic year shall be apportioned equally between the weeks in the period beginning with the benefit week [7, the first day of which coincides with, or immediately follows, the first day of that academic year and ending with the benefit week, the last day of which coincides with, or immediately precedes,] the last day of that academic year but excluding any benefit weeks falling entirely within the quarter during which, in the opinion of the Secretary of State, the longest of any vacation is taken and for the purposes of this sub-paragraph, "quarter" shall have the same meaning as for the purposes of the Education (Student Support) Regulations 2001;]

(b) in respect of the final academic year of a course (not being a course of a single year's duration), a loan which is payable in respect of that final academic year shall be apportioned equally between the weeks in the period beginning with [7. . .]—

[7(i) except in a case where (ii) below applies, the benefit week, the first day of which coincides with, or immediately follows, the first day of that academic year;

(ii) where the final academic year starts on 1st September, the benefit week, the first day of which coincides with, or immediately follows, the earlier of 1st September or the first day of the autumn term;]

and ending with [7the benefit week, the last day of which coincides with, or immediately precedes,] the last day of the course;

(c) in any other case, the loan shall be apportioned equally between the weeks in the period beginning with the earlier of—

(i) the first day of the first benefit week in September; or

[7(ii) the benefit week, the first day of which coincides with, or immediately follows, the first day of the autumn term,]

and ending with [7the benefit week, the last day of which coincides with, or immediately precedes, the last day of June],

and, in all cases, from the weekly amount so apportioned there shall be disregarded £10.]

[1(3) A student shall be treated as possessing a student loan in respect of an academic year where—

(a) a student loan has been made to him in respect of that year; or

(b) he could acquire such a loan in respect of that year by taking reasonable steps to do so.

(4) Where a student is treated as possessing a student loan under paragraph (3), the amount of the student loan to be taken into account as income shall be, subject to paragraph (5)—

(a) in the case of a student to whom a student loan is made in respect of an academic year, a sum equal to the maximum student loan he is able to acquire in respect of that year by taking reasonable steps to do so and either—

(i) in the case of a student other than one to whom head (ii) refers, any contribution whether or not it has been paid to him; or

(ii) in the case of a student who satisfies the additional conditions for a disability premium specified in paragraph 14 of Schedule 1 (applicable amounts), any contribution which has actually been paid to him;

(b) in the case of a student to whom a student loan is not made in respect of an academic year, the maximum student loan that would be made to the student if—

(i) he took all reasonable steps to obtain the maximum student loan he is able to acquire in respect of that year; and

(ii) no deduction in that loan was made by virtue of the application of a means test.

(5) There shall be deducted from the amount of income taken into account under paragraph (4)—

(a) the sum of [[8][[11] £303] per academic year] in respect of travel costs; and

[[4](b) the sum of [[9][[12] £390] per academic year] towards the costs of books and equipment,]

whether or not any such costs are incurred.]

AMENDMENTS

1. Social Security Amendment (Students) Regulations 1999 (SI 1999/1935) reg.2(5) (August 30, 1999, or if the student's period of study begins between August 1 and 29, 1999, the first day of the period).

2. Social Security Amendment (Students and Income-related Benefits) Regulations 2000 (SI 2000/1922) reg.3(7) (August 28, 2000, or if the student's period of study begins between August 1 and 27, 2000, the first day of the period).

3. Social Security Amendment (Students and Income-related Benefits) Regulations 2001 (SI 2001/2319) reg.3(1) and (3)(d) (August 27, 2001, or if the student's period of study begins between August 1 and 26, 2001, the first day of the period).

4. Social Security Amendment (Students and Income-related Benefits) Regulations 2001 (SI 2001/2319) reg.3(2) and (3)(d) (August 27, 2001, or if the student's period of study begins between August 1 and 26, 2001, the first day of the period).

5. Social Security Amendment (Students and Income-related Benefits) Regulations 2001 (SI 2001/2319) reg.4 (August 27, 2001, or if the student's period of study begins between August 1 and 26, 2001, the first day of the period).

6. Social Security Amendment (Students and Income-related Benefits) Regulations 2002 (SI 2002/1589) reg.3 (August 26, 2002, or if the student's period of study begins between August 1 and 25, 2002, the first day of the period).

7. Social Security Amendment (Students and Income-related Benefits) Regulations 2002 (SI 2002/1589) reg.5 (August 26, 2002, or if the student's period of study begins between August 1 and 25, 2002, the first day of the period).

8. Social Security (Students and Income-related Benefits) Amendment Regulations 2007 (SI 2007/1632) reg.3(3)(a) (September 1, 2007, or if the student's period of study begins between August 1 and 31, 2007, the first day of the period).

9. Social Security (Students and Income-related Benefits) Amendment Regulations 2007 (SI 2007/1632) reg.3(3)(b) (September 1, 2007, or if the stu-

dent's period of study begins between August 1 and 31, 2007, the first day of the period).

10. Social Security (Miscellaneous Amendments) (No.6) Regulations 2008 (SI 2008/2767) reg.4(9) (November 17, 2008).

11. Social Security (Students and Miscellaneous Amendments) Regulations 2009 (SI 2009/1575) reg.2(2) and (4)(b) (September 1, 2009, or if the student's period of study begins between August 1 and 31, 2009, the first day of the period).

12. Social Security (Students and Miscellaneous Amendments) Regulations 2009 (SI 2009/1575) reg.2(3) and (4)(b) (September 1, 2009, or if the student's period of study begins between August 1 and 31, 2009, the first day of the period).

DEFINITIONS

"academic year"—see reg.130.
"student loan"—*ibid.*

GENERAL NOTE

See the note to reg.66A of the Income Support Regulations. **3.390**

[1 Treatment of payments from access funds

136A.—(1) This regulation applies to payments from access funds that are not payments to which regulation 138(2) or (3) (income treated as capital) applies. **3.391**

(2) A payment from access funds, other than a payment to which paragraph (3) of this regulation applies, shall be disregarded as income.

(3) Subject to paragraph (4) of this regulation and paragraph 38 of Schedule 7, any payments from access funds which are intended and used for food, ordinary clothing or footwear [4. . .], household fuel, rent for which housing benefit is payable [2 or any housing costs] to the extent that they are met under regulation 83(f) or 84(1)(g) (housing costs) [2. . .], of a single claimant or, as the case may be, of [3 his partner], and any payments from access funds which are used for any council tax or water charges for which that claimant or [3partner is liable] shall be disregarded as income to the extent of £20 per week.

[4 (3A) In paragraph (3) "ordinary clothing or footwear" means clothing or footwear for normal daily use, but it does not include—

(a) school uniforms, or
(b) clothing or footwear used solely for sporting activities.]

(4) Where a payment from access funds is made—

(a) on or after 1st September or the first day of the course, whichever first occurs, but before receipt of any student loan in respect of that year and that payment is intended for the purpose of bridging the period until receipt of the student loan; or
(b) before the first day of the course to a person in anticipation of that person becoming a student,

that payment shall be disregarded as income.]

AMENDMENTS

1. Social Security Amendment (Students and Income-related Benefits) Regulations 2000 (SI 2000/1922) reg.3(8) (August 28, 2000, or if the student's period of study begins between August 1 and 27, 2000, the first day of the period).

2. Social Security Amendment (Residential Care and Nursing Homes) Regulations 2001 (SI 2001/3767) reg.2(2) and Pt II of Sch. para.13 (April 8, 2002).

3. Social Security (Working Tax Credit and Child Tax Credit) (Consequential Amendments) Regulations 2003 (SI 2003/455) reg.3 and Sch.2 para.17 (April 6, 2004, except in "transitional cases" and see further the note to reg.83 and reg.17 of the Income Support Regulations).

4. Social Security (Miscellaneous Amendments) Regulations 2007 (SI 2007/719) reg.3(6) (April 2, 2007).

DEFINITIONS

"access funds"—see reg.1(3).
"payment"—see reg.1(3).
"single claimant"—*ibid.*
"student loan"—see reg.130.

GENERAL NOTE

3.392 See the note to reg.66B of the Income Support Regulations.

[1 Treatment of fee loans

3.393 **136B.**—A loan for fees, known as a fee loan or a fee contribution loan, made pursuant to regulations made under article 3 of the Education (Student Support) (Northern Ireland) Order 1998, section 22 of the Teaching and Higher Education Act 1998 or section 73(f) of the Education (Scotland) Act 1980, shall be disregarded as income.]

AMENDMENT

1. Social Security (Students and Income-related Benefits) Amendment Regulations 2006 (SI 2006/1752) reg.5(4) (September 1, 2006, or if the student's period of study begins between August 1 and August 31, 2006, the first day of the period).

GENERAL NOTE

3.394 See the note to reg.66C of the Income Support Regulations.

Disregard of contribution

3.395 **137.**—Where the claimant or his partner is a student and, for the purposes of assessing a contribution to the student's grant [1 or student loan], the other partner's income has been taken into account, an amount equal to that contribution shall be disregarded for the purposes of assessing that other partner's income.

AMENDMENT

1. Social Security Amendment (Students) Regulations 1999 (SI 1999/1935) reg.2(6) (August 30, 1999, or if the student's period of study begins between August 1 and 29, 1999, the first day of the period).

DEFINITIONS

"claimant"—see Jobseekers Act s.35(1) and reg.88(1).
"contribution"—see reg.130.
"grant"—*ibid.*
"partner"—see reg.1(3).
"student loan"—see reg.130.

GENERAL NOTE

See reg.67 of the Income Support Regulations. 3.396

[1Further disregard of student's income

137A.—Where any part of a student's income has already been taken into account for the purposes of assessing his entitlement to a grant [2or student loan], the amount taken into account shall be disregarded in assessing that student's income.] 3.397

AMENDMENTS

1. Social Security (Miscellaneous Amendments) Regulations 1998 (SI 1998/563) reg.4(3) and (4)(f) (April 6, 1998).
2. Social Security Amendment (Students) Regulations 1999 (SI 1999/1935) reg.2(7) (August 30, 1999, or if the student's period of study begins between August 1 and 29, 1999, the first day of the period).

DEFINITIONS

"grant"—see reg.130.
"student loan"—*ibid.*

Income treated as capital

138.—[1(1)] Any amount by way of a refund of tax deducted from a student's income shall be treated as capital. 3.398

[1(2) An amount paid from access funds as a single lump sum shall be treated as capital.

(3) An amount paid from access funds as a single lump sum which is intended and used for an item other than food, ordinary clothing or footwear [4. . .], household fuel, rent for which housing benefit is payable [2or any housing costs] to the extent that they are met under regulation 83(f) or 84(1)(g) (housing costs) [2. . .], of a single claimant or, as the case may be, of [3his partner], or which is used for an item other than any council tax or water charges for which that claimant or [3partner is liable] shall be disregarded as capital but only for a period of 52 weeks from the date of the payment.]

[4 (4) In paragraph (3) "ordinary clothing or footwear" means clothing or footwear for normal daily use, but it does not include-

(a) school uniforms, or
(b) clothing or footwear used solely for sporting activities.]

AMENDMENTS

1. Social Security Amendment (Students and Income-related Benefits) Regulations 2000 (SI 2000/1922) reg.3(9) (August 28, 2000, or if the student's period of study begins between August 1 and 27, 2000, the first day of the period).

2. Social Security Amendment (Residential Care and Nursing Homes) Regulations 2001 (SI 2001/3767) reg.2(2) and Pt II of Sch. para.14 (April 8, 2002).

3. Social Security (Working Tax Credit and Child Tax Credit) (Consequential Amendments) Regulations 2003 (SI 2003/455) reg.3 and Sch.2 para.17 (April 6, 2004, except in "transitional cases" and see further the note to reg.83 and to reg.17 of the Income Support Regulations).

4. Social Security (Miscellaneous Amendments) Regulations 2007 (SI 2007/719) reg.3(7) (April 2, 2007).

DEFINITIONS

"access funds"—see reg.1(3).
"payment"—see reg.1(3).
"single claimant"—*ibid.*

GENERAL NOTE

3.399 On paras (2) and (3), see the note to reg.66B of the Income Support Regulations.

Disregard of changes occurring during summer vacation

3.400 **139.**—In calculating a student's income [1the Secretary of State] shall disregard any change in the standard maintenance grant occurring in the recognised summer vacation appropriate to the student's course, if that vacation does not form part of his period of study, from the date on which the change occurred up to the end of that vacation.

AMENDMENT

1. Social Security Act 1998 (Commencement No.11, and Savings and Consequential and Transitional Provisions) Order 1999 (SI 1999/2860 (C.75)) art.3(12) and Sch.12 para.2 (October 18, 1999).

DEFINITIONS

"period of study"—see reg.1(3).
"standard maintenance grant"—see reg.130.

GENERAL NOTE

3.401 See reg.69 of the Income Support Regulations.

PART IX

HARDSHIP

GENERAL NOTE

3.402 This Part deals with the circumstances in which a hardship payment of JSA will be made. A hardship payment can only be paid if a sanction has been imposed; or the claimant is waiting for a decision at the beginning of his claim as to whether he satisfies the labour market conditions in s.1(2)(a)–(c) of the Jobseekers Act; or payment of JSA has been suspended because a question has arisen as to whether the claimant satisfies the labour market conditions; or, in the case of a claimant who is in a "vulnerable group" (see reg.140(1)) only, a decision-maker has decided that he does not satisfy the labour market conditions. Hardship payments are not available in any other circumstances.

See reg.140 for the meaning of "hardship". Unless the claimant falls into a vulnerable group (see reg.140(1)), no hardship payment will be made for the first two weeks, however severe the person's hardship. If a hardship payment is made, it will be subject to a 40 per cent or 20 per cent reduction of the appropriate personal allowance for a single claimant (see reg.145). While hardship payments are being paid the claimant must continue to satisfy the other conditions of entitlement for income-based JSA and in addition will be required to sign a declaration of hardship (see reg.143).

See also the notes to s.20(4)–(6) of the Jobseekers Act on hardship payments where a sanction has been imposed.

Meaning of "person in hardship"

140.—(1) In this Part of these Regulations, a "person in hardship" means for the purposes of regulation 141 a claimant, other than a claimant to whom paragraph (3) or (4) applies [7or a member of a joint-claim couple and regulation 3E does not apply], who— 3.403

(a) is a single woman—
   (i) who is pregnant; and
   (ii) in respect of whom [5the Secretary of State] is satisfied that, unless a jobseeker's allowance is paid to her, she will suffer hardship; or
(b) is a single person who is responsible for a [14 child or young person], and [5the Secretary of State] is satisfied that, unless a jobseeker's allowance is paid to the single person, the [14 child or young person] will suffer hardship; or
(c) is a member of [12 a couple], where—
   [12 (i) at least one member of the couple is a woman who is pregnant; and]
   (ii) [5the Secretary of State] is satisfied that, unless a jobseeker's allowance is paid, the woman will suffer hardship; or
(d) is a member of a polygamous marriage and—
   (i) one member of the marriage is pregnant; and
   (ii) [5the Secretary of State] is satisfied that, unless a jobseeker's allowance is paid, that woman will suffer hardship; or
(e) is a member of [12 a couple] or of a polygamous marriage where—
   (i) one or both members of the couple, or one or more members of the polygamous marriage, are responsible for a child or young person; and
   (ii) [5the Secretary of State] is satisfied that, unless a jobseeker's allowance is paid, the child or young person will suffer hardship; or
(f) has an award of a jobseeker's allowance which includes or would, if a claim for a jobseeker's allowance from him were to succeed have included, in his applicable amount a disability premium and—
   (i) where the person has an award, a jobseeker's allowance is not payable [20 . . .] because it is suspended [20 or the award is

reduced in accordance with section 19 or 19A or regulation 69B]; and

(ii) [5the Secretary of State] is satisfied that, unless a jobseeker's allowance is paid, the person who would satisfy the conditions of entitlement to that premium would suffer hardship; or

(g) suffers, or whose partner suffers from a chronic medical condition which results in functional capacity being limited or restricted by physical impairment and [5 the Secretary of State] is satisfied that—

(i) the suffering has already lasted, or is likely to last, for not less than 26 weeks; and

(ii) unless a jobseeker's allowance is paid to the claimant the probability is that the health of the person suffering would, within 2 weeks of [5the Secretary of State] making his decision, decline further than that of a normally healthy adult and that person would suffer hardship; or

(h) does, or whose partner does, or in the case of a claimant who is married to more than one person under a law which permits polygamy, at least one of those persons do, devote a considerable portion of each week to caring for another person who—

(i) is in receipt of an attendance allowance [22 , the care component of disability living allowance at one of the two higher rates prescribed under section 72(4) of the Benefits Act or the daily living component of personal independence payment at the standard or enhanced rate in accordance with section 78 of the 2012 Act] [23 or armed forces independence payment]; or

(ii) has claimed either attendance allowance [22 , disability living allowance [23 armed forces independence payment] or personal independence payment] but only for so long as the claim has not been determined, or for, 26 weeks from the date of claiming, [1 whichever is the earlier; or

(iii) has claimed either attendance allowance or disability living allowance and has an award of either attendance allowance or the care component of disability living allowance at one of the two higher rates prescribed under section 72(4) of the Benefits Act for a period commencing after the date on which that claim was made,] [22 or

(iv) has claimed personal independence payment and has an award of the daily living component of personal independence payment at the standard or enhanced rate in accordance with section 78 of the 2012 Act for a period commencing after the date on which that claim was made,] [23 ; or

(v) has claimed and has an award of armed forces independence payment for a period commencing after the date on which that claim was made,]

and [5the Secretary of State] is satisfied, after taking account of the factors set out in [2paragraph (5)] in so far as they are appropriate to the particular circumstances of the case, that the person providing the care will not be able to continue doing so unless a jobseeker's allowance is paid to the claimant; or

(i) is a person or is the partner of a person to whom section 16 applies by virtue of a direction issued by the Secretary of State, except where the person to whom the direction applies does not satisfy the requirements of section 1(2)(a) to (c); or

(j) is a person—

(i) to whom section 3(1)(f)(iii) (persons under the age of 18) applies, or is the partner of such a person; and

(ii) in respect of whom [5the Secretary of State] is satisfied that the person will, unless a jobseeker's allowance is paid, suffer hardship.

[6(k) is a person—

(i) who, pursuant to the Children Act 1989, was being looked after by a local authority;

(ii) with whom the local authority had a duty, pursuant to that Act, to take reasonable steps to keep in touch; or

(iii) who, pursuant to that Act, qualified for advice and assistance from a local authority,

but in respect of whom (i), (ii) or, as the case may be, (iii) above had not applied for a period of three years or less as at the date on which he complies with the requirements of regulation 143; and

(iv) as at the date on which he complies with the requirements of regulation 143, is under the age of 21].

(2) Except in a case to which paragraph (3) [2 ...] [4 ...] [15 ...] [19 [20 . . .]] applies [8 or where the person in hardship is a member of a joint-claim couple and regulation 3E does not apply] a "person in hardship" means for the purposes of regulation 142, a claimant where [5the Secretary of State] is satisfied that he or his partner will suffer hardship unless a jobseeker's allowance is paid to him.

(3) In paragraphs (1) and (2) a "person in hardship" does not include a claimant who is entitled, or whose partner is entitled, to income support [13 or an income-related employment and support allowance] or [3 a claimant or a partner of a claimant] who falls within a category of persons prescribed for the purpose of section 124(1)(e) of the Benefits Act.

(4) Paragraph (1)(h) shall not apply in a case where the person being cared for resides in a [11 care home, an Abbeyfield Home or an independent hospital].

[4(4A) [20 . . .]]

[15(4B) [20 . . .]]

[19 (4C) [20 . . .]]

(5) Factors which, for the purposes of paragraphs (1) and (2), [5the Secretary of State] is to take into account in determining whether a person will suffer hardship are—

(a) the presence in the claimant's family of a person who satisfies the requirements for a disability premium specified in paragraphs 13 and 14 of Schedule 1 [1or [10an element of child tax credit in respect of a child or young person who is disabled or severely disabled within the meaning of regulation 8 of the Child Tax Credit Regulations 2002]];

(b) the resources which, without a jobseeker's allowance, are likely to be available to the claimant's family, the amount by which these resources fall short of the amount applicable in his case in accordance with regulation 145 (applicable amount in hardship cases), the amount of any resources which may be available to members of the claimant's family from any person in the claimant's household who is not a member of his family, and the length of time for which those factors are likely to persist;

(c) whether there is a substantial risk that essential items, including food, clothing, heating and accommodation, will cease to be available to the claimant or to a member of the claimant's family, or will be available at considerably reduced levels and the length of time those factors are likely to persist.

[21 (6) In paragraph (5)(b), "resources" does not include any sum, where applicable, specified in paragraph 6B(1) and (2) of Schedule 7 (sums to be disregarded in the calculation of income other than earnings—child tax credit and child benefit).]

AMENDMENTS

1. Jobseeker's Allowance (Amendment) Regulations 1996 (SI 1996/1516) reg.13 (October 7, 1996).

2. Jobseeker's Allowance (Amendment) Regulations 1996 (SI 1996/1516) reg.20 and Sch. (October 7, 1996).

3. Jobseeker's Allowance and Income Support (General) (Amendment) Regulations 1996 (SI 1996/1517) reg.25 (October 7, 1996).

4. Social Security Amendment (New Deal) Regulations 1997 (SI 1997/2863) reg.11 (January 5, 1998).

5. Social Security Act 1998 (Commencement No.11, and Savings and Consequential and Transitional Provisions) Order 1999 (SI 1999/2860 (C.75)) Arts 3(1) and (12) and Sch.12 para.2 (October 18 1999).

6. Jobseeker's Allowance (Amendment) Regulations 2000 (SI 2000/239) reg.2(4) (March 6, 2000).

7. Jobseeker's Allowance (Joint Claims) Regulations 2000 (SI 2000/1978) reg.2(5) and Sch.2 para.45(a) (March 19, 2001).

8. Jobseeker's Allowance (Joint Claims) Regulations 2000 (SI 2000/1978) reg.2(5) and Sch.2 para.45(b) (March 19, 2001).

9. Social Security Amendment (New Deal) Regulations 2001 (SI 2001/1029) reg.9(1) (April 9, 2001).

10. Social Security (Working Tax Credit and Child Tax Credit) (Consequential Amendments) Regulations 2003 (SI 2003/455) reg.3 and Sch.2 para.18 (April 6, 2004, except in "transitional cases" and see further the note to reg.83 and to reg.17 of the Income Support Regulations).

11. Social Security (Care Homes and Independent Hospitals) Regulations 2005 (SI 2005/2687) reg.3 and Sch.2 para.7 (October 24, 2005).

12. Civil Partnership (Pensions, Social Security and Child Support) (Consequential, etc. Provisions) Order 2005 (SI 2005/2877) art.2(3) and Sch.3 para.26(8) (December 5, 2005).

13. Employment and Support Allowance (Consequential Provisions) (No.2) Regulations 2008 (SI 2008/1554) reg.3(1) and (17) (October 27, 2008).

14. Social Security (Lone Parents and Miscellaneous Amendments) Regulations 2008 (SI 2008/3051) reg.11(14) (November 24, 2008).

15. Social Security (Flexible New Deal) Regulations 2009 (SI 2009/480) reg.2(8) (April 6, 2009).

16. Social Security (Flexible New Deal) Regulations 2009 (SI 2009/480) reg.2(8) (b) (October 5, 2009).

17. Jobseeker's Allowance (Sanctions for Failure to Attend) Regulations 2010 (SI 2010/509) reg.2(14) (April 6, 2010).

18. Jobseeker's Allowance (Mandatory Work Activity Scheme) Regulations 2011 (SI 2011/688) reg.16(f) (April 25, 2011).

19. Jobseeker's Allowance (Employment, Skills and Enterprise Scheme) Regulations 2011 (SI 2011/917) reg.9 (May 20, 2011).

20. Jobseeker's Allowance (Sanctions) (Amendment) Regulations 2012 (SI 2012/2568) reg.3 (October 22, 2012).

21. Social Security (Miscellaneous Amendments) Regulations 2013 (SI 2013/443) reg.4(1) and (10) (April 2, 2013).

22. Personal Independence Payment (Supplementary Provisions and Consequential Amendments) Regulations 2013 (SI 2013/388) reg.8 and Sch. para.16(1) and (4) (April 8, 2013).

23. Armed Forces and Reserve Forces Compensation Scheme (Consequential Provisions: Subordinate Legislation) Order 2013 (SI 2013/591) art.7 and Sch. para.10(1) and (4) (April 8, 2013).

DEFINITIONS

"Abbeyfield Home"—see reg.1(3).
"attendance allowance"—*ibid.*
"care home"—*ibid.*
"child"—see Jobseekers Act s.35(1).
"claimant"—*ibid.*
"couple"—see reg.1(3).
"independent hospital"—*ibid.*
"partner"—*ibid.*
"polygamous marriage"—*ibid.*
"week"—*ibid.*
"young person"—see reg.76.

GENERAL NOTE

Paragraph (1)

This lists those claimants who are eligible for hardship payments without any waiting period (the "vulnerable groups"). Note the exclusion in para.(3) of claimants who (or whose partners) are in a category who can claim income support (claimants who, or whose partners, are entitled to income support would in any event be excluded from JSA under s.3(1)(b) or (c) of the Jobseekers Act). 3.404

The categories are:

(i) a single claimant who is pregnant whom the decision-maker accepts will suffer hardship if no payment is made (sub-para.(a));
(ii) a single claimant who is responsible for (see reg.77) a child or a young person (see regs 1(3) and 76(3)) where the decision maker accepts that the child or young person will suffer hardship if no payment is made (sub-para.(b)). Note however, that where claimant is responsible for a child under the age of five, the claimant will be entitled to IS and therefore ineligible for a hardship payment under para.(3);
(iii) a member of a couple, or of a polygamous marriage, where the/a woman is pregnant and the decision-maker accepts that the woman will suffer hardship if no payment is made (sub-paras (c) and (d));
(iv) a member of a couple, or of a polygamous marriage, who is/are responsible (see reg.77) for a child or young person (see reg.76) and the decision- maker accepts that the child or young person will suffer hardship if no payment is made (sub-para.(e));
(v) people eligible for a disability premium in their income-based JSA and the decision-maker accepts that the person who qualifies for the disability premium would suffer hardship if no payment is made (sub-para.(f)). In contrast to the other sub-paragraphs, sub-para.(f) refers to a person who "has an award of " JSA which includes a disability premium (or whose claim, if successful, would include a disability premium). The intention would seem to be that this category does not apply if the reason for the non-payment of JSA is that the claimant has failed to satisfy the labour market

conditions (in such a case the person would not have an award of JSA and see head (i)). But if such a person having failed to satisfy the labour market conditions then makes a further claim for JSA, arguably he falls within sub-para.(f) because he has made a claim for JSA which were it to succeed would include a disability premium;

(vi) a claimant who, or whose partner, has a chronic medical condition resulting in his functional capacity being restricted by physical impairment which has lasted, or is likely to last, for at least 26 weeks and the decision-maker accepts that in the next two weeks the person's health is likely to "decline further than that of a normally healthy adult" and that that person will suffer hardship if no payment is made (sub-para.(g)). If such a person is incapable of work he will be eligible for income support and so will not qualify for a hardship payment (see para.(3));

(vii) a claimant who, or whose partner, "devotes a considerable portion of each week" to caring for someone (not in a residential care or nursing home, see para.(4)) who is in receipt of, or (in certain circumstances) has claimed attendance allowance, or the higher or middle rate care component of disability living allowance, or the daily living component of PIP, or armed forces independence payment, and the decision-maker accepts that the person will not be able to continue caring if no payment is made (sub-para.(h)). (*Note*: a person in this situation may well be eligible for income support, see paras 4–6 of Sch.1B to the Income Support Regulations.);

(viii) a claimant who, or whose partner, is under 18, the subject of a severe hardship direction and who satisfies the labour market conditions (sub-para.(i));

(ix) a claimant who, or whose partner, is under 18, but eligible for JSA and the decision-maker accepts that that person will suffer hardship if no payment is made (sub-para.(j)). (*Note*: a 16- or 17-year-old who is being sanctioned for an "offence" under s.19(2)(c) or (d) or s.19A(2)(a), (c), (d),(e), (f) or (g) of the Jobseekers Act will automatically be paid a reduced rate of JSA and will not need to rely on this provision: see reg.68.); and

(x) a person under the age of 21 who was being looked after by a local authority under the Children Act 1989 (or was the subject of certain other local authority duties under that Act) within the past three years (sub-para.(k)).

See para.(5) for the factors the decision-maker must consider when deciding whether a person will suffer hardship.

Note the requirement under reg.143 for the claimant to sign a written declaration as to why he will suffer hardship if no payment is made.

Paragraph (2)

3.405 If a person does not come within one of the categories listed in para.(1) he will only be entitled to a hardship payment after two weeks (reg.142(2), (4) and (5)) and if the decision-maker accepts that he or his partner will suffer hardship if no payment is made. Note the exclusions in para.(3). As regards para.(3), claimants who, or whose partners, are entitled to income support would in any event be excluded from JSA under s.3(1)(b) or (c) of the Jobseekers Act. See para.(5) for the factors the decision-maker must consider when deciding whether hardship will occur and reg.143 for the declaration the claimant will be required to sign.

Paragraph (5)

3.406 This lists factors that the decision-maker must consider when deciding whether a person will suffer hardship. The list is not exhaustive and the decision-maker should consider all the circumstances of the claimant and his family (if any). "Hardship" is not defined. The *Decision Makers Guide* suggests that it means "severe suffering or privation", and that "privation means a lack of the necessities of life" (para.35155).

The factors that the decision-maker must consider are whether a member of the claimant's family qualifies for a disability or (in "transitional cases" only—see the note to regs 83 and 17 of the Income Support Regulations) a disabled child premium, or the disabled child, or severely disabled child, element of child tax credit (sub-para.(a)); other available resources, including those which may be available to the claimant's family from anyone else in the claimant's household (sub-para.(b)); and whether there is a "substantial risk" that the claimant or a member of his family will go without essential items such as food, clothing, heating and accommodation, or that they will be available at "considerably reduced" levels, and if so, for how long (sub-para.(c)).

Sub-paragraph (a) is straightforward. Under sub-para.(b) the decision-maker has to take into account other resources that are likely to be available to the claimant or his family. Thus income and capital that is normally disregarded (e.g. disability living allowance) will be taken into account under sub-para.(b). But note that para.35181 of the *Decision Makers Guide* considers that JSA paid for an earlier period should not be taken into account. (Note that if the decision-maker does decide that the person is in hardship the normal income and capital rules will be applied when calculating the amount of a hardship payment; unlike urgent cases payments there are no special rules for the calculation of income and capital. However, the payment will be reduced by 40 or 20 per cent of the appropriate personal allowance for a single person of the claimant's age: see reg.145.) In addition, if there are any non-dependents (for example, a grown-up son or daughter) living in the claimant's household, any contribution that they might be expected to make will be considered. But the resources have to be available to the claimant. So, for example, if a payment from a pension fund will only be available in four weeks' time, or savings can only be cashed after a period of notice has been given, a hardship payment can be made until these resources become available (see paras 35185–35195 of *DMG*). Moreover, money that might be obtainable from credit facilities (e.g. a credit card or overdraft) should not be taken into account as such facilities are not resources but only increase the claimant's indebtedness (see para.35196 of *DMG*). The decision-maker also has to consider the length of time for which any other resources are likely to be available. Clearly the longer the period of time that JSA will not be payable (e.g. if a sanction of several weeks or months' duration has been imposed) the more likely it is that hardship will occur. Sub-paragraph (c) gives examples of essential items that the decision-maker should take into account but this does not exclude consideration of other items that may be essential to the particular claimant or a member of his family.

If the claimant is not in hardship when the claim is first made but the decision-maker decides that hardship will be established by a later date, the decision to impose the sanction (i.e. that JSA is payable at a nil rate for the sanction period) can be superseded with effect from that later date on the basis that it is anticipated that a relevant change of circumstances will occur under reg.6(1)(a)(ii) of the Social Security and Child Support (Decisions and Appeals) Regulations 1999 (see Vol.III).

[[1]Period when a person is not a person in hardship

140A.—[[7] . . .]] 3.407

AMENDMENTS

1. Social Security Amendment (New Deal) Regulations 1997 (SI 1997/2863) reg.12 (January 5, 1998).
2. Jobseeker's Allowance (Amendment) Regulations 2000 (SI 2000/239) reg.2(5)(a) (March 6, 2000).
3. Jobseeker's Allowance (Amendment) Regulations 2000 (SI 2000/239) reg.2(5)(b) (March 6, 2000).
4. Social Security Amendment (New Deal) Regulations 2001 (SI 2001/1029) reg.10(1) (April 9, 2001).
5. Social Security Amendment (New Deal) Regulations 2001 (SI 2001/1029) reg.10(2) (April 9, 2001).

6. Social Security (Flexible New Deal) Regulations 2009 (SI 2009/480) reg.2(9) (October 5, 2009).
7. Jobseeker's Allowance (Sanctions) (Amendment) Regulations 2012 (SI 2012/2568) reg.3 (October 22, 2012).

Circumstances in which an income-based jobseeker's allowance is payable to a person in hardship

3.408 **141.**—(1) This regulation applies to persons in hardship within the meaning of regulation 140(1), and is subject to the provisions of regulations 143 and 144.

(2) Subject to paragraph (3) a person in hardship [1, other than a person to whom regulation 46(1) (waiting days) applies, shall be treated as entitled to an income-based jobseeker's allowance for the period beginning with the [7 8th] day of the jobseeking period or,] if later, from the day he first becomes a person in hardship and ending on the day before the claim is determined where [2the sole reason for the delay] in determining the claim is that a question arises as to whether the claimant satisfies any of the conditions of entitlement specified in section 1(2)(a) to (c) [2provided he satisfies the conditions of entitlement specified in paragraph (d)(ii) of subsection (2) of section 1.]

(3) A person in hardship to whom paragraph (2) applies may be treated as entitled to an income-based jobseeker's allowance for a period after the date [1 . . .] referred to in that paragraph [1which is applicable in his case] but before the date the statement mentioned in regulation 143(1) is furnished where [3the Secretary of State] is satisfied that the claimant suffered hardship because of a lack of resources during that period.

(4) A person in hardship, except where the person has been treated as not available for employment in accordance with regulations under section 6(4) of the Act shall, subject to the conditions specified in regulation 143 (conditions for hardship payments), be entitled to an income-based jobseeker's allowance without satisfying the requirements of section 1(2)(a) to (c) of the Act provided he satisfies the other conditions of entitlement to that benefit.

(5) An income-based jobseeker's allowance shall be payable to a person in hardship even though payment to him of a jobseeker's allowance has been suspended in accordance with [4regulation 16 of the Social Security and Child Support (Decisions and Appeals) Regulations 1999] on the ground that a doubt has arisen as to whether he satisfies the requirements of section 1(2)(a) to (c), but the allowance shall be payable only if and for so long as the claimant satisfies the other conditions of entitlement to an income-based jobseeker's allowance.

(6) An income-based jobseeker's allowance shall be payable to a person in hardship even though [5 [6 his award of jobseeker's allowance has been reduced in accordance with section 19 or 19A or regulation 69B] but the allowance shall be payable only if and for so long as he satisfies the conditions of entitlement to an income-based jobseeker's allowance.

AMENDMENTS

1. Jobseeker's Allowance and Income Support (General) (Amendment) Regulations 1996 (SI 1996/1517) reg.26 (October 7, 1996).

2. Social Security and Child Support (Jobseeker's Allowance) (Miscellaneous Amendments) Regulations 1996 (SI 1996/2538) reg.2(9) (October 28, 1996).

3. Social Security Act 1998 (Commencement No.11, and Savings and Consequential and Transitional Provisions) Order 1999 (SI 1999/2860 (C.75)) Arts 3(1) and (12) and Sch.12 para.2 (October 18 1999).

4. Social Security Act 1998 (Commencement No.11, and Savings and Consequential and Transitional Provisions) Order 1999 (SI 1999/2860 (C.75)) arts 3(1) and (12) and Sch.12 para.8 (October 18, 1999).

5. Jobseeker's Allowance (Sanctions for Failure to Attend) Regulations 2010 (SI 2010/509) reg.2(15) (April 6, 2010).

6. Jobseeker's Allowance (Sanctions) (Amendment) Regulations 2012 (SI 2012/2568) reg.3 (October 22, 2012).

7. Social Security (Jobseeker's Allowance and Employment and Support Allowance) (Waiting Days) Amendment Regulations 2014 (SI 2014/2309) reg.3(1) and (2) (October 27, 2014).

Definitions

"claimant"—see Jobseekers Act s.35(1).
"entitled"—*ibid.*

General Note

The circumstances in which hardship payments can be made are set out in this regulation for claimants who can be paid immediately and in reg.142 for claimants who have to wait two weeks. No payment will be made under this regulation or reg.142 unless the claimant has signed the declaration required by reg.143 (but note para.(3) below) and provided information about the person in hardship (see reg.144). 3.409

Paragraph (2) applies where a question arises as to whether the claimant satisfies the labour market conditions in s.1(2)(a)–(c) of the Jobseekers Act (availability for work, signing a jobseeker's agreement, actively seeking work) when a claim is made. This has to be the only reason for the delay in deciding the claim; hardship payments will not be available if the delay is for some other reason (e.g. because there is a question whether the person has too much capital or income). If hardship is established a payment will be made until the claim is decided, except for the first three—or if the claimant's jobseeking period began on or after October 27, 2014 (see SI 2014/2309 regs 3 and 4(1))—seven waiting (see para.4 of Sch.1 to the Jobseekers Act and reg.46) if these apply. The claimant must continue to satisfy the other conditions of entitlement for income-based JSA in s.3 of the Jobseekers Act. A payment under para.(2) may also be made for the period before the claimant has completed a reg.143 declaration if the decision-maker accepts that he suffered hardship because of "a lack of resources" during that period (para.(3)). Once the decision-maker has decided the claim this paragraph no longer applies but the claimant may be eligible for hardship payments under para.(4).

Paragraph (4) covers a person who is not entitled to JSA because a decision-maker has decided that he does not satisfy the labour market conditions in s.1(2)(a)–(c) of the Jobseekers Act. But it does not apply if the person is treated as not available for work under reg.15 (full-time students, prisoners on temporary release, women in receipt of maternity pay or allowance, people treated as not available at the start of a claim). The person must be in hardship and continue to satisfy the other conditions of entitlement for income-based JSA. Hardship payments can start from the date of the decision-maker's decision and continue for as long as the person remains in hardship. There is no requirement that the claimant has appealed against the decision-maker's decision. Note that there is no equivalent of this provision in reg.142 (persons eligible for hardship payments after waiting period).

Paragraph (5) applies where payment of a person's JSA has been suspended 3.410

because a question has arisen as to whether he satisfies the labour market conditions. The person must be in hardship and continue to satisfy the other conditions of entitlement for income-based JSA. Hardship payments can be made until the suspension is lifted or the decision-maker decides that the claimant does not satisfy the labour market conditions. If the decision goes against the claimant he may be eligible for hardship payments under para.(4).

Under para.(6) a person can be paid hardship payments if a sanction has been applied, provided that he is in hardship and that he continues to satisfy the other conditions of entitlement for income-based JSA (including the labour market conditions). Payments under para.(6) can last as long as the sanction lasts.

See reg.145 for the amount of a hardship payment.

Further circumstances in which an income-based jobseeker's allowance is payable to a person in hardship

3.411 **142.**—(1) This regulation applies to a person in hardship who falls within paragraph (2) but not paragraph (1) of regulation 140 and is subject to the provisions of regulations 143 and 144.

(2) A person in hardship shall be treated as entitled to an income-based jobseeker's allowance for a period commencing on whichever is the later of—

[1(a) the 15th day following the date of claim disregarding any waiting days; or]

(b) [1. . .]

(c) the day the claimant complies with the requirements of regulation 143,

and ending on the day before the claim is determined where [1the sole reason for the delay] in determining the claim is that a question arises as to whether the claimant satisfies any of the conditions of entitlement specified in section 1(2)(a) to (c) [1provided he satisfies the conditions of entitlement specified in paragraph (d)(ii) of subsection (2) of section 1.]

(3) An income-based jobseeker's allowance shall be payable subject to paragraph (4) to a person in hardship even though payment to him of a jobseeker's allowance has been suspended in accordance with regulations made by virtue of [2section 21 of the Social Security Act 1998] (suspension of benefit) on the ground that a doubt has arisen as to whether he satisfies the requirements of section 1(2)(a) to (c) but the allowance shall be payable only if and for so long as the claimant satisfies the other conditions of entitlement to an income-based jobseeker's allowance.

(4) An income-based jobseeker's allowance shall not be payable in respect of the first 14 days of the period of suspension.

(5) An income-based jobseeker's allowance shall be payable to a person in hardship even though [3 his award of jobseeker's allowance has been reduced in accordance with section 19 or 19A or regulation 69B], but the allowance—

(a) shall not be payable under this paragraph in respect of the first 14 days of the period to which [3 the reduction] applies; and

(b) shall be payable thereafter only where the conditions of entitlement to an income-based jobseeker's allowance are satisfied.

AMENDMENTS

1. Social Security and Child Support (Jobseeker's Allowance) (Miscellaneous Amendments) Regulations 1996 (SI 1996/2538) reg.2(10) (October 28, 1996).

2. Social Security Act 1998 (Commencement No.11, and Savings and Consequential and Transitional Provisions) Order 1999 (SI 1999/2860 (c.75)) arts 3(1) and (12) and Sch.12 para.9 (October 18 1999).
3. Jobseeker's Allowance (Sanctions) (Amendment) Regulations 2012 (SI 2012/2568) reg.3 (October 22, 2012).

DEFINITION

"claimant"—see Jobseekers Act s.35(1).

GENERAL NOTE

See the notes to reg.141. This regulation applies to claimants who do not come within any of the categories listed in reg.140(1) and so have to wait for two weeks before any hardship payments can be made. 3.412

The circumstances in which hardship payments can be made under this regulation are similar to those in reg.141 (the differences are noted below), *except* that there is no provision for payment to claimants who have failed to satisfy the labour market conditions in s.1(2)(a)–(c) (compare reg.141(4)); there is only provision in para.(2) for payment where a question arises when a claim is made as to whether a claimant satisfies the labour market conditions and in para.(3) where a claimant's benefit has been suspended because of doubt as to whether these conditions are satisfied. Once a decison-maker has decided that the person does not satisfy the labour market conditions he will not be eligible for hardship payments if he is not in a "vulnerable group". This is the case even if the claimant is appealing against the decision-maker's decision.

Paragraphs (3) and (5) correspond to paras (5) and (6) in reg.141, except that in each case a hardship payment under this regulation is not payable for the first two weeks (see para.(4) and para.(5)(a)). Paragraph (2) is the equivalent of reg.141(2) except that under this regulation a hardship payment can only be made from the fifteenth day after the date of claim, or the eighteenth day if the "waiting days" apply (see para.4 of Sch.1 to the Jobseekers Act and reg.46) or from the day the claimant makes the declaration required by reg.143, whichever is the later. There is thus no discretion in the case of hardship payments under para.(2) of this regulation to make any payment for the period before a reg.143 declaration is signed (compare para.(3) of reg.141).

Conditions for hardship payments

143.—(1) A jobseeker's allowance shall not be payable in accordance with regulation 141 or, as the case may be, 142, except where the claimant has— 3.413

(a) furnished on a form approved for the purpose by the Secretary of State or in such other form as he may in any particular case approve a statement of the circumstances he relies upon to establish entitlement under regulation 141 or as the case may be regulation 142; and
(b) signed the statement.

(2) The completed and signed form shall be delivered by the claimant to such office as the Secretary of State may specify.

DEFINITION

"claimant"—see Jobseekers Act s.35(1).

Provision of information

144.—For the purposes of [1section 20(5) of and] paragraph 10(3) of Schedule 1 to the Act, a claimant shall provide to the Secretary of State information as to the circumstances of the person alleged to be in hardship. 3.414

AMENDMENT

1. Jobseeker's Allowance (Amendment) Regulations 1996 (SI 1996/1516) reg.14 (October 7, 1996).

DEFINITION

"claimant"—see Jobseekers Act s.35(1).

Applicable amount in hardship cases

3.415 **145.**—[1(1) The weekly applicable amount of a person to whom an income-based jobseeker's allowance is payable in accordance with this Part of these Regulations shall be reduced by a sum equivalent to 40% or, in a case where the claimant or any other member of his family is either pregnant or is seriously ill, 20% of the following amount]—

(a) where he is a single claimant aged less than 18 or a member of a couple or a polygamous marriage where all the members, in either case, are less than 18, the amount specified in paragraph 1(1)(a), (b) or (c), as the case may be, of Schedule 1 (applicable amounts);

(b) where he is a single claimant aged not less than 18 but less than 25 or a member of a couple or polygamous marriage where one member is aged not less than 18 but less than 25 and the other member or, in the case of a polygamous marriage each other member, is a person under 18 who is not eligible for an income-based jobseeker's allowance under section 3(1)(f)(iii) or is not subject to a direction under section 16, the amount specified in paragraph 1(1)(d) of Schedule 1;

(c) where he is a single claimant aged not less than 25 or a member of a couple or a polygamous marriage (other than a member of a couple or polygamous marriage to whom sub-paragraph (b) [2applies]) at least one of whom is aged not less than 18, the amount specified in paragraph 1(1)(e) of Schedule 1.

(2) [1. . .]

(3) A reduction under paragraph (1) or (2) shall, if it is not a multiple of 5p, be rounded to the nearest such multiple or, if it is a multiple of 2.5p but not of 5p, to the next lower multiple of 5p.

AMENDMENTS

1. Jobseeker's Allowance (Amendment) Regulations 1996 (SI 1996/1516) reg.15 (October 7, 1996).

2. Jobseeker's Allowance and Income Support (General) (Amendment) Regulations 1996 (SI 1996/1517) reg.28 (October 7, 1996).

DEFINITIONS

"claimant"—see Jobseekers Act s.35(1).
"couple"—see reg.1(3).
"polygamous marriage"—*ibid.*
"single claimant"—*ibid.*

GENERAL NOTE

3.416 Hardship payments of JSA are paid at a reduced rate. The reduction in benefit is 40 per cent of the appropriate personal allowance for a single claimant of that age, or 20 per cent if a member of the claimant's family is pregnant or seriously ill (not defined).

Payments made on account of suspended benefit

146.—(1) This regulation applies to a person to whom— 3.417

(a) payments of a jobseeker's allowance have been suspended in accordance with regulations made under [1section 21 of the Social Security Act 1998];

(b) an income-based jobseeker's allowance is paid under regulation 141 or 142.

(2) In the case of a person to whom—

(a) this regulation applies; and

(b) payments in respect of the benefit suspended fall to be made, any benefit paid or payable by virtue of regulation 141(5) or 142(3) shall be treated as having been paid on account of the suspended benefit and only the balance of the suspended benefit (if any) shall be payable.

AMENDMENT

1. Social Security Act 1998 (Commencement No.11, and Savings and Consequential and Transitional Provisions) Order 1999 (SI 1999/2860 (C.75)) arts 3(1) and (12) and Sch.12 para.9 (October 18, 1999).

GENERAL NOTE

This provides that hardship payments made while payment of a claimant's JSA was suspended will be taken into account if it is later decided that the suspension should be lifted, and only the balance of the benefit owing will be paid. In other cases (e.g. where hardship payments have been made because of a delay in deciding the claim for JSA) offsetting will be applied under the normal rules (see reg.5 of the Payments on Account, Overpayments and Recovery Regulations). 3.418

[1 PART IXA

HARDSHIP FOR JOINT-CLAIM COUPLES

Meaning of "couple in hardship"

146A.—(1) In this Part of these Regulations, a "couple in hardship" means for the purposes of regulation 146C, a joint-claim couple who are claiming a jobseeker's allowance jointly, other than a couple which includes a member to whom paragraph (3) or (4) applies, where— 3.419

(a) [4, at least one member of the joint-claim couple is a woman who is pregnant] and the Secretary of State is satisfied that, unless a joint-claim jobseeker's allowance is paid, she will suffer hardship; or

(b) one or both members of the couple are members of a polygamous marriage, one member of the marriage is pregnant and the Secretary of State is satisfied that, unless a joint-claim jobseeker's allowance is paid, she will suffer hardship; or

(c) the award of a joint-claim jobseeker's allowance includes, or would, if a claim for a jobseeker's allowance from the couple were to succeed, have included in their applicable amount a disability premium and—

(i) where the couple have an award, a joint-claim jobseeker's allowance is not payable [10 . . .] because it is suspended [10 or the award is reduced in accordance with section 19 or 19A or regulation 69B]; and

(ii) the Secretary of State is satisfied that, unless a joint-claim jobseeker's allowance is paid, the member of the couple who would have caused the disability premium to be applicable to the couple would suffer hardship; or

(d) either member of the couple suffers from a chronic medical condition which results in functional capacity being limited or restricted by physical impairment and the Secretary of State is satisfied that—

(i) the suffering has already lasted or is likely to last, for not less than 26 weeks; and

(ii) unless a joint-claim jobseeker's allowance is paid, the probability is that the health of the person suffering would, within two weeks of the Secretary of State making his decision, decline further than that of a normally healthy adult and the member of the couple who suffers from that condition would suffer hardship; or

(e) either member of the couple, or where a member of that couple is married to more than one person under a law which permits polygamy, one member of that marriage, devotes a considerable portion of each week to caring for another person who—

(i) is in receipt of an attendance allowance [11 , the care component of disability living allowance at one of the two higher rates prescribed under section 72(4) of the Benefits Act [12 , armed forces independence payment] or the daily living component of personal independence payment at the standard or enhanced rate in accordance with section 78 of the 2012 Act]; or

(ii) has claimed either attendance allowance [11 , disability living allowance [12 , armed forces independence payment] or personal independence payment], but only for so long as the claim has not been determined, or for 26 weeks from the date of claiming, whichever is the earlier; or

(iii) has claimed either attendance allowance or disability living allowance and has an award of either attendance allowance or the care component of disability living allowance at one of the two higher rates prescribed under section 72(4) of the Benefits Act for a period commencing after the date on which that claim was made, [11 ; or

(iv) has claimed personal independence payment and has an award of the daily living component of personal independence payment at the standard or enhanced rate in accordance with section 78 of the 2012 Act for a period commencing after the date on which that claim was made] [12 ; or

(v) has claimed and has an award of armed forces independence payment for a period commencing after the date on which that claim was made,]

and the Secretary of State is satisfied, after taking account of the factors set out in paragraph (6) in so far as they are appropriate to the particular circumstances of the case, that the person providing the care will not be able to continue doing so unless a joint-claim jobseeker's allowance is paid; or

(f) section 16 applies to either member of the couple by virtue of a direction issued by the Secretary of State, except where the member of the joint-claim couple to whom the direction applies does not satisfy the requirements of section 1(2)(a) to (c); or

(g) section 3A(1)(e)(ii) (member of joint-claim couple under the age of 18) applies to either member of the couple and the Secretary of State is satisfied that unless a joint-claim jobseeker's allowance is paid, the couple will suffer hardship;

(h) one or both members of the couple is a person—

(i) who, pursuant to the Children Act 1989, was being looked after by a local authority;

(ii) with whom the local authority had a duty, pursuant to that Act, to take reasonable steps to keep in touch; or

(iii) who, pursuant to that Act, qualified for advice or assistance from a local authority,

but in respect of whom head (i), (ii) or, as the case may be, (iii) above had not applied for a period of three years or less as at the date on which the requirements of regulation 146F are complied with; and

(iv) as at the date on which the requirements of regulation 146F are complied with, that member is, or both of those members are, under the age of 21.

(2) Except in a case to which paragraph (3), (4) [6 [10 . . .]] applies, a "couple in hardship" means for the purposes of regulation 146D, a joint-claim couple where the Secretary of State is satisfied, after taking account of the factors set out in paragraph (6) in so far as they are appropriate to the particular circumstances of the case, that the couple will suffer hardship unless a joint-claim jobseeker's allowance is paid.

(3) In paragraph (1) and (2), a "couple in hardship" does not include a couple one of whose members is entitled to income support [5 or an income-related employment and support allowance] or who falls within a category of persons prescribed for the purposes of section 124(1)(e) of the Benefits Act.

(4) Paragraph (1)(e) shall not apply in a case where the person being cared for resides in a [3 care home, an Abbeyfield Home or an independent hospital].

(5) [10 . . .]

[6 (5A) [10 . . .]]

[9 (5B) [10 . . .]]

(6) Factors which, for the purposes of paragraphs (1) and (2), the Secretary of State is to take into account in determining whether a joint-claim couple will suffer hardship are—

(a) the presence in the joint-claim couple of a person who satisfies the requirements for a disability premium specified in paragraphs 20H and 20I of Schedule 1;

(b) the resources which, without a joint-claim jobseeker's allowance, are likely to be available to the joint-claim couple, the amount by which these resources fall short of the amount applicable in their case in accordance with regulation 146G (applicable amount in hardship cases for joint-claim couples), the amount of any resources which may be available to the joint-claim couple for any person in the couple's household who is not a member of the family and the length of time for which those factors are likely to persist;

(c) whether there is a substantial risk that essential items, including food, clothing, heating and accommodation, will cease to be available to the joint-claim couple, or will be available at considerably reduced levels, the hardship that will result and the length of time those factors are likely to persist.]

AMENDMENTS

1. Jobseeker's Allowance (Joint Claims) Regulations 2000 (SI 2000/1978) reg.2(3) (March 19, 2001).

2. Social Security Amendment (New Deal) Regulations 2001 (SI 2001/1029) reg.9(2) (April 9, 2001).

3. Social Security (Care Homes and Independent Hospitals) Regulations 2005 (SI 2005/2687) reg.3 and Sch.2 para.8 (October 24, 2005).

4. Civil Partnership (Pensions, Social Security and Child Support) (Consequential, etc. Provisions) Order 2005 (SI 2005/2877) art.2(3) and Sch.3 para.26(9) (December 5, 2005).

5. Employment and Support Allowance (Consequential Provisions) (No.2) Regulations 2008 (SI 2008/1554) reg.3(1) and (18) (October 27, 2008).

6. Social Security (Flexible New Deal) Regulations 2009 (SI 2009/480) reg.2(10) (April 6, 2009).

7. Social Security (Flexible New Deal) Regulations 2009 (SI 2009/480) reg.2(10)(b) (October 5, 2009).

8. Jobseeker's Allowance (Sanctions for Failure to Attend) Regulations 2010 (SI 2010/509) reg.2(16) (April 6, 2010).

9. Jobseeker's Allowance (Employment, Skills and Enterprise Scheme) Regulations 2011 (SI 2011/917) reg.10 (May 20, 2011).

10. Jobseeker's Allowance (Sanctions) (Amendment) Regulations 2012 (SI 2012/2568) reg.4 (October 22, 2012).

11. Personal Independence Payment (Supplementary Provisions and Consequential Amendments) Regulations 2013 (SI 2013/388) reg.8 and Sch. para.16(1) and (5) (April 8, 2013).

12. Armed Forces and Reserve Forces Compensation Scheme (Consequential Provisions: Subordinate Legislation) Order 2013 (SI 2013/591) art.7 and Sch. para.10(1) and (5) (April 8, 2013).

GENERAL NOTE

3.420 This regulation makes provision corresponding to reg.140 for joint-claim couples.

[1Period when a joint-claim couple is not in hardship

3.421 **146B.**—[4 . . .]]

AMENDMENTS

1. Jobseeker's Allowance (Joint Claims) Regulations 2000 (SI 2000/1978) reg.2(3) (March 19, 2001).

2. Social Security Amendment (New Deal) Regulations 2001 (SI 2001/1029) reg.10(1) (April 9, 2001).

3. Social Security Amendment (New Deal) Regulations 2001 (SI 2001/1029) reg.10(2) (April 9, 2001).
4. Jobseeker's Allowance (Sanctions) (Amendment) Regulations 2012 (SI 2012/2568) reg.4 (October 22, 2012).

[1Circumstances in which a joint-claim jobseeker's allowance is payable where a joint-claim couple is a couple in hardship

146C.—(1) This regulation applies where a joint-claim couple is a couple in hardship within the meaning of regulation 146A(1) and is subject to the provisions of regulations 146E and 146F. 3.422

(2) Subject to paragraph (3), a couple in hardship referred to in paragraph (1), other than a couple in hardship where either or both members are persons to whom regulation 46(1) (waiting days) applies, shall be treated as entitled to a joint-claim jobseeker's allowance for the period—

(a) beginning with the [4 eighth] day of the jobseeking period or, if later, from the day the couple first becomes a couple in hardship; and
(b) ending on the day before the claim is determined,

where the sole reason for the claim being determined on that day and not earlier is that a question arises as to whether either or both members satisfy the conditions of entitlement in section 1(2)(a) to (c) provided the joint-claim couple satisfy the conditions set out in section 1(2B)(c).

(3) A couple in hardship to whom paragraph (2) applies may be treated as entitled to a joint-claim jobseeker's allowance for a period after the date referred to in that paragraph which is applicable in their case but before the date of the statement referred to in regulation 146E(1) is furnished where the Secretary of State is satisfied that that couple suffered hardship because of a lack of resources during that period.

(4) A couple in hardship, except where either or both members have been treated as not available for employment in accordance with regulations under section 6(4) shall, subject to the conditions specified in regulation 146E (conditions for hardship payments), be entitled to a joint-claim jobseeker's allowance without both members satisfying the requirements of section 1(2)(a) to (c) provided the joint-claim couple satisfy the other conditions of entitlement to that benefit.

(5) A joint-claim jobseeker's allowance shall be payable to a joint-claim couple who are a couple in hardship even though payment to the couple of a joint-claim jobseeker's allowance has been suspended in accordance with regulations made under section 21 of the Social Security Act 1998 on the ground that a doubt has arisen as to whether either joint-claimant satisfies the requirements of section 1(2)(a) to (c), but the allowance shall be payable only if and for so long as—

(a) the joint-claim couple satisfy the other conditions of entitlement to a joint-claim jobseeker's allowance; or
(b) one member satisfies those conditions and the other member comes within any paragraph in Schedule A1 (categories of members not required to satisfy conditions in section 1(2B)(b)).

(6) A joint-claim jobseeker's allowance shall be payable to a couple in hardship even though [2 3 the award of joint-claim jobseeker's allowance has been reduced in accordance with section 19 or 19A or regulation 69B] but the allowance shall be payable only if and for so long as—

(a) the joint-claim couple satisfy the other conditions of entitlement to a joint-claim jobseeker's allowance; or

(b) one member satisfies those conditions and the other member comes within any paragraph in Schedule A1 (categories of members not required to satisfy conditions in section 1(2B)(b)).]

AMENDMENTS

1. Jobseeker's Allowance (Joint Claims) Regulations 2000 (SI 2000/1978) reg.2(3) (March 19, 2001).

2. Jobseeker's Allowance (Sanctions for Failure to Attend) Regulations 2010 (SI 2010/509) reg.2(17) (April 6, 2010).

3. Jobseeker's Allowance (Sanctions) (Amendment) Regulations 2012 (SI 2012/2568) reg.4 (October 22, 2012).

4. Social Security (Jobseeker's Allowance and Employment and Support Allowance) (Waiting Days) Amendment Regulations 2014 (SI 2014/2309) reg.3(1) and (3) (October 27, 2014).

GENERAL NOTE

3.423 This regulation makes provision corresponding to reg.141 for joint-claim couples.

The increase from three to seven in the number of days at the beginning of a jobseeking period during which no hardship payment can be made (see para.(2)(a)) only applies where the claimant's jobseeking period began on or after October 27, 2014 (see SI 2014/2309 regs 3 and 4(1)).

[1Further circumstances in which a joint-claim jobseeker's allowance is payable to a couple in hardship

3.424 **146D.**—(1) This regulation applies to a couple in hardship falling within paragraph (2) but not paragraph (1) of regulation 146A and is subject to the provisions of regulations 146E and 146F.

(2) A couple in hardship shall be treated as entitled to a joint-claim jobseeker's allowance for a period commencing on whichever is the later of—

(a) the 15th day following the date of claim disregarding any waiting days; or

(b) the day on which regulation 146E is complied with,

and ending on the day before the claim is determined where the sole reason for the claim being determined on that day and not earlier is that a question arises as to whether either or both members of that couple satisfy the conditions of entitlement in section 1(2)(a) to (c) provided the joint-claim couple satisfy the conditions set out in section 1(2B)(c).

(3) A joint-claim jobseeker's allowance shall be payable, subject to paragraph (4), to a couple in hardship even though payment to them of a joint-claim jobseeker's allowance has been suspended in accordance with regulations made under section 21 of the Social Security Act 1998 (suspension of benefit) on the ground that a doubt has arisen as to whether either or both members of that couple satisfy the requirements of section 1(2)(a) to (c) of the Act but the allowance shall be payable only if and for so long as—

(a) the joint-claim couple satisfy the other conditions of entitlement to a joint-claim jobseeker's allowance; or

(b) one member satisfies those conditions and the other member comes within any paragraph in Schedule A1 (categories of members not required to satisfy conditions in section 1(2B)(b)).

(4) A joint-claim jobseeker's allowance shall not be payable in respect of the first 14 days of the period of suspension.

(5) A joint-claim jobseeker's allowance shall be payable to a couple in hardship even though [2 the award of joint-claim jobseeker's allowance has been reduced in accordance with section 19 or 19A or regulation 69B] but the allowance—

(a) shall not be payable under this paragraph in respect of the first 14 days of the period to which [2 the reduction] applies; and

(b) shall be payable thereafter only where the conditions of entitlement to a joint-claim jobseeker's allowance are satisfied or where one member satisfies those conditions and the other member comes within any paragraph in Schedule A1 (categories of members not required to satisfy conditions in section 1(2B)(b)).]

AMENDMENTS

1. Jobseeker's Allowance (Joint Claims) Regulations 2000 (SI 2000/1978) reg.2(3) (March 19, 2001).

2. Jobseeker's Allowance (Sanctions) (Amendment) Regulations 2012 (SI 2012/2568) reg.4 (October 22, 2012).

GENERAL NOTE

This regulation makes provision corresponding to reg.142 for joint-claim couples. **3.425**

[1Conditions for hardship payments to a joint-claim couple

146E.—(1) A joint-claim jobseeker's allowance shall not be payable in accordance with regulation 146C or, as the case may be, 146D, except where either member of the joint-claim couple has— **3.426**

(a) furnished on a form approved for the purpose by the Secretary of State or in such other form as he may in any particular case approve, a statement of the circumstances he relies upon to establish entitlement under regulation 146C or, as the case may be, regulation 146D; and

(b) signed the statement.

(2) The completed and signed form shall be delivered by either member to such office as the Secretary of State may specify.]

AMENDMENT

1. Jobseeker's Allowance (Joint Claims) Regulations 2000 (SI 2000/1978) reg.2(3) (March 19, 2001).

GENERAL NOTE

This regulation makes provision corresponding to reg.143 for joint-claim couples. **3.427**

[1Provision of information

3.428 **146F.**—For the purposes of section 20B(5) and paragraph 10(3) of Schedule 1 to the Act, a member of a joint-claim couple shall provide to the Secretary of State information as to the circumstances of the alleged hardship of that couple.]

AMENDMENT

1. Jobseeker's Allowance (Joint Claims) Regulations 2000 (SI 2000/1978) reg.2(3) (March 19, 2001).

GENERAL NOTE

3.429 This regulation makes provision corresponding to reg.144 for joint-claim couples.

[1Applicable amount in hardship cases for joint-claim couples

3.430 **146G.**—[2 (1) The weekly applicable amount of the joint-claim couple to whom a joint-claim jobseeker's allowance is payable in accordance with this Part of these Regulations shall be reduced by a sum equivalent to—

(a) 20% of the amount specified in paragraph 1(1)(e) of Schedule 1 in a case where a member of a joint-claim couple is—
   (i) either pregnant or seriously ill, or
   (ii) a member of a polygamous marriage and one of the members of that marriage is pregnant or seriously ill, or

(b) 40% of the amount specified in paragraph 1(1)(e) of Schedule 1 in all other cases.]

(2) A reduction under paragraph (1) shall, if it is not a multiple of 5p, be rounded to the nearest such multiple or, if it is a multiple of 2.5p but not of 5p, to the next lower multiple of 5p.]

AMENDMENTS

1. Jobseeker's Allowance (Joint Claims) Regulations 2000 (SI 2000/1978) reg.2(3) (March 19, 2001).
2. Social Security (Miscellaneous Amendments) (No.2) Regulations 2010 (SI 2010/641) reg.4(1) and (11) (April 13, 2010).

GENERAL NOTE

3.431 This regulation makes provision corresponding to reg.145 for joint-claim couples.

[1Payments made on account of suspended benefit

3.432 **146H.**—(1) This regulation applies to a joint-claim couple to whom—

(a) payments of a joint-claim jobseeker's allowance have been suspended in accordance with regulations made under section 21 of the Social Security Act 1998;

(b) a joint-claim jobseeker's allowance is paid under regulation 146C or 146D.

(2) In the case of a joint-claim couple to whom—

(a) this regulation applies; and

(b) payments in respect of the benefit suspended fall to be made,

any benefit paid or payable by virtue of regulation 146C(5) or 146D(3) shall be treated as having been paid on account of the suspended benefit and only the balance of the suspended benefit, if any, shall be payable.]

AMENDMENT

1. Jobseeker's Allowance (Joint Claims) Regulations 2000 (SI 2000/1978) reg.2(3) (March 19, 2001).

GENERAL NOTE

This regulation makes provision corresponding to reg.146 for joint-claim couples. 3.433

PART X

URGENT CASES

GENERAL NOTE

Part X (regs 147–149), which provided for "urgent cases" payments of JSA was revoked by the Social Security (Miscellaneous Amendments) (No.5) Regulations 2009 (SI 2009/3228) reg.2 with effect from January 25, 2010. 3.434

For the abolition of urgent cases payments generally, see the commentary to Pt VI of the Income Support Regulations.

PART XI

PART-WEEKS

Amount of a jobseeker's allowance payable

150.—(1) Subject to the following provisions of this Part, the amount payable by way of an income-based jobseeker's allowance in respect of part-week shall be calculated by applying the formula— 3.435

(a) where the claimant has no income—

$$\frac{(N \times A)}{7}; \text{ or}$$

(b) where the claimant has an income—

$$\frac{(N \times (A - I))}{(7)} - B,$$

where—

A is the claimant's weekly applicable amount in the relevant week;

B is the amount of any jobseeker's allowance, income support, maternity allowance, incapacity benefit [3 , severe disablement allowance or employment and support allowance] payable to any member of the claimant's family other than the claimant in respect of any day in the part-week;

I is the claimant's weekly income in the relevant week less B;

N is the number of days in the part-week.

[1 (1A) In relation to a joint-claim couple jointly claiming a joint-claim jobseeker's allowance, paragraph (1) shall have effect as if the references to the claimant were references to the joint-claim couple.

(1B) Where a joint-claim couple become, or cease to be, a joint-claim couple on any day other than on the first day of a benefit week, the amount payable by way of a joint-claim jobseeker's allowance in respect of that benefit week shall be calculated by applying the formula in paragraph (1).]

(2) Subject to the following provisions of this Part, the amount payable by way of a contribution-based jobseeker's allowance in respect of a part-week shall be calculated by applying the formula—

$$\frac{(N \times X) - Y}{(7)}$$

where—

X is the personal rate determined in accordance with section 4(1);

Y is the amount of any widow's benefit, [2 carer's allowance], training allowance and any increase in disablement pension payable in accordance with Part I of Schedule 7 to the Benefits Act (Unemployment Supplement) payable in respect of any day in the part-week;

N is the number of days in the part-week

(3) In this Part—

"part-week" means an entitlement to a jobseeker's allowance in respect of any period of less than a week;

"relevant week" means the period of 7 days determined in accordance with regulation 152.

AMENDMENTS

1. Jobseeker's Allowance (Joint Claims) Regulations 2000 (SI 2000/1978) reg.2(5) and Sch.2 para.48 (March 19, 2001).

2. Social Security (Miscellaneous Amendments) Regulations 2003 (SI 2003/511) reg.3(4) and (5) (April 1, 2003).

3. Employment and Support Allowance (Consequential Provisions) (No.2) Regulations 2008 (SI 2008/1554) reg.3(1) and (20) (October 27, 2008).

DEFINITION

"claimant"—see Jobseekers Act s.35(1).

Amount of a jobseeker's allowance payable where a person is in a residential care or nursing home

3.436 **151.**—[1 . . .]

AMENDMENT

1. Social Security Amendment (Residential Care and Nursing Homes) Regulations 2001 (SI 2001/3767) reg.2 and Sch. Pt II para.17 (April 8, 2002).

Relevant week

152.—(1) Where the part-week— 3.437

(a) is the whole period for which a jobseeker's allowance is payable or occurs at the beginning of an award, the relevant week is the period of 7 days ending on the last day of that part-week; or

(b) occurs at the end of an award, the relevant week is the period of 7 days beginning on the first day of the part-week; or

(c) occurs because a jobseeker's allowance [7 is reduced for any period in accordance with regulations 69, 69A or 69B], the relevant week is the 7 days ending immediately before the start of the next benefit week to commence for that claimant [2 or the joint-claim couple].

(2) [3 Except in a case to which paragraph (3) applies,] where a person has an award of a jobseeker's allowance and his benefit week changes, for the purpose of calculating the amounts of a jobseeker's allowance payable for the art-week beginning on the day after his last complete benefit week before the change and ending immediately before the change, the relevant week is the period of 7 days beginning on the day after the last complete benefit week.

[4 (3) Where a joint-claim couple have an award of a joint-claim job-seeker's allowance and their benefit week changes, for the purpose of calculating the amounts of a joint-claim jobseeker's allowance payable for the part-week beginning on the day after their last complete benefit week before the change and ending immediately before the change, the relevant week is the period of 7 days beginning on the day after the last complete benefit week.]

AMENDMENTS

1. Jobseeker's Allowance (Joint Claims) Regulations 2000 (SI 2000/1978) reg.2(5) and Sch.2 para.50(a)(i) (March 19, 2001).
2. Jobseeker's Allowance (Joint Claims) Regulations 2000 (SI 2000/1978) reg.2(5) and Sch.2 para.50(a)(ii) (March 19, 2001).
3. Jobseeker's Allowance (Joint Claims) Regulations 2000 (SI 2000/1978) reg.2(5) and Sch.2 para.50(b) (March 19, 2001).
4. Jobseeker's Allowance (Joint Claims) Regulations 2000 (SI 2000/1978) reg.2(5) and Sch.2 para.50(c) (March 19, 2001).
5. Jobseeker's Allowance (Sanctions for Failure to Attend) Regulations 2010 (SI 2010/509) reg.2(18) (April 6, 2010).
6. Jobseeker's Allowance (Mandatory Work Activity Scheme) Regulations 2011 (SI 2011/688) reg.16(g) (April 25, 2011).
7. Jobseeker's Allowance (Sanctions) (Amendment) Regulations 2012 (SI 2012/2568) reg.5(20) (October 22, 2012).

DEFINITION

"benefit week"—see reg.1(3).

Modification in the calculation of income

153.—For the purposes of regulation 150 (amount of jobseeker's allowance payable for part-weeks) a claimant's income and, in determining the 3.438

amount payable by way of an income-based jobseeker's allowance, the income of any person which the claimant is treated as possessing under section 12(4) or [1 regulation 88(4) or 88ZA(3)], shall be calculated in accordance with Parts VIII, and, where applicable, IX and X subject to the following changes—

(a) any income which is due to be paid in the relevant week shall be treated as paid on the first day of that week;

(b) in determining the amount payable by way of an income-based jobseeker's allowance, any jobseeker's allowance, income support, maternity allowance, incapacity benefit or severe disablement allowance under the Benefits Act [4 , universal credit] [3 or employment and support allowance] payable in the relevant week but not in respect of any day in the part-week shall be disregarded;

(c) in determining the amount payable by way of a contribution-based jobseeker's allowance, any widow's benefit, [2 carer's allowance], training allowance or any increase in disablement pension payable in accordance with Part I of Schedule 7 to the Benefits Act (Unemployment Supplement) which is payable in the relevant week but not in respect of any day in the part-week shall be disregarded;

(d) where the part-week occurs at the end of the claim, any income or any change in the amount of income of the same kind which is first payable within the relevant week but not on any day in the part-week shall be disregarded;

(e) where the part-week occurs immediately after a period in which a person was treated as engaged in remunerative work under regulation 52 (persons treated as engaged in remunerative work) any earnings which are taken into account for the purposes of determining that period shall be disregarded;

(f) where only part of the weekly amount of income is taken into account in the relevant week, the balance shall be disregarded.

AMENDMENTS

1. Jobseeker's Allowance (Joint Claims) Regulations 2000 (SI 2000/1978) reg.2(5) and Sch.2 para.51 (March 19, 2001).

2. Social Security (Miscellaneous Amendments) Regulations 2003 (SI 2003/511) reg.3(4) and (5) (April 1, 2003).

3. Employment and Support Allowance (Consequential Provisions) (No.2) Regulations 2008 (SI 2008/1554) reg.3(1) and (21) (October 27, 2008).

4. Universal Credit (Consequential, Supplementary, Incidental and Miscellaneous Provisions) Regulations 2013 (SI 2013/630) reg.30(1) and (6) (April 29, 2013).

DEFINITIONS

"the Benefits Act"—see Jobseekers Act s.35(1).

"claimant"—*ibid.*

Reduction in certain cases

3.439 **154.**—The reduction to be made in accordance with Part IX (Hardship) in respect of an income based jobseeker's allowance shall be an amount equal to one seventh of the reduction which would be made under that Part for a week multiplied by the number of days in the part-week.

Modification of section 15(2) of the Act

155.—[1 (1)] In its application to an income-based jobseeker's allowance [2 but not a joint-claim jobseeker's allowance] payable for a part-week, section 15(2)(d) shall have effect subject to the following modification— 3.440

"(d) any payment by way of an income-based jobseeker's allowance for that period or any part of it which apart from this paragraph would be made to the claimant—
(i) shall not be made, if the amount of an income-based jobseeker's allowance which would be payable for a period of less than a week is equal to or less than the proportion of the prescribed sum appropriate to the number of days in the part-week;
(ii) shall be at a rate equal to the difference between the amount which would be payable for a period of less than a week and the prescribed sum where that amount would be more than the prescribed sum."

[3 (2) In its application to a joint-claim jobseeker's allowance payable for a part-week, section 15(2)(d) shall have effect subject to the following modification—

"(d) any payment by way of a joint-claim jobseeker's allowance for that period or any part of it which apart from this paragraph would be made to the nominated member for the purposes of section 3B—
(i) shall not be made, if the amount of joint-claim jobseeker's allowance which would be payable for less than a week is equal to or less than the proportion of the prescribed sum appropriate to the number of days in the part-week;
(ii) shall be at a rate equal to the difference between the amount which would be payable for a period of less than a week and the prescribed sum where that amount would be more than the prescribed sum."]

AMENDMENTS

1. Jobseeker's Allowance (Joint Claims) Regulations 2000 (SI 2000/1978) reg.2(5) and Sch.2 para.52 (March 19, 2001).
2. Jobseeker's Allowance (Joint Claims) Regulations 2000 (SI 2000/1978) reg.2(5) and Sch.2 para.52(a) (March 19, 2001).
3. Jobseeker's Allowance (Joint Claims) Regulations 2000 (SI 2000/1978) reg.2(5) and Sch.2 para.52(b) (March 19, 2001).

PART XII

SPECIAL CATEGORIES

GENERAL NOTE

The text of the regulations in Pt XII, which mainly amend other regulations, has been omitted. The major special category for which the ordinary rules are altered is of share fishermen. These provisions have not been reproduced in previous editions. The substance is the same as Pt 9 of the JSA Regulations 2013 in Pt VI below, with some differences of drafting and arrangement and to take account of the specific nature of old style and new style JSA. Thus, regs 156–158 of the JSA Regulations 1996 equate to regs 67–69 of the JSA Regulations 2013 and regs 160–164 equate to 3.440A regs 70–74. Regulation 159 of the JSA Regulations 1996, deeming work as a share fisherman to be employed earner's employment for the purposes of ss.19 and 20 of the old style Jobseekers Act 1995 has no equivalent in the JSA Regulations 2013. Anyone dealing with an actual old style JSA case involving a share fisherman, rather than merely seeking general information, should take care to consult the text of the JSA Regulations 1996.

Regulation 163 of the JSA Regulations 1996 has the same effect as reg.75 of the JSA Regulations 2013, but the modification it makes is not incorporated into the text of s.2 of the old style Jobseekers Act 1995 in Pt I as it is into the new style Jobseekers Act 1995 in Pt VI.

PART XIII

MISCELLANEOUS

Recovery of Maintenance

Recovery orders

3.441 **169.**—(1) Where an award of income-based jobseeker's allowance has been made to a person ("the claimant"), the Secretary of State may apply to the court for a recovery order against the claimant's spouse [[1] or civil partner] ("the liable person").

(2) On making a recovery order the court may order the liable person to pay such amount at such intervals as it considers appropriate, having regard to all the circumstances of the liable person and in particular his income.

(3) Except in Scotland, a recovery order shall be treated for all purposes as if it were a maintenance order [[2] made by the family court].

(4) Where a recovery order requires the liable person to make payments to the Secretary of State, the Secretary of State may, by giving notice in writing to the court which made the order, the liable person, and the claimant, transfer to the claimant the right to receive payments under the order and to exercise the relevant rights in relation to the order.

(5) In this regulation—

the expressions "the court" and "recovery order" have the same meanings as in section 23 of the Act; and

"the relevant rights" means, in relation to a recovery order, the right to bring any proceedings, take any steps or do any other thing under or in relation to the order.

AMENDMENTS

1. Civil Partnership (Pensions, Social Security and Child Support) (Consequential, etc. Provisions) Order 2005 (SI 2005/2877) art.2(3) and Sch.3 para.26(10) (December 5, 2005).

2. Crime and Courts Act 2013 (Family Court: Consequential Provision) (No.2) Order 2014 (SI 2014/879) art.74 (April 22, 2014).

DEFINITION

"claimant"—see Jobseekers Act s.35(1).

General Note

See the note to s.23 of the Jobseekers Act. 3.442

Training Allowance

Persons in receipt of a training allowance

170.—[3 (1) A person who is not receiving training falling within paragraph (2) [5 and is not a qualifying young person or child within the meaning of section 142 of the Benefits Act (child and qualifying young person)] may be entitled to an income-based jobseeker's allowance without— 3.443

(a) being available for employment;
(b) having entered into a jobseeker's agreement; or
(c) actively seeking employment,

if he is in receipt of a training allowance [8 . . .].]

(2) Training falls within this paragraph if it is training for which persons aged under 18 are eligible and for which persons aged 18 to 24 may be eligible [2 secured by the [9 [10 Secretary of State] [11 . . .]] or by the [4 [6 Welsh Ministers]] and, in Scotland, provided] directly or indirectly by a Local Enterprise Company pursuant to its arrangement with, as the case may be, [7 Skills Development Scotland,] Scottish Enterprise or Highlands and Islands Enterprise (whether that arrangement is known as an Operating Contract or by any other name).

Amendments

1. Jobseeker's Allowance (Amendment) (No.2) Regulations 1998 (SI 1998/1698) reg.5 (August 4, 1998).
2. Social Security (Miscellaneous Amendments) (No.2) Regulations 2001 (SI 2001/652) reg.5(c) (March 26, 2001).
3. Social Security (Breach of Community Order) (Consequential Amendments) Regulations 2001 (SI 2001/1711) reg.2(4)(b) (October 15, 2001).
4. National Council for Education and Training for Wales (Transfer of Functions to the National Assembly for Wales and Abolition) Order 2005 (SI 2005/3238 (W.243)) art.9(2) and Sch.2 para.8(5) (April 1, 2006).
5. Social Security (Young Persons) Amendment Regulations 2006 (SI 2006/718) reg.3(8) (April 10, 2006).
6. Social Security (Miscellaneous Amendments) (No.7) Regulations 2008 (SI 2008/3157) reg.3(8) (January 5, 2009).
7. Social Security (Miscellaneous Amendments) Regulations 2009 (SI 2009/583) reg.4(3) (April 6, 2009).
8. Welfare Reform Act 2009 (Section 26) (Consequential Amendments) Regulations 2010 (SI 2010/424) reg.3(3) (March 22, 2010).
9. Apprenticeships, Skills, Children and Learning Act 2009 (Consequential Amendments to Subordinate Legislation) (England) Order 2010 (SI 2010/1941) art.5(5) (September 1, 2010).
10. Young People's Learning Agency Abolition (Consequential Amendments to Subordinate Legislation) (England) Order 2012 (SI 2012/956) art.5(7) (May 1, 2012).
11. Deregulation Act 2015 (Consequential Amendments) Order 2015 (SI 2015/971) art.2 and Sch.3 para. 4(6) (May 26, 2015).

DEFINITIONS

"employment"—see reg.4.
"training allowance"—see reg.1(3).

GENERAL NOTE

3.443A See the note to para.28 of Sch.1B to the Income Support Regulations.

Trade Disputes

Trade disputes: exemptions from section 15 of the Act

3.444 **171.**—Section 15(2) (trade disputes: effect on other claimants) shall not apply to a claimant during any period where—

(a) a member of the claimant's family is, or would be, prevented by section 14 from being entitled to a jobseeker's allowance; and
(b) that member is—
  (i) a child or young person; [2 . . .]
  (ii) [1incapable of work] or within the maternity period, and for this purpose "the maternity period" means the period commencing at the beginning of the 6th week before the expected week of confinement and ending at the end of the 7th week after the week in which confinement takes place [2 or
  (iii) has limited capability for work.]

AMENDMENTS

1. Jobseeker's Allowance (Amendment) Regulations 1996 (SI 1996/1516) reg.20 and Sch. (October 7, 1996).
2. Employment and Support Allowance (Consequential Provisions) (No.2) Regulations 2008 (SI 2008/1554) reg.3(22) (October 27, 2008).

DEFINITIONS

"child"—see Jobseekers Act s.35(1).
"claimant"—*ibid.*
"family"—*ibid.*
"trade dispute"—*ibid.*
"young person"—see reg.76.

GENERAL NOTE

3.445 See the note to s.15 of the Jobseekers Act.

Trade disputes: prescribed sum

3.446 **172.**—The prescribed sum for the purposes of section 15(2)(d) is [1£40.50].

AMENDMENT

1. Social Security Benefits Up-rating Order 2015 (SI 2015/457) art.20 (April 6, 2015).

General Note

Unlike in previous years this "prescribed sum" was not up-rated in April 2016. 3.446A

[1 SCHEDULE A1

Categories of Members of a Joint-claim Couple who are not Required to satisfy the Conditions in Section 1(2B)(b)

Interpretation

1.—In this Schedule, "member" means a member of a joint-claim couple. 3.447

Member studying full-time

[2 **2.**—(1) A member— 3.448

(a) who, at the date of claim, is [6 a qualifying young person within the meaning of] section 142 of the Benefits Act;

(b) who, at the date of claim, is a full-time student; or

(c) to whom (a) or (b) does not apply but to whom sub-paragraph (1A) or (2) does apply.

(1A) This sub-paragraph applies to a member who—

(a) as at the date of claim—

(i) had applied to an educational establishment to commence a full-time course of study commencing from the beginning of the next academic term or, as the case may be, the next academic year after the date of claim and that application has not been rejected; or

(ii) had been allocated a place on a full-time course of study commencing from the beginning of the next academic term or, as the case may be, the next academic year; and

(b) is either—

(i) [6 a qualifying young person within the meaning of] section 142 of the Benefits Act; or

(ii) a full-time student.

(2) This sub-paragraph applies to a member who has applied to an educational establishment to commence a full-time course of study (other than a course of study beyond a first degree course or a comparable course)—

(a) within one month of—

(i) the last day of a previous course of study; or

(ii) the day on which the member received examination results relating to a previous course of study; and

(b) who is either—

(i) [6 a qualifying young person within the meaning of] section 142 of the Benefits Act; or

(ii) a full-time student.]

(3) A member to whom any provision of regulation 13(2)(b) to (e) of the Income Support Regulations (persons receiving relevant education who are severely handicapped, orphans and persons estranged from their parents or guardian) applies.

Member caring for another person

3.—A member (the carer)— 3.449

(a) who is regularly and substantially engaged in caring for another person if—

(i) the person being cared for is in receipt of attendance allowance [19, the care component of disability living allowance at the highest or middle rate prescribed in accordance with section 72(3) of the Benefits Act [20 , armed forces independence payment] or the daily living component of personal independence payment at the standard or enhanced rate in accordance with section 78(3) of the 2012 Act]; or

(ii) the person being cared for has claimed attendance allowance but only for the period up to the date of determination of that claim, or the period of 26 weeks from the date of that claim, whichever date is the earlier; or

(iii) the person being cared for has claimed attendance allowance in accordance with section 65(6)(a) of the Benefits Act (claims in advance of entitlement), an award has been made in respect of that claim under section 65(6)(b) of that Act and, where the period for which the award is payable has begun, that person is in receipt of the allowance;

(iv) the person being cared for has claimed entitlement to a disability living allowance [20 , armed forces independence payment] [19 or personal independence payment] but only for the period up to the date of determination of that claim, or the period of 26 weeks from the date of that claim, whichever date is the earlier; or

(v) the person being cared for has claimed entitlement to the care component of a disability living allowance in accordance with regulation 13A of the Claims and Payments Regulations (advance claims and awards), an award at the highest or middle rate has been made in respect of that claim and, where the period for which the award is payable has begun, that person is in receipt of the allowance; [19 [20 . . .]

(vi) the person being cared for has claimed entitlement to the daily living component of personal independence payment in accordance with regulation 33 of the Universal Credit etc. Claims and Payments Regulations (advance claim for and award of personal independence payment), an award of the standard or enhanced rate of the daily living component has been made in respect of that claim and, where the period for which the award is payable has begun, that person is in receipt of that payment;] [20 or

(vii) the person being cared for has claimed entitlement to armed forces independence payment and an award has been made in respect of that claim and, where the period for which the award is payable has begun, that person is in receipt of that payment;]

(b) who is engaged in caring for another person and who is both entitled to, and in receipt of, [4 a carer's allowance].

4. A member to whom paragraph 3 applied, but only for a period of 8 weeks from the date on which that paragraph ceased to apply to him.

5. A member who, had he previously made a claim for, and had been entitled to, a jobseeker's allowance, would have fulfilled the conditions of paragraph 3, but only for a period of 8 weeks from the date on which he ceased to fulfil those conditions.

[15 Member treated as capable of work, or member entitled to statutory sick pay]

3.450 **6.**—A member who—

(a) [14 . . .]

(b) [14. . .]

(c) is treated as capable of work by virtue of regulations made under section 171E(1) of [16 the Benefits Act] (disqualification etc.); or

(d) is entitled to statutory sick pay.

[8 Member has limited capability for work

3.451 **6A.**—A person who—

(a) has limited capability for work under section 8 of the Welfare Reform Act; or

(b) is treated as having limited capability for work under regulations made under paragraph 1 of Schedule 2 to that Act; or

(c) is treated as not having limited capability for work under regulations made under section 18(1) of that Act (disqualification).]

[17 **6B.**—(1) Subject to sub-paragraph (2), a person who provides-

(a) a statement which complies with the rules in Part 1 of Schedule 1 to the Social Security (Medical Evidence) Regulations 1976,

(b) a self-certificate for a period of limited capability for work which lasts less than 8 days or in respect of any of the first 7 days of limited capability for work, or

(c) where it would be unreasonable to require a person to provide a statement in accordance with paragraph (a), such other evidence as the Secretary of State considers to be sufficient to show that the person has limited capability for work.

(2) Sub-paragraph (1) applies to a person for the period covered by evidence falling within that sub-paragraph.

(3) For the purposes of this paragraph-

(a) "limited capability for work" has the meaning given by section 1(4) of the Welfare Reform Act 2007; and

(b) "self-certificate" means a declaration made by the person in writing on a form approved for the purpose by the Secretary of State that the person has been unfit for work on a date or for a period specified in the declaration and may include a statement that the person expects to continue to be unfit for work on days subsequent to the date on which it is made.]

Members in employment living in residential care homes, nursing homes or residential accommodation

7.—[11 . . .] 3.452

Disabled workers

8.—[11 . . .] 3.453

Disabled students

9.—[14 . . .] 3.454

Deaf students

10.—[14 . . .] 3.455

Blind members

11.—[14 . . .] 3.456

Pregnancy

12.—A member who is a woman and who is incapable of work [8 or who has limited capability for work] by reason of pregnancy. 3.457

[12Members who have attained the qualifying age for state pension credit

13.—A member who has attained the qualifying age for state pension credit.] 3.458

Refugees

14.—A member who is a refugee within the definition in Article 1 of the Convention relating to the Status of Refugees done at Geneva on 28th July 1951 as extended by Article 1(2) of the Protocol relating to the Status of Refugees done at New York on 31st January 1967 and who— 3.459

(a) is attending for more than 15 hours a week a course for the purpose of learning English so that he may obtain employment; and

(b) on the date on which that course commenced, had been in Great Britain for not more than 12 months,

but only for a period not exceeding nine months.

[7 Members required to attend a court or tribunal

15.—(1) A member who is required to attend a court or tribunal as a justice of the peace, a party to any proceedings, a witness or a juror. 3.460

(2) In this paragraph, "tribunal" means any tribunal listed in Schedule 1 to the Tribunals and Inquiries Act 1992.]

Young persons in training

16.—A member who [6 is not a qualifying young person or child within the meaning of section 142 of the Benefits Act (child and qualifying young person) and who] is engaged in training and for this purpose "training" means training for which persons aged under 18 are eligible and for which persons aged 18 to 24 may be eligible [3 secured by the [13 [18Secretary of State [21 . . .]] or by the [5[9 Welsh Ministers]]] and, in Scotland, directly or indirectly by a Local Enterprise Company pursuant to its arrangements with, as the case may be, [10 Skills Development Scotland,] Scottish Enterprise or Highlands and Islands Enterprise (whether that arrangement is known as an Operating Contract or by any other name). 3.461

Trade disputes

17.—A member who is or would be prevented from being entitled to a jobseeker's allowance by virtue of section 14 (trade disputes) but only where that section does not prevent the other member from being so entitled.] 3.462

AMENDMENTS

1. Jobseeker's Allowance (Joint Claims) Regulations 2000 (SI 2000/1978) reg.2(4) and Sch.1 (March 19, 2001).

2. Social Security Amendment (Joint Claims) Regulations 2001 (SI 2001/518) reg.2(6) (March 19, 2001).

3. Social Security (Miscellaneous Amendments) (No.2) Regulations 2001 (SI 2001/652) reg.4 (March 26, 2001).

4. Social Security (Miscellaneous Amendments) Regulations 2003 (SI 2003/511) reg.3(4) and (5) (April 1, 2003).

5. National Council for Education and Training for Wales (Transfer of Functions to the National Assembly for Wales and Abolition) Order 2005 (SI 2005/3238 (W.243)) art.9(2) and Sch.2 para.8(6) (April 1, 2006).

6. Social Security (Young Persons) Amendment Regulations 2006 (SI 2006/718) reg.3(9) (April 10, 2006).

7. Social Security (Income Support and Jobseeker's Allowance) Amendment Regulations 2006 (SI 2006/1402) reg.2(6) (May 30, 2006).

8. Employment and Support Allowance (Consequential Provisions) (No.2) Regulations 2008 (SI 2008/1554) reg.3(23) (October 27, 2008).

9. Social Security (Miscellaneous Amendments) (No.7) Regulations 2008 (SI 2008/3157) reg.3(9) (January 5, 2009).

10. Social Security (Miscellaneous Amendments) Regulations 2009 (SI 2009/583) reg.4(3) (April 6, 2009).

11. Social Security (Miscellaneous Amendments) (No.5) Regulations 2009 (SI 2009/3228) reg.4(1)(b)(ii) (January 25, 2010).

12. Social Security (Equalisation of State Pension Age) Regulations 2009 (SI 2009/1488) reg.12 (April 6, 2010).

13. Apprenticeships, Skills, Children and Learning Act 2009 (Consequential Amendments to Subordinate Legislation) (England) Order 2010 (SI 2010/1941) art.5(5) (September 1, 2010).

14. Social Security (Miscellaneous Amendments) (No.5) Regulations 2010 (SI 2010/2429) reg.4(2)(a) (November 1, 2010).

15. Social Security (Miscellaneous Amendments) (No.5) Regulations 2010 (SI 2010/2429) reg.4(2)(b) (November 1, 2010).

16. Social Security (Miscellaneous Amendments) (No.5) Regulations 2010 (SI 2010/2429) reg.4(2)(c) (November 1, 2010).

17. Social Security (Miscellaneous Amendments) (No.3) Regulations 2011 (SI 2011/2425) reg.10(11) (October 31, 2011).

18. Young People's Learning Agency Abolition (Consequential Amendments to Subordinate Legislation) (England) Order 2012 (SI 2012/956) art.5(8) (May 1, 2012).

19. Personal Independence Payment (Supplementary Provisions and Consequential Amendments) Regulations 2013 (SI 2013/388) reg.8 and Sch. Pt 2 para.16(6) (April 8, 2013).

20. Armed Forces and Reserve Forces Compensation Scheme (Consequential Provisions: Subordinate Legislation) Order 2013 (SI 2013/591) art.7 and Sch. para.10(6) (April 8, 2013).

21. Deregulation Act 2015 (Consequential Amendments) Order 2015 (SI 2015/971) art.2 and Sch.3 para.4(7) (May 26, 2015).

DEFINITIONS

"armed forces independence payment"—see reg.1(3).
"attendance allowance"—*ibid.*
"the Benefits Act"—see Jobseekers Act s.35(1).
"course of study"—see reg.1(3).
"date of claim"—*ibid.*
"disability living allowance"—*ibid.*
"full-time student"—*ibid.*
"joint-claim couple"—see JSA s.1(4).
"personal independence payment"—see reg.1(3).
"qualifying age for state pension credit"—*ibid.*

"remunerative work"—reg.51(1).
"single claimant"—see reg.1(3).
"student"—see reg.130.
"the Universal Credit etc. Claims and Payments Regulations"—see reg.1(3).
"young person"—see regs 1(3) and 76.

GENERAL NOTE

See the note to reg.3D. 3.463

Many of the categories are similar to those in Sch.1B to the Income Support Regulations (people eligible for income support). See the notes to that Schedule.

In order to mirror the changes to Sch.1B to the Income Support Regulations made as a result of the introduction of ESA, paras 6(a) and (b), 9, 10 and 11 were revoked with effect from November 1, 2010. This will not, however, apply to joint-claim claimants who immediately before November 1, 2010 were entitled to JSA and to whom one of those provisions applied (reg.4(3) of the Social Security (Miscellaneous Amendments) (No.5) Regulations 2010 (SI 2010/2429)). This savings provision ceases to apply when the JSA award to which the couple were entitled before November 1, 2010 ends (reg.4(4) of the 2010 Regulations).

The new para.6B inserted on October 31, 2011 covers a member of a JSA joint-claim couple who provides evidence of his limited capability for work, without the need for that member to make a claim for ESA. Paragraph 6B will apply for the period covered by the evidence (see sub-para.(2)). Such evidence can take the form of a self-certificate for up to seven days, a medical certificate, or, where it would be unreasonable to require the person to provide the latter, such other evidence as the Secretary of State considers sufficient.

SCHEDULE 1 — **Regulations 83 and 84(1)**

APPLICABLE AMOUNTS

[9 Part I

Personal Allowances

1.—The weekly amounts specified in column (2) below in respect of each person or couple specified in column (1) shall be the weekly amounts specified for the purposes of regulations 83 [28 84(1), 86A and 86B] (applicable amounts and polygamous marriages). 3.464

(1) *Person or Couple*	*(2)* *Amount*
(1) Single claimant aged—	
(a) except where head (b) or (c) of this sub-paragraph applies, less than 18;	1. (a) [49£57.90];
(b) less than 18 who falls within paragraph (2) of regulation 57 and who—	(b) [49£57.90];
(i) is a person to whom regulation 59, 60 or 61 applies [1. . .]; or	
(ii) is the subject of a direction under section 16;	
(c) less than 18 who satisfies the condition in [33 paragraph 13(1)(a)] of Part 3;	(c) [49£57.90];
(d) not less than 18 but less than 25;	(d) [49£57.90];
(e) not less than 25.	(e) [49£73.10].
(2) Lone parent aged—	
(a) except where head (b) or (c) of this sub-paragraph applies, less than 18;	2. (a) [49£57.90];
(b) less than 18 who falls within paragraph (2) of regulation 57 and who—	(b) [49£57.90];

(1)	*(2)*
Person or Couple	*Amount*
(i) is a person to whom regulation 59, 60 or 61 applies [1. . .]; or (ii) is the subject of a direction under section 16;	
(c) less than 18 who satisfies the condition in [33 paragraph 13(1)(a)] [2of Part 3];	(c) [49£57.90];
(d) not less than 18.	(d) [49£73.10].
(3) Couple—	
(a) where both members are aged less than 18 and— (i) at least one of them is treated as responsible for a child; or (ii) had they not been members of a couple, each would have been a person to whom regulation 59, 60 or 61 (circumstances in which a person aged 16 or 17 is eligible for a jobseeker's allowance) applied or (iii) had they not been members of a couple, the claimant would have been a person to whom regulation 59, 60 or 61 (circumstances in which a person aged 16 or 17 is eligible for a jobseeker's allowance) applied and his partner satisfies the requirements for entitlement to income support [36 or an income-related employment and support allowance] other than the requirement to make a claim for it; or [1(iv) they are married [31 or civil partners]and one member a of the couple is person to whom regulation 59, 60 or 61 applies and the other member is registered in accordance with regulation 62; or (iva) they are married [31 or civil partners] and each member of the couple is a person to whom regulation 59, 60 or 61 applies; or] (v) there is a direction under section 16 (jobseeker's allowance in cases of severe hardship) in respect of each member; or (vi) there is a direction under section 16 in respect of one of them and the other is a person to whom regulation 59, 60 or 61 applies [1. . .], or (vii) there is a direction under section 16 in respect of one of them and the other satisfies requirements for entitlement to income support [36 or an income-related employment and support allowance] other than the requirement to make a claim for it;	3. (a) [49£87.50];
(b) where both members are aged less than 18 and sub-paragraph (3)(a) does not apply but one member of the couple falls within paragraph (2) of regulation 57 and either— (i) is a person to whom regulation 59, 60 or 61 applies [1. . .]; or (ii) is the subject of a direction under section 16 of the Act;	(b) [49£57.90];
(c) where both members are aged less than 18 and neither head (a) nor (b) of sub-paragraph (3) applies but one member of the couple— (i) is a person to whom regulation 59, 60 or 61 applies [1. . .]; or (ii) is the subject of a direction under section 16;	(c) [49£57.90];
(d) where both members are aged less than 18 and none of heads (a), (b) or (c) of sub-paragraph (3) apply but one member of the couple is a person who satisfies the requirements of [33 paragraph 13(1)(a)];	(d) [49£57.90];
[35 (e) where— (i) both members are aged not less than 18; or (ii) one member is aged not less than 18 and the	(e) [49£114.85];

(1)	(2)
Person or Couple	*Amount*
other member is a person who is— (aa)under 18, and (bb)treated as responsible for a child;]	
(f) where [[35] paragraph (e) does not apply and] one member is aged not less than 18 and the other member is a person under 18 who— (i) is a person to whom regulation 59, 60 or 61 applies [1. . .]; or (ii) is the subject of a direction under section 16; [[38] or (iii) satisfies requirements for entitlement to income support or who would do so if he were not a member of a couple, other than the requirement to make a claim for it; or (iv) satisfies requirements for entitlement to an income-related employment and support allowance other than the requirement to make a claim for it;]	(f) [[49]£114.85];
(g) where one member is aged not less than 18 but less than 25 and the other member is a person under 18— (i) to whom none of the regulations 59 to 61applies; or (ii) who is not the subject of a direction under section 16; and (iii) does not satisfy requirements for entitlement to income support [[36] or an income-related employment and support allowance] disregarding the requirement to make a claim for it;	(g) [[49]£57.90];
(h) where one member is aged not less than 25 and the other member is a person under 18— (i) to whom none of the regulations 59 to 61 applies; or (ii) is not the subject of a direction under section 16; and (iii) does not satisfy requirements for entitlement to income support [[36] or an income-related employment and support allowance] disregarding the requirement to make a claim for it.	(h) [[49]£73.10].

2.—[[30] . . .]
3.—[[29] . . .]

Part II

Family Premium

4.—[[30] . . .] 3.465

Part III

Premiums

5.—Except as provided in paragraph 6, the weekly premiums specified in Part IV of this Schedule shall for the purposes of regulations 83(e) and 84(1)(f), be applicable to a claimant who satisfies the condition specified in [[4 15] paragraphs 9A] to 17 in respect of that premium. 3.466

6.—Subject to paragraph 7, where a claimant satisfies the conditions in respect of more than one premium in this Part of this Schedule, only one premium shall be applicable to him and, if they are different amounts, the higher or highest amount shall apply.

[[16] **7.**—(1) Subject to sub-paragraph (2), the following premiums, namely—

(a) a severe disability premium to which paragraph 15 applies;
(b) an enhanced disability premium to which paragraph 15A applies;
(c) [[30] . . .]; and
(d) a carer premium in which paragraph 17 applies,
may be applicable in addition to any other premium which may apply under this Part of this Schedule.

(2) An enhanced disability premium in respect of a person shall not be applicable in addition to—

(a) a pensioner premium under paragraph 10 or 11; or
(b) a higher pensioner premium under paragraph 12.]

8.—(1) Subject to sub-paragraph (2) for the purposes of this Part of this Schedule, once a premium is applicable to a claimant under this Part, a person shall be treated as being in receipt of any benefit—

(a) in the case of a benefit to which the Social Security (Overlapping Benefits) Regulations 1979 applies, for any period during which, apart from the provisions of those Regulations, he would be in receipt of that benefit; and

[3(b) for any period spent by a claimant in undertaking a course of training or instruction provided or approved by the Secretary of State [35 . . .] under section 2 of the Employment and Training Act 1973, or by [37 Skills Development Scotland,] Scottish Enterprise or Highlands and Islands Enterprise under section 2 of the Enterprise and New Towns (Scotland) Act 1990 or for any period during which he is in receipt of a training allowance.]

(2) For the purposes of the carer premium under paragraph 17, a person shall be treated as being in receipt of [24 carer's allowance] by virtue of sub-paragraph (1)(a) only if and for so long as the person in respect of whose care the allowance has been claimed remains in receipt of attendance allowance, [46 the care component of disability living allowance at the highest or middle rate prescribed in accordance with section 72(3) of the Benefits Act [47 , armed forces independence payment] or the daily living component of personal independence payment at the standard or enhanced rate prescribed in accordance with section 78(3) of the 2012 Act].

Lone parent premium

3.467 **9.**—[4. . .]

[15 Bereavement Premium

3.468 **9A.**—[34 . . .]]

Pensioner premium for persons [40over the qualifying age for state pension credit]

3.469 **10.**—The condition is that the claimant—

(a) is a single claimant or lone parent who has attained [40 the qualifying age for state pension credit]; or
(b) has attained [40 the qualifying age for state pension credit] and has a partner; or
(c) has a partner and the partner has attained [40 the qualifying age for state pension credit] but not the age of 75.

Pensioner premium where claimant's partner has attained the age of 75

3.470 **11.**—The condition is that the claimant has a partner who has attained the age of 75 but not the age of 80.

Higher pensioner premium

3.471 **12.**—(1) [33 Subject to sub-paragraph (5), the] condition is that—

(a) the claimant is a single claimant or lone parent who has attained [40 the qualifying age for state pension credit] and either—
  (i) satisfies one of the additional conditions specified in paragraph 14(1)(a), (c), (e), (f) or (h); or
  (ii) was entitled to either income support or income-based jobseeker's allowance [12, or was treated as being entitled to either of those benefits and the disability premium was or, as the case may be, would have been,] applicable to him in respect of a benefit week within 8 weeks of [40 the date he attained the qualifying age for state pension credit] and he has, subject to sub-paragraph (2), remained continuously entitled to one of those benefits since attaining that age; or
(b) the claimant has a partner and—
  (i) the partner has attained the age of 80; or
  (ii) the partner has attained [40 the qualifying age for state pension credit] but not the age of 80, and the additional conditions specified in paragraph 14 are satisfied in respect of him; or
(c) the claimant—
  (i) has attained [40 the qualifying age for state pension credit];
  [3(ii) satisfies the requirements of either sub-head (i) or (ii) of paragraph 12(1)(a); and]
  (iii) has a partner.

(2) For the purposes of this paragraph and paragraph 14—

(a) once the higher pensioner premium is applicable to a claimant, if he then ceases, for a period of eight weeks or less, to be entitled to either income support or income-based jobseeker's allowance [12 or ceases to be treated as entitled to either of those benefits], he shall, on becoming re-entitled to either of those benefits, thereafter be treated as having been continuously entitled thereto;

(b) in so far as sub-paragraphs (1)(a)(ii) and (1)(c)(ii) are concerned, if a claimant ceases to be entitled to either income support or an income-based jobseeker's allowance [12 or ceases to be treated as entitled to either of those benefits] for a period not exceeding eight weeks which includes [40 the date he attained the qualifying age for state pension credit], he shall, on becoming re-entitled to either of those benefits, thereafter be treated as having been continuously entitled thereto.

[8(3) In this paragraph where a claimant's partner is a welfare to work beneficiary, sub-paragraphs (1)(a)(ii) and (2)(b) shall apply to him as if for the words "8 weeks" there were substituted the words "[32 104 weeks]".]

[12 (4) For the purposes of this paragraph, a claimant shall be treated as having been entitled to income support or to an income-based jobseeker's allowance throughout any period which comprises only days on which he was participating in an employment zone programme and was not entitled to—

(a) income support because, as a consequence of his participation in that programme, he was engaged in remunerative work or had income in excess of the claimant's applicable amount as prescribed in Part IV of the Income Support Regulations; or

(b) a jobseeker's allowance because, as a consequence of his participation in that programme, he was engaged in remunerative work or failed to satisfy the condition specified in section 2(1)(c) or in section 3(1)(a).]

[33 (5) The condition is not satisfied if—

(a) the claimant is a single claimant or a lone parent and (in either case) is a long-term patient;

(b) the claimant is a member of a couple or polygamous marriage and each member of the couple or polygamous marriage is a long-term patient; or

(c) the claimant is a member of a couple or a polygamous marriage and a member of that couple or polygamous marriage is—

(i) a long-term patient; and

(ii) the only member of the couple or polygamous marriage to whom sub-paragraph (1)(b) or (c) refers.]

Disability premium

13. [33 —(1) Subject to sub-paragraph (2), the] condition is that the claimant— **3.472**

(a) is a single claimant or lone parent who has not attained [40 the qualifying age for state pension credit] and satisfies any one of the additional conditions specified in paragraph 14(1)(a), (c), (e), (f) or (h); or

(b) has not attained [40 the qualifying age for state pension credit], has a partner and the claimant satisfies any one of the additional conditions specified in paragraph 14(1)(a), (c), (e), (f) or (h); or

(c) has a partner and the partner has not attained [40 the qualifying age for state pension credit] and also satisfies any one of the additional conditions specified in paragraph 14.

[33 (2) The condition is not satisfied if—

(a) the claimant is a single claimant or a lone parent and (in either case) is a long-term patient;

(b) the claimant is a member of a couple or polygamous marriage and each member of the couple or polygamous marriage is a long-term patient; or

(c) the claimant is a member of a couple or polygamous marriage and a member of that couple or polygamous marriage—

(i) is a long-term patient; and

(ii) is the only member of the couple or polygamous marriage to whom the condition in sub-paragraph (1)(b) or (c) refers.]

Additional conditions for higher pensioner and disability premium

14.—(1) The additional conditions specified in this paragraph are that— **3.473**

(a) the claimant or, as the case may be, his partner, is in receipt [25 the disability element or the severe disability element of working tax credit as specified in regulation 20(1)(b) and (f) of the Working Tax Credit (Entitlement and Maximum Rate) Regulations 2002] or mobility supplement;

(b) the claimant's partner is in receipt of severe disablement allowance;

(c) the claimant or, as the case may be, his partner, is in receipt of attendance allowance or disability living allowance or is a person whose disability living allowance is payable, in whole or in part, to another in accordance with regulation 44 of the Claims and Payments Regulations (payment of disability living allowance on behalf of third party);

[46 (ca) the claimant or, as the case may be, his partner, is in receipt of personal independence payment or is a person whose personal independence payment is payable, in whole or in part, to another in accordance with regulation 58(2) of the Universal Credit etc. Claims and Payments Regulations (payment to another person on the claimant's behalf);]

[47 (cb) the claimant or, as the case may be, the claimant's partner, is in receipt of armed forces independence payment or is a person whose armed forces independence payment is payable, in whole or in part, to another in accordance with article 24D of the Armed Forces and Reserve Forces (Compensation Scheme) Order 2011;]

(d) the claimant's partner is in receipt of long-term incapacity benefit or is a person to whom section 30B(4) of the Benefits Act (long term rate of incapacity benefit payable to those who are terminally ill) applies;

(e) the claimant or, as the case may be, his partner, has an invalid carriage or other vehicle provided to him by the Secretary of State under section 5(2)(a) of and Schedule 2 to the National Health Service Act 1977 or under section 46 of the National Health Service (Scotland) Act 1978 or provided by the Department of Health and Social Services for Northern Ireland under article 30(1) of the Health and Personal Social Services (Northern Ireland) Order 1972, or receives payments by way of grant from the Secretary of State under paragraph 2 of Schedule 2 to the Act of 1977 (additional provisions as to vehicles) or, in Scotland, under section 46 of the Act of 1978;

(f) the claimant or, as the case may be, his partner, is a person who is entitled to the mobility component of disability living allowance but to whom the component is not payable in accordance with regulation 42 of the Claims and Payments Regulations (cases where disability living allowance not payable);

[46 (fa) the claimant or, as the case may be, his partner, is a person who is entitled to the mobility component of personal independence payment but to whom the component is not payable in accordance with regulation 61 of the Universal Credit etc. Claims and Payments Regulations (cases where mobility component of personal independence payment not payable);]

(g) the claimant's partner was either—

(i) in receipt of long term incapacity benefit under section 30A(5) of the Benefits Act immediately before attaining pensionable age and he is still alive;

(ii) entitled to attendance allowance or disability living allowance but payment of that benefit was suspended in accordance with regulations under section 113(2) of the Benefits Act or otherwise abated as a consequence of [2the partner] becoming a patient within the meaning of regulation 85(4) (special cases), [46 ; or

(iii) entitled to personal independence payment but no amount is payable in accordance with regulations made under section 86(1) (hospital in-patients) of the 2012 Act]

and in either case the higher pensioner premium or disability premium had been applicable to the claimant or his partner;

[48 (h) the claimant or, as the case may be, his partner, is certified as severely sight impaired or blind by a consultant ophthalmologist.]

[48 (2) For the purposes of sub-paragraph (1)(h), a person who has ceased to be certified as severely sight impaired or blind on regaining his eyesight shall nevertheless be treated as severely sight impaired or blind, as the case may be, and as satisfying the additional condition set out in that sub-paragraph for a period of 28 weeks following the date on which he ceased to be so certified.]

Severe disability premium

3.474 **15.**—(1) In the case of a single claimant, a lone parent or a claimant who is treated as having no partner in consequence of sub-paragraph (3), the condition is that—

(a) he is in receipt of attendance allowance [46 , the care component of disability living allowance at the highest or middle rate prescribed in accordance with section 72(3) of the Benefits Act [47 , armed forces independence payment] or the daily living component of personal independence payment at the standard or enhanced rate in accordance with section 78(3) of the 2012 Act]; and

(b) subject to sub-paragraph (4), there are no non-dependants aged 18 or over normally residing with him or with whom he is normally residing; and

[11(c) no person is entitled to, and in receipt of, [24 a carer's allowance] under section 70 of the Benefits Act [52 or has an award of universal credit which includes the carer element] in respect of caring for him;]

(2) Where the claimant has a partner, the condition is that—

(a) the claimant is in receipt of attendance allowance [46 , the care component of disability living allowance at the highest or middle rate prescribed in accordance with section 72(3) of the Benefits Act [47 , armed forces independence payment] or the daily living component of personal independence payment at the standard or enhanced rate in accordance with section 78(3) of the 2012 Act]; and

(b) the partner is also in receipt of a qualifying benefit, or if he is a member of a polygamous marriage, all the partners of that marriage are in receipt of a qualifying benefit; and

(c) subject to sub-paragraph (4), there is no non-dependant aged 18 or over normally residing with him or with whom he is normally residing; and

(d) either—

(i) [11no person is entitled to, and in receipt of, [24 a carer's allowance] under section 70 of the Benefits Act [52 or has an award of universal credit which includes the carer element] in respect of] caring for either member of the couple or all the members of the polygamous marriage; or

(ii) a person is engaged in caring for one member (but not both members) of the couple, or one or more but not all members of the polygamous marriage, and in consequence is [11entitled to] [24 a carer's allowance] under section 70 of the Benefits Act [52 or has an award of universal credit which includes the carer element].

(3) Where the claimant has a partner who does not satisfy the condition in subparagraph (2)(b), and that partner is [48 severely sight impaired or blind or treated as severely sight impaired or blind] within the meaning of paragraph 14(1)(h) and (2), that partner shall be treated for the purposes of sub-paragraph (2) as if he were not a partner of the claimant.

(4) The following persons shall not be regarded as a non-dependant for the purposes of sub-paragraphs (1)(b) and (2)(c)—

(a) a person in receipt of attendance allowance [46 , the care component of disability living allowance at the highest or middle rate prescribed in accordance with section 72(3) of the Benefits Act [47 , armed forces independence payment] or the daily living component of personal independence payment at the standard or enhanced rate in accordance with section 78(3) of the 2012 Act];

(b) subject to sub-paragraph (6), a person who joins the claimant's household for the first time in order to care for the claimant or his partner and immediately before so joining the claimant or his partner satisfied the condition in sub-paragraph (1) or, as the case may be, (2);

(c) a person who is [48 severely sight impaired or blind or treated as severely sight impaired or blind] within the meaning of paragraph 14(1)(h) and (2).

(5) For the purposes of sub-paragraph (2), a person shall be treated [11 . . .]

(a) [11as being in receipt of] attendance allowance, or the care component of disability living allowance at the highest or middle rate prescribed in accordance with section 72(3) of the Benefits Act if he would, but for his being a patient for a period exceeding 28 days, be so in receipt;

[46 (aa) as being in receipt of the daily living component of personal independence payment at the standard or enhanced rate in accordance with section 78 of the 2012 Act if he would, but for regulations made under section 86(1) (hospital in-patients) of the 2012 Act, be so in receipt;]

[11(b) as being entitled to and in receipt of [24 a carer's allowance] [52 or having an award of universal credit which includes the carer element] if he would, but for the person for whom he was caring being a patient in hospital for a period exceeding 28 days, be so entitled and in receipt [52 of carer's allowance or have such an award of universal credit].]

(6) Sub-paragraph (4)(b) shall apply only for the first 12 weeks following the date on which the person to whom that provision applies first joins the claimant's household.

(7) For the purposes of sub-paragraph (1)(c) and (2)(d), no account shall be taken of an award of [24 carer's allowance] [52 or universal credit which includes the carer element] to the extent that payment of such an award is backdated for a period before [34 the date on which the award is first paid].

(8) A person shall be treated as satisfying this condition if he would have satisfied the condition specified for a severe disability premium in income support in paragraph 13 of Schedule

2 to the Income Support Regulations by virtue only of regulations 4 to 6 of the Income Support (General) Amendment (No.6) Regulations 1991 (savings provisions in relation to severe disability premium) and for the purposes of determining whether in the particular case regulation 4 of those Regulations had ceased to apply in accordance with regulation 5(2)(a) of those Regulations, a person who is entitled to an income-based jobseeker's allowance shall be treated as entitled to income support.

[20 (9) In sub-paragraphs (1)(c) and (2)(d), references to a person being in receipt of [24 a carer's allowance] [52 or as having an award of universal credit which includes the carer element] shall include references to a person who would have been in receipt of that allowance [52 or had such an award] but for the application of a restriction under section [39 6B or] 7 of the Social Security Fraud Act 2001 (loss of benefit provisions).]

[52 (10) For the purposes of this paragraph, a person has an award of universal credit which includes the carer element if the person has an award of universal credit which includes an amount which is the carer element under regulation 29 of the Universal Credit Regulations 2013.]

[16 Enhanced disability premium

3.475 **15A.**—[46 (1) Subject to sub-paragraph (2), the condition is that—

(a) the claimant; or

(b) the claimant's partner (if any),

is a person who has not attained the qualifying age for state pension credit and is a person to whom sub-paragraph (1ZA) applies.

(1ZA) This sub-paragraph applies to the person mentioned in sub-paragraph (1) where—

(a) the care component of disability living allowance is, or would, but for a suspension of benefit in accordance with regulations under section 113(2) of the Benefits Act or but for an abatement as a consequence of hospitalisation, be payable to that person at the highest rate prescribed under section 72(3) of the Benefits Act; or

(b) the daily living component of personal independence payment is, or would, but for a suspension of benefits in accordance with regulations under section 86(1) (hospital in-patients) of the 2012 Act, be payable to that person at the enhanced rate in accordance with section 78(2) of the 2012 Act] [47 ; or

(c) armed forces independence payment is payable to that person.]

[42 (1A) Where the condition in sub-paragraph (1) ceases to be satisfied because of the death of a child or young person, the condition is that the claimant is entitled to child benefit in respect of that person under section 145A of the Benefits Act (entitlement after death of child or qualifying young person).]

[33 (2) The condition is not satisfied where the person to whom sub-paragraph (1) refers is—

(a) a child or young person—

(i) whose capital if calculated in accordance with Part 8 of these Regulations in like manner as for the claimant, except as provided in regulation 106(1), would exceed £3,000; or

(ii) who is a long-term patient;

(b) a single claimant or a lone parent and (in either case) is a long-term patient;

(c) a member of a couple or polygamous marriage and each member of the couple or polygamous marriage is a long-term patient; or

(d) a member of a couple or polygamous marriage who is—

(i) a long-term patient; and

(ii) the only member of the couple or polygamous marriage to whom sub-paragraph (1) refers.]]

Disabled child premium

3.476 **16.**—[30 . . . 33]

Carer premium

3.477 **17.**—(1) Subject to sub-paragraphs (3) and (4), the condition is that the claimant or his partner is, or both of them are, [11entitled to] [24 a carer's allowance] under section 70 of the Benefits Act.

(2) [28 . . .]

[23 (3) Where a carer premium is awarded but—

(a) the person in respect of whose care the [24 carer's allowance] has been awarded dies; or

(b) in any other case the person in respect of whom a carer premium has been awarded ceases to be entitled [28 . . .] to [24 a carer's allowance],

the condition for the award of the premium shall be treated as satisfied for a period of eight weeks from the relevant date specified in sub-paragraph (3A) below.

(3A) The relevant date for the purposes of sub-paragraph (3) above shall be—
(a) [28 where sub-paragraph (3)(a) applies,] the Sunday following the death of the person in respect of whose care [24 a carer's allowance] has been awarded or the date of death if the death occurred on a Sunday;
(b) [28 . . .]
(c) in any other case, the date of which the person who has been entitled to [24 a carer's allowance] ceases to be entitled to that allowance.]

(4) Where a person who has been entitled to an invalid care allowance ceases to be entitled to that allowance and makes a claim for a jobseeker's allowance, the condition for the award of the carer premium shall be treated as satisfied for a period of eight weeks from the date on which—
[23(a) the person in respect of whose care the [24 carer's allowance] has been awarded dies;
(b) [28 . . .]
[28 (c) in any other case, the person who has been entitled to a carer's allowance ceased to be entitled to that allowance.]

Persons in receipt of concessionary payments

18.—For the purpose of determining whether a premium is applicable to a person under paragraphs 14 to 17, any concessionary payment made to compensate that person for the non-payment of any benefit mentioned in those paragraphs shall be treated as if it were a payment of that benefit. **3.478**

Person in receipt of benefit

19.—For the purposes of this Part of this Schedule, a person shall be regarded as being in receipt of any benefit if, and only if, it is paid in respect of him and shall be so regarded only for any period in respect of which that benefit is paid. **3.479**

PART IV

Weekly Amounts of Premiums Specified in Part III

3.480

Premium	*Amount*
20.—(1) [4. . .]	(1) [4 . . .]
(1A) [34 . . .]	(1A) [34 . . .];
(2) Pensioner premium for persons [40 who have attained the qualifying age for state pension credit]—	
(a) where the claimant satisfies the condition in paragraph 10(a);	(2) (a) [53£82.50];
(b) where the claimant satisfies the condition in paragraph 10(b).	(b) [53£122.70];
(c) where the claimant satisfies the condition in paragraph 10(c).	(c) [53£122.70];
(3) Pensioner premium for claimants whose partner has attained the age of 75 where the claimant satisfies the condition in paragraph 11;	(3) [53£122.70].
(4) Higher Pensioner Premium—	
(a) where the claimant satisfies the condition in paragraph 12(1)(a);	(4) (a) [53£82.50];
(b) where the claimant satisfies the condition in paragraph 12(1)(b) or (c).	(b) [53£122.70].
(5) Disability Premium—	
(a) where the claimant satisfies the condition in [33 paragraph 13(1)(a)];	(5) (a) [50£32.25];
(b) where the claimant satisfies the condition in [33 paragraph 13(1)(b) or (c)].	(b) [50£45.95].
(6) Severe Disability Premium—	
(a) where the claimant satisfies the condition in paragraph 15(1);	(6) (a) [50£61.85];
(b) where the claimant satisfies the condition in paragraph 15(2)—	(b)
(i) if there is someone in receipt of [24 a carer's allowance] or [2if any partner of the claimant] satisfies that condition by virtue of paragraph 15(5);	(i) [50£61.85];

Premium	*Amount*
(ii) if no-one is in receipt of such an allowance.	(ii) [50£123.70].
(7) [30 . . .]	(7) [30 . . .]
(8) Carer Premium.	(8) [50£34.60] in respect of each person who satisfied the condition specified in paragraph 17.]
[16 (9) Enhanced disability premium where the conditions in paragraph 15A are satisfied.]	[16 (9) (a) [30 . . .] (b) [50£15.75] in respect of each person who is neither— (i) a child or young person; nor (ii) a member of a couple or a polygamous marriage, respect of whom the in conditions specified in paragraph 15A are satisfied; (c) [50£22.60] where the claimant is a member of a couple or a polygamous marriage and the conditions specified in paragraph 15A are satisfied in respect of a member of that couple or polygamous marriage.]

[14 PART IVA

Premiums for Joint-claim Couples

3.481 **20A.**—Except as provided in paragraph 20B, the weekly premium specified in Part IVB of this Schedule shall, for the purposes of regulations 86A(c) and 86B(d), be applicable to a joint-claim couple where either or both members of a joint-claim couple satisfy the condition specified in paragraphs 20E to 20J in respect of that premium.

20B.—Subject to paragraph 20C, where a member of a joint-claim couple satisfies the conditions in respect of more than one premium in this Part of this Schedule, only one premium shall be applicable to the joint-claim couple in respect of that member and, if they are different amounts, the higher or highest amount shall apply.

[16 **20C.**—(1) Subject to sub-paragraph (2), the following premiums, namely—

(a) a severe disability premium to which paragraph 20I applies;
(b) an enhanced disability premium to which paragraph 20IA applies; and
(c) a carer premium to which paragraph 20J applies,

may be applicable in addition to any other premium which may apply under this Part of this Schedule.

(2) An enhanced disability premium in respect of a person shall not be applicable in addition to—

(a) a pensioner premium under paragraph 20E; or
(b) a higher pensioner premium under paragraph 20F.]

20D.—(1) Subject to sub-paragraph (2) for the purposes of this Part of this Schedule, once a premium is applicable to a joint-claim couple under this Part, a person shall be treated as being in receipt of any benefit—

(a) in the case of a benefit to which the Social Security (Overlapping Benefits) Regulations 1979 applies, for any period during which, apart from the provisions of those Regulations, he would be in receipt of that benefit; and
(b) for any period spent by a person in undertaking a course of training or instruction provided or approved by the Secretary of State under section 2 of the Employment and Training Act 1973, or by [37 Skills Development Scotland,] Scottish Enterprise or Highlands and Islands Enterprise under section 2 of the Enterprise and New Towns (Scotland) Act 1990, or for any period during which he is in receipt of a training allowance.

(2) For the purposes of the carer premium under paragraph 20J, a person shall be treated as being in receipt of [24 carer's allowance] by virtue of sub-paragraph (1)(a) only if and for so long as the person in respect of whose care the allowance has been claimed remains in receipt of attendance allowance, [46 the care component of disability living allowance at the highest or middle rate prescribed in accordance with section 72(3) of the Benefits Act or the daily living component of personal independence payment at the standard or enhanced rate in accordance with section 78(3) of the 2012 Act [47 or armed forces independence payment]].

Pensioner premium where one member of a joint-claim couple has attained [40 the qualifying age for state pension credit]

20E.—The condition is that one member of a joint-claim couple has attained [40 the qualifying age for state pension credit]but not the age of 75. **3.482**

Higher pensioner premium

20F.—(1) [33 Subject to sub-paragraph (5), the] condition is that one member of a joint-claim couple— **3.483**

(a) has attained [40 the qualifying age for state pension credit] but not the age of 80, and either the additional conditions specified in paragraph 20H are satisfied in respect of him; or

(b) has attained [40 the qualifying age for state pension credit] and—

(i) was entitled to or was treated as entitled to either income support or an income-based jobseeker's allowance and the disability premium was or, as the case may be, would have been applicable to him in respect of a benefit week within 8 weeks of [40 the date he attained the qualifying age for state pension credit] and he has, subject to sub-paragraph (2), remained continuously entitled to one of those benefits since attaining that age; or

(ii) was a member of a joint-claim couple who had been entitled to, or who had been treated as entitled to, a joint-claim jobseeker's allowance and the disability premium was or, as the case may be, would have been applicable to that couple in respect of a benefit week within 8 weeks of [40 the date either member of that couple attained the qualifying age for state pension credit] and the couple have, subject to that sub-paragraph (2), remained continuously entitled to a joint-claim jobseeker's allowance since that member attained that age.

(2) For the purpose of this paragraph and paragraph 20H—

(a) once the higher pensioner premium is applicable to a joint-claim couple, if that member then ceases, for a period of 8 weeks or less, to be entitled or treated as entitled to either income support or income-based jobseeker's allowance or that couple cease to be entitled to or treated as entitled to a joint-claim jobseeker's allowance, he shall or, as the case may be, that couple shall, on becoming re-entitled to any of those benefits, thereafter be treated as having been continuously entitled thereto;

(b) in so far as sub-paragraph (1)(b)(i) or (ii) is concerned, if a member of a joint-claim couple ceases to be entitled or treated as entitled to either income support or an income-based jobseeker's allowance or that couple cease to be entitled to or treated as entitled to a joint-claim jobseeker's allowance for a period not exceeding 8 weeks which includes [40 the date either member of that couple attained the qualifying age for state pension credit], he shall or, as the case may be, the couple shall, on becoming re-entitled to either of those benefits, thereafter be treated as having been continuously entitled thereto.

(3) In this paragraph, where a member of a joint-claim couple is a welfare to work beneficiary, sub-paragraphs (1)(b)(i) and (2)(b) shall apply to him as if for the words "8 weeks" there were substituted the words "[32104 weeks]".

(4) For the purposes of this paragraph, a member of a joint-claim couple shall be treated as having been entitled to income support or to an income-based jobseeker's allowance or the couple of which he is a member shall be treated as having been entitled to a joint-claim jobseeker's allowance throughout any period which comprises only days on which a member was participating in an employment zone scheme and was not entitled to—

(a) income support because, as a consequence of his participation in that scheme, he was engaged in remunerative work or had income in excess of the claimant's applicable amount as prescribed in Part IV of the Income Support Regulations; or

(b) a jobseeker's allowance because, as a consequence of his participation in that scheme, he was engaged in remunerative work or failed to satisfy the condition specified in section 2(1)(c) or the couple of which he was a member failed to satisfy the condition in section 3A(1)(a).

[33 (5) The condition is not satisfied if the member of the joint-claim couple to whom sub-paragraph (1) refers is a long-term patient.]

[33 Disability Premium

3.484 **20G.**—(1) Subject to sub-paragraph (2), the condition is that a member of a joint-claim couple has not attained [40 the qualifying age for state pension credit] and satisfies any one of the additional conditions specified in paragraph 20H.

(2) The condition is not satisfied if—

(a) paragraph (1) only refers to one member of a joint-claim couple and that member is a long-term patient; or

b) paragraph (1) refers to both members of a joint-claim couple and both members of the couple are long-term patients]

Additional conditions for higher pensioner and disability premium

3.485 **20H.**—(1) The additional conditions specified in this paragraph are that a member of a joint-claim couple—

(a) is in receipt of [26 the disability element or the severe disability element of working tax credit as specified in regulation 20(1)(b) and (f) of the Working Tax Credit (Entitlement and Maximum Rate) Regulations 2002] or mobility supplement;

(b) is in receipt of severe disablement allowance;

(c) is in receipt of attendance allowance or disability living allowance or is a person whose disability living allowance is payable, in whole or in part, to another in accordance with regulation 44 of the Claims and Payments Regulations (payment of disability living allowance on behalf of third party);

[46 (ca) is in receipt of personal independence payment or is a person whose personal independence payment is payable, in whole or in part, to another in accordance with regulation 58(2) of the Universal Credit etc. Claims and Payments Regulations (payment to another person on the claimant's behalf);]

[47 (cb) is in receipt of armed forces independence payment or is a person whose armed forces independence payment is payable, in whole or in part, to another in accordance with article 24D of the Armed Forces and Reserve Forces (Compensation Scheme) Order 2011;]

(d) is in receipt of long-term incapacity benefit or is a person to whom section 30B(4) of the Benefits Act (long-term rate of incapacity benefit payable to those who are terminally ill) applies;

(e) has been entitled to statutory sick pay, has been incapable of work or has been treated as incapable of work for a continuous period of not less than—

(i) 196 days in the case of a member of a joint-claim couple who is terminally ill within the meaning of section 30B(4) of the Benefits Act; or

(ii) 364 days in any other case,

and for these purposes, any two or more periods of entitlement or incapacity separated by a break of not more than 56 days shall be treated as one continuous period;

[36 (ee) has had limited capability for work or has been treated as having limited capability for work for a continuous period of not less than—

(i) 196 days in the case of a member of a joint-claim couple who is terminally ill within the meaning of regulation 2(1) of the Employment and Support Allowance Regulations; or

(ii) 364 days in any other case,

and for these purposes any two or more periods of limited capability for work separated by a break of not more than 12 weeks is to be treated as one continuous period;]

(f) has an invalid carriage or other vehicle provided to him by the Secretary of State under section 5(2)(a) of, and Schedule 2 to, the National Health Service Act 1977 or under section 46 of the National Health Service (Scotland) Act 1978 or provided by the Department of Health and Social Services for Northern Ireland under article 30(1) of the Health and Personal Social Services (Northern Ireland) Order 1972, or receives payments by way of grant from the Secretary of State under paragraph 2 of Schedule 2 to the Act of 1977 (additional provisions as to vehicles) or, in Scotland, under section 46 of the Act of 1978;

(g) is a person who is entitled to the mobility component of disability living allowance but to whom the component is not payable in accordance with regulation 42 of the Claims and Payments Regulations (cases where disability living allowance not payable);

[46 (ga) is a person who is entitled to the mobility component of personal independence payment but to whom the component is not payable in accordance with regulation 61 of the Universal Credit etc. Claims and Payments Regulations (cases where mobility component of personal independence payment not payable);]

(h) was either—

(i) in receipt of long-term incapacity benefit under section 30A(5) of the Benefits Act immediately before attaining pensionable age and he is still alive; or

(ii) entitled to attendance allowance or disability living allowance but payment of that benefit was suspended in accordance with regulations under section 113(2) of the Benefits Act or otherwise abated as a consequence of either member of the joint-claim couple becoming a patient within the meaning of regulation 85(4) (special cases), [46 or

(iii) entitled to personal independence payment but no amount is payable in accordance with regulations under section 86(1) (hospital in-patients) of the 2012 Act,]

and in either case, the higher pensioner premium or disability premium had been applicable to the joint-claim couple; or

[48 (l) is certified as severely sight impaired or blind by a consultant ophthalmologist.]

(2) [41 . . . [32 . . .]]

[48 (3) For the purposes of sub-paragraph (1)(i), a person who has ceased to be certified as severely sight impaired or blind on regaining his eyesight shall nevertheless be treated as severely sight impaired or blind, as the case may be, and as satisfying the additional condition set out in that sub-paragraph for a period of 28 weeks following the date on which he ceased to be so certified.]

Severe disability premium

20I.—(1) The condition is that— 3.486

(a) a member of a joint-claim couple is in receipt of attendance allowance [46 , the care component of disability living allowance at the highest or middle rate prescribed in accordance with section 72(3) of the Benefits Act [47 , armed forces independence payment] or the daily living component of personal independence payment at the standard or enhanced rate in accordance with section 78(3) of the 2012 Act] ; and

(b) the other member is also in receipt of such an allowance, or if he is a member of a polygamous marriage, all the partners of that marriage are in receipt of a qualifying benefit; and

(c) subject to sub-paragraph (3), there is no non-dependant aged 18 or over normally residing with the joint-claim couple or with whom they are normally residing; and

(d) either—

(i) no person is entitled to, and in receipt of, [24 a carer's allowance] under section 70 of the Benefits Act [52 or has an award of universal credit which includes the carer element] in respect of caring for either member or the couple or all the members of the polygamous marriage; or

(ii) a person is engaged in caring for one member (but not both members) of the couple, or one or more but not all members of the polygamous marriage, and in consequence is entitled to [24 a carer's allowance] under section 70 of the Benefits Act [52 or has an award of universal credit which includes the carer element].

(2) Where the other member does not satisfy the condition in sub-paragraph (1)(b), and that member is [48 severely sight impaired or blind or treated as severely sight impaired or blind] within the meaning of paragraph 20H(1)(i) and (2), that member shall be treated for the purposes of sub-paragraph (1) as if he were not a member of the couple.

(3) The following persons shall not be regarded as non-dependant for the purposes of sub-paragraph (1)(c)—

(a) a person in receipt of attendance allowance [46 , the care component of disability living allowance at the highest or middle rate prescribed in accordance with section 72(3) of the Benefits Act [47 , armed forces independence payment] or the daily living component of personal independence payment at the standard or enhanced rate in accordance with section 78(3) of the 2012 Act];

(b) subject to sub-paragraph (5), a person who joins the joint-claim couple's household for the first time in order to care for a member of a joint claim couple and immediately before so joining, that member satisfied the condition in sub-paragraph (1);

(c) a person who is [48 severely sight impaired or blind or treated as severely sight impaired or blind] within the meaning of paragraph 20H(1)(i) and (2).

(4) For the purposes of sub-paragraph (1), a member of a joint-claim couple shall be treated—

(a) as being in receipt of attendance allowance, or the care component of disability living allowance at the highest or middle rate prescribed in accordance with section 72(3) of the Benefits Act if he would, but for his being a patient for a period exceeding 28 days, be so in receipt;

(b) as being entitled to and in receipt of [24 a carer's allowance] [52 or having an award of universal credit which includes the carer element] if he would, but for the person for whom he was caring being a patient in hospital for a period exceeding 28 days, be so entitled and in receipt [52 of carer's allowance or have such an award of universal credit].

[46 (c) as being in receipt of the daily living component of personal independence payment at the standard or enhanced rate in accordance with section 78 of the 2012 Act if he would, but for regulations made under section 86(1) (hospital in-patients) of the 2012 Act, be so in receipt.]

(5) Sub-paragraph (3)(b) shall apply only for the first 12 weeks following the date on which the person to whom that provision applies first joins the joint-claim couple's household.

(6) For the purposes of sub-paragraph (1)(d), no account shall be taken of an award of [24 carer's allowance] [52 or universal credit which includes the carer element] to the extent that payment of such an award is back-dated for a period before [34 the date on which the award is first paid].

[20 (7) In sub-paragraph (1)(d), the reference to a person being in receipt of [24 a carer's allowance] [52 or as having an award of universal credit which includes the carer element] shall include a reference to a person who would have been in receipt of that allowance [52 or had such an award] but for the application of a restriction under section [39 6B or] 7 of the Social Security Fraud Act 2001 (loss of benefit provisions).]

[52 (8) For the purposes of this paragraph, a person has an award of universal credit which includes the carer element if the person has an award of universal credit which includes an amount which is the carer element under regulation 29 of the Universal Credit Regulations 2013.]

[16 Enhanced disability premium

3.487 **20IA.**—[46 (1) Subject to sub-paragraph (2), the condition is that in respect of a member of a joint-claim couple who has not attained the qualifying age for state pension credit—

(a) the care component of disability living allowance is, or would, but for a suspension of benefit in accordance with regulations under section 113(2) of the Benefits Act or but for an abatement as a consequence of hospitalisation, be payable at the highest rate prescribed under section 72(3) of the Benefits Act; or

(b) the daily living component of personal independence payment is, or would, but for regulations made under section 86(1) (hospital in-patients) of the 2012 Act, be payable at the enhanced rate in accordance with section 78(2) of the 2012 Act [47 or armed forces independence payment is payable].]

[33 (2) The condition is not satisfied if—

(a) paragraph (1) only refers to one member of a joint-claim couple and that member is a long-term patient; or

(b) paragraph (1) refers to both members of a joint-claim couple and both members of the couple are long-term patients.]]

Carer premium

3.488 **20J.**—(1) Subject to sub-paragraphs (3) and (4), the condition is that either or both members of a joint-claim couple are entitled to [28 . . .] [24 a carer's allowance] under section 70 of the Benefits Act.

(2) [28 . . .]

[23 (3) Where a carer premium is awarded but—

(a) the person in respect of whose care the [24 carer's allowance] has been awarded dies: or

(b) in any other case the member of the joint-claim couple in respect of whom a carer premium has been awarded ceases to be entitled [28 . . .] to [24 a carer's allowance],

the condition for the award of the premium shall be treated as satisfied for a period of eight weeks from the relevant date specified in sub-paragraph (3A) below.

(3A) The relevant date for the purposes of sub-paragraph (3) above shall be—

(a) [28 where sub-paragraph (3)(a) applies,] the Sunday following the death of the person in respect of whose care [24 a carer's allowance] has been awarded or beginning with the date of death if the death occurred on a Sunday;

(b) [28 . . .]

(c) in any other case, the date on which that member ceased to be entitled to [24 a carer's allowance].]

(4) Where a member of a joint-claim couple who has been entitled to an invalid care allowance ceases to be entitled to that allowance and makes a claim for a jobseeker's allowance jointly with the other member of that couple, the condition for the award of the carer premium shall be treated as satisfied for a period of eight weeks from the date on which—

[23(a) the person in respect of whose care the [24 carer's allowance] has been awarded dies;

(b) [28 . . .]

(c) [28 (c) in any other case, the person who has been entitled to a carer's allowance ceased to be entitled to that allowance.]

Member of a joint-claim couple in receipt of concessionary payments

20K.—For the purpose of determining whether a premium is applicable to a joint-claim couple under paragraphs 20H to 20J, any concessionary payment made to compensate a person for the non-payment of any benefit mentioned in those paragraphs shall be treated as if it were a payment of that benefit. 3.489

Person in receipt of benefit

20L.—For the purposes of this Part of this Schedule, a member of a joint-claim couple shall be regarded as being in receipt of any benefit if, and only if, it is paid in respect of him and shall be so regarded only for any period in respect of which that benefit is paid. 3.490

PART IVB

Weekly Amounts of Premiums Specified in Part IVA 3.491

Premium	*Amount*
20M.— (1) Pensioner premium where one member of a joint-claim couple [40 has attained the qualifying age for state pension credit] and the condition in paragraph 20E is satisfied.	(1)[53 £122.70].
(2) Higher Pensioner Premium where one member of a joint-claim couple satisfies the condition in paragraph 20F.	(2) [53 £122.70].
(3) Disability Premium where one member of a joint-claim couple satisfies the condition in paragraph [33 20G(1)].	(3) [51£45.95].
(4) Severe Disability Premium where one member of a joint-claim couple satisfies the condition in paragraph 20I(1)— (i) if there is someone in receipt of [24 a carer's allowance] or if either member satisfies that condition only by virtue of paragraph [16 20I(4)];	(4)(i) [51£61.85];
(ii) if no-one is in receipt of such an allowance.	(ii) [51£123.70].
(5) Carer Premium.	(5) [51£34.60] in respect of each person who satisfied the condition specified in paragraph 20J.]
[16 (6) Enhanced disability premium where the conditions in paragraph 20IA are satisfied.	(6) [51£22.60] where the conditions specified in paragraph 20IA are satisfied in respect of a member of a joint-claim couple.]

PART V

Rounding of Fractions

3.492 **21.**—Where an income-based jobseeker's allowance is awarded for a period which is not a complete benefit week and the applicable amount in respect of that period results in an amount which includes a fraction of one penny that fraction shall be treated as one penny.

AMENDMENTS

1. Jobseeker's Allowance (Amendment) Regulations 1996 (SI 1996/1516) reg.18 (October 7, 1996).
2. Jobseeker's Allowance (Amendment) Regulations 1996 (SI 1996/1516) reg.20 and Sch. (October 7, 1996).
3. Social Security and Child Support (Jobseeker's Allowance) (Miscellaneous Amendments) Regulations 1996 (SI 1996/2538) reg.2(11) (October 28, 1996).
4. Child Benefit, Child Support and Social Security (Miscellaneous Amendments) Regulations 1996 (SI 1996/1803) reg.44 (April 7, 1997).
5. Income-related Benefits and Jobseeker's Allowance (Personal Allowances for Children and Young Persons) (Amendment) Regulations 1996 (SI 1996/2545) reg.2 (April 7, 1997).
6. Income-related Benefits and Jobseeker's Allowance (Amendment) (No.2) Regulations 1997 (SI 1997/2197) reg.7(5) and (6)(b) (October 6, 1997).
7. Social Security Amendment (Lone Parents) Regulations 1998 (SI 1998/ 766) reg.14 (April 6, 1998).
8. Social Security (Welfare to Work) Regulations 1998 (SI 1998/2231) reg.14(3) (October 5, 1998).
9. Social Security Amendment (Personal Allowances for Children and Young Persons) Regulations 1999 (SI 1999/2555) reg.2(1)(b) and (2) (April 10, 2000).
10. Social Security and Child Support (Tax Credits) Consequential Amendments Regulations 1999 (SI 1999/2566) reg.2(2) and Sch.2 Pt III (October 5, 1999).
11. Social Security (Miscellaneous Amendments) Regulations 2000 (SI 2000/ 681) reg.4(3) (April 3, 2000)
12. Social Security Amendment (Employment Zones) Regulations 2000 (SI 2000/724) reg.4 (April 3, 2000)
13. Social Security Amendment (Personal Allowances for Children) Regulations 2000 (SI 2000/1993) reg.2 (October 23, 2000).
14. Jobseeker's Allowance (Joint Claims) Regulations 2000 (SI 2000/1978) reg.2(5) and Sch.2 para.53 (March 19, 2001).
15. Social Security Amendment (Breavement Benefits) Regulations 2000 (SI 2000/2239) reg.3(2) (April 9, 2001).
16. Social Security Amendment (Enhanced Disability Premium) Regulations 2000 (SI 2629) reg.5(c) (April 9, 2001).
17. Social Security Amendment (Joint Claims) Regulations 2001 (SI 2001/518) reg.2(7) (March 19, 2001).
18. Social Security Amendment (Bereavement Benefits) Regulations 2000 (SI 2000/2239) reg.3(2)(c) (April 9, 2001).
19. Social Security Amendment (Residential Care and Nursing Homes) Regulations 2001 (SI 2001/3767) reg.2 and Sch. Pt II para.18 (April 8, 2002).
20. Social Security (Loss of Benefit) (Consequential Amendments) Regulations 2002 (SI 2002/490) reg.2 (April 1, 2002).
21. Social Security Amendment (Residential Care and Nursing Homes) Regulations 2001 (SI 2001/3767) reg.2 and Sch. Pt II para.18 (as amended by Social Security Amendment (Residential Care and Nursing Homes) Regulations 2002 (SI 2002/398) reg.4(3)) (April 8, 2002).
22. Social Security Amendment (Personal Allowances for Children and Young Persons) Regulations 2002 (SI 2002/2019) reg.2 (October 14, 2002).

23. Social Security Amendment (Carer Premium) Regulations 2002 (SI 2002/2020) reg.3 (October 28, 2002).

24. Social Security (Miscellaneous Amendments) Regulations 2003 (SI 2003/511) reg.3(4) and (5) (April 1, 2003).

25. Social Security (Working Tax Credit and Child Tax Credit) (Consequential Amendments) Regulations 2003 (SI 2003/455) regs 1(9), 3 and Sch.2 para.20(b) (April 7, 2003).

26. Social Security (Working Tax Credit and Child Tax Credit) (Consequential Amendments) Regulations 2003 (SI 2003/455) regs 1(9), 3 and Sch.2 para.20(e) (April 7, 2003).

27. Social Security (Hospital In-Patients and Miscellaneous Amendments) Regulations 2003 (SI 2003/1195) reg.6 (May 21, 2003).

28. Social Security (Miscellaneous Amendments) (No.2) Regulations 2003 (SI 2003/2279) reg.3(3) (October 1, 2003).

29. Social Security (Removal of Residential Allowance and Miscellaneous Amendments) Regulations 2003 (SI 2003/1121) reg.4 and Sch.2 para.9 (October 6, 2003).

30. Social Security (Working Tax Credit and Child Tax Credit) (Consequential Amendments) Regulations 2003 (SI 2003/455) reg.3 and Sch.2 para.20 (April 6, 2004, except in "transitional cases" and see further the note to regs 83 and to 17 of the Income Support Regulations).

31. Civil Partnership (Pensions, Social Security and Child Support) (Consequential, etc. Provisions) Order 2005 (SI 2005/2877) art.2(3) and Sch.3 para.26(11) (December 5, 2005).

32. Social Security (Miscellaneous Amendments) (No.4) Regulations 2006 (SI 2006/2378) reg.13(10) (October 1, 2006).

33. Social Security (Miscellaneous Amendments) Regulations 2007 (SI 2007/719) reg.3(8) (April 9, 2007). As it relates to paras 15(2)(a) and 16, the amendment only affects "transitional cases". See further the note to reg.17 of the Income Support Regulations and the commentary below.

34. Social Security (Miscellaneous Amendments) (No.5) Regulations 2007 (SI 2007/2618) reg.2 and Sch. (October 1, 2007).

35. Social Security (Miscellaneous Amendments) Regulations 2008 (SI 2008/698) reg.4(14) (April 14, 2008).

36. Employment and Support Allowance (Consequential Provisions) (No.2) Regulations 2008 (SI 2008/1554) reg.3(1) and (24) (October 27, 2008).

37. Social Security (Miscellaneous Amendments) Regulations 2009 (SI 2009/583) reg.4(1) and (3) (April 6, 2009).

38. Social Security (Students and Miscellaneous Amendments) Regulations 2009 (SI 2009/1575) reg.3 (August 1, 2009).

39. Social Security (Loss of Benefit) Amendment Regulations 2010 (SI 2010/1160) reg.11(1) and (3) (April 1, 2010).

40. Social Security (Equalisation of State Pension Age) Regulations 2009 (SI 2009/1488) reg.13 (April 6, 2010).

41. Employment and Support Allowance (Transitional Provisions, Housing Benefit and Council Tax Benefit) (Existing Awards) (No.2) Regulations 2010 (SI 2010/1907) reg.26(1) and Sch.4 para.1A(3) (as amended by the Employment and Support Allowance (Transitional Provisions, Housing Benefit and Council Tax Benefit) (Existing Awards) (No.2) (Amendment) Regulations 2010 (SI 2010/2430) reg.15) (November 1, 2010).

42. Social Security (Miscellaneous Amendments) Regulations 2011 (SI 2011/674) reg.7(7) (April 11, 2011).

43. Social Security Benefits Up-rating Order 2012 (SI 2012/780) art.25(3) and Sch.13 (April 9, 2012).

44. Social Security Benefits Up-rating Order 2012 (SI 2012/780) art.25(5) and Sch.14 (April 9, 2012).

45. Social Security Benefits Up-rating Order 2012 (SI 2012/780) art.25(6) and Sch.15 (April 9, 2012).

46. Personal Independence Payment (Supplementary Provisions and Consequential Amendments) Regulations 2013 (SI 2013/388) reg.8 and Sch. para.16(1) and (7) (April 8, 2013).
47. Armed Forces and Reserve Forces Compensation Scheme (Consequential Provisions: Subordinate Legislation) Order 2013 (SI 2013/591) art.7 and Sch. para.10(1) and (7) (April 8, 2013).
48. Universal Credit and Miscellaneous Amendments (No.2) Regulations 2014 (SI 2014/2888) reg.3(3) (November 26, 2014).
49. Welfare Benefits Up-rating Order 2015 (SI 2015/30) art.9 and Sch.3 (April 6, 2015).
50. Social Security Benefits Up-rating Order 2015 (SI 2015/457) art.19(5) and Sch.10 (April 6, 2015).
51. Social Security Benefits Up-rating Order 2015 (SI 2015/457) art.19(6) and Sch.11 (April 6, 2015).
52. Universal Credit and Miscellaneous Amendments Regulations 2015 (SI 2015/1754) reg.15 (October 28, 2015).
53. Social Security Benefits (Adjustment of Amounts and Thresholds) Regulations 2016 (SI 2016/242) reg.3(1) and (2) (April 11, 2016).

DEFINITIONS

"attendance allowance"—see reg.1(3).
"the Benefits Act"—see Jobseekers Act s.35(1).
"child"—*ibid.*
"claimant"—*ibid.*
"couple"—see reg.1(3).
"disability living allowance"—*ibid.*
"family"—see Jobseekers Act s.35(1).
"invalid carriage or other vehicle"—see reg.1(3).
"lone parent"—*ibid.*
"mobility supplement"—*ibid.*
"non-dependent"—see reg.2.
"partner"—see reg.1(3).
"polygamous marriage"—*ibid.*
"preserved right"—*ibid.*
"single claimant"—*ibid.*
"welfare to work beneficiary"—*ibid.*
"young person"—see reg.76.

GENERAL NOTE

3.493 Here the details of the personal allowances and premiums for income-based JSA are set out. They follow a similar pattern to those for income support. But there are some differences. These are in relation to the qualifying conditions for the different rates of personal allowance paid where one or both members of a couple are under 18 (see para.1(3)) and the conditions for the pensioner and disability premiums.

See the notes to Sch.2 to the Income Support Regulations for discussion of the personal allowances and premiums where the rules are the same for JSA and income support. The note below just refers to the main differences.

Updating

3.493A Most of the amounts specified in paras 1, 20 and 20M have applied from April 6, 2015. In the past, they would have been up-rated each year under s.150(1)(k) SSAA 1992. However, on March 16, 2016, s.11 and Sch.1 of the Welfare Reform and Work Act 2016 came into force. As a result, the age-related amounts of contribution-based JSA (Sch.1 para.1(d)) and all the amounts specified in para.1 (Sch.1 para.1(e)) are frozen at their 2015/16 levels for four tax years (i.e. until April 6, 2020). The amounts of the pensioner premiums and higher pensioner premium in paras 20 and 20M were up-rated by over 5½ per cent (from £78.10 per week to £82.50 per week and from £116.00 per week to £122.70 per week) with effect from April 11, 2016 as a consequence of the so-called "triple lock" under which the state pension increases each year by the higher of inflation, the increase in average earnings or 2.5 per cent. The other amounts in paras 20 and 20M are not subject to the four-year freeze. However, they were not up-rated for 2016/17 as the Secretary of State decided that they had maintained their value in relation to prices as measured by the Consumer Prices Index over the 12-month period ending September 2015 (which had showed negative inflation of 0.1 per cent): see para.4.2 of the Explanatory Memorandum to SI 2016/230.

Paragraph 1

The conditions for the lower and higher rate of personal allowance for 16- or 17-year-olds who are single or lone parents match those that applied under income support before October 7, 1996 (see the 1996 edition of J. Mesher and P. Wood, *Income-related Benefits: the Legislation*). Similarly JSA, like income support, is paid at a lower rate for single people who are under 25. **3.494**

But in relation to couples there are some additional categories so that para.1(3) is even more complex than the pre-October 7, 1996 form of para.1(3) of Sch.2 to the Income Support Regulations. See heads (a)(iii), (a)(vii), (f)(iii), (g)(iii) and (h)(iii) where the fact that the other member of the couple would or would not be eligible for income support is an additional means of the couple qualifying or not qualifying for a higher rate. For an example of the potential unfairness caused by this see *CJSA/3009/2006* (where, at para.10, the Commissioner rejects an argument similar to the tentative suggestion in previous editions that the "and" at the end of head (f)(ii) should perhaps be read as if it were an "or"). Note also the new categories in heads (a)(iv) and (d).

Paragraphs 2–4

For a discussion of when the provisions abolishing JSA personal allowances for children and young persons, and the family premium, come into effect—and the "transitional cases" thereby created—see the notes to reg.83 and to reg.17 of the Income Support Regulations. In transitional cases, the personal allowance for a child or young person is £66.90 from April 6, 2015 and the family premium is £17.45 (see the Social Security Benefits Up-rating Order 2015 (SI 2015/457) art.19(3) and (4) and Sch.9). **3.495**

Paragraph 9A

This paragraph established a bereavement premium with effect from April 9, 2001. By reg.6 of the Social Security Amendment (Bereavement Benefits) Regulations 2000 (SI 2000/2239), it ceased to have effect from April 10, 2006. **3.496**

Paragraphs 10 and 11

The conditions for qualifying for a pensioner premium (for the rates see para.20; the premiums are paid at the same rate as the pensioner premiums for income support) differ from the income support rules to reflect the fact that income support claimants must be under 60, whereas JSA claimants must be below pensionable age (which for men is 65) (cf. s.124(1)(aa) of the Contributions and Benefits Act 1992 and s.1(2)(h) of the Jobseekers Act 1995). For the premium under para.10 to be payable the claimant must be 60 or over, or have a partner aged 60–74. If his partner is aged 75–79 the claimant will qualify for the premium under para.11. **3.497**

Paragraphs 12–14

Similarly, the rules for the higher pensioner and disability premiums differ from those for income support to reflect the fact that to be entitled to JSA the claimant has to be capable of work (s.1(2)(f) of the Jobseekers Act). Thus severe disablement allowance and long-term incapacity benefit (or short-term incapacity benefit at the higher rate payable to people who are terminally ill) remain qualifying benefits for the purpose of these premiums but only where it is the claimant's partner that receives them (see para.14(1)(b) and (d)). See also para.14(1)(g) (and note the differences from para.12(1)(c) of the Income Support Regulations). In addition, there is (obviously) **3.498** no equivalent to para.12(1)(b) of Sch.2 to the Income Support Regulations (claimant incapable of work for at least 52 weeks or 28 weeks in the case of terminal illness).

Paragraph 15

3.499 Note the saving provision in sub-para.(8). Regulations 4–6 of the Income Support (General) Amendment (No.6) Regulations 1991 are on pp.796–799.

Paragraph 16

3.500 Except in transitional cases (as to which, see the note to reg.17 of the Income Support Regulations), the disabled child premium was abolished with effect from April 6, 2004. For details of the position before that date see p.496 of Vol.II of the 2003 edition. In transitional cases, the disabled child premium was increased to £60.06 from the beginning of the first benefit week after April 6, 2015 by art.19(5) of, and Sch.10 to, the Social Security Benefits Up-rating Order 2015 (SI 2015/457). The transitional text of para.16 (as substituted with effect from April 9, 2007 by reg.3(8)(f) of SI 2007/719 and amended with effect from April 11, 2011 by reg.7(6) of SI 2011/674), and with effect from April 8, 2013 by reg.8 and Sch. para.16(7)(e) of SI 2013/388 and reg.7 and Sch. para.10(7)(e) of SI 2013/591, and with effect from November 26, 2014 by reg.3(3)(a)(iii) of SI 2014/2888) is as follows:

"Disabled Child Premium

16.—(1) Subject to sub-paragraph (2), the condition is that where the child or young person for whom the claimant or a partner of his is responsible and who is a member of the claimant's household is—

(a) in receipt of disability living allowance or is no longer in receipt of that allowance because he is a patient provided that the child or young person continues to be a member of the family;

[(aa) a young person who is in receipt of personal independence payment or who would, but for regulations made under section 86(1) (hospital in-patients) of the 2012 Act, be so in receipt, provided that the young person continues to be a member of the family;]

[(ab) a young person who is in receipt of armed forces independence payment;]

(b) [severely sight impaired or blind or treated as severely sight impaired or blind] within the meaning of paragraph 14(1)(h) and (2). [; or

(c) a child or young person in respect of whom section 145A of the Benefits Act (entitlement after death of child or qualifying young person) applies for the purposes of entitlement to child benefit but only for the period prescribed under that section, and in respect of whom a disabled child premium was included in the claimant's applicable amount immediately before the death of that child or young person, or ceased to be included in the claimant's applicable amount because of that child or young person's death.]

(2) The condition [in sub-paragraph (1)(a) [, (aa)] [, (ab)] or (b)] is not satisfied in respect of a child or young person—

(a) whose capital, if calculated in accordance with Part 8 of these Regulations in like manner as for the claimant, except as provided in regulation 106(1), would exceed £3,000; or

(b) who is a long-term patient."

SCHEDULE 2 **Regulations 83(f) and 84(1)(g)**

HOUSING COSTS

Housing costs

3.501 **1.**—(1) Subject to the following provisions of this Schedule, the housing costs applicable to a claimant are those costs—

(a) which he or, where he is a member of a family, he or any member of that family is, in accordance with paragraph 2, liable to meet in respect of the dwelling occupied as the home which he or any other member of his family is treated as occupying; and

(b) which qualify under paragraphs 14 to 16.

(2) In this Schedule—

"housing costs" means those costs to which sub-paragraph (1) refers;

[66 . . .]
[66 . . .]
"standard rate" means the rate for the time being [23 determined in accordance with] paragraph 11.

(3) For the purposes of this Schedule a disabled person is a person—

(a) in respect of whom a disability premium, a disabled child premium, a pensioner premium where the claimant's partner has attained the age of 75 or a higher pensioner premium is included in his applicable amount or the applicable amount of a person living with him; or

(b) who, had he in fact been entitled to a jobseeker's allowance or to income support, would have had included in his applicable amount a disability premium, a disabled child premium, a pensioner premium where the claimant's partner has attained the age of 75 or a higher pensioner premium; or

(c) who satisfies the requirements of paragraph 9A of Schedule 2 to the Income Support [1Regulations] (pensioner premium for person aged 75 or over) [32; [42 . . .]

(d) who is disabled or severely disabled for the purposes of section 9(6) (maximum rate) of the Tax Credits Act 2002] [42 or

[57 (e) who-

(i) is in receipt of an employment and support allowance which includes an amount under section 2(2) or (3) or 4(4) or (5) of the Welfare Reform Act (components); or

(ii) would be entitled to an employment and support allowance including an amount of a work-related activity component under section 2(3) of that Act (amount of contributory allowance: work-related activity component), but for the application of section 1A of the Act (duration of contributory allowance)]] [62; or

(f) who is entitled to an award of universal credit the calculation of which includes an amount under regulation 27(1) of the Universal Credit Regulations 2013 in respect of the fact that he has limited capability for work or limited capability for work and work-related activity, or would include such an amount but for regulation 27(4) or 29(4) of those Regulations].

(4) For the purposes of sub-paragraph (3), a person shall not cease to be a disabled person on account of his being disqualified for receiving benefit or treated as capable of work by virtue of the operation of section 171E of the Benefits Act (incapacity for work, disqualification etc.) [42 or disqualified for receiving employment and support allowance or treated as not having limited capability for work in accordance with regulations made under section 18 of the Welfare Reform Act (disqualification)].

[5 [37 Previous entitlement to income support [42, income-related employment and support allowance] or state pension credit]

1A.—(1) Where a claimant or his partner was in receipt of or was treated as being in receipt of income support [42 or income-related employment and support allowance] not more than 12 weeks before one of them becomes entitled to income-based jobseeker's allowance or, where the claimant or his partner is a person to whom paragraph 13(2) or (10) (linking rules) refers, not more than 26 weeks before becoming so entitled and— 3.502

(a) the applicable amount for income support [42 or income-related employment and support allowance] included an amount in respect of housing costs under [37 paragraphs 15 to 17] of Schedule 3 to the Income Support Regulations [41 or paragraphs 16 to 18 of Schedule 6 to the Employment and Support Allowance Regulations]; and

(b) the circumstances affecting the calculation of those housing costs remain unchanged since the last calculation of those costs,

the applicable amount in respect of housing costs for income-based jobseeker's allowance shall be the applicable amount in respect of those costs current when entitlement to income support [42 or income-related employment and support allowance] was last determined.

[37 (1ZA) Where a claimant or his partner was in receipt of state pension credit not more than 12 weeks before one of them becomes entitled to income-based jobseeker's allowance or, where the claimant or his partner is a person to whom paragraph 13(2) or (10) (linking rules) refers, not more than 26 weeks before becoming so entitled, and—

(a) the appropriate minimum guarantee included an amount in respect of housing costs under paragraphs 11 to 13 of Schedule II to the State Pension Credit Regulations 2002; and

(b) the circumstances affecting the calculation of those housing costs remain unchanged since the last calculation of those costs, the applicable amount in respect of housing costs for income-based jobseeker's allowance shall be the amount applicable in respect of those costs current when entitlement to state pension credit was last determined.]

[16 (1A) Where either member of a joint-claim couple was in receipt of or treated as being in receipt of income support [41 or income-related employment and support allowance] not more than 12 weeks before the couple becomes entitled to a joint-claim jobseeker's allowance, or, where either member is a person to whom paragraph 13(2) or (10) (linking rules) refers, not more than 26 weeks before becoming so entitled and—

(a) the applicable amount for income support [41 or income-related employment and support allowance] included an amount in respect of housing costs under paragraph 15 or 16 of Schedule 3 to the Income Support Regulations [42 or paragraphs 16 or 17 of Schedule 6 to the Employment and Support Allowance Regulations]; and

(b) the circumstances affecting the calculation of those housing costs remain unchanged since the last calculation of those costs,

the applicable amount in respect of housing costs for joint-claim jobseeker's allowance shall be the applicable amount in respect of those costs current when entitlement to income support [41 or income-related employment and support allowance] was last determined.]

[37 (1B) Where either member of a joint-claim couple was in receipt of state pension credit not more than 12 weeks before the couple becomes entitled to a joint-claim jobseeker's allowance, or, where either member is a person to whom paragraph 13(2) or (10) (linking rules) refers, not more than 26 weeks before becoming so entitled, and—

(a) the appropriate minimum guarantee included an amount in respect of housing costs under paragraphs 11 to 13 of Schedule II to the State Pension Credit Regulations 2002; and

(b) the circumstances affecting the calculation of those housing costs remain unchanged since the last calculation of those costs,

the applicable amount in respect of housing costs for joint-claim jobseeker's allowance shall be the amount applicable in respect of those costs current when entitlement to state pension credit was last determined.]

(2) Where, in the period since housing costs were last calculated for income support [41 or income-related employment and support allowance] [37 or (as the case may be) state pension credit], there has been a change of circumstances, other than a reduction in the amount of an outstanding loan, which increases or reduces those costs, the amount to be met under this Schedule shall, for the purposes of the claim for income-based jobseeker's allowance, be recalculated so as to take account of that change.]

Circumstances in which a person is liable to meet housing costs

3.503 **2.**—(1) A person is liable to meet housing costs where—

(a) the liability falls upon him or his partner [16 or, where that person is a member of a joint-claim couple, the other member of that couple,] but not where the liability is to a member of the same household as the person on whom the liability falls;

(b) because the person liable to meet the housing costs [1is not meeting them], the claimant has to meet those costs in order to continue to live in the dwelling occupied as the home and it is reasonable in all the circumstances to treat the claimant as liable to meet those costs;

(c) he in practice shares the housing costs with other members of the household none of whom are close relatives either of the claimant or his partner, [16 or, where that person is a member of a joint-claim couple, the other member of that couple,] and—

(i) one or more of those members is liable to meet those costs, and

(ii) it is reasonable in the circumstances to treat him as sharing responsibility.

(2) Where any one or more, but not all, members of the claimant's family are affected by a trade dispute, the housing costs shall be treated as wholly the responsibility of those members of the family not so affected.

Circumstances in which a person is to be treated as occupying a dwelling as his home

3.504 **3.**—(1) Subject to the following provisions of this paragraph, a person shall be treated as occupying as his home the dwelling normally occupied as his home by himself or, if he is a member of a family, by himself and his family and he shall not be treated as occupying any other dwelling as his home.

(2) In determining whether a dwelling is the dwelling normally occupied as the claimant's home for the purposes of sub-paragraph (1) regard shall be had to any other dwelling occupied by the claimant or by him and his family whether or not that other dwelling is in Great Britain.

(3) Subject to sub-paragraph (4), where a single claimant or a lone parent is a full-time student or is on a training course and is liable to make payments (including payments of mort-

gage interest or, in Scotland, payments under heritable securities or, in either case, analogous payments) in respect of either (but not both) the dwelling which he occupies for the purpose of attending his course of study or his training course or, as the case may be, the dwelling which he occupies when not attending his course, he shall be treated as occupying as his home the dwelling in respect of which he is liable to make payments.

(4) A full-time student shall not be treated as occupying a dwelling as his home for any week of absence from it, other than an absence occasioned by the need to enter hospital for treatment, outside the period of study, if the main purpose of his occupation during the period of study would be to facilitate attendance on his course.

(5) Where a claimant has been required to move into temporary accommodation by reason of essential repairs being carried out to the dwelling normally occupied as his home and he is liable to make payments (including payments of mortgage interest or, in Scotland, payments under heritable securities or, in either case, analogous payments) in respect of either (but not both) the dwelling normally occupied or the temporary accommodation, he shall be treated as occupying as his home the dwelling in respect of which he is liable to make those payments.

(6) Where a person is liable to make payments in respect of two (but not more than two) dwellings, he shall be treated as occupying both dwellings as his home only—

(a) where he has left and remains absent from the former dwelling occupied as the home through fear of violence in that dwelling or by a former member of his family and it is reasonable that housing costs should be met in respect of both his former dwelling and his present dwelling occupied as the home; or

(b) in the case of a couple or a member of a polygamous marriage where a partner is a full-time student or is on a training course and it is unavoidable that he or they should occupy two separate dwellings and reasonable that housing costs should be met in respect of both dwellings; or

(c) in the case where a person has moved into a new dwelling occupied as the home, except where sub-paragraph (5) applies, for a period not exceeding four benefit weeks [[36] from the first day of the benefit week in which the move occurs] if his liability to make payments in respect of two dwellings is unavoidable.

(7) Where—

(a) a person has moved into a dwelling and was liable to make payments in respect of that dwelling before moving in; and

(b) he had claimed a jobseeker's allowance before moving in and either that claim has not yet been determined or it has been determined but an amount has not been included under this Schedule and if the claim has been refused a further claim has been made within four weeks of the date on which the claimant moved into the new dwelling occupied as the home; and

(c) the delay in moving into the dwelling in respect of which there was liability to make payments before moving in was reasonable and—

(i) that delay was necessary in order to adapt the dwelling to meet the disablement needs of the claimant or any member of his family; or

[[33] (ii) the move was delayed pending [[58] local welfare provision or] the outcome of an application under Part 8 of the Benefits Act for a social fund payment to meet a need arising out of the move or in connection with setting up the home in the dwelling, and—

(aa) a member of the claimant's family is aged five or under,

(bb) the claimant's applicable amount includes a premium under paragraph 10, 11, 12, 13, 15 or 16 of Schedule 1 (applicable amounts), or

(cc) a child tax credit is paid for a member of the claimant's family who is disabled or severely disabled for the purposes of section 9(6) (maximum rate) of the Tax Credits Act 2002; or]

(iii) the person became liable to make payments in respect of the dwelling while he was a patient or was in residential accommodation,

he shall be treated as occupying the dwelling as his home for any period not exceeding four weeks immediately prior to the date on which he moved into the dwelling and in respect of which he was liable to make payments.

(8) This sub-paragraph applies to a person who enters residential accommodation—

(a) for the purpose of ascertaining whether the accommodation suits his needs; and

(b) with the intention of returning to the dwelling which he normally occupies as his home should, in the event, the residential accommodation prove not to suit his needs,

and while in the accommodation, the part of the dwelling which he normally occupies as his home is not let, or as the case may be, sub-let to another person.

(9) A person to whom sub-paragraph (8) applies shall be treated as occupying the dwelling

he normally occupies as his home during any period (commencing with the day he enters the accommodation) not exceeding 13 weeks in which the person is resident in the accommodation, but only in so far as the total absence from the dwelling does not exceed 52 weeks.

(10) A person, other than a person to whom sub-paragraph (11) applies, shall be treated as occupying a dwelling as his home throughout any period of absence not exceeding 13 weeks, if, and only if—

(a) he intends to return to occupy the dwelling as his home; and

(b) the part of the dwelling normally occupied by him has not been let or, as the case may be, sub-let to another person; and

(c) the period of absence is unlikely to exceed 13 weeks.

(11) This sub-paragraph applies to a person whose absence from the dwelling he normally occupies as his home is temporary and—

(a) he intends to return to occupy the dwelling as his home; and

(b) while the part of the dwelling which is normally occupied by him has not been let or, as the case may be, sub-let; and

(c) he is—

[27 (i) required, as a condition of bail, to reside—

(aa) in a dwelling, other than the dwelling he occupies as his home; or

(bb) in premises approved under [45 section 13 of the Offender Management Act 2007], or]

(ii) resident in a hospital or similar institution as a patient and is treated under regulation 55 as capable of work, or

(iii) undergoing or, as the case may be, his partner or his dependent child is undergoing, in the United Kingdom or elsewhere, medical treatment, or medically approved convalescence, in accommodation other than residential accommodation, or

(iv) following, in the United Kingdom or elsewhere, a training course, or

(v) undertaking medically approved care of a person residing in the United Kingdom or elsewhere, or

(vi) undertaking the care of a child whose parent or guardian is temporarily absent from the dwelling normally occupied by that parent or guardian for the purpose of receiving medically approved care or medical treatment, or

(vii) a person who is, whether in the United Kingdom or elsewhere, receiving medically approved care provided in accommodation other than residential accommodation, or

(viii) a full-time student to whom sub-paragraph (3) or (6)(b) does not apply, or

(ix) a person other than a person to whom sub-paragraph (8) applies, who is receiving care provided in residential accommodation, or

(x) a person to whom sub-paragraph (6)(a) does not apply and who has left the dwelling he occupies as his home through fear of violence in that dwelling or by a person who was formerly a member of [1 his] family, and

(d) the period of his absence is unlikely to exceed a period of 52 weeks or, in exceptional circumstances, is unlikely substantially to exceed that period.

(12) A person to whom sub-paragraph (11) applies is to be treated as occupying the dwelling he normally occupies as his home during any period of absence not exceeding 52 weeks beginning with the first day of that absence.

(13) In this paragraph—

(a) "medically approved" means certified by a registered medical practitioner;

(b) "patient" means a person who is undergoing medical or other treatment as an in-patient in a hospital or similar institution;

[29 (c) "residential accommodation" means accommodation which is a care home, an Abbeyfield Home or an independent hospital;]

(d) "training course" means such a course of training or institution provided wholly or partly by or on behalf of or in pursuance of arrangements made with, or approved by or on behalf of, [47 Skills Development Scotland,] Scottish Enterprise, Highlands and Islands Enterprise, a government department or the Secretary of State.

Housing costs not met

3.505 4.—(1) No amount may be met under the provisions of this Schedule—

(a) in respect of housing benefit expenditure; or

(b) where [16 a claimant] is [29 living in a care home, an Abbeyfield Home or an independent hospital except where he is living in such a home or hospital] during a temporary absence from the dwelling he occupies as his home and in so far as they relate to temporary absences, the provisions of paragraph 3(8) to (12) apply to him during that absence.

(2) Subject to the following provisions of this paragraph, loans which, apart from this para-

graph, qualify under paragraph 14 shall not so qualify where the loan was incurred during the relevant period and was incurred—

(a) after 7th October 1996, or

(b) after 2nd May 1994 and the housing costs applicable to that loan were not met in income support by virtue of the former paragraph 5A of Schedule 3 to the Income Support Regulations or paragraph 4(2)(a) of that Schedule in any one or more of the 26 weeks [[3]preceding] 7th October 1996, or

(c) subject to sub-paragraph (3), in the 26 weeks preceding 7th October 1996 by a person—

(i) who was not at that time entitled to income support; and

[[16](ii) who becomes, or whose partner becomes or, where that person is a member of a joint-claim couple, that couple become, entitled to a jobseeker's allowance after 6th October 1996 and that entitlement is within 26 weeks of an earlier entitlement to income support for the claimant or his partner or, as the case may be, either member of the joint-claim couple.]

(3) Sub-paragraph (2)(c) shall not apply in respect of a loan where [[16] a claimant] has interest payments on that loan met without restrictions under an award of income support in respect of a period commencing before 7th October 1996.

(4) The "relevant period" for the purposes of this paragraph is any period during which the person to whom the loan was made—

(a) is entitled to a jobseeker's allowance, or

(b) is living as a member of a family one of whom is entitled to a jobseeker's allowance,

together with any linked period, that is to say a period falling between two such periods of entitlement to a jobseeker's allowance, separated by not more than 26 weeks.

[[6](4A) For the purposes of sub-paragraph (4), a person shall be treated as entitled to a jobseeker's allowance during any period when he [[16], his partner or, where that person is a member of a joint-claim couple, the other member of that couple] was not so entitled because—

(a) that person [[16], his partner or, where that person is a member of a joint-claim couple, the other member of that couple] was participating in an employment programme specified in regulation 75(1)(a)(ii) [[17], in the Intensive Activity Period specified in regulation 75(1)(a)(iv) [[41] . . .]]; and

(b) in consequence of such participation that person, [[16], his partner or, where that person is a member of a joint-claim couple, the other member of that couple] was engaged in remunerative work or [[56] had income equal to or in excess of the amount of earnings calculated under regulation 56 or the applicable amount determined in accordance with regulations 83 to 86C, whichever applies].]

[[38] (4B) A person treated by virtue of paragraph 13 as being in receipt of a jobseeker's allowance for the purposes of this Schedule is not to be treated as entitled to a jobseeker's allowance for the purposes of sub-paragraph (4).]

(5) For the purposes of sub-paragraph (4)—

(a) any week in the period of 26 weeks ending on 7th October 1996 on which there arose an entitlement to income support shall be taken into account in determining when the relevant period commences; and

(b) two or more periods of entitlement and any intervening linked periods shall together form a single relevant period.

(6) Where the loan to which sub-paragraph (2) refers has been applied—

(a) for paying off an earlier loan, and that earlier loan qualified under paragraph 14 [[2]during the relevant period]; or

[[2](b) to finance the purchase of a property where an earlier loan, which qualified under paragraphs 14 and 15 during the relevant period in respect of another property, is paid off (in whole or in part) with monies received from the sale of that property;]

then the amount of the loan to which sub-paragraph (2) applies is the amount (if any) by which the new loan exceeds the earlier loan.

(7) Notwithstanding the preceding provisions of this paragraph, housing costs shall be met in any case where a claimant satisfies any of the conditions specified in sub-paragraphs (8) to (11) below, but—

(a) those costs shall be subject to any additional limitations imposed by the sub-paragraph; and

(b) where [[16] a claimant] satisfies the conditions in more than one of these sub-paragraphs, only one sub-paragraph shall apply in his case and the one that applies shall be the one most favourable to him. [[16], or, as the case may be, to the joint-claim couple of which he is a member].

(8) The conditions specified in this sub-paragraph are that—

(a) during the relevant period [[16] a claimant] or a member of his family acquires an interest ("the relevant interest") in a dwelling which he then occupies or continues to occupy as his home; and

(b) in the week preceding the week in which the relevant interest was acquired, housing benefit was payable to [16 a claimant] or a member of his family;

so however that the amount to be met by way of housing costs shall initially not exceed the aggregate of—

(i) the housing benefit payable in the week mentioned at sub-paragraph (8)(b); and

(ii) any amount included in the applicable amount of [16 a claimant] or a member of his family in accordance with regulation 83(f) [16, 84(1)(g), 86A(d) or 86B(e)] in that week;

and shall be increased subsequently only to the extent that it is necessary to take account of any increase, arising after the date of the acquisition, in the standard rate or in any housing costs which qualify under paragraph 16 (other housing costs).

(9) The condition specified in this sub-paragraph is that the loan was taken out, or an existing loan increased, to acquire alternative accommodation more suited to the special needs of a disabled person than the accommodation which was occupied before the acquisition by [16 a claimant].

(10) The conditions specified in this sub-paragraph are that—

(a) the loan commitment increased in consequence of the disposal of the dwelling occupied as the home and the acquisition of an alternative such dwelling; and

(b) the change of dwelling was made solely by reason of the need to provide separate sleeping accommodation for [45 persons] of different sexes aged 10 or over [45 but under the age of 20 who live with the claimant and for whom the claimant or the claimant's partner is responsible].

(11) The conditions specified in this sub-paragraph are that—

(a) during the relevant period [16 a claimant] or a member of his family acquires an interest ("the relevant interest") in a dwelling which he then occupies as his home; and

(b) in the week preceding the week in which the relevant interest was acquired, the applicable amount of [16 a claimant] or a member of his family included an amount determined by reference to paragraph 16 and did not include any amount specified in paragraph 14 or paragraph 15;

so however that the amount to be met by way of housing costs shall initially not exceed the amount so determined, and shall be increased subsequently only to the extent that it is necessary to take account of any increase, arising after the date of acquisition, in the standard rate or in any housing costs which qualify under paragraph 16 (other housing costs).

(12) The following provisions of this Schedule shall have effect subject to the provisions of this paragraph.

Apportionment of housing costs

3.506 5.—(1) Where the dwelling occupied as the home is a composite hereditament and—

(a) before 1st April 1990 for the purposes of section 48(5) of the General Rate Act 1967 (reduction of rates on dwellings), it appeared to a rating authority or it was determined in pursuance of sub-section (6) of section 48 of that Act that the hereditament, including the dwelling occupied as the home, was a mixed hereditament and that only a proportion of the rateable value of the hereditament was attributable to use for the purpose of a private dwelling; or

(b) in Scotland, before 1st April 1989 an assessor acting pursuant to section 45(1) of the Water (Scotland) Act 1980 (provision as to valuation roll) has apportioned the net annual value of the premises including the dwelling occupied as the home between the part occupied as a dwelling and the remainder,

the amounts applicable under this Schedule shall be such proportion of the amounts applicable in respect of the hereditament or premises as a whole as is equal to the proportion of the rateable value of the hereditament attributable to the part of the hereditament used for the purposes of a private tenancy or, in Scotland, the proportion of the net annual value of the premises apportioned to the part occupied as a dwelling house.

(2) Subject to sub-paragraph (1) and the following provisions of this paragraph, where the dwelling occupied as the home is a composite hereditament, the amount applicable under this Schedule shall be the relevant fraction of the amount which would otherwise be applicable under this Schedule in respect of the dwelling occupied as the home.

(3) For the purposes of sub-paragraph (2), the relevant fraction shall be obtained in accordance with the formula—

$$\frac{A}{A + B}$$

where—

"A" is the current market value of the claimant's interest in that part of the composite hereditament which is domestic property within the meaning of section 66 of the Act of 1988;
"B" is the current market value of the claimant's interest in that part of the composite hereditament which is not domestic property within that section.

(4) In this paragraph—

"composite hereditament" means—
(a) as respects England and Wales, any hereditament which is shown as a composite hereditament in a local non-domestic rating list;
(b) as respects Scotland, any lands and heritages entered in the valuation roll which are part residential subjects within the meaning of section 26(1) of the Act of 1987;

"local non-domestic rating list" means a list compiled and maintained under section 41(1) of the Act of 1988;
"the Act of 1987" means the Abolition of Domestic Rates Etc. (Scotland) Act 1987;
"the Act of 1988" means the Local Government Finance Act 1988.

(5) Where responsibility for expenditure which relates to housing costs met under this Schedule is shared, the amounts applicable shall be calculated by reference to the appropriate proportion of that expenditure for which the claimant is responsible.

Existing housing costs

6.—[66 . . .] 3.507

[66 Housing Costs]

7.—(1) Subject to the provisions of this Schedule, the [66 . . .] housing costs to be met in any particular case are— 3.508
(a) where the claimant has been entitled to a jobseeker's allowance for a continuous period of 39 weeks or more, an amount—
(i) determined in the manner set out in paragraph 9 by applying the standard rate to the eligible capital for the time being owing in connection with a loan which qualifies under paragraph 14 or 15; and
(ii) equal to any payments which qualify under paragraph 16(1)(a) to (c);
(b) in any other case, nil.

(2) For the purposes of sub-paragraph (1) [5 and subject to sub-paragraph (2A)], the eligible capital for the time being owing shall be determined on the date the [66 . . .] housing costs are first met and thereafter on each anniversary of that date.

(2A) Where a claimant or his partner ceases to be in receipt of or treated as being in receipt of income support [42 or income-related employment and support allowance] and one of them becomes entitled to income-based jobseeker's allowance in a case to which paragraph 1A applies, the eligible capital for the time being owing shall be recalculated on each anniversary of the date on which housing costs were first met for whichever of the benefits concerned the claimant or his partner was first entitled.]

[16 (2B) Where either member of a joint-claim couple ceases to be in receipt of or treated as being in receipt of income support [42 or income-related employment and support allowance] and that couple then become entitled to a joint-claim jobseeker's allowance in a case to which paragraph 1A(1A) applies, the eligible capital for the time being owing shall be recalculated on each anniversary of the date on which the housing costs were first met for whichever of the benefits concerned either member of the couple was first entitled to.]

(3) [66 . . .]
(4) [66 . . .]
(5) [66 . . .]
(6) [66 . . .]
(7) [66 . . .]

General exclusions from [66 paragraph 7]

8.—(1) [66 Paragraph] shall not apply where— 3.509
(a) the claimant or his partner [16 or either member of a joint-claim couple] [49 has attained the qualifying age for state pension credit];
(b) the housing costs are payments—
(i) under a co-ownership agreement;

(ii) under or relating to a tenancy or licence of a Crown tenant; or
(iii) where the dwelling occupied as the home is a tent, in respect of the tent and the site on which it stands.

(2) In a case falling within sub-paragraph (1), the housing costs to be met are—
(a) where head (a) of sub-paragraph (1) applies, an amount—
(i) determined in the manner set out in paragraph 9 by applying the standard rate to the eligible capital for the time being owing in connection with a loan which qualifies under paragraph 14 or 15; and
(ii) equal to the payments which qualify under paragraph 16;
(b) where head (b) of sub-paragraph (1) applies, an amount equal to the payments which qualify under paragraph 16(1)(d) to (f).

[18 The calculation for loans

3.510 **9.**—The weekly amount of [66 housing costs] to be met under this Schedule in respect of a loan which qualifies under paragraph 14 or 15 shall be calculated by applying the formula—

$$\frac{A \times B}{52}$$

where—
A = the amount of the loan which qualifies under paragraph 14 or 15;
B = the standard rate for the time being [24 applicable in respect of that loan].]

General provisions applying to [66 . . .] housing costs

3.511 **10.**—(1) [66 . . .]

(2) [66 . . .]

(3) Where for the time being a loan exceeds, or in a case where more than one loan is to be taken into account, the aggregate of those loans exceeds the appropriate amount specified in sub-paragraph (4), then the amount of the loan or, as the case may be, the aggregate amount of those loans, shall for the purposes of this Schedule, be the appropriate amount.

(4) Subject to the following provisions of this paragraph, the appropriate amount is £100,000.

(5) Where a person is treated under paragraph 3(6) (payments in respect of two dwellings) as occupying two dwellings as his home, then the restrictions imposed by subparagraph (3) shall be applied separately to the loans for each dwelling.

(6) In a case to which paragraph 5 (apportionment of housing costs) applies, the appropriate amount for the purposes of sub-paragraph (3) shall be the lower of—
(a) a sum determined by applying the formula—

$$P \times Q$$

where—
P = the relevant fraction for the purposes of paragraph 5, and
Q = the amount or, as the case may be, the aggregate amount for the time being of any loan or loans which qualify under this Schedule; or
(b) the sum for the time being specified in sub-paragraph (4).

(7) In a case to which paragraph 14(3) or 15(3) (loans which qualify in part only) applies, the appropriate amount for the purposes of sub-paragraph (3) shall be the lower of—
(a) a sum representing for the time being the part of the loan applied for the purposes specified in paragraph 14(1) or (as the case may be) paragraph 15(1); or
(b) the sum for the time being specified in sub-paragraph (4).

(8) In the case of any loan to which paragraph 15(2)(k) (loan taken out and used for the purpose of adapting a dwelling for the special needs of a disabled person) applies the whole of the loan, to the extent that it remains unpaid, shall be disregarded in determining whether the amount for the time being specified in sub-paragraph (4) is exceeded.

(9) Where in any case the amount for the time being specified for the purposes of subparagraph (4) is exceeded and there are two or more loans to be taken into account under either or both [1paragraphs 14 and 15], then the amount of eligible interest in respect of each of those loans to the extent that the loans remain outstanding shall be determined as if each loan had been reduced to a sum equal to the qualifying portion of that loan.

(10) For the purposes of sub-paragraph (9), the qualifying portion of a loan shall be determined by applying the following formula—

$$R \times \frac{S}{T}$$

where—

R = the amount for the time being specified for the purposes of sub-paragraph (4);
S = the amount of the outstanding loan to be taken into account;
T = the aggregate of all outstanding loans to be taken into account under paragraphs 14 and 15.

The standard rate

11.—[25 (1) The standard rate is the rate of interest applicable per annum to a loan which qualifies under this Schedule. **3.512**

[53 (2) Subject to the following provisions of this paragraph, the standard rate is to be the average mortgage rate published by the Bank of England in August 2010.

(2A) The standard rate is to be varied each time that sub-paragraph (2B) applies.

(2B) This sub-paragraph applies when, on any reference day, the Bank of England publishes an average mortgage rate which differs by [64 0.5 percentage points] or more from the standard rate that applies on that reference day (whether by virtue of sub-paragraph (2) or of a previous application of this sub-paragraph).

(2C) The average mortgage rate published on that reference day then becomes the new standard rate in accordance with sub-paragraph (2D).

(2D) Any variation in the standard rate by virtue of sub-paragraphs (2A) to (2C) comes into effect—

(a) for the purposes of sub-paragraph (2B) (in consequence of its first and any subsequent application), on the day after the reference day referred to in sub-paragraph (2C);
(b) for the purpose of calculating the weekly amount of housing costs to be met under this Schedule, on the day specified by the Secretary of State.

(2E) In this paragraph—

"average mortgage rate" means the effective interest rate (non-seasonally adjusted) of United Kingdom resident banks and building societies for loans to households secured on dwellings published by the Bank of England in respect of the most recent period for that rate specified at the time of publication;

"reference day" means any day falling after 1st October 2010.]

(3) [46 . . .]
(4) [39 . . .]
(5) [39 . . .]
(6) [39 . . .].]

Excessive housing costs

12.—(1) Housing costs which, apart from this paragraph, fall to be met under this Schedule shall be met only to the extent specified in sub-paragraph (3) where— **3.513**

(a) the dwelling occupied as the home, excluding any part which is let, is larger than is required by the claimant and his family and any child or young person to whom regulation 78(4) applies (foster children) and any other non-dependants having regard, in particular, to suitable alternative accommodation occupied by a household of the same size; or
(b) the immediate area in which the dwelling occupied as the home is located is more expensive than other areas in which suitable alternative accommodation exists; or
(c) the outgoings of the dwelling occupied as the home which are met under paragraphs 14 to 16 are higher than the outgoings of suitable alternative accommodation in the area.

(2) For the purposes of heads (a) to (c) of sub-paragraph (1), no regard shall be had to the capital value of the dwelling occupied as the home.

(3) Subject to the following provisions of this paragraph, the amount of the loan which falls to be met shall be restricted and the excess over the amounts which the claimant would need to obtain suitable alternative accommodation shall not be allowed.

(4) Where, having regard to the relevant factors, it is not reasonable to expect the claimant and his family to seek alternative cheaper accommodation, no restriction shall be made under sub-paragraph (3).

(5) In sub-paragraph (4) "the relevant factors" are—

(a) the availability of suitable accommodation and the level of housing costs in the area; and
(b) the circumstances of the family including in particular the age and state of health of its members, the employment prospects of the claimant and, where a change in accommodation is likely to result in a change of school, the effect on the education of any child or young person who is a member of his family, or any child or young person who is not treated as part of his family by virtue of regulation 78(4) (foster children).

(6) Where sub-paragraph (4) does not apply and the claimant (or other member of the family) was able to meet the financial commitments for the dwelling occupied as the home when these were entered into, no restriction shall be made under this paragraph during the first 26 weeks of any period of entitlement to a jobseeker's allowance nor during the next 26 weeks if and so long as the claimant uses his best endeavours to obtain cheaper accommodation or, as the case may be, no restriction shall be made under this paragraph on [11 supersession] during the 26 weeks from the date of the [11 supersession] nor during the next 26 weeks if and so long as the claimant uses his best endeavours.

(7) For the purposes of calculating any period of 26 weeks referred to in sub-paragraph (6), and for those purposes only, a person shall be treated as entitled to a jobseeker's allowance for any period of 12 weeks or less in respect of which he was not in receipt of a jobseeker's allowance and which fell immediately between periods in respect of which he was in receipt thereof.

(8) Any period in respect of which—

(a) a jobseeker's allowance was paid to a person, and

(b) it was subsequently determined on appeal [11, revision or supersession] that he was not entitled to a jobseeker's allowance for that period,

shall be treated for the purposes of sub-paragraph (7) as a period in respect of which he was not in receipt of a jobseeker's allowance.

(9) Heads (c) to (f) of sub-paragraph (1) of paragraph 13 shall apply to sub-paragraph (7) as they apply to [66 paragraph 7] but with the modification that the words "Subject to sub-paragraph (2)" are omitted and as if references to "the claimant" were references to the person mentioned in sub-paragraph (7).

Linking rule

3.514 **13.**—(1) Subject to [16 [54 sub-paragraph (2A)]] for the [1purposes] of this Schedule—

(a) a person shall be treated as being in receipt of a jobseeker's allowance during the following periods—

(i) any period in respect of which it was subsequently held, on appeal or [11revision], that he was so entitled to a jobseeker's allowance; and

(ii) any period of 12 weeks or less [13 or, as the case may be, 52 weeks or less,] in respect of which he was not in receipt of a jobseeker's allowance and which fell immediately between periods in respect of which

[2(aa) he was, or was treated as being, in receipt of a jobseeker's allowance,

(bb) he was treated as entitled to a jobseeker's allowance for the purposes of sub-paragraphs (5), (6) and (7), or

(cc) (i) above applies;]

(b) a person shall be treated as not being in receipt of a jobseeker's allowance during any period other than a period to which (a)(ii) above applies in respect of which it is subsequently held on appeal [11, revision or supersession] that he was not so entitled;

(c) where—

(i) the claimant was a member of a couple or a polygamous marriage; and

(ii) his partner was, in respect of a past period, in receipt of a jobseeker's allowance for himself and the claimant; and

(iii) the claimant is no longer a member of that couple or polygamous marriage; and

(iv) the claimant made his claim for a jobseeker's allowance within twelve weeks [13 or, as the case may be, 52 weeks,] of ceasing to be a member of that couple or polygamous marriage,

he shall be treated as having been in receipt of a jobseeker's allowance for the same period as his former partner had been or had been treated, for the purposes of this Schedule, as having been;

(d) where the claimant's partner's applicable amount was determined in accordance with paragraph 1(1) (single claimant) or paragraph 1(2) (lone parent) of Schedule 1 (applicable amounts) in respect of a past period, provided that the claim was made within twelve weeks [13 or, as the case may be, 52 weeks,] of the claimant and his partner becoming one of a couple or polygamous marriage, the claimant shall be treated as having been in receipt of a jobseeker's allowance for the same period as his partner had been or had been treated, for the purposes of this Schedule, as having been;

[16(dd) where the applicable amount of a member of a joint-claim couple was determined in accordance with paragraph 1(1) (single claimant) or paragraph 1(2) (lone parent) of Schedule 1 (applicable amounts) in respect of a past period, provided that the claim was made within twelve weeks of the joint-claimant becoming a member of the joint-claim couple, the joint-claim couple shall be treated as having been in receipt of a jobseeker's allowance for the same period as that member of the joint-claim couple had been treated, for the purposes of this Schedule, as having been;]

(e) where the claimant is a member of a couple or a polygamous marriage and his partner was, in respect of a past period, in receipt of a jobseeker's allowance for himself and the claimant, and the claimant has begun to receive a jobseeker's allowance as a result of an election by the members of the couple or polygamous marriage, he shall be treated as having been in receipt of a jobseeker's allowance for the same period as his partner had been or had been treated, for the purposes of this Schedule, as having been;

[6(ee) where the claimant—

(i) is a member of a couple or a polygamous marriage and the claimant's partner was, immediately before the participation by any member of that couple or polygamous marriage in an employment programme specified in regulation 75(1)(a)(ii) [17, in the Intensive Activity Period specified in regulation 75(1)(a)(iv) [48 or in the Flexible New Deal] [41 . . .]], in receipt of income-based jobseeker's allowance and his applicable amount included an amount for the couple or for the partners of the polygamous marriage; and

(ii) has, immediately after that participation in that programme, begun to receive income-based jobseeker's allowance as a result of an election under regulation 4(3B) of the Claims and Payments Regulations by the members of the couple or polygamous marriage,

the claimant shall be treated as having been in receipt of a jobseeker's allowance for the same period as his partner had been or had been treated, for the purposes of this Schedule, as having been;]

(f) where—

(i) the claimant was a member of a family of a person (not being a former partner) entitled to a jobseeker's allowance and at least one other member of that family was a child or young person; and

(ii) the claimant becomes a member of another family which includes that child or young person; and

(iii) the claimant made his claim for a jobseeker's allowance within 12 weeks [13 or, as the case may be, 52 weeks,] of the date on which the person entitled to a jobseeker's allowance mentioned in head (i) above ceased to be so entitled,

the claimant shall be treated as being in receipt of a jobseeker's allowance for the same period as that person had been or had been treated, for the purposes of this Schedule, as having been.

(2) [54 . . .]

[16(2A) Where a joint-claim jobseeker's allowance is payable to one member of a joint-claim couple in accordance with section 3B, both members of the couple shall be treated as receiving, or having received, a jobseeker's allowance for the purpose of this paragraph.

(2B) Where both joint-claimants claiming a jobseeker's allowance in respect of themselves have not been in receipt of a jobseeker's allowance for a period before they became a joint-claim couple, sub-paragraph (1) shall have effect in respect of that couple in relation to the period which is most favourable to the couple for the purposes of this Schedule.]

[4(3) For the purposes of this Schedule, where a claimant has ceased to be entitled to a jobseeker's allowance because he or his partner [16 or, where a claimant is a member of a joint-claim couple, the other member of that couple] is participating in arrangements for training made under section 2 of the Employment and Training Act 1973 or attending a course at an employment rehabilitation centre established under that section [45 or under the Enterprise and New Towns (Scotland) Act 1990], he shall be treated as if he had been in receipt of a jobseeker's allowance for the period during which he or his partner [16 or, where a claimant is a member of a joint-claim couple, the other member of that couple] was participating in such a course.]

[6(3A) For the purposes of this Schedule, a claimant who has ceased to be entitled to a jobseeker's allowance because—

(a) that claimant or his partner [16 or, where a claimant is a member of a joint-claim couple, the other member of that couple] was participating in an employment programme specified in regulation 75(1)(a)(ii) [17 in the Intensive Activity Period specified in regulation 75(1)(a)(iv) [40 . . .]] [12or in an employment zone programme] [48 or in the Flexible New Deal], and

(b) in consequence of such participation the claimant or his partner [16 or, where a claimant is a member of a joint-claim couple, the other member of that couple] was engaged in renumerative work or failed to satisfy the condition specified either in section 2(1)(c) [16, 3(1)(a) or 3A(1)(a)],

shall be treated as if he had been in receipt of a jobseeker's allowance for the period during which he or his partner [16 or, where a claimant is a member of a joint-claim couple, the other member of that couple] was participating in that programme [17 or activity].]

(4) Where, for the purposes of sub-paragraphs [6(1), (3) and (3A)], a person is treated as being in receipt of a jobseeker's allowance, for a certain period, he shall [10, subject to sub-paragraph (4A),] be treated as being entitled to a jobseeker's allowance for the same period.

[10 (4A) Where the appropriate amount of a loan exceeds the amount specified in paragraph 10(4), sub-paragraph (4) shall not apply except—

(a) for the purposes of paragraph [66 . . .] 7(1); or

(b) where a person has ceased to be in receipt of a jobseeker's allowance for a period of [35 104 weeks] or less because he or his partner is a welfare to work beneficiary.]

(5) For the purposes of this Schedule, sub-paragraph (6) applies where a person is not entitled to an income-based jobseeker's allowance by reason only that he has—

(a) capital exceeding £8,000; or

(b) income [54 equal to or] exceeding the applicable amount which applies in his case; or

[3(bb) a personal rate of contribution-based jobseeker's allowance that is equal to, or exceeds, the applicable amount in his case; or]

(c) both capital exceeding £8,000 and income exceeding the applicable amount which applies in his case.

(6) A person to whom sub-paragraph (5) applies shall be treated as entitled to a jobseeker's allowance throughout any period of not more than 39 weeks which comprises only days—

(a) on which he is entitled to a contribution-based jobseeker's allowance, statutory sick pay [42 , incapacity benefit or contributory employment and support allowance]; or

(b) on which he is, although not entitled to any of the benefits mentioned in head (a) above, entitled to be credited with earnings equal to the lower earnings limit for the time being in force in accordance with [9regulation 8A or 8B of the Social Security (Credits) Regulations 1975].

(7) Subject to sub-paragraph (8), a person to whom sub-paragraph (5) applies and who is either a person to whom regulation 13(4) applies (persons with caring responsibilities) or a lone parent shall, for the purposes of this Schedule, be treated as entitled to a jobseeker's allowance throughout any period of not more than 39 weeks following the refusal of a claim for a jobseeker's allowance made by or on behalf of that person.

(8) Sub-paragraph (7) shall not apply in relation to a person mentioned in that sub-paragraph who, during the period referred to in that sub-paragraph—

(a) is engaged in, or is treated as engaged in, remunerative work or whose partner is engaged in, or is treated as engaged in, remunerative work;

(b) is treated as not available for employment by virtue of regulation [41 15(1)(a)] (circumstances in which students are not treated as available for employment);

(c) is temporarily absent from Great Britain, other than in the circumstances specified in regulation 50 (temporary absence from Great Britain).

(9) In a case where—

(a) sub-paragraphs (6) and (7) apply solely by virtue of sub-paragraph (5)(b), and

(b) the claimant's income includes payments under a policy taken out to insure against the risk that the policy holder is unable to meet any loan or payment which qualifies under paragraphs 14 to 16,

sub-paragraphs (6) and (7) shall have effect as if for the words "throughout any period of not more than 39 weeks" there are substituted the words "throughout any period that payments are made in accordance with the terms of the policy".

(10) This sub-paragraph applies—

(a) to a person who claims a jobseeker's allowance, or in respect of whom a jobseeker's allowance is claimed, and who—

(i) received payments under a policy of insurance taken out to insure against loss of employment, and those payments are exhausted; and

(ii) had a previous award of a jobseeker's allowance where the applicable amount included an amount by way of housing costs; and

(b) where the period in respect of which the previous award of jobseeker's allowance was payable ended not more than 26 weeks before the date the claim was made.

(11) Where sub-paragraph (10) applies, in determining—

(a) [66 . . .]

(b) for the purposes of paragraph 7(1) whether a claimant has been entitled to a jobseeker's allowance for a continuous period of 39 weeks or more,

any week falling between the date of the termination of the previous award and the date of the new claim shall be ignored.

[8(12) Where the claimant's partner to whom this paragraph applies is a welfare to work beneficiary, sub-paragraphs (1)(a)(ii), [14 (1)(c)(iv),] (1)(d) and (1)(f)(iii) shall apply to him as if for the words "twelve weeks" there were substituted the words "[35 104 weeks]".]

[15 (13) For the purposes of sub-paragraph (1)(a)(ii), (1)(c)(iv), (1)(d) and (1)(f)(iii), the relevant period shall be—

(a) 52 weeks in the case of a person to whom sub-paragraph (14) applies;
(b) subject to sub-paragraph (12), 12 weeks in any other case.

(14) This sub-paragraph applies, subject to sub-paragraph (15), in the case of a person who, on or after 9th April 2001, has ceased to be entitled to a jobseeker's allowance because he or his partner or, where that person is a member of a joint-claim couple, the other member of that couple—

(a) has commenced employment as an employed earner or as a self-employed earner or has increased the hours in which he is engaged in such employment;
(b) is taking active steps to establish himself in employment as an employed earner or as a self-employed earner under any scheme for assisting persons to become so employed which is mentioned in regulation 19(1)(r)(i) to (iii); or
(c) is participating in—
  (i) a New Deal option;
  (ii) an employment zone programme;
  (iii) the self-employment route; [17 or
  (iv) the Intensive Activity Period specified in regulation 75(1)(a)(iv) [41 . . .]]

and, as a consequence, [56 that person, their partner or, where that person is a member of a joint-claim couple, the other member of that couple, was engaged in remunerative work or had income equal to or in excess of the amount of earnings calculated under regulation 56 or the applicable amount determined in accordance with regulations 83 to 86C, whichever applies].

(15) Sub-paragraph (14) shall only apply to the extent that immediately before the day on which the person ceased to be entitled to an income-based jobseeker's allowance or the joint-claim couple of which he was a member ceased to be entitled to a joint-claim jobseeker's allowance, his housing costs were being met in accordance with paragraph [66 . . .] 7(1)(a) or would have been so met but for any non-dependant deduction under paragraph 17.]

[22 (16) For the purpose of determining whether the linking rules set out in this paragraph apply in a case where a claimant's former partner was entitled to state pension credit, any reference to income-based jobseeker's allowance in this Schedule shall be taken to include also a reference to state pension credit.]

Loans on residential property

14.—(1) A loan qualifies under this paragraph where the loan was taken out to defray monies applied for any of the following purposes— **3.515**

(a) acquiring an interest in the dwelling occupied as the home; or
(b) paying off another loan to the extent that the other loan would have qualified under head (a) above had the loan not been paid off.

(2) For the purposes of this paragraph, references to a loan include also a reference to money borrowed under a hire purchase agreement for any purpose specified in heads (a) and (b) of sub-paragraph (1) above.

(3) Where a loan is applied only in part for the purposes specified in heads (a) and (b) of sub-paragraph (1), only that portion of the loan which is applied for that purpose shall qualify under this paragraph.

Loans for repairs and improvements to the dwelling occupied as the home

15.—(1) A loan qualifies under this paragraph where the loan was taken out, with or without security, for the purpose of— **3.516**

(a) carrying out repairs and improvements to the dwelling occupied as the home;
(b) paying any service charge imposed to meet the cost of repairs and improvements to the dwelling occupied as the home;
(c) paying off another loan to the extent that the other loan would have qualified under head (a) or (b) of this sub-paragraph had the loan not been paid off,

and the loan was used for that purpose, or is used for that purpose within 6 months of the date of receipt or such further period as may be reasonable in the particular circumstances of the case.

(2) In sub-paragraph (1) "repairs and improvements" means any of the following measures undertaken with a view to maintaining the fitness of the dwelling for human habitation or, where the dwelling forms part of a building, any part of the building containing that dwelling—

(a) provision of a fixed bath, shower, wash basin, sink or lavatory, and necessary associated plumbing, including the provision of hot water not connected to a central heating system;

(b) repairs to existing heating system;
(c) damp proof measures;
(d) provision of ventilation and natural lighting;
(e) provision of drainage facilities;
(f) provision of facilities for preparing and cooking food;
(g) provision of insulation of the dwelling occupied as the home;
(h) provision of electric lighting and sockets;
(i) provision of storage facilities for fuel or refuse;
(j) repairs of unsafe structural defects;
(k) adapting a dwelling for the special needs of a disabled person; or
(l) provision of separate sleeping accommodation for [45 persons] of different sexes aged 10 or over [45 but under the age of 20 who live with the claimant and for whom the claimant or the claimant's partner is responsible].

(3) Where a loan is applied only in part for the purposes specified in sub-paragraph (1), only that portion of the loan which is applied for that purpose shall qualify under this paragraph.

Other housing costs

3.517 **16.**—(1) Subject to the deduction specified in sub-paragraph (2) and the reductions applicable in sub-paragraph (5), there shall be met under this paragraph the amounts, calculated on a weekly basis, in respect of the following housing costs—

(a) payments by way of rent or ground rent relating to a long tenancy [34 . . .];
(b) service charges;
(c) payments by way of the rentcharge within the meaning of section 1 of the Rentcharges Act 1977;
(d) payments under a co-ownership scheme;
(e) payments under or relating to a tenancy or licence of a Crown tenant;
(f) where the dwelling occupied as the home is a tent, payments in respect of the tent and the site on which it stands.

(2) Subject to sub-paragraph (3), the deductions to be made from the weekly amounts to be met under this paragraph are—

(a) where the costs are inclusive of any of the items mentioned in [30 paragraph 6(2) of Schedule 1 to the Housing Benefit Regulations 2006] (payment in respect of fuel charges), the deductions prescribed in that paragraph unless the claimant provides evidence on which the actual or approximate amount of the service charge for fuel may be estimated, in which case the estimated amount;
(b) where the costs are inclusive of ineligible service charges within the meaning of [30 paragraph 1 of Schedule 1 to the Housing Benefit Regulations 2006] (ineligible service charges) the amounts attributable to those ineligible service charges or where that amount is not separated from or separately identified within the housing costs to be met under this paragraph, such part of the payments made in respect of those housing costs which are fairly attributable to the provision of those ineligible services having regard to the costs of comparable services;
(c) any amount for repairs and improvements, and for this purpose the expression "repairs and improvements" has the same meaning it has in paragraph 15(2).

(3) Where arrangements are made for the housing costs, which are met under this paragraph and which are normally paid for a period of 52 weeks, to be paid instead for a period of 53 weeks, or to be paid irregularly, or so that no such costs are payable or collected in certain periods, or so that the costs for different periods in the year are of different amounts, the weekly amount shall be the amount payable for the year divided by 52.

(4) Where the claimant or a member of his family—

(a) pays for reasonable repairs or redecoration to be carried out to the dwelling they occupy; and
(b) that work was not the responsibility of the claimant or any member of his family; and
(c) in consequence of that work being done, the costs which are normally met under this paragraph are waived,

then those costs shall, for a period not exceeding 8 weeks, be treated as payable.

(5) Where in England and Wales an amount calculated on a weekly basis in respect of housing costs specified in sub-paragraph (1)(e) (Crown tenants) includes water charges, that amount shall be reduced—

(a) where the amount payable in respect of water charges is known, by that amount;
(b) in any other case, by the amount which would be the likely weekly water charge had the property not been occupied by a Crown tenant.

Non-dependant deductions

17.—(1) Subject to the following provisions of this paragraph, the following deductions from the amount to be met under the preceding paragraphs of this Schedule in respect of housing costs shall be made— **3.518**

[28 (a) in respect of a non-dependant aged 18 or over who is engaged in any remunerative work, [67£94.50];

(b) in respect of a non-dependant aged 18 or over to whom paragraph (a) does not apply, [67£14.65].]

(2) In the case of a non-dependant aged 18 or over to whom sub-paragraph (1)(a) applies because he is in remunerative work, where the claimant satisfies [11 the Secretary of State] that the non-dependant's gross weekly income is—

(a) less than [67£133.00], the deduction to be made under this paragraph shall be the deduction specified in sub-paragraph (1)(b);

(b) not less than [67£133.00] but less than [67£195.00], the deduction to be made under this paragraph shall be [67£33.65];

(c) not less than [67£195.00] but less than [67£253.00], the deduction to be made under this paragraph shall be [67£46.20];

[1(d) not less than [67£253.00] but less than [67£388.00], the deduction to be made under this paragraph shall be [67£75.60];

(e) not less than [67£338.00] but less than [67£420.00], the deduction to be made under this paragraph shall be [67£86.10]].

(3) Only one deduction shall be made under this paragraph in respect of a couple or, as the case may be, the members of a polygamous marriage, and where, but for this sub-paragraph, the amount that would fall to be deducted in respect of one member of a couple or polygamous marriage is higher than the amount (if any) that would fall to be deducted in respect of the other, or any other member, the higher amount shall be deducted.

(4) In applying the provisions of sub-paragraph (2) in the case of a couple or, as the case may be, a polygamous marriage, regard shall be had, for the purpose of sub-paragraph (2), to the couple's or, as the case may be, all the members of the polygamous marriage's, joint weekly income.

(5) Where a person is a non-dependant in respect of more than one joint occupier of a dwelling (except where the joint occupiers are a couple or members of a polygamous marriage), the deduction in respect of that non-dependant shall be apportioned between the joint occupiers (the amount so apportioned being rounded to the nearest penny) having regard to the number of joint occupiers and the proportion of the housing costs in respect of the dwelling occupied as the home payable by each of them.

(6) No deduction shall be made in respect of any non-dependants occupying the dwelling occupied as the home of the claimant, if the claimant or any partner of his is—

(a) [65 severely sight impaired or blind or treated as severely sight impaired or blind] within the meaning of paragraph 14(1)(h) and (2) of Schedule 1 (additional condition for the higher pensioner and disability premiums); or

(b) receiving in respect of himself either—

(i) an attendance allowance, or

(ii) the care component of the disability living allowance [60 , [61 . . .]

(iii) the daily living component of personal independence payment] [61 , or

(iv) armed forces independence payment].

(7) No deduction shall be made in respect of a non-dependant—

(a) if, although he resides with the claimant, it appears to [11 the Secretary of State] that the dwelling occupied as his home is normally elsewhere; or

[2(b) if he is in receipt of [3a training allowance paid in connection with [45 youth training] established under section 2 of the Employment and Training Act 1973 or section 2 of the Enterprise and New Towns (Scotland) Act 1990; or]]

(c) if he is a full-time student during a period of study or, if he is not in remunerative work, during a recognised summer vacation appropriate to his course; or

(d) if he is aged under 25 and in receipt of [4an income-based jobseeker's allowance] or income support; or

(e) in respect of whom a deduction in the calculation of a rent rebate or allowance falls to be made under [30 regulation 74 of the Housing Benefit Regulations 2006] (non-dependant deductions); or

(f) to whom, but for paragraph (5) of regulation 2 (definition of non-dependant) paragraph (4) of that regulation would apply; or

(g) if he is not residing with the claimant because he has been a patient for a period in excess of [21 52] weeks, or is a prisoner, and for these purposes—

[31 (i) "patient" has the meaning given in paragraph 3(13)(b) and "prisoner" has the meaning given in regulation 85(4), and
(ii) in calculating any period of 52 weeks as a patient, any two or more distinct periods separated by one or more intervals each not exceeding 28 days shall be treated as a single period; [42 . . .]]

(h) if he is in receipt of state pension credit] [42 or

(i) he is aged less than 25 and is in receipt of [59 income–related] employment and support allowance which does not include an amount under section [43 . . .] 4(4) or (5) of the Welfare Reform Act (components)] [63; or

(j) if he is aged less than 25 and is entitled to an award of universal credit which is calculated on the basis that he does not have any earned income].

(8) In the case of a non-dependant to whom sub-paragraph (2) applies because he is in remunerative work, there shall be disregarded from his gross income—

(a) any attendance allowance [60 , disability living allowance [61 , armed forces independence payment] or personal independence payment] received by him;

(b) any payment made under [51 or by] the Macfarlane Trust, the Macfarlane (Special Payments) Trust, the Macfarlane (Special Payments) (No.2) Trust, the Fund, the Eileen Trust [50 , MFET Limited] [55 , the Skipton Fund, the Caxton Foundation] or the Independent Living [44 Fund (2006)] which, had his income fallen to becalculated under regulation 103 (calculation of income other than earnings), would have been disregarded under paragraph 22 of Schedule 7 (income in kind); and

(c) any payment which, had his income fallen to be calculated under regulation 103 would have been disregarded under paragraph 41 of Schedule 7 (payments made under certain trusts and certain other payments).

[63 (9) For the purposes of sub-paragraph (7)(j), "earned income" has the meaning given in regulation 52 of the Universal Credit Regulations 2013.]

Continuity with income support [42 or income-related employment and support allowance]

3.519 **18.**—(1) For the purpose of providing continuity between income support and a jobseeker's allowance—

(a) [66 . . .]

(b) had the award of a jobseeker's allowance been an award of income support and the housing costs which would then have been met would have included an additional amount met in accordance with paragraph 7 of Schedule 3 to the Income Support Regulations (add back), an amount equal to that additional amount shall be added to the housing costs to be met under this Schedule, but that amount shall be subject to the same qualifications and limitations as it would have been had the award been of income support; and

(c) for the purposes of any linking rule [2or for determining whether any qualifying or other period is satisfied], any reference to a jobseeker's allowance in this Schedule shall be taken also to include a reference to income support [42 or income-related employment and support allowance].

(2) Any loan which, had the claimant been entitled to income support and not a jobseeker's allowance, would have been a qualifying loan for the purposes of Schedule 3 to the Income Support Regulations by virtue of regulation 3 of the Income Support (General) Amendment and Transitional Regulations 1995 shall be treated also as a qualifying loan for the purposes of paragraph 14 or 15, as the case may be, of this Schedule; and for the purpose of determining whether a claimant would satisfy the provision of regulation 3(2) of those Regulations, a person in receipt of an income-based jobseeker's allowance shall be treated as being in receipt of income support.

Rounding of Fractions

3.520 **19.**—Where any calculation made under this Schedule results in a fraction of a penny, that fraction shall be treated as a penny.

AMENDMENTS

1. Jobseeker's Allowance (Amendment) Regulations 1996 (SI 1996/1516) reg.20 and Sch. (October 7, 1996).

2. Jobseeker's Allowance and Income Support (General) (Amendment) Regulations 1996 (SI 1996/1517) reg.29 (October 7, 1996).

3. Social Security and Child Support (Jobseeker's Allowance) (Miscellaneous Amendments) Regulations 1996 (SI 1996/2538) reg.2(12) (October 28, 1996).

4. Social Security and Child Support (Miscellaneous Amendments) Regulations 1997 (SI 1997/827) reg.4 (April 7, 1997).

5. Social Security (Miscellaneous Amendments) (No.4) Regulations 1997 (SI 1997/2305) reg.3 (October 22, 1997).

6. Social Security Amendment (New Deal) Regulations 1997 (SI 1997/2863) reg.13 (January 5, 1998).

7. Social Security (Non-Dependant Deductions) Regulations 1996 (SI 1996/2518) reg.4 (April 6, 1998).

8. Social Security (Welfare to Work) Regulations 1998 (SI 1998/2231) reg.14(4) (October 5, 1998).

9. Social Security Benefits (Miscellaneous Amendments) Regulations 1999 (SI 1999/714) reg.2(2) (April 5, 1999).

10. Income Support (General) and Jobseeker's Allowance Amendment Regulations 1999 (SI 1999/1921) reg.2(2) (August 2, 1999).

11. Social Security Act 1998 (Commencement No.11, and Savings and Consequential and Transitional Provisions) Order 1999 (SI 1999/2860 (C.75)) art.3(12) and Sch.12 (October 18, 1999).

12. Social Security Amendment (Employment Zones) Regulations 2000 (SI 2000/724) reg.4(4)(d) (April 3, 2000).

13. Social Security (Miscellaneous Amendments) Regulations 2001 (SI 2001/488) reg.12(b)(i) (April 9, 2001).

14. Social Security (Miscellaneous Amendments) Regulations 2001 (SI 2001/488) reg.12(b)(ii) (April 9, 2001).

15. Social Security (Miscellaneous Amendments) Regulations 2001 (SI 2001/488) reg.12(b)(iii) (April 9, 2001).

16. Jobseeker's Allowance (Joint Claims) Regulations 2000 (SI 2000/1978) reg.2(5) and Sch.2 para.54 (March 19, 2001).

17. Social Security Amendment (New Deal) Regulations 2001 (SI 2001/ 1029) reg.11 (April 9, 2001).

18. Income Support (General) and Jobseeker's Allowance Amendment Regulations 2001 (SI 2001/3651) reg.2(2) (December 10, 2001).

19. Social Security (Miscellaneous Amendments) Regulations 2002 (SI 2002/841) reg.6 (April 8, 2002).

20. Child Support (Consequential Amendments and Transitional Provisions) Regulations 2001 (SI 2001/158) reg.7(3) (in force in relation to any particular case on the day on which s.1 of the Child Support, Pensions and Social Security Act 2000 comes into force in relation to that type of case).

21. Social Security (Hospital In-Patients and Miscellaneous Amendments) Regulations 2003 (SI 2003/1195) reg.6(4) (May 21, 2003).

22. State Pension Credit (Consequential, Transitional and Miscellaneous Provisions) Regulations 2002 (SI 2002/3019) reg.30 (October 6, 2003).

23. Social Security (Housing Costs Amendments) Regulations 2004 (SI 2004/2825) reg.2(2) (November 28, 2004).

24. Social Security (Housing Costs Amendments) Regulations 2004 (SI 2004/2825) reg.2(3) (November 28, 2004).

25. Social Security (Housing Costs Amendments) Regulations 2004 (SI 2004/2825) reg.2(4) (November 28, 2004).

26. Social Security (Housing Costs Amendments) Regulations 2004 (SI 2004/2825) reg.2(5) (November 28, 2004).

27. Social Security (Housing Benefit, Council Tax Benefit, State Pension Credit and Miscellaneous Amendments) Regulations 2004 (SI 2004/2327) reg.6(a) (April 4, 2005).

28. Social Security (Housing Benefit, Council Tax Benefit, State Pension Credit and Miscellaneous Amendments) Regulations 2004 (SI 2004/2327) reg.6(b) (April 4, 2005).

29. Social Security (Care Homes and Independent Hospitals) Regulations 2005 (SI 2005/2687) reg.3 and Sch.2 para.9 (October 24, 2005).

30. Housing Benefit and Council Tax Benefit (Consequential Provisions) Regulations 2006 (SI 2006/217) reg.5 and Sch.2 para.8(4) (March 6, 2006).
31. Social Security (Hospital In-Patients) Regulations 2005 (SI 2005/3360) reg.6(4) (April 10, 2006).
32. Social Security (Miscellaneous Amendments) (No.4) Regulations 2006 (SI 2006/2378) reg.13(11)(a) (October 2, 2006).
33. Social Security (Miscellaneous Amendments) (No.4) Regulations 2006 (SI 2006/2378) reg.13(11)(b) (October 2, 2006).
34. Social Security (Miscellaneous Amendments) (No.4) Regulations 2006 (SI 2006/2378) reg.13(11)(c) (October 2, 2006).
35. Social Security (Miscellaneous Amendments) (No.4) Regulations 2006 (SI 2006/2378) reg.13(10)(b) (October 9, 2006).
36. Social Security (Miscellaneous Amendments) (No.5) Regulations 2006 (SI 2006/3274) reg.3 (January 8, 2007).
37. Social Security (Housing Costs and Miscellaneous Amendments) Regulations 2007 (SI 2007/3183) reg.4(2)(a) (December 17, 2007).
38. Social Security (Housing Costs and Miscellaneous Amendments) Regulations 2007 (SI 2007/3183) reg.4(2)(b) (December 17, 2007).
39. Social Security (Housing Costs and Miscellaneous Amendments) Regulations 2007 (SI 2007/3183) reg.4(2)(c) (December 17, 2007).
40. Social Security (Miscellaneous Amendments) Regulations 2008 (SI 2008/698) reg.4(15) (April 14, 2008).
41. Social Security (Students Responsible for Children or Young Persons) Amendment Regulations 2008 (SI 2008/1826) reg.3(5) (July 9, 2008).
42. Employment and Support Allowance (Consequential Provisions) (No.2) Regulations 2008 (SI 2008/1554) reg.3(25) (October 27, 2008).
43. Employment and Support Allowance (Miscellaneous Amendments) Regulations 2008 (SI 2008/2428) reg.41(3) (October 27, 2008).
44. Social Security (Miscellaneous Amendments) (No.6) Regulations 2008 (SI 2008/2767) reg.4(7) (November 17, 2008).
45. Social Security (Miscellaneous Amendments) (No.6) Regulations 2008 (SI 2008/2767) reg.4(10) (November 17, 2008).
46. Social Security (Housing Costs Special Arrangements) (Amendment and Modification) Regulations 2008 (SI 2008/3195) reg.2(1)(c) and (2) (January 5, 2009).
47. Social Security (Miscellaneous Amendments) Regulations 2009 (SI 2009/583) reg.4(3) (April 6, 2009).
48. Social Security (Flexible New Deal) Regulations 2009 (SI 2009/480) reg.2(12) (October 5, 2009).
49. Social Security (Equalisation of State Pension Age) Regulations 2009 (SI 2009/1488) reg.14 (April 6, 2010).
50. Social Security (Miscellaneous Amendments) (No.2) Regulations 2010 (SI 2010/641) reg.4(3)(e) (April 6, 2010).
51. Social Security (Miscellaneous Amendments) (No.2) Regulations 2010 (SI 2010/641) reg.4(8)(d) (April 6, 2010).
52. Social Security (Miscellaneous Amendments) (No.4) Regulations 2009 (SI 2009/2655) reg.4(13) (April 12, 2010).
53. Social Security (Housing Costs) (Standard Interest Rate) Amendment Regulations 2010 (SI 2010/1811) reg.2(1)(b) and (2) (October 1, 2010).
54. Social Security (Miscellaneous Amendments) Regulations 2011 (SI 2011/674) reg.7(7) (April 11, 2011).
55. Social Security (Miscellaneous Amendments) (No.3) Regulations 2011 (SI 2011/2425) reg.10(9) (October 31, 2011).
56. Social Security (Miscellaneous Amendments) (No.3) Regulations 2011 (SI 2011/2425) reg.10(13) (October 31, 2011).
57. Employment and Support Allowance (Duration of Contributory Allowance) (Consequential Amendments) Regulations 2012 (SI 2012/913) reg.4 (May 1, 2012).

58. Social Security (Miscellaneous Amendments) Regulations 2013 (SI 2013/443) reg.4(11)(a) (April 2, 2013).
59. Social Security (Miscellaneous Amendments) Regulations 2013 (SI 2013/443) reg.4(11)(b) (April 2, 2013).
60. Personal Independence Payment (Supplementary Provisions and Consequential Amendments) Regulations 2013 (SI 2013/388) reg.8 and Sch. Pt 2 para.16(8) (April 8, 2013).
61. Armed Forces and Reserve Forces Compensation Scheme (Consequential Provisions: Subordinate Legislation) Order 2013 (SI 2013/591) art.7 and Sch. para.10(8) (April 8, 2013).
62. Universal Credit (Consequential, Supplementary, Incidental and Miscellaneous Provisions) Regulations 2013 (SI 2013/630) reg.30(7)(a) (April 29, 2013).
63. Universal Credit (Consequential, Supplementary, Incidental and Miscellaneous Provisions) Regulations 2013 (SI 2013/630) reg.30(7)(b) (April 29, 2013).
64. Social Security (Miscellaneous Amendments) Regulations 2014 (SI 2014/591) reg.4(5) (April 28, 2014).
65. Universal Credit and Miscellaneous Amendments (No.2) Regulations 2014 (SI 2014/2888) reg.3(3)(b) (November 26, 2014).
66. Social Security (Housing Costs Amendments) Regulations 2015 (SI 2015/1647) reg.3 (April 1, 2016).
67. Social Security Benefits (Adjustment of Amounts and Thresholds) Regulations 2016 (SI 2016/242) reg. 3(3) (April 11, 2016).

DEFINITIONS

"Abbeyfield Home"—see reg.1(3).
"armed forces independence payment"—*ibid.*
"attendance allowance"—*ibid.*
"the Benefits Act"—see Jobseekers Act s.35(1).
"benefit week"—see reg.1(3).
"care home"—*ibid.*
"the Caxton Foundation"—*ibid.*
"claimant"—see Jobseekers Act s.35(1).
"close relative"—see reg.1(3).
"couple"—*ibid.*
"course of study"—*ibid.*
"co-ownership scheme"—*ibid.*
"Crown tenant"—*ibid.*
"disability living allowance"—*ibid.*
"dwelling occupied as the home"—*ibid.*
"the Eileen Trust"—*ibid.*
"employment zone programme"—*ibid.*
"family"—see Jobseekers Act s.35(1).
"the Fund"—see reg.1(3).
"housing benefit expenditure"—*ibid.*
"independent hospital"—*ibid.*
"the Independent Living Funds"—*ibid.*
"local welfare provision"—*ibid.*
"lone parent"—*ibid.*
"the Macfarlane (Special Payments) Trust"—*ibid.*
"the Macfarlane (Special Payments) (No.2) Trust"—*ibid.*
"the Macfarlane Trust"—*ibid.*
"MFET Limited"—*ibid.*
"non-dependant"—see reg.2.
"partner"—see reg.1(3).
"period of study"—*ibid.*
"personal independence payment"—*ibid.*

"polygamous marriage"—*ibid.*
"qualifying age for state pension credit"—*ibid.*
"remunerative work"—see reg.51(1).
"single claimant"—see reg.1(3).
"the Skipton Fund"—*ibid.*
"student"—see reg.130 and reg.1(3).
"training allowance"—see reg.1(3).
"universal credit"—*ibid.*
"water charges"—*ibid.*
"welfare to work beneficiary"—*ibid.*
"year of assessment"—*ibid.*

General Note

3.521 Most of this Schedule is very similar to Sch.3 to the Income Support Regulations, subject to some minor differences in the wording. See the notes to Sch.3. There are a few differences which reflect the fact that a claimant must satisfy the labour market conditions in order to be entitled to JSA. Thus there was no equivalent of para.8(2)(b) of Sch.3 in para.7 (note that para.8(2)–(5) of Sch.3 and para.7(3)–(7) were revoked on April 1, 2016, subject to a saving provision (see p.824)). See also the differences in para.3(11)(c)(i) and (ii) (person treated as occupying his home during temporary absences of up to 52 weeks). Note also in para.13 (linking rules) the additional category (from October 28, 1996) in sub-para.(5)(bb): person who is not entitled to income-based JSA because his contribution-based JSA equals or exceeds his applicable amount for income-based JSA; and that a carer in sub-para.(7) is defined by reference to reg.13(4) (person with caring responsibilities, see reg.4 for the definition of "caring responsibilities") rather than being restricted to a person who cares for someone receiving attendance allowance or disability living allowance, etc.

Note that in relation to, for example, satisfying the waiting periods for housing costs (from April 1, 2016, there is only one waiting period of 39 weeks, subject to a saving provision (see p.824)), periods during which hardship payments are being made will count, since hardship payments are payments of JSA. In addition, periods when a claimant is sanctioned will count towards the waiting period, since entitlement to JSA continues during the sanction, even though JSA is not paid. This will be so whether or not a hardship payment is made. But "waiting days" at the beginning of a JSA claim are not days of entitlement. The amendments made on March 19, 2001 are necessary because of the introduction of joint-claim jobseeker's allowance (see the notes at the beginning of the Jobseekers Act 1995 and to s.1(4) of the Act). Obviously there is no equivalent to these amendments in Sch.3 to the Income Support Regulations.

The transitional protection provisions in para.7 of Sch.3 to the Income Support Regulations have been omitted, but note the effect of para.18(1)(b) (para.7 of Sch.3 was revoked on April 1, 2016). Paragaph 18 is important for claimants transferring from income support or income-related ESA to jobseeker's allowance. For the equivalent of para.18(1)(c) where the transfer is to income support, see reg.32 of the Income Support (General) (Jobseeker's Allowance Consequential Amendments) Regulations 1996 (p.807) and para.20 of Sch.6 to the ESA Regulations 2008 in Vol.I of this series where the transfer is to ESA. See p.804 for reg.3 of the Income Support (General) Amendment and Transitional Regulations 1995 referred to in para.18(2) and see the note to para.7 of Sch.3. Note also the further transitional provisions in reg.87(4)–(6). For the linking rule where the claimant's former partner was entitled to state pension credit, see para.13(16), inserted with effect from October 6, 2003.

Note also that entitlement to either contribution-based or income-based JSA counts towards the waiting periods in paras 6 and 7 (there is now only one waiting period of 39 weeks, as para.6 has been revoked and para.7 has been amended with effect from April 1, 2016, subject to a saving provision (see p.824)). As the Commissioner points out in *CJSA 2028/2000* the words used are "a jobseeker's allowance" and so refer to either element of JSA.

SCHEDULE 3

[Revoked by the Social Security (Removal of Residential Allowance and Miscellaneous Amendments) Regulations 2003 (SI 2003/1121), reg.4 and Sch.2, para.10 with effect from October 6, 2003.] **3.522**

SCHEDULE 4

Applicable Amounts of Persons in Residential Care and Nursing Homes

[Revoked by Social Security Amendment (Residential Care and Nursing Homes) Regulations 2001 (SI 2001/3767) reg.2 and Sch. Pt II para.19 with effect from April 8, 2002.] **3.523**

SCHEDULE 4A

Applicable Amount of a Joint-Claim Couple where a Member is in a Residential Care or Nursing Home

[Inserted by Jobseeker's Allowance (Joint Claims) Regulations 2000 (SI 2000/1978) reg.2(5) and Sch.2, para.55 with effect from March 19, 2001 and revoked by Social Security Amendment (Residential Care and Nursing Homes) Regulations 2001 (SI 2001/3767) reg.2 and Sch. Pt II para.19 with effect from April 8, 2002.] **3.524**

SCHEDULE 5 **[[15] Regulations 85 and 85A]**

Applicable Amounts in Special Cases

3.525

Column (1)	*Column (2)*
1.—[[14] . . .]	**1.**—[[14] . . .]
[[14] Claimant who is a patient **1A.**—[[16] . . .]	**1A.**—[[16] . . .]
2.—[[12 17]. . .] **2.**—[[12 17]. . .]	
Claimants Without Accommodation **3.**—A claimant who is without accommodation.	**3.**—The amount applicable to him under regulation 83(a) (personal allowance) only.
Members of Religious Orders **4.**—A claimant who is a member of and fully maintained by a religious order.	**4.**—Nil
Specified Cases of Temporarily Separated Couples **5.**—A claimant who is a member of a couple and who is temporarily separated from his partner, where— (a) one member of the couple is— [[13] (i) not a patient but is residing in a care home, an Abbeyfield Home or an independent hospital, or] (ii) [[13] . . .] (iii) resident in premises used for the rehabilition of alcoholics or drug addicts, or (iv) resident in accommodation provided under section 3 of and	**5.**—Either— (a) the amount applicable to him as a member of a couple under regulation 83; or

Column (1)	*Column (2)*
Part II of the Schedule to, the Polish Resettlement Act 1947 (provision of accommodation in camps), (v) or participating in arrangements for training made under section 2 of the Employment and Training Act 1973, or section 2 of the Enterprise and New Towns (Scotland) Act 1990 or participating in an employment rehabilitation programme established under that section of the Act of 1973, where the course requires him to live away from the dwelling occupied as the home, or (vi) in a probation or bail hostel approved for the purpose by the Secretary of State, and (b) the other member of the couple is— (i)living in the dwelling occupied as the home, or (ii)a patient, or [13 (iii)residing in a care home, an Abbeyfield Home or an independent hoptial.]	(b) the aggregate of his applicable amount and that of his partner assessed under the provisions of these Regulations as if each of them were a single claimant, or a lone parent. whichever is the greater.
Polygamous Marriages where one or more partners are temporarily separated 6. Either— **6.**—A claimant who is a member of a polygamous marriage and who is temporarily separated from a partner of his, where one of them is living in the home while the other member is— [13 (a) not a patient but is residing in a care home, an Abbeyfield Home or or an independent hospital, or] (b) resident in premises used for the rehabilitation of alcoholics or drug addicts; or (c) attending a course of training or instruction provided or approved by the Secretary of State where the course requires him to live away from home; or (d) in a probation or bail hostel approved for the purpose by the Secretary of State.	(a) the amount applicable to the members of the polygamous marriage under regulation 84; or (b) the aggregate of the amount applicable for the members of the polygamous marriage who remain in the home under regulation 84 and the amount applicable in respect of those members not in the home calculated as if each of them were a single claimant, or a lone parent, whichever is the greater.
Single claimants temporarily in local authority accommodation **7.**—[11 . . .]	**7.**—[11 . . .]
Couples and members of polygamous marriages where one member is or all are temporarily in local authority accommodation **8.**—[11 . . .]	**8.**—[11 . . .]

Column (1)	*Column (2)*
Lone parents who are in residential accommodation temporarily **9.**—[11 . . .]	**9.**—[11 . . .]

Column (1)	*Column (2)*
Couples where one member is absent from the United Kingdom **10.**—[7(1)] Subject to paragraph 11, a claimant who is a member of a couple and whose partner is temporarily absent from the United Kingdom. applicable to the claimant in Great Britain under regulation 83 [9 . . .] as the case may be as if the claimant were a single claimant or, as the case may be, a lone parent.	**10.**—[7(1)] For the first four weeks of that absence, the amount applicable to them as a couple under regulation 83 [9 . . .] as the case may be and thereafter the amount
[7 (2) A claimant who is a member of a joint-claim couple and whose partner is temporarily absent from the United Kingdom— (a) in the circumstances prescribed in regulation 50(6A); (b) in any other circumstances.]	[7 (2) (a) For the first four weeks of that absence, the amount applicable to them as a couple under regulation 83 [9 . . .] and thereafter the amount applicable to the claimant in Great Britain under regulation 83 [9 . . .] as if the claimant were a single claimant; (b) The amount which would be applicable to the claimant under regulation 83 [9 . . .] if that claimant was a single claimant for the period commencing on the date of claim and ending on the day after the day on which the partner returns to the United Kingdom.]
Couple or member of couple taking child or young person abroad for treatment **11.**—(1) A claimant who is a member of a couple where either— (a) he or his partner is, or (b) both he and his partner are absent from [1United Kingdom] in the circumstances specified in sub-paragraph (2), (2) For the purpose of sub-paragraph (1), the specified circumstances are— (a) the claimant is absent from the United Kingdom but is treated as [5available for and actively seeking] employment in accordance with regulations 14(1) and 19(1); (b) the claimant's partner is absent from the United Kingdom and regulation 50(5) would have applied to him if he had claimed a jobseeker's allowance.	**11.**—For the first 8 weeks of that absence, the amount applicable to the claimant under regulation 83 [8 . . .], as the case may be, and, thereafter, if the claimant is in Great Britain the amount applicable to him under regulation 83 [8 . . .], as the case may be, as if the claimant were a single claimant, or, as the case may be, a lone parent

Column (1)	*Column (2)*
Polygamous marriages where any member is abroad **12.**—Subject to paragraph 13 a claimant who is a member of a polygamous marriage where— (a) he or one of his partners is, or (b) he and one or more of his partners are, or (c) two or more of his partners are, temporarily absent from the United Kingdom.	**12.**—For the first four weeks of that absence, the amount applicable to the claimant under regulations 84 to 87, as the case may be, and thereafter, if the claimant is in Great Britain the amount applicable to him under regulations 84 to 87, as the case may be, as if any member of the polygamous marriage not in the United Kingdom were not a member of the marriage.
Polygamous marriage: taking child or young person abroad for treatment **13.**—(1) A claimant who is a member of a polygamous marriage where— (a) he or one of his partners is, (b) he and one of his partners are, or [1(c) two or more of his partners are, absent from the United Kingdom in the circumstances specified in sub-paragraph (2).] (2) For the purposes of sub-paragraph (1) the specified circumstances are— (a) in respect of the claimant, [3 . . .] he is absent from the United Kingdom but is treated as available for and actively seeking employment in accordance with regulations 14(1) and 19(1); or [3(b)] one or more of the members of the polygamous marriage is absent from the United Kingdom and regulation 50(5) would have applied to the absent partner [1if he had claimed a jobseeker's allowance.]	**13.**—For the first 8 weeks of that absence, the amount applicable to the claimant under regulations 84 to 87, as the case may be, and thereafter, if the claimant is in Great Britain the amount applicable to him under regulations 84 to 87, as the case may be, as if any member of the polygamous marriage not in the United Kingdom were not a member of the marriage.
[6Partner of a person subject to immigration control **13A.**— (a) A claimant who is the partner of a person subject to immigration control. (b) Where regulation 84 (polygamous marriages) applies and the claimant is a person— (i) who is not subject to immigration control within the meaning of section 115(9) of the Immigration and Asylum Act; or	[12 **13A.**— (a) the amount applicable in respect of the claimant only under regulation 83(a), plus any amount which may be applicable to him under regulation 83(e) or (f) plus the amount applicable to him under regulation 87(2) or (3) or, as the case may be, regulation 85; (b) the amount determined in accordance with that regulation or regulation 85 in respect of the claimant and any partners of his who are not subject to immigration control within the meaning of section 115(9) of the Immigration

Column (1)	*Column (2)*
(ii) to whom section 115 of that Act does not apply by virtue of regulation 2 of the Social Security (Immigration and Asylum) Consequential Amendments Regulations 2000; and (iii) who is a member of a couple and one or more of his partners is subject to immigration control within the meaning of section 115(9) of that Act and section 115 of that Act applies to her for the purposes of exclusion frwom entitlement to income-based jobseeker's allowance.]	and Asylum Act and to whom section 115 of that Act does not apply for the purposes of exclusion from entitlement to jobseeker's allowance;]
Persons from abroad 14.—[6 person from abroad]	14.—[18 . . . nil]
[6Persons in residential accommodation 15.—(1) [11 . . .] (2) [10 . . .]	15.—(1) [11 . . .] (2) [10 . . .]]
Persons temporarily absent from a hostel, residential care or nursing home 16.—[8 . . .]	16.—[8 . . .]
Persons in residential care or nursing homes who become patients 17.—[8 . . .]	17.—[8 . . .]
[7 **Joint-claim couples where a claim is made other than jointly by both members** **17A.**—A joint claim couple and one member— (a) is a person to whom regulation 3E(2)(a) applies; (b) is a person to whom regulation 3E(2)(b) applies.]	[7 (a) The amount which would be applicable to the claimant under regulation 83 [10 . . .] if that claimant was a single claimant for the period commencing on the day on which the member of the couple who is not the claimant fails to attend at the time and place specified by the Secretary of State for the purposes of regulation 6 of the Claims and Payments Regulations and ending on the day on which that member does so attend; (b) The amount which would be applicable to the claimant under regulation 83 [10 . . .] if that claimant was a single claimant.]

Rounding of fractions

18.—Where any calculation under this Schedule or as a result of a jobseeker's allowance being awarded for a period less than one complete benefit week results in a fraction of a penny that fraction shall be treated as a penny. **3.526**

AMENDMENTS

1. Jobseeker's Allowance (Amendment) Regulations 1996 (SI 1996/1516) reg.20 and Sch. (October 7, 1996).

2. Jobseeker's Allowance and Income Support (General) (Amendment) Regulations 1996 (SI 1996/1517) reg.30 (October 7, 1996).

3. Social Security and Child Support (Jobseeker's Allowance) (Miscellaneous Amendments) Regulations 1996 (SI 1996/2538) reg.2(13) (October 28, 1996).

4. Child Benefit, Child Support and Social Security (Miscellaneous Amendments) Regulations 1996 (SI 1996/1803) reg.45 (April 7, 1997).

5. Social Security (Miscellaneous Amendments) Regulations 1997 (SI 1997/454) reg.2(15) (April 7, 1997).

6. Social Security (Immigration and Asylum) Consequential Amendments Regulations 2000 (SI 2000/636) reg.4 (April 3, 2000).

7. Jobseeker's Allowance (Joint Claims) Regulations 2000 (SI 2000/1978) reg.2(5) and Sch.2 para.56 (March 19, 2001).

8. Social Security Amendment (Residential Care and Nursing Homes) Regulations 2001 (SI 2001/3767) reg.2 and Sch. Pt II para.20 (April 8, 2002).

9. Social Security Amendment (Residential Care and Nursing Homes) Regulations 2001 (SI 2001/3767) reg.2 and Sch. Pt II para.20 (as amended by Social Security Amendment (Residential Care and Nursing Homes) Regulations 2002 (SI 2002/398) reg.4(3)) (April 8, 2002).

10. Social Security (Hospital In-Patients and Miscellaneous Amendments) Regulations 2003 (SI 2003/1195) reg.6 (May 21, 2003).

11. Social Security (Removal of Residential Allowance and Miscellaneous Amendments) Regulations 2003 (SI 2003/1121) reg.4 and Sch.2 para.11 (October 6, 2003).

12. Social Security (Working Tax Credit and Child Tax Credit) (Consequential Amendments) (SI 2003/455) reg.3 and Sch.2 para.20 (April 6, 2004, except in "transitional cases" and see further the note to reg.83 and to reg.17 of the Income Support Regulations).

13. Social Security (Care Homes and Independent Hospitals) Regulations 2005 (SI 2005/2687) reg.3 and Sch.2 para.10 (October 24, 2005).

14. Social Security (Hospital In-Patients) Regulations 2005 (SI 2005/3360) reg.6 (April 10, 2006).

15. Social Security (Miscellaneous Amendments) Regulations 2007 (SI 2007/719) reg.3(9)(a) (April 2, 2007).

16. Social Security (Miscellaneous Amendments) Regulations 2007 (SI 2007/719) reg.3(9)(b) (April 9, 2007).

17. Social Security (Miscellaneous Amendments) Regulations 2007 (SI 2007/719) reg.3(9)(c) (April 8, 2007).

18. Social Security Benefits Up-rating Order 2007 (SI 2007/688) art.24(8) and Sch.17 (April 9, 2007).

DEFINITIONS

"Abbeyfield Home"—see reg.1(3).
"care home"—*ibid.*
"child"—see Jobseekers Act s.35(1).
"claimant"—*ibid.*
"couple"—see reg.1(3).
"family"—see Jobseekers Act s.35(1).
"independent hospital"—see reg.1(3).
"lone parent"—*ibid.*
"partner"—*ibid.*
"patient"—see reg.85(4).
"person from abroad"—*ibid.*

"polygamous marriage"—see reg.1(3).
"prisoner"—see reg.85(4).
"relative"—see reg.1(3).
"single claimant"—*ibid.*
"young person"—see reg.76.

GENERAL NOTE

See the note to reg.85. 3.527

There are some differences between this Schedule and Sch.7 to the Income Support Regulations, mainly due to the different conditions of entitlement for JSA (see, e.g. paras 1 and 2).

[1 SCHEDULE 5A **Regulation 86C**

APPLICABLE AMOUNTS OF JOINT-CLAIM COUPLES IN SPECIAL CASES

3.528

Column (1)	*Column (2)*
Patients **1.**—[8 . . . **1A.**—[9 . . .]	 **1.**—[8 . . . **1A.**—[9 . . .]
Joint-claim couple without accommodation **2.**—A joint-claim couple who are without accommodation.	**2.**—The amount applicable to the couple under regulation 86A(a) (personal allowance) only.
Members of religious orders **3.**—A joint-claim couple who are both members of and fully maintained by a religious order.	**3.**—Nil.
Specified cases of temporarily separated joint-claim couples **4.**—A joint-claim couple who are temporarily separated where— (a) one member is— [7 (i) not a patient but is residing in a care home, an Abbeyfield Home or an independent hospital, or] (ii) [7 . . . (iii) resident in premises used for the rehabilitation of alcoholics or drug addicts; (iv) resident in accommodation provided under section 3 of, and Part II of the Schedule to, the Polish Resettlement Act 1947 (provision of accommodation in camps); (v) participating in arrangements for training made under section 2 of the Employment and Training Act 1973, or section 2 of the Enterprise and New Towns (Scotland) Act 1990 or participating in an employment rehabilitation	**4.**—Either— (a) the amount applicable to the joint-claim couple under

Column (1)	*Column (2)*
programme established under that section of the Act of 1973, where the course requires him to live away from the dwelling occupied as the home; or (vi) in a probation or bail hostel approved for the purpose by the Secretary of State, and (b) the other member is— (i) living in the dwelling occupied as the home; (ii) a patient; [7 (iii) residing in a care home, an Abbeyfield Home or an independent hospital.]	(b) the aggregate of the applicable amounts of both claimants assessed under the provisions of these Regulations as if each of them were a single claimant, whichever is the greater.
Polygamous Marriages where one or more members of the marriage are temporarily separated **5.**—A joint-claim couple where one member is a member of a polygamous marriage and is temporarily separated from a partner of his, where one of them is living in the home while the other member is— [7 (a) not a patient but is residing in a care home, an Abbeyfield Home or an independent hospital, or] (b) [7 . . .] (c) resident in premises used for the rehabilitation of alcoholics or drug addicts; (d) attending a course of training or instruction provided or approved by the Secretary of State where the course requires him to live away from home; or (e) in a probation or bail hostel approved for the purpose by the Secretary of State.	**5.**—Either— (a) the amount applicable to the joint-claim couple under regulation 86B; or (b) the aggregate of the amount applicable for the joint-claim couple in respect of the members of the polygamous marriage who remain in the home under regulation 86B and the amount applicable in respect of those members not in the home calculated as if each of them were a single claimant, whichever is the greater.
Joint-claim couples and members of polygamous marriages where one member is, or all are, temporarily in local authority accommodation **6.**—[6 . . .]	**6.**—[6 . . .]
Joint-claim couples where one member is absent from the United Kingdom **7.**—A joint-claim couple where one member is temporarily absent from the United Kingdom— (a) in the circumstances prescribed in regulation 50(6B);	**7.**— (a) The amount applicable to them as a couple under regulation 86A [2 . . .] for the relevant period prescribed in regulation 50(6B).
(b) in any other circumstances.	(b) For the first four weeks of that absence, the amount applicable to them as a couple under regulation

Column (1)	*Column (2)*
	86A [2. . .] as the case may be and thereafter the amount applicable to the claimant in Great Britain under regulation 83 [2 . . .] as the case may be as if that claimant were a single claimant.
Polygamous marriages where any member of the marriage is abroad **8.**—A joint-claim couple where one member is a member of a polygamous marriage and— (a)he, the other member or one of his partners is; (b) he, the other member and one or more of his partners are; or (c) the other member and one or more of his partners or two or more of his partners are, temporarily absent from the United Kingdom.	**8.**—For the first four weeks of that absence, the amount applicable to the joint-claim couple under regulations 86B to [2 86C], as the case may be, and thereafter, if the joint-claim couple are in Great Britain the amount applicable to them under regulations 86B to [2 86C], as the case may be, as if any member of the polygamous marriage not in the United Kingdom were not a member of the marriage.
Members of joint-claim couples in residential accommodation **9.**—[4 . . .]	**9.**—[4 . . .]
Members of joint-claim couples temporarily absent from a hostel, residential care or nursing home **10.**—[2 . . .]	**10.**—[2 . . .]
Members of joint-claim couples in residential care or nursing homes who become patients **11.**—[2 . . .]	**11.**—[2 . . .]

Rounding of fractions

12.—Where any calculation under this Schedule or as a result of a joint-claim jobseeker's allowance being awarded for a period of less than one complete benefit week results in a fraction of a penny, that fraction shall be treated as a penny.] **3.529**

AMENDMENTS

1. Jobseeker's Allowance (Joint Claims) Regulations 2000 (SI 2000/1978) reg.2(5) and Sch.2 para.57 (March 19, 2001).
2. Social Security Amendment (Residential Care and Nursing Homes) Regulations 2001 (SI 2001/3767) reg.2 and Sch. Pt II para.21 (April 8, 2002).
3. Social Security Benefits Up-Rating Order 2003 (SI 2003/526) art.23(9) and Sch.14 (April 7, 2003).
4. Social Security (Removal of Residential Allowance and Miscellaneous Amendments) Regulations 2003 (SI 2003/1121) reg.4 and Sch.2 para.12 (October 6, 2003).
5. Social Security (Hospital In-Patients and Miscellaneous Amendments) Regulations 2003 (SI 2003/1195) reg.6 (May 21, 2003).
6. Social Security (Miscellaneous Amendments) Regulations 2004 (SI 2004/565) reg.6 (April 1, 2004).

7. Social Security (Care Homes and Independent Hospitals) Regulations 2005 (SI 2005/2687) reg.3 and Sch.2 para.10 (October 24, 2005).

8. Social Security (Hospital In-Patients) Regulations 2005 (SI 2005/3360) reg.6 (April 10, 2006).

9. Social Security (Miscellaneous Amendments) Regulations 2007 (SI 2007/719) reg.3(10) (April 9, 2007).

General Note

3.530 This regulation makes provision corresponding to Sch.5 for joint-claim couples.

SCHEDULE 6 **Regulations 99(2), 101(2) and 106(6)**

Sums to be Disregarded in the Calculation of Earnings

3.531 [15 **1.**—(1) In the case of a claimant who has been engaged in remunerative work as an employed earner or, had the employment been in Great Britain, would have been so engaged—

(a) any earnings, other than items to which sub-paragraph (2) applies, paid or due to be paid from that employment which terminated before the first day of entitlement to a jobseeker's allowance;

(b) any earnings, other than a payment of the nature described in [17 sub-paragraph (2)(a) or (b)(ii)] paid or due to be paid from that employment which has not been terminated where the claimant is not—

(i) engaged in remunerative work, or

(ii) suspended from his employment.

(2) This sub-paragraph applies to—

[17 (a) any payment of the nature described in—

(i) regulation 98(1)(d), or

(ii) section 28, 64 or 68 of the Employment Rights Act 1966 (guarantee payments, suspension from work on medical or maternity grounds); and]

(b) any award, sum or payment of the nature described in—

(i) regulation 98(1)(f) or (g), or

(ii) section 34 or 70 of the Employment Rights Act 1996 (guarantee payments and suspension from work: complaints to employment tribunals),

including any payment made following the settlement of a complaint to an employment tribunal or of court proceedings.

1A.—If the claimant's partner has been engaged in remunerative work as an employed earner or, had the employment been in Great Britain, would have been so engaged, any earnings paid or due to be paid on termination of that employment by way of retirement but only if—

(a) on retirement the partner is entitled to a retirement pension under the Benefits Act, or

(b) the only reason the partner is not entitled to a retirement pension under the Benefits Act is because the contribution conditions are not satisfied.

[23 **1B.** If the claimant's partner has been engaged in remunerative work as an employed earner or, had the employment been in Great Britain, would have been so engaged, any earnings paid or due to be paid on termination of that employment by way of retirement but only if—

(a) on retirement the partner is entitled to a state pension under Part 1 of the Pensions Act 2014, or

(b) the only reason the partner is not entitled to a state pension under Part 1 of the Pensions Act 2014 is because the partner does not have the minimum number of qualifying years.]

2.—(1) In the case of a claimant to whom this paragraph applies, any earnings (other than items to which paragraph 1(2) applies) which relate to employment which ceased before the first day of entitlement to a jobseeker's allowance whether or not that employment has terminated.

(2) This paragraph applies to a claimant who has been engaged in part-time employment as an employed earner or, had the employment been in Great Britain, would have been so engaged; but it does not apply to a claimant who has been suspended from his employment.]

3.—Any payment to which regulation 98(1)(f) applies—

(a) which is due to be paid more than 52 weeks after the date of termination of the employment in respect of which the payment is made; or

(b) which is a compensatory award within the meaning of section [15 118(1)(b) of the Employment Rights Act 1996] for so long as such an award remains unpaid and the employer is insolvent within the meaning of section 127 of that Act.

4.—In the case of a claimant who has been engaged in remunerative work or part-time employment as a self-employed earner or, had the employment been in Great Britain, would have been so engaged and who has ceased to be so employed, from the date of the cessation of his employment any earnings derived from that employment except earnings to which regulation 95(2) (royalties etc.) applies.

5.—(1) In a case to which this paragraph applies, [7 £20.00] but notwithstanding regulation 88 (calculation of income and capital of members of claimant's family and of a polygamous marriage), if this paragraph applies to a claimant it shall not apply to his partner except where, and to the extent that, the earnings of the claimant which are to be disregarded under this paragraph are less than [7 £20.00].

(2) This paragraph applies where the claimant's applicable amount includes, or but for his being an in-patient [8 . . .] [13 . . .] would include, an amount by way of a disability premium under Schedule 1 (applicable amounts).

(3) This paragraph applies where—

(a) the claimant is a member of a couple, and—

(i) his applicable amount would include an amount by way of the disability premium under Schedule 1 but for the higher pensioner premium under that Schedule being applicable; or

(ii) had he not been an in-patient [8 . . .] [13 . . .] his applicable amount would include the higher pensioner premium under that Schedule and had that been the case he would also satisfy the condition in (i) above; and

(b) he or his partner [18 has not attained the qualifying age for state pension credit] and at least one is engaged in part-time employment.

(4) This paragraph applies where—

(a) the claimant's applicable amount includes, or but for his being an in-patient [8 . . .] [13 . . .] would include, an amount by way of the higher pensioner premium under Schedule 1; and

(b) the claimant or, if he is a member of a couple, either he or his partner has attained [18 the qualifying age for state pension credit]; and

(c) immediately before attaining that age he or, as the case may be, he or his partner was engaged in part-time employment and the claimant was entitled by virtue of sub-paragraph (2) or (3) to a disregard of [7 £20.00]; and

(d) he or, as the case may be, he or his partner has continued in part-time employment.

(5) [6 . . .].

(6) [6 . . .].

(7) For the purposes of this paragraph—

(a) except where head (b) or (c) applies, no account shall be taken of any period not exceeding eight consecutive weeks occurring—

(i) on or after the date on which the claimant or, if he is a member of a couple, he or his partner attained [18 the qualifying age for state pension credit] during which either was or both were not engaged in part-time employment or the claimant was not entitled to a jobseeker's allowance [16 , income support or an employment and support allowance]; or

(ii) immediately after the date on which the claimant or his partner ceased to participate in arrangements for training made under section 2 of the Employment and Training Act 1973 or section 2 of the Enterprise and New Towns (Scotland) Act 1990 or to participate in an employment rehabilitation programme established under that section of the 1973 Act;

(b) in a case where the claimant has ceased to be entitled to a jobseeker's allowance [16 , income support or an employment and support allowance] because he, or if he is a member of a couple, he or his partner becomes engaged in remunerative work, no account shall be taken of any period, during which he was not entitled to a jobseeker's allowance [16 , income support or an employment and support allowance], not exceeding the permitted period, occurring on or after the date on which the claimant or, as the case may be, his partner attained [18 the qualifying age for state pension credit];

(c) no account shall be taken of any period occurring on or after the date on which the claimant or, if he is a member of a couple, he or his partner attained [18 the qualifying age for state pension credit] during which the claimant was not entitled to a jobseeker's allowance [16 , income support or an employment and support allowance] because he or his partner was participating in arrangements for training made under section 2 of the Employment and Training Act 1973 or section 2 of the Enterprise and New Towns (Scotland) Act 1990 or participating in an employment rehabilitation programme established under that section of the 1973 Act;

[5 **6.**—In a case where the claimant is a lone parent and paragraph 5 does not apply, [7 £20.00].

7.—(1) In a case to which neither paragraph 5 or 6 applies to the claimant, and subject to sub-paragraph (2), where the claimant's applicable amount includes an amount by way of the carer premium under Schedule 1 (applicable amounts), [7 £20.00] of the earnings of the person who is, or at any time in the preceding eight weeks was, in receipt of [9 carer's allowance] or treated in accordance with paragraph 17(2) of that Schedule as being in receipt of [9 carer's allowance].

(2) Where the carer premium is awarded in respect of the claimant and of any partner of his, their earnings shall for the purposes of this paragraph be aggregated, but the amount to be disregarded in accordance with sub-paragraph (1) shall not exceed [7 £20.00] of the aggregated amount.

8.—Where the carer premium is awarded in respect of a claimant who is a member of a couple and whose earnings are less than [7 £20.00], but is not awarded in respect of the other member of the couple, and that other member is engaged in an employment—

(a) specified in paragraph 9(1), so much of the other member's earnings as would not when aggregated with the amount disregarded under paragraph 7 exceed [7 £20.00];

(b) other than one specified in paragraph 9(1), so much of the other member's earnings from such other employment up to £5 as would not when aggregated with the amount disregarded under paragraph 7 exceed [7 £20.00].

9.—(1) In a case to which none of paragraphs 5 to 8 applies to the claimant, [7 £20.00] of earnings derived from one or more employments as—

(a) [21 . . .]

[11 (aa) [21 . . .]]

[12 (ab) [21 . . .]]

[21 (a) a part-time fire-fighter employed by a fire and rescue authority under the Fire and Rescue Services Act 2004 or by the Scottish Fire and Rescue Service established under section 1A of the Fire (Scotland) Act 2005;]

(b) an auxiliary coastguard in respect of coast rescue activities;

(c) a person engaged part-time in the manning or launching of a lifeboat;

(d) a member of any [22 . . .] reserve force prescribed in Part I of [14 Schedule 6 to the Social Security (Contributions) Regulations 2001];

but, notwithstanding regulation 88 (calculation of income and capital of members of claimant's family and of a polygamous marriage), if this paragraph applies to a claimant it shall not apply to his partner except to the extent specified in sub-paragraph (2).

(2) If the claimant's partner is engaged in employment—

(a) specified in sub-paragraph (1), so much of his earnings as would not in aggregate with the amount of the claimant's earnings disregarded under this paragraph exceed [7 £20.00];

(b) other than one specified in sub-paragraph (1), so much of his earnings from that employment up to £5 as would not in aggregate with the claimant's earnings disregarded under this paragraph exceed [7 £20.00].

10.—Where the claimant is engaged in one or more employments specified in paragraph 9(1) but his earnings derived from such employments are less than [7 £20.00] in any week and he is also engaged in any other part-time employment, so much of his earnings from that other employment up to £5 as would not in aggregate with the amount of his earnings disregarded under paragraph 9 exceed [7 £20.00].

11.—Where the claimant is a member of a couple [1 . . .]—

(a) in a case to which none of paragraphs 5 to 10 applies, £10; but, notwithstanding regulation 88 (calculation of income and capital of members of a claimant's family and of a polygamous marriage), if this paragraph applies to a claimant it shall not apply to his partner except where, and to the extent that, the earnings of the claimant which are to be disregarded under this sub-paragraph are less than £10;

(b) in a case to which one or more of paragraphs 5 to 10 applies and the total amount disregarded under those paragraphs is less than £10, so much of the claimant's earnings as would not in aggregate with the amount disregarded under paragraphs 5 to 10 exceed £10.

12.—In a case to which none of paragraphs 5 to 11 applies to the claimant, £5.

13.—Notwithstanding the foregoing provisions of this Schedule, where two or more payments of the same kind and from the same source are to be taken into account in the same benefit week, because it has not been practicable to treat the payments under regulation 96(1)(b) (date on which income treated as paid) as paid on the first day of the benefit week in which they were due to be paid, there shall be disregarded from each payment the sum that would have been disregarded if the payment had been taken into account on the date on which it was due to be paid.

14.—Any earnings derived from employment which are payable in a country outside the United Kingdom for such period during which there is a prohibition against the transfer to the United Kingdom of those earnings.

15.—Where a payment of earnings is made in a currency other than sterling, any banking charge or commission payable in converting that payment into sterling.

16.—Any earnings which are due to be paid before the date of claim and which would otherwise fall to be taken into account in the same benefit week as a payment of the same kind and from the same source.

17.—Any earnings of a child or young person [10 . . .].

18.—[10 . . .]

[19 **19.**—(1) In the case of a contribution-based jobseeker's allowance, where by reason of earnings to which sub-paragraph (3) applies (in aggregate with the claimant's other earnings (if any) calculated in accordance with this Part) the claimant would (apart from this paragraph) have a personal rate of less than 10 pence, the amount of such earnings but only to the extent that that amount exceeds the claimant's personal rate less 10 pence.

(2) In the case of an income-based jobseeker's allowance, where earnings to which sub-paragraph (3) applies (in aggregate with the claimant's other income (if any) calculated in accordance with this Part) exceed the applicable amount less 10 pence, the amount of those earnings corresponding to that excess.

(3) This sub-paragraph applies to earnings, in so far as they exceed the amount disregarded under paragraph 9, derived by the claimant from employment as a member of any [22 . . .] reserve force prescribed in Part 1 of Schedule 6 to the Contributions Regulations in respect of a period of annual continuous training for a maximum of 15 days in any calendar year [22 or in respect of training in the claimant's first year of training as a member of a reserve force for a maximum of 43 days in that year.]

(4) In sub-paragraph (1), "personal rate" means the rate for the claimant calculated as specified in section 4(1) of the Act.]

20.—In this Schedule "part-time employment" means employment in which the person is not to be treated as engaged in remunerative work under regulation 52 or 53 (persons treated as engaged, or not engaged, in remunerative work).

21.—In paragraph 5(7)(b) "permitted period" means a period determined in accordance with regulation 3A of the Income Support Regulations, as it has effect by virtue of regulation 87(7) of these Regulations.

AMENDMENTS

1. Jobseeker's Allowance (Amendment) Regulations 1996 (SI 1996/1516) reg.19 (October 7, 1996).

2. Jobseeker's Allowance (Amendment) Regulations 1996 (SI 1996/1516) reg.20 and Sch. (October 7, 1996).

3. Jobseeker's Allowance and Income Support (General) (Amendment) Regulations 1996 (SI 1996/1517) reg.31 (October 7, 1996).

4. Child Benefit, Child Support and Social Security (Miscellaneous Amendments) Regulations 1996 (SI 1996/1803) reg.46 (April 7, 1997).

5. Social Security Amendment (Lone Parents) Regulations 1998 (SI 1998/ 766) reg.15 (April 6, 1998).

6. Social Security (Miscellaneous Amendments) Regulations 2000 (SI 2000/ 681) reg.12(b) (April 3, 2000).

7. Social Security Amendment (Capital Limits and Earnings Disregards) Regulations 2000 (SI 2000/2545) reg.3 and Sch. para.3 (April 9, 2001).

8. Social Security Amendment (Residential Care and Nursing Homes) Regulations 2001 (SI 2001/3767) reg.2(2) and Pt II of Sch. para.22 (April 8, 2002).

9. Social Security (Miscellaneous Amendments) Regulations 2003 (SI 2003/ 511) reg.3(4) and (5) (April 1, 2003).

10. Social Security (Working Tax Credit and Child Tax Credit) (Consequential Amendments) Regulations 2003 (SI 2003/455) reg.3 and Sch.2 para.22 (April 6, 2004, except in "transitional cases" and see further the note to regs 83 and to 17 of the Income Support Regulations).

11. Fire and Rescue Services Act 2004 (Consequential Amendments) (England)

Order 2004 (SI 2004/3168) art.36(4) (December 30, 2004) (in relation to England); Fire and Rescue Services Act 2004 (Consequential Amendments) (Wales) Order 2005 (SI 2005/2929 (W.214)) art.36(4) (October 25, 2005) (in relation to Wales). The amendment does not extend to Scotland.

12. Fire (Scotland) Act 2005 (Consequential Provisions and Modifications) Order 2005 (SI 2005/2060 (S.7)) art.3 and Sch. para.10(4) (August 2, 2005) (in relation to Scotland only; this amendment also revokes head (a) of para.9(1), again in relation to Scotland only).

13. Social Security (Care Homes and Independent Hospitals) Regulations 2005 (SI 2005/2687) reg.3 and Sch.2 para.12 (October 24, 2005).

14. Social Security (Miscellaneous Amendments) (No.4) Regulations 2006 (SI 2006/2378) reg.13(3)(c) (October 2, 2006).

15. Social Security (Miscellaneous Amendments) (No.5) Regulations 2007 (SI 2007/2618) reg.8(14) (October 1, 2007).

16. Employment and Support Allowance (Consequential Provisions) (No.2) Regulations 2008 (SI 2008/1554) reg.3(26) (October 27, 2008).

17. Social Security (Miscellaneous Amendments) (No.4) Regulations 2009 (SI 2009/2655) reg.4(14) (October 26, 2009).

18. Social Security (Equalisation of State Pension Age) Regulations 2009 (SI 2009/1488) reg.15 (April 6, 2010).

19. Jobseeker's Allowance (Members of the Reserve Forces) Regulations 2012 (SI 2012/1616) reg.2(7) (July 30, 2012).

20. Police and Fire Reform (Scotland) Act 2012 (Consequential Provisions and Modifications) Order 2013 (SI 2013/602) art.26 and Sch.2 para.74(4) (April 1, 2013).

21. Social Security (Miscellaneous Amendments) (No.3) Regulations 2013 (SI 2013/2536) reg.6(14) (October 29, 2013).

22. Social Security (Members of the Reserve Forces) (Amendment) Regulations 2015 (SI 2015/389) reg.3(6) (April 6, 2015).

23. Pensions Act 2014 (Consequential, Supplementary and Incidental Amendments) Order 2015 (SI 2015/1985) art.16(3) (April 6, 2016).

Definitions

"the Benefits Act"—see Jobseekers Act s.35(1).
"benefit week"—see reg.1(3).
"child"—see Jobseekers Act s.35(1).
"claimant"—*ibid.*, and reg.88(1).
"couple"—see reg.1(3).
"date of claim"—*ibid.*
"employment"—see reg.3
"employed earner"—see reg.3 and SSCBA s.2(1)(a).
"first year of training"—see reg.1(3).
"Great Britain"—see Jobseekers Act s.35(1).
"family"—*ibid.*
"partner"—see reg.1(3).
"polygamous marriage"—*ibid.*
"qualifying age for state pension credit"—*ibid.*
"remunerative work"—*ibid.*, and reg.51(1).
"self employed earner"—see reg.1(3) and SSCSA s.2(1)(b).
"young person"—see regs 1(3) and 76.

General Note

3.532 Before April 6, 2004 the income (but not the capital) of a child or young person who was a member of the claimant's family was aggregated with the claimant's, subject to the modifications in reg.106. Under the form of this Schedule in force at that time paras 1–13 and 19 did not apply to children or young persons (see the form of reg.88(2) then in force) and paras 17 and 18 only applied to children and young persons (see the 2003 edition of this volume for the old form of reg.88 and of paras 17 and 18 of this Schedule). However, with effect from April 6, 2004 (except in "transitional cases"—see the note to reg.83 and to reg.17 of the Income Support Regulations), amounts for children and young persons have been removed from income-based JSA; financial assistance to help with the cost of bringing up a child or young person is now provided through the child tax credit system, see Vol.IV of this series. As a consequence, the income of a child or young person is no longer aggregated with the claimant's (see the new form of reg.88 and the notes to that regulation) and so the disregards that applied to such income are no longer needed (although note that part of para.17 has been retained). The former disregards do however remain in force for "transitional cases"—see the note to reg.83 and to reg.17 of the Income Support Regulations.

For income-based JSA claimants who had an award of child tax credit before April 6, 2004 see reg.8 of the Social Security (Working Tax Credit and Child Tax Credit) (Consequential Amendments) Regulations 2003 (SI 2003/455) (as amended) on p.811 and the notes to that regulation.

The disregards in this Schedule are similar to those in Sch.8 to the Income Support Regulations but there are some differences, the main ones being the slight difference in the treatment of earnings where part-time employment has stopped (para.2) and the disregard in para.3. See the notes to Sch.8.

Note that where the claimant is a member of a couple, unless the £20 disregard in paras 5–10 applies (para.6 cannot in fact apply as it only applies to lone parents) the earnings disregard is £10 (para.11). Since October 7, 1996 this has also been the case for income support (replacing the previous £15 earnings disregard for long-term unemployed couples aged less than 60). For a single claimant the earnings disregard is £5 (unless the £20 disregard in paras 5–10 applies) (para.12).

Paragraphs 1, 1A, 1B and 2

See the notes to paras 1 and 2 of Sch.8 to the Income Support Regulations. **3.533**
However, note that in the case of JSA the disregard is slightly less extensive where part-time work has ceased before the first day of entitlement to benefit (see para.2). Under para.2 any employment protection payments referred to in reg.98(1)(f) (but see para.3 if the payment is due to be made more than 52 weeks after the termination of the employment) or (g) (including any payment made in settlement of an employment tribunal claim or court action) are taken into account, which is not the case for income support. It is not entirely clear why this different rule for JSA is being maintained (although the difference is of less significance since the October 2009 changes to paras 1 and 2 of Sch.8 to the Income Support Regulations and to para.1 of this Schedule), since the stated intention behind the October 2007 changes was to align the treatment of termination payments on all new claims to benefit.

Paragraphs 1A and 1B apply to a claimant's partner's earnings paid on termination of employment due to retirement. Such earnings will be disregarded in full, provided that the partner is retiring at pensionable age. For the equivalent income support provision see para.1A of Sch.8 to the Income Support Regulations. Under that provision the disregard applies if the partner has reached the qualifying age for state pension credit. The difference between the two provisions reflects the fact that it is possible for a person to claim JSA up to pensionable age (i.e. currently 65 in the case of a man), whereas a person who has reached the qualifying age for state pension credit is not entitled to income support. "Qualifying age for state pension credit" is defined in reg.1(3)—the effect of that definition is that the qualifying age was 60 but from April 2010 it will gradually rise in line with the staged increase in pensionable age for women until it reaches 65 in November 2018 (this equalisation of the state pension age for men and women was previously to have been completed by April 5, 2020 but the timetable for this in the Pensions Act 1995 has been accelerated with effect from April 2016 so that women's state pension age will now be 65 by November 2018; in addition, the increase in state pension age to 66 for both men and women has been brought forward—it will start to rise from 65 in December 2018 to reach 66 by October 2020, see s.1 of the Pensions Act 2011, and between 2026 and 2028 it will rise to 67 (see s.26 of the Pensions Act 2014)).

In *R(JSA) 8/03* the claimant, a supply teacher who worked part-time, claimed JSA at the beginning of the school summer holidays. The Commissioner accepts that unless it could be shown that the claimant had a cycle of work she had ceased to be engaged in employment at the time of her claim for JSA and so her earnings fell to be disregarded under para.2. Since she worked odd days with a number of schools on an irregular basis a cycle of work could not be established. See also *CIS 914/1997* and *CJSA 2759/1998* in the note to reg.5 of the Income Support Regulations under the heading "*Term-time only workers*" for other examples of circumstances in which a cycle of work had not, or had not yet, been established.

But when a part-time worker does have a recognisable cycle of work, *R(JSA) 2/03* holds that she is to be treated as engaged in part-time work for the whole of the cycle. The Commissioner considered that it would be odd if "engaged in . . . employment" had a different meaning in para.2 from the meaning in para.1 and that although para.20 (definition of "part-time work") was not well-drafted, the reference to reg.52 in his view made it plain that a person was to be regarded as engaged in part-time work in circumstances where she would be engaged in remunerative work if a greater number of hours per week were worked. [Note that in *R(JSA) 2/03* the Commissioner held that the claimant was to be regarded as engaged in part-time employment during the whole of the cycle by virtue of reg.51(2)(c) in accordance with the House of Lords' decision in *Banks v Chief Adjudication Officer* [2001] UKHL 33 (reported as *R(IS) 15/01*). In relation to JSA (although not income support) *R(JSA) 4/03* has since held that reg.51(2)(c) is inconsistent with Directive 79/7 and should be regarded as being of no effect (see the note to reg.51). The consequence is that reg.51(2)(b)(i) applies instead (see *R(JSA) 5/03* in the note to reg.51). However, this does not affect the reasoning in *R(JSA) 2/03* that a part-time worker with a recognisable cycle of work is to be regarded as engaged in employment during the whole of the cycle.] Thus the disregard in para.2 did not apply because the claimant had not ceased to be engaged in part-time employment. The claimant in *R(JSA) 2/03* was paid monthly for a 12-hour working week during term-time only. She had claimed contribution-based JSA and therefore the question was whether any of her earnings fell to be deducted under s.4(1)(b) of the Jobseekers Act (under s.2(1)(c) it is also a condition that the claimant should "not have earnings in excess of the prescribed amount"; the Commissioner did not find it necessary to decide this point in view of his decision on the attribution of her earnings for the purposes of s.4(1)(b) but he did point out that there appeared to be no statutory provision attributing earnings to any particular period for the purposes of s.2(1)(c)). The Commissioner holds, under reg.80(1) and applying *R(IS) 10/95*, that her earnings were paid "in respect of a month" and that under the form of reg.94(2)(a) as then in force they were to be taken into account for the period of a month beginning with the first day of the benefit week in which the earnings were due to be paid. The result was that the claimant was not entitled to JSA during the half-term holiday as her earnings exceeded her JSA applicable amount.

Paragraph 3

3.534 Under JSA, any payment for compensation for unfair dismissal under ss.112(4), 113, 117(3)(a), 128, 131 and 132 of the Employment Rights Act 1996 is disregarded if it is due to be paid more than 52 weeks after the end of the employment to which it relates (sub-para.(a)). In addition, any unpaid compensatory award under s.118(1)(b) of the 1996 Act where the employer is insolvent is also disregarded (sub-para.(b)).

Paragraph 19

3.535 The effect of para.19, as amended from April 6, 2015, is that earnings as a member of a reserve force from training (i) for a maximum of 43 days in the first year of training (see the definition of "first year of training" in reg.1(3)); or (ii) for a maximum of 15 days' annual continuous training in any calendar year, are disregarded to the extent that they would have the effect of reducing JSA entitlement to less than 10p per week. This disregard is in addition to the £20 disregard of earnings as a member of a reserve force in para.9(1)(d).

Note that a claimant is treated as available for work while engaged in such reservist training (see reg.14(1)(v)) and as actively seeking work in any week in which he is taking part in such training for three or more days a week (see reg.19(1)(y)).

The purpose of these amendments is to enable entitlement to JSA to continue while a claimant (or any partner: see reg.88(1)) is attending such training. Note also that reg.2 of the Social Security (Benefit) (Members of the Forces) Regulations 1975 (SI 1975/493) has been amended by reg.2(3) of the Social Security (Benefit) (Members of the Forces) (Amendment) Regulations 2012 (SI 2012/1656) with effect from July 30, 2012, in order to remove the prohibition on entitlement to JSA for serving members of the armed forces.

See reg.94(2C) which provides that earnings from such reservist training will be taken into account, where the training lasts for the number of days listed in column 1 of the table in reg.94(2C)(c), for the number of days listed in column 2 of the table; or in any other case, for the number of days that the training lasts. The period begins on the date that the earnings are treated as paid under reg.96 (see reg.94(2D)).

Paragraph 20

See *R(JSA) 2/03* in the note to para.2 above. **3.536**

[1 SCHEDULE 6A

SUMS TO BE DISREGARDED IN THE CALCULATION OF EARNINGS OF MEMBERS OF JOINT-CLAIM COUPLES

1.—(1) In a case to which this paragraph applies, [2 £20]; but notwithstanding regulation 88ZA (calculation of income and capital of members of a joint-claim couple), if this paragraph applies to one member of a joint-claim couple, it shall not apply to the other member except where, and to the extent that, the earnings of the member which are to be disregarded under this paragraph are less than [2 £20]. **3.537**

(2) This paragraph applies where the joint-claim couple's applicable amount includes, or but for one member being an in-patient [3 . . .] [5 . . .] would include, an amount by way of a disability premium under Schedule 1 (applicable amounts).

(3) This paragraph applies where—

(a) the joint-claim couple's applicable amount would include—

(i) an amount by way of the disability premium under Schedule 1 but for the higher pensioner premium under that Schedule being applicable; or

(ii) had a member of that couple not been an in-patient [3 . . .] [5 . . .], the higher pensioner premium under that Schedule and had that been the case, the joint-claim couple would also satisfy the condition in (i) above; and

(b) either member [8 has not attained the qualifying age for state pension credit] and at least one is engaged in part-time employment.

(4) This paragraph applies where—

(a) the joint-claim couple's applicable amount includes, or but for a member being an inpatient [3 . . .] [5 . . .] would include, an amount by way of the higher pensioner premium under Schedule 1; and

(b) either member has attained [8 the qualifying age for state pension credit]; and

(c) immediately before attaining that age either, or as the case may be both, members were engaged in part-time employment and the joint-claimant was entitled by virtue of sub-paragraph (2) or (3) to a disregard of [2 £20]; and

(d) either, or as the case may be both, members have continued in part-time employment.

(5) For the purposes of this paragraph—

(a) except where paragraph (b) or (c) applies, no account shall be taken of any period not exceeding eight consecutive weeks occurring—

(i) on or after the date on which either member attained [8 the qualifying age for state pension credit] during which either member was, or both members were, not engaged in part-time employment or either member was, or both members were, not entitled to a jobseeker's allowance or [7 , income support or an employment and support allowance]; or

(ii) immediately after the date on which either member ceased to participate in arrangements for training made under section 2 of the Employment and Training Act 1973 or section 2 of the Enterprise and New Towns (Scotland) Act 1990 or ceased to participate in an employment rehabilitation programme established under that section of the 1973 Act;

(b) in a case where either or both members have ceased to be entitled to a jobseeker's allowance or [7 , income support or an employment and support allowance] because either member becomes engaged in remunerative work, no account shall be taken of any period during which either or both members were not entitled to a jobseeker's allowance or [7 , income support or an employment and support allowance], not exceeding the permitted period, occurring on or after the date on which either member attained [8 the qualifying age for state pension credit];

(c) no account shall be taken of any period occurring on or after the date on which either member attained [8 the qualifying age for state pension credit] during which either or both members were not entitled to a jobseeker's allowance or [7 , income support or an employment and support allowance] because either or both members were participating in arrangements for training made under section 2 of the Employment and Training Act 1973 or section 2 of the Enterprise and New Towns (Scotland) Act 1990 or participating in an employment rehabilitation programme established under that section of the 1973 Act.

2.—(1) In a case where paragraph 1 does not apply to a member of a joint-claim couple and subject to sub-paragraph (2), where the joint-claim couple's applicable amount includes an amount by way of the carer premium under Schedule 1 (applicable amounts), [2£20] of the earnings of the person who is, or at any time in the preceding eight weeks was, in receipt of [4 a carer's allowance] or treated in accordance with paragraph 20J(2) of that Schedule as being in receipt of [4 a carer's allowance].

(2) Where the carer premium is awarded in respect of a joint-claim couple, the earnings of each member shall for the purposes of this paragraph be aggregated but the amount to be disregarded in accordance with sub-paragraph (1) shall not exceed [2 £20] of the aggregated amount.

3.—(1) In the case to which neither paragraph 1 nor 2 applies to a member of a joint-claim couple ("the first member"), [2 £20] of earnings derived from one or more employments to which paragraph 9 of Schedule 6 applies but, notwithstanding regulation 88ZA (calculation of income and capital of a joint-claim couple), if this paragraph applies to one member of a joint-claim couple it shall not apply to the other member except to the extent specified in sub-paragraph (2).

(2) If the other member is engaged in employment—

(a) specified in sub-paragraph (1), so much of his earnings as would not in aggregate with the amount of the first member's earnings disregarded under this paragraph exceed [2 £20];

(b) other than one specified in sub-paragraph (1), so much of his earnings from that employment up to £5 as would not in aggregate with the first member's earnings disregarded under this paragraph exceed [2 £20] .

4.—Where a member of a joint-claim couple is engaged in one or more employments specified in paragraph 3(1) but his earnings derived from such employments are less than [2 £20] in any week and he is also engaged in any other part-time employment, so much of his earnings from that other employment up to £5 as would not in aggregate with the amount of his earnings disregarded under paragraph 3 exceed [2 £20].

5.—[9 . . .]

6.—(1) In a case where none of paragraphs 1 to 5 apply, £10 but, notwithstanding regulation 88ZA (calculation of income and capital of joint-claim couples), if this paragraph applies to one member of a joint-claim couple, it shall not apply to the other member except where, and to the extent that, the earnings of the member which are to be disregarded under this sub-paragraph are less than £10.

(2) In a case where one or more of paragraphs 1 to 5 apply and the total amount disregarded under those paragraphs is less than £10, so much of the earnings of the member of a joint-claim couple as would not in aggregate with the amount disregarded under paragraphs 1 to 5 exceed £10.

7.—In this Schedule, "part-time employment" and "permitted period" shall bear the meanings prescribed respectively in paragraphs 20 and 21 of Schedule 6.]

AMENDMENTS

1. Jobseeker's Allowance (Joint Claims) Regulations 2000 (SI 2000/1978) reg.2(5) and Sch.2 para.58 (March 19, 2001).
2. Social Security Amendment (Capital Limits and Earnings Disregards) Regulations 2000 (SI 2000/2545) reg.3 and Sch. para.3 (April 9, 2001).
3. Social Security Amendment (Residential Care and Nursing Homes) Regulations 2001 (SI 2001/3767) reg.2(2) and Pt II of Sch. para.23 (April 8, 2002).
4. Social Security (Miscellaneous Amendments) Regulations 2003 (SI 2003/511) reg.3(4) and (5) (April 1, 2003).
5. Social Security (Care Homes and Independent Hospitals) Regulations 2005 (SI 2005/2687) reg.3 and Sch.2 para.13 (October 24, 2005).
6. Social Security (Miscellaneous Amendments) (No.4) Regulations 2006 (SI 2006/2378) reg.13(3)(d) (October 2, 2006).
7. Employment and Support Allowance (Consequential Provisions) (No.2) Regulations 2008 (SI 2008/1554) reg.3(27) (October 27, 2008).
8. Social Security (Equalisation of State Pension Age) Regulations 2009 (SI 2009/1488) reg.16 (April 6, 2010).
9. Jobseeker's Allowance (Members of the Reserve Forces) Regulations 2012 (SI 2012/1616) reg.2(8) (July 30, 2012).

DEFINITIONS

"employment"—see reg.3.
"joint-claim couple"—see JSA s.1(4).
"joint-claim jobseeker's allowance"—*ibid.*
"qualifying age for state pension credit"—see reg.1(3).
"remunerative work"—see reg.1(3) and reg.51(1).

SCHEDULE 7 **Regulation 103(2)**

SUMS TO BE DISREGARDED IN THE CALCULATION OF INCOME OTHER THAN EARNINGS

A1.—[*Omitted*] 3.538

[88 **A2.**—Any payment made to the claimant in respect of any travel or other expenses incurred, or to be incurred, by him in respect of his participation in the Mandatory Work Activity Scheme.]

[89 [96 **A3.** . . .]]

[95 **A3.**—Any payment made to the claimant in respect of any travel or other expenses incurred, or to be incurred, by him in respect of his participation in a scheme prescribed in regulation 3 of the Jobseeker's Allowance (Schemes for Assisting Persons to Obtain Employment) Regulations 2013.]

A4.—*[Omitted]*

A5.—*[Omitted]*

1.—Any amount paid by way of tax on income which is taken into account under regulation 103 (calculation of income other than earnings).

2.—Any payment in respect of any expenses incurred [27, or to be incurred,] by a claimant who is—

(a) by a charitable or voluntary organisation; or
(b) a volunteer,

if he otherwise derives no remuneration or profit from the employment and is not to be treated as possessing any earnings under regulation 105(13) (notional income).

[76**2A.**—Any payment in respect of expenses arising out of the [106 claimant participating as a service user].]

3.—In the case of employment as an employed earner, any payment in respect of expenses wholly, exclusively and necessarily incurred in the performance of the duties of the employment.

4.—In the case of a payment of [36 [94 [116 statutory paternity pay]] by virtue of Part 12ZA of the Benefits Act, statutory adoption pay by virtue of Part 12ZB of the Benefits Act,] [108 statutory shared parental pay by virtue of Part 12ZC of the Benefits Act,] statutory sick pay or statutory maternity pay or any remuneration paid by or on behalf of an employer to the claimant who for the time being is unable to work due to illness or maternity [36 or who is taking paternity leave [109 , adoption leave or shared parental leave]]—

(a) any amount deducted by way of primary Class 1 contributions under the Benefits Act;

(b) one-half of any sum paid by the claimant by way of a contribution towards an occupational or personal pension scheme.

5.—In the case of the payment of statutory sick pay or statutory maternity pay under Parts XI or XII of the Social Security Contributions and Benefits (Northern Ireland) Act 1992 [36, or a payment under any enactment having effect in Northern Ireland corresponding to a payment of [117 statutory paternity pay] [110 statutory shared parental pay or statutory adoption pay]]—

(a) any amount deducted by way of primary Class 1 contributions under that Act;

(b) one-half of any sum paid by way of a contribution towards an occupational or personal pension scheme.

6.—Any housing benefit [51 to which the claimant is entitled].

[38 **6A.**—(1) Any guardian's allowance.]

[43 **6B.**—(1) Any child tax credit.

(2) Any child benefit.]

[85 (3) Any increase in respect of a dependent child or dependent young person under section 80 or 90 of the Benefits Act where—

(a) the claimant has a child or young person who is a member of the claimant's family for the purposes of the claimant's claim for income-based jobseeker's allowance, and

(b) the claimant, or that claimant's partner, has been awarded a child tax credit.]

[73 **6C.**—(1) £1.20 in relation to each week in which child benefit is payable to the claimant at the enhanced rate in respect of a child or qualifying young person for whom the claimant is treated as responsible.

(2) 65 pence in relation to each week in which child benefit is payable to the claimant other than at the enhanced rate in respect of a child or qualifying young person for whom the claimant is treated as responsible (and if there is more than one, 65 pence in relation to each such child or young person).

(3) This paragraph does not apply to a claimant in relation to whom regulation 3 of, and Schedule 2 to, the Social Security (Working Tax Credit and Child Tax Credit) (Consequential Amendments) Regulations 2003 have effect.

(4) In this paragraph—

"child" and "qualifying young person" have the meanings given in section 142 of the Contributions and Benefits Act;

"treated as responsible" is to be construed in accordance with section 143 of that Act;

"the enhanced rate" has the meaning given in regulation 2(1)(a) of the Child Benefit (Rates) Regulations 2006.]

[74 **7.**—The mobility component of disability living allowance [100 or the mobility component of personal independence payment].]

8.—Any concessionary payment made to compensate for the non-payment of—

(a) any payment specified in paragraph 7 or 10;

[74 (b) income support;

(c) an income-based jobseeker's allowance; [104. . .]

(d) an income-related employment and support allowance] [104 ; or

(e) universal credit].

9.—Any mobility supplement or any payment intended to compensate for the non-payment of such a supplement.

10.—Any attendance allowance [101 , the care component of disability living allowance or the daily living component of personal independence payment] [29 . . .].

11.—Any payment to the claimant as holder of the Victoria Cross or George Cross or any analogous payment.

[46 **12.**—(1) Any payment—

(a) by way of an education maintenance allowance made pursuant to—

(i) regulations made under section 518 of the Education Act 1996;

(ii) regulations made under section 49 or 73(f) of the Education (Scotland) Act 1980;

[74 (iii) directions made under section 73ZA of the Education (Scotland) Act 1980 and paid under section 12(2)(c) of the Further and Higher Education (Scotland) Act 1992; [93 . . .]]

(b) corresponding to such an education maintenance allowance, made pursuant to—

(i) section 14 or section 181 of the Education Act 2002; or

(ii) regulations made under section 181 of that Act [93 ; or

(c) in England, by way of financial assistance made pursuant to section 14 of the Education Act 2002.]

(2) Any payment, other than a payment to which sub-paragraph (1) applies, made pursuant to—

(a) regulations made under section 518 of the Education Act 1996;

(b) regulations made under section 49 of the Education (Scotland) Act 1980; or

[74 (c) directions made under section 73ZA of the Education (Scotland) Act 1980 and paid under section 12(2)(c) of the Further and Higher Education (Scotland) Act 1992,]

in respect of a course of study attended by a child or a young person or a person who is in receipt of an education maintenance allowance [93 or other payment] made pursuant to any provision specified in sub-paragraph (1).]

[33 **12A.**—Any payment made to the claimant by way of repayment under regulation 11(2) of the Education (Teacher Student Loans) (Repayment, etc.) Regulations 2002.]

13.—In the case of a claimant to whom regulation 11 (part-time students) applies, any sums intended for any expenditure specified in paragraph (2) of regulation 131 (calculation of grant income) necessary as a result of his attendance on his course.

[42 **14.**—(1) Any payment made pursuant to section 2 of the Employment and Training Act 1973 or section 2 of the Enterprise and New Towns (Scotland) Act 1990 except a payment—

(a) made as a substitute for income support, a jobseeker's allowance, incapacity benefit [69 , severe disablement allowance or employment and support allowance];

(b) of an allowance referred to in section 2(3) of the Employment and Training Act 1973 or section 2(5) of the Enterprise and New Towns (Scotland) Act 1990;

(c) intended to meet the cost of living expenses which relate to any one or more of the items specified in sub-paragraph (2) whilst a claimant is participating in an education, training or other scheme to help him enhance his employment prospects unless the payment is a Career Development Loan paid pursuant to section 2 of the Employment and Training Act 1973 and the period of education or training or the scheme, which is supported by that loan, has been completed; or

(d) made in respect of the cost of living away from home to the extent that the payment relates to rent for which housing benefit is payable in respect of accommodation which is not normally occupied by the claimant as his home.

(2) The items specified in this sub-paragraph for the purposes of sub-paragraph (1)(c) are food, ordinary clothing or footwear, household fuel, rent for which housing benefit is payable, or any housing costs to the extent that they are met under regulation 83(f) or 84(1)(g) (housing costs), of the claimant or, where the claimant is a member of a family, any other member of his family, or any council tax or water charges for which that claimant or member is liable.

(3) For the purposes of this paragraph, "ordinary clothing or footwear" means clothing or footwear for normal daily use, but does not include school uniforms, or clothing or footwear used solely for sporting activities.]

15.—[59 (1) Subject to sub-paragraph (3) and paragraph 41, any relevant payment made or due to be made at regular intervals.]

(2) [59 . . .]

(3) [59 Sub-paragraph (1)] shall not apply—

(a) to a payment which is made by a person for the maintenance of any member of his family or of his former partner or of his children;

(b) to a payment made—

(i) to a person who is, or would be, prevented from being entitled to a jobseeker's allowance by section 14 (trade disputes); or

(ii) to a member of the family of such a person where the payment is made by virtue of that person's involvement in the trade dispute.

(4) [59 . . .]

(5) [59 . . .]

[34 (5A) In this paragraph, "relevant payment" means—

(a) a charitable payment;

(b) a voluntary payment;

(c) a payment (not falling within sub-paragraph (a) or (b) above) from a trust whose funds are derived from a payment made in consequence of any personal injury to the claimant;

(d) a payment under an annuity purchased—

(i) pursuant to any agreement or court order to make payments to the claimant; or

(ii) from funds derived from a payment made,

in consequence of any personal injury to the claimant; or

(e) a payment (not falling within sub-paragraphs (a) to (d) above) received by virtue of any agreement or court order to make payments to the claimant in consequence of any personal injury to the claimant.]

(6) [[29] . . .].

16.—[[60] . . .]

[[2]**16A.**—[[29] . . .].]

[[74] **17.**—Subject to paragraphs 38 and 39, £10 of any of the following, namely—

(a) a war disablement pension (except insofar as such a pension falls to be disregarded under paragraph 9 or 10);

(b) a war widow's pension or war widower's pension;

(c) a pension payable to a person as a widow, widower or surviving civil partner under any power of Her Majesty otherwise than under an enactment to make provision about pensions for or in respect of persons who have been disabled or have died in consequence of service as members of the armed forces of the Crown;

(d) a guaranteed income payment and, if the amount of that payment has been abated to less than £10 by a [[77] pension or payment falling within article 31(1)(a) or (b) of the Armed Forces and Reserve Forces (Compensation Scheme) Order 2005], so much of [[77] that pension or payment] as would not, in aggregate with the amount of [[77] any] guaranteed income payment disregarded, exceed £10;

(e) a payment made to compensate for the non-payment of such a pension or payment as is mentioned in any of the preceding sub-paragraphs;

(f) a pension paid by the government of a country outside Great Britain which is analogous to any of the pensions or payments mentioned in sub-paragraphs (a) to (d) above;

(g) a pension paid to victims of National Socialist persecution under any special provision made by the law of the Federal Republic of Germany, or any part of it, or of the Republic of Austria;

(h) any widowed mother's allowance paid pursuant to section 37 of the Benefits Act;

(i) any widowed parent's allowance paid pursuant to section 39A of the Benefits Act.]

18.—Where a claimant receives income under an annuity purchased with a loan which satisfies the following conditions—

(a) that the loan was made as part of a scheme under which not less than 90 per cent. of the proceeds of the loan were applied to the purchase by the person to whom it was made of an annuity ending with his life or with the life of the survivor of two or more persons (in this paragraph referred to as "the annuitants") who include the person to whom the loan was made;

(b) that the interest on the loan is payable by the person to whom it was made or by one of the annuitants;

(c) that at the time the loan was made the person to whom it was made or each of the annuitants had attained the age of 65;

(d) that the loan was secured on a dwelling in Great Britain and the person to whom the loan was made or one of the annuitants owns an estate or interest in that dwelling; and

(e) that the person to whom the loan was made or one of the annuitants occupies the accommodation on which it was secured as his home at the time the interest is paid,

the amount, calculated on a weekly basis equal to—

(i) where, or in so far as, section 369 of the Income and Corporation Taxes Act 1988 (mortgage interest payable under deduction of tax) applies to the payments of interest on the loan, the interest which is payable after deduction of a sum equal to income tax on such payments at the applicable percentage of income tax within the meaning of section 369(1A) of that Act;

(ii) in any other case the interest which is payable on the loan without deduction of such a sum.

19.—Any payment made to the claimant by a person who normally resides with the claimant, which is a contribution towards that person's living and accommodation costs, except where that person is residing with the claimant in circumstances to which paragraph 20 or 21 refers.

20.—Where the claimant occupies a dwelling as his home and the dwelling is also occupied by another person and there is a contractual liability to make payments to the claimant in respect of the occupation of the dwelling by that person or a member of his family—

[[66] (a) where the aggregate of any payments made in respect of any one week in respect of the occupation of the dwelling by that person or a member of his family, or by that person and a member of his family, is less than £20, the whole of that amount; or

(b) where the aggregate of any such payments is £20 or more per week, £20.]

21.—Where the claimant occupies a dwelling as his home and he provides in that dwelling board and lodging accommodation, an amount, in respect of each person for whom such accommodation is provided for the whole or any part of a week, equal to—

(a) where the aggregate of any payments made in respect of any one week in respect of such accommodation provided to such person does not exceed £20, 100% of such payments; or

(b) where the aggregate of any such payments exceeds £20, £20 and 50% of the excess over £20.

22.—(1) [19 Subject to sub-paragraphs (2) and (3)], except where [19 regulation 103(6)(b) (provision of support under section 95 or 98 of the Immigration and Asylum Act including support provided by virtue of regulations made under Schedule 9 to that Act in the calculation of income other than earnings) or] regulation 105(10)(a)(i) (notional income) applies or in the case of a payment made—

(a) to a person who is, or would be, prevented from being entitled to a jobseeker's allowance by section 14 (trade disputes); or

(b) to a member of the family of such a person where the payment is made by virtue of that person's involvement in the trade dispute,

any income in kind.

(2) The exceptions under sub-paragraph (1) shall not apply where the income in kind is received from the Macfarlane Trust, the Macfarlane (Special Payments) Trust, the Macfarlane (Special Payments) (No.2) Trust, the Fund, the Eileen Trust [80 , MFET Limited] [91 , the Skipton Fund, the Caxton Foundation] or the Independent Living [71 Fund (2006)].

[19 (3) The first exception under sub-paragraph (1) shall not apply where the claimant is the partner of a person subject to immigration control and whose partner is receiving support provided under section 95 or 98 of the Immigration and Asylum Act including support provided by virtue of regulations made under Schedule 9 to that Act and the income in kind is support provided in respect of essential living needs of the partner of the claimant and his dependants (if any) as is specified in regulations made under paragraph 3 of Schedule 8 to the Immigration and Asylum Act.]

[53 (4) The reference in sub-paragraph (1) to "income in kind" does not include a payment to a third party made in respect of the claimant which is used by the third party to provide benefits in kind to the claimant.]

23.—(1) Any income derived from capital to which the claimant is, or is treated under regulation 115 (capital jointly held) as, beneficially entitled but, subject to sub-paragraph (2), not income [1 derived] from capital disregarded under paragraph 1, 2, 4 to 8, 11 or 17 of Schedule 8.

(2) Income derived from capital disregarded under paragraph 2 or 4 to 8 of Schedule 8 but only to the extent of—

(a) any mortgage repayments made in respect of the dwelling or premises in the period during which that income accrued; or

(b) any council tax or water charges which the claimant is liable to pay in respect of the dwelling or premises and which are paid in the period during which that income accrued.

(3) The definition of "water charges" in regulation 1(3) shall apply to sub-paragraph (2) with the omission of the words "in so far as such charges are in respect of the dwelling which a person occupies as his home".

24.—Any income which is payable in a country outside the United Kingdom for such period during which there is prohibition against the transfer to the United Kingdom of that income.

25.—Where a payment of income is made in a currency other than sterling, any banking charge or commission payable in converting that payment into sterling.

26.—(1) Any payment made to the claimant in respect of a child or young person who is a member of his family—

(a) [57 pursuant to regulations under section 2(6)(b), 3 or 4 of the Adoption and Children Act 2002 or in accordance] with a scheme approved by the [74 Scottish Ministers under section 51A] of the Adoption (Scotland) Act 1978 (schemes for payment of allowances to adopters) [90 or in accordance with an adoption allowance scheme made under section 71 of the Adoption and Children (Scotland) Act 2007 (adoption allowances schemes)];

(b) [74 . . .]

[78 (ba) which is a payment made by a local authority in Scotland in pursuance of section 50 of the Children Act 1975 (payments towards maintenance of children);]

(c) which is a payment made by a local authority in pursuance of section 15(1) of, and paragraph 15 of Schedule 1 to, the Children Act 1989 (local authority contribution to a child's maintenance where the child is living with a person as a result of a [105 child arrangements] order);

[7 (d) which is a payment made by an authority, as defined in Article 2 of the Children Order, in pursuance of Article 15 of, and paragraph 17 of Schedule 1 to, that Order (contribution by an authority to child's maintenance);]

[49 (e) in accordance with regulations made pursuant to section 14F of the Children Act 1989 (special guardianship support services);]

[43 . . .]

[58 (1A) Any payment, other than a payment to which sub-paragraph (1)(a) applies, made to the claimant pursuant to regulations under section 2(6)(b), 3 or 4 of the Adoption and Children Act 2002.]

(2) [43 . . .]

[43 **26A.**—In the case of a claimant who has a child or young person—

(a) who is a member of his family, and

(b) who is residing at an educational establishment at which he is receiving relevant education,

any payment made to that educational establishment, in respect of that child or young person's maintenance by or on behalf of a person who is not a member of the family or by a member of the family out of funds contributed for that purpose by a person who is not a member of the family.]

[86 **27.**—Any payment made to the claimant with whom a person is accommodated by virtue of arrangements made—

(a) by a local authority under—

(i) section 23(2)(a) of the Children Act 1989 (provision of accommodation and maintenance for a child whom they are looking after),

(ii) section 26 of the Children (Scotland) Act 1995 (manner of provision of accommodation to child looked after by local authority), or

(iii) regulations 33 or 51 of the Looked After Children (Scotland) Regulations 2009 (fostering and kinship care allowances and fostering allowances); or

(b) by a voluntary organisation under section 59(1)(a) of the Children Act 1989 (provision of accommodation by voluntary organisations).]

28.—[8Any payment made to the claimant or his partner for a person ("the person concerned"), who is not normally a member of the claimant's household but is temporarily in his care, by—

(a) a health authority;

(b) a local authority [51 but excluding payments of housing benefit made in respect of the person concerned];

(c) a voluntary organisation; or

(d) the person concerned pursuant to section 26(3A) of the National Assistance Act 1948 [24 [74 . . .]

[111 (dza) the person concerned where the payment is for the provision of accommodation in respect of the meeting of that person's needs under section 18 or 19 of the Care Act 2014 (duty and power to meet needs for care and support);]

[103(da) a clinical commissioning group established under section 14D of the National Health Service Act 2006;

(db the National Health Service Commissioning Board; or]

(e) [103 . . .]]

[74 (f) a Local Health Board established under section 16BA of the National Health Service Act 1977 or established by an order made under section 11 of the Health Service (Wales) Act.]]

[67 **29.**—(1) Any payment made by a local authority in accordance with—

(a) section 17, 23B, 23C or 24A of the Children Act 1989,

(b) section 12 of the Social Work (Scotland) Act 1968, or

(c) section [87 22,] 29 or 30 of the Children (Scotland) Act 1995.

(2) Any payment (or part of a payment) made by a local authority in accordance with section 23C of the Children Act 1989 or section [87 22 or] 29 of the Children (Scotland) Act 1995 (local authorities' duty to promote welfare of children and powers to grant financial assistance to persons in, or formerly in, their care) to a person ("A") which A passes on to the claimant.

(3) Sub-paragraphs (1) and (2) are subject to the following provisions.

(4) Neither of those sub-paragraphs applies where the claimant is a person who is, or would be, prevented from being entitled to a jobseeker's allowance by section 14 (trade disputes).

(5) Sub-paragraph (2) applies only where A—

(a) was formerly in the claimant's care, and
(b) is aged 18 or over, and
(c) continues to live with the claimant.]

30.—(1) Subject to sub-paragraph (2), any payment received under an insurance policy, taken out to insure against the risk of being unable to maintain repayments on a loan which qualifies under paragraph 14 or 15 of Schedule 2 (housing costs in respect of loans to acquire an interest in the dwelling, or for repairs and improvements to the dwelling, occupied as the home) and used to meet such repayments, to the extent that it does not exceed the aggregate of—

(a) the amount, calculated on a weekly basis, of any interest on that loan which is in excess of the amount met in accordance with Schedule 2 (housing costs);
(b) the amount of any payment, calculated on a weekly basis, due on the loan attributable to the repayment of capital; and
(c) any amount due by way of premiums on—
 (i) that policy, or
 (ii) an insurance policy taken out to insure against loss or damage to any building or part of a building which is occupied by the claimant as his home.

(2) This paragraph shall not apply to any payment which is treated as possessed by the claimant by virtue of regulation 105(10)(a)(ii) (notional income).

31.—(1) Except where paragraph 30 [10or 31A] applies, and subject to sub-paragraph (2), any payment made to the claimant which is intended to be used and is used as a contribution towards—

(a) any payment due on a loan if secured on the dwelling occupied as the home which does not qualify under Schedule 2 (housing costs);
(b) any interest payment or charge which qualifies in accordance with paragraphs 14 to 16 of Schedule 2 to the extent that the payment or charge is not met;
(c) any payment due on a loan which qualifies under paragraph 14 or 15 of Schedule 2 attributable to the payment of capital;
(d) any amount due by way of premiums on—
 (i) an insurance policy taken out to insure against the risk of being unable to make the payments referred to in (a) to (c) above, or
 (ii) an insurance policy taken out to insure against loss or damage to any building or part of a building which is occupied by the claimant as his home;
(e) his rent in respect of the dwelling occupied by him as his home but only to the extent that it is not met by housing benefit; or his accommodation charge but only to the extent that the actual charge [29 exceeds] the amount payable by a local authority in accordance with Part III of the National Assistance Act 1948 [112 or Part 1 of the Care Act 2014 (care and support).]

(2) This paragraph shall not apply to any payment which is treated as possessed by the claimant by virtue of regulation 105(10)(a)(ii) (notional income).

[10**31A.**—(1) Subject to sub-paragraph (2), any payment received under an insurance policy, other than an insurance policy referred to in paragraph 30, taken out to insure against the risk of being unable to maintain repayments under a regulated agreement as defined for the purposes of the Consumer Credit Act 1974 or under a hire-purchase agreement or a conditional sale agreement as defined for the purposes of Part III of the Hire-Purchase Act 1964.

(2) A payment referred to in sub-paragraph (1) shall only be disregarded to the extent that the payment received under that policy does not exceed the amounts, calculated on a weekly basis, which are used to—

(a) maintain the repayment referred to in sub-paragraph (1); and
(b) meet any amount due by way of premiums on that policy.]

32.—(1) Subject to sub-paragraphs (2) and (3), in the case of a claimant [54 residing in a care home, an Abbeyfield Home or an independent hospital], any payment, [64 except a charitable or voluntary payment disregarded under paragraph 15] [62 . . .], made to the claimant which is intended to be used and is used to meet the cost of maintaining the claimant in that home [54 or hospital].

(2) This paragraph shall not apply to a claimant for whom accommodation in a [54 care home, an Abbeyfield Home or an independent hospital] is provided by

[113 (a) a local authority under section 26 of the National Assistance Act 1948 or section 59 of the Social Work (Scotland) Act 1968 [29. . .]; or
(b) a person other than a local authority under arrangements made with the person by a local authority in the exercise of the local authority's functions under section 18 or 19 of the Care Act 2014 (duty and power to meet needs for care and support).]

(3) The amount to be disregarded under this paragraph shall not exceed the difference between—

[29(a) the claimant's applicable amount; and]

(b) the weekly charge for the accommodation.

33.—Any social fund payment made pursuant to Part VIII of the Benefits Act.

[98 **33A.**—Any local welfare provision.]

34.—Any payment of income which under regulation 110 (income treated as capital) is to be treated as capital.

35.—Any payment under Part X of the Benefits Act (pensioner's Christmas bonus).

36.—In the case of a person who is, or would be, prevented from being entitled to a jobseeker's allowance by section 14 (trade disputes), any payment up to the amount of the prescribed sum within the meaning of section 15(2)(d) made by a trade union.

37.—Any payment which is due to be paid before the date of claim which would otherwise fall to be taken into account in the same benefit week as a payment of the same kind and from the same source.

38.—The total of a claimant's income or, if he is a member of a family, the family's income and the income of any person which he is treated as possessing under regulation 88(4) (calculation of income and capital of members of claimant's family and of a polygamous marriage) to be disregarded under regulations 132(2)(b) and 133(1)(c) (calculation of covenant income where a contribution assessed), regulation 136(2) (treatment of student loans) [21, regulation 136A(3) (treatment of payments from access funds)] and [63 paragraph 17] shall in no case exceed £20 per [4benefit week].

39.—Notwithstanding paragraph 38, where two or more payments of the same kind and from the same source are to be taken into account in the same benefit week, there shall be disregarded from each payment the sum which would otherwise fall to be disregarded under this Schedule; but this paragraph shall only apply in the case of a payment which it has not been practicable to treat under regulation 96(1)(b) (date on which income treated as paid) as paid on the first day of the benefit week in which it is due to be paid.

40.—[74 . . .]

41.—(1) Any payment made under [81 or by] the Macfarlane Trust, the Macfarlane (Special Payments) Trust, the Macfarlane (Special Payments) (No.2) Trust, the Fund, the Eileen Trust ("the Trusts") [82 , MFET Limited] [91 , the Skipton Fund, the Caxton Foundation] or the Independent Living [74 Fund (2006)].

(2) Any payment by or on behalf of a person who is suffering or who suffered from haemophilia or who is or was a qualifying person, which derives from a payment made under [81 or by] any of the Trusts to which sub-paragraph (1) refers and which is made to or for the benefit of—

- (a) that person's partner or former partner from whom he is not, or where that person has died was not, estranged or divorced [55 or with whom he has formed a civil partnership that has not been dissolved or, where that person has died, had not been dissolved at the time of that person's death];
- (b) any child or young person who is a member of that person's family or who was such a member and who is a member of the claimant's family.

(3) Any payment by or on behalf of the partner or former partner of a person who is suffering or who suffered from haemophilia or who is or was a qualifying person, provided that the partner or former partner and that person are not, or if either of them has died were not, estranged or divorced, [55 or, where the partner or former partner and that person have formed a civil partnership, the civil partnership has not been dissolved or, if either of them has died, had not been dissolved at the time of the death], which derives from a payment made under [81 or by] any of the Trusts to which sub-paragraph (1) refers and which is made to or for the benefit of—

- (a) the person who is suffering from haemophilia or who is a qualifying person;
- (b) any child or young person who is a member of that person's family or who was such a member and who is a member of the claimant's family.

(4) Any payment by a person who is suffering from haemophilia or who is a qualifying person, which derives from the payment under [81 or by] any of the Trusts to which sub-paragraph (1) refers, where

- (a) that person has no partner or former partner from whom he is not estranged or divorced, [55 or with whom he has formed a civil partnership that has not been dissolved], nor any child or young person who is or had been a member of that person's family; and
- (b) the payment is made either—
  - (i) to that person's parent or step-parent, or
  - (ii) where that person at the date of the payment is a child, a young person or a student who has not completed his full-time education, and had no parent or step-parent, to his guardian,

but only for a period from the date of the payment until the end of two years from that person's death.

(5) Any payment out of the estate of a person who suffered from haemophilia or who was a qualifying person, which derives from a payment under [81 or by] any of the Trusts to which sub-paragraph (1) refers, where—

(a) that person at the date of his death (the relevant date) had no partner or former partner from whom he was not estranged or divorced [55 or with whom he had formed a civil partnership that had not been dissolved], nor any child or young person who was or had been a member of his family; and

(b) the payment is made either—

(i) to that person's parent or step-parent, or

(ii) where that person at the relevant date was a child, a young person or a student who had not completed his full-time education, and had no parent or step-parent, to his guardian,

but only for a period of two years from the relevant date.

(6) In the case of a person to whom or for whose benefit a payment referred to in this paragraph is made, any income which derives from any payment of income or capital made under or deriving from any of the Trusts.

[48 (7) For the purposes of paragraphs (2) to (6), any reference to the Trusts shall be construed as including a reference to the Skipton Fund [92 , the Caxton Foundation] [82, MFET Limited] [56 and the London Bombings Relief Charitable Fund].]

42.—Any payment made by the Secretary of State to compensate for the loss (in whole or in part) of entitlement to housing benefit.

43.—Any payment made to a juror or a witness in respect of attendance at a court other than compensation for loss of earnings or for the loss of a benefit payable under the [74 benefit Acts].

44.—[72 . . .]

[68 **45.**—Any payment in consequence of a reduction of council tax under section 13 [99, 13A]or 80 of the Local Government Finance Act 1992 (reduction of liability for council tax).]

46.—[74 . . .]

[74 **47.**—(1) Any payment or repayment made—

(a) as respects England, under regulation 5, 6 or 12 of the National Health Service (Travel Expenses and Remission of Charges) Regulations 2003 (travelling expenses and health service supplies);

(b) as respects Wales, under regulation 5, 6 or 11 of the National Health Service (Travelling Expenses and Remission of Charges) (Wales) Regulations 2007 (travelling expenses and health service supplies);

(c) as respects Scotland, under regulation 3, 5 or 11 of the National Health Service (Travelling Expenses and Remission of Charges) (Scotland) (No.2) Regulations 2003 (travelling expenses and health service supplies).

(2) Any payment or repayment made by the Secretary of State for Health, the Scottish Ministers or the Welsh Ministers which is analogous to a payment or repayment mentioned in sub-paragraph (1).

48.—Any payment made to such persons entitled to receive benefits as may be determined by or under a scheme made pursuant to section 13 of the Social Security Act 1988 in lieu of vouchers or similar arrangements in connection with the provision of those benefits (including payments made in place of healthy start vouchers, milk tokens or the supply of vitamins).]

49.—Any payment made either by the Secretary of State for [65 Justice] or by the [74 Scottish Ministers] under a scheme established to assist relatives and other persons to visit persons in custody.

50.—Any payment (other than a training allowance) made, whether by the Secretary of State or by any other person, under the Disabled Persons (Employment) Act 1944 [42 . . .] to assist disabled persons to obtain or retain employment despite their disability.

51.—[97 . . .]

[74 **52.**—(1) If the claimant is in receipt of any benefit under Part 2, 3 or 5 of the Benefits Act, any increase in the rate of that benefit arising under Part 4 (increases for dependants) or section 106(a) (unemployability supplement) of that Act, where the dependant in respect of whom the increase is paid is not a member of the claimant's family.

(2) If the claimant is in receipt of any pension or allowance under Part 2 or 3 of the Naval, Military and Air Forces Etc. (Disablement and Death) Service Pensions Order 2006, any increase in the rate of that pension or allowance under that Order, where the dependant in respect of whom the increase is paid is not a member of the claimant's family.

53.—Any supplementary pension under article 23(2) of the Naval, Military and Air Forces

Etc. (Disablement and Death) Service Pensions Order 2006 (pensions to surviving spouses and surviving civil partners) and any analogous payment made by the Secretary of State for Defence to any person who is not a person entitled under that Order.]

54.—In the case of a pension awarded at the supplementary rate under article 27(3) of the Personal Injuries (Civilians) Scheme 1983 (pensions to [55 widows, widowers or surviving civil partners]), the sum specified in paragraph 1(c) of Schedule 4 to that Scheme.

55.—(1) Any payment which is—

(a) made under any of the Dispensing Instruments to a [55 widow, widower or surviving civil partner] of a person—

(i) whose death was attributable to service in a capacity analogous to service as a member of the armed forces of the Crown; and

(ii) whose service in such capacity terminated before 31st March 1973; and

[74 (b) equal to the amount specified in article 23(2) of the Naval, Military and Air Forces Etc. (Disablement and Death) Service Pensions Order 2006.]

(2) In this paragraph "the Dispensing Instruments" means the Order in Council of 9th December 1881, the Royal Warrant of 27th October 1884 and the Order by His Majesty of 14th January 1922 (exceptional grants of pay, non-effective pay and allowances).

[3**56.**—Any payment made [75 . . .] under section 12B of the Social Work (Scotland) Act 1968 [83 , or under sections 12A to 12D of the National Health Service Act 2006 (direct payments for health care)] [114 or under sections 31 to 33 of the Care Act 2014 (direct payments)] [39a or under regulations made under section 57 of the Health and Social Care Act 2001 (direct payments)].

57.—[42. . .]

58.—[42. . .]

59.—(1) Any payment specified in sub-paragraph (2) to a claimant who was formerly a full-time student and who has completed the course in respect of which those payments were made.

(2) The payments specified for the purposes of sub-paragraph (1) are—

(a) any grant income and covenant income as defined for the purposes of Chapter IX of Part VIII;

[17(b) any student loan as defined in Chapter IX of Part VIII;

(c) any contribution as defined in Chapter IX of Part VIII which—

(i) is taken into account in ascertaining the amount of a student loan referred to in head (b); and

(ii) has been paid.]]

[25 **60.**—[42. . .]].

[32 **60A.**—[42. . .].]

[6 **61.**—[42. . .].]

[12**62.**—(1) Subject to sub-paragraph (2), in the case of a person who is receiving, or who has received, assistance under [22 the self-employment route], any payment to that person—

(a) to meet expenses wholly and necessarily incurred whilst carrying on the commercial activity;

(b) which is used or intended to be used to maintain repayments on a loan taken out by that person for the purpose of establishing or carrying on the commercial activity,

in respect of which such assistance is or was received.

(2) Sub-paragraph (1) shall apply only in respect of payments which are paid to that person from the special account as defined for the purposes of Chapter IVA of Part VIII.]

[13**63.**—[42. . .].]

[14**64.**—Any payment [79 made with respect to a person on account of the provision of after-care under section 117 of the Mental Health Act 1983 or section 25 of the Mental Health (Care and Treatment) (Scotland) Act 2003 or the provision of accommodation or welfare services to which Part III of the National Assistance Act 1948 refers or to which the Social Work (Scotland) Act 1968 refers,] [115 or the provision of care and support under Part 1 of the Care Act 2014,] which falls to be treated as notional income made under paragraph (11) of regulation 105 above (payments made in respect of a person [54 residing in a care home, an Abbeyfield Home or an independent hospital]).]

65.—[*Omitted.*]

66.—[*Omitted.*]

[16**67.**—(1) Any payment of a sports award except to the extent that it has been made in respect of any one or more of the items specified in sub-paragraph (2).

(2) The items specified for the purposes of sub-paragraph (1) are food, ordinary clothing or footwear, household fuel, rent for which housing benefit is payable or any housing costs to

the extent that they are met under regulation 83(f) or 84(1)(g) (housing costs) [29 . . .], of the claimant or, where the claimant is a member of a family, any other member of his family, or any council tax or water charges for which that claimant or member is liable.

(3) For the purposes of sub-paragraph (2)—

"food" does not include vitamins, minerals or other special dietary supplements intended to enhance the performance of the person in the sport in respect of which the award was made;

"ordinary clothing and footwear" means clothing or footwear for normal daily use but does not include school uniforms or clothing or footwear used solely for sporting activities.]

[20 **68.**—Where the amount of a subsistence allowance paid to a person in a benefit week exceeds the amount of income-based jobseeker's allowance that person would have received in that benefit week had it been payable to him, less 50p, that excess amount.

69.—In the case of a claimant participating in an employment zone programme, any discretionary payment made by an employment zone contractor to the claimant, being a fee, grant, loan or otherwise.]

[35[41[84**70.**—(1) Any payment of child maintenance made or derived from a liable relative where the child or young person in respect of whom the payment is made is a member of the claimant's family, except where the person making the payment is the claimant or the claimant's partner.

(2) In paragraph (1)—

"child maintenance" means any payment towards the maintenance of a child or young person, including any payment made voluntarily and payments made under—

(a) the Child Support Act 1991;
(b) the Child Support (Northern Ireland) Order 1991;
(c) a court order;
(d) a consent order;
(e) a maintenance agreement registered for execution in the Books of Council and Session or the sheriff court books;

"liable relative" means a person listed in regulation 117 (interpretation) other than a person falling within sub-paragraph (d) of that definition.]]]

[26**71.**—Any discretionary housing payment paid pursuant to regulation 2(1) of the Discretionary Financial Assistance Regulations 2001.]

[37 [39 **72.**—(1) Any payment made by a local authority, or by the [74 Welsh Ministers], to or on behalf of the claimant or his partner relating to a service which is provided to develop or sustain the capacity of the claimant or his partner to live independently in his accommodation.]]

(2) For the purposes of sub-paragraph (1) "local authority" means—

(a) in relation to England, a county council, a district council, a London borough council, the Common Council of the City of London or the Council of the Isles of Scilly;
(b) in relation to Wales, a county council or a county borough council;
(c) in relation to Scotland, a council constituted under section 2 of the Local Government etc. (Scotland) Act 1994.]

[102 **72A.**—Armed forces independence payment.]

[39 **73.**—[42. . .].]

[40 **74.**—[42. . .].]

[107 **75.**—Any payments to a claimant made under section 49 of the Children and Families Act 2014 (personal budgets and direct payments).]

AMENDMENTS

1. Jobseeker's Allowance (Amendment) Regulations 1996 (SI 1996/1516) reg.20 and Sch. (October 7, 1996).

2. Jobseeker's Allowance and Income Support (General) (Amendment) Regulations 1996 (SI 1996/1517) reg.32 (October 7, 1996).

3. Income-related Benefits and Jobseeker's Allowance (Miscellaneous Amendments) Regulations 1997 (SI 1997/65) reg.2(4) (April 7, 1997).

4. Social Security (Miscellaneous Amendments) Regulations 1997 (SI 1997/454) reg.2(16) (April 7, 1997).

5. Income-related Benefits and Jobseeker's Allowance (Amendment) (No.2) Regulations 1997 (SI 1997/2197) reg.7(7) and (8)(f) (October 6, 1997).

6. Social Security Amendment (New Deal) Regulations 1997 (SI 1997/2863) reg.14 (January 5, 1998).
7. Social Security (Miscellaneous Amendments) Regulations 1998 (SI 1998/563) reg.7(1) and (2)(e) (April 6, 1998).
8. Social Security (Miscellaneous Amendments) Regulations 1998 (SI 1998/563) reg.7(3) and (4)(f) (April 6, 1998).
9. Social Security (Miscellaneous Amendments) Regulations 1998 (SI 1998/563) reg.13(2), (April 6, 1998).
10. Social Security (Miscellaneous Amendments) (No.3) Regulations 1998 (SI 1998/1173) reg.5 (June 1, 1998).
11. Social Security (Miscellaneous Amendments) (No.4) Regulations 1998 (SI 1998/1174) reg.4(a) (June 1, 1998).
12. Social Security (Miscellaneous Amendments) (No.4) Regulations 1998 (SI 1998/1174) reg.4(b) (June 1, 1998).
13. Social Security Amendment (New Deal) (No.2) Regulations 1998 (SI 1998/2117) reg.4(1) (September 24, 1998).
14. Social Security Amendment (New Deal) (No.2) Regulations 1998 (SI 1998/2117) reg.6(1) (September 24, 1998).
15. Social Security Amendment (Educational Maintenance Allowance) Regulations 1999 (SI 1999/1677) reg.2(1) and (2)(f) (August 16, 1999).
16. Social Security Amendment (Sports Awards) Regulations 1999 (SI 1999/2165) reg.6(4) (August 23, 1999).
17. Social Security Amendment (Students) Regulations 1999 (SI 1999/1935) reg.3(8) (August 30, 1999, or if the student's period of study begins between August 1 and 29, 1999, the first day of the period).
18. Social Security Amendment (Education Maintenance Allowance) Regulations 2000 (SI 2000/55) reg.2(1) and (2)(d) (February 7, 2000).
19. Social Security (Immigration and Asylum) Consequential Amendments Regulations 2000 (SI 2000/636) reg.4(9) (April 3, 2000).
20. Social Security Amendment (Employment Zones) Regulations 2000 (SI 2000/724) reg.3(3) (April 3, 2000).
21. Social Security Amendment (Students and Income-related Benefits) Regulations 2000 (SI 2000/1922) reg.3(10) (August 28, 2000, or if the student's period of study begins between August 1 and 27, 2000, the first day of the period).
22. Social Security Amendment (Employment Zones) (No.2) Regulations 2000 (SI 2000/2910) reg.4(1) and (2)(d)(i) (November 27, 2000).
23. Social Security Amendment (Bereavement Benefits) Regulations 2000 (SI 2000/2239) reg.3(3) (April 9, 2001).
24. Social Security (Miscellaneous Amendments) (No.3) Regulations 2001 (SI 2001/859) reg.6(3) (April 9, 2001).
25. Social Security Amendment (New Deal) Regulations 2001 (SI 2001/1029) reg.12 (April 9, 2001).
26. Social Security Amendment (Discretionary Housing Payments) Regulations 2001 (SI 2001/2333) reg.2(1) (July 2, 2001).
27. Social Security Amendment (Volunteers) Regulations 2001 (SI 2001/2296) reg.2 (September 24, 2001).
28. Children (Leaving Care) Act 2000 (Commencement No.2 and Consequential Provisions) Order 2001 (SI 2001/3070) art.3(5) and Sch.4 para.(c) (October 1, 2001).
29. Social Security Amendment (Residential Care and Nursing Homes) Regulations 2001 (SI 2001/3767) reg.2(2) and Pt II of Sch. para.24 (April 8, 2002).
30. Social Security Benefits Up-rating Order 2002 (SI 2002/668) art.22(10) (April 8, 2002).
31. Social Security (Miscellaneous Amendments) Regulations 2002 (SI 2002/841) reg.3(4) (April 8, 2002).
32. Social Security Amendment (Employment Programme) Regulations 2002 (SI 2002/2314) reg.2(5) (October 14, 2002).

33. Social Security (Miscellaneous Amendments) (No.2) Regulations 2002 (SI 2002/2380) reg.3(b) (October 14, 2002).

34. Social Security Amendment (Personal Injury Payments) Regulations 2002 (SI 2002/2442) reg.3 (October 28, 2002)

35. Social Security (Child Maintenance Premium and Miscellaneous Amendments) Regulations 2000 (SI 2000/3176) reg.2(2)(b) (in force in relation to any particular case on the day on which s.23 of the Child Support, Pensions and Social Security Act 2000 comes into force in relation to that type of case).

36. Social Security (Paternity and Adoption) Amendment Regulations 2002 (SI 2002/2689) reg.3(6) (December 8, 2002).

37. Social Security (Miscellaneous Amendments) Regulations 2003 (SI 2003/511) reg.3(2) (April 1, 2003).

38. Social Security (Working Tax Credit and Child Tax Credit) (Consequential Amendments) Regulations 2003 (SI 2003/455) reg.3 and Sch.2 para.23(a) (April 7, 2003).

39. Social Security (Miscellaneous Amendments) (No.2) Regulations 2003 (SI 2003/2279) reg.3(4) (October 1, 2003).

39a. Community Care, Services for Carers and Children's Services (Direct Payments) (England) Regulations 2003 (SI 2003/762) reg.11(2) and Sch.2 (April 8, 2003).

40. Social Security (Incapacity Benefit Work-focused Interviews) Regulations 2003 (SI 2003/2439) reg.16(a) (October 27, 2003).

41. Social Security (Child Maintenance Premium) Amendment Regulations 2004 (SI 2004/98) reg.3 (in force on: (i) February 16, 2004 in relation to any particular case in respect of which s.23 CSPSSA 2000 has come into force before February 16, 2004; (ii) where this does not apply, the day on which s. 23 comes into force in relation to that type of case; (iii) February 16, 2004 in relation to a person who is entitled to income support/income-based JSA on that date and who receives her first payment of child maintenance made voluntarily whilst entitled to income support/income-based JSA on that date; (iv) in such a case where the day that the first voluntary payment is received is after February 16, 2004, the day that payment is received; and (v) February 16, 2004 in relation to a person who makes a claim for income support/income-based JSA on or after that date and receives a payment of child maintenance made voluntarily on or after the date of that claim).

42. Social Security (Miscellaneous Amendments) Regulations 2004 (SI 2004/565) reg.5(3) (April 1, 2004).

43. Social Security (Working Tax Credit and Child Tax Credit) (Consequential Amendments) Regulations 2003 (SI 2003/455) reg.3 and Sch.2 para.23 (except sub-para.(a)) (April 6, 2004, except in "transitional cases" and see further the note to reg.83 and to reg.17 of the Income Support Regulations).

44. Social Security (Miscellaneous Amendments) (No.2) Regulations 2004 (SI 2004/1141) reg.4(1) and (2)(d) (May 12, 2004).

45. Social Security (Miscellaneous Amendments) (No.2) Regulations 2004 (SI 2004/1141) reg.4(3) and (4)(d) (May 12, 2004).

46. Social Security (Students and Income-related Benefits) Amendment Regulations 2004 (SI 2004/1708) reg.6(3) (September 1, 2004, or if the student's period of study begins between August 1 and August 31, 2004, the first day of the period).

47. Social Security (Miscellaneous Amendments) (No.3) Regulations 2004 (SI 2004/2308) reg.2(1) and (2)(b) (October 4, 2004).

48. Social Security (Miscellaneous Amendments) (No.3) Regulations 2004 (SI 2004/2308) reg.3(5) (October 4, 2004).

49. Social Security (Miscellaneous Amendments) (No.3) Regulations 2004 (SI 2004/2308) reg.4(3) and (4)(b) (October 4, 2004).

50. Social Security (Miscellaneous Amendments) Regulations 2005 (SI 2005/574) reg.2(9) (April 4, 2005).

51. Social Security (Miscellaneous Amendments) Regulations 2005 (SI 2005/574) reg.6(5) (April 4, 2005).

52. Mental Health (Care and Treatment) (Scotland) Act 2003 (Modification of Subordinate Legislation) Order 2005 (SSI 2005/445) art.2 and Sch. para.23(3) (Scotland); Mental Health (Care and Treatment) (Scotland) Act 2003 (Consequential Provisions) Order 2005 (SI 2005/2078) art.15 and Sch.2 para.17(4) (England and Wales) (October 5, 2005).

53. Social Security (Miscellaneous Amendments) (No.2) Regulations 2005 (SI 2005/2465) reg.3(8)(a) (October 3, 2005).

54. Social Security (Care Homes and Independent Hospitals) Regulations 2005 (SI 2005/2687) reg.3 and Sch.2 para.14 (October 24, 2005).

55. Civil Partnership (Pensions, Social Security and Child Support) (Consequential, etc. Provisions) Order 2005 (SI 2005/2877) art.2(3) and Sch.3 para.26(12) (December 5, 2005).

56. Income-related Benefits (Amendment) (No.2) Regulations 2005 (SI 2005/3391) reg.5(4) (December 12, 2005).

57. Social Security (Miscellaneous Amendments) (No.2) Regulations 2005 (SI 2005/2465) reg.3(8)(b) (December 30, 2005).

58. Social Security (Miscellaneous Amendments) (No.2) Regulations 2005 (SI 2005/2465) reg.3(8)(c) (December 30, 2005).

59. Social Security (Miscellaneous Amendments) (No.4) Regulations 2006 (SI 2006/2378) reg.13(12)(a) (October 2, 2006).

60. Social Security (Miscellaneous Amendments) (No.4) Regulations 2006 (SI 2006/2378) reg.13(12)(b) (October 2, 2006).

61. Social Security (Miscellaneous Amendments) (No.4) Regulations 2006 (SI 2006/2378) reg.13(12)(c) (October 2, 2006).

62. Social Security (Miscellaneous Amendments) (No.4) Regulations 2006 (SI 2006/2378) reg.13(12)(d) (October 2, 2006).

63. Social Security (Miscellaneous Amendments) (No.4) Regulations 2006 (SI 2006/2378) reg.13(12)(e) (October 2, 2006).

64. Social Security (Miscellaneous Amendments) Regulations 2007 (SI 2007/719) reg.3(11) (April 2, 2007).

65. Secretary of State for Justice Order 2007 (SI 2007/2128) Sch. para.16(2) (August 22, 2007).

66. Social Security (Miscellaneous Amendments) (No.5) Regulations 2007 (SI 2007/2618) reg.8(15) (April 7, 2008).

67. Social Security (Miscellaneous Amendments) Regulations 2008 (SI 2008/698) reg.4(16)(a) (April 7, 2008).

68. Social Security (Miscellaneous Amendments) Regulations 2008 (SI 2008/698) reg.4(16)(b) (April 14, 2008).

69. Employment and Support Allowance (Consequential Provisions) (No.2) Regulations 2008 (SI 2008/1554) reg.3(28) (October 27, 2008).

70. Social Security (Child Maintenance Amendments) Regulations 2008 (SI 2008/2111) reg.3(9) (October 27, 2008).

71. Social Security (Miscellaneous Amendments) (No.6) Regulations 2008 (SI 2008/2767) reg.4(7) (November 17, 2008).

72. Social Security (Miscellaneous Amendments) (No.6) Regulations 2008 (SI 2008/2767) reg.4(11) (November 17, 2008).

73. Social Security (Child Benefit Disregard) Regulations 2008 (SI 2008/3140) reg.3 (January 5, 2009; this regulation ceases to have effect on April 6, 2009).

74. Social Security (Miscellaneous Amendments) (No.7) Regulations 2008 (SI 2008/3157) reg.3(10) (January 5, 2009).

75. Social Security (Miscellaneous Amendments) Regulations 2009 (SI 2009/583) reg.4(12) (April 6, 2009).

76. Social Security (Miscellaneous Amendments) (No.4) Regulations 2009 (SI 2009/2655) reg.4(15)(a) (October 26, 2009).

77. Social Security (Miscellaneous Amendments) (No.4) Regulations 2009 (SI 2009/2655) reg.4(15)(b) (October 26, 2009).

78. Social Security (Miscellaneous Amendments) (No.4) Regulations 2009 (SI 2009/2655) reg.4(15)(c) (October 26, 2009).

79. Social Security (Miscellaneous Amendments) (No.4) Regulations 2009 (SI 2009/2655) reg.4(15)(d) (October 26, 2009).

80. Social Security (Miscellaneous Amendments) (No.2) Regulations 2010 (SI 2010/641) reg.4(3)(f) (April 6, 2010).

81. Social Security (Miscellaneous Amendments) (No.2) Regulations 2010 (SI 2010/641) reg.4(8)(e) (April 6, 2010).

82. Social Security (Miscellaneous Amendments) (No.2) Regulations 2010 (SI 2010/641) reg.4(12) (April 6, 2010).

83. Social Security (Miscellaneous Amendments) (No.2) Regulations 2010 (SI 2010/641) reg.4(13) (April 6, 2010).

84. Social Security (Miscellaneous Amendments) (No.4) Regulations 2009 (SI 2009/2655) reg.4(15)(e) (April 12, 2010).

85. Social Security (Miscellaneous Amendments) (No.5) Regulations 2010 (SI 2010/2429) reg.4(5)(a) (November 1, 2010).

86. Social Security (Miscellaneous Amendments) (No.5) Regulations 2010 (SI 2010/2429) reg.4(5)(b) (November 1, 2010).

87. Social Security (Miscellaneous Amendments) (No.5) Regulations 2010 (SI 2010/2429) reg.4(5)(c) (November 1, 2010).

88. Jobseeker's Allowance (Mandatory Work Activity Scheme) Regulations 2011 (SI 2011/688) reg.14(1)(d) and (2) (April 25, 2011).

89. Jobseeker's Allowance (Employment, Skills and Enterprise Scheme) Regulations 2011 (SI 2011/917) reg.14(1)(d) and (2) (May 20, 2011).

90. Adoption and Children (Scotland) Act 2007 (Consequential Modifications) Order 2011 (SI 2011/1740) art.2 and Sch.1 para.19(3) (July 15, 2011).

91. Social Security (Miscellaneous Amendments) (No.3) Regulations 2011 (SI 2011/2425) reg.10(9) (October 31, 2011).

92. Social Security (Miscellaneous Amendments) (No.3) Regulations 2011 (SI 2011/2425) reg.10(10) (October 31, 2011).

93. Social Security (Miscellaneous Amendments) (No.3) Regulations 2011 (SI 2011/2425) reg.10(14) (October 31, 2011).

94. Social Security (Miscellaneous Amendments) Regulations 2012 (SI 2012/757) reg.4(3) (April 1, 2012).

95. Jobseeker's Allowance (Schemes for Assisting Persons to Obtain Employment) Regulations 2013 (SI 2013/276) reg.11(1)(d) and (2) (February 12, 2013).

96. Jobseekers (Back to Work Schemes) Act 2013 s.1(14) (March 26, 2013).

97. Council Tax Benefit Abolition (Consequential Provision) Regulations 2013 (SI 2013/458) reg.3 and Sch.1 (April 1, 2013).

98. Social Security (Miscellaneous Amendments) Regulations 2013 (SI 2013/443) reg.4(12)(a) (April 2, 2013).

99. Social Security (Miscellaneous Amendments) Regulations 2013 (SI 2013/443) reg.4(12)(b) (April 2, 2013).

100. Personal Independence Payment (Supplementary Provisions and Consequential Amendments) Regulations 2013 (SI 2013/388) reg.8 and Sch. Pt 2 para.16(9)(a) (April 8, 2013).

101. Personal Independence Payment (Supplementary Provisions and Consequential Amendments) Regulations 2013 (SI 2013/388) reg.8 and Sch. Pt 2 para.16(9)(b) (April 8, 2013).

102. Armed Forces and Reserve Forces Compensation Scheme (Consequential Provisions: Subordinate Legislation) Order 2013 (SI 2013/591) art.7 and Sch. para.10(9) (April 8, 2013).

103. National Treatment Agency (Abolition) and the Health and Social Care Act 2012 (Consequential, Transitional and Saving Provisions) Order 2013 (SI 2013/235) art.11 and Sch.2 para.27(3) (April 1, 2013).

104. Universal Credit (Consequential, Supplementary, Incidental and

Miscellaneous Provisions) Regulations 2013 (SI 2013/630) reg.30(8) (April 29, 2013).

105. Child Arrangements Order (Consequential Amendments to Subordinate Legislation) Order 2014 (SI 2014/852) art.6 (April 22, 2014).

106. Social Security (Miscellaneous Amendments) Regulations 2014 (SI 2014/591) reg.4(6) (April 28, 2014).

107. Special Educational Needs (Consequential Amendments to Subordinate Legislation) Order 2014 (SI 2014/2103) art.4(1) (September 1, 2014).

108. Shared Parental Leave and Statutory Shared Parental Pay (Consequential Amendments to Subordinate Legislation) Order 2014 (SI 2014/3255) art.7(6)(a)(ii) (December 31, 2014).

109. Shared Parental Leave and Statutory Shared Parental Pay (Consequential Amendments to Subordinate Legislation) Order 2014 (SI 2014/3255) art.7(6)(a)(iii) (December 31, 2014).

110. Shared Parental Leave and Statutory Shared Parental Pay (Consequential Amendments to Subordinate Legislation) Order 2014 (SI 2014/3255) art.7(6)(b)(ii) (December 31, 2014).

111. Care Act 2014 (Consequential Amendments) (Secondary Legislation) Order 2015 (SI 2015/643) art.2 and Sch. para.9(3)(a) (April 1, 2015).

112. Care Act 2014 (Consequential Amendments) (Secondary Legislation) Order 2015 (SI 2015/643) art.2 and Sch. para.9(3)(b) (April 1, 2015).

113. Care Act 2014 (Consequential Amendments) (Secondary Legislation) Order 2015 (SI 2015/643) art.2 and Sch. para.9(3)(c) (April 1, 2015).

114. Care Act 2014 (Consequential Amendments) (Secondary Legislation) Order 2015 (SI 2015/643) art.2 and Sch. para.9(3)(d) (April 1, 2015).

115. Care Act 2014 (Consequential Amendments) (Secondary Legislation) Order 2015 (SI 2015/643) art.2 and Sch. para.9(3)(e) (April 1, 2015).

116. Shared Parental Leave and Statutory Shared Parental Pay (Consequential Amendments to Subordinate Legislation) Order 2014 (SI 2014/3255) art.7(6)(a)(i) (April 5, 2015).

117. Shared Parental Leave and Statutory Shared Parental Pay (Consequential Amendments to Subordinate Legislation) Order 2014 (SI 2014/3255) art.7(6)(b)(i) (April 5, 2015).

DEFINITIONS

"Abbeyfield Home"—see reg.1(3).
"access funds"—*ibid.*
"armed forces independence payment"—*ibid.*
"attendance allowance"—see reg.1(3).
"the Benefits Act"—see Jobseekers Act s.35(1).
"benefit week"—see reg.1(3).
"board and lodging accommodation"—*ibid.*
"care home"—*ibid.*
"the Caxton Foundation"—*ibid.*
"child"—see Jobseekers Act s.35(1).
"the Children Order"—see reg.1(3).
"claimant"—see Jobseekers Act s.35(1) and reg.88(1).
"claimant participating as a service user"—see reg.1(3G).
"concessionary payment"—see reg.1(3).
"contribution"—see reg.130.
"course of study"—see reg.1(3).
"disability living allowance"—*ibid.*
"dwelling occupied as the home"—*ibid.*
"the Eileen Trust"—*ibid.*
"employed earner"—see reg.3 and SSCBA s.2(1)(a).
"the Employment, Skills and Enterprise Scheme"—see reg.1(3).
"employment zone contractor"—*ibid.*

"employment zone programme"—*ibid.*
"family"—see Jobseekers Act s.35(1).
"the Fund"—see reg.1(3).
"a guaranteed income payment"—*ibid.*
"Immigration and Asylum Act"—*ibid.*
"independent hospital"—*ibid.*
"the Independent Living Fund (2006)"—*ibid.*
"Intensive Activity Period for 50 plus"—*ibid.*
"local welfare provision"—*ibid.*
"the London Bombings Relief Charitable Fund"—*ibid.*
"the Macfarlane (Special Payments) Trust"—*ibid.*
"the Macfarlane (Special Payments) (No.2) Trust"—*ibid.*
"the Macfarlane Trust"—*ibid.*
"the Mandatory Work Activity Scheme"—*ibid.*
"MFET Limited"—*ibid.*
"mobility supplement"—*ibid.*
"occupational pension scheme"—see Jobseekers Act s.35(1).
"partner"—see reg.1(3).
"partner of a person subject to immigration control"—see reg.85(4).
"payment"—see reg.1(3).
"personal independence payment"—*ibid.*
"personal pension scheme"—see Jobseekers Act s.35(1).
"qualifying person"—see reg.1(3).
"self-employment route"—*ibid.*
"shared parental leave"—*ibid.*
"the Skipton Fund"—*ibid.*
"sports award"—*ibid.*
"subsistence allowance"—*ibid.*
"student loan"—see reg.130.
"training allowance"—see reg.1(3).
"universal credit"—*ibid.*
"voluntary organisation"—*ibid.*
"war disablement pension"—*ibid.*
"war widow's pension"—*ibid.*
"war widower's pension"—*ibid.*
"young person"—see reg.76.

GENERAL NOTE

Most of the disregards in Sch.7 are the same as those in Sch.9 to the Income Support Regulations (with minor adjustments in the wording). See the notes to Sch.9. **3.539**

The only paragraphs in Sch.9 that were not reproduced in the original Sch.7 were paras 41 and 42 which related to compensation payments made as a consequence of the 1988 benefit changes and so were not relevant. In addition, there was no equivalent to para.57 of Sch.9 (backdated payments under reg.21ZB of the Income Support Regulations) (now revoked), but the disregard in para.12 of Sch.8 should have applied to such payments.

A single disregard of the various allowances, grants and other payments made under s.2 of the Employment and Training Act 1973 or s.2 of the Enterprise and New Towns (Scotland) Act 1990 to people participating in New Deals and other training and welfare to work schemes was introduced on April 1, 2004 to replace the separate disregards that had existed in respect of such payments under a number of the provisions in this Schedule (para.14). As a consequence of this change, those provisions have been revoked or amended. The revoked paragraphs are paras 57, 58, 60, 60A, 61, 63, 73 and 74; the paragraph that has been amended is para.50. See further the note to para.13 of Sch.9.

On para.62, see the note to reg.102C.

Paragraphs 41(4)(b)(i) and (ii) and 41(5)(b)(i) and (ii) include references to step-parents. Note that from December 5, 2005, references to "step" relationships and "in laws" are to be read as including relationships arising through civil partnership in any provision to which s.246 of the Civil Partnership Act 2004 applies. Section 246 is applied to paras 41(4)(b)(i) and (ii) and 41(5)(b)(i) and (ii) by art.3 of and para.63 of the Schedule to the Civil Partnership Act 2004 (Relationships Arising Through Civil Partnership) Order 2005 (SI 2005/3137).

The amendment to para.64 on October 26, 2009 brings it into line with the corresponding income support and ESA provisions (see para.66 of Sch.9 to the Income Support Regulations and para.56 of Sch.8 to the ESA Regulations 2008 respectively, see Vol.I of this series for the latter). Where a claimant lives in a care home, an Abbeyfield Home or an independent hospital, under reg.105(11) any payment made by a third party towards the cost of the claimant's or any partner's fees, counts as the claimant's income. The effect of the previous form of para.64 was that all such payments were then disregarded. The intention, however, was that only certain payments made by a health or local authority should be disregarded, hence the amendment.

Paragraphs A2–A3

3.540 Paragraph A2 provides for an income disregard of payments of expenses in respect of a person's participation in the Mandatory Work Activity Scheme. The original para. A3 contained the same disregard in relation to the Employment, Skills and Enterprise Scheme. However, a further para.A3 was inserted on February 12, 2013, and the original para.A3 has been treated as revoked from that date as a result of s.1(14) of the Jobseekers (Back to Work Schemes) Act 2013. This was because the Jobseeker's Allowance (Employment, Skills and Enterprise Scheme) Regulations 2011 (SI 2011/917) were held to be ultra vires by the Court of Appeal in *R (Reilly and Wilson) v Secretary of State for Work and Pensions* [2013] EWCA Civ 66. The appeal against this decision was allowed by the Supreme Court on October 30, 2013 (*R (on the application of Reilly and another) v Secretary of State for Work and Pensions* [2013] UKSC 68) but "on the basis only that the Jobseekers (Back to Work Schemes) Act 2013 has come into force" (the 2013 Act came into force on March 26, 2013). The new para.A3 provides that payments of expenses in respect of a person's participation in a scheme listed in reg.3 of the Jobseeker's Allowance (Schemes for Assisting Persons to Obtain Employment) Regulations 2013 (SI 2013/276) are ignored as income.

Paragraphs A1, A4 and A5

3.541 These paragraphs have not been included. This is because they only apply to pilot schemes in certain areas of the country.

Paragraph A1 was inserted by reg.16(1)(d) and (2) of the Jobseeker's Allowance (Work for Your Benefit Pilot Scheme) Regulations 2010 (SI 2010/1222) to provide for a disregard of payments for child care, travel and other expenses incurred in respect of the claimant's participation in the Work for Your Benefit Pilot Scheme as income. These Regulations came into force on November 22, 2010 and were to cease to have effect on November 21, 2013 but in fact were revoked on March 1, 2012.

Paragraph A4 was inserted by reg.13(1)(c) and (2) of the Jobseeker's Allowance (Supervised Jobsearch Pilot Scheme) Regulations 2014 (SI 2014/1913); its effect was that payments for child care, travel and other expenses incurred by a person who was participating in the Supervised Jobsearch Pilot Scheme would be ignored as income. These Regulations came into force on July 18, 2014 and ceased to have effect on April 30, 2015.

Paragraph A5 was inserted by reg.17(1)(c) and (2) of the Jobseeker's Allowance (18–21 Work Skills Pilot Scheme) Regulations 2014 (SI 2014/3117) and makes the same provision in relation to a person's participation in the 18–21 Work Skills Pilot Scheme. These Regulations came into force on November 25, 2014 and will cease to have effect two years after they came into force.

Paragraph 56

With effect from April 1, 2014, the disregard in para.56 is modified by art.2 of, and para.5 of the Schedule to, the Social Care (Self-directed Support) (Scotland) Act 2013 (Consequential Modifications and Savings) Order 2014 (SI 2014/513) so that the words "as a direct payment as defined in section 4(2) of the Social Care (Self-directed Support) (Scotland) Act 2013" are substituted for the words "under section 12B of the Social Work (Scotland) 1968". However, under art.3 of the Order, this modification does not apply if a payment is made under s.12B of the 1968 Act on or after April 1, 2014. **3.542**

SCHEDULE 8 **Regulation 108(2)**

CAPITAL TO BE DISREGARDED

A1.—*[Omitted]* **3.543**

[54 **A2.**—Any payment made to the claimant in respect of any travel or other expenses incurred, or to be incurred, by him in respect of his participation in the Mandatory Work Activity Scheme but only for 52 weeks beginning with the date of receipt of the payment.]

[55 [60 **A3.**— . . .]]

[59 **A3.**—Any payment made to the claimant in respect of any travel or other expenses incurred, or to be incurred, by him in respect of his participation in a scheme prescribed in regulation 3 of the Jobseeker's Allowance (Schemes for Assisting Persons to Obtain Employment) Regulations 2013 but only for 52 weeks beginning with the date of receipt of the payment.]

A4.—*[Omitted]*

A5.—*[Omitted]*

1.—The dwelling occupied as the home but, notwithstanding regulation 88, (calculation of income and capital of members of claimant's family and of a polygamous marriage), only one dwelling shall be disregarded under this paragraph.

2.—Any premises acquired for occupation by the claimant which he intends to occupy as his home within 26 weeks of the date of acquisition or such longer period as is reasonable in the circumstances to enable the claimant to obtain possession and commence occupation of the premises.

3.—Any sum directly attributable to the proceeds of sale of any premises formerly occupied by the claimant as his home which is to be used for the purchase of other premises intended for such occupation within 26 weeks of the date of sale, or such longer period as is reasonable in the circumstances to enable the claimant to complete the purchase.

4.—Any premises occupied in whole or in part by—

(a) a partner or relative of a single claimant or of any member of the family as his home where that person [50 has attained the qualifying age for state pension credit] or is incapacitated;

(b) the former partner of a claimant as his home; but this provision shall not apply where the former partner is a person from whom the claimant is estranged or divorced [35 or with whom he formed a civil partnership that has been dissolved].

5.—Where a claimant has ceased to occupy what was formerly the dwelling occupied as the home following his estrangement or divorce from [35 or dissolution of a civil partnership with] his former partner, that dwelling for a period of 26 weeks from the date on which he ceased to occupy that dwelling [22 or, where that dwelling is occupied as the home by the former partner who is a lone parent, for as long as it is so occupied].

6.—Any premises where the claimant is taking reasonable steps to dispose of those premises, for a period of 26 weeks from the date on which he first took such steps, or such longer period as is reasonable in the circumstances to enable him to dispose of those premises.

7.—Any premises which the claimant intends to occupy as his home, and in respect of which he is taking steps to obtain possession and has sought legal advice or has commenced legal proceedings with a view to obtaining possession, for a period of 26 weeks from the date on which he first sought such advice or first commenced such proceedings, whichever is earlier, or such longer period as is reasonable in the circumstances to enable him to obtain possession and commence occupation of those premises.

8.—Any premises which the claimant intends to occupy as his home to which essential repairs or alterations are required in order to render them fit for such occupation, for a period of 26 weeks from the date on which the claimant first takes steps to effect those repairs or alterations, or such longer period as is reasonable in the circumstances to enable those repairs or alterations to be carried out and the claimant to commence occupation of the premises.

9.—Any grant made to the claimant in accordance with a scheme made under section 129 of the Housing Act 1988 or section 66 of the Housing (Scotland) Act 1988 (schemes for payments to assist local housing authority and local authority tenants to obtain other accommodation) which is to be used—

(a) to purchase premises intended for occupation as his home; or

(b) to carry out repairs or alterations which are required to render premises fit for occupation as his home,

for a period of 26 weeks from the date on which he received such a grant or such longer period as is reasonable in the circumstances to enable the purchase, repairs or alterations to be completed and the claimant to commence occupation of those premises as his home.

10.—Any future interest in property of any kind, other than land or premises in respect of which the claimant has granted a subsisting lease or tenancy, including sub-leases or sub-tenancies.

11.—(1) The assets of any business owned in whole or in part by the claimant and for the purposes of which he is engaged as a self-employed earner or, if he has ceased to be so engaged, for such period as may be reasonable in the circumstances to allow for disposal of any such asset.

(2) The assets of any business owned in whole or in part by the claimant where—

(a) he is not engaged as a self-employed earner in that business by reason of some disease or bodily or mental disablement; but

(b) he intends to become engaged (or, as the case may be, re-engaged) as a self-employed earner in that business as soon as he recovers or is able to become engaged or re-engaged in that business,

for a period of 26 weeks from the date on which the claim for a jobseeker's allowance is made, or is treated as made, or if it is unreasonable to expect him to become engaged or re-engaged in that business within that period, for such longer period as is reasonable in the circumstances to enable him to become so engaged or re-engaged.

[[4](3) In the case of a person who is receiving assistance under [[12] the self-employment route], the assets acquired by that person for the purpose of establishing or carrying on the commercial activity in respect of which such assistance is being received.

(4) In the case of a person who has ceased carrying on the commercial activity in respect of which assistance was received as specified in sub-paragraph (3), the assets relating to that activity for such period as may be reasonable in the circumstances to allow for disposal of any such asset.]

12.—[[21]—(1) Subject to sub-paragraph (2),] any arrears of, or any concessionary payment made to compensate for arrears due to the non-payment of—

(a) any payment specified in paragraph 7, 9 or 10 of Schedule 7 (other income to be disregarded);

(b) [[48] an income-based jobseeker's] allowance or an income-related benefit under Part VII of the Benefits Act [[23], [[43] . . .] child tax credit, working tax credit [[63], universal credit], [[46] or an income-related employment and support allowance]];

[[1](c) [[32] . . .]]

[[16](d) any discretionary housing payment paid pursuant to regulation 2(1) of the Discretionary Financial Assistance Regulations 2001,]

but only for a period of 52 weeks from the date of receipt of the arrears of the concessionary payment.

[[21] (2) In a case where the total of any arrears and, if appropriate, any concessionary payment referred to in sub-paragraph (1) relating to any one of the specified payments, benefits or allowances amounts to £5, 000 or more (referred to in this sub-paragraph and in sub-paragraph (3) as the "relevant sum") and is—

(a) paid in order to rectify, or to compensate for, an official error as defined in regulation 1(3) of the Social Security and Child Support (Decisions and Appeals) Regulations 1999, and

(b) received by the claimant in full on or after 14th October 2001,

sub-paragraph (1) shall have effect in relation to such arrears or concessionary payment either for a period of 52 weeks from the date of receipt, or, if the relevant sum is received in its entirety during the award of an income-based jobseeker's allowance, for the remainder of that award if that is a longer period.

(3) For the purposes of sub-paragraph (2), "the award of an income-based jobseeker's allowance" means—

(a) the award either of an income-based jobseeker's allowance [[46], income support or of an income-related employment and support allowance] in which the relevant sum (or first part thereof where it is paid in more than one instalment) is received, and

(b) where that award is followed by one or more further awards which in each case may be either of an income-based jobseeker's allowance [46 , income support or of an income-related employment and support allowance] and which, or each of which, begins immediately after the end of the previous award, such further awards until the end of the last such award, provided that for any such further awards the claimant—

(i) is the person who received the relevant sum, or

(ii) is the partner of the person who received the relevant sum, or was that person's partner at the date of his death, or

(iii) in the case of a joint-claim jobseeker's allowance, is a joint-claim couple either member or both members of which received the relevant sum.]

13.—Any sum—

(a) paid to the claimant in consequence of damage to, or loss of, the home or any personal possession and intended for its repair or replacement; or

(b) acquired by the claimant (whether as a loan or otherwise) on the express condition that it is to be used for effecting essential repairs or improvements to the home,

and which is to be used for the intended purpose, for a period of 26 weeks from the date on which it was so paid or acquired or such longer period as is reasonable in the circumstances to enable the claimant to effect the repairs, replacement or improvements.

14.—Any sum—

(a) deposited with a housing association as defined in section 1(1) of the Housing Associations Act 1985 as a condition of occupying the home;

(b) which was so deposited and which is to be used for the purchase of another home, for the period of 26 weeks or such longer period as is reasonable in the circumstances to complete the purchase.

15.—Any personal possessions except those which have or had been acquired by the claimant with the intention of reducing his capital in order to secure entitlement to a jobseeker's allowance or to income support or to increase the amount of those benefits.

16.—The value of the right to receive any income under an annuity and the surrender value (if any) of such an annuity.

17.—Where the funds of a trust are derived from a payment made in consequence of any personal injury to the claimant [39 or the claimant's partner], the value of the trust fund and the value of the right to receive any payment under that trust.

[40 **17A.**—(1) Any payment made to the claimant or the claimant's partner in consequence of any personal injury to the claimant or, as the case may be, the claimant's partner.

(2) But sub-paragraph (1)—

(a) applies only for the period of 52 weeks beginning with the day on which the claimant first receives any payment in consequence of that personal injury;

(b) does not apply to any subsequent payment made to him in consequence of that injury (whether it is made by the same person or another);

(c) ceases to apply to the payment or any part of the payment from the day on which the claimant no longer possesses it;

(d) does not apply to any payment from a trust where the funds of the trust are derived from a payment made in consequence of any personal injury to the claimant.

(3) For the purposes of sub-paragraph (2)(c), the circumstances in which a claimant no longer possesses a payment or a part of it include where the claimant has used a payment or part of it to purchase an asset.

(4) References in sub-paragraphs (2) and (3) to the claimant are to be construed as including references to his partner (where applicable).]

18.—The value of the right to receive any income under a life interest or from a liferent.

19.—The value of the right to receive any income which is disregarded under paragraph 14 of Schedule 6 or paragraph 24 of Schedule 7 (earnings or other income payable in a country outside the United Kingdom).

20.—The surrender value of any policy of life insurance.

21.—Where any payment of capital falls to be made by instalments, the value of the right to receive any outstanding instalments.

[44 **22.**—(1) Any payment made by a local authority in accordance with—

(a) section 17, 23B, 23C or 24A of the Children Act 1989,

(b) section 12 of the Social Work (Scotland) Act 1968, or

(c) section 29 or 30 of the Children (Scotland) Act 1995.

(2) Any payment (or part of a payment) made by a local authority in accordance with section 23C of the Children Act 1989 or section 29 of the Children (Scotland) Act 1995

(local authorities' duty to promote welfare of children and powers to grant financial assistance to persons in, or formerly in, their care) to a person ("A") which A passes on to the claimant.

(3) Sub-paragraphs (1) and (2) are subject to the following provisions.

(4) Neither of those sub-paragraphs applies where the claimant is a person who is, or would be, prevented from being entitled to a jobseeker's allowance by section 14 (trade disputes).

(5) Sub-paragraph (2) applies only where A—

(a) was formerly in the claimant's care, and

(b) is aged 18 or over, and

(c) continues to live with the claimant.]

23.—Any social fund payment made pursuant to Part VIII of the Benefits Act.

[61 **23A.**—Any local welfare provision.]

24.—Any refund of tax which falls to be deducted under section 369 of the Income and Corporation Taxes Act 1988 (deductions of tax from certain loan interest) on a payment of relevant loan interest for the purpose of acquiring an interest in the home or carrying out repairs or improvements in the home.

25.—Any capital which under regulation 104 [25 . . .] or 136 (capital treated as income [25 . . .] and treatment of student loans) is to be treated as income.

26.—Where a payment of capital is made in a currency other than sterling, any banking charge or commission payable in converting that payment into sterling.

27.—(1) Any payment made under [52 or by] the Macfarlane Trust, the Macfarlane (Special Payments) Trust, the Macfarlane (Special Payments) (No.2) Trust, the Fund, the Eileen Trust [51 , MFET Limited] [29, the Skipton Fund] [57 , the Caxton Foundation] [36, the London Bombings Relief Charitable Fund] ("the Trusts") or the Independent Living [47Fund (2006)].

(2) Any payment by or on behalf of a person who is suffering or who suffered from haemophilia or who is or was a qualifying person, which derives from a payment made under [52 or by] any of the Trusts to which sub-paragraph (1) refers and which is made to or for the benefit of—

(a) that person's partner or former partner from whom he is not, or where that person had died was not, estranged or divorced [35 or with whom he has formed a civil partnership that has not been dissolved or, where that person has died, had not been dissolved at the time of that person's death];

(b) any child or young person who is a member of that person's family or who was such a member and who is a member of the claimant's family.

(3) Any payment by or on behalf of the partner or former partner of a person who is suffering or who suffered from haemophilia or who is or was a qualifying person, provided that the partner or former partner and that person are not, or if either of them has died were not, estranged or divorced [35 or, where the partner or former partner and that person have formed a civil partnership, the civil partnership has not been dissolved or, if either of them has died, had not been dissolved at the time of the death], which derives from a payment made under [52 or by] any of the Trusts to which sub-paragraph (1) refers and which is made to or for the benefit of

(a) the person who is suffering from haemophilia or who is a qualifying person;

(b) any child or young person who is a member of that person's family or who was such a member and who is a member of the claimant's family.

(4) Any payment by a person who is suffering from haemophilia or who is a qualifying person, which derives from a payment made under [52 or by] any of the Trusts to which sub-paragraph (1) refers, where—

(a) that person has no partner or former partner from whom he is not estranged or divorced [35 or with whom he has formed a civil partnership that has not been dissolved], nor any child or young person who is or had been a member of that person's family; and

(b) the payment is made either—

(i) to that person's parent or step-parent, or

(ii) where that person at the date of payment is a child, a young person or a student who has not completed his full-time education, and has no parent or step-parent, to his guardian,

but only for a period from the date of the payment until the end of two years from that person's death.

(5) Any payment out of the estate of a person who suffered from haemophilia or who was a qualifying person, which derives from a payment made under [52 or by] any of the Trusts to which sub-paragraph (1) refers, where—

(a) that person at the date of his death (the relevant date) had no partner or former partner from whom he was not estranged or divorced [35 or with whom he had formed a civil partnership that had not been dissolved], nor any child or young person who was or had been a member of his family; and

(b) the payment is made either—

(i) to that person's parent or step-parent, or

(ii) where that person at the relevant date was a child, a young person or a student who had not completed his full-time education, and had no parent or step-parent, to his guardian,

but only for a period of two years from the relevant date.

(6) In the case of a person to whom or for whose benefit a payment referred to in this paragraph is made, any capital resource which derives from any payment of income or capital made under or deriving from any of the Trusts.

[[33] **27A.**—[[36] . . .]]

28.—The value of the right to receive an occupational or personal pension.

29.—The value of any funds held under a personal pension scheme.

30.—The value of the right to receive any rent except where the claimant has a reversionary interest in the property in respect of which rent is due.

31.—Any payment in kind made by a charity or under [[52] or by] the Macfarlane Trust, the Macfarlane (Special Payments) Trust, the Macfarlane (Special Payments) (No.2) Trust, the Fund, the Eileen Trust [[51] , MFET Limited] [[56] , the Skipton Fund, the Caxton Foundation] or the Independent Living [[47] Fund (2006)].

[[26] **32.**—Any payment made pursuant to section 2 of the Employment and Training Act 1973 or section 2 of the Enterprise and New Towns (Scotland) Act 1990, but only for the period of 52 weeks beginning on the date of receipt of the payment.]

33.—Any payment made by the Secretary of State to compensate for the loss (in whole or in part) of entitlement to housing benefit.

34.—Any payment made to a juror or a witness in respect of attendance at a court other than compensation for loss of earnings or for the loss of a benefit payable under the [[48] benefit Acts].

35.—Any payment in consequence of a reduction [[45] . . .] of council tax under section 13 [[62] , 13A] or, as the case may be, section 80 of the Local Government Finance Act 1992 (reduction of liability for council tax), but only for a period of 52 weeks from the date of the receipt of the payment.

[[48] **36.**—(1) Any payment or repayment made—

(a) as respects England, under regulation 5, 6 or 12 of the National Health Service (Travel Expenses and Remission of Charges) Regulations 2003 (travelling expenses and health service supplies);

(b) as respects Wales, under regulation 5, 6 or 11 of the National Health Service (Travelling Expenses and Remission of Charges) (Wales) Regulations 2007 (travelling expenses and health service supplies);

(c) as respects Scotland, under regulation 3, 5 or 11 of the National Health Service (Travelling Expenses and Remission of Charges) (Scotland) (No.2) Regulations 2003 (travelling expenses and health service supplies),

but only for a period of 52 weeks from the date of receipt of the payment or repayment.

(2) Any payment or repayment made by the Secretary of State for Health, the Scottish Ministers or the Welsh Ministers which is analogous to a payment or repayment mentioned in sub-paragraph (1), but only for a period of 52 weeks from the date of receipt of the payment or repayment.

37.—Any payment made to such persons entitled to receive benefits as may be determined by or under a scheme made pursuant to section 13 of the Social Security Act 1988 in lieu of vouchers or similar arrangements in connection with the provision of those benefits (including payments made in place of healthy start vouchers, milk tokens or the supply of vitamins), but only for a period of 52 weeks from the date of receipt of the payment.]

[[49] **37A.**—Any payment made under Part 8A of the Benefits Act (entitlement to health in pregnancy grant).]

38.—Any payment made either by the Secretary of State for [[42] Justice] or by the [[48] Scottish Ministers] under a scheme established to assist relatives and other persons to visit persons in custody, but only for a period of 52 weeks from the date of receipt of the payment.

[[48] **39.**—Any arrears of supplementary pension which is disregarded under paragraph 53 of Schedule 7 (sums to be disregarded in the calculation of income other than earnings) or of any amount which is disregarded under paragraph 54 or 55 of that Schedule, but only for a period of 52 weeks from the date of receipt of the arrears.]

40.—Any payment (other than a training allowance [[26] . . .]) made, whether by the Secretary of State or by any other person, under the Disabled Persons (Employment) Act 1944 [[26] . . .] to assist disabled persons to obtain or retain employment despite their disability.

41.—Any payment made by a local authority under section 3 of the Disabled Persons (Employment) Act 1958 to homeworkers assisted under the Blind Homeworkers Scheme.

[41 **42.**—(1) Any sum of capital to which sub-paragraph (2) applies and—

(a) which is administered on behalf of a person by the High Court or the County Court under rule 21.11(1) of the Civil Procedure Rules 1998 or by the Court of Protection;

(b) which can only be disposed of by order or direction of any such court; or

(c) where the person concerned is under the age of 18, which can only be disposed of by order or direction prior to that person attaining age 18.

(2) This sub-paragraph applies to a sum of capital which is derived from—

(a) an award of damages for a personal injury to that person; or

(b) compensation for the death of one or both parents where the person concerned is under the age of 18.]

43.—Any sum of capital administered on behalf of a person [2. . .] in accordance with an order made under [24 section 13 of the Children (Scotland) Act 1995], or under Rule 36.14 of the Ordinary Cause Rules 1993 or under Rule 128 of the Ordinary Cause Rules, where such sum derives from—

(a) an award of damages for a personal injury to that person; or

(b) compensation for the death of one or both parents [2where the person concerned is under the age of 18].

44.—Any payment to the claimant as holder of the Victoria Cross or George Cross.

[14 **45.**—[26 . . .].]

[20 **45A.**—[26 . . .].]

[3**46.**—[26 . . .].]

[6**47.**—In the case of a person who is receiving, or who has received, assistance under [12 the self-employment route], any sum of capital which is acquired by that person for the purpose of establishing or carrying on the commercial activity in respect of which such assistance is or was received but only for a period of 52 weeks from the date on which that sum was acquired.]

[7**48.**—[26 . . .].]

49.—[*Omitted.*]

50.—[*Omitted.*]

[8 **51.**—(1) Any payment of a sports award for a period of 26 weeks from the date of receipt of that payment except to the extent that it has been made in respect of any one or more of the items specified in sub-paragraph (2).

(2) The items specified for the purposes of sub-paragraph (1) are food, ordinary clothing or footwear, household fuel, rent for which housing benefit is payable or any housing costs to the extent that they are met under regulation 83(f) or 84(1)(g) (housing costs) [19 . . .], of the claimant or, where the claimant is a member of a family, any other member of his family, or any council tax or water charges for which that claimant or member is liable.

(3) For the purposes of sub-paragraph (2)—

"food" does not include vitamins, minerals or other special dietary supplements intended to enhance the performance of the person in the sport in respect of which the award was made;

"ordinary clothing and footwear" means clothing or footwear for normal daily use but does not include school uniforms or clothing or footwear used solely for sporting activities.]

[30 **52.**—(1) Any payment—

(a) by way of an education maintenance allowance made pursuant to—

(i) regulations made under section 518 of the Education Act 1996;

(ii) regulations made under section 49 or 73(f) of the Education (Scotland) Act 1980;

[48 (iii) directions made under section 73ZA of the Education (Scotland) Act 1980 and paid under section 12(2)(c) of the Further and Higher Education (Scotland) Act 1992; [58 . . .]]

(b) corresponding to such an education maintenance allowance, made pursuant to—

(i) section 14 or section 181 of the Education Act 2002; or

(ii) regulations made under section 181 of that Act [58 ; or

(c) in England, by way of financial assistance made pursuant to section 14 of the Education Act 2002.]

(2) Any payment, other than a payment to which sub-paragraph (1) applies, made pursuant to—

(a) regulations made under section 518 of the Education Act 1996;

(b) regulations made under section 49 of the Education (Scotland) Act 1980; or

[48 (c) directions made under section 73ZA of the Education (Scotland) Act 1980 and paid under section 12(2)(c) of the Further and Higher Education (Scotland) Act 1992,]

in respect of a course of study attended by a child or a young person or a person who is in receipt of an education maintenance allowance [58 or other payment] made pursuant to any provision specified in sub-paragraph (1).]

[11 **53.**—In the case of a claimant participating in an employment zone programme, any discretionary payment made by an employment zone contractor to the claimant, being a fee, grant, loan or otherwise, but only for the period of 52 weeks from the date of receipt of the payment.

54.—Any arrears of subsistence allowance paid as a lump sum but only for the period of 52 weeks from the date of receipt of the payment.]

55.—*[Omitted.]*

[13 **56.**—Where an ex-gratia payment of £10, 000 has been made by the Secretary of State on or after 1st February 2001 in consequence of the imprisonment or internment of—

(a) the claimant;
(b) the claimant's partner;
(c) the claimant's deceased spouse [35 or deceased civil partner]; or
(d) the claimant's partner's deceased spouse [35 or deceased civil partner],

by the Japanese during the Second World War, £10, 000.]

[15 **57.**—(1) Subject to sub-paragraph (2), the amount of any trust payment made to a claimant or a member of a claimant's family who is—

(a) a diagnosed person;
(b) the diagnosed person's partner or the person who was the diagnosed person's partner at the date of the diagnosed person's death;
(c) a parent of a diagnosed person, a person acting in the place of the diagnosed person's parents or a person who was so acting at the date of the diagnosed person's death; or
(d) a member of the diagnosed person's family (other than his partner) or a person who was a member of the diagnosed person's family (other than his partner) at the date of the diagnosed person's death.

(2) Where a trust payment is made to—

(a) a person referred to in sub-paragraph (1)(a) or (b), that sub-paragraph shall apply for the period beginning on the date on which the trust payment is made and ending on the date on which that person dies;
(b) a person referred to in sub-paragraph (1)(c), that sub-paragraph shall apply for the period beginning on the date on which the trust payment is made and ending two years after that date;
(c) a person referred to in sub-paragraph (1)(d), that sub-paragraph shall apply for the period beginning on the date on which the trust payment is made and ending—
    (i) two years after that date; or
    (ii) on the day before the day on which that person—
        (aa) ceases receiving full-time education; or
        (bb) attains the age of [38 20],

    whichever is the latest.

(3) Subject to sub-paragraph (4), the amount of any payment by a person to whom a trust payment has been made, or of any payment out of the estate of a person to whom a trust payment has been made, which is made to a claimant or a member of a claimant's family who is—

(a) the diagnosed person's partner or the person who was the diagnosed person's partner at the date of the diagnosed person's death;
(b) a parent of a diagnosed person, a person acting in the place of the diagnosed person's parents or a person who was so acting at the date of the diagnosed person's death; or
(c) a member of the diagnosed person's family (other than his partner) or a person who was a member of the diagnosed person's family (other than his partner) at the date of the diagnosed person's death,

but only to the extent that such payments do not exceed the total amount of any trust payments made to that person.

(4) Where a payment as referred to in sub-paragraph (3) is made to—

(a) a person referred to in sub-paragraph (3)(a), that sub-paragraph shall apply for the period beginning on the date on which that payment is made and ending on the date on which that person dies;
(b) a person referred to in sub-paragraph (3)(b), that sub-paragraph shall apply for the period beginning on the date on which that payment is made and ending two years after that date;

(c) a person referred to in sub-paragraph (3)(c), that sub-paragraph shall apply for the period beginning on the date on which that payment is made and ending—
(i) two years after that date; or
(ii) on the day before the day on which that person—
(aa) ceases receiving full-time education; or
(bb) attains the age of [38 20],
whichever is the latest.

(5) In this paragraph, a reference to a person—
(a) being the diagnosed person's partner;
(b) being a member of the diagnosed person's family; or
(c) acting in the place of the diagnosed person's parents,
at the date of the diagnosed person's death shall include a person who would have been such a person or a person who would have been so acting, but for the diagnosed person [34 residing in a care home, an Abbeyfield Home or an independent hospital] on that date.

(6) In this paragraph—
"diagnosed person" means a person who has been diagnosed as suffering from, or who, after his death, has been diagnosed as having suffered from, variant Creutzfeldt-Jakob disease;
"relevant trust" means a trust established out of funds provided by the Secretary of State in respect of persons who suffered, or who are suffering, from variant Creutzfeldt-Jakob disease for the benefit of persons eligible for payments in accordance with its provisions;
"trust payment" means a payment under a relevant trust.]

[18 **58.**—The amount of a payment, other than a war pension [48 . . .], to compensate for the fact that the claimant, the claimant's partner, the claimant's deceased spouse [35 or deceased civil partner] or the claimant's partner's deceased spouse [35 or deceased civil partner]—
(a) was a slave labourer or a forced labourer;
(b) had suffered property loss or had suffered personal injury; or
(c) was a parent of a child who had died, during the Second World War.]

[22 [24 **59.**—(1) Any payment made by a local authority, or by the [48 Welsh Ministers], to or on behalf of the claimant or his partner relating to a service which is provided to develop or sustain the capacity of the claimant or his partner to live independently in his accommodation.]

(2) For the purposes of sub-paragraph (1) "local authority" means—
(a) in relation to England, a county council, a district council, a London borough council, the Common Council of the City of London or the Council of the Isles of Scilly;
(b) in relation to Wales, a county council or a county borough council;
(c) in relation to Scotland, a council constituted under section 2 of the Local Government etc. (Scotland) Act 1994.]

[24 **60.**—Any payment made under [49 . . .] [65 sections 31 to 33 of the Care Act 2014 (direct payments) or under] regulations made under section 57 of the Health and Social Care Act 2001 or under section 12B of the Social Work (Scotland) Act 1968 [53 , or under sections 12A to 12D of the National Health Service Act 2006 (direct payments for health care)].

[37 **61.**—Any payment made to the claimant pursuant to regulations under section 2(6)(b), 3 or 4 of the Adoption and Children Act 2002.]

[31 **61A.**—Any payment made to the claimant in accordance with regulations made pursuant to section 14F of the Children Act 1989 (special guardianship support services).]

62.—[26. . .].]

[25 **63.**—[26. . .].]

[64 **64.**—Any payments to a claimant made under section 49 of the Children and Families Act 2014 (personal budgets and direct payments).]

AMENDMENTS

1. Social Security and Child Support (Jobseeker's Allowance) (Miscellaneous Amendments) Regulations 1996 (SI 1996/2538) reg.2(14) (October 28, 1996).
2. Income-related Benefits and Jobseeker's Allowance (Amendment) (No.2) Regulations 1997 (SI 1997/2197) reg.7(9) and (10)(f) (October 6, 1997).
3. Social Security Amendment (New Deal) Regulations 1997 (SI 1997/2863) reg.15 (January 5, 1998).
4. Social Security (Miscellaneous Amendments) (No.4) Regulations 1998 (SI 1998/1174) reg.5(a) (June 1, 1998).
5. Social Security (Miscellaneous Amendments) (No.4) Regulations 1998 (SI 1998/1174) reg.5(b) (June 1, 1998).

6. Social Security (Miscellaneous Amendments) (No.4) Regulations 1998 (SI 1998/1174) reg.5(c) (June 1, 1998).
7. Social Security Amendment (New Deal) (No.2) Regulations 1998 (SI 1998/2117) reg.5(1) (September 24, 1998).
8. Social Security Amendment (Sports Awards) Regulations 1999 (SI 1999/2165) reg.7(5) (August 23, 1999).
9. Social Security Amendment (Education Maintenance Allowance) Regulations 2000 (SI 2000/55) reg.2(3) and (4)(d) (February 7, 2000).
10. Social Security (Miscellaneous Amendments) Regulations 2000 (SI 2000/681) reg.9 (April 3, 2000).
11. Social Security Amendment (Employment Zones) Regulations 2000 (SI 2000/724) reg.3(4) (April 3, 2000).
12. Social Security Amendment (Employment Zones) (No.2) Regulations 2000 (SI 2000/2910) reg.4(1) and (2)(d)(ii) (November 27, 2000).
13. Social Security Amendment (Capital Disregards) Regulations 2001 (SI 2001/22) reg.2 (February 1, 2001).
14. Social Security Amendment (New Deal) Regulations 2001 (SI 2001/1029) reg.13 (April 9, 2001).
15. Social Security Amendment (Capital Disregards and Recovery of Benefits) Regulations 2001 (SI 2001/1118) reg.2(1) (April 12, 2001).
16. Social Security Amendment (Discretionary Housing Payments) Regulations 2001 (SI 2001/2333) reg.2(2)(d) (July 2, 2001).
17. Children (Leaving Care) Act 2000 (Commencement No.2 and Consequential Provisions) Order 2001 (SI 2001/3070) art.3(5) and Sch.4 para.1(c) of (October 1, 2001).
18. Social Security Amendment (Capital Disregards) (No.2) Regulations 2001 (SI 2001/3481) reg.2 (November 19, 2001).
19. Social Security Amendment (Residential Care and Nursing Homes) Regulations 2001 (SI 2001/3767) reg.2(2) and Sch.1 Pt II of para.25 (April 8, 2002).
20. Social Security Amendment (Employment Programme) Regulations 2002 (SI 2002/2314) reg.2(6) (October 14, 2002).
21. Social Security (Miscellaneous Amendments) (No.2) Regulations 2002 (SI 2002/2380) reg.3(c) (October 14, 2002).
22. Social Security (Miscellaneous Amendments) Regulations 2003 (SI 2003/511) reg.3(3) (April 1, 2003).
23. Social Security (Working Tax Credit and Child Tax Credit) (Consequential Amendments) Regulations 2003 (SI 2003/455) reg.3 and Sch.2 para.24(a) (April 7, 2003).
24. Social Security (Miscellaneous Amendments) (No.2) Regulations 2003 (SI 2003/2279) reg.3(5) (October 1, 2003).
25. Social Security (Incapacity Benefit Work-focused Interviews) Regulations 2003 (SI 2003/2439) reg.16(b) (October 27, 2003).
26. Social Security (Miscellaneous Amendments) Regulations 2004 (SI 2004/565) reg.5(4) (April 1, 2004).
27. Social Security (Working Tax Credit and Child Tax Credit) (Consequential Amendments) Regulations 2003 (SI 2003/455) reg.3 and Sch.2 para.24(b) (April 6, 2004, except in "transitional cases" and see further the note to reg.83 and to reg.17 of the Income Support Regulations).
28. Social Security (Miscellaneous Amendments) (No.2) Regulations 2004 (SI 2004/1141) reg.3(1) and (2)(d) (May 12, 2004).
29. Social Security (Miscellaneous Amendments) (No.2) Regulations 2004 (SI 2004/1141) reg.3(7) and (8)(b) (May 12, 2004).
30. Social Security (Students and Income-related Benefits) Amendment Regulations 2004 (SI 2004/1708) reg.6(4) (September 1, 2004, or if the student's period of study begins between August 1 and August 31, 2004, the first day of the period).
31. Social Security (Miscellaneous Amendments) (No.3) Regulations 2004 (SI 2004/2308) reg.4(7) (October 4, 2004).

32. Social Security (Miscellaneous Amendments) Regulations 2005 (SI 2005/574) reg.6(6) (April 4, 2005).
33. Income-related Benefits (Amendment) Regulations 2005 (SI 2005/2183) reg.5 (August 5, 2005).
34. Social Security (Care Homes and Independent Hospitals) Regulations 2005 (SI 2005/2687) reg.3 and Sch.2 para.15 (October 24, 2005).
35. Civil Partnership (Pensions, Social Security and Child Support) (Consequential, etc. Provisions) Order 2005 (SI 2005/2877) art.2(3) and Sch.3 para.26(13) (December 5, 2005).
36. Income-related Benefits (Amendment) (No.2) Regulations 2005 (SI 2005/3391) reg.5(5) (December 12, 2005).
37. Social Security (Miscellaneous Amendments) (No.2) Regulations 2005 (SI 2005/2465) reg.3(9) (December 30, 2005).
38. Social Security (Young Persons) Amendment Regulations 2006 (SI 2006/718) reg.3(11) (April 10, 2006).
39. Social Security (Miscellaneous Amendments) (No.4) Regulations 2006 (SI 2006/2378) reg.13(13)(a) (October 2, 2006).
40. Social Security (Miscellaneous Amendments) (No.4) Regulations 2006 (SI 2006/2378) reg.13(13)(b) (October 2, 2006).
41. Social Security (Miscellaneous Amendments) (No.4) Regulations 2006 (SI 2006/2378) reg.13(13)(c) (October 2, 2006).
42. Secretary of State for Justice Order 2007 (SI 2007/2128) Sch. para.16(3) (August 22, 2007).
43. Social Security (Miscellaneous Amendments) Regulations 2008 (SI 2008/698) reg.4(17)(a) (April 14, 2008).
44. Social Security (Miscellaneous Amendments) Regulations 2008 (SI 2008/698) reg.4(17)(b) (April 7, 2008).
45. Social Security (Miscellaneous Amendments) Regulations 2008 (SI 2008/698) reg.4(17)(c) (April 14, 2008).
46. Employment and Support Allowance (Consequential Provisions) (No.2) Regulations 2008 (SI 2008/1554) reg.3(29) (October 27, 2008).
47. Social Security (Miscellaneous Amendments) (No.6) Regulations 2008 (SI 2008/2767) reg.4(7) (November 17, 2008).
48. Social Security (Miscellaneous Amendments) (No.7) Regulations 2008 (SI 2008/3157) reg.3(11) (January 5, 2009).
49. Social Security (Miscellaneous Amendments) Regulations 2009 (SI 2009/583) reg.4(13) (April 6, 2009).
50. Social Security (Equalisation of State Pension Age) Regulations 2009 (SI 2009/1488) reg.17 (April 6, 2010).
51. Social Security (Miscellaneous Amendments) (No.2) Regulations 2010 (SI 2010/641) reg.4(3)(g) (April 6, 2010).
52. Social Security (Miscellaneous Amendments) (No.2) Regulations 2010 (SI 2010/641) reg.4(8(f) (April 6, 2010).
53. Social Security (Miscellaneous Amendments) (No.2) Regulations 2010 (SI 2010/641) reg.4(13) (April 6, 2010).
54. Jobseeker's Allowance (Mandatory Work Activity Scheme) Regulations 2011 (SI 2011/688) reg.15(1)(d) and (2) (April 25, 2011).
55. Jobseeker's Allowance (Employment, Skills and Enterprise Scheme) Regulations 2011 (SI 2011/917) reg.15(1)(d) and (2) (May 20, 2011).
56. Social Security (Miscellaneous Amendments) (No.3) Regulations 2011 (SI 2011/2425) reg.10(9) (October 31, 2011).
57. Social Security (Miscellaneous Amendments) (No.3) Regulations 2011 (SI 2011/2425) reg.10(10) (October 31, 2011).
58. Social Security (Miscellaneous Amendments) (No.3) Regulations 2011 (SI 2011/2425) reg.10(14) (October 31, 2011).
59. Jobseeker's Allowance (Schemes for Assisting Persons to Obtain Employment) Regulations 2013 (SI 2013/276) reg.12(1)(d) and (2) (February 12, 2013).

60. Jobseekers (Back to Work Schemes) Act 2013 s.1(14) (March 26, 2013).
61. Social Security (Miscellaneous Amendments) Regulations 2013 (SI 2013/443) reg.4(13)(a) (April 2, 2013).
62. Social Security (Miscellaneous Amendments) Regulations 2013 (SI 2013/443) reg.4(13)(b) (April 2, 2013).
63. Universal Credit (Consequential, Supplementary, Incidental and Miscellaneous Provisions) Regulations 2013 (SI 2013/630) reg.30(9) (April 29, 2013).
64. Special Educational Needs (Consequential Amendments to Subordinate Legislation) Order 2014 (SI 2014/2103) art.4(2) (September 1, 2014).
65. Care Act 2014 (Consequential Amendments) (Secondary Legislation) Order 2015 (SI 2015/643) art.2 and Sch. para.9(4) (April 1, 2015).

Definitions

"Abbeyfield Home"—see reg.1(3).
"the Benefits Act"—see Jobseekers Act s.35(1).
"care home"—see reg.1(3).
"the Caxton Foundation"—*ibid.*
"child"—see Jobseekers Act s.35(1).
"claimant"—*ibid.*, and reg.88(1).
"concessionary payment"—see reg.1(3).
"dwelling occupied as the home"—*ibid.*
"the Eileen Trust"—*ibid.*
"the Employment, Skills and Enterprise Scheme"—*ibid.*
"employment zone contractor"—*ibid.*
"employment zone programme"—*ibid.*
"family"—see Jobseekers Act s.35(1).
"the Fund"—see reg.1(3).
"independent hospital"—*ibid.*
"the Independent Living Funds"—*ibid.*
"the London Bombings Relief Charitable Fund"—*ibid.*
"the Macfarlane (Special Payments) Trust"—*ibid.*
"the Macfarlane (Special Payments) (No.2) Trust"—*ibid.*
"the Macfarlane Trust"—*ibid.*
"the Mandatory Work Activity Scheme"—*ibid.*
"the Skipton Fund"—*ibid.*
"MFET Limited"—*ibid.*
"occupational pension"—*ibid.*
"partner"—*ibid.*
"payment"—*ibid.*
"personal pension scheme"—see Jobseekers Act s.35(1).
"policy of life insurance"—see reg.1(3).
"qualifying age for state pension credit"—*ibid.*
"qualifying person"—*ibid.*
"relative"—*ibid.*
"self-employed earner"—*ibid.*, and SSCBA s.2(1)(b).
"sports award"—see reg.1(3).
"subsistence allowance"—*ibid.*
"training allowance"—*ibid.*
"universal credit"—*ibid.*
"young person"—see reg.76.

General Note

Most of the disregards in Sch.8 are the same as those in Sch.10 to the Income Support Regulations (subject to some reordering and minor adjustments in the wording). See the notes to Sch.10. **3.544**

Paragraphs 32 and 33 of Sch.10 were not reproduced in the original Sch.8 as they are no longer relevant. There was also no equivalent of paras 47–49 of Sch.10, but see para.12 of this Schedule.

Note that in para.15 the disregard of the value of personal possessions does not apply if they have been acquired in order to reduce capital so as to gain jobseeker's allowance *or income support*. This avoids the question that might otherwise have arisen on a claimant transfering from income support to jobseeker's allowance whether if the acquisition had only been for the purposes of income support the disregard in para.15 applies. However, para.15 has not been amended to include an acquisition for the purposes of income-related ESA.

3.545 A blanket capital disregard of the various allowances, grants and other payments made under s.2 of the Employment and Training Act 1973 or s.2 of the Enterprise and New Towns (Scotland) Act 1990 to people participating in New Deals and other training and welfare to work schemes was introduced on April 1, 2004 to replace the separate disregards that had existed in respect of such payments under a number of the provisions in this Schedule. As a consequence of this change, those provisions have been revoked or amended. The revoked paragraphs are paras 45, 45A, 46, 48, 62 and 63; the amended paragraph is para.40. However note that if these payments do count as capital they are only ignored for 52 weeks from the date of receipt.

On paras 11(3) and (4) and 47, see the note to reg.102C and on paras 53 and 54, see the note to reg.42(5A) of the Income Support Regulations.

Paragraphs 27(4)(b)(i) and (ii) and 27(5)(b)(i) and (ii) include references to step-parents. Note that from December 5, 2005, references to "step" relationships and "in laws" are to be read as including relationships arising through civil partnership in any provision to which s.246 of the Civil Partnership Act 2004 applies. Section 246 is applied to paras 27(4)(b)(i) and (ii) and 27(5)(b)(i) and (ii) by art.3 of and para.64 of the Schedule to the Civil Partnership Act 2004 (Relationships Arising Through Civil Partnership) Order 2005 (SI 2005/3137).

Paragraph 55

3.546 This paragraph has not been reproduced as it only related to a pilot scheme to reduce under-occupation operating in three London boroughs (Croydon, Haringey and Newham) from April 3, 2000. It was added by reg.12 of the Social Security (Payments to Reduce Under-occupation) Regulations 2000 (SI 2000/637) on April 3, 2000 and provided that a payment made under the scheme would be ignored for 52 weeks from the date of payment. The pilot scheme lasted for three years and the Payments to Reduce Under-occupation Regulations ceased to have effect on March 31, 2003.

Paragraphs A2–A3

3.547 Paragraph A2 provides for a capital disregard of payments of expenses in respect of a person's participation in the Mandatory Work Activity Scheme for 52 weeks from the date the payment was received. The original para.A3 contained the same disregard in relation to the Employment, Skills and Enterprise Scheme. However, a further para.A3 was inserted on February 12, 2013, and the original para.A3 has been treated as revoked from that date as a result of s.1(14) of the Jobseekers (Back to Work Schemes) Act 2013. This was because the Jobseeker's Allowance (Employment, Skills and Enterprise Scheme) Regulations 2011 (SI 2011/917) were held to be ultra vires by the Court of Appeal in *R (Reilly and Wilson) v Secretary of State for Work and Pensions* [2013] EWCA Civ 66. The appeal against this decision was allowed by the Supreme Court on October 30, 2013 (*R (on the application of Reilly) v Secretary of State for Work and Pensions* [2013] UKSC 68) but "on the basis only that the Jobseekers (Back to Work Schemes) Act 2013 has come into force" (the 2013 Act came into force on March 26, 2013). The new para.A3 provides that payments of expenses in respect of a person's participation in a scheme listed in reg.3 of the Jobseeker's Allowance (Schemes for Assisting Persons to Obtain

Employment) Regulations 2013 are ignored as capital but only for 52 weeks from the date of receipt.

Paragraphs A1, A4 and A5

These paragraphs have not been included. This is because they only apply to pilot schemes in certain areas of the country. **3.548**

Paragraph A1 was inserted by reg.17(1)(d) and (2) of the Jobseeker's Allowance (Work for Your Benefit Pilot Scheme) Regulations 2010 (SI 2010/1222) to provide for a disregard of payments for child care, travel and other expenses incurred in respect of the claimant's participation in the Work for Your Benefit Pilot Scheme as capital but only for 52 weeks from the date the payment was received. These Regulations came into force on November 22, 2010 and were to cease to have effect on November 21, 2013 but in fact were revoked on March 1, 2012.

Paragraph A4 was inserted by reg.14(1)(c) and (2) of the Jobseeker's Allowance (Supervised Jobsearch Pilot Scheme) Regulations 2014 (SI 2014/1913); its effect was that payments for child care, travel and other expenses incurred by a person who was participating in the Supervised Jobsearch Pilot Scheme would be ignored as capital for 52 weeks from the date of receipt. These Regulations came into force on July 18, 2014 and ceased to have effect on April 30, 2015.

Paragraph A5 was inserted by reg.18(1)(c) and (2) of the Jobseeker's Allowance (18–21 Work Skills Pilot Scheme) Regulations 2014 (SI 2014/3117) and makes the same provision in relation to a person's participation in the 18–21 Work Skills Pilot Scheme. These Regulations came into force on November 25, 2014 and will cease to have effect two years after they came into force.

Paragraph 12

In relation to the April 2013 amendment to para.12, this only amends para.12(1)(b). It is not clear why para.12(3) has not been amended in the same way as para.7(3) of Sch.10 to the Income Support Regulations. **3.549**

Paragraph 60

With effect from April 1, 2014, the disregard in para.60 is modified by art.2 of, and para.5 of the Schedule to, the Social Care (Self-directed Support) (Scotland) Act 2013 (Consequential Modifications and Savings) Order 2014 (SI 2014/513) so that the words "as a direct payment as defined in section 4(2) of the Social Care (Self-directed Support) (Scotland) Act 2013" are substituted for the words "under section 12B of the Social Work (Scotland) 1968". However, under art.3 of the Order, this modification does not apply if a payment is made under s.12B of the 1968 Act on or after April 1, 2014. **3.550**

The Jobseeker's Allowance (Transitional Provisions) Regulations 1996

(SI 1996/2567)

For the text of these regulations, omitted here for reasons of space and relative infrequency of use, see Social Security: Legislation 2000: Vol.II: Income Support, Jobseeker's Allowance, Tax Credits and the Social Fund, pp.1054–1083. **3.551**

The Social Security (Miscellaneous Amendments) (No. 5) Regulations 2010

(SI 2010/2429)

Made by the Secretary of State under ss.123(1)(a), (d) and (e), 124(1)(e), 136(3) and (5)(b), 136A(3), 137(1) and 175(1), (3) and (4) of the Social Security Contributions and Benefits Act 1992, ss.2A(1), (3)(e), (4)(b) and (5), 15A(2)(a) and (4), 189(1), (4) and (5) and 191 of the Social Security Administration Act 1992, ss.12(1) and (4)(b), 35(1) and 36(2) and (4)(a) of, and para.8A(1) of Sch.1 to, the Jobseekers Act 1995, s.16 of the Employment Tribunals Act 1996, ss.15(3) and (6)(b) and 17(1) of the State Pension Credit Act 2002 and ss.17(1) and (3)(a) and (b), 24(1) and 25(3),(4) and (5)(a) of the Welfare Reform Act 2007

[In force November 1, 2010]

Amendments to the Jobseeker's Allowance Regulations 1996

3.552 **4.**—(1) The Jobseeker's Allowance Regulations 1996 are amended as follows.

(2) In Schedule A1 (categories of members of a joint-claim couple who are not required to satisfy the conditions in section 1(2B)(b)), subject to paragraph (3) below—

(a) the following provisions are revoked—

(i) paragraph 6(a) and (b) (member incapable of work),

(ii) paragraph 9 (disabled students),

(iii) paragraph 10 (deaf students), and

(iv) paragraph 11 (blind members);

(b) *[Omitted.]*

(c) *[Omitted.]*

(3) A provision revoked or amended by paragraph (2) continues to have effect in relation to a joint-claim couple as if that revocation or amendment had not been made where, immediately before 1st November 2010—

(a) the couple were entitled to a jobseeker's allowance, and

(b) that provision applied to a member of that couple.

(4) Paragraph (3) ceases to apply to a joint-claim couple upon termination of the jobseeker's allowance award that they were entitled to immediately before 1st November 2010.

GENERAL NOTE

3.553 See the note to Sch.A1 to the JSA Regulations.

The Jobseeker's Allowance (Mandatory Work Activity Scheme) Regulations 2011

(SI 2011/688)

The Secretary of State for Work and Pensions makes the following Regulations in exercise of the powers conferred by sections 123(1)(d) and (e), 136(3) and (5)(a) and (b), 137(1) and 175(3) and (4) of the Social Security Contributions and Benefits Act 1992, sections 30 and 146(1) and (2) of the Housing Grants, Construction and Regeneration Act 1996, sections 9 and 10 of the Social Security Act 1998 and sections 12(1), (4)(a) and (b), 17A(1), (2), (5)(a), (d) and (e) and (6) to (9), 20, 20A, 20B(4) to (6), 20E(3)(a), 21, 35(1) and 36(2) and (4) of, and Schedule 1 to, the Jobseekers Act 1995.

These Regulations are made with the consent of the Treasury in respect of provisions relating to section 30 (means testing in case of application by owner-occupier or tenant) of the Housing Grants, Construction and Regeneration Act 1996.

In respect of provisions in these Regulations relating to housing benefit and council tax benefit, organisations appearing to the Secretary of State to be representative of the authorities concerned have agreed that consultations need not be undertaken.

In accordance with section 172(1) of the Social Security Administration Act 1992, the Secretary of State referred the proposals for these Regulations to the Social Security Advisory Committee.

Arrangement of Regulations

Part 1

General

Part 2

Selection for and participation in the Mandatory Work Activity Scheme

Part 3

Sanctions

Part 4

Hardship

PART 5

Consequential amendments

11. Definitions
12. Notional income
13. Notional capital
14. Income to be disregarded
15. Capital to be disregarded
16. Further amendments of the Jobseeker's Allowance Regulations
17. Consequential amendments relating to sanctions
18. Consequential amendments relating to decisions and appeals
19. Consequential amendments relating to the Jobseeker's Allowance (Work for Your Benefit Pilot Scheme) Regulations 2010

PART 6

Contracting Out

20. Contracting out certain functions in relation to the Scheme

GENERAL NOTE

3.555 The Jobseekers (Back to Work Schemes) Act 2013 was designed to validate retrospectively the ESES Regulations that had been declared ultra vires by the Court of Appeal in *R (Reilly and Wilson) v Secretary of State for Work and Pensions* [2013] EWCA Civ 66 on the ground that the regulations failed to describe, rather than merely name, the schemes they purported to bring within s.17A. The Act was passed on the day on which the Secretary of State sought permission to appeal to the Supreme Court. On the day of the Court of Appeal's judgment (February 12, 2013) the ESES Regulations were replaced by the SAPOE Regulations, which set out the details of the schemes that had been named in the ESES Regulations.

The 2013 Act also sought to protect the operation of the MWAS Regulations from challenge on the basis that notices given to claimants under reg.4 were invalid in the same way as notices under reg.4 of the ESES Regulations in *Reilly and Wilson*, on which now see the decision of the Supreme Court ([2013] UKSC 68; [2014] 1 A.C. 453) and the decision of the three-judge panel of the Upper Tribunal in *SSWP v TJ (JSA)* [2015] UKUT 56 (AAC), discussed in detail in the introductory note to the 2013 Act. The Upper Tribunal concluded that the Supreme Court had been proceeding on an assumed factual basis that had been shown to be wrong in saying that in Mr Wilson's case the notice to participate in the scheme would have been vitiated by the failure to give him adequate information about the scheme in advance of the notice to enable him to make meaningful representations about whether the notice should be issued. It took the view that where the scheme in question was mandatory at the stage of referral as well as at the stage of participation after issue of a notice, there was no possibility of representations altering the decision to refer, so that no duty of fairness to provide prior information could arise. See the introductory note to the 2013 Act for a doubt about the Upper Tribunal's approach. The Secretary of State's appeal against the decision in *TJ*, on some issues at least, is listed to be heard in November 2015, at the same time as the appeal against the decision of Lang J in *R (Reilly (No.2) and Hewstone) v*

Secretary of State for Work and Pensions [2014] EWHC 2182 (Admin). However, the 2013 Act gave no protection to the MWAS Regulations against a vires challenge on the same grounds as in *Reilly and Wilson*. Such a challenge was rejected by Hickinbottom J in *R (Smith) v Secretary of State for Work and Pensions* [2014] EWHC 843 (Admin). He held that there was sufficient description of the scheme to meet the standard required by the Supreme Court. The reasons included that the prescription of the period of the scheme was relevant to its description under s.17A(1) and was not relevant only to subs.(2). The Court of Appeal in *Smith v Secretary of State for Work and Pensions* [2015] EWCA Civ 229 has affirmed that decision on essentially the same reasoning.

PART 1

GENERAL

Citation and commencement

1.—These Regulations may be cited as the Jobseeker's Allowance (Mandatory Work Activity Scheme) Regulations 2011 and shall come into force on 25th April 2011. **3.556**

Interpretation

2.—(1) In these Regulations— **3.557**

"the Act" means the Jobseekers Act 1995;

"claimant" means a person who claims a jobseeker's allowance, except that in relation to a joint-claim couple claiming a joint-claim jobseeker's allowance, it means either or both of the members of the couple;

"the Council Tax Benefit Regulations" means the Council Tax Benefit Regulations 2006;

"the Housing Benefit Regulations" means the Housing Benefit Regulations 2006;

"the Housing Renewal Grants Regulations" means the Housing Renewal Grants Regulations 1996;

"the Jobseeker's Allowance Regulations" means the Jobseeker's Allowance Regulations 1996;

"the Mandatory Work Activity Scheme" means a scheme within section 17A (schemes for assisting persons to obtain employment: "work for your benefit" schemes etc.) of the Act known by that name and provided pursuant to arrangements made by the Secretary of State that is designed to provide work or work-related activity for up to 30 hours per week over a period of four consecutive weeks with a view to assisting claimants to improve their prospects of obtaining employment;

"the Scheme" means the Mandatory Work Activity Scheme; and

"working day" means any day except for a Saturday, Sunday, Christmas Day, Good Friday or bank holiday under the Banking and Financial Dealings Act 1971 in England, Wales or Scotland.

(2) For the purpose of these Regulations, where a written notice is given by sending it by post is taken to have been received on the second working day after posting.

PART 2

SELECTION FOR AND PARTICIPATION IN THE MANDATORY WORK ACTIVITY SCHEME

Selection for participation in the Scheme

3.558 **3.**—(1) The Secretary of State may select a claimant who is aged at least 18 for participation in the Scheme.

(2) Only a claimant who is required to meet the jobseeking conditions may be required to participate in the Scheme.

Requirement to participate and notification

3.559 **4.**—(1) Subject to regulation 5, a claimant ("C") selected under regulation 3 is required to participate in the Scheme where the Secretary of State gives C a notice in writing complying with paragraph (2).

(2) The notice must specify—

(a) that C is required to participate in the Scheme;

(b) the day on which C's participation will start;

(c) that C's participation will be for four weeks;

(d) details of what C is required to do by way of participation in the Scheme;

(e) that the requirement to participate in the Scheme will continue until C is given notice by the Secretary of State that C's participation is no longer required, or C's award of jobseeker's allowance terminates, whichever is earlier;

(f) information about the consequences of failing to participate in the Scheme.

(3) Any changes made to the requirements mentioned in paragraph (2)(d) after the date on which C's participation starts must be notified to C in writing.

Circumstances in which requirement to participate in the Scheme ceases to apply

3.560 **5.**—(1) A requirement to participate in the Scheme ceases to apply to a claimant ("C") if—

(a) the Secretary of State gives C notice in writing that C is no longer required to participate in the Scheme, or

(b) C's award of jobseeker's allowance terminates,

whichever is earlier.

(2) The requirement ceases to apply on the day specified in the notice.

PART 3

SANCTIONS

Failure to participate in the Scheme

6.—A claimant ("C") is to be regarded as having failed to participate in the Scheme in accordance with these Regulations where C fails to comply with any requirement notified under regulation 4. 3.561

Regs 7 and 8 revoked by the Jobseeker's Allowance (Sanctions) (Amendment) Regulations 2012 (SI 2012/2568) reg.7 (October 22, 2012).

PART 4

HARDSHIP

Hardship

9.—(1) This paragraph applies to a claimant ("C") if, during the period in which C's jobseeker's allowance is not payable by virtue of regulation 8(2), C is a person in hardship within the meaning of regulation 140(1) or (2) (meaning of "person in hardship") of the Jobseeker's Allowance Regulations. 3.562

(2) Regulations 140 to 146 of the Jobseeker's Allowance Regulations have effect in relation to a person to whom paragraph (1) applies.

(3) *The amendment effected to reg 141(6) of the JSA Regulations has been taken into account in the text of that provsion.*

Hardship for joint-claim couples

10.—(1) This paragraph applies to a joint-claim couple if, during the period in which the sanctions referred to in regulation 8(3) apply, they are a couple in hardship within the meaning of regulation 146A(1) or (2) (meaning of "couple in hardship") of the Jobseeker's Allowance Regulations. 3.563

(2) Regulations 146A and 146C to 146H of the Jobseeker's Allowance Regulations have effect in relation to a couple to whom paragraph (1) applies.

(3) *The amendment effected to reg 146C(6) of the JSA Regulations has been taken into account in the text of that provision.*

PART 5

CONSEQUENTIAL AMENDMENTS

An amendment effected to reg.8A(5) of the Credits Regulations by reg.17(4) of this SI has been taken into account in Vol.I. 3.564

Amendments to regs 1(3), 25(1A), 47(4)(b)(ii), 105(10A), 113(3A), and Schs 7 and 8 of the JSA Regulations effected by regs 11–16 of this SI have been taken into account in the text of those provisions.

Amendments to regs 3(6), 6(2) and 7(8) of the Decisions and Appeals Regulations effected by reg.18 of this SI have been taken into account in Vol.III.

PART 6

CONTRACTING OUT

Contracting out certain functions in relation to the Scheme

3.565 **20.**—(1) Any functions of the Secretary of State specified in paragraph (2) may be exercised by, or by employees of, such person (if any) as may be authorised by the Secretary of State.

(2) The functions are any function under—

(a) regulation 4 (requirement to participate and notification);

(b) regulation 5(1)(a) (notice that requirement to participate ceases).

The Jobseeker's Allowance (Employment, Skills and Enterprise Scheme) Regulations 2011

(SI 2011/917) (*AS AMENDED*)

The Secretary of State for Work and Pensions makes the following Regulations in exercise of the powers conferred by sections 123(1)(d) and (e), 136(3) and (5)(a) and (b), 137(1) and 175(3) and (4) of the Social Security Contributions and Benefits Act 1992, sections 30 and 146(1) and (2) of the Housing Grants, Construction and Regeneration Act 1996, section 10, 79(1) and (4) and 84 of the Social Security Act 1998 and sections 12(1), (4)(a) and (b), 17A(1), (2), (5)(a), (d) and (e) and (6) to (9), 20, 20A, 20B(4) to (6), 20E(3)(a), 21, 35(1) and 36(2) and (4) of, and Schedule 1 to, the Jobseekers Act 1995.

These Regulations are made with the consent of the Treasury in respect of provisions relating to section 30 (means testing in case of application by owner-occupier or tenant) of the Housing Grants, Construction and Regeneration Act 1996.

In respect of provisions in these Regulations relating to housing benefit and council tax benefit, organisations appearing to the Secretary of State to be representative of the authorities concerned have agreed that consultations need not be undertaken.

In accordance with section 173(1)(b) of the Social Security Administration Act 1992, the Secretary of State has obtained the agreement of the Social Security Advisory Committee that the proposals in respect of these Regulations should not be referred to it.

(SI 2011/917) (as amended)

Arrangement of Regulations

General Note

3.567 In *R (Reilly and Wilson) v Secretary of State for Work and Pensions* [2013] EWCA Civ 66, the Court of Appeal quashed as unlawful these Regulations (SI 2011/917) ("the ESES Regulations") because the Secretary of State acted ultra vires in failing to provide sufficient detail about the various schemes in the Regulations to satisfy s.17A of the old style Jobseekers Act 1995. The Court also held that notices sent to claimants advising them that they were required to take part in a programme within the ESE Scheme did not comply with the requirements of reg.4 of these Regulations. The effect of the decision was that the DWP had no right to impose a sanction on claimants who had failed to meet their requirements.That decision was confirmed by the Supreme Court ([2013] UKSC 68; [2014]1 A.C. 453), which is now the authoritative basis for the principle involved.

The DWP immediately on the handing down of the Court of Appeal's decision issued the Jobseeker's Allowance (Schemes for Assisting Persons to Obtain Employment) Regulations 2013, SI 2013/276 ("the SAPOE Regulations"), which came into effect at 1845 on February 12, 2013 so that sanctions could be applied from the date those new Regulations came into force.

The Jobseekers Allowance (Back to Work) Act 2013 is designed retrospectively to validate the impugned ESES Regulations making actions which related to participation in these employment programmes effective, and providing that notices served under those Regulations informing claimants of requirements as to participation, and about consequences of failing to meet requirements, were effective. The provisions affect claimants where sanctions have been applied for failures to comply with the ESES Regulations and cases where the claimant has failed to comply with a requirement of the ESES Regulations but a decision to impose a sanction has not yet been taken. It aims to ensure that any such decisions cannot be challenged on the grounds that the ESES Regulations were invalid or the notices inadequate, notwithstanding the Court of Appeal's judgment, so that benefit sanctions already imposed or to be imposed stand, saving the public purse some £130 million which would otherwise have to be paid to claimants who had been, if the Court of Appeal decision had stood, treated unlawfully. The Act also aims to protect from challenge on the basis of the reasoning in *Reilly and Wilson* notices given under the MWAS Regulation (see the notes to those Regulations).

3.568 See the introductory note to the 2013 Act for the state of the case law current as at the date of publication on whether that Act has in law retrospectively validated these Regulations and notices issued under them prior to February 12, 2013 in relation to sanctioned claimants who had lodged appeals prior to March 26, 2013 as well as to other categories of claimant. The Court of Appeal in *SSWP v Reilly and Hewstone* and *SSWP v Jeffrey and Bevan* [2016] EWCA Civ 413 has decided that the 2013 Act was to be construed as having that effect, whether as "read down" under s.3 of the Human Rights Act 1998 or not, contrary to the view of the majority of the three-judge panel of the Upper Tribunal in *SSWP v TJ (JSA)* [2015] UKUT 56 (AAC). The Court of Appeal gave a declaration of incompatibility with art.6 of the ECHR in respect of claimants who had lodged appeals, but that does not affect the validity or continuing operation of the Act, including in its effect on the ESES Regulations (s.4(6) of the Human Rights Act 1998).

Section 1(14) of the 2013 Act also treats these Regulations as revoked by the SAPOE Regulations with effect from the day and time those SPAOE Regulations came into force: 18.45 on February 12, 2013. It does so in order that two sets of Regulations covering the same ground were not in force simultaneously. However, s.1(10) of the Act means that the original penalty provisions (on which see the text of those Regulations in the 2012/13 edition of this volume) continue to apply to failures occurring before the entry into force of the Jobseeker's Allowance (Sanctions) (Amendment) Regulations 2012 (SI 2012/2568), namely October 22, 2012, even if the penalty was imposed after that date.

One of the appeals in *MH v SSWP (JSA)* [2016] UKUT 199 (AAC), CJSA/3093/2014, concerned a notice to attend an interview issued by a Work Programme provider purportedly under reg.4(2) of the ESES Regulations on February 12, 2013 itself. This was the very day on which the Court of Appeal in *Reilly and Wilson* quashed the ESES Regulations and the notice must have been issued before the SAPOE Regulations came into force at 1845 on that day. The Secretary of State submitted in the Upper Tribunal that, regardless of the outcome of the litigation on the question of whether the 2013 Act did retrospectively validate the ESES Regulations (which has for the time being been determined by the Court of Appeal in *Reilly, Hewstone, Jeffrey and Bevan*), no sanction could be imposed under s.19A(2)(b) of the old style Jobseekers Act 1995 for a failure to comply with the requirement to participate in the scheme in accordance with the notice. That was because on February 12, 2013 the DWP had contacted all Work Programme providers to tell them that they no longer had delegated authority (under reg.17(2)) to issue "mandatory activity notices" such as the appointment letter in question. The category of cases covered by this reasoning is obviously exceptionally narrow. The validity of notices issued before February 12, 2013 will depend on the outcome of the litigation on the effect of the 2013 Act. For notices issued after 18.45 on February 12, 2013, see the notes to the SAPOE Regulations.

Part 1

General

Citation and Commencement

1.—These Regulations may be cited as the Jobseeker's Allowance (Employment, Skills and Enterprise Scheme) Regulations 2011 and shall come into force on 20th May 2011. **3.569**

Interpretation

2.—(1) In these Regulations— **3.570**

"the Act" means the Jobseekers Act 1995;

"claimant" means a person who claims a jobseeker's allowance, except that in relation to a joint-claim couple claiming a joint-claim jobseeker's allowance, it means either or both of the members of the couple;

"the Council Tax Benefit Regulations" means the Council Tax Benefit Regulations 2006;

[[1]"full-time student" has the same meaning as in regulation 1(3) of the Jobseeker's Allowance Regulations;]

"the Housing Benefit Regulations" means the Housing Benefit Regulations 2006;

"the Housing Renewal Grants Regulations" means the Housing Renewal Grants Regulations 1996;

"the Jobseeker's Allowance Regulations" means the Jobseeker's Allowance Regulations 1996;

[[1]New Enterprise Allowance" means an employment initiative provided in pursuance of arrangements made by or on behalf of the Secretary of State under section 2 of the Employment and Training Act 1973 designed to assist claimants into self-employed earner's employment;]

"the Scheme" means the Employment, Skills and Enterprise Scheme;

[[1]"self-employed earner's employment" has the same meaning as in the Benefits Act;]

"working day" means any day except for a Saturday, Sunday, Christmas Day, Good Friday or bank holiday under the Banking and Financial Dealings Act 1971 in England and Wales or in Scotland;

"the Employment, Skills and Enterprise Scheme" means a scheme within section 17A (schemes for assisting persons to obtain employment: "work for your benefit" schemes etc.) of the Act known by that name and provided pursuant to arrangements made by the Secretary of State that is designed to assist claimants to obtain employment or self-employment, and which may include for any individual work-related activity (including work experience or job search).

(2) For the purpose of these Regulations where a written notice is given by sending it by post it is taken to have been received on the second working day after posting.

AMENDMENT

1. Social Security (Miscellaneous Amendments) (No.2) Regulations 2011 (SI 2011/1707) reg.3 August 5, 2011).

PART 2

SELECTION FOR AND PARTICIPATION IN THE EMPLOYMENT, SKILLS AND ENTERPRISE SCHEME

Selection for participation in the Scheme

3.571 **3.**—The Secretary of State may select a claimant for participation in the Scheme.

Requirement to participate and notification

3.572 **4.**—(1) Subject to regulation 5, a claimant ("C") selected under regulation 3 is required to participate in the Scheme where the Secretary of State gives C a notice in writing complying with paragraph (2).

(2) The notice must specify—

(a) that C is required to participate in the Scheme;

(b) the day on which C's participation will start;

(c) details of what C is required to do by way of participation in the Scheme;

(d) that the requirement to participate in the Scheme will continue until C is given notice by the Secretary of State that C's participation is no longer required, or C's award of jobseeker's allowance terminates, whichever is earlier;

(e) information about the consequences of failing to participate in the Scheme.

(3) Any changes made to the requirements mentioned in paragraph (2)(c) after the date on which C's participation starts must be notified to C in writing.

Circumstances in which requirement to participate in the Scheme is suspended or ceases to apply

5.—(1) Where a claimant ("C") is— 3.573

(a) subject to a requirement to participate in the Scheme, and

(b) while C is subject to such a requirement, the Jobseeker's Allowance Regulations apply so that C is not required to meet the jobseeking conditions C's requirement to participate in the Scheme is suspended for the period during which C is not required to meet the jobseeking conditions.

(2) A requirement to participate in the Scheme ceases to apply to a claimant ("C") if—

(a) the Secretary of State gives C notice in writing that C is no longer required to participate in the Scheme, or

(b) C's award of jobseeker's allowance terminates,

whichever is earlier.

(3) Where paragraph (2)(a) applies, the requirement ceases to apply on the day specified in the notice.

[[1]Requirement to meet the jobseeking conditions

5A.—(1) A claimant who is participating in the Scheme is not required to meet the condition set out in section 1(2)(c) of the Act (conditions for entitlement to a jobseeker's allowance: actively seeking employment) if the claimant is also participating in New Enterprise Allowance. 3.574

(2) A claimant who is participating in the Scheme is not required to meet the conditions set out in section 1(2)(a) and (c) of the Act (conditions for entitlement to a jobseeker's allowance: available for and actively seeking employment) if the claimant is a full-time student.]

[[2](3) A claimant who is participating in the Scheme is not required to meet the conditions set out in section 1(2)(a) and (c) of the Act if the claimant has been discharged from detention in a prison, remand centre or youth custody institution, for one week commencing with the date of that discharge.]

AMENDMENTS

1. Social Security (Miscellaneous Amendments) (No.2) Regulations 2011 (SI 2011/1707) reg.3 (August 5, 2011).

2. Jobseeker's Allowance (Jobseeking and Work for Your Benefit) (Amendment and Revocation) Regulations 2012 (SI 2012/397) reg.3 (March 1, 2012).

PART 3

SANCTIONS

Failure to participate in the Scheme

6.—A claimant who fails to comply with any requirement notified under regulation 4 is to be regarded as having failed to participate in the Scheme. 3.575

Regs 7–10 revoked by the Jobseeker's Allowance (Sanctions) (Amendment) Regulations 2012 (SI 2012/2568) reg.7 (October 22, 2012).

PART 5

CONSEQUENTIAL AMENDMENTS

3.576 *Amendments to regs 1(3), 25(1A), 53, 105(10A), 113(3A), and Schs 7 and 8 of the JSA Regulations effected by regs 11–16 of this SI have been taken into account in the text of those provisions*

Reg.17, effecting an amendment to reg.7 of the Decisions and Appeals Regulations was revoked with effect from October 22, 2012 by the Jobseeker's Allowance (Sanctions) (Amendment) Regulations 2012 (SI 2012/2568) reg.7.

PART 6

CONTRACTING OUT

Contracting out certain functions in relation to the Scheme

3.577 **18.**—(1) Any function of the Secretary of State specified in paragraph (2) may be exercised by, or by employees of, such person (if any) as may be authorised by the Secretary of State.

(2) The functions are any function under—

(a) regulation 4 (requirement to participate and notification);

(b) regulation 5(2)(a) (notice that requirement to participate ceases);

[1 . . .]

AMENDMENT

1. Jobseeker's Allowance (Sanctions) (Amendment) Regulations 2012 (SI 2012/2568) reg.7 (October 22, 2012).

The Jobseeker's Allowance (Schemes for Assisting Persons to Obtain Employment) Regulations 2013

(SI 2013/276)

The Secretary of State for Work and Pensions makes the following Regulations in exercise of the powers conferred by sections 123(1)(d) and (e), 136(3) and (5)(a) and (b), 137(1) and 175(1), (3) and (4) of the Social Security Contributions and Benefits Act 1992, section 113(1) and (2) of, and paragraph 4 of Schedule 1A to, the Local Government Finance Act 1992, sections 12(1),

(4)(a) and (b), 17A(1), (2) and (5)(a) and (b), 20E(3)(a), 35(1) and 36(2) and (4) of the Jobseekers Act 1995 and sections 30 and 146(1) and (2) of the Housing Grants, Construction and Regeneration Act 1996 and sections 17(1) and (3)(a) and (b), 24(1) and 25(2) and (3) of the Welfare Reform Act 2007.

These Regulations are made with the consent of the Treasury in respect of provisions relating to section 30 (means testing in case of application by owner-occupier or tenant) of the Housing Grants, Construction and Regeneration Act 1996.

In respect of provisions in these Regulations relating to housing benefit and council tax benefit, in accordance with section 176(2) of the Social Security Administration Act 1992(7), it appears to the Secretary of State that by reason of the urgency of the matter it is inexpedient to undertake consultations with organisations appearing to the Secretary of State to be representative of the authorities concerned.

In accordance with section 173(1)(a) of the Social Security Administration Act 1992, it appears to the Secretary of State that by reason of the urgency of the matter it is inexpedient to refer the proposals in respect of these Regulations to the Social Security Advisory Committee.

Arrangement Of Regulations

PART 1

Schemes for Assisting Persons to Obtain Employment

Part 2

Consequential Amendments

PART 3

CONTRACTING OUT

17. Contracting out certain functions

GENERAL NOTE

3.579 See the annotations to the Jobseekers (Back to Work) Act 2013 and to s.17A of the old style Jobseekers Act 1995. It would seem that the schemes prescribed below are validly described for the purposes of s.17A within the principles laid down by the Supreme Court in *R (Reilly and Wilson) v Secretary of State for Work and Pensions* [2013] UKSC 68; [2014] 1 A.C. 453 and applied to the MWAS Regulations by Hickinbottom J in *R (Smith) v Secretary of State for Work and Pensions* [2014] EWHC 843 (Admin), as confirmed on appeal ([2015] EWCA Civ 229).

One of the appeals in *MH v SSWP (JSA)* [2016] UKUT 199 (AAC), CJSA/3094/2014, concerned a notice to attend an interview issued by a Work Programme provider on March 4, 2013, after the SAPOE Regulations had come into force. On some date from February 13–17, 2013, Jobcentre Plus on behalf of the Secretary of State had sent the claimant a WP05(C) letter to replace the WP05 letter originally sent in June 2011. Judge Wright accepted that there was no issue over the claimant having received the WP05(C) letter and held that, despite some clumsy use of words in references to revision of earlier notices, it evidenced a fresh decision to select the claimant for participation in the Work Programme scheme under reg.4(1). Then, through the combination of the WP05(C) letter and the appointment letter of March 4, 2013 (as allowed in the Upper Tribunal decision in *SSWP v TJ (JSA)* [2015] UKUT 56 (AAC): see the notes to the 2013 Act), sufficient notice had been given to meet the requirements of reg.5(2) in substance. Accordingly, the First-tier Tribunal's finding that the claimant had not shown a good reason for failing to comply with the requirement to participate in the scheme being accepted, a sanction under s.19A(2)(b) of the old style Jobseekers Act 1995 had to be imposed, but with the period adjusted because of the setting aside in CJSA/3093/2014 (see the notes to the ESES Regulations) of a previous sanction.

Citation and commencement

3.580 **1.**—These Regulations may be cited as the Jobseeker's Allowance (Schemes for Assisting Persons to Obtain Employment) Regulations 2013 and come into force on 12th February 2013 at 6.45pm.

Interpretation

3.581 **2.**—(1) In these Regulations—

"the Act" means the Jobseekers Act 1995;

"claimant" means a person who claims a jobseeker's allowance, except that in relation to a joint-claim couple claiming a joint-claim jobseeker's allowance, it means either or both of the members of the couple;

"the Council Tax Benefit Regulations" means the Council Tax Benefit Regulations 2006;

"the Housing Benefit Regulations" means the Housing Benefit Regulations 2006;

"the Housing Renewal Grants Regulations" means the Housing Renewal Grants Regulations 1996;

"the Jobseeker's Allowance Regulations" means the Jobseeker's Allowance Regulations 1996;

"working day" means any day except for a Saturday, Sunday, Christmas Day, Good Friday or bank holiday under the Banking and Financial Dealings Act 1971 in England and Wales or in Scotland.

(2) For the purpose of these Regulations where a written notice is given by sending it by post it is taken to have been received on the second working day after posting.

Schemes for Assisting Persons to Obtain Employment

3.—(1) The schemes described in the following paragraphs are prescribed for the purposes of section 17A(1) (schemes for assisting persons to obtain employment: "work for your benefit" schemes etc) of the Act. 3.582

(2) Day One Support for Young People is a scheme comprising up to 30 hours per week in a work placement for the benefit of the community and up to 10 hours per week of supported work search over a period of 13 weeks, for any claimant aged between 18 and 24 years who has less than 6 months work history since leaving full-time education.

(3) The Derbyshire Mandatory Youth Activity Programme is a scheme delivered in the Derbyshire Jobcentre Plus District comprising up to 30 hours per week of work-related activity for the benefit of the community and up to 6 hours per week of supported work search over a period of 8 weeks, for any claimant aged between 18 and 34 years.

(4) Full-time Training Flexibility is a scheme comprising training of 16 to 30 hours per week, for any claimant who has been receiving jobseeker's allowance for a continuous period of not less than 26 weeks ending on the first required entry date to the scheme.

(5) New Enterprise Allowance is a scheme designed to assist a claimant into self-employed earner's employment comprising guidance and support provided by a business mentor, access to a loan to help with start-up costs (subject to status) and a weekly allowance for a period of 26 weeks once the claimant starts trading.

(6) The sector-based work academy is a scheme which provides, for a period of up to 6 weeks, training to enable a claimant to gain the skills needed in the work place and a work experience placement for a period to be agreed with the claimant, and either a job interview with an employer or support to help participants through an employer's application process.

(7) Skills Conditionality is a scheme comprising training or other activity designed to assist a claimant to obtain skills needed to obtain employment.

(8) The Work Programme is a scheme designed to assist a claimant at risk of becoming long-term unemployed in which, for a period of up to 2 years, the claimant is given such support as the provider of the Work Programme considers appropriate and reasonable in the claimant's circumstances, subject to minimum levels of support published by the provider, to assist the claimant to obtain and sustain employment which may include work search support, provision of skills training and work placements for the benefit of the community.

[[1](8A) Community Work Placements is a scheme lasting up to 30 weeks, designed to assist a claimant who requires further support in order to obtain and sustain employment, in which participants undertake work placements for the benefit of the community and work-related activity.

(8B)[[2]. . .]].

(9) In this regulation—

[1"Learning Difficulty Assessment" has the same meaning as in section 139A of the Learning and Skills Act 2000;]

"self-employed earner" has the same meaning as in section 2(1)(b) of the Social Security Contributions and Benefits Act 1992; and

"work history" includes employment, voluntary work, internships and work experience.

AMENDMENTS

1. Jobseeker's Allowance (Schemes for Assisting Persons to Obtain Employment) (Amendment) Regulations 2013 (SI 2013/2584) reg.2 (November 5, 2013).

2. Social Security (Traineeships and Qualifying Young Persons) Amendment Regulations 2015 (SI 2015/336) reg.3 (March 27, 2015).

Selection for participation in a Scheme

3.583 **4.**—(1) The Secretary of State may select a claimant for participation in a scheme described in regulation 3.

(2) The scheme in which the claimant is selected to participate is referred to in these Regulations as "the Scheme".

Requirement to participate and notification

3.584 **5.**—(1) Subject to regulation 6, a claimant selected under regulation 4 is required to participate in the Scheme where the Secretary of State gives the claimant a notice in writing complying with paragraph (2).

(2) The notice must specify—

(a) that the claimant is required to participate in the Scheme;

(b) the day on which the claimant's participation will start;

(c) details of what the claimant is required to do by way of participation in the Scheme;

(d) that the requirement to participate in the Scheme will continue until the claimant is given notice by the Secretary of State that the claimant's participation is no longer required, or the claimant's award of jobseeker's allowance terminates, whichever is earlier; and

(e) information about the consequences of failing to participate in the Scheme.

(3) Any changes made to the requirements mentioned in paragraph (2)(c) after the date on which the claimant's participation starts must be notified to the claimant in writing.

Circumstances in which requirement to participate in the Scheme is suspended or ceases to apply

3.585 **6.**—(1) Paragraph (2) applies where a claimant is—

(a) subject to a requirement to participate in the Scheme; and

(b) while the claimant is subject to such a requirement, the Jobseeker's Allowance Regulations apply so that the claimant is not required to meet the jobseeking conditions.

(2) Where this paragraph applies the claimant's requirement to participate in the Scheme is suspended for the period during which the claimant is not required to meet the jobseeking conditions.

(3) A requirement to participate in the Scheme ceases to apply to a claimant if—

(a) the Secretary of State gives the claimant notice in writing that the claimant is no longer required to participate in the Scheme; or

(b) the claimant's award of jobseeker's allowance terminates,

whichever is earlier.

(4) If the Secretary of State gives the claimant a notice in writing under paragraph (3)(a), the requirement to participate in the Scheme ceases to apply on the day specified in the notice.

Exemptions from requirement to meet the jobseeking conditions

7.—(1) A claimant who is participating in the New Enterprise Allowance scheme described in regulation 3(5) is not required to meet the condition set out in section 1(2)(c) of the Act (conditions for entitlement to a jobseeker's allowance: actively seeking employment). 3.586

(2) A claimant who is participating in the Scheme is not required to meet the conditions set out in section 1(2)(a) and (c) of the Act (conditions for entitlement to a jobseeker's allowance: available for and actively seeking employment) if the claimant is a full-time student.

(3) A claimant who is participating in the Scheme is not required to meet the conditions set out in section 1(2)(a) and (c) of the Act if the claimant has been discharged from detention in a prison, remand centre or youth custody institution, for one week commencing with the date of that discharge.

(4) In this regulation, "full-time student" has the same meaning as in regulation 1(3) of the Jobseeker's Allowance Regulations.

Definitions

8.—*The amendments effected by this regulation have been taken into account in the text of the Jobseekers Allowance Regulations elsewhere in this volume.* 3.587

Notional income

9.—*The amendments effected by this regulation have been taken into account in the text of the Jobseekers Allowance Regulations elsewhere in this volume.* 3.588

Notional capital

10.—*The amendments effected by this regulation have been taken into account in the text of the Jobseekers Allowance Regulations elsewhere in this volume.* 3.589

Income to be disregarded

11.—*The amendments effected by this regulation have been taken into account in the text of the Jobseekers Allowance Regulations elsewhere in this volume.* 3.590

Capital to be disregarded

12.—*The amendments effected by this regulation have been taken into account in the text of the Jobseekers Allowance Regulations elsewhere in this volume.* 3.591

Amendments to the Income Support (General) Regulations 1987

13.—*The amendments effected by this regulation have been taken into account in the text of the Jobseekers Allowance Regulations elsewhere in this volume.* 3.592

Further amendments to the Jobseeker's Allowance Regulations

3.593 **14.**—*The amendments effected by this regulation have been taken into account in the text of the Jobseekers Allowance Regulations elsewhere in this volume.*

Amendments to the Employment and Support Allowance Regulations 2008

3.594 **15.**—*The amendments effected by this regulation have been taken into account in the text of the Employment and Support Allowance Regulations in Social Security Legislation 2014/15: Vol. I: Non Means Tested Benefits and Employment and Support Allowance*

Amendments to the Council Tax Reduction Schemes (Default Scheme) (England) Regulations 2012

3.595 **16.**—[*Omitted.*]

Contracting out certain functions

3.596 **17.**—(1) Any function of the Secretary of State specified in paragraph (2) may be exercised by, or by employees of, such person (if any) as may be authorised by the Secretary of State.

(2) The functions are any function under—

(a) regulation 5 (requirement to participate and notification); and

(b) regulation 6(3)(a) (notice that requirement to participate ceases).

The Jobseeker's Allowance (Habitual Residence) Amendment Regulations 2013

(SI 2013/3196)

The Secretary of State for Work and Pensions makes the following Regulations in exercise of the powers conferred by sections 4(5) and (12), 35(1) and 36(2) of the Jobseekers Act 1995.

The Secretary of State has not referred proposals in respect of these Regulations to the Social Security Advisory Committee, as it appears to him that by reason of the urgency of the matter it is inexpedient to do so.

[In force January 1, 2014]

REGULATION REPRODUCED

3.597 3. Saving

GENERAL NOTE

3.598 See the commentary to reg.85A of the Jobseeker's Allowance Regulations 1996 and reg.21AA of the Income Support Regulations

Saving

3.599 **3.**—The amendment in regulation 2 does not apply in relation to a claim for a jobseeker's allowance which is made or treated as made before these Regulations come into force.

The Jobseeker's Allowance (Supervised Jobsearch Pilot Scheme) Regulations 2014

(SI 2014/1913)

The text of these regulations is omitted here because they were only in force down to April 29, 2015. The regulations are set out in the Supplement to the 2014/15 edition. **3.600**

The Jobseeker's Allowance (18–21 Work Skills Pilot Scheme) Regulations 2014

(SI 2014/3117)

[In force November 25, 2014] **3.601**

The text of these regulations is omitted here because they only apply to claimants registered at Jobcentres in the Black Country, Devon, Somerset and Cornwall, Kent and Mercia. The regulations are set out in the Supplement to the 2014/15 edition.

PART IV

STATE PENSION CREDIT

The State Pension Credit Regulations 2002

(SI 2002/1792) (AS AMENDED)

Made by the Secretary of State under s.175(3) to (5) of the Social Security Contributions and Benefits Act 1992, ss.7(4A), 9(4A) and 11(1) and (4) of the Social Security Fraud Act 2001 and ss.1(5), 2(3), (4) and (6), 3(4) to (8), 4(3), 5, 6(2), 7(4) and (7), 9(4) and (5), 12(2) and (3), 15, 16(2) and 17(1) and (2) of the State Pension Credit Act 2002

ARRANGEMENT OF REGULATIONS

PART I

General

PART II

Entitlement and amount

PART III

Income

PART I

General

Citation, commencement and interpretation

4.2 **1.**—(1) These Regulations may be cited as the State Pension Credit Regulations 2002 and shall come into force on 6th October 2003.

(2) In these Regulations—

"the Act" means the State Pension Credit Act 2002;

"the 1992 Act" means the Social Security Contributions and Benefits Act 1992;

[26 "the 2012 Act" means the Welfare Reform Act 2012;]

[3 "adoption leave" means a period of absence from work on ordinary or additional adoption leave in accordance with section 75A or 75B of the Employment Rights Act 1996;]

"the appointed day" means the day appointed under section 13(3) of the Act;

[7 "the Armed Forces and Reserve Forces Compensation Scheme" means the scheme established under section 1(2) of the Armed Forces (Pensions and Compensation) Act 2004;]

[27 "armed forces independence payment" means armed forces independence payment under the Armed Forces and Reserve Forces (Compensation Scheme) Order 2011;]

"attendance allowance" means—

(a) an attendance allowance under section 64 of the 1992 Act;

(b) an increase of disablement pension under section 104 or 105 of the 1992 Act;

(c) [29. . .]

(d) [29. . .]

(e) a payment by virtue of article 14, 15, 16, 43 or 44 of the Personal Injuries (Civilians) Scheme 1983 or any analogous payment; or

[18 (f) any payment based on a need for attendance which is paid as part of a war disablement pension, or any other such payment granted in respect of disablement which falls within regulation 15(5)(ac);]

"benefit week" means the period of 7 days beginning on the day on which, in the claimant's case, state pension credit is payable;

[8 "board and lodging accommodation" means accommodation provided to a person or, if he is a member of a family, to him or any other member of his family, for a charge which is inclusive of—

(i) the provision of that accommodation, and

(ii) at least some cooked or prepared meals which both are cooked or prepared (by a person other than the person to whom the accommodation is provided or a member of his family) and are consumed in that accommodation or associated premises,

but not accommodation provided by a close relative of his or of his partner, or other than on a commercial basis;]

"care home" has the meaning it has for the purposes of the Care Standards Act 2000 by virtue of section 3 of that Act [2and in Scotland means a care home service];

[22 "care home service" has the meaning assigned to it by paragraph 2 of schedule 12 to the Public Services Reform (Scotland) Act 2010;]

[23 "the Caxton Foundation" means the charitable trust of that name established on 28th March 2011 out of funds provided by the Secretary of State for the benefit of certain persons suffering from hepatitis C and other persons eligible for payment in accordance with its provisions;]

"the Claims and Payments Regulations" means the Social Security (Claims and Payments) Regulations 1987;

"close relative" means a parent, parent-in-law, son, son-in-law, daughter, daughter-in-law, step-parent, step-son, step-daughter, brother, sister, [10 or if any of the preceding persons is one member of a couple, the other member of that couple]

[28 "contributory employment and support allowance" means an allowance under Part 1 of the Welfare Reform Act as amended by the provisions of Schedule 3, and Part 1 of Schedule 14, to the 2012 Act that remove references to an income-related allowance, and a contributory allowance under Part 1 of the Welfare Reform Act as that Part has effect apart from those provisions;]

[28 "contribution-based jobseeker's allowance" means an allowance under the Jobseekers Act 1995 as amended by the provisions of Part 1 of Schedule 14 to the 2012 Act that remove references to an income-based allowance, and a contribution-based allowance under the Jobseekers Act 1995 as that Act has effect apart from those provisions;]

[30 "couple" means—

(a) two people who are married to, or civil partners of, each other and are members of the same household; or

(b) two people who are not married to, or civil partners of, each other but are living together as a married couple;]

[1 "the Computation of Earnings Regulations" means the Social Security Benefit (Computation of Earnings) Regulations 1996;

"dwelling occupied as the home" means the dwelling together with any garage, garden and outbuildings, normally occupied by the claimant as his home including any premises not so occupied which it is impracticable or unreasonable to sell separately, in particular, in Scotland, any croft land on which the dwelling is situated;]

"Eileen Trust" means the charitable trust of that name established on 29th March 1993 out of funds provided by the Secretary of State for the benefit of persons eligible for payment in accordance with its provisions;

[16 "the Employment and Support Allowance Regulations" means the Employment and Support Allowance Regulations 2008;]

[19 "enactment" includes an enactment comprised in, or in an instrument made under, an Act of the Scottish Parliament [29 or the National Assembly for Wales];]

[6 "equity release scheme" means a loan—

(a) made between a person ("the lender") and the claimant;

(b) by means of which a sum of money is advanced by the lender to the claimant by way of payments at regular intervals; and

(c) which is secured on a dwelling in which the claimant owns an estate or interest and which he occupies as his home;]

[20 "foreign state retirement pension" means any pension which is paid under the law of a country outside the United Kingdom and is in the nature of social security;]

"the Fund" means moneys made available from time to time by the Secretary of State for the benefit of persons eligible for payment in accordance with the provisions of a scheme established by him on 24th April 1992 or, in Scotland, on 10th April 1992;

"full-time student" has the meaning prescribed in regulation 61(1) of the Income Support Regulations;

[12 "the Graduated Retirement Benefit Regulations" means the Social Security (Graduated Retirement Benefit) Regulations 2005;]

[7"a guaranteed income payment" means a payment made under article 14(1)(b) or article 21(1)(a) of the Armed Forces and Reserve Forces (Compensation Scheme) Order 2005;]

[17 "the Health Service Act" means "the National Health Service Act 2006];

"the Health Service (Wales) Act" means "the National Health Service (Wales) Act 2006";]

[28 "income-based jobseeker's allowance" means an income-based allowance under the Jobseekers Act 1995;]

[16 "income-related employment and support allowance" means an income-related allowance under Part 1 of the Welfare Reform Act (employment and support allowance);]

"the Income Support Regulations" means the Income Support (General) Regulations 1987;

[21 "independent hospital"—

(a) in England, means a hospital as defined by section 275 of the National Health Service Act 2006 that is not a health service hospital as defined by that section;

(b) in Wales, has the meaning assigned to it by section 2 of the Care Standards Act 2000; and

[22 (c) in Scotland, means an independent health care service as defined in section 10F(1)(a) and (b) of the National Health Service (Scotland) Act 1978;]]

[17 . . .]

[14 "the Independent Living Fund (2006)" means the Trust of that name established by a deed dated April 10, 2006 and made between the Secretary of State for Work and Pensions of the one part and Margaret Rosemary Cooper, Michael Beresford Boyall and Marie Theresa Martin of the other part;]

[17 . . .]

"the Jobseeker's Allowance Regulations" means the Jobseeker's Allowance Regulations 1996;

[25 "local welfare provision" means occasional financial or other assistance given by a local authority, the Scottish Ministers or the Welsh Ministers, or a person authorised to exercise any function of, or provide a service to, them, to or in respect of individuals for the purpose of—

(a) meeting, or helping to meet, an immediate short term need—

  (i) arising out of an exceptional event, or exceptional circumstances; and

  (ii) that requires to be met in order to avoid a risk to the well-being of an individual; or

(b) enabling individuals to establish or maintain a settled home, where those individuals have been or, without the assistance, might otherwise be—

  (i) in prison, hospital, a residential care establishment or other institution; or

  (ii) homeless or otherwise living an unsettled way of life;]

[11 "the London Bombings Relief Charitable Fund" means the company limited by guarantee (number 5505072) and registered charity of that name established on 11th July 2005 for the purpose of (amongst other things) relieving sickness, disability or financial need of victims (including families or dependants of victims) of the terrorist attacks carried out in London on 7th July 2005;]

"the Macfarlane (Special Payments) Trust" means the trust of that name, established on 29th January 1990 partly out of funds provided by the Secretary of State, for the benefit of certain persons suffering from haemophilia;

"the Macfarlane (Special Payments) (No.2) Trust" means the trust of that name, established on 3rd May 1991 partly out of funds provided by the Secretary of State, for the benefit of certain persons suffering from haemophilia and other beneficiaries;

"the Macfarlane Trust" means the charitable trust, established partly out of funds provided by the Secretary of State to the Haemophilia Society, for the relief of poverty or distress among those suffering from haemophilia;

[20 "MFET Limited" means the company limited by guarantee (number 7121661) of that name, established for the purpose in particular of making payments in accordance with arrangements made with the Secretary of State to persons who have acquired HIV as a result of treatment by the NHS with blood or blood products;]

[24 "paternity leave" means a period of absence from work on [34 . . .] paternity leave by virtue of section 80A or 80B of the Employment Rights Act 1996 [34 . . .];]

[13 "patient", except in Schedule II, means a person (other than a prisoner) who is regarded as receiving free in-patient treatment within the meaning of regulation 2(4) and (5) of the Social Security (Hospital In-Patients) Regulations 2005;]

"pension fund holder" means with respect to [15 an occupational pension scheme,] a personal pension scheme or retirement annuity contract, the trustees, managers or scheme administrators, as the case may be, of the scheme or contract concerned;

[26 "personal independence payment" means personal independence payment under Part 4 of the 2012 Act;]

"policy of life insurance" means any instrument by which the payment of money is assured on death (except death by accident only) or the happening of any contingency dependent on human life, or any instrument evidencing a contract which is subject to payment of premiums for a term dependent on human life;

"prisoner" means a person who—

(a) is detained in custody pending trial or sentence upon conviction or under a sentence imposed by a court; or

(b) is on temporary release in accordance with the provisions of the Prison Act 1952 or the Prisons (Scotland) Act 1989,

other than a person detained in hospital under the provisions of the Mental Health Act 1983, or in Scotland, under the provisions of the [9 Mental Health (Care and Treatment) (Scotland) Act 2003] or the Criminal Procedure (Scotland) Act 1995;

[19 "public authority" includes any person certain of whose functions are functions of a public nature;]

"qualifying person" means a person in respect of whom payment has been made from the Fund [4, the Eileen Trust [20, MFET Limited] [11, the Skipton Fund [23, the Caxton Foundation] or the London Bombings Relief Charitable Fund]];

[31 . . .]

[32 "shared parental leave" means leave under section 75E or 75G of the Employment Rights Act 1996;]

[5 "the Skipton Fund" means the ex-gratia payment scheme administered by the Skipton Fund Limited, incorporated on 25th March 2004, for the benefit of certain persons suffering from hepatitis C and other persons eligible for payment in accordance with the scheme's provisions;]

[28 "universal credit" means universal credit under Part 1 of the 2012 Act;]

[2 "voluntary organisation" means a body, other than a public or local authority, the activities of which are carried on otherwise than for profit;]

"water charges" means—

(a) as respects England and Wales, any water and sewerage charges under Chapter 1 of Part V of the Water Industry Act 1991;

(b) as respects Scotland, any water and sewerage charges under Schedule 11 to the Local Government Finance Act 1992;

in so far as such charges are in respect of the dwelling which a person occupies as his home;

[16 "the Welfare Reform Act" means the Welfare Reform Act 2007.]

(3) In these Regulations, unless the context otherwise requires, a member of [11 a couple] is referred to as a partner and both members are referred to as partners.

[31 (3A) References in these Regulations to a claimant participating as a service user are to—

(a) a person who is being consulted by or on behalf of—

(i) a body which has a statutory duty to provide services in the field of health, social care or social housing; or

(ii) a body which conducts research or undertakes monitoring for the purpose of planning or improving such services, in their capacity as a user, potential user, carer of a user or person otherwise affected by the provision of those services; or

[33 (ab) a person who is being consulted by or on behalf of—

(i) the Secretary of State in relation to any of the Secretary of State's functions in the field of social security or child support or under section 2 of the Employment and Training Act 1973; or

(ii) a body which conducts research or undertakes monitoring for the purpose of planning or improving such functions,

in their capacity as a person affected or potentially affected by the exercise of those functions or the carer of such a person;]

(b) the carer of a person consulted under [33 sub-paragraphs (a) or (ab)].]

(4) In these Regulations, unless the context otherwise requires, a reference—

(a) to a numbered section is to the section of the Act bearing that number;

(b) to a numbered Part is to the Part of these Regulations bearing that number;

(c) to a numbered regulation or Schedule is to the regulation in, or Schedule to, these Regulations bearing that number;

(d) in a regulation or Schedule to a numbered paragraph is to the paragraph in that regulation or Schedule bearing that number;

(e) in a paragraph to a lettered or numbered sub-paragraph is to the sub-paragraph in that paragraph bearing that letter or number.

AMENDMENTS

1. State Pension Credit (Consequential, Transitional and Miscellaneous Provisions) Regulations 2002 (SI 2002/3019) reg.23(a) (October 6, 2003).

2. State Pension Credit (Consequential, Transitional and Miscellaneous Provisions) (No.2) Regulations 2002 (SI 2002/3197) reg.2 and Sch. para.1 (October 6, 2003).

3. State Pension Credit (Transitional and Miscellaneous Provisions) Amendment Regulations 2003 (SI 2003/2274) reg.2(2) (October 6, 2003).
4. Social Security (Miscellaneous Amendments) (No.2) Regulations 2004 (SI 2004/1141) reg.2(a) (May 12, 2004).
5. Social Security (Miscellaneous Amendments) (No.2) Regulations 2004 (SI 2004/1141) reg.2(b)(iv) (May 12, 2004).
6. Social Security (Housing Benefit, Council Tax Benefit, State Pension Credit and Miscellaneous Amendments) Regulations 2004 (SI 2004/2327) reg.7(2) (October 4, 2004).
7. Social Security (Miscellaneous Amendments) Regulations 2005 (SI 2005/574) reg.2(1) (April 4, 2005).
8. Social Security (Miscellaneous Amendments) (No.2) Regulations 2005 (SI 2005/2465) reg.6(2) (October 3, 2005).
9. Mental Health (Care and Treatment) (Scotland) Act 2003 (Modification of Subordinate Legislation) Order 2005 (SSI 2005/445) art.2 and Sch. para.35(1) (October 3, 2005).
10. Civil Partnership (Pensions, Social Security and Child Support) (Consequential, etc. Provisions) Order 2005 (SI 2005/2877) art.2(3) and Sch.3 para.35(2) (December 5, 2005).
11. Income-related Benefits (Amendment) (No.2) Regulations 2005 (SI 2005/3391) reg.7(2) (December 12, 2005).
12. Social Security (Deferral of Retirement Pensions, Shared Additional Pension and Graduated Retirement Benefit) (Miscellaneous Provisions) Regulations 2005 (SI 2005/2677) reg.13(2) (April 6, 2006).
13. Social Security (Hospital In-Patients) Regulations 2005 (SI 2005/3360) reg.8(2) (April 10, 2006).
14. Independent Living Fund (2006) Order 2007 (SI 2007/2538) art.6(2) (October 1, 2007).
15. Social Security (Miscellaneous Amendments) (No.5) Regulations 2007 (SI 2007/2618) reg.10(2) (October 1, 2007).
16. Employment and Support Allowance (Consequential Provisions) (No.2) Regulations 2008 (SI 2008/1554) reg.4(2) (October 27, 2008).
17. Social Security (Miscellaneous Amendments) (No.6) Regulations 2008 (SI 2008/2767) reg.5(2) (November 17, 2008).
18. Social Security (Miscellaneous Amendments) (No.7) Regulations 2008 (SI 2008/3157) reg.4(2) (January 5, 2009).
19. Social Security (Miscellaneous Amendments) (No.4) Regulations 2009 (SI 2009/2655) reg.5(2) (October 26, 2009).
20. Social Security (Miscellaneous Amendments) (No.2) Regulations 2010 (SI 2010/641) reg.6(3)(a) (April 6, 2010).
21. Health and Social Care Act 2008 (Miscellaneous Consequential Amendments) Order 2010 (SI 2010/1881) art.5 (October 1, 2010).
22. Public Services Reform (Scotland) Act 2010 (Consequential Modifications of Enactments) Order 2011 (SI 2011/2581) art.2 and Sch.2 para.35 (October 28, 2011).
23. Social Security (Miscellaneous Amendments) (No.3) Regulations 2011 (2011/2425) reg.15(2) (October 31, 2011).
24. Social Security (Miscellaneous Amendments) Regulations 2012 (2012/757) reg.5(2) (April 1, 2012).
25. Social Security (Miscellaneous Amendments) Regulations 2013 (SI 2013/443) reg.6(2) (April 2, 2013).
26. Personal Independence Payment (Supplementary Provisions and Consequential Amendments) Regulations 2013 (SI 2013/388) reg.8 and Sch. para.27(2) (April 8, 2013).
27. Armed Forces and Reserve Forces Compensation Scheme (Consequential Provisions: Subordinate Legislation) Order 2013 (SI 2013/591) art.7 and Sch. para.23(2) (April 8, 2013).
28. Universal Credit (Consequential, Supplementary, Incidental and

Miscellaneous Provisions) Regulations 2013 (SI 2013/630) reg.33(2) (April 29, 2013).

29. Social Security (Miscellaneous Amendments) (No.3) Regulations 2013 (SI 2013/2536) reg.10(2) (October 29, 2013).

30. Marriage (Same Sex Couples) Act 2013 (Consequential Provisions) Order 2014 (SI 2014/107) art.2 and Sch.1 para.32 (March 13, 2014 for England & Wales only); Marriage and Civil Partnership (Scotland) Act 2014 and Civil Partnership Act 2004 (Consequential Provisions and Modifications) Order 2014 (SI 2014/3229) art.29 and Sch.6 para.23 (December 16, 2014 for the United Kingdom).

31. Social Security (Miscellaneous Amendments) Regulations 2014 (SI 2014/591) reg.7(2) (April 28, 2014).

32. Shared Parental Leave and Statutory Shared Parental Pay (Consequential Amendments to Subordinate Legislation) Order 2014 (SI 2014/3255) art.10(2)(b) (December 31, 2014).

33. Social Security (Miscellaneous Amendments) Regulations 2015 (SI 2015/67) reg.2(2) (February 23, 2015).

34. Shared Parental Leave and Statutory Shared Parental Pay (Consequential Amendments to Subordinate Legislation) Order 2014 (SI 2014/3255) art.10(2)(a) (April 5, 2015).

Definition

"claimant"—see SPCA 2002 s.17(1).

General Note

Paragraph (2)

"*Appointed day*": This date was October 6, 2003: see State Pension Credit Act 2002 (Commencement No.5) and Appointed Day Order 2003 (SI 2003/1766 (C.75)). 4.3

"Board and lodging accommodation": On the importance of establishing, in this context, the precise status of someone staying with the claimant (e.g. as sub-tenant, lodger or non-dependant), see *KC v Secretary of State for Work and Pensions (SPC)* [2012] UKUT 114 (AAC).

"Care home": Section 3(1) of the Care Standards Act 2000 provides that "an establishment is a care home if it provides accommodation, together with nursing or personal care" for various categories of person (e.g. the ill, the disabled, those with mental disorders and those with alcohol or drug dependency). An establishment is not a care home if it is a hospital, independent clinic or children's home, or if it is excluded by regulations (see Care Standards Act 2000 s.3(3) and Care Homes Regulations 2001 (SI 2001/3965) reg.3)). For the (slightly differently phrased) Scottish definition of "care home", see Regulation of Care (Scotland) Act 2001 s.2. This defines a "care home" as an establishment in which a care home service is provided, i.e. accommodation together with nursing, personal care, or personal support for people by reason of their vulnerability or need. See further *SA v Secretary of State for Work and Pensions (IS)* [2010] UKUT 345 (AAC); [2011] AACR 16.

"Close relative": This definition is in identical terms to that used in reg.2(1) of the Income Support (General) Regulations 1987 (SI 1987/1967), and therefore will presumably be interpreted in the same way. Thus "brother" and "sister" include half-brothers and half-sisters, and persons who are adopted cease to have any legal relationship with their birth family (*R(SB) 22/87*).

"Couple": This new streamlined definition is consequential upon the Marriage (Same Sex Couples) Act 2013—see further the Note at the start of this Volume.

"Dwelling occupied as the home": This also follows the income support definition: see para.2.27 above. See also *ED v Secretary of State for Work and Pensions* [2009] UKUT 161 (AAC), confirming that the basic meaning of this expression "does not extend to any land or other premises not occupied by the person in question, whatever the nature of the other premises" (at [17]). See further *PJ v Secretary of State for Work and Pensions* (SPC) [2014] UKUT 0152 (AAC), holding that "a person who chooses for financial reasons not to live in his usual home for a period of three years cannot say that during that period he normally occupies the property as his home" (at para.16).

"Full-time student": For analysis of the complex case law on this term in the context of income support, see the commentary to Pt VIII of the Income Support (General) Regulations 1987 (SI 1987/1967).

"Patient": This is the same definition as used for the purposes of income support (see reg.21(3) of the Income Support (General) Regulations 1987 (SI 1987/1967).

"Prisoner": This is also the same definition as used for the purposes of income support (see reg.21(3) of the Income Support (General) Regulations 1987 (SI 1987/1967).

Paragraph (3)

4.4 These Regulations adopt the traditional social security approach of treating married and unmarried couples in the same way for the purposes of assessing entitlement to the state pension credit. There is no definition in these Regulations as to what constitutes a married or unmarried couple. However, these terms are defined in the same way as for social security purposes in s.17(1) of the State Pension Credit Act 2002. On the approach to be taken, see the commentary to SSCBA 1992 s.137(1) above.

Part II

Entitlement and amount

[1 Disapplication of section 1(1A) of the Social Security Administration Act

4.5 **1A.**—Section 1(1A) of the Social Security Administration Act 1992 (requirement to state a national insurance number) shall not apply to a person who—

(a) is a person in respect of whom a claim for state pension credit is made;
(b) is subject to immigration control within the meaning of section 115(9)(a) of the Immigration and Asylum Act 1999;
(c) does not satisfy the conditions of entitlement to state pension credit as specified in section 1(2); and
(d) has not previously been allocated a national insurance number.]

Amendment

1. Social Security (National Insurance Number Information: Exemption) Regulations 2009 (SI 2009/471) reg.8 (April 6, 2009).

GENERAL NOTE

This provision ensures that there is no requirement for a National Insurance number (NINo) to be allocated to an individual who has no leave to enter or remain in the United Kingdom where that person is a partner of a legitimate benefit claimant. See also the earlier Commissioner's decision *CH/3801/2004*. 4.6

[1 Persons not in Great Britain

2. —(1) A person is to be treated as not in Great Britain if, subject to the following provisions of this regulation, he is not habitually resident in the United Kingdom, the Channel Islands, the Isle of Man or the Republic of Ireland. 4.7

(2) No person shall be treated as habitually resident in the United Kingdom, the Channel Islands, the Isle of Man or the Republic of Ireland unless he has a right to reside in (as the case may be) the United Kingdom, the Channel Islands, the Isle of Man or the Republic of Ireland other than a right to reside which falls within paragraph (3).

(3) A right to reside falls within this paragraph if it is one which exists by virtue of, or in accordance with, one or more of the following—

(a) regulation 13 of the Immigration (European Economic Area) Regulations 2006;

(b) regulation 14 of those Regulations, but only in a case where the right exists under that regulation because the person is—

(i) a jobseeker for the purpose of the definition of "qualified person" in regulation 6(1) of those Regulations, or

(ii) a family member (within the meaning of regulation 7 of those Regulations) of such a jobseeker;

[5 (bb) regulation 15A(1) of those Regulations, but only in a case where the right exists under that regulation because the claimant satisfies the criteria in regulation 15A(4A) of those Regulations;]

(c) Article 6 of Council Directive No.2004/38/EC; [5 . . .]

(d) [4 Article 45 of the Treaty on the Functioning of the European Union] (in a case where the person is seeking work in the United Kingdom, the Channel Islands, the Isle of Man or the Republic of Ireland) [5 ; or]

[5 (e) Article 20 of the Treaty on the Functioning of the European Union (in a case where the right to reside arises because a British citizen would otherwise be deprived of the genuine enjoyment of the substance of their rights as a European Union citizen).]

(4) A person is not to be treated as not in Great Britain if he is—

[8 (za) a qualified person for the purposes of regulation 6 of the Immigration (European Economic Area) Regulations 2006 as a worker or a self-employed person;

(zb) a family member of a person referred to in sub-paragraph (za) within the meaning of regulation 7(1)(a), (b) or (c) of those Regulations;

(zc) a person who has a right to reside permanently in the United Kingdom by virtue of regulation 15(1)(c), (d) or (e) of those Regulations;]

(g) a refugee within the definition in Article 1 of the Convention relating to the Status of Refugees done at Geneva on 28th July 1951, as extended by Article 1(2) of the Protocol relating to the Status of Refugees done at New York on 31st January 1967;

[6 (h) a person who has been granted leave or who is deemed to have been granted leave outside the rules made under section 3(2) of the Immigration Act 1971 (where that leave is—

(i) discretionary leave to enter or remain in the United Kingdom;

(ii) leave to remain under the Destitution Domestic Violence concession; or

(iii) leave deemed to have been granted by virtue of regulation 3 of the Displaced Persons (Temporary Protection) Regulations 2005;]

(hh) a person who has humanitarian protection granted under those rules;] [7 or]

(i) a person who is not a person subject to immigration control within the meaning of section 115(9) of the Immigration and Asylum Act 1999 and who is in the United Kingdom as a result of his deportation, expulsion or other removal by compulsion of law from another country to the United Kingdom;[3 . . .].

(j) [7 . . .]

(k) [7 . . .]

AMENDMENTS

1 Social Security (Persons from Abroad) Amendment Regulations 2006 (SI 2006/1026) reg.9 (April 30, 2006).

2. Social Security (Persons from Abroad) Amendment (No.2) Regulations 2006 (SI 2006/2528) reg.4 (October 9, 2006).

3. Social Security (Habitual Residence) (Amendment) Regulations 2009 (SI 1009/362) reg.4 (March 18, 2009).

4. Treaty of Lisbon (Changes in Terminology or Numbering) Order 2012 (SI 2012/1809) art.3 and Sch. Pt 2 (August 1, 2012).

5. Social Security (Habitual Residence) (Amendment) Regulations 2012 (SI 2012/2587) reg.4 (November 8, 2012).

6. Social Security (Croatia) Amendment Regulations 2013 (SI 2013/1474) reg.4(2) (July 1, 2013).

7. Social Security (Miscellaneous Amendments) (No.3) Regulations 2013 (SI 2013/2536) reg.10(3) (October 29, 2013).

8. Social Security (Habitual Residence) (Amendment) Regulations 2014 (SI 2014/902) reg.4 (May 31, 2014).

GENERAL NOTE

4.8 It is a fundamental requirement of entitlement to the state pension credit that the claimant "is in Great Britain" (SPCA 2002 s.1(2)(a)). In this context note *EC v Secretary of State for Work and Pensions* [2010] UKUT 93 (AAC); [2010] AACR 39, where it was held that state pension credit is a special non-contributory benefit within art.10a of Regulation 1408/71 and so is payable only to those living in Great Britain. In its original form this provision simply adopted the habitual residence test from the income support scheme as a means of determining whether a person was "in Great Britain" for the purposes of pension credit. This was then supplemented by the addition of the right to reside test as from May 1, 2004. However, as from April 30, 2006, the provision was recast in its current form (and has subsequently also been further amended). The new reg.2 reflects the evolution of the right to reside test and in particular the coming into force of Directive 2004/38. On the detail of the new provisions, see by analogy the commentary to the Income Support (General) Regulations 1987 (SI 1987/1967) reg.21AA). Note also the special dispensation for those temporarily absent from Great Britain (reg.3) and those being treated abroad under NHS provisions (reg.4).

For a full analysis of both the habitual residence and the right to reside rules, see the commentary to reg.21AA of the Income Support (General) Regulations 1987 in this volume.

The pre-April 30, 2006 version of reg.2 was considered by Commissioner Jacobs in *CPC/3588/2006* and by Commissioner Rowland in *CPC/1072/2006*; the claimant's appeal in the latter case was dismissed by the Court of Appeal in *Patmalniece v Secretary of State for Work & Pensions* [2009] EWCA Civ 621 and then by the Supreme Court ([2011] UKSC 11; [2011] AACR 34). The Supreme Court held that s.1 of the Act and reg.2 had to be read as a whole. The test under reg.2(2) was constructed in such a way that it was more likely to be satisfied by a UK national than by a national of another Member State. In terms of EU law, that meant that although it was not directly discriminatory on grounds of nationality, it was indirectly discriminatory and so had to be justified. The purpose of the right to reside test was to safeguard the UK's social security system from exploitation by those who wished to enter in order to live off income-related benefits rather than to work. That was a legitimate reason for the imposition of the test. It was independent of nationality, arising from the principle that only those who were economically or socially integrated with the host Member State should have access to its social assistance system. There was, therefore, sufficient justification for the discrimination arising from reg.2(2). The position of Irish nationals—who met the requirements of reg.2(2) even though they did not have a right to reside in the UK and were not habitually resident there—was protected by art.2 of the Protocol on the Common Travel Area. It was not discriminatory not to extend the same entitlement to the nationals of other Member States.

Commissioner Jacobs has analysed the post-April 30, 2006 version of reg.2 in **4.9**
CPC/2134/2007 and *CPC/3764/2007*. In *CPC/2134/2007* the claimant, a Lithuanian national, arrived in the UK in 2000, and unsuccessfully claimed asylum. She abandoned her asylum appeal when Lithuania joined the EU in May 2004. She claimed state pension credit in January 2006 but her claim was not decided until October 2006, when it was refused on the basis that she had no right to reside. Commissioner Jacobs acknowledged that the claimant had been in the UK for more than five years but ruled that she had no permanent right of residence. Pre-accession periods of residence could not be taken into account (following *GN (EEA Regulations: five years' residence) Hungary* [2007] UKAIT 00073). The claimant had not exercised any EU right either before or after accession.

In *CPC/3764/2007* Commissioner Jacobs likewise confirmed that a pre-accession period of residence by a Slovakian national between 1997 and 2004 could not be taken into account (see also *R(IS) 3/08*). The Commissioner also analysed in detail the argument of the claimant's representative based on proportionality, concluding that the circumstances were "not sufficiently exceptional to justify ignoring the terms of the legislation governing the right to reside" (at para.46).

See also *Secretary of State v AA* [2009] UKUT 249 AAC, where the issue was whether the claimant had a right to reside where he was a dependant of his son, who was in employment and held both British and Spanish nationality and with whom he had gone to live on a rent-free basis. Upper Tribunal Judge Rowland distinguished *McCarthy v Secretary of State for the Home Department* [2008] EWCA Civ 641, ruling that on a literal construction of the Immigration (European Economic Area) Regulations 2006 (SI 2006/1003) "a Spanish national is therefore an EEA national to whom regulation 6 applies, even if he or she also holds British nationality" (at [16]). In *HG v Secretary of State (SPC)* [2011] UKUT 382 (AAC), a decision issued after the judgment of the ECJ in *McCarthy v Secretary of State for the Home Department* (C-434/09). [2011] All E.R. (EC) 729, it was accepted that the claimant, a Polish national, was dependent upon her daughter, Mrs D. Judge Jacobs, taking the same approach as Judge Rowland in *Secretary of State v AA* [2009] UKUT 249 (AAC), held that Mrs D had a right to reside in the UK under the Immigration (EEA) Regulations 2006:

"9. The claimant is a family member of Mrs D under regulation 7(1)(c) as a dependent direct relative in her ascending line. As such, she has a right to reside under regulation 14(2) if Mrs D has a permanent right to reside. Mrs D has resided for the requisite period of five years to acquire that right under regulation 15(1)(a), provided two conditions are satisfied. One is that she is 'an EEA national'. She satisfies that condition by virtue of the definitions in regulation 2(1), under which an EEA national is a national of an EEA State other than the United Kingdom. Mrs D, as I have said, is Polish. The other condition is that she has resided in the United Kingdom in accordance with the 2006 Regulations.She would do so if she has resided as a worker. Under regulation 4(1)(a) a worker means 'a worker within the meaning of Article 39 of the Treaty'. The Secretary of State accepts that the evidence shows that Mrs D was a worker within the caselaw of the European Court of Justice. Article 39 is a Treaty provision and so free of the limitations on the scope of Directive 2004/38. There is, therefore, no impediment to Mrs D relying on that status for the purposes of the 2006 Regulations."

4.10 The decision of the Deputy Commissioner in *CPC/1433/2008* has been reversed by the Court of Appeal in *Pedro v Secretary of State for Work and Pensions* [2009] EWCA Civ 1358; [2010] AACR 18. The claimant was a 62-year-old Portuguese national who had come to the UK to live with her son, who worked here. She had largely been financially dependent upon him and had claimed JSA and later state pension credit. The Court of Appeal stressed that the aim of Directive 2004/38 was to strengthen the right of free movement in the EU. Furthermore, an EU citizen who wished to work in another state might be deterred from doing so if he knew that his elderly, but not then dependent, mother would not be regarded as his dependant for the purposes of art.2(2) were she to join him and later become dependent upon him. Thus no such impediment should be placed in his way (*Metock and Minister voor Vreemdelingenzaken en Integratie v Eind* (C-291/05) [2008] All E.R. (EC) 371). Whether someone had the status of a dependent family member was a question of fact (*Centre Public d'Aide Sociale, Courcelles v Lebon* (C-316/85) [1987] E.C.R. 2811). Article 2(2)(d) did not specify when the dependency had to have arisen, nor did it require that the relative had to be dependent in the country of origin. Accordingly, proof of the claimant's dependence on her son in the UK would suffice under art.2(2)(d), and as the tribunal had already found as a fact that she was dependent on him, she was entitled to state pension credit. On the importance of fact-finding where there is a claim of dependency on a relative, see also *LA v SSWP* [2010] UKUT 109 (AAC).

For a discussion of what may be needed to lose habitual residence, see *KS v SSWP* [2010] UKUT 156 (AAC), holding that a VSO volunteer who went to India for more than two years had not lost his UK habitual residence.

Secretary of State for Work and Pensions v LL (SPC) [2014] UKUT 0136 (AAC), concerning a Belgian pensioner supported in the UK by her daughter, who was unemployed at the material time, confirms that the effect of para.(2) and (3)(b)(ii) is that a right to reside is excluded for the family member of a jobseeker. See also *Secretary of State for Work and Pensions v LZ (SPC)* [2014] UKUT 0147 (AAC), holding that the lack of a registration certificate prevented the claimant (a 64-year-old Polish woman living with her brother in the UK) as an "extended family member" from being treated as the "family member" of her brother, with the consequence that she too had no right to reside.

For an illustration of a case in which self-employed was found to be "marginal and ancillary" (the claimant was self-publishing his life story) rather than "genuine and effective", see *SSWP v HH (SPC)* [2015] UKUT 0583 (AAC).

Paragraph (4)(i)

4.11 On the meaning of a "person subject to immigration control" within sub-para. (4)(i), see *OO v Secretary of State for Work and Pensions (SPC)* [2013] UKUT 335 (AAC). A spouse who falls within that definition is not treated as part of the claimant's household for SPC purposes, i.e. when calculating the claimant's applicable amount or income. The tribunal in this case had failed to distinguish between a spouse being "sponsored" for immigration purposes and a person being subject to a sponsorship undertaking (under immigration law, written sponsorship undertakings cannot apply to a spouse). The claimant's statement on his SPC claim form that his wife was sponsored to be in the UK was accurate (he had not stated that he had signed a written undertaking). The DWP, which had wrongly assumed that his wife was a person subject to immigration control (rather than having been given indefinite leave to remain, as in fact was the case), had failed to make proper enquiries as to her true immigration status. The resulting overpayment was, therefore, due to official error and was not recoverable. The entitlement decision was remitted to a new tribunal for detailed findings on the claimant's means which were required to determine his entitlement to SPC.

[[1] Persons temporarily absent from Great Britain

3.—A claimant's entitlement to state pension credit during periods of temporary absence from Great Britain is to continue for up to 13 weeks if— **4.12**

(a) the period of the claimant's absence from Great Britain is unlikely to exceed 52 weeks; and

(b) while absent from Great Britain the claimant continues to satisfy the other conditions of entitlement to state pension credit.]

AMENDMENT

1. Social Security (Miscellaneous Amendments) (No.4) Regulations 2008 (SI 2008/2424) reg.3(2) (October 6, 2008).

GENERAL NOTE

The original version of reg.3 provided for entitlement to state pension credit to be retained for up to four weeks of a temporary absence from Great Britain, or for up to eight weeks in certain circumstances. In October 2008 the rule was simplified and broadly brought into line with the provisions governing housing benefit. Claimants may now retain entitlement for up to 13 weeks, so long as they continue to satisfy the other conditions of entitlement, and need no longer specify the purpose of their absence. However, at the same time as relaxing this requirement, the Social Security (Miscellaneous Amendments) (No.4) Regulations 2008 (SI 2008/2424) also reduced the time limit for claiming state pension credit from 12 months to three months (by amending reg.19(3) of, and repealing para.12 of Sch.4 to, the Social Security (Claims and Payments) Regulations 1987 (SI 1987/1968). **4.13**

[[1] Persons temporarily absent from Great Britain on 6th October 2008

3A.—Where a claimant— **4.14**

(a) is already temporarily absent from Great Britain on 6th October 2008;

(b) had a continuing entitlement to state pension credit immediately before that day; and

(c) while absent from Great Britain, continues to satisfy the other conditions of entitlement to state pension credit,

the claimant's entitlement to state pension credit is to continue during that period of absence from Great Britain for up to 13 weeks.]

AMENDMENT

1. Social Security (Miscellaneous Amendments) (No.4) Regulations 2008 (SI 2008/2424) reg.3(3) (October 6, 2008).

GENERAL NOTE

4.15 See General Note to reg.3 above.

Persons receiving treatment outside Great Britain

4.16 **4.**—[2(1) For the purposes of the Act, a person who is receiving treatment at a hospital or other institution outside Great Britain shall be treated as being in Great Britain if the treatment is being provided—

(a) under section 6(2) of the Health Service Act (performance of functions outside England) or section 6(2) of the Health Service (Wales) Act (performance of functions outside Wales);

(b) pursuant to arrangements made under section 12(1) of the Health Service Act (Secretary of State's arrangements with other bodies), section 10(1) of the Health Service (Wales) Act (Welsh Ministers' arrangements with other bodies), paragraph 18 of Schedule 4 to the Health Service Act (joint exercise of functions) or paragraph 18 of Schedule 3 to the Health Service (Wales) Act (joint exercise of functions);

(c) under equivalent provision in Scotland or pursuant to arrangements made under such provision.]

[1(2) Paragraph (1) applies only where—

(a) the "person" is the claimant or his partner; and

(b) the claimant satisfied the conditions for entitlement to state pension credit immediately before he or, as the case may be, his partner, left Great Britain.]

AMENDMENTS

1. State Pension Credit (Consequential, Transitional and Miscellaneous Provisions) Regulations 2002 (SI 2002/3019) reg.23(b) (October 6, 2003).

2. Social Security (Miscellaneous Amendments) (No.6) Regulations 2008 (SI 2008/2767) reg.5(3) (November 17, 2008).

DEFINITION

"claimant"—see SPCA 2002 s.17(1).

GENERAL NOTE

4.17 This provision ensures that those pensioners who are being treated in hospitals abroad under NHS arrangements (e.g. in France or Germany, as a means of cutting waiting list times for certain types of surgery) retain their entitlement to state pension credit. There is no time limit on the dispensation of the normal rule requiring actual presence in Great Britain where such treatment is being received. The dispensation does not assist a pensioner who happens to fall ill while abroad and obtains treatment overseas.

Persons treated as being or not being members of the same household

4.18 **5.**—(1) A person is to be treated as not being a member of the same household as the claimant if—

(a) he is living away from the claimant and—

(i) he does not intend to resume living with the claimant; or

(ii) his absence is likely to exceed 52 weeks except where there are exceptional circumstances (for example the person is in hospital or otherwise has no control over the length of his absence), and the absence is unlikely to be substantially more than 52 weeks;

(b) he or the claimant is permanently in a care home [4or an independent hospital];

(c) he or the claimant is, or both are—

(i) detained in a hospital provided under [2 the provisions of the Mental Health Act 1983, the [3 Mental Health (Care and Treatment) (Scotland) Act 2003], or the Criminal Procedure (Scotland) Act 1995; or]

(ii) detained in custody pending trial or sentence upon conviction or under a sentence imposed by a court; or

(iii) on temporary release in accordance with the provisions of the Prison Act 1952 or the Prison (Scotland) Act 1989;

(d) the claimant is abroad and does not satisfy [2 . . .] regulation 3 (persons temporary absent from Great Britain);

(e) [5 . . .]

[6 (f) he is absent from Great Britain for more than 13 weeks;]

[1(g) [2. . .]

(h) he is a person subject to immigration control within the meaning of section 115(9) of the Immigration and Asylum Act 1999.]

[5 (1A) Paragraph (1)(d) and (f) shall not apply where a person is treated as being in Great Britain in accordance with regulation 4.]

(2) Subject to paragraph (1), partners shall be treated as members of the same household notwithstanding that they are temporarily living apart.

[6. . .]

AMENDMENTS

1. State Pension Credit (Consequential, Transitional and Miscellaneous Provisions) (No.2) Regulations 2002 (SI 2002/3197) reg.2 and Sch. para.2 (October 6, 2003).

2. State Pension Credit (Transitional and Miscellaneous Provisions) Amendment Regulations 2003 (SI 2003/2274) reg.2(5) (October 6, 2003).

3. Mental Health (Care and Treatment) (Scotland) Act 2003 (Modification of Subordinate Legislation) Order 2005 (SSI 2005/445) art.2 and Sch. para.35(2) (October 3, 2005).

4. Social Security (Care Homes and Independent Hospitals) Regulations 2005 (SI 2005/2687) reg.6 and Sch.5 para.2 (October 24, 2005).

5. Social Security (Miscellaneous Amendments) (No.4) Regulations 2006 (SI 2006/2378) reg.14(2) (October 2, 2006).

6. Social Security (Miscellaneous Amendments) (No.4) Regulations 2008 (SI 2008/2424) reg.3(4) (October 6, 2008).

DEFINITIONS

"appropriately qualified"—see para.(3) and reg.3(4).
"care home"—see reg.1(2).
"claimant"—see SPCA 2002 s.17(1).
"partners"—see reg.1(3).
"young person"—see para.(3) and reg.3(4).

GENERAL NOTE

4.19 This provision is modelled on the parallel rule relating to income support (see Income Support (General) Regulations 1987 (SI 1987/1967) reg.16), although the drafting is a little more straightforward. The starting point is that partners (i.e. members of a married or unmarried couple) are treated as members of the same household "notwithstanding that they are temporarily living apart" (para.(2)). In other words, membership of the same household does not cease simply because one partner is temporarily living elsewhere. This basic rule is then subject to the exceptions set out in para.(1), which replicate in part those that apply to income support.

Amount of the guarantee credit

4.20 **6.**—(1) Except as provided in the following provisions of these Regulations, the standard minimum guarantee is—

(a) [2£237.55] per week in the case of a claimant who has a partner;
(b) [2£155.60] per week in the case of a claimant who has no partner.

(2) Paragraph (3) applies in the case of—

(a) prisoners; and
(b) members of religious orders who are fully maintained by their order.

(3) In a case to which this paragraph applies—

(a) section 2(3) has effect with the substitution for the reference to the standard minimum guarantee in section 2(3)(a) of a reference to a [1 nil] amount; and
(b) except in the case of a person who is a remand prisoner, [1 nil] is the prescribed additional amount for the purposes of section 2(3)(b).

(4) Except in a case to which paragraph (3) applies, an amount additional to that prescribed in paragraph (1) shall be applicable under paragraph (5) if the claimant is treated as being a severely disabled person in accordance with paragraph 1 of Part I of Schedule I.

(5) The additional amount applicable is—

(a) except where paragraph (b) applies, [1£61.85] per week if paragraph 1(1)(a), (b) or (c) of Part I of Schedule I is satisfied; or
(b) [1£123.70] per week if paragraph 1(1)(b) of Part I of Schedule I is satisfied otherwise than by virtue of paragraph 1(2)(b) of that Part and no one is entitled to and in receipt of an allowance under section 70 of the 1992 Act [1, or has an award of universal credit which includes the carer element under regulation 29 of the Universal Credit Regulations 2013,] in respect of caring for either partner.

(6) Except in a case to which paragraph (3) applies, an amount additional to that prescribed in paragraph (1) shall be applicable—

(a) if paragraph 4 of Part II of Schedule I is satisfied (amount applicable for carers);
(b) in accordance with Part III of Schedule I (amount applicable for former claimants of income support or income-based jobseeker's allowance); or
(c) except where paragraph (7) applies, in accordance with Schedule II (housing costs).

(7) This paragraph applies in the case of a person who has been detained in custody for more than 52 weeks pending trial or sentence following conviction by a court.

(8) The amount applicable if paragraph 4 of Part II of Schedule I is satisfied is [1£34.60] per week, and in the case of partners, this amount is applicable in respect of each partner who satisfies that paragraph.

(9) In the case of a remand prisoner paragraph (6) shall apply as if sub-paragraphs (a) and (b) were omitted.

(10) In this regulation, "remand prisoner" means a person who, for a

period not exceeding 52 weeks, has been detained in custody on remand pending trial or, as a condition of bail, required to reside in a hostel approved under section 27(1) of the Probation Service Act 1993 or, as the case may be, detained pending sentence upon conviction.

AMENDMENTS

1. Universal Credit and Miscellaneous Amendments Regulations 2015 (SI 2015/1754) reg.16(2) (November 4, 2015).
2. Social Security Benefits Up-rating Order 2016 (SI 2016/230) art.6 (April 11, 2016).

DEFINITIONS

"the 1992 Act"—see reg.1(2).
"claimant"—see SPCA 2002 s.17(1).
"partner"—see reg.1(3).
"prisoner"—see reg.1(2).
"remand prisoner"—see para.(10).

GENERAL NOTE

Paragraph (1)

The general conditions of entitlement to state pension credit are set out in s.1 of the SPCA 2002, with the supplementary conditions for the guarantee credit component contained in s.2. The amount of the guarantee credit is the "appropriate minimum guarantee" for claimants with no income and the difference between that figure and the person's income in other cases (s.2(2)). The "appropriate minimum guarantee" is comprised of the "standard minimum guarantee" and such other amounts as may be prescribed. This provision sets out the amount of the "standard minimum guarantee" for individual claimants and couples respectively. The "standard minimum guarantee" therefore performs broadly the same function as the age-related personal allowance taken together with the former pensioner premium in the income support scheme before that was subject to amendments consequential upon the coming into force of the SPCA 2002. This figure is then aggregated together with other prescribed amounts as set out in the remaining paragraphs of this regulation and Sch.1 to these Regulations to produce the "appropriate minimum guarantee" (or applicable amount in income support terms). The calculation used to arrive at the final guarantee credit is then as provided for by s.2(2) of the SPCA 2002, as described above. 4.21

Subsections (2) and (3)

As with income support (see the Income Support (General) Regulations 1987 (SI 1987/1967) Sch.7 paras 7 and 8), prisoners and those fully maintained by their religious orders effectively have no entitlement to the guarantee credit, as their living costs are met from other sources. They also have a nil entitlement to the savings credit (reg.7(3)). 4.22

See further *CSPC/677/2007*, the lead case of several involving claims for state pension credit by nuns who were all members of a Carmelite closed order. Any income received by an individual nun was paid into a monastery account, which held the funds in common. Commissioner May QC held that in these circumstances the nuns were fully maintained by their order; no distinction could be made between those nuns who contributed their own income and those who had no income. Nor could any distinction be made between those orders which were self-maintaining and those which were not. The Commissioner also held that neither art.1 of Prot.1 nor art.8 of the European Convention on Human Rights was engaged.

Furthermore, in *Secretary of State for Work and Pensions v Sister IS and KM* [2009] UKUT 200 (AAC), where the claimants were Benedictine and Carmelite nuns, a three-judge panel of the Upper Tribunal ruled that: (1) the expression "religious order" in reg.6(2)(b) is to be read in the broader sense of that term found in dictionaries; it is not limited to those religious communities subject to a centralised authority or control; (2) the nuns in question were fully maintained from funds held by their orders, and that it did not matter from what source the funds originated (whether by their own work or any entitlement to benefits which contributed to the order's funds); and (3) it was possible to remove any element of religious discrimination (if there was one) in reg.6(2)(b) "by removing the reference to religion. That would leave the provision to apply to 'members of religious orders who are fully maintained by their order'."

The claimant's further appeal to the Court of Appeal was dismissed in *Scott v Secretary of State for Social Security* [2011] EWCA Civ 103; [2011] AACR 23. The Court held that the Upper Tribunal had not misdirected itself as to the proper construction of the phrase "fully maintained"; the proposition that "full maintenance" was only conceptually possible if the recipient of the funds was making no contribution could not be read into the Regulations. There was no doubt that the claimant was being "fully maintained" by her community when she made her claim. Her work was not for her own personal benefit, but exclusively for the trust, in return for which she received the benefit of bed and board under the trust arrangements in place. It followed that her maintenance was provided by the trust, rather than, as the Upper Tribunal had found, directly from her own efforts.

Subsections (4) and (5)

4.23 Section 2(7) of the SPCA 2002, which mirrors SSCBA 1992 s.135(5), requires an additional amount to be prescribed (for the purposes of calculating the "appropriate minimum guarantee") for severely disabled people. The qualifying criteria for this additional amount, which essentially performs the same function as the severe disability premium in the income support scheme, are set out in para.1 of Sch.1 to these Regulations.

Subsections (6)–(10)

4.24 Further additional amounts for the purposes of calculating the "appropriate minimum guarantee" are prescribed for carers, former claimants of income support or income-based jobseeker's allowance, and in respect of housing costs. The amount of the carer additional amount is set out in para.(8); the other additional amounts are detailed in Pt III of Sch.1, and Sch.2 to these Regulations respectively. Prisoners and fully maintained members of religious orders are not eligible for such additional amounts. Furthermore, those who have been detained in custody for more than 52 weeks pending trial or sentence following conviction are not eligible for housing costs. Note also that remand prisoners are in any event not eligible for the additional amounts prescribed for carers and for former claimants of income support or income-based jobseeker's allowance (paras (9) and (10)).

Savings Credit

4.25 7.—(1) The percentage prescribed for the purposes of determining—

(a) the maximum savings credit is [2 60 per cent];

(b) "amount A" in section 3(4) is [2 60 per cent];

(c) "amount B" in section 3(4) is [2 40 per cent].

(2) The amount prescribed for the savings credit threshold is [3£133.82] for a claimant who has no partner and [3£212.97] for a claimant who has a partner.

(3) The maximum savings credit shall be taken to be [2 nil] in the case of—

(a) prisoners; and
(b) members of religious orders who are fully maintained by their order.

[1(4) If a calculation made for the purposes of paragraph (1)(b) or (c) results in a fraction of a penny, that fraction shall, if it would be to the claimant's advantage, be treated as a penny; otherwise it shall be disregarded.]

AMENDMENTS

1. State Pension Credit (Consequential, Transitional and Miscellaneous Provisions) Regulations 2002 (SI 2002/3019) reg.23(d) (October 6, 2003).

2. Social Security Benefits Up-rating Order 2015 (SI 2015/457), art.21(3) and (6) and Sch.13 (April 6, 2015).

3. Social Security Benefits (Adjustment of Amounts and Thresholds) Regulations 2016 (SI 2016/242) reg.4(2) (April 11, 2016).

DEFINITIONS

"claimant"—see SPCA 2002 s.17(1).
"partner"—see reg.1(3).
"prisoner"—see reg.1(2).

GENERAL NOTE

4.26 See annotations to s.3 of the SPCA 2002 for a full explanation as to the calculation of the savings credit. This regulation prescribes the relevant percentages (para.(1)) for the purposes of that calculation, specifies the savings credit threshold for individuals and couples (para.(2)) and excludes prisoners and fully maintained members of religious orders (para.(3)).

[1 Limitation of savings credit for certain mixed-age couples

4.26A **7A.**—A person who is a member of a mixed-age couple, is not entitled to a savings credit unless one of the members of the couple—

(a) has been awarded a savings credit with effect from a day before 6th April 2016 and was entitled to a savings credit immediately before 6th April 2016, and
(b) remained entitled to a savings credit at all times since the beginning of 6th April 2016.]

AMENDMENTS

1. Pension Credit (Amendment) Regulations 2015 (SI 2015/1529) reg.2(2) (April 6, 2016).

DEFINITIONS

"couple"—see reg.1(2).

GENERAL NOTE

4.26B The first requirement for entitlement to the savings credit element of pension credit, as originally enacted, was that the claimant (or their partner) was at least 65 (State Pension Credit Act 2002, s.3(1)). However, as a result of amendments made by the Pensions Act 2014, there is no longer access to the savings credit element for those claimants reaching state pension age on or after April 6, 2016 unless they are a member of a couple where their partner reached state pension age before that date (known as "a mixed-age couple"). Section 3ZA of the 2002 Act provides the enabling power for entitlement to the savings credit to be so restricted and defines what is meant by a "mixed-age couple". This regulation specifies the conditions which must be met for a mixed-age couple to qualify for savings credit. Although the drafting of the regulation suggests that there are only two pre-conditions, in reality there are three. First, one member must have attained state pension age before April 6, 2016. Second, that person must have been entitled to savings credit immediately before April 6, 2016. Third, that individual must have been entitled to savings credit at all times since that date.

Special groups

4.27 **8.**—Schedule III shall have effect in the case of members of polygamous marriages and [1 persons serving a sentence of imprisonment detained in hospital].

AMENDMENT

1. Social Security (Persons Serving a Sentence of Imprisonment Detained in Hospital) Regulations 2010 (SI 2010/442) reg.4(2) (March 25, 2010).

GENERAL NOTE

4.28 Section 12 of the SPCA 2002 enables special provision to be made for members of polygamous marriages. Special provision for other persons is authorised by the general regulation-making powers in SSCBA 1992 s.175 which apply in this context by virtue of SPCA 2002 s.19(1).

Qualifying income for the purposes of savings credit

4.29 **9.**—For the purposes of section 3 (savings credit), all income is to be treated as qualifying income except the following which is not to be treated as qualifying income—

(a) working tax credit;
(b) incapacity benefit;
(c) a contribution-based jobseeker's allowance [2 . . .]
(d) severe disablement allowance;
(e) maternity allowance;
(f) payments referred to in regulation 15(5)(d) (maintenance payments).
[1 (g) contributory employment and support allowance.]

AMENDMENTS

1. Employment and Support Allowance (Consequential Provisions) (No.2) Regulations 2008 (SI 2008/1554) reg.4(3) (October 27, 2008).
2. Universal Credit (Consequential, Supplementary, Incidental and Miscellaneous Provisions) Regulations 2013 (SI 2013/630) reg.33(3) (April 29, 2013).

GENERAL NOTE

4.30 WTC and the other benefits and payments listed here are excluded from the definition of qualifying income for the purpose of calculating the savings credit under SPCA 2002 s.3.

In *CPC/4177/2005* Commissioner May QC dismissed a challenge to reg.9(d) based on Directive 79/7 (equal treatment). The Commissioner ruled that art.4 of the Directive was engaged for the purposes of the savings credit element of pension credit (but not for the guaranteed credit). The Commissioner then held that there was no discrimination and so no breach of art.4 of the Directive. However, the reasoning in this decision may be revisited in subsequent decisions–e.g. it is less than clear that it is permissible to "sever" pension credit into its constituent elements, given that jobseeker's allowance is treated as one benefit (see *Hockenjos v*

Secretary of State for Social Security [2001] EWCA Civ 624; [2001] 2 C.M.L.R. 51). It should also be noted that in *CPC/4177/2005* the claimant did not attend the Commissioner's oral hearing and was unrepresented.

In *CPC/4173/2007* the claimant, aged 76, lived with her husband, aged 61, who received incapacity benefit. Her husband's incapacity benefit did not count as qualifying income for the purposes of savings credit by virtue of reg.9(b). The claimant argued that this was discriminatory as a woman of the same age as her husband would have received retirement pension (which does count as qualifying income). Commissioner Howell QC held that reg.9 does not contravene art.14 of the European Convention, as there was no differential treatment by reason of status. The Commissioner also ruled that there was no breach of Council Directive 79/7/EEC on equal treatment, as the circumstances fell squarely within the exclusion in art.7, which related to the determination of pensionable ages. Moreover, the Sex Discrimination Act 1975 had no application in this context.

Assessed income period

10.—(1) For the purposes of section 6(2)(b) (circumstances in which the Secretary of State is prevented from specifying an assessed income period), the circumstances are— 4.31

(a) in the case of partners, one partner is under the age of 60; or
(b) state pension credit is awarded, or awarded at a higher rate, because an element of the claimant's retirement provision which is due to be paid to the claimant stops temporarily.
[[2] (c) that—
  (i) the Secretary of State has sent the claimant the notification required by regulation 32(6)(a) of the Claims and Payments Regulations; and
  (ii) the claimant has not provided sufficient information to enable the Secretary of State to determine whether there will be any variation in the claimant's retirement provision throughout the period of 12 months beginning with the day following the day on which the previous assessed income period ends.]

(2) The circumstances prescribed for the purposes of section 7(4) (circumstances in which assessed amounts are deemed not to change) are that—

[[4] (a) except where sub-paragraph (b) applies, the arrangements under which the assessed amount is paid contain no provision for periodic increases in the amount payable; or]
(b) the assessed income comprises income from capital other than income to which paragraph (7) applies.

(3) Paragraphs (4) and (5) do not apply where the assessed amount comprises income from capital.

(4) Where the Secretary of State is informed that the arrangements under which the assessed amount is paid contains provision—

(a) for the payment to be increased periodically;
(b) for the date on which the increase is to be paid; and
(c) for determining the amount of the increase, the assessed amount shall be deemed to increase from the day specified in paragraph (5) by an amount determined by applying those provisions to the amount payable apart from this paragraph.

[[3] (5) The day referred to in this paragraph is—

(a) in a case to which paragraph (5A) applies—
(i) where the first increased payment date is the day on which the benefit week begins, that day;
(ii) where head (i) does not apply, the first day of the next benefit week which begins after that increased payment date;
(b) in a case to which paragraph (5A) does not apply—
(i) where the second increased payment date is the day on which the benefit week begins, that day;
(ii) where head (i) does not apply, the first day of the next benefit week following that increased payment date.

(5A) This paragraph applies where the period which—
(a) begins on the date from which the increase in the assessed amount is to accrue; and
(b) ends on the first increased payment date,
is a period of the same length as the period in respect of which the last payment of the pre-increase assessed amount was made.

(5B) In paragraphs (5) and (5A)—
"increased payment date" means a date on which the increase in the assessed amount referred to in paragraph (4) is paid as part of a periodic payment [4 . . .]; and
"pre-increase assessed amount" means the assessed amount prior to that increase.]

(6) Except where paragraph (4) applies, the assessed amount shall be deemed to increase—
[3 (a) on the day in April each year on which increases under section 150 (1)(c) of the Administration Act come into force if that is the first day of a benefit week but if it is not from the next following such day; and]
(b) by an amount produced by applying to the assessed amount the same percentage increase as that applied for the purposes of additional pensions under section 150(1)(c) and 151(1) of the Administration Act.

(7) Where the assessed amount comprises income from capital, it shall be deemed to increase or decrease—
(a) on the first day of the next benefit week to commence [1on or after] the day on which the income increases or decreases; and
(b) by an amount equal to the change in the claimant's income produced by applying to his income changes made to the yields capital is deemed to produce, or to the capital amounts, specified in regulation 15(6), or to both if both are changed.

(8) [5 . . .]

AMENDMENTS

1. State Pension Credit (Consequential, Transitional and Miscellaneous Provisions) Regulations 2002 (SI 2002/3019) reg.23(e) (October 6, 2003).

2. State Pension Credit (Transitional and Miscellaneous Provisions) Amendment Regulations 2003 (SI 2003/2274) reg.2(6) (October 6, 2003).

3. State Pension Credit (Miscellaneous Amendments) Regulations 2004 (SI 2004/647) reg.3(2) and (3) (April 5, 2004).

4. State Pension Credit (Amendment) Regulations 2005 (SI 2005/3205) reg.2(2) (December 18, 2005).

5. Social Security (Miscellaneous Amendments) (No.4) Regulations 2006 (SI 2006/2378) reg.14(3) (October 2, 2006).

Definitions

"the Administration Act"—see SPCA 2002 s.17(1).
"assessed income period"—see *ibid.*
"benefit week"—see reg.1(2).
"claimant"—see SPCA 2002 s.17(1).
"increased payment date"—see para.(5B).
"partner"—see reg.1(3).
"pay day"—see para.(8).
"pre-increase assessed amount"—see para.(5B).
"retirement provision"—see SPCA 2002 ss.7(6) and 17(1).

General Note

The "assessed income period" was central to the original conception of the state pension credit. Recognising that the traditional weekly means test of income support has been an important factor in the relatively low take-up of that benefit amongst pensioners, the Government initially adopted a very different strategy for state pension credit. Section 6(1) of the SPCA 2002 imposed a duty on the Secretary of State to specify an assessed income period when making a decision on a state pension credit claim. In normal circumstances, the assessed income period was fixed at five years from the date that decision took effect (SPCA 2002 s.9(1)). The principle then was that changes in the pensioner's income during that period need not be reported and thus any increases in income did not, of themselves, result in disentitlement or run the risk of overpayments accruing. Instead, the claimant's income throughout the five-year period was deemed to be the same as the income at the outset (*ibid.*, and s.7(3)), subject to deemed cost of living increases (*ibid.* and s.7(4)). 4.32

See further *CPC/0206/2005*, discussed in the note to State Pension Credit Act 2002 s.7 and *CPC/1928/2005*, discussed in the note to s.9 of that Act.

However, as a result of the Pensions Act 2014, assessed income periods will be phased out as from April 2016. As a result, any change in retirement income will in future need to be reported to the Department when it occurs, triggering a review and change in benefit award where appropriate.

Paragraph (1)

Section 6(2) of the SPCA 2002 provides that the Secretary of State is prevented from specifying a standard assessed income period under s.6(1) in two categories of case. The first is where an assessed income period is already in force in the claimant's case by virtue of an earlier application of the s.6 rule. The second comprises "such other circumstances as may be prescribed" (SPCA 2002 s.6(2)(b)). This paragraph prescribes two such types of case. The first is where the claimant is a member of a couple and one partner is aged under 60. This inevitably increases the likelihood that they are in (or may re-enter) the labour market and so a five-year "deeming rule" may be inappropriate. The second is where there has been a temporary cessation of the claimant's retirement provision leading to an award (or higher award) of state pension credit. 4.33

Presumably the insertion of reg.10(1)(c) should be read as being preceded by the word "or" at the end of reg.10(1)(b).

Paragraph (2)

As explained in the General Note above, the normal rule is that the amount of income fixed at the date of claim (the "assessed amount") is deemed to be the claimant's income throughout the assessed income period, subject to cost of living increases (SPCA 2002 s.7(3) and (4)). The prescribed cost of living increases in a claimant's assessed income do not operate where there is no clause in the claimant's pension scheme or annuity contract which provides for such periodic increases in the amount payable. The assessed amount is also not periodically 4.34

uprated where it comprises income from capital (except income covered by para. (7) below).

Paragraphs (3)–(5)

4.35 Many occupational and personal schemes will include provisions for periodic (typically annual) increases in the amount payable, which also specify when such increases are to be paid and how they are to be calculated. Where the Secretary of State is informed that such arrangements exist, then para.(4) enables the claimant's assessed income to be increased accordingly, reflecting such improvements in pension provision. The increase is deemed to apply from the start of the benefit week if the increase under the pension scheme is due to be paid on that day or, failing that, from the start of the next benefit week (para. (5)). For cases not covered by para.(4), see para.(6). These provisions do not apply where the assessed income comprises income from capital (para.(3); see further para.(7)).

Paragraph (6)

4.36 In the event that the pension scheme does not include a provision which meets the criteria of para.(4), the default position is that the assessed amount is increased in line with the percentage increase stipulated by the Secretary of State as the amount by which additional pensions are to be increased.

Paragraph (7)

4.37 If the assessed amount comprises income from capital, it is deemed to increase (or decrease) in line with the tariff income rule under reg.15(6).

Retirement provision in assessed income period

4.38 **11.**—[1 (1) Where an element of a person's retirement provision ceases to be payable by one source but—

(a) responsibility for that element is assumed by another source, income from both those sources shall be treated as income from the same source; or

(b) in consequence of that element ceasing, income of a different description becomes payable from a different source, that income shall be treated as income of the same description from the same source as the element which ceased to be payable.

[1 (2) For the purposes of section 7(6) (meaning of retirement provision) of the Act, a foreign state retirement pension is to be treated as a benefit under the 1992 Act.]

AMENDMENT

1. Social Security (Miscellaneous Amendments) (No.2) Regulations 2010 (SI 2010/641) reg.6(4) (April 13, 2010).

DEFINITION

"retirement provision"—see ss.7(6) and 17(1) of the SPCA 2002.

GENERAL NOTE

4.39 The purpose of this provision is to ensure that the assessed income period continues notwithstanding the fact that responsibility for a pensioner's retirement provision changes (e.g. from one pension provider to another). The addition of para. (2) was designed to reverse the effect of *CPC/571/2008*.

End of assessed income period

12.—An assessed income period shall end [2 . . .] 4.40

(a) [2 at such time as] the claimant no longer satisfies a condition of entitlement to state pension credit;

(b) [2 at such time as] payments of an element of the claimant's retirement provision which is due to be paid to him stops temporarily or the amount paid is less than the amount due and in consequence his award of state pension credit is superseded under section 10 of the Social Security Act 1998;

(c) [2 at such time as] a claimant who has no partner is provided with accommodation in a care home [1 or an independent hospital] other than on a temporary basis [2;

(d) if, apart from this sub-paragraph, it would have ended on a date falling within the period specified in column 1 of the table in Schedule IIIA, on the corresponding date shown against that period in column 2 of that table.]

Amendments

1. Social Security (Care Homes and Independent Hospitals) Regulations 2005 (SI 2005/2687) reg.6 and Sch.5 para.3 (October 24, 2005).

2. State Pension Credit (Amendment) Regulations 2015 (SI 2015/1529) reg.2(3) (April 6, 2016).

Definitions

"assessed income period"—see SPCA 2002 ss.6, 9 and 17(1).
"care home"—see reg.1(2).
"claimant"—see SPCA 2002 s.17(1).
"partner"—see reg.1(3).
"retirement provision"—see ss.7(6) and 17(1) of the SPCA 2002.

General Note

The Assessed Income Period (AIP), a feature of pension credit from its introduction in 2003, removed the requirement for many recipients aged 65 and over to notify the DWP of changes to their retirement provision (i.e. savings and non-State pensions) during a set period. The maximum length of an AIP was 5 years in the case of recipients under the age of 75 when their AIP was set, but an indefinite period for those aged 75 or over. Changes which would increase the award could still be notified during an AIP and lead to a change in the award; changes that would reduce the award were assessed if they are notified, but the award itself was not changed until the end of the AIP. 4.41

Thus the normal rule was that the assessed income period would last for five years (SPCA 2002 s.9(1)). The primary legislation provides for various exceptions to this principle, namely where the claimant becomes (or ceases to be) a member of a couple, reaches the age of 65 or (in the case of a couple) where their partner attains 65 (ibid., and s.9(4)). The regulation originally provided for just three further and restricted circumstances in which that period will end before the expiry of five years—where the claimant no longer satisfies a condition of entitlement (para.12(a)), where there is a fall in income provided by way of retirement provision (para.12(b)), and where a single claimant goes into long-term care (para.12(c)). The underlying thinking is that instead of having to report the multitudinous changes of circumstances required under the income support scheme, state pension credit claimants will only have to report the sorts of significant life changes which have to be reported in any event for state pension purposes (e.g. bereavement, remarriage, moving into a care home).

As a result of the amendments made by the Pensions Act 2014 (see s.28), there is now a fourth and further situation in which assessed income periods will cease. This restriction is far more significant. The effect of the Pensions Act 2014 is to limit the application of the AIP legislation to decisions that took effect *before* April 6, 2016. Consequently, and as from April 6, 2016, no new AIPs have been or will be set. Where this change takes effect, any change in retirement provision must accordingly be reported by the claimant when it occurs, triggering an immediate review and (where appropriate) a change of the pension credit award. The position with AIPs already set before April 6, 2016 is that they will remain valid beyond that date, until such time as they end—whether through natural expiry, being phased out early, or under the existing rules on reporting changes of circumstances.

The effect of the new reg.12(d) is to bring to an end all pre-April 6, 2016 AIPs within 3 years (being the necessary time frame to achieve the annual expenditure savings agreed in the Government's 2013 Spending Round; the removal of the AIP is expected to generate savings of approximately £80 million per year by 2020/21). As a result, and as from April 2016, existing AIPs due to end on a date between April 2016 and March 2019 will run their course until they end (in whatever circumstances under the current rules); and existing AIPs that would otherwise be due to end after March 2019 will be brought forward to end on a specified date between July 2016 and March 2019. Consequently, by April 2019, the only AIPs still in existence should be those that were set indefinitely prior to April 6, 2016 (and where the claimants' circumstances have remained unchanged). The details of those AIPs which will be ended early are set out in a table to these Regulations, added as Schedule IIIA. Column 1 of the table in Sch.IIIA sets out the dates when these AIPs were originally due to be terminated, while Column 2 of Sch.IIIA provides the new dates on which they will now end. The Department's intention is that recipients with a fixed-term AIP which is to be ended early will receive a letter giving six months' advance notice of their revised end-date. The table contains several gaps between some of the months; the purpose of this which is to allow the Department's Operations branch to distribute and manage the prescribed volumes, including customer contact and explanation of benefit revision. As the fixed-term AIPs come to an end, the intention is that in future periodic case reviews will be conducted on those cases. These are generally conducted on a three-yearly basis, but the intervals for reviews are not set out in existing legislation and can therefore be applied more flexibly in practice.

The decision to abolish AIPs was taken as part of the 2013 Spending Round. The policy justification was that when AIPs were introduced, it was assumed that pensioners are more likely to have relatively stable income and capital. However, the Government has argued that this assumption has not proved to be correct. In particular, recent analysis suggests that pensioners' financial circumstances change more significantly than was anticipated (see DWP, *Abolition of Assessed Income Periods for Pension Credit; Impact Assessment*, October 2013, especially pp.10–11). As a result, fixing retirement provision for a long period has allowed some recipients to keep their benefit despite obtaining higher amounts of capital or new income streams—whereas if an AIP were not in place in these cases, the award would be either reduced or removed entirely.

Small amounts of state pension credit

4.42 **13.**—Where the amount of state pension credit payable is less than 10 pence per week, the credit shall not be payable unless the claimant is in receipt of another benefit payable with the credit.

DEFINITION

"claimant"—see SPCA 2002 s.17(1).

GENERAL NOTE

This applies the same de minimis rule as operates in the income support scheme (Social Security (Claims and Payments) Regulations 1987 (SI 1987/1968) reg.26(4)): see Vol.III). **4.43**

[1Part-weeks

13A.—(1) The guarantee credit shall be payable for a period of less than a week ("a part-week") at the rate specified in paragraph (3) if— **4.44**

(a) the claimant was entitled to [3 universal credit,] income support [2, an income-related employment and support allowance] or an income-based jobseeker's allowance immediately before the first day on which the conditions for entitlement to the credit are satisfied; and

(b) the claimant's entitlement to the credit is likely to continue throughout the first full benefit week which follows the part-week.

(2) For the purpose of determining the amount of the guarantee credit payable in respect of the part-week, no regard shall be had to any income of the claimant and his partner.

(3) The amount of the guarantee credit payable in respect of the part-week shall be determined—

(a) by dividing by 7 the weekly amount of the guarantee credit which, taking into account the requirements of paragraph (2), would be payable in respect of a full week; and then

(b) multiplying the resulting figure by the number of days in the part-week, any fraction of a penny being rounded up to the nearest penny.]

AMENDMENTS

1. State Pension Credit (Consequential, Transitional and Miscellaneous Provisions) Regulations 2002 (SI 2002/3019) reg.23(f) (October 6, 2003).
2. Employment and Support Allowance (Consequential Provisions) (No.2) Regulations 2008 (SI 2008/1554) reg.4(4) (October 27, 2008).
3. Universal Credit (Consequential, Supplementary, Incidental and Miscellaneous Provisions) Regulations 2013 (SI 2013/630) reg.33(4) (April 29, 2013).

DEFINITIONS

"a part-week"—see para.1.
"benefit week"—see reg.1(2).
"claimant"—see SPCA 2002 s.17(1).
"partner"—see reg.1(3).

GENERAL NOTE

This regulation provides for a simple means of ensuring continuity of payment for claimants transferring from income support or income-based jobseeker's allowance to state pension credit. Claimants in such circumstances are entitled to a part-week payment of the guarantee credit to take them up to the start of their first week on state pension credit. This part week payment is paid irrespective of the claimant's income (or that of their partner) (para.(2)). Note that there is no provision for part week payments of the savings credit. **4.45**

[1Date on which benefits are treated as paid

13B.—(1) The following benefits shall be treated as paid on the day of the week in respect of which the benefit is payable— **4.46**

(a) severe disablement allowance;
(b) short-term and long-term incapacity benefit;
(c) maternity allowance;
(d) contribution-based jobseeker's allowance [4 . . .]
[3 (e) contributory employment and support allowance.]

(2) All benefits except those mentioned in paragraph (1) shall be treated as paid on the first day of the benefit week in [2 . . .] which the benefit is payable.]

AMENDMENTS

1. State Pension Credit (Consequential, Transitional and Miscellaneous Provisions) Regulations 2002 (SI 2002/3019) reg.23(f) (October 6, 2003).
2. State Pension Credit (Consequential, Transitional and Miscellaneous Provisions) (No.2) Regulations 2002 (SI 2002/3197) reg.2 and Sch. para.3 (October 6, 2003).
3. Employment and Support Allowance (Consequential Provisions) (No.2) Regulations 2008 (SI 2008/1554) reg.4(5) (October 27, 2008).
4. Universal Credit (Consequential, Supplementary, Incidental and Miscellaneous Provisions) Regulations 2013 (SI 2013/630) reg.33(5) (April 29, 2013).

DEFINITION

"benefit week"—see reg.1(2).

GENERAL NOTE

4.47 This provision is a good example of the topsy-turvy principle of statutory drafting. The general rule, as enshrined in para.(2), is that a social security benefit is treated as being paid on the first day of the benefit week in which the benefit is payable. The "benefit week" is the period of seven days beginning on the day in which, in the claimant's case, the state pension credit is payable (reg.1(2)). The exceptions to this general principle are then listed in para.(1). Employment and support allowance, incapacity benefit, severe disablement allowance and jobseeker's allowance are all normally paid fortnightly in arrears from the date of claim (Social Security (Claims and Payments) Regulations 1987 (SI 1987/1968) regs 24(1), 26A(1) and 26C(1)). Maternity allowance is usually payable on Fridays (Social Security (Claims and Payments) Regulations 1987 (SI 1987/1968) reg.24(4)).

PART III

Income

Calculation of income and capital

4.48 **14.**—The income and capital of—
(a) the claimant; and
(b) any partner of the claimant,

shall be calculated in accordance with the rules set out in this Part; and any reference in this Part to the claimant shall apply equally to any partner of the claimant.

DEFINITIONS

"claimant"—see SPCA 2002 s.17(1).
"income"—see *ibid.*, and s.15.
"partner"—see reg.1(3).

GENERAL NOTE

On the definition of "income", see SPCA 2002 s.15(1) and regs 15–18 and reg.24 below. On the meaning of "capital", see regs 19–23 below. The normal rules on aggregating the income and capital resources of married and unmarried couples apply to state pension credit as to other means-tested benefits (SPCA 2002 s.5). 4.49

The approach to income is rather different to the income support scheme, under which claimants are required to report every element of their income and capital and any changes as they occur. For state pension credit purposes, the categories of income to be disclosed by claimants are set out in SPCA 2002 ss.15 and 16 and in this Part of the Regulations, taken together with Schs IV, V and VI, which deal with disregards and calculation. There is, therefore, no need to report forms of income which are not listed in these statutory provisions (e.g. charitable payments and compensation for personal injuries).

Income for the purposes of the Act

15.—(1) For the purposes of section 15(1)(e) (income), all social security benefits are prescribed except— 4.50

(a) disability living allowance;
[16 (aa) personal independence payment;]
[17 (ab) armed forces independence payment;]
(b) attendance allowance payable under section 64 of the 1992 Act;
(c) an increase of disablement pension under section 104 or 105 of the 1992 Act;
(d) a payment under regulations made in exercise of the power conferred by paragraph 7(2)(b) of Part II of Schedule 8 to the 1992 Act;
(e) an increase of an allowance payable in respect of constant attendance under paragraph 4 of Part I of Schedule 8 to the 1992 Act;
(f) any child special allowance payable under section 56 of the 1992 Act;
(g) any guardian's allowance payable under section 77 of the 1992 Act;
(h) any increase for a dependant, other than the claimant's partner, payable in accordance with Part IV of the 1992 Act;
(i) any social fund payment made under Part VIII of the 1992 Act;
(j) child benefit payable in accordance with Part IX of the 1992 Act;
(k) Christmas bonus payable under Part X of the 1992 Act;
[1(l) housing benefit;
[15 . . .]
(n) bereavement payment;
(o) statutory sick pay;
(p) statutory maternity pay;
[14 (q) ordinary statutory paternity pay payable under Part 12ZA of the 1992 Act;
(qa) [19 . . .]
[18 (qb) statutory shared parental pay payable under Part 12ZC of the 1992 Act;]
(r) statutory adoption pay payable under Part 12ZB of the 1992 Act;
(s) any benefit similar to those mentioned in the preceding provisions of this paragraph payable under legislation having effect in Northern Ireland.]

[13 (2) For the purposes of section 15(1)(f) (foreign social security benefits) of the Act, income includes—

(a) all foreign social security benefits which are similar to the social security benefits prescribed under paragraph (1), and

(b) any foreign state retirement pension.]

(3) Where the payment of any social security benefit prescribed under paragraph (1) is subject to any deduction (other than an adjustment specified in paragraph (4)) the amount to be taken into account under paragraph (1) shall be the amount before the deduction is made.

(4) The adjustments specified in this paragraph are those made in accordance with—

(a) the Social Security (Overlapping Benefits) Regulations 1979;

[8 (b) regulation 2 of the Social Security (Hospital In-Patients) Regulations 2005;]

(c) section 30DD or section 30E of the 1992 Act (reductions in in-capacity benefit in respect of pensions and councillor's allowances);

[9 (d) section 3 of the Welfare Reform Act (deductions from contributory allowance).]

(5) For the purposes of section 15(1)(j) (income to include income of prescribed descriptions), income of the following descriptions is prescribed—

[10 (a) a payment made—

(i) under article 30 of the Naval, Military and Air Forces Etc. (Disablement and Death) Service Pensions Order 2006, in any case where article 30(1)(b) applies; or

(ii) under article 12(8) of that Order, in any case where sub-paragraph (b) of that article applies;]

[4(aa) a guaranteed income payment;

(ab) a payment made under article 21(1)(c) of the Armed Forces and Reserve Forces (Compensation Scheme) Order 2005 [10, in any case where article 23(2)(c) applies];]

[10 (ac) any retired pay, pension or allowance granted in respect of disablement or any pension or allowance granted to a widow, widower or surviving civil partner in respect of a death due to service or war injury under an instrument specified in section 639(2) of the Income Tax (Earnings and Pensions) Act 2003, where such payment does not fall within paragraph (a) of the definition of "war disablement pension" in section 17(1) of the State Pension Credit Act 2002 or, in respect of any retired pay or pension granted in respect of disablement, where such payment does not fall within paragraph (b) of that definition;]

(b) a pension paid to victims of National Socialist persecution under any special provision made by the law of the Federal Republic of Germany, or any part of it, or of the Republic of Austria;

(c) payments under a scheme made under the Pneumoconiosis, etc. (Worker's Compensation) Act 1979;

(d) payments made towards the maintenance of the claimant by his spouse [6, civil partner, former spouse or former civil partner] or towards the maintenance of the claimant's partner by his spouse [6, civil partner, former spouse or former civil partner], including payments made—

(i) under a court order;

(ii) under an agreement for maintenance; or

(iii) voluntarily;

(e) payments due from any person in respect of board and lodging accommodation provided by the claimant [5 . . .];

[11 (f) royalties or other sums paid as a consideration for the use of, or the right to use, any copyright, design, patent or trade mark;] [2. . .]

[11 (g) any payment in respect of any—

(i) book registered under the Public Lending Right Scheme 1982; or

(ii) work made under any international public lending right scheme that is analogous to the Public Lending Right Scheme 1982;]

[2 (h) any income in lieu of that specified in—

(i) paragraphs (a) to (i) of section 15(1) of the Act, or

(ii) in this regulation;

(i) any payment of rent made to a claimant who—

(i) owns the freehold or leasehold interest in any property or is a tenant of any property;

(ii) occupies part of that property; and

(iii) has an agreement with another person allowing that person to occupy that property on payment of rent.]

[3(j) any payment made at regular intervals under an equity release scheme;]

[7 (k) PPF periodic payments.]

[12 (6) For the purposes of section 15(2) (deemed income from capital) and subject to regulation 17(8) (capital to be disregarded), a claimant's capital shall be deemed to yield a weekly income of—

(a) £1 for each £500 in excess of £10,000; and

(b) £1 for any excess which is not a complete £500.]

(7) [13 . . .]

(8) [13 . . .]

AMENDMENTS

1. State Pension Credit (Consequential, Transitional and Miscellaneous Provisions) Regulations 2002 (SI 2002/3019) reg.23(g) (October 6, 2003).

2. State Pension Credit (Transitional and Miscellaneous Provisions) Amendment Regulations 2003 (SI 2003/2274) reg.2(7) (October 6, 2003).

3. Social Security (Housing Benefit, Council Tax Benefit, State Pension Credit and Miscellaneous Amendments) Regulations 2004 (SI 2004/2327) reg.7(3) (October 4, 2004).

4. Social Security (Miscellaneous Amendments) Regulations 2005 (SI 2005/574) reg.2(2) (April 4, 2005).

5. Social Security (Miscellaneous Amendments) (No.2) Regulations 2005 (SI 2005/2465) reg.6(3) (October 3, 2005).

6. Civil Partnership (Pensions, Social Security and Child Support) (Consequential, etc. Provisions) Order 2005 (SI 2005/2877) art.2(3) and Sch.3 para.35(3) (December 5, 2005).

7. Social Security (Miscellaneous Amendments) Regulations 2006 (SI 2006/588) reg.4(2) (April 6, 2006).

8. Social Security (Hospital In-Patients) Regulations 2005 (SI 2005/3360) reg.8(3) (April 10, 2006).

9. Employment and Support Allowance (Consequential Provisions) (No.2) Regulations 2008 (SI 2008/1554) reg.4(6) (October 27, 2008).

10. Social Security (Miscellaneous Amendments) (No.7) Regulations 2008 (SI 2008/3157) reg.4(3) (January 5, 2009).

11. Social Security (Miscellaneous Amendments) Regulations 2009 (SI 2009/583) reg.5(2) (April 6, 2009).

12. Social Security (Deemed Income from Capital) Regulations 2009 (SI 2009/1676) regs 2 and 3 (November 2, 2009).

13. Social Security (Miscellaneous Amendments) (No.2) Regulations 2010 (SI 2010/641) reg.6(5) (April 13, 2010).

14. Social Security (Miscellaneous Amendments) Regulations 2012 (2012/757) reg.5(3) (April 1, 2012).

15. Council Tax Benefit Abolition (Consequential Provision) Regulations 2013 (SI 2013/458) reg.3 and Sch.1 (April 1, 2013).

16. Personal Independence Payment (Supplementary Provisions and Consequential Amendments) Regulations 2013 (SI 2013/388) reg.8 and Sch. para.27(3) (April 8, 2013).

17. Armed Forces and Reserve Forces Compensation Scheme (Consequential Provisions: Subordinate Legislation) Order 2013 (SI 2013/591) art.7 and Sch. para.23(3) (April 8, 2013).

18. Shared Parental Leave and Statutory Shared Parental Pay (Consequential Amendments to Subordinate Legislation) Order 2014 (SI 2014/3255) art.10(3)(b) (December 31, 2014).

19. Shared Parental Leave and Statutory Shared Parental Pay (Consequential Amendments to Subordinate Legislation) Order 2014 (SI 2014/3255) art.10(3)(a) (April 5, 2015).

DEFINITIONS

"the 1992 Act"—see reg.1(2).
"attendance allowance"—see *ibid.*
"board and lodging accommodation"—see *ibid.*
"capital"—see SPCA 2002 s.17(1).
"care home"—see reg.1(2).
"claimant"—see SPCA 2002 s.17(1).
"income"—see *ibid.*
"partner"—see reg.1(2).

GENERAL NOTE

Paragraph (1)

4.51 The presumption under SPCA 2002 s.15(1)(e) is that social security benefits count as income for the purposes of calculating entitlement to state pension credit. There is, however, an extensive list of exceptions here. Note also that there are disregards that apply to certain forms of income, as specified in reg.17(7) and Sch.IV below.

Paragraph (2)

4.52 This provision was amended in order to reverse the effect of *SSWP v JK* [2009] UKUT 55 (AAC). If income is received in a currency other than Sterling, the value of any payment is determined by taking the Sterling equivalent on the date that payment is made (reg.17(6)).

Paragraph (3)

4.53 The effect of this rule is that payments of prescribed social security benefits are taken into account gross, i.e. before any deductions are applied (e.g. under the Social Security (Claims and Payments) Regulations 1987 (SI 1987/1968) reg.35 and Sch.9). This is subject to the exceptions specified in para.(4).

Paragraph (5)

4.54 Section 15(1)(j) is a catch-all provision that enables the Secretary of State to prescribe other forms of income not caught by any of the other provisions. As regards board and lodging accommodation (sub-para.(5)(e)), and on the importance of establishing the precise status of someone staying with the claimant (e.g. as a sub-tenant, lodger or non-dependant), see *KC v Secretary of State for Work and Pensions (SPC)* [2012] UKUT 114 (AAC).

Paragraph (6)

The tariff income rule for state pension credit is markedly more generous to claimants than that which applies in the income support scheme. In particular, the assumed rate of return is halved. The rule for state pension credit is that the claimant is assumed to receive £1 per week for every £500 or part thereof over the threshold of £10,000. Thus a state pension credit claimant with £14,000 in savings will have a deemed income of £8 per week from that capital. A person of working age with £10,000 in capital is excluded from entitlement to income support. Note also that there is no upper capital limit for state pension credit, and that the threshold for the tariff income rule was raised to £10,000 for all claimants, and not just those in residential care and nursing homes, with effect from November 2, 2009. 4.55

Retirement pension income

16.—There shall be added to the descriptions of income listed in section 16(1) (retirement pension income) the following [1paragraphs]— 4.56

"(k) any sum payable by way of pension out of money provided under the Civil List Act 1837, the Civil List Act 1937, the Civil List Act 1952, the Civil List Act 1972 or the [1Civil List Act 1975];

[1(1) any payment, other than a payment ordered by a court or made in settlement of a claim, made by or on behalf of a former employer of a person on account of the early retirement of that person on grounds of ill-health or disability;]

[2(m) any payment made at regular intervals under an equity release scheme;]"

[4(n) any payment made under the Financial Assistance Scheme Regulations 2005.]

Amendments

1. State Pension Credit (Consequential, Transitional and Miscellaneous Provisions) (No.2) Regulations 2002 (SI 2002/3197) reg.2 and Sch. para.3 (October 6, 2003).

2. Social Security (Housing Benefit, Council Tax Benefit, State Pension Credit and Miscellaneous Amendments) Regulations 2004 (SI 2004/2327) reg.7(4) (October 4, 2004).

3. State Pension Credit (Amendment) Regulations 2005 (SI 2005/3205) reg.2(3) (December 18, 2005).

Definition

"income"—see SPCA 2002 ss.15 and 17(1).

General Note

Readers with republican tendencies will doubtless be reassured to see that pensions paid from the Civil List count as retirement pension income for the purposes of SPCA 2002 s.16(1). More prosaically, payments made by virtue of early retirement on ill-health grounds (other than those ordered by court or agreed under the settlement of a claim) also count. 4.57

Calculation of weekly income

17.—(1) Except where paragraph (2) and (4) apply, for the purposes of calculating the weekly income of the claimant, where the period in respect of which a payment is made— 4.58

(a) does not exceed a week, the whole of that payment shall be included in the claimant's weekly income;

(b) exceeds a week, the amount to be included in the claimant's weekly income shall be determined—
   (i) in a case where that period is a month, by multiplying the amount of the payment by 12 ad dividing the product by 52;
   (ii) in a case where that period is three months, by multiplying the amount of the payment by 4 and dividing the product by 52;
   (iii) in a case where that period is a year, by dividing the amount of the payment by 52;
   (iv) in any other case, by multiplying the amount of the payment by 7 and dividing the product by the number of days in the period in respect of which it is made.

(2) Where—
(a) the claimant's regular pattern of work is such that he does not work the same hours every week; or
(b) the amount of the claimant's income fluctuates and has changed more than once,

the weekly amount of that claimant's income shall be determined—
   (i) if, in a case to which sub-paragraph (a) applies, there is a recognised cycle of work, by reference to his average weekly income over the period of the complete cycle (including, where the cycle involves periods in which the claimant does no work, those periods but disregarding any other absences); or
   (ii) in any other case, on the basis of—
      (aa) the last two payments if those payments are one month or more apart;
      (bb) the last four payments if the last two payments are less than one month apart; or
      (cc) such other payments as may, in the particular circumstances of the case, enable the claimant's average weekly income to be determined more accurately.

(3) For the purposes of paragraph (2)(b) the last payments are the last payments before the date the claim was made or treated as made or, if there is a subsequent supersession under section 10 of the Social Security Act 1998, the last payments before the date of the supersession.

(4) If a claimant is entitled to receive a payment to which paragraph (5) applies, the amount of that payment shall be treated as if made in respect of a period of a year.

(5) This paragraph applies to—
[3 (a) royalties or other sums received as a consideration for the use of, or the right to use, any copyright, design, patent or trade mark;]
[3 (b) any payment in respect of any—
   (i) book registered under the Public Lending Right Scheme 1982; or
   (ii) work made under any international public lending right scheme that is analogous to the Public Lending Right Scheme 1982;] [1 and
(c) any payment which is made on an occasional basis.]

(6) Where payments are made in a currency other than Sterling, the value of the payment shall be determined by taking the Sterling equivalent on the date the payment is made.

(7) Income specified in Schedule IV is to be disregarded in the calculation of a claimant's income.

(8) Schedule V shall have effect so that—

(a) the capital specified in Part I shall be disregarded for the purpose of determining a claimant's income; and

(b) the capital specified in Part II shall be disregarded for the purpose of determining a claimant's income under regulation 15(6).

[1(9) The sums specified in Schedule VI shall be disregarded in calculating—

(a) the claimant's earnings; and

[3 (b) any amount to which paragraph (5) applies where the claimant is the first owner of the copyright, design, patent or trademark, or an original contributor to the book or work referred to in paragraph (5)(b).]

(9A) For the purposes of paragraph (9)(b), and for that purpose only, the amounts specified in paragraph (5) shall be treated as though they were earnings.]

(10) [1Subject to regulation [217B(6)] (deduction of tax and contributions for self-employed earners),] in the case of any income taken into account for the purpose of calculating a person's income, there shall be disregarded—

(a) any amount payable by way of tax;

(b) any amount deducted by way of National Insurance Contributions under the 1992 Act or under the Social Security Contributions and Benefits (Northern Ireland) Act 1992;

(c) [2. . .].

[1(11) In the case of the earnings of self-employed earners, the amounts specified in paragraph (10) shall be taken into account in accordance with paragraph (4) or, as the case may be, paragraph (10) of regulation 13 of the Computation of Earnings Regulations, as having effect in the case of state pension credit.]

Amendments

1. State Pension Credit (Consequential, Transitional and Miscellaneous Provisions) Regulations 2002 (SI 2002/3019) reg.23(h) (October 6, 2003).
2. State Pension Credit (Consequential, Transitional and Miscellaneous Provisions) (No.2) Regulations 2002 (SI 2002/3197) reg.2 and Sch. para.5 (October 6, 2003).
3. Social Security (Miscellaneous Amendments) Regulations 2009 (SI 2009/583) reg.5(3) (April 6, 2009).

Definitions

"claimant"—see SPCA 2002 s.17(1).
"Computation of Earnings Regulations"—see reg.1(2).
"income"—see SPCA 2002 s.17(1).

General Note

Paragraph (1)

This follows the precedent of income support by providing for the same simple method of converting payments of income into weekly equivalents (Income Support (General) Regulations 1987 (SI 1987/1967) reg.32(1)). This is subject to the special rules for irregular patterns of work (para.(2)) and for payments of royalties and other occasional payments (paras (4) and (5)). 4.59

In *R(PC) 3/08* the Commissioner rejected the Secretary of State's argument that "capital" has a special meaning in the state pension credit scheme. The

Commissioner held that the general rule applied, namely that a payment of income (there state retirement pension, paid four-weekly) did not metamorphose into capital until the expiry of a period equal in length to the period in respect of which it was paid. The Commissioner applied the general principle to that effect as stated in *R(IS)3/93*, notwithstanding the absence in the state pension credit scheme of an equivalent provision to reg.29(2) of the Income Support (General) Regulations 1987. The Commissioner held that the state pension credit system "must operate on an assumed notion of a period of attribution" (para.24).

See also *PS v Secretary of State for Work and Pensions (SPC)* [2016] UKUT 0021 (AAC), where the claimant had been paid arrears of his army pension in 2008, for a period going back to March 2006. The DWP subsequently sought to recover from the claimant an overpayment of pension credit, including the period from March 2006 to the date of receipt of the arrears. The First-tier Tribunal confirmed this decision. However, Judge Ward allowed the claimant's further appeal, ruling that for pension credit purposes income payable in arrears falls to be attributed *forward* from the date of receipt rather than *backwards* over the period in respect of which it was earned (see paras 14–17). In doing so Judge Ward followed *R(PC) 3/08* at para.24.

Paragraphs (2) and (3)

4.60 This is yet another variant on the various legislative measures devised to deal with the problematic question of accommodating those with irregular working patterns into a means-tested benefit system. The rule is modelled on but also departs from the traditional income support approach (see Income Support (General) Regulations 1987 (SI 1987/1967) reg.32(6)).

Paragraphs (4) and (5)

4.61 Royalties and other occasional payments are treated as paid in respect of a year, in contrast to the income support rule (Income Support (General) Regulations 1987 (SI 1987/1967) reg.30(2)).

Paragraph (6)

4.62 Any banking charges or commission payable when converting payments of income in other currencies into Sterling are disregarded (Sch.IV para.16).

Paragraph (7)

4.63 See the annotations to Sch.IV.

Paragraph (8)

4.64 Schedule V is divided into two Parts. Part I specifies those forms of capital which are to be disregarded for the purpose of calculating the claimant's income. This extensive list is modelled on Sch.10 to the Income Support (General) Regulations 1987 (SI 1987/1967). Part II contains a more limited list of categories of capital which are to be disregarded solely for the purposes of calculating notional income.

Paragraph (9)

4.65 This links to Sch.VI, which carries forward the standard £5, £10 and £20 disregards on earnings that apply in the income support scheme to the state pension credit system. However, there is no hours rule for state pension credit, so it matters not whether a pensioner is working under or over 16 hours a week.

Paragraph (10)

4.66 This is similar to the income support rule (see Income Support (General) Regulations 1987 (SI 1987/1967) reg.36(3)). The principal difference is that the income support rule applies to earnings, whereas this rule applies to all income. The income support rule permits a deduction from earnings representing 50 per cent of the amount of any occupational or personal pension scheme contributions. The parallel provision for state pension credit purposes is to be found in reg.17A(4A) below.

Paragraph (11)

See also reg.17B. 4.67

[[1]Treatment of final payments of income

17ZA.—(1) Save where regulation 13B applies, this regulation applies where— 4.68

(a) a claimant has been receiving a regular payment of income;

(b) that payment is coming to an end or has ended; and

(c) the claimant receives a payment of income whether as the last of the regular payments or following the last of them ("the final payment").

(2) For the purposes of regulation 17(1)—

(a) where the amount of the final payment is less than or equal to the amount of the preceding, or the last, regular payment, the whole amount shall be treated as being paid in respect of a period of the same length as that in respect of which that regular payment was made;

(b) where the amount of the final payment is greater than the amount of that regular payment—

(i) to the extent that it comprises (whether exactly or with an excess remaining) one or more multiples of that amount, each such multiple shall be treated as being paid in respect of a period of the same length as that in respect of which that regular payment was made; and

(ii) any excess shall be treated as paid in respect of a further period of the same length as that in respect of which that regular payment was made.

(3) A final payment referred to in paragraph (2)(a) shall, where not in fact paid on the date on which a regular payment would have been paid had it continued in payment, be treated as paid on that date.

(4) Each multiple and any excess referred to in paragraph (2)(b) shall be treated as paid on the dates on which a corresponding number of regular payments would have been made had they continued in payment.

(5) For the purposes of this regulation, a "regular payment" means a payment of income made in respect of a period—

(a) referred to in regulation 17(1)(a) or (b) on a regular date; or

(b) which is subject to the provisions of regulation 17(2).]

AMENDMENT

1. State Pension Credit (Miscellaneous Amendments) Regulations 2004 (SI 2004/647) reg.3(4) (April 5, 2004).

DEFINITIONS

"the final payment"—see para.(1)(c).
"regular payment"—see para.(5).

GENERAL NOTE

This regulation provides for the treatment of final payments of income. The rule applies whenever the claimant has been receiving a regular payment of income (a term which is wider than it first appears; see para.(5) and below), those payments come 4.69

to an end and a final payment is made (para.(1)). The basic rule is that where the final payment of income is less than or equal to the previous payment of income, then the whole of the final payment is attributed to the normal period for such payments (para.(2)(a); and see para.(3) for the date on which the final payment may be treated as paid). If, however, the final payment exceeds the usual or "regular payment", then it is treated as applying to a series of sequential periods, depending on the number of multiples involved (para.(2)(b); and see para.(4) for the dates on which such multiple payments may be treated as paid). Paragraph (5) defines "regular payment" by reference to reg.17(1) and (2); the effect of this is that irregular patterns of work may nevertheless give rise to a "regular payment" for the purpose of this provision (see reg.17(2)(b)(ii)).

[1Earnings of an employed earner

4.70 **17A.**—(1) For the purposes of state pension credit, the provisions of this regulation which relate to the earnings of employed earners, shall have effect in place of those prescribed for such earners in the Computation of Earnings Regulations.

(2) Subject to paragraphs [2(3), (4) and 4(A)], "earnings" in the case of employment as an employed earner, means any remuneration or profit derived from that employment and includes—

(a) any bonus or commission;

(b) any payment in lieu of remuneration except any periodic sum paid to a claimant on account of the termination of his employment by reason of redundancy;

(c) any payment in lieu of notice;

(d) any holiday pay;

(e) any payment by way of a retainer;

(f) any payment made by the claimant's employer in respect of expenses not wholly, exclusively and necessarily incurred in the performance of the duties of the employment, including any payment made by the claimant's employer in respect of—

(i) travelling expenses incurred by the claimant between his home and place of employment;

(ii) expenses incurred by the claimant under arrangements made for the care of a member of his family owing to the claimant's absence from home;

(g) the amount of any payment by way of a non-cash voucher which has been taken into account in the computation of a person's earnings in accordance with Part V of Schedule 3 to the Social Security (Contributions) Regulations 2001;

(h) statutory sick pay and statutory maternity pay payable by the employer under the 1992 Act;

[4 (i) [7 . . .] statutory paternity pay payable under Part 12ZA of the 1992 Act;

(ia) [7 . . .];]

[6 (ib) statutory shared parental pay payable under Part 12ZC of the 1992 Act;]

(j) statutory adoption pay payable under Part 12ZB of the 1992 Act;

(k) any sums payable under a contract of service—

(i) for incapacity for work due to sickness or injury; or

(ii) by reason of pregnancy or confinement.

(3) "Earnings" shall not include—

(a) subject to paragraph (4), any payment in kind;

(b) any payment in respect of expenses wholly, exclusively and necessarily incurred in the performance of the duties of the employment;
(c) any occupational pension;
(d) any lump sum payment made under the Iron and Steel Re-adaptation Benefits Scheme;
[[2](e) any payment of compensation made pursuant to an award by an employment tribunal in respect of unfair dismissal or unlawful discrimination.]
[[3] (f) any payment in respect of expenses arising out of the [[5] claimant participating as a service user]

(4) Paragraph (3)(a) shall not apply in respect of any non-cash voucher referred to in paragraph (2)(g).

[[2](4A) One half of any sum paid by a claimant by way of a contribution towards an occupational pension scheme or a personal pension scheme shall, for the purpose of calculating his earnings in accordance with this regulation, be disregarded.]

(5) In this regulation "employed earner" means a person who is gainfully employed in Great Britain either under a contract of service, or in an office (including elective office) with emoluments chargeable to income tax under Schedule E.]

AMENDMENTS

1. State Pension Credit (Consequential, Transitional and Miscellaneous Provisions) Regulations 2002 (SI 2002/3019) reg.23(i) (October 6, 2003).
2. State Pension Credit (Consequential, Transitional and Miscellaneous Provisions) (No.2) Regulations 2002 (SI 2002/3197) reg.3(1) (October 6, 2003).
3. Social Security (Miscellaneous Amendments) (No.4) Regulations 2009 (SI 2009/2655) reg.5(3) (October 26, 2009).
4. Social Security (Miscellaneous Amendments) Regulations 2012 (SI 2012/757) reg.5(4) (April 1, 2012).
5. Social Security (Miscellaneous Amendments) Regulations 2014 (SI 2014/591) reg.7(3) (April 28, 2014).
6. Shared Parental Leave and Statutory Shared Parental Pay (Consequential Amendments to Subordinate Legislation) Order 2014 (SI 2014/3255) art.10(4)(c) (December 31, 2014).
7. Shared Parental Leave and Statutory Shared Parental Pay (Consequential Amendments to Subordinate Legislation) Order 2014 (SI 2014/3255) art.10(4)(a) and (b) (April 5, 2015).

DEFINITIONS

"claimant"—see para.(2)(a).
"Computation of Earnings Regulations"—see reg.1(2).
"employed earner"—see para.(5).
"occupational pension scheme"—see SPCA 2002 s.17(1).
"personal pension scheme"—see *ibid.*

GENERAL NOTE

This provides a comprehensive definition of "earnings" for employed earners who claim state pension credit which is independent of the rules contained in the Social Security (Computation of Earnings) Regulations 1996 (SI 1996/2745). In contrast, reg.17B below specifically applies the 1996 Regulations to the assessment of the earnings of *self*-employed earners, subject to certain modifications. The rules governing employed earners in this regulation follow closely (but do not entirely mirror) those that apply to the definition of an employed earner's earnings for the purposes of income support (see Income Support (General) Regulations 1987 (SI 1987/1967) reg.35). 4.71

[1Earnings of self-employed earners

4.72 **17B.**—(1) For the purposes of state pension credit, the provisions of the Computation of Earnings Regulations in their application to the earnings of self-employed earners, shall have effect in so far as provided by this regulation.

(2) In their application to state pension credit, regulations 11 to 14 of the Computation of Earnings Regulations shall have effect as if—

[2(za) "board and lodging accommodation" has the same meaning as in [3 regulation 1(2)];]

(a) "claimant" referred to a person claiming state pension credit and any partner of the claimant;

(b) "personal pension scheme" referred to a personal pension scheme—

(i) as defined in section 1 of the Pension Schemes Act 1993; or

(ii) as defined in section 1 of the Pension Schemes (Northern Ireland) Act 1993.

(3) In regulation 11 (calculation of earnings of self-employed earners), paragraph (1) shall have effect, but as if the words "Except where paragraph (2) applies" were omitted.

(4) In regulation 12 (earnings of self-employed earners).

(a) paragraph (1) shall have effect;

(b) [5 the following paragraph shall be added after paragraph (1)]

"(2) Earnings does not include—

(a) where a claimant occupies a dwelling as his home and he provides in that dwelling board and lodging accommodation for which payment is made, those payments;

[5 (b) any payment made by a local authority to a claimant with whom a person is accommodated by virtue of arrangements made under—

(i) section 23(2)(a) of the Children Act 1989 (provision of accommodation and maintenance for a child whom they are looking after),

(ii) section 26 of the Children (Scotland) Act 1995 (manner of provision of accommodation to child looked after by local authority), or

(iii) regulations 33 or 51 of the Looked After Children (Scotland) Regulations 2009 (fostering and kinship care allowances and fostering allowances);]

(c) any payment made "by a voluntary organisation in accordance with section 59(1)(a) of the Children Act 1989 (provision of accommodation by voluntary organisations);

(d) any payment made to the claimant or his partner for a person ('the person concerned') who is not normally a member of the claimant's household but is temporarily in his care, by—

(i) a health authority;

(ii) a local authority;

(iii) a voluntary organisation;

(iv) the person concerned pursuant to section 26(3A) of the National Assistance Act 1948; [4 . . .]

[6 (iva) a clinical commissioning group established under section 14D of the National Health Service Act 2006;

(ivb) the National Health Service Commissioning Board; [7 . . .]]

(v) [6 . . .]

[4 (vi) a Local Health Board established under section 16BA of the National Health Service Act 1977 or established by an order made under section 11 of the Health Service (Wales) Act;]

[7"or

(vii) the person concerned where the payment is for the provision of accommodation in respect of the meeting of that person's needs under section 18 or 19 of the Care Act 2014 (duty and power to meet needs for care and support);]

(e) any sports award [2 being an award made by one of the Sports Councils named in section 23(2) of the National Lottery etc. Act 1993 out of sums allocated to it for distribution under that section]."

(5) In regulation 13 (calculation of net profit of self-employed earners)—

(a) for paragraphs (1) to (3), the following provision shall have effect—

"(1) For the purposes of regulation 11 (calculation of earnings of self-employed earners), the earnings of a claimant to be taken into account shall be—

(a) in the case of a self-employed earner who is engaged in employment on his own account, the net profit derived from that employment;

(b) in the case of a self-employed earner whose employment is carried on in partnership, his share of the net profit derived from that employment less—

(i) an amount in respect of income tax and of social security contributions payable under the Contributions and Benefits Act calculated in accordance with regulation 14 (deduction of tax and contributions for self-employed earners); and

(ii) one half of any premium paid in the period that is relevant under regulation 11 in respect of a retirement annuity contract or a personal pension scheme";

(b) paragraphs (4) to (12) shall have effect.

(6) Regulation 14 (deduction of tax and contributions for self-employed earners) shall have effect.]

AMENDMENTS

1. State Pension Credit (Consequential, Transitional and Miscellaneous Provisions) Regulations 2002 (SI 2002/3019) reg.23(i) (October 6, 2003).

2. State Pension Credit (Consequential, Transitional and Miscellaneous Provisions) (No.2) Regulations 2002 (SI 2002/3197) reg.3(2) (October 6, 2003).

3. Social Security (Miscellaneous Amendments) (No.2) Regulations 2005 (SI 2005/2465) reg.6(4) (October 3, 2005).

4. Social Security (Miscellaneous Amendments) (No.7) Regulations 2008 (SI 2008/3157) reg.4(4) (January 5, 2009).

5. Social Security (Miscellaneous Amendments) (No.5) Regulations 2010 (SI 2010/2429) reg.6 (November 1, 2010).

6. National Treatment Agency (Abolition) and the Health and Social Care Act 2012 (Consequential, Transitional and Saving Provisions) Order 2013 (SI 2013/235) art.11 and Sch.2 para.54(3) (April 1, 2013) (England and Wales only).

7. Care Act 2014 (Consequential Amendments) (Secondary Legislation) Order 2015 (SI 2015/643) reg.19(1) and (2) (April 1, 2015).

DEFINITIONS

"board and lodging accommodation"—see para.(2)(za).
"claimant"—see para.(2)(a).
"Computation of Earnings Regulations"—see reg.1(2).
"dwelling occupied as the home"—see *ibid.*
"personal pension scheme"—see para.(2)(b).
"retirement annuity contract"—see SPCA 2002 s.16(3).

GENERAL NOTE

4.73 The earnings of self-employed earners for the purposes of state pension credit are calculated in accordance with the Social Security (Computation of Earnings) Regulations 1996 (SI 1996/2745) (on which see Vol.I in this series), subject to the modifications made by this regulation. Thus the special rule relating to royalties does not apply (para.(3)), as special provision is made for such payments for the purposes of state pension credit (see reg.17(4) and (5)). There is also a more extensive list of disregards to be applied when calculating earnings (para.(4)).

In *CPC/3373/2007* Deputy Commissioner Poynter held that the state pension credit scheme does not permit a claimant to offset a loss from self-employment income against his other sources of income. There is no equivalent within the state pension credit scheme to what used to be s.380 of the Income and Corporation Taxes Act 1988 (now Income Tax Act 2007 s.64). Accordingly, where a claimant makes a loss on self-employed income, the net profit for the purposes of state pension credit is nil, and not a negative figure. But note also that on the particular facts of that case the Deputy Commissioner held that the Secretary of State had not shown a relevant changes of circumstances such as to justify a supersession of the award of benefit to the claimant.

Notional income

4.74 **18.**—[2 (1) A claimant who has attained the qualifying age shall be treated as possessing the amount of any retirement pension income—

(a) to which section 16(1)[7(za)] to (e) applies,
(b) for which no claim has been made, and
(c) to which the claimant might expect to be entitled if a claim for it were made,

but only from the date on which that income could be expected to be acquired if a claim for it were made.

(1A) Paragraph (1) is subject to paragraphs (1B) [3, (1CA) and 1(CB)].

(1B) Where a claimant—

(a) has deferred entitlement to retirement pension income to which section 16(1)(a) to (c) applies for at least 12 months, and
(b) would have been entitled to make an election under Schedule 5 or 5A to the 1992 Act or under Schedule 1 to the Graduated Retirement Benefit Regulations,

he shall be treated for the purposes of paragraph (1) as possessing the amount of retirement pension income to which he might expect to be entitled if he were to elect to receive a lump sum.

[3 (1C) Paragraphs (1CA) and (1CB) apply for the purposes of paragraph (1) (or, where applicable, paragraph (1) read with paragraph (1B)).

(1CA) Where a benefit or allowance in payment in respect of the claimant would be adjusted under the Social Security (Overlapping Benefits) Regulations 1979 if the retirement pension income had been claimed, he shall be treated as possessing that income minus the benefit or allowance in payment.

(1CB) Where a benefit or allowance in payment in respect of the claimant would require an adjustment to be made under the Social Security (Overlapping Benefits) Regulations 1979 to the amount of retirement pension income payable had it been claimed, he shall be treated as possessing that retirement pension income minus the adjustment which would be made to it.]

(1D) A claimant who has attained the qualifying age shall be treated as possessing income from an occupational pension scheme which he elected to defer, but only from the date on which it could be expected to be acquired if a claim for it were made.]

(2) Where a person, [5 who has attained the qualifying age], is a person entitled to money purchase benefits under an occupational pension scheme or a personal pension scheme, or is a party to, or a person deriving entitlement to a pension under, a retirement annuity contract, and—

(a) he fails to purchase an annuity with the funds available in that scheme where—

(i) he defers, in whole or in part, the payment of any income which would have been payable to him by his pension fund holder;

(ii) he fails to take any necessary action to secure that the whole of any income which would be payable to him by his pension fund holder upon his applying for it, is so paid; or

(iii) income withdrawal is not available to him under that scheme; or

(b) in the case of a retirement annuity contract, he fails to purchase an annuity with the funds available under that contract,

the amount of any income foregone shall be treated as possessed by him, but only from the date on which it could be expected to be acquired were an application for it to be made.

(3) The amount of any income foregone in a case to which either head (i) or (ii) of paragraph (2)(a) applies shall be the maximum amount of income which may be withdrawn from the fund.

(4) The amount of any income foregone in a case to which either head (iii) of paragraph (2)(a) or paragraph (2)(b) applies shall be the income that the claimant could have received without purchasing an annuity had the funds held under the relevant scheme or retirement annuity contract been held under a personal pension scheme or occupational pension scheme where income withdrawal was available and shall be determined in the manner specified in paragraph (3).

(5) In paragraph (2), "money purchase benefits" has the meaning it has in the Pensions Scheme Act 1993.

(6) [1 Subject to [4 the following paragraphs],] a person shall be treated as possessing income of which he has deprived himself for the purpose of securing entitlement to state pension credit or increasing the amount of that benefit.

[1 (7) Paragraph (6) shall not apply in respect of the amount of an increase of pension or benefit where a person, having made an election in favour of that increase of pension or benefit under Schedule 5 or 5A to the 1992 Act or under Schedule 1 to the Graduated Retirement Benefit Regulations, changes that election in accordance with regulations made under Schedule 5 or 5A to that Act in favour of a lump sum.

[7 (7ZA) Paragraph (6) shall not apply in respect of the amount of an increase of pension where a person, having made a choice in favour of that increase of pension under section 8(2) of the Pensions Act 2014, alters that choice in favour of a lump sum, in accordance with Regulations made under section 8(7) of that Act.

(7ZB) Paragraph (6) shall not apply in respect of the amount of an increase of pension where a person, having made a choice in favour of that increase of pension in accordance with Regulations made under section 10 of the Pensions Act 2014 which include provision corresponding or similar to section 8(2) of that Act, alters that choice in favour of a lump sum, in accordance with Regulations made under section 10 of that Act which include provision corresponding or similar to Regulations made under section 8(7).]

[4 (7A) Paragraph (6) shall not apply in respect of any amount of income other than earnings, or earnings of an employed earner, arising out of the [6 claimant participating as a service user]

(8) In paragraph (7), "lump sum" means a lump sum under Schedule 5 or 5A to the 1992 Act or under Schedule 1 to the Graduated Retirement Benefit Regulations.]

[7 (8A) In paragraph (7ZA), "lump sum" means a lump sum under section 8 of the Pensions Act 2014.

(8B) In paragraph (7ZB), "lump sum" means a lump sum under Regulations made under section 10 of the Pensions Act 2014.]

[2 (9) For the purposes of paragraph (6), a person is not to be regarded as depriving himself of income where—

(a) his rights to benefits under a registered pension scheme are extinguished and in consequence of this he receives a payment from the scheme, and

(b) that payment is a trivial commutation lump sum within the meaning given by paragraph 7 of Schedule 29 to the Finance Act 2004.

(10) In paragraph (9), "registered pension scheme" has the meaning given in section 150(2) of the Finance Act 2004.]

AMENDMENTS

1. Social Security (Deferral of Retirement Pensions, Shared Additional Pension and Graduated Retirement Benefit) (Miscellaneous Provisions) Regulations 2005 (SI 2005/2677) reg.13(3) (April 6, 2006).

2. Social Security (Miscellaneous Amendments) (No.4) Regulations 2006 (SI 2006/2378) reg.14(4) (October 2, 2006).

3. Social Security (Miscellaneous Amendments) (No.5) Regulations 2007 (SI 2007/2618) reg.10(3) (October 1, 2007).

4. Social Security (Miscellaneous Amendments) (No.4) Regulations 2009 (SI 2009/2655) reg.5(4) (October 26, 2009).

5. Social Security (Miscellaneous Amendments) (No.2) Regulations 2010 (SI 2010/641) reg.6(6) (April 6, 2010).

6. Social Security (Miscellaneous Amendments) Regulations 2014 (SI 2014/591) reg.7(4) (April 28, 2014).

7. Pensions Act 2014 (Consequential, Supplementary and Incidental Amendments) Order 2015 (SI 2015/985) art.24(2) (April 6, 2016).

DEFINITIONS

"claimant"—see SPCA 2002 s.17(1).
"income"—see *ibid*.
"lump sum"—see paras (8A) and (8B).
"money purchase benefits"—see para.(5).

"occupational pension scheme"—see SPCA 2002 s.17(1).
"pension fund holder"—see reg.1(2).
"personal pension scheme"—see SPCA 2002 s.17(1).
"qualifying age"—see SPCA 2002 s.1(6).
"retirement annuity contract"—see *ibid.*, and s.16(3).
"retirement pension income"—see SPCA 2002 ss.16 and 17(1).

General Note

This regulation provides for three types of notional income: certain forms of pension income which have not been applied for or have been deferred (para.(1)), income foregone under a money purchase benefits pension scheme or under a retirement annuity contract (paras (2)–(5)), and cases of income deprivation for the purpose of securing entitlement to (or increasing the amount of) state pension credit (para.(6)). Note also that Pt II of Sch.V lists various forms of capital which are to be disregarded in determining a person's notional income. **4.75**

Paragraph (1)

The general rule is that pension income which the claimant could expect to receive on application is to be deemed to be notional income. The reference to SPCA 2002 s.16(1)(za)–(e) has the effect of confining this provision to various categories of state retirement pension income under the SSCBA 1992 or its Northern Ireland equivalent. The inclusion of the cross-reference to s.16(1)(za) in subs.(1)(a) means that for the purposes of pension credit a person is to be treated as receiving their new state pension while they are deferring it. Notional income also includes income from an occupational pension scheme which the claimant has chosen to defer. Other forms of income from private pension arrangements may be caught by paras (2)–(5). **4.76**

Paragraphs (2)–(5)

These provisions mirror those that apply to income support (Income Support (General) Regulations 1987 (SI 1987/1967) reg.42(2A)–(2C); see further *BRG v SSWP (SPC)* [2014] UKUT 246 (AAC). **4.77**

Paragraph (6)

This is expressed in the same terms as the notional income and notional capital rules for income support, and so the same principles apply ((Income Support (General) Regulations 1987 (SI 1987/1967) regs 42(1) and 51(1)). **4.78**

Paragraphs (7ZA) and (7ZB)

The effect of these provisions is that a person who changes their choice of a weekly increase to a lump sum in respect of the new state pension is not penalised by being treated as still possessing the extra income. See further paras.(8A) and (8B) for definitions. **4.78A**

[1Calculation of capital in the United Kingdom

19.—Capital which a claimant possesses in the United Kingdom shall be calculated at its current market or surrender value less— **4.79**

(a) where there would be expenses attributable to sale, 10 per cent; and
(b) the amount of any encumbrance secured on it.]

Amendment

1. Social Security (Miscellaneous Amendments) (No.5) Regulations 2007 (SI 2007/2618) reg.10(4) (October 1, 2007).

Definitions

"capital"—see SPCA 2002 s.17(1).
"claimant"—see *ibid.*

General Note

4.80 This is in the same terms as the parallel provision in the income support scheme (see Income Support (General) Regulations 1987 (SI 1987/1967) reg.49.

Calculation of capital outside the United Kingdom

4.81 **20.**—Capital which a claimant possesses in a country outside the United Kingdom shall be calculated—

(a) in a case where there is no prohibition in that country against the transfer to the United Kingdom of an amount equal to its current market or surrender value in that country, at that value;
(b) in a case where there is such a prohibition, at the price which it would realise if sold in the United Kingdom to a willing buyer,

less, where there would be expenses attributable to sale, 10 per cent, and the amount of any encumbrance secured on it.

Definitions

"capital"—see SPCA 2002 s.17(1).
"claimant"—see *ibid.*

General Note

4.82 This is in the same terms as the parallel provision in the income support scheme (see Income Support (General) Regulations 1987 (SI 1987/1967) reg.50).

Notional capital

4.83 **21.**—[2(1) A claimant shall be treated as possessing capital of which he has deprived himself for the purpose of securing entitlement to state pension credit or increasing the amount of that benefit except to the extent that the capital which he is treated as possessing is reduced in accordance with regulation 22 (diminishing notional capital rule).]

[3 (2) A person who disposes of a capital resource for the purpose of—

(a) reducing or paying a debt owed by the claimant; or
(b) purchasing goods or services if the expenditure was reasonable in the circumstances of the claimant's case,

shall be regarded as not depriving himself of it.]

[1(3) Where a claimant stands in relation to a company in a position analogous to that of a sole owner or partner in the business of that company, he shall be treated as if he were such sole owner or partner and in such a case—

(a) the value of his holding in that company shall, notwithstanding regulation 19 (calculation of capital), be disregarded; and
(b) he shall, subject to paragraph (4), be treated as possessing an amount of capital equal to the value or, as the case may be, his share of the value of the capital of that company and the foregoing provisions of this Chapter shall apply for the purposes of calculating that amount as if it were actual capital which he does possess.

(4) For so long as a claimant undertakes activities in the course of the business of the company, the amount which he is treated as possessing under paragraph (3) shall be disregarded.

(5) Where under this regulation a person is treated as possessing capital, the amount of that capital shall be calculated in accordance with the provisions of this Part as if it were actual capital which he does possess.]

AMENDMENTS

1. State Pension Credit (Consequential, Transitional and Miscellaneous Provisions) Regulations 2002 (SI 2002/3019) reg.23(j) (October 6, 2003).
2. State Pension Credit (Consequential, Transitional and Miscellaneous Provisions) (No.2) Regulations 2002 (SI 2002/3197) reg.2 and Sch. para.6 (October 6, 2003).
3. State Pension Credit (Miscellaneous Amendments) Regulations 2004 (SI 2004/647) reg.3(5) (April 5, 2004).

DEFINITIONS

"capital"—see SPCA 2002 s.17(1).
"claimant"—see *ibid.*

GENERAL NOTE

Readers who are well acquainted with the income support system will be familiar with the concept of notional capital, that is capital which the claimant is deemed to possess even though he or she does not actually have such resources. This is, therefore, essentially an anti-avoidance provision in the context of means-tested benefits. Section 15(6) of the SPCA 2002 (which mirrors SSCBA 1992 s.163(5)) provides the legislative authority for such a rule in the state pension credit scheme. The notional capital rule enshrined in this regulation contains some parallels with the equivalent rule in the income support scheme (Income Support (General) Regulations 1987 (SI 1987/1967) reg.51), but is also different. In particular, the state pension credit rule operates only where there is a deprivation of capital with a view to claiming or increasing entitlement to benefit (para.(1)) or where the claimant is a sole trader or a partner in a business which is a limited company (paras (3) and (4)). There is, therefore, no equivalent to the income support rules governing failures to apply for capital which is available, payments to third parties by someone else on the claimant's behalf or retention of capital received on behalf of a third party (Income Support (General) Regulations 1987 (SI 1987/1967) reg.51(2) and (3)). 4.84

See also *MC v Secretary of State for Work and Pensions* [2010] UKUT 29 (AAC) for guidance on how the presumption of a resulting trust may operate in the context of a transaction between family members.

Paragraph (1)

The general rule is expressed in similar terms to Income Support (General) Regulations 1987 (SI 1987/1967) reg.51(1). The Secretary of State must accordingly show that: (1) the claimant has deprived him or herself of actual capital, and (2) this was done with the purpose of securing or increasing entitlement to state pension credit. As to (1), the traditional approach has been that "deprive" does not carry a special legal meaning and is a matter of ordinary English (*R(SB) 38/85, R(SB) 40/85*). However, these authorities will have to be applied with some care in the context of state pension credit as, unlike in the income support scheme, para.(2) below gives specific examples of what is not to be regarded as a deprivation. The supplementary benefit and income support case law on the claimant's purpose in making the deprivation will presumably apply equally here given the statutory language is the same in this respect (see commentary at para.2.364 above). There is, however, no express exception for capital for personal injuries compensation held in trust or administered by the court (contrast Income Support (General) Regulations 1987 (SI 1987/1967) reg.51(1)(a) and (c)). 4.85

Paragraph (2)

4.86 This is an interesting provision which has no direct parallel in the analogous rule that applies under the income support scheme (Income Support (General) Regulations 1987 (SI 1987/1967) reg.51). That said, it appears to be an attempt to illustrate what is not to be regarded as an act of deprivation. Thus, a disposal for the purpose of either reducing or paying a debt owed by the claimant, or in purchasing goods or services "if the expenditure was reasonable in the circumstances of the claimant's case", is not to be seen as a deprivation. Under the income support scheme, such disposals would be seen as a deprivation and the argument would then revolve around the claimant's purpose in making such a disposal. Typically the claimant would argue that the payment was solely for some other purpose, and not with a view to claiming or increasing entitlement to benefit. The position under the state pension credit scheme would appear to be different and perhaps weighted more in favour of the claimant. If the claimant is able to demonstrate that one of the circumstances in para.(2) applies, then there has been no deprivation and the issue as to the claimant's purpose need not be explored. This construction is strengthened by the repeal of the qualifying phrase "Without prejudice to the generality of paragraph (1)" as from April 5, 2004. That amendment also repealed the provision which automatically deemed a disposal by way of a gift to a third party to be a deprivation. However, it remains open to decision-makers and tribunals to find that such a gift was a deprivation made with the intent of securing (or increasing) entitlement to pension credit.

Paragraphs (3) and (4)

4.87 These two paragraphs establish an artificial method for dealing with one person companies and analogous enterprises. In summary, the value of the individual's shareholding itself is disregarded (para.(3)(a)) but the claimant is treated as possessing a proportionate share of the company's capital (para.(3)(b)). However, so long as the individual undertakes activities in the course of the business, the amount produced by para.(3)(b) is disregarded (para.(4)). See further the commentary on the parallel provisions in reg.51(4) and (5) of the Income Support (General) Regulations 1987 (SI 1987/1967).

Paragraph (5)

4.88 As the claimant's capital is to be calculated as though it were actual capital, it follows that notional capital is assumed to yield a weekly income on the basis set out in reg.15(6). It also means that any relevant capital disregards under reg.17(8) and Sch.V must be applied to the notional capital (by analogy with *CIS/231/1991*).

Diminishing notional capital rule

4.89 **22.**—(1) Where a claimant is treated as possessing capital under regulation 21(1) (notional capital), the amount which he is treated as possessing—

(a) in the case of a week that is subsequent to—
  (i) the relevant week in respect of which the conditions set out in paragraph (2) are satisfied, or
  (ii) a week which follows that relevant week and which satisfies those conditions,

shall be reduced by an amount determined under paragraph (2);

(b) in the case of a week in respect of which sub-paragraph (1)(a) does not apply but where—
  (i) that week is a week subsequent to the relevant week, and
  (ii) that relevant week is a week in which the condition in paragraph (3) is satisfied,

shall be reduced by the amount determined under paragraph (3).

(2) This paragraph applies to a benefit week where the claimant satisfies the conditions that—

(a) he is in receipt of state pension credit; and
(b) but for regulation [1 21(1)], he would have received an additional amount of state pension credit in that benefit week;

and in such a case, the amount of the reduction for the purposes of paragraph (1)(a) shall be equal to that additional amount.

(3) Subject to paragraph (4), for the purposes of paragraph (1)(b) the condition is that the claimant would have been entitled to state pension credit in the relevant week, but for regulation [1 21(1)], and in such a case the amount of the reduction shall be equal to the aggregate of—

(a) the amount of state pension credit to which the claimant would have been entitled in the relevant week but for regulation [1 21(1)];
(b) the amount of housing benefit (if any) equal to the difference between his maximum housing benefit and the amount (if any) of housing benefit which he is awarded in respect of the benefit week, within the meaning of regulation 2(1) of the Housing Benefit (General) Regulations 1987 (interpretation), which includes the last day of the relevant week;
(c) the amount of council tax benefit (if any) equal to the difference between his maximum council tax benefit and the amount (if any) of council tax benefit which he is awarded in respect of the benefit week which includes the last day of the relevant week, and for this purpose "benefit week" [2 means a period of 7 consecutive days beginning on a Monday and ending on a Sunday].

(4) The amount determined under paragraph (3) shall be re-determined under that paragraph if the claimant makes a further claim for state pension credit and the conditions in paragraph (5) are satisfied, and in such a case—

(a) sub-paragraphs (a) to (c) of paragraph (3) shall apply as if for the words "relevant week" there were substituted the words "relevant subsequent week"; and
(b) subject to paragraph (6), the amount as re-determined shall have effect from the first week following the relevant subsequent week in question.

(5) The conditions are that—

(a) a further claim is made 26 or more weeks after—
    (i) the date on which the claimant made a claim for state pension credit in respect of which he was first treated as possessing the capital in question under regulation [1 21(1)]; or
    (ii) in a case where there has been at least one re-determination in accordance with paragraph (4), the date on which he last made a claim for state pension credit which resulted in the weekly amount being re-determined; or
    (iii) the date on which he last ceased to be in receipt of state pension credit, whichever last occurred; and
(b) the claimant would have been entitled to state pension credit but for regulation [1 21(1)].

(6) The amount as re-determined pursuant to paragraph (4) shall not have effect if it is less than the amount which applied in that case immediately before the re-determination and in such a case the higher amount shall continue to have effect.

(7) For the purpose of this regulation—

(a) "relevant week" means the benefit week in which the capital in question of which the claimant has deprived himself within the meaning of regulation [[1]21(1)]—

(i) was first taken into account for the purpose of determining his entitlement to state pension credit; or

(ii) was taken into account on a subsequent occasion for the purpose of determining or re-determining his entitlement to state pension credit on that subsequent occasion and that determination or re-determination resulted in his beginning to receive, or ceasing to receive, state pension credit;

and where more than one benefit week is identified by reference to heads (i) and (ii) of this sub-paragraph the later or latest such benefit week;

(b) "relevant subsequent week" means the benefit week which includes the day on which the further claim or, if more than one further claim had been made, the last such claim was made.

AMENDMENTS

1. State Pension Credit (Consequential, Transitional and Miscellaneous Provisions) (No.2) Regulations 2002 (SI 2002/3197) reg.2 and Sch. para.7 (October 6, 2003).

2. Council Tax Benefit Abolition (Consequential Provision) Regulations 2013 (SI 2013/458) reg.4 and Sch.2 para.6 (April 1, 2013).

DEFINITIONS

"benefit week"—see reg.1(2).
"capital"—see SPCA 2002 s.17(1).
"claimant"—see *ibid.*
"relevant week"—see para.(7)(a).
"relevant subsequent week"—see para.7(b).

GENERAL NOTE

4.90 This diminishing notional capital rule is, in all material respects, identical to that which operates under the income support scheme (Income Support (General) Regulations 1987 (SI 1987/1967) reg.51A). Thus if the amount of notional capital has the effect of removing entitlement to state pension credit altogether, owing to the application of the tariff income rule in reg.15(6) above, that notional capital is to be treated as reducing each week in accordance with para.(1)(b) and (3). In such a case the weekly reduction is by a sum representing the aggregate of the state pension credit which would have been received in the absence of such notional capital plus the proportion of rent and council tax not met by housing benefit and council tax benefit respectively. In other cases, the interaction of the notional capital rule and the tariff income rule will reduce rather than extinguish entitlement to state pension credit. In this type of situation the notional capital is to be treated as reducing each week by the amount by which the state pension credit would be increased in the absence of such notional capital (para.(1)(a) and (2)). Paragraphs (4)–(6) provide for redetermination and recalculation in the event of a fresh claim being made.

Capital jointly held

4.91 **23.**—Where a claimant and one or more persons are beneficially entitled in possession to any capital asset they shall be treated as if each of them were entitled in possession to the whole beneficial interest therein in an equal share and the foregoing provisions of this Part shall apply for the purposes of calculating the amount of capital which the claimant is treated as possessing as if it were actual capital which the claimant does possess.

Definitions

"capital"—see SPCA 2002 s.17(1).
"claimant"—see *ibid.*

General Note

This provision is essentially in the same terms as the parallel and notoriously problematic provision in the income support scheme (see Income Support (General) Regulations 1987 (SI 1987/1967) reg.52). For a valuable reminder that in cases where capital is held jointly "the market value of such an interest in circumstances such as these is not by any means the same thing as half the entire value of the freehold with vacant possession", see *AM v SSWP* [2010] UKUT 134 (AAC), para.5, applying *R(IS) 5/07*. However, its impact in the context of state pension credit is likely to be much less as there is no capital rule as such. It will, however, have effect for the purpose of calculating the value of the claimant's capital for the purpose of attributing the deemed tariff income under reg.15(6). **4.92**

Income paid to third parties

24.—(1) Any payment of income, other than a payment specified in [1 paragraphs (2) or (3)], to a third party in respect of the claimant shall be treated as possessed by the claimant. **4.93**

(2) Paragraph (1) shall not apply in respect of a payment of income made under an occupational pension scheme or in respect of a pension or other periodical payment made under a personal pension scheme where—

(a) a bankruptcy order has been made in respect of the person in respect of whom the payment has been made or, to Scotland, the estate of that person is subject to sequestration or a judicial factor has been appointed on that person's estate under section 41 of the Solicitors (Scotland) Act 1980;
(b) the payment is made to the trustee in bankruptcy or any other person acting on behalf of the creditors; and
(c) the person referred to in sub-paragraph (a) and his partner does not possess, or is not treated as possessing, any other income apart from that payment.

[1 (3) Paragraph (1) shall not apply in respect of any payment of income arising out of the [2 claimant participating as a service user]

Amendments

1. Social Security (Miscellaneous Amendments) (No.3) Regulations 2011 (2011/2425) reg.15(4) (October 31, 2011).
2. Social Security (Miscellaneous Amendments) Regulations 2014 (SI 2014/591) reg.7(5) (April 28, 2014).

Definitions

"claimant"—see SPCA 2002 s.17(1).

"income"—see SPCA 2002 ss.15 and 17(1).
"occupational pension scheme"—see SPCA 2002 s.17(1).
"partner"—reg.1(3).
"personal pension scheme"—see *ibid.*

General Note

4.94 The claimant is deemed to possess income which is paid to a third party by someone in respect of the claimant. This is subject to the exceptions set out in para.(2), which is in identical terms to regs 42(ZA)(d) and 51(3A)(c) of the Income Support (General) Regulations 1987 (SI 1987/1967), which apply to notional income and notional capital respectively for income support purposes.

[1 Rounding of fractions

4.95 **24A.**—Where any calculation under this Part results in a fraction of a penny that fraction shall, if it would be to the claimant's advantage, be treated as a penny; otherwise it shall be disregarded.]

Amendment

1. State Pension Credit (Consequential, Transitional and Miscellaneous Provisions) Regulations 2002 (SI 2002/3019) reg.23(k) (October 6, 2003).

General Note

4.96 This reflects the normal rule for means-tested benefits (see Income Support (General) Regulations 1987 (SI 1987/1967) reg.27).

Part IV

Loss of benefit

Loss of benefit

4.97 **25.**—[*Omitted.*]

General Note

4.98 This regulation amends the Social Security (Loss of Benefits) Regulations 2001 (SI 2001/4022); the relevant changes are incorporated in Vol.III in this series.

SCHEDULES

SCHEDULE I **Regulation 6(4)**

Part I

Circumstances in which persons are treated as being or not being severely disabled

Severe disablement

4.99 **1.**—(1) For the purposes of regulation 6(4) (additional amounts for persons severely disabled), the claimant is to be treated as being severely disabled if, and only if—

(a) in the case of a claimant who has no partner—

(i) he is in receipt of attendance allowance [7, the care component of disability living allowance at the highest or middle rate prescribed in accordance with section 72(3) of the 1992 Act or the daily living component of personal independence payment at the standard or enhanced rate in accordance with section 78(3) of the 2012 Act [8 or armed forces independence payment]]; and

(ii) no person who has attained the age of 18 is normally residing with the claimant, nor is the claimant normally residing with such a person, other than a person to whom paragraph 2 applies; and

(iii) no person is entitled to and in receipt of an allowance under section 70 of the 1992 Act ([2 carer's allowance]) [10 , or has an award of universal credit which includes the carer element,] in respect of caring for him;

(b) in the case of a claimant who has a partner—

(i) both partners are in receipt of attendance allowance [7, the care component of disability living allowance at the highest or middle rate prescribed in accordance with section 72(3) of the 1992 Act or the daily living component of personal independence payment at the standard or enhanced rate in accordance with section 78(3) of the 2012 Act [8 or armed forces independence payment]]; and

(ii) no person who has attained the age of 18 is normally residing with the partners, nor are the partners normally residing with such a person, other than a person to whom paragraph 2 applies;

and either a person is entitled to, and in receipt of, an allowance under section 70 of the 1992 Act [10, or has an award of universal credit which includes the carer element,] in respect of caring for one only of the partners or, as the case may be, no person is entitled to, and in receipt of, such an allowance [10 under section 70, or has an award of universal credit which includes the carer element,] in respect of caring for either partner;

(c) in the case of a claimant who has a partner and to whom head (b) does not apply—

(i) either the claimant or his partner is in receipt of attendance allowance [7, the care component of disability living allowance at the highest or middle rate prescribed in accordance with section 72(3) of the 1992 Act or the daily living component of personal independence payment at the standard or enhanced rate in accordance with section 78(3) of the 2012 Act [8 or armed forces independence payment]]; and

[9 (ii) the other partner is certified as severely sight impaired or blind by a consultant ophthalmologist; and;]

(iii) no person who has attained the age of 18 is normally residing with the partners, nor are the partners normally residing with such a person, other than a person to whom paragraph 2 applies; and

(iv) no person is entitled to and in receipt of an allowance under section 70 of the 1992 Act [10, or has an award of universal credit which includes the carer element, in] respect of caring for the person to whom head (c) (i) above applies.

(2) A person shall be treated—

(a) for the purposes of sub-paragraph (1) as being in receipt of attendance allowance or, as the case may be, [7, the care component of disability living allowance at the highest or middle rate prescribed in accordance with section 72(3) of the 1992 Act or the daily living component of personal independence payment at the standard or enhanced rate in accordance with section 78(3) of the 2012 Act [8 or armed forces independence payment]], for any period—

(i) before an award is made but in respect of which the allowance [7or payment] is awarded; or

(ii) not covered by an award but in respect of which a payment is made in lieu of an award;

(b) for the purposes of sub-paragraph (1)(b) as being in receipt of attendance allowance or the care component of disability living allowance at the highest or middle rate prescribed in accordance section [172(3)] of the 1992 Act if he would, but for his being a patient for a period exceeding 28 days, be so in receipt;

[7 (ba) for the purposes of sub-paragraph (1)(b) as being in receipt of the daily living component of personal independence payment at the standard or enhanced rate in accordance with section 78 of the 2012 Act if he would, but for regulations made under section 86(1) (hospital in-patients) of that Act, be so in receipt;]

(c) for the purposes of sub-paragraph (1), as not being in receipt of an allowance under section 70 of the 1992 Act [10, or as having an award of universal credit which includes the carer element,] for any period before [5 the date on which the award is first paid].

[9 (3) For the purposes of sub-paragraph (1)(c)(ii), a person who has ceased to be certified as severely sight impaired or blind on regaining his eyesight shall nevertheless be treated as severely sight impaired or blind, as the case may be, and as satisfying the requirements set out in that sub-paragraph for a period of 28 weeks following the date on which he ceased to be so certified.]

[10 (4) For the purposes of this paragraph, a person has an award of universal credit which includes the carer element if the person has an award of universal credit which includes an amount which is the carer element under regulation 29 of the Universal Credit Regulations 2013.]

Persons residing with the claimant whose presence is ignored

4.100 **2.**—(1) For the purposes of paragraph 1(1)(a)(ii), (b)(ii) and (c)(iii), this paragraph applies to the persons specified in the following sub-paragraphs.

(2) A person who—

(a) is in receipt of attendance allowance [7, the care component of disability living allowance at the highest or middle rate prescribed in accordance with section 72(3) of the 1992 Act or the daily living component of personal independence payment at the standard or enhanced rate in accordance with section 78(3) of the 2012 Act [8 or armed forces independence payment]];

[9 (b) is certified as severely sight impaired or blind by a consultant ophthalmologist;

(c) is no longer certified as severely sight impaired or blind in accordance with head (b) but was so certified not more than 28 weeks earlier;]

(d) lives with the claimant in order to care for him or his partner and is engaged by a charitable or voluntary organisation which makes a charge to the claimant or his partner for the services provided by that person;

(e) is a partner of a person to whom head (d) above applies; or

(f) is a person who is [3 a qualifying young person or] child for the purposes of Part IX of the 1992 Act.

(3) Subject to sub-paragraph (4), a person who joins the claimant's household for the first time in order to care for the claimant or his partner and immediately before he joined the household, the claimant or his partner was treated as being severely disabled.

(4) Sub-paragraph (3) applies only for the first 12 weeks following the date on which the person first joins the claimant's household.

(5) A person who is not a close relative of the claimant or his partner and—

(a) who is liable to make payments on a commercial basis to the claimant or his partner in respect of his occupation of the dwelling;

(b) to whom the claimant or his partner is liable to make payments on a commercial basis in respect of his occupation of that person's dwelling; or

(c) who is a member of the household of a person to whom head (a) or (b) applies.

(6) Subject to paragraph 3(3), a person who jointly occupies the claimant's dwelling and who is either—

(a) co-owner of that dwelling with the claimant or the claimant's [1partner] (whether or not there are other co-owners); or

(b) jointly liable with the claimant or the claimant's partner to make payments to a landlord in respect of his occupation of that dwelling.

(7) Subject to paragraph 3(3), a person who is a partner of a person to whom sub-paragraph (6) applies.

3.—(1) For the purposes of paragraphs 1 and 2, a person resides with another only if they share any accommodation except a bathroom, a lavatory or a communal area, but not if each person is separately liable to make payments in respect of his occupation of the dwelling to the landlord.

(2) In sub-paragraph (1), "communal area" means any area (other than rooms) of common access (including halls and passageways) and rooms of common use in sheltered accommodation.

(3) Paragraph 2(6) and (7) applies to a person who is a close relative of the claimant or his partner only if the claimant or his partner's co-ownership, or joint liability to make payments to a landlord in respect of his occupation, of the dwelling arose either before 11th April 1988, or, if later, on or before the date upon which the claimant or the claimant's partner first occupied the dwelling in question.

PART II

Amount applicable for carers

4.—(1) For the purposes of regulation 6(6)(a), this paragraph is satisfied if any of the requirements specified in sub-paragraphs (2) to (4) are met. **4.101**

(2) A claimant is, or in the case of partners either partner is, or both partners are, entitled to an allowance under section 70 of the 1992 Act ([2 carer's allowance]).

(3) Where an additional amount has been awarded under regulation 6(6)(a) but—

(a) the person in respect of whose care the allowance has been awarded dies; or

(b) the person in respect of whom the additional amount was awarded ceases to be entitled or ceases to be treated as entitled to the allowance,

this paragraph shall be treated as satisfied for a period of eight weeks from the relevant date specified in sub-paragraph (4).

(4) The relevant date for the purposes of [1sub-paragraph (3) is]—

(a) the Sunday following the death of the person in respect of whose care the allowance has been awarded (or beginning with the date of death if the death occurred on a Sunday);

(b) where sub-paragraph (a) does not apply, the date on which the person who has been entitled to the allowance ceases to be entitled to that allowance.

5.—For the purposes of paragraph 4, a person shall be treated as being entitled to and in receipt of an allowance under section 70 of the 1992 Act for any period not covered by an award but in respect of which a payment is made in lieu of an award.

PART III

Amount applicable for former claimants of income support [6, income-based jobseeker's allowance or income-related employment and support allowance]

6.—(1) If on the relevant day the relevant amount exceeds the provisional amount, an additional amount ("the transitional amount") equal to the difference shall be applicable to a claimant to whom sub-paragraph (2) applies. **4.102**

(2) This sub-paragraph applies to a claimant who, in respect of the day before the relevant day, was entitled to either income support [6, an income-based jobseeker's allowance or an income-related employment and support allowance.]

(3) The relevant day is the day in respect of which the claimant is first entitled to state pension credit.

(4) The provisional amount means the amount of the appropriate minimum guarantee applicable to the claimant on the relevant day but for this paragraph.

(5) The relevant amount means the amount which, on the day before the relevant day, was the claimant's applicable amount—

(a) for the purposes of determining his entitlement to income support; [6 . . .]

(b) for the purpose of determining his entitlement to an income-based jobseeker's allowance,

less any of the following amounts included in it—

(i) any amount determined in accordance with paragraph 2 of Schedule 2 to the Income Support Regulations or paragraph 2 of Schedule 1 to the Jobseeker's Allowance Regulations;

(ii) any amount by way of a residential allowance applicable in accordance with paragraph 2A of Schedule 2 to the Income Support Regulations or paragraph 3 of Schedule 1 to the Jobseeker's Allowance Regulations;

(iii) any amount by way of family premium applicable in accordance with paragraph 3 of Schedule 2 to the Income Support Regulations or paragraph 4 of Schedule 1 to the Jobseeker's Allowance Regulations;

(iv) any amount by way of disabled child premium applicable in accordance with paragraph 14 of Schedule 2 to the Income Support Regulations or paragraph 16 of Schedule 1 to the Jobseeker's Allowance Regulations; and

(v) any amount in respect of a person other than the claimant or his partner by way of enhanced disability premium applicable in accordance with paragraph 13A of Schedule 2 to the Income Support Regulations [6, paragraph 7 of Schedule 4 to the Employment and Support Allowance Regulations] or paragraph 15A of Schedule 1 to the Jobseeker's Allowance Regulations [6; or

(c) for the purposes of determining his entitlement to income-related employment and support allowance.]

(6) In determining the relevant amount under sub-paragraph (5), the applicable amount shall be increased by an amount equal to the amount (if any) payable to the claimant in accordance with Part II of the Income Support (Transitional) Regulations 1987 (transitional protection) or regulation 87(1) of the Jobseeker's Allowance Regulations (transitional supplement to income-based jobseeker's allowance).

(7) If—

(a) paragraph 1 of Schedule 7 to the Income Support Regulations or paragraph 1 of Schedule 5 to the Jobseeker's Allowance [1 Regulations] applied to the claimant or his partner on the day before the relevant day; but

(b) paragraph 2(2) of Schedule 3 does not apply to the claimant or his partner on the relevant day;

then for the purposes of this paragraph the relevant amount shall be determined on the assumption that the provision referred to in sub-paragraph (7)(a) did not apply in his case.

(8) Subject to sub-paragraph (9), the transitional amount shall—

(a) be reduced by a sum equal to the amount (if any) by which the appropriate minimum guarantee increases after the relevant day;

(b) cease to be included in the claimant's appropriate minimum guarantee from the day on which—

(i) the sum mentioned in head (a) above equals or exceeds the transitional amount; or

(ii) the claimant or the claimant's partner ceases to be entitled to state pension credit.

(9) For the purposes of sub-paragraph (8), there shall be disregarded—

(a) any break in entitlement not exceeding 8 weeks; and

[4 (b) any amount by which the appropriate minimum guarantee of a patient is increased on 10th April 2006 by virtue of the substitution of paragraph 2 of Schedule 3.]

[1 (10) This sub-paragraph applies where the relevant amount included an amount in respect of housing costs relating to a loan—

(a) which is treated as a qualifying loan by virtue of regulation 3 of the Income Support (General) Amendment and Transitional Regulations 1995 or paragraph 18(2) of Schedule 2 to the Jobseeker's Allowance Regulation [6 or paragraph 20(2) of Schedule 6 to the Employment and Support Allowance Regulations]; or

(b) the appropriate amount of which was determined in accordance with paragraph 7(6C) of Schedule 3 to the Income Support Regulations as in force prior to 10th April 1995 and maintained in force by regulation 28(1) of the Income-related Benefits Schemes (Miscellaneous Amendments) Regulations 1995.

(11) Where sub-paragraph (10) applies, the transitional amount shall be calculated or, as the case may be, recalculated, on the relevant anniversary date determined in accordance with paragraph 7(4C) of Schedule II ("the relevant anniversary date") on the basis that the provisional amount on the relevant day included, in respect of housing costs, the amount calculated in accordance with paragraph 7(1) of Schedule II as applying from the relevant anniversary date and not the amount in respect of housing costs determined on the basis of the amount of the loan calculated in accordance with paragraph 7(4A) of that Schedule.

(12) The transitional amount as calculated in accordance with sub-paragraph (11) shall only be applicable from the relevant anniversary date.]

AMENDMENTS

1. State Pension Credit (Consequential, Transitional and Miscellaneous Provisions) (No.2) Regulations 2002 (SI 2002/3197) reg.2 and Sch. para.8 (October 6, 2003).

2. State Pension Credit (Transitional and Miscellaneous Provisions) Amendment Regulations 2003 (SI 2003/2274) reg.2(8) (October 6, 2003).

3. Social Security (Young Persons) Amendment Regulations 2006 (SI 2006/718) reg.6(3) (April 10, 2006).

4. Social Security (Miscellaneous Amendments) Regulations 2006 (SI 2006/588) reg.4(3) (April 10, 2006).

5. Social Security (Miscellaneous Amendments) Regulations 2007 (SI 2007/719) reg.4 (April 2, 2007).

6. Employment and Support Allowance (Consequential Provisions) (No.2) Regulations 2008 (SI 2008/1554) reg.4(7) (October 27, 2008).

7. Personal Independence Payment (Supplementary Provisions and Conse-

quential Amendments) Regulations 2013 (SI 2013/388) reg.8 and Sch. para.27(4) (a) (April 8, 2013).

8. Armed Forces and Reserve Forces Compensation Scheme (Consequential Provisions: Subordinate Legislation) Order 2013 (SI 2013/591) art.7 and Sch. para.23(4) (April 8, 2013).

9. Universal Credit and Miscellaneous Amendments (No.2) Regulations 2014 (SI 2014/2888) reg.3(4)(a) (November 26, 2014).

10. Universal Credit and Miscellaneous Amendments Regulations 2015 (SI 2015/1754) reg.16(3) (November 4, 2015).

General Note

Schedule I sets out the criteria for the award of additional guarantee credit amounts, on the same basis as under the income support scheme, for severely disabled pensioners (Pt I), for carers (Pt II) and for pensioners with entitlement to transitional additions (Pt III). Regulation 6 is the principal provision governing the guarantee credit and lists the actual weekly amounts for the principal additional elements. **4.103**

Paragraph 1

According to *CPC/2021/2008* (at [56]–[64]), the reference to a person being "in receipt of attendance allowance" is to be read as meaning "in actual receipt of attendance allowance" rather than being "entitled to but not actually in receipt of attendance allowance", notwithstanding the absence of a provision equivalent to para.14B of Sch.2 to the Income Support (General) Regulations 1987 (SI 1987/1967). **4.104**

Paragraphs 2 and 3

In *CPC/1446/2008*, Deputy Commissioner Wikeley considered whether a claimant was "residing with" a non-dependent within the meaning of Sch.1 paras 2 and 3. The Deputy Commissioner followed *CSIS/652/2003* in preferring *CSIS/2532/2003* to *CIS/185/1995* on the parallel income support rules. According to the Deputy Commissioner, a kitchen may therefore form part of shared accommodation even if the claimant personally does not visit the kitchen so long as he uses it in some other way (e.g. storage or for a third party to prepare meals). However, in *RK v SSWP* [2008] UKUT 34 (AAC) Judge Rowland was prepared to accept that a person does not necessarily share a kitchen merely because meals are prepared for him or her there. Judge Rowland also agreed with the outcomes of the appeals in *CSIS/185/1995*, *CIS/2532/2003*, *CSIS/652/2003* and *CPC/1446/2008* if not all of the reasoning. Judge Rowland took the view that "residing with" means "living in the same household as". On the facts a claimant who was confined to her bedroom in her son's house shared accommodation with her son and so normally resided with him, and so was not entitled to a severe disability premium. See further, *ST v Secretary of State for Work and Pensions* [2009] UKUT 269 (AAC). **4.105**

SCHEDULE II **Regulation 6(6)(c)**

Housing Costs

Housing costs

1.—(1) Subject to the following provisions of this Schedule, the housing costs applicable to a claimant in accordance with regulation 6(6)(c) are those costs— **4.106**

(a) which the claimant or, if he has a partner, his partner is, in accordance with paragraph 3, liable to meet in respect of the dwelling occupied as the home which he or his partner is treated as occupying; and

(b) which qualify under paragraphs 11 to 13.

(2) In this Schedule—

(a) "disabled person" means a person—
 (i) aged 75 or over;
 (ii) who, had he in fact been entitled to income support, would have satisfied the requirements of paragraph 12 of Schedule 2 to the Income Support Regulations (additional condition for the Higher Pensioner and Disability Premiums); or
 (iii) who—
  (aa) has not attained the age of [13 20] and for whom the claimant or his partner is responsible; [2and]
  (bb) is a person in respect of whom disability living allowance is payable or would be payable but for [12 suspension or abatement because the person becomes a patient]; [2 or]
  [32 (cc) is certified as severely sight impaired or blind by a consultant ophthalmologist or who is within 28 weeks of ceasing to be so certified;] [19 or
  (dd) is in receipt of an employment and support allowance which includes an amount under section 2(2) or (3) or 4(4) or (5) of the Welfare Reform Act (components) [26 or would be entitled to an employment and support allowance including an amount of a work-related activity component under section 2(3) of that Act (amount of contributory allowance: work-related activity component), but for the application of section 1A of that Act (duration of contributory allowance)]];[28 or
  (ee) is a person in respect of whom personal independence payment is payable or would be payable but for regulations under section 86(1) (hospital in-patients) of the 2012 Act [29 or is a person in respect of whom armed forces independence payment is payable]] [31; or
  (ff) is entitled to an award of universal credit the calculation of which includes an amount under regulation 27(1) of the Universal Credit Regulations 2013 in respect of the fact that he has limited capability for work or limited capability for work and work-related activity, or would include such an amount but for regulation 27(4) or 29(4) of those Regulations.]
(b) "housing costs" means those costs to which sub-paragraph (1) refers;
(c) "standard rate" means the rate for the time being [5 determined in accordance with] paragraph 9.

(3) For the purposes of sub-paragraph (2)(a), a person shall not cease to be a disabled person on account of his being disqualified for receiving benefit or treated as capable of work by virtue of the operation of section 171E of the 1992 Act (incapacity for work, disqualification, etc.) [19 or disqualified for receiving employment and support allowance or treated as not having limited capability for work in accordance with regulations made under section 18 of the Welfare Reform Act (disqualification)].

(4) In this Schedule, "non-dependant" means any person, except someone to whom sub-paragraph (5), (6) or (7) applies, who normally resides with the claimant.

(5) This sub-paragraph applies to—
(a) a partner of the claimant or any person under the age of [13 20] for whom the claimant or the claimant's partner is responsible;
(b) a person who lives with the claimant in order to care for him or for the claimant's partner and who is engaged for that purpose by a charitable or voluntary organisation which makes a charge to the claimant or the claimant's partner for the care provided by that person;
(c) the partner of a person to whom head (b) above applies.

(6) This sub-paragraph applies to a person, other than a close relative of the claimant or the claimant's partner—
(a) who is liable to make payments on a commercial basis to the claimant or the claimant's partner in respect of his occupation of the claimant's dwelling; [2or]
(b) [2. . .]
(c) who is a member of the household of a person to whom head (a) [2 . . .] above applies.

(7) This sub-paragraph applies to—
(a) a person who jointly occupies the claimant's dwelling and who is either—
 (i) co-owner of that dwelling with the claimant or the claimant's partners (whether or not there are other co-owners); or
 (ii) jointly liable with the claimant or the claimant's partner to make payments to a landlord in respect of his occupation of that dwelling;
(b) a partner of a person to whom head (a) above applies.

(8) For the purpose of sub-paragraphs (4) to (7) a person resides with another only if they share any accommodation except a bathroom, a lavatory or a communal area but not if each

person is separately liable to make payments in respect of his occupation of the dwelling to the landlord.

(9) In sub-paragraph (8), "communal area" means any area (other than rooms) of common access (including halls and passageways) and rooms of common use in sheltered accommodation.

Remunerative work

2.—(1) Subject to the following provisions of this paragraph, a person shall be treated for the purposes of this Schedule as engaged in remunerative work if he is engaged, or, where his hours of work fluctuate, he is engaged on average, for not less than 16 hours a week, in work for which payment is made or which is done in expectation of payment. **4.107**

(2) Subject to sub-paragraph (3), in determining the number of hours for which a person is engaged in work where his hours of work fluctuate, regard shall be had to the average of hours worked over—

(a) if there is a recognisable cycle of work, the period of one complete cycle (including, where the cycle involves periods in which the person does no work, those periods but disregarding any other absences);

(b) in any other case, the period of 5 weeks immediately prior to the date of claim, or such other length of time as may, in the particular case, enable the person's weekly average hours of work to be determined more accurately.

(3) Where, for the purposes of sub-paragraph (2)(a), a person's recognisable cycle of work at a school, other educational establishment or other place of employment is one year and includes periods of school holidays or similar vacations during which he does not work, those periods and any other periods not forming part of such holidays or vacations during which he is not required to work shall be disregarded in establishing the average hours for which he is engaged in work.

(4) Where no recognisable cycle has been established in respect of a person's work, regard shall be had to the number of hours or, where those hours will fluctuate, the average of the hours, which he is expected to work in a week.

(5) A person shall be treated as engaged in remunerative work during any period for which he is absent from work referred to in sub-paragraph (1) if the absence is either without good cause or by reason of a recognised, customary or other holiday.

(6) A person on income support or an income-based jobseeker's allowance for more than 3 days in any benefit week shall be treated as not being in remunerative work in that week.

(7) A person shall not be treated as engaged in remunerative work on any day on which the person is on maternity leave [[4], paternity leave [[33], shared parental leave] or adoption leave] or is absent from work because he is ill.

(8) A person shall not be treated as engaged in remunerative work on any day on which he is engaged in an activity in respect of which—

(a) a sports award has been made, or is to be made, to him; and

(b) no other payment is made or is expected to be made to him [[2], and for the purposes of this sub-paragraph, "sports award" means an award made by one of the Sports Councils named in section 23(2) of the National Lottery etc. Act 1993 out of sums allocated to it for distribution under that section.]

(9) In this paragraph "benefit week"—

(a) in relation to income support, has the same meaning as in regulation 2(1) of the Income Support Regulations;

(b) in relation to jobseeker's allowance, has the same meaning as in regulation 1(3) of the Jobseeker's Allowance Regulations.

Circumstances in which a person is liable to meet housing costs

3.—A person is liable to meet housing costs where— **4.108**

(a) the liability falls upon him or his partner but not where the liability is to a member of the same household as the person on whom the liability falls;

(b) because the person liable to meet the housing costs is not meeting them, the claimant has to meet those costs in order to continue to live in the dwelling occupied as the home and it is reasonable in all the circumstances to treat the claimant as liable to meet those costs;

(c) he in practice shares the housing costs with other members of the household none of whom are close relatives either of the claimant or his partner, and—

(i) one or more of those members is liable to meet those costs, and

(ii) it is reasonable in the circumstances to treat him as sharing responsibility.

Circumstances in which a person is to be treated as occupying a dwelling as his home

4.109 **4.**—(1) Subject to the following provisions of this paragraph, a person shall be treated as occupying as his home the dwelling normally occupied as his home by himself or, if he has a partner, by himself and his partner, and he shall not be treated as occupying any other dwelling as his home.

(2) In determining whether a dwelling is the dwelling normally occupied as the claimant's home for the purposes of sub-paragraph (1) regard shall be had to any other dwelling occupied by the claimant or by him and his partner whether or not that other dwelling is in Great Britain.

(3) Subject to sub-paragraph (4), where a claimant who has no partner is a full-time student or is on a training course and is liable to make payments (including payments of mortgage interest or, in Scotland, payments under heritable securities or, in either case, analogous payments) in respect of either (but not both) the dwelling which he occupies for the purpose of attending his course of study or his training course or, as the case may be, the dwelling which he occupies when not attending his course, he shall be treated as occupying as his home the dwelling in respect of which he is liable to make payments.

(4) A full-time student shall not be treated as occupying a dwelling as his home for any week of absence from it, other than an absence occasioned by the need to enter hospital for treatment, outside the period of study, if the main purpose of his occupation during the period of study would be to facilitate attendance on his course.

(5) Where a claimant has been required to move into temporary accommodation by reason of essential repairs being carried out to the dwelling normally occupied as his home and he is liable to make payments (including payments of mortgage interest or, in Scotland, payments under heritable securities or, in either case, analogous payments) in respect of either (but not both) the dwelling normally occupied or the temporary accommodation, he shall be treated as occupying as his home the dwelling in respect of which he is liable to make those payments.

(6) Where a person is liable to make payments in respect of two (but not more than two) dwellings, he shall be treated as occupying both dwellings as his home only—

(a) where he has left and remains absent from the former dwelling occupied as the home through fear of violence in that dwelling or of violence by a close relative or former partner and it is reasonable that housing costs should be met in respect of both his former dwelling and his present dwelling occupied as the home; or

(b) in the case of partners, where one partner is a full-time student or is on a training course and it is unavoidable that he or they should occupy two separate dwellings and reasonable that housing costs should be met in respect of both dwellings; or

(c) in the case where a person has moved into a new dwelling occupied as the home, except where sub-paragraph (5) applies, for a period not exceeding four benefit weeks [[15] from the first day of the benefit week where the move takes place on that day, but if it does not, from the first day of the next following benefit week] if his liability to make payments in respect of two dwellings is unavoidable.

(7) Where—

(a) a person has moved into a dwelling and was liable to make payments in respect of that dwelling before moving in; and

(b) he had claimed state pension credit before moving in and either that claim has not yet been determined or it has been determined but—

(i) an amount has not been included under this Schedule; or

(ii) the claim has been refused and a further claim has been made within four weeks of the date on which the claimant moved into the new dwelling occupied as the home; and

(c) the delay in moving into the dwelling in respect of which there was liability to make payments before moving in was reasonable and—

(i) that delay was necessary in order to adapt the dwelling to meet the disablement needs of the claimant, his partner or a person under the age of [[13] 20] for whom either the claimant or his partner is responsible; or

(ii) the move was delayed pending [[27] local welfare provision or] the outcome of an application under Part VIII of the 1992 Act for a social fund payment to meet a need arising out of the move or in connection with setting up the home in the dwelling; or

(iii) the person became liable to make payments in respect of the dwelling while he was a patient or was in a care home [[11] or an independent hospital],

he shall be treated as occupying the dwelling as his home for any period not exceeding four weeks immediately prior to the date on which he moved into the dwelling and in respect of which he was liable to make payments.

[11 (8) This sub-paragraph applies to a person who enters a care home or an independent hospital—

(a) for the purpose of ascertaining whether that care home or independent hospital suits his needs, and

(b) with the intention of returning to the dwelling which he normally occupies as his home should, in the event that, the care home or independent hospital prove not to suit his needs,

and while in the care home or independent hospital, the part of the dwelling which he normally occupies as his home is not let, or as the case may be, sub-let to another person.]

(9) A person to whom sub-paragraph (8) applies shall be treated as occupying the dwelling he normally occupies as his home during any period (commencing with the day he enters the [11 care home or independent hospital]) not exceeding 13 weeks in which the person is resident in the [11 care home or independent hospital], but only in so far as the total absence from the dwelling does not exceed 52 weeks.

(10) A person, other than a person to whom sub-paragraph (11) applies, shall be treated as occupying a dwelling as his home throughout any period of absence not exceeding 13 weeks, if, and only if—

(a) he intends to return to occupy the dwelling as his home; and

(b) the part of the dwelling normally occupied by him has not been let or, as the case may be, sub-let to another person; and

(c) the period of absence is unlikely to exceed 13 weeks.

(11) This sub-paragraph applies to a person whose absence from the dwelling he normally occupies as his home is temporary and—

(a) he intends to return to occupy the dwelling as his home; and

(b) while the part of the dwelling which is normally occupied by him has not been let or, as the case may be, sub-let; and

(c) he is—

[8 (i) detained in custody on remand pending trial or, as a condition of bail, required to reside—

(aa) in a dwelling, other than the dwelling he occupies as his home; or

(bb) in premises approved under [21 section 13 of the Offender Management Act 2007]

or, detained pending sentence upon conviction; or]

(ii) resident in a hospital or similar institution as a patient; or

(iii) undergoing or, as the case may be, his partner or a person who has not attained the age of [13 20] and who is dependent on him or his partner is undergoing, in the United Kingdom or elsewhere, medical treatment, or medically approved convalescence, in accommodation other than in a care home [11 or an independent hospital]; or

(iv) following, in the United Kingdom or elsewhere, a training course; or

(v) undertaking medically approved care of a person residing in the United Kingdom or elsewhere; or

(vi) undertaking the care of a person under the age of [13 20] whose parent or guardian is temporarily absent from the dwelling normally occupied by that parent or guardian for the purpose of receiving medically approved care or medical treatment, or

(vii) a person who is, whether in the United Kingdom or elsewhere, receiving medically approved care provided in accommodation other than a care home [11 or an independent hospital]; or

(viii) a full-time student to whom sub-paragraph (3) or (6)(b) does not apply; or

(ix) a person, other than a person to whom sub-paragraph (8) applies, who is receiving care provided in a care home [11 or an independent hospital]; or

(x) a person to whom sub-paragraph (6)(a) does not apply and who has left the dwelling he occupies as his home through fear of violence in that dwelling, or by a person who was formerly his partner or is a close relative; and

(d) the period of his absence is unlikely to exceed a period of 52 weeks or, in exceptional circumstances, is unlikely substantially to exceed that period.

(12) A person to whom sub-paragraph (11) applies is to be treated as occupying the dwelling he normally occupies as his home during any period of absence not exceeding 52 weeks beginning with the first day of that absence.

(13) In this paragraph—

(a) "medically approved" means certified by a medical practitioner;

(b) "training course" means such a course of training or instruction provided wholly or partly by or on behalf of or in pursuance of arrangements made with, or approved by or on behalf of [22 Skills Development Scotland], Scottish Enterprise, Highlands and Islands Enterprise, a government department or the Secretary of State.

Housing costs not met

4.110 **5.**—(1) No amount may be met under the provisions of this Schedule—

(a) in respect of housing benefit expenditure; or

(b) where the claimant is in accommodation which is a care home [11 or an independent hospital] except where he is in such accommodation during a temporary absence from the dwelling he occupies as his home and in so far as they relate to temporary absences, the provisions of paragraph 4(8) to (12) apply to him during that absence.

[1(1A) In paragraph (1), "housing benefit expenditure" means expenditure in respect of which housing benefit is payable as specified in regulation 10(1) of the Housing Benefit (General) Regulations 1987 but does not include any such expenditure in respect of which an additional amount is applicable under regulation 6(6)(c) (housing costs).]

(2) Subject to the following provisions of this paragraph, loans which, apart from this paragraph, qualify under paragraph 11 shall not so qualify where the loan was incurred during the relevant period and was incurred—

(a) after 1st October 1995, or

(b) after 2nd May 1994 and the housing costs applicable to that loan were not met by virtue of the former paragraph 5A of Schedule 3 to the Income Support Regulations in any one or more of the 26 weeks preceding 2nd October 1995; or

(c) subject to sub-paragraph (3), in the 26 weeks preceding 2nd October 1995 by a person—

(i) who was not at that time entitled to income support; and

(ii) who becomes, or whose partner becomes entitled to income support or an income-based jobseeker's allowance after 1st October 1995 and that entitlement is within 26 weeks of an earlier entitlement to income support or an income-based jobseeker's allowance of the claimant or his partner.

(3) Sub-paragraph (2)(c) shall not apply in respect of a loan where the claimant has interest payments on that loan met without restrictions under an award of income support in respect of a period commencing before 2nd October 1995.

(4) The "relevant period" for the purposes of this paragraph is any period during which the person to whom the loan was made—

(a) is entitled to income support, income-based jobseeker's allowance [19, income-related employment and support allowance] or state pension credit; or

(b) has a partner and the partner is entitled to income support, income-based jobseeker's allowance [19, income-related employment and support allowance] or to state pension credit;

together with any linked period, that is to say a period falling between two periods separated by not more than 26 weeks in which one of heads (a) or (b) above is satisfied.

(5) For the purposes of sub-paragraph (4), a person shall be treated as entitled to income support or, as the case may be, income-based jobseeker's allowance [19, state pension credit or income-related employment and support allowance], during any period when he or his partner was not so entitled because—

(a) that person or his partner was participating in an employment programme specified in regulation 75(l)(a)(ii) of the Jobseeker's Allowance Regulations, [18 or in the Intensive Activity Period specified in regulation 75(1)(a)(iv) of those Regulations]; and

(b) in consequence of such participation that person or his partner was engaged in remunerative work or—

(i) in the case of income support, had an income in excess of the claimant's applicable amount as prescribed in Part IV of the Income Support Regulations; or

(ii) in the case of state pension credit, the claimant's income exceeded the amount of his state pension credit entitlement.

(6) For the purposes of sub-paragraph (4)—

(a) any week in the period of 26 weeks ending on 1st October 1995 on which there arose an entitlement to income support such as is mentioned in that sub-paragraph shall be taken into account in determining when the relevant period commences; and

(b) two or more periods of entitlement and any intervening linked periods shall together form a single relevant period.

(7) Where the loan to which sub-paragraph (2) refers has been applied—

(a) for paying off an earlier loan, and that earlier loan qualified under paragraph 11 during the relevant period; or

(b) to finance the purchase of a property where an earlier loan, which qualified under paragraph 11 or 12 during the relevant period in respect of another property, is paid off (in whole or in part) with monies received from the sale of that property;

then the amount of the loan to which sub-paragraph (2) applies is the amount (if any) by which the new loan exceeds the earlier loan.

(8) Notwithstanding the preceding provisions of this paragraph, housing costs shall be met in any case where a claimant satisfies any of the conditions specified in sub-paragraphs (9) to [2(12)] below, but—

(a) those costs shall be subject to any additional limitations imposed by the sub-paragraph; and

(b) where the claimant satisfies the conditions in more than one of these sub-paragraphs, only one sub-paragraph shall apply in his case and the one that applies shall be the one most favourable to him.

(9) The conditions specified in this sub-paragraph are that—

(a) during the relevant period the claimant or his partner acquires an interest ("the relevant interest") in a dwelling which he then occupies or continues to occupy, as his home; and

(b) in the week preceding the week in which the relevant interest was acquired, housing benefit was payable to the claimant or his partner;

so however that the amount to be met by way of housing costs shall initially not exceed the aggregate of—

(i) the housing benefit payable in the week mentioned at sub-paragraph (9)(b); and

(ii) any additional amount applicable to the claimant or his partner in accordance with regulation 6(6)(c) in that week,

and shall be increased subsequently only to the extent that it is necessary to take account of any increase, arising after the date of the acquisition, in the standard rate or in any housing costs which qualify under paragraph 13 (other housing costs).

(10) The condition specified in this sub-paragraph is that the loan was taken out, or an existing loan increased, to acquire alternative accommodation more suited to the special needs of a disabled person than the accommodation which was occupied before the acquisition by the claimant.

(11) The conditions specified in this sub-paragraph are that—

(a) the loan commitment increased in consequence of the disposal of the dwelling occupied as the home and the acquisition of an alternative such dwelling; and

(b) the change of dwelling was made solely by reason of the need to provide separate sleeping accommodation for persons of different sexes aged 10 or over but under [13 20] who live with the claimant and are looked after by the claimant or his partner.

(12) The conditions specified in this sub-paragraph are that—

(a) during the relevant period the claimant or his partner acquires an interest ("the relevant interest") in a dwelling which he then occupies as his home; and

(b) in the week preceding the week in which the relevant interest was acquired, an additional amount was applicable under regulation 6(6)(c) in respect of the claimant or his partner which included an amount determined by reference to paragraph 13 and did not include any amount specified in paragraph 11 or paragraph 12;

so however that the amount to be met by way of housing costs shall initially not exceed the amount so determined, and shall be increased subsequently only to the extent that it is necessary to take account of any increase, arising after the date of acquisition, in the standard rate or in any housing costs which qualify under paragraph 13 (other housing costs).

(13) The following provisions of this Schedule shall have effect subject to the provisions of this paragraph.

Apportionment of housing costs

6.—(1) Where the dwelling occupied as the home is a composite hereditament and— 4.111

(a) before 1st April 1990 for the purposes of section 48(5) of the General Rate Act 1967 (reduction of rates on dwellings), it appeared to a rating authority or it was determined in pursuance of subsection (6) of section 48 of that Act that the hereditament, including the dwelling occupied as the home, was a mixed hereditament and that only a proportion of the rateable value of the hereditament was attributable to use for the purpose of a private dwelling; or

(b) in Scotland, before 1st April 1989 an assessor acting pursuant to section 45(1) of the

Water (Scotland) Act 1980 (provision as to valuation roll) has apportioned the net annual value of the premises including the dwelling occupied as the home between the part occupied as a dwelling and the remainder,

the additional amount applicable under this Schedule shall be such proportion of the amounts applicable in respect of the hereditament or premises as a whole as is equal to the proportion of the rateable value of the hereditament attributable to the part of the hereditament used for the purposes of a private tenancy or, in Scotland, the proportion of the net annual value of the premises apportioned to the part occupied as a dwelling house.

(2) Subject to sub-paragraph (1) and the following provisions of this paragraph, where the dwelling occupied as the home is a composite hereditament, the additional amount applicable under this Schedule shall be the relevant fraction of the amount which would otherwise be applicable under this Schedule in respect of the dwelling occupied as the home.

(3) For the purposes of sub-paragraph (2), the relevant fraction shall be obtained in accordance with the formula—

$$\left[^{34}\ \frac{A}{A + B}\right]$$

where—

"A" is the current market value of the claimant's interest in that part of the composite hereditament which is domestic property within the meaning of section 66 of the Act of 1988;

"B" is the current market value of the claimant's interest in that part of the composite hereditament which is not domestic property within that section.

(4) In this paragraph—

"composite hereditament" means—

(a) as respects England and Wales, any hereditament which is shown as a composite hereditament in a local non-domestic rating list;

(b) as respects Scotland, any lands and heritages entered in the valuation roll which are part residential subjects within the meaning of section 26(1) of the Act of 1987;

"local non-domestic rating list" means a list compiled and maintained under section 41(1) of the Act of 1988;

"the Act of 1987" means the Abolition of Domestic Rates, Etc. (Scotland) Act 1987;

"the Act of 1988" means the Local Government Finance Act 1988.

(5) Where responsibility for expenditure which relates to housing costs met under this Schedule is shared, the additional amounts applicable under this Schedule shall be calculated by reference to the appropriate proportion of that expenditure for which the claimant is responsible.

The calculation for loans

4.112 7.—(1) The weekly amount of housing costs to be met under this Schedule in respect of a loan which qualifies under paragraph 11 or 12 shall be calculated by applying the formula—

$$\left[^{34}\ \frac{A \times B}{52}\right]$$

where—

A = the amount of the loan which qualifies under paragraph 11 or 12;

B = the standard rate for the time being [6 applicable in respect of that loan].

[2(2) For the purposes of sub-paragraph (1) and subject to sub-paragraphs (3) and (4A), the amount of the qualifying loan—

(a) except where paragraph (b) applies, shall be determined on the date the housing costs are first met and thereafter on the anniversary of that date;

(b) where housing costs are being met in respect of a qualifying loan ("the existing loan") and housing costs are subsequently met in respect of one or more further qualifying loans ("the new loan"), shall be the total amount of those loans determined on the date the housing costs were first met in respect of the new loan and thereafter on the anniversary of the date housing costs were first met in respect of the existing loan.]

(3) Where the claimant or his partner—

(a) ceases to be in receipt of or treated as being in receipt of state pension credit; but
(b) within 12 weeks thereof, one of them subsequently becomes entitled again to the credit; and
(c) sub-paragraph (4) applies,

the amount of the qualifying loan shall be—

(i) the amount last determined for the purposes of the earlier entitlement; and
(ii) [[2]recalculated on the relevant date specified in sub-paragraph (4C)].

(4) This sub-paragraph applies if—

(a) the earlier entitlement included an amount in respect of a qualifying loan; and
(b) the circumstances affecting the calculation of the qualifying loan remain unchanged since the last calculation of that loan.

[[2] (4A) Where—

(a) the last day on which either the claimant or his partner were entitled to income support [[19], income-related employment and support allowance] or to an income-based jobseeker's allowance was no more than twelve weeks before—
   (i) except where head (ii) applies, the first day of entitlement to state pension credit; or
   (ii) where the claim for state pension credit was treated as made on a day earlier than the day on which it was actually made ("the actual date"), the day which would have been the first day of entitlement to state pension credit had the claim been treated as made on the actual date; and
(b) sub-paragraph (4B) applies,

the amount of the qualifying loan shall be the amount last determined for the purposes of the earlier entitlement and recalculated on the relevant date specified in paragraph (4C).

(4B) This sub-paragraph applies—

(a) where the earlier entitlement was to income support, if their applicable amount included an amount determined in accordance with Schedule 3 to the Income Support Regulations as applicable to them in respect of a loan which qualifies under paragraph 15 or 16 of that Schedule; [[19] . . .]
(b) where the earlier entitlement was to an income-based jobseeker's allowance, if their applicable amount included an amount determined in accordance with Schedule 2 to the Jobseeker's Allowance Regulations as applicable to them in respect of a loan which qualifies under paragraph 14 or 15 of that Schedule; [[19] or]

[[19] (c) where the earlier entitlement was to an income-related employment and support allowance, if their applicable amount included an amount determined in accordance with Schedule 6 to the Employment and Support Allowance Regulations as applicable to them in respect of a loan which qualifies under paragraph 16 to 18 of that Schedule, and]

where the circumstances affecting the calculation of the qualifying loan remain unchanged since the last calculation of that loan and in this paragraph, "qualifying loan" shall, where the context requires, be construed accordingly.

(4C) The recalculation shall take place—

(a) in a case where sub-paragraph (3) applies, on each subsequent anniversary of the date on which, for the purposes of sub-paragraph (2), housing costs were first met;
(b) in a case where sub-paragraph (4A) applies—
   (i) where housing costs under the earlier entitlement were being met in respect of more than one qualifying loan and the amounts of those loans were recalculated on different dates, on the first of those dates which falls during the award of state pension credit and on each subsequent anniversary of that date;
   (ii) in any other case, on each subsequent anniversary of the date on which housing costs were first met under the earlier entitlement;
(c) in the case of claims for state pension credit made between 6th October 2003 and 5th October 2004 and to which sub-paragraph (4A) does not apply—
   (i) where there are no housing costs to be met as at the date of claim but housing costs are to be met in respect of a qualifying loan taken out after the date of claim, on each subsequent anniversary of the date on which housing costs in respect of that loan were first met;
   (ii) in any other case, on each subsequent anniversary of the date on which the decision was made to award state pension credit.]

[[1](5) Where in the period since the amount applicable under this Schedule was last determined, there has been a change of circumstances, other than a reduction in the amount of the outstanding loan, which increases or reduces the amount applicable, it shall be recalculated so as to take account of that change.]

General provisions applying to housing costs

4.113 **8.**—(1) Where for the time being a loan exceeds, or in a case where more than one loan is to be taken into account, the aggregate of those loans exceeds the appropriate amount specified in sub-paragraph (2), then the amount of the loan or, as the case may be, the aggregate amount of those loans, shall for the purposes of this Schedule, be the appropriate amount.

(2) Subject to the following provisions of this paragraph, the appropriate amount is [34 £100,000].

(3) Where a person is treated under paragraph 4(6) (payments in respect of two dwellings) as occupying two dwellings as his home, then the restrictions imposed by subparagraph (1) shall be applied separately to the loans for each dwelling.

(4) In a case to which paragraph 6 (apportionment of housing costs) applies, the appropriate amount for the purposes of sub-paragraph (1) shall be the lower of—

(a) a sum determined by applying the formula—

$$[^{34}\ P \times Q]$$

where—

P = the relevant fraction for the purposes of paragraph 6, and

Q = the amount or, as the case may be, the aggregate amount for the time being of any loan or loans which qualify under this Schedule; or

(b) the sum for the time being specified in sub-paragraph (2).

(5) In a case to which paragraph 11(3) or 12(3) (loans which qualify in part only) applies, the appropriate amount for the purposes of sub-paragraph (1) shall be the lower of—

(a) a sum representing for the time being the part of the loan applied for the purposes specified in paragraph 11(1) or (as the case may be) paragraph 12(1); or

(b) the sum for the time being specified in sub-paragraph (2).

(6) In the case of any loan to which paragraph 12(2)(k) (loan taken out and used for the purpose of adapting a dwelling for the special needs of a disabled person) applies the whole of the loan, to the extent that it remains unpaid, shall be disregarded in determining whether the amount for the time being specified in sub-paragraph (2) is exceeded.

(7) Where in any case the amount for the time being specified for the purposes of sub-paragraph (2) is exceeded and there are two or more loans to be taken into account under either or both paragraphs 11 and 12, then the amount of eligible interest in respect of each of those loans to the extent that the loans remain outstanding shall be determined as if each loan had been reduced to a sum equal to the qualifying portion of that loan.

(8) For the purposes of sub-paragraph (7), the qualifying portion of a loan shall be determined by applying the following formula—

$$[^{34}\ R \times \frac{S}{T}]$$

where—

R = the amount for the time being specified for the purposes of sub-paragraph (1);

S = the amount of the outstanding loan to be taken into account;

T = the aggregate of all outstanding loans to be taken into account under paragraphs 11 and 12.

The standard rate

4.114 **9.**—[7 (1) The standard rate is the rate of interest applicable per annum to a loan which qualifies under this Schedule.

[24 (2) Subject to the following provisions of this paragraph, the standard rate is to be the average mortgage rate published by the Bank of England in August 2010.

(2A) The standard rate is to be varied each time that sub-paragraph (2B) applies.

(2B) This sub-paragraph applies when, on any reference day, the Bank of England publishes an average mortgage rate which differs by [31 0.5 percentage points] or more from the standard rate that applies on that reference day (whether by virtue of sub-paragraph (2) or of a previous application of this sub-paragraph).

(2C) The average mortgage rate published on that reference day then becomes the new standard rate in accordance with sub-paragraph (2D).

(2D) Any variation in the standard rate by virtue of sub-paragraphs (2A) to (2C) comes into effect—

(a) for the purposes of sub-paragraph (2B) (in consequence of its first and any subsequent application), on the day after the reference day referred to in sub-paragraph (2C);
(b) for the purpose of calculating the weekly amount of housing costs to be met under this Schedule, on the day specified by the Secretary of State(5).

(2E) In this paragraph—

"average mortgage rate" means the effective interest rate (non-seasonally adjusted) of United Kingdom resident banks and building societies for loans to households secured on dwellings published by the Bank of England in respect of the most recent period for that rate specified at the time of publication(6);

"reference day" means any day falling after 1st October 2010.]

(3) The Secretary of State shall determine the date from which the standard rate calculated in accordance with sub-paragraph (2) takes effect.

[17 . . .]

Excessive Housing Costs

10.—(1) Housing costs which, apart from this paragraph, fall to be met under this Schedule shall be met only to the extent specified in sub-paragraph (3) where— **4.115**

(a) the dwelling occupied as the home, excluding any part which is let, is larger than is required by the claimant, his partner (if he has one), any person under the age of [13 20] and any other non-dependants having regard, in particular, to suitable alternative accommodation occupied by a household of the same size; or
(b) the immediate area in which the dwelling occupied as the home is located is more expensive than other areas in which suitable alternative accommodation exists; or
(c) the outgoings of the dwelling occupied as the home which are met under paragraphs 11 to 13 are higher than the outgoings of suitable alternative accommodation in the area.

(2) For the purposes of heads (a) to (c) of sub-paragraph (1), no regard shall be had to the capital value of the dwelling occupied as the home.

(3) Subject to the following provisions of this paragraph, the amount of the loan which falls to be met shall be restricted and the excess over the amounts which the claimant would need to obtain suitable alternative accommodation shall not be allowed.

(4) Where, having regard to the relevant factors, it is not reasonable to expect the claimant and his partner to seek alternative cheaper accommodation, no restriction shall be made under sub-paragraph (3).

(5) In sub-paragraph (4), "the relevant factors" are—

(a) the availability of suitable accommodation and the level of housing costs in the area; and
(b) the circumstances of the claimant and those who live with him, including in particular the age and state of health of any of those persons, the employment prospects of the claimant and, where a change in accommodation is likely to result in a change of school, the effect on the education of any person below the age of [13 20] who lives with the claimant.

[21 (6) Where sub-paragraph (4) does not apply and the claimant or the claimant's partner was able to meet the financial commitments for the dwelling occupied as the home when these were entered into, no restriction shall be made under this paragraph during the first 26 weeks immediately following the date on which—

(a) the claimant became entitled to state pension credit where the claimant's housing costs fell within one of the cases in sub-paragraph (1) on that date; or
(b) a decision took effect which was made under section 10 (decisions superseding earlier decisions) of the Social Security Act 1998 on the ground that the claimant's housing costs fell within one of the cases in sub-paragraph (1),

nor during the next 26 weeks if and so long as the claimant uses his best endeavours to obtain cheaper accommodation.]

(7) For the purposes of calculating any period of 26 weeks referred to in sub-paragraph (6), and for those purposes only, a person shall be treated as entitled to state pension credit for any period of 12 weeks or less in respect of which he was not in receipt of state pension credit and which fell immediately between periods in respect of which he was in receipt thereof.

(8) Any period in respect of which—

(a) state pension credit was paid to a person, and
(b) it was subsequently determined that he was not entitled to state pension credit for that period,

shall be treated for the purposes of sub-paragraph (7) as a period in respect of which he was not in receipt of state pension credit.

(9) Any period which falls before the appointed day in respect of which a person was

entitled to income support or income-based jobseeker's allowance shall be treated, for the purpose of calculating any period of 26 weeks or as the case may be 12 weeks mentioned in sub-paragraphs (6) and (7), as a period in respect of which he was entitled to state pension credit.

(10) References to state pension credit in sub-paragraphs (6) and (7) shall be treated as including references to income support [19, income-based jobseeker's allowance and income-related employment and support allowance] in respect of any period which falls immediately before—

(a) the appointed day; or
(b) the day the claimant or his partner attains the qualifying age.

Loans on residential property

4.116 **11.**—(1) A loan qualifies under this paragraph where the loan was taken out to defray monies applied for any of the following purposes—

(a) acquiring an interest in the dwelling occupied as the home; or
(b) paying off another loan to the extent that the other loan would have qualified under head (a) above had the loan not been paid off.

(2) For the purposes of this paragraph, references to a loan include also a reference to money borrowed under a hire purchase agreement for any purpose specified in heads (a) and (b) of sub-paragraph (l).

(3) Where a loan is applied only in part for the purposes specified in heads (a) and (b) of sub-paragraph (1), only that portion of the loan which is applied for that purpose shall qualify under this paragraph.

Loans for repairs and improvements to the dwelling occupied as the home

4.117 **12.**—(1) A loan qualifies under this paragraph where the loan was taken out, with or without security, for the purpose of—

(a) carrying out repairs and improvements to the dwelling occupied as the home;
(b) paying any service charge imposed to meet the cost of repairs and improvements to the dwelling occupied as the home;
(c) paying off another loan to the extent that the other loan would have qualified under head (a) or (b) of this sub-paragraph had the loan not been paid off,

and the loan was used for that purpose, or is used for that purpose within 6 months of the date of receipt or such further period as may be reasonable in the particular circumstances of the case.

(2) In sub-paragraph (1), "repairs and improvements" means any of the following measures undertaken with a view to maintaining the fitness of the dwelling for human habitation or, where the dwelling forms part of a building, any part of the building containing that dwelling—

(a) provision of a fixed bath, shower, wash basin, sink or lavatory, and necessary associated plumbing, including the provision of hot water not connected to a central heating system;
(b) repairs to existing heating systems;
(c) damp proof measures;
(d) provision of ventilation and natural lighting;
(e) provision of drainage facilities;
(f) provision of facilities for preparing and cooking food;
(g) provision of insulation of the dwelling occupied as the home;
(h) provision of electric lighting and sockets;
(i) provision of storage facilities for fuel or refuse;
(j) repairs of unsafe structural defects;
(k) adapting a dwelling for the special needs of a disabled person; or
(l) provision of separate sleeping accommodation for persons of different sexes aged 10 or over but under age [13 20] who live with the claimant and for whom the claimant or partner is responsible.

(3) Where a loan is applied only in part for the purposes specified in sub-paragraph (1), only that portion of the loan which is applied for that purpose shall qualify under this paragraph.

Other housing costs

4.118 **13.**—(1) Subject to the deduction specified in sub-paragraph (2) and the reductions applicable in sub-paragraph (5), there shall be met under this paragraph the amounts, calculated on a weekly basis, in respect of the following housing costs—

(a) payments by way of rent or ground rent relating to a long tenancy [14 . . .];
(b) service charges;
(c) payments by way of rentcharge within the meaning of section 1 of the Rentcharges Act 1977;
(d) payments under a co-ownership scheme;

(e) payments under or relating to a tenancy or licence of a Crown tenant;
(f) where the dwelling occupied as the home is a tent, payments in respect of the tent and the site on which it stands.

(2) Subject to sub-paragraph (3), the deductions to be made from the weekly amounts to be met under this paragraph are—

(a) where the costs are inclusive of any of the items mentioned in paragraph 5(2) of Schedule I to the Housing Benefit (General) Regulations 1987 (payment in respect of fuel charges), the deductions prescribed in that paragraph unless the claimant provides evidence on which the actual or approximate amount of the service charge for fuel may be estimated, in which case the estimated amount;
(b) where the costs are inclusive of ineligible service charges within the meaning of paragraph 1 of Schedule I to the Housing Benefit (General) Regulations 1987 (ineligible service charges) the amounts attributable to those ineligible service charges or where that amount is not separated from or separately identified within the housing costs to be met under this paragraph, such part of the payments made in respect of those housing costs which are fairly attributable to the provision of those ineligible services having regard to the costs of comparable services;
(c) any amount for repairs and improvements, and for this purpose the expression "repairs and improvements" has the same meaning it has in paragraph 12(2).

(3) Where arrangements are made for the housing costs, which are met under this paragraph and which are normally paid for a period of 52 weeks, to be paid instead for a period of 53 weeks, or to be paid irregularly, or so that no such costs are payable or collected in certain periods, or so that the costs for different periods in the year are of different amounts, the weekly amount shall be the amount payable for the year divided by 52.

(4) Where the claimant or the claimant's partner—

(a) pays for reasonable repairs or redecorations to be carried out to the dwelling he occupies; and
(b) that work was not the responsibility of the claimant or his partner; and
(c) in consequence of that work being done, the costs which are normally met under this paragraph are waived, then those costs shall, for a period not exceeding eight weeks, be treated as payable.

(5) Where in England and Wales an amount calculated on a weekly basis in respect of housing costs specified in sub-paragraph (l)(e) (Crown tenants) includes water charges, that amount shall be reduced—

(a) where the amount payable in respect of water charges is known, by that amount;
(b) in any other case, by the amount which would be the likely weekly water charge had the property not been occupied by a Crown tenant.

[[1](6) In this paragraph—

(a) "co-ownership scheme" means a scheme under which a dwelling is let by a housing association and the tenant, or his personal representative, will, under the terms of the tenancy agreement or of the agreement under which he became a member of the association, be entitled, on his ceasing to be a member and subject to any condition stated in either agreement, to a sum calculated by reference directly or indirectly to the value of the dwelling;
(b) "Crown tenant" means a person who occupies a dwelling under a tenancy or licence where the interest of the landlord belongs to Her Majesty in right of the Crown or to a government department or is held in trust for Her Majesty for the purposes of a government department except (in the case of an interest belonging to Her Majesty in right of the Crown) where the interest is under the management of the Crown Estate Commissioners;
(c) "housing association" has the meaning assigned to it by section 1(1) of the Housing Associations Act 1985;
(d) "long tenancy" means a tenancy granted for a term of years certain exceeding twenty one years, whether or not the tenancy is, or may become, terminable before the end of that term by notice given by or to the tenant or by re-entry, forfeiture (or, in Scotland, irritancy) or otherwise and includes a lease for a term fixed by law under a grant with a covenant or obligation for perpetual renewal unless it is a lease by sub-demise from one which is not a long tenancy.]

Persons residing with the claimant

14.—(1) Subject to the following provisions of this paragraph, the following deductions from the amount to be met under the preceding paragraphs of this Schedule in respect of housing costs shall be made— **4.119**

[9 (a) in respect of a non-dependant aged 18 or over who is engaged in any remunerative work, [35£94.50];

(b) in respect of a non-dependant aged 18 or over to whom paragraph (a) does not apply, [35£14.65]

(2) In the case of a non-dependant aged 18 or over to whom sub-paragraph [2(1)(a)] applies because he is in remunerative work, where the claimant satisfies the Secretary of State that the non-dependant's gross weekly income is—

(a) less than [35£133.00], the deduction to be made under this paragraph shall be the deduction specified in sub-paragraph [14(1)(b)];

(b) not less than [35£133.00] but less than [35£195.00], the deduction to be made under this paragraph shall be [35£33.65];

(c) not less than [35£195.00] but less than [35£253.00], the deduction to be made under this paragraph shall be [35£46.20];

(d) not less than [35£253.00] but less than [35£338.00], the deduction to be made under this paragraph shall be [35£75.60];

(e) not less than [35£338.00] but less than [35£420.00], the deduction to be made under this paragraph shall be [35£86.10].

(3) Only one deduction shall be made under this paragraph in respect of partners and where, but for this sub-paragraph, the amount that would fall to be deducted in respect of one partner is higher than the amount (if any) that would fall to be deducted in respect of the other partner, the higher amount shall be deducted.

(4) In applying the provisions of sub-paragraph (2) in the case of partners, only one deduction shall be made in respect of the partners based on the partners' joint weekly income.

(5) Where a person is a non-dependant in respect of more than one joint occupier of a dwelling (except where the joint occupiers are partners), the deduction in respect of that non-dependant shall be apportioned between the joint occupiers (the amount so apportioned being rounded to the nearest penny) having regard to the number of joint occupiers and the proportion of the housing costs in respect of the dwelling occupied as the home payable by each of them.

(6) No deduction shall be made in respect of any non-dependants occupying the dwelling occupied as the home of the claimant, if the claimant or any partner of his is—

[32 (a) certified as severely sight impaired or blind by a consultant ophthalmologist, or who is within 28 weeks of ceasing to be so certified; or]

(b) receiving in respect of himself either—

(i) an attendance allowance; or

(ii) the care component of the disability living allowance27; [29 . . .]

(iii) the daily living component of personal independence payment];[29 or

(iv) armed forces independence payment.]

(7) No deduction shall be made in respect of a non-dependant—

(a) if, although he resides with the claimant, it appears to the Secretary of State that the dwelling occupied as his home is normally elsewhere; or

(b) if he is in receipt of a training allowance paid in connection with [21 youth training] under section 2 of the Employment and Training Act 1973 or section 2 of the Enterprise and New Towns (Scotland) Act 1990; or

(c) if he is a full-time student during a period of study or, if he is not in remunerative work, during a recognised summer vacation appropriate to his course; or

[2(cc) if he is a full-time student and the claimant or his partner has attained the age of 65;]

(d) if he is aged under 25 and in receipt of income support or an income-based jobseeker's allowance; or

[14 (dd) in respect of whom a deduction in the calculation of a rent rebate or allowance falls to be made under regulation 55 (non-dependant deductions) of the Housing Benefit (Persons who have attained the qualifying age for state pension credit) Regulations 2006; or]

(e) if he is not residing with the claimant because he has been [12 an in-patient residing in a hospital or similar institution] for a period in excess of [352] weeks, or is a prisoner; and in calculating any period of [352] weeks, any 2 or more distinct periods separated by one or more intervals each not exceeding 28 days shall be treated as a single period [10; or]

[10 (f) if he is in receipt of state pension credit;]

[19 (g) if he is aged less than 25 and is in receipt of [27 income-related] employment and support allowance which does not include an amount under section [20 . . .] 4(4) or (5) of the Welfare Reform Act (components).] [30; or

(h) if he is aged less than 25 and is entitled to an award of universal credit which is calculated on the basis that he does not have any earned income;]

(8) In the case of a non-dependant to whom sub-paragraph (1) applies because he is in remunerative work, there shall be disregarded from his gross income—

(a) any attendance allowance [[28], disability living allowance [[29], armed forces independence payment] or personal independence payment] received by him;

(b) any payment from the Macfarlane Trust, the Macfarlane (Special Payments) Trust, the Macfarlane (Special Payments) (No.2) Trust ("the Trusts"), the Fund, the Eileen Trust [[23], MFET Limited] [[25], the Skipton Fund, the Caxton Foundation] or the Independent Living [[20] Fund (2006)]; and

(c) any payment in kind.

[[30] (9) For the purposes of sub-paragraph (7)(h), "earned income" has the meaning given in regulation 52 of the Universal Credit Regulations 2013.]

Rounding of fractions

15.—Where any calculation made under this Schedule results in a fraction of a penny, that fraction shall be treated as a penny. **4.120**

AMENDMENTS

1. State Pension Credit (Consequential, Transitional and Miscellaneous Provisions) Regulations 2002 (SI 2002/3019) reg.23(l) (October 6, 2003).

2. State Pension Credit (Consequential, Transitional and Miscellaneous Provisions) (No.2) Regulations 2002 (SI 2002/3197) reg.2 and Sch. para.9 (October 6, 2003).

3. Social Security (Hospital In-Patients and Miscellaneous Amendments) Regulations 2002 (SI 2003/1195) reg.8(2) (May 21, 2003).

4. State Pension Credit (Transitional and Miscellaneous Provisions) Amendment Regulations 2003 (SI 2003/2274) reg.2(9)(a) (October 6, 2003).

5. Social Security (Housing Costs Amendments) Regulations 2004 (SI 2004/2825) reg.2(2) (November 28, 2004).

6. Social Security (Housing Costs Amendments) Regulations 2004 (SI 2004/2825) reg.2(3) (November 28, 2004).

7. Social Security (Housing Costs Amendments) Regulations 2004 (SI 2004/2825) reg.2(4) (November 28, 2004).

8. Social Security (Housing Benefit, Council Tax Benefit, State Pension Credit and Miscellaneous Amendments) Regulations 2004 (SI 2004/2327) reg.7(5)(a) (April 4, 2005).

9. Social Security (Housing Benefit, Council Tax Benefit, State Pension Credit and Miscellaneous Amendments) Regulations 2004 (SI 2004/2327) reg.7(5)(b)(i) (April 4, 2005).

10. Social Security (Housing Benefit, Council Tax Benefit, State Pension Credit and Miscellaneous Amendments) Regulations 2004 (SI 2004/2327) reg.7(5)(b)(ii) (April 4, 2005).

11. Social Security (Care Homes and Independent Hospitals) Regulations 2005 (SI 2005/2687) reg.6 and Sch.5 para.5 (October 24, 2005).

12. Social Security (Hospital In-Patients) Regulations 2005 (SI 2005/3360) reg.8(4) (April 10, 2006).

13. Social Security (Young Persons) Amendment Regulations 2006 (SI 2006/718) reg.6(4) (April 10, 2006).

14. Social Security (Miscellaneous Amendments) (No.4) Regulations 2006 (SI 2006/2378) reg.14(5) (October 2, 2006).

15. Social Security (Miscellaneous Amendments) (No.5) Regulations 2006 (SI 2006/3274) reg.4(1) (January 8, 2007).

16. Social Security (Miscellaneous Amendments) (No.5) Regulations 2007 (SI 2007/2618) reg.10(5) (October 1, 2007).

17. Social Security (Housing Costs and Miscellaneous Amendments) Regulations 2007 (SI 2007/3183) reg.5 (December 17, 2007).

18. Social Security (Miscellaneous Amendments) Regulations 2008 (SI 2008/698) reg.5 (April 14, 2008).

19. Employment and Support Allowance (Consequential Provisions) (No.2) Regulations 2008 (SI 2008/1554) reg.4(8) (October 27, 2008).

20. Employment and Support Allowance (Miscellaneous Amendments) Regulations 2008 (SI 2008/2428) reg.41(4) (October 27, 2008).

21. Social Security (Miscellaneous Amendments) (No.6) Regulations 2008 (SI 2008/2767) reg.5(4) (November 17, 2008).

22. Social Security (Miscellaneous Amendments) Regulations 2009 (SI 2009/583) reg.5(4) (April 6, 2009).

23. Social Security (Miscellaneous Amendments) (No.2) Regulations 2010 (SI 2010/641) reg.6(3)(b) (April 6, 2010).

24. Social Security (Housing Costs) (Standard Interest Rate) Amendment Regulations 2010 (SI 2010/1811) reg.2(1)(c) and (2) (October 1, 2010).

25. Social Security (Miscellaneous Amendments) (No.3) Regulations 2011 (2011/2425) reg.15(5) (October 31, 2011).

26. Employment and Support Allowance (Duration of Contributory Allowance) (Consequential Amendments) Regulations 2012 (SI 2012/913) reg.6 (May 1, 2012).

27. Social Security (Miscellaneous Amendments) Regulations 2013 (SI 2013/443) reg.6(3) (April 2, 2013).

28. Personal Independence Payment (Supplementary Provisions and Consequential Amendments) Regulations 2013 (SI 2013/388) reg.8 and Sch. para.27(5) (April 8, 2013).

29. Armed Forces and Reserve Forces Compensation Scheme (Consequential Provisions: Subordinate Legislation) Order 2013 (SI 2013/591) art.7 and Sch. para.23(5) (April 8, 2013).

30. Universal Credit (Consequential, Supplementary, Incidental and Miscellaneous Provisions) Regulations 2013 (SI 2013/630) reg.33(6) (April 29, 2013).

31. Social Security (Miscellaneous Amendments) Regulations 2014 (SI 2014/591) reg.7(6) (April 28, 2014).

32. Universal Credit and Miscellaneous Amendments (No.2) Regulations 2014 (SI 2014/2888) reg.3(4)(b) (November 26, 2014).

33. Shared Parental Leave and Statutory Shared Parental Pay (Consequential Amendments to Subordinate Legislation) Order 2014 (SI 2014/3255) art.10(5) (December 31, 2014).

34. Social Security Benefits Up-rating Order 2015 (SI 2015/457) art.21(4) and Sch.13 (April 6, 2015).

35. Social Security Benefits (Adjustment of Amounts and Thresholds) Regulations 2016 (SI 2016/242) reg.4(3) (April 11, 2016).

General Note

4.121 This Schedule, dealing with housing costs, follows the pattern of the income support scheme (Income Support (General) Regulations 1987 (SI 1987/1967) Sch.3).

Paragraph 3

4.122 On the application of para.3(b), see *Secretary of State for Work and Pensions v DP* [2009] UKUT 225 (AAC), confirming that "there had to be an immediate threat to the continued occupation of the home, not a theoretical possibility of this happening in the future" (agreeing with *CIS/14/1993*). See further *AH v SSWP* [2010] UKUT 353 (AAC).

Paragraph 4

4.123 The purpose of para.4 is to make it clear that "in general, for the purpose of entitlement to housing costs, a person is only occupying the dwelling normally occupied by him as his home if he is living there": *PJ v Secretary of State for Work and Pensions* (SPC) [2014] UKUT 0152 (AAC), [15]. The claimant and his wife had moved out of their flat as they could no longer afford the council tax. One of their daughters lived in the flat for a while, and when she was ill the claimant and/or his wife would stay overnight at the flat to look after her. However, they were staying over to care for the daughter in *her* home, and not because it was the *claimant's* home.

The amendment to para.4(6)(c) made by Social Security (Miscellaneous Amendments) (No.5) Regulations 2006 (SI 2006/3274) reg.4(1) does not apply to any person covered by reg.36(6) of the State Pension Credit (Consequential, Transitional and Miscellaneous Provisions) Regulations 2002 (SI 2002/3019) (i.e. persons entitled to income support immediately before the appointed day). In such cases para.4(6)(c) is to be read as if after "four benefit weeks" there were inserted "from the first day of the benefit week in which the move occurs": Social Security (Miscellaneous Amendments) (No.5) Regulations 2006 (SI 2006/3274) reg.4(2) and (3).

Paragraph 5

The concept of a "relevant period" in para.5(4) was analysed by Commissioner Jacobs in *CPC/3226/2005*. The claimant took out a mortgage in April 2004; later, in January 2005, he claimed pension credit which was awarded with effect from January 2004 but without any allowance for housing costs. The Commissioner, reversing the tribunal, confirmed the Secretary of State's decision, noting that "The conditions of entitlement have to be applied to the circumstances obtaining at the time covered by the award. Any of the claimant's relevant circumstances may have changed during the period for which the claim is made" (at [11]). **4.124**

The meaning of a "relevant period" within para.5(4) was considered further in *CPC/3992/2007*, where the Deputy Commissioner followed the reasoning in *CPC/3326/2005*. It followed that a claimant who applied for backdating of state pension credit at the Department's instigation received no help with his housing costs as the effect of the backdating was to bring the mortgage within the "relevant period". The Deputy Commissioner also considered other remedies that might be open to the claimant.

On the inter-relationship between para.5(2) (non-qualifying loans) and para.5(7) (modification where existing loan is paid off), see *CPC/3433/2007*.

For a useful discussion of the authorities, and confirmation that the test under para.5(10) is that "the satisfaction of the 'more suited' test requires some demonstration as to what the special needs are, and how the new accommodation caters better for them", see *MAA v Secretary of State for Work and Pensions* [2013] UKUT 593 (AAC), paras 31–44).

Paragraph 8

Note that the £100,000 limit is increased to £200,000 where the claimant or their partner was in receipt of housing costs under Pts 2 or 3 of the Social Security (Housing Costs Special Arrangements) (Amendment and Modification) Regulations 2008 (SI 2008/3195) and the claimant becomes entitled to state pension credit within 12 weeks of that entitlement ending: see reg.12(3) of the same Regulations. **4.125**

Paragraph 9

Note that according to art.21(6) and Sch.13 to the Social Security Benefits Uprating Order 2014 (SI 2014/516): **4.126**

> "The standard rate is to be the average mortgage rate published by the Bank of England in August 2010. It is to be varied each time that sub-paragraph (2B) applies such that the average mortgage rate published on the reference day then becomes the new standard rate in accordance with sub-paragraph (2D)."

The change in the definition of the standard rate in October 2010, referring to the average mortgage rate published by the Bank of England in August 2010, inevitably resulted in some claimants receiving less by way of financial support for housing costs through the pension credit scheme than previously. In *PB v Secretary of State for Work and Pensions (SPC)* [2014] UKUT 0069 (AAC) the claimant had been on income support since 1989 and as such had formerly had the benefit of housing costs at the actual (not standard) rate of interest and also transitional protection from the £100,000 loan cap. When the claimant transferred from income support to pension credit in 2004 he lost that transitional protection (which was not carried through to pension credit) and became subject to the standard interest rate. Judge Williams held in the particular circumstances of the case that he did not have jurisdiction, as there was no relevant appealable decision before the tribunal below. However, he went on to hold that, assuming there was an appealable decision and there was discrimination, such differential treatment was both justifiable and justified. The decision not to link transitional relief across from income support to pension credit did not evidence an infringement of rights that was manifestly without legal foundation, applying the test in *Humphreys v HMRC* [2012] UKSC 18; [2012] AACR 46.

Paragraph 11

4.127 In *CPC/3322/2007* Commissioner Jacobs examined the application of para.11 in the context of a 20-year mortgage involving deferred capitalised interest. The claimant's mortgage advance in 1989 was an amount of £40,000. By the time of the appeal the balance was £48,920 (including deferred interest). The claimant paid lower monthly repayments in the first 10 years of the term, during which deferred interest accrued, and higher monthly payments in the latter 10 years of the term. Setting aside the tribunal's decision, the Commissioner substituted his own decision to the effect that the claimant's housing costs were limited to the interest on a qualifying loan of £40,000.

Applying *R(IS) 14/01*, albeit with some hesitation on this first point, the Commissioner accepted that the deferral of interest amounted to a loan. Agreeing with both *R(IS) 14/01* and *CIS/141/1993*, the Commissioner also held that only the primary loan of £40,000 was used for the purpose of "acquiring an interest in the dwelling occupied as the home" within para.11(1)(a). If the current capital balance represented a single loan, it could be apportioned under para.11(3). The Commissioner applied the reasoning from the case law on income support as the state pension credit rules were evidently derived from those regulations (agreeing with *CJSA/888/1999*).

Paragraph 12

4.128 In practice the absence of documentation to support claims for loans taken out to pay for repairs and improvements is often a problem when the work in question was undertaken some years ago. As Judge Lane pointed out in *KWA v Secretary of State for Work and Pensions (SPC)* [2011] UKUT 10 (AAC), "the tribunal cannot pluck figures out of the air" (at para.7). Thus:

> "There are two principles which come into play where there is a lack of evidence on an issue. The first is that parties to tribunal proceedings have a duty to cooperate with the tribunal. If a party has not done all that he could reasonably do to provide evidence which lies within his purview, a tribunal is entitled to determine an issue dependent upon that evidence against him: *Kerr v Department for Social Development* [2004] UKHL 23, per Lady Hale of Richmond [62, 63]. The second is that if, at the end of the day, an issue cannot be resolved because of the lack of evidence, it will be decided against the party who had the burden of proving it. In this case, the burden is on the claimant" (at para.8).

Judge Lane also observed that "'repairs and improvements' must be carried out with a view to maintaining fitness for human habitation. That is a low standard. It does not reflect the highest standards of living a person may wish to have. Moreover, the work done is only a repair and improvement if it falls within one of the categories (a)–(l). There is no discretion to award housing costs in relation to works which do not fall within the headings set out" (at para.12).

The scope of para.12(2)(l) was considered by Judge Jacobs in *CPC/2038/2008*. A loan taken out to provide separate sleeping accommodation may be taken out before a child reaches the age of 10 and still be covered by this provision; how far in advance will depend on the circumstances of the particular case (broadly following *CIS/14657/1996* and *CIS/5119/2001* and not following *CIS/1678/1999*).

Paragraph 13

The treatment of service charges for the purposes of entitlement to pension credit was considered by the Commissioner in *R(PC) 1/07*. Tribunals cannot assume that where a proportion of service charges are met by the Supporting People programme, the balance necessarily constitute eligible housing costs under para.13. In *R(PC) 1/07* the evidence before the tribunals lacked "any detail of what the scheme manager did other than in relation to general counselling and support, and nowhere was there any indication of what proportion of his time a scheme manager spent on activities said to relate to the provision of adequate accommodation" (at para.18). The Commissioner agreed: 4.129

> "with the remark of the Commissioner in paragraph 9 of *CPC/968/2005* that a "broad approach" is called for: for example, a decision-maker or tribunal supplied with the terms of the lease relating to services and service charges, a breakdown of the service charges, details of what service charges (if any) are met by the Supporting People programme, and a statement from the scheme manager as to how his working time is usually divided up should normally be able to make a reasoned estimate of how much of the service charges in dispute are eligible or ineligible. Each case will, however, inevitably turn on its own facts and evidential requirements will vary" (at [23]).

See also *R(PC) 2/08*, which deals with several technical issues concerned with how an award of state pension credit should be adjusted for housing costs after estimated service charges have been finalised.

The case law on the treatment of eligible service charges was considered further in *DL v Secretary of State for Work and Pensions* [2013] AACR 22; [2013] UKUT 29 (AAC). This review of the authorities confirmed that charges for maintenance, repairs, cleaning, and utility charges for communal areas and gardens are eligible (*CIS/1459/1995*); charges for reserve fund contributions for accommodation costs are eligible (*CPC/968/2005* and *CIS/667/2002*); staffing costs fairly attributable to the provision of adequate accommodation based on what the staff actually do in the particular development or similar developments are eligible (*R(PC) 1/07* and *CPC/977/2007*); and other administrative costs, which cannot be neatly categorised, should be apportioned in the same ratio as eligible and non-eligible charges in the rest of the budget (*R(PC) 1/07* and *CPC/968/2005*), rather than in the same ratio as eligible and non-eligible charges in the staff costs budget only (as held in *R(IS) 2/07*).

On the meaning of "long tenancy" (see para.(6)(d)) under Scots law, see *NR v Secretary of State for Work and Pensions* [2013] UKUT 0647 (AAC), dealing with the requirement that the tenancy be capable of registration (see also R(H) 3/07). Judge J.N. Wright QC held that in principle this requirement did not apply in Scotland, because although a lease for 20 years or more requires to be registered to be effectual against singular successors (i.e. successors in title), under Scots law a tenancy might be enforceable only against the granter. This did not assist the tenant on the facts, as there was no written agreement, and Scots law requires a lease for more than one year to be in writing. The decision also confirms that caravan park periodical fees for mobile homes will normally fall under the housing benefit scheme.

SCHEDULE III

SPECIAL GROUPS

Polygamous marriages

1.—(1) The provisions of this paragraph apply in any case to which section 12 (polygamous marriages) applies if the claimant is taken to be "the person in question" for the purposes of that section. 4.130

(2) The following provision shall apply instead of section 3(1)—

"(1) The first condition is that, if the claimant is taken [1 . . .] to be "the person in question" for the purposes of section 12 (polygamous marriages)—

(a) the case is one to which that section applies; and
(b) any one or more of the persons falling within subsection (1)(c) of that section has attained the age of 65.".

(3) The following provision shall apply instead of section 4(1)—

"(1) A claimant is not entitled to state pension credit if, taking the claimant to be 'the person in question' for the purposes of section 12 (polygamous marriages)—
(a) the case is one to which that section applies; and
(b) any one or more of the other persons falling within subsection (1)(c) of that section is entitled to state pension credit.".

(4) The following provision shall apply instead of section 5—

"**5.—Income and capital of claimant, spouses, etc.**

(1) This section applies in any case to which section 12 (polygamous marriages) applies if the claimant is taken to be 'the person in question' for the purposes of that section.

(2) In any such case, the income and capital of each of the other persons falling within subsection (1)(c) of that section shall be treated for the purposes of this Act as income and capital of the claimant, except where regulations provide otherwise.".

(5) In regulation 6 (amount of the guarantee credit), for paragraph (1) there shall be substituted—

"(1) Except as provided in the following provisions of these Regulations, in a case to which section 12 (polygamous marriages) applies if the claimant is taken to be 'the person in question' for the purposes of that section the standard minimum guarantee is the sum of—
(a) [10£237.55] per week in respect of the claimant and any one spouse of the claimant's; and
(b) [10£81.95] per week in respect of for each additional spouse (whether of the claimant or that spouse) who falls within section 12(1)(c).".

(6) The maximum savings credit shall be determined on the assumption that the standard minimum guarantee is the amount prescribed for partners under regulation 6(1)(a).
(7) In regulation 7 (savings credit) for paragraph (2) there shall be substituted—

"(2) In any case to which section 12 (polygamous marriages) [2applies] if the claimant is taken to be 'the person in question' for the purposes of that section, the amount prescribed for the savings credit threshold is [10£212.97]."

(8) In regulations [6. . .],5, [16(8),] 10,12 and 14 and in paragraph [36(5)(b)(v)] of Schedule 1 and in Schedule 2, any reference to a partner includes also a reference to any additional spouse to whom this paragraph applies.
(9) For the purposes of regulation 6(5)(a) and (b), paragraph 1(1)(b)(i) of Part I of Schedule I is satisfied only if both partners and each additional spouse to whom this paragraph applies are in receipt of attendance allowance [8, the care component of disability living allowance at the highest or middle rate prescribed in accordance with section 72(3) of the 1992 Act or the daily living component of personal independence payment at the standard or enhanced rate in accordance with section 78(3) of the 2012 Act [9 or armed forces independence payment]].
(10) For the purposes of regulation 6(5)(a), paragraph 1(1)(c) of Part I of Schedule 1 is only satisfied if—
(a) both partners and each additional spouse to whom this paragraph applies all fall within either paragraph 1(1)(c)(i) or paragraph 1(1)(c)(ii); and
(b) at least one of them falls within paragraph 1(1)(c)(i); and
(c) at least one of them falls within paragraph 1(1)(c)(ii) but not paragraph 1(1)(c)(i); and
(d) either paragraph 1(1)(c)(iv) is satisfied or a person is entitled to and in receipt of an allowance under section 70 of the 1992 Act in respect of caring for one or more, but not all, the persons who fall within paragraph 1(1)(c)(i).
(11) Any reference in this paragraph to an additional spouse to whom this paragraph applies is a reference to any person who is an additional spouse (whether of the claimant's or of a spouse of the claimant's) falling within subsection (1)(c) of section 12 if the claimant is taken to be "the person in question" for the purposes of that section.

Persons serving a sentence of imprisonment detained in hospital

[4**2.** —[7 (1) Sub-paragraph (2) applies in the case of a claimant ("C") who satisfies either of the following conditions. 4.131

(1A) The first condition is that—

(a) C is being detained under section 45A or 47 of the Mental Health Act 1983 (power of higher courts to direct hospital admission; removal to hospital of persons serving sentences of imprisonment etc.); and

(b) in any case where there is in relation to C a release date within the meaning of section 50(3) of that Act, C is being detained on or before the day which the Secretary of State certifies to be that release date.

(1B) The second condition is that C is being detained under—

(a) section 59A of the Criminal Procedure (Scotland) Act 1995 (hospital direction); or

(b) section 136 of the Mental Health (Care and Treatment) (Scotland) Act 2003 (transfer of prisoners for treatment of mental disorder).]

(2) In the case of a claimant to whom paragraph (1) applies—

(a) section 2(3) has effect with the substitution of a reference to a nil amount for the reference to the standard minimum guarantee in paragraph (a) [5, and [10 nil] is the prescribed additional amount for the purposes of paragraph (b)] and

(b) the maximum amount of savings credit shall be taken to be [10 nil]]

AMENDMENTS

1. State Pension Credit (Consequential, Transitional and Miscellaneous Provisions) Regulations 2002 (SI 2002/3019) reg.23(m) (October 6, 2003).

2. State Pension Credit (Consequential, Transitional and Miscellaneous Provisions) (No.2) Regulations 2002 (SI 2002/3197) reg.2 and Sch. para.10 (October 6, 2003).

3. State Pension Credit (Transitional and Miscellaneous Provisions) Amendment Regulations 2003 (SI 2003/2274) reg.2(10) (October 6, 2003).

4. Social Security (Hospital In-Patients) Regulations 2005 (SI 2005/3360) reg.8(5) (April 10, 2006).

5. Social Security (Miscellaneous Amendments) Regulations 2006 (SI 2006/588) reg.4(4) (April 10, 2006).

6. Social Security (Miscellaneous Amendments) (No.4) Regulations 2008 (SI 2008/2424) reg.3(5) (October 6, 2008).

7. Social Security (Persons Serving a Sentence of Imprisonment Detained in Hospital) Regulations 2010 (SI 2010/442) reg.4(2) (March 25, 2010).

8. Personal Independence Payment (Supplementary Provisions and Consequential Amendments) Regulations 2013 (SI 2013/388) reg.8 and Sch. para.27(6) (April 8, 2013).

9. Armed Forces and Reserve Forces Compensation Scheme (Consequential Provisions: Subordinate Legislation) Order 2013 (SI 2013/591) art.7 and Sch. para.23(6) (April 8, 2013).

10. Social Security Benefits (Adjustment of Amounts and Thresholds) Regulations 2016 (SI 2016/242) reg.4(4) (April 11, 2016).

GENERAL NOTE

Paragraph 2

This paragraph was amended with effect from March 25, 2010 in response to the Court of Appeal's decision in *R. (on the application of D & M) v Secretary of State for Work and Pensions* [2010] EWCA Civ 18. The Court of Appeal had held that the previous wording meant that a person subject to an indeterminate sentence of imprisonment who was being detained in hospital for treatment for mental disorder would be eligible for DWP benefits when the tariff part of the sentence had been served. This was regarded as contrary to Government policy. The amended paragraph provides a revised form of words which is intended to ensure that such a person continues to be excluded from benefits when the tariff date has passed. 4.132

[1 SCHEDULE IIIA **Regulation 12**

Date on which certain fixed length assessed income periods end

4.132A

Column 1 *Period in which the assessed income period would end apart from regulation 12(d)*	*Column 2* *Date on which assessed income period is to end*
1st April 2019 to 14th April 2019	14th July 2016
15th April 2019 to 30th April 2019	28th July 2016
1st May 2019 to 14th May 2019	14th August 2016
15th May 2019 to 31st May 2019	28th August 2016
1st June 2019 to 14th June 2019	14th October 2016
15th June 2019 to 30th June 2019	28th October 2016
1st July 2019 to 14th July 2019	14th November 2016
15th July 2019 to 31st July 2019	28th November 2016
1st August 2019 to 14th August 2019	14th December 2016
15th August 2019 to 31st August 2019	28th December 2016
1st September 2019 to 14th September 2019	14th February 2017
15th September 2019 to 30th September 2019	28th February 2017
1st October 2019 to 14th October 2019	14th March 2017
15th October 2019 to 31st October 2019	28th March 2017
1st November 2019 to 14th November 2019	14th April 2017
15th November 2019 to 30th November 2019	28th April 2017
1st December 2019 to 14th December 2019	14th June 2017
15th December 2019 to 31st December 2019	28th June 2017
1st January 2020 to 14th January 2020	14th July 2017
15th January 2020 to 31st January 2020	28th July 2017
1st February 2020 to 14th February 2020	14th September 2017
15th February 2020 to 29th February 2020	28th September 2017
1st March 2020 to 14th March 2020	14th October 2017
15th March 2020 to 31st March 2020	28th October 2017
1st April 2020 to 14th April 2020	14th December 2017
15th April 2020 to 30th April 2020	28th December 2017
1st May 2020 to 14th May 2020	14th January 2018
15th May 2020 to 31st May 2020	28th January 2018
1st June 2020 to 14th June 2020	14th March 2018
15th June 2020 to 30th June 2020	28th March 2018
1st July 2020 to 14th July 2020	14th April 2018
15th July 2020 to 31st July 2020	28th April 2018
1st August 2020 to 14th August 2020	14th June 2018
15th August 2020 to 31st August 2020	28th June 2018
1st September 2020 to 14th September 2020	14th July 2018
15th September 2020 to 30th September 2020	28th July 2018
1st October 2020 to 14th October 2020	14th August 2018
15th October 2020 to 31st October 2020	28th August 2018
1st November 2020 to 14th November 2020	14th October 2018
15th November 2020 to 30th November 2020	28th October 2018
1st December 2020 to 14th December 2020	14th November 2018
15th December 2020 to 31st December 2020	28th November 2018
1st January 2021 to 14th January 2021	14th January 2019
15th January 2021 to 31st January 2021	28th January 2019
1st February 2021 to 14th February 2021	14th February 2019
15th February 2021 to 28th February 2021	28th February 2019
1st March 2021 to 14th March 2021	14th March 2019
15th March 2021 to 5th April 2021	28th March 2019]

AMENDMENT

1. State Pension Credit (Amendment) Regulations 2015 (SI 2015/1529) reg.2(4) (April 6, 2016).

General note

See the notes to reg.12 above and to s.2(6) of the State Pension Credit Act 2002. 4.132B

SCHEDULE IV **Regulation 17(7)**

Amounts to be Disregarded in the Calculation of Income other than Earnings

1.—In addition to any sum which falls to be disregarded in accordance with paragraphs 3 to 6, £10 of any of the following, namely— 4.133

(a) a war disablement pension (except insofar as such a pension falls to be disregarded under paragraph 2 or 3);

(b) a war widow's or war widower's pension;

[7 (ba) unless paragraph 1(a) or (b) applies, any payment described in regulation 15(5)(ac) (except insofar as such a payment falls to be disregarded under paragraph 2 or 3);]

(c) a pension payable to a person as a [6 widow, widower or surviving civil partner] under [7. . .]any power of Her Majesty other wise than under an enactment to make provision about pensions for or in respect of persons who have been disabled or have died in consequence of service as members of the armed forces of the Crown;

[4 (cc) a guaranteed income payment] [7 and, if the amount of that payment has been abated to less than £10 by a [8 pension or payment falling within article 31(1)(a) or (b) of the Armed Forces and Reserve Forces (Compensation Scheme) Order 2005], so much of [8 that pension or payment] as would not, in aggregate with the amount of [8 any] guaranteed income payment disregarded, exceed £10];

(d) a payment made to compensate for the non-payment of such a pension [4 or payment] as is mentioned in any of the preceding sub-paragraphs;

(e) a pension paid by the government of a country outside Great Britain which is analogous to any of the [4 pensions or payments mentioned in sub-paragraphs (a) to (cc) above];

(f) a pension paid to victims of National Socialist persecution under any special provision made by the law of the Federal Republic of Germany, or any part of it, or of the Republic of Austria.

2.—The whole of any amount included in a pension to which paragraph 1 relates in respect of—

(a) the claimant's need for constant attendance;

(b) the claimant's exceptionally severe disablement.

3.—Any mobility supplement under [7 article 20 of the Naval, Military and Air Forces Etc. (Disablement and Death) Service Pensions Order 2006] (including such a supplement by virtue of any other scheme or order) or under article 25A of the Personal Injuries (Civilians) Scheme 1983 or any payment intended to compensate for the non-payment of such a supplement.

[7 **4.**—Any supplementary pension under article 23(2) of the Naval, Military and Air Forces Etc. (Disablement and Death) Service Pensions Order 2006 (pensions to surviving spouses and surviving civil partners) and any analogous payment made by the Secretary of State for Defence to any person who is not a person entitled under that Order.]

5.—In the case of a pension awarded at the supplementary rate under article 27(3) of the Personal Injuries (Civilians) Scheme 1983 (pensions to [6 widows, widowers or surviving civil partners]), the sum specified in paragraph 1(c) of Schedule 4 to that Scheme.

6.—(1) Any payment which is—

(a) made under any of the Dispensing Instruments to a [6 widow, widower or surviving civil partner] of a person—

(i) whose death was attributable to service in a capacity analogous to service as a member of the armed forces of the Crown; and

(ii) whose service in such capacity terminated before 31st March 1973; and

[7 (b) equal to the amount specified in article 23(2) of the Naval, Military and Air Forces Etc. (Disablement and Death) Service Pensions Order 2006.]

(2) In this paragraph "the Dispensing Instruments" means the Order in Council of 19th December 1881, the Royal Warrant of 27th October 1884 and the Order by His Majesty of 14th January 1922 (exceptional grants of pay, non-effective pay and allowances).

7.—£10 of any widowed parent's allowance to which the claimant is entitled under section 39A of the 1992 Act.

[2**7A.**—£10 of any widowed mother's allowance to which the claimant is entitled under section 37 of the 1992 Act.]

8.—(1) Where the claimant occupies a dwelling as his home and he provides in that dwelling board and lodging accommodation, an amount, in respect of each person for whom such accommodation is provided for the whole or any part of a week, equal to—

(a) where the aggregate of any payments made in respect of any one week in respect of such accommodation provided to such person does not exceed £20.00, 100 per cent of such payments; or

(b) where the aggregate of any such payments exceeds £20.00, £20.00 and 50 per cent of the excess over £20.00.

(2) [5 . . .]

9.—If the claimant—

(a) owns the freehold or leasehold interest in any property or is a tenant of any property; and

(b) occupies a part of that property; and

(c) has an agreement with another person allowing that person to occupy another part of that property on payment of rent and—

(i) the amount paid by that person is less than £20 per week, the whole of that amount; or

(ii) the amount paid is £20 or more per week, £20.

10.—Where a claimant receives income under an annuity purchased with a loan, which satisfies the following conditions—

(a) that the loan was made as part of a scheme under which not less than 90% of the proceeds of the loan were applied to the purchase by the person to whom it was made of an annuity ending with his life or with the life of the survivor of two or more persons (in this paragraph referred to as "the annuitants") who include the person to whom the loan was made;

(b) that at the time the loan was made the person to whom it was made or each of the annuitants had attained the age of 65;

(c) that the loan was secured on a dwelling in Great Britain and the person to whom the loan was made or one of the annuitants owns an estate or interest in that dwelling;

(d) that the person to whom the loan was made or one of the annuitants occupies the dwelling on which it was secured as his home at the time the interest is paid; and

(e) that the interest payable on the loan is paid by the person to whom the loan was made or by one of the annuitants,

the amount, calculated on a weekly basis, equal to—

(i) where, or insofar as, section 369 of the Income and Corporation Taxes Act 1988 (mortgage interest payable under deduction of tax) applies to the payments of interest on the loan, the interest which is payable after deduction of a sum equal to income tax on such payments at the applicable percentage of income tax within the meaning of section 369(1A) of that Act;

(ii) in any other case the interest which is payable on the loan without deduction of such a sum.

11.—(1) Any payment, other than a payment to which sub-paragraph (2) applies, made to the claimant by Trustees in exercise of a discretion exercisable by them.

(2) This sub-paragraph applies to payments made to the claimant by Trustees in exercise of a discretion exercisable by them for the purpose of—

(a) obtaining food, ordinary clothing or footwear or household fuel;

(b) the payment of rent, council tax or water charges for which that claimant or his partner is liable;

(c) meeting housing costs of a kind specified in Schedule 2;

(d) [1. . .].

(3) In a case to which sub-paragraph (2) applies, £20 or—

(a) if the payment is less than £20, the whole payment; or

(b) if, in the claimant's case, £10 is disregarded in accordance with paragraph 1(a) to (f), [1 or paragraph 7] [2 or 7A] £10 or the whole payment if it is less than £10.

(4) For the purposes of this paragraph—

"ordinary clothing and footwear" means clothing or footwear for normal daily use, but does not include school uniforms, or clothing and footwear used solely for sporting activities; and

"rent" means eligible rent for the purposes of the Housing Benefit (General) Regulations 1987 less any deductions in respect of non-dependants which fall to be made under regulation 63 (non-dependant deductions) of those Regulations.

12.—Any increase in [7 pension or allowance under Part 2 or 3 of the Naval, Military and Air Forces Etc. (Disablement and Death) Service Pensions Order 2006] paid in respect of a dependent other than the pensioner's [7 . . .] [6 partner].

13.—Any payment ordered by a court to be made to the claimant or the claimant's partner in consequence of any accident, injury or disease suffered by [2the person] to whom the payments are made.

14.—Periodic payments made to the claimant or the claimant's partner under an agreement entered into in [2 . . .] settlement of a claim made by [2 that person] for an injury suffered by him.

15.—Any income which is payable outside the United Kingdom for such period during which there is a prohibition against the transfer to the United Kingdom of that income.

16.—Any banking charges or commission payable in converting to Sterling payments of income made in a currency other than Sterling.

17.—[7 . . .]

[3**18.** Except in the case of income from capital specified in Part II of Schedule V, any actual income from capital.]

AMENDMENTS

1. State Pension Credit (Consequential, Transitional and Miscellaneous Provisions) Regulations 2002 (SI 2002/3019) reg.23(n) (October 6, 2003).
2. State Pension Credit (Consequential, Transitional and Miscellaneous Provisions) (No.2) Regulations 2002 (SI 2002/3197) reg.2 and Sch. para.11 (October 6, 2003).
3. State Pension Credit (Transitional and Miscellaneous Provisions) Amendment Regulations 2003 (SI 2003/2274) reg.2(11) (October 6, 2003).
4. Social Security (Miscellaneous Amendments) Regulations 2005 (SI 2005/574) reg.2(7) and (8)(d) (April 4, 2005).
5. Social Security (Miscellaneous Amendments) (No.2) Regulations 2005 (SI 2005/2465) reg.6(5) (October 3, 2005).
6. Civil Partnership (Pensions, Social Security and Child Support) (Consequential, etc. Provisions) Order 2005 (SI 2005/2877) art.2(3) and Sch.3 para.35(4) (December 5, 2005).
7. Social Security (Miscellaneous Amendments) (No.7) Regulations 2008 (SI 2008/3157) reg.4(5) (January 5, 2009).
8. Social Security (Miscellaneous Amendments) (No.4) Regulations 2009 (SI 2009/2655) reg.5(5) (October 26, 2009).

GENERAL NOTE

This Schedule performs the same function in relation to state pension credit as Sch.9 to the Income Support (General) Regulations 1987 (SI 1987/1967) does in the context of income support, although the list of disregards is much less extensive (reflecting the different nature of state pension credit). **4.134**

Paragraph 1

See Income Support (General) Regulations 1987 (SI 1987/1967) Sch.9 para.16 (although that also includes widowed mother's allowance and widowed parent's allowance: see para.(7)). **4.135**

Paragraph 3

See Income Support (General) Regulations 1987 (SI 1987/1967) Sch.9 para.8. **4.136**

Paragraphs 4–6

See Income Support (General) Regulations 1987 (SI 1987/1967) Sch.9 paras 54–56. **4.137**

Paragraphs 7–7A

See Income Support (General) Regulations 1987 (SI 1987/1967) Sch.9 para.16(g) and (h). **4.138**

Paragraph 8

4.139 See Income Support (General) Regulations 1987 (SI 1987/1967) Sch.9 para.20.

Paragraph 9

4.140 This is a more generous provision than the nearest equivalent under the income support scheme. Income Support (General) Regulations 1987 (SI 1987/1967) Sch.9 para.19 provides that, for the purposes of income support, only the first £4 a week of income from a sub-tenant is disregarded (plus a slightly larger prescribed figure where the rent charged includes an amount for heating). This provision grants a state pension credit claimant in similar circumstances a disregard of up to £20 a week on payments from a sub-tenant or licensee.

Paragraph 10

4.141 See Income Support (General) Regulations 1987 (SI 1987/1967) Sch.9 para.17.

Paragraph 11

4.142 See Income Support (General) Regulations 1987 (SI 1987/1967) Sch.9 para.15 for the closest equivalent under the income support scheme.

Paragraphs 13–14

4.143 These are more generous rules than apply to income support. The rule there is that sums paid by way of personal injuries compensation and held under a trust are disregarded as capital (Income Support (General) Regulations 1987 (SI 1987/1967) Sch.10 para.12), but payments made out of the fund to the claimant count as income or capital in the normal way. The rule for state pension credit is that payments made in compensation for personal injuries under a court order or following a settlement do not count as income. The repeal of the word "final" in the first amendment to para.14 (so that it reads "in settlement of" and not "in final settlement of") presumably ensures that the benefit of this provision will be gained by pensioners who receive provisional awards of personal injuries damages under the Supreme Court Act 1981 s.32A.

Paragraphs 15–16

4.144 See Income Support (General) Regulations 1987 (SI 1987/1967) Sch.9 paras 23–24.

SCHEDULE V **Regulation 17(8)**

INCOME FROM CAPITAL

PART I

Capital disregarded for the purpose of calculating income

4.145 **1.**—Any premises acquired for occupation by the claimant which he intends to occupy as his home within 26 weeks of the date of acquisition or such longer period as is reasonable in the circumstances to enable the claimant to obtain possession and commence occupation of the premises.

[3 **1A.**—The dwelling occupied by the claimant as his home but only one home shall be disregarded under this paragraph.]

2.—Any premises which the claimant intends to occupy as his home, and in respect of which he is taking steps to obtain possession and has sought legal advice, or has commenced legal proceedings, with a view to obtaining possession, for a period of 26 weeks from the date on which he first sought such advice or first commenced such proceedings whichever is the earlier, or such longer period as is reasonable in the circumstances to enable him to obtain possession and commence occupation of those premises.

3.—Any premises which the claimant intends to occupy as his home to which essential repairs or alterations are required in order to render them fit for such occupation, for a period of 26 weeks from the date on which the claimant first takes steps to effect those repairs or alterations, or such longer period as is necessary to enable those repairs or alterations to be carried out.

4.—Any premises occupied in whole or in part—

(a) by a [6 person who is a close relative, grandparent, grandchild, uncle, aunt, nephew or niece of the claimant or of his partner] as his home where that person [18 has attained the qualifying age for state pension credit or is incapacitated];

(b) by the former partner of the claimant as his home; but this provision shall not apply where the former partner is a person from whom the claimant is estranged or divorced [9 or with whom he had formed a civil partnership that has been dissolved].

5.—Any future interest in property of any kind, other than land or premises in respect of which the claimant has granted a subsisting lease or tenancy, including sub-leases or sub-tenancies.

6.—(1) Where a claimant has ceased to occupy what was formerly the dwelling occupied as the home following his estrangement or divorce from [9, or dissolution of his civil partnership with,] his former partner, that dwelling for a period of 26 weeks from the date on which he ceased to occupy that dwelling or, where the dwelling is occupied as the home by the former partner who is a lone parent, for so long as it is so occupied.

(2) In this paragraph—

(a) "dwelling" includes any garage, garden and outbuildings, which were formerly occupied by the claimant as his home and any premises not so occupied which it is impracticable or unreasonable to sell separately, in particular, in Scotland, any croft land on which the dwelling is situated;

(b) "lone parent" means a person who has no partner and who is responsible for, and a member of the same household as, a child; and

(c) "child" means a person [12 who is a qualifying young person or] a child for the purposes of Part IX of the 1992 Act.

7.—Any premises where the claimant is taking reasonable steps to dispose of the whole of his interest in those premises, for a period of 26 weeks from the date on which he first took such steps, or such longer period as is reasonable in the circumstances to enable him to dispose of those premises.

8.—All personal possessions.

9.—The assets of any business owned in whole or in part by the claimant and for the purposes of which he is engaged as a self-employed earner or, if he has ceased to be engaged, for such period as may be reasonable in the circumstances to allow for disposal of those assets.

[1**9A.**—The assets of any business owned in whole or in part by the claimant if—

(a) he is not engaged as a self-employed earner in that business by reason of some disease or bodily or mental disablement; but

(b) he intends to become engaged (or, as the case may be, re-engaged) as a self-employed earner in that business as soon as he recovers or is able to become engaged, or re-engaged, in that business,

[3 . . .].]

10.—The surrender value of any policy of life insurance.

11.—The value of any funeral plan contract; and for this purpose, "funeral plan contract" means a contract under which—

(a) the claimant makes one or more payments to another person ("the provider");

(b) the provider undertakes to provide, or secure the provision of, a funeral in the United Kingdom for the claimant on his death; and

(c) the sole purpose of the plan is to provide or secure the provision of a funeral for the claimant on his death.

12.—Where an ex-gratia payment has been made by the Secretary of State on or after 1st February 2001 in consequence of the imprisonment or [2internment] of—

(a) the claimant;

(b) the claimant's partner;

(c) the claimant's deceased spouse [9 or deceased civil partner]; or

(d) the claimant's partner's deceased spouse [9 or deceased civil partner],

by the Japanese during the Second World War, an amount equal to that payment.

13.—(1) Subject to sub-paragraph (2), the amount of any trust payment made to a claimant or a claimant's partner [3 who is]—

(a) [3 . . .] a diagnosed person;

(b) [3a diagnosed person's partner or] was a diagnosed person's partner at the time of the diagnosed person's death;

(c) [3 . . .] a parent of a diagnosed person, a person acting in place of the diagnosed person's parents or a person who was so acting at the date of the diagnosed person's death.

(2) Where [3 a trust payment is made to]—

(a) [3 a person referred to in sub-paragraph (1)(a) or (b), that sub-paragraph] shall apply for the period beginning on the date on which the trust is made and ending on the date on which [3 that person] dies;
(b) [3 a person referred to in sub-paragraph (1)(c), that sub-paragraph] shall apply for the period beginning on the date on which the trust payment is made and ending two years after that date.

(3) Subject to sub-paragraph (4), the amount of any payment by a person to whom a trust payment has been made or of any payment out of the estate of a person to whom a trust payment has been made, which is made to a claimant or a claimant's partner [3 who is]—
(a) [3 . . .] the diagnosed person;
(b) [3 a diagnosed person's partner or] was a diagnosed person's partner at the date of the diagnosed person's death; or
(c) [3 . . .] a parent of a diagnosed person, a person acting in place of the diagnosed person's parents or a person who was so acting at the date of the diagnosed person's death.

(4) Where [3 a payment referred to in sub-paragraph (3) is made to]—
(a) [3 a person referred to in sub-paragraph (3)(a) or (b), that sub-paragraph] shall apply for the period beginning on the date on which the payment is made and ending on the date on which [3 that person] dies;
(b) [3 a person referred to in sub-paragraph (3)(c), that sub-paragraph] shall apply for the period beginning on the date on which the payment is made and ending two years after that date.

(5) In this paragraph, a reference to a person—
(a) being the diagnosed person's partner;
(b) acting in place of the diagnosed person's parents,

at the date of the diagnosed person's death shall include a person who would have been such a person or a person who would have been so acting, but for the diagnosed person [8 residing in a care home or independent hospital].

(6) In this paragraph—

"diagnosed person" means a person who has been diagnosed as suffering from, or who, after his death, has been diagnosed as having suffered from, variant [3 Creutzfeldt]-Jakob disease;

"relevant trust" means a trust established out of funds provided by the Secretary of State in respect of persons who suffered, or who are suffering, from variant [3 Creutzfeldt]-Jakob disease for the benefit of persons eligible for payments in accordance with its provisions;

"trust payment" means a payment under a relevant trust.

14.—[16 (1)] The amount of any payment, other than a war disablement pension or a war widow's or widower's pension, to compensate for the fact that the claimant, the claimant's partner, the claimant's deceased spouse [9 or deceased civil partner] or the claimant's partner's deceased spouse [9 or deceased civil partner]—
(a) was a slave labourer or a forced labourer;
(b) had suffered property loss or had suffered personal injury; or
(c) was a parent of a child who had died, during the Second World War.

[16 (2) In sub-paragraph (1), "war disablement pension" and "war widow's or widower's pension" include any payment described in regulation 15(5)(ac).]

15.—(1) Any payment made under [20 or by] the Macfarlane Trust, the Macfarlane (Special Payments) Trust, the Macfarlane (Special Payments) (No.2) Trust ("the Trusts"), the Fund, the Eileen Trust [19, MFET Limited] [4, the [15 Independent Living Fund (2006)] [10, the Skipton Fund [21, the Caxton Foundation] or the London Bombings Relief Charitable Fund]].

(2) Any payment by or on behalf of a person who is suffering or who suffered from haemophilia or who is or was a qualifying person, which derives from a payment made under [20 or by] any of the Trusts to which sub-paragraph (1) refers and which is made to or for the benefit of that person's partner or former partner from whom he is not, or where that person has died was not, estranged or divorced [9 or with whom he has formed a civil partnership that has not been dissolved or, where that person has died, had not been dissolved at the time of that person's death].

(3) Any payment by or on behalf of the partner or former partner of a person who is suffering or who suffered from haemophilia or who is or was a qualifying person provided that the partner or former partner and that person are not, or if either of them has died were not, estranged or divorced [9 or, where the partner or former partner and that person have formed a civil partnership, the civil partnership has not been dissolved or, if either of them has died, had not been dissolved at the time of the death], which derives from a payment made under [20 or by] any of the Trusts to which sub-paragraph (1) refers and which is made to or for the benefit of the person who is suffering from haemophilia or who is a qualifying person.

(4) Any payment by a person who is suffering from haemophilia or who is a qualifying person, which derives from a payment under [20 or by] any of the Trusts to which sub-paragraph (1) refers, where—

(a) that person has no partner or former partner from whom he is not estranged or divorced [9 or with whom he has formed a civil partnership that has not been dissolved], nor any child who is or had been a member of that person's household; and

(b) the payment is made either—

(i) to that person's parent or step-parent, or

(ii) where that person at the date of the payment is a child or a student who has not completed his full-time education and has no parent or step-parent, to any person standing in the place of his parent,

but only for a period from the date of the payment until the end of two years from that person's death.

(5) Any payment out of the estate of a person who suffered from haemophilia or who was a qualifying person, which derives from a payment under [20 or by] any of the Trusts to which sub-paragraph (1) refers, where—

(a) that person at the date of his death (the relevant date) had no partner or former partner from whom he was not estranged or divorced [9 or with whom he has formed a civil partnership that had not been dissolved], nor any child who was or had been a member of his household; and

(b) the payment is made either—

(i) to that person's parent or step-parent, or

(ii) where that person at the relevant date was a child or a student who had not completed his full-time education and had no parent or step-parent, to any person standing in place his parent,

but only for a period of two years from the relevant date.

(6) In the case of a person to whom or for whose benefit a payment referred to in this paragraph is made, any capital resource which derives from any payment of income or capital made under or deriving from any of the Trusts.

(7) For the purposes of sub-paragraphs (2) to (6), any reference to the Trusts shall be construed as including a reference to the Fund [5, the Eileen Trust [19, MFET Limited] [10, the Skipton Fund [21, the Caxton Foundation] and the London Bombings Relief Charitable Fund]].

(8) In this paragraph—

"child" means any person [12 who is a qualifying young person or] a child for the purposes of Part IX of the Contributions and Benefits Act (child benefit);

"course of study" means any course of study, whether or not it is a sandwich course and whether or not a grant is made for undertaking or attending it;

"qualifying course" means a qualifying course as defined for the purposes of Parts II and IV of the Jobseeker's Allowance Regulations;

"sandwich course" has the meaning given in regulation 5(2) of the Education (Student Support) Regulations 2001, regulation 5(2) of the Education (Student Loans) (Scotland) Regulations 2000 or regulation 5(2) of the Education (Student Support) Regulations (Northern Ireland) 2000, as the case may be;

"student" means a person, other than a person in receipt of a training allowance, who is attending or undertaking—

(a) a course of study at an educational establishment; or

(b) a qualifying course;

"training allowance" means an allowance (whether by way of periodical grants or otherwise) payable—

(a) out of public funds by a Government department or by or on behalf of the Secretary of State, [17 Skills Development Scotland,] Scottish Enterprise or Highlands and Islands Enterprise;

(b) to a person for his maintenance or in respect of a member of his family; and

(c) for the period, or part of the period, during which he is following a course of training or instruction provided by, or in pursuance of arrangements made with, that department or approved by that department in relation to him or so provided or approved by or on behalf of the Secretary of State, [17 Skills Development Scotland,] Scottish Enterprise or Highlands and Islands Enterprise,

but it does not include an allowance paid by any Government department to or in respect of a person by reason of the fact that he is following a course of full-time education, other than under arrangements made under section 2 of the Employment and Training Act 1973 or is training as a teacher [2. . .].

[7 **15A.**—[10. . . .]]

16.—[1(1)] An amount equal to the amount of any payment made in consequence of any personal injury to the claimant or, if the claimant has a partner, to the partner.

[1(2) Where the whole or part of the payment is administered—

[13(a) by the High Court or the County Court under rule 21.11(1) of the Civil Procedure Rules 1998, or the Court of Protection, or on behalf of a person where the payment can only be disposed of by order or direction of any such court;]

(b) in accordance with an order made under [13 . . .] rule 36.14 of the Ordinary Cause Rules 1993 or under rule 128 of those Rules; or

(c) in accordance with the terms of a trust established for the benefit of the claimant or his partner,

the whole of the amount so administered.]

17.—Any amount specified in paragraphs 18 to 20 [16 or 20B]—

(a) in a case where there is an assessed income period, until the end of that period or until the expiration of one year from the date of payment, whichever is the later; or

(b) in any other case, for a period of one year beginning with the date of receipt.

18.—Amounts paid under a policy of insurance in connection with the loss of or damage to the property occupied by the claimant as his home and to his personal possessions.

19.—So much of any amounts paid to the claimant or deposited in the claimant's name for the sole purpose of—

(a) purchasing premises which the claimant intends to occupy as his home; or

(b) effecting essential repairs or alterations to the premises occupied or intended to be occupied by the claimant as his home.

20.—(1) Any amount paid—

(a) by way of arrears of benefit;

(b) by way of compensation for the late payment of benefit; or

[24 (ba) personal independence payment;]

[25 (bb) armed forces independence payment;]

(c) in lieu of the payment of benefit;

[3 (d) any payment made by a local authority (including in England a county council), or by the [16 Welsh Ministers], to or on behalf of the claimant or his partner relating to a service which is provided to develop or sustain the capacity of the claimant or his partner to live independently in his accommodation] [23; or

(e) by way of local welfare provision including arrears and payments in lieu of local welfare provision; or

(f) in consequence of a reduction of council tax under section 13, 13A or 80 of the Local Government Finance Act 1992 (reduction of liability of council tax).]

(2) In paragraph (1), "benefit" means—

(a) attendance allowance under section 64 of the Contributions and Benefits Act;

(b) disability living allowance;

(c) income support;

(d) income-based jobseeker's allowance;

(e) housing benefit;

(f) state pension credit;

(g) [3 . . .]

(h) [3 an increase of a disablement pension under section 104 of the Contributions and Benefits Act (increase where constant attendance needed), and any further increase of such a pension under section 105 of that Act (increase for exceptionally severe disablement)];

(i) any amount included on account of the claimant's exceptionally severe disablement [3 or need for constant attendance] in a war disablement pension or [16 any other such amount described in regulation 15(5)(ac)].

[1(j) council tax benefit;

(k) social fund payments;

(l) child benefit;

(m) [3 . . .]

(n) child tax credit under the Tax Credits Act 2002;]

[14 (o) income-related employment and support allowance] [26;

(p) universal credit;]

[3**20A.**—(1) Subject to sub-paragraph (3), any payment of £5,000 or more to which paragraph 20(1)(a), (b) or (c) applies, which has been made to rectify, or to compensate for, an official error relating to a relevant benefit and has been received by the claimant in full on or after the day on which he became entitled to benefit under these Regulations.

(2) Subject to sub-paragraph (3), the total amount of any payment disregarded under—

(a) paragraph 7(2) of Schedule 10 to the Income Support (General) Regulations 1987;
(b) paragraph 12(2) of Schedule 8 to the Jobseeker's Allowance Regulations 1996;
[16. . .]
[14 or
(e) paragraph 11(2) of Schedule 9 to the Employment and Support Allowance Regulations,]
[16 (f) paragraph 9(2) of Schedule 6 to the Housing Benefit Regulations 2006;
(g) paragraph 22 of Schedule 6 to the Housing Benefit (Persons who have attained the qualifying age for state pension credit) Regulations 2006;
(h) paragraph 9(2) of Schedule 5 to the Council Tax Benefit Regulations 2006; [26 . . .]
(i) paragraph 22 of Schedule 4 to the Council Tax Benefit (Persons who have attained the qualifying age for state pension credit) Regulations 2006;] [26 or
(j) [27 paragraph 18] of Schedule 10 to the Universal Credit Regulations 2013;]

where the award during which the disregard last applied in respect of the relevant sum either terminated immediately before the relevant date or is still in existence at that date.

(3) Any disregard which applies under sub-paragraph (1) or (2) shall have effect until the award comes to an end.

(4) In this paragraph—

"the award", except in sub-paragraph (2), means—
(a) the award of State Pension Credit under these Regulations during which the relevant sum or, where it is received in more than one instalment, the first instalment of that sum is received; or
(b) where that award is followed immediately by one or more further awards which begins immediately after the previous award ends, such further awards until the end of the last award, provided that, for such further awards, the claimant—
   (i) is the person who received the relevant sum;
   (ii) is the partner of that person; or
   (iii) was the partner of that person at the date of his death;

"official error"—
(a) where the error relates to housing benefit [22 . . .] has the meaning given by regulation 1(2) of the Housing Benefit and Council Tax Benefit (Decisions and Appeals) Regulations 2001;
and
(b) where the error relates to any other relevant benefit, has the meaning given by regulation 1(3) of the Social Security and Child Support (Decisions and Appeals) Regulations 1999;

"the relevant date" means the date on which the claimant became entitled to benefit under the Act;

"relevant benefit" means any benefit specified in paragraph 20(2); and

"the relevant sum" means the total payment referred to in sub-paragraph (1) or, as the case may be, the total amount referred to in sub-paragraph (2).]

[16 **20B.**—Any arrears of supplementary pension which is disregarded under paragraph 4 of Schedule 4 (amounts to be disregarded in the calculation of income other than earnings) or of any amount which is disregarded under paragraph 5 or 6 of that Schedule.]

21.—Where a capital asset is held in a currency other than sterling, any banking charge or commission payable in converting that capital into sterling.

22.—The value of the right to receive income from an occupational pension scheme or a personal pension scheme.

23.—The value of a right to receive income from a under a retirement annuity contract.

[11 **23A.**—Where a person elects to be entitled to a lump sum under Schedule 5 or 5A to the 1992 Act or under Schedule 1 to the Graduated Retirement Benefit Regulations, or is treated as having made such an election, and a payment has been made pursuant to that election, an amount equal to—
(a) except where sub-paragraph (b) applies, the amount of any payment or payments made on account of that lump sum;
(b) the amount of that lump sum,

but only for so long as that person does not change that election in favour of an increase of pension or benefit.]

[30 **23AA**. Where a person chooses a lump sum under section 8(2) of the Pensions Act 2014 or in accordance with Regulations made under section 10 of that Act which include provision corresponding or similar to section 8(2) of that Act, or fails to make a choice, and a lump sum payment has been made, an amount equal to—

(a) except where sub-paragraph (b) applies, the amount of any payment or payments made on account of that lump sum;

(b) the amount of that lump sum,

but only for so long as that person does not alter that choice in favour of an increase of pension.]

[17 **23B.**—Any payment made under Part 8A of the 1992 Act (entitlement to health in pregnancy grant).]

[21 **23C.**—Any payments made [28 . . .]—

(a) [28 by virtue of regulations made under] section 57 (direct payments) of the Health and Social Care Act 2001;

[28 (b) as a direct payment as defined in section 4(2) of the Social Care (Self-directed Support) (Scotland) Act 2013; [29 . . .]

(c) [28 by virtue of regulations made under] sections 12A to 12C (direct payments for health care) of the National Health Service Act 2006] [29 or

(d) under sections 31 to 33 of the Care Act 2014 (direct payments).]

PART II

4.146 **[1Capital disregarded only for the purposes of determining deemed income]**

24.—The value of the right to receive any income under a life interest or from a life rent.

25.—The value of the right to receive any rent except where the claimant has a reversionary interest in the property in respect of which rent is due.

26.—The value of the right to receive any income under an annuity or the surrender value (if any) of such an annuity.

27.—[3 . . .]

28.—Where property is held under a trust, other than—

(a) a charitable trust within the meaning of the Charities Act 1993; or

(b) a trust set up with any payment to which paragraph 16 of this Schedule applies, and under the terms of the trust, payments fall to be made, or the trustees have a discretion to make payments, to or for the benefit of the claimant or the claimant's partner, or both, that property.

AMENDMENTS

1. State Pension Credit (Consequential, Transitional and Miscellaneous Provisions) Regulations 2002 (SI 2002/3019) reg.23(o) (October 6, 2003).

2. State Pension Credit (Consequential, Transitional and Miscellaneous Provisions) (No.2) Regulations 2002 (SI 2002/3197) reg.2 and Sch. para.12 (October 6, 2003).

3. State Pension Credit (Transitional and Miscellaneous Provisions) Amendment Regulations 2003 (SI 2003/2274) reg.2(12) (October 6, 2003).

4. Social Security (Miscellaneous Amendments) (No.2) Regulations 2004 (SI 2004/1141) regs 3(3) and 3(4)(d) (May 12, 2004).

5. Social Security (Miscellaneous Amendments) (No.2) Regulations 2004 (SI 2004/1141) regs 3(5) and 3(6)(d) (May 12, 2004).

6. Social Security (Housing Benefit, Council Tax Benefit, State Pension Credit and Miscellaneous Amendments) Regulations 2004 (SI 2004/2327) reg.7(6) (October 4, 2004).

7. Income-related Benefits (Amendment) Regulations 2005 (SI 2005/2183) reg.6 (August 5, 2005).

8. Social Security (Care Homes and Independent Hospitals) Regulations 2005 (SI 2005/2687) reg.6 and Sch.5 para.6 (October 24, 2005).

9. Civil Partnership (Pensions, Social Security and Child Support) (Consequential, etc. Provisions) Order 2005 (SI 2005/2877) art.2(3) and Sch.3 para.35(5) (December 5, 2005).

10. Income-related Benefits (Amendment) (No.2) Regulations 2005 (SI 2005/3391) reg.7(3) (December 12, 2005).

11. Social Security (Deferral of Retirement Pensions, Shared Additional Pension and Graduated Retirement Benefit) (Miscellaneous Provisions) Regulations 2005 (SI 2005/2677) reg.13(4) (April 6, 2006).

12. Social Security (Young Persons) Amendment Regulations 2006 (SI 2006/718) reg.6(5) (April 10, 2006).
13. Social Security (Miscellaneous Amendments) (No.4) Regulations 2006 (SI 2006/2378) reg.14(6) (October 2, 2006).
14. Employment and Support Allowance (Consequential Provisions) (No.2) Regulations 2008 (SI 2008/1554) reg.4(9) (October 27, 2008).
15. Social Security (Miscellaneous Amendments) (No.6) Regulations 2008 (SI 2008/2767) reg.5(5) (November 17, 2008).
16. Social Security (Miscellaneous Amendments) (No.7) Regulations 2008 (SI 2008/3157) reg.4(6) (January 5, 2009).
17. Social Security (Miscellaneous Amendments) Regulations 2009 (SI 2009/583) reg.5(4) and (5) (April 6, 2009).
18. Social Security (Equalisation of State Pension Age) Regulations 2009 (SI 2009/1488) regs 22 and 23 (April 10, 2010).
19. Social Security (Miscellaneous Amendments) (No.2) Regulations 2010 (SI 2010/641) reg.6(3)(c) (April 6, 2010).
20. Social Security (Miscellaneous Amendments) (No.2) Regulations 2010 (SI 2010/641) reg.6(2) (April 6, 2010).
21. Social Security (Miscellaneous Amendments) (No.3) Regulations 2011 (2011/2425) reg.15(6) and (7) (October 31, 2011).
22. Council Tax Benefit Abolition (Consequential Provision) Regulations 2013 (SI 2013/458) reg.3 and Sch.1 (April 1, 2013).
23. Social Security (Miscellaneous Amendments) Regulations 2013 (SI 2013/443) reg.6(4) (April 2, 2013).
24. Personal Independence Payment (Supplementary Provisions and Consequential Amendments) Regulations 2013 (SI 2013/388) reg.8 and Sch. para.27(7) (April 8, 2013).
25. Armed Forces and Reserve Forces Compensation Scheme (Consequential Provisions: Subordinate Legislation) Order 2013 (SI 2013/591) art.7 and Sch. para.23(7) (April 8, 2013).
26. Universal Credit (Consequential, Supplementary, Incidental and Miscellaneous Provisions) Regulations 2013 (SI 2013/630) reg.33(7) (April 29, 2013).
27. Social Security (Miscellaneous Amendments) (No.3) Regulations 2013 (SI 2013/2536) reg.10(4) (October 29, 2013).
28. Social Care (Self-directed Support) (Scotland) Act 2013 (Consequential Modifications and Savings) Order 2014 (SI 2014/513) art.2 and Sch. para.7 (April 1, 2014).
29. Care Act 2014 (Consequential Amendments) (Secondary Legislation) Order 2015 (SI 2015/643) reg.19(1) and (2) (April 1, 2015).
30. Pensions Act 2014 (Consequential, Supplementary and Incidental Amendments) Order 2015 (SI 2015/1985) reg.24(2) (April 6, 2016).

GENERAL NOTE

This Schedule includes many of the same disregards as are to be found in Sch.10 to the Income Support (General) Regulations 1987 (SI 1987/1967). However, the function of the two Schedules is conceptually different. The purpose of Sch.10 in the income support scheme is to provide for disregards to be applied in calculating the claimant's capital with a view to seeing whether the relevant capital threshold is exceeded. The purpose of this Schedule is to specify disregards which apply in the assessment of capital which is then used for calculating the claimant's income under the tariff income rule in reg.15(6), there being no capital rule as such in the state pension credit scheme. That said, the actual drafting of these provisions follows closely the parallel provisions in the income support schemes. But note also that the disregards in this Schedule are subdivided into two categories: those which are dis- **4.147** regarded for the purpose of calculating income (Pt I) and those disregarded—which are fewer in number—for the purpose of calculating notional income (Pt II).

Paragraph 1

4.148 See Income Support (General) Regulations 1987 (SI 1987/1967) Sch.10 para.2. The claimant's own home (Sch.2 para.1 of the 1987 Regulations) is disregarded for state pension credit purposes by para.1A below.

Paragraphs 2–3

4.149 See Income Support (General) Regulations 1987 (SI 1987/1967) Sch.10 paras 27–28.

Paragraphs 4–5

4.150 See Income Support (General) Regulations 1987 (SI 1987/1967) Sch.10 paras 4 and 5.

Paragraph (4)(a) provides for the disregard of the value of a second property where that property is occupied by someone who is aged 60 or over or is incapacitated and who is a relative of the pension credit claimant or their partner. Note that the original drafting of para.(4) meant that the disregard applied only if the occupier of the property was a close relative of the pension credit claimant himself (or herself). The amended formulation applies the disregard equally where the occupier is a close relative of the claimant's partner. The original wording reflected a drafting oversight, and the Minister has indicated that extra-statutory payments will be considered to anyone who lost out (*Hansard*, HC Vol. 421, col. 140W, May 10, 2004).

Paragraph 4(b) makes similar provision where the claimant's former partner occupies the property. This disregard is not available if the claimant is divorced or estranged from their ex-partner (or a civil partnership has been dissolved). On the meaning of "estranged", see *CPC/0683/2007*, following *R(IS) 5/05* and *CH/0177/2005*.

Paragraph 6

4.151 This applies the more generous housing benefit disregard (see, e.g. Housing Benefit (General) Regulations 1987 (SI 1987/1971) Sch.5 para.24) in preference to the more limited disregard in the Income Support (General) Regulations 1987 (SI 1987/1967) Sch.10 para.25. Thus the disregard on a former family home is for 26 weeks where the claimant moves out following a relationship breakdown, and beyond that time if the remaining partner is a lone parent (until such time as that status ceases).

Paragraph 7

4.152 See Income Support (General) Regulations 1987 (SI 1987/1967) Sch.10 para.26.

Paragraph 8

4.153 See Income Support (General) Regulations 1987 (SI 1987/1967) Sch.10 para.10 (although the qualification in the income support provision is not repeated here).

Paragraphs 9–9A

4.154 See Income Support (General) Regulations 1987 (SI 1987/1967) Sch.10 para.6(1) and (2).

Paragraph 10

4.155 See Income Support (General) Regulations 1987 (SI 1987/1967) Sch.10 para.15. See further *AB v SSWP* [2010] UKUT 343 (AAC), where the claimant wrote to the DWP asking for a recalculation of his pension credit and for it to be backdated, as he now realised that on his claim form he had declared details of the surrender value of a life insurance policy which should not have been counted as part of his capital resources. His benefit was recalculated as from the date of the letter. Judge Ovey held that the tribunal had erred in treating the information supplied by the claimant as a notification of a change of circumstances rather than revelation of a mistake in the calculation of the original award, and had further failed to consider whether there had been an official error in the making of that award.

Paragraph 11

This has no direct parallel under the income support scheme. **4.156**

Paragraph 12

See Income Support (General) Regulations 1987 (SI 1987/1967) Sch.10 para.61. **4.157**

Paragraphs 13–14

See Income Support (General) Regulations 1987 (SI 1987/1967) Sch.10 paras 64–65. **4.158**

Paragraph 15

See Income Support (General) Regulations 1987 (SI 1987/1967) Sch.10 para.22. **4.159**

Paragraph 16

Payments in respect of compensation for personal injuries are disregarded for both capital and income purposes (see also Sch.IV paras 13 and 14). Paragraph 16(2) deals with the specific example of funds held in court: see Income Support (General) Regulations 1987 (SI 1987/1967) Sch.10 paras 44 and 45. **4.160**

Paragraphs 17–19

These paragraphs are designed to fulfil broadly the same functions as the disregards Income Support (General) Regulations 1987 (SI 1987/1967) Sch.10 paras 3 and 8. These disregards, however, last for one year rather than the "26 weeks or such longer period as is reasonable in the circumstances" qualification that applies under the income support scheme. See *DH v SSWP* [2010] UKUT 241 (AAC), confirming that for the purposes of the disregard in paras 17(b) and 19 time runs from the actual date of receipt of the funds, regardless of whether the claimant is actually in the UK at the time in question. **4.161**

Paragraph 20

See Income Support (General) Regulations 1987 (SI 1987/1967) Sch.10 para.7. **4.162**

Paragraph 21

See Income Support (General) Regulations 1987 (SI 1987/1967) Sch.10 para.21. See also reg.17(6). **4.163**

Paragraph 22

See Income Support (General) Regulations 1987 (SI 1987/1967) Sch.10 para.(23). **4.164**

Paragraph 23AA

The effect of this provision is that an amount equal to the pre-tax amount of the lump-sum payment paid where a person changes their choice of payment of the new state pension is to be disregarded for life, so long as that person does not change their choice to a weekly increase. **4.164A**

Paragraphs 24–26

See Income Support (General) Regulations 1987 (SI 1987/1967) Sch.10 paras 13, 24 and 11 respectively. **4.165**

SCHEDULE VI **Regulation 17(9)**

SUMS DISREGARDED FROM CLAIMANT'S EARNINGS

4.166 **1.**—(1) In a case where a claimant is a lone parent, £20 of earnings.

(2) In this paragraph—

(a) "lone parent" means a person who has no partner and who is responsible for, and a member of the same household as, a child;

(b) "child" means a person [4 who is a qualifying young person or] a child for the purposes of Part IX of the 1992 Act.

2.—In a case of earnings from employment to which sub-paragraph (2) applies, £20.

(2) This paragraph applies to employment—

[9 (a) a part-time fire-fighter employed by a fire and rescue authority under the Fire and Rescue Services Act 2004 or by the Scottish Fire and Rescue Service established under section 1A of the Fire (Scotland) Act 2005;]

(b) as an auxiliary coastguard in respect of coast rescue activities;

(c) in the manning or launching of a lifeboat if the employment is part-time;

[1(d) a member of any territorial or reserve force prescribed in Part I of Schedule 6 to the Social Security (Contributions) Regulations 2001].

[1**2A.**—Where a person is engaged in one or more of the employments specified in paragraph 2 but his earnings derived from those employments are less than £20 in any week and he is also engaged in any other employment, so much of his earnings from that other employment as would not in aggregate with the amount of his earnings disregarded under paragraph 2 exceed £20.]

[2 **2B.**—Where only one member of a couple is in employment specified in paragraph 2(2), so much of the earnings of the other member of the couple as would not, in aggregate with the earnings disregarded under paragraph 2, exceed £20.]

3.—(1) If the claimant or one of the partners is a carer, or both partners are carers, £20 of any earnings received from his or their employment.

(2) In this paragraph the claimant or his partner is a carer if paragraph 4 of Part II of Schedule I (amount applicable for carers) is satisfied in respect of him.

4.—(1) £20 is disregarded if the claimant or, if he has a partner, his partner—

(a) is in receipt of—

(i) long-term incapacity benefit under section 30A of the 1992 Act;

(ii) severe disablement allowance under section 68 of that Act;

(iii) attendance allowance;

(iv) disability living allowance under section 71 to 76 of that Act;

(v) any mobility supplement under [6 article 20 of the Naval, Military and Air Forces Etc. (Disablement and Death) Service Pensions Order 2006](including such a supplement by virtue of any other scheme or order) or under article 25A of the Personal Injuries (Civilians) Scheme 1983; [5 . . .]

[1(vi) the disability element or the severe disability element of working tax credit under Schedule 2 to the Working Tax Credit (Entitlement and Maximum Rate) Regulations 2002; or]

[5 (vii) employment and support allowance; [7 . . .]]

[7 (viii) personal independence payment; [7 . . .]]

[8 (ix) armed forces independence payment; or]

[10 (b) is or are certified as severely sight impaired or blind by a consultant ophthalmologist.]

(2) Subject to sub-paragraph (4), £20 is disregarded if the claimant or, if he has a partner, his partner has, within a period of 8 weeks ending on the day in respect of which the claimant first satisfies the conditions for entitlement to state pension credit, had an award of income support [5, income-based jobseeker's allowance or income-related employment and support allowance] and—

(a) £20 was disregarded in respect of earnings taken into account in that award;

(b) the person whose earnings qualified for the disegard in employment after the termination of that award.

(3) Subject to sub-paragraph (4), £20 is disregarded if the claimant or, if he has a partner, his partner, immediately before attaining pensionable age—

(a) had an award of state pension credit; and

(b) a disregard under paragraph 4(1)(a)(i) or (ii) was taken into account in determining that award.

(4) The disregard of £20 specified in sub-paragraphs (2) and (3) applies so long as there is no break, other a break which does not exceed eight weeks—

(a) in a case to which sub-paragraph (2) refers, in a person's entitlement to state pension credit or in employment following the first day in respect of which state pension credit is awarded; or

(b) in a case where sub-paragraph (3) applies, in the person's entitlement to state pension credit since attaining pensionable age.

(5) [1. . .].

[1**4A.**—(1) £20 is the maximum amount which may be disregarded under any of paragraphs 1, 2, 3 or 4 notwithstanding that—

(a) in the case of a claimant with no partner, he satisfies the requirements of more than one of those paragraphs or, in the case of paragraph 4, he satisfies the requirements of more than one of the sub-paragraphs of that paragraph; or

(b) in the case of [3 couples], both partners satisfy one or more of the requirements of paragraphs 2, 3 and 4.

(2) Where, in a case to which sub-paragraph (1)(b) applies, the amount to be disregarded in respect of one of the partners ("the first partner") is less than £20, the amount to be disregarded in respect of the other partner shall be so much of that other partner's earnings as would not, in aggregate with the first partner's earnings, exceed £20.]

5.—Except where the claimant or his partner qualifies for a £20 disregard under the preceding provisions of this Schedule—

(a) £5 shall be disregarded if a claimant who has no partner has earnings;

(b) £10 shall be disregarded if a claimant who has a partner has earnings.

6.—Any earnings [1, other than any amount referred to in regulation 17(9)(b),] derived from any employment which ended before the day in respect of which the claimant first satisfies the conditions for entitlement to state pension credit.

[1**7.**—Any banking charges or commission payable in converting to Sterling payments of earnings made in a currency other than Sterling.]

AMENDMENTS

1. State Pension Credit (Consequential, Transitional and Miscellaneous Provisions) (No.2) Regulations 2002 (SI 2002/3197) reg.2 and Sch. para.13 (October 6, 2003).

2. State Pension Credit (Transitional and Miscellaneous Provisions) Amendment Regulations 2003 (SI 2003/2274) reg.2(13) (October 6, 2003).

3. Civil Partnership (Pensions, Social Security and Child Support) (Consequential, etc. Provisions) Order 2005 (SI 2005/2877) art.2(3) and Sch.3 para.35(6) (December 5, 2005).

4. Social Security (Young Persons) Amendment Regulations 2006 (SI 2006/718) reg.6(6) (April 10, 2006).

5. Employment and Support Allowance (Consequential Provisions) (No.2) Regulations 2008 (SI 2008/1554) reg.4(10) (October 27, 2008).

6. Social Security (Miscellaneous Amendments) (No.7) Regulations 2008 (SI 2008/3157) reg.4(7) (January 5, 2009).

7. Personal Independence Payment (Supplementary Provisions and Consequential Amendments) Regulations 2013 (SI 2013/388) reg.8 and Sch. para.27(8) (April 8, 2013).

8. Armed Forces and Reserve Forces Compensation Scheme (Consequential Provisions: Subordinate Legislation) Order 2013 (SI 2013/591) art.7 and Sch. para.23(8) (April 8, 2013).

9. Social Security (Miscellaneous Amendments) (No.3) Regulations 2013 (SI 2013/2536) reg.10(5) (October 29, 2013).

10. Universal Credit and Miscellaneous Amendments (No.2) Regulations 2014 (SI 2014/2888) reg.3(4)(c) (November 26, 2014).

DEFINITIONS

"attendance allowance"—see reg.1(2).
"child"—see para.1(2).

"claimant"—see SPCA 2002 s.17(1).
"lone parent"—see para.1(2).
"partner"—see reg.1(3).
"pensionable age"—see SPCA 2002 s.17(1).

GENERAL NOTE

4.167 This Schedule performs the same function in relation to state pension credit as Sch.8 to the Income Support (General) Regulations 1987 (SI 1987/1967) does in the context of income support. Thus the standard disregard on earnings is £5 a week for a single claimant and £10 a week for a couple (para.5). There are then various special cases (e.g. lone parents, carers, disabled claimants and those active pensioners who are still involved in various emergency services in a part-time capacity) where the disregard is £20 a week. Note that the maximum weekly disregard is £20 even where both members of a couple satisfy one of the tests for the maximum disregard (para.(4A)).

There is, however, one significant difference from income support: although the same earnings disregards apply, there is no 16-hours rule in the context of state pension credit. On the other hand, the low level of the earnings disregards is hardly an incentive for pensioners (or their partners) to work extra hours.

The typographical error in para.4(2)(b) ("disegard" for "disregard") appears in the original version of the Regulations and, as at the time of writing, has not been corrected.

PART V

THE SOCIAL FUND

The Social Fund Cold Weather Payments (General) Regulations 1988

(SI 1988/1724) (AS AMENDED)

Made by the Secretary of State under ss.32(2A) and 84(1) of the Social Security Act 1986 and s.166(1) to (3A) of the Social Security Act 1975

GENERAL NOTE

Section 138(2) of the Contributions and Benefits Act provides that payments may be made out of the social fund "to meet expenses for heating, which appear to the Secretary of State to have been or to be likely to be incurred in cold weather". That power has been used to make these Regulations and also the Social Fund Winter Fuel Payment Regulations 2000 (see below). 5.1

The cold weather payments scheme was introduced in April 1988 and, although there have been subsequent technical changes, has had substantially the same structure since November 1, 1991. That structure is as follows:

- Every postcode in Great Britain is linked to a weather station accredited by the Meteorological Office (see Schs 1 and 2).
- If a period of cold weather (i.e. seven consecutive days during which the average daily temperature is below 0°C) is forecast for, or recorded by, the weather station that is linked to a postcode district then any claimant whose home is in that district and who satisfies the conditions in reg.1A is entitled to a cold weather payment of (currently) £25.
- There is no need for a claim. However, a cold weather payment cannot be made after September 28 following the winter which included the period of cold weather (26 weeks beginning with March 31) (see reg.2(6)).

The decision to make a payment is made by a decision-maker but there is no notification in cases where a payment is not made. As it is not possible to make a claim, a person who does not receive a payment to which s/he thinks s/he is entitled, must request a negative decision before there is something to appeal against.

For a historical review of the Scheme see pp.338–353 of the 3rd edition of T. Buck, *The Social Fund—Law and Practice* (London: Sweet & Maxwell, 2009).

Citation, commencement and interpretation

1.—(1) These regulations may be cited as the Social Fund Cold Weather Payments (General) Regulations 1988 and shall come into force on 7th November 1988. 5.2

(2) In these Regulations, unless the context otherwise requires—

[11 "the 2012 Act" means the Welfare Reform Act 2012;]

[9 "the Act" means the Social Security Contributions and Benefits Act 1992;]

[7 "the Welfare Reform Act" means the Welfare Reform Act 2007;]

"the General Regulations" means the Income Support (General) Regulations 1987;

[4 "the Meteorological Office" means the Meteorological Office of the [10 Department for Business, Innovation and Skills];]

[9 . . .]

[2"claimant" means a person who is claiming or has claimed income support [6, state pension credit [7 , income-based jobseeker's allowance [11, income-related employment and support allowance or universal credit]]];]

[9 "cold weather payment" means a payment to meet expenses for heating made out of the social fund under section 138(2) of the Act and these Regulations;

"family" has the meaning given to it in section 137 of the Act and the General Regulations;]

[2"forecast" means a weather forecast produced by the Meteorological Office [4. . .] and supplied to the [8 Department for Work and Pensions] on a daily basis [4 between 1st November in any year and 31st March in the following year,] which provides the expected average mean daily temperature for a period of 7 consecutive days;

"forecasted period of cold weather" means a period of 7 consecutive days, during which the average of the mean daily temperature for that period is forecasted to be equal to or below 0 degrees celsius; and for the purposes of this definition where a day forms part of a forecasted period of cold weather it shall not form part of any other such forecasted period;]

"home" means the dwelling, together with any garage, garden and outbuildings normally occupied by the claimant as his home, including any premises not so occupied which it is impracticable or unreasonable to sell separately in particular, in Scotland, any croft land on which the dwelling is situated;

[4"income-based jobseeker's allowance" has the same meaning in these Regulations as it has in the Jobseekers Act 1995 by virtue of section 1(4) of that Act;]

[7"income-related employment and support allowance" means an income-related allowance under Part 1 of the Welfare Reform Act (employment and support allowance);]

[9 "income support" means income support under Part 7 of the Act;]

[6 . . .]

"mean daily temperature" means, in respect of a day, the average of the maximum temperature and minimum temperature recorded at a station for that day;

[2"overlap period" means any period of a day or days, where a day forms part of a recorded period of cold weather and also forms part of a forecasted period of cold weather;]

[6 . . .]

[9 . . .]

[4"postcode district" means a Post Office postcode district [5except in the case of any postcode district which is identified with an alpha suffix which shall, for the purposes of these Regulations, be treated as if it forms part of a postcode district which is identified without that suffix]];

"recorded period of cold weather" means a period of 7 consecutive days, during which the average of the mean daily temperature recorded for that period was equal to or below 0 degrees celsius; and for the purposes of this definition where a day forms part of a recorded period of cold weather it shall not form part of any other such recorded period;

[6 "state pension credit" has the meaning given by section 1(1) of the State Pension Credit Act 2002]

[4. . .]

[4"station" means a station accredited by the Meteorological Office at which a period of cold weather may be forecasted or recorded for the purposes of these Regulations;]

[11 "universal credit" means universal credit under Part 1 of the 2012 Act;]

[9 "winter period" means the period beginning on 1st November in any year and ending on 31st March in the following year.]

[6 . . .]

[1 (2A) [6 . . .]]

(3) In these Regulations, unless the context otherwise requires, a reference to a numbered regulation is to the regulation in these Regulations bearing that number and a reference in a regulation to a numbered paragraph or sub-paragraph is to the paragraph or sub-paragraph in that regulation bearing that number.

AMENDMENTS

1. Social Fund (Miscellaneous Amendments) Regulations 1990 (SI 1990/580) reg.3 (April 9, 1990).
2. Social Fund Cold Weather Payments (General) Amendment No.2 Regulations 1991 (SI 1991/2238) reg.2 (November 1, 1991).
3. Social Fund Cold Weather Payments (General) Amendment (No.2) Regulations 1992 (SI 1992/2448) reg.2 (November 1, 1992).
4. Social Fund Cold Weather Payments (General) Amendment Regulations 1996 (SI 1996/2544) reg.2 (November 4, 1996).
5. Social Fund Cold Weather Payments (General) Amendment Regulations 1997 (SI 1997/2311) reg.2 (November 1, 1997).
6. Social Fund Cold Weather Payments (General) Amendment Regulations 2005 (SI 2005/2724) reg.3 (November 1, 2005).
7. Employment and Support Allowance (Consequential Provisions) (No.2) Regulations 2008 (SI 2008/1554) reg.6(1) and (2) (October 27, 2008).
8. Social Fund Cold Weather Payments (General) Amendment Regulations 2008 (SI 2008/2569) reg.2(1) and (2) (November 1, 2008).
9. Social Fund Cold Weather Payments (General) Amendment Regulations 2010 (SI 2010/2442) reg.2(1) and (2) (November 1, 2010).
10. Transfer of Functions (Her Majesty's Land Registry, the Meteorological Office and Ordnance Survey) Order 2011 (SI 2011/2436) art.6 and Sch.2 para.6 (November 9, 2011).
11. Social Fund Cold Weather Payments (General) Regulations 1988 (SI 2013/248) reg.2(1) and (2) (November 1, 2013).

GENERAL NOTE

Most of the definitions in reg.1 are self-explanatory. The following merit additional comment. 5.3

"Home": The definition is the same as the definition of "dwelling occupied as the home" in reg.2(1) of the Income Support General Regulations. See the notes to that regulation.

"Forecasted period of cold weather": The definition covers any period of seven consecutive days (i.e. not necessarily a calendar week) during which the average of the mean daily temperature (as defined) for that period is forecasted to be equal to or less than 0°C. If a day falls into a forecasted period of cold weather it cannot count in any other forecasted period, but it can be part of a "recorded period of cold weather" (see the definition of that phrase and of "overlap period"). The possibility of relying on a forecast without having to wait until a period of cold weather has actually been recorded allows the cold weather payment to be made nearer to the time when the need to incur additional heating expenses arises.

"*Overlap period*": On the assumption that weather forecasts are occasionally correct, a day that falls within a "forecasted period of cold weather" will sometimes also fall within a "recorded period of cold weather". Such a day (or days) form an "overlap period". For the treatment of overlap periods, see reg.2(3)–(5).

"Recorded period of cold weather": The definition covers any period of seven consecutive days (i.e. not necessarily a calendar week) during which the average of the mean daily temperature (as defined) recorded for that period was equal to or less than 0°C. If a day falls into a recorded period of cold weather it cannot count in any other recorded period, but it can be part of a "forecasted period of cold weather" (see the definition of that phrase and of "overlap period"). The possibility of relying upon recorded temperatures means that a cold weather payment can be made in respect of a period of cold weather that was not forecast.

[1 10 Prescribed description of persons

5.4 **1A.**—(1) A cold weather payment may be made in the circumstances prescribed by regulation 2 to a person who satisfies the following conditions.

(2) The first condition is that, in respect of at least one day during the recorded or the forecasted period of cold weather specified in regulation 2(1)(a), the person has been awarded—

(a) state pension credit;
(b) income support;
(c) an income-based jobseeker's allowance; [13 . . .]
(d) an income-related employment and support allowance [13; or
(e) universal credit.]

(3) The second condition (which applies only if the person ("P") falls within paragraph (2)(b), [13 (c), (d) or (e)] is that, in respect of the day to which paragraph (2) relates—

(a) P's family includes a member aged less than 5;
(b) where P has been awarded income support, P's applicable amount includes one or more of the premiums specified in paragraphs 9 to 14 of Part 3 of Schedule 2 to the General Regulations;
(c) where P has been awarded a jobseeker's allowance, P's applicable amount includes one or more of the premiums specified in paragraphs 10 to 16 of Part 3 of Schedule 1 to the Jobseeker's Allowance Regulations 1996;
(d) P's child tax credit includes an individual element referred to in regulation 7(4)(a), (b), (d) or (e) of the Child Tax Credit Regulations 2002; [13 . . .]
(e) where P has been awarded an employment and support allowance, P's applicable amount includes—
    (i) one or more of the premiums specified in paragraphs 5 to 7 of Schedule 4 to the Employment and Support Allowance Regulations 2008, or
    (ii) an amount under section 4(2)(b) of the Welfare Reform Act [13; or
(f) where P has been awarded universal credit—
    (i) the award includes an amount under section 10(2) of the 2012 Act (child or qualifying young person who is disabled); or
    (ii) the award includes an amount under section 12(1) of the 2012 Act in respect of the needs or circumstances specified in section 12(2)(a) or (b) (limited capability for work or limited capability for work and work-related activity) or would do so if it did not include an amount in respect of the needs or circumstances specified in section 12(2)(c) (caring responsibilities for a severely disabled person).]

(4) The third condition (which does not apply to a person who comes [11 within] paragraph (3)(a) or (d)) is that the person does not reside in—

(a) a care home;
(b) an independent hospital;
(c) an establishment run by the Abbeyfield Society or by a body corporate or incorporate which is affiliated to that Society; or
(d) accommodation provided under section 3(1) of, and Part 2 of the Schedule to, the Polish Resettlement Act 1s947 (provision by the Secretary of State of accommodation in camps).

[13 (4A) In relation to a person who has been awarded universal credit, the third condition applies as if paragraph (4)(d) were omitted.]

(5) In paragraph (4) —
(a) "care home" in England and Wales has the meaning assigned to it by section 3 of the Care Standards Act 2000, and in Scotland means a care home service as defined by [12 paragraph 2 of schedule 12 to the Public Services Reform (Scotland) Act 2010];
(b) "independent hospital"—
(i) in England, means a hospital as defined by section 275 of the National Health Service Act 2006 that is not a health service hospital as defined by that section;
(ii) in Wales, has the meaning assigned to it by section 2 of the Care Standards Act 2000; and
(iii) in Scotland, means an independent healthcare service as defined in [12 section 10F(1)(a) and (b) of the National Health Service (Scotland) Act 1978].]

[13 (6) The fourth condition, which applies only where the person has been awarded universal credit and their award of universal credit does not include an amount under section 10(2) of the 2012 Act (child or qualifying young person who is disabled) is that—
(a) in a case where a cold weather payment is payable in relation to a recorded period of cold weather as mentioned in regulation 2(1)(a)(i), the person was not in employment or gainful self-employment on any day during that period; or
(b) in a case where a cold weather payment is payable in relation to a forecasted period of weather as mentioned in regulation 2(1)(a)(ii), the person is not in employment or gainful self-employment on the day when the Meteorological Office supplies the Department for Work and Pensions with the forecast.

(7) For the purpose of paragraph (6)—
(a) "employment" means employment under a contract of service, or in an office, including an elective office;
(b) a person is in gainful self-employment where—
(i) they are carrying on a trade, profession or vocation as their main employment;
(ii) their earnings from that trade, profession or vocation are treated as self-employed earnings for the purpose of regulations made under section 8(3) of the 2012 Act; and
(iii) the trade, profession or vocation is organised, developed, regular and carried on in expectation of profit.]

AMENDMENTS

1. Social Fund Cold Weather Payments (General) Amendment No.3 Regulations 1991 (SI 1991/2448) reg.2 (November 1, 1991).

2. Social Fund Cold Weather Payments (General) Amendment Regulations 1993 (SI 1993/2450) reg.2 (November 1, 1993).

3. Social Fund Cold Weather Payments (General) Amendment Regulations 1996 (SI 1996/2544) reg.3 (November 4, 1996).

4. State Pension Credit (Consequential, Transitional and Miscellaneous Provisions) Regulations 2002 (SI 2002/3019) reg.31 (October 6, 2003).

5. Social Security (Removal of Residential Allowance and Miscellaneous Amendments) Regulations 2003 (SI 2003/1121) reg.3 (October 6, 2003).

6. Social Fund Cold Weather Payments (General) Amendment Regulations 2004 (SI 2004/2600) reg.2 (November 1, 2004).

7. Social Security (Care Homes and Independent Hospitals) Regulations 2005 (SI 2005/2687) reg.9 (October 24, 2005).

8. Social Fund Cold Weather Payments (General) Amendment Regulations 2008 (SI 2008/2569) reg.2(1) and (3) (October 27, 2008).

9. Health and Social Care Act 2008 (Miscellaneous Consequential Amendments) Order 2010 (SI 2010/1881) regs 2 and 6 (October 1, 2010).

10. Social Fund Cold Weather Payments (General) Amendment Regulations 2010 (SI 2010/2442) reg.2(1) and (3) (November 1, 2010).

11. Social Fund Cold Weather Payments (General) Amendment Regulations (No.2) 2010 (SI 2010/2591) reg.3(1) November 1, 2010.

12. Public Services Reform (Scotland) Act 2010 (Consequential Modifications of Enactments) Order 2011(SI 2011/2581) art.2 and Sch.2 para.15 (October 28, 2011).

13. Social Fund Cold Weather Payments (General) Regulations 1988 (SI 2013/248) reg.2(1) and (3)–(6) (November 1, 2013).

Definitions

"the Act"—see reg.1(2).
"the General Regulations"—*ibid.*
"claimant"—*ibid.*
"family"—*ibid.*
"forecasted period of cold weather"—*ibid.*
"income-based jobseeker's allowance"—*ibid.*
"income support"—*ibid.*
"recorded period of cold weather"—*ibid.*

General Note

5.5 Regulation 1A sets out the four conditions which a claimant must satisfy in order to receive a cold weather payment. The second, third and fourth conditions do not apply to all claimants. However, where they apply, the conditions are cumulative so failure to satisfy any of them means that no cold weather payment can be made.

The first condition is that the claimant must actually have been awarded (i.e. an underlying entitlement will not suffice) SPC, IS, income-based JSA, income-related ESA or universal credit for at least one day in the relevant (forecasted or recorded) period of cold weather.

The second condition is that, unless the claimant has been awarded SPC, then—for that day—either:

- his or her family must include a child under five;
- the claimant has an award of child tax credit which includes an individual element for a disabled, or severely disabled, child or qualifying young person;
- (if the claimant has been awarded IS or income-based JSA) his or her applicable amount must include one of the pensioner or disability premiums;
- (if the claimant has been awarded income-related ESA) his or her applicable amount must include either one of the pensioner or disability premiums or the work-related activity component or the support component; or

- (if the claimant has been awarded universal credit) the award includes either the disabled child addition (i.e. the additional amount of the child element payable for a child or qualifying young person who is disabled); or the LCW element or the LCWRA element; or would include the LCW element if it did not include the carer element (see Vol.V). Those who qualify on the basis that their award includes the LCW element or the LCWRA element must also satisfy the fourth condition.

The third condition applies to claimants who do not have a child under five in their family and who do not have an award of child tax credit which includes one of the individual elements specified above. It is that the claimant does not reside in a care home or independent hospital (as defined in each case in para.(5)) or (for claimants who are not in receipt of universal credit: see para.(4A)) in an Abbeyfield Home or accommodation provided under the specified provisions of the Polish Resettlement Act 1947. **5.6**

The fourth condition applies to claimants who have an award of universal credit that does not include the disabled child addition (i.e. those who have limited capability for work or work-related activity (see above)). It is that the claimant is not in gainful employment or self-employment (as defined in para.(7)) during the period of cold weather in respect of which the cold weather payment is payable.

Since no claim for a cold weather payment is possible, the decision maker will identify qualifying claimants from Departmental records and make a payment automatically.

[1Prescribed circumstances

2.—(1) The prescribed circumstances in which [9 a cold weather payment may be made] are— **5.7**

(a) subject to paragraphs [5 (1A), (1B),] (3), (4) [6 , (5) and (6)]—

(i) there is a recorded period of cold weather at a station [3identified] in column (1) of Schedule 1 to these Regulations [4 . . .]; or

(ii) there is a forecasted period of cold weather at a station [3identified] in column (1) of Schedule 1 to these Regulations; [5 and]

[4(iii) [5 . . .]

(b) the home of the claimant is, or by virtue of paragraph (2)(b) is treated as, situated in a postcode district in respect of which the station mentioned in sub-paragraph (a)(i) or, as the case may be, (a)(ii) is the designated station.]

(c) [2 . . .]

[5(1A) For the purposes of paragraph (1)(a)(i), where a station identified in column (1) of Schedule 1 to these Regulations (in this paragraph and in paragraph (1B) referred to as "the primary station") is unable to provide temperature information in respect of a particular day, the mean daily temperature on that day—

(a) at the alternative station for that primary station specified in column (2) of Schedule 2 to these Regulations; or

(b) where there is no such alternative station specified, at the nearest station to that primary station able to provide temperature information in respect of that day,

shall be used to determine whether or not there is a recorded period of cold weather at the relevant primary station.

(1B) For the purposes of paragraph (1)(a)(ii), where the Meteorological Office is unable to produce a forecast in respect of a particular period at a primary station, any forecast produced in respect of that period—

(a) at the alternative station for that primary station specified in column (2) of Schedule 2 to these Regulations; or

(b) where there is no such alternative station specified, at the nearest station to that primary station able to provide temperature information for that period,

shall be used to determine whether or not there is a forecasted period of cold weather at the relevant primary station.]

(2) For the purposes of this regulation—

(a) the station [3identified] in column (1) of Schedule 1 to these Regulations is the designated station for the [4postcode districts] [3identified] in the corresponding paragraph in column (2) of that Schedule;

(b) where the home of the claimant is not situated within a [4postcode district] [3[4 . . .] identified] in column (2) of that Schedule, it shall be treated as situated within the [4postcode district] [4 . . .] nearest to it [3identified] in that column.

(3) Subject to paragraphs (4) and (5) where a recorded period of cold weather is joined by an overlap period to a forecasted period of cold weather a payment under paragraph (1) may only be made in respect of the forecasted period of cold weather.

(4) Where—

(a) there is a continuous period of forecasted periods of cold weather, each of which is linked by an overlap period; and

(b) the total number of recorded periods of cold weather during that continuous period is greater than the total number of forecasted periods of cold weather,

a payment in respect of the last recorded period of cold weather may also be made under paragraph (1).

[6 (5) Where—

(a) a claimant satisfies the conditions in regulation 1A and paragraph (1) in respect of a recorded period of cold weather, and

(b) a payment in respect of the recorded period of cold weather does not fall to be made by virtue of paragraph (4), and

(c) the claimant does not satisfy the conditions in regulation 1A in respect of the forecasted period of cold weather which is linked to the recorded period of cold weather by an overlap period,

a cold weather payment may be made in respect of that recorded period of cold weather.

(6) A cold weather payment may not be made after the end of the period of 26 weeks beginning with the last day of the winter period in which the period of cold weather concerned falls.]

AMENDMENTS

1. Social Fund Cold Weather Payments (General) Amendments No.2 Regulations 1991 (SI 1991/2238) reg.3 (November 1, 1991).

2. Social Fund Cold Weather Payments (General) Amendment No.3 Regulations 1991 (SI 1991/2448) reg.3 (November 1, 1991).

3. Social Fund Cold Weather Payments (General) Amendment (No.2) Regulations 1992 (SI 1992/2448) reg.3 (November 1, 1992).

4. Social Fund Cold Weather Payments (General) Amendment Regulations 1996 (SI 1996/2544) reg.4 (November 4, 1996).

5. Social Fund Cold Weather Payments (General) Amendment Regulations 1997 (SI 1997/2311) reg.3 (November 1, 1997).

6. Social Fund Cold Weather Payments (General) Amendment Regulations 2010 (SI 2010/2442) reg.2(1) and (4) (November 1, 2010).

DEFINITIONS

"the Act"—see reg.1(2).
"the General Regulations"—*ibid.*
"claimant"—*ibid.*
"family"—*ibid.*
"forecasted period of cold weather"—*ibid.*
"home"—*ibid.*
"income support"—*ibid.*
"overlap period"—*ibid.*
"postcode district"—*ibid.*
"recorded period of cold weather"—*ibid.*
"station"—*ibid.*

GENERAL NOTE

Regulation 2 prescribes the circumstances in which a cold weather payment is to be made. The principal rule is established by para.1(a) and (b): a period of cold weather (i.e. seven consecutive days) must be either recorded or forecast at the weather station relevant to the claimant's home. The two conditions are alternatives so that the cold weather payment is payable even if a forecasted period of cold weather does not materialise or if there is a recorded period of cold weather that was not forecast. 5.8

The relevant weather station will normally be the one listed for the relevant postcode district in Sch.1. However, if that weather station is unable to provide temperature information, the relevant station is the alternative station specified in Sch.2 or (if no alternative station is specified) the nearest station to the station listed in Sch.1 that is able to provide such information: see paras (1A) and (1B). There were originally 55 primary weather stations. That number was increased to 70 from November 1996, 72 from November 1997, 73 from November 2003, 74 from November 2006, 76 from November 2007, 85 from November 2009, 91 from November 2010 and 92 from November 2011. Those increases are intended to improve the sensitivity of the scheme.

Where a claimant's home is not in a postcode district listed in Sch.1, it is treated as being in the nearest such district: see para.(2)(b).

Paragraphs (3)–(5) are designed to prevent double payment. An individual day can only count as part of one recorded period of cold weather or one forecasted period of cold weather (see the definitions in reg.1(2)), although it can be part of both a recorded and a forecasted period. Where there is a recorded period of cold weather which coincides wholly or partly with the forecasted period, there is then an overlap period, again defined in reg.1(2). The general rule in those circumstances is that the cold weather payment is only payable for the forecasted period (para.(3)) because the policy is to make the payment before the extra heating is required if possible. That rule is subject to two exceptions:

- where there is a continuous series of overlapping forecasted periods and recorded periods which includes more recorded periods than forecasted periods, a cold weather payment can also be made for the final recorded period (para.(4)); and
- where para.(4) does not apply and the claimant does not satisfy the conditions in reg.1A for any day of the forecasted period, but does satisfy those conditions for at least one day of the recorded period, then a payment can be made for the recorded period (para.(5)).

Prescribed amount

5.9 **3.**—[1 . . .] The amount of the payment in respect of each period of cold weather shall be [2 3£25].

AMENDMENTS

1. Social Fund Cold Weather Payments (General) Amendment No.2 Regulations 1991 (SI 1991/2238) reg.4 (November 1, 1991).
2. Social Fund Cold Weather Payments (General) Amendment Regulations 1995 (SI 1995/2620) reg.2 (November 1, 1995).
3. Social Fund Cold Weather Payments (General) Amendment Regulations (No. 2) 2010 (SI 2010/2591) reg.2(1) November 1, 2010.

GENERAL NOTE

5.10 Payment is at the fixed rate of £25 for each week which counts under regs 1A and 2.

The weekly rate was originally set at £5 in 1988. It was then increased to £6 in February 1991, to £7 in November 1994 and to £8.50 in November 1995. For the periods from November 1, 2008 to March 31, 2009, and from November 1, 2009 to March 31, 2010, reg.3 was modified by, respectively, reg.3 of the Social Fund Cold Weather Payments (General) Amendment Regulations 2008 (SI 2008/2569) and reg.3 of the Social Fund Cold Weather Payments (General) Amendment Regulations 2009 (SI 2009/2649). In each case, the effect of the modification was that the weekly amount of £8.50 increased to £25 for any period of cold weather which began during either of the above periods. That increase was made permanent with effect from November 1, 2010.

Effect and calculation of capital

5.11 **4.**—[1 . . .]

AMENDMENT

1. Social Fund Cold Weather Payments (General) Amendment No.2 Regulations 1991 (SI 1991/2238) reg.5 (November 1, 1991).

GENERAL NOTE

5.12 There is no capital limit for cold weather payments.

SCHEDULES

Regulation 2(1), (1A) and (2)

[18 SCHEDULE 1

IDENTIFICATION OF STATIONS AND POSTCODE DISTRICTS

5.13

Column (1) *Meteorological Office Station*	*Column (2)* *Postcode Districts*
1. Aberporth	SA35-48, SA64-65.
2. Aboyne No 2	AB30-34, AB38, AB51-55, DD8-9.
3. Albemarle	DH1-7, DH9, DL4-5, DL14-17, NE1-13, NE15-18, NE20-21, NE23, NE 25-46, SR1-7, TS21, TS28-29.

Column (1) *Meteorological Office Station*	*Column (2)* *Postcode Districts*
4. Andrewsfield	CB1-5, CB10-11, CB21-25, CM1-9, CM11-24, CM77, CO9, RM4, SG8-11.
5. Auchincruive	DG9, KA1-26, KA28-30, PA20.
6. Aultbea No 2	IV21-22, IV26.
7. Aviemore	AB37, IV13, PH19-26.
8. Bainbridge	BD23-24, DL8, DL11-13.
9. Bedford	MK1-19, MK40-46, NN1-16, NN29, PE19, SG5-7, SG15-19.
10. Bingley, No 2	BB4, BB8-12, BB18, BD1-22, HD3, HD7-9, HX1-7, LS21, LS29, OL13-14, S36.
11. Boscombe Down	BA12, RG28, SO20-23, SP1-5, SP7, SP9-11.
12. Braemar No 2	AB35-36, PH10-11, PH18.
13. Brize Norton	OX1-6, OX8, OX10-14, OX18, OX20, OX25-29, OX33, OX44, SN7.
14. Capel Curig No 3	LL24-25, LL41.
15. Cardinham, Bodmin	PL13-18, PL22-35, TR9.
16. Carlisle	CA1-8, DG12, DG16.
17. Cassley	IV27-28, KW11, KW13.
18. Charlwood	BN5-6, BN44, GU5-6, ME6, ME14-20, RH1-20, TN1-20, TN22, TN27.
19. Charterhall	NE71, TD1-6, TD8, TD10-15.
20. Chivenor	EX23, EX31-34, EX39.
21. Coleshill	B1-21, B23-38, B40, B42-50, B60-80, B90-98, CV1-12, CV21-23, CV31-35, CV37, CV47, DY1-14, LE10, WS1-15, WV1-16.
22. Crosby	CH41-49, CH60-66, FY1-8, L1-40, PR1-5, PR8-9, PR25-26.
23. Culdrose	TR1-8, TR10-20, TR26-27.
24. Dunkeswell Aerodrome	DT6-8, EX1-5, EX8-15, EX24, TA21.
25. Dunstaffnage	PA30-31, PA34-35, PA37-38, PA62-65, PA67-75, PA80.
26. Dyce	AB10-16, AB21-25, AB39, AB41-43.
27. Edinburgh, Gogarbank	EH1-42, EH47-49, EH51-55, FK1-7, FK9-10, KY3, KY11-12.
28. Eskdalemuir	DG3-4, DG10-11, DG13-14, ML12, TD7, TD9.
29. Filton	BS1-11, BS13-16, BS20-24, BS29-32, BS34-37, BS39-41, BS48-49, GL11-13, NP16, NP26.
30. Fylingdales	YO13, YO18, YO21-22, YO62.
31. Glasgow, Bishopton	G1-5, G11-15, G20-23, G31-34, G40-46, G51-53, G60-62, G64, G66, G69, G71-78, G81-84, ML4-5, PA1-19, PA21-27, PA32.
32. Gravesend, Broadness	BR5-8, CM0, DA1-18, ME1-5, ME7-8, RM1-3, RM5-20, SS0-17.
33. Hawarden Airport	CH1-8, LL11-14, SY14.
34. Heathrow	BR1-4, CR0, CR2-9, E1-18, E20, EC1-4, EN1-5, EN7-11, HA0-9, IG1-11, KT1-24, N1-22, NW1-11, SE1-28, SL0, SL3, SM1-7, SW1-20, TW1-20, UB1-11, W1-14, WC1-2, WD1-2.
35. Hereford, Credenhill	GL1-6, GL10, GL14-20, GL50-53, HR1-9, NP7-8, NP15, NP25, SY8, WR1-11, WR13-15.

Column (1) *Meteorological Office Station*	*Column (2)* *Postcode Districts*
36. Herstmonceux, West End	BN7-8, BN20-24, BN26-27, TN21, TN31-40.
37. High Wycombe, HQ Air	HP5-23, HP27, OX9, OX39, OX49, RG9, SL7-9.
38. Hurn	BH1-25, BH31, DT1-2, DT11, SP6.
39. Isle of Portland	DT3-5.
40. Keele	CW1-3, CW5, CW12, ST1-8, ST11-12, ST14-21.
41. Kinloss	AB44-45, AB56, IV1-3, IV5, IV7-12, IV15-20, IV30-32, IV36.
42. Kirkwall	KW15-17.
43. Lake Vyrnwy No 2	LL20-21, LL23, SY10, SY15-17, SY19, SY21-22.
44. Langdon Bay	CT1-21, ME9-13, TN23-26, TN28-30.
45. Leconfield	DN14, HU1-20, YO11-12, YO14-17, YO25.
46. Leek, Thorncliffe	DE4, DE45, S32-33, SK13, SK17, SK22-23, ST9-10, ST13.
47. Lerwick	ZE1-3.
48. Leuchars	DD1-7, DD10-11, KY1-2, KY6-10, KY15-16, PH12, PH14.
49. Linton on Ouse	DL1-3, DL6-7, DL9-10, HG1-5, LS1-20, LS22-28, TS9, TS15-16, YO1, YO7-8, YO10, YO19, YO23-24, YO26, YO30-32, YO41-43, YO51, YO60-61.
50. Liscombe	EX16, EX35-36, TA22, TA24.
51. Little Rissington	CV36, GL54-56, OX7, OX15-17, WR12.
52. Llysdinam	LD1-8, SA19-20, SY7, SY9, SY18.
53. Loch Glascarnoch	IV4, IV6, IV14, IV23-24, IV63.
54. Loftus	SR8, TS1-8, TS10-14, TS17-20, TS22-27.
55. Machrihanish	KA27, PA28-29, PA41-49, PA60.
56. Marham	CB6-7, IP24-28, PE12-14, PE30-38.
57. Mona	LL33-34, LL42-49, LL51-78.
58. Morpeth, Cockle Park	NE22, NE24, NE61-70.
59. North Wyke	EX6-7, EX17-22, EX37-38, PL19-21, TQ1-6, TQ9-14.
60. Nottingham, Watnall	CV13, DE1-3, DE5-7, DE11-15, DE21-24, DE55-56, DE65, DE72-75, LE1-9, LE11-14, LE16-19, LE65, LE67, NG1-22, NG25, NG31-34.
61. Pembrey Sands	SA1-8, SA14-18, SA31-34, SA61-63, SA66-73.
62. Plymouth, Mountbatten	PL1-12, TQ7-8.
63. Redesdale Camp	CA9, DH8, NE19, NE47-49.
64. Rhyl No 2	LL15-19, LL22, LL26-32.
65. Rochdale	BL0-9, M24, M26, OL1-12, OL15-16, SK15.
66. Rostherne No 2	CW4, CW6-11, M1-9, M11-23, M25, M27-35, M38, M40-41, M43-46, M50, M90, PR7, SK1-12, SK14, SK16, WA1-16, WN1-8.
67. Rothamsted	AL1-10, EN6, HP1-4, LU1-7, SG1-4, SG12-14, WD3-7, WD17-19, WD23-25.
68. St. Athan	CF3, CF5, CF10-11, CF14-15, CF23-24, CF31-36, CF61-64, CF71-72, NP10, NP18-20, SA10-13.
69. St. Bees Head No 2	CA13-15, CA18-28.
70. Salsburgh	EH43-46, G65, G67-68, ML1-3, ML6-11.

Column (1) *Meteorological Office Station*	*Column (2)* *Postcode Districts*
71. Scilly: St. Marys Airport	TR21-25.
72. Shap	CA10-12, CA16-17, LA8-10, LA21-23.
73. Shawbury	SY1-6, SY11-13, TF1-13.
74. Sheffield	DN1-8, DN11-12, HD1-2, HD4-6, S1-14, S17-18, S20-21, S25-26, S35, S40-45, S60-66, S70-75, S80-81, WF1-17.
75. Skye: Lusa	IV40-49, IV51-56, PH36, PH38-41.
76. South Farnborough	GU1-4, GU7-35, GU46-47, GU51-52, RG1-2, RG4-8, RG10, RG12, RG14, RG18-27, RG29-31, RG40-42, RG45, SL1-2, SL4-6, SO24.
77. Stonyhurst	BB1-3, BB5-7, LA2, LA6-7, PR6.
78. Stornoway Airport	HS1-9.
79. Strathallan Airfield	FK8, FK11-19, G63, KY4-5, KY13-14, PH1-7, PH13.
80. Thorney Island	BN1-3, BN9-18, BN25, BN41-43, BN45, PO1-22, PO30-41, SO14-19, SO30-32, SO40-43, SO45, SO50-53.
81. Threave	DG1-2, DG5-8.
82. Tibenham Airfield	NR1-35.
83. Tiree	PA61, PA66, PA76-78, PH42-44.
84. Trawsgoed	LL35-40, SY20, SY23-25.
85. Tredegar, Bryn Bach Park No 2	CF37-48, CF81-83, NP4, NP11-13, NP22-24, NP44, SA9.
86. Tulloch Bridge	FK20-21, PA33, PA36, PA40, PH8-9, PH15-17, PH30-35, PH37, PH49-50.
87. Waddington	DN9-10, DN13, DN15-22, DN31-41, LN1-13, NG23-24, PE10-11, PE20-25.
88. Walney Island	LA1, LA3-5, LA11-20.
89. Wattisham	CB8-9, CO1-8, CO10-16, IP1-23, IP29-33.
90. Westonbirt	BA1-3, BA11, BA13-15, GL7-9, RG17, SN1-6, SN8-16, SN25-26.
91. Wick Airport	IV25, KW1-3, KW5-10, KW12, KW14.
92. Wittering	LE15, NN17-18, PE1-9, PE15-17, PE26-29.
93. Yeovilton	BA4-10, BA16, BA20-22, BS25-28, DT9-10, SP8, TA1-20, TA23.]

AMENDMENTS

1. Social Security Cold Weather Payments (General) Amendment Regulations 2000 (SI 2000/2690) reg.2 (November 1, 2000).
2. The Social Fund Cold Weather Payments (General) Amendment Regulations 2002 (SI 2002/2524) reg.2 (November 1, 2002).
3. Social Fund Cold Weather Payments (General) Amendment Regulations 2003 (SI 2003/2605) reg.2 and Sch.1 (November 1, 2003).
4. Social Fund Cold Weather Payments (General) Amendment (No.2) Regulations 2003 (SI 2003/3203) reg.2 (November 28, 2003).
5. Social Fund Cold Weather Payments (General) Amendment Regulations 2004 (SI 2004/2600) reg.3 (November 1, 2004).
6. Social Fund Cold Weather Payments (General) Amendment Regulations 2005 (SI 2005/2724) reg.4 and Sch.1 (November 1, 2005).
7. Social Fund Cold Weather Payments (General) Amendment Regulations 2006 (SI 2006/2655) reg.3 and Sch.1 (November 1, 2006).
8. Social Fund Cold Weather Payments (General) Amendment Regulations 2007 (SI 2007/2912) reg.3 and Sch.1 (November 1, 2007).

9. Social Fund Cold Weather Payments (General) Amendment Regulations 2008 (SI 2008/2569) reg.2(1) and (4) (November 1, 2008).
10. Social Fund Cold Weather Payments (General) Amendment Regulations 2009 (SI 2009/2649) reg.2(1) and (2) and Sch.1 (November 1, 2009).
11. Social Fund Cold Weather Payments (General) Amendment Regulations 2010 (SI 2010/2442) reg.2(1) and (5) (November 1, 2010).
12. Social Fund Cold Weather Payments (General) Amendment Regulations 2011 (SI 2011/2423) reg.2(1) and Sch.2 (November 1, 2011).
13. Social Fund Cold Weather Payments (General) Amendment Regulations 2012 (SI 2012/2280) reg.2(1) (November 1, 2012).
14. Social Fund Cold Weather Payments (General) Amendment (No.2) Regulations 2012 (SI 2012/2379) reg.2 (November 1, 2012).
15. Social Fund Cold Weather Payments (General) Amendment (No.2) Regulations 2013 (SI 2538/2013) reg.2(1) and Sch.1 (November 1, 2013).
16. Social Fund Cold Weather Payments (General) Amendment Regulations 2014 (SI 2014/2687) reg.2(1) and Sch.1 (November 1, 2014).
17. Social Fund Cold Weather Payments (General) Amendment Regulations 2015 (SI 2015/183) reg.2 (March 23, 2015).
18. Social Fund Cold Weather Payments (General) Amendment (No.2) Regulations 2015 (SI 2015/1662) reg.2(1) and Sch.1 (November 1, 2015).

DEFINITIONS

"Meteorological Office"—see reg.1(2).
"postcode district"—*ibid.*
"station"—*ibid.*

Regulation 2(1A)(a) and 2(1B)(a)

[13 SCHEDULE 2

SPECIFIED ALTERNATIVE STATIONS

5.14

Column (1) *Meteorological Office Station*	*Column (2)* *Specified Alternative Station*
Aberporth	Pembrey Sands
Albemarle	Redesdale Camp
Bingley, No 2	Stonyhurst
Boscombe Down	Westonbirt
Braemar No 2	Aboyne No 2
Capel Curig No 3	Lake Vyrnwy No 2
Cardinham, Bodmin	North Wyke
Carlisle	Keswick
Charlwood	Kenley Airfield
Coleshill	Pershore College
Crosby	Rhyl No 2
Culdrose	Scilly: St. Marys Airport
Dunstaffnage	Skye: Lusa
Edinburgh, Gogarbank	Strathallan Airfield
Eskdalemuir	Redesdale Camp
Gravesend, Broadness	Kenley Airfield
Hawarden Airport	Crosby
Heathrow	Gravesend, Broadness
Hereford, Credenhill	Pershore College
High Wycombe, HQ Air	Rothamsted

Column (1) *Meteorological Office Station*	*Column (2)* *Specified Alternative Station*
Hurn	Swanage
Keele	Shawbury
Kinloss	Lossiemouth
Lake Vyrnwy No 2	Shawbury
Langdon Bay	Gravesend, Broadness
Leconfield	Linton on Ouse
Linton on Ouse	Bramham
Liscombe	North Wyke
Llysdinam	Sennybridge No 2
Mona	Rhyl No 2
North Wyke	Okehampton, East Okement Farm
Redesdale Camp	Albemarle
Rhyl No 2	Crosby
Rochdale	Rostherne No 2
St. Athan	Mumbles Head
St. Bees Head No 2	Threave
Shap	Keswick
Sheffield	Nottingham, Watnall
Stonyhurst	Bingley, No 2
Thorney Island	Hurn
Threave	Dundrennan
Tiree	Skye: Lusa
Trawsgoed	Llysdinam
Tredegar, Bryn Bach Park No 2	Sennybridge No 2
Tulloch Bridge	Aviemore]

AMENDMENTS

1. Social Fund Cold Weather Payments (General) Amendment Regulations 1999 (SI 1999/2781) reg.3 and Sch.2 (November 1, 1999).
2. Social Fund Cold Weather Payments (General) Amendment Regulations 2003 (SI 2003/2605) reg.3 and Sch.2 (November 1, 2003).
3. Social Fund Cold Weather Payments (General) Amendment Regulations 2005 (SI 2005/2724) reg.5 and Sch.2 (November 1, 2005).
4. Social Fund Cold Weather Payments (General) Amendment Regulations 2006 (SI 2006/2655) reg.4 and Sch.2 (November 1, 2006).
5. Social Fund Cold Weather Payments (General) Amendment Regulations 2007 (SI 2007/2912) reg.4 and Sch.2 (November 1, 2007).
6. Social Fund Cold Weather Payments (General) Amendment Regulations 2008 (SI 2008/2569) reg.2(1) and (6) (November 1, 2008).
7. Social Fund Cold Weather Payments (General) Amendment Regulations 2009 (SI 2009/2649) reg.2(1) and (3) and Sch.2 (November 1, 2009).
8. Social Fund Cold Weather Payments (General) Amendment Regulations 2010 (SI 2010/2442) reg.2(1) and (6) (November 1, 2010).
9. Social Fund Cold Weather Payments (General) Amendment Regulations 2011 (SI 2011/2423) reg.2(2) and Sch.2 (November 1, 2011).
10. Social Fund Cold Weather Payments (General) Amendment Regulations 2012 (SI 2012/2280) reg.2(2) (November 1, 2012).
11. Social Fund Cold Weather Payments (General) Amendment (No.2) Regulations 2013 (SI 2538/2013) reg.2(2) and Sch.2 (November 1, 2013).
12. Social Fund Cold Weather Payments (General) Amendment Regulations 2014 (SI 2014/2687) reg.2(2) and Sch.2 (November 1, 2014).
13. Social Fund Cold Weather Payments (General) Amendment (No.2) Regulations 2015 (SI 2015/1662) reg.2(2) and Sch.2 (November 1, 2015).

DEFINITIONS

"Meteorological Office"—see reg.1(2).
"station"—*ibid.*

The Social Fund Winter Fuel Payment Regulations 2000

(SI 2000/729)

Made by the Secretary of State under ss.138(2) and (4) and 175(1), (3) and (4) of the Social Security Contributions and Benefits Act 1992 and ss.5(1)(a) and (i), and 189(1) and (4) of the Social Security Administration Act 1992 and s.16(1) and s.79(1) and (4) of, and para.3 of Sch.5 to, the Social Security Act 1998

[In force April 3, 2000]

GENERAL NOTE

5.15 In November 1997, the Government announced that all pensioner households would receive a one-off payment in the winter of 1998 (and another in 1999) towards their fuel bills. These payments would be in addition to any cold weather payments which might be awarded under the Social Fund Cold Weather Payments (General) Regulations 1998 (above). As is the case under those regulations, no separate claim needs to be made for a winter fuel payment. Entitlement simply depends on the person being ordinarily resident in Great Britain and over the qualifying age on at least one day in the "qualifying week" (see reg.1(2)).

The qualifying age was originally pensionable age (i.e. 60 for a woman and 65 for a man). However, in *R. v Secretary of State for Social Security Ex p. Taylor* (C–382/98)(ECJ, December 16, 1999), the ECJ held that the different qualifying ages for men and women constituted unlawful discrimination on the ground of sex contrary to Directive 79/7/EEC. The qualifying age was therefore equalised at 60 for both women and men from the winter of 2000–2001 and remained at that level until April 6, 2010 when the gradual process of increasing pensionable age for women began. The qualifying age is now the same as for state pension credit, i.e. pensionable age in the case of a woman, and in the case of a man, the age which is pensionable age for a woman born on the same day.

Citation, commencement and interpretation

5.16 **1.**—(1) These Regulations may be cited as the Social Fund Winter Fuel Payment Regulations 2000 and shall come into force on 3rd April 2000.

(2) In these Regulations—

[5 "care home" in England and Wales has the meaning assigned to it by section 3 of the Care Standards Act 2000, and in Scotland means a care home service as defined by [11 paragraph 2 of schedule 12 to the Public Services Reform (Scotland) Act 2010];]

[6 [12 13 "couple" means—

(a) two people who are married to, or civil partners of, each other and are members of the same household; or

(b) two people who are not married to, or civil partners of, each other but are living together as a married couple;]]

"free in-patient treatment" shall be construed in accordance with regulation [7 2(4) and (5) of the Social Security (Hospital In-Patients) Regulations 2005];

[8 "income-related employment and support allowance" means an income-related allowance under Part 1 of the Welfare Reform Act (employment and support allowance);]

[14 . . .]

[5 10 "independent hospital"—

(a) in England, means a hospital as defined by section 275 of the National Health Service Act 2006 that is not a health service hospital as defined by that section;

(b) in Wales, has the meaning assigned to it by section 2 of the Care Standards Act 2000; and

(c) in Scotland, means an independent healthcare service as defined in [11 section 10F(1)(a) and (b) of the National Health Service (Scotland) Act 1978];]

[9 "qualifying age for state pension credit" means—

(a) in the case of a woman, pensionable age; or

(b) in the case of a man, the age which is pensionable age in the case of a woman born on the same day as the man;]

"qualifying week" means in respect of any year the week beginning on the third Monday in the September of that year;

[5 . . .]

"partner" means a member of—

(a) [6 a couple]; or

(b) a polygamous marriage;

[5 . . .] and

[4 "state pension credit" has the meaning assigned to it by section 1 of the State Pension Credit Act 2002;]

[1 . . .]

[2 (3) [5 . . .] in these Regulations a person—

(a) is in residential care if, disregarding any period of temporary absence, he resides in—

[5 (i) a care home;

(ii) an independent hospital; or]

(iii) accommodation provided under section 3(1) of the Polish Resettlement Act 1947 (provision by the Secretary of State of accommodation in camps),

throughout the qualifying week and the period of 12 weeks immediately before the qualifying week;

(b) lives with another person if—

(i) disregarding any period of temporary absence, they share accommodation as their mutual home; and

(ii) they are not in residential care.

[5 . . .]

(4) In these Regulations, unless the context otherwise requires, a reference—

(a) to a numbered regulation is to the regulation in these Regulations bearing that number; and

(b) in a regulation to a numbered paragraph is to the paragraph in that regulation bearing that number.

AMENDMENTS

1. Social Fund Winter Fuel Payment (Amendment) Regulations 2000 (SI 2000/2864) reg.2(a)(1) (November 13, 2000).
2. Social Fund Winter Fuel Payment (Amendment) Regulations 2001 (SI 2001/3375) reg.2(2) (November 2, 2001).
3. Social Security (Removal of Residential Allowance and Miscellaneous Amendments) Regulations 2003 (SI 2003/1121) reg.5 (October 6, 2003).
4. Social Fund Winter Fuel Payment (Amendment) Regulations 2004 (SI 2004/2154) reg.2(a) (September 20, 2004).
5. Social Security (Care Homes and Independent Hospitals) Regulations 2005 (SI 2005/2687) reg.8 (October 24, 2005).
6. Civil Partnership (Pensions, Social Security and Child Support) (Consequential, etc. Provisions) Order 2005 (SI 2005/2877) art.2(3) and Sch.3 para.32 (December 5, 2005).
7. Social Security (Hospital In-Patients) Regulations 2005 (SI 2005/3360) reg.7 (April 10, 2006).
8. Employment and Support Allowance (Consequential Provisions) (No.2) Regulations 2008 (SI 2008/1554) reg.7(1) and (2) (October 27, 2008).
9. Social Security (Equalisation of State Pension Age) Regulations 2009 (SI 2009/1488) reg.19 (April 6, 2010).
10. Health and Social Care Act 2008 (Miscellaneous Consequential Amendments) Order 2010 (SI 2010/1881) regs 2 and 5 (October 1, 2010).
11. Public Services Reform (Scotland) Act 2010 (Consequential Modifications of Enactments) Order 2011(SI 2011/2581) art.2 and Sch.2 para.29 (October 28, 2011).
12. Marriage (Same Sex Couples) Act 2013 (Consequential Provisions) Order 2014 (SI 2014/107) reg.2 and Sch.1 para.28 (March 13, 2014). The amendment extends to England and Wales only (see SI 2014/107 art.1(4)).
13. Marriage and Civil Partnership (Scotland) Act 2014 and Civil Partnership Act 2004 (Consequential Provisions and Modifications) Order 2014 (SI 2014/3229) art.29 and Sch.6 para.19 (December 16, 2014). The amendment relates only to Scotland (see SI 2014/3229, art.3(4)) but is in the same terms as the amendments made in relation to England and Wales by SI 2014/107 (see point 12 above).
14. Social Security (Miscellaneous Amendments) Regulations 2015 (SI 2015/67) reg.4(1)(a) (February 23, 2015).

Social fund winter fuel payments

5.17 [[1]**2.**—(1) Subject to paragraphs (2) [[6] to (4)] and regulation 3 of these Regulations, and regulation 36(2) of the Social Security (Claims and Payments) Regulations 1987, the Secretary of State shall pay to a person who—

[[6] (a) in respect of any day falling within the qualifying week is—
   (i) ordinarily resident in Great Britain; or
   (ii) habitually resident in [[8] any of the countries listed in the Schedule to these Regulations]; and]

[[5] (b) in or before the qualifying week has attained the qualifying age for state pension credit,]

a winter fuel payment of—
   (i) £200 unless he is in residential care or head (ii)(aa) applies; or
   (ii) £100 if [[3] state pension credit] [[4] , an income-based jobseeker's allowance or an income-related employment and support allowance] has not been, nor falls to be, paid to him in respect of the qualifying week and he is—
   (aa) in that week living with a person to whom a payment under

these Regulations has been, or falls to be, made in respect of the winter following the qualifying week; or

(bb) in residential care.

(2) Where such a person has attained the age of 80 in or before the qualifying week—

(a) in paragraph (1)(i), for the sum of £200 there shall be substituted the sum of £300; and

[[2](b) in paragraph (1)(ii), for the sum of £100 there shall be substituted the sum of £200, except that—

(i) where he is in that week living with a person to whom a payment under these Regulations has been, or falls to be, made in respect of the winter following that week who has also attained the age of 80 in or before that week, or

(ii) where he is in residential care,

there shall be substituted the sum of £150.]

(3) Where such a person has not attained the age of 80 in or before the qualifying week but he is a partner of and living with a person who has done so, in paragraph (1)(i) for the sum of £200 there shall be substituted the sum of £300.]

[[6] (4) A person does not qualify for a winter fuel payment by virtue of falling within paragraph [[7] (1)(a)(ii)] above unless—

(a) they are a person to whom Council Regulation (EC) No 1408/71 on the application of social security schemes to employed persons, to self-employed persons and to members of their families moving within the Community, or Regulation (EC) No 883/2004 of the European Parliament and of the Council on the coordination of social security systems, applies; and

(b) they are able to demonstrate a genuine and sufficient link to the United Kingdom social security system.]

AMENDMENTS

1. Social Fund Winter Fuel Payment (Amendment) Regulations 2003 (SI 2003/1737) reg.2 (September 1, 2003).

2. Social Fund Winter Fuel Payment (Amendment) (No.2) Regulations 2003, (SI 2003/2192) reg.2 (September 3, 2003).

3. Social Fund Winter Fuel Payment (Amendment) Regulations 2004 (SI 2004/2154) reg.2(b) (September 20, 2004).

4. Employment and Support Allowance (Consequential Provisions) (No.2) Regulations 2008 (SI 2008/1554) reg.7(1) and (3) (October 27, 2008).

5. Social Security (Equalisation of State Pension Age) Regulations 2009 (SI 2009/1488) reg.20 (April 6, 2010).

6. Social Fund Winter Fuel Payment (Amendment) Regulations 2013 (SI 2013/1509) reg.2(1) and (2) (September 16, 2013).

7. Social Security (Miscellaneous Amendments) Regulations 2015 (SI 2015/67) reg.4(1)(b) (February 23, 2015).

8. Social Fund Winter Fuel Payment (Amendment) Regulations 2014 (SI 2014/3270) reg.2(1) and (2) (September 21, 2015).

DEFINITIONS

"qualifying week"—see reg.1(2).

"residential care"—see reg.1(3).

General Note

5.18 Regulation 2 sets out the conditions of entitlement to a winter fuel payment. A person qualifies if:

(a) He or she is either ordinarily resident in Great Britain, or in one of the countries listed in the Schedule to the Regulations, in the qualifying week (i.e. the week commencing on the third Monday in September (see reg.1(2)).

Claimants who qualify on the basis of habitual residence in a scheduled country must also fall within the personal scope of (EEC) or of Regulation (EC) 883/2004 and have a "genuine and sufficient link to the United Kingdom social security system": see para.(4) and the commentary on Regulation (EC) 883/2004 in Vol.III.

Until the winter of 2015/16, winter fuel payments were payable to people who were habitually resident in any EEA state (or Switzerland) rather than only to those who were habitually in a scheduled country. The effect of the amendment made by SI 2014/3270 with effect from September 21, 2015 is that those who are habitually resident in Cyprus, France, Greece, Malta, Portugal and Spain no longer qualify. According to the explanatory memorandum to SI 2014/3270 the average winter temperature (November to March) in the warmest part of the United Kingdom is 5.6°C. The policy is to exclude from entitlement those who are habitually resident in EEA states where the average winter temperature is warmer. The memorandum goes on to state:

> "7.7 DWP is aware there will be people who live in cold regions of "warm" countries who will not be eligible for a Winter Fuel Payment. However, we would have to implement the scheme on a regional basis throughout the EEA in order to make a Winter Fuel Payment for even some of these people. DWP considered this very carefully but concluded that it would introduce disproportionate complexity and administrative costs. Therefore, the scheme has to be administered on a countrywide basis using the average winter temperature for each EEA country to determine where Winter Fuel Payments will be payable."

It remains to be established whether the new restrictions are compatible with EU law.

For the winter of 2013/2014, the qualifying week ran from Monday, September 16 to Sunday, September 22, 2013, for the winter of 2014/2015 it ran from Monday, September 15 to Sunday, September 21, 2014; and for the winter of 2015/2016 it ran from Monday, September 21 to Sunday, September 27, 2015. For the winter of 2016/2017, it will run from Monday, September 19 to Sunday, September 25, 2016.

(b) He attains the qualifying age for state pension credit before the end of the qualifying week. The progressive increase in state pension age for women born after April 5, 1950 (to which the qualifying age for state pension credit is linked) means that, for the winter of 2012/2013, the claimant must have been born on or before July 5, 1951; for the winter of 2013/2014 s/he must have been born on or before January 5, 1952; and for the winter of 2014/2015 s/he will have to have been born on or before July 1952. Those born after those dates do not reach the qualifying age until—at the earliest—November 6 in each of those years.

People who meet these conditions may nevertheless be excluded from entitlement if reg.3 applies to them.

The drafting of reg.2 is quite unnecessarily opaque and must be read with reg.3

to be fully understood. Careful analysis discloses that, subject to what is said below about modification, it prescribes four rates of payment—£300, £200, £150 and £100—which apply as follows.

Claimants who live alone, or are the only person in their household who qualify for the winter fuel payment, receive either £200 (reg.2(1)(b)(i)) or £300 if they have reached the age of 80 by the end of the qualifying week (reg.2(2)(a)). Those rates do not apply to claimants in residential care. **5.19**

For claimants who live with another person, who also qualifies for a winter fuel payment (described in this note as a "qualifying person"), the position is more complicated:

- If the qualifying person is the claimant's *partner* and has been awarded SPC, income-based JSA or income-related ESA, then the claimant is excluded from entitlement (reg.3(1)(a)(i)). The effect, at least in the normal case where the couple do not live with a third (or fourth, etc.) person who is also a qualifying person, is that, as the claimant has been excluded, the partner becomes the only person in the household who qualifies for the payment and therefore receives the £200 rate under reg.2(1)(b)(i), or, if the partner or the claimant is over 80, the £300 rate under reg.2(2)(a) or reg.2(3) respectively.

- The converse also applies. Where it is the *claimant* who has been awarded SPC, income-based JSA or income-related ESA, and he/she lives with a partner who would otherwise be a qualifying person, then his or her partner is excluded from entitlement by reg.3(1)(a)(i) and it is therefore the claimant who is entitled to receive the £200 rate under reg.2(1)(b)(i).

- Subject to that, claimants who have *not* been awarded SPC, income-based JSA or income-related ESA, receive £100 (reg.2(1)(b)(ii)(aa). That appears to be the case even if the qualifying people have been awarded SPC, income-based JSA or income-related ESA, as long as they are not the claimant's partner. That rate is increased to £200 for a claimant aged 80 or over (reg.2(2)(b)), unless the qualifying person is also aged 80 or over, in which case it is increased to £150 reg.2(2)(b)(i).

- The rate payable where the claimant has been awarded SPC, income-based JSA or income-related ESA and lives with qualifying person, who is not his or her partner, and who has also been awarded SPC, income-based JSA or income-related ESA is unclear.

  The point turns on the meaning of the words "or head (ii)(aa) applies" in reg.2(1)(b)(i). Does head (aa) apply whenever a claimant lives with a qualifying person, or does it only apply when the additional requirement that the claimant has not been awarded SPC, income-based JSA or income-related ESA is satisfied? The former interpretation is the more natural: the additional requirement is contained in the main body of subpara.(ii) but not in head (aa) itself, so if it was intended to refer to it why not refer to the whole subparagraph rather than just head (aa)? But on that view, neither the claimant, nor the qualifying person receives a payment: reg.2(1)(b)(i) does not apply (because head (ii)(aa) does) and no other rate has been prescribed that expressly covers the situation in the first sentence of this bullet point. It cannot have been intended to leave two people, both of whom are reliant on income-related benefits, without a winter fuel payment that is paid to many people who are much better off financially. Therefore one is driven to the latter interpretation. On that view, head (ii)(aa) does not apply in the circumstances under discussion (because the claimant has an award of SPC, income-based JSA or income-related ESA for the qualifying week) and so the claimants (and the qualifying people) are entitled to £200 under reg.2(1)(b)(i) (if they are aged 79 or less) or £300 (if they are aged 80 or over).

The test for whether one person lives with another for these purposes, is established in reg.1(3)(b). It provides a person lives with another person if, disregarding any period of temporary absence, they share accommodation as their mutual home and are not in residential care (as defined below).

5.20 Claimants who are in residential care are only entitled if they have *not* been awarded SPC, income-based JSA or income-related ESA for the qualifying week, in which case they get £100 (reg.2(1)(b)(ii)(bb)) or, if they are 80 or over, £150 (reg.2(2)(b)(ii)). Claimants in residential care who do have an award of SPC, income-based JSA or income-related ESA for the qualifying week are excluded from entitlement. With effect from February 23, 2015, the new reg.3(1)(a)(iv)—which appears to have been introduced to address criticisms of the drafting made in previous editions—confirms that this is the case. People count as being in residential care if they have resided in a care home an independent hospital or a Polish Resettlement Home for a continuous period of at least 13 weeks ending with the last day of the qualifying week: see reg.1(3)(a). Temporary absences are disregarded when calculating the 13-week period.

The position is further complicated by the fact that the above rates of payment were temporarily modified by:

- reg.2 of the Social Fund Winter Fuel Payment (Temporary Increase) Regulations 2008 (SI 2008/1778) during "the 2008–09 winter" (defined as "the winter which follows the qualifying week beginning on 15th September 2008");
- reg.2 of the Social Fund Winter Fuel Payment (Temporary Increase) Regulations 2009 (SI 2009/1489) during "the 2009–2010 winter" (defined as "the winter which follows the qualifying week beginning on 21st September 2009"); and
- reg.2 of the Social Fund Winter Fuel Payment (Temporary Increase) Regulations 2010 (SI 2010/1161) during "the 2010-2011 winter" (defined as the winter which follows the qualifying week beginning on September 20, 2010).

On each occasion, the modifications took the form of a temporary increase in so that the £100 rate in regs 2(1)(b)(ii) became £125; the £100 figure in reg.2(2)(b) became £125; the £200 rate in regs 2(1)(b)(i), (2)(a) and (3), became £250; the £200 rate in reg.2(2)(b) became £275; the £150 rate in reg.2(2)(b) became £200; and the £300 rate in regs 2(2)(a) and 2(3) became £400.

Note that it is possible to be "ordinarily resident" in more than one country: see *CIS/1691/2014*.

Persons not entitled to a social fund winter fuel payment

5.21 **3.**—(1) Regulation 2 shall not apply in respect of a person who—

(a) is [5 throughout the qualifying week]—

[4 (i) a partner of, and living with, a person who attained the qualifying age for state pension credit in or before the qualifying week and to whom state pension credit, an income-based jobseeker's allowance or an income-related employment and support allowance has been, or falls to be, paid in respect of the qualifying week;]

(ii) receiving free in-patient treatment and has been receiving free in-patient treatment for more than 52 weeks; or

(iii) detained in custody under a sentence imposed by a court; or

[7 (iv) in residential care and is a person to whom state pension credit, an income-based jobseeker's allowance or an income-related employment and support allowance has been, or falls to be, paid in respect of the qualifying week; or]

(b) subject to paragraph (2), has not made a claim for a winter fuel payment [5 on or before the 31st March] following the qualifying week in respect of the winter following that week.

(2) Paragraph (1)(b) shall not apply where—

(a) a payment has been made by virtue of regulation 4(1) [5 on or before the 31st March] following the qualifying week in respect of the winter following that week; or

(b) regulation 4(2) applies.

[6 (3) No person is entitled to a winter fuel payment for the winter of 1997 to 1998, 1998 to 1999 or 1999 to 2000 unless they have made a claim for such a payment on or before 31st March 2014.]

AMENDMENTS

1. Social Fund Winter Fuel Payment (Amendment) Regulations 2000 (SI 2000/2864) reg.2(a)(ii) (November 13, 2000).

2. Social Fund Winter Fuel Payment (Amendment) Regulations 2004 (SI 2004/2154) reg.2(c) (September 20, 2004).

3. Employment and Support Allowance (Consequential Provisions) (No.2) Regulations 2008 (SI 2008/1554) reg.7(1) and (4) (October 27, 2008).

4. Social Security (Equalisation of State Pension Age) Regulations 2009 (SI 2009/1488) reg.21 (April 6, 2010).

5. Social Security (Miscellaneous Amendments) Regulations 2012 (SI 2012/757) reg.18 (April 1, 2012).

6. Social Fund Winter Fuel Payment (Amendment) Regulations 2013 (SI 2013/1509) reg.2(1) and (3) (September 16, 2013).

7. Social Security (Miscellaneous Amendments) Regulations 2015 (SI 2015/67) reg.4(1)(c) (February 23, 2015).

DEFINITIONS

"free in-patient treatment"—see reg.1(2).
"qualifying week"—*ibid.*

GENERAL NOTE

Regulation 3 excludes certain people from entitlement to a winter fuel payment even if they fall within reg.2(a) and (b). There are four categories: 5.22

(a) partners of people who were entitled to income support or income-based jobseeker's allowance throughout the qualifying week (reg.3(1)(a)(i)). This is to prevent double payment;

(b) people who, throughout the qualifying week, have been receiving free in-patient treatment (see the notes to reg.21(3) of the Income Support Regulations) for more than 52 weeks (reg.3(1)(a)(ii));

(c) people serving a custodial sentence throughout the qualifying week (reg.3(1)(a)(iii)). Note that the reference to "a sentence imposed by a court" excludes those in prison on remand;

(d) people in residential care who were entitled to state pension credit, income-based jobseeker's allowance or income-related employment and support allowance during the qualifying week; and

(e) anyone who does not automatically receive a winter fuel payment under reg.4 and who fails to claim it by March 31 in the following year. There is an exception for refugees to whom reg.4(2) applies. In *CIS 2337/2004*, Commissioner Jacobs held that the time limit in reg.3(1)(b) does not infringe claimants' rights under art.1 of the First Protocol to the European Convention on Human Rights even when a payment has been made without a claim in respect of previous years. The time limit did not deprive claimants of any rights but merely defined the scope of those rights. In *Walker-Fox v Secretary of State for Work and Pensions* [2005] EWCA Civ 1441 (*R(IS) 3/06*), the Court of Appeal held (overruling the decision of the Deputy Commissioner in *CIS/488/2004*) that the March 31 time limit applied for the winters of 2000/01 and 2001/02 in cases in which the claimant had to rely on Regulation 1408/71, even though the UK Government did not accept that there was an entitlement in such cases until July 2002 (i.e. after those time limits had expired). In this context, see also *CIS/3555/2004*. The final time limit for claiming a winter fuel payment for the winters of 1997/1998, 1998/1999 and 1999/2000 is March 31, 2014 (see para.(3)).

A claim for a winter fuel payment may be made using one of the forms at *http://www.gov.uk*. Typing the words "winter fuel payment claim" into the search box on the home page gives a link to the forms (one for those living in Great Britain and the other for those living in another EEA country or Switzerland). Proof of age will usually be required. Claiming in other ways may be acceptable, as long as it is done in writing, but—unless to do so would risk missing the absolute time limit for claiming—it is better to use the appropriate form, if possible.

Making a winter fuel payment without a claim

5.23 **4.**—(1) Subject to paragraph (2), the Secretary of State may [3 on or before the 31st March] of the year following the year in which the qualifying week falls make a winter fuel payment under regulation 2 in respect of the preceding winter to a person who (disregarding regulation 3(b)) appears from official records held by the Secretary of State to be entitled to a payment under that regulation.

(2) Where a person becomes entitled to income support [1[2 , state pension credit or an income-related employment and support allowance]] in respect of the qualifying week by virtue of a decision made after that week that section 115 of the Immigration and Asylum Act 1999 (exclusions) ceases to apply to him the Secretary of State shall make a winter fuel payment to that person under regulation 2 in respect of the winter following the qualifying week.

(3) Subject to paragraph (4), for the purposes of paragraphs (1) and (2) official records held by the Secretary of State as to a person's circumstances shall be sufficient evidence thereof for the purpose of deciding his entitlement to a winter fuel payment and its amount.

(4) Paragraph (3) shall not apply so as to exclude the revision of a decision under section 9 of the Social Security Act 1998 (revision of decisions) or the supersession of a decision under section 10 of that Act (decisions superseding earlier decisions) or the consideration of fresh evidence in connection with the revision or supersession of a decision.

AMENDMENTS

1. Social Fund Winter Fuel Payment (Amendment) Regulations 2004 (SI 2004/2154) reg.2(d) (September 20, 2004).

2. Employment and Support Allowance (Consequential Provisions) (No.2) Regulations 2008 (SI 2008/1554) reg.7(1) and (5) (October 27, 2008).

3. Social Security (Miscellaneous Amendments) Regulations 2012 (SI 2012/757) reg.18 (April 1, 2012).

Definition

"qualifying week"—see reg.1(2).

General Note

Regulation 4 empowers (but does not oblige) the Secretary of State to make winter fuel payments on the basis of Benefits Agency records and without an express claim being made. At the outset, the information in those records is deemed to be sufficient evidence of entitlement or non-entitlement (see reg.4(3)) but reg.4(4) permits the initial decision to be revised or superseded in the normal way if further information comes to light. Those who consider themselves to be entitled to a winter fuel payment but do not receive one automatically may make a claim for it, provided they do so by March 31 in the year following the qualifying week (see reg.3(1)(b)). In cases where the Secretary of State does not make an automatic payment, there is no right of appeal against that omission. This is because omitting to make a payment does not give rise to a "decision" against which there is a right of appeal (see *CIS/751/2005* and *CIS/840/2005*, the latter decision doubting the decision of the Deputy Commissioner in *CIS/4088/2004*). In *CIS/840/2005*, the Commissioner explained the point as follows: 5.24

> "9. . . . I do not consider that, where the Secretary of State does not decide to make a payment under regulation 4(1), he is obliged to issue a decision not to make a payment. Indeed, it seems to me that he is not entitled, before 31 March of the relevant year, to issue a decision not to make a payment to a person who may be entitled to one, because that person may still make a claim within the time allowed by regulation 3(1)(b) and might establish his entitlement on the claim. He can make a decision under regulation 4 to make a payment but otherwise it seems to me that he must leave matters open and await a possible claim."

And, of course, after March 31 the Secretary of State's power to make the payment ends in any event by virtue of reg.3(1)(b).

For the effect of reg.4(2) before June 14, 2007, see p.1246 of Vol.II of the 2007 edition. The paragraph now appears to be otiose following the revocation of reg.21ZB of the Income Support Regulations. However, it has not itself been revoked.

In *CIS 2497/2002* an argument was raised that the operation of reg.4 discriminated indirectly against men on the grounds of their sex contrary to Directive 79/7. The evidence was that those selected by the Secretary of State to receive a winter fuel payment without a claim had been identified from official records of those receiving social security benefits (including retirement pension) in the qualifying week. As the pensionable age for women is lower than that for men, it was argued that there would be significantly more women than men in that category. However, Commissioner Mesher rejected that argument on the basis that, even if the operation of the rules allowing the Secretary of State to make payments without a claim was discriminatory, the claimant had not been disadvantaged by reg.4 but by "the overall and identical time-limit [i.e. March 31, after the winter in question] set for claims and for the making of payments without a claim".

Revocations

5.—The Social Fund Winter Fuel Payment Regulations 1998, the Social Fund Winter Fuel Payment Amendment Regulations 1998 and the Social Fund Winter Fuel Payment Amendment Regulations 1999 are hereby revoked. 5.25

[1 Regulation 2

SCHEDULE

5.25A

Countries
Republic of Austria
Kingdom of Belgium
Republic of Bulgaria
Republic of Croatia
Czech Republic
Kingdom of Denmark
Republic of Estonia
Republic of Finland
Federal Republic of Germany
Republic of Hungary
Republic of Iceland
Republic of Ireland
Republic of Italy
Republic of Latvia
Principality of Liechtenstein
Republic of Lithuania
Grand Duchy of Luxembourg
Kingdom of the Netherlands
Kingdom of Norway
Republic of Poland
Republic of Romania
Slovak Republic
Republic of Slovenia
Kingdom of Sweden
Swiss Confederation.]

AMENDMENT

1. Social Fund Winter Fuel Payment (Amendment) Regulations 2014 (SI 2014/3270) reg.2(1) and (3) (September 21, 2015).

The Social Fund Maternity and Funeral Expenses (General) Regulations 2005

(SI 2005/3061) (AS AMENDED)

Made by the Secretary of State under sections 138(1)(a) and (4) and 175(1), (3) and (4) of the Social Security Contributions and Benefits Act 1992, after agreement by the Social Security Advisory Committee that proposals in respect of these Regulations should not be referred to it

[In force December 5, 2005]

ARRANGEMENT OF REGULATIONS

PART I

GENERAL

GENERAL NOTE

With effect from December 5, 2005, these Regulations replaced the Social Fund Maternity and Funeral Expenses (General) Regulations 1987 in their entirety. However, with a few exceptions, the effect was intended to consolidate those regulations and to produce a (greatly needed) simplification in the structure and wording of the rules for funeral payments. 5.27

The main changes were:

- a new definition of "couple" in reg.3(1) to reflect the coming into force of the Civil Partnership Act 2004. The definition has since been amended to reflect the coming into force of the Marriage (Same Sex Couples) Act 2013;
- a cosmetic change to the definition of "family" in reg.3(1). The definition now refers to "polygamous marriage" rather than a "polygamous relationship";
- the exclusion from the "immediate family member test" in reg.8(1) of students aged less than 19 who are in non-advanced education. Previously only those in advanced education were excluded (see reg.8(4)(a) of the former regulations);
- a large increase in the categories of people that are excluded from the "closer contact" test in reg.8(6)–(8) so that those categories are now the same as the categories of people who are exempt from the "immediate family member test" (cf. reg.8(8)(b) with reg.7(7) of the former regulations); and
- the metrification of references to distance.

PART I

GENERAL

Citation and commencement

1.—(1) These Regulations may be cited as the Social Fund Maternity 5.28

and Funeral Expenses (General) Regulations 2005 and shall come into force on 5th December 2005.

Revocation

5.29 **2.**—The Regulations specified in the Schedule are revoked to the extent specified there.

GENERAL NOTE

5.30 The Schedule has not been reproduced. Its effects are noted at paras 3.197 and 3.200–3.204 of the Supplement to the 2005 edition.

Interpretation

5.31 **3.**—(1) In these Regulations—

"the Act" means the Social Security Contributions and Benefits Act 1992;

[3 "the 1995 Act" means the Jobseekers Act 1995;

"the 2007 Act" means the Welfare Reform Act 2007;

"the 2012 Act" means the Welfare Reform Act 2012;]

[1 "the Employment and Support Allowance Regulations" means the Employment and Support Allowance Regulations 2008;]

"the Income Support Regulations" means the Income Support (General) Regulations 1987;

"the Jobseeker's Allowance Regulations" means the Jobseeker's Allowance Regulations 1996;

"absent parent" means a parent of a child who has died where—

(a) that parent was not living in the same household with the child at the date of that child's death; and

(b) that child had his home, at the date of death, with a person who was responsible for that child for the purposes of Part IX of the Act;

[2 "adoption agency" has the meaning given in section 2 of the Adoption and Children Act 2002;

"adoption order" means an order made under section 46 of the Adoption and Children Act 2002;]

"child" means a person under the age of 16 or a young person within the meaning of regulation 14 of the Income Support Regulations or, as the case may be, of regulation 76 of the Jobseeker's Allowance Regulations;

[5 "child arrangements order" means a child arrangements order as defined in section 8(1) of the Children Act 1989 which consists of, or includes, arrangements relating to either or both of the following—

(i) with whom the child is to live, and

(ii) when the child is to live with any person;]

"child tax credit" means a child tax credit under section 8 of the Tax Credits Act 2002;

"claimant" means a person claiming a social fund payment in respect of maternity or funeral expenses;

"close relative" means a parent, parent-in-law, son, son-in-law, daughter, daughter-in-law, step-parent, step-son, step-son-in-law, step-daughter, step-daughter-in-law, brother, brother-in-law, sister or sister-in-law;

"confinement" means labour resulting in the [2 birth] of a living child, or labour after 24 weeks of pregnancy resulting in the [2 birth] of a child whether alive or dead;

[4 6 "couple" means—

(a) two people who are married to, or civil partners of, each other and are members of the same household; or

(b) two people who are not married to, or civil partners of, each other but are living together as a married couple;]

"family" means—

(a) a couple and any children who are members of the same household and for whom at least one of the couple is responsible;

(b) a person who is not a member of a couple and any children who are members of the same household and for whom that person is responsible;

(c) persons who are members of a polygamous marriage who are members of the same household and any children who are also members of the same household and for whom a member of the polygamous marriage is responsible [3 except where the claimant is in receipt of universal credit,];

"family element" means—

(a) in a case where any child in respect of whom child tax credit is payable is under the age of one year, the amount specified in regulation 7(3)(a) of the Child Tax Credit Regulations 2002, or

(b) in any other case, the amount specified in regulation 7(3)(b) of those Regulations,

but subject to calculations of that amount made in accordance with the Tax Credits (Income Thresholds and Determination of Rates) Regulations 2002;

"funeral" means a burial or a cremation;

"funeral payment" has the meaning given in regulation 7(1);

[2 "guardian" means a person appointed as a guardian or special guardian under section 5 or 14A of the Children Act 1989;]

"health professional" means—

(a) a registered medical practitioner, or

(b) a registered nurse or registered midwife;

"immediate family member" means a parent, son or daughter;

"income-based jobseeker's allowance" has the same meaning as it has in the Jobseekers Act 1995 by virtue of section 1(4) of that Act;

[1 "income-related employment and support allowance" means an income-related allowance under Part 1 of the Welfare Reform Act (employment and support allowance);]

"occupational pension scheme" has the same meaning as in the Pension Schemes Act 1993;

[2 "parental order" means an order made under section 30 of the Human Fertilisation and Embryology Act 1990 or section 54 of the Human Fertilisation and Embryology Act 2008;]

"partner" means where a person—

(a) is a member of a couple, the other member of that couple;

(b) is married polygamously to two or more members of his household, any such member [3 except that paragraph (b) does not apply where the claimant is in receipt of universal credit,];

[2 "placed for adoption" has the meaning given in section 18 of the Adoption and Children Act 2002;]

"person affected by a trade dispute" means a person—

(a) to whom section 126 of the Act applies; or

(b) to whom that section would apply if a claim for income support were made by or in respect of him;

"prescribed time for claiming" means the appropriate period during which a Sure Start Maternity Grant or, as the case may be, a funeral payment, may be claimed pursuant to regulation 19 of, and Schedule 4 to, the Social Security (Claims and Payments) Regulations 1987;

[2 "qualifying order" has the meaning given in regulation 3A;

"residence order" means a residence order as defined in section 8, and made under section 10, of the Children Act 1989;]

[5 . . .]

"still-born child", in relation to England and Wales, has the same meaning as in section 12 of the Births and Deaths Registration Act 1926 and, in relation to Scotland, has the same meaning as in section 56(1) of the Registration of Births, Deaths and Marriages (Scotland) Act 1965;

"Sure Start Maternity Grant" is to be construed in accordance with regulation 5;

[3 "universal credit" means universal credit under Part 1 of the 2012 Act;]

"working tax credit" means a working tax credit under section 10 of the Tax Credits Act 2002.

[2 (1A) References in these Regulations to—

(a) section 5, 8, 10 or 14A of the Children Act 1989,

(b) section 2, 18, 46 or 66 of the Adoption and Children Act 2002,

are to be construed as including a reference to a provision (if any) in legislation which has equivalent effect in Scotland, Northern Ireland, the Channel Islands or the Isle of Man.]

(2) For the purposes of Part III of these Regulations, persons shall be treated as members of the same household where—

(a) they are married to each other, or in a civil partnership with each other, and are living in the same care establishment, or

(b) they were partners immediately before at least one of them moved permanently into such an establishment,

and at least one of them is resident in a care establishment as at the date of death of the person in respect of whom a funeral payment is claimed.

(3) In paragraph (2), "care establishment" means—

(a) a care home,

(b) an Abbeyfield Home, or

(c) an independent hospital,

as defined in regulation 2(1) of the Income Support Regulations [1 or regulation 2(1) of the Employment and Support Allowance Regulations].

(4) For the purposes of these Regulations—

(a) persons are to be treated as not being members of the same household in the circumstances set out in regulation 16(2) and (3)(a), (b) and (d) of the Income Support Regulations [1 , in regulation 156 of the Employment and Support Allowance Regulations] or, as the case may be, in regulation 78(2) and (3)(a) to (c) of the Jobseeker's Allowance Regulations;

(b) [3 except where the claimant is in receipt of universal credit,] a person shall be treated as a member of a polygamous marriage where, during the subsistence of that marriage, a party to it is married to more than one person and the ceremony of marriage took place under the law of a country which permits polygamy.

AMENDMENTS

1. Employment and Support Allowance (Consequential Provisions) (No.2) Regulations 2008 (SI 2008/1554) reg.8(1) and (2) (October 27, 2008).

2. Social Fund Maternity Grant Amendment Regulations 2010 (SI 2010/2760) reg.2 (December 13, 2010).

3. Social Fund (Maternity and Funeral Expenses) Amendment Regulations 2013 (SI 2013/247) reg.2 (April 1, 2013) (Note that the extraneous comma at the end of the definition of "partner" is required by SI 2013/247 and is not an editorial error).

4. Marriage (Same Sex Couples) Act 2013 (Consequential Provisions) Order 2014 (SI 2014/107) reg.2 and Sch.1 para.37 (March 13, 2014). The amendment extends to England and Wales only (see SI 2014/107, art.1(4)).

5. Child Arrangements Order (Consequential Amendments to Subordinate Legislation) Order 2014 (SI 2014/852) art.12(1) and (2) (April 22, 2014).

6. Marriage and Civil Partnership (Scotland) Act 2014 and Civil Partnership Act 2004 (Consequential Provisions and Modifications) Order 2014 (SI 2014/3229) art.29 and Sch.6 para.26 (December 16, 2014). The amendment relates only to Scotland (see SI 2014/3229 art.3(4)) but is in the same terms as the amendments made in relation to England and Wales by SI 2014/107 (see point 4 above).

GENERAL NOTE

Paragraph (1)

Regulation 3 defines the terms commonly used in these Regulations. Where relevant, these will be noted at the appropriate places in the commentary below. The following should, however, be noted: 5.32

"Close relative": The definition is narrower than the equivalent definitions in reg.2(1) of the Income Support Regulations and reg.1(3) of the Jobseeker's Allowance Regulations because, although it includes a "step-son-in-law" and a "step-daughter-in-law", it does not specify that the partner of a close relative is also a close relative. So, for example, the unmarried partner or civil partner of the claimant's son (or a person with whom the claimant's son lives as if they were civil partners) is a "close relative" for the purposes of IS and JSA but not of maternity grants or funeral payments. For the position of "half-blood" and adoptive relationships, see the commentary to reg.2(1) of the Income Support Regulations.

"Confinement": Note that a payment can be made for a stillbirth only if it occurs after the 24th week of the pregnancy.

"Couple": The definition is the same as for IS and JSA—see the note to the definition in reg.2(1) of the Income Support Regulations. In some circumstances where the members of a couple are living apart, they are deemed not to be members of the same household—see the note to para.(4)(a) below. For the position where at least one member of the couple lives in a "care establishment" see paras (2) and (3).

"Family": See the commentary on the definition of "family" in s.137(1) of the Contributions and Benefits Act. The definition in para.(1) is differently worded from that definition (which applies for IS purposes) and the equivalent definition in s.35(1) of the Jobseekers Act. But, subject to the commentary to para.(4)(a) below, the consequences of the definition are the probably the same for all claimants other than those in polygamous marriages and their

children (who are included in the definition for the purposes of maternity grants and funeral payments but not of IS or JSA). (For the circumstances in which a person is to be treated as a member of a polygamous marriage, see para.(4)(b).)

For the circumstances in which a person is "responsible" for a child see reg.4A below.

"Family element": For child tax credit generally, see Vol.IV. Under reg.7(2) of the Child Tax Credit Regulations 2002 ("the CTC Regulations"), the maximum rate of CTC is the aggregate of the family element and an individual element for each child or young person included in the claim. The family element is fixed by reg.7(3) of the CTC Regulations. From April 6, 2011, the family element has been £545 per annum. For the years from 2003/2004 to 2010/2011, it was £545 per annum unless one of the children included in the award was less than one year old, in which case it was £1090. Under regs 5(1)(a)(v) and 7(4)(a)(v), CTC must be payable at a higher rate than this to count as a qualifying benefit for, respectively, a maternity grant or a funeral payment. Note, however, that tax credit award letters sometimes (wrongly) attribute the childcare element of working tax credit to CTC (see, for example, para.4 of *CIS/1064/2004*). As this is not, in fact, part of CTC any childcare element appearing in the award letter should be disregarded when calculating whether CTC is paid at a rate in excess of the family element.

Where the claimant's award of CTC does not cover a full tax year, the comparison with the family element must be carried out on a "proportionate daily basis": see *CSG/607/2004* at para.21.

The definition of "family element" in reg.3 was considered in detail by the Upper Tribunal in *AM v SSWP (SF)* [2010] UKUT 344 (AAC). Following *CSG/607/2004* and *CIS/2303/2008*, Judge Wikeley held that child tax credit is payable at a rate higher than the family element when the level of the award is such that, after the application of the first taper (i.e. the 41 per cent (formerly 39 per cent (from April 6, 2008 to April 5, 2011) and 37 per cent (from April 6, 2003 to April 5, 2008)) taper provided for by Steps 3–7 of reg.8(3) of the Tax Credits (Income Thresholds and Determination of Rates Regulations) 2002 as amended), includes a sum attributable to an individual child element of CTC and not just sums attributable to the family element. That is so even if the actual cash amount of CTC paid appears to be just over the prescribed family element as a result of rounding by HMRC. Judge Wikeley also points out that the statement in previous editions of this work that:

> "In practice, CTC will only be payable at a rate at or below the level of the family element if the family's income (calculated in accordance with the Tax Credits (Definition and Calculation of Income Regulations) 2002) is over £50,000 *per annum* (see reg. 8(3) of the Tax Credits (Income Thresholds and Determination of Rates) Regulations 2002, particularly Steps 8–10)"

confuses that first taper with the second taper of 6.67 per cent that is applied to the family element once annual income exceeds £50,000pa under Steps 8–10 of reg.8(3) and disregards the "plateau effect" that occurs where a claimant's income is sufficient to reduce the individual child elements to nil under the first taper but does not exceed £50,000. He suggests that the commentary would be "would be more accurate, if perhaps more long-winded, if it read:

> 'In practice, CTC will only be payable at a rate above the family element (i.e. including at least some individual child element) where the family's income (calculated in accordance with the Tax Credits (Definition and Calculation of Income) Regulations 2002) is either below or at least (and depending on the precise circumstances) not very far above

> the initial threshold of £16,040 per annum, given the impact of the first taper of 37 pence [39 pence in 2010/2011 and 41 pence from 2011/2012] in the pound (see reg.8(3) of the Tax Credits (Income Thresholds and Determination of Rates) Regulations 2002, and particularly Steps 3–7).'"

In *GC v SSWP (SF)* [2010] UKUT 100 (AAC), it was accepted by the Secretary of State that the reference in reg.7 to "having an award" of CTC or WTC was to the award under s.14 TCA 2002, rather than the subsequent determination of entitlement under s.18 of that Act.

"Still-born child": The definition referred to is "a child which has issued forth from its mother after the 24th week of pregnancy and which did not at any time after being completely expelled from its mother draw breath or show any other signs of life."

Paragraphs (2) and (3)

For "*care home*", "*Abbeyfield Home*" and "*independent hospital*", see reg.2(1) of the Income Support Regulations and the commentary to that regulation. 5.33

Paragraph 4(a)

See the commentary to reg.16 of the Income Support Regulations. The general rule in that regulation (and reg.78 of the Jobseeker's Allowance Regulations and reg.156 of the ESA Regulations) is that family members are treated as continuing to be members of the same household even though one or more of them is temporarily living away from the others. That general rule is subject to the exceptions listed in paras (2) and (3) of reg.16. Previous editions of this work have expressed the view that the operation of para.(4)(a) is problematical because, whilst it incorporates the exceptions into the rules for maternity grants and funeral payments (other than the exceptions relating to residential care, which are dealt with in paras (2) and (3)) and goes further than reg.16 by deeming people within those exceptions *not* to be members of the same household, it does not incorporate the general rule. If that were correct, it would follow that, in cases that do not fall within the exceptions, the general law applies to the question of whether membership of a household endures through a temporary absence (see *England v Secretary of State for Social Services* [1982] 3 F.L.R. 222; *Taylor v Supplementary Benefit Officer (R(FIS) 5/85)*; *Santos v Santos* [1972] 2 All E.R. 246). However, in *SSWP v LD (IS)* [2010] UKUT 77 (AAC), the Upper Tribunal held that the general rule in reg.16(1) (or, by implication, in regs 78 and 156) does apply to maternity grants and funeral payments. Judge Levenson stated: 5.34

> "16. Regulation 3(4)(a) of the 2005 regulations refers to not being treated as a member of the same household in the circumstances set out in regulation 16(2) of the 1987 regulations. Those circumstances refer to paragraph 16(1) of the 1987 regulations not applying if paragraph 16(2) applies. The logic of this is that 16(1) is also incorporated into the story by the wording of regulation 3(4)(a). There is no doubt that before the deceased moved away from the claimant, they were partners living in the same household. The First-tier Tribunal was clearly satisfied, as am I, that the deceased was only temporarily living away from the claimant. Regulation 16(1) of the 1987 regulations requires that they continue to be treated as members of the same household. That being the case, they continued to be a couple for the purposes of regulation 7(8)(a) of the 2005 regulations."

In any event, the couple in that case continued to be members of the same household whilst living in different places.

Paragraph (4)(b)

This applies the usual social security rule regarding polygamous marriages (i.e. that the marriage is polygamous at any time during which it is actually, rather than potentially, polygamous) to maternity grants and funeral payments. 5.35

[1 Provision against double payment: Sure Start Maternity Grants

5.36 **3A.**—(1) In this regulation—

(a) "C" is the child in respect of whom a Sure Start Maternity Grant has been claimed;

(b) "first grant" is a first Sure Start Maternity Grant in respect of C;

(c) "second grant" is a second Sure Start Maternity Grant in respect of C.

(2) Subject to paragraph (3), a second grant may not be awarded if a first grant has been awarded.

(3) A second grant may be awarded to a person ("P") if the following conditions are satisfied.

(4) The first condition is that P—

(a) alone, or together with another person, has been granted a qualifying order; or

(b) falls within regulation 5(3)(b), (d), (e) or (f).

(5) The second condition is that P—

(a) has not already received a first grant; or

(b) was not, at the time a first grant was claimed, a member of the family of a person to whom a first grant has been paid.

(6) A qualifying order is one of the following types of order—

(a) an adoption order;

(b) a parental order;

(c) a [2 child arrangements] order.]

AMENDMENTS

1. Social Fund Maternity Grant Amendment Regulations 2010 (SI 2010/2760) reg.2 (December 13, 2010).

2. Child Arrangements Order (Consequential Amendments to Subordinate Legislation) Order 2014 (SI 2014/852) art.12(1) and (3) (April 22, 2014).

GENERAL NOTE

5.37 Paragraph (2) sets out the general rule is that only one maternity grant may be paid for any individual child. That rule is subject to the exceptions set out in paras (3)–(5).

From December 13, 2010, those exceptions allow a second maternity grant to be paid in circumstances where the claimant did not receive the first grant (and was not a family member of the person who received the first grant when that grant was claimed)—see para.(5)—and either:

- the claimant has been granted a "qualifying order" (defined by para.(6) as an adoption order, a parental order or a child arrangements order);
- the claimant is responsible for a child aged under 12 months in the circumstances set out in reg.5(3)(b) below;
- the claimant (or claimant's partner) has been appointed the guardian of a child under 12 months and is responsible for that child (i.e. where reg.5(3)(d) applies);
- the claimant (or claimant's partner) is responsible for a child aged under 12 months who has been "placed for adoption" by an "adoption agency" (i.e. where reg.5(3)(e) applies and see the commentary to that provision for the definition of the terms in quotation marks); or
- (in certain circumstances) the claimant (or claimant's partner) has adopted a child aged under 12 months under the laws of a country outside the UK (i.e. where reg.5(3)(f) applies).

The various types of "qualifying order" are defined further by reg.3(1). An "adoption order" is an order made under s.46 of the Adoption and Children Act 2002. A "parental order" is an order made under either s.30 of the Human Fertilisation and Embryology Act 1990 or s.54 of the Human Fertilisation and Embryology Act 2008 (which replaced s.30 with effect from April 6, 2010). Such an order provides for a child who has been born following a surrogate pregnancy to be treated in law as the child of the couple in whose favour it is granted. A "child arrangements order" is "a child arrangements order as defined in section 8(1) of the Children Act 1989 which consists of, or includes, arrangements relating to either or both of the following (i) with whom the child is to live, and (ii) when the child is to live with any person".

Note that, even if none of the above exceptions applies, only a lawful payment bars another payment—see *CG/30/1990*. So, where the first payment was made to the partner of the maternity grant claimant (who was the income support claimant) and not to her, this did not prevent her receiving a payment.

[1 Provision against double payment: funeral payments

4.—(1) Subject to paragraph (2), no funeral payment shall be made under these Regulations if such a payment has already been made in respect of any funeral expenses arising from the death of the same person. 5.38

(2) A further funeral payment may be made in respect of any funeral expenses arising from the death of a person in respect of which such a payment has already been made where—

(a) the decision pursuant to which the funeral payment was awarded has been revised; and

(b) the further amount of the award as revised, together with the amount of the funeral payment already paid in respect of the death of that person, does not exceed the amount of any funeral payment which may be awarded pursuant to regulation 9.]

AMENDMENT

1. Social Fund Maternity Grant Amendment Regulations 2010 (SI 2010/2760) reg.2 (December 13, 2010).

GENERAL NOTE

Only one funeral payment may be made in respect of any individual death. The one exception is where the decision to award the payment is revised so as to increase the amount of the claimant's entitlement after the original (smaller) payment has been made. In such a case, a further payment may be made (subject to the overall maximum prescribed by reg.9). 5.39

PART II

PAYMENTS FOR MATERNITY EXPENSES

[1 Persons to be treated as responsible for children

4A.—(1) For the purposes of this Part, subject to paragraph (4), a person ("P") is to be treated as responsible for a child if paragraph (2) or (3) applies. 5.40

(2) This paragraph applies if—

(a) P is receiving child benefit in respect of the child, unless P is a child in respect of whom another person is receiving child benefit; or

(b) no one is receiving child benefit in respect of the child but the child usually lives with P.

(3) This paragraph applies where P is receiving child benefit in respect of a child who is in receipt of child benefit in respect of another child in which case P is to be treated as responsible for both children.

(4) P is not to be treated as responsible for a child if the child is—

(a) being looked after by a local authority within the meaning of section 22 of the Children Act 1989, or section 93 of the Children (Scotland) Act 1995, unless the child usually lives with P; or

(b) detained in custody pending trial or sentence upon conviction or under a sentence imposed by a court.]

AMENDMENT

1. Social Fund Maternity Grant Amendment Regulations 2011 (SI 2011/100) reg.2 (January 24, 2011).

GENERAL NOTE

5.41 It is only possible for claimants to qualify for a maternity grant under regs.5(3)(b)–(e) below if they (or, sometimes, their partners) are "responsible for" the child in respect of whom the grant is to be made. From January 24, 2011 reg.4A defines the circumstances in which a person is to be treated as responsible for a child for the purposes of these Regulations.

The general rule is that the person receiving child benefit for the child is responsible. But that does not apply where a person is receiving child benefit for a child who is herself the parent of, and receiving child benefit for, another child. In those circumstances, the first person mentioned is responsible for both children. If no-one receives child benefit for the child, then the person with whom the child usually lives is responsible.

Under para.(4), no-one is responsible for—and therefore reg.5(3)(b)–(e) do not apply with respect to—children who are looked after by a local authority or are detained in custody. The only exception is where a child who is looked after by a local authority nevertheless usually lives with another person. In those circumstances, the person with whom the child usually lives is responsible.

[2 Entitlement

5.42 **5.**—(1) Subject to [3 regulations 5A and 6], a payment of £500 to meet maternity expenses (referred to in these Regulations as a "Sure Start Maternity Grant") shall be made in respect of a child or still-born child where the following conditions are satisfied.

(2) The first condition is that the claimant or the claimant's partner has, in respect of the date of the claim for a Sure Start Maternity Grant, been awarded—

(a) income support;

(b) state pension credit;

(c) an income-based jobseeker's allowance;

(d) working tax credit where the disability element or the severe disability element of working tax credit as specified in regulation 20(1)(b) and (f) of the Working Tax Credit (Entitlement and Maximum Rate) Regulations 2002(11) is included in the award;

(e) child tax credit payable at a rate higher than the family element; [4 . . .]

(f) an income-related employment and support allowance [4 ; or

(g) universal credit.]

(3) The second condition is that—

(a) the claimant or, if the claimant is a member of a family, one of the family is pregnant or has given birth to a child or a still-born child;

[3 (b) the child's parents are not partners at the date of the claim and the claimant—

(i) is the parent (but not the mother) of the child (who must not exceed the age of twelve months at the date of the claim), or is responsible for that parent, and

(ii) is responsible for the child;]

(c) the claimant or the claimant's partner—

(i) has been granted a qualifying order in respect of a child who does not exceed the age of twelve months at the date of the claim, and

(ii) is responsible for the child;

(d) the claimant or the claimant's partner—

(i) has been appointed the guardian of a child who does not exceed the age of twelve months at the date of the claim, and

(ii) is responsible for the child;

(e) a child who does not exceed the age of twelve months at the date of the claim has been placed for adoption with the claimant or the claimant's partner by an adoption agency and the claimant or the claimant's partner is responsible for the child; or

(f) the claimant or the claimant's partner has adopted a child who does not exceed the age of twelve months at the date of the claim and that adoption falls within section 66(1)(c) to (e) of the Adoption and Children Act 2002 (meaning of adoption).

(4) The third condition is that the claimant or the claimant's partner has received advice from a health professional—

(a) on health and welfare matters relating to the child (but this requirement does not apply where the claim is made after the birth of a still-born child); and

(b) where the claim is made before the child is born, on health and welfare matters relating to maternal health.

(5) The fourth condition is that the claim is made within the prescribed time for claiming a Sure Start Maternity Grant.]

AMENDMENTS

1. Employment and Support Allowance (Consequential Provisions) (No.2) Regulations 2008 (SI 2008/1554) reg.8(1) and (3) (October 27, 2008).

2. Social Fund Maternity Grant Amendment Regulations 2010 (SI 2010/2760) reg.2 (December 13, 2010).

3. Social Fund Maternity Grant Amendment Regulations 2011 (SI 2011/100) reg.2 (January 24, 2011).

4. Social Fund (Maternity and Funeral Expenses) Amendment Regulations 2013 (SI 2013/247) reg.2(4) (April 1, 2013).

GENERAL NOTE

Regulation 5 sets out the four conditions of entitlement for a one-off lump sum payment of £500 per child (see para.(1)) called a "Sure Start Maternity Grant". Those conditions are: 5.43

- the claimant (or the claimant's partner) must be in receipt of a qualifying benefit (para.(2));

- the claimant, (or, in some cases, the claimant's partner or a member of the claimant's family) must be either pregnant or, have given birth to a child, or have become responsible for a child aged less than 12 months in certain specified circumstances (para.(3));
- except in the case of a still-birth, the claimant (or the claimant's partner) must have received advice from a health professional (para.(4)); and
- the claim for the maternity grant must have been made within the time limit (para.(5)).

All four conditions must be satisfied to qualify for the grant. In addition there are restrictions on entitlement where the claimant (or the claimant's partner) is a person affected by a trade dispute (see reg.6) and, from January 24, 2011 (but subject to the transitional protection in reg.3 of SI 2011/100: see below) where another member of the claimant's family is under 16.

Qualifying benefits—paragraph (2)

5.44 These are listed in sub-paras (a)–(f) of para.(2) and are largely self-explanatory. For the family element of child tax credit, see the note to the relevant definition in reg.3. For working tax credit generally, see Vol.IV. WTC comprises eight separate elements, namely the basic, disabled, 30-hour, second adult, lone parent, childcare, severe disability and 50 Plus elements (see s.11 TCA 2002 and reg.3 of the Working Tax Credit (Entitlement and Maximum Rate) Regulations 2002 ("the WTC Regulations")). WTC is a qualifying benefit for a maternity grant if either the disability element (under reg.9 of the WTC Regulations) or the severe disability element (under reg.17) is included in the calculation of the claimant's "maximum annual rate of working tax credit" under reg.20 of the WTC Regulations. In contrast with the position for CTC, as long as one of those elements has been awarded, the rate at which WTC is paid does not matter as long as (presumably) the award is higher than nil.

The qualifying benefit must have been awarded to the claimant or to her partner. Whether or not a claimant has a partner is a matter of law, and her own views on the point are relevant factors to be taken into account but are not conclusive of that issue—see *CIS/2031/2003* in which the Commissioner advised tribunals that:

> ". . . the question of whether a claimant has a partner is intrinsic to the very question of entitlement to a grant and in an appeal against a refusal of a grant which depends on the question of entitlement to a qualifying benefit, a tribunal should always enquire whether the person applying for the grant has a partner".

In that appeal, the claimant was entitled to a maternity grant because her (undisclosed) partner had been entitled to IS at the relevant date, albeit not in respect of her.

To meet the condition in para.(2), it is necessary for a qualifying benefit to have been awarded "in respect of the date of claim". It is not necessary that the qualifying benefit should actually have been paid by that date. Further, although para.(1) (a) appears to require that a qualifying benefit "has . . . been awarded", an award of made *after* the date of the claim for the maternity grant but which covers the date of claim will suffice (see *SSWP v FS (IS)* [2010] UKUT 18 (AAC), para.27 and *GC v SSWP* [2010] UKUT 100 (AAC)). For what happens when a decision refusing a grant has been made and a qualifying benefit is subsequently awarded, see under "*Time limit for claims*" (below).

Pregnancy, birth and becoming responsible for a child under 12 months—paragraph (3)

5.45 When reg.5 was completely recast with effect from December 13, 2010, the main change was to extend the list of circumstances (now set out in para.(3)) in which a maternity grant can be made. That list now takes into account the decision of the Court of Appeal in *Francis v Secretary of State for Work and Pensions* [2005] EWCA Civ 1303, *R(IS) 6/06* (and see further p.1332 of Vol.II of the 2010/11 edition), which held that the refusal (under the former reg.5(1)(b)) of a maternity grant to a parent who had obtained a residence order (in circumstances in which a grant would have been made if she had obtained an adoption order) discriminated against her contrary to arts 8 and 14 of the ECHR. It also creates new entitlements to a maternity grant in the circumstances set out in sub-paras (b), (d), (e) and (f).

For the definitions of "family", parent" and "still-born child" see reg.3 and the commentary to that regulation. For "qualifying order" see regs 3(1) and 3A(6) and the commentary to the latter. For "responsible for the child" see reg.4A.

Sub-paragraphs (a)–(f) are alternative rather than cumulative so it is sufficient to satisfy any one of them. The issues to which they give rise will normally be simple ones of fact.

Sub-paragraph (a)—The phrase "is pregnant" in sub-para.(a) means that an advance payment can be made where a child is to be born to the claimant or a member of her/his family. In other cases, entitlement can only arise after the event. 5.46

Sub-paragraph (b)—was amended with effect from January 24, 2011 by SI 2011/100. Its original wording (which was in effect from December 13, 2010 to January 23, 2011) was as follows:

> "(b) the claimant is the parent (but not the mother) of a child not exceeding the age of twelve months at the date of the claim and is responsible for the child and the child's parents are not partners at the date of the claim;".

The effect of that wording was to confer entitlement on a father of a child under 12 months who is responsible for that child and who is not the partner of the child's mother. The amended wording continues to cover those circumstances but also confers entitlement where:

- the child is less than 12 months old;
- the mother or father of the child is a child her/himself; and
- the claimant is responsible for the mother or father and is also responsible for the child.

The drafting would have been clearer if the amendment had dealt with those two, very different, cases by using different sub-paragraphs.

Sub-paragraph (d)—"Guardian" is defined by reg.3(1) as "a person appointed as a guardian or special guardian under section 5 or 14A of the Children Act 1989".

Sub-paragraph (e)—"Adoption agency" is defined by reg.3(1) as having the meaning set out in s.2 of the Adoption and Children Act 2002. That Act provides that a local authority or a "registered adoption society" "may be referred to as an adoption agency". "Registered adoption society" is itself defined (subject to a proviso) as a "voluntary organisation which is an adoption society registered under Pt 2 of the Care Standards Act 2000 (c. 14). . .". Regulation 3(1) also defines "placed for adoption" by reference to s.18 of the 2002 Act which empowers an adoption agency to place a child for adoption with prospective adopters and, following such a placement, to leave the child with them as prospective adopters. 5.47

Sub-paragraph (f)—Section 66(1)(c)–(e) of the Adoption and Children Act 2002 covers:

- an adoption under the law of a country or territory outside the British Islands, in which the Hague Convention (i.e. the Convention on Protection of Children and Co-operation in respect of Intercountry Adoption, concluded at the Hague on 29th May 1993) is in force that has been certified in pursuance of Article 23(1) of that Convention (see also s.144 of the 2002 Act);
- an "overseas adoption" as defined by s.87 of the 2002 Act; and
- an adoption recognised by the law of England and Wales and effected under the law of any other country.

Double payments—Where sub-paras (b), (d), (e) or (f) apply, it will sometimes be possible for the claimant to be awarded a maternity grant even if such a grant has previously been paid to another person: see reg.3A.

Health and welfare advice—para.(4)

5.48 Under para.(4), either the claimant or her partner (if she has one) must have received advice on the health and welfare of the child from a "health professional" (as defined in reg.3) before a maternity grant can be paid. For obvious reasons, this requirement does not apply if the child is still-born (see sub-para.(a)). Where the claim is made before the birth of the child, advice must also have been given about the health of the mother.

Time limit for claims—para.(5)

5.49 Under para.(5), it is a condition of entitlement to a maternity grant that it should have been claimed within the time limit for doing so. That time limit is prescribed by the Claims and Payments Regulations (reg.19(1) and Sch.4 para.8) (see Vol.III) and depends upon which sub-paragraph of reg.5(3) is the basis for the claim. Where the claim is based on pregnancy or the birth of a child (reg.5(3)(a)), the time limit is the period beginning 11 weeks before the first day of the expected week of confinement and ending three months after the actual date of confinement. A claim based on the grant of a qualifying order (reg.5(3)(c)) must be made within three months after the date the order is made. A claim based on appointment as a guardian (reg.5(3)(d)), or placement for adoption (reg.5(3)(e)) must be made within three months after the date on which the appointment took effect or the placement was made. A claim based on a foreign adoption (reg.5(3)(f)) must be made within three months after the date on which the adoption either took effect or was recognised under UK law.

The time limit for claims based on reg.5(3)(b) is slightly more complex. From December 13, 2010 to January 23, 2011, the time limit was three months from the date of confinement. Since January 24, 2011 (when Sch.4 para.8 was further amended by reg.4 of SI 2011/100) the time limit has been three months from the date the claimant became responsible for the child.

The time limit in Sch.4 para.8 cannot be extended. However if a claim for a maternity grant is refused because (at the date of that claim) a qualifying benefit not yet been awarded then, as long as the qualifying benefit is claimed within 10 working days of the original claim for the maternity grant, a further claim made within three months of a subsequent award of the qualifying benefit is treated as made on the date of the original claim, or the date the qualifying benefit was awarded, whichever is later (Claims and Payments Regulations, regs 6(16)–(18) and (22)). When deciding whether the claim for the qualifying benefit was made within the 10 working day' limit, it is the date on which the claim form was received by the relevant office that counts. A claim for council tax benefit (or housing benefit) that is backdated and therefore "treated as made" within the 10-day period will not suffice—see *CIS/3416/2004* (a case about funeral payments, for which the rules are identical).

Another way of dealing with the problem caused by a subsequent award of a qualifying benefit is by seeking a revision of the earlier decision to refuse the original claim. Under reg.3(3) of the Decisions and Appeals Regulations (see Vol. III). the Secretary of State has power to revise that decision where the application for a revision is made within one month of the notification of the original refusal, or within the three months' time limit, whichever is later. So far those time limits are less generous to claimants than the rules in reg.6(16)–(18) of the Claims and Payments Regulations. The potential advantage of this route is that the time limit may be extended under reg.4 of the Decisions and Appeals Regulations up to 13 months from the date of notification of the original decision. If the qualifying benefit was not awarded until after the expiry of the primary time limit, that might amount to "special circumstances . . . as a result of [which] it was not practicable for the application to be made within the time limit"—see reg.4(4)(c) of those Regulations. Note, however, that there is no right of appeal against a refusal by the Secretary of State to extend time under reg.4 (see *R(TC) 1/05*).

Paragraph (2)

The amount of the payment is £500 per child. 5.50

[[1] [2] Entitlement where another member of the claimant's family is under the age of 16

5A.—(1) In this regulation— 5.51

(a) "C" means the child or still-born child in respect of whom a Sure Start Maternity Grant is claimed; and

(b) "existing member of the family" has the meaning given in paragraph (2) or, as the case may be, (3).

(2) Where a parent of C ("P") is under the age of 20 and a member of the claimant's family, "existing member of the family" means any member of the claimant's family who is also a child of P, apart from C or any other child born as a result of the same pregnancy as C.

(3) In any other case, "existing member of the family" means any member of the claimant's family apart from—

(a) C;

(b) any other child born as a result of the same pregnancy as C;

(c) any child whose parent is under the age of 20 and a member of the claimant's family.

(4) Subject to the following provisions of this regulation, a Sure Start Maternity Grant shall not be awarded if, at the date of claim, any existing member of the family is under the age of 16.

(5) Where C is one of two or more children—

(a) born or still-born as a result of the same pregnancy, or

(b) (if the claim is made before the confinement in a case where regulation 5(3)(a) applies) who are expected to be born as a result of the same pregnancy,

(c) the number of Sure Start Maternity Grants to be awarded is to be determined in accordance with paragraphs (6) and (7).

(6) Where at the date of claim no existing member of the family is under the age of 16 a Sure Start Maternity Grant is to be awarded in respect of each of the children mentioned in paragraph (5).

(7) Where at the date of claim any existing member of the family is under the age of 16 then—

(a) where each of those existing members of the family under the age of 16 was born as a result of separate pregnancies, a Sure Start Maternity Grant is to be awarded for all but one of the children mentioned in paragraph (5); and

(b) where two or more of those existing members of the family under the age of 16 were born as a result of a single pregnancy, the number of Sure Start Maternity Grants to be awarded in respect of the children mentioned in paragraph (5) is the number of children mentioned in paragraph (5) minus the maximum number of existing members of the family born as a result of a single pregnancy.]

AMENDMENTS

1. Social Fund Maternity Grant Amendment Regulations 2011 (SI 2011/100) reg.2 (January 24, 2011).

2. Social Fund Maternity Grant Amendment Regulations 2012 (SI 2012/1814) reg.2 (August 13, 2012).

General Note

5.52 From January 24, 2011, a maternity grant cannot generally be awarded if any "existing member of the family" is under the age of 16. That general rule is now stated in para.(4).

For the definition of "family" see the commentary to reg.3(1). "Existing member of the family" is defined by paras (2) and (3). The phrase normally means any member of the family apart from the child for whom the maternity grant is claimed ("C"), any other child born as a result of the same pregnancy as C and any child whose parent is under the age of 20 and a member of the claimant's family (para.(3)).

However, where C's parent ("P") is under 20 and the claim is made by another member of the family (i.e. normally, a grandparent), "existing member of the family" means any child of P, apart from C or any other child born as a result of the same pregnancy as C, who is also a member of the claimant's family (para.(2)). That definition has the effect that the a maternity grant can be awarded for C even if there are other members of the family (excluding children born as a result of the same pregnancy as C) who are under 16, as long as P is not the parent of those other family members.

5.53 Paragraph (6), taken together with para.(5), provides that where more than one child is born (or still born or expected to be born) as a result of the same pregnancy and there is no other family member under the age of 16, a maternity grant is payable for each child. Presumably this provision has been included out of an abundance of caution because the consequence appears to follow in any event. In those circumstances, the definition of "existing member of the family " in para.(3) would remove the other child born as a result of the same pregnancy from the scope of the restriction in para.(4) even if para.(6) did not exist.

Paragraph (7), taken together with para.(5), introduces a further exception the first time from August 13, 2012. Where more than one child is born (or still born or expected to be born) as a result of the same pregnancy, then a maternity grant is to be awarded in respect of the additional child or children born even if other existing members of the family are under 16. As the explanatory memorandum to SI 2012/1814 states:

> "For example, if a claimant has an existing child but then has twins, one further [maternity grant] will be paid on the basis that the claimant already has existing baby items from the first child but needs additional baby items in respect of the second twin. If they have one existing child and then have triplets, two more grants will be paid and so on."

Paragraph (7)(b) modifies that principle where there have been previous multiple births in the family (or, more technically, where two or more of the existing members of the family under the age of 16 were born as a result of a single pregnancy).

5.54 Regulation 3 of SI 2012/1814 (see below) contains transitional provisions which mean that claimants cannot take advantage of the more generous terms of the new reg.5A where:

- the claim is based on reg.5(3)(a), was made before the birth and before August 13, 2012 and the expected date of confinement is before October 29, 2012;
- the claim is based on reg.5(3)(a), was made after the birth and the birth took place before October 29, 2012;
- the claim is based on reg.5(3)(c) and the qualifying order was made before October 29, 2012;
- the claim is based on reg.5(3)(d) and the appointment as guardian took effect before October 29, 2012;

- the claim is based on reg.5(3)(e) and the child is placed for adoption with the claimant or the claimant's partner before October 29, 2012; and
- the claim is based on reg.5(3)(f) and the adoption took effect before October 29, 2012.

For claims affected by the transitional provisions, the former version of reg.5A continues to apply: see pp.1393–1394 of Vol.II of the 2012/13 edition.

In *LS v SSWP (SF)* [2014] UKUT 298 (AAC), it was submitted that reg.5A is ultra vires on the ground that the Secretary of State had not complied with the public sector equality duty in s.71 of the Race Relations Act 1976 as amended when making it. The Upper Tribunal (Judge Levenson) rejected that submission. The claimant was given permission to appeal to the Court of Appeal on November 19, 2014 but it is understood that the appeal is not being pursued.

Persons affected by a trade dispute

6.—(1) Where the claimant or the claimant's partner is a person affected by a trade dispute, a Sure Start Maternity Grant shall be made only if— 5.55

(a) in the case where the claimant or the claimant's partner is in receipt of income support or income-based jobseeker's allowance, the trade dispute has, at the date of the claim for that payment, continued for not less than six weeks; or

(b) in the case where the claimant or the claimant's partner is in receipt of—

 (i) working tax credit where the disability element or the severe disability element of working tax credit as specified in regulation 20(1)(b) and (f) of the Working Tax Credit (Entitlement and Maximum Rate) Regulations 2002 is included in the award, or

 (ii) child tax credit payable at a rate higher than the family element,

 the "relevant claim" was made before the beginning of the trade dispute.

(2) In paragraph (1)(b), the relevant claim means the claim in respect of which a tax credit of the type referred to in head (i) or (ii) of that sub-paragraph was awarded.

General Note

Regulation 3 defines "person affected by a trade dispute" by reference to s.126 of the Social Security Contributions and Benefits Act 1992: see the notes to that section. 5.56

If the claimant (or her/his partner) is affected by a trade dispute then there is no entitlement to a maternity grant unless, either, that dispute is of at least six weeks' duration or the family is entitled to one of the tax credits specified in sub-para.(b) by virtue of a claim made before the trade dispute started.

It may sometimes be difficult to tell when a trade dispute started, since the dispute is to be distinguished from the stoppage of work due to it.

Part III

Payments for Funeral Expenses

Funeral payments: entitlement

7.—(1) In these Regulations— 5.57

(a) "funeral payment" means a social fund payment to meet funeral expenses of a deceased person;

(b) "responsible person" means the person who accepts responsibility for the funeral expenses.

(2) Subject to regulation 8, a funeral payment shall be made where each of the conditions referred to in paragraphs (3) to (9) is satisfied.

(3) The first condition is that, in respect of the date of the claim for a funeral payment, the responsible person or his partner is a person to whom paragraph (4) applies.

(4) This paragraph applies to a person—

(a) who has an award of—

(i) income support,

(ii) state pension credit,

(iii) income-based jobseeker's allowance,

(iv) working tax credit where the disability element or the severe disability element of working tax credit as specified in regulation 20(1)(b) and (f) of the Working Tax Credit (Entitlement and Maximum Rate) Regulations 2002 is included in the award,

(v) child tax credit payable at a rate higher than the family element,

(vi) housing benefit, or

(vii) [3 . . .] [2 . . .

(viii) income-related employment and support allowance; or]

[3 (ix) universal credit.]

(b) [3 . . .]

(5) The second condition is that the deceased was ordinarily resident in the United Kingdom at the date of his death.

(6) The third condition is that the claim is made within the prescribed time for claiming a funeral payment.

(7) The fourth condition is that the claimant is the responsible person or the partner of the responsible person.

(8) The fifth condition is that—

(a) the responsible person was the partner of the deceased at the date of death; or

(b) in a case where the deceased was a child and—

(i) there is no absent parent, or

(ii) there is an absent parent who, or whose partner, is a person to whom paragraph (4) applied as at the date of death,

the responsible person was the person, or the partner of the person, responsible for that child for the purposes of Part IX of the Act as at the date of death; or

(c) in a case where the deceased was a still-born child, the responsible person was a parent, or the partner of a parent, of that still-born child as at the date when the child was still-born; or

(d) in a case where the deceased had no partner and neither sub-paragraph (b) nor (c) applies, the responsible person was an immediate family member of the deceased and it is reasonable for the responsible person to accept responsibility for those expenses; or

(e) in a case where the deceased had no partner and none of sub-paragraphs (b), (c) and (d) applies, the responsible person was either—

(i) a close relative of the deceased, or

(ii) a close friend of the deceased,

and it is reasonable for the responsible person to accept responsibility for the funeral expenses.

(9) The sixth condition is that the funeral takes place—

(a) in a case where paragraph (10) applies, in a member State of the European Union, Iceland, Liechtenstein [1, Norway or Switzerland];

(b) in any other case, in the United Kingdom.

[1 (10) This paragraph applies where the responsible person or his partner is—

(a) a worker for the purposes of Council Directive No.2004/38/EC;

(b) a self-employed person for the purposes of that Directive;

(c) a person who retains a status referred to in sub-paragraph (a) or (b) pursuant to Article 7(3) of that Directive;

(d) a person who is a family member of a person referred to in sub-paragraph (a), (b) or (c) within the meaning of Article 2 of that Directive; or

(e) a person who has a right to reside permanently in the United Kingdom by virtue of Article 17 of that Directive.]

AMENDMENTS

1. Social Security (Persons from Abroad) Amendment Regulations 2006 (SI 1026/2006) reg.8(2) (April 30, 2006).

2. Employment and Support Allowance (Consequential Provisions) (No.2) Regulations 2008 (SI 2008/1554) reg.8(1) and (4) (October 27, 2008).

3. Social Fund (Maternity and Funeral Expenses) Amendment Regulations 2013 (SI 2013/247) reg.2(5) (April 1, 2013).

GENERAL NOTE

For the legislative history of funeral payments see pp.1229–1230 of Vol.II of the 2005 edition. 5.58

This regulation, together with reg.8, governs the right to funeral payments. Regulation 7 sets out the conditions of entitlement and reg.8 makes supplementary provision and contains two exclusory rules which disqualify some claimants who would otherwise have been entitled.

Regulation 7 specifies six conditions of entitlement, all of which must be satisfied (para.(2)):

- the claimant (or her/his partner) must have an award of a qualifying benefit or be a person in respect of whom council tax benefit in the form of second adult rebate could be awarded (paras (3) and (4));
- the deceased must have been ordinarily resident in the UK (para.(5));
- a claim must have been made within the time limit (para.(6));
- the claimant (or her/his partner) must be a "responsible person" (para.(7));
- the responsible person must be sufficiently closely connected to the deceased (para.(8)); and
- the funeral must take place in the UK or (in certain circumstances) in another EEA state (paras (9) and (10)).

Each of these conditions requires consideration in more detail.

Qualifying benefit

Under paras (3) and (4), the benefits that qualify a claimant for a funeral payment include all those that are qualifying benefits for a sure start maternity grant (see the commentary to reg.5) with the addition of housing benefit and council tax benefit. 5.59

For the family element of child tax credit, see the note to the relevant definition in reg.3.

Before April 1, 2013, the first condition was also satisfied if the claimant (or her/his partner) was a person in respect of whom a second adult rebate could be awarded: see the former sub-para.(4)(b). Secondly adult rebate was an alternative form of council tax benefit, which was abolished with effect from that date. For further details of the position before April 1, 2013, see p.1397 of Vol.II of the 2012/13 edition.

5.60 The award of the qualifying benefit must be in respect of the date of claim for the funeral payment. See the notes to reg.5(1) and *GC v SSWP* (SF) [2010] UKUT 100 (AAC). Also note *CIS/2059/1995*. In that case the claimant's claim for a funeral payment had been rejected on the ground that he was not entitled to income support. However, the consequence of the Commissioner allowing his appeal against the decision refusing income support was that the basis for the rejection of his claim for a funeral payment had gone. Thus the tribunal's decision on that appeal, although sound when it was given, had become erroneous and it too had to be set aside.

A person "has an award" of income-based JSA (and therefore satisfies the condition in para.(4)(a)(iii)) while serving the waiting days (i.e. under Jobseekers Act 1995 Sch.1 para.4 and reg.46 of the JSA Regulations 1996) before entitlement to that benefit begins: *SSWP v SJ (IS)* [2015] UKUT 0127 (AAC).

The requirement that claimants should be in receipt of a qualifying benefit has been held not to infringe their Convention rights under the Human Rights Act 1998, see *CIS/3280/2001*, *CIS/1722/2002* and *Faith Stewart v SSWP* [2011] EWCA Civ 907, [2012] AACR 9, upholding *SSWP v FS (SF)* [2010] UKUT 18 (AAC). It has also been held that failure of the scheme to provide for the personal representative of an insolvent estate to be eligible for a payment was neither irrational nor an infringement of the Convention: see *RM v SSWP (IS)* [2010] UKUT 220 (AAC).

Ordinary residence in the UK

5.61 The deceased must be ordinarily resident in the UK at the date of his death. Ordinary residence "connotes residence in a place with some degree of continuity and apart from accidental and temporary absences" (see *R(P) 1/78*, para.7). As the requirement is one of ordinary residence, not presence, a claim can be made in respect of a UK resident who dies, for example, while on holiday abroad for the cost of the funeral in the UK (although the cost of transporting the body back to the UK would not be covered, except possibly under reg.9(2)(g)).

The time limit

5.62 Under Claims and Payments Regulations, reg.19(1) and Sch.4 para.9, the time for claiming a funeral payment begins on the date of the death and ends three months after the date of the funeral. Otherwise the rules in this area are the same as for maternity grants—see the note to reg.5.

The three-month time limit begins to run on the day after the funeral and ends on the day three months later that corresponds to the day of the month on which the funeral took place: see *SSWP v SC (SF)* [2013] UKUT 607 (AAC) in which the funeral took place on July 26, 2011 and the time limit ended on October 26, 2011 so that a claim made on October 27, 2011 was out of time.

Responsible person

5.63 The claimant (or her/his partner) must be a "responsible person", which is defined by para.(1)(b) as "the person who accepts responsibility for the funeral expenses".

In *CSB/488/1982*, it was held that the fact that someone else makes the arrangements does not mean that the claimant has not taken responsibility for the costs. The test is not who is responsible for arranging the funeral. The question is whether the claimant (or partner) has entered into a contractual relationship with the funeral director. Often the fact that the claimant's name appears on the funeral director's account will be sufficient evidence of that. But if someone else's name appears that does not necessarily mean that the claimant has not accepted responsibility because that person may, on a correct legal analysis, have been acting as the claimant's (or partner's) agent. In *CIS/12344/1996* the claimant's son made the funeral arrangements; his mother was unable to do so because of her age and the sudden death of her husband. The bill was in his name and he paid it before the claim for a social fund funeral payment was made. It is held that the son had been acting as agent for his mother and the fact that the account was addressed to him did not detract from this. The claimant had accepted responsibility for the funeral costs. In *R(IS) 6/98* the Commissioner retracts his statement in *CIS/12344/1996* that it was necessary for the undertakers to know of the agency. The concept of the "undisclosed principal" in the law of agency allowed an agency to exist even where this was not disclosed to the third party, provided that the agent had in fact had authority beforehand. But if there was no agency at the time the funeral debt was incurred, it was not open to a person to intervene later and claim to be legally responsible for the debt (although depending on the circumstances a novation may achieve that result, see below). In *VC v SSWP (IS)* [2010] UKUT 189 (AAC), the Upper Tribunal stressed the importance of making sufficient findings of fact as to the nature of any agreement between the claimant and any other putative responsible person.

Agency must be distinguished from a novation, or transfer, of the contract as occurred in *R(IS) 9/93*. The Commissioner follows *CSB/423/1989* in holding that if another person has initially made a contract with the undertakers the claimant may assume liability for the funeral costs by a novation of the contract under which the claimant assumes the other person's liability and the undertakers release the other person from his liability. The novation requires the consent of all three parties, but no consideration or further payment is necessary. Providing that the claimant comes within one of the heads of what is now sub-para.(e) and has assumed responsibility for the costs before the decision is made (or possibly before the claim is made) the condition is satisfied. Often, arrangements will be made without thinking about the legal niceties, and a commonsense view should be taken.

Legal issues can also arise if the closest relative lacks the legal capacity to accept a contractual liability to the undertakers. In *C1/01-02(SF)* the Commissioner had to decide whether a 16-year-old boy could legally "accept responsibility" for the expenses of his mother's funeral under the Northern Ireland equivalent of reg.7. She held that, in the particular circumstances of that case (where the claimant was the deceased's eldest child, 16-years old, had become the tenant of the family home and there was no other parent whose whereabouts were known) those expenses were a "necessary" for him so that he was obliged to pay a reasonable price for them under s.3 of the Sale of Goods Act 1979 even though he did not have capacity to make a binding contract to pay them.

Connection with the deceased

Paragraph 8 identifies the person who may claim a funeral expenses payment on the basis of how closely he or she was related to, or connected with, the deceased. There are two different hierarchies depending on whether the deceased was an adult or a child. 5.64

If the deceased was an adult then, under sub-para.(a), the claimant must be his or her partner. If the deceased had no partner at the date of death then, under sub-para.(d), the claim may be made by an "immediate family member" (i.e. a parent, son or daughter—see reg.3(1)) if it is reasonable for him or her to take responsibility for the funeral expenses. If the deceased dies without a partner or an immediate family member (or if there was an immediate family member but it is not reasonable for him or her to take responsibility for the funeral expenses), then, under subpara. (e), the claim may be made by a "close relative" (i.e. a parent, parent-in-law, son, son-in-law, daughter, daughter-in-law, step-parent, step-son, step-son-in-law, step-daughter, step-daughter-in-law, brother, brother-in-law, sister or sister-in-law—again see reg.3(1)) or a close friend. Again, a close relative or close friend, must show that it was reasonable for him or her to take responsibility for the funeral expenses. In the very rare case where the deceased's partner also dies before the deceased's funeral without making a claim for a funeral payment, then the deceased is treated as not having had a partner at the date of his or her death—see reg.8(4).

If the deceased was a child then the first question to ask is whether s/he was still-born. If so, then the claimant must be one of the child's parents or a person who was the partner of one of the child's parents at the date of the death (sub-para.(c)). If not, then the claimant must be the person responsible for the child at the date of death (or his or her partner), unless there is an absent parent (defined in reg.3(1)) who (or whose partner) was not receiving a qualifying benefit at the date of death (sub-para.(b)). If no-one qualifies under sub-paras (b) or (c) then, as for adults, the claimant must be an "immediate family member", or failing this, a "close relative" or a close friend. A person is responsible for a child if s/he is counted as such for the purposes of child benefit.

5.65 If there is more than one "immediate family member" then, unless the claimant is the deceased's partner, see also reg.8(1) and (2).

In any case where the claimant is a close relative (other than an immediate family member) or a close friend of the deceased, s/he must also establish that it was reasonable for him or her to accept responsibility for the funeral expenses. Regulation 8(5) states that this "shall be determined by the nature and extent of his contact with the deceased". *R(IS) 3/98* holds that in deciding this question, regard should be had to the person's relationship with the deceased as a whole and not just during the period immediately preceding the date of death. The claimant had claimed a funeral payment in respect of his late father whom he had not seen for 24 years. He was the only close relative. The Commissioner decided that the lack of contact over the previous 24 years did not automatically erase the contact they had had in the preceding 30 years. It was not unreasonable for a son to wish to pay his last respects to his father whatever the reasons for their estrangement. See also *CIS/13120/1996* (claimant divorced from the deceased only two weeks before his death after 40 years of marriage), a decision on the law as in force up to June 5, 1995 (although the actual result would be different on the current law). The fact that it is reasonable for one person to assume responsibility for the cost of a funeral does not mean that it is not reasonable for someone else to do so (*CIS/13120/196*).

If there is more than one close relative then see reg.8(6)–(8).

It will be apparent from the above that an ex-partner (or someone who is no longer treated as a partner), or a relative who is not a close relative, will have to qualify under the category of close friend. According to the Decision Makers Guide, in considering whether a person was a close friend of the deceased, the depth of the relationship will be more important than its duration. In *CIS/788/2003* the deceased was a boy who had died at the age of three months. The child's mother was herself a minor and the funeral directors refused to enter into a contract with her for that reason. The child's grandmother therefore undertook responsibility for the expenses and claimed a funeral payment. Commissioner Turnbull held that the grandmother could be treated as a "close friend" of the deceased. The Secretary of State had argued that as child benefit had been paid to the child's mother, she would have satisfied what is now reg.7(8)(b)(ii) if she had accepted responsibility for the funeral expenses and therefore that the words equivalent to "none of sub-paragraphs (b), (c) and (d) applies" in sub-para.(e) were not satisfied. The Commissioner rejected that argument. The provision about the receipt of child benefit "did not apply" because there was no real possibility of the mother taking responsibility for the funeral expenses. Neither the existence of a family relationship between the grandmother and the child nor the child's very young age prevented her from being treated as his "close friend" for the purposes of the regulation.

Place of funeral

"Funeral" is defined by reg.3(1) as "a burial or cremation". Paragraph (9) provides that the burial or cremation must take place in the UK unless the claimant is a worker for the purposes of Regulations 1612/68 or 1251/70, a member of the family of a worker for the purposes of Regulation 1612/68, a member of the family of a worker who has died and to whom Regulation 1251/70 applied, or a person who has a right to reside in the UK under Directives 68/360 or 73/148, in which case it may take place in the EU or one of the other specified EEA states. This wording now reflects the judgment of the ECJ in *O'Flynn v Adjudication Officer* (C–237/94) (*R(IS) 4/98*). For details of that litigation (which is now of historical interest only) see pp.1231–1232 in Vol.II of the 2005 edition. 5.66

For Regulations 1612/68 and 1251/70 and Directives 68/360 and 73/148, see the notes to the definition of "person from abroad" in reg.21 of the Income Support Regulations.

The effect of paras (9) and (10) is that where the funeral takes place in an EEA country, financial help with the costs of repatriating a dead body is available that would not be available where the funeral takes place in other countries. This has led to a number of attempts to argue that the rule (and its predecessor which required the funeral to take place in the UK) were unlawfully discriminatory. Apart from the *O'Flynn* case (noted above), these have all been unsuccessful:

- In *R. v Secretary of State for Social Security Ex p. Nessa, The Times*, November 15, 1994, the High Court rejected an argument that the predecessor rule was unlawful under the Race Relations Act 1976. Section 75 of that Act stated that it applied to acts done by ministers, as it applied to acts done by a private person. But Auld J held that acts of a governmental nature, such as the making of regulations, were not subject to the control of the 1976 Act as they were not acts of a kind that could be done by a private person.
- In *CIS/3150/1999* a challenge to the validity of the rule on the basis that it was ultra vires and irrational was rejected.
- In *CIS 4769/2001* the Commissioner rejected a challenge under the Human Rights Act: the rule was not directly discriminatory and the Commissioner was not persuaded either that there was any indirect discrimination against the claimant, a Muslim of Pakistani origin, or that, if there was such discrimination, it had not been established that it was not objectively justified.
- In *Esfandiari v Secretary of State for Work and Pensions* [2006] EWCA Civ 282 (*R(IS) 11/06*), the Court of Appeal also held the rule did not discriminate unlawfully against recent migrants. Giving the judgment of the Court, Carnwath LJ stated:

  "8. . . . I find it impossible to see this as a case of 'discrimination' in any relevant sense. The state made provision for a suitable burial in the UK for all those of inadequate means, regardless of personal characteristics or status. There was no obligation on the state to do so, and certainly no obligation to do more. It was open to each appellant to take advantage of this provision, but each chose not to do so for understandable, but entirely personal, reasons.

  9. The only way in which this can be represented as 'discriminatory' is by characterising them as members of a 'group', that of recent migrants to this country; and then finding 'indirect' discrimination, in that as a group (so it is assumed) they are more likely than other comparable groups to have retained family links with their countries of origin, and therefore more likely to want their loved ones to be buried there. Such reasoning seems to me, with respect, wholly artificial. Without demeaning the strength and sincerity of the wishes of these appellants as individuals, it is not obvious that recent migrants, as a group, are particularly likely to prefer a burial

in their country of origin, rather than in the country they have made their home. In any event there may be many other categories of people resident in this country, who, given the choice, might elect for a burial abroad for themselves or their loved ones, whether for religious, family, social or purely sentimental reasons. They may have spouses from another country, who have retained their native family links; they may have spent large parts of their lives in another country; they may have children who have moved to another country. Such wishes are understandable and to be respected; but it is not the job of the state to satisfy them. Nor does the sharing of such desires render those who have them a 'group' requiring special protection under Article 14."

- Alternatively, if the rule was regarded as discriminatory then that discrimination was objectively justified.

In *CIS/1335/2004*, the claimant's husband died while they were on holiday in Spain. Because she could not afford to have his body flown back to the UK, he was cremated in Spain. His ashes were then interred in England. The Commissioner confirmed the Secretary of State's decision to refuse a funeral payment. The "funeral" was the Spanish cremation and not the subsequent burial of ashes in the UK. Therefore, the actual cost of the burial did not qualify under reg.9(3)(a) and the other UK costs could only qualify as other funeral expenses under reg.9(3)(g) as incidental to, or consequential upon, the cremation in Spain if the claimant was in principle entitled to a funeral payment in respect of that cremation. That was not the case because the claimant was neither a migrant worker nor a family member of such a worker within the provisions set out in para.(10). The result was that the rule treated UK citizens less favourably than citizens of other Member States exercising rights in the UK under EU law. However, that discrimination was not unlawful under EU law or under ECHR art.14, taken together with art.1 of the First Protocol. From April 30, 2006 para.(10) applies to nationals of Switzerland as well as to nationals of Iceland, Liechtenstein and Norway—and to members of their families as defined by art.2 of the Rights of Residence Directive—as if those nationals were EU nationals (see reg.10(g) of SI 1026/2006).

Funeral payments: supplementary

5.67 **8.**—(1) Subject to paragraph (2), the claimant shall not be entitled to a funeral payment where the responsible person is an immediate family member, a close relative or a close friend of the deceased and—

(a) there are one or more immediate family members of the deceased;

(b) one or more of those immediate family members or their partners are not persons to whom regulation 7(4) applied as at the date of death; and

(c) any of the immediate family members referred to in sub-paragraph (b) was not estranged from the deceased at the date of his death.

(2) Paragraph (1) shall not apply to disentitle the claimant from a funeral payment where the immediate family member who meets the description specified in sub-paragraph (c) of that paragraph is at the date of death—

(a) a person who has not attained the age of 18;

(b) [1 a qualifying young person within the meaning of section 142 of the Act (child and qualifying young person);]

[2 (bb) a qualifying young person under section 10(5) (prescription of qualifying young person) of the Welfare Reform Act 2012;]

(c) a person who has attained the age of 18 but not the age of 19 and who is attending a full-time course of advanced education, as defined in regulation 61 of the Income Support Regulations, or, as the case may be, a person aged 19 or over but under pensionable age who is attending a full-time course of study, as defined in that regulation, at an educational establishment;

(d) a person in receipt of asylum support under section 95 of the Immigration and Asylum Act 1999;

(e) a member of, and fully maintained by, a religious order;

(f) being detained in a prison, remand centre or youth custody institution and either that immediate family member or his partner is a person to whom regulation 7(4) applied immediately before that immediate family member was so detained;

(g) a person who is regarded as receiving free in-patient treatment within the meaning of the Social Security (Hospital In-Patients) Regulations 1975, or the Social Security (Hospital In-Patients) Regulations (Northern Ireland) 1975, and either that immediate family member or his partner is a person to whom regulation 7(4) applied immediately before that immediate family member was first regarded as receiving such treatment; or

(h) a person ordinarily resident outside the United Kingdom.

(3) Paragraphs (4) to (8) apply for the purposes of regulation 7(8)(d) and (e).

(4) The deceased shall be treated as having had no partner where the deceased had a partner at the date of death and—

(a) no claim for funeral expenses is made by the partner in respect of the death of the deceased; and

(b) that partner dies before the date upon which the deceased's funeral takes place.

(5) Whether it is reasonable for the responsible person to accept responsibility for meeting the expenses of a funeral shall be determined by the nature and extent of his contact with the deceased.

(6) Paragraph (7) applies (subject to paragraph (8)) in a case where the deceased had one or more close relatives.

(7) If, on comparing the nature and extent of any close relative's contact with the deceased and the nature and extent of the responsible person's contact with the deceased, any such close relative was—

(a) in closer contact with the deceased than the responsible person,

(b) in equally close contact with the deceased and neither that close relative nor his partner, if he has one, is a person to whom regulation 7(4) applies,

the claimant shall not be entitled to a funeral payment.

(8) However paragraph (7) shall not apply where the close relative who was in—

(a) closer contact with the deceased than the responsible person, or (as the case may be)

(b) equally close contact with the deceased,

is at the date of death of a description specified in any of sub-paragraphs (a) to (h) of paragraph (2).

(9) In a case where the responsible person is the partner of the person who was a close relative, immediate family member or (as the case may be) close friend of the deceased, references in the preceding provisions of this regulation, and in regulation 7(8)(d) and (e), to the responsible person are to be construed as references to the responsible person's partner.

AMENDMENTS

1. Social Security (Miscellaneous Amendments) Regulations 2006 (SI 2006/588) reg.6 (April 10, 2006).

2. Social Fund (Maternity and Funeral Expenses) Amendment Regulations 2013 (SI 2013/247) reg.2(6) (April 1, 2013).

GENERAL NOTE

5.68 Apart from making supplementary provision that has already been noted in the commentary to reg.7, reg.8 contains two important exclusory rules.

The first, in para.(1), disentitles a claimant who was not the deceased's partner if there are any immediate family members of the deceased (other than those excluded under para.(2)) who, or whose partners, have not been awarded a qualifying benefit, unless they were estranged from the deceased.

The second, in paras (6)–(8), disentitles a claimant who was not the deceased's partner if any close relative (other than one excluded under para.(2)) either had closer contact with the deceased or had equal contact and was not (or his or her partner was not) in receipt of qualifying benefit. This is a separate test from that in para.(1) so that estrangement from the deceased is not directly relevant in a claim where there are no immediate family members (*CIS/3534/2007* and *MS v SSWP* [2009] UKUT (AAC) 201).

5.69 To avoid confusion between the two rules, it is necessary to pay close regard to the distinction between "immediate family members" and "close relatives". In everyday language a brother or sister, for example, might be regarded as an immediate family member. As defined in reg.3(1), however, the *only* "immediate family members" are parents, sons and daughters. As people in those categories are also "close relatives", *both* exclusory rules apply to them.

Other relatives, however, (i.e. brothers, sisters, sons-in-law, daughters-in-law, parents-in-law, brothers-in-law, sisters-in-law, step-parents, step-children and step-children-in-law) are "close relatives only" and not "immediate family members". For the reasons given below, the first exclusory rule does not usually apply to them. Except where they have claimed in circumstances where there is an immediate family member (i.e. where the immediate family member has not claimed because it is not reasonable for him or her to take responsibility got the funeral expenses), they will be subject to the second exclusory rule only.

Immediate family members not in receipt of a qualifying benefit

5.70 The first exclusory rule will normally only apply to claims by an "immediate family member". This is because, where there is an "immediate family member", a claim by a "close relative" or "close friend" is only possible in circumstances where it is not reasonable for the immediate family member to take responsibility for the funeral expenses (see reg.7(8)(e) and, e.g. *CIS/788/2003*).

The meaning of the provision corresponding to para.(1) in the 1987 Regulations was considered in *CIS/2288/1998*. Read as a whole, the paragraph means that the claimant is not entitled to a funeral payment if there is at least one (other) immediate family member who not estranged from the deceased and neither that family member nor his or her partner was in receipt of a qualifying benefit.

A further point arose in *CIS/1218/1998*. The claimant had applied for a funeral payment in respect of his late mother. His sister was not in receipt of a qualifying benefit. The tribunal decided that what is now para.(1)(b) referred to *both* the claimant and his sister and since he was in receipt of a qualifying benefit the disentitlement imposed by the paragraph did not apply. The AO appealed, contending that if the tribunal's interpretation was correct, no claim would ever be caught by the provision since it was a requirement under what is now reg.7(3) and (4) that the responsible person be in receipt of a qualifying benefit. In addition, there would be no need to exempt those immediate family members now listed in para.(2) from the operation of the provision. The Commissioner agreed; in his view the immediate family members referred to in sub-paras (a) and (b) did not include the responsible person.

"Estrangement" has "connotations of emotional disharmony" (*R(SB) 2/87*) and may exist even though financial support is being provided. In *C1/01–02(SF)*, the Commissioner stated that "[m]ere disagreement is not sufficient to constitute estrangement, there must be something akin to treating as a stranger for a sufficient period of time". On the facts of that case estrangement had taken place between the claimant's grandparents and his mother (who had a drink problem) "in that there was a deliberate decision to sever relationships due to the strong disapproval and anger which the grandparents felt about the deceased's drinking and the strong desire which they felt that this lifestyle should change and had to change before any relationships could be resumed." In *CIS/4498/2001* the claimant's deceased mother had suffered from senile dementia as a result of which she could not communicate with anyone or recognise family members and his sister—the other "immediate family member"—had lived in Australia for 10 years but had returned to Britain on at least three occasions because of her mother's ill-health. Quoting his earlier decision in *CIS/5321/1998*, Commissioner Henty stated: 5.71

> "The appropriate OED definition of 'estranged', accepted in *CIS/5119/97* is, 'to alienate in feeling or affection'. I might put a gloss on that such as 'not to be on speaking terms'. The evidence before the tribunal points, I think, not at so much as an alienation of feeling or affection—the emphasis being on 'alienation', a concept which involves some form of positive consideration—but a drifting apart which to my mind connotes something short of alienation. Of course a long period of 'drifting apart' may lead to the inference that there had been an alienation, but such is not, in my view, the case here'. Those considerations are equally applicable here. Had such a break down in relation occurred before the on set of the mother's incapacity, then estrangement there would have been. But the incapacity by itself is not estrangement, and neither is the fact that the sister had been in Australia for some 10 years."

In *CIS 1228/2004*, Commissioner Fellner held "that registering a death is [not] enough *in itself* to show that the person who does so *cannot* have been estranged from the deceased" (original emphasis).

In *CIS/4096/2005*, Commissioner Jupp reviewed the authorities on estrangement (in the context of reg.13(1)(d) of the Income Support Regulations) and concluded that there was no requirement of mutuality in feeling for estrangement to exist, as had been suggested by the Commissioner in *CIS/4498/2001*. Disharmony can arise from one person's attitude to another even though the other party may not wish the situation to be as it is. The position has to be judged from the point of view of (in the context of funeral payments) the surviving immediate family member who is being considered and not from the point of view of the deceased.

The concept of "estrangement" is also relevant to the capital disregard in para. (4) of Sch.10 to the Income Support Regulations, Sch.8 to the JSA Regulations and Sch.5 to the State Pension Credit Regulations. However, caution needs to be exercised when applying the caselaw on that provision to funeral payments. In *CPC/683/2007*, the Commissioner noted that "the language used in [that] legislation is attempting to identify those cases in which the relationship between the parties is such that it is appropriate for their finances to be treated separately for the purposes of benefit entitlement". That is not the same as the context in which estrangement needs to be considered on a claim for a funeral payment. 5.72

What happens if—as may well be the case even in relatively close families—the claimant simply does not know whether or not any of the other immediate family members or close relatives is in receipt of a qualifying benefit: where does the burden of proof lie? This was one of the issues considered by the House of Lords in *Kerr v Department for Social Development* [2004] UKHL 23 (*R 1/04 (SF)*). In that case, which concerned the Northern Ireland equivalent of the current reg.8, the claimant was the eldest of three brothers and a sister who, although living in the Belfast area, had not been in touch with each other for over 20 years. One of the brothers died and the claimant was traced by the police and agreed to accept financial responsibility for the funeral. He claimed a funeral payment which was refused without any enquiry by the Department into whether the surviving brother and sister had been awarded a qualifying benefit, an question which, of course, the Department was better placed to answer than the claimant. The issue was therefore whether Mr Kerr had to prove a negative—that neither his sister or brother were in receipt of a qualifying benefit—or whether the Department had to show that they were. Giving the judgment of the House, Baroness Hale said, in a passage which has profound implications for social security administration generally:

> "61. Ever since the decision of the Divisional Court in *R. v Medical Appeal Tribunal (North Midland Region), Ex p Hubble* [1958] 2 QB 228, it has been accepted that the process of benefits adjudication is inquisitorial rather than adversarial. Diplock J. as he then was said this of an industrial injury benefit claim at p.240:
>
> > 'A claim by an insured person to benefit under the Act is not truly analogous to a lis inter partes. A claim to benefit is a claim to receive money out of the insurance funds . . . Any such claim requires investigation to determine whether any, and if so, what amount of benefit is payable out of the fund. In such an investigation, the minister or the insurance officer is not a party adverse to the claimant. If analogy be sought in the other branches of the law, it is to be found in an inquest rather than in an action.'
>
> 62. What emerges from all this is a co-operative process of investigation in which both the claimant and the department play their part. The department is the one which knows what questions it needs to ask and what information it needs to have in order to determine whether the conditions of entitlement have been met. The claimant is the one who generally speaking can and must supply that information. But where the information is available to the department rather than the claimant, then the department must take the necessary steps to enable it to be traced.
>
> 63. If that sensible approach is taken, it will rarely be necessary to resort to concepts taken from adversarial litigation such as the burden of proof. The first question will be whether each partner in the process has played their part. If there is still ignorance about a relevant matter then generally speaking it should be determined against the one who has not done all they reasonably could to discover it. As Mr Commissioner Henty put it in decision *CIS/5321/1998*, 'a claimant must to the best of his or her ability give such information to the AO as he reasonably can, in default of which a contrary inference can always be drawn.' The same should apply to information which the department can reasonably be expected to discover for itself."

In this case, the claim was allowed because the Department had failed to ask Mr Kerr the necessary questions and could not "use its own failure to ask questions which would have led it to the right answer to defeat the claim" (at para.65). Baroness Hale also addressed the position which would have existed if both the claimant and the Department had done everything which was legally required of them but it had still not proved possible to ascertain the true position? In that case:

> "66. This will not always be sufficient to decide who should bear the consequences of the collective ignorance of a matter which is material to the claim. It may be that everything which could have been done has been done but there are still things unknown. The conditions of entitlement must be met before the claim can be paid. . . It may therefore become relevant to ask whether a particular matter relates to the conditions of entitlement or to an exception to those conditions. In

this case, the department argues that all the elements, including those in regulation 6(6) [equivalent to reg.8(7) of the current GB regulations], are conditions of entitlement, so that the claimant must bear the consequences of ignorance. The claimant argues that the conditions of entitlement are laid down in regulation 6(1), supplemented where relevant by paragraphs (2) and (5) [regs 7 and 8((4) and (5) of the current GB Regulations]. Paragraphs (3) and (4), which go together, and paragraph (6) [reg.8(1),(2) and (7) of the current GB regulations] are exceptions.

67. The structure and wording of the regulation support the claimant's case. Conditions (a), (b), (c) and (d) in regulation 6(1) are clearly established. The claimant qualifies as a 'close relative' under condition (e)(iv)(aa) but this also requires that it be reasonable for him to accept responsibility. Under regulation 6(5) the question 'whether it is reasonable for a person to accept responsibility for meeting the expenses of the funeral shall be determined by the nature and extent of that person's contact with the deceased'. The tribunal decided that it was reasonable for the claimant, as the eldest son who had grown up with his brother, to accept that responsibility, despite the fact that they had not been in contact with one another for many years. That conclusion is not challenged in this appeal, in my view rightly. For the reasons given earlier, there is a strong public interest in encouraging families to take responsibility for the speedy and seemly burial of their deceased relatives.

68. Regulation 6(3) provides that the person who has made himself responsible 'shall not be entitled' if there is a more appropriate immediate family member. That this is a disentitling provision is made clear by regulation 6(4), which states that 'Paragraph (3) shall not apply to *disentitle* the responsible person' (my emphasis) in the circumstances there set out. In the same way, paragraph 6(6) provides that if there is a close relative who is either in closer contact or in equally close contact and not receiving benefits or having capital, the responsible person 'shall not be entitled' to the payment. These paragraphs are therefore worded in terms of exceptions rather than qualifying conditions. If anything, this interpretation is supported by the legislative history given earlier, as the existence of a more suitable relative was added as an exception or qualification to the basic rule.

69. This, therefore, is a case in which the department should bear the burden of the collective ignorance and pay the claim."

Paragraph (2) sets out the circumstances in which the claimant may remain entitled to a funeral payment even if s/he has an immediate family member who is not in receipt of a qualifying benefit. These are largely self-explanatory and include where the immediate family member is under 18, a qualifying young person for child benefit purposes, in certain types of full-time education, in receipt of asylum support, ordinarily resident outside the UK or—in some circumstances—in hospital or in prison. 5.73

Closer contact

Under paras (6)–(8), if the responsible person is an immediate family member, another close relative or a close friend (see para.(3)), and the deceased had one or more close relatives (para.(6)), the nature and extent of their contact with the deceased will be compared (para.(7)). 5.74

This is a separate test from deciding whether it is reasonable for the person to have accepted responsibility for the funeral costs (see para.(5)), as confirmed in *R(IS) 3/98*. If any close relative had closer contact, the claimant will not be entitled to a funeral payment (para.(7)(a)). If the contact was equally close, a payment will also be refused if the close relative (or their partner) is not getting a qualifying benefit (see para.(7)(b)). But this rule does not apply if at the date of death the close relative concerned came within any of the categories listed in para.(2) (see above).

Close contact will be a question of fact in each case. It should be noted that the test involves having regard to the nature as well as the extent of the contact. Thus this will bring in issues of quality as well as quantity. *CIS/8485/1995* states that, when considering the question of contact with the deceased, tribunals should adopt a broad brush, commonsense approach. The amount of time spent with the deceased is only one factor, and the nature of the contact should be judged not just by visits, letters, etc. but also by the quality of the contact. So if the claimant's half-brother's unpredictable nature had affected his relationship with his late mother, that should have been taken into account in assessing the nature of his contact with her. The guidance given to decision-makers by the Decision Makers Guide is that they "should consider the overall nature and extent of the contact with the deceased given the circumstances of the individual. For example, domestic or work responsibilities may prevent a close relative from keeping in regular contact with the deceased but the nature of the contact may be equally as close as a close friend who visited every day." The guidance suggests that factors to be considered include the nature of the relationship, frequency of contact, type of contact, domestic or caring assistance given to the deceased, social outings and holidays, domestic or work responsibilities and estrangements or arguments with the deceased (paras 39181–39182).

5.75 As the Deputy Commissioner pointed out in *CIS/3534/2007*, whether or not the close relative was estranged from the deceased is not legally relevant to the test in para.(7). However, the existence of estrangement may be relevant as a matter of fact. It is suggested that a close relative who was not estranged from the deceased will normally have been in closer contact with the deceased than a close relative who was so estranged.

The question of how para.(7)(b) applies in the situation where none of the close relatives was in contact with the deceased at all—i.e. whether the phrase "in equally close contact" includes circumstances in which there was an equal lack of contact—was considered, obiter, by three members of the House of Lords in the *Kerr* case (above). Lord Scott was of the view that it did not. To read "equally close contact" as meaning "equal contact" was to rewrite the statutory language and to ignore the significance of the words "close" and "in"—one cannot be "in" a "close" lack of contact. Where there was no contact at all, then none of the sub-paras of what is now para.(7) was applicable. Further, the question was not whether any of the close relatives "had had close contact with the deceased in the past" but "whether they were 'in equally close contact' with him at the time of his death" (paras 26–35). By contrast Lord Hope held (at para.9) that the test in what is now para.(7)(b) was not necessarily limited to the state of affairs which existed at the time of the deceased's death:

> "Regulation [8(7)] assumes that where there is 'contact' the question of 'closeness' is put in issue, however slight or remote in time that may be. I do not find anything in the regulation to indicate that the contact must have been current at, or immediately before, the date of the deceased's death. The period of time during which a comparison of the nature and extent of the contact is to be undertaken is not specified. The conclusion which I would draw from this is that there is no restriction as to the time of this contact. In my opinion the first question which the adjudicator must ask himself is whether the relevant person had any 'contact' with the deceased at all at any time. If he did, the question of the relative 'closeness' of that contact in comparison with the contact of the responsible person can and must be asked and answered."

Baroness Hale (at para.70), whilst agreeing with Lord Scott that it was "harder to see how 'was . . . in equally close contact' can cover contact which ended 20 years earlier", preferred not to express any view on the issue. It is disappointing that when the regulations were re-drafted in 2005, the opportunity was not taken to clarify the point one way or another.

Amount of funeral payment

9.—(1) A funeral payment shall be an amount sufficient to meet any relevant expenditure less any amount which falls to be deducted under regulation 10. **5.76**

(2) In paragraph (1), "relevant expenditure" means any costs to which paragraph (3) applies which fall to be met or have been met by the responsible person (or a person acting on behalf of the responsible person), inclusive of any available discount on those costs allowed by the funeral director or by any other person who arranges the funeral.

(3) This paragraph applies to the following costs—

(a) where the deceased is buried—

(i) the necessary costs of purchasing a new burial plot for the deceased, together with an exclusive right of burial in that plot;

(ii) the fees levied in respect of a burial by the authority or person responsible for the provision and maintenance of cemeteries for the area where the burial takes place, or the fees levied by a private grave-digger, in so far as it is necessary to incur those fees;

(b) where the deceased is cremated—

(i) the fees levied in respect of a cremation by the authority or person responsible for the provision and maintenance of crematoria for the area where the cremation takes place in so far as it is necessary to incur those fees;

(ii) the cost of any medical references;

(iii) the cost of any necessary registered medical practitioner's certificates;

(iv) the fee payable for the removal of any device as defined for the purposes of the Active Implantable Medical Devices Regulations 1992 save that, where that removal is carried out by a person who is not a registered medical practitioner, no more than £20 shall be met in respect of that fee;

(c) the cost of obtaining any documentation, production of which is necessary in order to release any assets of the deceased which may be deducted from a funeral payment pursuant to regulation 10;

(d) where the deceased died at home or away from home and it is necessary to transport the deceased within the United Kingdom in excess of 80 kilometres (approximately 50 miles) to the funeral director's premises or to the place of rest, the reasonable cost of transport in excess of 80 kilometres;

(e) where transport is provided by a vehicle for the coffin and bearers and by one additional vehicle, from the funeral director's premises or the place of rest to the funeral and—

(i) the distance travelled, in the case of a funeral which consists of a burial where no costs have been incurred under sub-paragraph (a)(i) above, exceeds 80 kilometres; or

(ii) the distance travelled, in the case of any other funeral, necessarily exceeds 80 kilometres,

the reasonable cost of the transport provided, other than the cost in respect of the first 80 kilometres of the distance travelled;

(f) the necessary cost of one return journey for the responsible person, either for the purpose of making arrangements for, or for attendance at, the funeral; and

(g) any other funeral expenses which shall not exceed £700 in any case.

(4) Paragraphs (2) and (3) have effect subject to the following provisions.

(5) Paragraph (3)(a) does not apply to costs in connection with burial of the deceased's ashes (where he was cremated).

(6) All references to 80 kilometres shall be construed as applying to—

(a) in a case to which paragraph (3)(d) applies, the combined distance from the funeral director's premises or the deceased's place of rest to the place of death and of the return journey;

(b) in a case to which paragraph (3)(e) applies, the combined distance from the funeral director's premises or the deceased's place of rest to the funeral and of the return journey.

(7) The cost of items and services referred to in paragraph (3)(a), (b), (d) and (e) shall not include any element in the cost of those items and services which relates to a requirement of the deceased's religious faith.

(8) Paragraph (3)(e)(i) includes costs only to the extent that, together with the costs referred to under paragraph (3)(a)(ii), they do not exceed the costs which would have been incurred under—

(a) paragraph (3)(a)(i) and (ii), and

(b) where appropriate, paragraph (3)(e)(ii),

if it had been necessary to purchase for the deceased a new burial plot with an exclusive right of burial.

(9) Paragraph (3)(f) includes costs only to the extent that they do not exceed the costs which would have been incurred in respect of a return journey from the home of the responsible person to the location where the necessary costs of a burial or, as the case may be, cremation referred to in paragraph (3)(a) or (b) would have been incurred.

(10) Where items and services have been provided on the death of the deceased under a pre-paid funeral plan or under any analogous arrangement—

(a) no funeral payment shall be made in respect of items or services referred to in paragraph (3) which have been provided under such a plan or arrangement; and

(b) paragraph (3)(g) shall have effect in relation to that particular claim as if for the sum "£700", there were substituted the sum "£120".

GENERAL NOTE

5.77 Regulation 9 defines "relevant expenditure", i.e. the expenses that are eligible to be met by a funeral payment. Under para.(1) the amount of the funeral payment is the total relevant expenditure less any deduction that falls to be made under reg.10.

A payment can be made for the expenses that are listed in para.(3)(a)–(f) (except for those that have been met by a pre-paid funeral plan or similar arrangement (para.(10)(a)), together with up to £700 for other funeral expenses, or £120 if some of the funeral costs have been met under a pre-paid funeral plan or similar arrangement, (paras (3)(g) and (10)(b)). For funeral plans, see also reg.10(e) and the commentary on that provision.

It will be noted that some of sub-paras (a)–(f) in para.(3) contain an express limitation to "reasonable" costs and some do not (in others the word "necessary" is used). On a previous form of this provision *R(IS) 14/92* considered that the word "reasonable" should be read into the listed categories even where it was not expressed. But in *CIS/6818/1995* the Commissioner concluded that what was said about reasonableness in *R(IS) 14/92* was not an essential part of the decision. He expressed the view (which was also not necessary to his decision) that each sub-paragraph in what is now reg.8(3) contained its own complete test and that there was no room for any further conditions to be implied. In view of the quite specific nature of the items or services covered by para.(3)(a)–(f) it is suggested that the approach of *CIS/6818/1995* is to be preferred.

Any element in the burial or transport costs that relates to a requirement of the deceased's religious faith will not be met (para.(7))—see *CSIS/42/1996*, which held that a vigil is a requirement of the Roman Catholic faith.

Burial and cremation—paras 3(a) and (b)

Paragraph (3)(a)(i) allows "the necessary costs of purchasing a new burial plot for the deceased". The meaning of the word "necessary" in a predecessor of this paragraph was considered in *R(IS) 18/98*. The Commissioner decided that it implied that any expense over that which was properly required was to be excluded. However, its effect was not to require the purchase of the cheapest possible plot without regard to any other consideration. Account should be taken of the proximity to the deceased's residence while he was alive and of the deceased's religion, so that, for example a person of the Greek Orthodox faith was entitled to be buried in an area set aside for people of that faith. **5.78**

A funeral payment may be awarded for the cost of either a cremation or a burial but not both. Costs in connection with the burial of cremated ashes are not eligible (para.(5)).

See also in this context *CIS/1335/2004* discussed in the commentary to reg.7(10) (above).

Transport costs—paras (3)(d)–(f)

Paragraphs (3)(d) and (e) allow certain transport costs for distances (i.e. the combined distance of the outward and return journey (para.(3)), in excess of 80km (about 50 miles) to be met. For the calculation of the 80km, see para.(6). **5.79**

R(IS) 11/91 decided that the deceased's "home" in para.(3)(d) was the accommodation where he normally lived prior to his death, as opposed to his "home town".

Where the costs of transport and burial in an existing plot (i.e. usually away from where the deceased lived) exceed the purchase and burial costs of a new plot, plus any necessary transport costs (i.e. the costs of burying locally), para.(3)(e)(i) provides that such costs will be met up to the level of the local burial costs (para.(8))

Paragraph (3)(f) covers the necessary costs of one return journey for the responsible person for arranging the funeral or attending it. The journey is not restricted to a journey within the UK but see para.(9) which limits the costs that will be met to those of a return journey from the responsible person's home to the place where the "necessary" funeral costs would have been incurred (although the drafting is not entirely clear, it is understood that the intention is to restrict payment of travel costs to those that would have been incurred if the funeral had taken place in the UK). *CIS 16957/1996* decides that although sub-para.(f) refers to a "return journey" it did also apply where the claimant only undertook a single journey (her husband had died away from home and she had travelled home to attend the funeral). Others who are relatives of the deceased may be eligible for a community care grant for the cost of travel to and from a funeral in the UK (see Social Fund direction 4(b)(ii)). The applicant must be a member of a family containing a claimant in receipt of income support or income-based JSA.

Other expenses

The expenses to be covered by para.(3)(g) are not specified but will include items such as a funeral director's fees (including the cost of a coffin which cannot be met under either para.(3)(a) or (b)—see *CIS/2651/2003* and *CIS 2607/2003*), church fees or flowers. But there is no definition of funeral expenses and so any expense that is a funeral expense should be allowed. Thus, in *CIS/1345/2004*, **5.80**

Commissioner Williams held that "suitable funeral attire" might amount to a funeral expense within sub-para.(g). The test was not, as had been suggested by the Secretary of State, whether the expense was "wholly exclusively and necessarily required for the funeral". There was no basis in law for restricting the scope of the paragraph beyond the words actually used in the sub-para. The only tests for applying sub-para.(g) were:

"(i) Were the expenses in fact funeral expenses that took into account any relvant discounts?
(ii) If so, were the expenses met by the claimant or partner (or will they be)?
(iii) If so, were they of a nature covered by any of the provisions in regulation [9(3)(a) to (f)]?
(iv) If not, do they exceed the set sum?

If they do not, they are allowable."

It should be noted, however, that in *CIS/1924/2004*, Commissioner Fellner held that, although flowers were capable of amounting to a funeral expense within the sub-para., obituary notices and the cost of a memorial stone and flower container were not. There is a clear tension between these two decisions: if the *CIS/1345/2004* test had been applied to the items disallowed in *CIS/1924/2004*, it seems probable that some, at least, would have been allowed.

Under para.(3)(g) there is no limit on the funeral expenses that are to be met, other than the £700 (or £120) ceiling. There is therefore nothing to prevent para. (3)(g) being used to pay for the cost of items or services in para.(3)(a)–(f) that have not been fully met or to cover the cost of a religious requirement.

Payment of funeral expenses

5.81 A funeral payment will be made even if the costs have already been met by the claimant, his partner, or a person acting on their behalf. If the funeral costs have not been paid any funeral payment is to be made direct to the creditor—see reg.35(2) of the Claims and Payments Regulations.

Deductions from an award of a funeral payment

5.82 **10.**—(1) There shall be deducted from the amount of any award of funeral payment which would otherwise be payable—

(a) [4 subject to paragraph (1A)] the amount of any assets of the deceased which are available to the responsible person (on application or otherwise) or any other member of his family without probate or letters of administration, or (in Scotland) confirmation, having been granted;

(b) the amount of any lump sum due to the responsible person or any other member of his family on the death of the deceased by virtue of any insurance policy, occupational pension scheme or burial club, or any analogous arrangement;

(c) the amount of any contribution towards funeral expenses which has been received by the responsible person or any other member of his family from a charity or a relative of his or of the deceased;

(d) the amount of any funeral grant, made out of public funds, in respect of the death of a person who was entitled to a war disablement pension;

(e) in relation to a pre-paid funeral plan or any analogous arrangement—

(i) where the plan or arrangement had not been paid for in full prior to the death of the deceased, the amount of any sum payable under that plan or arrangement in order to meet the deceased's funeral expenses;

(ii) where the plan or arrangement had been paid for in full prior to the death of the deceased, the amount of any allowance paid under that plan or arrangement in respect of funeral expenses.

[4 (1A) For the purposes of regulation 10(1)(a), arrears of the following benefits payable to the deceased as at the date of death are excluded from the assets of the deceased—

(a) attendance allowance under Part 3 of the Act;
(b) bereavement allowance under Part 2 of the Act;
(c) carer's allowance under Part 3 of the Act;
(d) child benefit under Part 9 of the Act;
(e) child tax credit under section 8 of the Tax Credits Act 2002(8);
(f) council tax benefit under Part 7 of the Act;
(g) disability living allowance under Part 3 of the Act;
(h) employment and support allowance under—
 (i) Part 1 of the 2007 Act as amended by Schedule 3, and Part 1 of Schedule 14, to the 2012 Act (to remove references to an income-related allowance); or
 (ii) Part 1 of the 2007 Act as it has effect apart from the amendments made by Schedule 3, and Part 1 of Schedule 14, to the 2012 Act;
(i) exceptionally severe disablement allowance under Part 5 of the Act;
(j) guardian's allowance under Part 3 of the Act;
(k) housing benefit under Part 7 of the Act;
(l) incapacity benefit under Part 2 of the Act;
(m) income support under Part 7 of the Act;
(n) industrial death benefit under Part 5 of the Act;
(o) industrial injuries disablement benefit under Part 5 of the Act;
(p) jobseeker's allowance under—
 (i) the 1995 Act as amended by Part 1 of Schedule 14 to the 2012 Act (to remove references to an income-based allowance); or
 (ii) the 1995 Act as it has effect apart from the amendments made by Part 1 of Schedule 14 to the 2012 Act;
(q) maternity allowance under Part 2 of the Act;
(r) personal independence payment under Part 4 of the 2012 Act;
(s) reduced earnings allowance under Part 5 of the Act;
(t) severe disablement allowance under Part 3 of the Act;
(u) state pension credit under section 1 of the State Pension Credit Act 2002;
(v) state retirement pension under Parts 2 or 3 of the Act;
[6 (va) a state pension under Part 1 of the Pensions Act 2014;]
(w) universal credit under Part 1 of the 2012 Act;
(x) war disablement pension under an instrument specified in section 639(2) of the Income Tax (Earnings and Pensions) Act 2003(10) in respect of the death or disablement of any person;
(y) war widow's pension under an instrument specified in section 639(2) of the Income Tax (Earnings and Pensions) Act 2003 in respect of the death or disablement of any person;
(z) war widower's pension under an instrument specified in section 639(2) of the Income Tax (Earnings and Pensions) Act 2003 in respect of the death or disablement of any person;
(aa) widowed mother's allowance under Part 2 of the Act;
(bb) widowed parent's allowance under Part 2 of the Act;
(cc) widow's pension under Part 2 of the Act;
(dd) winter fuel payment under Part 8 of the Act;

(ee) working tax credit under section 10 of the Tax Credits Act 2002] [5;
(ff) armed forces independence payment under the Armed Forces and Reserve Forces (Compensation Scheme) Order 2011.]

(2) The amount of any payment made under [2 or by]—
(a) the Macfarlane Trust,
(b) the Macfarlane (Special Payments) Trust,
(c) the Macfarlane (Special Payments) (No.2) Trust,
(d) the Fund,
(e) the Eileen Trust,
(f) the Skipton Fund, [1 . . .]
(g) a trust established out of funds provided by the Secretary of State in respect of persons who suffered, or who are suffering, from variant Creutzfeldt-Jakob disease for the benefit of persons eligible for payments in accordance with its provisions, [1 [2 . . .]
(h) the London Bombings Relief Charitable Fund,] [2 [3 ...]
(i) MFET Limited,] [3 or
(j) the Caxton Foundation,]

shall be disregarded from any deduction made under this regulation.

(3) In paragraph (2), "the Macfarlane Trust", "the Macfarlane (Special Payments) Trust", "the Macfarlane (Special Payments) (No.2) Trust", "the Fund", "the Eileen Trust" [2 , MFET Limited] [1, "the Skipton Fund" [3 , "the London Bombings Relief Charitable Fund" and "the Caxton Foundation"]] shall have the same meaning as in regulation 2(1) of the Income Support Regulations.

AMENDMENTS

1. Income-related Benefits (Amendment) (No.2) Regulations 2005 reg.8 (December 12, 2005).
2. Social Security (Miscellaneous Amendments) (No.2) Regulations 2010 (SI 2010/641) reg.7 (April 6, 2010).
3. Social Security (Miscellaneous Amendments) (No.3) Regulations 2011 (SI 2011/2425) reg.18 (October 31, 2011).
4. Social Fund (Maternity and Funeral Expenses) Amendment Regulations 2013 (SI 2013/247) reg.2 (April 1, 2013).
5. Armed Forces and Reserve Forces Compensation Scheme (Consequential Provisions: Subordinate Legislation) Order 2013 (SI 2013/591) art.7 and Sch. para.32 (April 8, 2013).
6. Pensions Act 2014 (Consequential, Supplementary and Incidental Amendments) Order 2015 (SI 2015/1985) art.27 (April 6, 2016).

GENERAL NOTE

5.83 The amounts listed in reg.10 are deducted from the amount calculated under reg.9. Those amounts do not include the value of the deceased's estate but, by virtue of s.78(4) of the Administration Act any funeral payment from the social fund may be recovered from the estate (i.e. not just those assets available to the responsible person without a grant of probate or letters of administration: see para.(1)(a)) as if it were a funeral expense—see further the commentary to s.78 in Vol.III.

Paragraph (1) specifies the amounts that are to be deducted.

5.84 *Sub-paragraph (a)*: Under the Administration of Estates (Small Payments) Act 1965 certain sums can be distributed from the estate to beneficiaries without a grant of probate or letters of administration. The current limit is £5,000. In addition many statutes regulating Post Office and building society accounts, savings certificates, etc. (but not, after privatisation, Trustee Savings Bank accounts) allow payment to be made after the owner's death. There is a similar power for most social security benefits. One problem is that these provisions are generally merely permissive, so that payment cannot be demanded as of right. In *R(IS) 14/91* the Commissioner indicates that in straightforward cases it may be concluded that such an amount is available on application. However, the circumstances (e.g. some dispute between next of kin of equal status) may point to the opposite conclusion. *R(IS) 14/91* also decides that evidence of availability of assets from the date of death up to the date of the decision on the claim is relevant. Thus where the claim was made on the date of death, a sum of £1300 in the deceased's building society account was available, although the claimant did not obtain the money until a week later. Nor was that conclusion defeated by the fact that before the decision the claimant had distributed or spent most of the money.

In *PA v SSWP (SF)* [2010] UKUT 42 (AAC), the deceased left no partner or surviving close relatives. The funeral was arranged by his carer, who claimed a funeral payment as a close friend. That claim was refused, ultimately because he did not provide evidence of the deceased's estate, the Secretary of State drawing the inference that the amount available to the claimant was sufficient to extinguish any entitlement. Allowing the appeal, Judge Mesher pointed out that reg.10(1)(a) "does not contain a rule that the value of the deceased's estate or of any assets within the estate is always to be set against the amount of a funeral payment that would otherwise be awarded". It only applies where those assets are "available" and available "to the claimant or some member of this family". There was some evidence that the claimant had approached the deceased's bank to try to obtain the balance standing to the credit of his account. According to that evidence, Judge Mesher remarked (at para.11):

> "The bank said that if there was money in the account a cheque would be sent to the funeral directors. There was not in fact an indication that money would have been paid over to the claimant, a person apparently not entitled to any share of Mr O's estate and not an executor under a will or an administrator on intestacy. Nor was there a clear indication that such a person would be provided with a copy of the closing bank statement."

As there was no other evidence to suggest that the deceased had (or had in the past had) significant capital, and as the burden of proof on the issue was on the Secretary of State (para.14), Judge Mesher awarded the claimant a funeral payment on the basis that reg.10(1)(a) did not apply.

Funeral expenses are a first charge on the estate (*R(SB) 18/84*). If there are liquid assets in the estate, these may be immediately available for funeral expenses regardless of other debts. In *R(IS) 12/93* arrears of attendance allowance for the deceased were paid to the claimant as next of kin. The Commissioner holds that the arrears were available. Since they exceeded the cost of the funeral, no award was made. 5.85

However, from April 1, 2013, arrears of the benefits listed in para.(1A) (including attendance allowance) do not form part of the deceased's assets for these purposes and therefore no deduction can be made in respect of them under para.(1)(a).

In *TG v SSWP (SF)* [2015] UKUT 0571 (AAC), the claimant made an internet transfer of £2,500 from his late mother's bank account to his own shortly before his mother died on a Sunday afternoon. However, as Sunday was not a business day, the deceased's bank statements did not show the money leaving her account until the following day. Whether or not the claimant was entitled to a funeral payment depended upon whether the sum of £2,500 was an asset of the deceased at the time of her death.

Judge Rowley accepted the Secretary of State's submission in support of the appeal that ". . . where a transfer is ordered prior to death, notwithstanding that the transaction does not clear until after the death, the funds which are the subject of the transfer are, generally speaking, no longer 'assets of the deceased' available to the responsible person". That proposition was subject to any contrary provision in the contractual arrangements between the deceased and her bank. However, there was no such provision in *TG*. Rather, the evidence from the bank was that when one of its customers transferred funds using internet banking the funds would be applied to the payee's account within minutes even if the transfer were made on a non-business day, and even though, in those circumstances, the payment would only show on the customer's statement as being paid on the next following business day.

The claimant said that his mother had owed him the money and that he had made the transfer on her instructions. However, the First-tier Tribunal did not accept that the transfer represented a genuine reimbursement of money owed to the claimant. Rather, it viewed the transaction as a means of reducing the mother's estate prior to her death. Judge Rowley held that the motivation behind the transfer was irrelevant. The question to be determined was whether there were assets of the deceased that were available to the responsible person. If the transfer was validly made, then the transferred assets did not fall within reg.10(1)(a).

5.86 *Sub-paragraph (b):* For this sub-paragraph to apply, the amount must be due to the claimant or a member of his family (defined in reg.3(1)). Due must mean legally due. Sometimes such a member will have a clear legal entitlement under an insurance policy or a pension scheme. Sometimes trustees may have a discretion as to who should be paid a lump sum. In these circumstances no amount can be legally due until the trustees have exercised that discretion.

In *PA v SSWP* [2010] UKUT 157 (AAC), the deceased's daughter had taken out insurance policies on her mother's life. In England and Wales children do not have an insurable interest in the lives of their parents and it was therefore arguable that the proceeds of those policies were not "due" within the meaning of subpara. (b). However, Judge Levenson held that the insurance company had accepted the premiums and a court (or the regulatory institutions of the insurance industry) would have enforced payment. Even if what the daughter had entered into could not technically be an "insurance policy" it was an "analogous arrangement" within the subparagraph.

5.87 *Sub-paragraph (c):* This sub-paragraph provides for the deduction of any contribution towards funeral expenses which has been actually been received by the claimant or a family member from a charity or a relative. Payments from anyone else, or for other purposes, do not count. So, if a contribution is for expenses which are not funeral expenses (e.g. clothing to wear to the funeral), it is not included. *CIS/450/1995* decides that a genuine loan from a relative that is legally recoverable is not a "contribution" and is not caught by sub-para.(c).

As the total amount of the funeral payment will almost certainly be less than the actual cost of the funeral, the most likely reason for charities or family members to make such a contribution is to top-up the funeral payment. But, unless care is exercised, the probable effect will be to reduce that payment. Those wishing to make such contributions should wait until after the funeral payment has been awarded and paid. This is because it cannot then be said that the contribution "has been received": sub-para.(c) does not specify the date by which the contribution must "[have] been received" but logically it cannot be later than the date of the decision.

In *CSIS/534/2007*, the Commissioner rejects the suggestion, made in earlier editions, that if the contribution is made directly to the funeral director then it is arguable that it has not been "received by" the claimant. The Commissioner states (at para.11):

> "11. . . . The evidence is not clear whether it was paid directly by one or more of the claimant's relatives to the funeral director or to the claimant herself. I do not consider that this is a matter which is material for the application of regulation 10(1)(c). The claimant was the debtor for the purposes of the funeral account.

Whether a payment was made directly to the funeral directors or to her for transmission to the funeral directors, in my view, is neither here nor there in respect that it can properly, in my view, be said to have been received by the claimant as she was the debtor."

As there was no evidence of direct payment to the funeral director in *CSIS/534/2007*, at para.11 does not form part of the *ratio* of that decision. It is therefore only persuasive authority for tribunals. Despite that authority, the view expressed in previous editions is maintained. It is undoubtedly the case that a claimant who is liable to pay for a funeral account benefits from a contribution made directly to the funeral director by another person but that does not mean that s/he "receives" that contribution: as a matter of the ordinary use of the English language, s/he does not. This is not the only context in which social security law draws a distinction between payments made to a claimant and payments made to third parties for his or her benefit. For example, the notional income rules in reg.42(4) of the Income Support Regulations only make sense if that distinction is made. It would be anomalous for the amount of a funeral payment to depend upon whether friends or relatives pay their contributions to the claimant or to the funeral director. However, given the comments of the Commissioner in para.3 of *R(IS) 3/02* and the fact that the tribunal in *CSIS/534/2007* described the result of its own decision as "unfortunate", it is suggested that the anomaly is not so great as to require sub-para.(c) to be given a broader meaning than the wording strictly requires.

Sub-paragraph (d): This paragraph is straightforward. **5.88**

Sub-paragraph (e): Any amount payable under a pre-paid funeral plan or similar arrangement will be deducted. In order to avoid a double deduction, it is necessary to interpret this deduction as applying when a funeral plan pays a cash benefit to the responsible person or other relative of the deceased and reg.9(10) as applying where payment under the plan has been made direct to the funeral director. This interpretation is supported by the use of the words "[w]here items and services have been provided . . . under a pre-paid funeral plan . . ." in reg.9(10).

Paragraph (1A): Arrears of these benefits that had not been paid to the deceased at the date of her/his death do not count as "assets of the deceased" for the purposes of the rule in para.(1)(a).

Paragraphs (2) and (3): No deduction is to be made for payments received from these trusts. **5.89**

The Social Fund Maternity Grant Amendment Regulations 2012

(SI 2012/1814)

Made by the Secretary of State for Work and Pensions under ss.138(1)(a) and (4) and 175(1), (3) and (4) of the Social Security Contributions and Benefits Act 1992, the Social Security Advisory Committee having agreed that proposals in respect of these regulations should not be referred to it.

General Note

See the commentary to reg.5A of the Social Fund Maternity and Funeral Expenses (General) Regulations 2005 (above). **5.90**

Citation, commencement and interpretation

5.91 **1.**—(1) These Regulations may be cited as the Social Fund Maternity Grant Amendment Regulations 2012.

(2) They come into force on 13th August 2012.

(3) In these Regulations, "the principal Regulations" means the Social Fund Maternity and Funeral Expenses (General) Regulations 2005 and expressions defined in those Regulations have the same meaning in these Regulations.

Amendment of the principal Regulations

5.92 **2.**—*[For the amendments made by reg.2, see reg.5A of the Social Fund Maternity and Funeral Expenses (General) Regulations 2005]*

Transitional provisions

5.93 **3.**—(1) The substitution made by regulation 2 does not apply in a case where any of paragraphs (2) to (7) apply.

(2) This paragraph applies in a case where—

(a) the claimant falls within regulation 5(3)(a) of the principal Regulations;

(b) the claim is made before C's birth;

(c) the claim is made before 13th August 2012; and

(d) the expected date of confinement is before 29th October 2012.

(3) This paragraph applies in a case where—

(a) the claimant falls within regulation 5(3)(a) or (b) of the principal Regulations;

(b) the claim is made after C's birth; and

(c) C is born before 29th October 2012.

(4) This paragraph applies in a case where—

(a) the claimant falls within regulation 5(3)(c) of the principal Regulations; and

(b) the qualifying order is made before 29th October 2012.

(5) This paragraph applies in a case where—

(a) the claimant falls within regulation 5(3)(d) of the principal Regulations; and

(b) the appointment as guardian takes effect before 29th October 2012.

(6) This paragraph applies in a case where—

(a) the claimant falls within regulation 5(3)(e) of the principal Regulations; and

(b) C is placed for adoption with the claimant or the claimant's partner before 29th October 2012.

(7) This paragraph applies in a case where—

(a) the claimant falls within regulation 5(3)(f) of the principal Regulations; and

(b) the adoption referred to in that provision takes effect before 29th October 2012.

(8) In this regulation, "C" means the child or still-born child in respect of whom a Sure Start Maternity Grant is claimed.

PART VI

NEW STYLE JOBSEEKER'S ALLOWANCE

New Style Jobseekers Act 1995

(1995 c.18)

SECTIONS REPRODUCED

AS AMENDED BY THE WELFARE REFORM ACT 2012

PART I

THE JOBSEEKER'S ALLOWANCE

Entitlement

Work-related requirements

Income and capital

Trade disputes

Miscellaneous

An Act to provide for a jobseeker's allowance and to make other provision to promote the employment of the unemployed and the assistance of persons without a settled way of life. [June 28, 1995]

General Note

6.2 The form of the Act set out below (described in this volume as the new style Jobseekers Act 1995) is as amended in cases in which universal credit has come into operation, so that IBJSA has been abolished. See the annotation to reg.1 of the JSA Regulations 2013 for the cases in which that has taken place. Universal credit is not being brought into force on the same date throughout the country, but only in relation to specified claimants who are in specified places at the time of making a claim. Accordingly, although many crucial amendments can operate from April 29, 2013 onwards, the actual date on which they come into effect in any particular case will depend on whether the claimant at the date of the relevant claim comes within the universal credit system. In the AMENDMENTS sections below this is indicated by referring to a "trigger date" on or after April 29, 2013. The process of amendment and the commencement of amendments and repeals has been very complex. Although the text below has been checked as far as possible, mistakes may possibly remain (to be corrected in future editions), although it is hoped none that have any significant practical consequences.

To save space and complication, the only amendments identified below are those made in and under the Welfare Reform Act 2012, and subsequent amendments to this form of the Act. Previous amendments are not identified, but can be traced in the old style Jobseekers Act 1995 as reproduced in Part I of this volume. In the DEFINITIONS sections below, references to sections are to the new style Jobseekers Act 1995.

The essential difference between old style JSA and new style JSA is that there can be entitlement to the latter only on satisfaction of contribution conditions. The role of what was formerly IBJSA has been taken over by universal credit as a separate benefit.

PART I

THE JOBSEEKER'S ALLOWANCE

Entitlement

The jobseeker's allowance

1.—(1) An allowance, to be known as a jobseeker's allowance, shall be payable in accordance with the provisions of this Act. **6.3**

(2) Subject to the provisions of this Act, a claimant is entitled to a jobseeker's allowance if he–

(a) [1 . . .];
(b) has [2 accepted a claimant commitment];
(c) [1 . . .];
(d) satisfies the conditions set out in section 2;
(e) is not engaged in remunerative work;
(f) does not have limited capability for work;
(g) is not receiving relevant education;
(h) is under pensionable age; and
(i) is in Great Britain.

(2A) – (2D) [3 . . .].

(3) A jobseeker's allowance is payable in respect of a week.

(4) [3 . . .].

AMENDMENTS

1. Welfare Reform Act 2012 s.49(2) (trigger date on or after April 29, 2013).
2. Welfare Reform Act 2012 s.44(2) (trigger date on or after April 29, 2013).
3. Welfare Reform Act 2012 Sch.14 Pt 1 (trigger date on or after April 29, 2013).

DEFINITIONS

"claimant"—see s.35(1).
"claimant commitment"—see s.6A.
"Great Britain"—see s.35(1)
"limited capability for work"—see s.35(2) and Sch.1.
"pensionable age"—see s.35(1) and reg.2(1) of the JSA Regulations 2013 and SSCBA 1992 s.122(1).
"relevant education"—see s.35(2) and Sch.1.
"remunerative work"—*ibid.*, and JSA Regulations 2013, reg.42(1).
"week"—see s.35(1).

GENERAL NOTE

Subsection (2) sets out the basic conditions of entitlement to new style JSA. See the annotations to s.1(2) of the old style Jobseekers Act 1995 in Pt I of this volume for conditions (d)–(i), ignoring the references to IBJSA. The most important differences from old style JSA are that under condition (b), instead of having entered a jobseeker's agreement which remains in force, the claimant must have accepted a claimant commitment (on which see s.6A below) and that it is no longer a condition of entitlement that the claimant be available for and actively seeking employment. Equivalent requirements can be imposed under ss.6D and 6E, but a failure without **6.4** a good reason to comply with those requirements is a matter for an imposition of a sanction, rather than a determination that a condition of entitlement is no longer met. The only remaining conditions of entitlement specifically related to unemployment are that the claimant is not engaged in remunerative work (condition (e)) and must satisfy the contribution and earnings conditions under s.2 (condition (d)).

On remunerative work, see regs 42–44 of the JSA Regulations 2013. On limited capability for work, see para.2 of Sch.1 to this Act and regs 46, 46A and 47. On relevant education, see reg.45. On pensionable age, see reg.2(1). On presence in Great Britain, see reg.41.

The contribution-based conditions

6.5 **2.**—(1) The conditions referred to in section 1(2)(d) are that the claimant—

(a) has actually paid Class 1 contributions [3 or Class 2 contributions under Case G of Part 9 of the Social Security (Contributions) Regulations 2001] in respect of one ("the base year") of the last two complete years before the beginning of the relevant benefit year and satisfies the additional conditions set out in subsection (2);

(b) has, in respect of the last two complete years before the beginning of the relevant benefit year, either paid Class 1 contributions [3 or Class 2 contributions under Case G of Part 9 of the Social Security (Contributions) Regulations 2001] or been credited with earnings and satisfies the additional condition set out in subsection (3);

(c) does not have earnings in excess of the prescribed amount; [1. . .]

(d) [1. . .].

(2) The additional conditions mentioned in subsection (1)(a) are that—

(a) the contributions have been paid before the week for which the jobseeker's allowance is claimed;

(b) the claimant's relevant earnings for the base year upon which primary Class 1 contributions [3 or Class 2 contributions under Case G of Part 9 of the Social Security (Contributions) Regulations 2001] have been paid or treated as paid are not less than the base year's lower earnings limit multiplied by 26.

(2A) Regulations may make provision for the purposes of subsection (2)(b) for determining the claimant's relevant earnings for the base year.

(2B) Regulations under subsection (2A) may, in particular, make provision—

(a) for making that determination by reference to the amount of a person's earnings for periods comprised in the base year;

(b) for determining the amount of a person's earnings for any such period by—

(i) first determining the amount of the earnings for the period in accordance with regulations made for the purposes of section 3(2) of the Benefits Act, and

(ii) then disregarding so much of the amount found in accordance with sub- paragraph (i) as exceeded the base year's lower earnings limit (or the prescribed equivalent.

(3) The additional condition mentioned in subsection (1)(b) is that the earnings factor derived from so much of the claimant's earnings as did not exceed the upper earnings limit and upon which primary Class 1 contributions [3 or Class 2 contributions under Case G of Part 9 of the Social Security (Contributions) Regulations 2001] have been paid or treated as

paid or from earnings credited is not less, in each of the two complete years, than the lower earnings limit for the year multiplied by 50.

(3A) Where primary Class 1 contributions [3 or Class 2 contributions under Case G of Part 9 of the Social Security (Contributions) Regulations 2001] have been paid or treated as paid on any part of a person's earnings, subsection (3) above shall have effect as if such contributions had been paid or treated as paid on so much of the earnings as did not exceed the upper earnings limit.

(3B) Regulations may—

(a) provide for the first set of conditions to be taken to be satisfied in the case of persons—

(i) who have been entitled to any prescribed description of benefit during any prescribed period or at any prescribed time, or

(ii) who satisfy other prescribed conditions;

(3C) In subsection (3B)—

"the first set of conditions" means the condition set out in subsection (1)(a) and the additional conditions set out in subsection (2);

"benefit" means—

[2 (za) universal credit,]

(a) any benefit within the meaning of section 122(1) of the Benefits Act,

(b) any benefit under Parts 7 to 12 of the Benefits Act,

(c) credits under regulations under section 22(5) of the Benefits Act,

(d) a [1 . . .] jobseeker's allowance, [1 . . .]

(e) [1 . . .].

(4) For the purposes of this section—

(a) "benefit year" means a period which is a benefit year for the purposes of Part II of the Benefits Act or such other period as may be prescribed for the purposes of this section;

(b) "the relevant benefit year" is the benefit year which includes—

(i) the beginning of the jobseeking period which includes the week for which a jobseeker's allowance is claimed, or

(ii) (if earlier) the beginning of any linked period; and (c) other expressions which are used in this section and the Benefits Act have the same meaning in this section as they have in that Act.

AMENDMENTS

1. Welfare Reform Act 2012 Sch.14 Pt 1 (trigger date on or after April 29, 2013).
2. Welfare Reform Act 2012 Sch.2 para.35 (April 29, 2013).
3. JSA Regulations 2013 reg.75 (trigger date on or after April 29, 2013).

DEFINITIONS

"the Benefits Act"—see s.35(1).

"claimant"—*ibid.*

"earnings"—see s.35(3) and Sch.1 and reg.2(2) of the JSA Regulations 2013.

"earnings factor"—see sub.(4)(c) and SSCBA 1992 ss.22 and 23.

"jobseeking period"—see s.35(1) and regs 2(1) and 47 of the JSA Regulations 2013.

"linked period"—see s.35(2) and Sch.1 para.3 and reg.39 of the JSA Regulations 2013.

"lower earnings limit"—see subs.(4)(c) and SSCBA 1992 s.5(1)(a).

"prescribed"—see s.35(1).
"primary Class 1 contributions"—see subs.(4)(c) and SSCBA 1992 ss.6 and 8.
"upper earnings limit"—see subs.(4)(c) and SSCBA 1992 ss.122(1) and 5(1).
"week"—see s.35(1).
"year"—*ibid.*

General Note

6.6 See the annotations to s.2 of the old style Jobseekers Act 1995 in Pt I of this volume. The contribution conditions are essentially the same as for old style CBJSA. See reg.34 of the JSA Regulations 2013 for the prescription of relevant earnings for the purposes of subs.(2)(b) (the equivalent of reg.45A of the JSA Regulations 1996) and reg.35 (the equivalent of reg.45B of the JSA Regulations 1996) for a limited relaxation of the conditions in subs.(1)(a) and (2), as allowed by subss.(3B) and (3C). The condition that the claimant's earnings do not exceed a prescribed amount (subs.(1)(c)) has been retained. See reg.48 of the JSA Regulations 2013 for the prescribed amount, which is in effect the age-related applicable amount of benefit under s.4(1)(a) and reg.49, less any amounts that fall to be disregarded from the claimant's earnings. Note that only the claimant's own earnings are relevant. There is no provision for aggregating the earnings or other income of other members of the family or household. And capital is irrelevant. Earnings under the prescribed amount affect the amount of benefit payable under s.4 (s.4(1)(b) and reg.50 of the JSA Regulations 2013).

The condition previously in subs.(1)(d) of not being entitled to income support has been removed because by definition income support has ceased to exist for claimants to whom universal credit has started to apply. Since entitlement to new style JSA is only on a contributory basis there is no obstacle to being entitled to it at the same time as being entitled to universal credit.

Section 2 is modified in relation to its application to share fishermen by reg.69 of the JSA Regulations 2013. Since the modification applies only in those restricted cases it is not included in the text above. By contrast, the modification in reg.75 (covering volunteer development workers who have taken up the option of paying Class 2 contributions while abroad) is made general and is included.

The income-based conditions

6.7 **3.**—[1. . .].

Amendment

1. Welfare Reform Act 2012 Sch.14 Pt 1 (trigger date on or after April 29, 2013).

The conditions for claims by joint-claim couples

6.8 **3A.**—[1 . . .].

Amendment

1. Welfare Reform Act 2012 Sch.14 Pt 1 (trigger date on or after April 29, 2013).

Joint-claim couples: the nominated member

6.9 **3B.**—[1 . . .].

Amendment

1. Welfare Reform Act 2012 Sch.14 Pt 1 (trigger date on or after April 29, 2013).

Amount payable by way of jobseeker's allowance

4.—(1) In the case of a [1 . . .] jobseeker's allowance, the amount payable in respect of a claimant ("his personal rate") shall be calculated by— 6.10

(a) determining the age-related amount applicable to him; and
(b) making prescribed deductions in respect of earnings, pension payments, PPF payments and FAS payments.

(2) The age-related amount applicable to a claimant, for the purposes of subsection (1)(a), shall be determined in accordance with regulations.

(3) and (3A) [1 . . .].

(4) Except in prescribed circumstances, a jobseeker's allowance shall not be payable where the amount otherwise payable would be less than a prescribed minimum.

(5) The applicable amount shall be such amount or the aggregate of such amounts as may be determined in accordance with regulations.

(6) – (11A) [1. . .].

AMENDMENT

1. Welfare Reform Act 2012 Sch.14 Pt 1 (trigger date on or after April 29, 2013).

DEFINITIONS

"claimant"—see s.35(1).
"earnings"—see s.35(3).
"FAS payments"—see s.35(1).
"pension payments"—*ibid.*
"PPF payments"—*ibid.*
"prescribed"—*ibid.*
"regulations"—*ibid.*

GENERAL NOTE

See the annotations to subss.(1) and (2) of s.4 of the old style Jobseekers Act 1995 in Pt I of this volume. See reg.49 of the JSA Regulations 2013 for the age-related applicable amount (a higher rate for those aged 25 and over, a lower rate for under-25s). See the annotations to reg.79 of the JSA Regulations 1996 for the validity of this difference. On the deduction of earnings from the basic age-related amount under subs.(1)(b), see reg.50, requiring deduction of any earnings from employment or self-employment as calculated in accordance with Pt 7 of the Regulations, which brings in the disregards in the Schedule. If earnings equal or exceed the age-related amount, the claimant is not entitled to new style JSA at all (s.2(1)(c) and reg.48). On the deduction of pension and cognate payments over £50 per week, see reg.51 (the equivalent of reg.81 of the JSA Regulations 1996: see the annotations to that provision in Pt III of this volume). It appears that where this abatement process operates to make the amount of benefit payable nil, but s.2(1)(c) is still satisfied, the days affected will nonetheless count against the 182-day limit on entitlement in s.5. 6.11

Amount payable in respect of joint-claim couple

4A.—[1 . . .]. 6.12

AMENDMENT

1. Welfare Reform Act 2012 Sch.14 Pt 1 (trigger date on or after April 29, 2013).

Duration of a [1. . .] jobseeker's allowance

6.13 **5.**—(1) The period for which a person is entitled to a [1. . .] jobseeker's allowance shall not exceed, in the aggregate, 182 days in any period for which his entitlement is established by reference (under section 2(1)(b)) to the same two years.

(2) The fact that a person's entitlement to a [1. . .] jobseeker's allowance ("his previous entitlement") has ceased as a result of subsection (1), does not prevent his being entitled to a further [1 . . .] jobseeker's allowance if—

(a) he satisfies the contribution-based conditions; and

(b) the two years by reference to which he satisfies those conditions includes at least one year which is later than the second of the two years by reference to which his previous entitlement was established.

(3) Regulations may provide that a person who would be entitled to a [1. . .] jobseeker's allowance but for the operation of prescribed provisions of, or made under, this Act shall be treated as if entitled to the allowance for the purposes of this section.

AMENDMENT

1. Welfare Reform Act 2012 Sch.14 Pt 1 (trigger date on or after April 29, 2013).

DEFINITIONS

"contribution-based conditions"—see s.35(1).
"entitled"—*ibid.*
"prescribed"—*ibid.*
"regulations"—*ibid.*
"year"—*ibid.*

GENERAL NOTE

6.14 The maximum duration of new style JSA within any one jobseeking period is 182 days. A claimant can re-qualify under subs.(2) following the expiry of the 182 days, but on conditions which on the face of it would have led to the start of a new limit under subs.(1) anyway. See the annotations to s.5 of the old style Jobseekers Act 1995 in Pt I of this volume. Regulation 37(3) of the JSA Regulations 2013 (the equivalent of reg.47(4) of the JSA Regulations 1996) is apparently made under subs.(3). It provides that a day within a jobseeking period counts against the 182-day limit if the claimant satisfies the purely contribution conditions in s.2 and the amount of benefit payable has been reduced to nil following a sanction under s.6J or 6K or a fraud sanction. However, in those circumstances the provision appears to be unnecessary (and possibly ultra vires) because the effect of a reduction in the amount of benefit payable under s.6J or 6K to nil is not to remove entitlement. Similarly, the Social Security Fraud Act 2001 imposes restrictions on payability of benefit and does not remove entitlement.

The transition from old style JSA

6.15 In subss.(1) and (2) (the first reference), the references to jobseeker's allowance are, where art.13(1) and (2) of the Welfare Reform Act 2012 (Commencement No.9 and Transitional and Transitory Provisions and Commencement No.8 and Savings and Transitional Provisions (Amendment)) Order 2013 (as amended and set out in the 2014/15 Supplement) applies, to be read as if they included a reference to an old style contribution-based JSA award (art.12(4) of that Order).

Availability for employment

6.—[1. . .]. 6.16

AMENDMENT

1. Welfare Reform Act 2012 s.49(3) (trigger date on or after April 29, 2013).

Actively seeking employment

7.—[1. . .]. 6.17

AMENDMENT

1. Welfare Reform Act 2012 s.49(3) (trigger date on or after April 29, 2013).

Attendance, information and evidence

8.—[1. . .]. 6.18

AMENDMENT

1. Welfare Reform Act 2012 s.49(3) (trigger date on or after April 29, 2013).

The jobseeker's agreement

9.—[1. . .]. 6.19

AMENDMENT

1. Welfare Reform Act 2012 s.49(3) (trigger date on or after April 29, 2013).

GENERAL NOTE

Section 49(3) of the Welfare Reform Act 2012 also appears to revoke the substituted ss.9 and 10 introduced into the Jobseekers Act 1995 for the interim period by s.44(3). 6.20

Variation of jobseeker's agreement

10.—[1. . .]. 6.21

AMENDMENT

1. Welfare Reform Act 2012 s.49(3) (trigger date on or after April 29, 2013).

GENERAL NOTE

Section 49(3) of the Welfare Reform Act 2012 also appears to revoke the substituted ss.9 and 10 introduced into the Jobseekers Act 1995 for the interim period by s.44(3). 6.22

[1 *Work-related requirements*

Work-related requirements

6.—(1) The following provisions of this Act provide for the Secretary of State to impose work-related requirements with which claimants must comply for the purposes of this Act. 6.23

(2) In this Act "work-related requirement" means—
(a) a work-focused interview requirement (see section 6B);
(b) a work preparation requirement (see section 6C);
(c) a work search requirement (see section 6D);
(d) a work availability requirement (see section 6E).]

AMENDMENT

1. Welfare Reform Act 2012 s.49(3) (trigger date on or after April 29, 2013).

DEFINITION

"claimant"—see s.35(1).

GENERAL NOTE

6.24 Sections 6–6L replace ss.6–10 of the old style Jobseekers Act 1995 on jobseeking. They in the main set out what sort of work-related requirements can be imposed on which new style claimants, as well as the system for imposing sanctions (reductions in benefit) on claimants for failure to comply with those requirements and for other failures. The provisions are very similar to those in ss.13–28 of the Welfare Reform Act 2012 on universal credit (see Vol.V, *Universal Credit*), except that as in general all new style JSA claimants are subject to the work-related requirements regime, there is no need for the complicated provisions about what sort of requirements can be imposed on what sort of universal credit claimants. That is subject to the important qualification in reg.5 of the JSA Regulations 2013 (made under ss.6F(1) and 6H(1)(a)) that if a person is entitled both to new style JSA and to universal credit the work-related requirements under this Act do not apply, although a claimant commitment under s.6A below must still be accepted. Thus the control of conditionality and the imposition of sanctions appears to be restricted to universal credit, which could have bizarre results (see the annotations to reg.5). There is also a general exemption for recent victims of domestic violence (s.6H(5)–(6) and reg.15 of the JSA Regulations 2013) and for miscellaneous categories of deserving claimants specified in regs 16 and 16A.

Although s.6 refers only to work-related requirements as defined in ss.6B–6E, s.6G allows the Secretary of State to require claimants to participate in an interview for various related purposes, to provide information and evidence and to report specified changes in their circumstances. A failure for no good reason to comply with a requirement under s.6G can lead to a sanction and reduction of benefit under s.6K(2)(b). A failure for no good reason to comply with a work-related requirement can lead to a sanction and reduction of benefit under s.6K(2)(a), unless the circumstances fall within s.6J (higher-level sanctions).

Section 6A contains rules about the "claimant commitment", acceptance of which is a condition of entitlement under s.1(2)(b).

[1 Claimant commitment

6.25 **6A.**—(1) A claimant commitment is a record of a claimant's responsibilities in relation to an award of a jobseeker's allowance.

(2) A claimant commitment is to be prepared by the Secretary of State and may be reviewed and updated as the Secretary of State thinks fit.

(3) A claimant commitment is to be in such form as the Secretary of State thinks fit.

(4) A claimant commitment is to include—
(a) a record of the requirements that the claimant must comply with under this Act (or such of them as the Secretary of State considers it appropriate to include),

(b) any prescribed information, and
(c) any other information the Secretary of State considers it appropriate to include.

(5) For the purposes of this Act a claimant accepts a claimant commitment if, and only if, the claimant accepts the most up-to-date version of it in such manner as may be prescribed.]

AMENDMENT

1. Welfare Reform Act 2012 s.49(3) (trigger date on or after April 29, 2013).

DEFINITIONS

"claimant"—see s.35(1).
"prescribed"—*ibid.*

GENERAL NOTE

Under s.1(2)(b) it is one of the conditions of entitlement to new style JSA, as it is for universal credit, that the claimant has accepted a claimant commitment. Section 6A defines the nature of a claimant commitment and there are further provisions in regs 7 and 8 of the JSA Regulations 2013 about methods of acceptance and exceptions from the condition. 6.26

Note that when the important reg.5 of the JSA Regulations 2013 applies, because a new style JSA beneficiary is also entitled to universal credit, so that the work-related requirements in ss.6B–6I do not apply, s.6A is left untouched. But there is then a question what could be included in a JSA claimant commitment.

Subsections (1) and (2) define a claimant commitment as a record prepared by the Secretary of State (in such form as he thinks fit: subs.(3)) of a claimant's responsibilities in relation to an award of new style JSA. In particular, by subs.(4)(a), the record is to include the requirements that the particular claimant must comply with under the Act, in the main work-related and connected requirements (see ss.6B–6G). Those requirements can sometimes be to take specific action (e.g. to participate in a particular interview under s.6B or to take particular action to improve prospects of paid work under s.6C or to obtain paid work under s.6D), so that the document may need to be fairly detailed and subject to frequent change, although there is a discretion in subs.(4)(a) to omit requirements if appropriate. The process of review and updating under subs.(2) appears to be completely informal, in stark contrast to the process for variation of a jobseeker's agreement under s.10 of the old style Jobseekers Act 1995, so can accommodate that. Each updating will trigger a new requirement to accept the most up-to-date version. Subsection (4)(b) allows the record to contain any prescribed information. Regulations have not as yet prescribed any such information. Subsection (4)(c) allows the record to contain any other information (note, information, not a further requirement) that the Secretary of State considers appropriate. For the claimant commitment to serve the basic purpose discussed below, that information must at least include information about the potential consequences under the Act of receiving a sanction for failure to carry out a requirement.

Exceptions from the application of the basic condition in s.1(2)(b) are set out in reg.8 of the JSA Regulations 2013. The Act does not seek to define what is meant by acceptance of a claimant commitment beyond the provision in s.6A(5) that it must be the most up-to-date version that has been accepted in such manner as prescribed in regulations. Regulation 7 of the JSA Regulations 2013 provides for the time within which and the manner in which the claimant commitment must be accepted, but says nothing about what accepting the commitment entails in substance.

Since the commitment is the record of the particular claimant's responsibilities, 6.27
it does not seem that acceptance can mean much more than an acknowledgement of its receipt or possibly also that the claimant understands the implications of the

requirements set out. There can be no question of a claimant having to express any agreement with the justice or reasonableness of the requirements, let alone of the policy behind the imposition of "conditionality" in JSA and universal credit. Nor does acceptance seem to involve any personal commitment to carrying out the stated requirements. The obligation to comply with any requirements imposed under the new style Jobseekers Act 1995 does not rest on any contractual or consensual basis. It rests on the terms of the legislation. Further, a failure to comply with any requirement imposed by the Secretary of State is a matter for a potential sanction under s.6J or 6K, not for a conclusion that the basic condition of entitlement in s.1(2)(b) is no longer met. There is no direct sanction for a failure to comply with a requirement just because it is included in the claimant commitment, nor does such a failure show that the claimant commitment has ceased to be accepted in the sense suggested above.

The notion of the claimant commitment is in many ways at the heart of what "conditionality" is meant to achieve under new style JSA and universal credit. It looks on its face to be an expression of what Charles Reich in his classic essay *The New Property* 73 *Yale Law Journal* 733 (1964) called "the New Feudalism". The claimant not only has, as the price of securing entitlement to the benefit, to accept a defined status that involves the giving up of some rights normally enjoyed by ordinary citizens, but appears to have to undertake some kind of oath of fealty by accepting a commitment to the feudal duties of that status. However, in reality the claimant commitment is a much more prosaic, and more sensible, thing. In its interesting paper *Universal Credit and Conditionality* (Social Security Advisory Committee Occasional Paper No.9, 2012) the SSAC reported research findings that many claimants of current benefits subject to a sanctions regime did not understand what conduct could lead to a sanction, how the sanctions system worked (some not even realising that they had been sanctioned) and in particular what the consequences of a sanction would be on current and future entitlement. Paragraph 3.12 of the paper states:

> "The lessons to be learned from the research ought to be relatively straightforward to implement, although providing the appropriate training for a large number of Personal Advisers may present a considerable challenge:
>
> - claimants need to have the link between conditionality and the application of sanctions fully explained at the start of any claim
> - clear and unambiguous communication about the sanctions regime between advisers and claimants is vital at the start of any claim and must form a key element in the Claimant Commitment
> - claimants need to know when they are in danger of receiving a sanction and to be told when a sanction has been imposed, the amount and the duration
> - claimants need to know what actions they have to take to reverse a sanction – the process and consequences of re-compliance."

If one of the main aims of conditionality, of encouraging claimants to avoid behaviour that would impede a possible return to or entry into work and thus reducing the incidence of the imposition of sanctions or of more severe sanctions, is to be furthered, it therefore makes sense to build into the system a requirement to set out each claimant's responsibilities and the consequences of not meeting them in understandable terms. However, as the SSAC suggests, the nature of the personal interaction between personal advisers and claimants may be much more important than a formal written document in getting over the realities of the situation and in encouraging claimants to take steps to avoid or reduce dependence on benefit.

6.28 A similar line of thought seems to be behind what was set out in paras 65 and 66 of the joint judgment of Lords Neuberger and Toulson in *R (on the application of Reilly and Wilson) v Secretary of State for Work and Pensions* [2013] UKSC 68, [2014] 1 A.C. 453 in relation to the old style JSA regime, after noting the serious consequence of imposing a requirement to engage in unpaid work on a claimant on pain of discontinuance of benefits:

> "65. Fairness therefore requires that a claimant should have access to such information about the scheme as he or she may need in order to make informed and meaningful representations to the decision-maker before a decision is made. Such claimants are likely to vary considerably in their levels of education and ability to express themselves in an interview at a Jobcentre at a time when they may be under considerable stress. The principle does not depend on the categorisation of the Secretary of State's decision to introduce a particular scheme under statutory powers as a policy: it arises as a matter of fairness from the Secretary of State's proposal to invoke a statutory power in a way which will or may involve a requirement to perform work and which may have serious consequences on a claimant's ability to meet his or her living needs.
>
> 66. Properly informed claimants, with knowledge not merely of the schemes available, but also of the criteria for being placed on such schemes, should be able to explain what would, in their view, be the most reasonable and appropriate scheme for them, in a way which would be unlikely to be possible without such information. Some claimants may have access to information downloadable from a government website, if they knew what to look for, but many will not. For many of those dependent on benefits, voluntary agencies such as Citizens Advice Bureaus play an important role in informing and assisting them in relation to benefits to which they may be entitled, how they should apply, and what matters they should draw to the attention of their Jobcentre adviser."

However, how such principles might impact on the new style JSA and universal credit will have to be worked out in particular legislative contexts.

A sample claimant commitment for universal credit purposes has been produced by the DWP in response to a freedom of information request (available at: *https://www.gov.uk/government/publications/foi-query-universal-credit-claimant-commitment-example*) [Accessed May 26, 2014], or through a link in the universal credit part of the discussion forum on the Rightsnet website). The document puts things in terms of what the claimant says he or she will do. It is suggested above that that is not quite what the legislation requires, but there is obviously a tension with an attempt to use everyday and simple language. Nevertheless, the document is long and complicated. In the sample, there is no attempt to specify the precise length of the sanction that would be imposed for a failure for no good reason (the document says "without good reason") to comply with a requirement, but the maximum possible duration is included, plus the words "up to". It is arguable that this information is insufficiently precise.

There is some difficulty in working out what remedies a claimant would have who disagrees with the imposition of a requirement included in the claimant commitment. If the claimant declines to accept the Secretary of State's form of the record, at the outset of the claim or as later reviewed and up-dated, then any initial disallowance of the claim or subsequent supersession of an awarding decision would be appealable. However, it is not clear whether such an appeal could succeed on the basis that a requirement in fact included in the claimant commitment should not have been imposed. If the requirement was one whose imposition was prohibited by the legislation and the claimant was prepared to accept everything else, it is submitted that it could properly be concluded that the condition in s.1(2)(b) had been satisfied from the outset (compare the approach of Judge Rowland in *CJSA/1080/2002* and *GM v SSWP (JSA)* [2014] UKUT 057 (AAC) in holding that a claimant was to be accepted as satisfying a condition of attendance at a Jobcentre when he had in fact not attended after being informed that he was not entitled to JSA so that attendance was pointless: see the annotations to reg.23 of the JSA Regulations 1996). If it was a matter of the Secretary of State's discretion under s.6F(2), the result might be different. A claimant who accepts a claimant commitment under protest about some requirement may no doubt request the Secretary of State not to impose the challenged requirement and in consequence to review the claimant commitment, as mentioned in reg.7(2) of the JSA Regulations 2013. However, it appears that the claimant cannot appeal directly against either imposition of the requirement or the content of the claimant commitment or a refusal by the Secretary of State to remove a requirement and to review the claimant commitment. See the discussion in the note to s.6F below, which would apply equally to any of the kinds of decision mentioned. None of them are "outcome" decisions.

[1 Work-focused interview requirement

6.29 **6B.—**(1) In this Act a "work-focused interview requirement" is a requirement that a claimant participate in one or more work-focused interviews as specified by the Secretary of State.

(2) A work-focused interview is an interview for prescribed purposes relating to work or work preparation.

(3) The purposes which may be prescribed under subsection (2) include in particular that of making it more likely in the opinion of the Secretary of State that the claimant will obtain paid work (or more paid work or better-paid work).

(4) The Secretary of State may specify how, when and where a work-focused interview is to take place.]

AMENDMENT

1. Welfare Reform Act 2012 s.49(3) (trigger date on or after April 29, 2013).

DEFINITIONS

"claimant"—see s.35(1).
"prescribed"—*ibid.*

GENERAL NOTE

6.30 This section defines what a "work-focused interview" is and makes the related requirement "participation" in the interview. By virtue of s.6F(2)(a) below the Secretary of State has a discretion whether or not to impose the work-focused interview requirement, the exemptions from the imposition of work-related requirements in regs 16 and 16A of the JSA Regulations 2013 not applying to the work-focused interview requirement , although reg.15 (domestic violence) does apply.

Under subss.(2) and (3) regulations must prescribe the purposes, relating to work or work preparation, for which an interview may be required. The prescription, in very wide terms, is in reg.10 of the JSA Regulations 2013. That regulation, like s.6B, uses the word "work", not "paid work". There is no further provision about what participating in a work-focused interview entails. The Secretary of State is allowed under subss.(1) and (4) to specify how, when and where the interview is to take place, so that there is no straightforward limit on the number or frequency of the interviews that may be specified, or on the persons who may conduct the interview. The interviews must of course properly be for one of the purposes prescribed in reg.10. The requirement to participate in interviews cannot be used for punitive purposes or simply as a means of control of a claimant. No doubt it is also to be implied that only rational requirements may be imposed, so that a specification of two interviews in different places at the same time or so that they could not practically be co-ordinated could be disregarded as invalid (see the approach of Judge Rowland in *GM v SSWP (JSA)* [2014] UKUT 057 (AAC): notes to s.6A above). Rationality would also require that what was specified should not be incompatible with other requirements, in particular the work search and work availability requirements where there is no discretion under s.6F about their imposition. Thus, a claimant could not validly be required to attend so many interviews that it made it impossible to take work search actions for the hours specified under s.6D, unless there was a corresponding reduction in the s.6D requirements. These are rather extreme examples, which it is hoped would not arise in practice. Because, as discussed in the notes to s.6H, there is no right of appeal against an imposition of a work-related or connected requirement as such, the issues will normally arise in the course of appeals against reductions of benefit following a sanction for non-compliance, where the main focus will be on whether the claimant had a good reason for not complying with the requirement in question.

Note that the requirement, as for UC and now old style JSA, is not attendance at an interview at the specified time and date, but participation in it. This would appear to mean that a claimant can be required to participate in an interview over the telephone, providing that that manner of conducting it has been specified under subs.(4). However, in an ambiguous Parliamentary answer on November 24, 2015 (UIN 17005), the Minister of State, Priti Patel, said:

> "Under JSA, claimants are not sanctioned for failing to answer their telephone. In Universal Credit, claimants who have a prearranged telephone interview with their Work Coach, and who fail to participate without good reason, can be referred for a sanction decision."

There is no further provision about what participating in a work-focused interview entails. It must at least entail turning up at the place and time specified, although the decision of Judge Knowles in *SA v SSWP (JSA)* [2015] UKUT 454 (AAC) (see the notes to s.19A(2)(c) of the old style Jobseekers Act 1995 for full discussion) would indicate that tribunals should consider, in cases where the claimant arrives not very late, whether it is proportionate to the nature of all the circumstances to regard that as a failure to participate in an interview. There were all sorts of mitigating circumstances in *SA*, that may well not be present in other cases. The requirement to participate must also extend to making some meaningful contribution to the interview, but the limits will probably not be established until there have been some sanctions appeals that reach the Upper Tribunal. Behaviour that leads to the premature termination of the interview may well amount to a failure to participate (see the facts of *DM v SSWP (JSA)* [2015] UKUT 67 (AAC) in the notes to s.19A(2)(c) of the old style Jobseekers Act 1995). There may, though, in cases of uncooperative claimants or heavy-handed officials or a combination, be difficult questions about when an interview has ceased to exist, so that subsequent behaviour cannot be relevant to whether there has been a failure to participate (see *PH v SSWP (ESA)* [2016] UKUT 119 (AAC) on failing to submit to a medical examination). A failure for no good reason to comply with any work-related requirement is sanctionable under s.6K(2)(a). That is the context in which what amounts to a failure to comply will be identified, as well as what might amount to a good reason for non-compliance. For instance, there appear to be no provisions prescribing the length of notice of an interview to be given or how far a claimant can be required to travel, but there could plainly be a good reason for failing to comply with unreasonable requirements, especially if the claimant had attempted in advance to draw any problem with attendance to the Secretary of State's attention.

Note that under s.6G(1) the Secretary of State is empowered to require a claimant to participate in an interview relating to the imposition of a work-related requirement on the claimant or assisting the claimant to comply with a requirement. Under s.6G(3) he can require the provision of information and evidence for the purpose of verifying compliance with a work-related requirement and that the claimant confirm compliance in any manner. A failure for no good reason to comply with any of those connected requirements is also sanctionable under s.6K(2)(b).

[1 Work preparation requirement

6C.—(1) In this Act a "work preparation requirement" is a requirement that a claimant take particular action specified by the Secretary of State for the purpose of making it more likely in the opinion of the Secretary of State 6.31

that the claimant will obtain paid work (or more paid work or better-paid work).

(2) The Secretary of State may under subsection (1) specify the time to be devoted to any particular action.

(3) Action which may be specified under subsection (1) includes in particular—

(a) attending a skills assessment;
(b) improving personal presentation;
(c) participating in training;
(d) participating in an employment programme;
(e) undertaking work experience or a work placement;
(f) developing a business plan;
(g) any action prescribed for the purpose in subsection (1).]

AMENDMENT

1. Welfare Reform Act 2012 s.49(3) (trigger date on or after April 29, 2013).

DEFINITION

"claimant"—see s.35(1).

GENERAL NOTE

6.32 This section defines "work preparation requirement". The requirement is to take particular action specified by the Secretary of State for the purpose of making it more likely that the claimant will obtain paid work or obtain more or better-paid such work. Subsection (3) gives a non-exhaustive list of actions that may be specified, including under para.(g) any action prescribed in regulations. No such regulations have as yet been made. The list is in fairly broad terms, not further defined in the legislation, even "employment programme". The sorts of activities required do not themselves have to be paid, so long as they can legitimately be related to the purpose of improving prospects of paid work or more or better paid work (see below). So unpaid work experience or placements (e.g. as an intern) or voluntary work can be made mandatory. See the notes to s.6B above for the need for the co-ordination with the practical application of other work-related or connected requirements for the specification of any particular work preparation requirement to be rational.

The Secretary of State may under subs.(2) specify the time to be devoted to any particular action, but in practice this is likely to be less controversial than the similar power in s.6D(2) in relation to a work search requirement. Subsections (4) and (5) allow the making of regulations requiring limitations to be attached to the kind of work in relation to which the claimant has to take action. See reg.14 of the JSA Regulations 2013. By virtue of s.6F(2)(a) below the Secretary of State has a discretion whether or not to impose the work preparation requirement, the exemptions from the imposition of work-related requirements in regs 16 and 16A of the JSA Regulations not applying to the work preparation requirement.

A failure for no good reason to comply with a requirement under this heading to undertake a work placement of a prescribed description is sanctionable under s.6J(2)(a) (higher-level sanctions). Outside that limited category, failure for no good reason to comply with any work-related requirement is sanctionable under s.6K(2)(a). That is the context in which there will be exploration of what action can be said to make it more likely that the claimant will obtain paid work or more or better-paid work, since the addition of the Secretary of State's opinion in subs.(1) will not be allowed to take away the power of tribunals to reach their own conclusions on that matter. What amounts to a failure to comply will also be identified, as well as what might amount to a good reason for non-compliance. *JS v SSWP (ESA)* [2013] UKUT 635 (AAC), at para.15 suggests that if a claimant is patently not going to be able to obtain work at any stage or is already in an appropriate apprenticeship or placement no action could make it more likely that work or more work would be obtained, so that no action could legitimately be specified. However, in the present context it has to be considered whether prospects of obtaining paid or better paid work could be improved.

Note that under s.6G(1) the Secretary of State is empowered to require a claimant to participate in an interview relating to the imposition of a work-related requirement on the claimant or assisting the claimant to comply with a requirement. Under s.6G(3) he can require the provision of information and evidence for the purpose of verifying compliance with a work-related requirement and that the claimant confirm compliance in any manner. A failure for no good reason to comply with any of those connected requirements is also sanctionable under s.6K(2)(b).

[1 Work search requirement

6D.—(1) In this Part a "work search requirement" is a requirement that a claimant take— 6.33

(a) all reasonable action, and

(b) any particular action specified by the Secretary of State,

for the purpose of obtaining paid work (or more paid work or better-paid work).

(2) The Secretary of State may under subsection (1)(b) specify the time to be devoted to any particular action.

(3) Action which may be specified under subsection (1)(b) includes in particular—

(a) carrying out work searches;

(b) making applications;

(c) creating and maintaining an online profile;

(d) registering with an employment agency;

(e) seeking references;

(f) any other action prescribed for the purpose in subsection (1).

(4) Regulations may impose limitations on a work search requirement by reference to the work to which it relates; and the Secretary of State may in any particular case specify further such limitations on such a requirement.

(5) A limitation under subsection (4) may in particular be by reference to—

(a) work of a particular nature,

(b) work with a particular level of remuneration,

(c) work in particular locations, or

(d) work available for a certain number of hours per week or at particular times, and may be indefinite or for a particular period.]

AMENDMENT

1. Welfare Reform Act 2012 s.49(3) (trigger date on or after April 29, 2013).

DEFINITIONS

"claimant"—see s.35(1).

"regulations"—*ibid.*

GENERAL NOTE

6.34 This section defines "work search requirement", which is one of the requirements that, by virtue of s.6F(1)(a), the Secretary of State must impose on all new style JSA claimants, unless exempted by regulations. It is a requirement that a claimant take both all reasonable action (subs.(1)(a)) and any particular action specified by the Secretary of State (subs.(1)(b)) for the purpose of obtaining paid work or more or better-paid work. "Paid work" is not defined in the Act, nor is it defined in regulations for the specific purpose of s.6D. However, under the power in s.6I, regs 11 and 12 of the JSA Regulations 2013 deem the work search requirement not to have been complied with in certain circumstances and make references to "obtaining paid work". For those purposes, the extension in reg.3(7) to cover obtaining more or better paid work will apply, but this appears to add nothing of substance to the terms of s.6D itself. There is no further definition of what amounts to paid work. Thus it appears that both self-employment and employment can be considered under the ordinary meaning of the phrase "paid work" and that voluntary work or unpaid internship or work placements are excluded. However, according to the then Minister of State Esther McVey (House of Commons written answers April 2, 2014 and September 1, 2014), guidance to Jobcentre Plus staff is that JSA claimants (in contrast to universal credit claimants) are not to be mandated to apply for vacancies for zero hours contracts, apparently whether there is an exclusivity clause (made unenforceable from May 26, 2015 by the new s.27A of the Employment Rights Act 1996) or not. Thus no sanction under s.6J(2)(b) should arise from a failure to apply for such a vacancy.

Subsections (4) and (5) allow regulations to impose limitations on the kind of work search which can be required and also allow the Secretary of State to specify further limitations. Regulation 14 of the JSA Regulations 2013 contains the prescribed limitations, in terms of hours of work for carers and those with a disability, of the maximum time for travel to and from work and of the type of work recently undertaken. See the annotations to reg.14. There appears to be no limitation on the number of hours a week that work could involve while still falling for consideration, apart from in the cases of the particular categories of claimant identified in reg.14(5). Note also that reg.16 exempts claimants carrying out a variety of categories of worthwhile activity from the imposition or continued application of a work search requirement and that reg.15 exempts victims of domestic violence for a fixed period. Regulation 16A exempts claimants falling within the new reg.46A (extended period of sickness). See the annotations to those regulations.

What is all reasonable action under subs.(1)(a) for the purpose of obtaining paid work within any applicable limitations is obviously in general a matter of judgment. That includes a judgment about what counts as "action". The actions mentioned in subs.(3) might be a starting point, but other things could plainly count, such as carrying out research into the job market or potential for self-employment. No doubt just sitting and thinking falls the other side of the line, but can often form an essential element of the hours devoted to some more active action. But reg.12 of the JSA Regulations 2013 deems a claimant not to have complied with that requirement unless quite stringent conditions about the weekly hours devoted to work search are satisfied. See the annotations to reg.12 and remember that the sanction in s.6K(2)(a) can only be imposed when there was no good reason for the failure to comply. Paragraph 15 of *JS v SSWP (ESA)* [2013] UKUT 635 (AAC) suggests that if a claimant is patently not going to be able to obtain work at any stage or is already in an appropriate apprenticeship or placement no action could make it more likely that work or more work would be obtained, so that it could not be reasonable to take any further action. However, in the present context it has to be considered whether prospects obtaining paid or better paid work could be improved.

6.35 The particular action that can be specified by Secretary of State under subs.(1)(b) can, by subs.(3), include a number of actions, including under para.(g) those prescribed in regulations. No such regulation has yet been made. Where a claimant has been required to apply for a particular vacancy (which it seems can only fall under subs.(1)(b) rather than (1)(a)), reg.11 of the JSA Regulations 2013 deems the work search requirement not to have been complied with where the claimant fails to participate in an interview offered in connection with the vacancy. The specific sanction in s.6J(2)(b) for failing to comply with a requirement to apply for a particular vacancy can only be imposed when there was no good reason for the failure to comply.

Note that under s.6G(1) the Secretary of State is empowered to require a claimant to participate in an interview relating to the imposition of a work-related requirement on the claimant or assisting the claimant to comply with a requirement. Under s.6G(3) he can require the provision of information and evidence for the purpose of verifying compliance with a work-related requirement and that the claimant confirm compliance in any manner. A failure for no good reason to comply with any of those connected requirements is also sanctionable under s.6K(2)(b).

[1 Work availability requirement

6E.—(1) In this Act a "work availability requirement" is a requirement that a claimant be available for work. 6.36

(2) For the purposes of this section "available for work" means able and willing immediately to take up paid work (or more paid work or better-paid work).

(3) Regulations may impose limitations on a work availability requirement by reference to the work to which it relates; and the Secretary of State may in any particular case specify further such limitations on such a requirement.

(4) A limitation under subsection (3) may in particular be by reference to—

(a) work of a particular nature,
(b) work with a particular level of remuneration,
(c) work in particular locations, or
(d) work available for a certain number of hours per week or at particular times, and may be indefinite or for a particular period.

(5) Regulations may for the purposes of subsection (2) define what is meant by able and willing immediately to take up work.]

AMENDMENT

1. Welfare Reform Act 2012 s.49(3) (trigger date on or after April 29, 2013).

DEFINITIONS

"claimant"—see s.35(1).
"regulations"—*ibid.*

GENERAL NOTE

This section defines "work availability requirement", which is one of the requirements that, by virtue of s.6F(1)(a), the Secretary of State must impose on all new style JSA claimants, unless exempted by regulations (see in particular reg.15 of the JSA Regulations 2013 (domestic violence)). It requires in general that a claimant be able and willing immediately to take up paid work, or more or better-paid work. "Paid work" is not defined in the Act, nor is it defined in regulations for the specific purpose of s6E. However, under the power in s.6I, reg.13 of the JSA Regulations 2013 deems the work availability requirement not to have been complied with in certain circumstances and to have been satisfied in other circumstances and makes references to "paid work". For those purposes, the extension in reg.3(7) to cover obtaining more or better paid will apply, but this appears to add nothing of substance to the terms of s.6E itself. There is no further definition of what amounts to paid work. Thus it appears that both self-employment and employment can be considered under the ordinary meaning of the phrase "paid work" and that voluntary work or unpaid internship or work placements are excluded (but see s.6C on work preparation). For some suggestions as to a common sense approach to "immediately", see Simon Browne LJ in *Chief Adjudication Officer v David*, reported in *R(JSA) 3/01* (see the notes to reg.7 of the JSA Regs 1996 in Pt III). 6.37

Subsections (3) and (4) allow regulations to impose limitations on the kind of work for which a claimant can be required to be available and also allow the Secretary of State to specify further limitations. Regulation 14 of the JSA Regulations 2013 contains the prescribed limitations, in terms of hours of work for carers and those with a disability, of the maximum time for travel to and from work and of the type of work recently undertaken. See the annotations to reg.14. There appears to be no limitation on the number of hours a week that work could involve while still falling for consideration, apart from in the cases of the particular categories of claimant identified in reg.14(5).

Subsection (5) allows regulations to define what is meant in subs.(1) by being able and willing immediately to take up work. Regulation 16(1)(b) of the JSA Regulations 2013 uses this power to provide that claimants in any of the circumstances set out in reg.16(3), (4) or (5) are regarded as being available for work if able and willing to take up paid work immediately after the relevant circumstance ceases to apply. Regulation 13(1)(a) deems the work availability requirement not to be complied with if the claimant is not able and willing immediately to attend an interview in connection with finding paid work. Regulation 13(2)–(5) defines circumstances in which carers, those doing voluntary work and those in paid employment are to be treated as having complied with the requirement, where it is accepted that some longer notice than "immediately" is needed. Regulation 16A(3)–(6) now makes equivalent provision for claimants who fall within the new reg.46A (extended period of sickness).

6.38 It is notable, by contrast with the position that will be familiar to many readers from old style JSA and, before it, unemployment benefit, that being available for work is not a condition of entitlement to new style JSA, failure to satisfy which means that there can be no entitlement to benefit at all. Instead, a failure to comply with the work availability requirement, if the claimant is not exempted from it, is merely a potential basis for a sanction under s.6J or 6K. Under s.6J(2)(c) a higher-level sanction can be imposed if a claimant fails for no good reason to comply by not taking up an offer of paid work. Section 6K(2)(a) requires the imposition of a lower level sanction for a failure for no good reason to comply with any work-related requirement.

Note that under s.6G(1) the Secretary of State is empowered to require a claimant to participate in an interview relating to the imposition of a work-related requirement on the claimant or assisting the claimant to comply with a requirement. Under s.6G(3) he can require the provision of information and evidence for the purpose of verifying compliance with a work-related requirement and that the claimant confirm compliance in any manner. Under s.6G(4) he can require the reporting of any changes in the claimant's circumstances. A failure for no good reason to comply with any of those connected requirements is also sanctionable under s.6K(2)(b).

[1 Imposition of work-related requirements

6.39 **6F.**—(1) The Secretary of State must, except in prescribed circumstances, impose on a claimant—

(a) a work search requirement, and
(b) a work availability requirement.

(2) The Secretary of State may, subject to this Act, impose either or both of the following on a claimant—

(a) a work-focused interview requirement;
(b) a work preparation requirement.]

AMENDMENT

1. Welfare Reform Act 2012 s.49(3) (trigger date on or after April 29, 2013).

DEFINITIONS

"claimant"—see s.35(1).
"work availability requirement"—see ss.35(1) and 6E(1).
"work preparation requirement"—see ss.35(1) and 6C(1).
"work search requirement"—see ss.35(1) and 6D(1).
"work-focused interview requirement"—see ss.35(1) and 6B(1).
"work-related requirement"—see ss.35(1) and 6(2).

GENERAL NOTE

This section sets out the default position that any claimant of new style JSA is, unless exempted under reg.15, 16 or 16A of the JSA Regulations 2013, to be subject to the work search and work availability requirements. The imposition of the work-focused interview and the work preparation requirement is, subject only to a possible exemption under reg.15 (domestic violence), a matter for the discretion of the Secretary of State under subs.(2). The content of the requirements is set out in ss.6B–6E and associated regulations. Under s.6G(1) the Secretary of State is empowered to require a claimant to participate in an interview relating to the imposition of a work-related requirement or assisting the claimant to comply with a requirement. Under s.6G(3) he can require the provision of information and evidence for the purpose of verifying compliance with a work-related requirement, that the claimant confirm compliance in any manner and that the claimant report specified changes in circumstances. 6.40

See s.6H for the process of imposing a requirement.

Note the important reg.5 of the JSA Regulations 2013, under which, if a claimant is concurrently entitled to new style JSA and to universal credit, no work-related requirements under ss.6B–6I can be imposed, nor can any sanctions under s.6J or 6K operate.

[1 Connected requirements

6G.—(1) The Secretary of State may require a claimant to participate in an interview for any purpose relating to— 6.41

(a) the imposition of a work-related requirement on the claimant;
(b) verifying the claimant's compliance with a work-related requirement;
(c) assisting the claimant to comply with a work-related requirement.

(2) The Secretary of State may specify how, when and where such an interview is to take place.

(3) The Secretary of State may, for the purpose of verifying the claimant's compliance with a work-related requirement, require a claimant to—

(a) provide to the Secretary of State information and evidence specified by the Secretary of State in a manner so specified;
(b) confirm compliance in a manner so specified.

(4) The Secretary of State may require a claimant to report to the Secretary of State any specified changes in their circumstances which are relevant to—

(a) the imposition of work-related requirements on the claimant;
(b) the claimant's compliance with a work-related requirement.]

AMENDMENT

1. Welfare Reform Act 2012 s.49(3) (trigger date on or after April 29, 2013).

DEFINITIONS

"claimant"—see s.35(1).
"work-related requirement"—see ss.35(1) and 6(2).

General Note

6.42 This section gives the Secretary of State power to require a claimant to do various things related to the imposition of work-related requirements, verifying compliance and assisting claimants to comply: to participate in an interview (subss.(1) and (2)); for the purpose of verifying compliance, to provide specified information and evidence or to confirm compliance (subs.(3)); or to report specified changes of circumstances relevant to the imposition of or compliance with requirements. Such requirements do not fall within the meaning of "work-related requirement", but there is a separate ground of sanction under s.6K(2)(b) for failing for no good reason to comply. The Secretary of State is allowed under subs.(2) to specify how, when and where any interview under subs.(1) is to take place, so that the requirement to participate must at least entail turning up at the place and time specified, although the decision of Judge Knowles in *SA v SSWP (JSA)* [2015] UKUT 454 (AAC) (see the notes to s.19A(2)(c) of the old style Jobseekers Act 1995 in Pt I for full discussion) would indicate that tribunals should consider, in cases where the claimant arrives not very late, whether it is proportionate to the nature of all the circumstances to regard that as a failure to participate in an interview. There were all sorts of mitigating circumstances in *SA*, that may well not be present in other cases. The requirement to participate must also extend to making some meaningful contribution to the interview, but the limits will probably not be established until some sanctions appeals have reached the Upper Tribunal. Behaviour that leads to the premature termination of the interview may well amount to a failure to participate (see the facts of *DM v SSWP (JSA)* [2015] UKUT 67 (AAC) in the notes to s.19A(2)(c) of the old style Jobseekers Act 1995). There may, though, in cases of uncooperative claimants or heavy-handed officials or a combination, be difficult questions about when an interview has ceased to exist, so that subsequent behaviour cannot be relevant to whether there has been a failure to participate (see *PH v SSWP (ESA)* [2016] UKUT 119 (AAC) on failing to submit to a medical examination). The compulsory imposition of a sanction for a failure for no good reason to report specified changes in circumstances, to provide specified information or evidence or to confirm compliance with a work-related requirement is a new departure.

See s.6H for the process of imposing a requirement.

[1 Imposition of work-related and connected requirements: supplementary

6.43 **6H.**—(1) Regulations may make provision—

(a) where the Secretary of State may impose a requirement under the preceding provisions of this Act, as to when the requirement must or must not be imposed;

(b) where the Secretary of State may specify any action to be taken in relation to a requirement under the preceding provisions of this Act, as to what action must or must not be specified;

(c) where the Secretary of State may specify any other matter in relation to a such requirement, as to what must or must not be specified in respect of that matter.

(2) Where the Secretary of State may impose a work-focused interview requirement, or specify a particular action under section 6C(1) or 6D(1)(b), the Secretary of State must have regard to such matters as may be prescribed.

(3) Where the Secretary of State may impose a requirement under the preceding provisions of this Act, or specify any action to be taken in relation to such a requirement, the Secretary of State may revoke or change what has been imposed or specified.

(4) Notification of a requirement imposed under the preceding provisions of this Act (or any change to or revocation of such a requirement) is, if not included in the claimant commitment, to be in such manner as the Secretary of State may determine.

(5) Regulations must make provision to secure that, in prescribed circumstances, where a claimant has recently been a victim of domestic violence—

(a) a requirement imposed on the claimant under the preceding provisions of this Act ceases to have effect for a period of 13 weeks, and

(b) the Secretary of State may not impose any other requirement on the claimant during that period.

(6) For the purposes of subsection (5)—

(a) "domestic violence" has such meaning as may be prescribed;

(b) "victim of domestic violence" means a person on or against whom domestic violence is inflicted or threatened (and regulations under subsection (5) may prescribe circumstances in which a person is to be treated as being or not being a victim of domestic violence);

(c) a person has recently been a victim of domestic violence if a prescribed period has not expired since the violence was inflicted or threatened.]

AMENDMENT

1. Welfare Reform Act 2012 s.49(3) (trigger date on or after April 29, 2013).

DEFINITIONS

"claimant commitment"—see s.6A(1).
"prescribed"—see s.35(1).
"regulations"—*ibid.*
"work-focused interview requirement"—see ss.35(1) and 6B(1).
"work-related requirement"—see ss.35(1) and 6(2).

GENERAL NOTE

This section contains a variety of powers and duties in relation to the imposition by the Secretary of State of either a work-related requirement or a connected requirement under s.6G. It makes the imposition of a requirement and the notification to the claimant a moderately formal process, which raises the question of whether the decision of the Secretary of State to impose a requirement is a decision that is appealable to a First-tier Tribunal under s.12(1) of the SSA 1998, either as a decision on a claim or award or one which falls to be made under the WRA 2012 as a "relevant enactment" (s.8(1)(a) and (c) of the SSA 1998). However, if it is a decision not made on a claim or award, it is not covered in Sch.3 to the SSA 1998 (or in Sch.2 to the Decisions and Appeals Regulations 2013 (see Vol.III)), so is not appealable under that heading. The discussion in the note to s.12(1) of the SSA 1998 in Vol.III would indicate that, since the imposition of a requirement is not an "outcome" decision determining entitlement to or payability of new style JSA or the amount payable, it is not appealable under s.12(1)(a) as a decision on a claim or award. 6.44

Thus, it appears that a direct challenge to the imposition of any particular requirement, including any element specified by the Secretary of State and/or its inclusion in a claimant commitment under s.6 of this Act, can only be made by way of judicial review in the High Court, with the possibility of a discretionary transfer to the Upper Tribunal. Otherwise, a challenge by way of appeal appears not be possible unless and until a reduction of benefit for a sanctionable failure is imposed on the claimant for a failure to comply with a requirement. It must therefore be arguable that in any such appeal the claimant can challenge whether the conditions for the imposition of the requirement in question were met, with the result that, if that challenge is successful, the sanction must be removed. That appears to have been the assumption of the Supreme Court in *R (on the application of Reilly and Wilson) v Secretary of State for Work and Pensions* [2013] UKSC 68; [2014] 1 A.C. 453. At [29] of their joint judgment, Lords Neuberger and Toulson mentioned without any adverse comment Foskett J's holding at first instance that a consequence of a breach of a regulation requiring a claimant to be given notice of a requirement to participate in a scheme was that no sanctions could lawfully be imposed on the claimants for failure to participate in the scheme.

Subsection (1)

6.45 Regulations 16 and 16A of the JSA Regulations 2013 are made under para.(a), reg.15 on domestic violence falling more specifically under subss.(5) and (6). No regulations appear to have been made under paras (b) or (c) of subs.(1).

Subsection (2)

6.46 No regulations appear to have been made under this provision.

Subsection (3)

6.47 The inclusion of this express power to revoke or change any requirement, or any specification of action, is an indication of the formality entailed in the imposition of a requirement. However, there appears to be no restriction on the circumstances in which the Secretary of State may carry out such a revocation or change, subject of course to the legislative conditions being met for whatever the new position is. A mere change of mind without any change in circumstances or mistake or error as to the existing circumstances will do.

Subsection (4)

6.48 This provision allows the Secretary of State to notify the claimant of the imposition of any requirement, if not included in a claimant commitment under s.6A, in any manner. Thus, it may be done orally (or presumably even through the medium of mime), but it is a necessary implication that a requirement must be notified to the claimant. That in turn implies that, whatever the manner of notification, the content must be such as is reasonably capable of being understood by the particular claimant with the characteristics known to the officer of the Secretary of State (so perhaps the medium of mime will not do after all). Less flippantly, this principle may be important for claimants with sensory problems, e.g. hearing or vision difficulties. The expectation of course is that the requirements imposed under the Act will be included in the claimant commitment, one of whose aims is to ensure that claimants know and understand what is being required of them and the potential consequences of failing to comply. However, it is clear in law that the validity of a requirement is not dependent on inclusion in the claimant commitment. There is no such express condition and under s.6A(4)(a) the Secretary of State is only under a duty to record in the claimant commitment such of the requirements under the Act as he considers it appropriate to include. It may be that the fact that a requirement is not recorded in the claimant commitment could be put forward as part of an argument for there having been a good reason for failing to comply with the requirement.

Subsections (5) and (6)

6.49 The duty to make regulations providing that no work-related requirement or connected requirement under s.6G may be imposed for a period of 13 weeks on a claimant who has recently been a victim of domestic violence is carried out in reg.15 of the JSA Regulations 2013. Most of the meat is in the regulation, including the definition of "domestic violence", which has been amended since April 2013. See the annotations to reg.15 for the details. However, subs.(6)(b) does define "victim" to include not just those on whom domestic violence is inflicted but also those against whom it is threatened.

[1 Compliance with work-related and connected requirements

6I.—Regulations may make provision as to circumstances in which a claimant is to be treated as having— 6.50

(a) complied with or not complied with any requirement imposed under the preceding provisions of this Act or any aspect of such a requirement, or

(b) taken or not taken any particular action specified by the Secretary of State in relation to such a requirement.]

AMENDMENT

1. Welfare Reform Act 2012 s.49(3) (trigger date on or after April 29, 2013).

DEFINITIONS

"claimant"—see s.35(1).
"regulations"—*ibid.*
"work-related requirement"—see ss.35(1) and 6(1).

GENERAL NOTE

Under subs.(a) regulations may deem a claimant either to have or not to have complied with any work-related requirement or connected requirement under s.6G in particular circumstances. Regulations 11–13 of the JSA Regulations 2013 make use of this power, mainly in treating claimants as not having complied. No regulations appear to have been made as yet under subs.(b). 6.51

[1 Higher-level sanctions

6J.—(1) The amount of an award of jobseeker's allowance is to be reduced in accordance with this section in the event of a failure by a claimant which is sanctionable under this section. 6.52

(2) It is a failure sanctionable under this section if a claimant—

(a) fails for no good reason to comply with a requirement imposed by the Secretary of State under a work preparation requirement to undertake a work placement of a prescribed description;

(b) fails for no good reason to comply with a requirement imposed by the Secretary of State under a work search requirement to apply for a particular vacancy for paid work;

(c) fails for no good reason to comply with a work availability requirement by not taking up an offer of paid work;

(d) by reason of misconduct, or voluntarily and for no good reason, ceases paid work or loses pay.

(3) It is a failure sanctionable under this section if, at any time before making the claim by reference to which the award is made, the claimant—

(a) for no good reason failed to take up an offer of paid work, or

(b) by reason of misconduct, or voluntarily and for no good reason, ceased paid work or lost pay.

(4) For the purposes of subsections (2) and (3) regulations may provide—

(a) for circumstances in which ceasing to work or losing pay is to be treated as occurring or not occurring by reason of misconduct or voluntarily;

(b) for loss of pay below a prescribed level to be disregarded.

(5) Regulations are to specify—

(a) the amount of a reduction under this section;

(b) the period for which such a reduction has effect, not exceeding three years in relation to any failure sanctionable under this section.

(6) Regulations under subsection (5)(b) may in particular provide for the period of a reduction to depend on either or both of the following—

(a) the number of failures by the claimant sanctionable under this section;

(b) the period between such failures.

(7) Regulations may provide—

(a) for cases in which no reduction is to be made under this section;

(b) for a reduction under this section made in relation to an award that is terminated to be applied to any new award made within a prescribed period of the termination;

(c) for the termination or suspension of a reduction under this section.]

AMENDMENT

1. Welfare Reform Act 2012 s.49(3) (trigger date on or after April 29, 2013).

DEFINITIONS

"claimant"—see s.35(1).
"prescribed"—*ibid.*
"regulations"—*ibid.*
"work availability requirement"—see ss.35(1) and 6E(1).
"work preparation requirement"—see ss.35(1) and 6C(1).
"work search requirement"—see ss.35(1) and 6D(1).
"work-related requirement"—see ss.35(1) and 6(2).

GENERAL NOTE

6.53 Sections 6J and 6K set up a very similar structure of sanctions leading to reductions in the amount of JSA to that already imposed in the universal credit scheme by ss.26 and 27 of the WRA 2012. The main difference for new style JSA, apart from the omission of elements specifically linked to the particular nature of universal credit as a general income maintenance benefit, covering people in quite substantial work as well as those out of work for various reasons, is that "other" sanctions apart from higher-level sanctions are divided into only two levels (medium and low), rather than three. There are also similarities to the new ss.19–20 of the old style Jobseekers Act 1995 in operation from October 22, 2012 (see Pt I of this volume). The similarity there is in the creation of higher-level sanctions, here under s.6J, and of a lower level of other sanctions, here under s.6K, and in the stringency of the fixed periods and the amount of reductions to be imposed, in particular for higher-level sanctions. Section 6J also takes over a number of concepts that are very familiar from the history of unemployment benefit and JSA and on which a wealth of case-law authority has built up. On such concepts there will be reference to the discussion in the annotations to s.19 of the old style Jobseekers Act 1995 in Pt I. There are, however, some potentially significant differences in the wording of otherwise similar provisions as between the old style and the new style Jobseekers Act 1995, which will be noted below.

The central concept under these provisions is of a "sanctionable failure", which under s.6J(1) (subject to reg.28 of the JSA Regulations 2013) and s.6K(1), is to lead to a reduction in the amount of an award of new style JSA. For higher-level sanctions under s.6J, the reduction is in brief of 100 per cent of the claimant's entitlement under reg.49 for about 13 weeks for a first higher-level failure, 26 weeks for second such failure (or universal credit failure) within a year and 156 weeks for a third or subsequent such failure within a year. For other sanctions under s.6K the reduction is of the same amount, but generally for limited periods. As noted below, regulations set out the amount and period of the reduction. There is no discretion under either s.6J or 6K as to whether or not to apply a reduction if the conditions are met and no discretion under the regulations as to the amount and period of the reduction as calculated under the complicated formulae there. Regulation 28 of the JSA Regulations 2013, made under s.6J(7)(a), sets out limited circumstances in which no reduction is to be made for a sanctionable failure under s.6J. Those circumstances are not relevant to the sanctionable failures covered by s.6K.

See the notes to regs 18–21 of the JSA Regulations 2013 for the position where there has been a transition from old style JSA to new style JSA, either in the form of some unexpired period of reduction of old style JSA or the existence of a previous sanctionable failure under that legislation.

Sight must also never be lost of the important provision in reg.5(3) of the JSA 6.54
Regulations 2013, made under s.6J(7)(a) and s.6K(9)(a), that where a person is entitled to both universal credit and new style JSA, reductions of an award of JSA under ss.6J or 6K and the relevant part of the JSA Regulations 2013 do not apply. That appears to mean that, if such a claimant who has income from new style JSA topped up by universal credit commits a sanctionable failure, the amount of the JSA award cannot be reduced and only the amount of the universal credit top-up can be available for reduction under the universal credit sanctions provisions. See further the annotations to reg.5.

Another important common concept is that of a "good reason" for the conduct or failure to comply with a requirement under either form of the Jobseekers Act 1995 or the Welfare Reform Act 2012. Most of the definitions of sanctionable failures in ss.6J and 6K incorporate the condition that the failure was "for no good reason". Paragraph 14AA of Sch.1 to the new style Jobseekers Act 1995 allows regulations to prescribe circumstances in which a claimant is to be treated as having or as not having a good reason for an act or omission and to prescribe matters that are or are not to be taken into account in determining whether a claimant has a good reason. No regulations have been made under this power. There is no equivalent to reg.72 of the JSA Regulations 1996 (but the problem dealt with there is covered by the allowance of limitations of work search and work availability requirements in new style JSA).

Thus, the concept remains a fairly open-ended one, no doubt requiring consideration of all relevant circumstances but also containing a large element of judgment according to the individual facts of particular cases. The amount and quality of information provided to the claimant in the claimant commitment or otherwise about responsibilities under the new style Jobseekers Act 1995 and the consequences of a failure to comply will no doubt be relevant, especially in the light of the approach of the Supreme Court in paras 65 and 66 of *R (on the application of Reilly and Wilson) v Secretary of State for Work and Pensions* [2013] UKSC 68, [2014] 1 A.C. 453 (see the notes to s.6A above). Probably, in addition, as in the previously familiar concept of "just cause", a balancing is required between the interests of the claimant and those of the community of those whose contributions and taxes finance the benefit in question. See the extended discussion under the heading of "Without a good reason" in the note to s.19 of the old style Jobseekers Act 1995 in Pt I.

However, there is a potentially significant difference in wording. In ss.6J and 6K 6.55
the condition is that the claimant fails "for no good reason", not that the claimant acts or omits to act "without a good reason" (as in ss.19 and 19A of the old style Jobseekers Act 1995). It may eventually be established that these two phrases have the same meaning, but in the ordinary use of language the phrase "for no good reason" carries a suggestion that something has been done or not done capriciously or arbitrarily, without any real thought or application of reason. It could therefore

be argued that it is easier for a claimant to show that s/he did not act for no good reason and on that basis that the balancing of interests mentioned above could not be applicable. It would be enough that the claimant acted or failed to act rationally in the light of his or her own interests. It can of course be objected that such an argument fails to give the proper weight to the identification of what is a *good* reason and that it would seem contrary to the overall policy of the legislation if it was much easier to escape a new style JSA (or universal credit) sanction than an old style JSA sanction. On the other hand, it can be asked why Parliament chose to use a different phrase for the purposes of new style JSA and universal credit sanctions than "without a good reason" when the latter phrase could have fitted happily into s.6J and 6K. It is to be hoped that the ambiguity will be resolved in early decisions of the Upper Tribunal.

Subsections (2) and (3) set out what can be a sanctionable failure for the purposes of s.6J and higher-level sanctions. Subsections (4)–(7) give regulation-making powers. These provisions are substantially identical to s.26 of the Welfare Reform Act 2012 on universal credit with the omission of subs.(3) which is relevant only to the special case of a person being entitled to universal credit while in substantial work.

Subsection (2)

6.56 (a) It is a higher-level sanctionable failure for a claimant to fail for no good reason (on which see the note above) to comply with a work preparation requirement under s.6C to undertake a work placement of a description prescribed in regulations. Regulation 29(1) of the JSA Regulations 2013 prescribes Mandatory Work Activity as a work placement for the purposes of this provision. Regulation 29(2) as substituted with effect from April 29, 2013 provides a description of the nature of that scheme that is probably sufficient for the scheme to be validly prescribed for the purposes of subs.(2)(a) in accordance with the principles adopted by the Supreme Court in *R (on the application of Reilly and Wilson) v Secretary of State for Work and Pensions* [2013] UKSC 68; [2014] 1 A.C. 453. See also the decision of the Court of Appeal in *Smith v Secretary of State for Work and Pensions* [2015] EWCA Civ 229. The same amendment was made to reg.114 of the UC Regulations, but was by mistake omitted from the 2013/14 edition of Vol.V, *Universal Credit*.

Before undertaking a Mandatory Work Activity scheme can have become a work preparation requirement under s.6C it must have been specified for the claimant in question by the Secretary of State. The requirement is to take the action specified by the Secretary of State, so that the detail of the specification will be important in determining what amounts to a failure to comply with the requirement. There will be familiar issues, e.g. whether turning up to a scheme and then declining to co-operate or doing so only grudgingly amounts to a failure to comply. See *SA v SSWP (JSA)* [2015] UKUT 454 (AAC), discussed in the notes to s.19A(2)(c) of the old style Jobseekers Act 1995 in Pt I, on when turning up late (or some similarly minor infraction of the scheme's requirements) might not amount to a failure to participate in the scheme, regardless of issues of good reason. On what might be a good reason for not undertaking a scheme, see the example (no more than that) of a genuinely held fear preventing travel to the town where the scheme was to take place (*GR v SSWP (JSA)* [2013] UKUT 645 (AAC)).

(b) It is a higher-level sanctionable failure for a claimant to fail for no good reason (on which see the note above) to comply with a work search requirement under s.6D to apply for a particular vacancy for paid work. It would seem that for there to have been a requirement to apply for a particular vacancy the taking of that action must have been specified by the Secretary of State under s.6D(1)(b). See the note to s.6D for discussion of the meaning of "paid work" and of the guidance to Jobcentre Plus staff that claimants should not be required to apply for a vacancy involving a zero hours contract. Thus no sanction should arise under the present provision for failing to apply for such a vacancy, although if such a requirement was in fact imposed, it would be arguable that the nature of the contract, especially if prior to May 26,

2015 (Employment Rights Act 1996, s.27A) it contained an enforceable exclusivity clause, constituted a good reason for failing to apply. It appears in the nature of the word "vacancy" that it is for employment as an employed earner, or possibly some form of self-employment that is closely analogous to such employment, e.g. through an agency. In *MT v SSWP (JSA)* [2016] UKUT 72 (AAC) doubts were expressed whether registration with an employment agency could fall within s.19(2)(c) of the old style Jobseekers Act 1995, at least without evidence of some specific vacancy.

Regulation 11 of the JSA Regulations 2013 deems a claimant not to have complied with a requirement to apply for a particular vacancy for paid work where the claimant fails to participate in an interview offered in connection with the vacancy. Participation must at least entail turning up at the place and time for the interview and extend to making some meaningful contribution to the interview, but the limits will probably not be established until there have been some more sanctions appeals to the Upper Tribunal. Behaviour that leads to the premature termination of the interview may well amount to a failure to participate (see the facts of *DM v SSWP (JSA)* [2015] UKUT 67 (AAC) in the notes to s.19A(2)(c) of the old style Jobseekers Act 1995. There may, though, in cases of uncooperative claimants or heavy-handed officials or a combination, be difficult questions about when an interview has ceased to exist, so that subsequent behaviour cannot be relevant to whether there has been a failure to participate (see *PH v SSWP (ESA)* [2016] UKUT 119 (AAC) on failing to submit to a medical examination). That is the context in which what amounts to a failure to comply will be identified, as well as what might amount to a good reason for non-compliance. For instance, there appear to be no provisions prescribing the length of notice of an interview to be given or how far a claimant can be required to travel, but there could plainly be a good reason for failing to comply with unreasonable requirements, especially if the claimant had attempted in advance to draw any problem with attendance to the attention of the Secretary of State or the potential employer. Another example (no more than that) might a genuinely held fear preventing travel to the town where the interview was to take place (*GR v SSWP (JSA)* [2013] UKUT 645 (AAC). See the discussion in the note to s.19(2)(c) of the old style Jobseekers Act 1995 in Pt I for what might amount to refusing to apply. See also reg.28(1)(a) of the JSA Regulations 2013 excluding consideration of vacancies due to strikes arising from trade disputes.

(c) It is a higher-level sanctionable failure for a claimant to fail for no good reason **6.57** (on which see the note above) to comply with a work availability requirement under s.6E by not taking up an offer of paid work. See the note to s.6D for discussion of the meaning of "paid work" and for the approach to zero hours contracts. Since the requirement under s.6E is in the very general terms of being able and willing immediately to take up paid work, the relevance of not taking up an offer can only be in revealing an absence of such ability or willingness. Therefore, both any limitations under reg.14 of the JSA Regulations 2013 on the kinds of paid work that a claimant must be able and willing to take up immediately and the provisions of reg.13(2)–(5) on when a claimant is deemed to have complied with the requirement despite not being able to satisfy the "immediately" condition must be taken into account in determining whether a claimant has failed to comply with the requirement. See the discussion in the note to s.19(2)(c) of the old style Jobseekers Act 1995 in Pt I for what might amount to refusing or failing without a good reason to accept a situation, if offered, in any employment, but note that there may be differences between failing to accept a situation in employment and failing to accept an offer of paid work. See also reg.28(1)(a) of the JSA Regulations 2013 excluding consideration of vacancies due to strikes arising from trade disputes. An example (no more than that) of what might be a good reason for not taking up an offer might a genuinely held fear preventing travel to the town where the job was located (*GR v SSWP (JSA)* [2013] UKUT 645 (AAC).

(d) It is a higher-level sanctionable failure for a claimant to cease paid work or lose pay by reason of misconduct or voluntarily and for no good reason (on which see the note above). Subsection (3)(b) below covers such circumstances occurring before the claim for JSA is made, but this provision can apply while a claimant is in receipt of benefit and working at a level not sufficient to amount to "remunerative work" under s.1(2)(e). See the note to s.6D for discussion of the meaning of "paid work". See the note to subs.(4) below for discussion of the meanings of "misconduct" and "voluntarily and for no good reason", as well as of the implications of fixed and severe sanctions for losing pay apparently no matter what the amount of loss, subject to the possible application of exceptions in reg.28(1) of the JSA Regulations 2013. See reg.28(1)(b) (trial periods in work where the claimant attempts hours additional to a limitation under ss.6D(4) or 16E(3)); (d) (voluntarily ceasing paid work or losing pay because of a strike); (e) (voluntarily ceasing paid work or losing pay as a member of the regular or reserve forces); and (f) (volunteering for redundancy or lay-off or short-time). According to the then Minister of State Esther McVey (House of Commons written answers April 2, 2014), guidance to Jobcentre Plus staff is that if a JSA claimant leaves a zero hours contract there should be no sanction for misconduct or voluntarily ceasing work.

Subsection (3)

6.58 It is a higher-level sanctionable failure if before making the claim relevant to the award the claimant for no good reason failed to take up an offer of paid work (para.(a)) or by reason of misconduct or voluntarily and for no good reason ceased paid work or lost pay (para.(b)). A practical limit to how far back before the date of claim such action or inaction can be to lead to a reduction of benefit is set by regs 19(3) and 28(1)(c) of the JSA Regulations 2013. If the gap between the action or inaction and the date of claim is longer than or equal to the period of the reduction that would otherwise be imposed, there is to be no reduction. Thus a lot depends on whether it is a first, second or subsequent "offence" within a year. These two grounds of sanction are the most similar to the familiar unemployment benefit and JSA grounds now in s.19(2)(a), (b) and (c) of the old style Jobseekers Act 1995.

Under subs.(3)(a), see the discussion in the note to subs.(2)(c), but note that this sanction applies to any offer of paid work. Therefore, all questions of whether the work is suitable for the claimant and whether or not it was reasonable for the claimant not to take it up will have to be considered under the "no good reason" condition. See the introductory part of the note to this section for the meaning of that phrase as compared with "without a good reason".

Under para.(b), it would appear that misconduct and voluntarily ceasing work will have the same general meaning as misconduct and leaving employment voluntarily for the purposes of old style JSA and, before it, unemployment benefit. See the extensive discussion in the notes to s.19(2)(a) and (b) of the old style Jobseekers Act 1995 in Pt I. The scope of the sanction has to be slightly wider to take account of the possibility of becoming entitled to JSA while still working part-time. Ceasing paid work certainly has a significantly wider meaning than losing employment as an employed earner if it encompasses self-employment in addition, as suggested in the note to s.6D. The notion of ceasing paid work seems in itself wider than that of losing employment and to avoid difficulties over whether suspension from work without dismissal and particular ways of bringing a contract of employment to an end are covered. But remember that under reg.28(1)(f) of the JSA Regulations 2013 a reduction cannot be applied on the ground of voluntarily ceasing paid work where the claimant has volunteered for redundancy or has claimed a redundancy payment after being subject to lay-off or short-time working, although the action remains a sanctionable failure. See also the exceptions for voluntarily ceasing paid work or losing pay because of a strike arising from a trade dispute or as a member of the regular or reserve forces (reg.28(1)(d) and (e)). According to the then Minister of State Esther McVey (House of Commons written answers April 2, 2014), guidance to Jobcentre Plus staff is that if a JSA claimant leaves a zero hours contract there should be no sanction for misconduct or voluntarily ceasing work. However, it is hard to see the legal basis for such guidance. If a claimant did have employment (even though under a zero hours contract) and committed an act of misconduct that led to its loss, that would appear to be a sanctionable failure requiring a reduction of benefit in the absence of any legislative exemption. Similarly, ceasing such employment would appear to bring the legislation into play but the terms of the contract might contribute to a good reason for ceasing the employment.

The other particularly significant widening of the scope of the sanction as compared with those in old style JSA is in the application of this and the similar sanctions under previous subsections to losing pay as well as to ceasing paid work. This is necessary, both in relation to circumstances before the date of claim and later, because it is possible for a claimant to be entitled to new style JSA while still in some paid work.

Subsection (4)

Regulations may deem ceasing work or losing pay not to be by reason of misconduct or voluntarily in certain circumstances and may provide that loss of pay below a prescribed level is to be disregarded. No such regulations have been made. Regulation 28 of the JSA Regulations 2013 is made under the powers in subs.(7)(a) and only affects whether a reduction in benefit is to be imposed, not whether there is or is not a sanctionable failure. **6.59**

Subsections (5) and (6)

See regs 18 and 19 and 22–27 of the JSA Regulations 2013 for the amount and period of the reduction in benefit under a higher-level sanction. The three-year-limit is imposed in subs.(5)(b) and cannot be extended in regulations. **6.60**

Subsection (7)

Under para.(a), see reg.28 of the JSA Regulations 2013. Under para.(b), see reg.23. Under para.(c), see regs 24 and 25. **6.61**

[1 Other sanctions

6K.—(1) The amount of an award of a jobseeker's allowance is to be reduced in accordance with this section in the event of a failure by a claimant which is sanctionable under this section. **6.62**

(2) It is a failure sanctionable under this section if a claimant—

(a) fails for no good reason to comply with a work-related requirement;

(b) fails for no good reason to comply with a requirement under section 6G.

(3) But a failure by a claimant is not sanctionable under this section if it is also a failure sanctionable under section 6J.

(4) Regulations must specify—

(a) the amount of a reduction under this section;

(b) the period for which such a reduction has effect.

(5) Regulations under subsection (4)(b) may provide that a reduction under this section in relation to any failure is to have effect for—

(a) a period continuing until the claimant meets a compliance condition specified by the Secretary of State,

(b) a fixed period not exceeding 26 weeks which is—

(i) specified in the regulations, or

(ii) determined in any case by the Secretary of State, or

(c) a combination of both.

(6) In subsection (5)(a) "compliance condition" means—

(a) a condition that the failure ceases, or

(b) a condition relating to future compliance with a work-related requirement or a requirement under section 6G.

(7) A compliance condition specified under subsection (5)(a) may be—

(a) revoked or varied by the Secretary of State;

(b) notified to the claimant in such manner as the Secretary of State may determine.

(8) A period fixed under subsection (5)(b) may in particular depend on either or both the following—

(a) the number of failures by the claimant sanctionable under this section;

(b) the period between such failures.

(9) Regulations may provide—

(a) for cases in which no reduction is to be made under this section;

(b) for a reduction under this section made in relation to an award that is terminated to be applied to any new award made within a prescribed period of the termination;

(c) for the termination or suspension of a reduction under this section.]

AMENDMENT

1. Welfare Reform Act 2012 s.49(3) (trigger date on or after April 29, 2013).

DEFINITIONS

"claimant"—see s.35(1).
"regulations"—*ibid.*
"work-related requirement"—see ss.35(1) and 6(2).

GENERAL NOTE

6.63 See the introductory part of the annotations to s.6J for the general nature of the new style JSA sanctions regime under ss.6J and 6K and for discussion of the meaning of "for no good reason". Section 6K(1) and (2) requires there to be a reduction, of the amount and period set out in regulations, wherever the claimant has failed for no good reason to comply with any work-related requirement or a connected requirement under s.6G. There is no general discretion whether or not to apply the prescribed deduction, but that is subject to the rule in subs.(3) that if a failure is sanctionable under s.6J (and therefore potentially subject to the higher-level regime) it is not to be sanctionable under s.6K. Note also the important effect of reg.5 of the JSA Regulations 2013 (discussed in the note to s.6J) where a claimant is also entitled to universal credit.

While the duty and power under subs.(4) for regulations to provide for the amount and period of the reduction to be imposed is in fact more open-ended than that in s.6J(5), because it does not have the three-year limit, subss.(5)–(7) introduce the specific power (that did not of course have to be used) for regulations to provide for the period of the reduction for a particular sanctionable failure to continue until the claimant meets a "compliance condition" (subs.(6)) or for a fixed period not exceeding 26 weeks specified in regulations or determined by the Secretary of State or a combination of both. The 26-week limit in subs.(5)(b) appears not to have any decisive effect because a longer period could always be prescribed under subs.(4)(b), unless "may" in subs.(5) is to be construed as meaning "may only". In practice, the powers have been used in the JSA Regulations 2013 to set up a structure of medium-level (regs 17 and 20) and low-level (regs 17 and 21) sanctions. See the annotations to those regulations for the details.

The medium-level sanction, by virtue of the definition in reg.17, applies only to failures to comply with a work search requirement under s.6D(1)(a) to take all reasonable action to obtain paid work etc or to comply with a work availability requirement under s.6E(1). A failure to comply with a work search requirement under s.6D(1)(b) to apply for a particular vacancy attracts a higher-level sanction under s.6J(2)(b). The reduction period under reg.20 is 28 days for a first "offence" and 91 days for a second "offence" or subsequent offence within a year of the previous failure (which also includes medium-level universal credit sanctions).

The low-level sanction, by virtue of the definition in reg.17, applies where the claimant fails to comply with a work-focused interview requirement under s.6B(1), a work preparation requirement under s.6C(1), a work search requirement under s.6D(1)(b) to take any specified action specified by the Secretary of State or a connected requirement in s.6G. The reduction period under reg.20 lasts until the claimant complies with the requirement in question or the award of JSA terminates, plus seven days for a first "offence", 14 days for a second "offence" within a year of the previous failure and 28 days for a third or subsequent "offence" within a year (which also includes a low-level universal credit or employment and support allowance sanction). 6.64

For the purposes of reg.21, "compliance condition" is defined in subs.(6) to mean either a condition that the failure to comply ceases or a condition relating to future compliance. A compliance condition may be revoked or varied by the Secretary of State, apparently at will, and may be (not must be) notified to the claimant in such manner as the Secretary of State may determine (subs.(7)). But under reg.21 a compliance condition has to be "specified" by the Secretary of State. On the one hand, it is difficult to envisage it being decided that the Secretary of State can specify such a condition to himself, rather than to the claimant. On the other hand, it is difficult to envisage it being decided that a claimant who has in fact complied with a requirement has not met a compliance condition merely because the Secretary of State failed to give proper notice of the condition.

Note that reg.28 of the JSA Regulations 2013, prescribing circumstances in which no reduction is to be made for a sanctionable failure, does not apply to s.6K, only to s.6J.

Under para.(b) of subs.(9), see reg.23. Under para.(c), see regs 24 and 25.

[1 Delegation and contracting out

6L.—(1) The functions of the Secretary of State under sections 6 to 6I may be exercised by, or by the employees of, such person as the Secretary of State may authorise for the purpose (an "authorised person"). 6.65

(2) An authorisation given by virtue of this section may authorise the exercise of a function—

(a) wholly or to a limited extent;

(b) generally or in particular cases or areas;

(c) unconditionally or subject to conditions.

(3) An authorisation under this section—

(a) may specify its duration;

(b) may be varied or revoked at any time by the Secretary of State;

(c) does not prevent the Secretary of State or another person from exercising the function to which the authorisation relates.

(4) Anything done or omitted to be done by or in relation to an authorised person (or an employee of that person) in, or in connection with, the exercise or purported exercise of the function concerned is to be treated for all purposes as done or omitted to be done by or in relation to the Secretary of State or (as the case may be) an officer of the Secretary of State.

(5) Subsection (4) does not apply—

(a) for the purposes of so much of any contract made between the authorised person and the Secretary of State as relates to the exercise of the function, or

(b) for the purposes of any criminal proceedings brought in respect of anything done or omitted to be done by the authorised person (or an employee of that person).

(6) Where—

(a) the authorisation of an authorised person is revoked, and

(b) at the time of the revocation so much of any contract made between the authorised person and the Secretary of State as relates to the exercise of the function is subsisting, the authorised person is entitled to treat the contract as repudiated by the Secretary of State (and not as frustrated by reason of the revocation).]

AMENDMENT

1. Welfare Reform Act 2012 s.49(3) (trigger date on or after April 29, 2013).

DEFINITION

"person"—see Interpretation Act 1978 Sch.1.

GENERAL NOTE

6.66 This section allows the Secretary of State to authorise other persons (which word in accordance with the Interpretation Act 1978 includes corporate and unincorporated associations, such as companies) and their employees to carry out any of his functions under s.6–6I. Any such authorisation will not in practice cover the making of regulations, but may well (depending on the extent of the authorisations given) extend to specifying various matters under those sections. The involvement of private sector organisations, operating for profit, in running various schemes within the scope of the benefit system is something that claimants sometimes object to. Such a generalised objection, even if on principled grounds, is unlikely to amount in itself to a good reason for failing to engage with a scheme in question (although see the discussion in the note to s.6J on whether "for no good reason" has a restricted meaning). An objection based on previous experience with the organisation concerned or the nature of the course may raise more difficult issues. See also the discussion in *R(JSA) 7/03* plus *CSJSA/495/2007* and *CSJSA/505/2007.*

Jobseeker's agreement: reviews and appeals

6.67 **11.**—[*Repealed.*]

Income and capital

Income and capital: general

6.68 **12.**—(1) In relation to a claim for a jobseeker's allowance, the income and capital of a person shall be calculated or estimated in such manner as may be prescribed.

(2) A person's income in respect of a week shall be calculated in accordance with prescribed rules.

(3) The rules may provide for the calculation to be made by reference to an average over a period (which need not include the week concerned).

(4) Circumstances may be prescribed in which–

(a) a person is treated as possessing capital or income which he does not possess;
(b) capital or income which a person does possess is to be disregarded;
(c) income is to be treated as capital;
(d) capital is to be treated as income.

DEFINITIONS

"prescribed"—see s.35(1).
"week"—*ibid.*

Income and capital: income-based jobseeker's allowance

6.69 **13.**—[1 . . .].

AMENDMENT

1. Welfare Reform Act 2012 Sch.14 Pt 1 (trigger date on or after April 29, 2013).

Trade disputes

Trade disputes

14.—(1) Where— 6.70

(a) there is a stoppage of work which causes a person not to be employed on any day, and

(b) the stoppage is due to a trade dispute at his place of work,

that person is not entitled to a jobseeker's allowance for the week which includes that day unless he proves that he is not directly interested in the dispute.

(2) A person who withdraws his labour on any day in furtherance of a trade dispute, but to whom subsection (1) does not apply, is not entitled to a jobseeker's allowance for the week which includes that day.

(3) If a person who is prevented by subsection (1) from being entitled to a jobseeker's allowance proves that during the stoppage—

(a) he became bona fide employed elsewhere;

(b) his employment was terminated by reason of redundancy within the meaning of section 139(1) of the Employment Rights Act 1996, or

(c) the bona fide resumed employment with his employer but subsequently left for a reason other than the trade dispute,

subsection (1) shall be taken to have ceased to apply to him on the occurrence of the event referred to in paragraph (a) or (b) or (as the case may be) the first event referred to in paragraph (c).

(4) In this section "place of work", in relation to any person, means the premises or place at which he was employed.

(5) Where separate branches of work which are commonly carried on as separate businesses in separate premises or at separate places are in any case carried on in separate departments on the same premises or at the same place, each of those departments shall, for the purposes of subsection (4), be deemed to be separate premises or (as the case may be) a separate place.

DEFINITIONS

"employment"—see s.35(1) and reg.2(1) of the JSA Regulations 2013.
"entitled"—se s.35(1).
"trade dispute"—*ibid.*
"week"—*ibid.*

GENERAL NOTE

See the annotations to s.14 of the old style Jobseekers Act 1995 in Pt I of this Volume. 6.71

Effect on other claimants

15.—[1 . . .]. 6.72

AMENDMENT

1. Welfare Reform Act 2012 Sch.14 Pt 1 (trigger date on or after April 29, 2013).

Trade disputes: joint-claim couples

6.73 **15A.**—[1 . . .].

AMENDMENT

1. Welfare Reform Act 2012 Sch.14 Pt 1 (trigger date on or after April 29, 2013).

Persons under 18

Severe hardship

6.74 **16.**—[1 . . .].

AMENDMENT

1. Welfare Reform Act 2012 Sch.14 Pt 1 (trigger date on or after April 29, 2013).

Reduced payments

6.75 **17.**—[1. . .].

AMENDMENT

1. Welfare Reform Act 2012 Sch.14 Pt 1 (trigger date on or after April 29, 2013).

"Work for your benefit schemes etc.

Schemes for assisting persons to obtain employment: "work for your benefit schemes etc.

6.76 **17A.**—[1. . .].

AMENDMENT

1. Welfare Reform Act 2012 Sch.14 Pt 4, in so far as not already repealed by other Parts of Sch.14 (trigger date on or after April 29, 2013).

Section 17A: supplemental

6.77 **17B.**—[1. . .].

AMENDMENT

1. Welfare Reform Act 2012 Sch.14 Pt 4 (trigger date on or after April 29, 2013).

Persons dependent on drugs etc

Persons dependent on drugs etc.

6.78 **17C.**—[1. . .].

AMENDMENT

1. Welfare Reform Act 2012 s.60(1) (May 8, 2012).

Recovery of overpayments

18.—[*Omitted as amending s.71A of the Social Security Administration Act 1992*] 6.79

Denial of jobseeker's allowance

Higher-level sanctions

19.—[[1]. . .]. 6.80

AMENDMENT

1. Welfare Reform Act 2012 Sch.14 Pt 4 (trigger date on or after April 29, 2013), repealing the provision as substituted by s.46(1) with effect from October 22, 2012.

Other sanctions

19A.—[[1]. . .]. 6.81

AMENDMENT

1. Welfare Reform Act 2012 Sch.14 Pt 4 (trigger date on or after April 29, 2013), repealing the provision as substituted by s.46(1) with effect from October 22, 2012.

Claimants ceasing to be available for employment etc.

19B.—[[1]. . .]. 6.82

AMENDMENT

1. Welfare Reform Act 2012 Sch.14 Pt 4 (trigger date on or after April 29, 2013), repealing the provision as substituted by s.46(1) with effect from October 22, 2012.

Hardship payments

19C.—[[1]. . .]. 6.83

AMENDMENT

1. Welfare Reform Act 2012 Sch.14 Part 4 (trigger date on or after April 29, 2013), repealing the provision as substituted by s.46(1) with effect from October 22, 2012, if that substitution ever came into effect.

Exemptions from section 19 and 19A

20.—(1) – (3) [[2]. . .]. 6.84
(4)–(6) [[1]. . .].
(7) and (8) [[2]. . .].

AMENDMENTS

1. Welfare Reform Act 2012 Sch.14 Pt 3 (October 22, 2012).
2. Welfare Reform Act 2012 Sch.14 Pt 4 (trigger date on or after April 29, 2013).

Denial or reduction of joint-claim jobseeker's allowance

6.85 **20A.**—[1. . .].

AMENDMENT

1. Welfare Reform Act 2012 Sch.14 Part 3 (October 22, 2012).

6.86 **20B.**—[1. . .].

AMENDMENT

1. Welfare Reform Act 2012 Sch.14 Part 3 (October 22, 2012).

Sanctions for violent conduct etc. in connection with claim

6.87 **20C.**—[1. . .].

AMENDMENT

1. Welfare Reform Act 2012 Sch.7 Pt 6 (October 22, 2012), although the section appears never have to been brought into operation.

Section 20C: supplementary

6.88 **20D.**—[1. . .].

AMENDMENT

1. Welfare Reform Act 2012 Sch.7 Pt 6 (October 22, 2012), although the section appears never have to been brought into operation.

Miscellaneous

Contracting out

6.89 **20E.**—[1. . .].

AMENDMENT

1. Welfare Reform Act 2012 Sch.14 Pt 4 (trigger date on or after April 29, 2013).

Supplementary provisions

6.90 **21.**—Further provisions in relation to jobseeker's allowance are set out in Schedule 1.

Members of the forces

6.91 **22.**—(1) Regulations may modify any provision of this Act, in such manner as the Secretary of State thinks proper, in its application to persons who are or have been members of Her Majesty's forces.

(2) [1. . .].

(3) For the purposes of this section, Her Majesty's forces shall be taken to consist of such establishments and organisations in which persons serve under the control of the Defence Council as may be prescribed.

AMENDMENT

1. Welfare Reform Act 2012 Sch.14 Pt 4 (trigger date on or after April 29, 2013).

DEFINITION

"regulations"—see s.35(1).

Recovery of sums in respect of maintenance

23.—[[1]. . .]. 6.92

AMENDMENT

1. Welfare Reform Act 2012 Sch.14 Pt 1 (trigger date on or after April 29, 2013).

Effect of alteration of rates

24.—[*Omitted as amending the Social Security Administration Act 1992.*] 6.93

Age increases

25.—[[1]. . .]. 6.94

AMENDMENT

1. Welfare Reform Act 2012 Sch.14 Pt 1 (trigger date on or after April 29, 2013).

PART II

BACK TO WORK SCHEMES

The back to work bonus

26.—[[1]. . .]. 6.95

AMENDMENT

1. Welfare Reform Act 2012 Sch.14 Pt 1 (trigger date on or after April 29, 2013).

Employment of long-term unemployed: deductions by employers

27.—[*Omitted.*] 6.96

Expedited claims for council tax benefit and housing benefit

28.—[[1]. . .]. 6.97

AMENDMENT

1. Welfare Reform Act 2012 Sch.14 Pt 1 (trigger date on or after April 29, 2013).

Pilot schemes

29.—(1) Any regulations to which this subsection applies may be made so as to have effect for a specified period not exceeding 36 months. 6.98

(2) Any regulations which, by virtue of subsection (1), are to have effect for a limited period are referred to in this section as "a pilot scheme".

(3) A pilot scheme may provide that its provisions are to apply only in relation to—

(a) one or more specified areas or localities;
(b) one or more specified classes of person;
(c) persons selected—

(i) by reference to prescribed criteria; or
(ii) on a sampling basis.

(4) A pilot scheme may make consequential or transitional provision with respect to the cessation of the scheme on the expiry of the specified period.

(5) A pilot scheme ("the previous scheme") may be replaced by a further pilot scheme making the same, or similar, provision (apart from the specified period) to that made by the previous scheme.

(6) Subject to subsection (8), subsection (1) applies to—

(a) regulations made under this Act, other than—
(i) regulations made under section 4(2) or (5) which have the effect of reducing any age-related amount or applicable amount; or
(ii) regulations made under section 27;
(b) regulations made under the Administration Act, so far as they relate to a jobseeker's allowance;
(c) regulations made under Part VII of the Benefits Act (income-related benefits), other than any mentioned in subsection (7); and
(d) regulations made under the Administration Act, so far as they relate to income- related benefits payable under Part VII of the Benefits Act.

(7) The regulations referred to in subsection (6)(c) are—

(a) [*repealed*];
(b) [*repealed*];
(c) regulations under section 130(4) of that Act which have the effect of reducing the appropriate maximum housing benefit;
(d) regulations under section 131(10)(a) of that Act which have the effect of reducing the appropriate maximum council tax benefit; and
(e) regulations reducing any of the sums prescribed under section 135(1) of that Act.

(8) Subsection (1) applies only if the regulations are made with a view to [[1]testing the extent to which the provision made by the regulations is likely to promote—

(a) people remaining in work, or
(b) people obtaining or being able to obtain work (or more work or better-paid work).]

AMENDMENT

1. Welfare Reform Act 2012 s.49(4) (trigger date on or after April 29, 2013).

DEFINITIONS

"the Administration Act"—see s.35(1).
"the Benefits Act"—*ibid.*
"regulations"—*ibid.*

GENERAL NOTE

6.99 See the annotations to s.29 of the old style Jobseekers Act 1995 in Pt I of this volume.

Grants for resettlement places

6.100 **30.**—[*Omitted*].

PART III

MISCELLANEOUS AND SUPPLEMENTAL

Termination of awards

31.—[1. . .]. 6.101

AMENDMENT

1. Welfare Reform Act 2012 Sch.14 Pt 1 (trigger date on or after April 29, 2013).

Insolvency

32.—[*Omitted as amending the Social Security Administration Act 1992.*] 6.102

Offences

33.—[*Repealed.*] 6.103

Offences

34.—[*Repealed.*] 6.104

Interpretation

35.—(1) In this Act— 6.105

"the Administration Act" means the Social Security Administration Act 1992;

"applicable amount" means the applicable amount determined in accordance with regulations under section 4;

"benefit year" has the meaning given by section 2(4);

"the Benefits Act" means the Social Security Contributions and Benefits Act 1992;

"child" means a person under the age of 16;

"claimant" means a person who claims a jobseeker's allowance [2. . .];

"continental shelf operations" has the same meaning as in section 120 of the Benefits Act;

"contribution-based conditions" means the conditions set out in section 2;

[2. . .];

[4 "couple" means—

(a) two people who are married to, or civil partners of, each other and are members of the same household; or

(b) two people who are not married, or civil partners of, each other but are living together as a married couple otherwise than in prescribed purposes;]

"employed earner" has the meaning prescribed for the purposes of this Act;

"employment", [3. . .], has the meaning prescribed for the purposes of this Act;

[3. . .];

"entitled", in relation to a jobseeker's allowance, is to be construed in accordance with—
(a) the provisions of this Act relating to entitlement; and
(b) sections 1 of the Administration Act and section 27 of the Social Security Act 1998.

"family" means—
(a) a couple;
(b) a couple and a member of the same household for whom one of them is, or both are, responsible and who is a child or a person of a prescribed description;
(c) except in prescribed circumstances, a person who is not a member of a couple and a member of the same household for whom that person is responsible and who is a child or a person of a prescribed description;

"FAS payments" means payments made under the Financial Assistance Scheme Regulations 2005;

"Great Britain" includes the territorial waters of the United Kingdom adjacent to Great Britain;

[2. . .];

[3. . .];

"jobseeking period" has the meaning prescribed for the purposes of this Act;

[3. . .];

[2. . .];

"occupational pension scheme" has the same meaning as it has in the Pension Schemes Act 1993 by virtue of section 1 of that Act;

"pensionable age" has the meaning prescribed for the purposes of this Act;

"pension payments" means—
(a) periodical payments made in relation to a person, under a personal pension scheme or, in connection with the coming to an end of an employment of his, under an occupational pension scheme or a public service pension scheme; and
(b) such other payments as may be prescribed;

"personal pension scheme" means—
(a) a personal pension scheme as defined by section 1 of the Pension Schemes Act 1993;
(b) an annuity contract or trust scheme approved under section 620 or 621 of the Income and Corporation Taxes Act 1988 or a substituted contract within the meaning of section 622(3) of that Act which is treated as having become a registered pension scheme by virtue of paragraph 1(1)(f) of Schedule 36 to the Finance Act 2004; and
(c) a personal pension scheme approved under Chapter 4 of Part 14 of the Income and Corporation Taxes Act 1988 which is treated as having become a registered pension scheme by virtue of paragraph 1(1)(g) of Schedule 36 to the Finance Act 2004;]

"PPF payments" means any payments made in relation to a person—
(a) payable under the pension compensation provisions as specified in section 162(2) of the Pensions Act 2004 or Article 146(2) of the Pensions (Northern Ireland) Order 2005 (the pension compensation provisions); or
(b) payable under section 166 of the Pensions Act 2004 or Article

150 of the Pensions (Northern Ireland) Order 2005 (duty to pay scheme benefits unpaid at assessment date etc.);

"prescribed", except in section 27 (and in section 36 so far as relating to regulations under section 27), means specified in or determined in accordance with regulations;

"public service pension scheme" has the same meaning as it has in the Pension Schemes Act 1993 by virtue of section 1 of that Act;

"regulations" means regulations made by the Secretary of State;

"tax year", except in section 27 (and in section 36 so far relating to regulations under section 27), means the 12 months beginning with 6th April in any year;

"trade dispute" means any dispute between employers and employees, or between employees and employees, which is connected with the employment or non-employment or the terms of employment or the conditions of employment of any persons, whether employees in the employment of the employer with whom the dispute arises, or not;

[3. . .];

"week" means a period of 7 days beginning with a Sunday or such other period of 7 days as may be prescribed;

"work" has the meaning prescribed for the purposes of this Act;

[1"work availability requirement" has the meaning given by section 6E;

"work preparation requirement" has the meaning given by section 6C;

"work search requirement" has the meaning given by section 6D;

"work-focused interview requirement" has the meaning given by section 6B;

"work-related requirement" has the meaning given by section 6;]

"year", except in the expression "benefit year", means a tax year.

(1A) [4 . . .]

(2) The expressions "limited capability for work", "linked period", "relevant education" and "remunerative work" are to be read with paragraphs 2, 3, 14 and 1 of Schedule 1.

(3) Subject to any regulations made for the purposes of this subsection, "earnings" is to be construed for the purposes of this Act in accordance with section 3 of the Benefits Act and paragraph 6 of Schedule 1 to this Act.

AMENDMENTS

1. Welfare Reform Act 2012 s.49(5) (trigger date on or after April 29, 2013).
2. Welfare Reform Act 2012 Sch.14 Pt 1 (trigger date on or after April 29, 2013).
3. Welfare Reform Act 2012 Sch.14 Pt 4 (trigger date on or after April 29, 2013).
4. Marriage (Same Sex Couples) Act 2013 (Consequential and Contrary Provisions and Scotland) Order 2014 (SI 2014/516) art.2 and Sch.1 para.26 (March 13, 2014 in relation to England and Wales); Marriage and Civil Partnership (Scotland) Act 2014 and Civil Partnership Act 2004 (Consequential Provisions and Modifications) Order 2014 (SI 2014/3229) art.29 and Sch.5 para.12 (December 16, 2014 in relation to Scotland).

GENERAL NOTE

See the annotations to the relevant definitions in s.35(1) of the old style Jobseekers Act in Pt I of this volume. **6.106**

Regulations and orders

6.107 **36.**—(1) Any power under this Act to make regulations or orders, other than an order under section 8(3), 9(13, 16(4) or 19(10)(a), shall be exercisable by statutory instrument.

(1A) [1. . .]

(2) Any such power may be exercised—

(a) either in relation to all cases to which it extends, or in relation to those cases subject to specified exceptions, or in relation to any specified cases or classes of case;

(b) so as to make, as respects the cases in relation to which it is exercised—

(i) the full provision to which the power extends or any less provision (whether by way of exception or otherwise),

(ii) the same provision for all cases in relation to which it is exercised, or different provision for different cases or different classes of case or different provision as respects the same case or class of case for different purposes of this Act,

(iii) any such provision either unconditionally or subject to any specified condition.

(3) Where any such power is expressed to be exercisable for alternative purposes it may be exercised in relation to the same case for any or all of those purposes.

(4) Any such power includes power—

(a) to make such incidental, supplemental, consequential or transitional provision as appears to the Secretary of State, or (in the case of regulations made by the Treasury) to the Treasury, to be expedient; and

(b) to provide for a person to exercise a discretion in dealing with any matter.

(4A) [1. . .].

(5) Any power to make regulations or an order for the purposes of any provision of this Act is without prejudice to any power to make regulations or an order for the purposes of any other provision.

AMENDMENT

1. Welfare Reform Act 2012 Sch.14 Pt 4 (trigger date on or after April 29, 2013).

DEFINITION

"regulations"—see s.35(1).

Parliamentary control

6.108 **37.**—(1) Subsection (2) applies in relation to the following regulations (whether made alone or with other regulations)—

(a) regulations made under, or by virtue of, any provision of this Act other than—

(i) section [4. . .], 26, 29 or 40,

(ii) paragraph (b) of the definition of "pension payments" in section 35(1), or

(iii) paragraph 17 of Schedule 1,

before the date on which jobseeker's allowances first become payable;

[3(aa) the first regulations to be made under section 6J or 6K;]

(ab) [4. . .];
(b) the first regulations to be made under section 26;
(c) regulations made under section [1. . .], 29, paragraph (b) of the definition of "pension payments" in section 35(1) [2. . .] or paragraph 8B or 17 of Schedule 1.

(2) No regulations to which this subsection applies shall be made unless a draft of the statutory instrument containing the regulations has been laid before Parliament and approved by a resolution of each House.

(3) Any other statutory instrument made under this Act, other than one made under section 41(2), shall be subject to annulment in pursuance of a resolution of either House of Parliament.

AMENDMENTS

1. Welfare Reform Act 2012 s.47 (March 20, 2012).
2. Welfare Reform Act 2012 Sch.14 Pt 6 (May 8, 2012).
3. Welfare Reform Act 2012 s.49(6) (February 25, 2013).
4. Welfare Reform Act 2012 Sch.14 Pt 4 (trigger date on or after April 29, 2013).

DEFINITION

"regulations"—see s.35(1).

General financial arrangements

38. [*Omitted as not relevant*] **6.109**

Provision for Northern Ireland

39. [*Omitted as not relevant*] **6.110**

Transitional provisions

40.—(1) The Secretary of State may by regulations make such transitional provision, consequential provision or savings as he considers necessary or expedient for the purposes of or in connection with— **6.111**

(a) the coming into force of any provision of this Act; or
(b) the operation of any enactment repealed or amended by any such provision during any period when the repeal or amendment is not wholly in force.

(2) Regulations under this section may in particular make provision—

(a) for the termination or cancellation of awards of unemployment benefit or income support;
(b) for a person whose award of unemployment benefit or income support has been terminated or cancelled under regulations made by virtue of paragraph (a) to be treated as having been awarded a jobseeker's allowance (a "transitional allowance")—
   (i) of such a kind,
   (ii) for such period,
   (iii) of such an amount, and
   (iv) subject to such conditions,

   as may be determined in accordance with the regulations;
(c) for a person's continuing entitlement to a transitional allowance to be determined by reference to such provision as may be made by the regulations;
(d) for the termination of an award of a transitional allowance;

(e) for the review of an award of a transitional allowance;
(f) for a contribution-based jobseeker's allowance not to be payable for a prescribed period where a person is disqualified for receiving unemployment benefit;
(g) that days which were days of unemployment for the purposes of entitlement to unemployment benefit, and such other days as may be prescribed, are to be treated as having been days during which a person was, or would have been, entitled to a jobseeker's allowance;
(h) that days which were days of entitlement to unemployment benefit, and such other days as may be prescribed, are to be treated as having been days of entitlement to a contribution-based jobseeker's allowance;
(i) that the rate of a contribution-based transitional allowance is to be calculated by reference to the rate of unemployment benefit paid or payable.

DEFINITIONS

"entitled"—see s.35(1).
"regulations"—*ibid.*

GENERAL NOTE

6.112 Although the repeal of this provision was included in Pt 1 of Sch.14 to the Welfare Reform Act 2012 it was not brought into operation with rest of Pt 1 by the Commencement No.9 Order (SI 2013/983). So far as can be ascertained, the repeal has not been brought into operation by any subsequent Commencement Order, although the section appears to be redundant in the context of new style JSA.

Short title, commencement, extent, etc.

6.113 **41.**—(1) This Act may be cited as the Jobseekers Act 1995.

(2) Section 39 and this section (apart from subsections (4) and (5)) come into force on the passing of this Act, but otherwise the provisions of this Act come into force on such day as the Secretary of State may by order appoint.

(3) Different days may be appointed for different purposes.

(4) Schedule 2 makes consequential amendments.

(5) The repeals set out in Schedule 3 shall have effect.

(6) Apart from this section, section 39 and paragraphs 11 to 16, 28, 67 and 68 of Schedule 2, this Act does not extend to Northern Ireland.

SCHEDULE A1

[Repealed by the Welfare Reform Act 2012, s.60(1), with effect from May 8, 2012]

SCHEDULE 1

SUPPLEMENTARY PROVISIONS

Remunerative work

6.114 **1.**—(1) For the purposes of this Act, "remunerative work" has such meaning as may be prescribed.

(2) Regulations may prescribe circumstances in which, for the purposes of this Act—
(a) a person who is not engaged in remunerative work is to be treated as engaged in remunerative work; or
(b) a person who is engaged in remunerative work is to be treated as not engaged in remunerative work.

Limited capability for work

2.—(1) The question whether a person has, or does not have, limited capability for work shall be determined, for the purposes of this Act, in accordance with the provisions of Part 1 of the Welfare Reform Act 2007 (employment and support allowance) [3 or Part 1 of the Welfare Reform Act 2012 (universal credit) as the Secretary of State considers appropriate in the person's case]. **6.115**

(2) References in Part 1 of the Welfare Reform Act 2007 to the purposes of that Part shall be construed, where the provisions of that Part have effect for the purposes of this Act, as references to the purposes of this Act.

[3(3) References in Part 1 of the Welfare Reform Act 2012 to the purposes of that Part are to be construed, where the provisions of that Part have effect for the purposes of this Act, as references to the purposes of this Act.]

Linking periods

3.—Regulations may provide— **6.116**
(a) for jobseeking periods which are separated by not more than a prescribed number of weeks to be treated, for purposes of this Act, as one jobseeking period;
(b) for prescribed periods ("linked periods") to be linked, for purposes of this Act, to any jobseeking period.

Waiting days

4.—Except in prescribed circumstances, a person is not entitled to a jobseeker's allowance in respect of a prescribed number of days at the beginning of a jobseeking period. **6.117**

Periods of less than a week

5.—Regulations may make provision in relation to— **6.118**
(a) entitlement to a jobseeker's allowance, or
(b) the amount payable by way of such an allowance,
in respect of any period of less than a week.

Employment protection sums

6.—(1) In relation to any [3. . .] jobseeker's allowance, regulations may make provision— **6.119**
(a) for any employment protection sum to be treated as earnings payable by such person, to such person and for such period as may be determined in accordance with the regulations; and
(b) for any such period so far as it is not a period of employment, to be treated as a period of employment.

(2) In this paragraph "employment protection sum" means—
(a) any sum, or a prescribed part of any sum—
 (i) payable, in respect of arrears of pay, under an order for reinstatement or re-engagement made under the Employment Rights Act 1996;
 (ii) payable, by way of pay, under an order made under that Act for the continuation of a contract of employment;
 (iii) payable, by way of remuneration, under a protection award made under section 189 of the Trade Union and Labour Relations (Consolidation) Act 1992; and
(b) any prescribed sum which the regulations provide is to be treated as related to any sum within paragraph (a).

Pension payments

7.—Regulations may make provision, for the purposes of any provision of, or made under, this Act— **6.120**

(a) for such sums by way of pension payments to be disregarded for prescribed purposes;
(b) as to the week in which any pension payments are to be treated as having begun;
(c) for treating, in a case where—
   (i) a lump sum is paid to a person in connection with a former employment of his or arrangement are made for a lump sum to be so paid; or
   (ii) benefits of any description are made available to a person in connection with a former employment of his or arrangements are made for them to be made so available; or
   (iii) pension payments to a person are assigned, reduced or postponed or are made otherwise than weekly,

such payments as being made to a person by way of weekly pension payments as are specified in or determined under the regulations;
(d) for the method of determining whether pension payments are made to a person for any week and their amount.

Exemptions

6.121 **8.**—[4. . .].
6.122 **8A.**—[4. . .].
6.123 **8B.**—[5. . .].
6.124 **9.**—[4. . .].

Continuity of claims and awards: persons ceasing to be a joint-claim couple

6.125 **9A.**—[4. . .].

Continuity of claims and awards: persons again becoming a joint-claim couple

6.126 **9B.**—[4. . .].

Continuity of claims and awards: couple becoming to be a joint-claim couple

6.127 **9C.**—[4. . .].

Paragraphs 9A to 9C: supplementary

6.128 **9D.**—[4. . .].

Claims yet to be determined and suspended payments

6.129 **10.**—[4. . .].

Presence in and absence from Great Britain

6.130 **11.**—(1) Regulations may provide that in prescribed circumstances a claimant who is not in Great Britain may nevertheless be entitled to a [4. . .] jobseeker's allowance.

(2) Regulations may make provision for the purposes of this Act as to the circumstances in which a person is to be treated as being or not being in Great Britain.

Households

6.131 **12.**—Regulations may make provision for the purposes of this Act as to the circumstances in which persons are to be treated as being or not being members of the same household.

Responsibility for another person

6.132 **13.**—Regulations may make provision for the purposes of this Act as to the circumstances in which one person is to be treated as responsible or not responsible for another.

Relevant education

6.133 **14.**—Regulations may make provision for the purposes of this Act—
(a) as to what is or not be treated as relevant education; and
(b) as to the circumstances in which a person is or is not to be treated as receiving relevant education.

6.134 [2**14AA.**—For any purposes of this Act regulations may provide for—
(a) circumstances in which a person is to be treated as having or not having a good reason for an act or omission;

(b) matters which are or are not to be taken into account in determining whether a person has a good reason for an act or omission.]

Calculation of periods

15.—Regulations may make provisions for calculating periods for any purposes of this Act. **6.135**

Employment on ships etc.

16.—(1) Regulations may modify any provision of this Act in its application to any person who is, has been, or is to be— **6.136**

(a) employed on board any ship, vessel, hovercraft or aircraft,
(b) outside Great Britain at any prescribed time or in any prescribed circumstances, or
(c) in prescribed employment in connection with continental shelf operations, so far as that provision relates to a [4. . .] jobseeker's allowance.

(2) The regulations may in particular provide—

(a) for any such provision to apply even though it would not otherwise apply;
(b) for any such provision not to apply even though it would otherwise apply;
(c) for the taking of evidence, in a country or territory outside Great Britain, by a British consular official or other prescribed person;
(d) for enabling payment of the whole, or any part of a [4. . .] jobseeker's allowance to be paid to such of the claimant's dependants as may be prescribed.

Additional conditions

17.—Regulations may require additional conditions to be satisfied with respect to the payment of a jobseeker's allowance to any person who is, has been, or is to be, in employment which falls within a prescribed description. **6.137**

Benefits Act purposes

18.—Regulations may provide for— **6.138**

(a) a jobseeker's allowance;
(b) [4. . .];
(c) [4. . .],

to be treated, for prescribed purposes of the Benefits Act, as a benefit, or a benefit of a prescribed description.

Treatment of information supplied as information relating to Social Security

19.—Information supplied in pursuance of any provision made by or under this Act [1. . .] shall be taken for all purposes to be information relating to social security. **6.139**

AMENDMENTS

1. Welfare Reform Act 2012 Sch.14 Pt 6 (May 8, 2012).
2. Welfare Reform Act 2012 s.46(3)(b) (June 10, 2012, for purposes of making regulations; October 22, 2012).
3. Universal Credit (Consequential, Supplementary, Incidental and Miscellaneous Provisions Regulations 2013 (SI 2013/630) reg.10 (April 29, 2013).
4. Welfare Reform Act 2012 Sch.14 Pt 1 (trigger date on or after April 29, 2013).
5. Welfare Reform Act 2012 Sch.14 Pt 4 (trigger date on or after April 29, 2013).

DEFINITIONS

"the Benefits Act"—see s.35(1).
"employment"—see s.35(1) and JSA Regulations 2013 reg.2(1).
"Great Britain"—see s.35(1).
"jobseeking period"—*ibid.*
"pension payments"—*ibid.*
"regulations"—*ibid.*
"prescribed"—*ibid.*
"week"—*ibid.*

GENERAL NOTE

6.140 See the annotations to Sch.1 in Pt I of this volume, disregarding the references to IBJSA, for the general effect of paras 1, 2, 3, 4, 5, 6, 7, 11, 12, 13, 14, 14AA, 16 and 17. In relation to those provisions, note the following cross-references to the JSA Regulations 2013 for the purposes of new style JSA.

On para.1, see regs 42–45. On para.3, see regs 37–40 for jobseeking periods, linked periods and linking. On para.4, see reg.36 on waiting days. On para.5, see regs 64–65 on part-weeks. On para.6, see reg.58(1)(f)–(h) on treatment as earnings. The power in para.6(1)(b) has not been exercised. Under para.7, see reg.51 on pension payments. On para.11(2), see reg.41. The power in para.11(1) appears not to have been exercised in relation to new style JSA. The powers in paras 12 and 13 appear not to have been exercised in relation to new style JSA. On para.14, see reg.45 and note that this covers students of any age in full-time advanced education as well as 16–19 year-olds who count as "qualifying young persons" and anyone else on a course or training that is not compatible with a work-related requirement imposed on them. The powers in 14AA appear not to have been exercised in relation to new style JSA, consistently with the approach in universal credit. The power in para.16 appears not to have been exercised in relation to new style JSA. On para.17, see regs 67–75.

As well as inserting para.14AA, s.46(3) of the Welfare Reform Act 2012 also, in paras (a) and (c), purported to amend para.14B of Sch.1 and a heading preceding para.14B (and maybe thus preceding para.14AA). But s.30(1) of the Welfare Reform Act 2009 inserting para.14B and the heading appears never to have been brought into operation. Therefore (subject to correction in the future) those provisions have been omitted.

The Jobseeker's Allowance Regulations 2013

(SI 2013/378) (AS AMENDED)

Made by the Secretary of State for Work and Pensions under ss.2(1)(c), (2A) and (3B)(a), 4(1)(b), (2) and (4), 5(3), 6A(5), 6B(2), 6D(4), 6E(3) and (5), 6F(1), 6H(1)(a), (5) and (6), 6I, 6J(2)(a), (5) and (7), 6K(4), (5) and (9), 12(1) to (4)(a) and (b), 35(1) and (3) and 36(2) to (4) of, and Sch.1 to, the Jobseekers Act 1995, ss.5(1)(i) and (j) and (1A), 189(4), (5) and (6) and 191 of the Social Security Administration Act 1992, ss.171D, 171G(2) and 175(3) to (5) of the Social Security Contributions and Benefits Act 1992 and paras 2(3) and 3 of Sch.5 to the Welfare Reform Act 2012, the Social Security Advisory Committee having agreed that the proposal to make the regulations did not need to be referred to it.

ARRANGEMENT OF REGULATIONS

PART 1

GENERAL

PART 2

Claimant responsibilities

PART 3

Sanctions

PART 4

Information and evidence

PART 5

CONDITIONS OF ENTITLEMENT

PART 6

AMOUNTS OF A JOBSEEKER'S ALLOWANCE

PART 7

EARNINGS

PART 8

PART WEEKS

PART 9

SHARE FISHERMEN

PART 10

MODIFICATION OF THE ACT

GENERAL NOTE

These regulations govern eligibility for new style JSA. They came into force on April 29, 2013. But being made under the form of the Jobseekers Act 1995 as amended for the purposes of new style JSA and set out earlier in this Part (the new style Jobseekers Act 1995), they only have effect in relation to claimants to whom that form of the Act applies, i.e. unless and until the universal credit scheme is fully rolled out, to claimants who down to June 15, 2014 are within the "Pathfinder group" and from June 16, 2014 meet the gateway conditions (see below). It is only in relation to that group that income-based JSA has been abolished, so that reg.1(3) is triggered. New style JSA is a wholly contribution-based benefit for those who are out of work and are seeking employment. Those entitled to it whose resources are insufficient to meet needs will have to seek a top-up through universal credit. In the longer term, when the universal credit scheme is fully rolled out, the result will be a simpler system, since that will then be the only income-related benefit for persons of working age, rather than the current system of several income-related benefits each for different categories of claimant and administered by different authorities: income support, income-based JSA and income-related ESA (by DWP/Jobcentre Plus), tax credits (by HMRC) and housing benefit and council tax reduction (by local authorities). But until the universal credit scheme is fully rolled out, universal credit is an additional benefit rather than a benefit replacing all those other income related benefits. The roll-out of universal credit is slow and complicated. As the commentators to Vol.V in this series, *Universal Credit*, put it in the 2013/14 edition: 6.142

> "it is inherent in the design of Universal Credit that it overlaps with each of the older benefits it is eventually intended to replace. That overlap means that, in addition to the complication of the old and new systems existing side-by-side (including having two different and mutually exclusive benefits both called JSA and two called ESA), it is also necessary to have legislation defining which set

of rules applies to any particular claimant at any given time. That legislation is to be found first, in the Universal Credit (Transitional Provisions) Regulations ("the Transitional Provisions Regulations") which create a "Pathfinder Group" of claimants who, depending on where they live, may have to claim universal credit rather than one of the "legacy" benefits and, second, in a series of Commencement Orders that, even by the high standards set by past social security legislation, are bewilderingly complex."

The areas in which, and within them, the cases to which, new style JSA and these Regulations apply—initially the "Pathfinder" pilots replaced from June 16, 2014 by the gateway conditions for the persons affected in designated areas — are set by reg.1(2) and (3), read with the Transitional Provisions Regulations and the various Welfare Reform Act 2012 Commencement Orders noted in the annotation to reg.1(2) and (3), and the subject of fuller commentary in Pt 4 of Vol.V, *Universal Credit*. In respect of areas and cases in relation to which IBJSA has yet to be abolished (i.e. those outside the areas designated for the operation of the Pathfinder pilots and now the gateway conditions), entitlement to old style JSA (either or both CBSA and IBJSA) remain governed by the old style Jobseekers Act 1995 and the JSA Regulations 1996 as set out in Pts I and III of this volume.

Most of the key rules on new style JSA remain the same in terms of effect as those applicable to CBJSA in the JSA Regulations 1996, but the DWP considers that in drawing up the JSA Regulations 2013 "opportunities have been taken to make simplifications and improvements". In addition, the regulations specific to IBJSA are not carried into the 2013 Regulations. This means that material may be differently distributed within the same-numbered regulation in these Regulations as compared to the JSA Regulations 1996, or be found in a differently numbered one. In addition, in the JSA Regulations 2013, there is a regime of claimant commitments and sanctions analogous in some respects to those applicable to universal credit and new style ESA, some of which were foreshadowed in earlier amendments to the sanctions regime for old style JSA.

In the AMENDMENTS sections below, reference to the Jobseekers Act 1995 are to the new style Act set out above in this Part of the book.

PART 1

General

Citation, commencement and application

6.143 **1.**—(1) These Regulations may be cited as the Jobseeker's Allowance Regulations 2013.

(2) They come into force on 29th April 2013.

(3) They apply in relation to a particular case on any day on which section 33(1)(a) of the Welfare Reform Act 2012 (abolition of income-based jobseeker's allowance) is in force and applies in relation to that case.

General Note

6.144 Although these Regulations entered into force on April 29, 2013, they do not as yet apply throughout the country. They will only do so once there has been a full rolling out of universal credit and consequent total abolition of IBJSA.

Instead, the Regulations initially became applicable only in those "Pathfinder" areas where IBJSA had been abolished and only as regards certain types of case ("in a particular case . . . on any day on which section 33(1)(a) of the Welfare Reform Act 2012 (abolition of income-based jobseeker's allowance) is in force and applies in relation to that case": subs.(3)). Areas and types of case were to expand as the system moved to full roll out of universal credit and abolition of IBJSA and IRESA, then planned for 2017. See further, Pt I of Vol.V, *Universal Credit*, and below.

As at April 28, 2014, areas and types of case were those covered by provisions in each of the Welfare Reform Act 2012 Commencement Nos 9, 11, 13, 14 and 16 Orders (see Pt IV of Vol.V, *Universal Credit* for all except the No.16 Order). The post-code districts covered in this process and the relevant dates were set out in the 2015/16 and earlier editions and need not now be reproduced. New style JSA therefore became applicable in those areas under the conditions in art.4 of each Commencement Order (annotated more fully in Pt IV of Vol.V, *Universal Credit*) covering six classes of case. In relation to each, a key requisite was that the claimant met the criteria for being in the "Pathfinder Group". These were set out in regs 5–12 of the Universal Credit (Transitional Provisions) Regulations 2013 (SI 2013/386) (see Pt IV of Vol.V, *Universal Credit*). The initial groups in the Pathfinder pilots were single persons without children, being new claimants who would otherwise have claimed old style JSA, whether CBJSA alone, IBJSA alone or a combination of the two. **6.145**

The Transitional Provisions Regulations 2013 were revoked (with minor savings) and replaced, with effect from June 16, 2014, by the Universal Credit (Transitional Provisions) Regulations 2014 (SI 2014/1230), which omit the "Pathfinder Group" provisions that had been in the 2013 Regulations. Instead, the Welfare Reform Act 2012 (Commencement Nos 9, 11, 13, 14 and 16 and Transitional and Transitory Provisions (Amendment) Order 2014 (SI 2014/1452) repeated essentially the same rules about the commencement of the new regime, but under the name of "gateway conditions" (see the new Sch.5 to the No.9 Commencement Order). The No.17 Commencement Order (SI 2014/1583) extended the areas covered in phases through June and July 2014 to reach the No.13 relevant districts. Then the Welfare Reform Act 2012 (Commencement Nos 9, 11, 13, 14, 16 and 17 and Transitional and Transitory Provisions (Amendment) Order 2014 (SI 2014/1661) started from June 30, 2014 the process of expanding the categories of claimants covered, for instance abandoning the restriction to single claimants in certain areas and the rule that an award of old style ESA or JSA must not have terminated in the two weeks preceding the universal credit claim, and including recipients of tax credits or housing benefit. All of these regulations and orders are set out in the 2014/15 Supplement to the Social Security Legislation volumes (in the part relating to Vol.V, *Universal Credit*), taking in also the Nos 19 and 20 Commencement Orders. **6.146**

By April 30, 2015 the Commencement Orders had reached No.23. Of particular significance for the operation of the JSA Regulations 2013 was the announcement that a complete national roll out of universal credit, in four tranches starting in February 2015, was to take place for single people without responsibility for a child or young person who would otherwise have been eligible for old style JSA. The first two tranches of postcodes took the coverage down to district no.49. The third and fourth tranches are due to take effect from September to November 2015 and from December 2015 to April 2016. When completed, that will mean a national coverage for the operation of new style JSA, at least for a restricted category of claimant. That process was completed on time at least for single claimants. It has also been announced that the roll out to the "full digital service" for new claims by all categories of claimant and transfers on certain significant changes of circumstances will start in May 2016, to be completed in June 2018 (see Osborne, "Universal credit: full steam ahead" (2016) *Welfare Rights Bulletin* 251, p.4). **6.147**

The outcome of the May 2015 general election and the reappointment of Iain Duncan Smith as Secretary of State led to no fundamental review and pausing of that timetable, as had been proposed by some other parties. However, it may be that negotiations about the devolution of powers to Scotland, including some social security and revenue-raising functions, will create further delay. Following Mr Duncan Smith's resignation, his successor, Stephen Crabb, committed himself in his first published speech after appointment to the existing programme for universal credit. It remains to be seen what might emerge under Theresa May's premiership. On July 20, 2016, Damien Green, the new Secretary of State, announced that there was to be a "reshaping" of the universal credit rollout to full digital service, so that the completion of migration from existing benefits would not be completed before March 2022. But the rollout of five Jobcentres a month until June 2017 was to continue, to be expanded thereafter.

General interpretation

6.148 **2.**—(1) For the purposes of the Act and of these Regulations—

"employed earner" has the meaning it has in Part 1 of the Benefits Act by virtue of section 2(1)(a) of that Act;

"employment" includes any trade, business, profession, office or vocation, except in section 14 of the Act, where it means employed earner's employment within the meaning in the Benefits Act;

"jobseeking period" means the period described in regulation 37;

"pensionable age" has the meaning it has in Parts 1 to 6 of the Benefits Act by virtue of section 122(1) of that Act.

(2) In these Regulations—

"the Act" means the Jobseekers Act 1995;

"adoption leave" means a period of absence from work on ordinary or additional adoption leave by virtue of section 75A or 75B of the Employment Rights Act 1996;

"attendance allowance" means—

(a) an attendance allowance under section 64 of the Benefits Act;

(b) an increase of disablement pension under section 104 or 105 of the Benefits Act;

(c) a payment by virtue of article 14, 15, 16, 43 or 44 of the Personal Injuries (Civilians) Scheme 1983 or any analogous payment;

(d) any payment based on the need for attendance which is paid as an addition to a war disablement pension (which means any retired pay or pension or allowance payable in respect of disablement under an instrument specified in section 639(2) of the Income Tax (Earnings and Pensions) Act 2003);

"basic rate" has the same meaning as in the Income Tax Act 2007;

"benefit week" means a period of seven days ending with the end day unless, in any particular case or class of case, the Secretary of State arranges otherwise, and for these purposes "end day" means the day in column (2) which corresponds to the series of numbers in column (1) which includes the last two digits of the person's national insurance number—

(1)		(2)
00 to 19		Monday
20 to 39		Tuesday
40 to 59		Wednesday
60 to 79		Thursday
80 to 99		Friday;

"Claims and Payments Regulations 2013" means the Universal Credit, Personal Independence Payment, Jobseeker's Allowance and Employment and Support Allowance (Claims and Payments) Regulations 2013;

"close relative" means a parent, parent-in-law, son, son-in-law, daughter, daughter-in-law, step-parent, step-son, step-daughter, brother, sister or, if any of the preceding persons is one member of a couple, the other member of that couple;

"date of claim" means the date on which the claimant makes, or is treated as making, a claim for a jobseeker's allowance for the purposes of—

(a) regulation 6 of the Social Security (Claims and Payments) Regulations 1987; or

(b) regulation 20, 22 or 24 of the Claims and Payments Regulations 2013;

"earnings", for the purposes of section 35(3) of the Act, has the meaning specified—

(a) in the case of an employed earner, in regulation 58; or

(b) in the case of a self-employed earner, in regulation 60;

[2"first year of training" means a period of one year beginning with a person's first day of training.

"Health Service Act" means the National Health Service Act 2006;

"Health Service (Wales) Act" means the National Health Service (Wales) Act 2006;

"maternity leave" means a period during which a woman is absent from work because she is pregnant or has given birth to a child, and at the end of which she has a right to return to work either under the terms of her contract of employment or under Part 8 of the Employment Rights Act 1996;

"net earnings" means such earnings as are calculated in accordance with regulation 59;

"net profit" means such profit as is calculated in accordance with regulation 61;

"occupational pension" means any pension or other periodical payment under an occupational pension scheme but does not include any discretionary payment out of a fund established for relieving hardship in particular cases;

"partner" means, where a claimant—

(a) is a member of a couple, the other member of that couple;

(b) is married polygamously to two or more members of the claimant's household, any such member;

"paternity leave" means a period of absence from work on leave by virtue of section 80A or 80B of the Employment Rights Act 1996;

"payment" includes a part of a payment;

"remunerative work" has the meaning prescribed in regulation 42(1);

[4 "Scottish basic rate" means the rate of income tax of that name calculated in accordance with section 6A of the Income Tax Act 2007;

"Scottish taxpayer" has the same meaning as in Chapter 2 of Part 4A of the Scotland Act 1998;]

"self-employed earner" is to be construed in accordance with section 2(1)(b) of the Benefits Act;

[1"shared parental leave" means a period of absence from work on leave by virtue of section 75E or 75G of the Employment Rights Act 1996;]

"sports award" means an award made by one of the Sports Councils named in section 23(2) of the National Lottery etc. Act 1993 out of sums allocated to it for distribution under that section;

"training allowance" means an allowance (whether by way of periodical grants or otherwise) payable—

(a) out of public funds by a Government department or by or on behalf of the Secretary of State, Skills Development Scotland, Scottish Enterprise, Highlands and Islands Enterprise [3 . . .] or the Welsh Ministers;

(b) to a person for their maintenance or in respect of the maintenance of a member of their family; and

(c) for the period, or part of the period, during which the person is following a course of training or instruction provided by, or in pursuance of arrangements made with, that department or approved by that department in relation to them or provided or approved by or on behalf of the Secretary of State, Skills Development Scotland, Scottish Enterprise, Highlands and Islands Enterprise or the Welsh Ministers,

but it does not include an allowance paid by any Government department to or in respect of a person by reason of the fact that the person is following a course of full-time education, other than under arrangements made under section 2 of the Employment and Training Act 1973 or section 2 of the Enterprise and New Towns (Scotland) Act 1990, or the person is training as a teacher;

"voluntary organisation" means a body, other than a public or local authority, the activities of which are carried on otherwise than for profit;

"voluntary work" means work other than for a member of the claimant's family, where no payment is received by the claimant or the only payment due to be made to the claimant by virtue of being so engaged is a payment in respect of any expenses reasonably incurred by the claimant in the course of being so engaged;

"week" means, in the definition of "Work Experience" and in Parts 5, 6, 7, 9 and 10, a period of seven days;

"Work Experience" means a programme which consists of work experience, job search skills and job skills (and which is not employment), provided in pursuance of arrangements made by or on behalf of the Secretary of State under section 2 of the Employment and Training Act 1973, and which—

(a) subject to paragraph (b), is of between two and eight weeks duration; or

(b) is of between two and 12 weeks duration where, during the first eight weeks of the claimant's participation in Work Experience, and as a result of that participation, the claimant is offered and accepts an apprenticeship made under government arrangements made respectively for England, Wales or Scotland;

"young person" means a person who falls within the definition of "qualifying young person" in section 142 of the Benefits Act (child and qualifying young person).

AMENDMENTS

1. Shared Parental Leave and Statutory Shared Parental Pay (Consequential Amendments and Subordinate Legislation) Order 2014 (SI 2014/3255) art.29(2) (December 31, 2014).

2. Social Security (Members of the Reserve Forces) (Amendment) Regulations 2015 (SI 2015/389) reg.5(2) (April 6, 2015).

3. Deregulation Act 2015 (Consequential Amendments) Order 2015 (SI 2015/971) Sch.3 art.25 (May 26, 2015).

4. Social Security (Scottish Rate of Income Tax etc.) (Amendment) Regulations 2016 (SI 2016/233) reg.7(2) (April 6, 2016).

DEFINITIONS

"the Benefits Act"—see Jobseekers Act 1995 s.35(1).
"claimant"—*ibid.*
"couple"—*ibid.*
"family"—*ibid.* and reg.3(1), (3) and (5).
"occupational pension scheme"—see Jobseekers Act 1995 s.35(1).

GENERAL NOTE

This sets out key definitions for the application of these Regulations. It is, not, however, the sole provider of relevant definitions. Aside from s.35 of the new style Jobseekers Act 1995, important definitions are also to be found in regs 3, 4, 17 and 67 and occasionally within other provisions, in that last case generally defining a term used solely in that provision. See the notes to reg.2 of the Income Support (General) Regulations 1987 in Pt II of this volume for some entries. **6.149**

Further interpretation

3.—(1) Any reference to the claimant's family or, as the case may be, to a member of the claimant's family, is to be construed for the purposes of these Regulations as if it included, in relation to a polygamous marriage, a reference to any partner and to any child or young person who is treated by the Secretary of State as the responsibility of the claimant or their partner, where that child or young person is a member of the claimant's household. **6.150**

(2) In such cases and subject to such conditions or requirements as the Secretary of State may specify by means of a direction, any requirement imposed under these Regulations for a signature may be satisfied by means of an electronic signature (within the meaning given in section 7(2) of the Electronic Communications Act 2000).

(3) A person of a prescribed description for the purposes of the definition of "family" in section 35(1) of the Act is a young person.

(4) For the purposes of paragraph (d) of the definition of "couple" in section 35(1) of the Act, two persons of the same sex are to be regarded as living together as if they were civil partners only if they would be regarded as living together as husband and wife were they instead two persons of the opposite sex.

(5) In this regulation, "polygamous marriage" means any marriage during the subsistence of which a party to it is married to more than one person and the ceremony of marriage took place under the law of a country which permits polygamy.

(6) References in these Regulations to a person participating as a service user are to [1 . . .]—

(a) a person who is being consulted by or on behalf of—

(i) a body which has a statutory duty to provide services in the field of health, social care or social housing; or

(ii) a body which conducts research or undertakes monitoring for the purpose of planning or improving such services, in the person's capacity as a user, potential user, carer of a user or person otherwise affected by the provision of those services; or

[1(ab) a person who is being consulted by or on behalf of—

(i) the Secretary of State in relation to any of the Secretary of State's functions in the field of social security or child support or under section 2 of the Employment and Training Act 1973; or

(ii) a body which conducts research or undertakes monitoring for the purpose of planning or improving such functions,

in their capacity as a person affected or potentially affected by the exercise of those functions or the carer of such a person;]

(b) the carer of a person consulted under [1 sub-paragraphs (a) or (ab)].

(7) In these Regulations, references to obtaining paid work includes obtaining more paid work or obtaining better-paid work.

AMENDMENT

1. Social Security (Miscellaneous Amendments) Regulations 2015 (SI 2015/67) reg.2 (February 23, 2015).

DEFINITIONS

"the Act"—see reg.2(2).
"child"—see Jobseekers Act 1995 s.35(1).
"claimant"—*ibid.*
"couple"—*ibid.*
"family"—*ibid.*
"partner"—see reg.2(2).
"young person"—see reg.2(2).

GENERAL NOTE

6.151 This provides further definitions and interpretative provisions in addition to those in reg.2. Paragraphs (1) and (5) bring polygamous marriages within the ambit of the definitions of "couple" and "family" in s.35(1) of the 1995 Act.

PART 2

CLAIMANT RESPONSIBILITIES

GENERAL NOTE

6.152 Claimant responsibilities in new style JSA cover similar issues to the "labour market" conditions (entering into a jobseeker's agreement, availability for and actively seeking employment) in old style JSA, but with different consequences according to the different structure of the benefit.

For new style JSA these responsibilities are laid down in s.6–6L of the new style Jobseekers Act 1995 as set out earlier in this Part. These responsibilities – not all of which are imposed on all claimants – cover work-related requirements and connected requirements under s.6G. They should be set out in the claimant commitment (s.6A) acceptance of which is required of all claimants, other than those exempted by reg.8, as a condition of a entitlement. Work-related requirements are: a work-focused interview requirement (s.6B); a work preparation requirement (s.6C); a work search requirement (s.6D); and a work availability requirement (s.6E). Connected requirements, such as participation in an interview to verify and assist claimants' compliance with their claimant commitment, fall under s.6G. While acceptance of the claimant commitment is a condition of entitlement to new style JSA under s.1(2)(b) of the new style Jobseekers Act 1995, failure to meet an obligation set out in claimant commitment does not attract any sanction for that reason in itself. It is only non-compliance for no good reason with a requirement imposed under s.6B–6G that leads to a sanction involving a reduction in the amount of benefit payable (s.6J and 6K).

Regulations 5 and 6 below deal with the relationship of the work-related requirements and sanctions regime with universal credit entitlement. Regulations 7 and 8 deal with the acceptance of a claimant commitment. Regulations 9–14 deal with the content of work-related requirements. Regulations 15, 16 and 16A set out the circumstances when various work-related requirements are not to be imposed, reg.15 dealing with recent victims of domestic violence. Part 3 of the Regulations deals with sanctions, including circumstances in which a reduction in benefit is not to follow from the existence of a sanctionable failure.

Interpretation

4.—(1) In this Part— **6.153**

"relevant carer" means—

(a) a parent of a child who is not the responsible carer, but has caring responsibilities for the child; or

(b) a person who has caring responsibilities for a person who has a physical or mental impairment which makes those caring responsibilities necessary;

"responsible carer", in relation to a child, means—

(a) a person who is the only person responsible for the child; or

(b) a person who is a member of a couple where—

(i) both members of the couple are responsible for the child; and

(ii) the person has been nominated by the couple jointly as responsible for the child;

"responsible foster parent", in relation to a child, means—

(a) a person who is the only foster parent in relation to the child; or

(b) a person who is a member of a couple where—

(i) both members of the couple are foster parents in relation to the child; and

(ii) the person has been nominated by the couple jointly as the responsible foster parent;

"voluntary work preparation" means particular action taken by a claimant and agreed by the Secretary of State for the purpose of making it more likely that the claimant will obtain paid work, but which is not specified by the Secretary of State as a work preparation requirement under section 6C of the Act.

(2) The nomination of a responsible carer or responsible foster parent for the purposes of paragraph (1) may be changed—

(a) once in a 12 month period, beginning with the date of the previous nomination; or

(b) on any occasion where the Secretary of State considers that there has been a change of circumstances which is relevant to the nomination.

(3) Only one person may be nominated as a responsible carer or a responsible foster parent.

(4) The nomination applies to all of the children for whom the claimant is responsible.

DEFINITIONS

"child"—see Jobseekers Act 1995 s.35(1).

"claimant"—*ibid.*

"couple"—see Jobseekers Act 1995 s.35(1) and reg.3(4).

GENERAL NOTE

In addition to terms already defined in regs 2 and 3, this provides for the purposes of this Part (Pt 2 Claimant responsibilities) a number of important definitions: "relevant carer"; "responsible foster parent"; "responsible carer"; "voluntary work **6.154** preparation". See the notes to s.19 of the Welfare Reform Act 2012 and regs 85 and 86 of the UC Regulations in Vol.V, *Universal Credit*.

Application of regulations where there is dual entitlement

6.155 **5.**—(1) This regulation applies where a person is entitled to universal credit and a jobseeker's allowance.

(2) The work-related requirements under sections 6B to 6I of the Act and regulations 9 to16 of these Regulations do not apply to such a person.

(3) Reductions relating to the award of a jobseeker's allowance under section 6J or 6K of the Act and regulations 17 to 29 of these Regulations do not apply to such a person.

Definition

"the Act"—see reg.2(2).

General Note

6.156 This provision, made it appears under ss.6F(1), 6H(1)(a), 6J(7)(a) and 6K(9)(a) of the new style Jobseekers Act 1995, constitutes an important element in the structure of new style JSA and its relationship with universal credit. Paragraph (2) provides that where a claimant is entitled to both universal credit and JSA, the work-related and connected requirements regime applicable to new style JSA does not operate at all. Although para.(2) refers to work-related requirements only, the specific reference to the whole of s.6B–6I must bring s.6G (connected requirements) within its scope. The claimant will instead be subject to the comparable universal credit regime. See the UC Regulations 2013 regs 84–114 in Vol.V, *Universal Credit*. It appears that the claimant is still subject to the condition of entitlement of accepting a claimant commitment under s.1(2)(b) of the new style Jobseekers Act 1995, but it is not clear what could go into that document in terms of a statement of responsibilities under the Act. The document could of course contain other relevant information, but it might be that in the circumstances envisaged in reg.5, where the claimant will by definition have accepted a universal credit claimant commitment or been exempted from needing to accept one (in order to be entitled) the Secretary of State will consider the application of reg.8(b) (unreasonable to expect a claimant to accept a claimant commitment).

Paragraph (3) provides that reductions in the amount of new style JSA payable under the sanctions regime do not apply to a person who is also entitled to universal credit. At first sight that appears somewhat redundant in the light of para.(2). If a claimant cannot be subject to any work-related or connected requirements, there can be no failure to comply that can lead to a sanction. However, sanctionable failures under s.6J are not limited to such failures to comply, but also extend, for example, to the traditional categories of losing employment through misconduct or leaving voluntarily for no good reason. Paragraph (3) will also presumably apply where a sanctionable failure occurred while the new style JSA recipient was not entitled to universal credit, but the person becomes entitled to universal credit before a sanction and reduction decision is made. See reg.6 for the situation where a JSA reduction has already been applied.

The rather odd result appears to follow that if a claimant who is entitled to new style JSA, having satisfied the contribution conditions, and is also entitled to universal credit to top up the income from JSA, commits a sanctionable failure, the reduction in the amount of benefit payable can only eat into whatever is the amount of universal credit payable and not into the amount of JSA payable. Although the amount of the reduction to be applied under the universal credit sanctions regime is expressed in terms of a percentage (100 per cent or 40 per cent) of the claimant's standard allowance, the concept of a reduction cannot allow the amount of universal credit payable to be reduced below nil. By contrast, if a new style JSA recipient does not qualify for a top-up through universal credit, or has not claimed universal credit, reg.5 will not apply and the 100 per cent reduction of benefit following a sanction will be applied to the amount of JSA payable. Similarly, a universal credit recipient who does not qualify for new style JSA will receive correspondingly more in universal credit without that income to be counted, but will then have more benefit to be reduced following a sanction. Note that while a reduction in the amount of universal credit payable following a sanction is in operation, the claimant remains entitled to universal credit, even if nothing is being paid, so that reg.5 continues to apply.

Sanction ceases to apply to jobseeker's allowance

6.—(1) This regulation applies where— 6.157

(a) a person is entitled to a jobseeker's allowance;

(b) there is a reduction relating to the person's award of a jobseeker's allowance under section 6J or 6K of the Act;

(c) the person becomes entitled to universal credit; and

(d) the person remains entitled to a jobseeker's allowance.

(2) Any reduction relating to the person's award of the jobseeker's allowance is to cease being applied to the award of the jobseeker's allowance.

Definition

"the Act"—see reg.2(2).

General Note

Where a new style JSA reduction is in place following a sanction and the claimant then becomes entitled to universal credit as well as JSA, the JSA reduction ceases to apply. The person will instead be dealt with under the universal credit regime. See the UC Regulations 2013 reg.112 and Sch.11 in Vol.V, *Universal Credit*, which require any unexpired period of the sanction to be applied to the amount of universal credit otherwise payable. It is not clear whether, if the claimant subsequently ceases to be entitled to universal credit while some part of the original sanction period remains unexpired, the case falls within reg.30 below. Has there been a reduction under s.26 or 27 of the WRA 2012? 6.158

Claimant commitment – date and method of acceptance

7.—(1) For the purposes of section 1(2)(b) of the Act, a claimant who has accepted a claimant commitment within such period after making a claim for a jobseeker's allowance as the Secretary of State specifies is to be treated as having accepted that claimant commitment on the first day of the period in respect of which the claim is made. 6.159

(2) The Secretary of State may extend the period within which a claimant is required to accept a claimant commitment or an updated claimant commitment where the claimant requests that the Secretary of State review—

(a) any action proposed as a work search requirement or a work availability requirement; or

(b) whether any limitation should apply to those requirements,

and the Secretary of State considers that the request is reasonable.

(3) A claimant must accept a claimant commitment by one of the following methods, as specified by the Secretary of State—

(a) electronically;

(b) by telephone; or
(c) in writing.

DEFINITIONS

"the Act"—see reg.2(2).
"claimant"—see Jobseekers Act 1995 s.35(1).
"claimant commitment"—see Jobseekers Act 1995 s.6A.
"work availability requirement"—see Jobseekers Act 1995 ss.35(1) and 6E.
"work search requirement"—see Jobseekers Act 1995 ss.35(1) and 6D.
"writing"—see Interpretation Act 1978 Sch.1.

GENERAL NOTE

6.160 By virtue of s.1(2)(b) of the new style Jobseekers Act 1995 it is a condition of entitlement to new style JSA that a claimant has accepted a claimant commitment as described in s.6A. See the notes to s.6A for the nature of a claimant commitment (i.e. a record of the claimant's responsibilities in relation to an award of JSA) and what is entailed in accepting such a record. There are exceptions from that condition in reg.8 below. Regulation 7 deals with the time within which and the method by which a claimant commitment must be accepted. The relevant regulation-making power is in s.6A(5), which requires the most up-to-date version of a claimant commitment to be accepted "in such manner as may be prescribed". However, there appears to be no equivalent to s.4(7) of the Welfare Reform Act 2012 in relation to universal credit (see Vol.V), to allow regulations to specify circumstances in which a claimant is to be treated as having or as not having accepted a claimant commitment (s.6I does not give power as there is no requirement to accept a claimant commitment). There is therefore some doubt about the validity of paras (1) and (2), but as they operate in general beneficially towards claimants a challenge to their validity is unlikely.

Paragraph (1)

6.161 On a new claim, if the claimant commitment is accepted within the time specified by the Secretary of State (as extended under para.(2) if applicable), and by a method prescribed in para.(3), the condition of entitlement in s.1(2)(b) of the new style Jobseekers Act 1995 is deemed to be satisfied from the first day of the period claimed for. Otherwise, the condition would only be met from the date on which the acceptance by a prescribed method actually took place, as would be the case if para.(1) is not validly made. No-one is likely to object to para.(1) being given effect even if invalid. Under s.6A(2) of the Act, the Secretary of State may review and up-date a claimant commitment as he thinks fit and under s.6A(5) a claimant has to accept the most-up-date version. Such circumstances do not seem to fall within either paras (1) or (2), although para.(2) refers to a period within which a claimant is required to accept an up-dated claimant commitment and its possible extension. There is doubt whether an acceptance of an up-dated claimant commitment after a review strictly takes effect only from its actual date or from the date of the preparation of the up-dated version, but again no-one is likely to complain if the Secretary of State gives retrospective effect to an acceptance of an up-dated version within a specified time, as consistency would suggest is fair.

Paragraph (2)

6.162 This paragraph allows the Secretary of State, in defined circumstances, to extend the period within which a person is required (which is only in the sense of required in order to take advantage of giving a retrospective effect to the acceptance) to accept a claimant commitment or an up-dated version. It is arguable that no such authorisation is needed to allow the Secretary of State to extend any period as first specified under para.(1), so that the form of the restrictions in sub-paras

(a) and (b) may not matter too much. Those provisions purport to apply when a claimant has requested that the Secretary of State review any action proposed as a work search or work availability requirement (see s.6D and 6E of the new style Jobseekers Act 1995) or whether any limitation should apply to those requirements (see reg.14 below). The main difficulty with them, apart from the fact that s.6E contains no power for the Secretary of State to specify particular action in relation to a work availability requirement, is that the legislation contains no formal process of review of the "proposals" mentioned. The reference must presumably be to the power under s.6H(3) for the Secretary of State to revoke or change any requirement imposed under the Act or any specification of action to be taken and to a request to exercise that power in relation to action specified under s.6D or 6E. Those difficulties perhaps reinforce the argument for the Secretary of State being able to extend the period for acceptance of the claimant whenever it appears reasonable to do so, although that would involve giving no effective force to para.(2).

Paragraph (3)

This paragraph, as allowed by s.6A(5) of the new style Jobseekers Act 1995, requires that any acceptance of a claimant commitment can count for the purposes of s.1(2)(b) only if done electronically, by telephone or in writing, with the Secretary of State able to specify which in any particular case. "Electronically" will no doubt cover a range of methods. It seems bizarre that acceptance orally or otherwise face-to-face is not allowed, although the telephone is covered. Both methods are capable of being recorded in some permanent form. In so far as no account is taken of the circumstances of claimants with disabilities and the problem cannot be taken care of under reg.8 this provision must be vulnerable to a challenge under the Human Rights Act 1998 for discrimination contrary to art.14 of the European Convention on Human Rights. **6.163**

Claimant commitment – exceptions

8.—A claimant may be entitled to a jobseeker's allowance without having accepted a claimant commitment if the Secretary of State considers— **6.164**

(a) the claimant cannot accept a claimant commitment because they lack capacity to do so; or

(b) there are exceptional circumstances in which it would be unreasonable to expect the person to accept a claimant commitment.

DEFINITIONS

"claimant"—see Jobseekers Act 1995 s.35(1).

"claimant commitment"—see Jobseekers Act 1995 s.6A.

GENERAL NOTE

The condition of entitlement in s.1(2)(b) of the new style Jobseekers Act 1995 does not have to be met where the claimant either lacks the capacity to accept a claimant commitment (para.(a)) or there are exceptional circumstances in which it would be unreasonable to expect the claimant to accept a claimant commitment (para.(b)). Both provisions, but especially para.(b), contain elements of judgment. If "accepting" a claimant commitment has the restricted meaning suggested in the notes to s.6A of the Act, that will affect when it might be unreasonable to expect a claimant to do so. If a claimant would be unable or experience undue difficulty in accepting a claimant commitment by any of the methods required by reg.7(3), that would suggest that it would be unreasonable to expect the claimant to take those steps to accept the claimant commitment. In a case where a claimant is entitled to both new style JSA and universal credit, so that under reg.5 above no work-related or connected requirements can be imposed in relation to JSA, it is arguable that it would be unreasonable to expect the claimant to accept a JSA claimant commitment. **6.165**

Expected hours

6.166 **9.**—(1) The expected number of hours per week in relation to a claimant for the purposes of determining any limitations on work search or work availability requirements is 35 unless some lesser number of hours applies in the claimant's case under paragraph (2).

(2) The lesser number of hours referred to in paragraph (1) is—

(a) where—

(i) the claimant is a relevant carer, a responsible carer or a responsible foster parent; and

(ii) the Secretary of State is satisfied that the claimant has reasonable prospects of obtaining paid work, the number of hours, being less than 35, that the Secretary of State considers is compatible with those caring responsibilities;

(b) where the claimant is a responsible carer or a responsible foster carer for a child under the age of 13, the number of hours that the Secretary of State considers is compatible with their caring responsibilities for the child during the child's normal school hours (including the normal time it takes the child to travel to and from school); or

(c) where the claimant has a physical or mental impairment, the number of hours that the Secretary of State considers is reasonable in light of the impairment.

DEFINITIONS

"child"—see Jobseekers Act 1995 s.35(1).
"claimant"—*ibid.*
"relevant carer"—see reg.4(1).
"responsible carer"—*ibid.*
"responsible foster parent"—*ibid.*
"work availability requirement"—see Jobseekers Act 1995 ss.35(1) and 6E.
"work search requirement"—see Jobseekers Act 1995 ss.35(1) and 6D.

GENERAL NOTE

6.167 The identification of the expected number of hours under this provision is relevant to reg.12(1)(a) and (2) below (hours of work search needed to avoid being deemed not to have complied with the work search requirement under s.6D of the new style Jobseekers Act 1995) and reg.14(5) (limitations for certain claimants on the work for which they must be available and for which they must search).

The number of hours under para.(1) is 35, unless some lesser number is applicable under para.(2). Can the number be reduced to zero? Why not? Zero is a number and it is less than 35. There are three alternative categories in para.(2). Sub-paragraph (a) applies where the claimant is a relevant carer, a responsible carer or a responsible foster parent (all as identified in reg.4), and so has some substantial caring responsibility. Then, if the claimant nonetheless has reasonable prospects of obtaining paid work (including obtaining more or better paid work: reg.3(7)), the expected hours are what is compatible with those caring responsibilities. Sub-paragraph (b) applies where the claimant is a responsible carer for a child under the age of 13, when the expected hours are those compatible with the child's normal school and travel hours. Sub-paragraph (c) applies where the claimant has a physical or mental impairment (not further defined), when the expected hours are those reasonable in the light of the impairment.

Note that the application of the deeming of non-compliance with the work search requirement under reg.12(1) if the expected hours of action are not taken is subject to deductions under reg.12(2), including for temporary circumstances. Also note regs 15–16A on circumstances in which the work availability and work search requirements cannot be imposed or are moderated, particularly reg.16(4) (temporary circumstances etc) and regs 16(5) and 16A (unfitness for work for short periods).

Purposes of a work-focused interview

10.—The purposes of a work-focused interview are any or all of the following— **6.168**

(a) assessing the claimant's prospects for remaining in or obtaining work;
(b) assisting or encouraging the claimant to remain in or obtain work;
(c) identifying activities that the claimant may undertake that will make remaining in or obtaining work more likely;
(d) identifying training, educational or rehabilitation opportunities for the claimant which may make it more likely that the claimant will remain in or obtain work or be able to do so;
(e) identifying current or future work opportunities for the claimant that are relevant to the claimant's needs and abilities.

DEFINITION

"claimant"—see Jobseekers Act 1995 s.35(1).

GENERAL NOTE

This provision sets out the purposes of a work-focused interview for the purposes of the definition in s.6B(2) of the new style Jobseekers Act 1995. The purposes could probably not be set out more widely, especially given that obtaining paid work includes obtaining more or better paid work (reg.3(7)). It appears odd that reg.10 uses the word "work" and not "paid work", by contrast with the terms of ss.6C–6E and the regulations related to those sections. The difference may though be deliberate, taking account that s.6B only requires the purposes of the interview to be related to work or work preparation, so that an interview may legitimately include discussion of opportunities that would improve the claimant's prospects of obtaining unpaid work, e.g. as an intern or in voluntary work. Compare ESA Regulations 2008 reg.55 and UC Regulations 2013 reg.93, the latter of which is in terms of paid work. Arguably, even if there is no realistic prospect of a claimant obtaining any kind of work, the purpose of assessing those prospects or lack of prospects in an interview could still be fulfilled. **6.169**

Work search requirement: interviews

11.—A claimant is to be treated as not having complied with a work search requirement to apply for a particular vacancy for paid work where the claimant fails to participate in an interview offered to the claimant in connection with the vacancy. **6.170**

DEFINITIONS

"claimant"—see Jobseekers Act 1995 s.35(1).
"work search requirement"—see Jobseekers Act 1995 ss.35(1) and 6D(1).

General Note

6.171 This provision, made under s.6I(a) of the new style Jobseekers Act 1995, applies when the Secretary of State has required under s.6D(1)(b) that the claimant take the particular action of applying for a specified vacancy for paid work. A claimant who fails to participate in an interview offered in connection with the vacancy is deemed not to have complied with the work search requirement. See the notes to s.6D, and the notes to s.6B for "participation" in an interview.

Work search requirement: all reasonable action

6.172 **12.**—(1) A claimant is to be treated as not having complied with a work search requirement to take all reasonable action for the purpose of obtaining paid work in any week unless—

(a) either—

(i) for the purpose of obtaining paid work, the claimant takes action for the claimant's expected hours per week minus any relevant deductions; or

(ii) the Secretary of State is satisfied that the claimant has taken all reasonable action for the purpose of obtaining paid work despite the number of hours that the claimant spends taking such action being lower than the expected number of hours per week; and

(b) that action gives the claimant the best prospects of obtaining work.

(2) In this regulation "relevant deductions" means the total of any time agreed by the Secretary of State—

(a) for the claimant to carry out paid work in that week;

(b) for the claimant to carry out voluntary work in that week;

(c) for the claimant to carry out a work preparation requirement, or voluntary work preparation, in that week; or

(d) for the claimant to deal with temporary child care responsibilities, a domestic emergency, funeral arrangements or other temporary circumstances.

(3) For the purpose of paragraph (2)(b) the time agreed by the Secretary of State for the claimant to carry out voluntary work must not exceed 50% of the claimant's expected number of hours per week.

Definitions

"claimant"—see Jobseekers Act 1995 s.35(1).
"expected number of hours"—see reg.9.
"obtaining paid work'—see reg.3(7).
"voluntary work"—see reg.2(2).
"voluntary work preparation"—see reg.4(1).
"week"—see Jobseekers Act 1995 s.35(1).
"work preparation requirement"—see Jobseekers Act 1995 ss.35(1) and 6C(1).
"work search requirement"—see Jobseekers Act 1995 ss.35(1) and 6D(1).

General Note

6.173 In old style JSA, the claimant has to be "actively seeking employment", which is a condition of entitlement. For new style JSA, this has become the obligation to comply with a work search requirement, which is no longer a condition of entitlement, but a requirement failure to comply with which for no good reason leads to the sanction of reduction in benefit. Section 6D of the new style Jobseekers Act

1995 deals with what is entailed in that requirement, covering both taking all reasonable action for the purpose of obtaining paid work or more or better-paid work (subs.(1)(a)) and taking any particular action specified by the Secretary of State for that purpose (subs.(1)(b)). Further provision is made in ss.6F and 6H and in regs 14–16A below (limitations on the kind of work that a claimant must search for and circumstances in which the requirement cannot be imposed).

The present regulation, made under s.6I(a) of the Act, deems certain claimants not to have complied with a work search requirement under s.6D(1)(a) to take all reasonable action. Although in form reg.12 merely lifts the deeming of non-compliance if its conditions are met, there would be no point in making such detailed provision if claimants were not to be positively treated as having complied if the conditions are met. See the notes to s.6D and see reg.14 below for limitations on the kind of work that needs to be searched for. A failure for no good reason to comply with the requirement under s.6D(1)(a) can lead to a medium-level sanction under s.6K(2)(a) of the Act and reg.17 (para.(a) of the definition of "medium-level sanction") below.

To avoid the deeming a claimant must get within *both* sub-paras (a) *and* (b) of para.(1). Under (a), the primary rule in head (i) is that the claimant must spend at least the "expected number of hours per week" (reg.9), less deductions for work or work-related activities or various emergency, urgent or other temporary difficulties (para.(2), subject to the further condition about voluntary work in para.(3)), in taking action for the purpose of obtaining paid work. Note that the starting point of expected hours under reg.9 may be reduced from 35 to take account of regular caring responsibilities and physical or mental impairments. The time to count as a deduction under para.(2) must be agreed by the Secretary of State. The words might suggest that the agreement must come in advance of the activity that might qualify. However, it would seem unrealistic for claimants to predict, say, the future occurrence of domestic emergencies so as to seek the Secretary of State's agreement in advance. Thus, it would seem, and would be in line with the normal pattern of claimants signing a declaration that they have been seeking work in the previous fortnight, that a subsequent agreement will do (although no doubt it would be sensible for claimants to raise potential issues in advance where possible). It must be the case that, while the Secretary of State appears to have an open-ended discretion whether or not to agree to any particular hours being deducted under para.(2), on appeal against any sanction for failure to comply with the work search requirement under s.6D(1)(a) a tribunal is allowed to substitute its own judgment about what should have been agreed. Even if it were to be held that whatever had or had not been agreed by the Secretary of State has to control whether there had been a sanctionable failure, the reasonableness or otherwise of the Secretary of State's view would be relevant to whether a failure to comply was "for no good reason". The deductions for hours spent in paid work and voluntary work are important. Would para.(2)(d) allow the Secretary of State to allow short "holidays" from work search, under the heading of temporary circumstances or temporary child care responsibilities (cf. reg.19(1)(p) and (2) of the JSA Regs 1996)? Or would such an allowance fall more naturally under reg.16(4)(a) or (b) (work search requirement not to be imposed where it would be unreasonable to do so because of temporary child care responsibilities or temporary circumstances)?

However, if the claimant cannot meet the expected hours condition, which for most claimants will be for 35 hours per week, sub-para.(a) can nevertheless be satisfied under head (ii) if the claimant has taken all reasonable action for the purpose of obtaining paid work. This important provision must never be overlooked. It can render some of the rigours of head (i) irrelevant and can go some way to meet the criticism that, especially for those who have been unemployed for some time, it is impossible to fill 35 hours with meaningful work-search action week after week.

Under (b), the action under (a) must give the claimant the best prospects of obtaining work, which arguably in the context must mean paid work. Taken at face value, that condition imposes an almost impossibly high standard, because there will nearly always be something extra that the claimant could do to improve prospects of obtaining work. The condition must therefore be interpreted in a way that leaves some work for condition (a) to do and with some degree of common sense, taking account of all the circumstances, especially any factors that have led to a reduction in the expected hours below 35 or a deduction under sub-para.(a)(i), as well as matters such as the state of the local labour market, what the claimant has done in previous weeks and how successful or otherwise those actions were (see reg.18(3) of the JSA Regs 1996). The work search requirement in s.6D(1)(a) is only to take all reasonable action. The reference here to the best prospects of obtaining work cannot be allowed to make the test as set out in the primary legislation stricter than that. There will of course be considerable difficulty in checking on the precise number of hours spent in taking relevant action, depending on what might count as action (see the notes to s.6D), and in what might be required from claimants in the way of record keeping. It may be that it will be much easier to define non-compliance with the requirement in s.6D(1)(b) of the Act to take particular action specified by the Secretary of State, although such a failure will only attract a low-level sanction under s.6K(2)(a) and reg.17 (para.(c) of definition of "low-level sanction") below.

Work availability requirement: able and willing immediately to take up paid work

6.174 **13.**—(1) Subject to paragraph (2), a claimant is to be treated as not having complied with a work availability requirement if the claimant is—

(a) not able and willing immediately to attend an interview offered to the claimant in connection with obtaining paid work;

(b) a prisoner on temporary release in accordance with the provisions of the Prison Act 1952 or rules made under section 39(6) of the Prisons (Scotland) Act 1989.

(2) A claimant is to be treated as having complied with a work availability requirement despite not being able immediately to take up paid work, if paragraph (3), (4) or (5) applies.

(3) This paragraph applies where—

(a) a claimant is a responsible carer or a relevant carer;

(b) the Secretary of State is satisfied that as a consequence the claimant needs a period of up to one month to take up paid work, or up to 48 hours to attend an interview in connection with obtaining paid work, taking into account alternative care arrangements; and

(c) the claimant is able and willing to take up paid work, or attend such an interview, on being given notice for that period.

(4) This paragraph applies where—

(a) a claimant is carrying out voluntary work;

(b) the Secretary of State is satisfied that as a consequence the claimant needs a period of up to one week to take up paid work, or up to 48 hours to attend an interview in connection with obtaining paid work; and

(c) the claimant is able and willing to take up paid work, or attend such an interview, on being given notice for that period.

(5) This paragraph applies where a claimant is—

(a) employed under a contract of service;

(b) required by section 86 of the Employment Rights Act 1996, or by the contract of service, to give notice to terminate the contract;

(c) able and willing to take up paid work once the notice period has expired; and

(d) able and willing to attend an interview in connection with obtaining paid work on being given 48 hours notice.

DEFINITIONS

"claimant"—see Jobseekers Act 1995 s.35(1).
"obtaining paid work"—see reg.3(7).
"relevant carer"—see reg.4(1).
"responsible carer"—*ibid.*
"voluntary work"—see reg.2(2).
"work availability requirement"—see Jobseekers Act 1995 ss.35(1) and 6E.

GENERAL NOTE

In old style JSA, s.6 of the old style Jobseekers Act 1995 stipulates that a claimant satisfies the condition of entitlement of being available for work if willing and able to take up immediately any employed earner's employment and the JSA Regulations 1996 provide some exemptions from the "immediately" requirement (reg.5) and enable limitations to be placed on availability (regs 6–13A). For new style JSA, this has become the obligation to comply with a work availability requirement, which is no longer a condition of entitlement, but a requirement failure to comply with which for no good reason leads to the sanction of reduction in benefit. Section 6E of the new style Jobseekers Act 1995 deals with what is entailed in that requirement, in particular being able and willing immediately to take up paid work or more or better paid work. See reg.14 below for limitations on the kind of work for which a claimant must be available and regs 16 and 16A for other situations in which the "immediately" test is modified. **6.175**

Paragraph (1) of this regulation specifies that a prisoner on temporary release is to be treated as not available (sub-para.(b)). More generally it provides in sub-para.(a) that a claimant is not available for work if not able and willing immediately to attend an interview offered to the claimant in connection with paid work, unless (as provided in para.(2)) one of the exemptions from the "immediately" requirement set out in paras (3), (4) or (5) applies.

Under para.(2) a claimant who falls within paras (3), (4) or (5) is to be treated as complying with the work availability requirement, including as extended by para.(1). Paragraph (3) applies to those with child-care or other caring responsibilities who would need to take up to one month to take up paid work or up to 48 hours to attend an interview and are able and willing to do so if given that length of notice. Can para.(3)(b) allow claimants with caring responsibilities (noting that such claimants do not need to have sole or main responsibility) to have a holiday without needing to arrange some means of taking up work offers or interviews immediately? Or would such an allowance fall more naturally under reg.16(4)(a) or (b) (no need to be available immediately where work search requirement not to be imposed because it would be unreasonable to do so because of temporary child care responsibilities or temporary circumstances)? Paragraph (4) applies to claimants doing voluntary work (as defined in reg.2(2)), subject to the same conditions. Paragraph (5) applies to claimants in employment who are required to give notice to terminate their contract of employment and who are able and willing to take up paid work once that notice has expired and to attend an interview on 48 hours' notice.

Work search requirement and work availability requirement: limitations

14.—(1) Paragraphs (2) to (5) set out the limitations on a work search requirement and a work availability requirement. **6.176**

(2) A work search requirement and a work availability requirement must be limited to work that is in a location which would normally take the claimant—

(a) a maximum of one hour and 30 minutes to travel from home to the location; and

(b) a maximum of one hour and 30 minutes to travel from the location to home.

(3) Where a claimant has previously carried out work of a particular nature, or at a particular level of remuneration, a work search requirement and a work availability requirement must be limited to work of a similar nature, or level of remuneration, for such period as the Secretary of State considers appropriate; but

(a) only if the Secretary of State is satisfied that the claimant will have reasonable prospects of obtaining paid work in spite of such limitation; and

(b) the limitation is to apply for no more than three months beginning on the date of claim.

(4) Where a claimant has a physical or mental impairment that has a substantial adverse effect on the claimant's ability to carry out work of a particular nature, or in particular locations, a work search requirement or work availability requirement must not relate to work of such a nature or in such locations.

(5) In the case of a claimant who is a relevant carer or a responsible carer or has a physical or mental impairment, a work search and work availability requirement must be limited to the number of hours that is determined to be the claimant's expected number of hours per week in accordance with regulation 9(2).

DEFINITIONS

"claimant"—see Jobseekers Act 1995 s.35(1).
"date of claim"—see reg.2(2).
"obtaining paid work"—see reg.3(7).
"relevant carer"—see reg.4(1).
"responsible carer"—see reg.4(1).
"week"—see Jobseekers Act 1995 s.35(1).
"work availability requirement"—see Jobseekers Act 1995 ss.35(1) and 6E.
"work search requirement"—see Jobseekers Act 1995 ss.35(1) and 6D.

GENERAL NOTE

6.177 This regulation is made under ss.6D(4) and (5) (work search requirement) and 6E(3) and (4) (work availability requirement) of the new style Jobseekers Act 1995. It sets out limitations on the kind of work that a claimant can be required to search for or be able and willing immediately to take up. See regs 15, 16 and 16A for other situations in which those requirements cannot be imposed or the ordinary tests are modified.

Paragraph (2)

6.178 A work search or availability requirement cannot relate to work in a location where the claimant's normal travel time either from home to work or from work to home would exceed 90 minutes, subject to the further limitation in para.(4) for some disabled claimants. Travel times below that limit could be relevant in relation to a sanction for non-compliance with a requirement, on the question whether the claimant had no good reason for the failure to comply. On that question all circumstances could be considered, including the effect of any physical or mental impairment not serious enough to count under para.(4), whereas under this provision time is the conclusive factor unless the location is completely excluded under para.(4).

Paragraph (3)

A claimant who has previously carried out work of a particular nature or at a particular level of remuneration is to have the kind of work to be considered limited to similar conditions for so long as considered appropriate up to three months from the date of claim. But the rule only applies if and so long as the claimant will have reasonable prospects of obtaining paid work (or more or better paid work) subject to that limitation. **6.179**

Paragraph (4)

A claimant who has a physical or mental impairment (not further defined) which has a substantial adverse effect on their ability to carry out work of a particular nature or in particular locations (a significant additional condition over and above that of impairment or disability on its own) is to have the kind of work to be considered under the work search and work availability requirements limited to avoid such work. **6.180**

Paragraph (5)

This paragraph establishes an important limitation on the kind of work that can be considered, but only for the particular categories of claimant identified: those with child care responsibilities and those with physical or mental impairments. Those categories of claimant can only be required to search for or to be able and willing to take up work for no more than the number of hours per week compatible with those circumstances, as worked out under reg.9(2). So far as the work search requirement is concerned, this limitation appears to apply as much to the sort of work in relation to which the Secretary of State may specify particular action under s.6D(1)(b) of the new style Jobseekers Act 1995 as to the requirement under s.6D(1)(a) to take all reasonable action for the purpose of obtaining paid work or more or better paid work. **6.181**

Victims of domestic violence

15.—(1) Where a claimant has recently been a victim of domestic violence and the circumstances set out in paragraph (3) apply— **6.182**

(a) a requirement imposed on that claimant under sections 6 to 6G of the Act ceases to have effect for a period of 13 consecutive weeks starting on the date of the notification referred to in paragraph (3)(a); and

(b) the Secretary of State must not impose any other such requirement on that claimant during that period.

(2) A person has recently been a victim of domestic violence if a period of six months has not expired since the violence was inflicted or threatened.

(3) The circumstances are that—

(a) the claimant notifies the Secretary of State, in such manner as the Secretary of State specifies, that domestic violence has been inflicted on or threatened against the claimant by a person specified in paragraph (4) during the period of six months ending on the date of the notification;

(b) this regulation has not applied to the claimant for a period of 12 months before the date of the notification;

(c) on the date of the notification the claimant is not living at the same address as the person who inflicted or threatened the domestic violence; and

(d) as soon as possible, and no later than one month, after the date of the notification the claimant provides evidence from a person acting in an official capacity which demonstrates that—

(i) the claimant's circumstances are consistent with those of a person who has had domestic violence inflicted on or threatened against them during the period of six months ending on the date of the notification; and

(ii) the claimant has made contact with the person acting in an official capacity in relation to such an incident, which occurred during that period.

(4) A person is specified in this paragraph if the person is—

(a) where the claimant is, or was, a member of a couple, the other member of the couple;

(b) the claimant's grandparent, grandchild, parent, parent-in-law, son, son-in-law, daughter, daughter-in-law, step-parent, step-son, step-daughter, brother, step-brother, brother-in-law, sister, step-sister or sister-in-law; or

(c) where any of the persons listed in sub-paragraph (b) is a member of a couple, the other member of that couple.

(5) In this regulation—

[1"coercive behaviour" means an act of assault, humiliation or intimidation or other abuse that is used to harm, punish or frighten the victim;

"controlling behaviour" means an act designed to make a person subordinate or dependent by isolating them from sources of support, exploiting their resources and capacities for personal gain, depriving them of the means needed for independence, resistance or escape or regulating their everyday behaviour;

"domestic violence" means any incident, or pattern of incidents, of controlling behaviour, coercive behaviour, violence or abuse, including but not limited to—

(a) psychological abuse;
(b) physical abuse;
(c) sexual abuse;
(d) emotional abuse;
(e) financial abuse,

regardless of the gender or sexuality of the victim;

"health care professional" means a person who is a member of a profession regulated by a body mentioned in section 25(3) of the National Health Service Reform and Health Care Professions Act 2002;

"person acting in an official capacity" means a health care professional, a police officer, a registered social worker, the claimant's employer, a representative of the claimant's trade union or any public, voluntary or charitable body which has had direct contact with the claimant in connection with domestic violence;

"registered social worker" means a person registered as a social worker in a register maintained by—

[2 (a) the Health and Care Professions Council;]
(b) the Care Council for Wales;
(c) the Scottish Social Services Council; or
(d) the Northern Ireland Social Care Council.

AMENDMENTS

1. Social Security (Miscellaneous Amendments) (No.2) Regulations 2013 (SI 2013/1508) reg.4(1) and (2) (October 29, 2013).

2. Universal Credit and Miscellaneous Amendments Regulations 2014 reg.3(2) (April 28, 2014).

DEFINITIONS

"the Act"—see reg.2(2).
"claimant"—see Jobseekers Act 1995 s.35(1).
"couple"—*ibid.*
"victim of domestic violence"—see Jobseekers Act 1995 s.6H(6)(b).

GENERAL NOTE

This regulation, made as required by s.6H(5) and (6) of the new style Jobseekers Act 1995, exempts recent victims of domestic violence from the imposition of any work-related or connected requirements for a period of 13 weeks from the date of notification to the Secretary of State under para.(3)(a) and lifts the effect of any existing imposition for the same period. Equivalent provision has been made in the UC Regulations 2013 reg.98 (Vol.V of this series, but note that in error the October 2013 amendment was omitted) and JSA Regulations 1996 reg.14A (Pt III of the present volume). **6.183**

Section 6H(6) of the Act, while defining "victim of domestic violence" as a person on or against whom domestic violence had been inflicted or threatened, left the meaning of "domestic violence" and of what is to be treated as recent to regulations. Paragraph (2) of this regulation provides that a person has recently been a victim of domestic violence if no more than six months has elapsed since its infliction or threat. Initially, para.(5) required the meaning of "domestic violence" to be in terms of abuse which is specified on a particular page of the December 2005 Department of Health document *Responding to domestic abuse: a handbook for health professionals*. It was not very satisfactory for an important definition not only not to be set out in the Regulations, but to be in a publication that was difficult to find (the text was reproduced in the note to reg.98 of the Universal Credit Regulations in Vol.V). Also, its terms were perhaps not well-suited to the particular benefits context. The new definition in para.(5), expanded into various forms of abuse and into further definitions of coercive and controlling behaviour, is still very wide. That makes the specification in para.(3) of the circumstances in which reg.15 applies more important. See the notes to reg.14A of the JSA Regulations 1996 (Pt III) for further discussion of the definition.

Paragraph (3)

This paragraph lays down four quite restrictive conditions that must all be satisfied for reg.15 to apply. Under sub-para.(a) the claimant must have notified the Secretary of State of the infliction or threatening of domestic violence by a partner, former partner or family member or relative (as defined in para.(4)) within the previous six months. Under sub-para.(b), reg.15 must not have applied within the 12 months before the notification. Under sub-para.(c), the claimant must not on the date of the notification have been living at the same address as the person named as the assailant. Under sub-para.(d), the claimant must also provide, as soon as possible and no more than one month after the notification, evidence from a person acting in an official capacity (defined quite widely in para.(5)) both that the claimant's circumstances are consistent with having had domestic violence inflicted or threatened in the six months before notification and that the claimant had made contact (apparently not necessarily within the six months) with the person in relation to an incident of infliction or threat of domestic violence that occurred during the six months before notification. **6.184**

The transition from old style JSA

In para.(3)(b) the reference to reg.15 applying to the claimant is, where art.12(1) and (2) of the Welfare Reform Act 2012 (Commencement No.9 and Transitional and Transitory Provisions and Commencement No.8 and Savings and Transitional Provisions (Amendment)) Order 2013 (as amended and set out in the 2014/15 Supplement) applies, to be read as if it included a reference to the claimant having been treated as available for employment under reg.14A(2) or (6) of the JSA Regulations 1996 (art.12(3)(a) of that Order). **6.185**

Circumstances in which requirements must not be imposed

6.186 **16.**—(1) Where paragraph (3), (4) or (5) applies—

(a) the Secretary of State must not impose a work search requirement on a claimant; and

(b) "able and willing immediately to take up work" under a work availability requirement means able and willing to take up paid work, or attend an interview, immediately once the circumstances set out in paragraph (3), (4) or (5) no longer apply.

(2) A work search requirement previously applying to the claimant ceases to have effect from the date on which the circumstances set out in paragraph (3), (4) or (5) apply.

(3) This paragraph applies where—

(a) the claimant is attending a court or tribunal as a party to any proceedings or as a witness;

(b) the claimant is temporarily absent from Great Britain because they are—

(i) taking their child outside Great Britain for medical treatment;

(ii) attending a job interview outside Great Britain; or

(iii) receiving medical treatment outside Great Britain;

(c) it is within six months of the death of—

(i) where the claimant is a member of a couple, the other member;

(ii) a child for whom the claimant or, where the claimant is a member of a couple, the other member, is responsible; or

(iii) a child, where the claimant is the child's parent;

(d) the claimant is receiving and participating in a structured, recovery-orientated, course of alcohol or drug dependency treatment, for a period of up to six months (where the course is for more than six months, this sub-paragraph only applies for the first six months);

(e) the claimant is a person for whom arrangements have been made by a protection provider under section 82 of the Serious Organised Crime and Police Act 2005, for a period of up to three months (where the arrangements are for more than three months, this sub-paragraph only applies for the first three months).

(4) This paragraph applies where the Secretary of State is satisfied that it would be unreasonable to require the claimant to comply with a work search requirement, including if such a requirement were limited in accordance with section 6D(4) of the Act, because the claimant—

(a) has temporary child care responsibilities;

(b) is subject to temporary circumstances;

(c) is carrying out a public duty; or

(d) is carrying out a work preparation requirement or voluntary work preparation.

(5) This paragraph applies where the claimant—

(a) is unfit for work—

(i) for a maximum of 14 consecutive days after the date on which the evidence referred to in sub-paragraph (b) is provided; and

(ii) on no more than two such periods in any period of 12 months; and

(b) provides to the Secretary of State the following evidence—

(i) for the first seven days when they are unfit for work, a declaration made by the claimant in such manner and form as the Secretary of State approves that the claimant is unfit for work; and

(ii) for any further days when they are unfit for work, a statement given by a doctor in accordance with the rules set out in Part 1 of Schedule 1 to the Social Security (Medical Evidence) Regulations 1976 which advises that the person is not fit for work.

(6) In this regulation, "tribunal" means any tribunal listed in Schedule 1 to the Tribunal and Inquiries Act 1992.

DEFINITIONS

"the Act"—see reg.2(2).
"child"—see Jobseekers Act 1995 s.35(1).
"claimant"—*ibid.*
"Great Britain"—*ibid.*
"voluntary work preparation"—see reg.4(1).
"work availability requirement"—see Jobseekers Act 1995 ss.35(1) and 6E.
"work preparation requirement"—see Jobseekers Act 1995 ss.35(1) and 6C.
"work search requirement"—see Jobseekers Act 1995 ss.35(1) and 6D.

GENERAL NOTE

This regulation is made under s.6H(1)(a) of the new style Jobseekers Act 1995 in respect of the work search requirement and under s.6E(5) in respect of the work availability requirement. Any claimant falling under paras (3)–(5) cannot have a work search requirement imposed (para.(1)(a)) and any existing such requirement ceases to have effect (para.(2)). And the requirement in s.6E(2) to be able and willing immediately to take up work means able to take up work, or attend an interview immediately the relevant circumstance under paras (3)–(5) ceases to exist. Regulation 16 does not affect the imposition of the work-focused interview requirement and the work preparation requirement, although under s.6F(2) of the new style Jobseekers Act 1995 there is a discretion regarding whether or not to impose those requirements, under which all relevant circumstances must be considered. **6.187**

Paragraph (3)

Paragraph (3) lists a number of categories of claimant where the circumstances mean that the claimant could not be expected to look for or take up work or attend an interview, generally of a temporary and fairly clear-cut nature. Cases which fall outside para.(3) can come within the much more open-ended provisions in para.(4) subject to the additional express condition that it would be unreasonable to require the claimant to comply with a work search requirement in the circumstances. **6.188**

(a) Attending a court or tribunal (defined in para.(6)) as a party to proceedings or as a witness, apparently so long as the hearing continues for a party and so long as attendance is required for a witness.

(b) Temporary absence from Great Britain in connection with medical treatment or accompanying a child undergoing such treatment, or to attend a job interview abroad. This provision seems very narrowly drawn by comparison with reg.99(3)(c) of the UC Regulations on medical treatment, etc. It appears to be restricted to the claimant and a child of the claimant (whatever that precisely means) and does not extend to accompanying a partner or a young person who is a member of the family abroad for medical treatment. Nor is it clear that convalescence would come within "medical treatment". But reg.16 may still apply where reasonable through the operation of para. (4).

(c) The claimant's then partner, a child (but not a young person) for whom the claimant or partner was responsible or a child of the claimant has died within the previous six months.

(d) Attending a structured recovery-oriented course of alcohol or drug dependency treatment, for no more than six months.

(e) Having protection arrangements made under s.82 of the Serious Organised Crime and Police Act 2005 (protection of persons involved in investigations or proceedings whose safety is considered to be at risk), for no more than three months. Arrangements for protection are made by protection providers (e.g. Chief Constables, any of the Commissioners for Her Majesty's Revenue and Customs).

Paragraph (4)

6.189 In four sorts of circumstances the imposition of a work search requirement or the satisfaction of a work availability requirement, even as limited under and s.6D(4) of the Act and reg.14, can be further restricted where those circumstances make it unreasonable for the claimant to be required to comply with the requirement. Although, in contrast to reg.99(5) of the UC Regulations, there is no express reference to whether or not it would be reasonable to apply the usual "immediately" test under the work availability requirement, for para.(1)(b) to apply while circumstances identified in para.(4) exist some such reference must be implied. Sub-paragraph (a) applies if the claimant has temporary child care responsibilities (apparently for any child). Sub-paragraph (b) applies where the claimant is subject to any kind of temporary circumstances. Sub-paragraph (c) applies where the claimant is carrying out any kind of public duty (not further defined). Sub-paragraph (d) applies if the claimant is carrying out a work preparation requirement (s.6C(1) of the Act) or a voluntary work preparation requirement (reg.4(1)).

It is arguable that under sub-para.(b), or (a) where the claimant has some responsibility for care of a child, the application of the work search requirement and the "immediate" obligations of the work availability requirement can be lifted during a holiday. The crucial test is whether it is unreasonable to expect the claimant to comply with the normal requirements. Claimants in part-time work, not amounting to remunerative work under s.1(2)(e) of the new style Jobseekers Act 1995, will have statutory holiday entitlements and it is arguable, depending of course on all the circumstances (including the likelihood of some actual opportunity arising for the claimant in question during the holiday period), that that should be acknowledged in the JSA system. Regulation 19(1)(p) and (2) of the JSA Regulations 1996 allows claimants of old style JSA two weeks off from actively seeking employment within any 12 months if residing away from home, and see the notes to s.6 of the old style Jobseekers Act 1995 for extensive discussion of the operation of the condition of entitlement of availability for employment during a holiday. If some other member of the claimant's family is in work and contractually entitled to holiday, an argument about reasonableness could still perhaps be made.

Paragraph (5)

6.190 A claimant who is unfit for work (not further defined) and provides a self-certificate for the first seven days and, if requested, a statement from a doctor under the Medical Evidence Regulations (see Vol.I) for any further days falls within the basic rules in this regulation. But the benefit of para.(5) is limited to a period of no more than 14 days after the evidence is provided and to no more than two such periods in any 12 months. There is a possible extension of those restrictions under para.(4)(b).

Now see reg.16A for the terms on which there can be a similar lifting of restrictions for an extended period of sickness, up to 13 weeks. The application of reg.16A can follow on from a period under reg.16(5) but not vice versa (see the notes to reg.46A).

[[1]Further circumstances in which requirements must not be imposed

16A.—(1) This regulation applies in the case of a claimant who is treated as capable of work or as not having limited capability for work under regulation 46A (extended period of sickness). **6.190A**

(2) Where the Secretary of State is satisfied that it would be unreasonable to require the claimant to comply with a work search requirement—

(a) the Secretary of State must not impose a work search requirement on the claimant; and

(b) a work search requirement previously applying to the claimant ceases to have effect from the date on which the claimant is first treated as capable of work or as having limited capability for work under regulation 46A.

(3) Paragraph (4) applies where the Secretary of State is satisfied that it would be unreasonable to require the claimant to comply with a work availability requirement to be able and willing to—

(a) take up work; and

(b) attend an interview.

(4) Where this paragraph applies, "able and willing to take up work" under a work availability requirement means able and willing to take up paid work and to attend an interview, immediately once the claimant ceases to be treated as capable of work or as not having limited capability for work under regulation 46A.

(5) Paragraph (6) applies where the Secretary of State is satisfied that it would be—

(a) unreasonable to require the claimant to comply with a work availability requirement to able and willing to take up work; and

(b) reasonable to require the claimant to comply with a work availability requirement to be able and willing to attend an interview.

(6) Where this paragraph applies, "able and willing to take up work" under a work availability requirement means—

(a) able and willing to take up paid work immediately once the claimant ceases to be treated as capable of work or as not having limited capability for work under regulation 46A; and

(b) able and willing to attend an interview before the claimant ceases to be so treated.]

Amendment

1. Jobseeker's Allowance (Extended Period of Sickness) Amendment Regulations 2015 (SI 2015/339) reg.3(2) (March 30, 2015).

Definitions

"claimant"—see Jobseekers Act 1995 s.35(1).
"paid work"—see reg.3(7).
"work availability requirement"—see Jobseekers Act 1995 ss.35(1) and 6E.
"work search requirement"—see Jobseekers Act 1995 ss.35(1) and 6D.

General Note

This regulation, together with reg.46A, provides a new extension to the rules in regs 16(5) and 46. The latter provisions allow, no more than twice in any 12 months, qualification for new style JSA while the claimant is unfit for work for **6.191** a period of up to 14 days. Regulation 16(5) (with sub-paras (1) and (2)) prevents the application of the work search requirement and modifies the work availability requirement. Regulation 46, under similar but slightly more restrictive conditions, deems the claimant to satisfy the condition of entitlement in s.1(2)(f) of the new style Jobseekers Act 1995 (does not have limited capability for work). The new provisions can produce the same effect for an extended period of up to 13 weeks but only once in any 12 months.

Regulation 16A is directly linked to the application of reg.46A. By virtue of para.(1) it only applies to claimants who are treated under reg.46A as capable of work or as not having limited capability for work (and so satisfy the condition of entitlement in s.1(2)(f)). The assessment of the evidence about fitness to work therefore takes place under reg.46A. By contrast to the position under reg.16, the effect on the work search requirement and the work availability requirement is not automatic but depends on a determination that it would be unreasonable to require the claimant to comply with a work search requirement or to be able and willing to take up work and/or attend an interview.

Regulation 16A does not affect the imposition of the work-focused interview requirement and the work preparation requirement. However, under s.6F(2) of the new style Jobseekers Act 1995 there is a discretion regarding whether or not to impose those requirements, under which all relevant circumstances must be considered.

PART 3

SANCTIONS

Interpretation

6.192 **17.**—For the purposes of this Part—

"ESA sanctionable failure" means a failure by a claimant which is sanctionable under section 11J of the Welfare Reform Act 2007;

"higher-level sanction" means a reduction of a jobseeker's allowance in accordance with section 6J of the Act;

"low-level sanction" means a reduction of a jobseeker's allowance in accordance with section 6K of the Act for a sanctionable failure by the claimant to comply with—

(a) a work-focused interview requirement under section 6B(1) of the Act;

(b) a work preparation requirement under section 6C(1) of the Act;

(c) a work search requirement under section 6D(1)(b) of the Act (requirement to take action specified by the Secretary of State to obtain work); or

(d) a requirement under section 6G of the Act (connected requirements);

"medium-level sanction" means a reduction of a jobseeker's allowance in accordance with section 6K of the Act for a sanctionable failure by the claimant to comply with—

(a) a work search requirement under section 6D(1)(a) of the Act (requirement to take all reasonable action to obtain paid work); or

(b) a work availability requirement under section 6E(1) of the Act (requirement to be available for work);

"pre-claim failure" means a sanctionable failure listed in section 6J(3) of the Act;

"reduction period" means the number of days for which a reduction in the amount of an award of a jobseeker's allowance is to have effect;

"sanctionable failure" means a failure by a claimant which is sanctionable under section 6J or 6K of the Act;

"total outstanding reduction period" means the total number of days for which no reduction has yet been applied for all of the claimant's higher-level sanctions, medium-level sanctions, low-level sanctions and reductions to which regulation 30 applies;

"UC sanctionable failure" means a failure by a claimant which is sanctionable under section 26 or 27 of the Welfare Reform Act 2012.

DEFINITION

"the Act"—see reg.2(2).

GENERAL NOTE

The general structure of the sanctions regime for new style JSA is set out in ss.6J and 6K of the Jobseekers Act 1995. This regulation provides definitions of various terms for the purposes of the more detailed provisions in the rest of Pt 3. However, the definitions of "higher-level sanction", "medium-level sanction" and "low-level sanction" in fact provide substantive rules about what sorts of failures to comply with work-related and connected requirements give rise to each level of sanction, the consequences of which are identified in regs 19–21 below. 6.193

A "higher-level sanction" is one imposed under s.6J of the Act, which, although headed "higher-level sanctions", does not use those words in its text. A "medium-level sanction" is one imposed under s.6K(2)(a) for a failure to comply with either of two specific requirements: a requirement to take all reasonable action to obtain paid work under s.6D(1)(a) (work search requirement) or a requirement to be available for work under s.6E(1). A "low-level sanction" is imposed for failures to comply with any other work-related or connected requirement.

General principles for calculating reduction periods

18.—(1) Subject to paragraphs (3) and (4), the reduction period is to be determined in relation to each sanctionable failure in accordance with regulations 19, 20 and 21. 6.194

(2) Reduction periods are to run consecutively.

(3) Where the reduction period calculated in relation to a sanctionable failure in accordance with regulation 19, 20 or 21 would result in the total outstanding reduction period exceeding 1095 days, the number of days in the reduction period in relation to that failure is to be adjusted so that 1095 days is not exceeded.

(4) In determining the reduction period in relation to a sanctionable failure, a previous sanctionable failure, UC sanctionable failure or ESA sanctionable failure is to be disregarded if it—

(a) occurred in the [1 13] days immediately preceding the failure in question; and

(b) gave rise to a reduction under these Regulations, the Universal Credit Regulations 2013 or the Employment and Support Allowance Regulations 2013.

AMENDMENT

1. Universal Credit and Miscellaneous Amendments Regulations 2014 (SI 2014/597) reg.3(3) (April 28, 2014).

DEFINITIONS

"ESA sanctionable failure"—see reg.17.
"reduction period"—*ibid.*
"sanctionable failure"—*ibid.*
"total outstanding reduction period"—*ibid.*
"UC sanctionable failure"—*ibid.*

GENERAL NOTE

6.195 Under ss.6J(1) and 6K(1) of the new style Jobseekers Act 1995, the definition of "reduction period" in reg.17 and this provision, the way in which a sanction bites is through a reduction in the amount of an award of JSA for a period determined under regs 19–21 for each sanctionable failure. A sanctionable failure is a failure which is sanctionable under s.6J or 6K of the Act, but that is subject to the rule in reg.5 above that the new style JSA requirements and sanctions regime does not apply at all if the claimant is entitled to universal credit. This regulation contains some general rules on calculating the length of sanction periods, which is where the main differences between higher, medium and low-level sanctions lie.

Under para.(2) reduction periods for separate new style JSA sanctionable failures run consecutively. The effect of reg.30 below is that if a claimant ceases to be entitled to universal credit while a reduction period for a universal credit sanction is running and either continues to be or becomes entitled to new style JSA, the balance of the period is to be to applied to the JSA award. Thus any reduction period for a new JSA sanctionable failure would appear to have to run consecutively after the expiry of the former universal credit reduction period and not concurrently. There appears to be no equivalent provision for the effect of an outstanding ESA sanctionable failure.

The general rule in para.(2) is subject to the general overall three-year limit in para.(3). The drafting is fairly impenetrable but the upshot seems to be that if adding a new reduction period to the end of an existing period or, more likely, chain of reduction periods would take the total days in the periods over 1095 days the new reduction period is to be adjusted to make the total 1095 days exactly. The definition of "total outstanding reduction period" in reg.17 expressly brings in the effect of reg.30, where it applies, to count the outstanding balance of a universal credit reduction period towards the 1095-day limit.

6.196 Paragraph (4) applies in the main to situations in regs 19–21 where the length of a reduction period depends on whether there have been any previous sanctionable failures, including under universal credit and, for low-level sanctions, ESA. A sanctionable failure within the 13 days immediately preceding the sanctionable failure in question is to be disregarded for this purpose. What is not so clear is whether para.(4) also qualifies para.(3) to allow a total outstanding reduction period to exceed 1095 days. With effect from July 25, 2016, the rule in para.(4)(a) is to be incorporated directly in regs 19–21 (SI 2016/678).

Note also the circumstances prescribed in reg.28 where there is to be no reduction despite the existence of a sanctionable failure under s.6J (and not s.6K).

The transition from old style JSA

6.197 Articles 17 and 18 of the Welfare Reform Act 2012 (Commencement No.9 and Transitional and Transitory Provisions and Commencement No.8 and Savings and Transitional Provisions (Amendment)) Order 2013 (as amended and set out in the 2014/15 Supplement) set out some rules operating where a claimant was, before becoming entitled to new style JSA, subject to a reduction in benefit from old style JSA by reason of a sanction under ss.19 or 19A of the old style Jobseekers Act 1995 or reg.69B of the JSA Regulations 1996. Article 17 deals with the situation where the old style JSA award was not in existence immediately before the first day of entitlement under the new style JSA award. Article 18 deals with the situation where the old style JSA award continues as a new style award without any gap. Essentially the same rules are applied. Where the old style JSA reduction was made under s.19, the circumstances are to be treated as a failure sanctionable under s.6J of the new style Jobseekers Act 1995. Where the old style JSA reduction was made under s.19A or reg.69B, the circumstances are to be treated as a failure sanctionable under s.6K. Then a reduction is to be made to the new style JSA award in accordance with the present Regulations as modified by arts.17(4) and 18(4) and is to be treated as made under s.6J or 6K as appropriate. The reduction period is to be the same as that imposed by the old style JSA reduction decision, reduced by the number of days for which the old style JSA was reduced and (in the case of art.17) the number of days between the end of the old style JSA award and the first day of entitlement under the new style JSA award. Where art.17 applies, the references in reg.18(1) and (3) to regs 19, 20 and 21 are replaced by references to art.17 (art.17(4)). Where art.18 applies, they are replaced by references to art.18 (art.18(4)).

Higher-level sanction

19.—(1) Where the sanctionable failure is not a pre-claim failure, the reduction period for a higher-level sanction is— **6.198**

(a) 91 days, if sub-paragraphs (b) and (c) do not apply;

(b) 182 days, if in the [1364] days preceding the failure in question there was—

(i) another sanctionable failure giving rise to a higher-level sanction for which a 91 day reduction period applies; or

(ii) a UC sanctionable failure giving rise to a higher-level sanction under regulation 102(2) of the Universal Credit Regulations 2013 for which a 91 day reduction period applies; or

(c) 1095 days, if in that period of [1364] days there was—

(i) another sanctionable failure giving rise to a higher-level sanction for which a 182 day or 1095 day reduction period applies; or

(ii) a UC sanctionable failure giving rise to a higher-level sanction under regulation 102(2) of the Universal Credit Regulations 2013 for which a 182 day or 1095 day reduction period applies.

(2) But where—

(a) the other sanctionable failure referred to in paragraph (1) was a pre-claim failure; or

(b) the UC sanctionable failure referred to in paragraph (1) was a pre-claim failure under regulation 102(4) of the Universal Credit Regulations 2013,

it is to be disregarded in determining the reduction period in accordance with paragraph (1).

(3) Where the sanctionable failure for which a reduction period is to be determined is a pre-claim failure, the reduction period is the lesser of—

(a) the period which would be applicable to the claimant under paragraph (1) if it were not a pre-claim failure; or

(b) where the sanctionable failure relates to paid work that was due to last for a limited period, the period beginning with the day after the date of the sanctionable failure and ending with the last day of the limited period,

minus the number of days beginning with the day after the date of the sanctionable failure and ending with the day before the date of claim.

AMENDMENT

1. Universal Credit and Miscellaneous Amendments Regulations 2014 (SI 2014/597) reg.3(4) (April 28, 2014).

DEFINITIONS

"date of claim"—see reg.2(2).
"higher-level sanction"—see reg.17.
"pre-claim failure"—*ibid.*
"reduction period"—*ibid.*
"sanctionable failure"—*ibid.*
"UC sanctionable failure"—*ibid.*

GENERAL NOTE

6.199 Higher-level sanctions are applicable to failures under s.6J of the new style Jobseekers Act 1995 (see the definition in reg.17). Such failures fall outside the scope of regs 20 and 21 and no failures under s.6K can come within the present regulation. Note the effect of reg.28 in preventing there being any reduction in benefit in specified circumstances though there has been a sanctionable failure under s.6J. There is a distinction between "pre-claim failures", i.e. failures under s.6J(3) (before the relevant claim failing for no good reason to take up an offer of paid work or ceasing paid work or losing pay by reason of misconduct or voluntarily and for no good reason), and other failures.

The general rule in para.(1)(a) for non-pre-claim failures is that the reduction period is 91 days if there have been no other higher-level sanctionable failures (or equivalent universal credit failures) in the previous 364 days, 182 days if there has been one other such failure in that period and 1095 days if there have been two or more such failures in that period. That is subject first to the rule in para.(2) that pre-claim failures are disregarded for that purpose. It is also subject to the limit in reg.18(3) and to the disregard in reg.18(4) of sanctionable failures in the 13 days before the sanctionable failure in question. See the notes to regs 25 and 28 below for discussion of when a sanctionable failure can be said to have given "rise to a higher-level sanction" or not. That form of words appears to require that reduction of benefit has at least been initially imposed.

For pre-claim sanctionable failures, under para.(3) the number of days between the date of the failure and the date of the relevant claim is deducted from the number of days in the reduction period calculated as under para.(1). That is subject to the further rule that if the sanctionable failure relates to paid work that was due to last only for a limited period, the period down to the date when the work was due to end is substituted for the para.(2) period in the calculation. Presumably that is to give an incentive to people to take such work. See also reg.28(1)(c) removing the possibility of a reduction of benefit if the JSA claim is made outside the period of reduction that would otherwise have applied to the pre-claim failure.

The form of this regulation is to be amended with effect from July 25, 2016 by SI 2016/678 to clarify its operation and close some unintended gaps.

The transition from old style JSA

6.200 Where there is a sanctionable failure directly under the new style JSA legislation, a reduction of a new style award under art.17 or 18 of the Welfare Reform Act 2012 (Commencement No.9 and Transitional and Transitory Provisions and Commencement No.8 and Savings and Transitional Provisions (Amendment)) Order 2013 (as amended and set out in the 2014/15 Supplement) (see the notes to reg.18) or a reduction of an old style JSA award counts as a previous sanctionable failure for which the reduction period is the number of days equivalent to the length of the period which applied under the old style JSA legislation (art.19 of that Order). However, if a period of entitlement to old style JSA, old style ESA or income support has intervened since the end of the new style JSA reduction under arts 17 or 18, no account is to be taken of that reduction for the present purpose (art.19(3)(a)). The same applies to a reduction of an old style JSA award but only where there has subsequently been entitlement to universal credit, new style JSA or new style ESA followed by entitlement to old style JSA, old style ESA or income support (art.19(3)(b)).

Medium-level sanctions

20.—The reduction period for a medium-level sanction is— 6.201

(a) 28 days, if paragraph (b) does not apply; or

(b) 91 days, if in the [1364] days preceding the failure in question there was—

(i) another sanctionable failure giving rise to a medium-level sanction for which a 28 day or 91 day reduction period applies; or

(ii) a UC sanctionable failure giving rise to a medium-level sanction under regulation 103 of the Universal Credit Regulations 2013 for which a 28 day or 91 day reduction period applies.

AMENDMENT

1. Universal Credit and Miscellaneous Amendments Regulations 2014 (SI 2014/597) reg.3(5) (April 28, 2014).

DEFINITIONS

"medium-level sanction"—see reg.17.
"sanctionable failure"—*ibid.*
"reduction period"—*ibid.*
"UC sanctionable failure"—*ibid.*

GENERAL NOTE

By virtue of the definition of "medium-level sanction" in reg.17, this regulation applies to the failures for no good reason to comply with two particular work-related requirements to which the claimant in question is subject: the requirement under s.6D(1)(a) of the new style Jobseekers Act 1995 to take all reasonable action to obtain paid work (but note, not the requirement under s.6D(1)(b) to take particular action specified by the Secretary of State, where failure to comply with a requirement to apply for a particular vacancy for paid work falls within s.6J(2)(b) and the higher-level sanctions regime) and the work availability requirement in s.6E(1). Note in relation to the second category that a failure for no good reason to comply with a work availability requirement by not taking up an offer of paid work falls under s.6J(2)(c) and so is subject to a higher-level sanction and not to any sanction under s.6K (s.6K(3)). 6.202

The reduction period under para.(a) is 28 days if there have been no other medium-level sanctionable failures (or equivalent universal credit failures) in the previous 364 days and 91 days if there have been one or more such failures in that period. That is subject to the disregard in reg.18(4) of sanctionable failures in the 13 days before the sanctionable failure in question.

See the notes to regs 19, 25 and 28 for discussion of what sanctionable failures might or might not count for these purposes.

The form of this regulation is to be amended with effect from July 25, 2016 by SI 2016/678 to clarify its operation and close some unintended gaps.

The transition from old style JSA

Where there is a sanctionable failure directly under the new style JSA legislation, a reduction of a new style award under arts 17 or 18 of the Welfare Reform Act 2012 (Commencement No.9 and Transitional and Transitory Provisions and 6.203

Commencement No.8 and Savings and Transitional Provisions (Amendment)) Order 2013 (as amended and set out in the 2014/15 Supplement) (see the notes to reg.18) or a reduction of an old style JSA award counts as a previous sanctionable failure for which the reduction period is the number of days equivalent to the length of the period which applied under the old style JSA legislation (art.19 of that Order). However, if a period of entitlement to old style JSA, old style ESA or income support has intervened since the end of the new style JSA reduction under arts 17 or 18, no account is to be taken of that reduction for the present purpose (art.19(3)(a)). The same applies to a reduction of an old style JSA award but only where there has subsequently been entitlement to universal credit, new style JSA or new style ESA followed by entitlement to old style JSA, old style ESA or income support (art.19(3)(b)).

Low-level sanctions

6.204 **21.**—(1) The reduction period for a low-level sanction is the total of the number of days referred to in paragraphs (2) and (3).

(2) The number of days beginning with the date of the sanctionable failure and ending with—

(a) the day before the day on which the claimant meets a compliance condition specified by the Secretary of State;

(b) the day before the day on which the claimant is no longer required to take a particular action specified as a work preparation requirement by the Secretary of State under section 6C(1) of the Act; or

(c) the day on which the award of a jobseeker's allowance is terminated,

whichever is soonest.

(3) Whichever of the following number of days is applicable in the claimant's case—

(a) seven days, if sub-paragraphs (b) and (c) do not apply;

(b) 14 days, if in the [[1]364] days preceding the failure in question there was—

(i) another sanctionable failure giving rise to a low-level sanction for which a seven day reduction period applies;

(ii) a UC sanctionable failure giving rise to a low-level sanction under regulation 104 of the Universal Credit Regulations 2013 for which a seven day reduction period applies; or

(iii) an ESA sanctionable failure giving rise to a low-level sanction under regulation 52 of the Employment and Support Allowance Regulations 2013 for which a seven day reduction period applies; or

(c) 28 days, if in the [[1]364] days preceding the failure in question there was—

(i) another sanctionable failure giving rise to a low-level sanction for which a 14 day or 28 day reduction period applies;

(ii) a UC sanctionable failure giving rise to a low-level sanction under regulation 104 of the Universal Credit Regulations 2013 for which a 14 day or 28 day reduction period applies; or

(iii) an ESA sanctionable failure giving rise to a low-level sanction under regulation 52 of the Employment and Support Allowance Regulations 2013 for which a 14 day or 28 day reduction period applies.

AMENDMENT

1. Universal Credit and Miscellaneous Amendments Regulations 2014 (SI 2014/597) reg.3(6) (April 28, 2014).

DEFINITIONS

"compliance condition"—see Jobseekers Act 1995 s.6K(6).
"ESA sanctionable failure"—see reg.17.
"low-level sanction"—see reg.17.
"sanctionable failure"—see reg.17.
"UC sanctionable failure"—see reg.17.

GENERAL NOTE

The definition of "low-level sanction" in reg.17 above is in terms of the requirements failure to comply with which lead to a sanction at that level under s.6K of the new style Jobseekers Act 1995: (a) a work-focused interview requirement under s.6B(1) of the Act; (b) a work preparation requirement under s.6C(1); (c) a work search requirement under section 6D(1)(b) of the Act (requirement to take particular action specified by the Secretary of State to obtain paid work); or (d) a requirement under s.6G of the Act (connected requirements). In effect, the low-level sanction covers any sanctionable failure under s.6K not covered by a medium-level sanction, the higher-level sanction being restricted to sanctions under s.6J. 6.205

Note in relation to category (b) that a failure for no good reason to comply with a work preparation requirement in the form of undertaking a work placement of a prescribed description falls within s.6J(2)(a) and so is subject to a higher-level sanction and not to any sanction under s.6K (s.6K(3)). Note in relation to category (c) that a failure for no good reason to comply with a work search requirement to take particular action in the form of applying for a particular vacancy for paid work falls under s.6J(2)(b) and so is subject to a higher-level sanction and not to any sanction under s.6K (s.6K(3)).

The calculation of the reduction period under para.(1) is more complicated than that for higher and medium-level sanctions. It is made up of a period of flexible length depending on the ongoing circumstances under para.(2) plus a fixed period of days under para.(3) to be added to the para.(2) period.

The basic rule in para.(2) is that the period runs until any compliance condition specified by the Secretary of State is met. See the notes to s.6K(5) of the Act for the authorisation for this provision. A compliance condition is that the failure to comply ceases to exist (e.g. attending a work-focused interview) or as to future compliance. The condition must in accordance with s.6K(5)(a) and sub-para.(a)(i) be specified by the Secretary of State. Although s.6K(7)(b) allows the Secretary of State to notify a claimant of a compliance condition in such manner as he determines, the approach of the Supreme Court in *R (on the application of Reilly and Wilson) v Secretary of State for Work and Pensions* [2013] UKSC 68, [2014] 1 A.C. 453 might possibly be relevant to the substance of what must be specified, as discussed further in the notes to s.6K(5). The para.(2) period will also end if the award of JSA terminates. 6.206

Under para.(3) the additional number of days is seven if there have been no other low-level sanctionable failures (or equivalent ESA or universal credit failures) in the previous 364 days, 14 if there has been one such failure in that period and 28 if there have been two or more such failures in that period. That is subject to the disregard in reg.18(4) of sanctionable failures in the 14 days before the sanctionable failure in question.

See the notes to regs 19, 25 and 28 for discussion of what sanctionable failures might or might not count for these purposes.

The form of this regulation is to be amended with effect from July 25, 2016 by SI 2016/678 to clarify its operation and close some unintended gaps.

The transition from old style JSA

6.207 Where there is a sanctionable failure directly under the new style JSA legislation, a reduction of a new style award under art.17 or 18 of the Welfare Reform Act 2012 (Commencement No.9 and Transitional and Transitory Provisions and Commencement No.8 and Savings and Transitional Provisions (Amendment)) Order 2013 (as amended and set out in the 2014/15 Supplement) (see the notes to reg.18) or a reduction of an old style JSA award counts as a previous sanctionable failure for which the reduction period is the number of days equivalent to the length of the period which applied under the old style JSA legislation (art.19 of that Order). However, if a period of entitlement to old style JSA, old style ESA or income support has intervened since the end of the new style JSA reduction under arts 17 or 18, no account is to be taken of that reduction for the present purpose (art.19(3)(a)). The same applies to a reduction of an old style JSA award but only where there has subsequently been entitlement to universal credit, new style JSA or new style ESA followed by entitlement to old style JSA, old style ESA or income support (art.19(3)(b)).

Start of the reduction

6.208 **22.**—A reduction period determined in relation to a sanctionable failure takes effect from—

(a) where the claimant has not been paid a jobseeker's allowance for the benefit week in which the sanctionable failure occurred, the first day of that benefit week;

(b) where the claimant has been paid a jobseeker's allowance for the benefit week referred to in paragraph (a), the first day of the first benefit week for which the claimant has not been paid a jobseeker's allowance; or

(c) where the amount of the award of the jobseeker's allowance for the benefit week referred to in paragraph (a) or (b) is already subject to a reduction because of a previous sanctionable failure, the first day of the first benefit week in respect of which the amount of the award is no longer subject to that reduction.

Definitions

"benefit week"—see reg.2(2).
"reduction period"—see reg.17.
"sanctionable failure"—*ibid*.

General Note

6.209 This stipulates in which benefit week the relevant period of reduction appropriate to the sanctionable failure actually takes effect in relation to an award of JSA. Paragraphs (a) and (b) presumably refer to weeks for which the claimant has not yet been paid, so that a reduction can be applied. Paragraph (c), making the start of the reduction period run on from the end of an existing reduction period, follows from the principle that reduction periods for separate sanctionable failures run consecutively (reg.18(2)).

Reduction period to continue where award of jobseeker's allowance terminates

6.210 **23.**—(1) Where an award of a jobseeker's allowance terminates while there is an outstanding reduction period—

(a) the period continues to run as if a daily reduction were being applied; and

(b) if the claimant becomes entitled to a new award of a jobseeker's allowance before the period expires, that new award is subject to a reduction for the remainder of the total outstanding reduction period.

(2) Paragraph (3) applies where—

(a) an award of a jobseeker's allowance terminates before the Secretary of State determines that the amount of the award is to be reduced in accordance with section 6J or 6K of the Act in relation to a sanctionable failure; and

(b) that determination is made after the claimant becomes entitled to a new award of a jobseeker's allowance.

(3) Where this paragraph applies—

(a) the reduction period in relation to the sanctionable failure referred to in paragraph (2) is to be treated as having taken effect on the day before the previous award terminated;

(b) that reduction period is treated as having continued to run as if a daily reduction were being applied; and

(c) if the new award referred to in paragraph (2)(b) begins before that reduction period expires, that new award is subject to a reduction for the remainder of the total outstanding reduction period.

DEFINITIONS

"the Act"—see reg.2(2).
"reduction period"—see reg.17.
"sanctionable failure"—see reg.17.
"total outstanding reduction period"—see reg.17.

GENERAL NOTE

If an award of new style JSA terminates while there is an outstanding reduction period, subsequent days count as if an actual reduction of benefit were being applied (thus reducing the days outstanding in the period), so that on any further claim for JSA the claimant is subject to the reduction only for the remainder of the period, if any (para.(1)). If an award of new style JSA terminates before the Secretary of State has made a decision about a reduction for a sanctionable failure, but a new award is in place by the time the decision is made, the reduction period starts as if the decision had been made on the day before the previous award terminated, so that the new award of JSA will be reduced for the remainder of the total outstanding reduction period (paras (2) and (3)). This regulation presumably applies only to cases that fall outside reg.6 (JSA sanction transfers to universal credit when become entitled to universal credit while JSA entitlement continues). It is not clear whether a JSA sanction that has "ceased to apply" under reg.6 revives when entitlement to universal credit ceases. Is there then an "outstanding reduction period" for JSA purposes? **6.211**

Suspension of a reduction where a fraud sanction applies

24.—(1) A reduction in the amount of an award of a jobseeker's allowance in accordance with section 6J or 6K of the Act is to be suspended for any period during which section 6B or 7 of the Social Security Fraud Act 2001 applies to the award. **6.212**

(2) The reduction ceases to have effect on the day on which that period begins and has effect again on the day after that period ends.

DEFINITION

"the Act"—see reg.2(2).

Termination of a reduction

6.213 **25.**—(1) A reduction in the amount of an award of a jobseeker's allowance in accordance with section 6J or 6K of the Act is to be terminated where, since the date of the most recent sanctionable failure which gave rise to such a reduction, the claimant has been in paid work—

(a) for a period of at least 26 weeks; or

(b) for more than one period where the total of those periods amounts to at least 26 weeks.

(2) The termination of the reduction has effect—

(a) where the date on which paragraph (1) is satisfied falls within a period of entitlement to a jobseeker's allowance, from the beginning of the benefit week in which that date falls; or

(b) where that date falls outside a period of entitlement to a jobseeker's allowance, from the beginning of the first benefit week in relation to any subsequent award of a jobseeker's allowance.

(3) The claimant is in paid work for the purposes of paragraph (1) where their weekly earnings are at least equal to their expected number of hours per week calculated under regulation 9 multiplied by the national minimum wage which would apply for a person of the claimant's age under the National Minimum Wage Regulations 1999.

DEFINITIONS

"the Act" —see reg.2(2).
"benefit week" —*ibid.*
"sanctionable failure"—see reg.17.

GENERAL NOTE

6.214 Any reduction for any level of sanction or sanctions terminates where, since the date of the most recent sanctionable failure, the claimant has been in paid work for at least 26 weeks, not necessarily consecutive, with weekly earnings at least equal to the expected number of hours per week (see reg.9: normally 35) multiplied by the national minimum wage applicable to a person of the claimant's age under the National Minimum Wage Regulations 1999 (paras (1) and (3)). The 1999 Regulations were revoked and consolidated with subsequent amendments into the National Minimum Wage Regulations 2015 (SI 2015/621), which can therefore be taken as covered by the reference to the 1999 Regulations. The amendments with effect from April 6, 2016 (SI 2016/68) to implement the "national living wage" still use the term "national minimum wage" in the text of the Regulations. The UC Regulations 2013 are to be amended from July 25, 2016 by SI 2016/678 to up-date the references, but the amending regulations contain no equivalent for the JSA Regulations 2013. Paragraph (2) sets out the time the termination takes effect dependent on whether or not the day the 26-week period is up falls within or outside a period of entitlement to JSA. If within, termination takes effect from the beginning of the benefit week in which there fell the completion of the 26-week period. If outside, it takes effect from the beginning of the first benefit week of any subsequent JSA award.

Note that it does not matter how long the outstanding reduction period is. A claimant could have had a reduction period of 1095 days imposed, yet after 26 weeks' work the entire reduction disappears, just as much as if the reduction period affected were much shorter. But note also that this regulation does not take away the status of the sanctionable failure or failures that the reduction was based on. It merely terminates the reduction in benefit. Thus for the purpose of asking in the future whether there have been any other sanctionable failures within the previous 364 days of a new sanctionable failure (see regs 19–21) it might appear that all such sanctionable failures still count for those purposes. However, since the references in regs 19–21 are to other sanctionable failures "giving rise to" a sanction at the appropriate level, it is arguable that if there is no longer any reduction being imposed the sanctionable failure no longer gives rise to a sanction. But if a reduction period was initially actually imposed following the sanctionable failure in question, which is later terminated under reg.25, there is also an argument that the sanctionable failure did give rise to a sanction for the purposes of regs 19–21.

Amount of reduction for each benefit week

26.—Where it has been determined that an award of a jobseeker's allowance is to be reduced in accordance with section 6J or 6K of the Act, the amount of the reduction for each benefit week in respect of which a reduction has effect is to be calculated as follows. 6.215

Step 1

Take the number of days—

(a) in the benefit week; or

(b) if lower, in the total outstanding reduction period,

and deduct any days in that benefit week or total outstanding reduction period for which the reduction is suspended in accordance with regulation 24.

Step 2

Multiply the number of days produced by step 1 by the daily reduction rate.

Step 3

Deduct the amount produced by step 2 from the amount of the award of jobseeker's allowance for the benefit week.

Definitions

"the Act"—see reg.2(2).

"benefit week"—*ibid.*

"daily reduction rate"—see reg.27.

"total outstanding reduction period"—see reg.17.

General Note

This provides the means of calculating for each benefit week the amount of reduction. It translates the daily reduction rate under reg.27 into the appropriate amount for each benefit week, depending on the number of days on the week covered by the reduction period. 6.216

Daily reduction rate

27.—(1) The daily reduction rate for the purposes of regulation 26 is the amount applicable to the claimant under regulation 49 multiplied by 52 and divided by 365. 6.217

(2) The amount of the rate in paragraph (1) is to be rounded down to the nearest 10 pence.

General Note

The effect of this regulation is that the reduction in benefit under a sanction of any level, for the period affected, in substance takes away the whole of the benefit otherwise payable. That is because new style JSA provides no benefit over and above the age-related amounts prescribed for claimants under 25 and aged 25 6.218

or over in reg.49. It is possible that the operation of the calculation in para.(1) to translate the figure per week in reg.49 to a daily rate, involving a division by 365 whether in a Leap Year or not, coupled with the rounding down process in para.(2), could result in an amount to be deducted under reg.26 for a full benefit week which is lower than the age-related amount. However, whatever remains is unlikely to be paid to a claimant in the light of the rule in reg.52 that where the weekly amount of JSA is less than 10p it is not payable.

Failures for which no reduction is applied

6.219 **28.**—(1) No reduction is to be made in accordance with section 6J of the Act for a sanctionable failure where—

(a) the sanctionable failure is listed in section 6J(2)(b) or (c) of the Act (failure to apply for a vacancy for paid work or failure to take up an offer of paid work) and the vacancy has arisen because of a strike arising from a trade dispute;

(b) the sanctionable failure is listed in section 6J(2)(d) of the Act (ceases paid work or loses pay) and the following circumstances apply—

(i) the claimant's work search and work availability requirements are subject to limitations under sections 6D(4) and 6E(3) of the Act in respect of work available for a certain number of hours;

(ii) the claimant takes up paid work that is for a greater number of hours; and

(iii) the claimant voluntarily ceases that paid work, or loses pay, within a trial period;

(c) the sanctionable failure is listed in section 6J(3) of the Act (failures that occur before a claim is made) and the period of the reduction that would otherwise apply under regulation 19 is the same as or shorter than the number of days beginning with the day after the date of the sanctionable failure and ending with the day before the date of that claim;

(d) the sanctionable failure is that the claimant voluntarily ceases paid work, or loses pay, because of a strike arising from a trade dispute;

(e) the sanctionable failure is that the claimant voluntarily ceases paid work as a member of the regular forces or the reserve forces (within the meanings in section 374 of the Armed Forces Act 2006), or loses pay in that capacity; or

(f) the sanctionable failure is that the claimant voluntarily ceases paid work in one of the following circumstances—

(i) the claimant has been dismissed because of redundancy after volunteering or agreeing to be dismissed;

(ii) the claimant has ceased work on an agreed date without being dismissed in pursuance of an agreement relating to voluntary redundancy; or

(iii) the claimant has been laid-off or kept on short-time to the extent specified in section 148 of the Employment Rights Act 1996, and has complied with the requirements of that section.

(2) In this regulation—

"redundancy" has the same meaning as in section 139(1) of the Employment Rights Act 1996;

"strike" has the same meaning as in section 246 of the Trade Union and Labour Relations (Consolidation) Act 1992;

"trade dispute" has the same meaning as in section 244 of that Act.

DEFINITIONS

"the Act"—see reg.2(2).
"claimant"—see reg.2(2).
"sanctionable failure"—see reg.17.
"work availability requirement"—see Jobseekers Act 1995 ss.35(1) and 6E.
"work search requirement"—see Jobseekers Act 1995 ss.35(1) and 6D.

GENERAL NOTE

This is a significant provision in prescribing, under s.6J(7)(a) of the new style Jobseekers Act 1995, cases of sanctionable failure for which no reduction of benefit can be imposed. It is thus limited to the higher-level sanctions regime and does not apply to medium or low-level sanctions under s.6K, although the categories prescribed would not seem to be relevant to the s.6K conditions. Note that if a case comes within this regulation that does not affect the status of the sanctionable failure in question. But, in contrast to the circumstances discussed in the note to reg.25, if no reduction period was ever imposed, it must be strongly arguable that the sanctionable failure in question did not "give rise to" a higher-level sanction for the purposes of reg.19. There remains scope for argument that in some of the circumstances listed there is a good reason for the particular claimant's failure to comply with the requirement in question, so that there is not in fact a sanctionable failure. 6.220

The cases are as follows.

Sub-paragraph (a)

Where the sanctionable failure is failing for no good reason to apply for a particular vacancy for paid work or to take up an offer of paid work (new style Jobseekers Act 1995 s.6J(2)(b) or (c)), no reduction is to be imposed if the vacancy arose because of a strike arising from a trade dispute. "Strike" is defined in para.(2) by reference on to s.246 of the Trade Union and Labour Relations (Consolidation) Act 1992, where it means "any concerted stoppage of work". Paragraph (2) also adopts the meaning of "trade dispute" given there (thus displacing the definition in s.35(1) of the new style Jobseekers Act 1995): 6.221

"(1) In this Part a "trade dispute" means a dispute between workers and their employer which relates wholly or mainly to one or more of the following—
(a) terms and conditions of employment, or the physical conditions in which any workers are required to work;
(b) engagement or non-engagement, or termination or suspension of employment or the duties of employment, of one or more workers;
(c) allocation of work or the duties of employment between workers or groups of workers;
(d) matters of discipline;
(e) a worker's membership or non-membership of a trade union;
(f) facilities for officials of trade unions; and
(g) machinery for negotiation or consultation, and other procedures, relating to any of the above matters, including the recognition by employers or employers' associations of the right of a trade union to represent workers in such negotiation or consultation or in the carrying out of such procedures.

(2) A dispute between a Minister of the Crown and any workers shall, notwithstanding that he is not the employer of those workers, be treated as a dispute between those workers and their employer if the dispute relates to matters which—
(a) have been referred for consideration by a joint body on which, by virtue of provision made by or under any enactment, he is represented, or
(b) cannot be settled without him exercising a power conferred on him by or under an enactment.

(3) There is a trade dispute even though it relates to matters occurring outside the United Kingdom, so long as the person or persons whose actions in the United Kingdom are said to be in contemplation or furtherance of a trade dispute relat-

ing to matters occurring outside the United Kingdom are likely to be affected in respect of one or more of the matters specified in subsection (1) by the outcome of the dispute.

(4) An act, threat or demand done or made by one person or organisation against another which, if resisted, would have led to a trade dispute with that other, shall be treated as being done or made in contemplation of a trade dispute with that other, notwithstanding that because that other submits to the act or threat or accedes to the demand no dispute arises.

(5) In this section—

"employment" includes any relationship whereby one person personally does work or performs services for another; and

"worker", in relation to a dispute with an employer, means—

(a) a worker employed by that employer; or

(b) a person who has ceased to be so employed if his employment was terminated in connection with the dispute or if the termination of his employment was one of the circumstances giving rise to the dispute."

That is a fairly comprehensive definition, although as compared with s.35(1) of the old Style Jobseeker's Act 1995 (which will still be relevant for old style JSA) it does not cover disputes between employees and employees. It is possible that vacancies could arise because of industrial action short of a strike. There seems no good reason why claimants who on principle are not prepared to apply for such vacancies or accept offers should not also be protected. Perhaps it is arguable that in any event they have a good reason for failing to comply with the requirement in question, so that there is no sanctionable failure.

Sub-paragraph (b)

6.222 This provision protects current new style JSA claimants who take up work for a trial period, but is restricted to those who are required only to search for and be available for work subject to limitations as to hours of work under reg.14. It is made under s.6D(4) and 6E(3) of the Act. Then if such a claimant takes up work, or more work, for more than the hours of limitation for a trial period, but later voluntarily gives up that work or extra work or loses pay within the trial period, there is to be no reduction. As above, it would be arguable there was good reason for such action, so no sanctionable failure.

Sub-paragraph (c)

6.223 Where there is a pre-claim sanctionable failure and the reduction period normally applicable would expire on or before the date of the relevant JSA claim, there is to be no reduction. It may be that the same result is achieved by reg.19(3).

Sub-paragraph (d)

6.224 This provision provides the same protection as under sub-para.(a) for voluntarily ceasing paid work or losing pay because of a strike arising from a trade dispute.

Sub-paragraph (e)

6.225 Members of the armed forces, both regular and reserve forces, who voluntarily cease paid work as such or lose pay, cannot suffer a reduction on that ground, whatever the circumstances.

Sub-paragraph (f)

6.226 This provides protection in the same circumstances as prescribed in reg.71 of the JSA Regulations 1996 for old style JSA purposes, except that there the claimant is deemed not to have left employment voluntarily and so is not subject to any sanction. Here the claimant is merely protected from having a reduction of benefit imposed, subject to any argument that there was a good reason under general principles for voluntarily ceasing work, so no sanctionable failure.

Sanctionable failures under section 6J of the Act: work placements

[1**29.**—(1) A placement on the Mandatory Work Activity Scheme is a prescribed placement for the purpose of section 6J(2)(a) of the Act (sanctionable failure not to comply with a work placement). 6.227

(2) In paragraph (1) "the Mandatory Work Activity Scheme" means a scheme provided pursuant to arrangements made by the Secretary of State and known by that name that is designed to provide work or work-related activity for up to 30 hours per week over a period of 4 consecutive weeks with a view to assisting claimants to improve their prospects of obtaining employment.]

AMENDMENT

1. Universal Credit (Consequential, Supplementary, Incidental and Miscellaneous Provisions) Regulations 2013 (SI 2013/630) reg.39 (April 29, 2013).

DEFINITION

"the Act"—see reg.2(2).

GENERAL NOTE

In order for a higher-level sanction to be imposed under s.6J(2)(a) of the new style Jobseekers Act, the claimant must have failed for no good reason to comply with a work preparation requirement to undertake a work placement of a prescribed description. Paragraph (1) prescribes the Mandatory Work Activity Scheme and para.(2) gives a description of the scheme considered sufficient to meet the test in s.6J(2)(a). See the notes to that section for discussion of the validity of this regulation. 6.228

Sanctions where universal credit ends and the person is entitled to a jobseeker's allowance

30.—(1) This regulation applies where— 6.229

(a) a person ceases to be entitled to universal credit;

(b) there is a reduction relating to the person's award of universal credit under section 26 or 27 of the Welfare Reform Act 2012; and

(c) the person is entitled to a jobseeker's allowance.

(2) Any reduction relating to the award of the universal credit is to be applied to the award of the jobseeker's allowance.

(3) The period for which the reduction relating to the award of the jobseeker's allowance is to have effect is the number of days which apply to the person under regulation 102, 103, 104 or 105 of the Universal Credit Regulations 2013 minus any such days which—

(a) have already resulted in a reduction in the amount of universal credit; or

(b) fall after the date the award of universal credit was terminated and before the date on which the award of a jobseeker's allowance starts.

(4) The daily reduction rate for the reduction relating to the award of the jobseeker's allowance is the amount of the claimant's jobseeker's allowance multiplied by 52 and divided by 365.

(5) The claimant's award of a jobseeker's allowance is to be reduced by the daily reduction amount referred to in paragraph (4) for each day of the period referred to in paragraph (3).

DEFINITION

"claimant"—see Jobseekers Act 1995 s.35(1).

General Note

6.230 Where someone subject to one or more universal credit sanctions ceases to be entitled to universal credit and becomes entitled to new style JSA, the remaining reduction period applicable to the universal credit award carries over to reduce the JSA award. The remaining reduction period is calculated by deducting from the period imposed as regards universal credit: (i) the days for which universal credit has been in consequence reduced, and (ii) the days between the cessation of entitlement to universal credit and the beginning of entitlement to JSA. The JSA award must be reduced for each day of the remaining reduction period by the daily reduction amount set out in para.(4) (para.(5)), which appears to be the same as the standard reduction under reg.27.

See the notes to reg.6 above for a question whether, if a new style JSA sanction has transferred to universal credit under that provision and the claimant then ceases to be entitled to universal credit while there are still some unexpired days in the sanction period, reg.30 applies. It is arguable that there was not a reduction under s.26 or 27 of the WRA 2012 (para.(1)(b)), since the sanction was originally imposed under the JSA legislation.

PART 4

Information and evidence

Provision of information and evidence

6.231 **31.**—(1) A claimant must supply such information in connection with the claim for a jobseeker's allowance, or any question arising out of it, as may be required by the Secretary of State.

(2) A claimant must furnish such certificates, documents and other evidence as may be required by the Secretary of State for the determination of the claim.

(3) A claimant must furnish such certificates, documents and other evidence affecting their continuing entitlement to a jobseeker's allowance, whether that allowance is payable to them and, if so, in what amount, as the Secretary of State may require.

(4) A claimant must notify the Secretary of State—

(a) of any change of circumstances which has occurred which the claimant might reasonably be expected to know might affect their entitlement to a jobseeker's allowance or the payability or amount of such an allowance; and

(b) of any such change of circumstances which the claimant is aware is likely to occur.

(5) The notification referred to in paragraph (4) must be given as soon as reasonably practicable after the occurrence or, as the case may be, after the claimant becomes so aware, by giving notice of the change to an office of the Department for Work and Pensions specified by the Secretary of State—

(a) in writing or by telephone (unless the Secretary of State determines in any particular case that notice must be given in writing or may be given otherwise than in writing or by telephone); or

(b) in writing if in any particular case the Secretary of State requires written notice (unless the Secretary of State determines in any particular case to accept notice given otherwise than in writing).

(6) Where, pursuant to paragraph (1), a claimant is required to supply

information, they must do so when they participate in a work-focused interview under section 6B of the Act, if so required by the Secretary of State, or within such period as the Secretary of State may require.

(7) Where, pursuant to paragraph (2) or (3), a claimant is required to provide certificates, documents or other evidence they must do so within seven days of being so required or such longer period as the Secretary of State may consider reasonable.

DEFINITIONS

"the Act"—see reg.2(2).
"claimant"—see Jobseekers Act 1995 s.35(1).
"writing"—see Interpretation Act 1978 Sch.1.

GENERAL NOTE

Paragraphs (1) and (2)

See reg.7(1) of the Social Security (Claims and Payments) Regulations 1987 and the annotations to that provision in Vol.I. The general rule in reg.19 of the Universal Credit, Personal Independence Payment, Jobseeker's Allowance and Employment and Support Allowance (Claims and Payments) Regulations 2013 (see Vol.III) is that a person wishing to make claim for new style JSA is to attend an appropriate office at a time specified by the Secretary of State. If the person attends as specified and provides a properly completed claim form at the time or within any extra time allowed under reg.20(3) of the Claims and Payments Regulations 2013, the claim is treated as made on the later of the first day of the period claimed for or the date of first notification of an intention to claim (reg.20(1)). If the person does not attend or does not provide a properly completed claim form within time, the claim cannot be treated as made before the person does attend or provide a properly completed claim form. It therefore appears that, before an effective claim is made and the person becomes a "claimant" as defined in s.35(1) of the new style Jobseekers Act 1995, the Secretary of State's powers to require the person to provide information and evidence when attending to claim must rest on the appropriate parts of reg.4 of the Claims and Payments Regulations 2013 giving power for a claim form to instruct that information or evidence be provided and that a claim is not properly completed and is defective if such instructions are not complied with (see reg.4(1A) and (9)). Paragraphs (1) and (2) of the present regulation can only apply once an effective claim has been made, as is confirmed by the rule in para.(6) that information required under para.(1) is to be provided at a work-focused interview under s.6B of the Act. A person cannot be required to participate in such an interview until they have become a "claimant". The consequence of a breach of the requirements of paras (1) and (2) would seem to be as discussed in *R(IS) 4/93*, that the claim has to be decided in the absence of the information or evidence in question, which may mean that the claimant has failed to show qualification for benefit. **6.232**

Paragraph (3)

See reg.32(1A) of the Claims and Payments Regulations 1987. **6.233**

Paragraphs (4) and (5)

See reg.32(1B) of the Claims and Payments Regulations 1987. **6.234**

Alternative means of notifying changes of circumstances

32.—(1) In such cases and subject to such conditions as the Secretary of State may specify, the duty in regulation 31(4) to notify a change of cir- **6.235**

cumstances may be discharged by notifying the Secretary of State as soon as reasonably practicable—

(a) where the change of circumstances is a birth or death, through a local authority, or a county council in England, by personal attendance at an office specified by that authority or county council, provided the Secretary of State has agreed with that authority or county council for it to facilitate such notification; or

(b) where the change of circumstances is a death, by telephone to a telephone number specified for that purpose by the Secretary of State.

(2) In this regulation "local authority" has the same meaning as in section 191 of the Administration Act.

DEFINITION

"the Administration Act"—see Jobseekers Act 1995 s.35(1).

GENERAL NOTE

6.236 See reg.32ZZA of the Claims and Payments Regulations 1987. "Local authority" seems to be the same as a "relevant authority" there.

Information given electronically

6.237 **33.**—(1) A person may give any certificate, notice, information or evidence required to be given and in particular may give notice of a change of circumstances required to be notified under regulation 31 by means of an electronic communication, in accordance with the provisions set out in Schedule 2 to the Claims and Payments Regulations 2013.

(2) In this regulation, "electronic communication" has the meaning given in section 15(1) of the Electronic Communications Act 2000.

DEFINITION

"Claims and Payments Regulations 2013"—see reg.2(2).

GENERAL NOTE

6.238 See reg.32ZA of the Claims and Payments Regulations 1987.

PART 5

CONDITIONS OF ENTITLEMENT

The conditions and relevant earnings

6.239 **34.**—(1) A claimant's relevant earnings for the purposes of section 2(2)(b) of the Act are the total amount of the claimant's earnings equal to the lower earnings limit for the base year.

(2) For the purposes of paragraph (1), earnings which exceed the lower earnings limit are to be disregarded.

GENERAL NOTE

6.240 This replicates reg.47A of the JSA Regulations 1996 on what is now old style JSA. See the annotations to that regulation in Pt III of this volume. See the annotations to s.2 of the old style Jobseekers Act 1995 in Pt I of this volume for the meaning of terms such as "base year" and "lower earnings limit" and for the operation of the condition of entitlement in s.2(2)(b).

Relaxation of the first set of conditions

35.—(1) A claimant who satisfies the condition in paragraph (2) is to be taken to satisfy the first set of conditions if the claimant has— 6.241

(a) paid Class 1 contributions before the relevant benefit week in respect of any one tax year; and

(b) earnings equal to the lower earnings limit in that tax year on which primary Class 1 contributions have been paid or treated as paid which in total, and disregarding any earnings which exceed the lower earnings limit for that year, are not less than that limit multiplied by 26.

(2) The condition referred to in paragraph (1) is that the claimant, in respect of any week during the last complete tax year preceding the relevant benefit year, is entitled to be credited with earnings in accordance with regulation 9E of the Social Security (Credits) Regulations 1975 (credits for certain spouses and civil partners of members of Her Majesty's forces).

(3) In this regulation, "relevant benefit week" means the week in relation to which the question of entitlement to a jobseeker's allowance is being considered.

Definitions

"benefit week"—see reg.2(2).
"claimant"—see Jobseekers Act 1995 s.35(1).
"tax year"—*ibid.*
"the first set of conditions"—see Jobseekers Act 1995 s.2(3C).

General Note

See the annotations to the JSA Regulations 1996 reg.45B on what is now old style JSA. "The first set of conditions" in para.(1) refers to the contribution conditions in s.2(1)(a) and (2) of the new style Jobseekers Act. 6.242

Waiting Days

36.—(1) Paragraph 4 of Schedule 1 to the Act does not apply in a case where a person's entitlement to a jobseeker's allowance commences within 12 weeks of an entitlement of theirs to income support, incapacity benefit, employment and support allowance or carer's allowance coming to an end. 6.243

(2) In the case of a person to whom paragraph 4 of Schedule 1 to the Act applies, the number of days is [1 seven].

Amendment

1. Social Security (Jobseeker's Allowance and Employment and Support Allowance) (Waiting Days) Amendment Regulations 2014 (SI 2014/2309) reg.2(3) (October 27, 2014).

DEFINITIONS

"the Act"—see reg.2(2).
"week"—*ibid.*

GENERAL NOTE

6.244 Unemployment benefit was a daily benefit payable in respect of a six-day week. JSA is a weekly benefit. Nonetheless, through para.4 of Sch.1 to the new style Jobseekers Act 1995, as amplified by this regulation, it deploys the traditional concept of "waiting days".

There is no entitlement to new style JSA for a number of days (now seven, but previously three (see para.(2)) but alterable by regulations) at the start of a jobseeking period. On "jobseeking period" and the effect of "linking", see the notes to regs 37 and 38 below. Note further that the "waiting days" rule does not apply where the claimant's entitlement to JSA begins within 12 weeks of the ending of entitlement to income support, incapacity benefit, employment and support allowance or carer's allowance.

The amendment to increase the number of waiting days to seven does not apply where the relevant jobseeking period began before October 27, 2014 (reg.4(1) of the amending regulations). Seven days' worth of benefit is a substantial amount, so that the provision in the Social Security (Payments on Account of Benefit) Regulations 2013 (Vol.III) for the making of payments on account of benefit, in certain cases of financial need (restrictively defined), has become more important. However, the claimant has to repay the "advance" out of future payments of JSA.

The transition from old style JSA

6.245 In para.(1) the reference to jobseeker's allowance is, where art.12(1)(b) of the Welfare Reform Act 2012 (Commencement No.9 and Transitional and Transitory Provisions and Commencement No.8 and Savings and Transitional Provisions (Amendment)) Order 2013 (as amended and set out in the 2014/15 Supplement) applies and the claimant was entitled to old style JSA under reg.46(1)(a) of the JSA Regulations 1996 during what would otherwise have been waiting days when that award continued as an award of new style JSA, to be read as if it included a reference to the old style JSA award (art.12(3)(b) of that Order).

Jobseeking Period

6.246 **37.**—(1) For the purposes of the Act, but subject to paragraph (2), the "jobseeking period" means any period throughout which the claimant satisfies or is treated as satisfying the conditions specified in section 1(2)(b) and (e) to (i) of the Act (conditions of entitlement to a jobseeker's allowance).

(2) The following periods are not to be, or to be part of, a jobseeking period—

(a) any period in respect of which no claim for a jobseeker's allowance has been made or treated as made;
(b) such period as falls before the day on which a claim for a jobseeker's allowance is made or treated as made;
(c) where a claim for a jobseeker's allowance has been made or treated as made but no entitlement to benefit arises in respect of a period before the date of claim by virtue of section 1(2) of the Administration Act (limits for backdating entitlement), that period;
(d) any week in which a claimant is not entitled to a jobseeker's allowance in accordance with section 14 of the Act (trade disputes); or

(e) any period in respect of which a claimant is not entitled to a jobseeker's allowance because section 1(1A) of the Administration Act (requirement to state national insurance number) applies.

(3) For the purposes of section 5 of the Act (duration of a jobseeker's allowance), a day must be treated as if it was a day in respect of which the claimant was entitled to a jobseeker's allowance where that day—

(a) falls within a jobseeking period; and

(b) is a day—

(i) on which the claimant satisfies the conditions specified in section 2 of the Act (the contribution-based conditions) other than the conditions specified in section 2(1)(c) and (d) of the Act; and

(ii) on which a jobseeker's allowance is not payable to the claimant by virtue of sections 6J or 6K of the Act or by virtue of a restriction imposed pursuant to section 6B, 7, 8 or 9 of the Social Security Fraud Act 2001 (loss of benefit provisions).

DEFINITIONS

"the Act"—see reg.2(2).
"the Administration Act"—see Jobseekers Act 1995 s.35(1).
"claimant"—*ibid.*

GENERAL NOTE

This regulation, read with regs 38 and 39 below and para.3 of Sch.1 to the new style Jobseekers Act 1995, provides some relief to those whose unemployment is intermittent, interspersed with, say, periods of employment, of incapacity for work, of training for work or periods when pregnant. It uses, somewhat after the fashion of unemployment benefit and its notion of a "period of interruption of employment" (PIE), the concept of "linking" and "linked periods" where what would otherwise be separate jobseeking periods are fused into one and certain periods ("linked periods") do not "break" a jobseeking period, although they do not themselves form part of the jobseeking period. There are three particular purposes for which the concept of the jobseeking period is relevant: (a) in the identification of the tax years in which the two contribution conditions in s.2(1)(a) and (b) of the Act must be satisfied; (b) in the application of the waiting days rule in para.4 of Sch.1 to the Act only once in each jobseeking period; and (c) in the possibly redundant provisions in para.(3) about days which count towards the 182-day limit on a period of entitlement under s.5 of the Act. **6.247**

Regulation 37 provides the general definition of "jobseeking period" and some important exceptions. Regulations 38 and 39 deal with linking.

A "jobseeking period" is under para.(1) any period throughout which the claimant satisfies (or is treated as satisfying) the conditions of entitlement to JSA set out in the new style Jobseekers Act 1995, s.1(2)(b) and (e)–(i): accepted a claimant commitment; not in remunerative work; does not have limited capability for work; not receiving relevant education; under pensionable age; and in Great Britain. Note that reg.39 below treats certain days as ones meeting those conditions in respect of persons approaching retirement.

None of the periods listed in para.(2) can constitute or form any part of, a jobseeking period. A period for which no claim for JSA has been made cannot count, although the conditions of entitlement mentioned in para.(1) were objectively satisfied in that period (sub-para.(a)). Nor can any period prior to the day on which the claim for JSA is made or treated as made (sub-para.(b)). See reg.29 of the Claims and Payments Regulations 2013 for the circumstances in which a claim can be "backdated" up to three months and treated as made on the first day of the period claimed for, within that three-month limit. If the rule in reg.29 were a great deal more generous, no period **6.248** prior to the 12-month limit on entitlement before the date of claim (Social Security Administration Act 1992 s.1(2)) could form part of a jobseeking period (sub-para. (c)). Any week in which the claimant is not entitled to benefit under the trade dispute disqualification under s.14 of the new style Jobseekers Act 1995 does not count (sub-para.(d)). Nor does a day on which there is no entitlement by virtue of the provisions of s.1(1A) of the Administration Act connected with national insurance numbers.

Under para.(3), for the purpose only of the rules in s.5 of the Act limiting the duration of entitlement to 182 days, a day which would otherwise fall within a jobseeking period, but on which someone satisfying the two contribution conditions in s.2(2) is subject to a JSA sanction or a fraud sanction so that JSA is not payable, is nonetheless to be treated as a day of entitlement to JSA, so that it will count as one of the 182 days. This provision is arguably unnecessary because sanctions under s.6J and 6K of the Act and restrictions under the Social Security Fraud Act 2001 only affect the payability of benefit or the amount payable, not entitlement.

The transition from old style JSA

6.249 Regulation 37 as a whole is, where art.12(1) and (2) of the Welfare Reform Act 2012 (Commencement No.9 and Transitional and Transitory Provisions and Commencement No.8 and Savings and Transitional Provisions (Amendment)) Order 2013 (as amended and set out in the 2014/15 Supplement) applies, to be read as if a jobseeking period includes any period that formed part of a jobseeking period under reg.47 of the JSA Regulations 1996 and in para.(3) as if the reference to a day treated as a day on which the claimant was entitled to new style JSA included a reference to a day treated under reg.47(4) of the JSA Regulations 1996 as a day of entitlement to old style JSA (art.12(3)(c) of that Order).

Jobseeking periods: periods of interruption of employment

6.250 **38.**—(1) For the purposes of section 2(4)(b)(i) of the Act and for determining any waiting days—

(a) where a linked period commenced before 7th October 1996, any days of unemployment which form part of a period of interruption of employment where the last day of unemployment in that period of interruption of employment was no more than eight weeks before the date upon which that linked period commenced;

(b) where a jobseeking period or a linked period commences on 7th October 1996, any period of interruption of employment ending within the eight weeks preceding that date; or

(c) where a jobseeking period or a linked period commences after 7th October 1996, any period of interruption of employment ending within the 12 weeks preceding the day the jobseeking period or linked period commenced,

must be treated as a jobseeking period and, for the purposes of sub-paragraph (a), a day must be treated as being, or not being, a day of unemployment in accordance with section 25A of the Benefits Act (determination of days for which unemployment benefit is payable) and with any regulations made under that section, as in force on 6th October 1996.

(2) In this regulation—

"period of interruption of employment" in relation to a period prior to 7th October 1996 has the same meaning as it had in the Benefits Act by virtue of section 25A of that Act as in force on 6th October 1996;

"waiting day" means a day—

(a) at the beginning of a jobseeking period; and

(b) in respect of which a person is not entitled to a jobseeker's allowance.

DEFINITIONS

"the Act"—see reg.2(2).
"the Benefits Act"—see Jobseekers Act 1995 s.35(1).
"jobseeking period"—see reg.37(1).
"linked period"—see reg.39(2).

GENERAL NOTE

Some spells of unemployment are continuous, others intermittent. A jobseeking period can consist of a long chain of such spells, interspersed with spells of work or entitlement to certain other benefits. This regulation enables such a chain to go back to the unemployment benefit regime before October 7, 1996, when JSA was introduced, for the purposes of the contribution conditions and the waiting days rule. Then the relevant concept was a "period of interruption of employment" (PIE) and the regime worked on an eight-week linking rule where two or more ostensibly separate PIEs were fused into a single one where they were not more than eight weeks apart. New style JSA works on a 12-week linking period (see reg.39(1) and (3)). 6.251

Linking Periods

39.—(1) For the purposes of the Act, two or more jobseeking periods must be treated as one jobseeking period where they are separated by a period comprising only— 6.252

(a) any period of not more than 12 weeks;
(b) a linked period;
(c) any period of not more than 12 weeks falling between—
  (i) any two linked periods; or
  (ii) a jobseeking period and a linked period; or
(d) a period in respect of which the claimant is summoned for jury service and is required to attend court.

(2) Linked periods for the purposes of the Act are any of the following periods—

(a) to the extent specified in paragraph (4), any period throughout which the claimant is entitled to a carer's allowance under section 70 of the Benefits Act;
(b) any period throughout which the claimant is incapable of work, or is treated as incapable of work, in accordance with Part 12A of the Benefits Act;
(c) any period throughout which the claimant has, or is treated as having, limited capability for work for the purposes of Part 1 of the Welfare Reform Act 2007;
(d) any period throughout which the claimant was entitled to a maternity allowance under section 35 [[1]or 35B] of the Benefits Act;
(e) any period throughout which the claimant was engaged in training for which a training allowance is payable;
(f) a period which includes 6th October 1996 during which the claimant attends court in response to a summons for jury service and which was immediately preceded by a period of entitlement to unemployment benefit.

(3) A period is a linked period for the purposes of section 2(4)(b)(ii) of the Act only where it ends within 12 weeks or less of the commencement of a jobseeking period or of some other linked period.

(4) A period of entitlement to carer's allowance is a linked period only where it enables the claimant to satisfy contribution conditions for entitle-

ment to a jobseeker's allowance which the claimant would otherwise be unable to satisfy.

AMENDMENT

1. Social Security (Maternity Allowance) (Miscellaneous Amendments) Regulations 2014 (SI 2914/884) reg.6(2) (May 18, 2014).

DEFINITIONS

"the Act"—see reg.2(2).
"the Benefits Act"—see Jobseekers Act 1995 s.35(1).
"claimant"—*ibid.*
"jobseeking period"—see reg.37(1).
"training allowance"—see reg.2(2).
"week"—*ibid.*

GENERAL NOTE

6.253 Under para.(1), two or more jobseeking periods as defined in reg.37 must be fused into a single jobseeking period where separated by no more than 12 weeks, by a linked period (defined in para.(2)), by any period of not more than 12 weeks falling between any two linked periods or a jobseeking period and a linked period, or by a period in respect of which the claimant is summoned for jury service and is required to attend court. Thus, through the list of categories in para.(2) are the intermittently unemployed protected, while oscillating between unemployment and work or training, or unemployment and sickness/disability related inability to work, or unemployment and maternity or performing jury service, or caring, or any combination of these. Not all linked periods count as such for all purposes. Thus, a period of entitlement to a carer's allowance (para.(2)(a)) counts only to enable the JSA claimant to satisfy the JSA contribution conditions (new style Jobseekers Act 1995 s.2(2)(a) and (b)) that otherwise would not be satisfied (para.(4)). Similarly, to rank for the purposes of s.2(4)(b)(ii) (identifying the "relevant benefit year" for contributions conditions purposes as earlier than the start of the benefit year in which the JSA claim is made) a linked period counts only if it ended within 12 weeks of the start of a jobseeking period or another linked period (para.(3)). It is hard to see why this result is not already achieved by para.(1)(a) and (c).

Note that linked periods or intervening periods of 12 weeks or less cannot themselves form part of a jobseeking period.

Persons approaching retirement and the jobseeking period

6.254 **40.**—(1) The provisions of this regulation apply only to days—

(a) which fall after 6th October 1996 and within a tax year in which the claimant has attained the qualifying age for state pension credit (which is, in the case of a woman, pensionable age and in the case of a man, the age which is pensionable age in the case of a woman born on the same day as the man) but is under pensionable age; and
(b) in respect of which a jobseeker's allowance is not payable because the decision of the determining authority is that the claimant—
  (i) has exhausted their entitlement to a jobseeker's allowance;
  (ii) fails to satisfy one or both of the contribution conditions specified in section 2(1)(a) and (b) of the Act; or
  (iii) is entitled to a jobseeker's allowance but the amount payable is reduced to nil by virtue of deductions made in accordance with regulation 51 for pension payments.

(2) For the purposes of regulation 37(1) (jobseeking period) but subject to paragraphs (3), (4) and (5), any days to which paragraph (1) applies and in respect of which the person does not satisfy the condition specified in section 1(2)(b) of the Act (conditions of entitlement to a jobseeker's allowance), are to be days on which the person is treated as satisfying the condition in section 1(2)(b) and (e) to (i) of the Act.

(3) Where a person is employed as an employed earner or a self-employed earner for a period of more than 12 weeks, then no day which falls within or follows that period is to be a day on which the person is treated as satisfying those conditions, but this paragraph is not to prevent paragraph (2) from again applying to a person who makes a claim for a jobseeker's allowance after that period.

(4) Any day which is, for the purposes of section 30C of the Benefits Act, a day of incapacity for work falling within a period of incapacity for work is not to be a day on which the person is treated as satisfying the conditions referred to in paragraph (2).

(5) Any day which, for the purposes of Part 1 of the Welfare Reform Act 2007, is a day where the person has limited capability for work falling within a period of limited capability for work is not to be a day on which the person is treated as satisfying the conditions referred to in paragraph (2).

DEFINITIONS

"the Act"—see reg.2(2).
"the Benefits Act"—see Jobseekers Act 1995 s.35(1).
"claimant"—*ibid.*
"employed earner"—see reg.2(1).
"pensionable age"—*ibid.*
"self-employed earner"—see reg.2(2).
"tax year"—see Jobseekers Act 1995 s.35(1).
"week"—see reg.2(2).

GENERAL NOTE

This provision benefits persons (in practice only men: para.(1)(a)) for some days falling after October 6, 1996 during the tax year in which they reach the qualifying age for SPC. The days are ones in that tax year prior to actual attainment of pensionable age on which JSA is not payable because of exhaustion of entitlement, failure to satisfy one or both contribution conditions (new style Jobseekers Act 1995 s.2(1)(a) and (b)), or because the JSA amount has been reduced to nil under reg.51 because of pension payments. Any such days (other than those excluded by any of paras (3)–(5)) are to be days in a jobseeking period notwithstanding that no claimant commitment has been accepted. **6.255**

Days which were ones of incapacity for work within a period of incapacity for work cannot form part of a jobseeking period in this way (para.(4)). Nor can days of limited capability for work forming part of a period of limited capability for work (para.(5)). But both such situations rank as linked periods under reg.39(2)(b). Further, where someone works in employment or self-employment for more than 12 weeks, no day within or after that period can be treated as part of a jobseeking period in this way, but the protection afforded by paras (1) and (2) of the regulation can apply again after such a period when the person makes a claim for JSA (para.(3)).

Persons temporarily absent from Great Britain

41.—(1) For the purposes of the Act, a claimant must be treated as being in Great Britain during any period of temporary absence from Great Britain— **6.256**

(a) not exceeding four weeks in the circumstances specified in paragraph (2);
(b) not exceeding eight weeks in the circumstances specified in paragraph (3).

(2) The circumstances specified in this paragraph are that—

(a) the claimant is in Northern Ireland and satisfies the conditions of entitlement to a jobseeker's allowance;
(b) immediately preceding the period of absence from Great Britain, the claimant was entitled to a jobseeker's allowance; and
(c) the period of absence is unlikely to exceed 52 weeks.

(3) The circumstances specified in this paragraph are that—

(a) immediately preceding the period of absence from Great Britain, the claimant was entitled to a jobseeker's allowance;
(b) the period of absence is unlikely to exceed 52 weeks;
(c) the claimant continues to satisfy or be treated as satisfying the other conditions of entitlement to a jobseeker's allowance;
(d) the claimant is, or the claimant and any other member of their family are, accompanying a member of the claimant's family who is a child or young person solely in connection with arrangements made for the treatment of that child or young person for a disease or bodily or mental disablement; and
(e) those arrangements relate to treatment—
  (i) outside Great Britain;
  (ii) during the period whilst the claimant is, or the claimant and any member of their family are, temporarily absent from Great Britain; and
  (iii) by, or under the supervision of, a person appropriately qualified to carry out that treatment.

(4) A person must also be treated, for the purposes of the Act, as being in Great Britain during any period of temporary absence from Great Britain where—

(a) the absence is for the purpose of attending an interview for employment;
(b) the absence is for seven consecutive days or less;
(c) notice of the proposed absence is given to the Secretary of State before departure, and is given in writing if so required by the Secretary of State; and
(d) on their return to Great Britain the person satisfies the Secretary of State that they attended for the interview in accordance with their notice.

(5) For the purposes of the Act a claimant must be treated as being in Great Britain during any period of temporary absence from Great Britain if—

(a) the claimant was entitled to a jobseeker's allowance immediately before the beginning of that period of temporary absence; and
(b) that period of temporary absence is for the purpose of the claimant receiving treatment at a hospital or other institution outside Great Britain where the treatment is being provided—
  (i) under section 6(2) of the Health Service Act (performance of functions outside England) or section 6(2) of the Health Service (Wales) Act (performance of functions outside Wales);
  (ii) pursuant to arrangements made under section 12(1) of the

Health Service Act (Secretary of State's arrangements with other bodies), section 10(1) of the Health Service (Wales) Act (Welsh Minister's arrangements with other bodies), paragraph 18 of Schedule 4 to the Health Service Act (joint exercise of functions) or paragraph 18 of Schedule 3 to the Health Service (Wales) Act (joint exercise of functions); or

(iii) under any equivalent provision in Scotland or pursuant to arrangements made under such provision.

(6) For the purposes of the Act, a person must be treated as being in Great Britain during any period of temporary absence from Great Britain not exceeding 15 days where—

(a) the absence is for the purpose of taking part in annual continuous training as a member of any [1 . . .] reserve force prescribed in Part 1 of Schedule 6 to the Social Security (Contributions) Regulations 2001; and

(b) the person was entitled to a jobseeker's allowance immediately before the period of absence.

(7) In this regulation, "appropriately qualified" means qualified to provide medical treatment, physiotherapy or a form of treatment which is similar to, or related to, either of those forms of treatment.

AMENDMENT

1. Social Security (Members of the Reserve Forces) (Amendment) Regulations 2015 (SI 2015/389) reg.5(5) (April 6, 2015).

DEFINITIONS

"the Act"—see reg.2(2).
"child"—see Jobseekers Act 1995 s.35(1).
"claimant"—*ibid.*
"family"—*ibid.*
"week"—see reg.2(2).
"young person"—see reg.2(2).

GENERAL NOTE

This provision is made under para.11 of Sch.1 to the new style Jobseekers Act 1995, for the purposes of the condition of entitlement in s.1(2)(i). It is almost identical to reg.50 of the JSA Regulations 1996. See the annotations to that provision, ignoring those on joint-claim couples and on para.(3). Regulation 47 below deals with the effect in relation to the condition of entitlement in s.1(2)(f) (not having limited capability for work). Note also the protection in reg.41(6) in respect of absences for annual continuous training as a member of any reserve force. 6.257

The transition from old style JSA

In paras (2)(b), (3)(a) and (c), (5)(a) and (6)(b) the references to entitlement to jobseeker's allowance are, where art.12(1)(b) of the Welfare Reform Act 2012 (Commencement No.9 and Transitional and Transitory Provisions and Commencement No.8 and Savings and Transitional Provisions (Amendment)) Order 2013 (as amended and set out in the 2014/15 Supplement) applies, to be read as if they included a reference to entitlement under an old style JSA award (art.12(3)(d) of that Order). 6.258

Remunerative work

42.—(1) For the purposes of the Act, "remunerative work" means work— 6.259

(a) for which payment is made or which is done in expectation of payment; and
(b) in which a claimant is—
(i) engaged for 16 or more hours per week; or
(ii) where their hours of work fluctuate, engaged on average for 16 or more hours per week.

(2) For the purposes of paragraph (1), the number of hours in which a claimant is engaged in work is to be determined—
(a) where no recognisable cycle has been established in respect of a person's work, by reference to the number of hours or, where those hours are likely to fluctuate, the average of the hours, which they are expected to work in a week;
(b) where the number of hours for which they are engaged fluctuate, by reference to the average of hours worked over—
(i) if there is a recognisable cycle of work, the period of one complete cycle (including, where the cycle involves periods in which the person does not work, those periods but disregarding any other absences);
(ii) in any other case, the period of five weeks immediately before the date of claim or the date of supersession, or such other length of time as may, in the particular case, enable the person's average hours of work to be determined more accurately.

(3) In determining in accordance with this regulation the number of hours for which a person is engaged in remunerative work—
(a) that number must include any time allowed to that person by their employer for a meal or for refreshments, but only where the person is, or expects to be, paid earnings in respect of that time;
(b) no account must be taken of any hours in which the person is engaged in an employment or scheme to which any one of sub-paragraphs (a) to (e) of regulation 44(1) (person treated as not engaged in remunerative work) applies;
(c) no account must be taken of any hours in which the person is engaged otherwise than in an employment as an earner in caring for—
(i) a person who is in receipt of attendance allowance, the care component [1 . . .] the daily living component [1 or armed forces independence payment];
(ii) a person who has claimed an attendance allowance, [1 armed forces independence payment,] a disability living allowance or personal independence payment, but only for the period beginning with the date of claim and ending on the date on which the claim is determined or, if earlier, on the expiration of the period of 26 weeks from the date of claim;
(iii) another person and is in receipt of a carer's allowance under section 70 of the Benefits Act; or
(iv) a person who has claimed either an attendance allowance, [1 armed forces independence payment,] a disability living allowance or personal independence payment and has an award of attendance allowance, [1 armed forces independence payment,] the care component or the daily living component for a period commencing after the date on which that claim was made.

(4) In this regulation—
[1 "armed forces independence payment" means armed forces inde-

pendence payment under the Armed Forces and Reserve Forces (Compensation Scheme) Order 2013;]

"disability living allowance" means a disability living allowance under section 71 of the Benefits Act;

"care component" means the care component of disability living allowance at the highest or middle rate prescribed under section 72(3) of the Benefits Act;

"daily living component" means the daily living component of personal independence payment at the standard or enhanced rate referred to in section 78 of the Welfare Reform Act 2012;

"personal independence payment" means an allowance under Part 4 of the Welfare Reform Act 2012.

AMENDMENT

1. Armed Forces and Reserve Forces Compensation Scheme (Consequential Provisions: Subordinate Legislation) Order 2013 (SI 2013/591) art.7 and Sch. para.52 (April 8, 2013).

DEFINITIONS

"the Act"—see reg.2(2).
"the Benefits Act"—see Jobseekers Act 1995 s.35(1).
"claimant"—see reg.2(2).

GENERAL NOTE

This is much the same in substance as reg.51 of the JSA Regulations 1996, with some minor drafting changes to the list in para.(3)(c) of those whose care is to be ignored in calculating hours engaged in work. See the annotations to reg.51 in Pt III of this volume, ignoring those with respect to the claimant's partner, non-dependant, child or young person (relevant only for IBJSA). It is a condition of entitlement under s.1(2)(e) of the new style Jobseekers Act 1995 that a claimant is not in remunerative work. **6.260**

Persons treated as engaged in remunerative work

43.—(1) Except in the case of a person on maternity leave, paternity leave, [1 shared parental leave,] adoption leave or absent from work through illness, a person is to be treated as engaged in remunerative work during any period for which they are absent from work referred to in regulation 42(1) (remunerative work) where the absence is either without good cause or by reason of a recognised, customary or other holiday. **6.261**

(2) Subject to paragraph (3), a person who was, or was treated as being, engaged in remunerative work and in respect of that work earnings to which regulation 58(1)(c) (earnings of employed earners) applies are paid, is to be treated as engaged in remunerative work for the period for which those earnings are taken into account in accordance with Part 7.

(3) Paragraph (2) does not apply to earnings disregarded under paragraph 1 of the Schedule to these Regulations.

AMENDMENT

1. Shared Parental Leave and Statutory Shared Parental Pay (Consequential Amendments and Subordinate Legislation) Order 2014 (SI 2014/3255) art.29(3) (December 23, 2014).

DEFINITIONS

"adoption leave"—see reg.2(2).
"maternity leave"—*ibid.*
"paternity leave"—*ibid.*
"remunerative work"—see reg.42(1).
"shared parental leave"—see reg.2(2).

GENERAL NOTE

6.262 This is similar in substance to reg.52 of the JSA Regulations 1996. See the annotations in Pt III of this volume to para.(1) of that provision, ignoring provisions applicable in respect the claimant's partner and trade disputes (relevant only for IBJSA). It is a condition of entitlement under s.1(2)(e) of the new style Jobseekers Act 1995 that a claimant is not in remunerative work. Note also that para.(1) still refers to being absent from work without good cause when reg.52 of the 1996 Regulations has been amended to use the apparently currently favoured phrase "without a good reason".

Persons treated as not engaged in remunerative work

6.263 **44.**—(1) A person is to be treated as not engaged in remunerative work in so far as they are—

(a) engaged by a charity or a voluntary organisation or are a volunteer where the only payment received by them or due to be paid to them is a payment in respect of any expenses incurred, or to be incurred, if they otherwise derive no remuneration or profit from the employment;
(b) engaged on a scheme for which a training allowance is being paid;
(c) engaged in employment as—
[1(i) a part-time fire-fighter employed by a fire and rescue authority under the Fire and Rescue Services Act 2004 or by the Scottish Fire and Rescue Service established under section 1A of the Fire (Scotland) Act 2005];
(ii) [1. . .];
(iii) an auxiliary coastguard in respect of coastal rescue activities;
(iv) a person engaged part-time in the manning or launching of a lifeboat;
(v) a member of any [2 . . .] reserve force prescribed in Part 1 of Schedule 6 to the Social Security (Contributions) Regulations 2001;
(d) performing their duties as a councillor, and for this purpose "councillor" has the same meaning as in section 171F(2) of the Benefits Act;
(e) engaged in caring for a person who is accommodated with them by virtue of arrangements made under any of the provisions referred to in regulation 60(2)(b) or (c), and are in receipt of any payment specified in regulation 60(2)(b) or (c);
(f) engaged in an activity in respect of which—
(i) a sports award had been made, or is to be made, to them; and
(ii) no other payment is made or is expected to be made to them;
(g) engaged in the programme known as Work Experience.

(2) In this regulation, "volunteer" means a person who is engaged in voluntary work, otherwise than for a close relative, grand-parent, grand-child,

uncle, aunt, nephew or niece, where the only payment received, or due to be paid to the person by virtue of being so engaged, is in respect of any expenses reasonably incurred by the person in connection with that work.

AMENDMENTS

1. Social Security (Miscellaneous Amendments) (No.2) Regulations 2013 (SI 2013/1508) reg.4(1) and (3) (July 29, 2013).
2. Social Security (Members of the Reserve Forces) (Amendment) Regulations 2015 (SI 2015/389) reg.5(5) (April 6, 2015).

DEFINITIONS

"the Benefits Act"—see Jobseekers Act 1995 s.35(1).
"close relative"—see reg.2(2).
"remunerative work"—see reg.42(1).
"sports award"—see reg.2(2).
"training allowance"—*ibid.*
"voluntary organisation"—*ibid.*
"voluntary work"—*ibid.*
"Work Experience"—*ibid.*

GENERAL NOTE

This is similar in substance to reg.53 of the JSA Regulations 1996 and thus to reg.6 of the Income Support Regulations. See the annotations to those provisions in Pts II and III of this volume, ignoring any dealing with the claimant's partner or joint-claim couples (relevant only to IBJSA). Note that participation in the Mandatory Work Activity Scheme or a scheme prescribed in reg.3 of the Jobseeker's Allowance (Schemes for Assisting Persons to Obtain Employment) Regulations 2013 is not included in the list in para.(1), although it is in the list in reg.53 of the 1996 Regulations. It is a condition of entitlement under s.1(2)(e) of the new style Jobseekers Act 1995 that a claimant is not in remunerative work. **6.264**

Relevant education

45.—(1) For the purposes of the Act— **6.265**
(a) a person is to be treated as receiving relevant education if they are a qualifying young person[[1], unless the person is participating in a traineeship]; and
(b) [[1]except in circumstances where sub-paragraph (a) applies,] the following are to be treated as relevant education—
(i) undertaking a full-time course of advanced education; and
(ii) undertaking any other full-time course of study or training at an educational establishment for which a student loan, grant or bursary is provided for the person's maintenance or would be available if the person applied for it.

[[1](1A) In paragraph (1) "traineeship" means a course which—
(a) is funded (in whole or in part) by, or under arrangements made by, the—
(i) Secretary of State under section 14 of the Education Act 2002, or
(ii) Chief Executive of Skills Funding;
(b) lasts no more than 6 months;
(c) includes training to help prepare the participant for work and a work experience placement; and

(d) is open to persons who on the first day of the course have reached the age of 16 but not 25.]

(2) In paragraph (1)(b)(i), "course of advanced education" means—

(a) a course of study leading to—

(i) a postgraduate degree or comparable qualification;

(ii) a first degree or comparable qualification;

(iii) a diploma of higher education;

(iv) a higher national diploma; or

(b) any other course of study which is of a standard above advanced GNVQ or equivalent, including a course which is of a standard above a general certificate of education (advanced level), or above a Scottish national qualification (higher or advanced higher).

(3) A claimant who is not a qualifying young person and is not undertaking a course described in paragraph (1)(b) is nevertheless to be treated as receiving relevant education if the claimant is undertaking a course of study or training that is not compatible with any work-related requirement imposed on the claimant by the Secretary of State.

(4) For the purposes of paragraph (1)(b), a person is to be regarded as undertaking a course—

(a) throughout the period beginning on the date on which the person starts undertaking the course and ending on the last day of the course or on such earlier date (if any) as the person finally abandons it or is dismissed from it; or

(b) where a person is undertaking a part of a modular course, for the period beginning on the day on which that part of the course starts and ending—

(i) on the last day on which the person is registered with the provider of the course, or part of the course, as undertaking that part; or

(ii) on such earlier date (if any) as the person finally abandons the course or is dismissed from it.

(5) The period referred to in paragraph (4)(b) includes—

(a) where a person has failed examinations or has failed to complete successfully a module relating to a period when the person was undertaking a part of the course, any period in respect of which the person undertakes the course for the purpose of retaking those examinations or that module; and

(b) any period of vacation within the period specified in paragraph (4)(b) or immediately following that period except where the person has registered with the provider of the course, or part of the course, to attend or undertake the final module in the course and the vacation immediately follows the last day on which the person is to attend or undertake the course.

(6) A person is not to be regarded as undertaking a course by virtue of this regulation for any part of the period mentioned in paragraph (4) during which the following conditions are met—

(a) the person has, with the consent of the relevant educational establishment, ceased to attend or undertake the course because they are ill or caring for another person;

(b) the person has recovered from that illness or ceased caring for that person within the past year, but not yet resumed the course; and

(c) the person is not eligible for a grant or student loan.

(7) In this regulation, except where paragraph (8) applies, "qualifying young person" means a person who has reached the age of 16 but not the age of 20—

(a) up to, but not including, the 1st September following their 16th birthday; and

(b) up to, but not including, the 1st September following their 19th birthday, if they are enrolled in, or accepted for, approved training or a course of education—

(i) which is not a course of advanced education;

(ii) which is provided at a school or college or provided elsewhere but approved by the Secretary of State; and

(iii) where the average time spent during term time (excluding meal breaks) in receiving tuition, engaging in practical work, or supervised study, or taking examinations exceeds 12 hours per week.

(8) A person is not a "qualifying young person" within the meaning in paragraph (7) where they—

(a) are aged 19 and have not started the education or training or been enrolled or accepted for it before reaching the age of 19;

(b) fall within paragraph (7)(b) and their education or training is provided by means of a contract of employment; or

(c) are receiving universal credit, an employment or support allowance or a jobseeker's allowance.

(9) In this regulation—

"approved training" means training in pursuance of arrangements made under section 2(1) of the Employment and Training Act 1973 or section 2(3) of the Enterprise and New Towns (Scotland) Act 1990 which is approved by the Secretary of State for the purposes of this regulation;

"modular course" means a course which consists of two or more modules, the successful completion of a specified number of which is required before a person is considered by the educational establishment to have completed the course;

"student loan" means a loan towards a student's maintenance pursuant to any regulations made under section 22 of the Teaching and Higher Education Act 1998, section 73 of the Education (Scotland) Act 1980 or Article 3 of the Education (Student Support) (Northern Ireland) Order 1998, including in Scotland a young student's bursary paid under regulation 4(1)(c) of the Student's Allowances (Scotland) Regulations 2007.

AMENDMENT

1. Social Security (Traineeships and Qualifying Young Persons) Amendment Regulations 2015 (SI 2015/336) reg.5 (March 27, 2015).

DEFINITIONS

"the Act"—see reg.2(2).

"claimant"—see Jobseekers Act 1995 s.35(1).

GENERAL NOTE

It is a condition of entitlement to new style JSA that a person is not receiving relevant education (new style Jobseekers Act 1995 s.1(1)(g)). This regulation **6.266** stipulates who is to be treated as receiving it. The regulation combines in one place elements of exclusionary rules on children and young persons and students which were in the JSA Regulations 1996 split between regs 1(3), 54 (relevant education) and Ch.IX: students. But note that reg.45 applies only to young persons (i.e. those aged from 16–19) and not to children (i.e. those under 16). That is presumably because it is impossible for a child to have satisfied the contribution conditions for new style JSA in s.2(1)(a) and (b).

Paragraph (1)(a) is comparable to reg.54 of the JSA Regulations 1996 and reg.12 of the Income Support Regulations in that a qualifying young person (QYP) is generally to be treated as receiving relevant education, and thus excluded from JSA unless participating in a traineeship (defined in para.(1A)). A QYP is someone aged 16–19 meeting all of the criteria set out in para.(7), mainly to do with participation in a course of non-advanced education, but excluding those within one of the exempt heads in para.(8). Traineeships as defined and described in the new para.(1A) are short courses aimed at addressing the skills gaps that employers consider prevalent among young people, combining English and maths tuition when needed with work preparation training and a work experience placement. Such a course would be regarded as not one of advanced education so that a participant would fall within the meaning of QYP and be excluded from entitlement to new style JSA were it not for the new exception to sub-para.(a). The exception is to encourage voluntary take-up of the courses.

6.267 In addition, under para.(1)(b)(i) anyone not covered by sub-para.(a) undertaking a full-time course of "advanced education" (as fairly comprehensively defined in para.(2) to cover courses over secondary level) is receiving relevant education and excluded from JSA. When a person is regarded as undertaking a course varies according to whether it is modular or not. For a non-modular course, a person is regarded as undertaking a course from when the person starts undertaking the course until the last day of the course, or where the person has been dismissed from it or finally abandoned it, from the date of dismissal or abandonment (para.(4)(a)). For a modular course, a person is regarded as undertaking part of a modular course from when that part of the course starts until the last date on which they are registered with the course provider or the provider of that part for that part of the modular course, or where the person has been dismissed from it or finally abandoned it, from the date of dismissal or abandonment. With modular courses, the person is regarded as undertaking it during vacations other than the vacation following completion of the final module and also when undertaking the course for purposes of retaking failed examinations (paras (4)(b) and (5)).

Whether the course of advanced education is modular or non-modular, someone who has taken time out of the course with the consent of the educational establishment concerned because of illness or caring responsibilities (not defined), and who has now recovered or whose caring responsibilities have ended, can claim new style JSA until the day before the person resumes the course (subject to a maximum of one year). This does not apply if the person is eligible for a grant or student loan during this period (para.(6)).

Finally anyone aged 20 or over (or possibly 16–19 and not meeting the definition of QYP in para.(7)) undertaking a course of study or training which is not one of full-time advanced education must be treated as receiving relevant education if undertaking it is not compatible with the work-related requirements imposed on them by the Secretary of State (para.(3)).

Short periods of sickness

6.268 **46.**—(1) Subject to the following provisions of this regulation, a person who—

(a) [1 . . .] has been awarded a jobseeker's allowance, or is a person to whom any of the circumstances mentioned in section 6J(2) or (3) or 6K(2) of the Act apply;

(b) proves to the satisfaction of the Secretary of State that they are unable to work on account of some specific disease or disablement; and

(c) [1 during the period of their disease or disablement, satisfies] the requirements for entitlement to a jobseeker's allowance other than those specified in section 1(2)(f) of the Act (capable of work or not having limited capability for work),

is to be treated for a period of not more than two weeks, beginning on the day on which sub-paragraphs (a) to (c) are met, as capable of work or as not having limited capability for work, except where the claimant states in writing that for the period of their disease or disablement they propose to claim or have claimed employment and support allowance [1 or universal credit].

(2) The evidence which is required for the purposes of paragraph (1)(b) is a declaration made by the claimant in writing, in a form approved for the purposes by the Secretary of State, that they have been unfit for work from a date or for a period specified in the declaration.

(3) [1 Paragraph (1) does not apply to a claimant on more than two occasions in any one jobseeking period or, where a jobseeking period exceeds 12 months, in each successive 12 months within that period; and for the purposes of calculating any period of 12 months, the first 12 months in the jobseeking period commences on the first day of the jobseeking period.

(4) [1 Paragraph (1) does not apply to any person where the first day in respect of which they are unable to work falls within eight weeks after the day the person ceased to be entitled to statutory sick pay.

(5) [1 Paragraph (1) does not apply to a claimant who is temporarily absent from Great Britain in the circumstances prescribed by regulation 41(5).

[1(6) Paragraph (1) does not apply to any person—

(a) during any period where the person is treated as capable of work or as not having limited capability for work under regulation 46A (extended period of sickness); or

(b) where the first day in respect of which that person would, apart from this sub-paragraph, have been treated as capable of work or as not having limited capability for work under this regulation falls immediately after the last day on which the person is so treated under regulation 46A.]

AMENDMENT

1. Jobseeker's Allowance (Extended Period of Sickness) Amendment Regulations 2015 (SI 2015/339) reg.3(3) (March 30, 2015).

DEFINITIONS

"the Act"—see reg.2(2).
"Great Britain"—see Jobseekers Act 1995 s.35(1).
"jobseeking period"—see reg.37(1).
"writing"—see Interpretation Act 1978 Sch.1.

GENERAL NOTE

It is a condition of entitlement to new style JSA that the claimant does not have limited capability for work (new style Jobseekers Act 1995 s.1(2)(f)). This regulation permits persons unable to work on account of some specific disease or disablement to be entitled to JSA for up to two weeks on two occasions in any 12-month **6.269** period by treating them as capable of work or not having limited capability for work, unless they inform the Secretary of State in writing that they have claimed or propose to claim ESA. This regulation is now in the same terms as reg.55 of the JSA Regulations 1996. See further the annotations to that provision in Pt III of this volume, ignoring references to income support and SDA. Under para.(5) a person who is treated as being in Great Britain by virtue of reg.41(5) cannot use this provision, but can benefit from reg.47 below. There are to be mainly clarificatory amendments with effect from May 23, 2016 by the Jobseeker's Allowance (Extended Period of Sickness) Amendment Regulations 2016 (SI 2016/502).

Note that to take advantage of this provision, claimants need only to show that they are unable to work on account of some specific disease or disablement, which test is not further defined. Thus the convolutions of the ESA test for having limited capability for work are not incorporated. The ordinary everyday meaning of the words must be applied. Also, the claimant need not produce any evidence beyond a written declaration on the approved form of unfitness for work (para.(2) but see the conditions in reg.16(5)(b) discussed below), although it may be that in particular cases something more would be needed to satisfy the Secretary of State under para.(1)(b). The operation of reg.46 is voluntary in the sense that if a claimant declares in writing that they intend to or have claimed ESA, it does not apply (end of para.(1)).

Under reg.16(5), while a claimant is unfit for work (for up to 14 days no more than twice within 12 months) and provides a signed declaration for the first seven days and a doctor's statement for any subsequent days, no work search requirement can be imposed and there is no requirement to be able and willing immediately to take up work. Thus the claimant can satisfy the conditions of entitlement in s.1(2) of the new style Jobseekers Act 1995, provided that a claimant commitment has been accepted.

6.270 There has been some discussion of whether reg.46 can apply immediately at the beginning of the period covered by a claim for new style JSA. The question has been asked, for instance, whether a claimant previously entitled to ESA who has lost entitlement on being found not to have limited capability for work and is challenging that decision, who is therefore left to claim JSA, can take advantage of reg.46 (and/or now reg.46A) immediately, so as to be able to maintain the contention of having limited capability for work. Although once an appeal against the ESA decision is made ESA entitlement can be claimed until the appeal is determined, the question may be relevant while the claimant is waiting for the mandatory reconsideration process to take place. Whatever the position prior to March 30, 2015, when reg.46 was not in quite the same form as reg.55 of the JSA Regulations 1996, the difficulty now lies in reg.46(1)(a), which requires that the claimant "has been awarded" JSA, or has committed various sanctionable failures, and in reg.46(1)(c). The reference to an award in the past tense appears to require that there has been a decision that the claimant is entitled to new style JSA (even if benefit is not payable because of a sanction) without the operation of reg.46. The new formulation of reg.46(1)(c) also seems to support the notion of proof of inability to work arising in the course of any existing JSA award.

It may be that a claimant who disputes the finding of not having limited capability for work in claiming new style JSA could avoid any immediate practical problems. The ESA decision on that question appears not to be conclusive for new style JSA purposes. Regulation 40(1) of the Universal Credit, Personal Independence Payment, Jobseeker's Allowance and Employment and Support Allowance (Decisions and Appeals) Regulations 2013 (Vol.III), in contrast to reg.10 of the 1999 Decisions and Appeals Regulations, specifically restricts the conclusive effect of such ESA decisions to further ESA decisions. However, the Secretary of State could perfectly properly adopt the same view in determining that the claimant satisfies the specific condition of entitlement in s.1(2)(f) of the new style Jobseekers Act 1995 (does not have limited capability for work), even though the claimant might not accept that view. Then under reg.16(5) the claimant can be free of the work search requirement and be deemed to meet the work availability requirement by showing unfitness for work by appropriate evidence even though reg.46 does not apply. The claimant must though have accepted a claimant commitment (s.1(2)(b), subject to reg.8 of the present Regulations). The record in the claimant commitment of the requirements to be complied with must, by virtue of s.6A(4)(a), take account of the restrictions in the present Regulations on the work-related requirements that can be imposed, so that if reg.16(5) applied initially, the claimant commitment could not include any work search requirement or any obligation to be able and willing immediately to take up work.

Now see reg.46A, allowing the same effect as under reg.46 to operate for a more extended period. Under reg.46(6), the present provision cannot be used while reg.46A applies. Nor can a reg.46 period of deeming follow on immediately from a reg.46A period. However, the converse does not apply. An extended period of sickness under reg.46A may follow on from a reg.46 period, as seems sensible when prediction of the duration of unfitness to work may be very uncertain. It appears, though, from the definition of "the first day" in reg.46A(4), that any days covered by reg.46 will count against the 13-week limit under reg.46A.

The transition from old style JSA

Where art.13(1) and (2) of the Welfare Reform Act 2012 (Commencement No.9 and Transitional and Transitory Provisions and Commencement No.8 and Savings and Transitional Provisions (Amendment)) Order 2013 (as amended and set out in the 2014/15 Supplement) applies, reg.46 is to be read as if it included the additional provisions set out below (art.12(3)(e) of that Order). The introduction of a new para.(6) for all purposes by the 2015 amending regulations cannot be taken as having revoked this additional para.(6). The two must co-exist. **6.271**

"(6) Where—

(a) a person has been treated under regulation 55(1) of the Jobseeker's Allowance Regulations 1996 as capable of work or as not having limited capability for work for a certain period; and

(b) these Regulations apply to that person with effect from a day ("the relevant day") within that period,

the person is to be treated for the part of that period that begins with the relevant day as capable of work or as not having limited capability for work.

(7) Where paragraph (6) applies to a person and the conditions in paragraph (1)(a) to (c) are fulfilled in relation to that person on any day within the part of a period referred to in paragraph (6), the requirement of paragraph (1) to treat the person as capable of work or as not having limited capability for work is to be regarded as satisfied with respect to the fulfilment of those conditions on that day.

(8) For the purposes of paragraph (3), where paragraph (6) applies to a person, paragraph (3) is to apply to the person as though the preceding provisions of this regulation had applied to the person with respect to the person having been treated for a period, under regulation 55(1) of the Jobseeker's Allowance Regulations 1996 and paragraph (6), as capable of work or as not having limited capability for work."

[[1]Extended period of sickness

46A.—(1) This regulation applies to a person who— **6.270A**

(a) has been awarded a jobseeker's allowance or is a person to whom any of the circumstances mentioned in section 6J(2) or 6K(2) of the Act apply;

(b) proves to the satisfaction of the Secretary of State that they are unable to work on account of some specific disease or disablement;

(c) either—

(i) declares that they have been unable to work, or expect to be unable to work, on account of that disease or disablement for more than 2 weeks but they do not expect to be unable to work on account of that disease or disablement for more than 13 weeks; or

(ii) is not a person to whom regulation 46(1) (short periods of sickness) applies by virtue of paragraph (3) of that regulation;

(d) during the period of their disease or disablement, satisfies the requirements for entitlement to a jobseeker's allowance except those specified in section 1(2)(f) (capable of work or not having limited capability for work); and

(e) has not stated in writing that for the period of the disease or disablement they propose to claim or have claimed an employment and support allowance or universal credit.

(2) The evidence which is required for the purposes of paragraph (1)(b) in a case where paragraph (1)(c)(i) applies is—

(a) evidence of incapacity for work or limited capability for work in accordance with the Social Security (Medical Evidence) Regulations 1976 (which prescribe the form of a doctor's statement or other evidence required in each case; and

(b) any such additional information as the Secretary of State may request.

(3) The evidence which is required for the purposes of paragraph (1)(b) in a case where paragraph (1)(c)(ii) applies is a declaration made by the person in writing, in a form approved for the purposes by the Secretary of State, that the person has been unfit for work from a date or for a period in the declaration.

(4) Subject to the following paragraphs, a person to whom this regulation applies is to be treated as capable of work or as not having limited capability for work for the continuous period beginning on the first day on which the person is unable to work on account of the disease or disablement ("the first day") and ending on—

(a) the last such day; or

(b) if that period would otherwise exceed thirteen weeks, the day which is thirteen weeks after the first day.

(5) This regulation does not apply to a person on more than one occasion in any period of twelve months starting on the first day applying for the purpose of paragraph (4).

(6) Paragraphs (4) and (5) of regulation 46 apply for the purposes of this regulation as they apply for the purposes of paragraph (1) of regulation 46.]

AMENDMENT

1. Jobseeker's Allowance (Extended Period of Sickness) Amendment Regulations 2015 (SI 2015/339) reg.3(4) (March 30, 2015).

DEFINITIONS

"the Act"—see reg.2(2).
"writing"—see Interpretation Act 1978 Sch.1.

GENERAL NOTE

6.272 This provision, in conjunction with the new reg.16A, produces a similar (but not identical) effect to that under regs 46 and 16, which can extend to 13 weeks rather than two weeks but can only be relied on once within any 12 months, rather than twice (para.(5)). However, it can be relied on by a claimant who has exhausted the two periods allowed under reg.46 (see para.(1)(c)(ii)). There are to be mainly clarificatory amendments with effect from May 23, 2016 by the Jobseeker's Allowance (Extended Period of Sickness) Amendment Regulations 2016 (SI 2016/502).

See the note to reg.46 for the general background and reg.55ZA of the JSA Regulations 1996. For the reasons discussed in that note it seems that reg.46A also cannot be relied on at the outset of a claim but only where the claimant has been awarded new style JSA at least for some period and unfitness for work then intervenes. However, if a claimant were able to establish an initial entitlement on the basis discussed there, it is arguable that after the effect of reg.16(5) ran out after 14 days, the claimant could then rely on regs 46A and 16A for a further 11 weeks. The 13-week limit in reg.46A(4) runs from the first day on which the claimant is unable to work on account of the disease or disablement. That plainly goes back to any day on which reg.46 had effect. Although para.(4) on its face refers to the objective state of being unable to work, fairness would dictate that the 13-week period should not be regarded as having started to run before the claimant's inability to work was accepted by the Secretary of State under regs 46(1)(b) or 46A(1)(b).

As in reg.46 the test is whether the claimant is unable to work on account of some specific disease or disablement rather than the ESA test for having limited capability for work, although the claimant must, unless excluded from reg.46 by the "twice in 12 months" rule, declare that they have been, or expect to be, unable to work for more than two weeks and do not expect to be unable to work for more than 13 weeks (para.(1)(c)). The provision is thus aimed at those with a relatively short-term condition, who can be expected to return to the JSA regime. Those with more long-term conditions are still required to claim ESA. In contrast to reg.46, no doubt because of the longer period involved, in ordinary cases the claimant is required to produce evidence of incapacity for work or limited capability for work under the Medical Evidence Regulations (usually a doctor's statement) or such additional information as requested by the Secretary of State (para.(2)(a)). Claimants falling under para.(1)(c)(ii) and in effect having a third go under reg.46 are only required to produce a written declaration of unfitness (para.(3)). It appears at first sight odd to require evidence in the terms just mentioned but the form of statement prescribed in Pt.2 of Sch.1 to the Medical Evidence Regulations requires the doctor to record advice in terms of being or not being fit for work.

Regulation 46A directly allows the condition of entitlement in s.1(2)(f) of the new style Jobseekers Act 1995 to be satisfied. See reg.16A for the prohibition on imposing a work search requirement and on satisfaction of the work availability requirement while reg.46A applies. In contrast to reg.16, there is an additional condition for the production of this effect. It must be unreasonable to require the particular claimant to comply with any work search requirement or to comply with a work availability requirement to be able and willing to take up work and attend an interview.

Periods of sickness and persons receiving treatment outside Great Britain

47.—(1) A person— 6.273

(a) who has been awarded a jobseeker's allowance, or is a person to whom any of the circumstances mentioned in section 6J(2) or (3) or 6K(2) of the Act apply;

(b) who is temporarily absent from Great Britain in the circumstances prescribed by regulation 41(5);

(c) who proves to the satisfaction of the Secretary of State that they are unable to work on account of some specific disease or disablement; and

(d) but for their disease or disablement, would satisfy the requirements for entitlement to a jobseeker's allowance other than those specified in section 1(2)(f) of the Act (capable of work or not having limited capability for work),

is to be treated during that period of temporary absence abroad as capable of work or as not having limited capability for work, except where that person has stated in writing before that period of temporary absence abroad begins that immediately before the beginning of the period of that temporary absence abroad they have claimed employment and support allowance.

(2) The evidence which is required for the purposes of paragraph (1)(c) is a declaration made by that person in writing, in a form approved for the purposes by the Secretary of State, that they are unfit for work from a date or for a period specified in the declaration.

DEFINITIONS

"the Act"—see reg.2(2).
"Great Britain"—see Jobseekers Act 1995 s.35(1).
"writing"—see Interpretation Act 1978 Sch.1.

GENERAL NOTE

6.274 This is much the same as reg.55A of the JSA Regulations 1996. See the annotation to that provision in Pt III of this volume, ignoring references to joint-claim couples. It provides the same protection as reg.46, but without time-limit, to those entitled to new style JSA who satisfy reg.41(5) on temporary absence from Great Britain to receive treatment.

Prescribed amount of earnings

6.275 **48.**—The prescribed amount of earnings for the purposes of section 2(1)(c) of the Act (the contribution-based conditions) is to be calculated by applying the formula—

$$(A+D) - £0.01$$

where—

A is the age-related amount applicable to the claimant for the purposes of section 4(1)(a) of the Act; and

D is any amount disregarded from the claimant's earnings in accordance with the Schedule to these Regulations and either regulation 59(2) (calculation of net earnings of employed earners) or regulation 61(2) (calculation of net profit of self-employed earners).

DEFINITIONS

"the Act"—see reg.2(2).
"claimant"—see Jobseekers Act 1995 s.35(1).
"earnings"—see Jobseekers Act 1993 s.35(3).

GENERAL NOTE

6.276 It is a condition of entitlement to new style JSA that the claimant does not have earnings in excess of the prescribed amount (new style Jobseekers Act 1995 s.2(1)(c)). This regulation gives the set formula for determining that prescribed amount, which amount is not the same for everyone. The prescribed amount is a level equal to the total of the claimant's personal age-related rate JSA (determined in accordance with new style Jobseekers Act 1995 s.4 and with reg.49) (A in the formula) and the appropriate disregards from his earnings (D in the formula), minus one penny.

PART 6

AMOUNTS OF A JOBSEEKER'S ALLOWANCE

Weekly amounts of jobseeker's allowance

49.—(1) In the case of a jobseeker's allowance, the age-related amount applicable to a claimant for the purposes of section 4(1)(a) of the Act is— **6.277**

(a) in the case of a person who has not attained the age of 25, [1£57.90] per week;

(b) in the case of a person who has attained the age of 25, [1£73.10] per week.

(2) Where the amount of any jobseeker's allowance would, but for this paragraph, include a fraction of one penny, that fraction is to be treated as one penny.

AMENDMENT

1. Welfare Benefits Up-rating Order 2015 art.10 (SI 2015/30) (April 6, 2015).

DEFINITIONS

"the Act"—see reg.2(2).
"claimant"—see Jobseekers Act 1995 s.35(1).
"week"—see reg.2(2).

GENERAL NOTE

See the annotations to the similar reg.79 of the JSA Regulations 1996 in Pt III of this volume. **6.278**

Deductions in respect of earnings

50.—The deduction in respect of earnings which falls to be made in accordance with section 4(1)(b) of the Act is an amount equal to the weekly amount of the claimant's earnings calculated in accordance with Part 7. **6.279**

DEFINITIONS

"the Act"—see reg.2(2).
"claimant"—see Jobseekers Act 1995 s.35(1).
"earnings"—see Jobseekers Act 1993 s.35(3).

GENERAL NOTE

This is very much like reg.80 of the JSA Regulations 1996. See the annotations to that provision in Pt III of this volume. Section 4(1)(b) of the new style Jobseekers Act 1995 provides that the amount of JSA is to be the claimant's age-related amount (reg.49) subject to deductions for earnings (reg.50) and for pension payments and cognate payments (reg.51). **6.280**

Payments by way of pensions

51.—(1) The deduction in respect of pension payments, PPF payments or FAS payments which fall to be made in accordance with section 4(1)(b) of the Act is a sum equal to the amount by which that payment exceeds or, as the case may be, the aggregate of those payments exceed £50 per week. **6.281**

(2) Where pension payments, PPF payments or FAS payments first begin to be made to a person for a period starting other than on the first day of a benefit week, the deduction referred to in paragraph (1) has effect from the beginning of that benefit week.

(3) Where pension payments, PPF payments or FAS payments are already in payment to a person and a change in the rate of payment takes effect in a week other than at the beginning of the benefit week, the deduction referred to in paragraph (1) has effect from the first day of that benefit week.

(4) In determining the amount of any pension payments, PPF payments or FAS payments for the purposes of paragraphs (1) and (5), there are to be disregarded—

(a) any payments from a personal pension scheme, an occupational pension scheme or a public service pension scheme which are payable to the claimant and which arose in accordance with the terms of such a scheme on the death of a person who was a member of the scheme in question; and

(b) any PPF payments or FAS payments which—

(i) are payable to the claimant; and

(ii) arose on the death of a person who had an entitlement to such payments.

(5) Where a pension payment, PPF payment or FAS payment, or an aggregate of such payments, as the case may be, is paid to a person for a period other than a week, such payments are to be treated as being made to that person by way of weekly pension payments, weekly PPF payments or weekly FAS payments and the weekly amount is to be determined—

(a) where payment is made for a year, by dividing the total by 52;

(b) where payment is made for three months, by dividing the total by 13;

(c) where payment is made for a month, by multiplying the total by 12 and dividing the product by 52;

(d) where payment is made for two or more months, otherwise than for a year or for three months, by dividing the total by the number of months, multiplying the result by 12 and dividing the product by 52; or

(e) in any other case, by dividing the amount of the payment by the number of days in the period for which it is made and multiplying the result by seven.

DEFINITIONS

"the Act"—see reg.2(2).
"claimant"—see Jobseekers Act s.35(1).
"FAS payments"—*ibid.*
"occupational pension scheme"—*ibid.*
"payment"—see reg.2(2).
"pension payments"—see Jobseekers Act 1995 s.35(1).
"personal pension scheme"—*ibid.*
"PPF payments"—*ibid.*
"public service pension scheme"—*ibid.*
"week"—see reg.2(2).

GENERAL NOTE

See the annotations to the similar reg.81 of the JSA Regulations 1996 in Pt III of this volume. Section 4(1)(b) of the new style Jobseekers Act 1995 provides that the amount of JSA is to be the claimant's age-related amount (reg.49) subject to deductions for earnings (reg.50) and for pension payments and cognate payments under this regulation. 6.282

Minimum amount of a jobseeker's allowance

52.—Where the amount of a jobseeker's allowance is less than 10 pence a week that allowance is not payable. 6.283

PART 7

EARNINGS

Rounding of fractions

53.—Where any calculation under this Part results in a fraction of a penny that fraction must, if it would be to the claimant's advantage, be treated as a penny, but otherwise it must be disregarded. 6.284

Calculation of earnings derived from employed earner's employment

54.—(1) Earnings derived from employment as an employed earner are to be taken into account over a period determined in accordance with the following paragraphs and at a weekly amount determined in accordance with regulation 57 (calculation of weekly amount of earnings). 6.285

(2) Subject to the following provisions of this regulation, the period over which a payment is to be taken into account is to be—

(a) where the payment is monthly, a period equal to the number of weeks beginning with the date on which the payment is treated as paid under regulation 56 and ending with the date immediately before the date on which the next monthly payment would have been so treated as paid whether or not the next monthly payment is actually paid;

(b) where the payment is in respect of a period which is not monthly, a period equal to the length of the period for which payment is made; or

(c) in any other case, a period equal to such number of weeks as is equal to the number obtained (see paragraph (13)) by applying the formula—

$$\frac{E}{J + D}$$

where—

E is the net earnings;

J is the amount of jobseeker's allowance which would be payable had the payment not been made;
D is an amount equal to the total of the sums which would fall to be disregarded from that payment under the Schedule to these Regulations (sums to be disregarded in the calculation of earnings), as is appropriate in the claimant's case,

and that period is to begin on the date on which the payment is treated as paid under regulation 56.

[[1](3)(a) This paragraph applies where earnings are derived by a claimant as a member of a reserve force prescribed in Part 1 of Schedule 6 to the Social Security (Contributions) Regulations 2001—
(i) in respect of a period of annual continuous training for a maximum of 15 days in any calendar year; or
(ii) in respect of training in the claimant's first year of training as a member of a reserve force for a maximum of 43 days in that year.

(b) Earnings, whether paid to the claimant alone or together with other earnings derived from the same source, are to be taken into account—
(i) in the case of a period of training which lasts for the number of days listed in column 1 of the table in sub-paragraph (c), over a period of time which is equal to the number of days set out in the corresponding row in column 2 of that table; or
(ii) in any other case, over a period which is equal to the duration of the training period.

(c) This is the table referred to in sub-paragraph (b)(i)—

Column 1 *Period of training in days*	*Column 2* *Period of time over which earnings are to be taken into account in days*
8 to 10	7
15 to 17	14
22 to 24	21
29 to 31	28
36 to 38	35
43	42"

(4) The period referred to in paragraph (3) over which earnings are to be taken into account is to begin on the date on which they are treated as paid under regulation 56.

(5) Where earnings are derived from the same source but are not of the same kind and the periods in respect of which those earnings would, but for this paragraph, fall to be taken into account, overlap wholly or partly—
(a) those earnings are to be taken into account over a period equal to the aggregate length of those periods; and
(b) that period is to begin with the earliest date on which any part of those earnings would otherwise be treated as paid under regulation 56 (date on which earnings are treated as paid).

(6) In a case to which paragraph (5) applies, earnings falling within regulation 58 (earnings of employed earners) are to be taken into account in the following order of priority—

(a) earnings normally derived from the employment;
(b) any compensation payment;
(c) any holiday pay.

(7) Where earnings to which regulation 58(1)(b) or (c) (earnings of employed earners) applies are paid in respect of part of a day, those earnings are to be taken into account over a period equal to a day.

(8) Subject to paragraph (9), the period over which a compensation payment is to be taken into account is to be the period beginning on the date on which the payment is treated as paid under regulation 56 (date on which earnings are treated as paid) and ending—

(a) subject to sub-paragraph (b), where the person who made the payment represents that it, or part of it, was paid in lieu of notice of termination of employment or on account of the early termination of a contract of employment for a term certain, on the expiry date;
(b) in a case where the person who made the payment represents that it, or part of it, was paid in lieu of consultation under section 188 of the Trade Union and Labour Relations (Consolidation) Act 1992(73), on the latest of—
   (i) the date on which the consultation period under that section would have ended;
   (ii) in a case where sub-paragraph (a) also applies, the expiry date; or
   (iii) the standard date; or
(c) in any other case, on the standard date.

(9) The maximum period over which a compensation payment may be taken into account under paragraph (8) is 52 weeks from the date on which the payment is treated as paid under regulation 56.

(10) In this regulation—

"compensation payment" means any payment" to which regulation 58(4) (earnings of employed earners) applies;

""the expiry date" means in relation to the termination of a person's employment—

(a) the date on which any period of notice (which means the period of notice of termination of employment to which a person is entitled by statute or by contract, whichever is the longer, or, if they are not entitled to such notice, the period of notice which is customary in the employment in question) applicable to the person was due to expire, or would have expired had it not been waived;
(b) subject to paragraph (11), where the person who made the payment represents that the period in respect of which that payment is made is longer than the period of notice referred to in paragraph (a), the date on which that longer period is due to expire; or
(c) where the person had a contract of employment for a term certain, the date on which it was due to expire;

"the standard date" means the earlier of—

(a) the expiry date; and
(b) the last day of the period determined by dividing the amount of the compensation payment by the maximum weekly amount which, on the date on which the payment is treated as paid under regulation 56, is specified in section 227(1) of the Employment Rights Act 1996, and treating the result (less any fraction of a whole number) as a number of weeks.

(11) For the purposes of paragraph (10), if it appears to the Secretary of State in a case to which paragraph (b) of the definition of "expiry date" applies that, having regard to the amount of the compensation payment and the level of remuneration normally received by the claimant when they were engaged in the employment in respect of which the compensation payment was made, it is unreasonable to take the payment into account until the date specified in that paragraph (b), the expiry date is to be the date specified in paragraph (a) of that definition.

(12) For the purposes of this regulation the claimant's earnings are to be calculated in accordance with regulations 58, 59 and 63.

(13) For the purposes of the number obtained as mentioned in paragraph (2)(c), any fraction is to be treated as a corresponding fraction of a week.

AMENDMENT

1. Social Security (Members of the Reserve Forces) (Amendment) Regulations 2015 (SI 2015/389) reg.5(3) (April 6, 2015).

DEFINITIONS

"claimant"—see Jobseekers Act 1995 s.35(1).
"earnings"—see Jobseekers Act 1995 s.35(3).
"employed earner"—see reg.2(1).
"first year of training"—see reg.2(2).
"week"—*ibid.*

GENERAL NOTE

Paragraphs (1)–(7)

6.286 See also the notes to paras (1)–(4A) of reg.29 of the Income Support Regulations in Pt II of this volume, ignoring references to disregards.

These provisions specify how earnings from employed earner's employment are to be taken into account for the purpose of making the deduction from the claimant's age-related amount under s.4(1)(b) of the new style Jobseekers Act 1995 and reg.50, in particular deal with the period over which a payment is to be taken into account. The start of the period is identified under reg.56. The weekly amount to be taken into account is determined under reg.57. Regulation 58 defines what counts as earnings from employment: in general covering any remuneration or profit derived from the employment, with a number of specific inclusions. Regulation 59 specifies the deductions that are to be made in calculating the net earnings to be taken into account.

The general rules on "what period" are found in para.(2). Different rules, however, apply for earnings from annual continuous training as a member of a territorial or reserve force (paras (3) and (4)). Furthermore, where earnings from the same source but of a different kind overlap, the para.(2) rules are first applied to each kind and then that set by para.(5), so that they are to be taken into account over a period equal to the aggregate length of the periods determined for each under the general rules, beginning on the earliest date on which any of these earnings would be treated as paid in accordance with reg.56, with para.(6) setting an order of priority. Where compensation payments or holiday pay ("earnings to which regulation 58(1)(b) or (c)" apply) are paid in respect of part of a day they are to be treated as applicable to a day (para.(7)).

Paragraphs (8)–(11)

6.287 These provisions define the length of the period for which a "compensation payment" (defined in para.(10)) is to be taken into account. There is no equivalent to reg.29(4C) of the Income Support Regulations, so it seems that a compensation payment made on the termination of part-time employment will be taken into account as earnings for the period covered by the payment. The "maximum weekly amount" referred to in para.(8)(c)(ii) is the amount specified at the relevant time as the amount to be used in calculating the basic award for unfair dismissal and redundancy payments. The figure in effect from April 6, 2016 is £479 (2015, £475; 2014, £464).

Note *CJSA 5529/1997* in which the effect of reg.94(6) of the JSA Regulations 1996 (the equivalent of para.(8) here) was that the period to which the claimant's compensation payment was to be attributed ended before it started. On October 1, 1996 the claimant agreed with her employer that her employment would end on December 31, 1996 by way of voluntary redundancy. She was to receive a payment of £41,500 on January 4, 1997, which would not include any sum in lieu of notice. She claimed JSA with effect from January 1, 1997. The Commissioner states that the period for which the compensation period was to be taken into account ended on the "standard date". Under the equivalent of para.(10) here, the standard date was the earlier of the "expiry date" and what might be termed the "apportionment date". The expiry date in this case was no later than December 31, 1996 because the claimant was entitled to 12 weeks' (or three months') notice and the agreement for redundancy had been made on October 1, 1996 (see para.(a) of the definition of "expiry date" in para.(10))). The result was that there was no period in respect of which the compensation payment was to be taken into account and thus no period during which she was to be treated as in remunerative work after December 31, 1996.

Calculation of earnings of self-employed earners

55.—(1) Except where paragraph (2) applies, where a claimant's income consists of earnings from employment as a self-employed earner the weekly amount of their earnings is to be determined by reference to their average weekly earnings from that employment— 6.288

(a) over a period of one year; or
(b) where the claimant has recently become engaged in that employment or there has been a change which is likely to affect the normal pattern of business, over such other period as may, in any particular case, enable the weekly amount of their earnings to be determined more accurately.

(2) Where the claimant's earnings consist of any items to which paragraph (3) applies, those earnings are to be taken into account over a period equal to such number of weeks as is equal to the number obtained (see paragraph (5)) by applying the formula—

$$\frac{E}{J + D}$$

where—

E is the earnings;
J is the amount of jobseeker's allowance which would be payable had the payment not been made;
D is an amount equal to the total of the sums which would fall to be disregarded from the payment under the Schedule to these Regulations (earnings to be disregarded) as is appropriate in the claimant's case.

(3) This paragraph applies to—

(a) royalties or other sums paid as a consideration for the use of, or the right to use, any copyright, design, patent or trade mark; or

(b) any payment in respect of any—

(i) book registered under the Public Lending Right Scheme 1982; or

(ii) work made under any international public lending right scheme that is analogous to the Public Lending Right Scheme 1982,

where the claimant is the first owner of the copyright, design, patent or trade mark, or an original contributor to the book or work concerned.

(4) For the purposes of this regulation the claimant's earnings are to be calculated in accordance with regulations 60 to 62.

(5) For the purposes of the number obtained as mentioned in paragraph (2), any fraction is to be treated as a corresponding fraction of a week.

DEFINITIONS

"claimant"—see Jobseekers Act 1995 s.35(1).
"self-employed earner"—see reg.2(2).

GENERAL NOTE

6.289 See the notes to reg.30 of the Income Support Regulations in Pt II of this volume. Note the more general exception to the rule in para.(1)(a) that is hidden in reg.61(10) which allows the amount of any item of income or expenditure to be calculated over a different period if that will produce a more accurate figure.

Date on which earnings are treated as paid

6.290 **56.**—A payment of earnings to which regulation 54 (calculation of earnings derived from employed earner's employment) applies is to be treated as paid—

(a) in the case of a payment which is due to be paid before the first benefit week pursuant to the claim, on the date on which it is due to be paid; or

(b) in any other case, on the first day of the benefit week in which it is due to be paid or the first succeeding benefit week in which it is practicable to take it into account.

DEFINITIONS

"benefit week"—see reg.2(2).
"payment"—*ibid.*

GENERAL NOTE

6.291 See the annotations to reg.31(1) of the Income Support Regulations in Pt II of this volume in so far as they deal with earnings rather than with other income. The identification of the date on which a payment is due to be paid in effect identifies the start of the period as fixed under reg.54 for which it is to be taken into account at the rate fixed under reg.57.

Calculation of weekly amount of earnings

6.292 **57.**—(1) For the purposes of regulation 54 (calculation of earnings derived from employed earner's employment), subject to paragraphs (2) to (5), where the period in respect of which a payment of earnings is made—

(a) does not exceed a week, the weekly amount is to be the amount of that payment;

(b) exceeds a week, the weekly amount is to be determined—

(i) in a case where that period is a month, by multiplying the amount of the payment by 12 and dividing the product by 52;

(ii) in a case where that period is three months, by multiplying the amount of the payment by four and dividing the product by 52;

(iii) in a case where that period is a year, by dividing the amount of the payment by 52;

(iv) in any other case, by multiplying the amount of the payment by seven and dividing the product by the number equal to the number of days in the period in respect of which it is made.

(2) Where a payment for a period not exceeding a week is treated under regulation 56(a) (date on which earnings are treated as paid) as paid before the first benefit week and a part is to be taken into account for some days only in that week ("the relevant days"), the amount to be taken into account for the relevant days is to be calculated by multiplying the amount of the payment by the number of relevant days and dividing the product by the number of days in the period in respect of which it is made.

(3) Where a payment is in respect of a period equal to or in excess of a week and a part is to be taken into account for some days only in a benefit week ("the relevant days"), the amount to be taken into account for the relevant days is, except where paragraph (4) applies, to be calculated by multiplying the amount of the payment by the number of relevant days and dividing the product by the number of days in the period in respect of which it is made.

(4) Except in the case of a payment which it has not been practicable to treat under regulation 56(b) as paid on the first day of the benefit week in which it is due to be paid, where a payment of income from a particular source is or has been paid regularly and that payment falls to be taken into account in the same benefit week as a payment of the same kind and from the same source, the amount of that income to be taken into account in any one benefit week is not to exceed the weekly amount determined under paragraph (1)(a) or (b), as the case may be, of the payment which under regulation 56(b) (date on which earnings are treated as paid) is treated as paid first.

(5) Where the amount of the claimant's earnings fluctuates and has changed more than once, or a claimant's regular pattern of work is such that they do not work every week, paragraphs (1) to (4) may be modified so that the weekly amount of their earnings is determined by reference to their average weekly earnings—

(a) if there is a recognisable cycle of work, over the period of one complete cycle (including, where the cycle involves periods in which the claimant does no work, those periods but disregarding any other absences);

(b) in any other case, over a period of five weeks or such other period as may, in the particular case, enable the claimant's average weekly earnings to be determined more accurately.

DEFINITIONS

"benefit week"—see reg.2(2).
"claimant"—see Jobseekers Act 1995 s.35(1).

"payment"—see reg.2(2).
"week"—*ibid*.

General Note

6.292A See the annotations to reg.94 of the JSA Regulations 1996 in Pt III of this volume and also those to reg.32(1)–(6) of the Income Support Regulations in Pt II in so far as they deal with earnings rather than with other income.

Earnings of employed earners

6.293 **58.**—(1) Subject to paragraphs (2) and (4), "earnings" means in the case of employment as an employed earner, any remuneration or profit derived from that employment and includes—

(a) any bonus or commission;
(b) any compensation payment;
(c) any holiday pay except any payable more than four weeks after the termination or interruption of employment but this exception does not apply to a person who is, or would be, prevented from being entitled to a jobseeker's allowance by section 14 of the Act (trade disputes);
(d) any payment by way of a retainer;
(e) any payment made by the claimant's employer in respect of expenses not wholly, exclusively and necessarily incurred in the performance of the duties of the employment, including any payment made by the claimant's employer in respect of—
   (i) travelling expenses incurred by the claimant between their home and place of employment;
   (ii) expenses incurred by the claimant under arrangements made for the care of a member of their family owing to the claimant's absence from home;
(f) any payment or award of compensation made under section 112(4), 113, 117(3)(a), 128, 131 or 132 of the Employment Rights Act 1996 (the remedies: orders and compensation, the orders, enforcement of order and compensation, interim relief);
(g) any payment made or remuneration paid under section 28, 34, 64, 68 or 70 of the Employment Rights Act 1996 (right to guarantee payments, remuneration on suspension on medical or maternity grounds, complaints to employment tribunals);
(h) any award of compensation made under section 156, 161 to 166, 189 or 192 of the Trade Union and Labour Relations (Consolidation) Act 1992 (compensation for unfair dismissal or redundancy on grounds of involvement in trade union activities, and protective awards);
(i) the amount of any payment by way of a non-cash voucher which has been taken into account in the computation of a person's earnings in accordance with Part 5 of Schedule 3 to the Social Security (Contributions) Regulations 2001.

(2) "Earnings" does not include—
(a) subject to paragraph (3), any payment in kind;
(b) any periodic sum paid to a claimant on account of the termination of their employment by reason of redundancy;
(c) any remuneration paid by or on behalf of an employer to the claim-

ant in respect of a period throughout which the claimant is on maternity leave, paternity leave [2, shared paternity leave] or adoption leave or is absent from work because they are ill;

(d) any payment in respect of expenses wholly, exclusively and necessarily incurred in the performance of the duties of the employment;

(e) any occupational pension;

(f) any redundancy payment within the meaning of section 135(1) of the Employment Rights Act 1996;

(g) any lump sum payment made under the Iron and Steel Re-adaptation Benefits Scheme;

(h) any payment in respect of expenses arising out of the claimant's participation as a service user;

[1(i) any bounty paid at intervals of at least one year and derived from employment to which paragraph 6 of the Schedule to these Regulations applies.]

(3) Paragraph (2)(a) does not apply in respect of any non-cash voucher referred to in paragraph (1)(i).

(4) In this regulation, "compensation payment" means any payment made in respect of the termination of employment other than—

(a) any remuneration or emolument (whether in money or in kind) which accrued in the period before the termination;

(b) any holiday pay;

(c) any payment specified in paragraphs (1)(f), (g), or (h) or (2);

(d) any refund of contributions to which the person was entitled under an occupational pension scheme.

AMENDMENTS

1. Universal Credit and Miscellaneous Amendments Regulations 2014 reg.3(7) (April 28, 2014).

2. Shared Parental Leave and Statutory Shared Parental Pay (Consequential Amendments and Subordinate Legislation) Order 2014 (SI 2014/3255) art.29(4) (December 23, 2014).

DEFINITIONS

"the Act"—see reg.2(2).
"adoption leave"—*ibid.*
"claimant"—see Jobseekers Act 1995 s.35(1).
"employed earner"—see reg.2(1).
"employment"—see reg.2(1).
"family"—see Jobseekers Act 1995 s.35(1).
"maternity leave"—see reg.2(2).
"occupational pension"—*ibid.*
"occupational pension scheme"—see Jobseekers Act 1995 s.35(1).
"person participating as a service user"—see reg.3(6).
"shared parental leave"—see reg.2(2).
"week"—*ibid.*

GENERAL NOTE

See the annotations to the similarly worded reg.98 of the JSA Regulations 1996 in Pt III of this volume and those to reg.35 of the Income Support Regulations in Pt II, ignoring references to things not ranking as earnings being treated as income or capital, that are relevant only to income-related benefits. **6.294**

Calculation of net earnings of employed earners

6.295 **59.**—(1) For the purposes of regulation 54 (calculation of earnings of employed earners), the earnings of a claimant derived from employment as an employed earner to be taken into account are to be, subject to paragraph (2), their net earnings.

(2) There is to be disregarded from a claimant's net earnings, any sum, where applicable, specified in the Schedule to these Regulations.

(3) For the purposes of paragraph (1) net earnings are to be calculated by taking into account the gross earnings of the claimant from that employment less—

(a) any amount deducted from those earnings by way of—
  (i) income tax;
  (ii) primary Class 1 contributions payable under the Benefits Act; and
(b) half of any sum paid by the claimant in respect of a pay period (the period in respect of which a claimant is, or expects to be, normally paid by their employer, being a week, a fortnight, four weeks, a month or other longer or shorter period as the case may be) by way of a contribution towards an occupational or personal pension scheme.

DEFINITIONS

"the Benefits Act"—see Jobseekers Act 1995 s.35(1).
"claimant"—*ibid.*
"employed earner"—see reg.2(1).
"employment"—*ibid.*
"occupational pension scheme"—see Jobseekers Act 1995 s.35(1).
"personal pension scheme"—*ibid.*
"week"—see reg.2(2).

GENERAL NOTE

6.296 See the annotations to reg.36 of the Income Support Regulations in Pt II of this volume.

Earnings of self-employed earners

6.297 **60.**—(1) Subject to paragraph (2), "earnings", in the case of employment as a self-employed earner, means the gross receipts of the employment.

(2) "Earnings" does not include—

(a) where a claimant is involved in providing board and lodging accommodation for which a charge is payable, any payment by way of such a charge;
(b) any payment made to the claimant with whom a person is accommodated by virtue of arrangements made—
  (i) under section 22C(2), (3), (5) or (6)(a) or (b) of the Children Act 1989 (provision of accommodation and maintenance for a child whom the local authority is looking after);
  (ii) by a local authority under section 26 of the Children (Scotland) Act 1995 (manner of provision of accommodation to child looked after by local authority); or

(iii) by a local authority under regulation 33 or 51 of the Looked After Children (Scotland) Regulations 2009 (fostering and kinship care allowances and fostering allowances); or

(iv) by a voluntary organisation under section 59(1)(a) of the Children Act 1989 (provision of accommodation by voluntary organisations);

(c) any payment made to the claimant for a person ("the person concerned"), who is not normally a member of the claimant's household but is temporarily in the claimant's care, by—

(i) the National Health Service Commissioning Board;

(ii) a local authority but excluding payments of housing benefit made in respect of the person concerned;

(iii) a voluntary organisation;

(iv) the person concerned pursuant to section 26(3A) of the National Assistance Act 1948;

(v) a clinical commissioning group established under section 14D of the Health Service Act; [1 . . .]

(vi) a Local Health Board established by an order made under section 11 of the Health Service (Wales) Act; [1or

(vii) the person concerned where the payment is for the provision of accommodation in respect of the meeting of that person's needs under section 18 or 19 of the Care Act 2014 (duty and power to meet needs for care and support);]

(d) any sports award.

(3) In this regulation, "board and lodging accommodation" means—

(a) accommodation provided to a person or, if they are a member of a family, to them or any other member of their family, for a charge which is inclusive of—

(i) the provision of that accommodation; and

(ii) at least some cooked or prepared meals which are cooked or prepared (by a person other than the person to whom the accommodation is provided or a member of their family) and consumed in that accommodation or associated premises; or

(b) accommodation provided to a person in a hotel, guest house, lodging house or some similar establishment,

except accommodation provided by a close relative of theirs or of any other member of their family, or other than on a commercial basis.

AMENDMENT

1. Care Act 2014 (Consequential Amendments) (Secondary Legislation) Order 2015 (SI 2015/643) Sch. art.41 (April 1, 2015).

DEFINITIONS

"claimant"—see Jobseekers Act 1995 s.35(1).
"close relative"—see reg.2(2).
"employment"—see reg.2(1).
"family"—see Jobseekers Act 1995 s.35(1) and reg.3(1).
"Health Service Act"—see reg.2(2).
"Health Service (Wales) Act"—*ibid.*
"self-employed earner"—*ibid.*
"sports award"—*ibid.*
"voluntary organisation"—*ibid.*

General Note

6.298 See annotations to the similar reg.100 of the JSA Regulations 1996 in Pt III of this volume, ignoring references to payments being treated as other income, something relevant only to IBJSA, now abolished in cases in which new style JSA has come into operation.

Calculation of net profit of self-employed earners

6.299 **61.**—(1) For the purposes of regulation 55 (calculation of earnings of self-employed earners), the earnings of a claimant to be taken into account are—

(a) in the case of a self-employed earner who is engaged in employment on their own account, the net profit derived from that employment;

(b) in the case of a self-employed earner whose employment is carried on in partnership, or is that of a share fisherman within the meaning of regulation 67, the claimant's share of the net profit derived from that employment less—

(i) an amount in respect of income tax and of national insurance contributions payable under the Benefits Act calculated in accordance with regulation 62 (deduction of tax and contributions for self-employed earners); and

(ii) half of any premium paid in the period that is relevant under regulation 55 in respect of a personal pension scheme.

(2) There is to be disregarded from a claimant's net profit any sum, where applicable, specified in paragraphs 1 to 11 of the Schedule to these Regulations.

(3) For the purposes of paragraph (1)(a) the net profit of the employment is, except where paragraph (9) applies, to be calculated by taking into account the earnings of the employment over the period determined under regulation 55 (calculation of earnings of self-employed earners) less—

(a) subject to paragraphs (5) to (7), any expenses wholly and exclusively incurred in that period for the purposes of that employment;

(b) an amount in respect of—

(i) income tax; and

(ii) national insurance contributions payable under the Benefits Act, calculated in accordance with regulation 62 (deductions of tax and contributions for self-employed earners); and

(c) half of any premium paid in the period determined under regulation 55 in respect of a personal pension scheme.

(4) For the purposes of paragraph (1)(b), the net profit of the employment is to be calculated by taking into account the earnings of the employment over the period determined under regulation 55 less, subject to paragraphs (5) to (7), any expenses wholly and exclusively incurred in that period for the purposes of that employment.

(5) Subject to paragraph (6), no deduction is to be made under paragraph (3)(a) or (4) in respect of—

(a) any capital expenditure;

(b) the depreciation of any capital asset;

(c) any sum employed or intended to be employed in the setting up or expansion of the employment;

(d) any loss incurred before the beginning of the period determined under regulation 55;
(e) the repayment of capital on any loan taken out for the purposes of the employment;
(f) any expenses incurred in providing business entertainment.

(6) A deduction is to be made under paragraph (3)(a) or (4) in respect of the repayment of capital on any loan used for—
(a) the replacement in the course of business of equipment or machinery; and
(b) the repair of an existing business asset except to the extent that any sum is payable under an insurance policy for its repair.

(7) The Secretary of State must not make a deduction under paragraph (3)(a) or (4) in respect of any expenses where the Secretary of State is not satisfied that the expense has been incurred or, having regard to the nature of the expense and its amount, that it has been reasonably incurred.

(8) A deduction under paragraph (3)(a) or (4)—
(a) must not be made in respect of any sum unless it has been incurred for the purposes of the business;
(b) must be made in respect of—
   (i) the excess of any Value Added Tax paid over Value Added Tax received in the period determined under regulation 55;
   (ii) any income expended in the repair of an existing asset except to the extent that any sum is payable under an insurance policy for its repair;
   (iii) any payment of interest on a loan taken out for the purposes of the employment.

(9) Where a claimant is engaged in employment as a child-minder the net profit of the employment is to be one-third of the earnings of that employment, less—
(a) an amount in respect of—
   (i) income tax; and
   (ii) national insurance contributions payable under the Benefits Act, calculated in accordance with regulation 62 (deductions of tax and contributions for self-employed earners); and
(b) half of any premium paid in the period determined under regulation 55 in respect of a personal pension scheme.

(10) Notwithstanding regulation 55 and paragraphs (1) to (9), the Secretary of State may assess any item of a claimant's income or expenditure over a period other than that determined under regulation 55 provided that the other period may, in the particular case, enable the weekly amount of that item of income or expenditure to be determined more accurately.

(11) Where a claimant is engaged in employment as a self-employed earner and they are engaged in one or more other employments as a self-employed or employed earner, any loss incurred in any one of their employments is not to be offset against their earnings in any other of their employments.

DEFINITIONS

"the Benefits Act"—see Jobseekers Act 1995 s.35(1).
"claimant"—*ibid.*
"employed earner"—see reg.2(1).

"employment"—*ibid.*
"personal pension scheme"—see Jobseekers Act 1995 s.35(1).
"self-employed earner"—see reg.2(2).
"share fisherman"—see reg.67.

GENERAL NOTE

6.300 See the annotations to reg.38 of the Income Support Regulations in Pt II of this volume. Note the width of para.(10). See the annotation to reg.55 above.

Deduction of tax and contributions for self-employed earners

6.301 **62.**—(1) Subject to paragraph (2), the amount to be deducted in respect of income tax under regulation 61(1)(b)(i), (3)(b)(i) or (9)(a)(i) (calculation of net profit of self-employed earners) is to be calculated—

(a) on the basis of the amount of chargeable income; and

[[2](b) as if that income were assessable to income tax at the basic rate, or in the case of a Scottish taxpayer, the Scottish basic rate, of tax less only the personal reliefs to which the claimant is entitled under Chapters 2, 3 and 3A of Part 3 of the Income Tax Act 2007 as are appropriate to their circumstances;]

(2) If the period determined under regulation 55 is less than a year, the earnings to which the basic rate of tax is to be applied and the amount of the personal allowance deductible under paragraph (1) is to be calculated on a pro rata basis.

(3) Subject to paragraph (4), the amount to be deducted in respect of national insurance contributions under regulation 61(1)(b)(i), (3)(b)(ii) or (9)(a)(ii) is to be the total of—

(a) the amount of Class 2 contributions payable under section [[1] 11(2)] or, as the case may be, [[1] 11(8)] of the Benefits Act at the rate applicable at the date of claim except where the claimant's chargeable income is less than the amount specified in section 11(4) of that Act ([[1] small profits threshold]) for the tax year in which the date of claim falls; and

(b) the amount of Class 4 contributions (if any) which would be payable under section 15 of that Act (Class 4 contributions recoverable under the Income Tax Acts) at the percentage rate applicable at the date of claim on so much of the chargeable income as exceeds the lower limit but does not exceed the upper limit of profits and gains applicable for the tax year in which the date of claim falls.

(4) If the period determined under regulation 55 is less than a year—

(a) the amount specified for the tax year referred to in paragraph (3)(a) is to be reduced pro rata; and

(b) the limits referred to in paragraph (3)(b) are to be reduced pro rata.

(5) In this regulation "chargeable income" means—

(a) except where sub-paragraph (b) applies, the earnings derived from the employment less any expenses deducted under regulation 61(3)(a) or, as the case may be, (4);

(b) in the case of employment as a child minder, one-third of the earnings of that employment.

AMENDMENT

1. Social Security (Miscellaneous Amendments No.2) Regulations 2015 (SI 2015/478) reg.37 (April 6, 2015).
2. Social Security (Scottish Rate of Income Tax etc.) (Amendment) Regulations 2016 (SI 2016/233) reg.7(3) (April 6, 2016).

DEFINITIONS

"the Benefits Act"—see Jobseekers Act 1995 s.35(1).
"date of claim"—see reg.2(2).
"employment"—see reg.2(1).
"Scottish basic rate"—see reg.2(2)
"Scottish taxpayer"—*ibid.*
"tax year"—see Jobseekers Act 1995 s.35(1).

GENERAL NOTE

See the annotations to reg.39 of the Income Support Regulations in Pt II of this volume. **6.302**

Notional earnings

63.—(1) Subject to paragraph (2), any earnings which are due to be paid to the claimant but have not been paid to the claimant, are to be treated as possessed by the claimant. **6.303**

(2) Paragraph (1) does not apply to any earnings which are due to an employed earner on the termination of their employment by reason of redundancy but which have not been paid to them.

(3) Where a claimant's earnings are not ascertainable at the time of the determination of the claim or of any revision or supersession, the Secretary of State must treat the claimant as possessing such earnings as is reasonable in the circumstances of the case having regard to the number of hours worked and the earnings paid for comparable employment in the area.

(4) Subject to paragraph (5), where—

(a) a claimant performs a service for another person; and
(b) that person makes no payment of earnings or pays less than that paid for a comparable employment in the area,

the Secretary of State must treat the claimant as possessing such earnings (if any) as is reasonable for that employment unless the claimant satisfies the Secretary of State that the means of that person are insufficient for that person to pay or to pay more for the service.

(5) Paragraph (4) does not apply—

(a) to a claimant who is engaged by a charity or voluntary organisation or who is a volunteer if the Secretary of State is satisfied in any of those cases that it is reasonable for the claimant to provide those services free of charge;
(b) to a claimant who is participating in a work placement approved by the Secretary of State (or a person providing services to the Secretary of State) before the placement starts.

(6) Where a claimant is treated as possessing any earnings under paragraphs (1) or (2), regulations 54 to 62 apply for the purposes of calculating the amount of those earnings as if a payment had actually been made and as if it were actual earnings which the claimant does possess.

(7) Where a claimant is treated as possessing any earnings under paragraphs (3) or (4), regulations 54 to 62 apply for the purposes of calculating the amount of those earnings as if a payment had actually been made and as if they were actual earnings which the claimant does possess, except that—

(a) regulation 59(3) does not apply; and

(b) the claimant's net earnings are to be calculated by taking into account the earnings which the claimant is treated as possessing less the amounts referred to in paragraph (8).

(8) The amounts mentioned in paragraph (7)(b) are—

(a) where the period over which the earnings which the claimant is treated as possessing are to be taken into account is—

(i) a year or more, an amount in respect of income tax equivalent to an amount calculated in accordance with paragraph (11);

(ii) less than a year, the earnings to which the starting rate of tax is to be applied and the amount of the personal allowance deductible under this paragraph are to be calculated on a pro rata basis;

(b) where the weekly amount of the earnings which the claimant is treated as possessing is not less than the lower earnings limit, an amount representing primary Class 1 contributions under the Benefits Act, calculated by applying to those earnings the initial and main primary percentages in accordance with section 8(1)(a) and (b) of that Act; and

(c) half of any sum payable by the claimant in respect of a pay period by way of a contribution towards an occupational or personal pension scheme.

(9) Paragraphs (1), (3) and (4) do not apply in respect of any amount of earnings derived from employment as an employed earner, arising out of the claimant's participation as a service user.

(10) In this regulation, "work placement" means practical work experience which is not undertaken in expectation of payment.

[[1](11) For the purposes of paragraph (8)(a)(i), the amount is calculated by applying to those earnings the basic rate, or in the case of a Scottish taxpayer, the Scottish basic rate, of tax in the year of assessment less only the personal reliefs to which the claimant is entitled under Chapters 2, 3 and 3A of Part 3 of the Income Tax Act 2007 as are appropriate to the claimant's circumstances.]

AMENDMENT

1. Social Security (Scottish Rate of Income Tax etc.) (Amendment) Regulations 2016 (SI 2016/233) reg.7(4) (April 6, 2016).

DEFINITIONS

"the Benefits Act"—see Jobseekers Act 1995 s.35(1).
"claimant"—*ibid.*
"earnings"—see reg.2(2).
"employment"—see reg.2(1).
"employed earner"—*ibid.*
"occupational pension scheme"—see Jobseekers Act 1995 s.35(1).
"participation as a service user"—see reg.3(6).
"personal pension scheme"—see Jobseekers Act 1995 s.35(1).
"Scottish basic rate"—see reg.2(2)
"Scottish taxpayer"—*ibid.*
"voluntary organisation"—see reg.2(2).

GENERAL NOTE

The concept of notional income and capital is familiar from old style JSA and income support. It is also carried forward into universal credit (see reg.60 of the UC Regulations 2013). The concept is that in certain circumstances the benefits regime treats someone as possessing income or capital they do not actually have. This regulation applies that concept to earnings, capital being irrelevant in new style JSA. Note that under para.(9) none of this regulation's "notional earnings" rules applies to any amount of earnings derived from employment as an employed earner, arising out of the claimant's participation as a service user, on which see reg.3(6). See in general the annotations to reg.42 of the Income Support Regulations in Pt II of this volume, taking account of the differences noted above and below. 6.304

Paragraphs (1), (2) and (6)

Earnings as an employee due, but not yet paid, to the claimant are treated as being possessed by the claimant, unless they are earnings not yet paid but due to the claimant on the termination of their employment by reason of redundancy. They are to be calculated under regs 54–62 as if actually paid to and possessed by the claimant. 6.305

Paragraph (3)

Where the claimant's earnings are not ascertainable at the time of the relevant decision, revision or supersession, the claimant must be treated as possessing such earnings as is reasonable in the circumstances of the case having regard to the number of hours worked and the earnings paid for comparable employment in the area. This is a very general discretion. The decision-maker (or tribunal) must have regard to the number of hours worked and the going rate locally for comparable employment in deciding what is reasonable, but is not prevented from considering all relevant circumstances (*R(SB) 25/83, R(SB) 15/86, R(SB) 6/88*). Paragraphs (7), (8) and (11) govern the calculation of the amount to be taken into account, including the making of deductions to take account of income tax, national insurance contributions and pension contributions. Note that reg.59(3), on the making of such deductions from actual earnings from employment does not apply. 6.306

Paragraphs (4) and (5)

See the annotations to reg.42(6) and (6A) of the Income Support Regulations. These provisions apply where a claimant provides services for nothing or for less than the going rate and allow notional earnings of what is reasonable for the employment to be deemed, subject to the means of the person for whom the services are provided not being insufficient to pay any more than the actual rate. There are exceptions in para.(5), including where the claimant is participating in an approved work placement, as defined in para.(10). Paragraphs (7), (8) and (11) on calculation also apply here as for para.(3). 6.307

PART 8

PART WEEKS

Amount of a jobseeker's allowance payable

64.—(1) Subject to the following provisions of this Part, the amount payable by way of a jobseeker's allowance in respect of a part-week is to be calculated by applying the formula— 6.308

$$(N \times X) / 7$$

where—

X is the personal rate determined in accordance with section 4(1) of the Act;
N is the number of days in the part-week.

(2) In this Part—
"part-week" means any period of less than a week in respect of which there is an entitlement to a jobseeker's allowance;
"relevant week" means the period of seven days determined in accordance with regulation 65.

DEFINITIONS

"the Act"—see reg.2(2).
"week"—*ibid.*

Relevant week

6.309 **65.**—(1) Where the part-week—
(a) is the whole period for which a jobseeker's allowance is payable or occurs at the beginning of an award, the relevant week is the period of seven days ending on the last day of that part-week;
(b) occurs at the end of an award, the relevant week is the period of seven days beginning on the first day of the part-week; or
(c) occurs because a jobseeker's allowance is not payable for any period in accordance with sections 6J or 7K of the Act (circumstances in which a jobseeker's allowance is not payable), the relevant week is the seven days ending immediately before the start of the next benefit week to commence for that claimant.

(2) Where a person has an award of a jobseeker's allowance and their benefit week changes, for the purpose of calculating the amounts of a jobseeker's allowance payable for the part-week beginning on the day after their last complete benefit week before the change and ending immediately before the change, the relevant week is the period of seven days beginning on the day after the last complete benefit week.

DEFINITIONS

"the Act"—see reg.2(2).
"benefit week"—*ibid.*
"part-week"—see reg.64(2).

Modification in the calculation of income

6.310 **66.**—For the purposes of regulation 64 (amount of jobseeker's allowance payable for part-weeks), a claimant's income is to be calculated in accordance with Part 7 subject to the following changes—
(a) any income which is due to be paid in the relevant week is to be treated as paid on the first day of that week;
(b) where the part-week occurs at the end of the claim, any income or any change in the amount of income of the same kind which is first payable within the relevant week but not on any day in the part-week is to be disregarded;

(c) where the part-week occurs immediately after a period in which a person was treated as engaged in remunerative work under regulation 43 (persons treated as engaged in remunerative work) any earnings which are taken into account for the purposes of determining that period are to be disregarded;
(d) where only part of the weekly amount of income is taken into account in the relevant week, the balance is to be disregarded.

DEFINITIONS

"part-week"—see reg.64(2).
"relevant week"—see regs 64(2) and 65.

PART 9

SHARE FISHERMEN

GENERAL NOTE

This Part of the Regulations modifies the usual rules so as to deal with "share fishermen" (defined in reg.67). Individual annotations are not provided below. **6.311**

Share fishermen are paid by way of a share of the catch or the gross profits of the fishing boat. For contributions purposes they are treated as a special form of self-employed earner and pay a special Class 2 contribution. Normally, of course, those liable to pay Class 2 (self-employed earner's contributions) rather than Class 1 contributions (employed earner's contributions) would not be entitled to JSA where fulfillment of the key contribution conditions depends on paid and/or credited Class 1 contributions (new style Jobseekers Act 1995 s.2). Regulation 69 modifies s.2 to take in for purposes of qualifying for new style JSA the special Class 2 contributions paid by share fishermen at the rate applicable in accordance with reg.125(c) of the Social Security (Contributions) Regulations 2001 (SI 2001/1004).

Regulation 70 modifies the definition of "trade dispute" in s.35(1) of the new style Jobseekers Act 1995. Regulation 71(1) sets an additional condition with respect to the payment of JSA to a share fisherman in respect of any benefit week: where in any benefit week claimants have not worked as a share fisherman (partly defined in reg.71(2)) they must prove that they have not neglected to avail themselves of a reasonable opportunity of employment as a share fisherman. Regulation 71(3) sets an additional condition that where claimants are master or a member of the crew of a fishing boat of which either the master or any member of the crew is the owner or part owner, they must also prove that in respect of any period in that benefit week when they were not working as a share fisherman, the fishing boat did not put to sea with a view to fishing for one of the reasons specified in reg,71(3)(a)–(c) or that "any other good cause necessitated abstention from fishing" (reg.71(3)(d)). Hours of engagement in work as a share fisherman are not to be counted "in determining the number of hours in which a person is engaged in remunerative work for the purposes of establishing entitlement to a jobseeker's allowance" (reg.72). Regulation 73 deals with calculation of the earnings of share fishermen, effecting modifications to the wording of standard rules in these Regulations, enabling them to be applied differently in the case of share fishermen. Regulation 74 provides that the amount of JSA payable is to be determined under its provisions and not those in Pt 8 above. For this purpose it also affords a different definition of "benefit week" (reg.74(3)).

Interpretation

6.312 **67.**—In this Part—

"fishing boat" means a fishing vessel as defined by section 313 of the Merchant Shipping Act 1995;

"owner" has the same meaning as in the Social Security (Mariners' Benefits) Regulations 1975;

"share fisherman" means any person who—

(a) is ordinarily employed in the fishing industry otherwise than under a contract of service, as a master or member of the crew of any fishing boat manned by more than one person, and is remunerated in respect of that employment in whole or in part by a share of the profits or gross earnings of the fishing boat; or

(b) has ordinarily been so employed, but who by reason of age or infirmity permanently ceases to be so employed and becomes ordinarily engaged in employment ashore in Great Britain, otherwise than under a contract of service, making or mending any gear relevant to a fishing boat or performing other services ancillary to or in connection with that boat and is remunerated in respect of that employment in whole or in part by a share of the profits or gross earnings of that boat and has not ceased to be ordinarily engaged in such employment.

Special provisions in respect of share fishermen

6.313 **68.**—The Act and above provisions of these Regulations have effect in relation to share fishermen subject to the provisions of this Part.

Modifications of section 2

6.314 **69.**—(1) Section 2 of the Act (the contribution-based conditions) applies to share fishermen with the modifications set out in the following provisions of this regulation.

(2) After the words "Class 1 contributions" in each place where they appear there is to be inserted the words "or special Class 2 contributions".

(3) In subsection (4) after the definition of "the relevant benefit year" there is to be inserted the following definition—

> "special Class 2 contributions" means any Class 2 contributions paid by a share fisherman at the rate applicable to share fishermen in accordance with regulation 125(c) of the Social Security (Contributions) Regulations 2001.".

Modification of section 35

6.315 **70.**—(1) The definition of "trade dispute" in section 35(1) of the Act (interpretation) applies to share fishermen with the effect that the owner (or managing owner if there is more than one owner) of a fishing boat is to be treated as the employer of any share fisherman (other than themselves) ordinarily employed as master or member of the crew of, or making or mending any gear relevant to, or performing other services ancillary to or in connection with, that fishing boat, and any such share fisherman is to be treated as their employee.

(2) In this regulation, "managing owner" means that the owner of any ship or vessel who, where there is more than one such owner, is responsible for the control and management of that ship or vessel.

Additional conditions for payment of a jobseeker's allowance

71.—(1) It is to be an additional condition with respect to the payment of a jobseeker's allowance to a share fisherman in respect of any benefit week, that in respect of any period in that benefit week when they have not worked as a share fisherman, they prove that they have not neglected to avail themselves of a reasonable opportunity of employment as a share fisherman. **6.316**

(2) The following provisions apply for the purposes of the application of paragraph (1)—

(a) work as a share fisherman within the meaning of paragraph (1) includes any of the work specified in sub-paragraph (b) which—

(i) at the time of its performance is necessary for the safety or reasonable efficiency of the fishing boat, or is likely to become so necessary in the near future; and

(ii) it is the duty of the share fisherman (whether by agreement, custom, practice or otherwise) to undertake without remuneration other than by way of a share in the profits or gross earnings of the fishing boat, but any other work done to the fishing boat or its nets or gear is to be disregarded; and

(b) the work so included by sub-paragraph (a) is any work done to the fishing boat or its nets or gear by way of repairs (including running repairs) or maintenance, or in connection with the laying up of the boat and its nets and gear at the end of a fishing season or their preparation for a season's fishing.

(3) It is to be a further additional condition with respect to the payment of a jobseeker's allowance to a share fisherman in respect of any benefit week that, where they are master or a member of the crew of a fishing boat of which either the master or any member of the crew is the owner or part owner, they must also prove that in respect of any period in that benefit week when they were not working as a share fisherman, the fishing boat did not put to sea with a view to fishing, for the reason that—

(a) on account of the state of the weather the fishing boat could not reasonably have put to sea with a view to fishing;

(b) the fishing boat was undergoing repairs or maintenance, not being repairs or maintenance to which paragraph (2) relates;

(c) there was an absence of fish from any waters in which the fishing boat could reasonably be expected to operate; or

(d) any other good cause necessitated abstention from fishing.

(4) In this regulation, "benefit week" in relation to a jobseeker's allowance has the meaning it has in regulation 74 (share fisherman: amount payable).

Remunerative work

72.—In determining the number of hours in which a person is engaged in remunerative work for the purposes of establishing entitlement to a jobseeker's allowance, no account is to be taken of any hours in which a person is engaged in work as a share fisherman. **6.317**

Calculation of earnings

73.—(1) In the calculation of earnings derived from work as a share fisherman for the purposes of establishing entitlement to a jobseeker's allow- **6.318**

ance, the provisions of Part 7 apply subject to the following provisions of this regulation.

(2) Regulation 55 (calculation of earnings of self-employed earners) is to be omitted.

(3) For regulation 61 (calculation of net profit of self-employed earners) there is to be substituted the following regulation—

"Calculation of earnings derived from work as a share fisherman

61.—(1) Earnings derived from work as a share fisherman within the meaning of regulation 67 (interpretation) are to be calculated in accordance with the following provisions of this regulation.

(2) Any such earnings are to be treated as paid in the benefit week in respect of which they are earned.

(3) The amount of earnings to be taken into account in respect of any benefit week are to be the claimant's share of the net profit derived from the work as a share fisherman less—

(a) an amount in respect of income tax and national insurance contributions under the Benefits Act calculated in accordance with regulation 62 (deduction of tax and contributions for self-employed earners); and

(b) half of any premium paid in respect of a personal pension scheme.

(4) Subject to paragraph (5), there is to be disregarded from a claimant's share of the weekly net profit—

(a) £20; and

(b) the amount of any earnings specified in paragraphs 4 and 10 of the Schedule to these Regulations, if applicable.

(5) Where a share fisherman has earnings from work other than work as a share fisherman, and an amount is disregarded from those earnings in accordance with paragraph 5, 6 or 7 of the Schedule—

(a) if the amount so disregarded is £20, paragraph (4)(a) does not apply;

(b) if the amount so disregarded is less than £20, the amount disregarded under paragraph (4)(a) must not exceed the difference between the amount disregarded from those other earnings and [1£20].

(6) For the purposes of paragraph (3), the net profit is to be calculated by taking into account the earnings less, subject to paragraphs (7) to (9), any expenses relevant to that benefit week which were wholly, exclusively and necessarily incurred for the purposes of the employment.

(7) Subject to paragraph (8), no deduction is to be made under paragraph (6) in respect of—

(a) any capital expenditure;

(b) the depreciation of any capital asset;

(c) any sum employed or intended to be employed in the setting up or expansion of the employment;

(d) the repayment of capital on any loan taken out for the purposes of the employment;

(e) any expenses incurred in providing business entertainment.

(8) A deduction is to be made under paragraph (6) in respect of the repayment of capital on any loan used for—

(a) the replacement in the course of business of equipment or machinery; and

(b) the repair of an existing business asset except to the extent that any sum is payable under an insurance policy for its repair.

(9) No reduction is to be made under paragraph (6) in respect of any expenses where the Secretary of State is not satisfied that the expense has been incurred or, having regard to the nature of the expense and its amount, that it has been reasonably incurred.

(10) A deduction under paragraph (6)—

(a) must not be made in respect of any sum unless it has been incurred for the purposes of the business;

(b) must be made in respect of—

(i) the excess of any Value Added Tax paid over Value Added Tax received in the benefit week;

(ii) any expense incurred in the repair of an existing asset except to the extent that any sum is payable under an insurance policy for its repair;

(iii) any payment of interest on a loan taken out for the purposes of the employment.

(11) Notwithstanding paragraphs (1) to (10), the Secretary of State may calculate earnings or expenditure over a period other than the benefit week if the Secretary of State considers it is reasonable to do so having regard to all the facts of the case and in particular whether the earnings earned or expenditure incurred in respect of a benefit week are unusually high or low.

(12) In this regulation "benefit week" has the same meaning as in regulation 74 (share fishermen: amount payable)."

(4) In regulation 62 (deduction of tax and contributions for self-employed earners)—

(a) in paragraphs (1) and (3), for the words "regulation 61(1)(b)(i)" there is to be substituted the words "regulation 61(3)(a)";

(b) paragraphs (2) and (4) are to be omitted;

[[2](ba) in paragraph (3) for "Subject to paragraph (4), the" substitute "The";]

(c) in paragraph (5)(a) for the words "regulation 61(3)(a) or, as the case may be, (4)" there is to be substituted the words "regulation 61(6)";

(d) at the end of the regulation there is to be added the following paragraph—

"(6) For the purposes of paragraphs (1) and (3) the earnings to which the basic rate of tax is to be applied and the amount of personal relief deductible, the amount specified in section 11(4) of the Benefits Act, and the upper limit of profits and gains referred to in paragraph (3)(b), are to be apportioned pro rata according to the period over which the earnings are assessed in accordance with regulation 61.".

AMENDMENT

1. Social Security (Miscellaneous Amendments) (No.2) Regulations 2013 (SI 2013/1508) reg.4(4) (July 29, 2013).

2. Social Security (Scottish Rate of Income Tax etc.) (Amendment) Regulations 2016 (SI 2016/233) reg.7(5) (April 6, 2016).

Amount payable

74.—(1) The amount payable to a share fisherman by way of a jobseeker's allowance is to be calculated in accordance with regulations 49 to 51 (weekly amounts of jobseeker's allowance, deductions in respect of earnings and payments by way of pensions) and this regulation, and Part 8 does not apply. **6.319**

(2) Regulations 49 to 51 apply in respect of share fishermen so that the amount payable is calculated by reference to earnings earned and pension payments received in the benefit week.

(3) In this regulation "benefit week" means—

(a) in respect of the week in which the claim is made, the period of seven days beginning with the date of claim; and
(b) in respect of any subsequent week, the period of seven days beginning with the day after the last day of the previous benefit week.

PART 10

MODIFICATION OF THE ACT

Modification of section 2 of the Act

6.320 **75.**—Section 2 of the Act (the contribution-based conditions) applies with the modifications that after the words "Class 1 contributions" in each place where they appear there is to be inserted the words "or Class 2 contributions under Case G of Part 9 of the Social Security (Contributions) Regulations 2001".

DEFINITION

"the Act"—see reg.2(2).

GENERAL NOTE

6.321 This modifies s.2 of the new style Jobseekers Act 1995 (already modified by reg.69, above in making the special class 2 contributions paid by share fishermen count for the contribution conditions) so as to make count for JSA entitlement "Class 2 contributions under Case G of Part 9 of the Social Security (Contributions) Regulations 2001". These cover a "volunteer development worker": someone who is ordinarily resident in Great Britain or Northern Ireland (as the case may be), but employed outside Great Britain, who has been allowed to pay Class 2 contributions because HMRC has certified that it is consistent with the proper administration of the Benefits Act that, subject to the satisfaction of further conditions, that person should be entitled to pay Class 2 contributions under reg.151 of the Contributions Regulations. The modification is set out in the text of s.2.

SCHEDULE

Regulations 59(2) and 61(2)

SUMS TO BE DISREGARDED IN THE CALCULATION OF EARNINGS

6.322 **1.**—(1) In the case of a claimant who has been engaged in remunerative work as an employed earner or, had the employment been in Great Britain, would have been so engaged—
(a) any earnings, other than items to which sub-paragraph (2) applies, paid or due to be paid from the employment which was terminated before the first day of entitlement to a jobseeker's allowance;
(b) any earnings, other than a payment of the nature described in sub-paragraph (2)(a) or (b)(ii), paid or due to be paid from the employment which has not been terminated where the claimant is not—
(i) engaged in remunerative work; or
(ii) suspended from their employment.

(2) This sub-paragraph applies to—

(a) any payment of the nature described in—
(i) regulation 58(1)(d); or
(ii) section 28, 64 or 68 of the Employment Rights Act 1996 (guarantee payments, suspension from work on medical or maternity grounds); and
(b) any award, sum or payment of the nature described in—
(i) regulation 58(1)(f) or (h); or
(ii) section 34 or 70 of the Employment Rights Act 1996 (guarantee payments and suspension from work: complaints to employment tribunals),including any payment made following the settlement of a complaint to an employment tribunal or of court proceedings.

2.—(1) In the case of a claimant to whom this paragraph applies, any earnings (other than items to which paragraph 1(2) applies) which relate to employment which ceased before the first day of entitlement to a jobseeker's allowance whether or not that employment has been terminated. **6.323**

(2) This paragraph—
(a) applies to a claimant who has been engaged in part-time employment as an employed earner or, had the employment been in Great Britain, would have been so engaged;
(b) does not apply to a claimant who has been suspended from their employment.

3.—Any payment to which regulation 58(1)(f) applies— **6.324**
(a) which is due to be paid more than 52 weeks after the date of termination of the employment in respect of which the payment is made; or
(b) which is a compensatory award within the meaning of section 118(1)(b) of the Employment Rights Act 1996 for so long as such an award remains unpaid and the employer is insolvent within the meaning of section 127 of that Act.

4.—In the case of a claimant who has been engaged in remunerative work or part-time employment as a self-employed earner or, had the employment been in Great Britain, would have been so engaged and who has ceased to be so engaged, from the date of the cessation of their employment any earnings derived from that employment except earnings to which regulation 55(2) (royalties etc) applies. **6.325**

5.—In a case to which neither of paragraphs 6 and 7 applies to the claimant, £5. **6.326**

6.—£20 of the total earnings derived from one or more employments as— **6.327**
[1(a) a part-time fire-fighter employed by a fire and rescue authority under the Fire and Rescue Services Act 2004 or by the Scottish Fire and Rescue Service established under section 1A of the Fire (Scotland) Act 2005];
(b) [1 . . ..];
(c) an auxiliary coastguard in respect of coast rescue activities;
(d) a person engaged part-time in the manning or launching of a lifeboat;
(e) a member of any territorial or reserve force prescribed in Part I of Schedule 6 to the Social Security (Contributions) Regulations 2001.

7.—Where the claimant is engaged in one or more employments specified in paragraph 6 but their earnings derived from such employments are less than £20 in any week and they are also engaged in any other part-time employment, so much of their earnings from that other employment up to £5 as would not in aggregate with the amount of their earnings disregarded under paragraph 6 exceed £20. **6.328**

8.—Notwithstanding paragraphs 1 to 7 of this Schedule, where two or more payments of the same kind and from the same source are to be taken into account in the same benefit week, because it has not been practicable to treat the payments under regulation 56(b) (date on which earnings are treated as paid) as paid on the first day of the benefit week in which they were due to be paid, there is to be disregarded from each payment the sum that would have been disregarded if the payment had been taken into account on the date on which it was due to be paid. **6.329**

9.—Any earnings derived from employment which are payable in a country outside the United Kingdom for such period during which there is a prohibition against the transfer to the United Kingdom of those earnings. **6.330**

10.—Where a payment of earnings is made in a currency other than sterling, any banking charge or commission payable in converting that payment into sterling. **6.331**

11.—Any earnings which are due to be paid before the date of claim and which would otherwise fall to be taken into account in the same benefit week as a payment of the same kind and from the same source. **6.332**

12.—(1) Where by reason of earnings to which sub-paragraph (2) applies (in aggregate with the claimant's other earnings (if any) calculated in accordance with this Part) the claimant would (apart from this paragraph) have a personal rate of less than 10 pence, the amount **6.333**

of such earnings but only to the extent that that amount exceeds the claimant's personal rate less 10 pence.

(2) This sub-paragraph applies to earnings, in so far as they exceed the amount disregarded under paragraph 6, derived by the claimant from employment as a member of any [2 . . .] reserve force prescribed in Part 1 of Schedule 6 to the Social Security (Contributions) Regulations 2001 in respect of a period of annual continuous training for a maximum of 15 days in any calendar year [2 or in respect of training in the claimant's first year of training as a member of a reserve force for a maximum of 43 days in that year.]

(3) In sub-paragraph (1), "personal rate" means the rate for the claimant calculated as specified in section 4(1) of the Act.

6.334 **13.**—In this Schedule "part-time employment" means employment in which the person is not to be treated as engaged in remunerative work under regulation 43 or 44 (persons treated as engaged, or not engaged, in remunerative work).

AMENDMENTS

1. Social Security (Miscellaneous Amendments) (No.2) Regulations 2013 (SI 2013/1508) reg.4(5) (July 29, 2013).
2. Social Security (Members of the Reserve Forces) (Amendment) Regulations 2015 (SI 2015/389) reg.5(4) (April 6, 2015).

DEFINITIONS

"the Act"—see reg.2(2).
"benefit week"—*ibid.*
"claimant"—see Jobseekers Act 1995 s.35(1).
"date of claim"—see reg.2(2).
"earnings"—see Jobseekers Act 1995 s.35(3).
"employed earner"—see reg.2(1).
"employment"—*ibid.*
"Great Britain"—see Jobseekers Act 1995 s.35(1).
"payment"—see reg.2(2).
"remunerative work"—see regs 2(2) and 42(1).
"self-employed earner"—see reg.2(2).

GENERAL NOTE

6.335 The Schedule sets out – for the purposes of regs 59 and 62, dealing respectively with the calculation of earnings of employed earners and self-employed earners—a range of payments which are wholly or to a degree to be disregarded in calculating those earnings. The provisions are substantially equivalent to those in Sch.6 to the JSA Regulations 1996 (Pt III of this volume), excluding those relevant only to IBJSA. Paragraphs 1–4 of this Schedule equate to paras 1–4 (omitting para.1A). Paragraphs 5–7 on £20 or £5 disregards for various categories of employment are much simpler than paras 5–11 of Sch.6, mainly because the complication of having to take a partner's earnings into account is avoided. Paragraphs 8–11 equate to paras 13–16 of Sch.6. Paragraphs 12 and 13 equate to paras 19 (omitting sub-para. (3)) and 20 of Sch.6. See the annotation to Sch.6 of the JSA Regulations 1996.

INDEX

LEGAL TAXONOMY
FROM SWEET & MAXWELL

This index has been prepared using Sweet and Maxwell's Legal Taxonomy. Main index entries conform to keywords provided by the Legal Taxonomy except where references to specific documents or non-standard terms (denoted by quotation marks) have been included. These keywords provide a means of identifying similar concepts in other Sweet & Maxwell publications and online services to which keywords from the Legal Taxonomy have been applied. Readers may find some minor differences between terms used in the text and those which appear in the index. Suggestions to *sweetandmaxwell.taxonomy@thomson.com*.

(All references are to paragraph number)